International Encyclopedia of the SOCIAL SCIENCES

Volumes 9 and 10
Complete and Unabridged

International Encyclopedia of the SOCIAL SCIENCES

DAVID L. SILLS EDITOR

VOLUME 9

The Macmillan Company & The Free Press, New York
COLLIER-MACMILLAN PUBLISHERS, LONDON

L

[C O N T I N U E D]

LANGUAGE

I
THE PSYCHOLOGY OF LANGUAGE

The psychologist tends to look at language in the first instance as he would look at any other problem area. Unique or special problems are confronted as they arise, but there is no unequivocal case for or against a special psychology—one created for language alone. The best, or, perhaps, the only way to discuss the psychology of language at this time is to describe how psychologists have been looking at it. Much of what can be said receives consideration in other articles in these volumes. The present one can serve as an introduction to the other articles, and it will be concerned, in part at least, with an attempt to set the framework which marks psychological studies of language. Certain more specific problems will also be treated—problems which represent some of the writer's special interests and which are unlikely to receive extended discussion elsewhere.

Early interests of psychologists in language

Studies of language—or, as psychologists prefer to call it, verbal behavior, which applies to both spoken and written forms—began very early in the postphilosophical period in psychology. Several themes may be identified (see Carroll 1953).

The "word-association experiment." First, Wilhelm Wundt, often called the first experimental psychologist, was interested in language—but more from a naturalistic than from an experimental point of view. However, workers in his laboratory early took an interest in the "word-association experiment," the origin of which is usually attributed to Sir Francis Galton. Galton's pioneering work was carried out with himself as subject: he wrote down stimuli on slips of paper and later looked at each slip (on more than one occasion) and recorded the thoughts that were thereby elicited. He also timed these reactions and noted the tendencies for the same or different thoughts to occur on the several occasions on which he looked at each slip (Warren 1921).

The "word-association experiment," despite its early entrance into the psychological laboratory (some of the results obtained are still cited today; see e.g. Woodworth [1938] 1960), soon figured more prominently in clinical diagnostic work than in the experimental laboratory. While the associations made by pathological subjects and by normal subjects were often found to differ, on the average, the association method never reached a dominant position in the armamentarium of clinical techniques, in the detection of "complexes," or, except in classroom demonstrations, in the detection of "guilty knowledge," although it was applied to all of these problems. It is safe to say that until about 1950 it had fallen into relative neglect. In the years since 1950, however, interest in association methods has reached a very high level because of the demonstrated value of measured associations in predicting other verbal behavior [see Marshall & Cofer 1963; Noble 1963; *see also* ANALYTICAL PSYCHOLOGY *and the biography of* JUNG].

Verbal learning. The study of verbal learning was begun in the laboratory almost as early as the word association method. Hermann Ebbinghaus reported the first experiments in a classic monograph in 1885. Ebbinghaus, however, was not really concerned with general questions of language or verbal behavior; he was interested instead in the formation of associations, and he attempted to prevent such factors as meaning, meaningfulness, and connectedness from influencing his results by inventing and using the nonsense syllable. A vast outpouring of work on verbal learning followed Ebbinghaus' pioneer efforts (see e.g. McGeoch [1942] 1952; Conference . . . 1961; Conference . . . 1963), but current opinion is that verbal learning cannot be divorced from features of the subject's usual language. [See LEARNING, *article on* VERBAL LEARNING; *and the biography of* EBBINGHAUS.]

Mediational processes. A third concern in psychology's study of verbal behavior is the role verbal processes may have in *mediating* between stimuli and responses. Quite early (in the 1890s) there was an interest in "mediate association," the notion that while two terms may not be related directly to one another they may be linked by a third term. Thus, justice and war may not be directly associated, but they may be related if, when one thinks justice, he also thinks peace. The latter may lead to the word "war," thus serving to mediate between justice and war.

Mediational processes, especially verbal ones, have provided a mechanism whereby objective and behavioristic psychologists can account for forms of thought, stimulus and response equivalence, and other phenomena which are otherwise refractory to a simple analysis in terms of stimulus and response (Goss 1961*a*). Much of the impetus to this way of thinking came from studies of semantic conditioning, both in Russia and in the United States (Osgood 1953; Jenkins 1963), in which verbal behavior is given an important role in the control of other behavior (Luriia 1961; Dollard & Miller 1950). There has also been great interest in the possibilities for altering verbal behavior itself (and thus perhaps its control over other behaviors) by means of reinforcement and nonreinforcement (Krasner 1958) or by other means (Cofer 1957; 1960).

Psycholinguistics. The fourth, and final, major trend appeared in the early 1950s and was a convergence of psychology (especially learning theory), descriptive linguistics, and information theory. This convergence was facilitated by the Social Science Research Council and the Carnegie Corporation (Carroll 1953). Essentially, it amounted to the bringing together of linguists and psychologists (see Osgood 1963; Osgood & Sebeok 1954) so that each group could become familiarized with the techniques and concepts of the other. As a result, an interdisciplinary "field"—psycholinguistics—has sometimes been identified, although its methods and concepts perhaps tend to be more aggregations than mergers of the concepts and methods of the disciplines. "Psycholinguisticians" tend to retain their primary identifications as linguists or as psychologists. The development of the notion of a "generative grammar" (Chomsky 1957) in linguistics may well alter the character of psycholinguistics. [See LINGUISTICS.]

It must be pointed out that what has been said implies very little concerning language as a process of interindividual communication. It is obvious that communication is a major function of language, but from the present vantage point it seems that matters other than communication per se have engaged the interests of the major psychological students of language or verbal behavior, although studies of communication processes do go on. Also neglected in the foregoing account is speech perception and speech pathology, the study of which can yield important and useful information on a variety of problems. [See LANGUAGE, *article on* SPEECH PATHOLOGY; PERCEPTION, *article on* SPEECH PERCEPTION.]

Viewpoints concerning mediational events

A major theoretical concern among psychologists interested in verbal behavior has been the implicit events which may accompany overt speech production or writing. Cofer and Foley (1942) suggested that a mediating response underlies cases of stimulus equivalence (or transfer or generalization) among stimuli which are physically dissimilar. Thus, if a response is learned to a word like "fashion" and it transfers, without further training, to the word "style" or "mode," the transfer cannot be explained on the basis of the visual appearance or the sound of the words. The argument advanced, in essence, was that each of these words elicits, as a result of prior experience, a common reaction. If this reaction occurs when fashion is presented, it will be associated with the new response being learned to fashion. Since style and mode also elicit the common reaction, its occurrence when they are presented would also result in the appearance of the response newly learned to fashion. The common reaction mediates the transfer. Cofer and Foley stressed the relation of synonymity among words as an indication of the existence of common mediating reactions among them, but they also spoke of interword associations in such a way as to suggest that associations, also, might serve as mediators.

Osgood's views—representational mediation. Osgood (1953; 1961) has made the mediating reaction the basis of a theory of meaning. Two words mean the same thing to the extent that they share the capacity to arouse the same *representational mediator*. The conception is that, with respect to an object, there is behavior, R_t (for total behavior). A sign, e.g., a word, may be acquired in relation to the object; but to have meaning with reference to the object the sign must arouse some representative part of the R_t made to the object. The representational part would ordinarily be those features of, R_t which can readily be detached from the total and occur implicitly without interfering with other behavior.

This formulation led Osgood to make certain distinctions among word relations with respect to meaning. Thus, contrasting or opposite words (antonyms) cannot share common mediators and hence cannot have common meanings. This is because R_t with respect to objects or events must be very different in the case of antonyms. The representational mediators, in turn, would then be very different for antonyms. Thus, Osgood is forced to explain the fact that antonyms are often highly associated in word association tests (e.g., black–white, up–down) on the basis of a rote verbal habit rather than on the basis of common representational mediators. Similarly, he took the position that the existence of interword associations does not demonstrate, generally, the presence of common meanings. He also seemed to hold that transfer and generalization should ordinarily be predicated on common representational mediators rather than on common associations.

The semantic differential. As an index of a representational mediator, Osgood (see Osgood et al. 1957) emphasized the *semantic differential*. This is a technique by which a given word or concept (e.g., baby) is rated by a subject on each of a number of seven-point rating scales, the extremes of which are defined by polar adjectives. Thus, scales appear whose extreme points are designated by such adjective pairs as hot–cold, bad–good, active–passive, tense–relaxed. Factor analysis of the intercorrelations among such scales has usually yielded three more basic dimensions—evaluative (e.g., bad–good), activity (e.g., active–passive), potency (e.g., strong–weak). It is possible to describe a given word in terms of where its ratings fall in a semantic space defined by these three (and

perhaps other) dimensions. As these dimensions are believed to characterize the representational mediator, they are an index of its meaning. Osgood has referred to this as connotative (or emotional) meaning in contrast to denotative meaning.

Among psychological investigators of verbal behavior, Osgood has perhaps been the leader in emphasizing that meaning is a critical factor in verbal behavior and that a satisfactory account of language must deal with it. Others have not been convinced. Skinner (1957) has written a psychology of language in which the concept of meaning does not enter and which treats verbal behavior as a case of the operant. Skinner is concerned with the analysis of this operant (and the classes into which it may be divided) in terms of the variables (reinforcement, stimulus control, deprivation, aversive conditions) which control its strength. This is essentially a descriptive or positivistic procedure, representing an extrapolation of notions developed in the animal laboratory.

Association in mediation. More closely associated with the mainstream of the psychological study of verbal behavior, however, have been the investigators who have emphasized interword associations as the important problem. They have insisted that the test of what is important is not whether a conception explains meaning. Rather, they have argued that the extent to which predictions can be made of the behavior of words in a variety of situations is critical. In other words, they have held forth not the criterion that a conception of verbal behavior explains (or ignores) meaning but the criterion that a theory of verbal behavior must accept measures and procedures which correlate well with other phenomena in the verbal realm.

To give this approach (it can hardly be called a theory) some concreteness, we may describe an experiment made a number of years ago at the University of Minnesota (see Jenkins 1963 for references and discussion). This experiment (and many others as well) was designed, in part, to determine whether meaning (in Osgood's sense) or association is a more effective variable in predicting transfer in certain situations. Before discussing the experiment, we may turn first to a discussion of contemporary procedures of association tests.

Association tests. The word association test, as it has been typically used, consists of a list of words to which a subject reacts, one at a time, by saying or writing down the first other single word that comes to mind when he sees or hears a list (stimulus) word. This process is called free association since no restriction is imposed on what response the subject can give, save that his response must be a single word and that repetitions of the stimulus word are prohibited. Despite its name, the procedure is not to be confused with the free association procedure as used in psychoanalysis: the two techniques differ widely.

The word association test is usually given to a number of subjects (from fifty to one hundred are considered a minimum for the establishment of norms), and their responses are tabulated for each stimulus. When such tabulations are made (and the stimuli used are relatively common words) the typical result is this: one word is given by a substantial number of subjects, another by somewhat fewer subjects, a third by still fewer subjects, and so on until words are found that are given by only one subject. An illustration will clarify this situation. Suppose the stimulus word is "length," and we obtain responses from 56 subjects. In such a sample the most frequent, or primary, response is width, occurring 18 times (32 per cent), the next is long, occurring 5 times (9 per cent), the next are height and measure, tied at 4 occurrences each, and there are 6 responses, each occurring twice— short, depth, foot, line, measurement, distance. In addition, there are 13 responses each occurring but a single time.

This set of associations, and others like it, is often termed an association hierarchy, because the responses differ and may be ordered in accordance with their frequencies of occurrence to the stimulus word. Such hierarchies may differ in a number of properties. Thus, the primary frequency may vary considerably (e.g., table elicits chair as a primary from about 75 per cent of a group of U.S. college students, in contrast to the 32 per cent indicated above), and the difference between the primary and other responses themselves may vary. Likewise, the number of different words given to a stimulus varies; usually the higher the primary frequency the fewer other words there are, a fact dictated by arithmetic if we are dealing with a constant sample size.

These differences in associative frequency have been taken as a measure of association or habit strength, not only for the group, but, by inference, for the individual. Though it is by no means a certain inference, there is evidence which justifies it (cf. Russell 1961). At any rate, a number of experiments have been predicated on this inference.

The dominant association to length, as we have seen, is width. The dictionary records a number of meanings for the word "length," but width is not among them; measure, measurement, and distance are, however, approximations to the dictionary statement of some of the meanings of length. We may say that width is a prominent *associative* meaning of length, if we wish to, but it certainly does not qualify in a dictionary or denotative sense as a meaning of length. This, of course, illustrates Osgood's argument that associations are not the same as meaning.

Predictive value of associations. The question, however, may still be raised whether the associations are effective in mediating transfer (and other phenomena) and, if they are, how they compare with synonyms in doing so. To answer this question, the following experiment was performed.

Two lists were constructed, each consisting of a series of word pairs. The subject was required to learn the two lists in succession, and the interest lay in the transfer effects of learning the first list upon learning the second list. Response members of the pairs in the two lists were related in two ways. Some responses were antonyms, but highly associated; since meaning has been ruled out by Osgood as a factor in the interrelation of antonyms, these pairs test the role of association. Other response members of the pairs were synonyms which, according to the word association test, were not associated. These test the capacity of meaning to mediate transfer without association. There were also control pairs, in which the response members of the two lists were neither synonyms nor associates. Table 1 shows the general experimental plan. When compared to control pairs in List 2, the pairs having associative and synonym relations with pairs in List 1 showed the effects of positive transfer in List 2. The associated pairs tended to be learned in a somewhat superior fashion than the synonymous pairs. In this experiment, then, both the postulated factors were effective. One can say that common meaning may effect transfer but that transfer can occur without it if suitable associations are present.

Table 1 — Experimental plan

CONDITION	LIST 1	LIST 2
Associated	eagle—sickness	eagle—health
Synonyms	mutton—long	mutton—tall
Controls	needle—king	needle—close

Many other experiments have been carried out which have explored and demonstrated the role of associations in a variety of situations. Among the situations studied have been free recall, list learning and recall, semantic generalization, recognition of words (in the context of other words) after very brief or inadequate presentations, verbal discrimination, transfer, and concept formation (for references see Deese 1961; Jenkins 1963; Cofer 1957; 1960; and Marshall & Cofer 1963). The role of meaning has also been studied in some of these situations, and some conflict has arisen over whether meaning or association is the better concept or whether one can be reduced to the other (see Bousfield 1961; Osgood 1961). Since the role of mediation is critical to this work, whether interpreted in terms of meaning or association, a good deal of effort has been devoted to basic mediational processes and mechanisms (Jenkins 1963).

Associations in other tasks. Two further areas of inquiry may be discussed to demonstrate the interest of psychologists in the role of associations in such tasks as concept identification and problem solving.

Underwood and Richardson (see Marshall & Cofer 1963) selected a large number of words, to each of which they obtained "sensory" associations from a large group of college subjects. The subjects were carefully instructed as to the kind of association they were to give; thus it was pointed out that to such a stimulus word as "apple" responses like red, sour, or round would be appropriate; responses like tree, fruit, or seed would not meet the criteria for a sensory association. To each stimulus, sensory associations were arranged in a hierarchy according to frequencies, called "dominance levels" by the investigators.

It is possible then to present several words to a new group of subjects, each word having a sensory associate in common with the other words of the set. The subject is asked what these words have in common. For example, one might present the words "chalk," "milk," "paste," and "shirt" and ask what they have in common or in what way they are similar. The instructions here would not mention or suggest sensory attributes. An answer for the set just mentioned might be that they are or can all be white. The subjects are more successful in finding the expected solution for sets with high dominance levels than for sets with low dominance levels.

This finding suggests that in tasks of this kind solution will be more likely if the instances suggest the answer than if they do not. More generally, it is consistent with the idea that problem solution often derives from responses to the materials available. If the materials suggest available and appropriate responses, solution will be quick; if they do not, or if they suggest inappropriate or incorrect responses, solution may be delayed, impeded, or prevented altogether.

A somewhat similar analysis may be made of an experiment by Judson and Cofer (see Cofer 1957).

These investigators developed a number of four-word items; in each item, the subject was to exclude the word that did not go with or belong with the others. The critical items had two possible solutions. Thus, the item

skyscraper   temple   cathedral   prayer

can be solved by excluding prayer, as it is not a building, or by excluding skyscraper, as it has nothing to do with religion. In the investigation carried out, an important factor found to determine solution was the word order of the item. As the item is shown above, prayer is excluded more often than skyscraper. If, however, the positions of prayer and skyscraper are interchanged in the item as presented, then skyscraper is excluded more often than prayer. Evidently, associations are initiated by the first word of the item and reinforced by the next two words (which are ambiguous in that they refer both to buildings and to religion) so that the last item is typically seen as not belonging. With highly religious persons, however (as measured by church attendance), the nonreligion item tends to be excluded no matter what its position is. Thus, while word order itself is important to the dominance of the concept to be identified (and thus to the word to be excluded), dominance can also arise from other, perhaps more personal, sources.

Associations should influence behavior over a period of time if their importance is great. A demonstration that is relevant was made by Judson and Cofer (see Cofer 1957). The procedure was divided into two parts, separated by a six-week interval. In part 1, each subject was asked to give ten free associations to each of ten stimulus words. Only one of these sets of associations was used later, however. Suppose one stimulus word was music and the first four associates given by one subject were tune, song, instrument, and melody. In part 2, for this subject, tune was presented on a card along with three other words (each on a card) that were new to the experiment. The subject was told to pick one of the four words. If he was "correct" (i.e., he chose tune) he was told that he was right. If he was "wrong" (i.e., he picked one of the other words), he continued to pick until he chose tune. After performing satisfactorily on this set of cards, he was then shown four more cards containing song and three new words. This time, he simply made a choice, with no information being given as to its correctness. Then he was shown four more cards, containing instrument and three new words and made a choice (without information); then melody with new words and so on until his sequence of ten associates was used up. The question was, would the subject choose more often the words that he had associated with music after the first response (tune in the example) was said to be correct than he would choose the new words which were not part of the associative chain? As compared to the control group, the subjects answered this question affirmatively, indicating that the chain established in part 1 was still intact and that subsequent choices were influenced by the designation of the first word of the chain as correct.

Another way of investigating the role of associations in problem-solving behavior was used by Cofer, Judson and Gelfand (see Cofer 1957). In this experiment, the subjects were asked to solve certain problems. Prior to attempting the problems, the subject was taught several short lists of words. One of the lists contained a sequence of words, which, if active in the subject's mind at the time of problem solving, could influence the kind of solutions used in solving the problems. The results were suggestive, if not definitive. That is, for male subjects at any rate, the frequency with which one particular solution appeared for each task was augmented (as compared to controls), and this solution was the one to which the word list was related.

These experiments on concept formation and problem solving do not cover the entire range of these phenomena but, so far as they go, they do suggest that verbal associative processes can have an important effect in these tasks. And experiments such as these illustrate very pointedly what is meant by the role of verbal responses in mediating and controlling other behaviors. [*See* CONCEPT FORMATION *and* PROBLEM SOLVING.]

Work of the kind we have just described illustrates the influence of association tests, learning theory, and the interest in mediation processes in the control of behavior. Our description should be clear on one point: much of what we have said has been concerned essentially with single words and their relations to one another. Language involves more complex arrangements of words than this, and in psychology some attention has been paid to these complexities. Both linguistics and information theory contribute knowledge and techniques to considerations of this problem of complexity.

Contributions of information theory

Information or communication theory has contributed, in addition to a model of the communication process and a means of measuring the amount of information transmitted, the important concept of redundancy. In successive segments of a sequence of words taken from normal English, there are or may be dependency on what has gone before. In such cases, the listener (or reader) can often predict accurately what is to come, and when it comes its occurrence does not contribute any information (i.e., resolve any uncertainty) over and above what the listener or reader already has. [*See* INFORMATION THEORY.] Some of this redundancy arises from structural features of the language; other aspects of it may arise from semantic (associative?) features. In the sentence "Tom went to the ____" there are many items (such as movie, play, concert, game, exhibit) which can be inserted in the blank with equal appropriateness. However, all of them are nouns; we cannot insert pronouns, adverbs, adjectives, verbs, conjunctions, and prepositions if only one word is to be placed in the blank and the sentence is to end with that word. This is an example of structural redundancy: our choice is limited to nouns in filling the blank. We cannot use just any word in the language to do so. As the noun class contains a very large number of items, we still have many choices but we are, nonetheless, restricted by the grammatical situation (here a prepositional phrase which contains an article before the blank) to selection among those words which have the privilege of occurrence in the situation.

In many situations, it is easier to fill in blanks when they stand for items that have chiefly structural rather than semantic significance. Thus, it is more likely that the blank in the following "Tom ____ going to the play" will be replaced with the word "is" or "was" than it is that the blank in the first version would be replaced by any of the noun alternatives listed. There is, we may say, more redundancy in the case of is or was than there is in the blank in the noun phrase, although there is redundancy there also. With content words (nouns, adjectives, verbs, or adverbs), the semantic or associative context often severely limits the possible choices. Thus, in the sentence "Tom went to read the part in the ____" few choices (play, drama, for example) remain to the reader or hearer; redundancy here is high.

One of the advantages for learning that connected discourse has over unconnected words is conferred by its redundancy, both structural and semantic (Deese 1961). The influence of structural redundancy is perhaps confined to strings of words in which some features, at least, of the language are preserved. Strings of unrelated words, however, may be associatively or semantically related; thus there may be some redundancy in such terms.

It is clear that redundancy is an important feature of language; it is probably essential to accurate communication (especially in noisy channels), and, for memory, it is very helpful that large amounts of material can be coded (thus reducing the load on memory) in terms of redundant features (Miller 1956). That language is often used to code or categorize (Brown 1958) the environment is perhaps a feature of the greatest importance to intellectual functioning and to the role of language in the control of behavior.

Contributions of linguistics

It is probably fair to say that linguistics has had its greatest impact on psychology because of its knowledge of the structure of language and the rules that govern the structure. Phonemic and morphemic analysis has been instructive, but morphology and syntax are perhaps more provocative.

There are at least two fundamental issues that morphology and syntax raise for a psychology of language. First, it is clear that no theory of verbal behavior which confines itself to semantic and associative relations among words alone is complete. Mechanisms must be developed to cope with semantic and associative changes that undoubtedly occur in the context of other words, and syntactic restraints must be an important aspect of this context. Furthermore, no psychological theory of morphology or syntax has been presented as yet. Analysis so far has largely been confined to specific cues in speech or writing which might elicit word inflections or specific syntactic forms (Goss 1961*b*).

The second issue arises from the fact that at a descriptive level it is clear that speech regularities appear very early in the development of the child (Brown & Fraser 1963). Furthermore, many rule-abiding features of speech are known to occur widely, even though the speakers are unaware of the rules or of the fact that they are following rules. Young children display the operation of a general rule when they pluralize goose incorrectly as gooses or form the past tense of the verb "take" as "taked." Perhaps more subtle examples are found in the speech of adults. We all recognize that there is something wrong with the expression "the sheer two silk stockings" and would prefer to say "the two sheer silk stockings." We would have difficulty in formulating the rule that makes one expression acceptable, the other not. Despite its semantic nonsense, we can recognize the grammatical correctness of Chomsky's (1957) famous sentence, "colorless green ideas sleep furiously," or make the appropriate substitutions of nouns, verbs, and modifiers in such strings as "the glibs duxed the neglan gojeys." Semantic factors are not essential to the identification of grammaticalness or to the identification of parts of speech.

The facts are, then, that morphological and syntactical principles govern much speech and writing behavior and that many of them cannot be verbalized by a large number of adults and appear in the speech behavior of young children without explicit instruction. These features suggest that a psychological theory or account of morphology and syntax may have to include concepts of a higher order than those of stimulus and response and that explicit coding responses cannot be invoked to mediate these phenomena of grammar.

Structural linguistics has provided descriptions of these phenomena and has described the regularities that prevail in language. However, it has not presented a theory of the behavior involved. Recently, Chomsky (1957) and Miller (1962) have argued for a new conception.

This conception holds that, in addition to a phrase-structure grammar, there is also a set of transformational rules which, when used, modifies a statement from one type to another including the necessary morphophonemic changes. Thus, a sentence model exists which appears to be the basic form (the kernel) of adult utterances, but it is transformed systematically, as needed, by the use of transformational rules like the interrogative, the passive, the negative, and so on. More than one rule may be applied, as when a simple declarative sentence becomes a passive interrogative negative. For example, "Tom hits the girl" would become "Is not the girl being hit by Tom?" by the application of the appropriate transformations.

Chomsky, a linguist, has been explicit in asserting that a simple stimulus–response formation and habit utilization theory cannot, in his opinion, cope with this conception of grammar. Miller, a psychologist, seems to agree, and while he thinks work on association is important, he believes that the mechanisms underlying the transformational grammar can hardly be of the associational kind. A psychological theory of the development and use of transformational grammar has not been formulated, but if these authors are correct it would presumably involve high-order processes not readily reducible to association or meaning.

We have surveyed some of the major interests and problems characterizing psychologists' work on language. Beginning with the historical trends in the psychological study of language, we have concentrated on mediational processes, conceived from both a meaning and a word-association point of view. While some progress on problems related to mediational processes has been made, many questions and further problems remain. Psychological understanding of language in the sense of connected words has not progressed very far, although concepts and methods of information theory and linguistics have been found useful. Whether the rule using that is evident in the verbal behavior of both children and adults, conceived either in terms of conventional morphology and syntax or in terms of transformational grammar, can be reduced to the concepts of contemporary learning theory is a question to be decided in the near future.

CHARLES N. COFER

[*Directly related are the entries* COMMUNICATION; LINGUISTICS; LITERATURE. *Other relevant material may be found in* INFORMATION THEORY; PERCEPTION, *article on* SPEECH PERCEPTION.]

BIBLIOGRAPHY

BOUSFIELD, W. A.   1961   The Problem of Meaning in Verbal Learning. Pages 81–91 in Conference on Verbal Learning and Verbal Behavior, New York University, 1959, *Verbal Learning and Verbal Behavior: Proceedings.* Edited by Charles N. Cofer. New York: McGraw-Hill.

BROWN, ROGER   1958   *Words and Things.* Glencoe, Ill.: Free Press.

BROWN, ROGER; and FRASER, COLIN   1963   The Acquisition of Syntax. Pages 158–197 in Conference on Verbal Learning and Verbal Behavior, Second, Ardsley-on-Hudson, N. Y., 1961, *Verbal Behavior and Learning, Problems and Processes: Proceedings.* Edited by Charles N. Cofer and Barbara S. Musgrave. New York: McGraw-Hill.

CARROLL, JOHN B.   (1953) 1961   *The Study of Language: A Survey of Linguistics and Related Disciplines in America.* Cambridge, Mass.: Harvard Univ. Press.

CHOMSKY, NOAM   1957   *Syntactic Structures.* The Hague: Mouton.

COFER, CHARLES N.   1957   Reasoning as an Associative Process: III. The Role of Verbal Responses in Problem Solving. *Journal of General Psychology* 57:55–68.

COFER, CHARLES N.   1960   Experimental Studies of the Role of Verbal Processes in Concept Formation and Problem Solving. New York Academy of Sciences, *Annals* 91:94–107.

COFER, CHARLES N.; and FOLEY, JOHN P. JR.   1942   Mediated Generalization and the Interpretation of Verbal Behavior: I. Prolegomena. *Psychological Review* 49:513–540.

CONFERENCE ON VERBAL LEARNING AND VERBAL BEHAVIOR, NEW YORK UNIVERSITY, *1959*   1961   *Verbal Learning and Verbal Behavior: Proceedings.* Edited by Charles N. Cofer. New York: McGraw-Hill.

CONFERENCE ON VERBAL LEARNING AND VERBAL BEHAVIOR, SECOND, ARDSLEY-ON-HUDSON, N. Y., *1961*   1963   *Verbal Behavior and Learning, Problems and Processes: Proceedings.* Edited by Charles N. Cofer and Barbara S. Musgrave. New York: McGraw-Hill.

DEESE, JAMES   1961   From the Isolated Verbal Unit to Connected Discourse. Pages 11–31 in Conference on Verbal Learning and Verbal Behavior, New York University, 1959, *Verbal Learning and Verbal Behavior: Proceedings.* Edited by Charles N. Cofer. New York: McGraw-Hill.

DOLLARD, JOHN; and MILLER, NEAL E.   1950   *Personality and Psychotherapy: An Analysis in Terms of Learning, Thinking and Culture.* New York: McGraw-Hill. → A paperback edition was published in 1965.

GOSS, ALBERT E.   1961a   Early Behaviorism and Verbal Mediating Responses. *American Psychologist* 16:285–298.

GOSS, ALBERT E.   1961b   Acquisition and Use of Conceptual Schemes. Pages 42–69 in Conference on Verbal Learning and Verbal Behavior, New York University, 1959, *Verbal Learning and Verbal Behavior: Proceedings.* Edited by Charles N. Cofer. New York: McGraw-Hill.

JENKINS, JAMES J.   1963   Mediated Associations: Paradigms and Situations. Pages 210–245 in Conference on Verbal Learning and Verbal Behavior, Second, Ardsley-on-Hudson, N. Y., 1961, *Verbal Behavior and Learning: Problems and Processes: Proceedings.* Edited by Charles N. Cofer and Barbara S. Musgrave. New York: McGraw-Hill.

KRASNER, LEONARD   1958   Studies of the Conditioning of Verbal Behavior. *Psychological Bulletin* 55:148–170.

LURIIA, ALEKSANDR R.   1961   *The Role of Speech in the Regulation of Normal and Abnormal Behavior.* New York: Liveright.

McGEOCH, JOHN A.   (1942) 1952   *The Psychology of Human Learning.* 2d ed., revised by Arthur L. Irion. New York: Longmans.

MARSHALL, GEORGE R.; and COFER, CHARLES N.   1963   Associative Indices as Measures of Word Relatedness: A Summary and Comparison of Ten Methods. *Journal of Verbal Learning and Verbal Behavior* 1:408–421.

MILLER, GEORGE A.   1956   The Magical Number Seven, Plus or Minus Two: Some Limits on Our Capacity for Processing Information. *Psychological Review* 63:81–97.

MILLER, GEORGE A.   1962   Some Psychological Studies of Grammar. *American Psychologist* 17:748–762.

NOBLE, CLYDE E.   1963   Meaningfulness and Familiarity. Pages 76–119 in Conference on Verbal Learning and Verbal Behavior, Second, Ardsley-on-Hudson, N. Y., 1961, *Verbal Behavior and Learning, Problems and Processes: Proceedings.* Edited by Charles N. Cofer and Barbara S. Musgrave. New York: McGraw-Hill.

OSGOOD, CHARLES E.   (1953) 1959   *Method and Theory in Experimental Psychology.* New York: Oxford Univ. Press.

OSGOOD, CHARLES E.   1961   Comments on Professor Bousfield's Paper. Pages 91–106 in Conference on Verbal Learning and Verbal Behavior, New York University, 1959, *Verbal Learning and Verbal Behavior: Proceedings.* Edited by Charles N. Cofer. New York: McGraw-Hill.

OSGOOD, CHARLES E.   1963   Psycholinguistics. Pages 244–316 in Sigmund Koch (editor), *Psychology: A Study of a Science.* Volume 6: Investigations of Man as Socius: Their Place in Psychology and the Social Sciences. New York: McGraw-Hill.

OSGOOD, CHARLES E.; and SEBEOK, THOMAS A. (editors)   (1954) 1965   *Psycholinguistics: A Survey of Theory and Research Problems.* Bloomington: Indiana Univ. Press.

OSGOOD, CHARLES E.; SUCI, G. J.; and TANNENBAUM, P. H. (1957) 1961 *The Measurement of Meaning.* Urbana: Univ. of Illinois Press.

RUSSELL, WALLACE A. 1961 Assessment Versus Experimental Acquisition of Verbal Habits. Pages 110–123 in Conference on Verbal Learning and Verbal Behavior, New York University, 1959, *Verbal Learning and Verbal Behavior: Proceedings.* Edited by Charles N. Cofer. New York: McGraw-Hill.

SKINNER, B. F. 1957 *Verbal Behavior.* New York: Appleton.

WARREN, HOWARD C. 1921 *A History of the Association Psychology.* New York: Scribner.

WOODWORTH, ROBERT S. (1938) 1960 *Experimental Psychology.* Rev. ed. by Robert S. Woodworth and Harold Schlosberg. New York: Holt.

II

LANGUAGE DEVELOPMENT

Language development refers to the child's acquisition of his first language, usually under informal natural conditions. By the end of the first four years of life, children have mastered the essentials of this most distinctively human attribute. Given normal hearing and a normal brain, variations in rates of mastery are small. Indeed, so gifted in language learning are they that many children become skilled in more than one language in their early years. The evolution of a child's knowledge of his language is basic to his intellectual and social development, yet explanations of this process make demands on theories of human learning which have not yet been met.

Historical aspects. Studies of child language development in modern times fall into three phases. The first studies in the nineteenth century consisted primarily of parental diaries. Authors trained in linguistics (Gvozdev 1961; Leopold 1939–1949) have continued to use case studies. More than any other form of behavior, language reveals obvious internal patterning, and linguists have been loath to lose sight of these patterns by pooling quantitative measures of output. In the second phase of research, carried out by psychologists, standardized measuring methods of large samples were emphasized (McCarthy 1954). For the most part these studies have been atheoretical and have been concerned with variations in performance with age, sex, race, social class, and so on.

A landmark in modern research was Velten's (1943) application of Jakobson's (1941) theory of phonemic development. This theory proposed that changes in each child's linguistic system followed an orderly sequence of increasing differentiation of significant features; thus it related language development to perceptual development and provided a theoretical framework which made comparison of children in different linguistic environments possible.

Subsequent research, particularly on phonology and grammar, is a product of the mating of psychology and linguistics. The differences from the preceding phase lie in the later work's sensitivity to linguistic theories, respect for the systematic nature of the child's linguistic knowledge, and emphasis on inferences about the structures or rules which underlie the observed situational changes in verbal behavior.

Prelinguistic phase of infancy. By the end of the first year of life, the average child understands some adult speech and can execute some directions. At first, he merely responds to adult sounds by attention and then by making sounds himself. Later he comes to recognize gross differences between voices and may distinguish intonational contrasts. His gradual discrimination of the critical features in the speech of adults is probably the most important aspect of language learning, yet almost nothing is known about the growth of comprehension.

The infant at first makes sounds which are closely tied to feeding and breathing. His vocalizations become increasingly triggered by vocal stimulation from others. In the first three months cooing comes to be highly associated with vocal stimulation and can also be increased in frequency if followed by other forms of adult responsiveness. On the other hand, the actual sounds uttered seem to be autogenous, since the sounds of deaf children and of children who hear are indistinguishable before six months.

Cooing gradually gives way to the consonant–vowel sequences and repetitive patterns which sound to adults like the syllables of their own language. During the babbling period, there is a rich variety of vocal play by the normal child. Sometimes he persists in making sounds which are idiosyncratic and not present in the speech around him. Further, he readily produces sounds and sequences in the adult repertoire which he will be unable to produce again for years after he begins to use language.

The role of babbling in language development is controversial. A child who lives in a linguistically stimulating environment may babble a great deal, and he may be more fluent than average when language develops. Yet, contrary to popular belief, there is as yet no evidence that babbling is in any specific way practice for language development. Indeed, the formal properties of babbling and of speech are so different that they suggest somewhat distinct central processes in their production.

Semantic system

Early sentences. An average child uses meaningful utterances by the middle of the second year, and by the middle of the third year babbling virtually disappears in play except as a stylistic device.

At first these utterances vary considerably in both sound and meaning. They may be quite idiosyncratic. Because of the simplicity of the child's phonological system, there may be numerous homonyms if his vocabulary grows rapidly. Meanings are generalized readily, so that a given utterance might on various occasions mean "my coat," "my hat," "my baby carriage," "let's go for a walk," "bye-bye," and so on. Frequently there is a close integration with gesture.

If the first utterances are based on adult words, they may sometimes be very inclusive in reference ("bird") or very narrow ("Bobby"). Adult beliefs about the semantic contrasts needed by children may influence the words they use in talking with children. From the standpoint of adult meanings, the words used by children tend to refer to animal and human movements and to concrete items with characteristic shapes and sizes (Brown 1958). When the child's range of reference of a term is actually tested, it appears to depend on the variety of verbal contexts in which a word is heard and, to a lesser degree, on the variety of physical referents.

Conceptual changes. As the size of vocabulary increases, inevitably there is a change in the conceptual system. The number of semantic contrasts marked by vocabulary grows, and the referential range for each word must therefore narrow. A child might begin by calling all adults "papa," next use the word for his own father, and then later learn the word "adult," which has a similar referential range to the primitive "papa" (Leopold 1939–1949).

In this example, there has been more than a change in range. By the time the word "adult" is present, the child has a hierarchical system of superordinates. The criteria for each class have increased in specificity and changed in character, becoming less visual. Changes in the semantic system have in fact been only sketchily studied. They may include increases in the specificity of terms, increases in knowledge or in concept range as experience grows, a shift from sensorimotor to relational bases for concepts, and shifts in the verbal structure, so that antonyms, synonyms, superordinates, and other structural relations in the vocabulary reflect the critical contrasts employed in the language.

Studies of the deaf and other experimental research have suggested that conceptual development may have important nonverbal roots. Yet words give society a sure way of imposing its conceptual system. Societies differ considerably in the semantic contrasts marked by their vocabulary of kin, color, quantity, shape, time, space, and so on. The sanctions against deviant denotative use of these terms bring the child's comprehension, speech, and presumably his conceptual system into line with his language community.

Verbal relations. The basis of the child's system of relating words shifts by mid-primary school from sounds to meanings and grammatical features. The sound of a word is salient to the preschool child, who readily produces rhymes and alliterative sequences in word play. Words which sound alike are easily confused, leading to contaminations of meaning. On the other hand, children's greater interest in the sounds of words may facilitate the learning of a spelling system or the sound system of a second language. In contrast, adults, who tend to respond less to the sound and who are concerned more with meaning, are known to have greater difficulty with the phonology of a second language, although they may acquire vocabulary far more quickly.

As children mature, their vocabulary increasingly becomes organized in terms of grammatical and semantic replacement classes, and they become more able to isolate words from their situational and sentence contexts. Each word more readily elicits other words. Interverbal associations are more rapid, more fluent, more specific, and more predictable from the semantic and grammatical system. This high rate of mutual evocation of words may be a help in intelligence tests and in school tasks requiring verbal retention of information. Children vary considerably in their readiness to convert their experience—including nonverbal experience—into spontaneous verbal thought. This skill seems to be a consequence of the verbal milieu in which the child is reared, and hence is responsive to training (see Ervin-Tripp in Hoffman & Hoffman 1966).

Phonology

As soon as a child knows several meaningful utterances it is possible to study his phonological system. The units of this system are phonemes, which are constructs that represent the smallest distinguishable unit of speech and which account for the significant formal contrasts between utterances. A very primitive system is illustrated when a child has two words, such as "baba" and "tata." At this point there are three phonemes—one vowel and two consonants. Extrapolating from a small number of diary studies, we might expect the following changes to take place: (1) We might next find a system containing four consonant phonemes in which there is a contrast between the stop consonants and continuants. For example, the child might add /m/ and /n/, or /f/ and /s/ to the primitive system. At this point the consonant system would have two intersecting features—place of articulation (front versus back) and type of articulation (stop versus continuant). (2) In the vowels, probably a low versus high contrast will appear first, so the next vowel might be a single higher vowel, followed by a front–back contrast, as in /i/ versus /u/. (3) Typically, a contrast of position is followed by a voicing contrast. When voicing becomes significant, we might find both "dada" and "tata" with different meanings. (4) The consonant system will usually be more elaborate at the beginning of words, so that the number of contrasts may be greater there during the course of development. (5) Syllable repetitions, as in the example, usually decrease in the second year, and the length and variety of word-formation patterns increase. (6) Some sequential arrangements, such as consonant clusters (*ts*, *kr*, *pl*), are absent for a long time, even when the component phonemes are present (see Ervin-Tripp in Hoffman & Hoffman 1966).

This has been a description of the child's phonology in its own terms, but most observers are more likely to notice the mapping of the adult's system onto the child's when the child makes substitutions. Thus, in the above system with three phonemes and a *CVCV* syllable repetition pattern, any word acquired by the child must become either "tata" or "baba"—an extreme case to be sure. The most obvious substitution patterns are simple replacements, such as the mapping of both stops (*t, d*) and affricates (*ch, j*) onto stops when there is no stop–affricate contrast. The word formation pattern of the child may require omission of whole syllables or members of clusters. The conversion of "father" into "papa" is predictable for a child who has not yet developed a stop–fricative contrast (between /p/ and /f/), who has a *CVCV* syllable repetition rule, and who selects the adult stressed syllable.

The child with a simplified phonemic system sometimes has a preferred phonetic realization of a given phoneme and sometimes has random or free variation. In the first case, he might always

say [*t*] and never use [*d*] in articulation of "tata." In the latter case, especially common for vowels, he may oscillate unpredictably. A third possibility is that he may use each predictably in a given context. For instance, he may use [*d*] at the beginning of words and [*t*] in the middle to realize a single phoneme (Velten 1943).

Although the number of phonemes in children's systems usually is less than in adults', their substitution rules are not always simple and may baffle parents or teachers unfamiliar with phonemic analysis. For instance, some children have a rule making an initial consonant nasal if there is a nasal consonant anywhere in the adult model word, producing imitations like /ni/ for "green." There may be phonemic contrasts in the child's system which are absent in the adult system. Assimilation is very common in children's word-formation patterns, so that neighboring phonemes or successive syllables may influence each other. Yet all of these are orderly rules. The factors producing these idiosyncratic patterns are as yet unknown.

What makes a child's phonemic system change? Perhaps the presence of numerous homonyms encourages change; yet some children tolerate extensive homonymy when they have a large vocabulary combined with a very simple phonemic system and restricted word-formation rules. Understanding or hearing a phonemic distinction is not a sufficient condition for producing it, although each process evidently facilitates the other. Thus, in adults, acoustic discrimination is much sharper when the listeners have learned a corresponding discrete articulation. The teaching of reading and spelling and the alteration of phonology when children learn to speak second dialects and second languages might be much easier if teachers knew more about phonological development [see PERCEPTION, *article on* SPEECH PERCEPTION].

Grammar

Languages differ considerably in their organization of basic grammatical devices, so it will be necessary to study children's language development in many types of languages to establish well-founded generalizations. For example, in English, the constituent order (e.g., subject–verb–object) has a high degree of regularity; deviations are significant; and the selection of entries in the subject and object position is semantically important. In Russian, on the other hand, there may be much more variability in constituent order, since inflectional suffixes mark the relations indicated by constituent order in English. Children learning both languages show order regularities before they use markers such as inflection or function words consistently, but children learning highly inflected languages have been reported to learn inflections much earlier (Gvozdev 1961).

Simple syntax. From the very beginning of multiword sentences, children usually reveal order regularities in speech. Certain frequent words may occupy fixed positions. For instance, "where," "there," and "this" may always be in antecedent position, and "up," "on," and "off" in last position. Other words and phrases, such as "broken," "blue," "truck," "the truck," "the broken," then could occupy either position in complement to the fixed items. On the basis of position alone, one can identify primitive word classes and usually a nominal phrase also, which can expand one of the complement classes. From the examples it can be seen that these classes are idiosyncratic and do not correspond exactly to adult classes (Bellugi & Brown 1964).

How do primitive classes develop? They cannot be based simply on imitation, since at this stage children's imitations are at least as simple as their own spontaneous speech, and classes appear even if the adult language has variable order (Gvozdev 1961). They reflect order regularities when they exist in adult language, and in part they reflect semantic features of adult classes (Brown 1958). In their idiosyncratic features they clearly reveal creative and analogizing activity by the child and cannot be based on rote learning. The study of the child's interpretation of what he hears may provide the key to this enigma. But as yet there have been no true experiments on grammatical acquisition in the very young. There is disagreement as to the character of "rules" in children's early grammar and as to the relation between the comprehension system and speech.

Inflections and function words. During the period of simple syntax, English-speaking children employ function words like "the" at random, and as their frequency increases such anomalous sentences may appear as "I see the Mary." The order of mastery of both function words and inflections is influenced by their semantic obviousness.

In English, inflectional suffixes such as plurals are randomly present at first, but in highly inflected languages, such as Russian, often a single form is used before the period of random variation. In many languages there are some irregular inflections, such as "go–went," which are preserved because of their high individual frequency. Children do not usually learn these first, as tense contrasts

at least, even though they are frequent. Among English nouns and verbs, the largest variety of verbs have an inflectional suffix, such as "stop–stopped." It is these forms which are productive or generalized to new words by children. These analogies can be highly resistant to adult influence; typically, a form like "foots" can remain in a child's speech for months after he has learned the plural form.

Sometimes alternative inflections depend upon the preceding phoneme; for example, a plural is formed by "-s" in most cases, but by "-es" in some, as in "mats" versus "matches." Children use the most common form first, then both at random, before discovering the phonemic conditioning rule. During the period of random variation one finds forms such as "handses" and "toasteded" (Ervin-Tripp in Hoffman & Hoffman 1966).

Complex syntax. It is a common observation that children's sentences grow longer as they get older. This is a superficial effect of deeper changes. As we have seen, this increase is due in part to the systematic use of function words and suffixes. Some of the constituents which were optional in the simple grammars—such as verbs—may become obligatory in the more complex phrase structure. Potentially infinite expansions of coordinate and subordinate structures appear. These are all changes in the child's syntax itself; in addition, there may be increases in the amount of information a child can include in a given utterance. One might say that programming capacity increases with age.

In the course of these changes, it is not easy to establish criteria for mastery of the adult syntactic rules. Sometimes a given sentence in a child's speech has the appearance of an adult sentence, but it derives from a different syntax. For example, during the early stages in the development of negation, children commonly use "no" or "don't" as simple negativizing words, much like the plural. Later, as inflection of verbs appears, one may find "he doesn't goes." Eventually the child will arrive at the adult rule, which in the negative marks tense and person only in the auxiliary. The intermediate stages of the evolution of the negation rule can be inferred if one has appropriate tests or a sufficiently large text from a child and is willing to make such inferences.

At the age of six, there remain a number of constructions which are still absent in the speech of many children, such as nominalizations of simple verbs (Menyuk 1964). Some of these constructions may be rare in the colloquial speech used to children. Perhaps, on the other hand, they involve inherently more complex rules requiring conceptual maturation.

Children's syntactical rules are always inferred from behavior, but the study of comprehension, imitations, spontaneous speech, or other measures may give different results. Comparison of these varying measures may help in the analysis of such inferred processes. Each makes different demands on knowledge, much as recognition and recall make different demands on memory. Imitation, for example, requires phases of perceptions, storage, retrieval, and speech. At different ages imitations are structurally quite dissimilar. At first they appear to be markedly simplified by the child's speech production rules. Later, restrictions occur in the other phases of the process, but eventually the child can perceive and store even the mistakes which he hears (Ervin-Tripp in Hoffman & Hoffman 1966).

Language functions

Private functions. Vocalizing begins as an autogenous activity, and throughout life there exist varieties of speech in which listeners do not actively mediate the speaker's satisfactions. In babies these may include cooing, babbling, and at first, crying. Vocal play with sounds continues into the phase of organized speech. Babies vocalize when they see objects and when they engage in action, but around four and five such speech appears to have an implicit audience. Such monologues, for instance, decrease in isolation, are inhibited by strangers, and increase when difficulties are encountered (Vygotskii 1934). Eventually speech not only is a product of play but aids in its organization, perhaps being a precursor, as Vygotskii believed, of some aspects of covert thought.

Social functions. Social play—for example, in gestural games—may be at least as significant in the evolution of early language as demands for goods and services. Such play receives social rewards, and even a three-month-old infant may vocalize more if so reinforced. It thus becomes difficult to mark any point when one can say that vocalizing becomes intentional. The rhetorical question, ritual naming of objects, and many other vocal performances in the second year appear to be socially motivated and probably vary markedly according to milieu. True offering of information, addressed to lacunae in the listener's knowledge, demands mature social development, and difficulties can still be found in this function during the school years. Because of the heavy dependence of

these different functions on social milieu, it is particularly difficult to establish any generalizations in the absence of experimental research.

Children's speech changes according to the audience, the function, and the setting. The most extreme adaptation occurs in multilingual children, who by three can usually distinguish their languages appropriately. Yet even within a language there may be formal alternations, as in the suffixes "-in" and "-ing" in English, which mark subtle style shifts in the speech of American children.

In many languages there is a special form of speech used in addressing infants, which may be called baby talk, and involves changes in phonology, vocabulary, and syntax. Children may employ baby talk as a stylistic device depending on the listener or the role during play. In languages such as Japanese there may be many changes in syntax or vocabulary according to the age or status of the listener, and these are acquired by children only gradually during the school years. Optional features of syntax, such as use of qualifiers and subordination, may be affected by audience or function. Conversations with adults or expository speech in the schoolroom may draw on syntactic skills not usually employed in conversations with other children.

Schooling. Schooling may indeed mark the most radical change in language functions encountered by children. In the home and among friends the function and form of speech may be quite different—briefer, situationally imbedded, narrative, repetitive, topically limited, aimed at solidarity or aggression. In school, there is a demand for precision, independence from the speech situation, exposition, novelty, breadth of topics, and transmission of information. The latter functions demand more abstract vocabulary and greater use of grammatical structures that signal analytic differentiations. Written language, since it is private, with neither audience nor situational support, is at the farthest remove from the colloquial practice children bring to school (Vygotskii 1934).

Knowledge of language increases, of course, after early childhood. The everyday vernacular of the peer group, not parents, in the preadolescent years remains as our spontaneous adult speech. We acquire new vocabulary from travel, reading, and the acquisition of skills. Later, as our social relationships become more complex we may come to control a greater range of the structural facilities of the language and its stylistic alternatives for such varied purposes as persuasive, expository, and aesthetic discourse. But these changes usually do not occur in children who lack any secondary education. While it is true that all normal children master the essentials of language before they enter school, variations in the language functions provided by the family and school milieu affect markedly the extent to which children go beyond these essentials.

SUSAN M. ERVIN-TRIPP

[*Directly related are the entries* LEARNING, *article on* VERBAL LEARNING; LINGUISTICS. *Other relevant material may be found in* DEVELOPMENTAL PSYCHOLOGY; HEARING.]

BIBLIOGRAPHY

BELLUGI, URSULA; and BROWN, ROGER W. (editors) 1964 *The Acquisition of Language.* Monographs of the Society for Research in Child Development, Vol. 29, No. 92. Univ. of Chicago Press.

BERKO, JEAN; and BROWN, ROGER W. 1960 Psycholinguistic Research Methods. Pages 517–557 in Paul Mussen (editor), *Handbook of Research Methods in Child Development.* New York: Wiley.

BROWN, ROGER W. 1958 *Words and Things.* Glencoe, Ill.: Free Press.

CARROLL, JOHN B. (1957) 1960 Language Development. Pages 744–752 in *Encyclopedia of Educational Research.* 3d ed. New York: Macmillan.

GVOZDEV, A. N. 1961 *Voprosy izucheniia detskoi rechi* (Problems in the Language Development of the Child). Moscow: Akademiia Pedagogicheskikh Nauk RSFSR.

HOFFMAN, MARTIN L.; and HOFFMAN, LOIS W. (editors) 1966 *Review of Child Development Research.* Volume 2. New York: Russell Sage Foundation. → See especially the article by Susan Ervin-Tripp on "Language Development."

JAKOBSON, ROMAN 1941 *Kindersprache, Aphasie, und allgemeine Lautgesetze.* Uppsala (Sweden): Almqvist & Wiksell.

LEOPOLD, WERNER F. 1939–1949 *Speech Development of a Bilingual Child: A Linguist's Record.* Studies in the Humanities, Nos. 6, 11, 18, 19. Evanston, Ill.: Northwestern Univ. Press.

LEOPOLD, WERNER F. 1952 *Bibliography of Child Language.* Evanston, Ill.: Northwestern Univ. Press.

LEWIS, MORRIS M. (1936) 1952 *Infant Speech: A Study of the Beginnings of Language.* 2d ed., rev. New York: Humanities.

LEWIS, MORRIS M. (1963) 1964 *Language, Thought and Personality in Infancy and Childhood.* New York: Basic Books.

MCCARTHY, DOROTHEA 1954 Language Development in Children. Pages 492–630 in Leonard Carmichael (editor), *Manual of Child Psychology.* 2d ed. New York: Wiley.

MENYUK, PAULA 1964 Syntactic Rules Used by Children From Preschool Through First Grade. *Child Development* 35:533–546.

TEMPLIN, MILDRED 1957 *Certain Language Skills in Children: Their Development and Interrelationships.* Institute of Child Welfare, Monograph No. 26. Minneapolis: Univ. of Minnesota Press.

VELTEN, H. V. 1943 The Growth of Phonemic and Lexical Patterns in Infant Language. *Language* 19:281–292.

VYGOTSKII, LEV S. (1934) 1962 *Thought and Language.* Cambridge, Mass.: M.I.T. Press. → First published as *Myshlenie i rech'.*

III
SPEECH PATHOLOGY

Speech pathology is a branch of communications dealing with disorders of speech and language. Speech pathologists concern themselves with diagnosis, treatment, and prevention of speech and language disorders. Although speech pathology in Europe was once a branch of medicine, today, throughout most of the world, the field has developed as an independent speciality, in somewhat the same fashion that clinical psychology has emerged as an area separate from psychiatry. As is the case with clinical psychology, most training programs in speech pathology in the United States are a part of the graduate program offered by colleges of arts and science. A limited number of training programs are affiliated with colleges of education or colleges of medicine.

Unlike the general field of speech, which is concerned with improving the normal and slightly subnormal, the area of speech pathology focuses on defects of speech and language. Speech is considered to be defective when any one or combination of the following conditions exists: speech is lacking in intelligibility; speech differs so much from normal that it calls undue attention to itself, often with the result that listeners pay more attention to the speech deviations than to what the speaker is saying; speech behavior leads to the development of negative attitudes by the speaker toward his own speech, which in turn often interfere with his over-all adjustment.

Speech and language problems can be described in terms of the acoustic end product perceived by listeners or in terms of the etiology of the problem.

Problems of the acoustic end product

From the standpoint of the acoustic end product, speech and language problems can be considered under five general headings: delayed speech and language, defects of articulation, defects of voice, defects of rhythm, defects of symbolic formulation.

Delayed speech and language. Most normal children are able to speak their first word at approximately age one. Language comprehension and production increase along with articulation ability. By age eight the majority of children have learned to articulate all sounds correctly. Speech pathologists use the term *delayed speech* to describe the speech of children who either do not talk or who perseverate habits and patterns of infantile speech. If there is vocabulary deficiency, inadequate formulation of ideas, or retarded sentence structure, the term *delayed language* may be employed (Matthews 1957a, pp. 394–395). A well-accepted listing of causes is provided by Van Riper (1963) and includes mental retardation, hearing loss, faulty coordination resulting from disease or paralysis, prolonged illness during infancy, lack of motivation for speech, improper teaching methods employed by parents, confused hand preference, necessity for learning two or more languages simultaneously, shock during the speaking act, emotional conflicts, and aphasia.

The treatment of delayed speech depends upon the significant etiological factors. The child with a hearing loss may need a hearing aid. Other causative factors should be removed or lessened. Van Riper describes therapy procedures for delayed speech. In general these procedures attempt to provide a stimulating environment in which the child is "bombarded" by speech and is taught to associate speech sounds with meaningful people and objects.

Defects of articulation. Defects of articulation in general can be divided into four types: substitution, distortion, omission, and addition. Substitution errors consist of the replacement of one sound with another. A common example is the substitution of *w* for *r*, as in "wed" instead of "red," "twuck" for "truck," and "dwink" for "drink." Other common substitution errors are *w* for *l*, as in "weave" for "leave"; *th* for *s*, as in "thick" for "sick"; and *d* for *th*, as in "dis" for "this."

The second type of articulation error involves sound distortion. This can be observed in the *s* sound when it is faultily produced with a whistling component, nasal air escape, or slushiness. Distortions in the pronounciation of the English *r* are often produced by speakers who have learned English as a second language.

The omission type of articulation error is illustrated by the individual who omits the *r* sound and says "ed abbit" instead of "red rabbit."

The addition type of articulation error is seen in the inclusion of an *r* sound where it is not called for, as in "idear" for "idea."

Articulatory disorders are sometimes classified as functional or organic in terms of possible causal factors. Matthews (1957b) has summarized the literature relating mental retardation and articulation disorders. A frequent cause of articulation disorders is faulty training resulting from inadequate speech environment. If a child's speech model is defective, he is likely to learn defective

speech. (A detailed discussion of etiological factors in functional articulation disorders can be found in Van Riper 1963; Johnson et al. 1948; and Berry & Eisenson 1956.)

Although the majority of articulatory disorders are of functional origin, there are organic factors that can adversely affect articulation. West and his associates (1937) discuss in detail articulation disorders resulting from lesions of the central nervous system. Cleft palate, dental anomalies, structural disorders of the peripheral speech organs, and hearing loss can cause articulation disorders.

Where a structural abnormality contributes to an articulation disorder, the organic defect may need correction prior to speech therapy. Sometimes speech therapy may proceed in conjunction with the correction of the organic disorder. Often, complete correction of the structural anomaly is not possible but speech therapy may prove to be beneficial.

The correction of articulatory errors requires teaching the production and habitual use of sounds. As a rule the sound is taught first in isolation, then in combination with other sounds, and finally in words, sentences, and conversation. Milisen describes a variety of approaches to articulation therapy (Milisen et al. 1954).

Defects of voice. Defects of voice can include complete absence of voice as well as problems of pitch, volume, and quality. Voice may be lacking because of total or partial paralysis or removal of the vocal folds, or the vocal structures may be normal and the absence of voice may be a reflection of a hysterical condition.

Pitch may be inappropriate for the age and sex of the speaker. This would be illustrated by a male talking in an extremely high-pitched voice or a female talking with low pitch. Monotone consists of a sameness of pitch. The failure to vary pitch can not only result in a speech pattern that is dull and uninteresting to listen to; it can also interfere with speech intelligibility, inasmuch as certain aspects of meaning are conveyed by means of variations in pitch.

Just as pitch may be inappropriate, it is possible that volume, also, may be inappropriate. Volume may be so weak that it is difficult for listeners to hear what is being said, or it may be so loud that listeners experience a certain amount of discomfort. Normal speakers do not use exactly the same volume from beginning to end of a message. Just as there are normal variations in pitch, so there are normal variations in volume. The absence of these variations in volume would be considered a type of voice disorder.

The third general type of voice disorder consists of defects in quality. These defects are difficult to describe and should be heard to be fully appreciated. Defects of voice quality sometimes are labeled with such terms as "nasal," "hoarse," "husky," "breathy," "harsh," etc. The quality is considered defective when it is not only unpleasant to listen to but seriously detracts a listener's attention from the message of the speaker.

As is the case with articulatory disorders, there are both functional and organic causes of voice disorder. Imitation of poor speech models, psychological maladjustments, adolescent voice change, poor breathing habits, as well as laryngeal pathology, paralysis, and adenoidal obstructions, appear as causes of voice disorders.

In the case of any type of laryngeal pathology, voice therapy should not be attempted until a medical evaluation and laryngeal examination have been completed. Voice training often includes auditory training, to make the client aware of the differences, in both sound and "feel," between proper and improper use of the voice. Where the voice problem is related to emotional disturbances of any kind, psychological help may be necessary. In those instances where the vocal mechanism has been removed, the client may use an electrical or mechanical vibrator as a substitute for vocal-fold vibration or the client may learn esophageal speech, a technique that involves using air expelled from the esophageal tract as a source of sound vibration.

Defects of rhythm. Defects of rhythm can be described as repetitions, prolongations, or hesitations. Individual sounds, words, or phrases may be involved. Frequently the disruption in rhythm may be accompanied by facial grimaces, tics, or other bodily movements, which in time can become an intimate part of the disruptions of rhythm. Very frequently the disruptions in rhythm and the accompanying grimaces carry with them considerable fear and many negative attitudes on the part of the speaker. The speaker's fear that he will have problems with his speech often contributes to additional difficulties with speech rhythm.

Stuttering. More has been written on the topic of stuttering than on any other single disorder of speech. Matthews (1957*a*), in a brief summary of theories of stuttering, cites representatives of three broad theoretical viewpoints: (1) dysphemic theories, which suggest that stuttering is related to constitutional abnormality; (2) personality theories, which hold that stuttering is related to psychological maladjustment; and (3) developmental theories, which suggest that stuttering develops largely as the result of environmental conditions. Therapy approaches are influenced by the thera-

pist's theory concerning the etiology of stuttering. Those who view stuttering in terms of a general neurosis will employ some form of psychotherapy. A therapist who sees stuttering as the result of lack of cerebral dominance will seek ways of establishing a dominant gradient of excitation in the central nervous system. Environmental modification is the goal of many therapists, regardless of the theory of causation of stuttering they subscribe to. Van Riper (1963) not only summarizes much of the literature on etiology and treatment of stuttering but also outlines in detail a therapy approach widely employed in the United States. His therapy seeks to help the stutterer stop reinforcing his stuttering. An important aspect of this therapy consists of eliminating the stutterer's avoidance of feared situations and words.

Defects of symbolic formulation. The defects of symbolic formulation may be of both an expressive and a receptive type. Although defects of symbolic formulation are often categorized as either expressive aphasia or receptive aphasia, in actuality most patients who have difficulty with symbolic formulation have some difficulties in both the expressive and the receptive realm. Individuals with receptive aphasia may be able to hear a speaker say the word "chair" but will not be able to translate the sounds in this word into the concept of a piece of furniture on which a person may sit; they may be able to see and to recognize each of the five letters used in writing the word "chair" but be unable to translate the written letters into the concept of chair. The individual with an expressive type of aphasia may know what a chair is and be able to pronounce all of the sounds in the word "chair" but be unable to put these sounds together so they become a recognizable symbol of the concept "chair."

The treatment of aphasia involves re-education and retraining, which utilizes the past speech background of the patient as much as possible. A detailed discussion of therapy for aphasics can be found in Wepman (1951).

Negative attitudes and frustrations. Often the individual with a speech problem is handicapped by more than just the acoustic end product of his speech. Frequently the speaker's attitude toward his speech constitutes one of his most serious problems. In some instances the speaker may actually talk with a fairly high degree of intelligibility. However, if the speaker's attitude toward his own speech is apprehensive and fearful, he may experience a handicap far beyond what would normally result from the faulty articulation or faulty voice quality alone.

A speech problem not only can interfere with

defective communication in social development but also can lead to the frustration of not being able to make oneself understood and of constantly being made to feel different. Such feelings of frustration, difference, and inferiority can lead to personality problems and attitudes which may be more serious than the original speech problem itself. For this reason, speech pathologists must be interested in the total adjustment of the person who has a speech problem.

Etiology and therapy

If speech problems are examined from the standpoint of etiology, they can be categorized as organic or functional. In actuality it is extremely difficult to fit all speech problems neatly into one or the other of these two broad classifications. The two classifications are presented because they frequently appear in the literature.

Organic and functional factors. Speech problems arising from primarily organic causes would include speech associated with cleft palate, cerebral palsy, dental abnormalities, brain damage, hearing loss, or any other type of anatomical or neurological involvement affecting any of the mechanisms used in speech production.

Etiological factors of a nonorganic type would include lack of stimulation to speak, withdrawal tendencies associated with emotional disturbance, failure to have available good models of speech for imitation, mental retardation, faulty learning, etc. The organic and functional aspects frequently are intertwined. This can be seen in the individual who is aphasic because of brain damage. Because of his aphasia, he experiences considerable frustration. This frustration in turn leads to withdrawal behavior. Frustration and withdrawal behavior contribute to further deterioration of speech. Frequently it becomes difficult to separate the components of the speech problem that are of organic causation from those that represent some sort of functional overlay.

Therapy. The speech pathologist initiates therapy after a thorough diagnosis has been performed. This diagnosis often must include a medical examination, psychological assessment, and determination of hearing acuity. Dental and social-work information are often necessary before an adequate diagnosis can be made. Wherever possible, causative factors are removed or minimized. In the case of cleft palate, for example, surgical or dental procedures may be necessary to provide a mechanism adequate for speech production. In some instances it may be impossible to provide a mechanism that is completely normal. Under these circumstances methods must be found to compensate for the structural inadequacies. In the case of a severe hearing loss, it may be possible to provide sound amplification in the form of a hearing aid.

Articulatory disorders constitute the largest group of speech problems encountered in children. The majority of articulatory problems are not caused by anatomical, neurological, or other organic factors. Most articulatory problems can be traced to lack of stimulation, poor speech models, faulty learning, and other factors quite far removed from defects of the oral structures. An early step in treatment consists of describing adequately the nature of the speech deviation. The speech pathologist helps the individual with the speech problem to understand the detailed nature of the problem. In some cases this consists of the speech pathologist's helping a client become more aware of his speech errors. A client must learn to distinguish between the correct and incorrect speech productions. A wide variety of procedures will be employed to help the client articulate a sound correctly, to eliminate an undesirable component in voice quality, to produce a pitch level more appropriate to the age and sex of the client, etc. Frequently a client learns to make correct speech productions in isolated sounds or words but finds it difficult to carry over these new patterns into everyday speaking situations. Frequently the newly acquired speech skills result in a pattern of speech that sounds strange to the client. The speech pathologist often spends considerable time helping the client understand his feelings toward his speech problem, as well as his feelings toward the new speech patterns which he acquires. Often the attitude of a parent toward a child and toward the child's speech is a contributing factor. For this reason, speech pathologists frequently spend a good deal of their time in parent-counseling activities.

Because some voice disorders are associated with organic pathology, the speech pathologist may carry out some of his treatment procedures in cooperation with an otolaryngologist. Such collaborative therapy activities may be carried out with psychiatrists, clinical psychologists, plastic surgeons, and dentists, as well as classroom teachers. The speech pathologist cannot limit himself to a consideration of the mechanical aspects of sound production. His interest must be in the person with a speech problem. The modern practice of speech pathology makes comparatively little use of the tongue, lip, and jaw exercises that were prevalent in the field a decade ago.

Training in speech pathology. Standards for the training of speech pathologists have been established by the American Speech and Hearing Association. The association awards a certificate

of clinical competence to individuals who successfully complete the requirements for a master's degree in the field of speech pathology. This graduate
program includes didactic classroom instruction,
supervised clinic practice, and four years of successful practice, under supervision, in an environment where speech and language problems are
diagnosed and treated. Graduate training programs
in speech pathology in the United States are accredited by the American Board of Examiners in
Speech Pathology and Audiology of the American
Speech and Hearing Association. The association
is a clearinghouse for information regarding clinical facilities, training institutions, and other data
relative to the field of speech pathology.

JACK MATTHEWS

[*See also* MENTAL DISORDERS, *article on* ORGANIC AS-
PECTS. *Other relevant material may be found in*
HEARING; LANGUAGE, *article on* LANGUAGE DEVEL-
OPMENT; MENTAL RETARDATION; PERCEPTION, *article
on* SPEECH PERCEPTION.]

BIBLIOGRAPHY

BERRY, MILDRED F.; and EISENSON, JON 1956 *Speech
Disorders.* New York: Appleton.
JOHNSON, WENDELL et al. (1948) 1956 *Speech Handicapped School Children.* Rev. ed. New York: Harper.
MATTHEWS, JACK 1957a Speech Defects. Pages 391–424
in Chauncey M. Louttit (editor), *Clinical Psychology
of Exceptional Children.* 3d ed. New York: Harper.
→ First published in 1936.
MATTHEWS, JACK 1957b Speech Problems of the Men-
tally Retarded. Pages 531–551 in Lee E. Travis (edi-
tor), *Handbook of Speech Pathology.* New York:
Appleton.
MILISEN, ROBERT et al. 1954 The Disorder of Articula-
tion: A Systematic Clinical and Experimental Ap-
proach. *Journal of Speech and Hearing Disorders
Monograph Supplements,* No. 4.
VAN RIPER, CHARLES 1963 *Speech Correction Principles
and Methods.* 4th ed. Englewood Cliffs, N.J.: Prentice-
Hall. → First published in 1939.
WEPMAN, JOSEPH M. 1951 *Recovery From Aphasia.*
New York: Ronald Press.
WEST, ROBERT W.; ANSBERRY, MERLE; and CARR, ANNA
(1937) 1957 *The Rehabilitation of Speech.* 3d ed.
New York: Harper.

IV
LANGUAGE AND CULTURE

The key role of language in all human activities
has made it perhaps inevitable that the field of linguistics should represent a mingling of several
streams of interest. Modern linguistics has arisen
from the philological tradition, concerned basically
with the classical and modern written languages,
and from the anthropological tradition, which has
been concerned largely with preliterate peoples. The anthropologist has long recognized the

importance of language, not only as a tool for
more effective field work, but as a critical element
of the cultural fabric which he studies. Thus we
sometimes refer to "anthropological linguistics,"
which may be defined as the study of previously
unknown speech varieties in the context of their
cultures; the term contrasts the anthropological approach to language with philological, psychological,
or philosophical approaches. Alternatively, we may
wish to speak of "linguistic anthropology," focusing attention on language as one element of human
culture; the term is analogous to "social anthropology," "economic anthropology," and the like. The
older term "ethnolinguistics" may well be used to
refer to the same area of interest.

All writers in this field have struggled with the
expressions "language *and* culture" versus "language *in* culture," both of which are in common
use as titles for university courses, scholarly symposia, etc. "Language and culture" seeems to imply
a dichotomy, which we must then reject in the
light of our position that language is *part* of culture. But if we speak of "language in culture," we
then lack a separate name for all the other cultural
areas whose relationship to language we wish to
study. Perhaps the best solution is to give formal
recognition to what has most often been done in
practice and to use the word "culture" in two ways,
on two different levels of a semantic hierarchy.
Distinguishing these meanings by subscript numerals, $culture_1$, on the higher level of generality,
constitutes learned patterns of human habitual behavior. Language is included along with everything
else that contrasts with instinctive behavior. $Cul-
ture_2$, on a more specific level, is that part of
"$culture_1$," which is *not* verbal communication; in
this sense, "culture" contrasts with "language." In
most cases, the context of discussion will make it
clear whether we are referring to "$culture_1$," or
"$culture_2$," just as context normally eliminates confusion between "man_1" (opposed to "animal") and
"man_2" (opposed to "woman").

Taking the view that language is part of culture,
linguistic anthropologists have been concerned with
these basic questions: In what respects does language fit into the general conception of cultural
systems, and in what ways is it distinguished from
other components? What similarities are there between the internal structures of language and of
other branches of culture? What role does language play in the over-all functioning of culture?
In what way do language and culture reflect each
other's structure at a given point in time or influence each other over the span of history? What
techniques may we use to infer linguistic from

nonlinguistic behavior, or vice versa, either in terms of predicting the future or of reconstructing the past? At this moment, most of these questions still lack definitive answers; the rapid growth of ethnolinguistics, however, suggests that the near future will bring, if not answers to all questions, at least a more unified framework for discussion.

The cultural nature of language. Language is assured a position as a branch of culture by its distinctively patterned nature, by its restriction to the human species, and above all because languages are learned, not transmitted genetically. In spite of the fact that race and language frequently have a historical connection—so that many people who share ancestors also share a common language—such connections are in no way necessary. The nongenetic transmission of languages is vividly demonstrated by the linguistic "melting pot" of the United States, in which people of the most diverse racial backgrounds share common standards of English usage. However, the fact that individual languages are transmitted culturally, not genetically, does not rule out the possibility that mankind has certain unique inborn capacities for linguistic behavior. For some purposes, we may distinguish between *language*, an inherited set of capabilities, and *languages*, particular structures which are built on those capabilities by culture.

The distinctiveness of language. Language obviously stands apart from other communication systems used by humans or animals because of the magnitude of its resources. It is especially impressive to consider that every normal child, by the age of four or five, is capable of using the language of his community to produce a literally infinite number of meaningful utterances. We are far from understanding all of the characteristics of language or of the human nervous system which make this possible. Two things, however, are clearly important—man's ability to invent *symbols* and the *duality of patterning* in linguistic structure.

If we understand a *sign* to be anything from which the existence of something else may be inferred, then we may define a symbol as a special kind of sign—one with arbitrary, conventionally assigned meaning. Thus, black clouds are a sign of rain, the relationship being intrinsic; but a particular weather flag, as a conventional sign of rain, is a symbol. By the same token, the word "rain" is a symbol; our use of this particular word is conventional and subject to change. Other animals may learn to respond to many arbitrary signals, including words of human language, but it is uniquely human to have the ability to assign arbitrary meaning to signs, i.e., to *invent* symbols.

But language goes beyond other symbolic systems, such as those of gestures, in one very specific feature—the duality of patterning. The meaningful symbols of language—such as words and meaningful parts of words, called *morphemes*—are not indivisible, like a flag or a gesture, but are themselves built up of smaller units. These smaller units are the *phonemes* or sound units of spoken language, and they are meaningless in themselves. Every language uses a small number of these meaningless units—usually less than fifty—to build up a huge number of meaningful units. It is this two-level structuring which gives language a degree of efficiency that is qualitatively superior to, not merely quantitatively different from, other communication systems.

Similarities between language and culture. The identification of such building blocks of language as the phoneme and the morpheme has given linguistics great prestige among the branches of anthropology; it is sometimes said that linguists are the only social scientists to have identified the basic units of their subject matter. The method used in this process of identification is one which moves from the level of observation to the level of structure. First, raw data are classified in terms of a universal taxonomic grid; in studying sound systems, this is the phonetic classification. Then the investigator finds that some phonetic differences, in particular languages, are not associated with contrastive meaning; e.g., the meaning of the Spanish *día* ("day") is the same whether the initial *d* is pronounced as an occlusive (completely blocking the flow of air with the tongue and then releasing it), or as a fricative (letting air issue continuously between the tongue and the teeth). In every language, however, the linguist also finds that some phonetic differences *are* correlated with differences of meaning; e.g., the difference between occlusive and fricative, although nonsignificant in Spanish, is contrastive in English, serving to distinguish "day" from "they." The result of such observations is the replacement of phonetic classifications by phonemic classifications, unique for each language. The phoneme is defined simultaneously by the range of noncontrastive sound differences which it subsumes and by the contrasts which it displays with the other phonemes of the system.

This method of qualitative contrast, first applied in phonological study, has been successfully extended to the identification of morphemes, i.e., grammatical units; and many scholars have speculated about their applicability to other areas of culture. The terms *etic* and *emic* have been coined (after "phonetic" and "phonemic") to refer to the observational and structural levels, respectively, which might be distinguished in such areas as kinship, religion, music, art, and folklore. Such studies are still in their infancy, but they constitute one of the most interesting frontiers of anthropology, based as they are on the assumption that each branch of culture, or indeed culture as a whole, is, like language, an *internally cohesive* system.

The role of language in culture. Language is not merely one of several aspects of culture: it is, at the very least, *prima inter pares*, in that it makes possible the development, the elaboration, the transmission, and (particularly in its written form) the accumulation of culture as a whole. One can imagine handicrafts being taught by one generation to the next without the use of language; but social, legal, religious, political, or economic institutions are another matter. It is hard to imagine that a community of deaf-mutes (if they were deprived of such speech surrogates as writing) could carry on human social life.

But how, exactly, does language (or any other symbolic system) relate to experience? It is commonly said that symbols, like signs in general, "stand for" or "mean" something else. The definition of *meaning* itself clearly cannot be taken for granted. A variety of theoretical models for the concept of meaning, each one valuable for its own ends, has been proposed by philosophers, psychologists, and linguists of various persuasions. The model presented below is not intended to compete with others in defining the "real" nature of meaning, but it may be useful as a framework for ethnolinguistic discussion.

Structural linguists have customarily been extremely cautious in semantic matters, sometimes attempting to exclude them from linguistics altogether. Until very recently, a strictly behaviorist conception of meaning was much in vogue:

We have defined the *meaning* of a linguistic form as the situation in which the speaker utters it and the response which it calls forth in the hearer. . . . The situations which prompt people to utter speech include every object and happening in their universe. In order to give a scientifically accurate definition of meaning for every form of a language, we should have to have a scientifically accurate knowledge of everything in the speaker's world. . . . We can define the names of minerals, for example, in terms of chemistry and mineralogy, as when we say that the ordinary meaning of the English word *salt* is "sodium chloride (NaCl)," . . . but we have no precise way of defining words like *love* or *hate*, which concern situations that have not been accurately classified. . . . (Bloomfield [1933] 1951, p. 139)

These statements seem to imply a model of linguistic function with just two parts—on the one hand, the linguistic form, and on the other hand, the associated nonlinguistic events (and, presumably, contextual linguistic events as well). Thus the definition of the word "salt" would be, at least in part, the actual substance NaCl. But Bloomfield seems to ignore the essentially arbitrary association between the word "salt" and the substance NaCl, in that his model has no place for the human individuals or the human cultures which have chosen this particular linguistic form.

A more satisfactory model was provided some two thousand years ago by the Hindu philosopher Patañjali: "Concentrate separately on the word, the meaning, and the object, which are mixed up in common usage"—which a modern commentator explicates with this example—"When we utter the word 'elephant,' we find that the word, the meaning and the object are mixed up; the word lives in air, the meaning lives in mind, the elephant lives by itself" (Patañjali, *Aphorism* . . .). It is indeed true that the word "lives in the air," in the sense that it is transmitted as vibrations of air molecules. It is equally true that the actual elephant "lives by itself," i.e., exists independently of all human conventions of nomenclature. The only way that these two isolates are related, then, is through the human mind; and we may define meaning not as a "thing," but rather as the *relationship* which associates word and object.

This three-part model is more adequate than Bloomfield's but still does not clarify the relation of language and culture. In order to do so, we may expand the model still further. First, a division may be made between the observational, or etic, universe, to which "word" and "object" belong, and the structural, or emic, universe, within the human mind. Second, we may distinguish linguistic behavior from its subject matter or content (though

Figure 1 — The relation of language to culture

the subject matter may itself, as a special case, be linguistic behavior, as when linguists talk about language). The two dichotomies then intersect as shown in Figure 1.

In this figure, the arrows marked *a, b,* and *c* indicate relationships of importance to the ethnolinguist. Arrow *a* is the relationship which concerns him when he functions purely as a linguist: it may be thought of inductively, in terms of the process by which the investigator sets up a structure to account for his raw behavioral data, or deductively, as the process by which psychological patterns of linguistic competence give rise to observable linguistic performance. Arrow *b* is the analogous relationship that is investigated by the ethnographer: the actual objects and events which concern a particular human group are here linked, by induction or by deduction, to subjective patterns of organization. Finally, the set of arrows marked *c* represents the relationships to which we assign the term "meaning"; this is conceived of not as a direct connection between the utterance "elephant" and the flesh-and-blood *Elephas maximus*, but rather as a connection mediated by "elephant" as an item of the English lexicon and by "the elephant" as an item in the cultural inventory of English speakers.

There are two types of structural units which are linked by the relationships of meaning. The relevant linguistic units are not phonemes or morphemes, but units of a higher level, which are called *lexemes:* these are the minimum units which participate in arbitrary relationships of meaning. Thus, single morphemes like "green" and "house" are lexemes, but so also is the two-morpheme combination "greenhouse" (as opposed to "green house"), since it arbitrarily designates a particular kind of structure. There is still little agreement about structural units of cultural behavior; insofar as they can be identified, they are often called *sememes.* To be sure, there is not always a one-to-one correspondence between lexemes and sememes; people sometimes show culturally determined differences in behavior where their language provides no lexemic differentiation. However, the general regularity of lexeme–sememe correspondences reflects the close integration between language and the rest of culture, and it is in this way that language may be regarded as a key to culture as a whole.

Ethnosemantics. The study of vocabulary as a guide to the way in which members of a culture divide up their universe has received increasing attention, and the relativity of cultural classifications is emphasized with every new empirical study. Thus, where English vocabulary reflects its users' approach to spatial orientation with the four-way classification "north, south, east, west," the Indian languages of northwestern California reflect the functionally similar but incommensurable division "upriver, downriver, toward the river, away from the river." Anthropologists have begun to pay close attention to such lexemic systems, understanding that they reflect an emic view of the culture being studied, a view uncontaminated by the varying etic frameworks of outside observers. Various terms have been used to identify this study, such as "ethnoscience," "folk taxonomy," "structural semantics," and "ethnosemantics."

A further development in ethnographic semantics is generally known as "componential analysis." This method tries to answer the question, Given a particular set of taxonomic terms used by members of a culture, what are the criteria for applying the individual terms? Taking an example from kinship terminology, if some male collateral kin in generations above ego's are called "uncle" and some are called "cousin," what does one need to know in order to label a particular kinsman correctly? Attempts to answer such questions have resulted in the idea that terms may be conceived of as bundles of simultaneously occurring semantic components. Thus the term "uncle" is applied when the features of "maleness," "ascending generation," and "colineality" are simultaneously present. (A "colineal" in this case is a nonlineal kinsman all of whose ancestors are included in the ancestors of ego.) The term "cousin" is applied in a larger number of cases, but they include those where the features of "maleness," "ascending generation," and "ablineality" are simultaneously present. (An "ablineal" is a consanguineal kinsman who is neither a lineal nor a colineal.) This type of analysis, as applied to kin terms, results in definitions which are both more concise and more exact than the extensional definitions given in traditional ethnographies. Application of componential analysis to areas other than kinship holds great promise.

Language and world view. In addition to correspondences between vocabulary and cultural inventory, a much more controversial type of correlation between language and culture has been proposed. This involves, on one side, whole grammatical systems or subsystems, and, on the other side, whole philosophies or ways of life held to be characteristic of particular cultures (though often not brought to the level of conscious formulation). The interest of anthropologists was drawn to such correlations by Edward Sapir, who not only recognized a linguistic relativity, covarying with cultural relativity, but also postulated a linguistic determinism operating on culture:

Human beings do not live in the objective world alone, nor alone in the world of social activity as ordinarily understood, but are very much at the mercy of the particular language which has become the medium of expression for their society. . . . The fact of the matter is that the "real world" is to a large extent unconsciously built up on the language habits of the group. No two languages are ever sufficiently similar to be considered as representing the same social reality. The worlds in which different societies live are distinct worlds, not merely the same world with different labels attached.   (Sapir [1910–1944] 1949, p. 162)

Benjamin Lee Whorf, a student of Sapir, continued the exploration of the matter, although with less emphasis on the tyranny of language over culture. His position has become known as the "Whorfian hypothesis," which holds that "language patterns [and] cultural norms . . . have grown up together, constantly influencing each other. But in this partnership the nature of the language is the factor that limits free plasticity and rigidifies channels of development in the more autocratic way" (Whorf [1927–1941] 1956, p. 156). The deterministic role of language is easy to understand when we consider how much of culture is transmitted through the linguistic medium. However, the Whorfian hypothesis is easier to accept intuitively than to prove in a rigorous way; in particular, no correlations can be traced between language and world view until specific world views are themselves defined in terms of observable behavior. Whorf shows that Hopi linguistic structure is compatible with a world view involving a peculiar relation between subjective and objective experience; but he tends to assume, rather than to demonstrate, that the Hopi actually hold such a view of the world. Pending the outcome of extensive, strictly controlled, cross-cultural testing of the Whorfian hypothesis, we may limit our acceptance to the following modified formulation: "Insofar as languages differ in the ways they encode objective experience, language users tend to sort out and distinguish experiences differently according to the categories provided by their respective languages. These cognitions will tend to have certain effects on behavior" (Carroll 1963, p. 12).

Language and society.   While the studies mentioned above have regarded each language as a unified whole, another type of research has focused attention on the variation that exists within languages or within multilingual speech communities. Such variation, apart from that associated with geographical dialects or with the idiosyncrasies of individuals, is commonly found to be correlated with one or more socially defined factors, such as the social identity of the speaker, the addressee, or the person referred to, and the social context in which communication takes place. Study of the covariance between linguistic diversity and social structure thus constitutes the new field of sociolinguistics. The findings of this field are applicable, from the synchronic viewpoint, to the diagnosis and analysis of social encounters, and, from the diachronic viewpoint, to examination of the ways in which linguistic patterns and social systems each change under the influence of the other.

WILLIAM BRIGHT

[Directly related are the entries COGNITIVE THEORY; COMPONENTIAL ANALYSIS; LINGUISTICS; SEMANTICS AND SEMIOTICS; and the biographies of BLOOMFIELD; SAPIR; SAUSSURE; WHORF.]

BIBLIOGRAPHY

The most valuable reference that can be given for linguistic anthropology is Hymes 1964, *which contains not only a rich selection of papers in the field but also very extensive bibliographies.*

BLOOMFIELD, LEONARD   (1933) 1951 *Language.* Rev. ed. New York: Holt.

CARROLL, JOHN B. 1963 Linguistic Relativity, Contrastive Linguistics, and Language Learning. *IRAL: International Review of Applied Linguistics* 1:1–20.

DIEBOLD, A. RICHARD JR. 1964 [Review of] Sol Saporta (editor), *Psycholinguistics. Language* 40:197–260. → An extensive review of the whole field of psycholinguistics, including many matters of interest to linguistic anthropology.

HAMMEL, EUGENE A. (editor) 1965 Formal Semantic Analysis. *American Anthropologist* New Series 67, no. 5, part 2 (Special publication).

HYMES, DELL H. (editor) 1964 *Language in Culture and Society: Reader in Linguistics and Anthropology.* New York: Harper.

NIDA, EUGENE A. 1964 *Toward a Science of Translating.* Leiden (Netherlands): Brill. → Chapter 5, "Referential and Emotive Meanings," summarizes recent work in ethnosemantics.

PATAÑJALI *Aphorisms of Yoga.* Translated into English with a commentary by Shree Purohit Swāmi. London: Faber, 1938.

ROMNEY, A. KIMBALL; and D'ANDRADE, ROY GOODWIN (editors) 1964 Transcultural Studies in Cognition. *American Anthropologist* New Series 66, no. 3, part 2 (Special publication). → Contains contributions by linguists, anthropologists, and psychologists to problems of ethnosemantics.

SAPIR, EDWARD A. (1910–1944) 1949 *Selected Writings in Language, Culture, and Personality.* Edited by David G. Mandelbaum. Berkeley: Univ. of California Press.

WHORF, BENJAMIN L. (1927–1941) 1956 *Language, Thought and Reality.* Edited by John B. Carroll. Cambridge, Mass.: M.I.T. Press.

LAPLACE, PIERRE SIMON DE

Pierre Simon de Laplace (1749–1827), renowned French mathematician, was born in Beaumont-en-Auge, a village 4 miles west of Pont l'Évêque in Normandy. He was the second of two children of Pierre de Laplace, a syndic of the parish, who owned and farmed a small estate. When Laplace arrived in Paris, barely twenty years old, he had finished his studies and begun his own research. His ability soon impressed d'Alembert, whose disciple he was to become. D'Alembert's patronage secured Laplace a position as a teacher at the École Royale Militaire, where he remained until changes in the organization brought his teaching there to an end. In 1783 he became an artillery inspector (Duveen & Hahn 1957), and in this capacity he made the acquaintance of the young Bonaparte. A mutual respect developed, and from then on Laplace enjoyed Bonaparte's increasingly powerful support. The two became colleagues at the Académie des Sciences; as first consul, Napoleon appointed Laplace minister of the interior, a position he gave up shortly afterward to become chancellor of the Sénat Conservateur. In 1814, however, he turned against Napoleon; he was eventually made a marquis by Louis XVIII, a surprising but not uncommon turn of events in those troubled times.

Laplace achieved distinction not only in mathematics; it was his literary style that won him election to the Académie Française in 1816. His famous sentence on the hidden determinism of natural laws is a good example of his style:

If there were an intelligence that for a given instant could comprehend all the forces that animate nature and the condition of each being that composes it; if, moreover, this intelligence were sufficiently great to submit these data to analysis, it would create a single formula that would embrace both the movements of the vastest bodies of the universe and those of the smallest atoms: to this intelligence nothing would be uncertain, and the future, as the past, would be present to its eyes. ([1814] 1951, p. 4)

Although Laplace's work has literary elegance, his demonstrations are not always rigorous; often they are even obscure. He frequently wrote "it is clear that . . ." in place of long and difficult calculations.

Laplace presided over the famous Société d'Arcueil, one of the informal scientific societies that flourished in the nineteenth century. It took its name from Laplace's estate, where he and the great chemist Claude Louis Berthollet periodically received their students to discuss scientific questions in an informal atmosphere.

Although our primary concern here is with Laplace's contributions to probability and statistics, it is worth noting that the full scope of his work includes physics (the theory of capillary phenomena, the exact formula for the speed of sound), pure mathematics, and celestial mechanics (he was dubbed a "second Newton"). In probability and its applications Laplace systematized and further extended the scattered researches of his predecessors, bringing the subject to full flower in the third edition (1820) of his great treatise, *Théorie analytique des probabilités* (1812). This is why Todhunter wrote: "On the whole, the Theory of Probability is more indebted to him than to any other mathematician" ([1865] 1949, p. 464).

Laplace was not content to make important discoveries; he also thought it necessary to communicate them to a wide public. To this end he wrote two popular works addressed to the intelligent and educated general reader, *Exposition du système du monde* (1796) and *Essai philosophique sur les probabilités* (1814). Other French mathematicians have continued this practice; thus, Émile Borel thought it useful to write an analogous work, *Le hasard* (1914), which took into consideration the progress made since Laplace.

Generating functions and characteristic functions. Motivated by problems arising, for instance, in the mathematical treatment of games of chance, Laplace, in the epochal *Mémoire sur les suites* (1782), developed the general theory of a powerful power-series technique for solving finite-difference equations, or recurrence relations, which he termed the "method of generating functions" (*calcul des fonctions génératrices; ibid.*, p. 1). In Book 1, Part 1, of his *Théorie analytique des probabilités* (1812) he reproduced this *Mémoire* almost entirely, and in Book 2 he made repeated use of generating functions in solving a great variety of probability problems arising in the mathematical treatment of games of chance. The probability-generating function of a random variable, X—that is, the mean (or expected) value of t^x, where t is a "dummy" real variable—had already been used (without being named) by De Moivre, in studies of games of chance (1730, pp. 191–197; [1718] 1756, pp. 41–43), and by Simpson and Lagrange, in their studies of the distribution of the arithmetic mean of independent observations under various laws of error (Simpson 1756; 1757; Lagrange 1770–1773). However, it is Laplace's extensive discussion of generating functions (1782) and the applications of them in his *Théorie analytique des probabilités* that is the actual source of their widespread use in probability theory, combinatory analysis, and the solution of finite-difference equations and recurrence formulas (see David & Barton 1962; Feller 1950; Fréchet 1940–1943; Jordan 1939; Riordan 1958; Uspensky 1937). The invention of the characteristic function (*fonction caractéristique*) of the distribution of a random variable X (that is, the expected value of e^{itx}, where $i = \sqrt{-1}$) and the associated inversion formula for deducing the distribution function of a random variable from its characteristic function are often attributed to later writers, such as A. L. Cauchy, 1789–1857, and Henri Poincaré, 1854–1912. Laplace, however, introduced this very same (characteristic) function, without assigning it a name, and gave the associated inversion formula for the case of a discrete random variable, in article 21 of Book 1 of his *Théorie analytique des probabilités* (it also appears in *Oeuvres complètes*, vol. 7, pp. 83–84) and then employed such functions systematically in Book 2, Chapter 4 (cf. Molina 1930, arts. 3–4). The technical advantages possessed by the characteristic function permit simplification of many manipulations and proofs, although when X takes only integral values the generating function is usually adequate. [*See* PROBABILITY, *article on* FORMAL PROBABILITY.]

Bayesian inference. Laplace was apparently the first to have stated in a general form what is now called Bayes' theorem (*Théorie analytique* [1812] 1820, book 2, art. 1; Molina 1930, appendix I). Several scholars have deprecated Laplace's originality in this area of "probability of causes," or Bayesian inference. [*See* BAYESIAN INFERENCE *for a discussion of the probability of causes.*] But Laplace did introduce an essential innovation here. Bayes had considered only the case where the a priori probabilities are equal (as an evident hypothesis when one is ignorant of these probabilities); Laplace extended Bayes' theorem to cover the general case where these a priori probabilities are not necessarily equal. What has generally not been stressed enough is that Bayes' theorem—whether generalized or not—is really only an interpretation of a standard relationship for conditional probabilities. [*See* PROBABILITY, *article on* FORMAL PROBABILITY.] It is the interpretation of the formula itself that is important here. A discussion by Molina (1930) clearly establishes Laplace's position and demonstrates previous misunderstandings of it.

Normal distribution. Laplace should have the major credit for discovering and demonstrating the central role of the normal distribution in the mathematical theory of probability and for determining its principal mathematical properties [*see* DISTRIBUTIONS, STATISTICAL, *article on* SPECIAL CONTINUOUS DISTRIBUTIONS].

De Moivre in 1733 had shown how to employ integrals of the function $\exp(-t^2)$ to approximate sums of successive terms of the binomial expansion of $(a + b)^n$ when n is large, obtaining what we today call the normal approximation to the binomial probability distribution [*see* DISTRIBUTIONS, STATISTICAL, *article on* APPROXIMATIONS TO DISTRIBUTIONS]. (De Moivre's analysis is readily available in Smith [1929] 1959, pp. 566–575.) Laplace extended this approach in two important directions.

Approximations to the normal integral. He developed (1781) a general method for approximating an arbitrary definite integral by a series expansion in terms of integrals of the function $\exp(-t^2)$ and its derivatives, anticipating by a century the so-called Gram–Charlier Type A series expansion. He then utilized this technique to approximate various discrete and continuous probability distributions arising in games of chance and other problems in the calculus of probabilities. Remarking (1786a, p. 305) that the integral of $\exp(-t^2)$ arises so frequently that it would be useful to have a table of its values for a succession of limits of integration, Laplace provided (1785, sec. VI; 1805; [1812] 1820, book 1, art. 27) the now well-known power-series, asymptotic-series, and continued fraction expansions for integrals of the function $\exp(-t^2)$. These many results collectively constitute Laplace's first great contribution to the central role of the normal distribution today, and throughout their development the function $\exp(-t^2)$ seems to have been regarded exclusively as an approximating function —neither De Moivre nor Laplace appears to have regarded it or any corresponding expression as a law of error or even as a probability distribution in its own right.

Central limit theorem. Laplace's second great contribution to the establishment of the leading role of the normal distribution is his discovery and proof of what we today call the (classical) central limit theorem. De Moivre's result of 1733 is a special case of this theorem, as are many of Laplace's results in his papers of 1781, 1785, and 1786, but the theorem itself appears for the first time in the important *Mémoire* (1810, sec. VI), for the case of n independent errors from a common arbitrary symmetric discrete distribution on the interval $(-a, +a)$. Then (*ibid.*, sec. VI), by considering the discrete distribution corresponding to a fine subdivision of his double exponential law of error

(1774, sec. v), $\frac{1}{2}m \exp(-m|x|)$, he illustrated the extension of this important theorem to symmetric continuous distributions on the interval $(-\infty, +\infty)$. Gauss (1809, arts. 175–177) had deduced his law of error, $C \exp(-h^2x^2)$, and thence his development of the method of least squares, from the principle of the arithmetic mean. Laplace's central limit theorem provided an alternative justification, or "proof," of this law of error as the limit of the distribution of the sum of n independent random errors as $n \to \infty$ when the relative contribution of each to their sum tends to 0 as n increases, and thus he provided a valid basis for the method of least squares when the individual results involved "are each determined by a very large number of observations, whatever be the laws of facility of the errors of these observations," and hence "a reason for employing it in all cases" (1810, supplement, p. 353). [See Distributions, statistical, *article on* special continuous distributions; *see also* Linear hypotheses, *article on* regression.]

Laplace's proof had only the limited precision current in his time, but it was later made more rigorous and more general by Aleksandr Mikhailovich Liapunov, Paul Lévy, and others. Laplace's demonstration centers on the hypothesis that one deals with the *sum* of independent random variables, but in applications neither independence nor summation may be appropriate. Other functions of random variables can lead to other distributions; for example, if instead of a sum one deals with the greatest random variable, entirely different limit distributions can result (Fréchet 1927). One of these distributions has found application in flood protection, breaking strength of materials, and other areas (Gumbel 1958).

Estimation. Laplace's writings contain the seeds of ideas that have been carefully studied only in recent years: optimum point estimation, hypothesis testing, and confidence interval estimation. Laplace proposed (see 1774, sec. v) that when estimating a parameter, θ, one use that function $T = T(Y_1, Y_2, \cdots)$ of the observations $Y_1, Y_2, \cdots$ for which the mean (or expected) absolute error of estimation, $E[|T - \theta|]$, is a minimum for the given probability distribution of errors. For the case of three independent identically distributed observations he gave an explicit algorithm for finding such a function to use for estimating the location parameter of their common distribution, $f(y - \theta)$, when this is completely specified except for the value of θ. He subsequently extended (1781, sec. xxx) this procedure (which is the same as Pitman's method of "close estimation"—see Pitman 1939) to cover n independent observations in the one-parameter case. Gauss's reformulation (1821) of the method of least squares in terms of minimum mean-square error of estimation (i.e., min $E[(T - \theta)^2]$) stems directly from this earlier work of Laplace's.

Many modern statisticians see the problem of confidence intervals as one of providing a random interval that contains, with at least a specified probability, some parameter of the distribution sampled. Laplace, however, gave another—somewhat vague—interpretation of the interval (*Oeuvres complètes*, vol. 7, pp. 286–287). Major differences of opinion persist about the interpretation of such intervals. [See Bayesian inference; Estimation, *article on* confidence intervals and regions; Fiducial inference.]

Applications to demography. Laplace was not satisfied merely to describe useful statistical methods; he never stopped applying them, most particularly to demography. In this area he was preceded by the great naturalist Buffon, whose early career was in mathematics, although this is not generally known, and who solved the famous problem of the needle thrown onto a table covered with parallel lines. His "Essai d'arithmétique morale" of 1777 deals with demographic statistics; he notes, for example, the propensity that most people have to use round numbers in stating their age. Laplace, using more general and more precise mathematical methods and ideas, was able to treat demographic problems much more intensively. Buffon had already noted the general preponderance of male over female births; Laplace noted that during the years 1745–1785, 393,386 boys and 377,555 girls were born in Paris, and he proved that given certain natural hypotheses, the probability that the chance of a male birth would be more than $\frac{1}{2}$ is $1 - 1/N$; in this example N is a very large number, greater than 10^{72}. In an anomalous case cited by Buffon—the birth of 203 boys and 213 girls in the village of Vitteaux over a five-year period—the same probability is only about $\frac{1}{3}$. Laplace pointed out that there is no logical contradiction between the two cases, since it is only for large populations that the value of the sought probability is near unity—i.e., that the event is almost certain.

An exact census of the French population would have been a very difficult undertaking in Laplace's time, and he therefore tried to estimate the population indirectly, by a rather curious method. He used in the approximation the rough constancy of the ratio between total population and annual number of births, so that if the numerical value of the ratio is known, one need only multiply it by the number of births to obtain an estimate of the population. The government accepted his proposal that studies be made to determine annual births and total population for thirty *départements*, selecting in each *département* only those parishes whose mayors seemed sufficiently conscientious. On September 22, 1802 (the Republic's New Year's Day), the inhabitants of these parishes were counted, and the number of births in each of the three preceding years was also recorded. From the resulting ratio and an estimate of the total number of yearly births in France, Laplace estimated the population to be 25 million.

Laplace was also interested in statistics having to do with the duration of marriages and with life insurance. In addition, he studied the application of statistics to problems of social order, such as the validity of trial evidence and of court judgments, and the concept of "moral expectation." This concept, introduced by Daniel Bernoulli, is based on the observation that the richer a man is, the less concerned he is about any fixed moderate sum of money. Laplace added to this generalization the qualification "all other things being equal," meaning that the benefit to be calculated depends in general on an infinity of circumstances that are impossible to evaluate and that are relative to the individual who is calculating it [*see* UTILITY]. The work that Laplace did on trial evidence and court judgments has been especially controversial; J. L. F. Bertrand, in his caustic way, treated it with complete disdain, but Borel ([1914] 1948, pp. 251–262) felt that Bertrand was too harsh.

MAURICE FRÉCHET

[*Directly related is the entry* PROBABILITY. *Other relevant material may be found in* SOCIOLOGY, *article on* THE EARLY HISTORY OF SOCIAL RESEARCH; *and in the biographies of* GAUSS *and* MOIVRE.]

WORKS BY LAPLACE

1771 Recherches sur le calcul intégral aux différences infiniment petites, aux différences finies. Accademia delle Scienze di Torino, *Memorie* 4:273–375. → Volume 4 is dated "1766–1769."

(1774) 1891 Mémoire sur la probabilité des causes par les événements. Volume 8, pages 27–65 in Pierre Simon de Laplace, *Oeuvres complètes*. Paris: Gauthier-Villars. → Includes "Problème III: Déterminer le milieu que l'on doit prendre entre trois observations données d'un même phénomène" on pages 41–48.

(1781) 1893 Mémoire sur les probabilités. Volume 9, pages 383–485 in Pierre Simon de Laplace, *Oeuvres complètes*. Paris: Gauthier-Villars.

(1782) 1894 Mémoire sur les suites. Volume 10, pages 1–89 in Pierre Simon de Laplace, *Oeuvres complètes*. Paris: Gauthier-Villars.

(1785) 1894 Mémoire sur les approximations des formules qui sont fonctions de très grands nombres. Volume 10, pages 209–291 in Pierre Simon de Laplace, *Oeuvres complètes*. Paris: Gauthier-Villars.

(1786a) 1894 Suite du mémoire sur les approximations des formules qui sont fonctions de très grands nombres. Volume 10, pages 296–338 in Pierre Simon de Laplace, *Oeuvres complètes*. Paris: Gauthier-Villars.

(1786b) 1895 Sur les naissances, les mariages et les morts à Paris, depuis 1771 jusqu'en 1784, et dans toute l'étendue de la France, pendant les années 1781 et 1782. Volume 11, pages 35–46 in Pierre Simon de Laplace, *Oeuvres complètes*. Paris: Gauthier-Villars.

(1796) 1836 *Exposition du système du monde.* 2 vols. 6th ed. Paris: Bachelier.

(1805) 1880 Traité de mécanique céleste. Part 2: Théories particulières des mouvements célestes. Volume 4 in Pierre Simon de Laplace, *Oeuvres complètes*. Paris: Gauthier-Villars.

(1810) 1898 Mémoire sur les approximations des formules qui sont fonctions de très grands nombres et sur leur application aux probabilités. Volume 12, pages 301–345 in Pierre Simon de Laplace, *Oeuvres complètes*. Paris: Gauthier-Villars. → A supplement to the "Mémoire" appears on pages 349–353.

(1812) 1820 *Théorie analytique des probabilités.* 3d ed., rev. Paris: Courcier. → Also published as Volume 1 of *Oeuvres complètes de Laplace*.

(1814) 1951 *A Philosophical Study on Probabilities.* New York: Dover. → First published as *Essai philosophique sur les probabilités*.

Oeuvres complètes de Laplace. 14 vols. Paris: Gauthier-Villars, 1878–1912.

SUPPLEMENTARY BIBLIOGRAPHY

BOREL, ÉMILE (1914) 1948 *Le hasard.* New ed., rev. & enl. Paris: Presses Universitaires de France.

COLBERT-LAPLACE, A. 1929 Letter to Karl Pearson, Dated 16 February 1929. *Biometrika* 21:203–204.

DANTZIG, D. VAN 1955 Laplace, probabiliste et statisticien, et ses précurseurs. *Archives internationales d'histoire des sciences* 8:27–37.

DAVID, F. N. 1965 Some Notes on Laplace. Pages 30–44 in Jerzy Neyman and Lucien M. Le Cam (editors), *Bernoulli, 1713; Bayes, 1763; Laplace, 1813.* New York: Springer.

DAVID, F. N.; and BARTON, D. E. 1962 *Combinatorial Chance.* London: Griffin; New York: Hafner.

DUVEEN, DENIS I.; and HAHN, ROGER 1957 Laplace's Succession to Bézout's Post of Examinateur des Élèves de l'Artillerie. *Isis* 48:416–427.

EISENHART, CHURCHILL 1964 The Meaning of "Least" in Least Squares. *Journal of the Washington Academy of Sciences* 54:24–33.

FELLER, WILLIAM (1950) 1957 *An Introduction to Probability Theory and Its Applications.* Vol. 1. 2d ed. New York: Wiley.

FRÉCHET, MAURICE 1927 Sur la loi de probabilité de l'écart maximum. Polskie Towarzystwo Matematyczne, *Annales: Rocznik* 6:93–122.

FRÉCHET, MAURICE 1940–1943 *Les probabilités associées à un système d'évènements compatibles et dépendants.* Parts 1–2. Paris: Hermann.

GAUSS, CARL FRIEDRICH (1809) 1963 *Theory of Motion of the Heavenly Bodies Moving About the Sun in Conic Sections.* New York: Dover. → First published in Latin.

GAUSS, CARL FRIEDRICH (1821) 1880 Theoria combinationis observationum erroribus minimis obnoxiae. Pars prior. Volume 4, pages 1–26 in *Carl Friedrich Gauss Werke.* Göttingen (Germany): Dieterichsche Universitäts-Druckerei. → A French translation was published in Paris in 1855 under the title *Méthode des moindres carrés: Mémoires sur la combinaison des observations*.

GUMBEL, E. J. 1958 *Statistics of Extremes*. New York: Columbia Univ. Press.

JORDAN, CHARLES (1939) 1947 *Calculus of Finite Differences*. 2d ed. New York: Chelsea.

LAGRANGE, JOSEPH LOUIS (1770–1773) 1868 Mémoire sur l'utilité de la méthode de prendre le milieu entre les résultats de plusieurs observations; dans lequel on examine les avantages de cette méthode par le calcul des probabilités; et où l'on résout différents problèmes relatifs à cette matière. Volume 2, pages 173–234 in Joseph Louis Lagrange, *Oeuvres de Lagrange*. Paris: Gauthier-Villars.

LÉVY, PAUL 1925 *Calcul des probabilités*. Paris: Gauthier-Villars.

MACMAHON, PERCY A. 1915 *Combinatory Analysis*. Vol. 1. Cambridge Univ. Press.

MERRIMAN, MANSFIELD 1877 A List of Writings Relating to the Method of Least Squares, With Historical and Critical Notes. Connecticut Academy of Arts and Sciences, *Transactions* 4:151–232.

MOIVRE, ABRAHAM DE (1718) 1756 *The Doctrine of Chances: Or, a Method of Calculating the Probabilities of Events in Play*. 3d ed. London: Millar.

MOIVRE, ABRAHAM DE 1730 *Miscellanea analytica de seriebus et quadraturis. . . .* London: Tonson & Watts.

MOIVRE, ABRAHAM DE (1733) 1959 A Method of Approximating the Sum of the Terms of the Binomial $(a + b)^n$ Expanded Into a Series, From Whence Are Deduced Some Practical Rules to Estimate the Degree of Assent Which Is to Be Given to Experiments. Volume 2, pages 566–575 in David Eugene Smith, *A Source Book in Mathematics*. New York: Dover. → First published as "Approximatio ad summam terminorum binomii $(a + b)^n$ in seriem expansi."

MOLINA, E. C. 1930 Theory of Probability: Some Comments on Laplace's *Théorie analytique*. American Mathematical Society, *Bulletin* 36:369–392.

NEWMAN, JAMES R. 1956 Commentary on Pierre Simon de Laplace. Volume 2, pages 1316–1324 in James R. Newman (editor), *The World of Mathematics*. New York: Simon & Schuster.

PEARSON, KARL 1929 Laplace: Being Extracts From the Lectures Delivered by Karl Pearson. *Biometrika* 21:202–216.

PITMAN, E. J. G. 1939 The Estimation of the Location and Scale of Parameters of a Continuous Population of Any Given Form. *Biometrika* 30:391–421.

RIORDAN, JOHN 1958 *An Introduction to Combinatorial Analysis*. New York: Wiley.

SIMON, G. A. 1929 Les origines de Laplace: Sa généalogie, ses études. *Biometrika* 21:217–230.

SIMPSON, THOMAS 1756 A Letter to the Right Honourable George, Earl of Macclesfield, President of the Royal Society, on the Advantage of Taking the Mean of a Number of Observations, in Practical Astronomy. Royal Society of London, *Philosophical Transactions* 49:82–93.

SIMPSON, THOMAS 1757 An Attempt to Show the Advantage Arising by Taking the Mean of a Number of Observations in Practical Astronomy. Pages 64–75 in Thomas Simpson, *Miscellaneous Tracts on Some Curious, and Very Interesting Subjects in Mechanics, Physical-astronomy, and Speculative Mathematics*. London: Nourse.

SMITH, DAVID EUGENE (1929) 1959 *A Source Book in Mathematics*. 2 vols. New York: Dover.

TODHUNTER, ISAAC (1865) 1949 *A History of the Mathematical Theory of Probability From the Time of Pascal to That of Laplace*. New York: Chelsea.

USPENSKY, JAMES V. 1937 *Introduction to Mathematical Probability*. New York: McGraw-Hill.

WALKER, HELEN M. 1929 *Studies in the History of Statistical Method, With Special Reference to Certain Educational Problems*. Baltimore: Williams & Wilkins.

WHITTAKER, EDMUND 1949a Laplace. *Mathematical Gazette* 33:1–12.

WHITTAKER, EDMUND 1949b Laplace. *American Mathematical Monthly* 56:369–372.

WILSON, EDWIN B. 1923 First and Second Laws of Error. *Journal of the American Statistical Association* 18:841–851.

LASHLEY, KARL S.

Karl Spencer Lashley (1890–1958), American psychologist, was born in Davis, West Virginia, of middle-class English stock. His father, Charles Gilpin Lashley, was the manager of the family store in Davis and the founder of a small bank there; at various times he served in such political posts as mayor and postmaster. Lashley's mother, Maggie Blanche Spencer, was descended from Jonathan Edwards, the philosopher, theologian, and educator of American revolutionary times; she had been a country schoolteacher before her marriage. After that she continued to be an avid reader, amassing a personal library of more than 2,000 volumes, and was an informal "adult education" instructor in diverse subjects. She appears to have been responsible for cultivating Lashley's love of nature and of learning.

Except for four years, from 1894 to 1898, during which the family, afflicted with "gold fever," trekked to the west coast and Alaska, Lashley spent his early years in Davis. He showed signs of being a prodigy. During his elementary school years, his interest in nature and animal behavior was already evident in his collection of all sorts of plants and animals, including many pets. During this period, too, his marked mechanical aptitude became apparent; he expertly designed many gadgets, small and large, and made them in his own workshop.

Graduating from Davis High School at the age of 14, he entered the University of West Virginia, but because his high school was unaccredited he had to spend a year in preparatory work before becoming a freshman. Although vaguely inclined toward engineering, he enrolled, at his mother's wish, in a liberal arts program, intending to major in Latin or English. It was only to fill an unscheduled hour that he enrolled in a course in zoology taught by John Black Johnston (later dean at the University of Minnesota when Lashley taught there). This contact with Johnston crystallized his interest in zoology for, as he later wrote, "Within a few weeks in this class I knew that I had found my life's work" (Beach 1961).

After Lashley's freshman year Johnston left and was succeeded by Albert M. Reese, who appointed Lashley departmental assistant. In this role he found a fascinating Golgi series of frog brain sections and proposed to "draw all the connections between the cells." To his surprise, most of the cells were not stained and therefore not visible. He later commented, ". . . I think almost ever since I have been trying to trace those connections" (*ibid.*, p. 169). Lashley went on to take all the courses offered by Reese, the only zoologist on the faculty, but he got much of his education in zoology by independently working out projects for which Reese gave only the briefest instructions. Lashley's philosophy of education and handling of his own students reflected this experience with independent work.

In 1910, with a B.A. in zoology, Lashley went to work on a master's degree at the University of Pittsburgh, where he had been awarded a teaching fellowship in biology. It was here that he took his only formal course in psychology. This was a laboratory course in experimental psychology taught by Karl Dallenbach who later wrote, "Lashley was intensely interested and was the outstanding student in the class. . . . He showed in that course the promise that he later fulfilled" (*ibid.*, p. 170).

Lashley received his master's degree in June 1911 and went that summer to Cold Spring Harbor to do research on the variability in the number of cirri in the ciliate *Stylonychia*. (Cold Spring Harbor is a prominent Long Island center for biological research; during the summer months many outstanding academic biologists work there.) This research led to his appointment by H. S. Jennings as a teaching fellow in zoology at Johns Hopkins University. There Lashley worked with Jennings on paramecia and with S. O. Mast on the behavior of various invertebrates, taking his PH.D. in 1914 with a dissertation on inheritance in asexual reproduction of *Hydra*. During this period he also pursued his interest in psychology, working with Adolph Meyer, professor of psychiatry and director of the newly established Phipps Clinic, and with John B. Watson, then professor of psychology.

Watson's behavioristic approach had tremendous appeal for Lashley and led him to do postdoctoral work on vertebrate behavior. This work extended over three years, from 1914 to 1917, during which he slowly formulated and launched the rich program of research and writing he was to carry on

for the rest of his life. The first two years he held successive appointments in zoology as Bruce fellow and Johnston scholar but worked with Watson on a variety of problems: field experiments on reproductive behavior of terns (in the Dry Tortugas), acquisition of human motor skills, color vision in birds, conditioning of the salivary reflex, and effects of strychnine and other drugs on maze learning in rats.

While pursuing these experiments, Lashley became interested in the work of Shepard Ivory Franz, who was examining the behavior of brain-injured patients at Saint Elizabeths Hospital in Washington, D.C. Franz was also inaugurating work on the behavioral effects of experimental brain lesions in animals. After frequent journeys to Washington to observe this work, Lashley was permitted to study neurological cases in the wards and to acquire the necessary surgical and histological skills for performing studies of the neural basis of learning. Here he got started solidly on the research career that eventually brought him eminence and recognition.

By the fall of 1917 the United States had entered World War I, and many psychologists were in the army or heavily involved in war-related activities, but Lashley's vision was too poor to meet army standards. Therefore, when he had completed his period of postdoctoral training, he accepted a post at the University of Minnesota arranged by Robert M. Yerkes, who was slated to become chairman there at the war's end but never did. Morale in the department was not high, and after one year Lashley, taking a leave of absence, accepted a position with the U.S. International Hygiene Board. Although he was working once again with Watson, this time in a program dealing with public education on the dangers of venereal disease, this assignment was not a productive one, and in 1920 R. M. Elliott, the new chairman of the department of psychology, prevailed on Lashley to return to the University of Minnesota as assistant professor.

Lashley's intellectual pre-eminence and prolific research on brain function brought him rapid promotion: in 1924, at the age of 34, he was made a full professor. In 1926 he left Minnesota for Chicago, at first serving as research psychologist with the Behavior Research Fund at the Institute for Juvenile Research and later, in 1929, moving to a professorship at the University of Chicago. In 1935 he went to Harvard University as professor and in 1937 was made a research professor in neuropsychology, a title he held until his retirement in 1955. However, in 1942, in a joint arrangement with Yale University and certain private foundations, he moved to Florida as director of the Yerkes Laboratories of Primate Biology.

It has been said of Lashley that he was an "inspiring teacher who described all teaching as useless" (Beach 1961, p. 163). He himself frequently asserted that "those who need to be taught can't learn, and those who can learn don't need to be taught" (*ibid.*, p. 182). He applied this principle by eschewing formal teaching, often raising artificial barriers to registration in his courses. Because his research was so excellent, he managed better than any other academic psychologist of his time to stay out of the classroom. The few lectures he did give were usually stimulating, often exciting. And in seminars he had few peers; he was an impressive scholar, with a pleasant wit and a fascinating intellect. Like Mark Hopkins, however, he was at his best "on a log." He was always available to graduate students and postdoctoral fellows in his laboratory, and for scores of psychologists their informal contacts with Lashley were to be the most significant periods of their education. In this way Lashley was a great teacher even though fewer students, probably, have studied under him formally than under any other psychologist of distinction.

One other related characteristic of Lashley's deserves mention. This was his "go-it-alone" attitude toward research. He had fewer collaborators and published fewer joint papers than most other comparable scientists. Except for very routine work, he did all his own research, "running" his animals, doing data analysis, making histological reconstructions, and writing his own papers. He expected the same of others working with him. He never directed but only advised when his advice was asked. He felt strongly that research of quality must be carried out by scientists of quality, not by a host of assistants and graduate students. It is easy, therefore, to understand his dismay at the increasingly large amounts of money being employed in organized research. Writing in 1953 to Watson, Lashley said, "The money available for research now is rather shocking. The man who doesn't have $20,000 per year for research is probably intellectually honest. There are not enough competent men to spend the money" (*ibid.*, p. 180).

Work on brain function. Lashley's most productive phase was launched in his work with Franz. At first he merely took for granted the connectionism of Watsonian behaviorism and looked for the neural basis of the connections. This, however, proved elusive, for in study after study in the 1920s he obtained data suggesting a field theory rather than a connectionist theory of brain function.

Lashley's reasoning and his findings in these studies should be briefly summarized. Connectionist theory holds that complex behavior is made up of conditioned reflexes, each forming a connection through the conditioning process. The connection, Lashley reasoned, should have a definite locus in the brain just as a connection in a telephone system does; he, therefore, tried to find a definite localization of these connections. His basic technique was to train an animal to run a maze or make a discrimination both before and after he had made lesions of different sizes in various areas of the cerebral cortex. He then tested for such effects of the lesion as a deficit in retention or learning ability. Except for certain specific visual discriminations discussed below, he found no localization of function. Deficits were found, indeed, but they were not specific to any particular cortical areas. Instead, the degree of deficit depended on the amount of cortex removed rather than upon its locus.

W. S. Hunter and others argued that Lashley's reasoning was faulty, and the present author agrees. Hunter pointed out that mazes involve many different cues, as others had shown by depriving animals of various senses, and complex motor responses. Quite specific localization of connections in the brain could well exist, but so many different connections would be involved in a habit like maze running that one could statistically expect the results Lashley obtained. Lashley's experiments, therefore, were not crucial to the issue. But Lashley felt otherwise and believed that his experiments did disprove the existence of specific connections and required explanation in terms of field-theory concepts.

Thus, Lashley came to propose two concepts (or principles) for which he became widely known and which had considerable influence on subsequent research. The two concepts were *mass action* and *equipotentiality*. Both were presented in his 1929 monograph *Brain Mechanisms and Intelligence*. By mass action he referred to his finding that learning, or at least certain kinds of learning, is mediated by the cerebral cortex as a whole. This principle is based mainly on his studies of maze learning which showed that the efficiency of learning depends roughly on the amount of cortex present and not on any particular cortical locus.

The related concept of equipotentiality came out of his studies of vision and applies primarily to sensory systems. It refers to the ability of certain parts of a system to assume the functions of its other parts. Lashley had found, for example, that a rat can relearn a visual discrimination after the discrimination has been destroyed by a lesion of the visual cortex; also, a rat can discriminate visual stimuli perfectly when only a small remnant of its visual cortex remains intact. From such results he concluded that various parts of a system are "equipotential" for the mediation of a learned visual discrimination.

Other investigators have, of course, pursued the problems raised by Lashley's work and his interpretations. Using more sophisticated physiological and behavioral techniques than Lashley had at his disposal and giving more attention to the brain of the primate, they have found more localization of function than the principle of mass action would lead one to expect. Indeed, in the primate brain there is considerable localization of learned functions. Still, Lashley was largely correct. The localization is far from precise, and within large areas of localized function there are mass-action effects. As for equipotentiality, later investigations bear out the presence of this phenomenon within sensory systems. It is the interpretation rather than the fact that is in question, and there are now complex alternative explanations available. The problem, however, remains far from solved and is in nearly the same state as Lashley left it.

Work on sensory functions. In another major phase of Lashley's work, the study of sensory functions, he made considerable contributions to the study of the generalization of learned visual discriminations, much of the work being planned as tests of connectionist versus field theories. He also made contributions to neuroanatomy. Concentrating at first on the visual system, he traced neural connections between the retina and the lateral geniculate nucleus of the thalamus and between this nucleus and the cerebral cortex. Later he extended this kind of neuroanatomic analysis to other sensory systems. His papers on thalamocortical connections (1941) and on the microscopic structure of the cortex are classics in their fields. In them he showed that although there are point-to-point projections in sensory systems, these systems cannot be rigidly compartmentalized. Later work, with more refined techniques, has borne him out.

Work on neural functions. The final major aspect of Lashley's work was an attempt to construct a general theory of neural function. Here he was frustrated; his grand design was to develop a theory of how the brain works in perception and learning. Having held earlier that other simple theories were untenable, he now turned to various forms of field theory. Many of his experiments and, particularly, his later papers were concerned with tests of such theories. In the end he felt he had succeeded only in exploding the theories

proposed but not in devising one that would satisfactorily stand the test of experiment. He had to be content with the thought that he and his generation had only laid the groundwork for building a good theory at a later date. Despite his frustration in theory building, however, he adhered steadfastly to the belief that a satisfactory theory would some day be possible. In his last published article, "Cerebral Organization and Behavior," he made an impressive case for his claim that the study of "the organization [of] mental states does not reveal any operations which cannot be accounted for in principle by the mechanism of the brain" (1958, p. 15).

Not long after this was written, Lashley collapsed and died in Poitiers, France. He left over 100 papers of an experimental or theoretical nature, but no book—because he could never make a large-scale theory stand up. Without question, he was the twentieth-century pioneer in the experimental study of brain functions and behavior.

CLIFFORD T. MORGAN

[For the historical antecedents of Lashley's work, see the biographies of BROCA; FLOURENS; GALL. The relevant work of Lashley's contemporaries is discussed in the biographies of HUNTER; MEYER; WATSON; YERKES. For discussion of the development of Lashley's ideas, see NERVOUS SYSTEM; PSYCHOLOGY, article on PHYSIOLOGICAL PSYCHOLOGY; VISION.]

WORKS BY LASHLEY

1929   Brain Mechanisms and Intelligence: A Quantitative Study of Injuries to the Brain. Univ. of Chicago Press.
1930   Basic Neural Mechanisms in Behavior. Psychological Review 37:1–24.
1941   Thalamo-cortical Connections of the Rat's Brain. Journal of Comparative Neurology 75:67–121.
1958   Cerebral Organization and Behavior. Pages 1–18 in Association for Research in Nervous and Mental Disease, The Brain and Human Behavior: Proceedings. Baltimore: Williams & Wilkins.
The Neuropsychology of Lashley: Selected Papers. Edited by Frank A. Beach et al. New York: McGraw-Hill, 1960. → A posthumous collection containing papers published between 1915 and 1958.

SUPPLEMENTARY BIBLIOGRAPHY

BEACH, FRANK A. 1961 Karl Spencer Lashley: June 7, 1890–August 7, 1958. Volume 35, pages 163–204 in National Academy of Sciences, Biographical Memoirs. Washington: The Academy. → See pages 196–204 for a bibliography of Karl Lashley's works.

LASKI, HAROLD J.

Harold Joseph Laski (1893–1950), teacher, political scientist, and British Labour party leader, was born in Manchester, England, the second son of Nathan and Sarah Laski; his father was a prosperous cotton shipper, a prominent Liberal, and a leader of the orthodox Jewish community. The young Laski's intellectual gifts and his precocity were demonstrated by an article he wrote when he was 16 years old and still a student at the Manchester Grammar School. The article, "On the Scope of Eugenics," which appeared in the *Westminster Review* in July 1910, called forth a letter of congratulation from Sir Francis Galton. For six months after he left school, Laski pursued his interest in eugenics by studying with Karl Pearson at University College in London.

In the summer of 1911 he broke with his family by marrying a Gentile, Frida Kerry, who was eight years older than he, and in the fall of that year he began his undergraduate studies at New College, Oxford. After a year of reading science, he shifted to history; he studied under H. A. L. Fisher and Ernest Barker and was strongly influenced by the writings of F. W. Maitland. During his undergraduate days, Laski was active in the women's suffrage movement, in which his wife was deeply interested. In this connection he became a close friend of H. W. Nevinson and George Lansbury, then editor of the Labour newspaper, the *Daily Herald*. After receiving his degree in 1914, Laski spent the summer months writing articles for the *Herald* on Ireland and on constitutional issues that affected labor. When his attempt to enlist in the armed forces ended in medical rejection, he accepted a post as lecturer in history at McGill University in Montreal, Canada. While at McGill, he wrote his first book, *Studies in the Problem of Sovereignty* (1917).

Two years later, in 1916, as a result of a meeting with Felix Frankfurter, who became a lifelong friend, Laski accepted a post as instructor in history at Harvard University. For the next four years, Laski was a stimulating teacher and a lively member of the Harvard intellectual community. He wrote several books during this period, including *Authority in the Modern State* (1919) and *The Foundations of Sovereignty, and Other Essays* (1921); in these works he argued against the myth of the sovereign, omnicompetent state and defended the doctrine of political pluralism in a series of historical and analytical essays. The state, he maintained, is not the supreme association to whose will all other groups must bow, but is only one among many groups—corporations, unions, churches, societies of all kinds—with which it is engaged in a constant struggle for men's loyalty and obedience. Laski's pluralistic view of the state reflected the influence of Gierke, Maitland, and Figgis, as well as the antistatist and anti-idealist currents in political thought and action that were

strong before and after World War I. Even at this period, Laski's primary concern was with the freedom of workers' organizations from control by the "sovereign state," and in October 1919, he gave striking evidence of this concern by a public defense of the Boston policemen who were then engaged in a strike that had outraged the leaders of the community [*see* PLURALISM].

In 1920 Laski left Harvard and his many American friends, chief among whom was, perhaps, Justice Oliver Wendell Holmes, with whom he maintained close touch until Holmes's death. Laski accepted a post at the London School of Economics and Political Science, where, in 1926, he succeeded Graham Wallas as professor of political science. Laski taught at the School until his death 24 years later; he was so well known and so influential among students that his name and the London School became almost synonymous terms in the minds of many people, especially of students from America and from Asia and Africa.

After his return to England, Laski became increasingly involved in politics and political discussions and in writing for the *Nation*. He was active in the election campaign of December 1923, which led to the first Labour minority government. Yet he found time for the teaching and counseling of students and for writing his most comprehensive study of politics, *A Grammar of Politics* (1925). In this work he moved away from his earlier pluralism and adopted a position that might be called "socialized Benthamism." He now accepted the view he had previously rejected, that the state was "the fundamental instrument of society," and he argued that its purpose was to "satisfy, or organize the satisfaction of, the wants of men on the largest possible scale." Yet he indicated that he retained a good deal of suspicion of political power by advocating a large measure of decentralization, consultation with organized groups, and restraints on governmental action. This suspicion of state power reflected his belief that in practice its incidence was heavily weighted in favor of the interests of the wealthy and powerful members of society. Laski, now committed to a democratic or Fabian socialism, urged that political democracy was virtually meaningless unless it led forward to "economic democracy" or socialism [*see* ECONOMIC THOUGHT, *article on* SOCIALIST THOUGHT].

From 1925 on, he began to express doubts that the necessary major reforms of the economic and social systems could be attained by the methods of political democracy. In his book *Communism* (1927), for example, he argued that since the workers no longer accepted capitalism or regarded it as legitimate, the only alternative to revolution was a series of major concessions by the ruling class—acceptance of nationalization of essential industries, sharp curtailment of inheritance rights, comprehensive regulation of private business, and guarantees of adequate wages, working conditions, and educational and welfare opportunities. He was not optimistic about the willingness of capitalists to accept these moves toward a more equal society and to abdicate from power peacefully, and in *Liberty in the Modern State* (1930) he warned that the price of social conflict is always the destruction of freedom.

With the advent of the great depression, the rise of fascism in Europe, the collapse of the British Labour government in 1931, and the defection of Ramsay MacDonald, Philip Snowden, and James H. Thomas from the party, which left it leaderless and bewildered, Laski's hopes for a peaceful and gradual transition to socialism grew dim, and his doubts about the possibility of achieving socialism by constitutional and democratic means became much more intense. In a series of works written during the 1930s, such as *Democracy in Crisis* (1933), *The State in Theory and Practice* (1935), *The Rise of European Liberalism* (1936), and *Parliamentary Government in England* (1938), he abandoned his Fabianism in favor of the Marxist view that the contradictions of capitalism were insoluble and that a democratic political system was incompatible with a capitalism in crisis. On the basis of British, French, German, and Italian experience, Laski now argued that once the operations of political democracy threatened the continued existence of capitalism and interfered with the pursuit of profits, the ruling class would destroy democracy and the labor movement and would initiate an authoritarian regime. The liberal and socialist alternatives to the communist doctrine of the necessity of violent revolution would then become untenable, and revolutionary socialism and fascism (the political form of capitalism in decay) would thus be left as the only serious contenders for power.

These were the years of Laski's most intense involvement in politics. From 1937 to 1949 he was a member of the National Executive of the Labour party, where he was often critical of the moderate views and tactics of the party's leaders. During the late 1930s his public influence probably reached its high point; this was the period of the Left Book Club, directed by Victor Gollancz, John Strachey, and Laski. During the Spanish Civil War he joined such left-wing Labourites as Sir Stafford Cripps and Aneurin Bevan in the Unity Campaign and the popular front movement of all antifascist groups, which was condemned by the Labour party leaders and by the party conference in 1937.

From the fall of 1938 to the end of the summer of 1939 Laski was in the United States, where he taught at the University of Washington and delivered at Indiana University the lectures that were later published as *The American Presidency* (1940). Shortly after his return to England the war began. The London School of Economics was evacuated to Cambridge, and during the war years Laski divided his time between teaching, assisting Clement Attlee after he became deputy prime minister under Churchill in 1940, and traveling around the country to address Labour party meetings and give lectures at military camps. Although overwork led to a serious nervous breakdown in 1943, he soon resumed his many activities and his writing. His major wartime publications were *Reflections on the Revolution of Our Time* (1943) and *Faith, Reason, and Civilization* (1944); in these books, and in many articles and speeches, he urged the leaders of the Labour party to insist that the Churchill coalition government commit itself during the war to a program of major social and economic reforms that would be carried out when peace was restored. In the unity of groups and classes and the patriotic enthusiasm of the war years he saw an opportunity, which would never be repeated, of achieving what he called "a revolution by consent." If this opportunity were missed because the Labour leaders were unwilling to threaten to resign from the coalition government, the postwar world would be neither any better nor more hopeful than the world of the 1920s and would again move toward the choice that had confronted Europe in the 1930s—reaction or revolution, fascism or communism. Laski was criticized by many people, including some of his friends in England and America, for his wartime attacks on Churchill and for his criticisms of the inadequacies and weaknesses of Attlee and other Labour party leaders.

Although the electoral victory of Labour in 1945 was a great satisfaction to Laski, the triumph was marred for him by the growing tensions on the international scene, particularly between the United States and the Soviet Union, and by his failure to win a libel action that he had instituted during the 1945 campaign, when several newspapers reported that he had made a speech in which he advocated violent revolution in Great Britain. He wrote a long book on American society and politics, *The American Democracy* (1948), which struck many observers, including some liberals, as a curiously doctrinaire and outdated portrait of the American scene. Early in 1949, Laski made his final visit to the United States; in the course of a five-week tour of the country he delivered, under the auspices of the Sidney Hillman Foundation, the series of lectures later published as *Trade Unions in the New Society* (1949). In these lectures he urged the American trade unions to move forward to the creation of a strong labor party in order to safeguard and develop the American democratic tradition.

Although he had resigned in 1949 from the national executive of the Labour party and was worn out and ill, Laski campaigned strenuously in the 1950 general election. He died suddenly, only a few weeks after the election, on March 24, 1950.

The influence that Laski exerted by his teaching and writing was probably greatest in the 1930s; during the years of depression and the growing menace of fascism and international war, he was an impassioned advocate of socialism who combined social and economic radicalism with a deep attachment to many traditional British and American institutions and values. In this period his influence among students in both Britain and the United States was particularly great. After World War II and especially since his death, his reputation as a political theorist and analyst has been higher among students and intellectuals in Asian and African countries than among similar groups in the West.

HERBERT A. DEANE

[*For the historical context of Laski's work, see* SOCIALISM *and the biographies of* FIGGIS; GIERKE; MAITLAND.]

WORKS BY LASKI

(1916–1935) 1953 HOLMES, OLIVER W.; and LASKI, HAROLD J. *Holmes–Laski Letters: The Correspondence of Mr. Justice Holmes and Harold J. Laski, 1916–1935.* Edited by Mark DeWolfe Howe, with a foreword by Felix Frankfurter. 2 vols. Cambridge, Mass.: Harvard Univ. Press. → A paperback edition was published in 1963 by Atheneum.
1917 *Studies in the Problem of Sovereignty.* New Haven: Yale Univ. Press.
1919 *Authority in the Modern State.* New Haven: Yale Univ. Press.
(1921) 1931 *The Foundations of Sovereignty, and Other Essays.* New Haven: Yale Univ. Press.
(1925) 1957 *A Grammar of Politics.* 4th ed. London: Allen & Unwin.
(1927) 1935 *Communism.* London: Butterworth.
(1930) 1961 *Liberty in the Modern State.* 3d ed. London: Allen & Unwin.
(1933) 1934 *Democracy in Crisis.* London: Allen & Unwin.
(1935) 1956 *The State in Theory and Practice.* London: Allen & Unwin.
(1936) 1958 *The Rise of European Liberalism: An Essay in Interpretation.* London: Allen & Unwin. → A paperback edition was published in 1962 by Barnes and Noble.
1938 *Parliamentary Government in England: A Commentary.* New York: Viking.
1940 *The American Presidency: An Interpretation.* New York: Harper. → A paperback edition was published in 1958 by Grosset and Dunlap.
1943 *Reflections on the Revolution of Our Time.* New York: Viking; London; Allen & Unwin.
1944 *Faith, Reason, and Civilization: An Essay in Historical Analysis.* New York: Viking.
1948 *The American Democracy: A Commentary and an Interpretation.* New York: Viking.
(1949) 1950 *Trade Unions in the New Society.* London: Allen & Unwin.
(1951) 1962 *Reflections on the Constitution: The House of Commons, the Cabinet [and] the Civil Service.* Manchester (England) Univ. Press.

SUPPLEMENTARY BIBLIOGRAPHY

DEANE, HERBERT A. 1955 *The Political Ideas of Harold J. Laski.* New York: Columbia Univ. Press.
ELLIOTT, WILLIAM Y. 1928 *The Pragmatic Revolt in Politics: Syndicalism, Fascism, and the Constitutional State.* New York: Macmillan.
MAGID, HENRY M. 1941 *English Political Pluralism: The Problem of Freedom and Organization.* Columbia University Studies in Philosophy, No. 2. New York: Columbia Univ. Press.
MARTIN, KINGSLEY 1953 *Harold Laski, 1893–1950: A Biographical Memoir.* New York: Viking; London: Gollancz.

LATENT STRUCTURE

A scientist is often interested in quantities that are not directly observable but can be investigated only via observable quantities that are probabilistically connected with those of real interest. Latent structure models relate to one such situation in which the observable or manifest quantities are multivariate multinomial observations, for example, answers by a subject or respondent to dichotomous or trichotomous questions. Models relating polytomous observable variables to unobservable or latent variables go back rather far; some early references are Cournot (1838), Weinberg (1902), Benini (1928), and deMeo (1934). These models typically express the multivariate distribution of the observable variables as a mixture of multivariate distributions, where the distribution of the latent variable is the mixing distribution [*see* DISTRIBUTIONS, STATISTICAL, *article on* MIXTURES OF DISTRIBUTIONS].

Lazarsfeld (1950) first introduced the term *latent structure model* for those models in which the variables distributed according to any of the component multivariate distributions of the mixture are assumed to be stochastically independent. (Thus a latent structure model of a subject's answers to 50 dichotomous questions—the latent class model of this article—assumes that subjects fall into relatively few classes, called latent classes, with the variable that relates the subject to his class being the latent variable. The distribution of this latent variable, that is, the distribution of the subjects among latent classes, is the mixing distribution. Within each class it is assumed that the responses to the 50 dichotomous questions are stochastically independent.) A basic reference for the general form of latent structure models is Anderson (1959).

The present article—restricted to the case of dichotomous questions—emphasizes the problems of identifiability and efficient statistical estimation of the parameters of latent structure models, points out difficulties with methods that have been proposed, and summarizes doubts currently held about the possibility of good estimation.

The simplest of the latent structure models and almost the only one in which the problem of parameter estimation has been carefully addressed is the *latent class model*. In this model, each observation in the sample is a vector x with p two-valued items or coordinates, conveniently coded by writing each either as 0 or as 1. The latent class model postulates that there is a small number m of classes, called *latent classes*, into which potential observations on the population can be classified such that within each class the p coordinates of the vector x are statistically independent. This is not to say that all identical observations in the sample are automatically considered as coming from the same class. Rather, associated with each class is a probability distribution on the 2^p possible vectors x, such that the p coordinates of x are (conditionally) independent. An observation vector x thus has a probability distribution that is a mixture of the probability distributions of x associated with each of the latent classes.

An example of the above model comes from the study (Lazarsfeld 1950) of the degree of ethnocentrism of American soldiers during World War II. Because it is not known how to measure ethnocentrism directly, a sample of soldiers was asked the following three questions: Do you believe that our European allies are much superior to us in strategy and fighting morale? Do you believe that the majority of all equipment used by all the allies comes from American lend-lease shipment? Do you believe that neither we nor our allies could win the war if we didn't have each other's help?

Here $p = 3$ and x is the vector of responses to the three questions, with Yes coded as 1 and No coded as 0. A suitable latent class model would postulate that there are two latent classes (so that $m = 2$), such that within each class the answers to the three questions are stochastically independent. Postulating the existence of any more than two latent classes would, as will be seen later, lead to difficulties, since the parameters of such a latent class model could not be consistently estimated. The two latent classes would probably be composed of ethnocentric and nonethnocentric soldiers, respectively. However, this need not be the case, and in fact it may happen that the two latent classes will have no reasonable interpretation, let alone the hoped-for interpretation. This phenomenon of possible noninterpretability is characteristic not only of the latent class model but also of the factor analysis and other mixture-of-distributions models.

The latent class model. Let σ denote a subset (unordered) of the integers $(1, 2, \cdots, p)$, possibly the null subset ϕ. (Other subsets will, for concreteness, be denoted by writing their members in customary numerical order.) Let π_σ denote the probability that for a randomly chosen individual each coordinate of x with index a member of σ is a 1, and define $\pi_\phi = 1$. For example, $\pi_{2,7,19}$ is the probability that the second, seventh, and nineteenth coordinates of x are all 1, forgetting about—or marginally with respect to—the values of the other coordinates of x.

Since the order of coordinates is immaterial for such a probability, one is justified in dealing with the 2^p unordered σ's, but a specific order in naming the subset is helpful for exposition. The π_σ's are notationally a more convenient set of parameters than what might be considered the 2^p natural parameters of the multinomial distribution of x.

A concise description of the natural parameters of the distribution of x is the following. Let $\bar{\sigma}$ denote that subset of the integers $(1, 2, \cdots, p)$ which is the complement of σ. Let $\pi_{\sigma;\bar{\sigma}}$ denote the probability that for a randomly chosen individual each coordinate of x with index of a member of σ is a 1 and each coordinate of x with index a member of $\bar{\sigma}$ is a 0. The 2^p $\pi_{\sigma;\bar{\sigma}}$'s are the natural parameters of the multinomial distribution of x, since they are the probabilities of each of the 2^p possible observation values. For example, in the ethnocentrism case, $\pi_{1,2;3}$ would be the probability that the first two questions are answered Yes, while the third question is answered No. The π_σ's and $\pi_{\sigma;\bar{\sigma}}$'s are related by a nonsingular linear transformation.

Let ν_α be the probability that the observation vector x is a member of the αth latent class, where

LATENT STRUCTURE 35

$\alpha = 1, 2, \cdots, m$ and $\sum \nu_\alpha = 1$. Let $\lambda_{\alpha\sigma}$ be the probability that if $\boldsymbol{x}$ is a vector chosen at random from the αth class, then each coordinate of $\boldsymbol{x}$ with index a member of σ is a 1. Clearly $\pi_\sigma = \sum_\alpha \nu_\alpha \lambda_{\alpha\sigma}$.

Let σ_i denote the ith member of σ, with the members of σ arranged in some order, say numerical. The fundamental independence assumption of the latent class model then says that for each α

$$\lambda_{\alpha\sigma} = \prod_{\sigma_i\epsilon\sigma} \lambda_{\alpha\sigma_i}$$

for all σ. That is, the probability (conditional on $\boldsymbol{x}$ being in the αth latent class) of any given set of coordinates of $\boldsymbol{x}$ being all 1's is the product of the probabilities of each of these coordinates being a 1. Then

$$\pi_\sigma = \sum_{\alpha=1}^{m} \nu_\alpha \prod_{\sigma_i\epsilon\sigma} \lambda_{\alpha\sigma_i}$$

for all σ. These equations are called the *accounting equations* of the latent class model. Thus the $m(p+1)$ parameters of the model are the *latent parameters* $\lambda_{\alpha i}$ and the ν_α, $\alpha = 1, \cdots, m$, $i = 1, \cdots, p$. These completely determine the 2^p *manifest parameters*, the π_σ, via the accounting equations.

Parameter estimation. Suppose that the number of latent classes, m, is known to the investigator. (This assumption is made because it underlies all the theoretical work on the estimation of parameters of the latent class model. In practice m is unknown, but a pragmatic approach is to assume a particular small value of m, proceed with the estimation, see how well the estimated model fits the manifest data, and alter m and begin again if the fit is poor.) Then a central statistical problem is that of estimating the parameters of the model, the ν's and λ's, from a random sample of n vectors $\boldsymbol{x}$. (The typical sample in survey work is a stratified rather than a simple random sample. However, the problem of estimating latent parameters from such samples is much more complicated, and as yet has hardly been touched.)

Let n_σ be the number of vectors in the sample with 1's in each component whose index is a member of σ, and let $p_\sigma = n_\sigma/n$. If the model were simply a multinomial model with parameters the π_σ's, then the p_σ's would be maximum likelihood estimators of the π_σ's. If for each set of 2^p π_σ's there is a unique set of latent parameters, ν_α's and $\lambda_{\alpha i}$'s, $\alpha = 1, \cdots, m$, $i = 1, \cdots, p$, then the ν's and λ's are functions of the π_σ's, and evaluating these functions at the p_σ's as arguments will yield estimators (actually consistent estimators) of the latent parameters. But the "if" in the last sentence is most critical; it ⸺ the identifiability condition, common

to all models relating distributions of observable random variables to distributions of unobservable random variables. Consequently, most of the work on parameter estimation in latent class analysis is really a by-product of work on finding constructive procedures, that is, procedures that explicitly derive the unique latent parameters as function of the π's, for proving the identifiability of a latent class model associated with a given m and p. With such a constructive procedure available, one can replace the π's by their estimates, the p's, and use the procedure to determine estimates of the ν's and λ's. The following description of estimation procedures based on constructive proofs of identifiability will thus really be a description of the constructive procedure for determining the ν's and λ's from a subset of the π's.

Green's method of estimation. The earliest constructive procedure was given by Green (1951). Let $\boldsymbol{D}_i$ be the $m \times m$ diagonal matrix with $\lambda_{\alpha i}$, $\alpha = 1, \cdots, m$, on the diagonal, and let $\boldsymbol{L}$ be the $(p+1) \times m$ matrix with first row a vector of 1's and jth row ($j = 2, \cdots, p+1$) the vector of $(\lambda_{1,j-1}, \cdots, \lambda_{m,j-1})$. Let $\boldsymbol{N}$ be the $m \times m$ diagonal matrix with ν_α, $\alpha = 1, \cdots, m$, on the diagonal. For σ a subset of $(1, 2, \cdots, p)$, define $\boldsymbol{D}_\sigma = \prod_{\sigma_j\epsilon\sigma} \boldsymbol{D}_{\sigma_j}$. Form the matrix $\Pi_\sigma = \boldsymbol{L}\boldsymbol{N}\boldsymbol{D}_\sigma\boldsymbol{L}'$, where the prime denotes the matrix transpose. The (i,j)th element of this matrix is

$$\sum_{\alpha=1}^{m} \nu_\alpha \lambda_{\alpha i} \lambda_{\alpha j} \prod_{\sigma_k\epsilon\sigma} \lambda_{\alpha\sigma_k}.$$

If $i \neq j$ and $i,j \not\epsilon \sigma$ then the (i,j)th element of this matrix is the manifest parameter $\pi_{ij\sigma}$. Otherwise the (i,j)th element of this matrix can formally be defined as a quantity called $\pi_{ij\sigma}$, where the subscript of π may have repeated elements. Since π's with repeated subscripts are not manifest parameters and have no empirical counterpart but are merely formal constructs based on the latent parameters, they are not estimable directly from the n_σ's. However, Green provided some rules for guessing at values of these π's (one rule is given below) so that the matrix Π_σ can be partly estimated and partly guessed at, given data.

Let $\Pi_0 = \boldsymbol{L}\boldsymbol{N}\boldsymbol{L}'$, $\boldsymbol{N}^{\frac{1}{2}}$ be the $m \times m$ diagonal matrix with $\sqrt{\nu_\alpha}$, $\alpha = 1, \cdots, m$, on the diagonal, $\boldsymbol{D} = \sum_{k=1}^{m} \boldsymbol{D}_k$, and $\boldsymbol{A} = \boldsymbol{L}\boldsymbol{N}^{\frac{1}{2}}$. Then $\Pi = \sum_k \Pi_k = \boldsymbol{A}\boldsymbol{D}\boldsymbol{A}'$. Under the assumptions that $m \leqslant p + 1$, rank $\boldsymbol{A} = m$, and all the diagonal elements of $\boldsymbol{D}$ are different and nonzero, the following procedure determines the matrices $\boldsymbol{L}$ and $\boldsymbol{N}$ of latent parameters.

Factor Π_0 as $\Pi_0 = \boldsymbol{B}\boldsymbol{B}'$ and Π as $\Pi = \boldsymbol{C}\boldsymbol{C}'$. (The matrices $\boldsymbol{B}$ and $\boldsymbol{C}$ are not unique, but any factorization will do.) Let $\boldsymbol{T} = (\boldsymbol{B}\boldsymbol{B}')^{-1}\boldsymbol{B}'\boldsymbol{C}$. A complete principal component analysis of TT' will yield an orthogonal matrix Q, and it can be shown that $A = BQ$. Since the first row of L is a vector of 1's, the first row of A is an estimate of the vector $(\sqrt{\nu_1}, \cdots, \sqrt{\nu_m})$, so that N is easily determined. The matrix L is then just $AN^{-\frac{1}{2}}$.

The major shortcoming of this procedure is the problem of how to guess at values of the π's bearing repeated subscripts. No one has yet devised a rule which, when applied to a set of p's, will yield consistent estimators of L and N. For example, Green suggests using $p_{ii} = p_i^2 + \max_{j \neq i}(p_{ij} - p_i p_j)$ as a guess at π_{ii}. Yet in the case $m = 2$, $p = 3$ with latent parameters $\nu_1 = \nu_2 = .5$, $\lambda_{11} = .9$, $\lambda_{12} = .2$, $\lambda_{13} = .8$, $\lambda_{21} = .7$, $\lambda_{22} = .9$, $\lambda_{23} = .4$, if $i = 2$, $\max_{j \neq 2}(p_{2j} - p_2 p_j)$ is a consistent estimator of $-.07$, so that p_{22} is a consistent estimator of something smaller than π_2^2. But $\pi_{ii} \geq \pi_i^2$, so that p_{22} is not a consistent estimator of π_{22}.

Determinantal method of estimation. A matricial procedure that does not have the above shortcoming, since it involves only estimable π's, was first suggested by Lazarsfeld and Dudman (see Lazarsfeld 1951) and independently by Koopmans (1951), developed by Anderson (1954), and extended by Gibson (1955; 1962) and Madansky (1960). For ease of exposition, the procedure will be described only for the cases treated by Anderson.

Assume that $p \geq 2m + 1$. In that case, $2m + 1$ different items can be selected from the p items (say, the first $2m + 1$) and the following matrices of π's involving only these items formed. Let

$$\Pi^* = \begin{bmatrix} 1 & \pi_1 & \cdots & \pi_m \\ \pi_{m+1} & \pi_{1,m+1} & \cdots & \pi_{m,m+1} \\ \vdots & \vdots & & \vdots \\ \pi_{2m} & \pi_{1,2m} & \cdots & \pi_{m,2m} \end{bmatrix}$$

and let $\tilde{\Pi}$ be the matrix Π^* with the 1 replaced by π_{2m+1} and all the π's having the additional subscript $2m + 1$. Let Λ_1 be an $(m+1) \times (m+1)$ matrix with the first row a vector of 1's and the jth row $(j = 2, \cdots, m+1)$ the vector $(\lambda_{1,j-1}, \cdots, \lambda_{m,j-1})$, and let Λ_2 be an $(m+1) \times (m+1)$ matrix with first row a vector of 1's and the jth row $(j = 2, \cdots, m+1)$ the vector $(\lambda_{1,m+j-1}, \cdots, \lambda_{m,m+j-1})$. Let N and D_{2m+1} be defined as above. Then $\Pi^* = \Lambda_1 N \Lambda_2'$ and $\tilde{\Pi} = \Lambda_1 N D_{2m+1} \Lambda_2'$. Thus, if the diagonal elements of D_{2m+1} are distinct and if Λ_1, N, and Λ_2 are of full rank, then the diagonal elements of D_{2m+1} are the roots θ of the determinantal equation $|\tilde{\Pi} - \theta \Pi^*| = 0$.

Table 1

Parameter	Value	Asymptotic variance
ν_1	3/4	$1115.42/n$
λ_{11}	1/2	$39.00/n$
λ_{12}	1/3	$60.89/n$
λ_{13}	1/3	$4.96/n$
λ_{21}	1/4	$303.00/n$
λ_{22}	2/3	$611.53/n$
λ_{23}	1/4	$31.00/n$

If Z is the matrix of characteristic vectors corresponding to the roots $\theta_1, \cdots, \theta_m$, then the columns of $\Pi^* Z$ are proportional to the columns of Λ_1, with the constant of proportionality determined by the condition that the first row of Λ_1 is a vector of 1's. A similar argument using the transposes of $\tilde{\Pi}$ and Π^* yields Λ_2, and N is determined by $N = \Lambda_1^{-1} \Pi^* \Lambda_2'^{-1}$.

A difficulty with this procedure is that it depends critically on which $2m + 1$ items are chosen from the p items, on which of these $2m + 1$ is chosen to define Π^*, and on the allocation of the $2m$ items to the rows and columns defining Π^*. That is, it depends critically on the ordering of the items. There are no general rules available for an ordering of the items that will yield relatively efficient estimators of the latent parameters.

The most important shortcoming of this procedure and of its extensions (which involve more of the π's) is that there is no guarantee that when the procedure is used with a set of p's it will produce permissible estimates of the latent parameters, that is, estimates that are real numbers between 0 and 1. In four sampling experiments with $n = 1,000$, $m = 3$, and $p = 8$, Anderson and Carleton (1957) found that of 2,240 determinantal equations only 33.7 per cent had all roots between 0 and 1. Madansky (1959) computed the asymptotic variance of the determinantal estimates for the case $m = 2$, $p = 3$, a case in which these estimators, if permissible, are the maximum likelihood estimators of the latent parameters, and found the results presented in Table 1, where n is the sample size. Thus, sample sizes must be greater than 1,116 for the variance of the estimators of all the parameters to be less than 1.

Table 2

$$\pi_{123:\phi} = 10/192$$
$$\pi_{23:1} = 14/192$$
$$\pi_{13:2} = 17/192$$
$$\pi_{12:3} = 22/192$$
$$\pi_{3:12} = 19/192$$
$$\pi_{2:13} = 34/192$$
$$\pi_{1:23} = 35/192$$
$$\pi_{\phi:123} = 41/192$$

Table 3

Response pattern	Number observed
123;ϕ	2
23;1	3
13;2	4
12;3	4
3;12	4
2;13	7
1;23	7
ϕ;123	9

Rounding error also affects the estimates greatly. The parameters of the multinomial distribution for the above model are given in Table 2.

For a sample of size 40, if one had actually observed the expected number of respondents for each of the response patterns (rounded to the nearest integer), then the sample would have the composition shown in Table 3. Table 4 shows the p_σ's based on these data (π_σ being given for comparison). The determinantal estimates of the latent parameters are given in the third column of Table 5. (The fourth column will be discussed below.)

Partitioning method of estimation. A third estimation procedure (Madansky 1959) looks at the problem in a different light. Since the latent classes are defined as those classes within which the p components of the vector x are statistically independent, one might (at least conceptually) look at all possible assignments of the n observations into m classes and find that assignment for which the usual χ^2 test statistic for independence is smallest. The estimates of the latent parameters would then just be the appropriate proportions based on this best assignment. They would always be permissible. Although for finite samples they would not be identical with minimum χ^2 estimates, they would have the same asymptotic properties and thus be asymptotically equivalent to maximum likelihood estimates.

Madansky (1959) introduced another measure of independence, simpler to compute than χ^2, and found that the asymptotic efficiency of the estimators of the latent parameters from this procedure, in the example described above, is about .91. The obvious shortcoming of this idea is that it is too time consuming to carry out all the possible assign-

Table 4

σ	p_σ	π_σ
1	.425	.4375
2	.400	.4167
3	.325	.3125
12	.150	.1667
13	.150	.1406
23	.125	.1250
123	.050	.0521

ments, even for moderate samples on an electronic computer. In the example described above, for a sample of size 40 it took four hours of computation on the IBM 704 to enumerate and assess all the assignments into two classes. The resulting estimates are shown in the fourth column of Table 5.

Table 5 — Parameter estimates for two methods*

Parameter	Value	Determinantal estimate	Partitioning estimate
ν_1	.75	.23	.58
λ_{11}	.50	.82	.00
λ_{12}	.33	.23	.43
λ_{13}	.33	.42	.30
λ_{21}	.25	.30	1.00
λ_{22}	.67	.45	.35
λ_{23}	.25	.29	.35

* $n = 40$.

Source: Madansky 1959, p. 21.

Scoring methods. Current activity on estimation procedures for the latent class model (Henry 1964) is directed toward writing computer routines using the scoring procedure described by McHugh (1956) to obtain best asymptotically normal estimates of the latent parameters. The scoring procedure will yield estimators with the same large asymptotic variances as those indicated by the above example of the maximum likelihood estimators' asymptotic variances. Also, the scoring procedure has the same permissibility problem associated with it as did the determinantal approach described above. However, the problem can be alleviated for this procedure by using a set of consistent permissible estimators for initial values in the scoring procedure.

ALBERT MADANSKY

[*See also* SCALING. *Directly related are the entries* DISTRIBUTIONS, STATISTICAL, *article on* MIXTURES OF DISTRIBUTIONS; FACTOR ANALYSIS; STATISTICAL IDENTIFIABILITY.]

BIBLIOGRAPHY

ANDERSON, T. W. 1954 On Estimation of Parameters in Latent Structure Analysis. *Psychometrika* 19:1–10.
ANDERSON, T. W. 1959 Some Scaling Models and Estimation Procedures in the Latent Class Model. Pages 9–38 in Ulf Grenander (editor), *Probability and Statistics.* New York: Wiley.
ANDERSON, T. W.; and CARLETON, R. O. 1957 Sampling Theory and Sampling Experience in Latent Structure Analysis. *Journal of the American Statistical Association* 52:363 only.
BENINI, RODOLFO 1928 Gruppi chiusi e gruppi aperti in alcuni fatti collettivi di combinazioni. International Statistical Institute, *Bulletin* 23, no. 2:362–383.
COURNOT, A. A. 1838 Mémoire sur les applications du calcul des chances à la statistique judiciaire. *Journal de mathématiques pures et appliquées* 3:257–334.

deMeo, G. 1934 Su di alcuni indici atti a misurare l'attrazione matrimoniale in classificazioni dicotome. Accademia delle Scienze Fisiche e Matematiche, Naples, *Rendiconto* 73:62–77.

Gibson, W. A. 1955 An Extension of Anderson's Solution for the Latent Structure Equations. *Psychometrika* 20:69–73.

Gibson, W. A. 1962 Extending Latent Class Solutions to Other Variables. *Psychometrika* 27:73–81.

Green, Bert F. Jr. 1951 A General Solution for the Latent Class Model of Latent Structure Analysis. *Psychometrika* 16:151–166.

Henry, Neil 1964 The Computation of Efficient Estimates in Latent Class Analysis. Unpublished manuscript, Columbia Univ., Bureau of Applied Social Research.

Koopmans, T. C. 1951 Identification Problems in Latent Structure Analysis. Cowles Commission Discussion Paper: Statistics, No. 360. Unpublished manuscript.

Lazarsfeld, Paul F. 1950 The Logical and Mathematical Foundation of Latent Structure Analysis. Pages 362–412 in Samuel A. Stouffer et al., *Measurement and Prediction*. Princeton Univ. Press.

Lazarsfeld, Paul F. 1951 *The Use of Mathematical Models in the Measurement of Attitudes*. Research Memorandum RM-455. Santa Monica (Calif.): RAND Corporation.

Lazarsfeld, Paul F. 1959 Latent Structure Analysis. Pages 476–543 in Sigmund Koch (editor), *Psychology: A Study of a Science*. Volume 3: Formulations of the Person and the Social Context. New York: McGraw-Hill.

McHugh, Richard B. 1956 Efficient Estimation and Local Identification in Latent Class Analysis. *Psychometrika* 21:331–347.

McHugh, Richard B. 1958 Note on "Efficient Estimation. . . ." *Psychometrika* 23:273–274. → This is a correction to McHugh 1956.

Madansky, Albert 1959 *Partitioning Methods in Latent Class Analysis*. Paper P-1644. Santa Monica (Calif.): RAND Corporation.

Madansky, Albert 1960 Determinantal Methods in Latent Class Analysis. *Psychometrika* 25:183–198.

Weinberg, Wilhelm 1902 Beiträge zur Physiologie und Pathologie der Mehrlingsgeburten beim Menschen. *Pflüger's Archiv für die gesamte Physiologie des Menschen und der Tiere* 88:346–430.

LATIN AMERICAN POLITICAL MOVEMENTS

The dominant characteristic of twentieth-century Latin America is the pressure for fundamental change—social, economic, and political change. In several nations, governments committed to such change have come to power. Even in many of the nations where conservative oligarchies maintain their hold, the pressures for change are such that few governments have believed it wise to ignore them completely. Dynamic forces are at work: population growth, urbanization, industrial development, growth of labor unions, the appearance and increasing influence of certain political parties, and an increasing demand on the part of the underprivileged and depressed mass of people for a better material life ("the revolution in rising expectations"). These forces have promoted, and to some degree have been promoted by, the emergence of several radical or reformist political movements during this century. The major ones are the Mexican revolution, the Uruguayan reforms (Batllism), the *Apristas*, Peronism, the Vargas movement, the Christian Democrats, and Castroism.

General characteristics and influences

Considerable similarity exists among these movements. They advocate development and various economic reforms, a strong government and a larger role for government, especially in the economic and social areas, and social reforms (e.g., increased literacy, expanded educational opportunities, social welfare programs). They appeal to and in varying degrees involve the masses. They urge either a breaking down or a modifying of traditional class lines and concomitantly urge broader mass participation in national life. In their economics most movements embrace some form of socialism. They are nationalistic and, either as an aspect of nationalism or as a separate ingredient, they inveigh against economic and political imperialism. Their anti-imperialism may be simply a negative, anti-United States sentiment, or it may be an aspect of a more positive phenomenon: a prohemispheric or pro-Latin American sentiment.

Numerous differences also exist among the movements. Some have a well-developed theoretical or philosophical base (especially the *Apristas* and the Christian Democrats); others are primarily pragmatic. They differ in the stress put on certain goals. Perhaps the major differences concern means of achieving desired changes and the kind of society that would be created. These differences are the effect of several factors: the level of social, economic, and political development; the political situation; and the variety of attitudes, inclinations, and estimations of the individuals who provide or have provided both intellectual and practical leadership for the movements.

The stress that twentieth-century movements put on change places them in sharp contrast with the political thought that previously dominated Latin America. That thought, primarily European in origin, was the monopoly of the small elite that had enjoyed political and economic power and high social status since independence. Reflecting the interests of the elite, the earlier thought either defended the *status quo* or urged relatively minor change, usually of a political nature (e.g., changes in electoral laws). In those instances where the principles advocated cannot be termed "minor" (e.g., matters in the area of church–state relations), they did not call for fundamental changes, nor were the changes called for intended to affect the masses. Where concerned with economic matters, the earlier thought proposed relatively moderate changes. Comtean positivism, the single most influential line of political thought in late nineteenth-century Latin America, emphasized a free secular society and the idea that the growth of knowledge gradually promoted political freedom and economic improvement. In short, the earlier political thought—still dominant in some of the nations—did not advocate a restructuring or reorganization of society; the newer political thought does.

This article will focus first on general factors influencing the new political thought, and then on each of the twentieth-century political movements and the methods it endorsed or employed to promote change.

The factors that have molded or influenced the movements may be classified as primarily material or primarily intellectual. These, in turn, may be classified as indigenous or nonindigenous, positive or negative influences.

Material influences. The most obvious and the single most important material influence is negative and indigenous: the reaction against prevailing economic conditions. Indeed, this is usually the main goal of all the movements, for other goals are seen to be directly related to it. The movements insist that conditions must be changed and advocate a massive, multipronged program of economic development. To some degree the desire for economic development may be attributed to the positive, nonindigenous influence of the world's mature economies, since economically less-developed nations desire to have the same level of economic well-being and diversity of economic activity. (This desire does not mean, however, that Latin America accepts the economic principles of the mature economies.)

A second influence, also negative and indigenous, is the reaction against prevailing social conditions. A large part, in some cases a majority, of the population is cut off from national life, living in a depressed condition without opportunity to achieve a better status. The movements pledge to improve the lot of this segment of the population and appeal to it for support.

Prevailing political conditions are a third negative, indigenous influence. Democratic forms (con-stitutions which are often modeled after that of the United States and provide for separation of powers, bills of rights, political parties, elections, and a variety of special devices to ensure democratic government) have long existed, but in many of the Latin American nations political practice has been quite undemocratic. Further, government, whether military or civilian, has been *by* and *for* the small elite, usually ignoring the needs of the masses. All of the movements advocate change in the political process. They may not agree on the kind of political system or how it should function, but they do agree that government by them and based on their principles will not be government devoted to promoting and protecting the interests of the elite. It will be government for (although not necessarily by) the masses.

Another negative influence, both indigenous and nonindigenous, on all of the movements (except perhaps Batllism) is the resentment against the economic and political influence the United States has long had and still has in Latin America. Limitation, if not elimination, of U.S. influence is a goal of the twentieth-century movements. Proposed means of accomplishing this end include controls on foreign capital, nationalization of some or all foreign investment, closer cooperation among Latin American nations, and creation of a new inter-American organization. The extent and intensity of efforts to reduce U.S. influence vary, of course, from movement to movement and from time to time.

Intellectual influences. For the most part the programs put forward by the movements are not borrowed ones. Rather, they are a response to local conditions. Nevertheless, various "outside" ideas and events have influenced all of the movements. European socialism, including Marxism, has had a tremendous impact on most of the movements. The same is true of French, British, and United States liberal thought. The notion of Latin American unification can be traced back to the liberator Simón Bolívar, and the ideal has been embraced by a host of persons in succeeding years. Similarly, the *Aprista* emphasis on the development of an Indian or Indo-American culture has some roots in Latin American thought.

The economic and social reforms of President Franklin D. Roosevelt (the New Deal) had an impact on several of the movements. The same can be said of the British Labour party and the development program "Operation Bootstrap" carried out by Muñoz Marín in Puerto Rico. Since the end of World War II, the "new economics" of Raúl Prebisch and the United Nations

Economic Commission for Latin America has been the major influence on Latin American economic thought.

The major movements

The Mexican revolution and the Uruguayan reforms may be added to the list of general influences, since these movements preceded the others and have served as examples, if not as models. They will therefore be discussed first.

The Mexican revolution. The Mexican revolution, the foremost political movement of twentieth-century Latin America, began in 1910 under the leadership of Francisco I. Madero as a revolt against the dictatorship of President Porfirio Díaz. Its original objectives were entirely political, as epitomized by Madero's slogan, "Effective Suffrage! No Re-election!" As the revolt spread and its support increased, it became a full-blown social revolution. Economic and social objectives—land reform, economic development, restrictions on the church and foreign capital, integration of the Indians, destruction of the existing class structure and class barriers—were added to the political objectives. Civil war raged until 1916. Thereafter order was progressively restored, and implementation of the revolutionary program began on a nation-wide scale.

The revolutionary program. The revolution was pragmatic and evolutionary, not ideological. No master plan existed concerning the implementation of objectives. The revolution consisted of a series of acts, and often these acts were experiments. As Robert Scott says, "Mexico had no Marx to supply a theoretical, rational, and systematic model for its revolution. And somehow history failed to produce any single dominant personality who could perform this service. . . . Probably the movement was too big, too diverse, and too spontaneous to be identified with any one program or person" ([1959] 1964, p. 98). To answer the question "What was the Mexican revolution?" one must look at what was done.

The best place to begin is the constitution of 1917. That document expresses the objectives of the revolution and gives considerable insight into its philosophy. It is a hybrid, because ". . . it retained the ideals of liberalism while placing the interests of society and of the state above those of the individual" (Ross 1963, p. 89). Three articles are especially worthy of note. Article 3 assigns to the national government responsibility for providing free, public elementary education. The article reflects the importance attached to education by the revolutionary leaders and the anticlerical bent

of the revolution. Article 27 deals with landownership and the rights of foreign capital, limits the size of agricultural holdings, and asserts the nation's control over the subsoil. Property is held to have a "social function," with the rights of private property subordinated to "social welfare." The article expresses several tenets of the revolution: hostility to the *hacienda*, commitment to agrarian reform, determination to overhaul the prerevolutionary class structure based on landownership, anticlericalism (for the church was a large landowner), opposition to foreigners, and nationalism. Article 123 assigns to the state the task of promoting, protecting, and regulating the labor movement and spells out the economic and social rights of labor. "The basic principle of Article 123 was that labor was a status, a way of life, for which the minimum essentials were now constitutionally guaranteed, rather than an economic commodity, subject to the market vagaries of supply and demand" (Cline 1953, p. 169). The article reflects the role—both the right and responsibility—assigned to the state in promoting social welfare, the effort to enhance the position of the working class, and concern with industrialization and the urban sector of the economy.

An extensive land reform program was begun in the early 1920s. Under this plan, land, either government-owned or taken from persons owning more than 5,000 hectares, was distributed to landless peasants. While some land was given outright to the peasants, most of it was given to village communities, *ejidos*. The *ejido* is not a collective farm; rather, it is a form of landholding with historical antecedents both in Spain and in pre-Hispanic Mexico. *Ejido* land is divided among the families of the community and is worked by them as individual units. Although the *ejidatario* cannot alienate his land, he can pass it on to his heir. By the mid-1960s, 40 to 50 per cent of the cropland was in *ejidos*, and about 30 per cent was in small and medium-size private holdings (Needler 1964, pp. 21–22).

During the early years of the revolution relatively little was done in the economic area apart from land reform, despite the declared objective of economic development. Admittedly some actions were taken that had economic effects (for example, nationalization of agricultural lands, railroads, and petroleum), but they were socially and politically, not economically, motivated (Cline [1962] 1963, p. 231). And the few economic programs that were attempted were unsuccessful.

The desire for economic independence, plus the adverse effects of the great depression and World

War II, dramatized the need for action and led to the inauguration of a development program. One part of this program was to increase the tempo of land reform. Another part, the key, was industrialization, and through various inducements a high rate of industrial development has been achieved. Industrialization is, in large part, the result of a shift in Mexican attitudes toward foreign capital; it is no longer rejected, but is welcomed. This shift in attitude is only one manifestation of a more general phenomenon: moderation of the revolution. (Such moderation is typical of radical movements once they have achieved power and consolidated their position.) However, the government is at least partially enforcing "Mexicanization" laws, which require that Mexicans must own 51 per cent of all business enterprises.

The economic and social programs accomplished fundamental change. The class structure was revamped and the prerevolutionary landowning elite was replaced by a new upper class whose wealth is in industry, commerce, and finance. A large, predominantly urban and industrial middle class has developed. The urban and rural masses have benefited, although the benefits have been limited. However, there has been much upward mobility of individuals *between* classes, and it is primarily through such individual mobility that substantial improvements in the real standard of living of the urban and rural proletariats can result (Needler 1964, p. 31).

The political objectives of the revolution have been implemented. Governmental stability has been achieved. "Effective Suffrage! No Re-election!" has been effected. A fairly high level of democracy prevails. Government is sensitive to citizen wants. Opposition groups are free to organize and operate. Civil liberties exist.

Mexico's foreign policy is based on the principles and experiences of the revolution: national sovereignty, juridical equality of nations, self-determination, and nonintervention. The Estrada doctrine, a Mexican contribution to international legal ideas, asserts that granting or withholding of diplomatic recognition at a government's discretion constitutes interference in the affairs of another state. Recognition should, therefore, be automatic.

Theory and philosophy. Although not an ideological movement, the revolution was not devoid of political thought. A list of writers would include (but not be limited to) Andres Molina Enríquez, Jesús Silva Herzog, Graciano Sánchez, Vincente Lombardo Toledano, Manuel Gamio, Gilberto Loyo, Fernando Gonzales Roa, Daniel Cosio Villegas, and Gómez Morin.

Uruguayan reform (Batllism).   A much different but only slightly less important movement (Batllism) remade Uruguay during the first quarter of the twentieth century under the leadership of José Batlle y Ordónez. Like the Mexican revolution, Batllism was concerned with social, economic, and political problems. Also like the Mexican revolution, it was pragmatic, not ideological. Unlike the Mexican revolution it was a peaceful movement and did not touch the whole population; its impact was primarily urban.

The program.   The actions taken under Batllism earned for Uruguay the reputation of being one of the world's most advanced laboratories for political, social, and economic experimentation (Fitzgibbon 1954, pp. 96–97).

The social and economic aspects of Batllism— which constituted a high degree of state socialism —can be described by citing what was done during Batlle's two presidential terms, 1903–1907 and 1911–1915. His proposal for an eight-hour working day and a weekly rest period was enacted, as were laws to protect the worker's life and health and to encourage labor union activity. During Batlle's presidency elementary education was made obligatory and education at all levels was made free. New schools were constructed; a women's university was established. Foreign professors and technicians were brought to Uruguay, and scholarships were given for study abroad.

Various social service measures were also enacted. Laws were passed giving protection to women, children, the sick, and the elderly. Women were emancipated. Divorce was legalized. Tax was abolished on the earnings of the lowest-paid public officials and on the smallest pensions.

Furthermore, steps were taken to stimulate industry. Immigration was encouraged. A state insurance monopoly was created. The Bank of the Republic was nationalized. Several government-owned and government-operated industries were established to provide certain basic products at a low price and to reduce dependence on imports. Railroads, power facilities, meat-packing plants, and some other businesses were nationalized.

Although Batllism focused attention on urban, industrial problems, some attention was also given to the agricultural sector. Stock raising and agriculture received governmental assistance. Rural credit facilities were established. Agricultural research was promoted. Import duties on agricultural tools and machinery were removed. To some degree, the agricultural programs may have been a means of "buying" rural toleration, for Batlle was detested and opposed by the large landowners.

From the perspective of the second half of the twentieth century, Batlle's reforms may seem extremely mild, but for the first quarter of the twentieth century they were radical.

The political reforms were equally radical. Batlle saw a Uruguay plagued with political problems, e.g., dictatorship, instability, and civil strife. He blamed these problems on the domination and abuses of past presidents. To overcome the problems, Batlle proposed the abolition of the presidency and the establishment of a nine-member executive council (modeled on the Swiss collegial executive) with three of the seats assigned to the minority party. Further, he proposed that congressional elections be conducted on a proportional representation system. The proposal met with hostility, especially from his own party, and was not adopted until 1919 (after Batlle was out of office) —and then in limited form. The bi-partisan collegial executive was abandoned in 1933 but reestablished, and in the form Batlle envisioned, in 1951. Batlle's political reforms are largely responsible for the high level of democracy that prevails in Uruguay.

Theory and philosophy. Very little theoretical writing is associated with Batllism. Batlle's ideas are expressed in his articles in *El Día*, his newspaper. But the articles "do not form a very systematic whole, since he did not generally concern himself with the philosophical base of ideas" (Davis 1958, p. 103).

The "Apristas." Between the two world wars Peru produced a distinctive ideological party, the Alianza Popular Revolucionaria Americana (APRA), whose ideology was popularly known as *aprismo* and whose members were called *Apristas*. The party dates back to 1914, but it was not formally organized until 1931. Led by Victor Raúl Haya de la Torre, the *Apristas* have had an almost hemisphere-wide influence, and *Aprista*-type parties have been founded in these areas and countries: in Cuba, Partido Revolucionario Cubano (Auténtico); in Venezuela, Acción Democrática; in Costa Rica, Liberación Nacional; in Paraguay, Partido Febrerista; in Haiti, Mouvement Ouvrier et Paysan; and in Puerto Rico, the Popular Democratic Party. However, there was little contact between the *Aprista* parties during their formative years.

Aprismo was begun by a group of students at Lima's University of San Marcos who led a successful effort to reform the school. Their next step was to establish night schools for adults, in order to raise the economic and social level of the illiterate (Kantor 1953). The government suppressed the schools and exiled the student organizers, who then decided that political action was necessary and developed the *Aprista* ideology.

The ideology. *Aprismo* is a blend of ideas and ideals about the uniqueness of Latin America and democratic socialism. The aim is to create a "new" Peru and a "new" Latin America. The basic thesis is that Latin America is unique; it is different from the United States and Europe, and must cease imitating their institutions and create its own Indo-American culture. (The thesis is related to Haya's historical space–time theory, which holds that there is no single theory or explanation of history valid for all societies.) Its over-all plan consists of two parts: a "maximum program" for all Latin America and a "minimum program" for Peru only. The principles of the maximum program are integration or assimilation of the Indian population, opposition to imperialism, unification of the Latin American nations, a planned economy including nationalization of land and business, and democratic government.

Aprista thinkers stress the need to integrate the Indian into society. To the *Apristas*, Latin America will not realize its economic or political potential until the Indian has been integrated. Two conflicting cultures are said to exist in Latin America, one European, the other indigenous, or Indian. The result is instability. A stable society will be possible in Latin America only when the two clashing cultures are merged. The *Apristas* believe that their program would amalgamate the Indian and Europeanized sections and produce a *new*, integrated Indo-American culture containing elements from both (Kantor 1953). Integration would not be easy or quick, and to achieve it several actions would be necessary: free, state-controlled education, including technical education; agrarian reform (formation of cooperative farms, government authority to regulate land purchases and sales, programs to increase productivity, and dissemination of technical information); and laws to enhance the position of labor (wage and hour laws, retirement benefits, employment services, organization of unions).

Anti-imperialism is another major tenet. Indeed, the *Apristas* believe that the most important problem facing Latin America is that created by imperialistic penetration. Imperialism, held to be economic in nature, is explained in the following terms:

Outward expansion is inevitable in a highly industrialized country based on the capitalist system of production. As the *Apristas* see the process, capitalism forces an industrially developed country to seek raw materials in the underdeveloped areas of the world. At the same time, an industrial country must seek markets for the manufactured goods which cannot be consumed at home.   (Kantor 1953, pp. 37–38)

And in an alliance with local elites, foreign capital gained control of the Latin American economies. However, the *Apristas* do not reject foreign capital; they recognize that it has made a contribution and can continue to do so. But foreign capital must be controlled to ensure that it plays a "useful role." Without eliminating their opposition to imperialism, *Aprista* leaders have over the years moderated their statements on this subject.

The *Apristas* hold that unification of Latin America is the only means of combating imperialism and strengthening Latin America. They see Latin America as a single "natural unit." Existing boundaries have no justification, being mere carry-overs from the colonial period that perpetuate economic feudalism. *Apristas* insist that unification would not be difficult. There are, they say, more similarities than differences among the hemisphere's people. Unification is necessary for defense. Further, realization of increased economic and political strength should be sufficient to overcome any hurdles that may exist. Two strong but not insurmountable forces—U.S. imperialism and the elite—work against unification. Although opposed to U.S. imperialism, the *Apristas* are not anti-United States. They desire to cooperate with the United States, seeing cooperation as a benefit to both parties. And Latin American unification is seen as a means of promoting cooperation by putting Latin America and the United States on an equal footing.

Economic development is a goal. Originally nationalization of industry and land was posited as the ideal form of economic organization. However, nationalization was a long-range goal, and the means of achieving it was spelled out. Nationalization is another area in which *Aprista* doctrine has changed; a mixed economy is now envisioned.

Haya de la Torre and other Peruvian *Aprista* leaders insist that the political process must be democratic, and they refuse to use force to obtain power. One author states that the most conspicuous weakness of the Peruvian *Apristas* is their neglect of the means of achieving power (Kantor 1953, p. 1). Asked why the *Apristas* have not used force, Haya replied ". . . that although the *Apristas* were not pacifists, they were convinced that the experience of history demonstrated that the use of violence in politics exposed its users to the danger of degenerating into complete dependence upon violence . . ." (Kantor 1953, p. 56). However, not all *Aprista*-type parties have refused to use force.

In Venezuela, Acción Democrática joined with segments of the military to overthrow a government, and when it came into power, established a democratic political process.

The Peruvian *Apristas* endeavor to make their movement more than a political party, seeing themselves as soldiers in a crusade and as seekers of educational purification which will transform Peru into a modern, democratic nation. They want to establish a high standard of living, but even more important than that, they want to see a spiritual renovation within Peru which will create a new country based on a morally changed people (*ibid.*, p. 61). In short, they seek to make *aprismo* a way of life.

Theory and philoscphy.   The theory and philosophy of *aprismo* is expressed in countless works and by numerous writers. Of the writers, Haya de la Torre stands out. Others who should be mentioned include Manuel Seoane, Luis Alberto Sánchez, Alfredo Saco, and Carlos Mariategui (a founder of *aprismo* who later embraced international communism).

Peronism.   Argentina's Peronist movement began in 1945: the following year the movement's leader, Juan D. Perón, was elected president of Argentina; he and his program then dominated the nation until mid-1955. Although Peronism wrought change, the change was not as fundamental as in the Mexican revolution and Batllism or in the *Aprista* program. Nevertheless, Peronism had a tremendous impact on Argentina, and despite the dictatorial, corrupt nature of Perón's regime and its eventual collapse, its impact has not been eradicated—probably cannot be eradicated.

Some have labeled Peronism as fascism (Lipset 1960, pp. 173–176). Still others reject the label (Silvert 1963, pp. 361–366), and the latter individuals may have the better case. Granted Perón may have been favorably impressed by Franco's Spain and Mussolini's Italy and some of his statements had fascist or profascist overtones. But Peronism differed from European fascism in fundamental ways. Actually, Peronism was nonideological, despite the appearance of *justicialismo*—the so-called ideology of the movement. The term *justicialismo* did not appear until 1949 (Blanksten 1953), and the *justicialist* ideas were propounded after that. *Justicialismo*—the "balancing of forces" or "Third Position"—never passed beyond being whatever Perón did or said.

The program.   Peronism advocated the "economic independence of Argentina," and to this end a primarily industrial development program was pursued to free the country from dependence on agriculture, imports, and foreign capital. As part of the development program, and as part of the nationalism that characterized Peronism, the government nationalized some industries and took over foreign-owned transportation and communications facilities. In typical twentieth-century Latin American fashion, private property was held to have a "social function" and was subordinated to state regulation.

The heart of Peronism was the program of "social justice." That program was directed toward the great mass of workers (the *descamisados*), who lived in ignorance and poverty and whose minimum wants and needs were ignored by the privileged members of society (Edelmann 1965, p. 354). A large body of social and labor legislation was enacted. The social and economic rights of the masses were written into the 1949 constitution. The *descamisados* were molded into a political force and a source of support by Perón, who, in return, rewarded them with social and economic benefits, a voice in government, and a government that was sympathetic to their needs and wants. (Perón's wife, Evita, played a major role in the program of "social justice.") The benefits were achieved at a price in addition to their financial cost: a loss of freedom of action.

Perón attempted to export his movement, or at least his influence, through labor attachés in Argentine embassies in Latin America, through general publicity, and through contacts with military leaders in other Latin American nations. And although Peronist governments did not come to power elsewhere in Latin America, Perón's efforts had some political impact in other Latin American nations.

The program was, however, very limited. The land tenure system was not changed. Wealth was not redistributed. The pre-Perón social class structure was not overthrown. And a question may be raised if Peronism was anything more than a typical Latin American dictatorship. Davis, for example, says Peronism was simply "a shrewd mixture of militarism, economic planning, and a demagogic appeal to the underprivileged [cemented with] a long overdue program of labor and social legislation" (1958, p. 112). Certainly Perón "governed internally by juggling already existing power centers in a fashion typical of states in immediately prenational situations, and . . . the regime even toppled in traditional . . . Latin American style" (Silvert 1963, p. 366). The power centers referred to were the army, the church, the oligarchy, "foreign imperialists," the interior, the *porteños*, and a new one, labor.

But the importance of Peronism must not be underestimated. The workers saw a government aware of their needs that allowed them a certain degree of participation in the political process, and, perhaps equally important, even the integrated middle and upper classes were finally willing to admit the alienation of some of their fellow citizens. Most of all, Peronism convinced the workers that much *could* be done by government to improve their lot. As a result, Peronism—even without Perón—remains a political force in Argentina.

Theory and philosophy. Peronism, a pragmatic movement, at first borrowed from the Neo-Thomism of Nicolas Desiri, an Argentine priest and philosopher, and from the ideas of Hernán Benítez, whose writings appeared in the *Revista de la Universidad de Buenos Aires.* After 1949, Peronism sought to develop its own ideology, *justicialismo.* Three men in particular endeavored to make it a social and political philosophy: Raúl A. Mende, Julio Claudio Otero, and Luis C. A. Serras. However, it is in the speeches of Péron and his wife that one finds most of the ideas of Peronism.

The Vargas movement. The major twentieth-century political movement in Brazil was that of Getulio Vargas, who headed the government from 1938 to 1945 and from 1950 to 1954. In many respects, the Vargas and Perón movements are of the same species. Originally Vargas relied for support on the *tenentes* (a group of young officers and civilians), but gradually he expanded his base through appeals to the discontented. Shortly before the 1938 election, Vargas promulgated a new constitution (the *estado novo* constitution) with features resembling Portuguese corporatism and Italian fascism. But the resemblance "was rather superficial; . . . the *estado novo* . . . is better understood as the product of Brazilian social and political elements" (Davis 1958, p. 109).

The program. Vargas pushed economic development. The government built highways and railroads. A development commission was established to promote industry and commerce—Vargas' principal objective. Education was promoted. Social and labor measures were enacted. Of all the decisions made by Vargas, probably none had greater political implications than his determination to bring the working groups into the political arena. Vargas retained their approval through elaborate welfare programs and by imposing restrictions and obligations on business and management. At the same time he maintained strict federal control over the labor movement as a guarantee to the business community that labor would not be permitted to get out of hand (Johnson 1958, pp. 167–168).

The movement contained a strong element of nationalism. One expression of this nationalism was the law providing that two-thirds of the workers in every enterprise had to be Brazilian. Another expression, the most dramatic, was construction of the Volta Redonda steel plant.

The importance of the movement did not end with Vargas' death in 1954. The forces activated or promoted by him retain much political influence.

Theory and philosophy.   The Vargas movement evolved no political theory of its own. Vargas' speeches were pragmatic and opportunist, not theoretical. Francisco Campo's *O estado nacional*, published in 1940, was widely but wrongly viewed as the regime's fascist theory (Loewenstein 1942).

The Christian Democrats.   The Latin American political movement growing most rapidly in strength and influence is Christian Democracy. The movement is not new. The first Christian Democratic party was established in 1910 (in Uruguay), and since then Christian Democratic parties have been established in all the nations except Cuba, Haiti, Honduras, and Paraguay (Edelmann 1965, p. 355). Its growing influence is, however, a recent development (Szulc 1965). In 1958, a Christian Democratic party, COPEI, became the second largest party in Venezuela. In 1964, the Christian Democratic candidate, Eduardo Frei, was elected president of Chile, and the following year the party gained control of the lower house of congress.

The movement possesses a well-developed ideology, of European origin, adapted to fit the Latin American scene. It was greatly influenced by the writing of the Catholic philosopher Jacques Maritain, a spokesman for liberal Thomism. Frei is the leading Latin American spokesman of the movement.

The ideology.   Christian Democracy is based on the Christian ethic. More specifically, it is based on the tenets of Roman Catholicism, especially the encyclical *Rerum novarum*, issued by Pope Leo XIII in 1891. That encyclical, the so-called Magna Carta of labor, declared that laborers had the right to organize and the employer had an obligation to pay a fair wage.

Latin American Christian Democracy is reformist, and left of center or leftist. Its leaders are committed to achieving a social revolution through evolutionary means. Their objective is a society of social and Christian justice for all. They are committed to democracy—a political system *by* and *for* all the people. "Democracy," Frei writes, "will not be saved by those who, praising it as it now exists, petrify its abuses. Much less will it be saved by those who see only its defects and not its infinite

possibilities. . . . Our task is to realize the possibilities of democracy" (see statement in Pike 1964, p. 213). Frei argues that democracy does not in fact exist when a sizable portion of the population is not incorporated into society—a common phenomenon in Latin America. "In order to acquire and preserve the precious gifts of democracy it is necessary," Frei declares, "to incorporate this proletariat into the national existence" (*ibid.*, p. 217).

The programs of Latin American Christian Democratic parties differ from nation to nation. Some general comments may be made about the Chilean party, not because it is a "typical" Christian Democratic party but because of its political power. The Chilean Christian Democrats reject both capitalism and communism. They condemn capitalism as "merciless" and "degrading of human dignity" and brand communism as "totalitarian" and "undemocratic" (Bray 1965, p. 24).

They advocate a middle way, a "communitarian society," characterized by labor's involvement in management and ownership, and government action to prevent "economic concentration" (Sigmund 1963, p. 309). The 1963 Chilean Christian Democratic platform advocated a mixed economy, control of foreign investment, agrarian reform, and government reform. In the international sphere, the Chilean Christian Democrats desire to cooperate with the United States. At the same time, they insist that Latin America should have a stronger voice in world affairs and a broader range of international relations. Further, they urge the Latin American nations to cooperate among themselves. Frei is endeavoring to expand Chilean contacts with Europe. Also, he supports Latin American economic integration and is urging the creation of a common market for all of Latin America.

Theory and philosophy.   As noted earlier, a large measure of the Christian Democratic ideology is drawn from European sources. In addition to Frei, Latin Americans who have contributed to the ideology include Jaime Castillo, Jacques Chonchol, Julio Silva, Máximo Pacheco Gómez, Bernardo Leighton, Radomiro Tomic, and Rafael Caldera.

Castroism.   On New Year's Day, 1959, the Batista dictatorship in Cuba collapsed and Fidel Castro came to power. The victors, who had waged a guerrilla war since December 1956, were determined that "this was to be a thorough-going revolution. The institutions and groups which possessed sufficient power to block such a revolutionary course were to be neutralized and, if necessary, destroyed. Above all, the United States was not going to be able to impose limitations upon change" (Schneider 1964, pp. 27–28). And for the first time in Cuban history, a group of revolutionaries, after achieving power, began a full-scale social revolution instead of rewarding themselves with the spoils of government.

The program. A social revolution is a complex of actions. Only a few of the Cuban actions can be cited here.

The Agrarian Reform Law was passed just four months after Batista's fall. It had three objectives: to Cubanize and socialize the sugar industry, to give land to the landless, and to diversify agricultural production. The law provided for three types of holdings: state farms, sugar cooperatives (now scheduled to be converted into state farms), and small peasant properties. At present more than 70 per cent of the land is state owned.

Decrees during 1960 nationalized all large businesses, both Cuban and foreign. Since then additional businesses have been nationalized and a collective economy has emerged.

Beginning in 1962, emphasis was put on industrial expansion. However, after Castro's trip to Moscow in May 1963, Cuba accepted the principle of the international socialist division of labor, which led to a reversal of the revolution's original emphasis on agricultural diversification and industrialization (Hennessy 1964, p. 203). Now, as before 1959, emphasis is on sugar production.

Education has also received attention. An imaginative attack was made on adult illiteracy through the 1961 *alfabetismo* campaign. The public education system was reformed; teaching was nationalized; and private schools were suppressed. Emphasis in university education was placed on science and technology.

Evolution of Castroism. The Cuban revolution became a communist revolution. This statement is based on the view that "Castro was not a Communist for all practical purposes before he took power but decided to cast his lot with the Communists sometime afterward" (Draper 1965, p. 3).

Castro's "History Will Absolve Me" speech at his 1953 trial and the succeeding pamphlet provided the first insight into his objectives. He promised restoration of the 1940 constitution, a popularly elected government, and a relatively limited land reform program. "The most radical note in the speech . . . was perhaps a brief reference to the 'nationalization of the U.S.-owned electric and telephone companies' " (*ibid.*, p. 6). The "History Will Absolve Me" program was within the scope of traditional left-wing Cuban politics. The same judgment applies to the several pronouncements issued during the guerrilla war.

On December 2–3, 1961, Castro made his "I Am a Marxist–Leninist" speech. The speech was preceded by a host of actions indicating an increasing closeness between Castro and the communist bloc. Relations between Castro and the Cuban communists had not always been cordial; in the early 1950s they were strained. However, after Castro gained power, the communists not only supported him but also gave him the assistance of their trained cadres. At the same time Castro was gradually alienated from his moderate supporters, who consistently called for a slowing down of his efforts to turn society inside out (Burks 1963, p. 82).

With the "I Am a Marxist–Leninist" speech, Castroism obtained an ideology or philosophy. In and of itself Castroism was an armed struggle, not an ideology, and Castro gave very little attention to developing one for the movement. Rather, the movement borrowed or attached itself to existing ideologies and could change attachments (although it may no longer be able to do so).

Castro's identification with Marxism–Leninism put the Cuban revolution in a very different category from the other Latin American movements and led Castro to adopt means different from those used by the other movements. It also affected Cuban relations with the outside world. The identification with communism and the declared intention of exporting Castro-style revolutions have, more than anything else, made the United States and many Latin Americans hostile to Cuba.

Theory and philosophy. The numerous speeches and articles of Fidel Castro and his closest associates are the best source of the ideas or ideology of Castroism. Many of the speeches and articles have appeared in the Cuban periodicals *Cuba socialista, Revolución, Hoy,* and *Verde olivo.*

This article has focused on movements for relatively sharp reform or revolution. A more comprehensive treatment of significant political elements and groups would include an analysis of elements supporting the *status quo,* even though these elements perhaps do not constitute "movements." Hopefully, however, the article shows both the essence and the variation of the major twentieth-century Latin American political movements. In a very real sense, the essence is far greater than the variation. Furthermore, the movements, in their goals as well as in their means, resemble those found in other developing regions, and even the diversity of movements found in Latin America is similar to the diversity found in the new nations of Asia and Africa.

The ideas embodied in the twentieth-century movements stand in sharp contrast with the bulk of Latin America's nineteenth-century political thought. Nineteenth-century thought was nonindigenous, primarily imitative of European thought. The current movements are rooted in local social–economic–political conditions; hence, they are more realistic and practical as means of solving Latin American problems and restructuring Latin American society.

JAMES D. COCHRANE

[See also CARIBBEAN SOCIETY; CAUDILLISMO; MIDDLE AMERICAN SOCIETY; MODERNIZATION; REVOLUTION; SOCIAL MOVEMENTS; SOUTH AMERICAN SOCIETY.]

BIBLIOGRAPHY

ALEXANDER, ROBERT J. (1951) 1965 The Perón Era. New York: Russell.
BLANKSTEN, GEORGE I. 1953 Perón's Argentina. Univ. of Chicago Press.
BRAY, DONALD W. 1965 Chile Enters a New Era. Current History 48:21–25, 52.
BURKS, DAVID 1963 The Future of Castroism. Current History 44:78–83, 116.
CLINE, HOWARD F. (1953) 1963 The United States and Mexico. Rev. & enl. ed. New York: Atheneum; Cambridge, Mass.: Harvard Univ. Press.
CLINE, HOWARD F. (1962) 1963 Mexico: Revolution to Evolution, 1940–1960. New York: Oxford Univ. Press.
DAVIS, HAROLD E. 1958 Political Movements and Political Thought. Pages 94–118 in Harold E. Davis (editor), Government and Politics in Latin America. New York: Ronald.
DRAPER, THEODORE 1962 Castro's Revolution: Myths and Realities. New York: Praeger.
DRAPER, THEODORE 1965 Castroism: Theory and Practice. New York: Praeger.
EDELMANN, ALEXANDER T. 1965 Latin American Government and Politics: The Dynamics of a Revolutionary Society. Homewood, Ill.: Dorsey.
FITZGIBBON, RUSSELL H. (1954) 1966 Uruguay: Portrait of a Democracy. New York: Russell.
HENNESSY, C. A. M. 1964 Cuba: The Politics of Frustrated Nationalism. Pages 183–205 in Martin C. Needler (editor), Political Systems of Latin America. Princeton, N.J.: Van Nostrand.
JOHNSON, JOHN J. 1958 Political Change in Latin America: The Emergence of the Middle Sectors. Stanford Studies in History, Economics, and Political Science, Vol. 15. Stanford Univ. Press.
KANTOR, HARRY 1953 The Ideology and Program of the Peruvian Aprista Movement. California, University of, Publications in Political Science, Vol. 4, No. 1. Berkeley: Univ. of California Press.
LIPSET, SEYMOUR M. 1960 Political Man: The Social Bases of Politics. Garden City, N.Y.: Doubleday.
LOEWENSTEIN, KARL (1942) 1944 Brazil Under Vargas. New York: Macmillan.
NEEDLER, MARTIN C. 1964 Mexico: Revolution as a Way of Life. Pages 1–33 in Martin C. Needler (editor), Political Systems of Latin America. Princeton, N.J.: Van Nostrand.
PIKE, FREDERICK B. (editor) 1964 The Conflict Between Church and State in Latin America. New York: Knopf. → See especially Part 3, dealing with Roman Catholic social action and Christian democracy.
ROSS, STANLEY R. 1963 Mexico: Cool Revolution and Cold War. Current History 44:89–94, 116–117.
SCHNEIDER, RONALD M. 1964 Five Years of Cuban Revolution. Current History 46:26–33.
SCOTT, ROBERT E. (1959) 1964 Mexican Government in Transition. Rev. ed. Urbana: Univ. of Illinois Press.
SIGMUND, PAUL E. (editor) 1963 The Ideologies of the Developing Nations. New York: Praeger.
SILVERT, KALMAN H. 1963 The Costs of Anti-nationalism: Argentina. Pages 347–372 in American Universities Field Staff, Expectant Peoples: Nationalism and Development. Edited by Kalman H. Silvert. New York: Random House.
SZULC, TAD 1965 Communists, Socialists, and Christian Democrats. American Academy of Political and Social Science, Annals 360:99–103.

LATIN SQUARES
See EXPERIMENTAL DESIGN.

LAUDERDALE, JAMES MAITLAND

James Maitland, eighth earl of Lauderdale, (1759–1839) was a product of the famous Scottish educational system that flourished in the second half of the eighteenth century. He was a pupil of the great John Millar, of whom it was said that "to hear his lectures . . . students resort hither (i.e., to Glasgow) from all quarters of Britain." Among his contemporaries in Glasgow and Edinburgh Lauderdale numbered James Mill, Sydney Smith, Francis Jeffrey, Thomas Chalmers, Francis Horner, and Henry Brougham—to name but a few members of that amazing generation. Politically he allied himself with the Whig opposition to Pitt, a policy that long kept him from high government office, an honor he would without doubt have achieved had he been of the government party. Following his teacher he was a staunch defender of democratic principles at a time when the holocaust of the French Revolution encouraged an extreme reaction in England. However, it would be a mistake to place Lauderdale in the radical tradition; he advocated limited democracy, and he lived to oppose—in a rather inexplicable volte face—the moderate innovations suggested in the 1832 Reform Bill.

Lauderdale has a rightful place in the history of economics, although not perhaps as a major figure. This is a position comparatively recently achieved and is a consequence, as with so many reevaluations in the history of economics, of quite recent developments in economic analysis.

Lauderdale's most original contributions are to be found in his Inquiry Into the Nature and Origin of Public Wealth (1804). The frame of reference for this work is Adam Smith's Wealth of Nations, and in an important sense Lauderdale's *Inquiry* may be regarded as a commentary on Smith's classic. It is important to remember this when considering Lauderdale's position in the development of economic thought. Lauderdale is often regarded as being in basic opposition to the orthodox English classical school and as representing an entirely separate, although contemporary, stream of development. While there is an element of truth in this, Lauderdale's work should not be considered too far outside the mainstream of economic thought: he did have certain criticisms of Smith's orthodoxy, but in terms of policy—the belief in the competitive order and the minimization of interference with economic systems—Lauderdale was part of the classical school.

The central theme of the *Inquiry*—the nature of relations between individual and public well-being—is not as pathbreaking as Lauderdale thought. He was worried by the fact that a rise in total spending on a commodity might be accompanied by a decline in the physical volume of purchases. We would now consider the problem in terms of index numbers of output. Lauderdale, however, was forced to consider it in terms of the demand schedule and what is now called the elasticity of the schedule, and did so in a way that was highly sophisticated for the time. His emphasis on the role of utility in the determination of relative prices places him much more with the subjective school (Condillac, Say, A. Walras, S. Bailey) than with the classical writers.

Lauderdale also applied his analysis to the question of overproduction. He argued, in opposition to the central classical position—often described as a belief in Say's Law—that saving could, nationally, be carried too far and result in an over-all excess supply of goods. It is for this reason that some contemporary economists, like Alvin Hansen or H. L. McCracken, consider Lauderdale as an early forerunner of Keynes. This is a mistaken view: since Lauderdale assumed the equality of *planned* saving and investment, oversaving was for him the mere production of capital equipment. This is certainly not what is normally understood as the Keynesian dilemma of capitalism. However, it must be acknowledged that when Lauderdale applied his analysis to the economic effects of national debt policy he came very close to a modern understanding of the question.

Lauderdale also wrote on monetary questions and gave an early statement of the bullionist position in *Thoughts on the Alarming State of the Circulation and on the Means of Redressing the Pecuniary Grievances in Ireland* (1805). Later on he defended the Bullion Report—he was a member of the committee that prepared it—and pressed for the early resumption of cash payments. Rather paradoxically, he combined these orthodox monetary views with vivid fears of underconsumption.

BERNARD CORRY

[*For the historical context of Lauderdale's work, see the biography of* SMITH, ADAM; *for much later development of his ideas, see* INCOME AND EMPLOYMENT THEORY *and* UTILITY.]

WORKS BY LAUDERDALE

(1804) 1819 *An Inquiry Into the Nature and Origin of Public Wealth, and Into the Means and Causes of Its Increase.* 2d ed., enl. Edinburgh: Constable.

1805 *Thoughts on the Alarming State of the Circulation and on the Means of Redressing the Pecuniary Grievances in Ireland.* London: Longman; Edinburgh: Constable.

(1829) 1965 *Three Letters to the Duke of Wellington, on the Fourth Report of the Select Committee of the House of Commons, Appointed in 1828 to Enquire Into the Public Income and Expenditure of the United Kingdom.* New York: Kelley.

SUPPLEMENTARY BIBLIOGRAPHY

CANNAN, EDWIN (1893) 1953 *A History of the Theories of Production and Distribution in English Political Economy From 1776 to 1848.* 3d ed. London and New York: Staples.

CORRY, B. A. 1962 *Money, Saving and Investment in English Economics, 1800–1850.* New York: Macmillan.

PAGLIN, MORTON 1961 *Malthus and Lauderdale: The Anti-Ricardian Tradition.* New York: Kelley.

LAUNHARDT, WILHELM

Carl Friedrich Wilhelm Launhardt (1832–1918) was by training and profession a transportation engineer, but he is now remembered chiefly for his pioneer work in the application of mathematical techniques to economic problems. He lived and worked virtually all his life in Hanover, Germany, as professor of highway, railroad, and bridge construction at the Polytechnical College. He received an honorary engineering doctorate in 1903 from the Institute of Technology at Dresden in recognition of basic work done on the technical and economic problems of transportation, in particular, of railroads. Not all his economic thinking was original, of course; on questions of capital and interest, for example, his ideas in general followed those of Léon Walras and Stanley Jevons. But he made important contributions to welfare economics, to pricing policies for public utilities, to industrial-location and market-area analysis, and to transportation-engineering economics in the narrow sense, as well as doing original work on the labor-supply function (1885, pp. 88–97).

Welfare economics. Much of Launhardt's writing in the area of welfare economics, although embedded in price theory, often delves into side areas that anticipate recent developments. For instance, his treatment of "repeated exchange" and "exchange with continually changing prices" in its dependence on the number of market participants (1885, pp. 35–53) foreshadows the basic theme, if not the results, of Oskar Morgenstern's demand theory (1948) rather than being simply a version of Walrasian *tâtonnement*.

Knut Wicksell (1901) implied that Launhardt had supplied a pseudo proof of the proposition that pure, perfect competition leads to the greatest social income. However, Launhardt explicitly disagreed with this proposition; in fact, in criticism of Walras, he branded such a conclusion as a "grave error" (1885, pp. 27–33, 42–44).

Public utility pricing policies. Launhardt's analysis of railroad costing and pricing (e.g., 1885, pp. 189–205), while in the spirit of Walras and Jevons, has been acclaimed for its originality and clarity. His analysis is marred by the spurious definiteness that results from his assumption of specific function forms. He opposed private ownership of railroads, since he favored marginal-cost pricing and differential freight rates, and believed that overhead costs should be paid out of general taxation in a manner dictated by over-all fiscal policies. Similar studies had been done both by Jules Dupuit and by Émile Cheysson and Clément Colson. The latter two were contemporaries of Launhardt's and, like him, combined engineering with economics.

Industrial location and market area. In the words of Walter Isard (1956, pp. 143, 160), Launhardt "presented the first significant treatment of industrial location theory" and "the earliest systematic treatment of the market-area among competing firms" (see Launhardt 1885, pp. 149–214). Although Johann Heinrich von Thünen had previously discussed industrial location, varying the circumstances more than Launhardt was to do, still Launhardt's location theories contain the germs of ideas later developed by Alfred Weber, Tord Palander, and more recent theorists. For example, he sketched the pole principle: a geometric construction for finding locational equilibrium points (Isard 1956, pp. 254–287). In the Launhardt–Hotelling problem, however, Launhardt did not simultaneously vary price and location; that remained for Harold Hotelling (1929) to do.

Transportation-engineering economics. In the field of transportation-engineering economics, which lay closer to his main occupation, Launhardt investigated such matters as the influence of gradients and curves on railroad operating costs (1877) and the location-dependent "rentability" of highways and railroads.

EBERHARD M. FELS

[*For the historical context of Launhardt's work, see the biographies of* JEVONS; THÜNEN; WALRAS; *for discussion of the subsequent development of his ideas, see* SPATIAL ECONOMICS; WELFARE ECONOMICS; *and the biography of* WEBER, ALFRED.]

WORKS BY LAUNHARDT

1877   Die Betriebskosten der Eisenbahnen in ihrer Abhängigkeit von den Steigungs- und Krümmungsverhältnissen der Bahn. Supplement to Volume 4 of Edmund Heusinger von Waldegg (editor), *Handbuch für spezielle Eisenbahn-technik.* Leipzig: Engelmann.
1882   Die Bestimmung des zweckmässigsten Standortes einer gewerblichen Anlage. *Zeitschrift des Vereines deutscher Ingenieure* 26: cols. 105–116.
1885   *Mathematische Begründung der Volkswirthschaftslehre.* Leipzig: Engelmann.

SUPPLEMENTARY BIBLIOGRAPHY

HOTELLING, HAROLD   1929   Stability in Competition. *Economic Journal* 39:41–57.
ISARD, WALTER   1956   *Location and Space-economy: A General Theory Relating to Industrial Location, Market Areas, Trade and Urban Structure.* Cambridge, Mass.: Technology Press of M.I.T.; New York: Wiley.
MORGENSTERN, OSKAR   1948   Demand Theory Reconsidered. *Quarterly Journal of Economics* 62:165–201.
SCHNEIDER, ERICH   1959   Wilhelm Launhardt. Volume 6, pages 533–534 in *Handwörterbuch der Sozialwissenschaften.* Stuttgart (Germany): Fischer.
WICKSELL, KNUT   (1901) 1951   *Lectures on Political Economy.* Volume 1: General Theory. London: Routledge. → Translated from the third Swedish edition.

LAW

The articles under this heading deal mainly with the study of law, and with the relationship between law and society, as do also JURISPRUDENCE; LEGAL REASONING; PSYCHIATRY, *article on* FORENSIC PSYCHIATRY; PUBLIC LAW. *The articles listed under* LEGAL SYSTEMS *discuss and compare the major modern systems. Other branches of the law are dealt with in* ADMINISTRATIVE LAW; CANON LAW; CRIMINAL LAW; CONFLICT OF LAWS; CONSTITUTIONAL LAW; INTERNATIONAL LAW; MILITARY LAW. *The creation of law and its relations with political institutions are discussed in* ADJUDICATION; CONFLICT OF INTERESTS; JUDICIAL PROCESS; JUDICIARY; LEGISLATION; POLITICAL JUSTICE. *Relevant to the development of modern jurisprudence are the biog-*

raphies of AUSTIN; BLACKSTONE; BRANDEIS; CAR-
DOZO; COKE; DUGUIT; EHRLICH; FRANK; GIERKE;
GROTIUS; HAMILTON, WALTON H.; HAURIOU;
HOLMES; JELLINEK; KANTOROWICZ; KELSEN; LLEW-
ELLYN; MAINE; MAITLAND; MOORE; JOHN BAS-
SETT; POUND; RADBRUCH; SAVIGNY; SCHMITT;
VATTEL. *For a discussion of law and related prob-
lems in preliterate societies see* POLITICAL ANTHRO-
POLOGY; SANCTIONS.

I
THE SOCIOLOGY OF LAW

The broad aim of legal sociology is the extension of knowledge regarding the foundations of a legal order, the pattern of legal change, and the contribution of law to the fulfillment of social needs and aspirations. The special interest of sociology in these matters rests on the basic assumption that law and legal institutions both affect and are affected by the social conditions that surround them.

Within sociology, the study of law touches a number of well-established areas of inquiry. In criminology attention is given to the changing character of penal law, the assumptions upon which it rests, and the social dynamics of law enforcement and corrections. The sociology of law shares with political sociology a concern for the nature of legitimate authority and social control, the social bases of constitutionalism, the evolution of civic rights, and the relation of public and private spheres.

The roots of legal sociology lie mainly in jurisprudence rather than in the autonomous work of sociologists. In legal theory a "sociological school" emerged out of the work of such jurists as Rudolf von Jhering, Oliver Wendell Holmes, Léon Duguit, Eugen Ehrlich, and Roscoe Pound, all of whom felt the need to look beyond the traditional confines of legal scholarship. The sociologists Émile Durkheim, Max Weber, E. A. Ross, and W. G. Sumner, among others, contributed to the development of a sociological orientation among students of jurisprudence, in some cases by direct influence on legal writers such as Duguit and Pound.

Historical perspectives

Four basic motifs have been prominent in the intellectual history of legal sociology: historicism, instrumentalism, antiformalism, and pluralism.

Historicism. Historicism emphasizes the tracing of legal ideas and institutions to their historical roots; patterns of legal evolution are seen as un-planned outcomes of the play of social forces. Important illustrations of this approach are Henry Maine's *Ancient Law*, Oliver Wendell Holmes's *Common Law*, and the treatments of legal typologies and evolution in Émile Durkheim's *Division of Labor in Society* (1893) and various writings by Max Weber (see especially 1922*a*). The historicist emphasis has had two implicit objectives. First, historical study is a way of identifying legal anachronisms, especially in the reasoning behind a received rule or concept. Second, the analysis of an underlying historical trend (e.g., Maine's thesis regarding the movement of "progressive societies" from status to contract) can provide an illuminating context for the interpretation of contemporary issues.

Instrumentalism. The instrumentalist approach, associated with the names of Jeremy Bentham and Rudolf von Jhering, among nineteenth-century writers, as well as Roscoe Pound, calls for the assessment of law according to defined social purposes. It thus invites close study of what the law is and does in fact. The chief significance of instrumentalism is that it encourages the incorporation of social knowledge into law. For if laws are instruments, they must be open to interpretation and revision in the light of changing circumstances. Moreover, law is seen as having more than one function; not only is it a vehicle for maintaining public order and settling disputes, but it also facilitates voluntary transactions and arrangements, confers political legitimacy, promotes education and civic participation, and helps to define social aspirations.

Antiformalism. Sociological jurisprudence has gained much of its vitality from attacks upon the "unrealistic" nature of legal rules and concepts. A jurisprudence that emphasizes the purity of law as a formal system is fallible on two counts. First, legal rules are necessarily abstract and general; there is always a considerable gap between a system of general rules and its implementation, if only because the rules are applied by human agencies that have their own interests and problems. Second, any view of the legal order as an isolated system wrongly detaches it from the environment in which it is implicated. Failure to take account of the historical and cultural forces impinging upon the law not only distorts reality but gives the legal order an excessive dignity, insulates it from criticism, and offers society inadequate leverage for change. In pressing its criticism of legal abstractions, the antiformalist approach leads readily to a derogation of the importance and effectiveness of legal norms.

While antiformalism is congenial to an instrumentalist assessment of the legal tradition, it is out of sympathy with the more narrowly utilitarian image of man as an isolated, goal-seeking actor guided by a hedonic calculus. Instead, it encourages a fuller awareness of the *nonrational* springs of action, of human dependency on social support, and of the emergence of social systems that have a viability of their own. The antiformalist theme is prominent in the work of Eugen Ehrlich and of the American legal realists, but almost every analyst of the social or psychological foundations of law has struck the same note, albeit with varying emphasis.

Pluralism. In the history of legal sociology, "pluralism" refers to the view that law is located "in society"—that is, beyond the official agencies of government. Sociological skepticism of state law has led some legal scholars, notably Ehrlich, to deny that law is solely or even mainly made by government. Ehrlich held that law is endemic in custom and social organization; it is in the actual regularities of group life that we find the "living law." In context, this approach is more than an appeal to bring law into closer relation with social practice; it is an assertion that *authoritative* legal materials are to be found in the realities of group life. In other words, it questions the claim of the state to be the sole receptacle of legal authority.

The pluralist motif was further enhanced by the central place Ehrlich gave to the "inner order of associations" as a font of law; here his work recalls Otto von Gierke's treatment of the law of associations. Gierke stressed the reality of the autonomous collectivity, and in doing so he criticized not only the atomistic view of society and legal order as based upon individual will but also the legal notion of the association as a juridical fiction. Related ideas are found in the writings of Maurice Hauriou, who sought a legal reality in "the institution"—that is, in the association or enterprise (private as well as public) that has its own established authority and appropriate procedures.

The sociological approach. These intellectual tendencies have helped open up the boundaries of the legal order. They have enlarged the relevance of nonlegal ideas and findings to law and legal reasoning. On the other hand, they have had the common outcome of downgrading formal legal systems as significant social realities. In an important sense, the sociological school has been antilegal. It has sought to put law in its place by emphasizing the primacy of the social context and by seeking "the legal" outside of its conventional sphere. In so doing, the sociological perspective runs the risk of dissolving the concept of law into the broader concepts of social control and social order; the idea of a "living law," encompassing all the regularities of group life, offers no touchstone for the distinctively legal. Whatever the merits of the sociological school in having called attention to the need for a more realistic jurisprudence, the failure to offer a theory of the distinctively legal has been its cardinal weakness.

The distinctively legal

According to Max Weber, the distinctively legal emerges when "there exists a 'coercive apparatus,' i.e., that there are one or more persons whose special task it is to hold themselves ready to apply specially provided means of coercion (legal coercion) for the purpose of norm enforcement" ([1922*a*] 1954, p. 13). In other words, a legal norm is known by the probability that it will be enforced by a specialized staff. Thus Weber offers an operational definition of law that is meant to exclude all value judgments in the assessment of what is or is not law. Although he emphasizes coercion, Weber is careful to point out that the threat of physical force is not essential to legal action, for coercion may consist in the threat of public reprimand or boycott. Thus Weber's definition does not limit law to the political community; it allows for "extrastate" law, such as ecclesiastical law or the law of any other corporate group that is binding on its own members.

Weber's approach does have a certain rough utility, and it has the special virtue of being general enough to encourage the study of law in private associations. However, he offers no satisfactory theoretical ground for identifying the requirements of a legal order as he does. The availability of a specialized staff for the enforcement of norms may be highly correlated with the existence of a legal order and thus may serve as a reliable *indicator* of norms that have been selected for special treatment. However, it does not follow that this is what basically distinguishes legal from nonlegal norms and institutions.

Authoritative norms. An adequate theory of law must identify the distinctive *work done* by law in society, the special *resources* of law, and the characteristic *mechanisms* that law brings into play. In the quest for such a theory, little is gained from formulas that place coercive enforcement of norms at the center of legal experience. The key word in the discussion of law is *authority*, not coercion. The fundamental problems of jurisprudence stem from the puzzles and ambiguities associated with identifying the sources of authoritative rules, the authoritative application of rules, and the nature of authoritative change in existing rules.

Although the legal requirement of paying a tax certainly has some connection with the coercive consequences of refusal to pay, the character of the obligation is more decisive. A tax is *illegal* if it violates an authoritative order, and it is *nonlegal* if it lacks appropriate authority, regardless of whether the probability of coercion exists. Hence legality presumes the emergence of authoritative norms whose status as such is "guaranteed" by evidence of other, consensually validated, rules.

H. L. A. Hart has argued that, in stepping "from the pre-legal to the legal world," a society develops special rules for curing the defects of a social order based on unofficial norms (1961, p. 91). A regime of unofficial norms has a number of inherent limitations, including the difficulty of resolving uncertainties as to the existence or scope of a norm. No criterion or procedure is available for settling such issues. The distinctively legal emerges with the development of "secondary rules," that is, rules of authoritative determination. These rules, selectively applied, raise up the unofficial norms and give them a legal status.

The elementary legal act is this appeal from an *asserted* rule, however coercively enforced, to a *justifying* rule. This presumes at least a dim awareness that some reason lies behind the impulse to conform; furthermore this reason is founded not in conscience, habit, or fear alone but rather in the decision to uphold an authoritative order. The rule of legal recognition may be quite blunt and crude: The law is what the king or priest says it is. But this initial reference of a historically given social norm to a more general ground of obligation breeds the complex elaboration of authoritative rules that marks a developed legal order.

Resources of legal institutions.   The special work of law is to identify claims and obligations that merit official validation or enforcement. This may consist of nothing more than the establishment of a public record invested with a special claim upon the community's respect as a guide to action. When institutions emerge that do this work we can speak of a legal order. These institutions need not be specialized, and they may have no resources for coercive enforcement; it is essential only that their determinations affecting rights and duties are accepted as authoritative.

An authoritative act asserts a claim to obedience, and the reach of that claim determines whether and to what extent a legal system exists. Although a weak legal order rests on a narrow base of consent, it may be able to mobilize very large resources of intimidation and thus command wide, if grudging, submission. A strong legal order is the product of a more substantial consensus and summons more willing obedience; it is correspondingly less dependent on the machinery of coercion. There is thus an important difference between the strength of a *regime* and the strength of a *legal order*, although the sheer persistence of the former may greatly influence acceptance for its claim to speak with authority. Of course, coercion is an important and often indispensable *resource* for law, but so are education, symbolism, and the appeal to reason. Coercion does not make law, though it may indeed establish an order out of which law may emerge.

In much of his work Max Weber saw quite clearly the intimate relation of the legal and the authoritative. For example, his theory of authority and legitimacy contrasts the charismatic, the traditional, and the "rational legal," thus placing law in a context of evolving forms of authority (1922*b*, pp. 328 ff. in 1947 edition). In this analysis Weber views fully developed law as a system of governance by rules; he sees the distinctively legal obligation as a component of an impersonal order that exhibits a strain toward rationality. Thus when Weber actually used the concept of law, especially in his theory of bureaucracy, he greatly modified the significance of coercion.

Social foundations of legality

The view of law just sketched highlights the place of authority, consensus, and rationality in the legal order. In a developed legal order, authority transcends coercion, accepts the restraints of reason, and contributes to a public consensus regarding the foundations of civic obligation. To the extent that law is "the enterprise of subjecting human conduct to the governance of rules" (Fuller 1964, p. 106), it can be said that law aims at a moral achievement; the name of that achievement is *legality* or "the rule of law." Its distinctive contribution is a progressive reduction of the arbitrary element in positive law and its administration.

As an intellectual discipline, the sociology of law has a far broader compass than the study of "the requirements of justice which lawyers term principles of legality" (Hart 1961, p. 202). Not every society gives equal weight to the ideal of "control by rule" as against other ideals; and there is much else to be said about law in society. Still, law is so intimately associated with the realization of these special values that study of "the rule of law" must be a chief preoccupation of legal sociology. Indeed, a considerable amount of contemporary research, as we shall note below, falls within this topic.

The sociological study of legality presumes that the potential of law for realizing values is at best unevenly fulfilled. Legal decision making is carried on by living men in living institutions, who are subject to all the external pressures and constraints and all the inner sources of recalcitrance that frustrate the embodiment of abstract ideals in action. At the same time, some patterns of group life are more congenial than others to the rule of law. To discover which social conditions are congenial to the rule of law and which undermine it, and in what ways, is the main task of scientific inquiry in this field. Four topics provide a framework in which research on legality can be pursued: the transition from legitimacy to legality; rational consensus and civic competence; institutionalized criticism; and institutionalized self-restraint. While these topics are suggested by the experience of the Western world, their relevance is universal.

Legitimacy and legality.   The existence of legality presumes that the power exercised by public officials is "legitimate" power. This means that an appeal is made to some principle as a source of right—the right to dispose of community resources in a certain way and especially the right to issue orders and enforce them. Many different principles of legitimacy are possible—for example, divine will, democratic election, private property, hereditary succession, seniority, and special competence. What principle of legitimacy will be accepted depends on the nature of the group, its cultural heritage, and special historical circumstances. To trace the rise and decline of various principles of legitimacy is to touch on major themes of political and social history.

Legitimate power tends to be restrained. It is inherent in legitimacy that the will of the ruler, including the majority will of a democratic assembly, is not completely free. Nevertheless, many regimes properly classified as legitimate retain a very large amount of arbitrary rule. Legitimacy is only a first step toward legality. It can begin in a quite primitive fashion, meaning little more than unconscious acceptance of another's authority because he is thought to have communication with the gods or special magical powers or because he belongs to a noble family. Authority is primitive when power is legitimated by no more than a historically given public sentiment supporting a claim to rightful rule.

But legitimacy carries the lively seed of legality, implanted by the principle that the exercise of power must be justified. From this it is but a step to the view that reasons must be given to defend official acts. Reasons invite evaluation, and evaluation requires the development of public standards. At the same time, implicit in the fundamental norm that reasons should be given is the conclusion that where reasons are defective, authority is to that extent weakened and even invalidated.

The transition from legitimacy to legality requires the recognition that official acts can be questioned and appraised. The test is not whether the ruler is wise or good but whether his acts are justified by an explicit or implied grant of power. Most important, *legality goes beyond a gross justification of the right to hold office;* it gains strength and focus in proportion as the criterion of legitimacy is used to decide whether particular acts meet public standards of validity. For example, if conservation of natural resources is the purported foundation of rule making by a government agency, then that publicly acknowledged objective becomes available as a basis for criticizing specific rules and decisions.

Clearly some principles of legitimacy are more competent than others to sustain the ideal of legality. If power is justified on the basis of tradition, proprietorship, kinship, or hereditary succession, it is difficult to find the leverage for continuous, reasoned criticism. When prescriptive right gives way to an abstract principle, as in the case of justification by popular will, social utility, trusteeship, or even divine right, then the principle of legitimacy can be analyzed and acts assessed. The way is then open for an appeal to reason.

Rational consensus and civic competence.   Legality requires that the principles of legitimacy be firmly established in the community's habits of thought; hence the study of both the content and the *quality* of consensus has a special bearing on the social bases of the rule of law. Strictly speaking, there can be no purely rational consensus. However, it may be approximated under two related conditions: if the historically given, nonrational sentiments are themselves supportive of rational conduct, for example, when received modes of apprehending man and society encourage self-restraint and tolerance of ambiguity; and if there is broad opportunity for the emergence of a public opinion founded in the free play of interests and ideas. In other words, rational consensus presupposes a genuine public opinion rather than agreement based on manipulation, withholding of information, or unmitigated appeals to tradition.

Whatever contributes to rational consensus provides social support for legality. Decision making in the light of legality requires the continuous exercise of discriminating judgment, especially in the balancing of values, the elaboration of defensible rules, and the application of abstract principles to changing circumstances. While this work is largely carried on by a relatively small group of professionals, the capacity of the professionals to sustain and extend the ideals of legality depends on a parallel development of the public mind. The legal profession itself is not immune to influences that may undermine its commitment to the rule of law.

The consensus that sustains legality entails deepened public understanding of the complex meaning of freedom under law. This goes beyond passive belief or even commitment. It is an extension of civic competence—the competence to participate effectively in a legal order. This is manifested, for example, in an increased capacity to be patient with procedural niceties in the face of a desire to punish, to exercise impartial judgment, and to use principles of criticism against even the most favored leaders of government.

In a vital legal order something more is wanted than submission to law. A military establishment places very great emphasis on obedience to lawful commands, yet such a setting is hardly a model of the development of legality. So, too, a conception of law as the manifestation of awesome authority encourages a posture of submission and is fully compatible with arbitrary rule. In a community that aspires to a high order of legality obedience to law is not submissive compliance. The obligation to obey the law should be closely tied to the defensibility of the rules themselves and of the official decisions that enforce them.

Institutionalized criticism. If the ideals of legality are to be fulfilled, the capacity to generate and sustain reasoned criticism of the rules and of official discretion must be built into the machinery of lawmaking and administration. To this end, the Anglo–American legal tradition has relied heavily upon the availability of counsel, upon the adversary concept of the legal process, and upon the freedom of the judiciary and other officials to adopt a critical stance toward received law, both statutory and judge-made.

Sociological research in this area confronts the ideals of due process with the realities of institutional life. For example, the availability of counsel may be limited for large sectors of the population; the independence and objectivity of officials may be weakened by their social origins and commitments; and limitations of competence and resources may inhibit the judiciary from effective criticism

of rule making in private and public agencies. The possibility of effective criticism may largely depend upon the availability of *group* resources. The lone individual seeking justice—especially if he is poor and if his claim is subject to routine processing—has little opportunity to press for new interpretations of law or of administrative regulations. Group-based counsel, on the other hand, can develop specialized expertise as well as work out a strategy for legal change.

In the Anglo–American tradition, the adversary principle has a special place as a vehicle of institutionalized criticism. It lends legitimacy to partisan advocacy within the legal process, allowing and even encouraging the zealous pursuit of special interest by means of self-serving interpretations of law and evidence. The assumptions underlying the adversary principle have not been fully analyzed or tested, nor have variations or functional surrogates in other societies been adequately studied. Moreover, there is evidence that partisan advocacy is weakened by certain factors that are becoming increasingly common in "administered" societies. Among these are the commitment of tribunals to a positive outcome, as in family conciliation proceedings; reliance on experts and investigators who serve the court directly; the mandate to temper justice with treatment, as in juvenile hearings; and the routine handling of a large number of cases.

No doubt these new problems and contexts will lessen reliance on the adversary principle in some areas; more important, however, will be the development of new forms of advocacy and critical dialogue. Administrative agencies, both criminal and civil, are increasingly recognized as active centers for making laws and dispensing justice, although the visibility of such decisions is often quite low. Sociological study of organizations can trace the actual course of decision making and can identify the opportunities available, within the social structure of the agency, for increasing the visibility of decisions and developing new forms of institutionalized criticism.

Institutionalized self-restraint. Every officer of the law—policeman, president, legislator, attorney, judge, licensing commissioner, draft board member—is in some degree a magistrate. He exercises discretion and thereby affects the rights of citizens. The rule of law requires that this discretion be restrained, yet it also asks for independent judgments in the assessment of fact, the assignment of moral culpability, and the application of legal rules to particular circumstances. To achieve restrained discretion, more is needed than criticism of authority and pressure upon it. The system depends heavily on *self*-restraint and thus on social mechanisms for building in appropriate values and rules of conduct.

Historically, legal self-restraint has been supported by public consensus on the nature and limits of authority, professionalization of lawyers and other officials, and the evolution of clearly defined roles, such as that of the judge. But there is considerable variation in that achievement, and under modern conditions there is a need for more attention to the *organizational* sources of self-restraint as distinguished from mechanisms of socialization. Ethical conduct is mainly found in settings that nourish and sustain it, that is, where such conduct makes sense for the official in the light of the realistic problems he faces. To design such settings is properly the chief aim of the architect of legal institutions. As applied to the legal profession, this principle has been documented in a recent study of the New York City bar (Carlin 1966).

Law and social change

The preceding discussion of the social foundations of legality emphasizes the conditions that strengthen or weaken the rule of law. The same problem may be approached historically, placing the evolution of legality in a context of broad social change and relating it to the development of other social institutions, including culturally defined conceptions of authority and justice. Thus Max Weber was interested in the emergence of rationality as a principle of organization and decision making; he saw rationality as the key to modernization and traced its effects in many fields, including law.

In modern Western society the extension of legality to new institutions and settings occurs mainly *within* government, encompassing wider circles of officials and agencies, subjecting more decisions to review, and raising the standard of what constitutes fair procedure. The Scandinavian ombudsman, an official to whom the citizen can appeal directly when he feels wronged by a government agency, is a symbol of the demand for new modes of redress against a large and opaque government apparatus. Also evident is a tentative movement toward legal restraint of arbitrary decision in nongovernmental institutions, especially those that serve a general public, such as colleges, trade unions, and large business firms. These developments, fostered in large measure by the work of associations formed to advance group interests, reflect a growing public sensitivity to legal rights. The legal profession itself, both by scholarship and by the official statements of its professional organizations, has contributed to the critical assessment of official procedures. Nor should it be overlooked that modern organizations, as part of their greater effectiveness and rationality, have an increased capacity to support the machinery of due process.

There is, however, an underlying conflict between administration and legality. In the first place, procedural safeguards are costly in time, energy, and the risk that action will be inhibited. In the United States, for instance, the police must carry out their traditional tasks of surveillance and apprehension subject to many new legal rulings affecting search, arrest, and detention. Any organization that has a job to do, yet must meet standards of fairness, faces this tension. Second, an official who is preoccupied with the fair application of general rules—equal treatment under law—finds it difficult to deal with each problem or case on its merits, taking account of special circumstances and needs and adapting policies to desired outcomes. The modern quest, and one that requires much supportive research, is for variable standards of fairness, embodying basic principles of procedural justice with due regard for the distinctive needs of specialized institutions and programs.

Incipient law. The antiformalist posture of legal sociology has encouraged interest in the problem-solving practices and spontaneous orderings of business or family life. While this approach has tended to depreciate formal law, in principle it just as easily supports an emphasis on the *emergence* of formal law out of the realities of group life. Incipient law is implicit in the way in which public sentiment develops or in any increasingly stabilized pattern of organization; it refers to a compelling claim of right or a practice so viable and so important to a functioning institution as to make legal recognition in due course highly probable. Thus some of the private arrangements worked out in collective bargaining agreements, especially seniority rights and protection against arbitrary dismissal, may be seen as incipient law. However, the location of incipient law cannot rest solely on the prevalence of a practice or even the urgency of a claim; two parallel assessments are required. First, the social viability of the practice in question—its functional significance for group life and especially for new institutional forms—must be considered. Second, the contemporary evolution of relevant legal principles must be assessed to see whether the new norm can be absorbed within the received but changing legal tradition.

A focus on incipient legal change bridges the concepts of law and social order without confounding the two; it assumes that law does indeed have its distinctive nature, however much it may rely on social support or be responsible to social change. On the other hand, some law is seen as *latent* in the evolving social and economic order. For example, the trend toward strict liability for harm caused by defects in manufactured goods (weakening or eliminating the need to prove negligence) reflects changing technology, both in manufacture and distribution, as well as the increased capacity of large firms to absorb the attendant costs either by increasing productivity or by passing them on to the general public. Similarly, the growing importance of large-scale organizations carries with it the likelihood that new claims of right will emerge, based upon a new perception of organizational membership as a protectable status.

Law as a vehicle of social change.   For the most part, legal sociology has viewed law as a passive rather than active agent in social change. Law "responds" to new circumstances and pressures. However, especially in recent years the great social effects of legal change have been too obvious to ignore. The question is no longer whether law is a significant vehicle of social change but rather *how* it so functions and what special problems arise.

One way of approaching these problems is to consider the relative significance for social change of *legislation*, *administration*, and *common law*. Each has its special competence, and each has been dominant as a mode of change at different periods and in different branches of the law. In this context "common law" is not restricted to the Anglo–American legal tradition. Rather, it refers to any pattern of legal decision and evolution that relies on judicial creativity. Although this form of legal development is most explicitly recognized in what are called the "common-law" jurisdictions, in fact such creativity is inherent in the judicial process and plays an important part in the "code" jurisdictions of continental Europe (Friedmann [1944] 1960, pp. 483–486).

The common-law approach relies heavily upon tradition and the authority of the tribunal as sources of legitimacy. Judicial elaboration of abstract ideas, including reasoning by analogy, fits

new departures into a received system of concepts and rules. "Realist" criticism of common-law concepts has sometimes overlooked this social function of abstractions. Legal ideas are indeed often distant from the realities of social practice, but their very generality is useful for making new adaptations while preserving a sense of continuity and therefore of legitimacy.

The common-law method of change is mainly piecemeal and gradual. It can safeguard a precarious consensus by avoiding radical or sweeping change and by relying on studied indirection rather than unambiguous confrontation. On the other hand, judges who have the authority to interpret a basic statute, such as a written constitution, can provide leadership in some branches of the law, as United States history has shown. In such a case, public commitment to the statute reinforces the legitimacy of judicial decision.

The great weakness of common-law empiricism is the difficulty of working out comprehensive attacks on new problems, such as urban land use, industrial accidents, or labor–management relations. The common-law approach seems to work best when basic policy is settled and the need is for refinement of distinctions and adaptation of the policy to new settings.

Legislation is the most obvious way of bringing political will to bear for the purpose of effecting social change through law. Unlike courts, which are tied to tradition, legislatures are commonly perceived as legitimate agencies for innovation; they can muster better means of inquiry, and they can create administrative agencies to execute and elaborate legislative policy.

There are important continuities, as well as tensions, in the relation between legislation and common law. Where these continuities and tensions occur, jurisprudential problems of law and social change arise. For example, a series of statutes can be viewed as creating a new "field" of law (such as labor law or welfare law), with the result that authoritative concepts and doctrines emerge which go beyond the letter of the statutes and form starting points for legal reasoning. This work of interpretation and elaboration, using a common-law perspective, is carried on by administrative agencies as well as courts. Its effect is to institutionalize the statutory policy.

Although politics and legislation are the basic *sources* of legal change in modern society, the administrative agency is a characteristic and potent *vehicle* of that change. It can summon material and human resources, including moral dedication and professional zeal, for turning legislative policy into social reality. An administrative agency can contribute to law by detailed rule making, its own adjudications, the patterned course of discretion it adopts, the practical effect it has on the social structure, and the initiative it may take in proposing statutory changes. However, agencies differ markedly in their capacity to influence law and society. Much depends on whether the agency conceives of itself as active or passive; this in turn reflects the nature of its special constituency, if any, as well as the newness and popular appeal of the program, the initial resources it is given, and the relations it may develop with other agencies. Some agencies are captives of their constituencies, including groups they are supposed to regulate, and contribute little to legal development.

Perhaps the most basic resource of the law for fostering and guiding social change is the set of legal principles that can be invoked to justify action in their name. This is especially true of constitutional principles that contain ideals of civic right. Such ideals are usually only imperfectly embodied in the operative rules of a given time and place. For long periods the gap between the legal ideal and the legal reality may be accepted with passivity and even good will, but social change may bring with it new opportunities for more perfect embodiment of the ideal in practice and a quickened awareness of this possibility. The result is twofold: Energy for social change is enlarged by a sense of legitimacy, and those who attempt to defend the *status quo* are made vulnerable and placed on the defensive. Thus law both contributes to rising expectations and may, in due course, provide vehicles for their realization.

Major trends.   Several large-scale social changes have contributed to a vast increase in the tasks that must be assumed by a modern legal order. As kinship, fixed status, and community have declined as sources of social control, the drift has been toward a mass society marked by high rates of mobility, fragmented social experience, rising demands for short-run gratification, and more active participation by large numbers in hitherto insulated areas of social life. This trend has resulted in greatly increased pressure on formal agencies of regulation and service. A related development has been the emergence of the large organization as the representative institution of modern society; it depends upon, and also summons, mass participation in economic, political, and cultural life. A new "corporatism" brings with it many new problems for the law, including assessment of the social responsibilities of private associations, blurring of the distinction between private and public law, concern for the rights of association members, and regulation of competition and conflict when self-governing market mechanisms break down (Friedmann 1959).

A third significant trend has been the ascendance of social interests over parochial interests. The increasing interdependence of existence in modern society and correlative changes in values have weakened the claims of private interests and stimulated the quest for criteria of social worth. This is the foundation of what has been called the "socialization of law." As described by Pound (1959), the socialization of law is manifested in a growing tendency to impose limitations on the use and disposition of property, on freedom of contract, and on the power of creditors to exact satisfaction; in the movement toward liability without fault; and in many other legal rules and concepts. While this trend undermines the concept of the individual as a holder of abstract rights, it tends strongly to make the *person* an object of social and legal concern. This is reflected in much welfare legislation, which often begins as a way of solving a social problem and increasingly turns attention to the needs of persons.

Social research

Recent efforts to encourage the sociology of law have emphasized the need for empirical research and for a corresponding sense of relevance to contemporary social problems. The newer work is less interested in showing the limitations of law relative to other forms of social control than in bringing the expertise of social science to bear on the analysis of specific problems. It is likely that in the future legal sociology will be characterized by an affirmation of law rather than by a downgrading of it. This is especially true of research on the administration of justice. Studies of tribunals and other legal agencies may be narrowly concerned with efficient use of scarce resources, but they also tend to compare the ideal and the reality. As the "morality of law" (Fuller 1964) becomes a subject for empirical research, there will be a natural tendency to stress the contribution law can make to a moral order.

In line with this emphasis, much current research centers on social aspects of the administration of justice, as in studies of the jury (Kalven & Zeisel 1966; Simon 1967), patterns of law enforcement (Lindesmith 1965; Skolnick 1966), juvenile justice (Tappan 1947; Matza 1964), and the legal profession. Most of this work is normative as well as factual: It seeks out the conditions and processes that undermine or support proce-

58   LAW: The Sociology of Law

dural fairness and the recognition of basic rights. There is an implicit demand for fulfillment of legal ideals.

A more ambiguous attitude toward the moral significance of law is found in the sociology of deviance. Here the recent emphasis is on the law's role in *creating* deviance (Becker 1963). This occurs in two ways. First, the definition of what is "criminal" is a social process; and in borderline crimes, where consensus is weak, large numbers of people may find themselves classified as "criminals" as a result of political action by moralists. When this occurs, there is a strong tendency for illicit activity to continue, for that activity to take on more determinate criminal form, and for the quality of law enforcement to suffer. Second, a casual offender may be transformed into a committed deviant by the legal "processing" to which he is exposed, especially when he is systematically treated as a deviant and stigmatized as such. Under these circumstances law breeds illegality. The normative lesson is: To preserve the integrity of law it should be used with restraint in the control of personal conduct, especially where the specific harm is problematical and may be exceeded by the social costs of ineffective enforcement (Schur 1965).

Other research includes studies of public opinion and law (Cohen et al. 1958), legal forms and economic realities (Berle 1959; Macaulay 1963), judicial values and perspectives (Schubert 1960), the extension of legal or quasi-legal rights to members of "private governments," such as the large corporation (Eels 1962), and social history of legal ideas and institutions (Friedman 1965; Hall 1935; Hurst 1950; 1960; 1964). The comparative study of law and society is being stimulated by scholarly interest in the "developing" nations (Anderson 1963; Lev 1965), by the assessment of changes in communist society (Berman 1950; Hazard 1953; 1960), and by a marked tendency among some students of comparative law to take fuller account of social and political contexts (Von Mehren 1963).

The major problem of legal sociology remains the integration of jurisprudence and social research. Unless jurisprudential issues of the nature and functions of law, the relation of law and morals, the foundations of legality and fairness, and the role of social knowledge in law are addressed by modern investigators, the sociology of law can have only a peripheral intellectual importance.

PHILIP SELZNICK

BIBLIOGRAPHY

ANDERSON, JAMES N. D. (editor) 1963 *Changing Law in Developing Countries.* New York: Praeger.

ARENS, RICHARD; and LASSWELL, HAROLD D. 1961 *In Defense of Public Order: The Emerging Field of Sanction Law.* New York: Columbia Univ. Press.

BECKER, HOWARD S. 1963 *Outsiders: Studies in the Sociology of Deviance.* New York: Free Press.

BERGER, MORROE (1952) 1954 *Equality by Statute: Legal Controls Over Group Discrimination.* New York: Columbia Univ. Press.

BERLE, ADOLF A. 1959 *Power Without Property: A New Development in American Political Economy.* New York: Harcourt.

BERMAN, HAROLD J. (1950) 1963 *Justice in the U.S.S.R.: An Interpretation of Soviet Law.* Rev. & enl. ed. Cambridge, Mass.: Harvard Univ. Press. → First published as *Justice in Russia: An Interpretation of Soviet Law.*

CARLIN, JEROME E. 1962 *Lawyers on Their Own: A Study of Individual Practitioners in Chicago.* New Brunswick, N.J.: Rutgers Univ. Press.

CARLIN, JEROME E. 1966 *Lawyers' Ethics: A Survey of the New York City Bar.* New York: Russell Sage Foundation.

COHEN, JULIUS; ROBSON, REGINALD A. H.; and BATES, ALAN 1958 *Parental Authority: The Community and the Law.* New Brunswick, N.J.: Rutgers Univ. Press.

DAVIS, F. JAMES et al. 1962 *Society and the Law: New Meanings for an Old Profession.* New York: Free Press.

DICEY, ALBERT V. (1905) 1962 *Lectures on the Relation Between Law and Public Opinion in England, During the Nineteenth Century.* 2d ed. London and New York: Macmillan. → A paperback edition was published in 1962.

DURKHEIM, ÉMILE (1893) 1960 *The Division of Labor in Society.* Glencoe, Ill.: Free Press. → First published as *De la division du travail social.*

DURKHEIM, ÉMILE (1950) 1958 *Professional Ethics and Civic Morals.* Glencoe, Ill.: Free Press. → First published, posthumously, as *Leçons de sociologie: Physique des moeurs et du droit.*

EELS, RICHARD 1962 *The Government of Corporations.* New York: Free Press.

EHRLICH, EUGEN (1913) 1936 *Fundamental Principles of the Sociology of Law.* Translated by Walter L. Moll with an introduction by Roscoe Pound. Cambridge, Mass.: Harvard Univ. Press. → First published as *Grundlegung der Soziologie des Rechts.*

EVAN, WILLIAM M. (editor) 1962 *Law and Sociology: Exploratory Essays.* New York: Free Press.

FRIEDMAN, LAWRENCE M. 1965 *Contract Law in America: A Social and Economic Case Study.* Madison: Univ. of Wisconsin Press.

FRIEDMANN, WOLFGANG (1944) 1960 *Legal Theory.* 4th ed. London: Stevens.

FRIEDMANN, WOLFGANG 1959 *Law in a Changing Society.* Berkeley: Univ. of California Press.

FULLER, LON L. 1964 *The Morality of Law.* New Haven: Yale Univ. Press.

GEIGER, THEODOR (editor) 1964 *Vorstudien zu einer Soziologie des Rechts.* Berlin and Neuwied: Luchterhand. → See especially "Internationale Bibliographie der Rechtssoziologie" by Paul Trappe.

GURVITCH, GEORGES D. (1940) 1947 *Sociology of Law.* Preface by Roscoe Pound. London: Routledge. → First published in French.

HALL, JEROME (1935) 1952 *Theft, Law and Society.* 2d ed. Indianapolis, Ind.: Bobbs-Merrill.

HART, H. L. A. 1961 *The Concept of Law.* Oxford: Clarendon.

HAZARD, JOHN N. 1953 *Law and Social Change in the U.S.S.R.* London: Stevens.

HAZARD, JOHN N. 1960 *Settling Disputes in Soviet Society: The Formative Years of Legal Institutions.* New York: Columbia Univ. Press.

HURST, JAMES W. 1950 *The Growth of American Law: The Law Makers.* Boston: Little.

HURST, JAMES W. 1960 *Law and Social Process in United States History.* Ann Arbor: Univ. of Michigan Law School.

HURST, JAMES W. 1964 *Law and Economic Growth: The Legal History of the Lumber Industry in Wisconsin; 1836–1915.* Cambridge, Mass.: Harvard Univ. Press.

KALVEN, HARRY; and ZEISEL, HANS 1966 *The American Jury.* Boston: Little.

LEV, DANIEL S. 1965 The Lady and the Banyan Tree: Civil-law Change in Indonesia. *American Journal of Comparative Law* 14:282–307.

LINDESMITH, ALFRED R. 1965 *The Addict and the Law.* Bloomington: Indiana Univ. Press.

LLEWELLYN, KARL N. (1928–1960) 1962 *Jurisprudence: Realism in Theory and Practice.* Univ. of Chicago Press.

LLEWELLYN, KARL N. 1960 *The Common Law Tradition: Deciding Appeals.* Boston: Little.

MACAULAY, STEWART 1963 Non-contractual Relations in Business: A Preliminary Study. *American Sociological Review* 28:55–67.

MANNHEIM, HERMANN 1946 *Criminal Justice and Social Reconstruction.* London: Routledge.

MATZA, DAVID 1964 *Delinquency and Drift.* New York: Wiley.

POUND, ROSCOE 1959 *Jurisprudence.* 5 vols. St. Paul, Minn.: West. → Volume 1: *Jurisprudence: The End of Law.* Volume 2: *The Nature of Law.* Volume 3: *The Scope and Subject Matter of Law.* Volume 4: *Application and Enforcement of Law.* Volume 5: *The System of Law.* Volume 1 reviews the main literature of sociological jurisprudence.

RENNER, KARL (1929) 1949 *The Institutions of Private Law and Their Social Functions.* London: Routledge. → First published as *Die Rechtsinstitute des Privatrechts und ihre soziale Funktion: Ein Beitrag zur Kritik des bürgerlichen Rechts.*

SCHUBERT, GLENDON 1960 *Quantitative Analysis of Judicial Behavior.* Glencoe, Ill.: Free Press.

SCHUR, EDWIN M. 1965 *Crimes Without Victims.* Englewood Cliffs, N.J.: Prentice-Hall.

SIMON, RITA (JAMES) 1967 *American Jury—The Defense of Insanity.* Boston: Little.

SIMPSON, SIDNEY P.; and STONE, JULIUS (editors) 1948–1949 *Cases and Readings on Law and Society.* 3 vols. St. Paul, Minn.: West.

SKOLNICK, JEROME H. 1966 *Justice Without Trial.* New York: Wiley.

TAPPAN, PAUL W. 1947 *Delinquent Girls in Court: A Study of the Wayward Minor Court of New York.* New York: Columbia Univ. Press.

TIMASHEFF, NICHOLAS S. 1939 *An Introduction to the Sociology of Law.* Cambridge, Mass.: Harvard Univ., Committee on Research in the Social Sciences.

VINOGRADOFF, PAUL 1920–1922 *Outlines of Historical Jurisprudence.* 2 vols. Oxford Univ. Press. → Volume 1: *Introduction; Tribal Law.* Volume 2: *The Jurisprudence of the Greek City.*

VON MEHREN, ARTHUR T. (editor) 1963 *Law in Japan: The Legal Order in a Changing Society.* Cambridge, Mass.: Harvard Univ. Press.

WEBER, MAX (1922a) 1954 *Max Weber on Law in Economy and Society.* Edited, with an introduction and annotations by Max Rheinstein. Cambridge, Mass.: Harvard Univ. Press. → First published as Chapter 7 of *Wirtschaft und Gesellschaft.*

WEBER, MAX (1922b) 1957 *The Theory of Social and Economic Organization.* Edited by Talcott Parsons. Glencoe, Ill.: Free Press. → First published as Part 1 of *Wirtschaft und Gesellschaft.*

II
THE LEGAL SYSTEM

The comparative analysis of the social structures of legal systems has its historical roots in the study of comparative law. It is possible to draw an analytical distinction between the two disciplines. Comparative structural analysis is a sociological endeavor. Its subject matter is the organization of legal activity and the variable character of the groups and social roles involved in the legal process; its primary goal is the discovery and explanation of regularities in institutional structure and development. Comparative law, on the other hand, is a jurisprudential study. Its practitioners are interested in the normative content of various systems of law and are often motivated by a desire to seek the fairest and most effective means of ordering the legal relations between men. Nevertheless, the intimate connection between the two fields should not be overlooked. In one branch of comparative law the sociological element is particularly strong: students of comparative legal history have generally accepted the proposition that legal concepts and modes of legal thought reflect an underlying framework of social organization. Thus, legal historians have often viewed the normative content of law from a sociological perspective.

Origins of the structural approach

The sociological perspective is at least as old as the Enlightenment and Montesquieu's classic, *De l'esprit des lois* (1748). Montesquieu found the sources of law in climate and geography and in the social institutions and national character of a people.

The concept of national character pervades the work of Friedrich Karl Savigny, who is generally regarded as the founder of historical jurisprudence (Stone [1946] 1950, chapter 18). Savigny wrote in the context of a national debate regarding the proposed codification of German law. He argued that codification would destroy the peculiarly Germanic character of German law and that the loss of national distinctiveness would be disastrous because any system of law must truly reflect the spirit and genius of the institutions of a people. To document his views, he produced a series of scholarly volumes on Roman and German law that were designed to demonstrate the close correspondence between social and legal development in those nations.

From here it is but a short, logical step to our contemporary interest in the relation between the "positive" norms of the law of the state and the *de facto* norms which emerge from the institutions of the larger society. In American sociology this concern has independent roots in William Graham Sumner's interest in the mores, the folkways, and the stateways (1906), and in E. A. Ross's emphasis on social control (1901; see also F. J. Davis et al. 1962, chapters 1, 2). On a global scale, however, the dominant transitional figure was the Austrian jurist Eugen Ehrlich (1913).

The proposition that laws *ought* to reflect the peculiar character of a nation's social institutions is easily transformed into the closely related view that such a correspondence is desirable but has not been achieved. Ehrlich became disturbed by the failure of the conceptual apparatus of positive law to adequately reflect the "living law." For Ehrlich the living law is the *de facto* normative pattern that develops as competing social interests are resolved within the many groups and institutions constituting the "inner order" of a society.

In the English-speaking world the works of Sir Henry Sumner Maine (1861) had a profound impact on jurists and social scientists alike, since Maine attempted to trace both the evolutionary development of legal concepts and the social developments that produced them. Maine's posthumous influence extended to the Continent, where it played a role in shaping the thought of scholars within the emerging discipline of sociology.

Weber's comparative studies. Among those Continental scholars, Max Weber (1922) formulated the most comprehensive accounts of comparative legal structure. Weber's investigations were carried out as a part of his inquiries into the causes and consequences of the "rationalization" of the Western world. "Rationalization" in this context refers to the process by which an institution becomes systematically and logically elaborated according to general, analytical, and calculable principles.

Weber developed one of his characteristic ideal typologies for distinguishing the various types of legal thought found in the history of juristic development. He then elaborated one of Maine's fundamental ideas by showing that each type of legal thought is associated with a given form of legal organization and particularly with the structural location of legal specialists. Thus, for example, the logical rationality of Continental European conceptual jurisprudence is attributable to the influence of university-based professors who turned their philosophically trained intellects to the task of expounding the Roman law as a logically closed, abstract system.

Weber also examined the impact of variation in the structure of both governmental institutions and power relations among elite groups. He pointed out that the forms of legal development fostered by the university-based Romanists appealed to the interests of monarchs and bureaucrats in systematic administration and to the concerns of the rising capitalist class with the predictable protection of private rights.

Weber's account of comparative legal structure must also be seen in the context of his general interest in the rise and development of capitalist economic structure. His analysis of the role of law in capitalist development is effectively summarized in his treatment of the change in the concept of "special law." We may speak of special law when legal obligations apply differentially to different groups of people. According to Weber, special law originated in the differentiation of society into various status groups each with its traditional code and a degree of feudal independence from regulation by agents of the larger society. By contrast, the modern law of the centralized, bureaucratic state permits the different units of society to enter into legally binding contracts with each other. Thus, the power of the state is made to support bodies of special law created *de novo* by capitalists with interdependent interests.

Durkheim's theory of sanctions. Weber's theory converges with the ideas of the French sociologist Émile Durkheim (1893), who, following in a direct line of influence from Maine, was interested in the transition to a social order based upon contract.

Durkheim speculated that differences in legal structure so closely reflect underlying differences in social structure as to constitute indices of types of societies. In primitive societies the bonds of cohesion are formed by the global, undifferentiated norms of the "common conscience." In such a society, law is repressive; it operates through sanctions designed to obliterate offenses to the common conscience and heal its wounds. Over time, as social solidarity comes to depend more and more upon the interdependence of specialized units, the legal order also becomes differentiated. Bodies of specialized norms develop, which are backed by *restitutive* sanctions designed to restore the balance of interests between competing but interdependent social groups. The new type of law permits private groups to negotiate within the context of general normative limitations and to contractually create for themselves viable systems of enforceable legal obligations.

Thus, Durkheim and Weber converged in a common recognition of an important dimension of structural variation in legal systems, namely, the extent of reliance on private action to create legal obligation. At the same time, both recognized the critical importance of the problem of the articulation of the authority of the larger society with private legal obligations.

Problems of structural analysis

Given Western legal values, one problem area stands out as the central concern of comparative structural analysis: What are the various ways that legal systems relate to their social environment and, in particular, what are the structural correlates of legal independence?

Defining the system. The first problem is to establish an analytical boundary between the legal system and its environment by defining the term "legal system." This is a notoriously difficult problem. Not the least of the difficulties stems from the fact that definitions that are adequate to the task of defining law in modern states fail to include the law of societies in which legal relations are inextricably entangled in other institutional contexts. One solution is to define the legal system functionally, so that its existence is not made to depend upon a structurally distinct set of roles or upon groups such as courts or police.

Many functional definitions rely upon the concept of social control (F. J. Davis et al. 1962, chapter 2). Law is defined as a type of social control that relies on a particular form of enforcement, usually enforcement through the legitimate use of force. Parsons (1962) and others would rather treat enforcement as a political function, external to the legal system. The advantage of this strategy is that it focuses attention on the variable structural arrangements through which legal systems come to have access to sources of coercive power.

In this view, the peculiar province of law is in-

terpretation. Social integration is often attributed to normative controls. However, social norms are not sufficiently specific to provide authoritative guides to conduct. Further, consensus about norms is often accompanied by dispute about the facts to which norms are to be applied. Accordingly, procedures develop for issuing authoritative versions of ambiguous situations of conflict and for propounding binding rules tailored to the particularities of these situations. Enforcement, on the other hand, is a political problem, a problem of mobilizing sufficient power to implement legal decisions.

Those who insist on including enforcement within the legal system can reply that interpretation is a necessary component of any act of enforcement. Interpretation could never be isolated in any single differentiated institution. A viable research strategy must guard against the fallacy of neglecting the fact that consequential interpretive decisions are continually being made at many points in the social structure.

System and environment. However the boundaries of the legal system are drawn, the problem of conceptualizing relations with the environment remains. There are a variety of ways of viewing this problem, but in Western thought one approach has dominated analysis. The problem has been defined as one of accounting for the independence of the legal system. Western political philosophy has accorded a high place to the "rule of law." From a sociological perspective, the rule of law refers to a society with a differentiated legal system, free from domination by any other institutional complex. Where the rule of law prevails, the legal process is subordinate only to established, known, and universalistic rules. Given this value concern, the task of comparative sociology is to account for the social basis of the rule of law.

To this end, we may distinguish four types of relations between the legal system and its social environment. First, the legal system may be *undifferentiated*, that is, it may have no differentiated structural home. Thus, legal functions are performed only as a by-product of activity within other institutions. For example, among the Eskimos socially enforceable interpretations are implicitly made in the context of public curing ceremonies and popular assemblies and in ritualized combat of various sorts, but there are no specialized procedures for formally proclaiming enforceable decisions (Hoebel 1954, chapter 5).

Second, a system may be *subordinate*. In this case specialized formal procedures, involving specially designated personnel, are present but legal activities are controlled by other institutions. For example, justice may be dispensed by the king's ministers, as in ancient Egypt, or by priests subject to sacerdotal discipline, as in Sumer and Babylonia.

Third, a system may be *autonomous*. The legal practitioners may become so insulated from external controls as to become unresponsive to demands from other quarters. In these circumstances a legal system will develop according to an inner dynamic reflecting the dominant concerns of the practitioner group. Thus, for example, religious scholars may treat the law as a logical elaboration of theological concepts. The outstanding example of this is the development of the Semitic legal tradition.

The fourth category is the most complicated, as well as the most highly prized, in legal philosophy. Legal systems may be called *partially independent* when they are sufficiently insulated to permit independence in some spheres but not so protected as to prevent adaptive responses to the needs of other sectors of the society. The "ideal" form of partial independence is *procedural* independence. In this case, insulating mechanisms protect the day-to-day operation of the legal system and the interpretive process but do not make the system unresponsive to social interests, as formulated into general policies by legislatures and organized public opinion.

The concept of procedural independence must not be confused with the discredited idea that the judicial process can be purely mechanical or logical. American political science and legal realism have effectively shown that legal decisions necessarily involve choices between alternative policies. The difference between autonomy and procedural independence is that in the latter case adjudicators are responsive to policy premises originating outside the legal system.

Procedural independence is not only highly valued; it is also a crucially important case for sociological theory. Theorists as divergent as Weber (1922) and Engels (Marx & Engels 1848–1898, pp. 447–448 in 1949 edition) have stressed that procedural independence may contribute to the interests of particular social classes or institutions. An independent legal system, operating through the universalistic interpretation of established rules, is an efficient vehicle for legitimizing political domination. Further, such a system provides a set of stable expectations that facilitate economic calculation. A degree of procedural independence may emerge as a response to the conditions of stable economic relations, even in the face of considerable political domination of the legal process. For in-

stance, contractual arbitration in the Soviet Union became subject to the rule of law in order to foster accountability and stability in the relations between economic units (Berman 1950).

Law as social institution

The demand for stabilization of economic rights is only one of the forces supporting procedural independence. It is the task of comparative analysis to explicate the various structures and mechanisms that either insulate legal systems or make them vulnerable to external demands. Many protective devices are quite familiar; judicial tenure, judicial review, constitutional limitation, and judicial control over enforcement officials are obvious sources of judicial power. But from a sociological point of view the important question is, How are these mechanisms institutionalized? that is, How are they supported by concrete social arrangements?

A number of components of social structure are involved in the patterning of the relations between legal systems and other social institutions, but one factor has seemed especially important to sociologists. Comparative analysts have been particularly interested in the impact of the structure of professional specialization.

Legal specialists. The significance of the structural location and internal organization of professional groups is implicit in what has already been stated. Undifferentiated legal systems, having no specialized legal procedures, lack persons with special legal functions. Once a differentiated legal system develops, its character is profoundly affected by the social characteristics of its associated professionals. Indeed, one of the central propositions of comparative legal sociology is that autonomous and independent legal systems are supported by tightly organized professional groups, with an independent power base, whereas subordinate legal systems reflect the dependency and weakness of legal specialists.

Apart from this general proposition, it may also be asserted that specific characteristics of legal systems may be derived from attributes of professional groups. To take an obvious example, when adjudication is controlled by religious functionaries, then law is likely to have religious overtones.

Four major categories of legal specialists can be distinguished for present purposes. The first group may be broadly designated *adjudicators* and includes judges, magistrates, arbitrators, referees, hearing examiners, and similar functionaries. The second group consists of professional *advocates* of legal causes. The third group consists of legal *advisers*, such as the familiar English solicitor. Notaries, conveyancers, and other draftsmen, also, belong in this category, and their significance should not be underestimated. As Weber ([1922] 1954, pp. 72–201, 210) has shown, where private elements are strong in the legal system, these "auxiliary" jurists assume special importance. When the state assures the bindingness of private agreements, the drafters of legal documents may become legal innovators who play an important role in shaping legal development.

The fourth group consists of the legal *scholars* —the teachers, writers, historians, and commentators whose contributions have been very important in both the Roman and civil law and in many non-Western traditions as well.

The four categories of legal specialists may or may not be differentiated from each other in practice, and the type and degree of internal differentiation is one of the important structural features of a legal system. Another of Weber's hypotheses is that the intensely practical and empirical character of the common law reflects the fact that it developed at a time when teaching was not differentiated from legal practice; there were no specialized scholars to impart an abstract ideological content to the law.

Professional organization. The internal differentiation of the legal profession is only one organizational element among many within the profession. Patterns of professional recruitment and advancement, the organization of professional training, and the organization and control of professional practice may have important consequences for the operation of the legal system. The explanatory potential of these variables is illustrated in Ulf Torgersen's study of the small and declining political role of the Norwegian Supreme Court (1963). The relative insignificance of judicial review is attributable to the patterns of recruitment to the court, which has been increasingly dominated by career bureaucrats rather than private attorneys.

Tight professional control over recruitment, training, advancement, and practice, founded upon a monopoly of access to technical legal knowledge and a monopoly of the right to legal advocacy, is one major source of independence and autonomy. However, there are other sources of legal power. The independence of legal specialists may be supported by the sponsorship of representatives of other powerful groups. Thus, adjudicators may be insulated from the domination of economic interests by the sponsorship of governmental power, or vice versa.

Symbolic factors are often especially powerful in the legal sector. Legal specialists have rivaled religious functionaries in their capacity to assert successfully claims of special access to the sources of truth and right. Such claims have been supported by a variety of symbolic paraphernalia, ranging from magic and ritual to the more subtle trappings of modern judicial dignity. Ritualistic practices should not be discounted, but in modern liberal democracies the most important bulwark of legal independence has been the capture of the right to symbolically represent the limitation of governmental power. In this sense, the rule of law has supported itself; the independent professionals, who provide its social foundation, derive their influence in part from their symbolic embodiment of the normative regulation of power.

The legal process. Another approach to the articulation of the legal system and its social environment would eschew the abstract analysis of the structural location and internal organization of legal specialists in order to concentrate on the concrete transactions between legal specialists and representatives of other spheres.

These transactions include such processes as litigation, professional consultation, judicial enforcement, appointment or election to adjudicative office, and complaint to legal authorities.

According to this view, the proper strategy for comparative analysis is to study the structural arrangements that pattern interaction between legal specialists and others. The structural framework of legal transactions shapes their content and often provides leverage for either the legal system or its potential adversaries.

For example, one of the functions of formal legal procedure is to compel the parties to legal disputes to mold their concrete conflicts into issues subject to normative settlement. In so doing, the parties are forced to isolate normative issues and eliminate extraneous power factors. Power factors come to be defined as being outside of the scope of inquiry, and the adjudicator thus gains leverage on his clients.

On the other hand, the process of litigation is structured by the characteristics of cases that are preshaped by social organization before they come to the attention of legal authorities. Social structure generates a variety of types of conflict. Some conflict situations are channeled to the legal system; others are resolved in other contexts. Ready access to the legal system may depend upon a preferred position in the social order. Further, even among those who have ready access to the legal system, litigation is a strategic alternative to a variety of other modes of pressing interests. In consequence, legal officials are not always in a position to control the types of issues that come before them or the structural context within which issues are presented. Thus, litigation can be conceived of as a series of transactions between the legal system and other social components, which are structured in part by the legal system and in part by external factors. Other transactions are subject to similar analysis.

Evolution of legal systems

A third approach to comparative analysis may be described as evolutionary: How, and in what sequence of steps, have differentiated legal systems emerged?

In this respect, Durkheim's thought runs counter to Weber. Weber was concerned with the emergence of the modern state from its feudal predecessors, and in this context he stressed the lack of centralized machinery of enforcement in many preindustrial societies. Durkheim, in his insistence on the importance of repressive sanctions in primitive society, seems to assume that the existence of societal enforcement mechanisms is not problematical. The anthropologists and historians who are students of legal evolution cannot agree with him. They continually search for the analogues to the legal process in "stateless" societies and trace the development of differentiated legal systems based upon a state monopoly of legitimate enforcement power.

The gradual development of central legal machinery in Europe has been known to legal historians for some time (F. J. Davis et al. 1962, chapter 2; Wigmore 1928). Scholarly interest in the evolution of legal procedure has been reawakened recently, in part because of concern for the problems of world legal order. The sequence of development from primitive self-help to central enforcement of norms through a universalistic, normatively regulated procedure has intrigued those who are interested in the possibility of a similar development at the world level [see INTERNATIONAL LAW].

R. D. Schwartz and J. C. Miller (1964), in a cross-cultural study of 51 societies, have shown that three structural attributes of legal procedure combine in a systematic pattern that can be described as a cumulative scale. The representation of interests by third parties is found only in societies with both special police forces and third-party mediation of disputes. Police and mediation sometimes occur in the absence of representation, and sometimes mediation is found in the absence of

any police to carry out the orders of mediating agencies. In some societies none of these procedural devices is present. The authors also found that the elaboration of legal procedure as measured by position on the cumulative scale is associated with measures of societal complexity, suggesting an evolutionary sequence of development. The sequence suggested is consistent with Western legal development as it has been pieced together by juristic scholars. The earliest legal systems are barely legal. The closest approximations to legal institutions are the rules governing kin-organized feuding and the sets of traditional compensations for wrongs. Later, regular procedures for submitting feuds to arbitration develop, but even then the parties may need to resort to self-help for enforcement. With the monopolization of legitimate force in the hands of the state, the legal system may rely on a specialized police force for enforcement of adjudicative orders. Finally, given a forum for binding and enforceable arbitration, the stage is set for the full development of professional advocacy.

Growth of legal pluralism. Historians have paid particular attention to the first two steps in the process. Law is said to appear in fully differentiated form once there is centralized enforcement of binding adjudication. From the perspective of comparative structural analysis the third step, also, is crucial, for with the appearance of institutionalized representation comes powerful support for procedural independence. For the first time there exists a set of legal specialists whose interests are not identical with the interests of mediators. It is possible that the new representer group will be captured by a particular set of interests, but theoretically the requisite social supports are present for the introduction of pluralism into the structure of the legal system. Professional representation can bring to the day-to-day administration of justice effective legal advocacy of the full range of interests present in society.

One step to pluralism is the creation of a market for professional services, so that legal representation can be purchased without regard to the content of the claims one wishes to advance. This requires either a high degree of professional neutrality or heterogeneity in the backgrounds and interests of recruits to professional service.

The establishment of a market for legal services is not a sufficient condition for pluralism, since the professional market will reflect the imperfections and inequalities of the economic structure of society. Since the inequalities of the marketplace may be overcome by various procedural devices and by effective organization for legal advocacy, the variable organization of access to representation is one of the most important elements in the comparative study of modern legal systems.

Administrative law

In many instances ready access to the legal system has been promoted through the creation of administrative remedies, which permit rights to be secured by direct application to administrative agencies of government. Traditional courts and their sometimes cumbersome procedures are by-passed. At the same time, in their judicial activities the administrative agencies operate in at least a quasi-judicial fashion, preserving many of the forms of law and subjecting themselves to the rule of law. Administrative procedure tends to be more informal than traditional legal procedure, and is less likely to involve formal adversaries. It can therefore permit the adjudicator a relatively free hand to shape solutions that take into account the particularities of a given case. Yet, administrative procedure is normatively regulated, and the standards of impartiality and decision according to law apply.

The tremendous burgeoning of administrative law in the twentieth century is the most recent chapter in legal evolution. On this count, Durkheim's sense of evolutionary development fared well, for he successfully foretold the growth and elaboration of administrative law. For Durkheim administrative law was an integral part of the restitutive approach to law; the moral order, as represented by the common conscience, seemed to him less important than effective administration of a complicated network of obligations.

From this perspective, the growth of administrative law should be interpreted as consisting in the legalization of administration. It is simply an aspect of the process of bureaucratization that accompanies economic development. The increasing involvement of government in large-scale economic and welfare projects has been a worldwide phenomenon. The requirements of efficient administration and the interests of bureaucratic officials have combined to create pressure for the stabilization of rights and obligations.

Important as it is, the legalization of administration does not entirely account for the increasing domination of administrative law, for there has been a corresponding and converging development on the legal side. Many administrative tribunals have been created to operate in areas that have been exclusively within the jurisdiction of courts. Numerous boards, commissions, and authorities have sprung up to deal with various criminal actions and tort claims.

Again one may invoke the argument of efficiency. The administrative tribunal has numerous practical advantages: it is less costly to litigants; it permits a high volume of litigation; it permits adjudication by specialists who are both technically skilled in particular areas and well acquainted with the concrete, practical problems of administration; it permits individualized treatment of complicated situations. But efficiency is not a sufficient explanation, unless one can show that particular groups have an interest in efficient administration. In this context, the growth of democracy is crucial (Evan 1962). Populist governments are responsive to demands for efficient administration of programs designed to produce public welfare and economic development. In the United States, for example, the growth of administrative law has been stimulated by a tendency for social welfare legislation to become bogged down in courts and by a movement to temper all legal administration by the application of a philosophy of social welfare.

Despite its humanitarian credentials, the growth of administrative law is often viewed with alarm in countries with a strong legal tradition. It is not surprising that administrative law should be surrounded by controversy, for its emergence is a classic case of a process that is usually associated with social strain. Whenever a group claims that special expertise or special familiarity with problems gives it a right to perform functions that were traditionally handled at other social locations, conflict ensues. Conflict is heightened when the technical specialist claims that his expertise frees him from some of the normative restraints that have governed performance of the function in the past. Yet this is exactly the claim of emergent administrative systems. The very differentiation of the legal function appears threatened as legal systems lose functions to substantively specialized but multifunctional enforcement agencies. All these processes have still to be adequately studied by students of contemporary social organization.

LEON H. MAYHEW

[*Directly related are the entries* ADMINISTRATIVE LAW; CRIMINAL LAW; LEGAL SYSTEMS; POLICE; PUNISHMENT; SOCIAL CONTROL. *Other relevant material may be found in* JURISPRUDENCE; LEGAL REASONING; *and in the biographies of* BECCARIA; BLACK-

STONE; COKE; DURKHEIM; EHRLICH; HAURIOU; MAINE; MONTESQUIEU; SAVIGNY; WEBER, MAX.]

BIBLIOGRAPHY

BERMAN, HAROLD J. (1950) 1963 *Justice in the U.S.S.R.: An Interpretation of Soviet Law.* Rev. & enl. ed. Cambridge, Mass.: Harvard Univ. Press. → First published as *Justice in Russia: An Interpretation of Soviet Law.*

DAVIS, E. EUGENE 1962 Legal Structures in a Changing Society. Pages 196–226 in F. James Davis et al., *Society and the Law: New Meanings for an Old Profession.* New York: Free Press. → Summarizes, from a lawyer's point of view, the administrative problems of the contemporary United States court system.

DAVIS, F. JAMES et al. 1962 *Society and the Law: New Meanings for an Old Profession.* New York: Free Press. → A symposium in which sociologists collaborated with lawyers. Chapter 1, "The Sociological Study of Law," is especially useful for its summary of sociological interest in law in the United States since 1900.

DURKHEIM, ÉMILE (1893) 1960 *The Division of Labor in Society.* 2d ed. Glencoe, Ill.: Free Press. → First published as *De la division du travail social.*

EHRLICH, EUGEN (1913) 1936 *Fundamental Principles of the Sociology of Law.* Translated by Walter L. Moll with an introduction by Roscoe Pound. Cambridge, Mass.: Harvard Univ. Press. → First published as *Grundlegung der Soziologie des Rechts.*

EVAN, WILLIAM M. (editor) 1962 *Law and Sociology: Exploratory Essays.* New York: Free Press. → See especially "Public and Private Legal Systems," pages 165–184. Argues that the modern democratic state contains a plurality of legal orders.

HOEBEL, E. ADAMSON 1954 *The Law of Primitive Man: A Study in Comparative Legal Dynamics.* Cambridge, Mass.: Harvard Univ. Press.

MAINE, HENRY J. S. (1861) 1960 *Ancient Law: Its Connection With the Early History of Society, and Its Relations to Modern Ideas.* Rev. ed. New York: Dutton; London and Toronto: Dent. → A paperback edition was published in 1963 by Beacon.

MARX, KARL; and ENGELS, FRIEDRICH (1848–1898) 1962 *Selected Works.* Volume 2. Moscow: Foreign Languages Publishing House.

MONTESQUIEU (1748) 1962 *The Spirit of the Laws.* 2 vols. New York: Hafner. → First published as *De l'esprit des lois.*

PARSONS, TALCOTT 1962 The Law and Social Control. Pages 56–72 in William M. Evan (editor), *Law and Sociology: Exploratory Essays.* New York: Free Press.

ROSS, EDWARD A. 1901 *Social Control: A Survey of the Foundations of Order.* New York and London: Macmillan.

SCHWARTZ, RICHARD D.; and MILLER, JAMES C. 1964 Legal Evolution and Societal Complexity. *American Journal of Sociology* 70:159–169.

STONE, JULIUS (1946) 1950 *The Province and Function of Law: Law as Logic, Justice, and Social Control; a Study in Jurisprudence.* Sydney: Associated General Publications; Cambridge, Mass.: Harvard Univ. Press.

SUMNER, WILLIAM G. (1906) 1959 *Folkways: A Study of the Sociological Importance of Usages, Manners, Customs, Mores, and Morals.* New York: Dover. → A paperback edition was published in 1960 by the New American Library.

TORGERSEN, ULF 1963 The Role of the Supreme Court in the Norwegian Political System. Pages 221–244 in Glendon A. Schubert (editor), *Judicial Decision-making.* New York: Free Press.

WEBER, MAX (1922) 1954 *Max Weber on Law in Economy and Society.* Cambridge, Mass.: Harvard Univ. Press. → First published as Chapter 7 of Max Weber's *Wirtschaft und Gesellschaft,* published posthumously; Weber died in 1920. His earliest contributions to the sociology of law date from the 1890s, and the topic was rarely absent from his subsequent writings.

WIGMORE, JOHN H. (1928) 1936 *A Panorama of the World's Legal Systems.* 3 vols. Washington: Washington Law Book. → A historical survey of 16 legal systems.

III

THE LEGAL PROFESSION

The legal profession encompasses all those who in view of their special competence in matters of law assume a distinctive responsibility in the administration of a legal order. The nature and extent of this responsibility may vary, and its locus may be found in one or in several social roles: judges, advocates, counselors, draftsmen, teachers, scholars. Because of special issues connected with it, the topic of the judiciary is treated more extensively under other headings [see JUDICIAL PROCESS].

The legal profession attracts the interest of both students of the professions and students of law and government. Political scientists, legal scholars, historians, and political sociologists are mainly concerned with the role of lawyers in politics and in the administration of justice. Recent sociological writings approach the bar from the perspective of the study of professions, focusing on such problems as professional independence, ethics, careers, recruitment, and relations with clients. The sociology of law draws on all these approaches.

The profession and the law

Whatever approach one takes to the study of the legal profession, it cannot be fully understood unless it is seen in the light of the special functions it performs for law and legal institutions. Indeed, the development and character of a legal profession are closely related to the growth and orientations of the legal order which it serves and within which it operates.

Where law is simply an expedient for the settlement of disputes or the accommodation of conflicting interests, the work of the lawyer involves little more than mastery of some techniques of social adjustment. The legal profession develops most fully when law is viewed as an embodiment of values. Society then requires specialized group energies for the protection of its legal heritage and may find them in that occupation whose interests are identified with the preservation of legal skills and values. In this process, the legal craftsmen are transformed into a legal elite and assume the critical mission of maintaining the legal order and determining its subsequent development. Although values are at stake, a legal elite may not be necessarily called for when, as in ancient Greece or in imperial China, the values of law are not seen as distinct from the morality of the polity. In Athens the legal tasks of counsel and judge were performed by experienced citizens in the absence of any specialized legal profession. But the more the distinctiveness of law is emphasized and the more society aspires to legality, the greater is the need for an autonomous profession. The profession will require more or less independence and authority, depending upon the relative strength of community commitment to legal values.

While its role is partly fashioned in response to social needs, the legal profession carries much autonomous power over the orientations of the legal and social order. It may shape many features of a legal tradition. The growth of Roman law can thus be traced to the way in which *pontifices* and, later, praetors declared the law in private cases: by developing and extending formulas to be used as bases for actions at law, they created a system that allowed a continuing and highly pragmatic elaboration of legal ideas. The legal profession may also succeed in imprinting the value of law upon the community, as American arbitrators have done in the relations between labor and industry. It may even give a color of legality to moral norms and religious doctrines as did the rabbis in the Talmudic period and, in a different way, the canonists in the Roman Catholic church. Similarly, the inner weaknesses of the profession may breed corresponding weaknesses in the quality and authority of the legal order. This occurs when the profession becomes captured by the special interests it serves or when it so insulates itself as to weaken its participation in and responsibility for the solution of social problems. How competent the profession is to perform its role and what institutional means secure this capability are critical issues in the assessment of the legal profession.

Thus, the more developed a legal order, the more demands and responsibilities are placed upon its legal profession. The lawyer is called to bring a set of distinctive skills to his task. His special competence may be defined as an *expertise in the assessment of authoritativeness;* this follows from the special character of law as an authoritative order. Whatever kind of activity he may be involved in, the lawyer's distinctive contribution lies in his ability to formulate or criticize the *reasons* upon which the authority of claims, decisions, policies, or actions rests. This ability is not confined to the evaluation of lawfulness; it includes a capacity to unravel issues, to scrutinize the rationale of policies, and to explore the firmness and test the relevance of evidence and inferences. The true lawyer is a generalist: he conveys this quality in his very posture of self-confidence and in the forthrightness of his style (Riesman 1954). To what extent such skills can be developed, of course, always remains problematic. This will vary partly with the richness of the resources a legal tradition makes available in its techniques of reasoning and criticism and partly with the capacity of the profession itself to instill this competence in some, if only a few, of its members. But some expertise of that nature is essential if the lawyer is to perform his task: that is, to add to social and legal institutions this strain toward the rational and the justified, which is the source of growth and strength of the legal order (Kadish 1961).

Typical legal roles.   The legal profession is historically associated with the performance of some typical roles involving particular applications of this general expertise.

The *adjudicator* is responsible for making authoritative decisions on issues of right and responsibility in the light of legal principles. As the normative dimensions of adjudication rather than the mere settlement of disputes become more salient, there tends to be more pressure to reserve access to, and control of, this role to the legal profession.

The *advocate*, as a legal representative, carries out the task of pressing for the official recognition of claims of right. This role is closely tied to the adjudicative process, especially when the latter rests upon the adversary presentation of claims, as in the Anglo–American tradition. The significance of advocacy may however extend beyond the sphere of adjudication, especially when the law assumes a positive role in the fulfillment of human aspirations. The advocate may then acquire more direct functions in the formation of law; as a result new forms of advocacy will tend to develop in new institutional settings. The role of advocate is marked by conflict between the lawyer's responsibilities as an officer of the law and his commitment to the interests of his client. This is a source of strains not only for the lawyer, who may cope with them in a variety of ways, but also for the legal system as a whole. Different systems vary in the way they balance these conflicting duties, as well as in the degree to which they tolerate this ambivalence and allow for the free development of advocacy. Whereas partisanship has been a cornerstone of common-law procedure, Soviet Russian law has until recently tended to restrict the right to counsel, and to insist on the advocate's primary loyalty to the courts and the public interest (Hazard 1960).

The *counselor* or *draftsman* has the special burden of assisting in the solution of social and human problems, while at the same time preserving the ideals of the legal order. The more emphasis that is placed on law as a creator of opportunities, the more this role is likely to develop. Thus, the notaries of northern Italy became pioneers in the fashioning of the law merchant, or commercial law, and the creation of negotiable instruments; their influence can be compared to that of modern lawyers in the growth of corporate enterprise. This development has been particularly significant in the United States, where business counseling became a primary focus of law practice to a much greater extent than in any European country.

The *jurist* or legal scholar is in charge of the systematic analysis and criticism of legal doctrine. One characteristic of law, as compared with other systems of norms, is that it contains its own built-in principles of criticism; the extension and refinement of these principles is a major task of the jurist. He may also share with the practitioners the role of training future lawyers. Jurists provide the profession with an instrument of self-scrutiny. The authority of their opinions varies, being generally higher in continental European than in Anglo–American law. One of the most important sources of law in imperial Rome lay in the *responsa prudentium*, that is, opinions in which famous scholars answered difficult questions of law. Under Hellenic influence, these jurists founded a tradition of formal legal analysis and teaching, which contributed to the progressive systematization and codification of Roman law; the Valentinian Law of Citations in A.D. 426 conferred legal authority on their writings. The revival and reception of Roman law in the Middle Ages was also the work of a school of jurists, the glossators of northern Italy, later followed by the scholastic postglossators in France and Italy. The German school of *usus modernus pandectarum* continued this tradition and, until the end of the nineteenth century, adapted the Roman doctrines to provide Germany with a workable common law; much of this work was incorporated in the German civil code of 1900.

Jurisprudence also attempts to clarify the ideals and perspectives of the legal order, a function that may be more effectively performed when jurists are not too closely bound to the practicing profession. There is, however, no clear evidence on this point, although the case of American law schools may be suggestive. Because of weak ties to universities and a tendency to recruit teachers from the ranks of practitioners, American law schools have generally been oriented to the practical interests of the profession, with little concern for jurisprudence and broader issues pertaining to the quality and needs of the legal order.

Lawyers have also been called to assume many other roles, such as mediators, managers in private business, politicians, and public administrators. How extensively they participate in such roles, especially in government, may both affect and reflect the authority of the law. Of special importance is the character of their participation. Their only contribution may lie in the ability to accommodate interests and manipulate social structures, a kind of activity in which they would not significantly differ from any trained politician (Eulau & Sprague 1964). Or they may bring to public life some of their own distinctive commitments and competence and help evolve, in both private and public government, an orientation to orderly procedure and the ideals of legality.

Structure of the profession

To analyze the structure of the legal profession is to ask how the social organization of the profession affects the role it performs in the legal order. The focus here is on internal and external sources of weakness or strength.

Legal education. By controlling access to the profession and the training of future lawyers, legal education has an important bearing on the character of the profession and the orientations of the law. Whether the law becomes the property of a privileged class or of the whole polity depends to some extent upon criteria of access to the profession. When admission is limited to a narrow segment of society, the services of the profession may be oriented primarily to this clan. The more the legal career is viewed as an avenue to political power and social status, the more efforts will be made to keep access open, especially where there is strong antipathy toward the establishment of governmental elites. This has been evident in the United States (Hurst 1950). Although wide accessibility may make the law responsive to a larger range of interests, it may also create problems for the profession in its endeavor to preserve standards of quality. American attempts to raise educational standards of admission to the bar have met only limited success: the shift from apprenticeship to academic training has been accompanied by the development of a highly stratified system of education, with only relatively few high-standard university law schools at the top. The bottom consists of a large number of low quality, part-time schools that have weak or no university ties and seek merely to prepare the student for the bar examination.

Methods of legal training affect the skills and perspectives lawyers bring to their practice and thereby shape many features of the law. Max Weber has noted the relation between apprenticeship and the pragmatic responsiveness of the common law, as contrasted with the more intellectual and formalistic treatment of the law arising from university education in Europe (1922). Orientations to law are thus created, which confer on the legal order more or less rigidity or flexibility. Some can better preserve the "open texture" of the law, allowing law to incorporate social change while retaining its continuity; the Anglo–American system has been remarkable in this respect. Other orientations are apt to freeze the structure of legal rules and to paralyze processes of legal change; the academism of legal education in Europe—a tradition that dates back to the glossators—tends to promote this rigidity. Social reforms are then more likely to be sought by means outside the law, thus arousing critical problems for the stability of both the legal and the political order. This tendency can be observed in some civil-law countries, especially in South America.

In a more direct way, legal education may become a source of law. In the very act of ordering legal materials for pedagogical purposes, law is divided into branches, and these are organized around governing concepts. The institutes of Roman law were originally purely pedagogical instruments; however, by systematizing the principles of Roman law, they started a movement toward codification and became an authoritative source of the *Corpus juris civilis*. In the process of being taught, law is thus given a structure which reflects the changing emphases of positive law and the needs of the practitioners. But this structure also provides ideas and perspectives which may affect the capacity of the law to cope with social change. Thus, the disappearance of the law of persons as a separate branch of legal study tends to impoverish the resources of American law for recognizing new forms of status.

Even more significant for the legal order is the role of legal education in providing lawyers with distinctive modes of analysis and reasoning. The case method, as practiced in American law schools, may be peculiarly competent to impart these skills. It may also tend, however, to create a perspective in which law appears as an outcome of controver-

sies rather than a way of implementing values. More importantly, by identifying the main locus of law in appellate decisions, it may promote a restricted conception of the legal. Attention is diverted from the variety of ways and settings in which law can emerge and be administered. Even in its empirical focus on decisions, the case method overstresses the role of the judiciary, neglecting legislation and administrative decision making. It may thus limit the capacities of legal education to prepare lawyers for a period such as the present, when the role of law is being extended beyond its traditional confines.

Professional autonomy.   The integrity of the law depends in part upon its ability to respond to political demands while maintaining its commitment to reason and impartiality. A continuing problem for the practicing lawyer is to remain sensitive to social needs and interests without becoming their captive and to preserve his autonomy without withdrawing himself from practical concerns.

Captivity may, of course, take a crude form, as when a political regime seizes control over the profession in order to neutralize a potential source of criticism (Kirchheimer 1961). It can, however, develop in more subtle forms where the profession is otherwise left free to serve. The lawyer can become the captive of his clients' interests: an insecure practice, for example, makes it harder for him to resist pressures from clients for fear of losing them to competitors. This condition arises when the demand for legal services remains weak and intermittent, as it is among the lower classes, or when there is intense competition from other lawyers or from such groups as realtors and accountants, who encroach upon areas of practice requiring only low level and standardized skills (Carlin 1962). Captivity can also result from too intimate involvement in the affairs of particular clients. Lawyers may thus tie themselves to a small number of institutional clients who demand extensive and continuing services, or as "house counsel" (members of a legal department) they may become too closely identified with or too submissive toward the enterprise or agency which employs them.

Professional integrity may also be undermined in the lawyer's dealings with courts and government agencies. The lower the standards of these institutions or the more open they are to outside political influences, as lower courts often are, the more they create opportunities and pressures which may attenuate norms of professional conduct. Continual practice before an agency may also lead the lawyer to share the perspectives of its administrators.

A common consequence of captivity is to deprive the lawyer of his special identity: he is transformed into a manipulator of social and economic structures who is no longer committed to the use of distinctively legal methods or resources. In this process, he tends to become indistinguishable from the politician or the business operator. Law is then made to appear as simply an expedient for the promotion of special interests, and the distinction between law and politics is lost.

The lawyer can resist pressures by avoiding involvement or insecurity, but such avoidance entails its own difficulties. A too rigid insistence upon independence and distinctiveness may divorce the lawyer from his clients' problems and needs, thus weakening the contribution law might make to their solution. The lawyer may then find himself confined to the passive role of providing technical help in the event of legal trouble. Under such conditions, law tends to evolve into legalism. A special view of law is conveyed which stresses the formalism of the legal order and the obstacles it creates to effective problem solving. Law may thus be emptied of its moral and political significance and reduced to its purely technical and positivistic aspects. Paradoxically, in seeking to protect his autonomy the lawyer may so insulate himself as to weaken both his own authority and the authority of the law, perhaps eventually becoming a docile servant of corporate or political power. The history of the legal profession in Nazi Germany illustrates this process.

Organization of the bar. The profession has evolved a number of structural arrangements which can be more or less successful in securing a viable autonomy. Apart from its effectiveness in this regard, the social organization of the bar may also influence patterns of development in the law.

One organizational device is to create within the profession an elite specially charged with the protection of legal ideals. While this segment insulates itself from outside pressures, others in the profession are left free to respond to and accommodate the variety of demands that are made on the legal order. The British system has achieved this differentiation by developing a small and specialized class of barristers, who enjoy a monopoly of practice in the higher courts and deal with clients only through solicitors. The latter do most of the client counseling and take care of cases in the lower courts and government agencies (Jackson 1940). In the United States, the large law firms have developed a very high level of technical proficiency in legal work, have restricted their practice to the most stable and secure clientele, and have limited their contacts to the top levels of government and the judiciary (Smigel 1964). Special training institutions, such as the Inns of Court in Britain and the American Ivy League law schools, help to strengthen these elites, while sharing in their trusteeship for the legal order.

The services of the elite bar tend to benefit those most competent to pursue their interests through use of the legal process. Thus, a critical issue is whether the elite can preserve its loyalty to legal institutions and its responsibility for the law as a whole, for it runs the risk of becoming so identified with the aims of a special clientele as to restrict its concerns to those areas of the law that best serve these aims. This encourages a highly selective development of the law and impairs recognition of legal demands arising from other segments of society. Large American law firms have thus been strongly criticized for their too exclusive services to corporate interests and their loss of concern for general legal values (Berle 1933). Moreover, in the United States the large metropolitan bar is highly stratified, with little mobility or communication between the upper and lower strata (Carlin 1966). The more the elite is cut off from the lower levels of the profession and of government, the more difficult it becomes to incorporate in the legal order the demands that are brought to these levels.

Formal associations. The weaker the sense of common purpose is within the bar and the more threatening the conditions under which it operates, the more pressing is the need for instruments of self-scrutiny and control. The practicing profession has traditionally been organized into guildlike associations, such as the Inns of Court in Britain and the Ordre des Avocats in France, which have often been quite powerful in regulating the practice of law. In the United States, the organization of the bar used to consist exclusively of small local and voluntary associations with little cohesion and authority. It still remains today highly fragmented, and primarily concerned, even in the exercise of disciplinary control, with the protection of the profession against public intervention and lay encroachments. A movement of reform, starting in the 1870s, led to the establishment of state bar associations and later to the integration of some of these. In states which have an "integrated bar," membership is compulsory for all practitioners in the state, and the association can thus enjoy greater security and larger resources. The American Bar Association was created in 1878 and progressively developed into a federation of state and local groups. It has assumed a prominent role in the bar as a whole, elaborating standards of admission and canons of ethics and recommending reforms in the law and the administration of justice. In legal reform it collaborates with two specialized organizations of the profession, the American Judicature Society and the American Law Institute. The latter undertook to codify American common law in a "Restatement of the Law." This work is still in progress. Contributions of the Institute include the drafting of model acts and codes in various branches of the law.

Types of practice. The practice of law may take a variety of forms, some of which have already been mentioned. Lawyers may work on their own or associate in firms of various size. They may serve mainly discrete individuals or organizations and businesses; the role of family lawyers, such as attorneys in the field of probate and estate, tends to decline as the family loses its economic functions.

Not all areas of legal practice allow the same quality of work. For instance, workmen's compensation and, frequently, personal injury call mainly for mass production and standardized legal techniques. In other fields, such as criminal law and domestic relations, "marriage counseling" and political manipulation are often more salient than legal craftsmanship (O'Gorman 1963). The lawyer is then likely to feel frustrated and threatened in his professional identity. The character of the market for services may also affect professional integrity: lawyers can more easily preserve their dignity when they can count on a secure and regular clientele. Others, however, especially those with low-status clients, have to keep continually searching for business, establishing connections, and resorting to such expedients as "ambulance chasing," through which potential clients are located and advantage is taken of whatever claims and speculations can be aroused. In this very process they become deprofessionalized (Carlin 1962).

A new type of practice has begun to develop as organized groups, such as labor unions and trade associations, assume the function of providing to their members the services of their retained counsel. The special contribution of these groups lies in their ability to aggregate common interests and to articulate legal demands. Resources can then be mobilized to press these claims in a systematic way and thereby promote legal change.

The practice of law has become more specialized: lawyers specialize according to the class of clients they serve, the agencies with which they deal, or the branch of the law they handle. In the United States, this trend has been facilitated by the expansion of law firms (Smigel 1964). Specialization is particularly significant for the growth of legal doctrine in undeveloped areas of the law and where special government institutions must be made accountable and sensitive to social demands. Specialized lawyers have thus played an important role in the development of administrative law and labor law and in the extension of constitutional rights in the United States.

The explosion of advocacy

Modern social transformations tend to place new demands on the legal order and the legal profession. Government—public and private—is asked to perform tasks and satisfy needs that were formerly taken care of in more informal settings. Thus, in contrast to a rather passive role in the past, law and legal institutions are being summoned to participate more positively in the task of fulfilling human aspirations and accomplishing social purposes.

The effectiveness of law in this new role depends upon considerable expansion of social resources for legal criticism. Modern times may thus witness what has been termed an "explosion of advocacy," with corresponding demands for critical changes in the services of the legal profession. The lawyer is called upon to relinquish his passive stance and assume an active role in the transformation of privileges into rights and in the development of rationality and competence in government institutions (Cahn & Cahn 1964).

This enlarged responsibility will require greater initiative on the part of the profession in scrutinizing the variety of social settings where decisions are made affecting established or incipient rights. The traditional role of law schools and professional associations will need re-evaluation in this respect. More positive responsibilities may fall upon legal departments, in view of their growing role in public and private organizations. Special agencies, similar to the Scandinavian office of ombudsman, may also be designed to carry out this task of legal criticism.

Wherever government relies upon self-help for the assertion of claims and interests, the viability of the system will ultimately depend upon the legal competence of the citizenry, that is, its capacity to make effective use of the legal machinery. To promote this competence is one of the major tasks of the legal profession. One requirement is that the provision of legal services be extended.

Pressures on the profession to broaden its availability have been heightened by social demands for equality and political enfranchisement. It is unlikely, however, that the enlarged need for legal services can be fully met with existing institutions, such as legal aid and public defender offices. Serious limitations of available organized services can be seen in their dependence upon traditionally restricted sources of support, their routine treatment of cases, and their view of legal assistance as a form of public welfare ("The Availability of Counsel . . ." 1965).

As legal institutions become increasingly used and crowded, a new burden falls on the lawyer. The working of both law offices and tribunals comes to depend upon establishing standardized methods for the mass processing of cases. Thus the operation of rules and procedures tends to become a routine which escapes criticism and blocks adaptation to unusual cases and new experiences. Special efforts are then required of the lawyer in continually subjecting procedures to re-evaluation and in opening them to challenge and change.

However, more than a simple extension of legal services may be needed. The traditional model of individual representation and counseling may prove inadequate to the task of developing legal competence. New types of legal services must be evolved. Thus, the older emphasis on serving individual clients may have to be supplemented and in part replaced by *organizational advocacy*: here legal services are provided to an organization representing the common interests of a group or they are made available to members of the group through intervention by the organization. This transformation has already taken place in American industry, where organized labor has secured the services of specialized labor lawyers to support the legal interests of its constituents. Group services will have to expand if legal assistance is to be made effectively available ("The Availablity of Counsel . . ." 1965). Experience has shown that persons who are insecure and lack social support for the assertion of their claims need a representative organization to lend them its strength and resources. Neighborhood law firms and defense organizations such as the National Association for the Advancement of Colored People and the American Civil Liberties Union constitute a step in this direction. As these changes proceed, new specializations will develop within the legal profession, thus promoting the growth of new, still inchoate, fields of law.

Together with the growth of group representa-

tion, there is a drift away from the passive acceptance of individual cases as they come. This traditional approach is consistent with an adversary system in which the presentation of legal issues depends upon the development of specific controversies between defined interests. This system tends to divert attention from structural sources of injustice. As individual demands become organized, *strategic advocacy* develops: the lawyer can select and possibly generate issues for the purpose of challenging practices and pressing recognition of new rights (Cahn & Cahn 1964). In this process, adjudication becomes less dependent upon disputes and can address itself more directly to issues of policy and the broader interests at stake. Adversariness is then used as a way of clarifying policy problems; at the same time, the role of the *amicus curiae* develops, and there is greater reliance upon forms of declaratory relief, where questions of law are clarified without the necessity of deciding on the outcome of a particular dispute. More importantly, the growth of the law tends to be less contingent upon the more or less random occurrence of cases and to proceed along lines of more systematic planning.

PHILIPPE NONET AND
JEROME E. CARLIN

[*Directly related are the entries* JUDICIAL PROCESS; JUDICIARY; LEGAL SYSTEMS. *Other relevant material may be found in* CANON LAW; JURISPRUDENCE; LEGAL REASONING; LEGISLATION.]

BIBLIOGRAPHY

The Availability of Counsel and Group Legal Services: A Symposium. 1965 *U.C.L.A. Law Review* 12:279–463. → Contains a foreword and eight articles.

BERLE, A. A. JR. 1933 Modern Legal Profession. Volume 9, pages 340–346 in *Encyclopaedia of the Social Sciences*. New York: Macmillan.

BLAUSTEIN, ALBERT P.; and PORTER, CHARLES O. 1954 *The American Lawyer: A Summary of the Survey of the Legal Profession*. Univ. of Chicago Press. → Valuable as a bibliographical source.

CAHN, EDGAR S.; and CAHN, JEAN C. 1964 The War on Poverty: A Civilian Perspective. *Yale Law Journal* 73:1317–1352.

CARLIN, JEROME E. 1962 *Lawyers on Their Own: A Study of Individual Practitioners in Chicago*. New Brunswick, N.J.: Rutgers Univ. Press.

CARLIN, JEROME E. 1966 *Lawyers' Ethics: A Survey of the New York City Bar*. New York: Russell Sage Foundation.

EULAU, HEINZ; and SPRAGUE, JOHN D. 1964 *Lawyers in Politics: A Study in Professional Convergence*. Indianapolis, Ind.: Bobbs-Merrill.

HAZARD, JOHN N. 1960 *Settling Disputes in Soviet Society: The Formative Years of Legal Institutions*. New York: Columbia Univ. Press.

HURST, JAMES W. 1950 *The Growth of American Law: The Law Makers*. Boston: Little.

JACKSON, RICHARD M. (1940) 1964 *The Machinery of Justice in England.* 4th ed. Cambridge Univ. Press.

KADISH, SANFORD H. 1961 The Advocate and the Expert—Counsel in the Peno–Correctional Process. *Minnesota Law Review* 45:803–841.

KIRCHHEIMER, OTTO 1961 *Political Justice: The Use of Legal Procedure for Political Ends.* Princeton Univ. Press.

LASSWELL, HAROLD D.; and McDOUGAL, MYRES S. 1943 Legal Education and Public Policy: Professional Training in the Public Interest. *Yale Law Journal* 52:203–295.

O'GORMAN, HUBERT J. 1963 *Lawyers and Matrimonial Cases: A Study of Informal Pressures in Private Professional Practice.* New York: Free Press.

PLUCKNETT, THEODORE F. T. (1929) 1956 *A Concise History of the Common Law.* 5th ed. London: Butterworth. → See especially pages 79–289, "The Courts and Profession."

POUND, ROSCOE 1953 *The Lawyer From Antiquity to Modern Times: With Particular Reference to the Development of Bar Associations in the United States.* St. Paul, Minn.: West.

RIESMAN, DAVID 1954 *Individualism Reconsidered, and Other Essays.* Glencoe, Ill.: Free Press. → See especially pages 440–466, "Toward an Anthropological Science of Law and the Legal Profession."

SCHACHT, JOSEPH (1950) 1959 *The Origins of Muhammadan Jurisprudence.* Oxford: Clarendon.

SMIGEL, ERWIN O. 1964 *The Wall Street Lawyer: Professional Organization Man.* New York: Free Press.

WEBER, MAX (1922) 1954 *Max Weber on Law in Economy and Society.* Edited, with an introduction and annotations by Max Rheinstein. Cambridge, Mass.: Harvard Univ. Press. → First published as Chapter 7 of Max Weber's *Wirtschaft und Gesellschaft.*

IV
LAW AND LEGAL INSTITUTIONS

More scholarship has probably gone into defining and explaining the concept of "law" than into any other concept still in central use in the social sciences. Efforts to delimit the subject matter of law—like efforts to define it—usually fall into one of several traps that are more easily seen than avoided. The most naive beg the question and use "law" in what they believe to be its common-sense, dictionary definition—apparently without looking into a dictionary to discover that the word "law" has six entries in Webster's second edition, of which the first alone has 13 separate meanings, followed by five columns of the word used in combinations. German and French have even more complex ambiguities, since their comparable words (*Recht, droit*) include some dimensions for which English uses other words.

Sophisticated scholars, on the other hand, have been driven either to write treatises on the art and pitfalls of definition (Cohen & Hart 1955) or, like Stone (1964), to realize that in relation to a noetic unity like law, which is not represented by anything except man's ideas about it, definition can mean no more than giving the reader a set of mnemonics to remind him what has been talked about. It was Kant who said, "The lawyers are still seeking a definition of their concept of law." A century and a half later Stone stated that " 'law' is necessarily an abstract term, and the definer is free to choose a level of abstraction; but by the same token, in these as in other choices, the choice must be such as to make sense and be significant in terms of the experience and present interest of those who are addressed" (1964, p. 177).

Definitions of "law"

Even if we agree with Hart (1954) that the searches for definition and the concomitant search for security that they represent became serious only in the time of Austin (and Kant's remark would seem to belie this), it is apparent that schools of jurisprudence have risen, battled, and fallen on bastions erected on one meaning or another. Austin has permanently affected British jurisprudence by emphasizing the command aspect of a law and pointing out that the law is a command of the "sovereign" (itself an ambiguous concept). Since then lawyers have for generations and without signal success been arguing whether Austin's stipulations applied only to developed systems of "municipal" law and whether he himself really gave the point of command such primacy.

The American "realists" clustered around Oliver Wendell Homes's dictum that law is a prediction of what a court will enforce. Continental scholars tended to be more concerned with the moralistic "right" and "ought" aspects of the rules of law and have gone deeply into moral philosophy.

In the effort to define "law," some modern scholars like Hart (1954) conclude that there are three "basic issues": (1) How is law related to the maintenance of social order? (2) What is the relation between legal obligation and moral obligation? (3) What are rules and to what extent is law an affair of rules? Others (Stone 1966) describe several sets of attributes that are usually found associated with law. Accordingly, law is (1) a complex whole, (2) which always includes social norms that regulate human behavior. These norms are (3) social in character, and they form (4) a complex whole that is "orderly." The order is (5) characteristically coercive and (6) institutionalized. Law has (7) a degree of effectiveness sufficient to maintain itself. Anthropological studies of law in the non-Western world have followed a similar course. To cite one of the most vivid and orderly presentations, Pospisil (1958) examined several attributes of the law—the attribute of authority, that of intention of universal application, that of *obligatio* (the right–obligation cluster), and that of sanction. In his view, the "legal" comprises a field in which custom, political decision, and the various attributes overlap, though each may be found extended outside that overlapping field, and there is no firm line, but rather a "zone of transition," between that which is unquestionably legal and that which is not.

It was Kantorowicz (1958) who pointed out that there are many subjects, including some of a nonlegal nature, that employ a concept of law. He perceived that each needs a different definition of "law" if it is to achieve its purposes. He then proceeded to a more questionable point: it is for "general jurisprudence" to provide a background to make these differing definitions sensible—in short, it is the task of jurisprudence to elicit meaning from this cacophony of attempted definitions. Kantorowicz's method in jurisprudence is very like Pospisil's in anthropology. Instead of trying to find points for definition of law, Kantorowicz examined some characteristics of law that are vital to one or more of the specific definitions. Law is thus characterized by having a body of rules that prescribe external conduct (it makes little immediate difference to the law how one feels about it—the law deals in deeds). These rules must be stated in such a way that the courts or other adjudging bodies can deal with them. Each of the rules contains a moralizing or "ought" element—and Kantorowicz fully recognized that this "ought" element is culturally determined and may change from society to society and from era to era. Normative rules of this sort must, obviously, also be distinguished from the real uniformities by which men (sometimes with and sometimes without the help of courts and lawyers) govern their daily round of activity. Law is one of the devices by means of which men can reconcile their actual activities and behavior with the ideal principles that they have come to accept, and can do it in a way that is not too painful or revolting to their sensibilities and in a way which allows ordered (which is to say predictable) social life to continue. No act is wholly bad if it is "within the law"; no law is wholly good if it condones "immoral" action.

Rules.   Custom is a body of more or less overt rules which express "ought" aspects of relationships between human beings and which are actually followed in practice much of the time. Law has an additional characteristic: it must be what Kantorowicz calls "justiciable," by which he means

that the rules must be capable of reinterpretation, and be actually reinterpreted, by one of the legal institutions of society so that the conflicts within nonlegal institutions can be adjusted by an outside "authority."

It is widely realized that many peoples of the world can state more or less precise "rules" which are, in fact, the ideals in accordance with which they think they ought to judge their conduct. In all societies there are allowable lapses from rules, and in most there are more or less precise rules (sometimes legal ones) for breaking rules.

Legal institutions.   In order to make the distinction between law and other rules, it has been necessary to introduce furtively the word "institution." We must now make an honest term of it. A social institution can be defined as a group of people who are united (and hence organized) for some purpose; who have the material and technical means of achieving that purpose or at least of making rational attempts at it; who support a value system, ethics, and beliefs validating that purpose; and who repeat more or less predictable activities and events in the carrying out of the purpose (Malinowski 1945). With this rubric, all human activity can be viewed either as institutionalized or as random (and the degree of random behavior may be the most diagnostic feature of any society). It need hardly be added that "institutionalized" does not necessarily mean "approved" by the people who participate in the institutions.

With these ideas it is possible to distinguish legal institutions from nonlegal ones. A legal institution is one by means of which the people of a society settle disputes that arise between one another and counteract any gross and flagrant abuses of the rules of the other institutions of society. Every ongoing society has legal institutions in this sense, as well as a wide variety of nonlegal institutions.

It can be pointed out that some nonlegal institutions—the priestly, the psychiatric, and the like—serve the function of settling disputes. To make the distinction between legal and nonlegal, social scientists generally invoke the doctrine of coercion and use of force. Such a settlement is sensible because the legal institutions with which modern Western lawyers deal are usually associated with a political unit of which the state is one type. A political organization *ipso facto* supplies theorists with a "sovereign" of Austinian type and the "enforcement" predicated by Holmes and others. From this point of view, then, legal institutions must have two defining criteria: (1) they must settle the disputes that arise in other (nonlegal) institutions, and (2) they must be associated with (or even constitute) some sort of political organization. Obviously, for some purposes—particularly in the study of less-developed legal systems—the second criterion can and must be dropped; for most purposes of Western jurisprudence, just as obviously, it is probably necessary to retain it.

In carrying out the task of settling difficulties in the nonlegal institutions, legal institutions must have specific ways to (1) disengage the difficulties from the institutions of origin which they now threaten, (2) handle the difficulties within the framework of the legal institution, and (3) set the new solutions back within the processes of the nonlegal institutions from which they emerged. Indeed, the presence of such characteristics is a vivid index of the presence of a political organization.

There are, thus, at least two aspects of legal institutions that are not shared with other institutions of society. First, legal institutions alone must have some regularized way to interfere in the malfunctioning (and, perhaps, the functioning as well) of the nonlegal institutions in order to disengage the trouble case. Second, there must be two kinds of rules in the legal institutions—those which govern the activities of the legal institution itself (called "adjectival law" by Austin and "procedure" by most modern lawyers) and those which are substitutes for, or modifications or restatements of, the rules of the nonlegal institution that has been invaded (called "substantive law"). The above are only the minimal aspects that are shared by all known legal institutions.

Seen in this light, the distinction between law and custom is fairly simple. Customs are rules (more or less strict and with greater or less support of moral, ethical, or even physical coercion) about the ways in which people must behave if social institutions are to perform their tasks and society is to endure. All institutions (including legal institutions) develop customs. Some customs in some societies are *re*institutionalized at another level: they are restated for the more precise purposes of legal institutions. When this happens, therefore, law may be regarded as a custom that has been restated in order to make it amenable to the activities of the legal institutions. In this sense one of the most characteristic attributes of legal institutions is that some of these "laws" are about the legal institutions themselves, although most are about the other institutions of society, such as the familial, economic, political, and ritual.

Malinowski, by his little book *Crime and Custom*

in Savage Society (1926), has widely influenced lawyers with a faulty mode of distinguishing law from nonlaw. His idea was a good one; he claimed that law is "a body of binding obligations regarded as right by one party and acknowledged as the duty by the other, kept in force by the specific mechanism of reciprocity and publicity inherent in the structure of . . . society." His error was in equating what he had defined with the law. It is not law that is "kept in force by . . . reciprocity and publicity" ([1926] 1961, p. 58). It is custom as we have defined it here. Law is better thought of as "a body of binding obligations regarded as right by one party and acknowledged as the duty by the other" *which has been reinstitutionalized within the legal institution so that society can continue to function in an orderly manner on the basis of rules so maintained.* In short, reciprocity is the basis of custom; but the law rests on the basis of this double institutionalization.

Rights. One of the best ways to perceive the doubly institutionalized norms, or "laws," is to examine the smaller components as they attach to persons (either human individuals or corporate groups) and so to work in terms of "rights" and their reciprocal "obligations." In the framework of rights and duties, the relationships between law and custom, law and morals, law and anything else can be seen in a new light. Whether in the realm of kinship or contract, citizenship or property rights, the relationships between people can be reduced to a series of prescriptions with the obligations and the correlative rights which emanate from these prescriptions. In fact, thinking in terms of rights and obligations of persons (or role players) is a convenient and fruitful way of investigating much of the custom of many institutions. Legal rights are only those rights which attach to norms that have been doubly institutionalized; they provide a means for seeing the legal institutions from the standpoint of the persons engaged in them.

The phenomenon of double institutionalization of norms and therefore of legal rights has been recognized for a long time, but analysis of it has been only partially successful. Legal rights have their material origins in the customs of nonlegal institutions but must be *overtly restated* for the specific purpose of enabling the legal institutions to perform their tasks.

Sanctions. Many scholars, in comparative studies, have focused attention on the sanction for purposes of determining what is to be included in the "legal" field. Use of the term "sanction" has the advantage of allowing the scholar to beg the question of the Austinian sovereign. Sanction is generally understood to mean what the law itself says will or may happen to one found guilty of having transgressed a legal rule. The word is often used in common parlance to mean "the teeth in the law." When it is used as a verb, its true ambivalence becomes apparent. "To sanction" something is in ordinary usage not to interfere with someone's doing it; yet jurists also use it to mean "visit an evil on doing it," and social scientists have extended the word "sanction" far beyond its technical meaning for modern law. Radcliffe-Brown (1934a) described positive and negative sanctions for behavior, embracing not only penalization of nonconformity but also rewarding of conformity—and all this without specifying precisely who confers rewards or inflicts punishments.

The problem of sanction would seem to be better summarized in terms of legal institutions which, in some situations, apply specific types of correction to adjudged breaches of law. That is, the "sanction" is the body of rules according to which legal institutions interpose themselves for the purpose of maintenance of a social system so that living in it can be comfortable and predictable.

Law and social science

It is apparent that we must examine two further factors. First, what sort of definitions of law may be needed by the social sciences? Second, and related to this, how can social scientists go about investigating the legal institutions and the legalization of rights in any specific culture or in any concatenation of cultures?

The kernel of the social scientist's concept of law must be found, I believe, in the phenomenon of double institutionalization of rights: once within customary institutions, then again within the legal institutions. Therefore he is required absolutely to study both the legal institutions and the social institutions on which they feed—and only in this way can he ever make any progress with the thorny problem of the relationship between law and society.

The social scientist studying law is quite right when he considers the law a type of social superstructure to be judged by criteria or values of the social sciences. He is, however, quite wrong if he extends this position to mean that he need not consider what is known about the law on its own ground. The determining variables of the law may be considered as part of a social field; but equally so, the social field must be considered by jurisprudence. In short, what is required is a sort of stereoscopic vision, looking at data with the lens of

jurisprudence in one eye and the lens of social science in the other.

Seen thus stereoscopically, a legal right (and, with it, a law) is the restatement, for the purpose of maintaining peaceful and just operation of the institutions of society, of some but never all of the recognized claims of persons within those institutions; the restatement must be made in such a way that these claims can be more or less assured by the total community or its representatives. Only by so viewing legal rights can the moral, religious, political, and economic implications of law be fully explored.

In fact, a primary problem of all legal studies may be the intersecting of the law and the other institutions of society. This relationship is no mere reflection of society in the law: it must be realized, rather, that the law is always out of phase with society, specifically because of the duality of the statement and restatement of rights. Indeed, the more highly developed the legal institutions, the greater the lack of phase, which not only results from the constant reorientation of the primary institutions but is magnified by the very dynamics of the legal institutions themselves (Stone 1964, chapter 1, sec. 1).

Thus, it is the very nature of law and its capacity to "do something about" the primary social institutions that create the lack of phase. Moreover, even if one could assume perfect legal institutionalization, change within the primary institutions would soon jar the system out of phase again. What is less obvious is that if there were ever to be perfect phase between law and society, then society could never repair itself, grow and change, flourish or wane. It is the fertile dilemma of law that it must always be out of step with society but that people must always (because they work better with fewer contradictions, if for no other reason) attempt to reduce the lack of phase. Custom must either grow to fit the law or it must actively reject it; law must either grow to fit the custom or it must ignore or suppress it. It is in these interstices that social growth and social decay take place.

Social catastrophe and social indignation and resultant changes in custom are sources of much new law. With technical and moral change new situations appear that must be "legalized." This truth has particular and somewhat different applications to developed and to less highly developed legal systems. In developed municipal systems of law, in which means for institutionalizing behavior on a legal level are already traditionally concentrated in political decision-making groups such as legislatures, there is a tendency for the legal institution not to reflect custom so much as to shape it. As developed nations put more faith in their legislatures, nonlegal social institutions sometimes take a very long time to catch up with the law. On the other hand, in less-developed legal systems, it may be that little or no popular demand is made on the legal institutions, and therefore little real contact exists or can be made to exist between them and the primary institutions (Stone 1966, chapter 2, sec. 17). Law can become one of the major sources of innovation in society.

The social scientist's first task, then, is the analysis of the legal institutions to be found and their interrelationships with the nonlegal institutions of society. There may be courts as in some parts of indigenous Africa or indigenous Europe; there may be self-help, oracles, moots, town meetings, contests, and certain types of feuds (although most feuds do not correct the difficulty and feed the corrected situation back into the nonlegal institutions of society). The social scientist can examine the particular types of customs that are legalized in any particular society. He can begin the process of comparing the customs of mating and child rearing with the laws of marriage; the customs of trading with the laws of contract; the customs of interpersonal relations with the law of tort; the customs of approved behavior with criminal law.

And what will he find? He will find that the practice of law is a force by itself, a force for preserving and molding society that both has its roots irrevocably in social institutions and must supersede any particular historicoethnographic phase of them.

The social scientist's next task is the reporting and comparison of legal institutions *in the terms of the people who participate in those institutions* and the subsequent comparison of those terms with the terms in which other people live in analogous or similar institutions.

His third task is the exposition of what Hoebel (1954) has called the "postulates" of that people's law: the assumptions held about the "natural" ways of the world, most often without even a possibility of overt statement, by the people who live by a custom and a law. These postulates lie behind the law as they lie behind every other aspect of that people's activity. They are those "values," or unquestioned premises, on which a people bases not merely its behavior (including law) but its moral evaluation of behavior (including ethics). The postulates behind a legal system are congruent with the postulates behind the accompanying economic or religious system. What may seem blatant discrepancies and contradictions and, indeed, hypocrisies (as between Sunday school and the market place) are in fact no more than inadequate analyses of the postulates. A postulate lying behind Anglo–American law is that the human body is inviolably private unless marriage or certain contracts have been entered into; a postulate behind Eskimo law is that life is hard and that kinship, amity, or love between individuals cannot be allowed to override the welfare of the society. The postulates underlying a people's law also underlie the rest of its culture. Law cases provide one of the best mechanisms by which the ethnographer can capture these postulates and make them overt.

PAUL BOHANNAN

[See also JUDICIAL PROCESS; POLITICAL ANTHROPOLOGY; SANCTIONS.]

BIBLIOGRAPHY

ALLEN, CARLETON K. (1927) 1958 *Law in the Making.* 6th ed. Oxford Univ. Press.

BOHANNAN, PAUL 1957 *Justice and Judgment Among the Tiv.* Published for the International African Institute. Oxford Univ. Press.

COHEN, JONATHAN; and HART, H. L. A. 1955 Symposium: Theory and Definition in Jurisprudence. Pages 213–264 in Aristotelian Society, *Proceedings,* Supplementary Volume 29: Problems in Psychotherapy and Jurisprudence. London: Harrison.

COHEN, MORRIS R. 1950 *Reason and Law: Studies in Juristic Philosophy.* Glencoe, Ill.: Free Press. → A paperback edition was published in 1961 by Collier.

EHRLICH, EUGEN (1913) 1936 *Fundamental Principles of the Sociology of Law.* Translated by Walter L. Moll with an introduction by Roscoe Pound. Cambridge, Mass.: Harvard Univ. Press. → First published as *Grundlegung der Soziologie des Rechts.*

GLUCKMAN, MAX 1955 *The Judicial Process Among the Barotse of Northern Rhodesia.* Manchester Univ. Press; Glencoe, Ill.: Free Press.

HAAR, BAREND TER (1939) 1948 *Adat Law in Indonesia.* Translated and edited with an introduction by E. Adamson Hoebel and A. Arthur Schiller. New York: Institute of Pacific Relations, International Secretariat. → First published as *Beginselen en stelsel van het adatrecht.*

HART, H. L. A. 1954 Definition and Theory in Jurisprudence. *Law Quarterly Review* 70:37–60.

HART, H. L. A. 1961 *The Concept of Law.* Oxford: Clarendon.

HOEBEL, E. ADAMSON 1954 *The Law of Primitive Man: A Study in Comparative Legal Dynamics.* Cambridge, Mass.: Harvard Univ. Press.

JONES, HARRY W. 1962 Law and the Idea of Mankind. *Columbia Law Review* 62:753–772.

KANTOROWICZ, HERMANN 1958 *Definition of Law.* Edited by A. H. Campbell. Cambridge Univ. Press. → Published posthumously.

KANTOROWICZ, HERMANN; and PATTERSON, EDWIN W. 1928 Legal Science: A Summary of Its Methodology. *Columbia Law Review* 28:679–707.

LLEWELLYN, KARL N.; and HOEBEL, E. ADAMSON 1941 *The Cheyenne Way: Conflict and Case Law in Primi-*

tive Jurisprudence. Norman: Univ. of Oklahoma Press.

MALINOWSKI, BRONISLAW (1926) 1961 *Crime and Custom in Savage Society*. London: Routledge. → A paperback edition was published in 1959 by Littlefield.

MALINOWSKI, BRONISLAW 1945 *The Dynamics of Culture Change: An Inquiry Into Race Relations in Africa*. New Haven: Yale Univ. Press. → A paperback edition was published in 1961.

POSPISIL, LEOPOLD 1958 *Kapauku Papuans and Their Law*. Yale University Publications in Anthropology, No. 54. New Haven: Yale Univ., Department of Anthropology.

RADCLIFFE-BROWN, A. R. 1934a Sanction, Social. Volume 13, pages 531–534 in *Encyclopaedia of the Social Sciences*. New York: Macmillan. → Reprinted in the author's *Structure and Function in Primitive Society*.

RADCLIFFE-BROWN, A. R. 1934b Law, Primitive. Volume 9, pages 202–206 in *Encyclopaedia of the Social Sciences*. New York: Macmillan.

RADIN, MAX 1940 *Law as Logic and Experience*. New Haven: Yale Univ. Press.

STONE, JULIUS 1964 *Legal System and Lawyers' Reasonings*. Stanford Univ. Press.

STONE, JULIUS 1966 *Social Dimensions of Law and Justice*. Stanford Univ. Press.

TIMASHEFF, NICHOLAS S. 1939 *Introduction to the Sociology of Law*. Cambridge, Mass.: Harvard University, Committee on Research in the Social Sciences.

WILLIAMS, L. GLANVILLE 1945 International Law and the Controversy Concerning the Word "Law." *British Year Book of International Law* 22:146–163.

WILLIAMS, L. GLANVILLE 1945–1946 Language and the Law. *Law Quarterly Review* 61:71–86, 179–195, 293–303, 384–406; 62:387–406.

LAW ENFORCEMENT

See CRIME; PENOLOGY; POLICE; PUNISHMENT; SOCIAL CONTROL.

LAW, JOHN

John Law of Lauriston (1671–1729), economist, banker, merchant, and statesman, founded the first Bank of France and is generally held responsible for the Mississippi Bubble. He was born in Edinburgh, the son of a prosperous goldsmith–banker, who died when Law was only 13. However, his mother, who was distantly related to the duke of Argyll, saw to it that Law studied both theoretical and applied economics. Law was a handsome man with an engaging personality and the ability to make a favorable impression on important people. Nevertheless, he spent many years as a fugitive from British justice, having been sentenced to death in 1694 for killing a man in a duel. It was not until 1717 that he was pardoned by George I, and his extensive travels during his exile enabled him to study diverse economic institutions and conditions abroad.

Law's early interest in money and banking may well have been intensified by the adoption of William Paterson's plan for the Bank of England in 1694, since Paterson was a fellow Scot. Over the next 20 years Law was to spend much time and energy making proposals for the establishment of banks, both in Scotland and on the Continent, and these efforts eventually culminated in the founding of the first Bank of France.

The original proposal was outlined in two drafts for a privately owned Bank of France, which he sent in 1702 to Madame de Maintenon, the morganatic wife of Louis XIV. In a brief theoretical introduction, Law enumerated as components of the money supply: Bank of England stock, stock in the English and Dutch East India companies, exchequer notes, and Dutch government bonds—a concept of money supply that was destined to lead to his most calamitous mistakes in monetary policy. Each province of France would have a branch of the Bank, with a fixed allotment of capital, and notes payable to bearer would be redeemed at the parent Bank in Paris or at any one of the branches. Law argued that the Bank of France, like the Bank of Amsterdam and the Bank of England, would increase the money supply, lower the rate of interest (thereby raising the price of land and stimulating economic activity), reduce losses from fire and theft, eliminate shipments of specie from the provinces to Paris, and, through its notes, provide a safe and convenient medium of exchange for travelers. Law's project was not accepted: the French finance minister, Michel Chamillart, was also war minister and was preoccupied with military problems, and Madame de Maintenon's prejudice against Protestants and foreigners did not predispose her to support Law.

But Law did not have to wait long for another opportunity to propose a banking scheme. He was in Edinburgh in the summer of 1704, when Scotland was suffering a depression subsequent to the failure of William Paterson's Darien expedition. The suspension of specie payments by the Bank of Scotland in December 1704 intensified the crisis, and this stimulated Law to propose to the Parliament of Scotland in 1705 that a land bank be created. The proposal was published anonymously, as *Money and Trade Considered: With a Proposal for Supplying the Nation With Money*. At least 15 other tracts with surprisingly similar titles appeared in the same year or early in 1706. Law and the authors of the other tracts all attributed the crisis to scarcity of money, but Law was the only one who carefully formulated the theory underlying his proposal. He explained that value is determined by supply and demand and that the value of money is only a special case in value theory. The key to his monetary thought is his assumption of a state of disequilibrium, with large masses of idle factors of production, as a starting point for analysis.

Law presented at least 24 numerical examples to show that if the money supply were increased by notes issued for productive loans, employment and output (and, implicitly, the demand for money) would rise proportionately and the value of money would remain stable. He also argued that the notes of the land bank would have other advantages over metallic money in that they would be easier to transport, store, and count, while being equally divisible without loss of value and equally capable of receiving a stamp as metallic money. Moreover, the supply of bank notes, unlike that of metallic money, would be perfectly elastic. Yet another advantage that Law attributed to his scheme was that it would prevent any adverse effect on the balance of trade. Assuming that the international demand for goods was perfectly inelastic, he argued that debasing the coinage and marking up coins would render the balance of trade unfavorable and induce an outflow of specie, while the introduction of notes would avoid this consequence. Nor would the notes, unlike debasement of the coinage, create inflation. Although Law's scheme was favored by the duke of Argyll, the lord high commissioner, and the earl of Islay, it won active support from only two members of the Scottish Parliament.

Back in France, in 1706 Law submitted to Chamillart his "Treatise on Money and Commerce" ("Mémoire touchant les monnoies et le commerce"). It was dated November 18, 1706, and has remained not only unpublished but unused even by scholars; yet it is the best single presentation of Law's monetary theory. A most interesting aspect of the document is Chamillart's extensive and often shrewd commentary in the margins; these comments are noteworthy because they show that Chamillart detected the error in Law's argument that debasing or marking up the coinage would render the balance of trade unfavorable. Law's proposals that France adopt paper money, as superior to gold and silver, led to his expulsion from that country. Allegations that he was banished because of his success as a gambler are unfounded.

In the winter of 1712 Law was in Turin and presented several tracts on money and banking to Vittorio Amadeo II, duke of Savoy, who was deeply impressed by Law's intellectual power and monetary knowledge but who decided against a bank.

Later the duke urged Law to return to Turin, presumably to establish a bank, but Law declined.

In December 1713 Law returned to Paris and was soon again plying the French government with proposals for a bank. In July 1715 he came very close to convincing Desmarets, then finance minister, who rejected his project only because he could not stomach a bank that would be as completely dominated by one man as, he sensed, the proposed one would be dominated by Law. After the death of Louis XIV, Law convinced the duke of Orleans, the regent, of the desirability of a royal bank, and encountered his last defeat when the proposal was rejected by the Council of Finance on October 24, 1715. Shifting to the concept of a privately owned institution, Law obtained a charter for the General Bank, on May 2, 1716. It was the first Bank of France and the opening wedge for his System. The charter for the Bank was granted to "Mr. Law and his Company." Law drafted the charter and subscribed for one-fourth of the stock. As Desmarets had anticipated, the bank was completely dominated by Law—more so than any other national or central bank has ever been dominated by one man.

From the outset the General Bank was conservatively managed. There is no evidence that it ever failed to meet an obligation. During the 31 months of its operation its notes raised the money supply only about 3 per cent, and its deposits were infinitesimal. The General Bank discounted accepted bills of exchange drawn on Paris at 6 per cent from June 1716 through March 1718, when the rate was reduced to 4 per cent. While the Bank's discount rate was 6 per cent, the modal market rate on secured loans at Paris was 5 per cent, and the average rate was a trifle lower. From April to December 1718 the market rate moved irregularly downward but did not reach 4 per cent. The General Bank may have exerted some slight downward pressure on the rate of interest, but it did not end "usury."

In the beginning the business of the Bank was confined to Paris; but in the summer of 1716 custodians of public revenue in the provinces were instructed to accept and redeem Bank notes, and on October 7 they were ordered to remit to Paris exclusively in these notes. Consequently, even in the Bank's first year, notes were circulating in distant provinces, and the Bank achieved a national circulation far more quickly than did any other public bank in Europe before the nineteenth century.

It was early in 1717 that Law first became involved in the financial scheme eventually known as the Mississippi Bubble (Louisiana being commonly called Mississippi then). The financier Antoine Crozat, a neighbor and friend of Law's, decided to give up his Louisiana concession, having lost 1.25 million livres in four years. Convinced that only a company could raise the necessary capital, the government made no effort to dissuade Crozat. It was attempting to withdraw paper money from circulation; since this currency lessened confidence in Bank notes, Law favored deflating it. He thereupon devised a scheme to solve the government's financial problem and at the same time promote colonial trade—he proposed to establish a company to take over Louisiana and sell its stock for government paper money, to be converted into *rentes* and destroyed.

In August 1717 his Company of the West was chartered. Its shares were in denominations of 500 livres, and the capital was ultimately fixed at 100 million livres, payable in government paper money depreciated by about 60 per cent. Business was far better than in 1716, when the General Bank had been chartered, and many people believed that Louisiana offered possibilities of rich rewards. But they also knew that West India companies chartered under Richelieu and Colbert had failed miserably and that Crozat, one of the ablest and richest financiers in France, had just relinquished his Louisiana concession. Hence the stock was not fully subscribed until July 1718.

Thereafter the company's fortunes rose. In September 1718 it outbid all rivals for the lucrative monopoly on the importation, manufacture, and sale of tobacco, and in November it purchased the property and privileges of the Senegalese Company. Law was on his way. On May 26, 1719, the Company of the West absorbed the French East India Company and the China Company, thereby forming the Company of the Indies. In June the Africa Company was acquired.

Meanwhile, on December 4, 1718, the General Bank had been nationalized and its name changed to Royal Bank; nationalization was actually only a formality, since the crown had already bought 100 per cent of the stock. Control over the Bank remained in Law's hands, subject to approval by the regent (as had been the case up to that time). But notes could be issued only by royal decree and were guaranteed by the crown. In July 1719 the Company of the Indies was granted the right to farm the mints for nine years, and 25 of the 26 mints, the sole exception being the one at Lyons, became virtual branches of the Bank. In August, Law took over the general farm of indirect taxes, and in October he arranged for the Company of the Indies to refund the remaining public debt of 1,500 million livres at 3 per cent. On January 5,

1720, after having been "publicly" converted to Catholicism, Law became finance minister.

Law's System was complete, and he stood at the pinnacle of his power. After his fall he often said that he had had more power than any other uncrowned person had ever exercised in Europe, and he may have been right; for he controlled the colonial trade, the Royal Bank, the tobacco monopoly, the public debt, indirect taxes, and more than half of what is now the United States (excluding Alaska). In addition to being finance minister, he was the principal economic adviser and favorite of an absolute prince.

Law's India shares rose fiftyfold in about two years, most of the rise in the last half of 1719, when France experienced the greatest speculative orgy she has ever had. The first impetus to this speculative rise was the substantial profit from the tobacco monopoly; more important was Law's acquisition of the tax farm, since it was well known that many of the great fortunes in France had been made through tax farming. From the beginning Law encouraged speculation, and his advice was widely taken. Traders rushed in from the provinces and from many foreign countries. Hitherto prudent Frenchmen and even some families in other countries liquidated real property to buy Law's stock, and the mania extended down to the very poor, who staked their patrimonies and life savings on small fractions of shares. The *Nouveau mercure* of November 1719 reported that "some stockholders have died from surprise, others from joy, [while still others] have gone mad from calculating their profits." Law converted much of his own great fortune—most of which was a capital gain on his stock—into magnificent rural estates and town houses, thus advertising his wealth and whetting the public appetite for his shares. The speculative boom rested heavily on hopes of gain from the exploitation of Louisiana.

It was not only the exaggerated estimate of the natural riches of Louisiana that constituted an essential weakness of Law's System but also his conviction, which went back to at least 1702, that shares of stock are money. Believing this, Law pegged the price of his stock at 9,000 livres when it began falling in January 1720, thus not only monetizing the stock but making it a monetary standard. Sales of stock to the Bank far exceeded purchases, and the quantity of Bank notes in circulation rose so sharply that they occasionally fell below par in specie. On Law's initiative, pegging was discontinued by the stockholders on February 22, but a considerable decline in the price of Law's stock led to its resumption on March 20. Inflation was disastrous: from March 26 to May 1 note circulation increased by 1,470 million livres, or about 125 per cent, and during May the note issue reached a peak of 2,696 million livres. Pegging the stock cost more than the equivalent of half the public debt. (The government admitted in 1725 that the second round of pegging was ordered by the regent.) Commodity prices had risen more than 50 per cent in the major cities, and money wages lagged far behind.

Law then made a mistake that again derived from his erroneous belief that stock is money: he chose to deflate, rather than remove the peg on his stock. Although this deflation has been widely attributed to his enemies, a decree lowering the price of stock to 8,000 livres as of May 22, 1720, and by stages to 5,000 livres on December 1, was drafted by Law himself and corrected in his own hand. Bank notes were to be marked down 20 per cent on May 22 and by stages to 50 per cent by December 1. Consternation and panic reigned, intensified by an attempt by the Bank to collect all loans on stock. Yielding to the clamor of the populace, the regent dismissed Law, but this only increased the uncertainty. On May 27 the deflationary decree was repealed and the old rating of the Bank's notes restored, while the peg on stock was removed. The restoration of Law, at the end of May, to his former position in the Bank and the company was not accompanied by any restoration of public confidence, and his System was doomed.

From June to September of 1720, Law and the regent strove desperately to rehabilitate the System through drastic deflation of the Bank's notes. But the notes steadily lost favor, and by December the country had returned to a specie basis. In mid-December Law was permitted to leave France, and his tottering System collapsed.

Even Law's worst enemies and severest critics recognized that France had been suffering one of the worst crises in her history in June 1716, when the General Bank opened its doors. Commodity prices had been falling disastrously for a year and a half. Unemployment, bank failures, commercial bankruptcies, agricultural distress, and social unrest were rife. Pessimism filled the air. Law was at the head of a national bank and in a position to influence strongly the economic policy of an absolute prince. No other "Keynesian" economist has ever had such a golden opportunity.

What did Law accomplish? He not only ended unemployment but even induced a labor shortage and overfull utilization of plant capacity. Public and private obligations, hitherto chronically in arrears, were paid promptly. Despair gave way to optimism. The population of Louisiana rose almost tenfold; the burden of taxation was lightened; sinecures were reduced; and many fetters to trade were removed.

Many of Law's achievements were lasting. There was feverish construction of buildings—including a substantial number of magnificent structures in the Place Vendôme in Paris erected by Law himself. Large numbers of skilled workers and technicians were brought from abroad to establish new industries and improve old ones. The books of the tax farm were rationalized, subfarming was largely eliminated, and the administration was simplified and unified. Reform of the tax system was one of Law's most durable achievements. Dreams of wealth from Louisiana focused attention on the New World. Reflections on a new people and a new culture enlarged horizons, bred tolerance, and prepared the way for the Enlightenment.

But these gains were not without cost. During the boom commodity prices rose about 100 per cent in Paris and Bordeaux; 170 per cent in Marseilles, afflicted in 1720 by one of the worst plagues in French history; and 140 per cent in Toulouse, also affected by the plague. Creditors, pensioners, and other holders of passive rights suffered cruel losses, and the average decline of daily real wages in Paris, Marseilles, and Toulouse was 25 per cent. Holders of the Bank's notes and of shares of the Company of the Indies presented more than half a million claims (nearly four-fifths of which were from the provinces) to the commission that liquidated the System, and losses in the liquidation ran as high as 95 per cent. (Even for those who could prove they had exchanged coins for notes at the Bank the loss was two-thirds.) Many families were ruined; most were hurt. A surprising number of very poor people suffered crushing losses on small fractions of shares. Thousands of noble and well-to-do families in foreign countries lost major portions of their fortunes.

Law made serious mistakes in theory and practice and undertook far more than anyone should have. However many of his ideas have stood the test of time, and his integrity has withstood all assaults.

EARL J. HAMILTON

WORKS BY LAW

(1705) 1966 *Money and Trade Considered: With a Proposal for Supplying the Nation With Money.* New York: Kelley.

Oeuvres complètes. Edited by Paul Harsin. 3 vols. Paris: Sirey, 1934. → Contains much previously unpublished material.

Oeuvres de J. Law. Translated from the English by Étienne de Sénovert. Paris: Buisson, 1790.

SUPPLEMENTARY BIBLIOGRAPHY

BUVAT, JEAN 1865 *Journal de la régence (1715–1723)*. Edited by Émile Campardon. 2 vols. Paris: Plon. → Published posthumously.

DUTOT (1738) 1935 *Réflexions politiques sur les finances et le commerce*. 2 vols. Liége, Université de, Faculté de Philosophie et Lettres, Bibliothèque, Vol. 66–67. Paris: Droz.

FAIRLEY, JOHN A. 1925 *Lauriston Castle: The Estate and Its Owners*. Edinburgh: Oliver & Boyd.

[FORBONNAIS, FRANÇOIS V. D. DE] 1758 *Recherches et considérations sur les finances de France, depuis l'année 1595 jusqu'à l'année 1721*. 2 vols. Basel: Cramer. → Published anonymously.

HAMILTON, EARL J. 1936 Prices and Wages at Paris Under John Law's System. *Quarterly Journal of Economics* 51:42–70.

HAMILTON, EARL J. 1937 Prices and Wages in Southern France Under John Law's System. *Economic History* 3:441–461.

HEINRICH, PIERRE 1908 *La Louisiane sous la Compagnie des Indes, 1717–1731*. Paris: Guilmoto.

LA JONCHÈRE, ÉTIENNE LESCUYER DE 1720 *Système d'un nouveau gouvernement en France*. 4 vols. Amsterdam: Le Bon.

LEVASSEUR, ÉMILE 1854 *Recherches historiques sur le système de Law*. Paris: Guillaumin.

LÜTHY, HERBERT 1959–1961 *La banque protestante en France, de la révocation de l'Édit de Nantes à la Révolution*. 2 vols. Paris: S.E.V.P.E.N.

MANN, FRITZ K. 1913 Die Vorgeschichte des Finanzsystems von John Law. *Schmollers Jahrbuch für Gesetzgebung, Verwaltung und Volkswirtschaft im Deutschen Reiche* 37:1165–1229.

[MARMONT DU HAUTCHAMP, BARTHÉLEMI] 1739 *Histoire du système des finances, sous la minorité de Louis XV. pendant les années 1719 & 1720*. 6 vols. The Hague: Hondt. → Published anonymously.

[MARMONT DU HAUTCHAMP, BARTHÉLEMI] 1743 *Histoire générale et particulière du visa fait en France. . . .* 4 vols. The Hague: Scheurleer. → Published anonymously.

[MELON, JEAN-FRANÇOIS] (1734) 1739 *A Political Essay Upon Commerce*. Dublin: Woodward & Cox. → First published anonymously in French.

P. C. 1722 *Het leven en caracter van den heer Jan Law*. Amsterdam. → Published under this pseudonym.

[PARIS DUVERNEY, JOSEPH] 1740 *Examen du livre intitulé* Reflexions politiques sur les finances et le commerce. 2 vols. The Hague: Prevôt. → Published anonymously.

WOOD, JOHN P. 1824 *Memoirs of the Life of John Law of Lauriston, Including a Detailed Account of the Rise, Progress, and Termination of the Mississippi System*. Edinburgh: Black.

LAWS, CONFLICT OF

See CONFLICT OF LAWS.

LE BON, GUSTAVE

Although Gustave Le Bon (1841–1931) is most generally known for his book *The Crowd*, his career in fact had three overlapping phases, the successive focuses of his interest being anthropology and archeology, experimental and theoretical natural science, and only finally social psychology.

Le Bon received a doctorate of medicine without any vocation for the profession. He began his adult life with travels in Europe, north Africa, and Asia. From these travels there resulted a half-dozen books, chiefly on anthropology and archeology. The last of the works on these subjects, *Les monuments de l'Inde*, appeared in 1893, when Le Bon was 52.

However, when he was in his late thirties Le Bon's interests began to shift radically: he invented recording instruments (exhibited in 1878), studied racial variations in cranial capacity, analyzed the composition of tobacco smoke, published a photographic method for making plans and maps, as well as a treatise that put the training of horses on an experimental basis, and, finally, devoted more than ten years to research on black light, intra-atomic energy, and the equivalence of matter and energy. During this period, furthermore, Le Bon began the work in social psychology that was to become the predominant concern of the final phase of his career. *The Crowd* appeared in 1895, when he was 54.

It is, of course, chiefly by virtue of the works of this third phase that Le Bon belongs to the history of social science. But these works in social psychology have links not only with the books of the period of his travels but also with those of what might be called his scientific phase. Thus, when Le Bon dealt with pedagogy and politics, he carefully transposed to children and peoples what he had earlier learned about horses. Similarly, he claimed to support his ideas on the psychological hierarchy of races and sexes with material from his study of the variations in the volume of the brain.

Before sketching the main outlines of the doctrine underlying all of Le Bon's psychological work, one trait of this work—perhaps at the time the most original—should be stressed. He selected extremely concrete problems for study—for example, the socialist movement, the organization of education, colonial policy, the French Revolution, and World War I—but always sought to treat these problems in terms of scientific generalizations at the highest level of abstraction. This was nothing less than an attempt to synthesize Comte and Spencer with Michelet and Tocqueville. Le Bon was convinced that contingent events as well as social behavior are guided by eternal laws (1912, p. 322).

The unconscious. One of these eternal laws that Le Bon constantly invoked is the futility of rationality in the affairs of society: an idea does not prevail because it is true, but by virtue of psychological mechanisms that have nothing to do with reason, such as repetition and "mental contagion." These mechanisms permit an idea to penetrate into the unconscious, and it is only when an idea does become part of the unconscious that it becomes effective for action. This rudimentary theory of learning was first formulated when he was studying the training of horses and then extended to human education and to politics. His watchword was: let the conscious become the unconscious.

The principle that only the unconscious produces effective action applies, according to Le Bon, not only to individuals but also to whole peoples (or races, so long as it is well understood that what is meant are "historical races," created by the events of history, and not races in the anthropological sense). Thus a people, or a civilization, or a race, properly so-called, must have a national soul, that is, shared sentiments, shared interests, and shared ways of thinking. The national soul is produced by such nonrational mechanisms as suggestion and heredity; all metaphysical, religious, political, and social beliefs are so rooted in the national soul of each people. It is these deeply-rooted beliefs that govern institutions (*not* the inverse, as Tocqueville had imagined).

The vital implication of this theory for politics is that laws are illusory and ineffective if they lack a basis in the national psychology. Moreover, according to Le Bon, it is these fundamental beliefs that produce lack of understanding and intolerance between peoples and groups and thus account for the irreducibility of what may be called ideological conflicts and the inevitability of civil strife and international wars.

Hierarchies. Le Bon was perennially establishing hierarchies. Thus he asserted the existence of a hierarchy of races, based on psychological criteria (such as degree of reasoning ability, power of attention, mastery over instinctual drives; see the *Psychology of Peoples* 1894) and confirmed on anatomical grounds by the alleged greater differentiation of the superior races and the greater consequent incidence of individuals who rise above the mean. As a specific instance of such hierarchical ordering, Le Bon repeatedly compared the mental constitution of the Anglo–Saxon race with that of the Latin peoples, and down to World War I he considered the Anglo–Saxons superior in every way. He established a hierarchy of the sexes using the same kind of criteria. According to his system of evaluation, animals, the insane, socialists, children, degenerates, and primitives were inferior beings.

The crowd. He postulated another, very interesting kind of inferiority: this is the inferiority of the crowd, or of man in the crowd. Le Bon believed that the psychology of men in a crowd differs essentially from their individual psychology; they become simple automata, instances of a sort of new being. Their spirit is that of the crowd which, like every spirit, is part of the unconscious; but this is a very low-level part of the unconscious, archaic or primitive from a historical point of view and medullar from a physiological one.

The psychological characteristics of crowds, as analyzed at length in the celebrated *The Crowd*, may be grouped around three themes. The first and most general characteristic attributed by Le Bon to crowd behavior is that of unanimity; he called this the law of the mental unity of crowds and asserted it as a dogma. He saw this mental unity accompanied by an awareness of unanimity that has important consequences: dogmatism and intolerance, a feeling of irresistible power, and a sense of irresponsibility. The second characteristic of crowd behavior is its emotionality: the actions of the crowd are sudden, simple, extreme, intense, and very changeable, so betraying the feminine nature of crowds. The third descriptive theme is that the intellectual processes of crowds are rudimentary and mechanical: crowds are very credulous, their ideas are schematic, and their logic is infrarational and ignores the principle of noncontradiction.

How, then, does it happen that in a crowd situation even the most rational of men are transformed into brutes? Le Bon, like Tarde, who wrote on the same topic at the same time, offered two explanations: mental contagion and the role of leaders, who are often, but not always, described as agitators. But what do these explanations amount to? "Contagion is a phenomenon that is readily observed, but has not yet been explained, and had best be related to the phenomena of hypnotism . . ." (1895, p. 17). "The unconscious minds of the charmer and the charmed, the leader and the led, penetrate each other by a mysterious mechanism" (1910, p. 139). These tautologous passages suggest that on occasion Dr. Le Bon knew how to resort to the technique of the doctors in Molière.

To concentrate criticism on this particular problem of explanation would be misleading, for these theories of mental contagion and of the role of leaders are no more gratuitous, no more confused, and no more based on obsolete psychology than is the entire core of Le Bon's system. They may even have special merit, for it was precisely such arbitrary assertions of Le Bon that contained his happiest insights. He believed that "the action of a group consists mainly in fortifying hesitant beliefs. Any individual conviction that is weak is reinforced when it becomes collective" (1912, p. 102); or that, during World War I, "isolated individuals regained their military value when they rejoined a familiar group, but not when they were merged into other groups" (1916, p. 243). These are sentences that would not surprise us if they appeared in *The People's Choice* or in *The American Soldier*.

The fact remains that these two sentences went unnoticed. It was by the most reckless, the most false, and the most harmful of his theories that Le Bon exerted his greatest influence, in France and even more so abroad. In particular, the "law of the mental unity of crowds" was widely accepted and taught, and perhaps still is. Ironically, the fame of some men is based on their mistakes and thereby confronts their critics with a painful dilemma: either to blame such a man for the very things that made him popular or to praise him for contributions that would not have existed were it not for the mistakes.

JEAN STOETZEL

[*For the historical context of Le Bon's work, see the biographies of* TARDE; TOCQUEVILLE. *For discussion of the subsequent development of his ideas, see* COLLECTIVE BEHAVIOR.]

WORKS BY LE BON

1892 *L'équitation actuelle et ses principes: Recherches expérimentales.* Paris: Firmin-Didot.
1893 *Les monuments de l'Inde.* Paris: Firmin-Didot.
(1894) 1898 *The Psychology of Peoples.* New York: Macmillan. → First published as *Lois psychologiques de l'évolution des peuples.*
(1895) 1947 *The Crowd.* New York: Macmillan. → First published as *Psychologie des foules.* Translation of extract was provided by the editors. A paperback edition was published in 1960 by Viking.
(1898) 1965 *Psychology of Socialism.* New York: Fraser. → First published as *Psychologie du socialisme.*
1902 *Psychologie de l'éducation.* Paris: Flammarion.
1910 *Psychologie politique et la défense sociale.* Paris: Flammarion.
1911 *Les opinions et les croyances.* Paris: Flammarion.
(1912) 1913 *The Psychology of Revolutions.* London: Allen & Unwin. → First published as *La révolution française et la psychologie des révolutions.* Translation of extract in the text provided by the editors.
1913 *Aphorisme du temps présent.* Paris: Flammarion.
1916 *The Psychology of the Great War.* London: Allen & Unwin. → First published in the same year as *Enseignements psychologiques de la guerre européenne.* Translation of extract in the text provided by the editors.

WORKS ABOUT LE BON

MERTON, ROBERT K. (1960) 1963 The Ambivalences of Le Bon's *The Crowd.* Pages v–xxxix in Gustave Le Bon, *The Crowd.* New York: Viking.
PICARD, EDMOND 1909 *Gustave Le Bon et son oeuvre.* Paris: Mercure de France.

LE PLAY, FRÉDÉRIC

Frédéric Le Play (1806–1882), French sociologist, is best remembered for his development of a method of research and data presentation known as the monographic method and for his classification of families into patriarchal, stem, and unstable types. His ideas had an important influence on European sociology from about 1860 to 1940, and his work is still a major inspiration to Roman Catholic sociologists. Many concepts developed by Durkheim can be found in their initial crude form in Le Play's work.

Le Play was born in Normandy, the son of a petty customs officer. His father died when Le Play was only five, and shortly afterward he went to live with a rich uncle in Paris. Here, as he grew up, he became an avid listener to the intellectual discussions that took place in his uncle's salon. Le Play, however, was never to forget the harbor town of his birth. He seems to have greatly idealized the frugal existence his family led during the difficult years of the Napoleonic blockade; this may help to explain why, when he came to consider such problems as the maintenance of order, the avoidance of violence, and the demoralization of the poor, it was not in the increase of the standard of living that he saw the solution but in the strengthening of family ties.

Social philosophy

Le Play wrote his main work, *Les ouvriers européens* (1855), between 1829 and 1855. At that time a large section of the bourgeoisie had developed a fairly durable synthesis of aristocratic and bourgeois values. Abandoning Voltairean skepticism, it had adopted a largely ceremonial Catholicism, tempered by mild anticlericalism and theological indifference. The only dynamic elements in this outlook were respect for hard work and a stress on the need for rootedness (*enracinement*) in the locality of one's birth—a rootedness consecrated by the ownership of private property.

Few counterinfluences disturbed this prevailing climate of thought. The followers of Saint-Simon still constituted a very articulate intellectual minority, and it was in reaction to one of them, with whom Le Play traveled through Europe, that Le Play was led to develop and systematize the beliefs and attitudes instilled by his upbringing. For the Saint-Simonians, centralist and deductive in their approach, social disorder and pauperism were to be solved through the complete reintegration of society around the industrial order. Property was to be controlled by the industrialists (the creators of wealth), rather than by inheritors, and the industrialists were to be helped—"guided," Auguste Comte would say—by the priests of the positive science of society. The problem of power relations would be solved by the obviousness of right reason. Reason would organize the world, control nature, and promote progress, with the happiness of the individual following naturally from the welfare of society.

Le Play rejected this technocratic and optimistic view. He decided that there is no such thing as unilinear social progress—there can only be cycles of prosperity and corruption, the former inevitably engendering the latter. People in simple societies, like the fishermen of his childhood or the gentle folk of the Harz, may attain peace and contentment, but people in complex societies cannot escape strife and misery. Le Play believed that man has always known that the supreme good lies in social peace, on the one hand, and moral conduct, on the other; this was codified once and for all in the Decalogue. How, then, can one speak of inevitable progress when the principles of the Decalogue may have been followed in earlier periods of history only to be ignored in later ones? The best that could happen would be a revival of what has always been acknowledged to be the truth. The happiness of man does not reside in increased comforts and education but in recognizing the soundness of these principles of good conduct, in spite of the seductiveness of false doctrines, and in conforming his life to them.

It is interesting to note the dual orientation of Le Play's thought. There is, on the one hand, the importance of having the right ideas—a typical French approach, which culminated in the concept of the idea-force of the late-nineteenth-century psychologists and which was not without influence even on Durkheim. And yet, on the other hand, there is the belief in the effectiveness of sheer coercion when practiced by the righteous to preserve lesser men from temptation. It reflects the Roman Catholic oscillation between the stress on individual free will and the need for the church to protect man from himself. The function of the social scientist is to fight against false doctrines and through the use of the scientific method to prove the soundness of the simple eternal truths. Another interesting aspect of Le Play's thought, differentiating it from Saint-Simon's, Comte's, or Tocqueville's, is its resolutely homocentric quality: he focused upon the problem of individual happiness—or salvation, as a Puritan might say—rather than upon the "utility of the community," as Pareto was to phrase it. The use of the word "happiness"

(*bonheur*) is not accidental either, and Durkheim used this concept later in his discussion of anomie: *bonheur* is a state of inner harmony, with a definite sensualist tonality, rather than an external goal, like salvation. And *bonheur* is to be gained through control over man's essentially base nature (Durkheim would later speak, more neutrally, of the animal nature of man in contrast to his social nature). To achieve this control, man has as allies a divine force, the grace of God, and a social force, the family. When population size and density reach a certain level, thereby creating more complex problems of control (the exact terms of the equation are left unclear, but the critical level seems related to a more complex division of labor), the church and the state are to assist the family in its task. Insofar as men acting collectively can have any impact upon the happiness of the individual, they can do so only through the strengthening of the family.

Since industrialization had created pauperism and a rootless, marginal type of working class, the members of which were at the mercy of their base passions, the control and reintegration of that working class into the community of the righteous would be secured only by the consolidation of the working-class family and, more immediately, by its assimilation into the entrepreneur's family through the institution of patronage. Then the individual worker and his kin would have once more an opportunity for *bonheur*. Where Durkheim was to offer the professional organization as a means of alleviating the anomie that prevailed in economic life—a recommendation commonly made by French intellectuals, unless they belonged to the somewhat marginal Manchesterian group of Molinari—Le Play offered the family firm, in which the sting of the power relationship was removed by the fusion, in paternal-type relationships, of power with love. The rootlessness of the urban working class might be overcome through the device of permanent labor contracts and the fostering of property ownership by workers.

Le Play's theoretical interest in the variety of income sources in the workingman's budget (see Parsons et al. 1961, pp. 457–459) not only shows he rejected on empirical grounds the definition of working-class status as the nonownership of the means of production but also suggests his concern for a program of social action. The budgets itemized by Le Play often show the worker's family securing "profits" from home industries of which family members are the sole customers (owning a cow, rather than buying milk on the open market). Ideally, instead of private property being abolished, as advocated by the socialists, its ownership should be diffused, and more immediately, the workers should be encouraged and assisted by the entrepreneur in securing home ownership, since the latter is strategic to family stability.

Le Play's conception of the way in which the industrial world should be organized fitted very well with the romanticized version of the French family firm. He believed that in return for fealty and a nonbargaining approach to the labor contract, the family firm protected the worker from the vagaries of the market, through a conservative investment and sales policy—restricting expansion in times of boom and stretching out employment in times of depression, protecting the worker's family from want by provision of easily purchased homes and gardens and free social services.

The function of the employer, according to Le Play, was not so much to raise the standard of living of the worker as to provide him with moral leadership, help him acquire private property, and stimulate in him "the respect of the laws governing the family" (1864, vol. 2, p. 28). Property, in this context, whether house, land, or factory, is a visible symbol of the family, of its continuity and its moral fervor, rather than a mere means of production. Complete testamentary freedom is necessary to permit the transmission of family property, in its entirety, to the most deserving heir and, even more important, to prevent the destruction of the stability of the family itself. Not only may a parceled-out homestead be economically unviable but the breaking up of the estate will foster a break in the sibling solidarity, so indispensable to the preservation of the sound family structures, i.e., the patriarchal family and the stem family (for definitions, see below).

Le Play realized that the preservation of integral estates, the moral importance of which he had established, was in conflict with rules of the Code Civil, which enforce practically equal division among heirs. In his opinion, families faced with this dilemma had resolved it through a reduction in their fecundity, so that equal division would not destroy completely the holdings accumulated through years of hard work and thrift. This is his explanation for the decline of the French birth rate.

This deceptively simple mechanism—a bad decision by jurists may have widespread consequences for the reproduction policy of millions of families—underlines Le Play's belief in the power of good or bad political decisions to effect broad changes in the society in a one-way causal chain. Although this attribution of far-reaching demographic consequences to the Code Civil became widely popular,

it was, in the main, erroneous. The tendency to divide estates equally had existed in French families prior to the enactment of the Code Civil. Even aristocratic families, before the French Revolution, as Le Play's disciple Paul de Rousiers showed in the history of his own family (1934), tended to give equal shares to their children: Equal love for one's children must be symbolized by equal shares of property. Therefore, it was not inheritance laws that were responsible for the restriction of fecundity—such laws could be bypassed by any father who was able to make his children internalize his own conception of the importance of integral estates—but instead the relatively high degree of social mobility present in French society after the revolution.

Nevertheless, we can readily understand the great success of Le Play's ideas among the provincial aristocracy and among that section of the bourgeoisie which aspired to assimilate aristocratic patterns and protect its dynasties from the vagaries of the market and the competition of "upstarts." Strictures against the growth of central state power, suspicion of intellectuals, respect for local notables, belief that men are born unequal in their capacity to resist evil or do good—all this was highly pleasing to the *bien-pensants*. No wonder that for a century Le Playism has been a basic ideology for that group, becoming a major element in the development of one brand of Christian socialism; it is a most plausible version of conservative mythology, and its influence extended to Russia, Great Britain, Holland, Germany, and French Canada.

Le Play's sociology

So far we have dealt only with the ideological component in Le Play's work. But important though this is, it should not be allowed to obscure Le Play's major contributions to the growth of sociology as a science. These contributions cover three major areas: the theory of social control, the theory of social change, and research methodology.

Social control. For Le Play, the family is the chief agency of socialization and social control. The chances for the abuse of power that are inherent in any system of social control are here limited by the love of the parents for their children, who, in return, endure frustration more easily when it is meaningfully related to the family's welfare. The church and the state can at best only assist or complete the work done by the family in checking the base impulses of the child's raw nature. Indeed, the weaker the central government, the better is the opportunity for the family to develop its authority and improve its performance.

Le Play distinguished three main types of family structure: the patriarchal family; the unstable family; and an intermediate type, the stem family. In the patriarchal family the father characteristically keeps near him all his married sons and exercises supreme authority over them and their children. Property remains communal. The patriarch directs all work and accumulates whatever savings can be gathered once the traditional needs of all family members have been satisfied. Le Play saw this type of family as common among the pastoral peoples of the Orient, the Russian peasantry, and the Slavs of central Europe.

Le Play's unstable family resembles what is today called the isolated nuclear family. It is unstable because it has little resiliency in the face of economic hardship. It is typical of the industrial working class and is also to be found among the upper classes, mainly because of successional laws that compel the division of estates among heirs. Although this type of family permits a brilliant individual to gain great success, it compounds the risk of failure for the untalented.

The stem family is a type of patriarchal family in which only one of the heirs is retained in the family homestead; the others receive some form of dowry that enables them to establish themselves elsewhere. Nevertheless, for those who leave, the family homestead remains a ceremonial center, as well as a port in a storm. Thus, the stem family combines some of the flexibility and recognition of talent of the unstable family with the continuity and security of the patriarchal family.

Social change. Le Play's theory of social change is essentially dualistic. On the one hand, he attached enormous importance to beliefs and ideas; on the other, he seemed to stress a sort of technological determinism, rooted in the geographic environment.

Religious belief was given an especially important part in Le Play's theory of social change, although differences between individual doctrines were of little consequence to him. All human societies, he asserted, accept some form of the Decalogue, belief in which is a fundamental condition for the maintenance of order and solidarity. When these beliefs weaken, the society suffers—and when they vanish, the society vanishes with them. The diffusion of areligious and/or antireligious doctrines by intellectuals was, therefore, a major source of social disorganization; so were erroneous laws regarding succession, which made it difficult for families to maintain the continuity of the family estate; or political decisions such as those of Louis XIV regarding the centralization of the French

state; or beliefs, such as Rousseau's, in the inherent goodness of human nature. Such errors only show man incapable, of his own free will, of availing himself of the wisdom contained in the Decalogue. But these errors are a contingent factor, like the presence or absence of elite personalities—Plato's "divine men"—who create peace and order around them (and whom Le Play thought to be the best sources of information for the researcher). What can be taken for granted is that men will remain vulnerable to these errors, as well as remaining unequal in their capacity to create harmony around them.

The only causal process in history of which Le Play was certain was that prosperity always leads to the corruption of the elites, which leads in turn to the corruption of society. Corrupt social orders are purged by wars, which permit the more virtuous populations to assume political control over the more corrupt ones. The measure of this corruption is essentially the decline of paternal authority and the move away from the patriarchal and stem forms of family pattern toward the unstable form. Le Play's theory of social change belongs with the pessimistic, cyclical theories rather than with the optimistic, unilinear ones.

In contrast to the religious factor in social change or the impact of leadership and prosperity—which are essentially unpredictable in their incidence, if not in their consequences—the relationship between the family and its physical environment, as mediated by work patterns, seems to provide causal regularities susceptible of scientific inquiry. Steppe areas tend to produce stable patriarchal families; coastal fishing areas, stem families; and forests, unstable families (unless there happens to be rational exploitation of timber resources). Agriculture, if combined with proper succession laws, permits patriarchal families but usually produces stem families. The factory system, on the other hand, encourages unstable families among its workers, especially if the entrepreneurs do not fulfill their obligations of patronage. This was a major source of corruption in the prosperity engendered by industrialization.

Methodology. The monographic method is usually considered to be Le Play's unique contribution to the development of social science. Indeed, this method marks a twofold departure from the prevailing type of social science writing: first, it stresses immediate contact with the field data, collected with an eye to measurement, rather than relying on historical data or shrewd observations, as did Tocqueville or Taine; second, as Sorokin pointed out (1928, pp. 63–98), it introduces a selective principle for the collation and presentation of data that is derived from a theoretical schema—the primacy of family relationships in controlling behavior, the dependence of family relationships upon certain aspects of the environment and especially upon those which determine the type of work the family engages in, and the belief that all crucial family activities express themselves in a monetary form, which can be represented as a budget item.

No doubt the monographic method developed from the type of systematic reports that students of the School of Mines were supposed to make on their field trips, with emphasis upon those items which could be tabulated and counted. Another intellectual influence was the surveys and inquiries which were commissioned by the parliaments of France and Great Britain. And about the same time Le Play began his field work, Villermé was conducting his inquiries on poverty in French cities.

The unique thing about Le Play's method is that his work contains the beginning of statistical techniques which *later* led to sampling, as well as the beginning of index construction. (The family budget was used because it permitted accurate computation, and the rigorous itemization of budgets is probably the reason why the *Ouvriers européens* received a prize from the Académie des Sciences in 1855). However, the monographic method, as Le Play used it, was in fact a rejection of the system building of Saint-Simon and Comte, rather than an effective commitment to inductive and experimental thought. Le Play was turning the positivist approach against its inventors because he believed that in his day only scientific descriptions of social realities would render self-evident the one way to social harmony and individual happiness. For him social science was not a cumulative body of theoretical propositions; it was simply a way to make evident the eternal laws of social peace. If abstract reasoning should lead to statements that contradict these laws, then the reasoning must be false. And although Le Play at one time seemed to draw an analogy between fact gathering and parliamentary representation, he did not see the necessity for systematic sampling, because he felt that a few monographs were sufficient to convince the reader of the correctness of these basic moral laws. The accumulation of data is more a rhetorical device than an attempt at inductive proof. In order to verify the results of direct observation, one should consult with local leaders, who are best equipped to describe and interpret local customs and events.

The paradox of Le Play's methodology is that it is the invention of an antiempiricist. This inherent contradiction may explain why it failed to make as significant an impact upon scientific sociology as one might have expected.

Diffusion of Le Play's ideas

After the *Ouvriers européens*, Le Play turned essentially to propagandizing for social reform. Although he invoked the authority of the scientific method, rather than its logic, it is likely that he did render social science an important service by making the field of study a respectable one for the gentleman scholar, even though it meant contact with the lower classes in a context that precluded appropriate deference.

Le Play's follower Henri de Tourville was to complete the monographic method in 1886 by drawing up a "nomenclature"—a sort of sequential check list for describing the relationship of the family to its social and physical environment. The items to be covered were place, work, property system, forms of wealth, remuneration, savings, and the major social categories and organizations with which the family must deal—neighborhood, formal organizations, community, city, province, state, racial group —in essence, the outline of what was to become known as the community study.

However, the duality of Le Play's thought— idealist in its emphasis upon religious values, positivist in its emphasis upon geography and technology—led in 1886 to a split between his followers. The idealist component was developed into a predicating type of analysis, most notably by Charles de Ribbe, and again, more recently, into a philosophical–æsthetic type of essay writing, best exemplified by the work of Jean Lacroix.

The positivist group, represented by Tourville, de Rousiers, Robert Pinot, and Edmond Demolins, focused much more on the elements of a theory of the social system that were already implicit in the famous "nomenclature." Some, like Demolins, became much more openly positivist and stressed the geographical aspect of Le Play's theory of social change. They refused to condemn the industrial order as the source of social disorganization and came to challenge the belief that the stem family was the highest form of moral life. For them the model family was the "particularist" type, which they saw predominating in Scandinavian and Anglo-Saxon countries and which is essentially an optimistic version of what we would now call the isolated nuclear family. De Rousiers in particular, who visited the United States, gave the American family a good share of the credit for American enterprise and progress (see 1892). The analysis made by the positivist group of the relations between family type, on the one hand, and forms of government, types of economy and managerial policies, general styles of formal and informal organizations, and the school system, on the other, are often amazingly insightful and modern in content.

Neither wing of the Le Play school, however, had much impact upon French academic sociology, which was controlled by middle-class, anticlerical Durkheimians. The Le Play school was Roman Catholic and upper class in orientation. In fact, many of its members were aristocrats, for whom the field techniques of the monographic method, far from implying a threat to their social status, represented both a novel way of reaching out benevolently to the masses and an endorsement of the "facts," rather than a submission to the "theories" of bureaucrats or professors. The method fitted the antirational ideology of the traditional French upper classes, as displayed, for instance, in their predilection for the metaphysical philosophy of Henri Bergson.

This rejection of theory was the key weakness of the monographic method. It accumulated data which are supposed to speak for themselves but which, in the absence of comparative perspectives, say relatively little. However, the contemporary sociologist who wishes to compare these data with present-day equivalents will find in the monographs of the Le Play school a rich lode of "sociological fossils."

Influences on the literature. The first edition of the *Ouvriers européens* was published in 1855. "In order to avoid upsetting public opinion," it was published as a limited luxury edition, and the government presses in Paris handled the printing. The second edition was published in Tours in 1879, by the Mame publishing company, well known in France for its specialization in Roman Catholic literature.

The books that Le Play published after the *Ouvriers européens* are fundamentally works of special pleading, although claiming to be based on his past empirical research. The main ones are *La réforme sociale en France* (1864), *L'organisation du travail* (1870; an English translation appeared in 1872), *L'organisation de la famille* (1871*a*), *La paix sociale après le désastre* (1871*b*), *La constitution de l'Angleterre* (1875), and *La réforme de l'Europe et le salut en France* (1876). Part of Le Play's correspondence was published under the title *Voyages en Europe, 1829–1854: Correspondance* (1899).

A fairly extensive bibliography of Le Play's works can be found in *Textes choisis* (1947, pp. 59–60). Partial translations of the *Ouvriers européens* into English are to be found in Zimmerman and Frampton's *Family and Society* (1935, pp. 359–595). Extracts have been translated and reproduced in Riley's *Sociological Research* (1963, vol. 1, pp. 80–90) and in Parsons and his associates' *Theories of Society* (1961, pp. 457–459).

In 1856 the Société Internationale des Études Pratiques d'Économie Sociale was founded, with L. R. Villermé as its first president. It published a bulletin of its proceedings and in 1857 brought out ten volumes of "monographies" under the title: *Les ouvriers des deux mondes.* The bulletin of the society became in 1881 a review called *La réforme sociale.* This journal was conservative, Catholic, and largely anti-industrial. One of the better representatives of that tendency was de Ribbe, whose *La famille et la société en France avant la Révolution* (1873) is fundamentally a work of moralizing ideology.

Dissatisfied with the orientation of *La réforme sociale*, a group composed of Demolins, Tourville, de Rousiers, and Robert Pinot broke away in 1886 and founded *La science sociale*, under the editorship of Demolins. (In 1935 *La réforme sociale* and *La science sociale* merged to become *Les études sociales.*)

Among the works of the *Science sociale* group one may cite Demolins's *Les grandes routes des peuples: Essai de géographie sociale, comment la route crée le type social* (1901–1903). A more popular book by the same author was translated into English in 1898 (see 1897), with the title *Anglo-Saxon Superiority: To What It Is Due*; it ascribes the putative superiority of the Anglo-Saxons over the collectivistic societies of France and Germany to the particularistic family system and its stress upon self-reliance, progressive education, a responsible elite, and a noninterfering government. A crucial interest of Demolins was indeed education, which he wanted to reform along the lines of the English public school system. He founded the only successful progressive school that France has known, and it is described in his *L'éducation nouvelle: L'École des Roches* (1898).

Tourville was the theoretician of the *Science sociale* group. His most important work, besides the refinement of Le Play's nomenclature, was translated into English in 1907 as *The Growth of Modern Nations: A History of the Particularist Form of Society* (1905).

One of the most interesting writers of the *Science sociale* group was de Rousiers. He wrote one of the best statements of the group's position in his article "La science sociale," published in the

Annals of the American Academy of Political and Social Science (1894). His *American Life* (1892) and *The Labour Question in Britain* (1895) are among the best products of the Le Play school. In *The Labour Question* the monographic method reaches a new level of sophistication, through effective comparisons between the families of wage earners in different industries and between different types of productive organizations. Note also de Rousier's *Hambourg et l'Allemagne contemporaine* (1902), which brings a needed correction to Demolins's strictures on Germany as a collectivistic society, and *Une famille de hobereaux pendant six siècles* (1934).

Sociologists who wish to use monographies for a comparative historical perspective will consult with profit the extensive bibliography in Ferré's *Les classes sociales dans la France contemporaine* (1936, pp. 231–262), in particular the works of Jacques Valdour, who used participant–observer techniques. An addition to the Ferré bibliography should be the white-collar budgets in Henry Delpech's *Recherches sur le niveau de vie et les habitudes de consommation* (*Toulouse 1936–1938*) (1938).

One of the more fruitful uses of the budget method was made by the Durkheimian Maurice Halbwachs and is summarized in his work *L'évolution des besoins dans les classes ouvrières* (1933).

The most interesting offshoot of the Le Play school has been the work of Philippe Ariès, who has attempted to synthesize its approach with that of the Durkheim school, using a comparative historical approach rather than a strictly monographic one. His most important works are *Histoire des populations françaises* (1948) and *L'enfant et la vie familiale sous l'ancien régime* (1960), which was published in English as *Centuries of Childhood: A Social History of Family Life* in 1962.

Among commentaries on Le Play and his school must be cited Sorokin's *Contemporary Sociological Theories* (1928, pp. 63–98), *Recueil d'études sociales publié à la mémoire de Frédéric Le Play* (1956), and "Les cadres sociaux de la doctrine morale de Frédéric Le Play," by Andrée Michel (1963).

JESSE R. PITTS

[*For the historical context of Le Play's work, see the biographies of* COMTE *and* SAINT-SIMON; *for discussion of the subsequent development of Le Play's ideas, see* ANTHROPOLOGY, *article on* THE ANTHROPOLOGICAL STUDY OF MODERN SOCIETY; GEOGRAPHY, *article on* SOCIAL GEOGRAPHY; MODERNIZATION, *article on* SOCIAL ASPECTS; *and the biographies of* DURKHEIM *and* TOURVILLE.]

WORKS BY LE PLAY

(1855) 1877–1879 *Les ouvriers européens.* 2d ed. 6 vols. Tours: Mame. → Volume 1: *La méthode d'observation appliquée . . . à l'étude des familles ouvrières.* Volume 2: *Les ouvriers de l'Orient et leurs essaims de la Méditerranée.* Volume 3: *Les ouvriers du nord et leurs essaims de la Baltique et de la Manche.* Volumes 4–6: *Les ouvriers de l'Occident.* Part 1: *Populations stables.* Part 2: *Populations ébranlées.* Part 3: *Populations désorganisées.*

(1864) 1878 *La réforme sociale en France.* 2 vols. 6th ed. Tours: Mame.

(1870) 1872 *The Organization of Labor in Accordance With Custom and the Law of the Decalogue: With a Summary of Comparative Observations Upon Good and Evil in the Regime of Labor.* Philadelphia: Claxton. → First published in French.

(1871a) 1907 *L'organisation de la famille: Selon le vrai modèle signalé par l'histoire de toutes les races et de tous les temps.* 5th ed. Tours: Mame.

1871b *La paix sociale après le désastre.* Tours: Mame.

1875 *La constitution de l'Angleterre.* Tours: Mame.

1876 *La réforme en l'Europe et le salut en France.* Tours: Mame.

1899 *Voyages en Europe, 1829–1854: Correspondance.* Paris: Plon.

Textes choisis. Preface by Louis Baudin. Paris: Dalloz, 1947.

SUPPLEMENTARY BIBLIOGRAPHY

ARIÈS, PHILIPPE 1948 *Histoire des populations françaises.* Paris: Société d'Éditions Littéraires Françaises.

ARIÈS, PHILIPPE (1960) 1962 *Centuries of Childhood: A Social History of Family Life.* New York: Knopf. → First published as *L'enfant et la vie familiale sous l'ancien régime.*

DELPECH, HENRY 1938 *Recherches sur le niveau de la vie et les habitudes de consommation (Toulouse 1936–1938).* Paris: Sirey.

DEMOLINS, EDMOND (1897) 1898 *Anglo-Saxon Superiority: To What It Is Due.* New York: Scribner. → First published as *À quoi tient la supériorité des Anglo-Saxons.*

DEMOLINS, EDMOND 1898 *L'éducation nouvelle: L'École des Roches.* Paris: Firmin-Didot.

DEMOLINS, EDMOND 1901–1903 *Les grandes routes des peuples: Essai de géographie sociale, comment la route crée le type social.* 2 vols. Paris: Firmin-Didot.

FERRÉ, LOUISE 1936 *Les classes sociales dans la France contemporaine.* Paris: Hachette.

HALBWACHS, MAURICE 1933 *L'évolution des besoins dans les classes ouvrières.* Paris: Alcan.

MICHEL, ANDRÉE 1963 Les cadres sociaux de la doctrine morale de Frédéric Le Play. *Cahiers internationaux de sociologie* 34:47–68.

PARSONS, TALCOTT et al. (editors) (1961) 1965 *Theories of Society: Foundations of Modern Sociological Theory.* New York: Free Press.

Recueil d'études sociales publié à la mémoire de Frédéric Le Play. 1956 Paris: Picard.

RIBBE, CHARLES DE (1873) 1879 *La famille et la société en France avant la Révolution.* 4th ed. Tours: Mame.

RILEY, MATILDA W. (editor) 1963 *Sociological Research.* 2 vols. New York: Harcourt.

ROUSIERS, PAUL DE 1892 *American Life.* Translated by A. J. Herbertson. Paris: Firmin-Didot. → Published in French in the same year.

Rousiers, Paul de 1894 La science sociale. American Academy of Political and Social Science, *Annals* 4, no. 4:620–646.

Rousiers, Paul de (1895) 1896 *The Labour Question in Britain.* London and New York: Macmillan.

Rousiers, Paul de 1902 *Hambourg et l'Allemagne contemporaine.* Paris: Colin.

Rousiers, Paul de 1934 *Une famille de hobereaux pendant six siècles.* Paris: Firmin-Didot.

Société d'Économie Sociale, Paris *Les ouvriers des deux mondes.* → Published from 1857 to 1908.

Sorokin, Pitirim A. 1928 *Contemporary Sociological Theories.* New York: Harper. → A paperback edition was published in 1964 as *Contemporary Sociological Theories Through the First Quarter of the Twentieth Century.*

Tourville, Henri de (1905) 1907 *The Growth of Modern Nations: A History of the Particularist Form of Society.* London: Arnold. → First published as *Histoire de la formation particulariste: L'origine des grands peuples actuels.*

Zimmerman, Carle C.; and Frampton, Merle E. 1935 *Family and Society: A Study of the Sociology of Reconstruction.* London: Williams & Norgate; Princeton, N.J.: Van Nostrand.

LEADERSHIP

I

PSYCHOLOGICAL ASPECTS

The concept of leadership, like that of general intelligence, has largely lost its value for the social sciences, although it remains indispensable to general discourse. There is a great variety of ways in which one individual stands out from others in social situations and in which the one may be said, therefore, to be "leading" the others. So diverse are these ways that any one concept attempting to encompass them all, as "leadership" does, loses the specificity and precision that is necessary to scientific thinking. To call someone a leading artist may mean only that as writer or painter he enjoys greater public acclaim and probably greater sales than do others similarly engaged; but it may also mean that others are aware of him and that in subtle ways he exercises an influence upon them. In general, it is an essential feature of the concept of leading that influence is exerted by one individual upon another, or more commonly, that one or a few individuals influence a larger number. Influence, however, is itself a nonspecific term. One may be influenced by another's disapproved-of behavior to act antagonistically toward him or in a direction quite contrary to that he represents or advocates. It is usual in such circumstances to say

that one is driven to act thus, rather than led. "Leading" implies a shared direction, and this, in turn, often implies that all parties to the leadership relation have a common goal or at least similar or compatible goals; and as Hollander and Julian (1964) say, "leader influence suggests a positive contribution toward the attainment of these goals." Thus, any act of leading implies an interindividual relationship, and leading is one form of interindividual influence. Definition of the simplest unit of analysis in leadership as "the act of leading" has led to the identification of four basic elements in the relationship: (1) the *leader*, with his characteristics of ability and personality and his "resources relevant to goal attainment" (Hollander & Julian 1964); (2) the *followers*, who also have relevant abilities, personality characteristics, and resources; (3) the *situation* within which the relationship occurs; and (4) the *task* with which the interacting individuals are confronted. The nature of the leader–influence relationship and the characterization of the act of leading are to be understood in terms of interaction between these four sets of variables, each of which requires modest amplification.

The leader. Acts of leading may be very brief and of varying importance for long-term interaction, but the concept of leader implies a role relationship of some duration, although this duration is not so great or the role so unvarying as is often thought. A leader, however, is one who is repeatedly perceived to perform acts of leading. As Sherif (1962) points out, generally the leader position is occupied for a considerable time by the same individual. While what has been said thus far holds equally for animal and for human social action, the greater complexity of human interaction and our more detailed knowledge of the communication processes involved in it enable us to pursue this discussion more deeply if particular attention is paid to human interaction.

The group. It is appropriate here to introduce the concept of groups and to discuss leading as action occurring in groups.

The term "group" refers to two or more individuals interacting in the pursuit of common or compatible goals in such a way that the existence of many is utilized for the satisfaction of some needs of each (Cattell 1951; Gibb 1954). Leading may therefore be said to occur only within groups, and a leader may be seen to occupy a position within a group and to fulfill a group role. The principal characteristic of this role is that its occupants are accorded a high proportion of the group's resources of time and attention and are expected to perform a high proportion of initiating, decision-making, or leading acts; there is a disposition to "follow" them. Given agreement with these principles, there is still room for a variety of approaches to the identification of leaders in specific groups. Fortunately these different approaches do not frequently lead to identification of different leaders in a given group at a given time, but they do represent different emphases. One widely used approach, which owes much to the work of Hemphill (e.g., 1949), identifies leaders in terms of the relative frequency with which they perform defined acts of leading. This approach recognizes the fact that groups develop leadership hierarchies and that differentiation between successive levels is primarily in terms of frequency of leading. Only rarely, and then in highly structured organizations, does such an approach identify "the leader." Most groups have many leaders, and differentiation between leaders and followers is a question of drawing an arbitrary line on a frequency continuum.

A second approach seeks those who exercise influence (in a shared direction) over other individuals. It has been shown (Gibb 1950) that leaders may be reliably identified in terms of the extent of such influence, and this form of definition has been employed frequently. In an unpublished study Seeman and Morris (1950) suggested one possible definition of leadership that emphasizes the aspect of influence: leadership acts influence other persons in a shared direction. The position of leader is then defined in terms of relative degrees of influence.

One of the earliest definitions, still widely adopted, is that of Pigors (1935), who indicated that leadership is a concept applied to the personality–environment relation to describe the situation when a personality is so placed in the environment that his "will, feeling and insight direct and control others in the pursuit of a common cause."

An important variant of the influence criterion has been proposed by Cattell (1951). It is his suggestion that the measure of a leader's influence is to be sought not so much in his influence on other group members but in his influence upon total group locomotion or group "syntality" (characteristics, nature, or quality, analogous to individual personality), which is judged from the effectiveness of total performance of the group as group. While this view has important implications, it does not necessarily lead to different leader identification than the other approaches.

The source of power.   Cutting across these considerations in the identification of leaders in a group, and contributing significantly to the definition of the concept of leading, is the essential question of the source of the power to influence. The point at issue here will be understood most readily if thought is given to a group within a larger organization. Power within such a group frequently resides, in whole or in part, in a person appointed by the parent organization to exercise a power delegated to him by that organization. That such a person exercises influence over other group members, there can be no question; but the sources of the power, the nature of the relevant and effective sanctions, and the nature of the relation between influence agent and recipient are in this case qualitatively very different from those to be observed in a voluntary group or association. There seem to be specific advantages for clarity in maintaining this distinction (Pigors 1935) and in using the term "headship" for the former, reserving "leadership" for the latter only. While many characteristics differentiate headship and leadership (Gibb 1954), most basically these two forms of influence differ with respect to the source of the authority. In Sherif's words, "the leadership status itself is within a group and not outside of it" (1962). The leader's authority is spontaneously accorded him by his fellow group members, the followers. The authority of the head derives from some extragroup power that he has over members, who cannot meaningfully be called his followers. They accept his influence on pain of punishment derived from the larger organization, rather than following him in the promise of positive satisfaction derived from the achievement of mutually compatible goals. It is not suggested, of course, that headship and leadership are mutually exclusive, but neither are they coincident, as so much popular thinking suggests. It is a most significant consideration that, as Sherif (1962, p. 17) recognizes, "the leader is not immune from group sanctions if he deviates too far from the bounds of acceptable behavior prevailing in the group," while a head is independent of sanctions applied by the group, though he will in turn, of course, be subject to those applied by the larger organization to its members occupying this particular status. Thus, there is a sensitivity to the interaction between leader and followers that is not necessarily present in that between head and subordinates.

The followers.   Probably the most important thing to be said about the concept of followers is that they, too, fulfill active roles. They are not to be thought of as an aggregation minus the leaders. It is part of the intention of the group concept to imply that all members actively interact in the course of movement in a common direction. Leaders and followers are collaborators. The concepts of leading and following define each other. There can be no leading without following, and of course, no following without leading. Not all members of any given group will, at any particular time and with a particular leadership, be followers, but all members will at some times, under some conditions, be followers or they will forfeit their membership. Neither are followers exclusively confined to this role, any more than leaders are exclusively and always engaged in acts of leading. In fact, leaders and followers frequently exchange roles (Hollander 1961), and observation has shown that the most active followers often initiate acts of leading. Hollander and Julian (1964) suggest that it is an error to speak of an influence agent and an influence recipient as if they were distinct from one another, and this is well supported. The expectations of the follower and the acceptance he accords the leader may be as influential in the production of the act of leading as are the resources of the leader himself. This relation, although rather more subtle and less well taught, may be quite as important as the reciprocal sex roles so readily observable in any society.

The situation.   The term "situation" is used here to mean "the set of values and attitudes with which the individual or the group has to deal in a process of activity and with regard to which this activity is planned and its results appreciated. Every concrete activity is the solution of a situation" (Thomas & Znaniecki [1918] 1947, p. 76). The elements of the situation are (1) the structure of interpersonal relations within a group; (2) the characteristics of the group as group and taken as a unit; (3) the characteristics of the larger culture in which the group exists and from which group members have been drawn; (4) the physical conditions within which the group finds itself constrained to act; and (5) the perceptual representation, within the group and among its members, of these elements and the attitudes and values engendered by them. The situation is especially liable to modification through changes in interpersonal relations, the entrance of new members and departures of others, changes in physical conditions, and the like, which alter action possibilities and, consequently, the perceived probabilities of goal attainment or assessments of costs. Research (Stogdill 1948; Gibb 1954) has shown that a person does not become a leader solely by virtue of any particular pattern of personality traits but rather by possession of any attribute that, by virtue of its relevance to the situation and its situationally determined evaluation by other group members, establishes a relation of leading–following.

The task.   While the task must, in many respects, be regarded as an additional element of the situation, its separate significance in defining acts of leading is probably sufficient to justify separate identification. Research has not yet succeeded in establishing a taxonomy of tasks, even for small groups, that would permit exploration of the relation between task characteristics and other leadership variables. However, Carter (1953) has shown that as far as the differentiation of leaders is concerned, tasks are not discrete but may be grouped in "families." In his experiments, using the same groups, leading in intellectual tasks fell to quite different members than leading in tasks calling for the manipulation of physical objects. More recently Hemphill, during an investigation of motivation to lead, observed, "Group tasks set widely different demands or requirements for leadership. The nature of the task thus becomes an important consideration in the complex of motivational factors related to the attempt to lead. A task that repeatedly presents occasions where a decision must be made produces many attempted leadership acts" (1961, p. 212). Certainly it has been repeatedly observed that as a group moves from one task to another, the situational demands alter in such a way that different forms of participation assume leading qualities, and different members may, depending on the complex interaction of all the elements now under discussion, become influence agents and leaders.

To some degree the nature of the interaction of these elements has already been explicitly discussed or clearly implied, and little more need be said of it until particular theoretical formulations are discussed below. It will be clear, also, that any suggestion that leadership can be reduced to some specific ability or to a set of personal attributes has been abandoned (Lang 1964). The quality of leadership inheres, not in an individual, but in a role that is played within some specified social system. A satisfactory summary statement is that of Zaleznik and Moment:

Identifying leadership [or leading] as a particular kind of interaction event, rather than as a particular set of characteristics of a person, conforms to the temporal, sequential and patterned aspects of role performance. The individual who engages in leadership events becomes a sometimes leader. Thus, the group leader would be the person or persons who engaged in more leadership events than others. We would use the term *influence* as synonymous [*sic*] with leadership only when the term *intended* preceded it. Behavioral analysis describes the ways in which all members of an interacting group influence one another; we identify as leadership only those interaction events in which *intended* influences are consummated. (1964, p. 414)

Leadership as group function

It is now common for social psychologists and sociologists, without any real or implied contradiction of the above analysis of acts of leading, to view leadership as a characteristic of a group rather than of individuals or individual acts. "Leadership is probably best conceived as a set of functions which must be carried out by the group" (Gibb 1954). As Cartwright and Zander suggest, the contemporary view of leadership, which ". . . stresses the characteristics of the group and the situation in which it exists, . . . seeks to discover what actions are required by groups under various conditions if they are to achieve their goals or their valued states, and how different group members take part in these group actions. Leadership is viewed as the performance of those acts which help the group achieve its preferred outcomes" (1953, p. 492). As Secord and Backman (1964) then recognize, such an orientation to leadership has the clear implications (1) that acts of leading will almost inevitably be very varied indeed, depending upon the situation, the task, interpersonal evaluations, and perceptions and interactions of all of these; and (2) that acts of leading may be performed by any or all members of a group and that there is no force in the nature of the leadership relation itself, making for "focused" rather than "distributed" leadership. Furthermore, since groups have two primary "needs"—for goal achievement or achievement of "valued states" and for maintenance of the group—it is to be expected that two primary categories of acts of leading exist and that, in turn, two primary modes of leadership appear. Empirical evidence for this was offered by Bales (1953), who found in small goal-oriented discussion groups both "instrumental" and "social–emotional" leaders. Strong theoretical and empirical support for this view exists.

On this view, the provision of leadership in a group is a complex but limited aspect of the more general process of role differentiation, by which a group develops "specialists" in the performance of recurring functions. The complex of functional roles that characterizes leadership has been more fully studied than have other and probably comparable complexes—for example, that of political figure or ambassador—but it is, perhaps, questionable whether a more complete understanding of role will not supersede particular concern with leadership.

Current psychological theories

Two recent attempts (Berelson & Steiner 1964; Collins & Guetzkow 1964) to set out systematically what is known of leadership have indicated the limitation of this knowledge, and this is especially true with respect to an understanding of the process by which roles are differentiated and status or position established. Gibb (1949) observed that in newly formed groups some degree of leadership emerged within the first few minutes of interaction. The enigma of this phenomenon has still not been elucidated. While it can be confidently asserted (Collins & Guetzkow 1964) that "the greater the personal attraction of other group members to a single individual, the greater the power of that individual," there remains little understanding of the sources and nature of differential personal attraction.

Sociometry. A very large proportion of the research in leadership has made use of the sociometric method. This technique has developed greatly since the first valuable lead given by Moreno (1934) and the first sociometric study of leadership by Jennings (1943). It provides an easily accessible, relatively objective means of assessing interpersonal attitudes within a group, and by way of such linkages, it offers a means of mapping the interpersonal structure of a group [*see* SOCIOMETRY].

The simple but important recognition that different choice criteria could be incorporated in the sociometric question has led to very significant insights into the leadership of groups. The value of Jennings' varying the criteria from choices among group tasks to quite informal friendship choices (1947) cannot be overestimated. Role criteria in the study of leadership are now numerous, and the use of different criteria has shown that members of a group do often distinguish between those they like as friends and those they would wish to have as leaders (Hollander 1961, p. 34). The sociometric method has also demonstrated that interpersonal designation of leaders varies in any group from time to time as goals, tasks, and internal structure change.

In an attempt to explain the importance of sociometric technique to the study of leadership, Hollander (1961) has said that social interaction leads to an implicit interpersonal assessment, which the perceiver reaches by comparing task-related elements and behavior with some social standard. Parsons (1952) was responsible for a very significant advance when he indicated that persons interacting are objects to each other in an evaluational process, the elements of which are cognitive (what the object is) and cathectic (what the object means in an emotional sense). Leadership is such an evaluational relationship; the cognitive component is perception of another individual's instrumentality in need satisfaction, and an emotional tone derives from the as yet not understood processes of interpersonal attraction.

The principal theories of leadership are based in some sense upon the sociometric method. Of these, mention should certainly be made of interaction theory, of Hollander's work on "idiosyncrasy credit," and of Fiedler's "contingency theory."

General interaction theory. The important aspects of interaction theory have been stated as follows (Gibb 1958). First, groups are mechanisms for achieving individual satisfactions, and conversely, persons interact with other persons for the achievement of group satisfactions. Second, role differentiation, including that complex called leadership, is part and parcel of a group's locomotion toward its goals and, thus, toward the satisfaction of needs of individual members. Third, leadership is a concept applied to the interaction of two or more persons when the evaluation of one or some of the parties to the interaction is such that he or they come to control and direct the actions of the others in the pursuit of common or compatible ends. Any group is a system of interactions. Within this system a structure emerges as a result of the development of relatively stable sets of expectations for the behavior of each member, and these expectations are an expression of the member's interaction with all other members. Thus, the particular role an individual member achieves within the group is determined both by the functional or role needs of the group in a situation and by the member's particular attributes of personality, ability, and skill, which differentiate him perceptually from others in the group. Leadership is basically a function of personality and social system in dynamic interaction. Fourth, evaluation of one party to interaction by another is itself an integration of perceptual and emotional relationships; it is a product of perception of instrumentality in need satisfaction and of emotional attachment. This form of conceptualization leads to a recognition of a complex of emotional relationships, which in turn define a variety of leadership relations. Among these may be identified (1) patriarchal leadership, in which the person upon whom the members perceive themselves to be dependent is both loved and feared; (2) tyrannical leadership, where the emotional relationship is dominated by fear; and (3) "ideal," or charismatic, leadership,

in which the interpersonal relationship is characterized by love or affection. Insofar as attention is given only to the momentary capacity of a group to mobilize its resources for a particular task, the emotional quality of the relations to a leader may be irrelevant. But if the time dimension is admitted, then the cathexis of the parties of the interaction to one another seems inevitable. It is a part of this theory, then, that even if consideration is given only to those groups in which the sources of all influence and control are within the group (i.e., if headship situations are ignored), the concept of leadership still embraces a wide variety of interactional relationships, all of which must be expected to have quite different effects in terms of group behavior. This view of social interaction gives rise to a number of hypotheses concerning leadership for which there is already some evidence in sociological observations and in the findings of psychological experimentation. Among these is the observation that, under different conditions, a leader can have varying degrees of influence on the "locomotion" of his group.

Fiedler's contingency theory. Some aspects of interaction theory have been systematically elaborated and investigated by Fiedler and his associates (Fiedler 1964). The starting point of these investigations was the widely recognized fact that while one form of leadership was associated with effective group performance in one set of circumstances, there were circumstances in which a quite contrary form seemed most effective. For example, a number of studies had shown that human-relations-oriented, considerate, or democratic leader behavior promoted high morale and productively effective behavior in a wide variety of work groups. Yet, other studies had shown task-oriented, instrumental, or authoritarian leadership to be associated with productive efficiency in experimental groups. Further examination of this research revealed that "the prediction of group performance on the basis of these leader attributes is contingent upon the specific, situational context in which the leader operates" (*ibid.*, p. 154).

Fiedler chose to measure, as predictors of leadership effectiveness, "assumed similarity between opposites" (ASo) and "esteem for the least preferred co-worker." These rather esoteric measures acquire general meaning and significance by virtue of the fact that each can be shown to bear some relation to the rather more widely acceptable variables of "task-orientation" and "consideration." Individuals who differentiate sharply between their most and least preferred co-workers (low ASo) tend to be more oriented toward the task and more punitive. A person who sees even a poor co-worker in a relatively favorable manner (high ASo) is likely to behave in a way that shows consideration for others and promotes member satisfaction; he is also likely to be less directive.

In an early study Fiedler (1955) was able to show that the leaders' ASo scores and the performance of army and air-force crews were negatively associated for crews in which the leader sociometrically endorsed his "keyman" (e.g., the gunner on a tank-gunnery task) and were positively associated for crews in which the leader sociometrically rejected his keyman. Subsequently, Fiedler demonstrated that "The relationship between ASo scores and crew effectiveness . . . seemed to be contingent upon the sociometric choice pattern within the crew" (1964, p. 156).

Fiedler has also suggested that group situations may be described in terms of three dimensions: (1) affective leader–group relations; (2) task structure; and (3) position power. There is reason to believe that task structure and position power are not independent (1964, p. 162), and further elaboration of this model is sure to follow. The first of these dimensions reflects the extent to which the leader feels accepted by his group members. Task structure is defined in terms of four scales, developed by M. E. Shaw, which refer to the degree to which the correctness of a decision can be demonstrated, the clarity to members of the requirements of the task, the restriction of procedures by which the task may be accomplished, and the uniqueness of the "correct" solution. By "position power" is meant the extent to which the leader may dispense rewards, punishments, and sanctions, generally by virtue of authority given him by the organization within which the group operates, by tradition, or by any other formally recognized institution.

By dichotomizing each of these dimensions into high and low, Fiedler obtains eight descriptively different group-task situations. The results from many studies are then called upon to reveal the relationship between leadership style and group performance in each of these different situations. "In very favorable conditions, where the leader has power, informal backing [i.e., good leader–member relations], and a relatively well-structured task, the group is ready to be directed on how to go about its task" (ibid., p. 165), as is shown by the fact that the correlations between ASo scores and group effectiveness are large and negative. In other words, the controlling, managing, and directive leaders perform best in these conditions. And under very unfavorable conditions, where leader–member relations are poor, the task is unstructured,

and the leader lacks power, the managing, controlling leadership style also proves most effective. It is in moderately favorable conditions, where the group faces an unstructured or ambiguous task or where the leader's relations with group members are tenuous, that permissive, considerate leadership is most effective. It is probably not unimportant that the situation where the leader position is weak, the task ambiguous, but the leader well liked is characterized by considerate, permissive leadership; and, alternatively, when the leader is not well liked but the task is clearly structured and his position is strong, the leadership is generally authoritarian and task oriented. This fact suggests a need for further consideration of the summary concept of favorableness of the situation. However, there is reason enough to accept Fiedler's general hypothesis that "the type of leader attitude required for effective group performance depends upon the degree to which the group situation is favorable or unfavorable to the leader" (1964, p. 164).

Fiedler and Meuwese (1963) have also shown that a leader's ability scores correlate highly with group performance only if the leader is sociometrically accepted or liked, and this finding contains the essence of the contingency theory. The fact that a person may be identified as a leader in an uncohesive group and that the correlation between his ability and group performance may be negative suggests that when the group perceives its major task to be group maintenance, the identified leader will be one who attends primarily to the performance of maintenance functions rather than to the overt task.

Hollander's idiosyncrasy credit.   Within the context of an interaction theory that sees social behavior as dependent upon individual attributes, conditions of the situation, and "inputs to a dynamic system arising from their interaction," Hollander (1958) proposed a mediating construct of "idiosyncrasy credit," to explain the fact that leaders must conform to the norms of the group led and also must be a force for innovation. Basically this is made possible through the achievement of status, which is primarily a matter of the leaders' being perceived to conform to group expectancies in the areas of both high individual task performance and generalized characteristics (e.g., pleasant appearance). To the extent that a person is positively evaluated in both task competence and status external to the group, he accumulates "idiosyncrasy credit."

This represents an accumulation of positively disposed impressions residing in the perceptions of relevant others; it is defined operationally in terms of the degree to which an individual may deviate from the common expectancies of the group. In this view, each individual within a group—disregarding size and function, for the moment—may be thought of as having a degree of group-awarded credits such as to permit idiosyncratic behavior in certain dimensions *before* group sanctions are applied. (Hollander 1958, p. 120)

Against this credit, such deviant behavior as the individual indulges in is to be seen as a debit. For any given individual, then, the extent to which he is allowed to innovate will depend upon his status. So long as he does nothing to negate the perception of himself as task competent, motivated to belong to the group, and loyal to others' expectations of him, he may enjoy sufficient credit to challenge and change prevailing social patterns in the group. But Hollander (1961) points out that "in attaining this level, the particular expectancies applicable to him will have undergone change," so there is no guarantee that it will be appropriate or possible for him to continue in innovation; in fact, the converse is more likely to obtain.

This "mediating concept" of idiosyncrasy credit is consistent with and helps to explain leader rotation in the group as task and other features of the situation alter, for as Hollander says, "the task competent follower who conforms to the common expectancies of the group at one stage may become the leader at the next stage. And, correspondingly, the leader who fails to fulfill the expectancies associated with his position of influence may lose credits among his followers and be replaced by one of them" (*ibid.*, p. 45).

Summary of current theories. The principal insistence of interaction theories in any of these forms is that the major variables in terms of which leadership might be understood are (1) the leader's personality; (2) the needs, attitudes, and problems of followers; (3) the group itself, in terms of both interpersonal structure and syntality; and (4) the situation in terms of both the physical circumstances and the group task. Further, it is clearly understood that the investigator needs to deal with the perception of each of these variables by the leader and by other group members.

Personality and leadership

In the context of interaction theories there is room for a thorough exploration of the extent to which attributes of the leader are related to the process of leadership and to group performance. Probably the earliest "explanation" of leadership phenomena was given in terms of personal qualities that, while partially modifiable and learnable, characterized the individual and established his dominance of and influence in any situation. For a

time during the late 1940s, reaction against this view was so marked that psychology seemed to some to be in danger of offering a thoroughly "situational" view of leadership phenomena. The major influences in this reaction were Gibb's report of the situational shifting of leadership in small groups (1947) and Stogdill's study of the literature of personality traits (1948), which revealed that those personality traits which were leadership traits depended upon the situation and the requirements of the group. Each of these papers, however, was interactional rather than situational in theoretical orientation. And the interactional approach has opened the way for understanding the relation between personality and leadership, while at the same time ending the quest for generalized "leadership traits."

The early tendency to lean heavily to the side of situational determinacy in this process was most effectively checked by Carter and Nixon (1949), who showed that when the emergence of leadership was studied in a carefully controlled way, through tasks which fell into three distinct "families," the leadership varied considerably from task family to task family but that within families it was relatively stable and appeared to be determined by other, probably personality, factors. In the years since 1950 many studies have provided evidence that personality factors contribute to the emergence and maintenance of leadership status. This has been especially true of those studies in which the situational variance has not been relatively great.

Representative studies. As examples, four of these studies may be mentioned.

(1) Bass (1960, p. 172) reports that in initially leaderless discussion groups extremely authoritarian personalities, as measured by the California F scale, are least likely to exhibit successful leadership behavior. On the other hand, in these groups he observed a positive correlation between successful leadership and perceptual flexibility. But probably the most telling is the finding of Klubeck and Bass (1954) that persons who do not naturally exhibit successful leadership in such groups are unable to profit from brief coaching as to how to behave as leaders, and the conclusion that these persons seem to be limited by personality and would need to undergo change, probably through major psychotherapy, before they could be freed to behave as leaders.

(2) Borgatta, Couch, and Bales have presented findings that they describe as relevant to a "great man" theory of leadership (1954). They varied the composition of three-man groups working on the same tasks and showed that individuals who scored

high on a composite of intelligence, leadership ratings by fellow participants, participation rate, and sociometric popularity in one group were also high in three subsequent group sessions, where they interacted with different persons. Those who scored highest on this composite criterion in one group did so consistently, and it was evident that "great men" selected on the basis of their first session continue to have an influence on the relatively superior performance of the groups in which they subsequently participate. However, as Hollander comments, "the task setting was essentially constant with only the participants varying across sessions" (Hollander and Julian 1964).

(3) In somewhat similar vein Cattell and Stice (1954) offered four formulas for selecting leaders on the basis of personality. They differentiated four kinds of leaders: "persistent momentary problem solvers" or technical leaders, identified in terms of the frequency with which nonparticipant observers had judged the individual to have influenced the group; salient leaders, picked by the observers as most powerfully influencing the group in at least one of the 22 situations presented; sociometric leaders, identified by choice by fellow members; and elected leaders, who were named after formal election on one or more occasions in the course of the experimental interaction.

The personality profiles of leaders were compared with those of nonleaders, and eight personality factors showed differences in the same direction for all four categories. These were *C*, emotional maturity, or ego strength; *E*, dominance; *G*, character integration, or superego strength; *H*, social adventurousness; *N*, shrewdness; *O* (negative), freedom from anxiety; *Q3*, deliberate will control; and *Q4* (negative), absence of nervous tension. Differences between leader types were that technical leaders had higher general intelligence, *B*, and elected leaders were higher in *F*, surgency. Discussing these results, the authors indicate that the relationships revealed are consistent with both technical and nontechnical thinking about leadership and the influence process. For example, the timid, withdrawn, hesitant behavior associated with a low *H* score would not be conducive to leadership in any of the categories. The anxious, worrying cautiousness in dealing with people represented by high *O* would not inspire confidence. And where conscience is considered to be the "will of the group"—a regard for superindividual values—the selection of leaders with high *G* represents a gain for the group. [*See* TRAITS.]

(4) Some confirmation of this finding is to be found in a study by Borg (1960). He derived four factor scores from a variety of tests that were primarily measures of personality variables and related these to sociometric measures of six small-group roles. Twelve of his 24 correlation coefficients were significant at the .01 level. The predictor factor "assertiveness" was the most successful. A correlation of .46 was found between assertiveness scores and a composite leadership role derived from individual role measures of assertiveness, creativity, and leadership. It is interesting to observe that the predictor factor "power orientation" is consistently unassociated with this leadership composite and that a third predictor, "rigidity," dependent primarily on the California *F* scale, is consistently and significantly negatively associated with leadership, thus confirming Bass's results. As Borg himself points out (p. 115), his success in predicting especially the leadership-role scores may mean that even more can be achieved in this area if predictor instruments are further developed.

Summary of the literature. Despite the common promise of these studies and others like them, it cannot at this time be said that there is evidence for a predominant personality component in leadership. The best review of the literature in this area to date is that of Mann (1959). In the course of examining a number of relationships between the personality characteristics of the individual and the way he behaves or is perceived to behave in small groups, Mann presents a summary of the relationships between some aspects of personality and leadership, as follows.

Intelligence. After examination of 28 independent studies, the positive association of intelligence and leadership in small groups seems to be beyond doubt, although the median correlation is only .25; no reported coefficient exceeded .50; and just half of the results examined failed to establish the significance of this trend.

Adjustment. The association of personal adjustment and leadership was found in 22 studies. Again the over-all trend is clearly positive, with a median correlation of approximately .15 and no single correlation coefficient greater than .53.

Extraversion–introversion. Twenty-two different studies have suggested a median correlation between extraversion and leadership of .15, and the highest correlation reported is .42. Despite some difficulty in ensuring the real similarity of scales of similar title, there is evidence for the conclusion that "those individuals who tend to be selected as leaders are more sociable and outgoing."

Dominance. On the evidence of 12 studies, dominance, as measured by personality scales, is positively associated with leadership, having a median correlation around .20 and a highest reported correlation of .42. "Although the trend is not very strong, these data suggest that dominant or ascendant individuals have a greater chance of being designated leader."

Conservatism. Seventeen studies reveal that in general there is a negative association between conservatism and leadership. Mann found that the California *F* scale had been used ten times in the prediction of leadership and that on each occasion authoritarian persons had been rated lower on leadership.

Interpersonal sensitivity. The measurement of interpersonal sensitivity, or empathic ability, has been subject to much attention. Some caution is needed in attempting to summarize the 15 studies relating it to leadership, and Mann duly qualifies his summary judgment that "there appears to be a low but clearly positive relationship between interpersonal sensitivity and leadership."

Evaluation and other techniques. A further and even more important qualification of these results is made by Mann in pointing out that leadership is variously determined by one of three popular techniques: peer ratings, criterion measures, and observer ratings. The relationship of some of the above personality variables differs when these different measuring techniques are used for leadership. While the relationship between intelligence and leadership is independent of the technique of identifying leadership, that between adjustment and leadership is more closely associated with peer ratings or informal leadership than with either of the other forms; extraversion is more likely to characterize formal leaders determined by criterion measures. Further, Mann observes that "extraverted individuals are no more likely than introverted individuals to be rated as informal leaders by their peers." To a large extent the significance of this observation by Mann, based upon a careful scrutiny of the literature, is that it confirms, in principle at least, the Cattell and Stice proposal of different regressions of personality measures upon different measures of leadership.

The evidence of research to date is clear in demanding that future research attempting to relate personality variables to the exercise of influence in groups must make use of more refined concepts than that of leadership, and close attention must be given to the techniques used to assess both personality and influence relationships.

Leadership in the enduring group

Implicit in the recognition that leadership is situation contingent is the understanding that leader behavior varies with such group factors as organization structure and pattern of communication. Probably the most prominent determinant of variation in these structural respects is the duration of the group. Much of the research in the psychology of leadership has employed newly formed groups of short duration, while a great many of the groups with which social science generally concerns itself are those that endure for a considerable period and either have or achieve a significant history. Sherif and Sherif (1948) have done much to establish the fact that enduring groups develop an organization and structure that becomes a considerable determinant of group-related behavior; and, indeed, they discuss leadership within the context of such structures. Secord and Backman (1964) properly indicate that "in groups that have functioned long enough to develop stable structures and a certain routine much of the stability in leader personnel can be explained" in terms other than those of personality–situation interaction. [*See* Groups, *article on* GROUP FORMATION.]

In enduring groups it is patent that formal office structure usually remains relatively stable, continuing from one situation to another throughout a formal term. This cannot always be regarded as continuing leadership. Primarily because of the complex values of stable structure and because there is a culture-carried expectation that offices will be filled for predetermined periods, groups maintain a status structure even if it no longer corresponds to functional demands. One result of this culture-carried expectation of persisting organization is that the nature or emotional–relational quality of leadership will change. In the early stages of group development persons emerge as organizational leaders by virtue of their control over problem-related resources or they emerge as positively cathected leaders by virtue of both their command of resources and the readiness members show to relate themselves emotionally to others on the basis of first impressions (Gibb 1949; 1958). As interaction persists, structure is stabilized for a variety of reasons. With time, the early congruence of the cognitive relation to the person controlling resources and the positive cathexis of that same person is reduced. When stability of structure, then, is formalized so that offices are held for a stated time without reference to contemporary contributory strength in problem solving, leadership becomes less functional and the officeholder is supported by structural rigidity. His leadership may now be said to have become headship, and the dynamics of the group will almost certainly have become complicated by the emergence of new leaders, thrown up by the complex of forces, which now includes, of course, the behavior of the formal officeholders. The officeholders strive to maintain the satisfactions of office, whether these be simply of status or more complex, and in doing so their behavior becomes more coercive. Frequently this implies the establishment of power cliques or bureaucracies. Under such conditions the emotional quality of relations to the leader or head becomes less positive and the nature of the influence has changed. [*See* BUREAUCRACY.]

However, in other, simpler, and more direct ways, too, the time dimension, or history, has been seen to affect leadership. Klein (1956) has suggested that communication structure may become habitual and independent of the problem to be solved. A structure that has been successful repeatedly because problems have been similar will, she suggests, be persisted in even when problems become dissimilar, because of a preference for orderliness and routine. Bass (1960) has shown that the perceived status an individual brings into a group by virtue of past interaction in the group or in another, mutually known group directly affects his willingness to make attempts to lead and the success of such attempts. As Secord and Backman (1964) observe, the communication and status structures mutually reinforce each other and together constitute strong forces determining leadership. One's position in group structure, whether in the communication net or in the mutually perceived status hierarchy, greatly affects his opportunities and abilities to exercise influence. Obviously communication centrality and status position are not independent. Hopkins (1964) adduces considerable evidence for the proposition that "for any member of a small group, the higher his rank, the greater his influence."

Two final points of some significance have also been made by Secord and Backman (1964). First, once having achieved success in leadership, and through it having attained centrality and status, which in turn tend to establish their leadership, these leaders have the best opportunity to develop leadership skills, which further accentuate their positive evaluation. Second, because of the community value placed upon status and leadership directly, established leaders are highly motivated to maintain their roles, while reciprocally, their success spells satisfaction for their followers, whose involvement may be correspondingly reduced.

CECIL A. GIBB

[*Directly related are the entries* ELITES; POWER. *Other relevant material may be found in* ATTITUDES, *article*
on ATTITUDE CHANGE; AUTHORITY; GROUPS, *especially the article on* GROUP FORMATION; ORGANIZATIONS; PERSUASION; POLITICAL ANTHROPOLOGY, *article on* POLITICAL ORGANIZATION; POLITICAL MACHINES; POLITICAL PROCESS; ROLE; *and in the biography of* LEWIN.]

BIBLIOGRAPHY

BALES, ROBERT F. 1953 The Equilibrium Problem in Small Groups. Pages 111–161 in Talcott Parsons et al., *Working Papers in the Theory of Action.* Glencoe, Ill.: Free Press.

BASS, BERNARD M. 1960 *Leadership, Psychology, and Organizational Behavior.* New York: Harper.

BERELSON, BERNARD; and STEINER, GARY A. 1964 *Human Behavior: An Inventory of Scientific Findings.* New York: Harcourt.

BORG, WALTER R. 1960 Prediction of Small Group Role Behavior From Personality Variables. *Journal of Abnormal and Social Psychology* 60:112–116.

BORGATTA, EDGAR F. et al. 1954 Some Findings Relevant to a Great Man Theory of Leadership. *American Sociological Review* 19:755–759.

BROWNE, CLARENCE; and COHN, THOMAS S. (editors) 1958 *The Study of Leadership.* Danville, Ill.: Interstate Printers & Publishers.

CARTER, LAUNOR F. 1953 Leadership and Small-group Behavior. Pages 257–284 in Conference in Social Psychology, University of Oklahoma, 1952, *Group Relations at the Crossroads.* Edited by Muzafer Sherif and M. D. Wilson. New York: Harper.

CARTER, LAUNOR F.; and NIXON, MARY 1949 Ability, Perceptual, Personality, and Interest Factors Associated With Different Criteria of Leadership. *Journal of Psychology* 27:377–388.

CARTWRIGHT, DORWIN; and ZANDER, ALVIN (editors) (1953) 1960 *Group Dynamics: Research and Theory.* 2d ed. Evanston, Ill.: Row, Peterson; New York: Harper. → See especially pages 487–510, "Leadership and Group Performance: Introduction."

CATTELL, RAYMOND B. 1951 New Concepts for Measuring Leadership in Terms of Group Syntality. *Human Relations* 4:161–184.

CATTELL, RAYMOND; and STICE, GLEN F. 1954 Four Formulae for Selecting Leaders on the Basis of Personality. *Human Relations* 7:493–507.

COLLINS, BARRY E.; and GUETZKOW, HAROLD 1964 *A Social Psychology of Group Processes for Decisionmaking.* New York: Wiley.

FIEDLER, FRED E. 1955 The Influence of Leader–Keyman Relations on Combat Crew Effectiveness. *Journal of Abnormal and Social Psychology* 51:227–235.

FIEDLER, FRED E. 1964 A Contingency Model of Leadership Effectiveness. Volume 1, pages 149–190 in *Advances in Experimental Social Psychology.* Edited by Leonard Berkowitz. New York: Academic Press.

FIEDLER, FRED E.; and MEUWESE, W. A. T. 1963 Leader's Contribution to Task Performance in Cohesive and Uncohesive Groups. *Journal of Abnormal and Social Psychology* 67:83–87.

GIBB, CECIL A. 1947 The Principles and Traits of Leadership. *Journal of Abnormal and Social Psychology* 42:267–284.

GIBB, CECIL A. 1949 *The Emergence of Leadership in Small Temporary Groups of Men.* Publication No. 1392. Ann Arbor, Mich.: University Microfilms.

GIBB, CECIL A. 1950 The Sociometry of Leadership in Temporary Groups. *Sociometry* 13:226–243.

GIBB, CECIL A. 1954 Leadership. Volume 2, pages 877–920 in Gardner Lindzey (editor), *Handbook of Social Psychology*. Cambridge, Mass.: Addison-Wesley.

GIBB, CECIL A. 1958 An Interactional View of the Emergence of Leadership. *Australian Journal of Psychology* 10:101–110.

HEMPHILL, JOHN K. 1949 *Situational Factors in Leadership*. Monograph No. 32. Columbus: Ohio State Univ., Bureau of Educational Research.

HEMPHILL, JOHN K. 1961 Why People Attempt to Lead. Pages 201–215 in Luigi Petrullo and Bernard M. Bass (editors), *Leadership and Interpersonal Behavior*. New York: Holt.

HOLLANDER, E. P. 1958 Conformity, Status, and Idiosyncrasy Credit. *Psychological Review* 65:117–127.

HOLLANDER, E. P. 1961 Emergent Leadership and Social Influence. Pages 30–47 in Luigi Petrullo and Bernard M. Bass (editors), *Leadership and Interpersonal Behavior*. New York: Holt.

HOLLANDER, E. P.; and JULIAN, J. W. 1964 Leadership. Unpublished manuscript.

HOPKINS, TERENCE K. 1964 *The Exercise of Influence in Small Groups*. Totowa, N.J.: Bedminster Press.

JENNINGS, HELEN H. (1943) 1950 *Leadership and Isolation: A Study of Personality in Inter-personal Relations*. 2d ed. New York: Longmans.

JENNINGS, HELEN H. 1947 *Sociometry of Leadership, Based on the Differentiation of Psychegroup and Sociogroup*. Sociometry Monograph No. 14. New York: Beacon House.

KLEIN, JOSEPHINE 1956 *The Study of Groups*. London: Routledge; New York: Humanities.

KLUBECK, STANLEY; and BASS, BERNARD M. 1954 Differential Effects of Training on Persons of Different Leadership Status. *Human Relations* 7:59–72.

LANG, KURT 1964 Leadership. Pages 380–381 in Julius Gould and William L. Kolb (editors), *A Dictionary of the Social Sciences*. New York: Free Press.

MANN, RICHARD D. 1959 A Review of the Relationships Between Personality and Performance in Small Groups. *Psychological Bulletin* 56:241–270.

MEREI, FERENC 1949 Group Leadership and Institutionalization. *Human Relations* 2:23–39.

MORENO, JACOB L. (1934) 1953 *Who Shall Survive? Foundations of Sociometry, Group Psychotherapy and Sociodrama*. Rev. & enl. ed. Sociometry Monograph No. 29. Beacon, N.Y.: Beacon House.

PARSONS, TALCOTT (1952) 1953 The Superego and the Theory of Social Systems. Pages 13–29 in Talcott Parsons et al., *Working Papers in the Theory of Action*. Glencoe, Ill.: Free Press.

PETRULLO, LUIGI; and BASS, BERNARD M. (editors) 1961 *Leadership and Interpersonal Behavior*. New York: Holt.

PIGORS, PAUL 1935 *Leadership or Domination*. Boston: Houghton Mifflin.

ROSS, MURRAY G.; and HENDRY, CHARLES E. 1957 *New Understandings of Leadership: A Survey and Application of Research*. New York: Association Press.

SECORD, PAUL F.; and BACKMAN, CARL W. 1964 *Social Psychology*. New York: McGraw-Hill.

SEEMAN, MELVIN; and MORRIS, R. T. 1950 A Status Factor Approach to Leadership. Unpublished manuscript.

SHERIF, MUZAFER (editor) 1962 *Intergroup Relations and Leadership: Approaches and Research in Industrial, Ethnic, Cultural, and Political Areas*. New York: Wiley.

SHERIF, MUZAFER; and SHERIF, CAROLYN W. (1948) 1956 *An Outline of Social Psychology*. Rev. ed. New York: Harper.

STOGDILL, RALPH M. 1948 Personal Factors Associated With Leadership. *Journal of Psychology* 25:35–71.

STOGDILL, RALPH M. 1962 Intragroup–Intergroup Theory and Research. Pages 48–65 in Muzafer Sherif (editor), *Intergroup Relations and Leadership*. New York: Wiley.

THOMAS, WILLIAM I.; and ZNANIECKI, FLORIAN (1918) 1947 The Definition of the Situation. Pages 76–77 in Society for the Psychological Study of Social Issues, *Readings in Social Psychology*. New York: Holt. → Reprinted from Volume 1 of W. I. Thomas and F. Znaniecki, *The Polish Peasant in Europe and America*.

VERBA, SIDNEY 1961 *Small Groups and Political Behavior: A Study of Leadership*. Princeton Univ. Press.

ZALEZNIK, ABRAHAM; and MOMENT, DAVID 1964 *The Dynamics of Interpersonal Behavior*. New York: Wiley.

II
SOCIOLOGICAL ASPECTS

To most sociological writers leadership is the exercise of power or influence in social collectivities, such as groups, organizations, communities, or nations. This power may be addressed to any or all of three very general and related functions: establishing the goals, purposes, or objectives of the collectivity; creating the structures through which the purposes of the collectivity are fulfilled; and maintaining or enhancing these structures. Sociological studies have emphasized the last function, in part because it seems more amenable to empirical investigation, particularly in bureaucratic settings, where much of the research on leadership is conducted. This emphasis has implied an interest in the role of leadership in maintaining the integrity and viability of the collectivity against threats, both internal and external, in maintaining collective order and unity, in minimizing dissension and conflict, and in motivating members and fostering their acceptance of the collectivity, of its goals, and of leadership itself. Thus, most theories of leadership are conservative in that they are addressed to the maintenance of social systems rather than to their change. Although this is not an exclusive emphasis, it is consistent with a major concern in contemporary sociology with the problems of social order and stability.

The exercise of power or influence implies "making things happen" through others. Leaders may engage in a number of activities in furthering this purpose. They may coordinate, control, direct, guide, or mobilize the efforts of others. A recent focus on the leaders' role in motivating members implies that they may counsel, support, help, persuade, or elicit the participation of others in some degree of goal setting. Leaders may also cajole, manipulate, entice, reward, coerce, or harangue, although some writers exclude some of these activities from the definition of leadership. "Strictly speaking," according to Schmidt (1933, p. 282), "the relation of leadership arises only where a group follows an individual from free choice and not under command or coercion and, secondly, not in response to blind drives but on positive and more or less rational grounds."

Many of the above activities of leaders are concerned with the details of interpersonal relations. Leaders may also wield power in representing the collectivity in its external relations. Or they may make decisions and formulate policies on a broad scale without becoming directly involved in the details of their execution. Selznick (1957) applies the term "institutional statesman" to those organization leaders who look beyond questions of routine administration and productive efficiency to the broader philosophic implications of the collectivity and its role in the larger society. Organization statesmen assume responsibility for defining policy values and for developing a plan of organization that embodies these values. Similarly, Harbison and Myers (1959) employ the term "organization builders" for those leaders who devote themselves to *creating* organizations. These leaders are concerned as much with innovation as with collective stability. Leaders in developing nations, in particular, are concerned with change, with defining new collective goals and creating structures appropriate to these goals. Many of these leaders must also undertake the difficult task of establishing new social values in the context of traditional philosophies (Fourastié & Vimont 1956, p. 57).

Leadership defines, initiates, and maintains social structure. The social system is, so to speak, "programmed" through leadership. Understanding leadership, then, should be a simple and parsimonious approach to understanding the larger social system. Leadership can have consequences for the lives and welfare of large numbers of people, and, therefore, those who are concerned with the practical consequences of human actions must be concerned with leadership.

Important social values are also frequently associated with leadership conceptions, and attempts are made to legitimate social systems in terms of particular theories or ideologies of leadership. The drama of leadership can be seen in its consequences and in the behavior of some well-known leaders. History is personalized and dramatized through stories of leadership, and the names of famous or infamous leaders elicit strong feeling. But the drama associated with leadership, together with its apparent theoretical and practical import, gives it an appeal that may sometimes be deceptive. The "great man theory," according to which outstanding leaders determine the course of history, is one expression of this appeal. Models of ruling elites, which explain whole social systems in terms of power concentrated in the hands of relatively small and exclusive leadership groups, are similarly appealing in their simplicity and drama. "The whole history of civilized mankind," according to Mosca, "comes down to a conflict between the tendency of dominant elements to monopolize political power and transmit possession of it by inheritance . . ." ([1896] 1939, p. 65). The United States, according to Mills's more contemporary analysis (1956), is dominated by a "power elite" that is in command of the major organizations of society.

Sociological treatments of leadership have leaned heavily on conceptions applying to elites, to autocratic systems, and to rigid class or caste societies. Almost all of the literature on leadership, according to Bell, stems from the works of Aristotle and Machiavelli and is committed to "the image of the mindless masses and the image of the strong-willed leader" (1950, p. 396). Classical models of bureaucracy share with these elite conceptions an authoritarian bias in their emphasis on the exclusive prerogative of leaders to command and the unquestioning obligation of subordinates to obey (Weber 1922a).

According to Michels (1911), leadership and democracy are incompatible. Leadership inevitably becomes oligarchic, even in political organizations that start democratically and are committed to a democratic ideology. Leaders themselves are incapable of deflecting this historic process; democratic and idealistic leaders succumb eventually to the corruption inherent in power. Michels cites a number of arguments in support of the tendency toward oligarchy in social systems. First, the masses, through incompetence and apathy, cannot and do not want to participate actively in the political process; they prefer to be led. Second, democracy is structurally impossible in large and complex social systems; there is no way of arranging the systems so that the views of the many individual members can be heard and taken into account. The impracticality of democracy is especially apparent in organizations or nations undergoing conflict with others. Especially during periods of crisis, organizations need firm leadership and precise adherence to orders. Finally, the tendency toward oligarchy results from the character of leaders themselves and of the role they must play. Because of their cultural and educational superiority over the masses, leaders form a distinct elite. The status, perquisites, and privileges associated with the leadership role serve further to separate the leaders from the masses. In labor unions and socialist parties, for example, the life of the leaders becomes that of the petty bourgeois. Leaders therefore develop a vested interest in their positions, which they must protect. Furthermore, a personal lust for power, which is characteristic of leaders, intensifies their efforts to enhance their power, and leaders will resort to ulterior devices toward this end. In "democratic" parties leaders will employ emotional and demagogic appeals to manipulate the gullible masses. They will control the party press, using it to describe themselves in the most favorable light, while deriding their opposition within the party. They will exploit their special information and knowledge of the organization to outmaneuver opponents. And if, despite these tactics, the leaders should be overthrown, the new officeholders in their turn will undergo the inevitable "transformation which renders them in every respect similar to the dethroned tyrants. . . . The revolutionaries of today become the reactionaries of tomorrow" (Michels 1911, p. 195 in 1962 paperback edition).

Changes in the character of leadership

Many of the classical conceptions of leadership, including those in Weber's work on bureaucracies and in Michels' on political organizations, have proven valuable in analyses of contemporary social systems. Nonetheless, the changing character of societies over the years, and of leadership itself, has made apparent some of the limitations of these older conceptions. The emphasis in contemporary sociology on quantitative research has also contributed to changes in interpretations of the leadership process because of the need to develop conceptions that are operationally feasible as well as theoretically meaningful. At the same time, research findings themselves have led to reinterpretations of older conceptions.

The increasing numbers and complexity of organizations in modern industrial societies require large numbers of persons with high levels of technical and administrative expertise to play leadership roles. The demand for expert leaders reduces the suitability of those recruited on the basis of social status or of family connections. Achievement thus replaces ascription as the basis for placing leaders, and their recruitment spreads to all strata of society. Similarly, political criteria prevalent as the basis of recruitment during early stages in newly independent countries and in revolutionary

societies become less important in highly industrialized societies. Training centers for leaders are established in universities, business schools, and training institutes, and the possibility for careers in industrial leadership are opened to large numbers of persons. Management becomes professionalized. While these developments are most apparent in business and industrial organizations and in some agencies of government, they are also occurring in other organizations, including military establishments and labor unions (see Kerr et al. 1960).

Most of these changes imply a rationalization of leadership in organizations that is consistent with Weber's (1922a) model of bureaucratic leadership. However, further changes in the way leaders exercise control are likely to accompany this rationalization, and these represent a divergence from the classical bureaucratic model. For example, leaders may rely on discussion and persuasion rather than exclusively on command. Attempts may be made to elicit cooperation, sometimes by having organization members participate in the making of decisions that affect them in the work place. The rising level of education of the work force contributes to this trend. Furthermore, professional managers are more inclined than their predecessors to consider the results of social research, which have supported the growth of "human relations" approaches to leadership in organizations. At the same time, political developments, particularly in some European countries, have led to the introduction of schemes for co-management and of workers' councils, with varying degrees of success (Emery & Thorsrud 1964; Meister 1964; Sturmthal 1964). These developments may not be fully consolidated in any contemporary society, but at least incipient support can be found in many organizations for less autocratic approaches to leadership than those that were customary in the past. A survey in 14 industrialized and developing nations, for example, shows that managers overwhelmingly subscribe at least to the idea of participation in decision making, although they express skepticism about workers' capacities to assume the responsibilities consonant with democratic leadership (Haire et al. 1963).

Taken together, these developments imply the growth—actual in some places, potential in others—of new types of leadership in addition to those prevalent in the past. Partly as a consequence of this trend and of developments in research, sociological conceptions have been broadened. This can be observed in a number of related issues.

Leader power. Many of the limitations of traditional leadership conceptions stem from assumptions about the social context within which leadership operates and about the character of power, which is the essence of leadership. One such assumption is that the context is one of conflict, in which the relative power of leaders and others is at stake. It is further assumed that the total amount of power in a social system is a fixed quantity and that leaders and followers are engaged in a "zero-sum game"—that is, an increase in the power of one party must be accompanied by a corresponding decrease in the power of the other. Contemporary social scientists are more inclined than their predecessors to question the generality of these assumptions (Likert 1961; Parsons 1963; Tannenbaum 1966, pp. 95–100). The total amount of power in a relational system may grow, and leaders and followers may therefore enhance their power jointly. Total power may also decline, and all groups within the system may suffer corresponding decreases.

Another view common to traditional analyses argues that the leadership process is unilateral: one either leads or is led, is strong or is weak, controls or is controlled. Georg Simmel, in spite of his general adherence to the traditional conflict view of leadership, noted a more subtle interaction underlying the appearance of "pure superiority" on the part of the leader and the "purely passive being led" of the follower: "All leaders are also led; in innumerable cases the master is the slave of his slaves" ([1902–1917] 1950, p. 185; contrast *ibid.*, p. 193). Contemporary analyses of leadership are more likely than earlier ones to consider relationships of mutual as well as unilateral power, of followers influencing leaders as well as vice versa.

An accompanying change has taken place in analyses of the bases of leaders' power. Coercion has played a prominent role in traditional analyses, consistent with the presumed conflict between leaders and followers. According to the traditional view, leaders are obeyed out of fear of punishment or out of hope for reward. Machiavelli, for example, advised his prince concerning the proper balancing of injuries and benefits to subjects. The leader who finds it necessary to commit injuries should do so quickly in order to minimize resentment. On the other hand, he should dispense rewards in small doses over time so that their effects will be enjoyed longer.

Weber, however, argued that the stability of social systems depends on acceptance by followers of the right of leaders to exercise control. This implied *legitimate* authority; and Weber (1922b) defined three types, all of which share a prominent position in sociological analyses of leadership. The first type is *charismatic authority*, according to which leaders are thought to be endowed with extraordinary, sometimes magical powers. Charisma on the part of a leader elicits obedience out of awe. It is illustrated in its pure form by the prophet, the warrior hero, and the great demagogue. Second, *traditional authority* appertains to those who possess the right to rule by virtue of birth or class. The traditional leader is obeyed because he or members of his class or family have *always* been followed. Its pure type is illustrated by certain patriarchs, monarchs, and feudal lords. The third type, *legal authority*, applies to those who hold leadership positions because of demonstrated technical competence. Legal authorities act impersonally, as instruments of the law, and they are obeyed impersonally out of a sense of duty to the law. Leadership in the ideal-type bureaucracy is based exclusively on legal authority.

The character of leadership envisioned within Weber's framework is still consistent with many of the traditional analyses; his leaders are prophets, warriors, demagogues, patriarchs, lords, and bureaucrats. More recent analyses have stressed bases of power in addition to those outlined by Weber.

Simon, for example, points to the importance of *social approval*. Approval and disapproval represent forms of reward and punishment, but they deserve special consideration, since they are frequently dispensed not only by the designated leader but by others as well (1957, pp. 105–106). Thus, a subordinate may obey a leader not so much because of the rewards and punishments meted out by the leader as because of the approval and disapproval given by the subordinate's own peers. *Confidence* may represent a further basis for acceptance of leaders' authority (*ibid.*, p. 106): a subordinate may trust the judgment, and therefore accept the authority, of a leader in areas where the leader has great technical competence. French and Raven (1959) make a further distinction between influence of a leader based on confidence by subordinates in the leader's expert knowledge, on the one hand, and "informational influence" based on acceptance by subordinates of the logic of the arguments which the leader offers, on the other. An expert leader, then, may be followed not simply because he is an acknowledged authority but because his decisions, being based on expertise, are manifestly logical, appropriate, and convincing; that is, subordinates are persuaded that the decisions are correct. This view is related to human relations approaches, which stress control by facts as opposed to control by men. Such "fact control" relies on *understanding*, and it is illustrated by the participative leader who influences subordinates by helping them understand the facts of a situation so that they may jointly arrive at a course of action consistent with their own interests and that of the collectivity. Some of these conceptions represent radical departures from many traditional ones, assuming as they do an overriding community of interests between leaders and followers.

Leaders and followers. The term "leader" has traditionally implied a person clearly distinguished from others in power, status, visibility, and in any of a number of character traits, such as decisiveness, courage, integrity, and intelligence. However, contemporary changes in assumptions, in the direction of recognizing both mutual influence between leaders and followers and the possibility of increasing total power, have led to some lack of clarity in the lines of demarcation between leaders and others. Human relations and participative approaches to leadership, which de-emphasize status and stress the community of interests among all members of the collectivity, also blur the conceptual distinction between leaders and followers. The results of research have added to this ambiguity.

First, little evidence has been found for the existence of universal character traits that define the essential and distinguishing qualities of leadership. This has strengthened the position of those "situationalists" who argue that the relevance of a trait will depend on the specific situation in which leadership occurs. Furthermore, while leaders in similar situations may share *some* relevant characteristics, they are also very likely to differ on others, so that their total personalities will certainly differ. Research also suggests that traits (e.g., intelligence) that may suit an individual to some leadership roles are likely to be distributed continuously in a population rather than dichotomously. Nor is there any basis for assuming that the traits pertinent to many leadership roles are so rare that large numbers of persons differing widely in total personalities would be ineligible for leadership positions.

As a group, therefore, leaders need not be alike, nor need they be distinguished sharply from followers. These conclusions are consistent, in some of their implications, with the changing character of leadership itself, in which the broad recruitment and trainability of leaders is stressed. Leadership abilities need not be an exclusive possession of narrowly defined types or classes of individuals. Many persons, given proper training, can perform a wide range of leadership functions.

Research has had a further effect on the conceptual distinction between leaders and followers. In terms of the operational criteria used to define and measure leadership behavior, many presumed followers are found to act in some degree like leaders and vice versa. Furthermore, the *same* individual may manifest different degrees of leadership behavior. He may be a leader at one point in time, not at another. He may be a leader relative to certain areas of collective action, not others. Leadership, then, is best understood as a matter of degree; it may be distributed in varying degrees throughout a social system. These interpretations call attention to leadership as a social function rather than simply as a property of an individual. While persons who perform leadership functions must have appropriate skills and qualities of character if they are to perform well, the *distribution* of leadership in collectivities and the variety of situations in which leadership occurs suggest some variety in the types of persons who can fulfill leadership functions [*see* GROUPS, *article on* ROLE STRUCTURE].

The concept of leadership should be understood as encompassing a wide range of activities. It applies to the running of small groups and the governing of nations. It may concern the relatively diffuse process of influence in establishing norms of style or opinion—or it may involve specific orders in a chain of command. It includes supervision and statesmanship, routine administration and organization building. Interpretations of leadership as a sociological concept have changed over the years. The total effort of sociologists can be seen as an attempt to develop conceptions that apply to a variety of social systems, including those that prevailed in the past as well as those now emerging. The need for more general conceptions is also felt as a need to understand leadership within the widely differing social and political contexts that exist in the modern world.

ARNOLD S. TANNENBAUM

[*Directly related are the entries* DIFFUSION, *article on* INTERPERSONAL INFLUENCE; INDUSTRIAL RELATIONS; ORGANIZATIONS, *article on* THEORIES OF ORGANIZATIONS. *Other relevant material may be found in* ADMINISTRATION; AUTHORITY; DEMOCRACY; *and in the biographies of* MACHIAVELLI; MICHELS; MILLS; MOSCA; SIMMEL; WEBER, MAX.]

BIBLIOGRAPHY

For definitions, reviews, and discussions of leadership see Schmidt 1933; Gouldner 1950; Gibb 1954; Rouček 1947. Bass 1960 *provides a thorough review of laboratory research as well as the research on leadership in organizations. For a classic expression of the great man theory of leadership, see* Carlyle 1841. Plekhanov 1898 *offers a critique of the great man view. Critiques of elite theories can be found in* Dahl 1958 *and in* Harbison & Myers 1959, *which also presents a detailed discussion of changes in industrial management and in social and political leader-*

ship brought about by industrialization. Bendix 1956 *provides a review of traditional and more recent leadership ideologies as applied to industrial management in western and eastern Europe and the United States.* Dahrendorf 1957 *and* Parsons 1963 *discuss the issue of power in collectivities as a zero-sum game. Leadership under conditions of mutual influence and increasing total power (non-zero-sum) is illustrated by the principles of* "co-optation" Selznick 1949; *"participative management"* March & Simon 1958; *"interaction influence system"* Likert 1961; *"organic" as opposed to "mechanistic" organization* Burns & Stalker 1961; *and by the concept of high "total control"* Tannenbaum & Kahn 1957 *and* Tannenbaum 1966. *The trait theory of leadership remains controversial.* Rainio 1955, *in a review of some of the American and European literature, lists 99 traits that are presumed by various authors to represent the essential qualities of leadership. See* Bogardus 1934 *and* Urwick 1957 *for illustrations of the trait approach; see* Bavelas 1960 *for a critique.*

BASS, BERNARD M. 1960 *Leadership, Psychology, and Organizational Behavior.* New York: Harper.

BAVELAS, ALEX 1960 Leadership: Man and Function. *Administrative Science Quarterly* 4:491–498.

BELL, DANIEL 1950 Notes on Authoritarian and Democratic Leadership. Pages 395–408 in Alvin W. Gouldner (editor), *Studies in Leadership: Leadership and Democratic Action.* New York: Harper.

BENDIX, REINHARD 1956 *Work and Authority in Industry: Ideologies of Management in the Course of Industrialization.* New York: Wiley.

BOGARDUS, EMORY S. 1934 *Leaders and Leadership.* New York: Appleton.

BURNS, TOM; and STALKER, GEORGE M. 1961 *The Management of Innovation.* London: Tavistock.

CARLYLE, THOMAS (1841) 1928 *On Heroes, Hero-worship and the Heroic in History.* London: Oxford Univ. Press.

CARTWRIGHT, DORWIN 1965 Influence, Leadership, Control. Pages 1–47 in James G. March (editor), *Handbook of Organizations.* Chicago: Rand McNally.

DAHL, ROBERT A. 1958 A Critique of the Ruling Elite Model. *American Political Science Review* 52:463–469.

DAHRENDORF, RALF (1957) 1959 *Class and Class Conflict in Industrial Society.* Rev. & enl. ed. Stanford Univ. Press. → First published as *Soziale Klassen und Klassen-Konflikt in der industriellen Gesellschaft.* See especially pages 165–173 for a discussion of the issue of power in collectivities as a zero-sum game.

EMERY, FREDERICK E.; and THORSRUD, E. 1964 *Industrielt demokrati.* Oslo: Universitets-forlaget.

FOURASTIÉ, JEAN; and VIMONT, CLAUDE 1956 *Histoire de demain.* Paris: Presses Universitaires de France.

FRENCH, JOHN R. P.; and RAVEN, BERTRAM 1959 The Bases of Social Power. Pages 150–167 in Dorwin Cartwright (editor), *Studies in Social Power.* Research Center for Group Dynamics, Publication No. 6. Ann Arbor: Univ. of Michigan, Institute for Social Research.

GIBB, CECIL A. 1954 Leadership. Volume 2, pages 877–920 in Gardner Lindzey (editor), *Handbook of Social Psychology.* Cambridge, Mass.: Addison-Wesley.

GOULDNER, ALVIN W. (editor) 1950 *Studies in Leadership: Leadership and Democratic Action.* New York: Harper.

HAIRE, MASON; GHISELLI, EDWIN E.; and PORTER, LYMAN W. 1963 An International Study of Management Attitudes and Democratic Leadership. Pages 101–104 in International Congress for Scientific Management, Thirteenth, New York, 1963, *Proceedings.* New York: Council for International Progress in Management.

HARBISON, FREDERICK H.; and MYERS, CHARLES A. 1959 *Management in the Industrial World: An International Analysis.* Princeton University, Industrial Relations Section. New York: McGraw-Hill.

KERR, CLARK et al. 1960 *Industrialism and Industrial Man: The Problems of Labor and Management in Economic Growth.* Cambridge, Mass.: Harvard Univ. Press. → A second edition was published in paperback in 1964 by Oxford Univ. Press.

LIKERT, RENSIS 1961 *New Patterns of Management.* New York: McGraw-Hill.

MARCH, JAMES G.; and SIMON, HERBERT A. 1958 *Organizations.* New York: Wiley. → Contains an extensive bibliography.

MEISTER, ALBERT 1964 *Socialisme et autogestion: L'expérience yougoslave.* Paris: Éditions du Seuil.

MICHELS, ROBERT (1911) 1959 *Political Parties: A Sociological Study of the Oligarchical Tendencies of Modern Democracy.* New York: Dover. → First published as *Zur Soziologie des Parteiwesens in der modernen Demokratie.* A paperback edition was published in 1962 by Collier.

MILLS, C. WRIGHT 1956 *The Power Elite.* New York: Oxford Univ. Press.

MOSCA, GAETANO (1896) 1939 *The Ruling Class (Elementi di scienza politica).* New York: McGraw-Hill. → First published in Italian.

PARSONS, TALCOTT 1963 On the Concept of Political Power. American Philosophical Society, *Proceedings* 107:232–262.

PLEKHANOV, GEORGE (1898) 1940 *The Role of the Individual in History.* New York: International Publishers. → First published in Russian.

RAINIO, KULLERVO 1955 Leadership Qualities: A Theoretical Inquiry and an Experimental Study on Foremen. Suomalainen Tiedeakatemia, Helsingfors, *Toimituksia: Annales* Series B 95, no. 1.

ROUČEK, JOSEPH S. (1947) 1956 *Social Control.* 2d ed. Princeton, N.J.: Van Nostrand.

SCHMIDT, RICHARD 1933 Leadership. Volume 9, pages 282–287 in *Encyclopaedia of the Social Sciences.* New York: Macmillan.

SELZNICK, PHILIP 1949 *TVA and the Grass Roots: A Study in the Sociology of Formal Organization.* University of California Publications in Culture and Society, Vol. 3. Berkeley: Univ. of California Press.

SELZNICK, PHILIP 1957 *Leadership in Administration: A Sociological Interpretation.* Evanston, Ill.: Row, Peterson.

SIMMEL, GEORG (1902–1917) 1950 *The Sociology of Georg Simmel.* Edited and translated by Kurt H. Wolff. Glencoe, Ill.: Free Press.

SIMON, HERBERT A. 1957 Authority. Pages 103–118 in Industrial Relations Research Association, *Research in Industrial Human Relations: A Critical Appraisal.* New York: Harper.

STURMTHAL, ADOLF F. 1964 *Workers' Councils: A Study of Workplace Organization on Both Sides of the Iron Curtain.* Cambridge, Mass.: Harvard Univ. Press.

TANNENBAUM, ARNOLD S. 1966 *Social Psychology of the Work Organization.* Belmont, Calif.: Wadsworth.

TANNENBAUM, ARNOLD S.; and KAHN, ROBERT L. 1957 Organizational Control Structure: A General Descriptive Technique as Applied to Four Local Unions. *Human Relations* 10:127–140.

URWICK, LYNDALL 1957 *Leadership in the 20th Century.* New York: Pitman.

WEBER, MAX (1922a) 1957 *The Theory of Social and Economic Organization.* Edited by Talcott Parsons. Glencoe, Ill.: Free Press. → First published as Part 1 of *Wirtschaft und Gesellschaft.*

WEBER, MAX (1922b) 1961 The Three Types of Legitimate Rule. Pages 4–14 in Amitai Etzioni (editor), *Complex Organizations: A Sociological Reader.* New York: Holt. → First published in German.

III

POLITICAL ASPECTS

By the middle of the twentieth century, in new nations and old, social and economic changes had imposed on all regimes new demands that resulted in greatly augmenting the power of executive leaders. Prime ministers and presidents, not legislators, were asked to supply the innovation and integration that these situations demanded.

In democratic regimes the executive is no longer merely an arm of government but has become the organizing center of the political system itself. A parliamentary regime in France was transformed into Charles de Gaulle's executive rule. West German politics were stabilized by Konrad Adenauer's shrewd balancing. British politics, in the opinion of some, has been transformed from cabinet government to prime-ministerial government. In the United States the president and the presidential corps have become the fulcrum of politics.

In many emerging nations, democratic forms of government, which have only recently been instituted, are precariously sustained by dramatic executive leaders who rule by mass appeal and the exercise of broad political powers. Fragile identifications with the new national entities are nurtured by mass loyalty to the leader. By personifying the new national values and giving a relentless drive to development, executive leaders energize the mobilized advance of these societies.

Twentieth-century social thought has expressed the paradox that leadership is a solution to the problems of both excessive and insufficient political power. Strong executive leadership was offered as a solution to two general and characteristic maladies of political systems. First, the ideologists of authoritarian movements and regimes proposed strong leadership as a substitute for atrophied traditional primary-group identifications—community, church, family, etc. The breakdown of traditional norm-fostering groups, they argued, leaves society open to conflicts that could be overcome or avoided by strong identification with political leaders. This was a seminal explanation of fascist and communist movements in Western industrial systems and of nationalist movements in preindustrial, developing countries.

Another ideological premise was that only effective leadership can furnish integrative direction and action as a cure for the stalemated pluralism endemic to Western democratic systems. Competing interests wear down consensus and paralyze national decision making. The pathology of political pluralism, the argument ran, is *immobilism.* Under such conditions, only strong executive leadership can furnish decisive national purpose. The most striking recent illustration has been the ideological justification surrounding the presidency of de Gaulle in France. Weaker but nonetheless insistent echoes of this ideology reverberate in the justifications for increasing the powers of other democratic chief executives—the American president, the British prime minister, and the German chancellor.

This integrative function of leadership is fulfilled by two political role types. One is the national hero—the chief executive as personification and representative of the "general will" or "higher interest" of the nation. De Gaulle and the leaders of many emerging nations exemplify this type. Like Rousseau's legislator, such populist figures stand above politics and particular interests. The second is the executive as political broker or artful synthesizer, exemplified by Franklin D. Roosevelt, that is, the expert manager of interests and builder of coalitions.

These two roles are distinct but not mutually exclusive. Each has its relevance in different political systems at particular times. The "general will" spokesman is called into power when national consensus becomes problematical; the "broker" comes to power when a viable consensus exists, unthreatened by polarizing and uncompromisable conflicts—when the management of interest conflicts is the compelling need. To some extent every chief executive must fulfill both roles.

Leadership theory and political executives

The principal functions of chief executives may vary, but all are responses to leadership demands and expectations by the led. Hence, understanding of executive behavior depends in large measure on understanding the phenomenon called leadership.

Historically, the concept of leadership was derived from leadership in a religious sectarian setting or in groups of primary relationships. Sectarian followings inspired by prophetic figures have been at the genesis of many religious movements. Moses, Muhammad, Jesus, Calvin, and many others are illustrative. The solitary, dramatic personality who mobilized and inspired masses to new goals and methods of religious salvation became an important prototype of leadership.

This conceptual view was reinforced by research on historical and primitive governmental institutions, e.g., tribal chiefs and leaders of small city-states, vested with absolute authority. Such studies also contributed the notion of status and hierarchy to the concept of leadership. Power was vested in the *status*, as well as in the person, of a ruler. The personalization of leadership was thus further reinforced.

By the twentieth century several intellectual trends had already effected a change in this conception of leadership. First, the democratic revolution of the eighteenth and nineteenth centuries depersonalized the concept of authority. Power, prescribed and defined in constitutions and law, was vested in the *office*, not the person. The scope and jurisdiction of public officials were given limits in law, so that arbitrary power could be prevented. Rules about leadership succession were specified, to check seizures of power by violence. Office set boundaries to personal influence, and the institutionalization of the executive was firmly implanted.

Second, the positivistic influence of the social sciences drastically modified the concept of political leadership. The traditional "hero" disappeared in the face of new views of psychology. The prevailing instinct-and-trait psychology gave way before the critiques of Mead, Cooley, Dewey, and others and their conceptions of a variable human behavior molded by social interaction. Leadership came to be viewed, not as a set of fixed traits and attributes, biologically peculiar to some individuals, but as a role that satisfies mutual expectations of leaders and followers.

Building on this new, interactional emphasis, research in the social sciences (invigorated by experimental emphasis) added increasing sophistication to the concept of leadership. Situational and group components were strongly emphasized. The leadership role was found to vary with situations. Leaders are always, covertly or overtly, "preselected" by their supporters according to the situational needs of the group. Leadership is a nexus of need fulfillments that binds situational demands and group membership. Thus, during crisis situations groups are likely to select leaders who diagnose problems quickly and act decisively. During less critical periods, leaders who can maintain cohesion and regularity of group performance may be preferred.

Another factor was given emphasis: group goals. Leadership is a differentiated role that enables group purposes to be realized. Where a group is task oriented, leadership integrates the members so that individual needs and group performance can be enhanced. Groups with other purposes choose leaders of another type.

Much insight on leadership is derived from experimentation with and observation of small groups. However, problems arise when such "micro" research is elevated to the "macro" level of many political science concerns. Can insights about leadership that are derived from small-group situations be extrapolated to large units or systems as a whole? Certainly, small-group situations are not replications of nation-state political systems. The danger of such extrapolations has been widely recognized, but general agreement exists that small-group leadership can provide suggestive simulations and simplifications for studying larger units. [*See* GROUPS.]

Characteristics of executive leadership. Analysis of the leadership of chief executives or of national political executives poses special problems to the social science analyst. In contrast to leadership in small-group situations, executive leadership is distinguishable by at least the following: (1) it is leadership at a distance; (2) it has a multirole character; (3) it has a corporate character; (4) it functions in an institutional framework.

If leadership is an interactional relationship, then the relationship between the chief executive of a modern state and his public supporters has the unique character of being leadership at a distance, where neither leader nor follower has *direct* impact upon the other. The relationship is mediated by mass communications, organized groups, and individuals. The leader is linked to his supporters by people who play many roles on various levels of the political system. The relationship between followers and leader is at some remove and therefore indirect. When Harry Truman ordered an atomic bomb dropped on Hiroshima, he could not see the consequences of his decision on the victims nor could he receive the immediate feedback.

Executive behavior is multirole conduct, fulfilling a variety of expectations that flow from various clienteles—from those immediately around the executive, from political parties and political associations, from the various bureaucracies and their political networks, and from the general public. One of the major tasks facing a chief executive is maintaining these different roles in balance. Role expectations are met by various techniques of reconciliation, e.g., by assigning priorities to various roles, minimizing some and stressing others; by insulating incompatible ones from each other; by delegating some and reserving others. What we have come to call the "style" of leadership has its referents in patterns of role management.

Modern executive leadership is an organizational process. The American presidency, the French presidency, and the British office of prime minister are corporate entities, consisting of a sizable staff. In such an organizational context, "leadership" may be attributed to an individual but it is in reality a collective product of organizational activity. It is generically distinct from the leader–led relationships of small-scale situations.

In its organizational context, executive leadership presents a complex face. The chief executive today has become a symbolic individual, whose many roles are collectively filled by several men. If the chief executive is expected to make programmatic statements in some policy area, then corps of experts and speech writers are grouped to produce such a statement. Before the executive makes decisions, various people, playing specific and general roles, define the situation and its alternatives for him. His manifold duties are all largely carried out *in his name by others*. Executive leadership has become institutionalized.

This inner leadership group or staff may be called the executive elite. All executives are dependent upon such a collective formation to perform their tasks. In the United States, for example, it is composed of several groups, some formally organized and some informal. Included among these are the White House staff, the Bureau of the Budget, the Council of Economic Advisors, the National Security Council, and many specialists and *ad hoc* committees. Various presidents have organized and used these cadres in different ways, depending on their interpretations of their roles. In Great Britain, Churchill instituted the so-called Statistical Section, the prime minister's brain trust. Numerous cabinet committees have been established, as well as staff agencies to coordinate the work of the prime minister and the cabinet.

Finally, executive leadership is a process that operates within an institutional framework. At any given time there are prescribed norms that bound and define the scope of authority and the channels of its exercise. These limits are fairly elastic. The chief executive, by the style of his operation, stretches or contracts the boundaries of the position. When the boundaries are exceeded, crisis exigency must justify the practice. At other times, executive boundary aggrandizement is resisted and can be accomplished only by skillful political bargaining on the part of the chief executive.

Because of its corporate and institutional character, the office itself is not wholly dependent upon its occupant. A cumulative heritage of decision and expectation has established precedents that make much of an executive's conduct predictable. This cumulative institutionalization of the office supplies continuity to all executive positions. Cases of sudden death or disability of the chief executive have demonstrated that the office functions in the absence of its principal. Such situations dramatically illustrate the fact that, while in normal times the corporate entity called executive leadership is sensitive to situational demands, it also has a degree of trained "insensitivity" and routine which gives it stability and continuity.

Some doubts have been raised as to whether this cumulative institutionalization might jeopardize executive capacity for decision. The growth in personal agents and *ad hoc* groups testifies to the vigor with which executives strive to prevent over-encumbrance by bureaucratization.

Legitimations of executive behavior

The structure of executive leadership is complex because of its multirole, organizational, and institutional context. This complex structure relies on diverse legitimations for support. [*See* LEGITIMACY.] Generally, the democratic chief executive is legitimated by his identification with the central values of his social system, both nonpolitical and political; by the manner in which he is recruited; by the symbolic and effective representation he bestows; and by his decision-making performance.

Societal and political values. Chief executives are legitimated by their identification with the most pervasive goals in society—that is, their embodiment of a national consensus. Thus, Adenauer personified rebirth of the German republic, in keeping with a pre-Nazi, republican past. De Gaulle was in part legitimized by his absorption with a romantic restoration of French glory and power. The sacred values of the system, those beyond dispute, must be expressed and epitomized by the chief executive.

The *political* goals of the executive must conform to the traditional political value system. Even the most innovating and precedent-shattering presidents and prime ministers affirm their adherence to the traditional substantive political values of the system. In Western democracies the chief executives must also affirm their adherence to procedural values—popular consent, parliamentary representation, majority rule, and civil liberties. They must profess respect for, and act in accordance with, the traditional continuities of the system.

Recruitment. The manner in which executives are recruited and elected provides an important basis of their legitimation. In normal times their nomination and election reflect their acceptability to party elites and the general public. Recruitment methods chart career paths and provide a test of the skills regarded as requisite. Most American presidents have been middle-class professionals, usually chosen from the echelon of governors of the leading states. The path to the post of British prime minister has been open to those of a certain social status, educational background, and parliamentary and cabinet career. The path of political mobility reaffirms the central values of the system. [See POLITICAL RECRUITMENT AND CAREERS.]

In the United States, as an expression of American egalitarian beliefs, it was expected that a president should rise from humble origins. He would thus embody the American ideal of success by achievement and competence rather than because of family status. The same ethos influences presidential appointments to staff and cabinet.

During periods of crisis or stalemate, recruitment patterns are disrupted. Then chief executives may be co-opted from outside conventional grooves and without the usual political experience, as was the case with de Gaulle in France. Such deviations from established patterns are legitimated by crisis needs and have themselves become a "tradition."

Symbolic and effective representation. The chief executive must represent or appear to represent the public at large *and* its various component segments. He does this in several ways. A common method is the appointment of spokesmen of various groups to his cabinet and to leading offices. Another method gives group representation through an executive staff accessible to various interests.

Another facet of representation by a chief executive may be called "apparent" representation. This is expressed in the many subtle forms of symbolic recognition bestowed by the chief executive upon various groups in the population. When the prime minister of England sends messages to conventions and when the president of the United States greets group delegations of many kinds, they are conferring status and symbolic recognition.

Both apparent and effective representation by the executive are important, because there are general expectations of access and status. The chief executive's audience and clientele must be (at least in a symbolic way) *all* the consensual groups in the system. [See REPRESENTATION.]

Decision making. Finally, the chief executive is legitimated by his decision-making performance. Despite overarching "sacred" authority, the effective influence of the chief executive is tested by his capacity to carry out certain policies. The failure or success of his leadership depends upon his effectiveness in knitting together political influence so that it responds to functional demands of the system. It is to this decision-making aspect of executive leadership that the greatest analytical attention has been devoted in recent years. [See DECISION MAKING, *article on* POLITICAL ASPECTS.]

Dilemmas of legitimation. The more chief executives are expected to perform, the greater the contradictory pressures which confront them. Crises of legitimation arise when acute tensions develop between several levels of legitimation. A political position that is legitimized by sacred values for what it "is" encounters dilemmas when it is called upon to "do." Despite the secularizing separation between politics and religion, overmoralization of politics makes political tasks delicate. The holders of public office carry the burden of excessive expectations of rectitude and exemplary conduct, yet they are also expected to behave expediently in order to be responsive to public demands.

Another dilemma that confronts chief executives arises from the gap between the executive elite and the public. They must bridge the social and political distance between their special knowledge and the need for responsiveness by the public. The executives must wear different faces at different stages of the policy-making process: when they formulate policies; when they settle for those that are acceptable; and when they implement the accepted ones.

Another dilemma arises out of the conflict between the expectations of the status or position and the political capabilities to fulfill such expectations. Often the public simplifies and exaggerates expectations of executive action. Yet the modern executive in democratic societies is limited by law, administrative organization, group resistances, and the climate of opinion from fulfilling such expectations. Status and influence are not equivalents, and many chief executives fail because their power is not commensurate with their status.

Efforts to resolve these dilemmas of legitimation generate new roles for members of the executive elite. Executives need "buffers" and "catalysts," expert bargainers whose freewheeling, unofficial conduct, is screened off from usual scrutiny. The appearance of rectitude can be maintained as long as the occupational "dirty work" is performed by executive agents.

Dilemmas are also resolved by the executive's efforts to control public expectations. The modern chief executive has become a direct communicator with the public, in order to manage and control public attitudes effectively. The skillful use of the press, radio, and television by chief executives invites identification, which can then be used as a political weapon against resistant and parochial bureaucracies, groups of legislators, or group interests.

Research on executive behavior

Some twenty years ago a shock of realization occurred among students of executive behavior with the discovery that executive behavior deviated from its institutional prescriptions and descriptions. The rigid compartmentalization of government action implied in the separation of powers was found not to exist in fact. This principle, regarded by Montesquieu and Locke as a cardinal check to absolute power, did not realistically describe what occurred. Executive and legislative action closely interpenetrated. Moreover, the modern nation-state more and more demanded the closer integration of these functions, rather than their separation.

Dichotomous categories such as "politics" and "administration" were found to be inaccurate and insufficient for the explanation of decision making. "Administrative" behavior was found to be, not a discrete type of behavior, distinct from "political" activity, but part of a continuous stream of action in a large-scale organizational environment. [*See* ADMINISTRATION.]

While such older categorizations were thus discredited, newer concepts and models were developing, of deeper and more empirical explanatory power. Decision making and systems theory were two such models. Herbert Simon, Richard Snyder, and others elaborated decision-making models that dissected the individual, organizational, and situational components of decision making and linked them together in causal propositions. The focus of analysis shifted away from the policies themselves toward the complexities of the processes of policy making. The "how" of decisions gave more significant clues to the organization of influence in modern governmental structures than the metaphysical "what."

Not all effort was bent on model building. Much analysis of executive behavior took the form of case studies. Many of these were narrative and descriptive, designed to illustrate and depict the variegated paths of policy formation. Some contended that many of these case studies relied on recollection, hearsay, and other questionable evidence and therefore could not be considered more than illustrative. They were also criticized for their overemphasis on the idiosyncratic and the unique, a fragile basis for theory building. Despite such limitations, in the building stages of more systematic analysis, case studies communicated a sense of executive milieu that contributed to suggestive hypotheses. [*See* PUBLIC ADMINISTRATION.]

Another approach in analyzing executive behavior proceeded from institutional frameworks and demonstrated how executive behavior departed from such institutional presumptions. The work of Richard Neustadt and Don Price, among others, exemplified this category. This type of analysis was rich in insight about the interplay between the less formal and more formal factors which condition and influence executive authority.

Situational analysis. Still another way of analyzing executive behavior stressed situational factors. It proceeded from the multirole character of executive behavior in its organizational context as it confronted characteristic problem situations. Illustrative of this are the following situational typologies, derived from American governmental experience.

Executive decisions may be divided into three situational types: (1) crisis situations; (2) programmatic situations; (3) anticipatory situations. In each situation interest groups, the executive, and the presidential elite play varying roles.

Crisis situations. Under crisis conditions, public opinion is more aware of the situation, but legislative and interest-group involvement is less than in programmatic or anticipatory situations; and in these stress situations, executive discretion is greatest.

Crisis situations, which have become quite frequent in the post-1945 world, can be categorized as follows: bargaining crises (e.g., industrial disputes); legitimacy crises (e.g., the dismissal of MacArthur); crises of norms (e.g., scandals of various kinds, such as the Profumo affair); and, by far the most frequent and serious, national defense crises (situations which acutely threaten resources regarded as essential to national safety, e.g., the Cuban missile standoff and the Berlin airlift).

In crisis situations each system, in varying degrees, loses some of its pluralistic safeguards as the executive assumes broad discretion. The executive acquires exclusive control in defining the situation and in directing the appropriate measures. The normal institutional workings of decision making are reduced to an executive directorate consisting of a handful of people. The public is anxiously alert but little informed, while the legislative bodies and interest groups assume passive roles. In sum, crisis situations bring structural changes in the system that give the broadest of authority to the executive. [*See* CRISIS; CRISIS GOVERNMENT.]

Programmatic situations. Programmatic situations demand long-range and broad-gauge policies. They require strategic determinations of ends and means. When programmatic issues are faced, a moderate degree of legislative and bureaucratic involvement results and executive discretion is limited. The Marshall Plan of the United States and the European Defense Community decisions by European governments are examples.

Anticipatory situations. Anticipatory situations concern eventualities, not immediate situations. The likelihood of occurrence may not be great, but should the situation occur, a course of action will have been decided upon. Of all situations, these evoke the greatest legislative debate, the least public awareness, and the greatest interest-group concern. Executive discretion is severely limited under these conditions, because the costs of inaction arc difficult to foretell and the consequences are not close at hand.

Anticipatory situations are the result of previous crises. For example, the depression of the 1930s gave rise both to legislation and to administrative policies that anticipated a recurrence and were therefore designed to come into play when economic danger signals appeared. Programs such as the federal insurance of deposits in savings banks and the public works agendas to be used when unemployment reaches certain levels were created.

Problems of executive behavior

Within the three situational configurations described above, there are problems of executive behavior which flow from certain structural features of the system itself. Insufficient recognition has been given to the subgroups within the executive. It is traditional to think of the executive and governmental bureaucracy in hierarchic terms. In this view, the president or prime minister stands at the pinnacle of the executive, and below him are the administrators, ranged in a descending order of subordination. The enlargement of executive scope gave rise to centrifugal tendencies that diffused executive influence. The bureaucracies,

which ostensibly enlarge executive jurisdiction, in fact dilute and disperse executive influence. These bureaucratic groups have their own biases and often act autonomously and at variance with executive policies.

As a result, a problem that executives face is the "horizontal bargaining" *within* the executive. Not uncommonly the executive has to negotiate with his nominally subordinate agencies. Governmental bureaucracy is pluralistic, so that each bureaucracy has its own subvalues. Out of the long-accrued interdependence between the bureaucracies and legislative and economic interests, the bureaucrats have gained considerable independence of executive authority, and a growing political division occurs between the executive and the governmental bureaucracies normally under his jurisdiction. The internal politics of the executive in decision making has, perhaps, become more significant than executive–legislative relations. [*See* BUREAUCRACY *and* CIVIL SERVICE.]

At the outset of this article, the integrating and innovating functions of executive leadership in all political systems were stressed. These functions are closely related to the expectations of executive programs, i.e., the definition of broad political goals and specific legislative and administrative measures necessary to their fulfillment. Broad and consistent national programs for economic stability and growth, foreign policy strategy, defense postures, and welfare goals are expected of the chief executive. It is through these that the executive defines the situation for all the political actors.

The winning of acceptance for these programs demands accommodation to various political subgroups, whose focus is less on the general societal effects of legislative and administrative proposals than on the special effects these have upon their particular interests. This accommodation to specialized publics and interests is a serious executive problem. The "politics" of executive behavior is largely a matter of finding some synthesis, i.e., identity of interest or complementarity of roles, between the general viewpoint of the executive and the particular perspective of various groups.

In sum, despite institutionalized continuities, executive decision making forms not a single pattern but several situational patterns, in which the roles of bureaucracies, interest groups, parties, and legislators vary. The increase of both secular and acute crises has more sharply differentiated these modes of executive decision making.

The study of executive decision making reveals the several configurations of political systems as they respond to situational demands. In an era so prone to crisis as the present, the far-reaching consequences of crisis decision making deserve fuller attention than they have yet received. As we have seen, crisis decision making is not merely a slight shift but a change in configuration of the system itself. Studies are needed, both of these structural changes and of certain secondary effects, such as changes in elite recruitment, responses of the various bureaucracies, and capabilities of the executive for prompt decision making.

The subject of leadership and executive behavior in general should draw the increasing attention of social scientists. The gap between the significance of executive behavior and current explanatory methods calls for greater research attention. The wide use of aggregate data about executive behavior and of direct empirical studies of executives in various systems has not seriously begun. If executive centralization is the trend, it must be carefully analyzed so that its processes and consequences are better understood.

LESTER G. SELIGMAN

[*See also* POLITICAL EXECUTIVE. *Other relevant material may be found in* GOVERNMENT; POLITICAL BEHAVIOR; POLITICAL PROCESS; PRESIDENTIAL GOVERNMENT; PUBLIC POLICY.]

BIBLIOGRAPHY

ACHESON, DEAN 1956 Legislative–Executive Relations. *Yale Review* New Series 45:481–495.
BROWNLOW, LOUIS 1949 *The President and the Presidency.* Chicago: Public Administration Service.
BURNS, JAMES M. (1956) 1962 *Roosevelt: The Lion and the Fox.* New York: Harcourt.
CORWIN, EDWARD S.; and KOENIG, LOUIS W. 1956 *The Presidency Today.* New York Univ. Press.
FENNO, RICHARD F. JR. 1958 President–Cabinet Relations: A Pattern and a Case Study. *American Political Science Review* 52:388–405.
HERRING, E. PENDLETON 1940 *Presidential Leadership.* New York: Farrar & Rinehart.
HOBBS, EDWARD H. 1954 *Behind the President: A Study of Executive Office Agencies.* Washington: Public Affairs Press.
HOLCOMBE, ARTHUR M. 1954 Presidential Leadership and the Party System. *Yale Review* New Series 43: 321–335.
KAUFMAN, HERBERT 1956 Emerging Conflicts in the Doctrines of Public Administration. *American Political Science Review* 50:1057–1073.
KOENIG, LOUIS W. 1944 *The Presidency and the Crisis: Powers of the Office From the Invasion of Poland to Pearl Harbor.* New York: King's Crown Press.
LIPSON, LESLIE 1939 *The American Governor From Figurehead to Leader.* Studies in Public Administration, No. 9. Univ. of Chicago Press.
LITWAK, EUGENE 1961 Models of Bureaucracy Which Permit Conflict. *American Journal of Sociology* 67: 177–184.
LONGAKER, RICHARD P. 1956 The President as International Leader. *Law and Contemporary Problems* 21: 735–752.

MILTON, GEORGE F. (1944) 1965 *The Use of Presidential Power, 1789–1943.* New York: Octagon.
NEUSTADT, RICHARD E. 1955 Presidency and Legislation: Planning the President's Program. *American Political Science Review* 49:980–1021.
NEUSTADT, RICHARD E. 1956 The Presidency at Mid-century. *Law and Contemporary Problems* 21:609–645.
PROTHRO, JAMES W. 1956 Verbal Shifts in the American Presidency: A Content Analysis. *American Political Science Review* 50:726–739.
RANSONE, COLEMAN B. 1956 *The Office of Governor in the United States.* University: Univ. of Alabama Press.
REDFORD, EMMETT S. 1952 *Administration of National Economic Control.* New York: Macmillan.
ROSSITER, CLINTON L. (1956) 1960 *The American Presidency.* 2d ed. New York: Harcourt.
SCHUBERT, GLENDON 1957 The Public Interest in Administrative Decision-making: Theorem, Theosophy, or Theory? *American Political Science Review* 51: 346:368.
SELIGMAN, LESTER G. 1955 Developments in the Presidency and the Conception of Political Leadership. *American Sociological Review* 20:706–712.
SELIGMAN, LESTER G. 1956*a* The President Is Many Men. *Antioch Review* 16:305–318.
SELIGMAN, LESTER G. 1956*b* Presidential Leadership: The Inner Circle and Institutionalization. *Journal of Politics* 18:410–426.
SELIGMAN, LESTER G. 1956*c* The Presidential Office and the President as Party Leader. *Law and Contemporary Problems* 21:724–734.
SELVIN, HANAN C. 1960 *The Effects of Leadership.* Glencoe, Ill.: Free Press.
SILVA, RUTH C. 1956 Presidential Succession and Disability. *Law and Contemporary Problems* 21:646–662.
SMITH, M. BREWSTER 1952 Social Psychology and Group Processes. *Annual Review of Psychology* 3: 175–204.
SOMERS, HERMAN M. 1950 *Presidential Agency: OWMR, the Office of War Mobilization and Reconversion.* Cambridge, Mass.: Harvard Univ. Press.
STOGDILL, RALPH M. 1948 Personal Factors Associated With Leadership: A Survey of the Literature. *Journal of Psychology* 25:35–71.
STOKE, HAROLD W. 1941 Executive Leadership and the Growth of Propaganda. *American Political Science Review* 35:490–500.
TURNER, HENRY A. 1951 Woodrow Wilson: Exponent of Executive Leadership. *Western Political Quarterly* 4:97–115.
VERBA, SIDNEY 1961 *Small Groups and Political Behavior: A Study of Leadership.* Princeton Univ. Press.
WILDAVSKY, AARON B. 1964 *The Politics of the Budgetary Process.* Boston: Little.

LEARNING

In addition to the general articles under this heading, broad fields of learning phenomena are reviewed in FORGETTING; IMITATION; IMPRINTING; THINKING. *More specific concepts relevant to learning are discussed in* CONCEPT FORMATION; DRIVES; FATIGUE; INTELLIGENCE AND INTELLIGENCE TESTING; MOTIVATION; PROBLEM SOLVING; REASONING

AND LOGIC. *The role of learning in personal development is discussed in* DEVELOPMENTAL PSYCHOLOGY; INTELLECTUAL DEVELOPMENT; LANGUAGE, *article on* LANGUAGE DEVELOPMENT; MORAL DEVELOPMENT; SENSORY AND MOTOR DEVELOPMENT; SOCIALIZATION. *The role of learning in society is treated in* ADULT EDUCATION; EDUCATION; EDUCATIONAL PSYCHOLOGY; INTELLECTUALS; KNOWLEDGE, SOCIOLOGY OF; LITERACY; TEACHING; UNIVERSITIES. *The importance of learning is also emphasized in* MENTAL DISORDERS, TREATMENT OF. *Theories of learning are discussed in* GESTALT THEORY; INFORMATION THEORY; LEARNING THEORY; MODELS, MATHEMATICAL. *Some applications of learning are discussed in* BRAINWASHING; COMMUNICATION, MASS; COMMUNICATION, POLITICAL; PERSUASION; PROPAGANDA. *The measurement of learning is discussed in* ACHIEVEMENT TESTING; INTELLIGENCE AND INTELLIGENCE TESTING; RESPONSE SETS. *Of direct relevance to learning are the biographies of* BEKHTEREV; GUTHRIE; HULL; MONTESSORI; PAVLOV; SECHENOV; TOLMAN; WATSON.

I
INTRODUCTION

Learning has been defined (Kimble 1961) as a relatively permanent change in a behavioral tendency, which occurs as a result of reinforced practice. One purpose of this definition, as with any definition, is to delimit as precisely as possible a particular realm of discourse. Thus, a word or two appears to be in order with respect to topics that this definition specifically includes and excludes.

Changes in behavior occur as a result of many processes, not all of which are forms of learning. The above definition succeeds in eliminating most if not all of these changes. Behavioral changes occurring as a result of maturation are ruled out by the requirement of dependence upon practice. Changes resulting from motivational fluctuations are temporary and are eliminated by the reference to a permanent change. Changes in behavior that come under the heading of forgetting and experimental extinction are excluded by the reference to reinforced practice. Learning necessitates the appropriate use of reward or punishment. If these operations, collectively called reinforcement, are omitted, learning disappears; experimental extinction or "unlearning" takes place. The reference to reinforced practice is necessary to exclude such changes from the definition of learning.

Turning now to matters that the definition does not exclude, it should be noted that the definition says nothing about the kinds of behavioral changes that qualify as learning. There is, for example, no suggestion that learning always leads to an improvement in behavior: bad habits as well as good habits are encompassed by the definition. Similarly, acquired motives, attitudes, and values come within the scope of the definition as easily as do changes in language habits and motor skills. Finally, the use of the term "tendency" allows the definition to cover cases in which the products of learning do not immediately appear in performance. In this way the definition covers the numerous cases in which an individual learns something that may not be put to practical use for years. Someone might learn as a boy scout that moss typically grows on the north side of trees and that this information may be used to find one's way out of a forest when lost, but not actually perform any responses based on this information until much later, if ever. The distinction implicit in the previous statements, that between learning and performance, is basic to the psychology of learning. In general, learning refers to the establishment of tendencies; performance refers to the translation of these tendencies into behavior.

Historical background. Although ideas basic to the modern psychology of learning have existed for millennia, especially in the associationistic philosophies, the immediate antecedents of the scientific study of learning are to be found in the work of three scientists writing in the late nineteenth and early twentieth centuries: the German Ebbinghaus, the Russian Pavlov, and the American Thorndike [*see* EBBINGHAUS; PAVLOV; THORNDIKE].

Ebbinghaus. Ebbinghaus fathered the study of verbal rote learning (1885). As materials, he used meaningless three-letter, consonant–vowel–consonant, sequences, which have come to be called nonsense syllables. GOC, TER, and BIV are examples. Ebbinghaus constructed lists of these materials of various lengths, memorized them under various conditions, and attempted to recall them after various amounts of time. He discovered many of the laws of such learning, which remain valid today. It is of incidental interest that Ebbinghaus also appears to have been the first psychologist to make use of the ideas of statistics and probability.

Pavlov. Using dogs as subjects, Pavlov studied the simple form of learning that we now call classical conditioning (1927). The Pavlovian procedure consisted of presenting the dog with food or an acid solution, which made the animal salivate, shortly after the presentation of some neutral stimulus, such as a tone or light, which did not. After several such pairings, the dog came to salivate at the presentation of the neutral stimulus as if that stimulus had somehow become a substitute for food or acid. Pavlov was able to demonstrate many of the basic phenomena of conditioning. He also developed a quasi-neurological theory to account for such learning.

Thorndike. Thorndike also worked with lower animals, such as dogs, cats, and chickens, and studied what we now call instrumental learning. The most famous of Thorndike's studies were those in which cats learned to operate a latch to escape from a puzzle box and to obtain a bit of fish outside (Thorndike 1898–1901). On the basis of his observations in these studies, Thorndike was led to develop an influential theory of learning in which three hypotheses were central: (1) learning consists of the formation of connections between stimuli and responses; (2) learning is a gradual rather than a sudden or insightful process; and (3) learning depends not just upon practice but also upon reward and punishment. This last hypothesis Thorndike called the law of effect.

Taxonomy of learning

As these historical materials indicate, the scientific study of learning involves the use of widely different procedures. It is useful, in fact, to differentiate forms of learning in addition to those described above. The most important of these are considered here.

Classical conditioning. Many investigators make a distinction between forms of learning in which the subject's reactions lead to reward or punishment and those in which such events take place independently of the subject's behavior. The former arrangement defines instrumental learning; the latter identifies classical conditioning. The four most important aspects of the classical conditioning experiment may be described by referring to the example of Pavlovian conditioning mentioned above.

(1) *Unconditioned stimulus* (*US*)—any stimulus that at the outset of an experiment produces a regular reaction. In the typical Pavlovian experiment the *US* is food.

(2) *Unconditioned response* (*UR*)—the consistent reaction evoked by the *US* just referred to. In the Pavlovian experiments this was the salivation.

(3) *Conditioned stimulus* (*CS*)—a neutral stimulus paired with the *US* for experimental purposes. In the typical Pavlovian experiments, this was a light, buzzer, bell, or ticking metronome.

(4) *Conditioned response* (*CR*). After several pairings of the *CS* and *US*, a response resembling the *UR* may be elicited by the conditioned stimulus. This is the conditioned response, conditioned reaction, or conditioned reflex.

Studies of the conditioned reflex show that such learning is a very general process. Reactions that have been conditioned, in addition to salivation, include the galvanic skin response, the eyeblink, a blocking of the alpha rhythm of the brain, pupillary dilation, vasodilation and constriction, and secretion of various internal organs. It has also been demonstrated that the range of neutral stimuli to which such conditioning may take place is wide and includes all of the stimuli that the organism ordinarily perceives and some that it ordinarily may not perceive.

In discussing classical conditioning, two items of interpretation appear to be important. First, as the responses listed above suggest, the reactions modifiable by classical conditioning are often emotional reactions. Thus, classical conditioning appears to be the mechanism by which hopes, fears, attitudes, and other emotionally toned reactions are established. Second, it is important to restrict the application of the term "conditioning" to classical conditioning. The extension of the concept of conditioning to almost every form of learning, as some authors have done, leads to confusion.

Simple instrumental learning. Most learning situations differ from classical conditioning in that the organism's reactions are instrumental to the securing of reward or the avoidance of punishment —hence the name "instrumental learning." In purely physical terms, there are four possible relationships between a given response and reward and punishment: the response in question may (1) produce reward, (2) avoid a punishment, (3) lead to punishment, or (4) lead to the withholding of reward. The great majority of experimental work in simple instrumental learning involves the first two of these, reward learning and avoidance learning. We shall discuss reward learning here, postponing the treatment of avoidance learning until later.

A common device for the study of reward learning is the Skinner box. A representative version of this apparatus might consist of a chamber about one foot on a side. A lever extends into the box on one side. If the rat (the species most commonly studied in the Skinner box) presses the lever, a bit of food or a small dipper of water is automatically presented.

Investigations of simple instrumental learning employ two general procedures: free responding and discriminative. In the latter method a distinctive signal such as a light or tone or the insertion of the lever into the box is used to indicate when reward is available. If the animal presses the bar in the presence of the discriminative stimulus, reward occurs. Bar pressures at other times go unrewarded. In the free-responding situation, there is no discriminative stimulus to indicate when reward is available.

Schedules of reinforcement. Most investigations of learning in the Skinner box employ the free-responding procedure and some version of a partial-reinforcement schedule. The rat does not receive reward for every bar depression but is reinforced on a schedule that is defined either in terms of a temporal interval or in terms of a specified number of responses. Thus, there are both interval and ratio schedules of reinforcement. Moreover, the number of responses required for reinforcement or the temporal interval separating reinforcements may be fixed (regular) or variable (irregular). The combinations of these physical arrangements generate four basic schedules of reinforcement: (1) fixed interval, (2) variable interval, (3) fixed ratio, and (4) variable ratio. In the fixed interval schedule the animal is reinforced for the first response after a standard period of time, perhaps one minute. In the variable interval schedule the animal is rewarded for the first response after some average amount of time, such as one minute, but the intervals separating successive reinforcements vary widely around this average value. Similarly with ratio schedules, the fixed ratio schedule is one in which the animal is reinforced for the *n*th (for example, the fifteenth) response and the variable ratio schedule provides reward after some average, but varying, number of bar depressions. These schedules of reinforcement produce characteristic behavioral patterns that cannot be described within the scope of this article. The interested reader is referred to Skinner (1938), Ferster and Skinner (1957), or to any standard book on learning (for example, Hall 1966; Kimble 1961). One practical consequence of any partial reinforcement schedule is the estab-

lishment of great persistence in behavior. This is particularly true of the variable interval schedule. This schedule, therefore, is widely used in experiments in which many tests must be conducted. The investigation of stimulus generalization, which we shall discuss later, and the influence of drugs upon behavior are important examples.

Complex instrumental learning. The simple experimental situations typified by the Skinner box are relatively recent in the history of the scientific study of learning. Earlier investigations tended to use more complex situations, the multiunit maze being, by far, the most popular. The general abandonment of these procedures probably resulted from two difficulties: the complex instrumental learning situations were difficult to subject to automation; and, more importantly, the learning that takes place in such situations is so complex as to defy analysis. On the other hand, investigations of complex instrumental learning did lead to a preliminary statement of certain laws of learning and to the development of certain important concepts. One of the most important items in the first category was suggested by the fact that mazes tend to be learned in a backward order; the correct turns near the goal are learned first, and those near the starting point are learned last. This fact implies the existence of a *goal gradient* or delay of reinforcement gradient, which means that responses followed immediately by reward are learned more rapidly than those for which reward is delayed.

Habit family hierarchy. The most useful general concept to come from the study of complex instrumental learning is that of habit family hierarchy. Investigators of maze behavior, for example, noticed that the initial behavior of the rat in the maze was not merely random wandering but revealed certain dependabilities. The rat might show a consistent tendency to turn right rather than left, to proceed straight ahead rather than to make a turn at all, to prefer dim alleys to those more brightly illuminated, and to choose paths leading in the general direction of the home cage over those that lead in the opposite direction. Such observations suggested the general proposition that the learner comes to the learning situation with a repertoire of responses (habit family) that vary in strength (hierarchy). This made it possible to view complex instrumental learning as a reorganization of the habit family hierarchy.

Acquisition of motor skill. At the human level, an important form of learning is the acquisition of motor skill. Improvements in handwriting, baseball pitching, piano playing, and bicycle riding are familiar examples. The only caution that should be urged is that it is important to distinguish between skills that emerge as a result of learning and those that appear as a result of maturation. In the young child, walking is an example of the latter type of skill. Although we speak of "learning to walk," experimental studies have shown that this skill is almost entirely the result of maturation and that practice has relatively little to do with it.

As is the case in all other areas of learning, laboratory study has led to a refinement in methods and to the use of relatively standardized procedures. A very commonly used device for the study of motor learning is the pursuit rotor (rotary-pursuit apparatus). The pursuit rotor resembles a phonograph turntable. Its main feature is a motor-driven disc, which usually turns at the rate of 60 rpm. At a distance of four or five inches from the center, there is a small target approximately the size of a dime. The subject's task is to keep the point of a hinged stylus in contact with the target while the disc rotates. The measure of performance is the amount of time the subject keeps the point of the stylus in contact with the target.

Massed versus distributed practice. Some of the most important results obtained from pursuit rotor studies deal with the spacing of practice trials. In one investigation (Kimble & Shatel 1952), subjects received fifteen 50-second trials per day for ten days (see Figure 1). One group learned under conditions of massed practice, in which the trials were separated by 10-second rest pauses. The other group learned under conditions of distributed (spaced) practice, the trials being separated by rest pauses of 70 seconds. The results of the investigation were as follows: (1) Massed practice produces a serious interference with the acquisition of pursuit rotor skill. (2) Under either condition of practice, improvement continues for a long time. In Figure 1, it can be seen that even after 150 trials, the subjects under both conditions of practice still continue to show improvement. (3) The initial trials on any day's session show certain interesting characteristics. One of these is the phenomenon of warm-up, which is most conspicuously displayed in the later sessions of the subjects who learn under distributed practice. The first trials are quite inferior to the final trials of the preceding day, and it may take six or eight trials for the warm-up process to be complete and for the level of performance of the previous day to be reached. (4) Under conditions of massed practice, a different effect may appear at the beginning of each practice. This is an improvement in performance that apparently occurs as the result of rest and the disappearance of a fatiguelike state produced by massed practice. This phenomenon is most obvious in the early sessions under massed practice. In Figure 1 the straight lines through the massed-practice functions are fitted curves used to estimate what performance would have been on the first trial of a particular session if a day's rest had not intervened (open circles) and what it would have been on that same trial if there had been no need to warm up (filled circles). The difference between the open and closed circles is a measure of this improvement, technically called reminiscence. It is of interest that in this experiment reminiscence disappears late in learning. (5) If these subjects, who practice with their preferred hand, are tested for performance with their nonpreferred hand and if appropriate control procedures are employed, it is possible to demonstrate that the performance of the nonpreferred hand benefits considerably from practice with the preferred one. This characteristic of motor learning, called transfer of training, is very conspicuous in motor skills.

Rote verbal learning. As was mentioned at the outset of this article, one of the earliest forms of learning to receive scientific study was verbal learning, which Ebbinghaus began to investigate in the late nineteenth century. In its modern form the study of verbal learning takes two major forms, serial learning and paired-associate learning. Serial learning involves the memorization of lists, typically lists of nonsense syllables; paired-associate learning, as the name implies, involves the learning of pairs of items in the way one learns a foreign language vocabulary.

Both of these forms of rote learning are influenced in the same way by certain variables: (1) The manipulation of distribution of practice

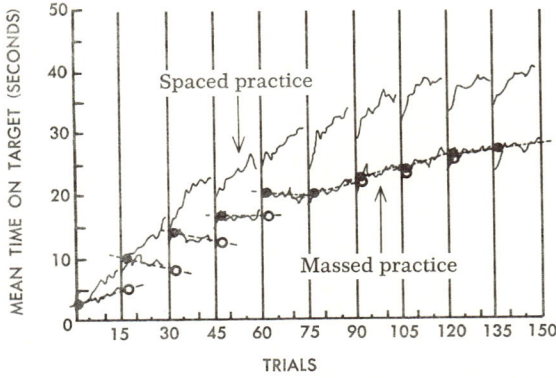

Figure 1 — Learning curves for a pursuit rotor task under spaced and massed practice

Source: Kimble & Shatel 1952, p. 356.

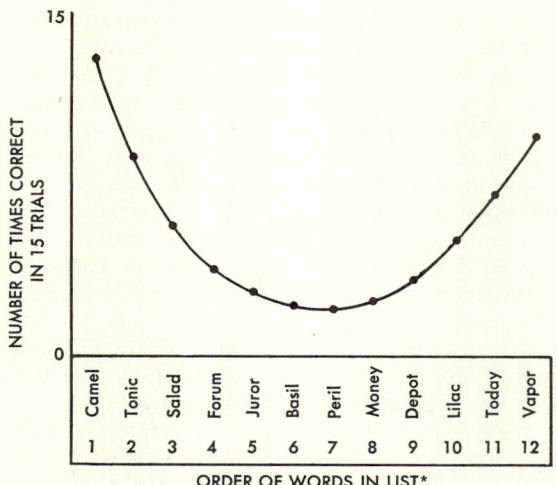

Figure 2 — A characteristic serial position function

* For purposes of illustration the words are listed along the base line.

leads, as in motor learning, to better performance under spaced practice than under massed practice; but typically the effect is of a much less impressive magnitude than in motor learning. (2) Both proceed much more rapidly with meaningful materials (for example, a list containing the words *house, robin, wagon, money, uncle,* etc.) than with nonsense materials (for example, a list containing the items TOZ, LUN, GIB, VUR, DEG).

Studies of serial learning have revealed characteristic differences in the ease of learning different portions of the list. The very first items are easiest; those at the end are next easiest; the most difficult items are those just after the middle of the list. This phenomenon, illustrated in Figure 2, may be referred to as a serial position function.

Interference phenomena. The paired-associate learning procedure has been particularly useful in the study of interferences of the kind thought to be responsible for normal forgetting. Suppose a subject learns the following pairs of words:

> table–bright
> dozen–forest
> value–camel
> willow–stone
> label–graze

He then learns these pairs:

> table–lozenge
> dozen–tempest
> value–blister
> willow–horse
> label–trial

Note that the stimulus words are the same in the two lists but that the responses are different. Re-

ferring to the stimulus and response words in the first list as *A* and *B,* respectively, the items in the second list can be referred to as *A* and *C.* This *A–B, A–C* relationship leads to great difficulty in remembering the *A–B* associations. The establishment of such interferences is commonly thought by psychologists of verbal learning to be the essential condition for forgetting.

Learning to learn. If subjects are required to learn a series of lists of verbal materials, they show a steadily improving ability as a function of the number of lists previously committed to memory (unless, as just noted, the lists are constructed to interfere with each other). The results typically obtained in experiments on learning to learn appear in Figure 3. Among the most important experimental demonstrations of this fact are the investigations of Harlow (1949). Harlow taught monkeys a series of several hundred discrimination

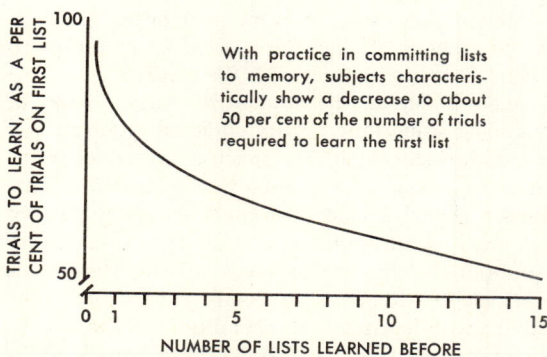

With practice in committing lists to memory, subjects characteristically show a decrease to about 50 per cent of the number of trials required to learn the first list

Figure 3 — Hypothetical function depicting "learning to learn" in a typical rote learning situation

problems. During the course of this experiment, the subjects improved to the point where they were solving new discriminations after just one trial.

Basic phenomena of simple learning

Most students of learning assume that the variety of forms of learning considered in the previous section all obey the same basic laws. For this reason, it has seemed expedient to most such students to study the basic properties of learning in simple situations, often with lower organisms as subjects. Thus, realistic presentations of what are regarded as the basic phenomena of learning (this section), as well as of its most fundamental laws (next section), must depend heavily upon studies of classical conditioning and simple instrumental learning.

Acquisition and the learning curve. During the course of practice, a subject's performance changes in a direction that indicates an increase in the strength of the underlying process. The phenomenon of habit acquisition is often represented in the form of a learning curve. The shape and direction of such functions depend upon the particular measure of learning employed. Idealized but typical functions appear in Figure 4. In what follows, we shall limit ourselves to a report of investigations where increases in the measure plotted reflect increases in the strength of a habit.

Extinction.   As mentioned earlier, and as will be developed in more detail later, learning requires the use of reinforcements; for example, allowing the subject the opportunity to obtain food or avoid punishment for performing the response to be learned. The omission of reinforcement leads to a reduction in performance that Pavlov called experimental extinction and is now more often referred to simply as extinction.

Spontaneous recovery.   If, following extinction, the subject is allowed a period of rest, there frequently occurs a spontaneous increase, or spontaneous recovery, in the strength of the previously extinguished response. This increase resembles the increase called reminiscence, which occurs in motor learning. Many theorists (for example, Hull 1951) regard both as reflecting the dissipation of some type of inhibitory process. What next happens to the strength of the spontaneously recovered response depends upon whether or not it is reinforced. The reintroduction of reinforcement leads to the rapid re-establishment of the full strength of the response. Omission of reinforcement leads to re-extinction. Figure 5 provides a graphic summary of the phenomena described.

Stimulus generalization.   Ordinarily, in a conditioning experiment the conditioned stimulus is precisely controlled. If the response is tested with other stimuli, the conditioned reaction may occur but in diminished strength. For example, Guttman and Kalish (1958) trained pigeons to peck at a disc illuminated with a light of 550 mμ and tested the reaction of the pigeon to lights of other colors. The measure of response strength employed was the rate of pecking. These investigators obtained results indicating that there is a generalization gradient (Figure 6 illustrates these findings). In general, such a gradient shows the transfer of response strength to stimuli similar to the training stimulus and a reduction in strength that is proportional to the difference between the training and test stimuli.

Discrimination.   The tendency for a response to generalize means that the subject fails to discriminate between similar stimuli. Discrimination between two stimuli may be obtained by presenting the two stimuli either together (allowing the organism to choose one) or in succession (allowing the organism to respond or not) and reinforcing responses to one stimulus and withholding reinforcement for responses to the other, provided that the organism's sensory mechanisms can detect the difference. Following such training, the subject

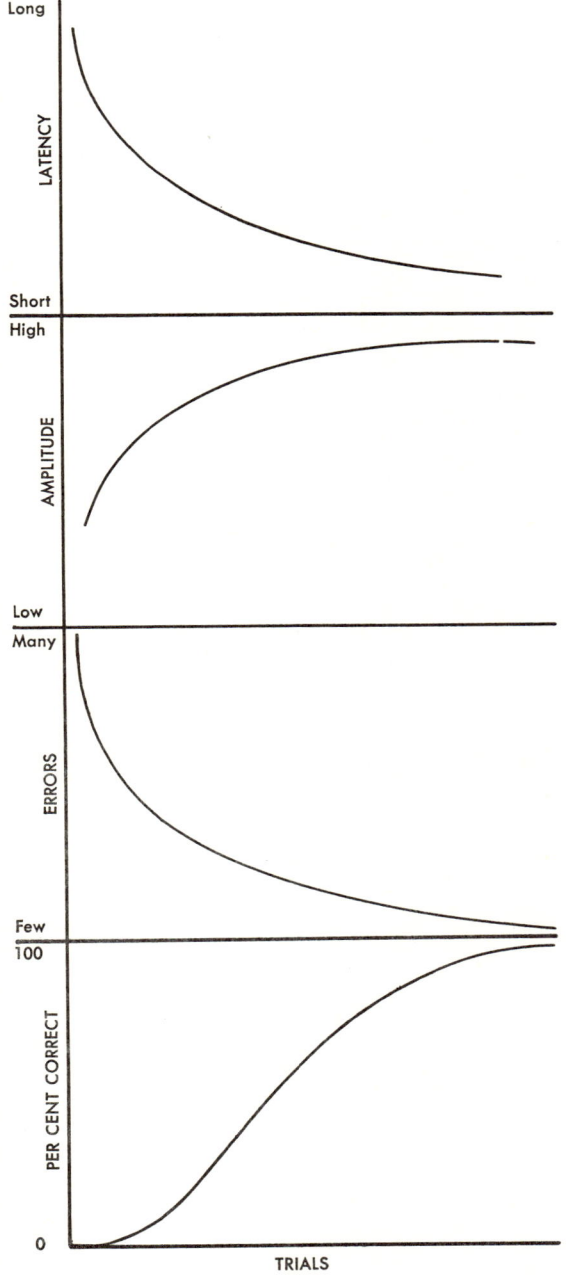

Figure 4 — Characteristic forms of learning curves for four different measures of performance

Figure 5 — Summary graph depicting acquisition, extinction, spontaneous recovery, reconditioning, and a second extinction

typically learns to respond to the reinforced stimulus but not to the other. It is clear that the establishment of a discrimination involves all of the basic phenomena discussed so far: Responses to the reinforced stimulus are *acquired* and then *generalized* to the nonreinforced stimulus. These latter responses are *extinguished* by nonreinforcement but presumably are subject to spontaneous recovery.

Concept formation. At a level much more complex than that of simple learning, it seems very likely that the formation of concepts entails a

Figure 6 — A generalization gradient

process of discrimination learning. A concept obviously involves a tendency to treat diverse things as identical (generalization) but to limit the extent of such indiscriminate reaction.

The laws of learning and performance

The major preoccupation of students of learning has been with the experimental manipulation of a variety of variables in an effort to determine their lawful relationship to learned changes in behavior. As we shall see, it is easy to list variables that have powerful effects upon performance in the learning situation. What is not so easy is to determine with certainty whether the effect is upon learning or performance. To illustrate this difficulty, suppose that two groups of rats learn a maze under conditions that are exactly alike except that one group learns after having been deprived of food for 24 hours and the other group learns after having been deprived of food for only 2 hours. The learning curves obtained on these two groups of subjects would surely be very different (see Figure 7). But is this difference a difference in learning or performance—or both? The obvious way to find out is to subdivide each group at some point when an impressive difference in behavior has been established, testing some previously very hungry animals when they are only moderately hungry and some previously moderately hungry animals when they are very hungry. Under controlled conditions and with the change in motivation, the performance of both groups changes immediately to what it would have been if the new condition of motivation had prevailed from the beginning (see Figure 7). In short, there is no evidence that motivation has any effect upon learning in an experiment of this sort. The influence, which is a powerful one, is entirely upon performance.

The difficulty in the experiment just described exists for every other variable that might be manipulated. Thus, in the sections to follow, we shall present several important regularities emerging from the experimental study of learning; but, except in connection with the first of these, we shall not return to the question whether the effect is on learning or performance. It will be sufficient to say that the current trend in the thinking of psychologists of learning is to assign more and more of these variables a role as determiners of performance rather than of learning.

Number of practice trials. By definition, learning depends upon practice; and it is obvious that the amount of practice must figure in some way in determining the amount of learning. There is considerable argument, however, about the kind of law involved (Kimble 1961, pp. 109–136). Some psychologists have maintained that all learning is, in some sense, insightful and occurs in just one trial; others have insisted that all learning represents the gradual strengthening of some underlying process. The learning–performance issue is a concern chiefly of the theorists who maintain that all learning is basically insightful, for the fact of the matter is that most learning curves reflect gradual improvements in performance. The general way out of this paradox taken by insight theorists has involved the assumption that learning involves numerous subskills that are acquired suddenly but after different amounts of practice, producing the appearance of gradual learning.

Amount of reinforcement. Obviously a practice trial, among other things, provides an occasion for the administration of reinforcement. Several of the best established laws of learning relate to reinforcement in some way. It is known, for example, that the amount of reinforcement is an

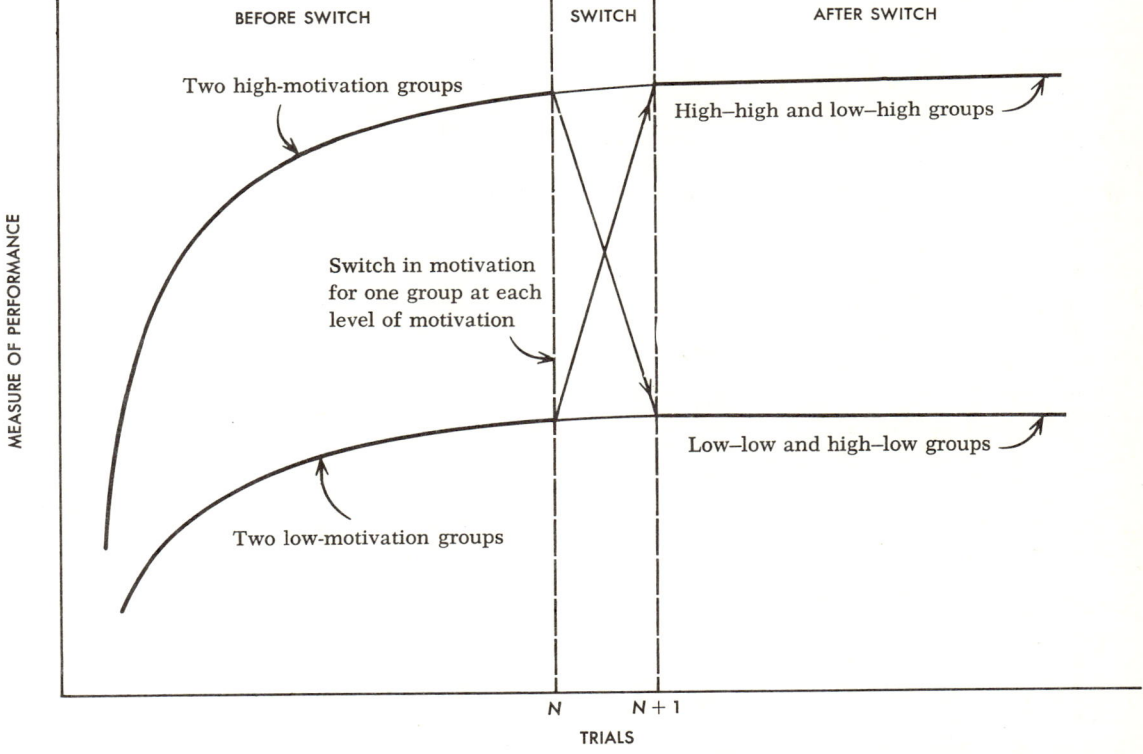

On trial $N + 1$, one low-motivation group is switched to high motivation and one high-motivation group is switched to low motivation

Figure 7 — Hypothetical learning curves showing that the effect of motivation is on performance, not on learning

important variable. Up to some limit, increasing amounts of reinforcement lead to improvements in performance, the characteristic function being negatively accelerated. The same results have been obtained for quality of reinforcement. Subjects learn more rapidly for a highly desirable reinforcer than for a less desirable one.

Delay of reinforcement. It is now well established that the time separating a response and its reinforcer is a very powerful variable in determining the progress of behavioral change in a learning situation. In general, the longer reinforcement is delayed following the execution of the response, the slower the rate of such change. What is most surprising in the results of such studies is that when extraneous sources of reinforcement are eliminated (for example, Grice 1948), it has been found that little if any learning occurs with delays greater than four or five seconds.

Secondary reinforcement. This last fact, of course, raises the question of what mechanisms have been at work in experiments in which subjects have learned with a fairly long delay of reinforcement. The commonly accepted answer is in terms of secondary reinforcement. A discussion of the details of secondary reinforcement would lead us far afield, but fortunately a nontechnical presentation of the argument will suffice. Suppose a rat runs a maze and at the end is restrained in a delay chamber for five minutes before being allowed access to the food used as a reinforcer. Suppose, further, that the rat learns the maze under these conditions, which obviously involve a delay of reinforcement much greater than the four or five seconds mentioned above. How are these two sets of facts to be brought into harmony? The argument in terms of secondary reinforcement goes this way: Cues in the delay chamber come to stand for food because they are always present just before food becomes available. Since these cues stand for food, they have some of the same characteristics as food, including the important characteristic of functioning as (secondary) reinforcers. Thus, the cues in the delay chamber serve as immediate (secondary) reinforcers and promote the progress of learning. The obvious implication of this argument is that if the cues preceding reinforcement varied from trial to trial, so that no stable association could be formed, there would be a serious disruption in the progress of learning.

The delay of reinforcement gradient is basic to the theoretical interpretation of a variety of phenomena in learning. For example, the backward order of elimination of blinds in a complex maze referred to earlier probably reflects the operation of this gradient. A gradient with all the features of the delay of reinforcement gradient also seems to apply to punishment. Miller (for example, 1959) has developed a theory of approach–avoidance conflict that is based on simultaneous operation of gradients based on reward and punishment.

The interstimulus interval. The experiments on delay of reinforcement described in the preceding section were all experiments in instrumental learning. A related variable in classical conditioning is the time between conditioned and unconditioned stimuli, often referred to as the interstimulus interval. Studies of this variable have produced relatively consistent results, which Figure 8 presents graphically. Two features of the interstimulus interval are important: (1) Backward conditioning, in which the unconditioned stimulus precedes the conditioned stimulus, leads to little or no conditioning. (2) The function for forward conditioning, in which the conditioned stimulus precedes the unconditioned stimulus, displays a conspicuous optimal interval; intervals either longer or shorter than the optimum produce inferior conditioning. For many response systems the optimal interval is in the neighborhood of .5 second. Recent investigations suggest that this optimal interval is more limited than was once thought. These studies (for example, Noble & Adams 1963; Noble & Harding 1963) have tended to indicate (1) that for lower animals the optimal interval is longer than .5 second and (2) that its duration may be different at different points in practice.

Other variables. The variables described above are representative of those studied in investigations of simple learning. A complete catalogue of such variables is beyond the scope of this report. Thus, we shall supplement the foregoing review by

Figure 8 — A characteristic interstimulus interval function

simply mentioning certain other variables and only briefly indicating their effect upon performance.

Motivation. As we have seen, motivation ordinarily facilitates performance in the learning situation. In some circumstances, however, motivation may energize tendencies that interfere with the response to be learned. Under these circumstances, motivation, particularly very strong motivation, may appear to interfere with learning.

Distribution of practice. As we have also seen, distribution of practice usually favors rapid learning. In some complex tasks, however, massed practice may aid in the elimination of initial errors and briefly speed the progress of learning.

Intensity of the unconditioned stimulus. The intensity of the unconditioned stimulus in classical conditioning behaves as the amount of reinforcement does in instrumental learning; the greater the intensity of the unconditioned stimulus, the more rapidly conditioning proceeds.

Intensity of the conditioned stimulus. The intensity of the conditioned stimulus usually has little effect on the speed of conditioning; but recent studies (Grice & Hunter 1964) show that when strong and weak conditioned stimuli are used in the same experiment with the same subjects, the effectiveness of this variable increases considerably.

A final point is that the effects of the variables mentioned in this and the preceding section interact; that is, the effect of one depends upon the values of the others. The precise nature of the interactions remains to be worked out for almost all combinations of variables.

The nature of reinforcement

The major theoretical issues in the psychology of learning are traceable to the opinions of E. L. Thorndike. As mentioned earlier, from Thorndike's studies of cats in a simple instrumental learning situation, Thorndike developed three important hypotheses about the nature of learning: learning is gradual rather than sudden; learning consists in the formation of stimulus–response connections; and at bottom, reinforcement entails the operation of rewards and punishments. This last idea is the one that we shall develop most fully in this section. As Thorndike put it:

The Law of Effect is that: Of several responses made to the same situation, those which are accompanied or closely followed by satisfaction to the animal will, other things being equal, be more firmly connected with the situation, so that, when it recurs, they will be more likely to recur; those which are accompanied or closely followed by discomfort to the animal will, other things being equal, have their connections with that situation weakened, so that, when it recurs, they will be less likely to occur. The greater the satisfaction or discomfort, the greater the strengthening or weakening of the bond.   ([1898–1901] 1911, p. 244)

This statement came in for severe criticism on two particular counts: (1) It was criticized as subjective and unscientific in that the terms "satisfaction" and "discomfort" appeared to entail commitments to a mentalism that the psychology of 1911 was struggling to escape. Thorndike, however, was on safer methodological ground than his critics realized for he offered a means of objectifying these terms that we find perfectly acceptable today. "By a satisfying state of affairs is meant one which the animal does nothing to avoid, often doing such things as attain and preserve it. By a discomforting or annoying state of affairs is meant one which the animal commonly avoids or abandons" ([1898–1901] 1911, p. 245).

(2) The law of effect was criticized as circular: that is, learning to approach some object (for example, food) could define an object as a satisfier that, in turn, could be used to explain the learning that served to define it as a satisfier in the first place. Although Thorndike himself was not particularly clear on how to deal with this criticism, later advocates of his general point of view (for example, Miller & Dollard 1941) provided an answer. In general, this answer is that the transparent circularity in the example above disappears when it is understood that the definition of a satisfier in a defining experiment of the type proposed by Thorndike establishes the object as a general satisfier that will function as a reinforcer in a variety of learning situations. That is, given that food functions as a reinforcer in one situation, it is possible to predict with a fair degree of certainty that it will function in a similar way in a host of others. The law of effect has survived these criticisms and now has become the position by which other interpretations of reinforcement are usually defined.

The law of effect. Before proceeding further with this discussion, it is important to make a distinction between empirical and theoretical versions of the law of effect. The empirical law of effect involves nothing more than the simple factual statement that there are objects, such as food, water, and escape from punishment, that function dependably as reinforcers. The theoretical law of effect, on the other hand, states (using Thorndike's terminology) that these events are reinforcers because they are satisfiers. Because of its factual status, the empirical law of effect is not an object of dispute. Arguments about the nature of reinforcement involve the theoretical law of effect.

The statement that all reinforcers are satisfiers or annoyers is merely one of several proposals that have been offered as to the ultimate nature of reinforcement. For purposes of exposition, it is convenient to identify three general classes of such proposals, which we shall call tension-reduction theory, stimulational theory, and reactional theory.

Tension-reduction theory. Tension-reduction theory maintains that the essential condition of reinforcement is the alleviation of a state of physiological or psychological tension. In the past, tension-reduction theory was so closely tied to Thorndike's theory that current usage tends to identify the law of effect with this position and often erroneously equates tension-reduction theory with reinforcement theory.

At different times, and in the hands of different authors, need-reduction, drive-reduction, and drive-stimulus–reduction theories of reinforcement have been offered. Need-reduction theory identifies reinforcement with the satisfaction of some physiological need (for example, food, water, or sex) that if not attained means that the individual or its species will perish. Although this theory is attractive because of its affinity to biological processes, certain facts make its acceptance impossible: (1) There are many rewards that appear to correspond to no biological need. These include rewards that satisfy such acquired motives as those for affection, dominance, and accomplishment. (2) Certain biological needs appear to involve no correlated reinforcer. One of these is the need for oxygen, which is present at very high altitudes but which does not seem to create a state of tension or drive. There is no evidence that the administration of oxygen under these circumstances is a reward.

Difficulties such as these led certain theorists (Hull 1943) to distinguish between need (a physiological condition) and drive (the psychological experience associated with needs) and to suggest that reinforcement is drive reduction rather than need reduction. We shall apply this distinction presently.

The drive-stimulus–reduction theory of reinforcement (Miller & Dollard 1941) suggests that drives are always intense stimuli and that drive reduction (assumed to be reinforcing) is a matter of stimulus reduction.

Stimulational theory. Stimulational theory maintains that particular stimuli are reinforcing and distinguishes itself from tension-reduction theory in these terms. Thus, food is a reinforcer because of its taste (not because it reduces hunger), and water is a reinforcer because of the stimulational aspects of drinking (not because it reduces thirst).

Reactional theory. Reactional theory stands in opposition to both tension-reduction theory and to stimulational theory and holds that it is the act of eating or drinking, rather than taste or drive reduction, that is essential to reinforcement.

Experimental tests. Disagreements among these various interpretations of reinforcement have led, over the years, to a wide variety of experimental tests designed to establish the validity of one particular interpretation. Typically, tension-reduction theory has provided the point of departure, and adherents of opposing theories have attempted to strengthen their theoretical positions by discrediting tension-reduction theory. For example, Sheffield and Roby (1950) demonstrated that rats will learn to run a simple maze for a reward consisting of saccharine dissolved in water. The significance of this finding derives from the fact that saccharine has no nutritional value, being eliminated from the body chemically unchanged. This suggests that it must be either the sweet taste of saccharine (stimulational theory) or the act of ingestion (reactional theory) that provides for reinforcement. Advocates of tension-reduction theory, however, were able to point out that although saccharine produces no reduction in need it may produce a reduction in drive. Thus, Miller (1963) reported that rats that were allowed to drink a saccharine solution subsequently ate less food than the control subjects, which were allowed to drink only water. Miller's interpretation was that the consumption of saccharine had led to a reduction of the hunger drive although obviously it had not altered the rats' need for food.

Similar problems for tension-reduction theory were provided by demonstrations that the opportunity to explore or to manipulate the environment is rewarding for lower animals. For example, Butler (1953) was able to show that rhesus monkeys will learn a discrimination for no other reward than the opportunity to see out of their normally closed cage. Other investigators (Harlow, Harlow, & Meyer 1950) demonstrated that monkeys learned to distinguish between manipulable and nonmanipulable objects apparently for no other reward than the opportunity to manipulate them. Still others (Kish 1955) showed that rats will learn a bar-pressing response to turn on a dim light or that they will learn a simple maze for the opportunity to explore a novel environment. For some of these demonstrations, but not all, tension-reduction theorists were able to deal with the problem by the postulation of a motive to explore or to manipulate and by the assumption that learning depended on the reduction of these drives. Obviously there are certain difficulties with such explanations in that they open the possibility of postulating a new motive for every demonstrable type of reward. On the other hand, it is known that some of these motives, for example, the exploratory motive, increase in strength with deprivation, as many other motives do. Such evidence makes the interpretation somewhat more acceptable in that it lends credence to the concept of an exploratory motive by providing independent evidence for it.

A special threat to tension-reduction theory has recently come in the form of demonstrations that rats will learn a variety of responses (the most common response is bar pressing) for a weak electrical stimulation of a variety of areas of the brain stem. The simplest interpretation of such a result is that such stimulation is somehow pleasant for the rat, and such demonstrations have been interpreted as a support for stimulational theory. On the other hand, Olds (1958) has shown that the effectiveness of brain stimulation depends in part upon the level of the rat's hunger and sex drives. This opens the possibility that brain stimulation reduces these and other motives.

At the same time that tension-reduction theorists were dealing with these attacks upon their position, they were also providing more positive evidence in support of their own position. A typical experiment is that of Miller and Kessen (1952). These investigators demonstrated that rats learned a simple discrimination for a reward provided by the introduction of food directly into the stomach by way of a fistula. Such learning took place in the absence of taste stimulation emphasized by stimulational theory and ingestive behavior emphasized by reactional theory. This appears to leave the alleviation of hunger (tension reduction) as the only remaining mechanism of reinforcement.

It is apparent that the variety of experimental tests described above did not succeed in establishing any particular theory as the obviously correct theory of reinforcement. This state of affairs has had two important consequences. One consequence is that certain theorists, most notably Collier (see, for example, Collier & Myers 1961), have made a strong case for the view that reinforcement entails a variety of mechanisms, probably all of those emphasized by the more specialized theories of reinforcement.

The other important consequence is the increased appeal of multiprocess theories of learning. Such theories propose that learning itself involves a number of subtypes and that the mechanisms of reinforcement differ for the various forms of learning.

Multiprocess theories. The most popular form of multiprocess theory is a two-process theory that maintains that the mechanisms of reinforcement are different for classical conditioning and instrumental learning. The position is that instrumental learning occurs as a result of reinforcement provided by tension reduction, whereas for classical conditioning all that is necessary is the contiguous occurrence of conditioned and unconditioned stimuli (or, in some versions, conditioned stimulus and unconditioned response).

One of the appealing features of two-process theory is the readiness with which it can be applied to avoidance learning, which is difficult to understand in terms of any single principle of reinforcement. Suppose we consider the following experimental arrangement: A rat is placed in a Skinner box and on each trial a light comes on and five seconds later an electric shock is applied to the animal's feet through an electrifiable grid in the floor, unless, in the meantime, the rat presses the bar. Rats are able to learn this response quite quickly. Two-process theory deals with this learning as follows. On the early trials, before the rat has learned to press the bar and avoid the shock, light and shock are paired on every trial as in classical conditioning. This pairing leads to a conditioning to the light of a fear reaction. On subsequent trials, the appearance of the light arouses fear in the subject, and this, in turn, leads to a heightened level of activity. In the course of such activity, sooner or later the animal presses the bar, terminating the light, reducing fear, and also avoiding the shock. The reduction in fear, which is contingent upon the cessation of the light, provides reinforcement for the bar-pressing reaction.

Psychopathology. Applications of learning theory to psychopathology, for example, those attempted by such theorists as Dollard and Miller (1950), have made important use of a two-process explanation in their descriptions of neurotic symptomology. Phobias are often interpreted as direct or symbolic representations of classically conditioned fear reactions; and neurotic behavior is viewed as avoidance behavior motivated by fear and reinforced by fear reduction.

GREGORY KIMBLE

[*See also* FORGETTING. *Other relevant material may be found in* ACHIEVEMENT TESTING; DRIVES; MOTIVATION; NERVOUS SYSTEM, *article on* BRAIN STIMULATION; STIMULATION DRIVES.]

BIBLIOGRAPHY

BUTLER, ROBERT A. 1953 Discrimination by Rhesus Monkeys to Visual-exploration Motivation. *Journal of Comparative and Physiological Psychology* 46:95–98.

COLLIER, GEORGE; and MYERS, LEONHARD 1961 The Loci of Reinforcement. *Journal of Experimental Psychology* 61:57–66.

DOLLARD, JOHN; and MILLER, NEAL E. 1950 *Personality and Psychotherapy: An Analysis in Terms of Learning, Thinking, and Culture.* New York: McGraw-Hill. → A paperback edition was published in 1965.

EBBINGHAUS, HERMANN (1885) 1913 *Memory: A Contribution to Experimental Psychology.* New York: Columbia Univ., Teachers College. → First published as *Über das Gedächtnis.* A paperback edition was published in 1964 by Dover.

FERSTER, C. B.; and SKINNER, B. F. 1957 *Schedules of Reinforcement.* New York: Appleton.

GRICE, G. R. 1948 The Relation of Secondary Reinforcement to Delayed Reward in Visual Discrimination Learning. *Journal of Experimental Psychology* 38:1–16.

GRICE, G. R.; and HUNTER, J. J. 1964 Stimulus Intensity Effects Depend Upon the Type of Experimental Design. *Psychological Review* 71:247–256.

GUTTMAN, NORMAN; and KALISH, HARRY L. 1958 Experiments in Discrimination. *Scientific American* 198, no. 1:77–82.

HALL, JOHN F. 1966 *The Psychology of Learning.* Philadelphia: Lippincott.

HARLOW, HARRY F. 1949 The Formation of Learning Sets. *Psychological Review* 56:51–65.

HARLOW, HARRY F.; HARLOW, M. K.; and MEYER, D. R. 1950 Learning Motivated by a Manipulation Drive. *Journal of Experimental Psychology* 40:228–234.

HILLMAN, BEVERLY; HUNTER, W. S.; and KIMBLE, G. A. 1953 The Effect of Drive Level on the Maze Performance of the White Rat. *Journal of Comparative and Physiological Psychology* 46:87–89.

HULL, CLARK L. 1943 *Principles of Behavior: An Introduction to Behavior Theory.* New York: Appleton.

HULL, CLARK L. 1951 *Essentials of Behavior.* New Haven: Yale Univ. Press.

KIMBLE, GREGORY A. 1961 *Hilgard and Marquis' Conditioning and Learning.* 2d ed., rev. New York: Appleton. → First published in 1940 as *Conditioning and Learning,* by Ernest R. Hilgard and Donald G. Marquis.

KIMBLE, GREGORY A.; and SHATEL, R. B. 1952 The Relationship Between Two Kinds of Inhibition and the Amount of Practice. *Journal of Experimental Psychology* 44:355–359.

KISH, GEORGE B. 1955 Learning When the Onset of Illumination Is Used as Reinforcing Stimulus. *Journal of Comparative and Physiological Psychology* 48:261–264.

MILLER, NEAL E. 1959 Liberalization of Basic S–R Concepts: Extensions to Conflict Behavior, Motivation and Social Learning. Volume 2, pages 196–292 in Sigmund Koch (editor), *Psychology: A Study of a Science.* New York: McGraw-Hill.

MILLER, NEAL E. 1963 Some Reflections on the Law of Effect Produce a New Alternative to Drive Reduction. Volume 11, pages 65–112 in *Nebraska Symposium on Motivation.* Edited by Marshall R. Jones. Lincoln: Univ. of Nebraska Press.

MILLER, NEAL E.; and DOLLARD, JOHN 1941 *Social Learning and Imitation.* New Haven: Yale Univ. Press; Oxford Univ. Press.

MILLER, NEAL E.; and KESSEN, M. L. 1952 Reward Effects of Food Via Stomach Fistula Compared With Those of Food Via Mouth. *Journal of Comparative and Physiological Psychology* 45:555–564.

NOBLE, MERRILL; and ADAMS, C. K. 1963 Conditioning in Pigs as a Function of the Interval Between CS and US. *Journal of Comparative and Physiological Psychology* 56:215–219.

NOBLE, MERRILL; and HARDING, G. E. 1963 Conditioning in Rhesus Monkeys as a Function of the Interval Between CS and US. *Journal of Comparative and Physiological Psychology* 56:220–224.

OLDS, JAMES 1958 Effects of Hunger and Male Sex Hormone on Self-stimulation of the Brain. *Journal of Comparative and Physiological Psychology* 51:320–324.

PAVLOV, IVAN P. (1927) 1960 *Conditioned Reflexes: An Investigation of the Physiological Activity of the Cerebral Cortex.* New York: Dover. → First published as *Lektsii o rabote bol'shikh polusharii golovnogo mozga.*

SHEFFIELD, FRED D.; and ROBY, THORNTON B. 1950 Reward Value of a Non-nutritive Sweet Taste. *Journal of Comparative and Physiological Psychology* 43:471–481.

SKINNER, B. F. 1938 *The Behavior of Organisms: An Experimental Analysis.* New York: Appleton.

THORNDIKE, EDWARD L. (1898–1901) 1911 *Animal Intelligence: Experimental Studies.* New York: Macmillan.

II
CLASSICAL CONDITIONING

Classical (or Pavlovian, respondent, or type-S) conditioning refers to any of a group of specific procedures that, when applied to an organism under appropriate conditions, result in the formation of the type of learned behavior known as the conditioned response. The term also refers to phenomena and relationships discovered through experiments using classical conditioning procedures. The adjective "classical" is used to distinguish these procedures from the more recently developed instrumental, or operant, conditioning procedures, which also lead to the formation of conditioned responses.

The Russian physiologist I. P. Pavlov was primarily responsible for the development of the methods and nomenclature of classical conditioning, and he discovered and described many of the most important associated phenomena (Pavlov 1927). The early writings of Pavlov had a profound influence on the development of behaviorism by John B. Watson, who considered classical conditioning to be the basis of acquisition of all learned behavior. The wide acceptance of behaviorism by American psychologists and the availability of two English translations of Pavlov's *Lectures on Conditioned Reflexes* (1923) in the late 1920s were followed by an increased and sustained output in the United States of published research on conditioning. However, most of this research was conducted by psychologists who used instrumental techniques more often than they used classical conditioning. Although Pavlov's methods and data were behavioral in nature, he treated them as bearing directly upon the physiology of the cerebral cortex. His theory of conditioning is, therefore, a theory of brain function. (The present article, however, will deal mainly with its more behavioral aspects.) The Russian work on conditioning since Pavlov has very largely followed the pattern set by him.

Characteristics. The following characteristics are principal features of classical conditioning. A response already within the repertory of the experimental subject is designated the unconditioned response (*UR*) and the stimulus that evokes it is called the unconditioned stimulus (*US*). Another stimulus, one that does not elicit the *UR* or any response similar to it, is designated the conditioned stimulus (*CS*). The *CS* and the *US* are presented repeatedly to the subject, either simultaneously or with the *CS* preceding but overlapping the *US* in time. A response similar to the *UR* that develops to the *CS* is called the conditioned response (*CR*). The change in this response to the *CS* from an initial zero magnitude or frequency to a positive magnitude or frequency following practice constitutes a learned acquisition that is called conditioning.

Pavlov and his collaborators used the dog as their experimental subject. Salivation was the *UR* to the *US* of food or dilute acid. The *CSs* were lights, sounds, or pressures systematically applied to the skin, and the *CR* was salivation. But Pavlov discovered that the sights and sounds produced accidentally by the experimenter and his apparatus might also become *CSs* or interfere with the process of conditioning. He found it necessary to develop techniques and apparatus for collecting and measuring the magnitude and latency of the salivary *CRs* and *URs* and for controlling the duration, magnitude, and time relations of the *CSs* and *USs*. These and similar procedures for isolation of the experimental subject and for control of the environment and measurement of responses are part of the technical procedures of classical conditioning.

Generality. Classical conditioning has very great generality. There is no apparent limit to the kinds of responses that can be conditioned in this manner or to the kinds of events that can serve as *CSs*. Any response that is evoked consistently by the *US* can be conditioned, and any stimulus that passes the initial test of neutrality can serve as a *CS*. Many stimuli fail this test, particularly when human beings are the subjects.

The generality of classical conditioning can be viewed also in terms of the level in the phyletic series and the chronological age of the organism in which conditioning first occurs. The few reports of classical conditioning of one-celled organisms have not been confirmed, and there is serious doubt that it is possible to achieve conditioning in these organisms. The evidence on conditioning of the worm is in similar confusion, and it is very doubtful that organisms without a true nervous system can be conditioned. With organisms higher in the phyletic series, who have a true nervous system, there is little question that they can be conditioned. Conditioning of infants of many species, including the human being, has been reported. There have also been reports of successful classical conditioning of the human fetus in the age range of 6.5–8.5 months.

Parameters of classical conditioning. It is possible to measure the latency, duration, and amplitude of a *CR* and also the frequency of its occurrence within a specified period of time. Ordinarily, only one or perhaps two of these measurements will be made concurrently, and whatever measure is applied to the *UR* will be applied also to the *CR* as a basis for comparison. Similar but not identical assessments of conditioning are obtained when different measures are used.

As conditioning develops over practice trials, the latency of the *CR* decreases, while the duration, the amplitude or magnitude, and the frequency of the *CR* increase. Eventually, each of these measures approaches an asymptotic level and does not change with further conditioning trials. The rates at which such asymptotic levels are approached vary with the measures used. It is common practice in experiments on classical *CRs* either to give all subjects an equal number of conditioning trials or to continue conditioning training until the same performance level has been attained by every subject. In the former case, individual differences between subjects show up in the variable level of conditioning attained, and in the latter case the differences appear in variations in the number of training trials required to reach the performance criterion. There are advantages and disadvantages to each of these procedures, but the results of any given experiment will depend upon this methodological consideration as well as upon the measurement procedures.

Temporal contiguity of stimuli. The rate or amount of conditioning and its relative difficulty are functions of the time relations between the *CS* and the *US*. Different names have been given to conditioned responses that are established under different time relations of the conditioned and un-conditioned stimuli.

Simultaneous conditioning. The simultaneous conditioned response is developed when the *CS* and the *US* are coincident or when the onset of the *CS* precedes the onset of the *US* by an amount of time just sufficient for the *CR* to occur. Exact simultaneity makes it impossible to follow the course of conditioning over each trial since there is no way to distinguish between the *CR* and the *UR*. If occasionally the *CS* is presented alone, the *CR* can be measured—but then these trials are extinction trials and interfere with conditioning. Since the acquisition process cannot be measured precisely in the simultaneous situation, it is standard procedure for the onset of the *CS* to precede the onset of the *US* and for the *CR* to be considered a simultaneous *CR*. The length of the interval between the onset of the *CS* and onset of the *US* that defines the simultaneous *CR* depends on the latency of the *UR*. For very fast striated-muscle responses, this interval ranges from a quarter of a second up to several seconds. For slow, or long-latency, responses, such as those of smooth muscle and glands, the interval varies from a few seconds up to thirty or more seconds.

Delayed conditioning. With the delayed conditioned response the interval between the onset of the *CS* and the onset of the *US* is longer than it is for the simultaneous *CR*, and the delayed *CR* also has a longer latency. Delayed *CR*s are subclassified into short delay and long delay *CR*s, depending upon the interval between onset of the *CS* and onset of the *US*.

Trace conditioning. The trace conditioned response is very similar to the delayed *CR*. The time relations for onset of the *CS* and onset of the *US* are identical. The time relations differ only with respect to the termination of the *CS*. For delayed conditioning, the *CS* overlaps the *US* and terminates either with it or some time after its onset. In trace conditioning the *CS* lasts as long as a *CS* in simultaneous conditioning, but it terminates a considerable time before the onset of the *US*. The trace *CR* has the same latency as the delayed *CR*, but because of the short duration of the *CS* it occurs in the time interval between the termination of the *CS* and the onset of the *US*. Since it is assumed in classical conditioning that no response occurs in the absence of a stimulus, it is assumed in this situation that there is a *trace* of the *CS* to which the *CR* is made.

Temporal conditioning. With the temporal conditioned response the *US* is presented alone at a constant rate. The time interval between successive presentations of the *US* functions as a *CS*. The *CR*

occurs just prior to the time at which the *US* is to be presented.

Backward conditioning. For the backward conditioned response, onset of the *CS* occurs after termination of the *US* and the *UR*. The *CR* occurs, of course, to the *CS*, after the prior occurrence of the *US* and the *UR*.

Pseudo conditioning. The pseudo conditioned response occurs without any impaired training trials of the *CS* and the *US*. First the *US* is presented alone for a series of trials. Then, after a short interval of time, the *CS* is presented alone. If a response similar to the *UR* occurs to the *CS*, it is called a pseudo conditioned response.

Effects of temporal variations. The simultaneous *CR* is acquired most rapidly and with the greatest ease. The first *CR* may occur on the second or third trial. Delayed and trace *CR*s are acquired with about equal difficulty if the time between the onset of the *CS* and that of the *US* is equal for both. Both are more difficult to establish than the simultaneous *CR*. For simultaneous, delayed, and trace conditioning the difficulty of conditioning increases as the time between the onset of the *CS* and that of the *US* increases. With long delay or long trace conditioning it is impossible to develop a *CR* unless a simultaneous *CR* is established first and training trials are then arranged in which the time interval between onset of the *CS* and onset of the *US* is gradually increased.

The temporal *CR* for short intervals of time is more readily established than the simultaneous *CR*. It may be acquired even when the interval between presentations of the *US* is as great as thirty minutes. It has not been studied extensively, but because it can be so easily acquired in standard simultaneous conditioning, it is necessary to vary the intervals between trials in a random sequence in order to prevent the occurrence of temporal conditioning.

The backward *CR* is more difficult to establish than are forward *CR*s. The difficulty of backward conditioning increases as the interval beween termination of the *US* and onset of the *CS* increases. The range over which this relation holds is small, since there is no evidence of backward conditioning for the longer time intervals between the onset of the *US* and the onset of the *CS* that are possible in delayed or trace forward conditioning.

Pseudo conditioning appears to depend upon the use of a very-high-intensity *US* that produces a large-magnitude, diffuse, emotional *UR*. The pseudo *CR* is neither as readily established nor as stable as a *CR* based upon equivalent practice with simultaneous conditioning procedures. Pseudo conditioning may be treated as a variant of backward conditioning, since presentation of the *US* precedes presentation of the *CS*. The efficiency of the method is low.

Other factors affecting conditioning. The study of other variables that affect the rate or speed of acquisition has been conducted primarily with simultaneous *CR*s. However, what evidence there is suggests that the effects of these variables on other types of *CR*s are similar. Distribution of practice, magnitude of the *US*, deprivation condition of the organism, physiological condition, neural condition, intensity of the *CS,* and the number of trials are independent variables that are well established as relating to acquisition.

Distributed versus massed practice. Some degree of distribution of practice provides the most rapid conditioning. The particular optimal distribution depends upon other variables, such as time relations, nature of the *US* and *CS*, and nature of the organism. The results universally show massed practice to be inferior to some form of distributed practice in speed of conditioning.

Magnitude of the unconditioned stimulus. Speed of conditioning increases with the magnitude of the *US* up to a point and thereafter declines with further increases in the magnitude of the *US*. This has been well established for *CR*s for which the *US* is food or electric shock.

Deprivation. The deprivation condition of the organism interacts with the magnitude of the *US* when the *US* is food. With very large magnitudes of *US* and fairly low degrees of deprivation, after only a few conditioning trials the subject may have received its total daily intake and become satiated. When the *US* is held constant at relatively small magnitudes and the period of deprivation increases, speed or amount of acquisition increases up to a point and then declines with further increase. This relation holds separately for food and for water, but there is probably an interaction between the two.

Deprivation is sometimes treated as a particular physiological condition, but physiological condition usually refers to endocrinological, biochemical, or drug conditions, and the effects of these on conditioning are complex.

Neural conditions. The effects of neural conditions are studied through application of the *CS* and *US* at different levels of the nervous system or through the use of conditioning procedures on organisms when varying levels of the nervous system are rendered functionless. Conditioning is possible if the *CS* is electrical stimulation of the sensory cortex or of the sensory tracts in the spinal cord. There is much evidence that conditioning will not occur if the *US* is direct stimulation of the motor cortex. The decorticate animal can be conditioned, but the weight of evidence is against the possibility of conditioning the spinal animal.

Stimulus intensity and complexity. Conditioning increases in rate and magnitude as the *CS* is increased in intensity from the stimulus threshold to the middle range of intensity but not to greater intensities. Conditioning at very high *CS* intensities has not been tested. Conditioning occurs at a greater magnitude and faster rate with compound *CS*s than with any one of the single component stimuli, whether the *CS*s are from the same or from different sense modalities. Variation in the characteristics of *CS*s makes it possible to study sensory thresholds and discriminations by conditioning procedures.

Transfer. Many instances of positive and negative transfer have been found in studies of classical conditioning. Transfer is usually positive when it is measured as a difference between performances under conditions that involve acquisition procedures. It is most often negative when it is measured as a difference between performance at a terminal level of acquisition and a subsequent performance that results from alteration of some variable present during acquisition. Positive transfer occurs for any subsequent *CR* elicited by a new *CS*, by a new *US*, or by both at the same time. The only instances of negative transfer under the above conditions occur when the *UR* and *CR* for the second treatment are the reverse of or are incompatible with those of the first conditioning treatment.

Stimulus generalization, response generalization, and incentive generalization are forms of positive transfer. Stimulus generalization refers to the occurrence of the *CR* to stimuli similar to the *CS* in the absence of specific training with those stimuli. Stimulus generalization declines as the degree of similarity along a given dimension (such as frequency of a tone in cycles per second) decreases. The form of stimulus-generalization gradients is not known because of serious technical difficulties in measuring stimulus generalization. Cross-modal stimulus generalization occurs only rarely. Response generalization can be studied only in limited fashion, such as from right to left side of body, but may also involve opposing responses when the *CR* is prevented from occurring. Incentive generalization refers to positive transfer of a *CR* that occurs following variation in the *US*, such as in the kind of food or in the frequency or locus of application of electric shock.

Extinction. The most striking transfer phenomenon is experimental extinction. This form of negative transfer occurs when, after acquisition, the US is omitted and the CS is presented alone under the same schedule as that used during acquisition. There is a progressive decrement in the magnitude and frequency of occurrence of the CR to the zero level. This phenomenon has led to a conception of reinforcement of the CR by the US. Empirical nonreinforcement refers to nothing more than the decrement of conditioning when the US is absent from the training procedure, and empirical reinforcement refers to nothing more than the original acquisition of the CR when the US is present in the training procedure and the reinstatement of the CR by reintroduction of the US following extinction. The theoretical views of reinforcement are many, and much of the study of extinction has been directed toward discovery of the reinforcement functions of the US.

With classical conditioning, there appears to be a positive relation between strength of conditioning and resistance to experimental extinction. The greater the amount of conditioning training and the larger the measures of CR magnitude, the greater the resistance to extinction. Any variable that increases the strength of a CR also increases its resistance to extinction. As the degree of extinction training is increased, the amount of training required to re-establish the CR is increased. There is even continued "silent" extinction beyond the zero level of CR: a greater amount of conditioning training is required to re-establish the CR than that required when just the zero extinction level is attained. If there is successive alternation of conditioning and extinction, each reversal requires fewer training trials, until a single trial of either the conditioning or the extinction procedure is sufficient to provide consistent response or response failure to the CS. Speed of extinction is greater for massed extinction trials than it is for distributed extinction trials. Extinction of a CR to one CS will increase the rate of extinction of the CR to a second CS that has not been given extinction training. This is called secondary extinction and is evidence of a generalization of extinction. Delay, trace, and pseudo CRs show more rapid extinction than do simultaneous CRs.

Although reintroduction of the US to the training procedure is the most efficient way to reverse experimental extinction, there are three other procedures that will also produce reversal. If the subject is removed from the experimental room at the time a zero level of extinction has been reached and is returned at a later time, the CS will evoke a CR. This recovery of the conditioned response is called spontaneous recovery. However, with sufficient extinction training there is no spontaneous recovery.

It is possible also to produce recovery of conditioning following extinction by presenting the US alone for a few trials. The CR will then be evoked by the CS presented alone.

Recovery of the CR following experimental extinction may also be produced by disinhibition. This occurs when a novel stimulus is presented in the laboratory at the termination of an extinction series. Disinhibition is a temporary phenomenon, and its magnitude is a function of the extent of extinction and the intensity of the disinhibiting stimulus.

Retention. The retention of classical CRs has received little study. What evidence there is indicates very high degrees of retention in animals who have experienced no conditioning for several years.

W. J. Brogden

[*Directly related are the biographies of* Pavlov *and* Watson. *Other relevant material may be found in* Forgetting.]

BIBLIOGRAPHY

Hilgard, Ernest R.; and Marquis, Donald G. (1940) 1961 *Hilgard and Marquis' Conditioning and Learning.* Revised by Gregory A. Kimble. 2d ed. New York: Appleton. → First published as *Conditioning and Learning.*

Pavlov, Ivan P. (1923) 1928 *Lectures on Conditioned Reflexes: Twenty-five Years of Objective Study of Higher Nervous Activity (Behavior) of Animals.* New York: International Publishers. → First published as *Dvadtsatiletnii opyt ob'jektivnogo izucheniia vysshei nervnoi deiatel'nosti (povedeniia) zhivotnykh.*

Pavlov, Ivan P. (1927) 1960 *Conditioned Reflexes: An Investigation of the Physiological Activity of the Cerebral Cortex.* New York: Dover. → First published as *Lektsii o rabote bol'shikh polusharii golovnogo mozga.*

Razran, G. 1961 The Observable Unconscious and the Inferable Conscious in Current Soviet Psychophysiology: Interoceptive Conditioning, Semantic Conditioning, and the Orienting Reflex. *Psychological Review* 68:81–147.

Stevens, S. S. (editor) 1951 *Handbook of Experimental Psychology.* New York: Wiley.

III
INSTRUMENTAL LEARNING

The concept of instrumental learning is a powerful one, primarily because it assists psychologists in their goals of predicting and controlling, or modifying, behavior. The concept is based on an empirically derived functional relationship between the probability of a response and the previous consequences of that response: while battles between theoreticians have not yet been fully resolved, it is generally useful to consider that the probability of a response to a stimulus situation is particularly likely to be strengthened if the response is followed by what may loosely be called a satisfying state of affairs.

This presentation will be chiefly concerned with applications and implications of instrumental, or operant, learning that may be of more general interest to social scientists; the technical aspects are covered elsewhere [see LEARNING, *article on* REINFORCEMENT].

Adherents of this position have maintained that most of the forms of behavior exhibited by infrahuman animals can be effectively analyzed in instrumental terms. A dog approaches when its name is called, horses respond to signals from their riders, cats "know" where to go for food, and cattle avoid an electrified fence, all because of the consequences of previous relevant behavior. Applying the techniques of instrumental conditioning in laboratory settings, experimental psychologists have succeeded in eliciting behavior of great complexity. B. F. Skinner has trained pigeons to engage in behavior that strikingly resembles table tennis. He and his colleagues have also, by reinforcing aggressive behavior, converted usually placid birds into "vicious" killers. The familiar reverse procedure, taming, is also accomplished by instrumental conditioning. Discriminations between colors, shapes, tones, and so forth, can be taught by differential application of reinforcements. For example, an animal can readily be trained to approach a green disc when a low-pitched tone is presented and to approach a red disc in response to a tone of higher frequency. A procedure as simple as this provides a most reliable means of ascertaining sensory capacities of animals. If, say, a food-deprived rat is given food whenever it presses a blue lever but is given no reinforcement when it presses a yellow lever of equal brightness, then equal rates of pressing the two levers would lead us to conclude that the animal cannot distinguish between the two colors. For the sake of simplicity this example has ignored both the possibility that in this instance reinforcement is not effective and the important finding that the kinesthetic and other stimulation resulting from a lever press may itself be reinforcing; recent studies indicate that almost any form of nonnoxious stimulation may possess, under certain specifiable conditions, extremely important reinforcing properties. [See LEARNING, *article on* DISCRIMINATION LEARNING.]

In terms of potential for generalization, few consequences of the learning process are more influential than what Harry F. Harlow (1949) has called "learning to learn." A monkey that has learned to make a particular discriminative response in a particular stimulus situation (e.g., to the "odd" stimulus in a three-stimulus array) has apparently learned not only that a particular response is rewarded in this situation but also that situations may have embedded in them stimulus properties which, if reacted to appropriately, lead to reinforcement. Thus, if "oddness" ceases to be relevant or reinforcing in this or other situations, a new principle will be sought (e.g., the largest object or the object on the far left of the array). Furthermore, this principle will be discovered far more readily if the animal has previously learned the value of learning.

There is good reason to believe that even some of the most "basic" forms of animal behavior are acquired through and maintained by instrumental conditioning. Copulation, for example, at least in those mammalian species in which it has been carefully studied, is apparently a product of learning. Rhesus monkeys without previous sexual experience have been observed to engage in considerable trial and error—males mounting males, and so on—before arriving at the usual preference for heterosexual intercourse. It is clear that "normal" sexual behavior becomes preferred simply because, for anatomical reasons, it is most likely to be reinforced. Statistically deviant forms of sexuality can be explained in exactly the same way: homosexual or autoerotic activity will tend to be repeated to the extent that it has been positively reinforced. A critical period for learning may exist: learning during a particular portion of the animal's life may be more influential than learning that takes place either earlier or later. Such a possibility would seem to hold greater promise for future research than speculations about the "mental health" of the deviant animals. [See IMPRINTING; SEXUAL BEHAVIOR.]

In a similar vein is the finding by Melzack and Scott (1957) that escaping from pain is a function of particular stimulus dimensions present early in life. It is apparently no longer safe to assume that if a stimulus–response bond is of sufficient biological importance, it is genetically transmitted. [See PAIN.]

As a final example of operant conditioning in infrahuman animals, let us consider what has been called "neurotic" behavior. After an animal has learned that a particular response (e.g., turning left in a T maze) is followed by positively reinforcing stimulation, the experimenter arranges for a strong electric shock, or other negative reinforcer, to be contingent upon the same response. If the experimenter has skillfully controlled his variables, he will have induced conflict. The frustrated animal will display fairly stereotyped behavior: going round in circles, "freezing," or showing other signs of acute and stressful indecision. Even if the shock apparatus is disconnected, the animal will continue to exhibit this behavior (which presumably serves to reduce anxiety) and may even starve to death unless "therapeutic" measures are taken. It is the compulsive self-destructive nature of the behavior and its origin in conflict that may justify the designation of "neurotic." Generalization to the human level must, of course, be undertaken with great caution. It should be noted that neurotic behavior can also be elicited by classical procedures. [*See* CONFLICT, *article on* PSYCHOLOGICAL ASPECTS.]

Instrumental conditioning in humans

B. F. Skinner chose to give to his seminal 1938 book the general title *The Behavior of Organisms*. No new principles, he suggests, need be invoked in order to study human behavior. There is good reason to believe that the human equivalents of the types of behavior described above are also attained, or at least maintained, by means of operant conditioning. Thus, for example, while a definitive experiment will probably never be conducted, it seems reasonable to assume that all forms of sexual behavior are learned by trial and error, by imitation, or by instruction. And both the tendency to imitate and the tendency to follow instructions can themselves be understood as functions of the organism's reinforcement history [*see* IMITATION].

Language. Perhaps the most important human skill from the standpoint of psychology is language. The initial babblings of the infant are random or semirandom; some sounds, like "ma," are easier to produce than others and will therefore be emitted at a relatively higher base rate. These babblings are differentially reinforced. Differential reinforcement simply means, in this case, that the mother —or other socializing agent—will find certain sounds more reinforcing than others and will behave in such a way as to increase the frequency of these sounds. "Ma," as a response, is strengthened; "ka" and "la" are not. The infant next learns that "ma" is reinforced only under certain conditions. Under other conditions (e.g., when only the father is present), "ma" is either ignored or is negatively reinforced. More complicated utterances can be built up in similar fashion. Thus, while the development of a repertoire of sounds and sound combinations that serve as responses to specific external or internal stimulus situations may be a prodigious feat, it is not a particularly mysterious one (Skinner 1957). Not all language is learned in this rather inefficient fashion. Many utterances result from imitation or from intentional instruction.

Recent experiments have revealed that the verbal behavior of adults can likewise be manipulated. Rates of emission, particular sounds, parts of speech, sentence length, and content are responsive to operant-conditioning procedures in which a smile or a nod provides quite effective reinforcement (see, for example, Portnoy & Salzinger 1964). It might also be pointed out here that operant conditioning is now being used by Lilly (1963) in an effort to teach bottle-nose dolphins to use the English language "intelligently." [*See* LANGUAGE, *article on* LANGUAGE DEVELOPMENT.]

Creativity. Another important kind of activity, creativity, is also susceptible to analysis in these terms. Here the key psychological, as distinguished from sociological, variable is novelty of response to a stimulus situation. Numerous studies (e.g., Maltzman et al. 1960) have demonstrated that the individual will learn to make novel responses if he is rewarded for doing so. A "motive" for originality is thus instilled just as readily as the "motive" for conformity is instilled in most of our educational institutions. The learned tendency to produce "original" responses, combined with the learned tendency to view one's productions critically, may be enough to explain even the highest achievements of human creativity. The fact that computer-type machines can be programmed to "create" music in a large variety of styles points in the same direction. [*See* CONFORMITY; CREATIVITY.]

Emotional behavior. Operant conditioning also provides a useful framework for studying those most complicated psychological processes, the emotions. Whether they are subjective states or physiological events, or both, emotions may be viewed as (*a*) responses to antecedent stimuli and (*b*) stimuli for consequent responses. As responses, emotions are learnable. It is extremely doubtful that the newborn infant has any emotions at all; he almost definitely is not afraid of the dark, or of falling, or of snakes; he does not love his mother, nor does he feel inferior. How are these emotions learned? It appears that no new principles need be invoked. A child observing his mother's frightened reactions to a thunderstorm may exercise his acquired tendency to imitate by manifesting similar signs of fright. These signs are reinforced by maternal solicitude. Studies indicate high correlations between the fears of children and of their parents (Hagman 1932).

As an extended hypothetical example, consider what is generally called love. The child may learn that the words "I love you" are often followed by more tangible rewards and that his own manifestations of "loving" behavior are followed by rewards from people in his environment. Consequently he may learn to seek out circumstances in which it is appropriate for such kinds of behavior to occur. He wants to love and be loved. The rewards of establishing a love relationship, which go far beyond the food and tactile stimulation that probably served as initial reinforcement, may include temporary freedom from corporal punishment, victory in a sibling rivalry, or erotic stimulation. With such a multitude of possible reinforcements, the child may readily learn those forms of behavior that elicit "loving" behavior from the people in his environment. And one particularly effective method for achieving this is to engage in "loving" behavior oneself. But since the well-socialized child has also probably learned that there are negative reinforcements for deceptive behavior, he must get himself to actually "feel" the emotion he is expressing. This necessary internal state is conditionable, but a classical conditioning model is probably more useful here than the operant model. [See AFFECTION; EMOTION; MORAL DEVELOPMENT; PERSONALITY, *article on* PERSONALITY DEVELOPMENT.]

Religiosity. One's religious convictions may likewise be regarded as nothing more than a complex set of learned responses to a complex set of stimuli. The objection that man is born with a knowledge of and reverence for God receives its strongest rebuttal from the practices of the major religions, whose emphasis on Sunday school and other forms of religious instruction seems at odds with such concepts as revelation or innate knowledge. The combination of formal religious training, informal parental inculcation (e.g., answering "God did it" to difficult questions in the natural sciences), and ubiquitous social pressures (e.g., the motto "In God We Trust" on U.S. currency) makes clear why so many children engage in religious behavior. Whether the mediator in such cases is the learned motive to conform or the learned motive to imitate, religious utterances and other religious activities tend to be positively reinforced. The intense emotionality that so often accompanies or defines the "religious experience" may result from the capacity of religion to satisfy such needs as dependency, affiliation, and (perhaps) erotic gratification, needs that may themselves be products of instrumental learning. Thus, to the extent that religiosity is inferred from behavior, principles of conditioning appear to be sufficient for a complete explanation. [See RELIGION.]

Mental illness. As a final example of the widespread applicability of these principles, we may consider those forms of behavior that characterize "mental illness." It is possible to regard the disordered or undesired behavior simply as a set of responses that have become progressively stronger because of their reinforcing consequences. This formulation holds true even if the behavior (nail-biting, cigarette smoking, destructive interpersonal relationships, self-degrading activities) appears to have negative consequences. The "reward" in such cases may be temporary relief from anxiety, satisfaction of abnormally strong learned needs to conform or not conform, to confirm a self concept, and so on. There may be a wide gap in complexity between a rat that makes the correct choice in a T maze and an accident-prone human, but it is possible to understand the behavior of both animals in terms of the same principles. [See MENTAL DISORDERS; NEUROSIS.]

Practical applications

In most sciences, including psychology, the goals of prediction and control, or modification, are inextricably related. While the foregoing paragraphs have emphasized the prediction of responses, the following examples refer specifically to the possibility of response modification or control.

Programmed instruction. The widespread adoption of "teaching machines" and other programmed instructional devices in schools all over the world attests to the ability of operant methods to establish the repertoire of stimulus–response bonds deemed necessary by society. Instead of the primary reinforcement of a pellet of food, so often used to control or shape the behavior of infrahuman animals, it has been found that such secondary reinforcers as "the feeling of success" are extremely effective for human students of all ages. There is nothing mysterious about these secondary reinforcers; their emergence can be predicted—or arranged—by virtue of their frequent association with primary rewards. So long as teacher shortages exist, programmed instructional devices will continue to be useful adjuncts to more conventional pedagogic techniques. But these devices are of far more than ancillary value. They provide advantages that are uniquely their own. Each student is permitted to proceed at his own rate and thus avoids either the boredom or the frustration that may result from the single-level approach so often necessary in crowded classrooms. Furthermore, the use of programmed materials largely does away with extrinsic rewards, such as grades and teacher-approval, by relying primarily on the reinforcing nature of the learning process itself. While many of their potentialities remain to be developed, it is difficult to conceive of any academic subject matter that cannot be taught, and taught effectively, by means of these methods. [See LEARNING, *article on* PROGRAMMED LEARNING.]

Behavior therapy. Principles of operant conditioning have also been found to be extremely useful in the modification of undesirable behavior. The behavior in question, whether it involves an isolated *S–R* connection (e.g., fear-responses to heights) or a complex pattern of behavioral tendencies from which some clinicians infer "neurosis" or "psychosis," can be altered by extinguishing the undesired response while building up a desired response (or set of responses) to the same stimuli. For example, homosexuality—a form of behavior that is notoriously resistant to traditional varieties of psychotherapy—often responds quite favorably to what is called behavior therapy (see, for example, Feldman & MacCulloch 1964). Procedures differ widely, but the following outline of treatment may be of illustrative value. The "patient" (a term which is particularly inappropriate in this context) is requested by the therapist to have a homosexual fantasy. When he signals that the fantasy has reached a peak of excitement, the individual receives a painful electric shock. This procedure is repeated over several sessions, with the result that in subsequent interviews, when it is clear to the patient that shock will not occur, he reports that homosexual thoughts and behaviors are gradually being extinguished. During the extinction process, heterosexual motives and activities are strengthened by means of familiar techniques of reinforcement. Early in the treatment, for example, the individual is directed to masturbate while engaging in heterosexual fantasies; before very long, an association develops between having an orgasm and visualizing a partner of the opposite sex. Within one year most individuals exposed to this form of treatment are behaving in ways acceptable to society and to themselves outside the therapist's office. New forms of undesirable behavior do not appear, and the proportion of "relapses" is far smaller than that encountered in other forms of treatment. [See MENTAL DISORDERS, TREATMENT OF, *article on* BEHAVIOR THERAPY; SEXUAL BEHAVIOR, *article on* HOMOSEXUALITY; *see also* Feldman & MacCulloch 1964.]

Obviously, behavior therapy is not simply symptom removal. Starting with the premises that the undesired behavior has been learned and that whatever has been learned can be unlearned, the method proceeds to instill new learnings as efficiently as possible. As a by-product of this counterconditioning, we may expect a reduction in the anxiety engendered by the behavior in question. This reduction, as measured, for example, by the galvanic skin reflex, will, in turn, tend to lower the frequency of pathological behavior. Alternatively the therapist may choose to attack the anxiety more directly by viewing it as a learned response to specifiable interpersonal or other stimuli. [See ANXIETY; PERSONALITY, *article on* THE FIELD.]

There appears to be no qualitative difference between the treatment of a simple self-destructive habit and of the most complex of neurotic constellations. Although some critics might accuse them of unjustified reductionism, proponents of behavior therapy would allege that the more conventional methods of treatment take longer and have a lower success rate because the necessary learning process is managed inexpertly, being incorrectly regarded as little more than an epiphenomenon of insight, catharsis, and so on.

The apparent therapeutic effectiveness of Skinnerian methods should not blind the reader to the equally stimulating applications of Pavlovian methodology to behavior therapy. The cautionary note should also be added that the number of individuals, the number of conditions treated, and the duration of follow-up studies are not yet sufficient to justify unreserved acceptance of the new methodology. Still, unlike certain other recent innovations in therapy, the use of conditioning is firmly based on a mass of quite unequivocal laboratory data. [See MENTAL DISORDERS, TREATMENT OF.]

Implications

As has been indicated, the principles and practices of instrumental conditioning provide useful tools for the prediction and control of behavior. This practical utility leads to a consideration of a number of quite crucial questions.

First, can a science of psychology exist entirely on the basis of prediction and control, without regard to the task of *understanding* behavior? The question virtually answers itself if the goals of understanding are made explicit. Although the wish to understand is, for some, based largely on intellectual curiosity rather than on the desire for practical applications, there are only two ways that one can persuasively confirm, test, or demonstrate understanding: by predicting or by controlling the phenomena he claims to understand. Furthermore, some psychologists wish to understand primarily because they wish to predict and control. It might also be pointed out here that the individual who wishes to apply psychological principles to his own betterment can do so by means of, and perhaps only by means of, that intelligent arrangement of stimulus–response contingencies called self-control. Clearly, the specification of empirical regularities in the occurrences of stimuli and responses eliminates the need for prior "understanding." The thoroughgoing adherent of the instrumental point of view might also claim that explanations of behavior in terms of the functioning of the central nervous system are likewise unnecessary.

Second, are there any forms of behavior that do not make sense within the framework of instrumental learning? Some writers have argued that behavior which is very complex requires a more complicated explanatory model; but complex behavior—including behavior that involves language —yields readily to instrumental analysis. Such analysis of a phenomenon is not, of course, logically identical to a valid causal explanation of it. Some also maintain that there are forms of complex behavior (referred to as "instinctive") that are genetically determined, but the realm of instinct seems to dwindle as more and more alleged instances yield to analysis in terms of prenatal or early postnatal conditioning. Certainly at the human level the concept of instinct seems no longer useful. On the other hand, there is no need to deny the existence of genetically transmitted unconditioned reflexes. [See GENETICS, *article on* GENETICS AND BEHAVIOR; INSTINCT.]

Perhaps the best objection to what might be called instrumental imperialism is that many kinds of behavior fit more readily into the framework of classical, rather than operant, conditioning. But it may be that these two categories are not really distinct from each other. To give a somewhat oversimplified example, Pavlov's dogs may have learned to salivate to the initially neutral stimulus because the response of salivation was "paid off" by the presentation of food.

A final consideration has to do with the ancient problem of free will versus determinism. If behavior is nothing but responses to stimuli, and if the stimuli determine the responses, then the concept of free will ceases to be necessary. The fact that different people may respond differently to the same stimulus is, of course, beside the point. The stimulus may not be the "same" at all, being contingent upon receptors, thresholds, and previous conditioning. And even if the stimuli *are* viewed as identical, response differences would be explicable by virtue of individual differences in reinforcement histories or physical abilities.

Because of the number and the complexity of the determining variables, some behavior may be, practically speaking, "unpredictable." But this practical limitation in no way justifies an explanation of such acts in terms of free will. Analogously, the result of a coin flip, while usually attributed to "chance," is the inevitable outcome of a set of variables: air currents, the force of the flip, the distance the coin is permitted to drop, and so on. While these variables can be ascertained only with great difficulty, we do not conclude that the coin has manifested free will. The same line of reasoning may be raised against those who invoke the physicists' principle of indeterminacy in support of the free-will position.

In short, as the instruments, methods, and concepts in the science of psychology become increasingly sophisticated, the number of unpredictable and uncontrollable human acts appears to be shrinking proportionally. The widespread application of conditioning procedures is not without its dangers. But the possible abuses of this powerful tool should not obscure the recognition of its potential advantages. It does not seem unrealistically optimistic to view instrumental conditioning as a way, perhaps *the* way, to elicit from human beings those forms of creative, satisfying, and socially useful behavior that the less-systematic educational methods have so conspicuously failed to obtain.

Instrumental conditioning is by no means a *new* method of behavioral development. Indeed, if its principles are valid, they were operating long before they were formulated. But the recent advances that have been reviewed herein suggest that these principles will play an increasingly pivotal role in twentieth-century psychology.

LAWRENCE CASLER

BIBLIOGRAPHY

FELDMAN, M. P.; and MACCULLOCH, M. J. 1964 A Systematic Approach to the Treatment of Homosexuality by Conditioned Aversion: Preliminary Report. *American Journal of Psychiatry* 121:167–171.

HAGMAN, ELMER R. 1932 A Study of Fears of Children of Pre-school Age. *Journal of Experimental Education* 1:110–130.

HARLOW, HARRY F. 1949 The Formation of Learning Sets. *Psychological Review* 56:51–65.

LILLY, JOHN C. 1963 Productive and Creative Research With Man and Dolphin. *Archives of General Psychiatry* 8:111–116.

MALTZMAN, IRVING et al. 1960 Experimental Studies in the Training of Originality. *Psychological Monographs* 74, no. 6.

MELZACK, RONALD; and SCOTT, T. H. 1957 The Effects of Early Experience on the Response to Pain. *Journal of Comparative and Physiological Psychology* 50:155–161.

PORTNOY, STEPHANIE; and SALZINGER, KURT 1964 The Conditionability of Different Verbal Response Classes: Positive, Negative and Nonaffect Statements. *Journal of General Psychology* 70:311–323.

ROGERS, CARL; and SKINNER, B. F. 1956 Some Issues Concerning the Control of Human Behavior. *Science* 124:1057–1066.

SKINNER, B. F. 1938 *The Behavior of Organisms: An Experimental Analysis.* New York: Appleton.

SKINNER, B. F. 1953 *Science and Human Behavior.* New York: Macmillan.

SKINNER, B. F. 1957 *Verbal Behavior.* New York: Appleton.

IV
REINFORCEMENT

The principle of reinforcement is not new. One form of that principle, the law of effect, dates back to Thorndike (1898–1901), who was one of the first systematic experimenters to observe that the development and maintenance of new instrumental performances are closely controlled by their environmental consequences. Thorndike theorized that an organism's behavior was "stamped in" when it was followed by a satisfying state of affairs. By a satisfying state of affairs, Thorndike meant a condition that the animal did nothing to avoid, and whose maintenance and renewal the animal sought. Although our language has developed in the interest of greater scientific objectivity, and our experimental methods have progressed in the direction of greater precision and analytical prowess, Thorndike's early observations on trial-and-error learning represent the foundations of modern effect, or reinforcement, theory.

In contrast to the trial-and-error, or instrumental, learning studied by Thorndike, Pavlov (1927) worked with classical conditioning procedures. Perhaps the best known example of Pavlov's work is salivary conditioning. A stimulus which does not initially elicit salivation (the conditioned stimulus: a bell or metronome, for example) is presented in close temporal conjunction with a substance that does elicit salivation when placed in the mouth (the unconditioned stimulus: food powder or dilute acid, for example). After several paired presentations of the conditioned and unconditioned stimuli —provided sufficient attention is given to the details of the conditioning procedure—the conditioned stimulus gains the power to elicit salivation as a conditioned response. Because the development and maintenance of the conditioned response are closely dependent upon presentation of the unconditioned stimulus, the latter has been called a reinforcing stimulus.

Generalizing from the above considerations, it can be said that both instrumental, or Thorndikean, and classical, or Pavlovian, reinforcers may be looked upon as critical events in a learning episode. Just as the occurrence of reinforcement "strengthens" behavior, so the omission of reinforcement "weakens" behavior. In both instrumental and classical conditioning, the elimination of behavior by removing the reinforcer responsible for its maintenance is called *extinction*. Space does not permit a detailed comparison between instrumental and classical conditioning procedures. The reader is referred to Kimble's revision of Hilgard and Marquis' *Conditioning and Learning* (1940).

While this discussion has stressed the importance of reinforcement in learned behavior, it should be noted that not all psychologists agree on this point. E. R. Guthrie (1935), for example, developed a theoretical system in which learning does not depend on reinforcement. Although Guthrie agreed with Thorndike that learning consists of the bonding or conditioning of responses to stimuli, Guthrie maintained that simple temporal contiguity of response and stimulus is sufficient. Thorndike, it will be recalled, stated that reinforcement, that is, the satisfying state of affairs, was necessary in addition to stimulus–response contiguity. Perhaps the most extensive stimulus–response reinforcement theory was developed by C. L. Hull (1943). The similarities and differences among the various theories of learning constitute a study in themselves—Hilgard's *Theories of Learning* (Hilgard & Bower 1948) should be consulted as a general reference. An indication of the type of research evolving from a theoretical concern with the nature of reinforcement is provided by Birney and Teevan's *Reinforcement* (1961), a collection of original papers—some classics—by prominent experimentalists.

Instrumental or operant behavior

Particularly important in the development of knowledge regarding the dynamics of reinforcement has been the work of B. F. Skinner (1938; 1953) and his colleagues. Skinner has adopted a nontheoretical, descriptive approach in his analysis of behavior, and the results of his work have had great practical and systematic significance. The methodology characteristic of Skinner's work has been analyzed and discussed by Sidman (1960) in his book *Tactics of Scientific Research*.

Instrumental, or operant, behavior may be defined as behavior that is under the control of its environmental consequences. Opening a door, walking across the street, speaking, etc., are examples of operant behaviors. When the consequence of a behavior serves to increase the frequency or probability of occurrence of the behavior, we refer to the consequence as *reinforcement*. *Positive reinforcement* involves the onset of some stimulus as the reinforcing consequence; *negative reinforcement* involves stimulus termination as the reinforcing consequence. Negatively reinforcing stimuli are often called aversive stimuli; it has been found that the onset of an aversive stimulus contingent upon a behavior will often decrease the probability of occurrence of that behavior. The reinforcement relationships just described are actually quite complex, and no simple statement will adequately summarize all of the detailed facts regarding positive and negative reinforcement. However, types of reinforcers and the ways in which they have been manipulated provide for some of the well-known behavioral paradigms.

Reward training. In reward training a positive reinforcer is contingent upon the occurrence of a response. Thorndike's experimental situation is a case in point; modern versions of the procedure involve such arbitrarily selected experimental behaviors as lever pressing, running in mazes and alleys, turning a wheel, jumping a gap, and, in humans, verbal behavior. Typical reinforcers that have been employed are food and water, for an animal appropriately deprived; the opportunity to engage in sexual activity or to explore a novel environment, money, praise, etc., have been used with humans.

Escape training. Negative reinforcement involves the termination of an aversive stimulus. The behavior which terminates that stimulus is called escape behavior. Arbitrarily selected behaviors like those mentioned above have been used to study the properties of negative reinforcement. The most frequently used negative reinforcer has been electric shock, although reproof, social isolation, etc., have been used with humans.

Avoidance training. While an escape-training paradigm involves the presentation of the aversive stimulus independent of the organism's behavior, a paradigm can be arranged in which some arbitrary response postpones or avoids the delivery of the aversive stimulus. Any response which does so is an avoidance response. Often a warning stimulus, such as a light or a buzzer, precedes by some predetermined period of time the scheduled occurrence of the aversive stimulus. In this arrangement, called discriminated avoidance, a response occurring between the onset of the warning stimulus and the scheduled onset of the aversive stimulus is the avoidance response. Typically, a response occurring during that interval terminates the warning stimulus and results in the avoidance of the aversive stimulus. Sidman (1953) has carefully studied an avoidance procedure, called nondiscriminated avoidance, in which no warning stimulus occurs. Instead, the aversive stimulus, such as electric shock, is scheduled to occur on a purely temporal basis. A response recycles a timer, and the shock is postponed. Ordinarily, more than one temporal interval is involved in this kind of experiment.

Punishment training. Punishment training involves the onset of an aversive stimulus contingent upon the occurrence of a response. An effective procedure for studying punishment has been employed by Azrin and is described by Azrin and Holtz (1965). Animals are trained to respond through the use of positive reinforcement. A punishment is then applied, and the local, transient, and permanent effects of punishment are studied.

This outline is necessarily brief and cannot do justice to the many detailed findings in the control of behavior through reinforcement contingencies. In order to explore further some of those findings, however, we may consider in more detail the positive reinforcement of operant behavior.

Reinforcement and chaining

Some of the important facts regarding reinforcement can be displayed by considering a laboratory example where a pigeon is trained to step on a treadle in the rear of an experimental chamber, then to peck on an illuminated plastic disk or key on the wall, and, finally, to approach and eat from a grain tray. The first step is the adaptation of a hungry pigeon to the experimental chamber. After the bird is in the chamber for several minutes, the food tray is raised, with the grain illuminated by a small overhead light. The tray is held in place until the bird sees and eats some grain. After the bird has eaten for several seconds, the tray is dropped away, out of reach of the bird, and the light is turned off. The procedure is repeated until the bird responds immediately to the lifting of the tray and the illumination of the grain. By temporally spacing tray presentations, we provide for the extinction of approach behavior when the tray is not in the lifted position.

For the next step, we illuminate the translucent plastic disk on the wall. The pigeon is trained to stay in the vicinity of the disk by means of a procedure known as *successive approximation*. In this procedure each movement of the bird is noted, and as soon as a movement occurs that brings him a little closer to the disk, the grain tray is immediately lifted for a few seconds and the bird is allowed to eat. When the bird is near the disk his finer movements are observed, and, again by successive approximation, we bring his beak closer and closer to the disk until he pecks it. Each closer approximation to the desired response of pecking the disk is immediately followed by, that is, *reinforced* with, access to the grain tray. Next, we darken the disk and permit the pigeon to peck. The grain tray is not lifted. Soon the key is illuminated and a peck is followed by the grain tray's being lifted. Several pecks at the dark disk are allowed, but none of them is reinforced with food. When the disk is illuminated, a peck produces grain. This procedure (that is, *discrimination training*) results in a rapid decrease in the frequency of pecking at the dark disk, with the maintenance of a high probability of pecking at the illuminated disk. In the final step, another example of successive approximation, we start with a dark disk. A movement by the pigeon in the direction of the treadle is immediately followed by illumination of the disk. The pigeon is allowed to peck the disk and eat from the tray. As before, when he pecks at the dark disk, the grain tray is not lifted. By the illumination of the disk, contingent on some preselected aspect of the bird's behavior, we get him closer and closer to, and finally stepping on, the treadle. The behavior sequence is complete. The pigeon steps on the treadle; the disk is illuminated; the pigeon pecks the disk; the grain tray is immediately raised for a few seconds; the pigeon approaches the tray, and sees and eats the grain.

Paradigm of behavior chain. The behavior chain may be written symbolically, as follows ("$S_x : R_x \longrightarrow$" indicates the stimulus, S_x, in the presence of which a specified response, R_x, will have a specified effect, that is, $\longrightarrow$, the production of a new stimulus):

$$S_4 : R_4 \longrightarrow S_3 : R_3 \longrightarrow$$

sight	step	key	peck
of	on	illumi-	at
treadle	treadle	nated	key

If the behavioral chain in question is "free running," that is, if the bird is permitted to run it through over and over (a recycling chain), we might specify another stimulus event, S_0. The dropping away of the grain tray, S_0, is "produced" by (more exactly, correlated with) R_1. Thus, S_0 becomes the stimulus event in the presence of which the bird emits R_0, approach to the treadle. The approach response R_0 produces S_4. Thus the chain is closed, forming a continuous behavioral sequence that might be expected to continue as long as deprivation (motivational) variables are effective, all else being equal.

Conditioned and primary reinforcers. In analyzing the sequence of events that we have just described, it is important to notice that the actual reinforcers maintaining the specific responses are light and sound rather than the ingestion of food. This is the distinction between *conditioned* and *primary* reinforcement. While the primary reinforcement, that is, the ingestion of food, is a necessary condition for maintaining the bird's over-all performance, the conditioned reinforcers are made instantaneously and precisely contingent on the exact form of behavior that we wish to maintain. Virtually all operant behavior is maintained by conditioned reinforcers such as sounds and lights analogous to those described above, rather than directly by primary reinforcers such as food, water, oxygen, etc.

Principles of reinforcement. The preceding demonstration illustrates the following important principles pertinent to the operation of reinforcement:

(1) The strength of the several components of the response chain—stepping on the treadle, pecking the key, approaching the food tray—is maintained by their immediately reinforcing consequences. This fact can be demonstrated by performing extinction operations within the chain. Suppose we permit the pigeon to step on the treadle; but now, unlike the previous situation, we do not illuminate the disk when the pigeon responds in this way. Since the disk is not illuminated, the pigeon does not peck at it; but ceasing to illuminate the disk also constitutes the removal of conditioned reinforcement for the initial chain link, that is, stepping on the treadle. As a consequence of that removal of reinforcement, we may note first an increase and then certainly a decrease in the dis-

---

$$S_2 : R_2 \longrightarrow S_1 : R_1$$

grain	approach	sight	eat
tray	tray	of	
rises		grain	

---

position of the bird to step on the treadle. The chain has been broken at its initial link. As a matter of fact, we could have broken the chain at any of its links by the simple expedient of removing the immediately reinforcing consequences of any of the responses making up the chain.

(2) Experiments of the kind just described demonstrate clearly the essential relationship among the several reinforcers of the chain. Food, the primary reinforcer that occurs at the end of the behavior sequence, is necessary to maintain the entire chain in strength, but each one of the several arbitrary links is closely controlled by the conditioned reinforcer that it immediately produces.

(3) A stimulus such as the illuminated response key serves a double function. Not only is it a reinforcer for the immediately preceding behavior, but it sets the occasion for the next response in the required sequence. Illumination of the key not only reinforces stepping on the treadle, but it also sets the occasion (that is, serves as a *discriminative stimulus*) for which a peck at the key will be reinforced. Implicit in the discriminative control by the illuminated disk is the corollary fact that when the disk is not illuminated, responses to it will have no further effect; the animal cannot progress any further in the chain. Since the animal's behavior is under the specific control of each stimulus element in the chain, it is this discriminative control by each stimulus element in the chain that keeps the sequential emission of the chain going.

(4) The chain is constructed by starting with its final component. After the final component

is securely developed, the next to the final one is added. When this is securely developed, another is added, and so on. In other words, the chain is built in a backward sequence. The reason for this procedure is readily appreciated if we take note of the fact that at the beginning of our training procedure we have at our disposal a single strong reinforcer, namely, the grain. The other events that finally serve as the conditioned link reinforcers are initially neutral and arbitrary events, such as light and sound. In order to establish such stimuli as conditioned reinforcers, it is necessary to associate them with already established reinforcers. Therefore, the compound stimulus, consisting of a flash of light illuminating the grain and the slap of the tray being raised, is established as a reinforcer through its association with the grain. It is thus capable of strengthening and maintaining peck responses on the illuminated disk. Note, however, that the illuminated disk is now correlated with the flash of the feeder light and the sound of the tray. By virtue of this association, the illuminated disk itself becomes a conditioned reinforcer and can be used to strengthen and maintain still an earlier member in the chain. Thus, practical considerations dictate the backward development of the sequence of conditioned reinforcers, and it is this development that makes advisable the backward development of a behavioral chain. A detailed review of positive conditioned reinforcement has been published by Kelleher and Gollub (1962).

Kinds of control through reinforcement

Continuous versus intermittent reinforcement. For many years the typical laboratory experiment involved the *continuous reinforcement* of the criterion response. Continuous reinforcement refers to a schedule of reinforcement in which the behavior in question is reinforced each time it occurs. It is clear that an analysis of behavior restricted to this experimental program can have limited applicability to the affairs of men. Men live in complicated societies. Their behaviors are not reinforced by automatic "grain trays," but are subject rather to the possible whims and fancies of such agencies of society as government bureaus, social groups, religious groups, and, perhaps most important for the day-to-day existence of most of us, other individuals at home, at work, and at play. If there is any outstanding characteristic of people either in groups or as individuals, it is that their behavior is complexly determined. As a consequence of this complex determination, behavior is reinforced on an intermittent basis when individuals interact. For this reason, the general problem of intermittent

reinforcement must occupy a central and crucial place in the experimental analysis of behavior, if the latter is to come to grips with the problems of human performance.

Intermittent reinforcement refers to the case where some of, rather than all, the occurrences of the specified response are followed by a reinforcer. The phrase *schedule of reinforcement* refers to the particular rule by which reinforcement is made contingent upon some occurrence of a response. Broadly speaking, there are two general schemes whereby reinforcers can be related to response emission. Within either of these schemes, not to mention those cases where they are combined, there are literally thousands of different schedules. Many of the simpler ones and some of the more complex ones have been extensively studied in the laboratory using both animal and human subjects.

Interval and ratio schedules. When a rule specifying the contingency between a response and its reinforcement involves the passage of time, we speak of *interval schedules*. For example, we may specify that reinforcement will occur on the first response following a fixed period of elapsed time since the last reinforcement. Such a schedule is referred to as a *fixed interval* schedule of reinforcement. On the other hand, when the contingency involves some number of responses we speak of *ratio schedules*. We may specify that reinforcement will occur following the emission of the *n*th response since the last reinforcement. This rule, specifying a fixed number of responses, is ordinarily referred to as a *fixed ratio* schedule of reinforcement. These are simple cases, but they exemplify the two broad classifications of response–reinforcement contingencies referred to as "interval" and "ratio" schedules. These two broad classifications of reinforcement contingencies produce behaviors that have markedly different properties.

Characteristics of ratio schedules. Fixed ratio schedules are generally characterized by high rates of response emission. As the reinforcer is made contingent upon successively higher and higher response requirements, sharp breaks in responding ordinarily develop. Initially, these breaks appear following a reinforcement and preceding the next ratio run. Later, when the ratio requirement has reached some relatively high number, breaks may occur at various places during the ratio run. An outstanding characteristic of ratio performance is that the organism is either not responding (pausing) or is responding at a relatively constant rate. If the ratio requirement is increased still further, responding becomes relatively sporadic; we refer to this condition as ratio strain.

It is no secret that a type of gambling machine, the slot machine, is designed in accordance with the principles of ratio behavior. The payoff frequency must be great enough so that the gambling behavior does not show marked strain. On the other hand, the exact ratio contingency must not be defined by the emission of a *fixed* number of responses. If that were the case, we would observe potential gamblers waiting for the other fellow to play until, of course, $N-1$ coins had been fed the machine. Then there would ensue a dash to the machine in order to make the payoff response. Instead, the slot machine is programmed according to a *variable ratio* schedule of reinforcement. In this case, reinforcement is again contingent upon the emission of a number of responses, but the number of responses required differs from reinforcement to reinforcement. A variable ratio schedule of reinforcement is less susceptible to the development of ratio strain. Although very large numbers of response occurrences may be required for some instances of reinforcement, other instances occur after very few responses. Through judicious selection of a sequence of ratio sizes in a variable ratio program, the slot machine may be made to show a consistent profit.

Characteristics of interval schedules. The properties of interval schedules are different from those of ratio schedules. Interval schedules often show intermediate rates of responding. In the fixed interval case mentioned earlier, one frequently observes a relatively smooth transition from a zero rate of responding immediately after a reinforcement to a fairly high rate of responding preceding the next reinforcement. The characteristic shape of the fixed interval, cumulative-response graph is referred to as a *fixed interval scallop*. As in the case of variable ratio reinforcement, we can specify a rule that defines the *variable interval* case. In a variable interval schedule of reinforcement, reinforcement availability is again made contingent upon elapsed time, but, unlike the fixed interval case, the periods of time that must elapse between the reinforcements vary in a random sequence around some selected value. By the careful selection of interval sizes and their exact order of occurrence, one can produce a nearly uniform rate of responding, if one desires to do so. In fact, there have been variable interval response graphs that were so regular, a straightedge would be required to detect deviations from regularity. It can be seen, then, that the schedule of reinforcement, to a considerable extent, serves to control the rate and pattern of response emission. Schedules also serve to determine the characteristics of extinction, when

reinforcements are no longer obtainable. A schedule of continuous reinforcement produces a relatively brief extinction curve, whereas a schedule of intermittent reinforcement may produce a protracted extinction curve characterized by a gradual transition from a high rate of responding to a zero rate after variable interval reinforcement, or gradually increasing periods of no responding punctuated by response bursts at a constant rate after ratio reinforcement.

Motivation. Schedules of reinforcement, to a large extent, account for some of the properties of behavior that are often referred to as "motivational." Individuals characterized as highly motivated or "driven" may in fact be individuals who are capable of sustaining high ratio requirements without obvious signs of strain. On the other hand, people who are characterized as lazy or indolent may be, in fact, individuals who are not capable of sustained performance on even a modest ratio requirement. While such characterizations must not be accepted on the basis of face validity, they do have the merit of suggesting methods of changing the behaviors of such individuals. In this way, the research of the animal laboratory can be brought to bear on the problems of human behavior. The reader interested in the details of reinforcement schedules should consult *Schedules of Reinforcement* by Ferster and Skinner (1957). [*See* DRIVES; MOTIVATION.]

Differentiation of new response forms. It has been seen that schedules of reinforcement can be utilized to control the rate and pattern of response emission. Another major function of reinforcement is to create "new" behavior. By the creation of new behavior, we do not mean the creation of something out of nothing, but rather the transition from one form of behavior into another. There are many examples from the world of human affairs. The powerful and accurate play of the professional golfer is created from the fumbling, awkward movements of the beginner. The changes characterizing such a transition in behavior are not simply quantitative in the sense that a change in response rate is quantitative. The professional golfer does not simply move faster or swing his club more often. Rather, his performance is qualitatively different from that of the beginner. It may be seen that the development of new behavior is often a problem in the acquisition of skills. We have already specified the essential process by which skills are acquired; that is, successive approximation. Once we can specify the form of the final behavior that we desire, we can, starting with almost any arbitrary performance, bring about the desired behavior by stages. The instructor, teacher, therapist, or any other individual who is concerned with the creation of new behavior in others must be capable of recognizing closer and closer approximations to the desired performance. In addition to recognizing these closer and closer approximations, he must have at his disposal a conditioned reinforcer that may be presented immediately upon the appearance of an acceptable intermediate performance. Verbal reinforcers such as "good" or "now you have it" are often used with humans. Improved control over the immediacy of reinforcement was one of the major considerations in the development of the new and very promising technique of programmed instruction or, as it is often called—with misplaced emphasis on the hardware—"teaching machines."

Differential reinforcement. The critical procedure in the development of new behavior involves a process known as *differential reinforcement*. Differential reinforcement refers to a procedure in which reinforcement is administered upon the occurrence of some behaviors and withheld upon the occurrence of other behaviors. The extremely powerful and precise control that may be gained over behavior through differential reinforcement is responsible for the success of the successive approximation technique. Since reinforcement may be made contingent upon either a qualitative or intensive property of a response, the procedure may be used to change the topographical characteristics of the response or its intensity.

Consider the example of a young child ignored by his parents. In searching for attention, he may emit a wide range of specific behaviors, differing enormously with respect to topography. Any of these behaviors that succeeds in gaining attention from the parents will be strengthened to some extent and become prepotent over the others. Attention is reinforcing. By the process of differential reinforcement, the parents can create a new and strong behavior pattern in the young child. It is no accident that in the practical case the new behavior pattern typically involves some element of aversiveness for the parent. The parent, after all, is a reinforceable organism. Termination of the child's aversive behavior serves to reinforce the parent's behavior, which, as we have noted, may likewise serve to reinforce the behavior of the child. It may be readily appreciated how a vicious feedback system may be developed. In order to gain attention from the parent, the child raises his voice or generally displays some other form of temperamental behavior. Because this behavior is aversive to the parent, the parent terminates it by responding to

the child. The attention thereby shown to the child reinforces the temperamental display. Through a process of adaptation to the aversive properties of the child's behavior, or simply because the parent may not want to "give in" so readily, attention may be withheld on some specific instance of a temperamental display. Since an increase in the intensity of a temperamental display will ordinarily establish a new level of aversiveness, it is likely that the parent will respond to that new level with immediate attention. As a result, a more intense form of the temperamental display is differentially reinforced. The end result of such a feedback system is one that most of us have seen at one time or another. The fundamental mistake made by the parent at the outset is to respond to (that is, reinforce) any form of behavior that has aversive properties for him. By withholding reinforcement under these conditions and responding with attention when some form of nonaversive behavior is emitted by the child, the whole problem can be avoided. On the other hand, starting with a child who has already developed in strength some form of aversive behavior, the principle of differential reinforcement may be used in order to short-circuit the development of the feedback system. Simple withholding of reinforcement on all temperamental displays by the child will produce eventual extinction of that form of behavior. Perhaps a more positive approach would be to combine extinction of intense forms of temperamental display with deliberate reinforcement of less and less intense exhibitions by the child. Ultimately, the child will have learned that attention, and hence satisfaction of his needs, will be forthcoming only when his request is stated moderately.

The dynamic properties of reinforcement

We have stressed the importance of immediacy in the effective use of reinforcement. A reinforcement that is delayed after the occurrence of the criterion behavior will ordinarily occur in close temporal proximity to some other behavior. Although there might be some tendency for the criterion behavior to be strengthened, maximal strengthening will occur with respect to the intervening behavior.

Superstition and uncontingent reinforcement. If the intervening behavior that is maximally strengthened is incompatible with the criterion behavior, we might, in fact, note a decrease in the strength of the criterion behavior. Perhaps the most dramatic example of the effect of uncontingent reinforcement is the well-known "superstition" experiment (Skinner 1948).

A hungry pigeon is placed in an experimental chamber, and the grain tray is operated at fairly frequent intervals, but independent of the animal's behavior. After a period of time, we note the development of some rather strong behavioral patterns during the intervals between reinforcement. Frequently, these behavior patterns appear quite bizarre. The pigeon, for example, may hop about on one leg while fluttering a wing, or the bird may dance furiously from one side of the box to the other while stretching its neck. The important point is that these behaviors have developed as a function of the uncontingent reinforcement: *Simply because the reinforcement has not been made experimentally contingent upon some specified response does not mean that the reinforcement was without effect.* In fact, what will always happen is the strengthening, by the reinforcement, of some chance behavior. By the process of differential reinforcement, the behavior that is accidentally reinforced may show some slow drift in topography. After a period of time, we actually might note a completely different topography from that which we observed earlier. As a general principle, we may state that the more immediate the reinforcement is with respect to the criterion response, the more highly stereotyped the criterion response is likely to be. Less immediate reinforcement will produce somewhat looser control, with a noticeable tendency for the criterion response to change in time. We may, as a matter of fact, make an experimental prediction about the superstition experiment just described. If the uncontingent reinforcers are presented at fairly frequent intervals, we will note the relatively rapid development of some arbitrary and perhaps bizarre behavior that will be fairly resistant to drift, that is, it will maintain a roughly similar topography over long periods of time. If the uncontingent reinforcements are delivered at less frequent intervals, we will note a susceptibility to change and drift in the accidentally reinforced behavior. In the extreme, if the uncontingent reinforcers are delivered at widely spaced intervals, then the drift becomes such a dominating characteristic of the behavior that we fail to notice a long-range strengthening effect of the reinforcement at all. Our conclusion, therefore, is that for reinforcement to be maximally effective it must follow the to-be-reinforced response without delay.

Reinforcement and deprivation. A second dynamic property of reinforcement is its relationship to deprivation. Some environmental events will be effective as reinforcers only if the organism has been deprived of some commodity. Food, for example, is effective in controlling the behavior of an animal only if that animal has been made hungry through food deprivation. Similarly, water can be used as a reinforcer only if the animal has been deprived of water. Other kinds of reinforcers, even at the level of lower organisms, can be effective in the absence of deprivation. Electric shock, for example, can serve as a very powerful negative reinforcer without the organism having been deprived of any commodity such as food or water. It is no accident that negative reinforcement is the most popular form of behavior control employed by the average person. It is easy to dispense in its varied forms, and it does not depend for its effect on some prior operation not under the control of the punisher, such as deprivation of the punishee. Many of us have met individuals who through some quirk of behavioral development are themselves positively reinforced by their own dispensation of negative reinforcement.

Novelty as a reinforcer.   There is now evidence to indicate that even at the level of the rat, a novel situation may serve to reinforce positively and to maintain exploratory behavior (Montgomery 1954). It is clear, however, that deprivation-independent reinforcers become more important as one ascends the phylogenetic scale. It has been demonstrated quite clearly that at the level of the monkey, behavior may be reinforced and maintained if the monkey has a brief opportunity to look out from an experimental chamber into a room that is occupied by other monkeys or by people (Butler 1953). Curiosity, then, is a motive in higher animals, and curiosity satisfaction is a potent reinforcer.

Generalized reinforcers.   Reinforcers such as food and water and oxygen are of obvious importance in the control of lower animals. Of course they can also serve to control the behavior of higher animals. Ordinarily, however, the behavior of higher animals is under the control of nonhomeostatic reinforcers. A child, for example, can be powerfully reinforced by some particular play activity or by some manipulatable novel object, such as a brightly colored toy or a plastic ring. Adult humans can be powerfully reinforced by a wide range of reinforcers that we refer to as *generalized* reinforcers. These may be defined as specific events or objects that can be used to reinforce a wide range of different behaviors across many motivational systems, both homeostatic and nonhomeostatic. In the life of human beings, the most obvious example of a generalized reinforcer is money. More subtle, but nonetheless just as powerful, are such reinforcers as praise, attention, and improvement in living standard and working conditions. It is interesting to note that "improvement in working conditions" can serve as a reinforcer for the behavior of lower animals also. It has been demonstrated, for example, that a pigeon will peck at one key when the sole consequence of behavior on that key is to change the schedule of reinforcement to a more favorable one on a second key (Findley 1958). A more favorable schedule may be defined either by a higher rate of reinforcement or less work per reinforcement.

Physiological mechanisms. Finally, a recent finding offers considerable promise for the laboratory study of the physiological mechanisms of reinforcement. It has been demonstrated by Olds and Milner (1954) that such animals as rats and cats will work to produce weak electrical stimulation of certain brain loci. The technique holds great promise for the study of the neural substrates of reward. Olds (1962) has recently summarized most of the studies on reward by electrical stimulation of the brain.

STANLEY S. PLISKOFF
AND CHARLES B. FERSTER

[Other relevant material may be found in DRIVES; MOTIVATION; NERVOUS SYSTEM, article on BRAIN STIMULATION; STIMULATION DRIVES; and in the biographies of GUTHRIE; HULL; PAVLOV; THORNDIKE.]

BIBLIOGRAPHY

AZRIN, N. H.; and HOLTZ, W. C. 1965 Punishment. Pages 380–447 in Werner K. Honig (editor), *Operant Behavior: Areas of Research and Application.* New York: Appleton.

BIRNEY, ROBERT C.; and TEEVAN, RICHARD C. (editors) 1961 *Reinforcement, an Enduring Problem in Psychology: Selected Readings.* Princeton, N.J.: Van Nostrand.

BUTLER, ROBERT A. 1953 Discrimination Learning by Rhesus Monkeys to Visual-exploration Motivation. *Journal of Comparative and Physiological Psychology* 46:95–98.

FERSTER, C. B.; and SKINNER, B. F. 1957 *Schedules of Reinforcement.* New York: Appleton.

FINDLEY, JACK D. 1958 Preference and Switching Under Concurrent Scheduling. *Journal of the Experimental Analysis of Behavior* 1:123–144.

GUTHRIE, EDWIN R. (1935) 1960 *The Psychology of Learning.* Rev. ed. Gloucester, Mass.: Smith.

HILGARD, ERNEST; and BOWER, GORDON H. (1948) 1966 *Theories of Learning.* 3d ed. New York: Appleton. → Ernest Hilgard was sole author of the previous editions.

HILGARD, ERNEST R.; and MARQUIS, DONALD G. (1940) 1961 *Hilgard and Marquis' Conditioning and Learning.* 2d ed., revised by Gregory A. Kimble. New York: Appleton.

HULL, CLARK L. 1943 *Principles of Behavior: An Introduction to Behavior Theory.* New York: Appleton.

KELLEHER, ROGER T.; and GOLLUB, LEWIS R. 1962 A Review of Positive Conditioned Reinforcement. *Journal of the Experimental Analysis of Behavior* 5:543–597.

MONTGOMERY, K. C. 1954 The Role of Exploratory Drive in Learning. *Journal of Comparative and Physiological Psychology* 47:60–64.

OLDS, JAMES 1962 Hypothalamic Substrates of Reward. *Physiological Reviews* 42:554–604.

OLDS, JAMES; and MILNER, PETER 1954 Positive Reinforcement Produced by Electrical Stimulation of Septal Area and Other Regions of Rat Brain. *Journal of Comparative and Physiological Psychology* 47:419–427.

PAVLOV, IVAN P. (1927) 1960 *Conditioned Reflexes: An Investigation of the Physiological Activity of the Cerebral Cortex.* New York: Dover. → First published as *Lektsii o rabote bol'shikh polusharii golovnogo mozga.*

SIDMAN, MURRAY 1953 Avoidance Conditioning With Brief Shock and No Exteroceptive Warning Signal. *Science* 118:157–158.

SIDMAN, MURRAY 1960 *Tactics of Scientific Research: Evaluating Experimental Data in Psychology.* New York: Basic Books.

SKINNER, B. F. 1938 *The Behavior of Organisms: An Experimental Analysis.* New York: Appleton.

SKINNER, B. F. 1948 "Superstition" in the Pigeon. *Journal of Experimental Psychology* 38:168–172.

SKINNER, B. F. 1953 *Science and Human Behavior.* New York: Macmillan.

THORNDIKE, EDWARD L. (1898–1901) 1911 *Animal Intelligence: Experimental Studies.* New York: Macmillan.

V

DISCRIMINATION LEARNING

Discrimination learning, or the acquisition of ability to respond differentially to objects in the environment, is of continuing interest to psychologists for both empirical and theoretical reasons. Its study provides an opportunity for exploring the sensory capacities of the nonverbal organism, as well as the possibility of relating the fields of learning, perception, and attention, a possibility that has motivated much of the theoretical speculation available on this subject. Before attempting to evaluate the progress made in this direction, however, it is helpful to outline the most common procedures used in studying the learning of discriminations, most of which have employed laboratory animals.

Simultaneous discrimination procedure. In a simultaneous discrimination procedure, the animal is usually confronted with two stimulus objects on each trial. These objects normally are alike in all respects except for variation on some given attribute such as brightness, color, or shape. The animal indicates its choice between them by some reaction such as picking one up, approaching one, or the like. A "correct" choice is rewarded with something desirable, perhaps a pellet of food. An incorrect choice is nonrewarded or even punished.

Initially, of course, the animal shows only a chance level of accuracy because it has no prior knowledge of which object is related to reward and which to punishment. With continued training, the percentage of successful choices may increase to the point where it is clear the animal has mastered the problem. When the appropriate experimental controls have been used, such performance is clear evidence that the animal is sensitive to the stimulus attribute under investigation. The experimenter may then decrease the difference between the two objects. As he continues to do this, the animal's accuracy again approaches a chance level. From these data, it is possible to determine the animal's differential sensitivity to values on this stimulus attribute.

Successive discrimination procedure. In a successive discrimination procedure, only one of the two stimulus objects is presented on a given trial, but each occurs equally often in a sequence of such trials. In a T maze, for example, the stimulus object is displayed at the choice point, and the animal has the alternatives of turning into either the right or left alley. If turning left is the correct and rewarded response to one of the objects, then turning right is the correct and rewarded response in the presence of the second object. Thus, a different reaction must be related to each of the two stimulus objects in order to master the successive discrimination.

Alternatively, the animal's choice may be between reacting and not reacting. In classical conditioning procedures, for example, the animal is required to make the conditioned response in the presence of one object, the positive stimulus, and to inhibit this response in the presence of a different object, the negative stimulus. This technique has been valuable in determining absolute thresholds, that is, the minimum amount of an attribute that the animal can detect. Once the discrimination is established, the intensity or amount of the positive stimulus is gradually reduced until the animal no longer responds to it.

Generalization and discrimination. Theoretical interest in discrimination learning has tended to concentrate on two opposing tendencies that the animal shows during training. If it has been trained to respond in some definite manner to one stimulus, it will generalize or transfer this tendency to respond to a wide variety of other similar stimuli. This occurs spontaneously, without any specific training with these new stimuli. This tendency to generalize is of considerable interest to the theorist because it is one obvious basis for the transfer of training. But at the same time it poses a problem

for him. He must not only indicate the conditions under which this tendency to generalize is aroused, but he must also explain why this generalization occurs for certain new stimuli but not for others.

An opposing tendency, however, is also evident during discrimination training. Using the procedures described above, the animal can be taught to make differential responses to two very similar stimuli, that is, stimuli that would otherwise evoke quite similar responses in accordance with the generalization tendency. But during the course of discrimination training this generalization tendency is suppressed. The animal now acts as though the two stimuli were perceived as being distinctly different. Thus, a focal problem for a theory of discrimination learning is to explain the disappearance or suppression of the tendency to generalize as a result of the training procedures used.

Hull's theory. One of the more influential accounts of discrimination learning was developed by Clark Hull (1943). This formulation has two unique features. First, it does not attempt to explain the tendency to generalize; instead it assumes that it is an innate and universal characteristic of all organisms. Second, it accounts for the partial suppression of this tendency during discrimination learning by postulating a second and opposing form of generalization.

Hull's basic formulation is that every time an animal's response to a stimulus object is followed by a reward, there is an increase in the probability that the animal will respond in the same way to that stimulus object the next time it is presented. This is the excitatory tendency, the tendency to respond. This excitatory tendency, however, is not specific to the rewarded stimulus. It generalizes or spreads to other stimuli in direct proportion to the degree of similarity they have to the rewarded stimulus. This differential spread is conceived of as a generalization gradient. The amount of excitatory tendency is greatest for the rewarded stimulus, but this amount diminishes along a continuum of decreasing stimulus similarity. Basically, this conception is a description of what is empirically observed in transfer-of-training studies.

The suppression of this generalization tendency during discrimination training is accounted for by postulating an opposing tendency. It is assumed that each time the animal's response to a stimulus is not rewarded there is an increase in the strength of an inhibitory tendency, the tendency to withhold or suppress the response in the presence of that stimulus. This inhibitory tendency also generalizes. It forms a gradient that has a maximum value at the nonrewarded stimulus and that diminishes in magnitude along a continuum of decreasing stimulus similarity.

In these terms, a conditioned discrimination can be conceived of in the following way. On some trials the animal is confronted by one stimulus and on the remainder of the trials by a second, similar stimulus. If it responds appropriately to the first stimulus, the positive one, it is rewarded. Thus, some amount of the excitatory tendency is associated with this stimulus and generalizes, although to a lesser degree, to the second stimulus. However, if the animal responds in the same way when this second or negative stimulus is presented, no reward is given. This results in a certain amount of inhibitory tendency becoming associated with the negative stimulus. This in turn generalizes, although to a lesser degree, to the positive stimulus. It is assumed that these successive interactions between excitatory and inhibitory processes continue during discrimination training until the following two conditions occur: (1) the excitatory tendency associated with the positive stimulus clearly outweighs the inhibitory tendency that has generalized to this stimulus, and (2) the converse is true for the negative stimulus. At this point the animal shows clearcut discrimination behavior by responding appropriately on each trial to the positive stimulus and withholding that response to the negative one.

When stated more exactly, this formulation has a wide range of implications concerning the rates of learning to be expected in various discrimination tasks, the types of transfer or transposition behavior that should occur, and the like. A sufficient number of these implications have received empirical support to justify considerable faith in this approach. At the same time, these empirical studies have indicated a number of weaknesses in the basic concepts of the formulation. Perhaps the most important of these weaknesses is the absence of any means of defining the degree of similarity between two stimuli independently of the observed generalization behavior of the animal. This suggestion of circularity in the system has led in large part to a number of alternative formulations of discrimination learning.

The concept of similarity.   In the psychological literature, stimulus similarity has been treated as a response-inferred construct. This means that the degree of similarity between two stimulus objects can be inferred only from the behavior of the animal with respect to them. If the stimuli are equivalent in the sense of producing comparable reactions, then, psychologically, they are highly similar for that animal. Phrased in this way, a theoretical account of the concept of similarity must state the conditions under which the animal will treat two stimulus objects as though they were equivalent. This can be done either in terms of assumptions about the make-up of the organism or in terms of the physical properties of the stimulus objects.

Organismic attributes.   One possible approach to this concept of similarity stems from the early work of Pavlov (1927). He claimed that similarity was largely a function of the neurological organization of the animal's cortex. Whether an animal perceives two stimuli as similar, as inferred from the generalization of behavior from one to the other, depends upon the spatial proximity of the sensory projections associated with these stimuli. If these are close together, considerable interaction or generalization can occur. With wider separations, the stimulus objects are perceived as independent or nonsimilar units. These neurological assumptions about the basis of similarity continue to have some influence in the physiological literature but have had little influence on psychological theorizing.

Stimulus attributes.   Recent theoretical interest has centered on the possibility of defining similarity in terms of overlap or of common elements in the two stimulus objects. This approach was prominent in the writings of Thorndike ([1913] 1921, chapter 4) and Guthrie (1935) but has been given a much more precise formulation in statistical learning theory (Estes 1959). The basic notion in this approach is that each stimulus object, plus the stimulus context in which it appears, is to be conceived of as potentially a population, or large set, of stimulus elements rather than as a single, unanalyzable unit. On a given trial the animal experiences only a randomly selected sample, or subset, of this potential population of elements that constitutes the object. This trial-to-trial variability in the sample of elements experienced is due to a number of factors; it stems in part from the impossibility of exactly reproducing the physical stimulus situation, in part from moment-to-moment variation in the state of an organism, in part from changes in the postural orientation of the animal with respect to the stimulus object, and so on. In order for the animal to experience all the elements in the population, it must be exposed repeatedly to the same stimulus object.

With two stimulus objects, of course, there are two populations of stimulus elements. Some of these elements may be common to the two populations, the rest being specific to one or the other. The proportion of common elements to the total number of elements in the combined populations is one possible measure of the degree of similarity between the two stimulus objects. The greater the proportion of overlapping elements, the greater is the degree of similarity.

The unique feature of this conception of similarity is that it does away with the need to assume that the animal has an innate tendency to generalize its learned behaviors. If an animal does transfer such a response from a training stimulus to a new one, it is because the populations of elements constituting the two objects have elements in common. These common elements were associated with the learned response during training with the first stimulus object. Consequently, there is a definite probability that they will evoke that same response when they again occur in the context of the new stimulus object. The probability that this generalization will occur increases as the proportion of overlapping elements in the two populations increases; the larger this degree of overlap, the more likely it becomes that any one sampling from the new stimulus object will contain a large number of them.

The assumptions underlying this conception of similarity have been stated mathematically in several recent formulations of statistical learning theory, making possible much more precise statements as to when generalization will occur and the amount of such transfer to be expected. As these predictions have considerable empirical support, it would appear that a real advance has been made in understanding the basis for psychological similarity.

Paradoxically, however, the success of this approach in predicting generalization has led to an impasse in attempting to apply the same assumptions to discrimination learning. If taken in its most literal form, this conception of similarity as being due to overlapping stimulus elements implies that an animal can never achieve a perfect discrimination between two similar stimulus objects, since their common elements would always be associated with each of the different responses, an implication that is clearly at variance with empirical observation.

Consequently, if this conception of similarity in terms of common elements is to apply to discrimination learning, as well as to generalization situations, additional assumptions must be made concerning these stimulus populations. One possibility is that their composition of elements is modified during discrimination training. In some sense the number of common elements is reduced, or at least their control over choice behavior is minimized [see GUTHRIE; THORNDIKE].

Selective attention. In a different context, the idea that the effective stimuli for behavior are modified or transformed during the course of learning has been discussed under the heading of selective attention. Two conceptualizations of this transformation process have been suggested. One of these involves the enrichment of, or additions to, the effective stimulus; the other emphasizes a reduction in the content of the stimulus.

Enrichment of the effective stimulus. The enrichment idea was clearly formulated by William James (1890, pp. 508 ff. in volume 1 of 1950 edition). He denied that the immediate sensory input from the stimulus object is the direct elicitor of choice behavior. Instead, he suggested that the effective stimulus is the complex of ideas, emotions, and other reactions that are associated with this sensory input. The main implication of this formulation is that the complexes associated with two stimulus objects may have proportionately less overlap and fewer common elements than do the immediate sensory experiences that give rise to them. Consequently, the tendency to generalize is reduced as these differentiating complexes develop during the course of learning. In more recent discussions of discrimination learning, this notion has been formulated somewhat more explicitly in terms of the concept of the "acquired distinctiveness of cues" (Miller & Dollard 1941).

Elimination of irrelevant cues. A more popular approach to the problem, however, is to view the stimulus transformation process as one in which the initial sensory inputs are gradually stripped of all irrelevant or nondifferentiating aspects. Only the differentiating, nonoverlapping aspects remain as the effective stimulus for the choice behavior. The simplest of these formulations postulates the learning of receptor-orienting behaviors. If, for instance, an animal looks at the top halves of two stimulus objects, the sensory input from them is likely to be quite different than if the animal looks at the bottom halves. Consequently, the animal may learn that certain receptor orientations lead to a more accurate discrimination than would be otherwise possible insofar as these sensory inputs contain a minimum number of common aspects and a maximum number of differentiating aspects. Learned orienting behaviors of this sort undoubtedly are involved in many types of discrimination, but the concept would seem to be of quite limited usefulness in situations where there is minimal need or opportunity for visual search procedures.

Stimulus coding. A number of alternative mechanisms have been proposed to account for the selective aspects of attention. These are variously referred to as "filter theory" (Broadbent 1961), "analyzer mechanisms" (Sutherland 1959), or "stimulus coding behaviors" (Lawrence 1963).

While these differ in many details, the general approach can be illustrated in terms of stimulus coding behaviors.

The stimulus coding formulation recognizes that the sensory input at any moment depends as much on the behavior of the organism as it does on the characteristics of the external stimulus object. For instance, the tactual sensations from a piece of sandpaper are quite different depending upon whether the individual merely places a finger tip on it or draws a finger rapidly across the surface. Thus, the effective stimulus to which the individual reacts is a joint function of his own behavior and the characteristics of the stimulus object.

In order to allow for both of these factors in determining the effective stimulus, the stimulus coding formulation assumes that the total sensory input from the discrimination situation is functionally divided into two parts. The first part corresponds to the stable, recurring aspects of the situation and the second part to the changing, variable aspects. In a successive discrimination, the stable part of the input may correspond to the characteristics of the room, the apparatus, and the like; the variable aspects may correspond to the characteristics of the stimulus objects to be discriminated.

It is assumed that the stable aspects of the situation become associated with, and control, an implicit, inferred coding response. When this coding response is elicited, it reacts on, or interacts with, the sensory input from the stimulus object. As a result of this interaction, a new input is generated which is called the "coded stimulus." When, as in discrimination learning, there are two different stimulus objects but only one coding response, two different coded stimuli are produced. These control the choice behavior.

In this schema, the characteristics of the coded stimuli change whenever there is a change in the coding response even though the stimulus objects remain constant. The coded stimuli are resultants from an interaction between a coding response and the immediate sensory inputs. A change in either the coding response or the immediate sensory inputs modifies the coded stimuli. The range of values the coded stimuli can assume, however, is limited by the actual properties of the sensory inputs. These latter are members of the interaction, and therefore the resultants cannot be independent of them. The implication is that these coded stimuli correspond to parts of, relationships within, or other limited aspects of the sensory input. But even with this restriction, the coded stimuli can vary greatly with changes in the coding response.

To complete the formulation, it is assumed that the coding response varies in a trial-and-error fashion during the initial stages of discrimination learning. Gradually, however, it shifts in that direction which tends to minimize the confusion and overlap between the coded stimuli. This is, of course, the direction that maximizes the accuracy of the discrimination. Thus, a dual learning process is always involved in a discrimination procedure: The animal must discover a coding response that produces highly distinctive coded stimuli, and at the same time learn which overt choice reactions are appropriate to these coded stimuli.

Formulations of this type offer a mechanism that permits the effective stimulus for behavior to be continuously modified throughout the course of learning. They permit the animal to react initially to the total stimulus input including the common, or overlapping, aspects. Thus, there can be the broad generalization characteristic of such situations. But with experience, the effective stimulus shifts in the direction that corresponds to the differentiating, nonoverlapping aspects of the stimulus objects. This ensures a high level of accuracy for the discrimination and offers a solution to the dilemma encountered in statistical learning theory. On the other hand, it is obvious that these formulations once again make stimulus similarity a direct function of the animal's own behavior.

Additional aspects. It should be emphasized, however, that even more precise and powerful theories of this type would not do justice to the wide range of empirical effects found during discrimination learning. The experimental literature contains many suggestions of changes in response selectivity, of heightened motivational effects, and of conflict resolution that largely fall outside the bounds of any of the theoretical approaches so far mentioned.

A clear example of changes in response selectivity is provided by the studies on learning set (Harlow 1959). These demonstrate that an animal can solve simultaneous discriminations with incredible rapidity after repeated experience with this class of problems. A sophisticated monkey requires only one or two information trials to reach a high level of mastery, whereas initially it required a prolonged training period to solve an equivalent problem. An analysis of this type of learning suggests that the increase in efficiency is in part due to the elimination of the response biases so prominent in the naive animal, for example, such biases as position preferences, alternation tendencies, or tendencies toward perseveration in a given response.

Motivational changes are apparent in studies on

contrast effects. Pavlov first demonstrated these in his studies on positive and negative induction. He found that once a successive discrimination was established by conditioning procedures, a series of presentations of the positive or rewarded stimulus object tended to strengthen and maintain the inhibitory tendencies evoked by the negative stimulus object. This was true even though the negative stimulus object was now followed by reward. Conversely, a series of presentations of the negative or nonrewarded stimulus object tended to strengthen and maintain the excitatory tendency evoked by the positive stimulus object, even though this was no longer rewarded. Descriptively, it is as though the animal has built up a set of contrasts as the result of discrimination training; experience with the positive stimulus object increases the undesirability of the nonrewarded behavior, and experience with the negative stimulus object enhances the desirability of the rewarded behavior. Comparable phenomena have been demonstrated with other types of discrimination training.

Related to these contrast effects are any number of phenomena that can be grouped in terms of conflict resolution. Perhaps the most dramatic of these is the change in behavior that occurs in experimental neurosis (Liddell 1956). After a successive discrimination is well established, the two stimulus objects are made more and more similar until the animal is unable to discriminate between them. Occasionally, under these conditions, the animal begins to show agitated and highly emotional behavior. This emotionality persists for long periods of time both in the experimental situation and in other contexts. Equally impressive are the abortive and stereotypic behaviors exhibited by animals who have been frustrated by being forced to respond in an unsolvable discrimination situation (Maier 1949).

This brief and highly selected survey of the many behavioral changes that occur during discrimination learning is sufficient to indicate the limitations of present theories on this subject. These formulations have been primarily concerned with developing appropriate concepts to deal with generalization phenomena, stimulus similarity, and selective attention. They obviously have not dealt adequately, as yet, with the phenomena of response selectivity, motivational changes, and conflict resolution.

DOUGLAS H. LAWRENCE

[*Other relevant material may be found in* ATTENTION; CONCEPT FORMATION; MODELS, MATHEMATICAL; PERCEPTION, *article on* PERCEPTUAL DEVELOPMENT; *and in the biography of* HULL.]

BIBLIOGRAPHY

ATKINSON, RICHARD C.; and ESTES, WILLIAM K. 1963 Stimulus Sampling Theory. Volume 2, pages 121–268 in R. Duncan Luce, Robert R. Bush, and Eugene Galanter (editors), *Handbook of Mathematical Psychology.* New York: Wiley.

BROADBENT, D. E. 1961 Human Perception and Animal Learning. Pages 248–272 in W. H. Thorpe and O. L. Zangwill (editors), *Current Problems in Animal Behaviour.* Cambridge Univ. Press.

ESTES, WILLIAM K. 1959 The Statistical Approach to Learning Theory. Volume 2, pages 380–491 in Sigmund Koch (editor), *Psychology: A Study of a Science.* New York: McGraw-Hill.

GUTHRIE, EDWIN R. (1935) 1960 *The Psychology of Learning.* Rev. ed. Gloucester, Mass.: Smith.

HARLOW, HARRY F. 1959 Learning Set and Error Factor Theory. Volume 2, pages 492–537 in Sigmund Koch (editor), *Psychology: A Study of a Science.* New York: McGraw-Hill.

HULL, CLARK L. 1943 *Principles of Behavior: An Introduction to Behavior Theory.* New York: Appleton.

JAMES, WILLIAM (1890) 1962 *The Principles of Psychology.* 2 vols. New York: Smith.

LAWRENCE, DOUGLAS H. 1963 The Nature of a Stimulus: Some Relationships Between Learning and Perception. Volume 5, pages 179–212 in Sigmund Koch (editor), *Psychology: A Study of a Science.* New York: McGraw-Hill.

LIDDELL, HOWARD S. 1956 *Emotional Hazards in Animals and Man.* Springfield, Ill.: Thomas.

MACKINTOSH, N. J. 1965 Selective Attention in Animal Discrimination Learning. *Psychological Bulletin* 64: 124–150. → A more recent and more easily accessible account of N. S. Sutherland's viewpoint and a review of the experimental evidence bearing on it.

MAIER, NORMAN R. F. 1949 *Frustration: The Study of Behavior Without a Goal.* New York: McGraw-Hill. → A paperback edition was published in 1961.

MILLER, NEAL E.; and DOLLARD, JOHN C. 1941 *Social Learning and Imitation.* New Haven: Yale Univ. Press; Oxford Univ. Press.

PAVLOV, IVAN P. (1927) 1960 *Conditioned Reflexes: An Investigation of the Physiological Activity of the Cerebral Cortex.* New York: Dover. → First published as *Lektsii o rabote bol'shikh polusharii golovnogo mozga.*

SUTHERLAND, N. S. 1959 Stimulus Analysing Mechanisms. Volume 2, pages 575–609 in Teddington, England, National Physical Laboratory, *Mechanisation of Thought Processes: Proceedings of a Symposium.* London: H.M. Stationery Office. → This is paper No. 2, session 4A, of the National Physical Laboratory Symposium No. 10. Reprinted in 1961.

THORNDIKE, EDWARD L. (1913) 1921 *Educational Psychology.* Volume 2: The Psychology of Learning. New York: Columbia Univ., Teachers College.

VI

AVOIDANCE LEARNING

In avoidance learning the organism comes to behave in an anticipatory or foresightful manner in order that unpleasant events no longer will occur. It learns to respond to certain cues or danger signals before painful or frightening stimuli can occur, and it performs acts that usually prevent the painful events from occurring. In the following account empirical generalizations are emphasized to demonstrate the wide variety of variables operating in avoidance learning. In some cases these generalizations are not very well established, and so they represent only the current state of affairs and are always subject to change as more experiments are reported. Avoidance learning represents an empirical focus today, and hundreds of experiments each year are completed in this area of science. Empirical findings have clearly outstripped adequate theoretical accounts of the avoidance learning process.

Avoidance training experiments of a scientific sort have, for obvious humanitarian and ethical reasons, been confined mainly to animal subjects. There have been few experiments in which human subjects were studied, and those experiments have yielded results quite similar to those obtained in animal experiments. There is every reason to believe that the variables in control of animal avoidance learning are not very different across mammalian species.

Two different types of training

Active avoidance. Imagine, if you will, a white rat placed by an experimenter (*E*) into a small training box. The floor of the box is an electrifiable grid of metal rods. At a height of 10 inches above the floor and hinged as a shelf to the side of the box is a small platform. The lid of the box is a transparent plastic plate, and above it is suspended a 60-watt lamp. *E* allows his subject *S*, the rat, to explore the box for a few minutes. Then training begins. *E* switches on the light above the rat box for a 30-second period. *S* continues his sniffing and exploring during the switching on and off of the light. *E* repeats the procedure 5 times, noting that *S* does not jump onto the platform. Then *E* switches on the light, waits for 5 seconds, and turns on the power supply which electrifies the metal grid floor of the box and shocks *S*. *S* squeals, rushes about, leaps into the air, and then, 12 seconds after the shock is turned on, jumps onto the platform where there is no shock. As *S* lands, *E* turns off the light. One minute later, the hinged shelf is momentarily lowered, dropping *S* onto the grid again. Then 2 minutes later, a second training trial is begun. The light goes on, and 5 seconds later the shock goes on. The rat leaps onto the platform 4 seconds after the shock goes on.

The rat's performance has improved in two trials of training. We say he is learning to *escape* from shock. After several escape training trials have gone by, *S* eventually will respond directly to the onset of the light, and he will jump onto the platform without the stimulus of shock. This jump is called an *avoidance* response. By this response, *S* *avoids* the shock, and since the light is turned off when he jumps onto the platform, he also *escapes* the light.

S has learned to respond in an anticipatory fashion in such a way that if he jumps quickly at the onset of the light he will never again receive the shock. This type of process is called *active* avoidance learning. *S* is taught *what to do* to minimize pain and distress. Note that he is punished for doing everything else but jumping onto the platform whenever the light goes on. He is, therefore, not being taught anything specific that he should *not do*. In the active avoidance training procedure, the light is usually called the *discriminative stimulus* (S^d), *cue*, or *signal*; the shock is called the *unconditioned stimulus* (*US*). Because the escape responses are instrumental in terminating the shock and the light and because the avoidance responses are instrumental in preventing the shock and terminating the light, they are often called *instrumental* responses. They change the environment in such a way as to make it more acceptable to the subject. They *operate* on the environment and so are often called *operants*.

Passive avoidance. A somewhat different yet very important avoidance training procedure produces *passive* avoidance learning. Passive avoidance training corresponds to our everyday conception of *punishment*. In this procedure *S* is taught specifically *what not to do*, but he is not taught *what to do*.

Imagine now that another white rat is placed by *E* on the platform of the small training box. This *S* is hungry, and *E* has placed a food pellet for him on the grid floor. After some hesitation, *S* scrambles down from the platform and eats the food pellet. *E* then picks *S* up and places him on the platform again. This time *S* jumps down more quickly than he did on the first trial, and he again eats a food pellet. After many trials, *S* shows stable food-getting behavior; he jumps down quickly and uniformly on each training trial. Now *E* can get rid of this instrumental response (jumping off the platform) by means of *passive* avoidance training. *E* electrifies the grid whenever *S* jumps down to get a pellet. Eventually, *S* will stay on the platform rather than jump down. *S* has learned to avoid shock by avoiding specific action. What *S* does when on the platform is *not* being specified by the training procedure, and so *anything* he does, as long as it does not lead him to the grid floor, goes unpunished.

Active and passive avoidance learning can take place under a wide variety of training procedures, and the characteristics of learning depend heavily on the type of procedure *E* uses.

Variants of the two types of training

Active avoidance.   Six important variants of the active avoidance procedure warrant discussion.

The method of gradual emergence.   By use of the general training conditions described under active avoidance, it can be shown that *S* will learn avoidance responses either very suddenly or very gradually by varying the training techniques. For example, when small movements or reflexive responses are selected by *E* to be the active avoidance responses, learning is slow and tortuous. Forepaw flexion responses in the dog often require several hundred training trials in order to establish them as reliable avoidance responses. The same is true of a tiny toe movement in human *Ss*. In contrast, massive movements that change the *S*'s environment are quick to emerge as reliable avoidance responses. Requiring a rat to jump onto a platform, as described above, requiring a dog to jump from one compartment of a box to another, or requiring a human *S* to push a knob a distance of 2 feet—all three are examples of efficient situations for producing sudden and reliable avoidance learning. A way of interpreting these findings is that medium-probability operants make the best avoidance responses, while high-probability, short-latency respondents (reflexes) make the poorest avoidance responses.

A characteristic of some avoidance responses is their persistence. In general, those training conditions leading to efficient learning also lead to a high degree of resistance to extinction. Such responses as the jumping onto a platform described above can persist over hundreds of trials without a shock being administered. This is not likely to be true of responses like forelimb flexion or toe flexion. The persistence of avoidance responses, as an empirical phenomenon, has extensive implications for studies of human neuroses. Long-lasting phobias, obsessive and compulsive behavior, and neurotic defenses of many types can be fruitfully analyzed in terms of the special experimental conditions that established such behavioral rigidity. Sometimes therapeutic treatments are deduced from such analyses. [*See* OBSESSIVE–COMPULSIVE DISORDERS; PHOBIAS.]

Other variables influencing the ease of active avoidance learning and, inversely, the ease of extinction are the S^d–*US* time interval, the intensity

of the *US*, the similarity of the S^d to the *US*, the immediacy of termination of the *US* and the S^d after the performance by *S* of the avoidance response, and the occurrence of events arousing responses that are incompatible with the required avoidance response. Usually, there is an optimum S^d–*US* interval for each type of avoidance response. If an avoidance response is a long-latency, complex operant, a long S^d–*US* interval of perhaps 5 to 10 seconds will be optimal. For short-latency, reflexive types of avoidance responses, short S^d–*US* intervals of around 1 to 2 seconds will be optimal. Usually, for a given type of avoidance response, lengthening the S^d–*US* interval beyond the optimal interval will facilitate extinction of the response when shock is no longer administered.

Shock intensity complexly influences avoidance learning. There is an optimum intensity for each type of response, and intensities lower or higher than the optimum will retard learning and facilitate extinction. The optimum intensity decreases as the complexity of the avoidance response increases. This is known as the Yerkes–Dodson law. When the S^d is frightening, learning is more rapid than when it is neutral. Thus, a mild shock used as an S^d will facilitate learning, as will a frightening buzzer. A nonfrightening light may be less efficient in controlling stable avoidances. Delaying either the termination of shock following an escape response, or the termination of the S^d following an avoidance response, or both, will retard avoidance learning, and even short delays of about 5 seconds may make it impossible for *S* to learn. Finally, some avoidance responses are incompatible with the innate fear responses of *S* and can interfere with correct responses as fear increases. For example, when *S* is a rat, we have to try to eliminate innate "freezing" reactions that often occur when the S^d becomes fear-arousing as a result of its association in time with the painful *US*. Often a rat will "freeze" when the S^d goes on and thus fail to avoid during the S^d–*US* time interval. He may escape easily as soon as the shock goes on if the shock is of an appropriate intensity for vigorous behavior arousal. One way of eliminating freezing is to decrease *US* intensity. Another way is to increase the S^d–*US* interval. Quite often, however, *S* fails to avoid in many experimental situations, and these failures have not yet been analyzed sufficiently by psychologists. Rather, they tend to be ignored as accidents or are attributed to unspecified individual differences. They represent an area of ignorance.

Most successful avoidance learning in the method of gradual emergence is characterized by a high level of fear and emotionality early in learning, when shocks are still being administered, followed by declining emotionality when the avoidance responses become reliable. Along with these correlated events, the topography of the avoidance responses themselves becomes stereotyped. When this stereotypy occurs, extinction is not easy to produce by constant elicitation of the responses.

The method of prior response shaping. In the method of prior response shaping, the S is first trained to escape the US without a signalizing S^d. After S is an expert escaper, the warning signal or S^d is paired with the US. Using this method, the avoidance responses are very much like the escape responses. In contrast, the method of gradual emergence often produces avoidance responses different in appearance from the escape responses from which they were derived.

Escape with short S^d–US interval. When the S^d–US interval is too short to allow avoidances, except on test trials when the S^d is presented without the US, very poor avoiding is produced along with reliable and short-latency escaping. The S is usually very fearful and emotionally disturbed.

The method of prior fear conditioning. In the method of prior fear conditioning, the S^d and US are paired closely in time on each trial, but there is at first no escape or avoidance response available to S. He merely learns to fear the S^d. After many trials, S is then allowed to terminate the S^d by means of a response in his repertory. If such a response is emitted in the presence of the S^d, the response is quickly adopted by S as a reliable avoidance response. On the other hand, S often does not make the required response, and so he never learns. Failures of this type are frequently produced by this method. Extinction of avoidance responses appears to occur more readily by this method than by the method of gradual emergence. This method is sometimes called the "acquired drive" experiment.

The Pavlovian method. In the Pavlovian procedure, E presents S with an S^d–US sequence repeatedly, but S cannot do anything either to prevent or to terminate the painful US. Instead, the US is omitted on test trials, and sometimes the S will demonstrate a consistent type of anticipatory or preparatory response pattern. Russian physiologists call this method "motor conditioning." When many test trials are run, we note that the US does not occur no matter what anticipatory responses may be evoked by the S^d. Thus, such trials are like avoidance-response trials in other methods. Despite this, very unstable learning occurs. Often the response consists of constantly varying struggling and diffuse emotional expressions.

The Sidman method. In the Sidman procedure,

no S^d is used (although one can be used). Instead, the US is regularly presented if S does not perform a particular response desired by E. If S does perform the required response, the US is delayed for a fixed time interval. The avoidance response thus "buys" shock-free time for S. Note that the US–US interval can be varied independently of the response–US interval. If an S^d is used, it can come anywhere in the US–US interval or in the response–US interval. This method can produce very stable avoidance responding and high resistance to extinction. There are, however, many individual failures of rats to learn. These failures can be reduced if the avoidance response is capable of terminating the US. This method is especially interesting because Ss often develop stable response rates, with the avoidance responses appearing at regular intervals. The responses appear to be under the control of some type of "internal time mechanism" that serves as an S^d substitute. As long as this mechanism elicits responses at interresponse time intervals less than the response–shock interval, S never receives a shock. The method is often viewed as revelatory of the build-up in time of "conditioned anxiety"; whenever the anxiety becomes intolerable during the response–shock interval, S makes another response. The similarity of this phenomenon to human compulsive neuroses is often pointed out.

Passive avoidance. Two major variants of the passive avoidance procedure will be discussed.

Punishment methods. There are two general types of punishment techniques. One technique used in the punishment method is illustrated by the general example given above to describe passive avoidance training in the rat. The rat is presented with a painful US contingent upon each jump from the platform to the grid floor of the training box.

The second technique, called the secondary aversive stimulus technique, establishes a previously neutral stimulus as an aversive CS (conditioned stimulus) by pairing it in time with several presentations of a painful or frightening US. When the CS evokes an acquired fear or anxiety reaction, called the "conditioned emotional response" (CER), the CS is then used to punish a specific type of behavior. The example we used above to illustrate passive avoidance learning would have been a secondary aversive stimulus technique if the rat, instead of being shocked for jumping down to the food, had been presented with a CS previously paired with shock.

Punishment procedures may be applied in an attempt to eliminate at least five different types of behavior: (1) an *instrumental* response previously established by rewards, illustrated by punishing the rat for jumping off the platform to get food; (2) an *instrumental* response previously established by punishment, illustrated by punishing a shock avoidance response with another frightening stimulus; (3) a *consummatory* response, such as eating, drinking, or copulating; (4) a complex, *instinctive* response pattern, such as nest building in birds; and (5) a simple *reflexive* reaction, such as an eyeblink. The results obtained by punishment procedures differ for each of these five categories.

First, when an instrumental response that has been previously established by rewards is punished, the outcome depends heavily on: (1) *duration* of the punishing stimulus—short-duration punishments that are presented after the response has occurred usually produce temporary suppression of the response and are followed by recovery of the response (sometimes to supernormal levels), while long-duration stimuli often suppress the punished behavior for long time intervals; (2) *intensity* of the punishing stimulus—low-intensity punishing stimuli will suppress behavior temporarily, but the behavior recovers, often to a level more vigorous than that prior to the use of punishment, but high-intensity punishing stimuli will often suppress behavior for long periods of time; (3) *delay* of punishment—the sooner the punishing stimulus is applied after an unwanted response has occurred the more effective will the punishment be, giving us what is known as the "temporal gradient of delay of punishment"; (4) *repeated exposure*—Ss often show some adaptation to repeated punishments, and, therefore, new punishments are often more effective than familiar ones, provided of course that their duration and intensities are equal; (5) *reward–punishment habituation* —if a response is simultaneously rewarded and punished and if the punishment is of low intensity and duration, sometimes the punishment will not only be ineffective in suppressing the response but will also be able to serve as a reward in its own right (this is similar to masochism in neurotic disturbances); (6) existence of a *rewarded alternative*—if alternative response A is punished and alternative B is quickly rewarded, the punishment will be very effective in suppressing A, but when there is no rewarded alternative to A, the response will recover more quickly from the suppressing effects of punishment; (7) *temporal discriminative alternatives*—the housebroken dog learns to urinate under condition A (outdoors) and never to urinate under condition B (indoors), provided that frequent punishment for B is followed quickly in time by no punishment for A (this is often referred to as "impulse control" training); (8) *temporal order* of reward and punishment—when a reward is followed regularly by punishment, the behavior leading to the reward is often suppressed, but if exactly the same behavior is evoked by punishment and then rewarded, the behavior can be strengthened, and S may come to tolerate the punishment or even to seek it out; (9) *species-specific* characteristics—a toy snake can be used to punish behavior in monkeys, but it does not bother a rat, for example; (10) the *resistance to extinction* of the response being punished—responses which would normally be extinguished quickly in the absence of reward will be suppressed more readily by punishment than will responses normally having a high resistance to regular extinction procedures.

Second, when an instrumental response that has been previously established as an active avoidance response is punished, the outcome is hard to predict. Sometimes the response intended by E to be suppressed by the punishment is actually energized. Probably this facilitation is produced most reliably when the punishing stimulus is very similar to or the same as that which was used as the US in the earlier avoidance training procedure. A good deal of ignorance exists in this field of study.

Third, when a consummatory response is punished, the suppression is very often long-lasting and emotionally disturbing. Punishment seems to be more effective when applied to this type of behavior than it is when used to suppress instrumental responses, for reasons that are at present quite mystifying.

Fourth, when punishment is used to suppress complex, species-specific, instinctive behavior patterns, the results are often confusing. Sometimes displacement occurs; that is, S shows behavior characteristics of another behavior pattern. Frightening an animal for courting behavior may induce nest-building behavior or other inappropriate acts.

Finally, little is known of the effects of punishment for specific reflexive behavior. This contingency happens frequently in everyday affairs, as when an involuntary act annoys others, but the phenomenon has not been studied systematically in the laboratory.

The CER method. The CER procedure differs from the punishment procedure in a subtle but evidently important way. No specific passive avoidance response is established. Thus, this method is similar to the punishment method. But, in contrast to the punishment method, the CER method does not apply a punishment to a specific response. Instead, a frightening, secondary aversive stimulus is added to the general surroundings of S for limited periods of time. Often the usual behavior in that environment is depressed in rate, or amplitude, or quickness. A typical example is as follows: a rat is trained to press a lever when he is hungry in order to obtain food pellets. After this lever pressing occurs at a reliable rate, the *CER* procedure is introduced. A previously neutral stimulus is now associated with shock in a special shock box (repeated *CS–US* pairings, with no escape or avoidance possible) and evokes a *CER*. When the *CER* stimulus is presented in the lever box, the lever-pressing rate often decreases. The *CER* stimulus is not presented contingent upon *S*'s lever-pressing response. Rather, it occurs without regard to the behavior being rewarded by food. Despite this, the instrumental behavior is often suppressed. Indeed, the *CER* technique may often produce suppression as effectively as does the punishment method.

One major value of the *CER* procedure has been in the assessment of psychologically active drugs. Often, tranquilizers have been shown to minimize the response suppression attendant on the *CER* stimulus, and the special characteristics of behavior during the suppression period in drugged *S*s can be of value in analyzing the action of the drug. The method has also been used to assess the level of fear controlled by a *CS*, assuming that the more the ongoing, appetitive, and instrumental behavior is suppressed, the more fear arousing is the *CS*. This dependent variable can then be related to events taking place during fear conditioning or to those occurring during avoidance training in which the same *CS* is used. For example, the S^d in avoidance training in situation A may not suppress appetitive behavior in situation B—thus leading to the conclusion that the S^d no longer arouses much fear. This finding has been correlated with observations of declining fear during stereotyped avoidance responding and with the finding that conditioned heart-rate elevation decreases during late phases of successful avoidance responding as the behavior becomes stereotyped. Thus, active and passive avoidance procedures can be combined to yield significant interrelationships between emotional reactions and instrumental responding.

Two of the most pressing questions concerning avoidance learning are theoretical ones. What mechanism produces the first avoidance response? What mechanism reinforces avoidance responses? Here, we are still in the dark. One explanatory scheme is cognitive. It argues that *S* comes to anticipate shock by virtue of S^d–*US* pairings and that *S* comes to know how to terminate shock by virtue

of escape responses. Then, by an insightful inference, *S* terminates the S^d by performing an avoidance response. Another explanatory scheme depends heavily on the James–Lange theory of emotion. It argues that the S^d–*US* pairings lead to conditioned fear (*CER*) in the presence of the S^d. When the *CER* is intense enough to be as arousing as the shock itself, then *S* does in the presence of the S^d what he has learned to do in the presence of the shock. He performs the escape response during the S^d–*US* interval, and so he comes to avoid. Avoidance responses remove the S^d, thus reducing the anxiety level, and so avoidances are reinforced by anxiety reduction. Finally, another explanatory scheme depends heavily on proprioceptive feedback arising from skeletal movements. It argues that *S* learns to avoid movements associated with shock, thus leaving *S* to perform only movements not associated with shock. Certain proprioceptive stimulus patterns acquire aversive properties during the escape training phase or, as in the Sidman method, during the phase of learning wherein the *US* is frequently presented. Avoidance of aversive proprioceptive stimulus patterns gradually "shapes up" the avoidance behavior. At the moment there seems to be no decisive evidence that would allow us to choose among the major explanatory alternatives. However, many current experiments are being aimed at the theoretical systems to probe their strengths and weaknesses in predicting important variables and phenomena.

RICHARD L. SOLOMON

[*Other relevant material may be found in* ANXIETY; DEFENSE MECHANISMS; ELECTROCONVULSIVE SHOCK; STRESS.]

BIBLIOGRAPHY

BRADY, JOSEPH V.; and HUNT, HOWARD F. 1955 An Experimental Approach to the Analysis of Emotional Behavior. *Journal of Psychology* 40:313–324.

DINSMOOR, JAMES A. 1954 Punishment: I. The Avoidance Hypothesis. *Psychological Review* 61:34–46.

ESTES, WILLIAM K. 1944 An Experimental Study of Punishment. *Psychological Monographs* 57, no. 3.

FERSTER, CHARLES B. 1958 Control of Behavior in Chimpanzees and Pigeons by Time Out From Positive Reinforcement. *Psychological Monographs* 72, no. 8.

GIBSON, ELEANOR J. 1952 The Role of Shock in Reinforcement. *Journal of Comparative and Physiological Psychology* 45:18–30.

GWINN, GORDON T. 1949 The Effects of Punishment on Acts Motivated by Fear. *Journal of Experimental Psychology* 39:260–269.

HOLZ, WILLIAM C.; and AZRIN, NATHAN H. 1961 Discriminative Properties of Punishment. *Journal of the Experimental Analysis of Behavior* 4:225–232.

KAMIN, LEON J. 1959 The Delay of Punishment Gradient. *Journal of Comparative and Physiological Psychology* 52:434–437.

KAMIN, LEON J.; BRIMER, C. J.; and BLACK, A. H. 1963 Conditioned Suppression as a Monitor of Fear of the CS in the Course of Avoidance Training. *Journal of Comparative and Physiological Psychology* 56:497–501.

KEEHN, J. D. 1959 On the Non-classical Nature of Avoidance Behavior. *American Journal of Psychology* 72:243–247.

LICHTENSTEIN, P. E. 1950 Studies of Anxiety: I. The Production of Feeding Inhibition in Dogs. *Journal of Comparative and Physiological Psychology* 43:16–29.

MASSERMAN, JULES H.; and PECHTEL, CURTIS 1953 Neuroses in Monkeys: A Preliminary Report of Experimental Observations. New York Academy of Sciences, *Annals* 56:253–265.

MILLER, NEAL E. 1960 Learning Resistance to Pain and Fear: Effects of Overlearning, Exposure, and Rewarded Exposure in Context. *Journal of Experimental Psychology* 60:137–145.

MOWRER, ORVAL H. 1960 *Learning Theory and Behavior.* New York: Wiley.

SHEFFIELD, FRED D. 1948 Avoidance Training and the Contiguity Principle. *Journal of Comparative and Physiological Psychology* 41:165–177.

SIDMAN, MURRAY 1953 Avoidance Conditioning With Brief Shock and No Exteroceptive Warning Signal. *Science* 118:157–158.

SOLOMON, RICHARD L. 1964 Punishment. *American Psychologist* 19:239–253.

SOLOMON, RICHARD L.; and BRUSH, ELINOR S. 1956 Experimentally Derived Conceptions of Anxiety and Aversion. Volume 4, pages 212–305 in Marshall R. Jones (editor), *Nebraska Symposium on Motivation.* Lincoln: Univ. of Nebraska Press.

SOLOMON, RICHARD L.; KAMIN, LEON J.; and WYNNE, LYMAN C. 1953 Traumatic Avoidance Learning: The Outcome of Several Extinction Procedures With Dogs. *Journal of Abnormal and Social Psychology* 48:291–302.

SOLOMON, RICHARD L.; and WYNNE, LYMAN C. 1954 Traumatic Avoidance Learning: The Principles of Anxiety Conservation and Partial Irreversibility. *Psychological Review* 61:353–385.

TURNER, LUCILLE H.; and SOLOMON, RICHARD L. 1962 Human Traumatic Avoidance Learning. *Psychological Monographs* 76, no. 40.

YERKES, R. M.; and DODSON, J. D. 1908 Relation of Strength of Stimulus to Rapidity of Habit Formation. *Journal of Comparative Neurology and Psychology* 18:459–482.

VII
NEUROPHYSIOLOGICAL ASPECTS

How the brain changes as a result of an organism's experiences, how it maintains its altered state through time, and how it influences future behavior in a modified but systematic manner are some of the most intriguing mysteries facing modern biology. Direct experimental study of this problem started shortly after the turn of the century, a time when substantial neuroanatomical knowledge had already accumulated, although the electrical techniques that evolved into those of modern day neurophysiology were then in their simplest, primitive stages. By the 1920s, two pioneering behavioral scientists, Lashley (1929) in the United States and Pavlov (1927) in Russia, were well along with their classical studies of learned behavior in animals and were attempting to relate their findings to the function of the brain.

Lashley, studying instrumental behavior in rats with experimentally created brain lesions, and Pavlov, theorizing about brain function from his studies of conditioned behavior in dogs, both focused their attention on the uppermost layer of the brain—the neocortex. The cortex, as it is more commonly called, gained early attention because of its greater size in man and the other higher animals. This anatomical fact suggested that the cortex might be particularly concerned with such complex neural processes as learning. It was not until the 1950s that investigations concerned with the physiology of the process of learning started to disengage themselves from the belief that the neocortex is exclusively responsible for the fixation of experience that permits new behavior patterns to be acquired.

From the standpoint of the nervous system, experience is some temporospatial pattern of transitory electrical activity in the nerve cells (neurons) of the brain. The basic neurophysiological question, then, is how can this evanescent neural activity modify the circuits of the brain so that they remain uniquely altered after the initiating physiological event has vanished. Any final understanding of this process requires answers to a number of interrelated and interlocking questions. First of all, how are the stimulus events that are to be learned electrophysiologically coded for introduction into the nervous system and transmission throughout the complex pathways of the brain? In what parts of the brain are the relevant coded messages integrated and stored for future use? How do electrical neural events, arising transitorily during initial learning, manage to induce a patterned and relatively permanent change in the brain, a change that is presumed to be chemical or structural? Finally, what is the physical nature of this semipermanent brain cell change, which can persist in neural tissue for years despite the active metabolic turnover in neurons, and how does this cellular change selectively modify the brain's subsequent functioning so that the organism's behavior can be an adaptive synthesis of past experience and current environmental demands? These are questions that have dominated research in the neurophysiology of learning.

Electrophysiological aspects

The nerve impulse. Any speculation about the physical basis of learning has of course been heavily influenced by the existing state of neurophysiological knowledge. The conspicuous electrical event that was first observed in the early studies of peripheral nerves was the nerve impulse, action potential, or spike, as it is variously called. This bioelectric activity is crucial in neural functioning and can be recorded from the stringlike extensions (fibers or axons) of all nerve cells. It is the nerve impulse, propagated along nerve fibers as the result of rapidly shifting chemical changes, that allows one neuron to influence the activity of other neurons with which it is in contact. At these points of contact (synapses), it is now known that the traveling nerve impulse induces the secretion of minute amounts of biochemical compounds (neurotransmitters) that, in turn, can influence the electrophysiological state of the next neuron in line. In this way, a nerve impulse can be initiated in the adjoining nerve cell.

It was early recognized that the basic nerve impulse was an all-or-none process. If the activation of a nerve cell reaches a given threshold, a spike of a predetermined size will be propagated at a given speed along the cell's axon. Further, once such a spike has developed and subsided (in several milliseconds at most), either in the initially stimulated neuron or in adjoining neurons via synaptic connections, there ensues a sequence of physiological changes (after potentials) that systematically influences the "firing" threshold of the cells for a brief time period. Over the span of about a tenth of a second, it is first more difficult and then easier to initiate a second spike. These were the primary facts of high-speed neural function that were available to behavioral scientists of the 1930s and early 1940s as they contemplated the overwhelming plasticity and long-term memory of the complex, multisynaptic brain.

Reverberating circuits and synaptic change. The first attempts to define the neurophysiological mechanisms that might provide the basis of learning were developed from these simple basics of brain function. Many more facts about the functioning of the central nervous system are now available, but the broad outlines of the generally accepted neurophysiological mechanism of learning have not changed in principle. It is still thought that nerve impulses, bombarding some combination of synapses in a pattern that is somehow appropriate to the task to be learned, bring about a change in the functional characteristics of the synapses and, thereafter, that particular pattern of nerve impulses will induce the response sequence that occurred during the original learning. Reverberating neuron circuits are thought capable of supplying the time necessary for the electrical activity to lead to

some form of permanent synaptic change that would account for the long-term behavioral changes that can follow a learning experience. Possibly the best-known statement of this point of view was that of the Canadian psychologist Donald O. Hebb, who suggested that the permanent neural changes might be based on the structural growth of appropriate axon endings at the synapse (Hebb 1949). His specific suggestion has yet to be proved or, for that matter, disproved.

Brain waves and electroencephalography. With improved electronic techniques that permit the direct study of brain activity, a variety of characteristics of brain function have been discovered. Neurophysiologists, for example, are looking with increased interest at the variety of slowly shifting electrical potentials that can be recorded throughout the central nervous system. Whereas the small spike of a primary nerve impulse, for example, can subside in less than a millisecond, these larger potentials can oscillate as slowly as several times a second. There are also even slower shifts of D.C. voltage, lasting seconds or even minutes. Certain of these slow potentials oscillate spontaneously even in the resting or sleeping brain. These are the brain waves seen in the well-known electroencephalogram (EEG). Although independently discovered in lower animals by R. Caton in England and A. Beck in Poland in 1875 and 1890, respectively, the EEG did not receive widespread attention until 1935, when the German psychiatrist Hans Berger reported that the same slow electrical rhythms were also evident in the human brain. The EEG remained largely a clinical tool, little used in behavioral research, until some of its neural and behavioral correlates started to be better understood because of the classic study made by the Italian neurophysiologist Giuseppe Moruzzi and his American collaborator, H. W. Magoun, in 1949. These investigators, together with many that followed them, showed that the EEG could serve as an indicator of arousal (or the lack of it) in the cortex as a whole or in restricted centers within the brain (Magoun 1958). As we shall see, behavioral scientists have subsequently started to use the EEG to evaluate the level of activity in various brain centers during different stages of learning.

Horizontal versus vertical organization

Aside from the more specific question of which particular structures within the brain may be necessary for learning, there is the prior but related question concerning the general flow of brain activities during complex behavior in general and learning in particular. General attitudes concerning this matter have shifted considerably during the half century or so since the beginning of direct laboratory study of brain mechanisms and learning.

Horizontal organization—association areas. The earliest point of view, and still the most common oversimplification of the facts, placed almost exclusive faith in the importance of the multilayered neocortex, which is conveniently located at the top of the central nervous system. As we have seen, the pattern of the phylogenetic development of the brain conspicuously pointed to the increased size of the cortex as the most likely source of control for such higher mental processes as learning. In its most traditional form, this corticocentric frame of reference also emphasized the horizontal organization of the neural substrate of learning, which is presumed to take place in the transcortical pathways that connect the sensory and motor areas of the neocortex. The so-called association areas, located between the sensory-input and motor-output areas, were assumed to supply pools of synapses where changes in transmission characteristics could afford new patterns of transcortical connections that would provide for the changing patterns of learned behavior. The highly influential Pavlovian theory of learning was like this in general form, the transcortical effects being visualized as irradiating neural influences between sensory and motor areas in the cortex.

Vertical organization. Along with the recent growth of interest in the role of subcortical structures in all varieties of behavior, there has developed a newer point of view, which emphasizes the vertical organization of the brain and the recurrent interactions between neural centers at all levels of the central nervous system, including the cortex. Possibly the most convincing evidence of the importance of extracortical pathways in learning has been reported from studies of animal conditioning in which the training was managed exclusively with direct electrical stimulation of sensory and motor areas in the cortex. After suitable pairing of sensory stimulation (*CS*) and motor stimulation (*US*), activation of the sensory electrode by itself led to the limb movement (now the conditioned response) that had occurred originally only when the motor electrode was stimulated (Doty 1961). Cutting transcortical connections between the two electrodes did not eliminate the conditioned response. That transcortical pathways are not necessary for such a newly developed neural circuit was further confirmed by studies in which similar electrophysiological conditioning was accomplished even though the sensory electrode was in one cerebral hemisphere, the motor electrode in the other, and the interhemispheric connections

(corpus callosum) completely severed (Doty & Giurgea 1961). While the cortex is certainly involved, in one way or another, in a variety of kinds of learned behavior, it appears to be substantially dependent on vertical interconnections that exist at all levels of the central nervous system.

Geography of the learning process

The recording of spontaneous EEG rhythms during simple learning situations, usually one form or another of classical conditioning, has shown that various parts of the brain are differentially active throughout successive stages of learning.

Alpha rhythm and alpha blocking. The use of brain wave changes to trace the shifts of brain activity during learning was initiated by an accidental observation of the French neurophysiologists G. Durup and A. Fessard in 1935. These investigators were studying the EEG alpha rhythm, a moderately slow wave form that can be recorded from the visual cortex of a resting animal during periods of reduced visual stimulation. This slow brain wave is arrested (alpha blocking) and replaced with a faster, lower voltage pattern following the onset of a bright light. This faster EEG pattern is what has since come to be known as the arousal pattern and, as discussed previously, is thought to indicate increased activity in the brain area concerned. Durup and Fessard were photographing examples of alpha blocking when they noticed that the click of the camera shutter started to induce the blocking even before the bright light was presented. They recognized that the click, by virtue of being paired with the light, had acquired the ability to influence the alpha waves. The conditioning-like properties of these paired sensory events attracted the attention of investigators throughout the world, and, with many modifications and elaborations, the study of spontaneous EEG changes during various conditioning procedures has since received widespread study (Morrell 1961*a*, pp. 444–451).

Localization of the arousal pattern. Early in conditioning, an EEG arousal pattern is seen widely throughout all levels of the brain. With further pairing of the conditioned and unconditioned stimuli, however, these generalized electrical changes start receding to areas, particularly cortical ones, that are related to the unconditioned stimulus and, finally, to areas concerned with the conditioned response. Since the arousal type of EEG is taken to mean that patterned or potentially integrating neural activity is taking place, widespread circuits apparently are active, or available, for use early in learning; as learning progresses, the cells and pathways involved become more localized along with the differentiation and refinement of the conditioned response.

Slow wave changes.   During the early period of diffuse brain activity, a subcortical EEG arousal pattern has been particularly noted in the reticular formation and limbic system and is thought by some to be related to attentional and motivational priming of the central nervous system, preparatory to learning, when the organism finds itself facing a novel situation. Two Hungarian investigators, K. Lissák and A. Grastyán, reported (1960) a specific type of slow wave change (theta) in the subcortical hippocampus during learning. They believe that this change, which arises during early training and subsides shortly before conditioning is complete, represents a suppression mechanism that damps distracting activity, both neural and behavioral, during the time that the learned response is being developed. When conditioning is complete, the EEG arousal pattern is seen most consistently in those connections between the thalamus and the neocortex that are topographically appropriate to the final learned response.

"Tagged" brain-wave changes.   Comparable findings have been reported recently from a similar, although slightly more elegant, experimental procedure in which tagged brain-wave changes, as they are called, are recorded during conditioning. In this type of study, a flashing or flickering light is used as the conditioned stimulus. If the flicker rate is not too divergent from the 10-per-second rate of the brain's alpha rhythm, EEG oscillations at about the same rate as the conditioned stimulus can be detected as they shift among different brain structures at various stages of the learning. While such a procedure was first reported about twenty years ago by M. N. Livanov and K. Poliakov in connection with a standard conditioning study, it has recently been put to more elaborate experimental use by the American research team of E. R. John and K. F. Killam (1960). These investigators recorded such frequency-specific EEG changes, as they are called, while cats were learning a differential discrimination problem in which two lights, flashing at different rates, were the positive and the negative stimulus. There were thus two frequency-specific changes to be sought in the brain wave record. The cats had to learn to perform an avoidance response to one flicker rate but not to the other. Under these conditions, the general sequence in which the tagged EEG changes appear in different brain structures during training was much the same as already discussed above. John and Killam, however, discovered one new phenomenon of con-

siderable interest. They found that when the flicker rate of the stimulus, and thus the tagged EEG rhythm seen in the visual cortex, matched the frequency of the EEG pattern recorded from certain subcortical structures, a correct response was more apt to be made. Discordance between the EEG frequencies at these two sites, on the other hand, was commonly correlated with either an error of omission or commission. It is as though the way the animal "reads" the stimulus or, for one reason or another, is "set" to respond to it is represented by the subcortical frequency, while the temporal events in the visual cortex are tied, of course, to the actual flickering stimulus being presented. The importance of an organism's expectancies or response set in conditioning situations is not a new idea (Sperry 1955), although it is presently receiving renewed consideration.

Evaluation of evidence.   While these bioelectric events indicate something about the widely shifting focuses of neural activity that occur during the course of even a simple learning experience, there is no compelling reason to believe that EEG changes of the type just discussed, no matter how meaningful their localization may appear to be, represent electrical changes that are necessarily associated with stimulus recognition or the eventual fixation of memory. For example, when EEG arousal occurs in its immediate vicinity, an individual cortical neuron may show increased transmission of nerve impulses, decreased transmission, or neither (Jasper et al. 1960). While conditioning systematically brings about statistical changes in the activities of single cells in particular brain areas, an invariant relation between the occurrence of a conditioned response and activity in a specific neuron thus far has not been reported. It may be, of course, that the performance of even a specific learned response by a particular subject does not always involve precisely the same individual neurons.

The hippocampus and memory.   Although much that we have considered indicates the diffuse nature of the neural substrate of learned behavior, scientists in several disciplines have become interested recently in the possibility that one subcortical structure, the hippocampus, contributes uniquely to the memory process. The hippocampus is in the rhinencephalon, the primitive portion of the forebrain. Recent interest in the hippocampus arose as the result of memory losses observed in human patients who had sustained damage to this brain structure as the result of either surgery or disease (Milner 1959). Such findings in man are particularly convincing since, in contrast to lower animals, one can be more confident that the deficit is in memory per se and not in some performance capacity that simply leaves the animal subject unable to demonstrate what has in fact been remembered. These neurological patients show a striking loss of recent memory, particularly if they are distracted while trying to memorize or have had no chance for repetitious practice. Retrograde amnesia for as long as a year prior to hippocampal damage is also seen in people with this type of brain lesion.

While no details are known about the manner in which the hippocampus might contribute to memory, one group of investigators discovered that electrophysiological activity in the hippocampal area of the cat did differ with correct and incorrect choices in a maze (Adey et al. 1960). The majority of studies employing hippocampally damaged animals, however, have failed to find the expected loss in learning ability when the operated subjects were measured on discrimination tasks or conditioned avoidance tests. It could be, however, that the failure to demonstrate a memory loss in animals with hippocampal lesions is due to the fact that tests of animal learning are typically the type that measure learning across a series of practice trials. This is the kind of repetitious training that, based on human studies at least, might minimize evidence of the surgically produced memory deficit. This explanation receives some support from the fact that mice, with chemically induced hippocampal damage, showed dramatic losses of recent memory when they were tested with a very simple learning task that they could have mastered in only a few practice trials (Flexner et al. 1963).

Mechanisms of memory storage

A variety of behavioral experiments support the notion that the early and late stages of the process of memory fixation are probably based on different physiological mechanisms (Gerard 1961). There is an early stage, which lasts for less than an hour and is easily disrupted by a variety of physiological insults to the brain, such as lowering its oxygen supply, cooling it, or bombarding it with electric current (Glickman 1961). Thereafter, the memory trace, or engram as it is sometimes called, becomes more rigidly fixed and cannot be disassembled so easily. As already discussed, these facts are usually taken to mean that the first evanescent steps in memory fixation are electrical in nature and then subsequently become anchored in some biochemical or structural alteration, most commonly presumed to be at the synapse.

Aside from these two well-recognized stages of memory fixation, sometimes called the dynamic and static stages of memory, there may be two additional critical time periods in the sequence of physical changes that underlie memory fixation. For one thing, chemical interference in the hippocampal area can eliminate a newly learned habit as long as a week after the original learning but not thereafter (Flexner et al. 1963). Finally, generalized brain trauma, such as a concussion, can disrupt the memory for events extending back for months and years prior to the injury. Yet, memory commonly remains intact for the stretch of years preceding this period of retrograde amnesia. There thus could be at least four successive steps in the process of memory storage: (1) an acute process, initiated at the time of learning and completed before an hour has passed; (2) a semiacute second process, at least in the hippocampal area, requiring some number of days; (3) a slowly developing third stage, completed over a period of months or years; and (4) a final, static stage of memory, which is not commonly open to disruption by either experimental or clinical influences. As Deutsch (1962) has pointed out, however, it is not clear that all these stages necessarily involve different physiological processes; they could represent, in part, different degrees of development in some common process. Finally, since it is not uncommon for the memories lost in retrograde amnesia to be retrieved when the patient recovers, it may well be that long-term memories are never really eliminated by generalized trauma to the brain but are only made unavailable for current use.

Dominant focus and postpolarization memory. In 1953, V. S. Rusinov discovered an electrophysiological procedure by which he was able to produce new temporary connections between sensory and motor cells in the cortex. He applied a mild anodal current to a small area of motor cortex in the rabbit and found, during this period of polarization, that a previously indifferent sensory stimulus, such as a novel tone, induced a discrete skeletal movement that was related topographically to the part of the motor area that was polarized. The polarizing current is thought to lower the excitability threshold of the motor cells that it influences and thus permit sensory activity in widespread brain areas to "drain," so to speak, through the polarized area and initiate motor activity appropriate to the polarized motor cells. Using a term originally suggested by A. A. Ukhtomskii in 1926, such an area of elevated excitability is called a dominant focus.

If a dominant focus is induced in the part of the motor area that, for example, initiates response pattern A (e.g., right foreleg flexion), the focus will help maintain previous conditioning if the conditioned response was pattern *A*. On the other hand, a conditioned response of pattern *B* is suppressed by the induction of dominant focus *A*. Such findings suggest that something like a dominant focus might be involved during the early stages of conditioning. The effect of a dominant focus persists for about thirty minutes after the anodal current is removed (postpolarization period), which matches reasonably well the time course of the early dynamic stage of memory as it is reported by some workers.

Frank Morrell (1961*b*), an American investigator, studied the activity of individual motor cells within the area of a dominant focus and started to analyze the fiber pathways, which are critical for this interesting phenomenon. He demonstrated, further, a degree of specificity for the 30-minute "memory" in the area of a previous dominant focus; the motor area can be activated during this postpolarization period only by a stimulus that has been presented during the period of polarization. Both transcortical and subcortical pathways were found to be necessary for the activation of the dominant focus by an effective stimulus event. Finally, perseverating activity of nerve impulses was not detected during the postpolarization period in the area of the dominant focus. This is contrary to what might have been expected if reverberating circuits of nerve impulses were responsible for the short-term maintenance of memory in the area. If the short-term phase of memory really is electrical in nature, this finding suggests that the process might be based on persistent graded potentials rather than on propagated nerve impulses. It is still possible, of course, that the early memory process is based on some other fragile biological process, which is possibly chemical and which is not apparent to the recording electrode of the neurophysiologist.

RNA and long-term memory. The physical basis of long-term memory is no better understood than the case of recent memory. As we have seen, the most popular idea is that some permanent change of a structural, or at least chemical, nature takes place at the synapses, and thereafter the routing or patterning of nerve impulse transmission is altered. No specific structural change at a synapse, associated with learning, has ever been demonstrated experimentally. In recent years, however, there has been growing interest in the possibility that changes in the ribonucleic acid (RNA) molecules of the nerve cell might be responsible for structural changes, at the synapse or elsewhere, that could then serve the purpose of long-term memory. This possibility, suggested by Joseph J.

Katz and Ward C. Halstead in 1950, now has received some indirect experimental support, although definite proof of such a mechanism is still lacking (Dingman & Sporn 1964). The general idea is that patterns of neural activity, impinging on a particular nerve cell, would shape the structure of complex RNA molecules within the cell. The RNA, as a regulator of protein synthesis in the cell, would thereafter perpetuate chemically coded protein molecules, thus rendering the cell, for example, maximally sensitive to the temporospatial pattern of neural activity that had originally induced the structural change in the RNA (Hydén 1962). How electrical neural activity could modify the structural pattern of RNA or how structurally coded RNA might then influence the synaptic characteristics of its neuron is still entirely speculative. Nevertheless, changes both in the concentration of RNA and in the specific chemical structure of RNA have been demonstrated in specific brain centers that have been subjected to high levels of neural activity or, more interestingly, have been involved in the learning of new patterns of behavior.

ROBERT A. McCLEARY

[*Other relevant material may be found in* NERVOUS SYSTEM; PSYCHOLOGY, *article on* PHYSIOLOGICAL PSYCHOLOGY; SENSES, *article on* CENTRAL MECHANISMS; STIMULATION DRIVES; *and in the biographies of* FLOURENS *and* LASHLEY.]

BIBLIOGRAPHY

ADEY, W. R.; DUNLOP, C. W.; and HENDRIX, C. E. 1960 Hippocampal Slow Waves: Distribution and Phase Relationships in the Course of Approach Learning. *A.M.A. Archives of Neurology* 3:74–90.

DEUTSCH, J. A. 1962 Higher Nervous Function: The Physiological Bases of Memory. *Annual Review of Physiology* 24:259–286.

DINGMAN, WESLEY; and SPORN, MICHAEL B. 1964 Molecular Theories of Memory. *Science* New Series 144:26–29.

DOTY, R. W. 1961 Conditioned Reflexes Formed and Evoked by Brain Stimulation. Pages 397–412 in Daniel E. Sheer (editor), *Electrical Stimulation of the Brain: An Interdisciplinary Survey of Neurobehavioral Integrative Systems.* Austin: Univ. of Texas Press.

DOTY, R. W.; and GIURGEA, C. 1961 Conditioned Reflexes Established by Coupling Electrical Excitation of Two Cortical Areas. Pages 133–151 in Council for International Organizations of Medical Sciences, *Brain Mechanisms and Learning: A Symposium.* Oxford: Blackwell; Springfield, Ill.: Thomas.

FLEXNER, JOSEFA B.; FLEXNER, L. B.; and STELLAR, E. 1963 Memory in Mice as Affected by Intracerebral Puromycin. *Science* New Series 141:57–59.

GERARD, R. W. 1961 The Fixation of Experience. Pages 21–35 in Council for International Organizations of Medical Sciences, *Brain Mechanisms and Learning: A Symposium.* Oxford: Blackwell; Springfield, Ill.: Thomas.

GLICKMAN, STEPHEN E. 1961 Perseverative Neural Processes and Consolidation of the Memory Trace. *Psychological Bulletin* 58:218–233.

HEBB, DONALD O. 1949 *The Organization of Behavior: A Neuropsychological Theory.* New York: Wiley.

HYDÉN, H. 1962 A Molecular Basis of Neuron–Glia Interaction. Pages 55–69 in Francis O. Schmitt (editor), *Macromolecular Specificity and Biological Memory.* Cambridge, Mass.: M.I.T. Press.

JASPER, H. H.; RICCI, G.; and DOANE, B. 1960 Microelectrode Analysis of Cortical Cell Discharge During Avoidance Conditioning in the Monkey. *Electroencephalography and Clinical Neurophysiology* (Supplement 13): 137–155.

JOHN, E. R.; and KILLAM, K. F. 1960 Studies of Electrical Activity of Brain During Differential Conditioning in Cats. Pages 138–148 in Society of Biological Psychiatry, *Recent Advances in Biological Psychiatry.* New York: Grune.

LASHLEY, KARL S. 1929 *Brain Mechanisms and Intelligence: A Quantitative Study of Injuries to the Brain.* Univ. of Chicago Press.

LISSÁK, K.; and GRASTYÁN, E. 1960 The Changes of Hippocampal Electrical Activity During Conditioning. *Electroencephalography and Clinical Neurophysiology* (Supplement 13): 271–277.

MAGOUN, HORACE W. (1958) 1963 *The Waking Brain.* 2d ed. Springfield, Ill.: Thomas.

MILNER, BRENDA 1959 The Memory Defect in Bilateral Hippocampal Lesions. *Psychiatric Research Reports* 11:43–58.

MORRELL, FRANK 1961a Electrophysiological Contributions to the Neural Basis of Learning. *Physiological Reviews* 41:443–494.

MORRELL, FRANK 1961b Effect of Anodal Polarization on the Firing Pattern of Single Cortical Cells. New York Academy of Sciences, *Annals* 92:860–876.

PAVLOV, IVAN P. (1927) 1960 *Conditioned Reflexes: An Investigation of the Physiological Activity of the Cerebral Cortex.* New York: Dover. → First published as *Lektsii o rabote bol'shikh polusharii golovnogo mozga.*

SPERRY, R. W. 1955 On the Neural Basis of the Conditioned Response. *British Journal of Animal Behaviour* 3:41–44.

VIII
VERBAL LEARNING

Research in the area of verbal learning is concerned with the experimental analysis of the acquisition and retention of verbal habits. The major emphasis in both experimentation and theory construction has been on rote learning, that is, the mastery of verbal materials in a prescribed arrangement. Studies of rote learning have provided the central body of empirical facts, analytic tools, and theoretical concepts dealing with verbal learning.

Historical developments

Early experimental studies. The first systematic experimental investigation of rote learning was carried out by the German psychologist Hermann Ebbinghaus, whose treatise *Memory* (1885) occupies an undisputed position as a classic in the field. Ebbinghaus set out to show that higher mental processes such as memory could be studied under strictly controlled experimental conditions and that they could be precisely measured. His conception of the processes of learning and memory was heavily influenced by the British empiricist doctrine of association by contiguity. In a monumental series of experiments, which were carried out with himself as the only subject, Ebbinghaus introduced procedures and methods of analysis which provided the point of departure for the subsequent development of the entire area of verbal learning. The large majority of Ebbinghaus' experiments were concerned with the acquisition and retention of series of discrete verbal units. In an effort to develop standardized materials that could be used interchangeably in a large variety of learning tasks, Ebbinghaus devised the nonsense syllable as the unit to be used in the construction of verbal series. (A nonsense syllable is a consonant–vowel–consonant combination devoid of dictionary meaning.) While such materials turned out to be far from equal in difficulty, the introduction of these materials was the first step toward the standardization and classification of the verbal units used in studies of rote learning. To provide a uniform standard of attainment with respect to which differences among tasks and conditions of practice could be evaluated, Ebbinghaus established the concept of a criterion of performance, for example, the errorless reproduction of an entire series. The number of repetitions or the amount of time required to reach this criterion could then be related to such variables as the length of the series or the temporal distribution of practice periods. A fixed criterion of performance also made it possible to evaluate retention after the cessation of practice; specifically, Ebbinghaus measured the amount of retention in terms of the amount of time saved in relearning a series relative to the time required for original acquisition. Using these methods of analysis, Ebbinghaus established a number of basic principles of acquisition and retention. His findings included evidence that the amount of practice time per item increases with the length of the series and that a strong positive relationship exists between the number of repetitions of a task and the degree of retention. Another famous product of Ebbinghaus' investigations is the classical curve of retention, which is characterized by a steep initial drop in retention immediately upon the end of learning, followed by more gradual losses thereafter.

Ebbinghaus' approach was soon adopted in other laboratories, and additional techniques for the study of rote verbal learning were developed rapidly. Among the early German investigators, G. E. Müller deserves special mention. In Müller's laboratory the first systematic studies of the processes of interference in retention were carried out. He was also responsible for many refinements in experimental technique, such as the use of an automatic exposure device for the presentation of learning materials (the prototype of the contemporary memory drum). Within less than two decades after the appearance of Ebbinghaus' pioneer investigations, the study of rote verbal learning had become a standard procedure in laboratories of experimental psychology.

American functionalists. In the United States the development of the area of verbal learning is historically tied to the functionalist movement, which helped to make the experimental study of learning a central concern of contemporary experimental psychology and which emphasized the application of psychological principles to problems of education. Although those working in the functionalist tradition put the discovery of empirical laws ahead of formal theory construction, there was a strong predilection for the analysis of the learning process in terms of principles of association. A discussion of the influence of the functionalist movement on the psychology of learning is provided by Hilgard ([1948] 1956, chapter 10). The associationist orientation permitted a ready translation of theoretical concepts and experimental operations into the language of stimulus–response psychology, which became widely accepted under the influence of behaviorism. Thus, the prevalent approach to problems of verbal learning became that of an associationistic stimulus–response psychology. With some important exceptions to be noted later, there was no strong commitment to formal theories of behavior.

A pragmatic orientation is apparent in the writings of the experimental psychologists who had a major influence on the development of the field of human learning. An exposition of the prevailing theoretical approach was given in Edward S. Robinson's *Association Theory Today* (1932). The broad definition of *association* as "the establishment of functional relations among psychological activities and states in the course of individual experience" (p. 7) was designed to accommodate the pursuit of a wide range of empirical questions within a common associationist framework. Robinson stressed the multiplicity of the laws of association and the necessity of reformulating such laws as functional relations between these multiple antecedent conditions on the one hand and measures of associative strength on the other.

The emphasis on functional relations led to the formulation of a program of *dimensional analysis* as a guide to experimental investigation. The essential objectives of such a program were first outlined by McGeoch (1936); a later systematic exposition of this approach may be found in an important article by Melton (1941). Learning situations vary continuously with respect to a manifold of descriptive characteristics or dimensions, and learning tasks can be ordered along these dimensions to provide the framework for the exploration of quantitative functional relations. Among the major axes of reference is the verbal–motor dimension; purely verbal tasks define one extreme and predominantly motor ones the other. A second dimension is defined by the degree to which the subject must discover the correct response and ranges from the acquisition of rote series to problem-solving situations. A third dimension refers to the degree to which mastery of a task requires a response to relational rather than to absolute properties of the stimuli.

Influence of conditioning theory. While dimensional analysis has provided a thread of continuity in empirical research, there have been important attempts to conceptualize the facts of verbal learning within the framework of general psychological theory. During the period between the two world wars an important landmark was the publication of the *Mathematico–Deductive Theory of Rote Learning* by Clark L. Hull and his associates (1940). In this analysis, the basic phenomena of serial rote learning are deduced from a set of postulates that were derived largely from the theory of classical conditioning. The effective strength of the associations linking the members of a verbal series was conceived as representing the balance of excitatory and inhibitory potentials, in accord with the dual-process interpretation of Pavlovian conditioning. With the aid of assumptions about the conditions governing the growth and decline of excitatory and inhibitory tendencies, specific quantitative predictions were made concerning the shape of the serial-position curve (level of performance as a function of the position of an item in a series), the effects of the temporal distribution of practice trials, and other properties of serial learning. Some of these predictions were confirmed experimentally; however, the scope of the theory is limited, and its influence has been declining with the rapid accumulation of empirical findings that fall outside its boundary conditions.

Another systematic application of principles of classical conditioning to verbal learning was proposed by Eleanor J. Gibson (1940). Gibson's analysis centered on the concepts of stimulus generalization and differentiation, which were adopted from conditioning theory. Stimulus generalization refers to the tendency for the conditioned response to be elicited by stimuli similar to the conditioned stimulus. The amount of generalization describes a gradient, that is, it is directly related to the degree of similarity between the training stimulus and the test stimulus. Differentiation refers to the reduction of generalization as a consequence of reinforcement of responses to the training stimulus and nonreinforcement of responses to other test stimuli. According to Gibson's analysis, speed of acquisition is determined by the rate at which differentiation among the stimulus items is achieved during practice. Thus, speed of learning should vary inversely with the degree of interstimulus similarity. In general, the experimental facts are consistent with this prediction. The theory also predicts, in accordance with principles of conditioning, that generalization tendencies recover spontaneously over time, with a consequent loss of differentiation. It follows that long-term retention, like speed of acquisition, should vary inversely with interstimulus similarity. However, this prediction has consistently failed to be confirmed. This lack of support for one of the critical deductions from the theory necessarily calls into question the validity of the basic postulates. The analytic power of the theory is also limited by the failure to consider the role of response generalization along with that of stimulus generalization. A comprehensive evaluation of the theory, which has exerted considerable influence on research in verbal learning ever since its publication, is provided by Underwood (1961).

Gestalt psychology. Although there has been wide agreement among investigators of verbal learning on the usefulness of associationist concepts in the formulation of empirical questions and theoretical issues, such agreement has been by no means general. A quite different approach is represented by exponents of the gestalt school of psychology, whose work in verbal learning was directed primarily at the validation of general principles of their theory. An exposition of this approach may be found in Koffka (1935, chapters 10–13). From the point of view of gestalt theory, learning and retention are governed by the same principles of organization that govern the formation of perceptual units. In the acquisition of verbal tasks, relationships such as similarity and proximity between the component items are considered critical in determining the readiness with which the organization required for mastery is achieved. The organizations developed during learning are, in turn, assumed to be preserved in the nervous system as memory traces, whose subsequent development is likewise governed by principles of organization. Re-exposure to part of an organized pattern activates the trace of the pattern and thus permits the recall of other component parts. Association is, therefore, interpreted as a special case of organization. Experimental studies initiated by gestalt psychologists have sought to demonstrate the applicability to verbal learning and memory of principles of perceptual organization. An example is provided by the studies of the effects of perceptual isolation. When a unique item is embedded in an otherwise homogeneous series, the unique or "isolated" item is recalled better than the average member of the homogeneous series. According to gestalt theory, the traces of the homogeneous items suffer assimilation and lose their identity, whereas the trace of the unique item remains distinctive and accessible. This dependence of recall on the relationship between items is interpreted as analogous to the salience of a perceptual figure against a homogeneous background. Alternative interpretations have been offered, for example, the differential susceptibility of isolated and homogeneous items to generalization. The conditions determining the isolation effect are still under investigation. This example illustrates the fact that crucial experiments permitting a clear-cut decision between gestalt and associationist interpretations have often been difficult to design. [*See* GESTALT THEORY.]

Recent developments. The two decades since the end of World War II have witnessed a rapid growth of activity in the field of verbal learning, with several new developments adding greatly to the diversity of experimental methods and theoretical concerns. Perhaps the most important trend is the convergence on common problems of research in psycholinguistics and in verbal learning. This development is reflected in the increased emphasis on the role of natural language habits in the analysis of verbal learning. A large amount of work has centered on the assessment of the effects on acquisition and retention of the associative hierarchies that are developed through linguistic usage. The method of free association (in which the individual is required to respond to each stimulus word with the first other word that comes to mind) and related normative techniques have been used to determine the structure of verbal associations characteristic of a given speech community. Learning tasks constructed on the basis of such norms are then used to evaluate the influence of pre-existing associative patterns on the formation of new verbal habits. Within this problem area a focus of special concern has been the study of mediational processes, that is, of the ways in which pre-existing associations serve to facilitate the establishment of connections between initially unrelated terms (see Jenkins 1963). The influence of contemporary linguistic analysis is also reflected in the growing number of investigations concerned with the role of grammatical habits in the acquisition and performance of verbal tasks. Largely under the influence of George A. Miller (e.g., 1962), much of the recent work has been directed at the exploration of the psychological processes suggested by the principles of transformational grammar.

In the experimental study of memory processes, several influences have converged to produce an upsurge of interest in short-term retention. Any a priori distinction between short-term and long-term memory is, of course, arbitrary; in practice the operational difference is between retention intervals of the order of seconds or minutes on the one hand and of hours, days, or weeks on the other. Rapid developments in the theory of communication and in the study of man–machine interaction have brought to the fore the question of man's capacity to process and to store continuously changing inputs of information; for example, in the performance of monitoring tasks incoming information has to be retained for critical periods of time to permit effective action. Thus, the study of short-term memory is an integral part of the analysis of the nervous system as a limited-capacity channel for the transmission of information. This general approach is well represented by the work of Broadbent (1958), who has introduced a number of influential new techniques for the measurement of short-term memory. The availability of the analytic methods of information theory has, of course, been of considerable value in bringing order to measures of immediate memory that are obtained with a wide variety of materials. Short-term memory also has continuing systematic significance for theories of the physiological basis of memory. A central concept of several influential theories is that of a transitory memory trace, which is assumed to fade or decay rapidly unless it is restored by repetition or rehearsal. The assumption of a short-lived immediate trace is characteristically supplemented by the postulation of a separate and distinct mechanism of long-term storage. A considerable amount of effort is being devoted to experimental tests of the dual-process conception. A systematic question on which agreement does not appear to be in sight as yet is whether the principles governing short-term and long-term memory are continuous or discontinuous. [See FORGETTING.]

Recent developments in verbal learning, as in several other special fields of psychology, include the construction of mathematical models for the description of circumscribed sets of data. Among the most influential approaches have been the stochastic models that treat acquisition as a probabilistic process. Very briefly, it is assumed that on any given learning trial (*a*) the organism samples the environmental events which constitute the stimulus situation; (*b*) all the stimulus elements sampled become connected to the response occurring contiguously with them; and (*c*) such association by contiguity occurs in an all-or-none fashion, that is, reaches maximal strength on a single trial. The probability of occurrence of the response increases as more and more stimulus elements are connected with it. While the most important applications of these models have been to discrimination learning and conditioning, the models have also been used for the acquisition of verbal associations as well. A point of major theoretical significance is the assumption made by stochastic models that association by contiguity occurs in an all-or-none fashion. If verbal stimuli function as single elements, it follows that associations are not built up gradually as a function of practice but, instead, change in probability from zero to one after a single occurrence. The assumption that associations may vary continuously in strength and are built up gradually through practice has been explicit or implicit in associationist interpretations of verbal learning. This assumption, which has been designated as the incremental hypothesis, has been challenged in recent years by exponents of the all-or-none position. Experimental tests to decide between these alternative conceptions have focused on the question of whether there is a growth in associative strength on practice trials prior to the first correct response. While it is fair to say that the evidence thus far has favored the incremental position, the issue cannot be regarded as finally settled (for a review see Postman 1963). The emergence of this controversial issue illustrates the recent trend toward the consideration of hypotheses about the nature of association and memory in the context of studies of verbal learning. [See MODELS, MATHEMATICAL.]

A brief survey of some representative experimental methods and findings in the area of verbal learning now follows. The evidence is grouped under the headings of acquisition, transfer of training, and retention. Detailed reviews and discussions of the relevant literature may be found in McGeoch (1942) and in the collections of papers edited by Cofer (Conference on Verbal Learning . . . 1961), Cofer and Musgrave (Conference on Verbal Learning . . . 1963), and Melton (Symposium . . . 1964).

Acquisition

It will be convenient to consider the analysis of the process of acquisition with reference to specific experimental procedures, each of which focuses on a different type of verbal performance.

Paired-associate learning. In the paired-associate method, the subject's task is to learn a prescribed response to each of a list of stimulus terms (much as in vocabulary learning). The characteristics of the stimulus and response terms can be varied independently. An important analytic advantage of the method is, therefore, that it permits the assessment of stimulus and response functions in the acquisition of associations. Progress in this task will depend on the extent to which the following requirements are met: (*a*) the stimulus terms are differentiated from each other; (*b*) the prescribed responses are available as integrated units in the subject's repertoire; and (*c*) stable associative connections are developed between the appropriate stimulus and response terms.

It is apparent that the requirements of the task with respect to the stimulus and response terms are not the same. Whereas the response terms must be recalled as prescribed, the stimulus terms need only be discriminated from each other and recognized as the occasions for the performance of the appropriate responses. The subject is free, therefore, to attend to only those characteristics of the stimulus which are minimally essential for the placement of the correct responses, that is, the subject can practice "stimulus selection." Recognition of this fact has led to the distinction between nominal and functional stimuli (Underwood 1963). The nominal stimulus refers to stimulus terms as specified by the experimenter for presentation to the subject; the functional stimulus refers to those characteristics of the stimulus which actually function as cues for the learner. The available evidence indicates that stimulus selection does, in fact, occur within the limits permitted by the requirements of the task; for example, when the stimulus is a compound composed of elements which vary in meaningfulness, there is a strong

tendency to select the more meaningful element as the functional cue.

The analysis of the components of the paired-associate task makes it useful to conceive of the total acquisition period as divided into two successive stages, namely, a response-learning stage and an associative stage (Underwood & Schulz 1960, pp. 92–94). During the former, the prescribed responses are established as integrated units available for performance; during the latter, the responses are linked to the appropriate stimuli. If the responses are items in the subject's pre-experimental repertoire, for example, familiar words, the response-learning stage reduces to a response-recall stage during which the subject learns to restrict his responses to the units in the list. The two stages certainly overlap in time. The distinction is, however, useful in the analysis of the conditions which influence performance in paired-associate learning.

Of the task variables which influence speed of acquisition, two will be singled out on the basis of the magnitude and reliability of their effects. These are (*a*) meaningfulness and (*b*) intralist similarity. In current usage, the term "meaningfulness" refers to several scaled characteristics of verbal units, such as the probability of a unit evoking an association within a limited period of time, the number of different associations evoked by the unit, etc. These indices tend to be closely related to each other and to the frequency of occurrence of the unit in the language (for a survey of measures of meaningfulness see Underwood & Schulz 1960). Intralist similarity may be either formal or semantic. Formal similarity is defined by the degree to which overlapping elements, such as letters, are used in the construction of different units included in a list; this variable is characteristically manipulated in lists composed of nonsense items. Semantic similiarity refers to the degree of synonymity and applies to lists composed of words.

Meaningfulness. The speed of paired-associate learning varies widely as a function of meaningfulness, but the relationship is much more pronounced when responses rather than stimuli are varied in meaningfulness (Underwood & Schulz 1960). From the point of view of the two-stage analysis of acquisition, it is clear that meaningfulness decisively influences the response-learning stage: the more fully a response unit conforms to prior linguistic usage the more readily it enters into association with new stimuli. There are two factors which may serve to reduce the effectiveness of the variable of stimulus meaningfulness: (*a*) stimulus selection may counteract the differences that exist in the nominal stimuli; (*b*) increases in stimulus meaningfulness may facilitate not only the formation of associative linkages with the prescribed responses but also the development of inappropriate associations with other responses. Thus, associative facilitation and interference may increase concurrently as a function of stimulus meaningfulness.

Intralist similarity. The effects of intralist similarity also differ depending on whether stimuli or responses are manipulated. In general, speed of acquisition varies inversely with the degree of similarity of the stimulus terms. As stimuli become less discriminable, the associative phase of learning is retarded. Variations in response similarity, on the other hand, have only small effects on the rate of learning, except for units of low meaningfulness. The usual absence of a large effect is attributable to the balance between two opposed influences: As responses become more similar, the amount of response learning is reduced; at the same time, individual responses become less discriminable from each other and the associative phase is prolonged.

Serial learning. Serial-learning tasks require the reproduction of a series of items in a prescribed order. The experimental procedure typically consists of the paced presentation of the successive members of the series, with the subject required to anticipate each item before it appears. Speed of acquisition varies reliably as a function of the ordinal position of the item in the series. The initial items are usually acquired first, the terminal items next, and the central items last. Thus, when percentage of correct responses during learning is plotted against serial position, a typical bow-shaped curve is obtained. Classical interpretations of serial learning (for example, that of Hull mentioned earlier) were based on the assumption that an individual member of the series serves a dual function during acquisition: it is the response to the immediately preceding item and the stimulus for the immediately following one. The bow-shaped serial position curve was attributed to interferences from incorrect associations among nonadjacent members of the series. Given certain assumptions about the number and strength of such remote associations, it can be shown that the total amount of interference should first increase and then decrease as a function of serial position. Recent experiments have, however, served to call the classical conception of serial learning into question. Some of the critical evidence comes from experiments in which the subject first learns a serial list and immediately there-

after a paired-associate list in which the pairs are composed of adjacent members of the serial list. If the mastery of the serial list depends on the establishment of a chain of sequential associations, pronounced facilitation should be found in the acquisition of the paired-associate list. A conclusive test of this prediction has proved difficult. Performance on the critical transfer task appears to be complexly determined and sensitive to procedural variations. The difficulties encountered by the classical hypothesis have raised questions about the nature of the functional stimulus in serial learning; for example, it has been suggested that each member of the series is associated to its ordinal position in the series rather than to the preceding item. This problem is receiving considerable experimental attention at the present time (Underwood 1963).

Free learning. The two methods discussed above require the establishment of prescribed links between verbal units, and, thus, they focus on the development of sequential associations. By contrast, the method of free learning yields information about the ordering and reproduction of verbal units when no sequential constraints are placed upon the subject. Under this method, a list of items, such as words, is presented to the subject, and he is then permitted to reproduce them in whatever order they occur to him (free recall). The method is useful in the investigation of preexperimental habits of classifying verbal units and of the process of recall (for general discussions see Deese 1961; Postman 1964). The major determinants of the amount of free recall are (*a*) the total learning time prior to the test of recall and (*b*) the number and strength of the preexperimental associations between the units in the list. The total learning time is the product of the list and the presentation time per item. The number of items recalled after a single exposure of a list remains approximately invariant with total learning time, that is, the number of items recalled increases with the length of the list and with the amount of study time per item, but a decrease in the value of one of these variables can be compensated for by an increase in the other. Thus, it is the total amount of time available for practice which is critical rather than the length of the task or the exposure rate per se. With length and rate held constant, the number of words recalled varies with the average degree of associative connection between the items in the list (as determined, for example, by the method of free association). In the absence of external constraints, recall performance reflects pre-existing associations and relations between the component units of the list. As free learning continues beyond a single presentation and recall, stable groupings of items are likely to be formed which are carried over from one test of recall to the next.

Transfer of training

Transfer of training refers to the influence of prior learning on the acquisition of new habits. The transfer effects may be positive or negative, depending on whether the earlier training facilitates or inhibits the mastery of the later task. In studies of verbal learning it has been conventional to distinguish between specific and general transfer effects. Specific transfer effects are those attributable to known similarity relations between successive tasks; general transfer effects represent the development of skills which cannot be ascribed to known similarity relations between tasks. General effects will be considered first.

General effects. When unrelated verbal lists are learned in the laboratory, the speed of acquisition typically increases, sharply at first and more gradually thereafter. Such progressive practice effects have been demonstrated for both paired-associate and serial learning. When learning sessions are held daily, the gains in performance are considerably greater within sessions than from one session to the next. A common interpretation of this finding is that the gains within a session are largely a matter of warm-up, that is, the development of postural adjustments, rhythms of responding, and other components of a set appropriate to the learning task. Such adjustments to the requirements of the task may be expected to be lost once the subject leaves the experimental situation. The changes which persist from one session to the next are attributed to "learning-to-learn," that is, the acquisition of higher-order habits or modes of attack which are relatively stable and persistent. According to this analysis, warm-up both develops and declines more rapidly than do the habits which constitute learning-to-learn. The possibility cannot be ruled out, however, that perceptual–motor adjustments are conditioned to the experimental situation and that components of learning-to-learn are forgotten.

Specific effects. The principles of specific transfer have been investigated primarily as a function of the similarity relations between the stimulus terms and/or the response terms of successive tasks. One general principle is that the amount of transfer, whether positive or negative, increases as the stimulus terms in successive tasks become more similar; stimulus identity is, therefore, the condition of maximal transfer. At a given level of similarity, the sign (positive or negative) and degree of transfer vary with the similarity, or strength of pre-existing associative connection, between successive responses. A large array of experimental findings may be subsumed under the following general principle: as the responses become increasingly dissimilar, the transfer effects shift from positive to negative. Thus, positive transfer is obtained when the successive responses learned to identical or similar stimuli are associatively related; negative transfer results when new unrelated responses are learned to old stimuli. These principles are, however, subject to modification by other factors, such as the readiness with which successive tasks can be differentiated from each other. For example, when old stimuli and old responses are re-paired, there is considerable negative transfer; even though the repertoire of responses remains the same, the identity of both stimuli and responses makes differentiation between successive tasks extremely difficult (for a discussion of methods and designs in the study of transfer see McGeoch 1942).

Retention

Retention refers to the persistence over time of changes produced by practice. It is apparent that retention is an integral component of acquisition; a habit can be mastered only if there is retention from one practice trial to the next. In the present context, however, the term retention refers to measurements of performance which are made after the end of a period of formal practice. The operational distinction between measures of acquisition and of retention is a convenient and, indeed, an essential one for investigation of the conditions of forgetting. The amount of retention is, of course, always inferred from specific measures of performance; the absolute level of performance will vary with the specific method of testing. Thus, after a given amount of practice, tests of recognition usually yield higher retention scores than do tests of recall, although the degree of discrepancy may vary widely as a function of the specific conditions of recall and recognition.

The basic empirical fact which theories of retention have sought to account for is the progressive decline in performance that occurs as a function of time after the end of practice. The position now held most widely attributes forgetting to the interference that develops between successively learned habits. Two major types of interference are distinguished, namely, retroactive inhibition and proactive inhibition. Retroactive inhibition refers to the interference produced by the acquisition of new habits between the end of practice and the test of retention; proactive inhibition occurs when earlier habits interfere with the retention of a more recent task. In both cases, the amount of interference varies with the similarity relations between successive tasks; specifically, the amount of interference is governed by the same conditions of intertask similarity as is negative transfer. Thus, negative transfer in acquisition, retroactive inhibition, and proactive inhibition are complementary manifestations of habit interference. Retroactive and proactive inhibition differ with respect to the development of interference effects over time. Whereas retroactive inhibition is present to its full extent immediately after acquisition of the interfering task, proactive inhibition develops gradually over time. Several specific mechanisms responsible for the observed interference effects have been identified experimentally. These include (*a*) the unlearning, in the sense of reduced availability, of old associations during the acquisition of new ones; (*b*) competition between incompatible responses at the time of recall which may cause performance to be blocked or a dominant error to displace a correct response; and (*c*) failure to differentiate between the members of alternative response systems at the time of recall (for a review of interference theory see Postman 1961).

The principles of retroactive and proactive inhibition have been established in experimental situations in which the conditions of interference can be fully controlled. Interference theory assumes that the same principles apply to forgetting outside the laboratory. For example, the forgetting of a verbal task would be attributed to interference from other verbal habits acquired both prior and subsequent to that task. Proactive inhibition is likely to play a larger role than retroactive inhibition to the extent that the number and strength of prior habits exceed those of subsequent habits.

Regardless of theoretical interpretation, certain facts about the long-term retention of verbal tasks are well supported by the experimental evidence. The single most important determinant of the amount of long-term retention is the degree of original learning, with resistance to forgetting a direct function of the degree of overlearning. It is essential, therefore, to hold the degree of original learning constant whenever the influence of other variables, such as meaningfulness or intratask similarity, on retention is to be evaluated. The evidence available thus far shows that the effects of such variables are minor relative to the sheer degree of original learning. The practical implication is that overlearning provides the most certain means of insuring the long-term stability of verbal habits.

LEO POSTMAN

[*See also* FORGETTING; LANGUAGE; *and the biographies of* EBBINGHAUS; HULL; MÜLLER, GEORG ELIAS.]

BIBLIOGRAPHY

BROADBENT, DONALD E. 1958 *Perception and Communication.* Oxford: Pergamon.

CONFERENCE ON VERBAL LEARNING AND VERBAL BEHAVIOR, NEW YORK UNIVERSITY, 1959 1961 *Verbal Learning and Verbal Behavior: Proceedings.* Edited by Charles N. Cofer. New York: McGraw-Hill.

CONFERENCE ON VERBAL LEARNING AND VERBAL BEHAVIOR, SECOND, ARDSLEY-ON-HUDSON, N.Y., 1961 1963 *Verbal Behavior and Learning; Problems and Processes: Proceedings.* Edited by Charles N. Cofer and Barbara S. Musgrave. New York: McGraw-Hill.

DEESE, JAMES 1961 From the Isolated Verbal Unit to Connected Discourse. Pages 11–31 in Conference on Verbal Learning and Verbal Behavior, New York University, 1959, *Verbal Learning and Verbal Behavior: Proceedings.* Edited by Charles N. Cofer. New York: McGraw-Hill.

EBBINGHAUS, HERMANN (1885) 1913 *Memory: A Contribution to Experimental Psychology.* New York: Columbia Univ., Teachers College. → First published as *Über das Gedächtnis.* A paperback edition was published in 1964 by Dover.

ESTES, WILLIAM K. 1959 The Statistical Approach to Learning Theory. Volume 2, pages 380–491 in Sigmund Koch (editor), *Psychology: A Study of a Science.* New York: McGraw-Hill.

GIBSON, ELEANOR J. 1940 A Systematic Application of the Concepts of Generalization and Differentiation to Verbal Learning. *Psychological Review* 47:196–229.

HILGARD, ERNEST R. (1948) 1956 *Theories of Learning.* 2d ed. New York: Appleton.

HULL, CLARK L. et al. 1940 *Mathematico–Deductive Theory of Rote Learning: A Study in Scientific Methodology.* New Haven: Yale Univ. Press; Oxford Univ. Press.

JENKINS, JAMES J. 1963 Mediated Associations: Paradigms and Situations. Pages 210–245 in Conference on Verbal Learning and Verbal Behavior, Second, Ardsley-on-Hudson, N.Y., 1961, *Verbal Behavior and Learning; Problems and Processes: Proceedings.* Edited by Charles N. Cofer and Barbara S. Musgrave. New York: McGraw-Hill.

KOFFKA, KURT 1935 *Principles of Gestalt Psychology.* New York: Harcourt.

McGEOCH, JOHN A. 1936 The Vertical Dimensions of Mind. *Psychological Review* 43:107–129.

McGEOCH, JOHN A. (1942) 1952 *The Psychology of Human Learning.* 2d ed., rev. New York: Longmans.

MELTON, ARTHUR W. 1941 Learning. Pages 667–686 in Walter S. Monroe (editor), *Encyclopedia of Educational Research.* New York: Macmillan.

MILLER, GEORGE A. 1962 Some Psychological Studies of Grammar. *American Psychologist* 17:748–762.

POSTMAN, LEO 1961 The Present Status of Interference Theory. Pages 152–179 in Conference on Verbal Learning and Verbal Behavior, New York University,

1959, *Verbal Learning and Verbal Behavior: Proceedings.* New York: McGraw-Hill.

POSTMAN, LEO 1963 One-trial Learning. Pages 295–335 in Conference on Verbal Learning and Verbal Behavior, Second, Ardsley-on-Hudson, N.Y., 1961, *Verbal Behavior and Learning; Problems and Processes: Proceedings.* Edited by Charles N. Cofer and Barbara S. Musgrave. New York: McGraw-Hill.

POSTMAN, LEO 1964 Short-term Memory and Incidental Learning. Pages 145–201 in Symposium on the Psychology of Human Learning, University of Michigan, 1962, *Categories of Human Learning.* Edited by Arthur W. Melton. New York: Academic Press.

ROBINSON, EDWARD S. 1932 *Association Theory Today.* New York: Century.

SYMPOSIUM ON THE PSYCHOLOGY OF HUMAN LEARNING, UNIVERSITY OF MICHIGAN, *1962* 1964 *Categories of Human Learning.* Edited by Arthur W. Melton. New York: Academic Press.

UNDERWOOD, BENTON J. 1961 An Evaluation of the Gibson Theory of Verbal Learning. Pages 197–223 in Conference on Verbal Learning and Verbal Behavior, New York University, 1959, *Verbal Learning and Verbal Behavior: Proceedings.* Edited by Charles N. Cofer. New York: McGraw-Hill.

UNDERWOOD, BENTON J. 1963 Stimulus Selection in Verbal Learning. Pages 33–75 in Conference on Verbal Learning and Verbal Behavior, Second, Ardsley-on-Hudson, N.Y., 1961, *Verbal Behavior and Learning; Problems and Processes: Proceedings.* Edited by Charles N. Cofer and Barbara S. Musgrave. New York: McGraw-Hill.

UNDERWOOD, BENTON J.; and SCHULZ, RUDOLPH W. 1960 *Meaningfulness and Verbal Learning.* Philadelphia: Lippincott.

IX
TRANSFER

The phrase "transfer of learning," or "transfer of training," refers to a class of phenomena that are aftereffects of learning. When some particular performance has been learned by an individual, the capability established by that learning affects to some extent other activities of the individual. The effects of the learning are said to transfer to these other activities. Having learned some performance, the individual may thereby be enabled to exhibit some additional, different performance that he could not do prior to learning. As more commonly used, transfer of training means that the individual is able to learn something else more readily than he could prior to the original learning (positive transfer) or that he is able to learn something else less readily than he could before the original learning (negative transfer).

Transfer of learning, since it is virtually always present as a learning effect, may reasonably be considered an essential characteristic of the learning process. Accordingly, it may be shown to play a role in a wide variety of human activities, including the learning of language, social customs, values, and attitudes and the acquisition of the human skills and knowledge that underlie practically all types of vocational activity. Transfer of learning is of particular importance in formal education. In the opinion of many educators, education should have transfer of learning, or "transferability of knowledge," as a recognized goal. It is generally agreed that the assessment of outcomes of education and training should include measures of transfer in addition to more direct measures of learning.

In studying the phenomenon of transfer of learning, investigators have employed a wide variety of situations and techniques. The work of experimental psychologists includes the exploration of such questions as (1) the degree of transfer resulting from the establishment of conditioned responses; (2) the specificity and limitations to transfer in the learning of simple perceptual and motor acts; (3) the occurrence of transfer between learned actions performed by different body members, such as the hand and foot; (4) the extent of bilateral transfer, as between actions performed by the left and right hands; (5) the occurrence of positive and negative transfer (called interference) in connection with the learning of verbal associates and sequences; (6) the positive transfer to a variety of specific novel situations resulting from the learning of principles; (7) the acquisition of a capability for transfer to novel discrimination problems in monkeys and human beings; and (8) the relation of transfer to the mediating effects of language in children. An interesting line of investigation has been undertaken by neurophysiologists in determining the conditions of transfer of training in animals with "split brains."

Educational aspects. In the field of educational research, studies have been concerned with the broad question of transfer of learning among the component subjects and topics that make up the school curriculum. Older studies arose from controversies over the doctrine of formal discipline, which held that certain subjects of the curriculum, such as Latin, geometry, and logic, derived a great part of their value from the general (that is, transferable) discipline they imparted to the mind, thus facilitating the learning of other subjects (Thorndike 1924). While this doctrine is probably quite true in the sense that certain capabilities acquired in school are much more widely transferable than others, the rationale for the choice of particular subjects was not a convincing one. At any rate, educational studies in the older tradition were concerned with such questions as whether transfer of training could be measured from the study of Latin to the study of English or from that of geometry to other fields necessitating the use of logical thinking.

More modern studies of educational transfer have concerned themselves with such questions as the extent to which certain kinds of within-subject learning transfer positively to advanced topics, such as the concept of the numberline to later mathematical topics, the discrimination of language sounds to the learning of foreign language utterances, etc. Additionally, there has been concern with the possibilities of negative transfer between the learning of such activities as the formal statements of verbal definitions and the later learning of advanced mathematical principles and between the learning of letter sounds and the acquisition of reading skill. Finally, there is an increasing interest in the exploration of the possibility of designing instruction to develop such highly transferable individual characteristics as thinking strategies, curiosity, and even creativity.

Observing and measuring transfer

The simplest observations of transfer of learning occur in the following ways. The individual is known to have learned a new performance, such as spelling the word *nation* in response to the oral direction, "Spell nation." It may now be found that the same child is able to learn to spell such words as *motion* and *lotion* much more rapidly than he learned to spell *nation*. The inference is that the child learns to spell *motion* more rapidly than he would have if he had not first learned to spell *nation*. Besides the specific outcome of the original learning, the performance of spelling *nation*, there has been another aftereffect of learning: some residual capability, which shows itself in the speeding up of the learning to spell a different word. A different example, illustrating negative transfer, is the following. An individual has moved to a new location and must learn two new telephone numbers, those of his office and his home. One is 643-2795, and the other is 297-6534. He has learned single telephone numbers previously, without a great deal of difficulty. But he now finds that he makes many errors in trying to learn these two numbers, tending to substitute one portion of one number for another portion of the other number. Over a period of time, he finds that, in his experience, learning these two new numbers turns out to be more than twice as difficult as learning any one number has been. There appears to be interference between the two learning tasks; in other

words, the inference is made that the learning of one number produces a negative transfer effect, which slows down the attainment of recalling the other number.

Design of transfer experiments. While neither of these sequences of observation and inference is unreasonable, it is apparent that certain variables are uncontrolled, and this generates a requirement for a more painstaking method of observing transfer in an experimental sense. Returning to the example of learning to spell, it is clear that for any given individual we do not really know how long it should take him to learn to spell either *nation* or *motion* because we do not know where learning begins. Possibly some peculiarity of his past learning makes *nation* a difficult word and *motion* an easy one. Accordingly, an experimental design for the measurement of transfer typically includes a pretest to measure the initial capabilities of the individual before learning begins. Still another possibility must be considered: perhaps the increase of facility at the second task (spelling *motion*) is engendered partly by increased motivation, partly by a "set" to learn, or partly by "warm-up" factors (Thune 1950), rather than by the specific effects of learning the first task (spelling *nation*). As a consequence, it is usually considered necessary to include in a transfer experiment a control condition for this set of "general" factors.

The typical schema for experimental study of transfer that results from these control requirements is one that uses two groups of individuals, either assumed or shown to be equivalent at the beginning of learning. Table 1 provides an example.

Table 1

Transfer group	Control group
1. Takes pretest on task 2	1. Takes pretest on task 2
2. Learns task 1	2. Learns a task of a sort very different from tasks 1 and 2 but requiring the same amount of time as task 1
3. Learns task 2	3. Learns task 2

When this design is used, an average difference in the ease of learning (often, the time to learn) of task 2 in the two groups is taken to be an indication of "specific" transfer of training from the learning of task 1 to the learning of task 2. This and other experimental designs for the study of transfer are discussed by Murdock (1957).

Quantification. The amount of transfer of learning is usually expressed as a percentage (Gagné et al. 1948). Should it be found that a second performance is learned no more readily than if the learning of a first performance had never occurred, transfer is said to be zero, or 0 per cent. If the second performance is found to be fully learned after the first performance has been learned, transfer is 100 per cent. Amounts between these extremes are, of course, often found. It is also possible to express negative transfer in this way; if a second performance takes half again as long to learn following initial learning of a first performance, the amount of transfer can be expressed as − 50 per cent. The use of percentages in expressing amount of transfer is, however, largely a matter of convenience and has no particular systematic significance for an understanding of the phenomenon.

Conditions of positive and negative transfer

The occurrence of transfer of training depends, by definition, on the occurrence of previous learning. For certain performances, such as the learning of a set of verbal associates, the evidence indicates that the amount of positive transfer obtained is directly related to the amount of initial learning (Gagné & Foster 1949; Mandler & Heinemann 1956). As for negative transfer, a somewhat more complex relationship has been found to hold: the amount of interference exhibited in the second task increases as the amount of practice on the initial task is increased to some intermediate amount (McGeoch 1952, pp. 335–339). As practice of the initial task continues, however, the interference with the second task decreases and may under some conditions come to yield positive transfer (Mandler 1954).

Effects of similarity. As a general rule, the amount of transfer (positive or negative) is influenced by the similarity of the performance initially learned to the second performance in which the occurrence of transfer is observed. For example, when a conditioned response is established to a tone of 1,000 cycles, the amount of positive transfer exhibited to tones differing in pitch from this original stimulus bears a direct relation to the degree of physical similarity of the second tone to the original one (Hovland 1937). According to Gibson's study (1941), when the two performances are such that negative transfer is found, the amount of such interference increases with the degree of similarity between the stimuli of the first and second tasks. There is an apparent paradox to these findings, whose resolution seems to depend upon a careful definition of what aspects of the two performances are being compared in similarity. According to Osgood (1949), the prediction of the direction of transfer (positive or negative) depends upon the differential specification of the stimuli of the two tasks and of their responses. A brief and partial summary of Osgood's conclusions may be given as follows. When tasks 1 and 2 contain identical responses, transfer is increasingly positive as the similarity of the stimuli of the two tasks increases. When tasks 1 and 2 contain identical stimuli, transfer is increasingly negative as the similarity of the responses of the two tasks decreases.

Despite the clarifying analyses that have been made, it is nevertheless apparent at the present time that the relation of transfer to the similarity of learned performances remains a perplexing and essentially unsolved problem. Two practical situations may serve as bench marks in consideration of what has yet to be understood about this relationship. (1) An individual first learns to drive a standard-shift automobile with the gearshift attached to the floor. A later model car comes equipped with the same type of transmission but with the gearshift attached to the steering column, so that first gear is now down rather than back, second gear is now up rather than forward and so on. Under these circumstances of apparent difference, the two tasks would nevertheless be judged as similar by almost any driver, and in fact the amount of positive transfer is close to 100 per cent. (2) The second situation is one in which a later model car comes equipped with a four-speed transmission; the gearshift, which is on the floor, must be pushed forward for first gear, backward for second gear, and so on. The situation in the second task is not only dissimilar; it may also be judged to have in it certain elements of reversal relative to the first task. It is a common experience that a considerable amount of negative transfer occurs under these conditions. Reversal of stimulus–response relationships has also been shown in laboratory tasks to produce large amounts of negative transfer (Lewis & Shephard 1950).

Mediational processes. Other limitations of the similarity principle in its present state of development are also shown by studies in which the performance acquired depends upon the learning of a mediational process.

Concept formation. The studies of Kendler and Kendler (1961) have shown that the performance of seven-year-old children who are required to learn a reversal of a discrimination task is markedly superior to the performance of four-year-olds on the same reversed task. These findings suggest that transfer occurs to the second task, which is dissimilar to the original task to the extent of requiring an opposite choice (the choice of a white square as opposed to a black one), because the older children are able to provide an implicit verbal mediator (such as "the opposite"); whereas the amount of transfer for the younger children is very small because they are unable to do this. Logically related are Harlow's studies of learning in monkeys (1949). These animals, over many practice periods, were able to acquire the capability of choosing "the odd one" of three objects, even though the particular objects used may have been highly dissimilar in physical appearance to those used during the original learning.

Acquisition of principles. The importance of mediational processes for transfer of training is also illustrated by a number of studies concerned with transfer of principles. Principles, whether verbally stated or not, relate classes of stimuli to classes of performance; accordingly, they remove the control of performance from the specific stimuli of the situation. If a principle is learned in connection with some particular performance, then it is to be expected that this principle will make possible broad transfer to an entire class of problem situations. In connection with card-trick and matchstick problems, as well as with other tasks, Katona (1940) showed that the acquiring of principles led to high degrees of transfer to classes of problems that differed from those of original learning in physical appearance. In contrast, learning to solve the original problems without acquiring such principles resulted in only small amounts of transfer to new problems. One meaning of "teaching for transfer" in educational settings appears to be the encouragement of principle learning as opposed to rote learning on the part of pupils.

Mechanisms of transfer

Although referred to by a single class name, it is fairly certain that the various phenomena called transfer of training represent several different kinds of events. The differences among them are to be found in the specific conditions that generate them and, consequently, in the kinds of mechanisms that may be inferred to account for them.

Stimulus generalization. When a conditioned response is established to a signaling stimulus, it is found that the same response, diminished in frequency or strength, is given to other stimuli differing from the initial one along some physical dimension. This finding, the phenomenon of stimulus generalization, has been obtained many times, and the previously cited results of Hovland (1937)

are typical. The underlying mechanism in this case appears to be a fairly dependable characteristic of the functioning central nervous system. The effects of stimulation on the nervous system are not highly specific but are generalized. The amount of this generalization may be markedly reduced by further conditioning contrasting stimulation that is positive in its effects with stimulation that is negative, a procedure referred to as discrimination training.

Transfer in associative learning. An association of words like *ready–joyful* or *small–klein* is frequently described by psychologists as an *S–R* (stimulus–response) association, in which the first member of the pair is called the stimulus member; through learning, this first member comes to elicit the second, or response, member. This form of learning has an extensive literature of its own that cannot be thoroughly summarized here (see McGeoch 1952; Underwood 1964). The following conclusions, which come from these investigations, however, have particular relevance to the phenomenon of transfer of training and to suggested underlying mechanisms.

One of these conclusions is that under many conditions, positive transfer occurs in the learning of verbal associates when previous learning "predifferentiates" the stimulus members (Gibson 1940; Gannon & Noble 1961). A second finding is that positive transfer is also a common occurrence when the response members of the paired associates have been made familiar through previous learning (Underwood & Schulz 1960). The mechanism of transfer suggested by these two findings is that the learning of paired associates is *not* simply a matter of associating an *S* and an *R*; it is better conceived as the "linking" of two performances, the first of which may be called "recognizing the stimulus member" and the second "uttering the response member." The thorough learning of these two different performances apparently transfers positively to the subsequent learning of the completed linking, or "association."

A third finding throws additional light on the process of association. Positive transfer in paired-associate learning is generated by previously learned mediating responses, which appear to serve the function of "coding" the stimulus member into the response member (McGuire 1961; Jenkins, 1963). The associate *hand* to the French word *main* may, for example, be mediated by the previously learned word *manual*. Still a third kind of previously learned performance, then, appears to be responsible for positive transfer; the ease of learning pairs of associates is markedly affected by the prior learning of what may be called a "coding performance."

The fourth conclusion that may be drawn from studies of associative learning has, in one form or another, been the subject of hundreds of experimental investigations. Negative transfer (interference) results when the learning of a pair of associates A–B is followed by the learning of the pair A–C, which has the same stimulus member but a different response member (Postman 1961; Underwood 1964). Although there is a great deal of evidence for this and related findings, it remains true at present that the mechanism by means of which such interference occurs has not been clearly delineated. The idea that there is "response competition" (Postman 1961) is a widely accepted view but seems little more than a renaming of the phenomenon of interference itself. A more promising possibility is the suggestion that the learning of a second response member also requires the complete erasure of the first from memory, that is, it extinguishes it after the fashion of extinction in a conditioned response (Barnes & Underwood 1959).

A quite different sort of hypothesis concerning the nature of negative transfer as it occurs in associative learning is receiving increasing attention. This is the proposition that the interference of a first task with a second (as in the arrangement A–B, then A–C) does not affect the learning of the second task at all but only its retention (Tulving 1964). This idea is consistent with the more general notion that the learning of each associate occurs in a single trial. Such a view, carried to its logical conclusion, would lead to the belief that negative transfer is essentially a process that reduces the probability of recall of learned associates in the phenomena called proactive interference and retroactive interference.

Transfer by means of concepts. The learning of relational concepts like "middle," "below," and "the odd one" and object concepts like "tree" and "door" has the effect of freeing performances from specific stimulus control. Having acquired a concept through learning, the individual is able to deal with a great variety of specific instances of the class that the concept represents. Particularly, it is true that the individual's performance can be correctly mediated by a concept, even though the specific instance to which he must respond has never been encountered during learning (cf. Kendler 1964; Gagné 1965). Concepts, therefore, are intimately bound with transfer of training. In order to demonstrate that an individual has learned

a concept, one must show that the effects of the learning will apply to not previously encountered members of the class of stimuli that are denoted by the concept's name. The mechanism by means of which the central nervous system accomplishes this feat of generalization is not well understood at present. This kind of capability is, of course, not restricted to human beings, although human conceptual behavior seems often to involve the use of language (Kendler 1964).

Transfer from principles. If principles are thought of as combinations of concepts, then for a similar reason they too provide the basis for transfer of training from the specific instances of learning to a large class of performances. The learning of a principle must be demonstrated by means of a test of transfer of training; it must be possible to show that the individual is able to apply the principle in a variety of situations that have not been specifically presented during learning (Gagné 1964). Hendrickson and Schroeder (1941) showed that the direct teaching of a principle in verbal form to high school students resulted in positive transfer to the task of hitting a target under water and that the transfer was greater than that produced by direct practice. Katona's findings (1940) concerning the transfer value of learning principles in the solution of card-trick and matchstick problems have been verified and elaborated by Hilgard and his colleagues (1953). To these laboratory studies concerning the effectiveness of principle learning for transfer must be added a great mass of unrecorded observations of teachers, who do not hesitate to assert that a principle such as is implied by the expression $a \cdot b + a \cdot c = a(b + c)$ accomplishes the job of knowledge transfer better than almost any number of specific examples like $2 \cdot 3 + 2 \cdot 4 = 2 \cdot 7$.

Transferability of learning

There are, then, a number of ways in which transfer can come about in behavior, ranging from the relatively specific stimulus generalization of a conditioned response to the very broad applicability of a principle. Whatever particular objective learning may have, it is reasonable to state that it will always be accompanied by an additional outcome of transfer of learning. So far as formal education is concerned, and even more broadly for the functioning of the human individual in society, the transferability of acquired knowledge and skill is often considered a more important goal than any number of specific learning accomplishments. For it is such transfer that makes it possible for the individual to solve new problems, to adjust to new situations, and to make novel inventions. Enthusiasm for transferability as an educational goal needs to be tempered by the reflection that transfer depends upon prior learning.

ROBERT M. GAGNÉ

[*Other relevant material may be found in* CONCEPT FORMATION; FORGETTING; RESPONSE SETS.]

BIBLIOGRAPHY

BARNES, JEAN M.; and UNDERWOOD, BENTON J. 1959 "Fate" of First-list Associations in Transfer Theory. *Journal of Experimental Psychology* 58:97–105.

GAGNÉ, ROBERT M. 1964 Problem Solving. Pages 293–323 in Symposium on the Psychology of Human Learning, University of Michigan, 1962, *Categories of Human Learning.* New York: Academic Press.

GAGNÉ, ROBERT M. 1965 *Conditions of Learning.* New York: Holt.

GAGNÉ, ROBERT M.; and FOSTER, H. 1949 Transfer to a Motor Skill From Practice on a Pictured Representation. *Journal of Experimental Psychology* 39:342–354.

GAGNÉ, ROBERT M.; FOSTER, H.; and CROWLEY, M. C. 1948 The Measurement of Transfer of Training. *Psychological Bulletin* 45:97–130.

GANNON, DONALD R.; and NOBLE, CLYDE E. 1961 Familiarization (*n*) as a Stimulus Factor in Paired-associate Verbal Learning. *Journal of Experimental Psychology* 62:14–23.

GIBSON, ELEANOR J. 1940 A Systematic Application of the Concepts of Generalization and Differentiation to Verbal Learning. *Psychological Review* 47:196–229.

GIBSON, ELEANOR J. 1941 Retroactive Inhibition as a Function of Degree of Generalization Between Tasks. *Journal of Experimental Psychology* 28:93–115.

HARLOW, HARRY F. 1949 The Formation of Learning Sets. *Psychological Review* 56:51–65.

HENDRICKSON, GORDON; and SCHROEDER, WILLIAM H. 1941 Transfer of Training in Learning to Hit a Submerged Target. *Journal of Educational Psychology* 32:205–213.

HILGARD, ERNEST R.; IRVINE, R. P.; and WIPPLE, J. E. 1953 Rote Memorization, Understanding, and Transfer: An Extension of Katona's Card-trick Experiments. *Journal of Experimental Psychology* 46:288–292.

HOVLAND, CARL I. 1937 The Generalization of Conditioned Responses: I. The Sensory Generalization of Conditioned Responses With Varying Frequencies of Tone. *Journal of General Psychology* 17:125–148.

JENKINS, JAMES J. 1963 Mediated Associations: Paradigms and Situations. Pages 210–257 in Conference on Verbal Learning and Verbal Behavior, Second, Ardsley-on-Hudson, N.Y., 1961, *Verbal Behavior and Learning: Problems and Processes, Proceedings.* New York: McGraw-Hill.

KATONA, GEORGE 1940 *Organizing and Memorizing.* New York: Columbia Univ. Press.

KENDLER, HOWARD H. 1964 The Concept of the Concept. Pages 211–236 in Symposium on the Psychology of Human Learning, University of Michigan, 1962, *Categories of Human Learning.* New York: Academic Press.

KENDLER, HOWARD H.; and KENDLER, TRACY S. 1961 Effect of Verbalization on Reversal Shifts in Children. *Science* 134:1619–1620.

LEWIS, DON; and SHEPHARD, ALFRED H. 1950 Devices for Studying Associative Interference in Psychomotor Performance: IV. The Turret Pursuit Apparatus. *Journal of Psychology* 29:173–182.

McGEOCH, JOHN A. 1952 *The Psychology of Human Learning.* 2d ed., rev. New York: Longmans. → The first edition was published in 1942 by Longmans.

McGUIRE, WILLIAM J. 1961 A Multiprocess Model for Paired-associate Learning. *Journal of Experimental Psychology* 62:335–347.

MANDLER, GEORGE 1954 Transfer of Training as a Function of Degree of Response Overlearning. *Journal of Experimental Psychology* 47:411–417.

MANDLER, GEORGE; and HEINEMANN S. 1956 Effect of Overlearning of a Verbal Response on Transfer of Training. *Journal of Experimental Psychology* 52:39–46.

MURDOCK, BENNET B., JR. 1957 Transfer Designs and Formulas. *Psychological Bulletin* 54:313–326.

OSGOOD, CHARLES E. 1949 The Similarity Paradox in Human Learning: A Resolution. *Psychological Review* 56:132–143.

POSTMAN, LEO 1961 The Present Status of Interference Theory. Pages 152–179 in Conference on Verbal Learning and Verbal Behavior, New York University, 1959, *Verbal Learning and Verbal Behavior: Proceedings.* New York: McGraw-Hill.

THORNDIKE, EDWARD L. 1924 Mental Discipline in High School Studies. *Journal of Educational Psychology* 15:1–22; 83–98.

THORNDIKE, EDWARD L.; and WOODWORTH, ROBERT S. 1901 The Influence of Improvement in One Mental Function Upon the Efficiency of Other Functions. *Psychological Review* 8:247–261; 384–395; 553–564.

THUNE, LELAND E. 1950 The Effect of Different Types of Preliminary Activities on Subsequent Learning of Paired-associate Material. *Journal of Experimental Psychology* 40:423–438.

TULVING, ENDEL 1964 Intratrial and Intertrial Retention: Notes Towards a Theory of Free Recall Verbal Learning. *Psychological Review* 71:219–237.

UNDERWOOD, BENTON J. 1964 The Representativeness of Rote Verbal Learning. Pages 47–78 in Symposium on the Psychology of Human Learning, University of Michigan, 1962, *Categories of Human Learning.* New York: Academic Press.

UNDERWOOD, BENTON J.; and SCHULZ, RUDOLPH W. 1960 *Meaningfulness and Verbal Learning.* Philadelphia: Lippincott.

X

ACQUISITION OF SKILL

In the scientific inquiry into the nature of skill, which has been largely conducted by experimental psychologists, operational definitions of skill are generally stated in terms of overt responses and controlled stimulation. Responses are subdivided into three types: verbal, motor, and perceptual, which typically stress speaking, moving, and judging, respectively. Common verbal tasks require the memorization of a list of words; motor tasks demand precise movements of the limbs and body; and perceptual tasks require discrimination of sensory information. Responses are evaluated or scored by means of errors, rates, pressures, amplitudes, time sharing, and information transmitted. Stimuli, on the other hand, are energy inputs to the operator and are expressed in units, such as frequency, length, time, and weight.

The study of skill has largely been confined to a relatively few laboratory tasks and trainers. The inquiry has been directed far less to the arts, the shop, and the playing field than to identifying variables that cut across many jobs and finding general laws that stand for many specific tasks. For example, practice, rest, feedback, and transfer are prominent variables.

The work of the skills psychologist may be divided into two parts. In his basic research, he seeks relevant variables, discovers empirical laws of relations between variables, and constructs theories to account for the laws. In his applied work, he takes part in selecting personnel for special jobs, helps to design display and control stations, and prescribes some of the training rules of educational programs.

World War II provided the impetus for an accelerated study of motor skill. It was necessary to select from hundreds of thousands of men a limited number to fly airplanes, aim gunnery equipment, etc. A battery of tests to determine psychomotor abilities was developed containing eight apparatus tests: tracking moving targets, setting dials, etc. A candidate's performance rank on these devices turned out to be very much related to his proficiency during later training for aircrew stations in air force schools. The devices used in the apparatus tests did not resemble air force or civilian hardware, yet they brought out basic learning and performance factors, such as reaction time, speed of movement, and pattern discrimination common to operable equipment. The great success of the apparatus tests in predicting later behavior led to the accelerated growth of both theoretical and applied studies of skills. One of the specific accomplishments was to provide an impetus to the laboratory study of what skills are and of how they are learned.

Tasks involving continuous responses. The major components of a typical research device involving continuous responses include (1) a visual display station, such as an oscilloscope; (2) a mechanical or electronic means for programming the display, such as the movement of a pip of light in some prescribed way; (3) a station with a control, such as an airplane stick, for the operator to compensate for pip movement; and (4) a means of measuring the operator's response output with respect to the stimulus input. Appropriate stick responses for spatial coordinates x and y balance or neutralize the programmed displace-

ments, and the pip remains quiet, centered, and under control. Ordinarily, several groups of operators or subjects are trained, each group under a special condition. One set of conditions may involve change in the properties of the apparatus; another set may involve change in the methods of training. Obvious *display* variations are changes in target speed and path complexity; simple *control* variations involve resistance to movement and amount of pip movement per unit of stick displacement. These and other variations have led to the discovery of quantitative relationships between responses and the conditions of practice. In addition, all of these variations are often treated by a systems approach in which the output of men and machines is expressed as a function of the input. Examples of maturing areas of application are the piloting of aircraft and submarines and target detection and identification in radar.

The training expert gives advice on schedules of practice: when, how long, how often. He decides on practice matters pertaining to individual tasks: their relative emphases and staging. He makes important recommendations on the operator's data-processing abilities and need for training aids. The operator may be in for long periods of vigilance, and he ought to detect faint or occasional signals; in addition, the operator is expected to make suitable decisions in the available time and to select and execute the proper response for the system. The expert's most critical analyses center on feedback (information about past performance) and the manner of its representation, since any solution for coding the feedback (which is essential) necessitates selecting a sensory modality and temporal, spatial, and numerical schedules of transformation.

Tasks involving discrete responses. One major premise underlying tasks involving discrete responses is that the next response (R) depends upon the knowledge of results of previous responses (KR), that is, $R = f(KR)$. The relations between KR and R are arbitrary, and transformations always obtain. For example, if a blindfolded person were directed to "Draw a 3-inch line," he need not be informed of his error after each and every attempt, nor are we compelled to report a $+\frac{1}{8}$ inch error as "too far by $\frac{1}{8}$ inch." It is possible, of course, to report any numerical error at any time.

As the line-drawing example shows, targets and responses need not be in continuous motion, although the variables of continuous and discrete types of tasks are quite similar. The task of learning to move levers and knobs through a critical distance has afforded a simple situation for study- ing the conditions regulating learning and per- formance. In these simple tasks, the simplest train of events is R_1, KR_1, R_2, KR_2, $\cdots$, R_n, KR_n; the timing can be anything at all. A few illustrations of typical findings will suffice: (1) the massing of trials produces faster learning than does spacing; (2) the occasional omission of KR does not preju- dice the effect of a later KR on the following R; and (3) even day or week intervals between R and KR do not necessarily impair the learning of R. The learning of R, however, is seriously handi- capped by (1) KRs which are vague ("You didn't do very well") and (2) KRs displaced from their normal position by another R, that is, R_1, R_2, KR_1, R_3, etc. Some investigators interpret the primary role of KR as reinforcing in much the same way that food can be used to shape the behavior of the hungry animal. Others interpret the primary role of KR as informational and treat it as a stimulus variable that serves as a representational code for the response or its effect.

Work tasks.   A man's output is dependent upon his recent and remote history of responding. His rate of work, for example, depends upon such obvious variables as work periods, rests, and loads. Rate also depends upon anticipated conditions of practice, rest, and load. According to the reactive inhibition theory of work decrement, decrement in performance is attributable to the build-up of re- active inhibition, and recovery in performance is attributable to the decay of inhibition. This theory is quite elaborate and effective; indeed, it explains a great deal more decrement data than do physio- logical-fatigue theories.

Among work tasks that have been studied are prolonged efforts at cranking, canceling letters of the alphabet, and packing small objects. The in- vestigation of vigilance, a related topic, arose with the introduction of radar—watching radar is as- sociated with infrequent, but critical, stimulation and with losses in performance at the critical moment. Losses in proficiency, however, may be caused by other means, a prominent one being response overload. Overload can be readily brought about by requiring reactions to more than one task. The breakdown in monitoring the incoming signals is intensified by increasing their number, compli- cating their constitution, or raising their frequency.

Forgetting.   A learned series of skilled proce- dures, such as an instrument check-out sequence, is much more susceptible to forgetting than a re- sponse that requires muscular coordination. The forgetting of a motor skill that may occur over periods of extended disuse is quickly overcome by comparatively few trials of retraining. Still, for- getting of even simple motor skills has been dem- onstrated, the phenomenon being more readily observed in changes in variance than in means.

Recent analyses of a person's ability to remem- ber a list of words have shown that a person is far less likely to forget than experiments since the 1890s have led us to believe. Recent work on verbal retention has made more use of meaningful mate- rial—one word per subject and normative informa- tion on word-association structures—and more use of recalling under conditions of controlled reten- tion environments. Retrieval of words from memory seems to depend strongly on free-association proc- esses. Cultural norms have been tabulated which show the probability (p) of any response word to a stimulus word, for example, for the stimulus word *thirsty*, the $p(R_1)$ for *water* (the most frequent response) is .35, the $p(R_2)$ for *drink* (the second most frequent response) is .30, etc. If a naïve stu- dent is taught the word *drink* (as one of several words in a list), later, in the presence of the word *thirsty*, if *drink* is not recalled, *water* is likely to intrude instead. The illustration shows the effects of language habits established some time ago on present recall behavior (Bilodeau 1966a).

The explanations of forgetting are nearly all related to interference theory, either retroactive or proactive. If the reader cannot quite recall the items of yesterday's breakfast, it may be that this morning's fare intrudes or otherwise interferes (*retroaction*); if the failure to recall can be traced to breakfasts prior to yesterday, then *proactive* agents are to blame. The bulk of the literature fa- vors retroaction as the mechanism of forgetting, but proaction is favored by present-day investi- gators.

Transfer of training.   An individual is never tested or required to perform under the very same conditions which constituted training. There is al- ways at least a small difference; sometimes there is a large one. The inquiry into the effects of these differences is called transfer of training. The ob- jective of any training program is to maximize the amount of transfer, although examination of actual instructional programs might make us wonder. The student might be trained to read to himself, but when tested he might be required to read orally; another's training might be characterized by his watching, testing by his performing. Generally, it is found that learning almost anything (referred to as Task A) facilitates the learning of almost any- thing similar (Task B). That is, the transfer is ordinarily positive in sign. Generally, it is less than 100 per cent in quantity. In order to obtain more than 100 per cent transfer, a training trial in Task *A* must be superior to a training trial in Task *B* when subsequently evaluated by the skill shown on Task *B*. Strictly speaking, more than 100 per cent transfer is most difficult to find. It appears that if Task *B* performance serves as the criterion, it is better to train at *B* and, if possible, avoid Task *A* from the start. Task *B*, however, in the hands of the novice may involve elements of danger or excessive expense, and so Task *A* may be substituted for Task *B* after all. For example, though it is probably true that the best training for helicopter piloting involves learning to fly the helicopter itself, the craft is dangerous and costly to operate. The ground trainers are inefficient, but if ten hours in them are actually worth five hours in the air, the 50 per cent transfer figure works to advantage.

The findings on negative transfer (detrimental effect of Task *A* upon the subsequent performance of Task *B*) are fairly clear. When Task *A* interferes with *B*, the interference is usually small and disappears quickly with additional practice on *B*. Indeed, there is even evidence to show that reversed forms of the same task involve the same psychomotor factors, and, further, there is no evidence for an individual trait of susceptibility to negative transfer. It can be speculated that to immunize oneself against negative transfer, or even to accelerate the normal processes of positive transfer, an exposure to any and many tasks is desirable. On the other hand, if a small amount of negative transfer includes one fatal error, the small amount should be considered most carefully.

Most psychologists believe that learning is an incremental process which could not take place without transfer. The number of constituent elements in two adjacent learning trials (A_1 and A_2) and the number of elements in common is believed to determine the amount of transfer. Because the events of training and education are never exactly reproduced in later life, a knowledge of the principles of transfer is of top priority for all users of applied skills research.

Composition rules. Skills have been analyzed and then synthesized by methods of probability, correlation, and geometry. A probability and a correlation model are sketched below to show how the reduction of skill to its components is accomplished in principle.

Probability model. Imagine that an operator views two meters whose pointers continually wander from center and that the pointers can be recentered by means of cranks for the left and right

The stippled portions of the instances of B (that is, B', B'', B''') represent the temporal overlap of A and B, the time during which both hands are on target simultaneously. If A and B are fixed at probabilities of .5, time sharing is maximum (.5) for B', minimum (0) for B'', and at chance (.25) for B'''.

Figure 1 — An illustration of three levels of coordination between skills A and B

hands. Figure 1 represents a polygraph record of the on–off target time for hands *A* and *B*. The total time represented is unity and, for simplicity only, the probability (p) for each hand's being on-target is arbitrarily fixed at .5. Three special cases of coordination are shown: for *A* and *B'* the time that both hands are on the target at the same time is maximum (.5); for *A* and *B''* it is minimum (0); and for *A* and *B'''* it is at the level of chance (.25). In each of these three cases, the hands are equally coordinated in the sense of equal proficiency at their separate tasks (.5); but in the sense of time sharing, the probability of the joint event $p(AB)$ ranges widely from 0 to .5. Somewhat surprisingly, many training situations yield results resembling *B'''* or chance time sharing, whatever the value of p. As a rule of thumb, the multiplicative formula $p(A) \times p(B)$ for independent events is used to produce a very good estimate of $p(AB)$. A better-than-chance score, then, is a show of positive coordination.

The multiplicative formula has a number of applications. If it is generalized to a three-part profile where, for example, $A = .90$, $B = .90$, and $C = .20$, the following predictions of their joint occurrence $[p(ABC)]$ are possible: the best prediction is

.90 × .90 × .20 = .16; instant improvement may be dramatically obtained through any increase in the poorest part at the expense of a better part, .70 × .90 × .40 = .25; the maximum possible score is $[\frac{1}{3}(.90 + .90 + .20)]^3 = .30$; the worst possible score in a rearranged profile is .00. The training objective now becomes one of raising the value of $p(ABC)$. The most common way is to raise the sum of the part probabilities through additional standard practice. A second possibility is to make a change in the profile of the component parts, while holding their sum constant. Still a third method would strive to break the multiplicative rule and replace it with better-than-chance pairing of events.

The correlation model. Another method of skills analysis intercorrelates the scores from (1) within a single task but from different stages of practice and (2) different tasks at the same or different stages of practice. The two techniques reveal the amounts of variance (the statistic σ^2) common to two or more variables and establish the degree of relationship. The questions at issue involve abilities, pre-experimental experience, integration of components into total task, and training procedures. To date most of this work has involved the correlations among length of time scores, such as time on target in tracking tasks.

Intratask analyses show relationships between (1) the first trial and successive later ones to be progressively lower and (2) adjacent trials to grow progressively larger. These patterns mean that the underlying composition of skill becomes simpler with increasing proficiency, for example, fewer abilities contribute to sophisticated than to naïve performance. Intertask analyses show that (1) predictor tests can provide better estimates for final than for initial criterion trials when the operator is skilled at both tasks; and (2) final level of criterion performance can be better predicted by extratask measures than by earlier levels of skill on the criterion-learning task.

EDWARD A. BILODEAU

[*Other relevant material may be found in* ATTENTION; CYBERNETICS; FATIGUE; FORGETTING.]

BIBLIOGRAPHY

ADAMS, JACK A. 1964 Motor Skills. *Annual Review of Psychology* 15:181–202.

ANDREAS, BURTON G. 1960 *Experimental Psychology.* New York: Wiley. → A college text; an introduction to the laboratory analysis of learning.

BILODEAU, EDWARD A. 1966a Retention. Pages 315–350 in Edward A. Bilodeau (editor), *Acquisition of Skill.* New York: Academic Press.

BILODEAU, EDWARD A. (editor) 1966b *Acquisition of Skill.* New York: Academic Press. → The book contains a survey of motor and verbal skills learning by a number of leading contributors to the field.

BILODEAU, EDWARD A.; and BILODEAU, INA McD. 1961 Motor-skills Learning. *Annual Review of Psychology* 12:243–280.

FITTS, PAUL M. 1964 Perceptual–Motor Skill Learning. Pages 243–285 in Symposium on the Psychology of Human Learning, University of Michigan, 1962, *Categories of Human Learning.* New York: Academic Press. → Definitions, taxonomies, models and other issues with a communication–computer flavor.

FLEISHMAN, EDWIN A. 1962 The Description and Prediction of Perceptual–Motor Skill Learning. Pages 137–175 in Robert Glaser (editor), *Training Research and Education.* Univ. of Pittsburgh Press. → A survey of work involving correlation and factor analysis.

SCOTT, MYRTLE G. (1942) 1963 *Analysis of Human Motion: A Textbook in Kinesiology.* 2d ed. New York: Appleton.

XI
LEARNING IN CHILDREN

Learning may be defined broadly to encompass relatively permanent behavior changes that result from experience. The experiential requirement usually implies that for the learning organism some changes in the associative properties of certain stimuli have taken place in such a way that the stimuli produce response effects that are different after training than before. Two general classes of empirical investigations in the area of children's learning may be cited. One type involves experimental manipulation of variables through laboratory investigation. Such studies have varied the number of conditioning trials, schedules of reinforcement, delay and magnitude of reinforcement, and motivational factors and have measured the resulting change in response or some attribute of response (Bijou & Baer 1960; Spiker 1960; Lipsitt 1963; White 1963; Rheingold & Stanley 1963; Munn 1946). The second category includes investigations of such training variables as familial or parental practices pertaining to feeding, toilet training, and effects of deprivation in infancy or in early childhood (McCandless 1961). The concepts of imprinting and trauma are not alien to this type of study, although little solid research with children is available on such matters.

Basic learning processes

Many of the experimental procedures used with animals and human adults have been adapted to the study of child behavior at all age levels. These studies generally indicate that for both classical (Pavlovian) conditioning and operant (Skinnerian) learning processes, the various parameters pertinent to conditioning in animals also control the occurrence and rate of conditioning in children.

Classical conditioning. It has been demonstrated that in classical conditioning in children, the time interval between the initially neutral stimulus (the conditioned stimulus, *CS*) and the initially effective response-producing stimulus (the unconditioned stimulus, *UCS*) is pertinent to the rapidity and strength of conditioning: there is an optimal interval of approximately half a second that varies somewhat with age and the nature of the response. A positive relationship has also been demonstrated between the drive or arousal level of the child and the rate of classical conditioning where that level has been variously defined by measures of muscular tension, tests of anxiety, or instruction-induced stress states. As in other organisms, it has been shown that the sensory modalities to which the *CS* and *UCS* are directed are pertinent to the conditioning process, as are the number of paired *CS–UCS* trials administered, and the nature of the tests used to measure the presence and strength of conditioning. In fact, the conclusion that conditioning has occurred often depends on the nature of these tests, including such procedural technicalities as whether interspersed test trials were administered among the training trials, whether conditioning was measured solely during extinction, or whether the response-recording apparatus permitted detection of subtle aspects of the reaction. In short, classical conditioning in the infant and child is a well-documented phenomenon, although knowledge of the variables affecting the phenomenon, including the age of the child, requires additional and extensive investigation. At present it appears quite likely, for instance, that there is an interaction between the age of the child and certain other parameters pertinent to the speed and strength of conditioning. One suggestion is that a younger child may require longer *CS–UCS* intervals for optimal conditioning than an older one.

Several investigators have recently established classical conditioning in neonates under rather well-controlled experimental conditions. Conditioning of appetitive responses is apparently obtained somewhat more easily than is classical conditioning of avoidance responses, at least under the levels of noxious stimulation that have been utilized. Some investigators have pointed out that fetal response to oral stimulation is developed neurophysiologically very early and that this response, and presumably its conditionability, has great survival value for the organism and the species. It can be pointed out, however, that certain withdrawal reactions to aversive stimuli also develop early and, under adverse circumstances, could play an important role in the survival of the organism. Again, investigations involving both appetitive and aversive processes in infants are much needed.

It may be added that the behavioral phenomenon of habituation has been well documented in infants and children, just as it has been with a wide variety of infrahuman organisms. Habituation is a progressive diminution of response that occurs as a result of repetitive presentation of a given stimulus. There may be, in fact, several different response–decrement phenomena, resulting from different conditions of stimulus presentation and varying histories of the organism, only one or some of which might be properly classified as learning processes.

Operant conditioning. Operant conditioning has also received considerable attention from investigators of child behavior. The systematic reinforcement of a response initially low in the child's hierarchy of responses importantly affects the rate at which that response will subsequently occur. Operant conditioning may involve the presentation of a "positive" event contingent on the desired response. Examples of such positive reinforcers would be the awarding of candy or the introduction of a signal indicating correctness of response. Alternately, "negative" reinforcement involves termination of an aversive stimulus contingent on occurrence of a response to be learned. Both kinds of reinforcement ultimately yield increases in the response to which the reinforcement is addressed. A third type of response-contingent event is the withdrawal of a positive reinforcer on the occasion of an undesired response. Automatic obliteration of a motion picture, for instance, has been shown to be most effective in terminating or suppressing undesired behavior, such as thumb sucking in children. The operant technique capitalizes on the well-known law of effect and has been shown under many experimental arrangements to exert powerful control over various kinds of behavior, including imitative responses, smiling, emission of expressions of courtesy, and language. It has been found that different types of reinforcement schedules (e.g., intermittent versus continuous) tend to produce different response patterns in children; these patterns result in differential susceptibility to extinction when the reinforcer is ultimately withdrawn.

Discrimination learning. Discrimination learning studies are another type of conditioning investigation having to do with effects of reinforcement in maintaining or generating certain kinds of behavior. These studies typically involve discrete trial procedures rather than techniques that permit the subject to respond at any time. In discrimination learning, the child is rewarded for choosing the correct manipulandum, or correct stimulus, among multiple opportunities present. Numerous parameters have been shown to influence the occurrence and rate of children's discrimination learning, including some variables that are unique to the articulate organism and, therefore, affect learning differently at different ages and in children of varying intelligence and social circumstances. Such studies of children's discrimination learning have contributed importantly to the development and extension of behavior theory; this seems to be particularly true in the areas of verbal learning and mediational (cognitive) effects upon performance.

It has been demonstrated in children that presenting the discriminative stimuli simultaneously generally produces more rapid learning than presenting the same stimuli successively, particularly if the response required is directed at or involves the manipulation of those stimuli. However, successive presentation and simultaneous presentation do not produce very different effects if the response is to be made to a locus removed from the stimulus source, such as buttons that are some distance away from the stimuli. Although psychophysical scaling of discriminative stimuli would be required for a meaningful comparison of the ease of discrimination learning in one sense modality with another, it appears that learning is more easily achieved when the discriminative cues involve variations in stimulus size and less easily achieved when the stimuli vary in color. Solid (stereometric) objects tend to be discriminated more rapidly than do two-dimensional representations of the same figures. Greater magnitudes of reward (including more preferred rewards) and lesser delays of reward produce more rapid learning than their opposites; recent data, however, suggest that the relationship may not be a monotonic one and that greater delays may result in better retention. Studies are needed of interactions of such incentive attributes of rewards as size and delay with factors affecting drive or arousal level, such as frustration. In some circumstances, increased delay of reward, for instance, may lead to poorer performance; but in other circumstances it is possible that such delay could increase frustration, which may in turn facilitate some aspect of performance, particularly those responses that are already prepotent.

Much new research on children's discrimination learning has dealt with effects of variables that have been historically of great interest to the general experimentalist but that only recently have been selected for extensive study by child psychologists. Some of these, for instance, pertain to the relative importance of positive and negative stimuli (i.e., reinforcement versus nonreinforcement) with most results indicating that both types of trial enhance performance.

Orientation behavior. White (1963) has noted that orientation behavior of children, or "observing responses," has been neglected by most experimenters, perhaps partly because this aspect of behavior is seldom included in formal learning theories. Because visual scanning of stimuli increases sharply at the onset of criterion performance in discrimination learning, an attentional shift important to the production of criterion or solution behavior is not unlikely. Studies of attentional behavior in discrimination learning as well as studies of observing behavior per se are becoming more frequent. In particular, a marked interest has recently arisen in the orientational behavior of human infants, wherein children from birth onward are provided with visual (and other) stimulation to which their reactions are recorded. It has been demonstrated that neonates respond differently to visual stimuli, depending primarily on the complexity of those stimuli, and that shifts in interest (defined in terms of length and frequency of fixation) occur with increasing age and experience. Since visual fixation occurs very early in life and is seemingly controlled by at least crudely specifiable stimulus attributes, there exists the intriguing possibility that attentional responses may be trained or conditioned very early through systematic reinforcement. Some writers, moreover, have suggested that visual orienting behavior of infants and the early changes in such behavior may be analogous to imprinting behavior found in lower organisms. Although much of this remains to be studied, the implication is that young human beings may "reach out" and follow with their eyes much as lower animals fixate upon and remain with objects that they encounter early [see ATTENTION; IMPRINTING].

Transfer of learning. Much work in children's discrimination learning has dealt with transfer of training. The phenomenon principally involved is that of generalization, whereby learning a certain response to a given stimulus predisposes the organism to respond to other similar stimuli, and proportionately so the greater the similarity.

Two general types of transfer of training, i.e., nonspecific and specific, have been extensively studied in children. Both of these are pertinent to the generalization of learning from one situation to another, whether from one laboratory situation to another, from the laboratory to "real life," or from one "real life" situation to another. Nonspecific transfer, variously referred to as "warm-up" or "learning to learn" depending upon the conditions used to induce it, refers to the subject becoming "set" to perform in certain prescribed ways. This type of transfer has to do with the skills involved in manipulating the response objects, viewing the stimuli properly, or merely relaxing and awaiting instructions. Quite possibly, such warm-up may impair as well as facilitate subsequent performance depending upon the requirements of the subsequent task. Specific transfer may also either facilitate or impair performance, and it refers to the influence of earlier task requirements on subsequent task performance, particularly to whether the previously learned task is similar or not to the subsequently learned task.

Many studies of specific transfer in both verbal and motor discrimination learning have been done with children. Much of the paired associate work with children has concentrated on the negative transfer phenomenon, created by retraining the subject to make new responses to stimuli to which other responses had been previously learned. Many of these paired associate studies, however, have dealt with verbal mediation that can produce either positive or negative transfer depending on the specific stimuli and responses involved. Some of these studies of proactive facilitation or interference deal with the phenomena of acquired distinctiveness or acquired equivalence. Acquired equivalence studies have demonstrated that children have more difficulty learning differential responses to stimuli to which they have previously learned similar names, whereas acquired distinctiveness studies have shown that if children have previously learned different names for the discriminative stimuli any subsequent learning of differential responses to the stimuli will be easier.

Transposition and verbal mediation. Considerable attention has focused on a special kind of training transfer in children—that known as transposition behavior. Typically, the child is first trained to select one of two or more stimuli simultaneously presented, such as the larger of a pair of circles; transposition is said to have occurred if the child, when confronted with a transfer task involving presentation of the larger stimulus together with a still larger one, chooses the largest rather than the specific stimulus to which response has been previously reinforced. Lower animals often show transposition when the transfer pair is very similar to the training pair but a breakdown

in such transposition when the test pair is more dissimilar. Several studies have shown that the same is true for young children, but total transposition tends to occur with older or more articulate children. Presumably, possession of a concept, such as "larger than," accounts for extension of transposition to the very dissimilar stimuli. Transposition attracts developmental interest because transposition behavior clearly tends to change with increasing chronological and mental age and because language skill seems to bear an important relationship to the phenomenon.

Corroborative evidence for the importance of verbality in discrimination learning is found in studies comparing "reversal shift" with "nonreversal shift" procedures. The typical experiment involves the presentation of stimuli varying in two dimensions, with one of these dimensions providing the cues pertinent to making the correct response. For instance, both size and brightness might be varied, the child being required to respond to the dark rather than the bright stimulus, regardless of size. A reversal shift would involve a change to making a bright response correct, while a nonreversal shift would make size the pertinent dimension. Nonreversal shift has been found easier for animals and young children; reversal shift is easier for adults and more articulate (or older) children. Presumably, verbal mediational factors, such as the subject informing himself covertly of the pertinent dimension, are crucial [*see* CONCEPT FORMATION].

The study of children's cognitive processes has been approached recently by many students of paired associate learning and verbal mediation. While much exploration remains to be done on the mechanisms by which verbal or symbolic responses mediate and control behavior, it has become increasingly apparent that children are excellent subjects for such study. Work with children should enable extensions of behavior theory that would not be possible otherwise. There is the interesting and not unlikely possibility, moreover, that studies of verbal learning in children, including the phenomena of associative clustering, free association, and other aspects of verbal expression, will illuminate important personality processes and anomalies. The suggestion does not seem amiss, for instance, that self-concepts (the responses that humans make to themselves about themselves) may be viewed as covert verbal responses which are learned according to the principles by which other responses are learned and that these self-conceptualizations may act as mediational responses to affect subsequent learning.

Effects of early experience

The study of children's learning and the lasting effects of such learning necessarily includes any documentation of sequelae of "crucial" life circumstances. Thus, any studies relating parent–child variables or institutional factors as antecedents to behavior of children fall within the scope of the present topic. Effects of traumatic experiences and psychodynamic hypotheses about such effects ultimately refer to learned changes in behavior that reflect familial or other social circumstances. One of the difficulties inherent in the study of the relationship between such early experiences and later behavior is that the behavioral phenomena must occur *in natura* to be the subject of study, since it is impossible or undesirable to produce such behavior deliberately. Consequently, factors other than those specifically investigated have the opportunity of producing effects on the behavior studied. For instance, it has been demonstrated that infants who were rated as being permissively fed engaged in more "reality play" at preschool age, whereas children who were rated as being rigidly fed engaged in more fantasy. While such a finding is interesting and suggestive and does support clinically held presuppositions about the influences of feeding schedules on children's behavior, the possibility exists that both rigidity in feeding and the occurrence of fantasy behavior in children are products of a common type of parenthood. This possibility necessarily attenuates the cause–effect relationship one would wish to infer from the data.

The same methodological weakness lies in the cross-cultural approach to collecting developmental data on effects of early-experience factors. For instance, it has been shown that there is a rather high negative correlation between the age of weaning and intensity of guilt feelings among members of a large number of cultures. While it is tempting, on the basis of such data, to conclude that guilt is produced by early weaning or oral frustration, it is possible that those cultures which reinforce guilt responses are also those which happen to wean early. Perhaps both guilt and early weaning are behavioral phenomena produced by some third causative factor. Another study related oral pessimism and optimism to age of weaning (whether before or after four months of age), and found that the oral pessimists tended to have been weaned earlier. A number of studies exist that, like those cited, implicate the age and style of weaning as causatively pertinent social determinants of later behavior, but few of these studies permit more than conjectural conclusions.

Toilet training. Another area of children's social training which involves a great investment of parental time and produces considerable conflict and anxiety is toilet behavior. Just as certain crucial interactions between parent and child may occur around oral activities when the child is in infancy, so later may the child's excretory activities become the focus of much parental attention. Studies suggest that toilet-training practices do constitute an important "arena" within which parents and children interact, often unpleasantly, to produce potentially lasting developmental effects. The earlier toilet training starts, the longer it takes to complete. Also, the earlier such training starts, the more annoying, frustrating, and generally unpleasant experiences there are likely to be between the parties involved. Rigid toilet training, along with a constellation of other restrictive parental attributes, seems to be associated with slower development, and mothers who are high in anxiety tend to start toilet training earlier than more relaxed mothers.

Deprivation of social stimulation. While effects of institutionalization and, in general, deprivation of social stimulation remain to a certain extent controversial, the bulk of evidence suggests that such experiences often produce serious emotional and intellectual deficits. The effects are not as controversial as is the specification of the real antecedent events producing these effects, e.g., whether the pertinent variable is separation from a mother or sheer reduction in human or environmental contacts. It does seem reasonable to assume that institutional and deprivational effects consist largely of sequelae to previous unfortunate learning circumstances [see INFANCY, *article on* THE EFFECTS OF EARLY EXPERIENCE].

LEWIS P. LIPSITT

[*See also* DEVELOPMENTAL PSYCHOLOGY; INTELLECTUAL DEVELOPMENT. *Other relevant material may be found in* INFANCY; INTELLIGENCE AND INTELLIGENCE TESTING; LANGUAGE, *article on* LANGUAGE DEVELOPMENT; PERCEPTION, *article on* PERCEPTUAL DEVELOPMENT; READING DISABILITIES; SENSORY AND MOTOR DEVELOPMENT; SOCIALIZATION; STIMULATION DRIVES.]

BIBLIOGRAPHY

BIJOU, SIDNEY W.; and BAER, DONALD M. 1960 The Laboratory–Experimental Study of Child Behavior. Pages 140–197 in Paul H. Mussen (editor), *Handbook of Research Methods in Child Development.* New York: Wiley.

LIPSITT, LEWIS P. 1963 Learning in the First Year of Life. Volume 1, pages 147–195 in Lewis P. Lipsitt and Charles C. Spiker (editors), *Advances in Child Development and Behavior.* New York: Academic Press.

McCandless, Boyd R. 1961 *Children and Adolescents: Behavior and Development.* New York: Holt.

Munn, Norman L. (1946) 1954 Learning in Children. Pages 374–458 in Leonard Carmichael (editor), *Manual of Child Psychology.* 2d ed. New York: Wiley.

Rheingold, Harriet L.; and Stanley, Walter C. 1963 Developmental Psychology. *Annual Review of Psychology* 14:1–28.

Spiker, Charles C. 1960 Research Methods in Children's Learning. Pages 374–420 in Paul H. Mussen (editor), *Handbook of Research Methods in Child Development.* New York: Wiley.

White, Sheldon H. 1963 Learning. Pages 196–235 in National Society for the Study of Education, Committee on Child Psychology, *Child Psychology.* Yearbook, Vol. 62, part 1. Univ. of Chicago Press.

XII
PROGRAMMED LEARNING

The term "programmed learning" is used to describe an instructional situation in which materials presented in a controlled sequence require the learner to respond in a way that meets specified criteria of the program objectives. Terms often used synonymously are "programmed instruction," "automated instruction," "automatic tutoring," or even "teaching machines."

Because of the control over responses and sequence of presentation, the materials are referred to as a "program." The responses made by the learner may be completing a statement with a word or words, writing an answer to a question, making a selection in a multiple-choice situation, imitating auditory or visual stimuli with oral or motor responses, stating agreement or disagreement, or solving a problem. The program may be presented to the learner through a mechanical device, known as a teaching machine, or in a book, known as a programmed textbook. The materials are programmed so that a tutorial situation is approximated without the immediate presence of a human tutor.

Programmed learning is viewed as a technological advancement in education and training developed in order to meet the increasing complexities in nearly all areas of human learning endeavor. In education, these complexities include the numbers to be educated, the rapidly expanding body of knowledge to be taught, and the special cases within a population—e.g., the intellectually gifted, the retarded, the delinquent, and the illiterate. Problems in management development and training–retraining associated with automation are concerns in business and industry to which the techniques of programmed learning are applicable.

History

Sidney L. Pressey. A device that could administer and score tests automatically was exhibited by Sidney L. Pressey in 1924. In a description of the uses of this device in his educational psychology classes at Ohio State University, Pressey also described the effectiveness of this machine for drill and recitation ([1926] 1960, pp. 35–41). The machine, which looked like a four-key typewriter, presented multiple-choice questions to the student. After the student had completed instruction through lectures and text reading, the machine was used to test his retention. The key corresponding to the student's choice for each item was pressed. If the student made the correct choice, the machine would present the next question; however, if the student chose incorrectly, the machine would not advance. The machine recorded the total number of key presses for the entire test. The immediate bringing into awareness of the correctness of a response provided more effective application of several of Thorndike's principles of learning than could the normal behaviors of the human teacher. Pressey observed that students who were tested by machine for weekly units of work showed higher achievement than students who took conventional tests.

Educators and trainers gave almost no consideration to the work done by Pressey and some of his students with the machine. After several years of effort modifying the device and applying it to several types of courses at different age levels, Pressey stopped working on the device and stated that education could not stay in a "crude handicraft stage" but would have to begin "quantity production methods" ([1932] 1960, pp. 47–51). He also predicted that new instruments and materials would be developed to facilitate research and sweeping advances in education and learning. Whether because of cultural inertia or other reasons, automated instructional devices failed to become established among educators and psychologists.

B. F. Skinner. More than twenty years later, in the 1950s, B. F. Skinner (1954, pp. 86–97) pointed out that education as a technology of learning did not approximate in its practice those principles observed and confirmed in learning research. Skinner stated that there were two principles of the learning process that had to be considered by those involved in teaching and training. The first, "contingencies of reinforcement," he described as a serious application of Thorndike's "law of effect" since it makes certain that desired responses appear in the student's behavior and that these responses are immediately reinforced. The second principle maintains that reinforcement should be arranged or "scheduled" so that the learner continues to make responses, i.e., so that the material keeps him interested. Responses that successfully approximated the criteria of learned behavior should be emitted by the learners, and any other responses would be considered a faulty arrangement of the stimuli presented to the learners.

On the basis of these principles Skinner stated that anyone wishing to control the learning situation so that the desired changes in behavior would occur must consider the following questions: (1) What responses are desired to meet the criterion of learning? (2) What sort of successive approximations in emitted responses will lead to the desired behavior? (3) What reinforcers are available in the particular situation? (4) How can the reinforcements be arranged so that behavior can be maintained in necessary strength?

It was obvious to Skinner that educational practice would have to change radically to be able to construct an instructional situation that would meet these requirements. For example, almost no provision was made for each learner to emit successive approximations of the desired behavior, nor was there any provision for the desired responses to be frequently and immediately reinforced. He observed that the reinforcements used in education *were* usually indirectly related, at best, to the responses desired for learning and that the contingencies of reinforcement, if considered at all, *are* arranged most haphazardly. The teacher as the primary reinforcing agent certainly was not adequate in most instructional situations. Some sort of device was needed.

A number of studies followed in which programs and machines were developed and tested, applying the principles described by Skinner. Programs in the areas of physics, remedial reading and vocabulary building, spelling, German, arithmetic, algebra, and psychology were involved. Various machines were designed and built for these programs. Much of this work was done under Skinner's direction and influence and reported by him a few years later (Skinner 1958, pp. 969–977).

The mechanism, or machine, had a number of features differing from Pressey's. The learner was required to compose his answer rather than select one from alternatives. Skinner argued that in step-by-step approximations plausible alternative choices presented to the learner can potentially strengthen unwanted responses. The machine would present only one frame, or item, to which the learner responded, and all other frames were out of sight. The machine would not advance to the next frame until the learner responded correctly on the current frame. Coding the correct answers into the machine made this feature automatic. With older subjects it was felt that the learner could himself make the comparison between his response and the

correct one and that precoded answers might make the program too rigid. These frames were on a disc, which revolved on a turntable; the frames were exposed one at a time, and the learner composed his answer on a strip of paper exposed in another opening. After making his response, he raised a lever that caused his response to move under a transparent cover and at the same time exposed the correct answer. Lowering the lever caused the disc to expose the next frame. The machine could only control the presentation of the program. This control is most vital in the learning situation, but it is the program or material being exposed that teaches.

The characteristics of this learning situation can be described as follows: (1) The student is forced to be active in the learning situation. Unlike less-controlled situations, such as lectures, text reading, movies, or television, he is forced to make responses to stimuli as they are presented to him. (2) He must give the correct response before proceeding further. Again, this differs from techniques where the next stimulus can be presented whether or not the student is ready to proceed. (3) Through the step-by-step approximation, it is apparent when the learner is ready for the next step. (4) With hints, suggestions, and promptings the program helps the learner to make the correct response. (5) Immediate reinforcement is given to each appropriate response. The exposure of the answer is reinforcement, and this immediate feedback is sufficient to maintain the strength of the behavior, i.e., "keep him going."

Norman A. Crowder. Somewhat different approaches to automated instructional devices began to appear in 1958. These differed from Skinner's mainly in what was termed *intrinsic* programming: it was not so important that errors be completely omitted from the learner's responses but that the program should adjust to the correct or incorrect response. Examples of this type of programming are the Tab Item, digital computers that adjust problems automatically according to the learner's responses, and Crowder's automatic tutoring devices. Since Crowder and Skinner represent the two major approaches to automated instruction in the developmental period, the comparison will be made between what Crowder has described as intrinsic programming and what has been discussed concerning Skinner's approach.

Crowder's intrinsic program goes beyond "knowledge of results" to an evaluation of the communication process between the learner and the program. Crowder stated that it is impossible to understand the learning process with specific material so completely that perfect step-by-step approximation can be constructed. To overcome this handicap he built into the program an evaluation of the learner's responses in order to make corrections when the learner does not adequately understand each step. A simple example of how this is done is Crowder's "TutorText" (1960, pp. 286–298). A problem is introduced and the learner makes a choice among the answers that are presented at the bottom of the page in a multiple-choice arrangement. Along with each choice is a page number to which he is referred on the basis of that answer. If his answer is a correct one, he is informed of that fact and is presented with the next step. If his answer is incorrect, his error will be pointed out and explained, and he is referred to the original problem again. The "AutoTutor" is a more complex mechanism, which presents microfilm, motion picture film, or both and records responses and response time on a paper tape. Crowder described what he calls greater flexibility both within and between program steps. "Within-step flexibility" refers to each item of a page or screen presentation, and this is a larger amount of material than is presented in one frame on Skinner's program. Crowder states that this larger amount of material, or flexibility, is necessary because of the complexity of the material and the complexity of the learners. The "between-items flexibility," sometimes referred to as "branching," is necessary because all incorrect responses represent a communication failure that needs correcting, and this can be done only by repeating some items or introducing special items to clear the misunderstanding.

Another major difference between the approaches of Skinner and Crowder is the question of response mode. Skinner emphasizes the necessity of the subject constructing his response rather than responding to a multiple-choice situation. Related to this difference is the fact that the steps from one frame to the next represent a wide jump in Crowder's intrinsic programming as opposed to the small steps in Skinner's linear programming.

Programmed learning criteria

Regardless of the differences between what has been described as linear programming and intrinsic programming, certain criteria can be established for both, which distinguish programming from other techniques and devices of instruction.

(1) Stimuli to which the learner must respond are presented to him. Active participation is required of the learner in contrast to the situations of the lecture, textbook, and audio–visual aids.

(2) The sequence of the material presented is highly controlled as a result of prior observation of its content within and between steps.

(3) A two-way communication is established, since immediate feedback is given by the program to the learner's response. The learner is aware of his progress at all times.

(4) Reinforcement or reward (usually this is immediate feedback) is used to keep the learner responding or interested.

(5) The learner responds to the program at his own rate; this then is similar to a tutorial situation.

(6) Learning occurs without a human instructor in the immediate situation.

Another way of contrasting the techniques of automated instruction with the more traditional educational methods is in the emphasis on what pays off for the learner rather than for the instructor. The lecturer, textbook writer, and the director of various audio–visual aids make use of those techniques which work for each in his own medium. In building a program the emphasis is on the learner's behavior at each step from beginning to end.

Research and development

The first reports of the use of programs in instruction began to appear in 1958, and most of the early reports were based on programs and machines developed and tested under Skinner's direction and influence. Much of this early effort was reported by Skinner in an article in *Science* which received a wide audience and gave impetus to the teaching-machine movement (Skinner 1958). In fact, the article was titled "Teaching Machines," and this was the first time these devices were given this label; the continued use of the term is an indication of the impact of that article.

Effectiveness of programmed instruction. The earliest research yielded some rather dramatic results that indicated a superiority of programmed instruction to more conventional techniques. This superiority was demonstrated in the significant differences found in the amount of time spent in learning and in learner performance.

The research and development in the next few years was phenomenal—a commentary on the value of this early effort and the tremendous need that many scholars felt existed for work in this direction. By 1964 more than two hundred research reports in programming appeared, directed toward the questions of whether programs do teach and, if so, which of the significant variables in the teaching–learning situation are under the control of the program.

The evidence leaves no doubt whether the programs teach: they do. Results of programs developed that use the models of Skinner, Crowder, or Pressey, as well as recent variations or combinations of these, contribute to this conclusion. Furthermore, learning occurs whether the program is presented by machine or in a text format. Learners varying in age from preschool to adult and in ability from the retarded and adult illiterate to advanced graduate student and practicing professional have been the subjects of these observations of program effectiveness. Programs have been used to teach motor, verbal, and perceptual skills at nearly every level of difficulty.

The question of whether programs teach more efficiently and effectively than other possible techniques was one of the first asked in research; in fact, most of the early research was concerned with a comparison of programmed instruction with conventional instruction. All but a few of these studies showed either a significant difference in favor of the program or no difference between the two. These observations were made with programs using the Skinnerian linear, or "shaping" model, the Crowder "intrinsic," or communication model, and the automated test model of Pressey. Although most of the programs constructed for these studies were of the linear type, enough programs employing the techniques of other models were used to indicate no inherent superiority of a particular set of techniques. It should be pointed out that these studies lacked the precision and thoroughness to warrant much confidence in them; the programs in most cases covered relatively small amounts of instructional material and generally were too crude and hastily developed to be exemplary of a desirable programming technology. Nevertheless, the results were such that most researchers felt that programs provided effective instruction, and because of the control over the teaching–learning situation inherent in the programming approach, their efforts were directed toward isolating those variables which make the instructional situation effective.

Analysis of the learning process. Most of the research has been done by psychologists and educational psychologists with the objective of basing a description of the learning process in instructional situations upon psychological principles of learning. Not since Thorndike had experimental psychologists interested in learning directed a concerted effort toward the application of learning principles in instruction. Because of techniques of behavioral analysis developed by Skinner and because of the respected position he enjoys among experimental psychologists, a great number of psy-

chologists were attracted to analysis of instruction through techniques of behavioral analysis developed in the laboratory. It was the application of the methodology to the applied situations in education and training, rather than a comparison of new and conventional instructional techniques, that attracted most psychologists. The major research, then, was concerned with isolating and describing the critical variables in the teaching–learning situation, using the method of behavioral analysis.

It was natural that many researchers began by attempting to replicate in modified form the earlier learning laboratory experiments and that the first of these were directed toward those variables found to be significant in Skinner's techniques of behavioral analysis. The techniques to be used for shaping the learner's responses, the effect of errors on this shaping process, the characteristics of the responses to be made by the learner, and the identification of the reinforcers in these learning situations were the problems covered in the early research; namely, how should the stimulus material be presented to the learner, in what mode and in what relationship to the stimulus should the learner's response be made, is confirmation of correct responses a reinforcement, and what effect does a high error rate have on learning?

Amount of information. A number of studies have focused upon varying the amount of information to which the learner is to respond. This amount ranged in scope from short statements to one or two paragraphs or even several pages of written material. The results of these studies are not easy to interpret; the amount of information is difficult to measure in terms of length alone and is not independent of the type of information transmitted. Generally the results favor smaller amounts, especially in the early steps of instruction. Since most of the studies used short programs involving a relatively small amount of information, critical tests of this question have yet to be made.

Sequence of information. Related to amount of information is the problem of how the information is to be sequenced. Should the information be arranged according to "expert" understanding of the specific material? Is there some logical pattern underlying the learning task that can be used in sequencing the material for instruction? Several experiments have failed to show any difference between ordered or random sequencing of the material, but these have been with short programs. A few studies that have been concerned with analyzing the material to identify categories of learning tasks for instructional sequencing appear as the major effort in attacking this area. By basing the instruction on the learner's present repertory and then proceeding through the material that has been sequenced according to the characteristic responses to be learned, the studies have made a major contribution to the technology of programmed learning.

Mode and importance of response. A relatively large number of experiments have been concerned with the response mode, i.e., overt responses, covert responses, multiple-choice responses, or reading the same material with no required response. In the great majority of studies no difference has been found between the three types of active responses, and evidence does not clearly indicate that active responding is superior to merely reading the material. The results, however, do show a relationship between errors during learning and some criteria of performance at the end of instruction. When response errors are made in the program, evidence suggests that those students required to make a correct response before proceeding further, ultimately perform at a higher level. Obviously, a short program with a low error probability would not yield much difference, especially if the performance criteria were not particularly sensitive.

In addition to the mode of response, the question of the relationship of the response to the material has been investigated, i.e., is the response critical to the material presented by the stimulus? Although only a few studies have been directed toward this question, the evidence indicates superior results from those programs in which critical response is required.

The nature of reinforcement. The research area receiving the major emphasis in the early work in programmed learning has been the application of the principle of reinforcement. What is reinforcing in the programming situation? Confirmation of correct responses is not clearly a reinforcer in all programming situations; the responses of some students do extinguish in the presence of confirmation while those of others fail to extinguish in the absence of confirmation. In several studies the effects of prompting—the correct response being shown to the learner, who is then required to repeat it—have been compared to those of confirmation, and in most of these studies prompting led to higher performance than confirmation. Obviously, reinforcement in the programming situation is related to the incentive conditions under which the learner is responding. One study suggests that the appearance of the frame in the machine is itself reinforcing. Other efforts to control responses have made highly desirable behaviors contingent upon making responses in a program. For example, a peer–tutor situation makes use of this by requiring

the student to learn in order to teach another student. This has been most successful in teaching adult illiterates to read and write. Nevertheless, the complex relationship of intrinsic and extrinsic reinforcers present in human learning situations makes the task of identifying effective reinforcers extremely difficult indeed.

Errors. One of the clearest results of the research has been recognition of the relationship between the number of errors and performance criteria. Programs with a lower probability of response errors tend to be related to ultimately higher criterion performance. The cause of a high rate of error obviously cannot be separated from other variables in the instructional situation; therefore, attempts to solve this particular problem become somewhat circular. There has been no adequate analysis of the effect of errors in intrinsic programs except an awareness that a learner's attitude tends to be negative when the error rate is high. Regardless of the type of program, the evidence indicates that errors need to be corrected immediately before proceeding.

Evaluation. Since the beginning of concerted research effort to describe the significant variables in the area of programmed learning, one is struck by the high proportion of studies in which no differences have been observed. It is clear that the variables involved in effective instruction have not been isolated and described. Many studies that have registered observable differences are counterbalanced by contradictory evidence in other research or lack sufficient replication to allow extrapolation to general instruction procedure. While the effort has been considerable, the period during which this work has occurred has been a brief one, the programs have covered only small amounts of material, and the instruments for evaluation have lacked precision.

Potential

Although positive contributions to an instructional technology from specific research efforts are few, the fact remains that never has the teaching–learning situation received the attention of so many experimentalists interested in human learning. Programmed learning represents an application of behavioral analysis techniques to the learning of meaningful material. The controlled observations possible through programmed learning are making possible more precise descriptions of behavior in the instructional situation than at any time previously. The necessity of evaluating instruction with stated objectives in behavioral terms and the effectiveness of the principles of active response and immediate reinforcement to instruction have been successfully demonstrated. From these beginnings a technology can be expected to develop which translates, in a systematic and highly generalizable way, the specified terminal behaviors into the form and sequence of the instructional task.

To many psychologists and educators the attraction of programming, and certainly the success of the approach thus far, has been the attention to laboratory research in learning. As noted earlier, however, the research in programming has been concerned with showing the influence of learning variables studied in the laboratory to applied learning situations; in general, the results of this research have been somewhat equivocal. Gagné (1962, pp. 85–86) has noted that the identification and arrangements of task components are more important in developing efficient and effective instructional situations than many of the variables studied in the learning laboratory, e.g., reinforcement, meaningfulness, distribution of practice, and so forth. Also, Melton (1959, pp. 100–101) has stated that laboratory research has not produced sufficient knowledge of different learning areas to allow an integration of possible generalizations to be highly useful in application. Melton also stated that there is yet no satisfactory taxonomical scheme to describe specific tasks that humans perform.

It is apparent that a number of factors are contributing to the absence of any rapid integration of a science of learning with an educational technology. The limited development of a science of learning, a taxonomy that allows placement of learning tasks in a dimensional matrix, the mutually exclusive efforts of the experimental and educational psychologists beween the 1930s and late 1950s, and the complex interaction of variables in an educational learning situation are some of the obstacles that have held back such an integration. By the mid-1960s, however, these obstacles seemed to be disappearing. Experimental psychologists were introducing into the laboratory problems from applied instructional situations, and experimental and educational psychologists were cooperating on research projects at an increasing rate. Programmed learning introduced a methodology for observing and controlling behavior in an instructional situation which attracted the experimentalist, and the programming technique proved to be an effective instructional instrument which attracted the educational psychologist. Clearly the effort was made to build an educational technology from a science of learning just as an engineering technology was built from basic sciences. Equally clear was the necessity for an area of transitional research to develop a taxonomy of tasks useful to technology and the science of learning.

Breadth of application. By 1965 there were more than a thousand programs published and available for purchase in the United States. Of these, approximately two-thirds were educational programs for courses or units within courses at all levels—elementary through graduate school. Programs were available for teaching beginning reading skills, mathematics at all levels, second-language reading and listening skills, spelling, grammar, punctuation, economic concepts, music fundamentals, statistics, genetics, biology, medicine, and physics. Many more programs were being developed or had been developed and were being used for limited objectives in specific classes. Programs were being used in other special situations, such as educational and vocational counseling, marriage counseling, interpersonal relationships, and the teaching of recreational skills.

Nearly three hundred programs in the field of business and industry were published and available by 1965; these included programs in areas of secretarial skills, management skills, bank teller skills, salesman training, and consumer training. Many more programs had been developed for the exclusive training of personnel of a particular company. Also, the military and the U.S. Public Health Service have developed a large number of programs to train their personnel.

Except in those cases in which the material presented or the response required demands a mechanical device, most programs are available in a text format. Language-listening skills, pitch discrimination, or the control of the responses of a small child are examples of such specific demands. The text format has provided economy and flexibility advantageous to programming's extended use in education, but the format probably has had a restraining effect on making broader application of the programming technique in education.

Use outside the United States. Because of the development of the programming technique in the United States, most research has taken place and the largest number of programs have been published there, but considerable effort in the research and development of programmed materials has been made in other countries. Considerable use of the techniques has been made in many European and Latin American countries, particularly in Great Britain, Germany, Sweden, the Soviet Union, the Netherlands, and Brazil. Much of the work has been done in these countries by following models of efforts in the United States. With the exception of the Soviet Union, a science of learning has not developed in other countries to the extreme that it has in the United States, a fact which has limited the use of the programming model elsewhere. Because of a highly developed psychology of learning and its differences from that in the United States, the Russians might be expected to make significant contributions to the programming field.

In 1963, two UNESCO-sponsored workshops, one in Nigeria and the other in Jordan, introduced programmed instruction to areas of the world where it may have special significance. The necessity for more efficient and effective methods of education and training is especially great in the so-called developing countries, but this necessity is compounded by the world-wide scarcity of teachers. The self-instruction feature of programming makes its potential obvious.

There is little doubt that programmed learning represents a significant union of the science of learning with the practical problems of learning management. Effective teaching and training devices have been constructed. These early devices undoubtedly are extremely crude in comparison to what may appear in the future. The limit and potential of the use of programming in education and training are far from being determined in this early stage of development. The more important contribution of programmed learning to teaching and training is the introduction of a technique for an experimental analysis of behavior. Through the technique the practical problems of learning management can be brought under control so that careful observation and precise descriptions of learner responses to stimulus materials in an instructional situation can be made.

RUSSELL W. BURRIS

[*Other relevant material may be found in* EDUCATIONAL PSYCHOLOGY; SIMULATION, *article on* INDIVIDUAL BEHAVIOR; *and in the biography of* THORNDIKE.]

BIBLIOGRAPHY

CENTER FOR PROGRAMED INSTRUCTION, NEW YORK 1962 *The Use of Programed Instruction in U.S. Schools: Report of a Survey of the Use of Programed Instructional Materials in the Public Schools of the United States During the Year 1961–1962.* New York: The Center. → Compiled and produced by the Center's Research Division in cooperation with the U.S. Department of Health, Education and Welfare.

CONFERENCE ON APPLICATION OF DIGITAL COMPUTERS TO AUTOMATED INSTRUCTION, WASHINGTON, D.C., *1961* 1962 *Programmed Learning and Computer-based Instruction: Proceedings.* New York: Wiley. → See especially John E. Coulson's contribution, "A Computer-based Laboratory for Research and Development in Education," on pages 191–204.

CROWDER, NORMAN A. 1960 Automatic Tutoring by Intrinsic Programming. Pages 286–298 in Arthur A. Lumsdaine and Robert Glaser (editors), *Teaching Machines and Programmed Learning: A Source Book.* Washington: National Education Association, Department of Audio–Visual Instruction.

GAGNÉ, ROBERT M. 1962 Military Training and Principles of Learning. *American Psychologist* 17:83–91.

GAGNÉ, ROBERT M. 1965 *The Conditions of Learning.* New York: Holt.

GALANTER, EUGENE (editor) 1959 *Automatic Teaching: The State of the Art.* New York: Wiley.

GLASER, ROBERT (editor) 1962 *Training Research and Education.* Univ. of Pittsburgh Press.

GREEN, EDWARD J. 1962 *The Learning Process and Programmed Instruction.* New York: Holt.

HOLLAND, JAMES G. 1960 Teaching Machines: An Application of Principles From the Laboratory. *Journal of the Experimental Analysis of Behavior* 3:275–287.

LUMSDAINE, ARTHUR A. 1961 *Student Response in Programmed Instruction: A Symposium on Experimental Studies of Cue and Response Factors in Group and Individual Learning From Instructional Media.* Washington: National Academy of Sciences–National Research Council.

LUMSDAINE, ARTHUR A.; and GLASER, ROBERT (editors) 1960 *Teaching Machines and Programmed Learning: A Source Book.* Washington: National Education Association, Department of Audio–Visual Instruction.

MAGER, ROBERT F. 1961 *Preparing Objectives for Programmed Instruction.* San Francisco: Fearon.

MELTON, ARTHUR W. 1959 The Science of Learning and the Technology of Educational Methods. *Harvard Educational Review* 29:96–106.

PRESSEY, SIDNEY L. (1926) 1960 A Simple Apparatus Which Gives Tests and Scores—and Teaches. Pages 35–41 in Arthur A. Lumsdaine and Robert Glaser (editors), *Teaching Machines and Programmed Learning: A Source Book.* Washington: National Education Association, Department of Audio–Visual Instruction. → First published in Volume 23 of *School and Society.*

PRESSEY, SIDNEY L. (1932) 1960 A Third and Fourth Contribution Toward the Coming "Industrial Revolution" in Education. Pages 47–51 in Arthur A. Lumsdaine and Robert Glaser (editors), *Teaching Machines and Programmed Learning: A Source Book.* Washington: National Education Association, Department of Audio–Visual Instruction. → First published in Volume 36 of *School and Society.*

PRESSEY, SIDNEY L. 1963 Teaching Machine (and Learning Theory) Crisis. *Journal of Applied Psychology* 47:1–6.

SCHRAMM, WILBUR L. 1962 *Programmed Instruction, Today and Tomorrow.* New York: Fund for the Advancement of Education.

SCHRAMM, WILBUR L. 1964 *The Research on Programed Instruction: An Annotated Bibliography.* U.S. Office of Education, Bulletin No. 35. Washington: U.S. Department of Health, Education and Welfare, Office of Education.

SKINNER, B. F. 1954 The Science of Learning and the Art of Teaching. *Harvard Educational Review* 24:86–97.

SKINNER, B. F. 1958 Teaching Machines. *Science* 128:969–977.

LEARNING THEORY

Since its emergence as a relatively distinct topic, learning theory has played a central role in psychology. Historically, many psychologists interested in the scientific understanding of behavior have worked with learning phenomena, while psychologists with major interests in areas other than learning, as well as workers in related disciplines, have considered learning to be a pervasive process that enters into quite diverse aspects of behavior. Widespread interest in learning theory has followed the recognition that the theoretical integration of facts and laws is an integral part of what is meant by scientific understanding and that theory serves useful organizational and conceptual functions. Objections to the theory aspect of learning theory have generally reflected disagreement concerning the schedule of the theorizing relative to the empirical development of the field, rather than questions of the ultimate desirability of theorizing about learning.

At the present time the kinds of activities subsumed under the rubric of learning theory present a rapidly changing and expanding pattern of interests. Because of this situation it is impossible to define or specify learning theory in any simple way. Indeed, neither "learning" nor "theory" is a term that is used with consistent meaning by those active in the area. Commonly, learning has been considered to be a process which results from practice and which is reflected as a more or less permanent change in behavior. In many traditional learning theories, learning has been carefully specified to be some sort of associationist process as distinguished from motivational, maturational, inhibitory, and fatigue processes. While learning is thus defined in some cases, even a cursory survey of those systems called learning theories reveals that they include motivational and inhibitory factors. In most such formulations, with the exception of mathematical theories of learning, consideration of motivational variables greatly overshadows concern with the more narrowly defined learning process itself. Thus, many learning theories are in reality theories of behavior, with the term "learning" more or less limiting the range of behavior included.

Similarly, the word "theory" is used in many ways, with an even greater range of meaning than is the case with "learning." At one extreme are theories which represent nonspecific verbal systems that better serve the "psychology of discovery" of the theorist than satisfy the basic requirement of theories with respect to the integration of data or generation of testable predictions. In this respect, it should be noted that the present discussion applies the term "theory" to a wide variety of formulations, without requiring that they meet criteria of testability, usefulness, or scope. At the other extreme are very specific uses of the term deriving from its usage in mathematical logic. In more restricted uses of the term, there are theories which represent, in varying degrees of quantitative elaboration, hypotheses about the interrelationships of systems of constructs, such as those of the intervening variable type. Further complicating the picture is the increasing use of the term "model" (Lachman 1960), which has a similar variable meaning.

It is obvious that no simple classification of learning theory is possible, and instead of an attempt to develop an arbitrary classificatory scheme attention will be directed, first, toward the development of learning theory and, second, toward a characterization of present approaches and formulations.

The development of learning theory

In the United States, systems or theories specifically concerned with learning and motivation began to emerge in the late 1930s and early 1940s. Coming from a background of "schools" of psychology, for example, structuralism, functionalism, gestalt psychology, and behaviorism, learning theory took the form of systematic positions organized around individuals who promulgated systems of constructs, principles, and research strategies in attempts to account for varying ranges of learning phenomena. Closely connected with this development were the controversies which arose about the basic nature of learning and reinforcement. These controversies, which came to dominate much of the activity in learning at that time, furthered the establishment and growth of the individualistic systems.

Major systems. The major systematic positions were the subject of Hilgard's influential book *Theories of Learning* (1948), the book itself being instrumental in establishing the term "learning theory" in common usage. Among the systems described by Hilgard were Thorndike's early connectionism, Guthrie's emphasis on contiguous conditioning as a basic principle of learning, Hull's attempt to develop a highly rigorous quantitative theory based on data from simple learning situations, and Tolman's cognitive, gestalt-influenced theory, which stressed "sign-learning." The contributions of Pavlov and Bekhterev certainly must be listed here also because of their tremendous influence on the development of learning theory and because of the importance of present-day neo-Pavlovian theory in the Soviet Union. [*See the biographies of* BEKHTEREV *and* PAVLOV.]

The learning theories of this period were characterized by Spence (1951) as being divided on two major issues: first, the nature of the concepts used to represent the hypothetical changes taking place in learning, and, second, the conditions believed to be necessary for these changes to take place.

Sign–significate versus stimulus–response. With respect to the first of these issues the comparison was between those (for example, Koffka, Köhler, Lewin, Tolman) who considered learning to reflect some kind of a perceptual reorganization or restructuring of the subject's cognitive field which corresponded to the stimulus relationships present in the environment; and those (for example, Guthrie, Thorndike, Hull) who conceived learning to be a modification of the strength of associations, habits, or response tendencies. The former were called S–S (sign–significate) theorists, the latter S–R (stimulus–response) theorists. The emphasis was directed, respectively, toward the effects of field conditions and other variables on perceptual organization and the relations between sensory events and toward the factors influencing the strength of associations, whether the associations were represented as empirical functional relationships or defined theoretical constructs. [*See the biographies of* GUTHRIE; HULL; LEWIN; THORNDIKE; TOLMAN; WATSON.]

Reinforcement versus contiguity. The second division was termed the reinforcement–contiguity issue. Here the distinctions concerned whether or not environmental aftereffects of behavior operated in some manner to change the strength of the learning process. Also involved were issues about the usefulness of special theories of reinforcement that attempted to identify the nature of the reinforcement or the manner in which the learning association was changed. Mention must also be made of two factor theories that generally postulated a classical–instrumental or autonomic–skeletal breakdown in which different kinds of learning were involved. These dual theories, which became increasingly popular, were held at various times by B. F. Skinner, Harold Schlosberg, O. H. Mowrer, and Kenneth Spence, among others. While many variations were proposed, contiguity principles were commonly paired with classical conditioning or with the conditioning of autonomic–

nervous-system responses, and reinforcement theory was usually paired with instrumental–skeletal responses.

Learning controversies. The learning theories and issues discussed above resulted in a great many disputes and controversies regarding the nature of learning, especially discrimination learning. Absolute and relational views of discrimination learning represented one such issue. The absolute position held that discrimination learning involves the strengthening or weakening of the response of approaching different aspects (discriminanda) of the total stimulus configuration, as a function of reinforcement and nonreinforcement; the relational position viewed discrimination learning as depending upon inherent perceptual-organizing tendencies, with the response always being to certain relational properties inherent in the stimulus configuration. This distinction also appeared in views of the nature of generalization and in analyses of transposition phenomena.

Another important controversy of the period centered on continuity and noncontinuity interpretations of discrimination learning, interpretations that were concerned with the question of whether an animal learns about environmental events which are being differentially reinforced but to which he is not responding differentially. The continuity position's answer to this question was, Yes; the noncontinuity answer, No. Interest in the problem declined because of the difficulty in testing the alternative positions that developed, although in a modified and less controversial form the general question of attention in discrimination learning remains an active area of interest. Finally, mention should be made of disputes regarding "latent learning," place (cognitive) versus response learning, and insight versus trial and error learning. [*See* LEARNING, *article on* DISCRIMINATION LEARNING; PERCEPTION, *articles on* PERCEPTUAL DEVELOPMENT *and* DEPTH PERCEPTION.]

The shift from major systems. It must be recognized that these positions and controversies occupied the major attention of learning theorists for a relatively long period during the growth of interest in learning phenomena and that much of the research of this time was in the context of these issues. Thus, the shift away from these formulations that began to be evident in the early 1950s marked a distinct change in both the direction and content of learning theory. This transition, which is clearly evident in a comparison of Hilgard's first (1948) and second (1956) editions of *Theories of Learning,* was due to a number of factors. Without detracting from the historical importance of these approaches or the recognition of their essential contribution to all aspects of current learning theory, it can be recognized that the problems and limitations of the systematic and controversy-oriented theory of that period were such as to lead to change. As psychology became more sophisticated about applying testability criteria to theories, the demand increased that concepts and constructs (or the systems and models into which they were incorporated) should have empirical reference. It became obvious that many of the positions and controversies that had been the focal points of debate were not formulated in a way that would provide clear-cut empirical predictions. In other words, with some exceptions these were systems at the verbal level that could not be translated into the clear-cut experimental manipulations necessary for unambiguous testing. While adequately representing general approaches and serving certain heuristic functions, many of the systems did not serve a desired function of theories—that of integrating and predicting laws. It was also recognized that one possible reason for their lack of specificity was the range of behavior included. It was found that with the existing state of empirical knowledge, learning, as an area, was much too complex to be adequately handled by these broad approaches.

By and large the systems were concerned with simple learning situations; for example, classical conditioning, instrumental learning, and simple discrimination learning. While many learning psychologists recognized the strategy of building from the simple to the complex, they were not satisfied with the pace, were skeptical of the system—controversy aspect of the activity, or felt that important variables were being neglected. These workers, therefore, applied some of the techniques and concepts to other areas of interest or became involved in different kinds of theorizing. The changes as they have developed have represented a distinct turn toward "smaller" theories that are more closely tied to empirical data and that often deal with a single or closely related group of phenomena. Thus, these "smaller" theories have not been based on the theoretical predictions of a few dominant theorists, instead, they have proliferated as phenomena or areas of investigation have been developed or have caught the interest of investigators. Concurrently, there has come a great increase in the use of the model and in the utilization of mediation process notions in all areas of theory construction.

Current learning theory. Current activity in learning theory cannot be simply classified along orthogonal dimensions, such as type of theorizing employed, type of learning phenomena involved, or experimental situations used. Rather than attempting to develop and justify a complex classificatory system, the following section will use broad categories that are intended only to serve a loose organizing function. Considered first are more general theories that have a relatively close relationship to the older systems; second, those which deal with classes of behavior or specific variables. In addition, theoretical activity concerned with traditional experimental learning situations, for example, classical conditioning, instrumental conditioning, discrimination learning, and verbal learning, is discussed, along with a brief consideration of more complex learning situations. It should be recognized that considerable overlap exists between these divisions and that many individual theories and areas of theoretical activity are omitted.

General approaches

While it is obvious that present-day learning theory is not primarily engaged in the elaboration of the theoretical structures of previous systems, the influence of older formulations is clearly represented in current work, and some theoretical activity has been rather directly derived from the "classical" positions. The latter has been the case more for S–R theory than for S–S approaches. There are several theoretical systems that are closely related to Hullian theory, and, similarly, the relationship of stimulus-sampling models to Guthrie's position is obvious. On the other hand, the influence of S–S theory is primarily evident in approaches that stress perceptual and cognitive variables, for example, perceptual models of discrimination learning and notions of cue utilization.

Modifications of S–R approaches. *Miller.* The changes in S–R approaches are exemplified by Miller's discussion of the "liberalization of S–R theory" (1959), which includes a consideration of the application of S–R concepts to central processes and the role of cybernetic-type feedback systems and attentional mechanisms in behavior. While admitting that postulation of central processes within an S–R framework reduces the difference between S–R and cognitive theory, Miller describes the S–R position as one that tends to apply the same laws to central processes as to peripheral stimuli and responses; this is in contrast to cognitive theory, which is characterized as being less specific about the laws involved. A characteristic of Miller's work has been his attempt to apply laboratory-developed theories and concepts to complex social-behavior situations, the application of his theory of approach–avoidance conflict behavior to diverse and complex human behavioral situations being a case in point. In a sense this is a "model" approach, since the attempt is to find isomorphism between the systems developed in simple animal learning situations and complex human behavior. This approach is to be contrasted with that which attempts to expand theories dealing with a restricted range of simple phenomena by gradually integrating variables and laws from other behavioral situations. [See CONFLICT, *article on* PSYCHOLOGICAL ASPECTS; CYBERNETICS.]

Spence. Spence's theory (e.g., 1956) developed from early collaborative work with Hull. Starting with a quantitative S–R account of discrimination learning, Spence has developed in his later work a system that is more systematic than Hull's theory and much more closely tied to empirical data. In contrast to Hull's broader, less empirically based approach, is Spence's detailed concern with such topics as (1) the fractional anticipatory goal response, which is proposed as the mechanism underlying incentive; (2) the role of frustration in partial reinforcement and extinction; and (3) his theory of emotionally based drive. A major objective of Spence's theorizing has been to develop formulations that would allow for the derivation of empirical relationships found in a variety of learning situations and that could, with the addition of "composition rules," extend to more complex learning phenomena. [See DRIVES, *article on* PHYSIOLOGICAL DRIVES.]

Mowrer. Another theorist to be considered in this section is Mowrer. His most recent formulation (1960) assigns a central role to the classical conditioning of implicit responses or emotional states, which are called hope, disappointment, fear, or relief, depending upon the nature of the reinforcer (positive or negative) and the relation of the stimulus to the reinforcer (signaling its presence or imminent onset, or absence or approaching cessation). Mowrer is one theorist who does not follow the trend toward more restricted theorizing; rather, he proposes that his basic explanatory principles will encompass a wide range of human learning phenomena.

Mathematical theories. Perhaps the most rapidly expanding area of learning theorizing is that of mathematical (stochastic) theories of learning. Two principal lines of development have generally been distinguished. Statistical learning theory, or stimulus-sampling theory, has used conceptions of the environmental stimulus situation to obtain

learning axioms and theorems about the changes that occur in response probabilities as a consequence of environmental events. Operator models, on the other hand, have been primarily concerned with those properties of response sequences that are a result of various transformation rules; assumptions about outcome effects and response classes appear in the nature of the particular model. Both approaches share similar features, such as the assumptions that the environmental outcomes associated with response alternatives change the distribution of choice probabilities and that probabilistic mechanisms govern response selections. Mathematical representations of learning have been quite successful in handling the data from some learning situations. Often, however, these situations have been specifically arranged to lend themselves to mathematical treatment and do not represent paradigms commonly used by other theorists. Further problems have been the relative difficulty of deciding when a particular formulation is appropriate and the fact that there are often a number of alternative assumptions or models that lead to essentially the same results. While promising advances have been made, the future of this approach will be determined by its success in overcoming obstacles and arriving at transsituational mathematical representations of basic learning processes. [See MODELS, MATHEMATICAL; *for a survey of this area, see* Sternberg 1963.]

Phenomena-centered theories

Turning to theories which tend to deal more with certain kinds of behaviors or classes of variables, brief mention will be made of several areas in which the general shift toward phenomena-centered theorizing is evident.

Curiosity behaviors and reinforcement. One trend that has developed since the 1950s has been the increasing attention directed toward exploratory, manipulative, and curiosity behaviors; and it is not surprising to find corresponding theoretical formulations which attempt to integrate the data of this area. One such theory is represented by the work of Berlyne (1960), who considers four variables to be of primary importance in stimulus-selection processes: novelty, uncertainty, degree of conflict, and complexity. The organism is presumed to direct attention both by central processes and by exploratory behavior (orienting responses, locomotor exploration, and investigatory responses) that alters the stimulus field. These variables are integrated with arousal-level concepts and further tied to reinforcement, for example, in that arousal reduction may be reinforcing. [See ATTENTION; STIMULATION DRIVES.]

Concern with the nature of the reinforcing event is characteristic of formulations dealing with the effects of novelty, exploratory behavior, curiosity, and similar stimulus variables and response patterns. To a large extent this concern has represented dissatisfaction with the tendency of older theories to expand their motivational and reinforcement notions from a single drive or drive mechanism and with their disposition to concentrate upon a few biogenic drives, for example, hunger. Also contributing to this interest has been the demonstration of the high reinforcing value of visual and manipulatory exploration. This work, in which Harlow has played a major role, has forced learning to attend to a new class of variables in a manner similar to the way in which gestalt psychology focused attention on a previously ignored set of perceptual phenomena. While theory concerned with novelty, curiosity, and similar variables has generally not reached the degree of specificity associated with some other areas of theorizing, it is an active and promising area that will undoubtedly become integrated with theories that presently do not deal with these variables to any great extent.

A similar situation exists with respect to investigations of the orienting reflex. Starting with Pavlov's original work, the orienting reflex has proved a rich topic for research in the Soviet Union and has been the focus of a great increase of interest in the United States. The orienting reflex, which is considered to be a functional, centrally organized and integrated system of somatic, visceral, and cognitive reactions, is evoked by changes in stimulation or "novel" stimuli. Sokolov, the most prominent worker in this field, has elaborated a neuronal model concerned with the properties of the orienting reflex (1960).

Verbal processes. Of similar interest is the concern with the role of verbal processes in learning. While these processes play a major role in some theories of discrimination learning, interest in verbal processes also serves as a more general framework within which many theoretical formulations are being made. Work in the Soviet Union is particularly noteworthy in this respect. Coming from the separate but related traditions of Pavlov and L. S. Vigotski, Soviet researchers have increasingly been concerned with the second (verbal) signaling system and its relationship to learning. Luria (1961) among others has been quite active

in theorizing about the verbal regulation of behavior, especially voluntary movements, with an emphasis on developmental factors both in normal and abnormal children. Note should also be made of the growing interest in relating conceptions of orienting reflex and feedback to theories of the development of voluntary action. [See CONCEPT FORMATION; LEARNING, *article on* VERBAL LEARNING.]

Punishment. Another area that has seen a large increase in theoretical activity is that concerned with the effects of punishment on behavior. It has become clear that punishment can have a wide variety of facilitatory, inhibitory, or suppressive effects depending upon the behavioral, situational, and punishment parameters involved, and a number of theorists have attempted to integrate these effects into existing theoretical structures or to develop principles which will link the various experimental findings. Thus, some theorists have discussed the conditioning of anticipatory punishment cues or have considered punishment to be a special case of avoidance learning, while others have emphasized the role of fear, the nature of the skeletal responses elicited by the punishment, or the stimulus properties of punishment. [See LEARNING, *article on* AVOIDANCE LEARNING.]

Developmental psychology. Another increasingly active area with import for learning theory is developmental psychology. The recent trend in this area has been a de-emphasis of normative, naturalistic observation and an increasing use of the experimental method. Correspondingly, there has been a turning away from the "grand" developmental theories as theories, although their utilization as a source of ideas continues. Thus, the conceptual framework and insightful observations of Piaget have occasioned intense interest in developmental psychology, and considerable effort is underway to translate the system and specific ideas into experimentally testable form. As this sort of experimental activity continues, developmental psychology seems destined to have closer ties to other areas of psychology. Indeed, those working in various content areas have also been moving toward developmental concepts. It appears obvious that learning theory must utilize, include, or become integrated with specific experimentally based developmental theory if it hopes to make significant progress in the future. [See DEVELOPMENTAL PSYCHOLOGY.]

Neurophysiology. Brief mention should also be made of the current work on the neurophysiological basis of learning. Although learning theory of the past has not emphasized physiological constructs to any great extent, this situation may well change as progress is made in understanding the neural basis of learning. It should also be noted that physiological theorizing has generally taken the form of hypotheses about the nature of the physiological or biochemical mechanisms involved. This is in contrast to learning theory in the United States, which has been much more inclined toward the use of systems involving defined concepts or constructs. Theorizing in both areas has felt the impact of the "model" approach, and some rapprochement may occur because of this. Learning theory in the Soviet Union has been much more closely tied to neurophysiological concepts. [*See* LEARNING, *article on* NEUROPHYSIOLOGICAL ASPECTS; NERVOUS SYSTEM.]

Other phenomena. Examples of theorizing can also be seen with learning phenomena of more limited scope. Thus, the effects of partial reinforcement in acquisition and extinction have served to trigger the development of "small" theoretical formulations that attempt to isolate the effective parameters in the experimental situation and to derive the effects from more basic learning phenomena, for example, stimulus generalization, or as special cases of more general learning theories. In some cases, empirical findings that have countered common sense expectations or the simple derivations of theory have served as the focal points of theoretical activity.

In these examples the phenomena-centered nature of current learning theory is evident, in contrast to the older formulations which tended to start with general principles or postulates concerning the nature of the learning or reinforcement process.

Current work in traditional areas

Classical conditioning. Contemporary theories concerned with classical conditioning have been summarized by Grings (1963). With some exceptions, for example, Razran's detailed schema, the primary theoretical work has been directed more toward various aspects of the conditioning process than toward the development of a general explanatory system of classical conditioning per se. Much of the interest in classical conditioning has been in its postulated role in other, presumably more complicated, kinds of behavior; for example, theorizing regarding incentive variables, such as the fractional anticipatory goal response, has made use of classical conditioning processes, or as Lachman (1960) discusses it, classical conditioning provides the model, that is, the inference rules, for fractional anticipatory goal response theory. Similar theorizing has developed with respect to (1) the consequences of frustration, with frustration being defined either as the blocking of an ongoing response or as the omission of a reward, as in partial reinforcement or extinction; and (2) behavioral situations involving the use of punishment. Thus, in many situations where events are conceptualized to mediate overt behavior, classical conditioning is postulated to play some role or to serve as an inference model for the mediation theory. It should be noted that this use of conditioning is in the *S–R* rather than the cognitive tradition. [*See* DRIVES, *article on* PHYSIOLOGICAL DRIVES; LEARNING, *article on* CLASSICAL CONDITIONING.]

Soviet work. In the Soviet Union, theorizing about classical conditioning has remained a major interest since the pioneering work of Pavlov (e.g., see Anokhin 1955). The characteristics of Pavlov's theorizing are well known, and while many of his specific notions regarding physiological structure and function have been abandoned or modified considerably, present-day learning theory in the Soviet Union retains a physiological orientation. The current Soviet emphasis on interoceptive conditioning, semantic conditioning, and the orienting reflex is reviewed in detail by Razran (1961). Especially noteworthy, in the present context, has been the theoretical development coming from Soviet interests in configural conditioning, the role of conditioning in verbal behavior, and the ontogenetic implications of their work.

Instrumental conditioning. Theorizing involving instrumental conditioning has taken several forms. The effects of various parameters upon instrumental learning have been of interest to theorists who have attempted to integrate empirical relationships into a more comprehensive theory, or who have tried to use the laws obtained in these simple situations to develop formulations which would make it possible to derive the data previously obtained from more complicated selective-learning paradigms. The relative simplicity of instrumental conditioning has been attractive to those who have found the more complicated situations difficult to analyze in a precise manner. Phenomena-centered theorizing is quite evident here, as in other behavioral situations. To mention only two such efforts: certain partial reinforcement effects in acquisition and extinction have been of theoretical interest, and Abram Amsel's analysis (1962) of frustrative nonreward effects has been based on data from instrumental conditioning. [*See* LEARNING, *article on* INSTRUMENTAL LEARNING.]

Avoidance learning. Perhaps the greatest amount of theorizing concerning instrumental behavior has taken place with respect to avoidance learning. These theoretical formulations have generally been concerned with the mediating role of anxiety or fear in avoidance behavior and with the reinforcement principles operating in the dual learning processes of (1) fear or anxiety and (2) the instrumental skeletal response. A comprehensive overview of this area is presented by Solomon and Brush (1956). More recent theorizing has been concerned with specific avoidance phenomena, again demonstrating the trend toward more molecular theorizing. [*See* LEARNING, *article on* AVOIDANCE LEARNING.]

Selective learning. The original work in selective (discrimination) learning was largely concerned with controversies regarding the nature of learning and reinforcement processes. While some of this type of work is still found, current interest has largely shifted to the various processes—attentional, verbal, etc.—which presumably mediate the learning. A closely related development has been the emphasis on phylogenetic and ontogenetic considerations, in terms of discrimination-learning performance and the relative use of the postulated mediational mechanisms. One of the most important developments in the discrimination-learning area has been the learning-set work of Harlow (1959). This research focused attention on discrimination procedures, demonstrated the relevance of this sort of research for more complex learning (for example, concept formation), and provided behavioral techniques that have proved useful in comparing human and infrahuman learning. Theoretical activity has been concerned with the nature of interfering tendencies or error factors.

A great deal of current activity is concerned with discrimination-learning "transfer" situations. A number of paradigms have been used to (1) compare the learning processes in human and infrahuman organisms, (2) explicate the nature of postulated mediating mechanisms, and (3) examine the mediational processes ontogenetically. Theoretical approaches that should be mentioned here include those of Luria (1961) and Kendler and Kendler (1962), both of which have tended to identify mediational processes with verbal behavior, and that of Zeaman and House (1963), which has developed from work with retarded children and which, although mathematical in nature, emphasizes the importance of attentional responses to stimulus dimensions. These formulations demonstrate several trends in discrimination-

learning theory. First, the use of multistage mediational models to account for the data; second, the increasing use of normal and retarded children as subjects; and third, as in the case of Zeaman and House, the emphasis on observing or attentional responses. Other theories proposed for selective learning include the observing–response formulation of Wyckoff (1952) and the analyzer-mechanism approach of N. S. Sutherland (1959). A succinct phrase which describes the basic process of concern in a number of these formulations is "selective attention," which can be conceived of in terms of stimulus–response relationships and laws or perceptual–cognitive processes. Approaches which attempt the integration of verbal-behavior relationships with discrimination-learning processes are also popular.

Verbal learning. An excellent discussion of the nature of theory in verbal learning is available in a paper by Gough and Jenkins (1963). These authors point out that verbal learning—the "rote" learning of material under laboratory conditions—did not develop from the learning theories of the 1940s but from the work of Ebbinghaus and the functionalist school of psychology. As an area, verbal learning has always been very closely tied to empirical data and methodological considerations, with little in the way of broad systematic theory. The theories that have developed have been concerned with specific verbal learning or retention phenomena and, as Gough and Jenkins point out, often have been called "analyses" rather than "theories." This lack of broad systematic formulations has led to the development of "small" testable theories, which have been quickly modified to reflect new experimental evidence. A listing of some recent theoretical formulations or analyses gives the flavor of the work. It has been proposed by Underwood and Schulz (1960) that paired-associate verbal learning can best be considered as a two-stage process involving response learning and stimulus–response associative stages. A considerable amount of research has demonstrated the usefulness of this conceptualization. Underwood (1957) has demonstrated that the role of proactive interference in laboratory learning is much greater than was previously assumed, an advance that has contributed to the understanding of forgetting and has led to important changes in methodology. Finally, the development of the interference theory of retroactive inhibition has witnessed the introduction of the concepts of differentiation or the discrimination of list membership and unlearning or extinction to account for discrepancies between interference theory and the obtained data. The close interplay between data and theory is apparent. [*See* FORGETTING; LEARNING, *article on* VERBAL LEARNING.]

Complex learning situations. Concept learning, skill learning, and problem solving are areas that have generally been considered to be more complex and harder to handle in terms of theory than those previously discussed. There are several dimensions of this complexity, for example, the ease or difficulty of dealing with discrete units of behavior or a limited number of basic processes and the necessity of considering sequential relationships. Until relatively recently, theorists were reluctant to deal with these situations, as demonstrated by the early discarding of problem-box situations for the simpler classical-conditioning and instrumental-learning procedures. The resurgence of interest in and of theorizing about these more complex areas has led to attempts to extend S–R and cognitive approaches to these phenomena, and, in some cases, it has led to new conceptual frameworks which bear little obvious relationship to traditional learning approaches.

Concept learning. Concept learning has, perhaps, remained closer to conventional learning research than the other areas mentioned. Kendler (1964) has pointed out that various learning models have been applied to concept learning. He lists S–R conceptions, operant conditioning, clustering, Piaget's methods of investigation, computer simulation of cognitive processes, and mathematical models as methods and models for the analysis of concept learning. [*See* CONCEPT FORMATION.]

Skill learning. In comparison to concept learning, theoretical activity regarding skill learning has been more removed from traditional learning theorizing. While issues such as the relative role of specific associations or cognitive sets in skill learning seem closely related to learning theory, the conceptual framework is not. Thus, the language of many models of skill learning is couched in terms of communication models, involving (1) notions of information processing, with subcategories of information translation, transmission, reduction, collation, and storage; (2) control-system models emphasizing feedback systems; and (3) adaptive-system models, with programs and memory systems which allow changes in the characteristics of the model with experience. [*See* LEARNING, *article on* ACQUISITION OF SKILL; *see also* Fitts 1964.]

Problem solving. Problem solving has long represented an area of controversy with S–R oriented theorists opposing gestalt-cognitive approaches. The S–R approach attempts to use such concepts as mediated generalization, response hierarchies, verbal mediators, and fractional anticipatory goal responses to account for problem-solving phenomena. Gestalt theory, on the other hand, emphasizes perceptual reorganization processes within the problem. One recent formulation or suggested framework, more in the gestalt than in the S–R tradition, has been the ahistorical, relatively rationally derived notions of Miller, Galanter, and Pribram (1960), which involve informational and feedback processes. [*See* PROBLEM SOLVING.]

The question as to what extent new language and methodological approaches are needed for theorizing in these complex areas remains to be determined. It seems evident, however, that information processing and feedback concepts of some sort will greatly influence learning theorizing in the future.

LEONARD E. ROSS

[*Directly related is the entry* LEARNING, *especially the articles on* CLASSICAL CONDITIONING, INSTRUMENTAL LEARNING, REINFORCEMENT. *Other relevant material may be found in* DRIVES; GESTALT THEORY; MOTIVATION.]

BIBLIOGRAPHY

AMSEL, ABRAM 1962 Frustrative Nonreward in Partial Reinforcement and Discrimination Learning: Some Recent History and Theoretical Extension. *Psychological Review* 69:306–328.

ANOKHIN, P. K. (1955) 1961 Features of the Afferent Apparatus of the Conditional Reflex and Their Importances for Psychology. Pages 75–103 in N. O'Connor (editor), *Recent Soviet Psychology.* New York: Liveright.

BERLYNE, D. E. 1960 *Conflict, Arousal, and Curiosity.* New York: McGraw-Hill.

FITTS, PAUL M. 1964 Perceptual–Motor Skill Learning. Pages 243–285 in Symposium on the Psychology of Human Learning, University of Michigan, 1962, *Categories of Human Learning.* New York: Academic Press.

GOUGH, PHILIP B.; and JENKINS, JAMES J. 1963 Verbal Learning and Psycholinguistics. Pages 456–474 in Melvin H. Marx (editor), *Theories in Contemporary Psychology.* New York: Macmillan.

GRINGS, WILLIAM W. 1963 Classical Conditioning. Pages 495–526 in Melvin H. Marx (editor), *Theories in Contemporary Psychology.* New York: Macmillan.

HARLOW, HARRY F. 1959 Learning Set and Error Factor Theory. Pages 492–537 in Sigmund Koch (editor), *Psychology: A Study of a Science.* Volume 2: General Systematic Formulations, Learning, and Special Processes. New York: McGraw-Hill.

HILGARD, ERNEST R. (1948) 1956 *Theories of Learning.* 2d ed. New York: Appleton.

KENDLER, HOWARD H. 1964 The Concept of the Concept. Pages 211–236 in Symposium on the Psychology of Human Learning, University of Michigan, 1962, *Cate-*

gories of Human Learning. New York: Academic Press.

KENDLER, HOWARD H.; and KENDLER, TRACY S. 1962 Vertical and Horizontal Processes in Problem Solving. *Psychological Review* 69:1–16.

KOCH, SIGMUND (editor) 1959 *Psychology: A Study of a Science.* Volume 2: General Systematic Formulations, Learning, and Special Processes. New York: McGraw-Hill.

LACHMAN, ROY 1960 The Model in Theory Construction. *Psychological Review* 67:113–129.

LURIA, ALEKSANDR R. 1961 *The Role of Speech in the Regulation of Normal and Abnormal Behavior.* New York: Liveright.

MILLER, GEORGE A.; GALANTER, E.; and PRIBRAM, K. H. 1960 *Plans and the Structure of Behavior.* New York: Holt.

MILLER, NEAL E. 1959 Liberalization of Basic S–R Concepts: Extensions to Conflict Behavior, Motivation and Social Learning. Pages 196–292 in Sigmund Koch (editor), *Psychology: A Study of a Science.* Volume 2: General Systematic Formulations, Learning, and Special Processes. New York: McGraw-Hill.

MOWRER, ORVAL H. 1960 *Learning Theory and Behavior.* New York: Wiley.

RAZRAN, GREGORY 1961 The Observable Unconscious and the Inferable Conscious in Current Soviet Psychophysiology: Interoceptive Conditioning, Semantic Conditioning, and the Orienting Reflex. *Psychological Review* 68:81–147.

SOKOLOV, EUGENE N. 1960 Neuronal Models and the Orienting Reflex. Pages 187–276 in *The Central Nervous System and Behavior: Transactions of the Third Conference.* Edited by M. A. B. Brazier. New York: Macy Foundation.

SOLOMON, RICHARD L.; and BRUSH, ELINOR S. 1956 Experimentally Derived Conceptions of Anxiety and Aversions. Volume 4, pages 212–306 in Marshall R. Jones (editor), *Nebraska Symposium on Motivation.* Lincoln: Univ. of Nebraska Press.

SPENCE, KENNETH W. 1951 Theoretical Interpretations of Learning. Pages 690–729 in Stanley S. Stevens (editor), *Handbook of Experimental Psychology.* New York: Wiley.

SPENCE, KENNETH W. 1956 *Behavior Theory and Conditioning.* New Haven: Yale Univ. Press.

STERNBERG, SAUL 1963 Stochastic Learning Theory. Volume 2, pages 1–120 in R. Duncan Luce et al. (editors), *Handbook of Mathematical Psychology.* New York and London: Wiley.

SUTHERLAND, N. S. 1959 Stimulus Analysing Mechanisms. Volume 2, pages 575–609 in Teddington, England, National Physical Laboratory, *Mechanisation of Thought Processes: Proceedings of a Symposium.* London: H.M. Stationery Office.

UNDERWOOD, BENTON J. 1957 Interference and Forgetting. *Psychological Review* 64:49–60.

UNDERWOOD, BENTON J.; and SCHULZ, RUDOLPH W. 1960 *Meaningfulness and Verbal Learning.* Philadelphia: Lippincott.

WYCKOFF, L. B. 1952 The Role of Observing Responses in Discrimination Learning. Part 1. *Psychological Review* 59:431–442.

ZEAMAN, DAVID; and HOUSE, BETTY J. 1963 The Role of Attention in Retardate Discrimination Learning. Pages 159–223 in Norman R. Ellis (editor), *Handbook of Mental Deficiency.* New York: McGraw-Hill.

LEAST SQUARES

See ESTIMATION *and* LINEAR HYPOTHESES.

LEGAL EVIDENCE

See PSYCHIATRY, *article on* FORENSIC PSYCHIATRY; STATISTICS AS LEGAL EVIDENCE.

LEGAL PROFESSION

See *under* LAW.

LEGAL REASONING

In countries like the United States and England, where thought about law has focused primarily on adjudication, legal reasoning is often identified with the intellectual processes by which judges reach conclusions in deciding cases. In countries like France and Germany, on the other hand, where thought about law has focused primarily on codification—that is, the creation of a complex and harmonious body of legal rules and concepts —legal reasoning is often identified with the intellectual processes by which the rationality and consistency of legal doctrines are maintained and justified. Since, as we shall see, both these types of reasoning are closely related to each other, we would define legal reasoning broadly enough to include them both; and indeed, we propose to broaden the definition still further to include also the types of reasoning used in other kinds of legal activity, such as making laws, administering laws, the trial (and not merely the decision) of cases in court, the drafting of legal documents, and the negotiation of legal transactions.

When legal reasoning is conceived of in these broader terms, it is seen to involve not only, and not primarily, the application of rules of formal logic but also other methods of exposition. To reason, according to dictionary definitions, may mean to give grounds (reasons) for one's statements, to argue persuasively, or to engage in discourse. Law, insofar as it has a distinctive subject matter and is founded on distinctive principles and purposes, has not only its own kinds of *logic* but also its own kinds of *rhetoric* and its own kinds of *discourse*, which are, of course, similar to the logic, rhetoric, and discourse of other social institutions and other scholarly disciplines but which nevertheless have certain distinctive characteristics.

In seeking to identify these distinctive characteristics, we must keep in mind that legal reasoning is not identical in all societies and that, in addition, the degree of its distinctiveness is not identical in all societies. In a theocracy, for example, legal reasoning may be closely related to sacerdotal reasoning; at one time the high priests of Israel found the law by consulting the breast-plates which they wore (the Urim and Thummim) —that is, their legal decisions were justified in terms of divine revelation. In a society that is undergoing a political revolution, such as the Soviet Union in the first years after 1917, legal reasoning may dissolve into the reasoning of politics and class struggle. These variations strongly suggest that in any society there is an intimate connection between the logic, rhetoric, and discourse of law and the dominant beliefs of the society concerning religion, politics, and other aspects of social life, including its beliefs about the nature of reasoning itself. Legal reasoning seems to be most distinctive in those societies that have experienced the emergence of a special professional class of lawmen, with its own special professional traditions and institutional values; here special modes of logic, rhetoric, and discourse seem to have as part of their functions the preservation and further development of the legal profession's traditions and values, although at the same time even in such societies the intimate connections between legal reasoning and other types of reasoning must be maintained if the legal profession is to retain the respect of the community as a whole.

Legal logic. Many Western jurists of the eighteenth and nineteenth centuries sought to make legal reasoning conform to syllogistic logic. The rules of law declared by legislatures, courts, and legal scholars were viewed as major premises, and the fact situations of particular cases or the terms of particular legal problems were viewed as minor premises. The decision of a case, or the resolution of a legal problem, was thought to follow inevitably from a proper juxtaposition of the major and minor premises. Given a rule or doctrine defining burglary, or contract, or any other basis of legal duty, it was thought only to be necessary to determine whether or not a particular act fell within the definition in order to determine whether or not legal responsibility should attach to it. It was supposed by many that if the entire body of law could be summarized in a set of rules, the sole remaining task of law would be to classify particular facts under one rule or another.

This mechanical model of the application of rules to facts did not go unchallenged even in its heyday. In Germany, Rudolf von Jhering ridiculed a "jurisprudence of concepts" (*Begriffsjurisprudenz*) and called for a conscious legal policy of evaluating the social and personal interests involved in the legal resolution of conflicts (*Interessenjurisprudenz*). Similarly, in the United States, Oliver Wendell Holmes, Jr., in some of his writings, viewed the logical form in which judges announced their conclusions as a veil covering their views of public policy. The life of the law has not been logic; it has been experience, Holmes stated in 1881. By "logic" Holmes indicated he meant "the syllogism" and "the axioms and corollaries of a book of mathematics"; by "experience" he meant "considerations of what is socially expedient."

However useful syllogistic logic may be in testing the validity of conclusions drawn from given premises, it is inadequate as a method of reasoning in a practical science such as law, where the premises are not given but must be created. Legal rules, viewed as major premises, are always subject to qualification in the light of particular circumstances; it is a rule of English and American law, for example, that a person who intentionally strikes another is civilly liable for battery, but such a rule is subject, in legal practice, to infinite modification in the light of possible defense (for example, self-defense, defense of property, parental privilege, immunity from suit, lack of jurisdiction, insufficiency of evidence, etc.). In addition, life continually presents new situations to which no existing rule is applicable; we simply do not know the legal limits of freedom of speech, for example, since the social context in which words are spoken is continually changing. Thus legal rules are continually being made and remade.

Also the "minor premises"—the facts of particular cases or the terms of particular legal problems—are not simply "there" but must be perceived and characterized, and this, too, requires interpretation and evaluation. Indeed, the legal facts of a case are not raw data but rather those facts that have been selected and classified in terms of legal categories.

Finally, the conclusion, that is, the application of the rule to the particular case or problem, since it is a responsible decision directly affecting particular people in particular situations, is never mathematically inevitable but always contingent upon the exercise of judgment. In the telling words of Immanuel Kant, "there is no rule for applying a rule"; that is, there are no rules that can tell us in advance, with certainty, how a particular judge (legislator, administrator, etc.) ought to resolve a concrete case or problem that is before him—and this would be true even though we were able to say in advance what rules are relevant to such a resolution. Once a legal conclusion is reached, it may often be stated in syllogistic form; but in the process of reaching it, the determination of the major and minor premises may have come last.

To say that legal reasoning cannot be reduced to the classical rules of formal logic is not, however, to deny that it has logical qualities. It is characteristic of legal reasoning that it strives toward consistency both of legal rules and of legal judgments; such a striving for consistency is implicit in the belief that law should apply equally to all who are subject to it and that like cases should be decided in a like manner. Even the judgments of the ancient Greek oracles were believed to reflect a hidden consistency. It is also characteristic of legal reasoning that it strives toward continuity in time; it looks to the authority of the past, embodied in previously declared rules and decisions, and it attempts to regulate social relations in such a way as to preserve stability. Finally, legal reasoning is dialectical reasoning; it is characteristically concerned with the weighing of opposing claims, whether expressed in legislative debate, in forensic argument, or the like. These three basic characteristics of legal reasoning impose upon it certain logical requirements.

The most pervasive form of legal logic is that of *analogy*, in the broad sense of the comparison and contrast of similar and dissimilar examples. Analogical reasoning is implicit in the striving for consistency; the striving for continuity (that is, historical consistency) also involves analogical reasoning, the analogies being found in past experience; similarly, the dialectical quality of legal reasoning involves comparison and contrast between the examples put forward by the opposing sides. (It should be noted that the term "analogy" also has a technical legal meaning, signifying the extension of a legal category to a situation which is "similar to" but not "the same as" those situations which the category "logically" includes; in contrast, we use the term "analogy" here more broadly and include under it the process by which it is determined that one situation is "the same as" another.)

In a legal system such as that of England or the United States, which stresses the authority of past judicial decisions (precedents), analogical reasoning in adjudication characteristically takes the form of (*a*) comparison of the fact situation before the court with the fact situations of previously decided cases in order to find a previously decided case whose fact situation is comparable; (*b*) extraction from the previously decided comparable case of the principle upon which that case was decided; and (*c*) application of that principle to the case at hand. It is generally recognized that each of these three steps is dependent upon the other two. Moreover, the second step—the extraction of the principle of the previous case—is complicated by the fact that the principle expressly relied on by the court in deciding the previous case is not necessarily binding upon future courts. Even under a strict doctrine of precedents, at least as understood in the United States, a court, although bound by the decisions in previous cases, may reject the reasons previously given for those decisions—as, for example, where much broader reasons were given than were required. In technical terms, the court is not bound by (may treat as mere *dictum*) any statement made in a previous comparable case which was not necessary to the decision in that case; and even a reason stated by the previous court as the necessary ground for its decision may be treated as dictum, and not binding, if the later court considers that the same decision could have been reached on other (better) grounds. Thus what is binding on future courts—the "holding" of the case—is determined in part by its subsequent application to similar fact situations.

Reasoning by *analogy of precedents* has been called by one writer "the basic pattern of legal reasoning." However, another characteristic method of legal reasoning—especially (but not exclusively) in legal systems that do not recognize the binding force of precedents—is to decide cases or resolve particular legal problems by *analogy of doctrines* expressed in statutes and in other forms of legal rules. To give an American example: in the latter part of the nineteenth century, most states enacted statutes giving married women the right to own their separate property, to make contracts, and to sue and be sued. Using the authority of such married women's acts, many courts overruled various earlier precedents which made a wife and husband incompetent to testify for or against each other, which made a husband liable for his wife's torts, which made one spouse not liable to conviction for stealing from the other, etc. These matters, although not dealt with specifically by the married women's acts, were sufficiently similar to the matters with which the married women's acts did deal that the policy of those acts was considered to be applicable. Such use of analogy of statute (or of legal doctrine) is especially prevalent in those countries of Europe in which the law is largely found in codes and in which the writings of leading legal scholars in interpreting the codes have more authority than judicial decisions.

Analogical reasoning, and especially reasoning

from analogy of decided cases, is sometimes said to be "inductive," as contrasted with "deductive" reasoning from legal rules. Such a characterization presupposes that the facts of cases are first analyzed and then legal principles are "inferred" from such facts. However, the distinction between the facts of a legal case and the legal principle governing those facts is not the same as the distinction sometimes drawn between the facts of a laboratory experiment and the hypothesis offered by the scientist to explain the facts. The facts of a legal case do not have an existence independent of the theory of liability applied to them. A collision between X and Y may be a "fact" which natural science can "explain"; but whether or not X should be legally liable to Y, or Y to X, depends on whether or not X or Y was "negligent" or was carrying on an "extrahazardous activity" or was otherwise engaged in liability-creating conduct. Thus, as suggested earlier, the same kind of judgment that is required to determine the applicable legal principle (liability for harm caused by negligence, liability for harm caused by extrahazardous activity) is also required to characterize the legally operative facts (X drove negligently, X was engaged in an extrahazardous activity). To contend that since liability is imposed in situation A (for example, harm caused by collision of aircraft with ground structures, regardless of fault, air travel being considered an extrahazardous activity), and since situation B (for example, harm caused by automobile travel) is (or is not) comparable to situation A, therefore liability should (or should not) be imposed in situation B is an example neither of deductive nor of inductive reasoning, although it contains elements of each. It is an example of reasoning applied to reach decisions for action and, like the reasoning of a physician or an engineer or a politician, is based on a very large variety of considerations, many of which cannot be fully articulated.

Although reasoning by analogy is the primary form of legal logic, it is not sufficient in itself to compel particular legal results. There is, indeed, a large area of indeterminacy in all analogical reasoning, since the criteria for selecting similarities and differences are left open to debate. A rigid definition confining the term "logic" to those propositions that necessarily follow from given premises might therefore exclude analogy altogether. According to an old proverb, " 'For example' is not proof." Yet analogical reasoning, despite its flexibility, does impose limits upon legal results even if it does not in itself compel them. In each society some similarities and differences are so strongly

felt that they cannot be denied. Moreover, particular legal doctrines often restrict the range within which analogies may be found. Most modern legal systems, for example, require that a criminal statute be interpreted much more "strictly" than a statute imposing only civil obligations; similarly, courts are generally more reluctant to extend analogies under rules of commercial law than under rules of personal injury law, since commercial rules are relied on in business transactions where a high degree of stability and predictability is desired. In addition, each legal system establishes procedures and methods for drawing analogies—such as adversary and investigative procedures or the method of precedent and the method of codification—and these procedures and methods are designed to prevent analogical reasoning from becoming arbitrary.

Analogical reasoning is, of course, a universal mode of reasoning and by no means unique to law. What is distinctive about law, in this respect, is the degree of emphasis placed upon the use of analogy and the development of special legal rules, procedures, and methods for drawing analogies. For law the method of analogy has the special virtue—as compared with syllogistic reasoning— of exposing the examples by which consistency, continuity, and the weighing of opposing claims and defenses are tested.

Legal rhetoric. We define rhetoric, following Aristotle, as referring not only to the art of persuasion through appeals to emotions but also to the art of public deliberation through appeals to reason and hence as a mode of reasoning. At the same time rhetoric is distinguished from logic, since logic is concerned with indicative statements that are considered to be either true or false ("propositions"), whereas rhetoric is concerned with subjunctive, normative, and imperative statements uttered in order to influence thought or action. The classical formula of logic: All men are mortal, Socrates is a man, therefore Socrates is mortal— might be rendered in rhetorical form as: If you would be a man, O Socrates, you must prepare yourself for death!

Legal rules, being stated usually in the indicative mood, give the deceptive appearance of being only logical propositions; yet on closer analysis it is apparent that they have a rhetorical significance at least equally as great as their logical significance. The statement, for example, that the intentional premeditated killing of a person with malice aforethought constitutes the crime of murder in the first degree and is punishable by life imprisonment or death is not only a "true proposition" concerning what *is* murder (assuming it has been authoritatively declared); it is also a warning to potential murderers, an assurance to potential victims, a mandate to law enforcement officials, and, in general, an expression of the desires and beliefs of the political community. Legal reasoning with respect to the crime of murder consists, therefore, not only in the logical analysis of its definition, involving the comparison of various kinds of homicide (for example, homicide committed from motives of mercy, in self-defense, in the heat of passion, negligently, etc.); it also consists in both legislative and forensic rhetoric ("the death penalty should be abolished"; "the defendant is not a murderer") as well as in other, less formal types of argumentative speech (for example, "a person should certainly not escape responsibility for murder just because he believed his act would benefit society").

As the logical aspect of legal reasoning focuses attention on legal *rules* and on the principles to be derived from decisions in analogous cases, so the rhetorical aspect of legal reasoning focuses attention on legal *activities*. As many writers have emphasized, law itself is not simply, or primarily, a body of rules but an activity, an enterprise. A principal purpose of this enterprise is to subject human conduct to the governance of rules (Fuller 1964); but for that purpose rules must be drafted, debated, voted, published, interpreted, obeyed, applied, enforced—all of which legal activities involve the use of rhetoric and not only of logic. Moreover, apart from activities connected with rule making, it is also a purpose of the legal enterprise to render decisions, as by the casting of votes, the issuance of orders, the handing down of judgments; and the rendering of such decisions, like the making of legal rules, is both a product and an expression of rhetorical utterance. In addition, legal reasoning is directed to the negotiation of legal transactions, the making of petitions or recommendations, the writing of legal opinions, the issuance of legal documents, and to a variety of other types of legal activities, all of which involve the use of language to induce a response in those to whom the language is addressed.

As the use of analogy is a characteristic and pervasive form of legal logic, so the appeal to authority is a characteristic and pervasive form of legal rhetoric. The nature of the authority to which appeal is made differs in different legal systems. It is said, for example, that in traditional Muslim law the authority of the Koran is decisive and that only a literal interpretation of its provisions is permissible. In Judaic law, on the other hand, with the development of the Talmud, there emerged the authority of leading rabbis who interpreted the Torah. In Roman law a similar authority was vested in leading jurists. We have already referred to the authority of judicial precedents in English and American law and of codes in modern continental European law. Probably the highest authority governing judicial decisions in most contemporary legal systems is that of statutes enacted by the legislature, although in the United States and some other countries the authority even of statutes must yield to that of constitutional provisions.

The appeal to authority in legal reasoning is not necessarily limited, however, to an appeal to legislation (whether embodied in statutes, codes, an authoritative book, or in a constitution), to judicial precedents, or to juristic commentaries on such legislation or precedents. In many legal systems— and perhaps in all—some room, at least, is left for appeal also to custom (that is, what is commonly done and what is commonly believed ought to be done) and to a sense of justice. Thus it is often said that there are four sources of law: legislation (including rules made by administrative authorities), precedent, custom, and equity. These four sources may also be viewed as four dimensions of law—legislation (and administrative rules) being directed to what should be done in the future, precedent being directed to what has been done in the past, custom being directed to outer social patterns and norms of behavior, and equity being directed to the inner sense of justice or fairness. Different legal systems, and different branches within a particular legal system, emphasize one or another of these four dimensions or sources or types of authority, and hence legal rhetoric is not uniform as between different legal systems or even within a single system. In American law, for example, the legislation-based rhetoric of a traffic regulation ("parked cars will be towed away") differs from the precedent-based rhetoric of a judicial decision ("this court has consistently held that the manufacturer is not liable to retail purchasers unless he is shown to have been negligent"); and both of these differ from the custom-based rhetoric of a negotiable instrument ("pay to the order of John Jones $1,000") or the equity-based rhetoric of a divorce decree ("the father may have the child visit him four times a year for a week at a time").

Legal discourse.   It is apparent that legal logic is itself a form of legal rhetoric. Legal rhetoric, in turn, is a form of legal discourse, whose functions go beyond that of influencing immediate thought and action and include the preservation and development of the legal traditions and values of the entire political–legal community as well as the traditions and values of the legal profession itself in societies where a legal profession exists.

The distinctive characteristics of legal discourse arise principally from the institution of *the hearing*, which is the basis of all legal activities, including not only adjudication but also legislation, administration, negotiation of legal transactions, and other legal activities. It is the opportunity of both sides to be heard that principally distinguishes adjudication from vengeance. Similarly, it is, above all, the opportunity to debate pending enactments that distinguishes legislation from mere commands, and it is the opportunity to petition for relief that distinguishes lawful administration from bureaucratic fiat. Even a unilateral legal act such as the writing of a will requires the draftsman to put himself in the position of third persons who might be called upon to interpret the will in the light of a dispute over its validity or meaning.

A legal hearing involves two qualities of discourse that are not necessarily present in nonlegal procedures of listening and speaking. The first quality may be described as formality, that is, the use of a deliberate and ceremonial form of discourse, which usually is reflected in a formal presentation of claims and defenses, formal deliberation of the court or other tribunal, and the formal rendering of a decision. The formalities of the hearing help to secure its objectivity, that is, its impartiality, internal consistency, restraint, and authority.

A second distinctive quality of discourse characteristic of a legal hearing is the tendency to categorize the persons and events that are involved. The specific, unique qualities of the dispute are named in general terms. John Jones is called "the plaintiff"; Sam Smith is called "the defendant"; the defendant is alleged, for example, to have broken a "lease" by causing certain "damage" to the leased "premises." These are the "legally operative facts." The "real" facts—Smith's obnoxious personal habits, the neighbors' gossip, the family feud, etc.—are excluded unless they can be brought into relevant legal categories. This helps to secure the generality of the hearing. For the issue is not whether John Jones or Sam Smith is the better man but rather whether the rights of a lessor, rights established by the law of the community, have been violated by a lessee.

The formulation of the dispute or problem in terms of general categories, and thus the viewing of the concrete facts *sub specie communitatis*, is organically derived from the hearing, although it is logically distinct from it. The dispute or the problem has challenged the existing legal rules; the parties have invoked a reformulation of them in the light of the concrete facts; and the court (if it is a judicial proceeding), or legislature (if it is a proposed statute), or administrative agency (if it is a new regulation that is sought), or lawyer (if it is a contract that is being negotiated or a will that is being drawn) is asked to reinterpret the existing rules or to create new rules in the light of the new dispute or new problem. Categorization of the specific, unique facts, carried out in the context of a deliberate and ceremonial presentation of claims and defenses with a formal procedure for interrogation, argument, and decision, helps to secure the generality and objectivity not only of the hearing but also of the reinterpreted or newly created rules and hence their acceptance by the community. At the same time, the legal vocabulary and techniques that are generated in this process provide a professional shorthand or jargon that is designed to contribute to the efficiency of legal procedures or to the fraternity of the legal profession, or to both, although it often has the effect of making both law and lawyers seem alien to the society that has produced them.

The circularity of legal reasoning. If law is seen, in the first instance, not as rules but as the enterprise of hearing, judging, prescribing, ordering, negotiating, declaring, etc., then it becomes possible to give a satisfactory explanation of what Jeremy Bentham called the tautology and circuity of legal terms and what H. L. A. Hart calls the "great anomaly of legal language—our inability to define its crucial words in terms of ordinary factual counterparts" (1953, p. 41). It is, indeed, true that legal reasoning characteristically appears to be circular. When it is said, for example, that a man has a "right" to something because someone has an "obligation" to transfer it to him, the "right" of the one and the "obligation" of the other seem to be merely two different terms for the same thing. Similarly, the word "crime" and the word "law" themselves seem to be only alternative ways of saying "right," "obligation," etc. Bentham wrote:

Each of these words may be substituted the one for the other. . . . The law directs me to support you—it imposes upon me the *obligation* of supporting you—it grants you the *right* of being supported by me—it converts into an *offence* the negative act by which I omit to support you—it obliges me to render you the *service* of supporting you. . . . This, then, is the connexion between these legal entities: they are only the law considered under different aspects; they exist as long as it exists; they are born and they die with it. . . . The legal terms seem to have no "empirical referents"—no "things" to which they "correspond." (*Bentham's Theory of Fictions*, pp. cxxix–cxxx)

The proliferation of interdependent legal terms referring to the same thing is due to the fact that the terms are not supposed to "refer" to "things" but instead to regulate a complex interrelationship of people engaged, actually or potentially, in legal activities of various kinds. From the standpoint of the child, support is a "right"; from the standpoint of the parent, it is an "obligation"; from the standpoint of the prosecutor, failure to fulfill the obligation may be a "crime." It is true that if there were no right there would be no obligation and no crime, and if there were no crime there would be no obligation and no right (or at least a different kind of obligation and right). But these (and many other) terms are needed to identify the complexity of the relationship between the child, the parent, and the state; they are needed especially when the relationship is described in abstract terms. The decision of the court may be simple enough: "Pay $25 a week for support of the child or go to jail."

It may seem senseless for courts or writers to go (as they sometimes do) from right to obligation to penalty as if in a logical sequence. Yet what may be senseless as a logical proposition may be sensible as a means of identifying the parties to a dispute and the nature of the disputed issue. To attack legal rules as question-begging is itself to beg the question of their function. Indeed, in some cases it is the function of judicial tautology and circularity to avoid giving a reason for a decision in a situation in which it is better to give no reason than to give the real reason. This is apt to be especially true of legal fictions, which are legal doctrines that state a legal result in terms of assumed facts that are known to be nonexistent. Here what are understood to be only analogies are consciously treated as identities, in order to preserve consistency of doctrine in the face of an unexplained inconsistent result. For example, a battery is traditionally defined as an unpermitted blow which the defendant intended to inflict on the plaintiff, but the courts nevertheless give a recovery to a person whom the defendant struck unintentionally while intending to strike another, applying the fiction that the defendant's intent to strike the third person is "transferred" to the person whom he in fact struck. Thus the original definition is preserved in form but its consequences are changed. In most cases, however, legal

tautologies and circularities are not intended to change the consequences of legal rules but are primarily a means of specifying the various aspects of legal relationships, often for procedural reasons. In any event, not only circular but also other "unscientific" qualities of law may often be understood if they are seen as part of the logic of analogy, the rhetoric of appeals to authority, and the discourse of formality and categorization that are the distinguishing characteristics of legal reasoning.

Legal reasoning and social science. Despite important insights into the nature and functions of legal reasoning contributed by such classical sociologists as Émile Durkheim and Max Weber (both of whom were legally trained), modern social science has left the subject largely to legal scholars. However, recent sociological studies of the professions have, following Weber, related legal reasoning to the need of the legal profession to have its own professional language; and in the last two decades many American political scientists have attempted to debunk legal reasoning as a disguise for judicial decisions reached on the basis of nonlegal considerations. More important, probably, at least in the long run, are studies by social scientists not of legal reasoning as such but of legal institutions, such as the jury system, civil rights legislation, criminal law enforcement, collective bargaining, the antitrust laws, etc., since such studies provide a necessary foundation for any generalizations about the relationship of legal reasoning to other types of reasoning. In the meanwhile, studies of legal reasoning by legal scholars —who are also social scientists—will continue to benefit from social science theories and methods directed to the study of social institutions generally, including legal institutions. Indeed, social science theories and methods sometimes have a direct impact on legal reasoning itself when they are introduced into legal proceedings through, for example, legislative hearings and, occasionally, court cases in which social scientists are called in as experts.

Social sciences other than law may, however, have more to learn from an understanding of legal reasoning than they have to contribute to such an understanding. Since law is a practical social science, in which principles of order and justice accepted by a given society are applied to the reaching of reasoned decisions for action, the legal profession (including legislators, judges, administrators, and legal scholars, as well as practicing lawyers) is highly sensitive to the relationship between theory and practice, and, more specifically, to the relationship between reasoning and the social context in which it takes place. Thus legal experience not only provides a wealth of data for investigation by social scientists but also has much to teach them concerning the nature of social science. Indeed, legal reasoning challenges the belief that any social science can properly avoid the question of its applicability to society; it challenges, therefore, the theory of a "value-free" social science based upon the methods of the physical sciences or of mathematics. Such a challenge is inherent in the emphasis which law places on the connection between what is said and the role of the speaker, as well as in the assumption implicit in law that a judgment affecting persons is not merely an observation or measurement of external facts but also a response to the language addressed to the person making the judgment, and that a proper judgment is itself addressed to the participants in the proceedings in which it is made.

HAROLD J. BERMAN

[See also ADJUDICATION; JUDICIARY; JURISPRUDENCE; LAW; LEGAL SYSTEMS; and the biographies of CARDOZO; COHEN; DURKHEIM; WEBER, MAX.]

BIBLIOGRAPHY

BENTHAM, JEREMY Bentham's Theory of Fictions. Introduction by C. K. Ogden. London: Routledge, 1932. → A selection of Bentham's unpublished writings.

BERMAN, HAROLD J. 1958 The Nature and Functions of Law: An Introduction for Students of the Arts and Sciences. New York: Foundation Press.

EVAN, WILLIAM M. (editor) 1962 Law and Sociology: Exploratory Essays. New York: Free Press.

FULLER, LON L. 1930–1931 Legal Fictions. Northwestern University Law Review 25:363–399, 513–546, 877–910.

FULLER, LON L. 1964 The Morality of Law. New Haven: Yale Univ. Press.

GENY, FRANÇOIS (1889) 1962 Méthode d'interprétation et sources en droit privé positif: Critical Essay. 2d ed. St. Paul, Minn.: West.

HART, HERBERT L. A. (1953) 1954 Definition and Theory in Jurisprudence. Law Quarterly Review 70:37–60.

HART, HERBERT L. A. 1961 The Concept of Law. Oxford: Clarendon.

LEVI, EDWARD H. 1949 An Introduction to Legal Reasoning. Univ. of Chicago Press.

LLEWELLYN, KARL N. 1960 The Common Law Tradition: Deciding Appeals. Boston: Little.

PERELMAN, CHAIM (1962) 1963 The Idea of Justice and the Problem of Argument. New York: Humanities. → First published in Hebrew.

PERELMAN, CHAIM; and OLBRECHTS-TYTECA, L. 1958 Traité de l'argumentation: La nouvelle rhétorique. 2 vols. Paris: Presses Universitaires de France.

ROSENSTOCK-HUESSY, EUGEN 1956–1958 Soziologie. 2 vols. Stuttgart (Germany): Kohlhammer. → Volume 1: Die Übermacht der Räume. Volume 2: Die Vollzahl der Zeiten.

STONE, JULIUS 1964 Legal System and Lawyers' Reasonings. Stanford Univ. Press.

VIEHWEG, THEODOR (1953) 1963 Topik und Jurisprudenz. 2d ed. Munich: Beck.

VON MEHREN, ARTHUR T. 1957 The Civil Law System: Cases and Materials for the Comparative Study of Law. Englewood Cliffs, N.J.: Prentice-Hall.

LEGAL SYSTEMS

I

COMPARATIVE LAW AND LEGAL SYSTEMS

Laws are different in different countries and often within the same country. This fact has given rise to that branch of jurisprudence which is known as comparative law (Rechtsvergleichung; droit comparé).

Precursors

While laws have been different through the ages, sustained scholarly concern about their diversity is hardly one hundred years old. An occasional interest in the diversity of laws has, of course, been shown every now and then, but systematic studies had their origin in the 1860s.

Comparative law could not be developed as a field of learning before the various local laws had come to constitute subject matters of academic learning. On the continent of Europe that was not the case until the high Middle Ages; in England it did not occur until the nineteenth century. But even the development of scholarly pursuits in the several legal systems did not immediately result in their comparative treatment. In fact, the way legal learning developed on the European continent constituted a hindrance to comparative observation.

The legal learning of the Roman Empire was lost in the barbarian invasions. In the course of the Middle Ages the crude customs of the Germanic invaders developed into bodies of law of considerable complexity and refinement, but they developed as customs of local courts of manifold kinds rather than as bodies of law that would be cultivated and elaborated by scholars. In England, the only medieval country where, in consequence of the Conquest, the growth of the law began to be centralized in the courts of the king, the law specialists were craftsmen rather than academic teachers and scholars. Only canon law, the law of the church, was given some attention by the scholars who came to gather in the emerging universities. A change occurred when Roman law was rediscovered and, from the twelfth century on, made the subject matter of academic teaching and writing, first in Bologna and then in the other rapidly growing and increasing universities. By the successive schools of the glossators (twelfth century) and post-glossators (thirteenth and fourteenth centuries), the humanists (sixteenth century), the Dutch and French jurists of the seventeenth and eighteenth centuries, the rationalist school of natural law, and, ultimately, the German Pandectists of the eighteenth and nineteenth centuries, the Roman law was transformed into the so-called civil law, which was taught in all the universities and was elaborated in scholarly treatises and dissertations, but which was not practiced anywhere in the form in which it was taught. The law that was actually applied in the courts was an amalgam of the civil law and local customs and statutes. The civil law of the scholars was thought of as a body of rules and principles of universal validity. The law in action differed from place to place. It was rarely regarded as worthy of the attention of the scholars. The law with which they were concerned was uniform. There was nothing with which to compare it. If views of the law differed, only one of them could be right. The actual laws that could have been compared were too limited in their spheres of application. What little comparative attention was paid to them was limited to a dry enumeration of differing rules. Even the great codifications of private law in Denmark–Norway (1683–1687), Sweden (1734), Prussia (1791–1794), and Austria (1811) evoked little interest on the part of the scholars. In France, on the other hand, Napoleon's codes (1804–1810) established themselves so firmly as the subject matter of professional treatment that the old civil law disappeared from the curriculum. The same concentration on new nationwide unified laws took place in consequence of the later codifications in Germany (1896), Switzerland (1907), Italy (1865–1942), and other countries. The vast task of expounding and elaborating the contents of the new codes absorbed the energies of the scholars. In each country legal science came to be nationalized in the sense of being nationally isolated. Scholars would look beyond the national borders only insofar as the national codification had been modeled upon that of another nation. French legal learning was thus looked to in Italy, the Netherlands, Spain, Latin America, and those other countries in which Napoleon's codes had served as models. German legal learning was influential where the local codes or laws had come under the influence of German scholarly writing, as in Austria, Switzerland, Scandinavia, and Japan.

In both periods, that of the civil law and that of the codes, Continental legal learning was primarily interested in "dogmatics." Starting with an authoritative text—in the civil-law epoch that of the corpus juris and in the later period that of the respective national code—the scholars busied themselves with the "interpretation" of these texts. The law laid down in the texts was regarded as being complete, that is, as providing the answer to every problem that would ever arise, provided one would only read and understand the text in the right way. Legal science was the science of properly interpreting the texts, just as theology consisted in the interpretation of the Scriptures. Under such an approach there was as little room for, and interest in, comparison of laws as there was in the comparison of religions.

In England the situation was similar but for different reasons. The centralized, well-organized, and politically powerful English bar had succeeded in resisting the onslaught of the Roman law. In the royal courts at Westminster, the various local customs were welded into the common law of England. The elaborators of the law were the practitioners, especially the judges. They were craftsmen, not academicians. English law was hardly taught in the universities; one learned it in apprentice fashion, by doing. To learn the practice of some outlandish law, say, of Scotland, was for the English lawyer of as little interest as it would have been for a shoemaker to learn carpentry.

Lawyers are not the only people interested in law. The law also attracts the interest of theologians, philosophers, and those who in English-speaking countries have come to be called jurists, that is, scholars who know the law and yet are interested in it not from the strictly professional point of view but from that of one who looks upon the law, so to speak, from the outside. The jurist is the man who is interested in the law's growth in history, in the values which it protects and promotes, in the machinery through which it functions, in the structure of its body, and in its role and functions in society. It was among philosophers and jurists that interest in comparative law was first exhibited. It is among sociologists, anthropologists, and political scientists that such interest is presently growing; but attitudes are changing also among the lawyers, especially the legal scholars. They have begun to develop a new jurisprudence within which comparative law is coming to play a constantly increasing role.

Among the precursors of modern comparative law students one might mention Aristotle, who engaged in the comparison of the constitutions of the Greek city-states. In the Middle Ages some canonist, legist, or theologian every now and then engaged in comparative observation of secular law and canon law. In later times the peculiar features of the law merchant attracted some attention.

Suddenly there appeared Montesquieu, almost without predecessor—and also to be without immediate successors. In *The Spirit of the Laws* (1748), the law is treated as a social phenomenon and the diversity of the laws is seen as being caused by diversities of the natural, historical, ethnical, political, and other factors of the social setting. In the early part of the nineteenth century, Montesquieu's ideas reappeared in the thinking of Hugo, Savigny, Eichhorn, and the other writers of the German historical school. In reaction to the natural-law jurists' belief in the possibility and desirability of a system of law that could be developed by reason and would be valid universally, they again emphasized the dependency of the laws upon the surrounding conditions, especially the peculiar spirit of each nation (the *Volksgeist*). Divided into the two hostile camps of Romanists and Germanists, the men of the historical school endeavored to replace the amalgam of Roman and Germanic traditions that characterized the *usus modernus pandectarum* by new systems of revitalized Roman or Germanic law. Comparisons between these two systems were, of course, incidental to the heated debates, and some attention had to be paid to the law of France, in which Germanic traditions had survived to a larger extent than in Germany, and to the laws of England and Scandinavia, where no wholesale reception of Roman law had taken place. Institutions of English public law had attracted attention ever since their praises had been sung by Montesquieu, and they were widely imitated on the Continent in the course of the revolutionary movements that were sparked by the events of 1789.

Montesquieu's insight into the interdependency of the law and other social factors was applied again by Sir Henry Maine, who was struck by similarities between the laws of ancient Rome and of India and by parallels in their development. Influenced by the Darwinist thought of his time, he ventured in his *Ancient Law* (1861) to formulate his famous "law" of universal sociolegal development from status to contract.

Modern comparative law

The interest of lawyers rather than jurists in the field of modern comparative law began with the foundation of the Société de Législation Comparée in 1869, the establishment of the Comité de Législation Comparée in the French Ministry of Justice in 1876, and the founding of the English Society of Comparative Legislation in 1898. The movement had its origin in practical considerations. It was believed that the ideas and experiences of foreign countries, especially new foreign legislation, should be made available for one's own national law making, which in the spirit of the time was identified with legislation. Translation and discussion of new foreign codes and laws thus constituted the principal field of activity of the small circle of interested specialists.

Comparative law rather than comparative legislation came to appeal to a widening circle of scholars in connection with the late nineteenth century's optimistic belief in the desirability and possibility of large-scale international unification of private law. Along with public and private international law, comparative law thus figured among the topics discussed at the annual meetings of the Institut de Droit International. The ideal of international legal unification also was the inspiring motive of the great international Congress of Comparative Law, held in Paris in 1900. With its large assembly of scholars from all over the world, the congress lived in the memories of the participants as the high point of what is nostalgically called *la belle époque du droit comparé*. From then on the work in the field grew more realistic. The development is reflected in the life work of Édouard Lambert, whose institute of comparative law at the University of Lyon (founded in 1920) constituted for some decades the center of painstaking, detailed research.

Practical interest in knowledge of law for purposes of legislation, international unification, and everyday law practice in international transactions, commercial and otherwise, continued to stimulate steadily increasing interest in the study of foreign laws. There also grew up new theoretical interest. The desire to discover the beginnings of the development of law as a general social phenomenon —a development which was widely regarded as having proceeded more or less unilineally—drew attention beyond Roman, Greek, or Germanic law to laws of more archaic character, as well as to the customs of primitive peoples. This new interest in "ethnological jurisprudence" and related matters was given a focus in the *Zeitschrift für vergleichende Rechtswissenschaft* (begun in 1878).

The more comparative law assumed the character of a social science, that is, a pursuit of systematic knowledge about law as a social phenomenon the study of which would have to reach beyond national boundaries, the more the workers in the field became aware of its difficulties. Where could one find a library containing all the necessary materials? What human mind could retain and organize them? A decisive step was taken in 1917 with the establishment of Ernst Rabel's institute of comparative law at the University of Munich and, nine years later in Berlin, the Kaiser Wilhelm (now Max Planck) institutes for foreign and international private law (now in Hamburg) and also for foreign and international public law (now in Heidelberg). At these institutes a comprehensive library was established, and there was assembled a team of specialists, who under Rabel's direction would advise drafters of new legislation and participants in international legal life and who would systematically observe legal developments the world over in order to gain theoretical insights and develop new methods of legal thinking and research. The impact of the innovation has been far-reaching. The establishment of the comparative law institutes coincided with and strengthened the change in method of German legal thought from conceptual–analytical jurisprudence to the new method of jurisprudence of interests with its emphasis upon knowledge of the facts of social life and of socially current evaluations of conflicting interests. Under such a method, limitation of scholarly concern to the phenomena of one's own nation is no longer possible.

The simultaneous shift in legal method that occurred in the United States was a principal cause of the rapid growth of American interest in comparative law or, as it is now frequently called, international legal studies. The growing involvement of the United States in world affairs, political and commercial, was another powerful motive.

Scholars like Roscoe Pound, John H. Wigmore, Ernst Freund, and H. W. Millar had been working since the turn of the century at breaking through "Mainstreetism" toward world-mindedness in legal learning. Their breadth of learning is reflected in the scope of their own work as well as in the Legal Philosophy Series, the Continental Legal History Series, and the Modern Criminal Science Series, which they promoted and edited. Effectively supported by the Ford Foundation, international legal studies have, since World War II, come to consti-

tute an essential part in the curriculum and the research programs of American university law schools. Cooperation with sociologists, economists, political scientists, anthropologists, and historians is being sought by the law scholars. What is still lacking in the United States is a great research institute on the pattern of the German Max Planck institutes.

In the United Kingdom, the study of comparative law was pioneered by Harold C. Gutteridge. It is now finding its place in the universities, where academic teaching of the law has come at a rapidly increasing pace to supplement, or to take the place of, the old-fashioned apprenticeship training. A center for research is provided at the Institute of Advanced Legal Studies in London, established in 1948.

In France, courses on the great legal systems of the world are offered at the university law schools; research is promoted through institutes, especially in Paris, Lyon, and Toulouse. In Italy, interest in comparative law is vigorously cultivated at a number of universities. Institutes and university faculties in Spain, Latin America, Scandinavia, Japan, Yugoslavia, and other countries are also active. In the Soviet Union, foreign legal developments are closely observed in the law institute of the Academy of Sciences.

Comparative law, being supranational, calls for international cooperation. An organizational instrument for cooperation is provided by the International Association of Legal Science, which is affiliated with UNESCO, and through its directorate, the International Committee of Comparative Law. International meetings of comparatists are sponsored by the International Academy of Comparative Law. Instruction is offered by the International Faculty for the Teaching of Comparative Law, which has its seat in Strasbourg, and the International University of Comparative Sciences in Luxembourg.

Methods and scope

In comparative legal research one may distinguish between micro-comparison and macro-comparison. The latter is concerned with the comparison of entire legal systems, such as the Anglo–American common law and the so-called civil law, or, within the civil law, the family of the so-called Romanist laws, that is, those based on the French and German patterns. Micro-comparison is concerned with detailed legal rules and institutions. The two approaches, of course, shade into each other, especially in the comparison of methods of procedure and of legal thought.

Micro-comparison.   In the earlier phase of the study of comparative law one tended to start out from particular institutions. One would, for instance, compare contract in Anglo–American and in civil law, or possessions in French and in German law, or the common-law doctrine of consideration and the civil-law concept of *causa*. In such a process one made two important discoveries: first, that seemingly identical terms rarely have the same meaning in different legal systems; second, that the same, or seemingly same, institution might perform different functions in different surroundings. The meaning of the Anglo–American term "contract," for instance, was found to differ in several respects from the term "contractus" of Romanist terminology and its modern counterparts. The institution of damages for tort was found to have a strictly compensatory function in German law, but both a compensatory and a punitive function in the common law. Thus, comparatists have increasingly come to incline toward the functional approach. Instead of starting with any particular rule or institution, one starts with a social problem and seeks to discover the rules or institutions by means of which the problem is resolved. What devices are, for instance, employed in different laws to provide for the orderly payment of the debts of a dead person, or to provide relief for the victims of unfair or sharp practices in business deals, or to provide for the security of title of purchasers of real estate? Such investigations are likely to indicate that, on the one hand, devices of considerable variety have been and can be used to achieve more or less identical purposes but, on the other hand, that the catalogue of technical devices available to legal designers is not unlimited.

Macro-comparison.   Macro-comparison of entire legal systems has sought, in the rare case of Max Weber or in such modern surveys as that of René David, to cover the world. Mostly, however, it has been concerned with the two great systems of Western civilization, the Anglo–American common law and the civil law.

Common law versus civil law.   Close inspection has shown that the characteristic differences between common law and civil law ought not to be expressed in the frequently used antitheses of codified versus uncodified law, or of statute law versus judge-made law, and even less in that between authoritarian versus libertarian law. Large sections of the law of civil-law countries, for example, the bulk of French or German administrative law, are neither codified nor even expressed in statutes, while big portions of English and American law have been brought together in comprehensive statutory codifications, as, for instance, the maritime and commercial laws of the United Kingdom or, in the United States, the uniform commercial code and the U.S. code of internal revenue. There exist, it is true, differences in the judicial attitudes toward such codifications, but they have their basis in that difference between the two great systems which is essential, namely, the difference between methods of legal thought.

The role of judicial precedent also differs less in the two systems than it was commonly believed to do. In theory, a common-law judge is bound by precedent, while a civil-law judge is not only free to ignore it but is supposed to take a fresh look at every individual case. In fact, judges in France or Germany pay such careful attention to precedent that entire sections of the law are judge-made, such as the French law of torts or that large body of German law which determines in great detail the commands of good faith and fairness which contracting parties are to observe toward each other. The older the code—the French civil code is 160 years old, the German civil code is about 70—the greater is the weight of the judicial gloss by which the text is overlaid. Common-law judges, on their side, are as well versed as their Continental brethren in the fine art of distinguishing upon the facts a new case from an unconformable precedent. Besides, in contrast to British courts, American courts no longer shy away from openly overruling a precedent that is regarded as no longer suitable.

As to the alleged contrast between civil-law authoritarianism and common-law espousal of liberty, it suffices to indicate that Switzerland is a civil-law country and Ghana is a common-law one, as was England in the days of Cromwell. And finally, it is a myth, though apparently an ineradicable one, that in civil-law criminal procedure the accused has to prove his innocence.

The essential difference between common law and civil law lies in the technical structure of court procedure, in the different conceptual framework within which legal thought moves, and in the underlying cause of these differences: the diversity of the personnel by which the machinery of the administration of justice is handled and guided.

Perhaps the most far-reaching discovery that has been made in comparative law research is Max Weber's observation that the climate of a society's legal system is ultimately determined by the kind of people by whom it is dominated, that is, as Weber calls them, the *honoratiores* of the law (1922). It makes a difference whether a legal system is dominated, as that of classical Rome, by gentlemen of leisure and high-ranking administrators, or, as the Islamic, by theologians, or, as the classical Chinese, by philosopher-bureaucrats. The common law grew up as the law of one set of centralized courts that was staffed with a small elite judiciary; this judiciary, in turn, was linked to that closely knit centralized bar from which it was drawn. The resulting common law reflects these surroundings: the mode of reasoning is that of analogy—policies are not always followed with consistency, nor are concepts always clean-cut; the law is thought of less as a body of norms of social conduct than as a set of rules of decision for the relatively few disputes that cannot be settled extrajudicially. Occasional obsolescence is not necessarily regarded as a serious evil, but, in general, those ex-barristers who occupy the bench are close to the course of affairs and know how to decide a concrete case that is presented to the court in oral contradictory trial by the members of a highly experienced bar.

What was decisive on the Continent was the absence of one central court. If the law was to keep abreast of changing conditions and to preserve a minimum of uniformity, guidance had to be exercised by the university law faculties, whose members for centuries constituted a supralocal community. Interpreting the book that was thought to constitute the theoretical basis of *the* law, they tended toward systematic arrangement, the elaboration of great principles, the logic of the syllogism, consistency of terminology, and an occasional remoteness from life. Efforts to adapt the law to changing social conditions were apt to be hidden behind controversies as to what should be the right interpretation of the authoritative text. Law being thought of as a set of rules of human conduct, it tended toward paternalistic guidance by those who would know best—the professors and the high-ranking officers in the service of the princes.

Today the scene has changed. On the Continent the establishment of central national courts has given great power to the judiciary, with a corresponding decline of the once leading role of learned doctrine. In the United States, on the other hand, the influence of the professors of the national law schools has come to be powerful in those branches of the law for which no uniform case law is created by a court of nationwide jurisdiction, that is, for all law other than that of the constitution of the United States and the body of federal statute law. With the breakdown of the centralized appellate jurisdiction of the Judicial Committee of the Privy Council, a similar develop-

ment has occurred in Britain. Legal education is being taken over by the universities, and their professors are becoming guides for the judges of the courts of England and the Commonwealth countries. These courts are now as independent of each other as the state supreme courts in the United States are and as the courts of the small jurisdictional units of the Continent once were. Subtle changes in the character of the law, substantive and procedural, are the consequence of these developments in both systems.

Socialist law. In macro-comparison of legal systems, much attention has recently been paid to the laws of the socialist countries, especially the Soviet Union. Western observers have raised the question of whether these laws constitute a legal system of their own or whether they should be regarded as a branch of the civil-law system. The answer depends upon what test one applies. If one looks to the content of the legal rules and the machinery by which they are administered, one will agree with the Soviet jurists that their laws constitute a system of their own, even if one regards the difference between socialist law and "bourgeois law" as less enormous than it is made to appear in Soviet theory. After all, the welfare-state idea has taken hold in Western countries. If, on the other hand, one looks to the conceptual framework of the law, especially as it appears in the codes, or if one is interested in the basic features of court organization and procedure, a lawyer trained in French, German, or Swiss law will find his way more easily than one trained in the common law. If one looks to the personnel of the administration of justice, he will observe attitudes considerably different from those of Western judges and lawyers, but he can also observe among his Eastern brethren a steadily growing tendency to look upon themselves as guardians of individual rights against arbitrariness.

The tasks of comparative law

The careful analysis of legal systems that is now being elaborated has resulted in a distrust of timeworn clichés. Even the distinction between common law and civil law must, we have learned, not be overestimated. It is a difference more in method and traditions than in content. Also, it applies more to private than to public law. The forms of democratic government and the legal devices to secure the citizen's participation in government and his protection against abuses of governmental power, democratic or authoritarian, are independent of the historical background of legal development.

Comparative law impressively demonstrates the unity of Western civilization, which has spread over the world and is transforming the once different civilizations of the East. Western laws have come to be the laws of Asia and Africa. They are influencing even family law, in which non-European traditions have held out longest. Except for disappearing traditions of family law and matters related thereto, there is now in the world not a single country whose law would not belong to one of the three systems of Western origin: civil law, common law, socialist law.

In both micro-comparison and macro-comparison, the comparatist has to do more than merely ascertain differences and similarities of legal norms and institutions. If he wishes to learn about the reasons he must investigate the social conditions under which the norms and institutions of the law have originated, under which they operate, and which they influence. The legal comparatist must become a social scientist. The difficulties of the task, which are already formidable in a strictly formal comparison, are multiplied. No wonder that performance has been lagging. However, beginnings have been made in micro-comparative as well as in macro-comparative studies, especially of subjects of private law and procedure.

The great creators of law have always been observers of social reality. The classical Roman jurists who patiently elaborated the legal norms which are necessary for the smooth functioning of an economic order of free enterprise were consistently engaged in what we today call social research. Medieval canonists sound like modern sociologists when they observe that papal efforts to suppress blood feuds by means of law had to fail because such means conflicted with the mores of the people. The ever-recurrent tendency of lawyers to regard law as a self-sufficient body of rules was carried *ad absurdum* by Montesquieu, Savigny, and such more recent legal scholars as Rudolf von Jhering, Henry Maine, Frederic W. Maitland, Otto von Gierke, and François Gény.

In the new jurisprudence of the mid-twentieth century, as it has been developed simultaneously in the United States (Roscoe Pound, John H. Wigmore, Karl Llewellyn), in Germany and Austria (Eugen Ehrlich, Max von Rümelin, Philipp von Heck), and in Scandinavia (Anders Vilhelm Lundstedt), and which is now tending to become as universal as the jurisprudence of concepts was in the latter part of the nineteenth century, the science of law has become a social science.

MAX RHEINSTEIN

[*See also* JURISPRUDENCE; LAW; PUBLIC LAW; *and the biographies of* EHRLICH; GIERKE; LLEWELLYN; MAINE; MAITLAND; MONTESQUIEU; POUND; SAVIGNY.]

BIBLIOGRAPHY

A concise but comprehensive discussion of comparative law, its background, and its problems is Gutteridge 1946. For a bibliography of books and articles published in English see Szladits 1955–1962 and annual supplements; for non-English periodical literature, see the Index to Foreign Legal Periodicals.

AMERICAN JOURNAL OF COMPARATIVE LAW 1961 *XXth Century Comparative and Conflicts Law: Legal Essays in Honor of Hessel E. Yntema.* Leiden (Netherlands): Sythoff.

American Journal of Comparative Law. → Published since 1952.

DAVID, RENÉ 1964 *Les grands systèmes de droit contemporains: Droit comparé.* Paris: Dalloz.

GUTTERIDGE, HAROLD C. (1946) 1949 *Comparative Law: An Introduction to the Comparative Method of Legal Study and Research.* 2d ed. Cambridge Univ. Press.

Index to Foreign Legal Periodicals. → Published since 1960.

INTERNATIONAL ASSOCIATION OF LEGAL SCIENCE, INTERNATIONAL COMMITTEE OF COMPARATIVE LAW, *Bulletin d'information.* → Published since 1955.

International and Comparative Law Quarterly. → Published since 1952.

Introduction à l'étude du droit comparé: Recueil d'études en l'honneur d'Edouard Lambert. 3 vols. 1938 Paris: Société Anonyme du Recueil Sirey.

MAINE, HENRY J. S. (1861) 1960 *Ancient Law: Its Connection With the Early History of Society, and Its Relations to Modern Ideas.* Rev. ed. New York: Dutton; London and Toronto: Dent. → A paperback edition was published in 1963 by Beacon.

MONTESQUIEU (1748) 1962 *The Spirit of the Laws.* 2 vols. New York: Hafner. → First published in French.

Rabels Zeitschrift für ausländisches und internationales Privatrecht. → Published since 1927.

Revue internationale de droit comparé. → Published since 1949.

SCHLEGELBERGER, FRANZ (editor) 1927–1939 *Rechtsvergleichendes Handwörterbuch für das Zivil- und Handelsrecht des In- und Auslandes.* 7 vols. Berlin: Vahlen.

SCHNITZER, ADOLF F. (1945) 1961 *Vergleichende Rechtslehre.* 2 vols., 2d ed., rev. & enl. Basel: Verlag für Recht und Gesellschaft.

SZLADITS, CHARLES 1955–1962 *A Bibliography on Foreign and Comparative Law: Books and Articles in English.* Published for the Parker School of Foreign and Comparative Law, Columbia University. 2 vols. Dobbs Ferry, N.Y.: Oceana. → Volume 1 contains a bibliography up to 1953, published in 1955; Volume 2, from 1953 to 1959, published in 1962. Supplemented annually.

WEBER, MAX (1922) 1954 *Max Weber on Law in Economy and Society.* Edited, with an introduction and annotations by Max Rheinstein. Cambridge, Mass.: Harvard Univ. Press. → First published as Chapter 7 of Max Weber's *Wirtschaft und Gesellschaft.*

Zeitschrift für ausländisches öffentliches Recht und Völkerrecht. → Published since 1929.

Zeitschrift für vergleichende Rechtswissenschaft. → Published since 1878.

II
COMMON LAW SYSTEMS

The term "common law" is used in a number of different senses. In medieval English law it denoted that law which was administered by the king's courts and which was, in principle at least, common to the whole realm. The common law, in this sense, was to be distinguished from the law administered in the local, county courts or in the feudal, barons' courts, which tended to be specialized or particularized by region; and it was also to be distinguished from autonomous bodies of law, like the law merchant, which were peculiar to certain classes of persons.

In another sense, however, the common law is set in opposition to statute law. The common law is rendered concrete and explicit in, and derives its juridical efficacy from, decisions of courts; whereas statute law, or legislation, is an emanation of the will of the sovereign parliament or legislature. In this same specific sense, the common law is also distinguished from codified law or code law (civil law). The common law is conceived of as a body of principles originally derived from customs which are either reflected in the judgments of the highest national courts or else contained in piecemeal statutes passed *ad hoc* to correct or extend those same decisions. Thus it is opposed to those systems of law which have been reduced to more or less permanent written form and organization through a single comprehensive piece of legislation or codification.

Insofar as the English-speaking countries have generally been able to resist comprehensive codification of their laws, we are led into the broadest and most popular meaning of the term common law—the law of the English-speaking countries as opposed to the (generally codified) civil law of continental Europe and of those countries in Latin America, Asia, and Africa that were politically influenced by, and whose legal systems were shaped by, continental Europe.

In yet another sense, the common law is opposed to equity—that body of law, distinct from the common law, which was administered by the lord chancellor, as "keeper of the king's conscience," through the chancery courts, in order to correct or ameliorate the harshness or rigidities of the common law as administered by the regular courts. Equity started as a series of principles and rules, reflecting considerations of fairness and natural justice, which were, in medieval times, of such flexibility and range as to warrant the latter-day charge that equity was "as long as the chancellor's foot." By the early nineteenth century, however, it had jelled into a fairly rigid system of precedents and judicial authorities distinguishable from the common law mainly in that it was administered by a separate judicial hierarchy, the chancery courts. The Judicature Acts of 1873–1875, which effected a wholesale organization of the English judicial structure, abolished the special chancery courts, and equity was formally fused with the common law into a single system of precedents administered by one system of courts.

Last, the term common law is sometimes used to denote the private law, i.e., that body of law governing relationships of private citizens *inter se* in which the public or state interests are normally minimal or else only peripheral (for example, the law of contracts, torts, personal property), in contradistinction to constitutional law and public law generally (for example, administrative law, labor law, antitrust law) in which the public interests are normally pervasive. This distinction is ceasing to be really meaningful in modern terms, as the state increasingly intrudes into areas of law originally considered as involving personal interests only.

Diffusion of the common law. It is true of the common law that English settlers proceeding overseas to found new colonies carry with them the law of England existing at the time of the first settlement, except insofar as that law may be obviously inapplicable to the new area. For example, the old common law rule of "ancient lights" might be considered inappropriate or unnecessary in newly settled areas without any tall buildings and therefore inapplicable and not automatically "received" as law on settlement. Through this device, whereby new content and meaning were poured into old formulas, the common law became the basic law of the United States and of those Commonwealth countries founded by settlement. In the case of those parts of the British colonial empire acquired by military conquest and already having a local population (indigenous people or non-British settlers), different principles were applied, usually involving the maintenance of the local private law, as, for example, in the case of India, South Africa, and the Province of Quebec.

Once the English common law was "received" into an overseas colony, it continued in force until such time as it was repealed, altered, modified, or added to by appropriate constitutional authority—whether by the British Parliament as the supreme imperial legislative authority, or by the Privy Council sitting in Westminster as the final appellate tribunal for the overseas empire, or by the colonial legislature and colonial courts acting within their respective jurisdictional limits and competence and subject to appropriate control by imperial constitutional agencies. These imperial controls disappeared, in the case of the American colonies, with the Declaration of Independence; and they virtually disappeared in the case of the self-governing Commonwealth countries with developing constitutional custom and convention. This was partly confirmed and recognized in statutory form with the Statute of Westminster (1931), a British statute, although some members of the Commonwealth (Australia and New Zealand, for example) still retain, by their choice, an appeal from their courts to the Privy Council. Insofar as the common law remains the basic private law of the various English-speaking countries today, it is by those countries' own decisions to maintain and even extend their historical legal inheritance. For these purposes it becomes necessary to consider the juridical institutions and techniques whereby the common law is applied and developed in these countries.

Institutions and techniques. The key element in the continued viability of the common law today is undoubtedly the existence of the *doctrine of precedent*. This doctrine establishes, first, the obligation of court jurisdictions to adhere to and apply the decisions of tribunals that are superior to them in the judicial hierarchy; and, second, the principle that the highest court in the land is bound by its own decisions. The first aspect seems obvious enough, since it is a natural consequence of the pyramidal structure of court organization in England and has the practical utility of ensuring uniformity and predictability of decisions by inferior and intermediate tribunals. The second aspect— the principle of *stare decisis* in the strict sense— although often regarded as a truism of common law jurisprudence, was actually formulated as a binding principle of the English common law only in 1898, in the London Tramways case decision. Since that time, however, it has been one of the major preoccupations of common law legal theory.

Quite apart from the issue of whether courts ought to be bound by past decisions, the "legal realist" school, which was very influential in American law schools in the period between the two world wars, raised the issue of whether courts, as a matter of *fact*, did bind themselves by past decisions. Led by such brilliant young scholars as Judge Jerome Frank and Karl Llewellyn in the early 1930s, the legal realists pointed to the substantial devices or stratagems available to courts to mitigate the effects of unwanted judicial decisions from earlier eras. Among these devices the legal realists identified the practice of "distinguishing" prior cases: focusing on assertedly new or different fact situations in the case before the court, in contrast to the fact present in those earlier cases that established the now unwanted principles of law. The legal realists also pointed to the widespread judicial inclination toward "shading" of earlier decisions, that is, giving some more weight than others by categorizing them as the decisions of "strong courts" or by focusing on individual judicial opinions, separate and distinct from the official opinion of the court, in cases in which more than one judicial opinion is filed. These individual opinions could be special concurring opinions or even dissenting opinions in the case of "prestige" jurists like Oliver Wendell Holmes of the United States Supreme Court. Opinions of the intellectual caliber and clarity of Holmes's great dissent in the Lochner case in 1905 became appeals to the future and were later expressly vindicated by United States Supreme Court majorities, as in *West Coast Hotel Company* v. *Parrish Company* (300 U.S. 379) in 1937.

It must be admitted that "distinguishing" prior decisions is immensely facilitated by the proliferation of individual opinion writing on final appellate tribunals in the common law world. Only the Privy Council, among these courts, still resolutely adheres to its practice of filing only a single *per curiam* opinion in each case.

The "distinguishing" of cases is also assisted by the plethora of separate common law jurisdictions of the present day, each turning out its own decisions. Consider the problem in the federal states of the English-speaking world. In the United States there are 50 autonomous private law jurisdictions; each is theoretically independent and separate from the other, and the supreme court of each state is the final appellate tribunal for cases arising there (except insofar as those cases also raise issues involving federal jurisdiction). Although the decisions of any one state supreme court are not, of course, binding on any other state, they may have a certain persuasive authority, and it is frequently possible to find lines of opposing decisions from different state supreme courts, thus opening up the way for a creative judicial choice—judicial policy making. Notwithstanding the 50 separate, and at times competing, state private law jurisdictions there are countervailing forces that point toward the unity of the common law in the United States. There is, first, the *Restatement of the Law* prepared by the American Law Institute (1953–1965). Although not "official," it brought together the best experts available (law professors, judges, and lawyers) and soon achieved a quasi-official status. The *Restatement* tried to present the consensus of private law among the then 48 states and thus performed an important unifying function among the 48 jurisdictions. It still enjoys high respect in most state courts. Another important unifying factor is the existence of great "national" law schools (Yale, Harvard, Columbia, Chicago, etc.), which consciously avoid stressing the law of their own particular state and can thereby teach a genuinely "national" common law that can draw on the best principles of the jurisprudence of the 50 separate state systems.

Emphasis upon the "distinguishing" of cases on the facts directs attention to the crucial role of facts in contemporary common law decision making. It is not merely that the orthodox view of the principle of a case (or *ratio decidendi*) is the rule enunciated by the judge plus the material facts in the case (Goodhart 1931). It is also that, under the influence of legal realist teachings, courts, in accepting the desirability and inevitability of judicial policy making (or judicial legislation) at the final appellate level, have increasingly accepted the desirability of having an adequate factual record in aid of such judicial legislation. This new emphasis has perhaps received its fullest outlet in American jurisprudence in the so-called "Brandeis Brief" method of adducing constitutional facts to the notice of the United States Supreme Court; but it has also had its effects in the private law.

It is in American constitutional law, of course, that the direct and avowed departure from the principle of *stare decisis* has been most marked, prompting Judge Owen Roberts to comment ruefully, on the overruling of earlier United States Supreme Court decisions, that this trend to court flexibility tended to "bring adjudications of this tribunal into the same class as a restricted railroad ticket, good for this day and train only" (*Smith* v. *Allwright*, 321 U.S. 649, 1944).

The common law and social change. The contemporary judicial disposition to depart from *stare decisis*—either by directly overruling past decisions or by "distinguishing" cases—emphasizes movement and growth in the positive law as the society in respect to which the positive law is to operate itself changes.

The American school of sociological jurisprudence, led by Roscoe Pound, was strongly influenced by the pragmatist teachings of William James and John Dewey. Sociological jurisprudence preached the necessary and proximate relationship, or symbiosis, between law and society—that is to say, the notion that the criteria for evaluating and appraising the positive law at any time must include (1) the extent to which that positive law in fact reflects the complex of interests pressed in society at that time, and (2) the extent to which the positive law has changed in measure with that society. The values to which a sophisticated legal system must give effect include both the interest in a reasonable stability of settled legal expectations and the interest in mobility and change in law, lest the positive law, if too unimaginatively and rigidly applied, should act as a brake on future social development.

The legal realists charged that in attempting to balance these two opposing principles the common law systems, certainly until the 1930s, overemphasized the interest in stability and predictability of legal relationships and forgot the maxim that "the life of the law has not been logic, but experience" (see, for example, the writings of Karl Llewellyn and Jerome Frank). The theories of most legal realists emphasized the law-making role of appellate judges. The recent emphasis on the more dynamic elements in law (see the work of Myres McDougal, Harold Lasswell, and others) represents, in addition, a return to an earlier common law philosophy, a philosophy which had, after all, so successfully transformed the common law from crude and unrefined custom, in the closed medieval society, into an instrument of social control amply suited to the resolution of conflicts and tensions in modern complex industrial civilization.

EDWARD McWHINNEY

[See also JURISPRUDENCE; LAW. *Directly related are the biographies of* BLACKSTONE; BRANDEIS; CARDOZO; COKE; FRANK; HOLMES; LLEWELLYN; POUND.]

BIBLIOGRAPHY

AMERICAN LAW INSTITUTE 1953–1965 *Restatement of the Law Second: Conflict of Laws.* Tentative Draft Nos. 1–13. Philadelphia: The Institute.

CARDOZO, BENJAMIN N. (1921) 1960 *The Nature of the Judicial Process.* New Haven: Yale Univ. Press.

DICEY, ALBERT V. (1885) 1959 *Introduction to the Study of the Law of the Constitution.* 10th ed. New York: St. Martins.

FRANK, JEROME (1930) 1949 *Law and the Modern Mind.* New York: Coward.

FRANK, JEROME 1949 *Courts On Trial.* Princeton Univ. Press. → A paperback edition was published in 1963 by Atheneum.

GOODHART, ARTHUR L. 1931 *Essays in Jurisprudence and the Common Law.* Cambridge Univ. Press.

HOLMES, OLIVER WENDELL (1881) 1963 *The Common Law.* Cambridge, Mass.: Harvard Univ. Press.

LLEWELLYN, KARL 1931 Some Realism About Realism: Responding to Dean Pound. *Harvard Law Review* 44: 1222–1264.

McDougal, Myres S.; Lasswell, Harold D.; and Vlasic, Ivan A. 1963 *Law and Public Order in Space.* New Haven: Yale Univ. Press.

Maitland, Frederic W. 1908 *The Constitutional History of England.* Cambridge Univ. Press.

Maitland, Frederic W. (1909a) 1936 *Equity.* Cambridge Univ. Press.

Maitland, Frederic W. (1909b) 1936 *The Forms of Action at Common Law.* Cambridge Univ. Press.

Plucknett, Theodore F. T. (1929) 1956 *A Concise History of the Common Law.* 5th ed., enl. & entirely rewritten. London: Butterworth.

Pound, Roscoe (1922) 1954 *An Introduction to the Philosophy of Law.* Rev. ed. New Haven: Yale Univ. Press.

Stone, Julius (1946) 1950 *The Province and Function of Law: Law as Logic, Justice, and Social Control; a Study in Jurisprudence.* Cambridge, Mass.: Harvard Univ. Press.

III
CODE LAW SYSTEMS

The term "code-law systems" is usually employed, as a legal term of art, with two different, if related, meanings. First, "code" refers to the reduction of the laws customarily observed by a particular people to a more or less permanent, organized, and written form through a comprehensive piece of legislation or *codification*. Strictly speaking, a "code" may denote a constitution or similar public-law enactment of fundamental laws; but more usually the term is limited to compilations of the private law (contracts, torts, property, agency, marriage, matrimonial property, and related matters), although many countries also have codifications of their criminal law, criminal procedure, civil procedure, and commercial law. It is in the general sense of there being a collection in a single, comprehensive statute of particular national laws on one or more main subjects that the code-law systems are normally opposed to uncodified, or common-law, systems. In the latter systems, in general, the private law at least remains an uncodified body of what were originally custom-derived rules or principles that purport to be reflected in the judgments of the highest national courts and in piecemeal statutes that may be passed *ad hoc* to correct or extend those judicial decisions.

In a second and more popular sense, the term "code-law systems" denotes the body of continental European civil law, which, as represented principally in the two major acts of codification of modern times, the French civil code (or Code Napoléon) of 1804 and the German civil code (Bürgerliches Gesetzbuch, or B.G.B.) of 1900, has spread throughout the world. The German civil

code of 1900 had a decisive influence on the drafting and adoption of the present Japanese civil code and on the precommunist Chinese code. The Code Napoléon has been widely copied or borrowed from in the codifications of the Middle East, former French Africa, and Latin America generally.

It is in this particular sense of referring to the substantive civil-law content of the two great western European acts of codification that the term "code-law systems" is normally distinguished from the common law of the English-speaking countries. The common law of England was carried by process of conquest, occupation, or settlement, to the original American states and to the British colonies overseas. With some modifications based on deference to existing local, customary law, in the case of certain countries having an indigenous, predominantly non-English or non-European population, the common law has remained in these countries even after British political power has formally and practically disappeared. Thus the common law is today the basic private law of Great Britain, the Commonwealth countries, and the United States. The term "common law" applies both where the common law has itself been codified—as is the case in most of the English-speaking countries in regard to commercial law and criminal law—and even where the law was originally Romanist (as in South Africa and Ceylon) and, while still formally uncodified, was transformed by successive decisions of the Privy Council in London into a semblance of the common law, case law system of precedents. An act of codification is always something of a revolutionary step in the sense that it represents a certain intellectual break with the past. Although all the codes purport to be merely a restatement of the old, pre-existing law, most of the great codifying commissions have used the opportunity to make innovations and changes in the old law; and the act of codification itself, in the sense that it involves reducing a large and hitherto unorganized mass of materials to comprehensive form, necessarily involves a certain clarification and streamlining of the existing law.

The great codifying projects have usually coincided with eras of great political or social change or upheaval, probably because in such periods it may be easier to obtain that minimum degree of consensus among the decision-making elite necessary to force such projects through to completion. It may be only in such periods that the conflicting pressures for stability and change can be satisfactorily reconciled to the point of reducing the laws to a single, comprehensive enactment. The French civil code was adopted in the wake of years of revolutionary turmoil in France and was one of the first projects of the Emperor Napoleon, who personally guided it through to completion, to the point of sometimes presiding himself at the sessions of the codifying commission. In Germany the codification movement only really got under way and received official blessing after the achievement of German political union, in federal form, in 1871; and codification was then looked upon as an instrument for assisting and furthering the spirit of national unity.

In the case of Quebec, the civil code of 1866 was adopted at the time of the pending political incorporation of French-speaking Roman Catholic Lower Canada into a Canadian confederation in which French Canadians would be heavily outnumbered by English-speaking Protestants: the codification of French Canada's civil law was viewed as a defensive measure to protect the distinctive social values and institutions of Quebec (for example, the family law, with its emphasis on the family unit with paternal control, the absence of any divorce, and the institution of the joint matrimonial property system) against the encroachment, after confederation, of an alien common law that was viewed as incorporating Anglo-Saxon Protestant values.

The modern Japanese and Chinese civil codes, with their large German civil law influences and derivations, were adopted as part of a deliberate policy of modernization or "Westernization" of basic social institutions, with a view to speeding large-scale industrialization and development.

The Soviet Russian civil code of 1922 was adopted at a time when governmental pressures in the Soviet Union were all for stability, clarity, and certainty in law, after the disastrously chaotic experiences in the era of free law finding from 1917 to 1921. During that period, the tsarist codes and laws had been largely swept away and Soviet judges and administrators were often bound by a no more sure and reliable criterion for decision than their own "spirit of revolutionary consciousness." The year 1922 also marked the introduction in the Soviet Union of the New Economic Policy, with an official relaxation of controls on economic activity and a new encouragement of entrepreneurial business activity and of foreign trade and investment in the country. It was, therefore, argued that a fixed and definite civil code—which manifestly, in its structure and organization and in a great deal of its substantive principles, too,

did not depart too much from the main continental European civil-law stream—would be an invaluable asset in promoting a more liberal Soviet official image, both at home and abroad.

Individual national codes differ widely, depending principally upon whether their makers have looked to the French or to the German civil code for their main intellectual inspiration. The Code Napoléon is direct, lucid, and often sparkling in structure and in language, reflecting perhaps both the inherently graceful qualities of the French language and the personality and techniques of its original drafting commission, whose members, essentially practicing lawyers, under some prodding from the Emperor Napoleon produced their final code in a matter of several months. The B.G.B., by contrast, is heavy, pedantic, and profuse, both in language and in drafting, reflecting in measure the essentially professorial and bureaucratic character of its main drafters and the years of research, public debate, and criticism that preceded its final adoption; for although the actual project for codification was put under way in 1874, with the appointment of the members of the codifying commission, it was not until 1896 that the final draft was completed and approved, to take effect from 1900. The Emperor Napoleon had said that his aim was to have the code so simple and convenient in its arrangement that the French peasant, reading it in its single, slim, pocket-book form by candlelight, would be able to know his legal rights; and so successful has the code been, from the viewpoint of legal writing, that Stendhal is said to have read a few pages of it each day to improve his literary style. The German code, by contrast, remains essentially a legal technician's code, without any particular claims to literary elegance or refinement of style.

This reference to a distinctive national psychology or personality—or *Volksgeist*, as Savigny called it—and its relationship to individual acts of national codification calls attention to the question of whether there are any particular periods in a nation's history that are especially ripe for codification, and perhaps it also poses the even more basic question of why some countries have achieved codes and others have not. In 1814, in reaction against the various French invasions and military occupations of the revolutionary and Napoleonic eras, Anton Thibaut and the German nationalist movement urged the immediate codification of German laws. Savigny, who opposed these pressures, argued that since a code existed primarily as a restatement or concretization of a nation's law it would act as a brake on national development if any nation should seek to codify its laws before it had reached its full political, social, and economic maturity. Savigny added a nationalistic argument to his injunction against any "premature" codification. He stated that, given the condition of German law at the opening of the nineteenth century, when only the loose, diffuse, and prolix Prussian code of 1794—an original project of Frederick the Great acting under the impulse of French rationalism—was available as a strictly Germanic model, any German act of codification, unless it were to be a reproduction in terms of the Code Napoléon, which had been carried into the Rhineland and other parts of Germany by Napoleon's armies, would require legal talents and resources beyond the then existing intellectual capacities of the German university law faculties.

It was far better, in Savigny's view, to keep the existing patchwork quilt of German law. In the Rhineland states, for example, the Code Napoléon would be retained; in Prussia and the areas under its control, the code of 1794; in the other states, the uncodified common law, or "received Roman law." The absorption of this uncodified law into Germany had taken place over the course of the fourteenth, fifteenth, and sixteenth centuries. In the process of that absorption and in the subsequent intensive study in the university law schools, it was progressively refined and restated. There is a particular irony in Savigny's argument against codification by appeal to *German* nationalistic traditions, since the received Roman law, which dominated so much of Germany at the opening of the nineteenth century, became ultra-*Roman* in content and character. Even the Code Napoléon, for example, while drawing heavily on the Roman law of southern France (or the *pays de droit écrit*), was still greatly influenced as to its substantive principles by the Germanic customary law of the northern provinces of France (or *pays de coutumes*).

A good part of the dynamics of a codification movement certainly comes from the spirit of rationalism. There have been powerful codification movements in both Great Britain and the United States. Bentham and his disciples, as part of their general law-reform movement in the early nineteenth century, launched a codifying project designed, in Bentham's own words, to render the law "cognoscible" to the layman. But the movement, except for some sustained influence in certain specialized areas of law, especially the criminal law and commercial law, and in the British colonies overseas, had largely petered out by the middle and late nineteenth century, probably because of the tenacious resistance of the vested professional interests of the judiciary and the practicing bar. The intellectual thoughtways of these special skill groups were attuned to that pragmatic, problem-by-problem development of legal principles inherent in the case-law system, and they were firmly opposed to any a priori postulation of principles through an act of codification. Since university teaching of law in England was very weak and largely unorganized until well into the nineteenth century, the practicing profession's influence was dominant in legal education through the Inns of Court, and this acted as a further intellectual barrier to codification.

In the United States the codification movement had its impact, represented in the great Field–Carter debate of the mid-nineteenth century; but the influence of codification has been very slow and, outside the commercial sphere, limited in area of impact. On the other hand, some factors have been very conducive to uniformity in the development of American private law, notwithstanding the existence of fifty formally separate and autonomous state jurisdictions. Especially important are the Restatements of American Law and the influence of the prestigious "national" law schools of the pattern of Yale and Harvard, which purport to teach a truly national, as distinct from a particularist or local law.

Once they have been drafted, there is a certain tendency for codes to become invested with a great deal of the seeming permanence, rigidity, and immutability of constitutions or similar fundamental laws. This particular truth, which had been observed by Savigny, seemed to be amply vindicated by the detailed history of the interpretation and application of the Code Napoléon during the nineteenth century. In France a highly conservative judiciary, aided by a strict and literal "grammatical" construction or exegesis of the text of the code, insisted on confining its practical application to a highly individualistic laissez-faire philosophy, at a time when France as a whole, speaking in social and political terms, had experienced a full-scale industrial revolution and had largely accepted collectivist or social democratic ideas. Yet, by the close of the nineteenth century the judiciary, aided by the work of a brilliant group of text writers and commentators, had begun systematically to reinterpret the Code Napoléon to take account of the new climate of an advanced industrial civilization, in which the code must operate. The operational tools for this transformation of the code were the new techniques of teleological interpretation (or interpretation in terms of social purposes), themselves products of Gény's call (1889) for free scientific research in law (*la libre recherche scientifique*). These developments in French code law in action parallel and anticipate the later realist and sociological emphases in North American jurisprudence.

Codes, like constitutions, if they are to be viable, must change with the society in which they operate; and this preferred relationship, or symbiosis, between law and society is assisted by the use of broad general formulas in drafting them. When the German Social Democrats were disposed to challenge the draft B.G.B. because of its alleged liberal, individualistic bias, the great jurist Rudolf Stammler was able to assure them that the lapidarian quality of the code's general provisions would make it continually adjustable to the community's own acceptance of social democratic ideas. The very generality of a code's key provisions—like the "due process" clauses in the fifth and fourteenth amendments to the United States constitution—enables new content to be poured into the old formulas. Thus the process of interpretation can serve to effect change and innovation in the law while avoiding the apparently radical step of direct legislative amendment.

EDWARD McWHINNEY

[*See also* CONSTITUTIONS AND CONSTITUTIONALISM; JURISPRUDENCE; LAW; *and the biographies of* MONTESQUIEU *and* SAVIGNY.]

BIBLIOGRAPHY

AMERICAN JOURNAL OF COMPARATIVE LAW 1961 *XXth Century Comparative and Conflicts Law: Legal Essays in Honor of Hessel E. Yntema*. Edited by Kurt H. Nadelmann, Arthur T. Von Mehren, and John N. Hazard. Leiden: Sythoff.

DAVID, RENÉ; and DE VRIES, HENRY P. (1957) 1958 *The French Legal System: An Introduction to Civil Law Systems*. Dobbs Ferry, N.Y.: Oceana.

DAVID, RENÉ et al. 1960— *Le droit français*. Paris: Libraire Générale de Droit et de Jurisprudence. → Two volumes have been published to date.

GENY, FRANÇOIS (1889) 1962 *Méthode d'interprétation et sources en droit privé positif: Critical Essay*. 2d ed. St. Paul, Minn.: West.

GREAT BRITAIN, FOREIGN OFFICE 1950–1952 *Manual of German Law*. 2 vols. London: H.M. Stationery Office.

HAZARD, JOHN N.; and SHAPIRO, ISAAC 1962 *The Soviet Legal System: Post-Stalin Documentation and Historical Commentary*. 3 vols. Dobbs Ferry, N.Y.: Oceana.

McWHINNEY, EDWARD 1958 *Canadian Jurisprudence: The Civil Law and Common Law in Canada*. Toronto: Carswell.

SAVATIER, RENÉ 1948 *Les métamorphoses économiques et sociales du droit civil d'aujourd'hui*. Paris: Dalloz.

SAVIGNY, FRIEDRICH KARL VON (1814) 1840 *Vom Beruf unserer Zeit für Gesetzgebung und Jurisprudenz*. 3d ed. Heidelberg (Germany): Mohr.

SCHLESINGER, RUDOLF B. 1950 *Comparative Law: Cases and Materials*. New York: Foundation Press.

VON MEHREN, ARTHUR T. 1957 *The Civil Law System: Cases and Materials for the Comparative Study of Law*. Englewood Cliffs, N.J.: Prentice-Hall.

IV
SOCIALIST LEGAL SYSTEMS—SOVIET LAW

Despite its stormy history, the Soviet legal system has acquired a definite character and gives evidence of being permanently established. Many of its features derive from prerevolutionary Russian origins and are therefore similar to those of other legal systems (especially the German and French), from which Russia borrowed in the nineteenth century. Other features, however, are peculiarly Soviet, reflecting the needs of a one-party state, a planned economy, and a social order directed toward a communist morality.

Development

In the first two decades after the Communist seizure of power, in 1917, Soviet legal institutions had to contend with the official Marxist–Leninist theory that law (like the state) is essentially a capitalist institution destined to wither away (literally, "die out") once socialism is established. This theory derived from the premise that the apparatus of political authority (the state) and the formal procedures and general rules enforced by such apparatus (law) are essentially instruments of domination by the ruling class. They would have to be retained during the period of proletarian dictatorship but would not be needed in the future classless society, which would regulate itself, like a family or a kinship society, by customary standards, by morality and common sense, and by a recognition of the identity of individual and social interests.

In the period of War Communism, 1917–1921, the new Soviet regime made strenuous efforts to eliminate the legal institutions of the prerevolutionary period and to usher in the new classless society as rapidly as possible. The formal political and legal institutions that were introduced were quite primitive in character and were thought to be very temporary. By 1921, however, the entire economy was at a standstill, and Lenin introduced the New Economic Policy (NEP); private trade was restored, foreign firms were invited to do business on the basis of "concessions," and the peasants were encouraged to sell the produce of their private holdings in the open market. The restoration of a certain degree of capitalism was thought to require also a restoration of law, and Lenin therefore sent his jurists to the prerevolutionary Russian codes, as well as to western European legal systems, to copy their provisions and adapt them to the new Soviet conditions.

In the 1920s there were promulgated codes of criminal law, criminal procedure, civil law, civil procedure, land law, labor law, and family law. These codes, as interpreted and developed by the judiciary, the bar, the Procuracy, the Ministry of Justice, and legal scholars, gave the Soviet Union a system of law comparable in its techniques and main outlines to those of Western countries. The system was hedged about, however, with provisions designed to prevent its being used contrary to the interests of the proletarian dictatorship.

Thus, article 1 of the Civil Code stated that the rights declared in the code should be protected by law "except in instances when they are exercised in contradiction to their social–economic purpose." Similarly, the Criminal Code, rejecting the "bourgeois" principle of *nullum crimen sine lege,* provided that an act not made punishable by a specific article of the code may, if it is socially dangerous, be punished under articles relating to analogous acts (the doctrine of analogy).

Other features of the law of the NEP that reflected a "proletarian" or "Leninist" orientation included severe limitations upon rights of private ownership, civil liability for causing personal injury regardless of the absence of fault on the part of the defendant, an administrative procedure for divorce by unilateral repudiation, and heavy penalties for "counterrevolutionary" acts or utterances. In addition, the legal system as a whole was rendered somewhat precarious by the theory that it was only part of a transition toward a socialist society in which law would die out.

With the end of the NEP in 1928, the introduction of the first Five-Year Plan, and the collectivization of agriculture, there came a return to the nihilistic and apocalyptic spirit of the earlier period of War Communism. Now, however, a more positive content was given to the notion of the dying out of state and law. These were to be replaced, it was declared, by the plan. The legal institutions of the NEP, although not formally abolished, now became in many respects obsolete. Communist party directives and police terror replaced law in many areas of economic and social life, and Stalin, in that period, built his personal machine for governing.

The spirit of Soviet law in the early 1930s was reflected particularly in the writings of E. B. Pashukanis, the leading jurist of that period, who in his "General Theory of Law and Marxism" (1927) had expounded the view that law in its very nature is based on the concept of reciprocal exchange of goods and hence is essentially a product of a market economy. In the early 1930s Pashukanis foresaw the imminent disappearance of law and argued that such law as continued to exist in the period of construction of the planned economy should have maximum political elasticity. "The utmost dynamic force is essential," he wrote in 1930. "Revolutionary legality is for us a problem which is ninety-nine per cent political" (*Soviet Legal Philosophy* 1951, pp. 279–280).

In the mid-1930s, however, there was once again a reaction against excessive dynamism. Stalin, in his "Report on the Draft Constitution," 1936, called for "stability of laws." With the adoption of the constitution in December 1936, socialism was declared to have been achieved; class antagonisms were said no longer to exist within the Soviet Union; but at the same time the new socialist era was said to require the strictest legality together with the strongest possible state power. The dying out of state and law was now postponed until the final stage of communism, after the end of "capitalist encirclement"—that is, when the whole world would be communist.

To this postponement Stalin added the "dialectical" doctrine that in order to pave the way for its own abolition the state must in the meanwhile become stronger and stronger. Thus the increase of terror against internal enemies—called agents of foreign imperialism—was given a theoretical justification, while at the same time the stabilization of the legal system could be promoted in those areas of social and economic life where terror was not considered necessary.

The dual system of law and terror that Stalin established in the mid-1930s is well symbolized by the fact that Pashukanis' nihilistic theories of law were denounced and he himself was shot as a counterrevolutionary. He was replaced as dean of the Soviet legal profession by Andrei Ia. Vyshinskii, who laid down the new party line about law in a series of articles and in a book on Soviet public law (1938). While defending party supremacy and the use of force against "enemies of the people," Vyshinskii attacked Pashukanis and other Soviet jurists for their attempt to reduce law to economics or to politics. He asserted that law has an "active, creative role" to play in the Soviet planned economy and that the reduction of law to politics would signify the ignoring of those tasks that stand before law, such as the tasks of legal protection of personal, property, family, testamentary, and other rights and interests (1938).

Under Vyshinskii's aegis the whole vocabulary of "rights," "duties," "legality," "contract," "ownership," "inheritance," "fault," "independence of the judiciary," "right to counsel," "burden of proof," and the like was carried over from the NEP period and rebaptized as "socialist both in form and in content." Moreover, the escape clauses of the NEP codes, such as article 1 of the Civil Code and the doctrine of analogy in criminal law, were greatly restricted in their application. In criminal law the element of personal guilt was emphasized as an essential element of crime. Liability for personal injury was now to be based on fault rather than on mere causation. A judicial procedure for divorce was introduced. Freedom of testation was increased, and the maximum 90 per cent inheritance tax was eliminated and replaced by a maximum 10 per cent notarial fee.

At the same time, "counterrevolutionaries" and "enemies of the people" were generally dealt with in secret administrative trials by the Special Board of the Ministry of Internal Affairs (MVD) or in a special secret procedure in the military courts. (The great purge trials of 1936–1938 were an exception to this rule.) Indeed, Vyshinskii developed theories to justify the application of special legal doctrines in political cases—for example, the theory that confessions have special evidentiary force in cases of counterrevolutionary crimes, since no person would confess to such a crime unless he were actually guilty!

The restoration of law as a positive feature of Soviet socialism was part of a general stabilization of social relations that occurred in the mid-1930s. It was related to the restoration of historical traditions, the re-emphasis of family stability, and the stress on Soviet patriotism, as well as to the recognition of the need for personal material incentives and for greater regularity and calculability in the administration of the economy. In the sphere of constitutional law, however, including choice of leaders, the legislative process, and civil liberties, "socialist legality" was largely a facade for Stalin's personal despotism.

After Stalin's death, in 1953, his successors denounced his "violations of socialist legality" and restricted very substantially the use of terror. They abolished the Special Board of the MVD and the special procedures in military courts for counterrevolutionary crimes. Hundreds of thousands of persons who had been convicted of counterrevolutionary crimes were released from labor camps and rehabilitated. Confessions were deprived of special evidentiary value, and the burden of proof was placed squarely on the prosecution in all criminal cases. The doctrine of analogy was eliminated from criminal law. New laws provided for the publication of all statutes and executive decrees having "general significance." There was also a slight narrowing of the law on counterrevolutionary crimes (renamed "state crimes"), although it remained a crime to defame the Soviet political and social system or even to possess written materials of such defamatory nature for the purpose of weakening Soviet authority. The regime in the labor camps (renamed labor colonies) was substantially reformed.

Even apart from political crimes, Soviet law underwent substantial liberalization in the years after Stalin's death. There was a re-examination of virtually every branch of law and a weeding out of most of the harshest features. Between 1958 and 1962 "Fundamental Principles" were enacted by the U.S.S.R. Supreme Soviet in the fields of criminal law, criminal procedure, civil law, civil procedure, and judicial administration. On the basis of these Fundamental Principles the various Soviet republics have begun to enact new codes in these fields. Draft "fundamental principles" of labor law were published in 1959 and were still under discussion in 1965, with new Fundamental Principles of family law in preparation as of that date. The new basic legislation has effected not only a general liberalization of the pre-existing law but also a significant systematization and rationalization.

Characteristics

Among the distinguishing features of the Soviet legal system is the institution of the Procuracy, which was established by Lenin in 1922 on the model of the old Russian Procuracy established by Peter the Great. The procurator-general of the U.S.S.R. and his subordinates at all levels have the function not only of indicting and prosecuting criminals but also of supervising legality generally. "General supervision" includes "protesting" administrative abuses to higher administrative authorities, as well as "protesting" erroneous judicial decisions to higher courts. Any citizen may complain about an abuse of his rights to the Procuracy, which is required to investigate and reply to the complaint and in proper instances to "protest" it. Thus, the Procuracy exercises a "watchdog" function, without having administrative powers of its own (apart from the power to indict for crime). It is a legal institution peculiarly adapted to a political system in which there is a high degree of central administrative regulation.

A second characteristic Soviet legal institution is the system of administrative adjudication of contract disputes between state economic enterprises and organizations. So-called *Arbitrazh* tribunals hear such disputes and resolve them on the basis of contract law, administrative regulations, and state economic plans. Where plans require enterprises to enter into contracts for supply of goods and the enterprises cannot agree on the terms, *Arbitrazh* tribunals will hold hearings and resolve the dispute. Most of the several hundred thousand cases decided annually by *Arbitrazh* involve, however, not these "pre-contract" disputes, but suits for specific performance or for damages for breach of contract.

A third distinguishing feature of the Soviet legal system is its heavy stress on the educational role of law. Both substantive and procedural law, in virtually all fields, is oriented toward the guidance, training, and disciplining of Soviet citizens to be loyal, responsible, and devoted to the aims of the society as formulated by the Communist party. A specific manifestation of this "parental" philosophy is the law of official crimes, which makes administrative and managerial personnel of state organizations criminally liable for intentional malperformance or negligent performance of their official duties.

The emphasis on the educational role of law is connected with the theory of the dying out of state and law once communism is achieved. In 1961 the achievement of the first stage of communism was promised within twenty years. At the same time the Stalinist theory that the state must get stronger and stronger in order to create the conditions for its demise was rejected. The 1961 Communist party program declared that the period of proletarian dictatorship was over and that Soviet society would take immediate (although very gradual) steps to replace the coercive machinery of the state by the persuasive, voluntary processes of popular social action. In accord with this theory, various paralegal bodies have been established—notably, informal "comrades' courts" in factories and apartment houses, which mete out reprimands and light fines for minor offenses, as well as "people's patrols" (*druzhiny*), which act as volunteer auxiliary police. In addition, people who lead an "antisocial, parasitic way of life" and "live on unearned income" are tried by collectives of workers or by the courts in a special administrative procedure and are subject to "resettlement" for two to five years in places where they must take socially useful jobs.

The adoption of these "antiparasite" laws in the major republics in 1961 coincided with a general increase in harsh penalties for serious crimes. Thus, in 1961 the death penalty was introduced for large-scale economic crimes, counterfeiting,

and illegal transactions in foreign currency. In 1962 repeated bribery of officials, rape committed by a group, and attempted homicide of a policeman or volunteer auxiliary policeman (*druzhinnik*) were added to the list of capital offenses. (Prior to 1961, only certain political crimes—treason, espionage, banditry, wrecking, terrorist acts—and murder committed under aggravating circumstances were subject to the death penalty in time of peace, and in 1958 the maximum period of confinement had been reduced from 25 to 15 years.)

Thus, as of the early 1960s there was a certain ambivalence in the Soviet legal system. On the one hand, many of Vyshinskii's theories justifying the use of terror were denounced, and socialist legality was proclaimed to extend to all spheres of Soviet life. On the other hand, the dualism of law and terror was replaced by a dualism of law and informal social pressure, and law itself, although applied with greater objectivity than ever before in Soviet history, reflected increased harshness in some areas and increased leniency in others. Soviet jurists rejected Vyshinskii's definition of law as a coercive instrument of state domination (embodying, Vyshinskii added, the will of the people); yet they were unable to find a new definition that corresponded to Marxist–Leninist theory, to the new conditions of Soviet life, and to the aspirations toward a communist society in which social influence and persuasion would replace formal rule and command.

HAROLD J. BERMAN

[*See also* COMMUNISM; MARXISM.]

BIBLIOGRAPHY

The major "classics" of Soviet legal theory in the period prior to Stalin's death have been translated in part by Hugh W. Babb in Soviet Legal Philosophy 1951. No one has emerged to replace Vyshinskii as dean of Soviet jurisprudence (1938). Among those scholars, formerly associated with Vyshinskii, who have been in the forefront of the reform movement since 1955 are M. S. Strogovich, S. A. Golunskii, A. A. Piontkovskii, and S. N. Bratus. Of the younger jurists who first came to prominence in the middle 1950s, O. S. Ioffe is perhaps the most outstanding. An extensive bibliography of Soviet legal writings may be found in Hazard & Shapiro 1962.

BERMAN, HAROLD J. (1950) 1963 *Justice in the U.S.S.R.: An Interpretation of Soviet Law.* Rev. & enl. ed. Cambridge, Mass.: Harvard Univ. Press. → Originally published as *Justice in Russia: An Interpretation of Soviet Law.*
BERMAN, HAROLD J. (compiler) 1966 *Soviet Criminal Law and Procedure: The R.S.F.S.R. Codes.* Cambridge, Mass.: Harvard Univ. Press.
GRZYBOWSKI, KAZIMIERZ 1962 *Soviet Legal Institutions: Doctrines and Social Functions.* Ann Arbor: Univ. of Michigan Press.

GSOVSKI, VLADIMIR 1948–1949 *Soviet Civil Law: Private Rights and Their Background Under the Soviet Regime.* 2 vols. Ann Arbor: Univ. of Michigan Press.

HAZARD, JOHN N. 1960 *Settling Disputes in Soviet Society: The Formative Years of Legal Institutions.* New York: Columbia Univ. Press.

HAZARD, JOHN N.; and SHAPIRO, ISAAC 1962 *The Soviet Legal System: Post-Stalin Documentation and Historical Commentary.* 3 vols. Dobbs Ferry, N.Y.: Oceana.

PASHUKANIS, E. B. 1927 *Obshchaia teoriia prava i marksizm* (General Theory of Law and Marxism). Moscow: Izdatel'stvo Kommunisticheskoi Akademii. → For a partial English translation see *Soviet Legal Philosophy,* 1951.

SCHLESINGER, RUDOLF (1945) 1951 *Soviet Legal Theory: Its Social Background and Development.* 2d ed. London: Routledge.

Soviet Legal Philosophy. 1951 Cambridge, Mass.: Harvard Univ. Press; Oxford Univ. Press. → A collection of major classics by V. I. Lenin and others, translated by Hugh W. Babb and published under the auspices of the Association of American Law Schools.

VYSHINSKII, ANDREI IA. (editor) (1938) 1948 *The Law of the Soviet State.* New York: Macmillan. → First published in Russian.

LEGENDS
See FOLKLORE.

LEGISLATION

I. NATURE AND FUNCTIONS   *Benjamin Akzin*
II. LEGISLATURES   *Ralph K. Huitt*
III. LEGISLATIVE BEHAVIOR   *John C. Wahlke*

I
NATURE AND FUNCTIONS

The term "legislation," in its narrowest modern usage, denotes the enactment of rules of law by specialized State agencies endowed with high authority and fairly representative of the general population; the term also denotes the rules that result from this process. In a wider sense, legislation includes, in addition, rules of general application enacted by executive, by subordinate administrative, by regional, and by local authorities. Rules of this kind are also known as secondary, or subordinate, or delegated legislation. At times, the term is used in a still broader meaning, in relation to rules stemming from other than State authorities (e.g., church or international legislation).

Legislation, thus understood, presupposes a fair degree of political and legal differentiation. It requires, first, a well-understood distinction between general norms intended to govern human conduct in an indefinite number of future instances and individual norms or commands intended to apply in a specific instance or in a strictly limited number of specific instances only. It requires, second, a well-established distinction between institutions authorized to issue general norms and those not authorized to do so; and more particularly, the setting up of a *central* agency equipped with this authority—the legislature in the proper sense of the word. It requires, third, a fair degree of consensus that norms thus enacted rank above most other legal rules found in the society. In more primitive legal systems, where such differentiation has not taken place and where society is largely regulated by rules to which metaphysical or customary origin is ascribed and which are regarded as beyond deliberate change by man-made institutions, one can hardly speak of legislation. And in those modern societies where differentiation of functions disappears in the plenitude of power wielded by an individual or by a small collective group—notably in some dictatorships—the concept of legislation as a distinct function suffers a serious setback.

Development of the concept

The term "legislation" derives from the Latin *lex*. The *lex*, once Roman law emerged from its primitive stage, was a distinct kind of legal rule of overriding authority and mainly of general application, expressly enacted by the people or on their behalf by some highly placed institutions (monarch, senate), singly or in combination. The same institutions were also regarded as entitled to modify or abrogate a *lex* once passed. It was therefore a term narrower than *ius*—the sum total of rules presumed to govern human conduct, whatever their authority, scope, or procedure of formation. It was, more precisely, an especially authoritative rule of the *ius civile* in the original meaning of the expression (i.e., the law which the State-organized society, *civitas*, provided for the regulation of conduct within itself), of what is called today "positive law" (i.e., imposed by the State) and of the *ius scriptum* (written, or enacted, law). Within this area of written positive law, the *lex* is a specific rule attributed to the highest law-making authority, which thus becomes *the* legislative authority par excellence. By definition, any other rule of positive law is viewed as subject to the *lex*, and if it acquires a status equal to a *lex*, it is said, in the language of Justinian's *Institutes* (I, II, 4), to "have the force of a lex" (*legis habet vigorem*).

Whether "nonpositive" law, which claims derivation from religion, from nature, from ethics, from reason, or from various ideological assumptions, is also subject to State-made legislative rules or, on the contrary, represents a "higher law" that states may not transgress, has remained a point of controversy in theory and still more in practice, ever since antiquity. Even custom and judge-made law were often regarded as immune from legislative interference, and not until the seventeenth century in England was the supremacy of legislation over the common law definitely acknowledged.

Several terms in various European languages—*loi, legge, ley, Gesetz, zakon,* and in English *a law* (as distinct from *the law*), but more precisely *statute, Act of Parliament, Act of Congress*—were coined to conform more or less to the historically developed meaning of *lex.* Upon closer observation, the criterion of generality appears in all of these to be rather incidental. The Romans had already noted that there are personal laws not intended to establish binding standards for future conduct (*leges . . . personales quae nec ad exemplum trahuntur*). Indeed, individual and special laws continue to form a considerable part of the legislative output in most civilized states. The decisive criterion for identifying legislation as a process and laws as the product of the process is increasingly the formal criterion of the identity of the enacting agency. In a curious reversal of roles, instead of legislation being explained as the activity which aims at the enactment of laws, we tend today to hold as laws those rules which are arrived at by the process of legislation.

Neither in antiquity nor in later times did specialists, let alone general usage, adhere strictly to the above meanings of the terms. In Rome *lex* was often used instead of *ius* to denote a whole area of jural regulation (e.g., *lex mancipi, lex commissoria*); and even another part of Justinian's codification (*Digest* I, III, 1) defines *lex* in a far broader manner than does his *Institutes. Lex* apparently had already become a highly popular expression, as overworked and used as indiscriminately as *law* in the English language today. In some other modern languages, the distinctiveness of the term is better preserved because, like Latin, they have a second term at their disposal (*loi–droit, legge–diritto, Gesetz–Recht, zakon–pravo*); but there, too, confusion is not unknown.

With the emergence of the Roman emperor and his appointees as the center of all governmental functions, a special legislative agency and its specific product, the *lex,* though maintained in theory, lost all practical importance. Different rules now stemmed largely from the same sources and from the same motivations; it hardly seems worthwhile, therefore, to pay much attention to formal differences between them. The influence of theology on

juristic theory in the centuries after Constantine's conversion to Christianity made the distinction even less meaningful. The three systems of the *ius naturale, ius gentium,* and *ius civile,* which the Romans were at such pains to keep distinct, tended to coalesce, the law of the church proper was added to them, and all four claimed ultimate legitimation by the same authority. Both enacted and customary rules of municipal law were occasionally described as *leges,* but so were the asserted principles of *ius gentium* and of *ius naturale,* as well as rules which claimed none but divine authority. Feudalism, too, contributed to this development. A device for maintaining social organization in the face of a weakened central power, it preserved no specific function as that power's sole prerogative but opened all of them, including the enactment of general rules, to the interplay of bilateral feudal relations; agreement and custom tended to rank above enactment in the legal structure. *Lex* and its plural *leges,* though at times used in contradistinction to *consuetudines,* extended beyond the particular rule and embraced a whole body of rules, being used in this sense concurrently with *jus. Lex Salica, lex Romana, lex civilis, leges Langobardorum,* and in private international law, *lex fori* and *lex contractus,* became technical expressions in which *lex* stood for *jus.*

From the eleventh century on, the revival of the original concept was stimulated by the universities, where Roman law dominated the jurists' thinking. The strengthening of the State at the expense of feudalism, which followed soon after, again lent reality to the distinction between higher-ranking and lower-ranking rules, and between individual and general ones. The *statutum* was defined as a written, general enactment, and the authority to enact statutes as the *potestas statuendi.* When exercised by the supreme political authority, it became the *potestas legis ferendi.* The *legis lator,* an expression known already in Rome and used there, as was the Greek *nomothetes,* mainly to denote an individual leader endowed with charisma or exceptional wisdom, like Moses or Solon or Lycurgus, appeared in a French source of the fourteenth century in its modern institutionalized meaning.

Further developments were again intimately connected with the gradual differentiation between the functions of various State agencies. As long as different rules emanating from the prince enjoyed similar status in the legal system, there was not much point in drawing formal distinctions between them. No doubt, certain restrictions were considered binding upon the princes of continental Europe, and some acts called in theory for the consent of representative assemblies. But in actual practice, most of these representative assemblies lost their powers, and the absolute power of the princes became prevalent, sweeping away before its authority all distinctions between basic and subordinate rules. Where, however, the representatives played an active part in the law-making machinery, e.g., in England, the Netherlands, Poland, the Italian and Hanseatic city-republics, and the Swiss cantons, the differentiation between rule-enacting agencies sharpened the differences between the resulting sets of rules. A rule which could be made only with the consent of a representative assembly and had to be modified in the same way was considered higher law than that enacted by mere executive authority. In monarchical countries such as England, the Netherlands, and Poland, this conception was somewhat blurred by the existence of the prince's "own right" or "prerogative"—a rival system of law impenetrable to the powers of the representative body. Nevertheless, there too the rules enacted by consent of representative bodies emerged as rules of higher authority, both in the consciousness of the population and in juristic practice. These were the rules that became increasingly identified as legislation, first in England and then in continental Europe.

In England special authority was early attributed to enactments agreed upon by the king and an assembly, soon to be divided into two houses. Thus arose the Act of Parliament, the first modern legislative act. The identity of the body which, in addition to the king, participated in the enactment; the procedure of this participation; and the social consensus symbolized by it lent special significance to the enactment. The contents of the act were of minor importance. Quite often its scope was general, but even where the same procedure was observed with respect to a measure of limited scope or applicability, the measure still enjoyed the same high degree of authority. Down to the seventeenth century there were many attempts to contest the special status of Acts of Parliament, to attribute a similar status to certain measures enacted on the king's sole authority, and to dispute the authority of Acts of Parliament to deviate from the common law; but by the end of that century the superiority of these acts over both king and common law stood unchallenged.

This concept of legislation, identified by the participation of a representative body in the enacting process and given a pre-eminent position in the State's scale of norms, remained virtually unchanged until the end of the eighteenth century. Both Continental and English philosophers and jurists adopted it and helped to spread it among the growing literate stratum of the population. A change ensued when the United States, followed by France, inaugurated the era of formal constitutions. These, wherever adopted, have displaced the ordinary laws, enacted through the legislative process, from their theoretical and moral pre-eminence in the legal structure, and—to the extent that the supremacy of the Constitution was accompanied by judicial or other sanctions—the displacement was of practical legal significance as well. Otherwise, legislation and its products—the laws, in the narrow meaning of the word—remained in their place, at or near the apex of the legal structure.

Secondary legislation

The stress of modern conditions has resulted in complications connected with (*a*) the complexities inherent in an industrial society, (*b*) a closer relationship between executive and legislature, (*c*) a generalized pattern of self-governing units, (*d*) the problem of meeting emergencies, and (*e*) the growth of modern dictatorships.

The complexities of modern society, combined with the increased social welfare purposes of the modern State, call for a vastly increased intervention by public authorities in areas of social relations which in former times had been regarded as lying outside the authorities' field of interest. Both administrative convenience and an increased sensitivity to the "rule of law" and the principle of equal treatment militate against exclusive reliance on *ad hoc* decisions, demanding instead regulation by general rules. But the very number of the general rules required, the complexity of their subject matter, and the specialized knowledge needed for their formulation make it difficult for the legislature to solve the problems incidental to their enactment. Willy-nilly, legislatures acquiesce nowadays to the enactment by administrative agencies of general rules, which but a few decades ago would have been regarded as reserved to legislation proper. [*See* DELEGATION OF POWERS.]

This trend was greatly assisted by a major change that has taken place in most countries of the world in the relations between legislatures and the top layers of the executive arm. No longer do these institutions represent two different principles of legitimacy and two different social groupings, often with opposing interests and credos and generally suspicious of each other's objectives, one centering on the prince, the nobility and the top bureaucracy; the other, on a broader group not intimately associated with the day-to-day conduct of public affairs. Nowadays the government, the top layer of the bureaucracy, and the legislature all trace their authority to the same source—the "people" (whatever the measure of reality or fiction behind this attribution)—and to a large extent share or reflect identical social interests. In those countries where some variety of the parliamentary regime prevails (i.e., one in which the heads of the executive are permanently answerable to the legislature and may be dismissed at the latter's discretion), it is the practice to place the direction of executive affairs in the hands of a group of persons who not only are for the most part members of the legislature enjoying the confidence of a majority of their fellow members, but are actually the leaders of that majority. In the circumstances, despite disagreements and mutual jealousies which still persist between executive and legislature, their conflicts can in no way be compared in intensity to those which marked the relations between the two in the days when they represented opposing principles of government and divergent social forces. In the modern State a large degree of basic unity of purpose and outlook between the legislature and the executive leadership replaces the fundamental lack of confidence which formerly existed between them.

This new situation explains why parliaments have largely abdicated their policy-making function to governments, whose lead they now tend to accept, but it explains more particularly why the former parliamentary reluctance to let executive agencies enact far-reaching general norms has considerably weakened. Many a statute is no more than an *enabling statute* authorizing the president, the cabinet, the minister, the subordinate executive department or officer to issue general rules within a very wide range of discretion. At times, special statutory provisions are aimed at exempting such rules and the decisions based on them from effective judicial review. Other general rules are issued by the executive without express authorization by statute, in the exercise of its powers under the Constitution, or of its police powers, or under the theory of the implied powers of government; and the legislature, as long as it does not disagree with the government on major questions of composition or policy, does not generally object. Action which in the former days of struggle between prince and parliament would have been resisted by the latter as usurpation of power, is now accepted as normal, inevitable, or even desirable, in the interest of good government.

This state of affairs is not without its influence on the judiciary and on academic jurisprudence:

courts have accepted it, and so have universities. In theory as well as in practice, the border line between legislation and regulations has become blurred, and regulations with more or less general contents are increasingly referred to as "secondary" or "subsidiary" or "delegated" legislation. Statutes passed by a parliamentary body are no longer the only form of legislation; they are distinguished merely by being "primary legislation." And the body itself is no longer the sole legislator; it is but the "primary legislator." In Britain this development has been most pronounced and, despite occasional protests from the traditionalist legal profession, is growing stronger. Other countries influenced by English law follow suit, and so do countries of the civil law tradition. In the United States, "delegation of legislative powers" is still rejected in principle, and the country's courts attempt to enforce this prohibition. But the factors that made for the practice elsewhere are active in the United States as well, and though the character of "legislation" is denied them, far-reaching general norms without much statutory guidance are becoming the rule.

Another kind of "secondary legislation," widespread in the modern world, is that indulged in by local authorities when making general rules within the scope of their jurisdiction. This trend goes back to medieval towns, many of which had representative institutions at a time when states were still governed autocratically, a circumstance which facilitated the conception of a difference between rules enacted by representative authorities and those made by executive authorities alone. Indeed, the very term "statute" was largely used to denote acts of self-governing local or regional authorities. But while, in premodern times, the jurisdiction of local authorities was often based on special arrangements and charters, it now conforms to a general State-wide pattern. In this pattern, the local authority consists of a predominantly elected representative body and of administrative personnel headed by an individual (mayor) or a small committee of officeholders with departmental responsibilities. Within this structure, the bifurcation into "higher" rules issued by the larger representative body and the acts of the "executive," bound by those rules, resembles the legislative–executive relationship within the State and justifies the designation by analogy of the "higher" local body as legislature and its output of general rules as legislation. In relation to the State, though, the rule-enacting activity in question is, of course, limited by State agencies and is subject to a variety of controls both before and after enactment. By no means can this activity pretend to "high" status within the total legal structure, however valued the principle of local self-government may be in current political thinking. At most, these acts too could be considered a kind of "secondary legislation" in the British sense. The special designation of "bylaws" points both to the analogy these rules bear to legislation and to the difference between them. [See LOCAL GOVERNMENT.]

The discussion of near-legislative activities by local authorities applies equally to representative regional authorities. The size of a regional entity, the scope of its authority, and the over-all status it enjoys in the politico-legal scheme of things do not theoretically affect the situation as described. In the United States this holds true of the school district as well as of the county, in England of the parish as well as of the county, in France of the *arrondissement* as well as of the *département* and the *région*.

It even holds true, to some extent, of regional entities in a federation which by courtesy, tradition, or formal enactment are accorded the dignity of statehood, whatever their precise designation (*states* in the United States, Australia, India, and Mexico; *republics* in the Soviet Union and Yugoslavia; *provinces* in Canada; *Länder* in Austria and the German Federal Republic; *cantons* in Switzerland). The scope of jurisdiction of these units is usually much wider, and within that scope they are much freer or altogether free from central controls; their status is anchored in the constitution and is often entrenched against interference by the federal legislature; and tradition or the letter of the constitution may describe them as "sovereign." Nevertheless, theirs too is an authority derived from a body politic larger than their own. Often there is the added limitation that in case of conflict, a federal statute will prevail over the product of the "member-state" legislation, thus relegating the latter to a clearly subordinate plane.

A further phenomenon which complicates the legislative picture is the emergency regulation. The ordinary regulation (variously known also as executive order, *décret*, *Verordnung*) and any action undertaken pursuant to it are characterized by being quite often an execution of a specific statute and, in any case, subject to statutory and constitutional provisions; this, as well as the sanction of judicial control of all regulatory activities, is the principal concomitant of the *rule of law*. However, genuine emergency conditions are apt to arise —mainly in connection with wars, internal disorders, severe economic crises, and major disasters—which make it imperative to allow for measures

that would be free from the time-consuming procedures accompanying modern legislation and yet might deviate from statutory and perhaps even from constitutional provisions. The proclamation by the executive of martial law, of a state of emergency, or of a state of siege has variously served in the past to justify such deviation from the normal rule of law pattern and is still occasionally resorted to, but whether or not accompanied by such proclamation, the emergency regulation (or emergency order) has become the main form of such exercise of executive powers in the twentieth century. Where war was concerned, Great Britain (until 1920) and the United States have found it possible to postpone the enactment of a suitable legal framework of emergency powers until the emergency has actually arisen and to do so by means of *ad hoc* legislation. Thus the British Defence of the Realm Act and the American Emergency Powers Act were passed in these countries in connection with the two world wars. In many other countries, however, where there are good grounds to fear a more instantaneous emergency, provision for such powers has been made ahead of time as part of the country's permanent structure, and even Great Britain now has the permanent Emergency Powers Act. The abuse of emergency powers that occurred in central Europe, notably in Germany, in the 1930s has made countries more cautious and has caused them to place emergency powers under increased parliamentary and judicial control. Nevertheless, even regulations passed under this conception of emergency powers approach legislation in the narrow sense of the word: they are not strictly bound by pre-existing statutory law; they enjoy a position of pre-eminence roughly approximating that of statutes; and they are held in check but little by judicial review. It is even more difficult than in the case of ordinary "secondary legislation" to ensure that the essential distinction between emergency regulations and parliamentary legislation be properly observed. [See also CRISIS GOVERNMENT.]

The previously noted complications arise even where the individuals and groups in control of the executive are willing to abide by the limitations placed on their powers and do not seek to overthrow the rule of law. Where this condition does not apply, the difficulties noted are aggravated, and the observer encounters a wholesale and deliberate trespassing by those who control the executive on what would be regarded as the normal domain of the legislature. Like those earlier regimes where power was highly concentrated, modern dictatorships, whether ideologically motivated or merely ambition-driven, whether totalitarian in their policies or fairly liberal, tend to obliterate the distinction between legislation and other procedures of law making. Representative legislative institutions are either abolished, or reduced in authority, or transformed into mere instruments whose composition and deliberations are wholly managed by the wielders of executive power. In either case the intrinsic importance of legislation and the distinction between it and other rules of law are diminished. [*See* TOTALITARIANISM.]

Structure of legislatures

The foregoing observations have shown that the body regarded specifically as the legislature bases its claim to higher legitimation on its being more fully representative than other public authorities. The actual mode of determining that body's composition, as well as the relative weight of the circles and interests thought worthy of representation, vary in accordance with the views prevailing at the time in the given society generally and among those who occupy the centers of power especially. A common characteristic of all properly differentiated legislatures is that they are *collective* bodies —an elementary device which makes fuller representativeness more likely and an excessive concentration of power less likely than would be possible in the case of a one-man legislature. *Appointment*, whether for a given period, for life, or even to a hereditary seat, was often practiced as a suitable mode of composing the legislature along with or instead of *election*, and this mode is still found in the mid-twentieth century in a number of "upper chambers," e.g., in Afghanistan, Canada, Ethiopia, Jordan, Luxembourg, the United Kingdom, and the Republic of South Africa.

Historically, the division of legislatures into two houses or chambers is a survival from the strongly estate-conscious medieval society, when deliberative bodies with partly legislative functions were organized by estates or groups of kindred estates. With the weakening of the estate as the prime integrating group and the strengthening of the direct links between the individual and the State, the "lower" chamber, based on some system of fairly wide and, most recently, near-universal adult suffrage, became the principal vehicle of mass representation, while the "upper" chamber was used to add an element of conservatism, moderation, or stability to the legislature. Conditions of eligibility and of voting were formulated more strictly in upper chamber elections, indirect elections were resorted to in the hope that they would screen out radical elements and make for a higher

level of expertness, and appointment was often practiced. All these methods could ensure weighted representation to social groups and interests favored by the regime. In federations, the device of the upper house is generally used to secure special representation of the federated entities, sometimes on the basis of equality irrespective of population numbers, thus affording the smaller autonomous units additional protection against encroachment by the larger ones. With the continuous growth of the idea that election by a larger proportion of the population furnishes the elected body a fuller measure of legitimate authority, the political importance and the formal attributes of upper houses gradually declined, except in some federal unions where they are regarded as the guardians of the federal principle. Several countries have dispensed with upper houses altogether, and the tendency seems to be spreading. In 1963, the list of countries with unicameral legislatures embraced a number of Latin American states, all unitary states with communist regimes, most of the new states in Africa and Asia, and Cyprus, Denmark, Finland, Greece, Israel, Lebanon, New Zealand, and Norway.

The shift from legislation

Legislation has constituted the principal business of parliamentary bodies almost from the beginning, a circumstance which so impressed political philosophers of the seventeenth and eighteenth centuries, especially Locke and Montesquieu, that they saw the creation of a specialized representative agency as principal participant in the legislative process to be a prominent characteristic of a well-ordered State. With modifications, this conception, an intrinsic part of the separation-of-powers doctrine, became the predominant practice, and representative parliaments became associated in the popular mind with the legislative power as such. In fact, however, this identity is by no means complete. In this article, some of the reasons have been set out which made parliaments lose much of their decisive role in the legislative process. In addition, parliaments in a number of countries occasionally share the legislative function with binding or advisory plebiscitary procedures (Australia, Austria, Denmark, France, Germany during the Weimar Republic, Italy, New Zealand, Norway, Switzerland, and—quite often—member states in federations) or with heads of State who may grant or withhold consent to a pending bill (United States, most other presidential republics, and constitutional monarchies of the nonparliamentary type). Nor can the representative character of parliaments always stand scrutiny. The not-quite-representative character of many an upper house has already been commented upon. Elections in which only part of the adult population was given the franchise and individual votes were given unequal weight were quite common until 1918. Since then, both practices have become less frequent, except in the form of assigning larger representation to rural than to urban constituencies—a practice still widespread. [*See* APPORTIONMENT.]

A newer problem is posed by parliamentary bodies in countries with communist, "popular-democratic," "guided-democratic," *caudillo*-type, and fascist regimes. There, parliaments are encountered which, though elected on an extremely broad suffrage basis and sometimes with an unusually large participation of voters, have their election process so encumbered with formal and factual restrictions on free discussion of issues and free choice of candidates, in an atmosphere so dominated by governmental and reigning-party pressure, that their representative character is doubtful in the extreme. The weaker a parliament's claim to be widely representative, the less foundation there is for its claim to have a preponderant part in legislation.

But even aside from these particular weaknesses, the significance of parliaments as legislative agencies has generally decreased. The connection between this development, the complexities involved in modern law making, and the greater unity of outlook between modern legislatures and executives, has been set out earlier. Even in the United States, where legislative activity proper is carried out more fully and more jealously by Congress and by the state legislatures than in most other countries, the national or state administrations initiate an ever-increasing portion of the more important bills. The American legislature is still in a position to deny clearance to a legislative measure desired by the administration, but less and less frequent are the cases in which, overriding a president's or a governor's veto, a legislature is able to enact a measure to which the administration objects. [*See* PRESIDENTIAL GOVERNMENT.] In other countries, to the extent to which parliaments are the expression of the voters' choice rather than of the governing group's pressure, legislation conforms to an even greater extent to the executive's desires. The executive's subordination to parliament is expressed mainly in the former's composition, so constituted as to ensure that the latter will confidently accept its guidance. Where parliamentary regimes are concerned, it is also expressed in formal votes denoting continuance or discontinuance of this confidence. But as long as a government enjoys a parliament's confidence, executive guidance of legislative business is accepted as a matter of course. [*See* PARLIAMENTARY GOVERNMENT.]

Nonetheless, parliaments, other than single-party ones, continue to exercise considerable influence on the specific contents of legislation. Bills introduced on the initiative of the government quite often undergo radical change as a result of discussion on the floor and in the committees of the legislature, and of public debate. Furthermore, bills are often introduced by the government or on its behalf as a result of opinions expressed in the legislature and of similar bills proposed by the opposition.

In matters of budgetary and finance legislation, special procedures have grown to hinder parliaments from seeking to please the voters by simultaneously advocating increased expenditures and decreased taxes—a double treatment necessary at times but dangerous when used indiscriminately. In several countries such devices were adopted as limiting parliament's opportunity to propose expenditures over and above those suggested by the government, making such increases conditional upon simultaneous provision for added revenues, or providing for a lengthened legislative procedure (such as an authorization and an appropriation act in the United States; the financial resolution in Great Britain). Long-term financial provisions such as the British Consolidated Fund, multiyear plans involving financing and enacted in advance, and authorization of economic activities controlled by the government and carried on through the intermediary of public corporations have further reduced the significance of the annual budgets handled by parliaments as part of their legislative routine. [*See* BUDGETING.]

Not only has the part of parliaments in the over-all legislative picture become smaller. Legislation has also become a less important, though not necessarily less time-consuming, part of parliamentary business. Its place has been taken largely by two other functions: the day-to-day control of governmental operation and the formalized, highly resonant expression of the grievances and aspirations of groups within the population. Speeches on the floor and in committee, interventions by members with appropriate ministers and their officials, questions or "interpellations," "points of order" and motions of different kinds ascending in intensity to the (British) motion of censure and the (continental European) motion of nonconfidence serve these various purposes. In the United States, some of these forms are not used, but their place is taken no less effectively by the formalized procedure of open hearings in legislative committees and the informal contact which members of the legislatures maintain with the press and other mass media so as to mobilize the latter in the service of causes to be supported or fought. Legislatures and their members thus become highly sensitive parts of the machinery of government, attuned to currents of popular opinion, capable of broadcasting their own moods to the population, and constantly pressing the resulting views on the administration.

If modern parliaments are still regarded largely as the legislative agencies par excellence and legislation is still represented as their principal business, this is, to some extent, an echo from the past, perhaps a reminder of a weapon parliaments hold in reserve to be used against the executive in some future contingency but hardly a fair description of the actual state of affairs. Those "legislatures" which have been deprived of the dynamic role of daily controllers and gadflies of the administration because of the utter subservience of their membership to the executive, and which have been reduced largely to legislative activity—again in an atmosphere of such subservience—lead but a shadowy existence. For obvious reasons, opposition groups and members in parliaments—wherever genuine opposition is allowed—are much freer from executive dominance than are groups and members that support the government of the day, both in their legislative and in their gadfly activities, and they appear by and large as the more dynamic part of the legislature. Only where party discipline is lax do members of the group pledged to support the government make themselves strongly felt in the conduct of parliamentary affairs. This is the case to a very marked extent in the United States and to some extent in Italy; such was the case in France during the Third and Fourth republics, and with respect to a few individualistic members of other parliaments (e.g., in Britain, Winston Churchill and Leopold Amery among the Conservatives; Stafford Cripps and Aneurin Bevan among Labour party members). [See PARTIES, POLITICAL.]

Legislative techniques

Typical of modern legislation is the elaborate procedure intended to avoid drafting errors and hasty decisions. Both the guiding ideas and the actual text of the original proposal may be suggested by an individual member of the legislature, by a group of members, by a partisan body, by an outside group primarily interested in the issue, by a government agency, or by experts to whom the task has been entrusted by one of the foregoing. Where formal introduction of bills by the government or a government minister is allowed, the role of the individual legislator in initiating legislation has been on the decrease, and so have his chances to have his bills considered on their merits or adopted. Legislative counsel, legislative reference services, and experts attached to specific legislative committees are growing in importance as media for assembling information, drafting documents, or otherwise assisting members and committees of the legislature. With the formal introduction of a text for consideration as a proposed piece of legislation, the text becomes a *bill*. In most legislatures, either members or the government (in the United States only members) are authorized to introduce bills.

Though subject to serious modification in detail, the legislative process commonly involves four stages. Upon formal introduction in parliament, the bill is either automatically turned over for consideration to an appropriate committee or first briefly discussed in plenary session (first reading) with a view to dismissal or to retention for further consideration. In Britain and some countries that closely follow British procedure, the next stage (second reading) takes the form of a debate in plenary session, which, in turn, is followed by consideration in committee (usually a smaller body chosen *ad hoc* or generally entrusted with matters of that kind, but in Britain often the "Committee of the Whole House"—i.e., the entire membership of the chamber proceeding in a less formal manner). In most other countries, consideration in a smaller committee comes first; and the second reading in the plenary session, with opportunity for detailed discussion and vote on individual sections of the bill, takes place only after it has been "reported out" by the committee or (in the United States) after the committee has been "discharged" from further consideration of it. (The discharge procedure is a remedy against undue dilatoriness on the part of the committee or the committee chairman.) Representatives of the government are usually heard by the committee, and in most countries other interested parties may also be heard (in the United States predominantly in open hearings, in other countries mainly behind closed doors). During the committee stage, especially when proceedings are held behind closed doors and do not involve the prestige of individual members, of parties, and of the government in the same measure as in public session, considerable changes are often introduced into the original text in response both to argument and to pressure. The last stage (third reading) usually involves a brief debate and, in most countries, concludes with a vote on the bill as a whole, although under British procedure the debate is more extensive and opportunity is given to decide on various amendments that have arisen out of committee proceedings.

Ordinarily, intervals of several days, weeks, or months separate these stages. Indeed, such intervals are regarded as desirable in order to permit thorough deliberation and to enable public reaction to make itself felt. But in emergencies legislatures resort to a "suspension of the rules," limiting debate, shortening the accepted intervals between stages, dispensing with committee consideration, and even passing the entire measure in the course of a single day.

Other decisions taken by legislatures are not to be confused with legislation proper. These include elections; votes of confidence, nonconfidence, and censure; votes of impeachment; expressions of approval or disapproval of administrative measures that require such action; procedural decisions of various kinds (including the determination of rules of procedure, or standing orders, under which the legislature operates); and especially declaratory resolutions of different kinds which may be morally and politically significant but have no binding force in strict law. In the United States Congress, it is important to distinguish between "joint resolutions," which are tantamount in their effect to statutes, and "concurrent resolutions," which in themselves have no legal effects. Where legislative agencies also have constitution-making and constitution-amending functions, procedures governing them should be distinguished from those involved in "ordinary" legislation.

Voting procedures differ greatly among the legislatures of the world and, depending upon circumstances, even in the same legislature. The vote may be taken by an informal estimate of the strength of the voiced (*viva voce*) approval and disapproval, by a "show of hands" or a "rising vote" estimated or actually counted, or by more formal counting ("division" in the British Parliament), by roll-call votes registered by name, or even by secret ballot. A simple majority of those voting, with abstentions not taken into account, is usually decisive, and most legislatures require either a low proportion of members to be present at deliberations or votes (quorum) or no quorum at all. The British House of Commons requires a quorum of only 40 members (out of 630 in 1963); the quorum requirements of both houses of the United States Congress of a majority of all members are among the strictest. There are, however, legislative and other decisions which require, to become effective, an absolute or an even higher majority of all members voting, of members present, or of the total membership.

Participation of other bodies in the formal legislative process is secondary in the modern State. Formal consultation of economic councils of various kinds takes place in some countries. Under some newer constitutions, an appropriate judicial or semijudicial body may be requested for its opinion if the constitutionality of the measure is doubtful (in Iran the Council of Ulemas, i.e., religious dignitaries, passes on the religious orthodoxy of the measure), and, if necessary, the bill is returned to the legislature. More widespread is the opportunity given to the head of state to withhold his consent to the bill, thereby either preventing its passage into law (absolute veto) or requiring its consideration anew by the legislature (suspensive veto).

Except in very special circumstances, publicity is a mark of modern legislative procedure. This publicity serves to enable public opinion and that of interested groups to make their weight felt before the final decision is taken, as well as to rally the public around the decision's results. The bill, after having been given the assent of all those whose participation is required, is certified, proclaimed (promulgated), and published, thus becoming *a law*, a statute.

Interpretation and codification of statutes

In most cases, a statute is restricted to a single subject matter, though this may be quite involved, present many aspects, and require subdivision into several sections or articles. As a rule, the adoption of a statute does not invalidate previous statutes, save insofar as they are expressly invalidated. But where a provision of an earlier statute is inconsistent with the provision of a later statute, the *later* rule should be applied (*lex posterior derogat priori*), unless the earlier rule is a special and the later a general one, in which case the special rule will prevail (*lex specialis derogat generali*). These and other principles of statutory interpretation are generally left to the courts, which follow certain traditional criteria and their own precedents; where statutes themselves contain rules of interpretation, these are to be followed, of course, but in no case are executive agencies to prescribe rules for the interpretation of statutes in states where the rule of law or the *principe de la légalité* prevails. [See JUDICIAL PROCESS.]

Where partial modification of an existing statute is desired, this is done mainly by an *amending* statute. When this has been done a number of times, or when provisions relating to a given subject matter are dispersed over several statutes (and perhaps over statutes, secondary legislation, and various forms of customary law), a patchwork pattern ensues which makes it difficult to grasp the exact requirements of the law. In the interest of clarification, *consolidated* statutes may then be adopted by the legislature or an up-to-date revision of the statutory material, to be done by experts, authorized by it. When the consolidation of the legal material is done in a particularly systematic and comprehensive manner and purports to regulate fully a very broad sector of social relations, the process is known as *codification* and the resulting product as a *code*. Codification may contain restatement of pre-existing statutory, customary, and judge-made law in diverse proportions, but also newly formulated rules that differ materially from the law previously in force. Several Oriental, Latin American, and European countries have adopted, virtually unchanged, codes that were previously enacted elsewhere, the most frequent models being the French, German, Italian, and Swiss codes. Such wholesale reception of foreign codes represents a variant of the well-known phenomenon of the reception of foreign law in general.

In its continental European meaning, a code, upon coming into force, is meant to displace all pre-existing law relating to the subject, thus rendering unnecessary inquiry into older sources and precedents, and simplifying access to the law. But in the United States pre-existing law, especially rules derived from the common law and from equity, continue to be regarded as in force, unless specifically conflicting with or expressly repealed by the code. In time, even consolidated and revised statutes as well as codes cease to be up to date: social changes and political aspirations result in partial amendments of the enacted material, and so do technical deficiencies in the original text as revealed in the course of its application. Furthermore, the best-planned and most detailed code or comprehensive statute is overgrown in time by judicial interpretation, even if—as in the case of countries outside of the common law sphere—its interpretation in the light of precode material is discouraged.

The above difference between English-speaking countries and others in regard to codification is related to the different attitudes which legal practitioners and scholars traditionally assume toward the relative places of enacted law and of customary law authoritatively formulated by a succession of judicial decisions. In civil law countries, legal thought considers law primarily the product of general enactments made by the legislators; custom is but one of the factors which the legislators may take into account; judicial decisions, however important in applying the law to concrete situations, are of merely interstitial significance in classifying, specifying, and sometimes stretching (by analogy, for instance) the general principles of the enactment to cover unforeseen combinations of circumstances—all of this under the guise of interpretation. In common law countries, law is primarily thought of as the body of rules evolved from a succession of judicial decisions on the basis of real or alleged custom, whereas legislation comes in interstitially, to fill the lacunae of the judge-made law or to adjust it to changing demands of society. The formal supremacy of the legislative rule is but reluctantly recognized in the English-speaking world, and wherever possible its significance is reduced by the tendency to interpret the enacted rule in the light of the common law. The difference is further accentuated by the tendency in civil law countries to interpret the enacted rule broadly, so as to bring under its sway as many concrete situations as possible, whereas common law countries tend to interpret the enacted rule narrowly and to continue applying judge-made law outside that narrow area. Basically, the common law attitude reflects the belief that the legislator is inherently a political agent interested in furthering his interests at the expense of true law, somehow related to "natural" law, of which the judge is the guardian, whereas civil law thinking has resigned itself to the acceptance of the legislator as the foremost exponent of the law. [*See* LEGAL SYSTEMS.]

Legislation and natural law

The foregoing section brings us back to the question of the relation of legislation, as the outstanding instance of a positive, i.e., State-imposed, law, to norms of human conduct which claim validity independently of State action. Where the role of legislator is entrusted to an elected assembly on a broad basis or to direct popular vote, the element of consensus enters the picture, and it is society as a whole that is assumed to impose the law on individual members and groups; still, there is a deliberate act of imposing a rule of conduct which previously could claim no validity. The question arises, in what relation the legislated rule, and positive law generally, stands to *natural law* or morality, that vague but intensely felt body of principles which in human consciousness divides the *just* from the *unjust*. In this confrontation, positive law enjoys great advantages: its contents are far more ascertainable, its formulators are tangible and certain, its sanction is secured by an organized and generally efficient machinery—all unlike the rules of natural law, the precise contents of which are doubtful, the originators and formulators of which are diffuse in the extreme, the sanctions of which are indefinite and uncertain. [*See* JUSTICE; NATURAL LAW.]

And yet, for all their weaknesses, natural law concepts—closely intertwined as they are with social *mores*, with rationalized interests and desires, with theological postulates, with individual conscience, and with the ensuing pattern of ethics accepted in society—exercise a permanent influence on positive law in general and on legislation in particular. Enacted rules of law are quite often a reflection of those natural law concepts which prevail at the time. And when positive law appears to one group or another to deviate from natural law, to be *unjust*, it is in the name of natural law, of justice, that changes in positive law are advocated and brought about more often than in the name of any other principle. This applies to partial changes in positive law, which can be accomplished in the forms provided for by the positive law itself, i.e., through the ordinary channels of new or amending legislation, of reglementation, of judicial interpretation, and of constitutional amendments. But it applies no less to such wholesale changes of the existing positive legal structure as are accomplished in disregard, even in violation, of these channels, i.e., to *revolutions*. Most revolutions which have a widely acknowledged ideological basis claim to be methods of adjusting the positive law to the true natural law as seen by the revolutionaries.

BENJAMIN AKZIN

[*See also* ADMINISTRATION; GOVERNMENT; INTEREST GROUPS; PARTIES, POLITICAL; POLITICAL EXECUTIVE; POLITICAL PROCESS; REPRESENTATION. *A guide to other relevant material may be found under* LAW.]

BIBLIOGRAPHY

AHMAD, MUSHTAQ 1959 *Legislatures in Pakistan.* Lahore: Univ. of the Panjab Press.

ALLEN, CARLETON K. (1927) 1964 *Law in the Making.* 7th ed. Oxford: Clarendon.

ALLEN, CARLETON K. (1945) 1956 *Law and Orders: An Inquiry Into the Nature and Scope of Delegated Legislation and Executive Powers in English Law.* 2d ed. London: Stevens.

AMELLER, MICHEL (editor) (1961) 1966 *Parlements: Une étude comparative sur la structure et le fonctionnement des institutions.* 2d ed., enl. Paris: Presses Universitaires de France.

ANDRADA, B. 1962 *Parlamentarismo e a evolução brasileira.* Belo Horizonte (Brazil): Alvarez.

BERMAN, DANIEL M. (1964) 1966 *In Congress Assembled: The Legislative Process in the National Government.* New York: Macmillan.

CAMPION, GILBERT F. (1929) 1958 *An Introduction to the Procedure of the House of Commons.* London: Macmillan.

CAMPION, GILBERT F.; and LIDDERDALE, D. W. S. 1953 *European Parliamentary Procedure: A Comparative Handbook.* London: Allen & Unwin.

CLAPP, CHARLES L. (1963) 1964 *The Congressman: His Work as He Sees It.* Garden City, N.Y.: Doubleday.

CRAIES, WILLIAM F. (1906) 1963 *Statute Law.* 6th ed. London: Sweet.

DAHL, ROBERT A. 1950 *Congress and Foreign Policy.* New York: Harcourt.

FINER, HERMAN (1932) 1961 *The Theory and Practice of Modern Government.* 4th ed. London: Methuen.

FRIEDMANN, WOLFGANG G. (1944) 1960 *Legal Theory.* 4th ed. London: Stevens.

FRIEDRICH, CARL J. (1937) 1950 *Constitutional Government and Democracy: Theory and Practice in Europe and America.* Rev. ed. Boston: Ginn. → First published as *Constitutional Government and Politics: Nature and Development.*

GALLOWAY, GEORGE B. 1953 *The Legislative Process in Congress.* New York: Crowell.

GRIFFITH, ERNEST S. (1951) 1961 *Congress: Its Contemporary Role.* 3d ed. New York Univ. Press.

GROSS, BERTRAM M. 1953 *The Legislative Struggle: A Study in Social Combat.* New York: McGraw-Hill.

HANSON, ALBERT H.; and WISEMAN, H. V. 1962 *Parliament at Work: A Case-book of Parliamentary Procedure.* London: Stevens.

HARRIS, JOSEPH (1964) 1965 *Congressional Control of Administration.* Garden City, N.Y.: Doubleday.

HART, H. L. A. 1961 *The Concept of Law.* Oxford: Clarendon.

HÅSTAD, ELIS 1957 *The Parliament of Sweden.* London: Hansard Society for Parliamentary Government.

HÖJER, CARL H. 1946 *Le régime parlementaire Belge de 1918 à 1940.* Stockholm: Almqvist & Wicksell.

ITALY, PARLAMENTO 1964 *Il parlamento nella storia d'Italia: Antologia storica della classe politica.* Edited by Giampiero Carocci. Bari (Italy): Laterza.

JENNINGS, W. IVOR (1939) 1960 *Parliament.* 3d ed. Cambridge Univ. Press.

KELSEN, HANS (1934) 1960 *Reine Rechtslehre.* With Supplement: *Das Problem der Gerechtigkeit.* 2d ed., rev. & enl. Vienna: Deuticke.

KING-HALL, STEPHEN; and ULLMANN, RICHARD K. 1954 *German Parliaments.* London: Hansard Society for Parliamentary Government.

LAPONCE, J. A. 1961 *The Government of the Fifth Republic: French Political Parties and the Constitution.* Berkeley: Univ. of California Press.

LEIBHOLZ, GERHARD (1929) 1960 *Das Wesen der Repräsentation und der Gestaltswandel der Demokratie im 20. Jahrhundert.* 2d ed. Berlin: Gruyter.

LIDDERDALE, D. W. S. 1951 *The Parliament of France.* London: Hansard Society for Parliamentary Government.

LOEWENSTEIN, KARL (1957) 1962 *Political Power and the Governmental Process.* Univ. of Chicago Press.

McCRACKEN, J. L. 1958 *Representative Government in Ireland: A Study of Dáil Éireann 1919–48.* Oxford Univ. Press.

MAXWELL, PETER B. (1875) 1962 *The Interpretation of Statutes.* 11th ed. London: Sweet.

MORE, S. S. 1960 *Practice and Procedure of Indian Parliament.* Bombay: Thacker.

MORRIS-JONES, WYNDRAETH H. 1957 *Parliament in India.* Philadelphia: Univ. of Pennsylvania Press.

Parliamentary Affairs. → Published since 1947 by the Hansard Society for Parliamentary Government, London.

POLLARD, ALBERT F. (1920) 1964 *The Evolution of Parliament.* 2d ed. London: Longmans; New York: Russell.

POUND, ROSCOE 1959 *Jurisprudence.* 5 vols. St. Paul, Minn.: West. → Volume 1: *Jurisprudence: The End of Law.* Volume 2: *The Nature of Law.* Volume 3: *The Scope and Subject Matter of Law.* Volume 4: *Application and Enforcement of Law.* Volume 5: *The System of Law.*

RAALTE, E. VAN 1959 *The Parliament of the Kingdom of the Netherlands.* London: Hansard Society for Parliamentary Government.

ROSS, ALF (1953) 1959 *On Law and Justice.* Berkeley: Univ. of California Press. → First published in Danish.

STONE, JULIUS (1946) 1950 *The Province and Function of Law: Law as Logic, Justice, and Social Control; a Study in Jurisprudence.* Cambridge, Mass.: Harvard Univ. Press.

SUTHERLAND, JABEZ G. (1891) 1943 *Statutes and Statutory Construction.* 3d ed. 3 vols. Chicago: Callaghan.

WAHLKE, JOHN C.; and EULAU, HEINZ (editors) 1959 *Legislative Behavior: A Reader in Theory and Research.* Glencoe, Ill.: Free Press.

WHEARE, KENNETH C. 1963 *Legislatures.* New York: Oxford Univ. Press.

II

LEGISLATURES

If legislation may be defined as making new rules of general applicability for the future, it should be evident that most, if not all, agencies of government legislate. The judge was probably the first public official to "discover" law, while the legislature, as a self-conscious lawmaking body, is a relatively late creation. The pressures of change induced by the industrial, technological, and scientific revolutions have made even the legislature inadequate, requiring it to lay down broad policy directives and delegate to administrative agencies the power to make actual rules.

If the legislature has no monopoly on legislation, it does at least have a distinct character of its own. Generally it is composed of one or two relatively large bodies of people who, technically at least, are peers. Their authority customarily is derived from some scheme of representation, most often the population living in a delimited geographical area, although there may be some other basis, such as class, or function performed in the system. Because all members are on the same footing and issues are decided by a majority vote, members tend to be or to become generalists, whatever their previous vocation. Except in some upper

houses based on class, members are politicians forced to face the recurrent hazards of the ballot box. These facts are important: they shape the institutional life of the legislature and the attitudes of its members, just as the bureaucracy and the judiciary are shaped institutionally by their own methods of recruitment and advancement and by the materials and methods of decision making on which they must rely.

Legislative structure

The structure of a legislature obviously affects its decision making, although structure is not necessarily the most important influence. There are essentially two models of legislative structure, the parliamentary and the congressional–presidential (referred to hereafter as the "congressional").

The parliamentary model. The crucial element in the parliamentary model is that the executive is selected by the legislature from among its own members. Presumably, then, the executive is responsible to the legislature. This responsibility may be enforced if the executive is allowed to stand only so long as it has the support of the legislature. The executive may in turn have the power to force the dissolution of the house to which it is responsible, thus requiring a new election. It should be obvious that this kind of responsibility is difficult to maintain toward more than one house. In England, where cabinet government emerged, the powers of the House of Lords withered away or were taken away by the House of Commons, as logically they should have been, until convention would not allow a lord to be prime minister (though he might still sit in the cabinet). There are systems, nevertheless, in which some responsibility falls to a second house, as it did in the French Third Republic and still does in some other systems, with predictable difficulties.

Most national legislatures in continental Europe are relatively recent creations or fairly complete overhauls of feudal institutions. In France, for instance, the States-General lay dormant for two centuries during the reigns of divine right monarchs; the National Assembly was a creature of revolution. The only legislature to survive to the present, adapting its procedures and distribution of powers without changing ancient forms, is the English Parliament. When William of Normandy conquered England in 1066, he imposed Norman feudal institutions, including the Curia Regis, a court of nobles who attended and advised him, and the Curia Regis Magnae, a great council that met usually three times a year to give counsel and present petitions. The permanent bureaucracy emerged from the former, while the seeds of Parliament took root in the latter. Knights first came to the Great Council in 1213, and virtually all elements were represented, after a fashion, in the Model Parliament of Edward I in 1295. The knights, burgesses, and lesser clergy, who represented the communities, met separately from the barons—who were summoned by name—and came in time to be the House of Commons.

It would be pleasant to relate that the members of Commons set about asserting themselves and followed a rational sequence of development to a system of responsible cabinet government—pleasant but not true. Actually, Commons frequently gave away its own tools, and the cabinet developed as a leadership group through necessity, because George I neglected his job. What has emerged nevertheless is a prototype of parliamentary government. The crown reigns but does not rule. The House of Lords sits and talks without power to bother anybody very much. In Commons the government is supreme, initiating legislation, controlling debate, and determining outcomes with the support of its disciplined majority, even when its margin of numerical superiority is quite thin. The notion that the House of Commons will overthrow a government that has lost its confidence is now a fiction. So, apparently, is the description of the prime minister as "first among equals"; a rather weak prime minister, Harold Macmillan, demonstrated that he could shuffle the membership of his cabinet without interference. It is also true, of course, that party leadership in England must consider the sentiments of its parliamentary members and of the country at large, as it probably must in any system and certainly must in a democratic one.

The government nevertheless can be responsible to the electorate because it is in fact in power: controlling the majority party. Its dominance is safeguarded by procedures that deny to the individual member an opportunity to build a personal following that might support him against his party's leadership, and the electorate demonstrates its understanding of the system by retiring the occasional rebel who tries. [See PARLIAMENTARY GOVERNMENT.]

Needless to say, there may be no end of variations on the parliamentary model. In Norway and the Netherlands and in the French Fifth Republic, ministers are prohibited from being members of parliament. They may have been members, they may run again when they are not ministers, but so long as they are in the government, they may be physically in the chamber but may not vote.

Structural differences may have less profound impact, however, than those induced by other variables in the system. Among the most important of these is the character of the party system. When more than two or three parties elect members to parliament and none has a majority, the coalition cabinet that, perforce, must be formed is likely to lack the stability and poise of a leadership confident of support. In the French Third Republic, where multiple parties could play musical chairs with cabinet seats without having to face a general election, governments fell with boring regularity. The fact that successive cabinets had little actual change of personnel was a consolation to the politicians but did little to increase the prestige of the system. In Germany under the Weimar Republic more than thirty parties reduced the regime to such impotence that the minority National Socialist party easily took power.

The problems faced by a multiparty parliament are enormously enlarged when one or more parties are antidemocratic in ideology and, thus, are determined to bring an end to the democratic game. Hemmed in at both ends of the political spectrum, the democratic parties are forced to mute legitimate differences if the system itself is to stand. Parliamentary government faced this problem in the French Third Republic, as it has in Italy since WORLD WAR II [see PARTIES, POLITICAL, *article on* PARTY SYSTEMS].

The congressional model. The daily operations of the U.S. Congress show a strong influence of British forms and procedure. For example, a speaker presides over the House of Representatives. The constitutional stipulation that revenue bills must originate in the lower house reflects hard British experience, as do the privileges and immunities which members take for granted. But such resemblances are superficial; the constitution fashioned a structure of power unlike the British one, and the forces of American life have strengthened and extended the differences. For example, the American speaker is as partisan as the British speaker is neutral.

The makers of the American constitution followed Locke and Montesquieu in attributing a separation of powers to the British system. More important, their colonial experience encompassed a more or less representative lower house pitted against the executive—the king's representative. Thus, they wrote into the constitution a prohibition against any person's serving simultaneously in both executive and legislative branches. This did not quite accomplish a separation of powers—the constitution provided for a certain commingling of powers, and in practice there has been even more.

Institutions, however, were separated with clean finality. When the Founding Fathers then gave the president and members of both houses fixed but different terms of office, they established conditions making continuous bargaining and compromise an imperative of the system.

British members of Parliament look to the bureaucracy for information, because its ministers are their own men; the same is not true for members of Congress. Congress recognized early that if it were to maintain its independence of, and a semblance of equality with, the executive, it must develop its own research tools. The answer was a system of standing committees, each, in time, coming to have a fairly clear subject-matter jurisdiction, which made it a little legislature within its own sphere of competence. Woodrow Wilson's observation at the end of the nineteenth century that "congressional government is committee government" is still true and seems likely to remain so, barring really fundamental changes in Congressional procedures. Each bill that becomes law must pass the committee test in each house; it may be the subject of hearings, debate, and amendment, or it may die without consideration. If it goes to the floor of either house, it will be promoted there by committee leaders, who also sit in conference with their counterparts of the other body of Congress, to compromise differences written into the bill by the respective houses. Committee chairmen, who gain their eminence through seniority on their committees and retain it so long as they are members, are thus powerful men indeed. Party leaders negotiate with them in a relationship that has more than a superficial resemblance to that of a medieval king and his feudal barons.

Power is further fragmented in Congress by the separation of the legislative and appropriations processes. The expenditure of public funds must first be authorized by legislation considered by the appropriate subject-matter committee in each house. No money can be spent, however, until there has been an appropriation, which is considered not by the legislative committees but by the two appropriations committees. Inasmuch as they may reduce the amount requested or deny funds altogether, they (and their subcommittees) exercise power and enjoy prestige not rivaled by many of the legislative committees.

Power vested in committee chairmen might still be harnessed to party purposes (the chairmen might sit on a party policy committee, for instance, and advance its program in their respective committees) if it were not for the localism of American politics. The constitution requires members of Congress to be residents of the states they represent, and in nearly all cases representatives reside in their districts. The major parties are not truly national; they are federations of state and local parties, held together by the exigencies of presidential politics, unable to help or hurt members of Congress very much. The individual member's constituency therefore is usually paramount; it can end his political life or furnish him a secure base independent of national party leadership. His policy preferences therefore tend to be an amalgam of interests; he may vote with a majority of his party on most issues because there is no conflict but reserve the right to proceed independently when he chooses. Thus, there are very few straight party-line votes in either house, and the president's floor leaders must learn to put together majorities however they can. Interest groups are in the thick of every fight, knowing full well that each contest is in a sense a new one [see PRESIDENTIAL GOVERNMENT].

Problems for research

Legislative–executive relations. The relationship of the legislature and the executive is crucial in any political system; yet analysis of it has not gone very deep. In England the House of Commons may harass its own minister through the question hour, but how much control can a minister who spends so much time on the floor exercise over his department? Indeed, how much does the legislature affect the performance of the bureaucracy in any country? In the republics of France the bureaucrats paid little heed to parliamentary charades. In the United States the oversight of administration is supposed to be a primary function of committees, but not much is known about the complex patterns of relationships that actually exist. Some committees apparently exercise no supervision; others participate as virtual partners in the most important decisions. Indeed, there probably is no more richly varied or complicated political relationship anywhere than that between the president and his establishment, on the one hand, and Congress, on the other. The initiative in legislation has passed over to the executive, but members of Congress share in it. Administration, the responsibility of the executive, is subjected to a variety of Congressional pressures, with results that defy measurement.

Answers to questions concerning legislative–executive relations had to wait for research interest to turn in that direction. In the early twentieth century students of the legislature were likely to devote themselves to formal descriptions of the institution and its procedures or to legal analyses of its powers and its relations with other organs of government. In the United States such writing was often value-laden; scholars could draw up "model" legislatures because they knew what a good legislature was like and what it should do. This willingness to prescribe, which extended to other public institutions as well, was a product of an earlier generation more confident of the efficacy of reform through structural change. And this trend has not by any means disappeared from American academic scholarship.

Legislative decision making. Beginning roughly with the 1930s, however, attention turned more and more to the political forces that shape legislative decisions—pressure groups, parties, constituencies; this research trend was to manifest itself somewhat later in other countries, particularly England. More recently, legislative research has begun to pry into the internal structure and group life of the legislative body and its subsystems.

A popular tool for this more behavioralistic approach was the case study of some slice of legislative life—the passage of a bill, say, or the activity of an interest group. The case study often gave fresh insights and, at its best, hypotheses worth more rigorous investigation. At its worst, it served as a substitute for analysis, piling up sterile recitals of what happened, which had no cumulative value. Other scholars turned to the public act of decision, the recorded vote, which had the virtue of being a quantifiable unit. With various indices (e.g., liberalism–conservatism, party cohesion, party loyalty) attempts were made to measure the relative weight of contending influences on Congressional decisions. These efforts increased in sophistication with the use of scaling, which tested whether a single attitudinal dimension (e.g., liberalism–conservatism) was in fact being tested, and cluster-bloc analysis, which made possible comparison of the votes of every member of the body on a set of issues with those of every other member.

Needless to say, a fatal flaw of the roll call vote is that it does not reveal vast portions of the legislative process. What finally happens on the floor may be simply the ratification of treaties negotiated elsewhere through bitter disputes. Students of this process face an array of fascinating problems— the relations of the leadership with the rank and file; the internal life of subsystems, such as committees, state delegations, friendship groups, and "classes" of legislators who enter the legislature at the same time; the influence of rules and procedures on legislative outcomes; the legislator's

perceptions of himself, other political actors, and the process; the relations of legislators with outsiders in the bureaucracy, press, interest groups, constituency; and many others. A host of impressions are easy to come by; what is necessary is that some patterns of behavior, individual and group, be identified and some hypotheses as to their relationships be formulated.

Whether they tried to answer such questions or merely sought to get the "feel" of the legislature, political scientists by the mid-1950s were going in person to the legislative chambers and offices. The days were past when a gifted scholar like Woodrow Wilson could write a classic on the American Congress from nearby Baltimore without ever having laid eyes on either house in session. In the United States especially, internships liberally financed by foundations provided for participant observation of national and state legislatures. They led in turn to the actual employment of academic scholars in legislative staff jobs. Interviewing became a popular technique. Usually this was unstructured and relatively informal but, increasingly, highly structured schedules of questions yielding quantifiable results were used with success.

Questions on process shifted their focus to include analysis of the legislative product as well. Were legislative outcomes actually affected differentially by changes in rules and procedures? Relating process to product suggested a different question: Does the legislature go about settling different categories of policy problems in systematically different ways?

Theory construction. As legislative research increased in systematic rigor and sophistication, the troubling question remained: Does it add up to anything? The testing of isolated hypotheses and the posing of problems for further research lead nowhere unless findings can be related to some tenable theory, even one of the "middle range" (to use Robert K. Merton's term). Theoretical endeavors were obstructed, however, by the difficulties posed by the data. On the one hand, roll call votes were so numerous that even a modest study of one Congress could be costly in time and money. To go back even a few congresses, sort out the votes by parties and other significant categories, and relate them to an evaluation of the significance of the votes was quite beyond the resources of research largely performed by individuals. Moreover, except for recorded votes there were few reliable records. Basic information, such as biographical and political data about members and analyses of the meaning of issues, was lacking altogether or hard to uncover. Tentative generalizations therefore lacked the crucial historical dimension, which could be supplied only by costly cooperative efforts to discover and store essential data and provide for easy retrieval.

Even if those tasks were accomplished and a reasonably useful theoretical model of a legislature constructed, there would still be no certainty that it had analytical value beyond the legislatures in a single system. A legislature is a part of a political system that in turn is a component of a larger social system. No model that ignored these relationships would make much sense. Obviously it matters what tasks the system assigns to the legislature. Again, the history of a people is important; it determines the level of their political sophistication and the kinds of divisions among the people the political process must bridge. Revolutions, civil wars, military defeats, are hard to assimilate. If the United States can see no end, a century later, to the passions stirred by its one civil war, how much of the difficulties of France should be attributed not to its governmental structure but to its tortured past?

Comparative analysis. If it should prove feasible and profitable to study political systems comparatively, can the same be said for political institutions like legislatures? Have developments in different countries been similar enough to suggest that there is an endemic need in a modern political system for such institutions? Do they perform similar enough functions for the system, do they affect the behavior of their members in ways enough alike, to make a comparative study of legislatures worthwhile? The same questions might be asked about parties, interest groups, bureaucracies, and so on; the issue is fundamental. Whatever the answer, research on legislatures has been almost wholly confined to single systems, with only some tentative comparisons of local legislatures within a system.

The role of modern legislatures

How effective is the modern legislature? This question has been asked earnestly and repeatedly in the twentieth century. The answer usually is that it is not very effective, that it has lost much ground to the executive. In the United States the criticism has been continuous and bitter. Ironically, the British Parliament, which is dominated by the executive and exercises little independent judgment compared to Congress, usually is discussed in deferential terms even by its critics. In any case, the common judgment is that the legislature was better suited to an earlier, more leisurely

day and that its appropriate task now is to react to executive initiative.

The question can be answered analytically only by relating the legislature to the political system of which it is a part. What functions does the legislature perform for the system—that is, what does it do that contributes to the adjustment or adaptation of the system, that is necessary to the maintenance of the system? It is self-evident that a legislature passes laws, but what is there about the enactment of legislation that is functional to the system? When the question of function is raised, it becomes apparent that to be a mere debating society is not contemptible if the debate is necessary to political education or stability. Performing routine chores for constituents is not degrading if the chores serve as a vital link between citizens and government. Legislation that does not accomplish its avowed purpose is not necessarily a sign of impotence; it may provide a symbolic victory for interests not strong enough to prevail. The lonely champion of a hopeless cause has not cried out in vain if he is the champion of the hopeless. Some of the legislative functions may be manifest, in the sense that their objective consequences for the system are intended and identified; some are latent, having unintended and unrecognized consequences. Whether manifest or latent, these functions contribute to the stability and maintenance of the system. It may be that there are common functions that all legislatures perform for their respective systems. If so, it seems likely also that there are functions performed by each legislature that are the products of the unique relationship between the particular institution and the system it serves.

RALPH K. HUITT

[See also ADMINISTRATION, *article on* THE ADMINISTRATIVE PROCESS; ELECTIONS, *article on* ELECTORAL SYSTEMS; JUDICIAL PROCESS; PARLIAMENTARY GOVERNMENT; PRESIDENTIAL GOVERNMENT; REPRESENTATION, *article on* REPRESENTATIONAL SYSTEMS.]

BIBLIOGRAPHY

BEER, SAMUEL H.; and ULAM, ADAM B. (editors) (1958) 1962 *Patterns of Government: The Major Political Systems of Europe.* 2d ed. New York: Random House.
FINER, HERMAN (1932) 1961 *The Theory and Practice of Modern Government.* 4th ed. London: Methuen. → See especially Part 4, "Legislatures," pages 367–572.
JENNINGS, W. IVOR (1939) 1960 *Parliament.* 3d ed. Cambridge Univ. Press.
KEEFE, WILLIAM J.; and OGUL, MORRIS L. 1964 *The American Legislative Process: Congress and the States.* Englewood Cliffs, N.J.: Prentice-Hall.

LIDDERDALE, D. W. S. 1951 *The Parliament of France.* London: Hansard Society.

TAYLOR, ERIC (1951) 1958 *The House of Commons at Work.* 3d ed. Harmondsworth, Middlesex (England): Penguin.

WHEARE, KENNETH C. 1963 *Legislatures.* New York: Oxford Univ. Press.

WILLIAMS, PHILIP 1954 *Politics in Post-war France: Politics and the Constitution in the Fourth Republic.* London: Longmans.

YOUNG, ROLAND A. 1958 *The American Congress.* New York: Harper.

III
LEGISLATIVE BEHAVIOR

In its most general connotation, "legislative behavior" refers to the activities of members of any representative body; in its commonest usage, however, it refers to activities of members of public representative bodies constituted by popular election.

Objectives and methods of study

The earliest relevant literature is the work of certain political philosophers prescribing various rules which they thought proper to guide legislators' actions, generally deduced from their conceptions of the proper functions of legislative institutions. Such literature includes Edmund Burke's familiar strictures concerning the desirability of representatives' being "free agents" instead of ambassadors from local interests (1774), numerous principles of behavior deduced by Jeremy Bentham from his conception of political and legislative functions (1817; 1843), and John Stuart Mill's arguments concerning the desirability of having representatives merely accept or reject proposals formulated by other agencies, or of responding to "free-forming" constituencies created by proportional-representation elections (1861).

Much current legislative behavior study is still concerned primarily with the functioning of legislative institutions, but in quite a different way. Instead of deducing norms of behavior from normative assumptions about legislatures' functions, it tends to discover, describe, and explain actually observable patterns of behavior which presumably are relevant to those functions. A. Lawrence Lowell, in the first modern empirical study of legislative behavior (1902), examined party-line voting in the British Parliament, the U.S. Congress, and several American state legislatures and based his work on implicit assumptions about the relationship between party voting and responsible legislative functioning. Julius Turner (1952), in comparing party with constituency factors in congressional voting, was more explicit about this

functional relationship, and David B. Truman (1959) not only explored the patterns of such influences in the U.S. Congress in still greater depth and precision but also sought more explicitly than previous investigators to identify and secure data concerning the legislative functions in question. A number of contemporary investigators, particularly Duncan MacRae, Jr. (1958), have explored overt and latent bases of cleavage and consensus underlying legislative voting, relating these either explicitly or implicitly to decision-making and value-allocating patterns characterizing the over-all legislative process.

The development of the "political behavior approach" influenced legislative behavior study as early and as much as it influenced any branch of political science. In the 1920s Stuart A. Rice (1928) and Herman C. Beyle (1931) had already suggested legislative roll calls as a fertile field of data to be explored by new, quantitative methods of analysis devised by them. The previously mentioned works of Turner and Truman, in fact, relied heavily on the methods of Rice and Beyle, respectively. E. Pendleton Herring's pioneering study of group representation in Congress (1929) and the "noninstitutional," "realistic" process studies stimulated in part by it (e.g., McKean 1938; Schattschneider 1935; Zeller 1937), while not precisely focused on legislators' behavior as such, nevertheless impelled attention to it by questioning the adequacy of purely formal and legal descriptions. The principal concern of these and many later writers, however, is still essentially "institutional," that is to say, related to questions about the structure and functions of the legislature or of the wider set of political institutions. They deal not so much with legisla*tors'* behavior as with legisla*tures'* activities, with legislative decisions rather than with legislators' choices. Their dependent variables tend to be process variables (e.g., characteristic ways of handling issues in different legislatures) or "output" variables (e.g., characteristic types of legislation produced under different circumstances). The behavioral indexes of such variables may be the aggregate voting of legislators on relevant roll calls, but the problem treated is that of relating the aggregate behavioral variable to some ecological, demographic, political, or other characteristic of the political or social system rather than explaining variations in behavior among individual legislators.

Of course, legislative decisions are definable only in terms of their component individual actions, so the behavior of individual legislators has in a sense had the theoretical status of 'intervening variable" between social, political, and other determinants of individual behavior (as independent variables) and legislative output and functioning (as dependent variables). But preoccupation with the aggregate of individual actions, the legislative decision, long inhibited scholars even from classifying legislators' behavior in terms of analytic concepts relevant to the explanation of individual behavior. The common practice was to make descriptive classifications in terms of those overt actions—above all the roll call vote—most directly and obviously related to the aggregate legislative decision. Even other categories of behavior which relate almost as clearly and directly to this function as do roll call votes (e.g., initiation or introduction of proposals, floor speeches, and actions in legislative committees) rarely were used to describe legislative behavior systematically.

Instead of inquiring into the antecedents of legislators' behavior, most research proceeded rather uncritically from assumptions about the bases of behavior, which were almost never made explicit. A simple *rationalistic model* pictured the legislator's activity as the outcome of individual means–ends calculations on his part. According to its simplest version, a legislator, knowing what "the public interest" is, acts in an effort to promote it. More complex versions envisage more demanding information-seeking and analytical efforts by him to discover what the "public interest" requires in specific instances and to assess the relative utility of various means of furthering it [see PUBLIC INTEREST]. The *group pressure model*, on the other hand, pictured the legislator acting primarily in response to specific cues or orders from external agencies—constituents, executives, pressure groups, lobbyists, political party agents, friends, relatives, and many others. These pressuring agencies might act out of selfish desire, out of reasoned conviction about the public interest, or other motives. And the legislator's motives for responding to the "pressure" might vary from plain fear to agreement in principle with the pressuring agent. But legislators' actions will in any case be seen as an arithmetic sum of the amounts and directions of the different pressures on them [see POLITICAL GROUP ANALYSIS]. Sometimes, particularly in normatively oriented works, these two models have been treated as the ideal and the perverse extremes of legislative behavior, with the actually observable behavior of "real" legislators in each case presumably lying somewhere between.

The inadequacy of such frameworks for the investigation of individual legislators' behavior was implied by one of the first types of behavioral study,

the tabulation of various social, economic, and political "background characteristics" of the individual legislators. This line of investigation, suggested as early as Lowell's time (Orth 1904), was pursued particularly by Charles S. Hyneman and his students (Hyneman 1940; Hyneman & Lay 1938), who made extensive inquiries into the occupation, political career, legislative tenure, and other characteristics of legislators in a number of American states over considerable time periods. Although, as Hyneman himself explicitly pointed out, there were few hypotheses and no clear theory about the relationship between background characteristics and legislative behavior, the assumption that some relationship did exist was made quite explicit. And it seemed clear to most scholars that this assumption fitted poorly with either rationalistic or group-pressure conceptions.

At the same time, increasing sophistication in more general conceptions of political structures and functions led to increasing awareness of hitherto neglected aspects of legislative behavior. For example, the many, varied "errand-boy" activities performed by legislators in many systems, informal but structured relationships among legislators (friendship, etc.), and numerous other aspects were seen to be as important for understanding the functioning of legislatures as were roll call votes. The importance of attitudinal dimensions of legislative behavior was emphasized by studies which viewed legislators' conceptions of themselves and their legislative jobs as the proximate indicators, if not the determinants, of their behavior (Silverman 1954).

It rapidly became accepted, therefore, that legislative behavior is social behavior in a particular institutional context, not atomistic rational calculation or mechanical reaction to mechanical impulsion or pressure. Increasingly the effort has been to conceptualize and explain legislative behavior more fully, both with respect to the amount and manner of its effect (as an independent variable) on legislative functioning and output and with respect to its relationship (as dependent variable) to other varieties or more general principles of human behavior. Recent studies, for example, have sought to relate the behavior of legislators to the group life of the society and to the role concepts of legislators as individuals (Patterson 1958) and to explain significant aspects of the observed behavior of legislators in terms of role theory (Wahlke et al. 1962), reference-group behavior (Michel 1964), or other social-psychological and psychoanalytical premises (Barber 1965).

Advances have also been made in surmounting

some of the methodological limitations which characterized earlier legislative behavior research. One limitation has been the failure to encompass the universe of public representative bodies. American social scientists, who have been responsible for most of this research, have generally confined their attention to American legislatures. Of the relatively few studies dealing with behavior in non-American legislatures, a disproportionate share are the product of American scholars (e.g., Aydelotte 1963; MacRae 1963). Although studies of behavior in American state legislatures and city councils are increasingly frequent (e.g., Zisk et al. 1965), research in America, as in other countries, has tended to concentrate on the national rather than on local or intermediate levels of government. There have been some important studies of behavior in international or supranational bodies, but they are relatively few (Alker & Russett 1965).

Moreover, despite the example of comparative analysis set by Lowell's pioneering venture, research has more often than not taken the form of case studies. There are numerous important exceptions, but, quantitatively speaking, the literature to date offers primarily studies of single legislatures rather than comparative studies, either of different legislatures or of single legislatures at different points in time. Research has often attempted to explain the historically unique features of particular events, decisions, or policy problems in a particular legislature. As a result, it is relatively difficult to establish generalizations by cumulating findings about legislative behavior even in a particular legislature, despite the qualitative richness of many available studies.

Another methodological limitation has been the tendency to utilize only the most obviously available types of data. Official documents, such as legislative journals and reports of debates, committee reports, newspaper accounts, and similar records provide a seemingly rich mine of data for a number of national legislatures, including the U.S. Congress, the British Parliament, the French National Assembly, and others, as well as for the United Nations General Assembly. Where such data have been readily available, a number of studies have been based on them. But, except for numerous roll call analyses, these studies have been more intuitive than systematic. Rarely have such data been subjected to content analysis or other objective techniques. Roll call analysis, however, has been developed with considerable methodological sophistication, so that various types of scalogram, factor, and other mathematical analyses of roll call data are by now familiar (Anderson et al. 1966).

Another frequently used type of documentary data is the legislative "blue book," or regularly published summary of memberships, legislative assignments, and limited biographical and other related information. A number of social background and recruitment studies have been based at least in part on these (e.g., Finer et al. 1961; Hyneman 1940; Hyneman & Lay 1938; Matthews 1954; 1960).

The most important methodological development in legislative behavior research since the beginnings of roll call analysis has been the use of new sources of data and new methods of gathering them. Systematic interviewing of whole legislative memberships or samples of them is perhaps the most widely used such method (e.g., Wahlke et al. 1962; Barber 1965). But direct observation, systematic surveillance, and participant observation, frequently in combination with systematic interviewing, have also produced some interesting findings (Crane 1959; Patterson 1958). Increasingly sophisticated methods of observing, recording, and analyzing data obtained by these methods promise further fruitful results.

Perhaps the most persuasive sign of methodological maturity in the field of legislative behavior research is the increasing frequency of efforts to combine many types of data, subjected to various types of analysis, in comprehensive assaults on theoretically important problems. Miller and Stokes (1963), for example, have combined survey and other data, utilizing imaginative statistical techniques, to investigate the problem of representation. Bauer, Pool, and Dexter (1963) have explored policy formulation in a broad context, also using a variety of data and techniques. It is fair to say, therefore, that by the middle 1960s legislative behavior had become an identifiable field of research and study, part of the mainstream of empirical political and social research; that scholars in the field were contributing their share of methodological innovations as well as utilizing techniques developed in other fields; and that research was becoming productive of findings relevant to theoretical interests well beyond the historical events and personages of the particular legislatures serving as research sites.

Dimensions of legislative behavior

The most striking characteristic of current legislative behavior research is the number of dimensions of behavior it envisages. Reference was made above to the categories of activity examined in legislative research. One important new category was revealed by the theoretical recognition (or recollection) that legislatures are, after all, political institutions. As such, legislatures in general are essentially patterns of behavior, and each specific legislature is a particular institutionalized group by virtue of the specific behavioral uniformities exhibited by each legislative generation and passed on from it to the next.

The uniformities which constitute the legislative institution have their roots in the constitutional and statutory definitions of legislative functions and tasks, but they go well beyond the formally prescribed behaviors. "Folkways" or "rules of the game," which include not only direct norms of behavior but also sanctions against violators, have been identified in a number of different representative bodies (Matthews 1960; Wahlke et al. 1962; Kornberg 1964). They prescribe such behavior as respect for fellow members' rights in the legislature and in politics; engaging in debate only when informed on a subject, and then with due restraint; standing ready to compromise rather than holding dogmatically to fixed positions; and so on. They have been shown to serve the functions of promoting cohesion and solidarity of the legislative group, channeling and restraining conflict, expediting the conduct of legislative business, etc. [see RULES OF THE GAME].

These norms enter into legislative behavior as major elements of the legislators' conceptions of the legislative role. They are the behaviors expected of individuals associated with the office or position of legislator, by legislators themselves and by their fellows. Besides "rules of the game" the legislative role includes norms concerning (1) the legitimate purpose of legislative activity (identifying social problems and inventing solutions to them, acting as broker between competing groups and interests, etc.), (2) the representational focus of the legislators' actions (the community collectively served by the whole legislature, the local community or constituency which elected the legislator, etc.), and (3) the style of representational judgment ("independent judgment," orders or advice from party leaders or powerful constituents, etc.). The legislature collectively gets work done because the job of legislator is perceived by all legislators in terms of such categories (even though there may be variation among members' conceptions of them).

Moreover, legislatures tend to develop roles obviously related to legislative task performance, to which the same principles apply. The positions of formal and semiformal leaders (speaker, committee chairmen, party leaders, whips, and so on) have role behaviors associated with them. In most legislatures there are also highly informal specialized roles that play an important part in the legislative process. One of these is the role of "subject-matter specialist," a status recognized by legislators, who tend to accept the advice or recommendations of such specialists not on the basis of their party affiliation, personal friendship, or political identification, but directly on the basis of their recognized "expertise" as knowledgeable, though nonprofessional, specialists. It has been demonstrated that such "experts" make their influence felt not just within their own party but among members of other parties as well (Wahlke et al. 1962, pp. 193–215).

Certain other relationships among legislators play a part in their legislative behavior even though they may be peripheral or irrelevant to legislative purposes and legislative roles as such. Friendship groups and cliques, for example, have been found to influence voting, debating, and other categories of behavior. Such groups may be based on affective social ties (ibid., pp. 216–235; Patterson 1959), on membership in a common state delegation (Truman 1959), or other nonlegislative social bases. These groups, which are never large (a dozen or more is unusual), tend to form within parties more than across party lines. There is an even stronger tendency for veteran legislator groups to be relatively impervious to newcomer legislators (who, as might therefore be expected, tend to form friendship groups among themselves).

Like social roles in general, legislative roles are conceived in terms of behavior appropriate for an individual in relation to some specific "significant other." In the case of the above-described rules of the game, the legislator's "significant other" comprises all his fellow legislators. But the legislative system (a network somewhat wider than just the legislature itself) includes numerous other classes of "significant others" with whom legislators interact with sufficient regularity to generate other components of the legislator's role. In most legislatures today these classes would include the chief executive and his representatives and aides, administrators, party officials (both within the legislative party leadership and in the broader party organization outside), lobbyists and other pressure-group representatives, and different categories of constituents.

One important dimension of legislative behavior, then, is the number of different categories of behavior which have analytically been found to be subsumed in legislative role concepts and manifested in legislative role behavior, and the amount and type of variation in these respects found empirically to occur between members of a given legislature and between patterns found in different legislatures.

A closely related dimension involves the synthesis of these components by individual legislators and its consequences for collective legislative action. The aggregative and individual behavior approaches intersect at this point. The aggregative approach sees it as a problem of assessing the relative significance of competing determinants of legislative decisions (e.g., parties versus pressure groups versus constituents). The individual approach sees it as a problem of determining which role cues have most salience for various legislators, which role sectors (e.g., expectations vis-à-vis executive agents, political party agents, lobbyists, etc.) will prevail where there may be role incongruity, or what cognitive and affective structure of individual attitudes will operate under what conditions. On this crucial point relatively little is known. With respect to individual legislative behavior, a beginning has been made at detecting, describing, and classifying individual role orientations in various role sectors—e.g., "trustee," "delegate," and "politico" orientations with respect to representational style (Wahlke et al. 1962)—and styles of conceiving and performing the legislative job in more general terms—e.g., "lawmakers," "advertisers," "spectators," and "reluctants" (Barber 1965). From the aggregative viewpoint, a number of assessments have been made of the degree of influence in particular instances of party, constituents, and other factors—e.g., the many investigations of party cohesion in roll call voting, beginning with Lowell's. There are as yet no instruments and measures for accurately determining the relative influence of such factors or the relative salience of different role concepts and their impact on behavior. Equally important is the theoretical need for more precise and comprehensive conceptualization in this area. It is, therefore, impossible to say with assurance why parties (or constituencies, or other agencies or factors) seem to affect legislative behavior enormously in one system but much less so in another, or even to determine the magnitude of such differences with any precision.

A final dimension, which has yet to receive much attention in research, is that of time—the duration of uniformities of behavior for individual legislators, as well as among groups of them, and the patterns and process of change and development over time. Secular trends in aggregate patterns have been shown to exist in many instances (Buchanan 1963; MacRae 1958), but stability in the behavior of individuals whose behavior constitutes the aggregate picture at any given moment has generally had to be assumed (Aydelotte 1963; Truman 1959). There is now some reason to believe that blocs and coalitions manifest themselves in a much smaller proportion of legislative business than has generally been believed (Riker & Niemi 1962). But the temporal mechanics of legislative behavior, whether in aggregate or individual terms, is another subject requiring considerable study.

Bases of legislative behavior

To account for variations in behavior along the dimensions described above obviously requires consideration of the mechanics and antecedents of individuals' behavior. Interpretation of behavior patterns identified in various cases is difficult without understanding this. For example, party cohesion was long explained in terms of party discipline, in the sense of more or less coercive activities by leaders, whips, and so on. But studies by Epstein (1960) of the British Parliament, by Dahl (1950) and Truman (1959) of Congress, and by others, point to the conclusion that disciplinary activity by party organizations is much less significant in this respect than are individual legislators' sentiments of party identification. The latter phenomenon must be comprehended within the same framework, to begin with, as the party identification of voters in general. Although it seems clear that other factors also enter in, it is by no means clear how or to what extent. Thus, there is conflicting evidence concerning whether American state legislators are more likely to cohere with their party if they are from safe or from competitive districts (Froman 1963; Sorauf 1963), and some evidence that deviation from party positions by CDU members in the West German Bundestag is traceable to the way in which the structure of interest groups in the party influences its nominations for proportional-representation, as against single-member, district seats (Rueckert & Crane 1962).

It does seem clear that legislators acquire basic elements of the legislative role conception as part of their general political socialization, and not from specific socialization into the legislative group, since all members of all legislatures so far examined on this point appear to recognize and conform to legislative expectations remarkably quickly and dependably upon entry into the legislature. It is not clear, however, whether this is because only certain types of persons, who, for reasons that are not yet known, will already have acquired the particular knowledge in question, are recruited for legislative service, or because general political socialization processes equip practically all members of a given culture with relevant norms that remain latent until called rapidly to consciousness by recruitment into the legislature. Socialization and recruitment studies to date offer little more than descriptive data about the occupational and social origins of legislators and their prelegislative political experience. [See POLITICAL RECRUITMENT AND CAREERS; SOCIALIZATION, *article on* POLITICAL SOCIALIZATION.]

The factors offered to account for variations in behavior fall into several identifiable classes, despite the paucity of theory and hypotheses about the exact linkages between the variables and the behavior to be explained.

Ecological and demographic characteristics of salient political units or environments of the legislator have long been presumed to affect his behavior. Reference has already been made to party competition in legislative districts as a possible influence on party identification and cohesion. The socioeconomic character of such units has also been considered an important factor of this kind. In American legislative research it has usually been assumed that the urban–rural character of the unit is the important characteristic in this respect, whereas in other systems the presumption has been that it is differences in social class (workers, businessmen, etc.) which are important. [See PARTIES, POLITICAL, *article on* PARTY UNITS.]

In neither case has it ever been made clear just how these variables are linked to legislative behavior. Social background and recruitment studies of the characteristics of legislators themselves sometimes imply that legislators individually tend to embody the ecological characteristics described. On the other hand, there is considerable evidence that, at least in American legislative bodies, legislators will in various ways reflect ecological and demographic characteristics of their districts, whatever their own individual backgrounds (Crane 1959). In any case, there is very little evidence for a simple deterministic view of the connection between individual socioeconomic background and individual legislative behavior.

From findings like those concerning the relationship between partisanship and party competition, it may well be inferred that structural and situational political variables have a great deal to do with variations of behavior among legislators. The finding in most American legislatures that constituents and constituency interests seem to have primary salience for most legislators similarly points to the importance of such factors. But there is no accepted theory or model of legislative behavior describing the mechanism by which such variables affect the individual legislators. And there is certainly no accepted explanation for the gross difference in such respects between legislatures.

Despite the fears of some early critics of be-

havioral studies of legislatures, it does seem that the unique personality and character of the individual legislator must be taken into account. An early, never replicated study in one American state (McConaughy 1950), for example, strongly suggested the psychological normality or well-adjustedness of legislators as compared with a matched sample of laymen. Barber (1965) has identified some differences of a psychological order among legislators. And Froman (1963) has shown that the unique "individuality" of Congressmen—elements of personality, outlook, style, etc., as well as views on issues and ideological orientations (if any)—leaves detectable traces in their legislative behavior.

The tasks of future legislative behavior research, then, include the elaboration of theories and concepts which will encompass the institution-forming uniformities of behavior within legislatures, the corollary differences and similarities between legislatures in these respects, and the differences in behavior among members within a legislature. Social-psychological frameworks such as role and reference-group theory appear to offer the most promise as guides to these tasks. But it seems clear from work to date that such guides will not by themselves provide answers to the important questions subsumed under the organizing questions— Why do legislators behave as they do, and what difference does it make in the legislative process?

JOHN C. WAHLKE

[*See also* COALITIONS; ELECTIONS; INTEREST GROUPS; LOBBYING; PARTIES, POLITICAL; REPRESENTATION, *article on* REPRESENTATIONAL BEHAVIOR. *Other relevant material may be found in* POLITICAL BEHAVIOR; POLITICAL PARTICIPATION; POLITICAL RECRUITMENT AND CAREERS; PUBLIC INTEREST; *and in the biographies of* KEY; LOWELL; RICE.]

BIBLIOGRAPHY

ALKER, HAYWARD R. JR.; and RUSSETT, BRUCE M. 1965 *World Politics in the General Assembly.* New Haven: Yale Univ. Press.

ANDERSON, LEE F.; WATTS, MEREDITH W.; and WILCOX, ALLEN R. JR. 1966 *Legislative Roll-call Analysis.* Evanston, Ill.: Northwestern Univ. Press.

AYDELOTTE, WILLIAM 1963 Voting Patterns in the British House of Commons in the 1840s. *Comparative Studies in Society and History* 5, no. 2: 134–163.

BARBER, JAMES D. 1965 *The Lawmakers.* New Haven: Yale Univ. Press.

BAUER, RAYMOND A.; POOL, ITHIEL DE SOLA; and DEXTER, L. A. 1963 *American Business and Public Policy: The Politics of Foreign Trade.* New York: Atherton.

BENTHAM, JEREMY (1817) 1818 *Plan of Parliamentary Reform: In the Form of a Catechism . . . .* London: Wooler.

BENTHAM, JEREMY (1843) 1962 Essay on Political Tactics. Volume 2, pages 291–373 in Jeremy Bentham, *Works.* Edited by John Bowring. New York: Russell.

BEYLE, HERMAN C. 1931 *Identification and Analysis of Attribute–Cluster–Blocs: A Technique for Use in the Investigation of Behavior in Governance. . . .* Univ. of Chicago Press.

BUCHANAN, WILLIAM 1963 *Legislative Partisanship: The Deviant Case of California.* Berkeley: Univ. of California Press.

BURKE, EDMUND (1774) 1920 *A Letter to the Sheriffs of Bristol.* Cambridge Univ. Press.

CRANE, WILDER W. 1959 The Legislative Struggle in Wisconsin: Decision-making in the 1957 Wisconsin Assembly. Ph.D. dissertation, Univ. of Wisconsin.

DAHL, ROBERT A. 1950 *Congress and Foreign Policy.* New York: Harcourt.

EPSTEIN, LEON D. 1960 British M.P.s and Their Local Parties: The Suez Cases. *American Political Science Review* 54:374–390.

EULAU, HEINZ; and SPRAGUE, JOHN D. 1964 *Lawyers in Politics: A Study in Professional Convergence.* Indianapolis, Ind.: Bobbs-Merrill.

FINER, SAMUEL E.; BERRINGTON, H. B.; and BARTHOLO-MEW, D. J. 1961 *Backbench Opinion in the House of Commons, 1955–59.* New York: Pergamon.

FROMAN, LEWIS A. 1963 *Congressmen and Their Constituencies.* Chicago: Rand McNally.

GLEECK, L. E. 1940 96 Congressmen Make Up Their Minds. *Public Opinion Quarterly* 4:3–24.

HERRING, E. PENDLETON 1929 *Group Representation Before Congress.* Washington: Brookings Institution.

HYNEMAN, CHARLES S. 1940 Who Makes Our Laws? *Political Science Quarterly* 55:556–581.

HYNEMAN, CHARLES S.; and LAY, HOUSTON 1938 Tenure and Turnover of the Indiana General Assembly. *American Political Science Review* 32:51–67, 311–331.

KORNBERG, ALLAN 1964 The Rules of the Game in the Canadian House of Commons. *Journal of Politics* 26:358–380.

KORNBERG, ALLAN 1966 Caucus and Cohesion in Canadian Parliamentary Parties. *American Political Science Review* 60:83–92.

LIJPHART, AREND 1963 The Analysis of Bloc Voting in the General Assembly: A Critique and a Proposal. *American Political Science Review* 57:902–917.

LOWELL, A. LAWRENCE 1902 The Influence of Party Upon Legislation in England and America. American Historical Association, *Annual Report* [1901] No. 1: 319–542.

McCONAUGHY, JOHN B. 1950 Certain Personality Factors of State Legislators in South Carolina. *American Political Science Review* 44:897–903.

McKEAN, DAYTON D. 1938 *Pressures on the Legislature of New Jersey.* New York: Columbia Univ. Press.

MacRAE, DUNCAN JR. 1958 *Dimensions of Congressional Voting: A Statistical Study of the House of Representatives in the Eighty-first Congress.* California, University of, Publications in Sociology and Social Institutions, Vol. 1, No. 3. Berkeley: Univ. of California Press.

MacRAE, DUNCAN JR. 1963 Intra-party Division and Cabinet Coalitions in the Fourth French Republic. *Comparative Studies in Society and History* 5, no. 2:164–211.

MATTHEWS, DONALD R. 1954 *The Social Background of Political Decision-makers.* Garden City, N.Y.: Doubleday.

MATTHEWS, DONALD R. 1960 *U.S. Senators and Their World.* Chapel Hill: Univ. of North Carolina Press.

MELLER, NORMAN 1960 Legislative Behavior Research. *Western Political Quarterly* 13:131–153.

MELLER, NORMAN 1965 Legislative Behavior Research Revisited: A Review of Five Years' Publications. *Western Political Quarterly* 18:776–793.

MICHEL, JERRY B. 1964 Legislative Decision Making: A Case Study of Reference Behavior. Ph.D. dissertation, Univ. of Texas.

MILL, JOHN STUART (1861) 1962 *Considerations on Representative Government.* Chicago: Regnery. → A reprint of the original edition.

MILLER, WARREN E.; and STOKES, DONALD E. 1963 Constituency Influence in Congress. *American Political Science Review* 57:45–56.

NAMIER, LEWIS B. (1929) 1957 *The Structure of Politics at the Accession of George III.* 2d ed. London: Macmillan; New York: St. Martins. → A paperback edition was published in 1961 by St. Martins.

ORTH, SAMUEL P. 1904 Our State Legislatures. *Atlantic Monthly* 94:728–739.

PATTERSON, SAMUEL C. 1958 Toward a Theory of Legislative Behavior: The Wisconsin State Assemblymen as Actors in a Legislative System. Ph.D. dissertation, Univ. of Wisconsin.

PATTERSON, SAMUEL C. 1959 Patterns of Interpersonal Relations in a State Legislative Group: The Wisconsin Assembly. *Public Opinion Quarterly* 23:101–109.

RICE, STUART A. 1928 *Quantitative Methods in Politics.* New York: Knopf.

RIKER, WILLIAM H.; and NIEMI, DONALD 1962 The Stability of Coalitions on Roll Calls in the House of Representatives. *American Political Science Review* 56:58–65.

ROBINSON, JAMES A. 1962 *Congress and Foreign Policymaking: A Study in Legislative Influence and Initiative.* Homewood, Ill.: Dorsey.

ROUTT, GARLAND C. 1938 Interpersonal Relationships and the Legislative Process. American Academy of Political and Social Sciences, *Annals* 195:129–136.

RUECKERT, GEORGE L.; and CRANE, WILDER W. 1962 CDU Deviancy in the German Bundestag. *Journal of Politics* 24:477–488.

SCHATTSCHNEIDER, ELMER E. 1935 *Politics, Pressures, and the Tariff: A Study of Free Private Enterprise in Pressure Politics, as Shown in the 1929–1930 Revision of the Tariff.* Englewood Cliffs, N.J.: Prentice-Hall.

SILVERMAN, CORINNE 1954 The Legislators' View of the Legislative Process. *Public Opinion Quarterly* 18:180–190.

SORAUF, FRANK J. 1963 *Party and Representation: Legislative Politics in Pennsylvania.* New York: Atherton.

TRUMAN, DAVID B. 1959 *The Congressional Party: A Case Study.* New York: Wiley.

TURNER, JULIUS 1952 *Party and Constituency: Pressures on Congress.* Johns Hopkins University Studies in Historical and Political Science, Series 69, No. 1. Baltimore: Johns Hopkins Press.

WAHLKE, JOHN C.; and EULAU, HEINZ (editors) 1959 *Legislative Behavior: A Reader in Theory and Research.* Glencoe, Ill.: Free Press.

WAHLKE, JOHN et al. 1962 *The Legislative System: Explorations in Legislative Behavior.* New York: Wiley.

ZELLER, BELLE 1937 *Pressure Politics in New York: A Study of Group Representation Before the Legislature.* Englewood Cliffs, N.J.: Prentice-Hall.

ZISK, BETTY H.; EULAU, HEINZ; and PREWITT, KENNETH 1965 City Councilmen and the Group Struggle: A Typology of Role Orientations. *Journal of Politics* 27: 618–646.

LEGITIMACY

Legitimacy is the foundation of such governmental power as is exercised both with a consciousness on the government's part that it has a right to govern and with some recognition by the governed of that right.

The concept of usurpation as the opposite of legitimacy has accompanied the concept of legitimate government since early medieval times and has helped to clarify it. Usurpers, after seizing power, have often tried to strengthen their positions by giving their governments a legitimate form, and these attempts to clothe a usurping power with legitimacy, whether successful or not, have often revealed what the standards of legitimacy are for a given society or civilization.

Revolutions, unlike usurpation or *coups d'état*, are not necessarily illegitimate. If they succeed they introduce a new principle of legitimacy that supersedes the legitimacy of the former regime. Under such circumstances recognition by the people will often be acquired only as the new government begins governing, and the process of becoming legitimate may include violence and terror. Foreign diplomatic recognition, while not essential, may help internal consolidation and therefore speed acceptance of the new pattern of legitimacy.

Governments, whether following traditional principles of legitimacy or establishing revolutionary ones, may lose their legitimacy by violating these principles. The desire for legitimacy is so deeply rooted in human communities that it is hard to discover any sort of historical government that did not either enjoy widespread authentic recognition of its existence or try to win such recognition. Because it is so universal a phenomenon, however, legitimacy is continuously endangered by the plurality of its patterns and sources. Rivals for power often automatically consider themselves legitimate and their opponents illegitimate. It is therefore difficult to talk about legitimacy in general terms; the different types must be discussed separately and specific examples given.

Types of legitimacy

The numerous historical types of governmental legitimacy may be classified into two broad groups: numinous and civil.

Numinous legitimacy. The dominion of a *god-king*, of which ancient Egypt offers perhaps the most impressive example, is the theological doctrine according to which every pharaoh is himself (among other things) the god Horus, son of Osiris. The doctrine seems to go back to the very origin of the empire. The underlying myth of the birth of Horus, repeated, as it were, in every accession to the throne, provided the Egyptian kingship with a powerful guarantee of identity and continuity, the appearance of eternity. The pharaoh is, as Henri Frankfort (1948) put it, the epiphany of the god, as distinct from the Hellenistic or late Roman institution of the apotheosis granted to an individual emperor (for example, Alexander the Great). The pharaoh's empire is god's empire. Obedience is not merely a political necessity but a religious obligation. Obviously, legitimacy of this sort is a matter of might rather than of right and transcends all juridical explanation.

The *godly origin* of the king, more specifically the king being the son of god, is a concept close to that of the godliness of the king. The early pharaoh was, indeed, both god and son of god. The phenomenon of being the son of god does not belong to antiquity alone, however; it constitutes an essential element of the Christian faith.

Divine vocation as a principle of legitimate government (whether temporal or spiritual) must be distinguished from divine origin. *Dominus noster Jesus Christus nos ad regnum vocavit* ("Jesus Christ our Lord called us to the throne"), claimed Henry IV in his struggle against Pope Gregory VII, and this understanding of the foundation of his office, and of his personal rulership as well, strictly followed the traditional pattern of the medieval Roman emperors. Charlemagne had considered himself as *a Deo coronatus* ("crowned by God"), and he also seems to have been the first king to attribute to himself the famous formula of *Dei gratia* ("by the grace of God"). The Christian *sacerdotium* ("priesthood") derived its legitimacy, and still does, from a source very similar to that of the *regnum* ("kingship"); according to official doctrine, the papal office is based on Christ's designation of St. Peter, which continues to sanctify and legitimize the rule of every successive pope. For centuries both king and priest were considered the embodiment of the institution of the vicariat. The controversy between them was not about their respective legitimacy as such, but rather about the question whether priestly coronation and consecration were of constituent or merely affirmative significance for the *regnum*.

Inspiration is a numinous basis of legitimate government that has not produced lasting governmental institutions to the degree the three previous bases have. Moses is the foremost example of numinous inspiration, and his name is cited in Christian political philosophy whenever government by inspiration and revelation is discussed. The later prophets of ancient Israel could be considered as performing the function in government that has since come to be called the opposition. Time and again prophecy (in the sense of a mission based on direct revelation of a superior will) has inspired powerful political movements, often of a revolutionary kind. The Puritan revolution is a prominent example. Such superior will is not necessarily of a divine nature; Marx, for example, refers to history, and the Bolshevik party is guided by the will of history, of which the party claims to have a (quasi-theological) scientific knowledge.

Civil legitimacy.   Civil legitimacy exists when a system of government is based on agreement between equally autonomous constituents who have combined to cooperate toward some common good. The polis is one paradigm, especially if understood in accordance with Aristotle, who defines it as "an aggregate of citizens, or in other words, of men possessing access to office and therefore either actual or possible rulers" (*Politics* III, 130). Medieval confederacies, viewed not as aggregates of citizens but as aggregates of autonomous estates, form another type of commonwealth, deriving their legitimacy from agreement, or *conjuratio*. Switzerland is an example of this type of commonwealth, the confederacy having survived Switzerland's transformation into a federal state. The institution of assemblies of estates (as for example, the French États Généraux, the old German Reichstag, or the unreformed English Parliament) is another example of an aggregate of autonomous entities, although it is of a very different structure and importance from the confederacy. Finally, every modern constitutional system, or more specifically, every system of representational government is founded either on a basic agreement to follow certain rules or at least on a justifiable assumption that a basic agreement to follow certain rules exists. These rules include the government's obligation to protect civil rights and liberties and to pursue the common good.

Modern constitutional government makes one characteristic of civil legitimacy particularly clear: governmental offices are ordered by trust rather than exercised by dominion. This characteristic is expressed in the institution of periodic elections. In recent times popular elections have become so predominant a criterion of legitimacy that almost every nation feels obliged to pay lip service to the institution of elections, no matter what its system of government [see ELECTIONS].

History and interpretations of the concept

Etymology.   The word *legitimus* is classical Latin, while *legitimitas* seems to occur first in medieval texts, and, even then, only rarely. The Roman form means lawful, according to law.

While the word was used in all spheres of juridical relations, there are definite political overtones: Cicero uses *legitimum imperium* and *potestas legitima* in the sense of powers or magistrates constituted by law. His concept of the *justus et legitimum hostis* ("enemy by right and by law") is revealing; this enemy is to be distinguished from a robber or pirate and is *legitimus* because treaties are concluded with him, and concluding treaties constitutes a common ground of law (*De officiis* III, 108). Occasionally Cicero's usage seems to approach the meaning of hereditary succession: he wrote of dominions given by the tyrant Dionysius to his son, as *quasi justam et legitimam potestatem* ("his by right and by law") (*De natura deorum* III, 84).

The medieval meaning is very different: *legitimus* is what conforms to ancient custom and to customary procedure. The word begins to be applied to persons: *electi sunt quatuor legitimi viri communi assensu* ("four duly constituted men were chosen by common consent") (from a monastery charter, quoted in Du Cange's *Glossarium mediae et infimae latinitatis*) which means qualified persons (*boni homines*) who can testify and guarantee some juridical action to which they give lawlike validity by their very presence, as custom requires. There is, indeed, something to be said for interpreting the medieval *lex* as indicating the particular customary procedure of an appropriate council or assembly composed of members of the family or the judiciary whose resolution or assent gives legitimacy to the respective decisions. *Legitima auctoritas* ("legal authority") is thus sometimes opposed to *regale preceptum* ("royal warrant") just as *legitima potestas* ("legal power") is opposed to *tyrannica usurpatio* ("dictatorial seizure of power"). In these cases the word legitimate points to the element of constituted rule and order, but included in the meaning is the assembly itself to which the rule refers. The 1338 Bavarian electoral law of Emperor Louis states that he who is elected by the electors *ex sola electione censeatur . . . pro vero et legitimo imperatore* ("by the sole process of election he shall be constituted . . . emperor in truth and in law") instead of having to wait for papal consecration and other sanctifying ceremonies. Here the meaning of *legitimus* appears to come very close to its modern sense by adding the element of consent to the original *veritas* of the elected emperor. This idea of consent is precisely the element of meaning which remains in modern usage. Popular consent, although not the whole essence of legitimate government, is one of its most important criteria.

Because the word legitimacy has had so many

different meanings, the kinds of problems considered relevant to a discussion of legitimacy have also varied. For example, Plato's idea of justice bears on the problem of legitimacy. The same is true of Aristotle's concept of the best constitution and his distinctions between good and bad forms of monarchy, aristocracy, and democracy (*Politics* III). In the course of the medieval revival of interest in Aristotle, his discussion of king and tyrant became particularly important. Later, Thomas Aquinas drew a much sharper line between king and tyrant than Aristotle had done and thus came close to a theory of legitimate and illegitimate government. (The king is pursuing the *bonum commune*, the tyrant his *bonum proprium*.)

Augustine.   Augustine declared that it was impossible for any community or government outside the City of God to be legitimate. Empires, he stated (*De civitate Dei* IV, 4), are big gangs of robbers. By turning Cicero's definitions against him, he claimed to prove that the Roman Empire had never been a *civitas* ("state") or *res publica* ("commonwealth") in the true meaning of those terms. He traced the origin of temporal government back to either Cain—the murderer—or Abel —a citizen of God's city. The two *civitates*, he insisted, share only a mutual enmity. There is one respect in which the worldly *civitas* seems to be justified: its desire for peace is a *bonum* ("good"), which through its imperfection points to the perfect and eternal peace of the heavenly city. Since legitimacy thus applies exclusively to the City of God, kingdoms must demonstrate that their subjects are Christ's people, just as kings must demonstrate that they are Christ's vicars. This need, which existed from the time of Augustine on through the Middle Ages, may explain a good deal of medieval political theology and "christology" (Kantorowicz 1957). It may also explain the similarity of claims made by the Roman church and the Roman Empire: *Extra civitatem Dei nulla legitimitas* ("No laws are binding save those of the City of God") [*see* AUGUSTINE].

Marsilius of Padua.   Marsilius rediscovered the concept of the polity as an autonomous entity not in need of spiritual approbation or interpretation. His *Defensor pacis* (1324) represented a bold revolution in political thought. He denied the church any right of dominion, and he based *regnum* and *imperium*, like any *principatus* ("civil power") on the constitution of the human society and the consent of the people, using Aristotle's explanation of the polis as his main source. His astonishing book served the cause of Louis of Bavaria in his struggle with Pope John XXII but did so in a com-

pletely novel way: the foundation of imperial legitimacy was neither God's institution and vocation nor the theory of *translatio imperii* ("imperial succession") but, instead, constitutional election. Marsilius thereby cut the bond of theological legitimation that had united church and empire for over five hundred years [*see* MARSILIUS OF PADUA].

John Locke.   Locke, the great revolutionary political thinker of seventeenth-century England, was, like Marsilius, an Aristotelian and a developer of a novel theory of civil legitimacy. While Marsilius' polemical attack was directed at papal domination and intervention, Locke's analysis of the nature of government started with an attack on the divine right of kings. He used Robert Filmer's *Patriarcha* as his text and demolished its arguments one by one in the first part of *Two Treatises of Government* (1690). Having destroyed the theory of the divine right of kings, he went on to build a totally different theory of government, according to which kingship was an office created by human agreement that served the common good of those agreeing to create it. Certainly, Locke's celebrated compact, from which political society originates, is concluded in order to preserve the natural rights of the contracting parties, but what matters more with regard to the question of legitimacy is that monarchy, as indeed all political institutions, is based on agreement and on the consent of the people. Locke served the cause of the Whig party and its Glorious Revolution against the Stuarts as Marsilius had served the Imperial party against the pope [*see* LOCKE].

Joseph de Maistre.   De Maistre was a leading nineteenth-century advocate of legitimism and a prime opponent of Locke and his revolutionary views. He argued that Locke's concept of law was actually the outcome of human agreement and not of natural right. Condemning Locke's interpretation, he claimed that man cannot make a constitution because *toute constitution est divine dans son principe*. De Maistre conceived of the divine right of kings in a dynastic sense; it is the royal *family* rather than the royal *office* that has been chosen by God. He gave no explanation of the origin of a given dynasty's power, other than through the paradoxical process of *usurpation légitime*. Royal families exist, he stated, and this fact is the most telling sign of their legitimacy. In this view hereditary succession is an essential element of legitimate rule. *Des constitutions politiques* (1809) served the cause of the Bourbon restoration and, more specifically, of Talleyrand's introduction of legitimist doctrine into Europe. Although legitimism as a political force ended in France with the

July revolution of 1830, legitimist ideas dominated nineteenth-century discussions of legitimacy.

Modern discussions

Modern scholarly discussions of legitimacy can best be covered by reviewing three writers who dealt with the general notion of legitimacy: Max Weber, Carl Schmitt, and Guglielmo Ferrero. (From this selection of a sociologist, a lawyer, and a historian, it is apparent that the problem of legitimacy is of concern to many disciplines other than political science.)

Max Weber.   Weber was the first to discover the universal applicability of the notion of legitimacy and therefore the first to use the term for classifying and comparing a great number of sociopolitical phenomena. The legitimists' preoccupation with dynastic succession had narrowed the meaning of the word "legitimacy," and this narrow usage had continued for almost a century. Weber's use of legitimacy helped deprive it of this specific historical connotation. Weber's typology of modes and sources of legitimacy forms part of his sociology of dominion (*Herrschaftssoziologie*) and is to be found in that monumental fragment *Wirtschaft und Gesellschaft* (1922). Legitimate dominion is not distinguished from illegitimate dominion. Instead, within the general framework of a value-free description of social patterns, the plurality of legitimacies becomes apparent. Weber seemed to assume that in legitimate dominion of any type, legitimacy is based on belief and elicits obedience. However, he did not discuss the general sense of legitimacy and instead concentrated on the pure types of legitimacy: the traditional, the charismatic, and the rational. His three types together cover the whole range of such phenomena. (Although these terms have provided the impetus for much empirical research, whether they provide the best classification of the empirical material they have helped unearth is still questionable.) By traditional legitimacy Weber understood mainly patriarchal and feudal forms of order and dominion. Here the objection may be made that the sanction of tradition plays its part in almost every kind of legitimacy, from constitutional systems to charismatic ones. Weber's notion of charisma is so closely associated with the uniqueness of prophets, heroes, and other leaders that it is difficult to understand the striking durability of certain historical systems based on the charisma either of kinship or of office. Weber himself had some doubts about the rationality of the third type: rational legitimacy. However, he never described the precise nature of the belief in legality which he placed at the bottom of legal and bureaucratic dominion. There is almost no place left in his system for civil government in its proper sense. Democratic legitimacy occurs only as a reversion of charismatic leadership and is another concept that cannot be handled in his system. Whether laws are granted or agreed upon did not basically affect Weber's defiant and somewhat bitter "realism" [*see* WEBER, MAX].

Carl Schmitt.   The problem of democratic legitimacy was, for obvious reasons, urgently discussed in the late years of the Weimar Republic. Schmitt's contribution to the discussion was his largely polemical treatise, *Legalität und Legitimität* (1932). The distinction between legality and legitimacy goes back to the French legitimist writers and is most sharply made in M. de Bonald's *Essai analytique sur les lois naturelles de l'ordre social* (1800). Although Schmitt did not define the terms of his title, he seemed to say that the state with parliamentary legislation lacks legitimacy altogether. "Fifty-one percent of parliamentary votes make for law and legality," he stated somewhat sarcastically, without ever asking why the remaining 49 per cent accept the majority decision, although this acceptance is, after all, the basic prerequisite of any constitutional system. Schmitt considered the plebiscitary elements of the Weimar constitution to be legitimizing factors, and he therefore pleaded that these factors be made the basis of an amended constitution. Schmitt's critics pointed out that his caesarist version of democracy was just as formalistic and neutral as to values as the parliamentary majority rule which he attacked (Kirchheimer & Leites 1932/1933). Schmitt's treatise both mirrored the lack of basic consent that characterized the Weimar Republic and was responsible for increasing that lack of consent [*see* SCHMITT].

Guglielmo Ferrero.   Neither Weber's pattern of rationality and legality nor Schmitt's notion about the plebiscitary legitimation of democratic leadership answered the basic question: What is the core of democratic legitimacy? One significant solution was offered by Ferrero, who described democratic legitimacy as resting on two "pillars": majority and minority, or government and opposition. His formula broke the spell of the Rousseauean fiction of a general will (*volonté générale*) and avoids the dangerous drawbacks of considering majority rule as the essence of democracy. Hopefully this illuminating concept will be tested by comparative studies.

Apart from the particular problems already mentioned, there are many important questions about legitimacy that deserve further study. Among them are the partly logical question of the universality of the concept and the partly ethical question of how to resolve conflicts of legitimacies both in theory and in practice.

DOLF STERNBERGER

[*See also* CHARISMA; DEMOCRACY; GENERAL WILL; MONARCHY; POLITICAL THEORY; SOCIAL CONTRACT.]

BIBLIOGRAPHY

BALON, JOSEPH 1959–1960 *Jus medii aevi.* 4 vols. Namur (France): Godenne. → See especially Part 2, "Lex jurisdictio."

BONALD, LOUIS GABRIEL AMBROISE DE (1800) 1817 *Essai analytique sur les lois naturelles de l'ordre social: Ou, du pouvoir, du ministre et du sujet dans la société.* 2d ed. Paris: Le Clère.

BRIE, SIEGFRIED 1866 *Die Legitimation einer usurpierten Staatsgewalt.* Heidelberg: Emmerling.

BRUNNER, OTTO 1962 Bemerkungen zu den Begriffen "Herrschaft" und "Legitimität." Pages 116–133 in *Festschrift für Hans Sedlmayr.* Munich: Beck.

CARLYLE, ROBERT W.; and CARLYLE, A. J. 1903–1936 *A History of Mediaeval Political Theory in the West.* 6 vols. New York: Barnes & Noble; London: Blackwood.

FERRERO, GUGLIELMO 1942 *The Principles of Power: The Great Political Crises of History.* New York: Putnam.

FIGGIS, JOHN N. (1896) 1922 *The Divine Right of Kings.* 2d ed. Cambridge Univ. Press. → First published as *The Theory of the Divine Right of Kings.* A paperback edition was published in 1965 by Harper.

FRANKFORT, HENRI 1948 *Kingship and the Gods: A Study of Ancient Near Eastern Religion as the Integration of Society and Nature.* Univ. of Chicago Press.

FRIEDRICH, CARL J. 1961 Political Leadership and the Problem of Charismatic Power. *Journal of Politics* 23: 3–24.

GIERKE, OTTO VON (1881) 1954 *Das deutsche Genossenschaftsrecht.* Volume 3: Die Staats- und Korporationslehren des Altertums und des Mittelalters und ihre Aufnahme in Deutschland. Graz (Austria): Akademische Druck- und Verlagsanstalt.

HECKEL, JOHANNES 1953 *Lex charitatis: Eine juristische Untersuchung über das Recht in der Theologie Martin Luthers.* Abhandlungen der Bayerischen Akademie der Wissenschaften, Phil.-hist. Klasse, New Series, vol. 36. Munich: The Academy.

KANTOROWICZ, ERNST H. 1957 *The King's Two Bodies: A Study in Mediaeval Political Theology.* Princeton Univ. Press.

KERN, FRITZ (1914) 1939 *Kingship and Law in the Middle Ages.* Oxford: Blackwell. → First published as *Gottesgnadentum und Widerstandsrecht im früheren Mittelalter.*

KIRCHHEIMER, O.; and LEITES, N. 1932/1933 Bemerkungen zu Carl Schmitts *Legalität und Legitimität. Archiv für Sozialwissenschaft und Sozialpolitik* 68: 457–487.

LOCKE, JOHN (1690) 1960 *Two Treatises of Government.* Cambridge Univ. Press.

MCILWAIN, CHARLES H. (1940) 1947 *Constitutionalism: Ancient and Modern.* Rev. ed. Ithaca, N.Y.: Cornell Univ. Press. → A paperback edition was published in 1958.

MAISTRE, JOSEPH DE (1809) 1959 *Des constitutions politiques et des autres institutions humaines.* Edited by Robert Triomphe. Univ. of Strasbourg, Faculté des Lettres, Publications, Series 2, Fasc. 21. Paris: Belles Lettres.

SCHMITT, CARL 1932 *Legalität und Legitimität.* Munich and Leipzig: Duncker & Humblot.

SCHRAMM, PERCY E. 1929 *Kaiser, Rom und Renovatio: Studien und Texte zur Geschichte des römischen Erneuerungsgedankens vom Ende des Karolingischen Reiches bis zum Investiturstreit.* 2 vols. Leipzig: Teubner.

STERNBERGER, DOLF 1962 *Grund und Abgrund der Macht: Kritik der Rechtmässigkeit heutiger Regierungen.* Frankfurt am Main: Insel-Verlag.

TAEGER, FRITZ 1957–1960 *Charisma: Studien zur Geschichte des antiken Herrscherkults.* 2 vols. Stuttgart: Kohlhammer.

WEBER, MAX (1922) 1956 *Wirtschaft und Gesellschaft* 4th ed., 2 vols. Tübingen: Mohr. → Part 1 has been translated as *The Theory of Social and Economic Organization* and published by the Free Press in 1957; Chapter 7 has been translated as *Max Weber on Law in Economy and Society* and published by Harvard University Press in 1954.

WINCKELMANN, JOHANNES 1952 *Legitimität und Legalität in Max Webers Herrschaftssoziologie.* Tübingen: Mohr.

WOLZENDORFF, KURT (1916) 1961 *Staatsrecht und Naturrecht in der Lehre vom Widerstandsrecht des Volkes gegen rechtswidrige Ausübung der Staatsgewalt.* Aalen: Scientia.

LEISURE

Some authors hold that leisure has existed in all civilizations at all periods. This is not the view that will be taken in this article. Time-out is of course as venerable an institution as work itself. But leisure has certain traits that are characteristic only of the civilization born from the industrial revolution.

In the earliest known societies, work and play alike formed part of the ritual by which men sought communion with the ancestral spirits. Both these activities, although their functions differed at the practical level, had the same kind of meaning in the essential life of the community. Religious festivals embodied both work and play. Moreover, work and play were often combined. Conflict between them was either inconsequential or nonexistent, since play entered into work and became part of it. However, it would be going too far to view the shamans or witch doctors, who were exempted from ordinary labor, as a primitive form of "leisure class" in Veblen's sense. Shamans and witch doctors undertake to perform magical or religious functions that are regarded as essential to the community. "Leisure" is not a term that can be applied to societies of the archaic period.

Nor was leisure, in the modern sense, to be found in the agrarian societies of recorded history.

The working year followed a timetable written in the very passage of the days and seasons; in good weather work was hard, in bad weather it slackened off. Work of this kind had a natural rhythm to it, punctuated by rests, songs, games, and ceremonies; it was synonymous with the daily round, and in some regions began at sunrise to finish only at sunset. After work came relaxation; but even then, it was hard to tell where one ended and the other began. In the temperate zones of northern Europe, during the long winter months, the period of hard work would give way to a kind of semi-active existence during which the struggle for survival was nearly always hard. The deadly cold was regularly accompanied by famine and disease. Inactivity, under such circumstances, was something to be endured; followed (as it too often was) by a train of misfortunes, it certainly had none of the characteristics of leisure as we understand it today.

The cycle of the year was also marked by a whole series of sabbaths and feast days. The sabbath belonged to religion; feast days, however, were often occasions for a great investment of energy (not to mention food) and constituted the obverse or opposite of everyday life. But the ceremonial aspect of these celebrations could never be disregarded; they stemmed from religion, not leisure. Accordingly, even though the major European civilizations knew more than 150 workless days a year, we cannot use the concept of leisure to analyze their use of time. Let us take the example of France. In his *Projet d'une dîme royale* (a revolutionary proposal for impartial direct taxation, which was published in 1707 and immediately suppressed) Sébastien Le Prestre de Vauban used the term "unemployed" to denote these workless days; among them he singled out the "holidays"; such days were often imposed by the church, against the will of the peasants and artisans, in order to promote the carrying out of spiritual obligations. Thus the poor man in one of La Fontaine's fables ("Le savetier et le financier") is made to complain that Monsieur le Curé "is always burdening us with a sermon on some new saint" (*ll.* 28–29). In France at the beginning of the eighteenth century, there were 84 "holidays" of this sort, and to these should be added an average of about 80 days a year on which work was impossible because of "illness, frost, or personal business" (Vauban [1707] 1943, p. 18). Thus by the end of the seventeenth century, according to Vauban, French peasants and artisans (some 95 per cent of the labor force) had to reckon with 164 workless days a year. In those poverty-stricken times the majority

of such days were not chosen; rather, they were imposed either by religious requirements or by lack of work.

Aristocratic and courtly leisure. Some authors, of whom de Grazia (1962) is representative, trace the origins of leisure to the way of life enjoyed by certain aristocratic classes in the course of Western civilization. But, in my opinion, neither the idle state of the ancient Greek philosophers nor even that of the gentry in the sixteenth century can be given the name of leisure. Such financially and socially privileged classes, cultured or not, paid for their own idleness with the work of their slaves, peasants, or servants. Such idleness cannot be defined in terms of its relation to work, since it neither complements nor rewards work but rather takes the place of work altogether. Of course, the aristocratic way of life has contributed in no small measure to the refinement of human culture; its ideal man was freed from work so none of his capacities, physical or mental, should fail to be developed to the highest level. In ancient Greece, philosophers associated this ideal with wisdom; Aristotle himself argued that the work of slaves (that is, almost any form of manual labor) was incompatible with nobility of mind, and it is significant that the Greek word for having nothing to do (*scholē*) also meant "school." The courtiers of Europe, after the end of the Middle Ages, both invented and extolled the ideal of the humanist and the gentleman. The idleness of the nobility never lost its connection with the very highest values of civilization, even though many of the nobles themselves might have been mediocrities or scoundrels. Nevertheless, "leisure" is not a suitable term for referring to the activities of these idle elites, since leisure in the modern sense presupposes work.

Modern leisure. For leisure to become possible in the life of the great majority of workers, two preconditions must exist in society at large. First, society ceases to govern its activities by means of common ritual obligations. At least some of these activities (work and leisure, among others) no longer fall under the category of collective rites but become the unfettered responsibility of the individual, even though the individual's choice in the matter may still, of course, be determined by more impersonal social necessities. Second, the work by which a man earns his living is set apart from his other activities; its limits are no longer natural but arbitrary—indeed, it is organized in so definite a fashion that it can easily be separated, both in theory and in practice, from his free time.

These two necessary conditions exist only in

the social life of industrial and postindustrial civilizations; their absence from archaic and traditional agrarian civilizations means the absence of leisure. When the concept of leisure begins to infiltrate the rural life of modern societies, it is because agricultural labor is tending toward an industrial mode of organization and because rural life is already permeated by the urban values of industrialization. The same can be said of the agrarian societies of the "third world," which are in the process of raising themselves to the preindustrial level.

Definition of leisure

Having outlined the nature of leisure in general, we can now proceed to a more specific definition, since the numerous studies of leisure made during the last thirty years allow us to describe with some exactitude how the concept may and may not be applied. In the first place, leisure should be distinguished from free time, that is, time left free not only from regular employment but also from overtime and from time spent in travel to and from the work place. Free time includes leisure, as well as all the other activities that take place outside the context of gainful employment. The personal needs of eating, sleeping, and caring for one's health and appearance, as well as familial, social, civic, and religious obligations, must all be attended to in one's free time. Leisure, by contrast, will be described here as having four basic characteristics, two of which can be called negative, since they refer to the absence of certain social obligations, and two positive, since they are defined in terms of personal fulfillment. In a 1953 survey of concepts of leisure based on a sample of French laborers and white-collar workers, it was found that, in nearly every case, these four characteristics were closely associated in the mind of the respondent.

Freedom from obligations.   Leisure is the result of free choice. To be sure, leisure is not the same thing as freedom, and it would be wrong to say that obligations have no part in leisure at all. However, leisure does include freedom from a certain class of obligations. It must, of course, be conceded that leisure, like other social phenomena, is subject to the operation of social forces. In the same way, since it is an activity, it must depend, like every activity, on social relationships and therefore on interpersonal obligations such as contracts or even agreements to meet at a certain time and place. It is likewise subject to the obligations that may be imposed by any of the groups and organizations, from athletic teams to film societies,

that minister to its needs. But leisure does imply freedom from those institutional obligations that are prescribed by the basic forms of social organization. With respect to these institutional obligations, the obligations arising from leisure, considered as a form of social organization, always have a secondary character from society's viewpoint, regardless of how heavy they may be. To employ a dialectical mode of reasoning, leisure both implies and presupposes the existence of the fundamental obligations that are its opposite; the latter must cease before the former can begin, and each can be defined only in terms of the other.

Leisure, then, consists first and foremost in freedom from gainful employment in a place of business; similarly, it implies freedom from study that is part of a school curriculum. Leisure also includes freedom from the fundamental obligations prescribed by other basic forms of social organization such as the family, the community, and the church. Let us call this class of institutional obligations "primary obligations." Conversely, when a leisure activity becomes part of one's job (like sport to an amateur turned professional), one's studies (like a film show that all members of the school must attend), one's family life (like a Sunday walk), or one's religious or political obligations (like a political mass rally), then its nature, from a sociological point of view, undergoes a change even when its technical content has not changed at all and it affords the same satisfactions as before.

Disinterestedness.   The disinterested character of leisure is the corollary, in terms of means and ends, of its freedom from primary obligations. Leisure is not motivated basically by gain, like a job; it has no utilitarian purpose, as do domestic obligations; unlike political or spiritual duties, it does not aim at any ideological or missionary purpose. True leisure precludes the use of any physical, artistic, intellectual, or social activity—in short, of any form of play—to serve any material or social end whatsoever, even though leisure, like any other activity, is subject to the laws of physical and social necessity.

It follows that, if leisure is governed in part by some commercial, utilitarian, or ideological purpose, it is no longer wholly leisure. Such leisure retains only part of its nature; we will therefore call it "semileisure." Under these conditions it is as if the circle of primary obligations partially obscured the circle of leisure; semileisure is the area where the two circles intersect. This situation exists when the athlete is paid for some of his appearances, the angler sells part of his catch, the gardener with a passion for flowers plants a few vegetables for his own consumption, or the ardent handyman repairs his own house; it can even happen when someone attends a municipal function more for the show than the ceremony, or when an office worker reads a highbrow novel so that he can let the head of his department know that he *has* read it.

Leisure and diversion.   We have defined what leisure is *not* by stating its relationship to the obligations and limits imposed by the basic forms of social organization. In order to define what leisure *is*, it is necessary to state its relationship to the needs of the individual, even when the individual fulfills these needs as a willing member of a group. In nearly all the empirical studies, leisure appears to be distinguished by a search for a state of satisfaction—a state that is sought as an end in itself. This activity is of a pleasure-seeking nature. To be sure, happiness is not simply a matter of leisure, since one can be happy while carrying out basic social obligations. But the search for contentment, pleasure, and delight is one of the fundamental characteristics of leisure in modern society. In this connection, Martha Wolfenstein (1951) has spoken of "fun morality." When the desired state of satisfaction either passes or begins to wear off, the individual tends to give up the activity in question. Nobody is tied to a leisure activity by material need or by moral or legal obligations, as is the case with the activities of getting an education, earning a living, or carrying out civic or religious ceremonies. Although social pressure or habit may run counter to his decision to give up, the question of whether or not he is contented weighs more heavily with the individual in his leisure than in any other form of activity. The prime condition of leisure is the search for a state of contentment; it is enough to say "That interests me." This state can consist in the denial of all tension, study, or concentration; but it can just as well consist in voluntary effort or even in the deferment of gratification. Whether the avocation involves battling against the elements, against a competitor, or against oneself, the effort of perfecting one's performance or one's wisdom can be greater than that spent on one's regular occupation and may even approach the intensity of religious discipline. But it is an effort and a discipline that is chosen voluntarily, in the expectation of an enjoyment that is disinterested. The search for diversion is so fundamental to leisure that when the expected delight or enjoyment fails to materialize, leisure itself is denatured—a situation that is summed up by such remarks as "It was

boring" or "It wasn't entertaining." Leisure, in such cases, is no longer wholly itself, but suffers impoverishment.

Leisure and personality.   All the manifest functions of leisure, to judge from their effect on the persons concerned, answer to individual needs, as distinguished from the primary obligations imposed by society. Thus leisure is directly associated both with the possibility that the individual may deteriorate (for instance, if he becomes an alcoholic), and with the fact that the individual is free to defend the integrity of his personality against the attacks of an urban industrial society that is becoming less and less natural and more and more regimented and run by the clock. It is associated with the realization, whether encouraged or discouraged, of unbiased human potentialities—in short, with the whole man. Such realization, whether or not it accords with social needs, is conceived as an end in itself.

The positive functions of leisure can be summed up as follows. (1) It offers the individual a chance to shake off the fatigue of work that, because it is imposed, interferes with his natural biological rhythms. It is a recuperative force, or at least an opportunity to do nothing. (2) Through entertainment, whether of a sort permitted or forbidden by society, leisure opens up new worlds, both real and imaginary, in which the individual can escape from the daily boredom of performing a set of limited and routine tasks. (3) Finally, leisure makes it possible for the individual to leave behind the routines and stereotypes forced on him by the workings of basic social institutions, and to enter into a realm of self-transcendence where his creative powers are set free to oppose or to reinforce the dominant values of his civilization. Leisure in the truest sense of the word fulfills all three of these basic functions and satisfies the human need that corresponds to each. Leisure that fails to offer all of these three kinds of choice at any time is leisure that, with regard to the needs of the human personality in modern society, must be considered seriously defective.

The sociology of leisure

The importance of leisure in the development of our civilization was foreseen by social thinkers from the very beginning of industrial society. In some contexts Marx treated work in itself as the first need of man, but in others he qualified this statement by adding that work would become fit for man only when it had been transformed by collective ownership, automation, great increases in free time, and the transcending of the antithesis between work and leisure by the creation of the unalienated "whole man." Comte and Proudhon differed from Marx in their conceptions of the society of the future, but all three attached great importance to conquering leisure by means of technological progress and social emancipation. And they all associated the growth of leisure with raising the workers' level of education and increasing the part played by them in public life.

The realities of leisure in the twentieth century, as sociologists have observed them in both socialist and capitalist societies, have turned out to be more complex and less easily defined. The first modern pamphlet in favor of leisure for the worker was written in Europe by Paul Lafargue (1883), who was a militant socialist; its title was *Le droit à la paresse* ("The Right to Be Lazy"). But it was in the United States that the foundations were laid for the sociology of leisure by Thorstein Veblen's *The Theory of the Leisure Class* (1899). Veblen analyzed the different types of idlers that he found among the bourgeoisie; he exposed the conspicuous consumption indulged in by the bourgeoisie in its quest for social status. But it was not until the 1920s and 1930s that there appeared, both in Europe and in the United States, the first empirical studies of leisure by sociologists. The introduction of the eight-hour day awakened both the hopes and the anxieties of social reformers, who wondered whether the extra free time would be used for self-improvement or for dissipation. In the U.S.S.R., the work of Strumilin (1925) inspired research on the "time budgets" of individuals, at the same time that the Soviet government developed an official policy on the organization of leisure. In 1924 the International Labor Office organized the first international conference on the free time of the worker; it was attended by 300 delegates from 18 nations. There was a general feeling that as the time spent on work decreased, leisure activities would have to become more organized (*International Labour Review* 1924). Research projects were launched in the United States; the most famous of them, by Robert and Helen Lynd (1929; 1937), devoted much space to the study of leisure activities, both traditional and modern, and to the way in which they were organized. In 1934 George A. Lundberg, in a study that has since become a classic, defined leisure as the *opposite* of those activities that are on the whole instruments to other ends rather than ends in themselves (Lundberg et al. 1934).

After World War II the sociology of leisure took on a new dimension and new levels of meaning. The United States was beginning to grapple with

the problems of mass society, namely, mass consumption and mass culture. In this new context the paradox of leisure nourished a whole new crop of studies. In 1950 David Riesman's *The Lonely Crowd* appeared, a work of which nearly one million copies have been printed and which has had a great influence not only in the United States but in every part of the world. Riesman argued in favor of the hypothesis that modern man, viewed in terms of his social character, has known only two revolutions. The first began with the Renaissance, when the "tradition-directed" man whose social character had been derived entirely from the community began to be governed by the norms and values of the family and so became "inner-directed." Finally, about the middle of the twentieth century, the second of these revolutions appeared in those countries that had entered the stage of mass consumption and mass culture. In this period man has begun to be governed by the norms and values conveyed by the mass media of communication on the one hand and by peer groups on the other. Under such circumstances man becomes "other-directed." Reflections on mass leisure were therefore central to Riesman's theoretical perspective. A few years later there appeared the first collections of readings on the topic of "mass leisure" (Larrabee & Meyersohn 1958; Rosenberg & White 1957). Finally, decisive progress was made in the empirical verification of these new ideas on the relationship of leisure and culture in mass society (see especially Havighurst & Feigenbaum 1959; Wilensky 1964).

In Europe, during the same period, the sociology of leisure has made almost equally remarkable progress; the work of Georges Friedmann, in particular, gives a special place to the role of leisure in "relocating" man in a civilization dominated by technology. In England B. S. Rowntree and G. R. Lavers' *English Life and Leisure* (1951) has inspired a whole series of sociological monographs and research studies that have evoked considerable response in other countries, especially Holland. Large-scale public-opinion polling from 1954 onwards on the way in which young people spend their leisure is beginning to result in vigorous government programs stressing character building and the provision of facilities for leisure. With these problems in mind, in 1953 Joffre Dumazedier began the research that finally resulted in *Vers une civilisation du loisir?* ("Towards a Civilization of Leisure?" 1962) and in *Le loisir et la ville* ("Urban Leisure") (Dumazedier & Ripert 1966).

In the socialist countries, likewise, the study of leisure has undergone expansion. For instance, in the U.S.S.R. during the period 1956–1962 the gradual replacement of the eight-hour working day by one of seven hours stimulated renewed inquiry, in the tradition of Strumilin, into time budgets and leisure-time activities (Prudenskii 1964; Petrosian 1965). The first empirical study of leisure in a socialist setting that made use of the very latest sociological research methods took place in Yugoslavia (Ahtik 1963). The empirical study of sociology has also taken remarkable strides forward in Poland, thanks to the efforts of the Center for the Study of Mass Culture, which is affiliated with the Polish Academy of Sciences.

Applications. The sociology of leisure has made it possible, for the first time, to draw empirical comparisons between the working class culture of different or contrasting political and economic systems. In 1956 the first comparative study of leisure in Europe was launched, dealing with the leisure of workers in six European cities, each in a different country. The countries included in the survey were Yugoslavia, Poland, France, Finland, Denmark, and the German Federal Republic.

The vitality of the sociology of leisure has given rise to a number of problem-oriented approaches. Leisure has been studied in its relation to work (Friedmann 1958; Riesman 1964), the family (Scheuch 1960; Anderson 1961), religion (Pieper 1948), politics (Lipset et al. 1956), and culture (Kaplan 1960; Dumazedier 1962; Wilensky 1964). It has been treated as a temporal framework (Prudenskii 1964; Petrosian 1965; Szalai 1966), a complex of activities (Littünen 1962), a system of values (de Grazia 1962), and in several other ways.

The sociology of leisure also exhibits great methodological variety; it is not marked by adherence to any particular method, but by use of any and all available methods. Thus, although empirical studies are more common, we find a strong historical tradition, from Veblen to Riesman and de Grazia. The most important project now in progress concerns time budgets; it is a comparative study, using national samples from the German Federal Republic, Belgium, Austria, France, Hungary, Poland, and the U.S.S.R., directed by Alexander Szalai, a Hungarian scholar, under the auspices of the European Center for Coordination of Research and Documentation in the Social Sciences.

It is to be expected that in the future the different industrial and preindustrial societies will stand in increasing need of research, especially in order to: (1) measure the effective limitations of time, distance, money, and so on, that are preventing the transformation of free time into genuine leisure in the life of numerous classes and categories of workers; (2) evaluate the resources available for leisure in the cultural development of whole societies.

In the postindustrial societies now entering the phase of mass consumption, specific problems have arisen, and will continue to arise with even greater intensity. It is the ambivalence of leisure values in popular culture that will pose the greatest problems to sociologists. Will commitment to leisure values be balanced by commitment to occupational, associational, political, and spiritual values, or will leisure threaten all these other values, thus placing in jeopardy the active participation of citizens in directing the future of their society? Finally, since leisure values are themselves diverse, will the values of entertainment and unfettered personal development join forces to create a new ideal of individual happiness and social well-being? Or, on the contrary, will the values of entertainment, artificially hypertrophied by an irresponsible commercial system, come to play, in certain countries, the role of a new "opiate of the people," while in certain other countries a unilateral and oppressive government policy for leisure activities risks truncating the complex phenomenon of leisure, encouraging boredom and malingering by way of reaction? In the last analysis, the whole future of man in industrial and postindustrial civilization is bound up with the answers to these questions. Today, they are the most important questions facing the sociology of leisure.

JOFFRE DUMAZEDIER

[*Directly related are the entries* LABOR FORCE, *article on* HOURS OF WORK; TIME BUDGETS. *Other relevant material may be found in* AUTOMATION; COMMUNICATION, MASS; GAMBLING; INDUSTRIAL RELATIONS; TIME; WORKERS; *and in the biographies of* LUNDBERG; MARX; VEBLEN.]

BIBLIOGRAPHY

AHTIK, VITO 1963 Participation socio-politique des ouvriers d'industrie yougoslaves. *Sociologie du travail* 5:1–23.

ANDERSON, NELS 1961 *Work and Leisure.* New York: Free Press.

CAILLOIS, ROGER (1958) 1961 *Man, Play and Games.* New York: Free Press. → First published as *Les jeux et les hommes.*

DE GRAZIA, SEBASTIAN 1962 *Of Time, Work and Leisure.* New York: Twentieth Century Fund.

DUMAZEDIER, JOFFRE 1962 *Vers une civilisation du loisir?* Paris: Éditions du Seuil.

DUMAZEDIER, JOFFRE; and RIPERT, A. 1966 *Le loisir et la ville.* Paris: Éditions du Seuil.

FRIEDMANN, G. 1958 *Le travail en miettes: Spécialisation et loisirs.* Paris: Gallimard.

HAVIGHURST, ROBERT J.; and FEIGENBAUM, KENNETH 1959 Leisure and Life-style. *American Journal of Sociology* 64:396–404.

HUIZINGA, JOHAN (1938) 1949 *Homo ludens: A Study of the Play-element in Culture*. London: Routledge. → First published in Dutch.

International Labour Review [1924], 9, no. 6.

KAPLAN, MAX 1960 *Leisure in America: A Social Inquiry*. New York: Wiley.

LAFARGUE, PAUL (1883) 1917 *The Right to Be Lazy, And Other Studies*. Chicago: Kerr. → First published as *Le droit à la paresse*.

LARRABEE, ERIC; and MEYERSOHN, ROLF (editors) (1958) 1960 *Mass Leisure*. Glencoe, Ill.: Free Press.

LIPSET, SEYMOUR M.; TROW, MARTIN A.; and COLEMAN, JAMES S. 1956 *Union Democracy: The Internal Politics of the International Typographical Union*. Glencoe, Ill.: Free Press. → A paperback edition was published in 1962 by Doubleday.

LITTÜNEN, YRJÖ 1962 Activity and Social Dependence. Unpublished manuscript. → Paper delivered before the World Congress of Sociology, Fifth, Washington, D.C., September 2–8, 1962.

LUNDBERG, GEORGE A. et al. 1934 *Leisure: A Suburban Study*. New York: Columbia Univ. Press.

LYND, ROBERT S.; and LYND, HELEN M. (1929) 1930 *Middletown: A Study in Contemporary American Culture*. New York: Harcourt. → A paperback edition was published in 1959.

LYND, ROBERT S.; and LYND, HELEN M. 1937 *Middletown in Transition: A Study in Cultural Conflicts*. New York: Harcourt. → A paperback edition was published in 1963.

MARX, KARL; and ENGELS, FRIEDRICH (1875–1891) 1959 *Critique of the Gotha Programme*. Moscow: Foreign Languages Publishing House. → Written by Marx in 1875 as "Randglossen zum Programm der deutschen Arbeiterpartei." First published with notes by Engels in 1891.

PETROSIAN, G. S. 1965 *Vnerabochee vremiia trudiashchikhsia v SSSR* (The Leisure Time of Workers in the USSR). Moscow: Ekonomika.

PIEPER, JOSEF (1948) 1960 *Leisure: The Basis of Culture*. New York: Pantheon. → First published as *Musse und Kult*.

PRUDENSKII, GERMAN A. 1964 *Vremia i trud* (Time and Work). Moscow: Mysl.

RIESMAN, DAVID 1950 *The Lonely Crowd: A Study of the Changing American Character*. New Haven: Yale Univ. Press. → An abridged paperback edition was published in 1960.

RIESMAN, DAVID 1964 *Abundance for What? And Other Essays*. Garden City, N.Y.: Doubleday.

ROSENBERG, BERNARD; and WHITE, DAVID M. (editors) 1957 *Mass Culture: The Popular Arts in America*. Glencoe, Ill.: Free Press.

ROWNTREE, BENJAMIN S.; and LAVERS, G. R. 1951 *English Life and Leisure: A Social Study*. London: Longmans.

SCHEUCH, ERWIN K. 1960 Family Cohesion in Leisure Time. *Sociological Review* 8:37–61.

STRUMILIN, STANISLAV G. 1925 *Problemy ekonomiki truda* (Problems of Labor Economy). Moscow: Izdatel'stvo "Voprosy Truda."

STRUMILIN, STANISLAV G. 1961 *Problemy sotsializma i kommunizma v SSSR*. Moscow: Izdatel'stvo Ekonomicheskoi Literatury.

SZALAI, ALEXANDER 1966 Trends in Comparative Time-budget Research. *American Behavioral Scientist* 9, no. 9:3–8.

VAUBAN, SÉBASTIEN LE PRESTRE DE (1707) 1943 *Projet d'une dîme royale*. Paris: Guillaumin. → Published in English in 1708 as *A Project for a Royal Tythe, or General Tax*.

VEBLEN, THORSTEIN (1899) 1953 *The Theory of the Leisure Class: An Economic Study of Institutions*. Rev. ed. New York: New American Library. → A paperback edition was published in 1959.

WILENSKY, HAROLD L. 1960 Work, Careers, and Social Integration. *International Social Science Journal*. 12:543–560.

WILENSKY, HAROLD L. 1961 Social Structure, Popular Culture and Mass Behavior: Some Research Implications. *Studies in Public Communication* 3:15–22.

WILENSKY, HAROLD L. 1964 Mass Society and Mass Culture: Interdependence or Independence? *American Sociological Review* 29:173–197.

WOLFENSTEIN, MARTHA (1951) 1960 The Emergence of Fun Morality. Pages 86–96 in Eric Larrabee and Rolf Meyersohn (editors), *Mass Leisure*. Glencoe, Ill.: Free Press.

LENIN

Vladimir Il'ich Ul'ianov (who in 1901 began to call himself Lenin) was born on April 22, 1870, in Simbirsk, now Ul'ianovsk, a provincial town on the Volga, one of six children in an educated middle-class family. When he died on January 21, 1924, near Moscow, he was acclaimed as "the greatest genius of mankind, creator of the Communist Party of the Soviet Union, founder of the Union of Soviet Socialist Republics, the leader and teacher of the peoples of the whole world." In different measure the events of his personal life, his intellectual life, and his active political life contributed to this metamorphosis.

His father, of lower middle-class origin, was a graduate of the university in Kazan and for many years taught mathematics and physics in secondary schools in the Volga region. In 1869 he was appointed a school inspector and, shortly afterward, director of the "people's schools" in Simbirsk province, thus earning the rank of nobleman. Ul'ianov's mother was a woman of indomitable character. Daughter of a country doctor with little money and a large family, she had received her schooling at home. The boy Vladimir, the second son, was an intelligent and conscientious student, and a good swimmer, skater, and chess player. He was much impressed by his father's talk of the "darkness" of life in the villages and of the arbitrary treatment of peasants by officials. A voracious reader, Ul'ianov became well acquainted at an early age with the writings of the great Russian authors, from Pushkin through Turgenev to Tolstoi, and was especially interested in the works of Nekrasov; he was also aware of such protorevolutionary writers as Belinskii, Herzen, Chernyshevskii, Pisarev, and Dobroliubov. But there was no hint in these early intellectual activities that he would become a revolutionary.

The first blow to young Ul'ianov's happy existence was the death of his father in 1886. An even worse shock was the arrest, in March 1887, of his elder brother, Alexander, whose brilliant research on worms at the university in St. Petersburg had promised a bright future but who, unknown to his family, had been active in terrorist revolutionary circles. Alexander was executed for having plotted the assassination of the tsar. The Ul'ianov family, shunned by local society, moved to a village not far from Kazan. Ul'ianov was admitted to the university in Kazan, though only on the strength of a character reference from the director of the Simbirsk Gymnasium, father of Alexander Kerenskii, the man Lenin was later to overthrow.

Ul'ianov was arrested in December 1887 for his part in a student demonstration against a university rule that enjoined students from forming organizations. Expelled from the university and forbidden to go abroad for study, he threw himself into preparation for external examinations and was finally permitted to take these in the spring of 1891, thus winning a first-degree diploma from the law faculty of the university in St. Petersburg. For two years he held a job in a Samara law office; at the same time he was studying Marxism and engaging in open criticism of the *narodniki*, activities which he continued in St. Petersburg, where he went in 1893 "in quest of the proletariat." By the spring of 1895 he had become well enough known to be sent by his comrades to visit Georgii Plekhanov, the "grandfather of Russian Marxism," in Geneva. Before his return he met Paul Lafargue, son-in-law of Karl Marx, and the veteran German Marxist Wilhelm Liebknecht but was unable to see the dying Friedrich Engels.

That fall young Ul'ianov joined with L. Martov (pseudonym of Iulii O. Tsederbaum) and a handful of other intellectuals to form the so-called Union of Struggle for the Emancipation of the Working Class, which planned to publish an illegal newspaper, *Rabochee delo* ("The Workers' Cause"). The first issue was confiscated, and Ul'ianov was among those arrested. Imprisonment prevented him from participating in the vigorous strike movement of 1896, but with the aid of books borrowed from the leading libraries of the capital he was able to continue his study and writing. In February 1897 he was released to make his arrangements for a three-year period of exile at the Siberian village of Shushenskoe in Yenisei province, near the modern coal basin of Kuznetsk. There he lived in a peasant hut, his main source of income being the government allowance of 8 rubles a month. A year later Nadezhda Krupskaia, whom he had met in St. Petersburg in 1894, arrived with her mother for a visit and was permitted to remain in Siberia on the condition that she and Ul'ianov be formally married.

In Siberia, he continued his feverish literary activity, in particular pursuing his study of the spread of capitalist relations in the peasant villages. Aware of serious gaps in his education, he undertook a systematic study of quite diverse philosophical views, while also broadening his knowledge of the writings of Marx and Engels. He completed his first major work, *The Development of Capitalism in Russia* (1899*a*), published under the pseudonym Vladimir Il'in. It was at this time also that he read Eduard Bernstein's *Die Voraussetzungen des Sozialismus und die Aufgaben der Sozialdemokratie* ("The Prerequisites of Socialism and the Tasks of Social Democracy"). Bernstein's thesis, revising some basic tenets of Marxism, shocked Ul'ianov profoundly, and he was no less outraged by the *Credo* of the "Economists." He issued his own *Protest* (1899*b*) against this penetration of Russia by the revisionist heresy, and it was adopted by a conference of exiles in Siberia (meeting ostensibly to celebrate a child's birthday).

Political achievements

From this time on, Ul'ianov's consuming passion was the organization of a disciplined Russian Marxist party capable of effectively combating all revisionist tendencies. To this end, he felt, it was necessary to found an all-Russian Marxist newspaper. Released from exile at the beginning of 1900 but forbidden to reside in either of the two capitals or in university or major industrial towns, he promptly applied for permission to go abroad and in July was able to leave for Switzerland. In Geneva, Plekhanov's insistence on controlling the proposed newspaper so offended Ul'ianov that the project almost fell through. However, a compromise was reached whereby Ul'ianov was permitted to arrange for the publication of *Iskra* ("The Spark") in Munich; there Krupskaia joined him in April 1901. The first number was printed (in Leipzig) in January 1901, and a monthly periodical, *Zar'ia* ("Dawn"), followed in December. It was in the course of this year that he began to sign his articles "Lenin."

It was in 1901 also that Lenin began to write his second—and most significant—major work, *What Is to Be Done?*, published at Stuttgart in March 1902. Meanwhile, disagreements between Lenin and his editorial colleagues in Switzerland multiplied; in particular, Lenin's insistence on emphasizing the "dictatorship of the proletariat" in connection with the formulation of an agrarian program irritated Plekhanov, who opposed Lenin's "polemics."

Mainly at Lenin's insistence it was decided to call the Second Party Congress to create an all-Russian party, a task at which the Minsk Congress of 1898 had failed. Lenin himself devoted immense effort, by voluminous correspondence with *Iskra* agents in Russia, to guarantee a workable majority of reliable delegates. The congress met in Brussels in the summer of 1903 but found it expedient to move to London. It was attended by 43 delegates, assigned 51 votes; of these, 44 could be counted on to support the *Iskra* position. With the support of his colleagues on the *Iskra* editorial board Lenin won adoption of his draft program, though two Economist delegates fought hard to include a reference to class consciousness as a precondition to establishment of the "dictatorship of the proletariat." However, a split developed among *Iskra* supporters over Lenin's effort to secure adoption of his version of the first paragraph of a party statute, embodying his conception of the dominance of a revolutionary elite. Despite the somewhat unexpected support of Plekhanov, Lenin's formulation was defeated; Martov's broader definition of party membership was adopted by a vote of 28–22, with one abstention. The subsequent withdrawal from the congress, over other issues, of the five delegates of the Jewish Bund and of two Economists changed the balance of strength. By vigorous caucusing Lenin was able to whip together a fairly solid bloc of 24 votes, which enabled him to carry the election of his candidates to the new editorial board of *Iskra* (now confirmed as the new party's "central organ") and to the new central committee. It was by virtue of these votes, not of the statistics of later party allegiance, that Lenin's followers for decades boasted the name *bol'sheviki* ("majority men").

Lenin's triumph was brief. Plekhanov soon abandoned Lenin's "hard" *Iskra* line, and control of the party and of its central committee passed to the *men'sheviki* ("minority men"). Lenin found himself doomed to years of bitter wrangling with his former colleagues. In the revolution of 1905 he was able to exercise almost no influence. He did not return to Russia until, with the October Manifesto, the autocracy had apparently surrendered. In Russia, he continued to denounce all socialists who would not follow him, and all liberals. After some wavering he supported boycott of the elections to the Duma, and he gave his blessing to, though he did not participate in, an abortive armed uprising in Moscow. After a few months of underground existence, of shifting from one hiding place to another, Lenin withdrew to the relative security of Finland. Pained by his failure to dominate the Fourth ("Unity") Congress of the Russian Social Democrats, in Stockholm (April–May 1906), he took some comfort from his successes at the Bolshevik-organized Fifth Congress in London (May 1907) and was considerably heartened by participation in the Stuttgart Congress of the Second International (August 1907), the first international congress he had ever attended. At the end of 1907 he abandoned his base in Finland and slipped back to Switzerland.

The next ten years were the bitterest and most difficult of Lenin's life. He became wholly occupied not with the direct struggle to combat capitalism and tsarism but with a preliminary, many-faceted battle to destroy the influence of all those who professed devotion to the cause of the proletariat, as he did, but who formulated its task in ways he considered unacceptable. Although Lenin was always ready to score a point at the expense of his rivals, he loudly and insistently denounced "opportunism" as the greatest brake on the progress of the socialist revolution. Thus, he worked himself into a position of almost total isolation within the revolutionary movement. This position, however, was ultimately to prove most advantageous to him. His name became one of the best known among the revolutionaries; but he was dissociated from all the failures of the other leading figures and thus was able, at a crucial moment, to offer fresh hope to the despairing.

In 1912, Lenin's Bolshevik adherents in Russia secured permission from the tsarist government to publish a newspaper called *Pravda* ("Truth"). Lenin at once moved from Switzerland to Cracow and then to Poronino, near the Austrian–Russian border. Here he could hope to keep in maximum contact with, and direct the policy of, the new organ. He could also supervise the activities of the "Bolshevik six" in the newly elected Fourth Duma. Lenin selected Roman Malinovskii to be their spokesman, unaware that he was on the police payroll. Although Bolsheviks from abroad were regularly arrested on their arrival in Russia, Lenin long remained obdurately blind to this circumstance, despite repeated protests from more sensitive friends.

On the outbreak of war in 1914 Lenin was arrested by the Austrian police on suspicion of espionage. The absurdity of the charge facilitated his release on condition that he return to Switzerland. There he remained, in devastating impotence, attending international socialist conferences at Zimmerwald and Kienthal, only to see the meager fruits of his vigorous efforts ruined by the subsequent defection of his allies. It is to this period that belongs the work of which Bolsheviks have remained most proud, *Imperialism, the Highest Stage of Capitalism*, completed in the summer of 1916.

At the end of January 1917, Lenin consoled himself—and all who would still heed him—with the thought that the tsar, fearing the outbreak of a bourgeois revolution in Russia, would not dare make a separate peace with Germany. Therefore, the war would continue, enormously enhancing the chances that Europe (*not* Russia) would begin the socialist revolution. Six weeks later, on March 15, 1917, to his surprise and delight Lenin learned from the Swiss newspapers that the Russian autocracy had collapsed and that a "Provisional Government" had been set up. A new danger loomed—the possibility that all elements in Russia might rally to the new regime. Lenin felt it was an urgent necessity that he reach Russia and prevent the Bolsheviks from making fools of themselves. The German government was likewise persuaded that Lenin's presence in Russia was an urgent need, though not for the same reasons. It was arranged, through Swiss intermediaries, that Lenin and other Russian exiles in Switzerland, whatever their political complexion, be permitted to travel incommunicado (on the "sealed train") across Germany. Via Sweden and Finland, Lenin reached Petrograd on the evening of April 16, 1917. From that moment, one might say, Lenin had no personal life, for his biography and the further history of the Russian Revolution became inextricably intertwined.

Lenin acknowledged that "Russia is now the freest country in the world"; yet he refused to take any part in enabling the new regime to establish itself. Instead he watched for every opportunity to overthrow it in the name of a new absolutism, "the dictatorship of the proletariat." He did seize power successfully on November 7, 1917, and thereafter, notwithstanding frequent vigorous opposition from tried associates, Lenin was in fact able to guide the ever-shifting policies of the new "Soviet" regime until he was incapacitated in May 1922 by a paralytic stroke. Sufficiently recovered to partially resume his duties, he was rendered wholly impotent by a second stroke and remained so for almost a year before his final, fatal stroke.

Major writings

The explanation of Lenin's political success cannot be found in his intellectual achievements, for he was of no significance as an abstract thinker. His most scholarly work, *The Development of Capitalism in Russia* (1899a), was simply a tract to prove definitively the folly of the *narodnik* concept of the role of the peasantry in Russia. He showed that the peasantry was ceasing to be a uniform mass and was splitting into capitalist and proletarian sectors (a development of which Witte and Stolypin became aware independently). In Lenin's view this process should be encouraged by the abolition of landlordism, which was slowing the development of capitalist relations in the village. Thus, the proletarian, "depeasantized," element in the countryside would strengthen the urban proletariat, whose lack of numbers was compensated for by its concentration, fitting it to lead a mass movement of the village poor to overthrow tsarism and capitalism together.

In *What Is to Be Done?*—directed against the *narodniki*, and against the Economists as well—Lenin developed the thought that the working class, left to its own spontaneous strivings, would never become socialist. Only the conscious effort of "educated representatives of the propertied classes," i.e., the Marxists, would be able to *divert* the labor movement, with its spontaneous trade-unionist striving, from under the wing of the bourgeoisie, and to bring it under the wing of revolutionary Social-Democracy." This viewpoint was embodied in the program adopted by the Second Congress, in preparation for which *What Is to Be Done?* had been published. It continued to dominate all Lenin's thinking and actions and is perhaps the very essence of "Leninism" as distinct from Marxism.

Imperialism, the Highest Stage of Capitalism has been hailed as "the most outstanding contribution to the treasury of creative Marxism" and as evidence of Lenin's stature as "a scholar of genius, a most conscientious researcher, and the greatest fighter for revolution" (Moscow [1960] 1963, p. 274). It did indeed assert as a scientific prediction that imperialism spells the doom of capitalism and, because it creates the objective conditions for world revolution, also represents the eve of socialist revolution. In other writings at this time, however, Lenin suggested that the "law of uneven development" might make possible the victory of socialism in a single country.

Even less original than *Imperialism* was his other famous tract, *State and Revolution* (1917*a*), written after the failure of the July uprising as a blueprint for the immediate future. He argued that the existing "hypocritically democratic" regime was merely a "dictatorship of the bourgeoisie" and must be replaced by a "dictatorship of the proletariat," a term that Lenin never ceased to think of as meaning dictatorship of the Bolsheviks. He was careful to emphasize the distinction between the two stages, "socialism" ("from each according to his abilities, to each according to his labor") and "communism" ("from each according to his abilities, to each according to his needs"), a distinction that Stalin was later to cause to be written into the 1936 constitution. Lenin believed that although social inequalities would persist under "socialism," it was impossible to attain to "communism" without an indefinitely prolonged period of "socialism."

Political realism

Lenin's forte was an extraordinary ability, found also in men such as Bismarck, to analyze a given practical situation and to give things an unexpected push in the general direction in which he wished them to move. He did not rely on abstract ideas as guides to policy; he attacked Trotsky for using "abstract (and therefore empty) words." Although, like many other Russian middle-class youths of his generation, he was impressed by the grandiose aspects of Marxism, he never fully committed himself to their implications as worked out in western Europe. On the morrow of his return to Russia in 1917 he denounced " 'Bolshevik' prerevolutionary antiques" on the grounds that they failed to grasp the "incontestable truth that a Marxist must take cognizance of real life, of the true facts of *reality*, and not cling to a theory of yesterday, . . . which like all theories . . . only *comes near* to embracing life in all its complexity. Theory . . . is grey, but green is the eternal tree of life" ([1917*b*] 1964, p. 45).

His leadership of the Bolsheviks during the revolution and in the still more chaotic years that ensued involved a shrewd following of events rather than a genuinely creative initiative. With the definite goal of seizure—and retention—of power in mind, he showed true realism, even adopting positions that to many seemed at the moment completely unrealistic.

His initial demand, in the "April Theses" (announced to his party colleagues the day after his arrival in Petrograd: see 1917*c*), for "all power to the Soviet" surely seemed ridiculous, for the Bolsheviks were only a small minority in the Petrograd Soviet. Yet it turned out to be the only way to save the Bolsheviks from joining the Soviet majority in support of the Provisional Government and thus to absolve them from responsibility in the eyes of the masses later when discontents and disappointments had accumulated. (To be sure, this demand involved the Bolsheviks in the premature July uprising, from whose consequences they were rescued, however, by the Kornilov affair.)

It was realism, too, that prompted Lenin to insist on an armed uprising in November rather than wait for the "uncertain voting" at the Second Congress of Soviets. He was aware, as some of his associates were not, that the masses were not swinging to active support of the Bolsheviks, that disappointments and weariness had bred tremendous apathy, and that there was no likelihood of serious opposition to any group that would act with vigor, particularly if it could wrap itself in the cloak of the soviets and would promise speedy convocation of the long-dreamt-of Constituent Assembly.

His extrication of Russia from the war, similarly, was not the realization of a plan thought out in advance; it was the result of realistic yielding to facts as they gradually became obvious to him. The initial "Appeal to the Peoples and Governments of All Warring Countries" (1917*d*) simply called for a general armistice (Lenin then rejected a separate one) and conclusion of the "democratic peace" that had been proposed by the Provisional Government. Only after weeks of silence on the part of the Allies did Lenin approve of separate negotiations with the Central Powers, and only on the same "democratic" terms. When it became clear that the Central Powers would not make a separate peace on the basis of no annexations and no indemnities, Lenin addressed pointed questions to a congress of army representatives: If negotiations were broken off, would the Germans, despite the winter weather, launch an offensive? If they did, could the army fight or would it flee in panic? Lenin was tempted by Wilson's Fourteen Points address, of January 8, 1918, to contemplate renewal of the war with practical assistance from the Allies. Even in the face of a German ultimatum, Lenin advised dragging out the negotiations in the hope that the expected German revolution would break out and save Russia. Only when Trotsky's defiant "no war, no peace" declaration precipitated the final rupture of the negotiations did Lenin begin to insist on immediate acceptance of the German terms, arguing that, no matter how onerous the

Brest-Litovsk terms were, they would leave the Bolsheviks in control of an amputated Russia, with a "breathing spell" to consolidate their power in preparation for the inevitable "revolutionary war" against the whole capitalist world.

This same realism showed in his handling of the peasant question. Rejecting as irrelevant the criticism that the original Bolshevik decree on the land problem meant scrapping the established Bolshevik program in favor of the policy advocated by the Socialist Revolutionaries, Lenin had exclaimed, "We must follow life." If the Bolsheviks were to remain in power, the peasant masses must be acquiescent; otherwise there would be no food for the towns. When, however, the peasants had clearly tired of accepting worthless Bolshevik paper in exchange for their surplus grain, Lenin promptly abandoned his principle that "the general and basic source of any right to the use of agricultural land is individual labor." He called for a crusade—not, of course, against the peasantry but against the "village bourgeoisie"—to "carry the class war into the countryside" with the aid of the "village poor" (*Polnoe sobranie sochinenii*, vol. 36, pp. 368–369).

His attitude toward the Constituent Assembly also reflected keen appraisal of the realities of the moment rather than any previously elaborated ideological position. At the moment of the seizure of power, when the Bolsheviks still needed the semblance of democracy and there was at least some hope that the Bolsheviks and their Left Socialist Revolutionary allies might win a slender majority, Lenin had been willing to gamble on permitting the election of a Constituent Assembly. When, however, despite Bolshevik control of the power centers, the elections went overwhelmingly against the Bolsheviks and their allies, he flatly declared, "The Soviets are superior to any parliament, to any Constituent Assembly" (*ibid.*, vol. 35, p. 140). After it had met for one night, Lenin announced, "We will not give up Soviet power for anything in the world," and the assembly was dissolved (*ibid.*, vol. 36, p. 242).

Wherever one turns in examining the various policies for which at various times he fought so vigorously, the same theme recurs. Never did Lenin argue for action on the basis of ideas he had advanced in his major theoretical works. In combating the "Left Communists" (April 1920), he wrote them off as "doctrinaires of revolution," adding that "God himself has ordained that for a time the young should talk such nonsense." In advocating the abandonment of the policy of confiscating all surplus grain, the basic step in the introduction of the New Economic Policy, he argued: "We know

that only agreement with the peasantry can save the socialist revolution in Russia, unless revolution begins in other countries. . . . [The] peasantry is not content with the form of relations we have established with it . . . and will not go on living this way. . . . [We] are sober enough politicians to say right out: 'Let's reconsider our policy in relation to the peasantry' " (*ibid.*, vol. 43, p. 59). In demanding at the Third Congress of the Third International that that body switch from the aggressive position he had urged on it a year earlier, he acknowledged:

When we began the international revolution . . . [it] seemed clear to us that without the support of international world revolution the victory of a proletarian revolution was impossible. . . . In other large, capitalistically more developed countries the revolution has not broken out even yet. . . .

What must we do now? We need fundamental preparation of the revolution and deep study of its concrete development in advanced capitalist countries. . . . As for our Russian Republic, we must take advantage of this brief breathing spell to adapt our tactics to the zigzag line of history. (*ibid.*, vol. 44, pp. 36–37)

In celebrating the fourth anniversary of the seizure of power, Lenin admitted:

We thought—or, it would be more accurate to say, we assumed without adequate consideration—that by direct orders of the proletarian state we could get state production and state distribution of products going on a communistic basis in a land of petty peasants. Life showed us our mistake. . . . Not directly on the basis of enthusiasm, but . . . on the basis of *personal* interest, on the basis of *individual* [or *personal*; in Russian, *lichnyi*] incentive, on the basis of economic calculation, will you labor to construct the first solid footbridge leading in a land of petty peasants by way of state capitalism to socialism; you will not otherwise attain to communism. . . . This is what life has told us. This is what the objective course of development of the revolution has told us. (*ibid.*, vol. 44, p. 151, italics added)

. . . It is individual incentive that raises production; we need increase in production above all and no matter what. (*ibid.*, vol. 44, p. 152)

This "lesson in tactics," far more than his so-called testament penned in the interval between his first and second strokes, was the real guideline Lenin left to his successors.

JESSE D. CLARKSON

[*For the historical context of Lenin's work, see* MARXISM *and* SOCIALISM; *and the biographies of* MARX *and* TROTSKY. *For discussion of the subsequent development of Lenin's ideas, see* COMMUNISM *and* IMPERIALISM.]

WORKS BY LENIN

The writings of Lenin listed below were first published in Russian.

(1899*a*) 1960 The Development of Capitalism in Russia: The Process of the Formation of a Home Market for Large-scale Industry. Volume 3, pages 23–607 in Vladimir I. Lenin, *Collected Works.* 4th ed. Moscow: Foreign Languages Publishing House.

(1899*b*) 1960 A Protest by Russian Social-Democrats. Volume 4, pages 167–182 in Vladimir I. Lenin, *Collected Works.* 4th ed. Moscow: Foreign Languages Publishing House.

(1902) 1961 What Is to Be Done? Volume 5, pages 347–529 in Vladimir I. Lenin, *Collected Works.* 4th ed. Moscow: Foreign Languages Publishing House.

(1916) 1964 Imperialism, the Highest Stage of Capitalism: A Popular Outline. Volume 22, pages 185–304 in Vladimir I. Lenin, *Collected Works.* 4th ed. Moscow: Progress.

(1917*a*) 1964 The State and Revolution: The Marxist Theory of the State and the Tasks of the Proletariat in the Revolution. Volume 25, pages 381–492 in Vladimir I. Lenin, *Collected Works.* 4th ed. Moscow: Progress.

(1917*b*) 1964 Letters on Tactics. Volume 24, pages 42–54 in Vladimir I. Lenin, *Collected Works.* 4th ed. Moscow: Progress.

(1917*c*) 1964 The Tasks of the Proletariat in the Present Revolution. Volume 24, pages 20–91 in Vladimir I. Lenin, *Collected Works.* 4th ed. Moscow: Progress. → This article contains Lenin's famous "April Theses."

(1917*d*) 1964 Report on Peace, October 26 (November 8). Volume 26, pages 249–253 in Vladimir I. Lenin, *Collected Works.* 4th ed. Moscow: Progress.

(1920) 1952 *"Left-wing" Communism: An Infantile Disorder.* Moscow: Foreign Languages Publishing House.

Collected Works. 4th ed. Vols. 1—. Moscow: Foreign Languages Publishing House; Progress, 1960—.

Polnoe sobranie sochinenii (Complete Works). 5th ed. Vols. 1–55. Moscow: Gosudarstvennoe Izdatel'stvo Politicheskoi Literatury, 1958–1965. → Translations in the text provided by Jesse D. Clarkson.

Selected Works. 12 vols. New York: International Publishers, 1935–1938.

SUPPLEMENTARY BIBLIOGRAPHY

BALABANOV, ANGELICA 1961 *Lenin.* Hanover (Germany): Literatur und Zeitgeschichte.

BUKHARIN, NIKOLAI I. 1925 *Lenin as a Marxist.* London: Communist Party of Great Britain.

HAIMSON, LEOPOLD H. 1955 *The Russian Marxists and the Origins of Bolshevism.* Cambridge, Mass.: Harvard Univ. Press.

KRUPSKAIA, NADEZHDA K. (1924) 1942 *Memories of Lenin (1893–1917).* London: Lawrence & Wishart. → First published in Russian.

LEFEBVRE, HENRI 1957 *La pensée de Lénine.* Paris: Bordas.

LUKÁCS, GYÖRGY 1924 *Lenin: Studie über den Zusammenhang seiner Gedanken.* Vienna: Malik.

MOSCOW, INSTITUT MARKSIZMA–LENINIZMA (1960) 1963 *Vladimir Il'ich Lenin: Biografiia.* 2d ed. Moscow: Gosudarstvennoe Izdatel'stvo Politicheskoi Literatury.

TROTSKY, LEON (1924) 1925 *Lenin.* New York: Blue Ribbon Books.

LESLIE, T. E. CLIFFE

T. E. Cliffe Leslie (1827–1882), Irish sociologist and economist, was born in County Wexford and educated at Trinity College, Dublin. After graduation in 1847 he studied law in London, where he attended the lectures of Sir Henry Maine and was influenced by Maine's emphasis on the historical approach to an understanding of institutions. He was a member of Lincoln's Inn and of the Irish bar, but he never practiced. In 1853 he was appointed to the chair of jurisprudence and political economy at Queen's College, Belfast, a post he held until his death. His academic duties required his presence in Belfast for only a few weeks in the year, and the larger part of the time he resided in London.

Leslie was a prolific writer of essays, most of which were reprinted. He never published a full-length book, and after his death a biographical sketch reported that while traveling on the Continent he had lost a partially completed manuscript of a comprehensive work on English economic and legal history. His first publication, in 1851, "Self-Dependence of the Working Classes Under the Law of Competition," read before the Dublin Statistical Society, was a youthful performance along conventional lines. It stressed the force of competition and showed none of the originality or break with conventional economics which marked his later writing. In 1856 appeared the only one of his professorial lectures to be printed as such: *The Military Systems of Europe Economically Considered*, a defense of voluntary enlistment as against compulsory military service. His concern with military problems, both in their narrower economic aspects and in their broader historical and sociological bearing, continued for over a decade.

Beginning in the late 1860s Leslie's writings were concentrated for several years on the land problem, particularly in Ireland. He opposed home rule for Ireland but championed land reform and was critical of what he called "insolent theories of race." Drawing upon observations from several visits to the Continent, which brought him in close touch with the French economist and politician Léonce de Lavergne, he stressed the advantages of small agriculture holdings. In his views of the land problem he generally defended laissez-faire policies, and his emphasis was on elimination of legislative abuses in taxation and property rights rather than on positive policies of social welfare. He attacked entail and primogeniture, urged taxation more equitable to workers, and supported extension of the political franchise.

In the 1870s Leslie's main interest turned to economic methodology, apparently as an outgrowth of a cross-fertilization between his studies of the land problem and the ideas of Sir Henry Maine. Leslie had, however, already attacked prevailing theory: in connection with a discussion of Irish conditions (1870*a*), he had repudiated the wages fund doctrine, and he repeatedly criticized it as not squaring with the historical facts of wage determination. He criticized the "vicious abstraction that has done much to darken economic inquiry" (1879*a*, p. 385), and he urged the importance of historical studies for an understanding of the workings of an economic system. In particular, he stressed that competition had not brought about the equalization that theory assumed, and he documented his thesis by repeated citations of geographical differences in agricultural wages in England and Ireland.

Leslie was an acute critic and a careful observer who was quick to see facts that did not square with the theories of classical economics. He did little, however, to present an organized alternative approach or to consider what modification of theory might explain these individual situations. Leslie is sometimes referred to as spokesman of the historical approach to economics in England, but this does not mean that he was part of an organized movement like the German historical school. His wide-ranging criticism of classical economics and his emphasis on the importance of institutions have much in common with the work of Thorstein Veblen.

Numerous references to Leslie by neoclassical economists in the 1880s and 1890s—in particular Henry Sidgwick, John Neville Keynes, and Alfred Marshall—suggest that he had some influence in softening the rigidity of the deductive economics of the classical tradition then dominant in England. His essays on the land problem are still important for the history of the controversy over the economic difficulties of Ireland, and his stimulating criticisms of the purely deductive approach to economics have timeless relevance.

FRANK W. FETTER

[*Directly related are the entries* ECONOMIC THOUGHT, *articles on* THE HISTORICAL SCHOOL *and* THE INSTITUTIONAL SCHOOL. *Other relevant material may be found in the biographies of* KEYNES, JOHN NEVILLE; MARSHALL; SIDGWICK.]

WORKS BY LESLIE

1856   *The Military Systems of Europe Economically Considered*. Belfast: Shepherd & Aitchison.
1870a   *Land Systems and Industrial Economy of Ireland, England, and Continental Countries*. London: Longmans.
(1870b) 1881   The Land System of France. Pages 291–312 in Cobden Club, *Systems of Land Tenure in Various Countries*. New York and London: Cassell.
(1871) 1872   Financial Reform. Pages 189–263 in Cobden Club, *Cobden Club Essays. Second Series*. 2d ed. London: Cassell.
1879a   *Essays in Political and Moral Philosophy*. Dublin: Hodges & Figgis; London: Longmans.
(1879b) 1888   *Essays in Political Economy*. Dublin: Hodges & Figgis; London: Longmans.

SUPPLEMENTARY BIBLIOGRAPHY

KEYNES, JOHN N. (1890) 1955   *The Scope and Method of Political Economy*. 4th ed. New York: Kelley.
MARSHALL, ALFRED (1890) 1961   *Principles of Economics*. 9th ed. New York and London: Macmillan.
MILL, JOHN STUART (1870) 1875   Professor Leslie on the Land Question. Volume 5, pages 95–121 in John Stuart Mill, *Dissertations and Discussions: Political, Philosophical, and Historical*. New York: Holt. → First published in Volume 13 of the *Fortnightly Review*.
Politico–Economical Heterodoxy: Cliffe Leslie. 1883 *Westminster Review* 120:470–500.
SIDGWICK, HENRY 1879   Economic Method. *Fortnightly Review* New Series 25:301–318.

LEVASSEUR, ÉMILE

Émile Levasseur (1828–1911) was the father of modern economic history in France. He was born into a family of jewelers in Paris, and he himself worked at the jeweler's trade. It was this experience which aroused his interest in economic history. After the revolution of 1848, as he put it, "I became interested in political and social problems and, with the eagerness of youth I embraced the republican idea" (quoted in Hauser 1911, p. 88).

He received his secondary schooling in a Paris *lycée* and then attended the École Normale Supérieure and passed the *agrégation des lettres*; it may be worth noting that he never received a degree in history. He advanced rapidly in his academic career. Initially he taught rhetoric at Alençon and Besançon, but in 1868 he was asked to introduce economic history into the curriculum of the Collège de France, and in 1872 a chair of economic history and geography was created for him. In 1871 he succeeded Louis Wolowski at the Conservatoire des Arts et Métiers, and in the very same year he founded, with Émile Boutmy and Ernest Renan, the École Libre des Sciences Politiques, where he taught until his death.

Levasseur's concern with incorporating the material, concepts, and methods of the social and economic sciences into the study of history represented a break with the historical tradition of his time. And not only did he broaden the traditional concept of history; he also brought history into the field of economics, following in the footsteps of the German historical school of economists in general and of Wilhelm Roscher in particular. Until the publication of Levasseur's *Recherches historiques sur le système de Law* (1854) and his *Histoire des classes ouvrières . . . avant 1789* (1859), political economy in France had been an abstract and speculative science; after Levasseur it became an area of historical research. He substituted historical criticism for theorizing and replaced abstractions with data derived from documents and the analysis of statistics.

To be sure, Levasseur made a fundamental distinction between what he called pure political economy, or economic science, and applied political economy, or "economic art"; his own sphere, economic history, was economic art. However, he saw the two aspects of political economy as interrelated: "Economic history is one of the branches of the history of civilization; it protects economic science from the errors of judgment that can result from abstraction, just as experience is a safeguard against the dangers of the mathematical method. In a way, economic history is political economy in action; it teaches, more or less clearly, the lesson of experience, and it is also ancillary to theory" (see Liesse 1914, pp. 348–349). Thus defined, political economy becomes a moral science, focused on man as the center of the whole economic process; he is both active principle and goal.

Of all the related sciences that Levasseur brought to bear on economic history, he singled out statistics as the most important. The publication of *La population française* (1889–1892) was, therefore, an even more important event in historiography than that of *Histoire des classes ouvrières*. For Levasseur, the object of statistics as a science was to make numerical data available to historians and economists. Indeed, he believed that statistics had become an indispensable tool for the historian.

Geography was another discipline Levasseur wished to see more closely connected with history. More than that, he made important contributions to the reorientation of the discipline and is considered one of the precursors of the great French geographers of the beginning of the twentieth century. In place of nomenclature and description, he substituted analysis of both present and future conditions. His 1879 report on the prospects of the proposed Panama Canal, made at the request of Ferdinand de Lesseps, is characteristic of this type of analysis: he calculated the traffic that could be expected and estimated the financial returns.

Finally, Levasseur considered what is now called sociology to be indispensable to the historian.

Levasseur made the following programmatic statement about the ways in which the economic historian should proceed:

Economic history, using documents from the past, statistics, archival material, and the descriptions of contemporaries, etc. aims to explain either a single aspect of the economy of a particular nation, or successive manifestations of such a single aspect in the economies of several nations, or else to present a comprehensive picture of all aspects of a particular national economy. . . . Economic history enables us to observe and follow the progress of economic phenomena in their social milieu, and to determine as accurately as possible the causes and effects of each nation's economic activity. . . . It shows how economic development is an integral part of the general evolution of all societies. (1898, pp. 25–26)

Levasseur's conception of economic history was humanistic, rather than mechanistic. Thus, in a lecture at the Collège de France in 1898, he considered the reasons why once-flourishing empires declined. The soil and climate had remained the same. It was man who had changed. Either he no longer had the skill to raise the produce that had made him rich, or social conditions had diverted him from his original goal. Levasseur explored this humanistic and synthetic concept in the five volumes of his *Histoire des classes ouvrières et de l'industrie* (1867a), which is his masterpiece and which after a century remains in large part valid.

Levasseur's economic concepts are no longer accepted, and sociology and statistics have undergone rapid transformations since his death. However, Levasseur was an important innovator and one who laid the groundwork for, and to some degree directly inspired, such important scholars as François Simiand, Henri Hauser, Marc Bloch, and Ernest Labrousse. French economic historians today still revere him.

CLAUDE FOHLEN

[*For the historical context of Levasseur's work, see* ECONOMIC THOUGHT, *article on* THE HISTORICAL SCHOOL; HISTORY, *article on* ECONOMIC HISTORY; *and the biography of* ROSCHER; *for discussion of the subsequent development of Levasseur's ideas, see the biographies of* BLOCH *and* SIMIAND.]

WORKS BY LEVASSEUR

1854 *Recherches historiques sur le système de Law.* Paris: Guillaumin.
1858 *La question de l'or: Les mines de Californie et d'Australie, les anciennes mines d'or et d'argent, ...* Paris: Guillaumin.

(1859) 1900–1901 *Histoire des classes ouvrières et de l'industrie en France avant 1789.* 2d ed., 2 vols. Paris: Rousseau. → First published as *Histoire des classes ouvrières en France depuis la conquête de Jules César jusqu'à la Révolution.*

1865 *La France industrielle en 1789.* Paris: Durand.

1866 *La prévoyance et l'épargne.* Paris: Hachette.

(1867a) 1903–1904 *Histoire des classes ouvrières et de l'industrie en France de 1789 à 1870.* 2d ed., 2 vols. Paris: Rousseau. → First published as *Histoire des classes ouvrières en France depuis 1789 jusqu'à nos jours.*

1867b *Du rôle de l'intelligence dans la production.* Paris: Hachette.

(1869) 1892 *Géographie de la France et de ses colonies (cours moyen).* 12th ed. Paris: Delagrave.

1872 *L'étude et l'enseignement de la géographie.* Paris: Delagrave.

1879 *Rapport sur le commerce et le tonnage relatifs au canal interocéanique.* Paris: Martinet.

1885 *La statistique officielle en France: Organisation, travaux, et publications des services de statistique des différents ministères, précédée d'un aperçu historique.* Nancy (France): Berger-Levrault.

1889–1892 *La population française: Histoire de la population avant 1789 et démographie de la France comparée à celle des autres nations au XIXᵉ siècle, précédée d'une introduction sur la statistique.* 3 vols. Paris: Rousseau.

(1898) 1900 *The American Workman.* Baltimore: Johns Hopkins Press. → First published as *L'ouvrier américain: L'ouvrier au travail, l'ouvrier chez lui, les questions ouvrières.*

1899 *L'organisation des métiers dans l'Empire Romain.* Paris: Giard & Brière.

1901 *L'enseignement de l'économie politique au Conservatoire des Arts et Métiers.* Paris: Chevalier-Marescq.

1902 *Les études sociales sous la Restauration: Saint-Simon et le saint-simonisme, Fourier et le fouriérisme.* Paris: Giard & Brière.

1907 *Questions ouvrières et industrielles en France sous la Troisième République.* Paris: Rousseau.

1911–1912 *Histoire du commerce de la France.* 2 vols. Paris: Rousseau. → Volume 1: *Avant 1789.* Volume 2: *De 1789 à nos jours.*

SUPPLEMENTARY BIBLIOGRAPHY

HAUSER, HENRI 1911 Émile Levasseur. *Revue historique* 108:88–91.

LÉVY, RAPHAËL-GEORGES 1911 Levasseur. *Revue des deux mondes* 5:96–131.

LIESSE, ANDRÉ 1914 Notice sur la vie et les travaux de M. Émile Levasseur. Académie des Sciences Morales et Politiques, *Séances et travaux* 181:337–361.

La vie scientifique: P. É. Levasseur. 1911 *Revue économique internationale* 3:396–418. → Contains a comprehensive bibliography.

LÉVY-BRUHL, LUCIEN

Lucien Lévy-Bruhl (1857–1939), French anthropologist, was born in Paris. He received a *doctorat ès lettres* from the École Normale Supérieure, and entered upon a brilliant university career, which was crowned by his nomination to the chair of history of modern philosophy at the Sorbonne in 1904. His lectures there were the basis of several of his books, notably those on Jacobi (1894) and Auguste Comte (1900). His lasting contributions, however, are his book *Ethics and Moral Science* (1903) and especially the six volumes he devoted to the study of what he called the primitive mentality.

Lévy-Bruhl's work is highly original, and it is hard to define precisely the influences on his thinking. His stress on the role of the emotions in psychic life may have derived from his studies of Jacobi. In the sociological aspects of his thought he was influenced by the ideas of Émile Durkheim. Yet Lévy-Bruhl also rejected some of Durkheim's ideas and carried on spirited controversies with Durkheim, who then dominated the French sociological school. Lévy-Bruhl could not accept all the implications of Durkheimian rationalism, but he did learn much from Durkheim's *Rules of Sociological Method.* In general, one might say that Lévy-Bruhl was influenced more in a negative than in a positive sense. He was nobody's disciple; indeed, he often defined his thinking by contrasting it to that of others, for instance, to that of the theorists of animism (Frazer, Tylor, and Spencer). But he was not indifferent to criticisms made of his theories, especially the objections of such sociologists as Durkheim and Mauss or of an anthropologist like Evans-Pritchard. His responsiveness to these criticisms caused changes in the orientation of his thought. Three major stages may be distinguished in his intellectual development: the first was marked by his work on morality; the second by his theories on the primitive mentality; and the third by the revisions and changes that he himself made in these latter theories.

Moral philosophy. In *Ethics and Moral Science* Lévy-Bruhl began by showing that all theoretical moralities (whether of metaphysical or scientific origin) are doomed to failure, because theory can be applied only to what is, not to what ought to be. They suffer also from the fact that they fail to take into account the variation of human nature in various civilizations. Morals do vary with time and place, and Lévy-Bruhl advocated that they be studied objectively and that their laws be discovered. On the basis of such scientific knowledge, a rational art and rules of conduct may be set up that will be valid solely in a specified sociological situation rather than claiming the universal validity of the theoretical moralities. Thus, already in this book Lévy-Bruhl was making a direct attack on the postulate of the unity of human nature and laying the foundations of a relativistic and pluralistic sociology.

The theory of the primitive mentality. Lévy-Bruhl's pluralism led him to suppose that several types of mentality can exist among men, that is, that their methods of thinking may vary basically from one society to another. The surest way to prove this, he believed, was to begin by comparing the mentality of civilized man with the mentality furthest removed from it.

He therefore studied the mental functions in so-called primitives, collecting and classifying a large number of documents on this subject. His first conclusion was that the mentality of primitives and that of people living in modern Occidental civilization differ not in nuance or degree but rather in kind. The anthropologists of the English animist school had believed that primitive peoples think or reason in the same way as civilized ones, although they may reason from mistaken premises. For Lévy-Bruhl the primitive man's very reasoning processes differ from ours; the primitive mentality is not simply a rudimentary or pathological form of the civilized. What makes for these differences is not the thought of the individual but collective representations. Ideally, the social scientist would establish the particular collective psychology of each society. Instead, in order to describe the primitive mentality Lévy-Bruhl took his documentation from all preliterate societies.

To the objections of those, like Marcel Mauss, who argued that these societies are not all alike, Lévy-Bruhl answered that for his purpose it was enough that they all share a characteristic that distinguishes them from us. When Evans-Pritchard reproached him with taking his examples from the books of travelers or missionaries, whose observations had not been made in conformity with the best ethnographical methods, he replied that it sufficed for him if the mentality of the peoples studied had been well understood. Evans-Pritchard did get Lévy-Bruhl to admit that he sometimes made savages appear more irrational than they actually are; he maintained, however, that it was not his intention to give a complete description of the life of primitive peoples but to highlight the differences between their mentality and ours.

The collective representations of primitives, he asserted, are essentially mystical, since they imply belief in forces or influences that are imperceptible to the senses. Mysticism pervades all their perceptions. Further, the primitive mentality is not governed exclusively by our laws of logic. Although it is not generally opposed to these laws, it does not shrink from violating especially the law against contradiction. This is why Lévy-Bruhl designated it as prelogical. The connections made by the primitive mind that fall outside of our principles of logic are governed by a principle that Lévy-Bruhl called the law of participation. According to this principle, a being or object can be both itself and at the same time something else. Participation cannot be explained by animism.

The conception of this mystical mentality based on participation led Lévy-Bruhl to more detailed analyses supported by a large number of concrete examples. He showed the effects of this mentality on the language of primitive peoples and on their way of conceiving the world. He described their occasionalist notion of causality and their way of looking at the human personality, distinguishing neither the human being (l'être même) from its "appurtenances," nor the body from the spirit or soul.

Between the primitive mind, which directly exhibits participation, and the civilized mind Lévy-Bruhl found intermediate stages in which participation can no longer be perceived directly but is represented or symbolized. He thus seems to have placed his dualism in an evolutionist perspective. But he took care to state that the mystical and prelogical mentality is never completely supplanted by the undisputed reign of logic. He held that in every human mind there is always some rational thought and some mystical thought. Reason alone cannot completely satisfy man. Lévy-Bruhl did not accept the charge that his was a doctrine of prelogism. For him there are not two mentalities that exclude one another; prelogical thought is not a stage antedating logical thought. Thus, such philosophers as Émile Bréhier maintained that Lévy-Bruhl's theory is actually more structuralist than evolutionist. And the phenomenologist Van der Leeuw interpreted it as postulating the mystical mentality and the logical mentality as two permanent structures of the human mind. In primitive man, the first dominates the second; in civilized man, it is the contrary.

Revisions in the theory. Lévy-Bruhl's first books on mental functions in primitive societies provoked a vigorous reply from Durkheim in his *Elementary Forms of the Religious Life* of 1912. Many further criticisms appeared in 1926–1927, in particular those of Larguier des Bancels, Raoul Allier, and Olivier Leroy. Lévy-Bruhl examined these objections seriously and was led to sharpen and revise his thought. As a result between 1931 and 1938 he published three further books on the same subject He now became more demanding as to the sources of his documentation, relying more frequently on the work of the best ethnographers. Also, without completely abandoning any of the basic concepts of his first analysis (mysticism, prelogical character, participation, occasionalism), he inverted their order of importance, putting mysticism ahead of the prelogical character. And, above all, he introduced a new principle of explanation that tended to dominate all the others, which he called "the affective category of the supernatural." He still maintained, to be sure, that primitive peoples are sometimes insensitive to contradiction, but he strongly affirmed that "the fundamental structure of the human mind is the same everywhere." Primitive men have concepts, but their knowledge is not rationally classified and organized, which leaves the field clear for "mystical preconnections" when the emotional, affective element supplements logical generalization. This colors their entire thinking, since for them ordinary experience is pervaded by mystical experience; similarly, for them the supernatural world, although different from the natural world, is not separate from it, and they pass unaware from one to the other. The prelogical is therefore explained by the mystical and this in turn by the predominance of affectivity over reason. Indeed, affectivity gives a special tonality to primitive representations, and it thus has that element of generality that makes it a category of thought.

In his last works Lévy-Bruhl reduced the study of primitive mentality entirely to an analysis of the mystic experience and the affective category of the supernatural that characterizes and explains it. He showed how this experience of the supernatural emerges mainly in the face of the unusual. He devoted other chapters to the various representations and beliefs marked by this affective category, for example, occult influences, beings and objects that bring bad or good luck, various rituals, magic, revelations as to the secret nature of things and animals, dreams, visions, the presence of the dead, and all of mythology and the techniques for participating in the mythical world.

In these books Lévy-Bruhl was also concerned with transitions between the primitive and the modern mentalities. He found such transitions especially in the development of prereligion into elaborated religion, or of myth into tale and folklore; but at the same time he emphasized more and more that both mentalities persist.

Hence the theory that at the outset seemed to postulate a principle of radical difference between the thinking of primitive and civilized peoples became more flexible. This evolution continued in the notes that Lévy-Bruhl was writing toward the end of his life and that probably would have become a book had he lived longer. These notes were collected and published after his death in a small

book entitled *Les carnets de Lévy-Bruhl* (1949). In it he stated that he was prepared to give up the term "prelogical," and he even questioned the specificity of the characteristics he had attributed to the primitive mentality.

Influence of Lévy-Bruhl. In addition to the phenomenological and structuralist extensions of Lévy-Bruhl's theory, mentioned above, the important influence it has had on the Jungian psychoanalysts should be pointed out: Aldrich (1931) has related the primitive mind to the archetypes of the unconscious. As for the fundamentals of the doctrine, however, few contemporary authors seem to accept a difference in kind between the primitive and the civilized mind. Lévy-Bruhl himself was on the point of giving it up, as may be seen in his posthumously published notebooks. But his analyses of participation play an important part in the thought of many philosophers and sociologists, for example, Przyluski (1940) and Roger Bastide (1953). Again, the advocates of a pluralist sociology, like Georges Gurvich, applaud Lévy-Bruhl's undermining of the classical unitary conception of the universality of modes of thinking. Lévy-Bruhl's doctrine may have few faithful disciples, but at least it compelled anthropologists to reflect on certain problems and in that sense gave a new direction to the study of primitive peoples.

JEAN CAZENEUVE

[*For the historical context of Lévy-Bruhl's work, see the biographies of* DURKHEIM; FRAZER; MAUSS; SPENCER; TYLOR. *For discussion of the subsequent development of his ideas, see* POLLUTION; RELIGION, *article on* ANTHROPOLOGICAL STUDY.]

WORKS BY LÉVY-BRUHL

1884   *L'idée de responsabilité.* Paris: Hachette.
1890   *L'Allemagne depuis Leibniz.* Paris: Hachette.
1894   *La philosophie de Jacobi.* Paris: Alcan.
(1900) 1903   *The Philosophy of Auguste Comte.* New York: Putnam; London: Sonnenschein. → First published in French.
(1903) 1905   *Ethics and Moral Science.* London: Constable. → First published as *La morale et la science des moeurs.*
(1910) 1926   *How Natives Think.* London: Allen & Unwin. → First published as *Les fonctions mentales dans les sociétés primitives.*
(1922) 1923   *Primitive Mentality.* New York: Macmillan. → First published as *La mentalité primitive.*
(1927) 1928   *The "Soul" of the Primitive.* New York: Macmillan. → First published as *L'âme primitive.*
(1931) 1935   *Primitives and the Supernatural.* New York: Dutton. → First published as *Le surnaturel et la nature dans la mentalité primitive.*
1935   *La mythologie primitive.* Paris: Alcan.
1938   *L'expérience mystique et les symboles chez les primitifs.* Paris: Alcan.
1949   *Les carnets de Lévy-Bruhl.* Paris: Presses Universitaires de France. → Published posthumously.

SUPPLEMENTARY BIBLIOGRAPHY

ALDRICH, CHARLES R. 1931 *The Primitive Mind and Modern Civilization.* New York: Harcourt.

ALLIER, RAOUL 1927 *Le non-civilisé et nous.* Paris: Payot.

BASTIDE, ROGER 1953 Contribution à l'étude de la participation. *Cahiers internationaux de sociologie* 14: 30–40.

BLONDEL, CHARLES 1926 *La mentalité primitive.* Paris: Stock.

BRÉHIER, ÉMILE 1949 Originalité de Lévy-Bruhl. *Revue philosophique* 139:385–388.

CAZENEUVE, JEAN 1961 *La mentalité archaïque.* Paris: Colin.

CAZENEUVE, JEAN 1963 *Lucien Lévy-Bruhl: Sa vie, son oeuvre, avec un exposé de sa philosophie.* Paris: Presses Universitaires de France.

DAVY, GEORGES (1931) 1950 *Sociologues d'hier et d'aujourd'hui.* 2d ed. Paris: Presses Universitaires de France.

ESSERTIER, DANIEL 1927 *Les formes inférieures de l'explication.* Paris: Alcan.

LEROY, OLIVIER 1927 *La raison primitive.* Paris: Geuthner.

PRZYLUSKI, JEAN 1940 *La participation.* Paris: Presses Universitaires de France.

SHAREVSKAIA, B. 1958 O metodologicheskoi i terminologicheskoi putanitse v voprosakh pervobytnogo myshleniia (Methodological and Terminological Confusions in the Question of the Mentality of Primitive Peoples). *Sovietskaia etnografiia* 6:61–75.

VAN DER LEEUW, G. G. 1940 *L'homme primitif et la religion.* Paris: Presses Universitaires de France.

LEWIN, KURT

Kurt Lewin (1890–1947) was born in Mogilno, Prussia. After studying at the universities of Freiburg and Munich, he completed his doctorate in philosophy at the University of Berlin in 1914. He taught in Berlin from 1921 to 1933, at which time he left Germany. In the United States he was a visiting professor at Stanford and at Cornell before becoming professor of child psychology in the Child Welfare Research Station of the State University of Iowa in 1935. In 1945 he left Iowa to found the Research Center for Group Dynamics at the Massachusetts Institute of Technology. He also served as a visiting professor at the University of California in Berkeley and at Harvard.

During his thirty years of scientific work, Lewin's theoretical interests and the focuses of his research shifted several times. At first he was concerned with the study and analysis of the cognitive processes of learning and perception; with the dynamics of individual motivation and emotion; and with the interpersonal processes of reward and punishment, conflict, and social influence. In his next phase, he conducted and stimulated research on group phenomena such as leadership, social cli-

mate, group standards, and values. Finally, he was led to an examination of the social restraints imposed on groups by technology, economics, law, and politics. Although his interests changed and developed, he nevertheless carefully adhered to a central theoretical tenet: that to represent and interpret faithfully the complexity of concrete reality situations requires continual crossing of the traditional boundaries of the social sciences, rather than a progressive narrowing of attention to a limited number of variables.

The theory that requires this interdisciplinary approach to psychological and social reality has at various times been referred to, by Lewin himself and by others, as "dynamic theory," "topological psychology," and "field theory." Field theory was Lewin's final preference. Briefly stated, it holds that events are determined by forces acting on them in an immediate field rather than by forces acting at a distance. Field theory may be characterized as a method of analyzing causal relations and building scientific constructs, that is, a theory about theory building, or a metatheory. At the same time, Lewin's field theory is a set of constructs, developed through empirical research, for describing and interpreting psychological and social phenomena.

Field theory as metatheory. The major tenets of field theory as metatheory for social science have been identified by Cartwright (1959, p. 7).

(1) The full empirical reality of human experience and behavior—not just certain abstract aspects that are most accessible or easy to manipulate—must be comprehended in a scientific manner. The observation of behavior in a real-life setting (what has been called naturalistic observation) and phenomenological analysis are procedures that may prevent scientific formalization from focusing on trivial aspects of human behavior.

(2) The language of concepts that is developed must be "two-faced," providing both a rigorous terminology for describing the behavioral events of the real world and a set of theoretical constructs that can be related to each other logically in the formulation of lawful regularities about the causation of behavioral events.

(3) The concepts must "fit" the nature of psychological phenomena, which they will not do if they are simply borrowed from physical or biological science. Presuppositions about the ultimate unity of science should not be allowed to distort the development of concepts that are intended to describe psychological phenomena (emotions, hopes, fears, illusions) rather than biological or physical processes.

(4) Lewin's *principle of concreteness* states that effects "can be produced only by what is 'concrete,' i.e., by something that has the position of an individual fact which exists at a certain moment" (1936, p. 32). From this important principle Lewin derived several of his basic ideas: that every behavioral event must be viewed as caused by several interdependent features of the total concrete situation of that moment; that the dynamics of a behavioral event cannot be adequately comprehended by the specialized concepts of a particular discipline or scientific specialty, for example, cognition, learning, economics, or political science; that the "life space" or concrete field of all coexisting psychological facts is quite different from the quantified dimensions of that situation; that causation is a contemporary process—"Since neither the past nor the future exists at the present moment it cannot have effects at the present" (*ibid.*, p. 35).

(5) Mathematics provides basic tools for developing a formal systematic theory of psychological processes, but this does not mean that all phenomena can be treated quantitatively. Non-Euclidean geometry seemed to Lewin the most appropriate mathematical tool for treating many empirical aspects of human behavior in terms of psychological space.

(6) Basic research that is generated by the need to develop field theoretical concepts should be of great practical value in the world of action. To Lewin this meant that there "is nothing as practical as a good theory." He demonstrated this again and again in his own contributions to the understanding of many critical social problems, such as autocracy, self-hatred, scapegoating, intergroup conflict, industrial inefficiency, conservative food habits, and child rearing. [*See* PREJUDICE.]

Experimental research. In his search for a comprehensive conceptual grasp of significant psychological events and processes Lewin instigated and led many research programs. Often they were carried on by his students after he himself had turned his attention to new problems.

His first research sequence began with an experimental critique of the work of Ach (1910) on "associative bonds" in the process of remembering. Lewin moved beyond structural concepts of remembering to such notions as intention to recall and expectation about events. Basic work was done by Ovsiankina (1928) and Zeigarnik (1927), who demonstrated experimentally that the tendency to recall interrupted tasks is stronger than the tendency to recall completed tasks and that there are forces acting toward resuming and completing interrupted activities.

This work on psychological interruption and on the forces acting toward resumption and completion led directly to another program of research that represents an early experimental investigation of motivational concepts. The research sought to discover whether the completion of a task different from the interrupted one can reduce the tendency to resume the interrupted one. In other words, can one task have substitute value for another? Lewin's students Lissner (1933) and Mahler (1933) demonstrated that tasks of different degrees of similarity and different degrees of reality have different types of substitute value. An important series of studies by Adler (1939), Cartwright (1942), and Sliosberg (1934) further developed this area of inquiry.

Lewin's interest in the internal dynamics of motivation led him to initiate another series of studies on the psychological process of satiation. Karsten (1928) and other students (Freund 1930; Kounin 1941; Seashore & Bavelas 1942) discovered that the time it takes to become satiated with a task depends on the over-all meaning context of the activity, on ego involvement in the activity, on the physiological state of the person, and on the degree of rigidity of interpersonal psychological systems.

Another important series of studies of motivational dynamics dealt with frustration and regression. Again, Lewin's plan of research was primarily carried out by others. Dembo's initial work in Berlin (1931) consisted of careful observational studies of the symptoms of emotional tension as contrasted to the symptoms of task- or problem-solving tension that occurred when subjects were assigned impossible tasks. The symptoms observed included anger, aggression, regression, substitution, and flight from reality. Later studies by Barker, Dembo, and Lewin (1941) and by Wright (1942) established important connections between frustration and intellectual regression as measured by the developmental level of play activity before and after frustration situations.

Dembo (1931) and Hoppe (1931) did valuable research on the concept of level of aspiration, and again other research developed from it. After Jerome Frank, one of Lewin's students, presented a summary in English of the German research (1935a; 1935b), a flood of studies by American investigators followed. The early research indicated that the experience of success or failure depends to a very significant degree upon the person's aspiration rather than upon some objective standard of performance. There was also clear evidence that the motivation for success or achievement of individuals leads them to set levels of aspiration that do not guarantee easy success. This line of inquiry has been the springboard for much of the current advanced theoretical work on social comparison processes, self-evaluation, and discrepancies between ideal self and actual self. [*See* ACHIEVEMENT MOTIVATION.]

The phenomena of decision making and conflict resolution were the focuses of another important series of investigations by Lewin and his students. These inquiries demonstrate the effect on decision making of the strength of the valences of the alternatives, the reality level of the choice situation, the difference in a choice between negative and positive alternatives, and attitudes of cautiousness and risk taking.

As Lewin's interests changed from individual to social psychology, his approach to decision making and conflict also changed. His famous series of studies of group decision making (1953) demonstrates the influence on individual behavior of participation in group discussions and decisions. Group discussion affects such phenomena as parental behavior, eating habits, and amount of effort on the production line. Later work on patterns of intergroup conflict derived from this work on individual decision making.

As he moved into social psychology, Lewin's research interests focused on the phenomena of social perception, social values, social influence, cooperation, and competition. In all these areas he instigated important research. His students demonstrated experimentally that the expectation or perception that another person is "warm" or "cold," high or low in power, or an insider or outsider greatly influences interpersonal attitudes and behavior (Kelley 1950; Pepitone 1950; Thibaut & Riecken 1955). [*See* PERCEPTION, *articles on* PERSON PERCEPTION *and* SOCIAL PERCEPTION.]

His move from Germany to the United States stimulated Lewin's interest in the comparative analysis of personal values as they relate to cultural differences and social norms. Several of Lewin's papers ([1935–1946] 1948, pp. 3–68) deal with the development of a definition of values and with approaches to change in cultural values. This was perhaps the beginning of his focus on the theory of planned change and social action, which became increasingly important in the later years of his career. His work on values moved from methodological work on the content of values (as developed in Kalhorn 1944; White 1951) to work on the development of the value of "fairness," which he conducted by means of experimental situations with children of different ages, and then

to an important series of studies on the development and functioning of group standards or group norms. The experimental field studies of the influence of group standards on work output in a factory (Coch & French 1948) and on behavior of residents in a housing project (Festinger et al. 1950) led to a basic theoretical paper in 1947 by Lewin (see in [1939–1947] 1963, pp. 188–237) on the quasi-stationary equilibrium as a tool for conceptual analysis of the field of forces determining behavior in a given social setting and situation. [*See* MORAL DEVELOPMENT.]

Perhaps Lewin's best-known contributions to social psychology and group dynamics are those focusing on authority and social influence. Initially, a series of children's groups were studied to see what effect different styles of leadership might have on the social–emotional atmosphere of a group, on its work productivity, and on the personal adaptation of members. There followed basic work on social influence, with laboratory studies of status hierarchy and communications channels; field studies of behavioral contagion and influence structures; and studies of the patterns and bases of influence in military units and in the working relations among the members of professional teams, such as those composed of psychiatrists, clinical psychologists, or social workers. [*See* LEADERSHIP.]

In the later years of his career, Lewin and his co-workers became interested in the problem of what they called psychological ecology. Thus, in his work on the maintenance and change of food habits (1943), Lewin constructed a theory of social channels and "gatekeepers" to account for the ecological processes by which particular foods reach the table and come in contact with the consumer. He showed that a number of cultural, economic, and technological factors combined to influence this series of decisions. This approach has been greatly developed and extended by Lewin's student and co-worker Barker, in his series of field studies of the psychological ecology of children and adults in a number of communities and a variety of social settings (Barker & Wright 1954).

Major concepts. In all his work, Lewin maintained an active interplay between the construction of theory and the concrete analysis of human behavior in all its complexity. It is possible here to indicate only briefly some of the concepts that became important in Lewin's comprehensive conceptual system. Probably the most widely known Lewinian concept is that of *psychological life space*. This fundamental notion refers to the totality of events or facts that determines the behavior of an individual at a given time. It is related to the basic tenet that causation is a contemporary process, and it has, therefore, created much active controversy in the field of psychotherapy. Defending the importance of this concept, one psychoanalyst (Ezriel 1956, p. 32) has asserted that the unconscious structures the analyst uncovers in working with a patient are *active in the present* and are not necessarily replicas of past realities and reactions.

The life space includes two major components: the person and the psychological environment. The latter is conceived to be the environment as it exists for the individual. Lewin assumed that an understanding of the interaction between the person and the psychological environment would permit the understanding and prediction of the person's behavior.

The concepts that Lewin developed to deal with the psychological and social processes of the life space can be classified as *structural* concepts, having to do with the arrangement and relationship of the parts of the life space, and *dynamic* concepts, dealing with tendencies toward change or resisting change. The basic structures of the life space are region and boundary, and derived from these are degree of differentiation, centrality, path, and psychological distance. The principal dynamic processes are interdependence, tension, force, field of forces, equilibrium, and power. Lewin also introduced two dimensions of the life space: a vertical dimension of degrees or levels of reality and a horizontal dimension of time perspective. Lewin's studies demonstrated that psychological processes vary with different levels of reality: the processes involved in assessing facts or expectations are different from those involved in fantasies or wishes. The use of the concept of time perspective was related to Lewin's field-theoretical stress on the interpretation and prediction of behavior in ahistorical terms.

When he first made contributions to social psychology, Lewin was content to treat the facts of interpersonal relations as social facts in the life space of each individual. For example, the fact of group membership and its implications for behavior then seemed quite satisfactorily represented as regions in the life space of the person. But as he added such new problems as group goals, group decision making, and group problem solving, it became necessary to relate life spaces to one another, that is, to construct a *social space* or a social field in which social, economic, political, and physical facts have objective, or at least intersubjective, reality, rather than only individual

psychological reality. In some of his final papers ([1939–1947] 1963, pp. 170–237), Lewin was beginning to grapple with the challenging problems of defining social space and social field-theory and of relating these concepts to those of psychological space. He was indicating some of the ways in which the behavioral sciences might go beyond empirical unity to the achievement of conceptual unity.

Social action and social problem solving. Lewin had a deep sensitivity to social problems and a commitment to use his resources as a social scientist to do something about them. Thus, in the early 1940s, he drew a triangle to represent the interdependence of research, training (or education), and action in producing social change. He saw every practical problem as requiring basic conceptual analysis, research, and a "change experiment." The concept of action-research as a method of planned social change was developed and clarified in the period when he was helping found the Commission on Community Interrelations of the American Jewish Congress and establishing the Research Center for Group Dynamics at MIT.

Lewin may well have been a bit optimistic when he asserted in 1945 that "leading practitioners" in government, agriculture, industry, education, and community life seemed to have an increasing awareness of the need for a "scientific level of understanding" and that they seemed to accept the dictum that "nothing is as practical as a good theory." Yet the success of the National Training Laboratories, which he helped establish in 1946 and 1947, does seem to vindicate his optimism. First held at Bethel, Maine, the summer after Lewin's death, these sessions have since expanded into a nationwide network serving the needs of professional men. They provide a link between these professional men and the resources of the behavioral sciences and the growing technology of re-education of attitudes, values, and behavior.

Persisting influence. Current research directly derived from Lewin's work is being carried on by Cartwright and his colleagues, who are working on the development and use of mathematical concepts that are coordinated with life-space phenomena; at the Research Center for Group Dynamics at the University of Michigan (it was founded by Lewin at MIT and moved to Michigan after his death) and at university centers founded by some of his students, for example, by Festinger, Schachter, Deutsch, Thibaut, and Kelley; by Barker and his colleagues, working on psychological ecology; by French, Bavelas, Marrow,

Cook, and others, who are coordinating organizational field experiments; and by Lippitt and his colleagues at the Center for Research on Utilization of Scientific Knowledge, the title of which is a key to its activities.

RONALD LIPPITT

[*See also* FIELD THEORY. *Other relevant material may be found in* DEVELOPMENTAL PSYCHOLOGY; GESTALT THEORY; GROUPS; SYSTEMS ANALYSIS, *article on* PSYCHOLOGICAL SYSTEMS; THINKING, *article on* COGNITIVE ORGANIZATION AND PROCESSES.]

WORKS BY LEWIN

1917   Die psychische Tätigkeit bei der Hemmung von Willensvorgängen und das Grundgesetz der Assoziation. *Zeitschrift für Psychologie* 77:212–247.

(1935–1946)   1948   *Resolving Social Conflicts: Selected Papers on Group Dynamics.* New York: Harper.

1936   *Principles of Topological Psychology.* New York: McGraw-Hill.

(1939–1947)   1963   *Field Theory in Social Science: Selected Theoretical Papers.* Edited by Dorwin Cartwright. London: Tavistock.

1941   BARKER, ROGER; DEMBO, TAMARA; and LEWIN, KURT *Frustration and Regression: An Experiment With Young Children.* University of Iowa Studies in Child Welfare, vol. 18, no. 1. Iowa City: Univ. of Iowa Press.

1943   Forces Behind Food Habits and Methods of Change. National Research Council, *Bulletin* 108:35–65.

(1945)   1948   LEWIN, KURT; and GRABBE, PAUL Conduct, Knowledge, and Acceptance of New Values. Pages 56–68 in Kurt Lewin, *Resolving Social Conflicts: Selected Papers on Group Dynamics.* New York: Harper. → First published in Volume 1 of the *Journal of Social Issues.*

1953   Studies in Group Decision. Pages 287–301 in Dorwin Cartwright and Alvin Zander (editors), *Group Dynamics: Research and Theory.* Evanston, Ill.: Row, Peterson. → Selections from writings first published between 1943 and 1947.

SUPPLEMENTARY BIBLIOGRAPHY

ACH, N.   1910   *Über den Willensakt und das Temperament: Eine experimentelle Untersuchung.* Leipzig: Quelle & Meyer.

ADLER, D. L.   1939   Types of Similarity and the Substitute Value of Activities at Different Age Levels. Ph.D. dissertation, State Univ. of Iowa.

BARKER, ROGER G.; and WRIGHT, HERBERT F.   1954   *Midwest and Its Children.* Evanston, Ill.: Row, Peterson.

CARTWRIGHT, DORWIN   1942   The Effect of Interruption, Completion and Failure Upon the Attractiveness of Activities. *Journal of Experimental Psychology* 31: 1–16.

CARTWRIGHT, DORWIN   1959   Lewinian Theory as a Contemporary Systematic Framework. Volume 2, pages 7–91 in Sigmund Koch (editor), *Psychology: The Study of a Science.* New York: McGraw-Hill.

COCH, LESTER; and FRENCH, JOHN R. P. JR.   1948   Overcoming Resistance to Change. *Human Relations* 1: 512–532.

DEMBO, TAMARA   1931   Der Ärger als dynamisches Problem. Untersuchungen zur Handlungs- und Affektpsychologie, 10. *Psychologische Forschung* 15:1–144.

DEUTSCH, MORTON   1954   Field Theory in Social Psychology. Pages 181–222 in Gardner Lindzey (editor), *Handbook of Social Psychology*, Volume 1: Theory and Method. Cambridge, Mass.: Addison-Wesley.

ESCALONA, SIBYLLE   1954   The Influence of Topological and Vector Psychology Upon Current Research in Child Development: An Addendum. Pages 971–983 in Leonard Carmichael (editor), *Manual of Child Psychology.* 2d ed. New York: Wiley.

EZRIEL, H.   1956   Experimentation Within the Psychoanalytic Session. *British Journal for the Philosophy of Science* 7:29–48.

FESTINGER, LEON; SCHACHTER, STANLEY; and BACK, KURT (1950)   1963   *Social Pressures in Informal Groups: A Study of Human Factors in Housing.* Stanford Univ. Press.

FRANK, JEROME D.   1935a   Individual Differences in Certain Aspects of the Level of Aspiration. *American Journal of Psychology* 47:119–128.

FRANK, JEROME D.   1935b   The Influence of the Level of Performance in One Task on the Level of Aspiration in Another. *Journal of Experimental Psychology* 18: 159–171.

FREUND, ALEX   1930   Psychische Sättigung im Menstruum und Intermenstruum. Untersuchungen zur Handlungs- und Affektpsychologie, 7. *Psychologische Forschung* 13:198–217.

HOPPE, FERDINAND   1931   Erfolg und Misserfolg. Untersuchungen zur Handlungs- und Affektpsychologie, 9. *Psychologische Forschung* 14:1–62.

KALHORN, JOAN   1944   Values and Sources of Authority Among Rural Children. Pages 99–152 in Kurt Lewin et. al., *Authority and Frustration.* University of Iowa Studies in Child Welfare, vol. 20. Iowa City: Univ. of Iowa Press.

KARSTEN, ANITRA   1928   Psychische Sättigung. Untersuchungen zur Handlungs- und Affektpsychologie, 5. *Psychologische Forschung* 10:142–254.

KELLEY, HAROLD H.   1950   The Warm–Cold Variable in First Impressions of Persons. *Journal of Personality* 18:431–439.

KOUNIN, JACOB S.   1941   Experimental Studies of Rigidity: 1–2. *Character and Personality* 9:251–282. → Part 1: The Measurement of Rigidity in Normal and Feeble-minded Persons. Part 2: The Explanatory Power of the Concept of Rigidity as Applied to Feeble-mindedness.

LEEPER, ROBERT W.   1943   *Lewin's Topological and Vector Psychology: A Digest and a Critique.* Eugene: Univ. of Oregon.

LISSNER, KATE   1933   Die Entspannung von Bedürfnissen durch Ersatzhandlungen. Untersuchungen zur Handlungs- und Affektpsychologie, 18. *Psychologische Forschung* 18:218–250.

MAHLER, WERA   1933   Ersatzhandlungen verschiedenen Realitätsgrades. Untersuchungen zur Handlungs- und Affektpsychologie, 15. *Psychologische Forschung* 18: 27–89.

OVSIANKINA, MARIA VON   1928   Die Wiederaufnahme unterbrochener Handlungen. Untersuchungen zur Handlungs- und Affektpsychologie, 6. *Psychologische Forschung* 11:302–379.

PEPITONE, ALBERT   1950   Motivational Effects in Social Perception. *Human Relations* 3:57–76.

SEASHORE, HAROLD C.; and BAVELAS, ALEX   1942   A Study of Frustration in Children. *Pedagogical Seminary and Journal of Genetic Psychology* 61:279–314.

SLIOSBERG, SARAH 1934 Zur Dynamik des Ersatzes in Spiel- und Ernstsituationen. Untersuchungen zur Handlungs- und Affektpsychologie, 19. *Psychologische Forschung* 19:122–181.

THIBAUT, JOHN W.; and RIECKEN, HENRY W. 1955 Some Determinants and Consequences of the Perception of Social Causality. *Journal of Personality* 24:113–133.

WHITE, RALPH K. 1951 *Value-analysis: The Nature and Use of the Method.* Glen Gardner, N.J.: Society for the Psychological Study of Social Issues.

WRIGHT, M. ERIK 1942 Constructiveness of Play as Affected by Group Organization and Frustration. *Character and Personality* 11:40–49.

ZEIGARNIK, BLUMA 1927 Das Behalten erledigter und unerledigter Handlungen. Untersuchungen zur Handlungs- und Affektpsychologie, 3. *Psychologische Forschung* 9:1–85.

LEXIS, WILHELM

Wilhelm Lexis (1837–1914), a German statistician and economist, made major contributions to the theory of statistics and its application, particularly in population research and economic time series. As a mathematician Lexis was deeply skeptical about the state of mathematical economics in his time. His criticism of certain contemporary work in mathematical economics led him to some fundamental observations on economic events and their interdependence.

Lexis was born in Eschweiler, near Aachen, Germany. His studies were widespread, and his interests ranged from law to the natural sciences and mathematics. He graduated from the University of Bonn in 1859, having written a thesis on analytical mechanics; he also obtained a degree in mathematics. For some time he did research in Bunsen's chemical laboratories in Heidelberg. In 1861, Lexis went to Paris to study the social sciences, and his studies led to his first major publication (1870), a treatise on French export policies. This work displays the feature that characterizes his later economic writings: a skepticism toward "pure economics" and toward the application of supposedly descriptive mathematical models which have no reference to economic reality. Even in this early work he insisted that economic theory should be founded on quantitative economic data. In Lexis' view an elaborate general economic equilibrium analysis, whose main problem was to match the unknowns with an equal number of equations, could make no contribution to the understanding or solution of economic problems and therefore should not be taken too seriously. He was one of a number of mathematically trained students of economics who, in the second half of the nineteenth century, became alienated from that discipline;

another, more famous one was Max Planck, who, after attempting to read Marshall's work, threw it away and changed his course of study for good (see Schumpeter 1954, pp. 957–958).

Lexis was appointed to the University of Strassburg in 1872. While there, he wrote his introduction to the theory of population (1875). From Strassburg he went to Dorpat in 1874, as professor of geography, ethnology, and statistics, and then to Freiburg in 1876, as professor of economics. His major contributions to statistics were made while he was at Freiburg (1876; 1877; 1879a), and he also published papers on economics at this time (1879b; 1881; 1882a; 1882b). After an interlude at the University of Breslau from 1884 to 1887, he was appointed professor of political science at the University of Göttingen.

Lexis' activities in his later years were remarkably diverse. An editor of the *Handwörterbuch der Staatswissenschaften*, the major German economic encyclopedia, he was also an active contributor, and he was director of the first institute of actuarial sciences in Germany. In the 1890s he published and edited several volumes pertaining to education, particularly to the university system (1893; 1901; 1902; 1904a; 1904b). Lexis' works on population research, economics, and statistics during the subsequent decade bring together and refine some of his earlier arguments (see 1903; 1906a; 1906b; 1908; 1914). He died in Göttingen during the very first days of World War I.

Statistics

Lexis' major contributions were in statistics. His statistical work originated in problems he encountered in population research (1875; 1879b; 1891; 1903), sociology (1877), and economics (1870; 1879a; 1908; 1914). In connection with his studies of social mass phenomena (1877) and the time series encountered in several of the social sciences (1879b), Lexis came upon problems concerning statistical homogeneity which apparently had been neglected up to then, although, as Bortkiewicz pointed out (1918), Dormoy (1874; 1878) developed similar ideas at about the same time. (Other possible forerunners of Lexis were Bienaymé [1855], Cournot [1843], and R. Campbell [1859].) Lexis credited Dormoy with having anticipated some of his ideas; nevertheless, it was Lexis who more or less independently gave a new direction to the analysis of statistical series and led statisticians in the shift of emphasis from the purely mathematical approach, with which Laplace is associated, to an empirical or inductive approach (see Keynes 1921, pp. 392 ff.). He also initiated the analysis of dispersion and variance in his attempts to develop statistics with which to evaluate qualitative changes in populations over time (see Keynes 1921; Pólya 1919).

Lexis showed that in the universe of social mass phenomena the conditions of statistical homogeneity (random sampling from a stable distribution) are seldom, if ever, fulfilled (1877; 1879a; 1879b). The underlying probability structure may well differ from one part of the sample to another because of special circumstances related to dispersion in space, time, or other factors. A universe in which individual samples are drawn from potentially different populations is now known as a *Lexis universe* (see, for example, Herdan 1966). To some extent Lexis' work was a reaction to the uncritical assumptions of homogeneity made in statistical work before his time—for instance, by Quetelet. As Keynes (1921) pointed out, Quetelet and others simply asserted, with little evidence, the probabilistic stability from year to year of various social statistics.

Lexis' work centered on the dispersion of observations around their local means and on the behavior of the means and dispersions over time. He devised statistics to measure the degree of stability of such time series and arrived at the useful generalization that these statistics would either confirm statistical homogeneity, indicating a *Bernoulli series*, or diverge from it, indicating a *Poisson series* or a *Lexis series*. (This terminology was developed by C. V. L. Charlier; see A. Fisher 1915, p. 117).

Lexis considered only dichotomous variates (male–female, living–dead, etc.), but the argument he advanced holds equally for numerical variates in the ordinary sense (see also Pólya 1919). In the following, Lexis' ideas are given in a generalized form.

Let x_{ij} $(i = 1, \cdots, n, j = 1, \cdots, m)$ be a set of n samples with m observations each, and let the arithmetic mean of the x_{ij} in sample i be $\bar{x}_i$ and the arithmetic mean of the x_{ij} over all n samples be $\bar{x}$. Similarly, let $a_{ij} = E(x_{ij})$, the expectation of x_{ij}, so that $\bar{a}_i = E(\bar{x}_i)$ and $\bar{a} = E(\bar{x})$. Lexis considered the following quadratic forms which measure dispersion in three different senses:

$$s_w^2 = \frac{1}{nm} \sum_i \sum_j (x_{ij} - \bar{x}_i)^2,$$

$$s_b^2 = \frac{1}{n} \sum_i (\bar{x}_i - \bar{x})^2,$$

$$s^2 = \frac{1}{nm} \sum_i \sum_j (x_{ij} - \bar{x})^2,$$

where s_b^2 has rank (degrees of freedom) $r_b = n - 1$, s_w^2 has rank $r_w = n(m - 1)$, and s^2 has rank $r = r_b + r_w = nm - 1$. (The subscripts "w" and "b" are used to indicate that s_w^2 comprises within sample dispersion and s_b^2 between sample dispersion.) Furthermore,

$$s^2 = s_b^2 + s_w^2.$$

If the n samples of m objects each are drawn at random from the same population, then the expected value of each observation equals the expected value of the sample mean and the expected value of the mean of all observations, that is,

$$a_{ij} = \bar{a}_i = \bar{a},$$

and statistical homogeneity is present. Repeated independent measurements of a distance and $n \times m$ drawings of balls from an urn with each ball returned after it is drawn are examples of such series. In this case the three quadratic forms, multiplied by appropriate constants, have the same expectations. Specifically, when statistical homogeneity holds,

$$E\left(\frac{n}{r}s^2\right) = E\left(\frac{n}{r_b}s_b^2\right) = E\left(\frac{n}{r_w}s_w^2\right),$$

and the common value is $1/m$ times the variance of the underlying population. A set of samples drawn under such conditions is known as a Bernoulli series (see, e.g., A. Fisher 1915).

It may, however, be the case that statistical homogeneity holds within the samples ($a_{i1} = a_{i2} = \cdots = a_{im}$) but not between samples—that is, the n samples may be random samples from different populations. In this case a Lexis series is generated (a supernormal series, in Lexis' terminology). Such a series is expected when, for example, each set of balls (one sample) is drawn from a different urn. Other examples of such series explain further the importance of the Lexis series: m observations made at time t_0, another m observations made at time t_1, and so forth, up to t_n, will give rise to a *time series* of $m \times n$ observations, where the ith sample (covering one period, t_i) may well come from a single population but where between different periods such changes occurred that statistical homogeneity is no longer preserved—that is, the samples come from different populations.

Similarly, social or economic samples of m observations drawn from n different geographical regions (nations) are likely to come from different statistical populations, although in each region (nation) the m observations of the sample come from the same distribution (*interregional series, in-*

ternational series). In short, if the over-all dispersion is caused not only by chance variations about a constant but also by trends and other systematic factors varying between samples, then a Lexis series will be generated. (A comprehensive and elementary treatment of Lexis series is given in Pólya 1919.)

We expect in this case that the variance between the samples will contribute relatively more to the over-all variance of the $m \times n$ observations than will the variance within the samples and that the expected value of an observation will equal the sample mean, whereas the sample mean is expected to differ from the mean of all observations. Further, although $a_{ij} = \bar{a}_i$, $\bar{a}_i \neq \bar{a}$ for at least some i, and

$$E \left(\frac{n}{r_w} s_w^2 \right) < E \left(\frac{n}{r} s^2 \right) < E \left(\frac{n}{r_b} s_b^2 \right).$$

Statistical homogeneity is not preserved.

Much less realistic, but a formal complement to the Bernoulli and Lexis series, is the Poisson series (a subnormal series, in Lexis' terminology). The Poisson model was developed as one that would generate higher within sample than between sample variability. In this case the jth observation of each sample is drawn from a fixed population, but the populations differ according to j. In short, $a_{1j} = a_{2j} = \cdots = a_{nj}$, but for a fixed i the a_{ij} are not all equal. Hence $\bar{a}_i = \bar{a}$, and there is no between sample variability coming from the a's. It follows that

$$E \left(\frac{n}{r_b} s_b^2 \right) < E \left(\frac{n}{r} s^2 \right) < E \left(\frac{n}{r_w} s_w^2 \right).$$

Other kinds of models leading to subnormal dispersion have also been considered.

Lexis proposed a statistic, based on the above quadratic forms, to describe the extent to which a given series is homogeneous, supernormal, or subnormal. The statistic, called the Lexis quotient, is

$$L = \frac{s_b^2/r_b}{s^2/r},$$

a monotone increasing function of another statistic, $(s_b^2/r_b)/(s_w^2/r_w)$, which might be used alternatively. A. A. Chuprov showed later (1922) that in the case of statistical homogeneity, $E(L) = 1$ and the variance of L is approximately $2/(n-1)$.

A further elaboration of this leads to significance tests. A first step in that direction is made by adding to and subtracting from the expected value of L its standard error, obtaining $1 \pm \sqrt{2/(n-1)}$. If L lies within the boundaries thus calculated, one may conclude with confidence of approximately two out of three that the statistical mass is homoge-

neous; if L is significantly larger than 1, one may conclude that the series was drawn from a Lexis universe; and if L is significantly smaller than 1, one may conclude that the series is Poisson.

The relevance and connections of the Lexis series and Lexis' L to the analysis of variance and the chi-square distribution were later shown by many authors. The formal connection between L and the χ^2 statistic of Pearson was elaborated by R. A. Fisher. Fisher showed that in the case of a $2 \times n$ classification the χ^2 statistic is just nL. [See Counted data; see also R. A. Fisher 1928; Gebelein & Heite 1951.]

The relation of the L-statistic to the F-statistic is very direct, and we may say that Lexis anticipated the F-statistic (see Coolidge 1921; Rietz 1932; Geiringer 1942a; 1942b; Gini 1956; Herdan 1966). Whereas in L one compares the variance between the samples to the variance of all $n \times m$ observations, that is,

$$L = \frac{s_b^2/r_b}{s^2/r},$$

in the F-statistic one compares the variance between the samples to the variance within the samples, that is,

$$F = \frac{s_b^2/r_b}{s_w^2/r_w}.$$

Furthermore,

$$L \gtrless 1 \qquad \text{if and only if} \qquad F \gtrless 1.$$

This concurrence is based on the previously stated equality

$$s^2 = s_b^2 + s_w^2.$$

Although the asymptotic distribution of the F-statistic as $m \to \infty$ was established by R. A. Fisher (1925, p. 97) and by W. G. Cochran (1934, p. 178) and generalized by M. G. Madow (1940), the same distribution was established for Lexis' L as early as 1876 by F. R. Helmert, using the method of characteristic functions.

Bortkiewicz extended the application of Lexis' theory of dispersion, and Chuprov (1922) extended Lexis' theory and gave it the most comprehensive treatment. Others influenced by Lexis were J. von Kries, H. Westergaard, and F. Y. Edgeworth, the only Anglo–American scholar closely familiar with statistical work on the Continent at that time (see Keynes 1921).

Economics

Lexis' contributions to economic theory were less appreciated than were his contributions to statistics; many economists, including Schumpeter, largely ignored them. Such a negative assessment of Lexis' work proves to be not entirely justified after closer examination of the reasons that led him to criticize certain aspects of the mathematical and "pure" economics of his contemporaries. His main contribution was a valid criticism of the work done at his time, particularly that of the Austrian school and the Lausanne school. His criticism was informed in part by the outlook of the historical school, which was prevalent in Germany, and accordingly he believed that it was necessary to incorporate in any theory of value and demand the element of time as well as the phenomenon of the recurrence of wants.

Lexis accepted Gossen's analysis of human behavior because Gossen appreciated all the shortcomings of any such theory. The criticisms Lexis made of the Austrian school seem contradictory but are only superficially so: he deplored the lack of mathematics in the work of some authors, especially Carl Menger, and found fault with the application of inappropriate mathematics in the work of others, especially Auspitz and Lieben.

Lexis regarded the concept of utility as being rather vague, since utility cannot be measured. He argued that to say that the utility of a good (set of goods) is equal to, larger than, or less than the utility of some other good permits a partial or complete preordering of utilities. Complementarity and substitution effects imply, however, subadditivity and superadditivity of utilities, which render futile any attempt to aggregate utilities and demand correspondences. Lexis questioned the convexity and continuity assumptions of preference orderings.

The controversy then raging over how to determine total utility given the marginal utility correspondences (a controversy between E. von Böhm-Bawerk and F. von Wieser) was correctly interpreted by Lexis and led him to a discussion of Gossen's other laws, most notably the equalization of marginal utilities. Any such theorem, he believed, must be hedged by a number of qualifications; it is particularly important to consider the time element connected with demand and consumption. Want and satisfaction are both felt and exercised over time. At one and the same time only a limited set of wants can be satisfied. One can eat, drink, sleep, and work, but these activities are to some extent mutually exclusive. Thus, the individual has to decide what sequence to follow in satisfying his set of wants. This sequence will be determined, according to Lexis, by the intensity of wants and by their periodicity, the most fundamen-

tal rhythms being the day, the year, and one lifetime. The demand of an individual will be classified and exercised accordingly. Intensive wants will be satisfied first, on a daily, yearly, or other basis, depending on the periodicity of recurrence of wants. Other, less intensive wants will be satisfied after full satisfaction of the intensive wants has been achieved. The implications are far-reaching but perhaps misleading; they have not been accepted by subsequent economists. Individual demand correspondences have to be defined by the period to which they relate, which in turn requires a reformulation of the theory of demand and implies the necessity of defining the demand for (consumption of) each good at different times as quantitatively different. This entails no theoretical difficulties in a general mathematical equilibrium analysis, but it does prevent the theory from having any operational value.

The concept of preferential ordering over time induced Lexis to observe that certain more intensive wants will be saturated whereas other, less intensive wants will be satisfied partially, implying satisfaction of zero marginal utility for the first set of wants and some positive marginal utility for the second. Lexis supported this conclusion by referring to economic reality. However, his statement about the equalization of marginal utilities turns out ultimately to be incorrect if we allow for errors of judgment, evaluations of uncertainties and risks, and diversity of attributes of each good for any individual.

Thus, Lexis' skepticism about the potential of the marginal utility theory in economics was based on the difficulty of measuring utility, the existence of subadditivities and superadditivities in utility correspondences, and the impossibility of aggregating individual preferences. The introduction of the time element into the theory of value and demand adds interesting arguments to general equilibrium analysis which imply, according to Lexis, obvious refutations of the equalization of marginal utilities. As a consequence of his skepticism, Lexis turned, in the rest of his economic work, to a rather dry description of economic events, which failed to be attractive to more speculative minds.

KLAUS-PETER HEISS

WORKS BY LEXIS

1870   *Die französischen Ausfuhrprämien im Zusammenhange mit der Tarifgeschichte und Handelsentwicklung Frankreichs seit der Restauration.* Bonn: Marcus.
1875   *Einleitung in die Theorie der Bevölkerungsstatistik.* Strassburg: Trübner.

1876 Das Geschlechtsverhältniss der Geborenen und die Wahrscheinlichkeitsrechnung. *Jahrbücher für Nationalökonomie und Statistik* 27:209–245.

1877 *Zur Theorie der Massenerscheinungen in der menschlichen Gesellschaft.* Freiburg im Breisgau: Wagner.

(1879a) 1942 *Über die Theorie der Stabilität statistischer Reihen (The Theory of the Stability of Statistical Series).* Minneapolis, Minn: WPA. → First published in Volume 32 of *Jahrbücher für Nationalökonomie und Statistik.*

1879b Gewerkvereine und Unternehmerverbände in Frankreich. Verein für Socialpolitik, Berlin, *Schriften* 17:1–280.

1881 *Erörterungen über die Währungsfrage.* Leipzig: Duncker & Humblot.

(1882a) 1890 Die volkswirthschaftliche Konsumtion. Volume 1, pages 685–722 in *Handbuch der politischen Oekonomie.* 3d ed. Edited by Gustav Schönberg. Tübingen: Laupp.

(1882b) 1891 Handel. Volume 2, pages 811–938 in *Handbuch der politischen Oekonomie.* 3d ed. Edited by Gustav Schönberg. Tübingen: Laupp.

1886 Über die Wahrscheinlichkeitsrechnung und deren Anwendung auf die Statistik. *Jahrbücher für Nationalökonomie und Statistik* 47:433–450.

1891 Bevölkerungswesen, II: Bevölkerungswechsel, 1: Allgemeine Theorie des Bevölkerungswechsels. Volume 2, pages 456–463 in *Handwörterbuch der Staatswissenschaften.* Jena: Fischer.

1893 *Die deutschen Universitäten: Für die Universitätsausstellung in Chicago 1893.* 2 vols. Berlin: Asher.

(1895a) 1896 *The Present Monetary Situation.* American Economic Association, Economic Studies, Vol. 1, No. 4. New York: Macmillan. → First published as *Der gegenwärtige Stand der Währungsfrage.*

1895b Grenznutzen. Volume 1, pages 422–432 in *Handwörterbuch der Staatswissenschaften: Supplementband.* Jena: Fischer.

1901 *Die neuen französischen Universitäten.* Munich: Academischer Verlag.

1902 Lexis, Wilhelm (editor) *Die Reform des höheren Schulwesens in Preussen.* Halle: Waisenhaus.

1903 *Abhandlungen zur Theorie der Bevölkerungs- und Moralstatistik.* Jena: Fischer. → Contains reprints of 1876 and 1879a.

1904a Lexis, Wilhelm (editor) *Das Unterrichtswesen im Deutschen Reich.* 4 vols. Berlin: Asher.

1904b *A General View of the History and Organisation of Public Education in the German Empire.* Berlin: Asher.

1906a Das Wesen der Kultur. Pages 1–53 in *Die allgemeinen Grundlagen der Kultur der Gegenwart. Die Kultur der Gegenwart,* vol. 1, part 1. Berlin: Teubner.

1906b *Das Handelswesen.* 2 vols. Sammlung Göschen, Vols. 296–297. Berlin: Gruyter. → Volume 1: *Das Handelspersonal und der Warenhandel.* Volume 2: *Die Effektenbörse und die innere Handelspolitik.*

1908 Systematisierung, Richtungen und Methoden der Volkswirtschaftslehre. Volume 1, pages I: 1–45 in *Die Entwicklung der deutschen Volkswirtschaftslehre im neunzehnten Jahrhundert.* Leipzig: Duncker & Humblot.

(1910) 1926 *Allgemeine Volkswirtschaftslehre.* 3d ed., rev. Die Kultur der Gegenwart, vol. 2, part 10, section 1. Berlin and Leipzig: Teubner.

(1914) 1929 *Das Kredit- und Bankwesen.* 2d ed. Sammlung Göschen, Vol. 733. Berlin: Gruyter.

SUPPLEMENTARY BIBLIOGRAPHY

Bauer, Rainald K. 1955 Die Lexissche Dispersionstheorie in ihren Beziehungen zur modernen statistischen Methodenlehre, insbesondere zur Streuungsanalyse (Analysis of Variance). *Mitteilungsblatt für mathematische Statistik und ihre Anwendungsgebiete* 7: 25–45.

Bienaymé, Jules (1855) 1876 Sur un principe que M. Poisson avait cru découvrir et qu'il avait appelé loi des grands nombres. *Journal de la Société de Statistique de Paris* 17:199–204.

Bortkiewicz, Ladislaus von 1901 Über den Präcisiongrad des Divergenzkoëffizienten. Verband der Österreichischen und Ungarischen Versicherungs-Techniker, *Mitteilungen* 5:1–3.

Bortkiewicz, Ladislaus von 1909–1911 Statistique. Part 1, Volume 4, pages 453–490 in *Encyclopédie des sciences mathématiques.* Paris: Gauthier-Villars.

Bortkiewicz, Ladislaus von 1915 Wilhelm Lexis [Obituary]. International Statistical Institute, *Bulletin* 20, no. 1:328–332.

Bortkiewicz, Ladislaus von 1917 Wahrscheinlichkeitstheoretische Untersuchungen über die Knabenquote bei Zwillingsgeburten. Berliner Mathematische Gesellschaft, *Sitzungsberichte* 17:8–14.

Bortkiewicz, Ladislaus von 1918 Der mittlere Fehler des zum Quadrat erhobenen Divergenzkoëffizienten. Deutsche Mathematiker-Vereinigung, *Jahresbericht* 27: 71–126.

Bortkiewicz, Ladislaus von 1930 Lexis und Dormoy. *Nordic Statistical Journal* 2:37–54.

Bortkiewicz, Ladislaus von 1931 The Relations Between Stability and Homogeneity. *Annals of Mathematical Statistics* 2:1–22.

Campbell, Robert 1859 On the Probability of Uniformity in Statistical Tables. *Philosophical Magazine* 18:359–368.

Chuprov, Aleksandr A. 1905 Die Aufgaben der Theorie der Statistik. *Jahrbuch für Gesetzgebung, Verwaltung und Volkswirtschaft im Deutschen Reich* 29: 421–480. → The author's name is given its German transliteration, Tschuprow.

Chuprov, Aleksandr A. 1922 Ist die normale Stabilität empirisch nachweisbar? *Nordisk statistisk tidskrift* 1:369–393. → The author's name is given its German transliteration, Tschuprow.

Cochran, W. G. 1934 The Distribution of Quadratic Forms in a Normal System, With Applications to the Analysis of Covariance. Cambridge Philosophical Society, *Proceedings* 30:178–191.

Coolidge, Julian L. 1921 The Dispersion of Observations. American Mathematical Society, *Bulletin* 27: 439–442.

Cournot, Antoine Augustin 1843 *Exposition de la théorie des chances et des probabilités.* Paris: Hachette.

Dormoy, Émile 1874 *Théorie mathématique des paris de courses.* Paris: Gauthier-Villars. → Also published in Volume 3 of *Journal des actuaires français.*

Dormoy, Émile 1878 *Théorie mathématique des assurances sur la vie.* 2 vols. Paris: Gauthier-Villars.

Edgeworth, F. Y. 1885 Methods of Statistics. Pages 181–217 in Royal Statistical Society, London, *Jubilee Volume.* London: Stanford.

FISHER, ARNE 1915 *The Mathematical Theory of Probabilities and Its Application to Frequency Curves and Statistical Methods.* Vol. 1. London: Macmillan.

FISHER, R. A. 1925 Applications of "Student's" Distribution. *Metron* 5, no. 3:90–104.

FISHER, R. A. 1928 On a Distribution Yielding the Error Functions of Several Well Known Statistics. Volume 2, pages 805–813 in International Congress of Mathematicians (New Series), Second, Toronto, 1924, *Proceedings.* Univ. of Toronto Press.

GEBELEIN, HAND; and HEITE, H.-J. 1951 *Statistische Urteilsbildung.* Berlin: Springer.

GEIRINGER, HILDA 1942a A New Explanation of Nonnormal Dispersion in the Lexis Theory. *Econometrica* 10:53–60.

GEIRINGER, HILDA 1942b Observations on Analysis of Variance Theory. *Annals of Mathematical Statistics* 13:350–369.

GINI, C. 1956 Généralisations et applications de la théorie de la dispersion. *Metron* 18, no. 1/2:1–75.

HELMERT, F. R. 1876 Ueber die Wahrscheinlichkeit der Potenzsummen der Beobachtungsfehler und über einige damit im Zusammenhange stehenden Fragen. *Zeitschrift für Mathematik und Physik* 21:192–218.

HERDAN, G. 1966 *The Advanced Theory of Language as Choice and Chance.* New York: Springer.

KEYNES, JOHN MAYNARD (1921) 1952 *A Treatise on Probability.* London: Macmillan. → A paperback edition was published in 1962 by Harper.

KRIES, JOHANNES VON (1886) 1927 *Die Principien der Wahrscheinlichkeitsrechnung: Eine logische Untersuchung.* 2d ed. Tübingen: Mohr.

MADOW, WILLIAM G. 1940 Limiting Distributions of Quadratic and Bilinear Forms. *Annals of Mathematical Statistics* 11:125–146.

PÓLYA, GEORG 1919 Anschauliche und elementare Darstellung der Lexisschen Dispersionstheorie. *Zeitschrift für schweizerische Statistik und Volkswirtschaft* 55:121–140.

RIETZ, H. L. 1932 On the Lexis Theory and the Analysis of Variance. *American Mathematical Society, Bulletin* 38:731–735.

SCHUMPETER, JOSEPH A. (1954) 1960 *History of Economic Analysis.* Edited by E. B. Schumpeter. New York: Oxford Univ. Press.

VON MISES, RICHARD 1932 Théorie des probabilités: Fondements et applications. Paris, Université de, Institut Henri Poincaré, *Annales* 3:137–190.

LIBERALISM

Liberalism is the belief in and commitment to a set of methods and policies that have as their common aim greater freedom for individual men. Early liberalism was identified with political parties or social classes and often with specific programs. Today, although some parties in Europe, Great Britain, and elsewhere bear the title Liberal, in contemporary usage the term "liberalism" refers to a system of thought and practice that is less specific than a philosophical doctrine and more inclusive than party principle. Liberalism is also too ecumenical and too pluralistic to be called, properly, an ideology. Contemporary liberalism is the product of centuries of development and of attitudes and responses widely shared among individuals. It can be described as: (1) a valuing of the free expression of individual personality; (2) a belief in men's ability to make that expression valuable to themselves and to society; and (3) the upholding of those institutions and policies that protect and foster both free expression and confidence in that freedom.

The term "liberal" probably first acquired its modern political connotation from the Liberales, a Spanish party that supported for Spain a version of the French constitution of 1791. As a coherent system of ideals and practical goals, however, liberalism first developed in England in the seventeenth and eighteenth centuries. Thereafter, liberal parties and liberal views, developing independently or derived from the English model, appeared in Europe, several British colonies, and elsewhere in the world.

Liberal thought and practice have stressed two primary themes. One is the dislike for arbitrary authority, complemented by the aim of replacing that authority by other forms of social practice. A second theme is the free expression of individual personality. Liberal movements and liberal thought have usually emphasized one theme more than the other, though seldom one to the virtual exclusion of the other. Much of liberal political and social theory has, in fact, been devoted to reconciling these two aims, especially with respect to their philosophical and practical implications.

Early liberalism emphasized freedom *from* arbitrary authority. One mode of attack was the assertion of free conscience and the demand for religious tolerance. Liberals have often been nonconformists in religion, secularists, skeptics, and even antireligious. In place of traditional authority they have supported the authority of reason and of demonstrated, rather than revealed, truth. Liberalism has stressed also the desirability of impersonal social and political controls: the rule of law and the market. Liberals have usually been individualists and pluralists and have supported local and group liberties and the methods of consent and persuasion.

Also vital to liberalism has been the goal of an active freedom, the ideal that the individual has the opportunity and the capacity for free expression. To this end, liberals have supported a more equal distribution of liberty, the abolition of monopolies, the destruction of aristocratic privilege, and a law that was general and founded upon rational principles. Liberals have argued also for the expansion of opportunity, including state intervention to equalize and increase the opportunities open to individuals. For all these reasons, liberalism has usually been "progressive," i.e., concerned with economic and social progress and favorable to science, technology, and pragmatic experimentalism.

The two most important objectives of liberalism —noninterference and enfranchisement—support each other but also conflict. The first objective, pursued to an extreme, would leave the individual at the mercy of nature, society, and group and economic power. The second, followed alone, leads ultimately to statism and technocracy. Liberalism is neither of the extremes. It is a reconciliation of the two goals, with the relation between them determined by the needs of a society and the means available to it. Thus, liberalism does not, in fact, include such disparate figures as Rexford G. Tugwell, John Dewey, and Ludwig von Mises. Each is in part illiberal. Liberalism requires a rational and conscientious reconciliation of two essential goals.

The heritage of liberalism

Liberalism, in both its classical and its more contemporary, or "revisionist," forms, is essentially a modern phenomenon. It is the heir of a rich tradition. Liberty, constitutionalism, and toleration were known to the ancient world, and the Western liberalism of England, Europe, and America is the beneficiary of several religious traditions, of Greek philosophy and literature, of Roman law and constitutionalism. In the ancient world, however, liberty was closely associated with religion, ethnic culture, and citizenship. Liberalism itself did not exist as a separate and self-sustaining tradition. Moreover, the line of descent from ancient to modern liberty is not a direct one. The liberalism that developed in England and Europe in the eighteenth and nineteenth centuries was, at that time, a unique occurrence, resulting from the convergence of social and political tendencies peculiar to a specific time and environment.

Liberalism benefited from medieval constitutionalism and from the religious traditions of the church and Western Christianity. English liberalism, because of the common law, the parliamentary tradition, and the peaceful character of the English Reformation, drew much from this background, a fact illustrated by the works of John Fortescue, Richard Hooker, and Edward Coke. On the Continent the same materials proved less usable, but they served in a limited way to legitimate ancient liberties, a measure of toleration, and the rule of law.

The Renaissance and the Reformation were important in fostering liberalism, especially through the contribution they made to individualism. The Protestant doctrine that each believer could communicate directly with God, without dependence upon priest or churchly hierarchy, was an important anti-institutional influence and therefore favorable to individualism. Ideals of personal sanctification and inwardness of moral life that earlier had been restricted to orders of monks, knights, and burghers were democratized during the fifteenth and sixteenth centuries. In addition, the Reformation and the Counter Reformation, by stressing internal energy, individual responsibility, and the need for reconstructing the worldly order, greatly stimulated individualism, despite the intentions of Luther and Calvin or St. Ignatius and Pope Paul III.

Political changes, especially during and after the Reformation, contributed ultimately to the rise of liberalism. Wars decimated nobilities, broke down settled relations between lord and commoner, engaged new groups in collective activity. The domestic and international policies of monarchs brought to prominence bureaucrats of common or semi-noble status, lawyers, town merchants, military adventurers, and scholars and scientists. The new nation-states fostered changes in law, in the economy, and in personal relations that increased commerce and the circulation of money, and the numbers of merchants, masters, and artificers. Not to be ignored is the further fact that many of these political changes entailed taxation, intervention, oppression, and suppression, which were important issues in later constitutional struggles and liberal protests.

From the policies of modern states, from economic change, and from a diffusion of culture and literacy came the small self-conscious middle class, which was the most important vehicle for liberal doctrine. Scientific discovery and technological innovation, capitalist methods of economic venture, modified legal concepts, and new forms of property worked reciprocally, especially from the sixteenth through the eighteenth centuries, to provide both the opportunity and the incentives for individual and group initiative. The consequence was the increase not only of a small commercial and industrial middle class but, even more important, the spread of attitudes hospitable to individual enterprise and to the creed of individual responsibility.

A comparatively rapid and wide diffusion of enlightened and cosmopolitan attitudes among social and political elites, as well as among burghers, professional men, merchants, and country gentry, was of enormous importance to the development of liberalism, especially in the later seventeenth and eighteenth centuries. This development depended upon and grew from the earlier humanism and enlightenment of the Renaissance and Reformation. But the earlier tradition had been restricted largely to the court, the city, and the clergy. During the eighteenth century the arts and the sciences, political life, and a comparatively sophisticated culture became accessible to a much wider circle. Many more read; many more discussed.

Liberalism, viewed in historical perspective, was the culmination of several broad social and political trends. It involved a change in the scope of individual aspirations and, perhaps more important, in the people who had them. Prior to the nineteenth century these aspirations were restricted to an elite of birth and wealth. Social environment, individual aspiration, and consciousness of capacity combined to produce, in the nineteenth century, a widely shared and politically potent liberal faith.

Classical liberalism

Liberalism, both as a doctrine and as a political program, developed most fully in England between the Glorious Revolution (1688) and the Reform Act of 1867. Liberalism was first a limited appeal for constitutional guarantees and individual rights. It became a positive theory of economic and political organization and a political program with broad national appeal extending to many groups and classes. Neither on the Continent nor in the United States did early liberalism develop in a similar fashion. The experience of England stands alone; and the term "classical liberalism" is ordinarily used with reference to England.

Liberalism in England first took the form of a demand for religious liberties and toleration, constitutionalism, and political rights. During the Puritan revolution and the Commonwealth, written constitutions were proposed and pamphlets published demanding a number of liberties. Digger and Leveller tracts, the pamphlets of John Lilburne, the more reflective *Commonwealth of Oceana* of James Harrington, and Milton's exalted defense of free speech in *Areopagitica* not only illustrate the scope of the constitutional controversy but also afford a sample of the political literature of the period. The revolution of 1688, the first "liberal revolution" in history, consolidated and gave definite constitutional form to the liberal gains of that century. The liberalism recognized and vindicated in 1689 was essentially negative in character, pro-

tecting groups and individuals *from* government, especially from the prerogatives of the crown. It was also aimed at securing chiefly political rather than economic objectives. Among those political objectives are some of the most important principles of liberal constitutionalism: the right of opposition, the rule of law, and the separation of powers. The settlement also included a recognition of important civil liberties by acts securing toleration, in 1688, and liberty of the press, in 1695. Locke's *Second Treatise of Government* and the American Declaration of Independence stand as the great monuments of this phase of liberalism. [*See* CONSTITUTIONS AND CONSTITUTIONALISM; *and the biography of* LOCKE.]

The constitutional settlement and civil peace gave enormous impetus to a second theme of classical liberalism: the theory and practice of economic liberty. The English liberal economists, led by Adam Smith, were neither the first nor the only group to erect a theory upon the postulate of laissez-faire, but they were the most influential. Their ideals were: in the juridical sphere, free contract and the rule of law; in the economic sphere, a self-regulating market, unrestrained either by monopoly or political intervention; and in the social sphere, voluntarism and collaboration for mutual benefit. The laissez-faire doctrine and the practical organization of the economy that the classical economists advocated greatly strengthened liberalism. They did so, first of all, because they broadened and democratized the values of liberalism, extending them to mercantile, commercial, and laboring classes. Second, they did so because they encouraged forms of social and economic activity that could substitute for more compulsive and bureaucratic techniques of regulation. Thus, the point of Adam Smith's "obvious and simple system of natural liberty" was not only that it was "free" and "impersonal" but—equally important—that it was a "system" allowing men to exert their energies both to their own and to the common benefit [*see* LAISSEZ-FAIRE; SMITH, ADAM].

The English utilitarians and their political allies completed the edifice of classical liberalism. Jeremy Bentham and James Mill accepted the market economy and especially the ideals it served. They accepted, for the most part, the aims but not the methods of the liberalism of 1689. They brought the two species of liberalism together by applying the concepts of utility and the market to politics and the tasks of constitutionalism. Arguing from the hedonistic calculus and the principle of equality, they advocated "the greatest good of the greatest number." They insisted in law and politics upon general rules that provide for a maximum of free choice and practical liberty for all, or as many as consonant with general utilitarian maxims. And they argued that only education and free speech, inclusive representation and an expanded suffrage, and the regular accountability of the governors to the governed—politics organized on the model of the free economy—could provide constitutional security and good government. English utilitarianism, as propounded by Bentham and James Mill, provided a philosophical foundation for political liberalism. It also unified economic liberalism with a theory of positive political action. Properly, this utilitarian doctrine deserves the title of the first comprehensive liberal philosophy [*see* BENTHAM; MILL; UTILITARIANISM].

Classsical liberalism in England owed much of its success to the fact that three liberal traditions—constitutionalism, economic liberalism, and utilitarianism—each developing in a different historic period and having a different group appeal, could be effectively joined in practical politics. Liberalism in England became a party with a broad appeal and sustained its appeal for many years. At the time of the corn law repeal (1846) liberalism in England had its broadest support, including many Whigs, Cobden and Bright liberals, utilitarians, and middle-class and working-class adherents. Probably this alliance marked the natural limits of the older liberalism. It also occupied the common meeting ground of several varieties of liberal program and ideology. Liberalism at this point in England achieved a maximum synthesis of its two competing themes: noninterference and enfranchisement.

Liberalism in Europe and America

Two vital conditions for a classical liberal synthesis existed only in England—a broad liberal movement and a powerful liberal party. In the United States the second condition was missing; on the Continent, the first.

In the United States classical liberalism did not exist, partly because conservatism in the European sense did not exist either. From Europe, Americans inherited the libertarian precepts of the Puritan revolution, the Whig settlement of 1689, and some liberal economic values. These were "received" in the colonial tradition and figured in the American Revolution, the Constitutional Convention, and, broadly, in the politics and jurisprudence of the developing nation. But they were a part of the national heritage and the spirit of the laws, not the self-conscious creed of a party or a class. Liberalism as such did not need to be vindicated, nor did

it have a specific role to play. Moreover, liberalism was mixed with other issues of democracy and equality, as, for instance, in the eras of Jefferson and Jackson. When, in the late nineteenth and early twentieth centuries, social Darwinism and natural-rights jurisprudence were erected into a creed of noninterference and supposed liberty, they were already "ideology" and not "utopia." America was, then, in large measure the unreflective inheritor of classical liberalism, especially the Lockean variety. Conscious or self-conscious liberalism in America came with the second phase of liberal development—the transition to a modern liberalism.

The classical liberal synthesis was sought in Europe but never fully achieved. Instead of developing into a broad and powerful movement and a comparatively effective political party, European liberalism remained fragmented and sectarian. Civil and religious strife and the slow development of commerce and industry contributed to this result. So did war. The state and the traditions of authority were too strong, liberalism too divided and weak, at the time when a liberal synthesis might have been realized. As a consequence, classical liberalism did not fully develop in Europe; instead several leading liberal creeds arose, which were usually doctrinaire in social philosophy and narrowly based in group support.

In Europe the primary task of securing and protecting the rule of law and constitutionally sanctioned liberties was more difficult. That task tended to become, for some European liberals, almost an end in itself, creating a liberal philosophy that Guido de Ruggiero (1925) has called "guarantism." Unfortunately, what needed to be guaranteed in the interests of constitutionalism were often ancient liberties and privileges that because of their oligarchic origins and reactionary tendency worked against a more common liberty and the general good. Consequently, one species of European liberalism was decidedly aristocratic, supporting not only liberty but also the inequitable privileges of localities, corporations, and social and religious groups. Montesquieu and Benjamin Constant afford good illustrations of aristocratic liberalism in political theory. The Restoration and the July Monarchy in France and the revolt of 1848 in Germany are historic tragedies of this divided heritage of European liberalism.

Rationalistic and utilitarian liberalism found expression, during the age of reason and afterward, primarily in an appeal for reform from above. The *philosophes* in France and German liberals such as Goethe and Herder adopted the goals of individualism, widened liberty, and a rational code of laws. They did not associate these objectives with political liberty or popular participation. For some the ideal was enlightened despotism and utilitarian standards, whatever the cost to particular and historic liberties or a constitutional tradition. The reform of civil and administrative institutions for liberal ends took precedence over the liberal method. And the liberal tradition was further divided within itself: some liberals espoused a despotic method, and others such as Rousseau, Fichte, and Mazzini sought the liberal spirit in a "general will" or "the people." Louis Bonaparte in France and Bismarck in Germany built much of their power upon this division.

In Europe there were liberal economic theorists, such as Jean Baptiste Say, Frédéric Bastiat, and Friedrich von Hermann; there were also middle-class political movements and parliamentary factions supporting laissez-faire and free trade. But Europe lacked the well-grown middle class and the economic, legal, and political environment needed to make the cause of economic freedom effective and, more important, to give liberalism a central direction. As a consequence, economic liberalism remained too long the creed of a part of the bourgeoisie and an intellectual preoccupation for scholars and a few publicists. Later, when economic liberalism was both possible and widely adopted— for instance, in the French Third Republic and in unified Italy—that policy served less fully the original liberal objectives of expanding liberty and equalizing opportunity. Economic circumstances made laissez-faire, as socialists protested, not a service to liberty as a whole but to the interests of a comparatively small number of economically advantaged individuals.

At an early stage, in Europe, liberalism failed because it was weak and divided. In the later decades of the nineteenth century it was "too late" for classical liberalism. This is not to say that liberalism was not a vitally needed political and doctrinal element of European society: it was. But liberalism had to appeal to a radically changed world, one in which democracy or republicanism, nationalism, and socialism were the popular gospels.

Modern liberalism

In the late nineteenth and early twentieth centuries classical liberalism and the traditions of thought and policy closely related to it were progressively modified. Later liberalism—especially in Great Britain and the United States, but to some extent almost everywhere in the modern world— has emphasized the positive rather than the nega-tive aspect of liberty: the opportunity to form and accomplish self-appointed goals, rather than freedom from the state. Along with this shifting of proximate goals of liberalism came an adoption of new methods. The central value of the liberated individual, of man as far as possible his own sovereign, did not change; the understanding of that value and of the means for achieving it did.

An important cause of this revision was the success of liberalism itself: the securing of a considerable measure of political and economic liberty and the conversion of liberalism from a sectarian demand for noninterference into a program of political and economic organization. Success raised not only the question, What next? but also, Liberty for whom? Aristocrats and the bourgeoisie now had substantially the bundle of rights they needed. The franchise gave them the means of self-defense. But the same concessions—even when granted—were not enough for the peasant or the worker. Effective liberty for them required more positive action by the state, a fact that conservatives, Catholic social theorists, and Marxian and other socialists pointed out emphatically.

Liberal reorientation came partly through challenge and response, from a need to meet political and philosophical criticism. Liberalism was itself a philosophical and reasonable doctrine and therefore responsive to the new theories of man and society announced by nineteenth-century scientists and made popular by parliamentary inquiry, governmental commissions, and the newspapers. Politics was also important. The varied appeals of Tory Democracy in England, Louis Bonaparte's imperialism in France, and monarchical socialism in Germany were political forces that could not be ignored. Nor could a liberalism that served principally the bourgeoisie of the French Second Republic or the textile manufacturers of Manchester prosper in an age of the expanded franchise, effective mass communications, and social consciousness. The liberalism that survived after 1848 had, perforce, to accommodate itself to democratic, nationalist, and socialist sentiment.

The growth of cities, of industry, and of national and world-wide commerce also forced revisions of the liberal position. Earlier liberal theory, with its individualistic premises, had contrived a model of man, his institutions, and society that minimized the facts of organizational power, of community cost and benefit, and of national history and common fate. Time progressively falsified that model, especially after the growth of the modern corporation and industrial technology. Great inequalities in market power made one man's economic freedom another's oppression. Similarly, free trade in commodities—such as child labor, slum housing, poisoned meat, and bad gin—made the common benefit of regulation obvious. Liberals split among themselves. One group argued for a remedy of abuses other than those perpetrated by the state. Another group clung to the dogmas of nonintervention and free trade. They made the means of liberalism into ends in themselves and liberalism itself into a conservative ideology. Thus, one heir of Bentham and Adam Smith is John Stuart Mill, and another is Herbert Spencer [see SPENCER].

With consciousness of changed circumstances came a major reassessment of the means to liberty. Later liberals assigned greater importance to the social environment within which liberty had to be realized. Their revision of liberalism followed from a recognition that certain forms of coercion and obstacles to liberty arise from society itself rather than the activities of officials. The revision had another important foundation. A society of great economic and social interrelatedness makes access to culture, the capacity to participate, and membership and status in natural and artificial groups increasingly important both to the pursuit of liberty and to its defense. Rousseau and Hegel, and, later, T. H. Green and John Dewey, all argued this theme. Man is in society, the point at which many impinging groups, institutions, and cultural influences intersect. Seldom can he effectively withdraw. He can realize and defend his liberty only by participation. But a live option of participation does not simply happen: it is a social product depending upon education, incentive, opportunity, and a supporting system of political and social values. Modern liberalism tends necessarily, therefore, to be closely associated not only with social reform but with democracy and popular participation.

The modern liberal's view of the individual is also different from the classical description. It was not merely that the life and goals that suited a Bentham or an English merchant would distress a Coleridge, a Cardinal Newman, and, indeed, even a John Stuart Mill. The earlier liberal view of human nature was two dimensional and overly rationalistic. Nineteenth-century sociology and psychology destroyed that view thoroughly. Modern liberalism has assimilated much of the critique. Liberals today see man not only as an individual in society but as a person with a continuing need for self-expansion and reintegration. For this reason the emphasis of modern liberalism is less upon external impediments to motion and more upon the individual person's subjective feeling of freedom and those circumstances that give to this feeling an objective reality in the experience of the individual. If a man does not feel free, he is not free. [See PERSONALITY, POLITICAL.]

One question that arises is whether modern, or "revised," liberalism can still appropriately be called liberalism. Liberty and equality, rights and powers are not the same things. Modern liberalism advocates collectivist means, invoking the state in aid of individuals and disadvantaged groups. It has adopted much of the program of democratic and socialist movements. Is modern liberalism still "liberal"? Three considerations argue that this query be answered with a qualified affirmative. In the first place, modern liberalism retains the same end of the autonomous individual that has guided all true liberalism. The means to that end and proximate ends have changed, but the final end remains the same. Second, those changes in method and policy that most writers identify with the expansion and modernization of liberalism have served not only to reduce arbitrary compulsion but also to extend the scope, equalize the distribution, and enrich the liberty enjoyed by individuals. Third, constitutional rights and the rule of law not only survive in the mixed regime of liberty, democracy, and the administrative state but have in some ways grown stronger. They are stronger to the extent that the mixed regime is a representative one—in which the state cannot be used as a tool for the purposes of any *one* group or class but must serve and be responsive and accountable to *all*. Certainly, modern liberalism invokes the coercive power of the state. In relation to the state itself men are, in some ways, less free to do with their own as they please. For this reason it is important that the options open to men be many and that the relations of state, society, and individual afford alternate ways of suiting means to essential ends. Pluralism, decentralization, and a variety of relations between the state and society answer to these needs. They probably afford men, given an established welfare state, a better marginal choice in distributing their energies and opting for one of several modes of liberty than ever before in history. [See WELFARE STATE.]

The future of liberalism

Although liberalism has been important to Western civilization, it may not continue to be so. Since the two world wars, many argue, liberalism has been in decline. Liberalism means less, so the argument runs, to the developing nations, to the semisocialist states of western Europe, to a world menaced with war and preoccupied with material benefit. Liberal parties and liberal ideology, it could also be argued, have served their function. The programs they supported have been adopted by others who have gone further. Historic liberalism survives only as a temper or mood of politics.

Liberal parties and liberal movements have been on the wane. In the British Commonwealth and Europe they have not fared well since World War II. Some maintain their electoral following, but mainly by altering their liberal stance. Specific movements, such as the neoliberalism of Germany and the Low Countries or the Mouvement Republicain Populaire of France, show an attrition of membership, unity, and purpose. The conclusion that liberalism as an *organized* party or self-conscious movement is for the present in decline is warranted by the facts. In no place, presently, are liberal parties or liberal movements gaining significantly in organized power or appeal.

Liberal policies have also received scant support among developing nations struggling for independence and material prosperity. The conditions that made Adam Smith's strategy of liberty suitable for England are missing today. Even such countries as Mexico and India, which seem determined to save liberty, are far from classical liberalism and even from more modern versions of liberalism. They are nationalistic and socialistic in many of their policies and are so by conscious intent and design.

The cold war has also weakened liberalism. In the short run, the communist challenge threatens liberty and constitutionalism directly. In the longer run, the danger is more insidious: external threats evoke response; and response demands collective effort. That effort is stimulated by nonliberal incentives and appeals: appeals to national purpose and common action and the incentives of a war economy. Liberty is not broken; but it shrinks. Liberalism is not vanquished; but it is not pursued. If, as John Stuart Mill said, "things left to themselves inevitably decay," the threat is greater than at first sight it appears. The danger to liberalism is not that it will be openly destroyed but that it will be forgotten or perverted.

From these facts it does not follow that liberalism is unimportant for the future. The importance of the liberal temper and of liberal principles applied to politics has not diminished; probably it has increased. Liberalism thrives on material prosperity, social peace, and common enlightenment. In the programs of the nations of western Europe immediately after World War II liberalism did not have a prominent place, nor has it been important in the programs of the developing nations. These nations have been engaged in creating the condi-

tions of material prosperity and economic security. Hopefully, their labor will eventually bear fruit in comparatively stable, pluralistic democracies and welfare economies capable of providing security and abundance for their populations. Such developments would not make liberalism outmoded. They would, in fact, make it possible and profitable: for they make it possible to realize liberty along with abundance and social justice; and they make the finer qualities of human relations increasingly accessible and valuable to all.

DAVID G. SMITH

[*See also* CONSERVATISM; CONSTITUTIONS AND CONSTITUTIONALISM; DEMOCRACY; EQUALITY; FREEDOM; LAISSEZ-FAIRE; UTILITARIANISM; WELFARE STATE; *and the biography of* MILL. *Other relevant material may be found in* ECONOMIC THOUGHT *and* POLITICAL THEORY.]

BIBLIOGRAPHY

DEWEY, JOHN (1927) 1957 *The Public and Its Problems.* Denver: Swallow.

GIRVETZ, HARRY K. (1950) 1963 *The Evolution of Liberalism.* Rev. ed. New York: Collier. → First published as *From Wealth to Welfare: The Evolution of Liberalism.*

HALÉVY, ÉLIE (1901–1904) 1952 *The Growth of Philosophic Radicalism.* New ed. London: Faber. → First published in French.

HARTZ, LOUIS 1955 *The Liberal Tradition in America.* New York: Harcourt.

HAYEK, FREDERICK A. VON 1960 *The Constitution of Liberty.* Univ. of Chicago Press; London: Routledge.

HOBHOUSE, LEONARD T. (1911) 1945 *Liberalism.* Oxford Univ. Press. → A paperback edition was published in 1964.

HUGHES, EMMET J. 1944 *The Church and Liberal Society.* Princeton Univ. Press.

KEYNES, JOHN M. 1926 *The End of Laissez-faire.* London: Woolf.

LASKI, HAROLD J. (1936) 1958 *The Rise of European Liberalism: An Essay in Interpretation.* London: Allen & Unwin. → A paperback edition was published in 1962 by Barnes & Noble.

LOCKE, JOHN (1689) 1963 *A Letter Concerning Toleration: Latin and English Texts. . . .* The Hague: Nijhoff. → First published as *Epistola de tolerantia.*

LOCKE, JOHN (1690) 1960 *Two Treatises of Government.* Cambridge Univ. Press.

MILL, JOHN STUART (1859) 1963 *On Liberty.* Indianapolis, Ind.: Bobbs-Merrill.

POLANYI, KARL 1944 *The Great Transformation.* New York: Farrar. → A paperback edition was published in 1957 by Beacon. Also published in 1945 by Gollancz under the title *Origins of Our Time.*

RUGGIERO, GUIDO DE (1925) 1927 *The History of European Liberalism.* Oxford: Collingwood. → First published as *Storia del liberalismo europeo.* A paperback edition was published in 1959 by Beacon.

WATKINS, FREDERICK 1948 *The Political Tradition of the West: A Study in the Development of Modern Liberalism.* Cambridge, Mass.: Harvard Univ. Press.

LIBERTY
See FREEDOM.

LIBIDO
See PSYCHOANALYSIS.

LIBRARIES
See under INFORMATION STORAGE AND RE-TRIEVAL.

LICENSING, OCCUPATIONAL

In labor markets in which the rule of free choice prevails, individuals may enter and leave occupations without securing the consent of private or public authorities. Occupational licensing limits the range within which free choice governs. Occupational licensing occurs where a profession, trade, or occupation may be legally practiced only by those who have been authorized to do so by some agency of government.

Occupational licensing should be distinguished from certification. In the former case, the law permits only licensed persons to practice; in the latter, anyone may practice but only certified persons may use the relevant occupational title in notifying the public that their services are available. It is also different from the licensing of businesses, although that sometimes involves occupational licensing implicitly.

Occupational licensing is extensive in the United States, where the licensing authorities are usually agents of the states or of municipalities, rather than of the federal government. The practice of a few occupations does require a federal license. Gellhorn (1956, p. 106) found that state licenses were required in one or more states for the practice of some eighty occupations. State legislatures and municipal legislative organs routinely receive proposals that additional occupations be licensed. In countries other than the United States, licensing is apparently less common but it does occur.

Justification. When legislatures enact occupational licensing legislation, they usually do so on grounds that the public health, safety, or morals are being protected. In the absence of provision for licensing, it is reasoned, incompetent practitioners will offer their services. Prospective buyers of these services are said not to be able to distinguish between qualified and unqualified persons, and this is considered to be especially true if consumers buy services of the particular kind only at infrequent intervals. Where the consequences of the employment of unqualified persons can be expected to be seriously adverse to the purchaser, and especially where the consequences of incompetently rendered service are irreversible, it is thought to be desirable that the state administer some examining or other procedure to determine who are qualified to practice, and prevent those who are unqualified from offering their services. The average quality of those permitted to practice is raised, and by the exclusion of "quacks" and incompetents the public is protected from the error of employing them.

Thus, occupations that are licensed are concentrated in the tertiary sector of the economy, in which self-employment is common and services are purchased by any given buyer only infrequently. Information about professional competency that is produced by employment over a long period is not easily available in such cases to would-be purchasers. (A sophisticated exposition of the reasons for licensing in the special case of medical care can be found in Arrow 1963.)

While there are some licensed occupations for which the foregoing line of reasoning is sensible, there are others for which it seems far-fetched.

Certification, although it permits anyone to practice, nevertheless diminishes uncertainty, as does licensing, by informing prospective buyers which of those in the occupation have successfully passed the state examination and which have not. Neither licensing nor certification reduces uncertainty to zero, because there is variance in the competency of those who are licensed or certified and consumers must still search out additional information.

The requests that come to legislatures that an occupation be licensed or that the qualifying standards of an already-licensed occupation be raised rarely come from coalitions of consumers but almost always from associations of practitioners of the occupation. These requests are almost always accompanied by the proposal that those who have already entered and are practicing the occupation be qualified *pro forma* and exempted from examination. Such a "grandfather clause" often appears in occupational licensing legislation; only those desiring to enter the occupation are subjected to the qualifying tests. It is also common for states and municipalities to appoint already-licensed practitioners to examining boards that determine whether applicants for entry into licensed trades and professions are qualified. In addition, professional and trade associations of those in licensed occupations are the most watchful and aggressive in preventing others from performing services the associations believe to be exclusively comprehended by their particular occupation.

The circumstances just described could reflect the desire of practitioners to assure consumers that they will secure only competent services. However, it is more likely that they reflect the hopes of practitioners for higher incomes, for licensing frequently causes the price of service and the earnings of practitioners in licensed occupations to be higher than they would be if the occupations were unlicensed.

Economic effects.   Whether economic effects occur depends upon the nature of the qualifying rules. If these do not check entry into the occupation, prices and earnings will be left unaffected. If entry is checked, they will be higher than they would have been had there been no licensing. The magnitude of the difference is determined by the degree to which the qualifying rules of licensure check entry and by the extent of change in the quantities of the relevant services that sellers are willing to sell and buyers are willing to buy as their prices change—that is to say, by the price elasticities of supply and demand. An estimate of the relative income effects of licensure in medicine and dentistry in the United States for the period 1929 to 1934 was made by Friedman and Kuznets (1945, chapter 4). The Friedman and Kuznets estimate is discussed by Lewis (1963, p. 114 ff.), who also makes a similar estimate for a more recent period.

Not all occupational licensing causes prices and earnings to rise, because in some licensed occupations almost all qualify and entry is not checked. This is the case if licenses are granted to all who are "of good moral character." Licensing arrangements of this kind are usually adopted in order to facilitate the administration of some standard of conduct by practitioners. Illustratively, a rule that in massage parlors men clients are to be separated from women clients can be conveniently enforced by the revocation of the licenses of masseurs who violate the rule. Most occupational licensing, however, does check entry, by imposing either explicit or implicit costs of entry in addition to those which would be incurred in the absence of licensing.

Explicit additional entry costs may include required general schooling, of some specified level; vocational or professional schooling, for some period or containing a specified content; successful performance upon written or oral examination; and employment for some period as an apprentice, with relatively low earnings. The explicit costs are the sum of tuition charges and other fees paid for schooling, and the income forgone that might have been earned if other employment had been taken during the required period of schooling and apprenticeship.

Implicit entry costs are, for example, a minimum-age qualification or a limitation on the number of licenses that will be issued. For those who do not qualify under such rules, the implicit cost of entry into the occupation is infinite.

Not infrequently, persons seeking to be licensed in some occupation are examined in subject matter that has no immediate relevance to the skills that will be ordinarily performed in it. In this way specialization in the acquisition of skill is discouraged. This is done, apparently, in order to prolong the period of training in preparation for the examination, thus increasing the cost of new entry into the occupation.

If the cost of entry is raised—either because incremental costs are imposed by licensure or for any other cause—fewer people will make themselves available to that occupation at every hypothetical level of relative earnings in it. In the conventional graphic representation of market schedules, a rise in entry costs shifts the supply schedule of labor in that occupation to the left. The point of intersection of the supply and demand schedules, which determines the price paid to labor in the occupation and (to a first approximation) the number who are employed in it, is now such that earnings in the trade will be higher and the number who are employed in it will be less than if there had been no increase in the cost of entry.

This is not to say that there are necessarily monopoly gains for those who are employed in the occupation. In principle, the rise in earnings will be just sufficient to compensate for the rise in entry costs. Those who have incurred the increased costs of entry will receive earnings that, when adjusted for the higher cost of entry, will just equal the earnings of those who are in similar occupations which are freely entered and for which licensure has not created an additional increment to the cost of entry.

But there will be monopoly gains—rents—for those in a licensed occupation who have *not* been required to incur the extra entry costs imposed by licensure or by higher qualifying standards. It is therefore understandable that practitioners in unlicensed occupations frequently propose that their occupations be licensed—with grandfather clauses that will qualify them *pro forma*—and that practitioners in licensed occupations propose higher qualifying standards for entry than those they were required to satisfy when they entered. Any increase in entry costs will check entry into the occupation and cause earnings to rise. This will produce rents for those already in the occupation, who are exempted from incurring the additional cost.

Rationing problem. If the licensing rules impose entry costs, a smaller number will be employed in the occupation than if there had been no licensing. But if licensing rules permit *all* who meet the qualifying standards to enter an occupation, there will be no explicit rationing problem. The number employed will be determined by the point of intersection of demand and supply schedules; the number making themselves available in the occupation will be just equal to the number whose services buyers want to buy, and the market will clear.

This may not be true, however, when explicit limits are put upon the number of licenses to be issued by the public authorities. This arrangement occurs in a minority of cases. In these cases, rationing may be necessary when, given the cost of entry and relative earnings in the licensed occupation, more qualify and seek to enter it than there are licenses available. Here the relevant agency of government must act on some principle that distinguishes those who will be granted a license from those who will be rejected. The rule may be of a first-come-first-served type—as when available licenses are issued to those who have waited longest for one—or it may be of some other nature. If the authorities, having predetermined the number of licenses they will issue, sell them by some auction procedure to the highest bidders, market processes will, of course, determine the distribution of licenses among prospective entrants to the occupation and the market will clear.

In some cases the authorities, after numerically limiting licenses to be issued for some occupation and rationing them among applicants for a nominal charge, have permitted these licenses to be privately transacted. Here the licenses, which give access to employment in the occupation exclusively to those who hold them, are capital assets whose values depend upon the time-discounted stream of monopoly rents (net earnings, over time, that exceed those that would be attached to the occupation if there were free access to it). The capital value of these licenses—that is to say, the prices at which they are transacted—may rise or fall in successive transactions. If their prices do change, it is because the future has not been perfectly foreseen by sellers or buyers in prior transactions with respect to any one or a number of relevant variables that affect the monopoly gains associated with the possession of a license.

Licensing checks on entry into an occupation only rarely use the strategy of explicit numerical limitation of licenses to be issued; the alternative device of imposing new entry costs is much more commonly employed. The latter device can be associated with the raising of standards of performance and qualification in the trade. The enforcement of numerical limits, on the other hand, can be defended only on the ground that unlimited entry will have adverse effects on third parties, for example, that unlimited numbers of taxis, competitively racing for customers, will cause accidents. Legislatures seem to find the defense-of-standards argument more attractive. If requirements for acquisition of the license exclude those who fall below some prescribed minimum of capacity or knowledge relevant to the service rendered in an occupation, the mean standard of performance by legal practitioners of a licensed occupation will, of course, be higher than if the occupation were unlicensed. In such a case, the mean quality of this service that is purchased by consumers will usually also be higher. But this result does not always occur. Whether it does depends on the substitute to which consumers have recourse when the law denies them access to low-priced, low-quality professional services.

The number of persons in licensed occupations is still a small proportion of all employed persons in the United States, but their relative numbers seem to be increasing as more and more legislatures respond to the overtures of practitioners and more and more occupations are licensed.

SIMON ROTTENBERG

[*See also* OCCUPATIONS AND CAREERS; PROFESSIONS.]

BIBLIOGRAPHY

ARROW, KENNETH J. 1963 Uncertainty and the Welfare Economics of Medical Care. *American Economic Review* 53:942–973.

FRIEDMAN, MILTON; and KUZNETS, SIMON 1945 *Income From Independent Professional Practice.* National Bureau of Economic Research, General Series, No. 45. New York: The Bureau.

GELLHORN, WALTER 1956 *Individual Freedom and Governmental Restraints.* Baton Rouge: Louisiana State Univ. Press.

LEWIS, H. G. 1963 *Unionism and Relative Wages in the United States: An Empirical Inquiry.* Univ. of Chicago Press.

ROTTENBERG, SIMON 1962 The Economics of Occupational Licensing. Pages 3–20 in Universities–National Bureau Committee for Economic Research, Conference, Princeton, N.J., 1960, *Aspects of Labor Economics.* National Bureau of Economic Research, Special Conference Series, No. 14. Princeton Univ. Press.

LIEBEN, RICHARD

See AUSPITZ, RUDOLF, AND LIEBEN, RICHARD.

LIFE CYCLE

The observer of life is always immersed in it and thus unable to transcend the limited perspectives of his stage and condition. Religious world views usually evolve pervasive configurations of the course of life: one religion may envisage it as a continuous spiral of rebirths, another as a crossroads to damnation or salvation. Various "ways of life" harbor more or less explicit images of life's course: a leisurely one may see it as ascending and descending steps with a comfortable platform of maturity in between; a competitive one may envision it as a race for spectacular success—and sudden oblivion. The scientist, on the other hand, looks at the organism as it moves from birth to death and, in the larger sense, at the individual in a genetic chain; or he looks at the cultural design of life's course as marked by rites of transition at selected turning points.

The very choice of the configuration "cycle of life," then, necessitates a statement of the writer's conceptual ancestry—clinical psychoanalysis. The clinical worker cannot escape combining knowledge, experience, and conviction in a conception of the course of life and of the sequence of generations—for how, otherwise, could he offer interpretation and guidance? The very existence of a variety of psychiatric "schools" is probably due to the fact that clinical practice and theory are called upon to provide a total orientation beyond possible verification.

Freud confessed only to a scientific world view, but he could not avoid the attitudes (often in contradiction to his personal values) that were part of his times. The original data of psychoanalysis, for example, were minute reconstructions of "pathogenic" events in early childhood. They supported an orientation which—in analogy to teleology—could be called *originology*, i.e., a systematic attempt to derive complex meanings from vague beginnings and obscure causes. The result was often an implicit fatalism, although counteracted by strenuously "positive" orientations. Any theory embracing both life history and case history, however, must find a balance between the "backward" view of the genetic reconstruction and the "forward" formulation of progressive differentiation in growth and development; between the "downward" view into the depth of the unconscious and the "upward" awareness of compelling social experience; and between the "inward" exploration of inner reality and the "outward" attention to historical actuality.

This article will attempt to make explicit those psychosocial insights that often remain implicit in clinical practice and theory. These concern the individual, who in principle develops according to predetermined steps of readiness that enable him to participate in ever more differentiated ways along a widening social radius, and the social organization, which in principle tends to invite such developmental potentialities and to support the proper rate and the proper sequence of their unfolding.

"Cycle" is intended to convey the double tendency of individual life to "round itself out" as a coherent experience and at the same time to form a link in the chain of generations from which it receives and to which it contributes both strength and weakness.

Strategic in this interplay are developmental crises—"crisis" here connoting not a threat of catastrophe but a turning point, a crucial period of increased vulnerability and heightened potential, and, therefore, the ontogenetic source of generational strength and maladjustment.

The eight stages of life

Man's protracted childhood must be provided with the psychosocial protection and stimulation which, like a second womb, permits the child to develop in distinct steps as he unifies his separate capacities. In each stage, we assume a new drive-and-need constellation, an expanded radius of potential social interaction, and social institutions created to receive the growing individual within traditional patterns. To provide an evolutionary rationale for this (for prolonged childhood and social institutions must have evolved together), two basic differences between animal and man must be considered.

We are, in Ernst Mayr's terms (1964), the "generalist" animal, prepared to adapt to and to develop cultures in the most varied environments. A long childhood must prepare the newborn of the species to become specialized as a member of a pseudo species (Erikson 1965), i.e., in tribes, cultures, castes, etc., each of which behaves as if it were the only genuine realization of man as the heavens planned and created him. Furthermore, man's drives are characterized by instinctual energies, which are, in contrast to other animals, much less bound to instinctive patterns (or inborn release mechanisms). A maximum of free instinctual energy thus remains ready to be invested in basic psychosocial encounters which tend to fix developing energies into cultural patterns of mutuality, reliability, and competence. Freud has shown the extent to which maladaptive anxiety and rage accompany man's instinctuality, while postulating

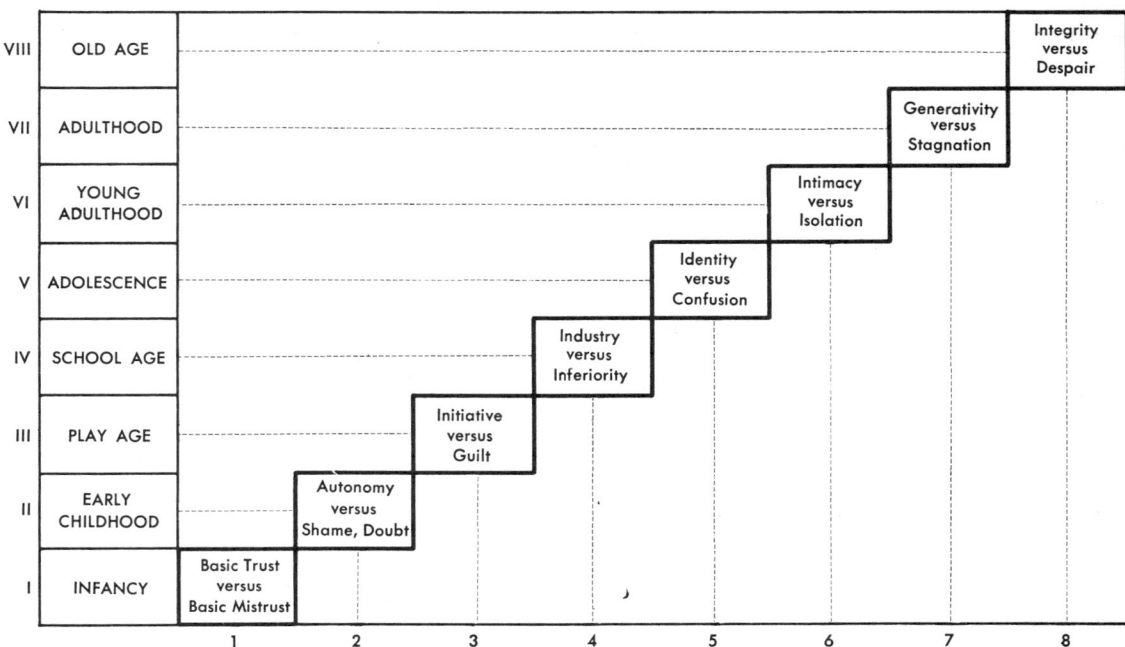

Figure 1 — Psychosocial crises in the life cycle

Source: Adapted from *Childhood and Society*, by Erik H. Erikson, Copyright 1950, © 1963 by W. W. Norton & Company. Reproduced with permission of W. W. Norton & Company, Inc. and Hogarth Press, Ltd.

the strength of the ego in its defensive and in its adaptive aspects (see Freud 1936; Hartmann 1939). We can attempt to show a systematic relationship between man's maladjustments and those basic strengths which must emerge in each life cycle and re-emerge from generation to generation (Erikson 1964).

In Figure 1, above, the various psychosocial crises and thus the ontogenetic sources of adaptation and of maladjustment are arranged according to the epigenetic principle. The diagonal signifies a successive development and a hierarchic differentiation of psychosocial strengths.

If a favorable ratio of basic trust over basic mistrust is the first step in psychosocial adaptation, and the second step a favorable ratio of autonomy over shame and doubt, the diagram indicates a number of fundamental facts. Each basic psychosocial trend (1, 2, etc.) meets a crisis (I, 1; II, 2; etc.) during a corresponding stage (I, II, etc.), while *all* must exist from the beginning in some form (broken line) and in later stages (solid lines) must continue to be differentiated and reintegrated with newly dominant trends. An infant will show something like autonomy from the time of birth

(I, 2), but it is not until the second year (II, 2) that he is ready to experience and to manage the critical conflict of becoming an autonomous creature while continuing to be dependent. At this time those around him will convey to him a cultural and personal version of the ratio of autonomy and dependence. The diagonal thus indicates a necessary sequence of such encounters but leaves room for variations in tempo and intensity.

The epigenetic pattern will have to be kept in mind as we now state for each stage: (*a*) the psychosocial crisis evoked by social interaction, which is in turn facilitated and necessitated by newly developing drives and capacities, and the specific psychosocial strength emanating from the solution of this crisis; (*b*) the specific sense of estrangement awakened at each stage and its connection with some major form of psychopathology; (*c*) the special relationship between all of these factors and certain basic social institutions (Erikson 1950).

Infancy (basic trust versus mistrust—hope). The resolution of the first psychosocial crisis is performed primarily by maternal care. The newborn infant's more or less coordinated readiness to incorporate by mouth and through the senses meets the mother's and the society's more or less coordinated readiness to feed him and to stimulate his awareness. The mother must represent to the child an almost somatic conviction that she (his first "world") is trustworthy enough to satisfy and to regulate his needs. But the infant's demeanor also inspires hope in adults and makes them wish to give hope; it awakens in them a strength which they, in turn, are ready and needful to have confirmed in the experience of care. This is the ontogenetic basis of hope, that first and basic strength which gives man a semblance of instinctive certainty in his social ecology.

Unavoidable pain and delay of satisfaction, however, and inexorable weaning make this stage also prototypical for a sense of abandonment and helpless rage. This is the first of the human estrangements against which hope must maintain itself throughout life.

In psychopathology, a defect in basic trust can be evident in early malignant disturbances or can become apparent later in severe addiction or in habitual or sudden withdrawal into psychotic states.

Biological motherhood needs at least three links with social experience—the mother's past experience of being mothered, a method of care in trustworthy surroundings, and some convincing image of providence. The infant's hope, in turn, is one cornerstone of the adult's faith, which throughout history has sought an institutional safeguard in organized religion. However, where religious institutions fail to give ritual actuality to their formulas they may become irrelevant to psychosocial strength.

Hope, then, is the first psychosocial strength. It is the enduring belief in the attainability of primal wishes in spite of the anarchic urges and rages of dependency.

Early childhood (autonomy versus shame, doubt —will power).   Early childhood sets the stage for psychosocial autonomy by rapid gains in muscular maturation, locomotion, verbalization, and discrimination. All of these, however, create limits in the form of spatial restrictions and of categorical divisions between "yes and no," "good and bad," "right and wrong," and "yours and mine." Muscular maturation sets the stage for an ambivalent set of social modalities—holding on and letting go. To hold on can become a destructive retaining or restraining, or a pattern of care—to have and to hold. To let go, too, can turn into an inimical letting loose, or a relaxed "letting pass" and "letting be." Freud calls this the anal stage of libido development because of the pleasure experienced in and the conflict evoked over excretory retention and elimination.

This stage, therefore, becomes decisive for the ratio of good will and willfulness. A sense of self-control without loss of self-esteem is the ontogenetic source of confidence in free will; a sense of overcontrol and loss of self-control can give rise to a lasting propensity for doubt and shame. The matter is complicated by the different needs and capacities of siblings of different ages—and by their rivalry.

Shame is the estrangement of being exposed and conscious of being looked at disapprovingly, of wishing to "bury one's face" or "sink into the ground." This potentiality is exploited in the "shaming" used throughout life by some cultures and causing, on occasion, suicide. While shame is related to the consciousness of being upright and exposed, doubt has much to do with the consciousness of having a front and a back (and of the vulnerability of being seen and influenced from behind). It is the estrangement of being unsure of one's will and of those who would dominate it.

From this stage emerges the propensity for compulsive overcompliance or impulsive defiance. If denied a gradual increase in autonomy of choice the individual may become obsessed by repetitiveness and develop an overly cruel conscience. Early self-doubt and doubt of others may later find their most malignant expression in compulsion neuroses or in paranoiac apprehension of hidden critics and secret persecutors threatening from behind.

We have related basic trust to the institutions of religion. The enduring need of the individual to have an area of free choice reaffirmed and delineated by formulated privileges and limitations, obligations and rights, has an institutional safeguard in the principles of law and order and of justice. Where this is impaired, however, the law itself is in danger of becoming arbitrary or formalistic, i.e., "impulsive" or "compulsive" itself.

Will power is the unbroken determination to exercise free choice as well as self-restraint in spite of the unavoidable experience of shame, doubt, and a certain rage over being controlled by others. Good will is rooted in the judiciousness of parents guided by their respect for the spirit of the law.

Play age (initiative versus guilt—purpose).   Able to move independently and vigorously, the child, now in his third or fourth year, begins to comprehend his expected role in the adult world and to play out roles worth imitating. He develops a sense of initiative. He associates with age-mates and older children as he watches and enters into games in the barnyard, on the street corner, or in the nursery. His learning now is intrusive; it leads him into ever new facts and activities, and he becomes acutely aware of differences between the sexes. But if it seems that the child spends on his play a purposefulness out of proportion to "real" purposes, we must recognize the human necessity to simultaneously bind together infantile wish and limited skill, symbol and fact, inner and outer world, a selectively remembered past and a vaguely anticipated future—all before adult "reality" takes over in sanctioned roles and adjusted purposes.

The fate of infantile genitality remains determined by the sex roles cultivated and integrated in the family. In the boy, the sexual orientation is dominated by phallic-intrusive initiative; in the girl, by inclusive modes of attractiveness and "motherliness."

Conscience, however, forever divides the child within himself by establishing an inner voice of self-observation, self-guidance, and self-punishment. The estrangement of this stage, therefore, is a sense of guilt over goals contemplated and acts done, initiated, or merely fantasied. For initiative includes competition with those of superior equipment. In a final contest for a favored position with the mother, "oedipal" feelings are aroused in the boy, and there appears to be an intensified fear of finding the genitals harmed as punishment for the fantasies attached to their excitability.

Infantile guilt leads to the conflict between unbounded initiative and repression or inhibition. In adult pathology this residual conflict is expressed in hysterical denial, general inhibition, and sexual impotence, or in overcompensatory exhibitionism and psychopathic acting-out.

The word "initiative" has for many a specifically American, or "entrepreneur," connotation. Yet man needs this sense of initiative for whatever he learns and does, from fruit gathering to commercial enterprise—or the study of books.

The play age relies on the existence of some form of basic family, which also teaches the child by patient example where play ends and irreversible purpose begins. Only thus are guilt feelings integrated in a strong (not severe) conscience; only thus is language verified as a shared actuality. The "oedipal" stage thus not only results in a moral sense restricting the horizon of the permissible, but it also directs the way to the possible and the tangible, which attract infantile dreams to the goals of technology and culture. Social institutions, in turn, offer an ethos of action, in the form of ideal adults fascinating enough to replace the heroes of the picture book and fairy tale.

That the adult begins as a playing child means that there is a residue of play acting and role playing even in what he considers his highest purposes. These he projects on a larger and more perfect historical future; these he dramatizes in the ceremonial present with uniformed players in ritual arrangements; thus men sanction aggressive initiative, even as they assuage guilt by submission to a higher authority.

Purpose, then, is the courage to envisage and pursue valued and tangible goals guided by conscience but not paralyzed by guilt and by the fear of punishment.

School age (industry versus inferiority—competence). Before the child, psychologically a rudimentary parent, can become a biological parent, he must begin to be a worker and potential provider. Genital maturation is postponed (the period of latency). The child develops a sense of industriousness, i.e., he begins to comprehend the tool world of his culture, and he can become an eager and absorbed member of that productive situation called "school," which gradually supersedes the whims of play. In all cultures, at this stage, children receive systematic instruction of some kind and learn eagerly from older children.

The danger of this stage lies in the development of a sense of inadequacy. If the child despairs of his skill or his status among his tool partners, he may be discouraged from further learning. He may regress to the hopeless rivalry of the oedipal situation. It is at this point that the larger society becomes significant to the child by admitting him to roles preparatory to the actuality of technology and economy. Where he finds, however, that the color of his skin or the background of his parents rather than his wish and his will to learn will decide his worth as an apprentice, the human propensity for feeling unworthy (inferior) may be fatefully aggravated as a determinant of character development.

But there is another danger: If the overly conforming child accepts work as the only criterion of worthwhileness, sacrificing too readily his imagination and playfulness, he may become ready to submit to what Marx called a "craft-idiocy," i.e., become a slave of his technology and of its established role typology.

This is socially a most decisive stage, preparing the child for a hierarchy of learning experiences which he will undergo with the help of cooperative peers and instructive adults. Since industriousness involves doing things beside and with others, a first sense of the division of labor and of differential opportunity—that is, a sense of the technological ethos of a culture—develops at this time. Therefore, the configurations of cultural thought and the manipulations basic to the prevailing technology must reach meaningfully into school life.

Competence, then, is the free exercise (unimpaired by an infantile sense of inferiority) of dexterity and intelligence in the completion of serious tasks. It is the basis for cooperative participation in some segment of the culture.

Adolescence (identity versus identity confusion—fidelity). With a good initial relationship to skills and tools, and with the advent of puberty, childhood proper comes to an end. The rapidly growing youths, faced with the inner revolution of puberty and with as yet intangible adult tasks, are now primarily concerned with their psychosocial identity and with fitting their rudimentary gifts and skills to the occupational prototypes of the culture.

The integration of an identity is more than the sum of childhood identifications. It is the accrued confidence that the inner sameness and continuity gathered over the past years of development are matched by the sameness and continuity in one's meaning for others, as evidenced in the tangible promise of careers and life styles.

The adolescent's regressive and yet powerful impulsiveness alternating with compulsive restraint is well known. In all of this, however, an ideological seeking after an inner coherence and a durable set of values can be detected. The particular strength sought is fidelity—that is, the opportunity to fulfill personal potentialities (including erotic vitality or its sublimation) in a context which permits the young person to be true to himself and true to significant others. "Falling in love" also can be an attempt to arrive at a self-definition by seeing oneself reflected anew in an idealized as well as eroticized other.

From this stage on, acute maladjustments due to social anomie may lead to psychopathological regressions. Where role confusion joins a hopelessness of long standing, borderline psychotic episodes are not uncommon.

Adolescents, on the other hand, help one another temporarily through much regressive insecurity by forming cliques and by stereotyping themselves, their ideals, and their "enemies." In this they can be clannish and cruel in their exclusion of all those who are "different." Where they turn this repudiation totally against the society, delinquency may be a temporary or lasting result.

As social systems enter into the fiber of each succeeding generation, they also absorb into their lifeblood the rejuvenative power of youth. Adolescence is thus a vital regenerator in the process of social evolution, for youth can offer its loyalties and energies to the conservation of that which it feels is valid as well as to the revolutionary correction of that which has lost its regenerative significance.

Adolescence is least "stormy" among those youths who are gifted and well trained in the pursuit of productive technological trends. In times of unrest, the adolescent mind becomes an ideological mind in search of an inspiring unification of ideas. Youth needs to be affirmed by peers and confirmed by teachings, creeds, and ideologies which express the promise that the best people will come to rule and that rule will develop the best in people. A society's ideological weakness, in turn, expresses itself in weak utopianism and in widespread identity confusion.

Fidelity, then, is the ability to sustain loyalties freely pledged in spite of the inevitable contradictions of value systems. It is the cornerstone of identity and receives inspiration from confirming ideologies and "ways of life."

Young adulthood (intimacy versus isolation—love). Consolidated identity permits the self-abandonment demanded by intimate affiliations, by passionate sexual unions, or by inspiring encounters. The young adult is ready for intimacy and solidarity—that is, he can commit himself to affiliations and partnerships even though they may call for significant sacrifices and compromises. Ethical strength emerges as a further differentiation of ideological conviction (adolescence) and a sense of moral obligation (childhood).

True genital maturity is first reached at this stage; much of the individual's previous sex life is of the identity-confirming kind. Freud, when asked for the criteria of a mature person, is reported to have answered: *"Lieben und Arbeiten"* ("love and work"). All three words deserve equal emphasis.

It is only at this stage that the biological differences between the sexes result in a full polarization within a joint life style. Previously established strengths have helped the two sexes to converge in capacities and values which enhance communication and cooperation, while divergence is now of the essence in love life and in procreation. Thus the sexes first become similar in consciousness, language, and ethics in order then to be maturely different. But this, by necessity, causes ambivalences.

The danger of this stage is possible psychosocial isolation—that is, the avoidance of contacts which commit to intimacy. In psychopathology isolation can lead to severe character problems of the kind which interfere with "love and work," and this often on the basis of infantile fixations and lasting immaturities.

Man, in addition to erotic attraction, has developed a selectivity of mutual love that serves the need for a new and shared identity in the procession of generations. Love is the guardian of that elusive and yet all-pervasive power of cultural and personal style which binds into a "way of life" the affiliations of competition and cooperation, procreation and production. The problem is one of transferring the experience of being cared for in a parental setting to an adult affiliation actively chosen and cultivated as a mutual concern within a new generation.

The counterpart of such intimacy, and the danger, is man's readiness to fortify his territory of intimacy and solidarity by exaggerating small differences and prejudging or excluding foreign influences and people. Insularity thus aggravated can lead to that irrational fear which is easily exploited by demagogic leaders seeking aggrandizement in war and in political conflict.

Love, then, is a mutuality of devotion greater than the antagonisms inherent in divided function.

Maturity (generativity versus stagnation—care). Evolution has made man the teaching and instituting as well as the learning animal. For dependency and maturity are reciprocal: mature man needs to be needed, and maturity is guided by the nature of that which must be cared for.

Generativity, then, is primarily the concern with establishing and guiding the next generation. In addition to procreativity, it includes productivity and creativity; thus it is psychosocial in nature. From the crisis of generativity emerges the strength of care.

Where such enrichment fails, a sense of stagnation and boredom ensues, the pathological symptoms of which depend on variations in mental epidemiology: certainly where the hypocrisy of the frigid mother was once regarded as a most significant malignant influence, today, when sexual "adjustment" is in order, an obsessive pseudo intimacy and adult self-indulgence are nonetheless damaging to the generational process. The very nature of generativity suggests that the most circumscribed symptoms of its weakness are to be found in the next generation in the form of those aggravated estrangements which we have listed for childhood and youth.

Generativity is itself a driving power in human organization. For the intermeshing stages of childhood and adulthood are in themselves a system of generation and regeneration given continuity by institutions such as extended households and divided labor.

Thus, in combination, the basic strengths enumerated here and the structure of an organized human community provide a set of proven methods and a fund of traditional reassurance with which each generation meets the needs of the next.

Various traditions transcend divisive personal differences and confusing conditions. But they also contribute to a danger to the species as a whole, namely, the defensive territoriality of the pseudo species, which on seemingly ethical grounds must discredit and destroy threateningly alien systems and may itself be destroyed in the process.

Care is the broadening concern for what has been generated by love, necessity, or accident—a concern which must consistently overcome the ambivalence adhering to irreversible obligation and the narrowness of self-concern.

Old age (integrity versus despair—wisdom). Strength in the aging and sometimes in the old takes the form of wisdom in its many connotations—ripened "wits," accumulated knowledge, inclusive understanding, and mature judgment. Wisdom maintains and conveys the integrity of experience, in spite of the decline of bodily and mental functions. Responding to the oncoming generation's need for an integrated heritage, the wisdom of old age remains aware of the relativity of all knowledge acquired in one lifetime in one historical period. Integrity, therefore, implies an emotional integration faithful to the image bearers of the past and ready to take (and eventually to renounce) leadership in the present.

The lack or loss of this accrued integration is signified by a hidden fear of death: fate is not accepted as the frame of life, death not as its finite boundary. Despair indicates that time is too short for alternate roads to integrity: this is why the old try to "doctor" their memories. Bitterness and disgust mask such despair, which in severe psychopathology aggravates senile depression, hypochondria, and paranoiac hate.

A meaningful old age (preceding terminal invalidism) provides that integrated heritage which gives indispensable perspective to those growing up, "adolescing," and aging. But the end of the cycle also evokes "ultimate concerns," the paradoxes of which we must leave to philosophical and religious interpreters. Whatever chance man has to transcend the limitations of his self seems to depend on his full (if often tragic) engagement in the one and only life cycle permitted him in the sequence of generations. Great philosophical and religious systems dealing with ultimate individuation seem to have remained (even in their monastic establishments) responsibly related to the cultures and civilizations of their times. Seeking transcendence by renunciation, they remain ethically concerned with the maintenance of the world. By the same token, a civilization can be measured by the meaning which it gives to the full cycle of life, for such meaning (or the lack of it) cannot fail to reach into the beginnings of the next generation and thus enhance the potentiality that others may meet ultimate questions with some clarity and strength.

Wisdom, then, is a detached and yet active concern with life in the face of death.

Conclusion

From the cycle of life such dispositions as faith, will power, purposefulness, efficiency, devotion, affection, responsibility, and sagacity (all of which are also criteria of ego strength) flow into the life of institutions. Without them, institutions wilt; but without the spirit of institutions pervading the patterns of care and love, instruction and training, no enduring strength could emerge from the sequence of generations.

We have attempted, in a psychosocial frame, to account for the ontogenesis not of lofty ideals but of an inescapable and intrinsic order of strivings, which, by weakening or strengthening man, dictates the minimum goals of informed and responsible participation.

Psychosocial strength, we conclude, depends on a total process which regulates individual life cycles, the sequence of generations, and the structure of society simultaneously, for all three have evolved together.

Each person must translate this order into his own terms so as to make it amenable to whatever kind of trait inventory, normative scale, measurement, or educational goal is his main concern. Science and technology are, no doubt, changing essential aspects of the course of life, wherefore some increased awareness of the functional wholeness of the cycle may be mandatory. Interdisciplinary work will define in practical and applicable terms what evolved order is common to all men and what true equality of opportunity must mean in planning for future generations.

The study of the human life cycle has immediate applications in a number of fields. Paramount is the science of human development within social institutions. In psychiatry (and in its applications to law), the diagnostic and prognostic assessment of disturbances common to life stages should help to outweigh fatalistic diagnoses. Whatever will prove tangibly lawful about the cycle of life will also be an important focus for anthropology insofar as it assesses universal functions in the variety of institutional forms. Finally, as the study of the life history emerges from that of case histories, it will throw new light on biography and thus on history itself.

ERIK H. ERIKSON

[*Directly related are the entries* ADOLESCENCE; AGING; DEVELOPMENTAL PSYCHOLOGY; EVOLUTION, *articles on* HUMAN EVOLUTION, CULTURAL EVOLUTION, *and* SOCIAL EVOLUTION; INFANCY. *Other relevant material may be found in* IDENTITY, PSYCHOSOCIAL; PSYCHOANALYSIS; SELF CONCEPT; SOCIALIZATION.]

BIBLIOGRAPHY

BÜHLER, CHARLOTTE (1933) 1959 *Der menschliche Lebenslauf als psychologisches Problem.* 2d ed., rev. Leipzig: Hirzel.

BÜHLER, CHARLOTTE 1962 *Values in Psychotherapy.* New York: Free Press.

ERIKSON, ERIK H. (1950) 1964 *Childhood and Society.* 2d ed., rev. & enl. New York: Norton.

ERIKSON, ERIK H. 1958 *Young Man Luther.* New York: Norton.

ERIKSON, ERIK H. 1964 *Insight and Responsibility.* New York: Norton.

ERIKSON, ERIK H. 1965 The Ontogeny of Ritualisation in Man. Unpublished manuscript.

FREUD, ANNA (1936) 1957 *The Ego and the Mechanisms of Defense.* New York: International Universities Press. → First published as *Das Ich und die Abwehrmechanismen.*

FREUD, ANNA 1965 *Normality and Pathology in Childhood: Assessment of Development.* New York: International Universities Press.

HARTMANN, HEINZ (1939) 1958 *Ego Psychology and the Problem of Adaptation.* Translated by David Rapaport. New York: International Universities Press. → First published as *Ich-Psychologie und Anpassungsproblem.*

MAYR, ERNST 1964 The Evolution of Living Systems. National Academy of Sciences, *Proceedings* 51:934–941.

WERNER, HEINZ (1926) 1965 *Comparative Psychology of Mental Development.* Rev. ed. New York: International Universities Press. → First published as *Einführung in die Entwicklungspsychologie.*

LIFE TABLES

The life table (also referred to as the mortality table) is a statistical device used to compute chances of survivorship and death and average remaining years of life, for specific years of age. The concept of the life table is applicable not only to humans (Spiegelman 1957) and other species of life (Haldane 1953; Ciba Foundation 1959) but also to items of industrial equipment (Dublin, Lotka, & Spiegelman [1936] 1949) and other defined aggregates subject to a measurable process of attrition. Life tables can also be developed further for computing the chances of other vital events in human life, such as marriage and remarriage, the birth of children, widowhood, illness and disability, and labor force participation and retirement (Spiegelman 1957); and they enter into a wide variety of annuity and life insurance computations (Hooker & Longley-Cook 1953–1957; Jordan 1952).

The conventional life table

The conventional form of a life table for the general population is illustrated in Table 1. The original data are recorded deaths and the census of population classified according to age (this step is not shown on the table). From these data were computed the *rates of mortality*, conventionally designated as q_x, for each year of age, x. These rates show the proportion of deaths occurring within the year of age among those who attain that age; the rates are usually shown per thousand ($1,000q_x$). For example, Table 1 shows that of every 1,000 who just attained age 0 (the newly born), 23.55 died before reaching their first birthday; similarly, of every 1,000 who attained age six, 0.53 died within that year of age. Typically, mortality rates for a general population start at a high point in the first year of life, fall rapidly to a minimum at about age ten, and then rise with advance in years. The rise is gradual to about age 40, and then becomes increasingly rapid; since the maximum attainable age for human beings is in the neighborhood of 110 years, life tables seldom go beyond that point.

Once one knows the mortality rates at each age of life, it becomes possible to compute the number of *survivors* (column l_x of the life table) and also the number of *deaths* (column d_x). It is usually most convenient to start the population life table with a base (radix) of 100,000 newborn individuals. In the example presented here, where there is a death rate of 23.55 per 1,000 at age 0, among the 100,000 newly born there must be 2,355 deaths in the first year of life. The number of survivors to attain age 1 is then $100,000 - 2,355 = 97,645$. With a mortality rate of 1.89 per 1,000 at age 1, among the 97,645 who attained that age there are

$$97,645 \times \frac{1.89}{1,000} = 185 \text{ deaths.}$$

The number of survivors to age 2 is then calculated in the same way:

$$97,645 - 185 = 97,460.$$

This procedure is continued to the end of the life table. Obviously, the number in the survivorship column, l_x, at any attained age is equal to the sum of the deaths in the d_x column for that and all higher ages.

To compute the *expectation of life* ($\overset{\circ}{e}_x$), or average future lifetime, for any attained age, it will be assumed that deaths, d_x, are uniformly distributed over the year of age, x. Equivalent to this is the

Table 1 — Life table for white females, United States, 1949–1951[a]

Year of age	RATE OF MORTALITY PER 1,000 Number dying between ages x and x + 1 among 1,000 living at age x	OF 100,000 BORN ALIVE Number surviving to exact age x	Number dying between ages x and x + 1	Number of years lived by the cohort between ages x and x + 1	Total number of years lived by the cohort from age x on, until all have died	Average number of years lived after age x per person surviving to exact age x[b]
x	$1,000q_x$	l_x	d_x	L_x	T_x	$\overset{\circ}{e}_x$
0	23.55	100,000	2,355	97,965	7,203,179	72.03
1	1.89	97,645	185	97,552	7,105,214	72.77
2	1.12	97,460	109	97,406	7,007,662	71.90
3	0.87	97,351	85	97,308	6,910,256	70.98
4	0.69	97,266	67	97,233	6,812,948	70.04
5	0.60	97,199	59	97,169	6,715,715	69.09
6	0.53	97,140	52	97,114	6,618,546	68.13
7	0.48	97,088	46	97,065	6,521,432	67.17
8	0.44	97,042	43	97,020	6,424,367	66.20
9	0.41	96,999	39	96,980	6,327,347	65.23
⋮	⋮	⋮	⋮	⋮	⋮	⋮
100	388.39	294	114	237	566	1.92
101	407.52	180	73	143	329	1.83
102	426.00	107	46	84	186	1.74
103	443.67	61	27	48	102	1.66
104	460.76	34	16	26	54	1.59
⋮	⋮	⋮	⋮	⋮	⋮	⋮

a. Based upon recorded deaths in the United States during the three-year period 1949–1951, recorded births for each year from 1944 through 1951, and the census of population taken April 1, 1950; for details, see U.S. Public Health Service 1959, pp. 149–158.

b. Represents complete expectation of life, or average future lifetime.

Source: U.S. Public Health Service 1954–1955, p. 18.

assumption that each of the persons dying lived one-half year after the last birthday. Thus, among the 294 in Table 1 who attained age 100, there were 114 deaths during that year of age, and these individuals lived $\frac{1}{2} \times 114$ years after their last birthday. Similarly, the 73 who died at age 101 lived $1\frac{1}{2}$ years each after attaining age 100, and the 46 who died at age 102 lived $2\frac{1}{2}$ years each after attaining age 100, and so on, to the last death. Altogether, the total number of years of life lived from age 100 on by the 294 who attained that age is $(\frac{1}{2} \times 114) + (1\frac{1}{2} \times 73) + (2\frac{1}{2} \times 46) + (3\frac{1}{2} \times 27) + \cdots = 566$. This is the figure for age 100 in the column headed T_x. Since the 294 who attained age 100 lived a total of 566 years from their 100th birthday until the death of the last survivor, the average remaining lifetime was

$$566 \div 294 = 1.92 \text{ years.}$$

This is more commonly known as the expectation of life, $\mathring{e}_x$; as an average, it is not applicable to any specific individual.

In Table 1 the life table symbols at the head of each column are defined by the terms above them. Reference has already been made to each, except L_x, which denotes the total number of years lived within the year of age by the number, l_x, who attain that age. It has been assumed that each of the persons dying lived only one half year after the last birthday. Accordingly, among the number, l_x, who attain age x, the years of life lived by those dying during that year of age is $\frac{1}{2}d_x$. The years of life lived by the survivors is l_{x+1}, which is equal to $l_x - d_x$. The sum of $\frac{1}{2}d_x$ and $l_x - d_x$ is the total number of years lived within that year of age. Thus,

$$L_x = l_x - \tfrac{1}{2}d_x.$$

Since T_x is the total number of years lived from age x on by those who attain age x, it follows that

$$T_x = L_x + L_{x+1} + L_{x+2} + \cdots$$

and also that

$$T_x = L_x + T_{x+1}.$$

It should be recognized that except for the mortality rates, which represent an actually observed situation, *all other columns of figures in the life table represent a hypothetical situation*. Thus, the survivorship column and the column of life table deaths show only the expected number of survivals and deaths for successive ages, on the assumption that the mortality rates observed during the specified calendar period continue without change over

time. The same assumption underlies the column of figures for expectation of life.

Life table formulas. It will be seen from the preceding discussion that the construction of life tables rests upon a small number of elementary assumptions, which can be summarized in the following formulas:

$$l_x - l_{x+1} = d_x,$$
$$q_x = \frac{d_x}{l_x}.$$

Moreover, it is evident that if p_x denotes the probability of surviving one year after attaining age x, then

$$p_x = \frac{l_{x+1}}{l_x} = \frac{l_x - d_x}{l_x} = 1 - q_x.$$

Similarly, if $_np_x$ denotes the probability of surviving n years after attaining age x, then

$$_np_x = \frac{l_{x+n}}{l_x} = 1 - {_nq_x},$$

where $_nq_x$ is the probability of dying within n years after attaining age x. Thus,

$$_nq_x = 1 - {_np_x} = \frac{l_x - l_{x+n}}{l_x}.$$

Another measure of mortality is the "force of mortality." This measure takes into account the fact that mortality varies continually with advance in age. In this sense, the rate of mortality in the brief instant after attaining exact age x will be different from that for the brief instant just before leaving age x to attain exact age $x + 1$. The force of mortality, μ_x, is the annual rate of loss of lives, corresponding to the loss, at any instant of time, per head surviving at that time. In terms of the calculus,

$$\mu_x = -\frac{1}{l_x} \cdot \frac{d\,l_x}{dx} = -\frac{d \log l_x}{dx},$$

where d/dx denotes the derivative of the specified function with respect to x.

The force of mortality at age x may be approximated by

$$\mu_x = \frac{l_{x-1} - l_{x+1}}{2l_x}$$

or, more closely, by

$$\mu_x = \frac{8(l_{x-1} - l_{x+1}) - (l_{x-2} - l_{x+2})}{12l_x}.$$

The relevant approximation formulas have been discussed by Jordan (1952, pp. 19–21).

Life table computation. The first task to be carried out in computing a life table for any specific population is to convert the *central death* rate, m_x—that is, the average annual death rate for persons of a given age—into a *mortality rate*, q_x, such as has already been described. A means of doing this is illustrated as follows. In any specified community, let D_x denote the number of deaths recorded within a calendar year of individuals at age x on last birthday (or average annual deaths for a calendar period). Also, let P_x denote the number of people at age x on last birthday on the mid-date of the calendar year or period; this is an approximation to the average number living and, therefore, to the number of years of life lived within the year of age. Then the central death rate at age x for the community is

$$m_x = \frac{D_x}{P_x}.$$

The problem is to convert the central death rate, m_x, into a mortality rate, q_x.

In the life table the number of years of life lived during the year of age x is L_x and deaths during age x number d_x, so that the central death rate m_x is

$$m_x = \frac{d_x}{L_x} = \frac{d_x}{l_x - \frac{1}{2}d_x}.$$

Since $d_x = l_x \cdot q_x$,

$$m_x = \frac{l_x \cdot q_x}{l_x - \frac{1}{2}l_x q_x} = \frac{q_x}{1 - \frac{1}{2}q_x}.$$

Solving for q_x yields

$$q_x = \frac{m_x}{1 + \frac{1}{2}m_x}.$$

In terms of the recorded (observed) deaths and population,

$$q_x = \frac{D_x/P_x}{1 + \frac{1}{2}D_x/P_x} = \frac{D_x}{P_x + \frac{1}{2}D_x}.$$

In practice, however, the mortality rates at the very early ages are usually computed on the basis of a population estimated from recorded births and deaths, since census data for this stage of life are usually unreliable. The risk of mortality in infancy is highest in the first month following birth, and decreases rapidly thereafter; accordingly, the assumption of a uniform distribution of deaths is not valid for the first year of age. For the terminal ages of life, the basic data are usually meager and unreliable; various artifacts are therefore used to compute these mortality rates. The mortality rates for the broad range of intervening ages are generally subjected to mathematical procedures of interpolation and graduation in order to produce a smooth progression of figures (Spiegelman 1955, p. 72). A complete life table shows the figures in each column for every age of life. An abridged life table shows figures for only selected ages, such as every fifth or tenth year of age.

Life tables directly from census data

Where death data are grossly inadequate or lacking, a life table may be approximated from the age distributions of population in two consecutive censuses, as in the following simplified example.

Assume two censuses, five years apart, with correct reporting of ages and with no migration. Then, clearly, the population at age $x + 5$ in the second census, P''_{x+5}, consists of survivors of the population five years younger at the time of the first census, P'_x. The ratio of P''_{x+5} to P'_x accordingly is a five-year survivorship rate for a population at age x last birthday. Assuming a uniform distribution of population over the year of age, this population is approximately at an average attained age $x + \frac{1}{2}$. Thus,

$$_5p_{x+\frac{1}{2}} = \frac{P''_{x+5}}{P'_x}.$$

Having arrived at a series of values of $_5p_{x+\frac{1}{2}}$ according to age, it is possible to work back to a series of mortality rates, q_x. In using this method, allowance may be made for migration (Mortara 1949).

There is also a method of life table estimation that can be used when a population age distribution is available from only one census (Stolnitz 1956). If there is good reason to believe that the size of the population of a community has been virtually stationary over time and that mortality according to age has remained essentially unchanged over time, then its age distribution is clearly very much like that of the life table column L_x. In other words, the number living, P_x, at age x last birthday is proportionate to L_x. Thus,

$$_5p_{x+\frac{1}{2}} = \frac{P_{x+5}}{P_x} = \frac{L_{x+5}}{L_x},$$

and q_x may be estimated, as in the case with two consecutive censuses.

Consider now a population that may be regarded as stable, in the sense that it is growing at a constant annual rate, r, and that mortality at each age is also constant over time. This growth results solely from an excess of births over deaths each year; there is no migration. Then, for an interval of five years,

$$P''_x = P'_x(1 + r)^5.$$

Likewise, P''_{x+5} consists of survivors of P'_x as before. It follows that

$$_5p_{x+\frac{1}{2}} = \frac{P''_{x+5}}{P'_x} = \frac{P''_{x+5}}{P''_x/(1+r)^5} = \frac{P''_{x+5}(1+r)^5}{P''_x},$$

so that use is made of the population at the second census only. Stolnitz generalized this approach by tracing the populations P''_{x+5} and P''_x from their respective births, $x + 5$ and x years previously, namely B_{x+5} and B_x. For this, he introduced survival factors to the same attained age x last birthday, namely S'_x and S''_x, and made use of the five-year survivorship ratio, $_5p_{x+\frac{1}{2}}$. Thus,

$$\frac{P''_{x+5}}{P''_x} = \frac{B_{x+5}}{B_x} \cdot \frac{S'_x}{S''_x} \cdot {}_5p_{x+\frac{1}{2}}.$$

Stolnitz shows how the birth ratio and the ratio of survival factors may be estimated from other experiences. With such estimates it becomes possible to compute $_5p_{x+\frac{1}{2}}$ from the age distribution of a single census.

Model life tables for developing areas. In the developing areas the problem is to estimate a life table for a population with scanty mortality data or from data gathered in a special survey. Since the mortality rate in infancy or the first few years of life is frequently indicative of the general level of mortality, such a rate may be used as the basis for estimation of life table values. Such an observed mortality rate, with suitable adjustment to enhance its validity, is used as a key to select one of a series of life table mortality rates (q_0, $_4q_1$, and $_5q_x$ for x at five-year intervals) from 40 theoretical model series (United Nations 1955a). These models were derived from a study of the patterns of mortality rates in existing life tables. For refinement, the series of life table mortality rates may be selected by interpolating among the models on the basis of the key rate. Further refinement is possible by computing from the equations used to derive the models. Although these model life tables of the United Nations have been subject to technical criticisms,

they are widely used (Gabriel & Ronen 1958; Kurup 1966). A more extensive set of model life tables, prepared at Princeton University, takes into account variations in the patterns of mortality between four broad geographic regions, defined as East, West, North, and South, in addition to variations in the level of mortality within each region (Coale & Demeny 1966).

Life tables directly from death data

As pointed out before, in a population that is virtually stationary, with mortality rates essentially unchanged over time, the age distribution corresponds closely to that in a life table. Only in such a situation is it feasible to cumulate the distribution of deaths according to age, starting with the highest age and noting the total for each age, running back to birth, in order to approximate the survivorship column of the life table. This approach is not applicable in any other situation, since the age distribution of deaths will be influenced by the age distribution of the population. Thus, a population with a large proportion of aged persons will have a large proportion of its deaths at the older ages, irrespective of the level of its mortality rates.

Multiple decrement tables

In a multiple decrement table, the survivorship column of the life table is split, in passing from one age to the next, into two or more component parts, on the basis of changes in status or of newly acquired characteristics (Jordan 1952, pp. 237, 251; Bailey & Haycocks 1946). One example is the case where the survivorship column is split, on the basis of marriage rates according to age, to distinguish those who marry from those who remain single. In another example, shown in Table 2, the

Table 2 — Example of a double decrement table, with decrements by death and by disability

	RATE OF MORTALITY PER 1,000		DISABILITY RATE PER 1,000[b]	Of 100,000 born alive[a]						
				NUMBER SURVIVING TO EXACT AGE x			ACTIVE LIVES DISABLED		NUMBER DYING BETWEEN AGES x AND x + 1	
Year of age, x	Among active lives	Among disabled lives	Among active lives	Total	As active lives	As disabled lives[c]	Between ages x and x + 1	Total	Among active lives	Among disabled lives
15	7.55	267	0.587	66,949	66,949	0	40	511	505	6
16	7.47	254	0.584	66,438	66,404	34	39	509	496	13
17	7.40	241	0.581	65,929	65,869	60	38	507	487	20
18	7.40	229	0.578	65,422	65,344	78	38	506	484	22
19	7.40	217	0.575	64,916	64,822	94	38	504	480	24
⋮	⋮	⋮	⋮	⋮	⋮	⋮	⋮	⋮	⋮	⋮

a. The radix in the source (100,000 at age 10) was changed to 100,000 at birth.
b. Per 1,000 active lives at exact age x.
c. Assuming no lives were disabled before age 15.

Source: Adapted from Hunter et al. 1932, p. 92.

Table 3 — Example of select and ultimate table, showing probabilities of remarriage during widowhood

| | YEARS ELAPSED SINCE HUSBAND'S DEATH | | | | | | |
Age at widowhood	0	1	2	3	4	5 or more	Attained age
35	0.0201	0.0490	0.0386	0.0376	0.0230	0.0163	40
36	0.0184	0.0449	0.0354	0.0345	0.0211	0.0149	41
37	0.0169	0.0412	0.0324	0.0316	0.0193	0.0137	42
38	0.0155	0.0377	0.0297	0.0290	0.0177	0.0126	43
39	0.0142	0.0345	0.0272	0.0266	0.0162	0.0115	44
	SELECT TABLE					ULTIMATE TABLE	

Source: Adapted from Myers 1949, p. 73.

survivorship column of the life table is split to show those who become permanently disabled lives apart from those who remain as active lives. This table shows, in addition to the numbers surviving to successive ages as active lives and as permanently disabled lives, the rates of mortality for each of these categories and the rates at which active lives become permanently disabled. The column of life table deaths is also split to show the number of deaths among the permanently disabled separately from that among the active. It is assumed that the number of newly disabled lives in any year of age is uniformly distributed over that year; consequently, they are exposed to the mortality rate of the disabled for an average of one half of a year.

Select tables

The life table has been described in terms of rates of mortality dependent only upon attained age; in describing multiple decrement tables, reference was made to rates of disability and of marriage according to attained age. In select tables, rates of mortality (or other rates) are shown on the basis of both the age at acquisition of a new characteristic and the duration since that acquisition (Jordan 1952, p. 26). This two-way classification constitutes a select table, since some selective process is present at the time of acquisition. For example, mortality rates for permanently disabled lives may be shown not only for the age at which disablement occurred but also separately for each subsequent year of disability. Another example of a select table is the two-way classification of rates of remarriage for widows, in relation to both age at widowhood and years since that event. Such a two-way classification of rates is shown in Table 3. In that table, remarriage rates after the fifth year of widowhood are shown only on the basis of attained age, since duration in this case is only of minor influence upon the rates. The table as a whole is known as a select and ultimate table. That portion showing rates according to duration since

widowhood is the select table; the ultimate table is that portion showing rates only according to attained age, since duration is no longer of any importance. Select and ultimate tables are used in life insurance mortality investigations. The choice of the number of durations to be shown for the select period is a matter of study in each experience.

Cohort or generation life tables

In the foregoing account of the conventional life table and the related multiple decrement and select tables, the rates of mortality and other rates of attrition were based upon observations during some specified year or other period. The hypothetical nature of the conventional life table with respect to the time period of observation has already been indicated. A realistic picture of the mortality and survivorship experience of a cohort traced from birth is obtained by observing these events each year in a generation born at the latest 100 years ago. In that way, a record would be obtained of the number surviving to successive ages in successive years and also of the corresponding number of deaths at each age; the mortality rates according to age in successive years may then be computed. After the last death, it would be possible to compute the average length of life of the generation and the average years of life remaining after each age. Such a table is called a generation life table, since it reflects the actual mortality rates of a cohort as it ages in successive years. The table derived from mortality rates for a calendar year or period is called a current life table (Dublin, Lotka, & Spiegelman [1936] 1949, p. 174; Jacobson 1964). Thus, the expectation of life computed from mortality rates observed in 1850 will understate the average length of life of the generation born that year, because of the reductions in mortality since then. In general, with the trend toward lower mortality, the expectation of life at birth computed from a current life table understates the average length of life of a newly born generation.

Further applications

In addition to the applications of the life table that are mentioned in the opening paragraph of this article, increasing use is being made of it as an analytic tool in social and economic problems. Several interesting and important examples may be cited in the field of demography (for references to examples, see Spiegelman 1955; 1957). John Durand (1960) made use of the United Nations model life tables, cited previously, as an adjunct in arriving at estimates of expectation of life at birth for the western Roman Empire. The life table is fundamental in the stable-population theory developed by A. J. Lotka (Dublin & Lotka 1925) and also in Lotka's work on the structure of a growing population (1931). In the field of education E. G. Stockwell and C. B. Nam (1963) prepared school life tables to show the joint effects of death and school dropouts on school attendance patterns. B. C. Churchill (1955) studied the mortality and survival of manufacturing, wholesale trade, and retail trade firms in the United States; in similar fashion A. J. Jaffe (1961) has used data from the censuses of manufactures in Puerto Rico to prepare survival curves according to the age of the establishment.

MORTIMER SPIEGELMAN

[*See also* MORTALITY; POPULATION; VITAL STATISTICS; *and the biographies of* GRAUNT; LOTKA.]

BIBLIOGRAPHY

A very elementary account of the essentials of the life table is given in Dublin, Lotka, & Spiegelman [1936] 1949. *A wholly nontechnical account of the life table, including double decrement and select tables, with brief descriptions of applications, will be found in* Spiegelman 1957. *The beginner in graduate study who has a nonmathematical background but a sense of arithmetic will find the chapter on the life table in* Barclay 1958 *a good introduction to the subject. A corresponding account of the life table, with some further development, is contained in* Pressat 1961. *U.S. Bureau of the Census* 1951 *provides step-by-step directions for elementary life table construction, as well as exercises for the beginning student. More technical is the exposition of the life table in* Benjamin 1959. *The student with a background in the calculus seeking a more comprehensive understanding of the life table, double decrement tables, and select tables may start with* Hooker & Longley-Cook 1953–1957; Jordan 1952. *The theoretical aspects of double and higher-order decrement tables are discussed in* Bailey & Haycocks 1946. *A firm understanding of the techniques of life table construction requires a good background in the means for estimating the exposed-to risk, as given in* Gershenson 1961, *and also for a grasp of the elements of graduation and interpolation, as given in* Miller 1946. *The principal techniques used in the construction of life tables are described in* Spiegelman 1955, *which also treats, in detail, the special situations at the early ages, where the assumption of a uniform distribution of deaths over the year of age is not applicable, and at extreme old age, where artifacts are used to complete the column of mortality rates.*

BAILEY, WALTER G.; and HAYCOCKS, HERBERT W. 1946 *Some Theoretical Aspects of Multiple Decrement Tables*. Edinburgh: Constable.

BARCLAY, GEORGE W. 1958 *Techniques of Population Analysis*. New York: Wiley.

BENJAMIN, BERNARD (1959) 1960 *Elements of Vital Statistics*. London: Allen & Unwin; Chicago: Quadrangle Books.

BRASS, WILLIAM 1963 The Construction of Life Tables From Child Survivorship Ratios. Volume 1, pages 294–301 in International Population Conference, New York, 1961, *Proceedings*. London: International Union for the Scientific Study of Population.

CHIANG, CHIN L. 1960 A Stochastic Study of the Life Table and Its Applications: 2. Sample Variance of the Observed Expectation of Life and Other Biometric Functions. *Human Biology* 32:221–238.

CHURCHILL, BETTY C. 1955 Age and Life Expectancy of Business Firms. *Survey of Current Business* 35, no. 12:15–19, 24.

CIBA FOUNDATION 1959 *Colloquia on Aging*. Volume 5: The Lifespan of Animals. Boston: Little.

COALE, ANSLEY J.; and DEMENY, PAUL 1966 *Regional Model Life Tables and Stable Populations*. Princeton Univ. Press.

DUBLIN, LOUIS I.; and LOTKA, ALFRED J. 1925 On the True Rate of Natural Increase. *Journal of the American Statistical Association* 20:305–339.

DUBLIN, LOUIS I.; LOTKA, ALFRED J.; and SPIEGELMAN, M. (1936) 1949 *Length of Life*. Rev. ed. New York: Ronald Press. → The 1936 edition was written by Dublin and Lotka only; citations in the text refer to the 1949 edition.

DURAND, JOHN D. 1960 Mortality Estimates From Roman Tombstone Inscriptions. *American Journal of Sociology* 65:365–373.

GABRIEL, K. R.; and RONEN, ILANA 1958 Estimates of Mortality From Infant Mortality Rates. *Population Studies* 12:164–169.

GERSHENSON, HARRY 1961 *Measurement of Mortality*. Chicago: The Society of Actuaries.

GREVILLE, T. N. E. 1966 *Methodology of the National, Regional, and State Life Tables for the United States: 1959–61*. Washington: National Center for Health Statistics.

HALDANE, J. B. S. 1953 Some Animal Life Tables. Institute of Actuaries, London, *Journal* 79:83–89.

HOOKER, PERCY F.; and LONGLEY-COOK, L. H. 1953–1957 *Life and Other Contingencies*. 2 vols. Cambridge Univ. Press.

HUNTER, ARTHUR et al. 1932 *Disability Benefits in Life Insurance Policies*. 2d ed. Actuarial Studies, No. 5. Chicago: Actuarial Society of America.

JACOBSON, P. H. 1964 Cohort Survival for Generations Since 1840. *Milbank Memorial Fund Quarterly* 42:36–53.

JAFFE, A. J. 1961 The Calculation of Death Rates for Establishments With Supplementary Notes on the Calculation of Birth Rates. *Estadística: Journal of the Inter-American Statistical Institute* [1961]:513–526.

JONES, J. P. 1962 *Remarriage Tables Based on Experience Under OASDI and U.S. Employees Compensation Systems*. Actuarial Study No. 55. Washington: U.S. Social Security Administration.

JORDAN, CHESTER W. 1952 *Society of Actuaries' Textbook on Life Contingencies*. Chicago: The Society of Actuaries.

KEYFITZ, NATHAN 1966 A Life Table That Agrees With the Data. *Journal of the American Statistical Association* 61:305–312.

KURUP, R. S. 1965 A Revision of Model Life Tables. Unpublished manuscript. → Paper presented at the second World Population Conference.

LOTKA, ALFRED J. 1931 The Structure of a Growing Population. *Human Biology* 3:459–493.

MILLER, MORTON D. 1946 *Elements of Graduation.* Chicago: Actuarial Society of America.

MORTARA, GIORGIO 1949 *Methods of Using Census Statistics for the Calculation of Life Tables and Other Demographic Measures.* Population Studies, No. 7. Lake Success, N.Y.: United Nations, Department of Social Affairs.

MYERS, ROBERT J. 1949 Further Remarriage Experience. Casualty Actuarial Society, *Proceedings* 36:73–104.

PRESSAT, ROLAND 1961 *L'analyse démographique.* Paris: Presses Universitaires de France.

SIRKEN, MONROE G. (1964) 1966 *Comparison of Two Methods of Constructing Abridged Life Tables.* Rev. ed. Series 2, No. 4. Washington: National Center for Health Statistics.

SPIEGELMAN, MORTIMER 1955 *Introduction to Demography.* Chicago: The Society of Actuaries. → See the references in Chapter 5 for materials on life tables.

SPIEGELMAN, MORTIMER 1957 The Versatility of the Life Table. *American Journal of Public Health* 47:297–304. → Contains a list of references.

STOCKWELL, EDWARD G.; and NAM, CHARLES B. 1963 Illustrative Tables of School Life. *Journal of the American Statistical Association* 58:1113–1124.

STOLNITZ, GEORGE J. 1956 *Life Tables From Limited Data: A Demographic Approach.* Princeton Univ., Office of Population Research.

UNITED NATIONS, DEPARTMENT OF SOCIAL AFFAIRS 1955a *Age and Sex Patterns of Mortality: Model Life Tables for Under-developed Countries.* Population Studies, No. 22. New York: United Nations.

UNITED NATIONS, DEPARTMENT OF SOCIAL AFFAIRS 1955b *Methods of Appraisal of Basic Data for Population Estimates.* New York: United Nations.

U.S. BUREAU OF THE CENSUS 1951 *Handbook of Statistical Methods for Demographers.* Washington: Government Printing Office.

U.S. PUBLIC HEALTH SERVICE 1954–1955 [Life Tables for 1949–1951.] U.S. National Office of Vital Statistics, *Vital Statistics: Special Reports* 41, no. 1; no. 2.

U.S. PUBLIC HEALTH SERVICE 1959 [Life Tables for 1949–1951.] U.S. National Office of Vital Statistics, *Vital Statistics: Special Reports* 41, no. 5:149–158.

U.S. PUBLIC HEALTH SERVICE 1961 *Guide to United States Life Tables, 1900–1959.* Bibliography Series, No. 42. Washington: Government Printing Office.

LIFE TESTING

See under QUALITY CONTROL, STATISTICAL.

LIKELIHOOD

The *likelihood function* is important in nearly every part of statistical inference, but concern here is with just the *likelihood principle*, a very general and problematic concept of statistical evidence. [*For discussion of other roles of the likelihood function, see* ESTIMATION; HYPOTHESIS TESTING; SUFFICIENCY.]

The likelihood function is defined in terms of the probability law (or density function) assumed to represent a sampling or experimental situation: When the observation variables are fixed at the values actually observed, the resulting function of the unknown parameter(s) is the likelihood function. (More precisely, two such functions identical except for a constant factor are considered equivalent representations of the same likelihood function.)

The likelihood principle may be stated in two parts: (1) the likelihood function, determined by the sample observed in any given case, represents fully the evidence about parameter values available in those observations (this is the *likelihood axiom*); and (2) the evidence supporting one parameter value (or point) as against another is given by relative values of the likelihood function (likelihood ratios).

For example, suppose that a random sample of ten patients suffering from migraine are treated by an experimental drug and that four of them report relief. The sampling is binomial, and the investigator is interested in the unknown proportion, p, in the population of potential patients, who would report relief. The likelihood function determined by the sample is a function of p,

$$\binom{10}{4} p^4 (1-p)^6, \qquad\qquad 0 \leqslant p \leqslant 1,$$

whose graph is shown in Figure 1. This likelihood function has a maximum at $p = .4$ and becomes very small, approaching 0, as p approaches 0 or 1. Hence, according to the likelihood principle, values of p very near .4 are supported by the evidence in this sample, as against values of p very near 0 or 1, with very great strength, since the corresponding likelihood ratios $(.4)^4(.6)^6/p^4(1-p)^6$ are very large.

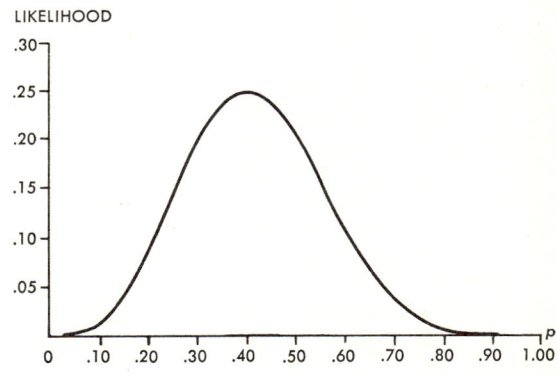

LIKELIHOOD

Figure 1 — The likelihood function $\binom{10}{4} p^4 (1-p)^6$

A different rule for sampling patients would be to treat and observe them one at a time until just four had reported relief. A possible outcome would be that just ten would be observed, with six reporting no relief and of course four reporting relief. The probability of that observed outcome is

$$\binom{9}{3} p^4 (1-p)^6, \qquad\qquad 0 \leqslant p \leqslant 1.$$

This function of p differs from the previous one by only a constant factor and hence is considered to be an alternative, equivalent representation of the *same* likelihood function. The likelihood principle asserts that therefore the evidence about p in the two cases is the same, notwithstanding other differences in the two probability laws, which appear for other possible samples.

Relation to other statistical theory. The likelihood principle is incompatible with the main body of modern statistical theory and practice, notably the Neyman–Pearson theory of hypothesis testing and of confidence intervals, and incompatible in general even with such well-known concepts as standard error of an estimate and significance level [*see* ESTIMATION; HYPOTHESIS TESTING].

To illustrate this incompatibility, observe that in the example two distinct sampling rules gave the same likelihood function, and hence the same evidence under the likelihood principle. On the other hand, different determinations of a lower 95 per cent confidence limit for p are required under the respective sampling rules, and the two confidence limits obtained are different. The likelihood principle, however, is given full formal justification and interpretation within Bayesian inference theories and much interest in the principle stems from recently renewed interest and developments in such theories [*see* BAYESIAN INFERENCE].

Finally, on grounds independent of the crucial and controversial Bayesian concepts of prior or personal probability, interest and support for the likelihood principle arises because most standard statistical theory fails to include (and clearly implicitly excludes) any precise general concept of evidence in an observed sample, while several concepts of evidence that many statisticians consider appropriate have been found on analysis to entail the likelihood axiom. Some of these concepts have become part of a more or less coherent widespread body of theory and practice in which the Neyman–Pearson approach is complemented by concepts of evidence often left implicit. Such concepts also appear as basic in some of Fisher's theories. When formulated as axioms and analyzed, these concepts have been discovered to be equivalent to the likelihood axiom and hence basically incompatible with, rather than possible complements to, the Neyman–Pearson theory.

General concepts of statistical evidence. The central one of these concepts is that of *condition-*

ality (or *ancillarity*), a concept that appeared first in rather special technical contexts. Another somewhat similar concept of evidence, which can be illustrated more simply here and which also entails the major part of the likelihood axiom, is the *censoring axiom:* Suppose that after interpretation of the outcome described with the second sampling rule of the example, it is discovered that the reserve supply of the experimental drug had been accidentally destroyed and is irreplaceable and that no more than ten patients could have been treated with the supply on hand for the experiment. Is the interpretation of the outcome to be changed? In the hypothetical possible case that seven or more patients reported no relief before a fourth reported relief, the sampling plan could not have been carried through even to the necessary eleventh patient: The change of conditions makes unavailable ("censored") the information whether if an outcome were to include more than six patients reporting no relief, that number would be seven, or eight, or any specific larger number. But in fact the outcome actually observed was a physical event unaffected, except in a hypothetical sense, by the differences between intended and realizable sampling plans. Many statisticians consider such a hypothetical distinction irrelevant to the evidence in an outcome. It follows readily from the general formulation of such a concept that the evidence in the observed outcome is characterized by just the function $\binom{9}{3} p^4 (1-p)^6$, $0 \leqslant p \leqslant 1$. More generally this censoring concept is seen to be the likelihood axiom, slightly weakened by disallowance of an arbitrary constant factor; the qualification is removable with adoption of another very weak "sufficiency" concept concerning evidence (see Birnbaum 1961; 1962; Pratt 1961).

Interpreting evidence. The only method proposed for interpreting evidence just through likelihood functions, apart from Bayesian methods, is that stated as part (2) of the likelihood principle above. The briefness and informality of these statements and interpretation are typical of those given by their originator, R. A. Fisher (1925; 1956), and their leading proponent, G. A. Barnard (1947; 1949; 1962). "Likelihood ratio" appears in such interpretations as a primitive term concerning statistical evidence, associated in each case with a nonnegative numerical value, with larger values representing qualitatively greater support for one parameter point against the other, and with unity (representing "no evidence") the only distinguished point on the scale. But likelihood ratio here is not subject to definition or interpretation in terms of other independently defined extramathematical concepts.

Only in the simplest case, where the parameter space has but two points (a case rare in practice but of real theoretical interest), are such interpretations of likelihood functions clearly plausible; and in this case they appear to many to be far superior to more standard methods, for example, significance tests. In such cases the likelihood function is represented by a single likelihood ratio.

In the principal case of larger parameter spaces, such interpretations can be seriously misleading with high probability and are considered unacceptable by most statisticians (see Stein 1962; Armitage 1963). Thus progress in clarifying the important problem of an adequate non-Bayesian concept of statistical evidence leaves the problem not only unresolved but in a positively anomalous state.

Another type of argument supporting the likelihood principle on non-Bayesian grounds is based upon axioms characterizing rational decision making in situations of uncertainty, rather than concepts of statistical evidence (see, for example, Cornfield 1966; Luce & Raiffa 1957).

Likelihoods in form of normal densities. Attention is sometimes focused on cases where likelihood functions have the form of normal density functions. This form occurs in the very simple and familiar problem of inferences about the mean of a normal distribution with known variance (with ordinary sampling). Hence adoption of the likelihood axiom warrants and invites identification with this familiar problem of all other cases where such likelihood functions occur. In particular, the maximum likelihood estimator in any such case is thus related to the classical estimator of the normal mean (the sample mean), and the curvature of the likelihood function (or of its logarithm) at its maximum is thus related to the variance of that classical estimator. In similar vein, transformations of parameters have been considered that tend to give likelihood functions a normal density shape (in problems with several parameters as well as those with only one). (See, for example, Anscombe 1964.)

Likelihoods in nonparametric problems. In nonparametric problems, there is no finite set of parameters that can be taken as the arguments of a likelihood function, and it may not be obvious that the likelihood axiom has meaning. However, "nonparametric" is a sometimes misleading name for a very broad mathematical model that includes all specific parametric families of laws among those allowed; hence in principle it is simple to imagine (although in practice formidably awkward to represent) the extremely inclusive parameter space containing a point representing each (absolutely) continuous law, and for each pair of such

points a likelihood ratio (determined as usual from the observed sample).

ALLAN BIRNBAUM

[*Other relevant material may be found in* DISTRIBUTIONS, STATISTICAL, *articles on* SPECIAL CONTINUOUS DISTRIBUTIONS *and* SPECIAL DISCRETE DISTRIBUTIONS.]

BIBLIOGRAPHY

ANSCOMBE, F. J. 1964 Normal Likelihood Function. Institute of Statistical Mathematics, *Annals* 26:1–19.

ARMITAGE, PETER 1963 Sequential Medical Trials: Some Comments on F. J. Anscombe's Paper. *Journal of the American Statistical Association* 58:384–387.

BARNARD, G. A. 1947 [Review of] *Sequential Analysis* by Abraham Wald. *Journal of the American Statistical Association* 42:658–664.

BARNARD, G. A. 1949 Statistical Inference. *Journal of the Royal Statistical Society* Series B 11:116–149.

BARNARD, G. A.; JENKINS, G. M.; and WINSTEN, C. B. 1962 Likelihood Inference and Time Series. *Journal of the Royal Statistical Society* Series A 125:321–375. → Includes 20 pages of discussion.

BIRNBAUM, ALLAN 1961 On the Foundations of Statistical Inference: I. Binary Experiments. *Annals of Mathematical Statistics* 32:414–435.

BIRNBAUM, ALLAN 1962 On the Foundations of Statistical Inference. *Journal of the American Statistical Association* 57:269–326. → Includes 20 pages of discussion. See especially John W. Pratt's comments on pages 314–315.

CORNFIELD, JEROME 1966 Sequential Trials, Sequential Analysis and the Likelihood Principle. *American Statistician* 20:18–23.

COX, D. R. 1958 Some Problems Connected With Statistical Inference. *Annals of Mathematical Statistics* 29:357–372.

FISHER, R. A. (1925) 1950 Theory of Statistical Estimation. Pages 11.699a–11.725 in R. A. Fisher, *Contributions to Mathematical Statistics.* New York: Wiley. → First published in Volume 22, Part 5 of the Cambridge Philosophical Society, *Proceedings.*

FISHER, R. A. (1956) 1959 *Statistical Methods and Scientific Inference.* 2d ed., rev. New York: Hafner; London: Oliver & Boyd.

LUCE, R. DUNCAN; and RAIFFA, HOWARD 1957 *Games and Decisions: Introduction and Critical Survey.* A Study of the Behavioral Models Project, Bureau of Applied Social Research, Columbia University. New York: Wiley.

PRATT, JOHN W. 1961 [Review of] *Testing Statistical Hypotheses* by E. L. Lehmann. *Journal of the American Statistical Association* 56:163–167.

STEIN, CHARLES M. 1962 A Remark on the Likelihood Principle. *Journal of the Royal Statistical Society* Series A 125:565–573. → Includes five pages of comments by G. A. Barnard.

LIMITED WAR

Limited war is a subjective and relative term that has gained currency chiefly to distinguish certain conflicts from wars fought for ends and by means that have impressed men as extreme. Limited wars are as old as the history of mankind. They have occurred among the most primitive and the most advanced peoples and in every civilization. The great majority of all international wars have been fought for ends far short of domination or annihilation and by means far short of the complete destruction of the enemy's armed forces or his society. In these respects even the two so-called total wars of this century—World War I and World War II—were significantly limited.

The *concept* of limited war is also old and ubiquitous in history. Primitive tribes, as well as the knights of the Middle Ages, have been conscious of explicit customs and rules of mutual restraint in the conduct of warfare. In ancient China, as well as eighteenth-century Europe, there were laws explicitly formulated to regulate warfare.

Yet the consciousness of limited war as a distinct kind of warfare, with its own theory and doctrine, has emerged most markedly in contrast to three major wars, waged between several major states, in behalf of popular national and ideological goals, by means of organized conscripted forces and massive firepower: the Napoleonic Wars, World War I, and World War II.

The detailed elaboration of a strategic doctrine of limited war, the formulation of specific plans for carrying out this doctrine, and the combined efforts of government, the military establishment, and private analysts and publicists to translate the doctrine into particular weapons and forces are developments peculiar to the nuclear age. They are products of the profound fear of nuclear war and the belief that the limitation of war must be carefully contrived, rather than left to inherent limitations upon military capabilities.

The principal exponents of limited war in the eighteenth century were (1) the principal military tacticians of wars of fortification and maneuver, like Vauban and Marshal de Saxe; (2) proponents of international laws to regulate and civilize war, like Vattel, who drew upon the principles of Grotius; and (3) political theorists like Rousseau and Fénelon, who saw war as a necessary, if rather indecisive, instrument for preserving a balance of power. In the latter half of the nineteenth century legal and balance-of-power theorists were somewhat overshadowed by the exponents of modern military power and glory, like Marshal Foch. Most of the leading military thinkers, with the notable exception of Karl von Clausewitz, were prophets of blitzkrieg and wars of annihilation. After World War I, proponents of international order, in their search for collective security and disarmament as methods of avoiding war, generally ignored the problem of limiting war. Liddell Hart, virtually the only exponent of a military strategy of limited war

between the two world wars, applied his prescriptions chiefly to Britain's situation.

After World War II, however, there was a great resurgence of interest in limited war among civilian analysts as well as military experts, particularly in the United States after the Korean War. The new exponents of limited war advocated the systematic control of military potential and of war as a useful, carefully restricted instrument of policy. On the most fundamental level they drew their inspiration from Clausewitz, who in expounding the theory of war as a continuation of diplomacy had related the scope and intensity of war to its political context with a profundity appreciated equally by Lenin and Mao Tse-tung. [*See the biography of* CLAUSEWITZ.]

A limited war is now broadly defined as a war that is fought for ends far short of the complete subordination of one state's will to another's and by means involving far less than the total military resources of the belligerents, leaving the civilian life and the armed forces of the belligerents largely intact and leading to a bargained termination. More narrowly, it is defined as a local nonnuclear war. Limited war is therefore a matter of degree. It is also a matter of perspective, since a war that is limited for one belligerent might be close to total for another. Furthermore, a limited war may be restricted in some respects and not in others. Thus, a civil war or insurrection may be fought by limited means for the total stake of controlling a government.

Yet despite the impossibility of defining limited war by simple and absolute criteria, it is not difficult, historically, to distinguish limited wars from wars of great scope and intensity.

Limited wars in history

The eighteenth century. The middle of the eighteenth century stands out as the first notable period of limited warfare in the history of the modern state system. In marked contrast to the preceding religious wars and the general wars revolving around Louis XIV's struggle for hegemony and to the subsequent French Revolution and Napoleonic Wars, the wars of this period generally consisted of short, duellike battles of maneuver fought for limited dynastic and territorial objectives, within a system where rough equilibrium of power was maintained by about five major states. The wars left civilian life relatively unaffected and altered the international status of the major countries only minimally or gradually.

The limited character of war in this period must be attributed largely to the economic and technological obstacles preventing the major states from destroying each other's armed forces and devastating or occupying each other's homelands. This in turn reflected the limited capacity of monarchies to organize armed forces and mobilize military potential. Furthermore, warfare was limited by the great role of sea power and by the fact that sea war did not ravish the land.

The limited warfare of the eighteenth century, however, cannot be attributed solely to the nature of military technology, since the technology was not very different then from that of the preceding and following periods of general war. It must also be attributed to the limited nature of the political ends for which states fought; to the equilibrium of power between the major participants, which restrained them from pushing an advantage too far; to the stilted, drill-field military tactics suited to keeping expensive and untrustworthy troops under control; to a general respect for laws of war distinguishing between combatants and noncombatants, belligerents and nonbelligerents; and to the prevailing social and political system, which made these political, legal, and military constraints congenial to the homogeneous ruling classes of Europe. Beyond these factors, the limitation of eighteenth-century warfare can be explained simply by the desire of rulers and ruled to avoid the chaos of the religious wars.

The nineteenth century. The Napoleonic period removed many of the political and social conditions of limited war. In undermining the *ancien régime* and introducing the concept of the "nation in arms," it prepared the way for a popular nationalism far less congenial to the limitation of war than the pragmatic *Realpolitik* of the eighteenth century.

Napoleon demonstrated the capacity of states to generate popular enthusiasm for war by nationalistic and ideological appeals and to translate this enthusiasm into unprecedented military power through mass conscription and the mobilization of industry and technology. By reconciling military discipline with individual initiative, he enabled states to use new tactics of camouflage, mobility, and destructive pursuit that gave war a new dynamism. He showed that where such decisive force could be exerted on land, sea war would cease to be a limiting factor and instead would become, through blockade and the destruction of commerce, a forerunner of total war against civilian life.

Nevertheless, the rest of the nineteenth century —notably from 1854 to 1870—was, again, a period of limited war, thanks largely to the absence of wars between the several major states (except the Crimean War, which was fought in a peripheral location). The latter half of the nineteenth century saw the unprecedented development in peacetime

of war plans, conscription, military logistics, and communications (notably railroads and telegraph) and a rapidly advancing military technology. Yet, the new potentialities of destruction inherent in these developments were not fully exploited or generally appreciated until World War I, although the American Civil War should have been a grim warning. Instead, Prussia's quick, limited victories in 1866 (against Austria) and 1871 (against France) were believed to be the models of future wars.

The two world wars. World War I was not deliberately undertaken as a general war. It became a world war because of diplomatic miscalculations, the interlocking network of alliance commitments, the inflexibility of mobilization plans and war plans, the prevailing assumption among the military that a general war was inevitable, the weakness of civilian control over the military, and the failure of the initial German offensive, followed by a war of attrition and stalemate that national animosities, fed by popular sentiment, made it difficult to terminate without victory. Consequently, even if the will to avoid general war had been stronger, war would have become general and extremely destructive without a systematic effort by governments to subject military planning and operations to over-all political direction under a strategy of limited war.

Yet few drew any such lessons from that shocking experience. Rather, it was generally assumed that unless war could be avoided by collective security and disarmament there would soon be another and even more devastating world war. The rise of the expansionist totalitarian powers, the fascist glorification of war, and the perfection and proliferation of more destructive weapons, including aerial bombardment, seemed to make this inevitable.

Actually, the fascist states preferred to satisfy their ambitions through intimidation and through quick, limited aggressions against negligible opposition; but the failure of the democratic states to contain these aggressions at the outset by limited means and their unwillingness to use force for limited ends assured the fulfillment of the prophecies of total war when the democratic states, contrary to Hitler's calculations, belatedly offered resistance in 1939 and when Japan, confronted with the American oil embargo and rearmament, launched what it regarded as a limited, preventive attack on Pearl Harbor.

The nuclear age. In the aftermath of World War II, the invention of nuclear weapons and the onset of the cold war raised a general feeling that only the United Nations and disarmament could prevent another total war. Yet, within a decade this opinion had been modified by the widespread conviction that the potential destructiveness of a nuclear war would deter a total war and by a concomitant surge of private and official interest in meeting a purported danger of limited wars.

This new attention to limited war has been justified by the occurrence of more than fifty limited wars of various kinds within twenty years after World War II. All of them were fought outside Europe, with the exception of the Greek civil war in 1945–1949 and the Hungarian rebellion in 1956. The great majority were internal wars; that is, wars that arose and were fought largely within the boundaries of a single state. Several of these were full-scale civil wars: in Greece; China in 1945–1949; Bolivia in 1949; Algeria in 1954–1962; Cuba in 1958–1959; the Congo in 1960–1963; Vietnam from 1959; and Indonesia in 1966.

A number of internal wars were, in communist parlance, "national liberation wars," supported from outside by the Soviet Union, Communist China, or other communist countries: in Greece; French Indochina in 1946–1954; Burma in 1948–1954; Malaya in 1948–1960; the Philippines in 1946–1954; and Vietnam. And one should add to this list two abortive rebellions against Soviet and Communist Chinese domination: in Hungary, and Tibet in 1956–1957. Although internal, most of these wars were major international political events because they determined the status of colonial holdings and/or affected the balance of power in the cold war.

Several of the approximately fifty limited wars arose from a direct invasion of the territory of one state by another state: the Korean War in 1950–1953; the Guatemalan war in 1954 (which, however, had many characteristics of an internal war); the Israeli–Egyptian war and the British–French invasion of Suez in 1956; and the Indian conquest of Goa in 1961. One might also categorize the Quemoy–Matsu conflict in 1954–1958 as an aborted interstate war. Like most of the internal wars, these interstate wars reflected the major political issues in the world since World War II: the national–colonial conflict and the communist–noncommunist conflict.

There were, also, a few interstate wars fought primarily by subversive means, but all of these except the war in Vietnam were low-level conflicts arising from indigenous national rivalries: Somalia–Ethiopia in 1960, Indonesia–Malaya in 1963, and Algeria–Morocco in 1963.

Some of the civil and internal wars were quite destructive—as in Greece, China, and Algeria—and total, rather than limited, in the sense that different regimes competed for complete control of a country. The Korean War, although limited from the American and Chinese standpoint, was virtually total from the standpoint of the North and South Korean regimes. Yet, all of these wars were strictly limited in geographical extent, the number of countries directly involved, and the scope and intensity of violence. Although a number of them involved either the United States or the Soviet Union, none involved both powers directly and simultaneously.

The limited nature of these wars can be partly explained by a variety of conditions that helped limit wars in previous periods of history: the limited or local nature of political issues at stake, the tactics of internal warfare, the limited military capacity of the belligerents, the one-sided nature of the contest, the pressure by allies for constraint, the fear of overcommitment at the expense of protecting prior interests elsewhere. The notable feature of this period, however, is that despite the global nature of the cold war and the depth and intensity of the over-all conflict of interests and aims, and despite the immense destructive power that the principal adversaries could inflict upon each other, the major communist and democratic powers did not bring their full military power to bear upon each other. Only in the Korean War did major Western and communist powers employ their armed forces in direct combat with each other. Therefore, the limitation of warfare since World War II must be largely attributed to the military abstinence and restraint practiced by the principal adversaries in the cold war.

A large part of the explanation of this military abstinence and restraint lies in the deterrent effect of the very capacity for mutual destruction that would make another general war so catastrophic. This deterrent effect, combined with a number of other military and political factors conducive to limitation, was most marked in the Korean War, where, contrary to all previous expectations in the West, an American–Communist Chinese conflict remained local and limited, with each side deliberately refraining from military actions that threatened to expand the war and both sides agreeing to an inconclusive termination.

The limited war in Vietnam is as notable an example as the Korean War of studied application by the United States of ascending gradations of limited force toward the achievement of a negotiated settlement on limited terms. It was even more notable, however, for evoking widespread popular approval of and insistence upon such limits.

The modern concept

The Korean War in time stimulated a new concept and strategic doctrine of limited war, which received additional impetus from the growth of Soviet nuclear striking power, the introduction of thermonuclear bombs and long-range missiles in Soviet and American arsenals, and the communists' explicit emphasis in the 1960s on national liberation wars.

According to this concept, the stability of the bipolar nuclear balance, resulting from the reluctance of the nuclear powers to use nuclear weapons except in retaliation against nuclear weapons, could not be relied upon to deter communist powers from supporting limited aggressions and might, in fact, encourage such aggressions because the United States might be deterred from using nuclear weapons first when it had no effective means of conventional resistance. Furthermore, if involved in a local conventional conflict, the United States and its allies might not be capable of controlling the escalation or expansion of such a war but would have to choose between defeat and a nuclear catastrophe. To deter such aggressions or to fight local wars effectively without incurring an intolerable risk of nuclear war, the United States, according to this thesis, would have to develop a capacity to fight different kinds of small wars successfully, with a diversified arsenal of conventional capabilities appropriate to various constraints upon weapons, targets, and the zone of combat, while holding open the lines of diplomatic communication to facilitate the termination of combat, probably short of a clear-cut military or political victory. This new concept of limited war was explicitly based on the principle, drawn from Clausewitz, that the conduct of war should be scrupulously disciplined by over-all political considerations, so that war will be an effective instrument of policy rather than an instrument of maximum destruction.

The concept of limited war did not find official favor with American Secretary of State Dulles; only in the last years of the Eisenhower administration were some concessions made to the idea. Instead, the administration stressed the alleged economic and military necessity of avoiding future Koreas by depending primarily on the American capacity to meet local conventional aggressions with strategic and tactical nuclear retaliation to deter little and big wars alike. This strategy—loosely called massive retaliation—was also adopted by allies of the United States in the North Atlantic Treaty Organization (NATO), who were equally anxious to substitute nuclear firepower for conventionally armed man power following their brief rearmament effort during the Korean War period.

In this period, however, a movement for strategic revision arose within the United States Army and Navy and among academic analysts and research organizations interested in military questions. According to this revisionist movement, the dependence of the West on nuclear weapons was increasingly incredible as a deterrent against the most likely forms of aggression; it would be ineffective or disastrous if deterrence should fail or be inapplicable; and it was inadequate as an instrument of policy in conflicts short of war (in which the Soviet Union could confront the United States and its allies with the choice between acquiescence and thermonuclear holocaust).

When President Kennedy and Secretary of Defense McNamara took office in 1961, they explicitly adopted the concept of limited war, which had emerged as a criticism of the prevailing strategy. Moreover, they instituted a far-reaching program to revise military policies so as to support a strategy of limited war. They created "special forces" to handle guerrilla warfare, urged a build-up of NATO's conventional capabilities in order to raise the threshold of effective resistance without resorting to nuclear war, and increased the capacity of the United States to transport armed forces by air to prevent or deter local wars. The key phrase used to describe this revised strategy was "flexible and controlled response."

The concept of flexible and controlled response, however, was applied beyond local nonnuclear war. It also embraced the concept of deliberately planning for the "option" of using nuclear weapons in a limited fashion, under constraints upon their number, type, and targets and in response to effective central political direction. Thus, the concept of limited war came to include even a controlled strategic "counterforce" war, in which the United States would try to confine nuclear exchanges to such military targets as missile bases, holding back its capacity to devastate Soviet cities, as an inducement to the Soviet Union not to attack American cities.

Whether or not a nuclear war could be kept limited, the unwillingness of the American government to relinquish this possibility was a striking indication of growing inhibitions against resorting to unlimited war or depending entirely on the "balance of terror" to deter armed conflict. It signified increasing reluctance to depend for deterrence upon a military response that it would not be rational to carry out.

There were signs that the nuclear-missile age had induced similar attitudes in Soviet civilian and military leaders. Premier Khrushchev led Soviet spokesmen in avowing that thermonuclear weapons, by deterring the "capitalist–imperialist" powers, had overruled the Marxist–Leninist dictum that the dictatorship of the proletariat could come about only by a violent clash of arms precipitated by imperialist desperation. Such a clash, he said, was no longer "fatalistically inevitable." On numerous occasions he and other Soviet leaders stressed the immense and intolerable damage that communist as well as "imperialist" powers would suffer in a nuclear war.

Although Chinese spokesmen did not disagree with this view, they differed with Soviet spokesmen in being more confident that the United States would be deterred by Soviet nuclear power from escalating national liberation wars and particularly from initiating the use of nuclear weapons.

Whether for effect or out of conviction, Soviet spokesmen continued to assert that any war between the Soviet Union and the United States would result in nuclear war and continued to deny the possibility that either a strategic or tactical nuclear war could be limited, but in the mid-1960s some Soviet military men began to publish criticisms and qualifications of these views.

Furthermore, communist doctrine had always emphasized political constraints on war and the cautious, flexible use of force. Mao Tse-tung's strategy of revolutionary war, which dominated Chinese thinking and remained the leading rationale of unconventional war, was suffused with concepts of limited war although its aim was total. By 1961 both Soviet and Chinese strategy emphasized the necessity of supporting "national liberation wars" (that is, internal wars promoting a communist takeover) and acknowledged the possibility of "local wars" outside Europe (that is, geographically restricted wars between states, which might or might not be limited in weapons) as a contingency to be deterred or frustrated.

Continuing problems

In the United States there emerged during the 1960s a broad consensus supporting the strategy of flexible and controlled response. America's European allies largely accepted the strategy as it applied outside Europe, but they were generally far more skeptical about the feasibility or utility of fighting a limited conventional war, let alone a limited nuclear war, in Europe. Their skepticism reflected differences of geography and was not likely to yield to American persuasion. Accordingly, they remained reluctant to build up NATO's conventional capabilities and were fearful that the emphasis on a strategy of limited conventional war would undermine the credibility of nuclear deterrence. France went furthest in openly criticizing the doctrine of flexible and controlled response and in acclaiming a doctrine of extended nuclear deter-

rence as a substitute for conventional resistance. Despite the German Federal Republic's twelve divisions and the six American divisions, the capacity of NATO's European-based forces to withstand the Soviet Union's forces in eastern Europe for more than a few days remained in doubt. France's withdrawal from NATO's integrated commands in 1966 only highlighted this situation.

The United States in the mid-1960s became increasingly preoccupied with the war in Vietnam. There the addition of concentrated firepower (including heavy strategic and tactical bombing) and regular ground warfare to guerrilla warfare and civic action fitted none of the previous concepts of limited war. Except for more detailed attention in the United States to the process of escalation, strategic thought about limited war seemed to have passed its phase of innovation.

Strategic quiescence, however, did not resolve outstanding differences in the West about the particular forces and strategies needed for deterrence, resistance, and the support of policy in crises short of war. What should be the purpose of NATO's conventional forces in Europe: to provide merely a "screening force" to detect an attack or to be a "tripwire" to sound the alarm for nuclear retaliation? to prevent an unopposed limited territorial grab? to force the enemy to pause long enough to consider the risk of a nuclear war? to withstand Soviet forces in Europe conventionally for days? months? Under what conditions, if any, should the West use nuclear weapons first? If nuclear weapons were used, how, if at all, could a bilateral nuclear war, especially one in Europe, be significantly limited in geographical extent, targets, and duration? What should be the function of tactical (that is, battlefield) weapons as opposed to longer-range nuclear weapons? Could either tactical or strategic nuclear exchanges be confined to "bargaining and demonstration"? How could such exchanges be kept under effective central command and political control?

The most hopeful thing about these unanswered and necessarily conjectural questions was that their very imponderability made a potential aggressor uncertain about the response to his incursions, and this uncertainty, combined with his awareness of the intolerable penalties of miscalculation, would itself be a powerful deterrent to rash moves. Indeed, notwithstanding the Korean War, throughout the cold war both the communist powers and the United States and its allies have exercised great caution in avoiding a direct military encounter with each other, afraid that any such encounter might expand into a thermonuclear war. Approaches to the brink of war, such as the Formosa Strait crisis in 1958, the Berlin crises in 1948–1949 and 1958–1962, and the Cuban crisis in 1962, show that this caution does not preclude dangerous tests of will and nerve, under the shadow of war. Yet, through such tests the major adversaries in the cold war seem to have learned the acceptable limits of pressure and counterpressure short of war. If the *détente* that developed after the Cuban missile crisis should last, it will be largely due to this mutual understanding, toward which the American doctrine and forces of limited war made a major contribution by bolstering American resolve to accept the risks of war in crises.

One of the serious questions for the future, however, is whether the deterrents that have developed in an essentially bipolar world would persist in a world in which there might be a number of additional significant centers of political decision and military power both inside and outside the two blocs. A more decentralized structure of international power and interests might weaken the existing deterrents against aggression and war and increase the danger of limited wars breaking out and expanding into major wars, especially if the initial belligerents owned nuclear weapons. In the light of this danger, the most challenging problem of limiting warfare in the future might be to extend to an eroding bipolar or multipolar world methods and concepts of deterring, confining, and restraining warfare that would be as effective as those that emerged in the first two decades after what one must hope was the last, and not just the latest, world war.

ROBERT E. OSGOOD

[*See also* DETERRENCE; NUCLEAR WAR; STRATEGY. *Other relevant material may be found under* INTERNATIONAL RELATIONS; MILITARY; WAR.]

BIBLIOGRAPHY

ARON, RAYMOND (1963) 1965 *The Great Debate: Theories of Nuclear Strategy.* Garden City, N.Y.: Doubleday. → First published as *Le grand débat: Initiation à la stratégie atomique.*

CLAUSEWITZ, KARL VON (1832–1834) 1943 *On War.* New York: Modern Library. → First published in German as *Vom Kriege,* in three volumes.

EARLE, EDWARD MEAD (editor) 1943 *Makers of Modern Strategy: Military Thought From Machiavelli to Hitler.* Princeton Univ. Press.

GARTHOFF, RAYMOND L. 1966 *Soviet Military Policy: A Historical Analysis.* New York: Praeger.

HALPERIN, MORTON H. 1963 *Limited War in the Nuclear Age.* New York: Wiley.

HSIEH, ALICE L. 1962 *Communist China's Strategy in the Nuclear Era.* Englewood Cliffs, N.J.: Prentice-Hall.

HUNTINGTON, SAMUEL P. (editor) 1962 *Changing Patterns of Military Politics.* New York: Free Press.

KAHN, HERMAN 1965 *On Escalation.* New York: Praeger.

KAUFMANN, WILLIAM W. 1964 *The McNamara Strategy.* New York: Harper.

KISSINGER, HENRY A. 1957 *Nuclear Weapons and Foreign Policy.* New York: Harper.

KISSINGER, HENRY A. 1965 *The Troubled Partnership: A Re-appraisal of the Atlantic Alliance.* New York: McGraw-Hill.

LIDDELL HART, BASIL H. (1929) 1954 *Strategy: The Indirect Approach.* New York: Praeger. → First published as *The Decisive Wars of History: A Study in Strategy.*

OSGOOD, ROBERT E. 1957 *Limited War: The Challenge to American Strategy.* Univ. of Chicago Press.

OSGOOD, ROBERT E. 1962 *NATO: The Entangling Alliance.* Univ. of Chicago Press.

ROPP, THEODORE 1959 *War in the Modern World.* Durham, N.C.: Duke Univ. Press. → A paperback edition was published in 1962 by Collier.

ROSENAU, JAMES N. (editor) 1964 *International Aspects of Civil Strife.* Princeton Univ. Press.

SCHELLING, THOMAS C. 1960 *The Strategy of Conflict.* Cambridge, Mass.: Harvard Univ. Press.

SOKOLOVSKII, VASILII D. (editor) (1962) 1963 *Military Strategy: Soviet Doctrine and Concepts.* Introduction by Raymond L. Garthoff. New York: Praeger. → First published in Russian.

VAGTS, ALFRED 1956 *Defense and Diplomacy: The Soldier and the Conduct of Foreign Relations.* New York: King's Crown.

WOLFE, THOMAS W. 1964 *Soviet Strategy at the Crossroads.* Cambridge, Mass.: Harvard Univ. Press.

WRIGHT, QUINCY (1942) 1965 *A Study of War.* 2d ed. Univ. of Chicago Press.

LINDSAY, A. D.

Alexander Dunlop Lindsay, Lord Lindsay of Birker (1879–1952), a political philosopher, was born in Scotland but spent most of his life in England as fellow and then as master of Balliol College, Oxford. After his retirement, he became the first principal of the University College of North Staffordshire (now the University of Keele). Because of his services to the Trades Union Congress and the Labour party, he was elevated to the peerage in 1945 and took the title of Baron Lindsay of Birker. In many ways, Lindsay's life followed the pattern originated by such Oxford idealist philosophers as T. H. Green; in other ways, he followed the lead of Benjamin Jowett, perhaps the most famous of Lindsay's predecessors as master of Balliol. Like Green, he attempted to combine the teaching of philosophy with the obligations imposed by citizenship—participation in actual administration as well as aiding the poor and teaching the disadvantaged; like Jowett, he thought that the first purpose of a university is to train public servants by sharpening their intellects and developing their will to control events. Lindsay also continued Balliol's Victorian tradition in that he preached in the college chapel and derived his politics as much from religion as from philosophy.

In the face of the assaults upon idealism made by Bertrand Russell, G. E. Moore, and Ludwig Wittgenstein, who redirected philosophical inquiry, Lindsay tacitly abandoned the traditional idealist attempt to base political ideas upon firm metaphysical grounds (for his specific criticism of modern British philosophy, see Lindsay 1951). Rather, he paraphrased idealist political ideas in terms derived from common sense, practical politics, and the language of classical political theory. The result was a persuasive statement of the "operative ideals" of modern constitutional democracies. Although Lindsay's work added little to what had already been said by Green and Bosanquet, he did prolong their influence by his restatement, which he based upon the points that had originally persuaded many people of the superiority of idealism over Victorian positivism and scientism, whether of the utilitarian or the social Darwinian varieties. As Talcott Parsons has indicated, idealism was an important source of modern sociology and political science. Idealist philosophers emphasized the importance of human groups, of collective representations, and the place of values in social action. No less important were idealist polemics against theories of human behavior that stress individual decisions taken on purely rational and self-interested grounds.

Lindsay's antipathy to doctrines stressing egotism was rooted in his family background. Both his parents were descended from Scottish families, aristocratic in origin but active in social work and in movements for the reform of religion and politics. His father was T. M. Lindsay, a distinguished church historian and principal of the United Free Church College at the University of Glasgow. Lindsay's first degree was from Glasgow University. Despite his failure to win a Snell exhibition at Balliol, he obtained a first class degree in greats and was elected president of the Oxford Union. Even as an undergraduate he was a member of the Fabian Society. After holding fellowships in philosophy at Glasgow and Edinburgh and assisting Samuel Alexander, professor of philosophy at Manchester, Lindsay was elected in 1906 to a fellowship at Balliol. In the period before World War I, he translated Plato's *Republic* (1907), wrote a number of prefaces to philosophical volumes in the Everyman's Library series, published short books on Henri Bergson (1911) and Kant (1913), and contributed to the influential volume, *Property: Its Duties and Rights* (1914), published by the Christian Social Union, an organization led by those of

Green's students who combined high-church theology with distaste for economic inequality. Lindsay married in 1907 and had two sons and a daughter.

After his service in World War I, Lindsay returned to Balliol and took an important part in establishing the new undergraduate degree in philosophy, politics, and economics. In 1922 he was elected professor of moral philosophy at Glasgow but returned to Oxford when he was elected master of Balliol in 1924. Although increasingly drawn into administration and university politics (he served a term as vice-chancellor of Oxford), he taught philosophy and preached in the Balliol chapel. Lindsay was among the few heads of Oxford colleges who supported the Labour party (1949). Probably the cause he cared for most was the Workers' Educational Association. In 1939 he was the Labour party candidate for a seat in Parliament that was won by Quinton Hogg, who had defended the Munich settlement of the previous year. During World War II, Lindsay often spoke on the radio and finished the first and, as it turned out, the only volume of his *Modern Democratic State* (1943), a work that displayed him at his best and was certainly preferable to his long book on Kant (1934*a*). After retiring as master of Balliol in 1948, he did much as first principal at Keele to institute a curriculum that put its stress on general education rather than on the specialized studies that until then were characteristic of English universities.

Lindsay's conception of political theory depended upon a series of distinctions that was designed to maintain the autonomy and, indeed, the primacy of ideas and values in the analysis of political action. Retreating from the metaphysical arguments of idealism, he nevertheless denied that the study of politics should center exclusively upon actual institutions or behavior. For Lindsay claimed that his position was neither metaphysical nor historical. He rejected the distinction between the state as studied by political theorists (in the form it ideally should have) and the state as studied by political scientists (in its actual form). Lindsay argued that these two views of the state are analytically and empirically inseparable.

Every state, he thought, is a historically conditioned association whose members share certain purposes, although these purposes need not be consciously recognized or fully realized. The laws, institutions, and moral and political practices of a society record its "operative ideals," that is, what it most values in its common life. Such preferences will be found to vary in the different historical types of states, such as the classical Greek democracies or medieval constitutional monarchies. What, in Lindsay's view, distinguishes the modern democratic state from all other types is the fact that in it the political organization that exercises a monopoly of organized force has as its function neither the creation of operative ideals nor their enforcement by coercion alone. The power of the state is properly used when, and only when, it corrects anomalies and harmonizes conflicts. The purpose of the state is to remove hindrances to the kinds of spontaneity and freedom that are compatible with the common purposes of society. It is significant that when Lindsay made this central argument in his two major works (1929; 1943) he did so by paraphrasing Bosanquet:

What Bosanquet seems to have done in his account of the general will is to have developed a hint of Rousseau's into a masterly account of the elaborate system of institutions and mutual relations which go to make up the life of society, to have insisted on its complexity and richness and vitality, its transcendence of what any one individual can conceive or express. This, he declares, in all its elaborateness and multifariousness *is* the community. It is less than that. That is the standard of legislation and what we ordinarily call state action. The business of politics is to take this elaborate complex of individuals and institutions for granted . . . and . . . [to] seek to remove the disharmonies which are threatening its life and checking its vitality.   ([1943] p. 244 in 1947 edition)

The state, in the narrow political sense, is, according to Lindsay, the hinderer of hindrances. The aim of its compulsion and the criterion of the success of that compulsion is the setting free of the spontaneity which is inherent in the life of society. Political machinery, general elections, legislatures, judges, and executives are endeavoring or ought to be endeavoring to express the spirit of a common social life.

Thus, Lindsay accepted certain distinctions that Bosanquet also had considered essential: the distinction between state and society, with primacy given to society; and that between the state, as an organization to which all must belong, and voluntary societies. These voluntary societies, traced by Lindsay to Puritan congregations, have the great merit of permitting individuals to have, within a limited sphere, real initiative, spontaneity, and liberty. But in the nature of things all such associations have purposes limited to the interests of their members. Voluntary associations, if left to themselves, come into conflict. It is the purpose of the state to eliminate such conflicts and to reconcile disagreements by reference to the operative ideals of society.

Lindsay, then, followed earlier idealists in a number of ways: he attempted to rescue by paraphrase and dilution a position that was essentially religious; he favored reconciliation and synthesis of the interests of different groups, rather than the admission of persisting conflicts and harsh choices between such interests; he refused to distinguish fact from value and argued that the social arrangements and moral practices of a society provide a meaningful guide to future decisions, both by conscientious individuals seeking to determine their obligations and by the state seeking to determine the proper sphere of its action. From this mode of analysis, however, Lindsay drew socialist conclusions, thus distinguishing his position from those of Green and Bosanquet.

MELVIN RICHTER

[*For the historical context of Lindsay's work, see* DEMOCRACY; PLURALISM; STATE; *and the biographies of* BOSANQUET *and* GREEN.]

WORKS BY LINDSAY

(1907) 1942 Introduction. In Plato, *Republic of Plato.* Translated by A. D. Lindsay. London: Dent; New York: Dutton.

1911 *The Philosophy of Bergson.* London: Dent.

(1913) 1914 *The Philosophy of Immanuel Kant.* London: Jack.

(1914) 1915 The Principle of Private Property. Pages 65–81 in *Property: Its Duties and Rights, Historically, Philosophically and Religiously Regarded.* 2d ed. London: Macmillan.

(1925) 1937 *Karl Marx's* Capital: *An Introductory Essay.* Oxford Univ. Press.

1927 *The Nature of Religious Truth: Sermons Preached in Balliol College Chapel.* London: Hodder & Stoughton.

1928 *General Will and Common Mind.* London: Hodder & Stoughton.

(1929) 1951 *The Essentials of Democracy.* 2d ed. Oxford Univ. Press.

1934a *Kant.* London: Benn.

1934b *The Churches and Democracy.* London: Epworth.

1940 *I Believe in Democracy: Addresses Broadcast in the B.B.C. Empire Programme on Mondays From May 20th to June 24th 1940.* Oxford Univ. Press.

(1943) 1959 *The Modern Democratic State.* Volume 1. Oxford Univ. Press.

1945 *The Good and the Clever.* Cambridge Univ. Press.

1949 The Philosophy of the British Labour Government. Pages 250–268 in Filmer S. C. Northrop (editor), *Ideological Differences and World Order: Studies in the Philosophy and Science of the World's Cultures.* New Haven: Yale Univ. Press.

1951 Philosophy as Criticism of Standards. *Philosophical Quarterly* 1:97–108.

SUPPLEMENTARY BIBLIOGRAPHY

GALLIE, W. B. 1960 *A New University: A. D. Lindsay and the Keele Experiment.* London: Chatto & Windus.

RICHTER, MELVIN 1964 *Politics and Conscience: T. H. Green and His Age.* Cambridge, Mass.: Harvard Univ. Press. → Provides a background for A. D. Lindsay's politics and philosophy.

LINEAGE
See KINSHIP.

LINEAR HYPOTHESES

I
REGRESSION

Regression analysis, as it is presented in this article, is an important and general statistical tool. It is applicable to situations in which one observed variable has an expected value that is assumed to be a function of other variables; the function usually has a specified form with unspecified parameters. For example, an investigator might assume that under appropriate circumstances the expected score on an examination is a linear function of the length of training period. Here there are two parameters, slope and intercept of the line. The techniques of regression analysis may be classified into two kinds: (1) testing the concordance of the observations with the assumed model, usually in the framework of some broader model, and (2) carrying out estimation, or other sorts of inferences, about the parameters when the model is assumed to be correct. This area of statistics is sometimes known as "least squares," and in older publications it was called "the theory of errors."

In the regression relations discussed in this article only one variable is regarded as random; the others are either fixed by the investigator (where experimental control is possible) or selected in some way from among the possible values. The relation between the expected value of the random variable (called the dependent variable, the predictand, or the regressand) and the nonrandom variables (called regression variables, independent variables, predictors, or regressors) is known as a regression relation. Thus, if a random variable Y, depending on a variable x, varies at random about a linear function of x, we can write

$$Y = \beta_0 + \beta_1 x + e,$$

which expresses a linear regression relation. The parameters β_0 and β_1 are the regression coefficients or parameters, and e is a random variable with expected value zero. Usually the e's corresponding to different values of Y are assumed to be uncorrelated and to have the same variance. If η denotes the expected value of Y, the basic relation may be expressed alternatively as

$$E(Y) = \eta = \beta_0 + \beta_1 x.$$

The parameters in the relation will be either unknown or given by theory; observations of Y for different values of x provide the means of estimating these parameters or testing the concordance of the simple linear structure with the data.

Linear models, linear hypotheses. A regression relation that is linear in the unknown parameters is known as a linear model, and the assertion of such a model as a basis for inference is the assertion of a linear hypothesis. Often the term "linear hypothesis" refers to a restriction on the linear model (for example, specifying that a parameter has the value 7 or that two parameters are equal) that is to be tested. The importance of the linear model lies in its ease of application and understanding; there is a well-developed body of theory and techniques for the statistical treatment of linear models, in particular for the estimation of their parameters and the testing of hypotheses about them.

Needless to say, the description of a phenomenon by means of a linear model is usually a matter of convenience; the model is accepted until some more elaborate one is required. Nevertheless, the linear model has a wide range of applicability and is of great value in elucidating relationships, especially in the early stages of an investigation. Often a linear model is applicable only after transformations of the independent variables (like x in the above example), the dependent variable (Y, above), or both [*see* STATISTICAL ANALYSIS, SPECIAL PROBLEMS OF, *article on* TRANSFORMATIONS OF DATA].

In its most general form, regression analysis includes a number of other statistical techniques as special cases. For instance, it is not necessary that the x's be defined as metric variables. If the values of the observations on Y are classified into a number of groups—say, p—then the regression relation is written $E(Y) = \beta_1 x_1 + \beta_2 x_2 + \cdots + \beta_p x_p$, and x_i may be taken to be 1 for all observations in the ith group and 0 for all the others. The p x-variables will then specify the different groups, and the regression relation will define the mean value of Y for each group. In the simplest case, with two groups,

$$E(Y) = \beta_1 x_1 + \beta_2 x_2,$$

where $x_1 = 1$ and $x_2 = 0$ for the first group, and vice versa for the second.

The estimation of the population mean from a sample is a special case, since the model is then just

$$E(Y) = \beta_0,$$

β_0 being the mean of the population.

This treatment of the comparison of different groups is somewhat artificial, although it is important to note that it falls under the regression rubric. Such comparisons are generally carried out by means of the technique known as the analysis of variance [see LINEAR HYPOTHESES, *article on* ANALYSIS OF VARIANCE].

When a regressor is not measured quantitatively but is given only as a ranking (for example, order in time of archeological specimens, social position of occupation), it may still provide a regression relation suitable for estimation or prediction. The simplest way to include such a variable in a relation is to replace the qualitative values (rankings) by arbitrary numerical scores, equally spaced (see, for example, Strodtbeck et al. 1957). More refined methods would use scores spaced according to some measure of "distance" between successive rankings; thus, in some instances the scores have been chosen so that their frequency distribution approximates a grouped normal distribution. Since any method of scoring is arbitrary, the method that is used must be judged by the relations based on it as well as by its theoretical cogency. Simple scoring systems, which can be easily understood, are usually to be preferred.

When both the dependent variable and the regression variable are qualitative, each may be replaced by arbitrary scores as indicated above. Alternative methods determine scores for the dependent variable that are most highly correlated (formally) with the regressor scores or, if the regressor scores for any set of data are open to choice, choose scores for both variables so that the correlation is maximized. The calculation and interpretation of the regression relations for such situations have been discussed by Yates (1948) and by Williams (1952).

Regression, correlation, functional relation. The regression relation is a one-way relation between variables in which the expected value of one random variable is related to nonrandom values of the other variables. It is to be distinguished from other types of statistical relations, in particular from correlation and functional relationships. [See MULTIVARIATE ANALYSIS, *articles on* CORRELATION.] Correlation is a relation between two or more random variables and may be described in terms of the amount of variation in one of the variables associated with variation in the other variable or variables. The functional relation, by contrast, is a relation between the *expected values* of random variables. If quantities related by some physical law are subject to errors of measurement, the functional relation between expected values, rather than the regression relation, is what the investigator generally wants to determine.

Although the regression relation relates a random variable to other, nonrandom variables, in many situations it will apply also when the regression variables are random; then the regression, conditional on the observed values of the random regression variables, is determined. Here the *expected value* of one random variable is related to the *observed values* of the other random variables. For a discussion of the fitting of regression lines when the regression variables are subject to error, see Madansky (1959). When more than one variable is to be considered as random, the problem is usually thought of as one of multivariate analysis [see MULTIVARIATE ANALYSIS].

History. The method of least squares, on which most methods of estimation for linear models are based, was apparently first published by Adrien Legendre (1805), but the first treatment along the lines now familiar was given by Carl Friedrich Gauss (1821, see in 1855). Gauss showed that the method gives estimators of the unknown parameters with minimum variance among unbiased linear estimators. This basic result is sometimes known as the Gauss–Markov theorem, and the least squares estimators as Gauss–Markov estimators.

The term "regression" was first used by Francis Galton, who applied it to certain relations in the theory of heredity, but the term is now applied to relationships in general and to nonlinear as well as to linear relationships.

The linearity of linear hypotheses rests in the way the parameters appear; the x's may be highly nonlinear functions of underlying nonrandom variables. For example,

$$\eta = \beta_0 + \beta_1 x_1 + \beta_2 x_1^2 + \beta_3 x_1^3$$

and

$$\eta = \beta_1 e^{x_1} + \beta_2 \tan x_1$$

both fall squarely under the linear hypothesis model, whereas

$$\eta = \beta_1 e^{\beta_2 x_1}$$

does not fit that model.

There is now a vast literature dealing with the linear model, and the subject is also treated in most statistical textbooks.

Application in the social sciences. There has been a good deal of discussion about the type of model that should be used to describe relations between variables in the social sciences, particularly in economics. Linear regression models have often been considered inadequate for complex economic phenomena, and more complicated models have been developed. Recent work, however, indicates that ordinary linear regression methods have a wider scope than had been supposed. For example, there has been much discussion about how to treat data correlated in time, for which the residuals from the regression equation (the e's) show autocorrelation. This autocorrelation may be the result of autocorrelation in the variables not included in the model. Geary (1963) suggests that in such circumstances the inclusion of additional regression variables may effectively eliminate the autocorrelation among the residuals, so that standard methods may be applied.

Further discussion of the applicability of regression methods to economic data is given by Ezekiel and Fox (1930, chapters 20 and 24) and also by Wold and Juréen (see in Wold 1953).

Investigators should be encouraged to employ the simple methods of regression analysis as a first step before turning to more elaborate techniques. Despite the relative simplicity of its ideas, it is a powerful technique for elucidating relations, and its results are easily understood and applied. More elaborate techniques, by contrast, do not always provide a readily comprehensible interpretation.

Assumptions in regression analysis. A regression model may be expressed in the following way:

$$E(Y) = \eta = \beta_0 + \beta_1 x_1 + \cdots + \beta_p x_p,$$
$$Y = \eta + e,$$

where Y is the random variable, η is its expected value, the x's are known variables, the β's are unknown coefficients, and e is a random error or deviation with zero mean. In the notation for variables, either fixed or random, subscripts are used only to distinguish the different variables but not to distinguish different observations of the same variable. The context generally makes the meaning clear. Thus, the above expression is an abbreviated form of

$$E(Y_j) = \eta_j = \beta_0 + \beta_1 x_{1j} + \beta_2 x_{2j} + \cdots + \beta_p x_{pj},$$
$$j = 1, 2, \cdots, n;$$
$$Y_j = \eta_j + e_j.$$

This model is perfectly general; however, in estimating the coefficients, it is usually assumed that the e_j are mutually uncorrelated and are of equal variance (homoscedastic).

If there is no regressor variable that is identically one (as in the two-sample situation described earlier), the β_0 term might well be omitted. This is primarily a matter of notational convention.

The additional assumption that the errors are normally distributed is convenient and simplifies the theory. It can be shown that, on this assumption, the linear estimators given by least squares are in fact the maximum likelihood (m.l.) estimators of the parameters. In addition, the residual sum of squares $\sum(Y - \hat{\eta})^2$ (see below) is the basis for the m.l. estimator of the error variance (σ^2).

Apart from the theoretical advantages of the assumption of normality of the e's, there are the practical advantages that efficient methods of estimation and suitable tests of significance are relatively easy to apply and that the test statistics have well-known properties and are extensively tabulated. The normality assumption is often reasonable in applications, since even appreciable departures from it do not as a rule seriously invalidate regression analyses based upon normality [*see* ERRORS, *article on* EFFECTS OF ERRORS IN STATISTICAL ASSUMPTIONS].

Some departures from assumptions may be expected in certain situations. For example, if some of the measurements of Y are much larger than others, the associated errors, either errors of measurement or errors resulting from uncontrolled random effects, may well be correspondingly larger, so that the variances of the errors will be heterogeneous (the errors are heteroscedastic). Again, with annual data it is to be expected that errors may arise from unobserved factors whose influence from year to year will be associated, so the errors will not be independent (but see Geary 1963). It is often possible in particular cases to transform the data so that they conform more closely to the assumptions; for instance, a logarithmic or square-root transformation of Y will often give a variable whose errors have approximately constant variance [*see* STATISTICAL ANALYSIS, SPECIAL PROBLEMS OF, *article on* TRANSFORMATIONS OF DATA]. This will amount to replacing the linear model for Y with a linear model for the transformed variable. In practice this often gives a satisfactory representation of the data, any departure from the model being attributed to error.

The method of least squares determines, for the parameters β_i in the regression equation, estimators that minimize the sum of squares of deviations of the Y-values from the values given by the equation. This sum of squares is

$$\sum(Y - \eta)^2 = \sum(Y - \beta_0 - \beta_1 x_1 - \cdots - \beta_p x_p)^2.$$

In the following discussion the estimated β's are denoted by b's, and the corresponding estimator of η is denoted by $\hat{\eta}$, so that

$$\hat{\eta} = b_0 + b_1 x_1 + \cdots + b_p x_p$$

and the minimized sum of squared deviations is $\sum(Y - \hat{\eta})^2$.

The method has the twofold merit of minimizing not only the sum of squares of deviations but also the variance of the estimators b_i (among unbiased linear estimators). Thus, for most practical purposes the method of least squares gives estimators with satisfactory properties. Sometimes such estimators are not appropriate—for example, when errors in one direction are more serious than those in the other—but those cases are usually apparent to the investigator.

The method of least squares applies equally well when the errors are heteroscedastic or even correlated, provided the covariance structure of the errors is known (apart from a constant of proportionality, which may be estimated from the data). The method can be generalized to take account of the general correlation structure or, equivalently, a linear transformation of the observations may be used to reduce the problem to the simpler case of uncorrelated homoscedastic errors. (Details may be found in Rao 1965, chapter 4.)

When the correlation structure is unknown, the method of least squares may still be applied. If the data are analyzed as though the errors are uncorrelated and homoscedastic, the estimators of the parameters will be unbiased, although they will be less precise than if based on the correct model.

On the other hand, if the assumed linear model is incorrect—for example, if the relation is quadratic in one of the variables but only a linear model is fitted—then the estimators are liable to serious bias.

Since the form of the underlying model is almost always unknown there is usually a corresponding risk of bias. This problem has been studied in various contexts, but there is still much to be done; see Box and Wilson (1951), Box and Andersen (1955), and Plackett (1960, chapter 2).

Simple linear regression

In the simple linear regression model the expected value of Y is a linear function of a single variable, x_1:

$$E(Y) = \eta = \beta_0 + \beta_1 x_1.$$

The parameter β_0 is the intercept, and the parameter β_1 is the slope, of the regression line. This model is a satisfactory one in many cases, even if a number of variables affect the expected value of Y, for one of these may have a predominating influence, and although the omission of variables from the relation will lead to some bias, this may not be important in view of the increased simplicity of the model.

In studying the relation between two variables it is almost always desirable to plot a scatter diagram of the points representing the observations. The x-axis, or abscissa, is usually used for the regression variable and the y-axis, or ordinate, for the random variable. If the regression relation is linear the points should show a tendency to fall near a straight line, though if the variation is large

this tendency may well be masked. Although for some purposes a line drawn "by eye" is adequate to represent the regression, in general such a line is not sufficiently accurate. There is always the risk of bias in both the position and the slope of the line. Because there is a tendency for the deviations from the line in both the x and y directions to be taken into account in determining the fit, lines fitted by eye are often affected by the scales of measurement used for the two axes. Since Y is the random variable, only the deviations in the y direction should be taken into account in determining the fit of the line. Often the investigator, knowing that there may be error in x_1, may attempt to take it into account. It should be understood that this procedure will give an estimate not of the regression relation but of underlying structure, which often differs from the regression relation. Another and more serious shortcoming of lines drawn by eye is that they do not provide an estimate of the variance about the line, and such an estimate is almost always required.

The method of least squares is commonly used when an arithmetical method of fitting is required, because of its useful properties and its relative ease of application. The equations for the least squares estimators, b_i, based on n pairs of observations (x_1, Y), are as follows:

$$b_1 = \sum Y(x_1 - \bar{x}_1) / \sum (x_1 - \bar{x}_1)^2,$$
$$b_0 = \bar{Y} - b_1 \bar{x}_1.$$

Here the summation is over the observed values, $\bar{x}_1 = \sum x_1 / n$, and $\bar{Y} = \sum Y / n$. (Note that the observations on x_1 need not be all different, although they must not all be the same.) The estimated regression function is

$$\hat{\eta} = b_0 + b_1 x_1.$$

The minimized sum of squares of deviations is

$$\sum (Y - \hat{\eta})^2 = \sum (Y - \bar{Y})^2 - b_1^2 \sum (x_1 - \bar{x}_1)^2$$
$$= \sum (Y - \bar{Y})^2 - b_1 \sum Y(x_1 - \bar{x}_1).$$

The standard errors (estimated standard deviations) of the estimators may be derived from the minimized sum of squares of deviations. Two independent linear parameters have been fitted, and it may readily be shown that the expected value of this minimized sum of squares is $(n-2)\sigma^2$, where σ^2 is the common variance of the residual errors. Consequently, an unbiased estimator of σ^2 is given by

$$s^2 = \sum (Y - \hat{\eta})^2 / (n - 2),$$

and this is the conventional estimator of σ^2. (The m.l. estimator of σ^2 is $\sum (Y - \hat{\eta})^2 / n$.) The sum of squares for deviations is said to have $n - 2$ degrees of freedom, representing the number of linearly independent quantities on which it is based.

The estimated variances of the estimators are est. var $(b_1) = s^2 / \sum (x_1 - \bar{x}_1)^2$ and est. var $(b_0) = s^2 \sum x_1^2 / [n \sum (x_1 - \bar{x}_1)^2]$, and the estimated covariance is est. cov $(b_0, b_1) = -s^2 \bar{x}_1 / \sum (x_1 - \bar{x}_1)^2 = -\bar{x}_1$ var (b_1).

Separate confidence limits for the parameters β_0 and β_1 may be determined from the estimators and their standard errors, using Student's t-distribution [see ESTIMATION, *article on* CONFIDENCE INTERVALS AND REGIONS]. If $t_{\alpha; n-2}$ denotes the α-level of this distribution for $n - 2$ degrees of freedom, the $1 - \alpha$ confidence limits for β_1 are $b_1 \pm t_{\alpha; n-2} s / \sqrt{\sum (x_1 - \bar{x}_1)^2}$. Confidence limits for the intercept, β_0, may be determined in a similar way but are not usually of interest. In a few cases it may be necessary to determine whether the estimator b_0 is in agreement with some theoretical value of the intercept. Thus, in some situations it is reasonable to expect the regression line to pass through the origin, so that $\beta_0 = 0$. It will then be necessary to test the significance of the departure of b_0 from zero or, equivalently, to determine whether the confidence limits for β_0 include zero.

When it is assumed that $\beta_0 = 0$ and there is no need to test this hypothesis, then the regression has only one unknown parameter; in such a case the sum of squares for deviations from the regression line, used to estimate the residual variance, will have $n - 1$ degrees of freedom.

When the parameters β_0 and β_1 are both of interest, a joint confidence statement about them may be useful. The joint confidence region is usually an ellipse centered at (b_0, b_1) and containing all values of (β_0, β_1) from which (b_0, b_1) does not differ with statistical significance as measured by an F-test (see the section on significance testing, below). [*The question of joint confidence regions is discussed further in* LINEAR HYPOTHESES, *article on* MULTIPLE COMPARISONS.]

Choice of experimental values. The formula for the variance of the regression coefficient b_1 shows that it is the more accurately determined the larger is $\sum (x_1 - \bar{x}_1)^2$, the sum of squares of the values of x_1 about their mean. This is in accordance with common sense, since a greater spread of experimental values will magnify the regression effect yet will in general leave the error component unaltered. If accurate estimation of β_1 were the only criterion, the optimum allocation of experimental points would be in equal numbers at the extreme ends of the possible range. However, the assumption that a regression is linear, although satisfactory over most of the possible range, is often likely

to fail near the ends of the range; for this and other reasons it may be desirable to check the linearity of the regression, and to do so points other than the two extreme values must be observed. In practice, where little is known about the form of the regression relation it is usually desirable to take points distributed uniformly throughout the range. If the experimental points are equally spaced, this will facilitate the fitting of quadratic or higher degree polynomials, using tabulated orthogonal polynomials as described below.

Confidence limits for the regression line. The estimated regression function is

$$\hat{\eta} = b_0 + b_1 x_1$$
$$= \bar{Y} + b_1 (x_1 - \bar{x}_1),$$

and corresponding to any specified value, x_{1*}, of x_1, the variance of $\hat{\eta}$ is estimated as

$$\text{est. var}\,(\hat{\eta}) = s^2 \left(\frac{1}{n} + \frac{(x_{1*} - \bar{x}_1)^2}{\sum (x_1 - \bar{x}_1)^2} \right).$$

Thus, for any specified value of x_1, confidence limits for η can be determined according to the formula

$$Y_L = \hat{\eta} \pm t_{\alpha; n-2} s \sqrt{\left(\frac{1}{n} + \frac{(x_{1*} - \bar{x}_1)^2}{\sum (x_1 - \bar{x}_1)^2} \right)}.$$

The locus of these limits consists of the two branches of a hyperbola, lying on either side of the fitted regression line; this locus defines what may be described as a confidence curve. A typical regression line fitted to a set of points is shown in Figure 1 with the 95 per cent confidence curve shown as the two inside upper and lower curves, Y_L.

The above limits are appropriate for the estimated value of η corresponding to a *given* value of x_1. They do not, however, set limits to the whole line. Such limits are given by a method developed by Working and Hotelling, as described, e.g., by Kendall and Stuart ([1943–1946] 1958–1966, vol. 2, chapter 28). [*See also* LINEAR HYPOTHESES, *article on* MULTIPLE COMPARISONS.] As might be expected, these limits lie outside the corresponding limits for the same probability for a single value of x_1. The limits may be regarded as arising from the envelope of all lines whose parameters fall within a suitable confidence region. These limits are given by

$$Y_{WH} = \hat{\eta} \pm s \sqrt{2 F_{1-\alpha; 2, n-2} \left(\frac{1}{n} + \frac{(x_{1*} - \bar{x}_1)^2}{\sum (x_1 - \bar{x}_1)^2} \right)},$$

where $F_{1-\alpha; 2, n-2}$ is the tabulated value for the F-distribution with 2 and $n - 2$ degrees of freedom at confidence level $1 - \alpha$. These limits, for a 95 per cent confidence level, are shown as a pair of broken lines in Figure 1.

Figure 1 — Regression line and associated 95 per cent confidence regions*

* The Y_P curves, although they appear straight in the figure, are hyperbolas like the other Y curves.

Source of data: Martin, Jean I., 1965, *Refugee Settlers: A Study of Displaced Persons in Australia.* Canberra: Australian National University.

The user of the confidence limits must be clear about which type of limits he requires. If he is interested in the limits on the estimated η for a particular value $x_{1°}$ or in only one pair of limits at a time, the inner limits, Y_L, will be appropriate, but if he is interested in limits for many values of $x_{1°}$ (some of which may not be envisaged when the calculations are being made), the Working–Hotelling limits, Y_{WH}, will be needed.

Application of the regression equation. The regression equation is usually determined not only to provide an empirical law relating variables but also as a means of making future estimates or predictions. Thus, in studies of demand, regression relations of demand on price and other factors enable demand to be predicted for future occasions when one or more of these factors is varied. Such prediction is provided directly by the regression equation. It should be noted, however, that the standard error of prediction will be greater than the standard error of the estimated points ($\hat{\eta}$) on the regression line. This is because a future observation will vary about its regression value with variance equal to the variance of individual values about the regression in the population. When standard errors are being quoted, it is important to distinguish between the standard error of the point $\hat{\eta}$ on the

regression line and the standard error of prediction. The estimated variance of prediction is

$$\text{est. var } (\hat{\eta}_P) = s^2 \left(1 + \frac{1}{n} + \frac{(x_{1°} - \bar{x}_1)^2}{\sum(x_1 - \bar{x}_1)^2} \right).$$

The outside upper and lower curves in Figure 1 are confidence limits for prediction, Y_P, based on this variance. Clearly, for making predictions of this sort there is little point in determining the regression line with great accuracy. The major part of the error in such cases will be the variance of individual values.

The formula for the standard error of $\hat{\eta}$ or $\hat{\eta}_P$ shows that the error of estimation increases as the x_1-value departs from the mean of the sample, so that when the deviation from the mean is large the variance of estimate can be so great as to make the estimate worthless. This is one reason why investigators should be discouraged from attempting to draw inferences beyond the range of the observed values of x_1. The other reason is that the assumed linear regression, even though satisfactory within the observed range, may not hold true outside this range.

Inverse estimation. In many situations the investigator is primarily interested in determining the value of x_1 corresponding to a given level or value, $\eta_°$. Thus, although it is still appropriate to determine the regression of the random variable Y on the fixed variable x_1, the inference has to be carried out in reverse. For example, if a drug that affects the reaction time of individuals is being tested at different levels, the reaction time Y will be a random variable with regression on the dose level x_1. However, the purpose of the investigation may be to determine a dose level that will lead to a given time of reaction on the average. The experimental doses, being fixed, cannot be treated as random, so that it is inappropriate to determine a regression of x_1 on Y, and such a pseudo regression would give spurious results. In such situations the value of x_1 corresponding to a given value of η has to be estimated from the regression of Y on x_1.

The regression equation can be rearranged to give an estimator of x_1 corresponding to a given value, $\eta_°$,

$$\hat{X}_° = (\eta_° - b_0)/b_1.$$

The approximate estimated variance of the estimator is

$$\text{est. var } (\hat{X}_°) \cong \frac{s^2}{b_1^2} \left(\frac{1}{n} + \frac{(\hat{X}_° - \bar{x}_1)^2}{\sum(x_1 - \bar{x}_1)^2} \right)$$
$$= \frac{s^2}{b_1^2} \left(\frac{1}{n} + \frac{(\eta_° - \bar{Y})^2}{b_1^2 \sum(x_1 - \bar{x}_1)^2} \right).$$

A more precise method of treating such a problem is to determine confidence limits for η given x_1 and to determine from these, by rearranging the equation, confidence limits for x_1. For the regression shown in Figure 1, the 95 per cent confidence curves (the inner curves, Y_L, on either side of the line) will in this way give confidence limits for x_1 corresponding to a given value of η. The point at which the horizontal line $Y = \eta$ cuts the regression line gives the estimate of x_1; the points at which the line cuts the upper and lower curves give, respectively, lower and upper confidence limits for x_1. This may be demonstrated by an extension of the reasoning leading to confidence limits. [*See* ESTIMATION, *article on* CONFIDENCE INTERVALS AND REGIONS.]

Sometimes, rather than a hypothetical regression value, η_*, a single observed value, y_* (not in the basic sample), is given, and limits are required for the value of x_1 that could be associated with such a value. The estimator $\hat{X}_*$ is given by

$$\hat{X}_* = (y_* - b_0)/b_1,$$

and its approximate estimated variance (which must take into account the variation between responses on Y to a given value of x_1) is

$$\text{est. var } (\hat{X}_*) \cong \frac{s^2}{b_1^2}\left(1 + \frac{1}{n} + \frac{(\hat{X}_* - \bar{x}_1)^2}{\sum (x_1 - \bar{x}_1)^2} \right).$$

Using this augmented variance, confidence limits on x_1 corresponding to a given y_* may be found. For more precise determination of the confidence limits for prediction, the locus of limits for y_* given x_1 may be inverted to give limits for x_1 given y_*. In Figure 1, the outer curves are these loci (for the 95 per cent confidence level); the 95 per cent limits for x_1 will be given by the intersection of the line $Y = y_*$ with these confidence curves for prediction.

Multiple regression

In many situations where a single regression variable is not adequate to represent the variation in the random variable Y, a multiple regression is appropriate. In other situations there may be only one regression variable, but the assumed relation, rather than being linear, is a quadratic or a polynomial of higher degree. Since both multiple linear regression and polynomial regression relations are linear in the unknown parameters, the same techniques are applicable to both; in fact, polynomial regression is a special case of multiple regression. The number of variables to include in a multiple regression, or the degree of polynomial to be applied, is to some extent a matter of judgment and convenience, although it must be remembered that a regression equation containing a large number of variables is usually inconvenient to use as well as difficult to calculate. With the use of electronic computers, however, there is greater scope for increasing the number of regression variables, since the computations are routine.

Consider the multiple regression equation

$$E(Y) = \eta = \beta_0 + \beta_1 x_1 + \cdots + \beta_p x_p,$$

with p regression variables and a constant term. The estimation of these $p + 1$ unknown parameters can be systematically carried out if β_0 is also regarded as a regression coefficient corresponding to a regression variable x_0 that is always unity. As in simple regression, the method of least squares provides unbiased linear estimators of the coefficients with minimum variance and also provides estimators of the standard errors of these coefficients. The quantities required for determining the estimators are the sums of squares and products of the x-values, the sums of products of the observed Y with each of the x-values, and the sum of squares of Y. The method of least squares gives a set of linear equations for the b's, called the *normal equations*:

$$b_0 t_{00} + b_1 t_{01} + \cdots + b_p t_{0p} = u_0$$
$$b_0 t_{10} + b_1 t_{11} + \cdots + b_p t_{1p} = u_1$$
$$\vdots \qquad \vdots \qquad \qquad \vdots \qquad \vdots$$
$$b_0 t_{p0} + b_1 t_{p1} + \cdots + b_p t_{pp} = u_p$$

where $t_{hi} = t_{ih} = \sum x_h x_i$ and $u_i = \sum Y x_i$. These equations can be written in matrix form as

$$\boldsymbol{Tb} = \boldsymbol{u},$$

where $\boldsymbol{T} = (t_{hi})$ and $\boldsymbol{u}$ is the vector of the u_i. The solution requires the inversion of the matrix $\boldsymbol{T}$, the inverse matrix being denoted by $\boldsymbol{T}^{-1}$ (with typical element t^{hi}). The solution may be written in matrix form as

$$\boldsymbol{b} = \boldsymbol{T}^{-1}\boldsymbol{u}$$

or in extended form as

$$b_0 = t^{00}u_0 + t^{01}u_1 + \cdots + t^{0p}u_p,$$

and so forth.

The variance of b_i is $t^{ii}\sigma^2$, and the covariance of b_i and b_j is $t^{ij}\sigma^2$. It should be remarked that in the special case of "regression through the origin"— that is, when the constant term β_0 is assumed to be zero—the first equation and the first term of each other equation are omitted; the constant regressor x_0 and its coefficient β_0 thus have the same status as any other regression variable.

When the constant term is included, computational labor may be reduced and arithmetical accuracy increased if the sums of squares and products are taken about the means. That is, the t_{hi} and u_i are replaced by

$$t'_{hi} = t_{hi} - \sum x_h \sum x_i/n = \sum(x_h - \bar{x}_h)(x_i - \bar{x}_i)$$

and

$$u'_i = u_i - \sum Y \sum x_i/n,$$

respectively. All the sums of products with zero subscripts then vanish, and the sums of squares are reduced in magnitude. The constant term has to be estimated separately; it is given by

$$b_0 = \bar{Y} - b_1\bar{x}_1 - b_2\bar{x}_2 - \cdots - b_p\bar{x}_p$$
$$= (\sum Y - b_1\sum x_1 - b_2\sum x_2 - \cdots - b_p\sum x_p)/n.$$

The computational aspects of matrix inversion and the determination of the regression coefficients are dealt with in many statistical texts, including Williams (1959); in addition, many programs for matrix inversion are available for electronic computers.

Effect of heteroscedasticity. When the error variance of the dependent variable Y is different in different parts of its range (or, strictly, of the range of its expected value, η), estimators of regression coefficients ignoring the heteroscedasticity will be unbiased but of reduced accuracy, as already mentioned. The calculation of improved estimators may then sometimes be necessary.

There are some problems in taking heteroscedasticity into account. Among them is the problem of specification: defining the relation between expected value and variance. Often, with adequate data, the estimated ($\hat{\eta}$) values from the usual unweighted regression line can be grouped and the mean squared deviation from these values for each group used as a rough measure of the variance. The regression can then be refitted, each value being given a weight inversely proportional to the estimated variance. Two iterations of this method are likely to give estimates of about the accuracy practically attainable. If an empirical relation between expected value and error variance can be deduced, this simplifies the problem somewhat; however, the weight for each observation has to be determined from a provisionally fitted relation, so iteration is still required.

To calculate a weighted regression, each observation Y_j $(j = 1, 2, \cdots, n)$ is given a weight w_j instead of unit weight as in the standard calculation. These weights will be the reciprocals of the estimated variances of each value. Then, if weighted quantities are distinguished by the subscript w,

$$t_{whi} = \sum wx_hx_i,$$
$$u_{wi} = \sum wYx_i,$$

and the normal equations are

$$b_{w0}t_{w00} + b_{w1}t_{w01} + \cdots + b_{wp}t_{w0p} = u_{w0}$$

and so on, or in matrix form

$$\boldsymbol{T}_w\boldsymbol{b}_w = \boldsymbol{u}_w.$$

The solution is

$$\boldsymbol{b}_w = \boldsymbol{T}_w^{-1}\boldsymbol{u}_w,$$

and the variances of the estimators b_{wi} are approximately $t_w^{ii}\sigma^2$.

When the weights are estimated from the data, as in the iterative method just described, some allowance has to be made in an exact analysis for errors in the weights. This inaccuracy will somewhat reduce the precision of the estimators. However, for most practical purposes, and provided that the number of observations in each group for which weights are estimated is not too small, the errors in the weights may be ignored. (For further discussion of this question see Cochran & Carroll 1953.)

Estimability of the coefficients. It is intuitively clear in a general way that the $p + 1$ regression variables included in a regression equation should not be too nearly linearly dependent on one another, for then it might be expected that these regression variables could be approximately expressed in terms of a smaller number.

More precisely, in order that meaningful estimators of the regression coefficients exist, it is necessary that the variables be linearly independent (or, equivalently, $\boldsymbol{T}$ must be nonsingular). That is, no one variable should be expressible as a linear combination of the others or, expressed symmetrically, no linear combination of the variables vanishes unless all coefficients are zero. Clearly, if only $p - r$ of the variables are linearly independent, then the regression relation may be represented as a regression on these $p - r$, together with arbitrary multiples of the vanishing linear combinations. From the practical point of view, this lack of estimability will cause no problems, provided that the regression on a set of $p - r$ linearly independent variables is calculated. Estimation from the equation will be unaffected, but for testing the significance of the regression it must be noted that the regression sum of squares has not $p + 1$ but $p - r$ degrees of freedom, and the residual has $n - p + r$.

However, if the lack of estimability is ignored, the calculations to determine the $p + 1$ coefficients either will fail (since the matrix $\boldsymbol{T}$, being singular, has no inverse) or will give misleading results (if an approximate value of $\boldsymbol{T}$, having an inverse, is used in calculation and the lack of estimability is obscured).

When the regression variables, although linearly independent, are barely so (in the sense that the matrix **T**, although of rank $p + 1$, is "almost singular," having a small but nonvanishing determinant), the regression coefficients will be estimable but will have large standard errors. In typical cases, many of the estimated coefficients will not differ with statistical significance from zero; this merely reflects the fact that the corresponding regression variable may be omitted from the equation and the remaining coefficients adjusted without significant worsening of the fit.

In this situation, as in the case of linear dependence, these effects are not usually important in practice; however, they may suggest the advisability of reducing the number of regression variables included in the equation. [*For further discussion, see* STATISTICAL IDENTIFIABILITY.]

Conditions on the coefficients. Sometimes the regression coefficients β_i are assumed to satisfy some conditions based on theory. Provided these conditions are expressible as linear equations in the coefficients, the method of least squares carries through and leads, as before, to unbiased estimators satisfying the conditions and with minimum variance among linear estimators. It will be clear that with $p + 1$ regression coefficients subject to $r + 1$ independent linear restrictions, $r + 1$ of the coefficients may be eliminated, so that the restricted regression is equivalent to one with $p - r$ coefficients. Thus, in principle there is a choice between expressing the model in terms of $p - r$ unrestricted coefficients or $p + 1$ restricted ones; often the latter has advantages of symmetry and interpretability.

A simple example of restricted regression is one in which η is a weighted average of the x's but with unknown weights, $\beta_1, \cdots, \beta_p$. Here the side conditions would be $\beta_0 = 0$, $\beta_1 + \cdots + \beta_p = 1$.

As the introduction of side conditions effectively reduces the number of linearly independent coefficients, such conditions are useful in restoring estimability when the coefficients are nonestimable. In many problems these side conditions may be chosen to have practical significance. For example, where an over-all mean and a number of treatment "effects" are being estimated, it is conventional to specify the effects so that their mean vanishes; with this specification they represent deviations from the over-all mean.

When a restricted regression is being estimated, it will often be possible and of interest to estimate the unrestricted regression as well, in order to see the effect of the restrictions and to test whether the data are concordant with the conditions assumed. The test of significance consists of comparing the $(p + 1)$-variable (unrestricted) regression with the $(p - r)$-variable (restricted) regression, in the manner described in the section on significance testing. This test of concordance is independent of the test of significance of any of the restricted coefficients.

Further details and examples of restricted regression are given by Rao (1965, p. 189) and Williams (1959, pp. 49–58). In the remainder of this article, the notation will presume unrestricted regression.

Missing values. When observations on some of the variables are missing, the simplest and usually the only practicable procedure is to ignore the corresponding values of the other variables—that is, to work only with complete sets of observations. However, it is sometimes possible to make use of the incomplete data, provided some additional assumptions are made. Methods have been developed under the assumption that (*a*) the missing values are in some sense randomly deleted, or the assumption that (*b*) the variables are all random and follow a multivariate normal distribution. Assumption (*b*) is treated by Anderson (1957) and Rao (1952, pp. 161–165). It is sometimes found, after the least squares equations for the constants in a regression relation have been set up, that some of the values of the dependent variable are unreliable or missing altogether. Rather than recalculate the equations it is often more convenient to replace the missing value by the value expected from the regression relation. This substitution conserves the form of the estimating equations, usually with little disturbance to the significance tests or the variances of the estimators.

The techniques of "fitting missing values" have been most fully developed for experiments designed in such a way that the estimators of various constants are either uncorrelated or have a symmetric pattern of correlations and the estimating equations have a symmetry of form that simplifies their solution. Missing values in such experiments destroy the symmetry and make estimation more difficult; it is therefore a great practical convenience to replace the missing values. Details of the method applied to designed experiments will be found in Cochran and Cox (1950). For applications to general regression models see Kruskal (1961).

The technique is itself an application of the method of least squares. To replace a missing value Y_j, a value $\hat{\eta}_j$ is chosen so as to minimize its contribution to the residual sum of squares. Thus, the estimate is equivalent to the one that would have been obtained by a fresh analysis; the calculation is simplified by the fact that estimates for only one or a few values are being calculated. The degrees of freedom for the residual sum of squares are reduced by the number of values thus fitted. For most practical purposes it is then sufficiently accurate to treat the fitted values as though they were original observations. The exact analysis is described by Yates (1933) and, in general terms, by Kruskal (1961).

Significance testing. In order to determine the standard errors of the regression coefficients and to test their significance, it is necessary to estimate the residual variance, σ^2. The sum of squares of deviations, $\sum(Y - \hat{\eta})^2$, which may readily be shown to satisfy

$$\sum(Y - \hat{\eta})^2 = \sum Y^2 - \boldsymbol{u}'\boldsymbol{T}^{-1}\boldsymbol{u}$$
$$= \sum Y^2 - \boldsymbol{b}'\boldsymbol{u},$$

is found under $p + 1$ constraints and so may be said to have $n - p - 1$ degrees of freedom; if the model assumed is correct, so that the deviations are purely random, the expected value of the sum of squares is $(n - p - 1)\sigma^2$. Accordingly, the *residual mean square*,

$$s^2 = \sum(Y - \hat{\eta})^2/(n - p - 1),$$

is an unbiased estimator of the residual variance. The variances of the regression coefficients are estimated by

$$\text{est. var } (b_i) = t^{ii}s^2,$$

and the standard errors are the square roots of these quantities. The inverse matrix thus is used both in the calculation of the estimators and in the determination of their standard errors. From the off-diagonal elements t^{hi} of the inverse matrix are derived the estimated covariances between the estimators,

$$\text{est. cov } (b_h, b_i) = t^{hi}s^2.$$

The splitting of the total sum of squares of Y into two parts, a part associated with the regression effects and a residual part independent of

them, is a particular example of what is known as the analysis of variance [*see* LINEAR HYPOTHESES, *article on* ANALYSIS OF VARIANCE].

Testing for regression effects. The regression sum of squares, being based on $p + 1$ estimated quantities, will have $p + 1$ degrees of freedom. When regression effects are nonexistent, the expected value of each part is proportional to its degrees of freedom. Accordingly, it is often convenient and informative to present these two parts, and their corresponding mean squares, in an analysis-of-variance table, such as Table 1.

In the table, the final column gives the expected values of the two mean squares; it shows that real regression effects inflate the regression sum of squares but not the residual sum of squares. This fact provides the basis for tests of significance of a calculated regression, since large values of the ratio of regression mean square to residual mean square give evidence for the existence of a regression relation.

Significance of a single coefficient. The question may arise whether one or more of the regression variables contribute to the relation anything that is not already provided by the other variables. In such circumstances the relevant hypothesis to be examined is that the β's corresponding to these variables are zero. A more general hypothesis that may sometimes need to be tested is that certain of the β's take assigned values.

The simplest test is that of the statistical significance of a single coefficient—say, b_i. The test will be of its departure from zero, if the contribution of x_i to the regression is in question. More generally, when β_i is specified, as, say, β_i^*, it will be relevant to test the significance of departure of b_i from β_i^*. The significance test in either case is the same; the squared difference between estimated and hypothesized values is compared with the estimated variance of that difference, which is $s^2 t^{ii}$.

The ratio $F = (b_i - \beta_i^*)^2/(s^2 t^{ii})$ has the F-distribution with 1 and $n - p - 1$ degrees of freedom if the difference is in fact due to sampling fluctuations alone; in this case, the F-statistic is just the square of the usual t-statistic. When β_i differs

Table 1 — Analysis-of-variance table for testing regression effects

Source	Degrees of freedom	Sum of squares	Mean square	Expected mean square
Regression	$p + 1$	$\sum b_i u_i$	$\dfrac{\sum b_i u_i}{p + 1}$	$\sigma^2 + \dfrac{\boldsymbol{\beta}'\boldsymbol{T}\boldsymbol{\beta}}{p + 1}$
Residual	$n - p - 1$	$\sum Y^2 - \sum b_i u_i = (n - p - 1)s^2$	s^2	σ^2
Total	n	$\sum Y^2$		

from β_i^* the F-statistic will tend to be larger, so that a right-tail test is indicated.

Testing several coefficients. To test a number of regression variables—or, more precisely, their regression coefficients—the method of least squares is equivalent to fitting a regression with and without the variables in question and testing the difference in the regression sums of squares against the estimated error variance. To choose a specific example, suppose the last q coefficients in a p-variable regression are to be tested. If the symbol S^2 is used to stand for sum of squares, the sum of squares for regression on all p variables may be written

$$S_p^2 = \boldsymbol{u}_p' \boldsymbol{T}_p^{-1} \boldsymbol{u}_p \, ,$$

with $p + 1$ degrees of freedom, and the corresponding sum of squares on the first $p - q$ variables as

$$S_{p-q}^2 = \boldsymbol{u}_{p-q}' \boldsymbol{T}_{p-q}^{-1} \boldsymbol{u}_{p-q}$$

with $p - q + 1$ degrees of freedom. The difference, a sum of squares with q degrees of freedom, provides a criterion for testing the significance of the q regression coefficients. The ratio

$$F = (S_p^2 - S_{p-q}^2)/(qs^2)$$

has, under the null hypothesis that the last q coefficients are zero, the F-distribution with q and $n - p - 1$ degrees of freedom. This simultaneous test of q coefficients may also be adapted to testing the departure of the q coefficients from theoretical values, not necessarily zero.

The significance test may be conveniently set out as in Table 2, where only the mean squares required for the significance test appear in the last column.

When $q = 1$, this test reduces to the test for a single regression coefficient, and the F-ratio

$$F = (S_p^2 - S_{p-1}^2)/s^2$$

is then identical with the F-ratio given above for making such a test.

Linear combinations of coefficients. Sometimes it is necessary to test the significance of one or more linear combinations of the coefficients—that is, to test hypotheses about linear combinations of the β's. A common example is the comparison of two coefficients, β_1 and β_2, say, for which the comparison $b_1 - b_2$ is relevant. The F-test applies to such comparisons also. Thus, for the difference $b_1 - b_2$, the estimated variance is $s^2(t^{11} - 2t^{12} + t^{22})$, and $F = (b_1 - b_2)^2/[s^2(t^{11} - 2t^{12} + t^{22})]$, with 1 and $n - p - 1$ degrees of freedom.

In general, to test the departure from zero of k linear combinations of regression coefficients the procedure is as follows. Let the linear combinations (expressed in matrix notation) be

$$\boldsymbol{\Gamma}' \boldsymbol{b},$$

where $\boldsymbol{\Gamma}$ is a $(p + 1) \times k$ matrix of known constants. Then the estimated covariance matrix of these linear combinations is

$$s^2 \boldsymbol{\Gamma}' \boldsymbol{T}^{-1} \boldsymbol{\Gamma},$$

and the F-ratio is

$$F = \boldsymbol{b}' \boldsymbol{\Gamma} (\boldsymbol{\Gamma}' \boldsymbol{T}^{-1} \boldsymbol{\Gamma})^{-1} \boldsymbol{\Gamma}' \boldsymbol{b}/ks^2,$$

with k and $n - p - 1$ degrees of freedom. Of course, this test can also be adapted to testing the departure of these linear combinations from pre-assigned values other than zero.

When the population coefficients β_i are in fact nonzero, the expected value of the regression mean square in the analysis of variance shown in Table 1 will be larger than σ^2 by a term that depends on both the magnitude of the coefficients and the accuracy with which they are estimated (see, for example, the last column of Table 1). Clearly, the greater this term, called the *noncentrality*, the greater the probability that the null hypothesis will be rejected at the adopted significance level. The F-test has certain optimum properties, but other tests may be preferred in special circumstances.

Table 2 — Analysis-of-variance table for testing several regression coefficients

Source	Degrees of freedom	Sum of squares	Mean square
Regression on p—q variables	$p - q + 1$	S_{p-q}^2	$\ldots$
Additional q variables	q	$S_p^2 - S_{p-q}^2$	$(S_p^2 - S_{p-q}^2)/q$
Regression on all p variables	$p + 1$	S_p^2	$\ldots$
Residual	$n - p - 1$	$(n - p - 1)s^2$	s^2
Total	n	$\sum Y^2$	

Multivariate analogues

Although hitherto only the regression of a single dependent variable Y on one or more regressors x_i has been discussed, it will be realized that often the simultaneous regressions of a number of random variables on the same regressors will be of importance. For instance, in a sociological study of immigrants the regressions of annual income and size of family on age, educational level, and period of residence in the country may be determined; here there are two dependent variables and three regressors.

Often the relations among the different dependent variables will also be of interest, or various linear combinations of the variables, rather than the original variables themselves, may be studied. The linear combination that is most highly correlated with the regressors may sometimes be relevant to the investigation, but the linear compounds will usually be chosen for their practical relevance rather than their statistical properties. [*For further discussion of multivariate analogues, see* MULTI-VARIATE ANALYSIS, *especially the general article,* OVERVIEW, *and the article on* CLASSIFICATION AND DISCRIMINATION.]

Polynomial regression

When the relation between two variables, x_1 and Y, appears to be curvilinear, it is natural to fit some form of smooth curve to the data. For some purposes a freehand curve is adequate to represent the relation, but if the curve is to be used for prediction or estimation and standard errors are required, some mathematical method of fitting, such as the method of least squares, must be used. The freehand fitting of a curvilinear relation has all the disadvantages of freehand fitting of a straight line, with the added disadvantage that it is more difficult to distinguish real trends from random fluctuations.

The polynomial form is

$$E(Y) = \eta = \beta_0 + \beta_1 x_1 + \beta_2 x_1^2 + \cdots + \beta_p x_1^p.$$

Being a linear model, it has the advantages of simplicity, flexibility, and relative ease of calculation. It is for such reasons, not because it necessarily represents the theoretical form of the relation, that a polynomial regression is often fitted to data.

Orthogonal polynomials. The computations in polynomial regression are exactly the same as those in multiple regression, except that some simplification of the arithmetic may be introduced if the same values of x_1 are used repeatedly. Then instead of using the powers of x_1 as the regression variables, these are replaced by orthogonal polynomials of successively increasing degree, so defined that the sum of products of any pair of them, over their chosen values, is zero.

This procedure has the twofold advantage that, first, all the off-diagonal elements of the matrix $\boldsymbol{T}$ are zero, so the calculation of regression coefficients and their standard errors is much simplified, and, second, the regression coefficient on each polynomial and the corresponding sum of squares can be independently determined.

Because it is common for investigators to use data with values of the independent variables equally spaced, the orthogonal polynomials for this particular case have been extensively tabulated. Fisher and Yates (1938) tabulate these orthogonal polynomials up to those of fifth degree, for numbers of equally spaced points up to 75. However, if the data are not equally spaced the tabulated polynomials are not applicable, and the regression must be calculated directly.

Testing adequacy of fit. The question of what degree of polynomial is appropriate to fit to a set of data is discussed below (see "Considerations in regression model choice"). If for each value of x_1 there is an array of values for Y, the variation in the data can be analyzed into parts between and within arrays by the techniques of analysis of variance [*see* LINEAR HYPOTHESES, *article on* ANALYSIS OF VARIANCE]. The sum of squares between arrays can be further analyzed into that part accounted for by regression and that part not so accounted for (deviation from regression). The adequacy of a polynomial fitted to the data is indicated by nonsignificant deviation from regression.

When there is but one observation of Y for each value of x_1, such an analysis is not possible. To test the adequacy of a pth-degree polynomial regression, a common though not strictly defensible procedure is to fit a polynomial of degree $p + 1$ and test whether the coefficient b_{p+1} of x_1^{p+1} is significant. Anderson (1962) has treated this problem as a multiple decision problem and has provided optimal procedures that can readily be applied.

Estimation of maxima. Sometimes a polynomial regression is fitted in order to estimate the value of x_1 that yields a maximum value of η. A detailed discussion of the estimation of maxima is given by Hotelling (1941). To give an idea of the methods that are used, consider a quadratic regression of the form

$$\hat{\eta} = b_0 + b_1 x_1 + b_2 x_1^2.$$

A maximum (or minimum) value of $\hat{\eta}$ occurs at the point $x_m = -b_1/2b_2$, and this value is taken as the estimated position of the maximum. Confidence limits for the position can be determined by means of the following device. If the position of the maximum of the true regression curve is ξ, then $\xi = -\beta_1/2\beta_2$, so that $\beta_1 + 2\beta_2\xi = 0$. Consequently the quantity

$$b_1 + 2b_2\xi$$

is distributed with mean zero and estimated variance

$$s^2(t^{11} + 4t^{12}\xi + 4t^{22}\xi^2).$$

The confidence limits for ξ with confidence coefficient $1 - \alpha$ are given by the roots of the equation

$$\frac{(b_1 + 2b_2\xi)^2}{s^2(t^{11} + 4t^{12}\xi + 4t^{22}\xi^2)} = F_{\alpha;1,n-3},$$

where $F_{\alpha;1,n-3}$ is the α-point of the F-distribution with 1 and $n - 3$ degrees of freedom, abbreviated below as F_α. The solution of this equation may be simplified by writing

$$g_{11} = \frac{F_\alpha s^2 t^{11}}{b_1^2}, \qquad g_{12} = \frac{F_\alpha s^2 t^{12}}{b_1 b_2}, \qquad g_{22} = \frac{F_\alpha s^2 t^{22}}{b_2^2},$$

so that the confidence limits become

$$X_L = x_m \frac{(1 - g_{12}) \pm \sqrt{(1 - g_{12})^2 - (1 - g_{11})(1 - g_{22})}}{1 - g_{22}}.$$

Note that these limits are not, in general, symmetrically placed about the estimated value $-b_1/2b_2$, since allowance is made for the skewness of the distribution of the ratio. Note also that the limits will include infinite values and will therefore not be of practical use, unless b_2 is significant at the α-level. In terms of the g-values, this means that g_{22} must not exceed 1.

When the regression model is a polynomial in two or more variables, investigation of maxima and other aspects of shape becomes more complex. [A discussion of this problem appears in EXPERIMENTAL DESIGN, article on RESPONSE SURFACES.]

Nonlinear models

In a nonlinear model the regression function is nonlinear in one or more of the parameters. Familiar examples are the exponential regression,

$$\eta = \beta_0 + \beta_1 e^{\beta_2 x_1},$$

and the logistic curve,

$$\eta = \frac{\beta_1}{1 + e^{-\beta_2 x_1}},$$

β_2 being the nonlinear parameter in each example. Such nonlinear models usually originate from theoretical considerations but nevertheless are often useful for applying to observational data.

Sometimes the model can be reduced to a linear form by a transformation of variables (and a corresponding change in the specification of the errors). The exponential regression with $\beta_0 = 0$ may thus be reduced by taking logarithms of the dependent variable and assuming that the errors of the logarithms, rather than the errors of the original values, are distributed about zero. If $Z = \log_e Y$ and $E(Z) = \zeta$, the exponential model with $\beta_0 = 0$ reduces to $\zeta = \log_e \beta_1 + \beta_2 x_1$, a linear model.

The general models shown above cannot be reduced to linear models in this way. For nonlinear models generally, the nonlinear parameters must be estimated by successive approximation. The following method is straightforward and of general applicability.

Suppose the model is

$$\eta = \beta_0 + \beta_1 f(x_1, \beta_2)$$

where $f(x_1, \beta_2)$ is a nonlinear function of β_2, and the estimated regression, determined by least squares, is

$$\hat{\eta} = b_0 + b_1 f(x_1, c).$$

If c_0 is a trial value of c (estimated by graphical or other means), the values of $f(x_1, c)$ and its first derivative with respect to c (denoted, for brevity, by f and f', respectively) are calculated for each value of x_1, with $c = c_0$. The regression of Y on f and f' is then determined in the usual way, yielding the regression equation

$$\hat{\eta} = b_0 + b_1 f + b_2 f'.$$

A first adjustment to c_0 is given by b_2/b_1, giving the new approximation

$$c_1 = c_0 + b_2/b_1.$$

The process of recalculating the regression on f and f' and determining successive approximations to c can be continued until the required accuracy is attained (for further details see Williams 1959).

The method is an adaptation of the *delta method*, which utilizes the principle of *propagation of error*. If a small change, $\delta\beta_2$, is made in a parameter β_2, the corresponding change in a function $f(\beta_2)$ is, to a first approximation, $f'(\beta_2)\delta\beta_2$. The use of this method allows the replacement of the nonlinear equations for the parameters by approximate linear equations for the adjustments. For a regression relation of the form

$$\eta = \beta_0 + \beta_1 e^{\beta_2 x_1},$$

Stevens (1951) provides a table to facilitate the calculation of the nonlinear parameter by a method similar to that described above, and Pimentel Gomes (1953) provides tables from which, with a few preliminary calculations, the least squares estimate of the nonlinear parameter can be read off easily.

Considerations in regression model choice

In deciding which of several alternative models shall be used to interpret a relationship, a number of factors must be taken into account. Other things being equal, the model which represents the predictands most closely (where "closeness" is measured in terms of some criterion such as minimum mean square error among linear estimators) will be used. However, questions of convenience and simplicity should also be considered. A regression equation that includes a large number of regression variables is not convenient to use, and an equation with fewer variables may be only slightly less accurate. In deciding between alternative models, the residual variance is therefore not the only factor to take into account.

In polynomial regression particularly, the assumed polynomial form of the model is usually chosen for convenience, so that a polynomial of given degree is not assumed to be the true regression model. Because of this, the testing of individual polynomial coefficients is little more than a guide in deciding on the degree of polynomial to be fitted. Of far more importance is a decision on what degree of variability about the regression model is acceptable, and this decision will be based on practical rather than merely statistical considerations.

Besides the question of including additional variables in a regression, for which significance tests have already been described, there is also the question of alternative regression variables. The alternatives for a regression relation could be different variables or different functions of the same variable—for instance, x_1 and $\log x_1$.

For comparison of two or more individual variables as predictors, a test devised by Hotelling (1940) is suitable, although not strictly accurate. It is based on the correlations between Y and the different predictors and of the predictors among themselves. For comparing two regression variables x_1 and x_2, the test statistic is

$$F = \frac{(u_1'/\sqrt{t_{11}'} - u_2'/\sqrt{t_{22}'})^2}{2s^2(1 - t_{12}'/\sqrt{t_{11}'t_{22}'})},$$

which is distributed approximately as F with 1 and $n - 3$ degrees of freedom. Here, as before,

$$u_i' = \sum Y(x_i - \bar{x}_i),$$
$$t_{hi}' = \sum (x_h - \bar{x}_h)(x_i - \bar{x}_i),$$

and s^2 is the mean square of residuals from the regression of Y on x_1 and x_2, with $n - 3$ degrees of freedom.

E. J. WILLIAMS

BIBLIOGRAPHY

ANDERSON, T. W. 1957 Maximum Likelihood Estimates for a Multivariate Normal Distribution When Some Observations Are Missing. *Journal of the American Statistical Association* 52:200–203.

ANDERSON, T. W. 1962 The Choice of the Degree of a Polynomial Regression as a Multiple Decision Problem. *Annals of Mathematical Statistics* 33:255–265.

BOX, GEORGE E. P.; and ANDERSEN, S. L. 1955 Permutation Theory in the Derivation of Robust Criteria and the Study of Departures From Assumption. *Journal of the Royal Statistical Society* Series B 17:1–26.

BOX, GEORGE E. P.; and WILSON, K. B. 1951 On the Experimental Attainment of Optimum Conditions. *Journal of the Royal Statistical Society* Series B 13:1–45. → Contains seven pages of discussion.

COCHRAN, WILLIAM G.; and CARROLL, SARAH P. 1953 A Sampling Investigation of the Efficiency of Weighting Inversely as the Estimated Variance. *Biometrics* 9:447–459.

COCHRAN, WILLIAM G.; and COX, GERTRUDE M. (1950) 1957 *Experimental Designs.* 2d ed. New York: Wiley.

EZEKIEL, MORDECAI; and FOX, KARL A. (1930) 1961 *Methods of Correlation and Regression Analysis: Linear and Curvilinear.* New York: Wiley.

FISHER, R. A.; and YATES, FRANK (1938) 1963 *Statistical Tables for Biological, Agricultural and Medical Research.* 6th ed., rev. & enl. Edinburgh: Oliver & Boyd; New York: Hafner.

GAUSS, CARL F. 1855 *Méthode des moindres carrés: Mémoires sur la combinaison des observations.* Translated by J. Bertrand. Paris: Mallet-Bachelier. → An authorized translation of Carl Friedrich Gauss's works on least squares.

GEARY, R. C. 1963 Some Remarks About Relations Between Stochastic Variables: A Discussion Document. Institut International de Statistique, *Revue* 31:163–181.

HOTELLING, HAROLD 1940 The Selection of Variates for Use in Prediction With Some Comments on the General Problem of Nuisance Parameters. *Annals of Mathematical Statistics* 11:271–283.

HOTELLING, HAROLD 1941 Experimental Determination of the Maximum of a Function. *Annals of Mathematical Statistics* 12:20–45.

KENDALL, MAURICE G.; and STUART, ALAN (1943–1946) 1958–1966 *The Advanced Theory of Statistics.* New ed. 3 vols. New York: Hafner; London: Griffin. → Volume 1: *Distribution Theory,* 1958. Volume 2: *Inference and Relationship,* 1961. Volume 3: *Design and Analysis, and Time-series,* 1966. Kendall was the sole author of the 1943–1946 edition.

KRUSKAL, WILLIAM H. 1961 The Coordinate-free Approach to Gauss–Markov Estimation and Its Application to Missing and Extra Observations. Volume 1, pages 435–451 in Symposium on Mathematical Statistics and Probability, Fourth, Berkeley, *Proceedings.* Berkeley and Los Angeles: Univ. of California Press.

LEGENDRE, ADRIEN M. (1805) 1959 On a Method of Least Squares. Volume 2, pages 576–579 in David Eugene Smith, *A Source Book in Mathematics.* New York: Dover. → First published as "Sur la méthode des moindres carrés" in Legendre's *Nouvelles méthodes pour la détermination des orbites des comètes.*

MADANSKY, ALBERT 1959 The Fitting of Straight Lines When Both Variables Are Subject to Error. *Journal of the American Statistical Association* 54:173–205.

PIMENTEL GOMES, FREDERICO 1953 The Use of Mitscherlich's Regression Law in the Analysis of Experiments With Fertilizers. *Biometrics* 9:498–516.

PLACKETT, R. L. 1960 *Principles of Regression Analysis.* Oxford: Clarendon.

RAO, C. RADHAKRISHNA 1952 *Advanced Statistical Methods in Biometric Research.* New York: Wiley.

RAO, C. RADHAKRISHNA 1965 *Linear Statistical Inference and Its Applications.* New York: Wiley.

STEVENS, W. L. 1951 Asymptotic Regression. *Biometrics* 7:247–267.

STRODTBECK, FRED L.; McDONALD, MARGARET R.; and ROSEN, BERNARD C. 1957 Evaluation of Occupations: A Reflection of Jewish and Italian Mobility Differences. *American Sociological Review* 22:546–553.

WILLIAMS, EVAN J. 1952 Use of Scores for the Analysis of Association in Contingency Tables. *Biometrika* 39:274–289.

WILLIAMS, EVAN J. 1959 *Regression Analysis.* New York: Wiley.

WOLD, HERMAN 1953 *Demand Analysis: A Study in Econometrics.* New York: Wiley.

YATES, FRANK 1933 The Analysis of Replicated Experiments When the Field Results Are Incomplete. *Empire Journal of Experimental Agriculture* 1:129–142.

YATES, FRANK 1948 The Analysis of Contingency Tables With Groupings Based on Quantitative Characters. *Biometrika* 35:176–181.

II
ANALYSIS OF VARIANCE

Analysis of variance is a body of statistical procedures for analyzing observational data that may be regarded as satisfying certain broad assumptions about the structure of means, variances, and distributional form. The basic notion of analysis of variance (or ANOVA) is that of comparing and dissecting empirical dispersions in the data in order to understand underlying central values and dispersions.

This basic notion was early noted and developed in special cases by Lexis and von Bortkiewicz [*see* LEXIS; BORTKIEWICZ]. Not until the pioneering work of R. A. Fisher (1925; 1935), however, were the fundamental principles of analysis of variance and its most important techniques worked out and made public [*see* FISHER, R. A.]. Early applications of analysis of variance were primarily in agriculture and biology. The methodology is now used in every field of science and is one of the most important statistical areas for the social sciences. (For further historical material see Sampford 1964.)

Much basic material of analysis of variance may usefully be regarded as a special development of regression analysis [*see* LINEAR HYPOTHESES, article on REGRESSION]. Analysis of variance extends, however, to techniques and models that do not strictly fall under the regression rubric.

In analysis of variance all the standard general theories of statistics, such as point and set estimation and hypothesis testing, come into play. In the past there has sometimes been overemphasis on testing hypotheses.

One-factor analysis of variance

A simple experiment will now be described as an example of ANOVA. Suppose that the publisher of a junior-high-school textbook is considering styles of printing type for a new edition; there are three styles to investigate, and the same chapter of the book has been prepared in each of the three styles for the experiment. Junior-high-school pupils are to be chosen at random from an appropriate large population of such pupils, randomly assigned to read the chapter in one of the three styles, and then given a test that results in a reading-comprehension score for each pupil.

Suppose that the experiment is set up so that P_1, P_2, and P_3 pupils (where $P_1 = P_2 = P_3 = P$) read the chapter in styles 1, 2, and 3, respectively, and that X_{ps} denotes the comprehension score of the pth pupil reading style s. (Here $s = 1, 2, 3$; in general, $s = 1, 2, \cdots, S$.) There is a hypothetical mean, or expected, value of X_{ps}, μ_s, but X_{ps} differs from μ_s because, first, the pupils are chosen randomly from a population of pupils with different inherent means and, second, a given pupil, on hypothetical repetitions of the experiment, would not always obtain the same score. This is expressed by writing

$$(1) \qquad X_{ps} = \mu_s + e_{ps}.$$

Then the assumptions are made that the e_{ps} are all independent, that they are all normally distributed, and that they have a common (usually unknown) variance, σ^2. By definition, the expectation of e_{ps} is zero.

Because differences among the pupils reading a particular style of type are thrown into the random "error" terms (e_{ps}), μ_s, the expectation of X_{ps}, does not depend on p. It is convenient to rewrite (1) as

$$X_{ps} = \mu + (\mu_s - \mu) + e_{ps},$$

where $\mu = (\sum \mu_s)/S$, the average of the μ_s. For simplicity, set $\alpha_s = \mu_s - \mu$ (so that $\alpha_1 + \alpha_2 + \cdots + \alpha_s = 0$) and write the structural equation finally in the conventional form

$$(2) \qquad X_{ps} = \mu + \alpha_s + e_{ps}.$$

Here α_s is the differential effect on comprehension scores of style s for the relevant population of pupils. The unknowns are μ, the α_s, and σ^2.

Note that this structure falls under the linear regression hypothesis with coefficients 0 or 1. For example, if $E(X_{ps})$ represents the expected value of X_{ps},

$$E(X_{p1}) = 1 \cdot \mu + 1 \cdot \alpha_1 + 0 \cdot \alpha_2 + 0 \cdot \alpha_3 + \cdots + 0 \cdot \alpha_s,$$
$$E(X_{p2}) = 1 \cdot \mu + 0 \cdot \alpha_1 + 1 \cdot \alpha_2 + 0 \cdot \alpha_3 + \cdots + 0 \cdot \alpha_s.$$

Consider how this illustrative experiment might be conducted. After defining the population to which he wishes to generalize his findings, the experimenter would use a table of random numbers to choose pupils to read the chapter printed in the different styles. (Actually, he would probably have to sample intact school classes rather than individual pupils, so the observations analyzed might be class means instead of individual scores, but this does not change the analysis in principle.) After the three groups have read the same chapter under conditions that differ only in style of type, a single test covering comprehension of the material in the chapter would be administered to all pupils.

The experimenter's attention would be focused on differences between average scores of the three style groups (that is, $\bar{X}_{\cdot 1}$ versus $\bar{X}_{\cdot 2}$, $\bar{X}_{\cdot 2}$ versus $\bar{X}_{\cdot 3}$, and $\bar{X}_{\cdot 1}$ versus $\bar{X}_{\cdot 3}$) relative to the variability of the test scores within these groups. He estimates the μ_s via the $\bar{X}_{\cdot s}$, and he attempts to determine which of the three averages, if any, differ with statistical significance from the others. Eventually he hopes to help the publisher decide which style of type to use for his new edition.

ANOVA of random numbers—an example. An imaginary experiment of the kind outlined above will be analyzed here to illustrate how ANOVA is applied. Suppose that the three P_s are each 20, that in fact the μ_s are all exactly equal to 0, and that $\sigma^2 = 1$ (setting $\mu_s = 0$ is just a convenience corresponding to a conventional origin for the comprehension-score scale).

Sixty random normal deviates, with mean 0 and variance 1, were chosen by use of an appropriate table (RAND Corporation 1955). They are listed in Table 1, where the second column from the left should be disregarded for the moment—it will be used later, in a modified example. From the "data" of Table 1 the usual estimates of the μ_s are just the column averages, $\bar{X}_{\cdot 1} = -0.09$, $\bar{X}_{\cdot 2} = 0.10$, and $\bar{X}_{\cdot 3} = 0.08$. The estimate of μ is the over-all mean, $\bar{X}_{\cdot\cdot} = 0.03$, and the estimates of the α_s are $-0.09 - 0.03 = -0.12$, $0.10 - 0.03 = 0.07$, and $0.08 - 0.03 = 0.05$. Note that these add to zero,

Table 1 — Data for hypothetical experiment; 60 random normal deviates

X_{p1}	$X_{p1} + 1$*	X_{p2}	X_{p3}
0.477	1.477	−0.987	1.158
−0.017	0.983	2.313	0.879
0.508	1.508	0.016	0.068
−0.512	0.488	0.483	1.116
−0.188	0.812	0.157	0.272
−1.073	−0.073	1.107	−0.396
−0.412	0.588	−0.023	−0.983
1.201	2.201	0.898	−0.267
−0.676	0.324	−1.404	0.327
−1.012	−0.012	−0.080	0.929
0.997	1.997	−1.258	−0.603
−0.127	0.873	−0.017	0.493
1.178	2.178	1.607	−1.243
−1.507	−0.507	0.005	−0.145
1.010	2.010	0.163	1.334
−0.528	0.472	−0.771	−0.906
−0.139	0.861	0.485	−1.633
0.621	1.621	0.147	0.424
−2.078	−1.078	−1.764	−0.433
0.485	1.485	0.986	1.245
Mean −0.09	0.91	0.10	0.08
Variance 0.83	0.83	1.03	0.78

* This column was obtained by adding 1 to each deviate of the first column.

as required. In ANOVA, for this case, two quantities are compared. The first is the dispersion of the three μ_s estimates—that is, the sum of the $(\bar{X}_{\cdot s} - \bar{X}_{\cdot\cdot})^2$, conveniently multiplied by 20, the common sample size. This is called the between-styles dispersion or sum of squares. Here it is 0.4466. (These calculations, as well as those below, are made with the raw data of Table 1, not with the rounded means appearing there.) The second quantity is the within-sample dispersion, the sum of the three quantities $\sum_p (X_{ps} - \bar{X}_{\cdot s})^2$. This is called the within-style dispersion or sum of squares. Here it is 50.1253.

This comparison corresponds to the decomposition

$$X_{ps} - \bar{X}_{\cdot\cdot} = (\bar{X}_{\cdot s} - \bar{X}_{\cdot\cdot}) + (X_{ps} - \bar{X}_{\cdot s})$$

and to the sum-of-squares identity

$$\sum_p \sum_s (X_{ps} - \bar{X}_{\cdot\cdot})^2$$
$$= \sum_p \sum_s (\bar{X}_{\cdot s} - \bar{X}_{\cdot\cdot})^2 + \sum_p \sum_s (X_{ps} - \bar{X}_{\cdot s})^2$$
$$= 20 \sum_s (\bar{X}_{\cdot s} - \bar{X}_{\cdot\cdot})^2 + \sum_p \sum_s (X_{ps} - \bar{X}_{\cdot s})^2,$$

which shows how the factor of 20 arises. Such identities in sums of squares are basic in most elementary expositions of ANOVA.

The fundamental notion is that the within-style dispersion, divided by its so-called *degrees of freedom* (here, degrees of freedom for error), unbiasedly estimates σ^2. Here the degrees of freedom for error are 57 (equals 60 [for the total number of

Table 2 — Analysis-of-variance table for one-factor experiment

(a) ANOVA of 60 random normal deviates

Source of variation	df	SS	MS	F	Tabled $F_{.05;2,57}$
Between styles	$3 - 1 = 2$	0.4466	0.2233	0.25	3.16
Within styles	$60 - 3 = 57$	50.1253	0.8794*		
Total	$60 - 1 = 59$	50.5719			

* Actually, σ^2 here is known to be 1.

(b) ANOVA of general one-factor experiment with S treatments

Source of variation	df	MS	EMS
Between treatments	$S - 1$	$\sum_{s=1}^{S} P_s (\overline{X}_{\cdot s} - \overline{X}_{\cdot \cdot})^2 / (S - 1)$	$\sigma^2 + \sum_{s=1}^{S} P_s \alpha_s^2 / (S - 1)$
Within treatments	$P_+ - S$*	$\sum_{s=1}^{S} \sum_{p=1}^{P_s} (X_{ps} - \overline{X}_{\cdot s})^2 / (P_+ - S)$*	σ^2
Total	$P_+ - 1$*	$\sum_{s=1}^{S} \sum_{p=1}^{P_s} (X_{ps} - \overline{X}_{\cdot \cdot})^2 / (P_+ - 1)$*	

* Here P_+ is used for $\sum_{s=1}^{S} P_s$ for convenience.

observations] minus 3 [for the number of μ_s estimated]). On the other hand, the between-styles dispersion, divided by its degrees of freedom (here 2), estimates σ^2 unbiasedly if and only if the μ_s are equal; otherwise the estimate will tend to be larger than σ^2. Furthermore, the between-styles and within-style dispersions are statistically independent. Hence, it is natural to look at the ratio of the two dispersions, each divided by its degrees of freedom. The result is the F-statistic, here

$$\frac{0.4466/2}{50.1253/57} = 0.25.$$

In repeated trials with the null hypothesis (that there are no differences between the μ_s) true, the F-statistic follows an F-distribution with (in this case) 2 and 57 degrees of freedom [see DISTRIBUTIONS, STATISTICAL, article on SPECIAL CONTINUOUS DISTRIBUTIONS]. Level of significance is denoted by "α" (which should not be confused with the totally unrelated "α_s," denoting style effect; the notational similarity stems from the juxtaposition of two terminological traditions and the finite number of Greek letters). The F-test at level of significance α of the null hypothesis that the styles are equivalent rejects that hypothesis when the F-statistic is too large, greater than its 100α percentage point, here $F_{\alpha;2,57}$. If $\alpha = 0.05$, which is a conventional level, then $F_{.05;2,57} = 3.16$, so 0.25 is much smaller than the cutoff point, and the null hypothesis is, of course, not rejected. This is consonant with the fact that the null hypothesis *is* true in the imaginary experiment under discussion.

Table 2 summarizes the above discussion in both algebraic and numerical form. The algebraic form is for S styles with P_s students at the sth style.

To reiterate, in an analysis of variance each kind of effect (treatment, factor, and others to be discussed later) is represented by two basic numbers. The first is the so-called *sum of squares* (SS), corresponding to the effect; it is random, depending upon the particular sample, and has two fundamental properties: (a) If the effect in question is wholly *absent*, its sum of squares behaves probabilistically like a sum of squared independent normal deviates with zero means. (b) If the effect in question is *present*, its sum of squares tends to be relatively large; in fact, it behaves probabilistically like a sum of squared independent normal deviates with *not* all means zero.

The second number is the so-called *degrees of freedom* (df). This quantity is not random but depends only on the structure of the experimental design. The df is the number of independent normal deviates in the description of sums of squares just given.

A third (derived) number is the so-called *mean square* (MS), which is computed by dividing the sum of squares by the degrees of freedom. When an effect is wholly absent, its mean square is an unbiased estimator of underlying variance, σ^2. When an effect is present, its mean square has an expectation greater than σ^2.

In the example considered here, each observation is regarded as the sum of (a) a grand mean, (b) a printing-style effect, and (c) error. It is conventional in analysis-of-variance tables not to have a line corresponding to the grand mean and to work with sample residuals centered on it; that convention is followed here. Printing-style effect and error differ in that the latter is assumed to be wholly random, whereas the former is not random but may be zero. The mean square for error estimates underlying variance unbiasedly and is a yardstick for judging other mean squares.

In the standard simple designs to which ANOVA is applied, it is customary to define effects so that the several sums of squares are statistically independent, from which additivity both of sums of squares and of degrees of freedom follows [see PROBABILITY, article on FORMAL PROBABILITY]. In the example, $SS_{between} + SS_{within} = SS_{total}$, and $df_b + df_w = df_{total}$. (Here, and often below, the subscripts "b" and "w" are used to stand for "between" and "within," respectively.) This additivity is computationally useful, either to save arithmetic or to verify it.

Analysis-of-variance tables, which, like Table 2, are convenient and compact summaries of both the relevant formulas and the computed numbers, usually also show *expected mean squares* (EMS), the average value of the mean squares over a (conceptually) infinite number of experiments. In fixed-effects models (such as the model of the example) these are always of the form σ^2 (the underlying variance) plus an additional term that is zero when the relevant effect is absent and positive when it is present. The additional term is a convenient measure of the magnitude of the effect.

Expected mean squares, such as those given by the two formulas in Table 2, provide a necessary condition for the F-statistic to have an F-distribution when the null hypothesis is true. (Other conditions, such as independence, must also be met.) Note that if the population mean of the sth treatment, μ_s, is the same for all treatments (that is, if $\alpha_s = 0$ for all s) then the expected value of MS_b will be σ^2, the same as the expected value of MS_w. If the null hypothesis is true, the average value of the F from a huge number of identical experiments employing fresh, randomly sampled experimental units will be $(P_+ - S)/(P_+ - S - 2)$, which is very nearly 1 when, as is usually the case, the total number of experimental units, P_+, is large compared with S. Expected mean squares become particularly important in analyses based on models of a nature somewhat different from the one illustrated in Tables 1 and 2, because in those cases it is not always easy to determine which mean square should be used as the denominator of F (see the discussion of some of these other models, below).

The simplest t-tests. It is worth digressing to show how the familiar one-sample and two-sample t-tests (or Student tests) fall under the analysis-of-variance rubric, at least for the symmetrical two-tail versions of these tests.

Single-sample t-test. In the single-sample t-test context, one considers a random sample, X_1, X_2, $\cdots$, X_P, of independent normal observations with the same unknown mean, μ, and the same unknown variance, σ^2. Another way of expressing this is to write

$$X_p = \mu + e_p, \qquad p = 1, \cdots, P,$$

where the e_p are independent normal random variables, with mean 0 and common variance σ^2. The usual estimator of μ is $\bar{X}.$, the average of the X_p, and this suggests the decomposition into average and deviation from average,

$$X_p = \bar{X}. + (X_p - \bar{X}.),$$

from which one obtains the sum-of-squares identity

$$\sum X_p^2 = \sum(X_p - \bar{X}.)^2 + \sum \bar{X}^2 + 2\bar{X}.\sum(X_p - \bar{X}.)$$
$$= \sum(X_p - \bar{X}.)^2 + P\bar{X}^2$$

(since $\sum(X_p - \bar{X}.) = 0$), a familiar algebraic relationship. Since the usual unbiased estimator of σ^2 is $s^2 = \sum(X_p - \bar{X}.)^2/(P-1)$, the sum-of-squares identity may be written

$$\sum X_p^2 = (P-1)s^2 + P\bar{X}^2.$$

Ordinarily the analysis-of-variance table is not written out for this simple case; it is, however, the one shown in Table 3. In Table 3 the total row is the actual total including all observations; it is of the essence that the row for mean is separated out.

Table 3

Effect	df	SS	EMS
Mean	1	$P\bar{X}^2$	$\sigma^2 + P\mu^2$
Error	$P-1$	$\sum(X_p - \bar{X}.)^2$	σ^2
Total	P	$\sum X_p^2$	

The F-statistic for testing that $\mu = 0$ is the ratio of the mean squares for mean and error,

$$\frac{P\bar{X}^2}{\sum(X_p - \bar{X}.)^2/(P-1)} = \frac{P\bar{X}^2}{s^2},$$

which, under the null hypothesis, has an F-distribution with 1 and $P-1$ degrees of freedom. Notice that the above F-statistic is the square of

$$\frac{\bar{X}.}{s/\sqrt{P}},$$

which is the ordinary t-statistic (or Student statistic) for testing $\mu = 0$. If a symmetrical two-tail test is wanted, it is immaterial whether one deals with the t-statistic or its square. On the other hand, for a one-tail test the t-statistic would be referred to the t-distribution with $P - 1$ degrees of freedom [see DISTRIBUTIONS, STATISTICAL, *article on* SPECIAL CONTINUOUS DISTRIBUTIONS].

It is important to note that a confidence interval for μ may readily be established from the above discussion [see ESTIMATION, *article on* CONFIDENCE INTERVALS AND REGIONS]. The symmetrical form is

$$\bar{X}. - \sqrt{F_{\alpha;1,P-1}}\, s/\sqrt{P} \leqslant \mu \leqslant \bar{X}. + \sqrt{F_{\alpha;1,P-1}}\, s/\sqrt{P}.$$

Alternatively, $F_{\alpha;1,P-1}$ can be replaced by the upper $100(\alpha/2)$ per cent point for the t-distribution with $P - 1$ degrees of freedom, $t_{\alpha/2;P-1}$.

Suppose, for example, that from a normally distributed population there has been drawn a random sample of 25 observations for which the sample mean, $\bar{x}.$, is 34.213 and the sample variance, s^2, is 49.000. What is the population mean, μ? The usual point estimate from this sample is 34.213. How different from μ is this value likely to be? For $\alpha = .05$, a 95 per cent confidence interval is constructed by looking up $t_{.025;24} = 2.064$ in a table (for instance, McNemar [1949] 1962, p. 430) and substituting in the formula

$$\text{Confidence}\left[34.213 - 2.064\left(\frac{\sqrt{49.000}}{\sqrt{25}}\right) \right.$$
$$\left. \leqslant \mu \leqslant 34.213 + 2.064\left(\frac{\sqrt{49.000}}{\sqrt{25}}\right) \right] = 0.95.$$

Thus,

$$\text{Confidence}\,[31.32 \leqslant \mu \leqslant 37.10] = 0.95.$$

This result means that if an infinite number of samples, each of size $P = 25$, were drawn randomly from a normally distributed population and a confidence interval for each sample were set up in the above way, only 5 per cent of the intervals would fail to cover the mean of the population (which is a certain fixed value).

Similarly, from this one sample the unbiased point estimate of σ^2 is the value of s^2, 49.000. Brownlee ([1960] 1965, page 282) shows how to find confidence intervals for σ^2 [see also VARIANCES, STATISTICAL STUDY OF].

Is it "reasonable" to suppose that the mean of the population from which this sample was randomly chosen is as large as, say, 40? No, because that number does not lie within even the 99 per cent confidence interval. Therefore it would be

unreasonable to conclude that the sample was drawn from a population with a mean as great as 40. The relevant test of statistical significance is

$$t = \frac{34.213 - 40.000}{7/5} = \frac{-5.787(5)}{7} = -4.134,$$

the absolute magnitude of which lies beyond the 0.9995 percentile point (3.745) in the tabled t-distribution for 24 degrees of freedom. Therefore, the difference is statistically significant beyond the $0.0005 + 0.0005 = 0.001$ level. The null hypothesis being tested was H_0: $\mu = 40$, against the alternative hypothesis H_a: $\mu \neq 40$. Just as the confidence interval indicated that it is unreasonable to suppose the mean to be equal to 40, this test also shows that 40 will lie outside the 99 per cent confidence interval; however, of the two procedures, the confidence interval gives more information than the significance test.

Two-sample t-test.   In the two-sample t-test context, there are two random samples from normal distributions assumed to have the same variance, σ^2, and to have means μ_1 and μ_2. Call the observations in the first sample $X_{11}, \cdots, X_{P_1 1}$ and the observations in the second sample $X_{12}, \cdots, X_{P_2 2}$. The most usual null hypothesis is $\mu_1 = \mu_2$, and for that the t-statistic is

$$\frac{\bar{X}._1 - \bar{X}._2}{s\sqrt{(1/P_1) + (1/P_2)}},$$

where the P's are the sample sizes, the $\bar{X}$'s are the sample means, and s^2 is the estimate of σ^2 based on the pooled within-sample sum of squares,

$$s^2 = \frac{1}{P_1 + P_2 - 2}\left\{ \sum_p (X_{p1} - \bar{X}._1)^2 + \sum_p (X_{p2} - \bar{X}._2)^2 \right\}.$$

Here $P_1 + P_2 - 2$ is the number of degrees of freedom for error, the total number of observations less the number of estimated means ($\bar{X}._1$ and $\bar{X}._2$ estimate μ_1 and μ_2, respectively). Under the null hypothesis, the t-statistic has the t-distribution with $P_1 + P_2 - 2$ degrees of freedom.

The basic decomposition is

$$X_{ps} - \bar{X}.. = (\bar{X}._s - \bar{X}..) + (X_{ps} - \bar{X}._s),$$

leading to the sum-of-squares decomposition

$$\sum_p \sum_s (X_{ps} - \bar{X}..)^2$$
$$= \sum_s P_s (\bar{X}._s - \bar{X}..)^2 + \sum_p \sum_s (X_{ps} - \bar{X}._s)^2.$$

Since s has only the values 1 and 2,

$$\bar{X}.. = \frac{P_1}{P_1 + P_2}\bar{X}._1 + \frac{P_2}{P_1 + P_2}\bar{X}._2,$$

Table 4

Effect	df	SS	EMS*
Style	1	$\sum P_s(\bar{X}._s - \bar{X}..)^2 = \dfrac{(\bar{X}._1 - \bar{X}._2)^2}{(1/P_1)+(1/P_2)}$	$\sigma^2 + \dfrac{(\mu_1 - \mu_2)^2}{(1/P_1)+(1/P_2)}$
Error	$P_1 + P_2 - 2$	$(P_1 + P_2 - 2)s^2$	σ^2
Total	$P_1 + P_2 - 1$	$\sum\sum (X_{ps} - \bar{X}..)^2$	

* Note that the expected mean square for style is σ^2 plus what is obtained by formal substitution for the random variables ($\bar{X}._1$, $\bar{X}._2$) in the sum of squares of their respective expectations (divided by df, which here is 1). This relationship is a perfectly general one in the analysis-of-variance model now under discussion, but it must be changed for other models that will be mentioned later.

and therefore

$$\sum_s P_s(\bar{X}._s - \bar{X}..)^2 = \frac{P_1 P_2}{P_1 + P_2}(\bar{X}._1 - \bar{X}._2)^2$$
$$= \frac{(\bar{X}._1 - \bar{X}._2)^2}{(P_1 + P_2)/P_1 P_2}$$
$$= \frac{(\bar{X}._1 - \bar{X}._2)^2}{(1/P_1) + (1/P_2)}.$$

The analysis-of-variance table may be written as in Table 4. The F-statistic for the null hypothesis that $\mu_1 = \mu_2$ is

$$\frac{(\bar{X}._1 - \bar{X}._2)^2/(P_1^{-1} + P_2^{-1})}{s^2} = \frac{(\bar{X}._1 - \bar{X}._2)^2}{s^2[(1/P_1) + (1/P_2)]},$$

and this is exactly the square of the t-statistic for the two-sample problem.

Note that the two-sample problem as it is analyzed here is only a special case (with $S = 2$) of the S-sample problem presented earlier.

The numerical example continued. Returning to the numerical example of Table 1, add 1 to every number in the leftmost column to obtain the second column and consider the numbers in the second column as the observations for style 1. Now $\mu_1 = 1$ and $\mu_2 = \mu_3 = 0$. What happens to the analysis of variance and the F-test? Table 5 shows the result; the F-statistic is 5.41, which is of high statistical significance since $F_{.01:2.57} = 5.07$. Thus, one would correctly reject the null hypothesis of equality among the three μ_s.

The actual value of μ is $\frac{1}{3} \cong 0.33$, and that of α_1 is $\frac{2}{3} \cong 0.67$. The estimate of μ is 0.36, and that of α_1 is 0.55.

With three styles, one can consider many contrasts—for example, style 1 versus style 2, style 1

versus style 3, style 2 versus style 3, $\frac{1}{2}$(style 1 + style 2) versus style 3. There are special methods for dealing with several contrasts simultaneously [see LINEAR HYPOTHESES, article on MULTIPLE COMPARISONS].

ANOVA with more than one factor

In the illustrative example being considered here, suppose that the publisher had been interested not only in style of type but also in a second factor, such as the tint of the printing ink (t). If he had three styles and four tints, a complete "crossed" *factorial design* would require $3 \times 4 = 12$ experimental conditions ($s_1t_1, s_1t_2, \cdots, s_3t_4$). From $12P$ experimental units he would assign P units at random to each of the 12 conditions, conduct his experiment, and obtain outcome measures to analyze. The total variation between the $12P$ outcome measures can be partitioned into four sources rather than into the two found with one factor. The sources of variation are the following: between styles, between tints, *interaction* of styles with tints, and within style–tint combinations (error).

The usual model for the two-factor crossed design is

$$X_{pst} = \mu + \alpha_s + \beta_t + \gamma_{st} + e_{pst},$$

where $\sum_s \alpha_s = \sum_t \beta_t = \sum_s \gamma_{st} = \sum_t \gamma_{st} = 0$, and the e_{pst} are independent normally distributed random variables with mean 0 and equal variance σ^2 for each st combination. The analysis-of-variance procedure for this design appears in Table 6. The α_s and β_t represent *main effects* of the styles and tints; the γ_{st} denote (two-factor) *interactions*.

Table 5 — One-factor ANOVA of 60 transformed random normal deviates

Source of variation	df	SS	MS	EMS	F
Between styles	2	8.9246	4.4623	$\sigma^2 + 20\sum_{s=1}^{3}\alpha_s^2/2$	5.41
Within styles	57	50.1253	0.8794	σ^2	
Total	59	59.0499			

Table 6 — ANOVA of a complete, crossed-classification, two-factor factorial design with P experimental units for each factor-level combination

Source of variation	df	SS	EMS
Between styles	$S-1$	$PT\sum_{s=1}^{S}(\bar{X}_{\cdot s\cdot}-\bar{X}...)^2$	$\sigma^2+PT\sum_s\alpha_s^2/(S-1)$
Between tints	$T-1$	$PS\sum_{t=1}^{T}(\bar{X}_{\cdot\cdot t}-\bar{X}...)^2$	$\sigma^2+PS\sum_t\beta_t^2/(T-1)$
Styles × tints (interaction)	$(S-1)(T-1)$	$P\sum_{s=1}^{S}\sum_{t=1}^{T}(\bar{X}_{\cdot st}-\bar{X}_{\cdot s\cdot}-\bar{X}_{\cdot\cdot t}+\bar{X}...)^2$	$\sigma^2+P\sum_s\sum_t\gamma_{st}^2/(S-1)(T-1)$
Within style–tint combinations	$ST(P-1)$	$\sum_{p=1}^{P}\sum_{s=1}^{S}\sum_{t=1}^{T}(X_{pst}-\bar{X}_{\cdot st})^2$	σ^2
Total	$PST-1$	$\sum_{p=1}^{P}\sum_{s=1}^{S}\sum_{t=1}^{T}(X_{pst}-\bar{X}...)^2$	

Interaction. The two-factor design introduces interaction, a concept not relevant in one-factor experiments. It might be found, for example, that, although in general s_1 is an ineffective style and t_3 is an ineffective tint, the particular combination s_1t_3 produces rather good results. It is then said that style interacts with tint to produce nonadditive effects; if the effects were additive, an ineffective style combined with an ineffective tint would produce an ineffective combination.

Interaction is zero if $E(X_{pst})=\mu+\alpha_s+\beta_t$ for every st, because under this condition the population mean of the stth combination is the population grand mean plus the sum of the effects of the sth style and the tth tint. Then the interaction effect, γ_{st}, is zero for every combination. Table 7 contains hypothetical data showing population means, $\bar{\mu}_{st}$, for zero interaction (Lubin 1961 discusses types of interaction). Note that for every cell of Table 7, $\bar{\mu}_{st}-(\bar{\mu}_s.-\mu)-(\bar{\mu}._t-\mu)=\mu=3$. (Here $\bar{\mu}..$ is written as μ for simplicity.) For example, for tint 1 and style $1, 3-(5-3)-(1-3)=3$.

One tests for interaction by computing F $MS_{\text{styles}\times\text{tints}}/MS_{\text{within style–tint}}$, comparing this F with the F's tabled at various significance levels for $(S-1)(T-1)$ and $ST(P-1)$ degrees of freedom.

Table 7 — Zero interaction of two factors (hypothetical population means $\bar{\mu}_{st}$)

Style \ Tint	1	2	3	4	Row means $(\bar{\mu}_s.)$
1	3	4	5	8	5
2	0	1	2	5	2
3	0	1	2	5	2
Column means $(\bar{\mu}._t)$	1	2	3	6	$3=\mu$

If there were but one subject reading with each style–tint combination (that is, if there were no replication), further assumptions would have to be made to permit testing of hypotheses about main effects. In particular, it is commonly then assumed that the style × tint interaction is zero, so that the expected mean square for interaction in Table 6 reduces to the underlying variance, and the $MS_{\text{styles}\times\text{tints}}$ may be used in the denominator of the F's for testing main effects. No test of the assumption of additivity is possible through $MS_{\text{within style–tint}}$, because this quantity cannot be calculated. However, Tukey (1949; see also Winer 1962, pp. 216–220) has provided a one-degree-of-freedom test for interaction, or nonadditivity, of a special kind that can be used for testing the hypothesis of no interaction for these unreplicated experiments of the fixed-effects kind. (See Scheffé 1959, pp. 129–134.)

The factorial design may be extended to three or more factors. With three factors there are four sums of squares for interactions: one for the three-factor interaction (sometimes called a second-order interaction, because a one-factor "interaction" is a main effect) and one each for the three two-factor (that is, first-order) interactions. If the three factors are A, B, and C, their interactions might be represented as $A \times B \times C$, $A \times B$, $A \times C$, and $B \times C$. For example, a style of type that for the experiment as a whole yields excellent comprehension may, when combined with a generally effective size of type and a tint of paper that has over-all facilitative effect, yield rather poor results. One three-factor factorial experiment permits testing of the hypothesis that there is a no second-order interaction and permits the magnitude of such interaction to be estimated, whereas three one-factor experiments or a two-factor experiment and a one-factor experiment do not. Usually, three-factor nonadditivity is difficult to explain substantively.

A large number of more complex designs, most of them more or less incomplete in some respect as compared with factorial designs of the kind discussed above, have been proposed. [See EXPERIMENTAL DESIGN; see also Winer 1962; Fisher 1935.]

The analysis of covariance

Suppose that the publisher in the earlier, style-of-type example had known reading-test scores for his 60 pupils prior to the experiment. He could have used these antecedent scores in the analysis of the comprehension scores to reduce the magnitude of the mean square within styles, which, as the estimate of underlying variance, is the denominator of the computed F. At the same time he would adjust the subsequent style means to account for initial differences between reading-test-score means in the three groups. One way of carrying out this more refined analysis would be to perform an analysis of variance of the differences between final comprehension scores and initial reading scores—say, $X_{ps} - Y_{ps}$. A better prediction of the outcome measure, X_{ps}, might be secured by computing $\alpha + \beta Y_{ps}$, where α and β are constants to be estimated.

By a statistical procedure called the *analysis of covariance* one or more antecedent variables may be used to reduce the magnitude of the sum of squares within styles and also to adjust the observed style means for differences between groups in average initial reading scores. If $\beta \neq 0$, then the adjusted sum of squares within treatments (which provides the denominator of the F-ratio) will be less than the unadjusted SS_w of Table 2, thereby tending to increase the magnitude of F. For each independent antecedent variable one uses, one degree of freedom is lost for SS_w and none for SS_b; the loss of degrees of freedom for SS_w will usually be more than compensated for by the decrease in its magnitude.

A principal statistical condition needed for the usual analysis of covariance is that the regression of outcome scores on antecedent scores is the same for every style, because one computes a single within-style regression coefficient to use in adjusting the within-style sum of squares. Homogeneity of regression can be tested statistically; see Winer (1962, chapter 11). Some procedures to adopt in the case of heterogeneity of regression are given in Brownlee (1960).

The regression model chosen must be appropriate for the data if the use of one or more antecedent variables is to reduce MS_w appreciably.

Usually the regression of outcome measures on antecedent measures is assumed to be linear.

The analysis of covariance can be extended to more than one antecedent variable and to more complex designs. (For further details see Cochran 1957; Smith 1957; Winer 1962; McNemar 1949.)

Models—fixed, finite, random, and mixed

In the example, the publisher's "target population" of styles of print consisted of just those 3 styles that he tried out, so he exhausted the population of styles of interest to him. Suppose that, instead, he had been considering 39 different styles and had drawn *at random* from these 39 the 3 styles he used in the experiment. His intention is to determine from the experiment based on these 3 styles whether it would make any difference which one of the 39 styles he used for the textbook (of course, in practice a larger sample of styles would be drawn). If the styles did seem to differ in effectiveness, he would estimate from his experimental data involving only 3 styles the variance of the 39 population means of the styles. Then he might perform further experiments to find the most effective styles.

Finite-effects models. Thus far in this article the model assumed has been the *fixed-effects* model, in which one uses in the experiment itself all the styles of type to which one wishes to generalize. The 3-out-of-39 experiment mentioned above illustrates a *finite-effects* model, with only a small percentage (8 per cent, in the example given) of the styles drawn at random for the experiment but where one has the intention of testing the null hypothesis

$$H_0: \mu_1 = \mu_2 = \cdots = \mu_{39}$$

against all alternative hypotheses and estimating the "variance," $\sigma_{\text{style}}^2 = \sum_{s=1}^{39} (\mu_s - \mu)^2 / (39 - 1)$ from $MS_b = 20 \sum_{s=1}^{3} (\bar{X}_{\cdot s} - \bar{X}_{\cdot \cdot})^2 / (3 - 1)$ and $MS_w = \sum_{s=1}^{3} \sum_{p=1}^{20} (X_{ps} - \bar{X}_{\cdot s})^2 / [3(20 - 1)]$.

Random-effects models. If the number of "levels" of the factor is very large, so that the number of levels drawn randomly for the experiment is a negligible percentage of the total number, then one has a *random-effects* model, sometimes called a components-of-variance model or Model II. This model would apply if, for example, one drew 20 raters at random from an actual or hypothetical population of 100,000 raters and used those 20 to rate each of 25 subjects who had been chosen at random from a population of half a million. (Strictly speaking, the number of raters and the number of subjects in the respective populations would have to be infinite to produce the random-effects model, but for practical purposes 100,000/20 and 500,000/25 are sufficiently large.) If every rater rated every subject on one trait (say, gregariousness) there would be $20 \times 25 = 500$ ratings, one for each experimental combination— that is, one for each rater–subject combination.

This, then, would be a two-factor design without replication, that is, with just one rating per rater–subject combination. (Even if the experimenter had used available raters and subjects rather than drawing them randomly from any populations, he would probably want to generalize to other raters and subjects "like" them; see Cornfield & Tukey 1956, p. 913.)

The usual model for an experiment thus conceptualized is

$$X_{rs} = \mu + a_r + b_s + e_{rs},$$

where μ is a grand mean, the a's are the (random) rater effects, the b's are (random) subject effects, and the e's combine interaction and inherent measurement error. The $20 + 25 + (20 \times 25)$ random variables are supposed to be independent and assumed to have variances as follows:

$$\text{var } a_r = \sigma_r^2, \quad \text{var } b_s = \sigma_s^2, \quad \text{var } e_{rs} = \sigma_e^2.$$

For F-testing purposes, a, b, and e are supposed to be normally distributed.

The analysis-of-variance table in such a case is similar to those presented earlier, except that the expected mean square column is changed to the one shown in Table 8.

Table 8

Effect	EMS
Rater	$\sigma_e^2 + 25\,\sigma_r^2$
Subject	$\sigma_e^2 + 20\,\sigma_s^2$
Error	σ_e^2

The F-statistic for testing the hypothesis that the main effect of subjects is absent (that $\sigma_s^2 = 0$) is MS_s / MS_{error}, where

$$MS_{\text{error}} = \frac{1}{19 \times 24} \sum \sum (X_{rs} - \bar{X}_r. - \bar{X}._s + \bar{X}..)^2.$$

Under the null hypothesis that $\sigma_s^2 = 0$, the F-statistic has an F-distribution with 24 and 19×24 degrees of freedom. (A similar F-statistic is used for testing $\sigma_r^2 = 0$.) An unbiased estimator of σ_s^2 is

$$\frac{1}{20}(MS_s - MS_{\text{error}})$$

with a similar estimator for σ_r^2. A serious difficulty with these estimators is that they may take negative values; perhaps the best resolution of that

difficulty is to enlarge the model. See Nelder (1954), and for another approach and a bibliography, see Thompson (1962).

Note that here it appears impossible to separate random interaction from inherent variability, both of which contribute to σ_e^2, the variance of the e's; in the random-effects model, however, this does not jeopardize significance tests for main effects.

In more complex Model II situations, the F-tests used are inherently different from their Model I analogues; in particular, sample components of variance are often most reasonably compared, not with the "bottom" estimator of σ^2, but with some other—usually an interaction—component of variance. (See Hays 1963, pp. 356–489; Brownlee [1960] 1965, pp. 309–396, 467–529.)

Mixed models. If all the levels of one factor are used in an experiment while a random sample of the levels of another factor is used, a *mixed model* results. Mixed models present special problems of analysis that have been discussed by Scheffé (1959, pp. 261–290) and by Mood and Graybill (1963).

Other topics in ANOVA

Robustness of ANOVA. Fixed-effects models are better understood than the other models and therefore, *where appropriate*, can be used with considerable confidence. Fixed-effects ANOVA seems "robust" for type I errors to departures from certain mathematical assumptions underlying the F-test, provided that the number of experimental units is the same for each experimental combination. Two of these assumptions are that the e's are normally distributed and that they have common variance σ^2 for every one of the experimental combinations. In particular, the common-variance assumption can be relaxed without greatly affecting the probability values for computed F's. If the number of experimental units does not vary from one factor-level combination to another, then it may be unnecessary to test for heterogeneity of variances preliminary to performing an ANOVA, because ANOVA is robust to such heterogeneity. (In fact, it may be unwise to make such a test, because the usual test for heterogeneity of variance is more sensitive to nonnormality than is ANOVA.) For further discussion of this point see Lindquist (1953, pp. 78–86), Winer (1962, pp. 239–241), Brownlee ([1960] 1965, chapter 9), and Glass (1966). Brownlee (1960) and others have provided the finite-model expected mean squares for the complete three-factor factorial design, from which one can readily determine expected mean squares for three-factor fixed, mixed, and random models.

Analysis-of-variance F's are unaffected by linear transformation of the observations—that is, by changes in the X_{ps} of the form $a + bX_{ps}$, where a and b are constants ($b \neq 0$). Multiplying every observation by b multiplies every mean square by b^2. Adding a to every observation does not change the mean squares. Thus, if observations are two-decimal numbers running from, say, -1.22 upward, one could, to simplify calculations, drop the decimal (multiply each number by 100) and then add 122 to each observation. The lowest observation would become $100(-1.22) + 122 = 0$. Each mean square would become $100^2 = 10,000$ times as large as for the decimal fractions. With the increasing availability of high-speed digital computers, coding of data is becoming less important than it was formerly.

A brief classification of factors. The ANOVA "factors" considered thus far are style of printing type, tint of ink, rater, and subject. Styles differ from each other qualitatively, as do raters and subjects. Tint of ink might vary more quantitatively than do styles, raters, and subjects—as would, for example, size of printing type or temperature in a classroom. Thus, one basis for classifying factors is whether or not their levels are ordered and, if they are, whether meaningful numbers can be associated with the factor levels.

Another basis for classification is whether the variable is manipulated by the experimenter. In order to conduct a "true" experiment, one must assign his experimental units in some (simple or restrictive) random fashion to the levels of at least one manipulated factor. ANOVA may be applied to other types of data, such as the scores of Englishmen versus Americans on a certain test, but this is an associational study, not a stimulus–response experiment. Obviously, nationality is not an independent variable in the same sense that printing type is. The direct "causal" inference possible from a well-conducted style-of-type experiment differs from the associational information obtained from the comparison of Englishmen's scores with those of Americans (see Stanley 1961; 1965; 1966; Campbell & Stanley 1963). Some variables, such as national origin, are impossible to manipulate in meaningful ways, whereas others, such as "enrolls for Latin versus does not enroll for Latin," can in principle be manipulated, even though they usually are not.

Experimenters use nonmanipulated, classification variables for two chief reasons. First, they may wish to use a factor explicitly in a design in order to isolate the sum of squares for the main effect of that factor so that it will not inflate the estimate of underlying variance—that is, so it will not make the denominator mean square of F unnecessarily large. For example, if the experimental units available for experimentation are children in grades seven, eight, and nine, and if IQ scores are available, it is wise in studying the three styles of type to use the three (ordered) grades as one fixed-effects factor and a number of ordered IQ levels—say, four—as another fixed-effects factor. If the experimenter suspects that girls and boys may react differently to the styles, he will probably use this two-level, unordered classification (girls versus boys) as the third factor. This would produce $3 \times 4 \times 2 \times 3 = 72$ experimental combinations, so with at least 2 children per combination he needs not less than 144 children.

Probably most children in the higher grades read better, regardless of style, than do most children in the lower grades, and children with high IQ's tend to read better than children with lower IQ's, so the main effects of grade and of IQ should be large. Therefore, the variation within grade–IQ–sex–style groups should be considerably less than within styles alone.

A second reason for using such stratifying or leveling variables is to study their interactions with the manipulated variable. Ninth graders might do relatively better with one style of type and seventh graders relatively better with another style, for example. If so, the experimenter might decide to recommend one style of type for ninth graders and another for seventh graders. With the above design one can isolate and examine one four-factor interaction, four three-factor interactions, six two-factor interactions, and four main effects, a total of $2^4 - 1 = 15$ sources of variation across conditions. In the fixed-effects model all of these are tested against the variation within the experimental combinations, pooled from all combinations. Testing 15 sources of variation instead of 1 will tend to cause more apparently significant F's at a given tabled significance level than would be expected under the null hypothesis. For any one of the significance tests, given that the null hypothesis is true, one expects 5 spurious rejections of the true null hypothesis out of 100 tests; thus, if an analyst keeps making F-tests within an experiment, he has more than a .05 probability of securing at least one statistically significant F, even if no actual effects exist. There are systematic ways to guard against this (see, for example, Pearson & Hartley 1954, pp. 39–40). At least, one should be suspicious of higher-order interactions that seem to be significant at or near the .05 level. Many an experimenter utilizing a complex design has worked extremely hard trying to interpret a spuriously significant high-order interaction and in the process has introduced his fantasies into the journal literature.

Studies in which researchers do not manipulate any variables are common and important in the social sciences. These include opinion surveys, studies of variables related to injury in automobile accidents, and studies of the Hiroshima and Nagasaki survivors. ANOVA proves useful in many such investigations. [See Campbell & Stanley 1963; Lindzey 1954; see also EXPERIMENTAL DESIGN, article on QUASI-EXPERIMENTAL DESIGN.]

"Nesting" and repeated measurements. Many studies and experiments in the social sciences involve one or more factors whose levels do not "cross" the levels of certain other factors. Usually these occur in conjunction with repeated measurements taken on the same individuals. For example, if one classification is school and another is teacher within school, where each teacher teaches two classes within her school with different methods, then teachers are said to be "nested" within schools. Schools can interact with methods (a given method may work relatively better in one school than in another) and teachers can interact with methods *within schools* (a method that works relatively better for one teacher does not necessarily produce better results for another teacher in the same school), but schools cannot interact with teachers, because teachers do not "cross" schools—that is, the same teacher does not teach at more than one school.

This does not mean that a given teacher might not be more effective in another school but merely that the experiment provides no evidence on that point. One could, somewhat inconveniently, devise an experiment in which teachers did cross schools, teaching some classes in one school and some in another. But an experimenter could not, for example, have boys cross from delinquency to nondelinquency and vice versa, because delinquency–nondelinquency is a personal rather than an environmental characteristic. (For further discussion of nested designs see Brownlee [1960] 1965, chapters 13 and 15.)

If the order of repeated measurements on each individual is randomized, as when each person undergoes several treatments successively in random order, there is more likelihood that ANOVA will be appropriate than when the order cannot be randomized, as occurs, for instance, when the learning process is studied over a series of trials.

Complications occur also if the successive treatments have differential residual effects; taking a difficult test first may discourage one person in his work on the easier test that follows but make another person try harder. These residual effects seem likely to be of less importance if enough time occurs between successive treatment levels for some of the immediate influence of the treatment to dissipate. Human beings cannot have their memories erased like calculating machines, however, so repeated-measurement designs, although they usually reduce certain error terms because intraindividual variability tends to be less than interindividual variability, should not be used indiscriminately when analogous designs without repeated measurements are experimentally and financially feasible. (For further discussion see Winer 1962; Hays 1963, pp. 455–456; Campbell & Stanley 1963.)

Missing observations. For two factors with levels $s = 1, 2, \cdots, S$ and $t = 1, 2, \cdots, T$ in the experiment, such that the number of experimental units for the stth experimental combination is n_{st}, one usually designs the experiment so that $n_{st} = n$, a constant for all st. A few missing observations at the end of the experiment do not rule out a slightly adjusted simple ANOVA, if they were not caused differentially by the treatments. If, for example, one treatment was to administer a severe shock on several occasions, and the other was to give ice cream each time, it would not be surprising to find that fewer shocked than fed experimental subjects come for the final session. The outcome measure might be arithmetical-reasoning score; but if only the more shock-resistant subjects take the final test, comparison of the two treatments may be biased. There would be even more difficulty with, say, a male–female by shocked–fed design, because shocking might drive away more women than men (or vice versa).

When attrition is not caused differentially by the factors one may, for one-factor ANOVA, perform the usual analysis. For two or more factors, adjustments in the analysis are required to compensate for the few missing observations. (See Winer 1962, pp. 281–283, for example, for appropriate techniques.)

The power of the F-test. There are two kinds of errors that one can make when testing a null hypothesis against alternative hypotheses: one can reject the null hypothesis when in fact it is true, or one can fail to reject the null hypothesis when in fact it is false. Rejecting a true null hypothesis is called an "error of the first kind," or a "type I error." Failing to reject an untrue null hypothesis is called an "error of the second kind" or "type II error." The probability of making an error of the first kind is called the *size* of the significance test and is usually signified by α. The probability of making an error of the second kind is usually signified by β. The quantity $1 - \beta$ is called the *power* of the significance test.

If there is no limitation on the number of experimental units available one can fix both α and β at any desired levels prior to the experiment. To do this some prior estimate of σ^2 is required, and it is also necessary to state what nonnull difference among the factor-level means is considered large enough to be worth detecting. This latter requirement is quite troublesome in many social science experiments, because a good scale of value (such as dollars) is seldom available. For example, how much is a one-point difference between the mean of style 1 and style 2 on a reading-comprehension test worth educationally? Intelligence quotients and averages of college grades are quasi-utility scales, although one seldom thinks of them in just that way. How much is a real increase in IQ from 65 to 70 worth? How much more utility for the college does a grade-point average of 2.75 (where $C = 2$ and $B = 3$) have than a grade-point average of 2.50? (For further discussion of this topic see Chernoff & Moses 1959.)

In the hypothetical printing-styles example (Tables 1 and 5) it is known that $\sigma^2 = 1$ and that the population mean of style 1 is one point greater than the population means of styles 2 and 3, so with this information it is simple to enter Winer's Table B.11 (1962, p. 657) with, for example, $\alpha = .05$ and $\beta = .10$ and to find that for each of the three styles $P = 20$ experimental units are needed.

In actual experiments, where σ^2 and the $\sum_{s=1}^{S} P_s \alpha_s^2$ of interest to the experimenter are usually not known, the situation is more difficult (see Brownlee [1960] 1965, pp. 97–111; McNemar [1949] 1962, pp. 63–69; Hays 1963; and especially Scheffé 1959, pp. 38–42, 62–65, 437–455).

Alternatives to analysis of variance

If one conducted an experiment to determine how well ten-year-old boys add two-digit numbers at five equally spaced atmospheric temperatures, he could use the techniques of regression analysis to determine the equation for the line that best fits the five means (in the sense of minimum squared discrepancies). This line might be of the simple form $\alpha + \beta T$ (that is, straight with slope β and intercept α) or it might be based on some other function of T. [*See* Winer 1962 *for further discussion of trend analysis; see also* LINEAR HYPOTHESES, *article on* REGRESSION.]

The symmetrical two-tail t-test is a special case of the F-test; $t_{df}^2 = F_{1, df}$. Likewise, the unit normal deviate (z), called "critical ratio" in old statistics textbooks when used for testing significance, is a special case of F: $z^2 = F_{1, \infty}$. The F-distribution is closely related to the chi-square distribution. [*For further discussion of these relationships, see* DISTRIBUTIONS, STATISTICAL, *article on* SPECIAL CONTINUOUS DISTRIBUTIONS.]

For speed and computational ease, or when assumptions of ANOVA are violated so badly that results would seem dubious even if the data were transformed, there are other procedures available (see Winer 1962). Some of these procedures involve consecutive, untied ranks, whose means and variances are parameters dependent only on the number of ranks; an important example is the Kruskal–Wallis analysis of variance for ranks (Winer 1962, pp. 622–623). Other procedures employ the binomial expansion $(p + q)^n$ or the chi-square approximation to it for "sign tests." Still others involve dichotomizing the values for each treatment at the median and computing χ^2. Range tests may be used also. [*See* Winer 1962, p. 77; McNemar (1949) 1962, chapter 19. *Some of these procedures are discussed in* NONPARAMETRIC STATISTICS.]

When the normal assumption is reasonable, there are often available testing and other procedures that are competitive with the F-test. The latter has factotum utility, and it has optimal properties when the alternatives of interest are symmetrically arranged relative to the null hypothesis. But when the alternatives are asymmetrically arranged, or in other special circumstances, competitors to F procedures may be preferable. Particularly worthy of mention are Studentized range tests (see Scheffé 1959, pp. 82–83) and half-normal plotting (see Daniel 1959).

Special procedures are useful when the alternatives specify an ordering. For example, in the style-of-type example it might be known before the experiment that if there *is* any difference between the styles, style 1 is better than style 2, and style 2 better than style 3 (see Bartholomew 1961; Chacko 1963).

It is also important to mention here the desirability of examining residuals (observations less the estimates of their expectations) as a check on the model and as a source of suggestions toward useful modifications. [*See* STATISTICAL ANALYSIS, SPECIAL PROBLEMS OF, *article on* TRANSFORMATIONS OF DATA; *see also* Anscombe & Tukey 1963.

Often an observed value appears to be so distant from the other values that the experimenter is tempted to discard it before performing an ANOVA. For a discussion of procedures in such cases, see STATISTICAL ANALYSIS, SPECIAL PROBLEMS OF, *article on* OUTLIERS.]

Multivariate analysis of variance. The analysis of variance is multivariate in the independent variables (the factors) but univariate in the dependent variables (the outcome measures). S. N. Roy (for example, see Roy & Gnanadesikan 1959) and others have developed a multivariate analysis of variance (MANOVA), multivariate with respect to both independent and dependent variables, of which ANOVA is a special case. A few social scientists (for example, Rodwan 1964; Bock 1963) have used MANOVA, but as yet it has not been used widely by workers in these disciplines.

JULIAN C. STANLEY

BIBLIOGRAPHY

ANSCOMBE, F. J.; and TUKEY, JOHN W. 1963 The Examination and Analysis of Residuals. *Technometrics* 5:141–160.

BARTHOLOMEW, D. J. 1961 Ordered Tests in the Analysis of Variance. *Biometrika* 48:325–332.

BOCK, R. DARRELL 1963 Programming Univariate and Multivariate Analysis of Variance. *Technometrics* 5:95–117.

BROWNLEE, KENNETH A. (1960) 1965 *Statistical Theory and Methodology in Science and Engineering.* 2d ed. New York: Wiley.

CAMPBELL, DONALD T.; and STANLEY, J. S. 1963 Experimental and Quasi-experimental Designs for Research on Teaching. Pages 171–246 in Nathaniel L. Gage (editor), *Handbook of Research on Teaching.* Chicago: Rand McNally. → Republished in 1966 as a separate monograph titled *Experimental and Quasi-experimental Designs for Research.*

CHACKO, V. J. 1963 Testing Homogeneity Against Ordered Alternatives. *Annals of Mathematical Statistics* 34:945–956.

CHERNOFF, HERMAN; and MOSES, LINCOLN E. 1959 *Elementary Decision Theory.* New York: Wiley.

COCHRAN, WILLIAM G. 1957 Analysis of Covariance: Its Nature and Uses. *Biometrics* 13:261–281.

CORNFIELD, JEROME; and TUKEY, JOHN W. 1956 Average Values of Mean Squares in Factorials. *Annals of Mathematical Statistics* 27:907–949.

DANIEL, CUTHBERT 1959 Use of Half-normal Plots in Interpreting Factorial Two-level Experiments. *Technometrics* 1:311–341.

FISHER, R. A. (1925) 1958 *Statistical Methods for Research Workers.* 13th ed. New York: Hafner. → Previous editions were also published by Oliver & Boyd.

FISHER, R. A. (1935) 1960 *The Design of Experiments.* 7th ed. London: Oliver & Boyd; New York: Hafner.

GLASS, GENE V. 1966 Testing Homogeneity of Variances. *American Educational Research Journal* 3:187–190.

[GOSSET, WILLIAM S.] (1908) 1943 The Probable Error of a Mean. Pages 11–34 in William S. Gosset, *"Student's" Collected Papers.* London: University College,
Biometrika Office. → First published in Volume 6 of *Biometrika.*

HAYS, WILLIAM L. 1963 *Statistics for Psychologists.* New York: Holt.

LINDQUIST, EVERET F. 1953 *Design and Analysis of Experiments in Psychology and Education.* Boston: Houghton Mifflin.

LINDZEY, GARDNER (editor) (1954) 1959 *Handbook of Social Psychology.* 2 vols. Cambridge, Mass.: Addison-Wesley. → Volume 1: *Theory and Method.* Volume 2: *Special Fields and Applications.* A second edition, edited by Gardner Lindzey and Elliot Aronson, is in preparation.

LUBIN, ARDIE 1961 The Interpretation of Significant Interaction. *Educational and Psychological Measurement* 21:807–817.

McLEAN, LESLIE D. 1967 Some Important Principles for the Use of Incomplete Designs in Behavioral Research. Chapter 4 in Julian C. Stanley (editor), *Improving Experimental Design and Statistical Analysis.* Chicago: Rand McNally.

McNEMAR, QUINN (1949) 1962 *Psychological Statistics.* 3d ed. New York: Wiley.

MOOD, ALEXANDER M.; and GRAYBILL, FRANKLIN A. 1963 *Introduction to the Theory of Statistics.* 2d ed. New York: McGraw-Hill. → The first edition was published in 1950.

NELDER, J. A. 1954 The Interpretation of Negative Components of Variance. *Biometrika* 41:544–548.

PEARSON, EGON S.; and HARTLEY, H. O. (editors) (1954) 1966 *Biometrika Tables for Statisticians.* Volume 1. 3d ed. Cambridge Univ. Press. → A revision of *Tables for Statisticians and Biometricians* (1914), edited by Karl Pearson.

RAND CORPORATION 1955 *A Million Random Digits With 100,000 Normal Deviates.* Glencoe, Ill.: Free Press.

RODWAN, ALBERT S. 1964 An Empirical Validation of the Concept of Coherence. *Journal of Experimental Psychology* 68:167–170.

ROY, S. N.; and GNANADESIKAN, R. 1959 Some Contributions to ANOVA in One or More Dimensions: I and II. *Annals of Mathematical Statistics* 30:304–317, 318–340.

SAMPFORD, MICHAEL R. (editor) 1964 In Memoriam Ronald Aylmer Fisher, 1890–1962. *Biometrics* 20, no. 2:237–373.

SCHEFFÉ, HENRY 1959 *The Analysis of Variance.* New York: Wiley.

SMITH, H. FAIRFIELD 1957 Interpretation of Adjusted Treatment Means and Regressions in Analysis of Covariance. *Biometrics* 13:282–308.

STANLEY, JULIAN C. 1961 Studying Status vs. Manipulating Variables. Phi Delta Kappa Symposium on Educational Research, *Annual Phi Delta Kappa Symposium on Educational Research:* [Proceedings] 2:173–208. → Published in Bloomington, Indiana.

STANLEY, JULIAN C. 1965 Quasi-experimentation. *School Review* 73:197–205.

STANLEY, JULIAN C. 1966 A Common Class of Pseudo-experiments. *American Educational Research Journal* 3:79–87.

THOMPSON, W. A. JR. 1962 The Problem of Negative Estimates of Variance Components. *Annals of Mathematical Statistics* 33:273–289.

TUKEY, JOHN W. 1949 One Degree of Freedom for Nonadditivity. *Biometrics* 5:232–242.

WINER, B. J. 1962 *Statistical Principles in Experimental Design.* New York: McGraw-Hill.

III
MULTIPLE COMPARISONS

Multiple comparison methods deal with a dilemma arising in statistical analysis: On the one hand, it would be unfortunate not to analyze the data thoroughly in all its aspects; on the other hand, performing several significance tests, or constructing several confidence intervals, for the same data compounds the error rates (significance levels), and it is often difficult to compute the over-all error probability.

Multiple comparison and related methods are designed to give simple over-all error probabilities for analyses that examine several aspects of the data simultaneously. For example, some simultaneous tests examine all differences between several treatment means.

Cronbach (1949, especially pp. 399–403) describes the problem of inflation of error probabilities in multiple comparisons. The solutions now available are, for the most part, of a later date (see Ryan 1959; Miller 1966). Miller's book provides a comprehensive treatment of the major aspects of multiple comparisons.

Normal means—confidence regions, tests

1. Simultaneous limits for several means. As a simple example of a situation in which multiple comparison methods might be applied, suppose that independent random samples are drawn from three normal populations with unknown means, μ_1, μ_2, μ_3, but *known* variances, $\sigma_1^2, \sigma_2^2, \sigma_3^2$. If only the first sample were available, a 99 per cent confidence interval could be constructed for μ_1:

$$(1) \quad \bar{X}_1 - 2.58\sigma_1/\sqrt{n_1} < \mu_1 < \bar{X}_1 + 2.58\sigma_1/\sqrt{n_1},$$

where $\bar{X}_1$ is the sample mean, and n_1 the size, of the first sample. In hypothetical repetitions of the procedure, the confidence interval covers, or includes, the true value of μ_1 99 per cent of the time in the long run. [*See* ESTIMATION, *article on* CONFIDENCE INTERVALS AND REGIONS.]

If all three samples are used, three statements like (1) can be made, successively replacing the subscript "1" by "2" and "3." The probability that all three statements *together* are true, however, is not .99 but .99 × .99 × .99, or .9703.

In a coordinate system with three axes marked $\mu_1, \mu_2,$ and μ_3, the three intervals together define a 97 per cent (approximately) confidence box. This confidence box is shown in Figure 1. In order to obtain a 99 per cent confidence box—that is, to have all three statements hold simultaneously with probability .99—the confidence levels for the three individual statements must be increased. One

Figure 1 — A confidence box

method would be to make each individual confidence level equal to .9967, the cube root of .99.

The simple two-tail test of the null hypothesis (H_0) $\mu_1 = 0$ rejects it (at significance level .01) if the value 0 is not caught inside the confidence interval (1). It is natural to think of extending this test to the composite null hypothesis $\mu_1 = 0$ *and* $\mu_2 = 0$ *and* $\mu_3 = 0$ by rejecting the composite hypothesis if the point (0,0,0) is outside the confidence box corresponding to (1). The significance level of this procedure, however, is not .01 but $1 - .9703$, almost .03. In order to reduce the significance level to .01, "2.58" in (1) must be replaced by a higher number. If this is done symmetrically, the significance level for each of the three individual statements like (1) must be .0033. In this argument any hypothetical values of the means, $\mu_1^*, \mu_2^*, \mu_3^*$, may be used in place of 0,0,0 to specify the null hypothesis; the point $(\mu_1^*, \mu_2^*, \mu_3^*)$ then takes the place of (0,0,0).

The same principles can be applied just as easily to the case where the three variances are not known but are estimated from the respective samples, in which case 1 per cent points of Student's t-distribution take the place of 2.58. Of course, any other significance levels may also be used instead of 1 per cent.

Pooled estimate of variance. The problem considered so far is atypically simple because the three intervals are statistically *independent*, so that probabilities can simply be multiplied. This is no longer true if the variances are unknown but are assumed to be equal and are estimated by a single *pooled* estimate of variance, $\hat{\sigma}^2$, which is the sum of the three within-sample sums of squares divided by $n_1 + n_2 + n_3 - 3$. This is equal to the mean square used in the denominator of an analysis-of-variance F [*see* LINEAR HYPOTHESES, *article on* ANALYSIS OF VARIANCE]. The conditions

$$\bar{X}_i - M\hat{\sigma}/\sqrt{n_i} < \mu_i < \bar{X}_i + M\hat{\sigma}/\sqrt{n_i}, \quad i = 1,2,3$$

(where M is a constant to be chosen), use the same $\hat{\sigma}$ and hence are *not* statistically independent. Thus, the probability that all three hold simultaneously is not the product of the three separate probabilities, although this is still a surprisingly good approximation, adequate for most purposes.

Critical values, M_α, have, however, been computed for $\alpha = .05$ and .01 and for any number of degrees of freedom $(n_1 + n_2 + n_3 - 3)$ of $\hat{\sigma}^2$. If M_α is substituted for M in the three intervals, the probability that all three conditions simultaneously hold is $1 - \alpha$ (Tukey 1953).

Exactly the same principles described for the problem of estimating, or testing, three population means also apply to k means. A table providing critical values M_α for $k = 2, 3, \cdots, 10$ and for various numbers of degrees of freedom, $N - k$, has been computed by Pillai and Ramachandran (1954). Part of the table is reproduced in Miller (1966). The square of M_α was tabulated earlier by Nair (1948a) for use in another context (see Section 7, below). This table is reproduced in Pearson and Hartley ([1954] 1966, table 19).

Notation. In the following exposition, "$\bar{X}_i$" and "μ_i" represent sample and population means, respectively $(i = 1, \cdots, k)$, "σ^2" the population variance, generally assumed to be common to all k populations, "$\hat{\sigma}^2$" the pooled sample estimate of σ^2, and "SE" the estimated standard error of a statistic (SE will depend on $\hat{\sigma}^2$, on the particular statistic, and on the sample sizes involved). The symbol "$\sum$" always denotes summation over i, from 1 to k, unless otherwise specified; N denotes $\sum n_i$, the total sample size, and "*ddf*" stands for "denominator degrees of freedom," the degrees of freedom of $\hat{\sigma}^2$.

2. Treatments versus control (Dunnett). Many studies are concerned with the *difference* between means rather than with the means themselves. For example, sample 1 may consist of *controls* (that is, observations taken under standard conditions) to be used for comparison with samples $2, 3, \cdots, k$ (taken under different treatments or nonstandard conditions), for the purpose of estimating the treatment effects, $\mu_2 - \mu_1, \cdots, \mu_k - \mu_1$. For $k = 3, 4, \cdots, 10$, for any number of denomi-

nator degrees of freedom, $N - k$, greater than 4, and for $\alpha = .05$ and .01, Dunnett (1955; also in Miller 1966) has tabulated critical values D_α such that with probability approximately equal to $1 - \alpha$, all $k - 1$ statements

$$|(\bar{X}_i - \bar{X}_1) - (\mu_i - \mu_1)| < D_\alpha SE,$$
$$i = 2, 3, \cdots, k,$$

will be simultaneously true—that is, all $k - 1$ effects $\mu_i - \mu_1$ will be covered by confidence intervals centered at $\bar{X}_i - \bar{X}_1$ with half-lengths $D_\alpha SE$, where $SE = \sqrt{(1/n_i) + (1/n_1)}\,\hat{\sigma}$.

The over-all probability is exactly $1 - \alpha$ if all k sample sizes are equal. It is not the product of $k - 1$ probabilities (obtained from Student's t-distribution) of the separate confidence statements, because these are not statistically independent; dependence comes not only from the common estimator of σ in all statements but also from the correlation ($\rho \cong .5$ for sample sizes roughly the same) between any two differences $\bar{X}_i - \bar{X}_1$ with $\bar{X}_1$ in common. Surprisingly enough, the product rule gives a close approximation just the same.

Viewed as restrictions on the point (μ_1, μ_2, μ_3) in three-space, the two (pairs of) inequalities for $k = 3$ define a confidence region that is the intersection of the slab bounded by two parallel planes, $\mu_2 - \mu_1 = \bar{X}_2 - \bar{X}_1 \pm D_\alpha SE$, and another slab at $45°$ to the first slab. This is illustrated in Figure 2, where for simplicity all n_i are assumed to be equal. The region is a prism that is infinite in length, is parallel to the $45°$ line $\mu_1 = \mu_2 = \mu_3$, and has a rhombus as its cross section.

Dunnett's significance test rejects the null hypothesis, H_0: $\mu_2 = \cdots = \mu_k = \mu_1$, in favor of the alternative hypothesis that one or more of the μ_i differ from μ_1 if the $k - 1$ confidence intervals do not all contain the value 0 or, equivalently, if

$$(2) \qquad |t_{i1}| = |\bar{X}_i - \bar{X}_1|/SE \geqslant D_\alpha$$

for any i $(i = 2, \cdots, k)$. If the null hypothesis is of the less trivial form $\mu_i - \mu_1 = d_{i1}$, where the d_{i1} are any specified constants, then d_{i1} is subtracted from the differences of sample means in the numerators of t_{i1}.

The probability of rejecting H_0 if it is true, called the *error rate experimentwise*, is exactly the stated α if all sample sizes are equal, and is approximately α for unequal n_i, provided the inequality is not gross. Dunnett (1955) showed that a design using equal n_i, $i = 2, \cdots, k$, but with n_1 larger in about the proportion $\sqrt{k-1} : 1$ is most efficient. Unfortunately this leads to true error rates exceeding the stated α if Dunnett's table is used, and it is then safer to substitute a Bonferroni t-statistic for Dunnett's D_α if k is as big as 6 or 10 (for Bonferroni t,

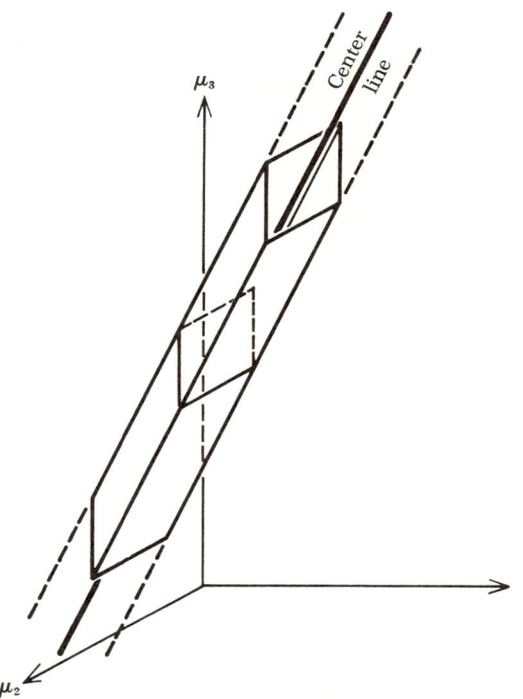

$$\mu_3$$

Center line

$$\mu_2$$

Figure 2 — Confidence region for Dunnett method

see Section 14, below; see also Miller 1966, table 2).

Simultaneous one-tail tests are of the same form as (2), above, except that the absolute-value signs are removed and an appropriate smaller critical value, D_α, also tabulated in Dunnett (1955), is used. The corresponding confidence intervals are one-sided, extending to infinity on the other side.

3. All differences—Tukey method. In order to compare several means with one another rather than only with a single control, a method of Tukey's (1953) is suitable. It provides simultaneous confidence intervals (or significance tests, if desired) for all $\binom{k}{2} = \frac{1}{2}k(k-1)$ differences, $\mu_i - \mu_j$, among k means.

A constant, T_α, is chosen so that the probability is at least $1 - \alpha$ that all $\binom{k}{2}$ statements

$$|(\bar{X}_i - \bar{X}_j) - (\mu_i - \mu_j)| < T_\alpha SE,$$

or, equivalently,

$$|t_{ij}| = |(\bar{X}_i - \bar{X}_j) - (\mu_i - \mu_j)|/SE < T_\alpha,$$

will be simultaneously true. Here SE is equal to $\sqrt{(1/n_i) + (1/n_j)}\,\hat{\sigma}$. The probability is exactly $1 - \alpha$ if the sample sizes are equal (Tukey 1953; Kurtz 1956; Kramer 1956).

Simultaneous confidence intervals for all the differences, $\mu_i - \mu_j$, are centered at $\bar{X}_i - \bar{X}_j$ with half-lengths $T_\alpha SE$. In a significance test of the null hypothesis, H_0, that the differences, $\mu_i - \mu_j$, have any specified (mutually consistent) values, d_{ij} (often 0), one substitutes d_{ij} for $\mu_i - \mu_j$ in the t-ratios and rejects H_0 if the largest ratio is not less than T_α.

The constant, T_α, is $R_\alpha / \sqrt{2} = .707R_\alpha$, where R_α is the upper α-point in the distribution of the Studentized range. Table 29 of Pearson and Hartley ([1954] 1966) shows R_α for $\alpha = .1$, .05, and .01, for values of k up to 20, and for any number of *ddf*. Briefer tables are found in Vianelli (1959) and in a number of textbooks—for example, Winer (1962). More extensive tables prepared by Harter (1960) can also be found in Miller (1966).

Geometrically, Tukey's $(1 - \alpha)$-confidence region can be obtained, for $k = 3$, by widening and thickening Dunnett's prism (Figure 2) in the proportion $T_\alpha : D_\alpha$ and then removing a pair of triangular prisms by intersection with a third slab. The cross section is hexagonal.

Tukey's multiple comparisons are frequently used after an F-test rejects H_0 but may also be used in place of F.

Simplified multiple t-tests. Simplified multiple t-tests, which were developed by Tukey, use the sum of sample ranges in place of σ and a critical value, T_α, adjusted accordingly. (See Kurtz et al. 1965.)

4. One outlying mean (slippage). In comparing k populations it may be desirable to find out whether one of them (which one is not specified in advance) is outstanding (has "slipped") relative to the others. Then using k independent treatment samples one may examine the differences, $\bar{X}_i - \bar{X}$, where $\bar{X} = \sum_{i=1}^{k} \sum_{j=1}^{n_i} X_{ij}/N = \sum n_i \bar{X}_i/N$. Let $\mu = \sum n_i \mu_i/N$.

Halperin provided critical values H_α such that with probability approximately $1 - \alpha$,

$$|(\bar{X}_i - \bar{X}) - (\mu_i - \mu)| < H_\alpha \sqrt{\frac{k}{k-1}\left(\frac{1}{n_i} - \frac{1}{N}\right)}\,\hat{\sigma}$$

simultaneously for $i = 1, \cdots, k$ (Halperin et al. 1955). The probability is exactly $1 - \alpha$ in the case of equal n_i. This provides two-sided tests for the null hypothesis that all $\mu_i = \mu$ and simultaneous confidence intervals for all the $\mu_i - \mu$, in the usual way. In case the table is not at hand, a good approximation to the right-hand side of the inequality is (upper $(\alpha/2k)$-point of Student's t) $\times \sqrt{(1/n_i) - (1/N)}\,\hat{\sigma}$.

Critical values for the corresponding one-sided test, to ascertain whether one of the means has slipped in a specified direction (for example, whether it has slipped down), were first computed by Nair (1952). David (1962a; 1962b) provides improved tables. A refinement of Nair's test and of Halperin's is presented by Quesenberry and David (1961). In Pearson and Hartley ([1954] 1966), tables 26a and 26b (and the explanation on p. 51) pertain to these methods, whereas table 26 is Nair's statistic.

5. Contrasts—Scheffé method. A *contrast* in k population means is a linear combination, $\sum c_i \mu_i$, with coefficients adding up to zero, $\sum c_i = 0$. This is always equal to a multiple of the difference between weighted averages of two sets of means— that is, constant $\times (\sum_h a_h \mu_h - \sum_j b_j \mu_j)$ with summations running over two subsets of the subscripts $(1, \cdots, k)$ having no subscript in common and with $\sum_h a_h = 1, \sum_j b_j = 1$. The simple differences, $\mu_h - \mu_j$, are special contrasts. Some other examples include contrasts representing a difference between two *groups* of means (for example, $\frac{1}{3}[\mu_2 + \mu_3 + \mu_5] - \frac{1}{2}[\mu_1 + \mu_4])$ or slippage of one mean (for example, $\mu_2 - \bar{\mu}$, since this is equal to $\{[k-1]/k\}\mu_2 - [1/k][\mu_1 + \mu_3 + \mu_4 + \cdots + \mu_k])$, or trend (for example, $-3\mu_1 - \mu_2 + \mu_3 + 3\mu_4$).

In an exploratory study to compare k means when little is known to suggest a specific pattern of differences in advance, any and all striking contrasts revealed by the data will be of interest. Also, when looking for slippage or simple differences one may wish to take account of some other, unanticipated, pattern displayed by the data.

Any of the systems of multiple comparisons discussed in sections 1–4 can be adapted to obtain tests, or simultaneous intervals, for all contrasts. For example, the $k-1$ simultaneous conditions $|(\bar{X}_i - \bar{X}_1) - (\mu_i - \mu_1)| < D_\alpha \sqrt{(1/n_i) + (1/n_1)}\, \hat{\sigma}$, where D_α represents the critical value of the Dunnett statistic as defined in Section 2, above, imply that every contrast, $\sum c_i \mu_i$, falls into an interval of half-length $D_\alpha \sum_2^k (|c_i| \sqrt{2/n_i})\, \hat{\sigma}$, centered at $\sum c_i \bar{X}_i$, in the case of equal sample sizes.

The following method, developed by Scheffé, however, is more efficient for all-contrasts analyses, because it yields shorter intervals for most contrasts. Scheffé proved that

$$\sqrt{(k-1)F} = \max[\sum c_i (\bar{X}_i - \mu_i)/SE],$$

the largest of all the (infinitely many) Studentized contrasts, where F is the analysis-of-variance F-ratio for testing equality of all the μ_i, and where $SE = \sqrt{\sum(c_i^2/n_i)}\, \hat{\sigma}$. Thus,

$$1 - \alpha = Pr\{F < F_\alpha\}$$
$$= Pr\{all \text{ Studentized contrasts} < \sqrt{(k-1)F_\alpha}\}$$
$$= Pr\left\{ \frac{\sum c_i (\bar{X}_i - \mu_i)}{SE} < \sqrt{(k-1)F_\alpha} \right.$$
$$\left. \text{for } all \text{ sets of } c_i \text{ with } \sum c_i = 0 \right\}.$$

Simultaneous confidence intervals for all contrasts, $\sum c_i \mu_i$, are centered at $\sum c_i \bar{X}_i$ and have half-lengths $SE\sqrt{(k-1)F_\alpha}$. The confidence level is *exactly* the stated $1 - \alpha$, regardless of whether sample sizes are equal.

For $k = 3$, any particular interval can be depicted in (μ_1, μ_2, μ_3)-space by a pair of parallel planes equidistant from the line given by $\mu_1 - \bar{X}_1 = \mu_2 - \bar{X}_2 = \mu_3 - \bar{X}_3$ through the point $(\bar{X}_1, \bar{X}_2, \bar{X}_3)$. Together these planes constitute all the tangent planes of the cylinder (in the "variables" μ_1, μ_2, μ_3),

$$\sum n_i [(\bar{X}_i - \bar{X}) - (\mu_i - \mu)]^2 = (3-1)\hat{\sigma}^2 F_\alpha,$$

where F_α has degrees of freedom $3 - 1$ and $n - 3$. This cylinder, like the prism of Figure 2, is infinite in length and equally inclined to the coordinate axes. (As in the case of the regions for Dunnett's and Tukey's procedures, the addition of the same constant to each of the coordinates X_1, X_2, X_3 of a point on the surface will move this point along the surface.) See Figure 3.

Significance test. A value of $F \geqslant F_\alpha$ implies $\sum c_i (\bar{X}_i - \mu_i) \geqslant SE\sqrt{(k-1)F_\alpha}$ for at least one contrast (namely, at least for the maximum Studentized contrast). Scheffé's multiple comparison test declares $\sum c_i \bar{X}_i$ to be statistically significant—that is, $\sum c_i \mu_i$ different from zero—for all those con-

Figure 3 — Confidence region for all contrasts (Scheffé)

trasts for which the inequality is true. Thus, one may test every contrast of interest, or every contrast that looks promising, and incur a risk of just α of falsely declaring any $\sum c_i \mu_i$ whatsoever to be different from zero; in other words, the probability of making no false statement of the form $\sum c_i \mu_i \neq 0$ is $1 - \alpha$, the probability of making one or more such statements is α. Of course, the Scheffé approach gives a larger confidence interval (or decreased power) than the analogous procedure if only a single contrast is of interest.

General linear combinations. Simultaneous confidence intervals, or tests, can also be obtained for all possible linear combinations, $\sum c_i \mu_i$, with the restriction $\sum c_i = 0$ lifted. Then Scheffé's confidence and significance statements for contrasts remain applicable, except that $(k - 1)F_\alpha$ is changed to kF_α and the numerator degrees of freedom of F are changed from $k - 1$ to k. (See Miller 1966, chapter 2, sec. 2).

A confidence region for all (standardized) linear combinations consists of the ellipsoid in the k-dimensional space with axes labeled $\mu_1, \mu_2, \cdots, \mu_k$, $\sum n_i (\bar{X}_i - \mu_i)^2 < kF_\alpha \hat{\sigma}^2$. For $k = 3$, any particular interval can be depicted in (μ_1, μ_2, μ_3)-space by a pair of parallel planes equidistant from the point $(\bar{X}_1, \bar{X}_2, \bar{X}_3)$. Together these planes constitute all the tangent planes of the confidence ellipsoid (in the "variables" μ_1, μ_2, μ_3).

Tukey (1953) and Miller (1966) also discuss the generalization of the application of intervals based on the Studentized range (referred to in Section 3, above) to take care of all linear combinations. Simultaneous intervals for all linear combinations can also be based on the Studentized maximum modulus (Section 1); half-lengths become $M_\alpha \sqrt{1/n} \hat{\sigma} \cdot \sum |c_i|$ (Tukey 1953).

All of these methods dealing with contrasts and general linear combinations are described in Miller (1966).

Further discussion of normal populations

6. Newman–Keuls and Duncan procedures. The Newman–Keuls procedure is a multiple comparison test for all differences. It does not provide a confidence region. The sample means are arranged and renumbered in order of magnitude, so that $\bar{X}_1 < \bar{X}_2 < \cdots < \bar{X}_k$. The first step is the same as Tukey's test; the null hypothesis is rejected or accepted according as $\bar{X}_k - \bar{X}_1$, the range of the sample means, is $\geq$ or $< T_{\alpha:k} SE$, where $T_{\alpha:k}$ is the upper α-point of Tukey's statistic for k means and $N - k$ *ddf*.

Accepting H_0 means that there is not enough evidence to establish differences between any of the population means, and the analysis is complete (all k means are then called "homogeneous"). On the other hand, if the null hypothesis is rejected, so that μ_k, the population mean corresponding to the largest sample mean, is declared to be different from μ_1, the population mean corresponding to the smallest sample mean, the next step is to test $\bar{X}_{k-1} - \bar{X}_1$ and $\bar{X}_k - \bar{X}_2$ similarly, but with $T_{\alpha:k-1}$ in place of $T_{\alpha:k}$ (the original pooled variance estimator $\hat{\sigma}^2$ and $N - k$ *ddf* are used throughout). A subrange of means that is not found statistically significant is called homogeneous. As long as a subrange is statistically significant, the two subranges obtained by removing in one case its largest and in the other case its smallest $\bar{X}_i$ are tested, using a critical value $T_{\alpha:h}$, where h is only the number of means left in the new subranges—but testing is limited by the rule that every subrange contained in a homogeneous range of means is not tested but is automatically declared to be homogeneous. The result of the whole procedure is to group the means into homogeneous sets, which may also be represented diagrammatically by connecting lines, as in the example presented in Section 10, below.

Critics of the Newman–Keuls method object that the error probabilities, such as that of falsely declaring $\mu_2 \neq \mu_5$, are not even known in this test; its supporters, however, argue that power should not be wasted by judging subranges by the same stringent criterion used for the full range of all k sample means.

Duncan (1955) goes a step further, arguing that even $T_{\alpha:h}$ is too stringent a criterion because the $\frac{1}{2}h(h - 1)$ differences between h means have only $h - 1$ degrees of freedom. He concludes that $T_{\gamma:h}$ should be used instead, where $1 - \gamma = (1 - \alpha)^{h-1}$. This further increases the power—and the effective type I error probability. For a study of error rates of Tukey, Newman–Keuls, Duncan, and Student tests, see Harter (1957).

7. General Model I design. The F-test in the one-way analysis of variance and the multiple comparison methods already discussed are based on the fact that *ddf* times $\hat{\sigma}^2/\sigma^2$ has a chi-square distribution and is independent of the sample means. This condition is also satisfied by the residual variance used in randomized blocks, factorial designs, Latin squares, and all Model I designs. Therefore, all these designs permit the use of the methods, and tables, of sections 1–6, to compare the means defined by any one factor, provided that these are independent.

In certain instances of nonparametric multiple comparisons and in certain instances of multiple comparisons of interactions in balanced factorial designs, where the (adjusted or transformed) observations are not independent but equicorrelated, the multiple comparison methods of sections 2–6 still apply: The use of the adjusted error variance, $(1 - \rho)\hat{\sigma}^2$, to compute standard errors fully compensates for the effect of equal correlations (see Tukey 1953; Scheffé 1953; Miller 1966, pp. 41–42, 46–47). Scheffé's method can also be adapted for use with unequal correlations (see Miller 1966, p. 53).

When several factors, and perhaps some interactions, are t-tested in the same experiment, the question arises whether extra adjustment should not be made for the resulting additional compounding of error probabilities. One method open to an experimenter willing to sacrifice power for strict experimentwise control of type I error is the conservative one of using error rates per t-test of $\alpha/$(number of t-tests contemplated), that is, using Bonferroni t-statistics (see Section 14). For experimentwise control of error rates in the special case of a 2^r factorial design, Nair (1948a) has tabulated percentage points of the largest of r independent χ^2's with one degree of freedom, divided by an independent variance estimator (Pearson & Hartley [1954] 1966, table 19). The statistic is equal to the square of the Studentized maximum modulus introduced in Section 1.

8. An example—juxtaposition of methods. Three competing theories about how hostility evoked in people by willfully imposed frustration may be diminished led Rothaus and Worchel (1964) to goad 192 experimental subjects into hostility by unfair administration of a test of coordination and then to apply the following "treatments" to four groups, each composed of 48 subjects: (1) no treatment (control); (2) fair readministration of the test, seemingly as a result of a grievance procedure (instrumental communication); (3) an opportunity for verbal expression of hostility (catharsis); (4) conversation to the effect that the test was unfair and the result therefore not indicative of failure on the subjects' part (ego support). After treatment all subjects were given another—

Table 1 — Analysis of variance of hostility scores

Source	df	Mean square	F-ratio
4 treatments	3	369.77	3.38*
3 subgroups	2	151.31	1.38
2 sexes	1	41.14	0.38
2 BIHS levels	1	2.68	0.02
All the interactions, none of them statistically significant	40		
4 replications (nested)	144	$109.54 = \hat{\sigma}^2$	

* Denotes statistical significance at the 5 per cent level.

fair—test of coordination. Each treatment group was subdivided into three subgroups, a different experimenter working with each subgroup. All subjects had been given Behavioral Items for Hostility Scales (BIHS) three weeks before the experiment.

The experimental plan was factorial: 4 treatments × 3 subgroups × 2 sexes × 2 BIHS score groups (high versus low) × 4 replications. The study variable, X, was hostility measured on the Social Sensitivity Scale at the end of the experiment.

The sample means (unordered) for the four treatment groups were $\bar{x}_1 = 47.08$, $\bar{x}_2 = 42.00$, $\bar{x}_3 = 48.53$, $\bar{x}_4 = 45.40$.

In fact, the numbers in Table 1 reflect an analysis of covariance. The mean squares shown are adjusted mean squares, the sample means are adjusted means, and $\hat{\sigma}^2$ has 143 df. But for the sake of simplicity of interpretation the data will be treated as if they had come from a $4 \times 3 \times 2 \times 2$ factorial analysis of variance. The estimated standard error for differences between two means, SE, is $\sqrt{[(1/48) + (1/48)] \times 109.54} = 2.136$.

Dunnett comparisons. The Dunnett method, with $\alpha = .05$, would be applied to the data of the experiment, as analyzed in Table 2. As indicated in Table 2, the one-tail test in the direction of the theory (H_1) under study declares μ_2 to be less than μ_1. Thus, the conclusion, if the one-sided Dunnett test and the 5 per cent significance level are adopted, is that instrumental communication reduces hostility but that the evidence does not confirm any reduction due to ego support or catharsis. If the two-tail test had been chosen, allowing for

Table 2 — Dunnett comparisons of control with three treatments, $\alpha = .05$

Pair	$\bar{x}_i - \bar{x}_j$	t-ratio: $\frac{\bar{x}_i - \bar{x}_j}{2.136}$	DUNNETT METHOD: TWO-SIDED Test: $D_\alpha = 2.40$	DUNNETT METHOD: TWO-SIDED Confidence interval (half-length = $2.136D_\alpha = 5.13$)	DUNNETT METHOD: ONE-SIDED Test: $D_\alpha = 2.08$	DUNNETT METHOD: ONE-SIDED Confidence interval (lower length = $2.136D_\alpha = 4.44$)
(1)–(2)	5.08	2.38	(near significance)	(−0.05,10.21)	*	(0.64,∞)
(1)–(3)	−1.45	−0.68	—	(−6.58,3.68)	—	(−5.89,∞)
(1)–(4)	1.68	0.79	—	(−3.45,6.81)	—	(−2.76,∞)

* Statistically significant at the 5 per cent level; all other comparisons do not reach statistical significance at the 5 per cent level.

Table 3 — All pairs, by Tukey and by Scheffé method, $\alpha = .05$

			TUKEY METHOD		SCHEFFÉ METHOD	
Pair	$\bar{x}_i - \bar{x}_j$	t-ratio: $\frac{\bar{x}_i - \bar{x}_j}{2.136}$	Test: $T_\alpha = 2.60$	Confidence interval (half-length = $2.136 T_\alpha = 5.55$)	Test: $\sqrt{3F_\alpha} = 2.80$	Confidence interval (half-length = $2.136\sqrt{3F_\alpha} = 5.98$)
(1)–(2)	5.08	2.38	—	(−0.47,10.63)	—	(−0.90,11.06)
(1)–(3)	−1.45	−0.68	—	(−7.00,4.10)	—	(−7.43,4.53)
(1)–(4)	1.68	0.79	—	(−3.87,7.23)	—	(−4.30,7.66)
(2)–(3)	−6.53	−3.06	*	(−12.08,−0.98)	*	(−12.51,−0.55)
(2)–(4)	−3.40	−1.59	—	(−8.95,2.15)	—	(−9.38,2.58)
(3)–(4)	3.13	1.47	—	(−2.42,8.68)	—	(−2.85,9.11)

* Statistically significant at the 5 per cent level; all other pairs do not reach statistical significance at the 5 per cent level.

a possible *increase* in hostility due to treatment, the conclusion would be that there is insufficient evidence to reject.

All pairs—Tukey and Scheffé methods. A comparison of all possible pairs of means by the methods of Tukey and Scheffé is shown in Table 3. The tests of Tukey and Scheffé in this case both discount $\bar{x}_1 - \bar{x}_3$ but declare $\bar{x}_2 - \bar{x}_3$ "significant." The conclusion is that instrumental communication leaves the mean hostility of frustrated subjects lower than ego support does, but no other difference is established; specifically, neither test would conclude that instrumental communication actually reduces hostility as compared with no treatment or that ego support increases (or reduces) it.

In addition to the simple differences, the data suggest testing a contrast related to the alternate hypothesis $\mu_2 < \mu_4 < \mu_1 < \mu_3$, for example, the contrast $-3\mu_2 - \mu_4 + \mu_1 + 3\mu_3$. (It is legitimate, for these procedures, to choose such a contrast after inspecting the data.) For the present example, $-3\bar{x}_2 - \bar{x}_4 + \bar{x}_1 + 3\bar{x}_3 = 21.27$; the SE for a Scheffé test is $\sqrt{(3^2 + 1^2 + 1^2 + 3^2)/48}\hat{\sigma} = \sqrt{10} \times 2.136 = 6.755$, and $t = 21.27/6.755 = 3.15$, statistically significant at the 5 per cent level ($3.15 > 2.80$). The conclusion is that $\mu_2 \leqslant \mu_4 \leqslant \mu_1 \leqslant \mu_3$ with at least one strict inequality holding. A Scheffé 95 per cent confidence interval for $-3\mu_2 - \mu_4 + \mu_1 + 3\mu_3$ is (1.36, 40.18). A Tukey test would not find this contrast statistically significant. For this analysis 2.136 is multiplied by $\frac{1}{2}(|-3| + |-1| + |1| + |3|) = 4$, instead of by $\sqrt{10}$, yielding 8.544. Thus, in this case $t = 21.27/8.544 = 2.49$, which is less than 2.60, and a confidence interval is (−0.94, +43.48).

The SE for individual $\bar{x}_i$, also used in slippage statistics, is $\sqrt{(1/48)\hat{\sigma}^2} = 2.136/\sqrt{2} = 1.510$. For $k = 4$, $M_{.05} = 2.50$, and simultaneous confidence intervals for the four μ_i are centered at the $\bar{x}_i$ and have half-lengths $2.50 \times 1.51 = 3.78$.

The 5 per cent critical value tabulated by Halperin et al. for two-sided slippage tests is 2.23;

thus $(\bar{x}_2 - \bar{x})/1.51 = 2.48$ is statistically significant, whereas the other three t-ratios for slippage are not. The conclusion of this test would be that mean hostility after instrumental communication is low compared with that after other treatments; no other treatment can be singled out as leaving hostility either low or high compared with that after other treatments.

An example of Newman–Keuls and Duncan tests is given in Section 10, below.

Other multiple comparison methods

9. Nonparametric multiple comparisons. The multiple comparison approach has been articulated with nonparametric (or distribution-free) methods in several ways [*for background see* NONPARAMETRIC STATISTICS].

For example, one of the simplest nonparametric tests is the sign test. Suppose that an experiment concerning techniques for teaching reading deals with school classes and that each class is divided in half at random. One half is taught by method 1, the other by method 2, the methods being allocated at random. Suppose further that improvement in average score on a reading test after two months is the basic observation but that one chooses to consider only whether the pupils taught by method 1 gain more than the pupils taught by method 2, or vice versa, and not the magnitude of the difference. If C is the number of classes for which the pupils taught with method 1 have a larger average gain than those taught with method 2, then the (two-sided) sign test rejects the null hypothesis of equal method effect when the absolute value of C is larger than a critical value. The critical value comes simply from a symmetrical binomial distribution.

Suppose now that there are k teaching methods, where k might be 3 or 4, and the classes are each divided at random into k groups and assigned to methods. Let C_{ij} $(i \neq j)$ be the number of classes for which the average gain in reading-test score for the group taught by method i is greater than that for the group taught by method j. Each C_{ij} taken separately has (under the null hypothesis that the corresponding two methods are equally effective) a symmetric binomial distribution which is approximated asymptotically by $\frac{1}{2}n + z\frac{1}{2}\sqrt{n} + \frac{1}{2}$, where n is the number of classes, z is a standard normal variable, and $\frac{1}{2}$ is a continuity correction. But to test for the equality of all k methods, the largest $|C_{ij}|$ should be used. The critical values of this statistic may be approximated by $T_\alpha \frac{1}{2}\sqrt{n} + \frac{1}{2}$, where T_α is the upper α point for Tukey's statistic with k groups and $ddf = \infty$.

The same procedure is feasible for other two-sample test statistics—for example, rank sums. An analogous method works for comparing $k - 1$ treatments with a control; in the teaching-method experiment, if method 1 were the control, this would mean using as the test statistic the maximum over $j \neq 1$ of $|C_{1j}|$ (or of C_{1j} in the one-sided case). For a discussion of this material, see Steel (1959).

Joint nonparametric confidence intervals may sometimes be obtained in a similar way. Given a confidence interval estimation procedure related to any two-sample test statistic with critical value S_α (see Moses 1953; 1965), the same procedure with S_α replaced by its multiple comparison analogue C_α yields confidence intervals with a joint confidence level of $1 - \alpha$.

A second class of nonparametric multiple comparison tests arises by analogy with normal theory analysis of variance for the one-way classification and other simple designs [see LINEAR HYPOTHESES, *article on* ANALYSIS OF VARIANCE]. The procedures start by transforming the observations into ranks or other kinds of simplified scores (except that the so-called permutation tests leave the observations unaltered). The analysis is conditional on the totality of scores and uses as its null distribution that obtained from random allocations of the observed scores to treatments. The test statistic may be the ordinary F-ratio on the scores, but modified so that the denominator is the exact over-all variance of the given scores. This statistic's null distribution is approximately F, with $k - 1$ and ∞ as degrees of freedom (where k is the number of treatments), or, equivalently, $k - 1$ times the F-test statistic has as approximate null distribution the chi-square distribution with $k - 1$ degrees of freedom. Similar adaptations hold for the Tukey test statistic and others. The approach may also be extended to randomized block designs; in another direction, the approach may be extended to compare dispersion, rather than location. Discussions of this material are given by Nemenyi (1963) and Miller (1966, chapter 2, sec. 1.4, and chapter 4, sec. 7.5).

A difficulty with these test procedures is that confidence sets cannot generally be obtained in a straightforward way.

A third nonparametric approach to multiple comparisons is described by Walsh (1965, pp. 535–536). The basic notion applies when there are a number of observations for each treatment or treatment combination. Such a set of observations is divided into several subsets; the average of each subset is taken. These averages are then treated by normal theory procedures of the kind discussed earlier.

For convenient reference, a few 5 per cent and 1 per cent critical points of multiple comparison statistics with $ddf = \infty$ are listed in Table 4.

Table 4 — Selected 5 per cent and 1 per cent critical points of multiple comparison statistics with $ddf = \infty$

k	DUNNETT $k-1$ versus one one-tail	DUNNETT two-tail	TUKEY all pairs range$/\sqrt{2}$	NAIR–HALPERIN outlier tests one-tail	NAIR–HALPERIN two-tail	SCHEFFÉ $\sqrt{\chi^2_{k-1}}$	DUNCAN
			5 per cent level				
2	1.64	1.96	1.96	1.39	1.39	1.96	1.96
3	1.92	2.21	2.34	1.74	1.91	2.45	2.06
4	2.06	2.35	2.57	1.94	2.14	2.80	2.13
5	2.16	2.44	2.73	2.08	2.28	3.08	2.18
6	2.23	2.51	2.85	2.18	2.39	3.23	2.23
			1 per cent level				
2	2.33	2.58	2.58	1.82	1.82	2.58	2.58
3	2.56	2.79	2.91	2.22	2.38	3.03	2.68
4	2.68	2.92	3.11	2.43	2.61	3.37	2.76
5	2.77	3.00	3.25	2.57	2.76	3.64	2.81
6	2.84	3.06	3.36	2.68	2.87	3.88	2.86

Table 5 — Frequency of church attendance of scientists in four different fields

Church attendance	(1) Chemical engineers	(2) Physicists	(3) Zoologists	(4) Geologists	Combined sample	Score u
Never	44	65	66	72	247	-1
Not often	38	19	21	30	108	0
Often	52	46	49	38	185	1
Very often	33	29	19	17	98	2
Sample size, n_i	167	159	155	157	$N = 638$	
$T_i = \sum$ Frequency $\cdot u$	74	39	21	0*	$T = 134$	
$\bar{u}_i = T_i/n_i$	0.443	0.245	0.136	0.000	$\bar{u} = 0.210$	
$1/n_i$	0.005988	0.006289	0.006452	0.006369	$1/N = 0.001567$	

* It is purely accidental that T_i exactly equals 0.

Source: Vaughan et al. 1966.

10. An example. As an illustration of some distribution-free multiple comparison methods, consider the following data from Vaughan, Sjoberg, and Smith (1966), who sent questionnaires to a sample of scientists listed in *American Men of Science* in order to compare scientists in four different fields with respect to the role that traditional religion plays in their lives. Table 5 summarizes responses to the question about frequency of church attendance and shows some of the calculations.

Using the data of Table 5, illustrative significance tests of the null hypothesis of four identical population distributions, against various alternatives, will be performed at the 1 per cent level.

The method of Yates (1948) begins by assigning ascending numerical scores, u, to the four ordered categories; arithmetically convenient scores, as shown in the last column of Table 5, are -1, 0, 1, and 2. Sample totals of scores are calculated—for example, $T_1 = 44(-1) + 38(0) + 52(1) + 33(2) = 74$, and the average score for sample i is $\bar{u}_i = T_i/n_i$. From the combined sample (margin) Yates computes an average score, $\bar{u} = T/N = .210$, and the variance of scores,

$$\sigma^2 = \frac{N}{N-1}(\text{average square} - \bar{u}^2),$$

giving $(638/637)\{[247(1) + 108(0) + 185(1) + 98(4)]/638 - .210^2\} = 1.2494$.

Yates then computes a variance between means, $T_1^2/n_1 + \cdots + T_4^2/n_4 - T^2/N = 17.05$, and the critical ratio used is either $F = (17.05/3)/1.2494$ or $\chi^2 = 17.05/1.2494 = 13.7$. The second of these is referred to a table of chi-square with 3 df and found significant at the 1 per cent level (in fact, $P = .0034$).

It follows that some contrasts must be statistically significant. The almost linear progression of the sample mean scores suggests calculating $3\bar{u}_1 + \bar{u}_2 - \bar{u}_3 - 3\bar{u}_4 = 1.438$. For the denominator, $(3^2/167 + 1^2/159 + 1^2/155 + 3^2/157)\sigma^2 = .1240 \times 1.2494 = .1549$, so that $\chi^2 = 1.438^2/.1549 = 13.35$, or its square root, $z = 1.438/\sqrt{.1549} = 3.65$. (This comes close to the value $\sqrt{13.7} = 3.70$ of the largest standardized contrast—see Section 5.) When 3.65 is referred to the Scheffé table (in Table 4, above) for $k = 4$, or when 13.35 is referred to a table of chi-square with 3 df, each is found to be statistically significant (in fact, $P = .0040$). The conclusion that can be drawn from this one-sided test for trend is that the population mean scores are ordered $\tilde{\mu}_1 \geqslant \tilde{\mu}_2 \geqslant \tilde{\mu}_3 \geqslant \tilde{\mu}_4$ with at least one strict inequality holding. Had a trend in this particular order been predicted ahead of time and postulated as the sole alternative hypothesis to be considered, $z = 3.65$ could have been judged by the normal table, yielding $P = .00013$. The two-tail version of this test is Yates's one-degree-of-freedom chi-square for trend (1948).

Another contrast that may be tested is the simple difference $\bar{u}_1 - \bar{u}_4 = .443 - .000$. Here $SE = \sqrt{[(1/167) + (1/157)] \times 1.2494} = .1243$, and $z_{14} = .443/.1243 = 3.57$. Because it is greater than 3.37, this contrast is statistically significant. Similarly, $z_{13} = (.443 - .136)/.1239 = 2.48$, but this is not significant at the 1 per cent level, and the other simple differences are still smaller.

If Tukey's test had been adopted instead of Scheffé's, the same ratios would be compared with the critical value 3.11 ($k = 4$, $\alpha = .01$). The conclusions would be the same in the present case. Tukey's method could also be used to test other contrasts.

In the present example, the Newman–Keuls procedure would also have led to the same conclusions about simple differences: $z_{14} = 3.57$ is called significant because it is greater than 3.11; then z_{13} (which equals 2.48) and z_{24} (which is still smaller) are compared with 2.91 and found "not significant," and the procedure ends. The conclusions may be summarized as follows:

$$\underline{.443 \quad\quad .245 \quad\quad .136} \quad\quad .000,$$

where the absence of a line connecting $\bar{u}_1$ with $\bar{u}_4$ signifies that $\bar{\mu}_1$ and $\bar{\mu}_4$ are declared unequal. It may be argued that a conclusion of the form "A, B, and C homogeneous, B, C, and D homogeneous, but A, B, C, and D not homogeneous" is self-contradictory. This is not necessarily the case if the interpretation is the usual one that A, B, and C *may* be equal (not enough evidence to prove them unequal) and B, C, and D may be equal, but A and D are not equal.

In Duncan's procedure the critical value 3.11 used in the first stage would be replaced by 2.76 (see Table 5), and the critical value 2.91 used at the second stage ($k = 3$) would be replaced by 2.68. Since $3.57 > 2.76$ but $2.48 < 2.68$, Duncan's test leads to the same conclusion in the present example as the Newman–Keuls procedure.

A Halperin outlier test would use max $|\bar{u}_i - \bar{u}|$, in this case $.443 - 2.10 = .233$, divide it by

$$\sqrt{4/3[(1/167) - (1/638)] \, 1.2494} = .08582,$$

and compare the resulting ratio, 2.72, with the critical value, 2.61 ($k = 4$, 1 per cent level). The next largest ratio is $(.210 - .000)/.08944 = 2.35$. The conclusion is that chemical engineers tend to report more frequent church attendance than the other groups, but nothing can be said about geologists. If the outlier contrasts had been tested as part of a Scheffé test for all contrasts, none of them would have been found significant at the 1 per cent level (critical value 3.37) or even at the 5 per cent level.

What would happen if unequally spaced scores had been used instead of -1, 0, 1, 2 to quantify the four degrees of religious loyalty? In fact, Vaughan and his associates described the ordered categories not verbally but as frequency of church attendance per month grouped into 0, 1, 2–4, 5+. Although we do not know whether frequency of church attendance is a linear measure of the importance of religion in a person's life, the scores (0, 1, 3, 6) could reasonably have been assigned. In the present case this would lead to essentially the same conclusions that the other scoring led to: The mean scores become 2.35, 2.08, 1.82, and 1.57, Yates's

χ^2 changes from 13.7 to 12.5, the standardized contrast for trend changes from $\sqrt{13.35}$ to very nearly $\sqrt{12.5}$, z_{14} changes from 3.57 to 3.36, and z_{13} and z_{24} again have values too small for statistical significance by Tukey's criterion or by Newman–Keuls'.

A fundamentally different assignment of scores —for example, 1, 0, 0, 1—would be used to test for differences in spread. It yields sample means, $\bar{u}_i$, of .461, .591, .548, .576, $\bar{u} = 0.541$ and a variance, σ^2, of .2484. Yates's analysis-of-variance χ^2 is $1.449/0.2484$, that is, only 5.83, so $P = .12$. Thus, no contrast is called significant in a Scheffé test (or, it turns out, in any other multiple comparison test at the 1 per cent significance level). In the present example these tests for spread are unreliable, because the presence of sample location differences, noted above, can vitiate the results of the test for differences in spread.

Throughout the numerical calculations in this section, the continuity correction has been neglected. In the case of unequal sample sizes it is difficult to determine what continuity correction would yield the most accurate results, and the effect of the adjustment would be slight anyway. When sample sizes are equal, the use of $|T_i - T_j| - \frac{1}{2}$ in place of $|T_i - T_j|$ is recommended, as it frequently (although not invariably) improves the fit of the asymptotic approximation used.

11. Comparisons for differences in scale. Standard multiple comparisons of variances of k normal populations, by Cochran (1941), David (1952), and others, utilize ratios of the $\hat{\sigma}_i^2$. These methods should be used with caution, because they are ultra-sensitive to slight nonnormality.

Distribution-free multiple comparison tests for scale differences are also available. Any rank test may be used with a Siegel–Tukey reranking [*see* NONPARAMETRIC STATISTICS, *article on* RANKING METHODS]. Such methods, too, require caution, because—especially in a joint ranking of all k samples—any sizable location differences may masquerade as differences in scale (Moses 1963).

Safer methods—but with efficiencies of only about 50 per cent for normal distributions—are adaptations of some tests by Moses (1963). In these tests a small integer, s, such as 2 or 3, is chosen, and each sample is randomly subdivided into subgroups of s observations. Let y be the range or variance of a subgroup. Then any multiple comparison tests may be applied to the k samples of y's (or log y's), at the sacrifice of between-subgroups information. The effective sample sizes have been reduced to $[n_i/s]$; if these are small (about 6), either a nonparametric test or, at any rate, log y's should be used. (Some nonparametric multiple comparison tests, such as the median test, have no power—that is, they cannot possibly reject the null hypothesis—at significance levels such as .05 with small samples. But rank tests can be used with several samples as small as 4 or 5.)

12. Multiple comparisons of proportions. A simultaneous test for all differences between k proportions $p_1, \cdots, p_k$, based on large samples, can be obtained by comparing

$$\text{Max} \frac{X_i/n_i - X_j/n_j}{\sqrt{\frac{N}{N-1}\left(\frac{1}{n_i}+\frac{1}{n_j}\right)\frac{X}{N}\left(1-\frac{X}{N}\right)}}$$

with a critical value of Tukey's statistic (Section 3), where X_i, $i = 1, \cdots, k$, denotes the number of "successes" in sample i and $X = \sum X_i$. Analogous asymptotic tests can be used for comparison of several treatments with a control and other forms of multiple comparisons. If X/N is small, the sample sizes must be very large for this asymptotic approximation to be adequate. (For a similar method see Ryan 1960.)

Small-sample multiple comparison tests of proportions may be carried out by transforming the counts into normal variables with known equal variances and then applying any test of sections 1–7 to these standardized variables (using $\infty \, ddf$). [See STATISTICAL ANALYSIS, SPECIAL PROBLEMS OF, article on TRANSFORMATIONS OF DATA; see also Siotani & Ozawa 1958.]

A $(1-\alpha)$-confidence region for k population proportions is composed of a $\sqrt[k]{1-\alpha}$-confidence interval for each of them. Simultaneous confidence intervals for a set of differences of proportions may be approximated by using Bonferroni's inequality (see Section 14). For a discussion of confidence regions for multinomial proportions, see Goodman (1965).

Some discussion of multiple comparisons of proportions can be found in Walsh (1965, for example, pp. 536–537).

13. Selection and ranking. The approach called selection or ranking *assumes* a difference between populations and seeks to select the population(s) with the highest mean—or variance or proportion —or to arrange all k populations in order [see SCREENING AND SELECTION; see also Bechhofer 1958]. Bechhofer, Kiefer, and Sobel (1967) have written a monograph on the subject.

Error rates, choice of method, history

14. Error rates and choice of method. In a significance test comparing two populations, the significance level is defined as

$$a = \frac{\text{number of type I errors}}{\text{number of comparisons when } H_0 \text{ is true}}$$

in repeated use of the same criterion. This is termed the *error rate per comparison*. The corresponding confidence level for confidence intervals is $1 - a$.

For analyses of k-sample experiments one may instead define the *error rate per experiment*,

$$a' = \frac{\text{number of type I errors}}{\text{number of experiments analyzed, when } H_0 \text{ is true}}.$$

This is related to what Miller (1966) terms the "expected error rate." For m (computed or implied) comparisons per experiment, $a' = ma$; $a = a'/m$ (see Stanley 1957).

Standard multiple comparison tests specify an *error rate experimentwise* (or "familywise"):

$$\alpha = \frac{\substack{\text{number of experiments, when } H_0 \text{ is true,}\\ \text{leading to any type I errors,}}}{\text{number of experiments analyzed, when } H_0 \text{ is true}}.$$

Miller refers to this as the "probability of a non-zero family error rate" or "probability error rate."

The only difference between a' and α is that α counts multiple rejections in a single experiment as only one error whereas a' counts them as more than one. Hence, $\alpha \leqslant a'$; this is termed *Bonferroni's inequality*.

On the other hand, it is also true that unless a' is large, α is almost equal to a', so that α and a' may be used interchangeably for practical purposes. For example, D_α for 6 treatments and a control, M_α for $k = 6$, and T_α for $k = 4$ ($\binom{4}{2} = 6$), are all approximately equal to the two-tailed critical value $|t|_{\alpha/6} = t_{\alpha/12}$ of Student's t. More generally, m individual comparisons may safely be made using any statistic at significance level α/m per comparison when it is desired to avoid error rates greater than α experimentwise; this procedure may be applied to comparisons of several correlation coefficients or other quantities for which multiple comparison tables are not available. Only when α is about .10 or more, or when m is very big, does this lead to serious waste. Then a' grossly overstates α, power is lost, and confidence intervals are unnecessarily long (see Stanley 1957; Ryan 1959; Dunn 1961).

Some authors refer to (α/m)-points as Bonferroni statistics and to their use in multiple comparisons as the Bonferroni method. Table 2 in Miller (1966) shows Bonferroni t-statistics, $(.05/2m)$-points of Student's t for various m and various numbers of ddf.

Bonferroni's second inequality (see **Halperin**

et al. 1955, p. 191) may sometimes be used to obtain an upper limit for the discrepancy $a' - \alpha$ and a second approximation to critical values for error rates α experimentwise. This works best in the case of slippage statistics and was used by Halperin and his associates (1955), Doornbos and Prins (1958), Thompson and Willke (1963), and others.

The choice between "experimentwise" and "per comparison" is largely a matter of taste. An experimenter should make it consciously, aware of the implications: A given error probability, a, per comparison implies that the risk of at least one type I error in the analysis is much greater than a; indeed, about $a \times m$ such errors will probably occur.

Perhaps analyses reporting error rates experimentwise are generally the most honest, or transparent. However, too dogmatic an application of this principle would lead to all sorts of difficulties. Should not the researcher who in the course of his career analyzes 86 experiments involving 1,729 relevant contrasts control the error rate *lifetimewise*? If he does not, he is almost bound to make a false positive inference sooner or later.

Sterling (1959) discusses the related problem of concentration of type I errors in the literature that result from the habit of selecting significant findings for publication [see FALLACIES, STATISTICAL, *for further discussion of this problem*].

There is another context in which the problem of choosing error rates arises: If an experimenter laboriously sets up expensive apparatus for an experiment to compare two treatments or conditions in which he is especially interested, he often feels that it would be unfortunate to pass up the opportunity to obtain additional data of secondary interest at practically no extra cost or trouble; so he makes observations on populations 3, 4, $\cdots$, k as well. It is then possible that the results are such that a two-sample test on the data of primary interest would have shown statistical significance, but no "significant differences" are found in a multiple comparison test. If the bonus observations thus drown out, so to speak, the significant difference, was the experimenter wrong to read them? He was not—the opportunity to obtain extra information should not be wasted, but the analysis should be planned ahead of time with the experimenter's interests and priorities in mind. He could decide to analyze his primary and subsidiary results as if they had come from separate experiments, or he could conduct multiple comparisons with an overall error rate enlarged to avoid undue loss of power,

or he could use a method of analysis which subdivides α, allocating a certain (large) part to the primary comparison and the rest to "data snooping" among the extra observations (Miller 1966, chapter 2, sec. 2.3).

Whenever it is decided to specify error rates experimentwise, a choice between different systems of multiple comparisons (different shapes of confidence regions) remains to be made. In order to study simple differences or slippage only, one of the methods of sections 2–4 above (or a nonparametric version of them) is best—that is, yields the shortest confidence intervals and most powerful tests, provided the n_i are (nearly) equal. But Scheffé's approach (see section 5) is better if a variety of contrasts may receive attention.

When sample sizes are grossly unequal, probability statements based on existing Tukey or Dunnett tables, computed for equal n's, become too inaccurate. Pending the appearance of appropriate new tables, it is better to use Scheffé's method, which furnishes exact probabilities. The Bonferroni statistics discussed above offer an alternative solution, preferable whenever attention is strictly limited to a few contrasts chosen ahead of time. Miller (1966, especially chapter 2, secs. 2.3 and 3.3) discusses these questions in some detail.

15. History of multiple comparisons. An early, isolated example of a multiple comparison method was one developed by Working and Hotelling (1929) to obtain a confidence belt for a regression line (see Miller 1966, chapter 3; Kerrich 1955). This region also corresponds to simultaneous confidence intervals for the intercept and slope [see LINEAR HYPOTHESES, *article on* REGRESSION]. Hotelling (1927) had already developed the idea of simultaneous confidence interval estimation earlier in connection with the fitting of logistic curves to population time series. In his famous paper introducing the T^2-statistic, Hotelling (1931) also introduced the idea of simultaneous tests and a confidence ellipsoid for the components of a multivariate normal mean.

The systematic development of multiple comparison methods and theory began later, in connection with the problem of comparing several normal means. The usual method had been the analysis-of-variance F-test, sometimes accompanied by t-tests at a stated significance level, a (usually 5 per cent), per comparison.

Fisher, in the 1935 edition of *The Design of Experiments*, pointed out the problem of inflation of error probabilities in such multiple t-tests and recommended the use of t-tests at a stated level a'

per experiment. Pearson and Chandra Sekar further discussed the problem (1936). Newman (1939), acting on an informal suggestion by Student, described a test for all differences based on tables of the Studentized range and furnished a table of approximate 5 per cent and 1 per cent points. Keuls formulated Newman's test more clearly much later (Keuls 1952).

Nair made two contributions in 1948, the one-sided test for slippage of means and a table for simultaneous F-tests in a 2^r factorial design. Also in the late 1940s, Duncan and Tukey experimented with various tests for normal means which were forerunners of the multiple comparison tests now associated with their names.

The standard methods for multiple comparisons of normal means were developed between 1952 and 1955 by Tukey, Scheffé, Dunnett, and Duncan. Tukey wrote a comprehensive volume on the subject which was widely circulated in duplicated form and extensively quoted but which has not been published (1953). The form of Tukey's method described in Section 3 for unequal n's was given independently by Kurtz and by Kramer in 1956. Also in the early and middle 1950s, some multiple comparison methods for normal *variances* were published, by Hartley, David, Truax, Krishnaiah, and others. Cochran's slippage test for normal variances was published, for use as a substitute for Bartlett's test for homogeneity of variances, as early as 1941 (see Cochran 1941).

Selection and ranking procedures for means, variances, and proportions have been developed since 1953 by Bechhofer and others.

An easy, distribution-free slippage test was proposed by Mosteller in 1948—simply count the number of observations in the most extreme sample lying beyond the most extreme value of all the other samples and refer to a table by Mosteller and Tukey (1950). Other distribution-free multiple comparison methods—although some of them can be viewed as applications of S. N. Roy's work of 1953—did not begin to appear until after 1958.

The most important applications of the very general methodology developed by the school of Roy and Bose since 1953 have been *multivariate* multiple comparison tests and confidence regions. Such work by Roy, Bose, Gnanadesikan, Krishnaiah, Gabriel, and others is generally recognizable by the word "simultaneous" in the title—for example, SMANOVA, that is, simultaneous multivariate analysis of variance (see Miller 1966, chapter 5).

Another recent development is the appearance of some Bayesian techniques for multiple comparisons. These are discussed by Duncan in the May 1965 issue of *Technometrics*, an issue which is devoted to articles on multiple comparison methods and theory and reflects a cross section of current trends in this field.

PETER NEMENYI

BIBLIOGRAPHY

The only comprehensive source for the subject of multiple comparisons to date is Miller 1966. *Multiple comparisons of normal means (and variances) are summarized by a number of authors, notably David 1962a and 1962b. Several textbooks on statistics—e.g., Winer 1962—also cover some of this ground. Many of the relevant tables, for normal means and variances, can also be found in David 1962a and 1962b; Vianelli 1959; and Pearson & Hartley 1954; these volumes also provide explanations of the derivation and use of the tables.*

BECHHOFER, R. E. 1958 A Sequential Multiple-decision Procedure for Selecting the Best One of Several Normal Populations With a Common Unknown Variance, and Its Use With Various Experimental Designs. *Biometrics* 14:408–429.

BECHHOFER, R. E.; KIEFER, J.; and SOBEL, M. 1967 Sequential Ranking Procedures. Unpublished manuscript. → Projected for publication by the University of Chicago Press in association with the Institute of Mathematical Statistics.

COCHRAN, W. G. 1941 The Distribution of the Largest of a Set of Estimated Variances as a Fraction of Their Total. *Annals of Eugenics* 11:47–52.

CRONBACH, LEE J. 1949 Statistical Methods Applied to Rorschach Scores: A Review. *Psychological Bulletin* 46:393–429.

DAVID, H. A. 1952 Upper 5 and 1% Points of the Maximum F-ratio. *Biometrika* 39:422–424.

DAVID, H. A. 1962a Multiple Decisions and Multiple Comparisons. Pages 144–162 in Ahmed E. Sarhan and Bernard G. Greenberg (editors), *Contributions to Order Statistics*. New York: Wiley.

DAVID, H. A. 1962b Order Statistics in Shortcut Tests. Pages 94–128 in Ahmed E. Sarhan and Bernard G. Greenberg (editors), *Contributions to Order Statistics*. New York: Wiley.

DOORNBOS, R.; and PRINS, H. J. 1958 On Slippage Tests. Part 3: Two Distribution-free Slippage Tests and Two Tables. *Indagationes mathematicae* 20:438–447.

DUNCAN, DAVID B. 1955 Multiple Range and Multiple F Tests. *Biometrics* 11:1–42.

DUNCAN, DAVID B. 1965 A Bayesian Approach to Multiple Comparisons. *Technometrics* 7:171–222.

DUNN, OLIVE J. 1961 Multiple Comparisons Among Means. *Journal of the American Statistical Association* 56:52–64.

DUNNETT, CHARLES W. 1955 A Multiple Comparison Procedure for Comparing Several Treatments With a Control. *Journal of the American Statistical Association* 50:1096–1121.

FISHER, R. A. (1935) 1960 *The Design of Experiments.* 7th ed. London: Oliver & Boyd; New York: Hafner.

FISHER, R. A.; and YATES, FRANK (1938) 1963 *Statistical Tables for Biological, Agricultural, and Medical Research.* 6th ed., rev. & enl. Edinburgh: Oliver & Boyd; New York: Hafner.

GABRIEL, K. R. 1966 Simultaneous Test Procedures for Multiple Comparisons on Categorical Data. *Journal of the American Statistical Association* 61:1081–1096.

GOODMAN, LEO A. 1965 On Simultaneous Confidence Intervals for Multinomial Proportions. *Technometrics* 7:247–252.

HALPERIN, M.; GREENHOUSE, S.; CORNFIELD, J.; and ZALOKAR, J. 1955 Tables of Percentage Points for the Studentized Maximum Absolute Deviate in Normal Samples. *Journal of the American Statistical Association* 50:185–195.

HARTER, H. LEON 1957 Error Rates and Sample Sizes for Range Tests in Multiple Comparisons. *Biometrics* 13:511–536.

HARTER, H. LEON 1960 Tables of Range and Studentized Range. *Annals of Mathematical Statistics* 31:1122–1147.

HARTLEY, H. O. 1950 The Maximum *F*-ratio as a Short-cut Test for Heterogeneity of Variance. *Biometrika* 37:308–312.

HOTELLING, HAROLD 1927 Differential Equations Subject to Error, and Population Estimates. *Journal of the American Statistical Association* 22:283–314.

HOTELLING, HAROLD 1931 The Generalization of Student's Ratio. *Annals of Mathematical Statistics* 2:360–378.

KERRICH, J. E. 1955 Confidence Intervals Associated With a Straight Line Fitted by Least Squares. *Statistica neerlandica* 9:125–129.

KEULS, M. 1952 The Use of "Studentized Range" in Connection With an Analysis of Variance. *Euphytica* 1:112–122.

KRAMER, CLYDE Y. 1956 Extension of Multiple Range Tests to Group Means With Unequal Number of Replications. *Biometrics* 12:307–310.

KRAMER, CLYDE Y. 1957 Extension of Multiple Range Tests to Group Correlated Adjusted Means. *Biometrics* 13:13–18.

KRISHNAIAH, P. R. 1965a On a Multivariate Generalization of the Simultaneous Analysis of Variance Test. Institute of Statistical Mathematics (Tokyo), *Annals* 17, no. 2:167–173.

KRISHNAIAH, P. R. 1965b Simultaneous Tests for the Equality of Variance Against Certain Alternatives. *Australian Journal of Statistics* 7:105–109.

KURTZ, T. E. 1956 An Extension of a Method of Making Multiple Comparisons (Preliminary Report). *Annals of Mathematical Statistics* 27:547 only.

KURTZ, T. E.; LINK, R. F.; TUKEY, J. W.; and WALLACE, D. L. 1965 Short-cut Multiple Comparisons for Balanced Single and Double Classifications. Part 1: Results. *Technometrics* 7:95–169.

McHUGH, RICHARD B.; and ELLIS, DOUGLAS S. 1955 The "Post Mortem" Testing of Experimental Comparisons. *Psychological Bulletin* 52:425–428.

MILLER, RUPERT G. 1966 *Simultaneous Statistical Inference.* New York: McGraw-Hill.

MOSES, LINCOLN E. 1953 Nonparametric Methods. Pages 426–450 in Helen M. Walker and Joseph Lev, *Statistical Inference.* New York: Holt.

MOSES, LINCOLN E. 1963 Rank Tests of Dispersion. *Annals of Mathematical Statistics* 34:973–983.

MOSES, LINCOLN E. 1965 Confidence Limits From Rank Tests (Reply to a Query). *Technometrics* 7:257–260.

MOSTELLER, FREDERICK W.; and TUKEY, JOHN W. 1950 Significance Levels for a *k*-sample Slippage Test. *Annals of Mathematical Statistics* 21:120–123.

NAIR, K. R. 1948a The Studentized Form of the Extreme Mean Square Test in the Analysis of Variance. *Biometrika* 35:16–31.

NAIR, K. R. 1948b The Distribution of the Extreme Deviate From the Sample Mean and Its Studentized Form. *Biometrika* 35:118–144.

NAIR, K. R. 1952 Tables of Percentage Points of the "Studentized" Extreme Deviate From the Sample Mean. *Biometrika* 39:189–191.

NEMENYI, PETER 1963 Distribution-free Multiple Comparisons. Ph.D. dissertation, Princeton Univ.

NEWMAN, D. 1939 The Distribution of the Range in Samples From a Normal Population, Expressed in Terms of an Independent Estimate of Standard Deviation. *Biometrika* 31:20–30.

PEARSON, EGON S.; and CHANDRA SEKAR, C. 1936 The Efficiency of Statistical Tools and a Criterion for the Rejection of Outlying Observations. *Biometrika* 28:308–320.

PEARSON, EGON S.; and HARTLEY, H. O. (editors) (1954) 1966 *Biometrika Tables for Statisticians.* Vol. 1. 3d ed. Cambridge Univ. Press. → Only the first volume of this edition has as yet been published.

PILLAI, K. C. S.; and RAMACHANDRAN, K. V. 1954 On the Distribution of the Ratio of the *i*th Observation in an Ordered Sample From a Normal Population to an Independent Estimate of the Standard Deviation. *Annals of Mathematical Statistics* 25:565–572.

QUESENBERRY, C. P.; and DAVID, H. A. 1961 Some Tests for Outliers. *Biometrika* 48:379–390.

ROESSLER, R. G. 1946 Testing the Significance of Observations Compared With a Control. American Society for Horticultural Science, *Proceedings* 47:249–251.

ROTHAUS, PAUL; and WORCHEL, PHILIP 1964 Ego Support, Communication, Catharsis, and Hostility. *Journal of Personality* 32:296–312.

ROY, S. N.; and BOSE, R. C. 1953 Simultaneous Confidence Interval Estimation. *Annals of Mathematical Statistics* 24:513–536.

ROY, S. N.; and GNANADESIKAN, R. 1957 Further Contributions to Multivariate Confidence Bounds. *Biometrika* 44:399–410.

RYAN, THOMAS A. 1959 Multiple Comparisons in Psychological Research. *Psychological Bulletin* 56:26–47.

RYAN, THOMAS A. 1960 Significance Tests for Multiple Comparisons of Proportions, Variances, and Other Statistics. *Psychological Bulletin* 57:318–328.

SCHEFFÉ, HENRY 1953 A Method for Judging All Contrasts in the Analysis of Variance. *Biometrika* 40:87–104.

SIOTANI, M.; and OZAWA, MASARU 1958 Tables for Testing the Homogeneity of *k* Independent Binomial Experiments on a Certain Event Based on the Range. Institute of Statistical Mathematics (Tokyo), *Annals* 10:47–63.

STANLEY, JULIAN C. 1957 Additional "Post Mortem" Tests of Experimental Comparisons. *Psychological Bulletin* 54:128–130.

STEEL, ROBERT G. D. 1959 A Multiple Comparison Sign Test: Treatments vs. Control. *Journal of the American Statistical Association* 54:767–775.

STERLING, THEODORE D. 1959 Publication Decisions and Their Possible Effects on Inferences Drawn From Tests of Significance—or Vice Versa. *Journal of the American Statistical Association* 54:30–34.

THOMPSON, W. A. JR.; and WILLKE, T. A. 1963 On an Extreme Rank Sum Test for Outliers. *Biometrika* 50:375–383.

Truax, Donald R. 1953 An Optimum Slippage Test for the Variances of *k* Normal Populations. *Annals of Mathematical Statistics* 24:669–674.

Tukey, J. W. 1953 The Problem of Multiple Comparisons. Unpublished manuscript, Princeton Univ.

Vaughan, Ted R.; Sjoberg, G.; and Smith, D. H. 1966 Religious Orientations of American Natural Scientists. *Social Forces* 44:519–526.

Vianelli, Silvio 1959 *Prontuari per calcoli statistici: Tavole numeriche e complementi.* Palermo: Abbaco.

Walsh, John E. 1965 *Handbook of Nonparametric Statistics.* Volume 2: Results for Two and Several Sample Problems, Symmetry, and Extremes. Princeton, N.J.: Van Nostrand.

Winer, B. J. 1962 *Statistical Principles in Experimental Design.* New York: McGraw-Hill.

Working, Holbrook; and Hotelling, Harold 1929 Application of the Theory of Error to the Interpretation of Trends. *Journal of the American Statistical Association* 24 (March Supplement):73–85.

Yates, Frank 1948 The Analysis of Contingency Tables With Groupings Based on Quantitative Characters. *Biometrika* 35:176–181.

LINEAR PROGRAMMING

See Operations research *and* Programming.

LINGUISTICS

I
THE FIELD

Linguistics has been called the science of language; but this definition begs the questions, What is scientific? What is language? Linguists themselves have not agreed; sometimes their answers have been quite narrow. If we are to consider the gamut of social science interests in language, we must adopt one of two approaches—either interpret "science of language" very broadly or conceive of it as part of some larger field.

In the first approach, "science" is taken in its broadest meaning, *Wissenschaft*, comprising all serious intellectual disciplines; "language" is taken as implicating all aspects of human speech. Linguistics is then truly the science of language, although as such it embraces work of both linguists and scholars in other disciplines. In the second approach, the "science of language" comprises only those kinds of knowledge for which linguists typically take responsibility. The science of language is then but part of a broader area of inquiry, the study of language; the science of language is linguistics proper, and the study of language may be called the field of linguistics.

The second approach is fairer to the present situation of linguistics. Linguistics is the indispensable basis for serious concern with any aspect of language, and its rapid growth is such that its effective scope may indeed come to equal the whole of the study of language. At present, the student of social science concerned with the place of language in human life must also consult other disciplines, perhaps including his own.

Our standpoint, then, will be that of the field of linguistics. We shall first sketch the development of linguistics within the context of the study of language, then characterize linguistics proper in terms of its scope and content today, and last discuss the import of its work with special reference to the social sciences.

Development of linguistics

The present expanding scope of linguistics is the outcome of a complex history. As a separately organized discipline, so named, linguistics is, however, quite young in English-speaking countries. The Linguistic Society of America was founded in 1924, and the Linguistics Association of Great Britain in 1965. Almost all of the independent departments of linguistics have appeared only since World War II. Indeed, "linguistics" has only recently displaced "philology" as a general name for the study of language, and "linguist" is still widely used by laymen for "polyglot" rather than for a member of a scientific discipline.

Early periods. Behind modern linguistics lies an accumulation of insight and knowledge that reaches to the early stages of human history. No known language is without at least some terms for facts of language and hence an elementary metalanguage of a protolinguistic sort. Such terms sometimes show close analysis of structural features; for the most part, however, the internal structures of language remain unconsciously known, and it is terms for uses and varieties of language that are elaborated. Every society indeed has terms, beliefs, attitudes, and knowledge concerning language that may be singled out as its *folk linguistics*. The character and extent of this folk linguistics are of interest as conditioning linguistic change and as part of the subject matter of ethnoscience. Where a separate discipline of linguistic study has emerged, the interaction between it and the folk linguistics of its society may also set some of the limits and directions of the discipline and hence interest the historian of science and the sociologist of knowledge. Some 2,500 years ago there began to appear disciplined studies of language that can be taken as heralding a stage of *national philologies*. In China,

India, and Greece, valued texts (the cultural arm, as it were, of expanding civilizations and aspiring states) came to be given special attention intended to preserve accurate knowledge of them and to aid in their use. These philologies were preceded by systems of writing, themselves embodiments of analysis of language. In the philologies, techniques of analysis became explicit, if with different emphases and differential success. The greatest achievement occurred in the Indian tradition (independently of writing), culminating in the work of Pāṇini (c. 500 B.C.). (Pāṇini was to influence the development of linguistics in Europe, once his work was made known there at the start of the nineteenth century.)

The Western study of language was shaped through most of its history by a tradition of philosophic thought and pedagogic grammars. In the classical world, analysis of language began amid controversies over the regularity or irregularity of language (*analogia : anomalia*), over language as part of nature or culture (*physis : nomos*), over relations between language and other subjects; and amid the establishment of Sophistic training and of educational institutions generally (see Robins 1951; Sandys 1903–1908; Marrou 1948). Etymological curiosity played a prominent part. A system of grammatical categories was evolved, based on the nature of Greek and then Latin. A great merit of the classical work was that it treated language structure integrally with language use; indeed, in education the grammarian was subordinate to the rhetor. Exclusive attention to the language (or languages) of an empire was a great limitation, shared by all early philologies. Given the social role of language study, this restriction was perhaps inevitable, but it was crippling to a general knowledge of language itself.

Early modern period.   In the medieval period of the West (during the intermittent periods of renaissance before that which bears the capitalized name) theoretical notions about the rational structure of language were elaborated and language's place in education and human life discussed (see Bolgar 1954; Robins 1951).

Skills that had begun in the classical world in the first renaissance of Greek literature—that of Alexandria—reached new heights in the Renaissance proper, and the tradition of classical philology which it founded provided the model for textual analysis and criticism in all fields, as well as models for grammars and dictionaries of the emerging national philologies in Europe. As the literary use and serious study of modern European languages grew, an empirical knowledge of languages from Asia, Africa, Oceania, and the New World slowly began to accumulate, especially through the field work of missionaries, history's first organized body of ethnographers. By the eighteenth century the growing body of information was considerable, and there were scientific expeditions whose mission included collection of linguistic data (see Gray 1939; Wonderly & Nida 1963).

Some criteria of relationship among languages had been sought earlier in attempts to harmonize the three great cultural languages (Hebrew, Greek, Latin) and to establish the origin of the peoples of the New World, as well as of modern European peoples. The search for relationships was abetted no doubt by the Biblical account of Babel, which (1) asserted original unity of all languages, and (2) left the details of differentiation open to discovery (see Borst 1957–1963; Metcalf 1964).

In this period the theoretical unity of human language was treated in the Cartesian rationalism of Leibniz and others, in British empiricism, Scottish "common sense," and French materialism. Indeed, as the intellectual foundations for the social sciences developed, the nature of language, posed as a problem of its origin in history and in the individual, engaged most major theorists— Hobbes, Locke, Rousseau, Adam Smith, Condillac, Herder, etc.—bearing as it did on the fundamental nature of man and the relationship between the natural and cultural worlds.

It is conventional to date the history of linguistics proper from the recognition of Sanskrit and the rise of diachronic linguistics, especially Indo-European studies, in the late eighteenth century and early nineteenth. This view (indeed, origin myth) preserves too much of the self-consciousness of an intellectual climate (romanticism, historicism) set off against the image of its predecessor, the Enlightenment. There was justice in the self-consciousness: in the study of language works were produced that became models and starting points for subsequent scholarship; with specialization, chairs, scholarly organizations, and journals increased quite dramatically. It is almost impossible, however, to fix any one point between the mid-eighteenth century and the mid-nineteenth century as decisive intellectually for the development of the successful methods of Indo-European study; Turgot, Rask, Bopp, Grimm, and Schleicher each has his claim to a contribution. Regarding theoretical views, some would now set aside much of the nineteenth-century effort, emphasizing the preceding rationalist inquiry as a more relevant predecessor. The work of Wilhelm von Humboldt thus comes to seem both an end point to developments of interest in the seventeenth and eighteenth centuries and a starting point for a strain of general linguistics in the nineteenth century.

No doubt the salience of periods of past linguistics will continue to change as modern linguistics changes. If we are to understand the history of linguistics, not for partisanship, but as a case in the comparative study of the general history of science and scholarship, one point is essential. Linguistic research, like social science research, proliferated as a sustained, organized, autonomous activity in the nineteenth century, but from an intellectual and empirical base in the general rise of scholarship and science in Europe as part of the expansion, at once intellectual and commercial, of its known world. With that rise began what can be truly called *general linguistics*, a linguistics which, while interdependent with the continued development of philologies and of specializations of other sorts, came to take as its compass all the languages of man. (On the place of linguistic thought in intellectual history, especially the place of language in human nature and culture, see Verburg 1952; Chomsky 1966; Cassirer 1923, chapter 1.)

Nineteenth century. The major study on nineteenth-century linguistics (actually a period approximately from the French Revolution to World War I) records it as the triumph of historical work, especially of comparative Indo-European (Pedersen 1924). From that standpoint the course of the century is one of increasing precision and power of historical method and of its very wide application. Indo-European studies held the center of the stage, partly because of their institutionalization in Prussia and subsequently elsewhere and partly because of the accident of cultural history that the languages prospective Indo-European specialists had to learn in school were the classical "languages of culture." Greek and Latin, together with their native languages and perhaps some other European language, gave these students intimacy with three or four branches of the language family they were to reconstruct. This cultural support and internal availability of data were not duplicated elsewhere. The Hungarian, Gyarmathai, had had the methodological insight to relate Hungarian and Finnish, in 1799 (see Pedersen [1924] 1962, pp. 105–106), but the languages of the family (Finno–Ugric) to which Hungarian belongs were scattered in Russia and the north, and scholars had to rely on cumulative field work. Moreover, there was no prestige in working out the relationship of one's mother tongue to the languages of poor "fish

eaters" (the heroic Turkish conquerors were more attractive as linguistic kin, thus leading much research into a blind alley). Indo-European scholars worked amid the rise of Oriental philology and of interest in the "wisdom from the East" symbolized by Sanskrit.

Among the main accomplishments of the period were the pioneering comparisons of Rask (who was not adequately recognized in his own day); the comparative grammar of Bopp; the recognition of regular patterns of sound change in Germanic by Grimm (and Rask); the etymological dictionaries of Pott and Fick; the method of reconstruction and the family-tree model (*Stammbaum*) of relationship of Schleicher; the more exact specification of regularities in change in sound and of the role of grammatical analogy of the *Junggrammatiker* and others of the 1870s (Ascoli, Verner, de Saussure, Brugmann); the wave model of relationship (*Wellentheorie*) of Schmidt, complementing that of the family tree. The first basis was laid for the historical study of many language families, both within and outside Indo-European (e.g., comparative grammars of Romance, Celtic, Dravidian, Bantu, Athapaskan). Near the end of the period, the great comparativist Meillet, while calling for attention to regularities independent of specific histories, could rightfully state that the principles already developed for the handling of regular sound change, analogy, and borrowing could continue to be fruitfully extended to all the language families of the world.

The traditions of anthropological philology also became established in this period, beginning perhaps with Herder's thesis of the individuality and the scientific and humanistic value of the language and literature of every people, whatever its stage of development. This attitude was to be freshly stated many times, for example, by Boas, a century later. Much anthropological study of language has indeed been the philology of peoples without philology of their own. In this sense anthropology has been the third of the great philological enterprises of European civilization, following upon and complementing classical and Oriental philology.

A master term for the study of language was *philology*, a putative "queen of the sciences" to some, although "linguistics," *linguistique*, and *Sprachwissenschaft* also were in use. Historical linguistics, requiring interpretation of texts, was often termed "comparative philology" in English-speaking countries; and since philologists proper produced the needed grammars and dictionaries, descriptive work also was often identified as "philology." Analogous to "classical philology," the study of contemporary European languages was labeled part of "modern philology" (*Neuphilologie*), and study of a particular set would be, e.g., not "Romance linguistics," but "Romance philology." In American anthropology, "philology" remained the common term into this century (e.g., Boas was retained by the Bureau of American Ethnology as "philologist"). In British usage and some learned American usage "philology" continued to serve until very recently. After World War I the trend among practitioners themselves to distinguish sharply between "philology" and "linguistics" was well established, however favorably the relationship between the two might be viewed (Pedersen [1924] 1962, p. 79). Philology might range far, but it remained inseparable from the study of texts and history, and linguistics was being defined as a more general study of language.

Looking back from the standpoint of contemporary linguistics, one sees in the nineteenth century important strands, which were largely neglected in accounts of the triumph of historical work. One is well known and the progenitor of continuing lines of work—linguistic geography and dialectology. It emerged in a rising wave of interest in geographical distributions in all the human sciences during the half-century embracing the turn of the twentieth century as midpoint. [*See* LINGUISTICS, *article on* THE SPEECH COMMUNITY.]

A second major trend in general linguistics stemmed from von Humboldt and others and sought cognitive import in an evolutionary typology of languages. Carried on by Schleicher, Steinthal, and others in various forms, the effort was later discarded amid a general rejection of evolutionary sequences of stages in the cultural sciences. The whole-language labels, such as isolating, agglutinating, inflectional, polysynthetic, and incorporating, were retained only for individual traits that might be compresent within one language.

The concern with typology was the main source of the attention paid to the structural cut of languages and to its possible import (witness the joint launching of the first journal in social psychology by Steinthal and Lazarus in 1860); and the cognitive interest was retained, but associated with grammatical categories and processes of individual languages, quite divorced from broad classes and stages. (Through Boas the interest became an intrinsic part of American linguistic anthropology.)

Typology was thus part of a third trend, the preparation in the nineteenth century of the structural outlook that was to dominate the twentieth.

In this outlook much was to depend on the approach taken to the sounds of speech. In the nineteenth century European languages often were taken as a norm, such that the sounds of "primitive" languages seemed odd and even to lack constant units—as so o' :n, projection of a lack of structure here betrayed an inadequate understanding of the nature of the primitive language being studied. Speech sounds were studied officially by a phonetics conceived as a natural science (*Naturwissenschaft*), not as a part of linguistics. Seeking universal objectivity through finer physical observation, phonetics plumbed a pit of variation, failing to see that universal invariants in language can be attained only through recognition of a patterning within language itself, and that within a language, objectivity of units is in the first instance intersubjective and qualitative. In the 1880s such a cultural (or psychological) approach to speech sounds was worked out in Kazan by Baudoin de Courtenay and Kruszewski and was independently adumbrated by Boas. Their insights became effective only later—that of the Kazan school in the work of de Saussure, Trubetskoi, and Jakobson, the Boasian heritage in Sapir's great paper, "Sound Patterns in Language" (1925). Meanwhile, the comparativists, by establishing ever more precisely the principle of invariance in historical reconstruction, anticipated and aided application of this principle in nonhistorical contexts. De Saussure's brilliant reconstruction of a part of the proto-Indo-European vowel system, for example, was not only confirmed a generation later by the discovery in Hittite of a phonological feature postulated purely on internal evidence in the reconstruction, but its treatment of relationships within and between languages as manifestations of an underlying invariant feature earlier in time is also quite the same in form as the treatment of variants within a language as manifestations of an underlying invariant compresent in time, i.e., as manifestations not of an origin but of a present system.

Twentieth century. Modern synchronic, structural linguistics emerged essentially after World War I. Despite the groundwork that had preceded it, the participants in its emergence saw not continuity but conflict. De Saussure viewed synchronic and diachronic study as antithetical—the one dealing in systems, the other in atomistic traits; and many subsequent structuralists rejected historical work, at least as practiced. At the same time, many historical scholars rejected the new descriptive approaches. Even in American linguistics, where both history and structure have often been of common concern, as the work of Sapir and Bloomfield shows, the issue has been debated (Hockett 1948, p. 188; Hymes 1964a, p. 600). In some circles, especially in Europe, conflict over this issue is perhaps only ending now.

The new movement was part of a general upheaval of intellectual interests after World War I and of the general shift from a primarily historical perspective to an interest in structure and form. With it came the definite triumph of "linguistics" as the general name for the study of language and the development of several different orientations toward the proper tasks of linguistics, often enough excluding portions of the general study of language by way of self-definition.

The first text of structural linguistics, the posthumous *Cours de linguistique générale*, published from lecture notes by students of de Saussure, ends with the maxim that linguistics has for its true and only object language itself (i.e., not facts of history, psychology, sociology, or whatever). De Saussure introduced the distinction *la langue : la parole*. It subsumes a variety of contrasts and has been variously interpreted and used, but the main import has been that the linguist's task is the study of *la langue*, the underlying system and social fact (de Saussure was influenced by Durkheim, as was Meillet), rather than the various aspects of speech and other uses of language that were understood as *la parole*.

Saussurean linguistics as such was maintained in Switzerland by Sechehaye, Frei, Godel, and others. In Denmark Hjelmslev drew inspiration from de Saussure (and also from Sapir) and developed with Uldall a methodological algebra, *glossematics*, which postulated the immanence of language and made no assumption as to its empirical reality. In Czechoslovakia two Russian scholars, Trubetskoi and Jakobson, collaborated to lead in the development of a structural outlook uniting synchronic and diachronic work and giving attention both to internal and external functions of language. The accomplishments included a distinctive methodology for phonological and grammatical analysis; basic examination of phonological typology in connection with a search for general laws; new emphasis on the diffusion of linguistic features, structurally interpreted; and analyses of social and poetic varieties of language. In England J. R. Firth advocated a flexible, encompassing descriptive approach, one shaped partly by the English tradition of phonetic research and partly by Malinowski's notion of the "context of situation." In the United States the matrix of structural

linguistics was in large part anthropological. Boas had prepared the way by his critique of existing generalizations about the nature of language in the light of American Indian evidence and by his insistence on the description of each language *sui generis*. (The major statement of his contribution is the 1911 introduction to the *Handbook of American Indian Languages*.) His student, Sapir, put field work with a multitude of Amerindian language structures to brilliant account in his *Language* (1921) and in his 1925 study established the basic principle of structural analysis for both American linguistics and ethnography. Around Sapir and Bloomfield gathered the subsequent leaders of professional linguistics. In the United States Bloomfield's *Language* (1933) was the first systematic exposition of the new descriptive approach, and it became the standard reference for a generation. Both Sapir and Bloomfield stressed the autonomy of language and linguistics. Sapir's *Language* is a masterful set of variations on the theme of the autonomy of grammatical form, and Bloomfield's book declares that the study of language has many times been approached, but never properly begun, because of failure to focus on language in its own right. Granting this autonomy, both saw larger implications for the results of linguistics, and indeed an interdependence with other disciplines—especially Sapir; in this respect, Bloomfield remained the more austere.

Each of these strands of structuralism has been labeled—the Geneva school, the Copenhagen school, the Prague school, the London school, the Yale school (although the differences between Sapir and his successor Bloomfield perhaps require recognition of two Yale schools). It must be remembered that distinguished linguists worked in the Netherlands, France, and elsewhere, without acquiring separate names and images, and that the labels are poor predictors of the work of individual scholars in the places named. The labels do serve as markers of salient intellectual emphases and outlooks. Differing intellectual contexts and assumptions led to sometimes acerbic exchanges in the first years after World War II; in particular, the stringent behaviorism dominant in the United States was set in method and attitude against the more open-minded empiricism found in Britain and against those influenced by phenomenology, logic, and dialectic on the Continent. There was salient skepticism, if not outright rejection, of the study of meaning, and there was antipathy to statements in terms of process in the Neo-Bloomfieldian camp. In the United States, the effective scope of linguistics became especially narrow for a time (see Joos 1957), in contrast to European outlooks and, indeed, the outlook of Boas and Sapir.

Recent trends and structural models

Developments within structural linguistics continue to hold the center of the stage. The main trend has been away from primary concern with phonology (whose conquest by structural methods was a main achievement of the 1920s and 1930s and in terms of which the battles of the day were fought) to concern with morphology, syntax, semantics, and, to some extent, stylistics, or poetics. In the 1940s and early 1950s great attention was given to the analysis of grammar in terms of morphology, the identification and distribution of forms. Especially in the United States there was an attempt to analyze grammar in terms analogous to those used in phonology, and insofar as possible, on the basis of the results of phonological analysis. This strategy of working upward from phonology fitted an emphasis on overt data (rather a "decoding" one) and a reluctance to deal with imputed entities. In the words of Joos, the maxim was "text signals its own structure." European scholars had usually taken the psychological reality of linguistic structure into account, as had Boas and Sapir; and glossematics began with the higher levels of text and grammar, working downward to phonology. In the late 1950s and the 1960s Noam Chomsky has stressed the centrality of grammar and the underlying mental abilities of users of language. His central point has been that structure in text is largely recognized not because overt signals are perceived but because users of a language apply their knowledge of grammatical structure. Chomsky's work, along with a general revival of interest in semantic work, has been the major force in bringing general American opinion into agreement to this extent with European and earlier American interests.

Models of language structure current on the American scene can be noted cursorily as follows:

(1) The Trager–Smith–Joos model, dominant in the early 1950s, treats phonology, grammar, and semology as coordinate and parallel in organization. Relations of language to culture and society are treated as questions of "metalinguistics." Language is associated with other communicative systems, such as *kinesics* (gesture and body motion) and *paralinguistics* (nonlinguistic phenomena of voice), within a general framework for the analysis of culture (Hall 1959).

(2) The *tagmemic* model, devised by Pike and subsequently developed by Longacre and others, has become the framework for descriptions from many different parts of the world, used especially by the members of the Summer Institute of Linguistics (a group devoted to translating the Bible). It treats phonology, grammar, and lexicon as coordinate hierarchies, parallel in organization. The concept of *tagmeme* treats as central the relation in grammar between a position and the class of elements that can occur in it, thus reintroducing and generalizing the notion of paradigm. Inspired by Sapir, Pike has sought to generalize linguistic methodology to make it applicable to cultural behavior (see Pike 1954). In doing so he has coined the terms "emic" and "etic" (from "phonemic" and "phonetic") for the difference between classifications of phenomena that are based on features validated internally in terms of the structure in question and classifications that are based on externally devised or generalized criteria.

Recent descriptive work done by Pike has emphasized use of matrices; by Longacre, analysis of strings and inclusion of transformations (1964).

(3) The "means–ends" model, as Jakobson (1963) has dubbed the original Prague school approach, has diffused into several lines of American research, largely through Jakobson's presence since the early 1940s. There is widespread acceptance of the notion and importance of distinctive features in phonology: the "letter size" units, or phonemes, are not ultimate constituents but bundles of contrasting components (e.g., voicing, produced by vibration of the vocal chords, versus voicelessness, or absence of vibration, which distinguishes the otherwise identical series of English stops /p t k/ : /b d g/). But not all linguists follow Jakobson in defining phonological features acoustically (in terms of the physical properties of the speech signal), some retaining definition in terms of articulation (where and how the sounds are produced); neither do all linguists follow him in supposing a proposed set of 12 phonological features to be adequate for describing all languages or in regarding distinctive features as always forming oppositions of a binary sort. Jakobson's analyses of grammatical categories in terms of distinctive semantic features have helped shape componential analysis; his work has influenced literary scholarship, ethnography, and psychology as well. [See COMPONENTIAL ANALYSIS.]

An enduring importance of the Prague school is that it always keeps the true social complexity of language in view as an object of linguistic study. In its conception a language is a dynamic "system of systems." A language is never a static, homogeneous system, but a developing set of interdependent, imperfectly adjusted subsystems, some of whose items are disappearing, some emerging. A language, moreover, is a set of means specialized to a multiplicity of communicative and social ends; for example, there are referential, expressive, and directive functions in speech; and literary, standard, and other varieties of a language. (On the history and present development of the Prague school, see Vachek 1964; 1966a; 1966b.)

(4) The most influential model both in the United States and abroad is that of *transformational–generative grammar*. As first formulated in the early 1950s by Zellig Harris (codifier of much post-war American method), transformations were a technique for syntax and text analysis serving to account for relations between sentences. Particularly telling have been the ways in which transformational analyses can account for the ambiguity of a sentence in terms of its derivation from two different underlying sentences; uncover an underlying difference between two superficially quite similar sentences; and integrate the productive systematic relations between different forms of sentence (e.g., actives, passives, negatives).

In the work of Harris' student, Chomsky, transformations have become part of a new model of language as a whole and of a program for radical recasting of previously held assumptions and goals. Analysis of the underlying "deep structure" of grammar is stressed; much of what was treated by earlier descriptive linguistics is relegated to "surface structure." Grammar shapes phonology rather than the reverse, and the phonological output of a grammar is specified in terms of distinctive features. (For the first influential monograph, see Chomsky 1957; for subsequent views, see Chomsky 1964; 1965; 1966.) The program is one of attack on behaviorist and positivist outlooks from a standpoint of rationalism and recent philosophy of science. The Neo-Bloomfieldian goal of an algorithm, a mechanical procedure for the analysis of a language, is shown to be futile, and earlier models of syntax are found inadequate to account for the actual facts of languages and the abilities that users of languages must have. Indeed, the goal of accounting for observed data is defined as mere *observational adequacy* (in effect, merely reporting the data). At the least, linguistics must aim for *descriptive adequacy*, an account of the knowledge that a fluent user of a language has of its structure, and which he or she can apply in producing and interpreting the infinite set of sentences of which a language is normally capable. What is crucial is the agreement of a grammar not with a corpus but with users' judgments of acceptable and unacceptable sentences. The true goal of linguistics

should be *explanatory adequacy*; that is, linguistics should characterize the nature of the equipment by means of which a child acquires such knowledge. To achieve the normal yet nearly miraculous result of an infinite capacity from a finite experience in but a few years, a child must be presumed to apply actively a native endowment, formulating theories to account for and go beyond the speech he hears. The rapidity and accuracy of a child's success, no matter what the language, indicate that all languages are of only one or a few fundamental types and that the contribution of the native endowment must be great. In this light the earlier emphasis in American linguistics on the diversity of languages is reversed in favor of an active search for universals.

The focus of linguistic theory is thus reformulated as *linguistic competence*, the knowledge of the ideally fluent user of language in an ideally homogeneous speech community. Theory is completed by an account of *linguistic performance*, comprising the various conditions—psychological, occasional, social—that modify and affect the expression of underlying competence. The critique of learning theory and behaviorism provides a new program for psychologists; the model of language stimulates new work in semantics and to some extent in stylistics and ethnography, although some lines of research into the social role of language are considered misguided or premature. It is fair to say that transformational–generative grammar has replaced Neo-Bloomfieldian work as the focus of attention today. Apart from the close-knit group centered about Chomsky and Halle, some linguists join transformational syntax with other approaches, especially in phonology; and some transformationalists abjure Chomsky's views of the psychological and philosophical import of the model (e.g., Harris, Henry Hiż).

(5) The *stratificational* model owes its name and central formulation to Sydney Lamb. It has attracted several leading linguists (e.g., Hockett, Gleason) and has affinities with the work of Halliday. Originating as a systematic explication of principles in earlier American descriptive work and as a response to needs in computer use, especially mechanical translation, the model treats language as four levels, or strata—semology, lexology, morphology, phonology. The elements of the several strata are related by realization rules, which may be traced either in speaking (semology to phonology) or in hearing (phonology to semology). The model thus is intended to represent the processes of a user of language in either activity (see Gleason 1964 and Lamb 1966 for other formalizations). As

with tagmemic analysis and the Harris–Hiż type of transformational analysis, there is interest in units larger than the sentence, such as whole narratives. The sememic analysis has close ties with work in componential analysis and ethnoscience.

(6) *System-structure* is a generic name for models derived from the Firthian heritage in Great Britain. The most notable of these models is what has come to be known as the "scale-and-category" grammar of M. A. K. Halliday and others (see Halliday et al. 1964; McIntosh & Halliday 1966). A special interest of the approach is its direct incorporation of questions of "institutional linguistics" (sociology of language) and its varied application to problems of language teaching, translation, analysis of style, and study of social dialect.

While models of the way grammars should best be written are the center of attention, other lines of linguistic work continue to develop, often revitalized in the light of structural principles; new interests emerge, often as applications and extensions of structural perspective; the concerns of the humanities and social sciences and of social institutions entail selective attention to the results and possible applications of linguistics. In short, controversy focused on structural models should not obscure the great variety of present-day linguistic activity. This variety can be grasped if one considers the three main ways, each cross-cutting the others, in which linguists may be grouped for purposes of congresses, journals, appointments, and so forth. There is affiliation with one or another of the structural approaches (some scholars affiliate with none); there are the subdisciplines, such as the phonetic sciences, lexicography, semantics, stylistics and poetics, onomastics, philology, dialectology, formal and mathematical linguistics, applied linguistics, anthropological linguistics, psycholinguistics, and sociolinguistics; and there are the groupings in terms of languages studied, whether in the sense of language family (Indo-European, Germanic, Algonquian linguistics) or area (African, Indian, Oceanic linguistics).

Distinctive constellations of approach, subdiscipline, and languages studied do occur, coupled with nationality or geographical region; but the overriding trends today are an internationalization and diffusion of interests and outlooks and a broadening and integration of them. Each major structural school, for example, has adherents in several countries, and a variety of links with subdisciplines and language families and areas. Moreover, each structural school has had a conception of structural linguistics as contributing to a larger enterprise, such as a general science of signs (semi-

ology, or semiotics), and as a link in the integration of the natural and social sciences, or at least as a strategic sector of social science; and such contributions are increasingly being realized.

Like many histories, this of linguistics has been rather Hegelian, moving from place to place and topic to topic as the "spirit" of the main advances moved. The main outlines might be caricatured in a Hegelian manner, describing the successive stages as "no language is known" (folk linguistics); "one language is known" (early national philology); "few languages are known" (later philology); and "many languages are known" (general linguistics). Yet any period comprises both the new and emerging and the old and steadily continuing, in a variety of forms, as has been indicated for the present state of linguistics. The nineteenth century was not all historical; the twentieth century is not all structural grammar; and if future linguistics builds on both in pursuit of a dominant functional concern with the place of language in human life, it will be in a spirit not of disregard of other concerns but of their integration. (On current trends, see Mohrmann et al. 1962; International Congress . . . 1963; Ivić 1965; *Current Trends in Linguistics*; *Biennial Review of Anthropology.*)

Content of linguistics

We must now take stock more exactly of the present content of linguistics. Linguistics proper can be defined by tasks that remain constant and characteristic. These central tasks are to describe languages, to classify them, and to explain their differences and similarities.

Descriptions of linguistic data. The descriptive task (understood as equivalent to analysis) is primary. In pursuing it, linguists may use a variety of means for determining data and may place data in a variety of frames of reference. To grasp this variety a general framework is needed. We shall adapt and enlarge one put forward by Hockett (1948, pp. 188–190; Hymes 1964a, pp. 600–601), distinguishing four kinds of means by which data are determined (contact, philological, reconstructive, theoretical) and four major frames of reference within which data are placed (syn-

Table 1 — Means and frames of reference for linguistic data

FRAMES OF REFERENCE	MEANS			
	Contact	Philological	Reconstructive	Theoretical
Synchronic				
Diachronic				
Diatopic				
Syncritic				

chronic, diachronic, diatopic, syncritic; Table 1 outlines this descriptive mode.

Means for determining linguistic data. Of the four kinds of means, *contact* subsumes first-hand observation, interviews, surveys, and experimentation in direct contact with users of a language—in short, the various forms of field work and laboratory work, including introspection into one's own speech habits. Such work has been most characteristic of descriptive linguistics and dialectology, and of anthropology, but the expanding role of psychologists and sociologists in the study of language must be noted (see Lounsbury 1953; Hymes 1959; Samarin 1967; Berko & Brown 1960; Ervin-Tripp 1964).

The *philological* methods are those used in the interpretation of the nature and transmission of written records, especially texts. Such methods are not limited to the study of classical languages or the languages of civilizations with writing. In the narrower sense that philological methods have come to have for some linguists, a field worker may find himself later in a philological relationship to his own materials; and in areas such as the New World the interpretation of records left by earlier investigators is indispensable for many languages no longer spoken. In the broader, earlier sense of philology, the method leads on into the general interpretation of texts for their cultural content as well as their linguistic form (see Sandys [1903–1908] 1958, vol. 1, pp. 4–13; Bernardini & Righi 1947; Hymes 1965; Malkiel 1966).

By *reconstructive* methods are meant those methods that use systematic variation in known languages (or dialects) to infer the presence and perhaps the patterning of features unknown in some other. When the evidence is from one language (or dialect) and the inference is to an earlier stage of it, the work is known as *internal reconstruction.* When the evidence is from two or more dialects or languages and the inference is to an earlier ancestral language, one usually speaks of the *comparative method.* Notice that in linguistics the term "comparative method" has this specialized use. Scholars in other fields have sometimes been misled into taking it as designating a general method of comparison, or as equivalent to such other techniques as the method of controlled comparison in social anthropology or the comparative method of nineteenth-century social evolution. Analogues to these in the study of language fall within the syncritic frame of reference and are quite distinct from what linguists speak of as the "comparative method" (see Bloomfield 1933; Hoenigswald 1960).

A less common form is that in which the infer-

ence is from a series of geographically linked languages or dialects to an intermediate or adjacent one; such use may count as a sort of reconstruction in space rather than time.

Theoretical methods concern aspects of data that are postulated by a general theory or inferred on theoretical grounds. A theoretical component is present in any description, although the extent to which it is recognized, if at all, may vary. Some examples are: that dialects be described in terms of the elements of a fixed over-all pattern; that distinctive features be binary; that rules specifying the phonological shapes of words be ordered (or unordered); that of two differing accounts the shorter is to be accepted; that of two differing accounts the more intuitively persuasive is to be accepted; and so forth.

Frames of reference. As frames of reference, linguists commonly distinguish "structural," "descriptive," or "synchronic" from "historical," or "diachronic," linguistics; linguistic geography, or dialectology, and typological comparison, together with general linguistics, often are distinguished as well. The implicit logic is to separate the primary description of languages from concern with change (through time) and with variation (in space), and from contrast and generalization independently of space and time. In adopting this scheme (somewhat relabeled for symmetry's sake), we recognize that no concise grouping can be wholly satisfactory and that the names must be somewhat arbitrary, designating as they do gross clusters of work that overlap and are internally diverse.

Synchronic description treats features (dialects, a language) with respect to a particular time, and, by implication, with respect also to a particular place. ("Structural" is used as a surrogate, but descriptions of the sort intended developed long before modern structuralism, and analysis within any frame of reference may be methodologically structural.) While other kinds of work may be strictly speaking "synchronic," the common connotation of the term in linguistics is that for the purpose at hand, data can be treated as coming from a single source and as essentially homogeneous or unified; in effect, "synchronic" means an idealized single case. The classical presentation of such a synchronic analysis is in the form of a grammar, texts, and dictionary. (For treatments of grammatical description, see Harris 1951; Hockett 1958; Gleason 1955; Bach 1964; Katz & Postal 1964; Longacre 1964; Martinet 1960; Robins 1964; Chomsky 1965; McIntosh & Halliday 1966; and the several approaches represented in the *Monograph Series on Languages and Linguistics* [see "Report of the Fifteenth Annual . . ." 1964] and the journal *Language*. On texts, see references in Hymes 1964*a*, p. 365; on dictionaries, p. 209.)

A synchronic structural description must choose or assume a particular norm—say, the standard speech of educated persons or the informal patois of lifelong inhabitants of a village. That is, any serious description must specify its boundary conditions—for whom and when and where it holds. Questions of contexts, purposes, and modes of use must enter (a point most consistently made by Firth and other British linguists such as Robins 1964; Halliday et al. 1964; Dixon 1965). Such questions are often distinguished as "functional," "structural" serving for the internal make-up of language. This usage, with its internal–external dichotomy, is not happy, however, since use must itself be structurally analyzed and since the point of structural analysis of the make-up of language is to treat features in terms of their functional relationships (e.g., sounds in terms of the contrasts into which they enter to distinguish utterances; see Sapir 1925). Considerations of structure and function apply throughout linguistics, and the extension of this joint scope is of special importance to the social sciences. It is better to specify the exact kind of structure and function in question, rather than to rely on a usage that implies a false discontinuity.

What the classical presentation of a description of use might be like is not yet known. Models for the description of language use have been often postulated, but actual analyses are rare. As prolegomena to such descriptions one can cite the framework employed by Halliday (Halliday et al. 1964) and the concept of an "ethnography of speaking" (Hymes 1962; 1964*b*). Restricting attention here to an idealized single case, one can say that an ethnography of speaking would identify and describe the speech events and sequences of speech acts recognized in a community and their distribution; their purposes and interactional norms (e.g., formal/informal); the relationships within speech events—who can participate as speakers and hearers, with regard to what settings, topics, message forms, channels, and codes; the patterning of messages in exchanges and sequences (conversations, curses, narrations, etc.); the hierarchies of functions (referential, expressive, rhetorical, poetic, and other) in such events; and the role of language with respect to other codes. No full accounts yet exist.

Diachronic description treats features (dialects, languages) in terms of time. Often one is concerned with changes in a single line of development, but features that remain stable may be of interest too; and the tracing of borrowings and their etymologies into earlier periods of other languages may become an objective of study. Among products of diachronic description are historical grammars, etymological dictionaries, statements of sound laws connecting stages of languages (e.g., Grimm's law), depictions of innovations leading to the present vocabularies of members of language groups, and so forth. Diachronic descriptions need not draw a hard line between so-called internal and external aspects of language change, and, indeed, for many purposes cannot do so. Beyond the question of what has occurred, questions of when, where, how, and why arise, requiring reference to uses, contexts, and values for their answers. It is not unusual, however, for a distinction to be drawn between *historical linguistics*, internal change, and *language history*, external events. (See chapters on language change in Sapir 1921; Bloomfield 1933; Hockett 1958; Gleason 1955; Martinet 1960; 1962; Hymes 1964*a*, parts 8 and 9.)

Diatopic description treats features (dialects, languages) in terms of space; it is thus inseparably associated with dialectology. Two observations must be made. First, dialectology is often synchronic description; important early work in Europe, for example, was motivated by concern for local forms of speech as against standard languages. There is also a European tradition of local ethnography that includes community speech as well as objects and practices. Second, diatopic description proper has not usually been undertaken for its own sake. Interest in the distribution of phenomena has often derived from diachronic questions of origin, spread, and loss. For dialects and languages, one may seek to infer an earlier location, migration, dispersion, or particular processes of formation. For features, one may seek to infer a particular history and also to sharpen a theory of linguistic change.

It remains that dialectology and linguistic geography require separate recognition, both analytically and for their special traditions of work. Earlier diatopic work most familiarly focused on sounds and words and produced atlases and maps. Recently there has been much recasting of earlier work in structural terms—e.g., analyzing the distribution of sounds in terms of phonological patterns (Hymes 1964*a*, p. 481).

A second kind of diatopic description is concerned not with geographic space but with social space. Earlier work was most concerned with the social dimension as it "horizontally" tied together several communities. Current work stresses "vertical" relations within communities, talking more of *social dialect* than of geographical dialect.

Such study may focus on the distribution of specific linguistic variables within a community; in doing so it gives special attention to the social valuation and role of these variables, for the light shed on the community as well as on processes of origin and diffusion (see Fischer 1958; Labov 1963; 1964). Description of variation in social space may also focus on all the varieties of speech to be found in a community—speech levels, men's speech and women's, baby talk, argots, and the like. The features of such forms of speech are specifiable structurally, but they appear here as aspects of the use of language within a universe that is defined first of all in social, not linguistic, terms. From an internal linguistic standpoint, cases of, say, men's versus women's speech appear only when the differences intrude into the normal description of a language, e.g., as constant differences in the phonological shape of lexical items or as obligatory alternates for inflectional elements. The speech appropriate to men and women presumably is differentiated in every society, however; it should be possible to describe how to "talk like a man" and "talk like a woman" everywhere. From the present standpoint one would inquire into the nature of the differentiation—whether or not it could be ignored in an ordinary grammar.

Such diatopic work is closely linked with description of use within a community. Indeed, in the description of a single community a full diatopic account and a synchronic ethnography of speaking differ only by an element of definition. An idealized synchronic account would restrict itself to a single variety of a language; but in fact every speech community has at least three (formal, conversational, slang). At the level of relations among a series of communities, however, or of relationships within a unit such as the nation, new complexities and types of problems emerge, so that the community-linked perspective of an ethnography of speaking can be considered part of a more general enterprise, the construction of an integrated theory of sociolinguistic description for social units of whatever scale and size.

Syncritic description compares dialects, languages, or features without regard to relative position in space and time. Such work is often called "typological," especially when the purpose is structural classification of whole languages or their subsystems. "Comparative" would be a natural term, had it not been pre-empted for a reconstruc-

tive method and, by extension, the particular kind of work to which that method contributes. Some British linguists indeed seek to recapture "comparative" for comparison of languages generally, including comparison for purposes of translation and language teaching (often called "contrastive linguistics" in the United States; see Halliday et al. 1964, pp. 111–112). *Syncritic* (from the Greek *synkrisis*, meaning "comparison") seems useful as a term that is both general and unambiguous, and so we introduce it here.

Syncritic description is undertaken sometimes simply to exhibit what diversity of structure may exist among languages, perhaps also to devise a classificatory scheme or measures for a scheme. Two particular purposes can be distinguished as *contrastive* and *generic*. A contrastive study sets out to specify differences, as in the characterizations of French and German by Bally or in the setting of Hopi against "Standard Average European" done by Whorf. (Whorf introduced the term "contrastive" in this use.) A generic study seeks significant commonalties in order to establish universals of language—underlying principles either true of all languages or so widely true independently of relationship in time and space as to require a general, rather than a historical, explanation (see Conference on Language Universals 1963; Martinet 1962; Chomsky 1965; references in Hymes 1964a, p. 661).

Syncritic description of uses and contexts also has contrastive and generic purposes, the contrastive being more salient. A notable example is Bernstein's model of two types of code, elaborated and restricted, which are characterized by differences that include the signaling of subjective intent in verbally explicit form versus its transmission extraverbally; the focusing of attention on verbal versus extraverbal channels; reliance on verbal persuasion versus authority; orientation toward personal discretion within roles versus status relationships and shared assumptions. The model has been most discussed with regard to class differences in England and the United States, but it has a more general application. For members of any class some situations may call for restricted code behavior; and it seems likely that aspects of socialization pertaining to whole societies can be contrasted in these terms. Other examples of syncritic work of this sort contrast types of verbal interaction as transactional or personal; types of bilingualism as coordinate or compound; types of speech situation as formal or informal; and the like. (These examples and related ones are discussed in articles by Bernstein,

Ervin-Tripp, and Gumperz in Gumperz & Hymes 1964, and in articles by Bloomfield, Gumperz, Ferguson, Diebold, and Garvin in Hymes 1964*a*.)

Each of the contrastive analyses might be directed toward generic purposes. Thus one might have a systematic comparison of baby talk or of men's and women's speech with a view to generalizations as to their places in human society as a whole. A further step would be to analyze and compare ranges and uses for whole languages or speech communities, seeking to identify recurrent patterns of function (independent of historical connection) and to integrate such patterns with the results of the contrastive typologies. Such an approach entails a consideration of the place of language among other modes of human communication and the comparison of human communication with communication in other species, treating language as a resource differentially allocated and adapted in human societies on a certain generic base.

Comments. The sketch of kinds of means and frames of reference requires two comments. First, the broad categories of means and frameworks do not conflict or stand in isolation. A way of determining data may contribute to any frame of reference; a frame of reference may make use of any means. Field work, for example, is often thought of as a means to synchronic description, but its purpose may be to place a language genetically or to trace the process of acculturation; to study relations among geographical or social dialects; to determine the distinctive cognitive style of a language or to substantiate a proposed universal of grammar. Synchronic description is often based on contact work, but one may write grammatical rules for philologically interpreted texts or a reconstructed language or specify theoretically the universal parameters of grammar. Desirable as such interplay is in principle, in practice it may be obscured by specialization and controversy (as it has been on some occasions in synchronic and diachronic work); but in the long run interest in knowledge of languages prevails, especially in the work of great scholars. Every means that can contribute information is likely to find a place; frames of reference are likely to prove complementary. Such unity in diversity appears most often in work on a group of languages, be it Romance (see Malkiel 1964*b*), Dravidian, or Algonquian. Most linguists being specialists in some language group, such work is a source of stability and strength to the field.

Second, an exact analysis of kinds of work and their interrelationships would require a greater number of dimensions, accurately and systemati-

cally named. One set would distinguish study of syntactics (relations of signs within a code), semantics (relations of signs to referents), and pragmatics (relations of signs to their users). (The distinctions are those of Morris; see Greenberg 1948; Hymes 1964*a*, pp. 27–31.) Our discussion has, in fact, consistently noted study of use (pragmatics) as well as study of codes (syntactics, semantics). A second set of distinctions concerns the underlying dimensions of time, space, social group, system, and function. For these, one can use the Greek forms *-chronic, -topic, -gelic, -systemic, -telic* together with a prefix to specify in what way each dimension is taken into account. Useful prefixes include *a-* : without reference to the dimension; *mono-* : one reference point; *bi-, tri-,* etc.: two, three, etc., reference points; *poly-* : multiple reference points; *pan-* : all reference points; *syn-* : treatment as having common reference point; *dia-* : treatment as having continuum, or linked series of reference points. Such dimensions and terms make terminologically convenient a large number of necessary distinctions. Thus, studies that treat the history of a language in terms of discrete stages (e.g., bichronic) can be distinguished from studies that treat it as a continuous development (diachronic). Within the context of synchronic descriptive theory, one can distinguish the complex adequacy of Prague school theory (diatopic, diagelic, polysystemic, polytelic) from descriptive theory that implies a wholly homogeneous description (monotopic, monoagelic, monosystemic, monotelic).

We have broached something of the tasks of classification and explanation; more must now be said about each.

Classification of languages. Languages are often classified by their common internal features (phonological, grammatical, lexical) and in one or another of three ways: as belonging to the same family, the same area, the same type. Although each way implies a different sort of process and explanation, the three need not be mutually exclusive; in a limiting case, a set of languages may all belong to the same family, area, and type at once.

When languages belong to the same family they share a *genetic relationship.* Specific features of each are explained as due to retention (perhaps much changed) from a common ancestor of all. English, Frisian, Dutch, German, Icelandic, Norwegian, Danish, Swedish (and extinct Gothic), for example, belong to the same family, Germanic, in virtue of their descent from a common ancestor that is called Proto-Germanic. As it happens, that ancestor can be shown to belong to an older family, Indo-European, whose common ancestor, Proto-Indo-European, may itself someday be shown convincingly to belong in yet an older family. The proportion of features that attest the genetic connection of languages may be quite small; what is required is that the presence of the features be inexplicable by chance or borrowing.

When languages are said to belong to the same language area (German *Sprachbund*), or convergence area, they share an *areal relationship*. Continued compresence in the same area may enable genetically related languages to maintain great commonalty of content through shared innovations and mutual borrowing, despite long divergence from their joint ancestor; these languages may even increase their commonalty after an earlier period of differentiation (see Hoenigswald 1960, pp. 155–157; Malkiel 1964a; Kroeber 1955). The most salient cases of areal relationship are those in which the languages are genetically unrelated. Thus the languages of the subcontinent of India belong to three distinct families (Indo-Aryan branch of Indo-European, Dravidian, Munda), but they share significant traits through sustained contact (Emeneau 1956; Hymes 1964a, pp. 642–650).

When languages are said to belong to the same type, one must notice what portion of their features is concerned. A *typological relationship* may be defined by one or a few traits of interest or by a distinct system or level (phonology, morphology, syntax, lexicon). Attempts to assign languages as wholes to types (a *language type* proper) have focused on grammatical or semantic characteristics or both. When specific features are investigated, a given language may, of course, fall together in type with quite different sets of other languages, depending on the features in question. (On genetic, areal, and typological classification, see references in Hymes 1964a, pp. 659–661, 651–653, 661–663, respectively.)

Classification of languages in terms of context and use is less well developed, a fact reflected in the absence of a comprehensive conventional terminology. There exists a scattering of individual terms not yet systematized. The dimensions of the subject can be sketched, however, along lines corresponding to those just followed, taking the genetic as concerned primarily with origin, the areal with co-occurrence, the typological as independent of either.

Some terms focus attention on languages as marked by their origin in particular circumstances of use. A *koiné* is a language that has arisen as a lingua franca by a merging of traits among a group of related dialects, as in the Greek *koiné* of Hellen-

istic times (from which the term comes). A *pidgin* arises by drastic reduction of one language, typically with admixture of another; it is by definition a second language to all who use it. A *creole* arises if a pidgin becomes and remains the first language for a group, expanding into a normal range of use. (Thus, by definition a creole was once a pidgin.) By virtue of their common origin in conscious invention, constructed languages intended for international auxiliary use (Esperanto, Interlingua, etc.) belong here.

Some terms group languages according to their relationships within a community or larger population. Some groups of Sephardic Jews in Greece, for example, used Greek at work, Hebrew in religious observances, and Spanish in family conversation. Together the three languages formed their linguistic (or verbal) repertoire. One general classification of the varieties forming a verbal repertoire distinguishes those associated with geographic and social differences and those associated with differences of activity, as *dialectal* and *superposed*, respectively. [*On this and other aspects of use, see* LINGUISTICS, *article on* THE SPEECH COMMUNITY.] Terms often distinguish range of use; "standard language : dialect" and "world language : vernacular" are two such pairs. The use of "language : dialect" has varied and is still unresolved, but the two terms are always correlated in such a way that dialect is the subordinate term—language indicating a variety with higher status or wider use or a set of dialects as a whole.

An important kind of co-occurrence is that analyzed by Ferguson (1959; Hymes 1964a, pp. 429–438) as *diglossia*: two mutually unintelligible forms of language are in use—one for government, literature, formal religion, and the like (the "High" form) and one for informal conversation, the home, and the like (the "Low" form). The two are part of the verbal repertoire of some, but not all, members of a society, many knowing only the Low form. The general description of language co-occurrence within nations has begun to be studied as a nation's *sociolinguistic profile* (Ferguson 1966).

Some terms specify use without necessary reference either to origin or co-occurrence. One such term is *lingua franca*, a language that serves as a common medium throughout a linguistically diverse region. *Standard language*, as a consciously codified form of language, belongs here, considered in terms of its intrinsic characteristics and associated attitudes and functions (see Garvin 1959; Hymes 1964a, pp. 521–526, with references). Indeed, all terms that designate components of a verbal repertoire or sociolinguistic profile may be specified and studied syncritically: the High and Low forms of a diglossia situation, languages of religion, trade languages, languages of conceal-ment, slang, etc., can all be studied both in terms of the social circumstances of their origin and in terms of their co-occurrence with other vari-eties of language.

The uses and imports of the modes of classifica-tion are varied but ultimately interrelated. Genetic classification has a certain priority, as a back-ground against which to interpret relationships of area and use and from which to guarantee the historical independence of cases for typological gen-eralizations. As a mode of explanation of resem-blances among languages, genetic classification has sometimes been set off against areal classification, as in the Boas–Sapir controversy (see Swadesh 1951; Hymes 1964a, pp. 624–637) and in the earlier California work of Dixon and Kroeber (see Hymes 1961a; 1964a, pp. 689–707). But in fact, the logic underlying the historical modes of classification makes them interdependent. This logic is to determine if corresponding features are (1) of independent origin (universals, convergent, chance), or (2) due to historical connection, and, if historical, whether (a) genetic ("cognate"), due to retention from a common ancestor, or (b) dif-fusional ("borrowed"). Neither genetic nor diffu-sional origin can be assumed; each must be proved, and proof of one excludes the other. Actual his-torical work must thus attend to both. There re-main questions concerning what explanation to assign to particular kinds and amounts of data. Well-integrated grammatical traits and basic vocab-ulary are the best, though not infallible, test of genetic connection. Despite a priori controversy, the work of the great students of linguistic prehis-tory is in practice one of cumulative inference from all the available evidence.

Although the languages of the world have been provisionally assigned to genetic groupings, such work is far from complete. For most parts of the world new and better descriptions of languages will permit deeper penetration of the past, as will reconstruction of protolanguages by the compara-tive method. Anthropologists (Swadesh, Greenberg, Haas, and others) have taken a leading role in this work, dealing with both proof of relationships and development of method for the great time depths and remote relationships that face students of linguistic prehistory. If data permit, beyond proof of relationship lies establishment of relative chronology (subgrouping) among the related lan-guages and of the location and perhaps some of the cultural content of the ancestral language. Proof of borrowing may also lead to knowledge of relative chronology of relationship and the earlier location and cultural content of languages. Such work may provide a framework and hypotheses for prehistoric research with other lines of evidence, and of course it provides many precise examples of regularities and complexities of change, exam-ples that have constantly been posed as problems for psychological and sociological explanation.

Studies of the American Indian languages of the Pacific Coast early revealed phonological areas where many distinct languages share systems con-taining few vowels and many consonants (includ-ing glottalized stops and voiceless laterals); and initial attempts to determine grammatical areas were made early in the century by Dixon and Kroeber. Neither in North America nor in the rest of the world outside Europe, however, has knowl-edge of areal connections gone beyond some notable individual studies. Increased interest in the struc-turing of interrelations of communities (such terms as "social field" and "intermediate societies") may stimulate increased attention to areal relationship as its linguistic counterpart (cf. Gumperz 1961).

Typological relationship may be linked to areal relationship, as when reconstruction of the Proto-Indo-European vowel system suggests a former areal tie with languages of the Caucasus or when it is proposed that proliferation of phonemes is correlated with fewness of speakers in areas of linguistic diversity, since persons in small commu-nities learn the languages of their neighbors as a result either of accommodation or of exogamy, and in either way introduce among themselves phonetic habits that come to enlarge the phono-logical system of their language. Most typological classification points in one of two directions. It seeks to explain recurrent types in terms of the limited possibilities and internal interdependence of linguistic systems (e.g., laws of the sort, "If A, then B") and to relate such types to underlying generic properties of the human mind; or it seeks to delineate types in terms of the selective drift within a given culture history, as distinctive of a society or as characteristic of a sociocultural type. (Findings with regard to Hopi, Navajo, and Wintu, for example, may be seen as manifestations of an underlying outlook common to primitive society that Redfield dubbed "participant maintenance.") The two directions seem to alternate in attention, interest in distinctiveness having given way re-cently to interest in what is common, considered apart from sociocultural adaptation; but underly-ing commonalty does not level the projecting differences that show languages engaged in the histories and lives of those who use them. Both interests are required to explain language.

Classifications as to use (often dubbed functional classifications) are of obvious importance to any concern with the varying roles of languages in culture, society, and personality. Choice and role of language are particularly important in nationalism, political identity, state formation, economic development, and in literacy, education, international communication; and they are also important for changes in the valuation of language itself relative to other modes of experience and communication. New analyses and syntheses of what is known are greatly needed, but they are only slowly beginning to appear (see Weinreich 1953; Ferguson & Gumperz 1960; Fishman et al. 1966, pp. 424–458; Ferguson 1966).

Each principal mode of classification in terms of internal content may seem linked to a different frame of reference—genetic to diachronic, areal to diatopic, typological to syncritic—but something of their interconnection has appeared. Any instance of classification can be put into all frames of reference by asking: What are the underlying descriptions? How did the relevant features come about? Where do they occur? What are their defining characteristics? And in pursuit of historical explanation, the emergence, persistence, and sometimes extinction of families, areas, types, and modes of use are interwoven (see Hoenigswald 1960). Pidgins and creoles, for example, pose problems for theory of genetic and areal relationship and for generic interpretation of typological resemblances. In sum, each mode of classification is useful, indeed indispensable, for particular questions: the major questions of linguistic explanation join together all of the modes. To generalize what Boas once wrote (with genetic classification in mind): "the problem of the study of language is not one of classification. . . . Our task is to trace the history of the development of human speech" ([1920] 1955, p. 212).

For any one language, its features can in principle be explained in terms of a portion common to all languages as languages (typological–generic), a portion retained from an ancestral stage (genetic), a portion acquired from other languages with which it has come into contact (diffusional), all of these portions having adapted to each other along distinctive lines (typological–contrastive) in certain circumstances of use. In Sapir's words, "The formal configuration of speech at any particular time and place is the result of a long and complex historical development, which, in turn, is unintelligible without constant reference to functional factors" ([1924] 1949, p. 152).

Explanation and import.   Descriptions and classifications go but part of the way in explaining linguistic data and their import. At the height of the historical approach to language the maxim was offered that the only explanation of a linguistic form is an earlier linguistic form. When the Neo-Bloomfieldian descriptive approach was dominant, some found it humorous to be asked to lecture on the nature of language. One asked of languages not "why" but "what." Such particularistic extremes set in relief the more common belief of linguists that in describing and classifying they also are illuminating something beyond the data in hand. How illumination is to come, what it should be, whether it is doggedly sought for or comfortably assumed—all yield much of the drama of the development of linguistics. The quest, most generally put, has been for meaning in particular texts and cultures, for the course of history, for characteristics of the human mind—in effect, for human nature as manifest in the concrete, in history, and in essence.

While the crucial role of language in human life makes its scientific study of perduring relevance to such goals, it remains true that most of the time most linguists seek the illumination of data within their own domain. "Why" questions, explicit or implicit, have a range of answers from the facts of a given language to general principles of structure, from facts of retention and borrowing to general processes of change. Each mode of description and classification implies explanation of some aspect of languages through the relationships it recognizes and discovers.

For our purpose, the critical point is reached when pursuit of explanation leads to relationships extending beyond language, when language is to explain or be explained in relation to other disciplines. Here questions of the unity and future of linguistics are most sharply posed. It is not that there are no questions of unity within linguistics proper, of the integration of different lines of purely linguistic work, but we can consider such questions only as they are entailed by the question of unity within the larger field of linguistics.

The field of linguistics

As must any discipline, linguistics proper must be master in its own house—literally, autonomous; but autonomy can be compatible with either isolation or integration. It is a striking fact that insistence on the independence of linguistics from other disciplines contributes to disunity within linguistics itself, for the independence is defined at the expense of some legitimate mode of studying linguistic data. Recognition of the unity of linguistics as a whole promotes recognition of its interdependence with other disciplines in the broader field of linguistics.

The many aspects of the import of linguistics and other disciplines for each other cannot be reviewed here; rather, we can consider what bases exist for integrating within a unified field of linguistics.

Unity and interdependence have long been recognized in principle, and often in practice, in the pursuit of historical explanation and philological interpretation, where one uses all there is to use. In the particular case, knowledge of customs, artifacts, social conditions, distributions, and environment plays a part inseparable from linguistic knowledge. The disciplines called upon to contribute include archeology, paleobotany, geography, folklore, comparative religion, numismatics, political and social history, and so forth. Where questions of the formation, movement, adaptation, specialization, obsolescence, and extinction of languages are concerned, dependence on social history is patent.

It is fair to say that the situation regarding unity is unclear outside the domain of historical explanation. A unity centered in structural analysis has gone far, integrating a great deal of work in linguistics proper, through recognition that structural formulations are prerequisite to many questions of history and use. There have been several efforts to base integration of a larger field on particular structural models (see references in Hymes 1964*a*, pp. 61–62), but none has prevailed. In other human sciences relevant to language one finds some use of linguistic models, some picking and choosing of linguistic results, some neglect of connection. The role of such disciplines in structural linguistics is similar; one finds some use of analytic models, some picking and choosing of results, some neglect or even denial of connection.

Such a situation may continue indefinitely. However, a larger unity within the field of linguistics can be attained; linguistic data must remain the focus, but the perspective brought to bear must encompass the gamut of relationships that determine the use of language.

The central requirement of such a perspective is that it focus on the integrity of the verbal message as an act. From such a focus there follows a series of consequences for conceptions of the object of analysis, consequences that have been partly indicated with regard to synchronic, diatopic, and syncritic description, but that must now be explicitly drawn.

(1) Linguistic description has focused on the form of languages, neglecting the structuring of their use (*la langue* as opposed to *la parole*). The social sciences, on the other hand, have usually been concerned with language use, neglecting form. Consequently, most attempts to integrate language with culture or society have inevitably failed, for the terms of the relationship have been conceived as disparate abstractions. A grammar and an ethnography both treat verbal messages as data, but, typically, neither studies messages as having an integral structuring of their own. The one abstracts certain aspects of form, the other certain aspects of content (other kinds of form), as if they were historically disjunct products. Having put asunder, one may try to join together, but the form and process of speech, wherein the relation of language to culture and society is mediated, the cambium, as it were, of both, has not been incorporated into either abstraction. A unified field of linguistics requires study of the patterning of speech as well as of codes.

(2) Structural description has usually defined its object synchronically as a single homogeneous code or the abilities of an ideally fluent user of such a code in an ideally homogeneous community. Such simplification is useful when models of internal structure are being devised and single codes are being described in their terms. Models of the structure of speech must allow for multiplicity of codes —quotation within messages and switching between messages (of bilinguals)—and specialization of codes in different topics, occasions, roles, and institutions. A unified field of linguistics should have as its natural unit of study the speech community rather than the individual code.

(3) Structuralists have usually considered the relation of language to other aspects of life as only supplementing what normally counts as language structure. One looks out from the linguistic account, seeing its features as subject to variation or additional rules and restrictions. The best models do envisage extension of structural description from sentences to larger units—paragraphs, narratives, even conversations, and the many recurrent routines that make daily speech so much more predictable than the infinite potential of language would suggest. Even so, much remains undiscerned until one looks at the linguistic account from the standpoint of its additional functions in social use. In general, one cannot predict such functions from

relations of structure as ordinarily described; rather, each level of organization (function) reveals new structural relationships among elements of those below it. Modal particles, for example, may show structural relationships only when seen to join with features of intonation to serve an expressive function. No internal linguistic relationship brings together greetings, terms of address, insults, curses, request forms, and so forth; only social rules can show each to be a set. Thus the lexicon and phrases of a language can be wholly analyzed structurally only from the standpoint of the social level, for some sets within the network of contrasts into which they enter are socially defined. Moreover, the usual structural account, normatively generalizing, omits as ungrammatical some sentences that specifically and acceptably do occur in a community.

In sum, social situations, relationships, and purposes bring into being and maintain linguistic (and nonlinguistic) features and relationships among them. A unified field of linguistics must consider the structures of languages from the standpoint of a description of their contexts of use.

(4) Structural descriptions have usually taken the functions of language for granted. They have focused on the organization of language in the service of reference. The latter term is used here as distinct from both denotation and meaning. One discovers the denotation of an expression in its application on particular occasions; its reference in a dictionary, which states criteria for its application; its meaning in the total import of the situation (see Firth 1935). In effect, most description has based itself on just those speech acts in which grammatical sentences are used with full referential force, neglecting the poetic or expressive facets of speech acts, for example, and the many messages in which (in Sapir's phrase) it is as if a powerful generator were hooked up to run an electric doorbell.

Descriptive theory has generally taken the social adaptation of language for granted as being everywhere the same. The images of one language per community and the infinite potential of any language (as well as the struggle against misconceptions of the adequacy of "primitive" languages) have led some to a militant egalitarianism that refuses to consider the obvious fact that the potentials of languages are not developed equally or in identical directions; that a language is often specialized in certain roles, not all; and that the valuation of even a native language may vary from community to community: free resource here, scarce good there; integral to unity here, easily

abandoned there; an object of pride here, without prestige, even disvalued, there; and so forth.

Models of internal structure may ignore these variations in adaptation: reference is indeed the central function underlying grammatical structure. It remains that a unified field of linguistics must take the functions of language (both in speech acts and in communities) as problematic, and it must develop the concepts and methods for their study. (On functions in speech acts, see Jakobson 1960; Hymes 1962; 1964b; on functions of languages, see Hymes 1961a; 1966; Ferguson 1966.)

The patterning of speech, from the standpoint of communities and contexts of use and the gamut of functions that speech serves in particular acts and groups, as men enact and transcend their situations, is a dimension of a "totalizing" approach (Sartre 1960) that calls for case studies and analytic comparisons going beyond any line of work familiar to us now; yet the need for such an approach can be indicated readily with regard to several problems.

Understanding the acquisition of language by children is of both theoretical and practical importance. Some seek to account for linguistic competence as the process of a child's learning to use any and all grammatical sentences in a language; but such a conception of a child's competence at once omits and idealizes. It omits, in that a child competent in all sentences still would be master of none, not knowing when, where, and how to speak, and about what, to whom, not sharing the attitudes and valuations of the community toward language. It idealizes, in that mastery even of internal structure is a matter of degree, affected at its root by social environment. To explain and affect the communicative competence of children requires the totalizing approach just indicated.

The relation of language to thought is persistently of concern. While the two are far from identical, experience and experimental evidence demonstrate that features of a language do shape behavior and thought. In the long run a language is shaped by the needs of its users, but in the short run the acquisition of experience through a particular language and the need to call on ready linguistic categories partly shape men. All men potentially perceive and think much the same; actually, they notice, store, and recall information mainly in familiar verbal grooves, although the aspects of life for which this is true may vary from society to society. In a multilingual world, moreover, a given language may be the matrix of thought to one person but only its superficial, occasional garb to another. The effect of a language on thought and behavior cannot be inferred from the language alone, but on the basis of a sociolinguistic description of its place in social and personal life (see Hymes 1966).

Verbal art—poetry, narration, oratory, rhetoric, dialectic—is universally made possible by language. A language, indeed, may be viewed as an aesthetic product (Sapir 1921). The forms possible to a verbal art are conditioned by the language, which is also the indispensable means to their study. With the new interest in metrics, poetics, and stylistics as approached through structural linguistics, and with the aid of folklore and anthropology, a truly comparative literature, global in scope, may emerge. And, if seen as not a matter of forms and texts alone but of symbolic action as well, verbal art becomes of special interest to the human sciences generally [see DRAMA; INTERACTION, *article on* DRAMATISM]. The aspects of human nature that underlie the universality of verbal art; the extent to which abilities are cultivated or left dormant, and why; differences in the valuation of language as an aesthetic medium, relative to others (music, dance, ritual, plastic arts) and to other concerns; the structuring of performances and the possibilities that such structures show major areal groupings, express particular aspects of social life, and reflect particular conceptions of the uses of language—all such concerns require an approach through texts as situated in contexts.

The question of the origin of language has returned to prominence, even though theory in this field is in one sense a myth, a projection into time of assumptions on the essential nature of language and its meaning for man. Linguistics proper can prescribe the elements, generic to all languages, whose origins are to be accounted for. (There is the possibility also that some elements of the last stage of the emergence of true language might be recoverable genetically.) A theory of origin must draw on all possible lines of evidence—biological, psychological, archeological—within a theory of the evolution of man. Since language emerges within an ongoing communication system, it is crucial to specify the conditions of selection that would have been operative. Comparison of human communication systems with those of primates is indispensable; so also is comparison of human communication systems among themselves. Studies that analyze comparatively the uses of language are also necessary, in that they bring into view not only what language may be used for but also what it need not be used for in the transmission of cul-

ture and cooperative activity (e.g., some societies seem not to require language for hunting or transmission of tool-making traditions). It is likely that a very limited code, less than true language, sufficed in small homogeneous groups until relatively late in prehistory.

With regard to linguistic conceptions of the unity of man, three perspectives can be distinguished—one envisaging unity through a common origin in the past, one envisaging unity in terms of a common essential nature of language in every time and place, and one envisaging a prospective unity in the context of an emerging world society. The three perspectives are complementary, but the first was more prominent in the nineteenth century (although carried on today in the work of Swadesh and others); the second has been more prominent with the emergence of structural linguistics in this century; and the third is coming into prominence with the increased attention, theoretical and practical, to a sociolinguistic approach. For a long period of human history the differentiation and dispersion of languages was the dominant process, but reintegration and mutual adaptation of languages within more complex social systems have increasingly superseded it. Indeed, genetic differentiation may never occur again. The processes of reintegration and mutual adaptation have accelerated within the same period that general linguistics has emerged, and many of the varied phenomena that attract sociolinguistic attention are aspects of the development of a single modern world—the correlated standardization of national languages; acculturation of dialects and of whole languages; the emergence of pidgins and creoles at the frontiers of mercantile activity and colonization; the efforts to construct rational international languages; the growth of language academies and bourgeois notions of correctness; the cultivation of intertranslatability among the languages of Europe; the challenge to the stable diglossia of older philological civilizations by proponents of "Low" forms of speech; the extension of writing and literacy; and so forth. If these phenomena are to be related within linguistic theory, that theory must approach communities, functions, uses, and adaptations in a way that indeed takes on the character of an evolutionary perspective.

In one view, to be sure, the concept of evolution does not apply to language after its origin. Certainly no subsequent biological selection is apparent (although suggestions concerning a genetic basis for a few sounds have been made). From the standpoint of sociocultural evolution the matter is different. In their make-up, use, and survival, languages have been part of the specific adaptations of societies to environments, cultural contacts, and internal changes. And if all languages are equivalent in fundamental structure and potential capacity, languages as actually developed and available to their users have come to differ in ways that correspond, in part, to general stages of the cultural history of man. One mark is development in terms of the metalinguistic function (language about language), as seen in the development of linguistics itself. Some grammatical features and phonological characteristics seem present at one or another level of sociocultural integration and not at others. Most clearly, the differentiation of society is necessarily accompanied by technical elaboration and differentiation in vocabulary and syntax of a novel order. Recently, such development has been carried to the point of providing the linguistic tools for universal science and an incipient world civilization. Science itself is a key factor, for the languages in which it can be conducted (the small subset that may be called "world" languages) share the novel obligation that there be a name for everything in the universe: botany must leave no plant unnamed, ornithology no bird, ethnology no tribe, and so forth. While mathematics and logic have become what may be considered "postlanguage" developments, it remains true that they must be interpreted in natural languages and can be interpreted only in a few of them. The ideal of universal translatability is most nearly realized in these languages (as languages into which translation is made). These languages of course confer no necessary superiority or advantage on any individual. A user of English may be less able to master experience verbally and less skilled in language use than a user of a language quite local in scope. Even so, these observations must be controversial as they stand, offending as they do the widespread belief in the equivalence of all languages in complexity and function (see Hymes 1961*a*; 1964*c*). The practical importance of such observations is manifest, however, in many issues of education and language policy, both in industrialized and industrializing nations. It should be clear that a modern evolutionary approach to society and culture fails to be adequate, theoretically or practically, if it excludes language.

Linguistics will play a part in the social sciences in the future if only because language so often must be the means of access to other things. Interest in language for its own sake as an aspect of man and society will continue to be an integral part of anthropology and psychology, and, increasingly, of sociology. The novel contributions that linguistic results and linguistic methods can make will be a constant source of such interest, but if an integration within a larger field of linguistics is to be realized, the social sciences themselves will have to contribute results and methods to the study of language. The prominence of the terms "ethnolinguistics," "psycholinguistics," and "sociolinguistics" since World War II augurs such a trend. While each term mediates between linguistics and a particular discipline, the set in total mediates between linguistics and the social sciences as a whole, drawing the two together. The outcome of such a unity will be a linguistics that is truly the science of language.

DELL HYMES

BIBLIOGRAPHY

BACH, EMMON W. 1964 *An Introduction to Transformational Grammars.* New York: Holt.

BERKO, JEAN; and BROWN, ROGER W. 1960 Psycholinguistic Research Methods. Pages 517–557 in Paul Mussen (editor), *Handbook of Research Methods in Child Development.* New York: Wiley.

BERNARDINI, ANTONIO; and RIGHI, GAETANO (1947) 1953 *Il concetto di filologia e di cultura classica dal Rinascimento ad oggi.* 2d ed. Bari (Italy): Laterza.

Biennial Review of Anthropology. → Published since 1955.

BLOOMFIELD, LEONARD (1933) 1951 *Language.* Rev. ed. New York: Holt.

BOAS, FRANZ 1911 Introduction. Part 1, pages 1–83 in Franz Boas (editor), *Handbook of American Indian Languages.* U.S. Bureau of American Ethnology, Bulletin No. 40. Washington: Government Printing Office.

BOAS, FRANZ (1920) 1955 The Classification of American Languages. Pages 211–218 in Franz Boas, *Race, Language and Culture.* New York: Macmillan. → First published in Volume 22 of *American Anthropologist* New Series.

BOLGAR, R. R. 1954 *The Classical Heritage and Its Beneficiaries.* Cambridge Univ. Press. → A paperback edition was published in 1964 by Harper.

BORST, ARNO 1957–1963 *Der Turmbau von Babel: Geschichte der Meinungen über Ursprung und Vielfalt der Sprachen und Völker.* Vols. 1–4. Stuttgart (Germany): Hiersemann.

CASSIRER, ERNST (1923) 1953 *The Philosophy of Symbolic Forms.* Volume 1: Language. New Haven: Yale Univ. Press.

CHOMSKY, NOAM (1957) 1964 *Syntactic Structures.* The Hague: Mouton.

CHOMSKY, NOAM 1964 *Current Issues in Linguistic Theory.* Janua Linguarum, Series Minor, No. 38. The Hague: Mouton.

CHOMSKY, NOAM 1965 *Aspects of the Theory of Syntax.* Massachusetts Institute of Technology, Research Laboratory of Electronics, Special Technical Report, No. 11. Cambridge, Mass.: M.I.T. Press.

CHOMSKY, NOAM 1966 *Cartesian Linguistics: A Chapter in the History of Rationalist Thought.* New York: Harper.

CONFERENCE ON LANGUAGE UNIVERSALS, DOBBS FERRY, NEW YORK, *1961* 1963 *Universals of Language: Report of a Conference.* Edited by Joseph H. Greenberg. Cambridge, Mass.: M.I.T. Press.

Current Trends in Linguistics. → Published since 1963.

DIXON, ROBERT M. W. 1965 *What Is Language? A New Linguistic Approach to Linguistic Description.* London: Longmans.

EMENEAU, MURRAY B. 1956 India as a Linguistic Area. *Language* 32:3–16.

ERVIN-TRIPP, SUSAN 1964 An Analysis of the Interaction of Language, Topic, and Listener. Pages 86–102 in John Gumperz and Dell Hymes (editors), *The Ethnography of Communication.* American Anthropologist, New Series, Vol. 66, No. 6, Part 2. Menasha, Wisc.: American Anthropological Association.

FERGUSON, CHARLES A. 1959 Diglossia. *Word: Journal of the Linguistic Circle of New York* 15:325–340.

FERGUSON, CHARLES A. 1966 National Sociolinguistic Profile Formulas. Pages 309–315 in UCLA Sociolinguistics Conference, Los Angeles, 1964, *Sociolinguistics.* Edited by William Bright. Janua Linguarum, Series Maior, Vol. 20. The Hague: Mouton.

FERGUSON, CHARLES A.; and GUMPERZ, JOHN J. (editors) 1960 *Linguistic Diversity in South Asia: Studies in Regional, Social, and Functional Variation.* Indiana Univ., Research Center in Anthropology, Folklore, and Linguistics, Publications, Vol. 13. Bloomington, Ind.: The Center.

FIRTH, JOHN R. (1935) 1957 The Technique of Semantics. Pages 7–33 in John R. Firth, *Papers in Linguistics, 1934–1951.* Oxford Univ. Press.

FISCHER, JOHN L. 1958 Social Influence on the Choice of a Linguistic Variant. *Word: Journal of the Linguistic Circle of New York* 14:47–56.

FISHMAN, JOSHUA A. et al. 1966 *Language Loyalty in the United States: The Maintenance and Perpetuation of Non-English Mother Tongues by American Ethnic and Religious Groups.* Janua Linguarum, Series Maior, Vol. 21. The Hague: Mouton.

GARVIN, PAUL L. 1959 The Standard Language Problem: Concepts and Methods. *Anthropological Linguistics* 1, no. 3:28–31.

GLEASON, HENRY A. (1955) 1961 *An Introduction to Descriptive Linguistics.* Rev. ed. New York: Holt.

GLEASON, HENRY A. 1964 The Organization of Language: A Stratificational View. Georgetown University, Washington, D.C., Institute of Languages and Linguistics, *Monograph Series on Languages and Linguistics* 17:75–95.

GRAY, LOUIS H. 1939 *Foundations of Language.* New York: Macmillan.

GREENBERG, JOSEPH H. 1948 Linguistics and Ethnology. *Southwestern Journal of Anthropology* 4:140–147.

GUMPERZ, JOHN J. 1961 Speech Variation and the Study of Indian Civilization. *American Anthropologist* New Series 63:976–988.

GUMPERZ, JOHN J.; and HYMES, DELL (editors) 1964 *The Ethnography of Communication.* American Anthropologist, New Series, Vol. 66, No. 6, Part 2. Menasha, Wisc.: American Anthropological Association.

HALL, EDWARD T. 1959 *The Silent Language.* Garden City, N.Y.: Doubleday. → A paperback edition was published in 1961 by Fawcett.

HALLIDAY, MICHAEL A. K.; McINTOSH, ANGUS; and STREVENS, PETER (1964) 1965 *The Linguistic Sciences and Language Teaching.* Bloomington: Indiana Univ. Press.

HARRIS, ZELLIG S. 1951 *Methods in Structural Linguistics.* Univ. of Chicago Press.

HOCKETT, CHARLFS F. 1948 Implications of Bloomfield's Algonquian Studies. *Language* 24:117–131.

HOCKETT, CHARLES F. 1958 *A Course in Modern Linguistics.* New York: Macmillan.

HOENIGSWALD, HENRY M. 1960 *Language Change and Linguistic Reconstruction.* Univ. of Chicago Press.

HYMES, DELL 1959 Field Work in Linguistics and Anthropology. *Studies in Linguistics* 14:82–91.

HYMES, DELL 1961a Functions of Speech: An Evolutionary Approach. Pages 55–83 in Frederick C. Gruber (editor), *Anthropology and Education.* Philadelphia: Univ. of Pennsylvania Press.

HYMES, DELL 1961b Linguistic Aspects of Cross-cultural Personality Study. Pages 313–359 in Bert Kaplan (editor), *Studying Personality Cross-culturally.* New York: Harper.

HYMES, DELL 1961c Alfred Louis Kroeber. *Language* 37:1–28.

HYMES, DELL 1962 The Ethnography of Speaking. Pages 13–53 in Anthropological Society of Washington, *Anthropology and Human Behavior.* Washington: The Society.

HYMES, DELL (editor) 1964a *Language in Culture and Society: A Reader in Linguistics and Anthropology.* New York: Harper.

HYMES, DELL 1964b Directions in (Ethno-) Linguistic Theory. Pages 6–56 in A. Kimball Romney and Roy D'Andrade (editors), *Transcultural Studies of Cognition.* American Anthropologist, New Series, Vol. 66, No. 3, Part 2. Menasha, Wisc.: American Anthropological Association.

HYMES, DELL 1964c A Perspective for Linguistic Anthropology. Pages 92–107 in Sol Tax (editor), *Horizons of Anthropology.* Chicago: Aldine.

HYMES, DELL 1965 Methods and Tasks of Anthropological Philology (Illustrated with Clackamus Chinook). *Romance Philology* 19:325–340.

HYMES, DELL 1966 Two Types of Linguistic Relativity. Pages 114–158 in UCLA Sociolinguistics Conference, Los Angeles, 1964, *Sociolinguistics.* Edited by William Bright. Janua Linguarum, Series Maior, Vol. 20. The Hague: Mouton.

INTERNATIONAL CONGRESS OF LINGUISTS, NINTH, CAMBRIDGE, MASS., *1961* 1963 *Trends in Modern Linguistics.* Edited by Christine Mohrmann et al. Utrecht (Netherlands): Spectrum.

IVIĆ, MILKA 1965 *Trends in Linguistics.* Janua Linguarum, Series Minor, No. 42. The Hague: Mouton.

JAKOBSON, ROMAN 1960 Closing Statement: Linguistics and Poetics. Pages 350–373 in Conference on Style, Indiana University, 1958, *Style in Language.* Edited by Thomas A. Sebeok. Cambridge, Mass.: Technology Press of M.I.T.

JAKOBSON, ROMAN 1963 Efforts Towards a Means–Ends Model of Language in Inter-war Continental Linguistics. Pages 104–108 in International Congress of Linguists, 9th, Cambridge, Mass., 1961, *Trends in Modern Linguistics.* Edited by Christine Mohrmann et al. Utrecht (Netherlands): Spectrum.

JOOS, MARTIN (editor) 1957 *Readings in Linguistics: The Development of Descriptive Linguistics in Amer-*

ica Since 1925. Washington: American Council of Learned Societies.

KATZ, JERROLD J.; and POSTAL, PAUL M. 1964 An Integrated Theory of Linguistic Descriptions. Cambridge, Mass.: M.I.T. Press.

KROEBER, A. L. 1955 Linguistic Time Depth Results So Far and Their Meaning. International Journal of American Linguistics 21:91–104.

LABOV, WILLIAM 1963 The Social Motivation of a Sound Change. Word: Journal of the Linguistic Circle of New York 19:273–309.

LABOV, WILLIAM 1964 Phonological Correlates of Social Stratification. Pages 164–176 in John Gumperz and Dell Hymes (editors), The Ethnography of Communication. American Anthropologist, New Series, Vol. 66, No. 6, Part 2. Menasha, Wisc.: American Anthropological Association.

LAMB, SYDNEY M. 1966 An Outline of Stratificational Grammar. Unpublished manuscript.

LONGACRE, ROBERT E. 1964 Grammar Discovery Procedure: A Field Manual. Janua Linguarum, Series Minor, No. 33. The Hague: Mouton.

LOUNSBURY, FLOYD G. 1953 Field Methods and Techniques in Linguistics. Pages 401–416 in International Symposium on Anthropology, New York, 1952, Anthropology Today: An Encyclopedic Inventory. Univ. of Chicago Press.

McINTOSH, ANGUS; and HALLIDAY, M. A. K. 1966 Patterns of Language. London: Longmans.

MALKIEL, YAKOV 1964a Some Diachronic Implications of Fluid Speech Communities. Pages 177–186 in John Gumperz and Dell Hymes (editors), The Ethnography of Communication. American Anthropologist, New Series, Vol. 66, No. 6, Part 2. Menasha, Wisc.: American Anthropological Association.

MALKIEL, YAKOV 1964b Distinctive Traits of Romance Linguistics. Pages 671–683 in Dell Hymes (editor), Language in Culture and Society: A Reader in Linguistics and Anthropology. New York: Harper.

MALKIEL, YAKOV 1966 Is There Room for "General Philology"? Pacific Coast Philology 1:3–11.

MARROU, HENRI I. (1948) 1956 A History of Education in Antiquity. London: Sheed & Ward. → First published in French.

MARTINET, ANDRÉ (1960) 1964 Elements of General Linguistics. Univ. of Chicago Press. → First published in French.

MARTINET, ANDRÉ 1962 A Functional View of Language. Oxford: Clarendon.

METCALF, GEORGE 1964 The Indo–European Hypothesis in the 16th and 17th Centuries. Paper prepared for Burg-Wartenstein Symposium, 25. Unpublished manuscript.

MOHRMANN, CHRISTINE et al. (editors) 1962 Trends in European and American Linguistics, 1930–1960. Utrecht (Netherlands): Spectrum.

PEDERSEN, HOLGER (1924) 1962 The Discovery of Language: Linguistic Science in the Nineteenth Century. Bloomington: Indiana Univ. Press. → First published in Danish.

PIKE, KENNETH L. 1954 Language in Relation to a Unified Theory of the Structure of Human Behavior. Part 1. Preliminary ed. Glendale, Calif.: Summer Institute of Linguistics.

[Report of the Fifteenth Annual Round Table Meeting on Linguistics and Language Studies.] ·1964 Georgetown University, Washington, D.C., Institute of Languages and Linguistics, Monograph Series on Languages and Linguistics 17.

ROBINS, ROBERT H. 1951 Ancient & Mediaeval Grammatical Theory in Europe With Particular Reference to Modern Linguistic Doctrine. London: Bell.

ROBINS, ROBERT H. 1964 General Linguistics: An Introductory Survey. London: Longmans.

ROMNEY, A. KIMBALL; and D'ANDRADE, ROY GOODWIN (editors) 1964 Transcultural Studies in Cognition. American Anthropologist, New Series, Vol. 66, No. 3, Part 2. Menasha, Wisc.: American Anthropological Association.

SAMARIN, WILLIAM 1967 Field Linguistics. New York: Holt.

SANDYS, JOHN E. (1903–1908) 1958 A History of Classical Scholarship. 3 vols. New York: Hafner.

SAPIR, EDWARD A. 1921 Language: An Introduction to the Study of Speech. New York: Harcourt.

SAPIR, EDWARD A. (1924) 1949 The Grammarian and His Language. Pages 150–159 in Edward A. Sapir, Selected Writings in Language, Culture and Personality. Edited by David G. Mandelbaum. Berkeley: Univ. of California Press.

SAPIR, EDWARD A. 1925 Sound Patterns in Language. Language 1:37–51.

SAPIR, EDWARD A. 1929 The Status of Linguistics as a Science. Language 5:207–214.

SARTRE, JEAN PAUL (1960) 1963 Search for a Method. New York: Knopf. → First published in French. A British edition was published as The Problem of Method.

SWADESH, MORRIS 1951 Diffusional Cumulation and Archaic Residue as Historical Explanations. Southwestern Journal of Anthropology 7:1–21.

VACHEK, JOSEF (1964) 1966 A Prague School Reader in Linguistics. Bloomington: Indiana Univ. Press.

VACHEK, JOSEF 1966a The Linguistic School of Prague: An Introduction to Its Theory and Practice. Bloomington: Indiana Univ. Press.

VACHEK, JOSEF (editor) 1966b Les problèmes du centre et de la périphérie du système de la langue. Travaux linguistiques de Prague, 2. Prague: Éditions de l'Académie Tchécoslovaque des Sciences.

VERBURG, PIETR A. 1952 Taal en functionaliteit: Een historisch-critische studie over de opvattingen aangaande de functies der taal vanaf de prae-humanistische philologie van Orleans tot de rationalistische linguistiek van Bopp. Wageningen (Netherlands): Veenman.

WEINREICH, URIEL 1953 Languages in Contact: Findings and Problems. New York: Linguistic Circle of New York.

WONDERLY, WILLIAM L.; and NIDA, EUGENE A. 1963 Linguistics and Christian Missions. Anthropological Linguistics 5, no. 1:104–144.

II

HISTORICAL LINGUISTICS

Although consecrated by over a century and a half of use, the term "historical linguistics," as a designation of a discipline, is something of a misnomer, because the most exciting and controversial operations of that discipline concern the reconstruction of language, i.e., prehistory, rather than documented history. For this reason, perhaps,

372 LINGUISTICS: Historical Linguistics

Saussure, in his search for a label that would neatly contrast with the newly discovered "synchronic" perspective, suggested the qualifier "diachronic," which, possibly as a result of its paleness, later proved less than successful (1916). In the mid-twentieth century, it might be most apposite to speak of "genetic linguistics" in reference to the entire domain, reserving the alternative designation "glottodynamics" for the hard core of general doctrine governing the analyst's major operations.

Historical linguistics is very often equated with "comparative linguistics"; to the extent that the tracing of genetic relationships involves some confrontation of an earlier with a later stage of the same language (of Old English, say, with Middle or Modern English), a measure of overlap is indeed unavoidable. For practical purposes, however, it seems advisable to refer to comparative linguistics only where several cognate languages—ideally, they should be observed at the same time level—are jointly analyzed in an effort to arrive at the parental tongue, as when proto-Central Algonquian is reconstructed from available records of Sauk and Fox, Cree, Menomini, and Ojibwa. Of course, it is equally legitimate to engage in the typological comparison of languages with no thought of historical reconstruction and regardless of the presence of any kinship ties—see Bally's classic confrontation of Modern German and Modern French (1932) and the currently fashionable "contrastive" grammars.

Historical and comparative linguistics reached their first peak of development in the nineteenth century, although there were some rudimentary attempts in western and central Europe from 1500 to 1800. Language history, in contrast, represents a relatively new genre of research; its roots are in broad-gauged introductory chapters to technically worded historical grammars. In terms readily understandable to layman and beginner alike, language history interweaves austere linguistic analyses with discussions—rarely devoid of grace—of social, economic, broadly cultural, demographic, and literary conditions prevailing at the successive time levels, allowing also for remarks on the philological state of transmission. At its best, as in Migliorini's masterpiece (1960), language history excels at tracing the vicissitudes of a single language viewed within the matrix of the corresponding highly literate national culture.

The individual facts ascertainable through the various analyses devised by historical linguists lend themselves to two entirely unrelated kinds of synthesis. Certain language forms can be lifted out of their original philological context (which alone, in most instances, made their secure identification possible) and can be arranged on a higher plateau of abstraction so as to illustrate broad aspects of a specific linguistic transformation, e.g., the development of sounds, derivational molds, lexical meanings, or syntactic structures from stage A to stage B of the given language. Climbing to a still higher level of generalization, the analyst is at liberty to abandon even the context of the specific language at issue and to cite the modifications observed, for the sake of their illustrative value, in a general methodology of linguistic change. On the other hand, the slivers and nuggets of information obtained through stringent linguistic (in particular, etymological) analysis may be deftly inserted, as highly prized items, in the grandiose mosaics pieced together by patient and versatile historians. These items of information are similar to the fragmentary bits of knowledge collected by physical anthropologists, archeologists, folklorists, and others who attempt to recapture the elusive past.

Traditionally, from the days of such pioneers as the Germanist Jacob Grimm and the Romanist Friedrich Diez to that towering Indo-Europeanist of the early twentieth century, Antoine Meillet, the two conspicuously parallel tools of research in diachronic linguistics have been the manual of historical grammar and the etymological dictionary—the one providing a tightly ordered macrocosm and the other a loose kaleidoscopic array of microcosms. The full-sized historical grammar—not infrequently a multivolume venture—embraced phonology (with excursuses into prosody or accentology), inflection, "word formation" (i.e., affixal derivation and composition or their counterparts in non-Indo-European languages), and syntax. These centered, in ever widening circles, on the word, the phrase, and the sentence. An abridged version was limited to phonology and inflection. Inflection and the "syntax of the word" are so closely adjacent that they tend to merge, and a few scholars have gone so far as to consolidate all of morphology and syntax into the single domain of "morphosyntax," which forms the hard, inalienable kernel of linguistics. Excursions into semantics, metrics (also, through the inclusion of tropes, rhetoric, or poetics), and stylistics—the last-mentioned more loosely organized and defined in a variety of ways—have at all times been regarded as optional rather than obligatory. Only in recent decades have grammatical and lexical studies drifted apart so sharply in techniques and appeal as to render problematic any joint ventures in the immediate future.

The relative stabilization of historical linguistics in the period 1850–1925 had the advantage of producing a far-reaching standardization in its terminology; this, in turn, by virtue of the comparability achieved, has invited and furthered at every step the confrontation of older and more recent studies, a procedure that has become more difficult in the last three decades. The long-unchallenged preeminence of central European scholarship in this field is mirrored by the wide acceptance of such technical terms as "umlaut" (metaphony) and "ablaut" (apophony), while other German labels, potentially just as helpful (e.g., *Lehnwort* "assimilated borrowing" versus *Fremdwort* "unassimilated borrowing"), have enjoyed no such popularity. Early standardization was particularly beneficial in certain special types of nonverbal symbolization, e.g., quotation marks for meaning, italics for quoted forms, boldface for transliteration into another alphabet, small capitals for an ancestral language (e.g., Latin versus Romance vernaculars), large capitals for epigraphic material, square brackets for phonetic transcription, asterisks for hypothetical forms, and, above all, the two directional signs: > "changes into" and < "descends from."

Before long, the success of these symbols led to a temporary staleness, except where the stagnation was relieved by the introduction of signs manufactured by the more aggressively imaginative structuralist school (e.g., slanted lines for "phonemicization"). Thus, few historically oriented scholars have bothered to discriminate typographically between two logically distinguishable hypothetical forms: (a) those undocumented, yet assumed to have existed (*) and (b) those expressly presented as nonexistent (₀). Again, although few experts would deny the sharp cleavage between phonology and morphology, historical linguists have failed to capitalize on the possibility of contrastive symbolization of phonological versus morphological shifts.

To the extent that genetic linguists are concerned with historical situations, unique by definition, they can resort to the device of "model formation" only on a limited scale. In a way, any reconstruction of genetic relationship between languages or dialects involves a generous measure of schematization aimed at eliminating those details that would tend to blur the broad outline. One can visualize an entirely different kind of model: instead of focusing attention on concrete territories (at historical stages) or avoiding any commitment to the speakers' habitat (at prehistoric stages), the analyst may decide to invent imaginary countries with a sharply profiled distribution of coastlines, wastelands, mountain chains, ports of entry, emporia, cultural shrines, etc. He can further posit a certain succession of political, socioeconomic, and strictly linguistic events (say, invasions, retreats into the

hilly inland, reconquest of coastal lowlands, splits into dialects) and project them onto the imaginary area, excogitating in abstract terms the likeliest concatenations of linguistic reactions to these pressures. By sharpening the analyst's alertness to possible and probable intricacies under artificial conditions that are relatively simplified, such schemata can prepare him for successful inquiries into real-life situations, incomparably more complex.

It should be emphasized that the postulate of historical uniqueness is not easy to reconcile with the search for evolutionary universals in the realm of language. However, the prospect of discovering such universals has for many decades been a source of constant titillation. One classic example is the often-observed correlation of word order (and comparable syntactic devices) with the available wealth of inflectional endings. Clarity and economy demand that, if relationships between members of a clause can no longer be expressed unequivocally by means of the endings (e.g., as a result of phonetic erosion), a stiffening of word order should provide an adequate substitute. Also, etymologists have discovered that, of all form classes, adjectives, on balance, tend to present lexical nuclei most resistant to identification. In addition, semanticists report that fluctuations and changes of meaning undergone by verbs exceed, as a rule, those to which a typical noun would be subject. The difficulty with trying to establish absolute universals is that each such attempt presupposes the testing of hundreds of languages. On the other hand, characteristic samples would suffice to identify tendential universals.

As in all evolutionary sciences, the question of purposeful, or oriented, change is at the heart of the philosophy underlying any genetic analysis of linguistic data. Linguists are sharply divided on this matter of teleology: the great Danish theorist Otto Jespersen and the founders of the Prague school categorically affirm the teleological principle (a few visualize a trend toward general improvement achieved through refinement, simplification, and economy); others, particularly Bloomfield (see 1933) and a whole generation of American linguists claiming allegiance to his doctrine, just as vehemently deny it. Discernibly different from the teleological approach, although occasionally confused with it, especially by opponents, is the idealistic slant (characteristic of Benedetto Croce's school in Italy and Karl Vossler's in Germany), which stresses the primacy of the speakers' thinking over their speech habits and grants them in the process a much wider margin of initiative and of control over linguistic change than would be accepted by believers in the pre-eminence of "blind forces" or those (such as Whorf) who view the configuration of a grammatical structure as a prime determinant of thinking and perception. The more literate the speaker and especially the writer, the stronger the case for the idealistic approach; in analyzing "graphemically" the comportment of ancient and medieval scribes, one can hardly fail to distinguish between what they aimed to achieve and what they actually accomplished.

Descriptive and historical linguistics

Basic to all operations in historical linguistics is the view which the analyst holds of the configuration of the speech community under study and of speech communities in general. This was clearly sensed by Bloomfield, who, in his influential book *Language* (1933), without disregarding the varying density of communication or denying the complexity of certain speech communities, impressed upon his readers the need to reckon with a far-reaching uniformity of speech habits. Similarly, in presenting the comparative method, he leaned toward favoring those situations that exhibit clear-cut dialect splits, without denying occasional alternatives. However, many younger scholars have recognized that the link holding together language communities is frequently mere similarity rather than actual homogeneity of speech habits, a point fraught with major implications for the geneticist. It is further held that bilingualism and even trilingualism are more widely disseminated the world over than is strict monolingualism, an assumption that demands flexibility in dealing with a multitude of diversified and changing situations. Thus, two groups speaking language X—one composed of members who have from infancy also mastered language Y and the other containing persons who happen to be constantly using language Z in certain social contexts—are unlikely to react identically to any incipient innovations spreading from a monolingual zone. (One also readily conceives of innovations arising at the intersection of languages.) One final argument in favor of fluidity in the object observed and elasticity in the method applied to its elucidation is the discovery that many areas commonly assigned *en bloc* to certain languages often lack such "natural boundaries" as might preserve a community of speakers in quasi-hermetic isolation. The emergence of such zones is due rather to conflation, i.e., to successive reapportionments of neighboring territories, each initially sheltering a different language or dialect. Therefore, unless perfect leveling subsequently ensues, one may detect beneath the present-day "roof"

bracketing the dialects remnants and splinters of their original phonic, grammatical, and lexical systems in almost kaleidoscopic confusion.

In linguistics, the relation of the descriptive (or synchronic) to the historical (or diachronic) perspective has been the subject of considerable speculation and discussion, the consensus being that descriptive analysis bears preponderantly on simpler, less opaque situations. From this nearly unanimous opinion several discrepant conclusions may be drawn. Some experts maintain that new techniques, such as the structural method, should be tried out first on horizontal, later on vertical, slices of linguistic material. There are those who visualize a historical structure as a succession of descriptive structures superimposed on one another. The main difficulty in designing such an edifice lies in the fact that certain features structurally less than significant at one evolutionary stage may suddenly acquire conspicuous importance during transition to the next stage. Thus, the descriptivist is free to assert that in words like *danc-er, kill-er,* the ending *-er* as the carrier of an identifiably specific meaning ("agent") represents a derivational morpheme, while in *hamm-er, pinc-er, rudd-er* the same sequence of sounds plays no comparable role. But the historical linguist, while acknowledging this distinction on certain temporal plateaus, must at all times reckon with the strong possibility of joint actions, inextricably interwoven, by homonymous genuine suffixes (such as the *-er* of *kill-er*) and mere suffixoids (the *-er* of *rudd-er*). One consensus is worth mentioning: from the minute inspection of any given state of a single language the experienced analyst can tentatively extract almost as much information on its earlier stages ("internal reconstruction") as he can from comparing that language "externally" with its congeners.

One way of doing justice to both perspectives has been to engage in a "stairway projection"; among the practitioners of this novel approach one may count such seasoned experimenters as Otto Jespersen (for English), Antoine Meillet (for Latin), and Walther von Wartburg (for French). This particular method of intricate surgery affords glimpses of the consecutive periods of the chosen language, slanted alternately in the descriptive and in the historical direction. The implication of this design is clearly that one may distinguish between periods of relative rest and stability and others marked by spells of stress and strain.

One salient difference between the descriptive and the historical approach in linguistics is that the former in most instances enables the researcher to operate with a finite corpus, an intentional selection over whose scope he retains a modicum of control, while the latter often bears on an irremediably fragmentary volume of data. The ability to work with lacunary material and a certain flair for filling in gaps thus become important prerequisites for success in linguistic reconstruction, just as they are for research in geology, paleontology, and paleobotany. Developments are contrastively symbolized by solid lines (documented) or broken lines (hypothesized); however, the latter do not invariably represent initial, prehistoric segments of trajectories. An archaic stage A may very well owe its transparency to the realistic, readily adjustable spelling habits of the scribes concerned; conversely, stage B, although temporally closer to the beholder, may become nebulous, because the scribes of that period, plagued by conservatism, or subject to an inferiority complex, may have endeavored stubbornly to cling to the orthographic norms of their predecessors ("etymological spelling"), while the actual speech processes ran their course with unabated speed; then again, stage C may mark a vigorous return to graphic realism, entailing the relative translucency of actual speech events. A vivid illustration of these three phases is provided by early Latin, late Latin, certain varieties of "low" and medieval Latin, and, on an overwhelming scale, the budding Romance vernaculars.

It also happens that some word of unmistakably Latin provenience which, judging from its "normal" transformations, must have been in constant use over two millennia, disappears from written records in the fifth century, only to re-emerge a thousand years later. In cases of this kind, the literary genres of the extant texts act as prisms or filters, often seemingly capricious. They may long repress a word, keeping it submerged until there arises some opportunity—socially or aesthetically controlled—for its definitive surfacing into the standard language.

Trajectories of linguistic change

Systematic inquiry into the configuration of trajectories has not yet outgrown the stage of trial and error. Where regular phonological change occurs, older notions of strictly gradual transitions do not apply. Between, say, the Latin $\bar{u}$, as in $p\bar{u}ru$, and the French $\ddot{u}$, as in pur, it is no longer admissible to posit an infinity of intermediate nuances of the stressed vowel without concurrently accepting some kind of cutoff point at which a vowel already markedly fronted, but still representing no more than an unusual variant within the phoneme $/\bar{u}/$, must have become a member, decreasingly erratic, of the sound family constituting the phoneme $/\ddot{u}/$.

In other words, structural thinking forces us to recognize the interaction of slow-working phonetic *rapprochements* and more or less sudden occasional jumps. This composite schema guarantees the semblance of a close-knit system to a language at any moment of its growth. Thus, the graduality of development—not superseded, but only qualified and hierarchized—remains a vitally important assumption. Significantly, the hypothesis that the shift $\bar{u} > \ddot{u}$, eminently characteristic of the transformation of provincial Latin into French, is traceable to the contributing agency of Gaulish cannot be refuted by the argument that the Celtic language in question lacked a fully developed $/\ddot{u}/$ in its own system. It would have sufficed for the local substratum language, at the start, to have slightly deflected the Latin $\bar{u}$ from its original status of a high back vowel in the direction of $\ddot{u}$, thus producing a kind of chain reaction or even an accelerated advance along a straight line.

In yet another context, the configuration of a trajectory of linguistic change, properly interpreted, may be revealing. If the changes due to associative interference were to be plotted on a chart, some of them might give the impression of a bizarre zigzagging curve. On such a chart a relatively level line may suddenly start climbing as a result of an outside pressure, a "disturbance," until it reaches a certain peak. Then the language's inner mechanism (e.g., the total weight of its inflectional paradigms) may begin to wipe out the irregularity, causing the line to drop until it reverts to its original direction. If in such an up-and-down movement, anteceding the advent of trustworthy written texts, the descending stage completely absorbs the effects of the ascending stage, it is quite impossible to detect the original disturbance. If the down movement falls short of counterbalancing the aberrancy or overcorrects it, there is bound to remain in its wake a residue of startling "exceptions." In case the irregularity happens to erupt at the very start of the written tradition, it may appear baffling in retrospect that the ancestral language and its eventual modern product should be in perfect mutual agreement while at such sharp variance with the intermediate step, which then, in fact, fails to perform any "mediation." Thus, the Latin third person singular imperfect ending -$\bar{\imath}bat$ (originally -$i\bar{e}bat$) cast off in early Romance speech -$ia(t)$, which to this day survives in Spanish as -ia, a safely predictable form, but paradoxically it produced instead, in early Old Spanish, -$i\acute{e}$, a variant difficult to reconcile either with its antecedent or with its sequel. Investigation (Malkiel 1959; 1964) has disclosed that the rise of -$i\acute{e}$ simply marks a minor temporary deflection (of ascertainable origin), ultimately neutralized, while the later form *-ia* represents far more faithfully the continuation of a basic trend.

Closely allied to the concern with the convolution of trajectories is the attempt, assuming a certain more or less steady rate of attrition in the core lexicon, to draw from parallel analyses tentative conclusions as to the degree of kinship between congeneric languages and the approximate date of their split. This approach, which rode the crest of a temporary vogue in the 1950s, has become known, broadly, as *lexicostatistics* and, with special application to dating, as *glottochronology*. Exaggerated claims, especially the attempt of some practitioners to place these techniques on the same pedestal as the rigorous study of sound correspondences, have led to quick disenchantment and virtual abandonment of the method.

Sound change

For better or worse, the vicissitudes of historical linguistics have been intimately linked with the theories of sound change. The recognition of regularity in these transmutations has been hailed as a milestone along the road to progress (cf. the radical programmatic statements of the "neogrammarians," or *Junggrammatiker*, circa 1870) or, more intransigently, as a touchstone of stringent scientific thinking. In the compressed classroom presentation of historical linguistics, lecturers have traditionally inclined toward concentrating on "regular sound changes" as the discipline's irreducible hard core. In the separate quarters of humanists and anthropologists alike, this rigid attitude has for decades contributed toward producing the impression of linguistics as a highly abstract subject, almost forbiddingly abstruse and, above all, divorced in its style and tone from cultural history, to say nothing of its aloofness from the realm of arts and letters. Moreover, because most provisional rules or "laws" admitted of a few exceptions and some of countless ones, there was for a while a widespread apprehension that the "regularists" were actually propounding some kind of mock science.

In reality, there exist several categories of sound change, each fairly autonomous—but not entirely so—and tied to diverse facets of human comportment and different levels of a speaker's consciousness. The immediate goal of linguists is to discover one workable formula for presenting these interconnections, however tenuous, and another for discovering the elusive ties of sound change categories to discrete mental processes.

The techniques of accurately circumscribing individual sound correspondences that are inherently limited in time and space can be traced to the nineteenth century. By contrasting the French *mer* ("sea") and *père* ("father") with their Latin prototypes *mare* and *patre*, the analyst learns that the Latin *a* tended, by and large, to yield *e* in French. Further refinement of this first approximation is within easy reach. The discrepant first vowels in *père* and *parrain* ("godfather") (originally *parrin*, from *patrīnus*) alert the observer to the possibility that the shift *a > e* hinges on a crucial accentual condition, while comparison of *père < pa-tre* with *part < par-te* dramatizes the share that the configuration of the stressed syllable may have had in an obvious bifurcation, depending on whether that syllable ended in a vowel or a consonant. By examining with scrupulous care all seemingly aberrant developments (amenable to observation with optimal results in Old French), the analyst isolates, step by step, the specific phonological ("internal") factors that must have presided over the evolution, erratic at first glance, of *(il)lāc* ("there") *> là*; *paupere* ("poor") *> povre* (modern *pauvre*); *clāuu* ("nail") *> clou; aqua* ("water") *> eaue* (modern *eau*); *palus* ("pole") *> pieus; caput* ("head") *> ch(i)ef*, etc. Comparably detailed breakdowns can be established for all other Latin sounds viewed in their transmission into a chosen "daughter language," and, by way of effective control, the linguist is free to reverse the perspective and select as a given the basic sound unit of the daughter language, assigning to himself the task of individuating its sources.

But this classification marks only a first step, yielding at best a tidily subdivided inventory of raw facts. The preliminary classification is nonexplicative, lacks statistical underpinning, fails to throw into bold relief parallels, convergences (including some that are partial or have been arrested), and, worse, concatenations of events, and does not begin to take into account other forms of sound shift. Such taxonomy disregards several broad or distinct categories of internal linguistic change. Moreover, it is not elastic enough to do justice to the various external pressures (demographic, social, educational) on evolutionary trends in speech and in the written word as well. It is in these directions— many of them affording fruitful contacts with a whole spectrum of other disciplines—that the chief advances of late-twentieth-century research are bound to lie.

The following are a few illustrations of research in progress and tempting prospects of investigation. Alongside regular phonetic change (akin to Sapir's "drift") scholars have placed sporadic shifts (also called spontaneous and saltatory), such as metathesis, the transposition of a sound or intermutation of two sounds, in contact or at a distance, haplology, the elimination of one or two successive segments partially identical, and certain dissimilatory processes. None of these, it has been argued, is confined to a specific locus or span of time, i.e., they are all, at least latently or tendentially, pantopic and panchronic. Granted the fundamental validity of this distinction, there arise several questions and second thoughts. Does the sound system of a language at a given stage—or, alternatively, its pattern of regular changes—typically stimulate or block sporadic shifts, or does it let them take their own course? Could it be true that, for all their uniqueness, regular sound changes, in any random selection, display such strong proclivities in a few characteristic directions that one discerns in them certain universals? Is it legitimate to grade the regularity of sound change (not as an ideal postulate, but as a bit of reality) and to contrast "strong" expectation of outcome, most likely to occur in monolithic societies, with "weak" predictability, attributable to, say, loose conflations of dialects, regional or social? Does such a state of prevalent weakness tend to intensify sporadic shifts and to invite even an excess of lexical contamination? Should frequency of lexical occurrence, or at least of incidence in actual speech, rank as a factor contributing to the degree of regularity, especially where a particularly unusual sequence of sounds falls into no broader pattern of immediate appeal? Can the exigencies of inflectional patterning slow down the pace of a sound change or counteract it to the point of weakening a phonetic "law"? Do other demands of this kind carry sufficient weight to set in motion or to accelerate potential and, especially, incipient sound changes? If the answer to the last two questions is affirmative, can one uphold the view that phonology operates in practically hermetic isolation? Specifically, is it still permissible to resolve the phenomena of genetic phonology into a neat interplay of sound relationships—to be precise, into an alternation of states of equilibrium and states of unrest or tension, to the virtual exclusion of all rival forces? Does it make sense to arrange sound changes in their presumed chronological succession (Richter 1934) without explicit forewarning that such sequences neither invariably presuppose nor necessarily imply the flow of one change from another or from the sum of all others already completed? Can one, in such contexts, ignore with impunity certain extraneous factors such as pressure of morphological paradigms and deflections from the straight course through associative lexical interference?

From earlier incidental mention it is clear that there are other kinds of change affecting linguistic form and, consequently, reflected in the sounds as the obligatory carriers of that form but not here caused by purely phonetic conditions. The most important of these supervenient categories of change is analogical. Speakers make adjustments bearing either on the configuration of a grammatical paradigm or on the shape of a single word; in the latter eventuality, both the radical and the affix are open to modification. Typically, such adjustments follow upon sound change; only by way of exception may one suspect them of impinging, as prime movers, upon sound development. Since analogical changes involve, by definition, associative interference, they seem to occur on a higher level of awareness than straight sound changes; thus they invite psycholinguistic analysis.

Sound symbolism constitutes yet another autonomous category, of slightly controversial status. To the extent that sounds, in symbolic context (and nowhere else), are credited with conveying messages of their own, this marginal category represents a tenuous bridge to semantic change, ordinarily removed from the realms of articulation, acoustics, and auditory perception. Sound symbolism may be absolute or relative. The former category prevails if the analyst attaches, cross-linguistically, an unvarying evocative value to, say, a high front vowel or to a hissing prepalatal consonant; the problem then is to ascertain whether speakers will allow words endowed with major connotative force, through such ingredients, to participate in normal sound shifts at the cost of heavy loss in suggestiveness. The effects of relative sound symbolism are conditioned by the given phonological system; thus, in a language generally averse to long consonants an occasional geminate may boast "expressive" value (which it would otherwise lack). Again, the language historian is curious to learn how speakers can maintain a word enhanced by such a feature in this privileged status amid the welter of pervasive transformations. At this juncture one welcomes contact with information theory.

Pressures for linguistic change

Entirely different from the classes of change are the categories of forces that are apt to produce changes of any kind. But the linguist's operational procedure in tackling this new problem remains essentially unaltered: again his dual task is first to isolate the forces in question and then to discover the closest available approximation to the formula for their interplay.

It is customary to divorce the internal from the external forces at the outset, notably because the separate inquiries into them seem to appeal to radically different minds. In the former group one can readily distinguish two drives, sometimes acting in polar opposition—one toward economy of effort, the other toward clarity. Economy, syntagmatically conceived, aims at the speech act; in paradigmatic perspective economy relates to the acquisition of, and sustained command over, neuromuscular skills. The former type determines the course of most assimilatory processes, contextual by definition (e.g., Latin *actu* > Italian *atto*) and governs the choice of those glides and buffer consonants that serve to smooth away troublesome contiguity (in Old Spanish viewed in its relation to Latin: *hŏnōrāre* > *onrar* > *on-d-rar* versus *fēmina* > *femna* > *fem-b-ra*). The latter type precipitates mergers of phonemes in the system where continued distinction between them would produce only a meager yield (/ā/ and /ē/ in older Parisian, /ɛ̄/ and /œ̄/ with increasing momentum in present-day Parisian). It also dooms to extinction minute groups of words displaying an infrequent sound or combination of sounds.

A groping search for increased clarity may be behind most dissimilatory and haplologic processes. It accounts, as would no other supposition, for the speakers' readiness to augment their vocabulary (in an effort to reduce lexical polysemy) and to accept longer and more cumbersome syntactic structures (in a recoil from ambiguity). It is perhaps at this point that the newly achieved refinement of transformational grammar would most benefit the classic researches conducted by geneticists. The same urge for increased clarity ultimately justifies the sometimes successful flight from harmful homonymy or from its mere threat—the nearest escape routes being substitute words borrowed from neighboring dialects and reinterpreted within one's own cultural heritage, and words freely invented.

After one deducts the two-pronged quest for maximum economy and clarity, it is the residue left that threatens to cause serious difficulty; the wisdom of applying to it some such pleasing blanket term as "expressivism" remains to be demonstrated, especially since it is doubtful whether, in the last analysis, one can reduce the remaining forces to a single denominator. One nucleus that cannot by any stretch of the imagination be subsumed under either economy or clarity contains those formations associated with special moods—playful, tender, or festive. In contemporary English the colloquially flavored compositional types, such as *hush-hush*, *ping-pong*, *riffraff*, *wishy-washy*, *pribbles and prabbles*, *topsy-turvy*, *mumbo jumbo* —sometimes originating in the nursery and displaying a strong admixture of onomatopoeia—admirably fit this description. In Slavic and Romance languages, formations involving strings of hypocoristic suffixes would qualify as a counterpart. The

Hebrew spoken in modern Israel, the twentieth century's linguistic melting pot par excellence, allows speakers the jocose lapse into the Ashkenazic rather than the officially favored Sephardic pronunciation for proper names affectionately uttered, thus proliferating doublets. On the other hand, one runs across a phenomenon such as hypercharacterization (i.e., the sharper, more explicit, even uneconomically generous marking of a major grammatical category—say, gender, number, or person). For instance, the Latin *socrus* ("mother-in-law"), hampered by its conspicuously uncharacteristic *-us*, is more neatly profiled with regard to gender (and sex) at the Romance stage through a new and far more appropriate ending (Italian, *suocera*; Spanish, *suegra*, etc.); cf. also the change of Latin *puppis* ("poop," "stern"), marred by an ending indeterminate as to gender, into the clear-cut Spanish *pop-a*. In such instances, the change is, of course, analogical, but the driving force behind it seems less easy to identify. It certainly can be neither economy nor any overflow of emotion, and one is hesitant, to say the least, to press into service a quest for heightened clarity. The propelling force, one suspects, is the speaker's endeavor to redesign selected portions of the language, to make the medium of transmission more pointed or so silhouetted as to be aesthetically more satisfying. Sapir's reference to the "cut" of a language comes to mind here—a fait accompli or a goal toward which speakers may strive.

The most familiar external forces whose impact will produce the various types of linguistic change are those resulting from contact between languages (occasionally one living and the other dead, but preserved in ritual or intensely studied) or regional and social dialects. Typically, a protracted transitional period of thoroughgoing bilingualism or plurilingualism is needed before the contact produces sizable results. In gauging any such impact on a specific language, the historian tries first to determine the principal layer of that language by inspecting the core structure of its grammar and those ingredients of its lexicon best known for their resistance, if not total immunity, to infiltration. Numerals, kinship terms, names of parts of the body, and grammatically functional words are typical examples of such elements. Once this frame of reference has been established, it becomes clear which layers, in the course of further study, will be labeled substrata and which superstrata—eloquent metaphors borrowed from geology and permitting a graphic projection of anteriority. Thus, vis-à-vis Great Russian, the numerous Finno–Ugric languages, now extinct or pushed back to the periphery of eastern Europe, constituted substrata; so did Coptic and, farther down the Nile valley in Egypt, the Greek *koinē* vis-à-vis Arabic, Frisian vis-à-vis Dutch in Holland, and French plus Canary Island Spanish vis-à-vis English in Louisiana. In the absence of any genuine symbiosis, it is doubtful whether American Indian languages may rank as substrata in relation to English in North America, as they indisputably do in relation to Spanish and Portuguese throughout Latin America. In the twilight hour between late Antiquity and the Middle Ages, Arabic in southern Spain and Frankish in northern Gaul represented superstrata in relation to divergent varieties of provincial Latin. To the extent that the Greeks tended to form independent cultural nuclei under the aegis of the expanding Roman Republic and later Roman Empire, their settlements qualify as examples of linguistic adstrata vis-à-vis Latin as well as the circum-Mediterranean indigenous languages.

Aside from such "vertical" relations, linguistic pressures operate "horizontally" across political borders and even at long distances through cultural diffusion. Thus, heavy clusters of Gallicisms are found not only in Spanish, Catalan, Italian, German, and Dutch, to say nothing of English, but also in languages occupying nonadjacent areas, such as Rumanian, Polish, Russian, and Swedish. Words are more easily borrowed than sounds, and affixes travel more rapidly than inflectional endings. A classic example of superimposed syntactic, semantic, and (probably) intonational patterns is provided by the multifarious Germanisms observable in eastern Switzerland's Romansh, a language descended from Raetian Latin.

Against the fairly trivial instances of direct, positive influence one may place the sorely neglected range of indirect or catalytic interferences. Thus, two early medieval Germanic kingdoms carved out of the ruins of the crumbling Roman Empire—that of the Suebi in Galician–Portuguese territory and that of the Burgundians in the Lyon–Geneva area —molded local Latin speech sparingly through loan words but exerted a powerful restraining influence by politically and culturally isolating their territories, at crucial junctures, from such centers of ceaseless linguistic innovation as Toledo and Paris.

An independent kind of external force comprises all sorts of nonlinguistic events potentially rich in linguistic reverberations. The invention of novel tools and machines may breathe new life into a moribund suffix serving to denote instruments. The emancipation of women the world over may develop dormant schemata (affixal, compositional, or otherwise derivational) for the designation of female agentials. A global vogue of formality or

familiarity (in clothing, dwellings, human relations, etc.) could hardly fail to revolutionize the system of forms of address and to affect even personal pronouns and possessive adjectives. The sections of the linguistic edifice most vulnerable to these influences are, then, the vocabulary, the derivational machinery (at the midway point between lexicon and grammar), plus a few pieces from the morphosyntactic tool kit.

Far beyond this boundary, the "idealistic" school of thought, entrenched in Italy and Germany only a generation ago (Vossler 1925), tended to assess very liberally the impact of changing modes of thinking on linguistic forms, extending that impact to the foundations of sentence structure. While the consensus of most generations of scholars has ascribed the disappearance of case endings to attrition, recognizing the rise of prepositional paraphrases as a relatively smooth replacement, the "idealists" preferred to view as prime mover the emergence of a new way of thinking (such as analytic rather than synthetic), crediting it with the manufacture of appropriate substitutes which eventually eroded the older grammatical framework. The advent of Christianity figured in these interpretations (especially in H. F. Muller's) as another favorite determinant of linguistic evolution. The idealistic position is thus diametrically opposed to that of Whorf, who, following Sapir (1921), mused that patterns of thinking may, in the first place, be molded by pre-existent grammatical structures.

The complex interaction of all these isolable forces can be illustrated with the differing, if reconcilable, answers to the classic question: What dooms a word to extinction? Plausible explanations offered either separately or in any number of free combinations include an excess of paradigmatic intricacy or phonological oddity in the fated word; the peril besetting the weaker of two conflicting homonyms; an intolerable dosage of polysemy; a sudden general demand at all levels of the given society for lexical rejuvenation or large-scale overhaul; the obsolescence of a specific cultural element (say, some container or garment) heretofore designated by the word at issue; the ineluctable effect of some socially controlled restriction (taboo, etc.); acceptance, through borrowing from the local prestige language, of a more attractive equivalent, as when the imported *Cousine* dislodged the native *Base* in eighteenth-century German.

Theories of linguistic change

For the projection of major phases of linguistic growth, and especially for signaling the relationship between cognate languages, experts in reconstruction have resorted either to the somewhat older "family-tree theory" (*Stammbaumtheorie*) or to the wave hypothesis. The former is associated with the name of Schleicher, that contemporary and counterpart of the evolutionist Darwin who actually refined rather than launched the "family-tree" concept (1861). It operates with a filiation chart reminiscent of those long favored in the life sciences. The filiation chart, germane in its verbalization and, even more, in its graphic suggestion to the physicists' and chemists' views of radiation, cannot be traced to any advocate earlier than Schuchardt (1866) and, in particular, Schmidt (1871). The inherently rigid family-tree diagram presupposes uniform speech communities and their sudden and clear-cut bifurcation. The more elastic wave diagram tends to dissolve any system (or, less orderly, any arsenal) of communication tools into its constituents, granting to each change, whether phonetic, morphosyntactic, or lexical, its own scope and history. Neither the lapse of time it demands nor the area it covers need be exactly identical with those involved in any comparable change. The latest thinking sees in these divergent hypotheses two complementary projections, neither satisfactory if applied in isolation. Regrettably, no theory apt to reconcile them and no technique capable of smoothly integrating their separate findings have so far been devised.

The wave theory has intrinsically tended to give unusual prominence to the territorial expansion of linguistic features, providing the logical justification for linguistic (*or* dialect) geography. The interest in dialect geography is now past its crest; for many decades it fed on its sentimental motivation, local patriotism, and its partisans' delight in open-air field work. Practitioners of this approach developed special methods for interviews, oral or written questionnaires, and the cartographic recording of field notes (linguistic atlases). Dialect geographers endowed with historical flair then proceeded to transform the geographic patterns laboriously established into bolder chronological sequences, calling themselves the geologists, paleontologists, or stratigraphers of human speech.

One extreme formulation of these assumptions, tastes, and techniques (the "age–area hypothesis") relies chiefly or even exclusively on territorial patterns in piecing together temporal successions. An attempt to schematize these procedures of "areal analysis" was undertaken by the small group of Italian "neolinguists," a school that produced a short flurry of activity from 1920 to 1950. A point that has hitherto not been satisfactorily investigated and yet clamors for imaginative inquiry is the wisdom of positing, alongside that "outer radiation" dear to dialect geographers and to diffusionists like Boas, some kind of "inner radiation" that might account in undulatory projections for the continuous restructuring of systems.

YAKOV MALKIEL

[*See also* HISTORY, *article on* CULTURE HISTORY; LINGUISTICS, *article on* THE SPEECH COMMUNITY; *and the biographies of* BLOOMFIELD; SAUSSURE; WHORF.]

BIBLIOGRAPHY

BALLY, CHARLES (1932) 1944 *Linguistique générale et linguistique française.* 2d ed. Bern: Francke.

BENVENISTE, ÉMILE 1966 *Problèmes de linguistique générale.* Paris: Gallimard.

BLOOMFIELD, LEONARD (1933) 1951 *Language.* Rev. ed. New York: Holt.

HYMES, DELL 1960 Lexicostatistics So Far. *Current Anthropology* 1:3–44. → Includes eight pages of "Comments" and "References."

KURYŁOWICZ, JERZY 1960 *Esquisses linguistiques.* Wroclaw (Poland): Zakład Narodowy Imienia Ossolinskich.

LEROY, MAURICE 1963 *Les grands courants de la linguistique moderne.* 2d ed. Brussels, Université Libre, Faculté de Philosophie et Lettres, Travaux, Vol. 24. Presses Universitaires de Bruxelles. → Contains a reliable account of nineteenth-century research.

MALKIEL, YAKOV 1959 Toward a Reconsideration of the Old Spanish Imperfect in -ía ～ -ié. *Hispanic Review* 27:435–481.

MALKIEL, YAKOV 1964 Initial Points Versus Initial Segments of Linguistic Trajectories. Pages 402–405 in International Congress of Linguists, Ninth, Cambridge, Mass., 1962, *Proceedings.* Janua linguarum, Series Maior, Vol. 12. The Hague: Mouton.

MARTINET, ANDRÉ 1955 *Économie des changements phonétiques: Traité de phonologie diachronique.* Bern: Francke.

MIGLIORINI, BRUNO 1960 *Storia della lingua italiana.* Florence: Sansoni.

RICHTER, ELISE 1934 *Beiträge zur Geschichte der Romanismen.* Zeitschrift für romanische Philologie, Supplement 82. Halle (Germany): Niemeyer.

SAPIR, EDWARD 1921 *Language: An Introduction to the Study of Speech.* New York: Harcourt.

SAUSSURE, FERDINAND DE (1916) 1959 *Course in General Linguistics.* New York: Philosophical Library. → First published (posthumously) as *Cours de linguistique générale.*

SCHLEICHER, AUGUST (1861) 1874–1877 *A Compendium of the Comparative Grammar of the Indo-European, Sanskrit, Greek and Latin Languages.* London: Trübner. → Selections from August Schleicher's *Compendium der vergleichenden Grammatik der indogermanischen Sprachen.*

SCHMIDT, JOHANNES 1871 *Die Verwandtschaftsverhältnisse der indogermanischen Sprachen.* Weimar (Germany): Böhlau.

SCHUCHARDT, HUGO 1866 *Der Vokalismus des Vulgärlateins.* Volume 1. Leipzig: Teubner.

VOSSLER, KARL (1925) 1932 *The Spirit of Language in Civilization.* London: Routledge. → First published as *Geist und Kultur in der Sprache.*

III
THE SPEECH COMMUNITY

Although not all communication is linguistic, language is by far the most powerful and versatile medium of communication; all known human groups possess language. Unlike other sign systems, the verbal system can, through the minute refinement of its grammatical and semantic structure, be made to refer to a wide variety of objects and concepts. At the same time, verbal interaction is a social process in which utterances are selected in accordance with socially recognized norms and expectations. It follows that linguistic phenomena are analyzable both within the context of language itself and within the broader context of social behavior. In the formal analysis of language the object of attention is a particular body of linguistic data abstracted from the settings in which it occurs and studied primarily from the point of view of its referential function. In analyzing linguistic phenomena within a socially defined universe, however, the study is of language usage as it reflects more general behavior norms. This universe is the speech community: any human aggregate characterized by regular and frequent interaction by means of a shared body of verbal signs and set off from similar aggregates by significant differences in language usage.

Most groups of any permanence, be they small bands bounded by face-to-face contact, modern nations divisible into smaller subregions, or even occupational associations or neighborhood gangs, may be treated as speech communities, provided they show linguistic peculiarities that warrant special study. The verbal behavior of such groups always constitutes a system. It must be based on finite sets of grammatical rules that underlie the production of well-formed sentences, or else messages will not be intelligible. The description of such rules is a precondition for the study of all types of linguistic phenomena. But it is only the starting point in the sociolinguistic analysis of language behavior.

Grammatical rules define the bounds of the linguistically acceptable. For example, they enable us to identify "How do you do?" "How are you?" and "Hi" as proper American English sentences and to reject others like "How do you?" and "How you are?" Yet speech is not constrained by grammatical rules alone. An individual's choice from among permissible alternates in a particular speech event may reveal his family background and his social intent, may identify him as a Southerner, a Northerner, an urbanite, a rustic, a member of the educated or uneducated classes, and may even indicate whether he wishes to appear friendly or distant, familiar or deferential, superior or inferior.

Just as intelligibility presupposes underlying grammatical rules, the communication of social information presupposes the existence of regular relationships between language usage and social structure. Before we can judge a speaker's social intent, we must know something about the norms defining the appropriateness of linguistically acceptable alternates for particular types of speakers; these norms vary among subgroups and among social settings. Wherever the relationships between language choice and rules of social appropriateness can be formalized, they allow us to group relevant linguistic forms into distinct dialects, styles, and occupational or other special parlances. The sociolinguistic study of speech communities deals with the linguistic similarities and differences among these speech varieties.

In linguistically homogeneous societies the verbal markers of social distinctions tend to be confined to structurally marginal features of phonology, syntax, and lexicon. Elsewhere they may include both standard literary languages, and grammatically divergent local dialects. In many multilingual societies the choice of one language over another has the same signification as the selection among lexical alternates in linguistically homogeneous societies. In such cases, two or more grammars may be required to cover the entire scope of linguistically acceptable expressions that serve to convey social meanings.

Regardless of the linguistic differences among them, the speech varieties employed within a speech community form a system because they are related to a shared set of social norms. Hence, they can be classified according to their usage, their origins, and the relationship between speech and social action that they reflect. They become indices of social patterns of interaction in the speech community.

Historical orientation in early studies

Systematic linguistic field work began in the middle of the nineteenth century. Prior to 1940 the best-known studies were concerned with dialects, special parlances, national languages, and linguistic acculturation and diffusion.

Dialectology. Among the first students of speech communities were the dialectologists, who charted the distribution of colloquial speech forms in societies dominated by German, French, English, Polish, and other major standard literary tongues. Mapping relevant features of pronunciation, grammar, and lexicon in the form of *isoglosses*, they traced in detail the range and spread of historically documented changes in language habits. Isoglosses were grouped into bundles of two or more and then mapped; from the geographical shape of such isogloss bundles, it was possible to distinguish the *focal areas*, centers from which innovations radiate into the surrounding regions; *relic zones*, districts where forms previously known only from old texts were still current; and *transition zones*, areas of internal diversity marked by the coexistence of linguistic forms identified with competing centers of innovation.

Analysis along these lines clearly established the importance of social factors in language change. The distribution of rural speech patterns was found to be directly related to such factors as political boundaries during the preceding centuries, traditional market networks, the spread of important religious movements, etc. In this fashion dialectology became an important source of evidence for social history.

Special parlances, classical languages.   Other scholars dealt with the languages of occupationally specialized minority groups, craft jargons, secret argots, and the like. In some cases, such as the Romany of the gypsies and the Yiddish of Jews, these parlances derive from foreign importations which survive as linguistic islands surrounded by other tongues. Their speakers tend to be bilinguals, using their own idiom for in-group communication and the majority language for interaction with outsiders.

Linguistic distinctness may also result from seemingly intentional processes of distortion. One very common form of secret language, found in a variety of tribal and complex societies, achieves unintelligibility by a process of verbal play with majority speech, in which phonetic or grammatical elements are systematically reordered. The pig Latin of English-speaking schoolchildren, in which initial consonants are transferred to the end of the word and followed by "-ay," is a relatively simple example of this process. Thieves' argots, the slang of youth gangs, and the jargon of traveling performers and other occupational groups obtain similar results by assigning special meanings to common nouns, verbs, and adjectives.

Despite their similarities, the classical administrative and liturgical languages—such as the Latin of medieval Europe, the Sanskrit of south Asia, and the Arabic of the Near East—are not ordinarily grouped with special parlances because of the prestige of the cultural traditions associated with them.

They are quite distinct from and often unrelated to popular speech, and the elaborate ritual and etiquette that surround their use can be learned only through many years of special training. Instruction is available only through private tutors and is limited to a privileged few who command the necessary social status or financial resources. As a result, knowledge of these languages in the traditional societies where they are used is limited to relatively small elites, who tend to maintain control of their linguistic skills in somewhat the same way that craft guilds strive for exclusive control of their craft skills.

The standard literary languages of modern nation-states, on the other hand, tend to be representative of majority speech. As a rule they originated in rising urban centers, as a result of the free interaction of speakers of a variety of local dialects, became identified with new urban elites, and in time replaced older administrative languages. Codification of spelling and grammar by means of dictionaries and dissemination of this information through public school systems are characteristic of standard-language societies. Use of mass media and the prestige of their speakers tend to carry idioms far from their sources; such idioms eventually replace many pre-existing local dialects and special parlances.

Linguistic acculturation, language shift.   Wherever two or more speech communities maintain prolonged contact within a broad field of communication, there are crosscurrents of diffusion. The result is the formation of a *Sprachbund*, comprising a group of varieties which coexist in social space as dialects, distinct neighboring languages, or special parlances. Persistent borrowing over long periods creates within such groups similarities in linguistic structure, which tend to obscure pre-existing genetic distinctions; a commonly cited example is the south Asian subcontinent, where speakers of Indo–Aryan, Dravidian, and Munda languages all show significant overlap in their linguistic habits.

It appears that single nouns, verbs, and adjectives are most readily diffused, often in response to a variety of technological innovations and cultural or religious trends. Pronunciation and word order are also frequently affected. The level of phonological and grammatical pattern (i.e., the structural core of a language), however, is more resistant to change, and loanwords tend to be adapted to the patterns of the recipient language. But linguistic barriers to diffusion are never absolute, and in situations of extensive bilingualism—

two or more languages being regularly used in the course of the daily routine—even the grammatical cores may be affected.

Cross-cultural influence reaches a maximum in the cases of pidgins and creoles, idioms combining elements of several distinct languages. These hybrids typically arise in colonial societies or in large trading centers where laborers torn out of their native language environments are forced to work in close cooperation with speakers of different tongues. Cross-cultural influence may also give rise to language shift, the abandonment of one native tongue in favor of another. This phenomenon most frequently occurs when two groups merge, as in tribal absorption, or when minority groups take on the culture of the surrounding majority.

Although the bulk of the research on speech communities that was conducted prior to 1940 is historically oriented, students of speech communities differ markedly from their colleagues who concentrate upon textual analysis. The latter tend to treat languages as independent wholes that branch off from uniform protolanguages in accordance with regular sound laws. The former, on the other hand, regard themselves primarily as students of behavior, interested in linguistic phenomena for their broader sociohistorical significance. By relating dialect boundaries to settlement history, to political and administrative boundaries, and to culture areas and by charting the itineraries of loanwords in relation to technical innovations or cultural movements, they established the primacy of social factors in language change, disproving earlier theories of environmental or biological determinism.

The study of language usage in social communities, furthermore, revealed little of the uniformity ordinarily ascribed to protolanguages and their descendants; many exceptions to the regularity of sound laws were found wherever speakers of genetically related languages were in regular contact. This led students of speech communities to challenge the "family-tree theory," associated with the neogrammarians of nineteenth-century Europe, who were concerned primarily with the genetic reconstruction of language history. Instead, they favored a theory of diffusion which postulates the spread of linguistic change in intersecting "waves" that emanate from different centers of innovation with an intensity proportionate to the prestige of their human carriers.

Thus, while geneticists regarded modern language distribution as the result of the segmentation of older entities into newer and smaller subgroups, diffusionists viewed the speech community as a dynamic field of action where phonetic change, borrowing, language mixture, and language shift all occur because of social forces, and where genetic origin is secondary to these forces. In recent years linguists have begun to see the two theories as complementary. The assumption of uniformity among protolanguages is regarded as an abstraction necessary to explain existing regularities of sound change and is considered extremely useful for the elucidation of long-term prehistoric relationships, especially since conflicting short-term diffusion currents tend to cancel each other. Speech-community studies, on the other hand, appear better adapted to the explanation of relatively recent changes.

Language behavior and social communication

The shift of emphasis from historical to synchronic problems during the last three decades has brought about some fundamental changes in our theories of language, resulting in the creation of a body of entirely new analytical techniques. Viewed in the light of these fresh insights, the earlier speech-community studies are subject to serious criticism on grounds of both linguistic and sociological methodology. For some time, therefore, linguists oriented toward formal analysis showed very little interest. More recent structural studies, however, show that this criticism does not affect the basic concept of the speech community as a field of action where the distribution of linguistic variants is a reflection of social facts. The relationship between such variants when they are classified in terms of usage rather than of their purely linguistic characteristics can be examined along two dimensions: the *dialectal* and the *superposed*.

Dialectal relationships are those in which differences set off the vernaculars of local groups (for example, the language of home and family) from those of other groups within the same, broader culture. Since this classification refers to usage rather than to inherent linguistic traits, relationships between minority languages and majority speech (e.g., between Welsh and English in Britain or French and English in Canada) and between distinct languages found in zones of intensive intertribal contact (e.g., in modern Africa) can also be considered dialectal, because they show characteristics similar to the relationship existing between dialects of the same language.

Whereas dialect variation relates to distinctions in geographical origin and social background, superposed variation refers to distinctions between different types of activities carried on within the same group. The special parlances described above form a linguistic extreme, but similar distinctions in usage are found in all speech communities. The language of formal speechmaking, religious ritual, or technical discussion, for example, is never the same as that employed in informal talk among friends, because each is a style fulfilling particular communicative needs. To some extent the linguistic markers of such activities are directly related to their different technical requirements. Scientific discussion, for instance, requires precisely defined terms and strict limitation on their usage. But in other cases, as in greetings, forms of address, or choosing between "isn't" and "ain't," the primary determinant is the social relationship between speakers rather than communicative necessity. Language choice in these cases is limited by social barriers; the existence of such barriers lends significance to the sociolinguistic study of superposed variation.

This distinction between dialectal and superposed varieties obviates the usual linguistic distinction between geographically and socially distributed varieties, since the evidence indicates that actual residence patterns are less important as determinants of distribution than social interaction patterns and usage. Thus, there seems to be little need to draw conceptual distinctions upon this basis.

Descriptions of dialectal and superposed variation relate primarily to social groups. Not all individuals within a speech community have equal control of the entire set of superposed variants current there. Control of communicative resources varies sharply with the individual's position within the social system. The more narrowly confined his sphere of activities, the more homogeneous the social environment within which he interacts, and the less his need for verbal facility. Thus, housewives, farmers, and laborers, who rarely meet outsiders, often make do with only a narrow range of speech styles, while actors, public speakers, and businessmen command the greatest range of styles. The fact that such individual distinctions are found in multilingual as well as in linguistically homogeneous societies suggests that the common assertion which identifies bilingualism with poor scores in intelligence testing is in urgent need of re-examination, based, as it is, primarily on work with underprivileged groups. Recent work, in fact, indicates that the failure of some self-contained groups to inculcate facility in verbal manipulation is a major factor in failures in their children's performances in public school systems.

Attitudes to language choice.   Social norms of language choice vary from situation to situation and from community to community. Regularities in attitudes to particular speech varieties, however, recur in a number of societies and deserve special comment here. Thieves' argots, gang jargons, and the like serve typically as group boundary maintaining mechanisms, whose linguistic characteristics are the result of informal group consensus and are subject to continual change in response to changing attitudes. Individuals are accepted as members of the group to the extent that their usage conforms to the practices of the day. Similar attitudes of exclusiveness prevail in the case of many tribal languages spoken in areas of culture contact where other superposed idioms serve as media of public communication. The tribal language here is somewhat akin to a secret ritual, in that it is private knowledge to be kept from outsiders, an attitude which often makes it difficult for casual investigators to collect reliable information about language distribution in such areas.

Because of the elaborate linguistic etiquette and stylistic conventions that surround them, classical, liturgical, and administrative languages function somewhat like secret languages. Mastery of the conventions may be more important in gaining social success than substantive knowledge of the information dispensed through these languages. But unlike the varieties mentioned above, norms of appropriateness are explicit in classical languages; this permits them to remain unchanged over many generations.

In contrast, the attitude to pidgins, trade languages, and similar intergroup media of communication tends to be one of toleration. Here little attention is paid to linguistic markers of social appropriateness. It is the function of such languages to facilitate contact between groups without constituting their respective social cohesiveness; and, as a result, communication in these languages tends to be severely restricted to specific topics or types of interaction. They do not, as a rule, serve as vehicles for personal friendships.

We speak of *language loyalty* when a literary variety acquires prestige as a symbol of a particular nationality group or social movement. Language loyalty tends to unite diverse local groups and social classes, whose members may continue to speak their own vernaculars within the family circle. The literary idiom serves for reading and for public interaction and embodies the cultural tradition of a nation or a sector thereof. Individuals choose to employ it as a symbol of their allegiance to a broader set of political ideals than that embodied in the family or kin group.

Language loyalty may become a political issue in a modernizing society when hitherto socially isolated minority groups become mobilized. Their demands for closer participation in political affairs are often accompanied by demands for language reform or for the rewriting of the older, official code in their own literary idiom. Such demands often represent political and socioeconomic threats to the established elite, which may control the distribution of administrative positions through examination systems based upon the official code. The replacement of an older official code by another literary idiom in modernizing societies may thus represent the displacement of an established elite by a rising group.

The situation becomes still more complex when socioeconomic competition between several minority groups gives rise to several competing new literary standards, as in many parts of Asia and Africa, where language conflicts have led to civil disturbances and political instability. Although demands for language reform are usually verbalized in terms of communicative needs, it is interesting to observe that such demands do not necessarily reflect important linguistic differences between the idioms in question. Hindi and Urdu, the competing literary standards of north India, or Serbian and Croatian, in Yugoslavia, are grammatically almost identical. They differ in their writing systems, in their lexicons, and in minor aspects of syntax. Nevertheless, their proponents treat them as separate languages. The conflict in language loyalty may even affect mutual intelligibility, as when speakers' claims that they do not understand each other reflect primarily social attitudes rather than linguistic fact. In other cases serious linguistic differences may be disregarded when minority speakers pay language loyalty to a standard markedly different from their own vernacular. In many parts of Alsace-Lorraine, for example, speakers of German dialects seem to disregard linguistic fact and pay language loyalty to French rather than to German.

Varietal distribution. Superposed and dialectal varieties rarely coincide in their geographical extent. We find the greatest amount of linguistic diversity at the level of local, tribal, peasant, or lower-class urban populations. Tribal areas typically constitute a patchwork of distinct languages, while local speech distribution in many modern nations takes the form of a dialect chain in which the speech of each locality is similar to that of adjoining settlements and in which speech differences increase in proportion to geographical distance. Variety at the local level is bridged by the considerably broader spread of superposed varieties, serving as media of supralocal communication. The Latin of medieval Europe and the Arabic of the Near East form extreme examples of supralocal spread. Uniformity at the superposed level in their case, however, is achieved at the expense of large gaps in internal communication channels. Standard languages tend to be somewhat more restricted in geographical spread than classical languages, because of their relationship to local dialects. In contrast to a society in which classical languages are used as superposed varieties, however, a standard-language society possesses better developed channels of internal communication, partly because of its greater linguistic homogeneity and partly because of the internal language loyalty that it evokes.

In fact, wherever standard languages are well-established they act as the ultimate referent that determines the association of a given local dialect with one language or another. This may result in the anomalous situation in which two linguistically similar dialects spoken on different sides of a political boundary are regarded as belonging to different languages, not because of any inherent linguistic differences but because their speakers pay language loyalty to different standards. Language boundaries in such cases are defined partly by social and partly by linguistic criteria.

Verbal repertoires. The totality of dialectal and superposed variants regularly employed within a community make up the *verbal repertoire* of that community. Whereas the bounds of a language, as this term is ordinarily understood, may or may not coincide with that of a social group, verbal repertoires are always specific to particular populations. As an analytical concept the verbal repertoire allows us to establish direct relationships between its constituents and the socioeconomic complexity of the community.

We measure this relationship in terms of two concepts: *linguistic range* and *degree of compartmentalization*. Linguistic range refers to internal language distance between constituent varieties, that is, the total amount of purely linguistic differentiation that exists in a community, thus distinguishing among multilingual, multidialectal, and homogeneous communities. Compartmentalization refers to the sharpness with which varieties are set off from each other, either along the superposed or the dialectal dimension. We speak of compartmentalized repertoires, therefore, when several languages are spoken without their mixing, when dialects are set off from each other by sharp isogloss bundles, or when special parlances are sharply distinct from other forms of speech. We speak of fluid repertoires, on the other hand, when transitions between adjoining vernaculars are gradual or when one speech style merges into another in such a way that it is difficult to draw clear borderlines.

Initially, the linguistic range of a repertoire is a function of the languages and special parlances employed before contact. But given a certain period of contact, linguistic range becomes dependent upon the amount of internal interaction. The greater the frequency of internal interaction, the greater the tendency for innovations arising in one part of the speech community to diffuse throughout it. Thus, where the flow of communication is dominated by a single all-important center—for example, as Paris dominates central France—linguistic range is relatively small. Political fragmentation, on the other hand, is associated with diversity of languages or of dialects, as in southern Germany, long dominated by many small, semi-independent principalities.

Over-all frequency in interaction is not, however, the only determinant of uniformity. In highly stratified societies speakers of minority languages or dialects typically live side by side, trading, exchanging services, and often maintaining regular social contact as employer and employee or master and servant. Yet despite this contact, they tend to preserve their own languages, suggesting the existence of social norms that set limits to freedom of intercommunication. Compartmentalization reflects such social norms. The exact nature of these sociolinguistic barriers is not yet clearly understood, although some recent literature suggests new avenues for investigation.

We find, for example, that separate languages maintain themselves most readily in closed tribal systems, in which kinship dominates all activities. Linguistically distinct special parlances, on the other hand, appear most fully developed in highly stratified societies, where the division of labor is maintained by rigidly defined barriers of ascribed status. When social change causes the breakdown of traditional social structures and the formation of new ties, as in urbanization and colonialization, linguistic barriers between varieties also break down. Rapidly changing societies typically show either gradual transition between speech styles or, if the community is bilingual, a range of intermediate varieties bridging the transitions between extremes.

JOHN J. GUMPERZ

[*See also* LANGUAGE, *article on* LANGUAGE AND CULTURE; *and* LINGUISTICS, *article on* HISTORICAL LINGUISTICS.]

BIBLIOGRAPHY

BARTH, FREDERIK 1964 Ethnic Processes on the Pathan–Baluch Boundary. Pages 13–20 in *Indo-Iranica: Mélanges présentés à Georg Morgenstierne, à l'occasion de son soixante-dixième anniversaire.* Wiesbaden (Germany): Harrassowitz.

BERNSTEIN, BASIL (1958) 1961 Social Class and Linguistic Development: A Theory of Social Learning. Pages 288–314 in A. H. Halsey et al. (editors), *Education, Economy, and Society.* New York: Free Press. → First published in Volume 9 of the *British Journal of Sociology.*

BLOOMFIELD, LEONARD (1933) 1951 *Language.* Rev. ed New York: Holt.

BROWN, ROGER W. 1965 *Social Psychology.* New York: Free Press.

GUMPERZ, JOHN J.; and HYMES, DELL H. (editors) 1964 The Ethnography of Communication. *American Anthropologist* New Series 66, no. 6, part 2.

HALLIDAY, MICHAEL A. K.; MCINTOSH, ANGUS; and STREVENS, PETER (1964) 1965 *The Linguistic Sciences and Language Teaching.* Bloomington: Indiana Univ. Press.

HAUGEN, EINAR I. 1956 *Bilingualism in the Americas: A Bibliography and Research Guide.* University, Ala.: American Dialect Society.

HAUGEN, EINAR I. 1966 *Language Conflict and Language Planning.* Cambridge, Mass.: Harvard Univ. Press.

HERTZLER, JOYCE O. 1965 *A Sociology of Language.* New York: Random House.

HYMES, DELL H. (editor) 1964 *Language in Culture and Society: A Reader in Linguistics and Anthropology.* New York: Harper.

JESPERSEN, OTTO (1925) 1964 *Mankind, Nation and the Individual, From a Linguistic Point of View.* Bloomington: Indiana Univ. Press. → First published as *Menneskehed, nasjon og individ i sproget.*

KURATH, HANS (editor) 1939–1943 *Linguistic Atlas of New England.* 3 vols. and a handbook. Providence, R.I.: Brown Univ. Press.

LABOV, WILLIAM 1966 The Social Stratification of English in New York City. Unpublished manuscript, Center for Applied Linguistics.

PASSIN, HERBERT 1963 Writer and Journalist in the Transitional Society. Pages 82–123 in Conference on Communication and Political Development, Dobbs Ferry, N.Y., 1961, *Communications and Political Development.* Edited by Lucian W. Pye. Princeton Univ. Press. → Contains a discussion of the relationship of national languages to political development.

WEINREICH, URIEL 1953 *Languages in Contact: Findings and Problems.* New York: Linguistic Circle of New York.

LINTON, RALPH

Ralph Linton (1893–1953), American cultural anthropologist, was one of the major contributors to the reconstruction of anthropology during the second quarter of the twentieth century. Trained in the traditions of the North American "historical school" of anthropology, Linton remained loyal throughout his career to the broad interests and general principles established by Franz Boas and other American anthropologists. But with the publication in 1936 of *The Study of Man*, which was quickly recognized by social scientists all over the world as a pioneering study of human behavior, he embarked on a series of creative and stimulating studies which provided new conceptions of social structure and cultural organization. He related these conceptions in a clear if somewhat simple manner to the biological individual and his personality and utilized them in his analyses of the processes of cultural change.

Linton belonged to the "third generation" of American academic anthropologists, succeeding such second-generation students of Putnam and Boas as Wissler, Dixon, Kroeber, Goldenweiser, Lowie, Sapir, and Radin. These academicians, together with a number of outstanding journeymen and masters involved more in field research than in teaching, had created a distinctive variety of anthropology. Like Tylor in England, they had a holistic approach to human studies which is still, thanks in part to Linton, a mark of American anthropology.

In the Americas much more than in Europe almost all anthropological study and training had been nurtured by experience in the field and disciplined by the empiricism required by field work on specific problems treating the temporal and spatial dimensions of culture. In dealing with the elements of local aboriginal development or culture history, most American anthropologists insisted that the combined skills of all the arts and sciences, as they may be relevant to the study of man, should be brought to bear on the task at hand. [*See* ETHNOGRAPHY.]

Linton's own teaching, writing, and research encompassed human biology, archeology, ethnography, ethnology, folklore, and regional and global cultural history. He contributed to all of these classical subfields of his discipline, although less significantly to physical anthropology, archeology, and folklore than to the others. He neglected technical developments in linguistics and approached the field with respectful diffidence, but he urged his students to become familiar with it, since he felt that it was the most scientific of the social disciplines. He did not emphasize statistical studies, nor did he use specialized mathematical methods in cultural or psychological anthropology, although he recognized these as legitimate activities. It was not any aversion to formalism or structuralism as such that made Linton shy away from these aspects of anthropology, for his approach to culture and to

personality studies was essentially formalistic and structural.

Like many other American anthropologists who began as archeologists, Linton's professional career started with a focus on artifacts. As a boy he had systematically collected arrowheads, and his interests in artifacts continued throughout his life as he privately gathered outstanding examples of African textiles and masks, Peruvian ceramics, and Oceanic sculpture. Linton's eidetic memory and extraordinary capacity for visual imagery enabled him to identify and compare artifacts from all over the world; and he could retrieve data from the masses of material he had read, explaining that often he could simply "turn the pages" in his mind and reread them.

Linton did his undergraduate work at Swarthmore College, a liberal institution to which his Philadelphia Quaker background led him. The college offered no studies in anthropology, but Linton was a good student in the natural sciences and an omnivorous reader in history and literature, and he decided, as he later recalled, that anthropology provided the most promising opportunity for a synthesis of varied fields. In 1912 and 1913 Linton joined field expeditions working in the American southwest and in Guatemala; and in the summer of 1915, after receiving his B.A., he discovered in New Jersey a prehistoric site of controversial importance, which he described in his first professional publications in the two following years. His graduate training at the University of Pennsylvania, where he obtained an M.A. in 1916, at Columbia University, and finally at Harvard University, where he completed his PH.D. in 1925, was heavily weighted on the side of archeology and physical anthropology. Linton had two more summers of archeological experience in the southwestern United States, one in 1916 for the American Museum of Natural History and another in 1919 following his return from army service in France. He embarked in 1920 on his doctoral research on the archeology of the Marquesas Islands.

Linton's two years in Polynesia proved a turning point in his career, for he found work with living Marquesans more rewarding than his study of the meager remains of their ancestors. His concern for archeological problems continued—he was later active in excavations in Ohio and Wisconsin, and his posthumously published reconstruction of global cultural history demonstrates the mastery he always maintained over the data of world prehistory (see 1955)—but from the early 1920s on, his primary interest was the study of contemporary peoples.

On his return from Polynesia in 1922 he joined

the staff of the Field Museum of Natural History in Chicago, working on Oceanic and American Indian materials and conducting a one-man ethnographic expedition to Madagascar and adjacent parts of east Africa from 1925 to 1927. The publications he prepared during his years as a curator in Chicago indicate that for him the main task of ethnology was not far removed from that of archeology—the reconstruction of human history through careful descriptive studies of the development and distribution of cultural traits. Thus, when Linton began his own teaching career, accepting the first tenure position in anthropology at the University of Wisconsin, in 1928, he had moved little beyond the range of interests which had preoccupied the two preceding generations of American anthropologists.

His early years in the department of sociology at Wisconsin (soon the department of sociology and anthropology) marked the major turning point in Linton's intellectual and professional progress. He suddenly acquired wide interests in the many dimensions of human behavior. The competent fieldworker, museum archeologist, and ethnologist became in a few years a leading American social scientist.

Linton was an excellent lecturer and teacher. Almost as soon as he arrived at Wisconsin he acquired a following of young scholars who had done their undergraduate work at the university; John Dollard, J. P. Gillin, E. A. Hoebel, Clyde Kluckhohn, Lauriston Sharp, and Sol Tax were among them. Although none of these completed his graduate training under Linton, they were nonetheless widely identified with him. A number of colleagues had a marked influence on Linton's thinking during his early years at Wisconsin. He said that Kimball Young, the social psychologist, had perhaps helped him most in developing his view of social organization and its relation to individual personality formation; but he also acknowledged his debt to other members of the department, as well as to the psychologists Clark Hull and Harry Harlow, the geneticist Michael F. Guyer, the political scientist John Gauss, and the ethicists F. C. Sharp and Eliseo Vivas. Students in the university's newly established Experimental College, while dealing with the large problems of order and change in the civilizations of classical Greece and modern America, were reading a wide range of materials bearing on cultural anthropology, and Linton participated in sessions on the nature and organization of culture and civilization that were unlike most anthropology courses of the day.

For a few years during the early 1930s A. R. Radcliffe-Brown, then a leader of the British functionalist school of social anthropology, taught at the University of Chicago, where Linton maintained informal connections. At that time Radcliffe-Brown was claiming in a somewhat doctrinaire manner that history is irrelevant to the real task of social anthropology, which is to study societies synchronically and induce general sociological laws through a comparison of the forms and functions of the social organizations of particular living societies. To Linton, the rejection of history, however fragmentary and insecure our knowledge of it may be, was anathema. However, his own field work had convinced him that the task of determining the functions of segments or complexes of cultural behavior as well as the functional interdependence of parts within the totality of a culture is a legitimate and essential one (1933). Furthermore, Linton himself was seeking regularities and general principles in the varied array of cultural experience in different times and places. Thus, in their intellectual objectives the two scholars were close together, however they differed as to means. Linton's correspondence of the period indicates that he deplored Radcliffe-Brown's considerable influence on younger members of the profession as a threat to the larger traditional concerns of American anthropology and one which he felt personally obligated to combat. However, the discussions which took place between the two men sharpened Linton's perceptions of Radcliffe-Brown's own special field of social structure and led him to argue for improved functional analyses which would take into account historical factors. Eventually this point of view largely prevailed on both sides of the Atlantic.

In the 1930s the new developments in psychiatry, psychology, European sociology, and functionalism began to influence American anthropologists, particularly Sapir, Benedict, Margaret Mead, and Hallowell. Physical anthropology and archeology, which had links to the natural sciences, and linguistics were beginning to develop rapidly and even in America were showing a strong tendency to go their separate ways. However, Linton's eclectic and wide-ranging approach to the study of man and his behavior enabled him to bring together some of these radically diverging historical, sociological, psychological, and biological interests which were dividing the anthropologists. His contributions to unity were open-ended; he found it unnecessary to impose any single closed, elaborate, or wholly consistent theoretical system on the social sciences.

Concept of culture. The work which Linton always considered his major contribution to anthropology, *The Study of Man* (1936), was written in a simple but lively style which attracted layman and scientist alike. While intended as a text, it lacked the apparatus of a school book, containing only two footnotes and an almost irrelevant bibliography prepared hastily by a student. Except for the absence of sections on religion and the arts (originally intended for inclusion but not completed), the work was representative of the main areas of Linton's interests and foreshadowed the main thrusts of his later thinking.

Following a short opening section on human origins and the biological and primate backgrounds to cultural behavior, later elaborated in *The Tree of Culture* (1955), Linton turned directly to the individual as he interacts in defined social contexts with other individuals: the network of learned and shared behavior of individuals—their culture—creates or maintains a community or society. He conceived of culture as both overt, or open to observation, and covert, with an inferred content of meanings, emotions, values, attitudes, "and so on."

While Linton could speak of "the mind" without blushing, he failed to deal effectively with cognition and other epistemological problems, seeing the mind as a wholly internal private sense organ rather than as a process or a product of the transaction of social business between the external and the inner worlds. As he later became involved more explicitly with psychoanalytic theory, Linton increasingly dealt with the category of covert behavior as though emotion is the prime ingredient and almost the sole source of data for the inner workings of the human personality, thus almost entirely neglecting cognitive processes.

Status and role.   Linton developed his concepts of "status" and "role" to deal with the discrete elements as well as the integrated aspects of society. By status he meant the place of an individual in society, defining it as a collection of rights and duties; by role he meant the dynamic aspect of behavior in a status, the putting into action of rights and duties (1936, pp. 113–114). Statuses and roles may be universal or specialized, depending on whether they are shared by all members of a society or only by a segment of the society. Roles appropriate to a given status are not necessarily performed in the same way by all those members of the society in that status, nor are they even performed identically by the same individual at different times. There may be recognized alternative ways of achieving particular customary goals: such alternative roles may arise within the society or they may be imported from without. Behavior in a role, according to Linton, is simply behavior appropriate to a particular recognized status.

Statuses or positions are, in Linton's view, either ascribed to the individual—that is, assigned at birth, on the basis of sex, caste, or other fixed characteristics—or they are achieved by the individual by virtue of his own effort. Roles also are of two kinds: "actual" roles—the way roles are in fact performed; and "ideal" roles—the normative patterns that serve as models for actual role performance. The total set of ideal roles constituted for Linton a social system. With this conception of roles, including child roles and those acquired as an adult, Linton laid the foundation of a theory of behavior that could bridge the gap between the individual and the cultural system.

Personality and culture.   Instead of systematically refining these ideas or attempting a synthesis along the lines developed in social psychology, Linton pursued his interest in the nature of the relation between the individual personality and society. In 1937 he went to Columbia University and began there a period of collaboration in seminars and publications with Abram Kardiner, a psychoanalyst. Their views were published, with documentary ethnographic analyses, in *The Individual and His Society* (Kardiner 1939) and *The Psychological Frontiers of Society* (Kardiner 1945). From this work emerged the concept of basic personality structure, or modal personality type—

. . . that personality configuration which is shared by the bulk of the society's members as a result of the early experiences which they have in common. It does not correspond to the total personality of the individual, but rather to the projective systems or, in different phraseology, the value–attitude systems which are basic to the individual's personality configuration. Thus the same basic personality types may be reflected in many different forms of behavior and may enter into many different total personality configurations. (Kardiner 1945, p. viii)

Somewhat disenchanted with the psychoanalytic approach, Linton expounded his own views in *The Cultural Background of Personality* (1945a), showing how each individual's experiences in a society—his performance of a particular set of more or less standardized cultural roles—produce what Linton then called the "status personality." The common elements of the status personalities found in a group of persons may be considered the basic personality type for a culture. Linton dealt with problems of deviation from type in a posthumously published volume, *Culture and Mental Disorders* (1956). While some anthropologists before Linton had been concerned with the individual, it was Linton's structural approach through status and role that did much to open the way for a retreat from the prevalent extreme reification of culture. [*See* AGE DIFFERENTIATION; CULTURE AND PERSON-

ALITY; INDIVIDUAL DIFFERENCES, *article on* SEX DIFFERENCES; NATIONAL CHARACTER; STATUS, SOCIAL.]

Hierarchy of interests.   Related to Linton's concern with culture and personality and the character structure of ethnic groups was his work on the cultural interests, orientations, and values of groups. He was dissatisfied with Benedict's conclusion, in her popular *Patterns of Culture* (1934), that the total behavior of a society or of most of its members may express, through a dominant cultural pattern or configuration, a single mode of feeling or world view heavily biased in a particular direction. While agreeing that cultures are configurations, Linton suggested that any culture exhibits a whole range of patterned "interests," each of which has a "rating" reflecting its importance relative to other interests of the group. Only empirical investigation can reveal which particular interest or set of interests dominates the others in a given period and so provides the culture with an over-all orientation (1936, chapters 20, 24, 25). Morris Opler and others later refined this idea through the concept of "themes."

In his later years, and particularly after he accepted a Sterling professorship at Yale University in 1946, Linton returned to a problem which had engaged him at Wisconsin, the question of cultural relativity and the possibility that all cultures may exhibit certain universal ethical or other values. He asserted that there are common denominators of behavior among all cultures and that these support common values which then must be described at a rather abstract level (1952; 1954).

Cultural change.   Linton's preoccupation with problems of culture history and culture change persisted from his first experience as an archeologist through his entire career; it even motivated his interest in the balanced relationships between the maturing individual and the changing culture in which he participates. Yet in his search for explanations of cultural change and transfer, Linton did not explore these relationships fully or systematically; rather, to explain the effective elements in change, acculturation, and social movements, he pointed to such general factors as the utility of the new, the compatibility of the new with the old, and the prestige of the innovator (1940). [See CULTURE, *article on* CULTURE CHANGE.]

Linton believed profoundly that the social sciences could become rigorous sciences and that their findings should inform the work of those dealing with current social problems (1945b, p. xiii).

However, he was not optimistic about the immediate prospects of modern civilization. His own creative innovations were widely recognized and he received the highest academic and professional honors from colleagues both within and outside his discipline. But he felt that this recognition of his work had been won in a rare period of freedom, one which could not last and which was already threatened by the bigotries which had appeared abroad and at home in his own lifetime. Expecting a "dark age," he dedicated *The Study of Man* (1936) to "the next civilization"; and almost two decades later he concluded *The Tree of Culture* (1955) in the same vein, expressing the hope that the social sciences would use this period of unusual freedom to prepare some "solid platform from which the workers of the next civilization might go on."

LAURISTON SHARP

[*Other relevant material may be found in the biographies of* BENEDICT; RADCLIFFE-BROWN; SAPIR.]

WORKS BY LINTON

1933   *The Tanala: A Hill Tribe of Madagascar.* Field Museum of Natural History, Publication No. 317, Anthropological Series, No. 22. Chicago: The Museum.

1936   *The Study of Man: An Introduction.* New York: Appleton.

1940   LINTON, RALPH (editor) *Acculturation in Seven American Indian Tribes.* New York: Appleton.

1945a   *The Cultural Background of Personality.* New York: Appleton.

1945b   LINTON, RALPH (editor) *The Science of Man in the World Crisis.* New York: Columbia Univ. Press.

1952   Universal Ethical Principles: An Anthropological View. Pages 645–660 in Ruth N. Anshen (editor), *Moral Principles of Action: Man's Ethical Imperative.* New York: Harper.

1954   The Problem of Universal Values. Pages 145–168 in Robert F. Spencer (editor), *Method and Perspective in Anthropology.* Minneapolis: Univ. of Minnesota Press.

1955   *The Tree of Culture.* New York: Knopf.

1956   *Culture and Mental Disorders.* Edited by George Devereux. Springfield, Ill.: Thomas.

SUPPLEMENTARY BIBLIOGRAPHY

BENEDICT, RUTH (1934) 1959 *Patterns of Culture.* 2d ed. Boston: Houghton Mifflin. → A paperback edition was published in 1961.

GILLIN, JOHN 1954 Ralph Linton. *American Anthropologist* New Series 56:274–281.

KARDINER, ABRAM 1939 *The Individual and His Society.* With a foreword and two ethnological reports by Ralph Linton. New York: Columbia Univ. Press.

KARDINER, ABRAM 1945 *The Psychological Frontiers of Society.* With the cooperation of Ralph Linton, Cora DuBois, and James West. New York: Columbia Univ. Press.

KLUCKHOHN, CLYDE 1958 Ralph Linton. National Academy of Sciences, *Biographical Memoirs* 31:236–253. → Includes a bibliography.

LIPPMANN, WALTER

Walter Lippmann was born in 1889 in New York City. His upper-middle-class family exposed him early to art, music, and literature. He attended Harvard University, where he completed the requirements for the A.B. degree in three years. His fourth year at Harvard was spent as an assistant to the philosopher George Santayana; and he graduated formally with the celebrated class of 1910, which included many others who later became prominent in the arts, the sciences, and public affairs.

An early desire to write—he had published several pieces of social criticism in the *Harvard Monthly*—turned him to journalism as a career. His first opportunity came through Lincoln Steffens, who went to Harvard in search of "the ablest mind that could express itself in writing" to help him with a series of muckraking articles for *Everybody's Magazine*.

Lippmann's accomplishments as a writer rapidly attracted the attention of those intellectual circles which were influential in the progressive climate of the prewar years. A short and disappointing stint as secretary to the socialist mayor of a city in upstate New York was followed by a brief period of free-lance writing for several magazines. But it was an invitation from Herbert Croly to join the editorial board of a new liberal journal, the *New Republic*, that provided Lippmann with a congenial and more permanent environment for his talents. No longer a socialist, yet one of the young "movers and shakers" whose intellectual vitality made the period immediately prior to World War I a seedtime of new ideas and limitless hope for the future, Lippmann found in the pages of the *New Republic* an outlet for articles on almost any topic about which he chose to write.

The *New Republic* became increasingly identified with President Wilson's policies, and in 1917 Lippmann was appointed executive secretary of a postwar planning group, the so-called House Inquiry. The following year he received a commission as captain in military intelligence to conduct propaganda on the western front. At the end of the war he was attached to the American Commission to Negotiate the Peace. In this capacity he prepared, in collaboration with Frank Cobb, then editor of the New York *World*, an elaborate memorandum on Wilson's Fourteen Points which served the American delegation as a basis for the peace discussions.

Lippmann was disappointed at the commitments and concessions made by the United States at the Versailles Peace Conference and soon returned to the *New Republic*. But shortly thereafter he took leave from the magazine to write *Public Opinion* and, upon finishing the book in 1922, was invited to become an editorial writer for the *World*. After Cobb's death in 1923, Lippmann was placed in charge of the paper's editorial page, and in 1929 he became its editor. Although some critics castigated his measured direction of the editorial page as evasion and pusillanimity, the *World* remained, until its end in 1931, in the forefront of those fighting against social and political injustice and for liberal reforms, both within American society and in international relations.

In 1931 Lippmann surprised many of his admirers by accepting an offer to write an independent column for the conservative and traditionally Republican *New York Herald Tribune*. He was evidently given a free hand to write as he pleased, but from 1936 on, his affiliations and connections were no longer with those individuals and groups generally called liberal or progressive. He had become, more than any other columnist or commentator, a spokesman of the American "establishment."

Intellectual development. Lippmann's years at Harvard had a deep and lasting effect on his intellectual development. He had come in contact there with socialist ideas and, for a short time, had been active in the socialist movement. He had also met William James, whose philosophy of pragmatism provided a necessary foil for Santayana's humanist idealism. And most important, he had met the English social scientist and Fabian ideologue Graham Wallas, whose *Human Nature in Politics* (1908) gave direction to Lippmann's early writings.

The more indirect influence of Sigmund Freud was at least as important as any other for Lippmann's work on public opinion and public morality. He had read Freud while writing *A Preface to Politics* (1913), and Freud's ideas seem to have played a most important part in making Lippmann aware of the obstacles to that full rationality which he deemed the goal of intellectual effort.

Finally, one cannot ignore the intellectual impact that his colleagues on the *New Republic* probably had on Lippmann. The editors had divergent ideas which had to be related to one another in order to give the magazine a semblance of unity. There was the centralist, Hamiltonian nationalism that Croly had articulated in *The Promise of American Life* (1909); but there was also the decentralist, Jeffersonian radicalism that Walter E. Weyl, another editor, expressed in *The New Democracy* (1912). Lippmann surely learned at the *New Republic* the tolerance in the face of conflicting ideas that he called "disinterestedness" and which he cherished so much.

Lippmann's own basic intellectual position is extremely difficult to describe, especially since, until his more advanced years, his political outlook rarely remained the same for long. The key to his successive political shifts may lie in Lippmann's statement that "every truly civilized and enlightened man is conservative and liberal and progressive" (1962, p. 11). The best we can do is to examine Lippmann's major works and to distinguish the different stages in his intellectual development.

Major works. Two of Lippmann's early books —*A Preface to Politics* (1913) and *Drift and Mastery* (1914)—testify to his shift from socialism and progressivism to pragmatic liberalism. *A Preface to Politics* is the more important work, for it also contains a protest against the empty formalism and legalism of much political discussion. Lippmann described the book as "a preliminary sketch for a theory of politics, a preface to thinking," and it is not surprising, given his training in philosophy, that he should have begun his writings on this epistemological note. The problem of how to think about things political continued to be a theme throughout his writings.

His basic premises in *A Preface to Politics* are that government is not a routine to be administered but a problem to be solved and that the desires of man, rather than artificially contrived institutional mechanisms, are the proper study of politics. Reason, he felt, must serve the dual purpose of setting direction to human wants and providing the tools for their satisfaction.

The uses of reason as a tool is the main theme of *Drift and Mastery.* Not traditional authority but the method of science must be harnessed to attain human goals. Only this method will permit different persons to agree on what the facts are and to reach the same conclusions. It alone can replace passion with intelligence. The failure of progressivism was its inability to understand the changes that the new industrialism had brought about. Science is "the culture under which people can live forward in the midst of complexity, and treat life not as something given but as something to be shaped" (1914, p. 275).

After World War I Lippmann came to doubt that it is possible, and even that it is desirable, to create a rational society. In *Liberty and the News* (1920), he still expressed a belief that democracy can function, provided the public is supplied with reliable and relevant information. Two years later, however, in *Public Opinion* (1922), he came close to questioning whether citizens can possibly make

rational, democratic decisions: the source of the difficulty in forming an intelligent public opinion is not man's irrationality but the necessity, inherent in the modern communications system, of condensing information into brief slogans. These slogans create a wall of stereotypes between the citizen and the issues to which he is expected to respond.

Lippmann's analysis of the public opinion process was remarkably advanced, considering that his contemporaries were still thinking in terms of such categories as "herd instinct" or "group mind." He recognized that both the external environment and man's own psyche are sources of errors that distort perceptions and opinions. Lippmann's use of the concept of stereotype in the analysis of public opinion was an original contribution and has remained a valuable one. Somewhat less original but very cogent was Lippmann's discussion of the role of the expert in public decision making. He did not consider the expert to be a mover and shaker in his own right; rather, he produces facts that may be helpful to those who do make decisions for the benefit of the mass. The mass, Lippmann concluded, is to all intents and purposes inarticulate— it does not decide issues; at most, it assents to or dissents from a proposition about a given issue.

While this denial of the possibility of genuine— in contrast with manipulated—democratic consensus is of course a prejudgment rather than a statement of fact, *Public Opinion* was predominantly analytical. Its sequel, *The Phantom Public* (1925), was frankly polemical. Here Lippmann asserted that the public's role in a democracy is a shadowy one, but he did not accept the conclusions of those conservative critics of democracy who celebrated the rule of an elite. However, his skepticism about the ability of the masses to decide on the merits of a question reflected his own disillusionment with the traditional theory of democracy. Unlike other critics, he became a skeptic moralist rather than an elitist. Morality is a relative, not an absolute, matter, determined at any given time by what men want rather than by what they know to be true, for "a code of the right and the wrong must wait upon a perception of the true and the false" (1925, p. 30). Since such perception is extraordinarily difficult, a code is virtually impossible to achieve.

Skeptic moralist though he had come to be, Lippmann could not accept a morality based on naked desires. Desires must be subjected to the moral test; and in the case of a humanistic morality appropriate to modern conditions, human experience rather than divine revelation must provide the criteria of good and evil. In his next major work, *A Preface to Morals* (1929), Lippmann sought to formulate a new public morality.

The moral test that Lippmann proposed for action was rationality and disinterestedness. Yet, having stated this moral imperative, he continued to doubt the multitude's ability to accept it. Statesmen and leaders would first have to re-educate the wants and desires of the many, and pending this outcome, these leaders must act on the basis of what the people will *in the end* consider good, rather than on the basis of their present desires.

A Preface to Morals in a sense reasserted Lippmann's faith in the rationality of man, tempered by psychological insight into man's volatility; it stated a belief in the possibility of responsible leadership but made the leaders subject to an ideal; and it excoriated current conditions as much as it expressed a new hope for the good society.

The appearance of the New Deal in America and of National Socialism in Germany presented a new challenge to Lippmann's thought. Initially his response to the New Deal was a favorable one, for the New Deal revived his old faith in the possibility of a rational ordering of society. In two small books, *The Method of Freedom* (1934) and *The New Imperative* (1935), his outlook was hopeful. But by 1937, in his *Inquiry Into the Principles of the Good Society*, his appraisal had changed. He identified the compensatory economy of the New Deal with the regimented economy of the totalitarian state, seeing both as evidence of the "collectivist heresy." Moreover, his old suspicion of irrational majorities was linked with a new fear of an irresponsible executive. Gradual collectivism, no less than any other collectivism, makes for arbitrary government.

True liberalism, he asserted in *The Good Society*, must insist on two social mechanisms that are threatened by the collectivist order—the free market and the law. With the market as the prime regulator of the division of labor, the state's function is limited to the administration of justice among men conducting their own affairs in terms of a common law of reciprocal rights and duties. Large public expenditures for education and public works are to be retained, as is protection against the hazards of a free economy, for liberalism is "radical in relation to the social order but conservative in relation to the division of labor in a market economy" (1937, p. 236). As to the role of the executive, society is so pluralistic and diversified that the statesman can only hope to reconcile social conflicts, but he cannot treat society as if it were an organization.

With the beginning of World War II, Lippmann's interest was diverted from problems of political theory to those of international affairs, and it was only with *Essays in the Public Philosophy* (1955) that he returned to his earlier concerns with the political order and democratic structure. The public philosophy, for Lippmann, is a set of positive precepts defining the law that is superior to arbitrary power. It can be discovered by any rational mind, and it is basic to Western institutions. It is the foundation of the good society and must be conscientiously cultivated and transmitted from generation to generation. The liberal democracies, Lippmann charged, have come dangerously close to ignoring the tradition of the public philosophy and accepting politics based on conflict and on interest as legitimate. But political conflict must have limits; and these, like the moral principles that must guide conduct, are to be discovered by reason.

If reason is sovereign, majority voting cannot be trusted, since the voters are too easily swept away by their passions and selfish interests. And their representatives are equally incapable of governing, for they are "insecure and intimidated men . . . [who] advance politically only as they placate, appease, bribe, seduce, or bamboozle, or otherwise manage to manipulate the demanding and threatening elements in their constituencies" (1955, p. 27). As in his first works, Lippmann turned to strong executive power as the practical way out— an executive power enlightened by rationality and constrained by natural law. Such an executive can rule in the interest of "the people"—namely, a "community of the entire living population, with their predecessors and successors" (1955, p. 32)— and not be subject to the whim of the voters.

HEINZ EULAU

[*See also* CONSERVATISM; DEMOCRACY; LIBERALISM; POLITICAL THEORY; PUBLIC OPINION; *and the biographies of* FREUD; JAMES; WALLAS.]

WORKS BY LIPPMANN

1913   *A Preface to Politics.* New York: Kennerley. → A paperback edition was published in 1962 by the University of Michigan Press.
1914   *Drift and Mastery: An Attempt to Diagnose the Current Unrest.* New York: Kennerley. → A paperback edition was published in 1961 by Prentice-Hall.
(1915) 1917   *The Stakes of Diplomacy.* 2d ed. New York: Holt.
1919   *The Political Scene: An Essay on the Victory of 1918.* New York: Holt.
1920   *Liberty and the News.* New York: Harcourt. → Reprinted in part from the *Atlantic Monthly.*
(1922) 1944   *Public Opinion.* New York: Macmillan. → A paperback edition was published in 1965 by the Free Press.

1925 *The Phantom Public*. New York: Harcourt.
1927 *Men of Destiny*. New York: Macmillan.
1928 *American Inquisitors: A Commentary on Dayton and Chicago*. New York: Macmillan.
(1929) 1952 *A Preface to Morals*. New York: Macmillan.
(1931–1932) 1932 *Interpretations: 1931–1932*. Edited by Allan Nevins. New York: Macmillan.
(1933–1935) 1936 *Interpretations: 1933–1935*. Edited by Allan Nevins. New York: Macmillan.
1934 *The Method of Freedom*. New York: Macmillan.
1935 *The New Imperative*. New York: Macmillan. → Contains two essays, "The Permanent New Deal" and "The New Imperative," both first published in 1935.
(1937) 1943 *Inquiry Into the Principles of the Good Society*. Rev. ed. Boston: Little.
1943 *U.S. Foreign Policy: Shield of the Republic*. Boston: Little.
1944 *U.S. War Aims*. Boston: Little.
1947 *The Cold War: A Study in U.S. Foreign Policy*. New York: Harper. → First appeared as a series of articles in the *New York Herald Tribune*.
1955 *Essays in the Public Philosophy*. Boston: Little.
1959 *The Communist World and Ours*. Boston: Little.
1962 Conservative, Liberal, Progressive. *New Republic* 146:10–11.

SUPPLEMENTARY BIBLIOGRAPHY

CHILDS, MARQUIS; and RESTON, JAMES (editors) 1959 *Walter Lippmann and His Times*. New York: Harcourt.
CROLY, HERBERT D. (1909) 1965 *The Promise of American Life*. Edited by Arthur M. Schlesinger, Jr. Cambridge, Mass.: Belknap Press.
EULAU, HEINZ 1951 Mover and Shaker: Walter Lippmann as a Young Man. *Antioch Review* 11:291–312.
EULAU, HEINZ 1952 Man Against Himself: Walter Lippmann's Years of Doubt. *American Quarterly* 4:291–304.
EULAU, HEINZ 1954 Wilsonian Idealist: Walter Lippmann Goes to War. *Antioch Review* 14:87–108.
EULAU, HEINZ 1956 From *Public Opinion* to *Public Philosophy*: Walter Lippmann's Classic Reexamined. *American Journal of Economics and Sociology* 15:439–451.
WALLAS, GRAHAM (1908) 1962 *Human Nature in Politics*. 4th ed. Gloucester, Mass.: Smith.
WEINGAST, DAVID E. 1949 *Walter Lippmann: A Study in Personal Journalism*. New Brunswick, N.J.: Rutgers Univ. Press.
WEYL, WALTER E. (1912) 1920 *The New Democracy*. Rev. ed. New York: Macmillan. → A paperback edition was published in 1964 by Harper.

LIQUIDITY PREFERENCE

"Liquidity preference" is a term that was coined by John Maynard Keynes in *The General Theory of Employment, Interest and Money* to denote the functional relation between the quantity of money demanded and the variables determining it (1936, p. 166). He also used this term, or such variants of it as "liquidity preference function" and "liquidity function," to denote more narrowly the relation between the quantity of money demanded and the rate of interest (see, for example, p. 168). Since the *General Theory* the term "liquidity preference" has come to be used to refer to the hypothesis or theory that the aggregate quantity of money demanded by the economy will, *ceteris paribus*, tend to be smaller the higher the rate of interest.

Keynes's analysis of the systematic and intimate relation between the demand for money and interest rates and its implications is generally acknowledged to be one of his major contributions to economics. It is one of the two main pillars on which the edifice of the *General Theory* rests, the other being the hypothesis that in a contemporary monetary economy, money prices and especially money wages tend to be rigid in the downward direction (see "Liquidity preference, monetary theory and monetary management," below).

The demand for money

Pre-Keynesian theories. Information about the history of theories of the demand for money may be found elsewhere [*see especially* MONEY, *articles on* QUANTITY THEORY *and* VELOCITY OF CIRCULATION; *see also* Marget 1938 *and* Patinkin 1956, pp. 373–472]. It will suffice to recall here that although monetary theorists had long recognized that money is a "store of value" as well as a "medium of exchange," prevailing theories of the demand for money before the *General Theory* tended to stress the role of money as a medium of exchange and the "transaction demand." The two major, broadly accepted formulations before the *General Theory* were that of Irving Fisher and that of the Cambridge school. Fisher (1911) started from the now well-known identity called Fisher's equation of exchange: $MV \equiv PT$, where M is the quantity of money in circulation, T is the volume of transactions, P is the price level, and V is the "transaction velocity of circulation." This equation is also frequently restated as $MV_y \equiv PX \equiv Y$, where X is "real income," Y is money income, and V_y is the "income velocity of circulation." From these identities Fisher derived his theory by hypothesizing (1) that at a given point of time V can be taken as constant (or at least as largely independent of M) and (2) that V tends to change, at best, very slowly over time, being largely determined by institutional and technological factors with a high degree of inertia. The major factors of this kind include the frequency of receipts and disbursements (intimately related in turn to the so-called income period, which is the length of the interval between the dates at which various types of income, such as wages, salaries, and dividends, are typically paid), the degree of synchronization of receipts and expenditures, prevailing financial arrangements, the rapidity of transportation, and so on. [See MONEY, *article on* VELOCITY OF CIRCULATION.]

By contrast, the so-called Cambridge school tried to put the explanation of the demand for money into the more familiar format of value theory, i.e., in terms of a demand-for-money equation, $M^d = kY$, an exogenously given supply of money, M, and a clearing-of-market equation, $M^d = M$, implying $M = kY$ (see, e.g., Pigou 1917; Marshall 1923). By comparing this equation with Fisher's equation above, one can readily see that $k = 1/V_y$, i.e., that k is the reciprocal of the velocity of circulation. Indeed, in analyzing the determinants of k and the reasons for its hypothesized stability, the Cambridge school tended to stress largely the same forces on which Fisher's theory rests.

The Fisher and Cambridge models are generally regarded as providing the definitive basis for the so-called "quantity theory of money," a view of very old standing according to which the price level, P, tends to be directly proportional to M. In order for this relationship to follow logically from these models, not only must M not affect V (or k), as those models imply, but also one must suppose that money is "neutral" in the wider sense that it does not affect any of the "real" variables of the system—inputs, outputs, and relative prices, including interest rates. Under this assumption, which, as shown below (see "The significance of liquidity theory under wage flexibility"), might provide a reasonable approximation under conditions of perfect wage and price flexibility, real income, X, may be taken as fixed at the "full employment" level, say $\bar{X}$. From either the Fisher or the Cambridge equation it then follows that

$$P = \left(\frac{V_y}{\bar{X}}\right)M = \left(\frac{1}{k\bar{X}}\right)M,$$

that is, the price level is proportional to the quantity of money, M.

It should be acknowledged that some of the writers in the Cambridge tradition did at times suggest that the demand for money might depend on wealth and that they did make some occasional references to the possible influence of interest rates (see, for example, Pigou [1917] 1951, p. 166; Lavington 1921, p. 30; Marshall 1923, chapter 4; for still earlier references, see Eshag 1963, pp. 13–14). But they failed to explore systematically the effect of interest rates on the demand for money and the implications of this effect. This failure is even more conspicuous in Fisher. He makes no mention of interest rates in his list of

factors affecting velocity, and although he makes fleeting mention of the "waste of interest" involved in holding money (1911, p. 152), one finds no reference to this passage in the index under the rubric "interest rates."

Two authors who anticipated Keynes in giving adequate recognition to the role of interest rates are Walras, in 1899, and Schlesinger, in 1914 (see Patinkin 1956, notes C and D), but their contributions were largely overlooked at the time. The most significant pre-Keynesian analysis of liquidity preference is generally acknowledged to be that of Hicks (1935), which, however, preceded the *General Theory* by but one year and was partly inspired by Keynes's earlier work, *A Treatise on Money*, published in 1930. This contribution to monetary theory, which in some respects has turned out to be even more influential for further developments than that of Keynes, will be touched upon below.

Keynes's theory. In chapters 13 and 15 of the *General Theory*, Keynes distinguished three "motives" for holding money. The first, the "transaction motive"—sometimes broken down into an income motive and a business motive—corresponds quite closely to the motives stressed by Fisher and the Cambridge school. Like his predecessors, Keynes did not regard transaction balances as being significantly affected by interest rates. The second motive is the "precautionary motive." Under this heading Keynes included balances not earmarked for some definite expenditure in the near future but held instead to "provide for contingencies requiring sudden expenditure and for unforeseen opportunities of advantageous purchases" (1936, p. 196). But why should these balances be kept in the form of idle cash instead of being invested in some kind of readily marketable securities, to be converted into cash if and when the contingency arises? The reason is that the market value of a debt instrument (or "bond"), if it is liquidated before its maturity, is uncertain, even if there is absolutely no risk of default. It depends on the market rate of interest prevailing at the future time of liquidation for loans having a duration equal to the remaining life of the bond: the higher this rate, the lower the market value. This uncertainty about the realization value of a bond would not by itself make bonds inferior to cash as a store of ready purchasing power if the sum of the uncertain liquidation value and the cash interest earned could be counted on to exceed the amount initially invested. However, there can be no such assurance, since between the times of purchase and liquidation interest rates could rise sufficiently to produce a capital loss in excess of the interest earned. Keynes suggested in particular that the likelihood of a net loss would be larger the smaller the yield of the bond originally acquired. This is because the smaller the yield, the smaller the rise in the rate of interest (in absolute as well as in percentage terms) that will produce a capital loss sufficient to wipe out the accrued interest earned. Furthermore, Keynes suggested that if the current rate is low by historical standards, it will usually be regarded as more likely to rise than to fall. He concluded that the lower the current rate, r, the stronger the incentive to hold precautionary reserves in the form of cash instead of securities. Therefore the (real) demand to hold money for precautionary reasons will tend to be inversely related to r. At the same time, somewhat surprisingly, Keynes did not appear to regard precautionary balances as very sensitive to r. Accordingly, much of the time he lumped together the demand for transaction and for precautionary reasons and regarded the sum, which he labeled M_1, as primarily controlled by—or a function of—current income. Thus, in his notation $M_1 = L_1(Y)$, where the function L_1 denotes the demand for money resulting from the transaction and precautionary motives.

The third and remaining source of demand for money is the speculative motive, a rather complex mechanism that Keynes had partly anticipated in *A Treatise on Money* (1930). In essence, speculative balances are balances held in cash rather than invested in (long-term) bonds, not just because of the risk that interest rates might rise but rather because of a definite expectation that the price of long-term bonds is likely to fall, and at a rate that more than offsets the interest earned by holding them. A person entertaining such an expectation would prefer to hold cash yielding nothing rather than invest it in what he regards as overpriced long-term bonds that would yield him a negative return. Since the price of long-term bonds varies inversely with long-term interest rates, we may equally well characterize speculative balances as those held by persons who regard the current long-term rate as untenably low and about to rise sufficiently rapidly.

The real significance of the speculative motive is that it may significantly impair, or even thwart altogether, efforts of the central bank to reduce long-term interest rates to the extent necessary to maintain investment at the level consistent with full utilization of resources (see "Liquidity preference, monetary theory, and monetary management," below). Normally, the central bank can expect to enforce lower long-term interest rates, or higher prices of long-term bonds, by buying such

bonds with newly created money. Suppose, however, that a large portion of the market holds definite views about the minimum maintainable level of the long-term rate and hence the maximum maintainable level of bond prices. If, then, the bank attempts to bid up the price of bonds to that maximum or beyond, it will find the public prepared to dump a large portion of its long-term bond holding. The bank will therefore have very little success in lowering the long-term rate, even though it is prepared to acquire a large volume of bonds and to expand the money supply correspondingly. What happens in this situation is that the increase in the money supply is absorbed, not by an increased transaction demand, but by an offsetting increase in the speculative demand, with a resulting fall in the velocity of circulation. In other words, the expansion in M, instead of achieving the desired expansion in income, Y, that would occur if V_y, the velocity of circulation, remained constant, tends to generate an offsetting change in V_y, with little effect on Y. A situation of this type has come to be known in the Keynesian literature as a "liquidity trap."

Keynes denoted speculative balances by M_2 and wrote the demand function for such balances as $M_2 = L_2(r)$, where L_2 is a decreasing function of r (1936, p. 199). This formulation—that M_2 increases as r falls—is somewhat misleading, since presumably M_2 should depend not on r as such but only on r in relation to the prevailing market expectations about the maintainable rate, say r^e. Nor can r^e be supposed to stay constant through time or to be uniquely related to r itself. Keynes's formulation might be defended as a useful "short run" approximation: at a given point in time, r^e can be taken as a constant or, at least, as changing more slowly than r. Hence, a fall in r would necessarily imply a fall *relative* to r^e and thus a rise in M_2 (*ibid.*, pp. 201–202). Under this interpretation, however, one should be aware that L_2 may be subject to significant shifts through time as a result of shifts in market expectations.

The sum of the transaction and precautionary demand, M_1, and the speculative demand, M_2, is the total demand for money proposed by Keynes: $M = M_1 + M_2 = L_1(Y) + L_2(r)$ (*ibid.*, p. 199). The Keynesian literature has tended to de-emphasize the sharp distinction between the three motives for holding money and to write the demand for money in the more general form $M = L(r, Y)$. There has also been a tendency to minimize the role of interest expectations, r^e, and to associate the liquidity trap with a low *absolute* level of the interest rate.

The implied relation between M and r for a

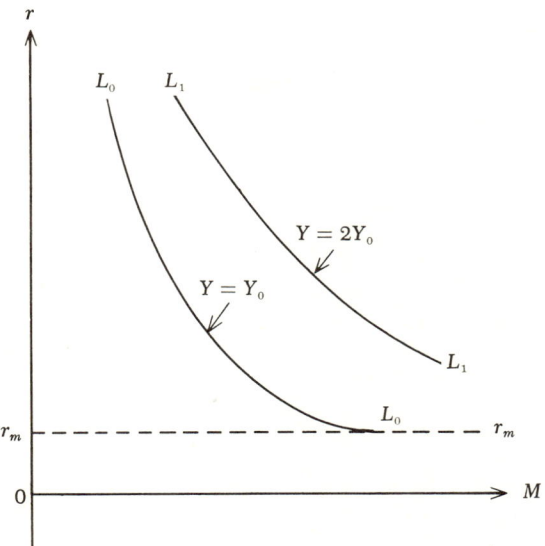

Figure 1 — Relation between the demand for money and the interest rate

given value of Y, say Y_0, is shown in Figure 1 by the curve labeled L_0L_0. (The choice of coordinates is dictated by the economists' peculiar convention, popularized by Marshall, of representing demand curves with the quantity demanded measured on the abscissa and the price on the ordinate.) The quantity of money demanded increases continuously as r falls, until, for some sufficiently low value, r_m, the liquidity trap is reached and the curve becomes horizontal (the demand becomes infinitely elastic). Alternatively, the demand curve might be drawn to approach the level r_m asymptotically. Just how low r_m may be depends somewhat on "institutional" factors and on whether r is understood to be the long-term or the short-term rate. But we can, with complete generality, place a lower bound on r_m: in a monetary economy, r_m can never be more negative than the (marginal) cost of storing money. In particular, when money is an intangible, the cost of storing it (at least in the form of bank deposits) is essentially zero, and therefore r_m cannot be (significantly) negative. Indeed, a negative r can be regarded as a premium paid by the lender to the borrower for carrying money over; for example, a short-term rate of -2 per cent per period means that the lender is willing to pay $100 to receive only $98 at the end of the period. If the cost of storing is less than 2 per cent, everybody would wish to borrow indefinitely large amounts, since by merely holding the money one would earn the excess of 2 per cent over storage costs. This implies in particular that with a zero

(marginal) storage cost, at a negative rate of interest the demand for money must become indefinitely large—or, equivalently, that no matter how large the quantity of money, r can never be negative. Hence, the demand curve must tend to approach a horizontal asymptote, $r = r_m$ (or possibly reach it from above for some finite M and become discontinuous). Furthermore, r_m cannot be lower than zero (quite generally, it cannot be more negative than the marginal cost of storing money), although it may well be higher, as in Figure 1.

The curve labeled L_1L_1 illustrates the effect on the demand for money of increasing Y, say from Y_0 to $2Y_0$ in Figure 1. Clearly, the demand for money must then be greater at any given rate r; that is, LL must shift to the right. The relation between L_0L_0 and L_1L_1 becomes especially simple if the demand function $L(r, Y)$ takes a more specialized form, which was suggested, for example, by Pigou (1917) and tested by Latané (1954; 1960) and which has been gaining favor in recent writings—namely, $M = k(r)Y = Y/V(r)$. This formulation provides an obvious bridge between Keynes's original formulation and the received Fisher and Cambridge models. It implies that for a given r the fraction k (or the velocity of circulation, V) will be constant but that k will tend to fall (or V to rise) as the rate of interest rises. In terms of Figure 1, it implies that L_1L_1 is obtainable from L_0L_0 by multiplying by 2 the abscissa value of L_0L_0 corresponding to any given r. More generally, it implies that the LL curve corresponding to any given Y is simply the graph of $k(r)$, up to a proportionality factor, Y. Similarly, the graph of $V(r)$, ·

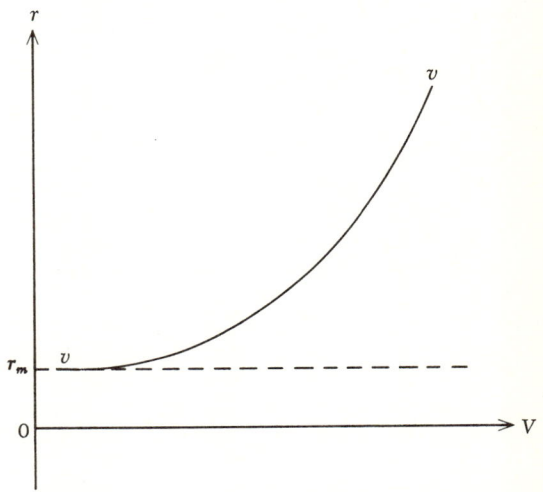

Figure 2 — Velocity of circulation and the interest rate

the velocity of circulation as a function of the interest rate, is the graph of the reciprocal of L_0L_0 up to a proportionality factor, $1/Y_0$. The general shape of the graph of $V(r)$ is shown by the vv curve of Figure 2.

Post-Keynesian developments. As indicated earlier, post-Keynesian developments of liquidity theory were inspired not only by Keynes's *General Theory* but at least as much by two germinal ideas advanced by Hicks (1935). Hicks's first suggestion was that the major reason why transactors hold money balances having little or no yield when they could invest them in a large number of income-yielding assets, some at least not significantly less safe than money, is to be found in the costs and the "bother" of the transactions necessary to move from money into earning assets and back to money (p. 19).

The portfolio approach. Hicks's second suggestion was that the theory of the demand for money must be developed out of a more general theory of the allocation of wealth among various assets. This theory, Hicks suggested, should be analogous to the standard theory of consumers' choice, except that the object of choice, instead of being consumption flows, would be the various stocks appearing on the asset and liability side of the balance sheet, and prices would be replaced by expected yields. He saw this substitution as presenting a real challenge, since yields in contrast to prices would have to be recognized as uncertain, and this uncertainty in turn would have important implications for the nature of choices.

Both ideas have been extensively pursued with the help of the emergence of the theory of choice under uncertainty [see DECISION MAKING, *article on* ECONOMIC ASPECTS]. At present the major differences of view between monetary theorists (and they are not very major) seem related to the relative importance assigned to each of Hicks's two ideas.

Among those who have pursued the portfolio, or wealth, approach, the formulation of Friedman (1956), developed in numerous writings, has been particularly influential [see MONEY, *article on* QUANTITY THEORY]. Friedman views the demand for money as being determined by wealth (broadly understood as the present value of expected net future receipts from all sources), by the distribution of wealth between human and nonhuman (i.e., marketable) wealth, by the expected yield of all major types of assets that are alternatives to money as ways of holding wealth, and by the "utility attached to the services rendered by money" relative to other assets—namely, bonds, equities,

and physical commodities. By combining this theory with his suggestion (1957) for ways of approximating wealth (or, more precisely, "permanent income," which is, however, essentially proportional to wealth as defined above) Friedman has endeavored to cast his theory in testable form and actually to test it (1959). He has concluded that his model fits the facts well, in that the demand for money increases with wealth and more than in proportion, although he can find little evidence that interest rates in fact play a significant role.

Other authors have been more concerned with developing and refining theoretical aspects of the Keynes–Hicks approach (see the very useful survey provided by Johnson 1962). Among their attempts, especially worth noting are the recent contribution of Turvey (1960) and the elegant formulation of the theory of choice between money and bonds of various maturities developed by Tobin (1958) along the lines of the modern theory of portfolio selection.

Transaction costs and the Neo-Fisherian approach. The portfolio approach suffers from one major inadequacy. As long as there exist any interest-bearing obligations that are issued by creditworthy borrowers and are of sufficiently short maturity—for example, redeemable on demand or on very short notice—it is impossible to explain why any portion of the portfolio should be held in the form of money, yielding less or nothing at all—except by explicit analysis of the role of transaction costs.

Even Keynes's stricture that, for sufficiently low interest rates, money may dominate bonds because of the uncertainty of the realization value cannot apply to short maturities or demand loans. These instruments dominate money in every possible dimension: they are equally safe, they yield an income, and they can be converted into the medium of exchange, if and when it is needed, at face value. Why, then, should anyone hold money, except for the very instant he receives a payment or is about to make one? The necessary and sufficient condition, as Hicks rightly pointed out, is that out-of-pocket costs and the effort required in moving from cash to bonds and back to cash exceed the yield. At first sight these transaction costs may appear too trivial to account for any substantial holding of cash, let alone for the observed cash holdings. (Aggregate cash holdings of U.S. consumers at the end of 1963 were estimated to represent slightly less than two months' income.) But this casual impression is misleading. It is well known, for instance, from the theory of optimum inventory holdings that transaction costs do account for a substantial portion of inventories held by business (which in the United States amount to some three months' sales). This parallel between business inventories and cash holdings is not fortuitous, for in many respects the holding of a stock of cash by transactors is closely analogous to the holding of a stock of goods by business. In fact, Allais (1947, chapter 8a) and Baumol (1952) pioneered in showing that the holding of cash balances could be analyzed by a straightforward application of the so-called lot-size formula of inventory theory: in order to avoid incurring too frequently the costs involved in transforming securities into cash, it pays to secure cash in a bulk or "lot" that will take care of expenditure requirements for a certain length of time, even though interest will be forgone on the amount withdrawn. Similarly, if a transactor is receiving money in a more or less continuous trickle, it will pay to accumulate a "lot" before investing it. The size of the lot, and hence the average cash balance held relative to the rate of outpayments (or receipts), which corresponds to the Cambridge k or to the reciprocal of the velocity of circulation, will be positively associated with the size of transaction costs and inversely associated with the rate of interest. Tobin (1956) refined and improved on this analysis, applying it more specifically to the consumer receiving his income in bulk at income-payment dates and spending it gradually over the income period.

Although these contributions are to be regarded as illustrative rather than as aimed at deriving an exact demand equation for money, they do point up one very fundamental principle. The amount that can be earned by investing an amount of cash, m, that will not be needed to meet expenditures for some span of time, t, in a security yielding r per cent per year, is approximately $m(tr - c)$, where c is the brokerage fee, if any, per dollar of investment. The investment will not be worthwhile unless this product exceeds the lump-sum cost of the two-way transaction, including both the out-of-pocket and the bother costs. To illustrate the order of magnitudes involved, suppose that a person earns $12,000 a year, paid monthly; he then receives $1,000 once a month. Suppose he spends these receipts at an even rate. He might then consider keeping half the sum for current expenditure and investing the remaining half, or $500, which he will not need until the first half is exhausted—that is, for half a month. Suppose the yield of a 15-day security, net of commissions, is 3 per cent per year; then all he stands to earn

from the transaction is $500 × .03/24, or a mere 62.5 cents. If the two-way transaction cost and bother exceeds this, he will invest none of the monthly receipts and thus will end up holding, on this account, an average cash balance of $500, or 1/24 of his (annual) income. Note that if he were paid twice as frequently—that is, $500 every two weeks—it would a fortiori not pay him to bother, and he would be holding an average cash balance of $250, or 1/48 of his income.

The conclusion to be drawn from these illustrations can be summarized as follows: In a money-using economy, transactors are paid in money and in turn must pay in money; lack of synchronization between receipts and payments gives rise to pools of money that will not be needed for some length of time. Given the rate of return and the cost and effort of transactions, it will not pay to invest such pools unless the product of their size and the length of the "idle" time exceeds some critical threshold level. Thus, the basic reason for holding idle cash balances is not that they provide a useful service but simply that it does not pay to shed them. Obviously, given the rate of interest, the extent to which it does not pay to shed idle money, and thus the average cash balance held, will depend on such institutional–technological factors as (a) transaction costs—the higher the cost, the smaller the incentive to shed; (b) the size and nature of the transactor's business —large transactors may be confronted with pools so large that it pays to shed them even for very short periods, and they may also have an incentive to set themselves up so as to minimize marginal transaction costs; and (c) the frequency of income payment and settlement dates—the greater the frequency, the smaller the average cash balance. But these are, by and large, precisely the factors emphasized by Fisher in explaining the determinants of the velocity of circulation. The new element is the recognition that given all these factors, the average cash balance demanded will tend to fall with the rate of interest, which provides the incentive to shed.

How does the Keynesian liquidity trap fit into this model? The first point to be noted is that Keynes's theory of the speculative demand suffers from his excessive concentration on long-term bonds as the alternative to cash, to the neglect of short-term instruments. The proposition that people will flee from long-term bonds when the price of those bonds is deemed to be untenably high seems valid enough, but the obvious abode for the funds accruing from moving out of long-term bonds should be short-term ones, not cash.

However, a massive endeavor to move from long-term into short-term instruments will unavoidably depress short-term rates, perhaps to such an extent that for many investors the investment will no longer be worth the effort. Thus, they may eventually end up holding cash, but because of the low level of short-term rates, not directly in response to the low level of long-term rates. In short, the central bank's endeavor to depress long-term rates by buying bonds and increasing the money supply can always be counted on to depress short-term rates. However, it may not be very successful in depressing long-term rates to the desired extent, except insofar as a persistent low level of the short-term rate may eventually persuade the public that the long-term rate is really not unreasonably low. A good example of such a development is provided by the United States in the late 1930s. Because of a sizable monetary expansion after 1932, by 1939–1940 the short-term rate on government bills had been driven down very nearly to zero (below 2/10 of 1 per cent), but the long-term rate on high-grade bonds was still hovering around 3 per cent (down from about 4.7 per cent in 1929). In this sense the Keynesian liquidity trap must still be acknowledged as a possible serious hindrance to the effectiveness of monetary policy. And in any event, the proposition that no market rate—long or short—can ever be negative retains its validity.

The theory that emerges from the preceding discussion emphasizes the flow of transactions (and therefore income rather than wealth) and interest rates, especially the short rate and the rate on savings deposits, as the main arguments of the demand function for money. It further suggests that the parameters of this function are largely determined by the forces emphasized by Fisher and should therefore tend to change at best slowly through time. Because the model represents an obvious blend of the motives emphasized by Fisher and by Keynes and Hicks, we have referred to it as the Neo-Fisherian approach (although this terminology is not in general use).

Although the contrast between the "portfolio" approach and the "transaction" approach has deliberately been emphasized here, it is well to recognize that the difference between these two models is minor—largely a matter of relative emphasis—both in principle and in terms of practical implications. In particular, these models concur in the conclusion that the demand for money should be "homogeneous of first degree in current prices"—that is, that a change in the price level, other things being equal, should give rise to a propor-tional change in the demand for money while leaving unaffected "real demand" (demand measured in terms of purchasing power over commodities).

Empirical verification.   Since the appearance of the *General Theory*, considerable effort has been devoted to assessing empirically the responsiveness of the demand for money to variations in interest rates and more generally to estimating demand functions for money and testing their stability (see, for the United States, Johnson 1962, pp. 354–357).

These investigations have tended to confirm that the demand for money is positively and closely associated with income or wealth or both and that a change in the price level tends to result in a proportional change in demand. They have also overwhelmingly tended to confirm that this demand is significantly responsive to changes in interest rates in the direction hypothesized by Keynes. The only significant exception in this regard is Friedman's results, cited in the section "The portfolio approach," above. His contrary conclusions, however, have been criticized for being very much dependent on the specific definition of money he uses (which includes means of payment and some, but not all, savings deposits), on the specific period chosen for his tests, and on his statistical techniques. They have also been criticized because his model, although it apparently fits the period from the second half of the last century to the late 1940s quite well, is not able to account for the very significant rise in velocity that has occurred since the beginning of the 1950s, concomitantly with the marked rise in interest rates. In particular, Meltzer (1963) and Brunner and Meltzer (1964), who otherwise fully sympathize with Friedman's basic theory, have found marked and significant interest-rate effects, whether one uses as additional variables income, or permanent income, or a measure of nonhuman wealth. The major novelty in their results is the strong showing of the nonhuman wealth variable as compared with current income, although these results contrast with those reported by other investigators using a different measure of wealth (e.g., Bronfenbrenner & Mayer 1960). On the whole, it seems fair to say that at the moment the evidence is not adequate for the fine discrimination between the wealth and the neo-Fisherian formulations of the demand for money.

Liquidity preference, monetary theory, and monetary management

The Keynesian revolution.   As suggested earlier, the two major analytical contributions of the *Gen-*

eral Theory are the hypotheses of liquidity preference and of wage rigidity. The systematic analysis of the implications of these two highly fruitful hypotheses and their interaction was made more powerful and incisive by a third novelty, which is primarily methodological. This is the development of "aggregative analysis," or what has since come to be known as macroeconomic analysis. Economists had long before been used to analyzing economic variables as reflecting the interaction of simultaneous relations, and the notion of equilibrium was used precisely to denote the value of the variables simultaneously satisfying all the relevant relations. However, before the *General Theory* this method of analysis was generally applied in so-called "partial equilibrium analysis," that is, the study of some portion of the economy—say, the market for a particular commodity or a group of interrelated commodities. The method had also been applied with some success, largely by Walras, to the economy as a whole in "general equilibrium analysis," which formally recognizes the interactions of all possible markets, treating the economy as a very large scale closed system of simultaneous equations. The novelty of aggregative analysis consists in lumping together a large number of commodities having common characteristics for the problem at hand and treating the aggregate as a single commodity. This approach makes possible the approximation of the whole economy with a small system of simultaneous relations, and, by permitting closer scrutiny and understanding of the interactions, it has proved to be highly fruitful.

Analysts of Keynes's work have correctly pointed out that none of these basic ingredients of the *General Theory*—liquidity preference, wage rigidity, or the aggregative approach—was entirely new. We have documented this point above with respect to liquidity preference. The novelty consisted in the masterly way in which the ingredients were blended, which enabled Keynes to provide an analytical explanation of the phenomenon of unemployment and its possible persistence in an advanced capitalistic economy and to shed new light on the role and limitations of monetary and fiscal policy in controlling the level of employment and prices. It is this achievement, and its enormous impact on economics, that has since come to be known as the Keynesian revolution.

The rest of this section, relying largely on aggregative analysis, endeavors to sketch out the role of liquidity preference, first under the classical assumptions of perfect wage and price flexibility and then in combination with the empirically far more relevant hypothesis of downward wage rigidity. Our focus is primarily on the significance of liquidity preference as seen *today*, some thirty years after the appearance of the *General Theory*, rather than on summarizing or criticizing Keynes's original formulation. Accordingly, in what follows, the post-Keynesian elaborations are freely drawn upon.

The basic model. In Keynes's *General Theory* and, more particularly, in later endeavors by other authors to formalize its message (e.g., Hicks 1937; Lange 1938; Modigliani 1944; 1963; Patinkin 1956), the whole economy is reduced (explicitly or implicitly) to four aggregates: aggregate output, X; labor, N; money, M; and bonds, B. For each of these aggregate commodities there is a "market" characterized by supply conditions, demand conditions, and the "clearing-of-market" or equilibrium requirement that demand must equal supply. Demand and supply, in turn, are controlled by three prices or terms of trade between each commodity and money: P, the price of output (the "price level"); W, the price of labor (the "wage rate"); and $1 + r$, the number of dollars obtainable next period by lending a dollar today, where r is the rate of interest. To understand the mechanism determining the level of economic activity in a given short interval and the role of liquidity preference, we must examine the structure of the four markets and their interaction.

The demand for output in the commodity market, usually referred to in the literature as "aggregate demand" and denoted here by X^d, is a central construct of Keynesian analysis. It has given rise to a voluminous literature, both theoretical and empirical, which can be summarized here very briefly, since it is covered in other articles [*see in particular* INCOME AND EMPLOYMENT THEORY; CONSUMPTION FUNCTION; INVESTMENT, *article on* THE AGGREGATE INVESTMENT FUNCTION]. Two sources of demand are distinguished: current consumption, C, and investment demand, I—i.e., demand for current output destined to increase the stock of productive capital. Thus, $X^d = C + I$. Theoretical considerations, and the empirical evidence, suggest that consumption in turn is primarily controlled by (a) the level of real income that, disregarding for the moment the fiscal activity of the government sector, can be equated with aggregate output, X; (b) net real private wealth, A; and possibly (c) the rate of interest, r. This can be formalized by means of the "consumption function," $C = \mathcal{C}(X, A, r)$. Investment demand can be taken to be positively associated with aggregate output and negatively associated with the rate of interest and the pre-existing stock of capital, K_0; thus,

$I = \mathcal{I}(r_0, X, K_0)$. Finally, net private real wealth, A, the sum of all privately held assets minus private debt, can be expressed as $A = K_0 + G/P$; that is, it consists of the stock of capital plus the money value of the outstanding government debt, G, deflated by the price level, P, to express it in terms of purchasing power over output.

The four equations given above can be conveniently reduced to a single one by first substituting for A in the consumption function and then substituting this function and the investment function into the definition of aggregate demand:

$$(1) \qquad X^d = \mathcal{C}\left(X, K_0 + \frac{G}{P}, r\right) + \mathcal{I}(r_0, X, K_0).$$

Next, we observe that in equilibrium, aggregate demand X^d must equal aggregate supply, or

$$(2) \qquad X = X^d.$$

We use this property to replace X with X^d in the right hand side of (1). The resulting equation contains X^d on both sides of the equality. We can, however, "solve" the equation explicitly for X^d, obtaining finally an expression of the form

$$(1') \qquad X^d = D\left(r, K_0, \frac{G}{P}\right),$$

which will be referred to hereafter as the aggregate demand relation. Note that aggregate demand, X^d, may be expected to be negatively associated with r. This is because an increase in r will reduce investment demand directly, and this reduction, in turn, will reduce aggregate demand even further by means of its depressing effect on consumption demand, which depends on total output—this is the so-called multiplier effect [see CONSUMPTION FUNCTION]. Insofar as investment demand itself depends on output, X^d may in fact not decrease continuously as r rises, but this complication will be ignored here.

To complete the description of the output market, we also need an "aggregate supply function." Aggregate supply, X, may be expected to be positively associated with (a) the price, P, at which firms can sell their output relative to the wage rate, W, they must pay, or P/W, and (b) with the pre-existing capital stock, K_0 (on the convenient approximation that the increment in the stock of capital resulting from current investment will not become productive until the next period); thus,

$$(3) \qquad X = S\left(\frac{P}{W}, K_0\right).$$

In the labor market, the aggregate demand for labor, N, can be inferred from the so-called aggregate production function, relating output, X, to the input of labor and the stock of capital, K_0. This function implies that N can be expressed in terms of X and K_0, say, $N = F(X, K_0)$. It is, however, more convenient to replace X in this equation with the right-hand side of (3), thus obtaining the "labor demand" equation

$$(4) \qquad N = \mathcal{N}\left(\frac{P}{W}, K_0\right).$$

The description of the supply side of the labor market is a somewhat more complex task, for it is here that we must formalize the Keynesian notion of "downward wage rigidity." In its broadest sense, this term connotes the absence of "wage flexibility," of a state of affairs in which money wages fall promptly whenever the supply of labor exceeds the demand for it and keep falling as long as the excess supply persists. In a narrower definition, it means that the current money wage will not be bid below some floor level, W_0 (reflecting the past history of the system), no matter how large the excess supply of labor—though it can be freely bid up in response to excess demand for labor. For present purposes, we shall rely on this narrower version, which we label "absolute" rigidity, because it is more readily formalized. However, the conclusion of the analysis below would not change qualitatively if the wage rate had some tendency to fall for sufficiently large unemployment and falling prices, as long as the reaction was sluggish and unsystematic. There can be little doubt that wage rigidity in this sense is, and has been for some time, a feature of free market economies.

To formalize the hypothesis of absolute wage rigidity we need to introduce the notion of a "potential supply of labor function," say, $\mathcal{E}(W/P)$, which gives the level of employment "desired," or labor force available, at any given real wage, W/P. Now, let E denote the actual level of employment. Then absolute wage rigidity can be expressed as follows:

$$(5) \quad (a)\ W = W_0, \qquad \text{if } \mathcal{N}\left(\frac{P}{W_0}, K_0\right) < \mathcal{E}\left(\frac{W_0}{P}\right),$$

$$(b)\ E = \mathcal{E}\left(\frac{W}{P}\right), \qquad \text{if } \mathcal{N}\left(\frac{P}{W_0}, K_0\right) \geqslant \mathcal{E}\left(\frac{W_0}{P}\right),$$

$$(6) \qquad E = N.$$

Line (a) of (5) states in essence that if at the rigid wage W_0 the demand for labor falls short of the potential supply, then the actual wage rate will coincide with W_0. Employment, being equal to the *demand* for labor as stated by (6), will then fall short of the potential supply, and the difference will represent the so-called involuntary unemployment. If, however, at W_0 the demand exceeds the potential supply, then line (b) of (5) becomes applicable: the floor level loses its relevance, and the actual wage will have to rise enough to equate the demand with the potential supply. This formulation of wage rigidity has the advantage that it can encompass wage flexibility as a limiting case, in which we assign to W_0 a value so small that the relevant portion of (5) will necessarily be line (b).

In the money market, the demand, M^d, can be expressed as $M^d = L(PX, PA, r)$, where L is, of course, the liquidity preference function that (in recognition of the two major points of view summarized in the section "Post-Keynesian developments" of liquidity preference) is written as a function of both money income (PX) and wealth (PA). By expressing A in terms of its components, K_0 and G, and using the property that a change in the price level should tend to give rise to a proportional change in the demand for money, the preceding equation can be rewritten as

$$M^d = PL(X, K_0 + G/P, r).$$

However, for the purpose of the graphical analysis that is developed below, we shall frequently find it convenient to rely on the specialized version $M^d = PX/V(r)$, where $V(r)$, it will be recalled, denotes the velocity of circulation as a function of the rate of interest. As to the supply side, unless otherwise specified, it will be assumed that money is created by the banking system in the process of purchasing debt instruments (bonds) issued either by the private sector or by the government, and that the total supply of money, M, is exogenously determined through central bank policy. Since in equilibrium we must have $M^d = M$, the description of the money market can be reduced to a single equation obtained by replacing M^d with M in the above equations:

$$(7) \qquad M = PL\left(X, K_0 + \frac{G}{P}, r\right),$$

or

$$(7') \qquad M = \frac{PX}{V(r)}.$$

Equations (1) to (7) involve seven endogenous variables: X^d, X, N, E, P, W, r. They therefore form a closed system whose solution describes the short-run equilibrium of the economy. This solution also depends, of course, on the parameters of the various equations, on initial conditions, such as K_0 and G, and on policy variables, of which in the present case there is but one, the money supply, M. The demand and supply for the remaining commodity,

namely, bonds, B, are not explicitly displayed in the system because, by a well-known principle called Walras's law, it can shown that the demand and supply for one commodity out of the set of all commodities are necessarily equal when all other markets are "cleared" (that is, when demand equals supply); we choose the bond market as the redundant one (Modigliani 1963).

With the help of this system we can now focus on the role of monetary forces, in particular that of liquidity preference, in the determination of equilibrium, beginning with the classical assumption of wage flexibility.

Wage flexibility. As already noted, under the assumption of wage flexibility the labor supply conditions are fully described by line (b) of equation (5). But this equation, together with that for labor demand, equation (4), and the equilibrium condition (6), turns out to involve only three variables: N, E, and P/W (or its reciprocal, the real wage). They therefore form a closed subsystem which can be solved independently of the rest. This solution yields the equilibrium real wage, $W\hat{/P}$ (where " ^ " denotes an equilibrium value), and employment, $\hat{N}$ (which is also "full employment" since it coincides with the labor supply). From (3) we can then infer the equilibrium or full-employment level of output, $\hat{X}$.

At this point it becomes useful to distinguish two possible cases, the one in which there is no national debt and the one in which there is.

No national debt. Referring back to the aggregate demand relation $(1')$, we observe that if G is zero, then the third argument of the aggregate demand function is necessarily zero, no matter what value P may take: in other words, *aggregate demand does not depend on the price level.* (This important implication, it should be noted, depends critically on the approximation implicit in the formulation of the consumption function, that aggregate consumption, C, depends only on *aggregate* net wealth, not on its distribution between households. Changes in the price level will of course affect the demand of individual consumers by causing redistributions of wealth between creditors and debtors, but our aggregative assumption implies that such redistributions will affect only the distribution of consumption between households, without affecting the total.) Since K_0 is a given initial condition, it can be seen that the right-hand side of $(1')$ contains only one variable, r. It follows that from $(1')$ we can infer the equilibrium value of r, $\hat{r}$, which makes the aggregate demand, X^d, equal to the aggregate supply, $\hat{X}$. Next, substituting $\hat{r}$ and $\hat{X}$ into the money-market equation

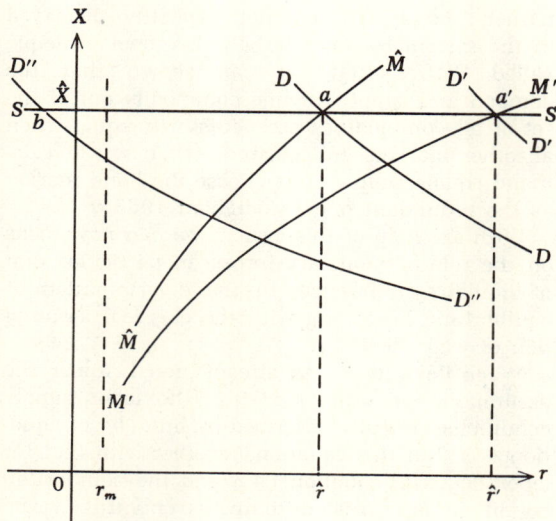

Figure 3 — Equilibrium under wage flexibility

(7), we can determine the price level $\hat{P}$ that equates the demand for money with the given supply (provided such a value of P exists; see below). Finally, from $\hat{P}$ and the equilibrium real wage, $W/\hat{P}$, we can infer the equilibrium money wage, $\hat{W}$.

The nature of the solution can be clarified by means of Figure 3, in which X is measured on the ordinate and r on the abscissa. The horizontal line labeled SS, cutting the ordinate at $\hat{X}$, represents the aggregate supply consistent with full employment —that is, with the clearing of the labor market. It is a horizontal line because, as should be apparent from the derivation above, the value of $\hat{X}$ does not explicitly depend on r. The curve labeled DD is the graph of the aggregate demand relation (1′), which is shown falling from left to right for the reasons stated earlier. Equilibrium in the commodity (and labor) market is thus represented by the point of intersection of the demand and supply curves, namely, point a, with coordinates $(\hat{X},\hat{r})$.

There remains to be shown the role of money and the money market in the determination of equilibrium. For this we refer back to equation (7′) and note that for a given value of M/P this equation expresses a relation between the two variables X and r. It is therefore amenable to graphical representation in our figure. Indeed, the shape of this graph can be readily inferred by solving (7′) for X to obtain $X = V(r)(M/P)$. Given M/P, the graph of this equation is simply that of $V(r)$, already shown in Figure 2, except for a proportionality fac-

tor and for the fact that the axes are interchanged, r now being measured on the abscissa instead of the ordinate. The result is a curve such as $M'M'$, which represents the locus of (7′) for an arbitrarily chosen value of the "real" money supply, $(M/P)'$. It rises from left to right because, as r increases and transactors are induced to economize on their cash holdings, the velocity of circulation increases, and thus a given "real" money supply is capable of financing a larger and larger volume of transactions, X.

It should be readily apparent that the curve corresponding to some other value of M/P, say, a value m times larger, can be obtained from the $M'M'$ curve by multiplying by the factor m the ordinate of the $M'M'$ curve corresponding to any given value of r. It follows that provided $\hat{r}$ (the abscissa of point a) is to the right of r_m there will be some unique value of M/P, say, $M/\hat{P}$, such that the corresponding MM curve will go through the point of intersection, a, of the other two curves. This unique curve is represented by $\hat{M}\hat{M}$ in the figure. Thus, with a real money supply $M/\hat{P}$, the money market as well as the commodity and labor markets will all be simultaneously cleared with the output $\hat{X}$ and the rate of interest $\hat{r}$. But this in turn means that, given the actual money supply M, the price level must tend to the equilibrium level $\hat{P}$, such that $M/\hat{P} = (M/\hat{P})$, or $\hat{P} = M/(M/\hat{P})$. Similarly, $\hat{W} = \hat{P}(W/\hat{P})$, where $(W/\hat{P})$ is the full-employment equilibrium real wage. A higher value of W and P would make the money supply inadequate to transact the full-employment income, unless the rate of interest were higher than $\hat{r}$. But a higher r would reduce the aggregate demand below the full-employment supply. This in turn would cause unemployment which, with flexible wages, would lead to a fall of W and hence of P to the equilibrium levels $\hat{W}$ and $\hat{P}$; the converse would be true for values of P and W below the equilibrium levels.

There are three main implications of this analysis to which attention must be called:

(a) Provided $\hat{r} > r_m$, the only economic effect of M is to determine the price level $\hat{P}$; furthermore, it is apparent from the derivation of the last paragraph that $\hat{P}$ is proportional to M, so that, in this sense, the quantity theory of money holds.

(b) The equilibrium value of P corresponding to a given M depends, not only on full-employment output $\hat{X}$, which controls the position of SS, and on slowly changing institutional factors determining the shape of $V(r)$, but also on r. As can be seen from Figure 3, the larger $\hat{r}$ is, the smaller will be the equilibrium real money supply. But $\hat{r}$, for a given $\hat{X}$, is in turn associated with the position of the aggregate demand relation, DD. A rise in the aggregate demand relation—reflecting an increase in consumption or investment demand or both at each level of income and of the interest rate—will result in an upward shift of the DD curve, and this in turn will move to the right the point of intersection, a, of aggregate demand and supply, increasing its r coordinate. Such a shift is illustrated by the curve $D'D'$ intersecting SS at a'. If in the face of such a shift the central bank does not force an appropriate contraction in M, excess demand will arise in the commodity and labor markets that will force wages and prices up. This will reduce the real money supply, lowering the MM curve, until a value of P is reached such that MM coincides with $M'M'$. If the price rise is to be avoided, the central bank must enforce an appropriate reduction in M (in the same proportion in which prices would rise otherwise). We deduce that once liquidity preference is recognized, if the monetary authority is concerned with maintaining the stability of the price level over time—as it must be if a monetary economy is to work smoothly—it must actively manage the money supply, enforcing a (relatively) larger money supply, and a smaller value of r, when demand tends to be slack and a relatively smaller supply, and higher r, when demand tends to be more active.

(c) Suppose, however, that in some period demand is slack and the DD curve is so depressed that it intersects SS at a value of r smaller than r_m, as illustrated by $D''D''$ intersecting SS at b in Figure 3. It is then apparent that there can be no possible value of M/P such that the corresponding MM curve will go through b, since regardless of the value of M/P, every MM curve must lie entirely to the right of r_m. In this situation, sometimes referred to as "the Keynesian case" or "the special Keynesian case," the economic system will not have any equilibrium solution (a set of prices and interest rates that can simultaneously equate all demands and supplies). If prices and wages are flexible, they will both tend to fall indefinitely under the pressure of excess supplies. But this fall, which under normal conditions would re-establish equilibrium by shifting MM up, can now never prove sufficient. By the same token, monetary policy also breaks down: there is no feasible expansion of the money supply sufficient to eliminate the excess supply of goods and labor.

Thus, from liquidity preference Keynes was able to derive the important and novel result that under certain conditions an economy using a token money

may simply break down, having no maintainable position of equilibrium (except through government fiscal policy or wage rigidity, which will be discussed below).

Positive national debt. The government debt, G, may consist of interest-bearing instruments (government bonds) or government fiat money or both, circulating along with or instead of the money created by the banking system. In any case, if G is positive, it is apparent from equation (1') that aggregate demand depends not only on r but also on P. In terms of Figure 3, equation (1') must now be represented by a *family* of curves, one for each value of P. For the sake of illustration, suppose that the curve DD in the figure corresponds to the received price level, P_0. It can readily be established that to a different value of P, say, $P_1 < P_0$, there will correspond a new DD curve higher and to the right, such as $D'D'$. This is because a fall in P will increase the real value of the government debt held by the public and hence the real net worth of the private sector. This in turn will tend to increase consumption demand, and hence total demand, for any given r. Conversely, a rise in P will shift DD downward and to the left.

This dependence of aggregate demand on P when G is not zero has come to be known in the literature as the "real-balance effect," and also as the "Pigou effect" because Pigou called attention to it in a very influential work (1947). However, the point had been made earlier by others, in particular by Scitovsky (1940). The main implication of the real-balance effect is that even with flexible wages the system *will* in general have a position of full-employment equilibrium. In other words, it rules out the possibility of the "Keynesian case" discussed above. To illustrate this point, suppose that corresponding to the received price, P_0, the aggregate demand function had the position $D''D''$ in the figure, which could not possibly intersect an MM curve on SS. Since the position of DD now *depends* on P, as P falls under the pressure of excess supply the DD curve will keep shifting to the right at the same time that MM shifts upward. Except under very special *ad hoc* assumptions, MM and DD will eventually intersect on SS at some point to the right of r_m.

This demonstration that, provided G is positive, a system with flexible wages will possess a position of full-employment equilibrium, contrary to Keynes's conclusion, has been seized upon by some of Keynes's critics as disposing of one of his most significant and novel results. They have concluded that underemployment equilibrium can arise only from wage–price rigidities. This view must be regarded as unwarranted, mainly for the following reasons: (*a*) Keynes's conclusion stands when $G = 0$. (*b*) Even when $G > 0$, the conclusion that a full-employment solution would exist is valid only under the assumption, implicit in the model, that falling prices do not generate perverse expectations of further falls, which would reduce demand. Furthermore, it ignores the likelihood that a violent deflation, which might be necessary to produce a sufficient increase in the real value of the national debt, would severely disrupt a monetary economy by producing wholesale debtors' insolvency. In view of these considerations, Pigou's demonstration has little practical relevance, as Pigou himself acknowledged ([1947] 1951, p. 251). Even if full employment could be re-established by sufficient deflation of prices and wages, it would be preferable to avoid this outcome by relying on the kind of fiscal policy devices, discussed in the next section, that one would have to fall back on when $G = 0$. To look at the matter in a slightly different light, wage and price rigidity, instead of hindering the working of a monetary economy, may provide it with a degree of price stability that in the long run contributes to its smooth working, even though this rigidity makes the task of successful monetary management more challenging.

Downward wage rigidity. The working of the system when the level of the rigid wage W_0 is sufficiently high to be at least potentially effective can be illustrated by Figure 4, which is a simple variant of Figure 3. For this purpose it is convenient to

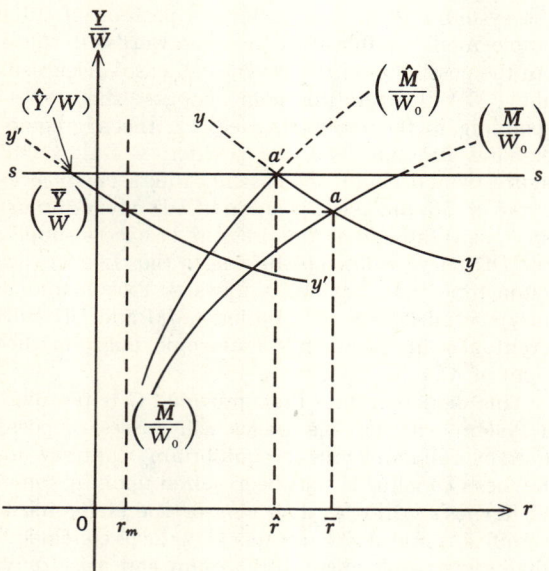

Figure 4 — Equilibrium with a rigid wage level (W_0)

introduce a new symbol to denote money income, Y, which is related to other variables of the system by the identity

$$(8) \qquad Y \equiv PX.$$

Also, for the sake of exposition we deal formally with the case $G = 0$, with some occasional reference to the (rather minor) modifications called for if this restriction is discarded.

We recall that with $G = 0$ the right-hand side of (1') contains only the variable r. From (1'), (2), and (3) we can then derive a relation between Y/W and r. Here Y/W is income measured in what Keynes called wage units (that is, income measured in terms of labor as a *numéraire*). We first solve equation (3) for P/W in terms of X and write the solution as

$$(3') \qquad P/W = \mathscr{P}(X),$$

a "Marshallian" short-run supply function indicating the price—in terms of the cost of labor—needed to call forth a given supply, X. Next, using (1') and (2), we can express X as a function of r. It follows that Y/W can itself be expressed as a function of r—say, $Y/W \equiv X(P/W) = X\mathscr{P}(X) = y(r)$. This equation is an obvious variant of the aggregate-demand relation (1'), shown as DD in Figure 3, except that output is expressed in wage units. Accordingly, its graph, shown by the yy curve of Figure 4, bears a close relation to that of DD in Figure 3, from which it differs only by the factor P/W. In particular, yy must fall from left to right if DD does, since P/W is an increasing function of X. The horizontal line ss again represents "full-employment output" in wage units, $(P\hat{/}W)\hat{X}$, where $P\hat{/}W$ and $\hat{X}$ can be inferred from the solution of the system under flexible wages. The portion of yy above ss has been dashed to indicate that it can never be "effective," since real income there exceeds the full-employment level.

The curve rising from left to right and labeled $\bar{M}/W_0$ is again derived from the money market equation (7'), on the assumption that the given money supply is $\bar{M}$. First solve (7') for PX, obtaining $PX = V(r)M$. Next replace M with $\bar{M}$ and divide both sides by W_0. This yields $Y/W_0 = V(r)(\bar{M}/W_0)$. Its graph must look like that of MM in Figure 3, for it is again the graph of $V(r)$ up to a proportionality factor M/W_0 (instead of M/P, as in Figure 3). It shows the level of income (in wage units) that can be transacted at each level of r, given the money supply in wage units.

If the yy curve and the money-market curve intersect in their effective range—below or on ss—as in Figure 4, then the coordinates of their point of intersection, labeled a, show the equilibrium value of income, $\bar{Y}/W$, and of the rate of interest, $\bar{r}$. If this intersection does not fall on ss, then the equilibrium is one of less than full employment. It is a position of *equilibrium* despite the presence of unemployment because, under wage rigidity, the excess supply of labor does not lead to any further adjustment (at least in the short run). By contrast, if wages were flexible, the excess supply would bid down W which, with $\bar{M}$ given, would raise $\bar{M}/W$, shifting the MM curve upward and moving its point of intersection with yy upward and to the left until it coincided with the full-employment point, a' in the figure. (If G is assumed to be positive, the fall in W will also tend to shift yy upward, moving a' to the right.)

Even under wage rigidity, output and employment could be increased by increasing the money supply, which, with W given at W_0, would raise M/W and hence the MM curve. In fact, provided that a' is to the right of r_m, there is an ideal money supply, $\hat{M}$, that produces an MM curve that intersects yy at a'. Alternatively, the goal of optimal monetary policy might be visualized as that of enforcing the rate of interest that would generate an aggregate demand equal to full-employment output, supplying whatever quantity of money is needed to enforce that rate. In terms of Figure 4, the rate of interest called for is, of course, $\hat{r}$ (which is the r coordinate of a'), and the corresponding quantity of money is again $\hat{M}$.

This analysis should help to show how the interaction of liquidity preference and wage rigidity makes the task of economic stabilization through monetary policy a highly complex and difficult one. In the absence of wage–price rigidities the concern of monetary policy would be reduced to the maintenance of price stability. And in the absence of liquidity preference the velocity of circulation could be counted upon to be sufficiently stable to make this task a relatively easy one. In a stationary economy it would call essentially for a stable money supply, whereas in an expanding economy it would call for a money supply that keeps pace with the growth of full-employment output, a growth that also appears to be characterized by a fair degree of stability.

But under wage rigidity, monetary policy has the double task of trying to achieve both price stability and full employment. Furthermore, because liquidity preference causes the velocity of circulation to vary with interest rates, the money supply needed to reach these goals will vary, relative to full-employment output, with variations in aggregate demand conditions. In terms of Figure 4,

a rise in consumption or investment demand relative to income will shift the yy curve to the right; a corresponding fall will shift it to the left. These shifts have to be countered by contrary adjustments of the money supply relative to the level of full-employment output. Furthermore, failure to adjust the money supply properly will tend to have asymmetrical consequences. An excessive money supply will still give rise to increases in prices that could have been avoided and that are largely irreversible. But too small a money supply will result in an insufficient aggregate demand that, aside from deflationary effects on the price level, will result in the waste and social scourge of unemployment.

Note also that the central bank's control over the price level is at best partial and largely unidirectional. The price level is anchored to the wage rate, which monetary policy can readily push up by being too expansive but which it can hardly hope to force down, except possibly through the painful and wasteful route of prolonged and widespread unemployment. Furthermore, if the minimum money wage—the W_0 of equation (5)—tends to be pushed up even before full employment is reached, whether through powerful unions or through partial bottlenecks or both, and if the rise tends to exceed the rate of increase of productivity, then monetary (as well as fiscal) policy will be faced with the unsavory choice between "creeping inflation" and chronic unemployment. Whether this dilemma is in fact a serious and real one revolves around the issue of the determinants of the over-all level of money wages, an issue that the Keynesian analysis has opened up but that is still far from settled. [See INFLATION AND DEFLATION; *see also* Phillips 1958.]

One other implication of the Keynesian framework, which can be only touched upon in this survey dealing primarily with monetary aspects, is that fiscal policy provides an alternative approach to the control of aggregate demand for economic stabilization [see FISCAL POLICY]. Fiscal policy can be accommodated in our macroeconomic model by adding government expenditure on goods and services as a component of aggregate demand in equation (1'), making consumption (and possibly investment) depend on taxes as well as on income produced, and adding an equation relating tax collection to income and tax rates. Without attempting to pursue this line here we may indicate that, in terms of Figure 4, fiscal policy—defined as policy concerned with the level of government expenditure and taxation—will affect the position and shape of the aggregate demand relation yy. An increase in expenditure will shift it upward and to the right; an increase in tax rates will shift it in the opposite direction. Thus, given a position of less than full employment equilibrium such as *a* in Figure 4, output and employment could be raised toward or up to the full-employment level by increased government expenditure, tax reductions, or both, which would shift the *yy* curve to the right.

The possibility of affecting equilibrium output and employment through fiscal tools becomes of critical importance in the special "Keynesian case," in which the aggregate demand is so depressed that the *yy* curve intersects *ss* to the left of the minimum achievable interest rate, r_m. In this case (illustrated by the curve *y'y'* in Figure 4) full employment, as we have seen, is beyond the reach of monetary policy, for no money curve can have points to the left of r_m. Fiscal policy is then the only effective tool of stabilization policy, at least until the *yy* curve has been shifted rightward enough to cut *ss* to the right of r_m.

Beyond this point—and, more generally, whenever the intersection of *yy* and *ss* is to the right of r_m—either fiscal or monetary tools can be used in the pursuit of full employment and price stability. Of course, both tools can be used simultaneously and in coordinated fashion. This should be clear from the fact that, in terms of Figure 4, fiscal policy acts basically on *yy* whereas monetary policy acts basically on the money curve. (The graphical apparatus of Figure 4 was chosen to illustrate the working of the system partly because of its convenience in isolating the *modus operandi* of monetary and fiscal policy.)

There is a substantial literature concerned with the analysis of the relative advantages and shortcomings of monetary and fiscal policy in terms of such criteria as reliability, response delays, ease of implementation, and reversibility (for monetary policy, see Johnson 1962, pp. 365–377; for fiscal policy see, e.g., Keiser 1964, part 5), effects on long-run economic growth (e.g., Smith 1957; Modigliani 1961), and, more recently, differential impact on the balance of payments (e.g., Mundell 1962). Because of the complexity of the problem it is not surprising that there have been substantial differences in points of view between economists favoring the use of one tool, or of some specific mix, and those favoring others. These differences can be traced in part to differences in the subjective valuation of different goals. But in part they revolve around disagreement about the empirical importance of the "Keynesian case" in which monetary policy becomes powerless to maintain or reestablish full employment, either because it is

ineffective in reducing interest rates any further (at least in the short run) or because the achievable reduction in interest rates is insufficient to induce the required expansion in investment and aggregate demand.

Liquidity preference, that is, the proposition that the demand for money is systematically and significantly affected by interest rates, has proved to be a major, lasting contribution to economic analysis, well supported by empirical evidence. From an analytical point of view its great significance lies in the implication that under certain conditions—the "special Keynesian case"—even an economy with flexible wages and prices might not possess a stable full-employment equilibrium. But beyond this fundamental theoretical contribution, the dramatic impact of the *General Theory* on economic theory and policy can be traced to its insightful analysis of the role of liquidity preference in a world of widespread wage and price rigidities. This analysis has led to a new understanding and fundamental reappraisal of the role of money and of the tasks and limitations of monetary and fiscal policy.

With downward wage rigidity (and even ignoring international trade) money cannot be regarded, even in first approximation, as "neutral," a mere veil having no effect on the economy other than the determination of the price level, except possibly when the money supply is excessive. Under conditions of less than full employment due to lack of demand, and barring the special Keynesian case, monetary policy plays a crucial role in the determination of income and employment. In the special Keynesian case, on the other hand, monetary policy breaks down, since it is incapable, at least in the short run, of affecting either output or prices.

FRANCO MODIGLIANI

BIBLIOGRAPHY

ALLAIS, MAURICE 1947 *Économie & intérêt: Présentation nouvelle des problèmes fondamentaux relatifs au rôle économique du taux de l'intérêt et de leurs solutions.* 2 vols. Paris: Librairie des Publications Officielles.

BAUMOL, WILLIAM J. 1952 The Transactions Demand for Cash: An Inventory Theoretic Approach. *Quarterly Journal of Economics* 66:545–556.

BRONFENBRENNER, MARTIN; and HOLZMAN, FRANKLYN D. 1963 Survey of Inflation Theory. *American Economic Review* 53:593–661.

BRONFENBRENNER, MARTIN; and MAYER, THOMAS 1960 Liquidity Functions in the American Economy. *Econometrica* 28:810–834.

BRUNNER, K.; and MELTZER, ALLAN H. 1964 Some Further Investigations of Demand and Supply Functions for Money. *Journal of Finance* 19:240–283.

ESHAG, EPRIME 1963 *From Marshall to Keynes: An Essay on the Monetary Theory of the Cambridge School.* Oxford: Blackwell.

FISHER, IRVING (1911) 1920 *The Purchasing Power of Money: Its Determination and Relation to Credit, Interest and Crises.* New ed., rev. New York: Macmillan.

FRIEDMAN, MILTON (editor) 1956 *Studies in the Quantity Theory of Money.* Univ. of Chicago Press. → See especially pages 5–21, "The Quantity Theory of Money—A Restatement," by Friedman.

FRIEDMAN, MILTON 1957 *A Theory of the Consumption Function.* National Bureau of Economic Research, General Series, No. 63. Princeton Univ. Press.

FRIEDMAN, MILTON 1959 The Demand for Money: Some Theoretical and Empirical Results. *Journal of Political Economy* 67:327–351.

HICKS, JOHN R. (1935) 1951 A Suggestion for Simplifying the Theory of Money. Pages 13–32 in American Economic Association, *Readings in Monetary Theory.* Philadelphia: Blakiston.

HICKS, JOHN R. 1937 Mr. Keynes and the "Classics": A Suggested Interpretation. *Econometrica* 5:147–159.

JOHNSON, H. G. 1962 Monetary Theory and Policy. *American Economic Review* 52:335–384.

KEISER, NORMAN F. 1964 *Macroeconomics, Fiscal Policy, and Economic Growth.* New York: Wiley.

KEYNES, JOHN MAYNARD (1930) 1958–1960 *A Treatise on Money.* 2 vols. London: Macmillan. → Volume 1: *The Pure Theory of Money.* Volume 2: *The Applied Theory of Money.*

KEYNES, JOHN MAYNARD 1936 *The General Theory of Employment, Interest and Money.* London: Macmillan. → A paperback edition was published in 1965 by Harcourt.

LANGE, OSKAR 1938 The Rate of Interest and the Optimum Propensity to Consume. *Economica* New Series 5:12–32.

LATANÉ, HENRY A. 1954 Cash Balances and the Interest Rate: A Pragmatic Approach. *Review of Economics and Statistics* 36:456–460.

LATANÉ, HENRY A. 1960 Income Velocity and Interest Rates: A Pragmatic Approach. *Review of Economics and Statistics* 42:445–449.

LAVINGTON, FREDERICK 1921 *The English Capital Market.* London: Methuen.

MARGET, ARTHUR W. 1938 *The Theory of Prices: A Re-examination of the Central Problems of Monetary Theory.* Vol. 1. Englewood Cliffs, N.J.: Prentice-Hall.

MARSHALL, ALFRED 1923 *Money, Credit and Commerce.* London: Macmillan.

MELTZER, ALLAN H. 1963 The Demand for Money: The Evidence From the Time Series. *Journal of Political Economy* 71:219–246.

MODIGLIANI, FRANCO (1944) 1951 Liquidity Preference and the Theory of Interest and Money. Pages 186–239 in American Economic Association, *Readings in Monetary Theory.* New York: Blakiston. → First published in Volume 12 of *Econometrica.*

MODIGLIANI, FRANCO 1961 Long Run Implications of Alternative Fiscal Policies and the Burden of the National Debt. *Economic Journal* 71:730–755.

MODIGLIANI, FRANCO 1963 The Monetary Mechanism and Its Interaction With Real Phenomena. *Review of Economics and Statistics* 45 (Supplement):79–107.

MUNDELL, ROBERT A. 1962 The Appropriate Use of Monetary and Fiscal Policy for Internal and External Stability. International Monetary Fund, *Staff Papers* 9:70–77.

PATINKIN, DON (1956) 1965 *Money, Interest, and Prices: An Integration of Monetary and Value Theory.* 2d ed. New York: Harper.

PHILLIPS, A. W. 1958 The Relation Between Unemployment and the Rate of Change of Money Wage Rates in the United Kingdom: 1861–1957. *Economica* New Series 25:283–299.

PIGOU, A. C. (1917) 1951 The Value of Money. Pages 162–183 in American Economic Association, *Readings in Monetary Theory.* Philadelphia: Blakiston.

PIGOU, A. C. (1947) 1951 Economic Progress in a Stable Environment. Pages 241–251 in American Economic Association, *Readings in Monetary Theory.* Philadelphia: Blakiston. → First published in Volume 14 of *Economica* New Series.

PIGOU, A. C. 1950 *Keynes's General Theory: A Retrospective View.* London: Macmillan.

SCITOVSKY, TIBOR 1940 Capital Accumulation, Employment and Price Rigidity. *Review of Economic Studies* 8:69–88.

SMITH, WARREN L. 1957 Monetary–Fiscal Policy and Economic Growth. *Quarterly Journal of Economics* 71:36–55.

TOBIN, JAMES 1956 The Interest-elasticity of Transactions Demand for Cash. *Review of Economics and Statistics* 38:241–247.

TOBIN, JAMES 1958 Liquidity Preference as Behavior Towards Risk. *Review of Economic Studies* 25, no. 2: 65–86.

TURVEY, RALPH (1960) 1961 *Interest Rates and Asset Prices.* New York: Macmillan.

LIST, FRIEDRICH

Friedrich List (1789–1846), German economist, was the son of a tanner from the free town of Reutlingen (Württemberg). Early in his life he absorbed the political ideas and doctrines of the Enlightenment, finding in them an excellent weapon against the rule of an arbitrary bureaucracy and the lingering restrictions of the age of the guilds. In the years following the defeat of Napoleon, he was able to give full scope to his liberal political ideas in his capacities as adviser to one of the leading statesmen of Württemberg, as professor of political economy at the University of Tübingen, and as editor of several periodicals.

With the rising tide of German reaction, however, his activity became suspect. When in 1819 he established an association of merchants and industrialists in Frankfurt am Main, the Handels- und Gewerbsverein, and advocated the abolition of internal German customs barriers, the officials of many German-speaking states, and especially Metternich, the Austrian chancellor, began to look upon him as a demagogue. In 1820 he was elected to the legislature of Württemberg. When he petitioned for an extension of local self-government and for publicity in judicial procedure, he was sentenced to ten months' imprisonment for attempting to undermine the stability of public institutions. He fled abroad in 1822 and led a wandering life for some years. In 1824 he returned to Germany and was promptly arrested. Released on the promise that he would emigrate to America—he had been invited by Lafayette—he sailed for New York in 1825.

In the United States, List engaged in various activities. He lived in Pennsylvania, first as an unsuccessful farmer, near Harrisburg, and then as the editor of a German newspaper, *Der Adler*, in Reading. He also discovered and successfully developed an anthracite coal mine near Tamaqua, Pennsylvania; the railroad he built to serve it—known as the Little Schuylkill Navigation Railroad and Canal Co.—was opened in November 1831 and was at the time the only railway line carrying both freight and passengers. At the same time he was a keen observer of the economic and political problems which beset the growing country; his entrepreneurial experiences confirmed his earlier doubts about the universal validity of Adam Smith's doctrines. He concluded that a protective tariff is indispensable for industrially underdeveloped countries. At the suggestion of Charles Ingersoll, vice-president of the Pennsylvania Society for the Promotion of Manufactures and the Mechanic Arts—the leading protectionist organization of the time—List wrote his "Outlines of American Political Economy" (1827). This was his first attempt at a systematic formulation of his views, and, indeed, it was the first attempt of any kind to draft a national system of political economy that was valid for early high capitalism. Copies of the "Outlines" were distributed to members of Congress, and the adoption of the Tariff Bill of 1828 was a direct consequence.

List supported the election campaign of Andrew Jackson in 1832 and was rewarded by being appointed American consul in Germany, serving first in Hamburg and then in Leipzig. While still American consul, he embarked on an ambitious plan to organize a German railway system. He contributed greatly to the development of the line between Leipzig and Dresden in 1837; it was one of the first railways on the Continent. The venture, although successful in itself, proved a source of personal and financial disappointment and even induced him to leave Germany for France.

It was in Paris in 1837 that List wrote his second systematic work, "Le système naturel de l'économie politique," which he submitted to the Académie des Sciences Morales et Politiques. The work was not rediscovered until 1925 and was published for the first time two years later in French and German (see *Schriften*, vol. 4). In this work, List deepened and expanded the theoretical system sketched in the "Outlines" and gave it, in addition, a historical basis. But the full results of his far-reaching studies and his international experiences were incorporated only in his best-known work on the subject of political economy, *The National System of Political Economy* (1841), which was written in Paris but appeared after List had finally returned to Germany in 1840. Beginning in 1843 he published *Das Zollvereinsblatt*, an influential review devoted to the dissemination of his ideas, which were by then both supported and confirmed by the rise of industrialism. He began to exercise an important influence on public opinion in Germany. However, financial worries, combined with the failure of his plan for an alliance between Germany and Great Britain, drove him to despair and led to his suicide.

In the nineteenth century List was the only economist, other than Karl Marx, who strongly emphasized the close interrelation of economic theory and political factors. He believed that economic doctrines have no abstract validity; he always examined accepted economic views and developed his own ideas in terms of concrete political areas at definite levels of economic development. He severely criticized the classical writers for not being aware of the great social and economic significance of the nation. For List, the nation is the most important link between the individual and mankind, whereas the economic principles of the classical school reflect the industrial and commercial supremacy of England in the nineteenth century and are inapplicable to the needs of underdeveloped but rising countries, such as nineteenth-century Germany, France, and the United States. Observing the destructive consequences of cheap British exports to the numerous small German states—consequences of the application of the English free-trade theory—List developed his countertheory of productive forces and of economic stages, related both to historical and cultural contexts. This was the basis of his later efforts to foster, by the development of railway systems, etc., the economic integration and industrial growth of the different German states that had been organized into the Zollverein (Customs Union) in 1834.

List's theory of protectionism, as presented in *The National System*, was actually only a small part of a much larger system in which he intended to deal with agricultural theory, the concept of balance between agriculture and industry within any economy, and the significance of the internal market. Unfortunately, his ideas were often not sufficiently clear, and his arguments were not always sound—the theoretical element in his basically historical approach was not adequate to the task he set himself. Consequently, his writings were often misunderstood. In the controversy over free trade, for example, some stressed List's argument that infant industries need protection if the nation's productive forces are to be developed, while others realized that free trade was List's ultimate goal. No one seemed to understand, however, that neither argument was central to List's concern. Rather, he wished to demonstrate that the growth of an economy is an organic process and that it is only because growth is organic that every nation has a temporary need for protection. Thus, List denied that the policy prescriptions of classical economic theory are absolute and asserted that a nation's best economic and commercial policy depends on its actual stage of development. The advisability of free trade is, therefore, a matter of politics and is not subject to a quasi-religious belief, as it was for the classical economists and as it is even today for many "neoliberals."

List's theory of economic stages is related to the pervasive eighteenth-century concept of harmony, for it is harmonic development that he saw realized in the *Normalnation*, the state of national development when productive forces are completely utilized. The fact that evolution proceeds from primitive conditions to the agricultural state, then to the agricultural-and-manufacturing state, and finally to the agricultural-manufacturing-and-commercial state may not only stimulate effort in underdeveloped nations but, if correctly interpreted, may also warn them against the dangers of underestimating the importance of agriculture and overestimating that of the most modern type of industry.

List was opposed to the individualistic–cosmopolitan orientation of classical economics, with its focus on value theory. He defended his organic doctrine of productive forces against the classical atomistic–materialistic approach, and he upheld his own concept of the cooperative aspects of the productive process against the classical stress on the division of labor. His dynamic approach and his consequent interest in the development of productive forces led him to his belief in the value of protective tariffs as a method whereby underdeveloped countries may exploit their natural resources and raise their economic level.

List's "Blicke in die Zukunft" (1846*a*), his vision of the political future, also manifests his concern for harmonic balance. He believed that the legal system of a developing nation should be preserved as a cultural prerequisite, as an ethical standard, and as a framework for political action both by individuals and by the people as a whole. Thus, the man who pioneered the Zollverein and heralded the politico–economic unity of the German nation had enough insight to anticipate the need to set limits to a possible German rise. Much more far-sighted than other political thinkers of his time, he predicted the inevitable division of the world into a few mighty empires. He foresaw the enormous growth of American population, industry, and power in the twentieth century, and he even anticipated the great impetus that Russia's "conditions of culture, constitution, law and administration" would need in order for her to become a world power. He therefore consumed his last energies in fighting—without mandate or title—for an Anglo–German alliance. Such an alliance with a united Germany would preserve England's hegemony and would save Europe from being crushed politically between the two rising world powers, Russia and the United States.

For a hundred years List's system was generally accepted without really being understood, even in Germany. Free traders, for example, thought he was a reactionary, although he was the founder of the movement that consolidated Germany commercially and that eventually destroyed more customhouses and more obstacles to trade than were swept away by the political whirlwinds of the American and French revolutions. The efforts to integrate Europe in the years after World War II, however, led to a reappraisal of his statement: "Commercial union and political union are twins; the one cannot come to birth without the other following" ([1846*b*] 1931, p. 276). Many passages in *The National System* can be easily adapted to the post-World War II situation by changing only the names of the states. It is even possible to maintain that List foresaw, strove for, and advocated a European common market; the German economic and political union of the nineteenth century was simply a preliminary stage.

Since World War II the Anglo-Saxon world has also become interested in the ideas that concerned List. Streeten (1959), for example, has stated that in *The National System* List clearly formulated the now widely discussed problem of "balanced growth" in underdeveloped countries. It is also recognized that List was one of the first economists to emphasize the importance of so-called social overhead capital (especially the means of transportation) as a necessary precondition for any economic development, be it in Germany in the nineteenth century or in the many underdeveloped countries of the world in the twentieth. Paul Samuelson (1960) has even placed List among the really important American economists, not only because he began formulating his theory of economic development during his stay in the United States but also because—like the majority of American economists of the past—he can be characterized by a protectionist tendency and a nationalist attitude. Thus, for the practical questions of the integration of Europe and the industrialization of underdeveloped countries, List's work remains of utmost importance, while as a theorist, he is significant as the originator of the historical theory of economic growth.

EDGAR SALIN AND RENÉ L. FREY

[*For discussion of the subsequent development of List's ideas, see* ECONOMIC THOUGHT, *article on* THE HISTORICAL SCHOOL; INTERNATIONAL INTEGRATION, *article on* ECONOMIC UNIONS; INTERNATIONAL TRADE CONTROLS.]

WORKS BY LIST

(1827) 1931 *Outlines of American Political Economy.* Volume 2, pages 95–156 in Friedrich List, *Schriften, Reden, Briefe.* Berlin: Hobbing.

(1841) 1928 *The National System of Political Economy.* London: Longmans. → First published in German.

(1846a) 1931 Blicke in die Zukunft. Volume 7, pages 482–494 in Friedrich List, *Schriften, Reden, Briefe.* Berlin: Hobbing. → First published as "Politik der Zukunft."

(1846b) 1931 Über den Wert und die Bedingungen einer Allianz zwischen Grossbritannien und Deutschland. Volume 7, pages 267–296 in Friedrich List, *Schriften, Reden, Briefe.* Berlin: Hobbing. → Translation of extract in the text provided by the editors.

Schriften, Reden, Briefe. 10 vols. in 12. Edited by Erwin von Beckerath et al. Berlin: Hobbing, 1927–1936. → Volume 1: *Der Kampf um die politische und ökonomische Reform: 1815–1825,* 1932. Volume 2: *Grundlinien einer politischen Ökonomie und andere Beiträge der amerikanischen Zeit: 1825–1832,* 1931. Volume 3: *Schriften zum Verkehrswesen,* 1929–1931. Volume 4: *Das natürliche System der politischen Ökonomie,* written in French in 1837, first published in French and German in 1927. Volume 5: *Aufsätze und Abhandlungen aus den Jahren 1831–1844,* 1928. Volume 6: *Das nationale System der politischen Ökonomie,* 1930. Volume 7: *Die politisch-ökonomische Nationaleinheit der Deutschen: Aufsätze aus dem Zollvereinsblatt und andere Schriften der Spätzeit,* 1931. Volume 8: *Tagebücher und Briefe: 1812–1846,* 1932. Volume 9: *Lists Leben in Tag- und Jahresdaten,* 1935. Volume 10: *Verzeichnisse zur Gesamtausgabe,* 1936.

SUPPLEMENTARY BIBLIOGRAPHY

BRINKMANN, CARL 1949 *Friedrich List.* Berlin: Duncker & Humblot.

EHEBERG, KARL T. VON 1883 Historische und kritische Einleitung zu Friedrich Lists *Nationalem System der politischen Oekonomie.* Pages 1–249 in Friedrich List, *Das nationale System der politischen Oekonomie.* 7th ed. Stuttgart (Germany): Cotta.

GEHRING, PAUL 1964 *Friedrich List: Jugend- und Reifejahre 1789–1825.* Tübingen (Germany): Mohr.

HÄUSSER, LUDWIG 1850 Friedrich Lists Leben. Volume 1 in Friedrich List, *Gesammelte Schriften.* Stuttgart and Tübingen (Germany): Cotta.

HIRST, MARGARET E. 1909 *Life of Friedrich List and Selections From His Writings.* With an introduction by F. W. Hirst. London: Smith; New York: Scribner.

LENZ, FRIEDRICH 1930 *Friedrich List, "die Vulgärökonomie" und Karl Marx nebst einer unbekannten Denkschrift Lists zur Zollreform.* Jena (Germany): Fischer.

LENZ, FRIEDRICH 1936 *Friedrich List: Der Mann und das Werk.* Munich and Berlin: Oldenbourg.

MEUSEL, ALFRED 1928 *List und Marx: Eine vergleichende Betrachtung.* Jena (Germany): Fischer.

NOTZ, WILLIAM (1925) 1926 Frederick List in America. *American Economic Review* 16:249–265. → First published in German in *Weltwirtschaftliches Archiv.*

OLSHAUSEN, HANS P. 1935 *Friedrich List und der deutsche Handels- und Gewerbsverein.* Jena (Germany): Fischer.

RITSCHL, HANS 1947 *Friedrich Lists Leben und Lehre.* Tübingen and Stuttgart (Germany): Wunderlich.

SALIN, EDGAR (1921) 1963 Friedrich Lists Lehre von den Wirtschaftsstufen und die Bedeutung der Typik. Pages 301–309 in Edgar Salin, *Lynkeus: Gestalten und Probleme aus Wirtschaft und Politik.* Tübingen (Germany): Mohr. → First published in Volume 45 of *Schmollers Jahrbuch.*

SAMUELSON, PAUL A. 1960 American Economics. Pages 31–50 in Ralph E. Freeman (editor), *Postwar Economic Trends in the United States.* New York: Harper.

SOMMER, ARTUR 1927 *Friedrich Lists System der politischen Ökonomie.* Jena (Germany): Fischer.

STREETEN, PAUL 1959 Unbalanced Growth. *Oxford Economic Papers* New Series 11:167–190.

LITERACY

Whenever the term "literacy" is used, a context is always implied. If the context is archeological, anthropological, or ethnographic, literacy usually refers to the cultural fact that writing has been invented and that the society contains a class, a caste, or an occupational group whose members keep accounts or preserve religious and moral precepts in written form or use writing for some other specific purpose. So used, literacy implies also the contrasting idea of *preliteracy*—a cultural stage in which writing has not yet been invented. The change from preliteracy to literacy—the spread of literate societies throughout the world—probably began in ancient Sumer during the fourth millennium B.C., through a gradual transition from pictography to the use of an alphabet.

If literacy is used in a historical or modern comparative context, then the implied contrast is with *illiteracy.* Literacy then refers to the degree of dissemination among a society's population of the dual skills of reading and writing. Here a "literate" society is one in which most adult members can read and write at least a simple message. In this context, England, the United States, Sweden, Denmark, the U.S.S.R., and Japan are among the literate societies, whereas Iraq, Haiti, and Nigeria, for example, can be called illiterate—or, at least, not yet literate—societies, even though they contain many highly educated persons.

Extent of literacy

As the great variation between countries with respect to illiteracy (Table 1) has become better known, concern about its consequences has greatly increased. For some, the existence of high levels of illiteracy detracts from the dignity of man and constitutes evidence of immense numbers of personal tragedies for the illiterate adults who are thereby prevented from escaping poverty and mental isolation. To others, illiteracy is primarily an obstacle to

peaceful and friendly international relations and to democratic processes within countries. Still others are aware that low levels of literacy act as brakes on the advance of countries along the paths of social and economic development and political power. These concerns have brought on a variety of efforts to gather detailed information on the extent of literacy in the world's countries and on the conditions under which the diffusion of literacy takes place.

From a world perspective, it is evident that in 1950, the latest date for which world-wide estimates are available, some 53 per cent of the world's population aged 10 and over were able to read and write a simple sentence; that is, in 1950 there were at least 800 million illiterates above the age of 10. The dissemination of literacy skills that has taken place since then is unlikely to have raised the per-

Table 1 — Illiteracy in selected census countries, by continent[a]

	PERCENTAGE OF ILLITERATES IN THE POPULATION AGED 10 AND OVER[b]			PERCENTAGE OF ILLITERATES IN THE POPULATION AGED 10 AND OVER[b]	
	Year	Per cent		Year	Per cent
Africa			**North America**		
Algeria	1948	82.1[c]	Costa Rica	1950	21.2
Egypt	1947	80.1[c]	Cuba	1953	22.1[c]
Gold Coast (Ghana)	1948	92.0	Dominican Republic	1950	56.8
Mozambique	1940	98.1	El Salvador	1950	60.9
Nigeria	1952/3	88.3	Guatemala	1950	72.0
Nyasaland	1945	91.1	Haiti	1950	89.5
Portuguese Guinea	1950	98.5	Honduras	1950	64.8
Union of South Africa	1946	55.3	Mexico	1950	43.2[d]
South America			Nicaragua	1950	62.6
Argentina	1947	12.6	Panama	1950	28.3
Bolivia	1950	68.9	**Asia**		
Brazil	1950	51.7	Burma	1953	30.1[e]
Chile	1952	19.9[c]	Ceylon	1946	42.2
Colombia	1938	44.2	India	1951	80.1
Ecuador	1950	43.7	Indonesia	1930	90.1
Paraguay	1950	31.8	Iraq	1947	89.1[f]
Peru	1940	56.6	Korea	1930	68.6
Venezuela	1950	47.8[c]	Malaya (incl. Singapore)	1947	56.1
Europe			Pakistan	1951	77.3
Bulgaria	1946	24.2[c]	Philippines	1948	40.2
Greece	1951	23.7	Thailand	1947	46.3
Italy	1951	14.4[c]	Turkey	1950	66.1
Poland	1931	23.1			
Portugal	1950	41.7			
Rumania	1948	23.2			
Spain	1950	14.2			
Yugoslavia	1948	25.4			

a. The reader is cautioned against insisting too closely on comparisons between countries whose literacy rates fall within the same decile range. Moreover, rates taken from international sources such as UNESCO (1957) are not always identical with rates calculated from statistical compendia, because persons whose ages are unknown may be omitted or included in the age group 10 and over.

b. Only countries with rates above 10 per cent about 1950 have been included.

c. Population aged 15 and over.

d. Population aged 6 and over.

e. Data for 252 towns only, based on a 20 per cent sample; population aged 16 and over.

f. Population aged 5 and over.

Sources: Calculated from official data (census, statistical compendia, etc.) for each country, or from international sources such as UNESCO 1957 and *Demographic Yearbook* 1960, pp. 434 ff.

Table 2 — *Illiteracy in the major world regions, 1930 and 1950, and in developed and under-developed countries, 1950*

PER CENT ILLITERATE OF ALL PERSONS
AGED 10 AND OVER[a]

	All countries		Developed countries[b]	Under-developed countries[b]
	1930	1950	1950	1950
World	59[c]	47	6	71
North America	4	2	2	
Europe	15	8	4	23
Oceania	14	11	1	88
U.S.S.R.	40	11	11	
South America	54	42	17	51
Middle America	59	48	22	53
Asia	81	70	2	75
Africa	88	88	56	91

a. The figures given in this table represent the weighted average obtained by combining the official and estimated rates for all the countries within the geographical division.

b. Developed countries are those with less than 50 per cent of their economically active males in agricultural pursuits, including hunting, fishing, and forestry; underdeveloped countries are those with 50 per cent or more of their economically active males in these pursuits. For a rationale of this division, see Davis (1951b, p. 8).

c. Abel and Bond (1929, p. 51) give a world average of 62 per cent for around 1920.

Sources: For 1930 Davis 1948, p. 614; for 1950 revisions have been made of Golden 1955, p. 2; for another set of 1950 estimates, see UNESCO 1957, p. 15.

centage to 60 or to have decreased the *number* of illiterates very much below 800 million, since population has grown very rapidly in this period. But, as Table 2 shows, the 1950 level represented a considerable *proportionate* gain over 1920 and 1930.

The literacy revolution. The world's transformation from largely illiterate to moderately literate began in the industrial nations of western Europe; the recent gains in world literacy reflect the entrance into this transition of an ever-increasing number of countries in many areas. As Table 1 shows, the differential spread of the literacy transition in 1950 suggests that today's countries can be arranged along a literacy scale that exhibits a definite pattern. The lowest rates exist in those areas that have completed the transition; the highest, in areas such as Ghana, Iraq, or Haiti, in which the transition has hardly begun; and between these two extremes fall all those countries, such as India, Pakistan, Bolivia, Paraguay, Mexico, and the Philippines, which are in the midst of the transformation.

The transformation from preponderantly illiterate to literate in the world's old industrial nations, which was accomplished in about 75 to 100 years, can be documented from official information and from estimates. At the beginning of the nineteenth century, although literacy and schooling were more

general than is often realized (Anderson & Bowman 1965, p. 345), at least half the adult population of England and Wales was illiterate; in 1850 the proportion had probably dropped to about 45 per cent. By 1910 illiteracy had been largely eliminated, with perhaps 5 per cent of the adults still illiterate and these concentrated in the older age groups; in 1914 0.8 per cent of the men and 1.0 per cent of the women signed the marriage register by mark (for all these estimates, see UNESCO 1957, pp. 177 ff.).

The decline of illiteracy in countries entering the literacy transition later can be shown by information for the U.S.S.R., Italy, and Greece. In Russia illiteracy declined very rapidly—from about 76 per cent in 1897, according to official census figures, to about 2 per cent in the early 1960s in the population aged 9 and over (United Nations, Statistical Office 1963, p. 312). In Italy and Greece the transition has been slower. In Italy, illiteracy among marriage registrants declined from 65.8 per cent in 1872 to 3.3 per cent in 1951 (UNESCO 1957, p. 169); illiteracy among persons 10 and over fell from 75 per cent, according to the 1861 census, to about 8 per cent, according to the 1961 census. In Greece illiteracy in the population aged 8 years and over declined from 60 per cent in 1907 to about 25 per cent in 1951 (UNESCO 1957, p. 90).

Because the world's transformation from illiterate to moderately literate had its start in the West and has been completed primarily in the world's urban–industrial countries, these nations have a disproportionate share of the world's literate population (Table 2). In some major areas of the world, such as India, Pakistan, and Egypt, the proportion of the adult population that is illiterate is still very high. In India the illiteracy rate for the population aged 10 and over declined from 95 per cent in 1881 to about 70 per cent in 1961, according to the 1961 census (*Demographic Yearbook*, 1964, p. 698). Whereas the decline of illiteracy in Pakistan and Egypt has followed about the same pattern as in India, some areas, such as Haiti, Mozambique, and Ghana (Table 1) have hardly begun the transition. Even the breakdown by continents understates the concentration of the literate population, because within both Asia and Africa the literate population is mainly in a few countries or in cities. For example, in 1950 Japan—the major highly literate nation of Asia exclusive of the U.S.S.R.—had only 6 per cent to 7 per cent of Asia's total population but at least 20 per cent of its adult literates. Future literacy gains for the world as a whole depend, then, very heavily on the degree to which the highly illiterate countries of the world become involved in this educational transformation.

Evaluating literacy data

Official literacy information can often be obtained from enumerations of total populations (census counts), though sometimes it is based on marriage registers, on tests given to military recruits, or on sample surveys. The results of these enumerations are usually made available in official sources. While minor census inaccuracies can rarely be detected, major inaccuracies in literacy enumeration are discoverable through careful evaluation or by check through independent estimates. For example, because past school enrollment rates for all countries correlate moderately highly with present literacy rates, for a specific country past enrollment rates provide one means of checking the accuracy of census results on literacy.

Definitions of literacy. Census definitions of literacy usually refer to the minimum level of literacy skills; hence they are relatively simple and clear. Yet they still differ slightly from country to country because the instructions to enumerators incorporate somewhat different conceptions of what constitutes the minimum level. In India, for example, government statisticians have instructed enumerators to count as literate only those who have the ability to read and write a simple message in any language, a definition proposed by the United Nations Population Commission. When these instructions are carried out by local schoolteachers, few persons are likely to be counted as literate who do not have the minimum skills. In 1930 Finland applied perhaps the strictest minimum definition: only those persons were classified as literate who passed a rather difficult test. Those who failed were divided into two categories, the semiliterates, that is, persons who could read and write but made orthographic errors, and the illiterates, who could neither read nor write (UNESCO 1957, p. 29). By contrast, in the Hong Kong census of 1961 (as in many others) a person who *said* that he was able to read a language was assumed by inference also to be able to write it and was classified as literate. The acceptance of what the enumerator is told may result in inflating the percentage literate or, in some special cases, lowering this percentage (Davis 1951*a*, p. 151).

Literacy proportions. Because of differences in definition and in enumeration procedure, no actual figure or proportion can be accepted with complete certainty for any area; however, for word-wide comparisons and analyses of literacy, we can profitably use a given proportion as an indicator of the literacy level achieved by a country. The use of literacy proportions as indicators makes it easier to take advantage of literacy proportions available from enumerations of such segments of the population as marriage registrants or recruits. For example, in the 1930s the proportions obtained by each of these enumeration procedures placed France among the highly literate nations of the world (UNESCO 1957, p. 22).

Even when we treat literacy proportions as indicators, it is still desirable to eliminate children from the calculations of rates and to compare rates for the same age groups—preferably 10 and over or 15 and over. Underdeveloped countries frequently have a large proportion of their population under 10 years and cannot manage to teach even the minimum literacy skills until about that age. However, in some cases (see Table 1) it is necessary, for lack of more detailed information, to use the rates for age groups 5 and over, 9 and over, or 15 and over as *estimates* for the age group 10 and over.

Obviously, *illiteracy* rates for the total population, as well as for persons aged 5 and over, are higher than for any of the older age groups; in India, for example, the rate for the total population in 1951 was 83.4 per cent, whereas for the population aged 10 and over it was 80.1 per cent. The rates for the age groups 10 and over and 15 and over are usually quite close; for example, in 1948 in the Philippines the illiteracy rate for each of these age groups was about the same.

For detailed comparisons between two countries, age-group differences and other variations in enumeration results—as in the number of persons returned as "literacy status unknown" or "age status unknown"—must be carefully examined. When literacy proportions are used as indicators, these variations create problems only in rare cases.

Use of estimates. Since some countries have never taken censuses and others have not taken a census for many years, an appraisal of the world's literacy status at one time, 1950, must rely to some extent on estimates. The fact that estimates are used need not imply inaccuracy; some estimates are superior in accuracy to the average census. If, for example, the estimate is derived from reasonably accurate census returns on literacy or from valid statistical noncensus information, or from both, it may be quite reliable. For instance, on the basis of school enrollment information it was estimated that the illiteracy rate for Iraq in 1950 would be 85 per cent of the population aged 10 and over; the census returns for 1953 showed 89.1 per cent illiterate for the population aged 5 and over, or about 85 per cent for the population aged 10 and over.

China and Indonesia present perhaps the most difficult problems of estimating literacy rates. For China there are no national census figures on illiteracy available, and because of the paucity of other accurate information estimates range from 50–55 per cent illiterate for the population aged 15 and over (UNESCO 1957, pp. 16–17) to 70–75 per cent for the population aged 10 and over (Golden 1955, *passim*). The estimate for Indonesia also requires special comment. The census returns of 1930 gave Indonesia an illiteracy rate of 90 per cent for the population aged 10 and over; this figure is so high that it raises doubts about the official estimate of 39 per cent for the population aged 13 to 45 (United Nations 1963c, p. 15). Other estimates for Indonesia suggest an illiteracy level of 80–85 per cent for persons aged 15 and over (UNESCO 1957, p. 39) and 75–80 per cent for the population aged 10 and over (Golden 1955, *passim*). But despite such occasional anomalies and the general impossibility of absolute exactness, world-wide comparisons and analyses can most usefully be undertaken.

The meaning of literacy figures

The unequal distribution of literacy skills in the world stems from the fact that behind a given level of literacy lies the whole institutional structure of a society, particularly the occupational structure. Hence, the sharp contrasts in literacy levels between developed and underdeveloped countries (see Table 2) reflect the differential spread of industrialism through the world; the slighter differences among countries at about the same level of industrial development indicate other differences in the countries' institutional structure. Transition from illiteracy to literacy for a whole country is accompanied usually by differential rates of transition within the population. Literacy skills are acquired more readily by young adults than by the aged; by those aiming for skilled occupations for themselves or their children; and by those—such as city dwellers—who have relatively easy access to the means of learning. In general, then, throughout the transition some literacy differentials within countries are predictable.

Literacy and economic development. The close connection between the prevalence of literacy skills among the adult population of a society and the nature of the society's occupational skills has been demonstrated in several ways. In the first place, the invention of writing itself was clearly connected with other changes in human societies, such as increased occupational differentiation and the emergence of the first true cities. In general, the presence or absence of writing has been used as a criterion to distinguish between civilizations and tribal societies. Further, it should be emphasized that no country's adult population became *preponderantly* literate until after the industrial revolution. Statistically, the dissemination of literacy and the changes in the occupational structure in today's industrial nations are very closely linked; the coefficients of correlation for these time series are all above .9, where 1.0 would indicate perfect correspondence (UNESCO 1957, pp. 177 ff.; Golden 1955, p. 3). Indeed, not only is mass literacy a recent phenomenon in any society, but it is still confined to a relatively few countries. For 1950 literacy rates of the countries and territories of the world and indicators of the degree of industrial development correlated better than .8 on a scale, where 1.0 would have indicated perfect correspondence (Golden 1955, p. 3; United Nations 1961, p. 42).

The transformation from an illiterate to a literate society is triggered, so most authors suggest, by pressures exerted on governments, on special groups, and on individuals by the changing conditions accompanying industrialization. But it is not easily achieved; the transition usually has taken at least 75 years, though in some spectacular cases only about 50 years. Some societies have at times diverted large shares of their means toward the diffusion of literacy, and others, small shares; as a result, in 1950 literacy progress in some countries was advanced and in others retarded, as compared with industrial change. For example, in 1950 Brazil and Yugoslavia were about equally developed (if industrial development is measured by the proportion of the male labor force in nonagricultural pursuits), yet Brazil had an illiteracy rate of more than 50 per cent whereas Yugoslavia's rate was only about 25 per cent for the population aged 10 and over. This retardation or advance, so several authors have suggested, can prove to be a handicap or an asset for a country's future economic progress (Davis 1955; Golden 1955; Anderson & Bowman 1965). A government's assessment of its country's educational position requires not only a knowledge of the literacy level achieved but also an evaluation of the literacy position in relation to the level of economic development.

HILDA H. GOLDEN

[*See also* CAPITAL, HUMAN; EDUCATION; RURAL SO-
CIETY.]

BIBLIOGRAPHY

ABEL, JAMES F.; and BOND, NORMAN J.   1929   *Illiteracy
in the Several Countries of the World.* Washington:
Government Printing Office.

ANDERSON, C. ARNOLD; and BOWMAN, MARY J. (editors)
1965   *Education and Economic Development.* Chicago: Aldine.

DAVIS, KINGSLEY   (1948) 1949   *Human Society.* New
York: Macmillan. → See especially pages 595–617,
"World Population in Transition."

DAVIS, KINGSLEY   1951a   *The Population of India and
Pakistan.* Princeton Univ. Press. → See especially pages
150–161, "Education, Language and Literacy."

DAVIS, KINGSLEY   1951b   Population and the Further
Spread of Industrial Society. American Philosophical
Society, *Proceedings* 95:8–19.

DAVIS, KINGSLEY   1955   Social and Demographic Aspects
of Economic Development in India. Pages 263–315
in Simon Kuznets, W. E. Moore, and J. J. Spengler
(editors), *Economic Growth: Brazil, India, Japan.*
Durham, N.C.: Duke Univ. Press.

Demographic Yearbook. → Issued annually by the United
Nations since 1948. See especially the 1960 and 1964
volumes. Data in Table 1 extracted from *Demographic
Yearbook* 1960, Copyright © United Nations 1961,
are reproduced by permission.

GINSBURG, NORTON S. (editor)   1961   *Atlas of Economic
Development.* Univ. of Chicago Press.

GOLDEN, HILDA H.   1955   Literacy and Social Change in
Underdeveloped Countries. *Rural Sociology* 20:1–7.

HARBISON, FREDERICK; and MYERS, CHARLES A.   1964
Education, Manpower, and Economic Growth. New
York: McGraw-Hill.

HAWKES, JACQUETTA; and WOOLLEY, LEONARD   1963   *Prehistory and the Beginnings of Civilization.* New York:
Harper. → See especially Part 2, Chapter 6 on "Languages and Writing Systems: Education."

LORIMER, FRANK   1946   *The Population of the Soviet
Union: History and Prospects.* Geneva: League of Nations. → See especially pages 79, 198–200.

McCLELLAND, DAVID C.   1966   Does Education Accelerate
Economic Growth? *Economic Development and Cultural Change* 24, no. 3:257–278.

RUSSETT, BRUCE et al.   1964   *World Handbook of Political and Social Indicators.* New Haven: Yale Univ.
Press. → See especially pages 221–226.

SJOBERG, GIDEON   1960   *The Preindustrial City: Past and
Present.* Glencoe, Ill.: Free Press. → See especially
pages 285–320.

SULLIVAN, HELEN   1933   Literacy and Illiteracy. Volume
9, pages 511–523 in *Encyclopaedia of the Social Sciences.* New York: Macmillan.

UNESCO   1952   *Basic Facts and Figures.* Paris: UNESCO.

UNESCO   1953   *Progress of Literacy in Various Countries.* Paris: UNESCO.

UNESCO   1957   *World Illiteracy at Mid-century: A Statistical Study.* Paris: UNESCO.

UNESCO   1964   *Economic and Social Aspects of Educational Planning.* Paris: UNESCO.

UNITED NATIONS, DEPARTMENT OF ECONOMIC AND SOCIAL
AFFAIRS   1961   *Report on the World Social Situation,
1961.* New York: United Nations.

UNITED NATIONS, DEPARTMENT OF ECONOMIC AND SOCIAL
AFFAIRS   1963a   *Report on the World Social Situation, 1963.* New York: United Nations.

UNITED NATIONS, ECONOMIC AND SOCIAL COUNCIL   1963b
UNESCO World Campaign for Universal Literacy.
Document E/3771. Unpublished manuscript.

UNITED NATIONS, STATISTICAL OFFICE   1963c   *Compendium of Social Statistics: 1963.* Statistical Papers,
Series K, No. 2. New York: United Nations.

WINSTON, SANFORD   1930   *Illiteracy in the United States.*
Chapel Hill: Univ. of North Carolina Press.

WORLD CONGRESS OF MINISTERS OF EDUCATION ON THE
ERADICATION OF ILLITERACY   1965   *Statistics of Illiteracy.* Paris: UNESCO.

LITERATURE

I. THE SOCIOLOGY OF
   LITERATURE   *Robert Escarpit*
II. THE PSYCHOLOGY OF
   LITERATURE   *Harold G. McCurdy*
III. POLITICAL FICTION   *James C. Davies*

I

THE SOCIOLOGY OF LITERATURE

The sociological approach to literature is by no
means an easy one. Like religion, sex, and art,
literature is protected by taboos both numerous
and powerful. To the cultured mind the study of
the writer as a professional man, of the literary
work as a means of communication, and of the
reader as a consumer of cultural goods is vaguely
sacrilegious.

Such a revulsion is all the more surprising, as
the concept of literature first appeared to describe
a sociocultural fact, not an aesthetic one. In Ter-
tullian's Latin, as well as in eighteenth-century
English or French, the word "literature" meant the
distinctive culture of those who belonged to the
social stratum of the *litterati*, "well-read people."
It meant practically nothing else in Dr. Johnson's
time and was still sporadically used in that sense
as late as the end of the nineteenth century, notably by Sainte-Beuve and William Dean Howells.

Even when the Germans—particularly Lessing
—evolved from their analysis of the written products of the human mind the objective notion of
Literatur as the art of expressing one's thoughts
in writing, on the one hand, and as the whole of
the works thus produced and published in a definite community, on the other, they never separated
the literary phenomenon from its social environment in time or space. For the group which gravi-
tated around the brothers August Wilhelm and
Friedrich von Schlegel and their pupil Madame de
Staël, literature was, in fact as in value, strongly
linked to, and even determined by, the two factors

of *Zeitgeist*, "the spirit of the time," and *Volksgeist*, "the national spirit." Madame de Staël was among the first to use the French word *littérature* in the new sense, in her book *De la littérature considérée dans ses rapports avec les institutions sociales* (1800).

Such a clearly stated doctrine, which ultimately elicited Taine's positivist criticism, also stirred up a romantic reaction whose spokesmen individualized and even divinized what came to be called literary creation, while ignoring or denying the collective aspects of the literary phenomenon. Late romanticism established the still current notion of the divine solitude of the writer in the act of "creating." Alfred de Vigny was the prototype of the poet, throwing his poems into the anonymous crowd like a shipwrecked sailor entrusting a bottle carrying his message to the shoreless sea, or escaping the bondage of society by self-destruction.

In fact, social consciousness and a sense of solitude often coexisted in the literary attitude of the nineteenth century, but the contradiction between them was not obvious to the romantics, some of the greatest of whom—such as Byron and Hugo—were keenly aware of their moral solitude yet never ignored the strong ties which united them with society. Nevertheless, literary criticism more and more shifted its emphasis from a collective to an individual outlook. Carlyle, in 1840, did stress the effects of literary reputation on a writer, but his representation of the man of letters as a hero can be considered the turning point of the movement from presociological to psychological criticism. Although William Hazlitt, in the 1820s, tried to recapture the "spirit" of the great literary ages, Sainte-Beuve and after him Matthew Arnold, in the second half of the nineteenth century, strove to reconstruct the personality of writers as perceived through their works.

Meanwhile, in Germany the new science of philology had awakened an interest in form and style which eventually opened a new approach to literature through the aesthetic analysis of the work of art. In the early twentieth century, Wilhelm Dilthey concretized this tendency into a doctrine which gave birth to a strong antisociological current which reigned almost unchallenged in many countries under the various shapes of formalism, *Stilforschung*, and aesthetic structuralism. France, however, remained steadfastly committed to the historical positivism of Taine.

Early attempts

Sociology long avoided the difficult job of analyzing literature. When sociologists—most of them

with a philosophical, not a literary turn of mind—touched on the subject, they included it in the wider categories of art, leisure, or communication, thus ignoring the specific characteristics of literature. Even Marx and Engels were extremely prudent in their handling of literary problems. Plekhanov, who was the first to offer a Marxist and a sociological theory of art (1899), did not treat literature satisfactorily.

There was a sociological tradition in Russian literary criticism. It was handed down from Belinski, a contemporary of Carlyle, through Pisarev, a contemporary of Taine, to the antiformalist critics of the Soviet era. But this "civic criticism," as it was called, merely rested on the assumption that a book must be judged by its revolutionary efficacy and by the degree of fidelity with which it represented historical reality. Most Marxists nowadays think this view much too simplistic to account for the complex nature of the literary phenomenon.

A true sociology of literature appeared only when literary critics and historians, starting from literature as a specific reality, tried to answer sociological questions by using current sociological methods. The difficulty was to formulate the questions. By the time an interest in sociology was awakened among literary specialists the habit had been formed of working on the writer as an individual or on the literary work as an isolated phenomenon but seldom on their relationship to the reading public.

As early as 1931 the German L. L. Schücking had tried to give an outline of a sociology of literary taste, but his attempt found little response. On the other hand, when the Hungarian György Lukács, after his conversion to a rather personal brand of Marxism, tried to base a method of critical analysis on a parallelism between the aesthetic patterns of the work of art and the contemporary economic structures of society, he certainly initiated a new type of sociological investigation in literary criticism (1961). The Lukácsian sociology of literature is widely followed in eastern and western Europe, particularly in France, where Lucien Goldmann may be said to have brought it to a high point of effectiveness (1950; 1964). It opened wide and numerous vistas on the social nature of literature, and no further studies on the subject can ignore it. Yet, although Lukács and his followers take into account society as the reality behind the appearances of literature, they still consider the work of art as an end in itself and neglect the part of the reader in literary communication. Indeed, they as much as ignore the very notion of literary communication.

Literary communication

Early sociological investigation in literature was stalemated by the antinomy between the ontological and phenomenological conceptions of literary criticism. Only when existentialism threw a new light on things was it possible to achieve a breakthrough. In that respect Jean-Paul Sartre's essay *What Is Literature?* (1948) may be considered a landmark. Sartre's idea, ostensibly very simple, was that the literary work—that is, the written product of the mind—only exists as such when it is read, since writing without reading is nonsense. An unread book is nothing but a handful of soiled paper. From this premise the inference is that the literary phenomenon cannot be the work of art itself, but rather the meeting and sometimes the clashing of two free acts, one of production and the other of consumption, with all their effects and side effects on moral and social relations. There is always another man in literature: a writer for a reader and a reader for a writer.

In fact, no fully satisfactory result may be obtained in investigating literature with sociological methods if one does not start from a clear idea of what in literary phenomena is fundamentally social.

There is danger in submitting the written product of the mind to purely aesthetic criteria. Although literature is an art, it is an impure one precisely because its main tools are language and writing. Whatever the aesthetic merits of a book may be, the sole fact that it is made up of words and letters—that is, of conventional symbols understood only in a given community, loaded with a semantic content and organized according to syntactic rules valid only for a definite body of population—provides it with an intellectual link to its society which far surpasses in strength if not in scope the links created by the purely sensuous, so-called language of art. The very nature of artistic values is thus inseparable from their actual or potential perception by a public. Instead of limiting the literary phenomenon to the isolated literary work, one should view it as an exchange between a writer and a reader through the medium of a book. Here again we find the familiar pattern of communication. But this pattern alone is insufficient for the needed sociological investigation.

As an instrument of communication the book does not work in a linear fashion. It does not go from one individual to another like a letter. The book appeared in the first millennium B.C., when new materials were found which were light enough to be carried about and smooth enough to allow quick and easy copying. However it is manufactured, a book is always defined by its two specific functions: multiplication and spatial dissemination of the written word. Although in some exceptional cases a book may have had only one reader, the mere fact that it *was* a book gave it an unlimited potential public. The writer may or may not imagine that public, which in turn may or may not be conscious of its own existence. We already know that the original notion of *litteratura* appeared in ancient Rome as a social characteristic when a highly educated reading public concentrated in a small area formed a community big enough to allow group consciousness. It fell into disuse at the beginning of the nineteenth century when many widely dispersed readers in all strata of society were unable to take stock of themselves as a community.

The literary milieu. Even in mass society the *litterati* of each ethnic, national, or social community still retain their group consciousness. Whether it is a motley and fast-changing *monde littéraire* as in France, a bright and sophisticated elite as in the United States, a pauperized intellectual aristocracy as in Spain, or a tight-knit union of writers or academy as in socialist countries, there is always a literary milieu in which ideas are exchanged, judgments passed, and values discussed.

The existence of such a milieu, the breeding ground of literary opinion, is and always has been inseparable from the very fact of literature. Other milieus are, of course, also touched by the literary work, but only the literary milieu has at its disposal the mental and verbal equipment, as well as the means of communication and expression, indispensable for fruitful and articulate intercourse.

In most cases the writer, who is also a reader, belongs to the literary milieu and takes part in the exchange of ideas and judgments. Even in the few cases when he lives apart from the literary world or belongs to an altogether different social set, he cannot escape being aware of the response of the literary milieu to his works and being influenced by it. Few writers are able to refrain from reading the reviews of their books, and those who do cannot ignore the reactions of their publishers, who in their turn are affected by literary opinion.

We are thus led to conceive of literature as a two-way communication in which an original message is broadcast by the writer to a community of readers, whose response to him takes the shape of thoughts, words, acts, and other messages, which react on one another and on the writer himself.

The pattern is made still more complicated by the fact that in normal circumstances many such messages are passed simultaneously to and fro and interfere with one another, while unsuspected readers or communities of readers beyond the social, educational, linguistic, or national borders may catch the message and unexpectedly add their own distortions to the jumble.

Last but not least, the literary milieu being part of a broader society and the writer being also a citizen, the whole network of literary intercourse is subject to all the conditions imposed by social life. In fact the amplitude, the significance, the richness—in short, the human worth—of literature depends to a large extent on the place occupied by the literary milieu and consequently by the writers in the society concerned, on their awareness of their situation, and on the assumption of the responsibilities implied by it. It was such a consideration which led Jean-Paul Sartre to make *engagement* the basis of all literary values.

Literary recognition and opinion

Since the writer exists as such only in the eyes of a reading community, the first problem to solve is that of recognition—that is, who is considered to be a writer by the reading public. The problem is easily understood from the following figures. If we count the names of all the writers retained by the historical memory of a given nation—that is, the writers mentioned in the histories of literature, the encyclopedias, the school or university curricula, the academic theses, the erudite articles published in specialized reviews, the papers read in symposia and congresses—we find that they represent about 1 per cent of the number who actually wrote and published literary books. (For example, in France between 1500 and 1900 about 1,000 out of 100,000 were remembered).

The severity of this elimination has been confirmed by the American psychologist Harvey C. Lehman, who conducted a poll among educated circles in the United States to find out which were the books of recognized importance. Out of the 733 "best books" by 488 authors named, Lehman found 337 books by 203 deceased authors and 396 books by 285 living authors (Lehman 1937). Many similar experiments have been conducted, and they all point to the fact that the historical image of literature in a given community includes a roughly equal number of contemporary and past writers. This means that the production of the more than 30 years which may be considered contemporary balances what remains of the production of several centuries. Furthermore, according

to the findings of the Centre de Sociologie des Faits Littéraires in Bordeaux, France, 90 per cent of the books are eliminated after 1 year and 99 per cent after 20 years. Similar conclusions may be reached through a study of reprints (Schulz [1952] 1960, pp. 104–105).

How, by whom, and according to what criteria is the selection made? A certain amount of contemporary literary recognition is of course necessary. In spite of persistent legends, no book was ever reclaimed after *total* failure at its first appearance. Yet, immediate success is by no means a guarantee of survival. A best seller may be forgotten within a year and a low-sale book remembered for centuries. The picture of a given literature revealed by the contemporary comments of past critics is quite different from the historical picture later presented at school; all students of literature have been told time and again of the instances of "bad taste" displayed by their forefathers.

Education plays an important part in the selection. For example, a survey of French army recruits (Institut . . . 1966) showed that the type of education determines the choice of "noteworthy" authors. French elementary education, with its republican and rationalistic traditions, strongly stresses the eighteenth century, while high school education, with its more bourgeois and conservative leanings, gives the seventeenth century a predominant position. In all cases the number of contemporary and past writers is fairly equal. However, the choices of the recruits with a low educational level were largely stereotyped: their choice of past authors reflected school memories; their choice of present authors bore the stamp of modern mass media. In contrast the choices of the university students were widely differentiated. Moreover, the higher the level of education, the narrower the chronological gap between past and contemporary authors. While in the case of nearly illiterate recruits there may be a "no man's land" of fifty years between the last of the deceased and the first of the living authors, in the case of highly educated recruits there is no gap, but rather a continuously increasing number of choices.

The opinion-leading group is not simply defined by education and social status; age is also important. Lehman (1945) showed that 40 is a critical age for the literary survival of a writer: works published after a writer reaches 40 are more easily forgotten than those published before. The reason is that most writers are recognized as such between the ages of 20 and 30 by readers belonging to a similar age group. This is the average recognition age for novelists. It may come earlier for lyric poets, and it always comes later for philosophers, a fact which leads to the delusion that poets are short-lived and philosophers hard to kill. In any case a writer seldom changes the clientele which ensured his initial success. The age group which first recognized him carries him along his career and offers him a support in literary opinion until shortly after the group reaches 40, and its influence is superseded by that of younger and more numerous readers. Therefore, about fifteen years after recognition all writers have an appointment with oblivion unless, as sometimes happens, they are taken up by the new opinion leaders and start a career afresh.

Another element which determines the composition of the opinion-leading group is the existence of social and political structures that limit literary exchange. Social stratification is a permanent structure of this type. A society in which the bulk of production is regulated by the demands of a moneyed minority is characterized by a very narrow opinion-leading group, which imposes its taste in wholesale fashion on the masses. The phenomenon is less perceptible in literature than in *haute couture* or in gastronomy, for instance, because reading is a more serious occupation than designing clothing or preparing food and the hold of the higher classes on it is less strong. But the moneyed minority delegates its powers to the hybrid stratum of the intellectuals who in fact belong to the working class but live—at least culturally—on the same level as the wealthy.

Class structure and political structure are, of course, strongly linked to one another, and the state imposes even more demanding limits on literary exchange than does the stratification system. A calculation based on the average age of writers in France (Escarpit 1965, pp. 27–29) shows that the rhythm of the literary generations (Peyre 1948) is determined by the succession of the various regimes in that country. Great reigns like that of Louis XIV in France or Elizabeth I or Victoria in Great Britain and new political eras like those which began in 1792 for France, in 1865 for the United States, and in 1871 for Germany are always marked by the establishment of a powerful and comparatively young (25 to 35) team of writers. This team expresses the national literature and blocks the way to fresh recognitions until it in turn is eliminated by age or by a new historical change.

Political influence is also exerted through the existence of national borders, which partition literary life by erecting various obstacles to the free flow of books. However, a customs barrier, although its role must not be minimized, seems nowadays to be one of the least insurmountable obstacles. Furthermore, national markets tend to expand, and some countries like the Netherlands have a foreign book market quite disproportionate to their actual literary production: in 1961 it was equal to that of France or West Germany. Yet even internationally we find an opinion-leading minority based on economic power. The United Kingdom and the United States, with their huge industrial and financial machines and their almost universal language, account for nearly two-thirds of the Western book market. On the other hand, they import few books and translate still fewer, being practically self-sufficient (Escarpit 1965).

For most other countries language is a more effective barrier than customs. The 1,200 million potential readers in the world (probably no more than 200 to 300 million of whom are habitual readers) are distributed in more than a hundred linguistic enclosures. Yet five languages (English, Russian, Spanish, German, and French) account for 75 per cent of the world book production and 40 per cent of the readers. All the other language units suffer either from a scarcity of readers or from a scarcity of writers (the case of Communist China is passed over for want of verified data). Translation in its present form and organization is not adequate to remedy this disparity, since much fewer than 10 per cent of the books published in the world are translated into another language and nearly 75 per cent of these come from English, Russian, French, and German.

In sum, the minority responsible for the literary recognition of writers and for the elaboration of literary opinion can be defined as the university-educated intellectuals belonging to the influential circles (moneyed class, "upper crust," high political or technical strata) of the five highly developed economic powers with an important mass of population and a widely spread language: the United States, the United Kingdom, the Soviet Union, Germany, and France—a bare ten or fifteen million people.

Literature in mass civilization

The above may seem a pessimistic view and a difficult one to reconcile with contemporary mass culture.

The problem is not really new even if its dimensions are. Several times in the history of written culture the book, as well as the literature it spread, went through sudden mutations, under the pressure of fresh masses of readers. With the spread of Christian culture, the book evolved from the connoisseurs' *volumen* of ancient Rome to the easily handled *codex*; then to the hand-printed book when a comparatively well-educated urban upper class enjoyed enough leisure to afford the already flourishing bookseller a commercially workable field; then to the machine-printed hardbound volume of the nineteenth century, when the triumph of the bourgeoisie and the establishment of the capitalist system allowed the creation of an actual market for cultural productions; and finally, in our own time, to the paperback.

The scale of readership changed from the hundred to the thousand, from the hundred thousand to the million. But the change was qualitative as well as quantitative. At each stage, the form of the book met the specific demand of the leading minority and was conceived for one definite type of literature. All the rest—that is, the actual cultural material consumed by the masses of people—was considered as despicable subliterature until the pressure of social changes brought about a shift in the opinion-leading group. This shift was both cause and effect of each technical mutation of the book and led to total revisions of literary values.

In the eyes of the Latin-reading clerk of the Middle Ages the chivalric tales written in the vulgar Romance language (hence the word "romance") were frivolous and meaningless subliterature, but those tales were transformed into legitimate, even noble, literature when printing shifted the responsibility of literary opinion to the urban upper class. The same happened to the novel; despised as "female reading" at the beginning of the eighteenth century, it became the absolute sovereign of literature in the nineteenth, when mechanized printing allowed editions of 100,000 copies for the triumphant middle class, as against the average 2,000 or 3,000 copies of the previous century.

Marginal reading material for the consumption of the masses has always existed side by side with official literature. Long made up of broadsheets, almanacs, and chapbooks disseminated by itinerant storytellers and hawkers, it now takes the shape of illustrated magazines, comics, and photonovels. This literature must not be underestimated, since great works originate in it when it is accepted by the officialdom of a new literary milieu, but it lacks the essential of literary communication: the feedback from the reader to the writer through the medium of the literary milieu.

This feedback is normally ensured not only by the diffuse crosscurrents existing in the literary milieu but by a network of specific institutions, among which literary criticism and book selling are predominant.

There is no such thing as literary criticism for popular literature like comics now or chapbooks in past centuries. Even when the popular paperbacks are devoted to the publication of recognized works the professional critics hesitate to review them, a fact often lamented by publishers. The literary critic serves less as a guide than as a voice of the cultured public's taste. He is, so to speak, a sample of the literary milieu. His judgments may reflect a great variety of aesthetic, political, or religious opinions, but they all bear testimony to a particular culture and way of life.

In the case of the bookseller one must distinguish the real bookshops, characterized by an autonomous commercial policy based principally on the sale of books, from the mere book outlets, exercising little or no responsibility in the choice of literary goods offered for sale. These outlets may range from newspaper stands to specialized departments in general or chain stores or even huge "book cafeterias."

The part played by the true bookseller in literary communication is an important one. He has to make a responsible choice from the overwhelming literary production. The wrong choices could dangerously burden his stock and clutter up his window, since after one year 90 per cent of what is produced is unsalable. The choices he makes for his stock are influenced by his current sales to all kinds of occasional customers, but those he makes for his window reflect the cultural image that his opinion-leading clientele has of itself. The greater the discrepancy between the composition of the stock and the contents of the window, the higher the efficiency of the bookseller as an intermediary in literary communication, but the narrower his field of influence (Escarpit & Robine 1963).

At ordinary points of sale there is practically no difference between the stock and the window, and the salesman transmits no response from the people who buy reading material in his shop. Such is the case in most places where books are sold. Surveys on the topography of book distribution show that bookshops selling quality books in a responsible way are concentrated in districts of the cities which are rarely visited by working people, at least during business hours.

A commercial policy in the majority of sales points cannot therefore be based on an awareness of the readers' reactions. Books are sold like any other industrial product. Their contents, as well as their presentations, are elaborated according to proved specifications—some of them age-old—

simply enhanced or glamorized by modern techniques. Analysis shows that the difference between the almanacs of past centuries and contemporary magazines lies mainly in language, paper, printing, color, and advertising; the contents—a mixture of horoscopes, amusements, sentimental stories, and recipes—are practically unchanged.

The publisher of mass-circulation books is thus confronted with a difficult problem. "Creative" publishing demands that he make numerous and necessarily hazardous experiments, offering the output of new talents to a responsive public. Yet he must, in view of the substantial capital involved, reduce the risks of his operation either by limiting the experimental field to the cultured elite or by abandoning the idea of "creative" publishing and strictly programming his production—that is, making it conform to the functional needs of a preselected mass market.

The latter solution leads to the exclusive publication either of semitechnical works like cookbooks and "do-it-yourself" manuals or of stereotyped reading matter ranging from the lowest kind of subliterature—comics, photonovels—to mechanically produced biographies and historical novels based on standard popular themes.

The former solution may seem more constructive, but it has a twofold drawback. The stock of time-proved classics to be reprinted is not inexhaustible—a few thousand at most—and the supply of contemporary best sellers that can be successfully tried out in the cultured network is very limited. Furthermore, these best sellers have been recognized as such by a public socially and culturally different from the mass public, and this leads to an imposition of literary values from without; a situation quite contrary to a real literary exchange. Such a "bestowed" literature is doomed either to intellectual sclerosis or to the paralyzing conventionality of officialdom.

The mass-distribution book (paperback, *livre de poche*, *Taschenbuch*, etc.) affords the technical means of a fresh mutation of the book as a means of cultural communication. Based on a combination of mass production and industrial design, it makes possible a substantial reduction of price, combined with a convenient size, a pleasant appearance, and quality contents. The principle was first successfully applied by Allen Lane when, in 1935, he founded the British Penguin series. During World War II the need to supply the widely scattered Allied forces with handy and cheap reading material accelerated the diffusion of the paperback, which by 1950 had spread all over the world, upsetting the traditional patterns of publishing. In the United States the revolution was particularly spectacular. In the 1940s a sale of over 100,000 copies for a single title was considered exceptional, while twenty years later several paperbacks sold well over a million copies a year.

Yet the paperback is nothing but a tool. It cannot solve all problems, and indeed it may raise some fresh ones. As a tool, it is useless and might even become dangerous unless attention is paid to the reactions and needs of the reading public.

The sociology of reading

No sociology of literature is therefore possible without a sociology of reading and of cultural consumption in general. Much has been done in that direction since Schücking's pioneer work on the sociology of literary taste. Such men as R. D. Altick (1957) opened the way to a historical field of investigation which is now widely explored. On the other hand, methods for the study of reading, *in vivo* so to speak, were borrowed from economics by P. Meyer-Dohm (1957) and from the sociology of leisure by J. Dumazedier and J. Hassenforder (1963).

Although the consumption of drama is quite different from that of the book, John Lough's studies of early theater audiences (1957) and J. Duvignaud's later and more complete work (1965) are also relevant to the sociology of reading.

The main obstacle to a sociology of reading is that, unlike a theater audience, a reading public is not easily defined. One must not mistake the various social circles concerned about literary work for the mass of actual readers, whose size, composition, coherence, and group consciousness vary with each book.

Any writer, consciously or not, addresses prospective readers when he writes; any publisher directs his publication toward an expected public when he plans the manufacture and distribution of the volume; both the writer and the publisher more or less belong to a milieu of possible readers. Each of those publics plays an essential part in the birth and life of the literary work, although few or none of its members may ever read it. There are, of course, instances of books written for a hundred readers and published in a comparatively narrow milieu of a few thousand persons but ultimately read by millions; however, the opposite case is much more common.

The cases of books reaching unexpected and even unsuspected publics beyond social, national, linguistic, or temporal barriers are becoming more numerous. Of course there must always be an environment of contemporary readers to accept a book at the outset, but even though the existence of such an environment is indispensable, its size and composition may have nothing to do with those of the wider or later groups which will ultimately ensure the success of the book. Indeed, in most cases the later success of a book is due to causes quite foreign to those of the initial success. While the set of readers which was first responsible for the literary recognition of the work shared the historical and cultural experiences of the writer, spoke the same language, and thought according to similar patterns, groups which have no direct contact with the writer's world have no other recourse than to substitute their own keys for the original ones in order to decode the text which is handed down to them.

In fact, reading any work outside the immediate social or historical vicinity of the writer—and a fortiori reading it in translation—implies a betrayal of the writer's intentions, since absolute fidelity would imply a complete reconstruction of the writer's psychological and social environment, a condition which may be partly and painstakingly fulfilled by scholars, but which is in no way compatible with current literary reading.

We must then admit that a literary work, insofar as it survives its time, is permanently reinterpreted and redigested by various groups of readers. Those synchronic or diachronic layers of meaning which are added to it together form its true historical personality. The literary death of a book occurs when no further interpretation or misinterpretation of it can be given. We are thus led to consider "creative treason" as one of the main keys to the literary phenomenon (Escarpit 1961). By "creative treason" we mean an unconscious or deliberate misconstruction of the author's actual intentions when he wrote the book. This reinterpretation may bring out a latent significance of the work of which the author himself may not have been aware or add an unsuspected meaning that can even replace the original one. The most typical examples are Swift's *Gulliver's Travels* and Defoe's *Robinson Crusoe*, which were originally intended as serious works, with a philosophical message, and are now widely read as children's books.

Obviously many books which had a tremendous but short-lived and localized success were never "betrayed" and died soon. Others, in contrast, starting from a comparatively narrow acceptance, continued for centuries to call up wider, deeper, and stronger responses. The question may be raised whether the likelihood of being betrayed is due to some specific quality of the work and not the audience. Such a surmise is quite plausible and points

to one of the ways in which the sociology of literature might help to found a system of literary values.

Such an objective is still beyond our grasp. We can for the time being only strive toward it along three lines of investigation. The first consists in studying the material conditions of reading so that its place in everyday life is clearly defined. According to the periods considered this may be done by historians or by sociologists. Applied to our time such a study may reveal the relationship of reading to the various forms of mass communication and cultural consumption like cinema, radio, television, records, etc. Another approach, mainly psychological or sociopsychological, tends to identify the various motivations and attitudes of readers according to sex, age, occupation, educational level, social class, IQ, etc. Typical patterns of behavior may thus be traced and linked to the factors that influence them. The third approach is through the study of the language of literary appreciation. A project for an international dictionary of literary terms was begun in 1962 by the International Comparative Literature Association. An effort is also being made—particularly in Bordeaux—to investigate the aesthetic vocabulary used by readers of the working class, in order to grasp the mechanism of literary appreciation among readers whose literary opinion is seldom voiced.

The aims and applications of the sociology of literature thus become clearer. Applied to past periods it may help to evolve a new type of historical criticism more directly linked to economic and social history than traditional formal criticism has been. Sociological criticism will never reveal the intimate nature of literary "creation" or supply a universal and eternal criterion of "beauty," but in spite of often stated ambitions, no criticism of any kind ever did or ever will.

More important still, the sociology of literature applied to contemporary problems may, on the one hand, help the persons or agencies responsible for book policy in the various regions of the world to take stock of the new problems raised by mass civilization and may, on the other hand, help the hitherto ignored masses of readers to gain aesthetic consciousness and claim their part of mankind's cultural heritage. It may ruffle a number of connoisseurs, comfortable in their minority culture, who would prefer to ignore what happens beyond their narrow intellectual circle. It may disturb more seriously and even revolt a number of writers who never wondered whence and whither the wind that blows through them. But no true lover of culture—

reader, critic, or writer—will suffer, in the long run, from a clear-sighted awareness of social realities.

ROBERT ESCARPIT

[See also COMMUNICATION, MASS; CREATIVITY; DRAMA; INTELLECTUALS; INTERACTION, article on DRAMATISM; SOCIAL SCIENCE FICTION; and the biography of LUKÁCS. A guide to other relevant material may be found under ART.]

BIBLIOGRAPHY

ALTICK, RICHARD D. 1957 The English Common Reader: A Social History of the Mass Reading Public, 1800–1900. Univ. of Chicago Press.

DUMAZEDIER, JOFFRE; and HASSENFORDER, JEAN 1963 Éléments pour une sociologie comparée de la production, de la diffusion et de l'utilisation du livre. Paris: Bibliographie de la France.

DUVIGNAUD, JEAN 1965 Sociologie du théâtre. Paris: Presses Universitaires de France.

ESCARPIT, ROBERT C. E. G. (1958) 1965 Sociology of Literature. Painesville, Ohio: Lake Erie College Press. → First published in French.

ESCARPIT, ROBERT C. E. G. 1961 "Creative Treason" as a Key to Literature. Yearbook of Comparative and General Literature 10:16–21.

ESCARPIT, ROBERT C. E. G. 1963 L'acte littéraire est-il un acte de communication? Filološki pregled (Belgrade) 1/2:17–21.

ESCARPIT, ROBERT C. E. G. (1965) 1966 The Book Revolution. Rev. ed. Paris: UNESCO; London: Harrap. → First published in French.

ESCARPIT, ROBERT C. E. G.; and ROBINE, NICOLE 1963 Atlas de la lecture à Bordeaux. Université de Bordeaux, Faculté des Lettres et Sciences Humaines, Centre de Sociologie des Faits Littéraires, Publications. Bordeaux: La Faculté.

GOLDMANN, LUCIEN 1950 Matérialisme dialectique et histoire de la littérature. Revue de métaphysique et de morale 55:283–301.

GOLDMANN, LUCIEN 1964 Pour une sociologie du roman. Paris: Gallimard.

HOGGART, RICHARD 1966 Literature and Society. American Scholar 35:277–289.

INSTITUT DE LITTÉRATURE ET DE TECHNIQUES ARTISTIQUES DE MASSE, UNIVERSITÉ DE BORDEAUX 1966 Le livre et le conscrit: Les jeunes recrues devant la lecture. → A survey of the reading habits of the recruits conducted by R. Escarpit and N. Robine at the Army Induction Center at Limoges.

LEHMAN, HARVEY C. 1937 The Creative Years: "Best Books." Scientific Monthly 45:65–75.

LEHMAN, HARVEY C. 1945 "Intellectual" Versus "Physical" Peak Performance: The Age Factor. Scientific Monthly 61:127–137.

LOUGH, JOHN 1957 Paris Theatre Audiences in the 17th and 18th Centuries. Oxford Univ. Press.

LUKÁCS, GYÖRGY 1961 Schriften zur Literatursoziologie. Edited by Peter Ludz. Berlin: Luchterhand.

MEYER-DOHM, PETER 1957 Der westdeutsche Büchermarkt. Stuttgart: Fischer.

PEYRE, HENRI 1948 Les générations littéraires. Paris: Boivin.

PICHOIS, CLAUDE 1961 En marge de l'histoire littéraire: Vers une sociologie historique des faits littéraires. Revue d'histoire littéraire de la France 61:48–57.

PLEKHANOV, GEORGII V. (1899) 1953 Art and Social Life. London: Lawrence & Wishart. → A collection of Plekhanov's principal writings on art and society. First published in Russian.

SARTRE, JEAN-PAUL (1948) 1949 What Is Literature? New York: Philosophical Library. → First published in French.

SCHÜCKING, LEVIN L. (1931) 1950 The Sociology of Literary Taste. London: Routledge. → First published in German.

SCHULZ, HANS FERDINAND (1952) 1960 Das Schicksal der Bücher und der Buchhandel: System einer Vertriebskunde des Buches. 2d ed., rev. & enl. Berlin: Gruyter.

STAËL-HOLSTEIN, GERMAINE DE (1800) 1959 De la littérature considérée dans ses rapports avec les institutions sociales. Edited by Paul van Tieghem. Geneva: Droz.

II
THE PSYCHOLOGY OF LITERATURE

The psychology of literature is an emerging, rather than an established, discipline. We can distinguish three aspects or stages in its development, although these are not sharply defined. First is the insertion of psychological questions and theories into the predominantly aesthetic or historical writing of students of literature. Second is the writing of psychologists who seek to explain and interpret literary works by means of theories and techniques developed in other contexts. Third is the psychological analysis of literature by those who try to adjust their method to the peculiar nature of the subject matter and who hope to make discoveries rather than to impose stock explanations. The present article, inevitably narrow in scope, will be organized loosely around these categories in an effort to sample the writings of the contemporary period.

As one of the most distinctive of human activities, literature would seem to be a natural focus of psychological inquiry. How it is produced, how it affects those who enjoy it, what it reveals concerning the author and his society—these are questions that have occupied major thinkers from early times. Psychology of literature is referred to in standard works on literary criticism, and a recent bibliography of the field lists thousands of relevant titles (Kiell 1963). Yet textbooks of psychology rarely mention either literature or psychology of literature. The paradox is partly explained by the positivistic restrictions of psychology and partly by the elusiveness of literature when approached by science.

Nature of literature. Some conception of literature necessarily precedes scientific study of it. Permanent material documents do exist that can be called repositories of literature, but these documents are simply a modern device for bringing author and reader together in the literary transaction. At an earlier time, essentially the same transaction took place by oral means, aided by gestures and pantomime and often by instrumental music, and nothing was stored in documents. Human memory and capacity for improvisation sufficed. The modern reader is a step removed from the early pantomime, but only a step. He can still turn the written words into spoken ones, and, if he is artistically sensitive, he is likely to do so. He can also, to some extent, experience the various kinds of imagery intended by the words, and, through the sound and imagery and temporal structure of the composition, participate in moods, attitudes, and values that may have acted as initiating and sustaining forces for the author. According to this view, literature is a process of expression by an author which induces a corresponding process of reception in a reader. The process in the reader is not necessarily equivalent to the process in the author, but it is such as to bind him to the author. Literature exists in that union. The author can, of course, be his own reader. This circular transaction, however, is typically not enough; the impulse of authorship moves toward communication.

Imperfect as this characterization of literature is, a scientific approach must be regulated by some such reflections; and since it appears that the literary process requires the scientific observer to be an intimate part of what he observes, it is evident that the methodological problem is grave.

Psychology in general discourse

The bulk of literary criticism falls in the first of the three categories mentioned above. Much of it does not pretend to be psychological. Some of it, however, consciously employs psychological language and theory to dress up, supplement, or govern the critical discussion. Rare are those works that are deeply imbued with psychology and are still, in the main, appreciative. An example is Bodkin's *Archetypal Patterns in Poetry* (1934). Exploring literature from a Jungian base, this book seeks to locate the meeting ground of author and reader in the universal symbols of the collective unconscious. The theory is not merely decorative; it controls the analysis throughout, although it is in turn controlled by mature literary taste.

The creative process. Lowes, in *The Road to Xanadu* (1927), an examination of Coleridge's vast reading as it contributed to the composition of his poetry, is more concerned with the author's part. The thesis that Lowes favors is that the poetic imagination is a variant of ordinary imagi-

nation, depending on the accumulation of miscellaneous images, the mingling and transformation of these in "the deep well of unconscious cerebration" (Henry James), their recovery in consciousness at the prompting of some stimulus, and their utilization in expression. Lowes's psychology is mainly British associationism. From Coleridge he draws such psychological phrases as "twilight realms of consciousness," "state of nascent existence in the twilight of imagination and just on the vestibule of consciousness," and "the streamy nature of associations, which thinking curbs and rudders." To this source of insight Lowes adds introspections of his own on dream and fantasy, and he acknowledges from personal experience that literary erudition and subliminal associative activity are not enough to produce a masterpiece of poetry. He does not explain the needed additional factor, but he refers to it under the terms "vision" and "will."

Lowes is not quite faithful to the author he admires. He reduces Coleridge's fundamental distinction between imagination and fancy to a mere intensity difference in the imaginative energy and ignores the distinction between primary and secondary imagination. For Coleridge, imagination is creative and esemplastic, making and shaping into organic unity, while fancy can only join together mechanically what imagination supplies. Fancy is thus removed some distance from the living I AM, "of imagination all compact," which stands at the source of all created things, whether universe (primary imagination) or poem (secondary). By the phrase "I AM" Coleridge designates the ultimate principle of God or the human soul. As the I AM of God creates the world, so the I AM of the human soul creates poetry. The poet's creative activity, "This light, this glory, this fair luminous mist, / This beautiful and beauty-making power," to use the words of his ode on "Dejection," is essentially joy, the joy of the soul in its own life. Coleridge's distinctions and the terms in which he makes them are the reaction of a poet to the inadequacy of Hartleian associationism for explaining poetry. In dwelling on association, Lowes, from Coleridge's point of view, would be regressing. From our point of view, Lowes may be seen as moving toward the new "associationism" of Freud, who has equally little room for the Coleridgean I AM but must agree with him that association depends more on recurring similar states of feeling than on ideas (Richards 1934, p. 68 in 1960 edition).

Poetry and dream. In agreement with Coleridge and Freud on the importance of feeling is Prescott, whose *The Poetic Mind* (1922) is an expansion of his earlier essays on the connection between poetry and dream. Prescott's agreement with Freud must not be overstressed. Like Freud he invokes the unconscious; distinguishes two modes of thought (practical and dreaming); closely identifies poetry with dream; emphasizes unfulfilled desire as the motive for both; makes use of the ideas of condensation, displacement, and projection; and otherwise shows an appreciation of Freudian principles. But, on the other hand, Prescott traces these principles to earlier sources, warns against the sterility of psychological science rigorously applied to literature, and takes particular exception to Freud's basic assumption that there is a latent dream content behind the manifest dream. For Prescott both literature and dream are direct, not cryptogrammic, expressions of the mind. He specifically compares poetic creation to sexual generation or the divine genesis of the universe.

Especially in his chapter on the formation of imaginary characters Prescott emphasizes the power of the mind to create. Fictional characters are held to be autogenous objectifications of the mind's tendencies. Although there are also exogenous characters, these exist in the literary composition because of their congruency with the author's desires. Prescott's emphasis has some relation to Coleridge's theory of the primacy of the I AM. That is, Prescott regards poetic creation as more than the concatenation and blending of ideas, whether in the Hartleian or the Freudian style—which would be what Coleridge calls "fancy"; it involves the vital participation of a real being, even to the extent of passing on to fictional characters a portion of real life. Thus it can happen that "the author divides himself to form characters" (Prescott 1922, p. 201 in 1959 edition).

Author types. One of Prescott's examples for the proposition that an author becomes divided into quasi-independent imaginary characters is the French dramatist François de Curel, studied by Binet. Unfortunately, Prescott does not consider Binet's later study of Paul Hervieu and his further reflections on this problem (Binet 1904).

Binet studied a number of contemporary authors by personal interview, including some formal testing, and by analysis of their lives and works. He attempted to sum up his impressions of the creative process by invoking two opposed mental forces, "imagination" and "critical function," the former tending to embody itself in more or less autonomous personal beings, the latter tending to inhibit or suppress this process. He put authors in three classes with respect to the relative strength of these

tendencies. There are those like de Curel, in whom the critical function is suspended during the period of creative activity and the imagination-produced characters use the writer as an amanuensis or sort of trance medium. There are those like Victorien Sardou, in whom the opposition between the two mental forces continues, but the critical function itself becomes one or more of the autonomous persons, participating in the dramatic dialogue with other persons more charged with the imaginative force. (Perhaps, to use a modern analogy, the case would be like that of a social psychologist serving as a "participant–observer" in some passionate social organization and using the opportunity to undermine the fully engaged members.) Finally, there are those like Hervieu, in whom the critical function remains in control so completely that the imaginary characters never achieve full autonomy, being themselves rather the puppets through which the voice of the master speaks. In all three types, however, according to Binet, the literary work reveals the personality of the producer.

Psychoanalytic explanation

As is evident from the preceding discussion, the psychoanalytic influence has been felt everywhere in the study of literature. A varied collection of essays showing this influence at its best has been edited by Phillips (1957). Yet, as the first shock of Freud's innovations has worn off, it has become apparent that the general theory of an emotional, orectic, unconscious origin of literature was not new and that the distinctive psychoanalytic explanatory apparatus—the Oedipus complex, polymorphous-perverse infantile sexuality, the devious dream work—as employed in the interpretation of individual literary works and their authors has yielded dubious results. Long before Freud, Dowden was explicitly pursuing the aim of deducing Shakespeare's personality from his dramas (1875). The psychoanalytic studies in this genre, in comparison, often seem less judicious. Probably the best is the Ernest Jones study, *Hamlet and Oedipus* (1949), which soberly develops the idea proposed by Freud that Hamlet and his creator could be explained by the Oedipus complex.

The seeming arbitrariness of psychoanalytic explanation stems from Freud's theory of the dream (1900), and, by extension, of literature. The dream is supposed to be a coded message from the unconscious. The code consists of certain stereotyped, universal symbols, plus many individual symbols produced by very complex dreamwork. These individual symbols cannot be decoded accurately without the aid of the dreamer's free associations. It is a technical fault that in the application of psychoanalysis to literature this theoretical point has often been overlooked, the author's literary "dream" being decoded without benefit of the required associations. But there are other reasons for distrust. For one thing, the Freudian approach at times has an uncomfortable resemblance to the cryptographic approach of the Baconians searching through the plays of Shakespeare for hidden evidence that their candidate, Francis Bacon (Lord Verulam), was the real author.

A more general reason is that literature seems in its basic constitution the very opposite of a cryptogram. Authors on the whole strive to express, not to conceal. It is true, no doubt, that a great literary work is thick with meaning, layer upon layer, and that some layers are more sharply articulated than others; but authors are aware of this and welcome the depth of meaning, in exactly the spirit of an orator who is glad for his voice to take on tremors and intonations that do not seem to be called for by the logic of his argument or the matter-of-factness of his vocabulary. The richness and subtlety of a literary work may elude an ordinary reader, but it is doubtful that such deficiency in sensitivity is to be repaired by imputing conscious or unconscious concealment to the author.

These strictures are not meant to disparage the merit of psychoanalysis as a vivifying influence on the study of literature. Recognition of the depth of literature and its relevance to the concerns of the psychiatrist (and vice versa) cannot be regarded as mistaken. Furthermore, the expansion of outlook engendered by psychoanalysis holds much promise for the future. Too huge for consideration here, but an illustration of the promise, is Jung's study of the Miller fantasies in *Symbols of Transformation* (1912).

Studies concerned with method

Imagery analysis.   To those who value simple and sharable method, the pioneer work of Spurgeon in *Shakespeare's Imagery* makes an instant appeal (1935). Definition of an image is difficult, but there can be practical agreement, she thinks, about these "word-pictures" in similes and metaphors, whether contained in a single word (as in *"ripeness* is all") or spread over a considerable portion of a dramatic scene. Once collected, the images can be classified and counted for the sake of answering various kinds of questions. Thus, she demonstrates that Shakespeare's imagery differs from Marlowe's and Bacon's; and she attempts to draw conclusions as to Shakespeare's favorite haunts (for example, gardens), particular experiences (for example,

noticing an eddy in the Avon below the eighteenth arch of the Old Clopton Bridge), and general character. Undoubtedly, at times she pushes inference too far. For example, from Shakespeare's many references to blushing and other quick emotional changes in fair-skinned faces she concludes that his own face was fair-skinned and of a fresh color. It is questionable whether we have, or can have, principles that fully justify such an argument.

Armstrong has extended Spurgeon's method to the study of image clusters in *Shakespeare's Imagination* (1946). For example, he finds that the images clustering around the goose symbol in many of the plays commonly refer to disease and penal restraint, and somewhat less commonly to music, bitterness, and seasoning. Several such image clusters are studied in detail. There seems to be no doubt that certain images tended to cohere in groups in the dramatist's mind, so strongly indeed that the almost inevitable concatenation often results in surprising turns of thought. Armstrong presses his analysis into (1) hidden images and (2) submerged themes. By the first he means the unspoken image latent in a spoken one (as when reference to wax points to the legend of Icarus); by the second, the adumbration of an understory by the images used in telling the obvious one (as when the Hostess in *Henry IV,* Part II, charges Falstaff with unfaithfulness in terms suggesting the Passion of Christ and the betrayal by Judas). Here he touches on an aspect of method which can hardly be reduced to simple counting and cataloguing. The manifold allusiveness of literature makes for a "thickness" which contrasts with the "thinness" of scientific writing. It is this "thickness" which especially baffles the search for perfectly mechanical procedures. Although Armstrong is convincing at this deeper level of analysis, he does not prescribe the conditions that enable him to be. One condition is obviously possession of the right knowledge, for example, knowledge of the New Testament. Other conditions may be inherently less definable, such as that vague but real thing, literary sensitivity.

Armstrong attempts to state some of the organizing principles of Shakespeare's thought and advances a general theory of imagination. With regard to Shakespeare, he infers that a primitive dualism of the warring opposites of life and death, love and hatred, governs the associations; that the extremely free, rapid, fluent associative activity leads to extraordinary combinations but without loss of organic unity; and that, although the surface of the dramas is relatively bare of religious reference, the depths are often permeated with imagery that gives religious quality to the whole. With regard to imagination in general, he accepts Freud's scheme of unconscious energies working up from a primitive level through a preconscious censorship to produce conscious elements, but he wishes to add to this a reverse direction of work to explain literary creation. He argues that the creator, in directing his will toward a certain achievement, focuses consciousness on obscure points and thus induces processes below the threshold to respond with a solution. The mid-region of the Freudian preconscious censorship (a phrase that may suggest to strict Freudians a misunderstanding of Freud) becomes for Armstrong a region of selective subconscious association where liberating as well as restricting functions occur. His theory thus tries to overcome a one-sided emphasis on pathogenic defense, repression, and disguise, in order to accommodate the full, open, creative expressiveness of artistic imagination.

Analysis of plot and and character.   Among American personality theorists, Murray has shown an unusual degree of interest in literature and has made a vital connection between literature and the clinic through his Thematic Apperception Test (TAT). The TAT stimuli (pictures) are used to elicit stories, and these are analyzed as revealing the personality of the storyteller, particularly his unconscious complexes (*Explorations* . . . 1938, esp. pp. 530–545). In an admirably concise paper Murray has drawn the parallel between TAT stories and literary masterpieces, as he argues from evidence that authors are reflected in their productions (1943). [*See* PROJECTIVE METHODS, *article on* THE THEMATIC APPERCEPTION TEST.]

Murray reports that experience with numerous college student subjects in the Harvard Psychological Clinic indicates that the personality revealed by analysis of major characters, repeated plots, etc., in TAT stories is consistent with what can be learned in other ways about an individual; for example, judges can successfully match autobiographies against corresponding TAT stories. He finds that TAT authors range from subjective egocentric to objective sociocentric, the former tending to identify consciously with their story heroes. His most definite examples of subjective egocentrism occurred most frequently among students majoring in English, but none of his TAT subjects exhibited the high degree of subjective egocentrism found in the literary geniuses Melville and Wolfe. From these facts it can be inferred that Melville and Wolfe must reveal themselves at least as fully as the students. Murray thinks that literary material can contain infantile complexes and Jungian

archetypes but notes that such unconscious patternings have their support and fulfillment in objective realities. For example, he finds that the Ishmael or social outcast theme, prominent in Melville and Wolfe, is rooted simultaneously in an infantile sense of rejection by the mother (a complex), in the low status of the literary artist in our culture (a sociological fact), and in a long, continuous development of the rebel or Satan myth in the West (a historical fact). In his opinion, analysis of literary works has general validity for personality study, since objective sociocentric authors also reveal themselves as much as the others, although with less awareness.

McCurdy is another worker with a similar interest in analysis of literature as a mode of personality research, and in a series of papers on various authors and a book on Shakespeare (1953) he has attempted to refine method and reach theoretical conclusions. A brief summary of these studies may be found in his textbook on personality (1961, pp. 413–427). McCurdy is phenomenological in outlook, and he views personality as a changing structure of relations between a self and its objects, particularly person objects; or, in other words, as a dynamic social system constituting a personal world. He is therefore inclined to regard a literary work of imagination as a description of the author's world, or at least a significant portion of it, and in analysis to concentrate on such obvious features as the characters and their interactions. To some extent, analysis of plot and character can be quantitative, and McCurdy has explored the possibilities. For example, in his study of the Brontë novels, he quantified the degree of resemblance between the characters by determining the amount of trait overlap in order to be more precise about types of characters and kinship lines between them. In the Shakespeare study, he arrived at weights to represent the relative importance of the characters by counting their speech lines and utilized these weights in several ways. One analysis led to the discovery that the average relative weights of characters within plays follow a simple exponential formula; and this result, which he also obtained for other authors, seems to point to a basic principle of personality organization. In spite of his interest in quantitative procedures, McCurdy would be the last to deny the validity of an impressionistic approach. In fact, he would insist that quantification must be kept subordinate to a nonmetrical understanding capable of grasping wholes, appreciating qualities, and judging values. His persistent hope has been that the study of personality through literature, while leaving room for quantitative and even experimental procedures, might encourage psychologists to recognize important realities that cannot easily be measured.

One can foresee an era of computer research in the psychology of literature, as quantitative methods are clarified and large-scale comparative studies are undertaken. The danger in such a stepping-up of quantification is that it may divert attention even more from the unquantifiable fundamentals of literature. That direction of development is relatively easy. What is harder and more essential is to keep near and draw nearer to the delicate, passionate, living processes of literary creation and exchange. If we could somehow bind our scientific energies to this far more difficult task, we might grow toward a richer form of knowing than hitherto achieved. In the meantime, we may at least take note of the great, apparently unremovable diversity of reader reaction to any given piece of literature (Richards 1929) and consider the problem which that poses for scientific consensus.

HAROLD G. MCCURDY

[See also AESTHETICS; CREATIVITY; DREAMS; FANTASY; PSYCHOANALYSIS.]

BIBLIOGRAPHY

ARMSTRONG, EDWARD A. (1946) 1963 *Shakespeare's Imagination: A Study of the Psychology of Association and Inspiration.* Lincoln: Univ. of Nebraska Press.

BINET, ALFRED 1904 La création littéraire: Portrait psychologique de M. Paul Hervieu. *L'année psychologique* 10:1–62.

BODKIN, MAUD (1934) 1948 *Archetypal Patterns in Poetry: Psychological Studies of Imagination.* New York: Oxford Univ. Press. → A paperback edition was published in 1963.

DOWDEN, EDWARD (1875) 1957 *Shakespeare: A Critical Study of His Mind and Art.* London: Routledge.

Explorations in Personality: A Clinical and Experimental Study of Fifty Men of College Age. By Henry A. Murray et al. 1938 London and New York: Oxford Univ. Press.

FREUD, SIGMUND (1900) 1953 *The Interpretation of Dreams.* 2 vols. London: Hogarth; New York: Macmillan. → First published as *Die Traumdeutung.* Constitutes Volumes 4 and 5 of *The Standard Edition of the Complete Psychological Works of Sigmund Freud.* A paperback edition was published in 1962 by Science Editions.

GHISELIN, BREWSTER (editor) 1952 *The Creative Process: A Symposium.* Berkeley: Univ. of California Press. → A paperback edition was published in 1955 by the New American Library.

HYMAN, STANLEY E. 1948 *The Armed Vision: A Study in the Methods of Modern Literary Criticism.* New York: Knopf. → A paperback edition was published in 1955 by Vintage Books.

JONES, ERNEST 1949 *Hamlet and Oedipus.* London: Gollancz. → A paperback edition was published in 1954 by Doubleday.

JUNG, CARL G. (1912) 1956 *Collected Works.* Volume 5: Symbols of Transformation: An Analysis of the Prelude to a Case of Schizophrenia. New York: Pantheon. → First published in German.

KIELL, NORMAN 1963 *Psychoanalysis, Psychology, and Literature: A Bibliography.* Madison: Univ. of Wisconsin Press.

LOWES, JOHN L. 1927 *The Road to Xanadu: A Study in the Ways of the Imagination.* New York: Houghton Mifflin. → A revised paperback edition was published in 1964.

McCURDY, HAROLD G. 1953 *The Personality of Shakespeare: A Venture in Psychological Method.* New Haven: Yale Univ. Press.

McCURDY, HAROLD G. 1961 *The Personal World: An Introduction to the Study of Personality.* New York: Harcourt.

MAURON, CHARLES (1950) 1963 *Introduction to the Psychoanalysis of Mallarmé.* Berkeley: Univ. of California Press. → First published in French.

MURRAY, HENRY A. 1943 Personality and Creative Imagination. Pages 139–162 in English Institute, *Annual: 1942.* New York: Columbia Univ. Press.

PHILLIPS, WILLIAM (editor) 1957 *Art and Psychoanalysis.* New York: Criterion.

PRESCOTT, FREDERICK C. 1922 *The Poetic Mind.* Ithaca: Cornell Univ. Press. → A paperback edition was published in 1959.

RICHARDS, IVOR A. 1929 *Practical Criticism: A Study of Literary Judgment.* London: Routledge; New York: Harcourt. → A paperback edition was published in 1956.

RICHARDS, I. A. (1934) 1962 *Coleridge on Imagination.* 3d ed. London: Routledge.

SPURGEON, CAROLINE F. E. (1935) 1961 *Shakespeare's Imagery, and What It Tells Us.* Cambridge Univ. Press.

III

POLITICAL FICTION

Politics has to do with the public exercise of power; political fiction, with the understanding and appraisal of those who are the subjects or objects of this exercise of power. Some writers of political fiction emphasize understanding, others appraisal. In the first case their work, if successful, approaches scientific theory in its insightful understanding of the dynamics of political power. In the second, mere appraisal without systematic understanding produces polemic or diatribe, which may nevertheless contribute expressively to understanding problems of power.

Fiction, political and nonpolitical

As the line between understanding and judging is often indistinct, so also is the line between fiction that is political and fiction that is not. Ever since political leaders first exercised power over the rest of society, writers have had the elite as subject matter—as Sophocles had in *Antigone*. Ever since ordinary citizens began to exercise overt power, notably during and after the Protestant Reformation and later the industrial revolution, writers have had the additional task of understanding and judging the public exercise of power by both elite and nonelite. This inherent, reciprocal, ancient relationship between the leader and the led, each as the subject and object of power, had not been clearly stated, let alone understood, before the modern activation of ordinary citizens. The infusion of psychological knowledge into culture, notably starting in the twentieth century with Freud, has made it possible to understand and judge political power with a penetration previously rare. Several bold, and a few successful, fictional efforts have been made in this direction. Some of the bolder and more successful ones are discussed below.

Even fiction that is political only by the vaguest of connections, allegorical or otherwise, has had enormous political impact. A very long and rambling Chinese novel, dating from the fifteenth century or before, *Shui hu chuan* (translated in 1933 by Pearl S. Buck under the title *All Men Are Brothers*), has among its themes brigandage, corruption of kings and princes, and the unending effort of valiant, lawless men to destroy the rich and powerful so that the poor and impotent might live in decency and justice. Even before the 1949 revolution a leading Chinese communist called this medieval novel the first communist writing, and it became a kind of guiding light for the revolutionary leaders during the decades before they got full power.

"Ward No. 6," Anton Chekhov's late-nineteenth-century short story about corruption and inefficiency in a lousy Russian hospital, had profound influence on Lenin, epitomizing for him one of the central justifications for the revolutionary drive for power. Comparable in their influence have been the eighteenth-century satires of Jonathan Swift (the most savage, perhaps, being his *Modest Proposal* for solving the population problem in Ireland by selling yearling Irish children to be served as a delicacy on the tables of English gentlemen) and the portrayals of social stench by Charles Dickens in his novels of poverty in Victorian England and by Victor Hugo in France. Harriet Beecher Stowe's polemical novel on early-nineteenth-century slavery in the American South, *Uncle Tom's Cabin* (1852), was itself a contributing cause of the American Civil War and almost a century later infused some animus into the African drive against colonialism following World War II.

Such polemical social fiction, however strong its influence on the climate of political opinion among elite and nonelite, does not, except by portraying the social context, contribute much to understand-

ing or judging political power. By the same token, some ostensibly political fiction, such as Anthony Trollope's *Phineas Finn* (1869), Émile Zola's *His Excellency* (1876), Edwin O'Connor's *The Last Hurrah* (1956), Allen Drury's *Advise and Consent* (1959), and Vladimir Dudintsev's *Not by Bread Alone* (1956), deals with rather peripheral aspects of power. João Guimarães Rosa's *The Devil to Pay in the Backlands* (1956), a Brazilian novel of backland banditry, is curiously reminiscent of the Chinese *All Men Are Brothers* in its preoccupation with primitive moral courage and the search for some justice in a lawless society.

Such fiction indeed involves political issues like corruption, personal integrity, and courage. But it relates these only peripherally to more central issues involved in the exercise of power. Or it only scratches the surface in areas where Dostoevski, Koestler, Orwell, and Mann have excavated deeply. There are books in running brooks, sermons in stones, and politics in everything, but there is also a continuous running babble of political fiction that signifies next to nothing.

The public exercise of power involves man in his relations with the state—that is, his relations with the government and with the citizenry, the public. These relations always include contact between individuals. The contact between one individual and another involves not only appraisal and understanding of the other individual but also appraisal and understanding of oneself.

The protest against unlimited power

The age-old questions of right and wrong, justice, and choice still endure. In recent decades they have been raised anew, in searching analyses of the individual himself, as the agent who chooses between right and wrong, just and unjust. The age-old rote exhortation to exercise power virtuously has in twentieth-century fiction been succeeded by a maturing comprehension of the intimate relations of one individual with others and with himself. Modern writers have boldly explored paths opened by psychologists of both intuitive and empirical orientation and with such modern knowledge have in effect analyzed ancient Greek and Judaic statements of the problem of political power. In the groping exploration of the nineteenth century the Russian Dostoevski had the Grand Inquisitor say in Spanish Seville that mankind wanted bread rather than liberty—wanted to survive but cared not for freedom. In the mid-twentieth century has come the rather antithetical observation that man and society can be enslaved and destroyed only (as Orwell seems to have said) if man, the social animal, is reduced to the point where his survival depends on the grace of an omnipotent Big Brother. To Dostoevski's assertion that men choose bread rather than liberty Orwell replies that this is so only in a tyranny and only when both are not available and choice is therefore impossible. As will be discussed, this thesis raises questions about the nature of man himelf.

Political fiction typically has been written in protest. It has originated not in abstract considerations of man's nature but in concrete appraisal of his circumstances. The protest, more often than not, has been against the social and political *status quo* and has favored some kind of utopia where the contemporary real and evil society and polity are replaced by the good. But with increasing frequency in the mid-twentieth century, the protest has radically criticized the good society envisioned by utopians. It has extrapolated from current developments to their logical conclusion in the polity that ends politics, when the exercise of power is unlimited and controls every human act. Orwell in *1984* finds the origin of this trend in the development of techniques of power by corrupt civilization. With a far more devastating analysis (which he seems to have abandoned in later writing), William Golding in *Lord of the Flies* (1955) finds it in the human soul, released from the restraints of civilization. Orwell says man is socially corrupted; Golding, in this novel, proclaims that man is innately corrupt. Each book is logical; each is equally incredible in its holistic analysis of political action as the product exclusively of either the environment or the organism. Both *1984* and *Lord of the Flies* have, however, set the focus of attention on the human psyche, the point where determining forces, external and internal, do their work and where choice—if the forces are not altogether determining—is made. And, as will appear later, Golding and others have proffered an explanation that is neither strictly environmental nor strictly organic but both.

The economic class struggle

Most political fiction involves status distinctions between people—differences of superiority and inferiority. In one major tributary of writing the status relation arising from economic inequality dominates the appraisal of political power.

A prototype is Thomas More's sixteenth-century *Utopia* (1516), a work of fiction that lacks two of the three classic ingredients of novels, plot and character, but expatiates on a setting that has since become a shibboleth. In Utopia the status distinctions of an England in transition from feudalism

to an open society are eliminated in a classless egalitarianism where virtually everyone enjoys the simplest provision of goods. The few who enjoy a little more do so only in consequence of their feudal but acknowledged exercise of political power, which includes authority not only to maintain order and national defense but also to allocate work. To keep the citizens from becoming accustomed to killing, the slaughter of livestock is done by slaves. People are punished as readily for the intent to commit a crime as for its commission. There are few laws and treaties, men being bound together by love, not words.

Deeply troubled as More was by the misery produced when feudally common pasture lands were enclosed and anti-Catholicism was rampant, his future good society looks like a serene early Christian communism. And it employs supposedly popular coercive measures having the gray-brown drabness and uniformity of the totalitarian slave-labor camps that actually came into being in the twentieth century. The election of top princes by high officials, of high officials by lesser ones, and of lower officials by citizens voting in family units seems more like feudalism stood on its head than like representative democracy. Reacting against the atavism of his time (a breakdown of community and law that seems to occur in all societies in transition), More could propose only a reversion to humanized, equalized, coerced feudalism.

In Émile Zola's *Germinal* (1885) the exploitation theme of More, deriving from English rural poverty, appears in a French industrial setting. The exploiters are not landowners enclosing once-common lands, thereby causing sheep to devour men (as More put it), but mine operators who work their miners to death. One part of the problem is the class system. The other part is the selfishness of man, whether bourgeois or proletarian. Zola abhorred the state of affairs in which the strong devour the weak, in which the lawless aim of each is to acquire power for himself, and in which the ability to love, sexually or otherwise, becomes a means of exploitation. Without resolving the issues of egoism, power, and love, Zola, in Marxist fashion, trusted the power of the proletariat to lay the basis for utopia in the next century by an avenging destruction of the bourgeoisie.

Later novelists have likewise reacted to the class crisis after industrialization, and they have similarly described despair and longed for utopia. The American nineteenth-century Populist Ignatius Donnelly in *Caesar's Column* (1890) carried the injustices of class exploitation to a point, a hypothetical century later, when wealth and political power are joined in the same ruling elite. In *The Iron Heel* (1907), Jack London began the reign of plutocrats soon after the last free election, in 1912, and continued it for three centuries.

Donnelly's solution, following a crisis that arouses the innocent but beastly urban mob, is for the good people to escape to Africa, where they set up their utopia built on brotherly love and protected by a high wall that keeps the outside world out. London's solution arises within man himself, in his reaction against degradation. And it emerges out of the most depressed and ignored class of menial laborers, the "people of the abyss," who join forces with the kept class of skilled workers and with a few natural geniuses motivated by "sheer love of man." Both Donnelly and London were Marxist in their critiques and utopian in their solutions. But London precociously presented a dilemma that has persisted: the relation between unsophisticated, ordinary man and the cosmic superman whom he sees as necessary to salvation from political repression.

London's striking work, like Zola's, avoids a sentimental belief in the simple goodness of mankind and probes more deeply into the human psyche. London clarified the problem of power with a prescience that portended Orwell. In *The Iron Heel* he envisioned new techniques for controlling the minds of the "masses," including a bomb plot faked by the government. He asserted: "Power is not God, not Mammon, but Power." And he had one of his plutocratic "oligarchs" say, "We will grind you revolutionists down under our heel, and we shall walk upon your faces" ([1907] 1958, p. 83). Some forty years later Orwell wrote, in *1984*, "If you want a picture of the future, imagine a boot stamping on a human face—forever" (1949, p. 268).

In *Martin Eden* (1908), London came closest to examining the mind and motivation of his idealized leaders, with their "sheer love of man." In this book the ordinary citizen becomes less an object of sympathy than of pity, and the Nietzschean element in the leader becomes more explicit. London has Martin Eden, torn asunder by his love of both the downtrodden *and* the distinguished, reflect: "Perhaps Nietzsche had been right. Perhaps there was no truth in anything, no truth in truth—no such thing as truth." Eden says, "I am a sick man. . . . It is my soul, my brain. I seem to have lost all values. I care for nothing. . . . It is too late now." And he drowns himself at sea.

By comparison with his contemporaries London, however lost he was, was not lost in a fog. In *The Octopus* (1901), by Frank Norris, the destructive aspects of capitalism come into false focus. It is all a battle of the interests against the decent, hard-working, bravely risk-taking farmers. London was caught between Scylla and Charybdis and knew it. For his contemporaries, like Norris and Donnelly, power remained a murky mystery, and they wallowed in it exquisitely.

For Paul Leicester Ford, power was neither a murky sea nor a rocky shore. It was something that one simply seized and used—like an adolescent grasping a gyrocompass but not trigonometry. The hero of his *Honorable Peter Stirling* (1894) wins both the governorship and a fair young lady, almost simultaneously. Stirling, in his long, stolid, and solid evolution from a boor to the beloved and just champion of the poor, shuns demagogy and observes neither more nor less than a firm respect for the just interests of the rich. Like London's hero in *The Iron Heel*, Stirling is animated by a pure love of mankind, but he works in a simple, sweet, manageable world.

Writing in a fictional milieu that took class conflict as a given, Ford and Norris (and Anthony Trollope in *Phineas Finn*) remained not seriously dismayed by the problem of power. Like a mad mariner, London pointed in anguish toward the twentieth century, which people had entered but were not yet in, and foresaw the techniques and consequences of complete social control.

The racial conflict

Another major tributary of political fiction deals with the kind of status that is not a consequence of property differences but of race. Writers have appraised this political problem in both the colonial and the intranational context. The issue is indeed raised by Shakespeare in *Othello* (c. 1604), and Swift's *Modest Proposal* (1729) protests the infrahuman status to which Englishmen relegated their Irish subjects. But it was not until the twentieth century, when E. M. Forster wrote his *Passage to India* (1924), that a broad and deep statement was made of the consequences of the conjunction of one race that calls itself master and another that acknowledges and protests its own subordination. Forster analyzed hierarchy by observing the effects of racial status as it was superimposed by conquest on a culture where status was already indigenously and meticulously imposed by caste and religion. He probed intimately into the relations between individuals who try to see others and themselves as individuals but who cannot escape the differences of status and are not much helped by the abstract egalitarianism of Christianity and Islam.

The basic conflict is not oversimplified but is reduced by Forster to that of loyalty and affection between individuals as they are inhibited and restricted by the bonds of religious, social, and national status. In the novel, Forster implicitly argues for the greater value of individual ties of affection, basing this on his supreme valuation of individuality as more important than religion, caste, and nation. Forster also wrote: "If I had to choose between betraying my country and betraying my friend, I hope I should have the guts to betray my country."

Poignant statements of the problem in an African context have been made by Alan Paton, in *Cry, the Beloved Country* (1948) and *Too Late the Phalarope* (1953). In both, individuals try to reach each other across the chasm of racial distinction. In the second, the sexual aspect, clearly present but not dominant in *A Passage to India*, becomes a central theme—the fascination of forbidden fruit and the spontaneity of physical interpersonal love, which closes its eyes to skin color.

The etiology of the endemic disease of racial tension, as it affects both individuals and politics, is classically stated and explored in these three novels. The dynamics as they operate within a nation have been inevitably stated in America, with its centuries-old dilemma of relations between whites and Negroes. These writings have had little overt political content, from Stowe's *Uncle Tom's Cabin* to Lillian Smith's *Strange Fruit* (1944) and Robert Penn Warren's *Band of Angels* (1955) and his epic poem *Brother to Dragons* (1953). The more recent work of Negro authors, written with an intensity that cannot ever be attained by white writers, has also been largely apolitical.

What is remarkable is the enormous political influence such fiction has had. It is not true that any one book (or any other force) has by itself impelled a social or political movement, but these writings have at times helped raise the strong winds of opinion to hurricane force. Literary discussion from the 1850s to the 1950s of race relations, in intranational, colonial, and latterly in foreign-aid contexts—e.g., William J. Lederer and Eugene Burdick's *The Ugly American* (1958)—indicates the persistence of this politically explosive issue. [*See* HUMAN RIGHTS.]

Political equality and individual dignity

A common theme of social novels with status preoccupation—whether it be economic or racial in origin—is the equality and dignity of the individual human being. The criticism of discrimination on the basis of class or race rests implicitly or explicitly on the belief in equal dignity or equal worth, regardless of bodily or economic circumstances over which the individual has no control.

Another category of writings reverses this theme and looks at what can happen when the principle of equality as the only end is assumed and any means appropriate to its achievement is morally justified. From Dostoevski in *The Possessed* (1871) to Henry James in *The Princess Casamassima* (1886) and Joseph Conrad in *The Secret Agent* (1907) the antianarchic critique of amoral equality has stressed the need for decency, honor, and integrity on the grounds that monistic egalitarianism produces only the destruction of orderly society and ultimately the nihilistic negation of the individual himself.

The egalitarian context in which these three novels were written is socioeconomic. They say in effect: What you people like More, Trollope, Chekhov, Hugo, and Dickens are talking about is all very well, but if you altogether succeed, what then? Are you quite sure your poor, sat-upon, proletarian egg will not be hatched a hawk?

The theme of racial equality has undergone a similar attack more recently, in a pair of novels: Robert Ruark's *Something of Value* (1955) and Nicholas Monsarrat's *The Tribe That Lost Its Head* (1956). With a querulous, lascivious dwelling on the terrors of extreme brutality, these novels present at most, and only by implication, a ritualistic solution to the dilemma of inequality (return to the decent, humane virtues of the aristocratic race), but they do succeed in presenting the problem in a crude fashion. The recoil by such as Dostoievski, Conrad, and Ruark at some of the consequences of equality poses the question of the exercise of power without stint in a society dedicated solely to the proposition that all men are created equal. These writings are reactionary without being atavistic: indeed they radically criticize the atavism resulting from unconstrained equality.

Opposition to anarchy and tyranny

The dialogue between the proponents and opponents of socioeconomic and racial equality skirts but never directly enters the area of political power exercised for its own sake. It deals with the adjective rather than the noun, with wealthy or racist power in politics rather than power itself.

The moral problem of political power itself was posed as early as the fifth century B.C., in Sophocles' *Antigone*. In the more abstract form of a man's relation to his God the problem was posed in the Biblical story of Job (probably fifth or fourth century B.C.), who achieved no peace until he surrendered to the divine will and recognized the gracious omnipotence of his almighty Lord. In Shakespeare's *Macbeth* (c. 1606) the conscience-less pursuit of power at last pricks the conscience of its pursuer, but his destruction is at the hands of society. In Herman Melville's *Billy Budd* (1891) authority (that is, sanctioned power) and simple human virtue come into conflict, virtue bowing to power. A variation of the Billy Budd theme occurs in Herman Wouk's *The Caine Mutiny* (1951), the difference being that the story ends well: both authority and humane justice prevail and all's well. In C. Virgil Gheorghiu's *Twenty-fifth Hour* (1950), law, authority, order, chaos, and the machine combine to destroy the individual.

These direct statements of the power problem do not, however, bore into its origins and its portents. Starting in the 1930s, a brilliant succession of novels has probed man's soul, with a skill showing the enormous impact of Freudian depth psychology. The proliferation of these remarkable works and their failure to fit into a chronological development makes it necessary to consider them by type rather than time.

In his *Brave New World* (1932), Aldous Huxley portrays a 26th-century utopia (or an antiutopia, if More's Utopia is deemed a good society) where people have become truly contented as a result of the elimination of disunity and disorder through the use of both eugenics and childhood conditioning. Only in a genetic sport, a man who developed in a neglected portion of the earth to which conditioning has not yet made its way, is the serene pattern disturbed. Both frightening and at times hilarious, the novel lacks the somber quality of later penetration into individual and social psychology. Karel Čapek's *War With the Newts* (1936) continues the theme of a conformist utopia, portraying a primordial, slimy horror that Huxley's happy English background fails to elicit in print.

André Malraux's *Man's Fate* (1933) is a poignant portent of intensified horror, as the jungles of psyche and society are more deeply explored. Instead of setting his story in European "mass" society, Malraux placed his picture of the human condition in an Asian context, the naked power contest in 1927 between Chiang Kai-shek and the Chinese communists, a conflict Malraux himself had witnessed. In *Man's Hope* (1938) he continued the argument, now set in the Spanish Civil War—which he again saw firsthand. *Man's Fate* is an almost despairing account of cynicism, both individual and governmental, of egocentricity, and of a tiny, nearly extinct spark of human compassion

that keeps man's fate from being quite hopeless. *Man's Hope*, in a kaleidoscopic, almost incomprehensible picture of air and land battles, seems to kindle the spark of compassion into a flickering flame that slightly warms both of the warring camps in Spanish society, and in human society in general.

Building at least systematically, if not actually, on the somewhat impersonal social accounts just discussed, the Italian writer Ignazio Silone increasingly personalized the power problem. In *Fontamara* (1934) and *Bread and Wine* (1937) the ordinary people are more fully drawn than are Malraux's. And a new feature—the top political leader, the chief of state—emerges somewhat dimly in the background. This character is absent or distant in the work of Huxley, Čapek, and Malraux. The dilemmas of ideology, utopia, simple affection among human beings (and its savage antithesis: sexual rape) are conjoined with a simple superstition among the peasantry that takes the form of fear of the leader combined with a feeling of his inevitability, his power, and his grace. Both the peasantry and the politically declassed members of the ruling elite are juxtaposed to the leader in passionate ambivalence.

Three later novels move the ruling class farther into the foreground and the ordinary citizenry into the background. Two of these are psychologically distinguished and logically brilliant; the other, with one or two exceptions, is unsurpassed in its psychological penetration. In *Animal Farm* (1946) and *1984*, George Orwell carries to their logical conclusions certain tendencies already well developed in modern industrial society. *Animal Farm*, the allegorical polity in which all animals are equal but the ruling elite of pigs is more equal than the other creatures, argues that ideology and social justice are trivial matters when they confront the lust for power. In *1984* simple, spontaneous, uncontrived, uninduced love, of course, loses the battle, and Winston Smith, mentally *in extremis*, betrays his beloved Julia and comes to love Big Brother himself.

The third of these three novels, Arthur Koestler's *Darkness at Noon* (1941), synthesizes the author's personal experiences in the Spanish Civil War, during which in 1937 he was in solitary confinement in a Seville prison for three months (two months incommunicado), and his earlier experiences as a communist and a newspaperman traveling as an honored guest in the Soviet Union.

The protagonist of the novel, Rubashov, is a composite of several Soviet leaders who were tried and executed during the Soviet purge trials of the late 1930s. He is a composite of ideologism, courage, intellectuality, opportunism, and atrophied compassion. His life deftly poses several fundamental questions of political power: What means justify what ends? What is truth? When may proximate falsehood be used in the interests of ultimate truth? What is the individual's usefulness, his dignity, and his value?

The book contains several tragedies: the destruction of love between man and woman, to serve party purposes; the exposure of a man's soul in ludicrous public display, to serve party purposes; and the destruction of a party faithful when his usefulness has passed. These tragedies are conjoined with two politically deeper ones: the growing compassion shown Rubashov by a never-seen fellow prisoner, an adherent of the old regime with whom he has nothing in common save uncultured humanity, and the inability of Rubashov to live outside the quite corrupt church of the Communist party, in which he has spent his life and the only thing to which he is dedicated aside from self. Neither the compassion of others nor fidelity to party saves him from destruction. In the end Rubashov can choose neither to stand with his fellow men nor to stand alone.

The early antiutopias of the 1930s and 1940s were relatively impersonal and dealt mainly with ordinary citizens. The more personal, and more real, accounts of Silone, Malraux, and Koestler move partially or completely from treatment of the ordinary to the extraordinary citizen, to the declassed member of the ruling elite. Two additional novels dealing with the same problems of unconstrained political power are fictionalized biographies of actual chiefs of state. Robert Penn Warren's *All the King's Men* (1946) follows closely the life of the American Huey P. Long, Louisiana's hypertrophied ruler without scruple in the 1930s. Peter Abrahams' *A Wreath for Udomo* (1956) fictionalizes the life of a prominent African chief of state whom Abrahams knew when both were in London as students and radical African nationalists.

Like Koestler's writing, *All the King's Men* juxtaposes a set of tragedies, the personal and political. There is the use and betrayal of people, the abuse of truth and the use of falsehood, the passionate sense of abstract justice combined with the enthusiasm for inducing a lawless personal dependency—revenge and grace without justice. The tragedy lies in the inability of the leader, Willie Stark, to extricate himself from the personal nest he has woven for himself and then befouled.

Though lacking the somber quality of *Darkness at Noon, All the King's Men* ends in deeper tragedy, because instead of being entrapped by circumstance—a party and its ideology—Willie Stark, like Macbeth, is unable to escape himself and death at the hands of a close associate.

A Wreath for Udomo similarly conjoins the personal and the political. Udomo is beloved by and loves a mature Englishwoman he meets in London. He betrays her by having an affair with a mutual friend. When he later gets established as leader of his newly liberated African nation, he sacrifices the life of an old friend and devoted follower, as the price for getting technical aid from the hated, white-ruled nation of South Africa. He is at last killed by tribal atavism, the fear-driven reaction to the modern ways Udomo is introducing.

Most of these antianarchic novels (from Dostoevski to Conrad) and antityrannic novels, often mislabeled antiutopias (from Huxley to Abrahams), were written in western Europe. Out of eastern Europe, in the post-Stalin era, has come a series of novels that offer the promise, and no more as yet, of the re-emergence of intensely political writing in the land that produced Dostoevski and Gogol. The new books remain timid, uncrafted products, still too close to tyranny itself to be able to appraise it freely. Among these are Vladimir Dudintsev's *Not by Bread Alone*, more concerned with public administration than with public policy; Abram Tertz's *The Trial Begins* (1960), which deals directly if crudely with Stalinist tyranny; and Alexander Solzhenitsyn's *One Day in the Life of Ivan Denisovich* (1963), which considers the theme of selfishness and the platitude of the endurance of the human spirit, but otherwise is undistinguished. It nevertheless is a milestone in the public recognition it has accorded the author in the Soviet Union, where he was nominated in 1963 for the Lenin Prize.

Nietzschean and anti-Nietzschean themes

There remains still another category of political novels, incongruous among those that oppose either anarchy or tyranny. These are the writings that implicitly or explicitly espouse and justify—or reject and condemn—a Nietzschean, individualist anarchism divorced from any social or socialist commitment. In a sense, these are antipolitical works.

A prototype of this genre is Stendhal's *The Red and the Black* (1830). Its protagonist Julien moves through life and through people's lives with a moral dedication to self that rises above any less exalted purpose. He pushes into boudoirs and the bureaus of business and government with a purity of heart that beguiles. At the end he faces trial with a moral courage and a refusal to compromise his principle that makes it easy to overlook the principle to which he was dedicated. If the pure in heart ever are to see their God, Julien saw his in himself and was by himself blest.

The Red and the Black is indeed a pure novel, unbesmirched by the dilemma between individual distinction and social service. If the solution for Martin Eden was the escape of private suicide, Julien went to his public execution with the courage of Socrates and Christ, the sole difference being in the diverse principles for which Julien and Socrates and Christ died.

Two more-recent novels echo the *Red and Black* theme, in one case with several inklings of awareness of the dilemma and in the other with no more than an inkling. Hermann Hesse's *Steppenwolf* (1927) is the story of an individualist who moves from the writing desk to the dance hall, discovers affection for others, but does not swerve dangerously from his self-dedication. For a while, nevertheless, he enjoys warming and being warmed by others.

Not so Dr. Zhivago, in Boris Pasternak's novel by that name (1957). With a dedication to self that rivals Julien's, Zhivago moves endlessly across the well-limned Russian landscape during and after the great revolution, sloughing off those whom he has used and who have become attached to him. He does it all with a remarkable sense of high purpose, blaming only the chaos and the Soviet system for his faults, that is, his inability to succeed altogether in his self-service. The critical enthusiasm with which the book was received after its official Soviet condemnation and the awarding of the Nobel Prize to its author reflected a pharisaical condemnation of Soviet communism and no understanding of the refusal of Pasternak to face the dilemma confronted by London, Koestler, and Orwell. In *Dr. Zhivago*, Nietzsche is not problematical but axiomatic.

Two individualistic American novels throw this issue into relief: James Gould Cozzens' *The Last Adam* (1933) and Ernest Hemingway's *For Whom the Bell Tolls* (1940). Both emphasize individual values and candidly make their protagonists into heroes. Both clearly indicate a commitment of these heroes to their communities. There is a consequent warmth in Cozzens' and Hemingway's characters that contrasts with the vibrating chill of Julien and Zhivago.

A brilliantly madcap Italian drama on egocentricity, Luigi Pirandello's *Six Characters in Search of an Author* (1922), mixes tragedy and comedy as his protagonists step in and out of character as concupiscent egoists exploiting one another and protesting their altruism. Obviously nonpolitical, this pungent play deeply influenced Gamal Abdel Nasser, who viewed the same prurient egoism on the other side of the Mediterranean as a prime cause of Egyptian political impotence before and after the 1952 revolution.

Two French novelists have written on the theme, in works that replace Pirandello's mordant laughter with a moan from the wounds of egoism that rises to a cry of mortal despair. The existentialist Jean-Paul Sartre in *The Age of Reason* (1945) has his characters search for private freedom, after liberty has been publicly betrayed in the Spanish Civil War. They seek it in the paradox of uncommitted love that exploits others for their companionship and passion but ends in solitude. At the last the central character muses that he is "alone but no freer than before. . . . this life had been given him for nothing, he was nothing and yet he would not change: he was as he was made" ([1945] see 1959, p. 342). In Sartre's *Troubled Sleep* (1949), set in France during the Nazi occupation in 1940, the search for freedom is similarly fruitless. To personal egoism is conjoined national egoism: man cares neither for man nor woman nor *Vaterland* nor *patrie*—and vice versa. All one can do, Sartre seems to say, is endure, clutching the thin coin of existentialism whose other side is nihilism.

The cry of Albert Camus is even more piercing. In *The Plague* (1947) he seems to argue with Sartre's morbid description of man's isolation. In an allegory of France during the Nazi occupation, he finds individual men who dedicate themselves warmly to a solidary, compassionate succoring of the plague-stricken community. Fear of fatal infection and mistrust of one's neighbors are overcome by the "craving for human contacts" and the identification with the dying. Society must endure, and with individual compassion for individuals it can endure. "The Stranger" in Camus's 1942 novel by that name is an emotionally empty man who kills without feeling, without even hatred, an alien in a community whose members remain individually and collectively united against their asocial fellow citizen. But in *The Fall* (1956), Camus appears to have surrendered to despair. There can be no conjunction of freedom and society. Solitude is unbearable, and man cannot bear freedom, a court sentence imposed on oneself by oneself. Man must be a slave, in a society where all are slaves to their own inescapable egoism. Lacking love, men are dragged through life by their almost impotent hypersexuality. Their common guilt can hold them together, but it only delays the solitude of death.

And in Ingmar Bergman's screenplays the theme is repeated in Scandinavian settings, with the sharp skill of London, Sartre, and Camus but without their resignation or despair. In *Wild Strawberries* (1957), a distinguished septuagenarian scientist, about to be honored for his dedicated pursuit of reality, in his dreams sees himself as indifferent, unloving and unloved, living in deadly solitude. "I'm dead, although I live." In the triad of screenplays *Through a Glass Darkly* (1961), *Winter Light* (1963), and *The Silence* (1963), the theme is reinforced: psychoanalytic understanding, piety, and sexual passion without love do become deathly futile and impotent. But, Bergman insists, men are capable of compassion.

The problem of free choice

Political fiction, like political science, has always been a product of the developing stage of culture in which it was written. Both fiction and science have drawn from the same intellectual sources and appraised the dilemmas of the time. When the very idea of limited government was taking shape, Sophocles in *Antigone* raised the radical issue of civil disobedience. In the twentieth century, when tyranny underwent another revival—perhaps unequaled since the savage sixteenth century of the Reformation and Counter Reformation—the theme of tyranny again became central.

But political fiction now reflects the infusion of new knowledge, notably from psychology and physiology. It has consequently produced an inquiry into the causes and consequences of tyranny that is remarkable in depth and suggestiveness. In so doing, political fiction has articulated analyses of problems that in contemporary writing in political science have had largely disjointed treatment: the relationship between the individual, his fellow men, his fellow citizens, and government; the concept of justice in which government is more than an arbiter between citizens; the problem of moral choice and free choice; and above all, the criteria for choice.

Indeed, to a great extent the new political theory of the twentieth century has been written in fictional form. Some writings already discussed and some not yet discussed show this sharply.

In *1984* Orwell develops his story and his theory by employing an almost classic Freudian thesis. Government, to control individual political loyalty, must sever ties of loyalty between individuals. The basic tie, says Orwell, following Freud, is the erotic one—physical love with its attendant personal affection. To break this tie, government must destroy physical desire. To do this, government must, in turn, reactivate the primordial individual desire for sheer survival and replace love between real people with the childish dependent love for the never-seen omnipotence that graciously or tyrannically permits survival and provides the means for survival. Heterosexual love is replaced with asexual, childish, dependent love, and political autonomy is replaced with political infancy. Justice is controlled by what through "doublethink" is called the Ministry of Love, where men are reduced to impotence.

Koestler in *Darkness at Noon* offers a more complicated set of hypotheses. Love and loyalty between individuals are indeed deadened by tyranny. But the problem of justice gets a less stark, more subtle and realistic, consideration than Orwell's brutal statement that power is a boot stamping on a human face forever. Justice now relates to means and ends. As object and subject the individual is considered by Koestler to be a commodity to be valued quite apart from his usefulness to the polity. But can man choose? With a vague, attenuated humanitarianism that becomes entangled with the justification of any efficient means to humane ends, Rubashov chooses only to condemn himself. A socialized, collectivized Nietzschean, he can exercise his will only by conforming to the will of the political party, which has become identical with the will of the leader. Koestler seems to say that men can be aware but not choose.

The problem of free moral choice (a tautology, at least in politics) gets precocious emphasis in Joseph Conrad's *Under Western Eyes* (1911). With or without the benefit of psychoanalytic theory, Conrad poignantly refines the problem. He indicates that the consequence of choice, when it destroys other people, is to destroy the chooser.

The criteria for choice are considered in two of the first works which deeply explore political behavior. In the theoretical dialogue between sexual and nonsexual love (eros and agape), both these novels employ depth psychology and argue against a simplistic Freudian erotism.

Franz Kafka in *The Castle* (1926) has his protagonist, K., use sex to get ahead, to try to get the attention of the leader, the unseen chief in the castle. The wretch K. fails because, like Julien and Zhivago, he is concentered all in self and at last can only throw himself on the infinite mercy that accompanies infinite power.

William Golding in *Free Fall* (1959) evidently rejects his earlier thesis in *Lord of the Flies* that beneath man's enculturation crouches only a primordial beast. He now argues that man cannot live alone, that he must live with and for other individuals, and that the dilemma of living for oneself and for others will persist and is the basis for guilt, which also will persist. Man is not altogether formed by either his genes or his environs: he can choose, with inevitable guilt, but without guilt he could never make choices that are right —that is, moral. He can never help establish a free society or free himself without considering the consequences of his choices both for himself and for others.

In so stating the criteria for choice, Golding avoids the surrender to divine will implicit in the Biblical Job and the modern *Castle*, to the will of the party and leader explicit in *Darkness at Noon* and *1984*, and to individually uncontrollable forces as in *Martin Eden*. *Free Fall* thus implies there is choice, that forces within and without the individual are not altogether uncontrollable, and that anxiety and guilt will inevitably accompany the exercise of choice. To this extent Golding indicates a way out of the dilemma so poignantly posed by London.

All these factors have been integrated in unequaled, necessarily epigrammatic form in a political novella of classic proportions, *Mario and the Magician* (1929) by Thomas Mann. In *Mario* are fully presented the leader, the citizenry that is led, and the citizen who kills the tyrant. The roots of tyranny are exposed in the leader's envy, contempt, and hatred for the public and in the public's moral obtuseness that considers politics a game at which they are irresponsible spectators. And using the need for people to huddle together, the leader isolates potential dissenters. In a brilliantly contrived denouement, Mann has the leader exploit and pervert sexual love and be undone by a young man whose revulsion at the leader seems to stem from the depths of the untutored, natural man. Mann in this rather short story does not explicate other political fiction; he epitomizes it.

If the themes of private and public egoism, tyranny, and free choice had not recurred in Russian, English, Italian, French, German, and Swedish writing, in contexts scattered over centuries and over the globe, one might argue that the condition was not universal but parochial. In Malraux and Golding, the dying despair of Dostoevski, Orwell, Pirandello, Sartre, Camus, Koestler, and Kafka is quickened by hope. Man need not just exist and then cease: he can elicit his own compassion and can redeem himself and his fellow men. Deepened psychological understanding need not just witness or contribute to the destruction of men and society; it can help build both. Man is helpless neither against the tyranny of his own egoism nor against the tyranny of egoism in the general public and its leaders.

Political fiction and political science

One conclusion from a look at political fiction is that the lines between fiction, theory, and fact are very indistinct. *Darkness at Noon*, a fiction piece about the great Soviet purges of the late 1930s, portended not only the factual account of them in Beck and Godin's *Russian Purge and the Extraction of Confession* (1951) but also the profound study of brainwashing in Lifton's *Thought Reform and the Psychology of Totalism* (1961). In a sense fiction here was a decade ahead of published fact and two decades ahead of systematic theory and observation. Koestler in turn was building on fact. Bukharin, one of the most distinguished victims of the 1938 purge, said at his trial: "When you ask yourself: 'If you must die, what are you dying for?'—an absolute black vacuity suddenly rises before you with startling vividness. There was nothing to die for, if one wanted to die unrepentant" (quoted in Daniels 1960, p. 389).

In raising basic issues of power in its political manifestations and of the ability and responsibility to make choices, political fiction has been working in the same garden as have political theory and political research. The far from accidental consequence is that political fiction has posed problems and stated solutions that are rarely behind, and often ahead of, the statement and resolution of these problems by more prosaic investigators. There is a relationship between Job's argument with his God, Antigone's with her king, and Winston Smith's with his Big Brother. There is a tie between Freudian theory, Marxian socioeconomic theory, and the writings of Koestler, Golding, and Bergman. Each supports and facilitates the understanding of the other. One very notable distinction is that the fiction writer puts the reader on guard, since the reader of fiction realizes that what is being written is not necessarily ultimate truth or exact fact. The nonfiction theorist or researcher in politics seldom so protects the reader. In this sense writers of political fiction are exercising a responsible moral choice as to the canons of scientific method that is too infrequently faced by writers of political science.

JAMES C. DAVIES

[*See also* ALIENATION; IDEOLOGY; INTELLECTUALS; SOCIAL SCIENCE FICTION; UTOPIANISM.]

BIBLIOGRAPHY

The examples of political fiction cited in the text are not included in the bibliography.

BECK, F.; and GODIN, W. [pseudonyms] 1951 *Russian Purge and the Extraction of Confession.* London and New York: Hurst & Blackett; New York: Viking.

BLOTNER, JOSEPH L. 1955 *The Political Novel.* Garden City, N.Y.: Doubleday. → Contains a comprehensive list of political novels.

CROSSMAN, RICHARD H. S. (editor) (1949) 1959 *The God That Failed.* New York: Harper. → A paperback edition was published in 1963.

DANIELS, ROBERT V. 1960 *The Conscience of the Revolution: Communist Opposition in Soviet Russia.* Russian Research Center Studies, No. 40. Cambridge, Mass.: Harvard Univ. Press.

DONNER, JÖRN (1962) 1964 *The Personal Vision of Ingmar Bergman.* Bloomington: Indiana Univ. Press. → First published as *Djävulens ansikte: Ingmar Bergmans filmer.*

HOWE, IRVING 1957 *Politics and the Novel.* New York: World.

LIFTON, ROBERT J. 1961 *Thought Reform and the Psychology of Totalism: A Study of "Brainwashing" in China.* New York: Norton.

LLEWELLYN, KARL N.

Karl Nickerson Llewellyn (1893–1962) was a leading exponent of "realism" in the field of jurisprudence. Applying the realistic method to commercial law, he produced the Uniform Commercial Code, now effective law in the United States. He also wrote on legal education, emphasizing craft skills and law as a liberal art; on the professional responsibility and organization of the bar; and on the sociology of law. He analyzed law-government as an institution and demonstrated that dispute settlement is the most reliable indicator of the law and values of a group. In addition, he wrote poetry, painted, and composed songs.

At Yale, where he studied both as an undergraduate and as a law student, his exposure to the ideas of William Graham Sumner, through the lectures of A. G. Keller, aroused Llewellyn's interest in patterns of behavior as fundamentals in societal structure. He was influenced by the fact-to-result analysis of cases used by Arthur L. Corbin and by the narrow-issue thinking of Wesley Hohfeld and Walter W. Cook. After teaching commercial law at Yale for two years, he went into practice in New York City, studying banking and business patterns as well as the crafts of counseling and advocacy. When he returned to Yale, his writings reflected his preoccupation with the relation of commercial practice and economics to law; his work also revealed his expanding interest in legal sociology.

He admired Holmes, Pound, Cardozo, Max Weber, and Eugen Ehrlich. Starting in the 1920s, he drafted legislation for the Commissioners on Uniform State Laws; at the same time, he examined the process of rule making in its theoretical and practical aspects. Llewellyn's move to Columbia in 1924 coincided with the ferment there concerning the merits of fact research and of the integration of law with the other social sciences. His major study of commercial doctrine, factual patterns, and the ways in which cases reflect social conditions, business practices, and styles of judicial decision led to his *Cases and Materials on the Law of Sales* (1930a), a classic introduction to the study of law; *The Bramble Bush* (1930b); and a set of lectures delivered in Germany and entitled "Einführung in das amerikanische Präjudizienrechtswesen."

His publication of "A Realistic Jurisprudence—The Next Step" (1930c) precipitated a controversy about the nature of realism. Llewellyn saw realism as a method of attacking legal problems by first looking at what was in fact being done by courts and other officials. In this connection, he insisted on the importance of narrow, factual categories and the temporary divorce of "is" from "ought." He read cases for their narrow holdings (the facts, precise legal issue, and result), testing whether the courts were doing what doctrine seemingly required. The objectives of this analysis were, first, an accurate statement of the operative law; second, a testing of the relation between that law and the life situation it encompasses; third, an evaluation of the policy thus reflected; and finally, a decision as to what the law ought to be, and its statement in a well-drafted legislative or judicial rule. He saw legal rules as vital to the guidance and control of behavior and urged that these rules explicitly state their reason and that they be accompanied by explanation of the policy on which they rest. He believed that the Janus-faced nature of precedent forces courts to make policy choices and that courts cannot operate effectively in our society without such leeway of choice. He urged recognition of this fact as a first step to better decisions. Few scholars have been more interested and more active in the process of rule making and in relating law to values, and none has been more falsely accused of being concerned only with the "is."

Already active in the Legal Aid Society and the American Civil Liberties Union, in the 1930s he also helped plan strategy for the National Association for the Advancement of Colored People. His commercial-law articles became increasingly concerned with the relation of judicial method, institutional structure, and practice to the development of doctrine.

A study he made with E. A. Hoebel of the law-government of the Cheyenne Indians resulted in *The Cheyenne Way* (1941), which broke ground in anthropological method. In *The Cheyenne Way*, Llewellyn departed from the traditional procedure of inferring the character of the law from the statements of informants; his methodological innovation was to try to determine what the effective law of the group was—what happened in actual conflict situations.

His writings in jurisprudence reflected his view of law-government as an institution with its own functions, values, crafts, and traditions. He used "law-government" to designate the total legal component of society. It includes the mechanics of dispute settlement; the allocation of the power to decide particular types of issues; and the formulation of substantive rules, whether by legislation, executive action, or judicial decision. The concept of law-government rejects the view that the law is simply a body of rules; instead, the law is considered to be a set of institutions.

In the 1940s Llewellyn's theories of rule making and his perception of the appellate process bore fruit in the style of organization and drafting of the Uniform Commercial Code. His insistence on preliminary analysis in terms of narrow issues and narrow factual categories proved its value in the resulting clarification of the policy considerations involved in this legislation. He also studied the law-government of pueblo groups and drafted legal codes for the Santa Ana and Santo Domingo pueblos. In 1944, as chairman of the Curriculum Committee of the Association of American Law Schools, he made a report, which has become a classic, analyzing legal crafts and skills as they relate to legal education (see Association of American Law Schools 1944). His Storrs lectures at Yale Law School foreshadowed Llewellyn's *Common Law Tradition: Deciding Appeals* (1960), a definitive statement of the appellate process. In 1948/1949, while a visiting professor at Harvard, he prepared a jurisprudence syllabus incorporating his view of law-government.

In 1951 he moved to the University of Chicago, attracted by the ideas of Edward H. Levi, dean of the law school. At Chicago he concentrated on the development of his jurisprudence syllabus, the refinement of materials on legal argument that he had been collecting since 1934, and the completion of his study of the process of appellate judging. His writings in legal education deal more directly with questions of craft, scope, and responsibility, and he explored further the relationship of law to the humanities, as well as to the behavioral sciences.

SOIA MENTSCHIKOFF

[See also JURISPRUDENCE; PUBLIC LAW, *and the biographies of* CARDOZO; HOLMES; POUND; SUMNER; WEBER, MAX.]

WORKS BY LLEWELLYN

1930a *Cases and Materials on the Law of Sales.* Chicago: Callaghan.

(1930b) 1951 *The Bramble Bush: On Our Law and Its Study.* New York: Oceana.

1930c A Realistic Jurisprudence: The Next Step. *Columbia Law Review* 30:431–465.

1931 What Price Contract? An Essay in Perspective. *Yale Law Journal* 40:704–751.

1936–1937 On Warranty of Quality, and Society. *Columbia Law Review* 36:699–744; 37:341–409.

1938–1939 On Our Case Law of Contract: Offer and Acceptance. *Yale Law Journal* 48:1–36, 779–818.

1940 The Normative, the Legal and the Law-jobs: The Problem of Juristic Method. *Yale Law Journal* 49:1355–1400.

1941a On the Problem of Teaching "Private" Law. *Harvard Law Review* 54:775–810.

1941b The Theory of Legal "Science." *North Carolina Law Review* 20:1–23.

1941 LLEWELLYN, KARL N.; and HOEBEL, E. ADAMSON *The Cheyenne Way: Conflict and Case Law in Primitive Jurisprudence.* Norman: Univ. of Oklahoma Press.

1944 Meet Negotiable Instruments. *Columbia Law Review* 44:299–329.

1960 *The Common Law Tradition: Deciding Appeals.* Boston: Little.

1962 The Study of Law as a Liberal Art. Pages 375–394 in Karl N. Llewellyn, *Jurisprudence: Realism in Theory and Practice.* Univ. of Chicago Press. → An address delivered on April 30, 1960.

Jurisprudence: Realism in Theory and Practice. Univ. of Chicago Press, 1962. → Contains essays first published between 1928 and 1960.

SUPPLEMENTARY BIBLIOGRAPHY

ASSOCIATION OF AMERICAN LAW SCHOOLS, COMMITTEE ON CURRICULUM 1944 The Place of Skills in Legal Education. *Columbia Law Review* 45:345–391. → Llewellyn served as chairman of the committee.

LOBBYING

If we had data on every government in every culture, we would probably find that lobbying in some form is an inevitable concomitant of government. The term originated in American governmental experience about 1830. Certain representatives of interest groups loitered in the lobbies off the assembly halls of the American Congress and state legislatures, hoping to get a chance to speak to legislators and thereby attempt to influence their decisions. As the term became part of the vernacular, it was broadened to include anyone who attempted to influence the decision of a governmental official. The term is currently used quite loosely, and often inappropriately, for all kinds of influence endeavors. Since it is popularly believed that lobbyists use improper methods in their attempts to influence officials, the term "lobbying" carries an unpleasant connotation to many minds.

Despite the imprecision of the current use of the term, some boundaries can be defined. (1) Lobbying occurs only in governmental decision making. Decisions made by private individuals, organizations, or corporations may be influenced by special interests, but the influence should not be called lobbying. (2) All lobbying is motivated by a desire to influence. Many actions and events may affect the outcome of governmental decisions, but if they are not accompanied by an intent to influence, there is no lobbying. (3) Lobbying implies the presence of an intermediary or representative as a communication link between citizens and governmental decision makers. A citizen who, of his own volition and by his own means, sends a message to a governmental decision maker is not considered a lobbyist even though he is attempting to influence governmental decisions. (4) All lobbying involves communication, for that is the only way that influence can be transmitted. Broadly defined, then, *lobbying is the stimulation and transmission of a communication, by someone other than a citizen acting on his own behalf, directed to a governmental decision maker with the hope of influencing his decision.*

Although most lobbyists do represent special-interest groups, or pressure groups, lobbying is not identical with interest-group behavior. For one thing, individuals as well as groups utilize lobbying. Second, interest groups engage in many activities in addition to lobbying; some groups, in fact, do not engage in lobbying at all. Third, individuals or groups with special interests may find direct representation without the intercession of lobbyists. Lobbying, then, is but one process or means of representation that individuals and groups might utilize.

Lobbying should be thought of as a process rather than as an organization. It is most helpful to think of it as a communication process by which lobbyists attempt to get governmental officials to accept the policy desires of lobbying clients. It is the lobbyist's job to create messages

and to choose means of transmission that are most likely to ensure clear and favorable reception of the message by the intended receiver. This means that the lobbyist must anticipate the predispositions of his intended receiver(s) and so act that the message will be favorably received with as little distortion as possible. He must take care that the message is not intercepted or blocked. He must choose a transmission channel that is open (has access), is not likely to be overloaded, and has a low noise level.

The origin of the term "lobbying" and its legal definition in the United States statute, the Federal Regulation of Lobbying Act of 1946, leads many persons to believe that lobbying applies only to legislative decisions. The definition given above suggests, however, that lobbying occurs just as readily with executive-branch officials as with legislators, and even to a certain extent with judicial officials. Empirical data for the United States national government show that executive-branch lobbying is just as prevalent as legislative-branch lobbying (Milbrath 1963, pp. 319–320; Cherington & Gillen 1962).

Patterns of lobbying

Although there have been studies of interest groups in a number of countries, studies of the lobbying process are relatively rare and nearly always confined to the United States. Consequently, little is known about how lobbying is conducted outside of the United States. It does seem clear, however, that only in the United States are large numbers of special political actors designated to play the role of lobbyist on a full-time, professional basis. Most of the persons who perform lobbying functions in other national cultures probably do so as a part-time activity while maintaining a major role as an interest-group official, labor union official, attorney, or corporation executive.

For lack of empirical evidence, one can only speculate on reasons for the greater emphasis on lobbying in the United States as compared with other countries. One possible reason is that representation of interests is more clearly built into the governmental system of other Western countries than into the American governmental system. Interest groups, in these other countries, are given seats on advisory boards or are consulted as a matter of course by ministers or bureau chiefs. In addition, interest groups often succeed in electing one or more of their own men to seats in the legislative body. Of course, these things also occur in American government, but the difference in emphasis is substantial. American interest groups believe they must take the initiative if they hope to be heard at decision time.

Another possible reason for the difference in lobbying between America and other Western countries is the difference in centralization of decision making in the government. In most Western governments, decision making is highly concentrated in the cabinet executive, whereas in the United States it is divided between the executive and the legislature, and sometimes between the state and national governments. A diffuse decision process, one that has many decision points, more likely requires continuous scrutiny and pressure by special interests in order to get a policy moved past each of these points. In a sense, lobbying must be used in a diffuse decisional system to avoid degeneration of the system into inaction or stalemate.

Differences in the political-party system also seem to affect lobbying. European parties are more closely allied with and based on interest groups (especially in multiparty systems). Generally, they also are more "responsible" (able and required to carry out their program when given power) than American parties. American parties are so heterogeneous that they must compromise group interests rather than clearly speak for them. Furthermore, American parties cannot be counted on for firm policy leadership. Interest groups in the United States have almost abandoned working through parties and instead have hired lobbyists to secure policy representation (Milbrath 1963, p. 200). By way of contrast, European interest groups are more likely than American interest groups to find political parties a useful means of representation and to depend to a lesser extent on lobbying (Beer 1958, p. 138).

During the initial stages of lobbying's development in the United States, some groups sought competitive advantage over other groups by sending a personal envoy (a lobbyist) to the seat of government. Lobbying at this stage was very much a function of the direct personal relationship between lobbyists and official decision makers. Groups with more competent lobbyists were more likely to have their messages accepted by government officials. Groups at a competitive disadvantage because they had no lobbyist were stimulated also to send a lobbyist envoy. Eventually, the seat of the national government, and also the seats of some state governments, became crowded with lobbyists clamoring for an opportunity to deliver direct personal messages to officials. Easy access for direct communication between lobbyist and

official, which had been possible with only a limited number of lobbyists, became very difficult. (Currently there are between eight hundred and one thousand registered lobbyists in Washington, D.C.)

Faced with a situation where the channels of direct communication with officials were constantly overloaded and seldom available, lobbyists turned to indirect communication methods. They sent messages through intermediaries who were thought to have better access, such as constituents or friends of the officials. They stimulated mass letter or telegram campaigns, hoping to impress officials with a ground swell of public sentiment for or against a policy. They launched massive public relations campaigns in the mass media, hoping to change (or maintain) political attitudes. This shift of tactics to indirect communication methods became known as "lobbying at the grass roots."

However, indirect methods also are limited in effectiveness. Grass-roots campaigns conducted by strong competitive groups often result in stalemate or *status quo*. Campaigns stimulated by lobbyists usually are detected as such by officials, and their potential impact is seriously discounted through knowledge of their nonspontaneous nature. Successful public relations campaigns require subtle management and are very expensive. As a result of these kinds of difficulties, the pendulum has begun to swing back from grass-roots lobbying.

Current lobbying methods in Washington, D.C. are a blend of direct and indirect methods of communication. Direct methods, such as personal presentation of viewpoints, are preferred by most lobbyists, but they cannot be relied on to get messages through to officials. Lobbyists turn to indirect methods when direct ones prove uncertain or unusable. In addition, lobbyists pay considerable attention to the problem of keeping their communication channels open. They employ various means of ingratiating themselves with officials to ensure that access will be speedy and direct when it is needed. Entertainment and bribery are not as widely used to ingratiate as is popularly supposed. They are not considered as rewards or favors by most officials, and bribery especially is dangerous to the careers of both officials and lobbyists (Milbrath 1963, chapter 13).

Lobbying occurs at all levels of government in the United States: city, county, and state as well as national. Research on state lobbying is scattered and uneven, while research on city and county lobbying is almost nonexistent. About three-fourths of the fifty states have a lobby-regulation or lobby-reporting law, but in most cases these laws are rather weakly enforced.

The scattered research evidence that exists on state lobbying suggests that lobbyists at the state level primarily employ direct methods of communication with officials. Competition for the time and attention of officials is less at the state level than at the national level. Consequently, state lobbyists do not find it so necessary to turn to the more expensive and less certain indirect methods that national lobbyists must employ.

Employing primarily direct methods, state lobbyists devote more time and resources to ingratiating themselves with officials and to keeping communication lines open. The reported incidence of entertainment and bribery is higher at the state level than at the national level. Furthermore, entertainment is considered more of a reward in state capitals than in Washington, D.C. Most state legislators do not establish residence at the seat of government, as most members of Congress do. Living in a hotel, the state legislator generally finds the prospect of spending an evening on a lobbyist's expense account much more appealing than does the overworked and overentertained member of Congress.

The study of lobbying

Lobbying is often studied within the context of some larger process. Four examples of such processes can be given. First, lobbying has been studied as a component of the legislative process (Herring 1929; Gross 1953). Second, it has been studied as a component of the process by which the total government arrives at a decision about a given bill or policy (Bailey 1950; Latham 1952; Bauer et al. 1963). Third, lobbying is a significant component of studies of the group process of politics (Bentley 1908; Truman 1951). Fourth, studies of the nature and activity of interest groups naturally incorporate lobbying activity as a part of total group activity (Garceau 1941; Kile 1948; Taft 1954; Eckstein 1960; Potter 1961).

A much smaller proportion of studies give direct and primary attention to lobbying per se; these fall into three categories. First, Congressional investigating committees have developed valuable information on lobbying in Washington, D.C., usually with a view to possible legislative changes in the regulation of lobbying. Two prominent examples are the House of Representatives Select Committee on Lobbying Activities, which was active in 1949 and 1950 and was chaired by Representative Frank Buchanan of Pennsylvania; and the Senate Special Committee to Investigate Political Activities, Lobbying, and Campaign Contributions, which was active in 1956 and 1957 and was chaired by Senator John McClellan of Arkansas. Second, some persons regard lobbying as a threat to free government and believe the process should be exposed from time to time to the glare of publicity. These journalistic exposés are usually more specific and polemical than general and scholarly; two book-length efforts are Crawford (1939) and Schriftgiesser (1951). Third, some recent scholarly work has focused directly on the lobbyist as political actor. Based on first-hand interview evidence, these studies describe the roles of lobbyists as mediators between groups and government and give detailed evaluations of methods and techniques used in the lobbying process (Milbrath 1963; Patterson 1963).

This last approach to the study of lobbying, deriving empirical data from the persons who practice lobbying, seems to shed most light on the subject. To date, such evidence is available only on Washington lobbyists and lobbyists in a few state governments such as Michigan (De Vries 1960) and Oklahoma (Patterson 1963). It is important that such evidence also be gathered in different national political systems. The role of lobbying in the policy-making process will be much better understood when comparisons using adequate and valid data are possible across national cultures.

Evaluation

The paucity of empirical data makes it difficult to give an adequate evaluation of the role of lobbying in the political process. It might be helpful, however, to list some of the utilities and disutilities of lobbying as a part of the political process.

One utility of lobbying is the service (primarily information) that lobbyists and lobby organizations provide to official decision makers. These services are often proclaimed as being free since they do not come directly out of the taxpayer's pocket. In another sense, however, the costs of lobbying are passed on to the public in the form of higher prices for goods and services. Since the public pays for the service in either case, the service should be evaluated according to its quality. The present system of lobbying services makes for considerable duplication and is clearly wasteful and time-consuming. Thus, even though officials make considerable use of this lobbying service, it probably could be obtained from alternative sources at a lower cost to the body politic.

On the other hand, there is something to be said for having alternative and duplicative sources of information and other services. An official who can turn to more than one source for information is less subservient to any one source. Dispensing with lobbying service probably would make Congress even more dependent on the executive, since Congress generally has fewer adequate information sources.

Perhaps the most useful service is the transmission and clash of viewpoints. This serves a creative function in alerting decision makers to all possible policy alternatives and mitigates a good deal of the waste and frustration involved in lobbying. Officials might find other sources for most services lobbyists provide, but they benefit quite clearly from the representational function that the lobbyist spokesmen for specific interests perform. Lobby groups and lobbyists were evolved as a part of government to fulfill this need for specific representation, a need that no other component of the political process is adapted to fill (Milbrath 1963, p. 313).

A major disutility of lobbying, in addition to waste, is its potential for corruption. Lobbyists usually represent persons seeking specific—therefore private—ends. Such private ends may coincide or be compatible with the public welfare, but, in many instances, they are not. An adequate political system reconciles these private ends to the public welfare, but it cannot do this if officials or lobbyists act corruptly. Corruption enters when the system responds to money or property instead of to votes alone; when personal pecuniary rewards are offered to or accepted by officials as they arrive at decisions; and when decisions are made in secret, thus foreclosing opportunity for dissent from the opposition.

Lobbying in Washington, D.C., has a relatively low incidence of corruption, not so much because of legal controls (which are relatively inadequate) but because of built-in systemic controls of the process. These systemic controls are integral to the total policy-making system. All of the actors in this system are interdependent; no man makes a governmental decision by himself. Furthermore, each actor is vulnerable; he can be punished by someone else if he does not perform according to expectations. Systems having interdependent, vulnerable actors naturally develop rules of the game so that actors may relate to one another with the least amount of friction. There is no room in the rules of such a system for corrupt or deceitful relationships between actors; the potential costs to other actors are too great. Actors who refuse to conform to these rules are readily ejected from the system (Milbrath 1963, part IV).

Lobbying is but one factor in the total policy-making process of any government. Seldom can the predominating influence on a policy decision be attributed to lobbying. Other influences—such as the desires of the voters, the cajolings of fellow officials, and the political philosophy of officials—generally outweigh the impact of lobbying. Yet lobbying makes a useful contribution by injecting the policy desires of special interests into the political system. The range of policy alternatives available to decision makers is probably broader, and the perceptions by officials of the potential impact of their decisions is probably clearer, because of lobbying activity. Assuming that this leads to better-informed and higher-quality decisions, the net contribution of lobbying to the political process is probably positive.

LESTER W. MILBRATH

[See also INTEREST GROUPS; LEGISLATION; POLITICAL FINANCING; POLITICAL GROUP ANALYSIS; REPRESENTATION; RULES OF THE GAME.]

BIBLIOGRAPHY

AMERICAN ACADEMY OF POLITICAL AND SOCIAL SCIENCE 1958 Unofficial Government: Pressure Groups and Lobbies. Edited by Donald C. Blaisdell. Annals, Vol. 319. Philadelphia: The Academy.
BAILEY, STEPHEN K. 1950 Congress Makes a Law: The Story Behind the Employment Act of 1946. New York: Columbia Univ. Press.
BAUER, RAYMOND A.; POOL, ITHIEL DE SOLA; and DEXTER, L. A. 1963 American Business and Public Policy: The Politics of Foreign Trade. New York: Atherton.
BEER, SAMUEL H. 1958 Group Representation in Britain and the United States. American Academy of Political and Social Science, Annals 319:130–140.
BENTLEY, ARTHUR F. (1908) 1949 The Process of Government: A Study of Social Pressures. Bloomington, Ind.: Principia.
CHERINGTON, PAUL W.; and GILLEN, RALPH L. 1962 The Business Representative in Washington. Washington: Brookings Institution.
CRAWFORD, KENNETH G. 1939 The Pressure Boys: The Inside Story of Lobbying in America. New York: Messner.
DE VRIES, WALTER D. 1960 The Michigan Lobbyist: A Study in the Bases and Perceptions of Effectiveness. Ph.D. dissertation, Michigan State Univ.
ECKSTEIN, HARRY H. 1960 Pressure Group Politics: The Case of the British Medical Association. London: Allen & Unwin; Stanford (Calif.) Univ. Press.
GARCEAU, OLIVER (1941) 1961 The Political Life of the American Medical Association. Hamden, Conn.: Shoe String Press.
GROSS, BERTRAM M. 1953 The Legislative Struggle: A Study in Social Combat. New York: McGraw-Hill.
HERRING, E. PENDLETON 1929 Group Representation Before Congress. Baltimore: Johns Hopkins Press.
KILE, ORVILLE M. 1948 The Farm Bureau Through Three Decades. Baltimore: Waverly.
LANE, EDGAR 1964 Lobbying and the Law. Berkeley: Univ. of California Press.

LATHAM, EARL 1952 *The Group Basis of Politics: A Study in Basing-point Legislation.* Ithaca, N.Y.: Cornell Univ. Press; Oxford Univ. Press.

MILBRATH, LESTER W. 1963 *The Washington Lobbyists.* Chicago: Rand McNally.

PATTERSON, SAMUEL C. 1963 The Role of the Lobbyist: The Case of Oklahoma. *Journal of Politics* 25:72–92.

POTTER, ALLEN M. 1961 *Organized Groups in British National Politics.* London: Faber.

SCHRIFTGIESSER, KARL 1951 *The Lobbyists: The Art and Business of Influencing Lawmakers.* Boston: Little.

TAFT, PHILIP 1954 *The Structure and Government of Labor Unions.* Cambridge, Mass.: Harvard Univ. Press.

TRUMAN, DAVID B. (1951) 1962 *The Governmental Process: Political Interests and Public Opinion.* New York: Knopf.

U.S. CONGRESS, HOUSE, SELECT COMMITTEE ON LOBBYING ACTIVITIES 1951 *Report and Recommendations on Federal Lobbying Act.* 81st Congress, 2d Session, House Report No. 3239. Washington: Government Printing Office.

U.S. CONGRESS, SENATE, SPECIAL COMMITTEE TO INVESTIGATE POLITICAL ACTIVITIES, LOBBYING, AND CAMPAIGN CONTRIBUTIONS 1957 *Final Report.* 85th Congress, 1st Session, Senate Report No. 395. Washington: Government Printing Office.

ZEIGLER, HARMON 1964 *Interest Groups in American Society.* Englewood Cliffs, N.J.: Prentice-Hall.

LOCAL FINANCE

Local governments and their financial structures have been subjected to heavy strains by the rapid population growth, urbanization, industrialization, and centralization of the past century. A local government is usually constrained by limited territorial jurisdiction, restrictions on the functions it can perform, ceilings on the amount of permitted taxes and debt, and restrictions on sources of revenue. Not only is its freedom limited, but often most of its actions are ordered, and its behavior then supervised, by the central government. It is no surprise that under these conditions local governments have responded sluggishly to the great technological and institutional changes of the past century. Few generalizations can be made about local finance, since each nation has a different constitution and each has many types of local governments; but one statement which holds for most of the world is that local governments have become weak relative to central governments.

The most common argument explaining the relative decline of local government is a financial one. It is asserted that the most tax-productive bases are pre-empted by central governments and that it is not feasible for a local government to raise its taxes, since industry and persons will respond by moving to other locations. This is far too simple. Throughout the world, localities can be found with almost every type of tax, and the burden of local taxes is highly variable among nations. The tremendous variation in behavior casts doubt on statements of necessary relationship. Localities do have greater financial problems than do central governments, but solutions that enable the localities to be vigorous and relatively autonomous are available. The relative decline of local government has been accompanied by a refusal fully to exploit purely financial solutions to problems, and it indicates that nonfinancial factors are more significant.

Among nations, the United States has one of the most active sets of local governments, but even in the United States the ratio of federal expenditures on civilian activity to state and local expenditures doubled in the first half of the twentieth century. Despite this relative decline of local governments, in absolute terms local governments have grown greatly in importance. In 1902 local expenditures were less than $900 million, and by 1964 they were over $45,000 million in current dollars. State expenditures increased even more dramatically, from $134 million in 1902 to $24,275 million in 1964. Per capita state and local expenditures increased from under $13 in 1902 to over $360 in 1964. These growth figures are dramatic, but they are accompanied, though to a lesser degree, by the world-wide phenomena of an outright transfer of some functions to central governments and of a shift of financial support to central governments, with a consequent absorption of authority by the central governments.

Given the wide range of experiences in degrees of centralization, any simple set of hypotheses would most likely be wrong. Unfortunately, there has been very little research in comparative local finance, so that sophisticated arguments are not available; therefore, we will have to be satisfied with rather general explanations of the relative decline of local government and finance.

Local government, like the horse and the candle, has been the victim of technology. High among the list of significant technological breakthroughs have been the transportation and communication revolutions, which have greatly reduced spatial costs. While these innovations have completely changed industrial structures, have made markets national and international in scope, and have made resources, as well as production centers, highly mobile, local governments have remained fixed in spatial jurisdiction.

The increase in the size of input and product markets has resulted in a great increase in the number of local governments that can affect the efficient operations of the markets. A system of roads can be crippled by poor design of one part, or inadequate education in one area may mean a poor labor force for another area to which the population moves. Therefore, the supply of inputs or the market possibilities of a firm in a city may be strongly affected by the behavior of many distant local governments which it cannot directly influence. Mass-production, standardized industry expanded throughout the nation, while local governments remained fixed. It is not surprising that pressures were strong to create uniformity of tax treatment and of public services in the various parts of the nation—a reasonable uniformity which has been effected by transfer of functions to central governments and by central subventions to local governments.

The goal of uniform public service throughout the nation is not restricted to those services which are inputs to industry; it extends to products going directly to households. Uniformity in consumption of public services would not necessarily lead to centralization, were it not for a second major factor. Fiscal resources are not uniformly distributed among local jurisdictions. If localities were to apply similar tax structures to their economic bases, very different yields would result. If they sought to vary their tax systems in order to realize somewhat equal per capita yields and similar levels of public services, they would have highly variable tax systems. This would have the undesirable consequences of complexity in taxation and nonuniform treatment. The latter might encourage mobile resources to move elsewhere to find another structure that might not tax them as severely. Achievement of uniformity in service without too much variation in tax structure requires the transfer of financing to a central government.

The simplest and most adaptable response of government to the changing economy is the design of a central administrative agency which can establish operational rules independent of past conventions and responsive to the new set of needs. This response has been the most common. The transfer of functions to a central government means a centralization of authority, control, and finance; but administration may be as widely dispersed as the pattern of local governments, or it may take an entirely new organizational form. From the point of view of attaining the most effective government response to the need for public services, this total centralization may be best; but the less radical solution of attempting to work through existing local governments is often adopted. Despite the relatively greater growth of the central administration, local administration is still important and

probably will remain so, especially in the United States, where the vitality of local government follows from the constitutionally imposed federal structure and from the structure of political parties, which have their strong base in state and local governments.

Types of arrangements

The nations of the world have invented many financial arrangements by which to support local governments; these arrangements can be ordered into a few categories.

Local taxes on differentiated bases. In the United States the major illustration of a separate tax base is the property tax. The federal government makes no use of the property tax, and state governments have been reducing their use of the tax. Some local governments, especially single-purpose districts like school districts and irrigation districts, are restricted to the property tax. Although the property tax is still the principal support of local government, it has declined in importance; its base has been progressively narrowed as more types of property have been removed from the base and other sources of support have been introduced.

Local reliance on the property tax is not uniform. The average property tax rate for the United States was estimated to be 1.4 per cent of market value of locally assessed property in 1962, but this varied from 2.7 per cent in Massachusetts to 0.5 per cent in South Carolina. Comparable variation exists in the percentage of local government revenues collected from property taxes.

Although property taxes have become relatively less important, their role as the distinctive local tax has resulted in extreme pressure to increase the property tax yield because of the increased demand for local services brought about by the rapid increase in urban population, especially in the number of school-age children. Although the demand for public services and property tax yields have increased, property tax payers have energetically sought to reduce their taxes through political action.

One way to reduce the property tax has been to introduce other financial sources, and these will be discussed below. Another way has been to limit the freedom of the local government in the use of the tax. This has taken the form of rate limits imposed by the state governments and of an erosion of the base through exemptions and poor administration. The property tax payer has been able to utilize his political power in the state capital to restrain local finance in one direction, but this has resulted in tax expansion in other directions.

Another political response to the increase in property taxes has been the adoption of fiscal profitability as a criterion for many local public policies, such as zoning, subdivision control, public facilities planning, and annexation.

In considering alternative land use developments, the local authority's analysts compute the property tax yields and the public expenditures associated with each alternative and then adopt the alternative with the maximum difference between property tax yields and public expenditures. Sometimes the analysis is more sophisticated, involving consideration of all the revenues to the local government and all the local expenditures requiring local finance. The results of the analysis almost always show low fiscal profitability in residential use by low-income families with school-age children and high fiscal profitability in industrial use requiring few transportation services, or in residential use by high-income families with few children. The outcome might be to encourage the development of clean industry and the residence of its executives and to discourage the workers employed in the plants from living in the area. Competitive behavior by all of the localities in the area would be self-defeating; on the other hand, if only a subset of the local governments adopted the criterion of fiscal profitability, then the entire area would develop inefficiently. Workers would travel longer distances, industry might not be optimally located, and so on.

The separate tax base does have the virtue of encouraging independent government, and certainly it has permitted American local government to be viable; but it has meant some loss in the efficiency of the operations of metropolitan areas. Although this separate (property) tax base is not likely to disappear, its role will decline because of the many defects of the tax per se and because of the endemic difficulties of independent financing of local governments. [See Taxation, article on property taxes.]

Shared bases with separate levies. Two types of base sharing are practiced. One form is that of complete independence between the levels of government; the bases need not be identical and the rates are independently determined. In the second type the base is identical, although rates may be independently determined, and often there is common administration. Both types are common in all nations.

An illustration of complete independence is the income tax. Although this is usually considered a central tax, many localities use it as well. In the United States in 1964, it was used by two-thirds of the states and by 30 cities. Although the states may define their base so as to approximate the federal base, the local income taxes tend to be payroll taxes. Because its narrower base gives rise to charges of inequity, the local income tax is not likely to be used widely.

A more common form of sharing of bases is under some joint administration, either restricted to the definition of the base or extending to collection. The property tax takes this form within the structure of local governments and in some countries is shared by local and national governments.

In the United States property may be appraised by the state or county, and each of the hundreds of local governments may then independently determine the rate it requires to satisfy its revenue requirements. In some cases a common appraisal of the property is required, while in others it is simply economical for one community to accept the appraisal of another. In either event, the set of taxes may often be collected in one bill and then allocated among the governments.

Although this procedure does limit the power of the government to determine the base most advantageous to it, it has the advantages of uniformity and administrative efficiency while allowing each local government to determine the level and distribution of services it prefers.

A somewhat more centralized tax shared by state and local governments in the United States is the general retail sales tax. Over two-thirds of the states have retail sales taxes, and several thousand local governments add tax supplements onto the state tax. There is a marked trend to adopt this tax structure, with administration by the state or local government and local government option to share in the base. Generally there is a ceiling on the local supplement, and sometimes a specific amount is stipulated. Under this structure the local government has formal freedom, but the incentives for all local governments to develop a uniform policy are great.

The trend has been to move from overlapping taxation of a common base, with independent definition of the base and rates, to joint definition of the base and common administration, with independent rates, and then on to more restrictive rules about rates.

Shared taxes. A shared tax is simply the transformation of a local supplement to a national tax into a simple assessment of the tax by the national government, with some share going to the local governments. This scheme is fairly common throughout the world, though of relatively less importance in the United States. Generally the transformation has taken the form of extending state administration of the tax, returning some of the proceeds to the local government which had been using it, e.g., the development of state motor-vehicle license taxes out of local personal property taxes assessed against automobiles. The initial impetus to shared taxes was the desire to achieve simplification and uniformity, but rules of sharing have become increasingly complex. Issues of need have been introduced into the formulas, so that it is often difficult to distinguish between a shared tax and an intergovernmental grant. Although, in principle, these two forms of financing are very different, experience has shown that if the central government has authority over the sharing formula, it will exercise its discretionary power and the local government will lose control over the size of its budget and sometimes even over the use of these shared funds.

Intergovernmental grants. The most completely centralized form of local financing is tax assessment and collection by the central government, with a transfer of funds to local governments for financing their services. This type of finance has grown most rapidly. Control over finance does not logically entail authority over local public services, but experience has shown that this has been the usual result. Generally, the three preceding forms allow fairly complete freedom to the local government in the allocation of its budget and often in determining the size of its budget. But even if no financial controls are exercised by the central government, localities may not have autonomy, since in many nations local governments are required to provide specific services which sometimes are prescribed in detail.

There are two general types of financial transfers from central governments, basically distinguished by the amount of discretion which remains with the local government in the allocation of the funds at its disposal.

Unconditional grants. The free unconditional grant in its purest form would be a simple transfer of funds from the central government, which is considered the most efficient taxing body, to the local government, which is considered the best decision-making body. If the problem confronting local government were simply financial, one would expect to see these unconditional grants play a major role. In fact, their role is trivial. Few countries use them, and where they do exist, as in England, they are not a major factor in local finance.

Local government has long advocated that grants be made as unconditionally as possible, in order to retain as much local autonomy as possible. But even where only minimum conditions are accepted as desirable, redistribution objectives are introduced into the criteria by which the grants are allocated among communities; and these originally very broad redistributional objectives readily become more specific and thereby influence the quality and types of public services to be encouraged.

Conditional grants. Conditional grants to local governments carry with them specific requirements for local government behavior. Since the conditions must be policed, extensive audit procedures accompany the grants. Local governments generally oppose this form of support, since they dislike the administrative supervision by the central government and they oppose its direct control of their budget.

The motives behind conditional grants are many. In some cases, especially that of the United States, it is not politically feasible to establish a central administration, but the same results are sought through imposing very specific conditions. Two other important motives are the encouragement of specific services and financial equalization.

The encouragement of specific services is obvious when the grant does not require the local government to contribute to the support of the service. Some local governments might deplore that the grant is directed toward their less urgent needs, but at least it will not divert their resources. But often the condition of the grant requires matching outlays from the local government. Since the local dollar spent on the subsidized service will buy proportionately more of that service, it is clear that budgetary allocations will be affected. There will be incentives to expand local support of the subsidized services. This budgetary distortion has been resented by local authorities. The encouragement of specific services through local matching provisions has become less important.

Financial equalization has become more important. Although this objective was never absent, initial matching grants were more favorable to the wealthier communities. More complex formulas have since been devised to take into account local needs, local fiscal resources, and local fiscal effort. Despite the increasing sophistication and complexity of formulas, no consensus has developed about an optimal formula. Subsidies distort; their administration will be lax if there is no burden on the local government; and if a burden is imposed, then the localities may not have the appropriate incentive to expand the service or equity may not be served.

Financing of local debt

Another aspect of local finance which has dramatically changed in many countries is the financing of local debt. Even in the United States, where a local government usually goes to the capital markets very much as private firms do, changes have occurred. Not only have debt limits become common and referendums by the voters often required, but the approval of a state agency as to technical or financial feasibility of the project now is often required. A further change has been the growth of loans by the central government to the local governments. In some countries almost all loans are centralized; in the United States the loan program is one of the instruments of intergovernmental transfers. The loan is often administered by the agency which administers the grant program and which may be carrying on services as well. State governments also extend loans to local governments.

Although the centralization of government and finances has been the most important recent structural change, another reorganization, concerning metropolitan government, may be of comparable importance, especially in the United States. A typical metropolitan area is made up of hundreds of governments. Some are the residuals of an agricultural economy of a half-century past, others are the many new suburban cities, and still more are the special-function governments ranging from a small-area police district to a regional air-pollution control board. Most of them have taxing powers, while some can finance themselves only by user charges. The conflicts among these governments have focused on the suburban–central city rivalry for financial bases. Central cities have charged that suburbanites work in the central cities and use all of their amenities while living in the suburbs, where they pay their local property taxes. The suburbs charge that they bear the heavy burdens of education and residential services while the fiscally rich industrial and commercial properties are in the central cities or industrial enclaves. Issues of equity in finance and service have inhibited agreements about urban development programs, and meanwhile the government of the metropolitan area has deteriorated.

The problems of metropolitan government and finance have been elaborated in great detail. Solutions have been of an *ad hoc* nature, e.g., a federal subsidy for urban renewal, a new government for a mass rapid-transit system, or an additional tax base. Despite the muddling-through procedures, there has been a great deal of experimentation.

In the past decade, user charges have increased sharply at the state and local levels. The metering of water and on-street parking has expanded as a revenue source, and the value of user charges as rationing devices is beginning to be understood. User charges not only help to bring about an effi-

cient rationing of limited public services, provide cues determining the scale at which services should be performed, and ease the financial plight of cities, but also lessen the conflict among governments. For example, if there is a charge on visiting the museum, it is irrelevant whether the school bus is discharging suburban or central city children: either school district would have to pay for cultural enrichment. Or it is unimportant if the parker is from the suburb or the central city if he pays the full incremental cost of making the street space available for his parked car. It is very likely that there will be a significant expansion of pricing of public services over a wide range of activities. [*See* PRICES, *article on* PRICING POLICIES.]

Innovations in local government arrangements have occurred in response to crises: many special authorities without taxing powers, or districts with taxing powers which move freely across old jurisdictional lines, have been created. From one perspective the *ad hoc* responses to crises have generated another layer of bureaucracies and assessing agencies, complicating still further the problems of rational management. But these governments are very fluid, their political bases are weak, and the possibilities of a more deliberative reshuffling of government and financial structures are not trivial. Metropolitan governments may develop out of the array of municipal governments and overlapping special districts and authorities, but it is likely that the state and federal governments will be the prime movers in metropolitan development and that the financial base of the metropolitan government may look very different from that of a mere composite of existing local governments.

JULIUS MARGOLIS

[*See also* LOCAL GOVERNMENT; TAXATION.]

BIBLIOGRAPHY

BRAZER, HARVEY E. 1962 Some Fiscal Aspects of Metropolitanism. Pages 61–82 in Guthrie S. Birkhead (editor), *Metropolitan Issues: Social, Governmental, Fiscal.* Syracuse Univ., Maxwell Graduate School of Citizenship and Public Affairs.

BURKHEAD, JESSE 1963 *State and Local Taxes for Public Education.* Syracuse Univ. Press.

DUE, JOHN F. 1963 *Taxation and Economic Development in Tropical Africa.* Cambridge, Mass.: M.I.T. Press.

Federalism and Economic Growth in Underdeveloped Countries: A Symposium, by Ursula K. Hicks et al. 1961 New York: Oxford Univ. Press.

HUMES, SAMUEL; and MARTIN, EILEEN M. 1961 *The Structure of Local Governments Throughout the World.* The Hague: Nijhoff.

MARGOLIS, JULIUS 1961 Metropolitan Finance Problems: Territories, Functions, and Growth. Pages 229–293 in Universities–National Bureau Committee for

Economic Research, *Public Finances: Needs, Sources, and Utilization.* Princeton Univ. Press.

MAXWELL, JAMES A. 1965 *Financing State and Local Governments.* Washington: Brookings Institution.

NETZER, DICK 1966 *Economics of the Property Tax.* Washington: Brookings Institution.

PHILIP, KJELD 1954 *Intergovernmental Fiscal Relations.* Copenhagen: Institute of Economics and History.

PREST, ALAN R. 1962 *Public Finance in Under-developed Countries.* London: Weidenfeld & Nicolson.

SIMON, HERBERT A. 1943 *Fiscal Aspects of Metropolitan Consolidation.* Berkeley: Univ. of California, Bureau of Public Administration.

U.S. ADVISORY COMMISSION ON INTERGOVERNMENTAL RELATIONS 1962 *Measures of State and Local Fiscal Capacity and Tax Effort.* Washington: Government Printing Office.

U.S. ADVISORY COMMISSION ON INTERGOVERNMENTAL RELATIONS 1964 *The Role of Equalization in Federal Grants.* Washington: Government Printing Office.

U.S. ADVISORY COMMISSION ON INTERGOVERNMENTAL RELATIONS 1965 *Metropolitan Social and Economic Disparities: Implications for Intergovernmental Relations in Central Cities and Suburbs.* Washington: Government Printing Office.

U.S. BUREAU OF THE CENSUS 1964 *Census of Governments: 1962.* Washington: Government Printing Office. → See especially Volume 5, *Local Government in Metropolitan Areas*, and Volume 6, No. 4, *Historical Statistics on Governmental Finances and Employment.*

LOCAL GOVERNMENT

Local government may be loosely defined as a public organization authorized to decide and administer a limited range of public policies within a relatively small territory which is a subdivision of a regional or national government. Local government is at the bottom of a pyramid of governmental institutions, with the national government at the top and intermediate governments (states, regions, provinces) occupying the middle range. Normally, local government has general jurisdiction and is not confined to the performance of one specific function or service.

This simple definition obscures wide variations in local governmental systems and operational patterns, and it should be supplemented by a system of classification for both description and analysis. In the past, local governments have been classified largely in terms of their formal structures. Thus, in the United States great stress was laid on the question of whether a local government had a mayor with broad executive powers or a mayor who was little more than a presiding officer of the city council (the strong versus the weak mayor "plans"); whether the council members divided among themselves administrative responsibility for the several aspects of local government (the commission plan); or whether the council employed a professional executive agent to administer the city's affairs and be accountable to the council (the city manager plan). Similar emphasis was placed on form and structure by authors attempting cross-national comparisons of local governmental systems. A perusal of the publications of the International Union of Local Authorities (e.g., *The Structure of Local Governments . . .*, Humes and Martin 1961) or of the contents of *The Municipal Yearbook* will indicate the dominant concern for structure. The *Yearbook*, for example, provides details on the organization of local government, but only in 1963 did it begin to provide data on local elections.

The formal structure of local government, important as it can be to the character of a system, is not the only nor even the most significant determinant of the style of local government. The quality and character of a local government are determined by a multiplicity of factors—for example, national and local traditions, customary deference patterns, political pressures, party influence and discipline, bureaucratic professionalism, economic resource controls, and social organization and beliefs. That a local government is located in a nation controlled by a communist party may be an infinitely more important fact than the structural forms it has. That an American city is located in the South, where Negroes occupy an inferior social position, may explain far more about the local government than its structure. The existence of a huge economic enterprise within a given municipality may be more determinative of the style and policies of a local government than its organization. And, it might be added, this may be as true in a totalitarian regime as in a democratic one.

There are hundreds of thousands of local governments in the world, and we lack sufficient information about their operational characteristics to make completely confident generalizations about the nature of local government or to isolate the most critical variables that shape it. In the process of moving toward surer understanding of the phenomenon it is useful to pursue answers to three basic questions about any local government. First, to what extent is there local self-government? For example, do the people of the community have an opportunity to participate in government through meaningful elections and to have access to public officials to express their opinions by organized and individual activity? Second, to what extent does the municipality have relative autonomy and discretionary authority to act? That is, is there a *deconcentration* of authority from the central government to the locality with little or no local discretion, or is there *decentralization* of authority with relative discretion to undertake programs on local initiative and with relative freedom from strict supervision and restriction from the central government? Third, is the local government a vital and significant force in the lives of the people? Is the government an institution with the will and the authority to undertake activities that deeply affect the lives of people, or is it so marginal an aspect of life that the citizenry is scarcely aware that it exists?

To facilitate discussion of local government in terms of these broad questions, five broad categories of local governmental systems may be postulated: (1) federal–decentralized, (2) unitary–decentralized, (3) Napoleonic–prefect, (4) communist, and (5) postcolonial. The meaning of each category will become clear in the discussion.

Federal–decentralized systems

Those federal systems which decentralize much authority to the regional governments that compose the federation also tend to be the nations that allow the broadest range of discretionary authority to local government. This is not true of all systems that are called federal, however, but only of those with actual decentralization. The Soviet government is formally organized along federal lines, but such decentralization of authority to the districts as exists occurs under strict central government controls; it is made abundantly clear that the sub-units of the Soviet system (the "republics" and their subdivisions) are in reality agents of the central government and the Communist party. In federal systems with much decentralization (for example, Australia, Canada, Germany, Switzerland, and the United States) the degree of autonomy of local government varies considerably from country to country, but in all cases a considerable degree of local independence prevails.

This variation extends deeper than the country-by-country comparison, for there is often much variation among individual states or provincial–regional governments as to the forms and authority of local government. For example, the closeness of supervision by administrative agencies of regional governments varies widely from fairly extensive reporting and oversight to almost none, except in cases of flagrant corruption. Likewise, certain states in the United States grant "home rule" to municipalities by statutory or state constitutional provisions that permit municipalities to alter their forms of government at will and that grant local authority to "make all laws and ordinances relating to municipal concerns," or broadly the "powers of local self-government," while in other states the municipality has to appeal to the state legislature for specific permission to undertake a particular program.

The idea of "home rule" as local independence is an ancient doctrine, but as a legal concept it originated in the late nineteenth century when American state legislatures interfered, often corruptly, with the functioning of local government. Gradually, home rule has extended, with varying degrees of effectiveness, to most of the states. Home rule does not grant total autonomy by any means, since legislatures through general law and the courts through interpretation still restrain local government. Nevertheless, the concept contradicts the principle of municipal inferiority that previously stood as a basic rule of law. In the late nineteenth century Judge John F. Dillon stated the classic principle of the status of the local government by saying that municipal corporations were completely creatures of the legislature which could control or even destroy municipalities at will. In the famous Dillon's Rule he stated:

It is a general and undisputed proposition of law that a *municipal corporation possesses and can exercise the following powers, and no others:* First, those granted in *express words;* second, those *necessarily or fairly implied* in or *incident* to the powers expressly granted; third, those essential to the accomplishment of the declared objects and purposes of the corporation—not simply convenient, but indispensable. Any fair, reasonable, substantial doubt concerning the existence of power is resolved by the courts against the corporation, and the power is denied. (Dillon [1872] 1911, vol. 1, sec. 237)

American courts no longer follow Dillon's Rule rigidly, although its fundamental precepts are still frequently drawn upon even in home rule states, when local and state jurisdictions are in conflict. Litigation and the threat of litigation are important restraints upon local independence.

In the United States all local legislative bodies and most chief executives are directly elected. Local government organization varies enormously —from the town meeting, where all registered voters may participate in basic decision making, to the highly bureaucratized governments of many large cities where mayors combat the inertia of professionalism and pluralistic stasis (see Sayre & Kaufman 1960; Dahl 1961; Banfield 1961). In some cities powerful political party machines control decision making by the formal officeholders; in others business elites have great power; in still others authority is widely dispersed to independent boards and commissions which are relatively invisible to the voters and partially beyond the control of the council or the mayor (for example, Los Angeles). Although it has commonly been thought that American small communities are highly democratic in the sense that the public has easy access to and much control over their representatives, research on local governmental operation suggests that this is not necessarily true (see Vidich & Bensman 1958; Presthus 1964). For example, survey research in American cities concerning the citizen's "subjective competence" (that is, a person's belief that he can exert significant influence upon his local government) indicated that two-thirds of the respondents felt a high degree of confidence in their political effectiveness, but there was no evidence of significant variation in terms of the size of the community from which the respondent came. Indeed, insofar as there was a variation, it favored the larger as opposed to the smallest cities (see Almond & Verba 1963, p. 235).

Swiss municipalities also have a wide area of local autonomy, although there are variations among the Swiss cantons (states) in this respect. The German-speaking cantons usually permit more discretion than do the Italian- and French-speaking ones. A high degree of local self-government prevails, particularly in the rural communities; in nine out of ten communes the municipal deliberative body is an assembly of all electors. In larger municipalities elective councils are employed, and under certain conditions a referendum may be used to submit questions to the vote of the people.

Other federal systems permit somewhat less local autonomy. In Australia, for example, local actions are subject to review by the state governor and ordinances are effective only after their approval by the governor, although there remains a general autonomy for the locality within the limitations of its local charter and the supervision of the state departments of local government. In Canada a considerable sphere of local autonomy exists, but not as much as traditionally prevails in the United States or Switzerland. An illustration of this is found in the decision of the provincial legislature of Ontario to form a new unit of metropolitan government in the Toronto area in 1953. The premier of Ontario warned that the legislature would act if the local communities failed to create some orderly method of coping with the problems of the metropolitan area, and when no action followed the legislature created a new governmental unit covering both the center city and its suburbs. While such action would be legally feasible in most (although not all) states in the United States, American political traditions of local independence make it nearly impossible to do this.

The local government system of the West German Federal Republic also has variations in local powers and procedures among the provincial governments (Länder), yet the over-all independence of local governments is considerable. The degree of independence does not match that in the United States or Switzerland, however. The burgomaster (roughly equivalent to a mayor) is a professional administrator and occupies a very strong position in the local government; significantly, he is not only a local official but a federal and state official as well, since the city performs certain functions for the higher jurisdictions. The supervision of local government from higher echelons is also fairly rigorous, and this has increased as the practice of the state's delegating certain functions for local performance has grown. It is perhaps suggestive of the representativeness of German local government that a far higher proportion of German respondents to an opinion survey indicated that they believed they could "do something about an unjust local law or regulation" than those who felt any competence to correct an unjust national law (Almond & Verba 1963, p. 185).

The vitality of local government in the federal–decentralized countries varies both within and among countries. In the United States the role of local government expanded greatly with the maturation of industrial society in the first half of the twentieth century; protective, regulatory, welfare, planning, economic promotion, cultural, and other activities were initiated or expanded. But the extent of expansion varies greatly with the size of the city, the area of the country, and even for adjacent cities. In the largest cities, where the functional expansion has been greatest, the hugeness and impersonal nature of the government probably make government appear to impinge less on the lives of the citizens than it does in fact. In smaller rural or suburban communities, local government ranges from the moribund to the fairly vital. Likewise in other nations the degree of vitality and impact of government varies widely. In the Swiss communities where a town-meeting style of government prevails, the sense of involvement and the level of participation are high. The English-speaking Commonwealth federal systems appear to have a range of variation in the vitality of local government that compares generally with that in the United States. [See FEDERALISM.]

Unitary–decentralized systems

Great Britain and the Scandinavian countries are examples of nations with unitary (that is, non-federal) governments which have a considerable degree of decentralization of autonomous power to localities. Although in all cases there is supervision by the central government, and although localities can take only such actions as authorized by the central government, local governments in these nations do have fairly wide responsibilities and make independent decisions about them. The independent status of the English city has a long history, as evidenced by ancient royal charters of cities. The first charters were just agreements by the king to recognize certain concessions that local leaders had bought or bargained for, but in time the charters became regularized and the basis of a considerable area of local discretion. As early as the fifteenth century merchant guilds and borough councils originated the rudiments of local self-government. Parliament remains the supreme source of local authority, but the practice of permitting local prerogatives is so firmly established that curtailment is always resisted and comes only after great deliberation. Nevertheless, there has been a considerable diminution of local independence since the nineteenth century. Although the functions of the municipality have in some respects been enlarged with the coming of new problems and public policies to meet them (for example, public housing), an extension of the central government's concern for formerly purely local matters has taken place simultaneously. Particularly in the fields where the central government has provided a percentage of the cost of programs through grants-in-aid, central government departments have greatly extended their control over local decisions. Centrally established minimum standards of performance have unquestionably raised the efficiency of local government, but at the same time they have curtailed the independence that once existed.

British local government is representative self-government. The local council is directly elected, although the local executive is not. The mayor (or chairman in certain local bodies) is chosen from among the council members, but he is not the chief executive in the same way that an American mayor is. The British mayor is more a ceremonial and presiding official than an active executive leader, and to the extent that he is the latter it is the result of his personal qualities or his political position. The major operating element of the British local council is the committee system, into which noncouncil members are co-opted as experts on aspects of policy covered by the particular committee. Although the council must ratify all committee actions before they are valid, the committees are the active elements in the process rather than the council as a whole. The town (or county) clerk also plays a significant role in local government in his relationship to the committees. It is he who prepares information for the committee and sets the agenda, but he is not a British parallel to the American city manager, for he is not directly given the function of overseeing administration. Traditionally clerks are not trained in administrative management but in the law, although their apprenticeship in local government necessarily emphasizes administrative matters, and as the problems of local government become more complex it increasingly falls to the clerk to provide expertise and to coordinate the diverse elements of local government.

Since the early nineteenth century local governments in the Scandinavian nations have been allowed a fair degree of autonomy. The list of powers for local government is extensive, and while regional appointees of the central government who are in some respects similar to the French prefect oversee local operations, the actual supervision is not strict and does not compare with that in nations with prefectoral systems. In Norway all actions involving expenditures must be cleared with the provincial governor before they can be carried out, which on the surface suggests that Norwegian local government may be less autonomous than that of Britain. In fact, however, Norwegian municipalities have somewhat more discretion, since the supervision is not strict. Norwegian local government is vital, has broad scope, and is a very important aspect of the nation's political–governmental system. Local government is a common recruiting ground for higher political office, and local forms and practices have been used as modes for creating regional institutions and practices. Denmark also has close supervision of fiscal matters, but the check on local government that this might imply is not apparently onerous. Local government is democratic, has a fairly wide range of discretion, but is somewhat less autonomous and vital than Norwegian local government. In Sweden local government activities are divided between those that are "free" of supervision, except on legal challenge, and those that are "regulated." Generally speaking, the free functions are those concerned with municipally provided utilities and cultural–recreational activities, whereas the regulated ones include a long list of functions extending from welfare services to town planning, local courts, and school administration. As in Norway and England there is extensive use of committees of the council for conduct of business. Finland's local governments have somewhat less discretionary authority and are subject to closer supervision, but the general pattern appears to be not markedly different from that in other Scandinavian nations. [See PARLIAMENTARY GOVERNMENT.]

Napoleonic–prefect systems

The peculiarity of this style of local government is that the central government places in subregions of the nation an agent of the national government to oversee, and if necessary to countermand, suspend, or replace local governments. The system is a direct survivor of the ancient institutions by which France attempted to create a centralized nation out of a scattered system of feudal fiefs, small cities, and ecclesiastical domains. The office of *intendant*, conceived by Richelieu in the early seventeenth century, was a means of extending the king's authority into the hinterland, where the thirty *intendants* were known as the "thirty tyrants." Animosity toward the office resulted in its dissolution in the French Revolution, but Napoleon restored it as the office of prefect, and it still flourishes in France today. In varying forms the office is commonly found in southern Europe and in Latin America, just as British forms are found in English-speaking nations.

In France the basic unit of local government is the commune, of which there are some 38,000, and each is under the supervision of a prefect of a *département* (of which there are 90) or under the intermediate control of a subprefect of an *arrondissement* (more than 300). (In some areas superprefects also provide regional supervision.) The commune is typically a small community, since most of France is rural, although cities are also organized as communes. There is a high degree of local interest in commune politics, and council elections are often heatedly contested. The mayor, who is chosen from the ranks of the council, has a wide range of executive authority; and although he is legally accountable to the council, he nevertheless is a powerful political force in the municipality. Initiative in fiscal matters and other policy issues is in the mayor's hands. The mayor and the council operate under the eye of the prefect or subprefect, however; and all commune actions are subject to review by the prefect, who may refuse to approve or may even dissolve the local council or remove the mayor. There are, on the average, some three hundred dissolutions per year,

although a major cause of this is irreconcilable disagreement within the council rather than conflict with the prefect.

It should not be assumed, however, that French local government is actually controlled from Paris. Prefects and subprefects have a considerable area of discretion, and they often find it wise to strike a political balance between themselves and the mayors, who are not entirely without weapons to deploy against a demanding prefect, for national political forces are often just barely beneath the surface of local politics. Many mayors are influential national political figures, and local politics is a common basis for a political career. Despite this countervailing force against centralization, local government in France remains far more subordinate and dependent than in such countries as the United States and England. Police and education, for example, are largely beyond local control; fiscal controls and subventions are deployed by prefects to bring commune policy in line. Interest and participation, however, run high in France. A British observer, granting that in England local government had more autonomy than it does in France, nevertheless found in France more interest in local matters and more vitality in local government (Chapman 1953, p. 221).

In other Mediterranean countries and in Latin America, where the prefectoral system prevails, there are many variations on the French pattern. In Spain and Italy, for example, there is considerably more centralization than in France. In Spain central government controls are rigorously applied to the more than nine thousand municipalities; the mayor is appointed by the central government, and he is the strongest force in local affairs. Portugal has a similar system of central control. In Italy the prefectoral system was a convenient device for extending the powers of the fascist system into the hinterland, and interestingly one of the consequences of the fascist interlude is that the prefect has greater power today than in the prefascist era (Fried 1963, p. 261). Local councils are popularly elected, but the mayor and the councils are well aware of the power of the prefect, who uses his position not only to provide general administrative supervision but to pursue political objectives as well —such as the curbing of the power of communists when they take over a local government. In rural areas particularly, local government is not a vital or popular institution; it is often considered by the people to be an element of nature to be endured— like drought or disease—not something from which benefits are likely to be derived.

In Latin America extensive supervision of local

government by officials similar to the prefect is common. In some countries the local mayor is appointed by the central government, and in others he is elected, but his actions and those of locally elective councils are subjected to extremely close control by the central government. Brazil, with its federal system, does not conform to this, however, and it has relatively little central or state government oversight of the details of local government operations. An essentially prefectoral system is also used in Japan, where, significantly, a large measure of the authority of the supervising administrator lies in his discretionary authority to grant subsidies to local government.

Communist systems

The local governmental systems of communist nations are, in general, examples of deconcentration of authority rather than decentralization. That is, the local governmental unit is an agency of the central government, and it functions as an integral element of the hierarchical administrative system of the state. The area of local independence is narrow and extends only to minor matters, whereas control devices are extensive and are rigorously applied. Local officials are well aware that their decisions must conform to an over-all design of higher authorities, and they know, too, that to divert budget funds to other purposes without permission may mean dismissal or even imprisonment. These systems are unique in that local governments are given a role in economic activities infinitely more extensive than in capitalist nations. Finally the discipline of the Communist party is a means of controlling policy in detail. As a supplement to and a check on the administrative system, the Communist party with its rigid discipline controls the key positions in government. Indeed, the Communist party's role is remarkably similar to that of the classic American local government party machine. Where a classic American machine acquired complete control, the formal distribution of authority was unimportant; what mattered was the internal discipline of the party through which decisions were made from the top to the bottom of the government (McKean 1940). The critical difference between the two situations is that the American boss system depends upon local insularity to maintain control, whereas the communist system utilizes the local party to carry out the program of the national party leaders.

Local government in the Soviet Union is subject to very intensive control, but the minute and stifling controls of the Stalin era are no longer used. The ponderous apparatus needed for detailed supervision of local operations from Moscow became so expensive and inefficient that in the 1950s efforts were made to decentralize to a limited extent. In the 1930s the rigidity of controls was such that a local bakery's request for a supplemental flour allotment was passed to higher and higher authority until it finally reached the desk of the premier, and he approved the request himself (Granick 1960, p. 162). Documents captured by the Germans in 1941, in the town of Smolensk, also reveal the manner in which the party was used to assert tight control by Moscow over local operations (Fainsod 1958).

The decentralizing tendencies of the 1950s and 1960s did not necessarily increase the degree of local self-government. As before, the locality elects large local soviets in which there is much discussion of local affairs, but apparently the decision-making power remains with the executive committee of the soviet rather than with the soviet members themselves. Local leaders are, however, permitted a wider range of discretion for which ultimately they are held responsible to their superiors. Evidence that the new policies did not involve a total change is the story in *Pravda* following the departure of Khrushchev from power. Khrushchev favored reinforced concrete blocks over bricks for construction and, as word of his attitude filtered down the hierarchy, local managers shut down brickworks regardless of local demand. Khrushchev's successors promised in *Pravda* to grant to local soviets power to "decide all local issues"; if this becomes a reality it will involve an enormous change in the traditional balance of political power in the U.S.S.R. [See COMMUNISM, *article on* SOVIET COMMUNISM.]

The Chinese commune is a striking experiment in devising local institutions to serve the purposes of a dedicated communist regime. The communes are at once instruments of economic planning, educational and cultural activity, and governmental control. In order to increase manpower, women are freed from child care and household work through provision of nurseries, common eating facilities, and "service centers" for clothing repair and other household chores. Millions of Chinese eat in public mess halls in both agricultural and urban communes. Local marginal industries are organized and operated by the commune. It is claimed that more than 500 million Chinese were in communes in 1960, but this probably includes many paper organizations. Nevertheless, the commune is potentially an impressive device in its totality of involvement of the citizen's life, the opportunities it offers for political control through propaganda, police, and tight party discipline, and its potential for economic production where man power so greatly exceeds all other forms of capital. It is an attempt to resolve China's age-old problem of balancing local initiative and central control—this time consistent with the requirements of an industrial revolution under rigid totalitarian control.

Yugoslavia offers a significantly different kind of communist local governmental system. Although the party and its discipline remain an important control factor, it is evident that a great degree of decentralization has been introduced. The Yugoslav commune has a bicameral council, one house being a political body elected by area and the other concerned with economic matters and representative of workers and farmers in their respective work units. The economic chamber is somewhat less powerful than the political one, since it acts on a more restricted range of issues; but on all basic economic questions, including the budget, the two chambers must agree. The central government has basic responsibility for the economic growth of the nation, and it grants funds for economic investment; yet the locality has some discretion about the form of development it desires and relative independence in the conduct of local enterprises once established. The municipal council sets basic standards of operation for all municipal economic organizations, and it appoints their managers; but the workers in the enterprises and their elected representatives have control over some aspects of operations. In addition to the workers councils, numerous other elected bodies deal with a broad range of subjects from education to social security. Periodic meetings of all voters who wish to participate allow for discussion of current questions, and under certain circumstances a referendum is possible, although it has been little used. In comparison with other communist systems, Yugoslavia has a high degree of decentralization and vitality. Local discretion and self government are, however, circumscribed by the existence of the party as a "guide" for local action. Yugoslavian leaders stress the importance of local self-government but at the same time emphasize the importance of the Leninist principle of "democratic centralism," which holds that minority views should give way to strict party discipline when basic decisions have been made. [See COMMUNISM, *article on* NATIONAL COMMUNISM.]

Postcolonial systems

The creation of new nations from former colonies involves varying degrees of change in local government. In some cases the imposition of a strong single-party political system subverts old patterns almost entirely; in others, where adjustment more than revolutionary change has been the theme, local government patterns have not altered drastically. The legacy of colonialism is omnipresent, however much the new leaders strive for complete breaks with the colonial past [see COLONIALISM]. The pre-existing systems of local government, closely supervised by colonial officials and native subordinate administrators, have often remained as the general pattern of local–central government relationships. The terminology and basic structures of the colonial local government system frequently persist for reasons of habituation and convenience, if no other. Some leaders of postcolonial nations do not have a simple alternative of returning to a precolonial local government system, both because the colonial powers undermined or abolished the old ways and because the old systems were incapable of dealing with the conditions of Westernized and modernized life. The original tribal and village systems or bureaucratized empires of the past were appropriate to a rural, self-sufficient, and isolated kind of social life or to conditions of minimal central control; but as these nations become urbanized and begin to develop integrated economies, the simple forms of the past are inappropriate. Although some of the ancient forms of tribal rulership were allowed to continue by some colonial powers, it was apparent to local residents that the real authority rested not with the traditional chiefs and elders councils but with the administrators, both native and colonial, who supervised local operations. Not the least important of the remnants of colonialism, then, is the simple continuance of the great authority of the outside supervisor; the creation of active local democracy is difficult under any circumstances but the more so when habits of central supervision are generations old.

Local government in these nations is beset by staggering social and economic problems. In the first place, many of the cities of Asia and Africa are not cities in the European sense; they lack the technology, organization, resources, and slowly developed institutions of the Western city and are often massive accumulations of squatters. Also, as new regimes the central governments tend to be politically unstable. Extraordinary poverty, severe difficulties associated with economic growth, and chronic overcrowding in the cities all produce a range of problems not faced in more modernized nations. For example, many Indian cities face a serious problem in dealing with the tens of thousands who perforce must sleep in the streets at night, and a common problem of the local Indian city corporation is the prevalence of beggars who are organized into self-protective groups to defend their rights. Interestingly, in certain African cities the analogue of the American boss system seems to have developed, where local politicians cater to ethnic minorities and attempt to provide assistance to the city newcomers in exchange for voting support. Remoteness of local communities where transportation is difficult means that many parts of the postcolonial nations have a high degree of local independence through default—the central government being unable to assert its potential authority. A few Near Eastern nations have suffered for long periods from a breakdown in local and national bureaucracy so that local services are not rendered and a semianarchic confusion prevails.

Although modernization is gradually prevailing over traditionalism throughout the postcolonial world, conflict between modernists and traditionalists is endemic [*see* MODERNIZATION]. Tradition in religion and in social organization is the enemy of rational bureaucratization and the extension of power by the new political parties of the developing nations; it is a battle between an old man in a gilded chair (the tribal chieftain) and a young man in a swivel chair (Cowan 1958, p. vi). The virtual elimination of the tribal chief as a man of authority, as in Ghana, is one pattern; whereas the retention of chiefs as significant factors, as in parts of Uganda, is another (Burke 1964). Where political parties are extremely powerful, for example, in Tunisia and Ghana, the forces of traditionalism have been hardest hit—although traditional forms have a way of surviving, partly because they tend to rest on kinship relations that are basic elements of the social fabric. In Morocco, for example, orders from the central government to establish local councils to direct local affairs meant that a few dominant families selected their leaders as the new ruling body. Likewise, commands by the Israeli government to resident Arab communities to create local governing councils produced a council of family elders based on kinship patterns.

There is much conscious effort in the postcolonial nations to improve the quality of local government performance, but much of this involves assertion of controls from above to get local action. In Pakistan, for example, the central government in its Basic Democracies Order of 1959 established a system of local government for all of Pakistan and, outwardly at least, encouraged the growth of local democracy. Yet the control of local operations by the central government is very close, and one observer has found that in a given area no less than 85 per cent of all issues on local council agendas

were put there by communications from the central government (Rahman 1962, p. 31). Inevitably the patterns of local governmental development in the postcolonial societies differ greatly, but the needs for economic growth and the extension of new national power to the hinterlands and in the rapidly growing cities have the tendency to produce as much central control as the regime finds possible. As a general rule the patterns are more like those of Richelieu's France than of Jefferson's United States.

The role of local government

Paradoxically, local government in the twentieth century seems to expand the number of functions it performs at the same time that it faces increasing central government supervision and a narrowing of its independence. As the problems of large and complicated cities and metropolitan areas grow, at least to the extent that financial means to cope with the problems exist, the city has greatly extended its role. Cultural activities expand simultaneously with programs on housing, redevelopment, air pollution control, and the recruitment of business enterprises. Many of the most dramatic and important of these functions are financed in good part by grants-in-aid from higher level governments, thereby decreasing local discretion at least to some extent. Also the expansion occurs simultaneously with a narrowing of distances between the central government and the municipality as the means of communication develop and as areas once isolated economically and politically become an integral part of a national economy and political system. It is therefore sometimes difficult to say whether local governments in a particular nation are now more or less significant agencies of government than they were in a simpler age.

In the case of the smaller communities there is not much doubt that increasing centralization has affected their range of discretion negatively. Although the capacity of a central government to control tends to dwindle with distance for the simple reason that remoteness prevents control, the growth of rapid communication tends to undercut this source of independence. Likewise, smaller communities caught up in the sprawl of metropolitan growth suddenly cease to be independent units and become entangled in the complications of over-all metropolitan areas. This leads to the development of regional institutions that in some degree may supplant or at least supplement local government, and it also tends to force local officials into governing in part through negotiation with officials from higher levels of government and with those of neighboring municipalities (Wood & Almendinger 1961).

Finally, it is important to note that the role of the municipal executive has grown greatly in the present century, owing to the same forces that have heightened the role of the executive in national government. The technological complexity of the problems being dealt with increases the power of the bureaucracy; and the diversity and diffusion of modern life also tend to lead to a stronger executive since, especially in larger cities, the chief executive seems to be the only functionary capable of controlling the bureaucracy, focusing public attention on key issues, and pressuring the various actors on the city scene to respond to the challenges a city faces.

DUANE LOCKARD

[*Directly related are the entries* CENTRALIZATION AND DECENTRALIZATION; CITY, *especially the article on* METROPOLITAN GOVERNMENT; LOCAL FINANCE; LOCAL POLITICS. *Other relevant material may be found under* COMMUNITY.]

BIBLIOGRAPHY

ADRIAN, CHARLES R. (1955) 1961 *Governing Urban America.* 2d ed. New York: McGraw-Hill.

ALDERFER, HAROLD F. 1964 *Local Government in Developing Countries.* New York: McGraw-Hill.

ALMOND, GABRIEL A.; and VERBA, SIDNEY 1963 *The Civic Culture: Political Attitudes and Democracy in Five Nations.* Princeton Univ. Press.

BANFIELD, EDWARD C. (1961) 1965 *Political Influence.* New York: Free Press.

BURKE, FRED G. 1964 *Local Government and Politics in Uganda.* Syracuse Univ. Press.

CHAPMAN, BRIAN LAING 1953 *Introduction to French Local Government.* London: Allen & Unwin.

CHAPMAN, BRIAN LAING 1955 *The Prefects and Provincial France.* London: Allen & Unwin.

COWAN, L. GRAY 1958 *Local Government in West Africa.* New York: Columbia Univ. Press.

DAHL, ROBERT A. (1961) 1963 *Who Governs? Democracy and Power in an American City.* New Haven: Yale Univ. Press.

DILLON, JOHN F. (1872) 1911 *Commentaries on the Law of Municipal Corporations.* 5 vols., 5th ed. Boston: Little.

FAINSOD, MERLE 1958 *Smolensk Under Soviet Rule.* Cambridge, Mass.: Harvard Univ. Press. → A paperback edition was published in 1963 by Random House.

FINER, HERMAN (1933) 1950 *English Local Government.* 4th ed. London: Methuen.

FRIED, ROBERT C. 1963 *The Italian Prefects: A Study in Administrative Politics.* Yale Studies in Political Science, Vol. 6. New Haven: Yale Univ. Press.

GOTTMANN, JEAN (1961) 1964 *Megalopolis: The Urbanized Northeastern Seaboard of the United States.* Cambridge: Massachusetts Institute of Technology Press.

GRANICK, DAVID 1960 *The Red Executive.* Garden City, N.Y.: Doubleday.

GREER, SCOTT A. 1962 *Governing the Metropolis.* New York: Wiley.

HUMES, SAMUEL; and MARTIN, EILEEN M. 1961 *The Structure of Local Governments Throughout the World.* The Hague: Nijhoff.

LETHBRIDGE, HENRY J. 1961 *China's Urban Communes.* Hong Kong: Dragonfly Books.

Local Government in the Twentieth Century. International Union of Local Authorities, Publication No. 72. 1963 The Hague: Nijhoff.

LOCKARD, DUANE 1963 *The Politics of State and Local Government.* New York: Macmillan.

MCKEAN, DAYTON D. 1940 *The Boss: The Hague Machine in Action.* Boston: Houghton Mifflin.

The Municipal Yearbook. 1963 Chicago: International City Managers' Association.

PRESTHUS, ROBERT V. 1964 *Men at the Top: A Study in Community Power.* New York: Oxford Univ. Press.

RAHMAN, A. T. RAFIQUR 1962 *Basic Democracy at the Grass Roots.* Comilla: Pakistan Academy for Village Development.

RAO, V. VENKATA 1960 *A Hundred Years of Local Self-government and Administration in the Andhra and Madras States 1850 to 1950.* Bombay: Local Self-government Institute.

ROBSON, WILLIAM A. 1954 *Great Cities of the World: Their Government, Politics, and Planning.* 2d ed., rev. & enl. London: Allen & Unwin.

SAYRE, WALLACE S.; and KAUFMAN, HERBERT 1960 *Governing New York City: Politics in the Metropolis.* New York: Russell Sage Foundation.

TINKER, HUGH 1954 *The Foundations of Local Self-government in India, Pakistan and Burma.* London: Athlone.

VIDICH, ARTHUR J.; and BENSMAN, JOSEPH 1958 *Small Town in Mass Society: Class, Power and Religion in a Rural Community.* Princeton Univ. Press.

VRATUŠA, ANTON et al. 1961 *The Yugoslav Commune. International Social Science Journal* 13:379–450.

WOOD, ROBERT C.; and ALMENDINGER, VLADIMIR V. 1961 *1400 Governments: The Political Economy of the New York Metropolitan Region.* New York Metropolitan Region Study, No. 8. Cambridge, Mass.: Harvard Univ. Press.

WRAITH, RONALD E. 1964 *Local Government in West Africa.* London: Allen & Unwin.

LOCAL POLITICS

Politics consists of the process by which goods, services, and privileges are allocated by government or the rules are established for their allocation by other social institutions. Local government is a political subdivision of a national or regional government which performs functions that are culturally defined as being "local" in character, which in nearly all cases receives its legal powers from the national or regional government but possesses some degree of discretion in the making of decisions and which normally has some taxing powers. Local politics, therefore, consists not merely of local activities which relate to national political matters, but it involves a degree of choice to be made within the boundaries of the local unit of government relative to the selection of office holders and the making and execution of public policy. These decisions are not necessarily made unilaterally through a local political system and its institutions. Often decisions are shared with other governments, and local political institutions and processes are commonly interwoven with those of neighboring localities and with regional and national political systems.

The patterns of politics at the local level are greatly varied. They assume a particular character in a particular locality according to the prevailing influences of ideology, social structure, and technology in the society. In primitive social systems there may be little in the way of recognized political institutions, but of those that do exist, the local political systems are often more important than the national so far as the typical citizen is concerned. In more complex societies, where governmental bureaucracies are specialized, where much is expected in the way of governmental functions, and where rapid means of transportation and communication exist, the activities and relative importance of local government become largely a function of ideology—the belief systems and traditions that condition the minds of a politically significant portion of the population. In some cases, as in Nazi Germany from 1933 to 1945, local government is of little importance; in others, as in the United States throughout its history, local government has been important in theory and quite important in practice.

In societies in which the concepts of change, "progress," specialization, or economic interdependence are little developed, local government is dominated by a politics of consensus. Traditional functions are accepted and honored. Politics may center largely on particular politicians, with the size and importance of personal followings determining political power. One of the functions of politics may be that of entertainment for the ordinary citizen who has little else to amuse him. Innovation is not expected from the local political process. The notions of ameliorating social problems or elevating the standard of living may be unrecognized or unaccepted concepts. African, Asian, and Latin American village societies tend to follow this pattern. Even in fairly complex, industrially developed societies, the dominant ideology in rural areas may call for this kind of function to be performed by local government. The village, in all societies, tends to have a politics based on face-to-face relationships, with the behavior of politicians tempered by considerations of the expectations of friends and neighbors.

In complex industrialized societies, local politics may be analyzed according to (1) images of the ideal function or goals of local government, (2) the degree to which local government is integrated with or insulated from the national political process, (3) the degree of autonomy of local government in relation to the national government in terms of discretionary powers in policy making, or (4) the distribution of power within the community.

Images of local government. The leaders in each community, irrespective of the amount of discretionary power vested in local government, seem to have an image of what the ideal community would be like and they seek to convert the image into reality. No one has attempted to develop a world-wide typology of such images, but some information concerning them is available. In primitive societies, the image is generally well established by a prevailing set of values and an absence of a desire for change: that which is—if uncorrupted by outside influences—is right.

In the United States, three types of images have been identified by Williams and Adrian (1963):

(1) Those designed to utilize government for specific policy goals constitute the first type; they can be divided into two subcategories, those with (a) production goals and (b) consumption goals. In the case of production goals, the common one in the United States is expressed in terms of "boosterism." The emphasis is upon public support for extending water supply, sewer lines, and other services into areas where industry or large commercial enterprises might locate, so as to help attract new jobs and broaden tax bases in the community. Land-use planning and controls designed to reserve sites for industrial parks, efforts to annex new territory suitable for industrial development, and special tax inducements for new industry are among the other attempts to lure new sources of wealth to the area and keep them there.

One special version of the production-oriented community is the "company town." This institution (in which the owners of a mine, lumber company, or factory own all property and businesses in the community) is disappearing in the United States. It so exclusively emphasized production goals or interests that it became unacceptable to the contemporary American culture. In some communities a single firm still dominates the local economy and takes a large part in social and political life. With the decline of locally owned industry and the dispersion of members of high-status "old" families, this pattern of *noblesse oblige* (and the development by these elites of a unique community and one attractive to live in) has become much less common.

Since the end of World War II the residential suburb has been more likely to emphasize consumption goals, i.e., more of life's amenities provided by local government than by the central city; these include effective sewage systems, palatable water supplies, beautiful parks, quiet traffic, good schools, imaginative recreation programs, and ornamental street lights. To maintain life styles desired by the politically dominant, there is likely to be interest in a comprehensive community plan to help clarify and program goals, as well as in effective land-use controls. Emphasis is generally upon the professional administration of these activities, with the council–manager plan often the preferred urban structure.

(2) A second type of community image calls for local government to perform, at a minimum level, only those traditional functions that are viewed as strictly necessary for the community, such as education, police, fire, and water services. This approach, sometimes called the "caretaker" image, is often associated in the United States with a low-tax ideology. All over the world it is associated with traditionalism and opposition to industrialism and the breaking down of established life styles.

(3) A third image of the proper role of local government, never dominant in the United States, is that of an instrument for the administration of central government policy with no local policy making. This is the prevailing image in countries where strong central control over local government is traditional, as it is in France and in many Asian nations.

Probably no single image is held exclusively in any given community of a complex society, although in some cases one is clearly dominant. Where images compete for acceptance, compromise seems to be the ordinary result, with some concessions to each of them.

Insulation or integration. The politics of local government may be closely tied to that of national politics or may be quite independent. In many democratic (e.g., Great Britain) and nondemocratic nations (e.g., the Soviet Union), national parties are active at the local level. On the other hand, in some democratic nations (e.g., the United States) or nondemocratic ones (e.g., some African states), national political party activity may be sharply separated from local.

In European democracies national parties commonly include in their platforms proposals relative to local government policies (although national and local elections do not necessarily coincide). It is assumed that politicians active at the local level are also committed to work for a national party. Whereas this is normal in European democracies, in the United States the pattern has been more complex. The American political arrangement in the last half of the nineteenth century was similar to that of European democracies. Political machines of that period were closely linked to national politics, and this remained the case past the mid-twentieth century in some cities, particularly in the East and in Chicago. But the reform movement that affected many communities, beginning in the 1880s or thereabouts, placed emphasis upon the separation of local from state and national politics. The result was a nonpartisan movement, based on the assumptions that local government issues are unrelated to the activities of national political parties and that the political aspects of recruitment for local offices should be reduced as much as possible. In the 1960s, even where party labels continue to appear on the ballot, it is common for local elections to be largely separated from other elections in terms of election dates, issues, and personnel. Parties continue to be important in most non-school-board and nonmunicipal elections and particularly in county and township elections. But because relatively few counties in the United States have meaningful two-party competition, even where the office seekers are active in a party, the real competition for office is often within a single party [see PARTIES, POLITICAL].

The amount of organization for politics at the local level has been declining in the twentieth-century United States and elsewhere. The great urban political machines that emerged during the period of rapid urbanization following the American Civil War were examples of near-complete political organization in a democracy. With their well-financed, ably led, city-wide party structure, they had ward, precinct, and block workers who looked after the party's interests and provided welfare services for party adherents. These machines achieved an intimacy concerning the problems, expectations, and political mood of constituents that rivaled that of the rural county and township machines, which also flourished during this period. [See POLITICAL MACHINES.]

The machines declined with the coming of alternative group associations (e.g., trade unions and ethnic and racial social and benevolent societies), middle-class reform efforts (especially to provide a secret ballot and accurate election results and to mobilize those who once believed it was unavailing to "fight city hall"), a higher living standard for a greater portion of the working class, and the professionalization of welfare services, particularly after 1933. Local politics in the United States is today characterized by the presence of few professional politicians. Candidates are commonly amateurs, recruited (sometimes self-recruited) from business, labor, or the professions, often by groups of lay citizens who have banded together into a part-time political-action group. Some candidates are clearly the choice of, and spokesmen for, particular interests (realtors, builders, merchants, labor unions), and the current pattern seems to encourage such candidates more than did the political machines. The boss's brokerage concept of the role of the councilman or mayor was broader than the concept of the guardianship of some specific interest. Political communication at the local level remains more on a face-to-face basis than it does for politics in general, but radio and television have become important, especially in the larger urban areas. Much communication is through associations that are only in part political, such as labor union locals, neighborhood associations, chambers of commerce, farm organizations, church lay groups, and community councils. The leaders of these organizations are also important opinion leaders, for many ordinary citizens rely upon them as sources of political guidance [see INTEREST GROUPS; POLITICAL CLUBS].

Discretionary decision-making powers. The variety of local politics is accounted for in part by the political stakes involved in local decisions, and these vary according to the social significance of decisions that can be made at the local level. In some traditional societies local politics may involve no expectation that the actors will make decisions affecting the allocation of goods, services, and privileges. In nations such as France through much of its modern history, where powers are centralized but political parties cannot provide effective leadership, or many Asian nations where innovation is encouraged by the central government, local politics may center on actors who seek to protect traditional local standards and values against the views and policies of the professional national bureaucracy.

In some countries, such as Great Britain and those of Scandinavia, where political parties seek to tie the various levels of government together in a common move toward agreed-upon governmental service goals, local politics tends to be oriented toward the activities of national parties. Political actives, rather than civil service specialists, provide the principal coordination in programs. In countries with a strong tradition of decentralized decision making, such as the United States, local politics combines showmanship, questions of relationships with national parties and state and national bureaucracies, and the settlement of many policy questions which are left to local governments by the states. Although the process of cooperative federalism, which has been developing for many decades in the United States, has reduced local autonomy in decision making, many decisions that affect the allocation of goods, services, and privileges are still made by actors in local political roles. As a result, the viewpoints of those who occupy particular offices are often important. But local politics is not necessarily on a higher plane in the United States because local government is a power center. The patterns of recruitment and contesting for office and of decision making may depend chiefly on whether or not there is consensus regarding the image of the proper policies for local government [see FEDERALISM].

The distribution of community power. A central problem in the analysis of local politics has been that of identifying the power holders. Studies designed to do this have generally ignored the question of how much power local governments actually are able to allocate (the amount available may, in theory at least, bear some relationship to the status levels of persons who become involved in the local political process). The concentration has been on identifying those who are wielders of power over whatever decisions can be made locally. By the mid-1960s questions of power were still of keen interest to social scientists, but many questions concerning its character remained unanswered. Among the issues the following were of critical importance:

(1) Is power deliberately used by an elite in a conspiracy to control society or is it essentially a socially useful device serving to provide an orderly social system? The conspiratorial theory stems from Marxian ideology and holds that a relatively few persons dominate local decision making for the benefit of the business and industrial leaders and middle-class citizens generally. In contrast, another theory holds that in a pluralistic democracy power may be distributed widely among various classes and groups in the community, with a variety of resources (e.g., money, votes, status, intensity of concern) as a basis for power. In support of the latter position, some have argued that the rising importance and numbers of functions of government have made the formal holders of elective office and the professional civil servants

powerful in their own right and not mere satraps for hidden leaders.

(2) Is the power structure monolithic or internally competitive? Early studies tended to find a monolithic pattern in which power holders met informally to decide policy relative to major items on the community agenda and to compromise any differences within the group. More recent studies indicate that power holders compete with one another, posing power against power, and negotiate with one another as diplomats and politicians. The concept of a "power structure," or simple pyramid of relatively powerful persons ranged in hierarchical order, is being replaced by that of a "power complex" of often competing persons from downtown businesses, neighborhood businesses, industry, organized labor, religion, education, politics, and sometimes other areas.

(3) Is power integrated or multinucleated? That is, are the power holders all in communication with one another, ordered in a single hierarchy, concerned with all major issues, and equally powerful in relation to all major issues? Or is power distributed functionally, so that those who have much to do with decisions about education policy, for example, overlap little or not at all with those in the fields of transportation, parks, or sewage disposal? Early studies (Robert and Helen Lynd in the 1920s, W. Lloyd Warner in the 1930s, and Floyd Hunter in the 1940s) tended to see an integrated structure. More recently, research reports indicate functional specialization, but whether the differences result from improved research techniques or from a changing distribution of power is not known.

(4) How are power holders to be distinguished from power users? A number of problems have arisen in efforts to identify those who are powerful in local politics. Some of these are problems of theory construction (Is a person powerful if his wants are anticipated and met even though he does not directly participate in a decision?); others are those of method (Can the powerful be identified more accurately by collecting and classifying the opinions of the supposedly knowledgeable or by observing the actors in particular decisions?). The study of local political power is complicated by the efforts of decision makers to anticipate the wants of those who are believed to be important or potentially powerful. It is also complicated, among other ways, by the fact that respondents and researchers have varying definitions and concepts of power and by the probability that a person asked to name the powerful cannot accurately identify them all and may overdiscount (or alternatively, exaggerate) the power of persons he disapproves of or regards as lacking a *legitimate right* to be powerful. In the 1960s research was continuing on the problem of analyzing local political power. Some of the most productive work in sociology and political science was taking place in this area [*see* COMMUNITY, *article on* THE STUDY OF COMMUNITY POWER; *see also* POWER].

Liberalism and conservatism. The concepts of liberalism and conservatism common in the Western world do not necessarily have the same meaning when applied to local politics as they do at the national level. The socialist, labor, and other reasonably well-disciplined parties of European democracies have tried to give the terms equivalent meanings at all levels of government. American national parties have not seriously attempted to bring local issues into their platforms or campaigns, and they have not themselves been clearly identified along a liberal–conservative continuum. In the twentieth century liberalism has become identified with the involvement of government in coping with a large variety of economic and social issues financed through a progressive tax system. While the social-service state has become the established pattern in the United States, home ownership has also become increasingly widespread. As a result studies have shown that persons who vote for liberal candidates for state and national offices may vote for conservatives at the local level, and vice versa. In particular, working-class homeowners with modest incomes sometimes oppose bond issues for capital outlays that would benefit them and vote for advocates of "caretaker" government, apparently because the cost of local government so clearly falls on the property owner. Sometimes they do this despite strong appeals for support of an issue or candidate by labor or other liberal leaders. Working-class persons have not pressed for social-service state and liberal reform programs (such as public housing or urban renewal) at the local level. Upper-middle-class persons, on the other hand, frequently are willing to spend local tax monies and subscribe to the images of "boosterism" and "amenities." As a result the terms liberal and conservative are often quite meaningless when applied to local government.

Local politics and democracy. Studies of local politics since the end of World War II indicate that the bulk of citizens in American democracy do not exert much individual influence, even at the local level. In fact, the pattern at the local level appears to be not much different from that at the national, despite the prevalence of nonpartisanship and the supposed significance of physical proximity to the decision makers. The level of information possessed by the typical citizen is low, citizens take their cues from various political leaders, and decisions seem to be largely the product of bargaining among leaders. Voter participation at the local level is typically lower than it is for national and state elections, and some scholars have been concerned about the high level of alienation at the local level, although evidence as to the significance of this, if it exists at all, is inconclusive. The indifferent do, however, seem to move toward the extremes of the political spectrum when they become activated, just as is the case in national elections. In the 1960s, then, the study of local politics leaves unanswered some questions that are important for democracy. Particularly, it is still uncertain how much citizen participation is necessary for healthy democracy at the local level, what form this participation should take for the viability of democracy, or to what degree present systems of local government provide adequate or satisfying representation and access to decision makers by all segments of the local population.

Charles R. Adrian

[*See also* Centralization and decentralization; City; Community; Local government; Political machines; Political participation.]

BIBLIOGRAPHY

Agger, Robert E.; Goldrich, Daniel; and Swanson, Bert 1964 *The Rulers and the Ruled: Political Power and Impotence in American Communities.* New York: Wiley.

Banfield, Edward C. (1961) 1965 *Political Influence.* New York: Free Press.

Dahl, Robert A. (1961) 1963 *Who Governs? Democracy and Power in an American City.* New Haven: Yale Univ. Press.

Decisions in Syracuse, by Roscoe C. Martin et al. Metropolitan Action Studies, No. 1. 1961 Bloomington: Indiana Univ. Press.

Form, William H.; and Miller, Delbert C. 1960 *Industry, Labor and Community.* New York: Harper.

Hunter, Floyd 1953 *Community Power Structure: A Study of Decision Makers.* Chapel Hill: Univ. of North Carolina Press. → A paperback edition was published in 1963 by Doubleday.

Janowitz, Morris (editor) 1961 *Community Political Systems.* New York: Free Press.

Long, Norton E. 1958 The Local Community as an Ecology of Games. *American Journal of Sociology* 64: 251–261.

Lynd, Robert S.; and Lynd, Helen M. (1929) 1959 *Middletown: A Study in American Culture.* New York: Harcourt.

Martin, Roscoe C. 1957 *Grass Roots.* University: Univ. of Alabama Press.

Michigan State University of Agriculture and Applied Science, Institute for Community Development and Services 1962 *Main Street Politics:*
Policy-making at the Local Level, a Survey of the Periodical Literature Since 1950. East Lansing, Mich.: The University.

Parsons, Talcott 1957 The Distribution of Power in American Society. *World Politics* 10: 123–143.

Pye, Lucian W. 1958 The Non-Western Political Process. *Journal of Politics* 20: 468–486.

Sayre, Wallace S.; and Kaufman, Herbert 1960 *Governing New York City: Politics in the Metropolis.* New York: Russell Sage Foundation.

Seeley, John R. et al. 1956 *Crestwood Heights: A Study of the Culture of Suburban Life.* New York: Basic Books.

Vidich, Arthur J.; and Bensman, Joseph 1958 *Small Town in Mass Society: Class, Power and Religion in a Rural Community.* Princeton Univ. Press.

Warner, W. Lloyd; and Lunt, Paul S. 1942 *The Status System of a Modern Community.* New Haven: Yale Univ. Press.

Williams, Oliver P.; and Adrian, Charles R. 1963 *Four Cities: A Study in Comparative Policy Making.* Philadelphia: Univ. of Pennsylvania Press.

Wood, Robert C. 1959 *Suburbia: Its People and Their Politics.* Boston: Houghton Mifflin.

LOCATION AND DISPERSION

See under Statistics, descriptive.

LOCATION THEORY

See Spatial economics. *Related material may be found in* Central place; Geography, *article on* statistical geography.

LOCKE, JOHN

John Locke made important contributions in the areas of epistemology, political theory, education, toleration theory, and theology; he also wrote on natural law and on various economic topics.

Born in 1632 in a Somerset village, he was the eldest and ultimately the only surviving child of a family of tradesmen and small landholders. His grandfather had been a tanner and clothier; his father was a notary with landholdings later inherited by his son. He kept his connections with his ramified west-country family and friends, most of whom were Whigs throughout the turbulent years of the later Stuart rule. After living for many years at Oxford and on the Continent, Locke made his headquarters in Essex in 1691 with his friend Lady Masham; in 1704 he was buried among the Mashams in the village church at High Laver.

Intellectual development. Locke studied at the Westminster School and Christ Church, Oxford, where in 1658 he was elected senior student (the equivalent of a fellow in other colleges) and taught moral philosophy. His academic duties were always light, and he consistently sought to lighten them still more, especially after 1666, when he met Lord Ashley (later Lord Shaftesbury), the great Whig leader; thenceforth Locke spent more time in London than at Oxford.

The political parliamentarianism of Locke's father may have influenced Locke's own ultimate Whiggery, which was strengthened by his association with Shaftesbury. Many west-country families, like Locke himself, became part of the "Shaftesbury connection" of Whigs, later supporting William of Orange in his successful coup. By all odds the most influential connection of Locke's life was with Shaftesbury, who quickened his early, though latent, interest in questions of political philosophy and practice. During his Shaftesbury years Locke sat on the Council of Trade and Plantations, an overseeing body for crown colonies, Ireland, and proprietary holdings in the New World. His interest in economic problems can be dated from that experience. Although he had been only on the fringes of the complicated politics of the late reign of Charles II, in 1683 Locke had to leave Oxford for good, a political refugee in Shaftesbury's wake.

Locke's intellectual development was marked by autonomy and autodidacticism. Evidently bored by his studies, he independently followed the medical curriculum at Oxford; though he never took his doctor's degree, he was qualified to practice medicine and did so, largely for the Shaftesbury family. He also studied chemistry in Robert Boyle's laboratory; in this way he came to know Boyle and eventually became an executor of his will. Other scientific friends were Richard Lower, Thomas Willis, and David Thomas; in 1688 he was elected a fellow of the Royal Society. Locke's "corpuscularianism," or atomic theory of matter, had much in common with Boyle's; his general curiosity and interest in "things" rather than in their names, as well as his experimental approach to social and scientific matters, can all be connected with his serious interest in the biological sciences. His medical empiricism was much like that of his associate Thomas Sydenham, one of the major experimental physicians of his day, who was especially interested in public health; both Sydenham and Locke voiced their awareness of the "unknowing," the "probabilism" involved in medical practice, notions which later influenced Locke's epistemology.

Locke's fear of Catholicism and absolutism had its roots in the English political scene and was deepened by several journeys to France, where persecution of the Huguenots was then intense. His Dutch sojourn, from 1683 to 1689, was voluntarily undertaken as a prudential flight from a government increasingly hostile to men of his political association and views: he was deprived of his studentship at Christ Church and even put on a proscription list of James II's real and supposed enemies hidden in Holland. During that time, Locke met many congenial thinkers who in different ways reflected his own biases and concerns: among others, Arminian broad-church theologians, all theorists of toleration; medical men interested in experiment and learned in a tradition other than his own, that of Cartesian medicine; publicists dedicated to the diffusion of both learning and information.

When Locke returned to England in 1689, it was to a government of which he could approve; by that time he himself had become an honored man and was recognized as a major thinker. Thenceforward, he devoted himself to studying and writing, while holding minor government offices and occasionally conferring with political leaders.

Writings. From the early 1660s Locke had written many short essays, evidently for his own clarification, on natural law, on the civil magistrate, on toleration. In 1669 these preoccupations fed into Lord Shaftesbury's *Fundamental Constitutions of Carolina*, written with the aid of Locke. (Although this item appears in Locke's collected works—see *The Works . . .*, vol. 10, pp. 175–199—it has been established that Shaftesbury was the principal author.) Locke's *Two Treatises* (1690a) were written, as we now know, at the time of the Exclusion crisis of 1679–1681, when Shaftesbury unsuccessfully attempted to exclude the duke of York from succession to the throne because he was a Catholic.

While Locke was in Holland, one of his publicist friends, Jean Le Clerc, persuaded him to write for his periodical: thus, in the *Bibliothèque universelle et historique*, a fortnightly review of issues and books of international interest, Locke published some book reviews—among others, one of Newton's *Principia*—as well as original works of his own, the chief of which was his abridgment of the then unpublished *Essay Concerning Human Understanding* (1690b).

In 1689–1690 Locke began his serious publishing career: *A Letter Concerning Toleration, Being the Translation of the* "Epistola de tolerantia" appeared in 1689 (*The Works . . .*, vol. 6, pp. 1–58); the *Two Treatises of Government* in 1689, bearing the date 1690; the *Essay Concerning Human Understanding* in the same year. From then on, Locke never ceased publishing: he continually revised and republished his *Essay*, also supervising its translation into French; between 1690 and 1704 he wrote three more letters on toleration (*The Works . . .*, vol. 6, pp. 59–574); in 1690, *Some Thoughts on Education* (*ibid.*, vol. 9, pp. 1–210);

in 1695, *The Reasonableness of Christianity* (*ibid.*, vol. 7, pp. 1–158); various defenses of the *Essay*; economic tracts; and paraphrases of Paul's Epistles. Much of the immediate stimulus to this work was topical: his study of education grew out of private letters to his friend Edward Clarke; the economic tracts all sprang from fiscal and commercial problems of the government; the later writings on toleration were called forth by attacks on his ideas and on William's efforts to solve the problem of dissent in England. Characteristically, however, even his topical writings contain elements of "philosophy," generalizations not required by the work's immediate polemical purpose.

Major contributions

Locke has often seemed a singularly disconnected thinker, an asystematic philosopher with occasional brilliant insights. Since the acquisition by the Bodleian Library of many Locke manuscripts from the Lovelace Collection, the development of Locke's interests and of his thinking can be more accurately traced than before; further, the ways in which his ideas, apparently so disparate, hang together has become clearer from study of the manuscripts. His earliest work was on natural law, which led him ultimately into his serious work on two branches of that large subject, political theory and human understanding. Though these two interests branched widely apart from one another and seemed far removed from his initial concern with the "covering" aspect of natural law, his friends expected, in vain, that he would eventually write a treatise about natural law, after he had completed his *Essay*. His early natural-law essays were written between 1660 and 1664 and deal with both the epistemological problem of knowing in natural law and with the natural law as a binding moral and social force; the essays show clear signs of Locke's later full-scale attack upon innateness and *consensus gentium*, as well as his incipient psychological sensationalism. As for moral natural law, Locke assumed it as a *donnée* from God, binding upon man's reason; this view remains rudimentary both in the *Second Treatise* ([1690a] 1960, pp. 283–446) and in Locke's other writings. In his manuscript treatises on the civil magistrate and on toleration, dating from the early years of the Restoration, Locke moved from a restrictive position to a more tolerant one, at first insisting on public order as a primary value and then stressing the irenic power of the civil magistrate, particularly in the regulation of religious practices. From these early works Locke's philosophical investigations emerged. They will be treated under several headings, with stress laid upon those elements of his thought most significant for the development of the social sciences: political theory, religious ideas, economic ideas, epistemology, psychology, educational theory.

Political thought. Locke's major contributions to political thought are in his *Second Treatise*, a document notoriously lacking in system, partly because of its remnant character, partly because of its connection with contemporary events, partly because of Locke's failure to rewrite it substantially for publication in 1689, ten years after its completion. Within its own time the work contained "dangerous" doctrines, some anathematized by decree in 1683, when Locke fled his country. By the time of its publication, however, it expressed the parliamentarian ideals of mixed government and separation of powers established in England by the political settlement reached after William's invasion. The origins of the tract seem to have been in the Exclusion crisis; it was designed to justify constitutional change, for which Locke undertook to investigate the origins and structure of civil (political) society. His polemical aim was to diminish popular acceptance of the patriarchalism which gave authority to much of the contemporary argument for absolutism; to do so, he postulated an original, direct relation of every man to God rather than to or through any political intermediary. Each man was in some sense God's "property": bypassing the notion of Adam as a model ruler of the social group, Locke postulated a state of nature regulated by laws derived from God, a state of nature in which men were equal and free before the Lord and each other. Paradoxically, the rule of law (in this case, the rule of the law of nature) was requisite for freedom; without such natural law man's "freedom" would have been anarchy. In this sense Locke's conception approached the anarchic state of nature postulated by Hobbes, although his insistence upon fundamental natural law saved him from Hobbes's pessimism about the lawlessness of basic human nature. From this natural condition, Locke inferred both a "law of reason," by which individuals reach and assent to social consensus, and the practical laws requisite to permit, even to insure, personal freedom [see NATURAL LAW]. Originally, in the state of nature, executive power of the natural law was vested in every individual; subsequently—whether suddenly or gradually is not made clear—men consented to live in a common society regulated by the communal executive power of the law of nature. Locke divided this communal power into three—the legislative, executive, and federative powers—with judicial decision a general power of the political commonwealth.

To effect the passage from the state of nature

to "civil society," Locke developed his important variation on the idea of property, which in turn graded into his theory of labor. From the natural-law postulate that a man has property in his own life, Locke derived the view that a man has property in the things necessary to the preservation of that life, so long as those things are rightfully his (that is, taken from the commonwealth at a point when the specific acquisition harmed or deprived no one else). A man has a right in himself and thus in his own labor; in turn, he has a right to what "he hath mixed his labor with," or a right to his property. A corollary of this is Locke's formulation of the labor theory of value, almost incidental to his argument: the value and the price of commodities in any society reflect the labor that has gone into them.

There are two sorts of relations between men, the first a natural social contract, entered into by the exercise of rational considerations of self-preservation, the second defined by rights in property. The function and end of government are the preservation of life, liberty, and property. One corollary of this formulation is that political rights derive from property and that the propertyless are either without political rights or are slaves. Such a conception of the commonwealth permits emphasis both on the common interest and on private holdings, which in Locke's essay (in line with seventeenth-century usage and notions of value) generally means land.

Without in any sense denying the importance and validity of a familial organization of society, Locke demonstrated that the power over children and dependents vested in the father (who shares it with the mother, interestingly enough) is simply a form of trusteeship: the guardian–father has certain obligations toward his children, especially to educate them; when the children reach full exercise of their reason, they are free "from subjection to the will and command of the father." The family was, for Locke, important in his theory of the origins of civil society, the conjunction of male and female being both a symbol of a wider assent and obligation and a primary stage in the voluntary community of mankind. Thus, even in families, arbitrary government is "impossible"; in commonwealths the necessary consent of each individual to enter into the bond of civil society (the social contract) eventuates in election, the choice of representatives charged to exercise legislative power. Legislative power is supreme in Locke's mixed government of separate legislative, executive, and federative powers. His assumption is that a man with political rights (by reason of his property in himself) enters into political life, inheriting with his property his obligations to the government that represents him. In turn, the government may not touch his property (i.e., levy taxes) without his consent through his representative. One implication of this formulation is a doctrine of resistance, or revolution, as expressed in the last chapter of the *Second Treatise*, the chapter which, above all others, made Locke objectionable to the government before 1688 and valuable to the government thereafter. Unlike the Protestant resistance-theorists of the sixteenth century, Locke did not base his revolutionary theory upon sanctions of conscience or religion; unlike the English parliamentarians of the 1640s, he did not base it on precedents in English law; unlike Algernon Sidney, he did not base it on a metaphysical and metapsychological natural right to liberty; rather, he advocated a restrained and considered revolution for the restoration of proper balance in the body politic. [*See* SOCIAL CONTRACT.]

Locke's theory of government emphasizes process, both the hypothetical process of human development from a state of nature to civil society and the processes of self-government. He therefore limited the number of specifiable elements in the proper commonwealth and was careful to leave ample room for adjustments to changing social needs. He was, in short, indicating a successful process of representative majority rule rather than setting up an exclusive structure for one. Hence, there are large areas of his thought which seem blank, either because he was unconcerned with total consistency or because he was concerned with leaving social alternatives open, especially in "matters of indifference."

Views on religion. His toleration theory, taken in conjunction with his religious views, demonstrates his appreciation of practical approaches. Thus, his *Letter Concerning Toleration* of 1689, Locke dealt with Christian toleration, "the chief characteristical mark of the true church." Since every man appears orthodox to himself, no one in his right or his wrong mind will accept as just the persecution of himself; furthermore, since in any case persecution cannot touch a man's inmost conviction, regardless of what he may say under stress, there is no practical merit in persecution. Locke politicized the problem of religious pluralism, assigning to the civil magistrate the protection of various rights (here defined as "life, liberty, and indolency of body") of members of a commonwealth. The care of souls was no more committed by God to the civil magistrate than the care of one man's conscience was committed to any other member of society. The magistrate's power consists only in civil force, which is irrelevant to any church (defined as "a voluntary society of men").

From the privileges of toleration, Locke excluded some—he excluded atheists from the benefits of the law, because they refuse to acknowledge its source—but he included idolators, men simply given to erroneous worship. Toleration is to be withheld from religious groups who deny it to others, a view supported by Locke's experiences in France, where persecution of Huguenots reached extremes between 1679 and 1685. Whenever religious assemblies endanger the public peace, then the civil magistrate, on civil grounds, may intervene against them; even then, however, he is not to interfere with their belief, which remains in the category of "things indifferent" and is therefore irrelevant to questions of public order. Although in this work Locke did not justify resistance, rebellion, or revolution for religion's sake, he made it plain that oppression of any kind naturally impels men toward sedition.

In *The Reasonableness of Christianity* Locke defended the Christian revelation against atheism and against natural religion without revelation, demonstrating by scriptural and historical authority the fact of Christ's messiahship. The tract defends the necessity of revelation against the idea of a sufficient natural religion, but at the same time it treats Christ's teachings as the fulfillment and explanation of the moral law of nature. Man's reason cannot by itself discover the full moral law of nature, but it can confirm it. Nowhere in the tract did Locke sanction a particular form of worship, but instead he endorsed a general scriptural Christianity to which, as it were, all Christians could subscribe. (For this, he was roundly attacked as being a deist.) In ways connected with his toleration theory and his epistemology, he adduced the uncertainties of man's perceptions and knowledge to support his minimal articles of faith, drawn from scriptural revelation and corroborated by the action of reason. [See CHRISTIANITY.]

Economic ideas. Locke's economic interests, stimulated during his early association with Shaftesbury, emerged long after in 1691 in *Some Considerations of the Consequences of the Lowering of Interest, and Raising the Value of Money* (*The Works . . .*, vol. 5, pp. 1–130) and in 1695 in *Further Considerations . . .* (*ibid.*, vol. 5, pp. 131–206). In these works, he advocated maintaining the interest rate and not devaluing the currency, on grounds of natural law. His economic laws were (1) that the intrinsic value of any piece of goods is not necessarily reflected in its price; (2) that its market value depends upon the proportion of supply and demand (which he called "quantity" and "vent"); (3) that price is determined by the amount of money relative to the supply and demand for a piece of goods. These laws permit prices to be set with some flexibility, according to varying conditions, and they rely upon a controlling notion in Locke's thought, that of self-regulation toward equilibrium. When it came to practice, as in the cases of the poor and of Irish manufactures, Locke advocated government intervention in economic affairs.

Psychology.   The aim of Locke's *Essay* (1690b) was to determine the limits of human knowledge, so that men might address themselves to problems within their power to solve. He set out to describe the process of human understanding, to inquire into probable knowledge, and to determine the nature of ideas. He concluded, very simply, that ideas have two sources, sensation and reflection upon ideas produced by sensation. It turns out, however, in the course of the book, that knowledge can also be intuitional and demonstrative, though in the discussion intuition tends to be assimilated to sensation and demonstration to reflection. Ideas may be either simple or complex: simple ideas are the result of sensation and reflection and are compounded of simple parts which can be found by analysis. Locke attributed reality to the external world and relied upon intuition to explain the relation between an idea and its referent in the external world. Knowledge derived by intuition (such as that of revelation) is "certain"; certain knowledge can also be derived from demonstration but less reliably than from intuition, since errors in reason and in memory may distort the result of demonstration. Locke's ontological proof of God's existence, much like Descartes's, is an example of the fusion of demonstration with intuition: that is, one's own existence is intuited, and from one's own existence God's can be demonstrated. He relied upon the skeptical provisionalism inherent in empirical investigations, both in his recognition of the role probability plays in human understanding and assessment of life and in his recognition of the idiosyncratic formation of each man's personal set of ideas. As in so much of his work, Locke took a middle position in the *Essay*, incorporating elements of skepticism and elements of idealism, combining what we now call behaviorism with gestalt principles. His empiricism embraced both the particular and the consensual: in the ongoing search for true knowledge individual men are required to check their ideas against those of the group, and the group does so against those of any given individual. [See GESTALT THEORY; THINKING.]

Locke's psychological principles are a by-product

of his effort to describe human understanding. His major hypothesis, that the mind is not equipped with innate ideas or principles but is at its formation a "white paper" (his translation of *tabula rasa*), was reached in part through his own empirical observation of children. He concluded that there are only two ways of human understanding, by sensation and by reflection on ideas derived from sensation. His whole notion of "understanding" is developmental; throughout the *Essay* he cited examples from his observation of the successive stages of men's lives. From his observation of children, he demonstrated that their understanding derives from their experience of the external and social world. Approximating modern notions of "control," Locke cited a great deal of evidence from his observation of human beings who were exceptional in that they lacked some "normal" element of apprehension or reflection—children, not yet developed to full powers; idiots; men born blind (including the famous philosophical example of a man who by an operation got his sight); men suffering from amnesia because their heads had been kicked by horses. In spite of their deficiencies, all such people entertained ideas that seemed to them as authentic as those "clear and distinct" ideas that are the hallmark of proper understanding. Madness, drunkenness, and dreaming interested Locke: the Cartesian criterion for human existence, consciousness, seemed to him too narrow to account for the existence of faultily conscious minds. His solution to the problem of identity turned on assumptions now associated with gestalt psychology: on the continuous existence of an organized body whose parts (including its intellectual store) shift over time in relation to one another. So "the night man" and "the day man," the drunken man and the sober man, the madman and the sane man may coexist in the same person, even though their control over consciousness may be intermittent or interrupted. To this notion may be connected Locke's idea of what are nowadays called "roles," the multiple relations, psychological and social (father, brother, son, son-in-law, servant, master, older, younger, etc.), possible and even inevitable in every man's experience. Memory (retention), the operation of which was never altogether accounted for in the Lockean philosophy or psychology, plays a major part in maintaining continuous personal identity. One of Locke's major psychological insights, that arbitrary mental connections are "stamped" on men's minds by the chance conjunctions of their experience, appears in the famous chapter on the association of ideas, an afterthought in his organization. There he demonstrated, by a kind of negative example, the supremacy of experience over rational powers: a man taught to dance in a room containing a trunk could never dance in the absence of a similar trunk; a man nearly axed in a doorway by a berserk village idiot could never go through a door without glancing behind him. So by experience, governing intellectual and emotional constellations are induced in individual minds. This doctrine and that of the *tabula rasa* underlie Locke's precepts for education. [*See* DEVELOPMENTAL PSYCHOLOGY; LEARNING; ROLE; SENSES.]

In the sense that he postulated ideas as originating in sensation, Locke's psychology is certainly mechanistic. His general concern, however, to establish the same organic interrelationship for the contents of the mind as for the members of the body or the state, tempers his mechanism with organic and developmental notions. Although he conceived of the body as made up of elements in a mechanistic organization, he saw that mechanism as having considerable feedback into its own individual, even idiosyncratic, development. Feedback is in turn not automatic, in his view, since the mind's judgment, the faculty which selects and arranges ideas in relation to one another, is also constantly at work during consciousness.

Locke's social conception of language may serve as a partial model for his ideas of how men understand as well as of how society functions: Although the designation of words is established by consensus, each man may alter it privately for himself alone, according to his individual associations of words and experience. Furthermore, though encountered as datum in each man's life, language is not rigid but is subject to modification over time by the social needs of the group using it.

Pedagogy. Locke's ideas of education follow from his psychology. The child inevitably grows into the man and should grow into as healthy a man as possible. Since each child is strongly individuated, no fixed regime works for all children, but Locke laid down general rules of education, chiefly applicable (as he wrote) to gentry sons whose duty was to undertake public service. Boys were to be educated at home, carefully fed, clothed, and taught to build and preserve good health. The father was to "imprint" obedience on his son but with such care and tact as to turn the child–subject naturally into his friend. Rewards and punishments were to be systematic but moderate (Locke outlawed beating, as making a child slavish). The father, tutor, and governor, charged with educating the child, were to be his moral exemplars; therefore, it was necessary for parents both to regulate themselves and to choose their surrogates with care. Though children must learn self-denial, some cravings may be gratified, especially since "craving" is so closely allied to "curiosity," nature's instrument to correct ignorance. So the child must be allowed to learn whenever ready and can often be cozened into learning by means of games and toys. Children's questions must always be answered truthfully, and conversation with them must be free of condescension. Instruction in the nature of reality —including the idea of God, excluding the idea of goblins—was to be undertaken early.

As for learning itself, Locke's program was practical: reading, writing, French, then Latin (for use, chiefly); geography, arithmetic, astronomy, geometry, chronology, history, ethics, civil law, rhetoric and logic, natural philosophy; then Greek and Latin as cultural subjects and, last of all, method. For learning by rote Locke had no use; he also advocated learning such practical subjects as trade and accountancy as well as recreations such as music, dancing, gardening, joinery—all useful to young men of property. Finally, the young man should travel, first at home and later abroad, before settling down to matrimony and his social and political obligations at the age of one and twenty.

Locke's originality and influence

In its day Locke's thought seemed strikingly "new," cast in a new language for any literate man to read; it had, naturally, many sources and analogues in ancient and contemporary thought. His skepticism and empiricism came from deep within the medical tradition; his attitude, and even the words he used, recall Sextus Empiricus and, more often, Montaigne, another essayist concerned with knowing, education, understanding, nescience, and probability. Locke had, too, a recognizably British stoicism, a preference for directness and plainness in morality and rhetoric; he often cited Seneca and the stoical writings of Cicero. His toleration theory derived from a long line of Protestant writers going back to Servetus and Erastus and exemplified by his Arminian friends; there are affinities between his view of church–state relations and the thought of Chillingworth, Falkland, and John Owen. His citations of natural law are to Hooker and Grotius, whose books he certainly knew, though he seems to have referred to them more out of piety and the need for authorities than from any desire to analyze their thought in relation to his own. Although he was a notable revisionist of the Cartesian epistemology and psychology, Locke's doctrine of ideas owes something to Descartes, his psychological theory of sensationalism shares elements of Carte-

sian mechanism, and his ontological proof of God's existence is brief and efficient partly because Descartes's similar proof was so thoroughly argued. Locke's nominalism had many sources: Greek empiricism, the Scotist tradition in scholasticism, and chiefly Francis Bacon and his followers in contemporary England.

However connected to other strands in the history of thought, Locke was characteristically original in pattern and device. His empirically argued rejection of innate ideas and principles, for example, in the first book of the *Essay* ran counter to traditional epistemologies ancient and modern. Among his contemporaries, both Cartesians and Cambridge Platonists, as well as most divines, postulated innateness as the basis of human knowing, relying on both Platonic and Stoical authorities. In psychology and epistemology a major contribution was his concept of the association of ideas, an involuntary experiential formation in the thought of individual men caused by the linkage of their simultaneous experiences. In economic thought his is the first full argument for the labor theory of value; his notions of property, revolution, and the social contract, though deriving from natural-law theory and resistance theory, are combined in a new interrelation and based upon assumptions of the rule of law that are neither narrowly legalistic nor generally metaphysical.

Across the range of Locke's topics of investigation his preoccupations are clear: his constant interest in the relation of thought to behavior, his concern for the balance of individual right and social obligation, his provisional attitudes to solutions, his distrust of dogmatism, his emphasis on equilibrium and self-stabilization. The last emphasis governs his notion of "power," according to which, even though a man is limited in his finite existence by certain conditional restraints, he is nonetheless free to exercise his mind and even his will. Notions of stabilization and equilibrium operate in his epistemology too, where individual understanding is, among other things, conceived as a constant altering of the balance and relationship between different experiences and ideas. Connected with this, one of Locke's personal behavior patterns makes some sense: from the 1650s until the 1690s Locke, wherever he was, joined or organized discussion groups in which ideas could be cooperatively investigated and idiosyncrasies modulated into a permissive consensus.

Locke's influence can hardly be overestimated; nor can it be accurately measured. His idealism, his concentration upon the autonomy of inward life found an extreme, though corrective, disciple in

Berkeley; his skepticism, in Hume. At first his *Essay* was fiercely attacked. Later, except for such idealists as Leibniz and his own pupil, the third earl of Shaftesbury, for most educated people the book seemed to provide as comprehensive a description and explanation of the mind's workings as Newton's of the workings of the cosmos. Locke's influence on deist thought, perceptible in his lifetime and deplored by him, was considerable both in England and in France; his notions of private education were often cited by eighteenth-century English gentlemen at home and in the colonies; his psychological principles were gradually absorbed into accepted belief and can be traced particularly in the work of eighteenth-century novelists (e.g., Richardson, Sterne, and Diderot). Voltaire's enthusiasm for Locke's ideas had considerable effect in popularizing them in prerevolutionary France. As for political thought, the American and French revolutions have been laid at his door: unquestionably his work was widely read in both countries by men concerned for their political rights, but how deeply they read it remains an open question. His epistemology inaugurated a "new way of ideas," his psychology certainly bore fruit in nineteenth- and twentieth-century psychological theory. Locke's works turn up in many auction lists of eighteenth-century private libraries and are found in the libraries of ancient educational institutions in England and America: Trinity College, Dublin, incorporated the doctrines of the *Essay* into its basic curriculum at an early stage, and Locke's influence at colonial Harvard has also been attested.

ROSALIE L. COLIE

[*See also* CIVIL DISOBEDIENCE; CONSENSUS; CONSERVATISM; CONSTITUTIONS AND CONSTITUTIONALISM; LEGITIMACY; NATURAL LAW; POLITICAL THEORY; SOCIAL CONTRACT; *and the biographies of* BACON; BURKE; HARTLEY; HOBBES; HUME.]

WORKS BY LOCKE

(1690a) 1960 *Two Treatises of Government.* Edited by Peter Laslett. Cambridge Univ. Press.
(1690b) 1959 *An Essay Concerning Human Understanding.* 2 vols. Edited by Alexander C. Fraser. New York: Dover.
Essays on the Law of Nature. Edited by Wolfgang von Leyden. Oxford: Clarendon, 1954. → Contains the Latin text with a translation.
The Works of John Locke. 10 vols. Aalen (Germany): Scientia Verlag, 1963. → A reprint of the 1823 edition.

SUPPLEMENTARY BIBLIOGRAPHY

AARON, RICHARD I. (1937) 1955 *John Locke.* 2d ed. Oxford: Clarendon.
BOURNE, HENRY R. FOX 1876 *The Life of John Locke.* 2 vols. London: King; New York: Harper.
CHRISTOPHERSEN, HANS O. 1930 *A Bibliographical Introduction to the Study of John Locke.* Norske-videnskaps-akademi i Oslo, Historisk-filosofisk Klasse, Skrifter, 1930: no. 8. Oslo: Dybwad.
CRANSTON, MAURICE W. 1957 *John Locke: A Biography.* New York: Macmillan.
DEWHURST, KENNETH 1963 *John Locke (1632–1704), Physician and Philosopher: A Medical Biography.* London: Wellcome Historical Medical Library.
GIBSON, JAMES (1917) 1960 *Locke's Theory of Knowledge and Its Historical Relations.* Cambridge Univ. Press.
GIVNER, DAVID A. 1962 Scientific Preconceptions in Locke's Philosophy of Language. *Journal of the History of Ideas* 23:340–354.
KING, PETER (1829) 1884 *Life and Letters of John Locke, With Extracts From His Journals and Common-place Books.* London: Bell.
LARKIN, PASCHAL 1930 *Property in the Eighteenth Century: With Special Reference to England and Locke.* London and New York: Longmans.
LOCKE, JOHN 1965 *The Library of John Locke.* Edited by John Harrison and Peter Laslett. Oxford Univ. Press.
MACPHERSON, CRAWFORD B. 1962 *The Political Theory of Possessive Individualism: Hobbes to Locke.* Oxford: Clarendon.
MANDELBAUM, MAURICE 1964 *Philosophy, Science, and Sense Perception: Historical and Critical Studies.* Baltimore: Johns Hopkins Press. → See especially Chapters 1 and 2 on John Locke.
OXFORD UNIVERSITY, BODLEIAN LIBRARY 1959 *A Summary Catalogue of the Lovelace Collection of the Papers of John Locke in the Bodleian Library,* by P. Long. Oxford Bibliographical Society, Publications, New Series, Vol. 8. Oxford Univ. Press.
POLIN, RAYMOND 1960 *La politique morale de John Locke.* Paris: Presses Universitaires de France.
SIMON, WALTER M. 1951 John Locke, Philosophy, and Political Theory. *American Political Science Review* 45:386–399.
TUVESON, ERNEST L. 1955 Locke and the Dissolution of the Ego. *Modern Philology* 52:159–174.
VIANO, CARLO A. 1960 *John Locke: Dal razionalismo all' illuminismo.* Turin (Italy): Einaudi.
YOLTON, JOHN W. 1956 *John Locke and the Way of Ideas.* Oxford Univ. Press.

LOGIC
See REASONING AND LOGIC.

LOGICAL POSITIVISM
See POSITIVISM.

LOMBROSO, CESARE

Born of Jewish parents in Verona, Cesare Lombroso (1835–1909), the Italian criminologist, was educated by the Jesuits; he received a degree in medicine from the University of Pavia in 1858 and a degree in surgery from the University of Genoa

in 1859. At various times he was an army physician and in charge of the insane at several hospitals, but his major positions, all at the University
of Turin, were those of professor of legal medicine
and public hygiene, 1876; professor of psychiatry
and clinical psychiatry, 1896; and professor of
criminal anthropology, 1906. Although he wrote
extensively about such diverse subjects as pellagra,
the nervous system, and genius, he came into
prominence with his major work, *L'uomo delinquente*, first published in 1876. The book went
through five editions in Italy and was translated
into various European languages, although never
into English.

Lombroso was influenced by French positivism,
German materialism, and English evolutionism.
In particular, he was influenced by Auguste Comte;
Charles Darwin; Bénédict Morel, the French alien-
ist who developed a theory of degeneracy; Bartolo-
meo Panizza, the Pavian comparative anatomist;
Carl Rokitanski, the Viennese pathologist; and Enrico Ferri, his principal younger colleague, who
suggested to him the term "the born criminal."

Although Lombroso was aware of the importance
of social and psychological factors in the causation
of crime, his primary emphasis was on the concept of the atavistic criminal. He believed the atavistic criminal to be a biological throwback to an
earlier stage of evolution, since inborn delinquency
was not natural to contemporary mankind but
peculiar to primitive races. The atavistic criminal
could be identified by various anatomical, physiological, and psychic stigmata, different kinds of
inborn delinquency being identifiable by different
patterns of stigmata.

Lombroso later modified his ideas about criminal typology. Because in the first edition of *L'uomo
delinquente* he had focused his attention so exclusively on such anatomical and anthropometric data
as skull measurements and facial asymmetries, he
had been led to an excessive emphasis on one type
of criminal and one theory of criminal causation,
atavistic criminality. In later editions he expanded
his investigations and consequently his theory,
adding degeneracy as a cause of criminality and
considering atavism to be a form of degeneracy.
Although his theoretical linking of atavism and
degeneracy was challenged by biologists, it did
widen his original narrow concept of the born
criminal, which had been the primary point of attack of his critics. Lombroso's investigations also
revealed that the born criminal had pathological
symptoms in common with the moral imbecile and
the epileptic, and this led him to expand his typology to include the insane criminal and the epileptic
criminal. The insane criminal type includes the

alcoholic, the mattoid, and the hysterical criminal.
Further additions to the typology include the crim-
inaloid—a criminal qualitatively similar to the
born criminal but differing quantitatively from him
—who had become a criminal more from precipitating external factors than from predisposing
internal ones; the pseudocriminal; the habitual
criminal; and the person who commits a crime of
passion.

Although Lombroso did not believe that all criminal behavior is of organic origin, there is no doubt
that he never completely relinquished his belief in
the existence of the born criminal type. However,
in the fifth and last edition of *L'uomo delinquente*
in 1896–1897 reduced his estimate of the proportion of this type to 40 per cent of the total
criminal population, and in his introduction to his
daughter Gina's summary of his work, *Criminal
Man* (1911), he reduced it still further. In response to suggestions by friends and attacks by
critics he also came to give more attention to factors in the physical and social environment of the
offender. For example, in *Crime: Its Causes and
Remedies* (1899) he not only revised the estimate
of the born criminal to 33 per cent of the criminal
population but also discussed social circumstances
which might be partially responsible for encouraging a variety of transmissible biological anomalies
that in turn would function within and affect the
social structure.

Lombroso was not entirely opposed to the death
penalty but believed it should be used only as a
last resort. He favored attempts to readjust the
criminal and suggested a doctrine of symbiosis of
crime, whereby society would make use of the
labor and aptitudes of offenders. Included in this
doctrine is the idea of the compensation of the
victims of crime from the proceeds of work done
by prisoners.

Lombroso's work influenced criminological thinking principally by redirecting emphasis from a
legalistic concern for crime to a scientific study
of the criminal. His approach is most evident in
the clinical criminology of Benigno Di Tullio and
his associates in Italy.

                                    MARVIN E. WOLFGANG

[*See also* CRIMINOLOGY; DELINQUENCY, *article on* PSY-
CHOLOGICAL ASPECTS; PENOLOGY; PSYCHOLOGY,
article on CONSTITUTIONAL PSYCHOLOGY; *and*
PSYCHOPATHIC PERSONALITY.]

WORKS BY LOMBROSO

(1876) 1896–1897 *L'uomo delinquente in rapporto all'-
antropologia, alla giurisprudenza ed alle discipline
carcerarie.* 5th ed., 3 vols. Turin (Italy): Bocca.
(1893) 1927 LOMBROSO, CESARE; and FERRERO, GUGLI-
ELMO *La donna delinquente, la prostituta e la donna*

normale. 5th ed. Turin (Italy): Bocca. → Partly translated as *The Female Offender* and published in 1958 by Philosophical Library.

(1897) 1907 *Genio e degenerazione: Nuovi studî e nuove battaglie.* Palermo (Italy): Sandron.

(1899) 1911 *Crime: Its Causes and Remedies.* Boston: Little. → First published in Italian. A bibliography of the writings of Lombroso on criminal anthropology appears on pages 453–464.

SUPPLEMENTARY BIBLIOGRAPHY

DI TULLIO, BENIGNO 1959 *Cesare Lombroso e la politica criminale moderna. La scuola positiva* Series 4th 1:495–508.

KURELLA, HANS G. (1910) 1911 *Cesare Lombroso: A Modern Man of Science.* London: Rebman. → First published in German.

LOMBROSO-FERRERO, GINA 1911 *Criminal Man According to the Classification of Cesare Lombroso.* New York and London: Putnam.

LOMBROSO-FERRERO, GINA (1915) 1921 *Cesare Lombroso: Storia della vita e delle opere.* 2d ed. Bologna (Italy): Zanichelli. → A short biography and a bibliography appear on pages 447–476.

MANNHEIM, HERMANN 1936 Lombroso and His Place in Modern Criminology. *Sociological Review* 28:31–49.

WOLFGANG, MARVIN E. 1960 Cesare Lombroso. Pages 168–227 in Hermann Mannheim (editor), *Pioneers in Criminology.* London: Stevens.

LONGFIELD, SAMUEL MOUNTIFORT

Samuel Mountifort Longfield (1802–1884), the Irish jurist, had only a brief career as a professional economist; he was the first occupant of the chair of political economy at Trinity College, Dublin, that Richard Whately founded when he was made archbishop of Dublin. Longfield held this professorship from 1832 to 1836 and then resigned to pursue a legal career.

It was in 1903 that Edwin R. A. Seligman (1915) drew attention to Longfield by referring to him as a "neglected" economist, and indeed he appears to have been virtually unread outside Ireland until then. His work certainly deserved belated recognition, even though it had not become part of the mainstream of economic thought, for in some aspects of that work, he was thirty—even sixty—years ahead of his time.

In establishing the determinants of value, Longfield emphasized cost of production as one determinant, and had a rudimentary conception of the importance of diminishing marginal utility of demand as the other determinant. Thus he spoke of price as indicating what the buyer with the least intense demand was willing to pay. The distribution of income, like diminishing marginal utility, was for Longfield a marginal problem—that of productivity. He enunciated a nicely symmetrical theory of factor payments, in the course of which he denied the importance of the cost of subsistence

for the level of wages. He asserted that the wage rate was governed instead by that unit of labor applied least efficiently in the production of any given quantity of a commodity. Nonetheless, like most of his contemporaries, Longfield rejected Malthusian population theory as determining the necessary cost of production of labor, asserting that ". . . to find out what is the cost of production of common labourers, appears to be a trifling with a serious subject" (1834b, pp. 202–203).

The cost of capital is the cost of sacrificing present commodities for future ones, and in suggesting the idea of the productivity of roundabout production, Longfield may well, as Seligman points out (1915, p. 113), have sketched a theory of interest that combined time preference and the productivity of capital. But again it was the most disadvantageously used machine—that is to say, the least productive—that determined the rate of interest. In the area of allocation theory Longfield did interesting work in the concept of comparative advantage. This and, even more, the marginalist aspects of his economic analysis may well be connected with the fact that Longfield had always been an able mathematician and in 1872 even published *An Elementary Treatise on Series* (Black 1947, p. 53).

It was consistent with his rejection of Malthus that Longfield did not share the gloom of some of the English classical school concerning economic evolution, and believed that technological improvements in agriculture could more than offset the effects of population increase. He not only advocated that Ireland be industrialized but also predicted that industrialization would over time result in such an increase in capital that the rate of profits would fall and the productivity, hence the real wage, of labor would rise.

Longfield was president of the Statistical and Social Inquiry Society of Ireland from 1863 to 1867, but made few contributions to its proceedings. In a paper to the society (1872b), he appears to have supported the idea of government intervention in economic matters, advocating pensions for the blind and the aged, state education, medical care regardless of demonstration of need, housing control, and state-provided clubrooms for workers.

ERSKINE MCKINLEY

[*For the historical context of Longfield's work, see the biography of* MALTHUS. *For discussion of the subsequent development of his ideas, see especially* WAGES, *article on* THEORY; *see also* CAPITAL.]

WORKS BY LONGFIELD

1834a *Four Lectures on Poor Laws.* Dublin: Curry.
(1834b) 1931 *Lectures on Political Economy.* Series of

Reprints of Scarce Tracts on Economic and Political Science, No. 8. London School of Economics and Political Science.

(1835) 1938 *Three Lectures on Commerce and One on Absenteeism.* Series of Reprints of Scarce Works on Political Economy, No. 4. London School of Economics and Political Science.

1872a *An Elementary Treatise on Series.* Dublin.

1872b The Limits of State Interference with the Distribution of Wealth, in Applying Taxation to the Assistance of the Public. *Journal of the Statistical and Social Inquiry Society of Ireland* 6:105.

SUPPLEMENTARY BIBLIOGRAPHY

BLACK, R. D. COLLISON 1945 Trinity College, Dublin, and the Theory of Value, 1832–1863. *Economica* New Series 12:140–148.

BLACK, R. D. COLLISON 1947 A History of the Society. Pages 1–47 in the Statistical and Social Inquiry Society of Ireland, Dublin, *Centenary Volume, 1847–1947.* Dublin: Eason.

SCHUMPETER, JOSEPH A. 1954 *History of Economic Analysis.* Edited by E. B. Schumpeter. New York: Oxford Univ. Press.

SELIGMAN, EDWIN R. A. (1915) 1925 An Economic Interpretation of the War. Pages 161–179 in Edwin R. A. Seligman (editor), *Essays in Economics.* New York: Macmillan. → First published in Seligman's *Problems of Readjustment After the War,* 1915.

VINER, JACOB 1932 The Doctrine of Comparative Costs. *Weltwirtschaftliches Archiv* 36:356–414.

VINER, JACOB 1933 Samuel Mountifort Longfield. Volume 9, pages 605–606 in *Encyclopaedia of the Social Sciences.* New York: Macmillan.

LONGITUDINAL STUDIES

See DEVELOPMENTAL PSYCHOLOGY; PANEL STUDIES; TIME SERIES.

LORIA, ACHILLE

Achille Loria (1857–1943), Italian economic theorist, was born and raised in Mantua and received his *laurea* in law at Bologna in 1877. Subsequently he came under the influence of Luigi Cossa at Pavia, Angelo Messedaglia at Rome, and Adolf Wagner at Berlin. In 1881 he was named professor of political economy at Siena, where he remained for ten years. In 1891 he moved to the University of Padua and in 1903 to the University of Turin, where he taught until his retirement in 1932. He was elected to the Accademia dei Lincei in 1901 and was appointed to the Senate in 1919.

Loria developed his theory from a wide range of predecessors—the English classical school, Marx, Darwin, the German historical school, and Luigi Cossa, a specialist in the history of economic theory. Loria was not, however, a simple eclectic, for he used borrowed ideas to formulate an original deterministic and mechanistic theory of economic

development and social history. From an intensive and extensive reading on landholding in the British Museum in 1882, when land reform in Ireland and England was being very earnestly debated, he came to the conclusion that the key to the historical process is the relationship between the productivity of land and the density of population. Loria contended that the relative scarcity of land leads to the subjugation of some members of society by others. Different forms of subjugation produce stages in the historical process: slavery, feudalism, high capitalism, and late capitalism. Thus, social and political phenomena are determined at each stage by basic economic and demographic circumstances.

This fundamental concept was developed in a large number of books, many of which were translated into foreign languages. In these works an effort was made to substantiate the theoretical statement by presenting empirical evidence, especially that derived from the experience of colonial countries like America. Loria placed great emphasis upon the importance of free land in the history of the United States. Reviews and discussions of his work in the *Political Science Quarterly* of Columbia University introduced his work to many historians and political scientists. Clearly his views had an impact upon Frederick Jackson Turner in the formulation of his theory regarding the role of the frontier in American life and upon Charles A. Beard in his investigations of the place of economic interests in American political behavior (Benson 1950). The wide interest in the works of Turner and Beard has meant that Loria has had a considerable indirect influence on the interpretation of American history.

SHEPARD B. CLOUGH

[*See also the biographies of* BEARD; TURNER.]

WORKS BY LORIA

1880 *La rendita fondiaria e la sua elisione naturale.* Milan: Hoepli.

1882 *La legge di popolazione ed il sistema sociale.* Siena: Sordomuti.

1884 *Carlo Darwin e l'economia politica.* Milan: Dumolard.

(1886) 1904 *The Economic Foundations of Society.* London: Sonnenschein; New York: Scribner. → First published as *La teoria economica della costituzione politica.*

1889 *Analisi della proprietà capitalista.* 2 vols. Turin: Bocca.

(1890) 1891 *Studi sul valore della moneta.* Turin: Bocca.

1892 *La terra ed il sistema sociale.* Verona and Padua: Drucker.

(1894) 1911 *Contemporary Social Problems.* London: Sonnenschein; New York: Scribner. → First published in Italian.

1899 *La costituzione economica odierna.* Turin: Bocca.

1900 *La sociologia, il suo compito, le sue scuole, i suoi recenti progressi.* Conferenze tenute all'Università di Padova, gennaio-maggio, 1900. Verona and Padua: Drucker.

1901 *Il capitalismo e la scienza: Studi e polemiche.* Turin: Bocca.

1902 *Marx e la sua dottrina.* Milan: Sandron.

1903 *Il movimento operaio: Origini, forme, sviluppo.* Milan: Sandron.

(1904) 1915–1920 *Verso la giustizia sociale (idee, battaglie ed apostoli).* 2 vols. Milan: Società Editrice Libraria.

1905 *La morphologie sociale.* Conférences tenues à l'Université Nouvelle de Bruxelles au mois de mars 1905. Brussels: Larcier; Paris: Giard & Brière.

(1909) 1914 *The Economic Synthesis: A Study of the Laws of Income.* London: Allen & Unwin. → First published in Italian.

(1910) 1934 *Corso di economia politica.* 4th ed., rev. Turin: Unione Tipografico–Editrice Torinese.

(1912) 1918 *The Economic Causes of War.* Chicago: Kerr. → First published as *Les bases économiques de la justice internationale.*

1921 *Aspetti sociali ed economici della guerra mondiale.* Milan: Vallardi.

1922 *I fondamenti scientifici della riforma economica: Studio sulle leggi della produzione.* Turin: Bocca.

1926 *Davide Ricardo.* Rome: Formíggini.

1927 *Ricordi di uno studente settuagenario.* Bologna: Zanichelli.

1935 *Dinamica economica: Studio sulle leggi delle variazioni.* Turin: Unione Tipografico–Editrice Torinese.

SUPPLEMENTARY BIBLIOGRAPHY

BENSON, LEE (1950) 1960 *Turner and Beard: American Historical Writing Reconsidered.* Glencoe, Ill.: Free Press. → See pages 2–40 on "Achille Loria's Influence on American Economic Thought."

EINAUDI, LUIGI 1932 *Bibliografia di Achille Loria.* Turin: La Riforma Sociale. → Published as a Supplement to Volume 43, no. 5 of *La Riforma Sociale.*

EINAUDI, LUIGI 1946 Achille Loria 1857–1943. *Economic Journal* 56: 147–150.

RICCI, UMBERTO 1939 *Tre economisti italiani: Pantaleoni, Pareto, Loria.* Bari: Laterza.

LOTKA, ALFRED J.

Alfred James Lotka (1880–1949) anticipated many of the ideas of cybernetics and did original work in demography, evolutionary processes, and self-renewing aggregates. Born in Austria of American parentage, he spent his boyhood in France and acquired his advanced education in England, Germany, and the United States. He was employed as a chemist, physicist, mathematician, and biologist until 1924, when he joined the Metropolitan Life Insurance Company. There he worked on tasks that made heavy demands upon his actuarial and demographic skills. Lotka's 95 technical papers and 6 books reflect his deductive acumen, imagination, pragmatism, precision, and erudition. These works,

as well as his magazine articles, also manifest a deep appreciation of the arts and humanities. He held the office of president of the Population Association of America and of the American Statistical Association and several posts in the International Union for the Scientific Study of Population.

His key concern was the set of processes underlying self-renewing aggregates and systems undergoing change, especially irreversible change; this interest prompted the work to which "the field of demography owes virtually its entire central core of analytical development" (Notestein 1950, p. 23). Having shown in 1907 how a closed population with fixed age distribution grows, Lotka (with F. R. Sharpe 1911) demonstrated how a closed population develops a stable age distribution and a characteristic rate of increase, thereby supplying the most powerful of the modern demographer's analytical tools, the stable population model. Building on this and later work, Lotka (with L. I. Dublin 1925) showed how to compute a stable age distribution and the "intrinsic" (or "true") rate of increase, a discovery meriting for him the title "father of demographic analysis" (Vincent 1950, p. 14). This study revealed how misleading crude rates of natural increase can be. Lotka subsequently published many studies of self-renewing aggregates, evolution of age distributions, indices of reproductivity, progeny of population elements, orphanhood, changes in fertility and family size, family extinction, mortality, and so on. Some of this work appeared in the revised editions of Dublin and Lotka's *The Money Value of a Man* and *Length of Life: A Study of the Life Table*, and a great deal was summarized in Lotka's *Théorie analytique des associations biologiques* (1934–1939).

Probably most representative of Lotka's thought is *Elements of Physical Biology* (1925). Appearing when few social scientists used mathematics, it informed some of them of the uses of differential equations, the mechanics of systems and subsystems and the uses of systemic theory, and an essentially cybernetic view of organismic behavior (Simon 1959, p. 494). The book was the source of certain central modern ideas, and it demonstrates Lotka's ability to discover significance in diverse phenomena. Even today it contributes to the understanding of statics and dynamics. The book focuses upon the mechanics of one of the "systems undergoing irreversible changes in the distribution of matter" among its several components, namely, the evolving "life-bearing system," which is made up of an assembly of biological species, among them man, and collections of certain inorganic materials. Having defined irreversibility and conceived of evolution as the redistribution of matter, Lotka described the fundamental equations of the kinetics of evolving systems, along with growth functions and constraints. Under "statics" he treated steady states and diverse equilibria (e.g., chemical, interspecies, moving); Le Châtelier's principle, displacement of equilibrium, homeostasis, stability conditions, and what is now called "comparative statics"; and the role of parameters which define the state of systems. Under "dynamics" he discussed "the progressive redistribution of the matter of the system" among "aggregations of living organisms" or "energy transformers," together with the inorganic background within which substance circulated and parameters could change, albeit very slowly. He described in detail the elements composing the apparatus which energy transformers use in coping with their external environments, among them depictors, receptors (including communicators), elaborators, epictors, effectors, adjusters, and "consciousness" involved in depictors and adjustors [see INFORMATION THEORY]. This nonteleological apparatus enables some organisms, especially man, to discriminate, select, and in some environments stem that increase in entropy which dominates irreversible systems; its influence may be accentuated by favorable orthogenesis.

JOSEPH J. SPENGLER

[*For discussion of the subsequent development of Lotka's ideas, see* COMPUTATION; CYBERNETICS; LIFE TABLES; POPULATION.]

WORKS BY LOTKA

1911   LOTKA, ALFRED J.; and SHARPE, F. R. A Problem in Age Distribution. *Philosophical Magazine* 21:435–438.
(1925) 1957   *Elements of Mathematical Biology.* New York: Dover. → First published as *Elements of Physical Biology.*
1925   LOTKA, ALFRED J.; and DUBLIN, LOUIS I. On the True Rate of Natural Increase. *Journal of the American Statistical Association* 20:305–339.
(1930) 1946   DUBLIN, LOUIS I.; and LOTKA, ALFRED J. *The Money Value of a Man.* Rev. ed. New York: Ronald.
1934–1939   *Théorie analytique des associations biologiques.* 2 vols. Paris: Hermann. → Volume 1: *Principes.* Volume 2: *Analyse démographique avec application particulière à l'espèce humaine.*
(1936) 1949   DUBLIN, LOUIS I.; LOTKA, ALFRED J.; and SPIEGELMAN, M. *Length of Life: A Study of the Life Table.* Rev. ed. New York: Ronald. → Spiegelman is a joint author of the revised edition only.

SUPPLEMENTARY BIBLIOGRAPHY

LOPEZ, ALVARO 1961 *Problems in Stable Population Theory.* Princeton Univ., Office of Population Research.
NOTESTEIN, FRANK W. 1950 Alfred James Lotka. *Population Index* 16:22–29. → Contains a bibliography.
SIMON, HERBERT A. 1959 [A Book Review of] *Elements of Mathematical Biology*, by Alfred J. Lotka. *Econometrica* 27:493–495.
VINCENT, PAUL 1950 Alfred J. Lotka: 1880–1949. *Population* 5:13–14.

LOTZE, HERMANN

Rudolf Hermann Lotze (1817–1881), German psychologist and philosopher, was born in Bautzen, Upper Lusatia. His father was a surgeon in the army of Saxony. In the confusion of the Napoleonic Wars, his family moved frequently, finding a permanent home only in 1818 in Zittau. There, in 1828, Lotze entered the excellent classical Gymnasium, graduating cum laude in 1834. In his last years at the Gymnasium, he wrote poetry, as well as a novelistic essay along the lines of Goethe's *Wilhelm Meister.* Strongly influenced by Goethe, and as yet unaware of the works of other thinkers, he began to develop what were to remain the essentials of his philosophy.

Lotze's lack of funds forced him to abandon his literary and other interests and prepare himself for a profession. Following in his father's footsteps, he began, in 1834, to study medicine at the University of Leipzig. He also studied philosophy under Christian H. Weisse, a friend of Fechner's and an adherent of the idealist philosophy of Schelling and Hegel. Lotze's later work was decisively influenced both by his medical and scientific training and by Weisse's idealist teaching.

He completed his study of medicine in 1838 with a dissertation entitled *De futurae biologiae principiis philosophicis.* As a scientist he vigorously opposed the medical mysticism implied in the concept of "vitality," replacing it with mechanistic explanations; as a philosopher, however, he denied that a mechanistic system of explanation is necessarily based on a materialist philosophy. He obtained a master's degree in philosophy at the same time as his medical degree.

Lotze practiced medicine in Zittau for a year, but he soon found the town too confining. Encouraged by his former professor, Weisse, he returned to Leipzig as an instructor in medicine and philosophy; he was appointed associate professor in 1843. While he was at Leipzig he produced the outlines of his scientific life work: the *Metaphysik* (1841), in which he broke with Hegelian idealism; the *Allgemeine Pathologie und Therapie als mechanische Naturwissenschaften* (1842); the *Logik* (1843*a*); and three articles for Rudolf Wagner's *Handwörterbuch der Physiologie*, "Leben, Lebenskraft" (1843*b*), "Instinct" (1844), and "Seele und

Seelenleben" (1846). In 1844 he accepted an appointment as full professor at Göttingen, occupying what had been Johann Friedrich Herbart's chair. He remained at Göttingen for 37 years until, at the urging of Eduard Zeller and Helmholtz, he accepted the chair vacated by Harms in Berlin. He died soon after his move to Berlin.

Lotze always remained both a scientist and a philosopher. His works are characterized, first, by his efforts to eliminate mysticism from science by using the causal–mechanistic method and, second, by his concern to dissociate mechanistic systematization from materialist–atheist philosophy. To Lotze intellectual achievement without faith was a *caput mortuum*, and science without causal–mechanistic systematization was not a science. Ultimately, to be sure, what concerned him was the ideal—what *ought* to be—and he saw the understanding of causal relationships simply as a condition for the realization of the ideal. Thus, mechanistic processes are indispensable to the existence of a phenomenon, but they are not its *raison d'être*. In this way Lotze tried to combine mechanistic systematization with ethical freedom, with what he called the dignity of subjectivity. In his own time his postulate of freedom, which went counter to the anti-idealist *Zeitgeist*, was not understood; his contemporaries availed themselves, instead, of the mass of physiological facts he cited —which clearly confirmed the dependence of the psychical on the physical—to support their materialist philosophy.

Lotze's *Allgemeine Physiologie des koerperlichen Lebens* appeared in 1851, and his *Medicinische Psychologie: Oder, Physiologie der Seele* in 1852. The latter is the first physiological psychology, the prototype of all later works bearing similar titles. In contrast to Fechner's parallelism, Lotze's psychology is a theory of interaction: sensation is produced by the mind "at the initiative of a neural state." Space is a mode of perception peculiar to the mind. A corollary to this theory of space perception is Lotze's theory of "local signs," which asserts that the world of external space is never simply perceived but rather reproduced by the mind.

His two-volume magnum opus, *Microcosmus* (1856–1864), has two aspects: it is both a polemic against materialist philosophy and an expansion of Lotze's psychology into a comprehensive anthropology. (Its German subtitle is "Versuch einer Anthropologie.") Exploring what he called education (*Bildung*), that is, the conditions under which a human being becomes human, he dealt with such subjects as national temperament, the evolution

of customs and morals, and the influences of home, family, division of labor, and so forth. He regarded the history of mankind as the history of the evolution of the human mind.

Lotze founded no school; he had no disciples. Yet he was a pioneer with some influence, for the friends and pupils he did have were men of scientific importance: Teichmüller, Stumpf, Konrad Langenbeck, and Georg E. Müller. Stumpf studied with Lotze in 1867–1868, and, after working with Franz Brentano in Würzburg for two years, he returned to Göttingen as an instructor. Müller took his doctorate with Lotze in 1873, became an instructor at Göttingen in 1876, and succeeded Lotze as professor there in 1881.

It is unlikely that anyone with an empirical, problem-oriented approach to psychology will find Lotze's work of direct relevance. But if he does not dismiss Lotze's work too readily as obsolete, he may find fertile suggestions there.

WILHELM J. REVERS

[*For discussion of the subsequent development of Lotze's ideas, see* PERCEPTION, *articles on* DEPTH PERCEPTION *and* PERCEPTUAL DEVELOPMENT.]

WORKS BY LOTZE

(1838) 1885 De futurae biologiae principiis philosophicis: Dissertatio inauguralis medica. Volume 1, pages 1–25 in Hermann Lotze, *Kleine Schriften.* Leipzig: Hirzel.

(1838–1881) 1885–1891 *Kleine Schriften.* 3 vols. Edited with an introduction by David Peipers. Leipzig: Hirzel.

1840 *Gedichte.* Leipzig: Weidmann.

1841 *Metaphysik.* Leipzig: Weidmann.

(1842) 1848 *Allgemeine Pathologie und Therapie als mechanische Naturwissenschaften.* 2d ed. Leipzig: Hirzel.

1843a *Logik.* Leipzig: Weidmann.

(1843b) 1885 Leben, Lebenskraft. Volume 1, pages 139–220 in Hermann Lotze, *Kleine Schriften.* Leipzig: Hirzel.

(1844) 1885 Instinct. Volume 1, pages 221–250 in Hermann Lotze, *Kleine Schriften.* Leipzig: Hirzel.

(1846) 1886 Seele und Seelenleben. Volume 2, pages 1–204 in Hermann Lotze, *Kleine Schriften.* Leipzig: Hirzel.

1851 *Allgemeine Physiologie des koerperlichen Lebens.* Leipzig: Weidmann.

1852 *Medicinische Psychologie: Oder, Physiologie der Seele.* Leipzig: Weidmann.

(1856–1864) 1894 *Microcosmus: An Essay Concerning Man and His Relation to the World.* 4th ed., 2 vols. Edinburgh: Clark. → First published as *Mikrokosmus: Ideen zur Naturgeschichte und Geschichte der Menschheit: Versuch einer Anthropologie,* in 3 volumes.

1857 *Streitschriften.* Volume 1: In Bezug auf Prof. I. H. Fichte's *Anthropologie.* Leipzig: Hirzel.

1868 *Geschichte der Aesthetik in Deutschland.* Akademie der Wissenschaft, Munich, Geschichte der Wissenschaften in Deutschland, Vol. 7. Munich: Cotta.

(1874) 1888 *Logic, in Three Books: Of Thought, of In-*
vestigation, and of Knowledge. 2d ed., 2 vols. Oxford:
Clarendon Press. → First published in German. Part 1
of Lotze's "System of Philosophy."
(1879) 1887 *Metaphysic, in Three Books: Ontology, Cos-*
mology and Psychology. 2d ed., 2 vols. Oxford: Clarendon Press. → First published in German. Part 2 of
Lotze's "System of Philosophy."
(1881) 1886 *Outlines of Psychology.* Boston: Ginn. →
First published in German.

SUPPLEMENTARY BIBLIOGRAPHY

BORING, EDWIN G. (1929) 1957 *A History of Experi-*
mental Psychology. 2d ed. New York: Appleton. → See
especially pages 261–270 on "Hermann Lotze."
BRETT, GEORGE S. (1912–1921) 1962 *Brett's History of*
Psychology. Edited and abridged by R. S. Peters. London: Allen & Unwin; New York: Macmillan. → An
abridged edition of the original three-volume publication, *A History of Psychology.* See especially pages
591–600 on Lotze's soul psychology.
FALCKENBERG, RICHARD F. O. 1901 *Hermann Lotze.*
Stuttgart: Fromann.
HALL, G. STANLEY 1912 *Founders of Modern Psychol-*
ogy. New York: Appleton. → See especially pages 65–
121 on "Rudolph Hermann Lotze."
HARTMANN, EDUARD VON 1888 *Lotze's Philosophie.* Leipzig: Friedrich.
MURPHY, GARDNER (1929) 1949 *Historical Introduction*
to Modern Psychology. Rev. ed. New York: Harcourt.
WENTSCHER, MAX 1925 *Fechner und Lotze.* Munich:
Reinhardt.

LOUIS, P. C. A.

Pierre Charles Alexandre Louis (1787–1872),
who did much to introduce the use of statistics into
medicine, was born the son of a vineyard proprietor
in the small town of Ay (Marne) in Champagne.
Although his father died when Louis was six, his
mother saw to her son's primary education. After
his schooling was over he was sent to a law office
to prepare for a legal career. In 1807, deciding that
the law was not to his liking, Louis began to study
medicine. He spent a year at Reims with a surgeon and then went to Paris to pursue his studies,
graduating in 1813 with a medical degree.

A chance encounter during a brief vacation in
his native town had an important effect on his
career. The comte de Saint-Priest, an emigré noble
in whose family Louis's aunt had been a governess,
was friendly with the Louis family and paid them
a visit. As governor of Podolia, Saint-Priest was in
the service of the tsar and persuaded Louis to
accompany him to Russia. After traveling about
that country for three years Louis settled in Odessa,
where he acquired a substantial practice and even
received a titular appointment as physician to the
tsar. In 1820 Odessa experienced a diphtheria epidemic, an event which led Louis not only to realize

the shortcomings in his knowledge of disease but to
give up his practice and return to Paris for further
study.

Six months in the Paris hospitals convinced
Louis that clinical medicine required a more precise basis than it had and that this could be
achieved by what he called the numerical method.
A.-F. Chomel, his friend and fellow student, was
attending physician at the Charité Hospital and
gave Louis the run of two wards of his service, as
well as the privilege of performing all the autopsies on the patients who died there. For six years
Louis worked at the hospital from three to five
hours a day, devoting at least two hours to each
autopsy and collecting over two thousand observations. In 1827 he retired to Brussels, where the cost
of living was lower, and spent a year tabulating
and analyzing his statistical data.

Some of his observations had been published
while he was still in Paris, and in 1825 Louis had
brought out his *Recherches anatomico-patholo-*
giques sur la phthisie, based on 123 cases. (Some
eighty were added to the second edition of 1843.)
By the time he returned to Paris in 1828 he had
acquired a reputation in medical circles. That year
he was sent, together with Armand Trousseau and
Nicolas Chervin, to investigate a yellow fever epidemic at Gibraltar. In 1828 his work on typhoid
fever was published and he became attending physician at La Pitié Hospital. Subsequently he was
also appointed to the Hôtel-Dieu; he served in these
institutions for many years. Louis's last important
publication was his critical analysis of the alleged
therapeutic effects of bloodletting, *Recherches sur*
les effets de la saignée dans quelques maladies in-
flammatoires (1835). In this book he employed the
numerical method to refute the views of François
Broussais on copious bloodletting in pneumonia
and other inflammatory diseases.

Louis married a daughter of the marquis de
Montferrier in 1832, when he was 45. For some
twenty years he carried on an ample consultation
practice in Paris. His only son, Armand, died of
tuberculosis in 1854, a loss from which Louis never
recovered.

The numerical method.   Louis's major contribution resides in his efforts to apply statistical analysis to problems of clinical medicine. His advocacy
and use of the *numerical method* served this end.
What Louis did was to study each patient as thoroughly as possible at the bedside and at autopsy,
employing rigorously the methodology already established by G. L. Bayle, René Th. H. Laënnec, and
others of the Paris school of clinicians and pathologists. Having carefully collected his observations he then grouped them in tabular form. From

these grouped and tabulated data inferences might be drawn concerning the relations between diverse clinical phenomena, the probability of their occurrence, the value of a given therapy, and other items. Although he had used his approach in his earlier publications on phthisis and typhoid fever, the numerical method was first fully presented in 1835 in Louis's therapeutic study, *Recherches sur les effets de la saignée* . . . , and in a special memoir *De l'examen des malades et de la recherche des faits généraux* (1837).

Essentially, Louis's numerical method was not new. The procedure had been employed some three decades earlier by Philippe Pinel to prove the value of his "moral treatment" of mental patients. It was also being employed in the 1820s and 1830s by physicians concerned with such public health problems as the causes of differential mortality and the effect on health of such factors as economic and social class, occupation, race, imprisonment, intemperance, or lack of proper sanitation. Furthermore, Louis's handling of numerical data was basically simple. If, as it is said, Louis was familiar with the work of Laplace on probability, there is no evidence that he ever used such knowledge in his statistical thinking. Like so many of his contemporaries he dealt with small numbers of observations and had no knowledge of how to establish the precision or validity of his results. There is no doubt that Louis was himself conscious of these difficulties; yet he did not seek statistical criteria of reliability, nor did he try to decide when the number of observations was large enough to avoid error.

Nevertheless, Louis has a significant place in the evolving application of statistical analysis to health problems. First of all, he recognized the basic importance of accurate observations. His insistence on good clinical records established a fundamental principle for statistical work in clinical medicine. Second, Louis made an important contribution as a teacher and a propagandist. Through his students, of whom a considerable proportion were foreigners (among them Americans), through the Société Médicale d'Observation (which several of his students founded in 1832), and through his writings Louis advocated and spread the idea of the numerical method, in spite of vigorous opposition. He envisaged the goal of a science of clinical medicine and pointed to the road that would lead to it.

GEORGE ROSEN

WORKS BY LOUIS

(1825) 1843 *Recherches anatomico-pathologiques sur la phthisie.* 2d ed. Paris: Baillière.

(1828) 1841 *Recherches anatomiques, pathologiques . . . sur la maladie connue sous les noms de fièvre typhoïde* . . . 2 vols., 2d ed. Paris: Baillière.
1835 *Recherches sur les effets de la saignée dans quelques maladies inflammatoires.* Paris: Baillière.
1837 De l'examen des malades et de la recherche des faits généraux. Société Médicale d'Observation, *Mémoires* 1:1–63.

SUPPLEMENTARY BIBLIOGRAPHY

ASTRUC, PIERRE 1932 Le centenaire de la Société Médicale d'Observation. *Progrès médical,* supplément illustré 9:73–87.
BÉCLARD, JULES-AUGUSTE 1878 *Notices et portraits: Éloges lus à l'Académie de Médecine.* Paris: Masson. → See especially pages 228–257.
GREENWOOD, MAJOR (the younger) 1936 *The Medical Dictator and Other Biographical Studies.* London: Williams & Norgate. → See especially pages 123–142.
OSLER, WILLIAM 1908 *An Alabama Student and Other Biographical Essays.* Oxford Univ. Press. → See especially pages 189–210.
ROSEN, GEORGE 1955 Problems in the Application of Statistical Analysis to Questions of Health: 1700–1800. *Bulletin of the History of Medicine* 29:27–45.
WOILLEZ, EUGÈNE J. 1873 *Le docteur Pierre Charles Alexandre Louis: Sa vie—ses oeuvres (1787–1872).* Paris: Dupont.

LOVE
See AFFECTION.

LOWELL, A. LAWRENCE

Abbott Lawrence Lowell (1856–1943), political scientist and president of Harvard University, was born into one of the great families of Boston society. The Lowells had been established in Massachusetts since 1639 and had contributed to American life a distinguished line of ministers, merchants, industrialists, philanthropists, jurists, and poets. Much of their philanthropy supported education, especially Harvard University, the Massachusetts Institute of Technology, and the Lowell Institute. When he graduated from Harvard College in 1877, A. Lawrence Lowell was the sixth in an unbroken series of generations of alumni.

After receiving an LL.B. from the Harvard Law School in 1880, Lowell opened a law office in Boston. When his practice proved unsuccessful, he began to write in his spare time, soon turning from legal topics to political science. A series of magazine articles, collected as *Essays on Government* (1889), received sufficient recognition to encourage him to begin work on a major study in comparative government, the two-volume *Governments and Parties in Continental Europe* (1896). From 1897 to 1900 he was a part-time lecturer at Harvard, and in 1900 he received a permanent appointment as professor of the science of government. His book *The Government of England* (1908) won praise on both sides of the Atlantic. Lowell was active in university affairs, and this led to his selection as president of Harvard in 1909, a post he held until 1933.

His basic approach to political science is stated on the opening page of *Essays on Government:* "The real mechanism of a government can be understood only by examining it in action." Studies were needed, therefore, to provide detailed descriptions of the actual operation of contemporary political structures. He observed, furthermore, that political parties, more than formal institutions, determine political practice.

Lowell's two major books were based on these themes. The one on continental Europe (1896) carefully described the formal political institutions of France, Italy, Germany, Austria–Hungary, and Switzerland and the way that the specific party system dominated the institutions of each country. The book on England (1908) provided a detailed review of the political life of that country, based on extensive interviews with political leaders as well as printed source material. These and less ambitious works discussing the management of legislation by parties and the impact of public opinion on party operations aroused contemporary enthusiasm. In the *English Historical Review* it was said that Lowell "has done for England what Mr. Bryce has done for the American Commonwealth" (Raleigh 1908, p. 809). Although succeeding generations may not rate Lowell's insights this highly, they will still find useful his precise portraits of how governments operated at the beginning of the twentieth century.

In his 24 years as president of Harvard, Lowell was particularly eager to enhance the stature of the undergraduate college. He modified the undergraduate curriculum by curtailing freedom in the choice of courses and by introducing the tutorial system to encourage individual work. He altered the structure of the college by the inauguration, in 1930, of the "house system," which split the undergraduate body into smaller residential and social units, on the model of the English universities. And despite his great identification with New England, he supported changes in admission rules and scholarship eligibility that opened Harvard to public school graduates from the entire country and transformed the college into a national institution.

Although Lowell aroused considerable liberal hostility when he supported the convictions of Sacco and Vanzetti, he was keenly sensitive to any encroachments on academic freedom. He strongly defended faculty members under attack by the public and by alumni for unpopular opinions—Hugo Münsterberg for pro-German attitudes during World War I, Zechariah Chaffee for liberal views during the "Red Scare" of the 1920s, and Harold Laski for his support of the police in the Boston police strike of 1919.

MILTON BERMAN

[*Other relevant material may be found in* PARTIES, POLITICAL; *and in the biographies of* BRYCE *and* MICHELS.]

WORKS BY LOWELL

1889   *Essays on Government.* Boston: Houghton Mifflin.
1896   *Governments and Parties in Continental Europe.* 2 vols. Boston: Houghton Mifflin.
1902   The Influence of Party Upon Legislation in England and America. American Historical Association, *Annual Report* [1901] no. 1:319–542.
(1908) 1912   *The Government of England.* 2 vols., new ed. New York: Macmillan.
(1913) 1926   *Public Opinion and Popular Government.* New ed. New York: Longmans.
1923   *Public Opinion in War and Peace.* Cambridge, Mass.: Harvard Univ. Press.
1934   *At War With Academic Traditions in America.* Cambridge, Mass.: Harvard Univ. Press.
1938   *What a University President Has Learned.* New York: Macmillan.

SUPPLEMENTARY BIBLIOGRAPHY

GREENSLET, FERRIS 1946 *The Lowells and Their Seven Worlds.* Boston: Houghton Mifflin.
MORISON, SAMUEL E. (editor) 1930 *The Development of Harvard University Since the Inauguration of President Eliot: 1869–1929.* Cambridge, Mass.: Harvard Univ. Press.
MORISON, SAMUEL E. 1936 The Lowell Administration. Pages 439–481 in Samuel E. Morison, *Three Centuries of Harvard: 1636–1936.* Cambridge, Mass.: Harvard Univ. Press.
RALEIGH, T. 1908 [A Book Review of] *The Government of England,* by A. Lawrence Lowell. *English Historical Review* 23:809–810.
YEOMANS, HENRY A. 1948 *Abbott Lawrence Lowell: 1856–1943.* Cambridge, Mass.: Harvard Univ. Press.

LOWIE, ROBERT H.

Robert H. Lowie (1883–1957), American anthropologist, was born in Vienna of a German mother and a Hungarian father. From the time he was ten he lived in New York City. In 1897 he entered City College, concentrating on Latin and Greek for the first two years and then on science. After he received his B.A. in 1901 he taught for three years in the New York public schools. Then he began graduate work in anthropology at Columbia University, studying primarily with Franz Boas; his minor field was psychology. He volunteered his services to Clark Wissler at the American Museum of Natural History and was sent by Wissler on his first field trip, to the Lemhi Shoshone, in 1906. In 1908 he received his PH.D. from Columbia, with a thesis on a subject in comparative mythology. Lowie spent most of his active professional life at two institutions: at the American Museum, from 1907 to 1917, and at the University of California at Berkeley, from 1917 until 1950. He married Luella Cole, a psychologist, in 1933. His last teaching position was at Harvard in the summer of 1955.

Lowie was exceedingly productive: his bibliography totals about four hundred separate pieces of writing—14 books, 18 monographs, 3 translations of monographs, 203 reviews, and numerous articles. Nearly all his works were on ethnology, but he did include some archeology in his *Introduction to Cultural Anthropology* (1934) and collected three volumes of texts in the Crow language. His many honors attest to the recognition of his contributions: he served as president of several major professional societies (the American Folklore Society, 1916–1917, the American Ethnological Society, 1920–1921, and the American Anthropological Association, 1935–1936); he was elected to the National Academy of Sciences in 1931; he received an honorary doctorate from the University of Chicago in 1941; he gave the Huxley lecture at the Royal Anthropological Institute in 1948; and he was awarded the Viking medal in the same year. He also served his profession as editor of the *American Anthropologist* from 1924 to 1933.

Approach to theory. Lowie's theoretical position was, in his own words, middle-of-the-road (*Selected Papers*, p. 13); for example, on the subject of the correlation of semantic categories in kinship terminologies, on the one hand, and social structure and behavior, on the other, he took a position somewhere in between Kroeber's historical one and the functional view propounded by Radcliffe-Brown. He refused to accept theories when he considered the supporting evidence to be weak, as in the case of Freudian interpretations of cultural behavior, for he insisted that ethnology is a science and that its theories must be supported by facts.

Of all Lowie's books, *Primitive Society* (1920) had the greatest impact on anthropology. Although Kroeber criticized the book for being too destructive of old theories and too little concerned with replacing them (Kroeber 1920), and although White repeatedly berated Lowie for being too harsh with L. H. Morgan (White 1943; 1944; 1945), *Primitive Society* dominated social organization theory until the almost simultaneous ap-

pearance of three new books, one by Lowie himself (1948), one by Murdock that appeared in 1949, and one by Lévi-Strauss, also in 1949. Lowie's 1920 book would have been great even if it had done nothing more than clarify terminology, but it contained so much more that graduate students reading it for the first time are often surprised to find that it anticipates much of current teaching.

Although Lowie used no explicit sampling technique, he was familiar with so wide a range of ethnographies that many of his global generalizations have since been confirmed by more refined methods. The broad scope of the book, which includes chapters on property, associations, rank, government, and justice, in addition to the discussion of kinship, is paralleled most closely by Hoebel's general textbook, published in 1949. Lowie's theoretical position in *Primitive Society* reflects that of the Boas historical school. While not denying independent invention and parallel and convergent evolution, especially in the field of economics, Lowie did reject the evolution of social organization proposed by L. H. Morgan and emphasized the dominant role of diffusion: "Creating nothing, this factor [diffusion], nevertheless makes all other agencies taper almost into nothingness beside it in its effect on the total growth of human civilization" ([1920] 1947, p. 434).

Lowie's *History of Ethnological Theory* (1937) shows more tolerance of the opinions of others than does *Primitive Society*. Although Lowie regarded many of the extreme diffusionist views and evolutionary sequences of the German *Kulturkreis* school as being undemonstrable, he nevertheless conceded (1937, p. 190) that the correlations the German anthropologists had obtained between feminine tillage, matrilocal residence, matrilineal descent, bride service, and monogamy were correct. These correlations have been confirmed statistically in recent years. Similarly, although Lowie had little use for Radcliffe-Brown's more general laws, he accepted the correlations Radcliffe-Brown had established among specific variables of kinship terminology and social organization. For instance, Radcliffe-Brown (1913) was the first to point out that in Australia four-section systems of social organization and marriage with a first cross-cousin were associated with one kind of kinship terminology, while eight-section systems and marriage with a second cross-cousin went with a different kind of kinship terminology.

Psychology and anthropology. Lowie maintained an interest in psychology throughout his life, mentioned it in many of his writings, and devoted a section of his *History of Ethnological*

Theory (1937, pp. 262–274) to it. He regarded psychology as the study of innate behavior, in contrast to the learned behavior of culture, and he pointed out that ethnological studies had shown that many kinds of behavior are in fact culturally determined, although they had previously been thought to be of genetic origin. At the same time he suggested that mythology and religion have common elements across cultures which are derived from dreams, and that these dreams may have some sort of biological basis. Lowie accepted Galton's notion that individual differences between members of the same society may be in part genetically determined, and even that there might be significant genetic differences between races, not in over-all ability but in special abilities, such as aptitude for music. He was among the first anthropologists to point out that cultural selection is a part of natural selection (1937, p. 267) and that it can in part determine which genes will be advantageous and which will be deleterious. He tended to distrust the sweeping Freudian generalizations of the early personality studies by ethnologists and never fully endorsed personality as an important subdiscipline within ethnology.

During World War II, Lowie taught an "area course" on Germany and the Balkans at Berkeley. This led to a book on Germany (1945), a field trip to Germany, Switzerland, and Austria in 1950/ 1951, and a second book on Germany in 1954. Lowie did a considerable amount of interviewing on the field trip, and he read a large amount of material on Germany, including self-evaluations by Germans. The 1954 book was concerned principally with describing the impact of the war on the personalities of German people.

Anthropological analysis. Lowie's many monographs on North American Indians, which were written for the most part while he was connected with the American Museum, are excellent. His field work on the Crow Indians goes far beyond the kind of cultural inventory that was common at the time and includes many insights into functional relationships. Take his description of the chaos that would result from an endogamous marriage within a single sib (or clan):

A Crow in such circumstances loses his bearings and perplexes his tribesmen. For he owes specific obligations to his father's relatives and others to his mother's, who are now hopelessly confounded. The sons of his father's clansmen ought to be his censors, whereas his mother's are bound to shield him from criticism; but now the very same persons are his joking-relatives and his clansmen. The dilemma affects others as well as himself. ([1948] 1960, p. 237)

The historical and comparative summaries at the end of his work on Plains Indian age-societies (1916a) were praised even by Boas, who was critical of so many historical reconstructions. They are still cited as among the best examples of the kind of comparative and historical interpretation produced by the Boas school.

It was in one of his early articles (1916b) that Lowie showed how well a balance can be preserved between historical and "sociological" (i.e. functional) interpretation of such data as kinship terminologies. Indeed, since more recent cross-cultural studies of kinship terminologies have largely ignored historical explanations, they have in this respect retrogressed from Lowie's position of 1916. However, in works by Naroll (1961; 1964), Naroll and D'Andrade (1963), and Driver (1966), Lowie's dual interpretation has been confirmed in applications to geographical distributions. It is an interpretation that can, in fact, be applied to almost all anthropological data.

Lowie wrote a number of articles in which he drew on more than one academic discipline (see *Selected Papers*, pp. 189–290) and in which he reached, among others, the following conclusions: that oral traditions are not reliable history and that a more accurate history can be inferred from careful comparative study in ethnology, archeology, linguistics, and physical anthropology; that all races are not necessarily equal in all inherited mental abilities just because they have not been proven to differ; that the concept of incorporeal property is common in primitive societies; that economic factors can explain only a minor part of cultural behavior; and that the progression from American Indian societies with the simplest form of government to the totalitarian state of the Inca was not a simple one. There was no unilineal development toward ever greater centralization of authority; for example, the Iroquois avoided military despotism because it would have conflicted with the separatism of their matricentered kinship organization.

Lowie's theory of evolution acknowledged the general increase in culture complexity through time and the increase in the efficiency of economic productivity, but it denied the inevitability of any universal increase in complexity and efficiency: particular races, languages, or cultures may either level off, retrogress, or become extinct rather than evolve toward greater complexity. Lowie also denied the inevitability of moral progress.

Lowie was early aware of the possibility and desirability of applying correlation techniques to cross-cultural variables, and in a book published in 1948 he also discussed the relation of correlation to the laws of evolution. Although he himself never applied the method of correlation to cross-cultural data, he praised Murdock's 1949 book for doing so. He was well aware of the essentials of scientific method in cross-cultural comparisons, such as the necessity of basing generalizations on representative samples. He pointed out also the lack of precise definition of the ethnic unit (society) and the equally vague definition of some of the variables (culture traits) being correlated. Rather than abandon quantitative methods entirely, Lowie argued for refinement of such definitions and caution in inferring time sequence or causality from correlations. In his books of world-wide scope he consistently cited sufficient evidence from every major world area, so that the generalizations he made have never been invalidated by statistics or even been challenged. In his comparative writings he made use of all the major explanations of resemblances in the culture inventories of ethnic units: universals, parallels, convergences, diffusions, and heritages from a common protoculture.

Most of Lowie's field work was done under the supervision of Clark Wissler of the American Museum of Natural History, who directed him to do reconnaissance in central Canada and the entire Great Basin area in the United States. When he was permitted to remain with the Crow Indians for a relatively long period of time, Lowie's field work was superb. His modest appraisal that his descriptions of material culture were not as competent as Wissler's may be correct, but his work on social organization and religion surely excelled that of his mentor and became a model for those who followed. He obtained most of his information from a small number of informants, but he occasionally used a larger number when he suspected significant individual differences, as in reports of visionary experiences. In addition to collecting material in English from competent bilinguals, he obtained three volumes of texts in the Crow language, thus preserving for the future a large amount of primary data.

HAROLD E. DRIVER

[See also ETHNOGRAPHY; INDIANS, NORTH AMERICAN; POLITICAL ANTHROPOLOGY; SOCIAL STRUCTURE; *and the biographies of* BOAS; KROEBER; MORGAN, LEWIS HENRY; RADCLIFFE-BROWN; WISSLER.]

WORKS BY LOWIE

1916a   Plains Indian Age-societies: Historical and Comparative Summary. Volume 11, pages 881–1031 in American Museum of Natural History, *Anthropological Papers.* New York: The Museum.

(1916b) 1960   Historical and Sociological Interpretations

of Kinship Terminologies. Pages 65–74 in Robert H. Lowie, *Selected Papers in Anthropology.* Edited by Cora DuBois. Berkeley: Univ. of California Press.

(1920) 1947   *Primitive Society.* New York: Liveright. → A paperback edition was published in 1961 by Harper.

(1921) 1960   A Note on Aesthetics. Pages 137–142 in Robert H. Lowie, *Selected Papers in Anthropology.* Edited by Cora DuBois. Berkeley: Univ. of California Press.

(1934) 1952   *An Introduction to Cultural Anthropology.* Rev. ed. New York: Farrar.

1937   *The History of Ethnological Theory.* New York: Farrar.

1942   *Studies in Plains Indian Folklore.* California, University of, Publications in American Archaeology and Ethnology, Vol. 40, no. 1. Berkeley: Univ. of California Press.

1945   *The German People: A Social Portrait to 1914.* New York and Toronto: Farrar.

(1948) 1960   *Social Organization.* New York: Holt.

1954   *Toward Understanding Germany.* Univ. of Chicago Press.

1959   *Robert H. Lowie, Ethnologist: A Personal Record.* Berkeley: Univ. of California Press.

Selected Papers in Anthropology. Edited by Cora DuBois. Berkeley: Univ. of California Press, 1960. → Thirty-three papers written or published between 1911 and 1957.

SUPPLEMENTARY BIBLIOGRAPHY

Bibliography of Robert H. Lowie. 1958   *American Anthropologist* New Series 60:362–375.

DRIVER, HAROLD E.   1966   Geographical–Historical versus Psycho–Functional Explanations of Kin Avoidances. *Current Anthropology* 7:131–182.

HOEBEL, E. ADAMSON   (1949) 1958   *Man in the Primitive World: An Introduction to Anthropology.* 2d ed. New York: McGraw-Hill.

KROEBER, A. L.   1920   [A Book Review of] *Primitive Society,* by Robert H. Lowie. *American Anthropologist* New Series 22:377–381.

LÉVI-STRAUSS, CLAUDE   1949   *Les structures élémentaires de la parenté.* Paris: Presses Universitaires de France.

MURDOCK, GEORGE P.   1949   *Social Structure.* New York: Macmillan. → A paperback edition was published in 1965 by the Free Press.

NAROLL, RAOUL S.   1961   Two Solutions to Galton's Problem. *Philosophy of Science* 28:16–39.

NAROLL, RAOUL S.; and D'ANDRADE, ROY G.   1963   Two Further Solutions to Galton's Problem. *American Anthropologist* New Series 65:1053–1067.

NAROLL, RAOUL S.   1964   Fifth Solution to Galton's Problem. *American Anthropologist* New Series 66:863–867.

RADCLIFFE-BROWN, A. R.   1913   Three Tribes of Western Australia. *Journal of the Royal Anthropological Institute of Great Britain and Ireland* 43:143–194.

RADIN, PAUL   1958   Robert H. Lowie: 1883–1957. *American Anthropologist* New Series 60:358–361.

WHITE, LESLIE A.   1943   Energy and the Evolution of Culture. *American Anthropologist* New Series 45:335–356.

WHITE, LESLIE A.   1944   Morgan's Attitude Toward Religion and Science. *American Anthropologist* New Series 46:218–230.

WHITE, LESLIE A.   1945   Diffusion vs. Evolution: An Anti-evolutionist Fallacy. *American Anthropologist* New Series 47:339–356.

LOYALTY

Loyalty can be defined as a feeling of attachment to something outside of the self, such as a group, an institution, a cause, or an ideal. The sentiment carries with it a willingness to support and act in behalf of the objects of one's loyalty and to persist in that support over an extended period of time and under conditions which exact a degree of moral, emotional, or material sacrifice from the individual. Josiah Royce captured most of the connotations of the term when he defined it as "the willing and practical and thorough going devotion of a person to a cause" (1908, pp. 16–17).

As used in political discourse, the concept of loyalty occupies the ground between patriotism and obligation. It is something less than the typically uncritical adulation' of one's own political group, often accompanied by rejective attitudes toward outsiders, which is the heart of patriotism. It is something more than the formal, rationally justified duty to obey law, which is the essence of obligation. Loyalty is cooler in emotional tone, more rational in its bases, and less comprehensive in its object than patriotism; and it is warmer, less rational, and more comprehensive than obligation.

Since loyalty is an attitude, it varies along the same dimensions as any other attitude: intensity, specificity, endurance, direction, content, and so forth. Loyalties emerge out of a social matrix, and the processes of loyalty formation, growth, and change are closely akin to those involved in the process of identification. When one is said to be loyal to a group, for example, it is tantamount to saying that he has identified himself with the group, that his membership in the group forms part of his own self-definition, and that he perceives his own interests and purposes as integrally connected with those of the group. Loyalty thus has both instrumental and affective components.

Political loyalties are those directed toward political objects that are of importance in the life of the political community. These objects include formal institutions, parties, interest groups, political leaders, social and economic classes, military organizations, constitutions, traditions, and symbols and myths which a population perceives as embodying or representing the community, history, and destiny which make them a distinct people. Political loyalties form part of a system's political culture—that particular constellation of normative, practical, and emotional orientations toward political things shared by the population of a political system (Almond & Verba 1963, chapter 1). Loyalties can be directed toward a variety of objects within the political system, and systems can easily and usefully be classified according to the strength, incidence, objects, and patterns of loyalties among the citizenry. [See POLITICAL CULTURE.]

Patterns of loyalty. Since loyalties sustain both the individual and the polity by laying the groundwork necessary for shared effort and unity of purpose, loyalty is a very old subject of political discourse, and virtually "all serious political writing regards the quality of loyalty as a good thing" (H. B. White, quoted in Grodzins 1956, p. 16). Classical Greek and Roman writers regarded loyalty as the supreme political virtue, and while few persons in the ancient states enjoyed the status of citizenship, those who did were taught to regard the role of citizen as the noblest of all roles. Duty to the state was the highest duty, and loyalty was the highest value. This evaluation of political loyalty and citizenship permeates the writings of Plato, Aristotle, Thucydides, and Plutarch. Early Christian writers, however, placed little value on loyalty to city or state; for them, religious salvation was the supreme goal, and loyalty to the church and creed that held the keys to that kingdom the highest loyalty. Between the fall of the Roman Empire and the rise of the nation-state, political loyalty, except in the form of the local and semipersonal loyalties of feudalism, mattered little to individuals. Machiavelli's reassertion of the primacy of political loyalty—his statement that he preferred his country to the safety of his soul—was considered blasphemous in the opinion of his time. The modern idea of mass political loyalty and the conception of the nation as the capstone and most comprehensive object of loyalty are really no older than the eighteenth century. They appeared with the French Revolution and reached their most passionate expression in Rousseau's plea for a "civil religion" (*Social Contract*, especially book 4, chapter 8).

Patterns of thought and behavior involving loyalty have been complex and contradictory since the end of the eighteenth century. On the one hand, a number of liberal internationalist thinkers have attacked loyalty to the nation-state as an outmoded and dangerous conception. They argue that increasing national interdependence requires a shift of loyalty away from the nation-state to the institutions and symbols of the international community. On the other hand, the totalitarian states of the twentieth century have demanded of their subjects a degree of concentrated loyalty toward national political leaders, institutions, and policies which is without precedent. Also, the creation of many new states in the underdeveloped areas of the world has meant a renewed growth of national loyalties at a time when such loyalties may be on the wane in the highly developed states.

It is characteristic of the advanced, complex, highly industrialized states that the loyalties of individuals tend to be numerous, segmental, and increasingly instrumental. The individual yields partial loyalty to many objects instead of giving all his devotion and allegiance to one or a very few objects. Similarly, peer-group loyalties increasingly supplant hierarchical affiliations. This is part of the meaning of the movement from "status to contract" [see the biography of MAINE] or from *Gemeinschaft* to *Gesellschaft* [see the biography of TÖNNIES]. One strand of modern social criticism laments this transformation in loyalty patterns as the "decline of community," while another welcomes it as the advent of an era of increased individual liberty.

Over and above these matters stands the dominant fact that no political system can long endure or enjoy much stability unless its citizens, and especially the elites, place a high value on political loyalty. Among the emerging nations, the development of sentiments of national loyalty and identification is a task of the highest priority (Pye 1962). Many of the emerging nations are riddled by tribal, ethnic, linguistic, and regional divisions. The inhabitants must be urged to abandon their parochial loyalties, and they must be imbued with a sense of affiliation with the national community and a willingness to obey the directives of central authority. Links must be forged in the minds of individuals between their personal interests and joys and the policies and institutions of the state. In order to do this, governments employ all the resources of propaganda and communication to reach the masses. Promoting nationalist ideologies, publicizing the activities and words of charismatic leaders, fomenting antagonism toward foreign governments and peoples, and developing programs of mass action and ritual participation are among the standard methods used in these attempts to build national loyalties. [See MODERN-IZATION.]

In a political system that has existed longer as an entity and reached a higher stage of political and economic development, the problem is not to create national loyalties but to maintain them. There, loyalty is both a product of the individual's direct identification with and involvement in the nation's history, symbols, institutions, and destiny and, indirectly, a product of the individual's private satisfactions. Rewards and satisfactions gained in the private sphere have a kind of spillover effect,

and political objects receive the benefits of the individual's gratitude for the joys of personal life. In addition, the level of communication and integration is higher in such states, and inhabitants are frequently exposed to political symbols and messages. The public schools carry the message of patriotism and loyalty to millions of children: after an extensive review of European and American experience, Merriam (1931) concluded that the public school had become the dominant agency for transmitting the themes of loyalty and "civil religion," having largely replaced the army, the church, the family, and patriotic rhetoric in performing this function. In such polities, through the processes of political socialization, attitudes of loyalty toward the nation are widely shared. The national political community forms a common reference point for nearly all citizens. [See SOCIALIZATION, article on POLITICAL SOCIALIZA-TION.]

Thus, loyalty is the ordinary condition. Although political loyalties are not prominent for most people most of the time, they are there in the background and can be evoked by the appropriate stimuli. Since loyalty is the ordinary condition—the atmospheric condition—active disloyalty is very difficult: custom, the climate of opinion, informal and formal sanctions, inertia, fear, the lack of clear alternative objects of loyalty—all these forces work to assure that even those who are not actively and intensely loyal are at least not *dis*loyal. Ordinarily, political authorities do not ask for more than that, for it is enough.

Multiple loyalties. Few persons are loyal to just one object. Most men move within a network of loyalties—to primary group, party, occupational group, clubs, and so forth. In the liberal–democratic states, these partial loyalties are not regarded as incompatible with a larger, comprehensive loyalty to the political community. In fact, these circles of particular loyalties are held to be the very foundation for firm loyalty to the nation (Grodzins 1956). This view, which is widely held among modern pluralistic theorists, is really a rediscovery of Burke's insistence that what holds society together and gives it meaning and richness is the multiplicity of its "little platoons," its primary associations of individuals. Individuals, then, are tied to the central symbols and agencies of the political system through a series of linkages formed by loyalties to smaller groups [see IDENTIFICATION, POLITICAL].

In an important study, Shils and Janowitz (1948) found that while goals and policies might be set by central political authorities, individuals acted in accordance with those policies not so much out of direct loyalty to the nation as in response to the smaller, primary groups in which they were involved. This was found to be the case within the German army during the Nazi period. The finding thus runs counter to the whole totalitarian conception of loyalty, which insists that all loyalty must be concentrated directly around one political center. As Mussolini stated the totalitarian conception of loyalty, "Fascism takes a man from his family at six, and gives him back to it at sixty." Contrary to this conception, it seems clear that lesser loyalties must exist even in totalitarian states and that these lesser loyalties constitute the individual's primary attachments. It is through them that he is tied to the state, and it is largely in response to them that he loyally accepts and executes his duties to the state.

The existence of multiple loyalties implies the constant possibility of conflicting loyalties. Hence, conflict of loyalties is a theme that entered political writing along with the subject of loyalty itself, and it is already present in the story of Abraham and Isaac and in the tragedy of Antigone. Conflicts of loyalty are especially important during times of rapid social change and when the state feels threatened from within and without. During such times, individuals are uncertain of the intentions and the reliability of others, and the old patterns of belief and affiliation conflict with the new patterns that are emerging. Governments are then likely to require formal professions of loyalty, to undertake investigations of loyalty, and to insist on public adherence to official ideology (see Brown 1958; Schaar 1957). Loyalty is equated with conformity, criticism with disloyalty. The concept of "loyal opposition," one of the supreme achievements of the liberal–democratic regimes, is placed in jeopardy.

Still, while conflicts of loyalty are dramatic and painful, it must be repeated that loyalty is the normal condition. Individuals, by processes similar to those subsumed under the theory of cognitive dissonance, tend to perceive their loyalties as mutually consistent, even when they might appear inconsistent to an observer. Or they tend to rationalize incompatible loyalty imperatives as not really incompatible after all.

In most political systems there is a measure of ambiguity as to just what one must be loyal to in order to be regarded as loyal. Does one owe loyalty to the nation? The government? Traditions and ideals? A mission? Rulers? Hence, actions which seem to be disloyal by one standard may be justified as entirely loyal by another. In all these ways, individuals are able to "save the appearances," to

regard themselves as loyal and to defend themselves against charges of disloyalty.

Political loyalty is supremely important both for individuals and for political communities, and many psychological mechanisms and social processes work to build and maintain it and to assure that loyalty rather than disloyalty or conflicts of loyalty will be the rule.

JOHN H. SCHAAR

[See also DUTY; IDENTIFICATION, POLITICAL; NATIONALISM. Other relevant material may be found in INTERNMENT AND CUSTODY; PERSONALITY, POLITICAL; SOCIAL CONTROL; and in the guide to the reader and the articles under COMMUNITY.]

BIBLIOGRAPHY

ALMOND, GABRIEL A.; and VERBA, SIDNEY 1963 The Civic Culture: Political Attitudes and Democracy in Five Nations. Princeton Univ. Press.
BLOCH, HERBERT A. 1934 The Concept of Our Changing Loyalties: An Introductory Study Into the Nature of the Social Individual. New York: Columbia Univ. Press.
BROWN, RALPH S. 1958 Loyalty and Security: Employment Tests in the United States. Yale Law School Studies, No. 3. New Haven: Yale Univ. Press.
CURTI, MERLE 1946 The Roots of American Loyalty. New York: Columbia Univ. Press.
DEWEY, JOHN (1922) 1950 Human Nature and Conduct: An Introduction to Social Psychology. New York: Modern Library.
DICKS, HENRY V. 1950 Personality Traits and National Socialist Ideology. Human Relations 3:111–154.
FREUD, SIGMUND (1921) 1955 Group Psychology and the Analysis of the Ego. Volume 18, pages 67–143 in The Standard Edition of the Complete Psychological Works of Sigmund Freud. London: Hogarth; New York: Macmillan. → First published in German.
GRODZINS, MORTON 1956 The Loyal and the Disloyal: Social Boundaries of Patriotism and Treason. Univ. of Chicago Press.
HOFFER, ERIC 1951 The True Believer: Thoughts on the Nature of Mass Movements. New York: Harper. → A paperback edition was published in 1958 by New American Library.
MEERLOO, JOOST A. M. 1954 The Psychology of Treason and Loyalty. American Journal of Psychotherapy 8: 648–666.
MERRIAM, CHARLES E. 1931 The Making of Citizens: A Comparative Study of Methods of Civic Training. Univ. of Chicago Press.
PYE, LUCIAN W. 1962 Politics, Personality, and Nation Building: Burma's Search for Identity. New Haven: Yale Univ. Press.
ROYCE, JOSIAH (1908) 1936 The Philosophy of Loyalty. New York: Macmillan.
SCHAAR, JOHN H. 1957 Loyalty in America. Berkeley: Univ. of California Press.
SCHACHTER, STANLEY 1959 The Psychology of Affiliation: Experimental Studies of the Sources of Gregariousness. Stanford Studies in Psychology, No. 1. Stanford Univ. Press.
SHERIF, MUZAFER; and CANTRIL, HADLEY 1947 The Psychology of Ego-involvements, Social Attitudes and Identifications. New York: Wiley; London: Chapman.

SHILS, EDWARD 1956 *The Torment of Secrecy: The Background and Consequences of American Security Policies.* Glencoe, Ill.: Free Press.

SHILS, EDWARD; and JANOWITZ, MORRIS 1948 Cohesion and Disintegration in the Wehrmacht in World War II. *Public Opinion Quarterly* 12:280–315.

WEST, R. G. RANYARD (1945) 1951 *Conscience and Society: A Study of the Psychological Prerequisites of Law and Order.* 2d ed. London: Methuen.

WEST, REBECCA (1947) 1964 *The New Meaning of Treason.* Rev. & enl. ed. New York: Viking. → First published as *The Meaning of Treason.*

LUBBOCK, JOHN

Sir John Lubbock (1834–1913) was an English biologist, anthropologist, and popular writer on science. His father, Sir John William Lubbock, was for forty years a distinguished member of the English scientific community and at the same time the successful head of the family banking establishment. The son achieved a similar kind of dual identity, adding to his scientific achievements a successful career in government.

Lubbock was essentially self-taught, although he did receive a certain amount of classical education. After entering the family banking business at the age of 14, he began to study natural history, following a program he had prepared himself. In the mid-nineteenth century the renaissance of natural history was an important event on the English intellectual scene; as a participant in this renaissance Lubbock was one of the first to investigate the social behavior of animals, and he published important studies in zoology and botany.

Apart from the mathematical and scientific interests of his father, the most compelling influence on Lubbock's development as a scientist was the relationship he established, while still an adolescent, with Charles Darwin. Darwin was then already a distinguished naturalist; he was also a friend of the elder Lubbock and his neighbor at Down. Darwin left no students and only a few protégés, of whom Lubbock was the first. Lubbock became an ardent supporter of Darwin's evolutionism when the *Origin of Species* was published in 1859. He was the youngest of that small articulate band whose reasoned and informed defense of the new doctrine led to its general acceptance within a decade; and all of his subsequent work was infused with the excitement of applying the theory of evolution.

Basic to all of his work was the underlying point of view that a science of human society is both necessary and possible: like other phenomena in nature, human society may be subjected to objective description leading to the formulation of general principles.

The discovery of man's great antiquity and the almost simultaneous publication of the principles of organic evolution by Darwin, in 1859, provided the essential theoretical elements for all of Lubbock's subsequent work in anthropology. Drawing upon an increasing body of data concerning the variation in human behavior, he constructed an over-all theory of cultural evolution that came to be the mainstay as well as the hallmark of English anthropology for almost half a century, even though his extreme position was rejected by more objective scholars. In *The Origin of Civilization and the Primitive Condition of Man* (1870) he developed a theory of the evolution of man and culture that rested on his equation of primeval man and the contemporary primitives. His extreme emphasis on the ideas of "natural progress" led him to arrange his materials (social, ethical, and technological) along a slowly ascending line leading to modern (nineteenth-century) perfection.

Lubbock's deserved reputation as a popularizer of developments in biology and anthropology, and the occasional innocence with which he approached fundamental problems in these fields, should not be permitted to conceal the significance of his own original contributions to both fields, especially to the nascent field of anthropology. He was the first to compile and synthesize the scattered data concerning the prehistory of Europe and North America, in a series of articles that formed the basis of his *Prehistoric Times* of 1865. But he believed that archeology is more than description and that it forms the link between geology and history. He clearly defined prehistoric archeology as a concern of anthropology and saw the reconstruction of past cultures as part of the evolutionary history of the continuous past rather than as the simple collection of monuments and antiquities. Prehistory was established as a science of man rather than an adjunct of classics or art history.

Lubbock drew upon ethnographic descriptions of contemporary "savages" to discover the use and cultural context of archeological materials. In reclassifying the stone tool categories formulated by Danish archeologists he coined the term "paleolithic" to designate the chipped tools found in caves and glacial gravels. He further suggested that these tools preceded a stage of development that he called "neolithic," characterized by the polished stone implements found in Danish peat bogs. Lubbock never accepted the revision of this scheme that was proposed by Mortillet.

On a practical level Lubbock used his parliamentary position and his private means to instigate the passage of the Ancient Monuments Act in order to protect the ancient monuments of Britain against destruction.

JACOB W. GRUBER

[For the historical context of Lubbock's work, see AN-THROPOLOGY, article on THE FIELD; and the biographies of DARWIN and TYLOR.]

WORKS BY LUBBOCK

(1865) 1913 Prehistoric Times as Illustrated by Ancient Remains and the Manners and Customs of Modern Savages. 7th ed., rev. London: Williams & Norgate.
(1870) 1912 The Origin of Civilization and the Primitive Condition of Man: Mental and Social Conditions of Savages. 7th ed. New York: Longmans.

WORKS ABOUT LUBBOCK

GRANT-DUFF, URSULA [Lubbock] (editor) (1924) 1934 The Life Work of Lord Avebury (Sir John Lubbock): 1834–1913. London: Watts.
HUTCHINSON, HORACE G. 1914 Life of Sir John Lubbock, Lord Avebury. 2 vols. London: Macmillan.
PUMPHREY, R. J. (1958) 1959 The Forgotten Man: Sir John Lubbock. Science 129:1087–1092. → First published in Notes and Records of the Royal Society of London.

LUKÁCS, GYÖRGY

György Lukács, literary critic and Marxist social theorist, was born in 1885 of wealthy Jewish parents in Budapest, then the second capital of the Austro–Hungarian monarchy. His father was a director of the Budapest Kreditanstalt, the leading bank in Hungary. A member of a remarkable generation of Hungarian Jewish intellectuals, many of whom later emigrated to Western countries and made their mark in the sciences and the humanities, Lukács received a cosmopolitan education. From adolescence he displayed a lively interest in European literature and a talent for literary criticism. His earliest critical writings date back to 1903 (when he was 18), and a two-volume study of the modern drama, written in Hungarian in 1908–1909, was published in 1911. In the same year Lukács issued the first German-language edition of any of his works, Die Seele und die Formen, which had been published in Hungarian in 1910, and from this time onward he partly abandoned his native Hungarian in favor of German as a medium of public and private discourse. (He came to be known widely by the German form of his name, Georg Lukacs.)

Early intellectual experience. A complex intellectual development carried Lukács from early involvement with the aestheticism fashionable be-fore 1914 to a prominent role in the German and east European communist movements after 1918. Prior to the outbreak of World War I, he shared with other central European intellectuals of his generation a pronounced distaste for politics and a commitment to the autonomy of art, not merely as an aesthetic principle but as a way of life. This attitude implied a criticism of bourgeois society, albeit its criteria were derived from Nietzsche and the aestheticism of the 1890s rather than from Marx. Like Thomas Mann, for whom, even in later years, he retained an admiration which Mann to some degree reciprocated, the youthful Lukács considered bourgeois society inherently hostile to the arts and specifically to the aesthetic claim to possession of certain intuitively apprehended truths about the nature of reality.

After early studies in Budapest, Lukács moved to Berlin and later to Heidelberg, where he stayed until 1916. During these prerevolutionary years he studied social science and philosophy, and in particular came under the influence of Max Weber and Georg Simmel, who introduced him to sociology. He was likewise influenced by the philosopher Emil Lask, who had constructed a logical bridge leading from the then dominant Neo-Kantianism to the phenomenological school founded by Edmund Husserl. At the same time, Lukács became acquainted with the literary critic Friedrich Gundolf, a member of the esoteric circle around the poet Stefan George, in which both the Nietzschean contempt for democracy and the aestheticist cult of the individual sensibility had been pushed to their farthest limits. The residual influences of this period were to plague Lukács in later years, when (after first going through a Hegelian phase) he had become a more or less orthodox Marxist.

Lukács's own account of this transformation, while not wholly trustworthy, lends due emphasis to the impact of the 1914–1918 war upon the generation of central European intellectuals to which he belonged and whose concerns he shared. In the preface (dated July 1962) to the new edition of his Theorie des Romans (an essay on the novel, drafted in 1914–1915, first published in a literary journal in 1916 and, expanded, in book form in 1920), he describes his wartime mood as one of despair, from which he was eventually rescued by the events of 1917—that is, by the Russian Revolution. Prior to this he had been tormented by the —as it seemed to him—depressing choice between the prospect of a German victory and the triumph of "Western civilization," which as a youthful Nietzschean he had learned to identify with soulless commercialism and materialism. This was also how the issue presented itself to conservative German intellectuals like Thomas Mann (see the latter's *Unpolitical Reflections*), but Mann gradually and hesitantly accepted Western democracy as the lesser evil, if not as a positive good, while Lukács opted for Lenin.

Heterodox Marxism.   Lukács's return to Budapest and his subsequent involvement in the Hungarian revolution of 1918–1919 coincided with a major change in his philosophical and political orientation: his acceptance first of Hegelianism and later of Marxism. Philosophically, the way for this conversion had been paved by his earlier rejection of Neo-Kantian epistemology insofar as it applied to the aesthetic realm, where, it appeared to him, intuitive apprehension of absolute truth is possible. Even as a youthful Neo-Kantian around 1910, he had not quite accepted the doctrine that knowledge of the empirical world does not extend to the nature of ultimate reality but is confined to phenomenal appearances, which in the last resort are the product of human understanding. He was not satisfied with this positivist interpretation of Kant, which Weber accepted, and for a while found solace in the belief that—in the arts at least—ultimate reality is cognizable through intuition of "pure essences." From about 1916 onward he came to believe that Hegel offered a way out of the impasse created by positivist science. The solution seemed to lie in treating the moral and aesthetic values (deemed by Weber and others to be wholly subjective) as entities located in the structure of reality and as such cognizable by philosophy, although not by empirical science. To this fundamental belief Lukács has adhered, with the necessary consequence that his Hegelianized Marxism has always appeared heretical to the adherents of Soviet orthodoxy, although not to Marxists faithful to the tradition of German idealism.

After brief involvement, as commissar for education, in the short-lived Hungarian communist regime of 1919, Lukács moved to Vienna, where as editor of the official party journal, *Kommunismus*, he came into conflict with the dominant faction. A dispute within the Hungarian Communist party over political tactics culminated in 1923 in the publication by Lukács of a collection of essays best known under the original, German title, *Geschichte und Klassenbewusstsein*. The appearance of this work initiated his new career as a semiheretical exponent of Marxism–Leninism, while at the same time it effectively ended his position as an official party spokesman. In later years he was to be an influential figure in the intellectual life of the Hungarian Communist party, but he never again held an official party position, and his utterances on literary and philosophical topics were henceforth regarded with suspicion by those Hungarian communist theoreticians (some of them his former pupils) who in 1923–1924 had committed themselves to the official Soviet interpretation of Marxism–Leninism.

Without going into the details of this controversy (a succinct account of which may be found in Watnick 1962) it can be said that Lukács's general orientation clashed with Lenin's pre-Hegelian (indeed, pre-Kantian) understanding of philosophy, while at the same time he pushed Lenin's implicitly elitist view of the Communist party's role to the point of paradox. In recovering the Hegelian dimension of Marx's own thought, Lukács had unwittingly transgressed upon Lenin's version of Engels' "dialectical materialism," with its naively pictorial interpretation of the role of consciousness. Philosophically speaking, he appeared to his Leninist critics as a left-wing Hegelian rather than a materialist. At the same time he allotted to the role of revolutionary "consciousness" an importance quite consonant with Lenin's own conception of the "vanguard." The consequences of this contradictory commitment were to pursue Lukács for years, down to the abortive Hungarian rebellion of 1956, which resulted in his temporary banishment and forced withdrawal from public life.

Acceptance of orthodoxy.   From 1933 to 1945 Lukács, like most other leading Hungarian communists, lived in Moscow, where he somehow escaped the great purge of 1936–1938. Those Hungarian communists who had sided against him in 1923–1924 (principally József Révai and László Rudas) had meanwhile become orthodox Stalinists, while Lukács himself—although from about 1932 the most doctrinaire of Leninists—paid only lip service to Stalin's "theoretical" contributions. He did, however, purge himself of his idealist errors by solemnly denouncing (in an address to the philosophical section of the Communist Academy in 1934) his 1923 work *Geschichte und Klassenbewusstsein* as an unwitting departure from Marxist–Leninist orthodoxy. After recalling the early influence upon him of Simmel and Max Weber, he named Georges Sorel as one of the pre-1914 writers who had reinforced his leanings toward what in 1934 he termed "romantic anticapitalism." Having stigmatized his earlier views as "objectively" counterrevolutionary, he paid a special tribute to the significance of Lenin's philosophical work, *Materialism and Empiriocriticism*.

This self-abasement set the tone for the literary productions of the following two decades, culminating in *Die Zerstörung der Vernunft* (1953*a*), a bulky 700-page diatribe against modern philosophy, couched in propagandist, indeed abusive, language. Its central thesis—the ideological decay of "bourgeois irrationalism," from Schelling via Nietzsche to the philosophers of the Third Reich—was worked out at such a primitive level that even some of his sympathizers in the West began to despair of Lukács.

Sociology of knowledge. An assessment of Lukács's significance as a forerunner of what is currently known as the sociology of knowledge must proceed from the recognition that as a theorist he has been primarily concerned with other than sociological topics. The "class consciousness" which appears in the title of his 1923 collection of essays (his only sustained excursion into sociopolitical theory) is not the empirical consciousness of the actual working class, but a political consciousness "imputed" to it (*zugerechnet*, to use his term) on extraempirical grounds. Lukács thus is not a sociologist, not even a Marxist sociologist. He took over from Marx the notion of social development through class conflict, culminating in a new type of society without classes, but did not attempt to apply it to the new postbourgeois reality around him. In particular he remained indifferent to the problem of social stratification in industrial society, as distinct from the issue of class relations in bourgeois society. As a critic of bourgeois culture he was content to rely on the Marxist analysis of capitalism. This furnished him with the assurance that industrialism could provide the economic basis for an organization of social life in which human labor would recover the dignity it had lost, and that human "alienation" (a term not explicitly employed by him in 1923, but inherent in his critique of "objectification") would be overcome.

Culture. The area where Lukács nonetheless has come to grips with genuinely sociological issues is that of culture. According to the Marxist hypothesis, a class with a genuine historical role is, among other things, the bearer of a new world view and ultimately of a new civilization. Lukács has tried to employ this concept in his voluminous writings on aesthetics. Basing his work on the principle that a particular outlook (variously described as "materialist" or "realist") has been shared by the bourgeoisie in its early revolutionary phase and the working class in its subsequent effort to build a higher culture, he has tried to safeguard the heritage of classical bourgeois realism. The antithesis of this classical realism is manifest, according to Lukács, in the various forms of modernism, which (in common with Soviet orthodoxy, although

in more sophisticated terms) he has denounced as "decadent."

Ideology. The ascription to the labor movement (and in particular to the Communist party as the supposed "vanguard" of this movement) of a viewpoint radically different from that of the collapsing bourgeois society furnished Lukács with a criterion for his definition of ideology. He attributed "false consciousness" (ideology) uniquely to the self-definition of the ruling class, while crediting the submerged revolutionary class with the possession of a "true consciousness," albeit imperfectly articulated and thus necessitating the separate existence of a "vanguard" of theorists in the shape of the Communist party. In principle the working class is held by Lukács to possess a theoretical insight into the historical situation superior to that of the bourgeoisie, although in the actual waging of political conflict this insight needs to be supplemented by the intellectual efforts of the Marxist party.

Objective knowledge. Dissatisfaction with this approach subsequently led Karl Mannheim (who in 1918–1919 had been acquainted with Lukács in Budapest but had not joined the communists) to develop the notion of the intelligentsia as a privileged floating stratum. Mannheim, like Lukács, had originally been induced by his reading of Weber and Simmel to question the possibility of objective truth in historical and social matters. As he saw it, all sociological statements were hopelessly compromised by sectional and party standpoints. Unlike Lukács, he did not seek a solution by identifying a particular standpoint (that of the rising proletarian class) with the attainment of absolute or objective insight. Rather, he contented himself with allotting to the intellectuals as a group the task of criticizing the sectional viewpoints of the major social classes. Lukács's work provided the chief stimulus for Mannheim's *Ideology and Utopia*, and in this sense he may be said to have been an important link between the sociology of Weber and Simmel and what later became known as *Wissenssoziologie*. But whereas Mannheim's "relational" doctrine seemed to issue in a species of relativism, Lukács retained the notion of a privileged intellectual standpoint, historically conditioned indeed (as all forms of thought must be), yet certifying its superiority over rival standpoints by virtue of its unique possession of insights enabling it to comprehend both its epoch and itself. Here we see the Hegelian heritage which had originally attracted the youthful Lukács to Marxism and subsequently to Leninism as the contemporary form of Marxism. All of this was too Hegelian for Soviet Marxists and their east European followers, yet it was also incompatible with what Lukács termed "bourgeois empiricism." Mannheim and others, although personally and doctrinally sympathetic to socialism, rejected the Hegelian–Marxist notion of a truth about history independent of, and superior to, the insights available to empirical sociology. The Marxian rejoinder (anticipated by Lukács in 1923) was to assert that, in thus rejecting philosophy, the sociology of knowledge had also relinquished the notion of an objective truth about history and society, leaving only partial truths relative to the standpoint of the observer and therewith seemingly opening the road toward a skepticism as boundless as it was hopeless. This theme was revived in the West after 1945, when impatience with the prospect of endless and pointless data accumulation carried a number of writers at least halfway toward the Hegelianized Marxism of the early Lukács—a tendency particularly marked among the Neo-Hegelian and Neo-Marxist schools in France and Italy.

In the central European context, the passions stirred by the 1923 controversy continued to be felt in the writings of Lukács's fellow heretic, Karl Korsch. They have likewise echoed in the historical and sociological studies published before and after the Hitler era by the scholars associated with the Frankfurt Institut für Sozialforschung—notably Max Horkheimer, T. W. Adorno, and Herbert Marcuse. The influence of the early Lukács is also discernible in the writings of such a noted literary critic of the Weimar period as Walter Benjamin, while a more distant echo may be discerned in the work of émigré scholars such as Leo Lowenthal of the University of California at Berkeley. From central Europe, the message of Lukács's Hegelianized Marxism was carried to France by the Rumanian-born scholar and literary critic Lucien Goldmann, whose studies of Pascal and Racine acquainted the French academic world with a new manner of treating literary subjects. Some of Goldmann's conclusions had been anticipated in 1934 by the Vienna-born scholar Franz Borkenau in an important, although neglected, work, *Der Übergang vom feudalen zum bürgerlichen Weltbild.* In contrast, Lukács paradoxically has not exercised any profound influence upon the younger generation of Marxist writers in central and eastern Europe since 1956. In general they have found him too orthodox for their taste and in particular too deeply wedded to the Leninist notions current in Soviet literature. These "revisionist" writers (e.g., the Austrian Ernst Fischer) tended to go beyond Lukács

in trying to construct a specifically Marxist doctrine of the social relevance of art. In philosophy, too, it was the existentialism of Sartre rather than the work of Lukács which, after the post-Stalin "thaw" of 1956, enabled the younger east European Marxists (e.g., the Polish writer Leszek Kolakowski) to free themselves from the ideological trammels of Leninism.

GEORGE LICHTHEIM

[*See also* LITERATURE, *article on* THE SOCIOLOGY OF LITERATURE; MARXIST SOCIOLOGY; *and the biographies of* HEGEL; LENIN; MANNHEIM.]

WORKS BY LUKÁCS

1903 Az új Hauptmann (The New Hauptmann). *Jövendő* [1903], August 23:29–32.
1906 A dráma formája (The Form of the Drama). *Szerda* [1906]:340–343.
1907 Gaugin. *Huszadik század* [1907]:559–562.
1908 Stefan George. *Nyugat* 2:202–211.
(1910) 1911 *Die Seele und die Formen.* Berlin: Fleischel. → First published as *A lélek és a formák (kisérletek).*
1911 *A modern dráma fejlödésének története* (The History of the Development of the Modern Drama). 2 vols. Budapest: Kisfaludy Társaság.
1914 Soziologie des modernen Drama. *Archiv für Sozialwissenschaft und Sozialpolitik* 38:303–345, 662–706.
(1920) 1963 *Die Theorie des Romans.* New ed., enl. Neuwied am Rhein (Germany): Luchterhand.
1923 *Geschichte und Klassenbewusstsein.* Berlin: Malik. → Contains essays first published between 1919 and 1922.
(1933) 1955 Mein Weg zu Marx. Pages 225–231 in *Georg Lukacs zum siebzigsten Geburtstag.* Berlin: Aufbau.
1934 Znachenie *Materializma i empiriokrititsizma* dlia bol'shevizatsii kommunisticheskikh partii (The Significance of *Materialism and Empiriocriticism* for the Bolshevization of Communist Parties). *Pod znamenem marksizma* 4:143–148.
(1935–1939) 1964 *Studies in European Realism.* New York: Grosset & Dunlap. → Contains essays first published in Hungarian and German.
(1946a) 1955 *Goethe und seine Zeit.* Berlin: Aufbau. → First published in Hungarian.
1946b *Nietzsche és a fasizmus* (Nietzsche and Fascism). Budapest: Hungaria.
(1947) 1965 *The Historical Novel.* New York: Humanities. → First published in book form as *A történelmi regény.* Parts 1 and 2 first appeared in Russian in 1937 in Volumes 7, 9, and 12 of *Literaturnyi kritik.* A paperback edition was published in 1963 by Beacon.
1948 *Der junge Hegel: Über die Beziehungen von Dialektik und Ökonomie.* Zurich and Vienna: Europa.
(1953a) 1954 *Die Zerstörung der Vernunft.* Berlin: Aufbau. → First published as *Az ész trónfosztása.* A third Hungarian edition was published in 1965.
(1953b) 1954 *Beiträge zur Geschichte der Ästhetik.* Berlin: Aufbau. → First published as *Adalékok az esztétika történetéhez.*
(1958) 1963 *The Meaning of Contemporary Realism.* London: Merlin. → First published as *Zur Gegenwartsbedeutung des kritischen Realismus.*
1961 *Schriften zur Literatursoziologie.* Edited by Peter Ludz. Berlin: Luchterhand.

Werke. Vol. 1—. Neuwied am Rhein (Germany): Luchterhand, 1963—. → A projected 12-volume work. Volumes 5, 6, 7, 9, 11, and 12 had appeared by 1966.

SUPPLEMENTARY BIBLIOGRAPHY

ADORNO, T. W. (1961) 1963 Erpresste Versöhnung: Zu
Georg Lukacs "Wider den missverstandenen Realis-
mus." Volume 2, pages 152–187 in T. W. Adorno,
Noten zur Literatur. Frankfurt am Main (Germany):
Suhrkamp. → First published in Volume 11 of *Der
Monat.*

*Georg Lukacs und der Revisionismus: Eine Sammlung von
Aufsätzen.* 1960 Berlin: Aufbau.

Georg Lukacs zum siebzigsten Geburtstag. 1955 Berlin:
Aufbau.

GOLDMANN, LUCIEN (1958) 1963 *Recherches dialectiques.* 3d ed. Paris: Gallimard. → See especially the
essay "Georg Lukacs: L'essayiste."

OLTVÁNYI, AMBRUS (compiler) 1955 Lukács György
írói munkássága (The Literary Works of György Lukács). *Irodalomtörténet* (Budapest) 43:402–420. → A
comprehensive bibliography of Lukács's writings from
1903 to 1955.

RÉVAI, JÓZSEF (1950) 1956 *Literarische Studien.* Berlin: Dietz. → First published as *Irodalmi tanulmá-
nyok.*

RÉVAI, JÓZSEF 1951 *La littérature et la démocratie populaire: À propos de Georg Lukacs.* Paris: Les Éditions de la Nouvelle Critique.

WATNICK, MORRIS 1962 Relativism and Class Consciousness: Georg Lukacs. Pages 142–165 in Leopold Labedz
(editor), *Revisionism: Essays on the History of Marxist Ideas.* New York: Praeger.

LUNDBERG, GEORGE

George Andrew Lundberg (1895–1966) was a
vigorous and influential advocate of the pursuit of
sociological knowledge by the method of natural
science. Much of his writing was devoted to stating
and clarifying the postulates of scientific thought,
the fundamental attributes of objective research,
and the applicability of such principles to sociological inquiry. He dedicated his academic career to
the view that there are no characteristics of social
phenomena and no features of scientific method
that would preclude rigorous adherence to that
method in the investigation of those phenomena.
He gave particular emphasis to two implications of
this position. First, he insisted that quantification
of sociological concepts is possible and that great
effort should be devoted to it. Second, he consistently argued that the achievement of scientific
competence requires that sociologists learn to
abandon traditional moralistic orientations toward
their subject matter (Lundberg et al. 1929, pp.
403–404).

During his lifetime great strides toward quantification were taken which Lundberg credited

chiefly to the impact of successful empirical work,
such as demographic studies, rather than to any
methodological arguments (1944a, p. 7). He was
far from sanguine in his last years, however, regarding the emancipation of contemporary sociologists from a legalistic–moralistic mode of thought,
and this alleged bondage became the central issue
of his final polemics.

Lundberg's positivism

Lundberg asserted that not all words have empirical referents but that people have responded to
them as if they did. The alleged distinction between
the "tangible" subject matter of the physical sciences and the supposedly "intangible" subject matter of the social sciences is merely a reflection of
the differential advancement of observational and
symbolizing techniques in the two fields; it is not
an intrinsic difference in the respective classes of
events being observed. Nothing essential is "left
out" when we study societal phenomena objectively,
although we often mourn the loss of feelings that
were associated with familiar but ambiguous terms
we have had to abandon. The operations by which
we measure characteristics of the phenomena we
study constitute definitions of those characteristics.
The same phenomena may be studied according to
various frames of reference, but these will lead to
different conclusions.

Exclusion of value judgments. Lundberg's conceptual approach was similar to that of the Vienna
circle, but he arrived at it independently. He attempted to show that all too many of the familiar-
sounding terms in the sociological vocabulary were
the sociological equivalent of the early chemist's
phlogiston—no more necessary to describe or explain social phenomena than phlogiston was to account for combustion.

The sociologist's central task, he said, is to gather
reliable data and from them to state principles—
i.e., predictable sequences of behavior within highly
standardized situations. Such principles can then
be used to explain events in other situations whose
significant departures from the standardized situation can be measured.

To be scientific, our analysis must be nonteleological. The physical sciences do very well without
the concept of values, Lundberg said, but social
scientists persist in transforming the verb "valuat-
ing" (which refers to discriminal or selective responding) into a noun, "values," and then they
hunt in vain for its ostensible referent (1941a,
p. 351). When critics accused him of "leaving out"
what is essentially human, Lundberg replied that

he was not denying the occurrence or importance of value judgments but only insisting that they are a kind of behavior and that standards of value are inferences from behavior. Thus defined, values are not inaccessible to scientific study (1941b, p. 84). Men have always had visions of the good life, and these have helped to shape human actions. Reliable assessment of the changing content of such visions is a prerequisite to their effective public implementation, and there now exist scientific procedures by which one can do this assessing better than it is done by traditional methods (1950a, pp. 110–111). Lundberg offered specific proposals for the study of human values (ibid., p. 105), but he continued to be accused of advocating a sociology that would "omit" this indispensable concept.

For some, this accusation gained plausibility from his perennial insistence that no science tells us what to do with the knowledge it creates. Scientific conclusions are statements of the probability of certain occurrences under clearly specified conditions, but they do not contain assessments of the "goodness or badness of the sequences described, *apart from specified standards.* The crucial point is that these standards are not themselves set by the scientific methods that result in the conditional scientific statements" (1950b, p. 265).

Social science and citizenship. In his presidential address to the American Sociological Society during World War II, Lundberg adamantly maintained that "it is more important than ever that we should not let the priority of our duties as citizens blind us to our functions as scientists" (1943a, p. 69). As a means of winning the war it was probably necessary, he conceded, to fabricate seriously distorted pictures of the world and of the nature of the enemy. Unfortunately, such pictures would persist, at least in part, for some time after the war and would influence the structure of the peace settlement. With a peace founded on illusion, another war was rendered likely (1944b, p. 89). It was vital that *social scientists themselves* not mistake the distortion for truth. Some of his statements illustrating this point were offensive to certain members of his audience and may have obscured his main message—that social scientists could hope to command public respect and thus be effective in an advisory role in regard to the peace settlement only if they were to demonstrate their scientific competence and objectivity (1944a, pp. 1–2).

Mindful of the impatience of others, Lundberg responded to the cliché that objective pursuit of abstract knowledge in such a crisis was like "lecturing on navigation while the ship goes down."

Because some men were content to keep on studying while their personal ships sank, he said, we have today some accumulated knowledge of navigation. We would not, had they joined the clamor for "short cuts to salvation whenever a storm occurred" (1943b, p. 199).

What bothered Lundberg most was the superficiality of the commitment of so many social scientists to the thoughtways of science. He lamented that in times of crisis many of us easily slip back "into the familiar personalistic–dramatic pattern of theology in which the forces of Good and Evil under their respective personal leaders again struggle for mastery" (1941b, p. 93). Not all scholars agreed with him when he spoke of the "theological and metaphysical nonsense" characterizing wartime discussions of "a highly subjective and relative concept called freedom." He held that "men are free when they feel free. They feel free when they are thoroughly habituated to their way of life" (1944a, p. 4). But some of his audience apparently felt dissatisfied with such a relativistic notion of freedom.

His unconventional views—for example, he had the temerity to argue that the understandable Jewish hostility to the German government exacerbated that government's hostility toward Jews—led to accusations that Lundberg had an anti-Semitic and profascist outlook, a product of his sociological positivism (Hartung 1944, pp. 340–341). If fascism means government by a self-appointed elite that suppresses all expressions of opposition, the accusation was clearly contradicted by Lundberg's lifelong insistence on the importance of distinguishing the role of scientist from the role of citizen and giving the scientist, in his role as citizen, no greater voice in public policy making than might be assented to by other citizens (1949, p. 10).

There is some indication that the accusation of anti-Semitism may have influenced Lundberg's subsequent choice of research topics, for although he had studied patterns of status differentiation and preferential association in the prewar years, he had not done previous research on minority groups as such or on ethnocentrism (Lundberg & Steele 1938; Larsen 1965a). He turned to these topics after the war, as if to substantiate his contention that moralistic and legalistic biases had heretofore tended to limit social science inquiry into these matters. As Lundberg saw it, numerous Jewish organizations striving to combat anti-Semitism pursue policies which actually aggravate it (1944c). The preventive for such ill-conceived programs is more adequate and more reliable knowledge, to which

Lundberg proposed to contribute (Lundberg & Dickson 1952).

Career and influence

Lundberg's polemics, less than persuasive to his accusers, were not his sole preoccupation in the postwar years. He also coauthored one of the leading introductory sociology textbooks (in its third edition at the time of his death), and he served as chairman of the department of sociology at the University of Washington during a period of rapid expansion of its faculty, its graduate program, and its research activities. Other facets of his postwar activities included writing the popular book *Can Science Save Us?* (1947) and editing a sociology series for a book publisher. Lundberg lectured on, and helped to promote, sociology in the Scandinavian countries, and, after concluding his administrative role at the University of Washington, he continued to teach there for a number of years before he retired. He was in demand as a lecturer at various universities and before nonacademic groups as well.

Before assuming the chairmanship at Washington, Lundberg had been on the faculties of the University of Pittsburgh, Columbia University, and Bennington College and had held appointments at Stanford, Brigham Young, and Minnesota. He had held research positions with federal and local welfare agencies and had been elected president of the Sociological Research Association and two regional sociological societies, as well as the American Sociological Society.

Lundberg was a graduate of the University of North Dakota, which also awarded him an LL.D. in 1958. He held the M.A. degree from Wisconsin and the PH.D. from Minnesota, which also awarded him its Distinguished Achievement Medal in 1951. He was editor of *Sociometry* from 1941 to 1947 and wrote some seventy articles, as well as several influential books.

At the time of Lundberg's retirement, Paul H. Furfey, one of his stanchest intellectual adversaries, paid him this tribute: "He has always made it seem obvious that winning an argument is unimportant, but that arriving at the truth is supremely important" (Larsen 1965a, p. 26).

WILLIAM R. CATTON, JR.

[*See also* LEISURE; POSITIVISM; VALUES.]

WORKS BY LUNDBERG

1929   LUNDBERG, GEORGE A.; BAIN, READ; and ANDERSON, NELS (editors) *Trends in American Sociology.* New York: Harper.

1934   LUNDBERG, GEORGE A. et al. *Leisure: A Suburban Study.* New York: Columbia Univ. Press.
1938   LUNDBERG, GEORGE A.; and STEELE, MARY Social Attraction-patterns in a Village. *Sociometry* 1:375–419.
1939   *Foundations of Sociology.* New York: Macmillan. → A revised and abridged paperback edition was published in 1964 by McKay.
1941a   The Future of the Social Sciences. *Scientific Monthly* 53:346–359.
1941b   Societal Pathology and Sociometry. *Sociometry* 4:78–97.
1941c   What Are Sociological Problems? *American Sociological Review* 6:357–369.
1943a   A Message From the President of the American Sociological Society. *American Sociological Review* 8:69–70.
1943b   Introductory Note. *Sociometry* 6:199 only.
1944a   Sociologists and the Peace. *American Sociological Review* 9:1–13.
1944b   Scientists in Wartime. *Scientific Monthly* 58:85–95.
1944c   Letter of March 1, 1944, to Dr. Zvi Cahn of the Nascent American Jewish Sociological Society. Unpublished manuscript.
(1947) 1961   *Can Science Save Us?* 2d ed. London: Longmans.
1949   Applying the Scientific Method to Social Phenomena. *Sociology and Social Research* 34:3–12.
1950a   Human Values: A Research Program. Washington State University, Pullman, *Research Studies* 18:103–111.
1950b   Can Science Validate Ethics? American Association of University Professors, *Bulletin* 36:262–275.
1952   LUNDBERG, GEORGE A.; and DICKSON, LENORE Selective Association Among Ethnic Groups in a High School Population. *American Sociological Review* 17:23–35.
(1958) 1963   LUNDBERG, GEORGE A.; SCHRAG, CLARENCE C.; and LARSEN, OTTO N. *Sociology.* 3d ed. New York: Harper.

SUPPLEMENTARY BIBLIOGRAPHY

HARTUNG, FRANK E.   1944   The Sociology of Positivism: Proto-fascist Aspects. *Science and Society* 8:328–341.
LARSEN, OTTO N.   1965a   The Art of George A. Lundberg as a Teacher. *Sociologiske meddelelser* 10:19–28.
LARSEN, OTTO N.   1965b   Publications of George A. Lundberg. *Sociologiske meddelelser* 10:6–18.

LUTHER, MARTIN

Although the Reformation was in its purest essence a religious movement, from the outset it also involved social, political, and economic forces and effected fundamental changes in many areas of life. The first of the magisterial reformers, Martin Luther (1483–1546), was pre-eminently concerned with theological matters, but his evangelical insight into the deepest meaning of the Christian gospel had tremendous implications for all aspects of social life and theory. Throughout his life he gave evidence of his concern for social action.

The operative principle of Luther's social ethics,

as expressed in his treatise entitled *Christian Liberty* (1520), was that religious faith must be active in love. The person precedes the action, for, as he asserted, "good works do not make a good man, but a good man does good works." The new spiritual life of a man who has come to a trusting faith in the gracious God revealed in Christ produces in him a spontaneous outflowing love for his fellow man. This love far transcends a mere prudential desire for the highest good and, like God's love, should not be dependent upon the worthiness or lovableness of the object. This ethical principle intensifies the force of conscience and the inner-directedness of the Christian in society, minimizing heteronomous controls.

Luther believed that all reality belongs to God's realm, for in the church God works through the Word of the Gospel for the spiritual good of man, and in the secular orders God works through men for the temporal good of man. Thus, such natural orders as the family, the various vocations, the state, and the organization of society in general are also divine orders. While historically they have shown development and are structurally subject to change, these natural orders have their origin in the divine will and are divinely ordained. This view allowed Luther to transcend the negative assessment of secular institutions characteristic of much medieval thought. Institutions such as marriage and state authority had been viewed merely as restraints necessitated by sin or as systems whose legality depended upon the sanction of the church. He viewed them positively as instruments of God's love and urged men to be thankful for them and to sustain them.

Luther held natural law to be the basis of the natural orders and of all secular authority, including that of non-Christian rulers. He understood this natural law to be the law of love implanted in man's consciousness and more clearly revealed in the Decalogue and refined in the Sermon on the Mount. Since communities are of divine ordinance, their good positive laws cannot be contrary to God's will; these laws are rooted in natural law and have a theonomous, or divinely obligating, character. Luther stressed emphatically the need to keep separate the secular and spiritual authorities, for the state is an authority that wields power and is exclusively concerned with the temporal order, while the church is a communion or priesthood of all believers responding to the gospel of God's love.

Luther's view of society and of man's culture, then, was dialectical. On the one hand, culture and society are theonomous insofar as they are sustained by the ever-present creative action of God, who initiates all, encompasses all, and rules over men. On the other hand, they are autonomous insofar as they are the product of man's own free, rational, responsible, cooperative action. Christians moved by love should participate in the social order and mend and improve it for the good of mankind. Because of his own foreshortened eschatology and preoccupation with ecclesiastical concerns, Luther did not invest effort in the systematic renovation or reorganization of society, as Calvin did, but his thought contained the basic elements for a constructive social philosophy.

In addressing himself to specific social issues, Luther at times reflected conservative views of long standing and at other times expressed novel ideas, which were ahead of his time and which found echoes in subsequent theorists. Although he was himself the son of a rising middle-class mining entrepreneur, he believed in the superior virtues of agrarian life over commerce. He opposed usury with vehemence and flayed the monopolies of ruthless large capitalists like the Fuggers and Medicis. He argued for the just-price theory and accepted the labor theory of value. He stressed the value of vocation to the active life and raised the *ordo naturalis* to the dignity of the *ordo spiritualis*. He opposed the mere giving of alms to beggars and urged that people sunk in poverty be given the means to help themselves. While encouraging support of the government and military service in the case of a just war of defense against an aggressor or an international lawbreaker, he insisted that under absolutely no circumstances could a Christian serve in an unjust cause or against his own conscience. It would seem that the highly organized and welfare-oriented social philosophies of such Lutheran lands as Denmark, Sweden, Norway, and Finland reflect generically the basic social thought of Luther. His pivotal faith in God gave him a certain detachment toward material wealth and a courageous attitude in the face of hostile political power and military threats—qualities that perhaps retain a basic relevance for modern social thought.

LEWIS W. SPITZ

[*See also* PROTESTANT POLITICAL THOUGHT; *and the biography of* CALVIN.]

BIBLIOGRAPHY

ERIKSON, ERIK H. (1958) 1962 *Young Man Luther: A Study in Psychoanalysis and History.* Austin Riggs Monograph No. 4. New York: Norton.

FORELL, GEORGE W. 1954 *Faith Active in Love.* New York: American Press.

HOLL, KARL (1911) 1959 *The Cultural Significance of the Reformation.* New York: Meridian. → First published as *Kulturbedeutung der Reformation.*

HUEGLI, ALBERT G. (editor) 1964 *Church and State Under God.* St. Louis, Mo.: Concordia.

LUTHER, MARTIN (1520) 192? *Christian Liberty.* Philadelphia: United Lutheran Publication House. → No date appears on the title page.

Luther's Works. 56 vols. St. Louis, Mo.: Concordia; Philadelphia: Muhlenberg, 1955–1965.

PAUCK, WILHELM (1950) 1961 *The Heritage of the Reformation.* Rev. & enl. ed. Glencoe, Ill.: Free Press.

RUPP, ERNEST G. 1953 *The Righteousness of God: Luther Studies.* London: Hodder & Stoughton.

LUXEMBURG, ROSA

Rosa Luxemburg (1870–1919) was one of the founders of the Social Democratic party of Poland and Lithuania, the leader of the left wing of the Social Democratic party (SPD) in Germany, and a prominent Marxist economic theorist. She was born in Zamosc but spent her childhood and youth in Warsaw. She came from a family of Polish-speaking Jewish merchants, and her mother brought her up in a liberal atmosphere, instilling in her a love of classical German culture. She grew up in a period when the tsarist government was increasing its political and religious oppression and when socialist activity was beginning in Poland.

While still in high school Rosa Luxemburg became active in the socialist movement, and in 1889 she was forced to flee abroad. She entered the University of Zurich with the intention of studying natural sciences but soon shifted to political economy. In addition to the university program, she studied the works of Adam Smith, Ricardo, Rodbertus, and, above all, Marx. In her doctoral thesis, *Die industrielle Entwicklung Polens* (1898; "The Industrial Development of Poland"), she argued that the development of industrial capitalism in the Polish kingdom depended heavily on the Russian market and that the economy of the Polish kingdom would never be more than a part of the tsarist economy. The analysis in this book formed the basis upon which the Polish Social Democratic party built its political program.

In order to be able to take part in the German socialist movement, she acquired German citizenship through a fictitious marriage with a German emigrant. From 1897 until her death she lived, except for short intervals, in Berlin.

Immediately upon her arrival in Germany she joined Karl Kautsky in the fight against Eduard Bernstein and his revisionist followers. Bernstein's thesis, "The movement is everything, the aim nothing," was incompatible with her belief that the struggle for political power was a necessary aim of the socialist movement. Her essays criticizing Bernstein's economic and political doctrines were collected in *Reform or Revolution* (1899).

In 1905 she returned to Warsaw under an assumed name to help the revolutionary movement there but was soon arrested. After her release from jail she went first to St. Petersburg and then to Finland, where she wrote the pamphlet *Massenstreik, Partei und Gewerkschaften* (1906; "General Strike, Party and Trade Unions"). The work contains a sociological analysis of the driving forces of social revolution and its mechanism—an analysis, on the one hand, of the role of the masses and, on the other hand, of the organization and role of the leaders. In this pamphlet she also developed the view that the general strike is the fundamental instrument in the struggle of the working class for power.

As the orthodox Marxists discussed their revolutionary experiences, particularly their experiences with political strikes, essential differences among them emerged. This led to a break between Luxemburg and Kautsky, which meant that the German Social Democratic party became divided into three groups: a right wing led by Bernstein, a center group led by Kautsky, and a left wing led by Luxemburg.

Beginning in 1907 she lectured at the Berlin school of the Social Democratic party. Both her earlier lectures on political economy and her later ones on economic history were published posthumously from her manuscripts, with the title *Einführung in die Nationalökonomie* (1925). Her most famous economic work, *The Accumulation of Capital* (1913), also grew out of these lectures.

The Accumulation of Capital may well be Luxemburg's most important contribution to the social sciences. The book has as its main theme the conditions of economic growth under capitalism, and its original contribution lies, therefore, in the field of economic theory. In Luxemburg's opinion, pure capitalism cannot create conditions adequate to maintain its own development. The main factor that gives capitalist production its dynamic power is the expansion toward noncapitalist areas, both underdeveloped countries and spheres of noncapitalist production within capitalist countries. This expansion comes about because capital accumulates, while at the same time demand within the capitalist society does not increase fast enough to absorb the increasing supply of goods.

During the imperialist phase of capitalism this difficulty is solved by the production of arms. The arms not only absorb domestic capital but also help create new markets in the colonies. The state's customs and tax policies also play an important part in the economic development of capitalism, especially in the period of imperialism. Luxemburg saw free international trade as only an episode in the history of capitalism and criticized Marx for disregarding the historical conditions that affected the accumulation of capital; she charged Marx with considering historical conditions important only in relation to the birth of capitalism and exclusively with reference to private accumulation. Luxemburg believed instead that the relations between capitalism and its precapitalist surroundings constitute a source of tension and international conflict. These lead to a series of wars and social revolutions that in turn start the process of the decline of capitalism. In the history of Marxist economic theory Luxemburg's work on the accumulation of capital has produced much theoretical and political polemics.

Initially, the reactions to *The Accumulation of Capital* were negative. Such theorists as Karl Kautsky, Otto Bauer, and Nikolai Bukharin not only rejected the major theory of the book but even questioned whether the problems investigated by Luxemburg were important ones. The first work in the literature of economics seriously to consider as well as to extend Luxemburg's theory of accumulation was Fritz Sternberg's *Der Imperialismus* (1926). Only with the Keynesian revolution was Luxemburg's theory, that lack of purchasing power causes a breakdown in the capitalist system, rehabilitated.

Luxemburg was again imprisoned during World War I, this time for her antimilitary activities. She devoted the three years she spent in jail to theoretical and journalistic writing. She wrote a book answering the critics of *The Accumulation of Capital*, a brief work on the crisis of social democracy (known as the "Junius Pamphlet"; see Luxemburg 1916), and the unfinished manuscript from which the posthumously published *Russian Revolution* (see in 1904–1922) was drawn. *The Russian Revolution* is one of the most controversial works in socialist political literature, where it occupies a position similar to that of *The Accumulation of Capital* in economic literature. Luxemburg acclaimed the October Revolution as the most important result of World War I, but this did not prevent her from criticizing Bolshevik practice. Thus, she deplored the fact that the postrevolutionary political system was a dictatorship not *of* the masses, but *over* the masses. She was disappointed that the large landholdings had been divided among the peasants, for she felt that this created a new and powerful class

of proprietors, i.e., enemies of socialism. She also disapproved of Bolshevik policy toward nationalities.

Upon her release from prison at the end of 1918, Luxemburg immediately joined the German revolution. Late that year she and Karl Liebknecht together founded the German Communist party and wrote its program. They were both arrested early in 1919 and were both assassinated by the soldiers in whose custody they had been placed.

TADEUSZ KOWALIK

[For *the historical context of Luxemburg's work, see* ECONOMIC THOUGHT, *article on* SOCIALIST THOUGHT; IMPERIALISM; MARXISM; SOCIALISM; *and the biographies of* BERNSTEIN; KAUTSKY; MARX.]

WORKS BY LUXEMBURG

(1894–1925) 1951 *Ausgewählte Reden und Schriften.* 2 vols. With a preface by Wilhelm Pieck. Berlin: Dietz.

1898 *Die industrielle Entwicklung Polens: Inaugural-Dissertation.* Leipzig: Duncker & Humblot.

(1899) 1951 *Reform or Revolution.* With an introduction by Hector Abhayavardhan. Bombay: Modern India Publications. → First published as *Sozialreform oder Revolution?*

(1904–1922) 1961 *The Russian Revolution* and *Leninism or Marxism?* With an introduction by Bertram D. Wolfe. Ann Arbor: Univ. of Michigan Press. → Two pamphlets, first published in German. *Leninism or Marxism?* was first published in 1904; *Die russische Revolution* was published posthumously in 1922, edited by P. Levi.

(1906) 1951 *Massenstreik, Partei und Gewerkschaften.* Volume 1, pages 157–257 in Rosa Luxemburg, *Ausgewählte Reden und Schriften.* Berlin: Dietz.

(1913) 1964 *The Accumulation of Capital.* New York: Monthly Review Press. → First published in German.

(1916) 1951 *Die Krise der Sozialdemokratie* (Junius-Broschüre). Volume 1, pages 258–399 in Rosa Luxemburg, *Ausgewählte Reden und Schriften.* Berlin: Dietz. → The 1916 edition was published under the pseudonym Junius.

1922–1928 *Gesammelte Werke.* Vols. 3, 4, and 6. Berlin: Vereinigung Internationaler Verlags-Anstalten. → Volumes 1, 2, and 5 were never published.

(1925) 1951 *Einführung in die Nationalökonomie.* Volume 1, pages 411–741 in Rosa Luxemburg, *Ausgewählte Reden und Schriften.* Berlin: Dietz.

SUPPLEMENTARY BIBLIOGRAPHY

ARENDT, HANNAH 1966 A Heroine of Revolution: [A Book Review of] *Rosa Luxemburg*, by J. P. Nettl. *New York Review of Books* 8, no. 5:21–27.

BUKHARIN, NIKOLAI I. (1926) 1927 *Der Imperialismus und die Akkumulation des Kapitals.* Berlin: Verlag für Literatur und Politik. → First published as *Imperialism i nakoplenie kapitala.*

CLIFF, TONY 1959 Rosa Luxemburg: A Study. *International Socialism: Quarterly for Marxist Theory* [1959]: no. 2–3.

FRÖLICH, PAUL (1939) 1940 *Rosa Luxemburg: Her Life and Work.* Translated by Edward Fitzgerald. London: Gollancz. → First published in German.

GROSSMANN, HENRYK 1929 *Das Akkumulations- und Zusammenbruchsgesetz des kapitalistischen Systems (Zugleich eine Krisentheorie).* Leipzig: Hirschfeld.

LAURAT, LUCIEN 1930 *L'accumulation du capital d'après Rosa Luxembourg, suivi d'un aperçu sur la discussion du problème depuis la mort de Rosa Luxembourg.* Paris: Rivière.

LENIN, VLADIMIR I. (1916) 1964 The Junius Pamphlet. Pages 305–319 in Vladimir I. Lenin, *Collected Works.* 4th ed. Volume 22: December 1915–July 1916. London: Lawrence & Wishart.

NETTL, JOHN P. 1966 *Rosa Luxemburg.* 2 vols. Oxford Univ. Press.

OELSSNER, FRED 1951 *Rosa Luxemburg: Eine kritische biographische Skizze.* Berlin: Dietz.

STERNBERG, FRITZ 1926 *Der Imperialismus.* Berlin: Malik.

STERNBERG, FRITZ 1929 Der Imperialismus *und seine Kritiker.* Berlin: Soziologische Verlagsanstalt.

M

MACAULAY, THOMAS BABINGTON

Thomas Babington Macaulay (1800–1859), English historian, essayist, and politician, was born at Rothley Temple, Leicestershire. His father, Zachary, one of the leading members of the "Clapham sect," was a stern evangelical who fought unremittingly for the abolition first of the slave trade and then of slavery itself. Macaulay's mother was the daughter of a Quaker bookseller and herself a devout evangelical. Thus, the young Macaulay, an astonishingly precocious boy, grew up in an atmosphere of piety, introspection, and humanitarian endeavor. He absorbed and retained the moral and ethical imperatives inculcated upon him; but much to the chagrin of his father, he never underwent a conversion experience and always remained wary of the emotional excesses, cant, and hypocrisy to which an experiential religion so easily lends itself.

At Trinity College, Cambridge, he distinguished himself as a classicist and a poet. He became a fellow of the college in 1824. While at the university, he triumphed as an orator in the Union Debating Society and began his brilliant career as an essayist. In the latter role, he first made his mark with his essay "Milton," which appeared in the *Edinburgh Review* of October 1825 ([1825–1844] 1963, vol. 1, pp. 150–194). It was indeed appropriate that in that essay, which made him famous overnight, he should have taken his place on the libertarian side of seventeenth-century English politics. Although Macaulay had been a mild Tory when he entered the university, he was a staunch Whig when he left, and in many ways his political stance was derived from his study of the constitutional conflicts of the seventeenth century.

In "Milton" and subsequent writings he transferred the theme of those conflicts to the decade of struggle between Whig and Tory before the passage of the Reform Act of 1832.

His early essays in the *Edinburgh Review* are richly caparisoned with wit, paradox, and antithesis, but as Bagehot justly remarked, "Macaulay is anything but a mere rhetorical writer, there is a very hard kernel of business in him." What gave his writings this "kernel of business" was his sturdy common sense, his fondness for Baconian induction, his suspicion of system making and *idées reçues*, and his ability to get to the root of the matter. These characteristics led him on occasion to anticipate some of the insights of twentieth-century social science; the results are still well worth sampling in some of his articles: "Thoughts on the Advancement of Academic Education in England" (1826), in which he presented a well-argued case against the collegiate system of Oxford and Cambridge and for a nonresidential university in an urban setting; "Social and Industrial Capacities of Negroes" (1827), in which Macaulay saw the roots of the Negro problem as fundamentally social and economic rather than in any sense innately "racial"; "Machiavelli" (*The Works of Lord Macaulay*, vol. 7, pp. 63–113), which, as Paul Lazarsfeld has pointed out (1957), contains an account of what is probably the first projective test recorded in the literature; "History" (*Works*, vol. 7, pp. 167–220), which makes an excellent case for writing the history of societies as a whole, rather than of wars, battles, diplomacy, and politics; "Mill on Government" (*Works*, vol. 7, pp. 327–371), which argues against the utilitarian theory of government persuasively enough to have convinced John Stuart Mill himself; and "Civil Disabilities of the Jews" (*Works,* vol. 8, pp. 1–17), which brilliantly places the problem of anti-Semitism into a historical context.

Macaulay was elected to Parliament in 1830. His speeches in favor of the Reform Bill in 1831 and 1832 gained him immense repute as an orator and secured for him, an outsider who lacked both wealth and noble birth, entry into the strongholds of Whig society. For him parliamentary reform was not merely a matter of expediency, although, to be sure, he emphasized that the aristocracy had better make timely political concessions to the middle classes if it wanted to avoid revolution. Reform was, rather, the latest inevitable stage in a series of historical developments that had resulted in a more widespread distribution of property, great increase of wealth, ever greater triumphs of science and industry, and a steady progress from rudeness to refinement. In other words, the Reform Act was merely one way of bringing political arrangements into alignment with an advancing state of society.

In 1834 Macaulay went to India as a member of the governor's Supreme Council. His personal motive for going was to make himself financially independent. In India he made two significant contributions. In 1835 he wrote the historic and still controversial "Minute on Indian Education" ([1831–1853] 1935, pp. 345–361), which proposed English as the principal language of instruction for any national system of education in India, so that Western science, culture, and technology could more easily be transmitted. And he was largely responsible for drawing up a uniform Indian penal code in 1837. Its substance was the English criminal law. Revised by Sir Barnes Peacock, it went into operation in 1862.

In 1838 Macaulay returned to England, and it was in the course of that year that he began seriously to plan his major literary work, which eventually appeared under the title *The History of England, From the Accession of James the Second, . . .* (1848–1861). He remained active in politics, was Secretary at War from 1839 to 1841, and sat in Parliament for most of the rest of his life.

The first two volumes of the *History* came out late in 1848, and it was appropriate that a work celebrating the bloodless revolution of 1688 and the establishment of English constitutional stability should make its appearance in the course of a year that had seen revolutionary violence on the continent of Europe, but not in England. In his *History* Macaulay showed himself to be a master of historical narrative.

The tour de force of the *History* is undoubtedly

"England in 1685," the first volume's famous third chapter which in the space of 150 pages surveys the nation's geography, population, resources, means of transport, and varied social classes and their occupations, as well as its army, navy, science, literature, and press. It is descriptive rather than analytical social history. Still, of its kind and of its time it remains a magnificent achievement.

The *History of England* is not without its defects. Macaulay's historical imagination was strong but limited. He approached the past from the vantage point of a more glorious present. He was, as S. R. Gardiner pointed out, a better judge of situations than of character. There are some distortions. But those who expect to find in the *History* a naively stated *parti pris* will look in vain.

The popular success of the *History* (volumes 3 and 4 appeared in 1855, a fifth volume posthumously in 1861) was immense and constituted a unique publishing phenomenon in nineteenth-century England. It appealed to the pride as well as the prejudices of its purchasers and was read with both pleasure and profit by an ever-growing literate public. In historiographical terms it marked, as Leopold von Ranke observed, the triumph of the Whig view of seventeenth-century English history over the Tory view, articulated by David Hume. But the recent tendency to categorize and then dismiss Macaulay as a "mere" Whig historian is giving way to a more balanced sense of his achievement.

Macaulay was awarded a peerage in 1857, the first English historian to be so honored.

JOHN CLIVE

[*For the historical context of Macaulay's work, see* HISTORY, *article on* SOCIAL HISTORY.]

WORKS BY MACAULAY

(1825–1844) 1963 *Critical and Historical Essays.* 2 vols. New York: Dutton.

1826 Thoughts on the Advancement of Academic Education in England. *Edinburgh Review* 43:315–341. → Published anonymously.

1827 [Social and Industrial Capacities of Negroes.] *Edinburgh Review* 45:383–423. → An anonymously published review of four papers.

(1831–1853) 1935 *Speeches by Lord Macaulay, With His "Minute on Indian Education."* Selected with an introduction and notes by G. M. Young. Oxford Univ. Press.

(1835–1837) 1946 *Lord Macaulay's Legislative Minutes.* Selected with a historical introduction by C. D. Dhaker. Oxford Univ. Press.

(1848–1861) 1913–1915 *The History of England, From the Accession of James the Second, ...* Edited by Charles Harding Firth. 6 vols. London: Macmillan.

The Works of Lord Macaulay. Albany edition, 12 vols London: Longmans, 1898. → Volumes 1–6: *History of*

England. Volumes 7–10: *Essays and Biographies.* Volumes 11–12: *Speeches, Poems and Miscellaneous Writings.*

WORKS ABOUT MACAULAY

BAGEHOT, WALTER (1856) 1950 Thomas Babington Macaulay. Volume 2, pages 198–232 in Walter Bagehot, *Literary Studies.* New York: Dutton.

BEATTY, RICHMOND C. 1938 *Lord Macaulay: Victorian Liberal.* Norman: Univ. of Oklahoma Press.

BRYANT, ARTHUR 1933 *Macaulay.* London: Davies.

CLIVE, JOHN 1960 Macaulay's Historical Imagination. *Review of English Literature* 1, no. 4:20–28.

FIRTH, CHARLES H. (1938) 1964 *A Commentary on Macaulay's* History of England. New York: Barnes & Noble.

GLADSTONE, WILLIAM E. (1876) 1879 Macaulay. Pages 265–341 in William E. Gladstone, *Gleanings of Past Years: 1843–1878.* Volume 1: Personal and Literary. London: Murray.

LAZARSFELD, PAUL F. 1957 The Historian and the Pollster. Pages 242–262 in Mirra Komarovsky (editor), *Common Frontiers of the Social Sciences.* Glencoe, Ill.: Free Press.

PAGET, JOHN 1861 *The New "Examen": Or, an Inquiry Into the Evidence Relating to Certain Passages in Lord Macaulay's* History *Concerning I. The Duke of Marlborough; II. The Massacre of Glencoe; III. The Highlands of Scotland; IV. Viscount Dundee; V. William Penn.* Edinburgh and London: Blackwood.

STEPHEN, LESLIE (1876) 1904 Macaulay. Volume 3, pages 227–271 in Leslie Stephen, *Hours in a Library.* New York and London: Putnam.

TREVELYAN, GEORGE O. (1876) 1932 *The Life and Letters of Lord Macaulay.* Oxford Univ. Press.

McCULLOCH, JOHN RAMSAY

John Ramsay McCulloch (1789–1864), economist and statistician, was born in Scotland, the son of a small landowner. He studied law in Edinburgh but soon abandoned that field in favor of political economy. His first publication, which appeared in 1816, called for a reduction of the rate of interest on the national debt on both theoretical and practical grounds and led to a correspondence with Ricardo. When Ricardo's *Principles* appeared in 1817, McCulloch immediately supplied a masterful digest of the book to the *Edinburgh Review,* the most popular quarterly of the day. For the next twenty years almost every issue of the *Review* carried an article by him. At the same time, he contributed to the *Scotsman,* and from 1818 to 1820 he edited this famous liberal paper.

In 1820 he went to London, where he taught economics privately. After Ricardo died in 1823, his friends and admirers chose McCulloch to deliver the Ricardo memorial lectures at a privately rented hall. These lectures were expanded into an outline of basic principles in the article on political economy for the new edition of the *Encyclopaedia Britannica* (1824*a*); in this article McCulloch equates Ricardo's brand of economics with the science itself. It was succeeded by a formal treatise, *The Principles of Political Economy* (1825), a work which had considerable vogue until J. S. Mill's work of the same title (1848) supplanted it. There followed *A Treatise on the Circumstances Which Determine the Rate of Wages* (1826), to which the Webbs later drew attention by calling McCulloch "the inventor of the wages fund doctrine" (Webb & Webb 1897). However, this doctrine is to be found in Adam Smith's writings, as well as in Ricardo's, and McCulloch did not contribute anything new to its presentation.

Academic security eluded him all his life. In 1828 he was appointed to an unendowed chair at the newly founded University College in London. He resigned the position in 1832 because no donor had come forward to endow the chair. Earlier an attempt to make him the first incumbent of a new chair of political economy at the University of Edinburgh had also been unsuccessful. At last, in 1838 he obtained a lifetime sinecure as comptroller of Her Majesty's Stationery Office. He took little part in the activities of the department and, although he had by then abandoned journalism, he continued to publish books and pamphlets on economic subjects.

It was McCulloch, more than any other man, who was responsible for Ricardo's enormous influence upon the economic thinking of the times. He was, however, more than Ricardo's spokesman; he was the greatest economic publicist of his day—so much so that all those who detested political economy invariably selected him as their whipping boy. He appears, Scots accent and all, as "McGroudy" in Carlyle; as "MacFungus" expounding "ecoonoomical science" in Peacock; and as "The Scot" in that old Victorian favorite *Noctes Ambrosianae,* by Christopher North. Today he is chiefly remembered as a prime example of the zealous, dogmatic disciple. But devoted disciple though he was, he did not endorse all of Ricardo's opinions: he condemned Ricardo's *volte face* on the question of technological unemployment; he never fully accepted the theory of comparative advantage; and he always qualified Ricardo's theory of profit. In later years he openly admitted defects in the Ricardian system.

An indifferent theorist, McCulloch appears at his best in his statistical and descriptive compendia rather than in his theoretical writings. His *Dictionary . . . of Commerce and Commercial Navigation* (1832), much of which was embodied in his later treatise *A Descriptive and Statistical Account of* the *British Empire* (1837), demonstrated his encyclopedic knowledge of the British economy, and it remains to this day an authoritative reference work. Moreover, he deserves to be regarded as the first professional historian of economic thought. *A Discourse on the Rise . . . of Political Economy*, first published in 1824 and then appended to his *Principles*, was the first attempt in any language to project a formal history of this subject. Later contributions to the historiography of economics consisted of an edition of Adam Smith's *Wealth of Nations* in 1828, with copious notes; an edition of the works of Ricardo in 1846, with a famous biography; numerous reprints of scarce tracts; and a celebrated *catalogue raisonné*, *The Literature of Political Economy* (1845a), based upon his own magnificent collection of economic works.

Unlike other members of Ricardo's circle, McCulloch did not subscribe to radicalism in politics, nor did he share the utilitarian enthusiasm for land reform. His outlook was that of a liberal Tory, optimistic but conservative. He always took exception to the gloomy implications of the Malthusian theory of population. He hesitated to condemn the poor laws entirely and, in contrast to most other economists of the day, disapproved of the Poor Law Amendment Act of 1834. Although a convinced free trader, he never joined Richard Cobden and John Bright in demanding immediate and total repeal of the corn laws. In his days as a journalist, he achieved notoriety as an apologist for the new factory system, but in later years he grew increasingly uneasy about the consequences of the industrial revolution.

MARK BLAUG

[*For the historical context of McCulloch's work, see the biography of* RICARDO.]

WORKS BY MC CULLOCH

1824a   *Political Economy.* Supplement, Volume 6, pages 216–278 in *Encyclopaedia Britannica.* Edinburgh: Constable.

1824b   *A Discourse on the Rise, Progress, Peculiar Objects, and Importance, of Political Economy: Containing an Outline of a Course of Lectures on the Principles and Doctrines of That Science.* Edinburgh: Constable. → Later appended to McCulloch 1825.

(1824c) 1921   *The Founding of the Political Economy Club.* Volume 6, page 41 in Political Economy Club of London, *Minutes of Proceedings, 1899–1920; Roll of Members and Questions Discussed, 1821–1920; With Documents Bearing on the History of the Club.* Centenary Volume. London: Macmillan. → The Johnsonian flavor of McCulloch's mind is best conveyed by his impromptu observations at the Political Economy Club and by letters in Ricardo 1817–1823.

(1825) 1886   *The Principles of Political Economy.* London: Ward.

(1826) 1868   *A Treatise on the Circumstances Which Determine the Rate of Wages, and the Conditions of the Labouring Classes. . . .* London: Longmans. → First published as *An Essay on the Circumstances. . . .*

(1832) 1882   *A Dictionary, Practical, Theoretical, and Historical, of Commerce and Commercial Navigation.* London: Longmans.

(1837) 1854   *A Descriptive and Statistical Account of the British Empire.* 4th ed., rev., 2 vols. London: Longmans. → First published as *A Statistical Account of the British Empire.*

(1845a) 1938   *The Literature of Political Economy.* London School of Economics and Political Science Series of Reprints of Scarce Works on Political Economy, No. 5. London School of Economics and Political Science.

(1845b) 1863   *A Treatise on the Principles and Practical Influence of Taxation and the Funding System.* 3d ed. Edinburgh: Black.

1848   *A Treatise on the Succession to Property Vacant by Death.* London: Longmans.

SUPPLEMENTARY BIBLIOGRAPHY

BLAUG, MARK   1958   *Ricardian Economics: A Historical Study.* Yale University Studies in Economics, No. 8. New Haven: Yale Univ. Press.

BONAR, JAMES   1895   John Ramsay McCulloch. Part 6, pages 1–5 in Bernard Quaritch (editor), *Contributions Towards a Dictionary of English Book-collectors.* London: Quaritch.

CANNAN, EDWIN   (1893) 1953   *A History of the Theories of Production and Distribution in English Political Economy, From 1776 to 1848.* 3d ed. London and New York: Staples.

HALÉVY, ÉLIE   (1901–1904) 1952   *The Growth of Philosophic Radicalism.* New ed. London: Faber. → First published in French.

MILL, JOHN STUART   (1848) 1961   *Principles of Political Economy, With Some of Their Applications to Social Philosophy.* 7th ed. Edited by W. J. Ashley. New York: Kelley.

RICARDO, DAVID   (1809–1823) 1951–1955   *Works and Correspondence.* Edited by Piero Sraffa. 10 vols. Cambridge Univ. Press. → Volumes 6 through 9 contain Ricardo's correspondence.

SMITH, ADAM   (1776) 1950   *An Inquiry Into the Nature and Causes of the Wealth of Nations.* 6th ed., 2 vols. Edited, with an introduction, notes, marginal summary, and an enlarged index, by Edwin Cannan. London: Methuen. → A paperback edition was published in 1963 by Irwin.

TAUSSIG, FRANK W.   (1896) 1932   *Wages and Capital: An Examination of the Wages Fund Doctrine.* London School of Economics and Political Science.

WEBB, SIDNEY; and WEBB, BEATRICE   (1897) 1920   *Industrial Democracy.* New ed. 2 vols. in 1. London and New York: Longmans.

McDOUGALL, WILLIAM

William McDougall (1871–1938) occupies a position in the history of psychology that is not easy to define. During the earlier part of his working life he was a central figure, in touch not only with all that was going on in psychology but also with anthropology and physiology as well. As time went on certain qualities of character and intellect tended to isolate him, and before he died he had moved to the fringes of the academic world, writing largely for laymen and associated in the minds of his fellow scientists with a discredited instinct theory, Lamarckian genetics, and parapsychology. He was aware of this and felt it deeply. "Similar abilities, energy, and sustained effort, applied in any other line of work, might well have brought considerable reward," he wrote in his autobiography. "The more I write, the more antagonism I seem to provoke" (1930, p. 223).

McDougall was born in Lancashire, England. A precocious student, he graduated from the University of Manchester at age 17. Two years later he went to Cambridge to study physiology, then as now a common approach to a medical qualification. His M.B., which he took in London in 1898, was not intended to lead to work as a physician. He had a few months of physiological research with Sherrington before returning to Cambridge, where his brilliant academic record had brought him a fellowship at St. John's College.

Almost immediately he was involved in a scientific expedition to the Torres Strait. W. H. R. Rivers, who was to influence so many Cambridge men, asked him to carry out psychological observations on the natives, and his wide-ranging mind was soon at home in the anthropological literature of his day. Darwin's influence at that time must have been so pervasive as to be unrecognizable, yet looking back we can see that it was the primary source of McDougall's thinking in many fields. On an expedition such as that to the Torres Strait the zoologists and botanists must have had the *Voyage of the Beagle* very much in mind, and the direction of their work was to identify the part played by various structures and activities in the adaptive economy of the species in which they occurred. This kind of interest, when it arises in psychology, forms part of the viewpoint which has been called functionalism to distinguish it from the psychological structuralism of Wundt and the quasi-physiological theories of behaviorism. It dominated the Anglo-Saxon world for a time and received its clearest expression in William James's great *Principles of Psychology*.

Returning to Cambridge, McDougall sampled the German and British philosophical psychologists of his period. Lotze attracted him but Wundt did not. The former was philosophical and tentative in his approach, with a bias against mechanism and an interest in psychological functioning; the latter was dogmatic in his claim that mental content is the only valid subject matter for psychology. On the advice of James Ward, professor of moral philosophy at Cambridge, McDougall went to Göttingen and studied under Georg E. Müller. He did not become a disciple but was attracted to color vision research. His work led him to reject the theories both of Hering and of Helmholtz, but his own theory did not constitute a major departure. Rather it was an attempt to supplement the views of Helmholtz so as to accommodate Hering's findings, by adding an evolutionary footnote. If McDougall had formulated his suggestion somewhat differently, as others did at the time, it would be acceptable today. [See VISION, *article on* COLOR VISION AND COLOR BLINDNESS.] At the same time he was concerned with the general nature of cerebral activity; here his views tended toward the theory, first put forward by Flourens, that the brain does not function as an enormous collection of individual pathways but is a unitary organ acting as a whole. This "mass action" theory may best be thought of as a protest against oversimplification. McDougall also displayed an interest in the relationship between mind and body which persisted throughout his life. He took a dualistic line and suggested that mental events as such may influence bodily processes. His views were unfashionable then, and, despite the rise of psychosomatic medicine, they have remained so. [See NERVOUS SYSTEM; PSYCHOSOMATIC ILLNESS.] They were also undoubtedly linked with his emerging interest in psychical research. He related his views in this connection to his "uncompromising arrogance" and to his inclination to support a theory merely because it was unpopular.

In 1904 McDougall went to Oxford as Wilde reader in mental philosophy. He had to give some forty lectures a year on topics of his own choosing, and the rest of the time was his own for research and writing. He did not feel at home in the Oxford atmosphere, but he did have a small laboratory in the department of physiology and some outstanding research students, including Cyril Burt and J. C. Flugel.

Some of his best work belongs to this period. His little *Physiological Psychology* appeared in 1905. It is not read now because later techniques and theories have dated it, but within its scope it was an admirably clear and objective piece of work, and its qualities highlight the diversity of McDougall's talents at this stage of his career. [See PSYCHOLOGY, *article on* PHYSIOLOGICAL PSYCHOLOGY.]

An Introduction to Social Psychology was published in 1908, and in it McDougall first propounded his influential instinct theory. The book ran through more than twenty editions in as many years and is perhaps as much undervalued today as it was overvalued then. In ethology and elsewhere, aspects of McDougall's position are now widely current, although restatement has done much to disguise them. To McDougall the fact that anthropologists could identify the adaptive role of social organizations and that zoologists could do the same for inherited patterns of behavior meant that at the human level also there is a mediating mechanism through which complex adaptive ways of behaving, both social and individual, can be transmitted, and that mechanism is instinct. An instinct, for McDougall, was not a built-in response pattern specified in detail—such as we see in the repertoire of solitary insects—but merely a tendency, under given conditions, to notice certain kinds of stimuli, to respond to them in ways that can best be specified by reference to some goal, and to experience a particular emotion if the response is delayed. Learning plays a great part in this mechanism both by diversifying and stabilizing the response. McDougall's later critics, using a much more limited definition of instinct, often did him an injustice by failing to give due weight to this last point.

The work was written rather quickly and was based on reading and reflection rather than actual research, but the argument was so persuasive that it soon established itself as one of the most widely read texts on either side of the Atlantic. The early acclaim for this vulnerable piece of work probably accounts in part for the vehemence with which it was later denounced. There also occurred during McDougall's lifetime, however, a change in the climate of opinion, which more than anything else was responsible for the curiously inverted nature of his career, with its early fame and later comparative obscurity. The functionalist approach, which derived from Darwin, became replaced by a more analytic and objective attitude. In psychology, the rise of behaviorism and associationist learning theory marked this change. McDougall found himself more and more out of step with his colleagues and, being the man he was, reacted polemically rather than creatively to the challenge.

Body and Mind, with its revealing subtitle, A History and a Defense of Animism, came out in 1911 and showed clearly that even before the rise of behaviorism there were expressions of hostility to mechanistic theories in the biological field. McDougall himself, who was not without insight into his own foibles, described the work as another characteristic championship of an unpopular view just because it was unpopular. Yet even then his

reputation as a scientist must have been very high. In 1912 he was elected a fellow of the Royal Society, one of the small number of psychologists ever to receive this honor.

World War I brought about some shift in the direction of McDougall's interests from pure research and speculation toward applied and clinical problems. Since he was medically qualified, it was natural that he should serve as a psychiatrist. Neither psychologist nor psychiatrist had much in the way of professional training in those days, and demarcation disputes did not arise. Many of the psychiatric casualties of World War I suffered from the hysterical condition known as shell shock. The methods which McDougall found most useful in treating psychiatric casualties confirmed his earlier belief in the value of Jung's work. He did not find it necessary to trace a breakdown to events in the early childhood of a patient but treated it as an inadequate reaction to an immediate situation. After the war he went to Jung in Zurich and underwent analysis. Writing of it later he said that his personality was so "hopelessly normal" that the process made very little difference to him. He remained, however, well disposed toward Jung.

In 1920 there appeared The Group Mind, a study in which the Darwinian ideas of the Introduction to Social Psychology were supplemented and elaborated by other ideas from analytic psychology and anthropology. It was conceived by its author to be the first part of his masterwork, and he had high hopes of being able to work out a single systematic treatment of his subject from its social and anthropological to its biological frontiers. His ideas, however, were far too speculative and his statement of them far too discursive to make what he had to say widely acceptable to his contemporaries. This seems to have been the turning point. Although McDougall was still to contribute much of value to psychology, the setback that he suffered at this stage seems to have done more than anything else to drive him into the byways. Although the size of his output remained considerable, its scientific content tended to decline.

It was perhaps a symptom of his unsettled state that he felt it would be a good idea to move from Oxford to Harvard. Münsterberg he had found congenial, and William James was probably, of all psychologists, the one he admired with fewest reservations. These were the names that represented Harvard to him, and he felt that he would find there a more sympathetic environment than anywhere else. It was an ill-judged move in many ways. The atmosphere had changed since the days of James and Münsterberg, the administrative arrangements were not what he had supposed, and in his frustration he may well have alienated some of his colleagues.

He began some animal experiments to test the Lamarckian hypothesis, and he published during this period two considerable but little read books—*Outline of Psychology* (1923) and *Outline of Abnormal Psychology* (1926). In a few years, however, the difficulties of Harvard became oppressive, and he made his final move, to Duke University in North Carolina. Duke had been recently founded and richly endowed, and it seemed to promise the independence and financial support required by a research scientist and something of the isolation demanded by a prophet. At any rate the change was a happy one, and McDougall settled down in his new home as contentedly as he could anywhere. He carried on his Lamarckian work, he supported psychical research, he built up a good psychology department, and he published extensively on a wide range of topics. It is not unfair to say, however, that judged by contemporary standards nothing of this later work is of first-rate importance.

McDougall's dogmatism and impatience are partly responsible, no doubt, for the fact that despite his brilliant gifts and tremendous industry he felt himself to have been a failure. He did arouse hostility where he need not have done, and, as has been pointed out, he lived through a period of rapid change in biological science and was out of step with events. More basic, however, as a reason for his difficulties seems to have been an emotionally toned refusal to look at human beings with the detachment and objectivity of the scientist. He was always a moralist and sometimes a metaphysician, so that his conclusions were as often a function of his personality as of his data.

JAMES DREVER

[*For the historical context of McDougall's work, see the biographies of* DARWIN; FLOURENS; HELMHOLTZ; HERING; JAMES; JUNG; LOTZE; MÜNSTERBERG; *for discussion of the subsequent development of his ideas, see* EMOTION; ETHOLOGY; INSTINCT; PARAPSYCHOLOGY; SOCIAL PSYCHOLOGY.]

WORKS BY MC DOUGALL

1905 *Physiological Psychology.* London: Dent.
(1908) 1950 *An Introduction to Social Psychology.* 30th ed., enl. London: Methuen. → A paperback edition was published in 1960 by Barnes and Noble.
(1911) 1938 *Body and Mind.* 8th ed. London: Methuen. → Previously published as *Body and Mind: A History and a Defense of Animism.*
1920 *The Group Mind: A Sketch of the Principles of Collective Psychology, With Some Attempt to Apply Them to the Interpretation of National Life and Character.* New York and London: Putnam. → A sequel to McDougall's *Introduction to Social Psychology.*
1923 *Outline of Psychology.* New York: Scribner.
1926 *Outline of Abnormal Psychology.* New York: Scribner.
1930 *Autobiography.* Volume 1, pages 191–223 in *A History of Psychology in Autobiography.* Worcester, Mass.: Clark Univ. Press.

SUPPLEMENTARY BIBLIOGRAPHY

ROBINSON, ANTHONY L. 1943 *William McDougall, M.B., D.Sc., F.R.S.: A Bibliography, Together With a Brief Outline of His Life.* Durham, N.C.: Duke Univ. Press.
SMITH, MAY 1939 William McDougall: Bibliography. *Character and Personality* 7:184–191.

MACHIAVELLI, NICCOLÒ

Niccolò Machiavelli (1469–1527) was an Italian political and military theorist, civil servant, historian, playwright, and poet.

The Machiavellis, an ancient middle-class family of Florence whose income came from landed property, had been reduced to near poverty at the time of Machiavelli's birth. His father was a doctor of law. Machiavelli seems to have been carefully educated in humanistic studies, although he never learned Greek. He entered Florentine government service in 1498, at the age of 29, as second chancellor and secretary of the Ten of Liberty and Peace, an executive committee concerned with domestic as well as military and foreign affairs. During his 14-year tenure he was engaged in numerous and sometimes lengthy diplomatic missions which took him to France, Switzerland, and Germany. His dispatches and reports contain ideas that anticipate many of the doctrines of his later works.

Military affairs were a continuing preoccupation of Machiavelli's. Not only was the famous militia ordinance of 1506 his, but also the responsibility for implementing it, in the capacity of secretary of the specially constituted Nine of the Militia. When the Florentine government was threatened in 1512 with the restoration of the Medici by Spanish forces, Machiavelli skillfully mobilized an army of twelve thousand conscripts to withstand the invasion; however, the amateur citizen-soldiers proved ineffectual before seasoned troops.

With the restoration of the Medici, Machiavelli was briefly imprisoned and tortured. Upon release he was banished from Florence to live in impoverished retirement on the small estate his family owned at Sant'Andrea. After 13 years of political inactivity he was recalled to government service by the Medici in 1525, but two years later the Medici were overthrown, and the new republic again excluded Machiavelli from office. He died in 1527, receiving the last rites of the church.

Machiavelli was a good father and an affectionate if unfaithful husband. Scrupulously honest, he was also generous and tolerant and had unusual courage and integrity. He excelled in witty conversation and storytelling. As much a poet as a man of practical affairs, he was a dedicated republican who desired only to serve Florence rather than any particular party. He was an extraordinary literary artist and has long been recognized for his masterful prose style; as the author of the comedy *Mandragola* (see 1509–1527) he has been acclaimed the equal of Molière.

Method. Machiavelli was neither a system builder nor a philosopher in a technical sense. In no single treatise did he rigorously expound his theory of man and government. His views are presented in a diffuse and impressionistic fashion, scattered through a number of different works. At the same time, there is system and remarkable consistency to his ideas, even if the coherence is not the most obvious and depends to a degree upon imaginative reconstruction by the sensitive reader.

Among Machiavelli's particular achievements was his attempt to discover an order in political activity itself, not in some external standard or cause. He examined politics in a detached, rational manner, analyzing the ways power can be acquired and maintained. He showed the kinds of actions that in varying situations will lead to political success or failure. Although he was not concerned with moral and political obligation or with the analysis of moral and political concepts, a conception of a good society does inform most of his political writings.

The sources of his approach are a matter of conjecture. He probably owed less to the traditional philosophers than to nonphilosophical classical writers—in particular, to Livy, Tacitus, Plutarch, Xenophon, Polybius, Vegetius, and Frontinus. Machiavelli was not alone among his contemporaries in abandoning a moralistic approach to human behavior for a rational and objective one: the influence of Platonism resulted generally in increasing efforts to reduce activity to an inherent order and these efforts in turn led to the scientific revolution of the seventeenth century (Cassirer 1927). That Machiavelli lived in a city whose very life was finance and commerce may also help to explain his method, which had some of the characteristics of a business calculation of profit and loss. Another possible influence was the increasing conceptual-

ization of government policy, since the thirteenth century, in terms of a notion of public utility: the Holy Roman Emperor Frederick II (1194–1250), Philip IV of France (1268–1314), and some Italian legalists held that the security and well-being of the state at times necessitated official acts which under ordinary circumstances would be considered morally reprehensible. Machiavelli was heir to this late medieval tradition.

Machiavelli was essentially concerned with ascertaining the conditions of political success, and he sought to do so by determining what kinds of acts have proved beneficial and what kinds detrimental to the (political) actors who performed them. In *The Prince* and the *Discourses*, written between 1513 and 1521 (see 1532*a*), he demonstrated the soundness of certain political precepts by using a kind of calculus: he cited numerous examples, drawn from history and from the events of his own time, that would support a particular proposition about the conditions of political success, and he then searched for further examples that would appear to negate the same maxim; only after careful scrutiny of the "negative" cases did he decide whether they really were in fact negative or only appeared to be so because of very different circumstances. He used this method for military precepts, in these works and in *The Art of War* (1521). Again, his penchant for discovering general patterns is evident in his *History of Florence*, completed in 1525 (1532*b*), in which he sought to establish causal relationships in place of mere chronology. It is a pioneer work in modern western European historical writing.

The inspiration for the method may well have been two books with which he was familiar—the *Dictorum factorumque memorabilium* of Valerius Maximus, a compendium of ancient examples to illustrate human behavior, which was dedicated to the first century emperor Tiberius, and the *Strategemata* of Frontinus, a catalogue of military stratagems of the latter part of the same century. Whatever the sources, the method differs markedly from that of classical and medieval political theory. In a way, Machiavelli's approach anticipates the inductive method of Francis Bacon, which, much like an adversary proceeding, entails the collection of positive and negative examples and their resolution.

Theory of man. Crucial to Machiavelli's political theory is his concept of man's nature. From his own shrewd observation and omnivorous reading of history, he concluded that man's nature is changeless—were it not changeless, generalizations about politics could not be made—and that it is essentially evil. (Unlike Plato and Aristotle, Machiavelli used the concept of human nature in a descriptive rather than a normative sense.)

Man's innate evil qualities are such, however, that they do not preclude the possibility of cooperative human endeavor; indeed, some of these very qualities facilitate social cooperation. Man's basic traits are the following: he is a creature of insatiable desires and limitless ambition, and his primary desire is for self-preservation; he is short-sighted, judging most commonly by the immediacy of reward rather than the remote consequences of his actions; he is imitative, inclined to follow the example of authority figures; and he is inflexible, so that behavior patterns established through imitation can be changed only to a limited extent.

Given these traits, the outlook for social cooperation may appear dim, but this is not so: men's desire for self-preservation and their very short-sightedness make them peculiarly susceptible to manipulation by civic leaders, and as stated above, their imitativeness predisposes them to accept the conditioning provided by leadership and organization. Furthermore, under conditions of necessity, when their lives are threatened by a hostile physical environment or by an act of aggression, men's desire for self-preservation moves them to act cooperatively and even virtuously: they prove to be industrious, courageous, and self-denying. Even after an immediate threat to survival has been overcome, social virtues can be maintained by astute leadership and rational social organization. In other words, Machiavelli differentiated between an original (evil) and a second (socially benevolent) nature, between natural and socially acquired characteristics.

Man's essentially evil nature, then, is raw material that may be molded or conditioned by leadership and organization; although, to be sure, the original nature of the material limits its malleability. Man is capable of socialization, and more or less desirable characteristics can be imprinted on his original nature by education, in the sense of conditioning. Civil society is the great school of mankind. Human behavior can be vitally affected by the structure of the social environment, by the socially established ends that canalize human desire. All men are to some extent creatures of convention rather than merely natural men; indeed, neither an absolutely natural nor an absolutely conventional man can exist, any more than either an absolutely evil or an absolutely good man is possible. All men fall somewhere along a scale between these extremes. It seemed plausible to Machiavelli that good and evil are roughly in equilibrium in the

world, although their distribution may vary from age to age, each quality being in some periods concentrated in particular societies, and in other periods dispersed.

Values. The supreme end of politics, in Machiavelli's view, is the public utility, the security and well-being of the community rather than the moral goal imputed to politics by previous thinkers. When he assessed the validity of political precepts by examining the consequences of particular political acts, he treated moral acts like any other kind, from a strictly instrumental point of view. The social and political consequences of acts always interested him more than the moral intent of the actors, and he argued that in human affairs the consequences of acts are bound to be both good and evil. Basically, he was not concerned with the problems of moral philosophy, and he accepted the fact that a life of action is necessarily one of moral dilemma and paradox. Perhaps Machiavelli's one important moral insight, never explicitly articulated, is that the very conditions of personal morality are dependent upon the security afforded by the immorality of the state.

This does not mean that Machiavelli condoned violations of personal morality or that he was himself immoral. He did distinguish between moral and immoral acts in the conventional sense. He never suggested that some people are innately superior to others, thereby having a right to dominate and enslave. He was usually careful to affirm that the common good upon occasion excuses rather than justifies immoral means. Violation of the standards of personal morality is excusable only when necessary for the public utility. Statesmen must know how to act iniquitously for the sake of the common good; but violence, cruelty, and deception should never become ends in themselves, and they should always be rationally controlled.

While Machiavelli himself was not above moral reproach, he was born and died a Christian and was neither depraved nor unprincipled. His attacks on the church were anticlerical rather than antireligious, being directed against the scandalous lives of the popes and their political activities. He did compare contemporary Christianity unfavorably with the paganism of the ancients, but he criticized Christianity primarily because it had become the means to socially undesirable ends—the subjection of the many to an avaricious minority— and called for a return to some kind of original creed. While he dwelt upon the socially pragmatic value of religion he did not view it from this standpoint alone.

The highest end to be pursued by man, according

to Machiavelli, is glory. Glory is conferred by acts that are remembered and cherished by mankind. The brief but glorious life of an individual or commonwealth is worth far more to Machiavelli than a lengthy mediocre existence. Mere success or reputation arising from great power or wealth has far less value than true glory. The greatest glory is to be won (in order of decreasing importance) by founding religions, by establishing commonwealths, by commanding armies, and by creating literature.

True glory depends upon the *virtù* of an individual or a people. Machiavelli's term is ambiguous, but what he seems most often to have had in mind is the pattern of conduct of the soldier in battle who displays foresight, self-discipline, constancy, determination, purposefulness, decisiveness, bravery, boldness, and vigor. War is only the archetypal struggle between *virtù* (the manly) and *fortuna* (the changeable, unpredictable, and capricious), for in fact all of life is such a contest. Rational control over the physical and social environments, so essential for human survival and well-being, depends upon the opposition of *virtù* to *fortuna*. By virtuous action men can control at least some part of their lives and limit the whims of chance.

Machiavelli again studied history to discover the conditions that produced the greatest possible amount of *virtù* in a commonwealth and the consequent achievement of glory. He decided that the most virtuous leaders and peoples were those of classical antiquity, particularly of republican Rome. The *virtù* of a people, he believed, depends entirely on education, while that of a prince or leader tends to be inborn but shaped by education. A republicanism in which liberty flourishes, defended by a citizens' army, is the atmosphere most conducive to the exercise of *virtù;* under these conditions political power will be the greatest and most durable, and the political order will be the most stable. The basic elements in Machiavelli's conception of political success, then, are glory, *virtù*, and liberty. Machiavelli lamented the decline of *virtù* in his own age; he condemned its luxurious, commercial life and directed his efforts to the problem of restoring the conditions of glory.

Conflict and corruption. Conflict is a vital concept in Machiavelli's political thought. He accepted conflict as a universal and permanent condition of society, stemming from human nature. The traditional classical and medieval view had been that social conflict is not a natural condition, and many classical and medieval thinkers had tried to design a type of social organization that would eliminate contention. The conception of social conflict as unnatural ran parallel to the Aristotelian concept that matter at rest is more natural than matter in motion. Machiavelli abandoned the former of these ancient modes of thought with his notion of the naturalness of social conflict, although the latter was not discarded until the next century with Galileo's revolutionary insight that the natural state of matter is motion.

The basic manifestation of social conflict, according to Machiavelli, is the perennial struggle between the common people and the great and powerful. While this is clearly a notion of class struggle involving economic factors, Machiavelli's explanation of the struggle is not couched in economic terms. The primary cause of domestic strife and of war between states is, as he saw it, a lust for power and domination. Within any state, the overwhelming majority seek security for their persons and possessions, while a handful, either a hereditary aristocracy or a commercial oligarchy, desire to dominate the masses.

Inspired by Polybius, Machiavelli believed that such conflict is not only natural but that it may be turned to socially useful ends. Virtuous commonwealths exhibit this kind of conflict no less than do corrupt ones. The difference lies not in the presence of conflict in the one and the absence in the other, or even in the degree of conflict, but in the quality of conflict in each.

Conflict in a virtuous commonwealth takes place within certain bounds: it is limited by a patriotic dedication to the common good that supersedes narrow self-interest, by a willingness to respect law and authority, and by an aversion to the use of violence and nonlegal activity. Republican Rome, Machiavelli's ideal of the virtuous commonwealth as described in the *Discourses*, exemplified this kind of limited conflict in that the struggle between patricians and plebeians was institutionalized through the Senate and the popular assemblies with their tribunes. The very strength and unity of the republic together with the citizens' liberties depended upon the continued contest.

By contrast, Florence, as analyzed in the *History of Florence*, is Machiavelli's prototype of the corrupt state. In such a state, society becomes atomized; each man is for himself. Religious sentiment declines, and with it civic honesty, the spirit of civic duty, and respect for authority. Factionalism and conspiracy are rife, and government is the successive captive of the most powerful cliques. *Virtù* decays; avarice proliferates; indolence, luxury, and economic inequalities rend the social fabric. Corruption is likely to develop in an overly successful society that knows peace and prosperity for a lengthy period. With the lack of challenge to survive, with well-being and leisure, men turn to private advantage; laws are no longer vigorously observed and enforced or adjusted to compensate for new conditions. Prevention of corruption requires a return to first principles, a periodic renovation of the civic order. Even the greatest vigilance and most prudent statesmanship, however, will not stem the tide of decay forever. Change is the way of all things, and the best-ordered commonwealths —for example, Rome and Sparta—are bound to decline.

Government and politics. The most important contrivance at man's command for containing and canalizing man's egoistic nature toward socially desirable ends is, according to Machiavelli, the state. By means of the state man can create the conditions for security and well-being.

Although Machiavelli frequently used medical imagery to describe the state, his conception of it actually resembles a mechanism more than an organism. The state has no higher end or spiritual purpose, nor does it have a life or personality apart from the people who constitute it. What has come to be called "reason of state," an expression Machiavelli himself never employed, is the calculated and prudent policy of statesmen to advance the secular aims of the governed, not a superrationality.

In *The Prince* and the *Discourses* Machiavelli presented a twofold classification of states based on the number who rule—the polar types being monarchies and republics. Monarchies may be limited (France), despotic (Turkey), or tyrannical (Syracuse); republics may be mass (Athens) or balanced (Rome). Of the balanced republics, in turn, two principal types exist—aristocratic (Venice) and democratic (Rome). On the basis of the Florentine experience Machiavelli distinguished two unstable forms intermediate between monarchies and republics, which might best be called oligarchy and plebiscitary monarchy. Machiavelli also classified states in other respects: according to the way power is acquired; according to their tendencies to expansion (Rome) or preservation (Sparta), to corruption (Florence) or *virtù* (Roman Republic); and according to whether the constitution originates with a single lawgiver (Sparta) or develops over time and with experience (Rome).

Machiavelli had, of course, elaborate prescriptions for successful government. Good government rests upon the foundation of a strong military establishment for protection against the external enemy. The life, property, family, and honor of each citizen must be safeguarded against interference from other citizens. General economic prosperity should be encouraged, individual economic aggrandizement prevented, and luxury strictly regulated. Adequate recognition must be given to the meritorious among the citizens, and advancement in the service of the state should be open to those who seek honor and glory. The best government draws upon and utilizes the skills of the governed, and the best state is one in which rank corresponds to ability.

These ends can be realized most fully in a republic patterned after the Roman one, which had a mixed constitution and such institutions as dictatorship in times of emergency, censorship, public accusations, popular assemblies, sumptuary laws, and a citizens' army. Republics, however, cannot be established everywhere; the form of the state should be suited to the conditions of a particular society. Moreover, the successful founding of any commonwealth depends on the presence of a single individual of the greatest *virtù* and prudence.

Any well-ordered state is, according to Machiavelli, a rational organization in which citizens know with a high degree of certainty the legal consequences of their actions, i.e., what they can and cannot do with impunity. Hence, central to Machiavelli's proposals for successful government is a rational system of law that will eliminate arbitrary rule by guaranteeing legal equality, by providing regularized procedures for the redress of grievances, by prohibiting retroactive laws, and by executing all laws vigorously and efficiently. Civil law should establish a state religion for the inculcation and maintenance of civic virtue. Law should also institute a citizens' army that will have a genuine stake in the common good and that will serve as a prime means of civic education, instilling citizens with a respect for authority, patriotism, and martial virtues.

Machiavelli's description of the model army in *The Art of War* gives a clearer picture of his concept of a rational society than does the *Discourses*. Since he viewed domestic politics as a kind of warfare and dealt with political matters as a general might deal with the problem of defeating an enemy, it is not surprising that he wrote about politics as classical military theorists wrote about war. Military stratagems are translated into political maxims of the same calculating objectivity, and a rationally organized and commanded army serves as a model of a rational social organization.

Most political situations, Machiavelli believed, are conspiratorial or counterconspiratorial, and conspiracy is primarily of a military character. The political art is akin to the military art with its premium upon secrecy, planning and preparedness, estimation of factors, flexibility, rapidity and decisiveness of execution, surprise, and deception.

These qualities characterize the conspiratorial methods necessary for founding or radically reforming a state and the counterconspiratorial methods required for maintaining a state (since conspiracy must be prevented by avoiding the hatred and contempt of the governed). Prior to Machiavelli, only military theorists had dealt in detail with the problems of conspiracy; in the *Discourses* (see III, vi), he formulated the West's first general theory of political conspiracy.

Not only did Machiavelli liken political situations to military ones and the art of politics to the military art, but he also considered political and military leadership to be similar. Political leadership resembles the creative activity of the general who organizes, disciplines, trains, and leads an army to victory. That *virtù* is the cardinal quality of political leadership as well as of successful generalship is significant. The political virtuoso is rational, calculating, and eminently self-controlled, plays many roles with aplomb, and is prudent enough to identify his own interest with the well-being of those he seeks to manage. Machiavelli's heroes are the ancient founders and the soldier-statesmen of the Roman Republic. He particularly admired the moderate, liberal-minded, and humane military genius Scipio Africanus Major.

Good internal government and successful foreign policy are carried on essentially in the same way. A state's foreign policy is advanced either by diplomacy or war. The familiar roster of necessary qualities is attached to skillful diplomacy—foresight, initiative, decisiveness, flexibility, and deception. Negotiation is the technique of the ambassador, who must be ready to persuade, temporize, or intimidate, as occasion demands. If negotiation fails, war may well be unavoidable. Careful military preparations must be made in peacetime because sooner or later war is inevitable, given man's nature. Machiavelli preferred a war with limited objectives and gains to total war.

Significance and influence. Although few would deny Machiavelli a foremost place among Western political thinkers, his reputation, all too often based on *The Prince* alone, has long rested on his description of the stratagems by which political power can be seized and conserved without regard for moral ends. Consequently, for centuries he has been vilified as devil's disciple and despots' tutor. More favorable appraisals have appeared in recent years: he is being discovered as the first political scientist, the first modern political theorist, or the first liberal. But these positive labels again contain only half-truths. One does find in Machiavelli's

thought harbingers of science, modernity, and liberalism. Yet it must not be forgotten that he had one foot firmly planted in the classical world, and this classical aspect of his work has had a considerable influence. The seventeenth-century English classical republicans—Harrington, Neville, and Sidney—found in Machiavelli theories of limited republican government and of a citizens' militia, and bequeathed them to the American constitutional fathers. Montesquieu came upon the Machiavelli of the *Discourses* in England, and his imprint is seen throughout the *Considérations sur les causes de la grandeur des Romains et de leur décadence* and also in *L'esprit des lois*, which in turn fired the radical Rousseau, the conservative Burke, and the liberal Tocqueville. Bodin, Hobbes, Spinoza, and Hegel all recognized Machiavelli's genius.

Machiavelli has also been vitally important as a military thinker. Because of his revival in *The Art of War* of the classical stress upon military training, discipline, and organization, he is unquestionably the father of modern military science, who directly or indirectly influenced practitioners and theorists from Maurice of Nassau to Clausewitz.

Today, Machiavelli is of importance as a forerunner of the rationalism of the Enlightenment. Notwithstanding his pessimism about human nature and cynicism about human behavior, he was not without hope. He never lost his vision of a good society and his faith that men could in part shape their destinies. Relevant to the social scientific concerns of our own time are his views on the integrative function of conflict, the instrumental value of law and ideology in shaping society, the role of conspiracy, and the political craft in general. A careful study of his military image of politics may help us to perceive more readily the inadequacy of our own comparable image of the political.

NEAL WOOD

[*See also* LEADERSHIP; POWER; SOCIAL CONTRACT; STATE; *and the biographies of* BODIN; CLAUSEWITZ; HARRINGTON; HEGEL; HOBBES; KAUṬILYA; MONTESQUIEU; ROUSSEAU; SHANG YANG; SPINOZA.]

WORKS BY MACHIAVELLI

(1504–1549) 1965 *Chief Works and Others.* 3 vols. Durham, N.C.: Duke Univ. Press.

(1506–1549) 1963 *Lust and Liberty: The Poems of Machiavelli.* With notes and introduction by Joseph Tusani. New York: Obolensky.

(1509–1527) 1961 *Literary Works: Mandragola; Clizia; A Dialogue on Language; Belfagor; With Selections From the Private Correspondence.* Edited and translated by J. R. Hale. Oxford Univ. Press.

(1521) 1965 *The Art of War.* Edited with an introduction by Neal Wood. Indianapolis: Bobbs-Merrill.

(1532*a*) 1950   *The Prince* and *The Discourses*. With an introduction by Max Lerner. New York: Modern Library.

(1532*b*) 1960   *History of Florence and of the Affairs of Italy, From the Earliest Times to the Death of Lorenzo the Magnificent.* With an introduction by Felix Gilbert. New York: Harper.

(1532*c*) 1950   *Discourses.* With an introduction and notes by Leslie J. Walker. 2 vols. New Haven: Yale Univ. Press.

The Historical, Political, and Diplomatic Writings. 4 vols. Boston: Osgood, 1882.

SUPPLEMENTARY BIBLIOGRAPHY

BARON, HANS   1955   *The Crisis of the Early Italian Renaissance: Civic Humanism and Republican Liberty in an Age of Classicism and Tyranny.* 2 vols. Princeton Univ. Press.

BAYLEY, CHARLES C.   1961   *War and Society in Renaissance Florence: The* De militia *of Leonardo Bruni.* Univ. of Toronto Press.

CASSIRER, ERNST   (1927) 1964   *The Individual and the Cosmos in Renaissance Philosophy.* Translated and with an introduction by Mario Domandi. New York: Barnes & Noble. → First published as *Individuum und Kosmos in der Philosophie der Renaissance.*

CHABOD, FEDERICO   (1924–1955) 1958   *Machiavelli and the Renaissance: Essays.* London: Bowes & Bowes. → First published in Italian.

GILBERT, ALLAN H.   1938   *Machiavelli's Prince and Its Forerunners: The Prince as a Typical Book de Regime Principum.* Durham, N.C.: Duke Univ. Press.

GILBERT, FELIX   1965   *Machiavelli and Guicciardini: Politics and History in Sixteenth-century Florence.* Princeton Univ. Press.

HEXTER, J. H.   1964   The Loom of Language and the Fabric of Imperatives: The Case of *Il principe* and *Utopia. American Historical Review* 69:945–968. → See especially Hexter's discussion of the concept of "lo stato" in Machiavelli's work.

MEINECKE, FRIEDRICH   (1924) 1962   *Machiavellism: The Doctrine of Raison d'État and Its Place in Modern History.* New York: Praeger. → First published as *Die Idee der Staatsräson in der neueren Geschichte.*

POST, GAINES   1964   *Studies in Medieval Legal Thought: Public Law and the State, 1100–1322.* Princeton Univ. Press.

RAAB, FELIX   1964   *The English Face of Machiavelli: A Changing Interpretation. 1500–1700.* With a foreword by Hugh Trevor-Roper. London: Routledge.

RIDOLFI, ROBERTO   (1954) 1963   *The Life of Niccolò Machiavelli.* Univ. of Chicago Press. → First published in Italian.

STRAUSS, LEO   1959   *Thoughts on Machiavelli.* Glencoe, Ill.: Free Press.

VILLARI, PASQUALE   (1877–1882) 1892   *The Life and Times of Niccolò Machiavelli.* 2 vols. New ed., rev. & enl. London: Unwin. → First published in Italian.

WHITFIELD, JOHN H.   1947   *Machiavelli.* Oxford: Blackwell.

MACHINE TABULATION
See COMPUTATION.

MACHINES, POLITICAL
See POLITICAL MACHINES.

McILWAIN, CHARLES H.

Charles Howard McIlwain, political scientist and historian, was born in Saltsburg, Pennsylvania, in 1871. He received a B.A. degree from Princeton in 1894. Three years later he was admitted to the Pennsylvania bar, but shortly thereafter he accepted a post as teacher of Latin and history in a private school. His knowledge and interest in the fields of Latin, history, and law, which later found expression in his writings on English constitutional development and ancient and medieval political thought, were sharpened and refined during his study for the doctorate at Harvard from 1901 to 1903. In 1911 McIlwain was appointed assistant professor of history and government at Harvard and was promoted to a full professorship only five years later, which was quite extraordinary at the time. In 1927 he was named Eaton professor of the science of government, and he held this chair until his retirement in 1946. During an active teaching career which spanned almost half a century, he lectured at numerous universities, including Oxford. In 1936 he was elected president of the American Historical Association.

McIlwain was profoundly disturbed by the divorce of political science and history. The disciplines were brought together, especially at Harvard, through the force and originality of McIlwain's scholarship. The dominance of political theory, and its historical orientation, in the Harvard department of government is in large measure a legacy from McIlwain. His influence was strongly felt by scholars of his own day—Edward Corwin and George Sabine, to name but two—and the work of more recent theorists, such as Louis Hartz and Leonard Levy, reflects the continuing impact of McIlwain's approach to the study of political thought.

Historical roots of judicial activism.   Avoiding the pitfall of reading the present into the past, McIlwain justly prided himself on his ability to interpret medieval writers such as Henry de Bracton and John Fortescue in terms of their own thinking and experience. His insight into juristic thought in England during the Middle Ages greatly contributed not only to a general understanding of the period but also to a clarification of political concepts such as constitutionalism and sovereignty. The unique and phenomenal discretionary power enjoyed by the American judiciary cannot be explained in the absence of an understanding of its historical roots in English jurisprudence. Addressing himself to this problem, McIlwain argued in *The High Court of Parliament* (1910) that medieval English courts exercised similar powers. He hammered home the point that medieval judicial activism was due to a *fusion*, not a *division*, of governmental powers. It is therefore a misconception to regard the High Court of Parliament as a court of justice which, in addition to its judicial function, exercised legislative powers. The distinction between legislation and adjudication was simply not recognized, thereby allowing the lower courts, as well as Parliament, to exercise both types of powers.

The fusion of powers in governmental institutions spawned not only judicial activism but also what might well be considered its natural outgrowth, judicial review. It is only within the context of McIlwain's interpretation of the character of governmental powers in seventeenth-century England that Sir Edward Coke's famous statement that "in many cases the common law will controul acts of Parliament" ([1610] 1826, p. 375) is reconcilable with his earlier declarations that Parliament's power is absolute (in [1644] 1817, pp. 28–36). The apparent paradox vanishes when one realizes that Coke was not invoking judicial authority against legislative sovereignty, but holding that common law, as higher law, is binding upon the ordinary courts and the High Court of Parliament alike.

Constitutionalism. The crux of McIlwain's concern was the true meaning of constitutionalism. Throughout his writings he championed the principles of medieval constitutionalism, perhaps most effectively in a thin volume which has become a classic, *Constitutionalism: Ancient and Modern* (1940). He defined constitutional government as government limited by law. It embodies the basic distinction, so clearly drawn by Bracton, between *gubernaculum* and *jurisdictio*, between discretion and law. The same concept was echoed by Coke in his famous Case of Proclamations. "It is a grand prerogative of the King," Coke declared, "to make proclamation . . . [yet] the King hath no prerogative but that which the law of the land allows him" ([1656] 1826, p. 299). In a word, within the bounds of higher law, the king is supreme. Bodin, too, developed views of sovereignty that recognized both the absolute power of the sovereign to make ordinary laws and the limitation of the sovereign by fundamental law; McIlwain therefore regarded Bodin as a constitutionalist [see BODIN].

Against this concept, McIlwain critically posed the more modern view of constitutionalism, that is, that constitutional government must be founded upon a division of powers which effectively restrains governmental action. This view—which is,

in McIlwain's opinion, historically unsound—obscures the distinction between control and limitation. Constitutional government must be strengthened to survive in the modern world, not enfeebled by checks and balances which dissipate its powers and render it ineffectual. While McIlwain believed that responsible and effective constitutional government necessitates the removal of balances, he emphasized that the limits beyond which no government can legally go must be strengthened. In a vein strikingly similar to the legal absolutists' position in the United States today, McIlwain declared, "I frankly want to rely on the earlier, the sounder, yes the medieval principle, that there are some individual rights that even a people's government can never touch" (1917–1937, p. 263). He placed complete reliance upon the judiciary to hold the line.

Viewed from a functional approach, McIlwain's juristic concept of constitutionalism is subject to major criticism. Intent upon demonstrating that the medieval *idea* of supreme, limited government embodied the true principle of constitutionalism, McIlwain was little concerned with the problem of the power relations necessary *actually* to limit government. Clearly, a balance of power within government may hamper governmental responsibility and effectiveness; however, it appears to be equally true that government cannot be effectively limited if it does not reflect a division of power among groups and classes within the community. Indeed, during the Middle Ages constitutionalism was actually operative only in those periods when the king was restrained by the power of the ecclesiastical authorities and the feudal landowners.

Convinced of the merits of the medieval distinction between control and limitation of government, McIlwain was naturally critical of the doctrine of separation of powers and the doctrine of checks and balances, both of which clearly violate this distinction. His argument would have been on firmer ground if he had not ignored the important question of whether government can be effectively limited in the absence of institutionalized controls.

PETER BACHRACH

[For the historical context of McIlwain's work, see CONSTITUTIONS AND CONSTITUTIONALISM; and the biography of COKE.]

WORKS BY MC ILWAIN

1910   *The High Court of Parliament and Its Supremacy: An Historical Essay on the Boundaries Between Legislation and Adjudication in England.* New Haven: Yale Univ. Press.
(1917–1937) 1939   *Constitutionalism and the Changing World: Collected Papers.* Cambridge Univ. Press.

1918 Introduction. In James I, King of England, *The Political Works of James I.* Cambridge, Mass.: Harvard Univ. Press.

1923 *The American Revolution: A Constitutional Interpretation.* New York: Macmillan. → A paperback edition was published in 1958 by Cornell University Press.

(1932) 1959 *The Growth of Political Thought in the West, From the Greeks to the End of the Middle Ages.* New York: Macmillan.

(1940) 1947 *Constitutionalism: Ancient and Modern.* Rev. ed. Ithaca, N.Y.: Cornell Univ. Press. → A paperback edition was published in 1958.

SUPPLEMENTARY BIBLIOGRAPHY

COKE, EDWARD (1610) 1826 Dr. Bonham's Case. Volume 4, part 8, pages 355–383 in Great Britain, Courts, *The Reports of Sir Edward Coke.* London: Butterworth.

COKE, EDWARD (1644) 1817 *The Fourth Part of the Institutes of the Laws of England Concerning the Jurisdiction of the Courts.* . . . London: Clarke. → Published posthumously.

COKE, EDWARD (1656) 1826 Proclamations. Volume 6, part 12, pages 297–299 in Great Britain, Courts, *The Reports of Sir Edward Coke.* London: Butterworth. → Published posthumously.

MacIVER, ROBERT M.

Sociologist, political theorist, philosopher, university administrator, and humanist, Robert Morrison MacIver was born in Stornoway, Scotland, in 1882. He will be remembered in the history of Western thought for having set forth systematically the fundamental moral, sociological, and philosophical principles of democratic institutions and processes.

Although he sought answers to the perennial theoretical problems of social, political, and moral philosophy that seem to defy ultimate solution, MacIver did not eschew concern for the mitigation of immediate social problems. He attempted to demonstrate by precept that sociological insights can be practicably applied to such pressing problems as labor relations, economic reconstruction, internationalism and peace, intergroup conflicts, religion, academic freedom, social work, juvenile delinquency, and effective utilization of manpower resources. He was vice-chairman of the Canadian War Labor Board in World War I and director of the City of New York Juvenile Delinquency Evaluation Project from 1956 to 1961, and he contributed effectively to the leadership of the Social Science Research Council, the Russell Sage Foundation, and the National Manpower Council.

MacIver's very important contribution to political theory is his view of the state as an agency of human purpose. The state, he argued, is an association established by the community for the regulation of the external conditions of the social order. It is thus an instrumentality within a more inclusive unity. Its essential tasks are to establish order and to respect personality, but it is a creature of society and is bound by the value systems that men live by and for. MacIver revealed the intimate relations between political structures and processes, on the one hand, and human values, on the other.

MacIver's contributions to sociology may be viewed as fourfold. First, he systematically developed and fruitfully exploited an impressive network of fundamental sociological concepts. Second, he helped stem the tide of excessive positivism and raw empiricism in American sociology, especially through his insistence on theory as a methodological tool. The progress of science, he suggested, is the progress of thought. Every scholar should be at the same time a specialist in his own field and a thinker about a larger one (1960, p. 30). Third, he reaffirmed the view of man as a creative human being with subjective hopes, feelings, aspirations, motives, ideals, and values. Life, he insisted, is expansively creative. Finally, he demonstrated that sociological writing can be clear, artistic, and literate. To an area of confusion and literary and intellectual chaos, MacIver brought both clarity of thought and felicity of expression.

Especially important in MacIver's sociological system are his classification of social interests, the distinction between community and association, the concept of social evolution, the harmony theory of the relation between society and individuality, and the differentiation between the institutions concerned with means (civilization) and the world of ends (culture).

The classification of social interests, particularly the distinction between like and common interests, has proved of immense value in clarifying the nature of interindividual relationships, the bases of group organization, and the nature of the social bond. The distinction between community as the matrix of social organization and associations as specific organizations which grow and develop within that matrix is the keystone of MacIver's political doctrines. To sociologists the distinction has proved significant in permitting a more precise definition of the problem of social solidarity and in providing a framework for a deeper understanding of the nature of a pluralistic or multigroup society.

MacIver's reaffirmation of the validity of the concept of social evolution, in the face of the bitter attacks upon it by anthropologists such as Goldenweiser, anticipated by many years the resurgence of interest in and the defense of the concept by Julian Steward and other American anthropologists, as well as by sociologists such as Talcott Parsons (1964), Robert Bellah (1964), S. N. Eisenstadt (1964). Numerous insights have stemmed from MacIver's tracing of a pattern of social change from the primitive type of functionally undifferentiated society, wherein life is of a communal nature, to the more evolved, functionally diverse, and institutionally and associationally differentiated social entity, wherein the basis of individual relationships is less communal and more associational and wherein personality becomes more developed and more expansive.

Important, too, is MacIver's resolution of the timeworn controversy of the relationship between the individual and society. Rejecting both social contract theories and organismic theories, he stressed the fundamental harmony between individuality and society, recognizing, at the same time, that this harmony is far from perfect. Sociality and individuality, he asserted in one of his most successful formulations, develop *pari passu*.

Also significant is the distinction between the world of means (civilization) and the world of ends (culture). The terms are unfortunate because of the more traditional connotations of "civilization" and "culture," but the emphasis on the difference between means and ends provides numerous analytical insights into the processes of social change and a better understanding of the functions of various social institutions. It indicates the areas of social life to which one may properly apply the concept of progress.

MacIver was an inspiring teacher. He had an impact on students at Aberdeen University, the University of Toronto, Barnard College, and Columbia University. At Columbia he held for more than twenty years the chair of Lieber professor of political philosophy and sociology. He served as president of the New School for Social Research in 1963/1964. He received advanced degrees from the universities of Edinburgh and Oxford and numerous honorary degrees.

In his Kurt Lewin memorial award address of 1961, MacIver stated: "In every area of scientific research we have often to depend on degrees of probability, on approximations, on indirect approaches, and such procedures can yield results of considerable importance. There are many ranges between certitude and ignorance, and nearly all we know about human beings and human activities lie within these ranges" (1962a, pp. 89–90). He has not been afraid to face "the paradox of knowledge," namely, that "the only things we know as im-

mutable truths are the things we do not understand," while "the only things we understand are mutable and never fully known" (1938, p. 124).

HARRY ALPERT

[*See also* ACADEMIC FREEDOM; CAUSATION; NEIGHBORHOOD; PREJUDICE, *article on* SOCIAL DISCRIMINATION; PUBLIC INTEREST; STATE.]

WORKS BY MAC IVER

(1917) 1935 *Community: A Sociological Study; Being an Attempt to Set Out the Nature and Fundamental Laws of Social Life.* 3d ed. London: Macmillan.

1919 *Labor in the Changing World.* New York: Dutton.

(1921) 1956 *The Elements of Social Science.* 9th ed., rev. London: Methuen.

(1926) 1955 *The Modern State.* Oxford Univ. Press.

1930a Jean Bodin. Volume 2, pages 614–616 in *Encyclopaedia of the Social Sciences.* New York: Macmillan.

1930b The Trend to Internationalism. Volume 1, pages 172–188 in *Encyclopaedia of the Social Sciences.* New York: Macmillan.

1931a *The Contribution of Sociology to Social Work.* New York: Columbia Univ. Press.

1931b *Society: Its Structure and Changes.* New York: Long & Smith.

1932 Interests. Volume 8, pages 144–148 in *Encyclopaedia of the Social Sciences.* New York: Macmillan.

1933 Maladjustment. Volume 10, pages 60–63 in *Encyclopaedia of the Social Sciences.* New York: Macmillan.

1934a Social Pressures. Volume 12, pages 344–348 in *Encyclopaedia of the Social Sciences.* New York: Macmillan.

1934b Sociology. Volume 14, pages 232–246 in *Encyclopaedia of the Social Sciences.* New York: Macmillan.

1935 Graham Wallas. Volume 15, pages 326–327 in *Encyclopaedia of the Social Sciences.* New York: Macmillan.

1937 *Society: A Textbook of Sociology.* New York: Farrar & Rinehart. → A rewriting of MacIver 1931b.

1938 The Social Sciences. Pages 121–140 in *On Going to College: A Symposium.* New York: Oxford Univ. Press.

1939 *Leviathan and the People.* University: Louisiana State Univ. Press.

1942 *Social Causation.* Boston: Ginn. → A paperback edition was published in 1964 by Harper.

(1947) 1961 *The Web of Government.* New York: Macmillan.

1948 *The More Perfect Union: A Program for the Control of Inter-group Discrimination in the United States.* New York: Macmillan.

(1949) 1961 MacIVER, ROBERT M.; and PAGE, CHARLES H. *Society: An Introductory Analysis.* New York: Holt. → Book 3 (Chapters 22–29) is an unusually extensive treatment of social change in a general textbook.

1952 *Democracy and the Economic Challenge.* New York: Knopf.

1955a *Academic Freedom in Our Time.* New York: Columbia Univ. Press.

1955b *The Pursuit of Happiness: A Philosophy for Modern Living.* New York: Simon & Schuster.

1960 *Life: Its Dimensions and Its Bounds.* New York: Harper.

1962a *Disturbed Youth and the Agencies. Journal of Social Issues* 18, no. 2:88–96.

1962*b* *The Challenge of the Passing Years: My Encounter With Time.* New York: Simon & Schuster. → A paperback edition was published in 1963 by Pocket Books.

1964 *Power Transformed.* New York: Macmillan.

1966 *The Prevention and Control of Delinquency: A Strategic Approach.* New York: Atherton.

SUPPLEMENTARY BIBLIOGRAPHY

ALPERT, HARRY (editor) 1953 *Robert M. MacIver: Teacher and Sociologist.* Northampton, Mass.: Metcalf Printing and Publishing Company. → An evaluation by eight former students.

ALPERT, HARRY (1954) 1964 Robert M. MacIver's Contributions to Sociological Theory. Pages 286–292 in Morroe Berger, T. Abel, and C. H. Page (editors), *Freedom and Control in Modern Society.* New York: Octagon Books.

BELLAH, ROBERT N. 1964 Religious Evolution. *American Sociological Review* 29:358–374.

COLUMBIA UNIVERSITY, COMMISSION ON ECONOMIC RECONSTRUCTION 1934 *Economic Reconstruction: Report.* Robert M. MacIver, Chairman. New York: Columbia Univ. Press.

EISENSTADT, S. N. 1964 Social Change, Differentiation and Evolution. *American Sociological Review* 29:375–386.

PARSONS, TALCOTT 1964 Evolutionary Universals in Society. *American Sociological Review* 29:339–357.

SPITZ, DAVID (1954) 1964 Robert M. MacIver's Contributions to Political Theory. Pages 293–313 in Morroe Berger, T. Abel, and C. H. Page (editors), *Freedom and Control in Modern Society.* New York: Octagon Books.

MACKINDER, HALFORD

Sir Halford John Mackinder (1861–1947) was both an academic geographer and a practicing politician. After reading physical science and modern history at Oxford, he served that university's pioneer extension scheme for adult education. He was deeply convinced of the value of this missionary effort to spread knowledge more widely in England. He lectured up and down the country between 1885 and 1893 on what he called "the new geography." He was a natural orator, and he preached his geographical gospel with zeal and fervor.

At that time the subject of geography did not occupy a high place in British or American education; it had little or no prestige in the universities. The fame of Mackinder's Oxford extension lectures reached the Royal Geographical Society of London. In January 1887 he was invited to lecture to the society on the scope and methods of geography. In the discussion after the lecture he defined geography as "the science of distribution, the science, that is, which traces the arrangement of things in general on the earth's surface" (1887, p. 160) and urged that physical and political geography be combined. An examination of the lecture shows that many notions that are now commonplace in geographical teaching were first enunciated by Mackinder.

Mackinder had a special mission for geography that still has considerable importance: in the 1887 lecture he said that "one of the greatest of all gaps lies between the natural sciences and the study of humanity. It is the duty of the geographer to build one bridge over an abyss which in the opinion of many is upsetting the equilibrium of our culture" (p. 145). In the same year that he gave this lecture Mackinder was appointed to a readership in geography at Oxford; he claimed that he was the first Oxford reader in geography since Hakluyt, the Elizabethan. As a result of Mackinder's efforts, the school of geography was established at Oxford in 1899; this was the first British university department of geography.

The idea of the region was an implicit part of Mackinder's argument for geography as an academic discipline. At Oxford one of his regular annual courses was always concerned with the analysis of a particular region. His *Britain and the British Seas* (1902) is one of the few classics of modern geographical literature. This book was the first of a series planned by Mackinder to present "a picture of the physical features and condition of a great natural region, and to trace their influence upon human societies" (1902, p. 7). By their efforts at Oxford both Mackinder and his successor, A. J. Herbertson, placed the study of regions in the forefront of geographical work. Mackinder also taught that geography is a unity which should not be split into fragments. These ideas about the unity of geography as a subject and the necessity for basing it on integrated studies of regions are the foundations upon which modern British academic geography has been built.

In January 1904 Mackinder read a paper entitled "The Geographical Pivot of History" to the Royal Geographical Society. He was then still teaching at Oxford but had just been elected director of the London School of Economics. Mackinder described a central part of Eurasia as "the pivot area," a term he later changed to "heartland." In his lecture he laid down two principles. The first was that since the modern improvement of steam navigation, the world had become one and, in so doing, had also become one closed political system. The second and main point of his argument concerned the importance to the world of the modern expansion of Russia. He asserted that "the pivot region of the world's politics" is

"that area of Euro-Asia which is inaccessible to ships," and is controlled by Russia (1904, p. 434). If the world is regarded as a unit, he argued, combinations of power "are likely to rotate round the pivot state, which is always likely to be great, but with limited mobility as compared with the surrounding marginal and insular powers" (pp. 436–437). In the discussion after the lecture Mackinder bluntly asserted that the development for the first time in recorded history of a great stationary population in the steppes constituted a revolution in the world (p. 442). In 1919 Mackinder expanded his paper into a book, *Democratic Ideals and Reality*, which was described by J. Russell Smith as "a tract addressed to the Peace Conference at Versailles" (1945, p. 148). It contains the famous warning: "When our Statesmen [at Versailles] are in conversation with the defeated enemy, some airy cherub should whisper to them from time to time saying: "Who rules East Europe commands the Heartland: Who rules the Heartland commands the World-Island: Who rules the World-Island commands the World" ([1919] 1942, p. 150).

Between the two world wars Mackinder's theory of the heartland received little attention in the English-speaking world; but it was closely examined in Germany, where it became a basic idea among the students of geopolitics (*Zeitschrift für Geopolitik, passim*). General Karl Haushofer (1937) described Mackinder's 1904 paper as the greatest of all geographical world views. During World War II, Mackinder's idea of the heartland received considerable attention in both Britain and America. In 1943 Mackinder, then 82 years of age, restated his heartland theory, with modifications, in an article in *Foreign Affairs*. He believed that his concept of the heartland was even more valid than it had been forty years earlier, and he boldly asserted that ". . . if the Soviet Union emerges from this war as conqueror of Germany, she must rank as the greatest land Power on the Globe. Moreover, she will be the Power in the strategically strongest defensive position. The Heartland is the greatest natural fortress on earth. For the first time in history it is manned by a garrison sufficient both in number and quality" (1943, p. 601).

Mackinder's writings on land power can be compared with those of Mahan on the influence of sea power [*see the biography of* MAHAN]. It has been suggested that modern air power destroyed the validity of the arguments of both Mahan and Mackinder. But Mackinder in 1919, and again in 1943, used the coming of air power to support his older thesis. He also stated his conviction that the conquest of the air gave the world's unity a new significance for all mankind. W. Gordon East, in a reasoned commentary of Mackinder's theories in the light of more recent events, similarly insisted that Mackinder's "geopolitical thinking is still relevant to the task of winning the peace" (1950, p. 93).

Mackinder's interest in politics led him to become a practicing politician, and he was a member of Parliament from 1910 to 1922. He also served as British high commissioner for South Russia in 1919–1920. But his achievements in politics are not as memorable as his pioneer research in the field of applied geography. He created modern British geography as a university subject. He can be regarded as a founder of several of its branches, especially that of political geography, but he steadfastly believed in the unity of the subject as a whole. He wanted geography to enlighten the practical affairs of daily life. In his own words, "geography must underlie the strategy of peace if you would not have it subserve the strategy of war" (1931, p. 335).

EDMUND W. GILBERT

[*See also* GEOGRAPHY, *article on* POLITICAL GEOGRAPHY.]

WORKS BY MACKINDER

1887 On the Scope and Methods of Geography. Royal Geographical Society, *Proceedings* 9:141–174. → Includes 14 pages of discussion.

(1902) 1930 *Britain and the British Seas.* 2d ed. Oxford: Clarendon.

1904 The Geographical Pivot of History. *Geographical Journal* 23:421–444. → Includes seven pages of discussion.

(1919) 1942 *Democratic Ideals and Reality: A Study in the Politics of Reconstruction.* London: Constable; New York: Holt.

1931 The Human Habitat. *Scottish Geographical Magazine* 47:321–335.

1935 Progress of Geography in the Field and in the Study During the Reign of His Majesty King George the Fifth. *Geographical Journal* 86:1–12.

1943 The Round World and the Winning of the Peace. *Foreign Affairs* 21:595–605.

SUPPLEMENTARY BIBLIOGRAPHY

EAST, W. GORDON 1950 How Strong Is the Heartland? *Foreign Affairs* 29:78–93.

GILBERT, EDMUND W. 1951 Seven Lamps of Geography: An Appreciation of the Teaching of Sir Halford J. Mackinder. *Geography* 36:21–43. → Contains a bibliography.

GILBERT, EDMUND W. 1961 *Sir Halford Mackinder, 1861–1947: An Appreciation of His Life and Work.* London: Bell.

HAUSHOFER, KARL 1937 *Weltmeere und Weltmächte.* Berlin: Zeitgeschichte Verlag.

Smith, J. Russell 1945 Heartland, Grassland, and Farmland. Pages 148–160 in Hans W. Weigert and Vilhjalmur Stefansson (editors), *Compass of the World: A Symposium on Political Geography.* New York: Macmillan.

Unstead, J. F. 1949 H. J. Mackinder and the New Geography. *Geographical Journal* 113:47–57.

McLENNAN, JOHN FERGUSON

John Ferguson McLennan (1827–1881), Scottish lawyer and theorist of social evolution, was born in Inverness and died in Hayes Common in Kent. He was educated at King's College, Aberdeen, graduating with distinction in 1849. He went on to Cambridge, where he stayed until 1855 without taking a degree. In 1857 he was called to the Scottish bar, and in 1871 he was made parliamentary draughtsman for Scotland. In 1874 Aberdeen University conferred on him an honorary doctor of laws degree. McLennan's later life was marred by continual ill health, and much of his work was published posthumously, edited first by his brother Donald and then by W. Robertson Smith. After these two had died, the remaining manuscripts were edited by McLennan's widow, Eleanora, and a friend, Arthur Platt.

McLennan's legal studies led him to an interest in "symbols," i.e., survivals in contemporary cultures of previous legal and customary behavior. He noted, for example, that even as late as the nineteenth century Scottish law was replete with feudal concepts. Another of the striking survivals that McLennan described and elaborated upon was the custom of simulated bride capture: as it occurred in ancient Rome, he suggested, it was a symbol of the actual practice of earlier times.

His attempt to account for such survivals led to a theory of the evolution of social forms. In this context he proposed a sequence of familial development in which matrilineal kinship preceded patrilineal. He suggested this sequence independently of J. J. Bachofen, who first proposed it. He defended his theories, sometimes acrimoniously, against the views of Maine, Morgan, Lubbock, Spencer, and even of Mr. Gladstone. Because McLennan saw contemporary primitive peoples as representing various stages of arrested social development, he believed that historical reconstruction consists in noting trait survivals and discovering functional explanations for them. Thus, when customs appeared to be nonfunctional, he attempted to deduce the earlier context in which they had arisen and in which they *had* been functional. When, for example, the levirate—wherein a man inherits his brother's widow—was found to coexist with polyandry in any society, one could conclude that polyandry was a necessary precondition for the levirate. McLennan developed his entire scheme of social evolution on this principle.

McLennan is chiefly remembered for his invention of the terms *exogamy* and *endogamy*, and for his analysis of totemism. These concepts emerged from his general scheme of evolution, which ran as follows: Originally, tribes were promiscuous, children being affiliated with the social group rather than with their biological parents. Harsh conditions of existence led to female infanticide. Because of the resulting sex imbalance, and also because these early tribes were always warring, capture came to be the prevailing method of obtaining wives. The corollary of bride capture was exogamy, which obliged men to seek marriage partners outside of their own social group. Such marriages were of the archaic polyandrous type, where no regulated relationship existed among the male partners of one woman. Since paternity could not be biologically determined, kinship was traced through females only.

According to McLennan's scheme, the capture of foreign women and matrilineal kinship furthered the recognition of subtribal divisions. These new social units continued to be exogamous, while for the larger tribal group, endogamy became possible. It should be noted that McLennan never clarified the identity of the social units involved; Morgan, in rebuttal of McLennan, insisted that the subtribal units were clans. Nevertheless, McLennan's conception of this early stage of polyandry did take cognizance of what later ethnologists have called local exogamy and the rules of residence attending upon marriage.

As the archaic form of polyandry was transformed into fraternal polyandry, the levirate became common practice. Kinship could then be established through males, and the way was paved for monogamy and polygyny. The thread of functional reasoning runs through all of this deductive reconstruction, but the ethnographic information on which McLennan based his evolutionary scheme was inadequate and resulted, therefore, in incorrect deductions. Moreover, the assumption of universal stages of social evolution based on no criteria other than kinship rendered his arguments circular. It is fair to say that McLennan was not unique in his faults, which stemmed not so much from his own inadequacies as from the currently accepted mode of evolutionary analysis. His critics were guilty of the same errors.

Of his debates with these critics, the only one

that retains its significance is that with Morgan, on the meaning of kinship terms. McLennan (1876) argued—against the views of Morgan in his *Systems of Consanguinity and Affinity of the Human Family* (1871)—that kinship terms are not indicative of consanguineous relationships but express "degrees of respect" based on "age and station." This point—that the terms refer to statuses and not to blood relationships—is now accepted; but anthropologists are still divided into those who follow Morgan and attach great significance to terminology and those who, perhaps unwittingly, follow McLennan in thinking that its importance is overrated.

McLennan's ideas concerning totemism were also part of his parallelist emphasis. He saw the totemic symbols attached to kinship groups as survivals of an earlier, localized worship of fetishes, and the worship of animals, plants, and eventually, of anthropomorphic gods was seen in terms of survivals derived from totemism. Exogamy caused totemic identifications to be dispersed, because they were transmitted through the female line. According to McLennan, totems became gods—often associated with a particular locality—when patrilineal descent groups were formed. His idea of totemism as the most primitive form of religion had wide influence. It is echoed in the work of Freud and Durkheim, and it directly influenced the thinking of Frazer (1887), Jevons (1896), and Robertson Smith (1885; 1889). Robertson Smith, a close friend and collaborator, interpreted the religious and social evolution of the Semitic peoples in accordance with McLennan's theories. Tylor (1899) was one of the first of many to criticize McLennan's totemic theories of the origins of religion. He insisted that totemism is of "far greater importance in sociology than religion, connected as it is with the alliance between clans which ensues from the law of exogamy." This, together with Tylor's opinion that totemism is an expression of man's tendency to classify the universe, represents the most influential modern view (see Lévi-Strauss 1962).

J. R. Fox

[*For the historical context of McLennan's work, see* Kinship; *and the biographies of* Bachofen; Lubbock; Maine; Morgan, Lewis Henry; Spencer; Tylor. *For discussion of the subsequent development of his ideas, see the biographies of* Durkheim; Frazer; Freud; Smith, William Robertson; Westermarck.]

WORKS BY MCLENNAN

1857 Law. Volume 13, pages 253–279 in *Encyclopaedia Britannica.* 8th ed. Edinburgh: Black.

1865 *Primitive Marriage: An Inquiry Into the Origin of the Form of Capture in Marriage Ceremonies.* Edinburgh: Black.

(1865–1876) 1886 *Studies in Ancient History.* New York: Macmillan. → Includes McLennan 1865, 1866b; and 1876.

1866a Bride Catching. *Argosy* 2:31–42.

1866b Kinship in Ancient Greece. *Fortnightly Review* 4:569–588, 682–691.

1867 *Memoir of Thomas Drummond. . . .* Edinburgh: Edmonston & Douglas.

1868 Totem. Supplement, pages 753–754 in *Chamber's Encyclopedia.* London: Chambers.

1869–1870 The Worship of Animals and Plants. *Fortnightly Review* New Series 4:407–427, 562–582; 7: 194–216.

(1876) 1886 Classificatory System of Relationship. Pages 247–315 in John Ferguson McLennan, *Studies in Ancient History.* New York: Macmillan.

1877a Exogamy and Endogamy. *Fortnightly Review* New Series 21:884–895. → A rejoinder by Herbert Spencer appears on pages 895–902.

1877b The Levirate and Polyandry. *Fortnightly Review* New Series 21:694–707.

1885 *The Patriarchal Theory.* Edited and completed by Donald McLennan. London: Macmillan. → Published posthumously.

1896 *Studies in Ancient History: Second Series.* Edited and completed by Eleanora A. McLennan and A. Platt. London: Macmillan. → Published posthumously.

SUPPLEMENTARY BIBLIOGRAPHY

Bachofen, Johann J. (1861) 1948 *Das Mutterrecht.* 2 vols. Basel: Schwabe.

Durkheim, Émile (1912) 1954 *The Elementary Forms of the Religious Life.* London: Allen & Unwin; New York: Macmillan. → First published as *Les formes élémentaires de la vie religieuse, le système totémique en Australie.* A paperback edition was published in 1961 by Collier.

Frazer, James G. (1887) 1910 *Totemism and Exogamy.* 4 vols. London: Macmillan. → See especially "Totemism" in Volume 1, pages 1–87.

Freud, Sigmund (1913) 1959 Totem and Taboo. Volume 13, pages ix–162 in *The Standard Edition of the Complete Psychological Works of Sigmund Freud.* London: Hogarth; New York: Macmillan. → First published in German.

Jevons, Frank B. (1896) 1914 *An Introduction to the History of Religion.* 6th ed. London: Methuen.

Leach, Edmund R. 1961 *Rethinking Anthropology.* London School of Economics and Political Science Monographs on Social Anthropology, No. 22. London: Athlone. → See especially Chapter 1.

Lévi-Strauss, Claude (1962) 1963 *Totemism.* Boston: Beacon. → First published as *Le totémisme aujourd'hui.*

Lowie, Robert H. 1937 *The History of Ethnological Theory.* New York: Farrar & Rinehart. → See especially Chapter 5.

Lubbock, John (1870) 1912 *The Origin of Civilization and the Primitive Condition of Man: Mental and Social Conditions of Savages.* 7th ed. New York: Longmans. → Chapter 3 is devoted almost entirely to McLennan's theories.

Maine, Henry Sumner (1861) 1960 *Ancient Law: Its Connection With the Early History of Society, and Its Relations to Modern Ideas.* Rev. ed. New York: Dutton; London and Toronto: Dent. → A paperback edition was published in 1963 by Beacon.

MAINE, HENRY SUMNER (1875) 1893 *Lectures on the Early History of Institutions*. 6th ed. London: Murray.

MORGAN, LEWIS H. 1871 *Systems of Consanguinity and Affinity of the Human Family*. Smithsonian Contributions to Knowledge, Vol. 17, art. 2, Publication No. 218. Washington: Smithsonian Institution.

MORGAN, LEWIS H. (1877) 1964 *Ancient Society*. Cambridge, Mass.: Belknap. → A long note to Chapter 6 deals with McLennan.

SMITH, WILLIAM ROBERTSON (1885) 1903 *Kinship and Marriage in Early Arabia*. New ed. London: Black.

SMITH, WILLIAM ROBERTSON (1889) 1959 *The Religion of the Semites*. New York: Meridian. → First published as *Lectures on the Religion of the Semites*.

SPENCER, HERBERT (1876) 1925 *The Principles of Sociology*. New York: Appleton. → Volume 1, Part 3, "Domestic Institutions," is a long dialogue with McLennan.

TYLOR, EDWARD B. 1899 Remarks on Totemism, With Especial Reference to Some Modern Theories Respecting It. *Journal of the Royal Anthropological Institute of Great Britain and Ireland* 28:138–148.

WESTERMARCK, EDWARD A. (1889) 1922 *The History of Human Marriage*. 5th ed., rev. New York: Allerton. → Criticizes McLennan's notion of "primitive promiscuity."

MACROECONOMICS

See INCOME AND EMPLOYMENT THEORY; INTEREST; LIQUIDITY PREFERENCE; MONEY.

MADISON, JAMES

James Madison (1751–1836), fourth president of the United States, from 1809 to 1817, was the principal framer of the constitution of 1787. It was Madison who made the first preliminary move toward the drafting of the constitution by sponsoring the Annapolis Convention of 1786. The constitution embodied his conviction that liberty and the rights of property could best be harmonized and secured in a federal republic, with powers divided between subordinate states and a supreme federal government, each with internal checks and balances to prevent the rise of arbitrary power. According to Madison, republican government required that representatives be elected directly (or, perhaps, in one house, indirectly) by the great body of the people; otherwise the republic would degenerate into an aristocracy or an oligarchy. Government so organized, he believed (relying to some extent on Hume), would be progressively safer to liberty and property as the territorial area was enlarged, since diversity of regional interests and of population would prevent any national majority—whether moved by a common property interest, by political or religious passion, or swayed

by an ambitious leader—from gaining power and oppressing the minority. He believed that the acquisition and protection of property is the ruling force in political faction and that the need to protect liberty and restrain power is a pressing one. These concepts, which he presented to the Philadelphia Convention of 1787, persuaded delegates fearful of the excesses of democracy to place their trust in democratic self-government. His voluminous notes of debates furnish the principal record of the convention.

In Congress Madison introduced the first ten amendments to the constitution, designed to enlarge its libertarian provisions into a bill of rights. In presenting these amendments he placed heaviest emphasis on freedom of religion, speech, and press. The religious guarantee was based on his modification of the 1776 Virginia Declaration of Rights, which discarded "toleration" and affirmed absolute rights of conscience, and on his successful "Memorial and Remonstrance Against Religious Assessments" (1785) for support of teachers of religion; such assessments, he asserted, were tantamount to an establishment of religion. His expectation that "independent tribunals of justice" would form "an impenetrable bulwark" against every encroachment on constitutional liberties was dashed by the enactment and savage enforcement of the Sedition Act of 1798. Consequently he wrote the Virginia Resolutions of 1798, which asserted the right of the states, in case of a deliberate and dangerous violation of the federal compact, to interpose collectively "for arresting the progress of the evil." Widespread interpretation of this as an assertion of the right to nullify acts of Congress led to his "Report on the Resolutions" (1799–1800), likewise adopted by the Virginia legislature, which defined interposition as an exertion of influence within the terms of the constitution but denied interposition any judicial force. The "Report" was notable for its assertion that freedom of the press exempted the press from punishment for licentiousness and its denial that the federal government had power to punish crimes under the common law of England.

In the famous *Federalist* No. 10, Madison systematized his earlier discussions of political faction. By that term he did not refer to political parties of the modern type but to the united activities of a majority or minority of the people "actuated by some common impulse of passion, or of interest, adverse to the rights of other citizens, or to the permanent and aggregate interests of the community" (Hamilton, Madison & Jay [1787–1788] 1961, p. 57). The unsteadiness and injustice of state governments, resulting from a factious spirit, had led to the breakdown of public trust and increasing alarm for private rights. The latent causes of faction, he believed, lie in the nature of man, especially men's varying capacities for acquiring property and its consequent unequal distribution. Liberty feeds faction, but limiting liberty is a greater evil than faction. The remedy, therefore, lies in controlling the effects of passion through checks and divisions of governments.

Madison had a deterministic view of human conduct and was essentially a pragmatist, committed to no particular school of political thought but intensely devoted to preserving the Union, maintaining a broadly based republican government, and protecting human rights. In the furtherance of national policy, his tendency was to rely upon coercive measures. In the first Congress, he sponsored a moderate protective tariff (though generally preferring free trade), advocated counterdiscrimination against British navigation acts injurious to American shipping, and worked unofficially to help repel senatorial encroachments on the president's powers. Madison and Hamilton were equally committed to full payment of depreciated Revolutionary War claims, but Madison resisted Hamilton's policy of full payment to speculators who purchased claims, urging that a share should go to the original holders, mostly impoverished veterans. This initiated the political alignment that developed into Hamiltonian federalism and Jeffersonian democracy. Hamilton's sweeping interpretation of the power to spend for the general welfare likewise prevailed over Madison's attempt to limit spending to subjects covered by the other enumerated powers—a view which did not prevent him, as president, from inaugurating government distribution of smallpox vaccine.

Jay's 1794 treaty with England blocked Madison's counterdiscrimination policy, but maritime restrictions continued and the Napoleonic Wars provoked wholesale seizures of American ships by both belligerents. In striking contrast with President Jefferson's defensive shipping embargo, Madison in his first month as president made identical offers to England and France: that if the power addressed would cease its aggressions against American commerce, and the other continued them, he would ask Congress to declare war against the continuing offender. Without knowing of these offers, Congress in effect gave them legal force by the Macon Bill No. 2 of 1810, leading to the War of 1812 with England.

Except during his student days at Princeton and the major portion of his years in public office,

Madison spent his entire life on his extensive estate, Montpelier, in the Virginia Piedmont. He pioneered in modern scientific agriculture and warned of the future dangers from world-wide overpopulation and man's upsetting of the balance of nature. Although strongly opposed to slavery, he lived by its fruits. The apparent happiness of his slaves, he told Harriet Martineau, was an illusion, concealing the degradation inherent in the institution. Believing that white Americans would permanently deny rights to which freedmen were entitled, he advocated the freeing of all slaves through government purchase—to be financed by western land sales—and voluntary resettlement in Liberia and other separate communities. The final years of his life were devoted to his work as rector of the University of Virginia and to preparing polemical articles combating South Carolina's nullification doctrine.

IRVING BRANT

[See also REPRESENTATION, article on REPRESENTATIONAL SYSTEMS; and the biographies of HAMILTON and JEFFERSON.]

WORKS BY MADISON

(1751–1836) 1962– *Papers.* Edited by William T. Hutchinson and William M. E. Rachal. Univ. of Chicago Press. → The first of a projected series of volumes.
(1769–1836) 1900–1910 *The Writings of James Madison, Comprising His Public Papers and His Private Correspondence,* . . . 9 vols. Edited by Gaillard Hunt. New York: Putnam.
(1785) 1904 Memorial and Remonstrance Against Religious Assessments. Pages 183–191 in James Madison, *The Writings of James Madison, Comprising His Public Papers and His Private Correspondence,* . . . Volume 2: 1783–1787. New York: Putnam.
(1787–1788) 1961 HAMILTON, ALEXANDER; MADISON, JAMES; and JAY, JOHN *The Federalist.* Edited with introduction and notes by Jacob E. Cooke. Middletown, Conn.: Wesleyan Univ. Press. → See also the 1961 John Harvard Library edition, under the editorship of Benjamin F. Wright and Irving Brant, for assignment of authorship.
(1789) 1904 June 8: Amendments to the Constitution. Pages 370–389 in James Madison, *The Writings of James Madison, Comprising His Public Papers and His Private Correspondence,* . . . Volume 5: 1787–1790. New York: Putnam.
(1799–1800) 1906 Report on the Resolutions. Pages 341–406 in James Madison, *The Writings of James Madison, Comprising His Public Papers and His Private Correspondence,* . . . Volume 6: 1790–1802. New York: Putnam.
1966 *Notes of Debates in the Federal Convention of 1787.* With an introduction by Adrienne Koch. Athens: Ohio Univ. Press.

SUPPLEMENTARY BIBLIOGRAPHY

BRANT, IRVING 1941–1961 *James Madison.* 6 vols. Indianapolis, Ind.: Bobbs-Merrill. → Volume 1: *The Virginia Revolutionist.* Volume 2: *The Nationalist:*

1780–1787. Volume 3: *Father of the Constitution: 1787–1800.* Volume 4: *Secretary of State: 1800–1809.* Volume 5: *The President: 1809–1812.* Volume 6: *Commander in Chief: 1812–1836.*

BRANT, IRVING 1961 Settling the Authorship of *The Federalist. American Historical Review* 67:71–75.

BURNS, EDWARD M. 1938 *James Madison: Philosopher of the Constitution.* Studies in History, Vol. 1. New Brunswick, N.J.: Rutgers Univ. Press.

MOSTELLER, FREDERICK; and WALLACE, DAVID L. 1963 Inference in an Authorship Problem: A Comparative Study of Discrimination Methods Applied to the Authorship of the Disputed Federalist Papers. *Journal of the American Statistical Association* 58:275–309.

U.S. CONSTITUTIONAL CONVENTION, 1787 (1911) 1937 *The Records of the Federal Convention of 1787.* 4 vols., rev. ed. Edited by Max Farrand. New Haven: Yale Univ. Press.

MAGIC

The article under this heading discusses witchcraft and sorcery as well as magic. Related material will be found under POLLUTION; RITUAL; *and in the articles mentioned in the guide to* RELIGION. *The biographies of* DURKHEIM; FRAZER; KLUCKHOHN; MALINOWSKI; MAUSS; *and* NADEL *should also be consulted.*

The relation of magic to religion and to science provided fuel for early anthropological speculation. All students of primitive religion have had to face the question in some form or other. It has proved difficult to circumscribe the subject of magic with any degree of precision. If, as is often the case, the subjects of *mana*, taboo, totemism, and ritual are included, the discussion of magic easily dissolves into comparative religion.

In recent years, apart from a notable work on taboo (Steiner 1956), there has been a lack of interest in magic, although the work of Lévi-Strauss on primitive thought (1962; 1964) promises to revive discussion. In the past 30 years anthropologists have concentrated on describing and analyzing the moral and religious ideas and institutions of particular peoples in great detail. In these studies the great philosophical issues of magic, science, and religion, which exercised thinkers in the nineteenth and early twentieth centuries, have receded into the background. There has been great interest in specific institutions, such as sorcery and witchcraft, which may be regarded as the social dimensions of magic. Although theoretical formulations in these fields have not kept pace with the greatly increased area of knowledge, such contributions as those of Evans-Pritchard (1937), Kluckhohn (1944), and Nadel (1952) have had important repercussions.

In historical terms, there can be seen a development from attempts to single out isolated and exotic instances of belief or practice in order to buttress a highly abstract philosophical position (such as Frazer's work) to an effort to place all magical acts in their proper context within the totality of moral and religious ideas, institutions, and practices of a culture.

For nineteenth-century thinkers like Tylor (1871), McLennan (1865–1876), Spencer (1876–1896), and Lang (1901), the question of greatest interest was the origins of magic as related to the origins of religion. Their works were attempts to understand how early man was led in the direction of superstition by faulty observation and reasoning. This line of inquiry led to Lévy-Bruhl's famous work on primitive mentality (1910). Frazer (1890) was also working on evolutionary premises. Theories regarding the evolution of religion or science from magic are no longer in vogue, but Frazer's work will remain one of the most sustained efforts to penetrate the difficulties of the subject. Frazer regarded magic as an earlier, primitive form of both religion and science. He observed rightly that primitive practice is often based on excellent observation of natural phenomena and involves a theory of causality. He therefore felt that there was a basic similarity between magic and science. The only difference was that for a variety of reasons the mistaken assumptions and erroneous conclusions of magic were veiled from the observer and did not shake his beliefs.

The basic principles of magic, according to Frazer, were two: the law of similarity and the law of contagion. According to the first principle, like produces like, so that sticking pins into a doll is like sticking arrows into the enemy; and according to the law of contagion, prolonged or intimate contact produces identity, so that the enemy's nail parings and hair can be treated as if they represented him.

Evans-Pritchard (1933) has remarked that if Frazer had observed what the natives did rather than what they thought, he would have been less inclined to draw similarities between scientists and witch doctors. He would also have seen the difference between scientific methods and traditional arts.

While anthropologists were skeptical about the attempt to reduce the exuberant complexity of primitive ritual and magic to two principles of thought, the initial impact of Frazer's ideas was considerable, especially beyond the circles of academic anthropology. In retrospect, Frazer's work is generally regarded as having one crippling difficulty: similar customs and practices from all cultures of the world were collected and examined under common labels. Since the labels and their relations exemplified Frazer's own thinking on the subject, the data merely filled the preconceived receptacles and did not add to the analysis of the phenomena in any one culture (Leach 1961).

Since Frazer, every major writer on primitive religion has struggled with "magic," and every major monograph has provided more material on this elusive subject. Durkheim (1912), for instance, distinguished magic and religion on the assumption that religion presupposed a church or a *congregation*, while the magician worked alone and merely had a *clientele*.

Malinowski wrote in a different vein. In his article "Magic, Science and Religion" (1925), he argued, in Frazerian terms, for the necessity of distinguishing among these fields, but on a non-evolutionary basis. Magic, he suggested, is related to anxiety. In ordinary, everyday economic pursuits there is no magic. But when the outcome of the enterprise is uncertain and there is danger involved, the native has recourse to magic. Moreover, magic is directed to specific ends and differs from religion in not being concerned with the worship of spiritual beings.

As Malinowski pointed out, the natives of the Trobriand Islands are perfectly able to distinguish the sphere of magic from that of technology. Thus, although every step of the cultivation process is marked by magical rites, there is no question of giving up one's own efforts to cultivate gardens and attempting to grow the food by magic alone. On the contrary, they know that even after having spent their best efforts on cultivation, some unpredictable act of nature may destroy their crops. Thus, argued Malinowski, the native has his "scientific technology" clearly distinguished from the sphere of magic. It is against the unpredictable that magic is utilized. Natives would consider it laughable to do otherwise.

This pragmatic point of view expressed by Malinowski has had many supporters. (We may observe also that the relation which he posits between anxiety and ritual harks back to psychoanalytic theory.) But the utilitarian basis of these theories has recently been severely questioned. It has become clear that the facts of ethnography do not fall into place as neatly as Malinowski had thought. Some features of magic, of Australian increase ceremonies, or of totemism don't make sense in simple utilitarian terms. Malinowski wrote, for instance, that ". . . food is the primary link between the primitive and providence. . . . The road from the wilderness to the savage's belly and conse-

quently to his mind is very short" ([1925] 1948, pp. 26–27). But in the magical repertoire of aboriginal Australians there are "increase ceremonies" for all kinds of nonutilitarian categories—for instance, mosquitoes—and simple pragmatic explanations for such complicated facts would be naive.

Malinowski had specifically dismissed the views of Mauss, who had argued (see Lévi-Strauss 1950) that magic is a special application of the forces of sacred powers, like *mana*, some conception of which is found in every society. For Mauss, *mana* was, in fact, a connection between religion and magic. Magic comes from religion into the realm of everyday life, where its end is action.

Malinowski, in denying the role of *mana*, attempted to place the emphasis again on pragmatic functions. He asked, ". . . what is *mana*, this impersonal force of magic supposed to dominate all forms of early belief? Is it a fundamental idea, an innate category of the primitive mind, or can it be explained by still simpler and more fundamental elements of human psychology . . . ?" These fundamental elements turn out to be merely "a blend of utilitarian anxiety about the most necessary objects of his surroundings. . . . With our knowledge of what could be called the totemic attitude of mind, primitive religion is seen to be nearer to reality and to the immediate practical life interests of the savage" ([1925] 1948, pp. 4–5).

Lévi-Strauss (1950) upholds Mauss and is concerned to redress the balance in favor of an argument that the inner logic of religious ideas is not utilitarian and that their logic has to be understood in their own terms. Features of primitive belief must be examined not by imputing our materialist viewpoint to the idealized native but in terms of the position of such ideas and symbols in the total tapestry of customary belief and practice. Thus, Lévi-Strauss agrees with Mauss and notes that the concept of *mana* is truly like a common denominator for concepts of the "sacred" and is, indeed, intimately related to magic. The conclusion here is that to understand magic, we must understand the refractions of the concept of the sacred in the culture.

Magic, then, is not a uniform class of practices and beliefs which can be immediately discerned in every society. On the contrary, it is best regarded as an aspect of religious belief and practice that takes its special force from the antecedent and deeply rooted recognition in many societies of supernatural or divine power. The place given to the practical use of such powers for everyday purposes such as healing or assuring luck and fertility —which in very general terms we may refer to as magic—differs from society to society.

Witchcraft and sorcery also involve the belief in supernatural powers, and sorcery in particular may be regarded as a specialized branch of offensive magic. What is said about magic and religion holds true for witchcraft and sorcery as well: it is imperative to place these beliefs and practices within the context of the total supernatural belief system of the culture in question. It will then be feasible to raise the question of whether there is logic in this madness and to what extent the different parts of the supernatural system show structure, division of labor, and specialization of function.

Sorcery and witchcraft

The terms "sorcery" and "witchcraft" refer to practices and supernatural beings which are part and parcel of the European Christian tradition. Their use in anthropology involves an essential widening of their meaning to cover a great many beliefs and practices from other cultures which have proved difficult to classify. The conceptual categories involved in such supernatural beings and practices are sometimes so unique to particular peoples that the translation of concepts from one cultural idiom into another becomes a difficulty of the first magnitude. Is "witchcraft" similar to the "evil eye"? Is a European witch the "same" as an Islamic djinn or a Hindu yakṣa? These questions about the similarities and differences between belief systems of different cultures remain largely unresolved.

With the above general reservations, it may be noted that in the area of witchcraft and sorcery, the empirical and theoretical distinctions made by Evans-Pritchard (1937) in his analysis of the ideas of the Azande have won general acceptance. The conceptual distinction made by the Azande has been observed in numerous other African cultures. The distinction turns on the nature of witches. According to Azande theories, "witches" are ordinary members of society who have inherited special supernatural powers to harm others and who may be completely unconscious of their evil potentialities. The Azande have consistent and developed physiological theories to explain just where in the human body such powers lie. They also have their special ways of consulting oracles to discover who among them carries the power, the reason for the attack, and how the danger is to be averted. Among the Azande these witches who are singled out by their fellow men are sharply distinguished from "sorcerers." Sorcerers are men who have learned the particular techniques of handling special substances and charms whereby they can affect others. While the witches' supernatural powers are innate

and unconscious, sorcery is an acquired technique and is conscious. In one case a person fully unconscious of his guilt may be publicly accused as a "witch" and by the use of oracles may be confirmed as such, whereas in the other case, at least in theory, there is a conscious agent responsible for certain incidents who may or may not be accused of evil intentions.

These distinctions have thrown light upon anthropological field information beyond the Azande material from which they were developed. Sorcery theory and practice are evidently very widespread on all continents; but witchcraft, with its direct accusations of certain individuals who may be totally unaware of what they are accused of, is a more remarkable and less widespread phenomenon. Apart from the celebrated medieval European and New England examples, cases of witchcraft accusation from parts of Middle America (Nash 1960) and central and east Africa also have been described. On the whole, the term "witchcraft," in the narrow sense, has not been used to describe related phenomena in the Near East and south Asia.

The above definitions make it possible to distinguish a gradation of witchcraft belief ranging from the fully developed dogmas that certain people become witches in some form (which may be embellished with detailed stories of their secret meetings and activities) to vague feelings that certain people might possess occult powers (such as the evil eye) to cause some harm, even though they may not be directly accused. The latter fear, in various degrees, is very widespread in the Mediterranean region as well as the Near East and south Asia, even though these powers are not usually described as "witchcraft."

It should be underlined that this distinction between sorcery and witchcraft lies entirely within the region of ideas and that there may be no "objective" basis to either set of beliefs. In other words, although it should be theoretically possible to observe the sorcerer at his work, and although external evidence could be produced in the form of magical substances, special bundles, and the like, it is also quite possible that while there may be widespread fear of sorcery, it may in fact never be practiced by anybody. In this sense, in the study of both sorcery and witchcraft we are almost entirely concerned with the analysis of supernatural beliefs.

Cultural and structural approaches

Although descriptive works of high quality are now numerous, little progress has been made by anthropologists into the systematic analysis of customary belief systems. The dilemma has remained: how far are belief systems to be related to and analyzed in terms of the economic and social structures of the groups in question? Or if such systems are not directly related to economic and social structures, are there internal logical and categorical features which produce consistency and form in belief systems? The differences between these approaches have made themselves felt in the emphasis placed on the cultural or structural aspects of these phenomena.

Internal features of belief systems.   The cultural approach to witchcraft and sorcery has underlined the consistency or logical closure of such systems: thus witchcraft and sorcery ideas are theories of causation concerning good and evil in human society. When a misfortune takes place, it can be explained by witchcraft or sorcery. This explanation in turn involves the necessity of discovering the agents of causation, i.e., those witches and sorcerers responsible. Thus, beginning with a theory of causation, one is led to techniques of divination. These, in turn, necessitate the development of the arts of healing and defense. Hence, ideas regarding witchcraft and sorcery become part of a coherent and consistent set of ideas regarding the nature of events in the world. Since these ideas have very wide ramifications and are inextricably related to the thought, language, and customary behavior of the societies in question, convictions regarding witches, sorcerers, and magic cannot be contradicted on simple rational or empirical grounds. They are rooted deep in the nature of social life.

There has been little analysis of the total "design" of supernatural belief systems, even though witnesses in the field have generally taken their coherence for granted. The "design" means here the characteristics, roles, rights, and obligations of supernatural beings, their organization and relations with each other and with human society at large. It also includes the methods whereby they may be approached, communicated with, appeased, angered, or utilized. It seems clear that all societies have a design of this nature whereby a division of labor between different sections of the supernatural is effected.

An example of the operation of such a system is to be seen among the Sinhalese villagers of Ceylon. In these communities the world of supernatural beings has both Buddhist and Hindu features. The Buddha and his monks, who are held in high esteem, are seen to help man's prospects in the next existence or in eternity, whereas the Hindu-influenced pantheon of supernatural beings is seen to hold sway over the present life and worldly prospects of men. Within this general framework, however, the supernatural beings who deal with this world are divided into gods and goddesses who are thought to ensure long life, well-being, and fertility, on the one hand, and demons and demonesses who are thought to wreak havoc and to bring infertility, suffering, and death, on the other. Oversimplifying, their relations can be seen as the forces of light and darkness, or those of good and evil.

The place of magic in this picture becomes clear when we observe the elaborate precautions which are taken on the threshing floors at harvest time. The threshing floor is treated as the temple–residence of the gods and goddesses who try to increase the yield. The small circle becomes the battleground for the gods and demons over the fertility of the lands and the yield of the harvest. The demons and demonesses are feared to be hovering outside its borders, aiming to attack the grain on the threshing floor and to steal it. Special magical precautions are taken to please the gods and repulse the demons. Indeed, until recently Sinhalese peasants in the interior spoke a special language, which the demons could not comprehend, when they entered the sacred precincts of their threshing floors.

It is in this context that the role of sorcery is also seen most clearly. Just as there are elaborately developed techniques of communicating with the supernatural in the threshing floor to appease the gods and hold the demons at bay, there are also techniques, said to be very dangerous, to achieve the opposite. Logically, if the achievement of the good is within the bounds of human influence, so is the working of evil. Hence, Sinhalese villagers fully believe that some people can activate the demons against them by special offerings and incantations. Thus, sorcery is part of the very foundations of the total belief system of the villagers. And further, if there is sorcery, and if there are demons who are active, then men must seek magical protection. Indeed, the great theatrical art of ritual healing—directed specifically against sorcery—is one of the most noteworthy and developed aspects of folk culture among the Sinhalese (Wirz 1954; Yalman 1964).

Such precise linking of supernatural cause and effect, white magic and sorcery, sorcery and ritual healing is not always clearly visible in the detailed description of supernatural designs, but it appears likely that further analysis will reveal similar logical interlinkages in most primitive religions. As Evans-Pritchard observes for the Azande, "witchcraft, oracles and magic are like three sides of a triangle" (1937, p. 387).

The attempt to understand fully the inner workings of the mind of even the most primitive peoples is an obvious prerequisite to the analysis of their supernatural beliefs, behavior, and rituals. Without such penetration into what appear to be irrational and alien mentalities, all observations are bound to be superficial, rash, or wrong. The process of understanding the minds of others is partly a matter of insight and freedom from prejudice, and although the discipline of anthropology has gone far in this direction, there is much room for improvement. In any case, the objective and respectful attempt to understand the inner logic in what superficially appears meaningless or illogical cannot be taken for granted. But the further question must also be raised of whether the linked and orderly system of ideas presented to us is really that of the native, or whether the order is artificially imposed on the phenomena by the mind of the anthropological observer. This issue is a difficult one, resting near the precipice of metaphysics, but its difficulty does not prevent the observation that the heuristic assumption of "system" in primitive ideologies has proved to be very fruitful. The claim regarding the systematic nature of primitive ideas is always open to further verification, but as yet no anthropologist has been able to sustain an argument based on the senselessness or illogicality of primitive beliefs.

In the meantime, further developments toward the understanding of belief systems have derived from structural linguistics. These are based on the desire not only to understand belief systems in a general way but also to go beyond the generalities and analyze the detailed features of belief systems on the model of communication systems (Lévi-Strauss 1964). Proponents of this approach maintain that belief and ritual systems have elements of order and internal structure because they form the framework for human communication. Lévi-Strauss (1955) has recommended examining the most minute details of primitive myths, as if they were literary texts. Other anthropologists have suggested that the sequences of ritual may be susceptible to the type of analysis that is applied to sequences of sounds in modern linguistics (Yalman 1964). These developments in the fields of mythology and ritual have an important bearing on magic, witchcraft, and sorcery; but as yet they remain promising methods rather than well-rounded and well-supported theoretical and analytic positions (Leach 1964). Their aim is the clarification of the structure of the language of mythology and ritual. Thus, they are formal analyses divorced both from Marxist opinions regarding the primacy of the social structure over systems of ideas and from the Freudian assumptions concerning the effects of the unconscious. Whether this line of inquiry will

prove effective remains to be seen (Lévi-Strauss 1963).

Structural aspects. We turn now to the effect of the beliefs in sorcery and witchcraft on social relations. The direct or veiled accusation of a person or a group is a critical element in the sorcery and witchcraft complex. Wherever these beliefs occur, we may expect a great elaboration of supernatural weapons of offense and defense against sorcerers and witches and these accusations.

There have been attempts to relate overt accusations of witchcraft and sorcery to the morphology of kinship or social groups. It is suggested that such accusation of evil intent of one person by another must run along the lines of stress in the structure of social groups. There is undoubtedly much truth in this statement, and it is confirmed by the widespread feeling among people of many cultures that institutions such as the evil eye, witches, and sorcery spring directly from one of the most powerful human sentiments, jealousy. This is merely a different way of expressing the strained social relations between the accuser and the accused. This is why jealousy and envy are so often given as the reason for the supernatural attack (Wilson 1951a). Witchcraft accusations that reveal both secret and unconscious envy as well as overt suspicions may be regarded as particularly clear symptoms of strain in the social structure.

One of the most interesting studies of this problem is by Nadel (1952). For purposes of precise comparison he selects two pairs of societies: the Nupe and Gwari of Nigeria, and the Korongo and Mesakin of the Sudan. Each pair is similar in most cultural respects but differs in a few critical structural features. Thus, in the Nigerian pair Nupe women are often traders, and their economic interest and activities put a well-recognized strain on husband–wife relations. Among the Gwari, the economic problems do not exist, and the strains are absent. Accordingly, although both cultures firmly believe in witchcraft, among the Nupe witches are conceived of as women, and witch associations are said to resemble women's trade associations. The Gwari, on the other hand, conceive of their witches as being both male and female.

In the second pair there is greater contrast. According to Nadel, the Korongo have no witchcraft beliefs at all, whereas the Mesakin are said to be totally obsessed by witchcraft. In general structural form the two groups are similar, except for some critical features which are singled out by Nadel. Both groups are matrilineal. Among the Korongo the age-class system permits easy mobility through the numerous classes for young men, whereas among the Mesakin there are fewer grades and they remain closed and rigid. Among the latter, mobility is curtailed and is replaced by competition and hostility between the generations. The Korongo have no witch problems, whereas among the Mesakin most witchcraft accusations occur among maternal kin—more specifically, between mother's brother and sister's son, who are placed in positions of the most intense competition in the age-grade system.

In such theories the ideology and practice of witchcraft are related with some precision to areas of anxiety and stress in the social fabric. All these theories are based on the incidence of witchcraft accusations between individuals in certain specific social roles. But, for obvious reasons, statistical evidence of sufficient depth and range in connection with such highly charged issues is difficult to collect and evaluate.

Middleton and Winter (1963) have raised some important questions regarding both the coherence of dogma and the structural aspects of witchcraft and sorcery. Accepting the notion that witchcraft and sorcery have coherent doctrines which explain events in social life, they argue that sorcery and witchcraft beliefs are exhaustive systems of supernatural explanation. When found in the same society, moreover, they are opposed explanations. Theoretically, then, one set should be redundant; but in fact most African societies, they argue, have both systems of dogma. If so, they suggest, witchcraft and sorcery must fit in with different aspects of the social structure, and this hypothesis is related to the different natures of witchcraft and sorcery.

Since sorcery is a voluntary matter and merely a technique which can be learned, anybody may be in a position to use it for offense or defense. Moreover, depending upon the motives of the sorcerer, it is not innately evil. On the other hand, witchcraft is by definition an innate matter, usually evil, in which the alleged witch has no choice. For this reason Middleton and Winter suggest that witchcraft accusations are more characteristically made against persons who are in *ascribed* roles, such as involuntary membership in unilineal descent groups where the individual acquires his position by virtue of his birth, whereas sorcery accusations tend to be made against persons in *achieved* statuses and are more characteristic of the nonunilineal aspects of societies.

Thus, among Lugbara lineages, the women who come in as wives are incorporated into their husbands' patrilineages and become full members.

Even if they leave the husband, their future children legally continue to belong to his patrilineage. In this context the elaborate ideology of witchcraft is linked to women, and witches are always said to be females. Among the Nyoro, on the other hand, people live in mixed nonunilineal neighborhoods, the women are not incorporated into patrilineages, most social positions are voluntary, and there is a developed technology of sorcery rather than witchcraft.

Even though the specific application of these ideas is illuminating, it is difficult to generalize from them to witchcraft beliefs at large. For there is always an ascribed aspect to social status, and it appears difficult to evaluate the witchcraft of complex communities in early New England, medieval Europe, or present-day Indian communities of Middle America and South America in these terms.

Apart from the question of tension in social relations, the psychological aspects of witchcraft beliefs are another dimension of the facts. If witchcraft beliefs are regarded as unrealistic fantasies—a weak theoretical position from the point of view of anthropology—then some similarity and connection may be seen between witchcraft, sorcery, and infantile fantasies. But since these ideas, however unrealistic, are collective fantasies, their explanation can be related in any meaningful fashion only to collective infantile experiences. The question remains interesting but open.

The dogmas of witchcraft, sorcery, and magic are also relevant to the social control and inheritance systems of certain societies. Among the Trobriand Islanders the power of sorcery was an important weapon which buttressed the position of the chief. Although commoners had access to sorcerers, the chief could call upon the services of many in different districts and thereby extend his authority. Frazer has reported similar instances of the use of supernatural means to secure extensive reinforcement of traditional political organizations. The divine kingship of the Shilluk is one of the well-known instances (Evans-Pritchard 1948).

In some societies where witchcraft is regarded as an innate quality in certain individuals, there are theories of its inheritance. In some cases when the main line of descent, for purposes of family organization, is in the male line, witchcraft is thought to run in the female line.

Magic and social change

Ideas about magic and supernatural creatures play a vital explanatory role as organized and institutionalized systems of public belief in traditional societies. They explain disease, injustice, misfortune, and death. Social reformers often feel that education may be used as the most potent weapon against such superstitions. It is true that modern education attacks these customary systems by providing alternative explanations for events and, probably more important, by undermining the authority of the spokesmen for the traditional system.

However, it is ironic that the fundamental changes in traditional society which permit the establishment of modern educational systems also bring about greater insecurity and increased tensions in social relations. Under such conditions, there is an even greater urge to turn to such supernatural weapons and beliefs as are available. It is notorious that modern governments in parts of Africa which have forbidden such practices as divination, the poison oracles, and similar traditional observances as being mere superstitions have naturally been seen as aligned with the forces of evil. For if the government prevents the use of appropriate traditional antiwitchcraft defensive weapons, they in effect frustrate the witch hunters and thereby materially contribute to the increase of witches. Hence, at least for parts of Africa, observers note that notwithstanding modernization, witches are felt to be more active and there is increased interest in modern movements of witch finders.

Magic, witchcraft, and sorcery are rooted in traditional customary ideas whereby cultures categorize and order the universe around them. As such, they not only are intertwined with every aspect of culture, thought, and language but also provide coherent and systematic means to influence the world in which man lives. For the anthropologist such belief systems provide essential material for the understanding of the metaphysics of non-Western cultures. They may also lead to a better understanding of the structured aspects of customary thought.

Ideas regarding witchcraft and sorcery appear strange in a rationalist period such as ours, but we should recall what immense sway such beliefs have held over very sophisticated and highly intelligent men. We must be guarded in our haste to dismiss these ideas of the supernatural. Rather, we must understand the very roots which provide the strength of conviction for such beliefs.

All knowledge rests on some degree of trust and respect. In modern societies the specialized task of developing knowledge and examining the basis of knowledge is given to thinkers and scientists in institutions of learning. Those not directly involved with a particular branch of investigation—if they understand its language at all—take their conclusions on trust. The respect in which the institution is held is an important aspect of this trust. Similarly, the knowledge of supernatural powers, of gods and goddesses, of demons and demonesses, of sorcerers and witches in all primitive societies derives from respected traditions and institutions and from men who have proved themselves worthy of trust. Commonly shared beliefs are at the basis of communal sentiments, and hence beliefs which appear primitive and totally illogical to the Western observer not only rest on dogma but also take added strength from the fact that they are part of the moral foundations of the society in which they are found.

NUR YALMAN

BIBLIOGRAPHY

DURKHEIM, ÉMILE (1912) 1954 *The Elementary Forms of the Religious Life.* London: Allen & Unwin; New York: Macmillan. → A paperback edition was published in 1961 by Collier.

EVANS-PRITCHARD, E. E. 1933 The Intellectualist (English) Interpretation of Magic. Cairo, Jāmiʿat al-Qāhirah, Kullīyat al-Ādāb, *Bulletin of the Faculty of Arts* 1:282–311.

EVANS-PRITCHARD, E. E. (1937) 1965 *Witchcraft, Oracles and Magic Among the Azande.* Oxford: Clarendon.

EVANS-PRITCHARD, E. E. 1948 *The Divine Kingship of the Shilluk of the Nilotic Sudan.* Cambridge Univ. Press.

FORTUNE, REO F. (1932) 1963 *Sorcerers of Dobu: The Social Anthropology of the Dobu Islanders of the Western Pacific.* Rev. ed. London: Routledge.

FRAZER, JAMES (1890) 1955 *The Golden Bough: A Study in Magic and Religion.* 3d ed., rev. & enl. 13 vols. New York: St. Martins; London: Macmillan. → An abridged edition was published in 1922 and reprinted in 1955.

GUITERAS-HOLMES, CALIXTA 1961 *Perils of the Soul: The World View of a Tzotzil Indian.* New York: Free Press.

HUBERT, HENRI; and MAUSS, MARCEL (1904) 1960 Esquisse d'une théorie générale de la magie. Pages 1–141 in Marcel Mauss, *Sociologie et anthropologie.* 2d ed. Paris: Presses Universitaires de France. → First published in Volume 7 of *Année sociologique.*

KLUCKHOHN, CLYDE 1944 *Navaho Witchcraft.* Harvard University, Peabody Museum of American Archaeology and Ethnology, Papers, Vol. 22, No. 2. Cambridge, Mass.: The Museum.

KLUCKHOHN, CLYDE; and LEIGHTON, DOROTHEA [CROSS] (1946) 1951 *The Navaho.* Oxford Univ. Press.

LANG, ANDREW 1901 *Magic and Religion.* London: Longmans.

LEACH, EDMUND R. 1961 Golden Bough or Gilded Twig? *Dædalus* 90:371–387.

LEACH, EDMUND R. 1964 Telstar et les aborigènes, ou *La pensée sauvage. Annales; économies, sociétés, civilisations* 19:1100–1116.

LÉVI-STRAUSS, CLAUDE (1950) 1960 Introduction à l'oeuvre de Marcel Mauss. Pages ix–lii in Marcel Mauss, *Sociologie et anthropologie*. 2d ed. Paris: Presses Universitaires de France.

LÉVI-STRAUSS, CLAUDE (1955) 1963 The Structural Study of Myth. Pages 206–231 in Claude Lévi-Strauss, *Structural Anthropology*. New York: Basic Books. → A revision of an article first published in English in Volume 68 of the *Journal of American Folklore*.

LÉVI-STRAUSS, CLAUDE (1962) 1966 *The Savage Mind*. Univ. of Chicago Press. → First published in French.

LÉVI-STRAUSS, CLAUDE 1963 Réponse à quelques questions. *Esprit* 31:628–653.

LÉVI-STRAUSS, CLAUDE 1964 *Le cru et le cuit*. Paris: Plon.

LÉVY-BRUHL, LUCIEN (1910) 1951 *Les fonctions mentales dans les sociétés inférieures*. 9th ed. Paris: Presses Universitaires de France.

McLENNAN, JOHN FERGUSON (1865–1876) 1886 *Studies in Ancient History*. New York: Macmillan. → Includes *Primitive Marriage* (1865).

MALINOWSKI, BRONISLAW (1925) 1948 Magic, Science and Religion. Pages 1–71 in Bronislaw Malinowski, *Magic, Science and Religion, and Other Essays*. Glencoe, Ill.: Free Press.

MARWICK, M. G. 1950 Another Modern Anti-witchcraft Movement in East Central Africa. *Africa* 20:100–112.

MARWICK, M. G. 1952 The Social Context of Cewa Witch Beliefs. *Africa* 22:120–135, 215–233.

MÉTRAUX, ALFRED (1958) 1959 *Voodoo in Haiti*. New York: Oxford Univ. Press. → First published as *Le voudou haïtien*.

MIDDLETON, JOHN; and WINTER, EDWARD H. (editors) 1963 *Witchcraft and Sorcery in East Africa*. London: Routledge.

NADEL, S. F. 1952 Witchcraft in Four African Societies: An Essay in Comparison. *American Anthropologist* New Series 54:18–29.

NASH, MANNING 1960 Witchcraft as Social Process in a Tzeltal Community. *América indígena* 20:121–126.

SMITH, WILLIAM ROBERTSON (1889) 1956 *The Religion of the Semites: The Fundamental Institutions*. New York: Meridian. → First published as the first series of *Lectures on the Religion of the Semites*.

SPENCER, HERBERT (1876–1896) 1925–1929 *The Principles of Sociology*. 3 vols. New York: Appleton.

STEINER, FRANZ 1956 *Taboo*. New York: Philosophical Library.

THOMAS, NORTHCOTE W. 1926 Witchcraft. Volume 28, pages 755–758 in *Encyclopaedia Britannica*. 13th ed. Chicago: Benton.

TYLOR, EDWARD B. (1871) 1958 *Primitive Culture: Researches Into the Development of Mythology, Philosophy, Religion, Art and Custom*. 2 vols. Gloucester, Mass.: Smith. → Volume 1: *Origins of Culture*. Volume 2: *Religion in Primitive Culture*.

WILSON, MONICA H. 1951a *Good Company: A Study of Nyakyusa Age-villages*. Published for the International African Institute. Oxford Univ. Press.

WILSON, MONICA H. 1951b Witch Beliefs and Social Structure. *American Journal of Sociology* 56:307–313.

WIRZ, PAUL 1954 *Exorcism and the Art of Healing in Ceylon*. Leiden (Netherlands): Brill.

YALMAN, NUR 1964 The Structure of Sinhalese Healing Rituals. Pages 115–150 in Conference on Religion in South Asia, University of California, Berkeley, 1961, *Religion in South Asia*. Edited by Edward B. Harper. Seattle: Univ. of Washington Press.

MAHAN, ALFRED THAYER

Alfred Thayer Mahan (1840–1914) was an American naval officer who wrote extensively on naval strategy and the history of sea power. From his studies of naval warfare he drew principles of strategy that greatly influenced the development and employment of naval forces during the first half of the twentieth century. As a historian he studied the relations of sea power and history, and he developed a philosophy of history in which the concept of force played a major role.

Mahan was born at West Point, New York, where his father was a professor of military engineering at the United States Military Academy. Mahan chose the navy for his profession and, graduating from the United States Naval Academy in 1859, saw active service in the American Civil War. At its conclusion, he continued his navy career and traveled widely. There was little indication during these years of the intellectual importance he was to attain.

Mahan was selected in 1885 to lecture on naval strategy, tactics, and history at the newly established Naval War College. He probably received the assignment because he wrote "The Gulf and Inland Waters," a competent volume appearing in 1883 as a part of a larger history of the American Civil War. His duties at the war college forced him to crystallize his thoughts on sea power and history. It was not his intention to do original research but rather to use the best historical works available to investigate his chosen field. From his lectures came the basis for his most important work, *The Influence of Sea Power Upon History: 1660–1783*, which appeared in 1890. There followed in 1892 *The Influence of Sea Power Upon the French Revolution and Empire: 1793–1812* and in 1905 *Sea Power in its Relations to the War of 1812*. He also wrote biographies and biographical sketches, as well as several interpretative articles upon events of his time.

A large number of his professional colleagues in the United States Navy did not recognize the importance of the task Mahan had set for himself. By his own choice, he retired from the navy in 1896 to pursue his literary career. He was a member of the naval war board that provided advice on strategy during the Spanish–American War. As a representative at the First International Conference at The Hague, he spoke against prohibiting poison gas, because he thought it inconsistent with permitting the use of the submarine torpedo. He was also instrumental in persuading American delegates not to sign the convention establishing the Hague Permanent Court of Arbitration until a reservation was added safeguarding the traditional position of the United States against European involvement in the Americas and American involvement in Europe.

Concepts of naval strategy. Mahan defined sea power as the ability of a nation to control movement across the sea. He claimed that this control is the most potent factor in national prosperity and in the course of history. The components of a nation's sea power are geographical factors and national resources, the character of its people and its government, and its diplomatic and naval policies.

From his studies Mahan derived several strategic principles, having to do with the concentration of force, the choice of the correct objective, and the importance of lines of communications. Reduced to more concrete terms these principles mean that a nation should construct a battle fleet that has as its main objective the ability to destroy an enemy battle fleet. French naval history in the seventeenth and eighteenth centuries and the American experience during the War of 1812 led him to believe that cruiser warfare and raids against merchant shipping were of secondary importance. Until Mahan, however, such warfare had been the basic naval strategy of the United States.

Mahan's works appeared at a time when national rivalries were producing the international crises that culminated in World War I and when technological developments made possible the *Dreadnought*-type battleship which had only big guns. His works were avidly read by the British, the Japanese, and the Germans. In his own nation, he exerted influence in part by his writings and in part by his close friendship with such leaders as Theodore Roosevelt and Henry Cabot Lodge.

Mahan's theories of sea power remained cogent in naval strategy until the middle of the twentieth century. After World War II his concepts of sea power required modification. He had studied naval rivalries and fleet actions; consequently, his theories were applicable primarily when two or more powers were contesting the control of the sea. His principles did not easily fit the post-World War II situation in which the United States, controlling the sea, confronted the Soviet Union, controlling a large land mass. Nonetheless, his principles are still valuable in military analyses.

Military power and theory of history. It was perhaps inevitable that Mahan, with his background and professional concerns, should see military force as playing a dominant role in history. To him history was the revelation of the plan of Providence. An integral part of this plan was the use of military force to preserve civilization and to right moral wrongs. It followed, therefore, that a nation could not blindly accept arbitration on all questions, for such arbitration might involve compromises on moral issues. Although Mahan saw history as a plan, he did not deny the individual a role: a military leader or a statesman can, by correct decision and action, shape events, but his power is limited by the materials with which he must work. Mahan, in his presidential address to the American Historical Association in 1902, issued a warning against too much research on detail, urging instead a careful grouping of facts and parts that would yield the truth of the whole.

Mahan was widely read in his own day. His emphasis on the role of the military and his call for expansion found resonance in the nationalism and imperialism of his time. While the basis of his philosophy was an orthodox, and even fundamentalist, Protestantism, the results of his thoughts were acceptable to the evolutionists of "the survival of the fittest" school. Historians feel that Mahan overstressed sea power and neglected the importance of other factors, but Mahan's contributions have not been erased. The strategic value of his principles has declined with the advent of the missile age and the nuclear weapon. Yet as both a historian and a strategist, Mahan influenced his own age and left a legacy of value to the future.

FRANCIS DUNCAN

[*For discussion of the subsequent development of Mahan's ideas, see* MILITARY POLICY *and* STRATEGY; *and the biography of* DOUHET.]

WORKS BY MAHAN

1883   *The Navy in the Civil War.* Volume 3: The Gulf and Inland Waters. New York: Scribner.

(1890) 1963   *The Influence of Sea Power Upon History: 1660–1783.* New York: Hill & Wang.

(1892) 1898   *The Influence of Sea Power Upon the French Revolution and Empire: 1793–1812.* 10th ed. Boston: Little.

(1897) 1899   *The Life of Nelson: The Embodiment of the Sea Power of Great Britain.* 2d ed., rev. Boston: Little.

(1897) 1918   *The Interest of America in Sea Power: Present and Future.* Boston: Little.

1899   *Lessons of the War With Spain, and Other Articles.* Boston: Little.

(1900) 1905   *The Problem of Asia and Its Effect Upon International Policies.* Boston: Little.

1902   *Retrospect and Prospect: Studies in International Relations, Naval and Political.* Boston: Little.

(1905) 1919   *Sea Power in Its Relations to the War of 1812.* Boston: Little.

1907   *From Sail to Steam: Recollections of Naval Life.* New York: Harper.

1909   *The Harvest Within: Thoughts on the Life of the Christian.* Boston: Little.

(1910) 1919 *The Interest of America in International Conditions.* Boston: Little.

1912 *Armaments and Arbitration: Or, the Place of Force in the International Relations of States.* New York: Harper.

SUPPLEMENTARY BIBLIOGRAPHY

DUNCAN, FRANCIS 1957 Mahan: Historian With a Purpose. United States Naval Institute, *Proceedings* 83: 498–503.

HUNTINGTON, SAMUEL P. 1954 National Policy and the Transoceanic Navy. United States Naval Institute, *Proceedings* 80:483–493.

LIVEZEY, WILLIAM E. 1947 *Mahan on Sea Power.* Norman: Univ. of Oklahoma Press. → Contains a comprehensive bibliography.

MAINE, HENRY SUMNER

Sir Henry Sumner Maine (1822–1888) was a lecturer on jurisprudence at Oxford and Cambridge, the founder of anthropological jurisprudence as an aspect of comparative law, a legal historian, and a colonial statesman. His enduring contribution to the social sciences is to be found in his formulation of the concept of ideal polar types and its uses in the comparative analysis of social phenomena.

Status and contract.   In his works, especially in *Ancient Law* (1861), Maine contrasted early societies in which social relations are dominated by *status* with "progressive" (complex) societies in which social relations are predominantly determined by *contract.* By status Maine meant "a condition of society in which all the relations of Persons are summed up in the relations of Family" ([1861] 1960, p. 99). These relations are ascribed to the individual as a member of a kinship group. By contract Maine meant individual obligation arising "from the free agreement of individuals."

Although Maine explicitly declared that he could recognize no evidence that proved any society to be entirely destitute of the concept of contract, his major proposition was that in early societies the individual creates few or no rights for himself and few or no duties. Rather, he is subject to the traditional rules that govern his status and to new rules which are issued as commands by the head of his household.

Maine held that the primitive kinship group is patrilineal and autocratic. The commands of the household headman are the authoritative expression of the *patria potestas.* "In truth, in the primitive view, Relationship is exactly limited by Patria Potestas. Where the Potestas begins, Kinship begins; . . . here we have the reason why the descend-ants of females are outside the limits of archaic kinship" (*ibid.*, p. 88).

The polar opposite to the patriarchally dominated, kinship-determined condition of status is the kind of social system exemplified by the complex Roman society during the time of Justinian. This kind of system is marked by contract-determined relations wherein the first person promises to perform acts or to observe certain forbearances and wherein a second person signifies his expectation that the first party will fulfill the proffered promise. The mental act of consensus is theoretically separated from the external formality of the ritual of the pact or convention (e.g., in transfers of possessions), and an obligation has been added which receives the full support of legal enforcement. This is true contract.

Maine wrote in the intellectual climate of eighteenth-century and nineteenth-century social evolutionism, and accordingly he set his model in an evolutionary mold. His polar types were designed not only to represent extremes in a range of variable social forms but also to describe development in the dimension of time. Hence the famous formula: ". . . we may say that the movement of the progressive societies has hitherto been a movement *from Status to Contract*" (*ibid.*, p. 100).

Because Maine worked exclusively with written historical records, his documentation of the evolutionary process was limited almost entirely to the Greco–Roman juridical experience. He judiciously defended this on the grounds that data on other ancient civilizations were scanty or altogether missing and that in any event Roman notions have so permeated most later systems as to preclude comparative study of crucial variations. Maine anticipated the concept of multilinear evolution when he expressed his belief that there can be no theory that accounts universally for the evolution of all social phenomena. Nonetheless, Maine concluded that "it may be reasonably believed that the history of ancient Roman Contracts is, up to a certain point, typical of the history of this class of legal conceptions in other ancient societies" (*ibid.*, p. 199).

In accordance with the concept of multilinear evolution, Maine proceeded to describe the steps by which the transformation from status to contract occurred. The life of ancient man in its earliest phases knew no custom, Maine believed, but was controlled by a regimen of caprice—the commanding judgments of the patriarchal family head or the king. These took the form of themistes —judgments on the individual case under the directive of divine inspiration. ". . . It must be distinctly understood," Maine held, "that they are not laws, but judgments . . . they cannot be supposed to be connected by any thread of principle; they are separate, isolated judgments" (*ibid.*, p. 3).

Subsequently, in the process of social evolution the heroic king lost his sacred power and was politically displaced by a class of aristocrats who were not themselves royalty. In Maine's account, the early councils of aristocrats, although they abjured the claim to divine inspiration (except in Asia), nonetheless established the claim that they alone knew the body of principles in accordance with which quarrels were to be settled. In short, they became the repositories and administrators of *law.* Theirs was the "epoch of customary law."

The next phase, called by Maine the "Era of Codes," followed the invention of writing. The reduction of law to the written word ended the "spontaneous" growth of law, and all subsequent legal development was the product of deliberate effort to close the gap between changing society and frozen codes.

Maine was not content to assert the idea of social evolution; he undertook to demonstrate evolutionary mechanisms. The instruments of legal change, which permitted the modification of the forms of archaic law and the growth of modern law, were examined by him in great detail, under the rubrics of fictions, equity, and legislation.

Particularly significant is Maine's treatment of legal fiction, defined as any assumption which conceals, or affects to conceal, the fact that a rule of law has undergone alteration, its letter remaining unchanged while its operation is modified. Fiction makes legal change possible at a time when it cannot be overtly admitted that change is possible. Maine considered fiction to be a more primitive device than equity, which followed. Equity is distinguished by the fact that there is recourse to a new body of principles which are believed to have universal validity (as in *jus gentium* and natural law). It exists alongside the pre-existing civil law but supersedes it. The last mechanism of change to be developed was legislation. It differs from all previous sources of law, in Maine's view, because its obligatory force is independent of its principles. Its authority derives from an external body, existing as fiat.

In early twentieth-century social science, particularly in anthropology, Maine's theory of comparative law fared rather badly. Although he enjoyed some first-hand knowledge of the village community in India, there are no references in his *Ancient Law*

to contemporary nonliterate tribal society. Maine was content to interpolate a hypothetical state of universal social organization from the materials of ancient Greece and Rome. He had nothing to say about customs and law in any known primitive society.

To the modern social scientist, Maine's customless society is not only empirically nonexistent but theoretically impossible. It has not been difficult for ethnographers to prove invalid Maine's assumption of the initial universality of patrilineal, patriarchal social organization, characterized by absolute submergence of the individual within the corporate whole. Of 564 nonliterate societies in G. P. Murdock's "World Ethnographic Sample" (1957), less than half (44 per cent) are patrilineal, one-third are bilateral, and one-sixth are matrilineal (Aberle 1961, p. 665). The very simplest of these primitive societies tend to be neither patrilineal nor matrilineal. Furthermore, detailed examination of actual primitive systems has demonstrated that the patriarchal authoritarianism of the *patria potestas*, as it was known in early Rome, is not a common characteristic of primitive patrilineality.

Recent empirical anthropology, following R. H. Lowie (1920), has demonstrated also the extent of nonkinship groupings (clubs, fraternities, voluntary associations) and relationships in primitive society. Anthropologists have thoroughly established that Maine was wrong in his dogmatic assumption that the kin bond was the sole initial basis of political union and that its later subversion by the establishment of local contiguity as the basis of common political action was an antipathetic revolution. Geography as well as kinship is now known to be a more or less important factor in all sociopolitical systems.

Tort and crime. A second major formulation of polar opposites advanced by Maine was the contrast between the law of tort and the law of crime. "If therefore," he wrote, "the criterion of a *delict, wrong,* or *tort* be that the person who suffers it, and not the State, is conceived to be wronged, it may be asserted that in the infancy of jurisprudence the citizen depends for protection against violence or fraud not on the Law of Crime but on the Law of Tort" ([1861] 1960, p. 218). The test is the law of responsibility for initiation and carrying through of legal action; it is a test of procedure. Although there is a good deal more of criminal law in the law of primitive societies than Maine imagined, Maine's contrast is essentially correct. The general trend of the law, from primitive to civilized, is toward an increasing shift of procedural responsibility from the individual as a member of a kinship group to the public officer as representative of the society at large.

Maine's influence. In spite of the antievolutionary reaction that almost submerged Maine, along with Lewis Henry Morgan, Tylor, and other social evolutionists of the late nineteenth century, Maine's working tool of ideal polar types was never wholly lost. Morgan used it to formulate his contrast of *societas* and *civitas*. Émile Durkheim used it to contrast the hypothetical isolated society of absolute homogeneity, bound by "mechanical solidarity," with the interdependent community ("the social organ") bound by the "organic solidarity" of interrelated, differentiated units. Through Durkheim, and through Tönnies' contrast of *Gemeinschaft* and *Gesellschaft*, Maine's influence on current French, German, and American sociology is clear.

As anthropology extends its interests beyond the illiterate tribe to the peasant community in the setting of civilization, interest in Maine is being renewed. The folk–urban continuum of Redfield and his followers is Maine's model with a new content. The extensive study of village communities in India and elsewhere, which burgeoned in the years following World War II, has revived Maine's work of comparative contrast, *Village-communities in the East and West* (1871).

In like manner, the current revival of interest in social evolution among anthropologists, as expressed in the writings of V. Gordon Childe, Leslie White, Julian H. Steward, and Marshall Sahlins, lends new vitality to Maine's work.

Above all, the problem of the economic and social development of recently independent underdeveloped nations has forced Maine's basic ideas once more to the fore. Economists, anthropologists, and sociologists have written extensively and emphatically to impress administrators of economic-development programs that African and Asian economic systems function as by-products of noneconomic institutions.

The most vigorous response to Maine's thought, relating to mid-twentieth century interests, is found in the writings of F. S. C. Northrop and his associates. Northrop goes beyond Maine, to hold that the concept of contract is a unique Roman invention, the product of Stoic lawyers creating, in the tradition of Greek mathematics, an imageless, logical–realistic universal concept. He attributes to the concept of contract the same significance for Western politico–legal development that the imageless constructs of Western scientific thought have for technical advancement and considers modern-

ization possible only if status-type social systems are replaced with universal contract relations.

In contrast, such men as Roscoe Pound and Morris Cohen, in their work earlier in this century with reference to trends within Western society, stressed countercontract developments in social and labor legislation that limit individual freedom of contract. Examples are workmen's compensation and minimum wage acts. Similarly, the standardization of contract terms in landlord–tenant, mortgage, insurance and other contracts is seen by some writers as substituting a group status-determinant for self-determination. Thus, when applied empirically to modern society, Maine's model is no more adequate than it proved to be when applied to actual primitive societies. In other words, contemporary empiricists have demonstrated that Maine's concept taken as absolute historical dogma will not stand up in detail; however, this does not mean that it may not be highly useful as a model of ideal types.

E. ADAMSON HOEBEL

[*For the historical context of Maine's work, see* EVOLUTION, *article on* CULTURAL EVOLUTION; JURISPRUDENCE; LAW; MODERNIZATION. *For discussion of the subsequent development of his ideas, see the biographies of* DURKHEIM; POUND; REDFIELD; TÖNNIES.]

WORKS BY MAINE

(1861) 1960 *Ancient Law: Its Connection With the Early History of Society, and Its Relations to Modern Ideas.* Rev. ed. New York: Dutton; London and Toronto: Dent. → A paperback edition was published in 1963 by Beacon.

(1871) 1890 *Village-communities in the East and West, to Which Are Added Other Lectures, Addresses, and Essays.* New ed. London: Murray.

(1875) 1897 *Lectures on the Early History of Institutions.* 7th ed. London: Murray. → A sequel to the author's *Ancient Law.*

SUPPLEMENTARY BIBLIOGRAPHY

ABERLE, DAVID F. 1961 Matrilineal Descent in Cross-cultural Perspective. Pages 655–727 in David M. Schneider and Kathleen Gough (editors), *Matrilineal Kinship.* Berkeley: Univ. of California Press.

BOHANNAN, PAUL 1963 *Social Anthropology.* New York: Holt.

GRANT DUFF, MOUNTSTUART E. 1892 *Sir Henry Maine: A Brief Memoir of His Life.* New York: Holt.

GRAVESON, R. H. 1940/1941 The Movement From Status to Contract. *Modern Law Review* 4:261–272.

HOEBEL, E. ADAMSON 1964 Status and Contract in Primitive Law. Pages 284–294 in F. S. C. Northrop and Helen H. Livingston (editors), *Cross-cultural Understanding: Epistemology in Anthropology.* New York: Harper.

LOWIE, ROBERT H. (1920) 1947 *Primitive Society.* New York: Liveright. → A paperback edition was published in 1961 by Harper.

Murdock, George P. 1957 World Ethnographic Sample. *American Anthropologist* New Series 59:664–687.

Northrop, F. S. C. 1964 Toward a Deductively Formulated and Operationally Verifiable Comparative Cultural Anthropology. Pages 194–222 in F. S. C. Northrop and Helen H. Livingston (editors), *Cross-cultural Understanding: Epistemology in Anthropology.* New York: Harper.

Redfield, Robert 1955 *The Little Community: Viewpoints for the Study of a Human Whole.* Univ. of Chicago Press. → A paperback edition was published in 1962.

Seagle, William (1941) 1946 *The History of Law.* 2d ed. New York: Tudor. → First published as *The Quest for Law.* See especially pages 252–277 in the 1941 edition, "The Omnipotence of Contract."

Smith, Joseph C. 1964 The Theoretical Constructs of Western Contractual Law. Pages 254–283 in F. S. C. Northrop and Helen H. Livingston (editors), *Cross-cultural Understanding: Epistemology in Anthropology.* New York: Harper.

Stone, Julius (1946) 1950 *The Province and Function of Law: Law as Logic, Justice, and Social Control; a Study in Jurisprudence.* Cambridge, Mass.: Harvard Univ. Press. → See especially pages 451–484 on "Social Types and Legal Types."

MAITLAND, FREDERIC WILLIAM

Frederic William Maitland (1850–1906), English legal historian and jurist, was born in London and died at Las Palmas in the Canary Islands, where ill-health had compelled him to winter since 1898. He was born into a family of intellectual distinction: his father was successively a fellow of Trinity College, Cambridge, a barrister, and secretary to the civil service commissioners; his mother was a daughter of a physicist, J. F. Daniell, a fellow of the Royal Society; his paternal grandfather, Samuel Roffey Maitland, barrister, clergyman, and for a short time the Archbishop of Canterbury's librarian at Lambeth Palace, London, was the author of 37 works, among them a remarkable book on medieval heresies (1832) that, in its skeptical attitude to accepted beliefs and its insistence on documentary proof, curiously anticipates the salient characteristics of his grandson's approach to history. From this grandparent, Maitland inherited, at the age of 16, a small property at Brookthorpe in Gloucestershire, which made him financially independent. In 1886 he married a niece by marriage of Sir Leslie Stephen (whom he commemorated in *The Life and Letters of Leslie Stephen* 1906), who was also the sister of H. A. L. Fisher, the historian and politician.

Education and academic career. With an excellent grounding in German from his governesses that was to serve him well in later life, Maitland went to Eton College in 1863, where his school life was unremarkable and unremarked, and then in 1869 to Trinity College, Cambridge. There he abandoned his first interest, mathematics, in favor of moral and mental sciences, in which he was bracketed first in the final examination in 1872. A long-distance runner for his university and a skilled oarsman for his college, he was also president of the Union Society and already noted for his fluent and witty speech. Called to the bar as a member of Lincoln's Inn in 1876, he was professionally engaged for eight years afterward in the work of conveyancing and equity; his first publication, in 1879, "The Law of Real Property" (see *Collected Papers,* vol. 1, pp. 162–201), entered a sardonic plea for the abolition of cumbrous procedures, however sacrosanct the passage of time had apparently made them. Not until 1926 was this reform belatedly accomplished.

Maitland was slow to find his true vocation and to realize that to him the history of the law was much more attractive than its practice. Nevertheless, his course was being set by three essays: "The Laws of Wales: The Kindred and the Blood Feud" in 1881, "The Criminal Liability of the Hundred" in 1882, and "The Early History of Malice Aforethought" in 1883 (*ibid.,* pp. 202–229, 230–246, 304–328). Furthermore, he had in these years taken the momentous step of reading legal records in the Latin shorthand of the original manuscripts at the Public Record Office in London and as a result edited his first book, *Pleas of the Crown for the County of Gloucester Before the Abbot of Reading . . . 1221* (1884). Seeking entrance to academic life, he was rejected by Oxford but accepted by Cambridge in 1884 as reader in English law. He produced a magnificent three-volume edition of *Bracton's Note Book* (1887), defraying the cost of publication himself. It contained a collection of some two thousand legal actions between 1217 and 1240 that had been made for the great thirteenth-century judge Henri de Bracton to use in writing his monumental treatise *De legibus et consuetudinibus Angliae* (1569). This scholarly achievement led to Maitland's appointment as Downing professor of the laws of England at Cambridge in 1888.

The legal historian. Before Maitland's time, the history of English law had suffered from three main defects: its expositors, among whom the most worthy was John Reeves (*History of the English Law* 1783–1829), were overwhelmed by the austere technicalities of the law as it existed in their day and in consequence produced quite unreadable factual surveys; they isolated the subject from all other departments of learning; and they saw no need to place it against its European background. Maitland wrought the great metamorphosis. Although he mastered the facts with infinite patience and used them constantly to provide concrete illustrations for his generalizations, he was interested above all else in the pattern of legal thought, particularly as it revealed itself in the origin and development of legal institutions. He insisted that the study of law, far from being a narrow, specialized discipline, provides the indispensable means of understanding the political, constitutional, social, economic, and religious history of the English people; he emphasized the value of comparative law, whether Roman and Germanic, Norman and French, Welsh and Scandinavian, and he placed the law of England firmly in the mainstream of European jurisprudence. In sharp contrast to William Stubbs, Maitland possessed the rare quality of mind that could free itself from the fetters of traditional concepts, whether about church or state, and reveal the way people of past eras defined the truth, thus making "the thoughts of men of the past thinkable to us."

Common law. To advance the knowledge of the history of English law, in 1887 he helped to found the Selden Society in London, and he sustained the burden of editing its early volumes until it had firmly established itself. Thus, he edited volume 1 of *Select Pleas of the Crown* (1888), *Select Pleas in Manorial and Other Seignorial Courts* (1889), and *The Court Baron* (1891a), and he provided the introduction to *The Mirror of Justices* (1895). These volumes helped to prepare the way for the incomparable *History of English Law Before the Time of Edward I* (1895). Though ostensibly a joint work with Sir Frederick Pollock, this work was written entirely by Maitland except for a section on Anglo-Saxon law. Soon after, Maitland made his own investigations into the dark terrain of pre-Conquest England in his *Domesday Book and Beyond* (1897). In 1903 he committed the Selden Society to the formidable task of printing the Year Books, which recounted the arguments of counsel in the king's courts from the first years of Edward I's reign until the time of the early Tudors, and he himself edited three of them and coedited three (1903–1951). To assist the reader, Maitland made an elaborate study of the complicated accidence of law French and this has ever since elicited the praise of grammarians. Whether discussing the knotty problem of law enforcement (1885) or the obdurate persistence of custom (1898a) or compiling the charters of the borough of Cambridge (1901a), he never failed to focus a new and brilliant light upon

the many facets of English society in the Middle Ages. [*See* LEGAL SYSTEMS, *article on* COMMON LAW SYSTEMS.]

Canon law. Although not anticlerical, Maitland was, in his own words, "a dissenter from all churches" and remarkably free from ecclesiastical presuppositions. His *Roman Canon Law in the Church of England* (1898b) revealed a whole library of theological books as invalid: it controverted the Anglican legend of the Reformation, which had been espoused by Stubbs, by showing that English ecclesiastical courts had regarded papal law as authoritative and had failed to observe it in practice only because of state intervention. [*See* CANON LAW.]

Comparative law. To discover the interplay between English common law and Roman law before the fourteenth century, Maitland examined in minute detail, in *Select Passages From the Works of Bracton and Azo* (1895), how much the English judge was indebted to the jurist of Bologna. At Cambridge in his Rede lecture, *English Law and the Renaissance* (1901), he looked again at the influence of Roman law, this time in Tudor England. To support his distinction between the concept of the trust and what was known abroad as the legal corporation, he translated part of the third volume of Otto Friedrich von Gierke's *Das deutsche Genossenschaftsrecht* under the title of *Political Theories of the Middle Age* (1900) [*see* GIERKE].

The history of Parliament. Although unappreciated at the time, it is now beyond question that Maitland's introduction to the parliament rolls of 1305, printed as *Records of the Parliament Holden at Westminster* (1893), abandoned the long-hallowed belief that the early parliament was a "national assembly of estates" and introduced the modern conception that it was essentially "the king's council" in one of its many forms. Maitland here achieved another breakthrough, another destruction of old habits of thought, and his brilliant essay has formed the starting point of a whole series of parliamentary studies, still vigorously pursued.

Literary style. As an artist in words, Maitland followed no conventions and is himself inimitable. The severity of the subject matter and the vast erudition needed to cope with it did not prevent him from attaining a beautiful clarity in exposition. He seems to take the reader into his confidence and to converse with him, charming him with his exquisite sense of the perfect word and phrase, his happy epigrams, his gay humor. Yet he has been termed the "historian's historian," and it is true that it was not simply literary merit that made him known to a wide circle: he probed deep below the surface in his preoccupation with analysis and rarely committed himself to writing narrative, although he did this with felicity in his chapter, "The Anglican Settlement and the Scottish Reformation" (1903).

Recognition. In the range of his interests, the fineness of his intellect, and the considerable bulk of what he wrote in barely twenty-five years, Maitland has no match among English historians. He was honored in his lifetime with doctorates from Cambridge (at the age of 41, while still serving that university), Oxford, Glasgow, Moscow, and Cracow; he was one of the first fellows of the British Academy; he was elected an honorary fellow of Trinity College, Cambridge, and a bencher of Lincoln's Inn; he was awarded the James Barr Ames medal by the Harvard law faculty. So highly was he revered that after his death, notes of his lectures were reassembled and published as *The Constitutional History of England* (1908), *Equity* (1909a), and *The Forms of Action at Common Law* (1909b).

Not all his views have been beyond dispute— for example, those on the garrison theory of borough origins, the superficiality of Bracton's knowledge of Roman law, the nature of corporations, the stability of the common law at the time of the Renaissance, and the Elizabethan religious settlement. Nevertheless, his reputation has increased, not dwindled, during the last sixty years: a historian can be paid no higher compliment.

G. O. SAYLES

[*See also* PARLIAMENTARY GOVERNMENT *and* PLURALISM.]

WORKS WRITTEN, EDITED, OR TRANSLATED BY MAITLAND

1884   GREAT BRITAIN, CURIA REGIS *Pleas of the Crown for the County of Gloucester Before the Abbot of Reading . . . 1221.* Edited by Frederic W. Maitland. London: Macmillan. → Text in Latin.

1885   *Justice and Police.* London: Macmillan.

1887   GREAT BRITAIN, COURTS *Bracton's Note Book.* Edited by Frederic W. Maitland, 3 vols. London: Clay. → A collection of cases decided in the reign of Henry III, annotated by a lawyer of that time, seemingly Henri de Bracton. Text in Latin.

1888   GREAT BRITAIN, CURIA REGIS *Select Pleas of the Crown.* Volume 1: A.D. 1200–1225. Edited for the Selden Society by Frederic W. Maitland. London: Quaritch. → Latin text and English translation on opposite pages.

1889   MAITLAND, FREDERIC W. (editor) *Select Pleas in Manorial and Other Seignorial Courts.* Volume 1: Reigns of Henry III. and Edward I. Edited for the Selden Society. London: Quaritch. → Latin text and English translation on opposite pages.

1891a   MAITLAND, FREDERIC W.; and BAILDON, WILLIAM P. (editors) *The Court Baron: Being Precedents for Use in Seignorial and Other Local Courts . . .* Edited for the Selden Society. London: Quaritch.

1891b   GREAT BRITAIN, CURIA REGIS *Three Rolls of the King's Court in the Reign of King Richard the First: A.D. 1194–1195.* Pipe Roll Society, London, Publications, vol. 14. With an introduction and notes by Frederic W. Maitland. London: Wyman.

(1893) 1964   GREAT BRITAIN, PARLIAMENT *Records of the Parliament Holden at Westminster on the Twenty-eighth Day of February, in the Thirty-third Year of the Reign of King Edward the First (A.D. 1305).* Edited by Frederic W. Maitland. New York: Kraus.

1895   Introduction. In Andrew Horn, *The Mirror of Justices.* London: Quaritch.

(1895) 1952   POLLOCK, FREDERICK; and MAITLAND, FREDERIC W. *The History of English Law Before the Time of Edward I.* 2 vols., 2d ed. Boston: Little.

1895   BRACTON, HENRI DE; and AZZO OF BOLOGNA *Select Passages From the Works of Bracton and Azo.* Edited for the Selden Society by Frederic W. Maitland. London: Quaritch.

1897   *Domesday Book and Beyond: Three Essays on the Early History of England.* Cambridge Univ. Press.

1898a   *Township and Borough.* Cambridge Univ. Press.

1898b   *Roman Canon Law in the Church of England: Six Essays.* London: Methuen.

(1900) 1958   Introduction. In Otto von Gierke, *Political Theories of the Middle Age.* Translated with an introduction by Frederic W. Maitland. Cambridge Univ. Press. → Gierke's work was first published in 1881 as "Die publicistischen Lehren des Mittelalters," a section of Volume 3 of Gierke's *Das deutsche Genossenschaftsrecht.*

1901a   CAMBRIDGE (ENGLAND), CHARTERS *The Charters of the Borough of Cambridge.* Edited by Frederic W. Maitland and Mary Bateson. Cambridge Univ. Press.

(1901b) 1957   English Law and the Renaissance. Pages 135–151 in Frederic W. Maitland, *Selected Historical Essays.* Cambridge Univ. Press.

(1903) 1934   The Anglican Settlement and the Scottish Reformation. Pages 550–598 in *Cambridge Modern History.* Volume 2: The Reformation. New York: Macmillan.

1903–1951   GREAT BRITAIN, YEAR BOOKS, 1307–1327 *Year Books of Edward II.* 24 vols. Edited for the Selden Society. London: Quaritch. → Volumes 1–3 were edited by Frederic W. Maitland, Volume 4 by F. W. Maitland and G. J. Turner, and Volumes 5 and 7 by W. C. Bolland, F. W. Maitland, and L. W. Vernon Harcourt.

1906   *The Life and Letters of Leslie Stephen.* London: Duckworth.

1908   *The Constitutional History of England.* Cambridge Univ. Press.

(1909a) 1936   *Equity.* Cambridge Univ. Press.

(1909b) 1936   *The Forms of Action at Common Law.* Cambridge Univ. Press.

The Collected Papers of Frederic William Maitland. 3 vols. Edited by H. A. L. Fisher. Cambridge Univ. Press, 1911.

The Letters of Frederic William Maitland. Edited by C. H. S. Fifoot. Cambridge, Mass.: Harvard Univ. Press, 1965.

Selected Essays. Edited by H. D. Hazeltine, G. Lapsley, and P. H. Winfield. Cambridge Univ. Press, 1936.

Selected Historical Essays. Chosen and introduced by Helen M. Cam. Cambridge Univ. Press, 1957.

SUPPLEMENTARY BIBLIOGRAPHY

BELL, H. E. 1965 *Maitland: A Critical Examination and Assessment.* London: Black; Cambridge, Mass.: Harvard Univ. Press.

BRACTON, HENRI DE (1569) 1915–1942 *De legibus et consuetudinibus Angliae.* 2 vols. New Haven: Yale Univ. Press.

DELANY, VINCENT T. H. (editor) 1957 *Frederic William Maitland Reader.* Dobbs Ferry, N.Y.: Oceana.

FISHER, HERBERT A. L. 1910 *Frederic William Maitland, Downing Professor of Laws of England: A Biographical Sketch.* Cambridge Univ. Press.

MAITLAND, SAMUEL R. 1832 *Facts and Documents Illustrative of the History, Doctrine and Rites of the Ancient Albigenses and Waldenses.* London: Rivington.

PLUCKNETT, T. F. T. 1958 *Early English Legal Literature.* Cambridge Univ. Press. → See especially "Maitland's View of Law and History" on pages 1–18.

REEVES, JOHN (1783–1829) 1880 *Reeves' History of the English Law, From the Time of the Romans to the End of the Reign of Elizabeth* [1603]. 5 vols. Philadelphia: Murphy.

SCHUYLER, ROBERT L. 1952 The Historical Spirit Incarnate: Frederic William Maitland. *American Historical Review* 57:303–322.

SMITH, ARTHUR LIONEL 1908 *Frederic William Maitland.* Oxford: Clarendon.

MAJORITY RULE

The term "majority rule" stands for a rule of decision making within a specified group. At its simplest, the rule requires that the vote of each member shall be counted as equal to that of every other and that no vote or decision by a minority may override that of a majority. By extension, majority rule is sometimes contrasted with any rule requiring that decisions be unanimous or by any number larger than a simple majority. According to this extended version, then, not only may a minority never override a majority but also it can never *check* a majority: a majority vote is conclusive for the whole group. It is common to distinguish this usage by referring to it as "bare majority" rule, rule by "simple majority," or "strict majoritarianism." Within democratic regimes most of the controversies about majority rule relate to whether it is desirable to apply the "bare majority" rule at some particular stage of the political process, or even whether the ethical premises of democracy demand its application. For electoral purposes it is common, especially where a two-party system prevails, to permit choice (election) by a plurality that is less than a majority. Strictly speaking, this procedure violates the majority principle, and such devices as run-off elections are often used to increase the probability that the elected candidate will have majority support.

History of theory and practice

Among the ancient Greeks, democracy entailed rule by majority vote of a popular assembly, of which all adult male citizens were members. Even in democratic Athens, however, there were institutional as well as practical limits on the power of majorities. A select group determined the agenda of the assembly, thus playing a significant role in framing the issues. Moreover, many important officials were selected by lot rather than by vote. This practice tended to limit the power of an organized majority or of a class or interest that comprised a majority, because in accordance with the laws of chance it gave proportionate representation to minority groups, as simple majority rule fails to do.

During the medieval period, whether in the great council of the church, in abbey chapter, or in secular parliament, decision by a bare or simple majority was slow to gain acceptance in practice and even slower to be vindicated in principle. The concurrence of all, the unanimity principle, seems universally to have been considered the ideal for positive action. It was common, however, to recognize that action could not be taken *against* the expressed wishes of a majority. (In this basic sense, majority rule prevailed.) The result was a kind of rule by "concurrent majorities" (Calhoun [1851] 1953, pp. 16–31). Typically, there was no fixed, mechanical formula for determining when a decision could be made, but unanimity was sought even if it could be obtained only by the process of wearing down and shouting down the dissenters—or by resort to threats or physical force. It was not until the sixteenth century that the ideal of unanimity and the practice of "veto groups" (the requirement of concurrence of the representatives of each town, county, etc.) gave way to the rule that the vote of a majority of individual representatives should prevail for positive as well as for negative action. Doubtless the rising individualism of this period, reinforced by the practical necessities of a state in which legislation was playing a far more important role than it had in the medieval period, led to this development.

The doctrine that the state should be based upon the consent of the majority of the people and that the specific acts of government should express the will of the majority (of adult males) was most systematically expounded and justified in the writings of John Locke (1690). Locke's fundamental position was founded upon the equality principle, which he assumed to be self-evident and which seemed to him to dictate the majority principle as opposed to any form of minority rule. Popular acceptance of this decision-making rule, he felt, was based upon both convenience and the superior strength of a majority.

This theory spread rapidly and became the foundation of political liberalism. Rousseau adopted it, with the important refinement that he specifically indicated that the support of more than a bare majority for all important political decisions should be insisted upon, unless the urgency of reaching a decision dictated otherwise [see ROUSSEAU]. In England, Jeremy Bentham and the Utilitarian school accepted the equalitarian principle unquestioningly and, as a corollary, accepted also the rule that for all political decisions the concurrence of a majority should be a sufficient as well as a necessary condition [see BENTHAM]. The theory and practice of constitutional democracy, however, as it spread throughout most of the Western world in the nineteenth and twentieth centuries, generally recognized certain individual and minority rights and gave them some form of constitutional protection, thus placing limitations on bare majorities. [See CONSTITUTIONS AND CONSTITUTIONALISM.]

Contemporary issues

Today, within the context of democratic principles, majority rule as the rule for decision making is the subject of continuing analysis and discussion from two points of view. One debate relates to whether it is legitimate, from the point of view of the democratic ethic, to require more than a bare majority for certain decisions. The other area of discussion deals with the question of whether majority rule is, in any sense of that difficult word, the best, most "rational" technique for expressing the equality principle, maximizing satisfaction, or attaining any other posited objective of democratic government.

Merits of majoritarianism.   Various writers have argued that the essence of the democratic ethic requires that the will (vote) of a simple majority should always prevail over the opposition. Any other rule, they urge, places a minority in a position to frustrate a majority and thus, in a sense, to rule. Accordingly, the logical and only legitimate derivative of the equalitarian, democratic assumption is held to entail bare majority rule.

Others defend the same decision-making rule on more pragmatic grounds. They maintain that a requirement, for any purpose, of more than a simple majority places undesirable obstacles in the way of government. The dice are sufficiently loaded against progressive change without placing in the hands of self-interested or traditionally oriented minorities a powerful instrument of obstructionism. As long as opportunity for free association, discussion, and deliberation prevails, they argue, the rights of minorities will not be trampled upon. In a fluid and pluralistic society, a majority will not consist of a solid, fixed interest but will be made up of shifting coalitions of groups well aware of the fact that tomorrow they may be part of a minority and, therefore, sensitive to the interests and rights of minorities.

Opponents of strict majoritarianism advance numerous arguments. First, they point out that the majoritarian principle might be used to destroy the conditions of its own existence, such as freedom of association and expression. Moreover, other individual rights widely accepted as fundamental, such as the right to freedom of religion, the protection of fair procedure ("due process"), or property rights, might not always be respected by the majority. They also contend that bare majority rule is potentially unfair: it does not really institutionalize the equality principle, for instead of giving to the minority its rightful proportionate weight, it gives it none at all. The strict majoritarian position is questioned on still another ground: not only does it fail to give weight to minorities; it also takes no account of the intensity of interest or demand. Finally, quite apart from the equality principle, the desirability of rule by a bare majority may be challenged on purely pragmatic grounds. Where feelings are intense, a decision to override a large minority poses a serious threat to basic consensus. On the question of racial segregation in United States public schools, for instance, the minority feels so intensely that the basis for law and order itself is threatened when the attempt is made to compel complete integration.

Majoritarians have frequently argued in an abstract manner that renders at least part of their position so unrealistic as to be inapplicable in real life. If it is the majority that should in all situations and at every turn rule, because of the principle of political equality, presumably it is the majority of the electorate who should rule. In other words, nothing short of direct democracy could satisfy this condition, for representatives do not always express the will of the majority of their constituents. Even if each representative did always vote the wishes of a majority of his constituents and if all constituencies contained exactly the same number of voters, the majority might not rule because minorities might be unevenly dispersed among the electoral districts. Moreover, on most questions that confront legislatures, many or most of the voters have no opinion, as opinion surveys are continually showing. The majority principle under these circumstances leads to pursuit of a will-o'-the-wisp. From these and similar considerations emerges the conclusion that the principle of political equality cannot lead to any clear and invariable rule for decision making. What institutional and voting arrangements should be adopted becomes a pragmatic matter, whether the goal is to reflect the desires of the greatest number of voters or whether different objectives, such as preservation of consensus and other conditions for continuing democracy and giving effect to intensity as well as numbers of opinions or desires, are taken into account.

Rational decision making. The other approach from which the problem of majority rule is currently being studied is a refinement of one of the arguments enumerated above, using the techniques of mathematics and of game theory. Even with models assuming rational men (defined as men who know what they want and pursue their ends by the most efficient means available), it appears that majority rule is not always an optimal decision-making process—that is, it does not maximize satisfaction. In particular, where the problem is one of allocation of goods, the results of majority decisions may be quite fortuitous, because everything depends upon the procedure adopted for proposing alternatives and submitting them for decision. Moreover, under certain circumstances, majority decisions may consistently lead to results that are less satisfactory (e.g., by the standard of the "Pareto optimum") than decisions arrived at in some other way (Buchanan & Tullock 1962, chapter 12; Ward 1961).

Serious problems could arise where voters' preferences are socially intransitive—that is, where the ways in which different voters would rank a series of possible choices are scrambled rather than patterned. For example: X prefers A to B, B to C, and A to C. Y prefers B to C, C to A, and B to A. Z prefers C to A, A to B, and C to B. It will be seen that a majority prefer A to B and B to C. It would seem, then, that the community, if it is rational, prefers A to C. But in fact a majority prefer C to A; and this result (known as the "voters' paradox") would be arrived at by the normal legislative procedure of voting on each of the possible pairs in turn (Arrow 1951, p. 3). This analysis suggests an important question: How often are preferences affecting political decisions in fact distributed in

this socially intransitive fashion? Currently data bearing on this question are almost wholly lacking [see Decision making].

Evaluation

It has been shown that it would be impossible to carry majority rule to its logical conclusion—to insist that all public policies be determined by majority will. Further, many arguments have been adduced that suggest serious ethical and practical limitations to the principle. Although the shortcomings of the principle are increasingly recognized, disagreement and sheer puzzlement as to desirable substitutes still prevail. Clearly no single alternative is acceptable. Beyond this point, generalization becomes difficult. Liberal democrats are widely agreed that individual and minority rights should have some protection against tyrannous majorities. Most constitutional democracies today seek to give a special status to some of these rights, protecting them from infringement by simple majorities. The government of Great Britain comes closer than most to enthroning simple majorities, yet even there the House of Lords remains as a slight check upon pure majoritarianism, while strong traditions of constitutional morality, fair play, and respect for minority rights place even more effective checks upon majorities. Many contend that informal checks are enough and that legal checks, whether in the form of requirements for extraordinary majorities or of the concurrence of different branches of a government responsible to separate constituencies, are unnecessary and undesirable. Some would cite the British experience in support of this position, but others would maintain that all depends upon the conditions of the country in question. In France under the Fourth Republic, for instance, institutional arrangements not very different from those that prevail in Britain permitted (and some would say encouraged) a degree of governmental instability that eroded consensus and respect for government to the point that the regime collapsed.

Granted, however, that constitutional devices to limit majorities may be desirable, it is difficult to show what devices are best, even under a given set of circumstances. Protection for the freedoms necessary for the continued effective functioning of majority rule are easily defended, but even here there is room for dispute as to means. It is difficult to determine whether requirements for extraordinary majorities, for bicameralism, or for the separation of powers are more or less likely to give proper weight to intense desires and to maximize satisfaction. Such devices do, however, have one important virtue, from the democratic point of view: they compel delay, giving time for deliberation; they force the majority, or those who are seeking governmental action, to try to win support for their proposal. This process is likely to contribute to the dissemination of information, to analysis of the probable effects of alternative courses of action, and to considered judgment of the various values and disvalues that may be involved. On such questions, however, one must rely at best on highly qualitative judgments. The need for research in this area is great.

Since modern industrial societies are typically highly pluralistic, majorities for any course of action can normally be obtained only by aggregating the support of a number of powerful groups. This process requires educational campaigns, argumentation, and deliberation. In itself it may meet the needs pointed out in the criticisms of majoritarianism, and it may do so without offering minority interests the opportunities for obstructionism provided by the numerous constitutional restraints embodied in, say, the constitution of the United States.

With respect to the shortcomings of the majority principle as a means for solving allocation problems in a way that maximizes satisfaction, a similar dilemma appears. It is easier to criticize the principle than to offer a better one. Here, again, the need for research and speculative imagination is great. Can ways be found to obtain fairer results without sacrificing the protection that majority rule provides against a consolidated and tyrannous minority? Can this be done without also giving up the values of popular interest and participation in the policy-making process? Ideally, different decision-making rules would be demanded for different situations, depending upon such variables as the type of question to be decided and the nature of the prevailing party and pressure-group systems.

One concluding point helps place the subject in perspective. Relatively small groups whose members view each other with respect and as equals tend to make their decisions unanimously, especially on important matters and, where unanimity is impracticable, to approach it as closely as possible. At the other extreme, small groups whose consensus is low are also likely to insist upon unanimity, more from mutual distrust than from mutual respect. In large groups unanimity is impracticable. If consensus is high, as in Great Britain, the polity may tolerate rule by simple majority. Where the society is more heterogeneous,

or the divisions are sharper, concurrence by more than a simple majority will often be required and will, in fact, be essential for the preservation of a viable polity.

J. ROLAND PENNOCK

[*See also* CONSENSUS; DEMOCRACY; ELECTIONS; EQUALITY; LIBERALISM; REPRESENTATION.]

BIBLIOGRAPHY

ARROW, KENNETH J. (1951) 1963 *Social Choice and Individual Values.* 2d ed. New York: Wiley.

BATY, THOMAS 1912 The History of Majority Rule. *Quarterly Review* 216:1–28.

BLACK, DUNCAN 1958 *The Theory of Committees and Elections.* Cambridge Univ. Press.

BUCHANAN, JAMES M.; and TULLOCK, GORDON 1962 *The Calculus of Consent: Logical Foundations of Constitutional Democracy.* Ann Arbor: Univ. of Michigan Press.

CALHOUN, JOHN C. (1851) 1953 *A Disquisition on Government, and Selections From the Discourse.* New York: Liberal Arts Press. → Published posthumously.

CLARKE, MAUDE V. (1936) 1964 *Medieval Representation and Consent: A Study of Early Parliaments in England and Ireland With Special Reference to the Modus Tenendi Parliamentum.* New York: Russell.

DE GRAZIA, ALFRED 1963 *Apportionment and Representative Government.* New York: Praeger. → A paperback edition was published in 1963 by the American Enterprise Institute.

FRIEDRICH, CARL J. 1942 *The New Belief in the Common Man.* Boston: Little. → See especially Chapter 4.

HEINBERG, JOHN G. 1932 Theories of Majority Rule. *American Political Science Review* 26:452–469.

KENDALL, WILLMOORE 1950 Prolegomena to Any Future Work in Majority Rule. *Journal of Politics* 12:694–713.

LINDBLOM, CHARLES E. 1965 *The Intelligence of Democracy: Decision Making Through Mutual Adjustment.* New York: Free Press.

LOCKE, JOHN (1690) 1964 *The Second Treatise of Government: An Essay Concerning the True Original, Extent, and End of Civil Government.* Pages 283–446 in John Locke, *Two Treatises of Government.* Cambridge Univ. Press.

McCLOSKY, HERBERT 1949 The Fallacy of Absolute Majority Rule. *Journal of Politics* 11:637–654.

MIMS, EDWIN JR. 1941 *The Majority of the People.* New York: Modern Age.

PENNOCK, J. ROLAND 1952 Responsiveness, Responsibility and Majority Rule. *American Political Science Review* 46:790–807.

RANNEY, J. AUSTIN; and KENDALL, WILLMOORE 1951 Democracy: Confusion and Agreement. *Western Political Quarterly* 4:430–439.

RIKER, WILLIAM H. 1961 Voting and the Summation of Preferences: An Interpretive Bibliographical Review of Selected Developments During the Last Decade. *American Political Science Review* 55:900–911.

ROUSSEAU, JEAN JACQUES (1762) 1962 *The Social Contract.* New York: Oxford Univ. Press. → First published in French. See especially Book 4, Chapter 2.

WARD, BENJAMIN 1961 Majority Rule and Allocation. *Journal of Conflict Resolution* 5:379–389.

MAJUMDAR, D. N.

D. N. Majumdar (1903–1960) was born of Bengali parents. He obtained a first-class master's degree in anthropology from the University of Calcutta in 1924. The training that he received there was in both cultural and physical anthropology, and to the end of his life he retained a broad interest in both the physical and the cultural aspects of the science of man. A large number of his papers and two of his books deal with anthropometric and serological studies among the tribes and castes of Uttar Pradesh, Gujarat, and Bengal.

"General anthropology" was not a mere slogan for Majumdar; it reflected his firm conviction that a unified science of man is not only desirable but also possible. Thus, in his analyses of social stratification in India, he emphasized the need to examine racial factors. Earlier H. H. Risley, in *The Tribes and Castes of Bengal* (1891a; 1891b) and *The People of India* (1908), had asserted a relationship between race and social groups in India; Majumdar gave further support to this view by his own extensive investigations. He showed that in Uttar Pradesh those castes which constitute "clusters," being close to each other in the hierarchy of castes, also fall within a narrow range of biometric variation (1949). Similarly, in his unpublished studies of growth among the schoolchildren of Uttar Pradesh, he included a sociocultural factor as a significant variable.

The greater part of Majumdar's published work is ethnographic in nature and consists of accounts of the Ho (Bihar), the Khasa, the Korwa, the Tharu, and the so-called criminal tribes (all of Uttar Pradesh), the Gond (Madhya Pradesh), and the Bhil (Gujarat). He published monographic studies of both the Ho (1937) and the Khasa (1962). He knew the Khasa best and spent 22 summers doing field work among them.

Majumdar considered these studies to be contributions to cultural anthropology; he regarded social anthropology as a subdiscipline within cultural anthropology and not as an alternative frame of reference for the study of human social behavior. His approach to the study of culture was that of a functionalist. He went to England in 1933 to work for his doctorate at Cambridge, and he was awarded his degree in 1935. While in England he attended Malinowski's seminar at the London School of Economics and came under his abiding influence. Majumdar was also much influenced by the writings of Ruth Benedict (e.g., Majumdar 1944a). He stressed the integrated character of culture and maintained that cultural

stresses and strains are the outcome of a disturbance in a culture's "base." The "base" of a culture, he wrote (1937), is a function of four variables, namely, man, area, resources, and cooperation. If the disturbance is not of too fundamental a nature, a culture has a tendency to absorb the shock and revert to its original character; if otherwise, it changes to attain a new equilibrium (1958). His view of culture was thus essentially "integrationist," though not static.

Majumdar was the first formally trained Indian anthropologist to study the impact of nontribal cultures upon the ways of life of Indian tribes. This early interest in cultural change led him, in the 1950s, to welcome the emergence in India of rural anthropology. He played a notable part in this new field of research and produced one of the first book-length village studies in India (1958).

He also pleaded for the application of the findings of social science to the task of national reconstruction. As a member of the Research Programmes Committee of the National Planning Commission, he emphasized the help which anthropologists and sociologists could give to the administration by studying the problems of backward communities and by assessing the impact of government-sponsored projects of community development. His posthumous book on the Khasa (1962) contains a detailed discussion of the community development program in Jaunsar-Bawar (Uttar Pradesh).

It was Majumdar's deep belief in the utility of applied sociological research which made him undertake, in 1954, a survey of the industrial city of Kanpur in Uttar Pradesh (1960a). In this, as in many other personal and academic attitudes, he reflected the strong influence of Western social science. Although he did not visit the United States until 1952–1953, when he attended a Wenner–Gren Foundation symposium on anthropology and lectured at Cornell University, from quite early in his life he was receptive to ideas emanating from American universities. Thus, in his very first book (1937) he underscored the importance of studying the psychological dimension of human behavior, particularly in the acceptance and rejection of innovations.

Majumdar's ethnographic works are characterized by a richness and precision of detail, but they lack theoretical sophistication. This is probably due to the fact that almost the whole of his work in physical as well as in cultural anthropology was of a pioneering nature. More than any other individual of his generation, he endeavored to place anthropological studies in India on a scientific footing. The success he achieved, considering the circumstances, was considerable.

At the time of his death, Majumdar was professor of anthropology and dean of the faculty of arts at the University of Lucknow. When he died, a book on polyandry among the Khasa was about to be published; at least one more (a village study) was ready for the publisher; and a research project on growth among schoolchildren in Uttar Pradesh was in progress. He was editor of the *Eastern Anthropologist*, a journal he founded in 1947. All these activities bear testimony to the breadth of his academic interests.

T. N. MADAN

[*Directly related are the entries* ASIAN SOCIETY, *article on* SOUTH ASIA; CASTE; *and the biographies of* BENEDICT *and* MALINOWSKI.]

WORKS BY MAJUMDAR

(1937) 1950   *The Affairs of a Tribe: A Study in Tribal Dynamics.* New & enl. ed. Lucknow: Universal Publishers. → First published as *A Tribe in Transition: A Study in Culture Patterns.*

1944a   *The Fortunes of Primitive Tribes.* Lucknow: Universal Publishers.

(1944b) 1961   *Races and Cultures of India.* 4th ed., rev. & enl. New York and Bombay: Asia Pub. House.

1947   *The Matrix of Indian Culture.* Lucknow: Universal Publishers.

1949   MAHALANOBIS, P. C.; MAJUMDAR, D. N.; and RAO, C. R. Anthropometric Survey of the United Provinces, 1941: A Statistical Study. *Sankhyā: The Indian Journal of Statistics* 9:89–324.

1950   *Race Realities in Cultural Gujarat: Report on the Anthropometric, Serological and Health Survey of Maha Gujarat.* Bombay: Gujarat Research Society.

(1956) 1960   MAJUMDAR, DHIRENDRA N.; and MADAN, T. N. *An Introduction to Social Anthropology.* New York and Bombay: Asia Pub. House.

1958   *Caste and Communication in an Indian Village.* Bombay: Asia Pub. House.

1960a   *Social Contours of an Industrial City: Social Survey of Kanpur; 1954–1956.* New York and Bombay: Asia Pub. House.

1960b   MAJUMDAR, DHIRENDRA N.; and RAO, CALYAMPUDI R. *Race Elements in Bengal: A Quantitative Study.* With a foreword by P. C. Mahalanobis. New York and Bombay: Asia Pub. House.

1962   *Himalayan Polyandry: Structure, Functioning and Culture Change; A Field-study of Jaunsar-Bawar.* New York and Bombay: Asia Pub. House. → Published posthumously.

SUPPLEMENTARY BIBLIOGRAPHY

RISLEY, HERBERT H.   1891a   *The Tribes and Castes of Bengal: Ethnographic Glossary.* 2 vols. Calcutta: Bengal Secretariat Press.

RISLEY, HERBERT H.   1891b   *The Tribes and Castes of Bengal: Anthropometric Data.* 2 vols. Calcutta: Bengal Secretariat Press.

RISLEY, HERBERT H.   (1908) 1915   *The People of India.* 2d ed. Calcutta: Thacker.

MALINOWSKI, BRONISLAW

Bronislaw Kaspar Malinowski (1884–1942) was a Polish-born social anthropologist whose professional training and career, beginning in 1910, were based in England. Through his scientific activities, especially his methodological innovations, he was a major contributor to the transformation of nineteenth-century speculative anthropology into a modern science of man. As a fieldworker, a scholar, a theorist, and above all, a brilliant and controversial teacher and lecturer, he played a decisive part in the formation of the contemporary British school of social anthropology. An accomplished polemicist, he also attracted a wide audience to anthropology as a field of knowledge. Early in his own development he came to view anthropology as a field-oriented science, in which theory and the search for general laws must be based on intensive empirical research involving systematic observation and detailed analyses of actual behavior in living, ongoing societies. His principal field work was carried out among the Papuo-Melanesian people of the Trobriand Islands, located off the coast of New Guinea.

Malinowski's primary scientific interest was in the study of culture as a universal phenomenon and in the development of a methodological framework that would permit the systematic study of specific cultures in all their particularities and open the way to systematic cross-cultural comparison. He reacted strongly against the speculative reconstructions of both evolutionists and diffusionists and against the atomistic treatment of traits and trait complexes torn from their cultural contexts (1926a; 1929a; 1931a). In *The Dynamics of Culture Change* (1945) he insisted that culture change must be subjected to observation and analysis of the total interactive situation. [*See* CULTURE, *article on* CULTURE CHANGE.]

Malinowski was the originator of a functionalist approach to the study of culture. Although the idea of "function" is a key concept throughout his work—from his early scholarly research on the Australian aboriginal family (1913) to his final theoretical statement in *A Scientific Theory of Culture* (1944a)—his use of the term was open-ended, exploratory, and subject to continual modification. He treated culture as the assemblage of artifacts and organized traditions through which the individual is molded and the organized social group maintains its integration and achieves continuity. But he also treated culture as an instrumental reality and emphasized its derivation from human needs, from the basic universal needs of the individual organism to the highly elaborated and often specialized needs of a complex society. In his view functionalism was a research tool, "the prerequisite for field-work and for the comparative analysis of phenomena in various cultures" (1944*a*, p. 175), that permitted the study of aspects of culture and the analysis of culture in depth. Through the intermediate analysis of institutions, a functionalist approach revealed the multilevel relationships between man as a psychobiological organism and man's creation, culture. [*See* FUNCTIONAL ANALYSIS.]

For purposes of research and exposition, Malinowski treated each culture as a closed system and all cultures as essentially comparable. However, he made little use of the comparative method, except illustratively. Rather, he treated the empirical study of a specific culture as a contribution to the understanding of the universal phenomenon of culture. In *Argonauts of the Western Pacific* he stated that the ethnographer's final goal must be

to grasp the native's point of view, his relation to life, to realize *his* vision of *his* world. We have to study man, and we must study what concerns him most intimately, that is, the hold which life has on him. . . . In each culture we find different institutions. . . . To study the institutions, customs, and codes or to study the behaviour and mentality without the subjective desire of feeling by what these people live, of realising the substance of their happiness—is, in my opinion, to miss the greatest reward which we can hope to obtain from the study of man. . . . Perhaps as we read the account of these remote customs there may emerge a feeling of solidarity with the endeavours and ambitions of these natives. Perhaps man's mentality will be revealed to us, and brought near, along some lines which we never have followed before. Perhaps through realising human nature in a shape very distant and foreign to us, we shall have some light shed on our own.   (1922*a*, p. 25 in the 1961 edition)

Malinowski regarded residence among the people under study, competent use of the native language, observation of the small events of daily life as well as the large events affecting the community, sensitivity to conflict and shades of opinion, and a consideration of each aspect within the context of the whole culture as indispensable conditions to ethnographic work and, indirectly, to the sound development of theory. His demands on the fieldworker are very high; what is continually captivating is his expectation of the ethnographer's involvement simultaneously with "these natives" and with "man." [*See* ETHNOGRAPHY.]

Intellectual background.   Malinowski was born in Cracow in the region of Poland that was then politically part of the Austro–Hungarian empire. His father, Lucyan Malinowski, 1839–1898, an emi-

nent Slavic philologist, was instrumental in bringing modern linguistic studies to Poland and also did work in ethnography and folklore (Symmons-Symonolewicz 1959). Bronislaw Malinowski grew up at a time and in a setting in which central European intellectuals were deeply aware not only of their special cultural heritage (which led many to an intense political nationalism) but also of the multilingual, multicultural milieu in which they moved. Malinowski had a gift for language, and like many intellectuals of his background, he had a wide command of modern languages, including Polish, Russian, German, French, English, Italian, and Spanish. In terms of his background, it is illuminating that his scientific interest in language centered on language as a mode of behavior and on problems of culturally determined meaning. In the same period that Franz Boas returned to the field to study types of speech, using new recording devices, Malinowski predicted the use of sound film for the study of "fully contextualized utterances" (1935*a*, vol. 1, p. 26).

His early experience certainly contributed to his assumptions about cultural uniqueness and the comparability of all cultures, assumptions that are not fully spelled out or tested in his work. They are, of course, crucial to his use of a single primitive culture, that of the Trobriands, as his vehicle of methodological exploration and analysis. However, in seminar discussions he drew—and encouraged his students to draw—on a wide range of complex cultures for contrast and comparison. Both forms of exposition delighted him.

Malinowski's initial training was in physics and mathematics, in which he took his PH.D. in 1908 at the Jagellonian University in Cracow. Ill health, which pursued him all his life, forced him to terminate work in these fields. Then, "as the only solace to his troubles," he began to read, in English, the three-volume edition of Frazer's *The Golden Bough* and discovered that "anthropology . . . is a great science, worthy of as much devotion as any of her elder and more exact sister studies" (1925*a*, pp. 93–94 in the 1954 edition).

For a brief period he studied at the University of Leipzig (where his father had earlier received his doctorate) and, working under Wilhelm Wundt and Karl Bücher, came in contact with current ideas of experimental psychology and historical economics. But in 1910, when he went to England as a postgraduate student at the London School of Economics, he already had his research on Australian aboriginal culture under way (Barnes 1963, p. xii) and probably his book on primitive religion and forms of social structure, later published in Poland (1915*a*).

Work on kinship. British anthropology was lively and contentious then, and Malinowski's work was responsive to the crosscurrents of thought. *The Family Among the Australian Aborigines* (1913) is a magnificent tour de force in its use of a vast patchwork of source materials to make the point (doubtful to those who looked upon the peoples of Australia as the living exemplars of an earlier stage of man) that these peoples had "individual marriage." Characteristically, Malinowski had another aim: "It is not *the* actual relationship, or *the* individual family, or 'family in the European sense'. . . . It is the aboriginal Australian individual family, with all its peculiarities and characteristic features, which must be constructed from the evidence" ([1913] 1963, p. 8). Westermarck's influence on his thinking is clear [*see the biography of* WESTERMARCK]. But he also raised the question of how to "find in all this complexity the structural features, the really essential facts, the knowledge of which in any given society would enable us to give a scientifically valid description of kinship" (*ibid.*, p. 198). Family and kinship, the unique culture and the universally applicable method, these are constant themes in his work.

This study is chiefly valuable today as a period piece and as a source book on Malinowski's thinking at the outset of his career. However, his handling of the data and choice of subject matter are measures of his virtuosity and unerring ability to select as the carrier of his own ideas a problem attractive to fellow scientists and a wider audience as well. [*See* KINSHIP.]

Field research. His interest now shifted to field research in New Guinea, an area that was being opened up by A. C. Haddon, W. H. R. Rivers, C. G. Seligman, and others who influenced his thinking. His training in scientific method and the fine detail of his scholarly work peculiarly fitted him for a part in developing the new techniques of intensive field research. Mainly through Seligman's efforts, he obtained a Robert Mond Travelling Studentship (University of London) and a Constance Hutchinson Scholarship (London School of Economics). Thus equipped, he went out to New Guinea via Australia, where he attended a meeting of the British Association as a guest of the Commonwealth government (which later made him a supplementary grant). In view of the cost of modern field research, it is enlightening to realize that over the six-year period 1914–1920, he had available for field work, data collection, and writing "little more than £250 a year" (1922a, p. xix in the 1961 edition).

His first expedition, September 1914 to February 1915, was to the Mailu of Toulon Island. Already familiar with the structure of Melanesian languages—in *Coral Gardens and Their Magic* (1935a, vol. 1, p. 453), Malinowski described his progress in learning these languages—he spent four weeks in Port Moresby working on pidgin English and Motu, the lingua franca used by the Mailu. His report on the Mailu (1915b), together with his Australian researches, earned him his D.SC. in 1916. But in later years he discounted this first field work. He found the Mailu "coarse and dull" (1922a, p. 34 in the 1961 edition). What excited his interest were their accounts of the Massim, to the east, from whom came handsome objects, lively songs and dances, and fearful tales of sorcery and cannibalism. Yet his report on the Mailu is of interest, since it documents not only his use of a conventional framework but also his attempt to use new kinds of ethnographic subject matter (for example, his observations of daily life), his difficulties in coming to grips with the problems of working in an ongoing society, and his leap ahead in recognizing essential conditions for field work. The necessity of working through an interpreter and an intermediate language was a particular source of frustration.

Returning to Australia, he paused briefly on Woodlark Island, where he hoped to work later. Instead, his second expedition, from June 1915 to May 1916, took him to the Trobriand Islands. He set up his tent in Omarakana, the village in which he began his work. By September he had dispensed with an interpreter and was using Kiriwinian, the Trobriand language. But he could follow fast conversation and take notes in the language only on his second Trobriand field trip, from October 1917 to October 1918, after he had organized his first year's notes (1935a, vol. 1, p. 453).

Between field trips he wrote his first account of the culture, "Baloma: The Spirits of the Dead in the Trobriand Islands" (1916). In retrospect, it is clear that he had now found his subject, his style of work, and his characteristic mode of presentation. In this essay he described in vivid detail the afterlife of the spirits (*baloma*), their relations to the living, their return visits at feasts in their honor, and their reincarnation. In one digression he discussed magic spells, the use of ancestral names in magic, and the inheritance of magic in this matrilineal, patrilocal society. Another dealt with Trobriand ignorance of physiological paternity and his struggle in the field to clarify Trobriand belief. In the final section he discussed the fieldworker's problem of bringing order into the "chaos of facts"—here referring to the diversity of views, the different levels of knowledge, and the various types of emotional response among different individuals. Fresh from the field, he was convinced that "no 'natives' [in the plural] have ever any belief or any idea; each one has his own ideas and his own beliefs" (1925a, p. 240 in the 1954 edition). The ethnographer, studying the "social dimension" in all its complexity, must find ways of systematizing the diversity of formulations and of extricating ideas and beliefs from native behavior and the institutions in which they are embedded. He wrote that "field work consists only and exclusively in the interpretation of the chaotic social reality, in subordinating it to general rules" (ibid., p. 238). [See FIELD WORK.] Finally, he defined the opposition between "individual ideas" and "the dogmas of native belief, or the social ideas of a community" that must be "treated as invariably fixed items" (ibid., p. 244), and so he laid the groundwork for his later discussions of myth, magic, and religion. But even as he acknowledged his indebtedness to Durkheim and his school, he rejected the concept of "collective ideas" as incompatible with the reality of the "aggregate of individual souls" in a community (ibid., pp. 273–274, n. 77). This highly selective way of handling the theories of his predecessors, in which he transformed what he accepted, was characteristic of Malinowski's approach, especially in his polemical writings.

This essay exhibits the mosaic quality that is typical of Malinowski's exposition. He stated a theme, he developed it in narrative form around an institution, a set of institutions, or the activities relevant to an aspect of the culture, and at different stages, he interpolated data on other aspects, other activities. Thus, step by step he progressed toward abstraction. On a larger scale the whole of the work on the Trobriands forms a very elaborate mosaic, no part of which stands wholly alone. The successive discussions are not serially linked; instead, his analysis grows by expansion and elaboration, over time, with the elaboration of his own thinking in the process of organizing the data. Yet each work, like this first long essay on the spirits of the dead, is characteristic of the whole.

A large part of Malinowski's work consists in the attempt to develop principles and create models for just this intermediate stage of interpretation, using Trobriand culture as his laboratory. One of the persistent criticisms of his work is that it is "overloaded with reality" (Gluckman 1947, p. 15). But it is with the ordering of this reality that he was concerned.

Career in London. In October 1918 Malinowski returned from the field to Australia. There he married Elsie Masson. He did not immediately go back to London but for reasons of health spent a period on Tenerife in the Canary Islands, where he worked on *Argonauts of the Western Pacific*.

He had first begun to lecture at the London School of Economics in 1913; in the early 1920s he again began to give short courses. In 1924 he was appointed to a readership in anthropology and in 1927 to the first chair in anthropology at the University of London. With the publication of *Argonauts* (1922a) his position as a scientist was secure, and he began to acquire an international reputation. The next 15 years, 1923–1938, were his most productive ones as a writer and as a teacher who drew into his seminars an ever-increasing number of talented and mature students, research workers, and professionals from various fields.

Describing Malinowski's relations to his students, Audrey I. Richards wrote:

He tended to regard them rather as a team engaged on a joint battle than as a number of individuals with different interests and needs. They learnt a particular method of work and a particular theoretical interest, rather than a body of detailed facts. . . . It was in seminars that his teaching gifts were best displayed. These weekly discussions became famous, and attracted students of the most different types. Colonial officers on leave valued Malinowski's live approach. . . . Senior research students came from many parts of the world, and Malinowski would often flash retorts in four or five different languages. University lecturers sat side by side with the veriest amateurs. . . . There was a curious kindling touch in all he did, and a rare power of evoking ideas in others. (1943, p. 3)

Malinowski's teaching methods reflected his own quick responsiveness and his need for response in others. Intellectual pretense he treated with caustic contempt, but he had unexpected resources of patience and gentleness in his relations with able, still inexperienced and self-doubting students. As more mature students progressively measured themselves against his standards of intellectual complexity, skill, and originality, he could be in turn ruthlessly witty at their expense, provocative, and devastatingly critical of what he valued most in them, their capacity for independent judgment. His most able students in time responded with anger and self-assertion mixed with admiration and devotion, a complex of attitudes that is evident in their later, very careful assessments of his work (Firth 1957; Gluckman 1947).

Malinowski's publications in his London years fall into several groups which, while overlapping, indicate his varied interests.

First, there are his major works on the Trobriand Islanders. *Argonauts of the Western Pacific* is an analysis of Trobriand economics through the study of overseas trading expeditions in the highly formalized *kula* ring, in which the circular exchange of "valuables" provided a setting for trade and communication [*see* ECONOMIC ANTHROPOLOGY]. *The Sexual Life of Savages in Northwestern Melanesia* (1929*b*) is an exposition of the individual's induction into the adult life of marriage and the family. Here Malinowski worked out in the field what he had glimpsed through his study of the Australian aboriginal family, and even today it is one of the most detailed and acute analyses of how, in one primitive society, cultural tradition molds individual behavior in the most highly emotionally charged aspect of personal life. *Coral Gardens* (1935*a*), Malinowski's most sophisticated and self-critical work, deals with the organization of Trobriand social life through activities related to horticulture, the place of magic in the belief system, and the integrative aspects of gardening. In this work Malinowski also presented the most sustained exposition of his linguistic approach through analyses of gardening spells.

In a second group of publications, including "Magic, Science and Religion" (1925*a*), *Crime and Custom in Savage Society* (1926*b*), *Myth in Primitive Psychology* (1926*c*), and *The Foundations of Faith and Morals* (1936*a*), he took up, and on several occasions returned to, topics that had long provided controversial issues. Each statement is, among other things, a demonstration of the transforming effect of detailed field work on the criteria of what is relevant to the delineation of a problem. Perhaps in no other context does Malinowski give such clear evidence of his position as a transition figure in social science. For in these essays he breaks new ground not in his choice of topic but in his dazzling use of field data. Yet, though he looks forward in this, he remains linked to the past in his use of very limited data to generalize about primitive culture and man.

Magic, science, and religion. In his handling of science, magic, and religion, Malinowski essentially accepted the traditional Western conception of a dual reality—the reality of the natural world, grounded in observation and rational procedures that lead to mastery, and supernatural reality, grounded in emotional needs that give rise to faith. Unlike Frazer, for example, Malinowski derived science not from magic but from man's capacity to organize knowledge, as demonstrated by Trobriand technical skills in gardening, shipbuilding, etc. In contrast, he treated magic, which coexisted with these skills, as an organized response to a sense of limitation and impotence in the face of danger,

difficulty, and frustration. Again, he differentiated between magic and religion in defining magical systems as essentially pragmatic in their aims and religious systems as self-fulfilling rituals organized, for example, around life crises. Significantly, he differentiated between the individual character of religious experience and the social character of religious ritual. In his analysis he linked myth to magic and religion, not as an explanation but as evidence of the authenticity of the magical act and the religious dogma. Particularly illuminating is his discussion of the use of public magic in the Trobriands as an initiating act in the organization of stages of work. *The Foundations of Faith and Morals* represents an attempt to apply hypotheses based on primitive cultures to the problems of European societies [*see* MAGIC; *see also* Nadel 1957].

Anthropology and psychology. Throughout his career Malinowski sought for a systematic psychology on which he could draw in establishing a dynamic relationship between man and culture. In the 1920s Freudian theory had a profound, if somewhat diffuse, influence on his thinking. As Meyer Fortes has pointed out (Firth 1957, pp. 157–188 *passim*), Freud's hypothesis about the Oedipal situation provided Malinowski with a psychological framework for developing his own analysis of the relationship of father, son, and maternal uncle in Trobriand culture. Although he later turned against psychoanalysis, such publications as "The Psychology of Sex" (1923*a*), "Psycho-analysis and Anthropology" (1924), *The Father in Primitive Psychology* (1927*a*), and *The Sexual Life of Savages* (1929*b*), in which he incorporated much of the earlier material, indicate the creative use he made of psychoanalytic concepts and some of the difficulties he faced in trying to transform psychological into cultural process. Even though Malinowski derived culture ultimately from man's needs, he eventually gave precedence to cultural tradition as the primary influence in the molding of the individual. In his last years at Yale he was attracted by Hullian learning theory (1944*a*); in fact, however, it had little effect on the core of his thinking. [*See* CULTURE AND PERSONALITY.]

Culture change. In the late 1920s Malinowski began to turn his attention to problems of culture change and the development of a "practical anthropology" as a field tool. Although he himself was called on for expert advice and his students, working in Africa, were brought face to face with the difficulties of research in rapidly changing societies, his approach was essentially schematic and exploratory (1945). Aside from a four-month trip in 1934 to visit his students' field sites in Africa, he lacked the crucial experience of relevant field work.

Career in the United States. In 1938 Malinowski came to the United States on sabbatical leave. The death of his wife in 1935 after a long illness had broken the thread of his personal life in London. This was not his first visit to America. In 1926 he spent some months there at the invitation of Lawrence K. Frank of the Laura Spelman Rockefeller Memorial. At that time he traveled, taught briefly at the University of California, and visited the Hopi Indians in the Southwest. In 1933 he delivered the Messenger lectures at Cornell University. In 1936 he came as a delegate of the University of London to the Harvard Tercentenary celebration, at which he delivered an address on culture as a determinant of behavior (1936b; 1937) and was awarded an honorary D.SC.

After October 1939 he was at Yale University, first as visiting professor, from 1939 to 1940, and then as Bishop Museum visiting professor, from 1940 to 1942. His marriage to Valetta Swann, the painter, in 1940 opened the way to new companionship and happiness.

Nevertheless, the years at Yale were very difficult ones. In the United States he was a stranger, celebrated and sometimes lionized, but a man in exile. For the most part, his Yale students were far less mature than his students in London. They were unfamiliar with his work, and his European point of view seemed no less exotic to most of them than American manners seemed to him. The necessity of beginning his teaching from the beginning again did not stimulate him. The simplified form in which he presented his theoretical system in *A Scientific Theory of Culture* (1944a) reflects his detachment. His strictly theoretical presentations (1926a; 1929a; 1929c; 1929d; 1931a), though elegant, are somewhat bare in comparison with those in which he was arguing or working toward abstraction, but his last and most extended statement is also curiously tentative.

In the 1930s he had become progressively alarmed at the dangers presented by totalitarianism. Like many intellectuals, he worked unsparingly to alert people to the possibility of "a period of dark ages, indeed the darkest ages of human history" (1944a, p. 15). Advised not to return to wartime England, he worked passionately on behalf of the democratic cause and a postwar international world order.

In 1940, in spite of ill health, he began a new field project, a study of marketing among the Zapotec of Oaxaca. He planned a series of studies, each from a special stance, and made two field

trips in the summers of 1940 and 1941. In between, he worked closely with a young Mexican colleague, Julio de la Fuente, an experienced and accomplished fieldworker. The work promised methodological innovations. In 1942 he received a permanent appointment at Yale, effective in October. He died on May 16 of that year, in the midst of ongoing work.

Assessment. Malinowski's place in anthropology is as yet exceedingly difficult to assess. In the years since his death, much of his theoretical work has been bypassed. Certain of his ideas that made him a storm center in the 1920s have been so fully incorporated into anthropological thinking that his exposition now appears unnecessarily didactic. He was an innovator, but the very necessity of breaking through older conceptions kept his attention focused on issues and problems that were absorbed or transformed by the new methods of observation and analysis and the new theoretical formulations that developed out of his own work and that of his students. Nadel pointed out that "at some stage, someone must ask, and attempt to answer, those 'big' questions if empirical work is to proceed systematically and fruitfully" (1957, p. 190). The necessity of doing so in ways that were relevant to a field-oriented science kept Malinowski a generalist even as he trained his students to become specialists. Nadel spoke for others among Malinowski's students when he said, "Today, we have grown much more modest, but also more conscious of the need for precision and solid empirical evidence" (*ibid.*, p. 189). It was Malinowski's breadth of vision that made this advance possible.

The contribution which his students, even the most critical of them, value is his comprehension of the total field situation and his ability to communicate to others the complex interplay of problem and reality. The actual period of time Malinowski spent in the field was astonishingly brief —only two and one-half years in New Guinea. But in one sense his lifework was a continual renewal and re-creation of this experience.

His method of institutional analysis made it possible for him to express, through a model, certain core ideas of his theory: the integrity of each culture; the complex interrelationship of the society, the culture, and the individual; the grounding of culture in the human organism (in man's needs and capacities and in the individual as the carrier of culture); and the systematic nature of culture as a phenomenon. He treated the institution as the unit of analysis; whatever its difficulties in application, it indicates how complex any "unit" of analysis must be.

Malinowski's theoretical framework is a major contribution. However, no anthropologist today is prepared to make the dizzying leap from the particular to the universal that characterized his attempt to create an effective methodology. There are essential intermediate steps. These involve, for example, intensive studies of process within and across cultures and over time. We require also fine-grained systematic comparison of intensively studied cultures and cultural process. Today we are acquiring the tools (for example, the sound-film recording devices Malinowski himself foresaw as necessary in studies of communication) that are making more delicate and systematic research feasible. Malinowski's search for an adequate psychology was a step toward broadening the base of empirical research. But collaboration among all the relevant sciences will be necessary. The study of culture is crucial to, but not in itself sufficient for, the development of a science of man.

Malinowski's attempt to formulate theory on the basis of limited data places him in extreme contrast with his older contemporary Franz Boas, as does his almost exclusive preoccupation with a theory of culture. Boas had a very broad experience, beginning early in his career, in planning for and administrating research, in much of which he was personally involved, in the whole field of anthropology. Necessarily, he worked within a comparative framework in space and time, and with full awareness of the importance of carefully recorded detail. Like Malinowski, he had the natural scientist's commitment to the formulation of general laws, but in his case, concern for long-term gains made him extremely dubious of the value of theoretical formulations based on partial evidence.

In the history of a science it is necessary to take into account the temperamental as well as the experiential differences among innovators. It is possible that the tensions necessary for the development of new thinking arise from just such differences. Malinowski's impact on a whole generation of anthropologists—like that of Boas—was a measure of his capacity as a thinker and a teacher to evoke in others a clear perception of the state of the science and confidence in the value of their own work. It remains to be seen whether their successors can resolve these tensions through research that will shape new aims.

RHODA MÉTRAUX

WORKS BY MALINOWSKI

1912a The Economic Aspect of the Intichiuma Ceremonies. Pages 81–108 in *Festskrift tillegnad Edvard Westermarck i Anledning av hans femtioårsdag den 20 november 1912.* Helsingfors (Finland): Simelli.

1912b Plemienne zwiazki w Australii (Tribal Male Associations of the Australian Aborigines). Akademja Umiejetnosci, Krakow, Wydział Filologiczny, Wydział Historycznofilozoficzny, *Bulletin international . . .* [1912]:56–63.

(1913) 1963 *The Family Among the Australian Aborigines: A Sociological Study.* New York: Schocken.

1915a Wierzenia pierwotne i formy ustroju społecznego (Primitive Religion and Forms of Social Structure). Cracow (Poland): Akademja Umiejetnosci.

1915b The Natives of Mailu: Preliminary Results of the Robert Mond Research Work in British New Guinea. Royal Society of South Australia, *Transactions* 39:494–706.

(1916) 1948 Baloma: The Spirits of the Dead in the Trobriand Islands. Pages 125–227 in Bronislaw Malinowski, *Magic, Science and Religion, and Other Essays.* Glencoe, Ill.: Free Press. → First published in Volume 46 of the *Journal of the Royal Anthropological Institute of Great Britain and Ireland.*

1918 Fishing in the Trobriand Islands. *Man* 18:87–92.

1920a Classificatory Particles in the Language of Kiriwina. London, University of, School of Oriental and African Studies, *Bulletin* 1, no. 4:33–78.

1920b Kula: The Circulating Exchange of Valuables in the Archipelagoes of Eastern New Guinea. *Man* 20:97–105.

1920c War and Weapons Among the Natives of the Trobriand Islands. *Man* 20:10–12.

1921 The Primitive Economics of the Trobriand Islanders. *Economic Journal* 31:1–16.

(1922a) 1960 *Argonauts of the Western Pacific: An Account of Native Enterprise and Adventure in the Archipelagoes of Melanesian New Guinea.* London School of Economics and Political Science, Studies, No. 65. London: Routledge; New York: Dutton. → A paperback edition was published in 1961 by Dutton.

1922b Ethnology and the Study of Society. *Economica* 2:208–219.

1923a The Psychology of Sex in Primitive Societies. *Psyche* 4:98–128.

(1923b) 1948 The Problem of Meaning in Primitive Languages. Pages 228–276 in Bronislaw Malinowski, *Magic, Science and Religion, and Other Essays.* Glencoe, Ill.: Free Press.

1923c Psycho-analysis and Anthropology [Letter to the Editor]. *Nature* 112:650–651.

1924 Psycho-analysis and Anthropology. *Psyche* 4:293–332.

(1925a) 1948 Magic, Science and Religion. Pages 1–71 in Bronislaw Malinowski, *Magic, Science and Religion, and Other Essays.* Glencoe, Ill.: Free Press. → A paperback edition was published in 1954 by Doubleday; citations in the article are to this edition.

1925b Complex and Myth in Mother-right. *Psyche* 5:194–216.

1925c The Forces of Law and Order in a Primitive Community. Royal Institution of Great Britain, London, *Proceedings* 24:529–547.

1925d Forschungen in einer mutterrechtlichen Gemeinschaft (Auf den Trobriand-Inseln, östlich von Neu-Guinea, Südsee). *Zeitschrift für Völkerpsychologie und Soziologie* 1:45–53.

1926a Anthropology. Supplementary volume 1, pages 131–140 in *Encyclopaedia Britannica.* 13th ed. Chicago: Benton.

(1926b) 1961 *Crime and Custom in Savage Society.* London: Routledge.

1926c Myth in Primitive Psychology. London: Routledge; New York: Norton.

1926d Anthropology and Administration [Letter to the Editor]. Nature 118:768.

1926e The Life of Culture. Psyche 7, no. 2: 37–44.

1926f Primitive Law and Order. Nature 117 (Supplement):9–16.

1926g The Role of Myth in Life. Psyche 6, no. 4:29–39.

1927a The Father in Primitive Psychology. London: Routledge.

(1927b) 1928 The Life of Culture. Pages 26–46 in Grafton Elliot Smith et al., Culture: The Diffusion Controversy. London: Routledge.

1927c Lunar and Seasonal Calendar in the Trobriands. Journal of the Royal Anthropological Institute of Great Britain and Ireland 57:203–215.

1927d Prenuptial Intercourse Between the Sexes in the Trobriand Islands, N.W. Melanesia. Psychoanalytic Review 14:20–35.

(1927e) 1953 Sex and Repression in Savage Society. London: Routledge; New York: Harcourt. → A paperback edition was published in 1955 by Meridian.

1928 The Anthropological Study of Sex. Volume 5, pages 92–108 in International Congress for Sex Research, First, Berlin, 1926, Verhandlungen. Berlin: Marcus & Weber.

1929a Social Anthropology. Volume 20, pages 862–870 in Encyclopaedia Britannica. 14th ed. Chicago: Benton.

(1929b) 1962 The Sexual Life of Savages in Northwestern Melanesia: An Ethnographic Account of Courtship, Marriage, and Family Life Among the Natives of the Trobriand Islands, British New Guinea. New York: Harcourt.

(1929c) 1962 Kinship. Pages 132–150 in Bronislaw Malinowski, Sex, Culture and Myth. New York: Harcourt.

(1929d) 1962 Marriage. Pages 1–35 in Bronislaw Malinowski, Sex, Culture and Myth. New York: Harcourt.

1929e Practical Anthropology. Africa 2:22–38.

1930a Kinship. Man 30:19–29.

1930b Parenthood: The Basis of Social Structure. Pages 113–168 in Victor F. Calverton and Samuel D. Schmalhausen (editors), The New Generation: The Intimate Problems of Modern Parents and Children. New York: Macaulay.

1930c Race and Labour. Listener 4, Supplement no. 8.

1930d The Rationalization of Anthropology and Administration. Africa 3:405–430. → Includes a résumé in French.

1931a Culture. Volume 4, pages 621–645 in Encyclopaedia of the Social Sciences. New York: Macmillan.

1931b The Relations Between the Sexes in Tribal Life. Pages 565–585 in Victor F. Calverton (editor), The Making of Man: An Outline of Anthropology. New York: Modern Library.

1931c Science and Religion. Pages 65–81 in Science & Religion: A Symposium. London: Howe.

1932 Pigs, Papuans, and Police Court Perspective. Man 32:33–38.

1933 The Work and Magic of Prosperity in the Trobriand Islands. Mensch en maatschappij 9:154–174.

1934 Stone Implements in Eastern New Guinea. Pages 189–196 in Essays Presented to C. G. Seligman. London: Routledge.

(1935a) 1965 Coral Gardens and Their Magic. 2 vols. Bloomington: Indiana Univ. Press.

1935b Preface. In Friedrich Lorentz et al., The Cassubian Civilization. London: Faber.

1936a The Foundations of Faith and Morals: An Anthropological Analysis of Primitive Beliefs and Conduct With Special Reference to the Fundamental Problems of Religion and Ethics. Oxford Univ. Press.

1936b Culture as a Determinant of Behavior. Scientific Monthly 43:440–449.

1936c The Deadly Issue. Atlantic Monthly 158:659–669.

1936d Native Education and Culture Contact. International Review of Missions 25:480–515.

1937 Culture as a Determinant of Behavior. Pages 133–168 in Harvard Tercentenary Conference of Arts and Sciences, Cambridge, Mass., 1936, Factors Determining Human Behavior. Cambridge, Mass.: Harvard Univ. Press.

1938a The Anthropology of Changing African Cultures. Pages vii–xxxviii in Methods of Study of Culture Contact in Africa. International Institute of African Languages and Cultures, Memorandum 15. Oxford Univ. Press.

1938b A Nation-wide Intelligence Service. Pages 81–121 in Charles Madge and Tom Harrisson (editors), First Year's Work, 1937–1938, by Mass-observation. London: Drummond.

1939a The Group and the Individual in Functional Analysis. American Journal of Sociology 44:938–964.

1939b The Present State of Studies in Culture Contact: Some Comments on an American Approach. Africa 12:27–47.

(1941a) 1948 An Anthropological Analysis of War. Pages 277–309 in Bronislaw Malinowski, Magic, Science and Religion, and Other Essays. Glencoe, Ill.: Free Press. → First published in Volume 46 of the American Journal of Sociology.

1941b War—Past, Present and Future. Pages 21–31 in American Historical Association, War as a Social Institution: The Historian's Perspective. Edited by Jesse D. Clarkson and Thomas C. Cochran. New York: Columbia Univ. Press.

1941–1942 Man's Culture and Man's Behavior. Sigma Xi Quarterly 29:182–196; 30:66–78.

1942 The Scientific Approach to the Study of Man. Pages 207–242 in Ruth N. Anshen (editor), Science and Man: Twenty-four Original Essays. New York: Harcourt.

1944a A Scientific Theory of Culture, and Other Essays. Chapel Hill: Univ. of North Carolina Press. → A paperback edition was published in 1960 by Oxford Univ. Press.

1944b Freedom and Civilization. With a preface by Valetta Malinowska. New York: Roy.

(1945) 1949 The Dynamics of Culture Change: An Inquiry Into Race Relations in Africa. New Haven: Yale Univ. Press. → A paperback edition was published in 1961.

1957 MALINOWSKI, BRONISLAW; and FUENTE, JULIO DE LA "La economía de un sistema de mercados en México": Un ensayo de etnografía contemporánea y cambio social en un valle Mexicano. Acta antropológica, Epoca 2, Vol. 1, no. 2. Mexico City: Escuela Nacional de Antropología e Historia, Sociedad de Alumnos.

Magic, Science and Religion, and Other Essays. Glencoe, Ill.: Free Press, 1948. → Contains essays published between 1916 and 1941. An abridged paperback edition was published in 1954 by Doubleday.

Sex, Culture and Myth. New York: Harcourt, 1962. → Contains essays first published between 1913 and 1941.

SUPPLEMENTARY BIBLIOGRAPHY

BARNES, J. A. 1963 Introduction. In Bronislaw Malinowski, *The Family Among the Australian Aborigines: A Sociological Study.* New York: Schocken.

FIRTH, RAYMOND (editor) (1957) 1964 *Man and Culture: An Evaluation of the Work of Bronislaw Malinowski.* New York: Harper.

GLUCKMAN, MAX (1947) 1949 *An Analysis of the Sociological Theories of Bronislaw Malinowski.* Rhodes-Livingstone Papers, No. 16. Oxford Univ. Press.

KABERRY, PHYLLIS M. (1945) 1958 Introduction. In Bronislaw Malinowski, *The Dynamics of Culture Change: An Inquiry Into Race Relations in Africa.* New Haven: Yale Univ. Press.

LEACH, EDMUND R. 1965 Frazer and Malinowski. *Encounter* 25, no. 5:24–36.

LEE, DOROTHY D. 1940 A Primitive System of Values. *Philosophy of Science* 7:355–378.

LEE, DOROTHY D. (1949) 1959 Being and Value in a Primitive Culture. Pages 89–104 in Dorothy D. Lee, *Freedom and Culture: Essays.* Englewood Cliffs, N.J.: Prentice-Hall. → First published in the *Journal of Philosophy.*

LEE, DOROTHY D. (1950) 1959 Codifications of Reality: Lineal and Nonlineal. Pages 105–120 in Dorothy D. Lee, *Freedom and Culture: Essays.* Englewood Cliffs, N.J.: Prentice-Hall. → First published in *Psychosomatic Medicine.*

LOWIE, ROBERT H. 1937 *The History of Ethnological Theory.* New York: Farrar & Rinehart.

LOWIE, ROBERT H. 1947 Biographical Memoir of Franz Boas: 1858–1942. National Academy of Sciences, Washington, D.C., *Biographical Memoirs* 24:303–322.

MURDOCK, GEORGE P. 1943 Bronislaw Malinowski. *American Anthropologist* New Series 45:441–451.

NADEL, S. F. 1957 Malinowski on Magic and Religion. Pages 189–208 in Raymond Firth (editor), *Man and Culture: An Evaluation of the Work of Bronislaw Malinowski.* London: Routledge.

RADCLIFFE-BROWN, A. R. 1946 A Note on Functional Anthropology. *Man* 46:38–41.

RICHARDS, AUDREY I. 1943 Bronislaw Kaspar Malinowski: Born 1884–Died 1942. *Man* 43:1–4.

SYMMONS-SYMONOLEWICZ, KONSTANTIN 1958 Bronislaw Malinowski: An Intellectual Profile. *Polish Review* 3, no. 4:55–76.

SYMMONS-SYMONOLEWICZ, KONSTANTIN 1959 Bronislaw Malinowski: Formative Influences and Theoretical Evolution. *Polish Review* 4, no. 4:17–45.

SYMMONS-SYMONOLEWICZ, KONSTANTIN 1960 Bronislaw Malinowski: Individuality as a Theorist. *Polish Review* 5, no. 1:53–65.

MALNUTRITION

See FAMINE *and* FOOD.

MALTHUS, THOMAS ROBERT

Thomas Robert Malthus (1766–1834) was born ten years before the publication of Adam Smith's *Wealth of Nations,* and his work as an economist belongs to the broad tradition established by Smith's treatise. After being privately educated, Malthus entered Jesus College, Cambridge, where he was elected to a fellowship at the age of 27. He took orders in 1797 and held a curacy for a short period. He married in 1805 and shortly thereafter was appointed professor of modern history and political economy at the East India Company's college at Haileybury, the first appointment of its kind in England. He died at Haileybury in 1834, the year that saw the passage of a new poor law inspired by his writings.

Malthus' father was a friend of Rousseau and shared the optimistic belief of Condorcet and William Godwin that nothing stood in the way of a regime of ideal equality but private ignorance and public inertia: propaganda and education were therefore the means for bringing about perfect happiness. The younger Malthus disagreed and argued that the effort to realize the perfect human society would always founder on the tendency of population to outrun the food supply. His father urged him to put his ideas on paper, and in 1798 Malthus published a long pamphet entitled *An Essay on the Principle of Population, as It Affects the Future Improvement of Society; With Remarks on the Speculations of Mr. Godwin, M. Condorcet, and Other Writers.* There was nothing original in Malthus' argument. It had all been said before, albeit with less force. Nevertheless, Malthus was attacking the dominant contemporary view, which saw underpopulation rather than overpopulation as a problem. When the first census, in 1801, produced evidence of a sharp rise in population growth in recent decades, Malthus decided to take advantage of the change in the climate of opinion by turning his pamphlet into a book (published in 1803) with a new subtitle that implied a change in emphasis: *A View of Its Past and Present Effects on Human Happiness With an Inquiry Into Our Prospects Respecting the Future Removal or Mitigation of the Evils Which It Occasions.* What had started out as an occasional tract against certain dangerous ideas held by some contemporary thinkers had become a full-scale treatise on the subject of demography. Further revised editions of the book were published at regular intervals during his lifetime, the sixth edition appearing in 1826.

Although Malthus' fame in the nineteenth century was based squarely on his theory of population, his modern reputation with economists rests rather on his prescient opposition to the Ricardian doctrine of the impossibility of "general gluts." As Keynes put it in *The General Theory:* "Ricardo conquered England as completely as the Holy Inquisition conquered Spain," in consequence of which, "The great puzzle of Effective Demand with which Malthus had wrestled vanished from economic literature" (1936, p. 32). Malthus' ideas on gluts, or, as we would now say, business depressions, were embodied in his *Principles of Political Economy*, first published in 1820. Other minor but significant publications on strictly economic questions are *An Inquiry Into the Nature and Progress of Rent* (1815); *The Measure of Value Stated and Illustrated* (1823); and *Definitions in Political Economy* (1827).

Demographic ideas.   Malthus' theory of population is baldly stated in the first two chapters of the *Essay*. These pages are brilliantly written in terse phrases and striking images, and they help us to understand why the book captured the imagination of its first readers, rousing a storm of controversy that never died down during Malthus' lifetime. The thesis itself is familiar enough, although all of its implications are not immediately evident: population, *when unchecked*, increases in a geometrical ratio, while the food supply at best increases in an arithmetical ratio; hence, population tends to increase up to the limits of "the means of subsistence." This is *the* principle of population that Malthus maintained against all his critics. He realized, of course, that in the real world there are checks that prevent population from increasing beyond the food supply. The checks are of two kinds: "positive" checks that show up in the death rate, such as war, famine, and pestilence; and "preventive checks" that show up in the birth rate, such as abortions, infanticide, and birth control. Both checks are the consequences of lack of food, which may, indeed, be regarded as the ultimate check on population growth that is always in operation.

Such was Malthus' argument in the first edition of the *Essay*. Its weakness was quickly discovered by Godwin, who pointed out that the working classes in the richer countries seemed to be maintaining themselves at a level considerably above the physical minimum of existence, without benefit of either the positive or the preventive checks. Malthus, realizing that he had trapped himself by denying the possibility of any rise in the standard of living, quietly gave way in the second edition of the *Essay* by recognizing the existence of a new preventive check, namely, "moral restraint." He defined "moral restraint" as postponement of the age of marriage accompanied by strict sexual continence before marriage, and, while the other checks were frequently described as "misery" or "vice," the new preventive check was allowed to stand alone without any pejorative tag attached to it. For the first time a hopeful note crept into the argument, although Malthus himself always remained pro-

foundly pessimistic about the capacity of mankind to regulate its numbers by the exercise of prudential restraint. Few readers realized that he had really abandoned his original thesis, and Malthus did nothing to help them appreciate the escape clause that had now been built into the doctrine.

Any critic who produced evidence of subsistence increasing faster than population without signs of "misery" or "vice" was silenced by the logical implication that the working class must be practicing "moral restraint," a phenomenon included in the theory. This left the critic with no reply other than to show that the average age of marriage had not increased or that the rate of illegitimate births had not fallen. Since contemporary population statistics were not adequate to verify such assertions, Malthus had furnished himself with an impregnable defense. There were a few critics who attacked the theory by questioning the notion that birth control constitutes "vice." Malthus' argument here was simply that birth control must be wrong, since man, being naturally indolent, could hardly be expected to work or save if it were made so easy for him to escape the consequences of his "natural passions." He was confident of the support of contemporary opinion in lightly dismissing what were later called neo-Malthusian checks, "both on account of their immorality and their tendency to remove a necessary stimulus to industry" ([1798] page 512 in 1878 edition).

Some hostile critics realized the futility of denying that unchecked populations tend to increase at a geometrical rate, inasmuch as no one had ever observed the growth of an unchecked population. Instead, they attacked the idea that the food supply could not possibly keep pace with the irrepressible tide of population. Here Malthus had recourse to the principle of diminishing returns in agriculture —in fact, he was one of the first to state this general principle in so many words. Since this principle soon became an integral part of orthodox political economy via Ricardo's theory of rent, it was difficult to criticize Malthus on this score [*see* RICARDO]. We realize now that Malthus was actually appealing not to the impeccable Ricardian law of diminishing returns to variable factor increments in a situation of given technical knowledge, but to a questionable historical law of diminishing returns from technical progress in agriculture. But the distinction between statics and dynamics was so little understood in those days—even Ricardo switched easily from static analysis to historical generalization, sometimes in the same sentence— that Malthus had no difficulty in meeting criticism along these lines.

The utter simplicity and familiarity of the ideas involved, calling neither for new concepts nor for new facts, was the essence of Malthus' popular appeal. All he seemed to be doing was to bring together a few familiar facts of life and to deduce the necessary consequences of these facts. Surely it was true that population nearly always multiplied up to the limits of the available food supply. And surely, where living standards had improved, the gain was necessarily precarious and always liable to disappear in a new spurt of population growth. Was it not self-evident that an unchecked multiplication of human beings must quickly lead to an impossible situation, whatever the plausible rate of increase of the means of subsistence? The contrast that Malthus drew between the two kinds of mathematical progression carried the hypnotic persuasive power of an advertising slogan. It was easy to see—"a slight acquaintance with numbers will show," as Malthus said—that even the smallest finite sum growing at the smallest *compound* rate must eventually overwhelm even the largest possible finite sum growing at the highest *simple* rate, so that, whatever the initial situation, there must soon be "standing room only." *Quod erat demonstrandum!*

It did not hurt the Malthusian theory that it justified the resistance of the upper classes to all efforts to reform existing social and political institutions: for if poverty had its roots in the unequal race between population and subsistence, only the working class itself, by practicing prudential restraint, could improve its·own conditions. Even the working-class newspapers of the day accepted the desirability of prudential restraint and condemned birth control devices. The Malthusian theory of population was widely appealing: it neatly explained the existence of poverty; it exposed the visionary panaceas of reformers; it enabled everyone to pontificate on questions of public policy; it rationalized the subsistence theory of wages, to which all contemporary economists subscribed; lastly, it underlay Ricardo's preoccupation with the land-using bias of economic progress, and Ricardo was the foremost economist of the day. Any one of these factors would have been enough to make a theory influential. Put together, they fully account for Malthus' astonishing success, a success that has few parallels in the history of ideas.

Despite all the attractive features of the Malthusian theory, it is doubtful, however, whether it would have received so wide a hearing if there had not also been a population explosion in the last two decades of the eighteenth century. Strangely enough, when Malthus published the first edition of the *Essay* in 1798, he shared the general belief of his day that the population of England had actually increased little in the eighteenth century. The census of 1801 showed how wrong everyone had been, and later generations credited Malthus with prophetic foresight in warning of the dangers of overpopulation as early as 1798. But, in fact, Malthus made no effort, nor was it his intention, to explain the unprecedented population explosion, even in the later versions of the *Essay.* Furthermore, it is evident that he did not provide the tools for such an explanation. The Malthusian theory emphasizes birth and marriage rates, whereas the population explosion of the 1780s was a more complicated phenomenon of rising birth rates in new factory districts and falling death rates in rural areas and congested towns. Unfortunately, the demographic data of the period, based as they are on defective registration of baptisms and burials, are so unreliable that modern authorities are still not agreed on whether the industrial revolution largely created its own labor force by a demand pull on births or whether improved sanitation, nutrition, and housing produced a supply push through a fall in the death rate. The fact remains, however, that Malthus makes a poor guide to the causes of the population explosion that gave such prominence to his views.

Permanent influence. Malthus' magisterial influence on public opinion lasted until the last decades of the nineteenth century. By that time, the record of sustained economic growth, the rise in the standard of living, and the decline in fertility in Western countries made disparagement of the Malthusian doctrine as common as praise had been before. Every schoolboy at the turn of the twentieth century could prove that Malthus had gone wrong by underestimating both the potentialities of technical progress and the possibility of family limitation by birth control devices. As far as it goes, of course, this is a perfectly valid refutation of the Malthusian theory, but it is so obvious now that it is hardly worth stating. One can make a much stronger case against Malthus.

The Malthusian theory of population is a perfect example of metaphysics masquerading as science. So long as we hold with Malthus that birth control is morally reprehensible, the history of population growth in the last two centuries proves him right: nothing has stemmed the tide of human numbers but "misery" and "vice." If, on the other hand, we consider birth control morally defensible, Malthus is vindicated again: "moral restraint" in the larger sense of the phrase is one of the checks that has limited the tendency of population to outstrip the food supply. The Malthusian theory cannot be refuted because it can be applied to any actual or any conceivable population change: it purports to say something about the real world, and what it says must be true by definition of its own terms.

By the 1920s, the Malthusian theory had lost almost all of its earlier prestige. Indeed, the Malthusian specter of overpopulation had given way to the Keynesian specter of underpopulation. But since World War II, the problem of underdeveloped countries has brought Malthus back into favor. Most underdeveloped countries today have the worst of both worlds: the typical high birth rates of agrarian economies and the typical low death rates of urbanized industrialized economies. Economic development will in time cure these difficulties, as they were cured in industrial Europe, but for the next few generations these countries face the alternative of the Malthusian checks of famine and disease or voluntary family limitation in opposition to prevailing religious mores. The name of Malthus is still bandied about in debates on population policies in Asia, Africa, and Latin America, although it is difficult to believe that the Malthusian theory has much relevance to the discussion of modern population problems. It sheds no light on the causes of declining fertility in developing societies; it tells us little about the demographic relationship between fertility and mortality; it is silent on the economic and social consequences of changes in the age distribution of a population; and it is of no help in framing policies for areas of heavy population pressure. Be that as it may, there is no doubt that the revival of interest in the Malthusian doctrine in our own day makes it one of the longest-lived social theories of all times. And, popular interest apart, demographers can never ignore him or forget him, for, with all his errors, Malthus put the problem of population growth on the map.

MARK BLAUG

[*For the historical context of Malthus' work, see* INCOME AND EMPLOYMENT THEORY; POPULATION, *article on* POPULATION THEORIES; *and the biography of* CONDORCET. *For discussion of the subsequent development of Malthus' ideas, see* POPULATION, *articles on* OPTIMUM POPULATION THEORY *and* POPULATION POLICIES; *and the biographies of* RICARDO *and* MARX.]

WORKS BY MALTHUS

(1798) 1960 *On Population.* New York: Modern Library. → First published in pamphlet form as *An Essay on the Principle of Population.* A paperback edition was published in 1963 by Irwin.
1815 *An Inquiry Into the Nature and Progress of Rent, and the Principles by Which It Is Regulated.* London: Murray.
(1820) 1964 *Principles of Political Economy Considered With a View to Their Practical Application.* 2d ed. New York: Kelley.
1823 *The Measure of Value Stated and Illustrated, With an Application of It to the Alterations in the Value of the English Currency Since 1790.* London: Murray.
1827 *Definitions in Political Economy.* London: Murray.

SUPPLEMENTARY BIBLIOGRAPHY

BLAUG, MARK 1962 *Economic Theory in Retrospect.* Homewood, Ill.: Irwin. → Reviews the theoretical issues in the inconclusive debate between Ricardo and Malthus, and lists additional readings on both sides of the question. Also considers Malthus' employment theory.
BONAR, JAMES (1885) 1924 *Malthus and His Work.* 2d ed. London: Allen & Unwin; New York: Macmillan.
BONER, H. A. 1955 *Hungry Generations: The 19th-Century Case Against Malthusianism.* New York: King's Crown Press; Oxford Univ. Press.
CANNAN, EDWIN (1893) 1953 *A History of the Theories of Production and Distribution in English Political Economy From 1776 to 1848.* 3d ed. London and New York: Staples.
GLASS, D. V. (editor) 1953 *Introduction to Malthus.* London: Watts; New York: Wiley. → Contains useful background material, as well as a reprint of Malthus' "Summary View of the Principle of Population," which he contributed to the *Encyclopaedia Britannica* in 1830.
KEYNES, JOHN MAYNARD 1936 *The General Theory of Employment, Interest and Money.* London: Macmillan.
McCLEARY, GEORGE F. 1953 *The Malthusian Population Theory.* London: Faber. → Contains a spirited defense of Malthus' ideas on population.
NEWMAN, JAMES R. 1956 Commentary on Thomas Robert Malthus. Volume 2, pages 1189–1191 in James R. Newman (editor), *The World of Mathematics: A Small Library of the Literature of Mathematics From A'h-mosé the Scribe to Albert Einstein.* New York: Simon & Schuster.
SMITH, KENNETH 1951 *The Malthusian Controversy.* London: Routledge. → Reviews the great nineteenth-century debate on the Malthusian doctrine.
UNITED NATIONS, DEPARTMENT OF SOCIAL AFFAIRS, POPULATION DIVISION 1953 *The Determinants and Consequences of Population Trends.* Population Studies, No. 17. New York: United Nations. → Covers succinctly the history of population theory before and after Malthus.

MAN

See ANTHROPOLOGY; EVOLUTION; RACE.

MAN, HENDRIK (HENRI) DE

Hendrik (Henri) de Man (1885–1953), a Flemish-born socialist militant, was led by his long and disheartening experience with the stultified proletariat and bureaucratized socialist movements of Belgium, Germany, and England to question the doctrinal and pragmatic adequacy of that radical Marxism to which he had early subscribed. His searing experience during World War I of man's capacity for self-sacrifice and of the role of national identity precipitated a major reformulation of socialist ideology, presented in his works *Psychology of Socialism* (1926) and *Die sozialistische Idee* (1933). This critique from the left could not be dismissed as mere bourgeois propaganda and, moreover, answered to the radical discontent with socialist practice reflected at that time in the defection of militants to the communist movement.

De Man's essential argument concerned the inadequacy of Marxist theory to account for contemporary trends within the socialist movement—above all, the unacknowledged collapse of chiliastic expectations that a socialist society would be ensured by means of the proletarian conquest of power. In political reality, the widening split between socialist practice and theory was leading to the covert sanctioning of reformist accommodation to the Western bourgeois order, a process that was merely veiled by the increasingly unrealistic revolutionary ideology. At the same time, the Russian experience demonstrated that orthodox Marxism could engender a tyrannical and Philistine sham egalitarianism.

The basic cause of the discrepancy between theory and practice was, de Man argued, the utilitarian explanation of behavior, which Marxism had inherited from classical economics. In interpreting all significant human action as the product of the maximization of advantages, "scientific socialism" had misinterpreted its own nature. This was strikingly demonstrated by its failure to explain such an anomaly as the absence of a class-conscious socialist movement in America and by the interpretation of the European movement as a response to economic conditions per se rather than to the conjunction of these conditions with invidious social distinctions.

De Man believed that if the autonomous role of values were recognized, it would also become evident that the development of a socialist society involved not only revolutionizing outward relations to the means of production but also infusing the work role itself with socialist values. This insight informed de Man's pioneer study in industrial sociology, *Joy in Work* (1927). Further, he held that an ideology that justified socialism in terms of values rather than class interests would more clearly establish the manifold goals of the socialist movement and would facilitate its coming to political power by furnishing a cogent basis for rallying nonproletarian support.

These ideological considerations received concrete political expression in the form of the *plan du travail* with which de Man returned to Belgium in 1933 from the University of Frankfurt, shaken by the overthrow of that *Sozialdemokratie* in which he had invested his greatest hope of reformation. The new plan of action, which defined a minimal program necessary to resuscitate the economy—essentially a substantial public works program and public control of the principal credit institutions—and which called for political support from all segments of the population suffering from the hegemony of finance capitalism, revived the *élan* of the Belgian socialist party. But with the onset of a financial crisis in 1935 the party, in effect, sacrificed integral *planisme* in order to participate in progressive coalition governments, in which de Man occupied strategic ministerial positions.

In the late 1930s de Man, frustrated by the evanescence of "structural reform" and unsuited by temperament to the compromises of political practice, called for radical revision of parliamentary government in the direction of what he termed authoritarian democracy, capable of sustained and resolute action. He also diverged from his fellow socialists in his fidelity to the appeasement policy; upon the Nazi conquest, he issued a manifesto in which he celebrated the cessation of the ineffective political role of the socialist movement and recommended a rigidly neutralist policy toward the occupying power (1940). Within a year de Man had to acknowledge the bankruptcy of his desperate attempt to construe Nazism in the image of socialism, and he thereupon completely withdrew from public life. He found ultimate refuge in Switzerland and after the war was convicted *in absentia* for treason. Generalizing from the ruin of his life's ambitions, he concluded that the socialist movement could not transcend its capitalist environment; in the general decadence the responsible individual could hope only that it would be possible to preserve the patrimony of the ages despite the convulsions of the historical "zone of catastrophe."

If the political circumstances of the 1930s robbed de Man's ideological reformulation of its force, the folly of the war years guaranteed that none thereafter would speak in his name. Yet postwar developments have moved socialism in the direction he indicated, and perhaps the perspicacity of this sociological socialist is best indicated by his insistence that responsible socialism must make ideological provision for the positive implementation of the rights of man in industrial society.

PETER DODGE

[*For the historical context of de Man's work, see* MARXISM *and* SOCIALISM; *for discussion of the subsequent development of his ideas, see* INDUSTRIAL RELATIONS *and* MARXIST SOCIOLOGY.]

WORKS BY DE MAN

(1926) 1928 *Psychology of Socialism.* London: Allen & Unwin. → First published as *Zur Psychologie des Sozialismus.*

(1927) 1929 *Joy in Work.* London: Allen & Unwin. → First published as *Der Kampf um die Arbeitsfreude.*

1933 *Die sozialistische Idee.* Jena (Germany): Diederich.

1940 *Manifesto. Gazette de Charleroi* [1940], July 3.

1941 *Après coup: Mémoires.* Brussels and Paris: Toison d'Or.

1948 *Cavalier seul: Quarante-cinq années de socialisme européen.* Geneva: Cheval Ailé. → A significantly re-written and enlarged version of de Man 1941.

1951 *Vermassung und Kulturverfall: Eine Diagnose unserer Zeit.* Bern: Francke.

SUPPLEMENTARY BIBLIOGRAPHY

DODGE, PETER 1966 *Beyond Marxism: The Faith and Works of Hendrik de Man.* The Hague: Nijhoff. → Includes a bibliography.

JONG, FRITS DE 1952 Aanvaardbare vernieuwing? *Socialisme en democratie* 9:187–200.

KÄHLER, OTTO H. 1929 *Determinismus und Voluntarismus in der Psychologie des Sozialismus Hendrik de Mans.* Dillingen an der Donau (Germany): Schwäbische Verlagsdruckerei.

PESKI, ADRIAAN M. VAN 1963 Hendrik de Man: Ein Wille zum Sozialismus. *Hamburger Jahrbuch für Wirtschafts- und Gesellschaftspolitik* 8:183–204.

PFAFF, A. A. J. 1956 *Hendrik de Man: Zijn wijsgerige fundering van het moderne socialisme.* Antwerp and Amsterdam: Standaard Boekhandel.

MANAGEMENT

See ADMINISTRATION, *article on* THE ADMINISTRATIVE FUNCTION; BUSINESS MANAGEMENT; INDUSTRIAL RELATIONS; OPERATIONS RESEARCH.

MANDATE

See REPRESENTATION *and* TRUSTEESHIP.

MANDEVILLE, BERNARD

Bernard Mandeville (1670?–1733), English political satirist, was born in (or near) Rotterdam. He was educated there at the Erasmian School and, at the age of 15, matriculated at the University of Leiden. There his studies included medicine and philosophy. The early influence on Mandeville of mechanistic philosophy—Descartes and Gassendi—was later reinforced by a reading of Hobbes. The fourth generation of a medical family, Mandeville took his M.D. in 1691 and followed his father's specialization in nervous and digestive disorders. By 1699 he had moved this practice to England, settled, and married there. He published a dialogue on his speciality, *A Treatise of the Hypocondriack and Hysterick Diseases* (1711; enlarged in 1730),

but even before this work appeared he had begun a second career as a satirist and wit, an anatomist of individual and social behavior.

Among Mandeville's early poems, translations, and dialogues—all published anonymously—was *The Grumbling Hive: Or, Knaves Turn'd Honest* (1705), a pamphlet describing in verse a thriving, vicious beehive: "Millions endeavouring to supply / Each other's Lust and Vanity" ([1714–1729] 1957, volume 1, p. 18). Each part is vicious, but the whole hive is wealthy and powerful. It is a dissatisfied, grumbling hive until, miraculously reformed, it becomes virtuous, contented, and, consequently, impoverished and depopulated. Since vice is as much a cause of greatness as hunger is of eating, "fools only strive / To make a Great an Honest Hive"; proponents of the Golden Age "must be as free, / For Acorns, as for Honesty" (*ibid.*, volume 1, pp. 36–37). In 1714 Mandeville explained the poem in "An Enquiry Into the Origin of Moral Virtue" and twenty "Remarks," entitling the now substantial work *The Fable of the Bees: Or, Private Vices, Publick Benefits.* In 1723 he expanded the work again, enlarging the "Remarks" and adding "An Essay on Charity and Charity-schools" and "A Search Into the Nature of Society." A second volume, *The Fable of the Bees, Part II* (a series of explanatory dialogues), appeared in 1729. Mandeville reiterated and corrected his views in *An Enquiry Into the Origin of Honour, and the Usefulness of Christianity in War* (1732).

Mandeville's outrageous paradox—"private vices, publick benefits"—involves a series of suggestive explanations. The vices of luxury (unnecessary consumption), pride (vain and fashionable display), greed, envy, and avarice (self-interest in various forms) all contribute to prosperity. To supply the luxury of a scarlet coat requires many manufacturing and trading operations—an extensive division of labor (see [1714] 1957, volume 1, pp. 356–358; volume 2, pp. 142, 284). A nation that restricts the consumption of foreign luxuries to achieve frugality will instead reduce its own prosperity because the countries that export those luxuries will no longer be able to import its own goods (*ibid.*, volume 1, pp. 107–116). Mandeville's descriptions of the economic benefits of vice, crime, and (limited) natural disaster approach the modern concept of a self-regulating economic system (*ibid.*, volume 1, pp. 85–89, 359–364). Among the benefits of the scheme proposed in *A Modest Defence of Publick Stews* is a self-regulating supply of prostitutes (1724, pp. 64–65).

Although his objections to meddling with trade make Mandeville a forerunner of laissez-faire

([1714] 1957, volume 1, pp. 299–300; volume 2, p. 353), he advocated not only that private property be secured, justice be impartially administered, and trade, agriculture, and fishery be promoted but also that the government manage taxes and prohibitions to maintain a favorable balance of trade (*ibid.*, volume 1, pp. 115–117, 197, 248–249). Private vices may be made public benefits through skillful management by a wise politician (*ibid.*, volume 1, p. 169).

Mandeville's argument was annoying because he insisted that vices are not the consequences of social decadence but rather the very motives on which a flourishing, civilized, powerful society depends; simultaneously, he insisted that these vices are obviously incompatible with virtue (or Christianity), which requires a self-denying endeavor to benefit others or to be good (*ibid.*, volume 1, pp. 48–49; volume 2, pp. 16–19, 109–110). Not only is virtue contrary to human instinct; but society is not, as Shaftesbury had argued, based on man's natural sociability. Society is founded on the difficulty men have in gratifying their appetites (self-preservation) and is made possible by their susceptibility to praise (self-love) and their capacity for hypocrisy. Men have been socialized by politicians and moralists who, by flattery, have produced the moral virtues, especially honor and shame, and thus induced men to conform to the fashionable social code, profess virtue, and disguise their passions even though they cannot conquer them. But Mandeville's functional analysis of social institutions does not depend upon the existence of mythical dexterous politicians, for, as he explains, morality, language, government, arts, and sciences—all social institutions—are "the joynt Labour of many Ages" (*ibid.*, volume 2, pp. 128, 238–243, 266–269, 285–290, 318–323; 1732, p. 41).

The *Fable*'s vigorous wit and social satire, like the similar mockery of Erasmus and La Rochefoucauld, was intended to encourage men to examine their own motives instead of censuring others. Especially in his *Free Thoughts on Religion* (1720), Mandeville followed Bayle in skeptically arguing for toleration and against priestcraft, in particular clerical politics. He pointed out that most men believe about God what they have been taught from infancy, but few men live according to their professed beliefs. Atheists, whether abstruse philosophers or aristocratic libertines, are few and harmless (1720, pp. 4–6).

Mandeville's *Fable of the Bees* was widely read in the eighteenth century. Berkeley denounced it for libertinism and atheism; Francis Hutcheson objected to its egoistic reduction of morality.

Hutcheson's pupil Adam Smith rejected Mandeville's moral theory but was influenced by the general tendencies of the *Fable* toward laissez-faire economics and the description of the division of labor. Luxury was a widely discussed eighteenth-century problem; Voltaire's treatment of it is derived from the *Fable*. Both Hume and Rousseau mention Mandeville; both are indebted to him.

M. M. GOLDSMITH

[*For the historical context of Mandeville's work, see the biographies of* DESCARTES *and* HOBBES; *for discussion of the subsequent development of his ideas, see* LAISSEZ-FAIRE; *and the biographies of* HUME; ROUSSEAU; SMITH, ADAM.]

WORKS BY MANDEVILLE

1705 *The Grumbling Hive: Or, Knaves Turn'd Honest.* London: Ballard. → Later incorporated into *The Fable of the Bees.*
(1711) 1730 *A Treatise of the Hypocondriack and Hysterick Diseases.* 3d ed. London: Tonson. → First published as *A Treatise of the Hypocondriack and Hysterick Passions.*
(1714) 1957 *The Fable of the Bees: Or, Private Vices, Publick Benefits.* Edited by F. B. Kaye. 2 vols. Oxford: Clarendon. → The introduction and notes by Kaye include a biography, a critical and historical evaluation, and an annotated bibliography.
(1720) 1723 *Free Thoughts on Religion, the Church, and National Happiness.* London: Brotherton.
(1724) 1740 *A Modest Defence of Publick Stews: Or, an Essay Upon Whoring, as It Is Now Practis'd in These Kingdoms.* London: Scott & Browne.
1732 *An Enquiry Into the Origin of Honour, and the Usefulness of Christianity in War.* London: Brotherton.

SUPPLEMENTARY BIBLIOGRAPHY

MAXWELL, J. C. 1951 Ethics and Politics in Mandeville. *Philosophy* 26:242–252.
ROBERTSON, JOHN M. 1907 *Pioneer Humanists.* London: Watts. → See especially pages 230–270 on "Mandeville."
ROSENBERG, NATHAN 1963 Mandeville and Laissez-faire. *Journal of the History of Ideas* 24:183–196.
STEPHEN, LESLIE (1876) 1949 *History of English Thought in the Eighteenth Century.* 3d ed. 2 vols. New York: Smith. → A paperback edition was published in 1962 by Harcourt.
VINER, JACOB 1958 Introduction to Bernard de Mandeville, *A Letter to Dion* (1732). Pages 332–342 in Jacob Viner, *The Long View and the Short: Studies in Economic Theory and Policy.* Glencoe, Ill.: Free Press.

MANGOLDT, HANS KARL EMIL VON

Hans Karl Emil von Mangoldt (1824–1868), German economist, was born in Dresden. After studying law and political science at the universities of Leipzig and Geneva, he took his doctorate in political science at the University of Tübingen with a dissertation entitled "Über die Aufgabe,

Stellung und Einrichtung der Sparkassen" (1847; "On the Purpose, Position, and Establishment of Savings Banks"). He returned to Dresden after obtaining his doctorate.

It was some years before Mangoldt entered upon an academic career. Between 1847 and 1850 he held a post in the ministry of foreign affairs but had to resign for political reasons. After spending two years in Leipzig studying political economy, he became editor of the *Weimarer Zeitung* in 1852. However, his political convictions again made it necessary for him to resign his position. The publication of his *Lehre vom Unternehmergewinn* in 1855 won him an appointment as *Privatdozent* of political economy at the University of Göttingen, and in 1858 he was promoted to associate professor. In 1862 he was appointed professor of political science and political economy at the University of Freiburg (Breisgau). Only four years after he moved there he died of a heart attack.

Mangoldt's principal works, *Die Lehre vom Unternehmergewinn* (1855) and *Grundriss der Volkswirthschaftslehre* (1863), are outstanding works of nineteenth-century German economics. Yet at the time that he wrote, the significance of his contributions was more fully appreciated in England than in Germany. The neglect and even rejection of economic theory that prevailed in Germany after the rise of the historical school diminished the impact of Mangoldt's ideas on economists in German universities, who lacked the well-grounded theoretical tradition of their Anglo-Saxon colleagues.

In England, Mangoldt's theory of international values—a highly original extension of Ricardo's theory of comparative costs—aroused the interest of F. Y. Edgeworth, who discussed it at length in the *Economic Journal* (1894); and his doctrine of entrepreneurial profit was mentioned approvingly by Alfred Marshall in the latter's exposition of his theory of quasi-rent: "It has indeed been shown by a long series of writers, among whom Senior and Mill, Hermann and Mangoldt are conspicuous, that much of what is commonly called profits ought rather to be regarded as belonging to a special class of income derived from 'a differential advantage in producing a commodity'; that is, the possession by one or more persons of facilities for production that are not accessible to all" ([1890] 1961, vol. 2, p. 462). Indeed, Mangoldt was one of the first economists who endeavored to establish entrepreneurial profit as a special category of income alongside wages, interest, and rent.

Mangoldt's theory of prices, as expounded in the first edition of the *Grundriss*, is truly a pioneer achievement of lasting value. With a precision not attained by any other author prior to 1863, he set forth the static theory of price formation on the assumption of free atomistic competition in supply and demand; the form of his presentation remains valid today. Cournot had employed curves of supply and demand as far back as 1838, but there is no reason to assume that Mangoldt was acquainted with Cournot's work; Edgeworth was probably right when he described Mangoldt as "one of the independent discoverers of the mathematical theory of Demand and Supply" (see 1891–1921, pp. 52–53). Yet Mangoldt went far beyond Cournot, and this is his truly original contribution. He did not confine himself to determining the existence of an equilibrium price but set forth the special features of price formation that arise from various forms of the supply curve and the demand curve and pointed out that there may be several equilibrium prices. He also described the process of transition from disequilibrium to an equilibrium price. Yet Mangoldt's most significant contribution to price theory is, no doubt, the analysis of price formation for the case of joint demands or for the case of joint supplies or for the case of both. Ideas and modes of thought initiated here were not developed further until Alfred Marshall took them up.

Mangoldt's important pioneering achievements were not appreciated in Germany. Although the second edition of the *Grundriss*, edited by F. Kleinwächter in 1871, after Mangoldt's death, appeared without any of the geometrical apparatus of the first edition, the book failed to gain a wider market. Only today do we begin to realize the significance of Mangoldt's contribution as an important link in the chain of great German theoretical achievements of the nineteenth century.

ERICH SCHNEIDER

[*For the historical context of Mangoldt's work, see the biographies of* COURNOT; EDGEWORTH; MARSHALL.]

WORKS BY MANGOLDT

1847   Über die Aufgabe, Stellung und Einrichtung der Sparkassen. Dissertation, Univ. of Tübingen.
1855   *Die Lehre vom Unternehmergewinn: Ein Beitrag zur Volkswirthschaftslehre.* Leipzig: Teubner.
(1863) 1871   *Grundriss der Volkswirthschaftslehre.* 2d ed. Stuttgart (Germany): Maier. → A chapter of this work, "Das Tauschverhältniss der Güter im allgemein," was translated as "The Exchange Ratio of Goods" and published in Volume 11 of the *International Economic Papers*.

SUPPLEMENTARY BIBLIOGRAPHY

EDGEWORTH, FRANCIS Y. (1891–1921) 1963 *Papers Relating to Political Economy.* New York: Franklin. → Contains and reviews articles which appeared in the *Economic Journal* from 1891 to 1921.

EDGEWORTH, FRANCIS Y. 1894 The Theory of International Values. *Economic Journal* 4:35–50, 424–443, 603–638. → Reprinted in Edgeworth 1891–1921.

HUTCHISON, TERENCE W. (1953) 1962 *A Review of Economic Doctrines, 1870–1929.* 2d ed. Oxford: Clarendon.

MARSHALL, ALFRED (1890) 1961 *Principles of Economics.* 9th ed., 2 vols. New York and London: Macmillan.

MANIC–DEPRESSIVE DISORDERS

See DEPRESSIVE DISORDERS.

MANNHEIM, KARL

Karl Mannheim (1893–1947), German sociologist, was born in Budapest. He attended school in that city and then studied at the universities of Berlin, Budapest, Paris, and Freiburg before going to the University of Heidelberg, where he habilitated as a *Privatdozent* in 1926. At that time Heidelberg was still the major intellectual center of the German academic world. Alfred Weber, Heinrich Rickert, Marianne Weber, Friedrich Gundolf, Ernst Kantorowicz, and Emil Lederer were among its major personalities. The spirit of Max Weber, who had died in 1920, dominated the atmosphere, and the youthful brilliance of György Lukács in his pre-Marxist period had not been forgotten. Mannheim lived and worked in Heidelberg until he was called to the professorship of sociology at the University of Frankfurt in 1930. He remained at that post until the spring of 1933, when, following the coming to power of the National Socialists, he took refuge in Great Britain. There he was lecturer in sociology at the University of London (London School of Economics) from 1933 to 1945; and from 1945 until his death, he was professor of the sociology and philosophy of education in the Institute of Education at the same university.

Mannheim's work falls into two main phases, which correspond approximately to his German and his British careers. In the first phase the sociology of knowledge—its methodological legitimation, its epistemological implications, and its substantive application—formed his main field of work. In the second phase the study of the structure of modern society came to the fore. In these latter studies he combined macrosociological and microsociological concerns with an explicit interest in social policy.

Sociology of knowledge

Mannheim's early writings expressed his struggle against the inheritance of German idealism. They were attempts to revise its epistemology in an instrumentalist direction and constituted a critique of its conception of intellectual history as an autonomously developing sequence of ideas. In this first phase of his work Mannheim was much influenced by the tradition of historicism and by the Marxist model of society; no less fundamental to his thought was his interest, derived from the classics of German sociological thought and from Marxism, in the structure and determinants of agreement and disagreement, of consensus and dissensus.

Mannheim went further than Marx and Tönnies: they saw society split by class conflict and class interest or by mutual distrust; Mannheim thought that the cleavages existed at deeper levels as well. Mannheim saw social cleavages not merely as divergences of interest but as divergences of modes of thought, of the categories in which events are conceived, and even, indeed, of the very criteria of validity. In "Competition as a Cultural Phenomenon" (1929) and *Ideology and Utopia* (1929–1931) he set forth his views on the profundity of the cleavages in styles of thought which had developed in modern times.

The profundity of these cleavages led Mannheim to formulate the distinction between "particular" and "total" conceptions of ideology. He was always concerned with the re-establishment of consensus: believing that the disintegration of the social order had penetrated into the epistemological and ontological spheres, he desired to lay the foundations for a comprehensive "perspective" which would transcend the partial perspectives associated with particular social positions. In *Ideology and Utopia* and in his article "Wissenssoziologie" he sought an epistemological solution (the article is incorporated in the English and American editions). Independently of Durkheim's and Lévy-Bruhl's relativization and "sociologization" of the categories of thought, Mannheim asserted that the fundamental categories are functions of divergent interests, aspirations, and *Weltanschauungen*, which are in turn related to social status, role, and position; he sought a way out in what he called "relationism." He insisted that the truth of a proposition cannot be assessed without regard for the "values and position of the subject . . . and the social content"; he did not take seriously the possibility of autonomous, disinterested, and disciplined intellectual action. The historicist view that each age has its own distinctive problems, views of the world, and conceptions of the good and true; the Marxist view that there are "bourgeois" and "proletarian" truths; and the idea of *Weltanschauung*, developed in the writings of Dilthey and Spranger, all came together in Mannheim's thought in the 1920s.

Mannheim's earliest formulation of relationism, in "On the Interpretations of 'Weltanschauung'" (1923), prefigured the whole concern and intellectual position of his German period. This essay represents an effort to legitimate a mode of understanding intellectual works as manifestations, expressions, or parts of something else. He regarded the *Weltanschauung* of an individual, school, or epoch as the nonrational matrix from which every particular work was an emanation. A major task of the analysis of particular works was, therefore, to discern their "style." According to this approach, style consists of features which a work shares with other works, which each part of a work shares with each other part of the work, and which intellectual works share with nonintellectual manifestations of a *Weltanschauung*. Thus, the problem with which Mannheim was concerned was the subsumption of a particular work under the pattern of other works like it and of the style of the *Weltanschauung* as a whole. Each particular intellectual work was treated —and *accounted for*—as related to or derived from something else.

Although Mannheim first applied this conception to art history, its implications for the next stage of his thought were patent. In two essays, "The Problem of a Sociology of Knowledge" (1925) and "Ideologische und soziologische Interpretation der geistigen Gebilde" (1926), he advanced to the treatment of moral works, mainly works of political and social philosophy, and to the "sociological approach." Whereas the "ideological" interpretation of intellectual works treated them simply as derivable from other intellectual works which preceded them and as generated by a process internal to the mind, the sociological approach purported to go further. It claimed that intellectual works are generated in response to the needs of the class or group to which their creators belong, as it is confronted with "practical" tasks and challenges to its position by other classes or groups. However much he sought to distinguish his own view from Marxism, he never fully escaped from the Marxist categories of *Unterbau* and *Überbau*.

The question may be asked, Did he really succeed, in this first phase of his work, in freeing himself from the ideological interpretation he tried to transcend? Much of his subsequent sociological analysis of political and cultural beliefs, not least that in his major substantive work, "Conservative Thought" (1927), consisted in relating particular beliefs to more general patterns of belief or *Weltanschauungen*. His work became sociological through scattered assertions that particular views are correlated with particular value orientations, characteristic of particular roles or statuses—for example, membership in particular social classes or the practice of particular occupations or styles of life. In this period he attempted fewer correlations

with social structural variables than with the culture or value orientations of classes or occupational strata. His "sociological" interpretations of political and social beliefs remained ideological. Nonetheless, the specification of the social group which possesses a particular culture or *Weltanschauung* did represent a genuinely sociological extension of the ideological approach, rather than its replacement or negation.

The sociological variables Mannheim used in this phase of his career were largely derived from Marxism, e.g., "declining classes," "ascendant classes," "threatened classes," "newly self-conscious classes," etc., although he also cited generations, sects, and parties as the structural bearers of different *Weltanschauungen*. In *Ideology and Utopia* he asserted, for example, that "uprooted" and "unintegrated" revolutionary groups think intuitively and lay little or no stress on historical development; that conservative groups think morphologically; that liberal–humanitarian strata stress the openness of the future and the progressive realization of ethical values; and that oppressed strata, which are chiliastic, expect immediate and sharply disjunctive changes.

The correlations were at best no more than correlations. Mannheim avoided the task of causal imputation and of a differentiated analysis of the process or mechanism through which ideas and social position are connected. In the main he committed himself to nothing more than the assertion that thought is "existentially connected" (*seinsverbunden*) with social position. His work was characterized by insights of great penetration, both into the interconnections between diverse elements in a given *Weltanschauung* and also, if more rarely, into the correlations of these elements with "positions" in society.

The contradictory combination of a persistent idealism with the Marxist negation of idealism by "standing it on its head" remained basic in Mannheim's thought throughout his German period. It was a contradiction which he did not overcome and of which he was unaware. His continuous insistence that the "internalist" (ideological) view is wrong and his failure to recognize how much of it he himself retained led to his failure to perceive the partial autonomy of intellectual traditions and the institutional structure in which autonomous intellectual activity is effectuated. By constantly stressing that intellectual activities are responses to current practical–political situations, which are "nonintellectual," he was precluded from a sociological analysis of the institutional structures of intellectual activity, which make possible the continuity of intellectual traditions. (His one effort to study the social processes that are immanent in intellectual continuity and change, "The Problem of Generations" [1928], remained very general and vague and was never assimilated into his sociology of knowledge.)

There were other reasons why Mannheim's sociology of knowledge failed. What he meant by "knowledge" was largely normative and metaphysical beliefs, ideas about the nature and right organization of society, and interpretations of history. He never came to grips with the natural sciences, that is, with science as that term is understood in English-speaking countries. Scientific knowledge as a body of systematically verified beliefs remained at the margin of his interests. The influence of science and of scientific, research-based technology on social structure passed unnoticed before him. This omission made it easier for him to neglect the element of continuity and the processes of internally instigated innovation within an intellectual pattern. His denial that there is anything like a "self-contained intellect which evolves by and from itself" and his equal insistence that every change in a pattern of thought corresponds to "a change in the position of the group" required that intellectual interest and criteria of truth other than the successful mastery of life situations also be denied.

In the three years between the publication of *Ideology and Utopia* and his departure from Germany, Mannheim's transition from the sociology of knowledge to the macrosociological and microsociological study of social structure began to become visible. Much influenced by Max Weber's ideas about bureaucracy, he wrote an essay, "Über das Wesen und die Bedeutung des wirtschaftlichen Erfolgsstrebens" (1930), in which he analyzed the psychological correlates of the bureaucratic career and the bureaucratization of modern society and adumbrated his later interest in a pragmatic educational policy. His interest in personality and culture and in the "planning of personality" also appeared here for the first time. He also wrote a book on the intelligentsia, which was unpublished in his lifetime. (It was published posthumously in 1956, as *Essays on the Sociology of Culture*.) In the final section of that book, entitled "The Democratization of Culture," he presented an original analysis of the postulates of the democratic outlook, setting forth for the first time his later more fully developed views about fundamental democratization and the deterioration of the rationality and solidarity of elites.

The structure of modern society

After Mannheim went to England, he ceased almost entirely to study doctrinal beliefs and their social correlates. His epistemological interests, which had foundered in inconclusiveness, were largely discontinued. (For example, his distinction, in *Man and Society in an Age of Reconstruction* [1935], of three modes of thought—thought at the level of discovery, at the level of invention, and at the level of planning—avoided all questions of epistemological validity.) Nonetheless, certain earlier themes continued to preoccupy him in this second stage of his career; dissensus, the conflict of classes, the disagreements of doctrines, and the irreconcilability of political movements still engaged his mind, although the particular contexts changed in which these phenomena were seen. While in his first phase his attention was preponderantly directed to the reconciliation of contending and antithetical interpretations of events and criteria of truth, the main aim of the macrosociology of his second period was the delineation of the contemporary dissensus, the disclosure of its causes, and the discovery of the means of its displacement by a new consensus.

Another line of continuity may be seen in his attitude toward sociology. Although in his second phase he came much closer to the scientific aspirations of empirical sociology, he never fully resigned himself to them. He became more sympathetic to the largely ahistorical, sociological, and social-psychological research of the period, but he never ceased to insist on the necessity of a "dynamic" and "historical" sociology. The natural-science model of knowledge remained alien to him and was never integrated into his thought.

In both periods he looked upon sociology as a potential cure for the ills of society. Just as the sociology of knowledge had been intended to emancipate intellectuals from extreme partisanship and from particularistic perspectives ([1929–1931] 1954, pp. 97–104), so a sociologically oriented education and sociologically oriented planning became the means, in his second phase, of overcoming dissensus and of avoiding the dangers of totalitarianism. His historicism led him to underemphasize the elements of identity between various societies, and he therefore believed that modern mass society is afflicted with a degree of dissensus such as no other society had ever suffered. But instead of focusing his attention on the dissensus of the intellectuals, he now stressed the dissensus of social strata and political groups.

Mannheim added some variants of his own to the German sociological tradition which derived from Tönnies and Simmel and which emphasized the disintegration of modern urban society. Unlike his predecessors, who characterized bourgeois society as uniform throughout its history, Mannheim distinguished between the stages of minority democracy and mass democracy. Several elements, not previously considered in the older diagnosis of the perpetual crisis resulting from unbridled conflicts of individual and collective desires, were added by him: the concentration of authority, the bureaucratization of work, "functional rationalization," increased integration ("increasing interdependence"), and "fundamental democratization." The concomitance of these major processes resulted in the democratization of access to positions within elites. Through these processes individuals who lacked practical and experienced judgment moved into the political elites at the very time that more and more of social life had become dependent on the decisions of these elites.

Mannheim stressed the intensification of demands which accompanied the democratization of political participation and the consequent increase in the frequency of unrealistic and unfulfillable demands. Yet the first years of his sojourn in Great Britain changed the accent of his thought. His outlook became more optimistic and more concrete. The increased optimism was manifested in his effort to promulgate a pattern of democratic planning. The enhanced concreteness arose in part from his increased interest in empirical sociological and social-psychological research. It was also related to the much greater matter-of-factness of discussions of social and political problems in Great Britain, where political differences were not invariably reduced to metaphysical and *weltanschauliche* differences. He became more sympathetic to psychoanalysis and better acquainted with it. He also became increasingly interested in educational techniques—that is, the possibility of transforming conduct through scientifically based educational techniques. This interest, encouraged by Sir Fred Clarke, the director of the University of London Institute of Education, brought him into a greater intimacy with the practical problems of education. His dislike of the prototype of the generally educated man espoused by German idealism had already, in his German period, caused him to reach out toward more practical types of education, which would be concerned with fitting individuals for differentiated social roles. His growing interest in planning strengthened his interest in education as preparation for participation in a democratic consensus.

His membership in an unusual group called the Moot, which met quarterly and which included Joseph Oldham, long active in Church of England affairs and social reform; Alec Vidler, a notable Anglican theologian and historian, then dean of Windsor Chapel; T. S. Eliot; J. Middleton Murry;

and other literary and academic men, civil servants and theologians, made him more sensitive to religious belief and its possible role in the planned democracy of the future than he had ever been before. It was to this group that he presented a long paper, "Towards a New Social Philosophy: A Challenge to Christian Thinkers by a Sociologist" (1943). Mannheim argued that laissez-faire has exhausted its possibilities; as a result of fundamental democratization and the process of functional rationalization, the free play of forces in the economy has lost its powers of self-equilibration. Man's capacity for autonomous and responsible individual judgment has weakened at the very time that greater demands for such judgment are being placed on him. The irrationality generated by these two processes has increased the danger of totalitarianism. The "primordial images" which have directed the life experiences of men through the ages have vanished, and nothing has taken their place. Conduct, in consequence, "falls to pieces," and only "disconnected fragments of unintegrated behaviour patterns" remain.

In the final product of his constructive imagination, *Freedom, Power, and Democratic Planning* (1950), Mannheim defined the principal task as the creation of a society-wide "spontaneous" consensus, which would permit planning to be carried out effectively. In Germany he had shared many of the general views of democratic socialism, and in the 1930s he came to accept the inevitability and desirability of planning. To prevent planning from becoming totalitarian, self-restraint in collective demands and confinement of popular participation in the exercise of power to specific occasions were necessary. The indispensable condition for such restraint and limitation was consensus, and the two paths to consensus were, first, pedagogy, and, second, a readiness to accept and even to arouse religious sensibility and the moral attitudes called forth by religious experience. He saw the function of religion as helping man to restrain himself through spontaneously experienced moral norms and therewith to stabilize a social framework which would permit a modicum of freedom in a society that had to be planned in order to exist. Society in its latest phase needed a spiritual purpose, to avoid having a purpose imposed on it by a totalitarian elite. Thus, it became necessary to plan religion— not by prescribing a theology, but by the planned provision of institutional settings in which religious experience could flourish.

Mannheim's influence

Although he was an extraordinarily stimulating teacher, Mannheim had few intellectual descendants: his Frankfurt students were scattered and their incipient careers broken; at the London School of Economics, students interested in empirical research found him insufficiently at home in the then prevailing techniques, and there were very few equipped to do the kind of historical and macrosociological work that was Mannheim's forte. During World War II the teaching of sociology ceased in England, and Mannheim was thereby deprived of the opportunity to influence the new generation of sociologists. In Germany the long suspension of social scientific work resulted in an attrition of the culture required to sustain Mannheim's kind of sociology, and when social scientific work was resumed after the war, the older tradition had been lost and Mannheim's prewar macrosociological writings did not appear relevant to current interests.

The sociology of knowledge as practiced by Mannheim has found no succession. Its only manifestations are Ernst Kohn Bramstedt's dissertation, *Aristocracy and Middle-classes in Germany* (1937), Hans Gerth's "Die sozialgeschichtliche Lage der bürgerlichen Intelligenz um die Wende des 18. Jahrhunderts" (1935), and Hans Speier's "Die Geschichtsphilosophie Lassalle's" (1929). Much work has been done since World War II which may be said to fall within the jurisdiction of the sociology of knowledge broadly conceived, yet very little of it bears the impress of Mannheim's thought.

More recent works like Thomas S. Kuhn's *Structure of Scientific Revolutions* (1962) and Michael Polanyi's *Personal Knowledge* (1958), which have carried very far the systematic analysis of patterns of thought and their modes of change, owe nothing to Mannheim's analyses of *Weltanschauungen*. Similarly, Mircea Eliade and Claude Lévi-Strauss, in work on the fundamental categories of thought, owe much to Jung, Durkheim, and Mauss; they owe practically nothing to Mannheim. Latent-structure analysis, which was developed by Paul F. Lazarsfeld and others for the analysis of attitude-survey data and which offers great possibilities of development for the analysis of the structure of beliefs, is also independent of Mannheim's influence.

The situation is somewhat different with regard to the study of ideologies: there can be little doubt that the prominent place which this kind of work is now beginning to occupy in sociological analysis owes something to the fact that Mannheim brought the term "ideology" to the attention of sociologists. His influence in this area is a product less of anything specific he said about the problems of ideology than of the fact that he dwelt on them long and seriously. Similarly, the study of the political and social role of intellectuals and of the institutional systems of intellectual life, as carried on by

Theodor Geiger, Robert K. Merton, Joseph Ben-David, Talcott Parsons, Helmuth Plessner, Martin Trow, Lewis Coser, A. H. Halsey, and others, owes some of its impetus to Mannheim's concern with these subjects.

Mannheim's macrosociological views of contemporary large-scale society have had a more receptive audience and a more enduring influence. They were in harmony with an already established tradition in the analysis of modern urban society, and their appearance coincided with the emergence of the influence on sociology of Marxism and of Max Weber's writings on bureaucracy and capitalism. Also, they appeared at a time of troubled interest in the causes of the breakdown of liberal societies and the emergence of populistic totalitarian regimes and movements. Mannheim's very term "mass society" focused attention on certain unique features of modern large-scale societies, and his emphasis on the significance of bureaucratization and democratization in government, industry, commerce, and culture created one of the major themes of contemporary sociological thought.

Mannheim's "morphological" approach, derived partly from German historicism, partly from Marxism, and partly from Weber's broad categories and comparative studies, made him one of the first proponents of the macrosociological approach in the world of English-language sociology. Here again, it was his inclination to think of society as a whole, rather than his specific hypotheses, which led to macrosociology. He was vague in his formulations, and there is a tantalizing ambiguity in nearly everything he wrote. Yet, he dealt with very important subjects. The adage which asserts that the mistakes of a distinguished mind are more interesting than the truths of a mediocre one was true of Mannheim. He had in large measure the rare gift of touching on vital and enigmatic things.

EDWARD SHILS

[*Directly related are the entries* IDEOLOGY; INTEGRATION, *article on* CULTURAL INTEGRATION; INTELLECTUALS; KNOWLEDGE, SOCIOLOGY OF; MASS SOCIETY; POLITICAL SOCIOLOGY; SOCIAL MOVEMENTS. *Other relevant material may be found in* CONSERVATISM; EDUCATION, *article on* THE STUDY OF EDUCATIONAL SYSTEMS; ELITES; GENERATIONS; HISTORY, *articles on* THE PHILOSOPHY OF HISTORY *and* INTELLECTUAL HISTORY; MARXIST SOCIOLOGY; PLANNING, SOCIAL; REVOLUTION; *and in the biographies of* DILTHEY; GEIGER; LUKÁCS; MARX; SCHELER; SIMMEL; TÖNNIES; WEBER, ALFRED; WEBER, MAX.]

WORKS BY MANNHEIM

(1922–1940) 1953 *Essays on Sociology and Social Psychology.* Edited by Paul Kecskemeti. London: Routledge; New York: Oxford Univ. Press.

(1923) 1952   On the Interpretations of "Weltanschauung." Pages 33–83 in Karl Mannheim, *Essays on the Sociology of Knowledge*. New York: Oxford Univ. Press. → First published as "Beiträge zur Theorie der Weltanschauungsinterpretation."

(1923–1929) 1952   *Essays on the Sociology of Knowledge*. Edited by Paul Kecskemeti. New York: Oxford Univ. Press.

(1925) 1952   The Problem of a Sociology of Knowledge. Pages 134–190 in Karl Mannheim, *Essays on the Sociology of Knowledge*. New York: Oxford Univ. Press.

1926   Ideologische und soziologische Interpretation der geistigen Gebilde. *Jahrbuch für Soziologie* 2:424–440.

(1927) 1953   Conservative Thought. Pages 77–164 in Karl Mannheim, *Essays on Sociology and Social Psychology*. London: Routledge; New York: Oxford Univ. Press. → First published as "Das konservative Denken."

(1928) 1952   The Problem of Generations. Pages 276–320 in Karl Mannheim, *Essays on the Sociology of Knowledge*. New York: Oxford Univ. Press. → First published as "Das Problem der Generationen."

(1929) 1952   Competition as a Cultural Phenomenon. Pages 191–229 in Karl Mannheim, *Essays on the Sociology of Knowledge*. New York: Oxford Univ. Press. → First published as "Die Bedeutung der Konkurrenz im Gebiete des Geistigen."

(1929–1931) 1954   *Ideology and Utopia: An Introduction to the Sociology of Knowledge*. New York: Harcourt; London: Routledge. → A paperback edition was published in 1955 by Harcourt. Part 1 is an introductory essay. Parts 2–4 are a translation of *Ideologie und Utopie* (1929); Part 5 is a translation of "Wissenssoziologie" (1931).

1930   Über das Wesen und die Bedeutung des wirtschaftlichen Erfolgsstrebens: Ein Beitrag zur Wirtschaftssoziologie. *Archiv für Sozialwissenschaft und Sozialpolitik* 63:449–512.

(1935) 1940   *Man and Society in an Age of Reconstruction: Studies in Modern Social Structure*. Revised and considerably enlarged by the author. New York: Harcourt. → First published as *Mensch und Gesellschaft im Zeitalter des Umbaus*.

(1939–1943) 1950   *Diagnosis of Our Time: Wartime Essays of a Sociologist*. London: Routledge.

(1943) 1950   Towards a New Social Philosophy: A Challenge to Christian Thinkers by a Sociologist. Pages 100–165 in Karl Mannheim, *Diagnosis of Our Time: Wartime Essays of a Sociologist*. London: Routledge.

1950   *Freedom, Power, and Democratic Planning*. New York: Oxford Univ. Press. → Published posthumously.

1956   *Essays on the Sociology of Culture*. Oxford Univ. Press. → Published posthumously.

SUPPLEMENTARY BIBLIOGRAPHY

BRAMSTEDT, ERNST KOHN   (1937) 1964   *Aristocracy and Middle-classes in Germany: Social Types in German Literature, 1830–1900*. Rev. ed. Univ. of Chicago Press.

GERTH, HANS H.   1935   Die sozialgeschichtliche Lage der bürgerlichen Intelligenz um die Wende des 18. Jahrhunderts. Unpublished manuscript.

KUHN, THOMAS S.   1962   *The Structure of Scientific Revolutions*. Univ. of Chicago Press. → A paperback edition was published in 1964.

LENK, KURT   1963   Die Rolle der Intelligenzsoziologie in der Theorie Mannheims. *Kölner Zeitschrift für Soziologie und Sozialpsychologie* 15:323–337.

MERTON, ROBERT K.   (1941) 1957   Karl Mannheim and the Sociology of Knowledge. Pages 489–508 in Robert K. Merton, *Social Theory and Social Structure*. Rev. ed. New York: Free Press.

MILLS, C. WRIGHT   (1940) 1963   Methodological Consequences of the Sociology of Knowledge. Pages 453–468 in C. Wright Mills, *Power, Politics and People: The Collected Essays of C. Wright Mills*. New York: Oxford Univ. Press.

POLANYI, MICHAEL   1958   *Personal Knowledge: Towards a Post-critical Philosophy*. Univ. of Chicago Press.

SPEIER, HANS   1929   Die Geschichtsphilosophie Lassalle's. *Archiv für Sozialwissenschaft und Sozialpolitik* 61:103–127, 360–388.

MANORIAL ECONOMY

The word *manoir* was used in Normandy in the eleventh century to designate the residence of a lord, the point of concentration of his economic and social power, and the place where the products of his lands were collected and where his men performed the services they owed him. In 1086, when Norman clerks drew up the inventory known as the *Domesday Book* for William the Conqueror, they used the word *manoir* as the key term in their descriptions of English estates. The word became part of the vocabulary of England. The expression "manorial economy" thus signifies, for Anglo-Saxon historians, a certain mode of economic organization of men and the land that developed during the feudal period. Continental historians usually employ the term "seignorial economy."

Earliest manifestations.   The first clear image of the manorial system appears from documents drawn up in the ninth century in northern France, western Germany, and Lombardy describing the landed estates of large monasteries and the way in which they were managed. The French scholar Benjamin Guérard published the oldest and most complete of these inventories, which was drawn up before 829 for the monastery of Saint-Germain-des-Prés in Paris. He made the first analysis of manorial economy at that period; the work of subsequent medievalists has added precision to his analysis.

These immense monastic estates were divided for management purposes into large units known as *villae;* their centers (*curtis*) corresponded exactly to the *manoir* in the Anglo-Norman vocabulary of the eleventh century. A more or less compact assemblage of cultivated and uncultivated land, covering hundreds and often thousands of hectares, was attached to the residence of the lord. This enormous landed estate was divided into two portions, each having entirely different economic functions.

The larger part, which comprised all the woods and pastures, most of the meadows and vineyards, and large tracts of arable land, formed the domain proper (*terra indominicata*). The master of the *villa* kept direct operation of this in his own hands and received all its produce.

The rest of the land was broken up into a number of operating units of much smaller size. Each of these, containing only a few hectares of plowland and sometimes a bit of meadow and vineyard, was attached to the lot where the family of the peasant lived (*mansus*). Each family of workers managed this farm and took what it produced, in exchange for certain obligations to the lord. This was a holding. The oldest inventories make a distinction between two types of *mansi*: one called free, the other servile. There were also two large legal categories among the peasant population: the freemen and the slaves. However, no perfect agreement existed between the status of the tenure and that of the peasants who operated it: some freeholdings were occupied by households of slaves and vice versa.

This division of the lord's land into two parts, the domain and the individual holdings, was in response to operating requirements. The central problem of management was a problem of manpower. The very low level of farming technique and the wretched inefficiency of farm tools made it necessary to employ a large number of laborers to make the fields and vineyards sufficiently productive. But the rural regions of Europe were very sparsely inhabited in the ninth century and there was insufficient money in circulation to permit regular use of wage labor. On the other hand, the reduction in traffic in slaves had made it impossible, by the ninth century, to base the operation of great aristocratic domains on the employment of human chattels, as had been done in previous epochs.

A set of domestic slaves was still maintained at the lord's residence at the center of the *villa*, but they were too few to farm the vast cultivated fields of the reservation at the time of major operations: haymaking, harvesting, vintage, ditching and fencing, cultivating the vineyards and, above all, plowing. Moreover, this team of domestics had to be re-formed periodically. The chief function of the holdings was to ensure periodical renewal of this group of domestics and provide it with supplementary unpaid labor services. The tenures known as servile were probably originally set up by the lord in order that some of his slaves might lead a family life on each such *mansus*. This separate settlement had two advantages.

The slave family had to get its food from its own holding. The lord was thus relieved of its maintenance. To be sure, this meant the loss of a part of the productive power of the family, but only a part. The tenant slaves continued to work for him without pay. The women were employed in the domestic workshops of the *villa* and produced pieces of cloth at home. The head of the family had to do any tasks given him during three days a week. The first function of the tenure was to provide the master with unpaid, half-time domestics.

Further, the married slaves, established by pairs in family homes, begot children and raised them until they were of an age to work. From these children the lord recruited the servants for full-time service in his house. Thus, the existence of servile tenures promoted the operation of a type of slave economy in an economic and social *ambiance* in which the slave markets were no longer regularly supplied.

As for the tenures known as free, whether they too had been set up by the lord on his own lands or were peasant farms that had once been independent and had been annexed to the *villa* in one way or another, they were generally more extensive than the servile tenures, for the peasant families holding them had a larger proportion of their time available for working their farms and usually kept work animals. The economic function of these freeholdings was a different one. To some extent they provided income, delivering a portion of their produce to the lord in the form of dues—in kind or in money. Their main contribution to the economy of the *villa*, however, was likewise labor. This took two forms: (1) a piece of land from the domain, assigned each year to each holding, had to be cultivated and its entire produce turned in; (2) at fixed times, for a certain number of days, the tenants, with their teams, had to be at the service of the lord and help the household servants in the work of plowing and cartage.

The system described above seems to have been fairly widespread in the ninth century in the regions between the Loire and the Rhine, and in the Po Valley. There it represented a developed form of the great aristocratic estates of the Roman era. From that time on, it seems to have spread gradually in the Germanic regions and in England. It was, in fact, perfectly adapted to a social structure in which slavery was in the process of dissolution but in which a sharp distinction was maintained in the peasant world between the free and the unfree, and in which a strong aristocracy, religious or secular, held huge tracts of land and completely dominated those who labored on the land. The economy was certainly not entirely closed (the existence of regular dues in money proves that the tenures, as well as the great estates, were normally engaged on the market), but labor productivity was low, population sparse, and the circulation of money very slow. The manorial system, whose basic nexus was the association of the holdings to the work of the domain, made possible the operation of the great grain-producing estates on which the power of the aristocracy rested.

Development under feudalism. Between the tenth and thirteenth centuries, in the rural regions of western Europe, the political power of the landholding aristocracy was strengthened and the old forms of slavery disappeared. The peasants were still divided into two legal categories: (1) the "free" peasants, subject only to the territorial lord's powers of justice and police; and (2) the personal dependents—serfs, *hommes de corps*, *Leibeigene*, villeins—hereditarily attached to a private master. The most significant changes took place in production. Great progress in rural techniques brought about a sharp improvement in the yield of human labor, and, as a result, a continual growth of population and acceleration in exchange and in the circulation of money. The manorial economy adapted to this evolution in the environment.

England. The new forms of the manorial economy appear most clearly in thirteenth-century England. An abundance of documents, well exploited by economic historians, gives us the following picture of the structure of the manor on the landed estates of the great English religious foundations.

The heart of the manor was the domain, a large unit whose production was to a great extent intended for sale, for at that time there were large markets for grain and wool. The peasant holdings ranged around the domain. Some of them were free, and their obligations consisted almost exclusively of dues. The others, which were closely associated in the work of the domain, fell into two groups. (1) Some, granted to men known as *bordarii*, were too small to provide full sustenance for the family that occupied them. Their holders were required to give one or more days of unpaid labor on the domain of the manor; additional days were worked for payment. (2) The tenures granted to *villani*, on the other hand, corresponded in size to the labor power and needs of a peasant household having a plow and team. Their obligations were much heavier. There was a multiplicity of dues which transferred a large portion of the produce of the land to the seignorial house. Above all, there were various kinds of *corvée*, or forced labor: the tenant and his livestock were summoned to perform both definite tasks and what was called

"week work"—the obligation to go to work on the domain a certain number of days each week. On some manors, during the heaviest work of harvesting and haymaking, this duty could extend to all the people living on the holding and to every working day. In addition, in the thirteenth century *villani* and *bordarii* were held to have no liberty. Accordingly, they were excluded from the jurisdiction of the public courts and subject to the private justice of the manor. They paid a number of personal taxes, by means of which the lord appropriated a part of the money they earned.

On these manors, therefore, the association for work between the domain and the individual holdings remained unbroken. On the contrary, during the thirteenth century the link seems to have become tighter: the managers of the great monastic estates, eager to increase production on the domains in order to have more to sell, were stricter in exacting the *corvée* and tried to extend such work. However, the *corvée* never was sufficient to get the work of the domain done. Part, often the major part, of the labor was done by a set of full-time servants and by workers for wages. The *bordarii* were regularly hired on the days they were not required to do unpaid work, and so were the poor peasants of the village, who were looking for supplementary resources. The growth of this rural proletariat in the thirteenth century favored recourse to paid labor; it kept the level of wages very low while the price of food rose, thus increasing the profits of the large estates.

It should be added that the manorial organization described in the ecclesiastical documents did not by any means characterize all seignorial lands. On most English manors the part played by statute laborers in working the domain was very slight or nonexistent; servants and wage laborers constituted the entire labor force.

The Continent. On the Continent—in France, the Low Countries, Germany, and Italy—the statute labor required from tenants diminished during the eleventh and twelfth centuries. By the thirteenth century, it had very often disappeared completely or was only two, three, or four days a year. Dues, collected in money for the most part, had taken its place. The old tenures, many of which had broken up and disintegrated, thus yielded only money income. The very large number of new holdings set up on the vast expanses of newly cultivated land had for the most part been exempted from *corvées* since their inception. Further, changes in the price level had in effect reduced the money dues, the most common obligation. By the thirteenth century, the obligations of the tenures had become trifling. Finally, emancipations had greatly reduced the number and cost of personal dependents.

But although the old manorial system was no longer very profitable to the aristocracy, they gained by other means. By taxes on inheritances and sales of tenures, by tithes on harvests, by tallage (*taille*, a periodical tapping of the capital in chattels of the peasant households), the lords took virtually all the money earned by a more numerous and more productive peasantry. Further, great investment operations—extensions of vineyards and cattle raising and, in Italy, of the *coltura promiscua*—introduced contracts of a new type binding the rural laborers to the lords. The latter contributed the land and the capital but kept the greater part of the profits.

However, the lords had not turned into mere passive receivers of income from the land. The almost complete disappearance of forced labor had not diminished the economic importance of the management of their domains, whose value had been considerably increased by the advances in rural production. But this large-scale seignorial farming was now based on the use of domestics and hired labor; it was furthered by the opening of the market for agricultural products and by the growth of the rural proletariat.

Final forms of the manorial economy. The last parts of the framework of manorial organizations were gradually destroyed in Europe during the thirteenth and fourteenth centuries by the extension of leaseholding (contracts of *fermage*). Under this system certain economic powers were ceded for short periods to an intermediary in exchange for payments fixed in advance. It was employed very early for the collection of certain seignorial rents. On the Continent it was employed by the greatest lords in the operation of their domains from the end of the twelfth century on. For an annual payment the lands of the domain, all the means for cultivating them, and, in particular, what was left of statute labor, were granted for some years, under certain guarantees, to a farming entrepreneur—the community of the peasants of the village, the former bailiff, a bourgeois capitalist, or even an ordinary peasant who had enough ability to take over the operation of all the great domain. Use of this procedure spread very widely during the fourteenth century and soon got to England.

At that time, the dominant tendencies in rural economy were reversed almost everywhere. Rural population was rapidly decreasing. The resultant rise in agricultural wages, coupled with the fall in grain prices, tolled the knell of the large-scale agricultural operation based on wage labor. From that time on, the extension of leaseholdings was accompanied by division of the great domains into small holdings. Leaseholds and farm contracts calling for payment in kind (*métayage*) were for much smaller tracts, corresponding to the means of production of a family helped by a few domestics. At the same time, political and social disorders did away with almost all survivals of personal servitude. In eastern Germany, however, certain political conditions, producing a re-formation of serfdom, intervened to promote the rise of large estates based on the *corvée*, namely, the *Gutsherrschaften*, the longest-lasting form of manorial economy.

GEORGES M. DUBY

[*See also* FEUDALISM. *Other relevant material may be found in* LAND TENURE.]

BIBLIOGRAPHY

ABEL, WILHELM 1962 *Geschichte der deutschen Landwirtschaft vom frühen Mittelalter bis zum 19. Jahrhundert.* Stuttgart (Germany): Ulmer.

BLOCH, MARC (1931) 1952–1956 *Les caractères originaux de l'histoire rurale française.* New ed. 2 vols. Paris: Colin. → Volume 2, *Supplément établi d'après les travaux de l'auteur (1931–1944)*, was written by Robert Dauvergne.

The Cambridge Economic History of Europe From the Decline of the Roman Empire. Volume 1: *The Agrarian Life of the Middle Ages.* 1941 Cambridge Univ. Press.

DUBY, GEORGES 1962 *L'économie rurale et la vie des campagnes dans l'occident médiéval (France, Angleterre, Empire, IX–XV siècles): Essai de synthèse et perspectives de recherches.* 2 vols. Paris: Aubier.

SLICHER VAN BATH, BERNARD H. (1960) 1963 *The Agrarian History of Western Europe: A.D. 500–1850.* London: Arnold. → First published in Dutch.

MANPOWER

See LABOR FORCE; WORKERS; *see also* CAPITAL, HUMAN.

MAPS

See CARTOGRAPHY *and* GRAPHIC PRESENTATION.

MARETT, ROBERT RANULPH

Robert Ranulph Marett (1866–1943) was one of a number of classically trained scholars in England (Frazer, Andrew Lang, and Myres were others) who at the end of the nineteenth century were attracted to the then developing subject of anthropology. Marett's own interest in anthropology was originally stimulated by his preparations for the Oxford University Green moral philosophy prize, which in 1893 was to be given to an essay on the ethics of savage races. At the time a tutor in philosophy at Exeter College, Marett won the prize, and so came into the orbit of E. B. Tylor. Marett was to spend almost his entire academic life at Oxford (from 1928 until his death he occupied the post of rector of Exeter College).

He remained essentially an "armchair" anthropologist, although he conducted some archeological excavations on his native island of Jersey. His major interests lay in the field of primitive religion. His theories of a "preanimistic" stage of religion were a development of Tylor's concept of "animism," but he insisted also upon the psychological component of religious belief. Unlike the heavy, comparative treatises of many of his contemporaries, most of Marett's books were initially lectures and addresses. He excelled in the nicely illustrated argument which examines in brief compass a new idea, approach, or observation. Marett's initial reputation was acquired through one such paper, delivered to the British Association for the Advancement of Science in 1899, "Pre-animistic Religion." Coming at a time when the psychological component of behavior was receiving growing recognition, the central idea—that a diffuse religious feeling probably preceded Tylor's postulated creed of "belief in spiritual beings"—was accepted by a number of English and German scholars and received the distinction of a lengthy discussion in Wundt's *Völkerpsychologie*, where it was translated as "der Marettische Präanimismus." The paper was included in Marett's first collection of essays, *The Threshold of Religion* (1900), which contains many of his key and most original ideas.

Anthropology, a popular general account reprinted many times in the following decades, was published in 1912, and a second collection of essays and addresses, *Psychology and Folk-lore*, in 1920. Marett was invited to give the Gifford lectures at St. Andrew's University in 1931/1932, and these were published in two volumes—the first, *Faith, Hope and Charity in Primitive Religion* (1932), dealing with religious sentiment in primitive societies, and the second, *Sacraments of Simple Folk* (1933), with primitive rituals. A final collection of essays, *Head, Heart & Hands in Human Evolution*, appeared in 1935, followed the next year by a biography of Tylor.

Marett viewed anthropology as a broad, coordinated study centrally concerned with "man in evolution." He stated many times that anthropology is based on Darwinian theory, but his was a humanized Darwinism, which insisted upon the unity of human nature that underlies the diversity of behavior: "Darwinism is the touch of nature that makes the whole world kin" (1912, p. 11). In view of the importance which is generally ascribed to

Tylor's introduction into anthropology of the concept of "culture," it is interesting to observe that Marett, Tylor's pupil and great admirer, did not begin to make any distinctive use of this concept before he wrote the papers published in *Psychology and Folk-lore* (1920), by which time it was also being developed by other writers, notably in the United States. The methodologically more diffuse concept "custom" was, for Marett, more important; he viewed behavior in primitive society as essentially "custom-bound," and primitive religion as "mobbish."

Marett criticized Tylor's and Frazer's theories concerning religion and magic for their "intellectualism" and pointed out the absurdity of regarding the "savage" as a kind of "primitive philosopher"; yet, in his own theories he perhaps did little more than substitute notions of primitive faith or religious "feeling" for their notions of primitive creed or their postulated theories about nature. For Marett, the original "stuff" of religion was "supernaturalism," a matter of emotion rather than of intellect; "that basic feeling of Awe, which drives a man ere he can think or theorise upon it, into personal relations with the Supernatural" ([1900] 1929, p. 15). Both magic and religion spring from this original, undifferentiated category of experience (which he called "magico–religious"), the former in practices antithetical to the common good, the latter in practices or beliefs in harmony with it. The concepts of taboo and mana gave Marett ethnographic evidence for such elemental apprehension of the supernatural, "mana" referring to it in a positive mode, "taboo" in a negative mode. This taboo–mana formula, delineating a belief in impersonal forces, Marett adopted for his own minimum definition of religion. He also referred to this wider category of belief by the term "animatism," in order to distinguish it from Tylor's "animism," defining it as "the attribution of life and personality to things, but not of a separate apparitional soul" (British Association . . . 1912, p. 262).

The teaching of anthropology in Oxford had started in 1884, with Tylor's appointment as reader, but he had extremely few pupils, and it was not until 1905, with the setting up of a committee for anthropology and the inauguration of a diploma in anthropology (in which Marett was actively concerned), that the subject obtained wider recognition in the university and a regular flow of students began. Marett held the post of reader in social anthropology from 1908 until 1934, when a chair was created, which Marett occupied for one year, until Radcliffe-Brown, who had already been appointed, was able to take up his duties. Despite his own lack of field experience, Marett held that the teaching of anthropology should be directed toward field work; the teaching of prospective colonial administrators was started at Oxford shortly after the diploma course was inaugurated, and a number of the students (including A. C. Hollis, R. S. Rattray and C. K. Meek) later made important contributions to anthropology while holding appointments in the colonial service.

M. J. Ruel

[Other relevant material may be found in Magic; Religion; and in the biographies of Frazer; Mauss; Tylor.]

WORKS BY MARETT

(1900) 1929 The Threshold of Religion. 4th ed. London: Methuen.
1912 Anthropology. New York: Holt.
1915 Magic. Volume 8, pages 245–252 in Encyclopaedia of Religion and Ethics. Edited by James Hastings. Edinburgh: Clark.
1920 Psychology and Folk-lore. London: Methuen.
1932 Faith, Hope and Charity in Primitive Religion. Oxford: Clarendon.
1933 Sacraments of Simple Folk. Oxford: Clarendon.
1935 Head, Heart & Hands in Human Evolution. London: Hutchinson.
1936 Tylor. New York: Wiley.
1941 A Jerseyman at Oxford. Oxford Univ. Press. → An autobiography.

SUPPLEMENTARY BIBLIOGRAPHY

British Association for the Advancement of Science 1912 Notes and Queries on Anthropology. 4th ed. Edited by Barbara Freire-Marreco and J. L. Myres. London: Routledge. → The first edition was published in 1874; a sixth and revised edition in 1954.
Custom Is King: Essays Presented to R. R. Marett on His Seventieth Birthday, June 13, 1936. 1936 Edited by L. H. Dudley Buxton. London: Hutchinson. → Includes a bibliography of Marett's scientific writings.
Evans-Pritchard, E. E. 1965 Theories of Primitive Religion. Oxford: Clarendon.
Rose, Herbert J. 1943 Robert Ranulph Marett, 1866–1943. British Academy, London, Proceedings 29:357–370.
Wundt, Wilhelm (1900–1909) 1911–1929 Völkerpsychologie: Eine Untersuchung der Entwicklungsgesetze von Sprache, Mythus und Sitte. 10 vols. Leipzig: Engelmann.

MARGINAL PRODUCTIVITY
See Production; Productivity; Wages.

MARKET RESEARCH

I
MARKET ANALYSIS

Market analysis is concerned with predicting the size and location of markets as measured by sales. The term is sometimes used as a synonym for "market research," which is more accurately defined to include the entire range of methods and techniques employed not only for the delineation of the sizes and shapes of markets but also for the evaluation of tactics and strategies useful for developing and exploiting markets.

While market analysis and advanced methods of sales forecasting derive from the relatively young fields of statistics, survey methodology, and econometrics, the practice of prediction—commercial prediction no less than any other kind—has a very long history. Before the Delphic liturgy was defined, the auguries were divined from the livers of bulls and the entrails of doves; and the ambiguities of the oracle may not have been less than some of the forecasts that today trumpet tomorrow's fortunes.

The process and the outcome of sales forecasting command general interest among business managers, since sales volume constitutes the most important source of income for all but a narrow class of (financial) enterprises; and it is basic for corporate planning with respect to plant, personnel, and investment. Marketing plans and the allocation of promotional budgets are, of course, importantly influenced by expectations of the level and distribution of market opportunities.

The methods of market measurement. In measuring markets, one is concerned with both industry and enterprise concepts—total generic product sales in an area, loosely referred to as "market potential," and enterprise or brand sales, which are some proportion of industry sales. This is the "market share" of the firm or brand. The sales forecasts of particular companies normally depend on estimates of market potential (itself sometimes an inference from a general economic forecast), which are then adjusted for the firm's expected market share.

Methodological discussions of market analysis usually focus on sales or market potential. In practice, of course, it is not always obvious what the most appropriate definition of "market" or "product" is. One speaks of markets in various contexts: the "gasoline market," for example, of which the "high octane market" is a segment. The "petroleum market" and the "liquid fuels market" are broader concepts—but narrower than the "energy sources market." Similarly, one often hears of the "high price" and "low price" markets, the "New York," the "west coast," and the "export" market. In estimating market potentials it is important to choose the relevant definition, but this choice is often influenced by the data available. [See Markets and industries.]

While successful forecasting depends on gauging the effects of changes in the firm's marketing policy, on competitive behavior, and on the consequences of future events that may transform the environment, business planning often starts from estimates of present (recent) sales. It is common practice to estimate potential market size by taking recent industry volume as the first approximation to the measure of expected market size. Even this is not always easy. Not only are there difficulties in establishing a relevant definition of "industry," but data on recent industry sales are not as readily available as one might expect. Census data of various sorts offer authoritative figures on production and sales volume of fairly broadly defined product classes in the United States, but these tabulations do not appear at frequent intervals. More frequent compilations of industry statistics are by-products of excise taxes (e.g., gasoline and tobacco in the United States) and/or import duties. Other sources of industry sales-volume data are sometimes found in the publications and the archives of trade associations and of advertising media. Many firms find it useful to subscribe to one or more of the commercial subscription services that collect panel data from households and/or dealers for certain kinds of products. These panels provide much more detailed information on product movement—by brand, price level, and type of outlet, for example —than is available by other means. Finally, of course, it is possible to undertake special surveys of product volume and use.

In the absence of industry sales figures, and in order to avoid the expense of direct data collection, corollary or proxy data may be used to estimate market potentials. Data on complementary goods, for example, can serve this purpose—the market potential of automobile batteries for replacement can be estimated from data on the distribution of cars, sales of electrical appliances will be related to and limited by the number and location of wired homes.

Whatever the data sources of the market potential estimates, they are often available only on a national basis. One of the tasks of market analysis is to make the conversion to local and regional estimates. The conversion is characteristically made by distributing national figures in proportion to such measures as population, income, number of employees, and value added by manufacture, which are available for smaller geographic units.

The technology of sales forecasting. It is customary in the literature of forecasting to distinguish between short-term and long-term forecasting, although there is only rough agreement on definitions. "Short term" clearly refers to the monthly or quarterly outlook and many practitioners would include the annual forecast. "Long term" can safely

be attached to 10-year forecasts, but many technicians would so classify any predictions whose horizon is greater than one year. Forecasts for three years and five years are sometimes categorized as "intermediate range." Much (most) of the technology of forecasting is common to predictions of the various planning horizons, although truly long-range forecasts (e.g., for 10 and 15 years) depend heavily on trend analysis of such fundamental variables as population, productivity, income distribution, political developments, and leisure—all of which change slowly and are assumed to be stable in forecasts for any period up to a few years.

While few analysts would enthusiastically endorse Alphonse de Lamartine's observation that "History teaches everything, even the future," the fact is that the experience of yesterday and today constitutes all we know about tomorrow. The technology of forecasting includes methods for identifying relevant historical data and for manipulating them in ways which may make the record more meaningful and illuminating. The art of forecasting largely consists in interpreting historical data and in specifying those future events that will condition tomorrow's performance.

There are numerous ways of categorizing sales forecasting methods. It is convenient here to distinguish among the following: "judgment forecasts," including sales-force estimates; market surveys; market tests; time series analysis, including curve fitting; and regression analysis. While these various techniques are sometimes presented as mutually exclusive and alternative analytical tools, in practice full reliance is seldom placed on any single method; two or more approaches often supplement each other. Certainly, the forecast ultimately accepted as the basis for company planning almost always will reflect the intuitive estimates of senior management.

Judgmental approaches. Hardly anyone will quarrel with the assertion that intuition and judgment dominate the practice of sales forecasting. Ease, cheapness, and flexibility all combine to support the use of predictions of sales volume which rest unabashedly on the judgment of one or more persons in the firm. Judgment forecasts, whether made by individuals or committees, are dominated by the experience, perception, and intuition of the forecasters. The process cannot be separated from the performer(s) and replication is impossible. However inelegant the method may appear, impressionistic evidence suggests that the more rigorous statistical forecasting methods continue to play a subsidiary role in business planning.

Judgment forecasts are sometimes based on

sales-force estimates of future sales. It is hoped that sales personnel (and their managers) are familiar with the needs and circumstances of customers and the relative strength of competitive offerings. In some companies sales representatives systematically interview customers concerning their spending plans. Rarely, however, are sales-force estimates the sole basis of a company's forecast. Substantial editing is generally contributed by corporate staff and senior management.

While it is often claimed that salesmen (and their supervisors) are unduly optimistic and therefore generate faulty forecasts, evidence is hard to come by. It is not obvious that such a bias should consistently attach to their estimates, since the estimators' interest will be a function both of the character of the compensation plan and the particular use to be made of the forecast.

Market surveys.   Whereas sales-force estimates rely on a survey of the forecasts of sales personnel, a more recent development has been that of the survey of buyer intentions. The market survey rests on a sample of potential buyers whose attitudes and/or intentions to purchase are solicited in person or by mail or telephone.

The survey has enormous appeal as a forecasting aid. It seems plausible that buyers should know (and be able and willing to say) what and whether they plan to buy in the future—especially if the future is not too distant. But this view assumes that consumers can predict what the future will be like as well as what they will choose to do if the future is as they expect it to be. Evidence on the validity of these assumptions is uncertain.

The Survey of Consumer Finances was initiated in 1946 by the Board of Governors of the Federal Reserve System (Juster 1964). These surveys, covering intentions to purchase durable goods (e.g., houses, automobiles, and major household appliances), are among the best-known and most thoroughly analyzed materials in the literature of forecasting. They are in many respects models of methodological nicety and generally far surpass ordinary commercial standards—and costs—of market investigation. Despite the relatively long history of these surveys and the superior methods and skills of the investigators, one must still characterize the method as more promising than certain. What does seem clear is that the survey method is best adapted to products involving relatively large expenditures and a fairly high degree of planning for purchase. In the case of family expenditures, homes and automobiles most clearly meet these conditions. In the case of industrial markets, expenditures for capital goods (e.g., expensive machinery and new

plant construction) obviously qualify. Indeed, surveys of spending plans for industrial capital goods have tended to yield more accurate forecasts than those for consumer goods.

Market testing.   Another method used to estimate market potential is the market test. Employed primarily for new products and invading brands, the market test is essentially an "experiment" which eschews direct questioning of respondents in favor of measuring their behavior. Market experiments are not feasible for all product categories, and they are expensive even when confined, as they usually are, to one or a few markets. The test is most commonly employed for packaged consumer goods items—the frequently purchased branded food, drug, and household supply products of relatively low price and high turnover. Market tests by and large amount to "tryouts" in one or a few markets—typically cities or metropolitan areas—which are selected as test locations because they are considered to be representative and relatively self-contained and have trade outlets and advertising media which are amenable to experimentation.

Virtually nothing is publicly available on the predictive value of the test market as a forecasting method. Test marketing is above all else a private affair. One infers that it provides useful, if not precise, information from the fact that successful and sophisticated enterprises continue to employ the method. At the same time, some conspicuous commercial failures suggest that test marketing is far from infallible as a basis for estimating market potential. In an article on the predictive power of test marketing, the author concluded:

Despite its shortcomings, test marketing has provided a certain degree of service to marketing management. It has, without question, considerably narrowed the range of new product sales prediction error over forecasts arrived at by judgment, even experienced judgment. From a management point of view, however, for a technique as expensive as test marketing, and one that exposes the company's future hand to competitors, it would seem that we have a right to expect a much greater measure of reliability and accuracy. (Gold 1964, p. 16)

Time series analysis.   Among the most frequently employed statistical forecasting techniques is that of time series analysis, which probes the record of past sales behavior in search of patterns that may be extrapolated. Historical sales, economic, and social data constitute time series which can be analyzed by statistical techniques of various kinds. But when measured against the task, the statistical tools are rudimentary and, some statisticians believe, of dubious value. One persistent approach seeks indicating or "leading" series which signal the direction and, hopefully, the extent of movement in the "following" or "lagging" series. While experience has dampened the hope that many companies can find consistently reliable lead–lag relationships, the search has not abated and empiricism rules.

Past sales patterns are sometimes mechanically projected by methods of curve fitting and trend analysis. The results are extremely sensitive to the particular formulas chosen and are perhaps most often used in combination with the forecasters' best guesses about the state of key variables in the future and often with a substantial dash of reasoning by analogy.

Forecasting for the month or the quarter ahead is frequently characterized by relatively mechanical projections of recent sales, usually "smoothed" by one statistical device or another. The availability of computers and developments such as exponentially weighted projections of past sales, the weights declining as one incorporates earlier and earlier data, promise better short-term forecasts and improved inventory control in situations of highly complex inventory assortments and relatively strong seasonal demand.

In all forecasting it is well to have some criterion of success and, particularly, a measure of the extent to which forecasts do little but exploit the tendency for sales figures to show inertia, each period tending to be close to the experience of the immediately preceding period. This interest in a criterion underlies the so-called "naive models." The simplest of such models is the "no-change" model, that is, the forecasted sales for the period ahead will equal the sales of the current period. A somewhat more complex formulation would be that the direction and rate of change, rather than the absolute value, will persist. (These are, of course, simple methods of extrapolation.) Naive models have been used mainly as standards for evaluating alternative forecasting methods. Nonetheless, the notion underlying naive models can be expressed in various autoregressive statistical methods that have some promise of improving judgmental forecasts, even for periods as long as a year.

Regression analysis. Regression analysis, in its many forms, attracts increasing interest and use. The underlying idea is to exploit the statistical relationship evidenced in the past between the variable to be forecast and the so-called independent variables (e.g., income, population, prices) that may be related to it. There are numerous regression

analyses "explaining" the sales of various products, in the sense of showing a statistical relationship between sales and the independent variables. The prediction problem is then shifted from the dependent variables (sales) to the independent variable(s). Occasionally, of course, a lagged relationship can be shown to exist. Predicting from a regression analysis assumes stability of the past statistical relationships. As in all other statistical forecasting techniques, intuition and judgment are required to allow for changes in basic conditions that are neither reflected in historical data nor embraced by the statistical model.

The advent of the computer has made it possible to undertake more sophisticated (complex) manipulations of data than ever before. Computer programs make feasible the exponential smoothing of time series, stepwise multiple regression, the solution of systems of multiple regression equations, and simulation. But while the contributions of the computer promise wider use of complex forecasting techniques and offer improved opportunities for experimenting and testing alternative methods, the millennium is not yet.

Status and prospect. Despite the enthusiasm for sales forecasting and the exhortations that it constitutes the basis if not, indeed, the essence of business planning, the record is neither clear nor impressive. Accurate forecasting is still a wish rather than a fact. Distressingly little published information is available on the degree to which actual sales conform to forecast sales. One survey in the United States reported that there was an average deviation of 8 per cent between forecasts and actuals in 1955, but the average performance masks a wide range of deviations within and between industry groups (American Management Association 1956, p. 148).

In an English study Carter and Williams suggest some of the difficulty of making accurate sales predictions in the case of new ventures. In 57 per cent of the cases examined where expected and actual yields were at variance, the explanation was associated with "unforeseen changes of demand, or changes in the price of competing product." They properly observed:

The importance of changes in demand can be seen. Many of these were changes in the demand for an intermediate product, deriving from a change in the nature of, or the demand for, some final products of other industries. Given the long period which must often elapse between the final decision to go ahead with a new plant and the sale of its first product, it is clearly unreasonable to expect many of these complex changes in demand to be foreseen; market research is not an answer to everything. (1958, pp. 90–91)

Limited information on European experience indicates mixed results, although the record of the "Munich Business Test" on quarterly forecasts of turning points is encouraging (see Theil 1958, chapters 4, 5).

There is an extensive literature on market analysis and sales forecasting, but most of it is preoccupied with technique and much of it is hortatory. And as Lorie observed a few years ago:

Progress comes most rapidly in any pragmatic discipline when adequate testing devices are available for measuring the success of current theories and procedures. Only by such testing is it possible to discard what has not succeeded and to cling to what has succeeded, for the purposes of further elaboration and refinement. These facts are considered self-evident in the field of meteorology, where most of the practitioners make their living by forecasting. As a consequence, a very extensive literature devoted to problems of evaluation has developed during the last seventy-five years. (1957, p. 177)

Unfortunately, the evaluation of sales forecasts is not general in the literature, and it is not common in industrial practice. Much too little is known about the predictive value of alternative techniques. The most sanguine would agree that there is much to be learned and that the task of prediction is to be approached with humility. Performance offers ample opportunity for improvement. The recording of methods and specific quantified forecasts with subsequent comparison with experience is certainly to be encouraged, not only as a means of educating technicians, but also as an opportunity for evaluating them.

JOHN E. JEUCK

BIBLIOGRAPHY

AMERICAN MANAGEMENT ASSOCIATION, MARKETING DIVISION 1956 *Sales Forecasting: Uses, Techniques, and Trends.* Special Report No. 16. New York: The Association.

CARTER, CHARLES F.; and WILLIAMS, BRUCE R. 1958 *Investment in Innovation.* Oxford Univ. Press.

FERBER, ROBERT 1960 The Railroad Shippers' Forecasts and the Illinois Employers' Labor Force Anticipations: A Study in Comparative Experience. Pages 181–199 in Universities–National Bureau Committee for Economic Research, *The Quality and Economic Significance of Anticipations Data.* National Bureau of Economic Research, Special Conference Series, No. 10. Princeton Univ. Press.

GOLD, JACK A. 1964 Testing Test Market Predictions. *Journal of Marketing Research* 1, no. 3:8–16.

HUMMEL, FRANCIS E. 1961 *Market and Sales Potentials.* New York: Ronald Press.

JUSTER, FRANCIS T. 1964 *Anticipations and Purchases: An Analysis of Consumer Behavior.* Princeton Univ. Press.

LORIE, JAMES H. 1957 Two Important Problems in Sales Forecasting. *Journal of Business* 30:172–179.

McLAUGHLIN, ROBERT L. 1962 *Time Series Forecasting: A New Computer Technique for Company Sales Forecasting.* Chicago: American Marketing Association.

NATIONAL INDUSTRIAL CONFERENCE BOARD 1964 *Forecasting Sales.* Studies in Business Policy, No. 106. New York: The Board.

SPENCER, MILTON H.; CLARK, COLIN G.; and HOGUET, PETER W. 1961 *Business and Economic Forecasting: An Econometric Approach.* Homewood, Ill.: Irwin.

THEIL, HENRI (1958) 1961 *Economic Forecasts and Policy.* 2d ed., rev. Amsterdam: North-Holland Publishing.

II
CONSUMER RESEARCH

Consumer research, or marketing research, is the systematic gathering, recording, and analyzing of data and problems related to the marketing of goods and services. The "first law" of marketing has been expressed as "Make what people want to buy; don't merely try to sell what you happen to make." This dictum reflects the existence of a society in which consumers can and do exercise considerable freedom of choice in purchasing.

Present interest in the consumer can be viewed against a historical background of concern with two other factors: production and sales. Concern with production grew in importance during the industrial revolution and reached a peak in the most advanced countries in the early part of the twentieth century with the introduction of assembly lines and mass production methods. Then, as manufacturing efficiency increased and unit costs decreased, the need to dispose of the fruits of mass production gradually shifted management's attention to sales. Later, with the increase in competition for the buyer's dollar within the market, sellers found that they had to take an interest in the consumer and, thus, turned to marketing research to find out what it is that people want to buy. By telling the seller what people want to buy, the researcher helps him plan more efficiently, avoid failures (thus lowering costs to consumers), and provide consumers with a much wider choice of products.

Definition. The first and most important step in any marketing research undertaking is to define the problem. A clear statement of the problem is sometimes more than half the answer. Sometimes, too, after the problem is clearly outlined, it becomes obvious that the answer is already known or may cost too much to obtain. However, the cost of *not* having the answer must also be considered. If it is high, research may pay off. But if the price of being without the answer is minimal, marketing research may be uneconomical.

Once the problem has been defined and agreement has been reached as to what kinds of measurement will yield acceptable answers, the researcher designs his experiment. There are two basic ways of obtaining information about consumers: one is to ask them directly about their awareness, attitudes, and *opinions;* the other is to observe their actual *behavior* (other than verbal behavior). Depending upon the problem and the need for a precise answer, the opinion test (sometimes called "consumer jury") may be entirely adequate. This approach is often used because it is quick, relatively inexpensive, and often provides useful guidance for marketing decisions. Its major drawback is that consumers do not always do what they say they will, for a variety of reasons.

Motivation research.   In an attempt to obtain better answers about why consumers act as they do, marketing researchers sometimes engage in motivation research (MR). The basic assumptions of MR are that people often have unconscious motivations and that indirect questioning and various projective devices may be more effective than direct questions.

In a study by Haire, for example, women were asked to describe a hypothetical individual solely on the basis of reading a grocery list prepared by that individual. There were two such lists, differing only in one item. One list included a reference to "regular grind coffee," and the other list referred to "instant coffee." Reactions to the second list showed that a significant number of women believed that the use of instant coffee characterized its user as "lazy." Once the reason for the product's lack of acceptance had been identified, the next step was to conduct an educational campaign, pointing out to housewives that by reducing food-preparation time, they could be with their families more—a use of the saved time that the experimenter assumed was consistent with the housewives' values (Haire 1950).

Other examples of such techniques include:

(*a*) *Word association.* ("Tell me the first word that comes into your mind when I say 'margarine.'")

(*b*) *Incomplete sentences.* (The respondent is asked to complete a sentence such as "The main reason my family doesn't have soup more often is _____.")

(*c*) *Balloon cartoons.* (An example would be a comic strip drawing of two men in conversation. The balloon above one of the men might read: "John, I've been thinking about buying a station wagon." The balloon above John's head is blank, and the respondent is asked to suggest John's response.)

(*d*) *Narrative projection.* (Character descriptions are followed by questions about the kinds of attitudes or purchasing behavior that might be expected from the individuals described.)

(*e*) *Involuntary attention tests.* (The respondent is asked to look at one of two stimuli, and the one he picks up and examines first is assumed to be more interesting.)

There is little doubt that for certain kinds of problems, and particularly for certain kinds of products and services about which people are sensitive (such as personal-care items or small loans), the techniques of motivation research are appropriate and even necessary. But to claim, as some proponents did during the 1950s, that these techniques are the only way to measure attitudes properly is to go to extremes. The violent arguments of that era between the quality-oriented, small-sample MR specialists and the more traditional, quantity-oriented, big-sample researchers (dubbed "mere nose counters" by the MR group) have largely ceased. It became clear that MR, although it contributed many lasting insights and methods that eventually influenced even the most traditional researchers, was not the ultimate key to a complete understanding of human behavior.

Sampling.   In most marketing research projects, once the problem has been defined, the next step is to decide how the sample of respondents is to be selected and how large the sample should be. It is important that the sample be free from systematic bias that could influence the conclusions. For example, a pre-election political survey of voter preference in upper-income suburbs would very probably be biased in favor of one political party; hence the sample findings could be quite different from the outcome of the actual election [*see* SAMPLE SURVEYS].

In marketing research it is not always desirable to sample from the total population. For example, if we wish to study reactions to a brand of hair tonic, we would be wise to qualify respondents as tonic users before proceeding to interview them about their reactions. Going still further, we might want to talk only to heavy users. For a wide variety of frequently purchased products it has been shown that the 50 per cent of buyers who are heavy buyers account for 80 to 90 per cent of total sales volume (Twedt 1964).

Since about half the population uses hair tonic, a fourth of the total population (the top half of users) accounts for nearly 90 per cent of all hair tonic consumption. There is increasing evidence that this relationship is not limited to packaged goods; the same basic pattern of purchase concentration is shown in sales of gasoline to credit card customers, in tolls for residential long-distance telephone calls, and even in sales of fractional horsepower motors to industrial buyers.

Since consumption varies by individual and by household, it seems appropriate to let each respondent "vote with his pocketbook" by weighting his response according to the amount of the given product he consumes. Suppose, for example, that research has been conducted to determine whether a package for cake mix should have a red or a blue background for package illustration. From hypothetical data in Table 1, one sees that although the total sample gives a majority vote to the package with the red background, the correct marketing decision would be to choose the blue background, since it is clearly more appealing to the heavy users, who account for about 85 per cent of total cake mix purchased.

Table 1 — Package-background preferences of cake-mix users*

	PREFERENCE	
	Red background	Blue background
Light users	450	50
Heavy users	150	350
Total	600	400

* Based on a sample of 1,000 cake-mix users (500 heavy users and 500 light users).

Questionnaires. After the necessary decisions have been made as to the purpose of the survey and who the respondents will be, it is necessary to make up a questionnaire. Questionnaires are often designed with a few general, bland questions at the beginning in order to establish rapport between interviewer and respondent. It is essential to ask the questions in such a way that the answer to a given question does not bias succeeding questions. For this reason many researchers build questionnaires by writing each question on a separate card, moving the cards around until a smooth sequence is achieved, and then transferring the questions to a regular questionnaire format. In major surveys the questions are "pretested" on a small group of 25 to 50 respondents, whose answers are not included in the final tabulations but are analyzed to see if the questions are clear and unambiguous. Revisions are made, and the questionnaire is again pretested. It is not unusual for a survey to go through as many as a dozen revisions before the questionnaire is finally approved (Payne 1951).

Precoding and tabulation. The next step is to precode the questionnaires by assigning to, and printing next to, each question the appropriate code for machine tabulation of responses. Questionnaires can now be designed for optical scanning by machine, with the answers converted directly to either punched cards or magnetic tape; the cards or tape can be programmed to produce a page of "print-out" that is used as photographic copy for the final research report. The enormous economies in human time and the accompanying error reduction through elimination of tedious copying and hand tabulation and computing make it obvious that these developments will continue. The great potential economies of the computer in marketing research are not its only value; a beneficial side effect is that in order to use the computer to its maximum efficiency, the entire research project, including the final tabulations, must be thought through in advance, and this usually results in uncovering mistakes in planning at a time when they can be more easily corrected.

Quality control in field interviewing. Questionnaire surveys are usually made by interviewing organizations that specialize in this type of work. A list of such firms, and of others that offer a broader variety of services, including consulting, experimental design, and preparation of the final report with recommendations for action, is contained in *Bradford's Directory of Marketing Research Agencies*, which lists 350 firms in the United States and abroad (Bradford 1965–1966).

After the interviewing organization has been selected, it is customary to hold a briefing session with the project leader, the interviewing supervisors, and the interviewers in order to give detailed instructions on how the interview is to be conducted. Any questions the interviewers have should be answered at this time. Often they will be told not to proceed after the first day of interviewing until the field supervisor has had an opportunity to review the quality of work done during that day.

As the field work is progressing, or immediately after it is completed, 10 to 20 per cent of the interviews are validated in one of several ways: reinterview, a telephone call, or by mail. During these follow-up procedures, the supervisor verifies that the interview actually took place, and a few key questions may be repeated to check for report consistency. When the work of a given interviewer seems irregular, all the interviews turned in by that person are rechecked. If, as occasionally happens, it develops that the interview was not made and that the questionnaire has been faked, the interviewer is not employed again by the same organization. One of the weakest links in the entire data-gathering and data-processing chain is the failure to validate questionnaires properly [see QUALITY CONTROL, STATISTICAL].

Recommendations for action. If the objectives of a research survey have been clearly defined, the right questions asked of the right people in order to answer these objectives, and the field work properly supervised, the two remaining tasks—tabulation and analysis, and report preparation—should be fairly routine. There are, however, two major conflicting viewpoints about the extent to which the researcher should make firm recommendations for marketing action.

One group of marketing executives tends to regard the researcher primarily as a technician from whom only "the facts" are wanted, with no interpretation or conclusions about appropriate courses of action. The other viewpoint is reflected by Theodore Levitt of Harvard University, who says,

Expertness [in marketing research] encompasses much more than the elaboration and use of formal techniques in research and analysis. More than anything else it should be viewed as involving imaginative audacity in the interpretation of data and events and in formulating positive action-oriented proposals for management's consideration. . . . Too often nothing is permissible in the way of making policy or entertaining ideas unless the data are so unambiguously in favor of proposed policies or ideas that even the elevator operator can see their merit. (1962, pp. 187–190)

Observing behavior. Most of the discussion up to this point relates to the gathering of opinions through survey research. There are many other ways in which marketing research can be conducted. Observing and recording consumer behavior takes many forms. Legibility tests of an advertisement, for example, can be made by determining the amount of illumination or length of exposure required to allow reading of the sales message. It is even possible to measure behavior which the respondent is not consciously aware of, such as pupillary dilation while viewing a product or an advertising stimulus. Or suppose that we wish to determine the proportion of consumers that will read the statement of ingredients on the package label of a new food product. It is a simple matter to observe shoppers at the moment of buying and record the number of seconds they examine each package before selecting it.

Another major method of behavioral research in marketing is to conduct controlled advertising and sales tests in selected areas. Two cities may be matched, for example, on the basis of their previous sales of a given product. An advertising campaign may then be undertaken in one city, and a different campaign (or perhaps no advertising) employed in the other city. After a predetermined time period sales results are compared for the two cities. Variations of this method may include much more complex statistical procedures and may involve factorial and Latin-square experimental designs, with many cities or retail outlets included in the test. The measures may be actual sales, the proportion of consumers who are aware of a given brand name, or the proportion who can recall specific sales points about the product. [See EXPERIMENTAL DESIGN.]

Subjects for marketing research. The most common research activities of 1,660 companies are shown in Table 2.

Table 2 — Market research activities*

Activity	Companies involved (per cent)
Sales and market research:	
Development of market potentials	68
Market share analysis	67
Determination of market characteristics	67
Sales analyses	66
Establishment of sales quotas	57
Distribution and costs studies	52
Test markets, store audits	37
Consumer panel operations	27
Sales compensation studies	44
Studies of premiums, coupons, sampling, deals	29
Product research:	
New product acceptance	63
Competitive product studies	65
Product testing	57
Packaging research	45
Business economics and corporate research:	
Short-range forecasting (to 1 year)	62
Long-range forecasting (over 1 year)	59
Studies of business trends	58
Profit and/or value analysis	53
Plant and warehouse locational studies	44
Diversification studies	49
Purchase of companies, sales of divisions	44
Export and international studies	39
Linear programming	35
Operations research	29
Program evaluation review technique studies	18
Employee morale studies	32
Advertising research:	
Motivation research	30
Copy research	37
Media research	47
Evaluation of advertising effectiveness	48

* Based on activities of 1,660 companies.

Source: American Marketing Association 1963.

Advertising research. Advertising research is a special application of marketing research but employs many of the same techniques and methods. The task of advertising research usually is to find answers to one or more of the following questions: (1) What shall we say? (2) How shall we say it? (3) Where, when, and how often shall we say it? (4) How well did we communicate the intended message? These questions are investigated, respectively, in motivation research, copy research, media research, and evaluation research [see ADVERTISING, *article on* ADVERTISING RESEARCH].

Growth of marketing research departments. Of 1,660 companies surveyed more than half reported having a marketing research department (American Marketing Association 1963). Research departments are most common among companies that manufacture consumer goods (62 per cent have them), industrial companies (60 per cent), and publishers and broadcasters (57 per cent). The bigger the company, the more likely it is to have a research department. The research department is a fairly recent addition to corporate staffs; more than half of the departments in the survey had been formed since 1955. Even the companies that do not have formal marketing research departments carry on such research, either through their own personnel or through outside consulting firms. Between 1960 and 1965 marketing research budgets as a percentage of sales increased for both consumer and industrial companies.

It is clear that marketing research has matured greatly since 1955 and that it has gained increased acceptance from business management. It is also true that marketing research has not yet reached its full potential.

DIK TWEDT

[*Directly related are the entries* ADVERTISING *and* CONSUMERS. *Other relevant material may be found in* INTERVIEWING, *article on* SOCIAL RESEARCH.]

BIBLIOGRAPHY

Readers interested in more detailed consideration of the various aspects of marketing research are referred to Wales & Ferber 1956, an annotated bibliography of more than 1,600 references covering 28 major areas. For current developments in the United States and abroad, see the three leading professional journals: Journal of Marketing, Journal of Marketing Research, *and* Journal of Advertising Research.

AMERICAN MARKETING ASSOCIATION 1963 *A Survey of Marketing Research: Organization, Functions, Budget, Compensation.* Edited by Dik W. Twedt. Chicago: The Association.
BRADFORD, ERNEST S. (editor) 1965–1966 *Bradford's Directory of Marketing Research Agencies and Management Consultants in the United States and the World.* 11th ed. Middleburg, Va.: Bradford.

HAIRE, MASON 1950 Projective Techniques in Marketing Research. *Journal of Marketing* 14:649–656.
Journal of Advertising Research. → Published since 1960.
Journal of Marketing. → Published since 1936.
Journal of Marketing Research. → Published since 1964.
LEVITT, THEODORE 1962 *Innovation in Marketing: New Perspectives for Profit and Growth.* New York: McGraw-Hill.
PAYNE, STANLEY L. 1951 *The Art of Asking Questions.* Studies in Public Opinion, No. 3. Princeton Univ. Press.
TWEDT, DIK W. 1964 How Important to Marketing Strategy Is the "Heavy User"? *Journal of Marketing* 28, no. 1:71–72.
WALES, HUGH G.; and FERBER, ROBERT (1956) 1963 *A Basic Bibliography on Marketing Research.* Chicago: American Marketing Association.

MARKETS AND INDUSTRIES

The market is the stage on which economic actors—firms, households, and unions—meet and make key economic decisions for society. Out of the process of market exchange come the prices, wages, and profits that serve to determine the allocation of the economy's resources and the distribution of the national income.

The market is thus a central concept in economics. It is, however, an elusive concept. It may mean merely the geographical place where exchange takes place—a nodal point where buyers and sellers meet to exchange goods and services. But the concept of the market as economists use it also embraces the whole set of circumstances that surround the process of exchange, and indeed it concerns as well the outcomes of the process of exchange. Thus we speak of market structure and market behavior and market price. Firms and households may take conditions in the market as external to them, and such conditions affect their behavior. But this behavior in turn affects market results and, indeed, may determine what is the market.

The market in the most general sense is the entire web of interrelationships between buyers, sellers, and products that is involved in exchange. The appropriate definition of the market depends upon which aspects of this web are of interest at the time; for different problems there are different appropriate definitions.

Historically and in much of common usage "the market" means a place where buyers and sellers meet to buy and sell goods. But while this usage serves well enough to identify the Fulton Fish Market, it provides little insight into what is meant by the used-car market, the stock market, the labor market, the mortgage market, or the black market in Japanese yen. Within the market, however defined, buyers and sellers negotiate the exchange of goods or services. A market definition may focus upon what the products are, as the market for cement, aluminum cable, or wheat. In this usage it is common to speak of the market as an industry. Alternatively, however, it may focus upon who the buyers are, as, for example, the market for loans to Chicago borrowers. It may focus upon who the sellers are, as the market for engineers or the market in which the integrated oil companies operate. Market definition may focus upon the rules by which the market is run, as in an auction market, or upon when goods are to be exchanged, as in the distinction between a present and a futures market. Finally, geographical definition may concern where buyers or sellers reside or do business as well as where they meet to exchange. In this sense the New York Stock Exchange is often regarded as an international securities market.

None of these bases for definition is without interest some of the time. In general, differences in focus will lead to differences in designation of which transactions belong in a market. The market is a concept with many dimensions.

The market in economic theory

Economists use the word "market" in two substantially different senses. While they have etymological precedent for this—the Latin root *mercatus* means either the place of or the method of contact between buyers and sellers—the result is often confusion.

The first sense in which economists use the word concerns the general conditions under which buyers and sellers exchange goods and services. The conditions may be summarized in a series of alternative theoretical market structures, such as "perfect competition," "monopoly," "oligopoly," and "monopolistic competition." [*See* COMPETITION; MONOPOLY; OLIGOPOLY.] These theoretical structures, or models, make assumptions about such things as the number of sellers and buyers and their perceptions of each other and yield predictions about market behavior. In turn this predicted behavior leads to predictions about market results: what will be the prices, quantities, and qualities of outputs that emerge from the market. Market structure is not one-dimensional, but it is often convenient to think of different market structures as differing from one another in terms of the kind and degree of competition that they lead to.

The second sense in which the word is used is to delineate the boundaries (usually geographic) that identify specific groups of buyers, sellers, and commodities. This concept of the market is designated *extent of the market*. In this sense we define the fluid-milk market for the New York City area or the upper Midwest cement market by an appropriate map.

Up to a point these two usages are both separate and separable. One does not need geographic boundaries to derive predictions about how, for example, a perfectly competitive market works in equating demand and supply, nor does one need theoretical models of market structure to describe or delimit the Fulton Fish Market. The need to confront these separate aspects of a market arises whenever economists wish to use economic theories of market structure to make predictions about the behavior or performance of real-world markets; it arises as well if they wish to use observed data about real-world markets to test the predictions of their theories; it arises, further, if one wishes to use economic conclusions about market behavior and performance in establishing or enforcing public policies that relate to the behavior of actual industries or firms. Since these are among the important uses of economics, it arises often.

The number of participants in the market is held to be a key factor in market structure, and thus in market behavior and in market results. The number of participants in a market will, however, vary as we change the boundaries of the market. Market structure and market extent are thus interrelated in applications. The great hazard in analyses of economic markets is the circular, or prediction-determining, definition.

Defining market extent by its structure.   Most well-defined theories of market structure contain implicit rules for delineating which transactions belong in the market. Using such implicit rules is superficially an appealing way to solve a difficult problem. Except in rare cases it proves quite unsatisfactory. Consider market definitions under perfect competition and under monopoly.

Under perfect competition.   A central prediction of the theory of perfect competition is that the price of all transactions will tend to uniformity, allowing for differences in transportation costs. Empirically, the boundaries of a *perfectly competitive market* may be established by searching for the area over which transactions occur at common prices. This definition of a market has an honored past and a wide range of contemporary acceptance. It is the definition used by Cournot (1838, chapter 4), popularized by Alfred Marshall (1890, p. 327 in 1920 edition), and repeated in leading contemporary texts (Stigler 1942, p. 92 in 1947 edition).

One drawback of this definition is that actual price behavior in such a market cannot be used to test the prediction of uniformity of prices. A more serious difficulty concerns the interpretation of transactions that occur at other than the adjusted common price. Do they represent transactions in a different market or do they provide evidence that this market is in fact not a perfectly competitive one? The implications of these two possibilities are totally different. In U.S. law, for example, the merger of two firms is legal if they are in quite separate markets but may be illegal if they are in the same, imperfectly competitive market. Using uniform price behavior to define market extent would be satisfactory if such behavior were a common implication of all theories of market structure; this, however, is not the case.

Under monopoly. The theoretical model of monopoly comprehends a situation in which there is but a single seller of the commodity (or a group of sellers who act as if they were under a single coordinated management). The implicit market for a monopolized product consists of all transactions in the commodity in which the monopolist is the seller. It is *not* a prediction of the theory that the price need be uniform among all customers, since the monopolist can discriminate among buyers. It is a prediction of the theory of discriminating monopoly that prices will be uniform only among subgroups of customers who can resell the commodity or among whom demand elasticities are approximately equal. Were we to apply the implicit competitive definition of a market in a situation that is, in fact, that of a discriminating monopolist, the group of transactions which occur at a common price would represent only a small part of the total relevant market.

The major deficiency of defining a market on the basis of theories of market structure is that different market structures contain different implicit rules for definition of the market. Indeed, their reason for being is that they make different predictions about market results. To define the market according to the price behavior exhibited destroys any possibility of using the market so defined to say anything about price behavior, and it prejudges the question of which market structure is the relevant one for making predictions. An empirically useful market definition must be independent of the alternative theoretical models of market structure, if we wish to test or to apply those theories.

Defining market extent by demand and supply alternatives. Any particular buyer or seller has a definable set of alternative sources of supply or demand which he considers available to him. From his point of view the relevant market is the set of these alternatives. This kind of individualized definition of a market would be of little general use if there were not important clusters of buyers and sellers for whom the relevant market was approximately the same; suppose there are such groups and that it is thus feasible to define markets that apply to significant numbers of transactions.

As a logical matter, market extent defined in this way may also be circular. The perceptions of, for example, a buyer as to which are the real alternative sources of supply depend upon the prices that prevail. A housewife who says she will never go across town to shop for food means it only within limits. A big enough "sale" will change her view. Thus if prices are, in fact, uniform as among sellers, the radius of the market extent around a customer will be much smaller than the market to which he might turn if prices were not uniform. Some Californians buy cars in Detroit if prices on the west coast get too far out of line.

Empirical approximations to definition

While as a logical matter there is no satisfactory definition of a market that identifies the relevant transactions independent of the market results, reasonable markets do exist in many commodities. While everything in principle depends upon everything else, in many cases the interactions and feedbacks are small enough to be negligible. Bicycles and sports cars are not in the same market, although there conceivably exists a set of prices that would lead to large-scale substitution of one for the other. As a practical matter cement is so rarely sold outside of a radius of 200 miles from the factory that a regional cement market may be defined.

The basic empirical problem of market definition is to define the range of alternatives to which a buyer or seller may *practicably* turn and to identify the sets of transactions whose outcomes are sufficiently interrelated that to subdivide them further invites error. One definition of an industry is as "a gap in the chain of substitutes"; a parallel definition of a market is as "a gap in the chain of alternatives." As a logical matter it has been argued that industries do not exist (Triffin 1940) and that all firms must be viewed either alone or as part of a generally interdependent network. Most economists reject this nihilistic view and believe the industry is a useful aggregate concept. Similarly, the market is a useful aggregation of sets of related transactions.

Suppose we seek an empirical approximation of the set of real, practicable alternatives. We must ask: "Real alternatives to whom?" One may focus upon the products or the sellers that are real alternatives to a particular group of buyers, one may instead ask what are the alternative sources of demand to a group of sellers, or one may ask what are the products that are effective substitutes for a particular product. There are, indeed, many aspects of each of these different ways of looking at the set of alternatives. Consider the producer of a given product: he may at one time be concerned with the group of other sellers of this product; at another time he may be concerned with other products that are technologically similar so that they represent real alternatives to him in production; at still another time he may be concerned with different products that his customers may regard as substitutes for his product. Of the hundreds of possible ways of defining sets of alternatives, two are of major interest to students of economic markets and how they work.

The first is *the real alternative sources of supply available to a defined group of buyers*. We may ask, for example, what are the sources of supply of credit available to the small businessman; we may be concerned with the sources of supply of safety glass to automobile manufacturers; or we may be concerned with the sources of supply of automobiles in the $1,500–$2,500 price range to buyers living in Peoria. Much of the public concern with competition is concerned with preserving a sufficient number of independent sources of supply so that every group of customers has genuine alternative sources of supply. The legislative concern evidenced in the major antitrust laws is centrally concerned with preserving effective competition in markets defined in this way.

The second is *the group of relevant rivals to a particular seller*. This concept of the market is crucial to understanding the market behavior of sellers. The number of rivals that a seller has and the nature of the interactions between them are hypothesized to be major determinants of the price and product patterns that emerge in an industry. Indeed, the very concept of an industry rests upon the identification of a group of sellers in substantial rivalry (actual or potential) with one another. Economists largely concerned with industrial structure and behavior regard this focus as central to the definition of the market.

Implicit in each of these definitions is the notion that a distinct "product" or group of products exists. The classification of products into meaningful "industries" is a major concern of the U.S. Bureau of the Census and other statistical agencies. The recognition that for different purposes

different clusters of products are relevant has led to the development in the United States of a Standard Industrial Classification (SIC) at several levels of aggregation. There are seventy-eight "2-digit" industries, hundreds of "3-digit" industries, and several thousand "4-digit" industries. By appropriate recombinations of the 4-digit industries a very much larger number of industries may be defined. The focus of the SIC is on the supply side rather than the demand side, and SIC industries are more nearly appropriate to the identification of interrelated sellers than of alternatives to buyers.

Markets defined in these ways overlap but do not coincide. Every transaction involves a buyer, a seller, and a well-defined product. It may, however, be a transaction in several different markets. Consider, for example, the purchase of a new compact Chevrolet by an individual living in St. Louis. From the buyer's point of view the relevant alternative products may have been any of four or five models of new cars or any of a number of used cars in the same price range. (The list of alternatives will certainly not include a truck or a tractor and almost certainly will not include a new Cadillac.) The relevant sellers will be the new- and used-automobile dealers in a definable geographic region centered largely on St. Louis, as well as private sellers with whom the buyer may make contact.

To the General Motors Company the transaction appears in a very different light. Its rivalry with Ford and Chrysler and American Motors for the new-car dollar is nation-wide and includes Buicks and Cadillacs as well as Chevrolets. At the same time, the compact-car market—in which the various American manufacturers are in open competition with certain foreign manufacturers, particularly Volkswagen—involves a different set of rivalries.

From the product point of view, the transaction occurred in SIC industry 37, Transportation Equipment; in industry 371, Motor Vehicles and Motor Vehicle Equipment; and in industry 3717, Motor Vehicles and Parts. Even the smallest of these is a substantially comprehensive classification including the manufacturing or assembling of (among other things) passenger automobiles, trucks, ambulances, and fire engines and also including the parts that make up such motor vehicles, such as axles, radiators, drive shafts, exhaust systems, universal joints, and automobile bumpers. For many purposes SIC 3717 is much too broad; an automobile muffler and an automobile bumper are not in any sense substitute products. The statistical problem of industry definition is made complex by the fact that some firms make a large variety of such component products and others specialize. For other purposes the definition of industries in the SIC is too narrow. Multiproduct firms may operate in many industries, and their wage policies and their labor market negotiations may extend across industry lines. All production workers of American Motors, whether they are making cars or refrigerators, are covered by contract negotiations with the United Automobile Workers.

The market to buyers. Major impetus to empirical definition of markets in the United States has been a by-product of the Anti-merger Act of 1950 (the so-called Celler–Kefauver Act). It made very general a prohibition on mergers "where in any line of commerce in any section of the country, the effect of such acquisition may be substantially to lessen competition, or to tend to create a monopoly."

A first step in every one of the cases involving this statute is the definition of the relevant market. Pathbreaking opinions in a series of antitrust decisions have sharpened the notion of what is a relevant market, as well as defining the legal issues involved. It is clear that one can always define a sufficiently localized geographical area in such a way that there is but one seller of a particular product; conversely, one can usually define an area so broadly as to make the effect on competition appear trivial. Every merger leads to the disappearance of one seller. But one out of how many? For example, the 1961 merger of the Continental Illinois National Bank and the City National Bank reduced the number of banks in the 200 S. block of LaSalle Street, Chicago, from 2 to 1, the number of business district banks from 16 to 15, and the number of banks in the Chicago Metropolitan Area from 219 to 218. For the whole United States there were about 14,000 commercial banks. After the merger there was one less.

Recent court opinions have established guidelines:

. . . the boundaries of the relevant market must be drawn with sufficient breadth to include competing products . . . to recognize competition where, in fact, competition exists. (*Brown Shoe Co.* v. *U.S.*, 370 U.S. 294, 326, 1962)

The relevant market is the area to which customers *can* practicably turn for supplies. (Paraphrase of *U.S.* v. *Philadelphia National Bank*, 374 U.S. 321, 1963)

The proper question, . . . is not where is the customer located, but what is the geographic area of effective competition for his patronage. (*U.S.* v. *Manufacturers Hanover Trust Co.*, CCH Trade Cases 71,708, pp. 80,744, 1965)

A relevant geographic market cannot be defined, however, solely on the basis of where . . . banks have actually done business, or even where customers have actually turned for their banking needs. The market must be drawn also on the basis of potential competition. . . . Where could customers practically turn for alternative sources of supply? (*ibid.*, pp. 80,746)

These are sensible guidelines; implementing them is hard. The problem is in relating observation to guideline. A customer buys from a particular seller for any or all of a number of reasons: it may be habitual, it may be convenient, it may be a matter of some indifference, or, importantly, it may be necessary. Defining the relevant choices of the buyer is in fact defining the group of sellers from one of whom it is necessary that they buy. Put differently, if we can define sellers from whom it is impracticable to buy, we have defined sellers outside of the relevant market. If one is to base empirical delineation of the extent of a market upon observations of which sellers are in fact utilized by buyers, the key problem is to differentiate the factor of necessity from that of convenience.

A housewife in a moderate-sized city will in general have a dozen or more supermarkets at which she may conveniently shop, and another dozen at which she might shop if there were any real reason to do so. In fact she will usually tend to shop at two or three, because, other things being equal, she has certain preferences. Indeed she may only shop at one. But this one is an explicit or an implicit choice from the larger set of practicable choices. It is the larger group that constitutes her real opportunities and that defines the market.

The determinants of a customer's choice of a supplier may in general be several. Some of these are (1) portability of the product, (2) cost of transportation of the product, (3) information about the availability and conditions of supply of the product, (4) acceptability of the customer to the seller, (5) price of the product, (6) convenience, and (7) chance and habit. These factors may be related to one another: for example, while there are limits to the geographic range over which fresh milk and live lobsters can be transported without spoiling, these limits may be extended by increasing costs of delivery. Refrigerated trucks and railroad cars extend the markets for fresh produce, some Maine lobsters are shipped to the Midwest by air (but none are shipped to San Francisco), and so on. Similarly, information can be gathered, but at some cost and some inconvenience. What is of concern in defining markets is the distinction between the first four listed factors (singly or in interaction), which represent real limits on practicable alternatives, and the last three, which represent instead the bases of choices among real alternative sources of supply.

As a practical matter geographic market definition becomes relatively easy when one of the first four considerations exercises a dominant limitation on sources of supply. Consider a few examples. For commodities such as cement, for which transportation cost per unit is a high fraction of unit value, the geographic limits on choice of suppliers is very clear. It is easy to define the relevant cement market for a given customer. The relevant housing market for an individual is delimited by distance from his work, by his income, and in some cases, additionally, by his race. The market for a business loan for a small business is effectively limited to those financial institutions that will accept local credit evaluations. Such a small borrower is typically limited to his home city or a portion thereof. Purchase of a used car tends to be limited more by available information than by anything else. On the other hand, well-organized markets in securities make the supplier from whom one buys 100 shares of General Motors stock a matter of substantial indifference. The borrowing of $1 million for working capital by a national corporation is not practically limited to any small geographic region.

Observing from whom each of the individual members of a large group purchases will tend to define the relevant geographic market if transportation cost, portability of product, information, or acceptability provides a binding constraint on available alternatives. Chance, convenience, and habit will average out over a large group, and over time variations in price will average out as well. The fact that over 90 per cent of all loans to businesses with assets of less than $50,000 are made by banks in the same city, county, or metropolitan area strongly suggests that the relevant geographic market is limited. Of customers with assets of over $100 million, only one-third borrow from local banks. (As this example suggests, one can perhaps *infer* geographic limitation by observed behavior. This is a complex matter of statistical estimation, discussion of which is inappropriate to this article.) Where no binding limitations of these kinds can be identified, geographical delineation of market extent is virtually impossible.

The market to the seller. Identifying the relevant rivals to a particular seller is typically a very much easier matter than identifying markets for customer groups, particularly for manufacturers of major commodities. But not always. Some forty firms in the United States manufacture electrical equipment, but only six of them manufacture tur-

bine generators, only four manufacture meters, about a dozen manufacture industrial control equipment. And General Electric and Westinghouse are clearly in rivalry with General Motors in the manufacture and sale of refrigerators, though they are no part of the automotive industry.

In practice the relevant group of rivals has to be defined in the context of a particular problem. With respect to price determination, of primary concern in many cases, sellers who regard each other's commodities as close substitutes and employ consciously parallel price policies clearly are in the same market. Products whose prices move closely together over a sufficient period of time to permit other influences to vary are usually regarded as in the same market, and the suppliers of them are considered to form an industry. Again, difficulties in precise definition exist but need not prevent reasonable estimation of related groups of suppliers who sell in the same market.

The many markets for a commodity. Consider the market(s) for business loans. A Federal Reserve Board survey in 1955 revealed over 1.2 million outstanding loans by some 7,000 U.S. member banks, amounting in aggregate to over $30,000 million. Most of these loans were very small: over 1 million were for less than $25,000, and they accounted for only one-sixth of the dollar total. On the other hand, 42,000 of these loans were for over $100,000, and they accounted for two-thirds of the total dollars of outstanding loans. There is no doubt that there is a national market for very large loans. There is also little doubt that small loans are largely limited to local markets. There are thus hundreds of local markets and a national market as well. (There may be regional markets in addition.) Let us consider the definition of one such local market, that for the Chicago Metropolitan Area (CMA).

In a total of 20,500 loans representing about

Table 1 — Loans involving CMA bank or borrower (millions of dollars)*

Location of bank \ Location of borrower	In CMA	Not in CMA	All
In CMA	1,125 (16.5)	1,224 (2.5)	2,349 (19.0)
Not in CMA	756 (1.5)		
All	1,881 (18.0)		

* Number of loans in thousands in parentheses.

Source: Special unpublished tabulation from Federal Reserve Board 1955 loan survey.

Table 2 — Loans under $100,000 involving CMA bank or borrower (millions of dollars)*

Location of bank \ Location of borrower	In CMA	Not in CMA	All
In CMA	215 (14.8)	36 (2.3)	251 (17.1)
Not in CMA	20 (0.8)		
All	235 (15.6)		

* Number of loans in thousands in parentheses.

Source: Special unpublished tabulation from Federal Reserve Board 1955 loan survey.

$3,105 million in value, either borrower or bank was located in the CMA. What fraction of this business was in the CMA "local loan" market? Table 1 shows this total business classified by location of bank and borrower. For only $1,125 million were both bank and borrower in the CMA. Chicago-located borrowers borrowed $756 million from other banks, and Chicago banks loaned $1,224 million to other borrowers. Some of the loans for which both bank and borrower were located in the CMA were very large loans, in which dealing with a local bank was a matter of convenience rather than necessity. Table 2 presents all loans with an outstanding balance of less than $100,000. Of these about 15,000 loans, representing $215 million, were between CMA banks and CMA borrowers. Judge MacMahon (in the Manufacturers Hanover case) suggested that only business loans under $100,000 should be considered limited to the local market. If he is correct, then the transactions in the CMA local market of $215 million are but a small fraction of the total transactions involving Chicago banks or Chicago customers.

Definition of a local market for loans no doubt requires more sophisticated measures than merely the address and size of loan used here. One would wish to pay attention to the size of the borrower, the nature of his business, his other sources of funds, and so on. Further, one would wish to consider nonbank suppliers of funds as well. But the illustration is suggestive.

Does it really matter how one defines a market? In some cases it matters very much. For example, in the CMA bank illustration the share of the market of the four largest suppliers (called the 4-firm concentration ratio) varies enormously as the definition of the market is changed. For 1955, the four largest Chicago banks made 84 per cent of the dollar volume of business loans of banks in the

CMA, 42 per cent of the dollar volume of loans to CMA located borrowers, but only 25 per cent of the dollar volume of loans of under $100,000 to CMA borrowers. These are major differences in terms of the relevant theoretical model to apply: 84 per cent is in the range where monopolistic models are often invoked; 25 per cent is near the competitive level. These differences are also important in terms of the legal status under antitrust laws. To take a different example, failure to recognize the geographical limits to the economical shipment of cement would lead to the conclusion that the U.S. cement industry has dozens of small sellers. In fact regional cement markets are highly concentrated and in some cases have but a single supplier.

The concept of a market is multidimensional and it is complex, but reasonably accurate delineation of markets is required if economic theory is to be brought into contact with economic observation. No single definition serves the many uses to which the concept is put; the relevant definition must be suited to the particular application required. Logical difficulties exist in attempting to define market extent independent of market behavior and market performance. Notwithstanding these difficulties, there is scope for approximations to the extent of relevant markets. These require both care in formulation and sophistication in empirical estimation. No greater barrier exists to the fruitful application of economic theory than the failure to forge the links to observable data. The operational definition of economic markets is such a link.

PETER O. STEINER

[See also ANTITRUST LEGISLATION.]

BIBLIOGRAPHY

COURNOT, ANTOINE AUGUSTIN (1838) 1960 Researches Into the Mathematical Principles of the Theory of Wealth. New York: Kelley. → First published in French.
MARSHALL, ALFRED (1890) 1936 Principles of Economics. 8th ed. New York and London: Macmillan. → A two-volume variorum edition was published in 1961.
STIGLER, GEORGE J. (1942) 1960 The Theory of Price. Rev. ed. New York: Macmillan.
TRIFFIN, ROBERT 1940 Monopolistic Competition and General Equilibrium Theory. Harvard Economic Studies, Vol. 67. Cambridge, Mass.: Harvard Univ. Press.

MARKOV CHAINS

A Markov chain is a chance process having the special property that one can predict its future just as accurately from a knowledge of the present state of affairs as from a knowledge of the present together with the entire past history.

The theory of social mobility illustrates the idea. Considering only eldest sons, note the status of successive generations of a particular male line in a society divided into three classes: upper, middle, and lower. If we assume the movement of a family among the three social classes is a chance process —governed by probabilistic laws rather than deterministic ones—several possibilities present themselves. An independent process represents a perfectly mobile society: the probability that a man is in a particular class depends in no way on the class of his father. At the other extreme is a society in which the probability that a man is in a particular class depends on the class of his father, that of his grandfather, that of his great-grandfather, etc.

A Markov chain is a process of intermediate complexity: the probability that a man is in a given class may depend on the class of his father, but it does not further depend on the classes of his earlier antecedents. For instance, while upper-class and middle-class fathers may have different probabilities of producing sons of a given class, an upper-class father whose own father was also upper class must have the same probability of producing a son of a given class as does an upper-class father whose father was, say, lower class. (This example will be used to illustrate each concept introduced below.)

No chance process encountered in applications is truly independent—in particular, no society is perfectly mobile. While in the same way no natural process exactly satisfies the Markov chain condition, many of them come close enough to make a Markov chain model useful.

Formal definitions.   For an exact formulation of the Markov chain concept, introduced in 1907 by the Russian mathematician A. A. Markov, imagine a system (family, society, person, organism) that passes with each unit of time (minute, hour, generation) from one to another of the s states $E_1, E_2, \cdots, E_s$. (Upper class, E_1, middle class, E_2, and lower class, E_3, are the states in the social mobility example.) Assume that a chance process governs the evolution of the system; the chance process is the collection of probability laws describing the way in which the system changes with time. The system is that which undergoes change; a particular analysis may involve many systems of the same kind (many families, or many societies, etc.), all obeying the same process or set of probability laws.

Since the system passes through various states in sequence, time moves in jumps, rather than continuously; hence the integers $1, 2, 3, \cdots$ provide a natural time index. Denote by $P(E_k|E_i, E_j)$ the conditional probability that at time $n + 2$ the system is in state E_k, given that at times n and $n + 1$ it was in states E_i and E_j in that order; and similarly for longer or shorter conditioning sequences of states. We make the usual assumption that the conditional probabilities just defined do not depend on n (that is, the conditional probabilities do not change as time passes). The process is a Markov chain if $P(E_k|E_i, E_j) = P(E_k|E_j)$, $P(E_l|E_i, E_j, E_k) = P(E_l|E_k)$, $P(E_m|E_i, E_j, E_k, E_l) = P(E_m|E_l)$, etc.

The *transition probabilities* $p_{ij} = P(E_j|E_i)$ determine the fundamental properties of the Markov chain; they form an s by s *transition matrix* $\boldsymbol{P} = (p_{ij})$, the basic datum of the process. (A matrix such as $\boldsymbol{P}$ that has only nonnegative entries and has rows summing to 1 is called a stochastic matrix.)

An independent process can be considered a special sort of Markov chain for which $p_{ij} = p_j$ (that is, the p_{ij} do not depend on i): the rows of $\boldsymbol{P}$ are all the same in this case. The *second-order transition probabilities* provide a second example of information contained in $\boldsymbol{P}$. If the system is presently in state E_i, then the conditional probability that it will pass to E_j and then to E_k in the next two steps is $P(E_j|E_i)P(E_k|E_i, E_j) = p_{ij}\,p_{jk}$; hence the conditional probability that the system will occupy E_k two time units later is

$$p_{ik}^{(2)} = \sum_{j=1}^{s} p_{ij}\,p_{jk}.$$

(Summing over the index j accounts for all the possible intermediate states.) But this second-order transition probability $p_{ik}^{(2)}$ is just the (i,k)th entry in $\boldsymbol{P}^2$ (the matrix $\boldsymbol{P}$ times itself in the sense of matrix multiplication).

Table 1

	E_1	E_2	E_3
E_1 (upper class)	.448	.484	.068
E_2 (middle class)	.054	.699	.247
E_3 (lower class)	.011	.503	.486

Social mobility in England and Wales is approximately described by a Markov chain with transition matrix shown in Table 1. (These numbers must, of course, be arrived at empirically. The problem of estimation of transition probabilities is discussed later.) For example, a middle-class man has chance .054 of producing a son (recall that only eldest sons are considered here) who enters the upper class. Now the chance that a man in the upper class has a middle-class grandson is $p_{12}^{(2)} = (.448 \times .484) + (.484 \times .699) + (.068 \times .503) = .589$, while the chance that a man in the middle class has a middle-class grandson is $p_{22}^{(2)} = .639$.

Notice that these last two probabilities are different, which raises a point often misunderstood. The Markov chain definition prescribes that an upper-class man with upper-class antecedents must have the same chance of producing a middle-class son as an upper-class man with lower-class antecedents has. But influence—stochastic influence, so to speak—of a man on his grandson, which does exist if $p_{12}^{(2)} \neq p_{22}^{(2)}$, is entirely consistent with the definition, which requires only that the grandfather exert this influence exclusively through the intermediate generation (the father).

To describe natural phenomena by Markov chains requires idealization; the social mobility example carried through here makes this obvious. Since Markov chains allow for dependence, however, they can with satisfactory accuracy account for the evolution of diverse social, psychological, biological, and physical systems for which an independent chance process would make too crude a model. On the other hand, Markov chains have simple enough structure to be mathematically tractable.

As another example of an approximate Markov chain, consider sociological panel studies. A potential voter is asked his party preference each month for six months preceding an election; his answer places him in state E_1 (Republican), E_2 (Democrat), or E_3 (undecided). The voter's progress among these states (approximately) obeys the Markov rule if, in predicting his August preference on the basis of his previous ones, one can without (essential) loss disregard them all except the most recent one, namely that for July (and similarly for the other predictions). In learning theory, Markov models have proved fruitful for describing organisms that change state from trial to trial in response to reinforcement in a learning process. (See Bibliography for applications in such areas as industrial inspection, industrial mobility, sickness and accident statistics, and economics.)

Mathematical analysis. The transition matrix $\boldsymbol{P}$ determines many of the characteristics of a Markov chain. We have seen that the (i,j)th entry $p_{ij}^{(2)}$ of $\boldsymbol{P}^2$ is the conditional probability, given that the system is in E_i, that it will be in E_j two steps later. In the same way, the nth *order transition probability* $p_{ij}^{(n)}$, the conditional probability that the system will occupy E_j after n steps if it is now in E_i, is the (i,j)th entry in $\boldsymbol{P}^n$. But $\boldsymbol{P}$ alone does not determine the absolute probability $a_i^{(n)}$ that at time n the system is in state E_i. For this we need $\boldsymbol{P}$ and the *initial probabilities* $a_i^{(1)}$.

The probability that the system occupies states E_i and E_j respectively at times n and $n+1$ is

$a_i^{(n)} p_{ij}$; adding over the states possible at time n, we conclude that $\sum_i a_i^{(n)} p_{ij} = a_j^{(n+1)}$, or, if $\boldsymbol{a}^{(n)}$ denotes the row vector $(a_1^{(n)}, \cdots, a_s^{(n)})$, $\boldsymbol{a}^{(n)} \boldsymbol{P} = \boldsymbol{a}^{(n+1)}$. More generally, the mth order transition probabilities link the absolute probabilities for time $n + m$ to those for time n: $\sum_i a_i^{(n)} p_{ij}^{(m)} = a_j^{(n+m)}$ or $\boldsymbol{a}^{(n)} \boldsymbol{P}^m = \boldsymbol{a}^{(n+m)}$. Thus the absolute probabilities $a_i^{(n)}$ are completely determined, via the relation $\boldsymbol{a}^{(n)} = \boldsymbol{a}^{(1)} \boldsymbol{P}^{n-1}$, by the transition probabilities p_{ij} and the initial probabilities $a_i^{(1)}$. In other words, $\boldsymbol{P}$ and $\boldsymbol{a}^{(1)}$ completely specify the probability laws of the Markov chain.

Chains with all $p_{ij} > 0$. The most important mathematical results about Markov chains concern the stability of the $a_i^{(n)}$ and the behavior of $p_{ij}^{(n)}$ for large n. Although some of the p_{ij} may be zero, suppose they are all strictly greater than zero. (Later this restriction will be lifted and other chains considered.) One expects that for large n, $p_{ij}^{(n)}$ should not depend much on i—the effect of the initial state should wear off. This is indeed true: there exist positive numbers $p_1, \cdots, p_s$ such that $p_{ij}^{(n)}$ is close to p_j for large n ($\lim_{n \to \infty} p_{ij}^{(n)} = p_j$ for all i and j). It follows that $a_i^{(n)} = \sum_k a_k^{(1)} p_{ki}^{(n-1)}$ approaches $\sum_k a_k^{(1)} p_i = p_i$ as n becomes large, so that the absolute probabilities $a_i^{(n)}$ stabilize near the p_i, no matter what the initial probabilities $a_i^{(1)}$ are.

The numbers p_i have several important mathematical properties, which in turn have probability interpretations. Clearly they sum to one: $\sum_i p_i = 1$. Moreover, if n is large, $\sum_i p_{ki}^{(n)} p_{ij}$ is near $\sum_i p_i p_{ij}$, while $p_{kj}^{(n+1)}$ is near p_j. Since $\sum_i p_{ki}^{(n)} p_{ij} = p_{kj}^{(n+1)}$, we have $\sum_i p_i p_{ij} = p_j$, or, with $\boldsymbol{p} = (p_1, \cdots, p_s)$, $\boldsymbol{p} \boldsymbol{P} = \boldsymbol{p}$. Therefore the p_j solve the system

$$(1) \quad \begin{aligned} \sum_{i=1}^{s} p_i p_{ij} &= p_j, \qquad j = 1, 2, \cdots, s, \\ \sum_{i=1}^{s} p_i &= 1 \end{aligned}$$

of $s + 1$ equations in s unknowns. Since it turns out that this system has but one solution, the limits p_j can be found by solving it, and this is the method used in practice. The vector $\boldsymbol{p}$ for the social mobility example is $(.067, .624, .309)$. Whatever a man's class, there is probability near .309 that a descendant a great many generations later is in the lower class.

The quantities p_j connect up with the absolute probabilities $a_j^{(n)}$. If $\boldsymbol{a}^{(n)} = \boldsymbol{p}$, then $\boldsymbol{a}^{(n+1)} = \boldsymbol{a}^{(n)} \boldsymbol{P} = \boldsymbol{p} \boldsymbol{P} = \boldsymbol{p}$, and similarly $\boldsymbol{a}^{(m)} = \boldsymbol{p}$ for all m beyond n. In other words, if the system has at a given time probability exactly p_j of being in state E_j (for each j) then the same holds ever after. For this reason, the p_j are called a set of *stationary probabilities*;

since the solution to (1) is unique, they form the only such set.

Thus a system evolving according to the laws of the Markov chain has long-range probability approximately p_j of being in E_j; and if the probability of being in E_j at a particular time is exactly p_j, this relationship is preserved in the future. The law of large numbers gives a complementary way of interpreting these facts. Imagine a large number of systems evolving independently of one another, each according to the laws of a common Markov chain. No matter what the initial states of the many systems may be, after a long time the numbers of systems in the various states will become approximately proportional to the p_j. And once this state of affairs is achieved, it will persist, except for fluctuations that are proportionately small if the number of systems involved is large. In the social mobility example, the proportions in the three classes of a large number of family lines will eventually be nearly 067:624:309.

A system setting out from state E_i is certain to return again to E_i after one or more steps; the expected value of the number of steps until first return turns out to be $1/p_i$, a result that agrees qualitatively with intuition: the lower the probability of a state the longer the average time between successive passages through it. There exist also formulas for the expected number of steps to reach E_j for a system starting in E_i. In the example from mobility theory, the mean time to pass from the lower class to the upper class is 26.5 generations, while the mean for the return trip is but 5.6 generations (which should be a lesson to us all).

Other Markov chains. In the analysis sketched above, it was assumed that the p_{ij} were all strictly greater than zero. More generally, the same results hold even if some of the p_{ij} equal zero, provided the Markov chain has the property that the states all communicate (for each i and j there is an n for which $p_{ij}^{(n)} > 0$) and provided also that there is no periodicity (no integer m exceeding 1 exists such that a passage from E_i back to E_i is possible in n steps only if n is divisible by m). Such a chain is called ergodic. The results can also be reformulated to cover nonergodic chains.

The theory extends in still other useful ways. (a) A chance process is a Markov chain of second order if the probability distribution of future states depends only on the two most recently visited states: $P(E_l|E_i, E_j, E_k) = P(E_l|E_j, E_k)$, $P(E_m|E_i, E_j, E_k, E_l) = P(E_m|E_k, E_l)$, etc. These processes contain ordinary Markov chains as a special case and make possible a more precise description of some phenomena. The properties derived above carry over to chains of second (and higher) order. (b) If, for instance, the system is a population and the state is its size, there are then infinitely many possible states. The theory generalizes to cover such examples, but the mathematics becomes more difficult; for example (1) becomes a system of infinitely many equations in infinitely many unknowns. (c) Continuous time, rather than time that goes in jumps, is appropriate for the description of some systems—for example, populations that change state (size) because of births and deaths that can occur at any instant of time. Such processes in principle admit an approximate description within the discrete-time theory: one observes the system periodically (every year or minute or microsecond) and ignores the state occupied at other time points. However, since such an analysis is often unnatural, an extensive theory of continuous-time processes has grown up.

Statistical analysis. One may believe a given process to be a Markov chain—or approximately a Markov chain—because of his knowledge of the underlying mechanism. Or he may hypothesize that it is a Markov chain, hoping to check this assumption against actual data. Under the Markov assumption, he may want to draw from actual data conclusions about the transition probabilities p_{ij}, which are the basic parameters of the model. In other words, statistical problems of estimation and hypothesis testing arise for Markov chains just as they do for independent processes [*see* ESTIMATION; HYPOTHESIS TESTING].

Suppose one observes n systems (governed by a common Markov chain), of which n_i start in state E_i, and follows each of them through one transition. If n_{ij} is the number that step from E_i to E_j, so that $\sum_j n_{ij} = n_i$, then the log-likelihood function is $\sum_{i,j} n_{ij} \log p_{ij}$; maximizing this function with the s constraints $\sum_j p_{ij} = 1$ gives the natural ratios n_{ij}/n_i as the maximum likelihood estimators of the p_{ij}. The numerical matrix given for the social mobility example was obtained in this way from a sample of some 3,500 father–son pairs in England and Wales. If the n_i are large, the estimators are approximately normally distributed about their mean values p_{ij}. By seeing how far the n_{ij}/n_i differ from putative transition probabilities p_{ij}, one can test the null hypothesis that these p_{ij} are the true parameter values. The statistic appropriate for this problem is $\sum_{i,j}(n_{ij} - n_i p_{ij})^2/n_i p_{ij}$; it has approximately a chi-square distribution with $s(s-1)$ degrees of freedom if the n_i are large.

Other tests are possible if the systems under observation are traced for more than one step. Suppose n_{ijk} is the number of the systems that start in E_i, step to E_j, and then step to E_k. If the process is a Markov chain, then (a) the chance that the second step carries the system from E_j to E_k does not depend on the initial state E_i and (b) the transition probabilities for the second step are the same as those for the first.

Let a dot indicate an index that has been summed out; for example, $n._{ij} = \sum_k n_{kij}$ is the number of systems that are in states E_i and E_j at times 2 and 3, respectively (with the state at time 1 completely unspecified). Assuming (a), one can test (b) by comparing the estimators $n_{ij}./n_{i}..$ of the transition probabilities for the first step with the estimators $n._{ij}/n._{j}.$ of the transition probabilities for the second step. And one can test (a) itself by comparing the ratios $n._{jk}/n._{j}.$ (the estimated second-step transition probabilities) with the ratios $n_{ijk}/n._{jk}$ (the estimated second-step transition probabilities, allowing for possible further influence of the initial state); if (a) holds, $n_{ijk}/n_{ij}.$ should, independently of i, be near $n._{jk}/n._{j}.$; thus one can check on the Markov chain assumption itself.

This statistical analysis, based on following a large number of independently evolving systems through a small number of steps, really falls under the classical chi-square and maximum likelihood theory. There is also a statistical theory for the opposite case, following a small number of systems (perhaps just one) through many steps. Although the estimates and tests for this case have forms similar to those for the first case, the derivation of their asymptotic properties is more involved.

The statistical analysis of Markov chains may be extended in various directions. For example, a mode of analysis in which *times of stay* in the states are considered, together with transition probabilities, is discussed by Weiss and Zelen (1965).

PATRICK BILLINGSLEY

[*Other relevant material may be found in* PANEL STUDIES; SOCIAL MOBILITY.]

BIBLIOGRAPHY

ANDERSON, T. W.; and GOODMAN, LEO A. 1957 Statistical Inference About Markov Chains. *Annals of Mathematical Statistics* 28:89–110. → A detailed treatment of the problem of many short samples.

BILLINGSLEY, PATRICK 1961 Statistical Methods in Markov Chains. *Annals of Mathematical Statistics* 32: 12–40. → A review paper covering the problem of one long sample from a Markov chain. Contains a large bibliography.

BLUMEN, ISADORE; KOGAN, MARVIN; and McCARTHY, PHILIP 1955 *The Industrial Mobility of Labor as a Probability Process.* Cornell Studies in Industrial and Labor Relations, Vol. 6. Ithaca, N.Y.: Cornell Univ. Press. → A detailed empirical study of mobility problems.

FELLER, WILLIAM 1950–1966 *An Introduction to Probability Theory and Its Applications.* 2 vols. New York: Wiley. → A classic text covering continuous-time processes as well as chains with infinitely many states. Excellent examples. The second edition of the first volume was published in 1957.

GLASS, D. V.; and HALL, J. R. 1954 Social Mobility in Great Britain: A Study in Inter-generation Changes in Status. In D. V. Glass (editor), *Social Mobility in Britain.* London: Routledge. → This is the source of the original data for the social mobility example.

GOODMAN, LEO A. 1961 Statistical Methods for the Mover–Stayer Model. *Journal of the American Statistical Association* 56:841–868.

GOODMAN, LEO A. 1962 Statistical Methods for Analyzing Processes of Change. *American Journal of Sociology* 68:57–78. → This and the preceding paper treat modifications of the Markov model for mobility problems.

JAFFE, JOSEPH; CASSOTTA, LOUIS; and FELDSTEIN, STANLEY 1964 Markovian Model of Time Patterns of Speech. *Science* 144:884–886.

KEMENY, JOHN G.; and SNELL, J. LAURIE 1960 *Finite Markov Chains.* Princeton, N.J.: Van Nostrand. → Contains both theory and examples. This is the source of the figures for the social mobility example.

PRAIS, S. J. 1955 Measuring Social Mobility. *Journal of the Royal Statistical Society* Series A 118:56–66. → This is the source of the analysis of the social mobility example.

WEISS, GEORGE H.; and ZELEN, MARVIN 1965 A Semi-Markov Model for Clinical Trials. *Journal of Applied Probability* 2:269–285.

International Encyclopedia of the SOCIAL SCIENCES

DAVID L. SILLS EDITOR

VOLUME 10

The Macmillan Company & The Free Press, New York
COLLIER-MACMILLAN PUBLISHERS, LONDON

MANUFACTURED IN THE UNITED STATES OF AMERICA

1 2 3 4 5 6 7 8 9 10

REPRINT EDITION 1972

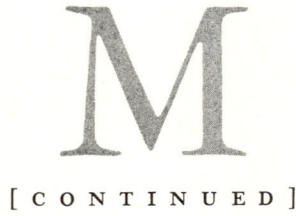

M

[C O N T I N U E D]

MARRIAGE

I. FAMILY FORMATION .... Robert F. Winch
II. COMPARATIVE ANALYSIS ... Gloria A. Marshall
III. MARRIAGE ALLIANCE ...... Louis Dumont

I
FAMILY FORMATION

The beginning of family formation may be either marriage or parenthood. It should not be concluded from the fact that sexual intercourse is a prerequisite for pregnancy that all peoples regard marriage or the establishing of a man–woman relationship as the first step in family formation. Indeed, according to Bohannan (1963, p. 73) the matricentric family, consisting of a woman and her children, is "both more nearly universal and more elementary than is the nuclear family," consisting of a marital couple plus any children they may have. In some societies it is thought proper that marriage should precede pregnancy, while in others the reverse sequence is regarded with favor; in the extreme case marriage is viewed as irrelevant to family formation. However, it seems safe to assert that in most societies the nuclear family is thought to be well launched only when both conditions are met.

Cultures also vary according to whether they emphasize marital solidarity over lineal solidarity or vice versa. Societies with strongly developed extended family systems emphasize lineal solidarity over marital solidarity. In such societies family formation is scarcely a meaningful concept: since the marriage of a man and woman and the coming of their progeny represent the carrying on of a continuous line, these events may signal the establishing of a new household but not the formation of a new family.

In this article the topic of family formation will be treated with reference to the nuclear family. Marriage will therefore be considered as the focus of the process of family formation, and mate selection as one of its most problematic features.

Definitions. From the functional point of view, the family is the one social system that all societies look to for the replacement of their members. However, from the structural point of view, the word "family" is used to refer not only to the marital couple and their children but also to the larger kin group; accordingly, it will be necessary to draw some structural distinctions. The "extended family" includes a nuclear family plus lineal and collateral kinsmen; to the extent that a society emphasizes rights and obligations among kinsmen who are not in the same nuclear family, it is spoken of as having an "extended family system." On the other hand, a "nuclear family system" is said to exist in a society in which the rights and obligations among those in the larger kin group are given little emphasis relative to the claims among members of the same nuclear family.

It should be emphasized that the term "family," whether it applies to a nuclear or an extended family, is not equivalent to the term "household" —the aggregate of persons occupying a common dwelling unit, whether or not those persons are kinsmen. In Western societies the nuclear family is frequently also a household while the parental couples are in their younger and middle years and before their children attain adulthood. However, many other arrangements are possible, and some are institutionalized. For example, in South Africa it has been the practice for decades for the husband-father to be away from his nuclear family for years at a time. A common type of household among

Negroes in the Caribbean and in the United States consists of a working woman, her children, and her mother. In traditional China the ideal household included the nuclear family of the head of the household plus his unmarried daughters, his sons with their nuclear families, his sons' unmarried daughters, his sons' sons with their nuclear families, and so on through all living generations; in practice, however, not many Chinese families could afford households of such size.

Marriage may be defined as a culturally approved relationship of one man and one woman (monogamy), of one man and two or more women (polygyny), or of one woman and two or more men (polyandry), in which there is cultural endorsement of sexual intercourse between the marital partners of opposite sex and, generally, the expectation that children will be born of the relationship ("polygamy" is the term that subsumes both polygyny and polyandry). "Homogamy" refers to the marriage of persons of similar characteristics, which is also known as "assortative" or "assortive" mating; "heterogamy" is the marriage of persons of different characteristics; and "hypergamy" is a marriage in which the husband is of higher social status than the wife. The term "endogamy" refers to marriage between persons belonging to the same social group, whereas in "exogamy" the partners come from different groups.

Marriage and legitimacy. By definition marriage is a relationship within which sexual intercourse is legitimate. In general, a woman who cohabits with a man has a legitimate status in relation to that man only if she is known to be married to him. Common-law marriage (recognized in the United Kingdom and in the United States) and the consensual union (recognized in the Caribbean) are forms of man–woman relationship that carry less than full cultural approval and legitimacy. Points of interest to American, as well as to English, courts in establishing whether or not a common-law marriage exists include: mutual agreement of the man and woman to take each other as husband and wife; cohabitation and presentation of themselves as a married couple to friends, neighbors, and the general public; and reputation, that is, the recognition by the community that the two are husband and wife.

The Caribbean pattern of the consensual union differs from the common-law marriage of Anglo-Saxon countries in that the former is not a legally recognized marriage. Various writers have held that except for this lack of legal sanction the consensual union carries no social stigma and therefore is quite as acceptable among the people prac-

ticing it as is legal marriage. More recent analyses by Blake (1961) and by Goode (1960), however, have concluded that there is general recognition among Caribbean societies that consensual unions are less legitimate and hence less desirable than legal marriages. Goode argues that whereas legal marriage is recognized throughout Caribbean societies as the legitimate form, there is variation among the social strata of these societies in the degree of norm commitment, with the consequence that persons in the lower strata tend to be generally less committed to familial norms than persons in the upper strata. The more frequent occurrence of consensual unions among the lower social strata than among the upper is seen as a reflection of the class-linked variation in the degree of commitment to familial norms. [See CARIBBEAN SOCIETY.]

Legitimacy affects the offspring of the marriage as well as the spouses themselves. In asserting what he called the "principle of legitimacy," Malinowski (1929) stated that in all societies a socially recognized father has been regarded as indispensable to the child. A legal marriage, then, gives a woman a socially recognized husband and her children a socially recognized father. According to Zimmerman (1947), the penalties attached to illegitimacy vary directly with the power of the extended family; thus, the penalties are heavy in societies characterized by the extended-family system and light where the nuclear family prevails. From a sociological point of view, the significance of legitimacy is that it is a necessary condition for the family to carry out its function of position-conferring. In this sense, the critical meaning of bastardy is not that the child has *low* status but rather that he lacks *any* position and status in his society. [See ILLEGITIMACY.]

Variations in familial organization. Cultural expectations pertaining to marriage are affected by variations in familial organization. In Western civilization it appears that the power of the family and the size of the effective kin group (i.e., of the familial structure) have varied inversely with the complexity of the society of which the effective kin group is a part. Zimmerman (1947), who extensively analyzed the civilizations of ancient Athens and Rome, reports that in the early stages of both of these civilizations (i.e., when both societies were relatively simple) there existed what he calls the "trustee" type of familial organization; whereas in their late (and, to Zimmerman, decadent) stages, Athens and Rome developed much more complex societies and simpler familial structures, which he describes as "atomistic." The kernel of Zimmerman's distinction lies in the locus of power. Where the trustee type of family exists, much power is located in the extended family. The head of the family, as the responsible center of familial authority, influences the behavior of the family members, and the extended family feels responsible for the behavior of its members. Where the atomistic type of family prevails, much power is located outside the kin group in specialized institutions. As the family loses power, its structure shifts from the extended family system to the nuclear family system. In the process of making this shift, according to Zimmerman, the divorce rate goes up and the birth rate goes down. Arguing that there are other lines of development than those of the West noted by Zimmerman, Goode (1963) holds, as we shall see below, that whether the divorce rate goes up as a society becomes more complex depends on the nature of the familial structure at the start of the process.

One way of formulating variation in the family's power and size is to speak of its functioning as a political unit. Moreover, the family may show variation in other kinds of functioning. In some settings the family is the basic economic unit that creates and distributes goods and services. In many settings it is the principal social unit responsible for socializing and educating the young. And in some settings, especially where ancestor worship is practiced, the family carries out the religious function. In general, as societies become more complex, specialized societal structures develop for the carrying out of these functions, with the result that the family loses some of its functions; indeed such a state of affairs is the meaning of societal complexity.

Taking account of Asian and African as well as Western societies, Goode (1963) agrees that most family systems of the world are moving toward a small-family system based on the nuclear family. Because the traits of non-Western family systems are so varied, however, he believes there will be marked differences in the direction of this change as the predicted convergence takes place. Thus, in African tribal societies where matrilineal systems are strong and divorce is common, Goode reasons that urbanization will be accompanied by a reduction in the conditions that have made divorce easy.

Mate selection

The functional emphasis in modern sociology leads the observer to anticipate that criteria for the choice of a mate will be related to the roles the mate is expected to enact and, perhaps, that the mate will be chosen by the incumbent of that social position most influenced by the quality of the mate's performance. There is some evidence to support such a set of functional expectations, but of course the empirical world is always less tidy than the social scientist's model.

The extended family system. In the extended family system it is common for members of the nuclear family to work in teams of kinsmen. Under this condition the mate-selective process is frequently a means of recruiting workers, and hence the members of the extended family have a lively interest in the work-related qualifications of a kinsman's prospective mate. Thus it is not unusual for responsible senior members of the extended family to select a son's spouse and to employ such familially relevant criteria as the industry and prospective fecundity of a potential daughter-in-law. For families of higher status, the standing of a girl's family becomes more important than her manual skills. Irrespective of status, however, the extended family system makes the procuring of a mate a matter of moment to a wide circle of kinsmen. It is consistent with this kind of family organization that mate selection should be a task calling for experienced perception and shrewd bargaining. Moreover, in order that their plans should not be thwarted by the passions of the young, the older people institute devices such as early marriage and efficient chaperonage (Goode 1959).

On the other hand, where the extended family is not highly functional and where the nuclear family system prevails, it is frequently thought to be inappropriate for members of the extended kin group to exhibit lively interest in the marital choices of family members, and even the influence of parents is reduced. Under these conditions the criteria for mate selection are more likely to include attributes having primary appeal to the nubile pair—physical beauty, sexual attractiveness, and congeniality. The response to one or more of these attributes comes to be subsumed under the rubric of love. The diminution of relatives' influence in mate selection is not, of course, a categorical matter but rather one of degree. By their own religion, ethnicity, and social status, as well as by their own choice of location of residence and of schools, parents continue to influence their youngsters' choice of spouses.

Traditional China provides an example of mate selection carried on by the family for familial purposes. When a son married, the preferred arrangement was for him to bring his bride into his parental home. The parents expected the bride to perform two important functions: to bear children, preferably sons, and to assist her mother-in-law in the performance of domestic chores. As the boy was growing up, he looked to his parents to provide him with a wife. The parents expected the son to accept whatever bride they chose, and they condemned vigorously any disposition on the son's part to make his own marital selection, especially if the son tried to do so on the basis of love. It was generally agreed that young people of marriageable age were too inexperienced to have sound judgment in such an important undertaking. Since most of the bride's time was to be spent assisting her husband's mother, functional considerations dictated that the latter was the most interested party in the marriage; appropriately, therefore, she was usually the most active person in selecting her son's wife. Thus, arranged marriages were customary, and it was not unusual for a young man to meet his bride for the first time at the wedding ceremony. Traditional China made extensive use of the "go-between," or marriage broker. This occupation served two useful functions: marriage brokers made it their business to have extensive and detailed information about marriageable young people; and they made it possible for families to enter into and break off negotiations without loss of face (Hsu 1948; Lang 1946; Levy 1949).

With industrialization came pressure for changes in Chinese family law. This was evident as early as the Boxer Rebellion at the beginning of the twentieth century, and new codes were promulgated in 1930 and 1931 (well before the communist revolution in China) that reflected Western standards —more emphasis on the nuclear family and less on the extended family, a reduction in male authority, and a closer approximation to legal equality of the sexes. However, the law retained a feature of Chinese filial piety: the obligations to one's parents superseded the obligations to one's children. In these matters the communist revolution has represented not so much a break with the past as a continuation of trends already under way (Yang 1959). Although reliable information on postrevolutionary China is still scanty, it appears that whereas the communist regime officially deplores both Western and traditional Chinese ways, love marriages are common, and the influence of the extended family is continuing to wane.

The nuclear family system. As specialized social structures spring up, take over functions from the family, and become societally important and individually rewarding, the resulting reduction in the functional importance of the extended family removes incentives for maintaining an extended family system. At the same time there are four functions inherent in the nuclear family that come to the fore as being relevant in mate selection.

These functions are: providing emotional gratification in the marital and parental relationships; providing identity and a social status in the societal system to individuals who enter the family by birth, adoption, or marriage—a function to be known here as position-conferring; performing such tasks as cleaning, bringing in supplies, and disposing of waste products, which may be subsumed under maintenance of the household; and child rearing, especially with respect to the parental functions of nurturance and control.

Of these four functions emotional gratification is most explicitly recognized in American culture as relevant to mate selection, and apparently this is so, to an increasing degree, in the middle-class subcultures of western Europe. There can be little doubt that convictions are widespread in the United States and western Europe that a couple should be "in love" before considering marriage and that legal codes are obsolete if they fail to provide for divorce on the ground of chronic marital conflict. Love as a mate-selective criterion invites idiosyncratic interpretation in the sense that, for instance, one man may be attracted to a demurely diffident girl whereas another finds the vivaciously extroverted girl irresistible.

As a mate-selective criterion, position-conferring (especially when phrased as status-conferring) evokes ambivalent responses. In many middle-class settings a girl who is thought to have married for money rather than for love risks social condemnation (Indian culture, by contrast, has had the tradition that it is good for a girl to marry into a subcaste of higher standing than her own). If a girl marries for love *plus* status improvement, however, she is said to have married "well," and the durability of the Cinderella legend suggests that there is little novelty in this theme. The woman's social status depends so largely on her husband's occupational performance that, for her, mate selection is sometimes spoken of as a "mobility bet." Such evidence as exists on this matter for the United States indicates that most marriages are between persons of roughly equal social status.

Although all four of the functions mentioned above are relevant to mate selection, a young couple considering marriage can usually check the suitability of each other only with respect to emotional gratification. This may have something to do with the emphasis given love as a criterion. In the premarital setting of early adulthood the other three functions can usually be no more than the focuses of guesswork. It is difficult for a young woman to foresee how a particular man will fare in the occupational sweepstakes and in being a model for their sons. Predictions are similarly difficult for the young man with respect to how a woman will manage their house and mother their children.

Where marriages are voluntary rather than arranged, there is need of some means for marriageable young men and women to meet and to select each other. The practice of dating is societally rational in the sense that it affords this opportunity. On the other hand, dating as a prelude to mate selection has been criticized on the ground that the leisure-time activities of dating fail to provide an adequate setting in which to test prospective spouses with respect to maritally relevant criteria, especially with respect to the functions of household maintenance and child rearing.

In sum, a reduction of functions in the extended family is accompanied by a reduction in the rights and obligations among extended kin that constitute the extended family system. This reduction in the significance of blood relationships shifts the emphasis from the extended family to the nuclear family. Marital solidarity replaces cognatic (both lineal and collateral) solidarity, and love becomes a criterion of mate selection.

Principles of preferential mating

Let us designate as "ego" a person of reference, that is, a person from whose point of view we shall consider certain relationships. All societies designate categories of persons whom ego may not marry, and frequently there are additional categories of persons whom it would be regrettable, but not totally forbidden, for ego to marry. Usually there are implicit, if not explicit, categories of persons whom it would be desirable for ego to marry. These negative and positive expectations can be subsumed under the "principle of incest avoidance" and the "principle of ethnocentrism." We shall speak of the set of persons whom ego is permitted to marry in any given sociocultural setting as ego's field of eligible spouse candidates or, in shorter form, as ego's "field of eligibles." European social scientists use the term "isolate" to refer to the field of eligibles.

The principle of incest avoidance. Every society has a prohibition against incest, that is, against sexual relations between persons who are closely related. Although the precise relationships that are viewed as incestuous vary from one society to another, they regularly include the mother–son, the father–daughter, and the brother–sister relationships, that is, all heterosexual relationships within the nuclear family except, of course, the marital relationship. The principle of incest avoidance re-

fers to the set of prohibitions existing in every culture to prevent ego from marrying someone too close to him in the kinship system.

Just how the principle of incest avoidance works out varies from one setting to another. In traditional China it was prohibited for ego to marry anyone with the same surname, and in that populous land with few surnames this rule proscribed hundreds of thousands of otherwise eligible spouse candidates. In northern India there was a tradition that marriage was not possible with someone removed from ego by less than seven degrees on the father's side or less than five degrees on the mother's; a more common rule in India prohibits marriage between relatives linked to a common ancestor within five degrees on the father's side and three on the mother's (Goode 1963, p. 210). In some societies ego is encouraged to marry a cross-cousin (e.g., mother's brother's daughter) but prohibited from marrying a parallel cousin (e.g., mother's sister's daughter). Prior to 1793 it was illegal in Connecticut for ego to marry the sister of his deceased wife; but among the ancient Hebrews there was the custom of the levirate, by which a man was enjoined to marry the widow of his deceased brother if the brother had died without a son. The record shows a very few isolated cases where persons of opposite sex from the same nuclear family were permitted to marry. An example is the brother–sister marriage among the Ptolemies of ancient Egypt. Apparently the practice in these few exceptions functioned to keep power within ruling families. [*See* INCEST.]

Ethnocentrism and homogamy. Whereas the principle of incest avoidance prevents ego from marrying someone too close to him in the kinship system, the principle of ethnocentrism prevents his marrying someone too different from him with respect to a number of social characteristics. In other words, ethnocentrism is a force tending toward endogamous and homogamous marriages.

Sumner ([1906] 1959, chapter 1) used the term ethnocentrism to refer to the set of attitudes shared by members of a tribe or other social group to the effect that the members of that group and any others like them were seen as the center of the civilized world and had, therefore, the correct and desirable set of social characteristics. Thus, ethnocentric attitudes lead to the condemnation of outsiders to the degree that they are recognized as differing from one's group. The minimum degree of social distance on the Bogardus scale is indicated by an affirmative response to the query as to whether or not the respondent would be willing to accept a person with a specified characteristic to close kinship by marriage. Traditionally, the castes of India have been endogamous, as have the sub-altern categories of subcaste, section, and subsection. According to Kapadia ([1955] 1958, p. 118), these endogamous restrictions limited a Hindu's field of eligibles to 50 to 300 families. In 1949, however, the Hindu Marriages Validity Act stipulated that no marriage of Hindus could be invalidated because of caste or sect differences between the parties concerned. Expert opinion is divided as to the likelihood that caste endogamy will break down.

In accordance with the principle of ethnocentrism there is evidence that in American society ego tends to select a spouse similar to himself with respect to race, religio-ethnic identification, socioeconomic status, and other social characteristics. In the United States the most conspicuously homogamous dimension of mate selection is race. Interracial marriages are still prohibited by law in a number of the Southern states; moreover, even where such laws do not exist, or where they have been repealed, there is little evidence of enthusiasm for such marriages. Various studies have shown the proportion of racially heterogamous marriages to be under one per cent. [*See* ASSIMILATION.]

The second dimension of ethnocentric preference and prohibition is that of religio-ethnic identification, which includes cultural as well as religious elements. Classifying the 1957 population of the United States into the three major religious categories (Protestant, Catholic, and Jewish), the U.S. Bureau of the Census found that approximately 94 per cent of the married persons had spouses in the same religious categories as themselves. If religious endogamy had not been practiced, and if, therefore, matings had been entirely random with respect to religious affiliation, the proportion having spouses in the same religious category as themselves would have been about 56 per cent (Winch [1952] 1963, p. 331). There is evidence that in heterogeneous communities the probability that ego will marry outside his religious category is greater when his category constitutes a small proportion of the community rather than a large proportion. If the religious category has a highly distinctive ethnic identity (e.g., Catholics who are Spanish-speaking in an English-speaking community), the probability of ego's marrying endogamously is increased.

A third dimension of ethnocentric preference is that of socioeconomic status. Commonly used indexes of socioeconomic status are occupation, income, and number of years of schooling. Numerous studies have shown that people tend to select their spouses from their own socioeconomic strata

with respect to all three of these indexes (several are cited in Winch [1952] 1963, pp. 336–338). Other characteristics with respect to which people tend to mate homogamously are age, previous marital status, and location of residence. Systematic research supports the common observation that young people tend to select young mates and older people choose older spouses. No doubt it is partially because of this fact that there is a tendency for people to marry others who are like themselves with respect to previous marital status: divorced men tend to marry divorcees; single persons tend to marry those who have not previously been married; and widows and widowers tend to marry each other. Another common-sense observation that has been supported by research concerns residential propinquity: ego is more likely to marry someone living nearby than someone living far away (Winch [1952] 1963, pp. 322–324, 339–345).

Since people are not randomly distributed through communities but rather tend to live near and to work with others of similar social characteristics, one would expect mate selection to be somewhat homogamous, whether or not there are any sanctions enforcing endogamy. Of course there are sanctions of varying degrees of intensity: for example, in American culture sanctions are quite intense with respect to race, less so with respect to religion and socioeconomic status, and virtually nonexistent with respect to residential propinquity.

Homogamy may also be considered on a more psychological level. For example, there is evidence that spouses tend to resemble each other in level of intelligence, in values (e.g., religious and aesthetic), and in attitudes (e.g., toward birth control and toward communism). When spouses are tested by paper-and-pencil methods, they appear to resemble each other somewhat, but not greatly, with respect to traits of temperament and personality. However, data gathered by other methods, such as interviews and projective methods, lead to the contrary conclusion that, at least in such traits as dominance and dependence, spouses tend to be complementary rather than similar. At present this seeming paradox is unresolved, although the answer may be that the homogamy apparent in paper-and-pencil tests is an artifact resulting from the effort of people to represent themselves to be as attractive as possible—what is called the "social desirability" effect (Winch 1958; [1952] 1963, chapter 18).

Differentiation of sex roles

The simple fact that only women can bear children causes every society to recognize some differentiation between the behavior of men and of women. Beyond the behavioral differences that are directly attributable to anatomy and physiology, however, cultures vary greatly in the degree to which they view human behavior as being properly sex differentiated.

From a study of 224 societies, Murdock (1937) has found that men tend to engage in such active and mobile tasks as hunting, fishing, trapping, and lumbering, whereas women tend to specialize in more sedentary but equally important tasks, such as gathering fuel and fruits and cooking and preserving meat and fish. More generally, it is possible to conceptualize two criteria that distinguish masculine from feminine tasks. Tasks assigned to men usually require physical exertion and strength, or spatial mobility and absence from home for considerable periods of time, or both. By contrast, feminine activities are typically less demanding of great strength, although perhaps requiring a considerable output of energy, and will involve only a few hours at a time away from home.

Analysis of these differences leads to the conclusion that the sharpness with which a culture distinguishes between masculine and feminine sex roles will be related to the importance it attaches to tasks requiring one or both of the two masculine task characteristics. Military activity is one obvious example that involves both of the masculine criteria; thus it is argued that a highly military-oriented culture will be one that draws a sharp distinction between properly masculine activities and those that are properly feminine. The converse inference is that to the degree that a society's important tasks do not call for either of the criteria distinguishing masculine activities, there will be no basis for developing highly differentiated sex roles. As nonhuman power has taken over most of the heavy tasks in the industrial societies, the proportion of the total labor force that is classified as "white collar" has greatly increased. And white-collar occupations, especially those not requiring travel, can be carried on as well by women as by men. Thus, if Western cultures have been "feminized" over the past century or so, as some writers have claimed, the present analysis would interpret such a trend as a consequence of the increased use of nonhuman power.

Sex dominance in the marital dyad. What are the conditions that result in the dominance of one spouse over the other? The opportunity for dominance exists in a dyad when resources desired by one member are controlled by the other, that is, when one is dependent upon the other. Resources may be viewed broadly to include both material goods, such as food, and intangibles, such as a compliment.

Where no organizational feature exists to determine otherwise, it appears that men have usually dominated women. The reasons for this originate in the two criteria differentiating masculine from feminine pursuits and in their anatomical and physiological bases. A woman with small children has greater need of a man to take care of her than the man has need of her. His care may be viewed as a resource, and by granting or withholding that resource, the man can dominate the woman. This is a state of affairs that has been remarked by social scientists from Aristotle through E. A. Ross and Willard Waller and is perhaps best known to contemporary readers under the rubric of the "principle of least interest": that is, the person in a relationship who has the least to lose through the termination of the relationship is in a position to demand more from others and thus to dominate them in exchange for his continued participation. Aside from this situation of unilateral dependence, other possibilities are mutual interdependence, where the resources are not available to either one unless they cooperate, and mutual independence, where each has control over his own resources.

With respect to organizational features, W. G. Sumner and A. G. Keller have remarked that where the bridal couple lives has bearing on which is the dominant sex and therefore that matrilocal marriage is a condition favorable to the relative standing of women. In traditional China, the favored pattern was patrilocal, and a wife was expected to obey her husband; masculine dominance was mitigated, however, in the case of adoptive marriage. According to this pattern, a man having no son might seek a young man (who was usually of somewhat lower social rank) to take the older man's family name, marry the older man's daughter, and live matrilocally.

Studies of marriage

During the second quarter of the twentieth century there was a good deal of concern about the state of the family in the Western world. There was evidence that divorce rates had risen, that the family had lost functions to other social structures, that the birth rate had fallen, that certain totalitarian regimes were trying to bring about the disintegration of the family, and that broken families were spawning delinquent children. Family disorganization was widely viewed as a social problem; probably for this reason, numerous studies were undertaken to discover the determinants, or at least some correlates, of what was variously called marital "adjustment," marital "happiness," and marital "success."

Although these studies did not undertake to distinguish very sharply among the three terms just noted, it does seem useful to differentiate them as follows. There are two kinds of marital adjustment, one pertaining to the role and the other to the psyche of the performer. An actor is adjusted to a marital or any other kind of role to the degree that he knows the expectations that define the role and, under the appropriate conditions, can produce the behaviors expected. On the other hand, he is adjusted psychically to the degree that the energy he invests in the role performance is commensurate with the gratification derived from it. Marital "happiness" refers to the subjective response of the actor to marriage and thus is related to psychic adjustment; however, one can be psychically adjusted when both output of energy and input of gratification are low, whereas presumably happiness requires at least a moderately high level of gratification. The term marital "success" implies the existence of a goal of marriage, and whatever goals there may be—avoidance of divorce, procreation, personality development of the spouses—seem to be more clearly conceived by those who write about marriage than by the participants whose behavior the writers describe.

Much of the research on marriage has been concerned with marital adjustment—that is, both with the aptitude to carry out the marital role and with the capacity to derive commensurate gratification from the performance. Kirkpatrick has surveyed a large number of studies and has reported the variables he finds that have correlated most consistently with what is here called marital adjustment. He has divided these variables into two sets: those that were clearly operating before the marriage and those that may or may not have been. Presumably the determinants of marital adjustment are more likely to come from the former set. Kirkpatrick ([1955] 1963, p. 389) presents the following premarital factors as having shown the strongest and most consistent association with high marital adjustment: happiness of parents' marriage; adequate length of acquaintance, courtship, and engagement; adequate sex information in childhood; personal happiness in childhood; approval of the marriage by parents and others; adjustment in engagement and normal motivation toward marriage; ethnic and religious similarity of the spouses; high social and educational status; maturity (marriage in the late twenties rather than in the teens or early twenties); similar chronological age of the spouses; and harmonious affection with parents during childhood.

Factors that may have become operative during marriage, rather than before, and therefore are regarded as part of the complex of marital adjust-

ment rather than among its determinants are early and adequate orgasm capacity, especially of the wife; confidence in the spouse's affection and satisfaction with degree of affection shown; equalitarian rather than patriarchal marital relations, with special reference to the role of husband; mental and physical health; and harmonious companionship based on common interests and accompanied by a favorable attitude toward the marriage and the spouse (Kirkpatrick [1955] 1963, p. 394).

ROBERT F. WINCH

[*See also* FAMILY; NUPTIALITY; *and the biographies of* BURGESS; MALINOWSKI; SUMNER; WALLER; WESTERMARCK.]

BIBLIOGRAPHY

BLAKE, JUDITH 1961 *Family Structure in Jamaica: The Social Context of Reproduction.* New York: Free Press.

BOHANNAN, PAUL 1963 *Social Anthropology.* New York: Holt.

GOODE, WILLIAM J. 1959 The Theoretical Importance of Love. *American Sociological Review* 24:38–47.

GOODE, WILLIAM J. 1960 Illegitimacy in the Caribbean Social Structure. *American Sociological Review* 25: 21–30.

GOODE, WILLIAM J. 1963 *World Revolution and Family Patterns.* New York: Free Press.

HSU, FRANCIS L. K. 1948 *Under the Ancestors' Shadow: Chinese Culture and Personality.* New York: Columbia Univ. Press.

KAPADIA, KANAILAL M. (1955) 1958 *Marriage and Family in India.* 2d ed. Bombay: Oxford Univ. Press.

KIRKPATRICK, CLIFFORD (1955) 1963 *The Family as Process and Institution.* 2d ed. New York: Ronald Press.

LANG, OLGA 1946 *Chinese Family and Society.* New Haven: Yale Univ. Press.

LEVY, MARION J. 1949 *The Family Revolution in Modern China.* Cambridge, Mass.: Harvard Univ. Press.

MALINOWSKI, BRONISLAW (1929) 1962 Marriage. Pages 1–35 in Bronislaw Malinowski, *Sex, Culture and Myth.* New York: Harcourt.

MURDOCK, GEORGE P. 1937 Comparative Data on the Division of Labor by Sex. *Social Forces* 15:551–553.

SUMNER, WILLIAM GRAHAM (1906) 1959 *Folkways: A Study of the Sociological Importance of Usages, Manners, Customs, Mores, and Morals.* New York: Dover. → A paperback edition was published in 1960 by New American Library.

WINCH, ROBERT F. (1952) 1963 *The Modern Family.* Rev. ed. New York: Holt.

WINCH, ROBERT F. 1958 *Mate-selection: A Study of Complementary Needs.* New York: Harper.

YANG, CH'ING-K'UN 1959 *The Chinese Family in the Communist Revolution.* Cambridge, Mass.: M.I.T. Press.

ZIMMERMAN, CARLE C. 1947 *Family and Civilization.* New York: Harper.

II
COMPARATIVE ANALYSIS

Every society has rules governing the assumption of the conjugal roles of husband and wife; there are also discernible rights accruing to and obligations incumbent upon the individuals who assume these roles. Marriage in all societies thus brings about a change in the jural status of the parties to the contract. Where marriage is defined by the state, it is possible to describe most of its jural entailments by reference to one or more legal codes adopted by that state. However, among many of the peoples studied by anthropologists, the jural tenets governing marriage cannot be ascertained by reference to codes laid down by a state and hence must be derived from the study of the recurrent patterns of behavior and of folk models that prescribe ideal behavior.

Marriage entails not only a change in the jural status of the individuals who enter the roles of husband and wife but also a change in the lawful status of specifiable consanguineal kinsmen of the individual partners. In fact, it is the linkage of groups as well as of individuals that is crucial to the formulation of the difference between marriage and its social analogues. Only marriage creates (or maintains) affinal relationships between the kinsmen of individuals who claim the roles of husband and wife (see Fortes 1959, p. 209). Even where it is socially admissible for individuals to *presume* conjugal status—that is, where they may assume the husband–wife roles without their actions being legitimated according to prevailing jural rules—this presumption of status does not generate lawful relations of affinity between kinsmen of the "spouses" concerned.

The importance of affinity to an understanding of marriage is made clear through a consideration of the nature of kinship. The social relations subsumed under the concept of kinship are of two fundamental types which, though referable to the biological processes of heterosexual mating and procreation, cannot be reduced to biology. Those social relationships based on parenthood and descent or, more precisely, on parenthood and filiation, are generally termed consanguineal relationships. All persons related by socially defined direct or shared descent are consanguineal kinsmen (P. Bohannan 1963, chapter 4). These "blood relatives" are distinguished in all societies from affinal relatives, i.e., those whose kinship status is fundamentally grounded "in law." Human mating is everywhere socially regulated, and adult mating for the purpose of procreation is normally preceded by the creation of *jurally derived kinship ties* between the mating pair and between certain of their respective consanguineal relatives. The continuance of publicly acknowledged affinal kinship depends on adherence to prescriptions and proscriptions delimited by the particular society under consideration. Whereas many societies make no provision for the legal severance of consanguineal

kinship bonds, they all provide for the severance —"by law"—of those which are based "in law."

Societies differ considerably with respect to the rules governing the way in which the roles of husband and wife should be assumed, with respect to the specific rights and obligations which accrue to persons in these roles, and with regard to the behavioral and jural attributes of the other affinal roles created by marriage. Nonetheless, most anthropologists have regarded the institution of marriage as a universal in human societies, and many have attempted to provide definitions of marriage sufficiently general to encompass its various manifestations.

The fact that marriage is closely linked to parenthood has led many scholars, including Westermarck, Malinowski, and Radcliffe-Brown, to propose definitions of marriage which center on what Malinowski termed "the principle of legitimacy." Thus, Radcliffe-Brown writes: "Marriage is a social arrangement by which a child is given a legitimate position in the society, determined by parenthood in the social sense" (1950, p. 5). The general, though by no means universal, acceptance of this formulation is indicated by the fact that *Notes and Queries on Anthropology* defines marriage in an essentially similar, but by implication more limited, manner: "Marriage is a union between a man and a woman such that children born to the woman are the recognized legitimate offspring of both partners" (British Association for the Advancement of Science 1951, p. 110).

Edmund R. Leach was among the first to argue that a definition of marriage in terms of legitimacy is too limited. In his opinion, any attempt at a universal definition of marriage is inevitably "vain," since the "institutions commonly classed as marriage are concerned with the allocation of a number of distinguishable classes of rights" (1961a, p. 107). Leach suggests that in most cases the institution of marriage serves to allocate rights to either or both spouses; in some cases it serves primarily to allocate rights to the husband and his wife's brothers.

Despite Leach's arguments against a universal definition of marriage, his formulations stimulated two fresh attempts at universal definitions. Prince Peter of Denmark suggested that in light of Leach's propositions, marriage should be defined as "the socially recognized assumption by man and woman of the kinship status of husband and wife" (Peter, Prince of Denmark 1956). The task of the anthropologist would then be to ascertain and delineate the particular rights and obligations associated with these kinship roles in the particular societies being studied.

H. Fischer (1956) called this definition tautological, on the grounds that the Oxford and Webster dictionaries defined "husband" and "wife" respectively by phrases such as "a married man" and "a married woman." In a discussion of Nayar marriage, Gough agrees and reaffirms the heuristic value of a definition of marriage based on "the principle of legitimacy." In an attempt to overcome the difficulties inherent in any formulation which defines marriage as a union of "*a man* and *a woman*," and in an attempt to provide a substantive definition for the concept of legitimacy, Gough suggests that marriage be defined as "a relationship established between a woman and one or more other persons, which provides that a child born to the woman under circumstances not prohibited by the rules of the relationship is accorded full birth-status rights common to normal members of his society or social stratum" (1959, p. 32).

Her effort to refine the older, more general "principle of legitimacy" definition has yielded one which, on close examination, is equally inadequate. Operating with such a definition, no investigator could classify as married any *particular* woman who had assumed the jurally recognized kinship role of wife but who had not borne children. Of course, the conditions under which a child would be accorded "full birth-status rights" *could* be elicited by the investigator. However, for any given case, the researcher would have to await the birth—or perhaps the conception—of a child before he could ascertain whether conditions entailed in the husband–wife relationship had been violated. Furthermore, Gough's definition implies that in any society each person having "full birth-status rights" is the child of a relationship which can be termed marriage. Among various peoples of the world, "full birth-status rights" accrue to persons born of relationships which *are not* recognized as marriage according to prevailing jural rules.

If a universal definition of marriage is to be formulated, it would seem that the one proposed by Prince Peter should serve as a model. Fischer's criticism of Prince Peter's definition may be disregarded, since dictionary definitions are usually unsatisfactory bases for discussions of roles. The roles of husband and wife must be defined in terms of the essential rights and obligations and the behavioral attributes entailed in them in any particular society. Gough and Fischer are justified in their concern that confronted with different forms of mating, the anthropologist employing Prince Peter's definition would be unable to decide which institutions should be referred to as "marriage," as "concubinage," etc. However, if the statement were modified so as to define marriage as the *jurally valid and socially (or publicly) recognized* assumption of the kinship roles of husband and wife, there would be few or no problems concerning the distinction between marriage and its socially recognized alternatives. Such a proviso emphasizes that the publicly acknowledged kinship roles created by marriage—as opposed to its alternatives—derive support from the juridico–political domain of the society. Of course, there may be more than one jurally valid way of assuming the roles of husband and wife—as is the case in some present-day African states which recognize marriages contracted according to one or more sets of "customary laws" as well as marriages contracted in accordance with legal codes based on European models.

It would appear that the cross-cultural study of marriage must rest on the premise that all societies recognize kinship roles which are founded "in law" as well as those which are based ultimately on actual, assumed, or presumed genetic relationships. Fundamental to the understanding of the concept of "lawfully based" kinship is the fact that human mating is everywhere subject to socially derived regulations. While it is normally expected that marriage will lead to parenthood, the roles of husband and wife need not be defined by reference to children who will come to be regarded as legitimate offspring of individuals in these roles. The roles of husband and wife should be defined in terms of the rights and obligations which attach to them, and marriage must be defined as the lawfully or jurally recognized assumption of these roles.

Choice of spouses

In all societies, socially derived limitations are placed on the range of persons from among whom spouses may be chosen. Regulations which prescribe marriage outside a stipulated group are referred to as *rules of exogamy*. Kin groups such as lineages, or territorial groups such as bands or villages, may constitute exogamous units. Societies possessing corporate unilineal descent groups usually prescribe that a person select as spouse someone from a descent group other than his own. In some cases the selection may be made from among persons within the descent group but outside specified degrees of relationship. Among the Gisu of east Africa, for example, it is the minimal patrilineage, comprising persons who trace their descent from an ancestor three to five generations removed from the oldest living generation, which constitutes the exogamous unit.

Every society prohibits heterosexual mating between certain "close" consanguineal relatives. This prohibition is referred to as the *incest taboo*, and ordinarily it proscribes mating between relatives who stand to each other in the relationships of mother and son, father and daughter, and brother and sister. In many societies the incest taboo is extended to various other kinsmen in the parental and filial generations. Among some royal or ruling groups, as in dynastic Egypt and in Polynesia, relatives ordinarily prohibited from mating may be preferred as marriage partners. The mating of close relatives is also permitted in some societies on specified ritual occasions.

A *rule of endogamy* exists where the field of possible spouses is limited to persons within an individual's territorial and/or social group. The castes of traditional India are the most often cited example of endogamous groups. Other societies also prescribe marriage among persons of the same social stratum. Among the Swazi of south Africa, where lineage exogamy prevails and where royalty marries royalty, there are frequent subdivisions of the royal lineage so as to make possible otherwise prohibited marriages. A number of studies indicate that in the absence of explicit prescriptions, it is posssible to discover endogamous tendencies within social or territorial groups of various size and scale.

In addition to proscriptions associated with incest and exogamy, societies usually prohibit marriage between certain other categories of persons. In some instances slaves cannot marry freemen. Where age sets are a feature of social organization, as among the Nuer, a man may be prohibited from marrying the daughter of another man in his age set.

Societies which prescribe that a spouse be chosen from among one or more designated categories of persons have been said to possess *closed marriage systems*. Those in which such prescriptions do not exist have been characterized as having *open marriage systems*. The designation of a marriage system as "closed" is not meant to suggest total absence of choice in the process of mate selection. This point is illustrated by Klass (1966), who shows that in Bengal (and in other parts of India), while caste affiliation delimits the broad category of persons from which a spouse is chosen, a man who must choose husbands for his daughters or "wards" does so from within a relatively narrow selection of eligible males known to certain of his kinsmen.

The most frequently cited closed marriage systems are found among the indigenous societies of Australia. Some of these societies, for example the Kariera, practice what anthropologists term "symmetrical cross-cousin marriage," wherein pairs of

local groups engage in the "simultaneous or nearly simultaneous exchange of women" (Leach 1961a, p. 59). The male members of the two groups concerned exchange their "sisters" for "wives." Ideally, a male ego marries his mother's brother's daughter, who may at the same time be his father's sister's daughter and the sister of his own sister's husband.

Among the Murngin of Australia is found a type of asymmetrical cross-cousin marriage wherein marriage with the mother's brother's daughter is preferred and marriage with the father's sister's daughter is proscribed. In this society and others practicing matrilateral cross-cousin marriage, a localized descent group gives wives to one or more other such groups and receives wives from a different set of such groups. In Murngin society there are descent groups which are allied through ties of kinship and ritual. Moreover, each pair of such allied groups stands in balanced opposition to another similar pair with which it exchanges women on a *nonexclusive* basis. Since men do not marry within their own moiety, any male ego and his mother's brother are in opposite moieties. Ego's group *receives* wives from and gives prestations to his mother's brother's group. Ego's mother's brother's group receives wives from and gives prestations to the group with which ego's group is allied. This latter group is the one containing ego's mother's mother's brother, who, of course, stands in the relationship of mother's brother to ego's own mother's brother. It can be said, therefore, that in Murngin society the "mothers' brothers" stand in the relation of "wife givers" to their sisters' sons (see Leach 1961a, pp. 68–72).

Claude Lévi-Strauss, Edmund R. Leach, Louis Dumont, and others have discussed the economic and political implications of this and other forms of "cousin marriage." Leach (1961a, pp. 54–104) has shown that where matrilateral cross-cousin marriage prevails, there exist permanent status differences between wife-giving and wife-receiving groups and has demonstrated that the marriage system is not insulated from other domains in the society. In fact, he argues that marriage alliance in such situations is but one of "many continuing relationships between paired local descent groups." Political and economic relationships are reflected in and sustained by the system of matrilateral cross-cousin marriage.

In open marriage systems, the only group of persons unequivocally proscribed as marriage partners are those to whom the incest taboo is extended. There are no normative prescriptions relating to groups from which spouses should be chosen. Nonetheless, many studies indicate that demographic, ecological, and sociological factors enter into the choice of spouse. Age, residential propinquity, class, religion, ethnicity, education, and occupation have been isolated as important determinants in the choice of marital partners. Likewise, parents and peer groups are often instrumental in delimiting for each individual the field from which a spouse will be chosen.

The transfer of rights at marriage

Marriage involves the allocation of rights and obligations among the parties to the agreement. A number of anthropologists have attempted to classify the various rights which are known to be allocated at marriage in different societies.

In discussing the jural element in marital and other kinship relations, Radcliffe-Brown (1950, p. 12) distinguishes personal rights (*jus in personam*) from possessive rights (*jus in rem*). A right *in personam* confers on an individual or a group the power to order the performance of certain duties by another individual or group. Rights *in rem* constitute claims on an object or person such that any encroachment on the object or person constitutes a violation of the "possessor's" rights. In most societies husbands and wives have personal rights in each other: either spouse may claim certain duties of the other. It is also common to find that a husband has "possessive" rights in relation to his wife. Her seduction, her abduction, or her murder would constitute a serious infringement of her husband's rights.

In an important contribution to the literature on marriage, Laura Bohannan (1949) distinguishes two classes of rights in females which may be allocated at marriage. Rights *in uxorem* (rights in a woman as wife) are distinguished from rights *in genetricem* (rights in a woman as mother).

In her discussion of Dahomean marriage, Bohannan shows that rights over a woman's sexual powers and certain of her domestic services were transferred from a woman's patrilineage to the man or woman who made the appropriate bride-wealth payments. In most of the "types" of Dahomean marriage, rights to any children a woman might bear during the course of her marriage were also transferred from a woman's patrilineage to that of her husband. Distinct classes of marriage payments were necessary to the transfer of each of these two classes of rights. However, in certain "types" of marriage, rights *in genetricem* were retained by the woman's natal patrilineage; this might occur in cases where a lineage was faced with a shortage of male heirs and one of the daughters of the lineage was given in marriage to

a man who agreed to make all the bride-wealth payments except those which would have given him jural authority over children of the marriage. Moreover, the marriage of a woman of the royal lineage never involved the transfer of rights *in genetricem* to the lineage of her husband (L. Bohannan 1949).

Even though it is usually rights in women which are in the forefront of marital negotiations, Leach has pointed out that marriages also serve to allocate rights in and over men (1961a, pp. 107–108). He suggests that a marriage may serve to do the following:

(1) To establish the legal father of a woman's children.

(2) To establish the legal mother of a man's children.

(3) To give the husband a monopoly of the wife's sexuality.

(4) To give the wife a monopoly of the husband's sexuality.

(5) To give the husband partial or monopolistic rights to the wife's domestic and other labor services.

(6) To give the wife partial or monopolistic rights to the husband's labor services.

(7) To give the husband partial or total rights over property belonging or potentially accruing to the wife.

(8) To give the wife partial or total rights over property belonging or potentially accruing to the husband.

(9) To establish a joint fund of property—a partnership—for the benefit of the children of the marriage.

(10) To establish a socially significant "relationship of affinity" between the husband and his wife's brothers.

Leach thus focuses attention on rights in and regarding children, sexuality, domestic and economic services, and property. In the last instance, he suggests that marriages may establish between groups of men mutual interdependencies which could entail any of the above rights as well as others of a political nature.

Where there are corporate kin groups, the allocation of rights at marriage is usually effected by and between at least two such groups. In the case of first marriages, it is usual that the groups into which the husband and wife were born are parties in this rearrangement of social relations.

Where recruitment to the corporate kin groups is based on patrilineal descent, normally the rights over a woman's sexuality and procreative capacities that are held by her natal group are transferred at marriage to the groom and his natal group. Thus, whereas prior to marriage any sexual offense against a woman constitutes a violation of rights held by *her* kin group, after marriage such an offense is an infringement of the groom's rights. Similarly, whereas children born to a woman outside marriage would fall under the jural authority of her natal kin group, those born after marriage are subject to the authority of, and have rights in, the groom's kin group.

Total rights over the bride's domestic and economic services are seldom transferred from her natal group to her husband or his kin group. The woman herself, as an adult member of the society, may retain some control over the dispensing of these services. Often her kin group retains the right to call upon these services. Among the Yoruba of Nigeria, for example, rights in the bride's sexuality, rights over her procreative powers, and partial rights over her domestic services are acquired at marriage by the groom and his patrilineage. However, a woman maintains control over her economic powers and resources, and her natal lineage retains the right to call upon her domestic services in certain circumstances. She is called upon to buy and prepare food at times when deities associated with her lineage must be propitiated, and on the death of a member of her lineage, she is expected to be of service in various ways.

This raises another point: in most societies possessing corporate patrilineages, a married woman does not usually relinquish all her rights in her natal lineage. She may retain some proprietary rights therein, and she usually remains under the religious protection of her lineage ancestors. Moreover, a woman's lineage may have the right to reclaim control over her sexual and procreative powers should there be a breach of the marital agreement on the part of her husband. While these statements are generally true, there are some patrilineal societies in which a married woman becomes virtually "absorbed" into her husband's lineage. According to Gluckman (1950), a married woman among the Zulu of south Africa had virtually no rights outside her husband's lineage; once a woman was married, her natal lineage forfeited virtually all authority over her.

Whatever rights are transferred to the husband or his lineage may be temporarily or permanently reallocated by him or his lineage. The most common example of this is the practice of "wife-lending" found among the Kipsigis and others. The fact that a man may permit another to have access to his wife's sexuality is proof of his monopoly over her sexual capacities. In some societies, a man

who is impotent may choose a sexual partner for his wife in order that she may bear children. Where this is so, the husband is the lawful father of the children, even though he is not the genitor. Where a female is permitted to assume the role of husband, she bestows her rights of sexual access to her wife on a man of her own or of her wife's choice.

In matrilineal societies, rights over the procreative capacities of women are held in perpetuity by their kin groups while partial or total rights in their sexuality are transferred at marriage to their husbands. Customarily, the husbands also attain rights to the domestic services of their wives. Among the Bemba of east central Africa, for example, a husband has monopoly over his wife's sexuality, but the children of any marriage belong to their mother's matrilineage and are therefore under the jural authority of the adult males of that group. A wife keeps her husband's house and contributes her labor to his agricultural pursuits.

Marriages and the exchanges of goods and/or services occasioned thereby are sometimes processual events extending over considerable periods of time. The rights and obligations entailed in the marriage may be allocated in serial fashion, the timing of their transfer being dependent on the transfer of the appropriate goods and services. In such cases, the exchange of goods and services may commence during the period of betrothal and continue even after the formal transfer of certain rights has taken place.

Where goods and services are exchanged as part of the marriage procedure, certain of these may be regarded as necessary prestations without whose exchange a transfer of rights will not take place. Others are contingent prestations which, although part of the contract, are not essential to the exchange of jural authority and the assumption of marital rights and obligations. As Fortes says, they constitute the "means of winning and preserving the goodwill of those with the power to transfer marital rights" (1962, p. 10).

The most general terms used to describe prestations entailed in the marital contract are those of *bridewealth* (or bride-price) and *dowry*. The former refers to gifts presented by the groom's kin group to that of the bride, and the latter describes gifts made by the bride's kin group to that of the groom. The dowry is the more familiar to Westerners, since for centuries it has been a part of the marriage contract in Europe. However, both bridewealth and dowry have been reported for various parts of the world.

Throughout history, the transfer of rights at

marriage has been enshrined in ritual and ceremony. This is a correlate of the fact that marriage transactions are always "publicly" acknowledged. The ceremonies which take place in effect call forth "the public" to bear witness to the lawfulness of the transactions. The sanctions which emanate from the jural domain of the society are strengthened by the incorporation of rituals associated with the religious realm of the society.

Concurrent marriages. The transfer of rights at marriage and the rituals associated with this transfer signify the assumption of new roles by the parties involved. In societies which permit *polygyny* or *polyandry*—marriages entailing a plurality of wives or of husbands, respectively—one of the partners to a marriage assumes the role of co-wife or co-husband along with the role of husband or wife.

In polygynous marriages, the husband usually acquires the same categories of rights in each of his wives. In patrilineal societies, a man is the legitimate father of all his wives' children, even though his rights over the wives' sexuality may be assigned to or "usurped by" other men. The children of polygynous marriages may or may not have equal claims on their father's property. In any case, each wife considers herself the guardian of her children's rights within the family created by the polygynous marriage.

Where polyandry is practiced, by definition a man does not have exclusive rights in his wife's sexuality. He may or may not have claims over the children which she bears him. Among the Sinhalese, rights over the wife's sexuality are partially vested in the first husband. The sexual rights of the other husbands are exercised with the consent of the first husband and the wife. A husband has claims over those of the wife's children whom he has fathered, and the children have legitimate claims over the property of their respective fathers. All the children have equal claims to the properties owned by their mother.

Among the Nayar of south India, a ritual marriage ceremony, called the *tāli* rite, bestowed upon a group of men of appropriate caste the right of access to a woman's sexuality. The completion of the *tāli* rite marked a girl's transition to womanhood. Thereafter, when she attained appropriate age, she could begin to enter into relationships, termed *sambandham* unions, with a number of men, for whom she might bear children. Rights over a Nayar woman's procreative powers were retained by her matrilineage, which had jural authority over her children. Nonetheless, in order for a child to have "full birth-status rights" in his

mother's lineage, he had to have an acknowledged father. A man acknowledged the paternity of a child by bearing certain expenses associated with its delivery. This man could be any one of those with whom the mother had entered into a *sambandham* union. In cases of doubtful paternity, a woman's current "visiting husband" could be forced by an assembly of persons in the neighborhood to make the birth payments. "But if no man of appropriate rank could be cited as potential father, woman and child were expelled from their lineage and caste" (Gough 1959, p. 30).

The levirate and the sororate. In many societies, an individual may assume the role of husband or wife in order to secure rights for a kinsman. Where the "true" *levirate* prevails, upon the death of a husband, it is the duty of one of his brothers to marry the widow, and any children born to the union are counted as the progeny of the deceased man. Certain of the "ghost marriages" found among the Nuer resemble the levirate. A man could marry a woman "to the name of" a brother who died childless, and the offspring of the union would be designated as children of the deceased. These practices differ from the custom of adelphic widow inheritance, wherein a man marries his deceased brother's widow and bears children who are counted as his own. Where the "true" *sororate* prevails, the husband of a barren woman marries her sister, and at least some of the children born to the union are counted as those of the childless wife. The term "sororate" is also used in reference to the custom whereby, upon the death of a wife, her kin supply a sister as wife for the widower. In the latter case, however, any children born to the woman are recognized as her own.

Affinal relationships. The transfer of rights at marriage not only signals the couple's assumption of new conjugal roles but also serves to establish or perpetuate affinal relationships between consanguineal kinsmen of the spouses. Often associated with affinal roles are behavioral attributes commonly subsumed under the categories of "joking relationships" and "avoidance relationships." Radcliffe-Brown (1952, pp. 90–116) has argued that the respect implied in avoidance practices and the formalized disrespect demonstrated by joking relationships are expressions of alliance or consociation. The actors in roles characterized by joking or by avoidance have divergent interests which could generate conflict between them and thereby undermine the bases of their common interests. The institutionalization of avoidance and joking serves to minimize the chance of the development of openly hostile relations between the parties.

The most widespread of the avoidance practices are those which restrict contact between a husband or wife and the mother-in-law and/or father-in-law. Such restrictions on contact may also extend to actual or classificatory brothers or sisters of the father-in-law or mother-in-law. Among the patrilineal Swazi of south Africa, a wife is prohibited from coming into face-to-face contact with her husband's father and those of his male relatives of the same generation resident in the compound. A man behaves in similar fashion toward his mother-in-law, but the likelihood of such contact is minimized by their residence in different compounds and often in different villages.

Joking relationships most commonly exist between a man or woman and affinal relatives of opposite sex in the spouse's generation. These relationships are characterized by the use of intimate names, the use of language otherwise considered lewd or abusive, and, in some cases, by indulgence in sexual play.

Affinal relatives are often expected to give assistance to one another in times of exigency. In many societies where political functions are vested in roles defined primarily by kinship criteria, affinal relatives serve to minimize open conflict between their respective consanguineal kin groups. They might serve, as among the Tiv of Nigeria, as emissaries of peace in cases of latent or open conflict between two lineages.

The linkage of individuals through marriage leads to the creation of new groups or, in Nadel's terminology, to the creation of new sets of bounded social relationships and thereby constitutes a phase in the developmental cycle of kin groups. As Radcliffe-Brown has pointed out, the eventual result of most marriages is that new sets of individuals are linked through common descendants.

Ultimately, the fission of kin groups can often be traced to relations generated by marriage. This process is evident in many societies where lineages (or, for that matter, ramages) are a feature of social organization. When adult members of a lineage segment occupy a common residence along with their spouses and children, the process of incorporation of additional coresidents through marriage often eventually leads to the founding of households in other locations. In the course of time, the founders of such households and their descendants may come to form new lineage segments.

Postmarital residence

In some societies, spouses are expected to live together throughout the period of their marriage; in others, they may be members of separate domestic groups and only visit each other's residences.

The "residence rules" outlined by anthropologists refer to situations in which husbands and wives are members of the same domestic unit. *Neolocal* residence predominates when couples establish independent domestic units after marriage. Residence is characterized as *virilocal* when most couples in a society join a domestic group in which the husband resided prior to marriage or in which he rather than the wife has proprietary or other claims. Residence is called *uxorilocal* when couples join the domestic group to which the wife was attached prior to the marriage or in which the wife rather than the husband has claims. The above terms may be compounded with others to describe more precisely the nature of the domestic group joined by the couple. Thus, *viripatrilocal* residence refers to domicile in a domestic group whose core includes the groom's father. *Uxorimatrilocal* residence refers to domicile in a group whose core includes the bride's mother. The term *avunculocal* is used to describe residence in a group whose core includes the groom's mother's brother.

Data collected by Goodenough (1956) and J. L. Fischer (1958) among the Nakanai of New Britain show that the classification of postmarital residence patterns is not as straightforward as some might assume. Their data also illustrate that there is no simple correlation between particular residence rules and particular rules for recruitment to descent groups. Goodenough shows that in this matrilineal society, a man takes his bride to live in the village in which his father resides. The couple lives there so long as the groom's father is alive, and they may remain after the father's death, particularly if the father is without sisters' sons who would be his jural heirs. More often, however, after the father's death, the couple moves to the residence of the husband's matrilineage, in which he has hereditary land rights. A man whose father is deceased takes his bride to live with the group which includes the man who acted as father-surrogate at the time of the marriage. Goodenough shows that even where ideal residence patterns suggest one or more prevailing modes of residence, the actual choices which couples make may depend on economic and other factors.

Fischer, who also worked on the island of Truk and who arrived at a classification of residences significantly different from Goodenough's, has suggested that residence be elicited for individuals than rather for married couples. He suggests that every person in a household has a "kin sponsor" and that his relationship to this sponsor most appropriately describes the residence pattern for that individual.

While Fischer's suggestion has some merit for the classification of residence patterns for entire populations, attention cannot be shifted from the fact that in most societies the major spatial arrangements of individuals are associated with marriage. Moreover, the kinds of rearrangements which do occur have important implications for many kinds of social relations. It has been shown, for example, that the study of the developmental cycle of domestic groups touches on virtually all aspects of social structure and that postmarital residence patterns are crucial to the understanding of the development of domestic groups (Goody 1958).

Alternatives to marriage

Marriage is a process or event signifying the assumption of the roles of husband and wife in accordance with jural tenets prevalent in the society or stratum of society to which the parties belong. In contemporary societies, marriages are contracts which must be formally legitimized by the state. A state may provide that for purposes of inheritance, or for other specified purposes, persons who are not legally married to each other but who share a common domicile and who otherwise demonstrate a claim to conjugal status may be accorded some or all rights associated with legal marriage. Similarly, a state may choose to recognize marriages contracted according to rules formulated prior to its existence by some or all of the groups which constitute it. Such is the case in various parts of the world where formerly autonomous or semiautonomous political entities have come together to form modern nation-states.

Unions other than lawful marriage are known to have existed in stateless societies as well as in states which did not make the legitimization of marriages their official concern. Yet it seems particularly characteristic of modern societies that there are individuals who, for various reasons, assume some or all of the obligations and rights associated with the roles of husband and wife without entering into legal marriage. Reference has already been made to the fact that one of the crucial ways in which such unions differ from marriage is that they do not create lawful kinship ties between consanguineal relatives of the couple.

These "consensual unions" occur in different frequencies in different modern societies. In the United States, in the Caribbean, and in other areas where such unions occur with relatively high frequency among certain socioeconomic classes and/or ethnic groups, research has centered primarily on family organization, and consensual unions are often regarded as but one aspect of over-all "family instability." The result is that while many hypotheses have been offered to account for the matrifocal or matricentric family which, in some areas, is one structural correlate of consensual unions, few students have offered hypotheses which explicitly attempt to account for the origin and/or persistence of such unions.

M. G. Smith (1962) has presented a wealth of statistical data in support of his hypothesis that specific mating patterns underlie the various forms of family organization in the Caribbean. He has demonstrated that the pattern of consensual mating underlies the matrifocal family in that area. However, he does not deal with the origin and persistence of the mating patterns themselves. Nevertheless, the data suggest that demographic and economic factors are important determinants of these patterns. For example, where the sex ratio is altered by the necessity that males migrate to find work, women often enter into extramarital unions with single or married men who remain behind. Such alliances may or may not entail coresidence.

Consensual unions may constitute a stage in the development of domestic groups and as such are not so much alternatives as preludes to marriage. In parts of the Caribbean where great prestige is attached to church marriages followed by festivities requiring the outlay of large sums of money, couples often assume the roles of husband and wife by mutual consent until such time as they can afford a religious marriage ceremony. Thus, many couples establish a common domicile and bear children before they enter into matrimony "before the eyes of man and of God."

This raises an important point. Even though, in most parts of the modern world, marriages may be contracted without religious ceremonies, historically marriage was the concern of religious institutions before it became the official concern of the state, and most religious doctrines still include prescriptions and proscriptions regarding marriage. Where the influence of religious tradition is particularly strong, civil marriages may be regarded as little more than alternatives to or complements of "true marriage." One of the consequences of this, as evidenced in parts of the Caribbean, is that couples enter into extramarital relationships until such time as they can finance the religious and convivial ceremonies as well as fulfill the legal requirements for marriage.

Marital stability and divorce

The ambiguities entailed in the concept of marital stability have been succinctly stated by David Schneider:

Stability may be defined in terms of the change of rules or expectations over time or in terms of the degree to which the rules or expectations are conformed to. Stable marriage may be defined as stable jural relations irrespective of conjugal relations, as stable conjugal and jural relations, or simply as stable conjugal relations. (1953, p. 56)

Thus, divorce, defined as the lawful dissolution of jural ties established at marriage, may occur relatively infrequently even though separation and other breaches in conjugal relations occur relatively frequently. In traditional Nuer society, the jural bonds established by marriage were stable; divorce, signified by the return of bridewealth, was rare. On the other hand, conjugal separation was relatively frequent. Max Gluckman (1950) was one of the first anthropologists to deal with the factors which contribute to the jural stability of marriage in preindustrial societies. His data on the Lozi and the Zulu led him to the hypothesis that the stability of jural relations established by marriage is correlated with the presence of patrilineages. He argued that where the "principle of father-right" prevailed, as among the Zulu, there was a complete and final transfer of women into their husbands' lineages (from which their children obtained their legal rights), and he suggested that this fact accounted for the virtual absence of divorce in such societies.

In a reconsideration of the Gluckman hypothesis, Fallers pointed out that not all patrilineal societies provide for the absorption of women into their husbands' lineages. He suggests that where women retain rights in their natal patrilineages, patriliny contributes to the jural *instability* of marriage by dividing the loyalties of spouses. Fallers (1957) found among the Busoga a relatively high incidence of divorce, which he attributed in part to the fact that loyalties to natal lineages undermined the bonds established at marriage.

Leach (1961a, pp. 114–123), Cohen (1961), and others have contributed to the discussions of marital stability begun by Gluckman, Schneider, and Fallers. However, there is yet to be undertaken the quantitative and comparative analyses required for a definitive statement on the determinants of stability in the jural aspects of marriage. Whether the aim is to isolate the determinants of differential rates of divorce within a single society or to account for the differences in the divorce rates reported for various societies, care must be taken to insure that the data utilized are in fact representative of the populations discussed. Moreover, more attention must be given than has been in the past to the limits of the utility of numerical data, which, at best, can be considered reliable for relatively short time spans.

The separation of spouses is usually taken as an index of instability in conjugal relations. However, it should be obvious that separation can only be taken as indicative of the disintegration of conjugal bonds when the coresidence of spouses is a societal norm. Even in these cases, separation does not always signal instability in conjugal relations. Among the Yoruba, it is common to find women living and working in one place while their husbands live and work in another. So long as these women are not known to have committed adultery, and so long as they fulfill certain responsibilities to their husbands and their husbands' lineages, their conjugal relations are not necessarily impaired.

The distinction drawn by Schneider between stability in conjugal relations and stability in the jural aspects of marriage relations is useful in the analysis of marriage in contemporary societies. For example, it would be useful to make such a distinction in discussions of marriage patterns in the Caribbean and in the United States. As has been pointed out, among some of the lower-class populations in these areas, consensual mating is common. Not all the parties to consensual unions are persons who have never been legally married. In fact, where the economics of divorce are a deterrent to the lawful dissolution of marriage, consensual unions are often an alternative to divorce and remarriage. Hence, the jural relations established at marriage are often maintained even though conjugal relations are completely or partially severed.

Most of the societies whose marriage systems are described in the anthropological literature are now incorporated into independent states. The very existence of these states signals changes in the rules regarding the establishment of marital contracts, since all contemporary states reserve the right to define what types of union constitute legal marriage.

There is general agreement that the economic and demographic changes taking place in the "developing areas" are also effecting changes in traditional marriage systems. However, Goode (1963) has pointed out the difficulties involved in isolating cause–effect relationships between changes in a society's family patterns, including marriage, and changes in its economic organization. Considerable refinement in research strategies is necessary before it will be possible to state with confidence the extent to which, the precise ways in which, and the specific points at which the spread of industrial technologies and the growth of cities impinge upon or serve to undermine traditional family structures and marriage patterns.

Some of the studies of marriage found in the anthropological literature provide convenient points of departure for investigations of changes in the rules and behavior associated with marriage in different parts of the world. However, it is obvious that analyses of changing patterns of marriage require the collection of a larger body of quantifiable data than is available in most existent anthropological studies of marriage. Whereas most of the marriage systems described in the anthropological literature lent themselves to representation in terms of mechanical models, such models are becoming increasingly inadequate as representations of particular systems and as bases for comparative studies. The rules governing the establishment of marriage contracts, the factors influencing the choice of spouses, the rights and obligations entailed in conjugal roles, and the behavior of persons in these roles are sufficiently variable in any one system to require partial or total representation by means of statistical models. With the construction of such models, we can begin the assessment of the directions and rates of change in marriage systems and the isolation of the specific variables which account for these changes.

GLORIA A. MARSHALL

BIBLIOGRAPHY

BOHANNAN, LAURA 1949 Dahomean Marriage: A Revaluation. *Africa* 19:273–287.

BOHANNAN, PAUL 1963 *Social Anthropology*. New York: Holt.

BRITISH ASSOCIATION FOR THE ADVANCEMENT OF SCIENCE 1951 *Notes and Queries on Anthropology*. 6th ed. London: Routledge. → The first edition was published in 1874. The sixth edition was revised and rewritten by a committee of the Royal Anthropological Institute of Great Britain and Ireland.

CHRISTENSEN, HAROLD T. (editor) 1964 *Handbook of Marriage and the Family*. Chicago: Rand McNally.

CLARKE, EDITH 1957 *My Mother Who Fathered Me: A Study of the Family in Three Selected Communities in Jamaica*. London: Allen & Unwin.

COHEN, RONALD 1961 Marriage Instability Among the Kanuri of Northern Nigeria. *American Anthropologist* New Series 63:1231–1249.

EVANS-PRITCHARD, E. E. 1951 *Kinship and Marriage Among the Nuer*. Oxford Univ. Press.

FALLERS, L. A. 1957 Some Determinants of Marriage Stability in Busoga: A Reformulation of Gluckman's Thesis. *Africa* 27:106–123.

FISCHER, H. T. 1956 For a New Definition of Marriage. *Man* 56:87 only.

FISCHER, JOHN L. 1958 The Classification of Residence in Censuses. *American Anthropologist* New Series 60:508–517.

FORTES, MEYER 1959 Descent, Filiation and Affinity: A Rejoinder to Dr. Leach. *Man* 59:193–197, 206–212.

FORTES, MEYER (editor) 1962 *Marriage in Tribal Societies*. Cambridge Papers in Social Anthropology, No. 3. Cambridge Univ. Press.

GLUCKMAN, MAX 1950 Kinship and Marriage Among the Lozi of Northern Rhodesia and the Zulu of Natal. Pages 166–206 in A. R. Radcliffe-Brown and Daryll Forde (editors), *African Systems of Kinship and Marriage*. Oxford Univ. Press.

GOODE, WILLIAM J. 1963 *World Revolution and Family Patterns*. New York: Free Press.

GOODE, WILLIAM J. (editor) 1964 *Readings on the Family and Society*. Englewood Cliffs, N.J.: Prentice-Hall.

GOODENOUGH, WARD H. 1956 Residence Rules. *Southwestern Journal of Anthropology* 12:22–37.

GOODY, JACK R. 1956 A Comparative Approach to Incest and Adultery. *British Journal of Sociology* 7:286–305.

GOODY, JACK R. (editor) 1958 *The Developmental Cycle in Domestic Groups*. Cambridge Papers in Social Anthropology, No. 1. Cambridge Univ. Press.

GOUGH, E. KATHLEEN 1959 The Nayars and the Definition of Marriage. *Journal of the Royal Anthropological Institute of Great Britain and Ireland* 89:23–34.

KLASS, MORTON 1966 Marriage Rules in Bengal. *American Anthropologist* New Series 68:951–970.

LAWRENCE, WILLIAM; and MURDOCK, GEORGE P. 1949 Murngin Social Organization. *American Anthropologist* New Series 51:58–66.

LEACH, EDMUND R. 1961a *Rethinking Anthropology*. London School of Economics and Political Science, Monographs on Social Anthropology, No. 22. London: Athlone.

LEACH, EDMUND R. 1961b Asymmetric Marriage Rules, Status Difference, and Direct Reciprocity: Comments on an Alleged Fallacy. *Southwestern Journal of Anthropology* 17:343–351.

LÉVI-STRAUSS, CLAUDE 1949 *Les structures élémentaires de la parenté*. Paris: Presses Universitaires de France.

LOWIE, ROBERT 1933 Marriage. Volume 10, pages 146–154 in *Encyclopaedia of the Social Sciences*. New York: Macmillan.

MALINOWSKI, BRONISLAW (1929) 1962 Marriage. Pages 1–35 in Bronislaw Malinowski, *Sex, Culture and Myth*. New York: Harcourt.

MOGEY, JOHN (editor) (1962) 1963 *Family and Marriage*. Leiden (Netherlands): Brill. → First published in Volume 3 of the *International Journal of Comparative Sociology*.

PETER, PRINCE OF DENMARK 1956 For a New Definition of Marriage. *Man* 56:48 only.

RADCLIFFE-BROWN, A. R. 1950 Introduction. Pages 1–85 in A. R. Radcliffe-Brown and Daryll Forde (editors), *African Systems of Kinship and Marriage*. Oxford Univ. Press.

RADCLIFFE-BROWN, A. R. 1951 Murngin Social Organization. *American Anthropologist* New Series 53:37–55.

RADCLIFFE-BROWN, A. R. (1952) 1961 *Structure and Function in Primitive Society: Essays and Addresses.* London: Cohen & West; New York: Free Press.

RADCLIFFE-BROWN, A. R.; and FORDE, DARYLL (editors) 1950 *African Systems of Kinship and Marriage.* Published for the International African Institute. Oxford Univ. Press.

SCHNEIDER, DAVID M. 1953 A Note on Bridewealth and the Stability of Marriage. *Man* 53:55–57. → For the ensuing discussion on this topic, see the articles numbered 122, 223, and 279 in Volume 53 of *Man,* by E. E. Evans-Pritchard, Max Gluckman, and E. R. Leach, respectively; see also the articles numbered 96, 97, and 153 in Volume 54 of *Man,* by Max Gluckman, William Watson, and E. R. Leach, respectively.

SCHNEIDER, DAVID M. 1965 Some Muddles in the Models: Or, How the System Really Works. Pages 25–85 in Conference on New Approaches in Social Anthropology, 1963, Cambridge, *The Relevance of Models for Social Anthropology.* Edited by Michael Banton. Association of Social Anthropologists, Monograph No. 1. London: Tavistock.

SMITH, M. G. 1953 Secondary Marriage in Northern Nigeria. *Africa* 23:298–323.

SMITH, M. G. 1962 *West Indian Family Structure.* Seattle: Univ. of Washington Press.

WINCH, ROBERT; McGINNIS, ROBERT; and BARRINGER, HERBERT (editors) (1953) 1962 *Selected Studies in Marriage and the Family.* Rev. ed. New York: Holt.

III
MARRIAGE ALLIANCE

All societies prohibit marriage with certain relatives, but some societies complement this prohibition by prescribing, or preferring, marriage with other relatives. In this way two kinds of cousins are sometimes distinguished, marriage being prohibited between those who are children of siblings of the same sex ("parallel cousins"), while it is prescribed between children of siblings of opposite sex ("cross-cousins"). This disposition is generally accompanied by exogamy. This article attempts to sum up recent developments in the theory of cross-cousin marriage.

Descent and alliance

The expression "marriage alliance," in which "alliance" refers to the repetition of intermarriage between larger or smaller groups, denotes what amounts to a special theory of kinship, a theory developed to deal with those types of kinship systems that embody positive marriage rules, though it also affords certain general theoretical insights regarding kinship. Two points may be noted at the outset: (1) The combination of the positive marriage rule with exogamy, or at the very least with a prohibition against marriage between parallel cousins, is essential to the type of system under description here; a preference for marriage with

the father's brother's daughter, as found among some Islamic peoples, is a quite different phenomenon. (2) The approach here presented is essentially common to several writers, though an element of personal interpretation is inevitable.

In the initial stages of kinship studies, the reconstruction of fanciful marriage rules (or mating arrangements) as having supposedly existed in the past was widely used in order to explain seemingly strange ways of classifying relatives (kinship terminologies). This practice has brought discredit, in the eyes of some, to the study of both marriage rules and terminologies. In 1871 Lewis Henry Morgan made two assumptions: (1) terminology reflects behavior, and hence, (2) if a terminology cannot be understood from present behavior, it must be because the behavior it reflects belongs to the past. [*See the biography of* MORGAN, LEWIS HENRY.]

Quite apart from the difficulty of reconstructing past behavior, anthropological thought in this matter is still ethnocentric. The underlying assumption is that all peoples entertain the same *ideas* about kinship; their classifying of relatives in different ways is, therefore, due to differences in *behavior.* Fully excusable in Morgan, such an assumption is less so today.

W. H. R. Rivers recognized the link between an actual marriage rule (symmetrical cross-cousin marriage) and a certain type of terminology (often called "bifurcate merging"). For Rivers, the marriage rule was the cause, the terminology the effect, and he saw his task as explaining the marriage rule itself. [*See the biography of* RIVERS.] Once again, terminology reflects behavior, and again historical speculation is called in, this time to discover the "origin" of one item, which is in fact essentially a normative trait. In our time the different features of a kinship system are, in practice, often considered in isolation or are hierarchized according to what is assumed to be their degree of reality or determinativeness. This tendency, if not found in such crudity as in the past, still exerts considerable pressure even on the best minds, and that it constitutes a major obstacle to the understanding of certain kinship systems can be shown by the example of Australian kinship, a classical subject for kinship theory. In Australian section systems, descent is overstressed; the reasons that may elsewhere justify this emphasis are here misplaced, for it prejudices the consideration of other elements in the system.

In writing about Australian kinship systems, authors vie with each other in stressing that in

KARIERA

ARANDA
(North)

AMBRYM
(Balap)

Figure 1

symmetrical cross-cousin marriage arrangements, double descent is always present or implied. This is unobjectionable in itself, but in the literature it is accompanied by a bias which makes itself obvious by repetition, whether it be in B. Z. Seligman's attempt to reduce the "type of marriage" to "forms of descent" (1928, p. 534), however strange the latter forms may appear, or in Radcliffe-Brown's overemphasis upon descent, or in Murdock's outbidding of Radcliffe-Brown in this respect. Radcliffe-Brown was not content with finding an underlying matrilineal exogamy in his classic Australian patrilineal systems and with seeing in what is now called "double descent" a widespread principle of Australian kinship. He claimed that his second kind of exogamous group actually "existed," whereas he had only inferred it (1931, pp. 39, 439); the point is insisted upon by Goody (1961, pp. 6 ff). It is perplexing later on to find Murdock opposing Radcliffe-Brown, while praising the same discovery in others; but the crux of the matter is that in Murdock's opinion Radcliffe-Brown had not gone far enough in stressing descent and descent groups, for Radcliffe-Brown had maintained, at another level, the primacy of individual relationships and marriage rules over the arrangement of groups (Murdock 1949, pp. 51 ff.).

Actually, the hypothesis of underlying matrilineal exogamy among the Kariera and Aranda accounts for the allocation of alternate generations to different groups. Among them, the patrilineal group is conceived not as a unity over a continuous series of generations but as a duality made up of two alternate generation-sections, called by different names and following different marriage rules (the grandson falling back, so to speak, into the grand-

father's section). This is the simple, concrete sociological fact, widespread in Australia. If we take this for granted, together with intermarriage between the named sections, we can in each case draw a simple diagram of the whole tribe. In Figure 1 the sign [=] denotes intermarriage in both directions, the letters A, B, etc., represent patrilineal groups, and the numbers 1 and 2 are used for the two alternating generation-sections in each patrilineal group. The system of Ambrym (Balap) is easily represented in the same fashion (Deacon 1927). All three systems represent variations on the same theme, the number of patrilineal groups being respectively two, four, and three, the number of sections four, eight, and six. Each of the three systems may be conceptualized as forming a single whole through a regular chain of intermarriage and patrilineal descent. The differences in the arrangement follow necessarily from the numbers of groups (for details, see Dumont 1966). I do not pretend that a second unilineal principle cannot be said to underlie these systems, but only that the above is a simpler view of them. Let us now turn to the general theory that, like the above analysis, recognizes intermarriage as a basic element in those systems which possess a preferential or prescriptive marriage rule.

Lévi-Strauss

We must neglect the scholars who had previously advanced the distinction and description of the types of cross-cousin marriage (e.g. Fortune 1933; Wouden 1935) and start with the general theory of Lévi-Strauss. His monumental book *Les structures élémentaires de la parenté* (1949) goes far beyond our limits. Josselin de Jong (1952) has provided an able summary of the book, while Leach (1961) and Needham (1960) have sympathetically, but sharply, criticized its detail. Our concern here is only with its leading ideas.

From the present point of view, the work is first of all a comparative study of positive marriage rules, informed by a general theory of kinship. Preferential marriage rules and marriage prohibitions are accounted for within an integrated body of theory. The prohibition of incest is recognized as universal; it is seen as a basic condition of social life. A man cannot take in marriage the women who are his immediate kin; on the contrary, he has to abandon them as wives to others and to receive from others his wife or wives. Lévi-Strauss considers this situation as a universal principle which lies beyond sociological explanation—and which implies an opposition between consanguinity and affinity as the cornerstone of kinship systems. He views marriage as predominantly a process of exchange (between one man and other men or between one domestic group and others), and he sees in positive marriage rules devices through which this exchange is directly regulated, giving rise to what he has called "elementary" structures.

Let us note that a kinship system is viewed here, starting from its basis in the incest prohibition, as an entirety resting on an opposition and not as a mere collection of features in which one feature might, for a priori reasons, be considered to determine the others. Abstractly, a kinship system is taken as combining a number of features (descent, inheritance, residence, affinity), and an effort is made to characterize the whole by the relations that prevail between the different features. Thus, a system is called harmonic if all transmission between generations takes place in one and the same line, dysharmonic if some features are transmitted patrilineally, others matrilineally. The rule of cross-cousin marriage, where it exists, correlates with this. Theoretically three types may be distinguished: bilateral, matrilateral, and patrilateral. In bilateral cross-cousin marriage, the spouse is at the same time mother's brother's child and father's sister's child. Two intermarrying groups exchange women as wives and thus constitute a self-sufficient unit. Lévi-Strauss has called this form "closed" or "restricted" exchange (*échange restreint*) and correlated it with dysharmonic transmission. In opposition to this type, he has stressed the quite different properties and implications of matrilateral cross-cousin marriage. This type had been less clearly recognized by previous writers, though he does not consider the Dutch literature on Indonesia in which the type had been characterized (e.g. Fischer 1935;

1936; Wouden 1935). In this type, a man marries his mother's brother's daughter; a given line B takes wives from a line A and gives wives to a line C, generation after generation. Intermarriage is thus asymmetrical, and if the society is conceived as a number of discrete groups giving and receiving women in marriage, the simplest system is that of a circle: at the end of the series, Z receives from Y and gives to A (called the "circulating connubium" by the Dutch scholars). This is what Lévi-Strauss calls "generalized exchange." In opposition to the closed type, it requires at least three groups and may accommodate any number of groups. This type correlates with harmonic transmission, which may be either matrilineal or patrilineal. Here the identity of the intermarrying group emerges from the network of relationships, for one group is not closely dependent on any other single group, nor are two successive generations distinguished. Relatives belonging to different generations within the same group of affines are terminologically equated. Since intermarriage is directionally oriented—a group does not receive wives from the group to which it gives its daughters—there is a probability of difference of status between wife-givers and wife-takers. For a discussion of the further consequences, see Leach (1961, chapter 3; cf. Fischer 1935).

The third type, the patrilateral, is only cursorily treated in Lévi-Strauss's treatise; it appears there as a kind of abortive crossbreed between the first two types and is omitted here because it is somewhat controversial (Needham 1958b; Lane 1962).

Some of the objections that have been leveled at Lévi-Strauss's theory can be briefly mentioned. One, forestalled by Lévi-Strauss, is that he argues exclusively about viripotestal societies; another is that his idea of marriage is naive, although this is beside the point, since he was actually concerned solely with the forms and implications of intergroup marriage. A more radical criticism can be directed at the fundamental character and explanatory value of "exchange" in Lévi-Strauss's scheme (discussed in Wolfram 1956). To view the prohibition of incest as the basis for the opposition between consanguinity and affinity appears tautological to those who think of consanguinity itself as fundamental and self-explanatory or appears insufficient to those who would like a psychological explanation. Viewing marriage as an exchange may be questioned on two counts. First, it introduces an arbitrary analogy between women and chattels, women being supposed, for instance, to be universally the most prized of "valuables." Second, "exchange" here tends to be given so wide and indeterminate a meaning as to be practically devoid of content. While this is true of "indirect exchange" and even more so of "reciprocity," the notion of exchange is certainly useful within limits. In still another critique of Lévi-Strauss, Homans and Schneider (1955) argue, in the last analysis, that to look at kinship systems as wholes having explanatory value in relation to their parts is to resort to "final causes." This critique has itself been carefully refuted by Needham (1962).

Developments

Since 1949 the Lévi-Straussian theory has been tested and has undergone partial modifications and developments. To mention only the major themes, we have first the clear-cut distinction, advocated by Needham, between prescription and preference in marriage rules. He claims that prescription alone has "structural entailments" in the total social system, and that Lévi-Strauss has dealt only with prescription or at any rate should have done so (Needham 1962). "Prescription" is here defined more as the characteristic of a system than as simply a marriage rule: it involves the combination of a rule prescribing some relatives and prohibiting others, a corresponding terminological distinction, and a sufficient degree of observation of the rule in practice (Needham 1958a, p. 75; 1958b, p. 212). The advisability of the distinction has been challenged by R. B. Lane (1962, p. 497). At first sight the distinction seems justified, and there is no objection to isolating a clear-cut type of "prescriptive alliance." That there is a danger of underestimating the importance of other types is apparent from the exacting criteria by which the author excludes the recognition of forms of patrilateral intermarriage as "prescriptive" in his sense (Needham 1958b). These latter forms, like preferential marriage in general, do have "structural entailments" of a kind, as we shall see. Moreover, the two forms are not easily distinguishable; the distinction, so presented, is more one of levels than of systems (for a recent clarification of this question, see Maybury-Lewis 1965).

The main development has probably been a refinement of the concept of alliance and the substitution of a more structural for a more empirical notion. At the start the theory, although anchored in the notion of complementarity, was in large part concerned with the exchange or circulation of women between the major exogamous components of the society. To begin with, three authors have asserted that the units which may be said to exchange women are, in concrete cases, smaller than the exogamous units. In 1951 Leach sternly insisted—with empirical, if somewhat dogmatic, good sense—that the agents arranging marriages are as a rule the males of the local descent groups, as distinct from the wider exogamous units and from the "descent lines" used in terminological diagrams and often unwittingly reified by the analyst into actual groups (see Leach 1961, p. 56; cf. Needham 1958a). Quite logically, Leach went on to criticize the assumption that a matrilateral marriage rule should necessarily result in the groups intermarrying "in a circle," an idea which Needham, on the other hand, tried to refine (1958a; 1962). A criticism from Berting and Philipsen may also be noted: to be meaningful, they suggest, the "marriage cycles" must be limited in number, and the people themselves must be aware of them (Needham 1961, p. 98). While such "alliance cycles" (Needham) do meaningfully exist in some cases, their existence does not exhaust the function or meaning of marriage alliance. On this all our authors agree, for Lévi-Strauss (1962, p. 333) himself recently recognized—if my interpretation is correct—that "conscious rules" have emerged from recent research as more important than their results in terms of "exchange." Leach had pointed out that, in the absence of cycles, the basic relationship is "one of the many possible types of continuing relationship between paired local descent groups" (1961, p. 101). Elsewhere, while marriage alliance does not result in a system of exchange at the level of the group as a whole, it is an integral part of the system of categories and roles as conceived by the people studied (Dumont 1957, pp. 22, 34).

Needham has gone furthest in submitting Lévi-Straussian structuralism to criticism from the inside and in referring the "mediating" concepts of exchange and reciprocity back to that of (distinctive) opposition (1960, p. 103). The more fundamental "integration" is not that of groups but rather that of the categories as it occurs within the social mind: the marriage rule is part and parcel of this system of ideas. Like everything else, social relationships are defined by classification. Studying the "symbolic order" of the Purum and others, Needham (1958a) found that asymmetrical intermarriage, although it could not function with less than three intermarrying or "alliance groups," can be dualistically conceptualized (wife-givers and wife-takers) in accordance with an over-all dualist scheme. Here are found "structural entailments" different from the group arrangements on which attention had first focused. The expression "marriage alliance" thus covers both the general phenomenon of mental integration and the particular phenomenon of group integration.

In its restricted field this truly structural theory alone transcends the bias inherent in our own culture. Such expressions as "cross-cousin marriage" are technically useful but basically misleading. Real understanding is reached when the marriage rule understood as marriage alliance is seen as giving affinity the diachronic dimension that we tend to associate only with descent and/or consanguinity. By this means we are able to transcend the limitations of thinking based upon our own society and make comparisons in terms of the basic concepts involved (consanguinity and affinity).

Much remains to be done. Certainly the implications of marriage alliance for status, economy, and political organization (i.e., the physiology of the system) should be worked out (Leach 1961, chapter 3). But even regarding the morphology, our analyses are as yet imperfectly structural; we still take too much for granted in the study of terminologies. Before attempting ambitious (re)constructions, the basis in comparative data must be strengthened and extended, and we must obtain a clearer view of the limits of the logical integration of features, or conversely, of the plasticity and tolerance of systems, which can in some cases go so far as to deny in effect the ideological primacy postulated above in principle.

Louis Dumont

BIBLIOGRAPHY

Deacon, A. Bernard 1927 The Regulation of Marriage in Ambrym. *Journal of the Royal Anthropological Institute of Great Britain and Ireland* 57:325–342.

Dumont, Louis 1957 *Hierarchy and Marriage Alliance in South Indian Kinship.* London: Royal Anthropological Institute.

Dumont, Louis 1966 Descent or Intermarriage? A Relational View of Australian Section Systems. *Southwestern Journal of Anthropology* 22:231–250.

Fischer, H. T. 1935 De aanverwantschap bij enige volken van de Nederlands–Indische Archipel. *Mensch en maatschappij* (Amsterdam) 11:285–297, 365–378.

Fischer, H. T. 1936 Het asymmetrisch cross-cousin-nuwelijk in Nederlandsch Indië. *Tijdschrift voor Indische taal-, land- en volkenkunde* 76:359–372.

Fortune, R. F. 1933 A Note on Some Forms of Kinship Structure. *Oceania* 4:1–9.

Goody, Jack R. 1961 The Classification of Double Descent Systems. *Current Anthropology* 2:3–26. → Includes comments by 13 scholars on pages 13–21; see especially R. B. Lane's comments on page 16.

Homans, George C.; and Schneider, David M. 1955 *Marriage, Authority, and Final Causes: A Study of Unilateral Cross-cousin Marriage.* Glencoe, Ill.: Free Press.

Josselin de Jong, Jan P. B. de 1952 *Lévi-Strauss's Theory on Kinship and Marriage.* Mededelingen van het Rijkmuseum voor Volkenkunde, No. 10. Leiden (Netherlands): Brill.

Lane, Robert B. 1962 Patrilateral Cross-cousin Marriage. *Ethnology* 1:467–499.

Leach, Edmund R. 1961 *Rethinking Anthropology.* London School of Economics and Political Science, Monographs on Social Anthropology, No. 22. London: Athlone.

Lévi-Strauss, Claude 1949 *Les structures élémentaires de la parenté.* Paris: Presses Universitaires de France.

Lévi-Strauss, Claude (1962) 1966 *The Savage Mind.* Univ. of Chicago Press. → First published in French.

Maybury-Lewis, David H. P. 1965 Prescriptive Marriage Systems. *Southwestern Journal of Anthropology* 21:207–230.

Murdock, George P. 1949 *Social Structure.* New York: Macmillan. → A paperback edition was published in 1965 by the Free Press.

Needham, Rodney 1958a A Structural Analysis of Purum Society. *American Anthropologist* New Series 60:75–101.

Needham, Rodney 1958b The Formal Analysis of Prescriptive Patrilateral Cross-cousin Marriage. *Southwestern Journal of Anthropology* 14:199–219.

Needham, Rodney 1960 A Structural Analysis of Aimol Society. *Bijdragen tot de taal-, land- en volkenkunde* (The Hague) 116:81–108. → Text is in Dutch and English.

Needham, Rodney 1961 Notes on the Analysis of Asymmetric Alliance. *Bijdragen tot de taal-, land- en volkenkunde* (The Hague) 117:93–117.

Needham, Rodney 1962 *Structure and Sentiment: A Test Case in Social Anthropology.* Univ. of Chicago Press.

Radcliffe-Brown, A. R. 1931 The Social Organization of Australian Tribes. *Oceania* 1:34–63, 206–246, 322–341, 426–456.

Seligman, Brenda Z. 1928 Asymmetry in Descent, With Special Reference to Pentecost. *Journal of the Royal Anthropological Institute of Great Britain and Ireland* 58:533–558.

Wolfram, E. M. S. 1956 The Explanation of Prohibitions and Preferences of Marriage Between Kin. Ph.D. dissertation, Oxford Univ. → See especially Chapter 8, "The Explanation of Incest and Marriage Regulations."

Wouden, F. A. E. van 1935 *Sociale structuurtypen in de Groote Oost.* Leiden (Netherlands): Ginsberg.

MARSH, GEORGE PERKINS

George Perkins Marsh (1801–1882), an American geographer, is known today primarily as the founding father of the conservation movement. His contemporaries regarded him as the most comprehensive American scholar of the time. His enduring contributions to knowledge stemmed from an unusual combination of historical and ecological insights. As a social historian, Marsh broke new ground in treating the story of mankind as the history of the use and misuse of resources.

As an ecologist, he saw the history of nature com-mingled with that of man and traced the motives, the techniques, and the consequences of man's impact on the earth. Although he was not a trained naturalist, Marsh manifested an extraordinary awareness of the fragile interdependence of all aspects of nature, physical and biological, and of their multiform significance for mankind.

The scion of a patrician family in frontier Ver-mont, Marsh graduated from Dartmouth College and practiced law in Burlington, meanwhile en-gaging in business—farming, lumbering, woolen manufacturing, railroad development, marble quar-rying—and in politics. He served in the state legis-lature and for six years in Congress. As a reward for services to the Whig and Republican parties, he was appointed United States minister to Turkey from 1849 to 1853 and to Italy from 1861 to 1882, the latter an unequaled tenure of office. This dip-lomatic career gave him an opportunity to travel widely and made possible the leisure essential for his scholarly work.

Marsh's first contributions were in linguistics. Attracted by new developments in the study of Teutonic languages, folklore, and cultural origins, he edited the first Icelandic grammar in English, delved into the history and literature of Old Norse and related tongues, and became the American promoter for C. C. Rafn's monumental *Antiquitates americanae*, a collection of Icelandic sagas bearing on the Iceland–Greenland–Vinland settlements. Marsh's historical studies of the English language were the standard texts during the 1860s, and he was in continual demand as editor, adviser, and critic of dictionaries, including the *New English Dictionary*. Familiarity with an extraordinary range of source materials in twenty languages made Marsh a first-rate, if not profoundly original, ety-mologist.

His work as a scientific middleman was of more lasting significance. In the House of Representa-tives, Marsh helped to create, to staff, and to shape the Smithsonian Institution, guiding its early ven-tures in archeology and in natural science and guarding its research endowment against congres-sional incursions. He himself added animal speci-mens from Turkey, Egypt, and Palestine to the Smithsonian collections. On his return from Turkey he strongly urged the introduction of camels as beasts of burden in the American West—an enter-prise initially successful but aborted by the Civil War.

A utilitarian zeal directed and inspired Marsh's best work. As early as the 1840s he publicly ad-vocated measures of physical improvement and conservation: the establishment of nurseries for forestry research and the regulation of logging to prevent excessive and flashy runoff and consequent flooding and desiccation. Not until he returned to Italy in 1861, however, did Marsh bring together the materials he had long been collecting into a systematic analysis of man's manipulation of the natural environment. Published in 1864, *Man and Nature* showed how man differs from nature, how nature operates within itself, and what happens to woods and waters, mountains and deserts, when men clear, farm, dam, and build.

In surveying man's impact, conscious and un-conscious, Marsh did not overlook the improve-ments but stressed the accompanying and resulting damage. Technology had enabled man to derange natural balances and might ultimately, Marsh feared, reduce the surface of the earth "to such a condition of impoverished productiveness, of shat-tered surface, of climatic excess, as to threaten the depravation, barbarism, and perhaps even extinc-tion of the species" ([1864] 1965, p. 44). *Man and Nature* was the first book to controvert the Ameri-can myth of an inexhaustible earth. Its immediate impact was more moral than practical, but by 1907, when it had gone through three editions, the basic principles of *Man and Nature* were embodied in the national conservation program.

In geography, Marsh is also important as an early and effective critic of environmental deter-minism, then popularized in the works of Arnold Guyot. How could man be viewed as the product of environment, when man himself had the power to alter that environment—and had in fact done so over most of the earth's surface? The mistakes man had made through ignorance or greed could, Marsh thought, in most cases be rectified by apply-ing scientific principles of land management, by avoiding waste, and by public control of resources.

DAVID LOWENTHAL

[*For discussion of the subsequent development of Marsh's ideas, see* CONSERVATION.]

WORKS BY MARSH

1856   *The Camel: His Organization, Habits, and Uses, Considered With Reference to His Introduction Into the United States.* Boston: Gould & Lincoln.
(1860a) 1885   *Lectures on the English Language.* Rev. ed. New York: Scribner.
1860b   The Study of Nature. *Christian Examiner* 68: 33–62. → An unsigned article.
(1862) 1898   *The Origin and History of the English Lan-guage, and of the Early Literature It Embodies.* Rev. ed. New York: Scribner.
(1864) 1965   *Man and Nature: Or, Physical Geography as Modified by Human Action.* Edited by David Lowen-thal. Cambridge, Mass.: Harvard Univ. Press. → See

the introduction to the 1965 edition by David Lowenthal. Revised editions were published between 1874 and 1907 as *The Earth as Modified by Human Action*.

WORKS ABOUT MARSH

KOOPMAN, HARRY L. 1892 *Bibliography of George Perkins Marsh*. Burlington, Vt.: Free Press Association.

LOWENTHAL, DAVID 1958 *George Perkins Marsh: Versatile Vermonter*. New York: Columbia Univ. Press.

MARSH, CAROLINE C. 1888 *Life and Letters of George Perkins Marsh*. Vol. 1. New York: Scribner.

MARSHALL, ALFRED

Alfred Marshall (1842–1924) is one of the great names in the development of contemporary economic thought, and the book by which he is most widely known—*Principles of Economics*—is one of the high points in the literature of social science. His influence was enormous; so much so that the first 25 years of twentieth-century economics may be described as the "age of Marshall" and subsequent developments as extensions of and countermovements to his influence. Moreover, even when due allowance is made for the natural progress of economic science since Marshall's time, it is remarkable how much of the Marshallian framework remains. These well-known points require restatement because the positive effects of the Marshallian influence are questioned today as perhaps never before. One could agree with criticisms if they were merely objections to the view sometimes expressed that "it's all in Marshall," meaning that little or no progress has been made in economics since he wrote. It would indeed be deplorable if scientific ideas worked out almost one hundred years ago were still the last word. (An analogy with the positions of Marx and Freud is appropriate here.) However, much of the contemporary criticism goes deeper than this; it argues that the Marshallian tradition checked the development of economics by diverting attention from real issues (by which is primarily meant macrotheory) much as Ricardo was alleged to have done in an earlier generation. The merit of these criticisms will be examined carefully later in this article.

Alfred Marshall was born in Clapham—then a leafy London suburb—in 1842. His father, John Marshall, held the respectable middle-class position of cashier in the Bank of England, and the family lived in modest comfort. Marshall's father was of a rather severe, evangelical frame of mind, almost a textbook example of what is loosely called Victorianism, and closely supervised his son's education. This paternal control and repression had a marked and lasting effect on Marshall; his pronounced tendency toward hypochondria, his unwillingness to commit himself unequivocally in print without massive documented qualification, his fear of indolence and idleness, and his ultimate rejection of "pure pleasure" activities (such as mathematics) have their roots in the experiences of his early years. His education was planned as basically a preparation for ordination in the Anglican church. He was expected to go up to Oxford with a classics scholarship, which would lead to a fellowship and a church living. However, he rejected this plan—rebelling not against orthodox theology but against further study of the classics— and with funds borrowed from an uncle proceeded to St. John's, Cambridge, where he read mathematics. Marshall was one of the best mathematics students of his generation in England (in 1865 he was second wrangler in the tripos examination). This is an important point to bear in mind in evaluating his ambivalent attitude toward the use of mathematical methods in economics—in any event, his criticisms were not based on ignorance. Marshall came into economics with much more mathematics training than did Jevons or Walras.

After graduation Marshall was elected to a fellowship in mathematics and gradually came under the influence of a group of philosopher-dons who were increasingly concerned with the social problems of industrial England. Marshall's interests centered initially on philosophy and ethics, which were then still at the frontier of social science, but worry about social conditions and the realization that poverty was at the root of many social evils led him into economics. Indeed, to Marshall the problem of poverty was not only central to the study of economics but its ultimate rationale. As he later wrote in the *Principles*, "the study of the causes of poverty is the study of the causes of the degradation of a large part of mankind" ([1890] 1961, vol. 1, p. 3).

In 1877 he married Mary Paley, a former student of his and one of the first women to be educated at Cambridge. Upon his marriage he was forced to resign his fellowship. He was for a short while principal and professor of political economy at the then University College of Bristol, became a fellow at Balliol in 1883 (after the requirement of celibacy had been eliminated), and the following year returned to Cambridge, to the chair of political economy vacated by Henry Fawcett; there he reigned until his retirement in 1908, when he was succeeded by his star pupil, A. C. Pigou.

Marshall's published output was not large, especially considering that he was active almost until the time of his death. Several books—*The Pure*

Theory of Foreign Trade and *The Pure Theory of Domestic Values* (1879*a*), *Principles of Economics* (1890), *Industry and Trade* (1919), *Money, Credit & Commerce* (1923), and *The Economics of Industry* (1879*b*), written jointly with Mary Marshall (which he tried to have withdrawn for complex personal reasons not bearing on its merit), a handful of articles, mainly reprinted in the *Memorials of Alfred Marshall* (1925), edited by Pigou; and a series of official memoranda and evidence before royal commissions (contained in *Official Papers*, a volume published in 1926) make up his total written contribution.

Marshall's reluctance to commit himself to print —the *Principles* did not appear until he was 48— makes it difficult to assess his originality. Ideas first published in the 1890s, such as Marshall's statement of the theory of marginal utility, had been worked out and presented orally by him in the late 1860s, i.e., before the publication of the theory in the works of Jevons, Walras, and Menger. As J. M. Keynes put it in his famous obituary of Marshall, "The task of expounding the development of Marshall's economics is rendered difficult by the long intervals of time which generally separated the initial discovery and its oral communication to pupils from the final publication in a book to the world outside" (1924, p. 322).

Intellectual background. Efforts to disentangle the various influences on Marshall's thinking as an economist are made difficult by his modesty—his desire to emphasize the continuity of thought—and also by his rather confused accounts of these influences. Marshall's first reading in economics was Ricardo and Mill; he described his early efforts as attempts to translate the ideas of these writers into differential equations. The most important single influence was surely Mill's *Principles of Political Economy* (1848), and a good way to get perspective on Marshall's contribution is to compare the two *Principles*. Also, what little mathematical economics then existed was open to Marshall, although it was not to most of his contemporaries. He clearly learned a lot from Cournot —especially about the use of continuous functions in economics. Thünen's *Der isolierte Staat* (1826–1863), with its hints of marginal productivity analysis, was also influential. German (Hegelian) philosophy and the historical school of economists are commonly mentioned as influencing him (Marshall studied in Germany for a year). However, it is difficult to see concrete evidence of these systems of thought in his work. There is no dialectic and no historicism, although in his concern with empirical investigation he was closer to the histor-

ical school than to the English classical school. His emphasis on the continuity of growth and his perpetual references to biology suggest the influence of social Darwinism—acquired through Herbert Spencer.

Methods

Much of the discussion of Marshallian economics deals with his methods of analysis. These methods are not particular hypotheses or models proposed by Marshall but, rather, represent ways of setting up a problem or partitioning it so that it can be solved. The central Marshallian method is usually termed "partial analysis" or "partial equilibrium analysis" and is often loosely referred to as the *ceteris paribus* approach. The Marshallian partial equilibrium approach is frequently contrasted with the method of general equilibrium associated with Léon Walras, and the contrast is usually considered unfavorable to Marshall. Indeed, this approach is sometimes regarded as one of the major weaknesses Marshall bequeathed to economic science. Since the question of partial versus general equilibrium has loomed so large in the literature, some discussion of the central issues is imperative. As Marshall realized, the general equilibrium approach is not *de facto* a fruitful approach to such practical problems as measuring the effect of an import duty on the price of a commodity or the effect of a fall in the final product price on the demand for a particular grade of labor. It is not very helpful to be told that "everything depends on everything else" and that a change in one parameter will have effects throughout an economic system. Partial analysis is a method by which an economy is partitioned so that the main effects of a parameter shift in a particular micromarket can be highlighted without considering the spillover into other markets; hence, this method also ignores the feedback effects from the spillover. There are, of course, obvious dangers inherent in this method, but the answer lies, not in the general equilibrium approach, but in better specification of the partial model. [*See* ECONOMIC EQUILIBRIUM *and the biography of* WALRAS.]

Let us take a specific example to illustrate the use of the *ceteris paribus* approach of partial equilibrium analysis and the related concept of comparative statics. We can draw up a demand schedule for a commodity and show the amount demanded per unit of time as a decreasing function of the price of the good. The relationship is *ceteris paribus*, i.e., it assumes that other factors influencing demand—such as the price of substitutes—are given, as are factors such as incomes, tastes, and expectations. In a free market, if an equilibrium exists it will be where supply equals demand. If one of the *ceteris paribus* conditions is relaxed, the demand curve shifts, and the new partial equilibrium solution is then considered. This leads to the comparison of the two sets of equilibrium values of the variables under discussion. The method of comparing equilibrium solutions is called comparative statics because it does not permit the tracing of the time paths (between the two points of equilibrium) of the variables involved. [*See* STATICS AND DYNAMICS IN ECONOMICS.]

Marshall's ultimate objective was to develop a full-fledged theory of dynamic change and growth. In the preface to his *Principles* he wrote, "The main concern of economics is . . . with human beings who are impelled, for good and evil, to change and progress. Fragmentary statical hypotheses are used as temporary auxiliaries to dynamical—or rather biological—conceptions: but the central idea of economics, even when its Foundations alone are under discussion, must be that of living force and movement" ([1890] 1961, vol. 1, p. xv). The immediate objective of Marshall's formal analysis was more limited: namely, the comparison of static equilibrium positions. Yet, even within this restrictive framework he was able, by his use of the time-period concept, to approximate dynamic analysis. His approach was to divide the adjustment, say, of price to changing demand or supply conditions into a series of adjustment periods. These periods should be regarded as measured by operational, not clock, time—the market period for one sector or industry may be (in terms of clock time) a longer one than the market period for another industry. The important consideration is which *ceteris paribus* assumptions are relaxed in successive periods.

Marshall's time division is as follows: the market period, the short period, and the long period. The market period takes the production of the commodity in question as fixed, so that supply can vary only if sellers have a reserve price for their own product. The condition for equilibrium (for all time periods) is that the market be cleared, i.e., that demand equal supply. Short-run equilibrium considers supply to be partially adaptable, in the sense that increased production can occur but capital equipment and certain other overhead items are held constant. In modern economics, analysis of this short period with partial adaptation is equivalent to an analysis of the law of variable proportions, although it is not certain that Marshall himself was precisely clear about the distinction between variable proportions and returns to scale. The Marshallian long period allows for optimal capital stock adjustment. The

market is cleared within a framework in which supply can be considered to be fully adaptable because all factors (excluding entrepreneurship) have adjusted to the situation. It was by means of this differential adjustment of supply that Marshall restated, within the supply and demand framework, his theory of value. The classical emphasis on costs is now seen as a particular hypothesis: that in long-run adjustment there are constant returns to scale.

Figure 1 illustrates this. *SS* is the fixed-stock supply curve (on the assumption of zero reserve price); *S'S'* the short-run supply curve and *S"P* the long-run supply curve. With demand at *DD*, the long-run price is *OP*. Now let demand rise to *D'D'*. Then long-run equilibrium price will again be *OP*, but price will pass through the stages *OP"* and *OP'*, and quantity will increase. [*See* DEMAND AND SUPPLY.]

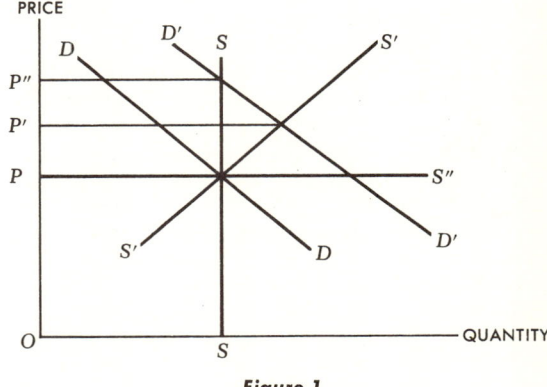

Figure 1

Marshall also hinted at the analysis of a fourth time period, in which factor supplies are allowed to adjust to changes in their underlying determinants. In the absence of innovation, in this period the economy reaches the full equilibrium solution for a stationary state.

Marshall was cautious and basically skeptical about the use of mathematics and theoretical statistics in economics; for better or worse, he did not foresee the mushrooming of mathematical economics and econometrics. The Marshallian attitude—which became embodied in the Cambridge tradition and especially in the work of Pigou and Keynes—is seen in the *Principles*, where the mathematical statements are in footnotes and in a mathematical appendix. The grounds for minimizing the formal use of mathematics in the final presentation (although not in preparation) were twofold: first, the need to communicate; and second—and much more important—the fear that sets of equations necessarily omit or distort many relevant influences and considerations. Marshall set out the matter squarely in a letter to A. L. Bowley dated February 27, 1906:

[A] good mathematical theorem dealing with economic hypotheses was very unlikely to be good economics: and I went more and more on the rules—(1) Use mathematics as a shorthand language, rather than as an engine of inquiry. (2) Keep to them till you have done. (3) Translate into English. (4) Then illustrate by examples that are important in real life. (5) Burn the mathematics. (6) If you can't succeed in 4 burn 3. This last I did often.   ([1925] 1956, p. 427)

Marshall had grave doubts as to the reasonableness of the assumptions underpinning the then existing techniques of theoretical statistics (which meant, basically, regression analysis) when applied to social science data. He had no doubts, however, about the need to be steeped in the empirical facts of any situation under analysis. He always emphasized deep statistical and historical knowledge of the area being investigated and referred again and again to the complexity of economic problems and the naïveté of simple hypotheses. Like Adam Smith, Marshall had a profound knowledge of the workings of economic systems. When asked, for example, by the Gold and Silver Commission of 1887/1888, "Do you speak with knowledge . . . of the working classes?" he replied (somewhat pompously but with all honesty), "I speak from personal observation ranging over many years, and a study of almost everything of importance that has been written on the subject" (*Official Papers*, p. 99).

Marshall's oft-quoted definition of economics—"the study of man in the ordinary business of life"—was not an attempt to demarcate the discipline precisely from other social sciences. Marshall's basic view on the scope of economics is best expressed in the sentence "The less we trouble ourselves with scholastic inquiries as to whether a certain observation comes within the scope of economics, the better" ([1890] 1961, vol. 1, p. 27). He used the term "ordinary business of life" to emphasize the point that economics is not the study of the workings of a fictional economy populated by abstract economic men: it is concerned with the real world around us.

Contributions to theory

Marshall's central theoretical contribution was the working out of the rigorous economics of the stationary state. For Marshall this was not, of course, the ultimate end of economics—it was indeed but the preface. To point the way to the conclusion—the working out of a full-fledged growth model—Marshall interlarded his stationary-state framework with bits and pieces of the dynamic process. It is this mixture that makes Marshall's *Principles* such difficult reading for some.

Theory of demand. Marshall developed utility theory for two reasons: first, to place restrictions on demand functions; and second, to create what he hoped would be powerful tools of welfare economics. The Marshallian demand curve relates the demand for a commodity per unit of time to its own price. The relationship is *ceteris paribus*; in particular, other prices and incomes are assumed constant. There are certain ambiguities in this statement of inclusions within *ceteris paribus*, but for the moment these are set aside. Marshall's generalized "law of demand" states that the price of a good and the quantity demanded are inversely related. This restriction on demand functions is derived a priori from the form of the utility function that he postulated, which is laid out most clearly in the mathematical appendix to the *Principles*. He used an additive, cardinal utility function; this means that one may think of utility as being a measurable quantity (although in practice Marshall spoke of it as being only indirectly measurable, at the margin, by price) and also that the total utility that a consumer derives from his consumption of goods and services is the sum of the individual utilities derived from the consumption of each item in his budget. Symbolically, we have

$$U = \sum_{i=1}^{n} U_i,$$

where U_i is the utility derived from the consumption of the ith commodity and U is total utility.

The basic restriction given by the additive nature of the function is that interrelationships between goods are excluded (all cross-partial derivatives are zero). Further, the law of diminishing marginal utility operates with respect to each good; this means that extra units consumed of a given commodity will increase total utility at a decreasing rate. Thus, the addition to total utility induced by the nth unit of a commodity will be less than the increase in utility induced by the $(n-1)$st unit. In terms of the function above,

$$MU_i = \frac{dU}{dX_i} > 0; \qquad \frac{d^2U}{dX_i^2} < 0.$$

It is assumed that the consumer seeks to maximize utility, given incomes and prices. The principle of substitution comes into full play here. By substituting at the margin, a consumer reaches his maximum utility point. Maximizing the utility function, subject to the budget constraint (i.e., that the quantities of all goods and services purchased multiplied by their respective prices equals total income), yields the well-known Marshallian first-order conditions for a maximum. These can be stated in the following equivalent terms:

(1) $\quad \dfrac{MU_i}{MU_j} = \dfrac{P_i}{P_j}$, $\qquad$ for all i and j,

(2) $\quad \dfrac{MU_i}{P_i} = \dfrac{MU_j}{P_j} = \cdots = \lambda$,

(3) $\quad MU_i = P_i \lambda$, $\qquad$ for all i.

Here P_i represents the price of commodity i, and the constant term λ represents the marginal utility of income. A fall in the price of commodity i must lead to more of the commodity's being bought; this must be so to keep the equalities listed in eqs. (1) to (3). That formulation (as Marshall realized) avoids the implications of the income effects of a price change—this is the purpose of assuming constant marginal utility of income. [See UTILITY.]

Rigorously applied, the Marshallian assumptions appear to restrict elasticities of demand to unity, but it is clear from the body of the *Principles* that Marshall did not contemplate this restriction.

Strictly speaking, a *ceteris paribus* demand curve requires that real income be held constant as price changes, so as to eliminate from the analysis the income effect of the price change. Holding money income constant is insufficient, since the real value of money income is its command over commodities and if commodity prices change, this changes also. Marshall solved this problem intuitively, by talking in terms of money income but postulating small changes in the prices of commodities that make up a small portion of the consumer's budget, so that the error involved in using money income is "of the second order of small quantities" ([1890] 1961, vol. 1, p. 132). Milton Friedman has since put the demand curve on a more satisfactory analytic footing.

But for Marshall the object of demand theory was not just to place testable restrictions on demand functions; he also regarded the demand curve and the allied concept of consumer surplus as powerful tools of welfare economics. We shall consider this aspect after we have looked at Marshall's contribution to production theory and the theory of the firm.

Theory of production. Marshall spoke in terms of "real costs" when considering costs of production. By "real" he meant ultimately the disutility of both the labor and the waiting involved in producing and bringing a commodity to market. The emphasis on real cost seems to contrast with the Austrian notion of opportunity cost, but in fact it

is easy to reconcile the two concepts. In any case, in spite of Marshall's emphasis, he rather too easily assumed the equality of real and money costs and proceeded with his analysis in terms of the latter. Central to his theory of cost and production is the principle of substitution, which works here the same way it does in his consumer theory. The entrepreneur substitutes at the margin until the total cost of a given output is at a minimum or, what is the same thing, until the output from a given set of inputs is maximized. [See COST.]

Marshall was confused about the so-called laws of production and especially about the distinction between what has come to be called "variable proportions" and returns to scale; so, of course, was the whole profession until Viner's classic article of 1931. Marshall tended to compare decreasing returns with increasing returns, as though they were similar. Although he postulated that diminishing returns were historically connected with agriculture and with a situation in which the labor–capital input had grown relative to (fixed) land, he did not see the logical connection between the principle of substitution and the law of variable proportions. Increasing returns, looked at in an analytic manner, occur where increase in output is proportionately greater than the simultaneous increase of all inputs. In the course of his discussion of increasing returns, Marshall made the crucial distinction between internal and external economies, from which the whole notion of externality started. Internal economies are "those dependent on the resources of the individual houses of business" in an industry, while external economies are "dependent on the general development of the industry." Internal economies, where present, produce a falling long-run marginal cost curve for a firm, and hence threaten the stability of competition. Marshall realized this, and his "life cycle" theory of entrepreneurship was meant as a partial explanation of the survival of competition. External economies, on the other hand, are compatible with competition but raise serious welfare problems. [See EXTERNAL ECONOMIES AND DISECONOMIES.]

Central to Marshall's discussion of the theory of the firm is the concept of the representative firm—a notion which is not only tenuous and vague but apparently unnecessary for Marshall's own purposes, as critics like Lionel Robbins were quick to point out. Marshall's definition of the representative firm gets us nowhere; it is only by specifying the problem with which he was trying to cope that we see the purpose of the concept.

Two questions in particular worried Marshall. First, in the real world, firms clearly are capable of expanding at falling marginal cost, yet industries do not become monopolized. Marshall's answer lies partially in the representative firm. The second, a closely related problem, concerns the estimate of the supply price of a product where industry output is taken as a given but the group of firms making up the industry are in a life cycle of birth, growth, decay, and death. According to Marshall's theory, the entrepreneurial life cycle prevents the continuing expansion of any *one* firm—an idea more appropriate to the days of small business than to those of the large corporation, where management is not dynastic. But apart from Marshall's exercise in social evolution, we still have the interesting problem, with disequilibrium at the firm level, of estimating supply price and, more generally, the industry supply curve. In contemporary economics the static solution to these problems, under perfect competition, is to sum the firms' marginal cost curves to obtain the industry supply curve. This supply price is equal to any firm's marginal cost; for Marshall, however, with his continual search for the dynamic solution, this answer was inadequate. A firm picked at random would not necessarily be typical in the sense that its costs would correctly reflect the sustainable degree of efficiency and level of economies for its aggregate output. It might be a firm about to disappear or one in the very early stages of growth. The answer, Marshall believed, was to identify a "typical" or representative firm. [*See* FIRM, THEORY OF THE.]

What is the typical market structure in Marshall's world? Nowhere in his work do we find the perfectly elastic demand curve of the current textbook version of perfect competition. It is clearly not monopoly (for Marshall reserves this case for special treatment), but it is doubtful whether, as has recently been suggested, the typical Marshallian market can be interpreted as monopolistically competitive in Chamberlin's sense. In spite of Marshall's remark that in the short run firms may have to lower price to increase sales, his basic view is that price is a parameter in the typical firm's plans.

Theory of distribution.   Marshall's theory of distribution is outlined on two levels. On the assumption of fixed coefficients (such as Walras assumed in the first edition of the *Elements*), Marshall worked out his theory of joint demand. In this case there is no substitution within a given productive process; the principle of substitution is inoperative, and hence the marginal productivity theory is not applicable. To divide up the total product among the cooperating factors in the case of fixed proportions, Marshall used the law of derived demand: "The demand schedule for any factor of production

of a commodity can be *derived* from that of the commodity by subtracting from the demand price of each separative amount of the commodity the sum of the supply prices for corresponding amounts of the other factors" ([1890] 1961, vol. 1, p. 383). But at best this is a clumsy approach, and it did not represent Marshall's basic position. More generally he worked out a complete marginal productivity theory, and although he expressly denied that it was a theory of distribution, we must take this as typical Marshallian caution. His objections to regarding marginal productivity as a theory of wages were twofold: first, supply conditions must be included in the analysis; and second, to the extent to which labor and capital are in fixed proportions, it is not possible to identify the marginal product.

The concept of quasi rent, which filled an important gap in classical analysis, is also important for Marshallian distribution theory. Rent theory explained the return to fixed land, but there was nothing in classical analysis to explain the return to capital equipment already in existence. Marshall used the term "quasi rent" to explain rewards to any factors in inelastic supply and specifically applied the analysis to capital equipment in the short run. [*See* RENT.]

Equilibrium conditions.   We have already discussed Marshall's division of the problem of price determination into a series of different time-period equilibrium positions. The general rule is that the longer the period of adaptation allowed, the more responsive is supply to price changes. To the extent to which long-run supply is perfectly elastic, Marshall saw a correlation with the classical cost-of-production theory of value. We have still to consider Marshall's conditions for market stability;

Figure 2

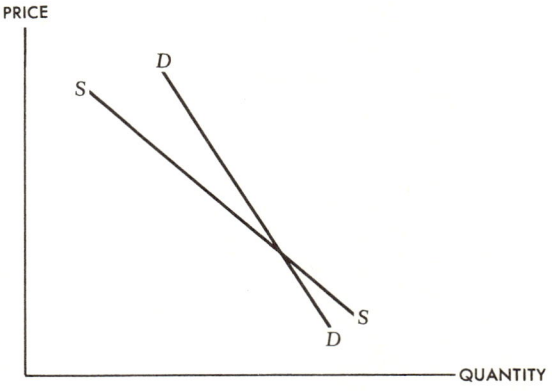

PRICE

QUANTITY

Figure 3

these appear to differ significantly from those laid down by Walras and Hicks, which are commonly studied in elementary dynamics. Marshall's conditions for a micromarket to be stable are as follows: (*a*) for quantity smaller than equilibrium quantity, demand price must be greater than supply price; (*b*) for quantity larger than equilibrium quantity, demand price must be less than supply price.

If a market that has "normal" demand and supply relationships, i.e., a downward-sloping demand curve and an upward-sloping supply curve, is stable in the Walras–Hicks sense, it is also stable in Marshall's sense. Divergences of interpretation occur, however, in other cases. Figure 2 shows a market where both stability conditions are satisfied. At price P_1, which is above equilibrium, excess demand is negative (the Hicksian condition) and quantity bought is less than equilibrium, with demand price, OP_1, greater than supply price, OP_2. The market shown in Figure 3 is stable in terms of Marshall's conditions but unstable in terms of the Walras–Hicks conditions (e.g., for price above equilibrium it has excess demand).

Which specification is correct cannot be determined a priori but is a matter for empirical investigation. It is clear that the two solutions assume different behavioral reactions of buyers and sellers. More important, perhaps, the notion of a supply curve has to be specified much more carefully. [*See* DEMAND AND SUPPLY *and* ECONOMIC EQUILIBRIUM.]

Marshall also attempted to formalize and explain Mill's work on the conditions for equilibrium—and the suitability of equilibrium—in foreign trade. He did this by using the techniques of offer curves. His work in this field was not formally published until 1923, when parts of it were appended to his *Money, Credit & Commerce*. However, it was circulated privately, through the efforts of Henry Sidgwick.

Welfare economics. Marshall's contributions to welfare economics, while suggestive in terms of contemporary thought, contain some of his most doubtful analysis. Here Marshall relaxed his customary caution in the face of complex situations, in an effort to promote certain policy measures. In general his welfare economics supported the classical view that a regime of free markets maximizes welfare (utility). Marshall called this the doctrine of maximum satisfaction; his demonstration consisted of showing that for each micromarket the sum of surpluses is maximized. A monopolized market involves a suboptimal position because the sum of surpluses is lessened. The surpluses summed include both consumer and producer surpluses, or rents. In Figure 4 the free market price is P_0 with quantity Q_0. The sum of consumer surplus and producer surplus is *CAB*. Let the market be monopolized and price and output be P_1, Q_1; total surplus is then reduced to *BCDE*. [*See* CONSUMER'S SURPLUS.]

However, Marshall stated two important exceptions to the doctrine of maximum satisfaction and free competition. First, he considered it to be an empirical fact that although utility is an increasing function of a person's real income, the rate of increase diminishes. As Marshall put it bluntly in the mathematical appendix to the *Principles*, "Every increase in his means diminishes the marginal degree of utility of money to him" ([1890] 1961, vol. 1, p. 838). Thus, it followed that, all other circumstances being the same, a redistribution of income from rich to poor would increase total satisfaction.

Much more important, perhaps, is Marshall's second ground for modifying the doctrine of max-

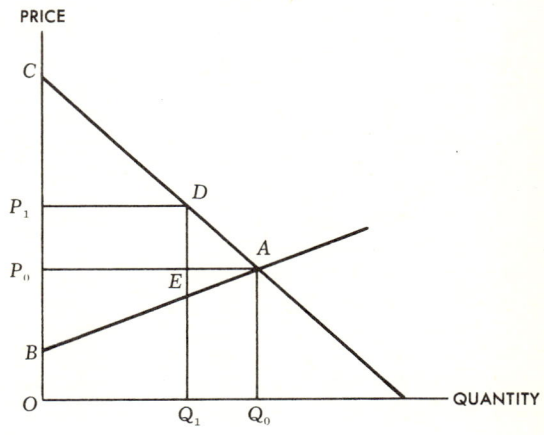

PRICE

QUANTITY

Figure 4

imum satisfaction. This is that satisfaction can be increased by taxing increasing-cost industries and subsidizing decreasing-cost industries. His analysis runs entirely in terms of consumer surplus, with all its weaknesses, and can easily be seen to depend on the slopes of the supply curves. However, the whole theory of externality and divergences between private and social benefits developed from Marshall's discussion, especially his exposition of the decreasing-cost case.

Monetary theory. Marshall is sometimes alleged to have neglected the monetary and, more generally, the aggregative framework within which his theory of value worked. This is a mistaken view. In his *Principles* Marshall is at pains to make clear that the core of that book presupposes a monetary framework, and he deals explicitly with this framework in other contributions. The two important sources for his views on money are *Money, Credit & Commerce*, written toward the end of his life, and, much more important, his *Official Papers*. This latter consists of a series of memoranda and evidence presented before royal commissions.

Official Papers contains the core of Marshall's monetary theory. The most important elements of his contributions in this area are the following: the so-called Cambridge equation and his development of a credit cycle through disequilibrium between real and monetary interest rates. Marshall is often regarded as the founder of the Cambridge approach to monetary theory. In essence, this theory postulates a stable demand function for money, with real income (or wealth) as the prime argument in the function. *Ceteris paribus*, such an approach will give a proportionate relationship between changes in the supply of money and changes in the general level of prices. [*See* MONEY, *article on* QUANTITY THEORY.] This approach was formalized by Pigou (1917) in a famous article [*see the biography of* PIGOU] and elaborated by Keynes in his *Tract on Monetary Reform* (1923). Marshall made it absolutely clear, however, that changes in the other factors—in the volume of activity and the demand for money—may well dominate the relationship, especially in periods of economic crisis. His other contribution to the field is the spelling out of a mechanism connecting real and money rates of interest, through which divergences between the two generate a credit cycle.

The view, mentioned at the beginning of this article, that Marshall diverted economics from a proper consideration of macroeconomics is largely a result of Keynes's treatment of Marshall in *The General Theory* (1936). His treatment there contrasts widely with his assessment of Marshall's monetary economics in his famous obituary of Marshall. The reasons for this dramatic *volte-face* are complex and cannot be discussed here; all that can be said is that in retrospect the "Keynesian revolution" appears to be more an extension of the Marshallian tradition than an attempt to reverse it.

BERNARD CORRY

[*For the historical context of Marshall's work, see the biographies of* COURNOT; JEVONS; MENGER; MILL; RICARDO; THÜNEN; *for discussion of the subsequent development of his ideas, see the biographies of* KEYNES, JOHN MAYNARD; PIGOU; ROBERTSON.]

WORKS BY MARSHALL

(1879a) 1930 *The Pure Theory of Foreign Trade* and *The Pure Theory of Domestic Values*. Series of Reprints of Scarce Tracts in Economic and Political Science, No. 1. London School of Economics and Politcal Science. → Privately printed in 1879.

(1879b) 1889 MARSHALL, ALFRED; and MARSHALL, MARY P. *Economics of Industry*. London: Macmillan.

(1890) 1961 *Principles of Economics*. 9th ed. 2 vols. New York and London: Macmillan. → A variorum edition. The eighth edition is preferable for normal use.

1919 *Industry and Trade: A Study of Industrial Technique and Business Organization, and of Their Influences on the Conditions of Various Classes and Nations*. London: Macmillan.

(1923) 1960 *Money, Credit & Commerce*. New York: Kelley.

(1925) 1956 *Memorials of Alfred Marshall*. New York: Kelley. → Contains essays on Marshall by J. M. Keynes, F. Y. Edgeworth, C. R. Fay, E. A. Benians, and A. C. Pigou; selections from Marshall's writings; and a bibliography of his works prepared by J. M. Keynes.

Official Papers. London: Macmillan. 1926. → Papers dated 1886–1903.

SUPPLEMENTARY BIBLIOGRAPHY

KEYNES, JOHN MAYNARD 1923 *A Tract on Monetary Reform*. London: Macmillan.

KEYNES, JOHN MAYNARD (1924) 1951 Alfred Marshall: 1842–1924. Pages 125–217 in John Maynard Keynes, *Essays in Biography*. New ed. → First published in Volume 34 of the *Economic Journal*. A paperback edition was published in 1963 by Norton.

KEYNES, JOHN MAYNARD 1936 *The General Theory of Employment, Interest and Money*. London: Macmillan. → A paperback edition was published in 1965 by Harcourt.

MILL, JOHN STUART (1848) 1961 *Principles of Political Economy, With Some of Their Applications to Social Philosophy*. 7th ed. Edited by W. J. Ashley. New York: Kelley.

PIGOU, A. C. (1917) 1951 The Value of Money. Pages 162–183 in American Economic Association, *Readings in Monetary Theory*. Philadelphia: Blakiston.

PIGOU, A. C. 1953 *Alfred Marshall and Current Thought*. London: Macmillan.

SCHUMPETER, JOSEPH A. (1941) 1965 Alfred Marshall, 1842–1924. Pages 91–109 in Joseph A. Schumpeter,

Ten Great Economists From Marx to Keynes. New York: Oxford Univ. Press.

Scott, William R. 1925 Alfred Marshall, 1842–1924. British Academy, London, *Proceedings* 11:446–457.

Stigler, George J. 1941 *Production and Distribution Theories: 1870 to 1895.* New York: Macmillan. → See especially Chapter 4.

Thünen, Johann H. von (1826–1863) 1930 *Der isolierte Staat in Beziehung auf Landwirtschaft und Nationalökonomie.* 3 vols. Jena (Germany): Fischer.

Viner, Jacob (1931) 1952 Cost Curves and Supply Curves. Pages 198–232 in American Economic Association, *Readings in Price Theory.* Chicago: Irwin. → First published in Volume 3 of the *Zeitschrift für Nationalökonomie.*

MARSILIUS OF PADUA

Marsilius of Padua (c. 1275–c. 1343) is known primarily as the author of the *Defensor pacis*, a bold antipapal tract dedicated to Emperor Louis IV of Bavaria in 1324 during his controversy with Pope John XXII. Although contemporary condemnations name John of Jandun as coauthor, internal evidence and incongruence with John's known political statements (Gewirth 1948) argue for its ascription to Marsilius alone. The *Defensor* is revolutionary in denying the clergy jurisdiction of any kind and in subordinating them completely to the state. The political concepts it brings to the support of these contentions are neither so "modern" nor so original as has sometimes been claimed. All are anticipated in some fashion somewhere in the long and complex medieval tradition. Yet, because Marsilius' argument leads him to special emphases, and because he richly develops, with ingenious use of Aristotle, ideas briefly enunciated by canonists and by other publicists, he is the first to present in elaborated theoretical form views that were to be fundamental to much of modern political thought. Even though the teaching of the *Defensor* is not free of ambiguity, no other medieval writing offers so vigorous or so complete a theory of popular sovereignty.

Jurisdiction in state and church. Marsilius argued that clerical pretensions to rule destroy the state (*civitas* or *regnum*), which, with its specialization of economic, military, governmental, and priestly "parts," is indispensable to "living and to living well." The survival of the state depends on effective government by a single unified "ruling part" (*pars principans*), and since the proper function of the clergy is not government but teaching (Christ having forbidden them all coercion), clerical rule of any sort, over anyone, destroys the unity of the government and deprives men of "the sufficient life." In this world divine law is without

direct sanction. It is only by authority of the human *legislator* that infractions can be brought to judgment.

All that is "truly law" on earth is the expression of the will of the legislator—the citizens of each community as a whole or their "weightier part" (*valentior pars*), the citizen body including all free adult males. The "weightier part" is weightier through "quality" as well as quantity of persons, but Marsilius argued that the more people who participate in legislation, the better the laws will be. Legislation by the multitude normally results in justice, because all but the singularly malicious or ignorant naturally wish to preserve the state and are able to discern the common benefit and to judge proposals. The legislator also establishes or selects the government or ruler. This may be one man or several but should in almost every instance be elective rather than hereditary. The legislator has the power to correct and even to depose the ruler. Although at times Marsilius seems to imply that the delegation of power to the ruler is all but absolute, his statements on correction and deposition are unequivocal.

Denying the divine institution of the papacy and of the episcopacy, Marsilius provides that in a Christian community the legislator select from candidates those to be priests and bishops, appoint them to pastorates, and control their exercise of office. A general council, elected by the several legislators of the Christian world and composed of both clerics and learned laymen (the laymen voting if the clerics are not unanimous), determines the articles of faith. Only by decree of the human legislator do conciliar decisions become binding. For convenience the council or "the faithful human legislator without a superior" appoints a "head bishop" to act as president and executive secretary of the council. Custom alone argues the choice of the bishop of Rome. Although early in the *Defensor* Marsilius expressed a preference for a plurality of sovereign states, the idea of a "primary" or "universal" "faithful human legislator" and "a ruler by its authority" suggests the empire, and in the *Defensor minor* of 1342, written at the court of Louis, the "human legislator" becomes the "Roman prince."

Formation of Marsilius' views. In the molding of Marsilius' concepts the fifth book of Aristotle's *Politics* played a significant part. Also of importance in the genesis of his attitudes was his youth in Padua, a city sovereign *de facto*, republican in constitution, and often in conflict with the clergy. His being a physician and not a lawyer or theologian no doubt had much to do with the freshness of his attack. Acquaintance with the work of French publicists seems probable from his years at the University of Paris, and familiarity with corporation law, from his position as rector of the university in 1313 (Lewis 1963, p. 564). Although he associated with Averroists, their influence on his ideas of church and state is impossible to ascertain.

Influence. Papal condemnations, including the excommunication of Marsilius (and John of Jandun) in 1327, established the reputation of the *Defensor* for the next three centuries. A principal charge in papal attacks on Wycliffe, and later on Luther, was that they borrowed Marsilius' doctrine. In the circumstances, conciliarist writers used the *Defensor* with caution. It was first printed (in Basel in 1522) to serve the Protestant cause, and in 1535 Thomas Cromwell paid most of the cost of printing an English translation. Through Richard Hooker, who cited it and shared some of its doctrines, it probably had an influence on John Locke, and so, indirectly, played an important part in carrying ideas of popular sovereignty from the medieval to the modern world.

JANE E. RUBY

[*For the historical context of Marsilius' work, see the biographies of* AQUINAS; ARISTOTLE; GERSON.]

WORKS BY MARSILIUS

(1324) 1951–1956   *Marsilius of Padua: The Defender of Peace.* Translated and introduced by Alan Gewirth. 2 vols. New York: Columbia Univ. Press. → Volume 1: *Marsilius of Padua and Medieval Political Philosophy.* Volume 2: *The Defensor pacis.* Volume 2 was written in 1324, and first printed in 1522 as *Defensor pacis.*
(1342) 1922   *The "Defensor minor" of Marsilius of Padua.* Edited by C. Kenneth Brampton. Birmingham (England): Cornish.

SUPPLEMENTARY BIBLIOGRAPHY

GEWIRTH, ALAN   1948   John of Jandun and the *Defensor pacis. Speculum* 23:267–272.
LAGARDE, GEORGES DE   (1934) 1948   *Marsile de Padoue, ou le premier théoricien de l'état laïque.* 2d ed. Paris: Presses Universitaires de France.
LEWIS, EWART   1963   The "Positivism" of Marsiglio of Padua. *Speculum* 38: 541–582.
PRÉVITÉ-ORTON, CHARLES W.   (1935) 1937   Marsilius of Padua. British Academy, London, *Proceedings* 21: 137–183.
SCHOLZ, RICHARD   1937   Marsilius von Padua und die Genesis des modernen Staatsbewusstseins. *Historische Zeitschrift* 156:88–103.

MARX, KARL

Karl Marx (1818–1883) was born in Trier in the Prussian Rhineland. His alienation from his family when he had scarcely passed adolescence foreshadowed the social isolation of his later years.

His father, a lawyer, was as concerned as he was impressed with his son's "demonic genius," as he called it, and feared that young Marx's passion for poetry and philosophy would consume him both physically and morally. The elder Marx and his wife were Jewish, but for social reasons they were converted to Christianity. The younger Marx's awareness of his ethnic background aroused in him a certain self-consciousness; this may have been one source of his sense of marginality, his ambivalence toward society, and eventually of his conflicting qualities—thinker and prophet, scientist and moralist.

Although Marx received his doctorate in philosophy from the University of Jena at the age of 23, his association with the Young Hegelians, and with Bruno Bauer in particular, precluded his appointment to a university position in Germany; indeed, Bauer lost his own post at the university in Bonn as a result of questioning the historicity of the New Testament. Marx thus became a "degraded bourgeois," deprived of a stable source of income and dependent for his livelihood and that of his wife and children on the generosity of his lifelong friend, Friedrich Engels, the son of a wealthy cotton manufacturer. (Marx's wife, Jenny von Westphalen, was of noble parentage but had no dowry.) At the age of 25, Marx left Germany and, except for a brief stay in Cologne in 1848–1849, lived the rest of his life in exile: in Paris from 1843 to 1845, in Brussels from 1845 to 1848, and finally in London. As early as 1845 he renounced his Prussian citizenship, and since he failed to acquire British citizenship by naturalization, for the greater part of his life he was something of a pariah.

Intellectual background. Marx's childhood and youth fall in that period of European history when the reactionary powers of the Holy Alliance were attempting to eradicate from post-Napoleonic Europe all traces of the French Revolution. There was, at the same time, a liberal movement in Germany that was making itself felt. The movement was given impetus by the July Revolution in France, and its chief representatives were the poets of the Junge Deutschland, among them Ludwig Börne and Heinrich Heine. In the late 1830s a further step toward radical criticism was made by the Young Hegelians, that group with which Marx became formally associated when he was studying law and philosophy at the University of Berlin.

Although he was the youngest member of the Young Hegelians—who included, in addition to Bauer, such thinkers as Ludwig Feuerbach, Arnold Ruge, and Moses Hess—Marx inspired their confidence, respect, and even admiration. They saw in him a "new Hegel," or rather a powerful anti-

Hegelian, who might successfully turn the dialectics of the master against his own conservative teachings in the fields of religion, politics, and law. Marx had already showed his determination to do so in his doctoral dissertation (1841), which dealt with the philosophical positions of Democritus and Epicurus; especially in the supplementary notes, he made his earliest attempt at a radical, albeit muted, criticism of Hegel, asserting, as Epicurus had argued against Democritus, that what is needed is a morally clear way of life rather than ideology or empty hypotheses.

The intensive study of Spinoza, Leibniz, and Hume provided Marx with a spiritual armory for the elaboration of a positive conception of democracy that went far beyond the notions held at that time by radicals in Germany. It was from Spinoza rather than from Hegel that Marx learned to reconcile necessity and freedom. Therefore, when he undertook to destroy Hegel's metaphysics of "the State," Marx was well prepared to integrate a rational ethics with his own sociological and revolutionary doctrine. His early rejection of Hegel's political philosophy was unconditional and permanent; yet stripped of its "idealistic" content, Hegel's dialectic continued to influence Marx as a way of analyzing his subject matter, namely society.

Marx's adherence to a radical view of democracy was also based on the study of such historical events as the revolutions in England, France, and America. From these historical studies he concluded that democracy must normally and inevitably culminate in communism, following a transitory stage of proletarian democracy (the "dictatorship of the proletariat"). After his conversion to communism Marx began his prolonged studies of economics; but while he was still developing from a liberal into a communist, he learned more from Spinoza and Feuerbach, Saint-Simon and Babeuf, Thomas Hamilton and Tocqueville, Weitling and Proudhon, Owen and Fourier, than from Smith or Ricardo.

Contributions to socialist thought. Although the epoch to which Marx belonged has its beginnings in the French Revolution, its historical dimensions coincide with those of the whole era of industrial and social revolutions and extend into our own time; hence the lasting appeal of a body of teachings that is by no means free from theoretical ambiguities.

The originality of Marx's thought lies in his immense efforts to synthesize, in a critical way, the entire legacy of social knowledge since Aristotle. His purpose was to achieve a better understanding of the conditions of human development and with this understanding to accelerate the actual process by which mankind was moving toward an "associa-

tion, in which the free development of each is the condition for the free development of all" (1848). The desired system would be a communist society based on rational planning, cooperative production, and equality of distribution and, most important, liberated from all forms of political and bureaucratic hierarchy.

This dual commitment—to scholarly understanding and to political action—created constant difficulty for Marx. He was often aware that his intense passion for reading and studying interfered with his activity on behalf of the political movement with which he identified himself. In his scholarly work the exposition and analysis are frequently interrupted by partisan outbursts of irony and sarcasm, by bitter indictments of the capitalist class and the social system based upon its dominance.

Political economy was only one of the social-scientific disciplines that Marx intended to explore and then subject to criticism; the others were law, morals, and politics. He intended to treat each of these disciplines (and perhaps others also) in "separate pamphlets." But the thoroughness with which he undertook his studies of the great economists and the delays in his scholarly work that arose from the need to make a living as a penny-a-liner prevented him from elaborating even one of these projects. *Capital*, subtitled "A Critique of Political Economy," although a work of enormous dimensions, is the fruit of only partially completed research. However, before the age of thirty, Marx produced a number of works which together provide a relatively adequate outline of his "materialist conception of history." Among these, the most important are *The Holy Family* (1845a), *The German Ideology* (in collaboration with Engels, 1845–1846), *The Poverty of Philosophy* (1847), and *The Communist Manifesto* (1848). To these must be added an unfinished work, first published in 1932 with the title *Economic and Philosophical Manuscripts of 1844* (see 1844a), which shows with particular clarity the connections between the various ideas Marx was later to elaborate in *Capital*.

In these works, Marx sketched out his theory of society and history. He repudiated Hegelian and post-Hegelian speculative philosophy, and building on Feuerbach's anthropological naturalism, he developed instead a humanist ethics based on a strictly sociological approach to historical phenomena. Drawing also on French materialism and on British empiricism and classical economics, Marx's theory sought to explain all social phenomena in terms of their place and function in the complex systems of society and nature, without recourse to what he considered metaphysical explanations ("primary causes"). Clearly outlined in these early writings, this eventually became a mature socio-logical conception of the making and development of human societies.

At the beginning of *A Contribution to the Critique of Political Economy* (1859), Marx summed up in a dozen aphorisms the general results of the investigation he had undertaken in the 1840s and asserted that these results were the "guiding thread" of his further studies. Here are the beginning and the end of this justifiably celebrated and controversial passage:

In the social production which men carry on they enter into definite relations that are indispensable and independent of their will; these relations of production correspond to a definite stage of development of their material powers of production. The sum total of these relations of production constitutes the economic structure of society—the real foundation, on which rise legal and political superstructures and to which correspond definite forms of social consciousness. The mode of production in material life determines the general character of the social, political and spiritual processes of life. It is not the consciousness of men that determines their existence, but, on the contrary, their social existence determines their consciousness. . . . In broad outlines we can designate the Asiatic, the ancient, the feudal, and the modern bourgeois methods of production as so many epochs in the progress of the economic formation of society. The bourgeois relations of production are the last antagonistic form of the social process of production . . . ; at the same time the production forces developing in the womb of bourgeois society create the material conditions for the solution of that antagonism. This social formation constitutes, therefore, the closing chapter of the prehistoric stage of human society. ([1859] 1913, pp. 11–13)

Marx's "materialistic method" is well exemplified by his treatment of the concept of "alienation"—a spiritual concept in Hegel's philosophy that had already been modified in Feuerbach's anthropology. In the "Paris Manuscripts of 1844" (1844*a*), Marx conceived of alienation as a phenomenon related to the structure of those societies in which the producer is divorced from the means of production and in which "dead labor" (capital) dominates "living labor" (the worker). A systematic elaboration of the concept appears in *Capital* under the heading "fetishism of commodities and money." But the ethical germ of this conception can be found as early as 1844 in the two essays Marx published in the *Deutsch–französische Jahrbücher:* "On the Jewish Question" (1844*b*) and "Contribution to the Critique of Hegel's Philosophy of Right" (1844*c*). There Marx unequivocally rejected and condemned "the state" and "money," and he invested the proletariat with the "historical mission" of emancipating society as a whole. The identity of Marx's early

political views with the theoretical analysis in *Capital* is evident in the manner in which the argument of *Capital* is brought to a close. Describing the "historical tendency of capital accumulation," Marx quoted the prophetic statement in the *Communist Manifesto:* "What the bourgeoisie . . . produces, above all, are its own gravediggers. Its fall and the victory of the proletariat are equally inevitable." Similarly, in ending the preamble of his inaugural address to the International Working Men's Association (1864), Marx launched the same summons that ends the *Manifesto:* "Workingmen of all countries, unite!"

Although this summons seems to contradict his assertion of the "historical necessity" of communism, in the very real unity of sociology and ethics the contradiction vanishes. The proletariat is enjoined to unite in order to transform society, and its recognition of the consequences of such unity for the achievement of its historical mission becomes part of the "historical necessity" of the process; by this recognition, the proletariat confirms the process.

In accordance with the maxim, formulated in his "Theses on Feuerbach" (1845*b*), that man must prove the truth of his thinking in practice, Marx neglected his scientific work for long periods in order to participate in the class struggles of his time. He did so not without regret, for he considered his scholarly studies the most valuable form of participation in the social struggle. His more direct intervention was, of course, mainly literary in character—his several hundred articles in German, British, and American newspapers and journals; and the various addresses and manifestoes he wrote for the Working Men's International. Among his writings on the political events of his time are some unquestionable masterpieces of this genre: *The Class Struggles in France* (1850); *The Eighteenth Brumaire of Louis Bonaparte* (1852); *Secret Diplomatic History of the Eighteenth Century* (1856); *Herr Vogt* (1860); "Address" to the First International (1864); *The Civil War in France* (1871); the *Critique of the Gotha Programme* (1875). In every line he wrote, whether intended for publication or not, his ultimate singleness of purpose is clearly evident.

This is particularly true of his magnum opus, *Capital*, whose scope transcends its outline of political economy as well as its critique of economics. At the same time that Marx defined the ultimate aim of the work as "[laying] bare the economic law of motion of modern society," he had in mind a thorough and systematic criticism of a type of society, namely capitalism. In spite of its truncated character, *Capital* is monumental in its construction and grandiose in its purpose. It is in *Capital* (even more than in Marx's philosophical writings) and particularly in the posthumously published *Grundrisse* (1857–1858), that the serious student will find the key to Marx's dialectical method as it contrasts with the method of Hegel. Moreover, *Capital*, to a greater extent than Marx's political writings, reveals the reason for the celebrated "failure" of Marxian predictions: the reason lies not so much in the inadequacy of Marx's social and economic theory as in the expectations he based on it. However, in the last analysis these expectations rest on the individual search for perfection and liberty.

Marx's influence. Marx's teachings have been expanded and diffused in two ways that are, in effect, opposed to each other. The first is "Marxism" as an ideology, i.e., a dogmatic systematization of Marx's ideas for political purposes, expressed as party doctrine or state religion, and disseminated by its supporters; the second form is a growing body of research and scholarly activity in various branches of the social sciences that has been illuminated by Marx's theoretical discoveries. When Marx himself noticed that his admirers were showing the first signs of "Marxism," he rebuked them unequivocally and asserted, as Engels reported in several letters (e.g., to Bernstein and Conrad Schmidt): "I am not a Marxist." However, he tolerated and even supported Engels' efforts to win acceptance for *Capital* in academic circles. Inadvertently, Engels thus became the first "Marxist" and the cofounder of the Marxist ideology, whose manifesto was Engels' *Anti-Dühring* (1878). Marx was thereafter acclaimed as the founder of the new science of socialism and was credited by Engels with two scientific discoveries—the materialistic concept of history and the theory of surplus value.

Engels' efforts to popularize Marx's ideas led to the schematization of some of Marx's basic propositions; he claimed to have extended Marx's methodological and critical approach, so that it embraced nature as well as history. With their followers, the distortion of Marx's thought went further still. While Marx considered his general theory to be a scientific method of investigating the transient nature of every economic system and placed his confidence in proletarian class consciousness as an agency of change, "Marxism," particularly in its Leninist version, has become a party ideology. This transformation is reflected in the substitution of the coercive direction of political elites for the spontaneous activity and con-

sciousness of the producing class; paradoxically, these "Marxist" elites have transformed Marx's theoretical propositions into norms of political action.

The relevance of Marx's theories for the social sciences has been the subject of much fruitful debate. In a kind of osmotic process, Marx's theories have been incorporated into the social sciences at the same time that they have stimulated important countertheories. A significant event in this process was Sorel's critique of Durkheim (Sorel 1895), in which he praised the "materialist theory of sociology" according to which the various social systems—political, philosophical, religious—must be considered as interdependent and as having a common base; Sorel believed that what Marx assigned to sociology as its major subject for investigation was the underlying system of production and exchange and the conflict of classes.

Marxist social science developed in Germany, stimulated by the work of Rudolf Stammler (1896), and it was in response to Stammler that Max Weber began his influential studies of the Marxian thesis concerning the relationship between the economy and other social institutions. In Italy Marxist theories were discussed in several universities under the leadership of Antonio Labriola, Giovanni Gentile, and Benedetto Croce, and in France such discussions were stimulated by François Simiand. Thomas G. Masaryk, while he was a university professor in Prague, produced a large work of analysis and criticism of Marx's sociological method and hypotheses (1898). The international character of the "debate with the ghost of Marx" may be further illustrated by the fact that in tsarist Russia numerous books and periodicals paid increasing attention to "scientific socialism" even before Plekhanov and Lenin appeared on the scene. In the United States the influence of Marx's ideas is evident in the writings of Albion W. Small, George H. Mead, Thorstein Veblen, and Joseph Schumpeter, among others.

Since World War I, Marx's theories have not only stimulated sociological work in general but have also given impetus to a new field of sociological inquiry, the sociology of knowledge, exemplified by the works of Max Scheler and Karl Mannheim.

The process of incorporating Marx's ideas into the social sciences in Western countries contrasts vividly with the unsure attempts by "Marxist" regimes to invent and decree a "Marxist" sociology. The efforts of these regimes unwittingly confirm one of Marx's major hypotheses—that the dominant ideas of a society are those of its ruling class.

MAXIMILIEN RUBEL

[*See also* COMMUNISM; ECONOMIC THOUGHT, *article on* SOCIALIST THOUGHT; MARXISM; MARXIST SOCIOLOGY; SOCIALISM; *and the biographies* BERNSTEIN; DURKHEIM; ENGELS; HEGEL; HUME; LENIN; LUKÁCS; MANNHEIM; MASARYK; MEAD; PROUDHON; SAINT-SIMON; SCHELER; SCHUMPETER; SIMIAND; SMALL; SOREL; SPINOZA; TOCQUEVILLE; VEBLEN; WEBER, MAX.]

MARX'S WRITINGS

WORKS BY MARX

(1841) 1927–1929 Über die Differenz der demokratischen und epikureischen Naturphilosophie. Pages 3–144 in Karl Marx and Friedrich Engels, *Historisch-kritische Gesamtausgabe: Werke, Schriften, Briefe.* Section 1, Volume 1, part 1: Werke und Schriften bis 1844. Frankfurt am Main (Germany): Marx-Engels Verlag. → Written in 1841, the text with some notes was first published posthumously in 1902.

(1843) 1953 Kritik des hegelschen Staatsrechts. Pages 20–149 in Karl Marx, *Die Frühschriften.* Stuttgart (Germany): Kröner.

(1844a) 1964 *Economic and Philosophic Manuscripts of 1844.* New York: International Publishers; London: Lawrence & Wishart. → Written in 1844 but first published posthumously in German in 1932. Sometimes referred to as the "Paris Manuscripts of 1844."

(1844b) 1963 On the Jewish Question. Pages 1–40 in Karl Marx, *Early Writings.* London: Watts. → First published in Volume 1/2 of the *Deutsch-französische Jahrbücher.*

(1844c) 1963 Contribution to the Critique of Hegel's Philosophy of Right: Introduction. Pages 41–59 in Karl Marx, *Early Writings.* London: Watts. → First published in Volume 1/2 of the *Deutsch-französische Jahrbücher.*

(1844d) 1963 *Early Writings.* Translated and edited by T. B. Bottomore. London: Watts. → First published in German. Contains "On the Jewish Question"; "Contribution to the Critique of Hegel's Philosophy of Right"; and "Economic and Philosophic Manuscripts."

(1845a) 1956 *The Holy Family.* Moscow: Foreign Languages Publishing House. → First published as *Die heilige Familie.*

(1845b) 1935 Theses on Feuerbach. Pages 73–75 in Friedrich Engels, *Ludwig Feuerbach and the Outcome of Classical German Philosophy.* New York: International Publishers. → First published in German.

(1845–1846) 1939 MARX, KARL; and ENGELS, FRIEDRICH *The German Ideology.* Parts 1 and 3. With an introduction by R. Pascal. New York: International Publishers. → Written in 1845–1846, the full text was first published in 1932 as *Die deutsche Ideologie* and republished by Dietz Verlag in 1953.

(1847) 1963 *The Poverty of Philosophy.* With an introduction by Friedrich Engels. New York: International Publishers. → First published as *Misère de la philosophie.*

(1848) 1964 MARX, KARL; and ENGELS, FRIEDRICH *The Communist Manifesto.* New York: Washington Square Press. → First published in German.

(1849) 1962 Wage Labour and Capital. Volume 1, pages 74–97 in Karl Marx and Friedrich Engels, *Selected Works.* Moscow: Foreign Languages Publishing House. → First published as "Lohnarbeit und Kapital" in the *Neue Rheinische Zeitung.*

(1850) 1964 *The Class Struggles in France: 1848–1850.* New York: International Publishers. → A series of articles first published as "Die Klassenkämpfe in Frankreich 1848 bis 1850" in the *Neue Rheinische Zeitung: Politisch-ökonomische Revue.*

(1852) 1964 *The Eighteenth Brumaire of Louis Bonaparte.* New York: International Publishers. → First published in German.

(1856) 1899 *Secret Diplomatic History of the Eighteenth Century.* Edited by Eleanor Marx Aveling. London: Sonnenschein. → First published as "Revelations of the Diplomatic History of the Eighteenth Century" in the *Sheffield Free Press.*

(1857–1858) 1953 *Grundrisse der Kritik der politischen Ökonomie.* Berlin: Dietz. → Written in 1857–1858; first published posthumously by the Marx-Engels-Lenin Institute, Moscow, in 1939–1941. A partial English translation was published in 1965 as *Pre-capitalist Economic Formations* by International Publishers.

(1857–1859) 1959 MARX, KARL; and ENGELS, FRIEDRICH *The First Indian War of Independence: 1857–1859.* Moscow: Foreign Languages Publishing House. → A collection of articles written for the *New York Daily Tribune.* Also includes articles dated 1853 and notes from a manuscript of the 1870s.

(1859) 1913 *A Contribution to the Critique of Political Economy.* Chicago: Kerr. → First published as *Zur Kritik der politischen Ökonomie.*

(1860) 1953 Herr Vogt. Berlin: Dietz.

(1861–1863) 1952 *Theories of Surplus Value: Selections.* New York: International Publishers. → A selection from the volumes first published between 1905 and 1910 as *Theorien über den Mehrwert*, edited by Karl Kautsky, taken from Karl Marx's preliminary manuscript written between 1861–1863 for a projected fourth volume of *Capital.*

(1861–1866) 1961 MARX, KARL; and ENGELS, FRIEDRICH *The Civil War in the United States.* 3d (Centennial) ed. New York: International Publishers. → A paperback edition was published in 1964 by Citadel Press.

(1864) 1937 Address and Provisional Rules of the Working Men's International Association. Pages 27–44 in *Founding of the First International: A Documentary Record.* New York: International Publishers.

(1867–1879) 1925–1926 *Capital: A Critique of Political Economy.* 3 vols. Chicago: Kerr. → Volume 1: *The Process of Capitalist Production.* Volume 2: *The Process of Circulation of Capital.* Volume 3: *The Process of Capitalist Production as a Whole.* The first volume was published in 1867. The manuscripts of Volumes 2 and 3 were written between 1867 and 1879. They were first published posthumously in German in 1885 and 1894.

(1871) 1963 *The Civil War in France.* With an introduction by Friedrich Engels. Moscow: Foreign Languages Publishing House. → First published in English. A paperback edition was published in 1964 by International Publishers.

(1875) 1959 MARX, KARL; and ENGELS, FRIEDRICH *Critique of the Gotha Programme.* Moscow: Foreign Languages Publishing House. → Written by Marx in 1875 as "Randglossen zum Programm der deutschen Arbeiterpartei." First published with notes by Engels in 1891.

SELECTIONS FROM MARX'S WORKS

Die Frühschriften. Stuttgart (Germany): Kröner, 1953.

Marx on China, 1853–1860: Articles From the New York Daily Tribune. With an introduction and notes by Dona Torr. London: Lawrence & Wishart, 1951.

MARX, KARL; and ENGELS, FRIEDRICH *Revolution in Spain.* New York: International Publishers, 1939. → A collection of articles first published in the *New York Daily Tribune*, *Putnam's Magazine*, the *New American Encyclopedia*, and *Der Volksstaat*.

MARX, KARL; and ENGELS, FRIEDRICH *The Russian Menace to Europe: A Collection of Articles, Speeches, Letters and News Dispatches*. Edited by Paul W. Blackstock and Bert F. Hoselitz. Glencoe, Ill.: Free Press, 1952. → Contains materials written between 1848–1894.

MARX, KARL; and ENGELS, FRIEDRICH *Karl Marx and Frederick Engels on Britain*. Moscow: Foreign Languages Publishing House, 1953. → Contains a collection of the most important writings of Marx and Engels, written between 1844–1895, dealing with England.

MARX, KARL; and ENGELS, FRIEDRICH *Karl Marx and Frederick Engels; Letters to Americans 1848–1895: A Selection*. New York: International Publishers, 1953.

MARX, KARL; and ENGELS, FRIEDRICH *Karl Marx and Frederick Engels: Selected Correspondence*. Moscow: Foreign Languages Publishing House, 1956. Contains material dated 1843–1895.

MARX, KARL, and ENGELS, FRIEDRICH *On Colonialism*. Moscow: Foreign Languages Publishing House, 1960. → Contains a collection of works by Marx and Engels written between 1850–1894.

MARX, KARL; and ENGELS, FRIEDRICH *Selected Works*. 2 vols. Moscow: Foreign Languages Publishing House, 1962.

Selected Writings in Sociology and Social Philosophy. 2d ed. Edited by T. B. Bottomore and M. Rubel, with a foreword by Erich Fromm. New York: McGraw-Hill, 1964. → Contains works written by Marx between 1844–1875.

COLLECTED WORKS

MARX, KARL; and ENGELS, FRIEDRICH *Historisch–kritische Gesamtausgabe: Werke, Schriften, Briefe*. 12 vols. Edited by David Rjazanov and V. Adoratskij, commissioned by the Marx–Engels Institute, Moscow. Frankfurt am Main, Berlin, and Moscow: Marx–Engels Verlag, 1927–1935.

MARX, KARL; and ENGELS, FRIEDRICH *Karl Marx, Friedrich Engels: Werke*. Vols. 1– . Berlin: Dietz, 1956– . → Volumes 1–19, 22–31 of a contemplated 36-volume edition.

SUPPLEMENTARY BIBLIOGRAPHY

ADLER, MAX 1922 *Die Staatsauffassung des Marxismus: Ein Beitrag zur Unterscheidung von soziologischen und juristischen Methoden*. Marx-Studien, Vol. 4, part 2. Vienna: Wiener Volksbuchhandlung.

ADLER, MAX (1930–1932) 1964 *Soziologie des Marxismus*. 3 vols. Vienna: Europa. → First published as *Lehrbuch der materialistischen Geschichtsauffassung*. Volume 1: *Grundlegung der materialistischen Geschichtsauffassung*. Volume 2: *Natur und Gesellschaft*. Volume 3: *Die solidarische Gesellschaft*.

Archiv für die Geschichte des Sozialismus und der Arbeiterbewegung. → Published between 1910–1930.

BERLIN, ISAIAH (1939) 1963 *Karl Marx: His Life and Environment*. 3d ed. New York: Oxford Univ. Press.

BERNSTEIN, EDUARD (1899) 1909 *Die Voraussetzungen des Sozialismus und die Aufgaben der Sozialdemokratie*. Stuttgart (Germany): Dietz.

[BLECH, WILLIAM J.] 1939 *Elements of Marxian Economic Theory and Its Criticism*, by William J. Blake [pseud.]. New York: Cordon.

BUKHARIN, NIKOLAI I. (1921) 1965 *Historical Materialism: A System of Sociology*. Translated from the 3d Russian edition. New York: Russell. → First published as *Teoriia istoricheskogo materializma*.

DRAPER, HAL 1962 Marx and the Dictatorship of the Proletariat. Institut de Science Économique Appliquée, *Cahiers* Fifth Series: Études de Marxologie 6:5–73.

DUNAYEVSKAYA, RAYA 1958 *Marxism and Freedom From 1776 Until Today*. New York: Bookman.

ENGELS, FRIEDRICH (1878) 1959 *Anti-Dühring: Herr Eugen Dühring's Revolution in Science*. 2d ed. Moscow: Foreign Languages Publishing House. → First published as "Herrn Eugen Dührings Umwälzung der Wissenschaft" in a series of articles in *Vorwärts* (Leipzig). Translated from the 3d German edition of 1894.

ENGELS, FRIEDRICH (1892) 1925 Marx, Heinrich Karl. Volume 6, pages 496–500 in *Handwörterbuch der Staatswissenschaften*. 4th ed. Jena (Germany): Fischer.

FROMM, ERICH (editor) 1961 *Marx's Concept of Man*. New York: Ungar.

GURVITCH, GEORGES (1950) 1963– La sociologie de Karl Marx. Volume 2, pages 220–322 in *La vocation actuelle de la sociologie*. 2d ed., rev. Paris: Presses Universitaires de France.

HILFERDING, RUDOLF (1904) 1949 Böhm-Bawerk's Criticism of Marx. Pages 119–196 in Eugen Böhm-Bawerk, *Karl Marx and the Close of His System*. New York: Kelley. → First published in German.

HIRSCH, HELMUT 1963 Marxiana judaica. Institut de Science Économique Appliquée, *Cahiers* Fifth Series: Études de Marxologie 7:5–22.

HODGES, DONALD C. 1965 Engels' Contribution to Marxism. *Socialist Register* 2:297–310.

HOOK, SIDNEY (1936) 1958 *From Hegel to Marx: Studies in the Intellectual Development of Karl Marx*. New York: Humanities. → A paperback edition was published in 1962 by the University of Michigan Press.

KAMENKA, EUGENE 1962 *The Ethical Foundations of Marxism*. London: Routledge; New York: Praeger.

KAUTSKY, KARL (1906) 1918 *Ethics and the Materialist Conception of History*. Chicago: Kerr. → First published in German.

KELSEN, HANS (1920) 1923 *Sozialismus und Staat: Eine Untersuchung der politischen Theorie des Marxismus*. 2d ed., enl. Leipzig: Hirschfeld.

KORSCH, KARL (1923) 1930 *Marxismus und Philosophie*. 2d ed. Leipzig: Hirschfeld.

KORSCH, KARL (1938) 1963 *Karl Marx*. New York: Russell.

LICHTHEIM, GEORGE (1961) 1964 *Marxism: An Historical and Critical Study*. 2d rev. ed. London: Routledge.

LUKÁCS, GYÖRGY (1919–1922) 1923 *Geschichte und Klassenbewusstsein: Studien über marxistische Dialektik*. Berlin: Malik.

MARCUSE, HERBERT (1941) 1955 *Reason and Revolution: Hegel and the Rise of Social Theory*. 2d ed. New York: Humanities; London: Routledge. → A paperback edition was published in 1960 by Beacon.

Marxismusstudien. 4 vols. Evangelische Studiengemeinschaft, Schriften. 1954–1962 Tübingen (Germany): Mohr.

MASARYK, THOMAS G. (1898) 1964 *Die philosophischen und soziologischen Grundlagen des Marxismus: Studien zur socialen Frage*. Osnabrück (Germany): Zeller.

MATTICK, PAUL 1962 Marx and Keynes. Institut de Science Économique Appliquée, *Cahiers* Fifth Series: Études de Marxologie 5:113–212.

MAYER, HENRY 1960 Marx, Engels and the Politics of the Peasantry. Institut de Science Économique Appliquée, *Cahiers* Fifth Series: Études de Marxologie 3:91–152.

MEHRING, FRANZ (1918) 1948 *Karl Marx: The Story of His Life*. London: Allen & Unwin. → First published in German. A paperback edition was published in 1962 by the University of Michigan Press.

NAVILLE, PIERRE 1957 *De l'aliénation à la jouissance: La genèse de la sociologie du travail chez Marx et Engels*. Paris: Rivière.

NIKOLAEVSKII, BORIS I.; and MAENCHEN-HELFEN, OTTO 1936 *Karl Marx: Man and Fighter*. Philadelphia: Lippincott.

OLLMAN, BERTELL 1967 Marx's Conception of Human Nature. Unpublished manuscript.

PAGE, CHARLES (1940) 1964 *Class and American Sociology: From Ward to Ross*. New York: Octagon Books.

PLAMENATZ, JOHN P. (1954) 1961 *German Marxism and Russian Communism*. 3d ed. London: Longmans.

PLEKHANOV, GEORGII V. (1895) 1947 *In Defense of Materialism: The Development of the Monist View of History*. London: Lawrence & Wishart. → First published in Russian.

POPPER, KARL R. (1945) 1963 *The Open Society and Its Enemies*. 4th rev. ed. 2 vols. Princeton Univ. Press. → Volume 1: *The Spell of Plato*. Volume 2: *The High Tide of Prophecy: Hegel, Marx and the Aftermath*.

RUBEL, MAXIMILIEN 1956 *Bibliographie des oeuvres de Karl Marx: Avec en appendice un répertoire des oeuvres de Friedrich Engels*. Paris: Rivière. → A *Supplément* was published in 1960.

RUBEL, MAXIMILIEN 1957 *Karl Marx: Essai de biographie intellectuelle*. Paris: Rivière.

SCHUMPETER, JOSEPH A. (1942) 1950 *Capitalism, Socialism, and Democracy*. 3d ed. New York: Harper; London: Allen & Unwin. → A paperback edition was published by Harper in 1962.

SOREL, GEORGES 1895 Les théories de M. Durkheim. *Devenir social* 1:1–26, 148–180.

STAMMLER, RUDOLF (1896) 1924 *Wirtschaft und Recht nach der materialistichen Geschichtsauffassung: Eine sozialphilosophische Untersuchung*. 5th ed. Berlin: de Gruyter.

WEBER, MAX (1907) 1922 R. Stammlers "Überwindung" der materialistischen Geschichtsauffassung. Pages 291–359 in Max Weber, *Gesammelte Aufsätze zur Wissenschaftslehre*. Tübingen (Germany): Mohr.

ZEITLIN, IRVING MORDECAI 1967 *Marxism: A Re-examination*. Princeton: Van Nostrand.

Zeitschrift für Sozialforschung. → Published between 1932 and 1941. Title changed to *Studies in Philosophy and Social Science* with Volume 8, No. 3. It represented (until 1938) a serious attempt to develop a Marxian sociology in nondogmatic terms.

MARXISM

This article deals with the origins and development of the political doctrine of Karl Marx. Marxism is also discussed in ECONOMIC THOUGHT, *article on* SOCIALIST THOUGHT; MARXIST SOCIOLOGY; SOCIALISM; *and in the biography of* MARX. *Contemporary political and economic aspects are discussed in* COMMUNISM; COMMUNISM, ECONOMIC ORGANIZATION OF. *Also related are* PLANNING, ECONOMIC, *article on* EASTERN EUROPE; WORKERS. *The biographies of* BERNSTEIN; ENGELS; FANON; KAUTSKY; LANGE; LENIN; LUKÁCS; LUXEMBURG; MAN; MILLS; OSSOWSKI; *and* TROTSKY *describe different intellectual developments after Marx. For the biographies of other socialist thinkers, see under* SOCIALISM.

Like other schools of socialism that arose in the early nineteenth century, Marxism was a response to the economic and social hardships accompanying the growth of Western industrial capitalism. If in recent decades it has attracted most of its adherents in countries hardly touched by industrial capitalism, this is the result of a tortuous ideological history.

The intellectual heritage from which Marxism drew its insights, attitudes, and concepts is a synthesis of many ideological currents of the early and middle nineteenth century. They include the basic assumptions of the democratic faith and the slogans of the French Revolution; indeed, Marxism asserts that this revolution was betrayed by the very class which made it and will only be fulfilled by the proletariat through socialism. Hence, Marxism also embraces the syndrome of attitudes associated with workers' protest movements and socialism. Further, Marxism embodies the empiricism or "materialism" of Bacon, Hobbes, and Helvétius. From Rousseau and the romantics it has taken a strongly ambivalent attitude toward past and present institutions, together with a strong commitment to historicism and its Hegelian form —dialectics. Finally, this mixture is seasoned with the anthropocentrism of Feuerbach, the economic doctrines of Smith and Ricardo, and the class-war theories of Michelet and other historians of the French Revolution.

As a syndrome of attitudes, Marxism might be described as a synthesis of radicalism, optimism, and a commitment to science: it is radical in criticizing contemporary social institutions and practices as stupid and inhuman; it is optimistic in expecting, eventually, the creation of a "good society" worthy of man's highest potentials; it is committed to science not only because it wishes to analyze society but also because it is convinced that the scientific investigation of the social forces active in the contemporary world will confirm both its radicalism and its optimism.

Doctrine

Marxism is a dialectical theory of human progress. It regards history as the development of man's effort to master the forces of nature and, hence, of production ("economic interpretation of history"). Since all production is carried out within social organization, history is the succession of changes in social systems, the development of human relations geared to productive activity ("modes of production"), in which the economic system forms the "base" and all other relationships, institutions, activities, and idea systems are "superstructural."

History is progress because man's ability to produce, his "forces of production," continually increase. It is regression because in perfecting the forces of production man creates a more and more complex and oppressive social organization, seemingly beyond human control (the "production relations"), the central feature of which is the division of society into classes. Classes are defined by their relations to the essential means of production: the ruling class is that group of men who own the means of production; those who are propertyless are forced to function as the laboring class. Like Rousseau, Marx was profoundly interested in exploring the inequalities of men because he shared his belief that there can be no democracy as long as there are inequality and special interests.

Progress, thus, is a mixed blessing. Nor is it unilinear, for in the history of man different elements of the complicated social system continually become dysfunctional to each other. In particular, the production relations, originally in tune with a given state of the forces of production, lag behind the latter and come to retard their further development. From a promoter of progress the ruling class turns into a useless parasite. But when the old production relations have turned into a dead shell, mankind assures the march of progress by remaking the social system in revolutionary violence, giving leadership to the class wielding the most advanced means of production. According to the Marxist scheme of history, mankind has gone through three or four major modes of production since an initial golden age of primitive communism: ancient slave society, feudalism, and capitalism (to which Marx added, in some of his works, Asiatic society as a distinct mode of production).

Capitalism, the last form of society torn by a class struggle, represents the peak of human development so far. On the one hand, it has created and amassed unprecedented wealth, which, if used rationally, could assure the material well-being of all mankind. Yet, by virtue of its own laws of operation, capitalism cannot utilize its means of production rationally but must match the accumulation of capital with the accumulation of misery and chaos. Again, while it has promoted constitutional government and the rights of man, the formal rights and equalities of liberal regimes are vitiated by actual inequalities and ultimate dehumanization: formally free, man has been converted into a commodity, whose labor power, talents, and personality are for sale on the free market. The resolution of these contradictions will be produced by capitalism itself. Its own economic laws not only produce chaos and crisis but also narrow the social basis of capitalism by casting the mass of the population into the proletariat. At a crisis point the exploited will rise in revolution, expropriate the ruling class, replace commodity production with an economy based on national planning, and abolish all class divisions in society.

Supporting the optimistic prognosis of revolutionary Marxism is the image of the proletariat as the "chosen people," who, because of their place in society, their state of organization, and their spontaneous grasp of reality ("class consciousness") can be expected to rise above all narrow interests, loyalties, and ideologies and liberate mankind forever from the curse of property and class.

Development

Marxist doctrine was spelled out concisely in the *Communist Manifesto*. This pamphlet was written shortly before the outbreak of the 1848 revolution, which Marx and Engels were confident would lead to the socialist revolution of the proletariat. The failure of 1848 forced them to explain what had prevented this act of deliverance. In subsequent political commentaries, they emphasized complicating factors left out of the more abstract analysis of capitalism: the role of precapitalist classes in European politics, especially the petty bourgeoisie; the baneful role of demoralized workers (*Lumpenproletariat*); the role of the state as an independent political force; and the role of nations. Many ideas contained in these political writings were never fully integrated with general Marxist theory. Indeed, Marx's major work on the capitalist system remained a fragment; and he died before he had time to give a systematic presentation of such a central concept as social class.

Another task made necessary by the failure of 1848 was to elaborate a political strategy for the proletarian movement. Here Marxism came to emphasize the differences between long-range and short-range objectives. Socialism was defined as the maximal goal, while the minimal goal was the liberation of capitalism from feudal and absolutist residues of a political, economic, or social nature. A more intermediate goal—the dictatorship of the proletariat—received scant mention in Marx's writings.

Problems of political strategy became more important because, after inauspicious beginnings, Marxist doctrine was in time accepted as the party ideology of the European labor movement. There is irony in this merger because the workers' movement which finally accepted Marxist ideology was in many ways different from the proletariat as Marx and Engels had described and idealized it in 1847–1848. It tended toward reformism, had faith in constitutional democracy, and, as the first mass party of modern history, became thoroughly bureaucratized. Ulam (1960) cogently argues that Marxism at that time was no longer a suitable ideology for the European labor movement. Hence, its adoption raises puzzling questions which cannot be pursued here.

Suitable or not, the merger of the ideology with the movement was a turning point because, with it, Marxism became a formal ideology, a guide to thought and action, a holy writ and catechism. Henceforth, it tended toward doctrinal rigidity. The growing discrepancy between revolutionary theories and actual party policies lent Marxism a note of hypocrisy, while a widening gap between assumptions and reality had the effect of ideological blinders on those who wanted to use Marxism as a tool for comprehension. Moreover, once Marxism was accepted as party doctrine, its adherents, beginning with Engels, extended the doctrine into areas of inquiry to which Marx himself had not applied it. Marx had thought to encompass with his theory contemporary society and all of human history. Engels sought to integrate Darwinian theory and all natural science with Marxism and to raise Marxist theories to the level of a universal philosophy. For Marx the ultimate determinant of the course of history was man and his needs, but for Engels it came to be matter and its motion. Yet, it was the ideas of Engels which set the tone for orthodox Marxism of both the social democratic and communist persuasions. The sociopsychological dynamics behind both this extension of the doctrine and its transformation into a holy writ still need to be explored.

Conflicting interpretations

As soon as Marxism was accepted as the doctrine of the European labor movement, it became a matter of controversy among its followers, partly because the work of Marx and Engels had remained unfinished in many details, but even more because of social changes that had occurred. The ensuing debates dealt with issues of strategy, focusing on the problem of maturity, i.e., the task of defining the point at which a society might be ripe for the proletarian revolution. Engels alluded to the problem by wondering about the paradox that the proletarian revolution might be impossible as long as it was necessary and unnecessary once it became feasible. Problems of organization and tactics also provided material for controversies. Discussions of these and many related issues are still going on within Marxism, even though the same questions are asked in changing circumstances.

Of the controversies raging before World War I, the bitterest was unrelated to strategy or organization. It arose instead out of the growing unrealism of Marxist doctrine. The spread of economic prosperity and constitutional government belied Marxist prognoses about the intensification of crises and misery; and the revolutionary slogans of the *Communist Manifesto* sounded incongruous when uttered by the moderate leaders of the Second International.

To resolve the discrepancy, the "revisionists" proposed a thoroughgoing change of Marxist doctrines so as to make them reflect current conditions, modern scientific insights, and social democratic aims and policies. Revisionism came close to being a repudiation of Marxist ideas; and it can be regarded as the first in a long series of steps away from Marx made by democratic socialists since the turn of the century. Their antagonists in the Second International insistently upheld the letter of Marxist doctrines, identifying loyalty to the writ of Marx with loyalty to the workers' movement. The method of bridging the gap between theory and reality was by denying its existence, meanwhile reinterpreting Marx's revolutionary theories so as to make them yield reformist counsel. For most Marxists committed to democratic socialism, this was an ideological rear-guard action, because the predominant trend in the socialist movement has been to follow the revisionists in their repudiation of Marx.

While the revisionists sought to change theories in order to align them with reality and the orthodox denied the need for such realignment, a radical wing of the Marxist movement, which arose after the turn of the century, attempted to bridge the gap between theory and practice by leading the workers' movement back to the revolutionary orientation of the *Communist Manifesto*. This wing became the nucleus of communism; most of its leaders joined communist parties, if only for short periods.

The radical Marxists asserted that despite profound changes in the capitalist world since the days of Marx—especially "imperialism" (the export of capital and of capitalism to dependent countries overseas)—the basic contradictions of capitalism had remained; hence also the inevitability and necessity of the revolution Marx had predicted. Disagreements among the radicals arose over many issues, the most divisive one being the question of organization. One faction, of which Rosa Luxemburg was the outstanding spokesman, saw the roots of "reformism," i.e., democratic socialism, in the bureaucratization of the workers' movement, which they thought stifled revolutionary initiative and proletarian class consciousness. Against them, Lenin and his Bolsheviks believed that revolution making should be subject to rational management (bureaucracy), and they held, moreover, that by itself, spontaneously, the proletariat would not be able to attain class consciousness; hence their emphasis on leadership by an enlightened elite organized in bureaucratic fashion in the party, which should function as the general staff of the proletarian revolution. Leninist Marxism thus focuses on the task of manipulating the masses through leaders who have acquired insight into the politically necessary and possible by applying Marxist categories to the analysis of their society.

New ideological problems were bound to arise when a Marxist party was founded in Russia toward the end of the nineteenth century, because most of the conditions to which Marxism originally had been a response were absent in that country. The very fact that Marxism could find acceptance among Russian revolutionaries is an interesting ideological development, which deserves explanation in another context. Russia's economic backwardness and repressive political system exacerbated problems of timing, leadership, organization, political alliances, and related issues, considerably straining the entire framework of Marxist concepts. For instance, the notion that the bourgeoisie cannot fulfill the ideological promises of the bourgeois revolution was a central tenet of Marx and Engels. But Lenin's idea that the bourgeoisie will not carry out or even initiate "its own" revolution (which will instead have to be accomplished by the proletariat and its allies) requires very bold use of Marxist class terminology. In its mature form Bolshevism takes even greater liberties with the original Marxist conception when it assigns to colonial and other dependent nations a significant role in the hoped-for "proletarian" revolutions. Underdeveloped nations here assume some of the traits which Marx had attributed to the industrial workers of the West. But as a consequence, the "proletarian revolution" itself turns into something very different from what Marx had assumed

it to be. Originally thought of as the act of taking over the mature industrial establishment created (and mismanaged) by capitalism, it now can take over nothing but a backward economy and culture; this leads to the paradoxical conclusion that the proletarian state (a "superstructural" phenomenon) will have to begin constructing its own economic "base," making use of "capitalist" methods in doing so.

In their controversies over policy and organization, the different factions of Russian Marxism emphasized those portions of the ideology which seemed to support their views, at the expense of other portions. Lenin and his Bolsheviks were so intent on reaching their goal, the proletarian revolution, that they amended Marx's revolutionary timetable beyond recognition; this led to the accusation that they were Blanquists rather than Marxists. The more cautious Mensheviks, in turn, seemed so concerned with following the timetable provided by Marx that Lenin accused them of postponing socialism and the revolution *ad calendas Graecas* and thus betraying the cause of the proletariat.

The schism which split Russian Marxism into two hostile social-democratic parties was extended to the entire world-wide movement in the years from 1914 to 1920. Disagreements over the proper attitudes a Marxist should take toward the war and the Russian Revolution divided Marxism irreconcilably into socialists and communists, each creating their own international federation of parties. The most important issue between them was their difference of attitude toward the Bolshevik seizure of power and method of governing. The communists regarded their state as the pioneer of the international workers' movement. The socialists saw in it an ill-timed and irresponsible adventure which discredited the Marxist movement. In subsequent decades, the communist–socialist split hastened the process by which democratic socialism came to dissociate itself from Marxist ideology. [*See* Socialism.]

Marxism as the ideology of a ruling party

Once in power, the Russian communists sought to use Marxism as a guidebook for the further road toward socialism and for managing a proletarian dictatorship. The difficulties they encountered and the sketchiness of the hints Marx and Engels had provided for solving these problems led to new and sharp controversies among the communists themselves, in which the broadest spectrum of Marxist concepts was once again discussed from divergent points of view. With Stalin's rise to power the debate was forcibly closed, and his own views were imposed as dogma over all communist parties. The substance of this dogma, based on Leninist principles, might be summarized as follows: Marxism is both scientific truth and ideology—the ideology of the working class. The Communist party alone possesses full scientific insight and expresses the true interests of the workers. Hence, only he who is loyal to the party can be loyal to the proletariat, in tune with the course of history, or capable of grasping the truth. Nothing can be true which contradicts the party. Further, official Soviet doctrine justifies the communist state, its policies and social structure, as a proletarian dictatorship and a true democracy engaged in "constructing socialism." Marxism here has turned into a theory of state defending, as virtually perfect, a regime violating all the libertarian and egalitarian values expressed by Marx. The success with which Marxist concepts have been used to fashion a conservative and authoritarian doctrine of this kind is a major achievement in ideology making. In the Soviet Union this has recently been supplemented by a program for the "transition to communism," which is an obvious attempt to tone down expectations. Calling for little significant change in present-day Soviet society, it signals the withering away of utopia on this branch of Marxist ideology. Finally, contemporary communist ideology incorporates a program for the further spread of the "proletarian" revolution. But although the workers in the industrialized countries have not been written off formally, in effect the communist movement has now substituted the colonial and other dependent nations in the historic role which Marx attributed to the proletariat of the capitalist world.

The function of the ideology in communist political systems has been the subject of much controversy. Many scholars (echoing communist dogma) see Marxism–Leninism as the master plan guiding all communist thought, actions, and institutions. Others assert that it is no more than rationalization which easily adapts to any changes in policy. However contradictory, both theories have some plausibility but are easily refuted in their exaggerated forms.

Marxist ideology, as amended by Lenin and his successors, did inspire the men who made communist revolutions and has influenced communist regimes and institutions even more directly than the ideas of Rousseau and Locke have shaped the institutions of the French and American republics. Although the ideology becomes primarily rationalization after the communist seizure of power, it

does remain the language of politics, meaning not only a code of communications for the political elite but also the conceptual frame of reference used for cognitive and ethical self-orientation. It thus determines both analysis and action, if only negatively, that is, as ideological blinders and as a brake ("bad conscience") on freedom of action. [See IDEOLOGY.]

A doctrine which is meant to serve as a useful aid to cognition must be realistic and flexible, whereas a doctrine functioning as a communications code need only be rigid. These and other conflicting functions of the ideology strain it. Primarily, perhaps, the ideology functions as a legitimation device, implying not only an exercise in public relations to attain legitimacy among the citizens but, even more important, a continual attempt by the party leaders to convince themselves of their own legitimacy; more generally, it functions as an ideological exoskeleton for insecure bureaucrats in a vast and powerful administrative machine. The implication is that communist leaders in making doctrinal pronouncements speak more to themselves than to their citizenry, and least of all to the outside world. This phenomenon of self-encouragement or self-legitimation, observable in all societies, has been unduly neglected by contemporary communications theory.

Ideological strains

Since World War II, communist parties have come to power in close to a dozen countries of eastern Europe, Asia, and the Caribbean area. These various Marxist–Leninist regimes came to power by widely divergent methods and, once installed, faced very different tasks because of the great differences in the cultures, economic development, political traditions, and social structures of the countries concerned. If to these variations in national interests and outlooks of the several communist regimes one adds the bitter memory of past disagreements and injuries, plus the normal political rivalries between groups and personalities within a large group of states, it is not astonishing that sharp conflicts arose in the communist camp, straining relations between the different regimes and within each communist party. Given the relations between politics and ideology within the communist movement, these disagreements sooner or later had to become doctrinal and thus turned into questions of fundamental principle. Hence, the dialogue between Tito and Stalin, between Khrushchev and Mao, and between revisionists and dogmatists in every communist party led to a discussion of not only basic problems in revolutionary strategy and socialist construction but also of the most fundamental concepts of Marxism–Leninism.

The resulting differences within the communist world are today as deep as the schism between Mensheviks and Bolsheviks half a century ago. Moreover, the issues under discussion are similar to those which divided Russian Marxism at that time, even though the circumstances and the concrete reference points have changed. The unity of the communist movement is as irretrievably gone as was the unity of European Marxism at the time of the October Revolution. As a result, what 15 years ago seemed well-established dogma is now subject to doubt. Within some of the communist societies, party dogmas today are also being criticized in the name of science, while the practices of communist governments and the rhetoric which justifies them are challenged in the name of Marxist humanism. In short, official ideology is assailed from several directions. Two tendencies are likely to result from this multiple onslaught. Official ideological output may turn increasingly into empty, meaningless political oratory, ritually incanted on suitable ceremonial occasions but as removed from life as Sunday sermons and Independence Day speeches. At the same time, a genuine dialogue conducted between and within the several communist parties over a sufficient period of time might serve to reinvigorate Marxist ideology, especially in communist parties that have not yet come to power, even though it may also lead many former adherents to repudiate this ideology. [See the articles under COMMUNISM.]

Marxism in the noncommunist world

Although the communist movement (or movements, as one must now write) claims to be the legitimate heir of Marxist ideology, Marxism continues to exist, in the Western world, as a non-communist ideology. To be sure, most socialist parties have gone far in severing their ties with Marxism. Yet interest in it has increased in certain intellectual circles. Most of this is roundly critical and, especially in its recent intensified form, is a function of the cold war. The variety of points of view from which Marxism, or what is understood to be Marxism, has been criticized cannot be summarized here. But some of the recent interest has been sympathetic. This may have been stimulated by the collaboration of many diverse elements with communists and socialists during and shortly after World War II. In addition, political, economic, racial, and other difficulties that have beset the

Western world since the war have increased many intellectuals' awareness of defects in their social system. For anyone focusing his attention on negative aspects of contemporary social life, Marxism offers considerable attraction, principally because of two elements: one is the message of inevitable doom derived from the analysis of the capitalist economy; the other is the humanist ethic of Marxism—the emphasis on the evil features of a commercial civilization, the romantic anger at institutions and practices that degrade, oppress, or exploit some men, and the sanguine belief in the inherent goodness of mankind, which under favorable circumstances can and will free itself from inhibiting and corrupting institutions. In the last decade or two interest in this humanist philosophy of Marx and in the early writings in which it is expressed has increased rapidly. Finally, there is some increase in the interest social scientists have in Marx as a precursor of contemporary social science: some of his methodological contributions are only now receiving recognition.

ALFRED G. MEYER

BIBLIOGRAPHY

See the bibliographies following the articles on ENGELS; LENIN; and MARX for their major works.

BLOOM, SOLOMON F. 1941 The World of Nations: A Study of the National Implications in the Work of Karl Marx. New York: Columbia Univ. Press.

CHAMBRE, HENRI (1959) 1963 From Karl Marx to Mao Tse-tung: A Systematic Survey of Marxism–Leninism. New York: Kennedy. → First published in French.

COLE, G. D. H. 1953–1960 A History of Socialist Thought. 5 vols. New York: St. Martins; London: Macmillan. → Volume 1: Socialist Thought: The Forerunners 1789–1850, 1953. Volume 2: Marxism and Anarchism 1850–1890, 1954. Volume 3: Second International 1889–1914, 2 parts, 1956. Volume 4: Communism and Social Democracy 1914–1931, 2 parts, 1958. Volume 5: Socialism and Fascism 1931–1939, 1960.

DANIELS, ROBERT V. 1960 The Conscience of the Revolution: Communist Opposition in Soviet Russia. Russian Research Center Studies, No. 40. Cambridge Mass.: Harvard Univ. Press.

FETSCHER, IRING (1956) 1959 Von Marx zur Sowjetideologie. 4th ed. Frankfurt am Main: Diesterweg.

Fundamentals of Marxism–Leninism. 2d ed., rev. (1959) 1963 Moscow: Foreign Languages Publishing House. → First published as Osnovy marksizma–leninizma.

GAY, PETER 1952 The Dilemma of Democratic Socialism: Eduard Bernstein's Challenge to Marx. New York: Columbia Univ. Press. → A paperback edition was published in 1962 by Collier.

GREGOR, A. JAMES 1965 A Survey of Marxism: Problems in the Philosophy and Theory of History. New York: Random House.

HAIMSON, LEOPOLD H. 1955 The Russian Marxist & the Origins of Bolshevism. Russian Research Center

Studies, No. 19. Cambridge, Mass.: Harvard Univ. Press.

KOLARZ, WALTER (1959) 1964 *Books on Communism: A Bibliography.* 2d ed. New York: Oxford Univ. Press.

LABEDZ, LEOPOLD (editor) 1962 *Revisionism: Essays on the History of Marxist Ideas.* New York: Praeger.

LEHMBRUCH, GERHARD (1956) 1958 *Kleiner Wegweiser zum Studium der Sowjetideologie.* Bonn: Gesamt-deutscher Verlag. → A revised and enlarged edition of H. Gollwitzer and G. Lehmbruch's *Kleiner Wegweiser zum Studium des Marxismus–Leninismus.*

LICHTHEIM, GEORGE (1961) 1964 *Marxism: An Historical and Critical Study.* 2d ed., rev. London: Routledge. → A paperback edition was published by Praeger in 1965.

MARCUSE, HERBERT (1941) 1955 *Reason and Revolution: Hegel and the Rise of Social Theory.* 2d. ed. New York: Humanities; London: Routledge. → A paperback edition was published in 1960 by Beacon.

MARCUSE, HERBERT 1958 *Soviet Marxism: A Critical Analysis.* New York: Columbia Univ. Press. → A paperback edition was published in 1961 by Vintage.

MEYER, ALFRED G. 1957 *Leninism.* Russian Research Center Studies, No. 26. Cambridge, Mass.: Harvard Univ. Press. → A paperback edition was published in 1962 by Praeger.

MITRANY, DAVID 1951 *Marx Against the Peasant: A Study in Social Dogmatism.* Chapel Hill: Univ. of North Carolina Press.

PLAMENATZ, JOHN P. (1954) 1961 *German Marxism and Russian Communism.* New York: Longmans.

RAMM, THILO 1955 *Die grossen Sozialisten als Rechts-und Sozialphilosophen.* Stuttgart: Fischer.

ROSENBERG, ARTHUR (1932) 1939 *A History of Bolshevism: From Marx to the First Five Years' Plan.* London and New York: Oxford Univ. Press. → First published in German.

RUBEL, MAXIMILIEN 1956 *Bibliographie des oeuvres de Karl Marx: Avec en appendice un répertoire des oeuvres de Friedrich Engels.* Paris: Rivière. → A 74-page supplement was added in 1960.

SCHORSKE, CARL E. 1955 *German Social Democracy, 1905–1917: The Development of the Great Schism.* Cambridge, Mass.: Harvard Univ. Press.

SCHWARTZ, BENJAMIN I. 1951 *Chinese Communism and the Rise of Mao.* Cambridge, Mass.: Harvard Univ. Press.

TIMASHEFF, NICHOLAS S. 1946 *The Great Retreat: The Growth and Decline of Communism in Russia.* New York: Dutton.

TUCKER, ROBERT C. 1961 *Philosophy and Myth in Karl Marx.* Cambridge Univ. Press.

ULAM, ADAM B. 1960 *The Unfinished Revolution: An Essay on the Sources of Influence of Marxism and Communism.* New York: Random House.

WETTER, GUSTAVO A. (1948) 1959 *Dialectical Materialism: A Historical and Systematic Survey of Philosophy in the Soviet Union.* New York: Praeger. → First published as *Il materialismo dialèttico sovietico.*

MARXIST SOCIOLOGY

Karl Marx introduced into the social sciences of his day a new method of inquiry, new concepts, and a number of bold hypotheses to explain the rise, development, and decline of particular forms of society; all of which came to exercise, in the later decades of the nineteenth century, a profound and extensive influence upon the writing of history, political science, and sociology. Marx was also a man of action, a revolutionary, whose political creed stood in a complex and uneasy relationship to his scientific investigations, and his followers, the Marxists of various hues, have tended toward one or the other limit of his ideas, to doctrinal exposition, or to the furtherance of a science of society. Marxist sociology has been one of the principal battlefields in this conflict between objective science and political commitment.

Marx's contributions

On the side of scientific method, Marx made two important contributions. One was to adopt, and to maintain consistently in his work, a view of human societies as wholes or systems in which social groups, institutions, beliefs, and doctrines are interrelated and have to be studied in their interrelations rather than treated in isolation, as in the conventional separate histories of politics, law, religion, or thought. The second contribution was the view of societies as inherently mutable systems, in which changes are produced largely by internal contradictions and conflicts, and the assumption that such changes, if observed in a large number of instances, will show a sufficient degree of regularity to allow the formulation of general statements about their causes and consequences.

Historical materialism. Marx's ideas, which played an essential part in the formation of modern sociology, had been adumbrated in the works of earlier thinkers as diverse in other respects as Hegel, Saint-Simon, and Adam Ferguson, all of whom greatly influenced Marx; and they resemble in some aspects the ideas which Comte and Spencer propounded in their attempts to lay the foundations of sociology. But Marx elaborated his conception of the nature of society, and of the appropriate means to study it, in a more precise, and above all more empirical, fashion than did his predecessors. He introduced an entirely new element by attributing to the characteristics of the economic system and to the derived relations between social classes a predominant influence in determining the structure of each society. It was this feature of Marx's method, to be known subsequently by the somewhat misleading term "historical materialism," which was widely accepted by later sociologists as offering a more promising starting point for exact and realistic investigations of the causes of social change than could be found in such notions as the three stages of man's intellectual development (Comte) or the process of superorganic evolution (Spencer).

Social class and social conflict. Marx's theories followed to a great extent from the above methodological conceptions, which he referred to as the "guiding thread" in his studies (1859, preface). The significance of the economic system of society was elaborated in a theory which traced the formation of the principal social groups—the classes—to the forms of ownership of the means of production and the forms of labor of nonowners. The idea of social change resulting from internal conflicts was developed in a theory of class struggles which made social classes the principal, if not the sole, agents of political activity; and this conception in turn led to the distinction between ruling and oppressed classes and to a distinctive theory of the state. The conviction that social changes display a regular pattern led Marx to construct, in broad outline, a historical sequence of the main types of society, proceeding from the simple, undifferentiated society of "primitive communism" to the complex class society of modern capitalism; and he sketched an explanation of the great historical transformations which demolished old forms of society and created new ones in terms of economic changes which he regarded as general and constant in their operation.

Although this theoretical scheme was intended to have a universal character, Marx actually employed it in a partial manner. His own researches were limited almost entirely to the nineteenth-century capitalist societies, and he gave only fragmentary accounts of the other types of society, in brief allusions in *Capital*, in newspaper articles and correspondence, and in manuscripts which were published after his death (see especially 1857–1858). Furthermore, some of his most important theoretical ideas were derived immediately from the observation of modern societies, and they fit closely only these particular societies. His theory of social classes applies in the main to the formation and development of the modern bourgeoisie and proletariat; it is not so helpful when applied to the phenomena of a caste system. Clearly, the theory of social conflict originated in an interpretation of the French Revolution, the materials for which had been prepared by earlier historians, and it was developed further by observation of the class struggles which accompanied the growth of the labor movement in western Europe.

The concept of ideology, similarly, originated in Marx's criticism of some contemporary social doctrines—utilitarianism, the "critical philosophy" of the Young Hegelians, political economy in some

of its aspects—which he regarded as concealing or distorting the real relationships between men and the actual social conflicts in the European societies of his time (Marx & Engels 1845–1846). It is not a concept which Marx brought, or tried to bring, within the framework of a general sociological theory of knowledge. This intense preoccupation with the origins and development of industrial capitalism is, indeed, a feature of Marx's theories which helps to account for the interest which they still excite. It has enabled Marxists to represent his thought as a modern philosophy that is closely linked with the progress of science and industry, and it has enabled sociologists to discover in it the elements of a theory of industrialization and economic growth.

Marx's influence in the nineteenth century

Marx's scientific writings were not widely noticed or criticized during his lifetime, and he became known principally as the author of a political doctrine expounded in the *Communist Manifesto* in 1848 and as one of the animators of the International Working Men's Association. Furthermore, the early expounders of his ideas, other than Friedrich Engels, were themselves political leaders of the growing working class movement in Europe—men such as August Bebel, Karl Kautsky, and Eduard Bernstein in Germany; Jules Guesde and Paul Lafargue in France—rather than scholars.

Only in the late 1880s did Marx's theories begin to claim the serious attention of academic social scientists. The first major work of sociology to recognize his importance and to display the influence of his thought was Ferdinand Tönnies' *Community and Society* (1887). In this book Tönnies expounded his distinction between two forms of society—"community" (*Gemeinschaft*) and "association" (*Gesellschaft*)—which has become one of the classic themes of sociology. His debt to Marx is indicated by the importance which he assigned to the system of production in determining these different forms of society and by the character of his analysis of modern capitalism. Much later Tönnies published an excellent short study of Marx's life and work (1921), in which he examined more fully the nature and limitations of Marx's contribution to sociology.

A more general recognition by the German academic world of Marx's importance as a sociological thinker became apparent in the 1890s with the publication of a long essay by Werner Sombart on Marx's theory of modern capitalism, books by Rudolf Stammler and Thomas G. Masaryk on the methodological foundations of his theories, and numerous discussions in scholarly journals. At this time Marx's work also began to be discussed by eminent scholars in other European countries: in Italy by Antonio Labriola (1895–1896), Benedetto Croce (in several essays which are collected in Croce 1900), Giovanni Gentile, and Vilfredo Pareto; and in France by Georges Sorel, who expounded Marx's theories in a number of articles from 1894 onward and published in his journal, *Le devenir social*, some notable essays on Marx by European scholars as well as his own reviews, from a Marxist standpoint, of the work of contemporary sociologists. Marx's sociology also figured prominently in the contributions to the first international congress of sociology held in 1894.

Divergence of Marxism and sociology

By the beginning of the twentieth century, therefore, Marx had been generally accepted as the author of a profound and original system of sociology, yet in the following period the influence of Marxism upon sociology diminished rather than increased. Many of the writers who had first drawn attention to the importance of Marx's theories—among them Croce, Sorel, and Pareto—now became severe critics of Marxist thought and advanced new social and historical theories which, however much they might owe to the initial shock which Marx's ideas had produced, were conceived in an entirely different fashion. On the other hand, a number of influential Marxist thinkers came to regard more critically the claims of sociology as a positive science and to insist more strongly upon the character of Marxism as a revolutionary social philosophy.

In the early 1900s only the small but distinguished group of thinkers who became known later as the Austro-Marxists were engaged in an attempt to set forth and develop the sociological elements in Marx's thought. Max Adler (1925), a philosopher deeply influenced by Neo-Kantianism, represented Marx as having established the epistemological foundations of social science, as Kant had done for the natural sciences; he saw in Marxism a sociological system of causal explanation. Another member of the group, Karl Renner (1904), produced what is still the outstanding Marxist contribution to the sociology of law, a study of the effect of economic forces and social changes upon the working of modern legal institutions. The writings of the Austro-Marxists, however, did not arrest the growing divergence between Marxism and sociology, which appears most clearly in the contrast between the work of Max Weber and Pareto in sociology and the fresh expositions of

Marxist thought by Karl Korsch and György Lukács.

Sociology—Weber and Pareto. Marxism was unquestionably one of the strongest influences upon the work of Max Weber, much of which is devoted either to testing, in a particular context, some part of Marx's theories, or to reassessing in a more general way his concepts and methods. In the first of these directions, Weber's best-known study is that on the origins of modern capitalism (1904–1905), which is intended to show that a body of religious ideas (the Protestant ethic) played a vital part in the development of European capitalism, alongside the economic changes and the rise of a new class, through the inculcation of new attitudes toward wealth, science, and work. From this first revision of Marx's economic interpretation of history, Weber went on to examine on a wider scale the social influence of religious ideas, to amend and supplement the Marxist theory of classes, to outline a radically different theory of political power, and to suggest an interpretation of modern European history as a movement, not toward socialism but, rather, toward greater bureaucratic regulation.

In the sphere of methodology, Weber's preoccupation with historical materialism is evident in his discussion (1907) of a book by Stammler and especially in an editorial in the *Archiv für Sozialwissenschaft und Sozialpolitik* in 1904, in which he observed that while the materialist conception of history should be rejected as a comprehensive *Weltanschauung*, the interpretation of historical events from the aspect of their economic conditioning or relevance may be accepted as a useful methodological principle, above all in the study of modern societies.

The impression made by Marxist ideas is equally clear in the earlier writings of Pareto, who singled out, as Marx's chief contribution to sociology, the theory of class conflict (1902–1903). This provided the basis for Pareto's own later elaboration of the idea of the struggle between elites for political power, which became the vital element in an interpretation of history directly opposed to that of Marx. Pareto replaced the idea of the progressive development of class systems by a cyclical theory of the rise and fall of elites, and concentrated attention upon the conditions of social equilibrium rather than the causes of social change.

Marxist philosophy. Both Weber and Pareto aspired, though in different ways and with varying success, to establish sociology as an objective social science. Korsch and Lukács, on the other hand, questioned the possibility, and also the value, of such an objective science, and they expounded Marxism as a philosophy of society which approaches every problem from the point of view of the working class.

Korsch, in *Marxismus und Philosophie* (1923), began by criticizing those thinkers who had regarded Marxism either as a set of methodological rules or as a system of universal causal laws, that is, as a general sociology in the positivist sense. According to him, Marxism includes both empirical and philosophical elements, but the latter are those which distinguish it clearly from other social theories. It is empirical in the sense that it deals with real social movements in modern society and is not in flagrant contradiction with actual events; it is philosophical in the sense that it interprets the facts by means of a conception of history as a process which will terminate in a "classless society." Because of this vision of the future which it contains, it is above all a theory of social revolution which expresses the outlook, and reflects the practical social activity, of a revolutionary class.

In similar fashion Lukács argued, in several of the essays collected in *Geschichte und Klassenbewusstsein* (1919–1922), that Marxism is not to be regarded as an objective interpretation of man's social history—still less as a scientific theory of social evolution—but as an interpretation, from the standpoint of the revolutionary working class, of the historical origins and development of capitalist society. Both writers insisted upon the opposition between Marxism and sociology. For them, Marxism is essentially a theory of history concerned with unique sequences of events and taking account both of objective conditions and of subjective human strivings. Sociology, on the other hand, by its ambition to establish general social laws, in the first place turns man into an object and discounts the subjective aspects of human action and, second, substitutes for the view of society as a historical process the conception of an unvarying system of social relationships which is to be discovered in every form of society.

This idea of Marxism did not find favor with the orthodox Marxist–Leninists, whose opinions were authoritatively expressed at that time through the Third Communist International. However, there were few scholars among the orthodox who attempted to set out an alternative version or to meet the sociological criticisms of Marxism on their own ground. The most important of them was undoubtedly Nikolai Bukharin, whose exposition of historical materialism (1921) is noteworthy for the serious attention which it gives to the difficulties arising from the claim that Marxism is at the same time an objective social science and the doctrine of a particular social class, and for its discussions of some of the more important criticisms of Marx.

During the early 1900s, the intellectual and political influence of Marxism and the discussions of Marx's sociological theories were largely confined to the continental European countries. In Britain, Marxism made little impact upon sociology, either then or later. The influence of Marxism was greater in the early development of American sociology, but it was soon overshadowed. Thorstein Veblen is the most notable of those who turned to Marx as a source of powerful and radical ideas, which he then developed in his own fashion in theories of the influence of technology upon social structure (1899) and of the rise to power of the engineers (1921). Albion W. Small, who assigned to Marx a place as the Galileo of the social sciences, also played a large part in introducing Marxist ideas and was himself strongly influenced by Marx in working out his theories of social conflict.

Marxist influence since the 1930s

In the period from the early 1930s to the present day, the lines of thought distinguished above have continued and have been enriched by new studies. A number of Marxist writers have upheld the opposition between Marxism and sociology, and they have found new evidence for their views in Marx's early manuscripts, which began to be published in 1932. Thus, Korsch expounded his ideas more fully, but in the same form, in a study of Marx (1938) that was contributed to a series on the great sociologists. A few years later Herbert Marcuse (1941), in a study of the relations between Marx and Hegel, represented Marx's thought as the culminating achievement of the Hegelian dialectical method, as a "critical philosophy" of society which Marcuse contrasted with the positive philosophy and sociology of Comte. The same general view of the nature of Marx's thought, inspired in this case by Lukács, is to be found in the work of Lucien Goldmann on the methods of the social sciences (1959) and on the social context and the literary expression of Jansenism in France (1955); and it has recently been expounded at length by Jean-Paul Sartre (1960), who argued that sociology, as an empirical discipline, either stands opposed to, or must be comprehended within, Marxism, which alone makes possible an understanding of the historically changing totality of social life.

Mainstream of sociology. In the mainstream of sociological thought, many writers continued to turn to Marx's work as a source of specific ideas and problems which they could develop along new lines. One of the most important ideas which was thus reassessed was that of ideology. It had already attracted the attention of Marxist writers at the end of the nineteenth century, and Franz Mehring's *Die Lessing-Legende* (1893) is the first major attempt to make use of Marx's theories in the interpretation of literary styles. But it was not until a quarter of a century later that Marxist literary criticism revealed its full scope in the work of Lukács, beginning with the publication of *Die Theorie des Romans* (1920) and continuing with his studies of nineteenth-century European realism (1935–1939) and of the historical novel (1947).

Another Marxist writer who was greatly preoccupied with problems of ideology in a broader sense is Antonio Gramsci, much of whose work was done during his imprisonment by the Italian fascist government and has become generally known and influential only since the 1950s. Gramsci was especially concerned with the nature of the cultural dominance exercised by a ruling class, to which he attributed much greater importance than other Marxists had done, and, on the other hand, with the means by which the working class in a capitalist society might resist bourgeois cultural influences while developing its own forms of expression in literature, art, and thought. The notion of "social hegemony" which he introduced was meant to emphasize the interdependence of economic, political, and cultural elements in class conflicts; and his studies of the role of intellectuals, of the educational system, and of other aspects of culture (Gramsci 1949), inspired by this idea, were highly original contributions to the discussion of the old Marxist problem of the relations between "base" and "superstructure" in social life.

The notion of ideology also provided the central theme in the work of Karl Mannheim, who envisioned his task as the elaboration of a general sociology of knowledge from Marx's one-sided criticism of bourgeois ideologies, as a means of understanding the ideological and political conflicts of the twentieth century. Mannheim's writings were symptomatic of a deep concern with the problems of ideology which has lasted until the present time and has produced a number of notable works, from the brilliant critical study by Ernst Grünwald (1934) to the historical survey, dealing at length with Marx and Nietzsche, by Hans Barth (1945).

Theories of class structure.   Mannheim was exceptional in attributing such overwhelming importance to the problems of ideology, and it is through other concepts—particularly those of class and conflict—that Marx has had his chief influ-

ence upon modern sociology. All the major theories of class structure, from those of Max Weber, Joseph Schumpeter, and Theodor Geiger up to those of the present day, have begun from Marx's formulation of the question and have been more or less strongly influenced in their conclusions by Marx's own results. Among recent writers, few have been prepared to abandon entirely Marx's model of the class system; but most of them have introduced modifications and have questioned Marx's explanations and predictions. Raymond Aron (1950; 1964), C. Wright Mills, and Ralf Dahrendorf (1959) reject, as inconsistent with the evidence, the constant association between economic ownership and political power which is a basic postulate of Marx's theory, and they draw attention in particular to the alternative bases of political power in societies where private ownership of industrial wealth is nonexistent. Marshall (1934–1962), Lockwood (1958), Lockwood and Goldthorpe (1963), and Mills (1951) examine the changing composition of the main social classes during the past century, especially the changes in the position of the middle classes, and show how these changes affect the relations between classes in a manner of which Marx's theory takes no account.

Class conflict.   Most recent sociologists have criticized Marx's theory of class conflict, especially that part of it which asserts the inevitability of working-class revolutions in capitalist societies and the eventual cessation of conflict in a society without classes. The critics, such as Dahrendorf (1959) and Aron (1964), argue that the growing differentiation of functions and the increasing separation between the economic, political, and other spheres in the advanced industrial societies have removed the basis for the coalescence of industrial, political, and ideological conflicts in massive class struggles, and that revolutionary movements have in fact disappeared from these societies. At the same time, they assert that some forms of conflict are unavoidable in any large and complex society and that a society without intergroup conflict, such as Marx envisaged, is sociologically impossible. The work of these writers shows, however, the extent to which the Marxist theory of conflict has influenced recent sociology; it has restored to the center of attention the problems of conflicting interests and values and of the strains produced by social change, which had been neglected in those theories, previously in the ascendant, that were chiefly concerned with consensus, integration, and social order.

Communist countries.   It might have been anticipated that with the spread of Marxism as a political creed in eastern Europe and Asia after 1945, there would be some revival of Marxist sociology in the countries concerned. However, so far this has not taken place. The later years of Stalin's rule were not propitious for any kind of sociology, and Soviet Marxism became increasingly occupied with adapting conventional formulas to political circumstances rather than with developing philosophical or sociological arguments; it was even less concerned with encouraging empirical investigations into Soviet society.

Since Stalin's death there has been a resurgence of sociological research in communist countries, but it is not in any obvious respect inspired by Marxist ideas. Much of the research is concerned with problems which are to be found in all industrialized, or rapidly industrializing, societies—technological change, productivity, urban growth, delinquency, education, and leisure—and it is carried out by the same methods that are used elsewhere. Only in a few instances, where there is some significant difference in the institutional setting of the problems, as in studies of the workers' councils in Yugoslavia, does the Marxist theoretical system appear to have any importance in shaping the investigations.

In the sphere of theoretical sociology, the contributions from communist countries have been few, and they have often revealed the difficulty of maintaining the Marxist system intact. A good example may be found in one of the most distinguished of these contributions: the last work published by the Polish sociologist Stanislaw Ossowski (1957), in which a profound reappraisal of Marx's theory of class leads to conclusions which do not differ widely from those reached by sociologists elsewhere. Ossowski recognizes that substantial changes have occurred in the class structure of capitalist countries, and he observes, in particular, that in all the modern industrial societies the political authorities increasingly determine the system of social stratification, rather than being determined by it, as a rigorous Marxist view would maintain. He also considers and criticizes the arguments which have been put forward, on opposite sides, for regarding both the United States and the Soviet Union as "classless societies." Perhaps his most important contribution, however, is to distinguish the various conceptions of class which were incorporated into Marx's theory, to establish the tentative character of Marx's synthesis, and to show its potentialities for further development so long as it is not accepted as dogma. Ossowski's book may be seen, to some extent, as the harbinger of a more creative period of Marxist thought in communist countries.

Defining Marxist sociology

The record of the encounter between Marxism and sociology since the 1880s shows plainly that while they are distinct, and even opposed, they have never ceased to have a powerful influence upon each other. Marxism is more than a system of sociology; it is a philosophy of man and society, as well as a political doctrine. Sociology, as it has mainly developed in the present century, is an attempt to describe impartially, to measure exactly, and to connect by means of scientific generalizations the diverse phenomena of social life. Even if it be held that a "philosophical anthropology" underlies every major system of theoretical sociology, as Karl Löwith does in his illuminating comparison of Weber and Marx (1932), Marxism still retains a distinctive character; no other body of social thought has become, in this way, the unique doctrine of a political movement and finally the orthodoxy of a ruling party. No other theory, therefore, has been so liable to end in dogmatic assertion and estrangement from social science.

Betwixt Marxism and sociology, the place of Marxist sociology is variable and uncertain. In one sense, Marxist sociology could be regarded as the sociology of those thinkers (for example, Nikolai Bukharin and Max Adler) who, on other grounds, are Marxist in their general philosophical or political outlook. It would then be of the same kind as any other school of sociology—let us say Thomist or Hindu sociology—which is based directly upon a philosophical world view. But it would still be affected by, and would have to respond to, the findings of empirical social research; and at some stage Marxists would be led to consider, as has happened in recent years, whether in fact there can be a separate Marxist sociology any more than there can be a separate Marxist physics.

In a broader sense, however, Marxist sociology might be regarded as including the work of all those thinkers who attach prime importance, in the investigation and explanation of social events, to the role of economic interests, relations between classes, and intergroup conflicts, without necessarily agreeing with the particular conclusions that Marx himself reached. But this category may seem too broad, since it would include those, from Weber and Pareto up to the recent sociologists discussed above, who have acknowledged Marx's outstanding importance as a thinker and have turned to his work for concepts and hypotheses, but who have revised or rejected so much of his system that it would be eccentric to refer to them as Marxists.

Lastly, Marxist sociology may be treated as a methodology, as a persistent critique of the aims and methods of the social sciences. In this form it has undoubtedly been prominent and important, as the writings of Lukács, Marcuse, and Sartre bear witness; but here it becomes not so much Marxist sociology as Marxist "anti-sociology."

T. B. BOTTOMORE

[See also ALIENATION; KNOWLEDGE, SOCIOLOGY OF; LEISURE; MARXISM; STRATIFICATION, SOCIAL, *articles on* SOCIAL CLASS *and* THE STRUCTURE OF STRATIFICATION SYSTEMS; *and the biographies of* CROCE; LENIN; LUKÁCS; LUXEMBURG; MANNHEIM; MARX; MILLS; OSSOWSKI; PARETO; SOMBART; TÖNNIES; TROTSKY; WEBER, MAX.]

BIBLIOGRAPHY

ADLER, MAX 1925 *Kant und der Marxismus.* Berlin: Laub.

ARON, RAYMOND 1950 Social Structure and the Ruling Class. *British Journal of Sociology* 1:1–16, 126–143.

ARON, RAYMOND 1960 Classe sociale, classe politique, classe dirigeante. *European Journal of Sociology* 1: 260–281.

ARON, RAYMOND 1964 *La lutte de classes.* Paris: Gallimard.

BARTH, HANS 1945 *Wahrheit und Ideologie.* Zurich: Manesse.

BUKHARIN, NIKOLAI I. (1921) 1926 *Historical Materialism: A System of Sociology.* London: Allen & Unwin. → First published as *Teoriia istoricheskogo materializma.*

CROCE, BENEDETTO (1900) 1922 *Historical Materialism and the Economics of Karl Marx.* London: Allen & Unwin; New York: Macmillan. → First published as *Materialismo storico ed economia marxistica.*

DAHRENDORF, RALF 1959 *Class and Class Conflict in an Industrial Society.* Stanford Univ. Press. → A greatly revised and expanded edition of a book first published in German in 1957.

FROMM, ERICH (editor) 1961 *Marx's Concept of Man.* New York: Ungar.

GOLDMANN, LUCIEN 1952 *Sciences humaines et philosophie.* Paris: Presses Universitaires de France.

GOLDMANN, LUCIEN 1955 *Le dieu caché.* Paris: Gallimard.

GOLDMANN, LUCIEN 1959 *Recherches dialectiques.* Paris: Gallimard.

GRAMSCI, ANTONIO (1919–1937) 1959 *The Modern Prince, and Other Writings.* New York: International Publishers.

GRAMSCI, ANTONIO 1949 *Gli intellettuali e l'organizzazione della cultura.* Turin: Einaudi.

GRÜNWALD, ERNST 1934 *Das Problem der Soziologie des Wissens.* Vienna and Leipzig: Braumüller.

KORSCH, KARL (1923) 1930 *Marxismus und Philosophie.* 2d ed. Leipzig: Hirschfeld.

KORSCH, KARL 1938 *Karl Marx.* London: Chapman.

LABRIOLA, ANTONIO (1895–1896) 1908 *Essays on the Materialistic Conception of History.* Chicago: Kerr. → First published in Italian.

LICHTHEIM, GEORGE 1961 *Marxism: An Historical and Critical Study.* New York: Praeger.

LOCKWOOD, DAVID 1958 *The Blackcoated Worker.* London: Allen & Unwin.

LOCKWOOD, DAVID; and GOLDTHORPE, J. H. 1963 Affluence and the British Class Structure. *Sociological Review* 11:133–163.

LÖWITH, KARL (1932) 1960 Max Weber und Karl Marx. Pages 1–67 in Karl Löwith, *Gesammelte Abhandlungen zur Kritik der geschichtlichen Existenz.* Stuttgart: Kohlhammer.

LUKÁCS, GYÖRGY (1919–1922) 1923 *Geschichte und Klassenbewusstsein: Studien über marxistische Dialektik.* Berlin: Malik.

LUKÁCS, GYÖRGY (1920) 1963 *Die Theorie des Romans: Ein geschichtsphilosophischer Versuch über die Formen der grossen Epik.* 2d ed., enl. Neuwied am Rhein (Germany): Luchterhand.

LUKÁCS, GYÖRGY (1935–1939) 1964 *Studies in European Realism.* New York: Grosset & Dunlap. → Contains essays first published in Hungarian and German. First published in English in 1950.

LUKÁCS, GYÖRGY (1947) 1965 *The Historical Novel.* New York: Humanities. → First published in book form in Hungarian as *A történelmi regény.* Parts 1 and 2 first appeared in 1937 in volumes 7, 9, and 12 of *Literaturnyi kritik.*

MARCUSE, HERBERT (1941) 1955 *Reason and Revolution: Hegel and the Rise of Social Theory.* 2d ed. London: Routledge. → A paperback edition was published in 1960 by Beacon.

MARCUSE, HERBERT 1958 *Soviet Marxism: A Critical Analysis.* New York: Columbia Univ. Press. → A paperback edition was published in 1961 by Vintage.

MARSHALL, T. H. (1934–1962) 1964 *Class, Citizenship, and Social Development: Essays.* Garden City, N.Y.: Doubleday. → A collection of articles and lectures first published in England in 1963 under the title *Sociology at the Crossroads and Other Essays.* A paperback edition was published in 1965.

MARX, KARL (1844) 1963 *Early Writings.* Translated and edited by T. B. Bottomore. London: Watts.

MARX, KARL (1844–1875) 1964 *Selected Writings in Sociology and Social Philosophy.* 2d ed. Edited by T. B. Bottomore and M. Rubel with a foreword by Erich Fromm. New York: McGraw-Hill.

MARX, KARL (1845) 1956 *The Holy Family.* Moscow: Foreign Languages Publishing House. → First published as *Die heilige Familie.*

MARX, KARL (1857–1858) 1953 *Grundrisse der Kritik der politischen Ökonomie.* Berlin: Dietz. → Written in 1857–1858. First published posthumously by the Marx–Engels–Lenin Institute, Moscow, in 1939–1941. A partial English translation was published as *Precapitalist Economic Formations* in 1965 by International Publishers.

MARX, KARL (1859) 1913 *A Contribution to the Critique of Political Economy.* Chicago: Kerr. → First published as *Zur Kritik der politischen Ökonomie.*

MARX, KARL; and ENGELS, FRIEDRICH (1845–1846) 1939 *The German Ideology.* Parts 1 and 3. With an introduction by R. Pascal. New York: International Publishers. → Written in 1845–1846; first published in German in 1932.

MEHRING, FRANZ (1893) 1953 *Die Lessing-Legende: Zur Geschichte und Kritik des preussischen Despotismus und der klassischen Literatur.* Berlin: Dietz.

MILLS, C. WRIGHT 1951 *White Collar: The American Middle Classes.* New York: Oxford Univ. Press. → A paperback edition was published in 1956.

Ossowski, Stanislaw (1957) 1963 *Class Structure in the Social Consciousness.* London: Routledge; New York: Free Press. → First published as *Struktura klasowa w społecznej świadomości.*

Pareto, Vilfredo (1902–1903) 1965 *Les systèmes socialistes.* 3d ed. Paris: Droz. → Constitutes Volume 5 of Pareto's *Oeuvres complètes.*

Renner, Karl (1904) 1949 *The Institutions of Private Law and Their Social Functions.* London: Routledge. → First published in German in *Marx-Studien* under the pseudonym J. Karner.

Sartre, Jean-Paul 1960 *Critique de la raison dialectique, précédée de question de méthode.* Paris: Gallimard. → An English translation of the prefatory essay, "Question de méthode," was published in 1963 by Knopf as *Search for a Method.*

Tönnies, Ferdinand (1887) 1957 *Community and Society (Gemeinschaft und Gesellschaft).* Translated and edited by Charles P. Loomis. East Lansing: Michigan State Univ. Press. → First published in German. A paperback edition was published in 1963 by Harper.

Tönnies, Ferdinand 1921 *Marx: Leben und Lehre.* Jena (Germany): Lichtenstein.

Veblen, Thorstein (1899) 1953 *The Theory of the Leisure Class: An Economic Study of Institutions.* Rev. ed. New York: New American Library. → A paperback edition was published in 1959.

Veblen, Thorstein 1921 *The Engineers and the Price System.* New York: Huebsch.

Weber, Max (1904–1905) 1930 *The Protestant Ethic and the Spirit of Capitalism.* Translated by Talcott Parsons, with a foreword by R. H. Tawney. London: Allen & Unwin; New York: Scribner. → See especially pages 35–92. First published in German. The 1930 edition has been reprinted frequently.

Weber, Max (1904–1917) 1949 *The Methodolgy of the Social Sciences.* Glencoe, Ill.: Free Press. → First published in German. See especially pages 50–113, "Objectivity in Social Science and Social Policy."

Weber, Max (1907) 1922 R. Stammlers "Überwindung" der materialistischen Geschichtsauffassung. Pages 291–359 in Max Weber, *Gesammelte Aufsätze zur Wissenschaftslehre.* Tübingen (Germany): Mohr.

Wiatr, Jerzy J. 1964 Political Sociology in Eastern Europe: A Trend Report and Bibliography. *Current Sociology* 13, no. 2.

MASARYK, THOMAS G.

Thomas G. Masaryk (1850–1937), Czechoslovakian statesman and social theorist, was born in Hodonin on the Moravian–Slovakian border. His father, a Slovak, was a coachman on one of the imperial estates; his mother came from a small Moravian town. He studied first at the Gymnasium in Brno, but after a conflict with the Roman Catholic church he left there and attended the Gymnasium in Vienna. Later, at the University of Vienna he wrote his dissertation, "Das Wesen der Seele bei Plato" (1876), under the philosopher Franz Brentano. In 1877 he studied with Gustav Theodor Fechner at the University of Leipzig, but Masaryk was influenced less by Fechner than by Charlotte Garrigue, a music student whom he met at Leipzig and later married. She came from a well-to-do American Unitarian family, whose religious faith had been shaped by Theodore Parker, and her religious views helped Masaryk define his own. Through her he also gained an understanding of English philosophy and American society: Locke, Hume, Mill, and Spencer influenced his thought, and American institutions guided his social and political aspirations. Masaryk acknowledged the extent of his debt to his wife by taking Garrigue as his middle name.

In 1879 Masaryk became *Privatdozent* of philosophy at the University of Vienna. His interests centered on sociology and on Czech political life. His first important book was *Der Selbstmord als sociale Massenerscheinung der modernen Civilisation* (1881). In this work he attempted to deal with suicide as a social phenomenon and to support his conclusions statistically. According to Masaryk, Europe was then in a period of high suicide rates. This could be directly attributed to a decline of monotheistic religion and thus was the "fruit of progress, of education, of civilization" (p. 146).

When the Czech university was established at Prague in 1882, Masaryk was called there as extraordinary professor of philosophy. He held his post for 32 years. During those years he helped to form the political and moral ideas of a significant part of the Czech and South Slav intelligentsia, although before 1914 he was not popular among the Czechs. His opposition to the Catholic church, on the one hand, and to Marxism, on the other, his pronounced Westernism, and his "realistic" moderation in political and national demands prevented him from exercising a wider influence.

While a professor in Prague, Masaryk published his *Versuch einer konkreten Logik: Klarifikation und Organisation der Wissenschaften* (1885), his last scholarly work. From then on, most of his work was more directly concerned with moral and political education. He founded and edited several journals, among them *Athenaeum* and *Naše doba* ("Our Epoch"), and a political weekly, *Čas* ("Time"). He was active politically as a member of the Austrian Reichsrat, representing first the Young Czech party, from 1891 to 1893, and later, from 1907 to 1914, the tiny Progressive party (more generally known as the Realist party), which he had founded.

Masaryk's political activities reflected the themes of his writings published during these years, in which he discussed Czech nationalism and deplored the deficiencies of the Marxist approach to basic social problems (1895; 1896; 1898). He knew

Russia from both studies and travels and wrote two volumes interpreting Russian culture, history, and religion (1913). He planned but never completed a third volume, on Dostoevski, whom he regarded as the key author for an understanding of Russia and whose philosophy and outlook he totally rejected.

Masaryk's own nationalism revived and extended the ideas underlying the work of the first modern Czech historian, František Palacký. Masaryk saw the Czech national awakening in the nineteenth century as a continuation of the Hussite reformation of the fifteenth. And the movement of the Bohemian Brethren, in his view, encompassed the highest aspirations of the Czech nation and of the whole of mankind. This vague, moral nationalism was sharply criticized by professional Czech historians like Jaroslav Goll and Josef Pekař.

In 1914 Masaryk left Prague, and during World War I he became the leading propagandist urging the establishment of independent small nations (1918) and the identification of Czech national traditions with those of Western democracy. He made London the center of his activities and in 1917–1918 visited Russia and the United States. It was his plan to create a Czechoslovakia in which Czechs and Slovaks would be united on the strength of ethnic principles and Germans and Magyars would be included on the basis of historical principles; his views prevailed at the Versailles peace conference. He was elected the first president of Czechoslovakia in 1918 and was continuously re-elected until he resigned in 1935 for reasons of ill health. Until 1948 he was revered as the "father of his country," but because of his strong anti-Bolshevik stand the post-1948 communist regime has been sharply critical of him.

HANS KOHN

WORKS BY MASARYK

1876 Das Wesen der Seele bei Plato. Ph.D. dissertation, Univ. of Vienna.
1881 *Der Selbstmord als sociale Massenerscheinung der modernen Civilisation.* Vienna: Konegen.
(1885) 1887 *Versuch einer konkreten Logik: Klarifikation und Organisation der Wissenschaften.* Vienna: Konegen. → First published as *Základové konkrétní logiky.*
(1895) 1935 *Česká otázka: Snahy a tužby národního obrození* (The Czech Question: Efforts and Aspirations Towards the National Rebirth). 4th ed. Prague: Čin.
(1896) 1920 *Karel Havlíček: Snahy a tužby politického probuzení* (Karel Havlíček: Efforts and Aspirations Towards the Political Awakening). 3d ed. Prague: Laichter.
(1898) 1935 *Otázka sociální: Základy marxismu sociologické a filosofické* (The Social Question: The Sociological and Philosophical Foundations of Marxism). 3d ed. Prague: Čin.
(1913) 1955 *The Spirit of Russia: Studies in History, Literature and Philosophy.* Rev. & enl. ed., 2 vols. New York: Macmillan. → First published in German.
1918 *The New Europe: The Slav Standpoint.* London: Eyre & Spottiswoode.
(1925) 1927 *The Making of a State: Memories and Observations, 1914–1918.* New York: Stokes; London: Allen & Unwin. → First published as *Světová revoluce za války a ve válce, 1914–1918.*
(1931–1933) 1944 *Masaryk on Thought and Life: Conversations With Karel Čapek.* New York: Macmillan. First published as *Hovory s T. G. Masarykem.*

SUPPLEMENTARY BIBLIOGRAPHY

Festschrift Th. G. Masaryk zum 80. Geburtstage. 2 vols. 1930. Bonn: Cohen.
LUDWIG, EMIL (1935) 1936 *Defender of Democracy: Masaryk of Czechoslovakia.* New York: Robert McBride. First published as *Gespräche mit Masaryk: Denker und Staatsmann.*
NEJEDLÝ, ZDENĚK (1930–1935) 1949–1950 *T. G. Masaryk.* 2d ed., 2 vols. Prague: Orbis.
SETON-WATSON, ROBERT W. 1943 *Masaryk in England.* New York: Macmillan.

MASS BEHAVIOR

See COLLECTIVE BEHAVIOR *and* MASS PHENOMENA.

MASS COMMUNICATION

See COMMUNICATION, MASS.

MASS CULTURE

See COMMUNICATION, MASS; MASS SOCIETY.

MASS MEDIA

See COMMUNICATION, MASS.

MASS PHENOMENA

The term "mass phenomena" as it is used in this article is intended to cover the same range of behavior as that denoted by two frequently used similar expressions: "collective behavior" and "mass behavior." Under this general rubric a number of more specific terms have commonly been employed to refer to the five major subtypes of mass phenomena: (1) apathy, (2) panic, (3) mob, (4) craze, and (5) social movement. These major subtypes are in turn divisible into still finer subclassifications, denoted by a miscellany of terms which have come to be used conventionally to describe local varieties of unique forms. Thus some mob situations are commonly labeled "riots," as in "race riots," and certain others are referred to as "lynchings"; some social movements are called "revitalization movements," and these are still further classified by local terms, such as "cargo cults" (Oceania), "nativistic movements" (American Indians), etc. The nomenclature for mass phenomena is so vast and so intricately related to varying criteria that there is no reason to review or attempt to rationalize it in detail here. It should be noted that there are also other terms, like "mass hysteria," which crosscut this natural historian's nomenclature. These terms draw attention to certain psychological or social attributes which several types of mass phenomena have in common and which they sometimes share with behavior that is not included under the category of mass phenomena.

Definition.   Although there seems to be an intuitive recognition by most observers that all of these forms of human behavior have something in common which justifies treating them as a unit, the efforts to define this commonality are not always in agreement. Smelser has provided a definition in his book, *Theory of Collective Behavior:* "we define collective behavior as mobilization on the basis of a belief which redefines social action" ([1962] 1963, p. 8). Brown (1954) in his discussion of the varieties of mass phenomena suggests a set of dimensions for their classification (size, frequency and regularity of congregation, frequency and regularity of polarization of attention, and continuity of identification of individuals with the group), but he provides no definition. Any definition must not only state common features of the various referents of the term but must also state common features which nonmembers of the class do not possess. Certainly the term "mass phenomenon" cannot be taken to refer to all attributes of a large group of people (however "large" may be defined); otherwise, we should have to include culture, acculturation, culture change, population growth, voting behavior, rumor circulation, and many other social and cultural attributes and processes under the rubric of mass phenomena. Neither can we comfortably include all situations in which a large group of people is collected in one place, or in which many people are simultaneously the target of communication: not all audience or crowd behavior will fall within the intuitive boundaries of the concept. Nor can we be satisfied with a definition that emphasizes a single psychological or social process—such as fear or mobilization—without regard to the size (or "mass") of the group involved.

If we keep these considerations in mind, it would appear that Smelser's definition is nearly adequate to our needs. But its emphasis on mobilization makes it difficult to include the disaster syndrome (including shock, apathy, disorientation, and the very opposite of mobilization of a group for action). Thus I suggest the following, somewhat less analytical, definition: *"Mass phenomenon" signifies that class of social event in which a large number of people at the same time behave in a way which constitutes a notable interruption of their routine, socially sanctioned role behavior.*

The varieties of mass phenomena.   Let us now consider how the characteristics recognized by the above definition are manifested in the subclasses of mass phenomena to which I have referred.

Apathy and the disaster syndrome.   The disaster syndrome occurs after a major catastrophe, usually physical, has destroyed important features of a group's natural and/or cultural environment, frequently with severe casualties. In this case the interruption of routine behavior implies the virtual cessation of any kind of adaptive behavior. Initially, the surviving population appears to be in a state of shock: people are passive, emotionally numb, relatively insensitive to physical pain, apathetic, disoriented, unable to understand the magnitude of the disaster, and unresponsive beyond minimal survival action; little mutual aid is undertaken, and remedial action is often trivial. After minutes or hours—and perhaps longer—as aid enters from outside the disaster area, the survivors become less apathetic and enter into a suggestible stage in which, under leadership, they can begin to engage in rescue, repair, and other useful activities. Eventually the syndrome moves into a euphoric stage of mutual aid in reconstruction, and at last it tapers off into the culturally standardized routine. [*See also* DISASTERS. *For discussion of the disaster syndrome see* Wallace 1956a.]

Panic.   Panic occurs when a group is subjected to an overwhelming and imminent threat to which escape appears to be the only effective response, and when escape routes are perceived to be inadequate to accommodate all of the group before the impact of the threatened event. In such a situation, the group structure disintegrates into an "every-man-for-himself" state of anarchy: individual escape tactics are apt to be chosen impulsively, with little foresight and with restricted attention to the real environment; jamming is likely to occur at the exits from the situation, with attendant injury, loss of life, and increased slowing of the escape flow. The interruption here is twofold: first, the abandonment of group structure by individuals (even though the group itself may have had a plan for handling the problem by reducing the threat or by orderly escape); and second, the severe constriction of perceptual and cognitive functions of individuals under the stress of fear.

Mob. The mob is an angry group which attacks and attempts to injure or destroy an object (usually a person or persons or some item of material culture identified with some human being or group). It differs from a military or police force insofar as the members of the mob are not performing socially sanctioned roles and insofar as the attack is not undertaken as an implementation of a rational policy concerted by the mob's members (although, to be sure, there may be a leader who, unknown to the rank and file, is exciting and directing the mob, carrying out a policy of his own or of some other group). The interruption of routine behavior here is the abandonment of the socially sanctioned roles of peaceable, law-abiding private citizens and the assumption of primitive judgmental and punitive roles which are carried out with minimal concern for justice (as locally defined) or for long-term consequences.

Craze. The craze is a short-lived rush, by many persons, to worship, to touch, or to acquire some object (human or material) or characteristic of value. In its milder forms it may be referred to as a "fad"—a clothing style, a type of haircut, a dance; in more extreme expression it may be termed a "craze" (proper)—such as the adulation of a popular singer by thousands of screaming fans, a kind of financial investment, or a rush to settle new lands or to exploit unclaimed mineral resources. The interruption here is the abandonment of previous objects of interest and the substitution for them, by many people at the same time, of a standardized object. [*See* FASHION.]

Social movement. The social movement (or revitalization movement), whether religious or political and whether revolutionary or reformative, is by definition an organized effort to induce the members of a community to abandon certain customs or practices and to adopt different ones. The participants in the movement, starting with the prophet or leader, then his disciples, and eventually at least some followers, do in fact change their ways and the distribution of their energies. In every social movement, therefore, there is an interruption of a routine and the substitution of a new pattern of behavior, rationalized by reference to an ideology. The aim of the movement, of course, may be to accomplish a much more extensive interruption and to institute a much more pervasive new system than ever is accomplished. [*See* SOCIAL MOVEMENTS.]

Phenomena not considered. It may be pointed out that in the above discussion we have left out certain phenomena which are included in some treatments. Thus, for instance, we have not treated crowds per se as examples of mass phenomena, because many crowds are engaged in perfectly routine, standardized activities. Thus, for instance, we do not treat as a mass phenomenon the audience at sports events, at theaters, and at religious ceremonials because it is an organized group interacting with another group (the performers) in a patterned, culturally institutionalized way, even in cases (as at political rallies, voodoo rituals, or Holy Roller types of religious revival) where the behavior is excited or hysterical in a technical sense. Similarly, crowds on arteries of transportation, in markets, or in military units, however poorly or well organized, are not treated as mass phenomena, because the behavior involved is perfectly explicable and predictable from a knowledge of the culture. Nor do we consider the gross characteristics and social activities of vast aggregates —like "the masses," "the consumer," "the proletariat," "the Negro," or "the Southern white"— as mass phenomena in themselves.

The reader may, however, note that while the behaviors which have been treated as mass phenomena do have in common the feature of interruption of routine, they range from the nonpurposeful, inactive, maladaptive extreme of the disaster syndrome, through grades of increasingly purposeful, active, adaptive behavior, to the social movement, which is eminently purposeful, active, and adaptive. In the next section we shall take up the question of explanation, not only for the mass phenomenon in general, but for the occurrence of its varieties.

Explanations of mass phenomena. Explanations —and predictions—of mass phenomena usually invoke a mixture of psychological and sociological principles. Sometimes efforts are made to provide purely sociological explanations; these efforts, however, are generally justified by pointing out the deficiencies of early psychological theories that postulated "herd instincts," "the group mind," and the atavistic vulnerabilities of civilized men. Although such appeals to supposed universal psychological tendencies are fruitless as guides for research, the "pure" sociological approach merely reintroduces psychology through the back door via definitions of "social" concepts in terms of sentiments, goals, values, needs, and so forth. It seems wisest to make use explicitly of both psychological and sociological variables, evaluating the utility of each by more or less operational criteria.

On the most generic level, the following conditions seem to be required for the occurrence of any mass phenomenon: (1) a certain type of information must be presented to the members of the target group, approximately simultaneously; (2) the type of information which is presented must describe a difference between the individual's present situation and that which either has obtained in the past or very probably will obtain in the future; (3) the difference must be sufficient to constitute a dramatic gain, or loss, of important values (such as life, health, or self-respect); (4) the present or future loss must be perceived as avoidable, or the future gain as achievable, if something is done. The resultant action is, in fact, the behavior described as the mass phenomenon.

Further conditions need to be specified before it is possible to predict what that action will be. Important classes of such conditions are, first, the precise nature of the threat, disaster, or future gain; and, second, the existing cultural system of the target group—its goals, its fears, its ontological beliefs, its social organization, and its modal personality structure.

Apathy and the disaster syndrome. In a major disaster or in a situation of threat from which no escape route can at the moment be perceived, the mass action is, in effect, no action, or apathy: the only relief from the awareness of an unchangeable contrast between good past and bad present, or good present and bad future, is denial or withdrawal from awareness of reality as thus defined. The disaster syndrome, the cultural situation of universal demoralized individual behavior resulting from anomie, and the fictional social condition of an impending world's end described in Nevil Shute's popular novel *On the Beach* are examples of the apathetic response. It is worth noting that panic does not occur under these conditions.

Panic. Where the catastrophe has not yet occurred and there is still a possibility—but a narrow and diminishing one—of escape, panic occurs instead of apathy. The action involved is frequently precipitate physical flight, but other activities may represent the appropriate mode of escape: the selling of property, as in a financial crash or in a neighborhood threatened with invasion by an unwanted social group; or the hoarding of food in anticipation of shortages.

Mob. Where a catastrophe may occur but is not imminent, and where its likelihood is believed to be increased by the actions or inaction of some other person or group who is not believed to be responsive to the fears of the threatened group, a likely response is mob action. Mob action is also likely where an important goal is believed to be achievable but blocked by the action or inaction of some nonresponsive social group. The critical factor here seems to be the group's belief that the disparity between present and future (whichever way the balance lies—good present and bad future or bad present and good future) can be resolved only if some weak and evil persons are injured or destroyed. In the mob situation, furthermore, it is possible for the group to find relief for their feelings of guilt in scapegoating, that is, attributing to others those faults, often irrelevant to the precipitating issue, whose recognition in themselves would cause the members of the mob to feel further discomfort. [See PREJUDICE.]

Craze. In the craze, the members of the group seem to be driven by both a hope for some desirable thing and a fear of being left behind while others enjoy themselves. In a sense the craze is a "positive" panic: the urgency of the situation lies not in the imminence of danger, escape from which becomes less likely with each passing moment, but in the availability of a benefit, access to which may be reduced in the near future.

Social movement. The social (or revitalization) movement is the most positive, most organized, and most deliberate of the mass phenomena. In polar contrast to apathy, the participants in such a movement must maintain an effective social organization over considerable periods of time. The social movement defines the present as a transfer point between an undesirable past and a glorious future. It mounts a carefully calculated campaign, by a mixture of religious and political procedures, to transform society from an evil to a good condition. In the social movement, the character of the existing culture is closely relevant to what happens. Prevailing beliefs about the mechanisms of change are apt to determine the form of—but not to precipitate—the movement. Thus, among Jews the belief in a Messiah, and among Muslims the belief in the Mahdi, have heavily colored the movements that have occurred among these peoples; the Melanesian "myth dream" of their ancestors returning with cargo and the Christian concept of the millennium have shaped many of the movements in their respective parts of the world. [See MILLENARISM; NATIVISM AND REVIVALISM.]

It should finally be pointed out that mass phenomena of different types can follow one another in sequence in a given group. Thus, an apathetic phase following the awareness of disaster may be succeeded by a revitalization movement; a rioting mob may be swept by panic; an enthusiastic meeting of participants in a craze may turn into a riot if the object of the craze is withheld; and so on. It follows from the definition and from the general statement of conditions that a mass phenomenon, once established, can readily be transmuted in form as the nature of the information given to the group is varied.

ANTHONY F. C. WALLACE

[Directly related is the entry COLLECTIVE BEHAVIOR. Other relevant material may be found in GROUPS; INTERACTION; SOCIAL PSYCHOLOGY.]

BIBLIOGRAPHY

The bibliography on mass phenomena is extensive and diffuse. Smelser 1962 contains the most useful general bibliography on the topics considered in this article, except for the subject of apathy, which is not treated. The National Academy of Sciences–National Research Council has published a series of monographs on disaster behavior, including the apathetic reaction, and maintains a large card catalogue of works on disaster. See also the bibliographies of COLLECTIVE BEHAVIOR and DISASTERS.

BLUMER, HERBERT   1957   Collective Behavior. Pages 127–158 in Joseph B. Gittler (editor), Review of Sociology: Analysis of a Decade. New York: Wiley.

BROWN, ROGER W.   1954   Mass Phenomena. Volume 2, pages 833–876 in Gardner Lindzey (editor), Handbook of Social Psychology. Cambridge, Mass.: Addison-Wesley.

FESTINGER, LEON; RIECKEN, HENRY W.; and SCHACHTER, STANLEY   1956   When Prophecy Fails. Minneapolis: Univ. of Minnesota Press.

QUARANTELLI, ENRICO   1954   The Nature and Conditions of Panic. American Journal of Sociology 60:267–275.

SMELSER, NEIL J.   (1962) 1963   Theory of Collective Behavior. London: Routledge; New York: Free Press.

WALLACE, ANTHONY F. C.   1956a   Tornado in Worcester. Washington: National Research Council.

WALLACE, ANTHONY F. C.   1956b   Revitalization Movements. American Anthropologist New Series 58:264–281.

MASS SOCIETY

"Mass society" is best understood as a term denoting a model of certain kinds of relationships that may come to dominate a society or part of a society. Terms like "mass production" and "mass communication" refer to activities that are intended to affect very large numbers of people who are seen, for these purposes, as more or less undifferentiated units of an aggregate or "mass." Similarly, a "mass society" is one in which many or most of the major institutions are organized to deal with people in the aggregate and in which similarities between the attitudes and behavior of individuals tend to be viewed as more important than differences. Societies or institutions organized in this way are said to have a "mass character," and the life of individuals in such societies is said to be governed primarily by "mass relations."

The structure of mass society

Large populations do not by themselves produce mass relations, although mass relations are less likely among small populations. In the past, large societies were divided into many segments with relatively clear boundaries separating each segment from the other. Even though a society contained thousands of villages, all of them much alike, it was not a mass society because human relations centered on the village and supported the integrity of the village as a social unit.

Unlike the village-based society, the mass society does not help to sustain spontaneously evolving and durable social units. "Mass" in its simplest sense means an aggregate of people without distinction of groups or individuals. In mass production, for example, workers are organized according to the logic of specialization and control rather than as members of social groups or as distinct persons, and production is geared to a market of similarly undifferentiated people. Mass production, of course, involves a highly structured mass, by virtue of the division of labor and administrative organization, and it is therefore to be distinguished from the unstructured mass represented, for example, by the aggregate of unemployed workers. Moreover, some industries have more of a mass character than others: the assembly-line system of automobile factories is much more conducive to the emergence of the mass than is the craft-based system of printing (Blauner 1964). Nevertheless, the mass character of the market is a decisive factor in the organization of most manufacturing industries.

It is not so much the large size of the population as it is the large scale of activities that favors mass relations. Where the scale of activity is very great, it is more likely that the social relations which individuals bring with them or develop will be easily ignored or transformed by the dictates of technical efficiency or effective control. Thus, mass relations are likely to emerge where large-scale activities predominate, as in nationwide organizations, markets, audiences, and electorates.

The decline of community.   Large-scale activities favor the emergence of the mass because they tend to develop at the expense of communal relations. The local community comes to provide for fewer of its members' needs and therefore cannot maintain their allegiance. The rural community no longer is isolated and self-sufficient. As it becomes dependent on the city, and particularly on national markets and organizations, the rural community loses its significance and cohesion. The city does not develop the communal life that was formerly provided by the rural community. The individual who migrates to the city does not enter the community as a whole, nor is he likely to enter a subcommunity of the city. The urban subcommunity loses its coherence as a result of the increasing scale and specialization of common activities. Instead of affiliation with a community, the urban resident frequently experiences considerable social isolation and personal anonymity.

Ethnic and religious groups also tend to lose their coherence as their members are drawn into large-scale organizations and arenas. Individuals derive less of their social identity, style of life, and social values from their ethnic and religious background. As ethnic cultures come in contact with mass culture, they cease to preserve their unique qualities. Religious groups tend to de-emphasize their theological and liturgical differences. The particular religious affiliation loses its significance for both religious and secular beliefs and conduct. Even if people continue to associate primarily with coreligionists, this has little influence on the quality of their lives or on the manner of their participation in the larger society.

Like local, ethnic, and religious communities, class-based communities tend to lose their importance and coherence where the whole population is incorporated into large-scale activities. Social classes weaken as sources of distinctive values, styles of life, and social identity; and they increasingly resemble one another in the beliefs, values, and interests of their members. Class distinctions are leveled, and class boundaries are blurred. Class consciousness and class solidarity dissolve into mass consciousness and mass solidarity. The lower classes are increasingly brought into arenas of communication, politics, and consumption previously limited to the higher classes. Class differences in opportunities and modes of participation that remain are no longer believed to be desirable or permanent. Common symbols of the good life and of rights and obligations replace class-differentiated concepts. Classes remain as categories of people who differentially share in common ways of life rather than as self-conscious groups with distinctive ways of life. Status strivings and anxieties abound, but this testifies to the ambiguity of status where fixed social hierarchies no longer exist.

The ascendance of organization. Mass organizations replace communal groups as the characteristic units of society. Mass organizations are large and formal, but some large and formal organizations exhibit more of a mass character than do others. The additional features that constitute a mass character include a membership that is structured primarily by administrative devices rather than through social relations, and, correlatively, activity that is mobilized from the center rather than generated through various groups within the organization (Selznick 1952). Mass organizations do not build on the primary relations of members,

nor do they support and facilitate primary relations among members. The result is a relatively unmediated and depersonalized relationship between the membership and the organization. Where the organization seeks a highly active membership, as in certain kinds of mass parties, intense identifications with the organization may be created. Most mass organizations do not seek a mobilized membership, however, and do not possess the symbols or other resources for mobilization. Instead, they are content with passive support from their members, who in turn acquire little social identity from the organization. Solidarity tends to be weak under these conditions, and symbolic or personal gratifications correspondingly slight. Unlike membership in communities, membership in mass organizations tends to be a fragile bond because relations are impersonal and leveled. This weakness is indicated by high rates of mobility of members, as they respond to opportunities for greater benefits and to new interests elsewhere.

As mass organizations replace communities, so do "mass arenas" displace local arenas. Mass arenas, including national markets and electorates, are spheres of activity common to all sections of the population. Like mass organizations, mass arenas are managed from the center rather than structured through social relations. They are managed primarily through the mass media of communication, since only in this way can an entire population be presented simultaneously with the same objects of attention. People participate in mass arenas by selecting from among the alternatives presented through the mass media. Since the alternatives are standardized in order to reach the entire population simultaneously and since they are directed to individuals as undifferentiated members of the society, participation transcends the individual's social relations (Blumer 1939).

Mass equalitarianism. Pervading all kinds of mass relations is a common normative orientation of equalitarianism. All members of mass society are equally valued as voters, buyers, and spectators. Numerical superiority therefore tends to be the decisive criterion of success. In the political realm this means the number of votes; in the economic realm it is the number of sales; and in the cultural realm it is the size of the audience. Mass equalitarianism is strengthened by the attenuation of the social bases of inequality, notably membership in ethnic and religious groups and especially in social classes. In contrast to the equalitarianism of small numbers, as in friendships, mass equalitarianism emphasizes the similarities of individuals rather than the uniqueness of persons.

Mass equalitarianism is also linked to the bureaucratization of organization. Mass organization simultaneously encourages the bureaucratic centralization of governing powers and the leveling of social differences among the governed (Weber 1906–1924). The incorporation of all sections of the population into large-scale activities summons centralized organization for coordination and control. Mass bureaucracies favor the leveling of social differences in the interest of efficiency. By treating everyone alike, according to functionally rational rules and procedures, mass bureaucracies foster equalitarianism. However, bureaucratic recruitment on the basis of professional competence raises new hierarchies. To be sure, careers open to talent are in greater harmony with equalitarian beliefs than is selection according to family and property. But professional elites are nevertheless elites and thereby introduce new social distinctions. This is a source of strain in modern society; in the political realm, for example, there is a tension between planning by experts and participation by mass electorates [see ELITES].

Mass equalitarianism is expressed in the populist character of mass society. Whatever is believed to express the popular will or to meet the most widely shared expectations is considered legitimate (Shils 1956). Political regimes strive to be popular regimes, whether they are dictatorial or constitutional. While this popular legitimation of authority centers in the polity, it pervades all kinds of social institutions. Populism places a premium on the capacity of leaders to create and placate popular opinion. Those who are effective in mobilizing large numbers of people have great power, and this generally means the leaders of mass parties. The mass leader seeks to embody and reflect popular desires; masses, not elites, are the ultimate sources of legitimation in mass society. This leads elites to make themselves readily accessible to popular pressures: that is, they are forced to be responsive not only to periodic expressions of public opinion through regular channels such as elections, but also to momentary and *ad hoc* representations of whatever is claimed to be popular.

Leaders, of course, do not seek merely to respond to mass opinion. They also try to control it. Since they lack firm bases of independent authority, their control tends to take the form of manipulation and mobilization rather than command. The very presence of large numbers of only loosely organized and committed people summons efforts of leaders to manipulate and mobilize them. For if elites are highly accessible to mass pressures, so are masses readily available for mobilization by elites. People are receptive to direct appeals from remote elites, because they are poorly attached to proximate sym-

bols and relationships and increasingly caught up in distant events and activities (Kornhauser 1959).

Mass movements. As mass society develops, there is a growing cleavage between those who continue to be integrated in local groups and those who have already been incorporated into mass relations. In part this is a difference between the old classes and the new classes—craftsmen versus industrial workers, independent entrepreneurs versus industrial managers, free professionals versus members of professional staffs, and so forth. Increasingly isolated from the larger society, members of the declining classes readily come to believe that they are the victims of it. More generally, the locally attached, in their resentment of the ascendancy of big cities, big government, big business, and big labor, become receptive to the appeals of mass movements directed against the forces of mass society.

Then there is the growing number of people who have been detached from communal relations but who are not, or not yet, incorporated into mass relations. It is likely to include, among others, new migrants to the cities, new workers in the factories, and, generally, the younger and newly mobile members of the society. In the absence of strong group ties, they are less constrained and more restless than those who continue to be rooted in communal groups or those who have been fully incorporated into mass relations. These poorly attached and unintegrated people are readily available for activistic modes of intervention in political life and for participation in mass movements that promise them full membership in the national society.

Thus, modern mass movements are characteristically composed of people who either seek entry into mass society or seek to reverse the processes of mass society. Like mass organizations, mass movements do not build on existing social relations but instead construct direct ties between participants and leaders. When a mass society has successfully incorporated most sections of the population into its central institutions, mass movements may become less widespread. In a highly developed mass society, mass participation is institutionalized in the form of mass organizations, especially mass parties, but also mass unions and similar associations, universal suffrage, extensive publicity of political men and events, and the official symbolism of popular government [see SOCIAL MOVEMENTS].

Criticism of mass society

Early critics. The concept of mass society had its major intellectual origin in the nineteenth-century criticism of the revolutionary changes in European (and especially French) society. Many thinkers believed that the decisive social tendency was the change from aristocratic to democratic society. It was not simply that a shift occurred in the class composition of governing groups. More fundamental was the shift that these thinkers perceived in the bases of social order. Formerly, standards of value and conduct had been assumed to exist as part of a natural order of society; in democratic society, by contrast, the arbitrary will and opinion of the masses were replacing established standards.

Early representatives of this kind of social criticism of the democratization of society were Catholic thinkers like Joseph de Maistre and the vicomte de Bonald. Following the ascendancy of portions of the middle classes, marked by such events as the accession in 1830 of Louis Philippe, the bourgeois king, in France and the passage of the 1832 Reform Act in England, liberal thinkers adopted mass society ideas, not to defend the old order but to assess the strengths and weaknesses of the new order. Thus, Tocqueville (1835) moved from a fairly hopeful analysis of the possibilities of preserving standards in a democratic society (in light of his examination of America) to a more pessimistic view of the matter following the 1848 revolution in France. Even so influential a liberal thinker as J. S. Mill found himself in wide agreement with Tocqueville's more pessimistic diagnosis of democratic culture. Burckhardt and Nietzsche, among many other late nineteenth-century romantic thinkers, sought to interpret changes in European society as the erosion of culture. Ortega (1930) later formulated a highly popular version of this view.

This aristocratic criticism of the development of nineteenth-century society profoundly influenced democratic criticism of the development of twentieth-century society. Where the first centered on the intellectual defense of elite values against the rise of mass participation, the second developed as a defense of democratic values against the rise of totalitarianism. The defensive posture of the aristocratic thinkers was adopted by democratic thinkers who, having won the nineteenth-century war of ideas and institutions, now sought to preserve their gains against the totalitarian challenge. Thus, such students of totalitarianism as Lederer (1940), Mannheim (1935), Fromm (1941), Neumann (1942), Arendt (1951), and Kornhauser (1959) see in the fragmentation of society the opportunity for new forms of domination based on the mobilization of large populations.

Two kinds of analysis closer to the social sciences have contributed significantly to the development of the idea of mass society during the past century. One is the effort to distinguish between traditional and modern societies, a line of analysis that has become a central theoretical perspective of sociology. An early formulation of this perspective was Maine's distinction between societies dominated by status relations of kinship and those dominated by contract relations of individuals. Tönnies (1887), in his highly influential analysis of *Gemeinschaft* and *Gesellschaft*, elaborated Maine's thesis. Further evolution of this line of analysis is to be found in Durkheim's theory of social solidarity and anomie (1893; 1897) and in Max Weber's treatment of traditional and bureaucratic authority (Weber 1906–1924). What made this kind of sociological theory relevant to the idea of mass society was its analysis of the atomization and depersonalization of social organization resulting from modernization. This became a central thesis of urban sociology, as in the writings of Simmel (1902–1903), Park (1916–1939), and Wirth (1933–1953). [*See* COMMUNITY–SOCIETY CONTINUA.]

The development of mass psychology provided still another source of ideas about mass society (Reiwald 1949). Gustave Le Bon, Scipio Sighele, and Gabriel Tarde were leading students of mass behavior at the turn of the century. In their analysis of the heightened suggestibility and manipulability of people no longer constrained by communal ties and traditional authorities, these theorists contributed to the social psychology of mass society. This line of analysis was given a more sociological and less polemical cast by American students of what came to be called "collective behavior" (Blumer 1939) [*see* COLLECTIVE BEHAVIOR]. Many of these themes from sociology and social psychology were drawn together in Mannheim's critical analysis (1935) of the effects of the "fundamental democratization" and "growing interdependence" of society.

A common perspective unites these theories and makes them part of the history of the idea of mass society. It is a view of modern society as containing certain fundamental pathological tendencies, which are believed to inhere in its development. The theory of mass society adds to such concepts as "democratic society," "urban society," and "industrial society" an emphasis on the socially disintegrative effects of democratization, urbanization, and industrialization. Foremost among these effects are the decline of community and authority and the spread of pseudo-community and pseudo-authority.

Pseudo-community. During the 1920s and 1930s, a number of American sociologists reported on various aspects of modern life and generally stressed the anonymity and atomization of persons in contemporary society. Following World War II, this portrait of modern life was subject to considerable criticism on the grounds that primary relations are much in evidence in the factory, the army, and other allegedly impersonal organizations. Kinship networks, neighborhood bonds, and local activity were observed in a number of urban and suburban settings, and primary-group mediation of mass communications was shown to prevail over completely atomized audiences. Such observations suggest that the decline of community is at most relative to the condition of premodern society (Greer 1958).

There is much more to the problem of community than the question of the mere presence or absence of personal attachments and communal bonds. Students of mass society assert that the *functions* of primary groups are weakened under conditions of modern society, not that primary groups are absent. The decreasing role of primary relations in the social organization of mass society and their increasing *isolation* from the larger society weaken them as sources of meaning and support for the individual in the larger society. Moreover, they are more easily broken because they receive less support from the institutional framework of society. Both weaknesses stem from the attenuation of the *links* between primary relations and the major functional areas of society.

The isolation of primary relations creates the need for more inclusive bonds of solidarity and gives rise to a search for new forms of community. The barriers to community thrown up by the mass character of society heighten receptivity to the appeals of pseudo-community. This hypothesis has been applied to otherwise widely diverse social contexts. The German middle-class youth movement at the beginning of the century made the "return to *Gemeinschaft*" its cardinal article of faith. The Nazi movement subsequently inscribed the "folk community" on its ideological banner and won many adherents on the strength of this appeal. The totalitarian mass movement is only the most dramatic and extreme case of pseudo-community. Much more mundane cases have been examined in the context of American life. For example, campaigns of mass persuasion exploit themes of community and personalization (Merton 1946), and programs of "human relations" in industry exploit unfulfilled needs for social bonds and participation in the interest of greater worker efficiency (Mayo 1933). These ideologies and programs simulate but do not create community, and consequently they make people more available for manipulation and mobilization. They exploit a general dilemma facing the individual in mass society: either he demands highly personalized meaning from the mass enterprise and suffers frustration, or he withholds commitment to it and suffers loss of identity.

"Social alienation," "false personalization," "enforced privatization," and similar notions found in the writings on mass society point, however unsteadily, to the pathology of community in modern society (Nisbet 1953; Riesman 1950). This concern with the *quality* of social relations—the fabrication of symbols and relations, the exploitation of unfulfilled needs for personal response, and related matters—marks the perspective of mass analysis. As a perspective, it invites attention to the various distorted forms and expressions of the search for community, to the social conditions that promote them, and to the consequences for individuals and institutions that flow from them.

Pseudo-authority. The decline of authority accompanies the decline of community. For the loosening of the various cohesive groupings that make up a society is at the same time the dissolution of the authority of these groups over the individual. Traditional standards and customary authorities anchored in kinship, church, and community are replaced by bureaucratic systems of legal and political control. The rationalization of authority liberates the individual from the often harsh and always close constraints of the cohesive group; however, it also removes the direction and support supplied by such a group but not by the large and impersonal bureaucracy.

Many students of such relatively democratic political societies as those of England and the United States have been quick to criticize this conception of the bureaucratic society on the grounds that it fails to see the pluralist character of these societies, especially the dispersion of power and authority among diverse and independent social groups. Thus, interest-group activity and influence are found to be extensive on all levels of government; power and authority in many local communities are observed to be widely distributed among competing groups; and party loyalties are reported to possess considerable stability. Such findings appear to contradict notions of contemporary society as a condition of social and political atomization (Bell 1960).

Mass theorists question, however, whether these observations in fact confirm a continuing vitality of social pluralism, or whether the pluralist group structure is not itself subject to the forces of mass society. Social pluralism undoubtedly receives a certain impetus from the elaborate functional differentiation of the large-scale industrial society: the proliferation of specialized occupational groups is the principal case in point. But since these associations are specialized, tend to be nationwide, and often do not incorporate the work group or other social relations of the individual, they are transformed into mass organizations (Nisbet 1953; Selznick 1952).

Moreover, the interests underlying the formation of diverse organizations tend to be creatures of a complex and specialized economy that splits the person from the role, so that they possess only a limited capacity to elicit broad or deep personal commitment. If the interests are not very substantial and distinct, the organized representation of interests that constitutes a pluralist system will be correspondingly insubstantial and amorphous. The affluent society and welfare state also reduce the urgency of these interests. New sources of disaffection appear in the mass society, but they are not readily articulated and mitigated by means of pluralist organization and bargaining.

Whether or not mass theorists are correct in this particular argument, the general principle is clear: "the differentiation . . . which disintegrates is very different from that which brings vital forces together" (Durkheim [1893] 1960, p. 353). The functional differentiation of structures may increase efficiency, but it simultaneously may disintegrate what was a viable social entity without creating the conditions for the formation of new social entities. A great deal depends upon whether a given social function can sustain a social identity or whether the function is so specialized or otherwise limited that it cannot provide sufficient meaning to summon commitment.

As organizations become very large, specialized, and removed from the network of social relations of their members, they lose their authoritative character. The modern trade union, for example, appears less capable of providing meaning and identity to its members than occupational associations of former times, so that its power may seem more arbitrary and less authoritative. When similar processes occur in the church, profession, corporation, and other secondary groups, the society begins to lose its pluralism and experiences a general dissolution of authority.

The decline of authoritative standards and leadership creates anxiety and insecurity; feelings of aimlessness and lack of social direction become widespread. Such a state of anomie generates the quest for new authority and heightens receptivity to pseudo-authority. As in the case of the search for community, mass analysts try to identify the symptoms and consequences of inappropriate and inauthentic responses to genuine needs for authoritative standards and direction. The rise of charismatic leadership testifies to this need. But of greater significance is the quality of this leadership—whether it is the carrier of new values or merely the popularity of a demagogue or celebrity. Where mass media of communication and the techniques of manipulation and mobilization are highly developed, it hardly suffices to say that popular enthusiasm is sufficient to demonstrate a charismatic relationship. The conditions of mass society facilitate the fabrication of charisma in the absence of value commitment on the part of either leaders or masses.

More generally, whenever the claim to authority is based substantially on the manipulation of symbols rather than on the invoking of standards, one may speak of pseudo-authority. What concerns mass analysts are situations in which there is a marked discrepancy between the symbols and the substance of authority. The claim that public opinion is authoritative under conditions of modern mass democracy is a case in point. Where public opinion becomes a slogan for whatever is believed to be popular, rather than a process and product of public deliberation and discussion, it is a form of pseudo-democracy. This is a powerful tendency in mass society because of the difficulties of making and eliciting personal responses in mass arenas and bureaucratic institutions. The ease of mass manipulation and the difficulty of public deliberation favor the symbols of democracy without the substance, especially where the symbols are widely stereotyped in terms that do not invite close scrutiny or comparison with actual experience (Selznick 1952).

The most extreme manifestation of manipulated and mobilized opinion is found in totalitarian systems. The unanimous elections, the staged demonstrations, and the mass indoctrination programs reveal the possibilities of pseudo-democracy. Totalitarianism itself is greatly facilitated by the existence or creation of masses of people who are not attached to independent social groups. Indeed, the study of totalitarianism is instructive because it shows how the effort to mobilize a whole population actually *requires* the destruction of bonds of authority and community and their replacement by ideological organizations. However, the ultimate reliance of totalitarian regimes on the use of force testifies to the limits of this strategy of mobilization. Moreover, mass conditions do not by themselves produce totalitarianism. The existence of modern technology plus the availability of large numbers of socially unintegrated people make totalitarianism possible, but a number of other conditions must be present to prepare the way for totalitarianism.

Theories of mass society are sometimes said to be prophecies of despair (Bell 1960; Shils 1962). But they need not be so construed. That the mass analyst tends to be a pathologist of contemporary society in no way denies the existence in that society of creative and value-sustaining social forces. Properly incorporated into social science, the concepts of mass society invite analysis of the conditions under which mass processes are strong or weak. Thus, mass analysis may take on new significance in alerting students of non-Western societies to certain pathologies of social development. Perhaps more important for social thought than any particular proposition of mass society is the concern this perspective represents for assessing the *quality* of culture and social institutions. If social science is to pursue this kind of inquiry, however, it will have to renew its communication with the humanities. For if the idea of mass society has greatly influenced social science, its formulation and development have been to a considerable extent the work of philosophy, history, and literature.

WILLIAM KORNHAUSER

[*See also* COMMUNICATION, MASS; DEMOCRACY; TOTALITARIANISM; *and the biographies of* BURCKHARDT; DURKHEIM; MAINE; MANNHEIM; MAYO; ORTEGA Y GASSET; TOCQUEVILLE; TÖNNIES; WEBER, MAX.]

BIBLIOGRAPHY

ARENDT, HANNAH (1951) 1958 *The Origins of Totalitarianism.* 2d ed., enl. New York: Meridian.

BELL, DANIEL (1960) 1962 *The End of Ideology: On the Exhaustion of Political Ideas in the Fifties.* 2d ed., rev. New York: Collier.

BLAUNER, ROBERT 1964 *Alienation and Freedom: The Factory Worker and His Industry.* Univ. of Chicago Press.

BLUMER, HERBERT (1939) 1951 Collective Behavior. Pages 167–222 in Alfred M. Lee (editor), *New Outline of the Principles of Sociology.* 2d ed., rev. New York: Barnes & Noble.

DURKHEIM, ÉMILE (1893) 1960 *The Division of Labor in Society.* Glencoe, Ill.: Free Press. → First published as *De la division du travail social.*

DURKHEIM, ÉMILE (1897) 1951 *Suicide: A Study in Sociology.* Glencoe, Ill.: Free Press. → First published in French.

FROMM, ERICH (1941) 1960 *Escape From Freedom.* New York: Holt.

GREER, SCOTT (1958) 1964 Individual Participation in Mass Society. Pages 329–342 in Roland Young (editor), *Approaches to the Study of Politics: Twenty-two Contemporary Essays Exploring the Nature of Politics*

and Methods by Which It Can Be Studied. Evanston, Ill.: Northwestern Univ. Press.

KORNHAUSER, WILLIAM 1959 *The Politics of Mass Society.* Glencoe, Ill.: Free Press.

LE BON, GUSTAVE (1895) 1947 *The Crowd.* New York: Macmillan. → First published as *Psychologie des foules.*

LEDERER, EMIL 1940 *State of the Masses: The Threat of the Classless Society.* New York: Norton.

MANNHEIM, KARL (1935) 1940 *Man and Society in an Age of Reconstruction: Studies in Modern Social Structure.* New York: Harcourt. → First published as *Mensch und Gesellschaft im Zeitalter des Umbaus.*

MAYO, ELTON (1933) 1946 *The Human Problems of an Industrial Civilization.* 2d ed. Boston: Harvard Univ., Graduate School of Business Administration, Division of Research. → A paperback edition was published in 1960 by Viking.

MERTON, ROBERT K. 1946 *Mass Persuasion: The Social Psychology of a War Bond Drive.* New York: Harper.

NEUMANN, SIGMUND (1942) 1965 *Permanent Revolution: Totalitarianism in the Age of International Civil War.* 2d ed. New York: Praeger. → First published as *Permanent Revolution: The Total State in a World at War.*

NISBET, ROBERT A. 1953 *The Quest for Community: A Study in the Ethics of Order and Freedom.* New York: Oxford Univ. Press.

ORTEGA Y GASSET, JOSÉ (1930) 1961 *The Revolt of the Masses.* London: Allen & Unwin. → First published in Spanish.

PARK, ROBERT E. (1916–1939) 1952 *Human Communities: The City and Human Ecology.* Collected Papers, Vol. 2. Glencoe, Ill.: Free Press.

REIWALD, PAUL 1949 *De l'esprit des masses.* Neuchâtel and Paris: Delachaux & Niestlé.

RIESMAN, DAVID 1950 *The Lonely Crowd: A Study of the Changing American Character.* New Haven: Yale Univ. Press. → An abridged paperback edition was published in 1960.

SELZNICK, PHILIP (1952) 1960 *The Organizational Weapon: A Study of Bolshevik Strategy and Tactics.* Glencoe, Ill.: Free Press.

SHILS, EDWARD 1956 *The Torment of Secrecy: The Background and Consequences of American Security Policies.* Glencoe, Ill.: Free Press.

SHILS, EDWARD 1962 The Theory of Mass Society. *Diogenes* 39:45–66.

SIMMEL, GEORG (1902–1903) 1950 The Metropolis and Mental Life. Pages 409–424 in Georg Simmel, *The Sociology of Georg Simmel.* Edited and translated by Kurt H. Wolff. Glencoe, Ill.: Free Press. → First published in German.

TOCQUEVILLE, ALEXIS DE (1835) 1945 *Democracy in America.* 2 vols. New York: Knopf. → First published in French. A paperback edition was published in 1961 by Vintage and by Schocken.

TÖNNIES, FERDINAND (1887) 1957 *Community and Society (Gemeinschaft und Gesellschaft).* Translated and edited by Charles P. Loomis. East Lansing: Michigan State Univ. Press. → First published in German. A paperback edition was published in 1963 by Harper.

WEBER, MAX (1906–1924) 1946 *From Max Weber: Essays in Sociology.* Translated and edited by Hans H. Gerth and C. Wright Mills. New York: Oxford Univ. Press.

WIRTH, LOUIS (1933–1953) 1956 *Community Life and Social Policy: Selected Papers.* Univ. of Chicago Press.

MATHEMATICAL STATISTICS
See STATISTICS.

MATHEMATICS

The history of mathematics, and to some extent its content, can be thought of as involving three major phases. Ancient mathematics, covering the period from the earliest written records through the first few centuries A.D., culminated in Euclidean geometry, the elementary theory of numbers, and ordinary algebra. Equally important, this phase saw the evolution and partial clarification of axiomatic systems and deductive proofs. The next major phase, classical mathematics, began more than 1,000 years later, with the Cartesian fusion of geometry and algebra and the use of limiting processes in the calculus. From these evolved, during the eighteenth and nineteenth centuries, the several aspects of classical analysis. Other contributions of this phase include non-Euclidean geometries, the beginnings of probability theory, vector spaces and matrix theory, and a deeper development of the theory of numbers. About a hundred years ago the third and most abstract and demanding phase, known as modern mathematics, began to evolve and become separate from the classical period. This phase has been concerned with the isolation of several recurrent structures of analysis worthy of independent study —these include abstract algebraic systems (for example, groups, rings, and fields), topological spaces, symbolic logic, and functional analysis (Hilbert and Banach spaces, for example)—and various fusions of these systems (for example, algebraic geometry and topological groups). The rate of growth of mathematics has been so great that today most mathematicians are familiar in detail with the major developments of only a few branches of the subject.

Our purpose is to give some hint of these topics. The reader interested in a somewhat more detailed treatment will find the best single source to be *Mathematics: Its Content, Methods, and Meaning,* the translation of a Russian work (Akademiia Nauk S.S.S.R. 1956). Other general works are Courant and Robbins (1941), Friedman (1966), and Newman (1956). More specific references are given where appropriate. We do not here discuss probability, mathematical statistics, or computation, even though they are especially important mathematical disciplines for the social sciences, because they are covered in separate articles in the encyclopedia.

Ancient mathematics

The history of ancient mathematics divides naturally into three periods. In the first period, the pre-Hellenic age, the beginnings of systematic mathematics took place in ancient Egypt and in Mesopotamia. Contrary to much popular opinion, the mathematical developments in Mesopotamia were deeper and more substantial than those in Egypt. The Babylonians developed elementary arithmetic and algebra, particularly the computational aspects of algebra, to a surprising degree. For example, they were able to solve the general quadratic equation, $ax^2 + bx + c = 0$. An authoritative and readable account of Babylonian mathematics as well as of Greek mathematics is presented by Neugebauer (1951).

The second period of ancient mathematics was the early Greek, or Hellenic, age. The fundamentally new step taken by the Greeks was to introduce the concept of a mathematical proof. These developments began around 600 B.C. with Thales, Pythagoras, and others, and reached their high points a little more than a century later in the work of Eudoxus, who is responsible for the theory of proportions, which in antiquity held the place now held by the modern theory of real numbers.

The third period is the Hellenistic age, which extended from the third century B.C. to the sixth century A.D. The early part of this period, sometimes called the golden age of ancient mathematics, encompassed Euclid's *Elements* (about 300 B.C.), which is the most important textbook ever written in mathematics, the work on conics by Apollonius (about 250 B.C.), and above all the extensive and profound work of Archimedes on metric geometry and mathematical physics (Archimedes died in 212 B.C.). The second most important systematic treatise of ancient mathematics, after Euclid's *Elements*, is Ptolemy's *Almagest* (about A.D. 150). Ptolemy systematized and extended Greek mathematical astronomy and its mathematical methods. The mathematical sophistication of Archimedes and the richness of applied mathematics evidenced by the *Almagest* were not equaled until the latter part of the seventeenth century.

Classical analysis

The intertwined and rapid growth of mathematics and physics during the seventeenth, eighteenth, and nineteenth centuries centered in a major way on what is now called classical analysis: the calculus of Newton and Leibniz, differential and integral equations and the special functions that are their solutions, infinite series and products, functions of a complex variable, extremum problems, and the theory of transforms. At the basis of all this are two major ideas, *function* and *limit*. The first evolved slowly, beginning with the correspondence, established in the Cartesian fusion of the two best-developed areas of ancient mathematics, between algebraic expressions and simple geometric curves and surfaces, until we now have the present, very simple definition of the term "function." A set f of points in the plane (ordered pairs of numbers) of the form (x, y) is called a function if at most one y is associated with each x. If (x, y) is a member of f, it is customary to write $y = f(x)$; x is sometimes called the independent variable and y the dependent variable, but no causal meaning should be read into this terminology.

The notion and notation may be generalized to more than one independent variable; if g is a set of ordered triples (x, y, z) with at most one z associated with each pair (x, y), then $z = g(x, y)$ is called a function of two arguments. Since the most general notion of function can relate any two sets of objects, not just sets of numbers, it is sometimes desirable to emphasize the numerical character of the function. Then f is said to be a real-valued function of a real variable; here the term "real" refers to real numbers (in contrast to complex numbers, which will be discussed later).

Although a real-valued function has been defined as a set of ordered pairs of numbers, (x, y), where the domain of x is is an unspecified set of numbers, the subsequent discussion of functions is mostly confined to the familiar case in which the domain of x is an interval of numbers. Even when the discussion applies more generally, it is helpful to keep the interval case in mind.

A desire to understand limits was apparent in Greek mathematics, but a correct definition of the concept eluded the Greeks. A fully satisfactory definition, which was not evolved until the nineteenth century (by Augustin Louis Cauchy), is the following: b is the limit of f at a if and only if for every positive number ϵ there is a positive number δ such that, when the absolute value of $x - a$ is less than δ and greater than 0 (that is, $0 < |x - a| < \delta$), the absolute value of $f(x) - b$ is less than ϵ (that is, $|f(x) - b| < \epsilon$). In other words, b is the limit of f at a if x can be chosen sufficiently close to a (but not equal to a) to force $f(x)$ to be as close to b as desired. Symbolically, this is written $\lim_{x \to a} f(x) = b$. The limit of f at a may exist even though $f(a)$ is not defined; moreover, when $f(a)$ is defined, b may or may not equal $f(a)$. If it does—that is, if $f(x)$ is "near" $f(a)$ whenever x is "near" a—then f is

Figure 1 — Approximation of the derivative of f(x)

said to be continuous at a. If f is continuous at each a in an interval, f is said to be continuous over that interval.

The calculus.   The calculus defines two new concepts, the derivative and the integral, in terms of function and limit. They and their surprising relationship serve as the basis of the rest of mathematical analysis.

The derivative.   The first definition arises as the answer to the question "Given a function f, what is its slope (or, equivalently, its direction or rate of change) at any point x?" For example, suppose that $y = f(x)$ represents the distance, y, that a particle has moved in x units of time; then what is the rate of change of distance—the instantaneous velocity—at time x? If h is a short period of time, then an approximate answer is the distance traversed between x and $x + h$, that is, $f(x + h) - f(x)$, divided by the time, h, taken to travel that distance (see Figure 1). The approximation is better the smaller the value of h, which suggests the definition of the rate of change of f at x as the limit of this ratio as h approaches 0, that is,

$$\lim_{h \to 0} \frac{f(x + h) - f(x)}{h}.$$

This limit, if it exists, is denoted by $f'(x)$ (or by $df(x)/dx$ or by dy/dx) and is called the *derivative* of f at x. If $f'(x)$ exists, then f can be shown to be continuous at x, but the converse is not true in general.

One of the earliest and most important applications in the social sciences of the concept of a derivative has been to the mathematics of marginal concepts in economics. For example, let x represent output, $C(x)$ the cost of output x, and $R(x)$ the revenue derived from output x; then $C'(x)$ and

$R'(x)$ (or $dC(x)/dx$ and $dR(x)/dx$) are the marginal cost and marginal revenue, respectively. Marginal utility, marginal rate of substitution, and other marginal concepts are defined in a similar fashion. Many of the fundamental assumptions of economic theory receive precise formulation in terms of these marginal concepts.

The integral. The second concept in the calculus arises as the answer to the question "What is the area between the graph of a function f and the line $y = 0$ (the horizontal axis, or abscissa, of the coordinate system) over the interval from a to b?" (Regions below the abscissa are treated as negative areas to be subtracted from the positive ones above the abscissa; see Figure 2.) The solution, which will not be stated precisely, involves the following steps: the abscissa is partitioned into a finite number of intervals; using the height of the function at some value within each interval, the function is approximated by the resulting step function; the area under the step function is calculated as the sum of the areas of the rectangles of which it is composed; and, finally, the limit of this sum is calculated as the widths of the intervals approach zero (and, therefore, as their number approaches infinity). When this limit exists, it is called the *Riemann integral* of f from a to b and is symbolized as $\int_a^b f(x)\,dx$. It can be shown that the Riemann integral exists if f is continuous over the interval; it also exists for some discontinuous functions. For more advanced work, the concept of the length of an interval is generalized to the concept of the *Lebesgue measure* of a set, and the Riemann integral is generalized to the *Lebesgue integral*. Roughly, the vertical columns used to approximate the area in the Riemann integral are replaced in the Lebesgue integral by horizontal slabs.

Although the interpretation of the integral as an extension of the elementary concept of area is

Figure 2 — Approximation of the integral of f(x)

important, even more important is its relation (called the fundamental theorem of the calculus) to the derivative: Consider $F(x) = \int_a^x f(u)\,du$ as a function of the upper limit, x, of the interval over which the integral is computed; it can then be proved that the derivative of this function, $F'(x)$, exists and is equal to $f(x)$. Put another way, the rate of change at x of the area generated by f is equal to the value of f at x; or put still another way, the operation of taking the derivative undoes the operation of integration. This fact plays a crucial role in the solution of many problems of classical applied mathematics that are formulated in terms of derivatives of functions.

Introductions to the calculus and elementary parts of analysis are Apostol (1961–1962) and Bartle (1964).

Implicit definitions of functions. An algebraic equation such as $2x^2 - 5x - 3 = 0$ implicitly defines two numbers (namely, the two values of x, 3 and $-\frac{1}{2}$) for which the equality holds. Other algebraic equations implicitly define sets of numbers for which they hold.

A functional equation is an equality stated in terms of an unknown function; it implicitly defines those functions (as in the algebraic case, there may be more than one) that render the equality true.

Ordinary differential equations. Suppose it is postulated that the amount of interest (that is, the rate of change of money at time t) is proportional to (that is, is a constant fraction, k, of) the amount, $f(t)$, of money that has been saved. (This is the case of continuous compound interest.) Then f satisfies the equation $f'(t) = kf(t)$. This is a simple example of an *ordinary differential equation*, the solution of which is any function having the property that its derivative is k times the function. The solutions are $f(t) = f(0)\exp(kt)$, where $f(0)$ denotes the initial amount of money at time $t = 0$. Another simple economic example is the differential equation that arises from the assumption that marginal cost always equals average cost (that is, $dC(x)/dx = C(x)/x$) which has the solution that average cost is constant, that is, that $C(x) = kx$ for some constant, k.

Some laws of classical physics are formulated as second-order, linear, ordinary differential equations of the form

$$f''(t) + P(t)f'(t) + Q(t)f(t) = R(t),$$

where f'' is the derivative of f' (f'' is called the second derivative of f) and P, Q, and R are given functions. If, for example, f denotes distance, then this differential equation asserts that at each time t, a linear relation holds among distance, velocity, and acceleration. A vast literature is concerned with the solutions to this class of equations for different restrictions on P, Q, and R; most of the famous special functions used in physics—Bessel, hypergeometric, Hankel, gamma, and so on—are solutions to such differential equations (see Coddington 1961).

Partial differential equations. Many physical problems require differential equations a good deal more complicated than those just mentioned. For example, suppose that there is a flow of heat along one dimension, x. Let $f(x,t)$ denote the temperature at position x at time t. With t fixed, one can find the rate of change (the derivative) of temperature with changes in x; denote this by $\partial f(x,t)/\partial x$ and its second derivative with respect to x by $\partial^2 f(x,t)/\partial x^2$. These are called partial derivatives. Similarly, holding x fixed, the derivative with respect to t is denoted by $\partial f(x,t)/\partial t$. According to classical physics, temperature changes due to conduction in a homogeneous one-dimensional medium satisfy the following *partial differential equation*:

$$\frac{\partial f(x,t)}{\partial t} = \frac{k}{\rho\sigma}\frac{\partial^2 f(x,t)}{\partial x^2},$$

where k is the thermal conductivity, ρ the density, and σ the specific heat of the medium. Problems involving two or more independent variables (usually, time and some or all of the three space coordinates)—fluid flow, heat dissipation, elasticity, electromagnetism, and so on—lead to partial differential equations. Their solution is often very complex and requires the specification of the unknown function along a boundary of the space. This requirement is called a boundary condition. (See Akademiia Nauk S.S.S.R. [1956] 1964, chapter 6.)

Integral equations. Some physical problems lead to *integral equations*. In one type, functions g and K of one and two variables, respectively, and a constant, λ, are given, and the problem is to find those functions, f, for which

$$f(x) = g(x) + \lambda \int_a^b K(x,y)f(y)\,dy.$$

This equation is called Fredholm's linear integral equation or the inhomogeneous linear integral equation. Basically, it asserts that the value of some quantity f at a point x is equal to an impressed value, $g(x)$, plus a weighted average of its value at all other points. Integral equations arise in empirical contexts for which it is postulated that the value of a function at a point depends on the behavior of the function over a large region of its domain. Thus, in the example just considered the value of f at x depends on the in-

tegrand $K(x,y)f(y)$ integrated over the interval (a,b). There is a large body of literature dealing with the solution of various types of integral equations, especially those of interest in physics and probability theory.

Functional equations. Although both differential and integral equations (and mixtures of the two, called integrodifferential equations) are examples of functional equations, that term is often restricted to equations that involve only the unknown function, not its derivatives or integrals. A simple, well-known example is $f(xy) = f(x) + f(y)$, which implicitly defines those functions that transform multiplication into addition. If f is required to be continuous, then the solutions are $K\int_1^x dz/z$, where K is a positive constant; this integral is called the natural logarithm. The choice of K is usually referred to as the selection of the base of the logarithm.

Difference equations are functional equations of special importance in the social sciences. They arise both in the study of discrete stochastic processes (in learning theory, for example) and as discrete analogues of differential equations. Here the unknown function is defined only on the integers (or, equivalently, on any equidistant set of points), not on all of the real numbers, and so the function is written $f_n = f(n)$, where n is an integer. The equation states a relation among values of the unknown function for several successive integers. For example, the second-order, linear difference equation—the analogue of the second-order, linear, ordinary differential equation, described above—is of the form

$$f_{n+2} + P_n f_{n+1} + Q_n f_n = R_n.$$

In some probabilistic models of the learning process it is postulated (or derived from more primitive assumptions) that the probability of a particular response on trial $n + 1$, denoted by p_{n+1}, is some function of p_n and of the actual events that occurred on trial n. The simplest such assumption is the linear one, that is, $p_{n+1} = \alpha p_n + \beta$, where α and β are parameters that depend upon the events that actually occur. If there is a run of trials during which the same events occur, so that α and β are constant, then the solution to the above first-order, linear difference equation is

$$p_k = \alpha^k p_0 + \frac{(1 - \alpha^k)}{1 - \alpha}\beta.$$

When different events occur on different trials, the equation to be solved becomes considerably more complex. An introduction to difference equations is Goldberg (1958).

Given a functional equation—in the most general sense—the answer to the question of whether a solution exists is not usually obvious. Exhibiting a solution, of course, answers the question affirmatively, but often the existence of a solution can be proved before one is found. Such a result is known as an *existence theorem*. If a solution exists, it is also not usually obvious whether it is unique and, if it is not unique, how two different solutions relate to one another. A statement of the nature of the nonuniqueness of the solutions is known, somewhat inappropriately, as a *uniqueness theorem*. Some rather general existence and uniqueness theorems are available for differential and integral equations, but in less well understood cases considerable care is needed to discover just how restrictive the equation is.

A general work on functional equations is Aczél (1966).

Three other areas of classical analysis. Three other branches of classical analysis will be briefly discussed.

Extremum problems. For what values of its argument does a function assume its maximum or its minimum value? This type of problem arises in theoretical and applied physics and in the social sciences. In its simplest form, a real-valued function f is defined over some interval of the real numbers, and the problem is to find those x_0 for which $f(x_0)$ is a maximum or a minimum. If f is differentiable and if x_0 is not one of the end points of the interval, a necessary condition is that $f'(x_0) = 0$; moreover, x_0 is a local maximum if $f''(x_0) < 0$ and a local minimum if $f''(x_0) > 0$. (These statements should be intuitively clear for graphs of simple functions.) From these results it is easy to find, for example, which rectangle has the maximum area when the perimeter is held constant: it is the square whose sides are each equal to a quarter of the perimeter.

A much more difficult and interesting problem— the subject of the *calculus of variations*—is to find which function (or functions) f of a given family of functions causes a given function F of f (known as a *functional*) to assume its maximum or minimum value. For example, let f be a continuous function that passes through two fixed points in the plane, and let $F(f)$ be the surface area of the body that is generated by rotating f about the abscissa. A question that may be asked is "For which f (or f's) is $F(f)$ a minimum?" A major tool in the solution of this problem is a second-order, ordinary differential equation, known as Euler's equation, that f must necessarily satisfy (just as the solution x_0 to the simpler problem necessarily satisfies $f'(x_0) = 0$). (See Akademiia Nauk S.S.S.R. [1956] 1964, chapter 8.)

Within the past twenty years new classes of extremum problems have been posed and partially solved; they are mainly of concern in the social sciences, and they go under the names of linear, nonlinear, and dynamic programming. An example of a linear programming problem is the following diet problem. Each of several foodstuffs, $f_1, f_2, \cdots, f_k$, contains known amounts of various nutritional components, such as vitamins and proteins. Let f_{ij} be the amount of component j in food f_i, $j = 1, 2, \cdots, n$, and let a_j be the minimum amount of component j acceptable in the diet. If x_i is the amount of food f_i in the diet, the diet will be acceptable only if the following n inequalities are fulfilled:

$$x_1 f_{1j} + x_2 f_{2j} + \cdots + x_k f_{kj} \geqq a_j, \quad j = 1, 2, \cdots, n.$$

If p_i denotes the price of food f_i, the problem is to choose the x_i so as to minimize the cost,

$$x_1 p_1 + x_2 p_2 + \cdots + x_k p_k,$$

while fulfilling the above linear inequalities. [*See* PROGRAMMING.]

Functions of a complex variable. One of the most beautiful subfields of analysis is the theory of functions of a complex variable, which was developed in the nineteenth century, starting with the work of Cauchy. It has been significant in the growth of several two-dimensional, continuous physical theories, including parts of electromagnetism, hydrodynamics, and acoustics, but so far its applications in the social sciences have been mainly restricted to mathematical statistics, as in the concept of the characteristic function of a probability distribution. A complex number, z, is of the form $z = x + iy$, where x and y are real numbers and $i = \sqrt{-1}$. Sums and products are defined in such a way that the resulting arithmetic reduces to that of the ordinary numbers when $y = 0$. Because a point (x,y) in the plane can be (usefully) identified with the complex number $x + iy$, functions from the plane into the plane can be interpreted as complex-valued functions of a complex variable. If the derivative of such a function exists at all points of a region, derivatives of all orders exist and the function can be expressed as a convergent *power series* of the form $a_0 + a_1 z + a_2 z^2 + \cdots$ for some circle of z's within that region. It is clear from this result that the mere supposition that the derivative exists is a much stronger condition for complex-valued functions than for ordinary numerical functions. Such functions, which are called *analytic*, are very strongly constrained—among other things, specifying an analytic function over a small region determines it completely—and this fact has been effectively exploited to solve many two-dimensional problems of theoretical and practical interest. Interestingly, the theory cannot be neatly generalized beyond two dimensions. An introductory work on functions of a complex variable is Cartan (1961).

Integral transforms. Suppose that f is any continuous, real-valued function defined over an interval from a to b and that K is a fixed, continuous, real-valued function of two variables, the first of which is also on the interval from a to b; then $I(f,y) = \int_a^b K(x,y)f(x)\,dx$ is called an *integral transform* of f. If K satisfies certain restrictions, knowing I is equivalent to knowing f. Nevertheless, if K is carefully chosen, I may have convenient properties not possessed by f. For example, if $a = 0$, $b = \infty$, and $K(x,y) = e^{-xy}$, then I, which is then known as the *Laplace transform* and which is closely related to the moment-generating function of statistics, has the property that it converts certain integrals (convolutions) of two functions into multiplications of their transforms. In statistics such a convolution represents the distribution of the sum of two independent random variables. Another well-known and important example is the *Fourier transform*, which is used widely in statistics, and to a lesser extent in probabilistic models of behavior, to obtain a probability distribution from its characteristic function.

Theory of numbers

Despite several intellectual crises that led mathematicians to introduce new types of numbers into mathematics, it was not until about a hundred years ago that numbers were treated as being something other than intuitively understood. The natural numbers, $1, 2, 3, \cdots$, and their ratios, the positive rationals, are ancient concepts. The Greeks first noted their incompleteness when they showed that they are inadequate to represent $\sqrt{2}$, the length of the diagonal of a square whose side is of length 1. Certain irrational numbers had to be added, and later 0, negative numbers, and complex numbers were added so that certain classes of equations would all have solutions. To clarify this patchwork and to understand the uniqueness of the additions, nineteenth-century mathematicians undertook the axiomatization of various aspects of the number system. Perhaps the most subtle step was the definition of irrational numbers in terms of sets of rational numbers (roughly, the set of all rationals less than the irrational to be defined).

The axiomatization of numbers is not really the mainstream of the "theory of numbers." When one sees a book or course with that title, it usually refers to the study of properties of the natural numbers, mainly the prime numbers. Recall that

an integer is prime if it is divisible only by 1 and itself; the first few primes are 3, 5, 7, 11, and 13. In addition to the many results that can be proved directly (some of which were known to the ancients), such as that every integer can be represented uniquely as the product of powers of primes and that there are infinitely many primes, other results have depended upon the application of deep results from analysis. For example, parts of the theory of functions of a complex variable were used to show that the number of primes not larger than n divided by the number $n/\ln n$, where $\ln n$ is the natural logarithm of n, that is, $\int_1^n dx/x$, is a ratio that approaches 1 as n becomes large. Not only has this work greatly increased the depth of understanding of integers, but it has fed back into analysis and was one of the factors leading to the development of parts of contemporary abstract algebra.

Many applications of mathematics (for example, in statistics) involve counting the number of distinct events or objects that satisfy certain conditions; often these counting problems are quite difficult. Theorems providing explicit formulas or recursion schemes are called combinatorial theorems. One of the earliest important examples was the binomial theorem for the expansion of $(a + b)^n$, which is now part of every elementary algebra course. [*See* PROBABILITY, *article on* FORMAL PROBABILITY.]

A general introduction to the theory of numbers is Ore (1948).

Algebra

Classically, algebra was the theory of solving equations expressed in terms of the four arithmetical operations—addition, subtraction, multiplication, and division. The linear and quadratic equations of elementary algebra are familiar examples. Historically, the expression of mathematical problems in the form of equations, using letters to stand for the unknown numbers, was a major step in clarifying and simplifying the mathematical nature of many kinds of problems. Perhaps the most important consequence of the introduction of letters and the use of equations was the extension of routine methods of calculation to quite complicated settings. The introduction of algebraic equations probably ranks in importance in the history of ideas with the earlier invention, probably first by the Babylonians, of the place-value system of notation for numbers; such a system was needed to develop simple algorithms for performing arithmetical computations.

The general theory of algebraic equations, the elementary parts of which are studied in high school, has a long and distinguished history in mathematics. The proof by Niels Henrik Abel in 1824 that solutions of an algebraic equation of degree five or greater, where the degree is the highest exponent of any term in the equation, cannot be expressed in terms of radicals (that is, expressions definable in terms of square roots) was one of the most important mathematical results of the first half of the nineteenth century. Another result of basic importance is the fundamental theorem of algebra, which was first proved in the eighteenth century but which was proved rigorously only in the last half of the nineteenth century. This theorem asserts that every algebraic equation always has at least one root that is a real or a complex number. Also of great significance were the proofs that not all numbers are roots of algebraic equations; numbers that are not such roots are called transcendental numbers. The most famous proofs of this sort are Charles Hermite's (in 1873) that e is transcendental and F. Lindemann's (in 1882) that π is transcendental.

Orderings. Much of the work in algebra during the present century has been devoted to generalized mathematical systems that are characterized not in terms of the four fundamental arithmetic operations but in terms of generalizations of these operations and of the familiar ordering relations of "less than" and "greater than."

In a number of the social sciences the theory of binary relations has received extensive application. From an algebraic standpoint a *binary relation structure* may be characterized as consisting of a set A and a set R of ordered pairs (x, y), where x and y are both elements of A. Such an R is called a binary relation on A. A relation R is said to be a *partial ordering* of A when it is reflexive, antisymmetric, and transitive—that is, when it satisfies the following three properties: *reflexive*: for every x in A, xRx; *antisymmetric*: for every x and y in A, if xRy and yRx, then $x = y$; *transitive*: for every x, y, and z in A, if xRy and yRz, then xRz. If R is also connected in A (that is, if for any two elements x and y in A with $x \neq y$, either xRy or yRx) then R is said to be a *complete* or *simple ordering* or, sometimes, a *linear ordering* of A. The concept of a complete ordering is a direct abstraction of the order properties of "$\leqslant$" with respect to the real numbers. A familiar use of the concept of an ordering relation is in utility theory, particularly in the classical theory of demand in economics, in which it is assumed that each individual has an ordering relation over the set of commodity bundles or, more generally, over the set of alternatives with which he is presented. The general concept of ordering relations also has far-ranging applications

in the theory of measurement within psychology and sociology, and more general binary relations have been extensively applied in anthropology in the study of kinship systems.

Partial orderings can be extended in another direction by imposing additional conditions to obtain *lattices*, which have also been used in the social sciences. In a different direction, but still within the framework of binary relations, is the *theory of graphs*, in which no restrictions are placed on the binary relation, R. Applications of graph theory have been made to social-psychological and sociological problems, especially to provide a mathematical method for representing various kinds of relationships between persons.

Groups, rings, and fields. Another direction of generalization of classical algebra has been to what are called groups, rings, and fields. A *group* is a set A together with a binary operation, $\circ$, satisfying the following axioms. First, the operation $\circ$ is associative, that is, for x, y, and z in A, $x \circ (y \circ z) = (x \circ y) \circ z$. Second, there is an element e, called the identity, of the set A such that for every x in A, $x \circ e = e \circ x = x$. And, finally, for each element x of A there is an inverse element x^{-1} such that $x \circ x^{-1} = e$. It is obvious that if A is taken as the set of integers, $\circ$ as the operation of addition, e as the number 0, and the inverse of x as the negative of x, then the set of integers is a group under the binary operation of addition. The theory of groups has had profound ramifications in other parts of mathematics and in the sciences, ranging from the theory of algebraic equations to geometry and physics. The reason for the fundamental importance of group theory is perhaps best summarized by stating that a group is the appropriate way to formulate the very important concept of symmetry. In the range of applications of group theory just mentioned, the underlying thread is the concept of symmetry, whether it is in the symmetry of the roots of an equation or the symmetry properties of the fundamental particles of physics. As a simple example, consider the finite group of rotations 90°, 180°, 270°, and 360°. A square does not change its apparent orientation under such a rotation about its center, but an equilateral triangle does. This group of rotations is the symmetry group of rotations for a square but not, of course, for an equilateral triangle. Although the methods and results of group theory have not yet had special applications of depth in the social sciences, they are important to many of the general mathematical results that have been applied.

The theories of rings and fields represent rather direct generalization of arithmetical properties of the number system. The theory of groups is fundamentally a generalization of the concept of a single binary operation, such as addition or multiplication, whereas rings and fields are algebraic systems that have two fundamental operations. The most familiar example of a field or of a ring is the set of rational numbers or of real numbers with respect to the operations of addition and multiplication.

Boolean algebras.   Algebraic aspects of the theory of sets have been studied under the heading of Boolean algebras. The concept of an algebra of sets, that is, a collection of sets closed under union and complementation, is fundamental in the modern theory of probability, where events are interpreted as sets of possible outcomes and numerical probabilities are assigned to events. [*See* Probability, *article on* formal probability.]

Isomorphism and homomorphism.   It should be mentioned that certain very general mathematical concepts find their most natural definition and application in modern algebra. One of the most important concepts is that of the isomorphism of two mathematical systems. An *isomorphism* is a one-to-one mapping of a system A onto a system B in which the operations and relations of A are preserved under the mapping and have the same structure as the operations and relations of system B. If the mapping is not one-to-one but the operations and relations are preserved, then it is called a *homomorphism*. A well-known application of the concept of isomorphism in the social sciences is in theories of fundamental measurement in which one shows that an appropriate algebra of empirical operations is isomorphic to some numerical algebra. It is this isomorphism that permits the direct application of computational methods to the results of measurement.

Introductory works on algebra, both for this and for the next section, are Birkhoff and MacLane (1941) and Mostow, Sampson, and Meyer (1963).

Vector spaces and matrix algebra

Linear algebra is one of the most important generalizations of classical elementary algebra. The objects to which the operations of addition and multiplication are applied are now matrices, vectors of an n-dimensional space, and linear transformations (an $n \times n$ matrix is a particular representation of a linear transformation in n-dimensional space). More particularly, linear algebra arises as a generalization of the linear equations so familiar in elementary algebra, and historically one of the most important tasks of linear algebra has been to find solutions of systems of linear equations. As many research workers in the social sciences know,

the numerical solution of linear equations can be an extremely laborious and difficult affair when the number of equations is large. The set of coefficients of a system of linear equations gives rise to the concept of a rectangular array of numbers, which is precisely what a matrix is. An algebra of matrices in terms of addition and multiplication may be constructed; the distinguishing feature of this algebra, as compared with the algebra of the real numbers, is that multiplication is not commutative—that is, **AB** is not usually equal to **BA**, and the product of two nonzero matrices can be zero.

The intuitive geometric concept of a vector may be represented by a column or row of n numbers, and an algebra of vectors, which bears a close resemblance to the algebra of numbers, may be constructed. Simple (linear) transformations of vectors, such as rotations and stretches of the coordinate system in space, can be interpreted as multiplication by matrices. The interaction between the geometrical intuitions about n-dimensional space and the algebraic techniques of calculation provided by linear algebra and the theory of matrices have made them powerful tools in the application of mathematics to many parts of science. These applications have been particularly prominent in statistics (for example, in factor analysis), as well as in economics, where it is often useful to treat n-dimensional bundles of commodities as vectors.

Topology and abstract spaces

Intuitively, a topological transformation of a geometrical figure or object is a deformation that introduces neither breaks nor fusions in the object. Put more exactly, a topological transformation is one that is one-to-one, is continuous, and has a continuous inverse. If one starts with a circle—perhaps the best example of a simple closed curve—one can deform it topologically into an ellipse or into the shape of a crescent, but one cannot deform it topologically into a figure eight, for example, because then two distinct points of the circle are fused as the intersection point of the eight. Also, one cannot deform it into a straight line segment, because to do so would introduce a break in the circle. Many familiar qualitative geometrical properties are topological invariants in the sense that they are not altered (are invariant) under topological transformations. Examples are the property of being inside or outside a closed figure in the plane; the property of a surface being closed, such as the surface of a sphere or an ellipsoid; or the property of the dimension of an object. For example, the surface of a sphere cannot be topologically transformed into a one-dimensional curve or a three-dimensional sphere. We shall not attempt here to give an exact definition of continuity as it is used in topology; we simply remark that it is a reasonable generalization of the concept of continuity used in analysis.

Topological methods and results have far-reaching applications in many branches of mathematics, but as yet the methods themselves have not been directly applied in those parts of the social sciences concerned extensively with empirical data. The most direct applications have been in economics, where topological fixed-point theorems have been of great importance in investigating the conditions guaranteeing the existence of a stable equilibrium in a competitive economy. The classical example of a fixed-point theorem—first proved by L. E. J. Brouwer, at the beginning of this century—states that for every topological mapping of an n-dimensional sphere into itself there is always at least one point that maps into itself, that is, remains fixed. Familiar examples of such mappings are rotations in two or three dimensions for which the center of the rotation is the fixed point of the transformation.

Topological space.   As a typical example of abstraction in modern mathematics, the initial concept of a topological transformation of familiar geometrical figures has led to the general abstract notion of a topological space. Roughly speaking, a *topological space* consists of a set, X, and a family, $\mathscr{T}$, of subsets of X, called *open sets*, for which the following four conditions are satisfied: the empty set is in $\mathscr{T}$; X is in $\mathscr{T}$; the union of arbitrarily many sets each of which is in $\mathscr{T}$ is also in $\mathscr{T}$; and the intersection of any finite number of sets from $\mathscr{T}$ is also in $\mathscr{T}$. The concept of an open set is a generalization of the notion of an open interval of real numbers (an interval that does not include its end points). For example, the natural topology of the real line is the family of open intervals together with the sets that are formed from arbitrary unions and finite intersections of open intervals. Generally speaking, the notion of open set is used to express the idea of continuity. The important thing about a continuous function is that it does not jumble neighboring points too much, and this requirement may be expressed by requiring of a topological transformation that open sets be mapped into open sets and that the inverse of an open set be an open set.

Metric space.   Other kinds of abstract spaces have come into prominence in the development of topology. Perhaps the most important is the concept of a metric space. A set, X, together with a distance function, d, that maps pairs of points into real numbers is called a *metric space* if d satisfies the following conditions: $d(x, y) = 0$ if and only if $x = y$, that is, the distance between x and y is 0 if and only if x and y are the same point; $d(x, y) \geqslant 0$, which asserts that distance is a nonnegative real number; $d(x, y) = d(y, x)$, that is, distance is symmetric; and, finally, $d(x, y) + d(y, z) \geqslant d(x, z)$, which is known as the triangle inequality. The concept of a metric space has had important applications in many parts of mathematics and is a fundamental concept in modern mathematics. It has been applied in recent work in scaling theory in psychology and sociology, particularly to the problems of multidimensional scaling, and also in certain areas of mathematical economics [*see* SCALING]. It is clear that the notion of a metric space generalizes, in a very natural way, the concept of distance in Euclidean space.

A typical metric problem raised in the social sciences is this: Given data in the form of "distances" among a finite set of points, what is the smallest dimensional Euclidean space within which the points can be embedded so that these distances equal the Euclidean or some other preassigned metric of that space? Recently this problem has been effectively generalized by permitting certain transformations of the "distances" that preserve their metric property. Little has yet been done about embeddings in non-Euclidean spaces.

An introductory work on topology is Hocking and Young (1961).

Foundations

As was remarked above, the concept of a rigorous mathematical proof originated in ancient Greek mathematics. The modern formal axiomatic method, characteristic of twentieth-century mathematical research and one of the most important topics to be clarified in modern research on foundations of mathematics, is conceptually very close to the approach followed in Euclid's *Elements*. The main difference is that the primitive concepts of the theory are now treated as undefined or meaningless. All that is assumed about them must be formally expressed in the axioms. In contrast, in the *Elements* primitive concepts such as those of point and line are given an interpretation or meaning from the very beginning. This modern conception originated with David Hilbert, who provided the first complete, modern axiomatization of geometry in 1889. It is customary to say that the concepts of the theory are implicitly defined by the axioms. What is not recognized often enough is that the collection of axioms together *explicitly* defines the theory embodied in the concepts. Thus, in slightly more exact phrasing, the axioms of Euclidean geometry define the theory of Euclidean geometry by defining the phrase "is a model of Euclidean geometry." In the same fashion, the axioms of group theory define the theory of groups by specifying what kinds of objects are called groups or, in other words, what kinds of objects are models of the theory of groups (here we are using the term "model" in the logical or mathematical sense).

A more particular aim of foundational research has been to provide a set of axioms that would serve as a basis for the main body of mathematics. At least three major positions on the foundations of mathematics have been enunciated in the twentieth century; they differ in their conception of the nature of mathematical objects.

Intuitionism.   Intuitionism holds that in the most fundamental sense mathematical objects are themselves thoughts or ideas. The intuitionist holds that one can never be certain that he has correctly expressed the mathematics when it is formalized as a mathematical theory. As part of this thesis, the classical logic of Aristotle, in particular the law of excluded middle, has been challenged by Brouwer and other intuitionists because it permits the derivation of purely existential, nonconstructive statements about mathematical objects. In particular the validity of classical *reductio ad absurdum* proofs depends upon this logical law. Although intuitionists express themselves in a way which suggests a psychological analysis of mathematics, it should be emphasized that their conception of mathematical objects as thoughts has not been seriously explored by any intuitionists from the standpoint of scientific psychology.

Platonism.   A second view of mathematics, the Platonistic one, is that mathematical objects are abstract objects that exist independently of human thought or activity. Those who hold that set theory or logic itself provides an appropriate foundation for mathematics (adherents of logicism) usually adopt some form of Platonism in their basic attitude. From the standpoint of working mathematics, set theory—and thus Platonism—has been the most influential conception of mathematics in this century. Set theory itself originated in the late nineteenth century with the revolutionary work of Georg Cantor. Its foundations were called into question by Bertrand Russell's discovery of a simple paradox which arises in considering the set of all objects that are not members of themselves. If it is supposed that to every property there corresponds the set of objects having this property, then a contradiction within classical logic may easily be derived by considering the set whose members are those and only those sets that are not members of themselves. An apparently satisfactory foundation for set theory, which avoids this and related paradoxes, was formulated in 1908 by Ernst Zermelo, and with suitable technical extensions it provides a satisfactory basis for most of the mathematics published in this century.

Formalism.   The third influential position on the foundation of mathematics, called formalism, was developed by Hilbert and others. This view is that the primary mathematical objects are the symbols in which mathematics is written. This carries to the extreme the development of the axiomatic method begun by the Greeks. Under the formalist account the interpretation and use of mathematics must then be given from outside pure mathematics. From a psychological or behavioral standpoint, there is much that is appealing about formalism, but again little effort has yet been made to relate the detailed results and methods of formalism to theoretical or experimental work in scientific psychology.

Relevance of research on foundations.   In view of the high degree of agreement about the validity of most published pieces of mathematics, the skeptical social scientist may question the real relevance of these varying views about the foundations of mathematics to working mathematics itself. There is a highly invariant content of mathematics recognized by almost all mathematicians, including those concerned with the foundations of mathematics, and this invariant content is essentially untouched by radically different philosophical views about the nature of mathematical objects. A reasonable conjecture is that future research in the foundations of mathematics will attempt to capture this invariant content by concentrating on the character of mathematical thinking rather than on the nature of mathematical objects.

One other important aspect of foundational research in the twentieth century is the fundamental work on mathematical logic, in particular the attempt by Gottlob Frege, A. N. Whitehead, Bertrand Russell, and others to reduce all of mathematics to purely logical assumptions. These efforts have led to great clarification of the nature of mathematics itself and to vastly increased standards of precision in talking about mathematical proofs and the structure of mathematical systems. Of major importance were the deep results of Kurt Gödel (1931) on the logical limitations of any formal system rich enough to express elementary number theory. His results show that any such formal system must be essentially incomplete in the sense that not all true sentences of the theory can be proved as theorems.

An introductory work on foundations is Kneebone (1963).

Mathematics applied to social sciences

Applications of mathematics to specific social science problems are described, and detailed references are given, elsewhere in this encyclopedia. That material is not repeated here; several reasonably general references are Allen (1938), Coleman (1964), Kemeny and Snell (1962), Luce (1964), Luce, Bush, and Galanter (1963–1965), Samuelson (1947). Suffice it to say that these applications involve only fragments of the whole of mathematics, and they have not been as successful as those in the physical sciences. The reasons are many, among them these: the effort so far expended is much less; the basic empirical concepts and variables have not been isolated and purified to the same degree; mathematics grew up with and was to some extent molded by the needs of physics, and so it may very well be less suited to social science problems if these problems are of a basically different character from those of physics; a typical social science problem appears to involve more variables than one is accustomed to handling in physics; and, finally, social scientists are generally not extensively trained in mathematics.

A social scientist who attempts to formulate and solve a scientific problem in mathematical terms is often disappointed with the mathematics he can find. This may happen simply because a mathematical system appropriate to his problem does not seem to have been invented, or, as is more common, the definite and often quite complex mathematical system that he happens to want to understand in depth has not been investigated in any detail. In this century especially, mathematicians have tended to focus on very general classes of systems, and the theorems concern properties that are true of all or of large subclasses of them; however, these results do not usually provide much detailed information about any particular member of the class.

As an example, the axioms of group theory are not categorical—that is, two groups need not be isomorphic. Therefore, theorems about groups in general tell one little about the specific properties of a particular group. But this is what is of interest when a particular group is used to represent an empirical structure, as in modern particle physics.

When this happens, it is necessary for the applied mathematician to carry out considerable mathematical analysis to achieve the understanding he needs to answer scientifically interesting questions.

We have already discussed two parts of mathematics in which highly specific systems have been explored in depth: classical analysis and matrix algebra. A primary motivation for this detailed work was the needs of physical science. In fortunate instances, a problem may be formulated in terms of one of these systems, in which case specific results can sometimes be extracted from the existing literature. Examples where this has been done are in the application of matrix algebra to factor analysis and of Markov chains (a part of probability theory) to several areas, including learning, social interaction, and social structure [see FACTOR ANALYSIS; MARKOV CHAINS].

Theory as detailed as this, however, is not typical of contemporary mathematics. We have in mind such active areas as associative and nonassociative algebras, homological algebra, group theory, topological groups, algebraic topology, rings, manifolds, and functional analysis.

The generality of contemporary mathematics can be seductive in that it invites sophistic treatments of scientific problems. It is often not difficult to find some general branch of mathematics within which to cast a specific social or behavioral problem without, however, actually capturing in detail the various constraints of the problem. Without these constraints few explicit results and predictions can be proved. Nevertheless, the real emptiness of such endeavors can be shrouded for the unwary in the impressive symbolism and ringing terms of whatever mathematics it is that is not being seriously used.

If the growth of the social sciences parallels at all that of the physical sciences, they will study in detail various systems, which, although of peripheral mathematical interest, are of substantive interest. Indeed, some examples already exist, including these: (1) Just as classes of maximum and minimum problems have been formulated and solved in the physical sciences, other classes have arisen in the social sciences, such as linear, nonlinear, and dynamic programming, game theory, and statistical decision theory. (2) Various mathematical structures that may correspond to (parts of) empirical structures have been investigated, for example, aspects of the theory of relations and the closely related theory of graphs, matrix algebra, and concatenation algebras, which arose in the study of grammar and syntax. (3) Underlying the success of much physical theory is the fact that many variables can be represented numerically. The theories that account for this in physics are not suitable for the social sciences, but alternative possibilities are under active development, particularly in terms of theories of fundamental and derived measurement. The mathematics is reasonably involved, although for the most part the proofs are self-contained. (4) Although the theory of stochastic processes is a well-developed part of probability theory, a number of the processes that have found applications in the social sciences had not previously been studied by probabilists; their properties have been partially worked out in the social science literature. Among the most prominent examples are the nonstationary processes that have arisen in learning theory. Some of these postulate that on each trial one of several operators Q_i transforms a response probability into the corresponding probability on the next trial. Two special cases have been most adequately studied. One assumes that the Q_i are linear operators and the other assumes that the operators commute with one another—that is, $Q_i Q_j = Q_j Q_i$. [*See* LEARNING.]

As increasing use is made of mathematics in the social sciences, one may anticipate the investigation of very specific mathematical systems and, ultimately, the isolation of interesting abstract properties from these systems for further study and generalization as pure mathematics.

R. DUNCAN LUCE AND PATRICK SUPPES

BIBLIOGRAPHY

ACZÉL, J. 1966 *Lectures on Functional Equations and Their Applications.* New York: Academic Press.

AKADEMIIA NAUK S.S.S.R., MATEMATICHESKII INSTITUT (1956) 1964 *Mathematics: Its Content, Methods, and Meaning.* Edited by A. D. Aleksandrov, A. N. Kolmogorov, and M. A. Laurent'ev. 3 vols. Cambridge, Mass.: M.I.T. Press. → First published in Russian.

ALLEN, R. G. D. (1938) 1962 *Mathematical Analysis for Economists.* London: Macmillan.

APOSTOL, TOM M. 1961–1962 *Calculus.* 2 vols. New York: Blaisdell.

BARTLE, ROBERT G. 1964 *The Elements of Real Analysis.* New York: Wiley.

BIRKHOFF, GARRETT; and MACLANE, SAUNDERS (1941) 1965 *A Survey of Modern Algebra.* 3d ed. New York: Macmillan.

CARTAN, HENRI (1961) 1963 *Elementary Theory of Analytic Functions of One or Several Complex Variables.* Reading, Mass.: Addison-Wesley. → First published in French.

CODDINGTON, EARL A. (1961) 1964 *An Introduction to Ordinary Differential Equations.* Englewood Cliffs, N.J.: Prentice-Hall.

COLEMAN, JAMES S. 1964 *Introduction to Mathematical Sociology.* New York: Free Press.

COURANT, RICHARD; and ROBBINS, HERBERT (1941) 1961 *What Is Mathematics? An Elementary Approach to Ideas and Methods.* Oxford Univ. Press.

FRIEDMAN, BERNARD 1966 What Are Mathematicians Doing? *Science* 154:357–362.

GÖDEL, KURT (1931) 1965 On Formally Undecidable Propositions of the *Principia mathematica* and Related Systems. I. Pages 4–38 in Martin Davis (editor), *The Undecidable: Basic Papers on Undecidable Propositions, Unsolvable Problems and Computable Functions.* Hewlett, N.Y.: Raven. → First published in German in Volume 38 of the *Monatshefte für Mathematik und Physik.*

GOLDBERG, SAMUEL 1958 *Introduction to Difference Equations: With Illustrative Examples From Economics, Psychology, and Sociology.* New York: Wiley. → A paperback edition was published in 1961.

HOCKING, JOHN G.; and YOUNG, GAIL S. 1961 *Topology.* Reading, Mass.: Addison-Wesley.

KEMENY, JOHN G.; and SNELL, J. LAURIE 1962 *Mathematical Models in the Social Sciences.* Boston: Ginn.

KNEEBONE, G. T. 1963 *Mathematical Logic and the Foundations of Mathematics: An Introductory Survey.* New York: Van Nostrand.

LUCE, R. DUNCAN 1964 The Mathematics Used in Mathematical Psychology. *American Mathematical Monthly* 71:364–378.

LUCE, R. DUNCAN; BUSH, ROBERT R.; and GALANTER, EUGENE (editors) 1963–1965 *Handbook of Mathematical Psychology.* 3 vols. New York: Wiley.

MOSTOW, GEORGE; SAMPSON, JOSEPH H.; and MEYER, JEAN-PIERRE 1963 *Fundamental Structures of Algebra.* New York: McGraw-Hill.

NEUGEBAUER, OTTO (1951) 1957 *The Exact Sciences in Antiquity.* 2d ed. Providence, R.I.: Brown Univ. Press.

NEWMAN, JAMES R. (editor) 1956 *The World of Mathematics.* 4 vols. New York: Simon & Schuster.

ORE, ØYSTEIN 1948 *Number Theory and Its History.* New York: McGraw-Hill.

SAMUELSON, PAUL A. (1947) 1958 *Foundations of Economic Analysis.* Harvard Economic Studies, Vol. 80. Cambridge, Mass.: Harvard Univ. Press.

MAURRAS, CHARLES

Charles Marie Photius Maurras (1868–1952), French man of letters, was born in Martigues, near Marseille. He entered public life supporting both Frédéric Mistral's *Félibrige* and Jean Moréas, with whom he joined in 1891 in founding the École Romane, a literary movement designed to defend "a common ideal of Romanity." He became the apostle of integral nationalism, having coined the term in 1900.

Reacting against the dominant relativism and eclecticism of his time, Maurras set out from skeptical and agnostic premises to find some solid basis for thought, style, and action in historical realities which, he argued, having worked in the past, might be expected to work again. He rediscovered the classical ideals of order, hierarchy, and discipline and insisted that they alone provide an escape from nihilism into the positive realm of "organizing empiricism"—a method of solving current problems in terms of past experience.

Transferred from literary to sociopolitical grounds, Maurras's *empirisme organisateur* turned him against what he considered the dissolvent and anarchic qualities of liberal individualism which had triumphed in the French Revolution. He thought France was in a state of decadence and attributed this to its abandonment of traditions identified with the old regime, campaigning against Protestants, Jews, and metics—all those alien agents of change and corruption to whom the revolution had given free rein in France. When, in the late 1890s, the scandals that periodically shook the Third Republic culminated in the Dreyfus affair, Maurras set out to elaborate a doctrine which might spark a reaction against the existing disorder and provide the basis of a national revival. Based upon penetrating if frequently unhistorical criticism of the republic and parliament, his critique asserted the necessity of a return to the historical sources of French intellectual and political success: the classical tradition of the seventeenth century and the monarchy. True patriotism, conscious of these conditions of national prosperity and greatness, demanded, he believed, a return to the stability and continuity which only hereditary monarchy could provide. This was the program of integral nationalism to which he soon converted the founders of the Ligue d'Action Française, a young, pragmatic, and patriotic movement dedicated to France's political and intellectual regeneration. Henceforth, the story of Maurras was that of the Action Française; he became its moving spirit, and most of his writings were published in the review (1899–1914) and the newspaper (1908–1944) of that name.

Despite his insistence that politics must take precedence over everything else (*Politique d'abord!*), the Action Française was less a political than a didactic and literary movement. The doctrine it taught combined traditionalism, regionalism, and corporatism and elaborated the picture of a society that was free of democratic sham, individualistic anarchy, and the struggles of political parties and that was ruled in a stable way by a monarch and by an elite of talent and birth who would consider only the interests of the nation, not those of particular interest groups. The negative aspects of Maurrasist doctrine were more convincing than its program, and its criticism of the republic and its institutions provided rich ammunition for all other critics. When written into legislation at Vichy (particularly in 1940–1941), Maurras's views proved anachronistic and unworkable.

Nevertheless, the Action Française provided an intellectual structure to which the French right could refer; Maurras's doctrine synthesized the ideas of nineteenth-century conservatives from Bonald to La Tour du Pin and influenced several generations of France's middle and upper classes. Its newspaper never ceased to warn against Germany, against a Red peril—not so much a peril of social revolution as of national disunity—against the popular front of 1936, and, thereafter, against war and warmongers—at a time of national division and unpreparedness to which its own campaigns had contributed a good deal. A steadfast supporter of Philippe Pétain after 1940, though as steadfastly anticollaborationist (his ideas inspired much of Vichy's nationalist isolationism), Maurras was condemned in 1945 to life imprisonment. In prison, as out, his pugnacity and the stream of his writings never ceased. When his sentence was commuted in 1952 to forced residence in a private clinic, Maurras publicly thanked President Vincent Auriol, congratulating him for finally granting him the freedom that was his due and suggesting the expiatory execution of the minister "responsible for the excesses committed at the Liberation." He died a few months later, still bellicose but reconciled with the church he had abandoned as a youth.

Maurras's destructive effect on the democratic and parliamentary ideology has been immense, his constructive influence slight. Yet his ideas affected the nationalists of all Latin nations, and there are strong traces of Maurrasism in Salazar's Portugal and de Gaulle's France. The Action Française has been and still is well represented in the Académie Française (in 1964, by three of its leaders), and many still respect its ideas in the breach if not in the observance. Still, the movement Maurras led is now but a memory and a sect. Responsible for much of its success between the wars, Maurras also bears the responsibility for its eventual failure. His intellectual elitism made for overemphasis of the written word, and his authoritarianism brought him into conflict with the Roman Catholic church he professed to admire (not for its Christianity but for its enduring power) and with the royalty he professed to serve (less out of personal loyalty than for theoretical reasons). The deafness which rid him at an early age of faith in God or nature grew steadily worse, isolating him and encouraging his pessimistic and intolerant dogmatism. Younger followers deserted, were excommunicated, or simply drifted away. But this very dogmatism gave him the strength needed to repeat tirelessly and to elaborate endlessly ideas which have left their mark on France and on the Latin world.

EUGEN WEBER

[See also NATIONALISM.]

WORKS BY MAURRAS

1931   *Au signe de Flore.* Paris: Oeuvres Représentatives.
1950   *Le Mont de Saturne.* Paris: Quatre Jeudis.
Oeuvres capitales. 4 vols. Paris: Flammarion, 1954.

SUPPLEMENTARY BIBLIOGRAPHY

BUTHMAN, WILLIAM 1939 *The Rise of Integral Nationalism in France.* New York: Columbia Univ. Press.
DIMIER, LOUIS 1926 *Vingt ans d'Action Française.* Paris: Librairie Nouvelle.
JOSEPH, ROGER; and FORGES, JEAN 1953 *Biblio-iconographie générale de Charles Maurras.* 2 vols. Paris: Roanne.
MASSIS, HENRI 1961 *Maurras et notre temps.* Paris: Plon.
NOLTE, ERNST 1963 *Der Faschismus in seiner Epoche.* Munich: Piper.
ROUDIEZ, LEON 1957 *Maurras jusqu'à l'Action Française.* Paris: Bonne.
TANNENBAUM, EDWARD R. 1962 *The Action Française.* New York: Wiley.
WEBER, EUGEN 1962 *Action Française.* Stanford Univ. Press.
WRIGHT, GORDON (1960) 1962 *France in Modern Times.* London: Murray; Chicago: Rand McNally.

MAUSS, MARCEL

Marcel Mauss (1872–1950), French sociologist, was born in Épinal (Vosges) in Lorraine, where he grew up within a close-knit, pious, and orthodox Jewish family. Émile Durkheim was his uncle. By the age of 18 Mauss had reacted against the Jewish faith; he was never a religious man. He studied philosophy under Durkheim's supervision at Bordeaux; Durkheim took endless trouble in guiding his nephew's studies and even chose subjects for his own lectures that would be most useful to Mauss. Thus Mauss was initially a philosopher (like most of the early Durkheimians), and his conception of philosophy was influenced above all by Durkheim himself, for whom he always retained the utmost admiration; by Kant, to whose work Durkheim introduced him; and by two philosophers at Bordeaux, O. Hamelin, a rationalist, and the more empirically minded A. Espinas, then concerned with the collective origin of arts, customs, and technology—subjects about which Mauss was later to write. The philosophical atmosphere was Neo-Kantian. Mauss placed third in the national *agrégation* competition of 1895 and decided to devote himself to research.

He studied the history of religion at the École Pratique des Hautes Études under Louis Finot, Sylvain Lévi, Auguste Carrière, and A. Meillet in the Section des Sciences Historiques et Philologiques and under Alfred Foucher, Israël Lévi, and Léon Marillier in the Section des Sciences Religieuses. Meillet and Lévi, together with Célestin Bouglé, were among his closest friends. In 1897–1898 he made a study tour to Leiden, Breda, and Oxford, where he worked with Tylor. He then studied Sanskrit and Indian texts and, as Foucher's assistant from 1900 to 1902, taught the history of the religion and philosophy of pre-Buddhist India, in 1901 succeeding Marillier to the chair in the history of the religion of "noncivilized" peoples, which he occupied for the rest of his career. He taught, in addition, at the Collège de France from 1930 to 1939. In 1925 he helped to found, and then became joint director of, the Institut d'Ethnologie de l'Université de Paris, which, by virtue of the instruction it provided and the publications it sponsored, contributed considerably to the development of field work by younger anthropologists. Mauss lectured at the Institut on ethnography until 1939, encouraging field workers to "take trouble to be exact, complete" and to have a sense for "facts and the relations between them," for "proportions and connexions" (1947, p. 5). (Apart from a brief voyage to Morocco, Mauss himself did no field work.)

Mauss worked very closely with Durkheim. In addition to their major joint work, "De quelques formes primitives de classification" (Durkheim & Mauss 1903), he compiled statistical tables for Durkheim's study of suicide, and they collaborated in writing reviews. It was, on the whole, Mauss who, with his greater sense of the concrete, had an eye for the illuminating fact, while the theoretical interpretation generally originated with Durkheim. The notion of "total social facts," commonly attributed to Mauss (Lévi-Strauss [1950] 1960, pp. xxiv ff.), was, according to Georges Davy (1958), born of their collaboration arising from the study of some documents of Boas and was subsequently applied by Mauss. It is indicative of the cooperative nature of the work done by the brilliant young scholars whom Durkheim had assembled around the journal *Année sociologique* (published in 12 volumes between 1898 and 1913) that almost all of Mauss's major work in this period was written in collaboration: with Hubert he published "Essai sur la nature et la fonction du sacrifice" in 1899, "Esquisse d'une théorie générale de la magie" in 1904, and "Introduction à l'analyse de quelques phénomènes religieux" in 1908; with Beuchat he published "Essai sur les variations saisonnières des sociétés eskimos" in 1906; and with Fauconnet he published an important encyclopedia article on sociology in 1901.

Mauss also took a major part in editing the *Année* from the time of its foundation, directing the religious sociology section with Hubert, collaborating on several other sections, and contributing a vast number of reviews and notes, to which he rightly attached great importance. World War I tragically decimated the *Année sociologique* group, and, after Durkheim's own early death, Mauss inherited the leadership of the group. He twice revived the journal (in the 1920s and in the 1930s) and devoted much of his time to editing posthumously published works by Durkheim, R. Hertz, Hubert, and others, thereby reducing his own output.

Mauss's most important post-World War I writings may be divided into two broad categories. First, there are the major ethnological studies: the great *Essai sur le don* of 1925, "Effet physique chez l'individu de l'idée de mort suggérée par la collectivité (Australie, Nouvelle-Zélande)" of 1926, "Les techniques du corps" of 1936, and "Une catégorie de l'esprit humain: La notion de personne, celle de 'moi'" of 1938. Second, there are writings of a methodological and programmatic character on the social sciences: "Rapports réels et pratiques de la psychologie et de la sociologie," which was a presidential address to the Société de Psychologie in 1924, "Divisions et proportions des divisions de la sociologie" of 1927, and "Fragment d'un plan de sociologie générale descriptive" of 1934. In addition, Mauss published other brief studies on a variety of subjects, among them the origins of the notion of money, the Melanesian potlatch, contract among the Thracians, joking relationships, the "Legend of Abraham," forms of civilization, social cohesion in polysegmentary societies, technology, the problem of nationality, and the sociology of Bolshevism.

Mauss also led an active political life. Like Durkheim, he supported Dreyfus and Zola, and he was a leading member of the Dreyfusard Groupe des Étudiants Collectivistes. He was closely associated with the socialist leaders, in 1904 helping them to found *L'humanité*, to which he contributed, taking part in strikes and supporting socialist candidates in elections. He was also much involved in the "popular universities" and the cooperative movements. The evolutionary, pluralist, and liberal quality of his socialism, akin to that of Jaurès, can be seen in the "Conclusions" to *The Gift* ([1925] 1954, pp. 63–81), where he stressed both the loss in terms of the quality of human relationships that

occurs when exchange becomes purely economic and the need to restore the older themes of "freedom and obligation in the gift, of generosity and self-interest in giving" (*ibid.*, p. 66).

Although Mauss is chiefly known as an ethnologist and historian of religion, he was in fact a polymath, one of the last encyclopedic minds, and had an extraordinary range of ethnographic and linguistic knowledge (his pupils said "Mauss knows everything"). Lévy-Bruhl (1951, p. 4) described his conversation and lectures as full of "new and fruitful ideas of which others made theses and books." His career was brutally ended by the German occupation, which for a second time deprived him of friends and colleagues and affected the balance of his mind. He never completed projected books on money, prayer (but see Mauss 1909), and the nation (the manuscripts of which were probably destroyed), and he never synthesized his many-sided and scattered work.

Contributions to theory. Mauss's theoretical contributions derive mainly from his concrete application and refinement of Durkheim's precept, "The essential thing is to unite not many facts, but facts at once typical and well-studied," as well as the precept laid down in the article written with Fauconnet (which was a sort of Durkheimian charter) that the sociologist must connect "collective representations" (i.e., collective ways of acting and thinking) with features of the social structure or with one another (1901, p. 172).

Thus the study of the Eskimos explores the relations between morphological factors, on the one hand, and legal and moral systems, domestic economy, and religious life on the other. Mauss related the crowded conditions in which the Eskimos lived in the winter to the development among them of a real community of ideas, to "a strong religious and moral unity of mind," which he contrasted with the social atomization, the extreme "moral and religious impoverishment" that accompanied the dispersal in summer ([1906] 1960, p. 470). Similarly, the classic study with Durkheim of primitive classification attempts to find the origin of classifications (such as space, time, hierarchy, number, class, etc.) in the social structure by establishing formal correspondences between social and symbolic classifications among Australian aborigines, among the Zuni, and in traditional China: thus "even ideas so abstract as those of time and space are, at each point in their history, closely connected with the corresponding social organization" (Durkheim & Mauss [1903] 1963, p. 88). The elucidation of these formal correspondences is of considerable theoretical interest and suggestiveness, however questionable may be the causal chain that is postulated, the causal role given to affectivity, and the differentiation of cognitive operations from the content of thought (see Needham 1963). It was the first sociological study of classification and opened up the question, still immensely fruitful, of the relationship between symbolic classification and social structure.

Other examples of Mauss's practice of Durkheimian precepts are the study of magic, analyzed as a social phenomenon and defined as *"every rite which does not form part of an organised cult,"* being "private, secret, mysterious and tending at the margin towards the forbidden rite" (Hubert & Mauss [1904] 1960, p. 16); the study of sacrifice, analyzed as "a means of communication between the sacred and profane worlds, through the mediation of a victim, that is, of a thing that in the course of the ceremony is destroyed" (Hubert & Mauss [1899] 1964, p. 97); the study of the concept of the self, offering no more than a sketch of "the series of forms which this concept has assumed in the life of men in societies, according to their systems of law, their religions, their customs, their social structures and their modes of thought" (Mauss [1938] 1960, p. 335); and the studies of the social determinants of mourning rites (Mauss 1921), of the lust to die, and of uses of the body.

It is, however, *The Gift* that must rank as Mauss's masterpiece. It is the supreme example of the study of "total social facts," being concerned with a limited range of social phenomena seen as a totality, with "wholes, with systems in their entirety" ([1925] 1954, p. 77), namely, "prestations," or systems of exchange, which are "in theory voluntary, disinterested and spontaneous, but are in fact obligatory and interested" (*ibid.*, p. 1). He focused on a comparative study of forms of contract and exchange in Polynesia, Melanesia, and northwest America, with supplementary reference to evidence from early Roman, Hindu, and Germanic literature. The central hypotheses of the study are that "the archaic form of exchange," with its three obligations of giving, receiving, and repaying, is an aspect of almost all societies (and should be resurrected in our own), that it maintains and strengthens social bonds (cooperative, competitive, and antagonistic), and that by studying it concretely in its totality in the societies chosen, "we have been able to see their essence, their operation and their living aspect, and to catch the fleeting moment when the society and its members take emotional stock of themselves and their situation as regards others" (*ibid.*, pp. 77–78). Gift exchange is revealed as at once religious, legal, moral, economic, aesthetic, morphological, and mythological in significance:

the obligations it involves are symbolically expressed in myth and imagery and take the form of an interest in the objects exchanged, but these objects "are never completely separated from the men who exchange them; the communion and alliance they establish are well-nigh indissoluble. The lasting influence of the objects exchanged is a direct expression of the manner in which subgroups within segmentary societies of an archaic type are constantly embroiled with and feel themselves in debt to each other" (*ibid.*, p. 31). Apart from its considerable ethnographic interest, *The Gift* was the first systematic and comparative study of gift exchange and the first elaboration of the relation between patterns of exchange and the social structure.

In general, it may be said that Mauss's theoretical contributions result from putting Durkheimian sociology to work, de-emphasizing its least acceptable features (the latent mysticism of the group, the crowd psychology, the identification of historical origin and analytical simplicity) and demonstrating its considerable explanatory power.

Influence. Mauss's influence is particularly difficult to measure because of his deep involvement in collaborative work with Durkheim and others. He was the Durkheimians' ethnographic adviser, and his part in the studies of magic, social morphology (1906), and primitive classification was of crucial importance in the development of Durkheim's own sociology of religion and knowledge. One may likewise assert, but not measure, his influence on other Durkheimians (such as Marcel Granet) and upon those who came under their collective influence, including historians (such as Lucien Febvre and Marc Bloch) and psychologists (such as Charles Blondel).

He had a direct influence, however, on French ethnology, inspiring such figures as A. Métraux, M. Leenhardt, M. Griaule, G. Dumézil, R. Bastide, and L. Dumont. He has been a major influence on Lévi-Strauss, who has written about him in terms which overstate Mauss's theoretical divergence from Durkheim (Lévi-Strauss 1945; 1950). Lévi-Strauss values above all Mauss's method, best illustrated in *The Gift*, of treating a total social fact as a symbolic system to be deciphered. Lévi-Strauss sees this approach as "inaugurating a new era for the social sciences" ([1950] 1960, p. xxxv), for it may be generalized to the whole of social life. Thus social life may be understood as a system of transactions between groups and between individuals, the rationale of which can be established by techniques analogous to those of structural linguistics. According to Lévi-Strauss, it is the great misfortune of modern ethnology that Mauss did not exploit his discovery; he himself applied it in his theory of the exchange basis of cross-cousin marriage, which, he maintains, shows that in the field of kinship "the analogy with language, so strongly affirmed by Mauss, has permitted the discovery of precise rules, according to which there are formed, in any society whatever, cycles of reciprocity, whose mechanical laws are thenceforth known, permitting the use of deductive reasoning and offering the promise of a vast science of communication of which anthropology will be a part" ([1950] 1960, p. xxxvi). Leacock (1954) sees Mauss's work as more old-fashioned, condemning particularly its sociologism and evolutionism.

The Gift is Mauss's best-known work outside France, and indeed it is the only one that has made any impact in the United States; its theoretical suggestiveness seems by no means spent. Also influential have been the seminal studies of magic, sacrifice, and, increasingly, primitive classification. Mauss's influence is especially hard to identify in these areas because his work has entered into the common theoretical inheritance, often operating through the medium of colleagues and disciples. He appears particularly to have influenced the following anthropologists: A. R. Radcliffe-Brown, B. Malinowski (both of whom in different ways distorted his somewhat refined Durkheimianism), E. E. Evans-Pritchard, R. Firth, M. J. Herskovits, W. Lloyd Warner, and R. Redfield, among others. More generally, his influence is especially apparent in the anthropological work emanating from Oxford (via Evans-Pritchard) and in the work of the Leiden school (especially F. D. E. van Ossenbruggen and J. P. B. de Josselin de Jong). But the rich possibilities of his work have still to be fully exploited.

STEVEN LUKES

[*See also* ETHNOGRAPHY; EXCHANGE AND DISPLAY; MAGIC; MYTH AND SYMBOL; RITUAL; SOCIAL STRUCTURE; *and the biographies of* BLOCH; DURKHEIM; FEBVRE; GRANET; HERSKOVITS; MALINOWSKI; MÉTRAUX; POLANYI; RADCLIFFE-BROWN; REDFIELD.]

WORKS BY MAUSS

(1899) 1964 HUBERT, HENRI; and MAUSS, MARCEL *Sacrifice: Its Nature and Function.* Univ. of Chicago Press. → First published as "Essai sur la nature et la fonction du sacrifice" in Volume 2 of *Année sociologique.*
(1899–1905) 1909 HUBERT, HENRI; and MAUSS, MARCEL *Mélanges d'histoire des religions.* Paris: Alcan. → A collection of previously published articles. See especially the preface.
1901 FAUCONNET, PAUL; and MAUSS, MARCEL *Sociologie.* Volume 30, pages 165–176 in *La grande encyclopédie: Inventaire raisonné des sciences, des lettres et des arts.* . . . Paris: Société Anonyme de La Grande Encyclopédie.

(1903) 1963 DURKHEIM, ÉMILE; and MAUSS, MARCEL *Primitive Classification.* Translated and edited with an introduction by Rodney Needham. Univ. of Chicago Press. → First published as "De quelques formes primitives de classification" in Volume 6 of *Année sociologique.*
(1904) 1960 HUBERT, HENRI; and MAUSS, MARCEL *Esquisse d'une théorie générale de la magie.* Pages 1–141 in Marcel Mauss, *Sociologie et anthropologie.* 2d ed. Paris: Presses Universitaires de France. → First published in Volume 7 of *Année sociologique.*
(1906) 1960 *Essai sur les variations saisonnières des sociétés eskimos: Étude de morphologie sociale.* Pages 389–477 in Marcel Mauss, *Sociologie et anthropologie.* 2d ed. Paris: Presses Universitaires de France. → With the collaboration of H. Beuchat. First published in Volume 9 of *Année sociologique.*
1908 HUBERT, HENRI; and MAUSS, MARCEL *Introduction à l'analyse de quelques phénomènes religieux. Revue de l'histoire des religions* 58:163–203.
1909 *La prière. I: Les origines.* Unpublished manuscript. → The beginning of a larger work; distributed privately.
1921 *L'expression obligatoire des sentiments: Rituels oraux funéraires australiens. Journal de psychologie* 18:425–434.
(1924) 1960 *Rapports réels et pratiques de la psychologie et de la sociologie.* Pages 281–310 in Marcel Mauss, *Sociologie et anthropologie.* 2d ed. Paris: Presses Universitaires de France. → First published in *Journal de psychologie normale et pathologique.*
(1925) 1954 *The Gift: Forms and Functions of Exchange in Archaic Societies.* Glencoe, Ill.: Free Press. → First published as *Essai sur le don: Forme et raison de l'échange dans les sociétés archaïques.*
(1926) 1960 *Effet physique chez l'individu de l'idée de mort suggérée par la collectivité (Australie, Nouvelle-Zélande).* Pages 311–330 in Marcel Mauss, *Sociologie et anthropologie.* 2d ed. Paris: Presses Universitaires de France. → First published in *Journal de psychologie normale et pathologique.*
1927 *Divisions et proportions des divisions de la sociologie. Année sociologique* New Series [1924–1925]: 98–173.
1934 *Fragment d'un plan de sociologie générale descriptive. Annales sociologiques* Series A 1:1–56.
(1936) 1960 *Les techniques du corps.* Pages 363–386 in Marcel Mauss, *Sociologie et anthropologie.* 2d ed. Paris: Presses Universitaires de France. → First published in *Journal de psychologie.*
(1938) 1960 *Une catégorie de l'esprit humain: La notion de personne, celle de "moi."* Pages 331–362 in Marcel Mauss, *Sociologie et anthropologie.* 2d ed. Paris: Presses Universitaires de France. → First published (in French) in Volume 68 of the *Journal of the Royal Anthropological Institute of Great Britain and Ireland.*
1947 *Manuel d'ethnographie.* Paris: Payot. → Based on a course given annually from 1926 to 1939 at the Institut d'Ethnologie de l'Université de Paris.
Sociologie et anthropologie. 2d ed. Paris: Presses Universitaires de France, 1960. → A collection of essays first published between 1904 and 1938.

SUPPLEMENTARY BIBLIOGRAPHY

DAVY, GEORGES 1958 In Memoriam: Émile Durkheim. *Année sociologique* 3d Series [1957–1958]:vii–x.
GUGLER, JOSEF 1961 *Die neuere französische Soziologie: Ansätze zu einer Standortbestimmung der Soziologie.* Neuwied (Germany): Luchterhand.

GUGLER, JOSEF 1964 Bibliographie de Marcel Mauss. *Homme* 64:105–112. → The most complete bibliography of Mauss's publications (excluding those in socialist journals and the numerous notes and reviews in the *Année sociologique* and the *Notes critiques–Sciences sociales*). Includes not only his writings but also summaries of his comments at meetings of academic societies and congresses.

LEACOCK, SETH 1954 Ethnological Theory of Marcel Mauss. *American Anthropologist* New Series 56:58–73. → Selected bibliography appended.

LÉVI-STRAUSS, CLAUDE 1945 French Sociology. Pages 503–537 in Georges Gurvitch and Wilbert E. Moore (editors), *Twentieth Century Sociology*. New York: Philosophical Library.

LÉVI-STRAUSS, CLAUDE (1950) 1960 Introduction à l'oeuvre de Marcel Mauss. In Marcel Mauss, *Sociologie et anthropologie*. 2d ed. Paris: Presses Universitaires de France. → The most important study of Mauss to date. Contains a selected bibliography.

LÉVY-BRUHL, H. 1951 In Memoriam: Marcel Mauss. *Année sociologique* 3d series [1948–1949]:1–4.

MERLEAU-PONTY, MAURICE (1953) 1960 De Mauss à Claude Lévi-Strauss. Pages 145–169 in Maurice Merleau-Ponty, *Éloge de la philosophie, et autres essais*. Paris: Gallimard.

NEEDHAM, RODNEY 1963 Introduction. In Émile Durkheim and Marcel Mauss, *Primitive Classification*. Univ. of Chicago Press.

MAXIMUM LIKELIHOOD

See ESTIMATION.

MAYO, ELTON

While the published writings of Elton Mayo (1880–1949) now seem to be mainly of historical interest, he personally had an enormous influence in the development of industrial sociology and psychology and in the stimulation of men who have made major contributions to research and theory.

Mayo was particularly influenced by the writings of the psychologist Pierre Janet. He combined an interest in psychoneuroses and what he termed "obsessive thinking," derived from his study of Janet, with the approach to culture and social structure of the social anthropologists Bronislaw Malinowski and A. R. Radcliffe-Brown. In research methods he adapted the interviewing methods of clinical psychologists to the field methods of the anthropologists and brought them to bear on studies of industrial organizations.

Mayo was born in Adelaide, Australia, the second of seven children. He came from a family of professional men. In the process of finding his vocation, Mayo ranged widely in space and experience: from medical student to newspaperman to laborer to businessman, from Scotland to west Africa and back to Australia. From the printing business, he turned to the study of psychology at Adelaide University. A psychiatric treatment program he and a collaborator organized toward the end of World War I to deal with soldiers suffering from shell shock led to his appointment in 1919 to the newly established chair of philosophy at the University of Queensland.

Rockefeller and Carnegie foundation grants brought him to the United States and supported his first research in human relations in industry, which he began while at the University of Pennsylvania. The site of his first research in this field was a textile mill.

The most productive period of his life began in 1926, when he accepted a position at Harvard University's Graduate School of Business Administration. In association with Lawrence J. Henderson, an eminent biological chemist and devotee of Pareto, Mayo organized a research team to study the psychological and social problems of industrial workers. The aim from the beginning was to follow these problems wherever they led, without regard to customary disciplinary boundaries.

In 1927 Mayo launched the now famous Western Electric research program. He worked particularly with Fritz J. Roethlisberger, William J. Dickson, and T. North Whitehead, and it was they who produced the principal research reports of the studies carried on at the Hawthorne Works in Chicago. As director of the program, Mayo had the task of handling the diplomacy involved in making such an unprecedented research effort acceptable within a company, and he also made important contributions to the design of the research program and to the interpretation of the results (see *Management and the Worker* by Roethlisberger & Dickson 1939).

While Mayo was primarily interested in problems of individual adjustment, he recognized the necessity of examining such individual problems in the context of organizations and social structure. He was instrumental in bringing W. Lloyd Warner to Harvard and worked closely with him in launching the Yankee City study. At the same time, Warner became consultant to the Western Electric research program and there stimulated the analysis of problems of group and organizational structure.

In all his writings Mayo was concerned with two basic ideas, one dealing with the nature of society, the other dealing with the problems of individuals. He argued that the industrial revolution had destroyed traditional society in which people responded to each other in terms of established routines. The breakdown in these traditional understandings had led to widespread conflict in industry and society. The traditions of old could not be re-established, and, therefore, the only solution must be to build an adaptive society in which an administrative elite, trained in social understandings and skills, would resolve human as well as technical problems.

He saw workers suffering from a form of anomie, the failure to find a satisfactory place for themselves in the world of work, with a consequent involvement in obsessive reveries in which they brooded unproductively over their problems. For dealing with these problems of obsessive thinking, he had great faith in the therapeutic relationship in which the individual is encouraged to talk out his problems freely to an interested listener.

Although Mayo directed the Western Electric research program, the principal research fruits of that program bear little relation to Mayo's ideas about social integration, obsessive thinking, and psychotherapy. To be sure, *Management and the Worker* does devote chapters to the personnel-counseling program, a direct outgrowth of Mayo's ideas, but that program was later abandoned by the company and never served as a model for other companies. Furthermore, few research men today consider a personnel-counseling program of much importance in dealing with problems of human adjustment in industry. The principal fruits of the Western Electric studies are found in those parts of *Management and the Worker* which deal with informal relations among workers, with worker–management relations, and with the methods for gathering systematic observational and interviewing data upon behavior in organizations. These contributions provided the foundation for the very rapid development of research on organizational behavior in the two decades following publication of that book in 1939.

Mayo, as the father of research on the human problems of industry, also became the principal target for attack. Critics argued that there was no place in his philosophy for conflict, that he sought to achieve organizational harmony through the subordination of individual and group interests by the administrative elite, and that he did not understand the role of unions in a free society. Mayo's supporters replied that he had no illusions about the possibility of establishing perfect harmony in any industrial society. He simply observed that there is so much destructive conflict that it is well to seek better ways of handling human problems. While Mayo has been charged with being anti-union, it might be more accurate to say that he was simply indifferent to unions. In his most productive period of work with Western Electric, the company had only a weak company union. Al-

though unions had become a prominent part of the industrial scene long before Mayo's death, he did not think they fundamentally altered those human problems of industry that interested him, and he never integrated unions into his thinking about industry.

Mayo was not a systematic theoretician. He had a wide-ranging mind and creative social abilities. Few men have contributed as much as he to the establishment of new fields of social research and teaching. He was a behavioral scientist long before the term became popular.

WILLIAM F. WHYTE

[*See also* GROUPS, *article on* THE STUDY OF GROUPS; INDUSTRIAL RELATIONS; ORGANIZATIONS, *article on* THEORIES OF ORGANIZATIONS; WORKERS; *and the biographies of* HENDERSON; JANET; MALINOWSKI; RADCLIFFE-BROWN.]

WORKS BY MAYO

(1933) 1946   *The Human Problems of an Industrial Civilization.* 2d ed. Boston: Harvard Univ., Graduate School of Business Administration. → A paperback edition was published in 1960 by Viking.
1945   *The Social Problems of an Industrial Civilization.* Boston: Harvard Univ., Graduate School of Business Administration.
1947   *The Political Problem of Industrial Civilization.* Boston: Harvard Univ., Graduate School of Business Administration.
1948   *Some Notes on the Psychology of Pierre Janet.* Cambridge, Mass.: Harvard Univ. Press.

SUPPLEMENTARY BIBLIOGRAPHY

BENDIX, REINHARD; and FISHER, LLOYD H.   1949   The Perspectives of Elton Mayo. *Review of Economics and Statistics* 31:312–319.
HOMANS, GEORGE C.   1949   Some Corrections. *Review of Economics and Statistics* 31:319–321.
ROETHLISBERGER, FRITZ J.; and DICKSON, WILLIAM J. (1939) 1961   *Management and the Worker: An Account of a Research Program Conducted by the Western Electric Company, Hawthorne Works, Chicago.* Cambridge, Mass.: Harvard Univ. Press. → A paperback edition was published in 1964 by Wiley.
URWICK, LYNDALL F.   1960   *The Life and Work of Elton Mayo.* London: Urwick.
WARNER, W. LLOYD et al.   1941–1959   *Yankee City Series.* 5 vols. New Haven, Conn.: Yale Univ. Press.

MEAD, GEORGE HERBERT

The work of George Herbert Mead (1863–1931), one of the leading figures in pragmatism, has had a profound impact on the development of American social science. Despite the lavish praise of Dewey and Whitehead, most philosophers tended to neglect him, because his ideas were not readily accessible during his lifetime. He was reluctant to set down in writing views that were still being formed; he published no books, and many of his articles dealt with education, psychology, and sociology. Communicating most effectively in oral discourse, Mead developed his thoughts in extemporaneous lectures at the University of Chicago, where he taught from 1893 to the time of his death. Although his style was involved and labored and even his admirers acknowledged difficulties in deciphering his sentences, the classes were well-attended; and his influence upon colleagues and students, especially in sociology and social psychology, is readily discernible in their writings. Four posthumous volumes have been pieced together by devoted students from stenographic notes of his lectures, fragmentary manuscripts, and tentative drafts.

Pragmatism represents an attempt to reformulate conceptions of man and his place in the universe in terms of the revolutionary implications of scientific method and of evolutionary theory. Mead viewed evolution as the process of meeting and solving problems and scientific method as the evolutionary process grown self-conscious. The characteristics of various species develop as organisms come to terms with life conditions, and Mead wanted to account for the emergent properties of man—thinking in abstractions, self-consciousness, and purposive and moral conduct. He contended that these attributes rest on the development of language, a form of social interaction that evolves among human beings as they meet the exigencies of living in groups.

Thus, Mead's central hypothesis made social psychology basic to his philosophical work. His approach was behavioristic, although not in the narrow sense of John B. Watson: man is to be studied in terms of his deeds, covert as well as overt. Since, however, each person is involved in a succession of joint enterprises with others, his acts can best be regarded as segments of larger transactions. Social psychology is the study of regularities in individual behavior that develop from participating in groups. Mead also stressed the temporal dimension—the extension of individual and group activities over time.

Analysis of the "act"

Society is an ongoing process and consists of social acts. By *social act* Mead meant a transaction involving two or more persons among whom there is a division of labor. The contributions of various individuals are coordinated to achieve objectives that bring gratifications of some sort to each. Unlike the instinctive cooperation found among social insects, concerted action among human beings is characterized by a high degree of flexibility. The

participants build up a social act as they continuously adjust to one another and to the demands of the developing situation. Should there be drastic environmental change, entirely novel patterns may emerge. Such concurrence among separate and independently motivated individuals is made possible by *role taking*, the ability of each to visualize his own performance from the standpoint of the others. Each person is able to comprehend the entire transaction, locate himself within it, and regulate his own contributions to fit into the larger pattern. Coordination depends, then, on the self-control of each actor. In highly institutionalized transactions, collaboration is facilitated insofar as the participants share a common perspective; each of them takes the role of a *generalized other*.

The execution of a social act is a communicative process; transactions of all kinds develop in the reciprocating adjustments of the participants. Mutual orientation is built up and maintained in a continuous interchange of gestures. A *gesture* is any perceptible sound or movement which indicates to a second party the inner experiences or intentions of the first; any act may become a gesture when an observer responds to it in terms of what it represents. Speech, which consists of vocal gestures, is of special importance. Since a speaker is able to hear his own remarks in much the same manner as his audience, the establishment of mutual understanding becomes easier. A gesture that has the same meaning for two or more people is a *significant symbol*, and language consists of such conventional sounds. Those who are associated in common activities eventually develop a universe of discourse, which facilitates their subsequent collaboration.

Although each deed is a fragment of a larger social act, it is also an episode in the life of an individual. Mead's basic unit of analysis is the *act*, which is initiated by some want and is directed toward its satisfaction through the use of suitable elements of the environment. All behavior can be broken down, for purposes of analysis, into a series of acts. Each act has a history; it is constructed as an organism makes a succession of adjustments to conditions (external and internal) that are undergoing constant change. Overt behavior is usually only the final phase of an act; in most cases it is preceded by a number of preparatory adjustments, including various subjective experiences. An act is teleological; it is not a mere sequence of passing events but an organized whole directed toward an end. To study such processes Mead proposed the concepts of impulse, perception, manipulation, and consummation. An *impulse* is a disturbance, any lack of adjustment between the organism and its milieu—pique over an imagined slight, hunger pangs, or concern over a difficult task to be faced. *Consummation* is the elimination of the disturbance. In his study of motivation, then, Mead developed an approach resembling some of the more recent tension-reduction models. His scheme was comprehensive, and his concepts made it possible to show the relationship between organic needs, external stimulation, conscious intent, and overt movements.

Between the terminal points of the act lie *perception* and *manipulation;* it is through these processes that various features of the environment become involved in the act. An organism is in continuous interaction with its milieu, and activity is redirected in response to a succession of sensory cues. Perception is selective: not everything in the environment is noticed. An *object* is something that is essential to the completion of the act, and a person is sensitized to whatever will enable him to carry out activity that is already under way. Both perception and manipulation rest upon hypotheses. An object is approached in terms of expectations: a person anticipates what would happen if he were to move forward and touch it. For this reason Mead referred to perception as a "collapsed" or "telescoped" act. What is perceived depends in part upon what is anticipated; these hypotheses are then tested and confirmed in manipulation, the handling of objects as tools.

The hypotheses upon which perception and manipulation rest are derived from the meanings of objects. For pragmatists *meaning* is primarily a property of behavior and only secondarily a property of the objects themselves. Meanings are stable relationships between an organism and a class of objects, defined in the manner in which the latter are characteristically handled. Physical attributes are important because they set limitations upon what can be done. Most meanings are subject to social control in that the anticipated reactions of other people place additional restrictions on usage. Approaching sacred objects without sufficient deference, for example, elicits outraged protests. Such expectations are incorporated into the organization of the act. Members of each species select out of their environment objects that are essential to their survival and organize responses toward them; the world view of human beings is necessarily anthropomorphic and social. But pragmatism is not solipsistic. Reality is objectified through activity, but the orientations which support such activity are subject to reality testing. Hypotheses that turn out to be unreliable are rejected, and objects are redefined.

Once an act is under way, it generally proceeds to consummation. One of the major contentions of pragmatists is that *thinking* is a form of behavior that occurs when activity is interrupted. The interference may arise from an external barrier, a disability of the organism, or an absence of necessary objects. When an act is blocked, a number of secondary adjustments take place, including emergency mobilization (emotion) and conscious reflection; and through these processes a delayed act may eventually be completed. Any impulse that is not immediately consummated is transformed into an *image*, which serves as the basis for reflection. Images are acts that fail to issue in overt behavior, acts that are innervated but not carried out. Each image may be regarded as a plan of action, one possible way of completing the interrupted act. A perplexed individual experiences a succession of images, and reflective thought is an imaginative rehearsal—a comparison and evaluation of alternative routes to consummation. Mentality may be regarded as the ability to anticipate the consequences of projected lines of action and to respond to them prior to commitment to overt action. Thinking, then, is problem-solving activity in which trial and error takes place in the imagination.

Once a person has mastered a language, images and objects may be designated by symbols; alternative plans of action are labeled, and their consequences are examined verbally. *Consciousness* is inner discourse, subvocal linguistic communication. While thinking is a private experience, it takes place through significant symbols; it is therefore behavior organized from the standpoint of a generalized other. The use of language transforms the effective environment to which human beings adjust. By using words, one can manipulate meanings outside the contexts in which they have developed and even make up more complex meanings. Foresight and planning are greatly facilitated. With symbols one can isolate certain experiences and hold on to them, pick out other relevant meanings, or emphasize a particular image while rejecting others. Language also makes possible the formulation of complex plans, broad schemes in which diverse and even antagonistic tendencies may be coordinated and a sequence of operations performed. *Mind* for Mead was internal symbolic communication, and it is this type of cognitive activity that computer engineers are now attempting to reconstruct. Modern decision theory describes regularities in the selection process.

Analysis of the "self"

Mead is best known for his theory of the *self*. The self is not one's body but a perceptual object. Since most acts are components of larger transactions, the actors are interdependent; the impulses of one cannot be consummated without the co-operation of his associates. Each participant therefore becomes concerned over the possible reactions of the others to himself, for he cannot afford to do anything that will jeopardize their support. Each person forms an object of himself through role taking, by reviewing his intended conduct from the standpoint of those with whom he is involved in a common venture. Mead's discussion was rendered unnecessarily difficult by his use of the term "self" to designate three different referents: (1) the perceptual object formed of oneself in a particular historical context, (2) the process of self-control, and (3) one's personality.

Voluntary conduct is constructed in a sequence of adjustments in which a person responds to himself as well as to the rest of his perceptual field. To study this process Mead proposed the concepts of the *I* and the *Me;* these terms refer not to agents but to phases of activity. The "Me" is the object one forms of oneself from a conventional standpoint, and the "I" is the reaction of the unique individual to the historical situation as he perceives it. Typical inclinations to react differ from person to person; in fact, the succession of "I's" constitutes the basis of individuality. In speaking of behavior as being built up in the interaction of the "I" and the "Me," Mead was stressing the seriated character of human conduct. If an impulse (I) is not immediately carried out, it is transformed into an image (Me), which in turn elicits another reaction (I). For example, if a man believes that his wife is disparaging his efforts (Me), he may want to beat her (I). As he refrains from striking, he imagines himself administering the beating (Me). Since he views himself from the standpoint of a group in which wife beaters are condemned, he reacts with disgust (I), and this inhibits one route to consummation. Frustrated and hurt (Me), he reacts with determination to demonstrate his competence through a superlative performance (I). Thus, an individual's line of conduct is constructed as he adjusts to a succession of organic states, perceptual objects, images, and anticipated reactions of other people. Self-control is part of the ongoing social current; each person adjusts in advance to the situation in which he is involved and thereby facilitates cooperation. In this process self-consciousness provides the basis for corrective measures. For Mead, as for Norbert Wiener, autonomy depends upon feedback; without it one becomes a creature of impulse or is subject to drift or external control. A crucial feature of feedback in self-control is that the object is formed from a standpoint shared with other people. The fact that all participants control themselves from the same perspective (generalized other) makes concerted action possible.

A human being is not born with a mind and self-discipline; these capacities develop gradually as the child comes to terms with the demands of group life. The meanings of objects and gestures are products of experience; appropriate ways of handling things and of speaking are shaped largely by the consistent responses of elders, who provide instructions, serve as models, and reinforce the accepted modes of conduct. Mead emphasized two especially important contexts for socialization. In *play* young children assume specific roles and imitate individuals they know—mother, postman, salesclerk. In so doing they begin to appreciate the perspectives of others. By repeating such role taking the child is able to build up an orientation toward himself as an object of a certain sort. But effective self-control develops only in the *game*— or in any other enterprise that requires teamwork. In games the responses of others are organized, and activity proceeds according to rules. The contributions expected of each player are standardized into impersonal roles. Furthermore, successful participation requires the ability to assume multiple positions vis-à-vis oneself: one must be ready to take the role of any other player. Through repeated participation in such transactions, the child learns to adopt a point of view that is shared by all other participants (generalized other), a perspective that transcends that of particular individuals.

Although Mead saw human beings as inextricably involved in groups, he stressed the importance of individuality. Each person, although a product of society, retains his distinctiveness, for he incorporates the generalized other from a unique standpoint. As one develops the capacity for conscious communication, one achieves greater independence from others and greater discreteness as an individual. For each person self-realization is attained through the consummation of a distinct set of impulses; what brings fufillment to one individual will not necessarily satisfy another. Furthermore, each person has a unique impact upon his community. Even when he is complying with conventional norms, he does so in his own style. The contributions of a genius are often striking and extensive and therefore more readily discernible, but everywhere allowances have to be made for the idiosyncrasies of the less talented. Thus, through self-assertion, each individual alters somewhat the social pattern in which he participates.

As a social philosopher Mead had a deep bias toward amelioration through understanding. The son of a Congregationalist minister in Ohio, he may have been influenced by the climate of opinion of his community, a station of the Underground Railroad and locale of the first college to admit women. He believed that progress takes place through the constant meeting and solving of problems. Social institutions, like everything else in nature, are continually evolving, but men can direct this process through intelligent action. Scientific method provides the most efficient way of solving problems and should be used to facilitate human adaptation. The ideal society is one in which there is maximum participation by all members, one in which each person understands all the others and still retains his individuality. This ideal, while imperfectly realized, is constantly being approximated. Mead believed that history is on the side of progress and that eventually a brotherhood of man will emerge.

Since pragmatism is an application of scientific method to philosophical problems, it is not surprising that Mead's position is so much like the developing outlook of the natural and social sciences. Mead was a thinker who was ahead of his time. His views on matter, space, time, and relativity are similar to those of modern theoretical physics; and his discussion of meaning resembles P. W. Bridgman's work on operational definitions. Many of the ideas Mead developed at the turn of the century are now widely accepted in social psychology: the selective and seriated character of perception, cognition through linguistic symbols, role enactment, decision processes, autonomy through feedback, personal identity, reference groups, and socialization through participation. Because of the congruence of Mead's views with current trends, it seems likely that increasing attention will be directed to his work. Many implications of his position still remain to be explored.

TAMOTSU SHIBUTANI

[For the historical context of Mead's work, see INTERACTION, article on SOCIAL INTERACTION; SOCIOLOGY, article on THE DEVELOPMENT OF SOCIOLOGICAL THOUGHT; and the biographies of DARWIN; DEWEY; HEGEL; JAMES; MARX; PARK; PEIRCE; SMITH, ADAM; SULLIVAN; THOMAS. For discussion of the subsequent development of Mead's ideas, see COMMUNICATION; DEVIANT BEHAVIOR; KNOWLEDGE, SOCIOLOGY OF; ROLE, article on SOCIOLOGICAL ASPECTS; SELF CONCEPT; SEMANTICS AND SEMIOTICS; SYSTEMS ANALYSIS, article on SOCIAL SYSTEMS; and the biographies of ANGELL; BECKER; BURGESS; COOLEY; FOLLETT; MERRIAM; MEYER; WALLER.]

WORKS BY MEAD

(1932) 1959 The Philosophy of the Present. La Salle, Ill.: Open Court.
1934 Mind, Self and Society From the Standpoint of a Social Behaviorist. Edited by Charles W. Morris. Univ. of Chicago Press. → Contains a complete bibliography.
1936 Movements of Thought in the Nineteenth Century. Univ. of Chicago Press.
1938 The Philosophy of the Act. Univ. of Chicago Press.
Selected Writings. Edited with an introduction by Andrew J. Reck. Indianapolis, Ind.: Bobbs-Merrill, 1964.

SUPPLEMENTARY BIBLIOGRAPHY

BLUMER, HERBERT 1966 Sociological Implications of the Thought of George Herbert Mead. American Journal of Sociology 71:534–544, 547–548.
CLAYTON, ALFRED S. 1943 Emergent Mind and Education: A Study of George H. Mead's Bio-social Behaviorism From an Educational Point of View. New York: Columbia Univ., Teachers College.
KOLB, WILLIAM L. 1944 A Critical Evaluation of Mead's "I" and "Me" Concepts. Social Forces 22:291–296.
LAGUNA, GRACE A. DE 1946 Communication, the Act, and the Object, With Reference to Mead. Journal of Philosophy 43:225–238.
LEE, GRACE C. 1945 George Herbert Mead: Philosopher of the Social Individual. New York: King's Crown Press.
NATANSON, MAURICE 1956 The Social Dynamics of George H. Mead. Washington: Public Affairs Press. → Contains an extensive list of secondary sources.
STRONG, SAMUEL M. 1939 A Note on George H. Mead's The Philosophy of the Act. American Journal of Sociology 45:71–76.

MEAN VALUES

See STATISTICS, DESCRIPTIVE, article on LOCATION AND DISPERSION.

MEASUREMENT

See CONTENT ANALYSIS; ECONOMETRICS; EVALUATION RESEARCH; PANEL STUDIES; PSYCHOMETRICS; SCALING; SOCIOMETRY; STATISTICS; STATISTICS, DESCRIPTIVE, article on LOCATION AND DISPERSION; STRATIFICATION, SOCIAL, article on THE MEASUREMENT OF SOCIAL CLASS; SURVEY ANALYSIS.

MECHANISMS

See DEFENSE MECHANISMS and FUNCTIONAL ANALYSIS.

MEDIATION

See DIPLOMACY; LABOR RELATIONS; INTERNATIONAL CONFLICT RESOLUTION; NEGOTIATION.

MEDICAL CARE

I. ETHNOMEDICINE Charles C. Hughes
II. SOCIAL ASPECTS William A. Glaser
III. ECONOMIC ASPECTS Rashi Fein

I
ETHNOMEDICINE

Judging from paleopathological evidence, diseases of one kind or another have always afflicted man. Indeed, given the nature of life and the nature of disease, it could not be otherwise; for disease is but an expression of man's dynamic relationship with his environment. And even as there has always been sickness, accident, deformity, and anxiety to trouble man, so, too, has there been an organized, purposeful response by society to such threats. In all human groups, no matter how small or technologically primitive, there exists a body of belief about the nature of disease, its causation and cure, and its relations to other aspects of group life. There also exist therapeutic and preventive practices, many of which are empirically efficacious by standards of modern medicine, although often not for the reasons advanced by folk belief. The variability of societies and cultural systems impedes easy generalization about the nature of "primitive" or "folk" medicine (cf. Ackerknecht 1942a), but one common characteristic is its close integration with other institutions of the society. Religion, medicine, and morality are frequently found together in the behavioral act or event, and "folk medicine" becomes "social medicine" to an extent not found in industrialized societies.

The term "ethnomedicine" will be used to refer to those beliefs and practices relating to disease which are the products of indigenous cultural development and are not explicitly derived from the conceptual framework of modern medicine. In this light, most of the following discussion focuses on the non-Western, nonindustrialized societies of the world, although it is clear that in "modern" societies as well there exist beliefs and practices relating to disease and its treatment which are based on magical or religious conceptions rather than on those of scientific medicine.

Theory of disease.   Man, everywhere, devises or divines causes for the significant events in his life. The afflictions which beset body and mind are explained in both naturalistic and supernaturalistic terms. A cut finger, a broken limb, a snake bite, a fever, the halting speech and wandering mind of senility—all may be regarded as sometime hazards in life. To explain such events there is always some conceptual framework founded in common-sense empiricism. But often a wound does not heal, a sickness does not respond to treatment, and the normally expected and predictable does not happen. In such cases another order of explanation is employed, one which attempts to come to terms with the more basic *meaning* of the event in metaphysical perspective. For most non-Western societies this transcendent explanation for the occurrence of disease tends to figure more pervasively in the total body of medical lore and practice than does

the empirical framework. One reason is the greater incapacitation and mortality from disease in the underdeveloped world than in highly industrialized societies. In addition, this reality is coupled with the comparative inadequacy of ethnomedical techniques and knowledge for dealing with these common threats to the existence of the group and the person.

Widespread throughout the world are five basic categories of events or situations which, in folk etiology, are believed responsible for illness: (1) sorcery; (2) breach of taboo; (3) intrusion of a disease object; (4) intrusion of a disease-causing spirit; and (5) loss of soul (Clements 1932). Not every society recognizes all five categories; indeed, many groups are selective in the emphasis placed upon one or a combination of causes. For example, the Eskimo most frequently trace the origin of diseases to soul loss and breach of taboo, while the malevolence of sorcerers or witches is especially emphasized in many African cultures. Usually, however, these categories are more useful in analytically characterizing the etiological beliefs of a particular group than in describing the content of an entire belief system. This would be the case where a disease is believed to be caused by the intrusion of an object which *contains* a spirit, and it is the latter to which primary causative influence is attributed (e.g., Hallowell 1935).

The Greeks were not alone in viewing disease as a manifestation of disharmony in man's over-all relation to the universe. "Health" is rarely, if ever, a narrowly restricted conception having its locus only in the well-being of the individual body. In discussing conceptions of illness among a west African people, Price-Williams gives a modern illustration:

In common with a great many other people, Tiv do not regard "illness" or "disease" as a completely separate category distinct from misfortunes to compound and farm, from relationship between kin, and from more complicated matters relating to the control of land. But it would be completely erroneous to say that Tiv are not able, in a cognitive sense, to recognize disease. As Bohannan has said: "The concept of a disease is not foreign to the Tiv: mumps, smallpox, . . . yaws and gonorrhoea are all common and each has a name." What is meant is that disease is seldom viewed in isolation.   (1962, p. 125)

Such a notion is widely found, as in certain American Indian groups, where bodily or mental affliction is often viewed as an indicator of moral transgression, in thought or in deed, against the norms of society. Indeed, man is frequently thought of as continuous with both the social and nonsocial aspects of his environment, and what happens in his surroundings affects his bodily well-being. Not only a person's own actions, therefore, but also those of kinsmen or neighbors can cause sickness. Such an etiological conception has obvious implications for treatment. For example, if the curative technique includes magically based dietary restrictions, they may apply to all members of the patient's family; a breach of the restriction by any of these people will undermine the patient's health. Similarly, as among the Thonga of South Africa, sexual relations between any of the inhabitants of the patient's village can aggravate his condition, and some Eskimo groups feel that the patient's family should do no work during the period of convalescence for fear of giving offense to the spirit causing the sickness.

The belief that by his own actions a man can influence the state of his fellow's health also has malevolent implications, as in the practice of witchcraft and sorcery. Frequently this may be an important factor deciding the success or failure of attempts at introducing new medical programs in underdeveloped societies. Cassel (1955) cites as an illustration the Zulu, who believe that only sorcerers and witches have the ability to transmit disease, particularly diseases which show themselves in symptoms normally associated with pulmonary tuberculosis. Progress in one community's acceptance of a Western-styled health program was brought to an abrupt halt when a physician tried to introduce the medical concept of contagion. He traced the course of tuberculosis through a family, showing how one person had been the original source of the disease in the group and had therefore been the agent responsible for sickness in all the others. The cautious cooperation of the family elder immediately turned into a hostile rejection, which was assuaged only after the doctor had retracted his apparent accusation that the daughter of the family was a witch.

A theory of disease implies a theory of normality. Yet the "normal" is in no way easy to define for all times and places. Aside from questions of a "statistical" versus a "functional" basis for normality, there is the cultural definition. Afflictions common enough in a group to be endemic, though they be clinical deformities, may often be accepted simply as part of man's natural condition. Ackerknecht (1946), for example, has noted that the Thonga believe intestinal worms, with which they are pervasively affected, to be necessary for digestion; the Mano, also of Africa, feel that primary and secondary yaws are so common that they say, "That is no sickness; everybody has that." North Ama-

zonian Indians, among whom dyschronic spirochetosis is prevalent, accept its endemicity to such an extent that its victims are thought to be normal, and individuals who have not had the disfiguring disease are said to be looked upon as pathological and consequently unable to contract marriage. It is culture, not nature, that defines disease, although it is usually culture *and* nature which foster disease.

Recent behavioral science research has attempted to go beyond a "phenomenological" orientation in investigation of cultural theories of disease and has sought analytic categories which would relate particular emphases in a theory of disease to other aspects of social and cultural life. A striking example of this type of investigation is the work of John Whiting and Irvin Child (1953). Using a wide sample from the ethnographic "laboratory," these investigators found high correlations between certain aspects of child-rearing practices and dominant themes in etiological beliefs related to disease, more particularly, between the hypothesized degree of anxiety generated during the socialization process—the degree of "negative fixation"— and a theory of disease which reflects these anxieties. Thus, harsh weaning is highly associated with oral explanations for onset of disease: these would include consumption of food, drink, or poison by the sick individual or oral activity on the part of others, such as incantations and spells. Societies in which independence training is characteristically fraught with emotional hazards tend also to have "dependence" explanations of illness. These include soul loss or spirit possession. "Aggression explanations" for disease are highly associated with societies in which training for handling aggressive impulses leaves a residue of unresolved anxiety, and they are expressed in theories which ascribe the cause of a disease to the patient's disobedience or aggression toward spirits, to aggressive wishes on the part of the patient or another person, to introjection of poison other than by mouth, or to harm by magical weapons or objects.

Theory and practice of treatment. Therapeutic practices in ethnomedicine address themselves to both supernatural and empirical theories of disease causation. Ackerknecht has said that primitive medicine is "magic medicine" (1942*b*); certainly much of it is, and, insofar as supernatural causes are involved, therapeutic regimes are based on countervailing supernatural powers or events. Thus, the powerful shaman or healer attempts to recover the soul lost or stolen by a human or supernatural agent. The intrusion of a disease object or disease-causing spirit is treated by extraction or exorcism, and diseases which come as punishment for breach of taboo are usually treated by divination or confession of the infraction. Forgiveness and re-establishment of harmony with the moral and supernatural order are thus important outcomes of the therapy.

In folk medicine, however, there is more to treatment than magical or religious ritualization, however effective this may be psychosocially in providing emotional catharsis and reassurance. All human groups have a pharmacopoeia and at least rudimentary medical techniques; some groups, indeed, are exceptional in their exploitation of the environment for medicinal purposes and in the degree of their diagnostic and surgical skills (Ackerknecht 1942b; Sigerist 1951; Laughlin 1963). The trephining done by the Inca, Masai surgery, the anatomical knowledge of the Aleut and the Eskimo, and the extensive drug repertory of west African tribes are familiar examples. In addition to trephining, numerous other types of surgery and bonesetting are found, as well as massages, bloodletting, dry cupping, bathing, inoculation, and cauterization. It has been estimated that from 25 to 50 per cent of the non-Western pharmacopoeia is empirically effective. In fact, our knowledge of the therapeutic efficacy of a large number of modern drugs is derived from the experience of primitive peoples: opium, hashish, hemp, coca, cinchona, eucalyptus, sarsaparilla, acacia, kousso, copaiba, guaiac, jalap, podophyllin, quassia, and many of the tranquilizers and psychotomimetics now used in psychiatric therapy and research.

A great part of the task of folk medicine, however, and especially of preventive medicine, is borne by cultural practices which, although oriented to different social purposes, have important functional implications for health. Thus, notable hygienic purposes are served by many religious and magical practices, such as avoidance of the house in which a death has occurred, theories of contagious "bad body humors" which necessitate daily bathing, distinctions of "hot" and "cold" food and water which require boiling or cooking, hiding of fecal and other bodily waste through fear of their use by sorcerers or witches, and numerous others.

Other cultural practices inadvertently relevant to health have a more general ecological basis. These may include customs regarding cosmetics and clothing or house styles and settlement patterns. Regardless of their value to the archeologist, the middens of ancient sedentary communities have rather baleful implications for the public health of the times. Changing economic incentives and circumstances which disrupt the adaptation of a cultural activity to its environment frequently create health hazards. May (1960) provides a striking illustration of the intersection between cultural and ecological factors in North Vietnam. Dwellers on the plains lived in low, squat houses in which they sheltered their cattle on one side and did their cooking on the other. When these rice growers moved into the hills they constructed houses according to the same general plan. In the hills, however, the incidence of malaria among them became so high as to limit further such movement, despite governmental encouragement. The people themselves ascribed the calamity to the ill will of the hill deities. In fact, however, the incidence of malaria was low among the indigenous hill people, who constructed their houses on stilts, sheltered their animals underneath, and did their cooking inside the house. Several factors were apparently instrumental in the latter case in keeping down the spread of malaria from the mosquito vector found in the hills; flight ceiling of *Anopheles minimus* is restricted to about ten feet above the ground, and, despite its preference for human blood, the presence of animals underneath the house and of smoke inside the house (where the cooking was done) created an unrealized protection for human inhabitants.

The study of folk medicine has important theoretical implications for the persistent question of a "magical" versus a "scientific" orientation among non-Western peoples. Erasmus (1952), utilizing data from South American Indian populations, contends that the inductive epistemological framework of folk medicine is essentially similar in structure to that of modern scientific medicine, but that the latter differs chiefly in its amenity to generalization and degree of predictive success. In folk medicine the chances of "natural" recovery are in favor of predictive successes, but, more often than in modern medicine, the theoretical propositions lying behind such predictions are merely coincidentally rather than functionally related to the phenomenon in question. Thus, the recooking, before eating, of food that has been left standing overnight is done on the basis of the need to dispel the dangerous quality of "coldness" in the food, but in fact such recooking destroys enterotoxin-producing staphylococci.

The possible implications for a sociology of knowledge are apparent: so long as any activity or set of activities produces a sufficiently high proportion of predictive successes, there will be little elaboration or alteration of the conceptual framework orienting the activity. Cognitive frameworks relating to disease are instruments in the total process of adaptation; they change, evolve, and respond when their viability and acceptability are challenged. Only when folk etiology fails too often and in too many areas to give pragmatic and especially psychodynamic satisfaction does it yield to other frameworks, autochthonous or adopted from outside.

Disease, medicine, and culture. Some knowledge of diseases, their classification and etiology, is part of all cultural systems (e.g., Lieban 1962; Rubel 1960; Price-Williams 1962). Investigators have analyzed disease categories in an attempt to understand the structure of the conceptual world of different peoples. The use of componential analysis, the investigation of semantic interrelationships of terms, has been applied to words for sicknesses (cf. Frake 1961). Aside from illustrating the extent to which concern with disease is elaborated in a folk nosology, such work also emphasizes a more general point: an effective cultural response to disease requires patterned discrimination and categorization of disease symptoms, even if treatment is based largely on methods of trial and error. Diagnostic categories, however crude, serve the purpose of directing sustained attention and reflection to the appearance of disease syndromes, thus providing empirical data for inferences about the probable effectiveness of one type of treatment or another. Undoubtedly this constitutes a kind of inadvertent experimental approach (see, e.g., Laughlin 1963; Erasmus 1952).

Theories of disease generally have major relevance to the moral order, that is, to the control of man's behavior in society. Disease is frequently seen as a warning sign, a visitation from punishing agents for a broken taboo, a hostile impulse, or an aberrant urge to depart from the approved way. In a series of classical papers, Hallowell (e.g., 1963) has analyzed the function of anxieties over sickness among the Ojibwa Indians of North America, and other investigators have looked at the same problem in different cultural settings (e.g., Lieban 1962). Sickness is often interpreted as the supernaturals' way of indicating an act or intention of socially disruptive behavior. Especially in societies lacking strong centralized sociopolitical institutions, the occurrence and imminence of disease—with the belief that it represents punishment for aberrant, dissocial impulse or action—can be functionally important in maintaining group cohesion and restraining disruptive tendencies.

The therapeutic practices attendant upon occurrence of disease may also have socially cohesive results. Although such therapy may often be medically effective, it may serve ancillary functions in the total organization of the society. Typically, the curative session (and often the diagnostic occasion as well) involves not only the patient and the healer but also the patient's family and neighbors. Often the therapy involves confession by the patient, and under such conditions the confession may well relieve him of diffuse as well as focused anxieties and guilt. When followed by concrete expiatory acts, it may also give him a chance to participate in his own treatment through action. (It is doubtful whether such curative rites do more than provide temporary symptom relief—but the same can be said of much modern psychotherapy.) At the same time group cohesion is often enhanced, for such confessions dramatize fundamental social values by illustrating the harm that can come from social deviance. They provide a setting in which all participants are enveloped in the aura of forgiveness and, through stress on the protection afforded by adherence to group values, assurance of good health. In short, the therapeutic context is usually explicitly a social context, and during the course of the therapy the reciprocal psychosocial involvement of the patient with his fellows is ritually underscored. As noted above, if therapeutic directives for behavior are issued, they frequently apply to the group, or selected members of the group, as well as to the patient; and if successful recovery is as dependent upon good thoughts as upon effective techniques—as frequently happens—then the assembled company must be devoid of ill wishes and hostilities toward not only the patient but also each other. The curative rite may thus serve in multiple ways as an occasion for reintegration of the group around common social values.

The practice of folk medicine is variously institutionalized. In all societies some rudimentary medical knowledge is an aspect of enculturation, but beyond this general protection there is always a specialist. Sometimes the specialist's role is a full-time activity, but more frequently it is combined with other principal roles appropriate for the practitioner. In some societies there are more complex social arrangements than the simple dyadic relationship between healer and patient. Even as the kin and covillagers of the patient may be explicitly involved in the curative process, so too there may be a society of healers or several societies of healers devoted to diagnosis and cure of various diseases. In west Africa there are found, for example, specialized associations of healers of smallpox or snake bite; each association possesses its own rules of qualification, initiation, and procedure (Harley 1941).

Folk medicine in change. Folk medicine does not easily change under the impact of sustained contact with the industrialized world, or even as a result of deliberate attempts to introduce new conceptions of disease and hygiene. Paul (1955), Foster (1962), and others have documented the variety of factors that may impede or altogether prevent the successful introduction of a modern health program, even of so simple an innovation as the boiling of drinking water. Such factors include ecological considerations, as well as functional efficiency in domestic tasks, the social structure, the status and prestige of the innovator, and the perception of threat or advantage to the recipient. The proper role of the healer may be differently defined; in India, for example, the medical practitioner must assure the patient of recovery, and any admission of uncertainty (even couched in the form of probability) is not allowed. Rudimentary physical testing may be impossible or difficult in a non-Western context. In societies where blood, for example, is thought of as a nonregenerative substance, to take samples for testing is tantamount to inflicting deliberate harm.

It has been found to be easier to introduce behavioral changes than changes in belief about the nature of illness, its cause, and prevention. Domestic hygiene and community health may be bettered by the public health worker who influences a change in habits while not disturbing the underlying belief system. One reason for this has been mentioned above: belief systems, particularly those centered on critical areas of social value, serve more than a single cognitive function. Because they interrelate with religious and magical systems, as well as with the moral order of the society, they impart a deeper sense of resignation and acceptance of events than does an alien concept treating of a germ theory of illness. The value system of a culture provides a more satisfying answer to the question, "Why did I and not my neighbor get sick?" than does an explanation phrased in terms of communicability of a disease, thresholds of resistance, host, agent, and environment.

Yet in many instances modern medicine does get accepted; and one of the reasons is its demonstrably greater effectiveness in the treatment and prevention of many diseases. But even such acceptance is often compromised by the existence of alternative diagnostic and therapeutic frameworks: one relating to those diseases for which it is felt modern medicine is more effective, and the second relating to diseases conceived to be unamenable to modern medical treatment. The first is often applied to sicknesses introduced by the Europeans (such as tuberculosis, measles, smallpox, and others of a communicable nature), while in the second group are traditionally endemic diseases and, especially, ailments having a large component of psychological or psychophysiological involvement.

But in the extremity of fear for a patient's life even such distinctions as these are often disregarded, and the ill person may be taken to a modern medical facility after indigenous healers have done their best—taken either to be cured or left to die. Every hospital, and not just those in non-Western, "underdeveloped" countries, will admit patients brought too late for the course of disease to be halted even by the most advanced techniques of scientific medicine. Disease being an unequivocal threat to life, adaptive responses are many and sometimes override ingrained belief, either of folk medicine on the one hand or modern medicine on the other. In this light, given the avowedly limited role of scientific medicine in society—together with the inevitability of disease—elements of folk medicine will no doubt everywhere persist, even as they do in Europe and the United States, so long as there is uncertainty of outcome or technical ineffectiveness in alleviating pain, prolonging life, and guaranteeing cure.

CHARLES C. HUGHES

[See also HEALTH and ILLNESS. Directly related are the entries ANTHROPOLOGY, article on APPLIED ANTHROPOLOGY; MAGIC; POLLUTION; RELIGION.]

BIBLIOGRAPHY

ACKERKNECHT, ERWIN H. 1942a Primitive Medicine and Culture Pattern. Bulletin of the History of Medicine 12:545–574.

ACKERKNECHT, ERWIN H. 1942b Problems of Primitive Medicine. Bulletin of the History of Medicine 11:503–521.

ACKERKNECHT, ERWIN H. 1946 Natural Diseases and Rational Treatment in Primitive Medicine. Bulletin of the History of Medicine 19:457–497.

ACKERKNECHT, ERWIN H. 1965 History and Geography of the Most Important Diseases. New York: Hafner.

CASSEL, JOHN 1955 A Comprehensive Health Program Among the South African Zulus. Pages 15–41 in Benjamin D. Paul (editor), Health, Culture, and Community. New York: Russell Sage Foundation.

CLEMENTS, FORREST E. 1932 Primitive Concepts of Disease. California, University of, Publications in American Archaeology and Ethnology 32, no. 2:185–252.

DUBOS, RENÉ (1959) 1961 Mirage of Health, Utopias, Progress, and Biological Change. New York: Harper.

DUBOS, RENÉ 1965 Man Adapting. New Haven: Yale Univ. Press.

ERASMUS, CHARLES J. 1952 Changing Folk Beliefs and the Relativity of Empirical Knowledge. Southwestern Journal of Anthropology 8:411–428.

FOSTER, GEORGE M. 1962 Traditional Cultures, and the Impact of Technological Change. New York: Harper.

FRAKE, CHARLES O. 1961 The Diagnosis of Disease Among the Subanun of Mindanao. American Anthropologist New Series 63:113–132.

HALLOWELL, A. IRVING 1935 Primitive Concepts of Disease. American Anthropologist New Series 37:365–368.

HALLOWELL, A. IRVING 1963 Ojibwa World View and Disease. Pages 258–315 in Iago Galdston (editor), *Man's Image in Medicine and Anthropology*. New York Academy of Medicine, Institute of Social and Historical Medicine, Monograph No. 4. New York: International Universities Press.

HARLEY, GEORGE W. 1941 *Native African Medicine: With Special Reference to Its Practice in the Mano Tribe of Liberia*. Cambridge, Mass.: Harvard Univ. Press.

HUGHES, CHARLES C. 1963 Public Health in Non-literate Societies. Pages 157–233 in Iago Galdston (editor), *Man's Image in Medicine and Anthropology*. New York Academy of Medicine, Institute of Social and Historical Medicine, Monograph No. 4. New York: International Universities Press.

KUHN, THOMAS S. 1962 *The Structure of Scientific Revolutions*. Univ. of Chicago Press.

LAUGHLIN, WILLIAM S. 1963 Primitive Theory of Medicine: Empirical Knowledge. Pages 116–140 in Iago Galdston (editor), *Man's Image in Medicine and Anthropology*. New York Academy of Medicine, Institute of Social and Historical Medicine, Monograph No. 4. New York: International Universities Press.

LIEBAN, RICHARD W. 1962 The Dangerous Ingkantos: Illness and Social Control in a Philippine Community. *American Anthropologist* New Series 64:306–312.

MAY, JACQUES M. 1960 The Ecology of Human Disease. New York Academy of Sciences, *Annals* 84:789–794. → A paper delivered at a conference on culture, society, and health held and sponsored by the New York Academy of Sciences and the Research Institute for the Study of Man.

PAUL, BENJAMIN D. (editor) 1955 *Health, Culture, and Community: Case Studies of Public Reaction to Health Programs*. New York: Russell Sage Foundation.

PRICE-WILLIAMS, D. R. 1962 A Case Study of Ideas Concerning Disease Among the Tiv. *Africa* 32:123–131.

RUBEL, ARTHUR J. 1960 Concepts of Disease in Mexican-American Culture. *American Anthropologist* New Series 62:795–814.

SIGERIST, HENRY E. 1951 *A History of Medicine*. Volume 1: Primitive and Archaic Medicine. New York: Oxford Univ. Press.

WHITING, JOHN W. M.; and CHILD, IRVIN L. 1953 *Child Training and Personality: A Cross-cultural Study*. New Haven: Yale Univ. Press. → A paperback edition was published in 1962.

II
SOCIAL ASPECTS

Medical care is the application of scientific knowledge and technique to solving the physical and emotional problems of man. To a physician, medical care denotes the body of diagnostic and therapeutic theory and procedure developed to understand, cure, and prevent diseases. A social scientist, however, defines medical care as a system of social institutions in a larger social structure. Since medical care is given by specialized personnel, it presents to the social scientist several problems in the sociology of professions. Since much medical care is given in organized settings, it can also be studied from the viewpoint of the sociology of formal organizations.

The demand for medical care

Medical institutions cannot originate without a market. Anthropological evidence suggests that recognition of physical and emotional problems by potential patients is universal among the world's populations: whether he is a Western city dweller or a peasant in an underdeveloped country, the human being is aware of discomfort and an inability to perform his normal social roles. However, the decision to take practical action and the choice of remedies vary widely according to the social system and according to the individual's statuses in each social system.

Religion and science. The meaning of illness and the practical action deemed appropriate in a society derive from the prevailing bodies of religious and scientific thought. In many underdeveloped countries, widespread beliefs attribute injuries and illness to alienation from divine forces or from social obligations. For remedies appropriate to the imputed causes, large numbers of people may rely on personal rituals or on the guidance of priests and folk practitioners. Where Western medical institutions have been imported into such societies by governments or missionaries, they may be used by only the small minority that is urban and Westernized (Williams & Scharff 1960, p. 18).

Extensive public use of medical care depends on widespread acceptance of certain doctrines about God and man: human life on earth should be preserved; the alleviation of physical discomfort does not contradict divine intent but may even serve God's will; practical action to save life is not inconsistent with divine purpose or church obligations. These doctrines have been prominent in Christianity, classical Islam, and Judaism. For these reasons, public utilization of therapeutic and preventive medicine has been widespread in the ancient Middle East and in the modern West. As Western religions spread in Asia, Africa, and Latin America, or as contrary traditional religions are redefined to tolerate or encourage the alleviation of discomfort by practical secular action, public utilization of scientific medical institutions increases.

In many societies, the prevailing religious and scientific beliefs define illnesses differently and, thus, teach a range of responses. For example, externally visible injuries and infections may be attributed to mundane events, while internal physical and mental malfunctions are believed to originate supernaturally. Since direct physical remedies are considered appropriate for the former and magical or propitiatory methods are alone believed efficacious for the latter, the population may bring its surgical and infectious problems to the Western-style doctor and hospital, while retaining clergymen and folk practitioners for internal and mental illnesses.

The referral of particular categories of people is often a function of religious belief. For example, folk religion in some Arab and Asian countries assumes that the evil eye and divine wrath fall particularly heavily upon babies and children. Therefore, pediatric illnesses may be thought irremediable; few children are brought for medical care; and pediatrics remains an undeveloped specialty in medicine (Cameron 1960; Williams & Scharff 1960, pp. 18, 32, 34).

Other social determinants. The demand for medical care varies with other broad characteristics of society, such as the general levels of urbanization, literacy, prosperity, and industrialization. Poverty breeds disease and neglect, and consequently the world's numerous underdeveloped countries have potentially huge numbers of patients (Brockington 1958, part 2). Illiteracy prevents many citizens from learning where to find medical care, and services are often inaccessible in the rural areas, where much of the population lives. However, as information spreads about the availability and efficacy of medical installations, public use increases. As urbanization rises, so does the number of patients; in the cities of underdeveloped countries, vast throngs of ill persons tax the outpatient clinics and inpatient wards of public hospitals (McGibony 1961, pp. 51–52; Mazen 1961, pp. 40, 72, 273–275).

Within each country, social class and literacy appear to correlate with the use of medical care. The lower and poorer social classes may have the greatest number of physical and mental problems. But the higher classes make greater use of medical services because of their greater understanding of medical services, their social sophistication, and their ability to pay (Kadushin 1964). The problem varies by social class: for example, in the developed countries, coronary disease and ulcers are found more often among the upper class, infections and tuberculosis more often among the lower class (Freeman et. al. 1963, chapter 14 *passim;* Susser & Watson 1962, chapter 3).

Family structure. The demand for medical care is affected in several ways by family structure. In the Muslim countries and in some others, religion and custom decree that women are to work and live solely within the family circle. Therefore, women hesitate to visit the hospital and particularly to become inpatients, since this would involve immodest contact with male strangers. More men than women use medical services in the Muslim countries, but the opposite is true elsewhere, particularly in the West (compare Mazen 1961, pp. 213–214 and Fehler 1961, p. 397). Medical specialties involving female modesty, particularly obstetrics and gynecology, are developed far more in the West than in the countries with sheltered women.

In preindustrial societies, the breadwinner is indispensable to provide current income, and the mother cannot easily be spared from her family duties. Thus, young adults may postpone medical care, particularly if inpatient hospitalization is likely, and medical services are used predominantly by children, the elderly, and severely ill young adults. However, in some underdeveloped countries, babies and young children occupy such a subordinate position in the family that they are brought for medical care much less often than adults (Stever 1961, p. 335). In general, the utilization of medical services is higher in the industrial countries, not only because family nursing is deemed less efficacious than expert hospital or clinic treatment, but also because employers expect efficient performance and because urban living conditions make home care difficult. The modernization of underdeveloped countries includes the establishment of Western-style medical institutions and the propagation of Western health norms, and consequently the foregoing cross-national differentials in the utilization of medical care will diminish.

Medical practice

Since every society has the functional problems of explaining illness to the sick and their families and of guiding practical action, each society develops a body of medical theory from its basic ideas about the universe, life, and man. These theories vary in their empirical utility and in their implications for remedial treatment. Some of the principal civilizations—notably, European, Islamic, Indian, and Chinese—derived considerable and still influential systems of medical theory from their religions and ontologies (Castiglioni 1927).

Each of the principal medical traditions became institutionalized in the form of a theoretical literature, recognized practitioners, and educational techniques for transmitting knowledge and remedial skill from one generation of practitioners to the next. Much of the training has been didactic, but some—particularly in the Greek–Islamic–Western tradition—has made the neophyte an apprentice or observer of a practitioner at work.

Western medicine. Transmitted to Europe by certain medieval Italian universities, Greek–Islamic medicine ultimately proved the most productive in empirical knowledge and in therapeutic success. Several characteristics of European thought and society seem to have been crucial conditions for its growth. First, much of Western scientific thought has been inductive and empiricist, and some of this thinking contributed to medicine. Thus, although deductive and metaphysical theory was not absent from Western medicine, and although the speculative system builders vigorously fought new trends, simultaneously there developed a medical tradition of observation, experimentation, and critical verification of facts and therapies. Western medical knowledge and remedies—particularly in recent centuries—have been under continuous revision in the light of new evidence, to a degree found in no other medical tradition. Furthermore, the empiricist spirit of Western medicine has resulted in a tradition of medical education in hospital wards and experimental laboratories, to a degree found nowhere else (Shryock [1936] 1947, especially chapters 1–11).

Second, religions in much of the world insist on preserving the complete body of the deceased person, usually as a condition for his heavenly salvation. But Christianity distinguishes more clearly between soul and body, and it pictures the salvation of the soul while the body rots. Therefore, Christianity has been able to tolerate the widespread use of autopsies, while most other religions discourage them, and much of the physiological and therapeutic knowledge of Western medicine has resulted from post-mortem examinations. Potentially productive medical traditions in other societies, such as Islam, have been stunted because the dominant religions forbade autopsies.

A third reason for the greater success of the Western medical tradition has been the West's technical inventiveness. This approach industrialized the West's economy. But even before the industrial revolution, the West's gadget-consciousness introduced into its medical research and practice extremely fruitful diagnostic and therapeutic devices, such as the microscope and thermometer. During the nineteenth and twentieth centuries, the industrial revolution has enabled Western medicine to employ even more complex devices, such as the X ray or the anesthetic equipment essential for thoracic surgery, which could not be invented by the world's numerous preindustrial societies.

Finally, the West has had a long tradition of bureaucratic organization. In this respect, of course, the West has not been unique; but its distinctive achievement was to apply such methods to the financing, staffing, and dissemination of med-

ical care. Nationwide systems of public health regulation, hospitals, medical education, and health insurance evolved under the auspices of churches, governments, and voluntary associations. All the foregoing variables—cumulative scientific knowledge, technology, and extensive formal organization—have combined in recent centuries to produce a highly developed system of medical care in the West and, increasingly, through cultural diffusion, in other societies.

Doctor and patient

The individual doctor renders medical care to the individual patient in a variety of settings: the patient's home, the doctor's office, hospitals, or polyclinics. The relationship between doctor and patient in the West is thought of by social scientists as a special case in the sociology of professional–client relationships.

American sociologists' thinking about the doctor–patient confrontation has been greatly influenced by a theoretical model suggested by Talcott Parsons (Parsons 1958; Parsons & Fox 1952). The sick person, according to this model, is temporarily exempt from his normal social roles but is expected to perform certain well-defined patient roles. The doctor specializes in diagnosing and solving the patient's problems in accordance with the social norms of his profession, and he has the social responsibility of controlling the patient for the good of society and of the patient himself. The patient is expected to obey the doctor and strive for recovery in accordance with the expectations of each stage of his treatment. Gradually the dependence of patient upon doctor diminishes, and the patient resumes his normal family and economic roles.

Parsons' analysis pictures an intelligent and ambitious patient and presupposes the achievement-oriented social system of the West. Research needs to be done in order to determine its applicability in non-Western societies with different values and with large proletariats possessing less ambition and more pessimistic medical prognoses. [See PROFESSIONS.]

Occasionally social scientists have observed the relationships between doctor and patient in hospitals and private offices, and they have attempted to trace the clinical consequences of the social structures governing this two-person interaction. For example, the class differences between doctor and patient have been found to affect the success of their clinical relationship: since the less educated patient is less able to communicate with the doctor in the latter's own vocabulary, he is asked to give fewer reports, and he receives fewer explanations and fewer instructions for home care than do patients of higher social classes (Freeman et al. 1963, chapter 11 *passim*). Another example of research on the social conditions governing relations between doctor and patient is Burling's finding that the patient's confidence in the doctor increases if the patient is not socially isolated but enjoys close personal relations with family members and with other patients (Burling et al. 1956, chapter 3).

Many of the clinical decisions of the doctor have been found to depend on his own social relations within the medical profession and within the larger, lay community. For example, the doctor's ethnicity, family origins, and prior educational career—as well as his professional skill—affect the types of colleague networks and hospitals that he will join, and these contacts will determine the quality of his facilities, the skill of his consultants, and the affluence of his practice (Hall 1946). Adoption of new drugs—and possibly other innovations —by the individual doctor occurs earlier and more often if the doctor is closely related to a network of colleagues, and the adoption pattern for the network is led by certain doctors with a proclivity for adopting new things generally (Coleman et al. 1959).

The hospital

In many societies, all patients are treated in their homes by family members, with occasional visits by the priest or medicine man or with occasional visits by the patient to the medicine man. Among a few preindustrial peoples—such as the early Hebrews and some contemporary African tribes—the medicine man maintains beds where he can watch and treat patients in proximity to his own medical supplies or religious shrines. However, only a few civilizations have produced hospitals in large number and as important centers of medical care.

Certain conditions in the social structure seem essential for the existence of an extensive and important hospital system. The society must have skill in creating and running organizations. The religious and other social beliefs must legitimize the diversion of substantial resources for the treatment and maintenance of sick strangers. Sick people and their families must accept the idea of living away from home under the control of strangers. Finally, the society must produce and train enough people qualified to work in hospitals and must motivate them to care for sick strangers.

Extensive hospital programs occurred in the past under the ancient Hebrews, in ancient India during a period of synthesis between Buddhism and Hinduism, and in medieval Islam. Religion was a powerful motive in all three societies, since it taught that human life should be saved, that illness was a remediable blight upon life, and that scientific knowledge could properly be applied in combating disease. Resources were readily available for hospitals, and the Hebrew and Muslim religions preached that private charity for the poor and sick were necessary conditions for salvation. Islam and India were ruled by governments which recognized that large cities could not be run efficiently without therapeutic and custodial centers. Furthermore, both Islam and India, during the periods of their hospital programs, had experience in creating networks of formal organizations—in Islam as a result of ecclesiastic work and in both countries as a result of powerful and active governments.

However, the hospital programs soon declined in all three societies because the necessary social conditions were incomplete. Hospitals require dedicated staffs, and none of these religions preached the duty or desirability of lifetime careers of caring for sick strangers. In fact, the caste taboos of Brahmanical Hinduism discouraged a large number of employees from working in the same place and from giving all necessary care to the general public. None of these countries had monastic traditions, and thus, the church could not run hospitals when the state was conquered by foreigners— in the Hebrew and Muslim cases—or when the state lost interest in running hospitals—as in India and the unconquered parts of Islam.

The role of Christianity. Christianity has been far more conducive to the development of hospitals than other world religions. Like the others that encouraged limited hospital programs, Christianity preached the value of human life and the desirability of preserving it through applied science. But above all, Christianity provided the doctrinal and organizational basis for hospital staffs. Humble and charitable care of the sick and poor was commended as one of the principal paths to salvation. Instead of sheltering women and thus discouraging nursing careers—as did Islam—Christianity encouraged unmarried women to do charitable work among the public and even to live away from home if necessary. Not only did Christianity legitimize hospital employment by laywomen; the Catholic church organized brotherhoods of monks and orders of nuns who nursed hospital inpatients as their apostolic mission. Employing bureaucratic procedures learned in large part from the government of the Roman Empire, the church organized hospitals, financed them through its extensive fund-raising machinery, and maintained them. Thus, Christianity's ecclesiastic structure produced a continuity in hospital affairs regardless of the fluctuations in state policy.

For many centuries, European hospitals were run by the church or by associations of laymen affiliated with the church, and they were staffed by nuns. For much of their history they were custodial institutions, where sick and dying people were maintained and given religious guidance. Greek–Islamic therapy was introduced when some of the medieval nursing monks attended southern Italian medical schools. Thereafter, hospital systems created and maintained by the church also became the workshops of doctors and centers of medical education. European hospitals became secularized as the function of religion changed in Western social structure, as medical science became more successful and influential, and as lay governments became more powerful and more responsive to their citizens' demands for social welfare. In the late Middle Ages the church forbade monks to practice surgery and restricted their other medical work; lay physicians were welcomed into the hospitals and soon commanded all their medical practices (Rosen 1963).

Secularization of hospitals. Between the Reformation and the present day, many church-affiliated hospitals have been taken over by governments, and many new hospitals have been created by governments or by secular owners. Even after these transfers to government, Catholic nuns and Protestant deaconesses continued to work in hospitals; however, a new occupation of trained lay nursing arose in the late nineteenth century, and these nurses have been taking over the numerous jobs that cannot be filled by the now contracting religious orders. Church-affiliated hospitals staffed by nuns can still be found in countries where the church must seek new converts and retain the loyalty of its own communicants, such as in non-Christian societies and in the Western countries with mixed religions (for example, Germany, Holland, Switzerland, and the United States).

As Western medical care spreads throughout the world, so does the Western hospital in its present secularized form. However, a serious obstacle is the recruitment of enough lay graduate nurses in non-Christian societies. Christian values seem to be an important recruitment motivation for lay nurses, just as they have been for nursing nuns.

It is evident from unpublished research by the present author that underdeveloped countries without large Christian minorities have great difficulty in staffing their hospitals.

The rise of scientific medicine. Since the hospital is organized to protect and treat sick people,

its goals, structure, and functions depend on the current state of medical science. As a result of the great medical advances of recent centuries, the Western hospital has been transformed. Previously, the hospital was a charitable establishment to care for the helpless and protect society from the infected. In order to perform such work, only a small staff of supervisors and unskilled attendants was needed; only a few doctors visited, to give quick treatments or to perform occasional clinical experiments. Since these were custodial institutions for the poor and since the wealthy could afford home visits by doctors, the higher classes were treated and housed in their homes. Because infection and pain were common in hospitals, much of the public avoided surgery and feared hospitalization.

Modern medicine learned to classify diseases and distinguish among the treatments for each; the hospital needed to separate patients according to disease for distinctive treatment by category, and therefore, modern hospitals became departmentalized. The understanding of sterile technique and the introduction of antiseptics reduced cross-infections, made surgery and obstetrics safe, and increased therapeutic success and public confidence. Surgery also became more successful and popular because of the introduction of anesthetics. Surgical facilities grew in hospitals, and surgeons gained prestige and wealth. The wards became places for continuing treatment and were recognized as places of potential but preventable cross-infections. Scientific nursing education was introduced, closer controls were instituted over lower nursing ranks, and nursing staffs were greatly increased in size. The introduction of laboratories, operating theaters, and many ancillary services increased the size of paramedical staffs and raised the cost of hospitals. Since medical specialists needed to treat their patients by means of these facilities, members of higher social classes were hospitalized. The physical appearance of existing hospitals was improved, and private hospitals originated. Since specialty training required acquaintance with the advanced techniques found in hospitals, large and disciplined medical staffs were created, and many hospitals added educational and research goals to their mission of patient care. To administer such large and complex organizations, there developed new occupations specializing in hospital management; to supply the hospitals there arose new and immensely profitable pharmaceutical and equipment industries.

Hospital organization. Within individual countries—and particularly in the United States—social scientists have studied interpersonal processes within hospitals, using the same concepts that they apply to any other organizations. For example, American sociologists have long been interested in latent social processes and in the entire set of functions and dysfunctions resulting from certain institutional arrangements. Thus, American medical sociologists have not only studied the manifest hospital structure and its successes but have pointed out the presence of latent processes with paradoxical outcomes. The hospital, they say, is manifestly dedicated to the provision of means for treating patients successfully. However, every organization requires an administrative structure to arrange its resources economically and to control deviant behavior. Thus, therapeutic and administrative structures exist simultaneously in the hospital, each with its own priorities and personnel. Emphasizing one set of goals (such as administrative order) is dysfunctional for maximization of the other structure's goals (such as patient care), and conflicts occur between the two lines of authority (such as the lay administrators and the doctors). Several studies of mental hospitals note the dilemma of combining organizational imperatives and therapy: the custodial structure necessary to control patients and maintain order is dysfunctional for mental care. [*See* ORGANIZATIONS, *article on* ORGANIZATIONAL GOALS; *see also* Freeman et al. 1963, chapter 10, and Reader 1959.]

A specialist in administrative medicine might primarily study the formal organization of hospitals, but sociologists—whether observing factories, schools, or hospitals—search for the informal social structures that may substantially deviate from the formal chain of command and that may powerfully influence the system in action. Some American medical sociologists have been participant–observers in hospital wards. They have described the informal social system among patients, and they have identified how this informal ward society alternately raises and lowers the morale of individual patients and alternately supports and disturbs each patient's relationships with the hospital staff (e.g., Fox 1959). From such research in mental hospitals has come the advice that the individual patient's recovery depends not only on treatment received during the hours reserved for formal therapy but also on harmonious relationships involving all patients and staff members throughout the day. The successful "therapeutic communities" are said to have democratic decision making, full communication of ideas and grievances, stable and rewarding careers among staff members, a proper balance between freedom and control, and an ideal combination of self-reliance and group support (Stanton 1954).

Quality of medical care

From the viewpoint of the social sciences, medical care is a strategic area for studying the institutionalization of social values and of applied scientific technique. However, from the viewpoint of the public and of an increasing number of medical practitioners, the proper task of the social sciences is to evaluate and improve the quality of care. Therefore, many medical organizations have retained social scientists to gather information and give advice. Some of the resultant studies deal with the training of doctors and nurses: the formal and informal organization of the curriculum, of the student community, and of the hospital are found to promote student learning in some ways and to inhibit it in others; and this information has been used by curriculum planners and administrators in the improvement of their instruction.

Determinants of good care. Several studies have attempted to locate elements in the social organization of medical care that affect the quality of treatment. Usually this research involves collaboration by physicians and social scientists: the former identify the actions constituting "good medical care," while the social scientists contribute knowledge about research techniques and ideas about the possible determinants of good care. For example, O. L. Peterson and his associates (1956) observed the work of general practitioners and concluded that class standing in medical school, length of preparatory education, exposure to refresher courses, and other experiences are strongly related to several indicators of good care. Contrary to common beliefs, involvement in medical society affairs, prestigious hospital appointments, hours of work, and certain other variables were found to have little relationship to good care in this sample.

In an ambitious study of ten hospitals, Basil S. Georgopoulos and Floyd C. Mann (1962, chapters 5 and 8) discovered that certain social attributes of the hospital correlated more strongly with quality of care than did other commonly credited determinants, such as the volume of material facilities, size of budget, number of beds, and ratio of personnel to beds. The organizational characteristics associated with good care were: high coordination throughout the hospitals, harmonious relations among departments and between doctors and nurses, lower absenteeism among graduate nurses, and efficient but congenial management. In another organizational study of hospitals, Melvin Seeman and John W. Evans (1961) found that the informal social organization of the ward affects the clinical performance of interns and nurses: where power inequalities and other forms of social distance are greater, efficiency and skill are lower.

Some social research methods have been used to gather expert opinions about the nature and sources of good care. For example, Milton C. Maloney and his associates (1960) used survey techniques to get a sample of expert opinion about the quality of care: they asked doctors about the care the doctors obtained for themselves and for their families. These expert judges preferred treatment by full-time specialists in metropolitan medical centers.

Doubtless applied social research will become an increasingly recognized fact of medical care in all countries. Modern medicine is devoting more attention to the "stress diseases" and other medical conditions that seem related to social roles. The organizational problems of medical care are rising because of increased costs, scarcities of personnel and of services, and because of the demands by social planners for greater efficiency and economy in medical administration. Teamwork among clinicians, administrators, and social scientists may consequently become commonly accepted as the means to a common goal of better quality care.

WILLIAM A. GLASER

[Directly related are the entries HEALTH; MEDICAL PERSONNEL; PUBLIC HEALTH. Other relevant material may be found in MENTAL DISORDERS, TREATMENT OF; MENTAL HEALTH; PSYCHIATRY.]

BIBLIOGRAPHY

Interest in social determinants of medical care first entered the literature of the field through the writings of several leading medical historians (e.g., Sigerist 1960; Shryock 1936) and through research in epidemiology and public health (see the bibliographies for the articles on these two topics).

Sociologists, social psychologists, and other social scientists began to write about medical care only in recent decades. Much of their work has been designed to provide practical information for psychiatric hospitals, the curriculum committees of medical and nursing schools, epidemiologists, and other medical practitioners with practical problems requiring knowledge of the facts. However, some research has been designed by social scientists to test hypotheses derived from their own disciplines. The voluminous American literature is summarized in Freeman et al. 1963, and some of the principal studies are reprinted in Jaco 1958. Research by social scientists is also well advanced in Great Britain, where a group of specialists in "social administration" provide facts and advice about all aspects of social policy, including health (Susser & Watson 1962). Similar work is beginning elsewhere: for example, König & Tönnesmann 1958 summarizes the research in Germany. Bibliographies of the American and European literature are provided by Freidson 1961/1962 and Pearsall 1963. Much of the social research on the quality of care is summarized by Anderson & Altman 1962.

Several writers on public health and administrative medicine have summarized the health problems and forms of medical organization in the world (e.g., Brockington 1958). As yet, no social scientist has written a general survey of the variations in the social organization of medical care throughout the world.

As social scientists have written more about medical care, their ideas have become more widely accepted in the writings of clinicians, and particularly by psychiatrists. An increasing number of writings by physicians, nurses, and medical administrators about the proper management of medical organizations and about the proper treatment of patients incorporate concepts and generalizations about the effects of the patient's family settings, the community's culture, the social relationships between patient and clinician, the personality traits of persons experiencing stress and social isolation, and so on (e.g., Balint 1957).

ANDERSON, ALICE J.; and ALTMAN, ISIDORE 1962 *Methodology in Evaluating the Quality of Medical Care: An Annotated Selected Bibliography, 1955–1961.* Univ. of Pittsburgh Press.

BALINT, MICHAEL 1957 *The Doctor, His Patient and the Illness.* London: Pitman Medical Publishers.

BROCKINGTON, C. FRASER 1958 *World Health.* Harmondsworth (England): Penguin. → Includes an account of the first ten years of the World Health Organization.

BURLING, TEMPLE; LENTZ, EDITH M.; and WILSON, ROBERT N. 1956 *The Give and Take in Hospitals: A Study of Human Organization in Hospitals.* New York: Putnam.

CAMERON, ALICK 1960 Folk-lore as a Medical Problem Among Arab Refugees. *Practitioner* 185:347–353.

CASTIGLIONI, ARTURO (1927) 1958 *A History of Medicine.* 2d ed. New York: Knopf. → First published as *Storia della medicina.*

COLEMAN, JAMES; MENZEL, HERBERT; and KATZ, ELIHU 1959 Social Processes in Physicians' Adoption of a New Drug. *Journal of Chronic Diseases* 9:1–19.

FEHLER, J. 1961 Verweildauer im allgemeinen Krankenhaus. *Krankenhaus* (Stuttgart, Germany) 53:397–403.

FOX, RENÉE C. 1959 *Experiment Perilous.* Glencoe, Ill.: Free Press.

FREEMAN, HOWARD E.; LEVINE, SOL; and REEDER, LEO G. (editors) 1963 *Handbook of Medical Sociology.* Englewood Cliffs, N.J.: Prentice-Hall.

FREIDSON, ELIOT 1961/1962 The Sociology of Medicine: A Trend Report and Bibliography. *Current Sociology* 10/11:123–192.

GEORGOPOULOS, BASIL S.; and MANN, FLOYD C. 1962 *The Community General Hospital.* New York: Macmillan.

HALL, OSWALD 1946 The Informal Organization of the Medical Profession. *Canadian Journal of Economics and Political Science* 12:30–44.

JACO, E. GARTLY (editor) 1958 *Patients, Physicians and Illness: Sourcebook on Behavioral Science and Medicine.* Glencoe, Ill.: Free Press.

KADUSHIN, CHARLES 1964 Social Class and the Experience of Ill Health. *Sociological Inquiry* 34, no. 1: 67–80.

KÖNIG, RENÉ; and TÖNNESMANN, MARGARET (editors) 1958 *Probleme der Medizin-Soziologie.* Cologne (Germany): Westdeutscher Verlag.

McGIBONY, JOHN R. 1961 Health Care in India: Its Patterns and Problems. *Hospitals* 35, no. 10:40–44; no. 11:47–52.

MALONEY, MILTON C.; TRUSSELL, RAY E.; and ELINSON, JACK 1960 Physicians Choose Medical Care: A Sociometric Approach to Quality Appraisal. *American Journal of Public Health* 50:1678–1686.

MAZEN, AHMED KAMEL 1961 Development of the Medical Care Program of the Egyptian Region of the United Arab Republic. Ph.D. dissertation, Stanford Univ.

PARSONS, TALCOTT 1958 Definitions of Health and Illness in the Light of American Values and Social Structure. Pages 165–187 in E. Gartly Jaco (editor), *Patients, Physicians and Illness: Sourcebook in Behavioral Science and Medicine.* Glencoe, Ill.: Free Press.

PARSONS, TALCOTT; and FOX, RENÉE (1952) 1958 Illness, Therapy, and the Modern Urban Family. Pages 234–245 in E. Gartly Jaco (editor) *Patients, Physicians and Illness: Sourcebook in Behavioral Science and Medicine.* Glencoe, Ill.: Free Press. → First published in Volume 8 of the *Journal of Social Issues.*

PEARSALL, MARION 1963 *Medical Behavioral Science: A Selected Bibliography of Cultural Anthropology, Social Psychology, and Sociology in Medicine.* Lexington: Univ. of Kentucky Press.

PETERSON, OSLER L. et al. 1956 An Analytical Study of North Carolina General Practice: 1953–1954. *Journal of Medical Education* 31, no. 12, part 2.

READER, GEORGE G. 1959 Medical Sociology With Particular Reference to the Study of Hospitals. Volume 2, pages 139–152 in World Congress of Sociology, Fourth, *Transactions.* London: International Sociological Association.

ROSEN, GEORGE 1963 The Hospital: Historical Sociology of a Community Institution. Pages 1–36 in Eliot Freidson (editor), *The Hospital in Modern Society.* New York: Free Press.

SEEMAN, MELVIN; and EVANS, JOHN W. 1961 Stratification and Hospital Care. *American Sociological Review* 26:67–80, 193–204.

SHRYOCK, RICHARD H. (1936) 1947 *The Development of Modern Medicine.* New York: Knopf.

SIGERIST, HENRY E. 1960 *On the Sociology of Medicine.* New York: MD Publications.

STANTON, ALFRED H. 1954 *The Mental Hospital: A Study of Institutional Participation in Psychiatric Illness and Treatment.* New York: Basic Books.

STERN, BERNHARD J. 1941 *Society and Medical Progress.* Princeton Univ. Press.

STEVER, ROBERT C. 1961 Medical Impressions From India and Nepal. *Journal of Medical Education* 36:330–337.

SUSSER, MERVYN W.; and WATSON, WILLIAM 1962 *Sociology in Medicine.* Oxford Univ. Press.

WILLIAMS, CICELY D.; and SCHARFF, J. W. 1960 *An Experiment in Health Work in Trengganu, Malaya.* Beirut: American Univ., School of Public Health.

III
ECONOMIC ASPECTS

The economic aspects of medical care encompass a broad and diverse area. It can include discussion of medical care utilization by various income groups, licensing arrangements, incomes of practitioners, fee structures, and so forth. This discussion will be limited to three topics: (1) some of the special characteristics that distinguish medical care from other goods and services; (2) the various alternative mechanisms for financing medical care services utilized at the present time;

(3) general economic problems related to alternative patterns of financing.

Special characteristics

Medical care, although generally viewed as a consumption commodity, has come to have a special status among the wide variety of such goods and services. This status affects its organization, the amount of resources it commands, and the patterns used in its financing.

Social-psychological factors. The view that medical care is somehow "different" is mainly an outgrowth of what may be called social-psychological factors. Medical care is felt to be (and obviously often is) intimately related to health and to life itself. The public associates medical care with dramatic lifesaving procedures, with the treatment of potentially fatal illness, and with the alleviation of suffering and pain. Since life is not considered a luxury commodity, those things which are believed to be associated with its preservation, e.g., medical care, have come to be considered a "human right." As a consequence, it is felt that the amount of medical care received—that the right to life or the prevention of pain—should not depend on the individual's income and purchasing power. Actual practice, of course, is often at wide variance with beliefs and declarations in this area.

Unpredictability of need. A number of significant economic distinctions between medical care and most other goods also impel the public to the view that the financing and organization of medical care should be treated differently from the financing of other goods and services. Perhaps of primary importance is the fact that illness, and consequently the need for care, is unpredictable for the individual, although it is predictable for the group. The individual, therefore, finds it impossible to anticipate the frequency of medical care, the amount he will need, and the costs that will be associated with such care. Furthermore, the economic burden imposed may be extreme—the illness may be severe and the economic consequences catastrophic. Not knowing the costs, he cannot save the appropriate amount in advance of an illness of unknown severity that may occur at some unknown time and with unknown frequency. This matter assumes increased significance, since real limitations exist on the possibility of postponing medical care purchases.

Although postpayment over a period of time would be a possible remedy for part of the problem, difficulties with that device are many: (1) illness may affect both short-run and long-run earning power and thus make such postpayment difficult, perhaps impossible; (2) the service rendered cannot be repossessed if there is a failure to meet payments; (3) the individual may feel that he has little or nothing to show for the medical care received, i.e., he is no better off than before he became ill and is simply back to the pre-illness state, to which he feels he might have returned even without the care; (4) treatment may involve discomfiture and pain, neither of which is certain to make one feel well disposed to those who rendered the treatment and thus to meeting periodic payments to the provider of care; (5) the individual does not consider that he is continuing to derive benefits from the service rendered in the past—as contrasted with the continuing pleasures derived from the purchase of consumer durables and other goods.

Externalities. A second characteristic of medical care services not shared by most other commodities involves externalities. These are present when benefits (or costs) accrue to others because the individual takes a particular action. The purchase of some types of medical services clearly involves such externalities. This is most evident in the case of communicable disease. All of us derive benefits from the immunization of others and from the prevention and treatment of the communicable diseases that affect them. The benefits to society, therefore, exceed the individual consumer's benefits. Conversely, there are costs to individuals when disease is not controlled in some other part of the population. The matter of externalities can be viewed even more broadly if we include satisfaction as well as dollar benefits in our consideration. If others are crippled, sick, or disabled, and if we are made uncomfortable by knowing about or seeing these conditions, then the benefits to society of rehabilitation or cure exceed the benefits accruing to the individual who is rehabilitated or cured. The increase in social satisfaction should, therefore, also be included in the calculus.

Economic theory has shown that where positive externalities (external benefits) exist, the individual underinvests in the commodity, from society's standpoint. Thus the private sector underinvests, insofar as there is insufficient philanthropy or absence of compulsion. This characteristic becomes one of the bases for public intervention in the health sector and is one of the reasons that government is often the major financing agent for certain types of health expenditures. [See EXTERNAL ECONOMIES AND DISECONOMIES; WELFARE ECONOMICS.]

Investment. Yet another special feature of medical care is implied by the use, in the preceding paragraph, of the term "invest." Medical care is in part a consumption commodity, but also in part an investment good. The purchase of medical care today increases the level of health and thus raises productivity in the future. Such sacrifice of current consumption in order to raise future output is the essence of all investments. Thus, the term "investment" need not be applied solely to expenditures on material capital. Accordingly, the analysis of public policy toward medical care can be cast in an investment framework.

Quality assessment problems. An additional significant distinction between medical care and other services is the consumer's relative inability to judge the quality of the product he is purchasing. This matter has even greater importance when it is recognized that sins of omission or commission on the part of the physician or persons working under his direction may have serious and non-reversible consequences. Even *ex post* evaluation of quality by the consumer is difficult, and the satisfaction or dissatisfaction with the medical care provided may, therefore, be based on various extraneous factors. Since medical care may involve more serious matters than are involved in the purchase of other consumer goods, and since the search to find quality care is more difficult than with other goods, some measure of protection is afforded the consumer by licensing arrangements. In this manner authorities "guarantee" some presumed minimum level of competence. The economic issues in such licensing arrangements are many, since, depending on the standards set and the responsibility of those who provide licenses, supply may be artificially and unnecessarily restricted, with consequent increase in prices for services and in incomes of practitioners not sufficiently compensated for by increase in quality of care. [See LICENSING, OCCUPATIONAL.]

Alternative financing mechanisms

The special characteristics of medical care have played a role in inducing governments to participate actively in the medical care sector. The form that such participation has taken has differed greatly and is a product of institutional and ideological constraints. Nevertheless, the role of government in the health sector and in financing health care is acknowledged in all countries. This role often takes the form of government participation in funding or distributing medical care for specific categories in the population. These categories of persons may be defined by specified health characteristics (e.g., the blind, the disabled), by age characteristics (e.g., the aged, children), by economic status (e.g., the indigent, the medically indigent), or by other special characteristics that define a particular population group (e.g., veterans, migrant workers). On occasion, combinations of these characteristics are utilized to determine eligibility, and individuals must then meet more than one criterion. Government participation and support, of course, need not be confined to categories of persons and in some countries covers the total resident population.

Voluntary insurance (United States). Voluntary health insurance has developed as one method of financing designed to meet the problem of unpredictability of illness and the need for medical care. The insurance principle lends itself to application in the health area, although it is relatively difficult to apply to certain health expenses and to certain population groups. This type of financing is most highly developed in the United States, where hospital insurance and surgical–medical insurance are provided both by nonprofit plans and by commercial insurance companies.

The expansion of private voluntary health insurance in the United States began in the 1930s with the development of Blue Cross plans for hospital coverage (with backing by the American Hospital Association) and Blue Shield plans for surgical–medical insurance (with backing by the organized medical profession). These plans are nonprofit and serve local areas (usually entire states), although national coordination is provided.

Commercial insurance companies entered the field in the late 1930s, largely through group coverage and utilizing arrangements for reimbursement of charges up to specified amounts rather than for provision of specified services (as in the nonprofit hospitalization plans). Commercial carriers competed successfully with the Blue Cross and Blue Shield plans. In part this was because the "Blues" used community rating: the rates charged for each of the various contracts offered were the same for all groups in a community. Commercial carriers used experience rating, wherein the rates charged any single group varied with the experience of that group. As a consequence, low-risk groups and individuals often found it advantageous to deal with a commercial carrier where premiums reflected their own experience and utilization of services rather than the average experience, including that of the high risks, in a community. The greater the number of low risks who left the "Blues," the higher the insurance rates rose for those remaining. Thus those who previously found themselves on "the margin" now found it advantageous to shift to commercial carriers. This mechanism could, in theory, continue indefinitely. It is one of the important considerations in the social insurance area and is often used to argue

for a compulsory element in social insurance. As a result of the force of this process, experience rating is now widely used even by those plans which originally rejected it on philosophic grounds. With experience rating, high-risk groups (e.g., the aged) find that the rates charged are higher than would be the case under community rating and that it becomes more difficult to participate in the plan.

This problem, as well as a number of other conditions, led the United States to institute, effective in 1966, a public system of health insurance, as part of its social insurance system, providing for limited financing of some medical care for persons 65 years of age and older. The pressure for such a system of insurance was also heightened by the fact that the aged often are not members of groups eligible for group insurance coverage. Insurance rates for individuals are significantly higher than group rates (and not only because the employer frequently pays a portion of the premium under group coverage). The high medical expenses of the aged and their relatively low financial resources compound the problems of finance. [*See* AGING, *article on* ECONOMIC ASPECTS.]

It is estimated that in 1965 about 80 per cent of the civilian population in the United States had some insurance protection against the costs of basic hospital care, about 75 per cent had some surgical expense protection, and almost 60 per cent were eligible for some additional coverage for in-hospital physician visits. Although the benefits met about 70 per cent of the total cost of hospital care, only about one-third of total consumer expenditures for personal health care were met by insurance. In the United States, health expenditures are financed largely by the private sector: of the $37,000 million of national health expenditures in 1964 (5.8 per cent of the gross national product), 74 per cent came from the private sector and only 26 per cent from the government—equally divided between the federal government on the one hand and state and local governments on the other. About 50 per cent of all personal health service expenditures were paid for by the recipient of the services (or his family), while third parties (government, insurers, etc.) paid for the remainder.

The problem of high-risk groups under experience rating in a voluntary insurance plan can be solved by a compulsory insurance program or direct government provision or financing of services. However, the traditional arguments that are used by those who favor approaches involving more government participation go beyond the solution of the difficulties that some groups and individuals face under experience rating. They include matters such as ease and economic efficiency of administration, comprehensiveness of care, coverage of the total population (including those groups that voluntary insurance finds it difficult or inefficient to reach or whose economic status is so low as to inhibit purchase of insurance), more ready control of inflation in medical care costs, increased equity in financing of care, and more possibility of increasing emphasis on certain aspects of medical services, e.g., preventive care. The success with which any of these objectives would be met would depend upon the particular characteristics of the health insurance or financing plan. The social security characteristic of a plan does not in itself guarantee comprehensiveness of coverage, quality of service, control of inflation in medical care prices, equity in financing, and so forth. Just as the voluntary private health insurance system can take many different forms and thus meet different problems, raise different issues, and resolve basic questions in different ways and with varying degrees of success, so too can each alternative basic system for financing or providing care.

National Health Service (United Kingdom). One type of approach to the financing and provision of medical care services is that employed in the United Kingdom under the National Health Service. Medical care services (rather than reimbursements) are provided all residents. The major costs of the program are financed out of general revenues, although small weekly contributions are paid by workers and employers. Some cost sharing by the patient for medicines and selected other items is also provided for. All residents are eligible for such services as general and specialized care, dental care, and hospitalization. The services are provided by doctors and druggists who are under contract to the National Health Service and by public hospitals owned by the central government. The physician receives a payment for each person on his rolls. This capitation method of payment of physicians encourages patients to have a continuing relationship with a particular general practitioner. The capitation method of payment, as contrasted with a payment for services rendered, is considered not only to be a good financial arrangement but also to represent a basic philosophical approach to medicine which is believed to have advantages that go beyond ease of administration.

The United Kingdom thus has a pattern of financing and organizing medical care substantially different from that of the United States, or from that which the latter will employ for those 65 years of age and over. Perhaps 85 per cent of all health expenditures in the United Kingdom are paid for by third parties, a much larger percentage than in the United States. The amount of resources allocated

to health services in the United Kingdom (4.2 per cent of a lower GNP) also differs from that in the United States (as indicated previously, 5.8 per cent of GNP). It is not clear, however, what part of these, and other, intercountry differences is attributable to differences in relative price levels (i.e., the relative costs of health services as compared with other goods and services in each country), differences in efficiency in the health sector, differences in levels of health and "needs," differences in quality of care, and differences in real resources devoted to health care. But it is clear that there do exist wide differences in the percentage of GNP devoted to health services in various countries. The significance and implications of these differences have yet to be thoroughly examined, but they do not seem to be related to the prevailing patterns or sources of finance or to the significance of the government sector in the health area.

Basic alternatives. The three main patterns of nonmarket provision of medical benefits in the various countries are (1) provision of direct services through facilities owned and operated by the government or by a social insurance fund; (2) services provided to patients, with the provider of services being paid directly by the government or fund; (3) reimbursement of fees paid directly by patients to providers of the services. As will be discussed below, the need for rationing of services still remains under the various arrangements, and patients are, therefore, often called upon to share the costs of the services rendered.

While a number of countries provide comprehensive medical services to all residents (although patients may pay part of the cost of the service provided), and an additional number of countries provide various selected therapeutic services, the particular benefits available and the mechanisms by which care is financed, provided, and organized differ greatly. In some countries medical services are provided to parts of the population under social insurance arrangements; in others, benefits are provided through membership in sickness funds to which employees, government, and (in some countries) employers contribute and in which membership is compulsory for certain categories of persons. Particular financing mechanisms are not necessarily tied to particular organizational arrangements, and thus many different combinations exist.

Economic problems

Need for rationing. Whatever the organizational pattern for distributing and financing medical care, the absence of a perfectly operating market for medical care presents certain difficulties. Although medical care is often viewed as a basic human right, few scientific standards exist to define the amount of care that an individual "needs" or should utilize (i.e., the health benefits associated with given amounts of care). However great the public dissatisfaction with the medical care received, it is a fact that some individuals tend to utilize more services than they require or are believed to require. Furthermore, changes in the price of medical care services do tend to change levels of utilization. Declines in price are associated with increases in usage. Although an increase in utilization is often one of the purposes of government in creating systems that reduce price or provide insured health benefits, allocation problems remain. If society were to allocate sufficient resources to medical care so that no choice need be made between care for the individual who is dying but can be saved and the hypochondriac who wants reassurance (that is, if we were prepared to meet all increases in, and levels of, utilization), then rationing of medical resources would not be required. But such a situation is neither conceivable nor, given competing demands on resources, desirable. Thus rationing becomes imperative, and since society is willing to make some interpersonal utility comparisons regarding who needs care, the rationing scheme must incorporate the public's judgments.

Nevertheless, since there is little scientific agreement on desirable utilization rates (or on the relationship between utilization rates and levels of health), it is difficult to agree upon, set, and control such rates and to develop medically "optimal" rationing devices. In the absence of control of usage, budgetary, physical, and personnel shortages often appear, particularly because consumers often demand more care than the authorities have estimated would be the case. Attempts to balance resource limitations (including budgetary considerations) against the private decisions to visit physicians, to enter hospitals, and to utilize medical care in quantities determined by the individual (the balancing of "scarcity" and "human right") have always been necessary and have seldom been easy to achieve.

Were the health sector treated as most other services are generally treated, this particular problem would not exist. If consumers, out of their own budgets and without public or private subsidization, chose to "overutilize" services (judged by some scientific standard), this would be fully acceptable. The price mechanism would serve as a rationing device and, however "foolish" some might feel these expenditures to be, the consumer would be sovereign.

Since government plays a role in the health field, even if in many cases it is limited to support for construction of physical resources (e.g., hospitals), or to training of personnel (e.g., supporting education), or to financing of certain types of care (e.g., for needy or aged persons), the government must be involved in the development of rationing devices to replace market forces. The same need exists, of course, when private physicians offer charity care.

Controlling utilization. The problem of "overutilization" (which can be viewed as the problem of scarcity) arises in all medical care financing mechanisms. The mechanisms of control when there is governmental involvement or control by a voluntary insurance carrier may, of course, differ. It is true that for many services waiting time, inconvenience, and even loss of income serve as deterrents to use. Even so, the use of "free" (but not costless) services may exceed the necessary, or "need," level. Therefore, additional monetary deterrents are often used, in the attempt to control overutilization. In particular, they are used to influence the consumer's choice between different types of care, e.g., office calls rather than house calls, home care rather than hospital care. Payment of some percentage of the costs (e.g., of hospital care) or in the form of some fixed charge (e.g., for a house call) is often instituted in order to induce the consumer to ration the care he seeks and in order to lead him toward those types of care which utilize less of society's economic resources. Such charges are also often made for prescription drugs. Since the use of such drugs is governed largely by the physician rather than by the patient, these charges may be instituted primarily as a device to cut the costs financed by the program rather than in order to change consumer behavior (although they do this as well).

The difficulty, sometimes unrecognized, with these procedures is that the money deterrent has a differential impact on individuals, depending greatly upon their "taste" and need for medical care, the accessibility of medical care, their total income, and the prices of other goods and services. What may be a small deterrent for some (perhaps the "optimal" deterrent from the point of view of the third party that finances the service or from the point of view of society) may represent a great deterrent for others and a trivial deterrent for still others. Income and price considerations thus reenter the medical market place, although with less impact than would be the case in the absence of third-party payments. Furthermore, it is clear that the conflict recurs between encouragement to use services in the "correct" quantities and rationing of care. No single level of fixed charges applying to all members of the population and designed to deter unnecessary use, but not to inhibit necessary use, can be the correct level for each individual. The operational consequences of the fixed charge will vary with a number of institutional considerations. It cannot be presumed that the consequences are necessarily severe (if maintaining accessibility is the primary goal) or are necessarily minor (if cutting utilization is the primary goal). The fixed charge in third-party payments does illustrate the fact that it is difficult to define that part of medical care which society considers a luxury and that part which is considered a need. With scarce resources a trade-off between goals is required—and difficult to determine.

Future developments in the provision and financing of medical care will be related to developments in medicine itself and to the acquisition of additional knowledge concerning the relationship between medical care and health and between health and productivity. The growing ability of medicine to prevent illness and to care for and rehabilitate the sick will bring increased pressures on the health sector. In most nations the role of government in health is likely to increase. In part this will take the form of intervention in the financing of services via social insurance or other arrangements. The financial responsibility, as well as the special characteristics, of medical care outlined earlier will result in government's assuming an increasing responsibility in the determination of the total amount of manpower and resources devoted to health and medical care and to the allocation of resources within the health sector itself.

The meeting of this responsibility will involve an increased reliance on new evaluative techniques. In recent years, partly as a result of the pressures for health expenditures and for planning of medical care in the less developed countries, and partly as a result of the refinement of benefit–cost analysis, the analysis of medical care has acquired an increasingly analytic economic content. In this approach, health and medical care are viewed in an economic context, and medical care programs are evaluated in relation to their cost and their potential impact on productivity through lower levels of morbidity and mortality. The economic value of man as a producer lies at the heart of the analysis, and the costs of various diseases are calculated in terms of the direct costs of treatment and medical care and the indirect costs to the economy of loss of productive power.

Decisions concerning the allocation of resources

to the health sector will, of course, not be based solely on the measurement of pecuniary costs and benefits. Nevertheless, such measurements are of assistance. It can, therefore, be anticipated that as understanding of the methodology of benefit–cost analysis grows, it will be increasingly used in governmental evaluation, planning, and budgeting processes.

RASHI FEIN

BIBLIOGRAPHY

The World Health Organization (Geneva) periodically issues publications on the level of health and on the financing and organization of health services in particular countries.
KLARMAN, HERBERT E. 1965 The Economics of Health. New York: Columbia Univ. Press.
Social Security Bulletin. → Published since 1938. Regularly contains articles on the economic aspects of medical care.
U.S. DEPARTMENT OF HEALTH, EDUCATION, AND WELFARE 1964 Social Security Programs Throughout the World: 1964. Washington: Government Printing Office.
WINSLOW, CHARLES E. A. 1951 The Cost of Sickness and the Price of Health. Geneva: World Health Organization.

MEDICAL PERSONNEL

I. PHYSICIANS Eliot Freidson
II. PARAMEDICAL PERSONNEL Eliot Freidson

I
PHYSICIANS

The physician is the most prominent among members of the generally recognized professions. He is seen by the public as possessing a higher standard than any other professional, and by the sociologist as the virtual prototype of his kind. While it would be a great mistake to confound what is peculiar to medicine with what is characteristic of professions in general, the study of physicians does offer the sociologist the opportunity to test both the truth and the utility of various orientations toward the concept of a profession.

One orientation sees a profession as an aggregate of people finding identity in sharing values and skills absorbed during the course of intensive training through which they all have passed in order to become professionals. In this view the professional is primarily a particular kind of person; one determines whether or not an individual "is" a professional by determining whether or not he has internalized certain given professional values. One explains a "bad" professional by reference to his inferior education, his defective character, or similar variables. In short, one explains the behavior of members of a profession by reference to individual attributes and experiences bearing on conformity to a given set of norms.

Another orientation sees the profession as a group of workers joined together on the most general level by virtue of sharing a particular position in society and by common participation in a given division of labor. More specifically, the behavior of the profession is interpreted by reference to the way in which its work life is organized and the pressures toward conformity or deviance implicit in that organization. Here, the general assumption is that one defines a professional by his status, irrespective of the norms to which he subscribes, and explains his behavior by reference to the work structure in which he participates.

One difficulty in assessing the virtues of each of these orientations is the fact that there has been little attempt at testing them by sustained and detailed analysis of any single profession. And there has been little of the comprehensive comparative analysis that must be the ultimate goal of the sociology of medicine. Furthermore, because one of the marked characteristics of established professions is their relative freedom from lay intervention, from the conventional discipline exercised by industrial employers, and from the detailed directives of crafts unions, both organization and structure have been difficult to perceive. Professional organization is usually taken to be synonymous with the formal professional association, and the actual organization of work or practice has gone largely unnoticed.

This article, by attempting a detailed analysis of the medical profession and by focusing particularly on the way the performance of medical work is controlled, will try to clarify both the sociological characteristics of the medical profession and some of the issues germane to the sociology of the professions. (For a more extended analysis, see Freidson 1966.) Because of the paucity of systematic empirical studies from other countries, it is regrettably necessary to run the risk of parochialism and concentrate on medicine in the United States.

Medicine and the state

The foundation on which the analysis of a profession must be based is its relationship to the ultimate source of power and authority in modern society—the state. In the case of medicine, much, though by no means all, of the profession's strength is based on legally supported monopoly over practice. This monopoly operates through a system of licensing that bears on the privilege to hospitalize patients and the right to prescribe drugs and order laboratory procedures that are otherwise virtually inaccessible to the layman. It is the state that grants this monopoly, the exact form of which varies widely throughout the world.

In the United States the profession, through its private associations, has very largely been given the right to determine how political and legal power bearing on medicine shall be exercised (see especially Hyde et al. 1954). In such countries as Great Britain, where the state has set up a national health system, representatives of the independent and private professional associations sit on both policy-making and administrative boards and negotiate with the state on various issues influencing practice (Stevens 1966). In the national health system of the Soviet Union there is no really private or independent representation of the profession that can negotiate with the state, although advisory and administrative councils do include physicians (Field 1967).

Clearly, the economic and political autonomy of the medical profession varies from country to country. What seems invariant, however, is its technological or scientific autonomy, for everywhere the profession appears to be left fairly free to develop its special area of knowledge and to determine what are "scientifically acceptable" practices. In national state health systems, although laymen do serve in policy-making and administrative positions, physicians tend to be administrative heads of practicing units and to be responsible for the determination of technical standards of equipment, procedures, and performance. Thus, while the profession may not be everywhere free to control the *terms* of its work, it is free to control the *content* of its work. Similarly, it is free to control the technical instruction of its recruits.

Medical training

The medical profession, quite as much as most sociologists, considers medical education to be the major single factor determining the performance of the practicing professional. By the content of his education the student is "socialized" to become a physician. The assumption is that in the course of such an education a new kind of person is created. Medical education in the United States is perhaps unparalleled by any other conventional professional training in its duration, its detail, and its rigidity. Medical school lasts four years after undergraduate college, followed by a fifth year of supervised practice in an accredited teaching hospital (the internship), and even more years for those seeking certification as specialists. It would seem reasonable to think that such intensive exposure in fact molds the student into a particular kind of person. The Columbia University study of medical education (Merton et al. 1957) sought to demonstrate that the student, in the course of his training, develops a conception of himself as a doctor, absorbs the knowledge he needs in order to be secure enough to deal with patients without too much anxiety, and attains the capacity to cope with basic uncertainty in clinical practice.

Nonetheless, the students' perspective on their educational experience differs from that of their instructors. Indeed, one may expect there to be some kind of conflict between students and faculty by the very nature of their different roles. It is the unique contribution of the University of Kansas study (Becker et al. 1961) that it demonstrated the clash of perspectives in medical school and showed that the differences in orientation leading to "restriction of production" are not limited to industrial organizations. The consequences of this for the educational process were followed up in some detail. But the study also emphasized that the existence of this clash of orientations did not mean that there was nothing in common between the performance of students and the demands of faculty. It was discovered that two dominant values, held by the faculty, were adopted by the students and used by them to guide their learning experience and select their careers. These were the values of *medical responsibility* and of *clinical experience* (*ibid.*, chapters 12 and 13).

The value of medical responsibility refers to the traditional ideals of medicine, according to which the physician holds the life of a patient in his hands. It is the personal responsibility held by the physician working directly with a patient that requires him to take the blame for bad results. In the Kansas study, it was found that this value was impressed on the student by frequent faculty lectures about the way in which mistakes of omission or commission endanger the patient's life. Furthermore, faculty members frequently asked students how they would handle an emergency so as to avoid serious consequences to the patient. The value also featured in the organization of the training hospital, where the hierarchy of medical staff was ordered by differential access to medical responsibility, so that the unlicensed student was restricted to routine work having little relationship to life-or-death issues and the highest-status person was free to carry out the most complicated and dangerous procedures.

Clinical experience refers to first-hand contact with patients and disease. Such contact is the ultimate justification for deciding to use one procedure for a treatment rather than another, and the experience so gained is valued because it provides a basis for therapeutic choice that is believed to be superior not only to the abstract considerations posed in textbooks but even to general, scientifically verified knowledge. It was observed in the course of the Kansas study that argument from experience was unanswerable except by the same type of argument from someone with greater experience.

These two values, Becker and his colleagues argued, order the choices the student makes from the range of experience offered by the medical school. These choices limit and direct his efforts in ways not anticipated or approved by the faculty. One of the student's most difficult problems is to select from the enormous mass of facts presented to him the information he is really to learn, for he cannot learn all of it. The idea of clinical experience, it was suggested, guides his selection of facts and information, leading him to discount basic science and focus on classes in which instructors give practical information not found in books— information that adds to his store of vicarious experience. By the same token, he struggles for personal clinical experience in his training, seeking opportunities for expanding it and deprecating routines he has already mastered. Similarly, he seeks tasks in which medical responsibility is apparent—reflecting some risk or danger—and avoids those in which it is not. And, finally, he responds positively to some patients as cases presenting him with valued responsibility and experience, and to others negatively as cases that take up a great deal of time without any valuable recompense (Becker et al. 1961, chapters 14 and 16).

The evidence seemed to show that choice of career also hinges on how far specialties provide the opportunity for medical responsibility and clinical experience. Thus, a desirable specialty is one which offers a wide variety of experience and in which responsibility is symbolized by the possibility of killing or disabling patients in the course of making a mistake. Internal medicine, general surgery, and pediatrics are therefore the most popular specialties, although the potentially "mechanical" character of surgery and the necessity of liking to work with children in pediatrics qualify their desirability for some students. At the other extreme, specialties like dermatology and allergy are unpopular because they are thought to involve little danger (and therefore little responsibility) or little variety (*ibid.*, chapter 20). National surveys of medical students in the United States have accumulated a fair amount of data on specialty choice, most of which are compatible with this interpretation of the values underlying the choices of the majority of students. In the case of those choosing the less popular specialties—the best-investigated of which is public health (Coker et al. 1966)—specification of more detailed patterns of values is of course necessary.

Empirical types of practice

Unmentioned in the course of the discussion of medical training is one element of great relevance to performance: the technical knowledge and skill learned by the student. Here, it is necessary to say only that the student does in fact gain command over a great deal of knowledge and skill; what we must dwell on is the fact that this knowledge and skill is not necessarily retained or used after graduation from medical school. While in a modern industrial country like the United States all physicians share the same basic technical education, they do not all practice in the same way. In the few systematic studies of medical practice that have been made, the association found between medical education and subsequent performance was at best very weak. While the available evidence is scanty and poor, it points to variation in the organization of practice—that is, in the organized setting in which the professional works—as a more important influence than medical education or variation in performance. (For a summary of this material, see Freidson 1963; for the parallel case of the lawyer, see Carlin 1966.) Indeed, the analysis of work organization or practice is a critical problem for the sociology of the professions.

The central issue in the analysis of work is how performance is controlled. This issue constitutes a special problem for the analysis of professional work because professions, unlike other occupations, have successfully gained freedom from control by outsiders. Indeed, a profession is said to control its own performance. This is a rather unusual arrangement, worth understanding both in itself, as one type of control, and in its bearing on how, in our complex world, freedom and autonomy can be joined with responsibility. Let us examine the various organized practices in which medical work takes place to see how control over performance can be exercised. (For a more extensive examination, see Freidson 1963.)

One type of practice that is frequently held up as the ideal by professionals is one in which the individual is an entrepreneur, free to do what his own conscience and knowledge dictate. This is so-called solo practice. While pure forms of solo practice are quite rare—invoking it as a norm reflects the individualistic ideology of the profession more than it reflects reality—we might ask what conditions must be met to assure that individuals practicing entirely on their own conform to professional standards. Assurance of adequate performance on the part of solo practitioners seems to require exceedingly careful recruitment policies and extraordinarily effective educational procedures. In essence, the practitioner must be able to resist all temptations to ethical or technical lapses by virtue of his inner resources alone, resources which must also motivate him to continue to keep up-to-date. In solo practice the burden of control rests solely on individual motivation and capacity.

Much more common than solo practice in the United States today is practice involving a loose network of interdependent practitioners who refer cases to each other—an informal organization that has been described as a "colleague network" (Hall 1946). Backed by a stable clientele relatively loyal to them, the practitioners in such a network control access to that clientele and thus access to work on the part of new young practitioners. In the rather well-organized case he studied, Hall showed how an "inner fraternity" of practitioners controlled access to practice settings and desirable patients and how, through the mechanism of sponsorship, newcomers were obliged both to take on minor tasks and to turn to their sponsors for consultation. While it may be doubted that professional services in large cities can be wholly dominated by any single informal fraternity, the sociometric studies of Coleman and his colleagues (1966) suggest that there are systematic and persistent patterns of interrelationships among practitioners even in so loosely organized a system as exists in the United States. These patterns of interaction suggest two of the most important prerequisites for control of the practitioner's performance by colleagues rather than by clients: by referring patients to each other, each practitioner has the opportunity to *observe* some of the other's performance; by being economically and technically interdependent, each practitioner has some leverage to *influence* the other's performance.

Finally, one may mention the less primitive structures of practice that are characteristic of some European countries and are represented in the United States by large group practices and university clinics. These are essentially bureaucratic organizations, although the variations in actual administrative detail are countless. We may point to one logically distinct type of bureaucracy that has received some theoretical attention in the literature because of its systematic deviation from the classical rational–legal model of bureaucracy. It has been called *professional* bureaucracy, and it has been characterized as a form of organization in which the hierarchy of professional practitioners is set apart from the hierarchy of the administration itself or (as in many European countries) a form of organization in which all important positions of organizational authority are filled by professionals. In both cases, professional work is free from the exercise of the authority of nonprofessionals even though the working professionals are technically subordinates in a bureaucratic system and lack the freedom of the entrepreneur. The exact theoretical importance of such a logical construct and the degree to which it mirrors enough of reality to be useful are by no means clear, but by pointing to the bureaucratic elements of organization it does indicate that here, more than in other forms of practice, physicians are in a position of interdependence that implies opportunities to observe and to exercise influence over one another's performance. Of all the types of practice reviewed, the bureaucratic type provides the best opportunity for professional self-regulation. Indeed, this is the type exemplified by high-prestige academic institutions in the United States and elsewhere.

Analytical types of practice

Thus far, it has been suggested that there is a range of practice organizations, from purely individual practice to bureaucratically organized practice. To understand how colleagues or clients may gain access to observe and influence performance, it is useful to distinguish those features of practice which determine both the source and the content of control. In this way it becomes possible to analyze the differential significance in the division of labor of various forms of specialization. The lay client's perspective on the service he seeks differs from that of the colleague group of professionals: this may be taken as axiomatic. Let us therefore distinguish practices by the degree to which they are amenable to lay or colleague control. It is clear that two types of medical practice form the logical extremes of the medical division of labor. At one extreme is practice wholly dependent on lay choice for its existence: it may be called *client-dependent* practice. Such a practice survives by using its own resources to attract and satisfy a lay clientele. Since the client uses lay standards in deciding that he needs professional services and in evaluating the services he gets, the practice must conform to lay standards in order to be patronized. Furthermore,

when wholly dependent on client choice, the practice cannot be observed by colleagues, nor is its survival dependent on their cooperation. In consequence, all the pressure on the practice is toward conforming to lay rather than professional standards. At the other extreme is *colleague-dependent* practice. It does not attract its own lay clientele but, rather, obtains clients through the referrals of other colleagues. Thus, in order to survive it must honor the prejudices of colleagues, and so is likely to conform more to professional than to lay standards.

How closely do actual practices conform to these logical types? The logical extreme of client-dependent practice does not seem fully applicable to any professional practice, although the "independent" solo neighborhood or village general practitioner comes close to it. Also close are specialists who must attract a clientele directly and do not have to make everyday use of hospital facilities—for example, in urban areas in particular, some internists, pediatricians, ophthalmologists, and gynecologists. In these instances lay standards may be expected to have some force. Empirical examples of the logical extreme of colleague-dependent practices are easier to find in modern medicine. Specialists like pathologists and radiologists, for instance, are almost completely dependent upon colleague referrals and therefore have little need for such client-oriented techniques as a good bedside manner. Here, we should expect considerably greater pressure to honor colleague rather than lay or patient standards.

This typology is based on the division of labor within the profession and is therefore applicable to analysis of the control of performance of individual practitioners in any kind of organized practice, from solo to bureaucratic. It might be pointed out, however, that in bureaucratically organized practice it is frequently the organization as a unit, not individual practitioners, that attracts a clientele and that all practitioners in the organization are therefore dependent on it for their work. Insofar as the organization is of the "professional" type discussed above, this means that dependence on it is actually dependence on the colleagues running it. Encouragement to meet professional standards of performance will therefore be considerably stronger than encouragement to meet lay standards. And insofar as work is at once more visible and amenable to control in such an organization than in less well-organized forms of practice, it is here that we should expect to find the highest professional standards. Indeed, it is the general opinion of teachers of medicine in the United

States, Great Britain, and elsewhere that this is the case, although adequate evidence to test this opinion has not yet been gathered.

All else being equal, then, we may hypothesize that colleague-dependent practices, in which the physician's performance is observable to and his work dependent on colleagues, will also be most likely to conform to professional standards. Insofar as bureaucratic practice is colleague-dependent, the same conclusion may be drawn for it. But this conclusion masks several assumptions the truth of which is not self-evident: first, that colleagues will exert control over performance; second, that the mechanisms of control used by colleagues are effective; third, that standards are homogeneous throughout the profession. The remainder of this article will explore these assumptions.

Professional regulation

Variation in the organization of medical practice bears on such necessary conditions for the exercise of professional regulation as the observability of performance to colleagues and the structural vulnerability of the practitioner to control by colleagues. However, while observability and dependence are necessary conditions for the effective exercise of supervision, they are not sufficient. What is needed in addition is the willingness to exercise supervision and exert effective influence over performance. What slender evidence there is suggests that rather less influence over performance is exercised than the organization of practice actually allows, and that the little regulation which does exist has properties that establish and maintain organized differences in performance standards.

The basic property of the system of control that seems to exist in the United States is its reliance upon what Carr-Saunders and Wilson, speaking of British medicine, call the "boycott"—that is, the refusal by individual practitioners to enter into a referral or collaborative relationship with those of whom they do not approve (1933, p. 403; see also Hyde et al. 1954). This device does not control the boycotted person's behavior so much as it pushes him outside the boundaries of observability and influence, to practice as he wishes in the company of those with similar standards. There seems to be a certain reluctance to exert active influence over another's performance—a reluctance that results in avoiding him rather than in seeking to change him.

There is, unfortunately, little systematically collected empirical information bearing on the process of supervision and control among physicians. A study by Freidson and Rhea (1963; 1965) of a large academically oriented group practice in the United States indicated that while performance was visible along the axes dictated by the interdependence of specialties within the over-all division of labor, each practitioner tended to keep his complaints about others to himself, so that what he could observe of others' performance in the division of labor was not transmitted to other colleagues. Since bits of information were scattered piecemeal through the colleague group, no really organized control of performance could be initiated unless a man behaved so outrageously as to personally offend everyone. Furthermore, attempts at control were largely individual and hortatory, and there were no control devices intermediate between remonstration and outright ejection from the organization (the latter being the structural equivalent of the boycott). While the physicians studied were aware of the looseness of supervision and control in this ostensibly well-organized practice, they were inclined to feel it adequate and appropriate for ordinary circumstances.

Another American study (Goss 1961; 1963) is particularly instructive because it was done in a setting into which supervision was built. There were clear bureaucratic as well as professional supervisory responsibilities allocated through hierarchical ranks. The superior physician in the hierarchy had the right and perhaps even the obligation to review case records and evaluate case management. Furthermore, he had the right to give advice to subordinates about the way a case should be handled, even when advice was not solicited. However, even though the supervisor was officially responsible for the care given to patients in his unit and therefore had the formal right to order that certain procedures be followed for a case, he very rarely gave such orders. Instead, he gave advice, which incurred no obligation to obedience. The only obligation the subordinate had was to consider the advice in the light of his personal experience with and responsibility for the case. So long as he could justify his management of the case by reference to medical knowledge and his clinical experience, and so long as it was he who took personal responsibility for the outcome, he could reject the advice of his superior. In short, even here, where supervisory inspection of performance was routine, the exercise of control over performance was quite loose and permissive. If this is so in hierarchically organized practice settings, it should be even more the case in the informal, small-scale community practices that are far more common in medicine. Thus, we may say that the medical profession, which has gained freedom from regulation by others, regulates itself in ways whose effectiveness is not self-evident. The analytical problem here is to understand what contributes to shaping this peculiar process of regulation and to point up its structural consequences.

Professional values

Obviously, when a social structure *permits* certain kinds of behavior but that behavior does not occur, we must explore the situation further to explain why it does not. Our first question might be why, in such a loose system, the physician does not routinely abuse his privilege. Here, the internalization of general professional values postulated by Parsons (1951, chapter 10) seems a plausible explanation. Parsons defines the professional as someone who is supposed to be recruited and licensed on the basis of his technical competence rather than his ascribed social characteristics; to use generally accepted scientific standards in his work rather than particularistic ones; to restrict his work activity to areas in which he is technically competent; to avoid emotional involvement and to cultivate objectivity in his work; and to put his client's interests before his own [*see* PROFESSIONS]. These normative expectations are intended by Parsons to apply to all professions, not only to medicine, since he treats the medical practitioner as the archetype of the professional. But it may be objected that the same expectations are applicable to all technical service occupations, not only to professions. Plumbers, too, are supposed to be recruited and licensed on the basis of achievement, to employ universalistic standards in their work, to be functionally specific and affectively neutral. And while plumbers are expected to make enough money from their work to gain a decent income (just as are physicians), they are not expected to do this by cheating the customer. Thus, such values constitute only the most general foundation of conscientiousness in occupational practice.

Our second question, however, may be more specific to the medical profession. Why, if it so conscientious, does it not exercise more regulation over its members' performance? Such an extraordinarily loose regulatory structure has been explained by Carr-Saunders and Wilson (1933, pp. 399–400) and by Parsons (1951, pp. 470–471) by reference to the character of professional work. Instead of a set routine, medicine requires the exercise of complex judgment; instead of caution, the taking of risks. Therefore, regulation can only be loose. But of all the old established professions medicine is the one most based on fairly precise and detailed scientific knowledge. Indeed, the practice of medicine involves considerably less uncertainty than many other technical occupations. As the use of the doctrine of *res ipsa loquitur* in American courts implies, there are some very clear rights and wrongs in medicine, even if there are also some uncertainties, and these rights and wrongs have not brought forth any formal regulatory mechanisms from the profession as such (as opposed to concrete organizations like teaching hospitals, in which regulatory mechanisms do exist). Without denying that there is a degree of uncertainty, we must conclude that the precision possible in much of modern medicine and the trivial routine of much of everyday medical practice call into question the adequacy of explaining the peculiarly loose structure of controls to be found in the profession by reference to the character of its work. However, it may be that the peculiar nature of the work of the practicing professional encourages a characteristic *sense* of uncertainty that reflects considerably more special values than those described by Parsons.

One such value is that of independence, or autonomy, which is significant for physicians in countries as different as Finland and the United States. Insofar as this value refers to social and economic independence, it reflects the entrepreneurial and individualistic ideology of the bourgeoisie, who are the prime source from which physicians are recruited in virtually all industrial countries. Insofar as the value refers to technical or professional independence—that is, the freedom to practice one's craft without interference, advice, or regulation by others—it seems more closely related to a state of mind encouraged by the character of professional work.

The aim of the practitioner is not knowledge but action, and while successful action is the aim, the tendency is to assume that any action at all is better than none. Furthermore, to take action requires faith in oneself and even a will to believe in whatever one does instead of maintaining a skeptical detachment. Dealing with individual and concrete cases, the practitioner is inclined to emphasize indeterminacy rather than lawful regularity and to be radically pragmatic, relying more on the results he associates with his own actions than on theory. These seem to be the orientations that contribute to the emphasis on clinical experience mentioned earlier in connection with medical education.

Given that the work of the medical practitioner is with individuals and that it is believed to be based on individual clinical experience, it follows that responsibility for the work can be perceived only as individual and personal. In assuming that responsibility, the practitioner does gain gratitude for success, but he also gains reproach for failure. Given the risk of blame, he evidences a certain sensitivity and defensiveness in the face of any outsider's evaluation of his performance. This defensiveness is manifested in imputing more uncertainty to the work than in fact exists and in insisting on using his own personal, clinical experience as the ultimate criterion for evaluating his own performance. Thus, collective responsibility for regulation is diminished, and the inclination to rely on individual responsibility and personal experience is augmented.

These, of course, are merely suggestions of the complex task that has still to be done in picking out and interrelating strands of what might be called the ideology of the practicing professional. Instead of dwelling on values of such generality that they have doubtful analytical utility for understanding the quality of professional self-regulation, sociologists should determine the specific values attached to different types of professional work. Such an approach would supply one of the critical elements for an adequate explanation of the peculiarities of professional organization.

Informal organization of the profession

Even without detailed information it seems possible to suggest that the notion of informal organization serves as a vital link between the formal structure given to the American medical profession by the national, state, and county medical associations (see Hyde et al. 1954) and professional performance in the concrete setting of medical practice. By focusing on the characteristic way in which practitioners assert control over each other's performance, one can delineate the relation of one local practice to another and the loose groupings of practices that both carve up a community and extend outside its boundaries. When these informal groupings and the mechanisms of control they express are seen to be intertwined with the formal structure of the profession as a whole, much more of the character of the profession can be understood than by reference to formal associations and codes alone.

Recalling that ordinarily the ultimate mechanism of control is the personal boycott, we can begin to indicate the informal structure of the profession by following out the implications of the boycott's operation on the interrelations of practitioners. Let us assume that individual practitioners are free to select the work they will undertake and to choose the colleagues with whom they will work in the division of labor. In this situation, control of professional standards is exercised largely by willingness to work with one man and to exclude another. But since exclusion as such neither changes a man nor prevents him from working, one may assume that he will eventually find a circle whose standards are such that he is not excluded.

There is thus a tendency for the control process to develop a stable set of colleague networks or fraternities. Each network, by the nature of its creation, is fairly homogeneous within itself. Its members share about the same professional standards, participate in each other's work, and participate in, if not dominate, the particular organizations and practices in which they work. But while each colleague network is likely to be fairly homogeneous, many differences are likely to exist *between* networks by virtue of the process of selection and rejection that differentiates them into separate networks. Thus there is not only likely to be little interaction between many contiguous networks, but also marked differences in technical and normative standards and in the practices and institutions in which the members of each network participate.

In a structure of this nature there is comparatively little opportunity for those in one network to be very much aware of the existence of other standards; and even when awareness may exist, there is little leverage by which one network could influence another because each has severed connections with the other and is independent of the other. Since it is a segregating process that leads to and maintains such networks, and since the individual's behavior is less regulated by such a process than classified and assigned to a self-maintaining collectivity of like people, we can see how within a single profession, even one quite free of lay interference, organized variations in professional performance can occur. While there are certainly social links between adjacent fraternities in the form of practitioners with connections in both, it does not seem to require a very large city to find individual practitioners who know nothing about each other.

The characteristic control mechanism of professional regulation, then, paradoxically operates to place offenders beyond the control of those who disapprove of their performance. Moreover, the informal organization of internally homogeneous colleague networks segregated from interaction with each other sustains, if not reinforces, the differences in standards between networks. Apart from civil suit, which is a nonprofessional source of control over practice, and regulatory devices established in the limited milieu of teaching hospitals, all that is left to concerned members of the profession in the United States is exhortation and, it is hoped, instruction by means of articles in professional journals that may or may not be read and that, if read, may or may not be influential on behavior.

What has been suggested, in short, is that the disjunctive process of social control characterizing the concrete, everyday practice of American physicians creates an informal structure of relatively segregated, small circles of practitioners, the extremes of which are so isolated from each other that the conditions necessary for each influencing the other's behavior are missing. Furthermore, the mechanism of control that produces and sustains this situation is no aberration—rather, it is characteristic of the profession, an outcome of its organization and of the way it sees itself and its work. The consequence is that a single profession can contain within itself, and even encourage, markedly different ethical and technical standards of performance, limited in a very superficial way by the minimal standards imposed by selective recruitment, a basic core of training required for licensing, and the writings of the leaders of the medical profession.

Tasks of a sociology of medicine

The problems of analysis described in this article are not unique to the sociology of medicine but affect the sociology of professions in general. If they can be solved for medicine, we will have taken a long step toward solving them for all professions. The central problem here, as in the study of society in general, is social control. The problem is particularly important for the professions because by definition they are free of the controls common to most occupations. In addressing the problem of control, it was necessary to assess the role of the state and of politico–legal institutions, the manifest and latent functions of professional education, the organization of work, the control processes operating in work, and the norms or values that bear on the exercise of social control in work. The outcome of that analysis was the suggestion that a fragmented structure underlies the serene façade of unity and homogeneity implied by the notion of a single profession joined by common values and a community of identity.

To extend, correct, and refine such a trial analysis of the organization of medical work is one of the prime tasks of a sociology of medicine. In the course of extending it, one would be led quite naturally into a more detailed examination of another major problem of analysis: the client–practitioner relationship. This problem, too, might be seen as one of control. The practitioner wants the client to seek him out for professionally appropriate reasons,

without visiting quacks and without untoward delay. He wants the client to accept his recommendations and follow them scrupulously. In seeking compliance on the part of his client, the professional cannot always rely on his influence as an expert. The character of this influence and of practitioner–client interaction has barely been explored in other than psychological terms, and poses a challenge both to the taxonomy of types of social influence and to the conceptualization of social interaction.

Finally, we may mention a problem of analysis that has not yet received much attention—the role of the professional in creating and defining his own work. In the case of medicine (more than of law or religion) this analytical problem has been confounded by the reification of "scientific knowledge," a viewpoint in which disease is taken to exist independently of human action and the physician is regarded as merely a diagnostician and therapist of what is objectively "there." However, disease that exists independently of human awareness and action is irrelevant to the sociologist, while biologically nonexistent "disease" in which people believe is quite relevant. What is sociologically relevant is a social definition of disease or any other kind of deviance, not the biological fact or fancy. If this premise be adopted, then it follows that physicians are responsible for the *social creation* of disease in the course of "discovery" and diagnosis [see HEALTH]. It would follow, further, that in medical practice the social organization of work biases the way in which diseases are created and shapes the way in which patients are managed and even created by diagnosis. Thus, a major task of the sociology of medicine is to study the causes and consequences of physicians' conceptions of disease, showing how disease as a social object is created or formed by medical institutions (Scheff 1966). If this task should be performed as something independent of the conventional study of the process of scientific discovery, and with different premises, we will have come a long way toward understanding the social institutions of medicine as one of the modern professions.

ELIOT FREIDSON

[See also HEALTH; ILLNESS; MEDICAL CARE; PROFESSIONS; PUBLIC HEALTH; SCIENCE, *article on* SCIENTIFIC COMMUNICATION; *and the biography of* HENDERSON.]

BIBLIOGRAPHY

BECKER, HOWARD S. et al. 1961 *Boys in White: Student Culture in Medical School.* Univ. of Chicago Press.

CARLIN, JEROME 1966 *Lawyers' Ethics: A Survey of the New York City Bar.* New York: Russell Sage Foundation.

CARR-SAUNDERS, ALEXANDER; and WILSON, P. A. (1933) 1964 *The Professions.* London: Cass.

COKER, ROBERT E. JR. et al. 1966 Medical Careers in Public Health. *Milbank Memorial Fund Quarterly* 44:143–258.

COLEMAN, JAMES S. et al. 1966 *Medical Innovation: A Diffusion Study.* Indianapolis, Ind.: Bobbs-Merrill.

FIELD, MARK G. 1967 *Soviet Socialized Medicine: An Introduction.* New York: Free Press.

FREIDSON, ELIOT 1961/1962 The Sociology of Medicine: A Trend Report and Bibliography. *Current Sociology* 10/11:123–192.

FREIDSON, ELIOT 1963 The Organization of Medical Practice. Pages 299–319 in Howard E. Freeman, Sol Levine, and Leo G. Reeder, *Handbook of Medical Sociology.* Englewood Cliffs, N.J.: Prentice-Hall.

FREIDSON, ELIOT 1966 The Sociology of Medicine: A Structural Approach. Unpublished manuscript.

FREIDSON, ELIOT; and RHEA, BUFORD 1963 Processes of Control in a Company of Equals. *Social Problems* 11:119–131.

FREIDSON, ELIOT; and RHEA, BUFORD 1965 Knowledge and Judgment in Professional Evaluations. *Administrative Science Quarterly* 10:107–124.

GOSS, MARY E. W. 1961 Influence and Authority Among Physicians in an Out-patient Clinic. *American Sociological Review* 26:39–50.

GOSS, MARY E. W. 1963 Patterns of Bureaucracy Among Hospital Staff Physicians. Pages 170–194 in Eliot Freidson (editor), *The Hospital in Modern Society.* New York: Free Press.

HALL, OSWALD 1946 The Informal Organization of the Medical Profession. *Canadian Journal of Economics and Political Science* 12:30–44.

HYDE, DAVID R. et al. 1954 The American Medical Association: Power, Purpose, and Politics in Organized Medicine. *Yale Law Journal* 63:938–1022.

MERTON, ROBERT K. et al. (editors) 1957 *The Student–Physician.* Cambridge, Mass.: Harvard Univ. Press.

PARSONS, TALCOTT 1951 *The Social System.* Glencoe, Ill.: Free Press.

SCHEFF, THOMAS J. 1966 Typification in the Diagnostic Practices of Rehabilitation Agencies. Pages 139–147 in Marvin B. Sussman (editor), *Sociology and Rehabilitation.* Washington: American Sociological Association.

STEVENS, ROSEMARY 1966 *Medical Practice in Modern England: The Impact of Specialization and State Medicine.* New Haven: Yale Univ. Press.

II

PARAMEDICAL PERSONNEL

The term "paramedical" refers to occupations whose work is both organized around tasks of healing and ultimately controlled by the authority of physicians. Ultimate control by medical authority is manifested in a number of ways. First, much of the technical knowledge learned by paramedical workers during the course of their training and used during the course of their work tends to be discovered, enlarged upon, and approved by physicians. Second, the tasks performed by paramedical workers tend to assist, rather than directly replace, the focal tasks of diagnosis and treatment. Third,

paramedical workers tend to be subordinate in that their work tends to be performed at the request or "order" of, and is often supervised by, physicians. Finally, the prestige assigned to paramedical occupations by the general public tends to be less than that assigned to physicians.

The paramedical occupations may be distinguished from established professions by their relative lack of autonomy, responsibility, authority, and prestige. However, the fact that they are by definition organized around an established profession and in varying degrees partake of some, but never all, of the elements of professionalism allows us to distinguish them from many other occupations and, indeed, argue that they represent a sociologically distinct form of occupational organization.

Furthermore, it may be noted that paramedical occupations are not adequately distinguished by reference to their health-related tasks. Occupations usually called paramedical do participate in a functional division of labor, but what is distinct about this division of labor is that it is ordered by the authority of a prime profession. Other occupations which may actually perform some of the same technical tasks but which stand in a different relationship to the dominant profession (as does, for example, a herbalist compared to a pharmacist) are not called paramedical, but rather quack or irregular. Differences between the paramedical and the quack do not necessarily arise from the actual tasks each performs, but rather from the relations each has to the dominant profession. Thus, the paramedical worker is less easily distinguished technologically, by the relation of his work to that of others, than sociologically, by his relation to medical authority.

However, distinct as it is, this "paraprofessional" pattern is not common. For example, while there is a fairly elaborate division of labor revolving around law, it would not be appropriate to use the term "paralegal" for bailiffs, accountants, clerks, real estate brokers, and bankers in the same way that we use "paramedical" for nurses and laboratory technicians. Nor does the prefix seem properly employed to designate the division of labor connected with any other established profession. Medicine alone seems to have imposed such definite order on the occupations surrounding it. We can but guess the reasons for this, citing such variables as the comparative specificity and technical complexity of the tasks involved, which can only be exercised in a medical setting. Whatever the reason, this mode of organizing a division of labor is taxonomically distinct, and if it is true that labor is in general being "professionalized," the paramedical model may become more widespread in the future. Both practically and conceptually it is worth close study. How did it develop? What are its present characteristics?

Development of the division of labor

A division of labor in the task of diagnosing and treating human ills has always existed in one form or another in every human society. There have always been diagnosticians, herbalists, midwives, and nurses, even if only on a part-time, amateur basis. However, the distinctive division of labor labeled paramedical—which is to say, one organized around the authority of the medical profession —is relatively new and is complex only in the highly industrialized societies of the world where the modern medical profession arose. Even in these countries it varies a great deal in the completeness of its integration around and control by the medical profession. Unfortunately, there are few adequate cross-national comparisons of the organization of health workers to provide even the basic descriptive information necessary for analysis, and so much of the indication of the types and sources of variation must be based on scattered bits of information (for one comparison, see Glaser 1966).

In Europe a distinctly paramedical division of labor, organized around the authority of a medical man, had begun to emerge at least by the time of the development in cities of the corporate guild and the university. The city provided the population density necessary for the support of a variety of *full-time* specialists, thereby allowing true occupations to arise. The guild provided the health-related occupations with a workable type of organization through which a distinct occupational identity, visible to officials and public alike, could slowly be established and through which they could press for exclusive rights to that identity and the work it involved. However, the right to have something of a monopoly of title and function—that is, to be licensed—and to control in a fairly strict way access into and progress through the occupational career was obtained from the state. Thus, the occupation gained organization, but it also became subject to assignment, by a political process, to a relatively well defined *official* position in a larger division of labor—a position that could involve enforced subordination to members of quite another guild.

The significance of the university in this situation is that occupations trained in one had a stronger claim, by virtue of their aura of learning and science, to a superordinate position in the occupational structure. University training gave phy-

sicians and surgeons a strong political position for persuading the state to subordinate to them such competitors as apothecaries, grocers, and barbers, and to allow them to prosecute irregular practitioners. This could be so even when it was doubtful that the actual knowledge and skill of the average university-trained practitioner in those days equipped him to practice any better than his self-taught or apprenticed competitor.

With the development of the university and the guild in European cities, then, there arose a rudimentary structure of full-time health workers, organized, at least in part, under the supervision of physicians and surgeons. For centuries this organization was highly unstable, weakened from within by undisciplined competition and from without by the persistence of a great variety of irregular practitioners (see King 1958; Turner 1959). As is the case with the health services in the nonindustrial countries of today, the medical division of labor was fairly stable only in those parts of cities where a well-to-do gentry was likely to patronize it. In the city slums and in the countryside the poor and the peasantry persisted in relying on their own folk remedies, their own, largely part-time practitioners, and, on occasion, itinerant irregulars; the first two being part of their own culture, the last exploiting the naïvete of that culture. There were in essence two health systems: the dominant one was rooted in the peasant culture, while the other, which was available only to a minority, owed its greater prestige to its origins in the learned traditions of Western civilization. Before the latter could become at once stable and universal, the former had to be destroyed or at least severely restricted. Not until the twentieth century in Europe and North America did anything emerge resembling a stable and extensive division of labor dominated by physicians, that is to say, a genuine paramedical division of labor. In the nonindustrial countries of the world today, such a structure does not yet exist to any great degree.

Modern developments. The prime prerequisite for the development of a stable and extensive division of labor that is distinctively paramedical seems to be the eradication of great qualitative differences in culture and education among the major social strata of a society. This seems to be so because health services are used mostly on a voluntary basis. People choose to use one health service rather than another, and if only one organized service is available, they can choose not to use it and rely on their own informal resources instead. In this sense, while the application of political power can drive out of practice all but officially licensed workers, it cannot make people use them. It seems no mere coincidence that the irregular health services declined greatly in industrialized countries about the same time that the institution of compulsory universal education arose. Contributory to this process, but by no means enough by itself (as experience in nonindustrial countries today indicates), was the rise of scientific medicine, which was capable for the first time in history of alleviating many complaints and symptoms consistently and predictably.

By the twentieth century the medical profession was at last able to establish a secure mandate to provide a central health service. In England the rural general practitioner had been drawn into regular medical ranks. In Russia the feldsher had been in part replaced by and in part subordinated to the physician. In the United States the many different kinds and qualities of practitioners, all democratically calling themselves doctor, had been reduced to some uniformity. Control over the focal tasks of diagnosis and prescription was thereby secured (Sigerist 1935), and by virtue of its major role as arbiter in the application of new scientific discoveries, the profession could order around itself the proliferating new technical personnel.

Some historical specialties, such as dentistry, survived fairly independently of the paramedical division of labor. Others, such as pharmacy and optometry, were not fully integrated into the paramedical division of labor, remaining at least partially independent of it. Still others, such as bonesetting and, in the United States, midwifery, were taken over by the physician himself, laymen and amateurs being driven out of practice. Others, the most prominent of which is nursing, maintained an ancient function while being brought firmly under medical control. And finally, with some few exceptions, such new specialties as laboratory technology, which arose with the new medical science and technology inside the walls of the hospital and medical school, developed unequivocally as part of an established paramedical division of labor.

Today's paramedical division of labor is therefore a specifically historical construction, with some *functionally* related occupations falling inside it and some outside it; not all of the very old or the very new occupations fall inside it. The source of whatever order may be found in this division of labor seems to lie in the character of the relationships to be found between medicine, other occupations, and prospective lay clientele—central to which, perhaps, is the possibility of functional autonomy.

Relations with the medical profession. The interoccupational relations of paramedical workers can be seen clearly only as part of a larger, evolving structure that embraces physicians, health workers who are not part of the paramedical division of labor, and the institutions in which medical and nonmedical health services are provided. One of the major variables mediating interoccupational relations in the health services seems to be *functional autonomy*—the degree to which work can be carried on independently of organizational or medical supervision and to which it can be sustained by attracting its clientele independently of organizational referral or referral by other occupations, including physicians. On the whole, the more autonomous the occupation and the greater the overlap of its work with that of physicians, the greater is the potential for conflict, legal or otherwise. Such conflict is to be seen between chiropractors and physicians in the United States, homeopaths and physicians in the Soviet Union, and "native" practitioners and physicians in virtually all nonindustrial countries.

The most interesting conflicts, however, occur *within* the paramedical division of labor during the course of the growth of new occupations capable of attaining functional autonomy. In the United States, where the movement toward professional status is strong and extensive and there are not enough physicians to perform all the traditional functions demanded of them, such conflict is common; it focuses on the question of whether or not nonphysicians are to be allowed to offer health services independently of medical supervision. The outcome has been, in such increasingly successful cases as that of the clinical psychologist, virtual independence in practice, limited only by the legal inability to prescribe drugs. Impelled by the force of professionalization, the growth of new techniques and new occupations to practice them seems to be giving a new shape to the paramedical division of labor. Some years ago it could be visualized quite simply as a pyramid, with the physician at the apex. However, in the present-day United States the pyramid seems to be changing into a less clear-cut structure, at the top of which is a plateau along which are ranged physicians as well as other relatively autonomous, but consulting and cooperating, new professionals.

Recruitment and training

Obviously the paramedical division of labor is a stratified system, the occupations of which are in varying degrees integrated around the work of the physician. All occupations in the system are given less prestige than the physician by the society at large. It follows that the socioeconomic status of those recruited into all paramedical occupations is likely to be lower than the status of those recruited into medicine itself. Furthermore, there is a hierarchy of prestige and authority among the ranks of paramedical workers; nurses, for example, are higher than attendants and technicians. This hierarchy is also likely to be reflected in the socioeconomic backgrounds of the workers. In the grossest comparison between physicians and paramedical workers, the latter are to a disproportionate degree women and from the less valued ethnic, racial, and religious groups. With the special exception of sex, those differences in background and personal characteristics are also likely to be ranged in an order corresponding to the general hierarchy of prestige and authority.

Variability of training. Training follows a variable pattern, its order roughly paralleling the prestige, independence, and imputed responsibility of the work (see Wardwell 1963). Patterns of training range from the one extreme of professional schools associated with universities, requiring a full higher education before several years of training, to the other extreme of brief, informal, on-the-job training. Between these extremes are many types of training, varied according to the length of study, the formality and abstractness of the curriculum, and the type of institutional arrangement, such as attendance at hospital training schools or proprietary technical schools, apprenticeships in various institutions, and the like. In the United States, where the university is a considerably less clearly defined institution than elsewhere, more paramedical education with professional trappings is to be found. In Europe technical training schools quite separate from the university are more likely to exist, for the education of even the high-prestige, more independent paramedical occupations.

The paramedical ranks tend to be ordered by the length and type of training required by the occupation: the longer the training and the more formal and the closer to the university it is, the higher is the occupation's position in the division of labor. It follows from this that the higher the position, the greater must be the investment of time and energy in training, the less casual can be the recruitment, and the greater must be the commitment to the occupation. Recruitment to the many low-skill positions in the paramedical division of labor seems, by and large, to be a simple function of the demand for unskilled service workers willing to do unpleasant work. Recruitment to the higher-skill positions, however, is considerably more problematic, especially in those occupations traditionally filled by women.

The position of women. Nursing is a fairly well-documented example of problems of recruit-ment and training in the paramedical occupations (see Corwin & Taves 1963). The problem in nursing is not that of attracting people to undergo training as such, for quite a few women begin training; it lies in recruiting women who will stay in training and subsequently pursue a lifetime career in the occupation. The essential difficulty here is that women are likely to be torn between the commitment to work and the commitment to marriage and family. This conflict has been discerned in nursing students and seems to be closely related to school dropouts and subsequent job turnover.

Leaders of nursing in the United States have attempted to contend with the problem by emphasizing the professional qualities of the occupation, presumably hoping to create a stronger "professional" commitment to work that might outweigh family considerations (Strauss 1966). The problem, however, seems to be inherent in the position of women in the labor force and does not seem soluble by professionalization. Even in the case of that most professional of professions, namely medicine, only a modest proportion of women in the United States who are qualified to practice medicine actually do so. One might therefore suspect that a more likely solution for a social system such as that of the United States would be found in changing the organization of the job so as to accommodate it to the demands of marriage and family.

In European countries the position of women in the medical and paramedical labor force is quite different, apparently because of national differences in the occupational roles of women that make a professional career highly desirable among women of the *haute bourgeoisie*, small but significant differences in the class system, and, finally, the level of industrialization and the general standard of living. The last consideration brings up another aspect of recruitment and training in the paramedical division of labor. Clear evidence is lacking, but general opinion seems to be that it is becoming more and more difficult to recruit people to the paramedical jobs that require considerable investment of time and money in technical training. If this is so, it might be understood as a symptom of a larger process of advanced industrialization.

Emphasis on professionalism. In the earlier stages of industrialization, the health services constituted a major and conspicuous source of social and economic mobility to which those willing and able to invest in specialized training could aspire. However, in later stages the demand for skilled technical services has developed markedly in other segments of the economy, thereby providing a considerably wider universe of opportunity than that which existed earlier. As older, fairly closely organized systems, requiring relatively extensive investment in training but offering relatively inflexible career lines, the health services, medical as well as paramedical, seem handicapped in competing for a limited pool of potential workers. Part of the pervasive emphasis on professionalism within the paramedical division of labor in the United States seems to be an attempt to increase the attractiveness of the work and thereby aid in recruiting the best possible workers.

However, the emphasis on professionalism is likely to be strong only during the course of training, which is where the leaders of the occupation are most likely to be influential. Inasmuch as professionalism tends to emphasize intellectual and technical skill, there is the danger of dissatisfying students whose motives for entering the occupation are not so much intellectual as humanitarian—a danger that has been observed in nursing schools. Furthermore, inasmuch as professionalism tends to emphasize the dignity and autonomy of the worker, it is likely that upon leaving school and entering the everyday institutions of work, which are generally not controlled by the leaders of the occupation, the erstwhile student, who has been imbued with professionalism, is in for what has been called "reality shock." If the student's indoctrination has been thorough, his relations with other occupations in the paramedical hierarchy are likely to be somewhat difficult and personally disillusioning.

Paramedical personnel in the hospital

It has been implied that the greatest opportunity for developing functional autonomy seems to exist for those occupations that can operate outside the walls of such medically organized institutions as clinics and hospitals. The nursing profession, whose leaders in the United States have with great energy sought to establish unique skills and fully professional status, seems fated nonetheless to remain subject to the doctor's orders, in part because a nurse's work is largely carried out in the hospital. In this, however, the nurse is not unique: the largest part of the paramedical division of labor grew up within such organizations and may be expected to persist and proliferate within them in the future. It is for this reason that once we leave the broad societal level of analysis of the paramedical division of labor to undertake the analysis of everyday work, we find ourselves

in the community agency, the clinic, and, most extensively studied of all, the hospital.

All hospitals are complex organizations coordinating a number of tasks and forming the focus for a number of distinct, usually overlapping goals. Given the fact that hospitals are fairly stable and spatially fixed, it is no accident that the paramedical occupations working within them have been studied far more than those working outside in the community at large, where the bulk of health services are actually provided. Thus, we have a severely limited view of paramedical as well as medical work. Among studies of hospital personnel, the nurse in the general hospital is the most frequent subject, and the attendant or aide in the mental hospital ranks second. We have little systematic empirical information about virtually all other paramedical workers. Handicapped as we are, the nurse and attendant between them do present us with a view of the range of workers, from the most professional to the least. By reviewing their respective positions, we can obtain some hints about the kinds of analytical problems posed by the work of paramedical personnel.

The nursing profession. It is difficult to speak of nursing as a single occupation, because the training and work situations of nursing are so variable. Training in the United States can vary from a three-year hospital-nursing-school program to a four-year college program and even to programs leading to the doctorate (Davis et al. 1966). On the job, nurses in some American and European hospitals are preoccupied with bedside patient care and virtually all housekeeping tasks; however, in larger American teaching hospitals nurses are characteristically engaged in supervising the lesser personnel who give bedside care and do the housekeeping. Furthermore, there are major differences in the organization of hospitals in which nurses work: in most hospitals throughout the world the medical staff constitutes the only significant hierarchy, but in some of the larger American hospitals the medical hierarchy is paralleled by that of a nonmedical administrative staff. In the latter case the nurse's traditional subordination to the physician becomes complicated by subordination to another hierarchy. The two lines of authority may make quite different, even opposing, demands on her, thereby introducing into her work more strain than has existed traditionally (see Croog 1963).

However, the problem of two lines of authority in hospitals has been overemphasized, particularly in light of the fact that the development of an administrative hierarchy provides the nurse with a better opportunity for mobility than exists when a medical hierarchy alone is present. The possibility of moving up into an administrative hierarchy is common for many occupations, including medicine, but it seems particularly significant for paraprofessional occupations. By their nature such occupations are technically subordinate: success within the occupation does not remove that subordination, and movement into the superordinate occupation is not usually possible. Only by forsaking the particularistic skills of the occupation and moving into administrative positions can that subordination be escaped. While administrative positions may in fact not be superordinate to professional staff positions, they may at least run parallel to the professional positions and attain equality with them.

We can therefore understand why it is that nurses who are preoccupied with attaining a fully independent status attempt to pass over as "dirty work" the skills of bedside care (i.e., what was once called nursing) to lesser workers and to specialize in administrative work (see Hughes 1958). Recalling the problems involved in recruiting students who can become committed to nursing as a career and the attempt to create such commitment by emphasizing professionalism, we are led into an interesting dilemma: if women become committed to nursing by becoming "professionalizers," their commitment makes them prone to forsake the work for which they were recruited in the first place.

That dilemma, however, is more characteristic of nursing in the United States than elsewhere, reflecting a national emphasis on social mobility and professionalization. Furthermore, it refers to one of the better-established paramedical occupations and more particularly to those members of the occupation in the United States who have been trained in and work in the high-prestige, academically oriented institutions. As such, it is hardly representative of the total range of paramedical occupations and their dilemmas. The cross-national comparison presented by William Glaser (1963) suggests that the more common problems of paramedical occupations are not really represented by American nursing studies. What is needed most is insight into the less trained, less mobile occupations. Unfortunately, about all we have to provide us with this insight are studies of attendants and aides in American mental hospitals.

The attendant.   The essential problem posed by the hospital attendant, and presumably by other relatively untrained personnel in similar positions in the division of labor, is his failure to satisfy the expectations of his professional supervisors. This difficulty may be the more important because the attendant is in the most continuous and intimate contact with the patient and therefore may in fact have greater influence on the patient than the supervising professionals. Thus, his "custodial" orientation to his patients is deplored, and a more "therapeutic" orientation is expected.

The cause of the attendant's deficiencies seems to stem from at least two sources. First, his job is, in the most immediate sense, one of keeping order—minimizing dirt, destruction or waste of property, and personal injury and allowing housekeeping, therapeutic, and other services to be carried out on a predictable and efficient schedule. In the nature of the case this is a custodial responsibility, requiring something of a custodial attitude. If health institutions are to be run relatively economically, such an attitude on the part of those responsible for the hour-by-hour care of resident patients seems necessary and inevitable.

It is the second element that is more variable— the way in which the attendant perceives his patients, their illness, and his relationship to them. Almost by definition, as a paramedical worker without formal training, the attendant is likely to adopt a view similar to that of the layman. The problem is not lay attitudes as such but *which* lay attitudes the attendant adopts. A great many studies of American state mental hospitals suggest that attendants adopt an attitude of punitiveness and contempt toward patients and of antagonism toward the expectations of the professional staff. Part of this attitude, as noted already, stems from the job the attendant has to do, as well as from the feeling that the more remote professional staff does not really understand how difficult it is to keep order or even how to keep order. Another part, however, seems to reflect more than anything else the average "unenlightened" American layman's conception of the mentally ill (see Strauss et al. 1964).

Attendants from other cultures may have entirely different conceptions of the mentally ill and behave quite differently, as Caudill's analysis of the *tsukisoi* in Japan (1961) and Parsons' discussion of a Neapolitan hospital (1959) suggest. Even in the United States, when the illness involved is not as stigmatized as mental illness, lay attitudes of unskilled aides can be supportive rather than punitive, sympathetic rather than hostile. In this sense, precisely what is "unprofessional" about such lower-order workers can be as much a virtue as a vice.

Indeed, that same less-professional character

enables the paramedical worker to accomplish what the professional cannot, that is, the paramedical worker can draw into treatment patients who would otherwise be evasive and hostile to organized health services. Many studies from around the world, particularly those summarized by Simmons (1958), indicate that patients of humbler origins than that of physicians feel more comfortable dealing with such paramedical workers as nurses, feldshers, and midwives, who are closer to their own class and culture. Furthermore, lower-status patients seem more easily "educated" by paramedical personnel than by physicians, not only because they can enter into rapport more easily but also because they are more prone to "speak the same language" and to adjust themselves to the patient's expectations.

This lesser social distance from patients seems to be particularly critical in circumstances where the contact between patient and health worker is voluntary and casual, rather than forced and desperate, and where status differences are quite marked, linguistically, culturally, and socially. Indeed, it appears that it is the need on the part of lower-status patients for consultants who are more nearly equal to them and who operate in a manner compatible with their culture that modern irregular practitioners have risen to serve. To the extent that paramedical personnel become professionalized, they may lose their advantage in dealing with lower-status patients. However, to the extent that the paramedical worker's success with those patients is predicated on lay attitudes, his relations with supervising professionals are certain to be problematic. This is one of the major dilemmas of paramedical work.

ELIOT FREIDSON

[*See also* MENTAL DISORDERS, TREATMENT OF, *article on* THE THERAPEUTIC COMMUNITY.]

BIBLIOGRAPHY

CAUDILL, WILLIAM 1961 Around the Clock Patient Care in Japanese Psychiatric Hospitals: The Role of the *tsukisoi. American Sociological Review* 26:204–214.

CORWIN, RONALD G.; and TAVES, MARVIN J. 1963 Nursing and Other Health Professions. Pages 187–212 in Howard Freeman et al., *Handbook of Medical Sociology.* Englewood Cliffs, N.J.: Prentice-Hall. → A review of many American studies of nursing.

CROOG, SIDNEY H. 1963 Interpersonal Relations in Medical Settings. Pages 241–271 in Howard Freeman et al., *Handbook of Medical Sociology.* Englewood Cliffs, N.J.: Prentice-Hall. → A review of studies of interoccupational relations in American hospitals.

DAVIS, FRED et al. 1966 Problems and Issues in Collegiate Nursing Education. Pages 138–175 in Fred Davis (editor), *The Nursing Profession: Five Sociological Essays.* New York: Wiley.

FREIDSON, ELIOT 1961/1962 The Sociology of Medicine: A Trend Report and Bibliography. *Current Sociology* 10/11:123–192. → Contains a brief review of the field and a fully annotated and classified international bibliography.

GLASER, WILLIAM A. 1963 American and Foreign Hospitals: Some Sociological Comparisons. Pages 37–72 in Eliot Freidson (editor), *The Hospital in Modern Society.* New York: Free Press. → A sketch of the different international settings in which paramedical personnel work.

GLASER, WILLIAM A. 1966 Nursing Leadership and Policy: Some Cross-national Comparisons. Pages 1–59 in Fred Davis (editor), *The Nursing Profession: Five Sociological Essays.* New York: Wiley.

HUGHES, EVERETT C. 1958 *Men and Their Work.* Glencoe, Ill.: Free Press. → Seminal essays on the study of occupations, many referring to paramedical and medical workers.

KING, LESTER S. 1958 *The Medical World of the Eighteenth Century.* Univ. of Chicago Press. → Contains a few excellent essays on interoccupational relations in English medicine of the sixteenth through the eighteenth centuries.

PARSONS, A. 1959 Some Comparative Observations on Ward Social Structure: Southern Italy, England and the United States. *Ospedale psichiatrico* 2:3–23.

SIGERIST, HENRY E. 1935 The History of Medical Licensure. *Journal of the American Medical Association* 104:1057–1060.

SIMMONS, OZZIE G. 1958 *Social Status and Public Health.* Pamphlet No. 13. New York: Social Science Research Council.

STRAUSS, ANSELM 1966 The Structure and Ideology of American Nursing: An Interpretation. Pages 60–180 in Fred Davis (editor), *The Nursing Profession: Five Sociological Essays.* New York: Wiley.

STRAUSS, ANSELM et al. 1964 *Psychiatric Ideologies and Institutions.* New York: Free Press.

TURNER, ERNEST S. 1959 *Call the Doctor.* New York: St. Martins. → A social history of medicine in England, somewhat popular, but containing more data on practice and practitioners than conventional academic studies.

WARDWELL, WALTER I. 1963 Limited, Marginal and Quasi-practitioners. Pages 213–239 in Howard Freeman et al., *Handbook of Medical Sociology.* Englewood Cliffs, N.J.: Prentice-Hall. → A review of American materials on pharmacists, dentists, podiatrists, optometrists, clinical psychologists, osteopaths, chiropractors, and others.

MEDICAL PSYCHOLOGY
See CLINICAL PSYCHOLOGY.

MEDICAL SOCIOLOGY
See EPIDEMIOLOGY; HEALTH; ILLNESS; MEDICAL CARE; MEDICAL PERSONNEL; MENTAL DISORDERS, TREATMENT OF, *article on* THE THERAPEUTIC COMMUNITY; MENTAL HEALTH, *article on* THE CONCEPT; PUBLIC HEALTH. *Related material may be found under* OCCUPATIONS AND CAREERS; PROFESSIONS.

MEINECKE, FRIEDRICH

Friedrich Meinecke (1862–1954) was the most important German historian to follow Ranke and Burckhardt. He developed Dilthey's concept of history of ideas; he followed the philosophy of historicism, first outlined by Ernst Troeltsch and Benedetto Croce, to its logical conclusion; and finally, he achieved a synthesis of historical thought and political action by becoming one of the moral leaders in Germany's return to democracy after 1945.

Sources of thought.   Meinecke was born in the town of Salzwedel in Prussian Saxony but was brought up in Berlin in solid, middle-class surroundings. As a student, he was stirred by the personality of Bismarck and influenced by the sense of discipline and courage found in the Prussian state. But Meinecke was impressed by the classical humanism of German literature and music, poetry, and philosophy as well as by the spirit of Potsdam.

After leaving the Gymnasium, Meinecke entered the University of Berlin, determined to become a historian. There he was initiated into the techniques of historical methodology which Leopold von Ranke and his school had perfected. Meinecke accepted not only their methods but also their general frame of reference; i.e., that the proper subject of study for the historian is conflict among the great powers. He attended the lectures of Johann G. Droysen and Wilhelm Dilthey; Heinrich von Sybel and Heinrich von Treitschke directed his scholarly pursuits.

A speech defect from which he suffered throughout his life made Meinecke choose the career of secluded archivist rather than academic teacher, and in "this dusty trade" he felt at home for many years. Among his fellow archivists was one of the masters of institutional and comparative history, Otto Hintze, who exercised considerable influence on Meinecke. Although Meinecke was shy and withdrawn by nature, his special gifts were soon recognized. In 1893 he was asked to become editor of the *Historische Zeitschrift*, Germany's most important historical review.

History of ideas.   In these early years of apprenticeship, Meinecke was already concerned with the world of political ideas. He formulated the task of the historian in this manner: "Ideas, carried and transformed by living personalities, [constitute] the canvas of historical life" (*Erlebtes . . .* p. 117). This sentence represents the core of Meinecke's *Ideengeschichte*. He first put this conviction to the test when he wrote the biography

(1896–1899) of Hermann von Boyen, the Prussian minister of war who, in 1814, introduced military conscription. It was a pioneering attempt to make the arid facts of military history a part of the history of ideas.

Meinecke's biography established Boyen's niche in history and Meinecke's own reputation as one of the most promising talents in Germany's academic world. His appointment as professor of modern European history at Strasbourg in 1901 was evidence of his immediate recognition. There, in the southwestern corner of Germany, Meinecke encountered some of the best minds then active in that country: Max Weber, Ernst Troeltsch, Heinrich Rickert, and many others, and they made him aware of the limitations of his earlier perspectives. One of Meinecke's characteristics was his never-failing capacity for growth; in Strasbourg, and after 1908 in Freiburg, he shed much of his Prussian parochialism.

For more than a decade Meinecke remained fascinated by the problems and paradoxes of German history, especially the years from 1789 to 1848. In his next work, *Weltbürgertum und Nationalstaat* (1908), he endeavored to show how cosmopolitanism and nationalism had become deeply intertwined in the complex development of nineteenth-century Germany. He showed how both elements could be found in the ideas of Fichte, Novalis, Schlegel, Hegel, and Ranke, and how early German nationalism was made up of politically inconsistent cultural components. As Meinecke saw it, the universalistic tendencies of German thinkers were put to the test in 1848, and the revolution failed because of the incapacity of many Germans to come to grips with the realities of power politics. In this perspective, Bismarck and what he stood for became essential to the German quest for national unity. Hegel, Ranke, and Bismarck were the great liberators who freed the German mind from its romantic mists and created a realistic attitude toward the state.

Meinecke thus traced the philosophical and literary origins of the ideology of the nation-state and went beyond the traditional borderlines of political history. His works were soon recognized as masterpieces in a new field, the biography of ideas or, as it were, of two ideas. He was at his best when analyzing the major polarities in Western thought: order and freedom, nationalism and universalism, power and ethics, "is" and "ought," uniqueness and recurrence. He became the historian of political ideas par excellence, founding a new school of historical thought, and developing a unique style—

subtle, sensitive, and highly expressive of the countless variations and mutations which political ideas produce as they develop.

In Freiburg, Meinecke moved into the political arena for the first time. Abandoning the conservative leanings of his earlier years, he joined the right wing of the liberal party, the National Liberals. His goal was the widening of the foundation of the nation-state to include the ever-growing masses of industrial labor. His initial attempt was timorous and lacking in energy; he approved of representative government, not as an end in itself, but as a means to an end—that of enabling Germany to play her role as a world power.

The nature and justification of power. In 1913 Meinecke accepted an appointment at the University of Berlin. At the outbreak of World War I he was at first uncritically committed to Germany's imperialistic aspirations. Only slowly did it dawn on him that this conflict harbored consequences surpassing by far the significance of previous engagements between feuding European nations. As the horizon around Germany grew darker, however, Meinecke's perceptions became more piercing. His keen political analysis and counsel, in turn, began to be sought after by the more thoughtful statesmen of Germany; Richard von Kühlmann, secretary of state in the Foreign Office, and Theobald von Bethmann-Hollweg, the hapless chancellor, discussed with Meinecke the unsolved problems of Germany's domestic situation and the chances for a negotiated peace. He began to work for a peace by compromise and without territorial gains for any of the great powers. He also bent his efforts toward more equitable political representation for the working class. But although his advice was heard in many quarters, it was little heeded.

More important than Meinecke's remedies for specific problems, however, was his emergent comprehension that the nation-state in which he had so strongly believed was no longer a sufficient answer to the political exigencies of the twentieth century. New questions crowded his mind: what was power? what was Germany's relationship to the rest of the Western world? what lay behind the great conflict that seemed to be splitting the Occident? Meinecke could not accept the Marxist–Leninist interpretation of the crisis, since world revolution and the revolt of the masses appeared to him as the predominant threats to Western civilization. On the other hand, by the time the war ended he realized that the old, aristocratic Germany was doomed. The downfall of imperial Germany in 1918 filled him with grief but not with despair. He accepted the Weimar Republic as a necessity and was ready to work for a new democratic Germany.

Meinecke's doubts about the nature and justification of power, aroused by World War I, were crystallized in his book *Machiavellism* (1924). Meinecke admitted that it was the extreme manifestations of power politics during World War I that had opened his eyes to the dangers of politics divorced from any ethical code. The Treaty of Versailles only served to deepen the lesson; it led him into a historical investigation of theories of the nature and function of power in human life, beginning with Machiavelli, through Bodin and Rohan, to Frederick the Great, Hegel, Ranke, and Treitschke. There are those who consider the book to be a history of Machiavellianism; others view it as an attempt to surmount the teachings of Machiavelli. Neither of these interpretations hits the mark; more nearly, the book is Machiavellianism considered with a guilty conscience. Meinecke could not subscribe to Burckhardt's and Acton's thoroughgoing condemnation of power; neither could he any longer assent to the idolatry of power found in Hegel and Treitschke. The result is a dichotomy, a separation of ethics and power that defies reconciliation: the creed of the statesman, said Meinecke, must embody both the interest of the state and the fundamental moral principles of mankind.

Historicism. There is a mood of philosophical reflection in *Machiavellism* which foreshadows an even more complex enterprise—a study of the genesis of historical thought. In Berlin, Meinecke lived in close contact with Troeltsch, who considered the historical outlook in its most comprehensive sense as characteristic of the twentieth century. In 1922 Troeltsch published *Der Historismus und seine Probleme*. After Troeltsch's death in 1923, his work on this subject was continued by Meinecke. However, Meinecke's perspective was somewhat narrower: as a historian he was more interested in the origins of historical thought than in its significance for the future of Western civilization. In 1936 he published *Die Entstehung des Historismus* ("The Origins of Historicism"). It is the third of his significant contributions to the history of ideas, completed when Meinecke was well past his seventieth year but dating back to very early reflections on the element of individuality, or uniqueness, in historical life.

German historians had long been hostile to positivistic attempts to reduce human development to "scientific laws"; such attempts, they contended, violate two of the most precious elements in history: spontaneity and uniqueness. Meinecke shared this interpretation of human life and traced it from the late seventeenth century to the twentieth. He defined "historicism" in the following manner: "the essence of historicism consists in replacing a general and abstract contemplation of human affairs by an individual one" (*eine individualisierende Betrachtung*) ([1936] 1959, p. 2). He did not hesitate to call this concentration on uniqueness the highest achievement in the contemplation of things human. This was an extreme stand, denying both the sociological ideal-type (as Max Weber conceived it) and the ethical norm of universal validity.

Die Entstehung des Historismus begins with an analysis of Shaftesbury, Leibniz, and Vico; it moves into an evaluation of the historiography of the Enlightenment, with special emphasis on Voltaire, Montesquieu, Hume, and Gibbon. From English preromanticism it switches to Möser, Winckelmann, Herder, and Goethe, and it ends with an epilogue on Ranke. Critics have pointed out, with justice, that this history of historicism ends at the moment when the movement really came into its own and that it describes its growth but not its flowering. Likewise, the problem of relativism (inherent in the idea of uniqueness) versus absolute and perennial values is stated by Meinecke but by no means elucidated or solved. Nevertheless, the book marks an important advance in the long discussion among historians, social scientists, and philosophers of the proper subject and the meaning of history.

The German catastrophe. Meinecke might have tried to answer some of these questions more conclusively had it not been for the general conditions of his time. When this book on historicism was published, Hitler had triumphed in Germany. Meinecke had fought with courage against the rise of National Socialism, both in the press and from his chair at the University of Berlin. Some of his close associates were ousted and silenced. Many of Meinecke's students were obliged to flee the country, and in 1935 Meinecke relinquished the editorship of the *Historische Zeitschrift*. But he was perhaps most oppressed by the foreboding of a second world war. His correspondence clearly reveals that he was one of the few German scholars who never compromised with the authorities and who had the courage to state frankly in his letters what he was not allowed to say in public.

An indefatigable worker, Meinecke spent these years working on his memoirs; they hold a certain charm but do not rank with his contributions to intellectual history. The war did not spare him: he suffered the same privations, the hunger, and bombings, as millions of others. Finally he fled from Berlin, shortly before it fell to the Russians. Once more his mind turned to the enigma of German history, especially to the questions that have puzzled so many observers: how could the advent of Hitler be explained? and further, to what extent was Germany responsible for the greatest retrogression in European civilization since the days of the Black Death?

Meinecke's answers were given in a small book, *The German Catastrophe* (1946). He began his analysis with the statement that National Socialism must be understood against the background of our entire Western civilization, against the conflict between the old society and the new industrial masses. And he did not spare those forces which had once elicited his praise: the Prussian state and the German bourgeoisie. The Prussian state, he wrote, had permeated the nation with its militaristic attitude; the bourgeoisie had closed its mind to democratic forms of government, which alone could have brought a reconciliation between itself and the working class. He accounted for the success of a demoniac figure like Hitler by indicating the German social interests which had tried to manipulate the "revolution of nihilism" only to become its victims.

This new approach, an attempt to combine intellectual and social history, is also apparent in other essays that Meinecke wrote after 1945, especially in his comparison of Burckhardt and Ranke (1948a) and in his appraisal of the revolution of 1848 (1948b). They reveal, if nothing else, an indomitable will to continue the task of the historian in a world changed beyond recognition from the well-grounded security into which Meinecke had been born.

When a large part of the student body revolted against the oppression of the communist-controlled University of Berlin, it found in Meinecke the leader to head an independent institution—the Free University of Berlin. To have heralded and ushered in so momentous an action is surely one of Meinecke's titles to lasting fame. His contributions to modern historiography have proved surprisingly durable and have reached well beyond the confines of Germany. They have been emulated, corrected, and improved in Austria, Italy, and, more especially, in the United States, where some of his students carry on his work.

GERHARD MASUR

[*See also* HISTORY; NATIONALISM; POWER; *and the biographies of* BURCKHARDT; CROCE; DILTHEY; HEGEL; HINTZE; MACHIAVELLI; RANKE; TREITSCHKE; TROELTSCH.]

WORKS BY MEINECKE

1896–1899 *Das Leben des Generalfeldmarschalls Hermann von Boyen.* 2 vols. Stuttgart: Cotta.

(1908) 1962 *Weltbürgertum und Nationalstaat: Studien zur Genesis des deutschen Nationalstaates.* Edited with an introduction by Hans Herzfeld. Munich: Oldenbourg.

(1924) 1962 *Machiavellism: The Doctrine of Raison d'État and Its Place in Modern History.* New York: Praeger. → Originally published as *Die Idee der Staatsräson in der neueren Geschichte.* Contains a general introduction to Friedrich Meinecke's work by Werner Stark.

(1936) 1959 *Werke.* Volume 3: Die Entstehung des Historismus. Munich: Oldenbourg. → The translation of the extract in the text was provided by Gerhard Masur.

(1946) 1950 *The German Catastrophe: Reflections and Recollections.* Cambridge, Mass.: Harvard Univ. Press. → First published in German. A paperback edition was published in 1963 by Beacon.

(1948*a*) 1954 Ranke and Burckhardt. Pages 141–156 in Hans Kohn (editor), *German History: Some New German Views.* Boston: Beacon. → First published in German.

(1948*b*) 1951 Year 1848 in German History: Reflections on a Centenary. Pages 668–686 in Herman Ausubel (editor), *Making of Modern Europe.* Volume 2: Waterloo to the Atomic Age. New York: Dryden. → First published as "1848: Eine Säkularbetrachtung."

Erlebtes: 1862–1919. Stuttgart: Koehler, 1964. → The translation of the extract in the text was provided by Gerhard Masur.

Werke. 6 vols. Munich: Oldenbourg, 1957–1962. → Volume 1: *Die Idee der Staatsräson in der neueren Geschichte.* Volume 2: *Politische Schriften und Reden.* Volume 3: *Die Entstehung des Historismus.* Volume 4: *Zur Theorie und Philosophie der Geschichte.* Volume 5: *Weltbürgertum und Nationalstaat: Studien zur Genesis des deutschen Nationalstaates.* Volume 6: *Ausgewählter Briefwechsel.*

SUPPLEMENTARY BIBLIOGRAPHY

STERLING, RICHARD W. 1958 *Ethics in a World of Power: The Political Ideas of Friedrich Meinecke.* Princeton Univ. Press. → Contains a bibliography of Friedrich Meinecke's writings and books and articles about him.

MEMORY

See FORGETTING *and* LEARNING.

MENGER, CARL

Carl Menger (1840–1921), economic theorist and founder of the Austrian school of marginal analysis, was both the most influential and the least read of the major figures who gave economic theory the shape it preserved from about 1885 to 1935. There is little doubt that it was his immediate disciples who cast microeconomic theory into the form which, in its essentials, it still retains. Of the three founders of modern utility analysis, he alone not only based his work on a long tradition and presented the outlines of his theory in a form which for some time could not be bettered, but also succeeded in creating a school which continued to develop his ideas. Menger exerted a widespread influence, mainly through his avowed disciples in many countries, despite the fact that his two main books were not reprinted for 50 years or translated into English for 79 years. His work also had an effect on the only important rival school of the period—the neoclassical Cambridge tradition. At an early stage, Alfred Marshall, founder of the Cambridge school, had evidently studied Menger's work much more assiduously than is suggested by the few references to Menger (most of which were dropped from later editions) in Marshall's *Principles.* (Marshall's personal copy of Menger's *Grundsätze,* with a detailed marginal commentary in Marshall's hand, is preserved in the Marshall Library at Cambridge.)

Menger was born in Neu Sandec, Galicia (then in the Austrian part of Poland), the descendant of a professional family that had earned the prefix "von" (Menger himself dropped it in early adulthood). In the well-stocked library of his father, a practicing lawyer, Menger and his two brothers became acquainted early with the literature on social and economic questions; one brother, Anton Menger, was a legal philosopher and historian of socialist doctrine.

Menger studied law at the universities of Vienna and Prague and finally took his doctorate at the University of Cracow in 1867. Apparently he had done some journalistic work in Vienna and Lemberg before taking the degree, and afterward he entered the press section of the prime minister's office in Vienna, a position which was frequently a springboard to high public office. In that position, apparently as a result of having to write market reports, Menger developed an interest in price theory. The recent publication of his annotations to Rau's *Grundsätze der Volkswirthschaftslehre* ([1870] 1963) suggests that it was mainly his critical analysis of this textbook exposition of classical doctrine that led Menger, from 1867 on, to develop his own value theory. In his extensive reading, Menger must have found ample material in the early nineteenth-century German and French economic literature on which to build a fully developed utility analysis. (The utility tradition was not as strongly preserved in the English literature.) It now appears that the literature on which he was able to draw included also the work of an Austrian economist, J. Kudler (whose textbook, *Die Grundlehren der Volkswirthschaft* 1846, he had probably used at the university), and one work by Cournot. Menger's sources, however, did not include the work of the author who had the most completely anticipated him, Gossen's *Entwickelung der Gesetze des menschlichen Verkehrs . . .* , published in 1854.

The results of Menger's studies appeared in his *Principles of Economics* (1871), the work on which his fame mainly rests. Described as the "first, general part" of an intended comprehensive work on economic theory, it remained his sole major publication in this field during his lifetime. In somewhat copious but always clear language, it provided a much more thorough account of the relations between utility, value, and price than is found in any of the works of Jevons and Walras, who at about the same time laid the foundation of the "marginal revolution" in economics.

The book gained for Menger first a lecturership and, in 1873, the position of extraordinary professor at the University of Vienna. For some years he published nothing more, apparently because of his appointment in 1876 as tutor to the 18-year-old crown prince of Austria, the ill-fated Archduke Rudolf. For two years Menger accompanied Rudolf on extensive travels through Germany, France, and the British Isles. He seems to have assisted the crown prince in the composition of a pamphlet (anonymously published in 1878) which attempted a critical examination of the role played by the higher Austrian aristocracy. The pamphlet caused some stir when in 1906, 17 years after the death of the archduke, his authorship was discovered.

The real beginning of Menger's long and very effective career as a teacher came with his appointment in 1879 to a full professorship at the University of Vienna. During the next 24 years he expended most of his energy on his general lectures to law students (which he appears to have rewritten every year), and he was particularly attentive to those few students who voluntarily chose economics as their field of special work. His teaching was interrupted only twice by bursts of literary activity. The first of these was connected with his second major book, *Problems of Economics and Sociology* (1883). Here he undertook to vindicate the importance of theory in the social sciences. This was an effort that seemed necessary to him in view of the complete indifference or even hostility which most of his German colleagues, influenced by the antitheoretical attitude of the "younger historical school" in economics, had shown toward his

attempt in the *Principles* to reconstruct economic theory.

To understand the aim of the *Problems* and the nature of the great controversy to which it gave rise, it is necessary to appreciate the character of the school against which it was directed. The "younger historical school" is somewhat misnamed: unlike von Savigny and the older historical school of jurisprudence, or even Roscher and the "older historical school" in economics, this "younger" school was not interested in history as the study of unique events but regarded historical study as the empirical approach to an eventual theoretical explanation of social institutions. Through the study of historical development it hoped to arrive at the laws of development of social wholes, from which, in turn, could be deduced the historical necessities governing each phase of this development. This was the sort of positivist–empiricist approach which was later adopted by American institutionalists (differing from similar, more recent efforts only in that it made little use of statistical technique), and which is better described (as by Popper) as historicism.

It was against this use of history as a means of discovering empirical laws that Menger undertook to defend what he considered to be the proper function of theory—reconstructing the structure of social wholes from their parts by the procedure called methodological individualism by Schumpeter, or the "compositive method" by Menger himself. It is essentially what today is called microtheory. Menger was greatly interested in history and the genesis of institutions, and he was anxious mainly to emphasize the different nature of the task of theory and the task of history proper and to prevent a confusion of their methods. The distinction, as he elaborated it, considerably influenced the later work of Rickert and Max Weber. Perhaps the most important part of his discussion was the clear recognition, first, that the object of all social theory is the tracing of what are now usually called the unintended consequences of individual actions (Menger's term was the *unbeabsichtigte Resultante*), and, second, that in this effort the genetic and the functional aspects could not be separated ([1883] 1963, pp. 163, 180, 182, 188). In expounding and illustrating this view he went far beyond the limit of economics and dealt particularly with the genesis of law.

The nature of the dispute has often been confused by the fact that Menger, in arguing against what he regarded as the dominant pseudohistorical school in economics, maintained ideas which had reached him through the historical school in law.

These ideas can be traced back to Mandeville, David Hume, and the later eighteenth-century Scottish philosophers, although the degree to which Menger was directly acquainted with these eighteenth-century sources is not clear. It is worth noting that Menger always had a great interest in the history of economic theory and used it with much didactic skill in his lectures as an introduction to the problems of modern economic theory.

The *Problems* was unfavorably and condescendingly reviewed by Gustav Schmoller, the head of the younger historical school of economists; Menger replied to Schmoller's criticism in a passionate brochure, *Die Irrthümer des Historismus in der deutschen Nationalökonomie* (1884). This was the beginning of the celebrated *Methodenstreit* (dispute on method). Emotions ran high; younger men on both sides joined in; and the dispute produced a cleavage between German and Austrian economics, traces of which were to be felt for decades. In a number of articles during the following few years Menger dealt mainly with problems arising out of the dispute, except for his only other contribution to pure economic theory, the article "Zur Theorie des Kapitals," published in 1888 (see *Collected Works*, vol. 3, pp. 133–183).

Menger emerged a second time from his academic seclusion in 1892 to join the discussion on the reform of the Austrian currency. His active participation in discussions of policy was foreshadowed in the very same year by his article on money (see *Collected Works*, vol. 4, pp. 1–2) for the new German encyclopedia of political science. The article was itself a substantial treatise, which devoted much space to the evolution of money but also emphasized the factors determining the amount of money held by individuals, and which laid the foundations for a theory of the value of money on which later Austrian economists, such as Wieser, Von Mises, and Weiss were able to build. No less important, however, are his memorandum and his oral evidence to the Austrian currency commission and various articles which he published in 1892 and in the next few years.

But while such special occasions led Menger to literary production, his teaching appears to have precluded progress on the great treatise which he hoped would replace his first work. Therefore, in 1903, he prematurely resigned his professorship in order to devote himself entirely to this task. But although he continued to work on it during the remaining 18 years of his life and at one stage seems to have come close to his goal, he continued his efforts after his powers had begun to fail, with the result that he left nothing that was readily publishable at his death. His son included part of the manuscript material in a second edition of the *Grundsätze*, which appeared in 1923. But the publication of more of the manuscript material has proved to be a very difficult task which so far has not been accomplished.

Menger built up over the years one of the greatest private libraries in the field of social science, which in 1911 he estimated at something like 25,000 volumes. The sections dealing with the social sciences and anthropology were sold after his death to the Commercial University (now Hitotsubashi University) in Tokyo, which published a catalogue of it in two parts, one in 1926 and the other in 1955.

In an assessment of Menger's influence it should be noted that his ideas were introduced into anthropology by Richard Thurnwald, one of his students.

FRIEDRICH A. VON HAYEK

[*For the historical context of Menger's work, see* ECONOMIC THOUGHT, *articles on* THE HISTORICAL SCHOOL, THE AUSTRIAN SCHOOL, *and* THE INSTITUTIONAL SCHOOL; *and the biographies of* COURNOT; GOSSEN; JEVONS; SCHMOLLER; WALRAS. *For discussion of the subsequent development of Menger's ideas, see* UTILITY; *and the biographies of* THURNWALD; VON MISES, LUDWIG; WEBER, MAX; WIESER.]

WORKS BY MENGER

(1870) 1963 *Carl Mengers erster Entwurf zu seinem Hauptwerk* Grundsätze *geschrieben als Anmerkungen zu den* Grundsätzen der Volkswirthschaftslehre *von Karl Heinrich Rau.* With an Introduction by Yuzo Yamada. Tokyo: Bibliothek der Hitotsubashi Universität. → Written in 1870 and published posthumously.

(1871) 1950 *Principles of Economics: First General Part.* Edited by James Dingwall and Bert F. Hoselitz, with an Introduction by Frank H. Knight. Glencoe, Ill.: Free Press. → First published as *Grundsätze der Volkswirthschaftslehre.* The second complete German edition was published in 1923.

(1883) 1963 *Problems of Economics and Sociology.* Edited with an introduction by Louis Schneider. Urbana: Univ. of Illinois Press. → First published as *Untersuchungen über die Methode der Socialwissenschaften und der politischen Oekonomie insbesondere.*

1884 *Die Irrthümer des Historismus in der deutschen Nationalökonomie.* Vienna: Holder.

1892 *Beitrage zur Währungsfrage in Oesterreich–Ungarn.* Jena (Germany): Fischer.

Carl Mengers Zusätze zu Grundzüge der Volkswirthschaftslehre. With an introduction by Emil Kauder. Tokyo: Bibliothek der Hitotsubashi Universität, 1961. → Published posthumously.

The Collected Works of Carl Menger. 4 vols. Series of Reprints of Scarce Tracts in Economic and Political Science, No. 17–20. London School of Economics and Political Science, 1933–1936. → Volume 1: *Grundsätze der Volkswirtschaftslehre* (1871) 1934. Volume 2: *Untersuchungen über die Methode der Socialwis-*

senschaften . . . , (1883) 1933. Volume 3: *Kleinere Schriften zur Methode und Geschichte der Volkswirthschaftslehre* (1884–1915) 1935. Volume 4: *Schriften über Geldtheorie und Währungspolitik* . . . (1889–1893) 1936. Contains a biographical introduction by von Hayek in Volume 1, and a complete list of Menger's known writings in Volume 4 1933–1936.

SUPPLEMENTARY BIBLIOGRAPHY

ANTONELLI, ÉTIENNE 1953 Léon Walras et Carl Menger à travers leur correspondance. *Économie appliquée* 6:269–287.

BLOCH, HENRI S. 1937 *La théorie des besoins de Carl Menger.* Paris: Librairie Générale de Droit et de Jurisprudence.

BLOCH, HENRI S. 1940 Carl Menger: The Founder of the Austrian School. *Journal of Political Economy* 48: 428–433.

FEILBOGEN, S. 1911 L'école autrichienne d'économie politique. *Journal des économistes* Sixth Series 31:50–57, 214–230, 375–388.

HOWEY, RICHARD S. 1960 *The Rise of the Marginal Utility School: 1870–1889.* Lawrence: Univ. of Kansas Press.

KAUDER, EMIL 1953 The Retarded Acceptance of the Marginal Utility Theory. *Quarterly Journal of Economics* 67:564–575.

KAUDER, EMIL 1957 Intellectual and Political Roots of the Older Austrian School. *Zeitschrift für Nationalökonomie* 17:411–425.

KAUDER, EMIL 1959 Menger and His Library. *Keizai kenkyu* (Economic Review), Hitotsubashi University 10:58–64.

KAUDER, EMIL 1961 Freedom and Economic Theory: Second Research Report on Menger's Unpublished Paper. *Hitotsubashi Journal of Economics* 2:67–82.

KAUDER, EMIL 1962 Aus Mengers nachgelassenen Papieren. *Weltwirtschaftliches Archiv* 89:1–28.

SCHUMPETER, JOSEPH A. (1921) 1960 Carl Menger: 1840–1921. Pages 80–90 in Joseph A. Schumpeter, *Ten Great Economists, From Marx to Keynes.* New York: Oxford Univ. Press. → First published in German in Volume 1 of *Zeitschrift für Volkswirtschaft und Sozialpolitik,* New Series.

STIGLER, GEORGE J. 1941 *Production and Distribution Theories: The Formative Period.* New York: Macmillan. → See especially pages 134–157 on "Carl Menger."

WEISS, FRANZ X. 1924 Zur zweiten Auflage von Carl Mengers Grundsätzen. *Zeitschrift für Volkswirtschaft und Sozialpolitik* New Series 4:134–154.

WIESER, FRIEDRICH 1923 Karl Menger. Volume 1, pages 84–92 in *Neue österreichische Biographie: 1815–1918.* Vienna: Wiener Drucke.

YEAGER, LELAND B. 1954 The Methodology of Henry George and Carl Menger. *American Journal of Economics and Sociology* 13:233–238.

MENTAL ABILITY

See INTELLIGENCE AND INTELLIGENCE TESTING.

MENTAL DISORDERS

General considerations underlying the study of mental disorders are discussed in the articles under this heading. Concepts of direct relevance are also discussed in ANXIETY; DEFENSE MECHANISMS; STRESS. *General categories of mental disorders are reviewed in the articles* NEUROSIS; PSYCHOSIS; *specific disorders are discussed in* CHARACTER DISORDERS; DEPRESSIVE DISORDERS; HYSTERIA; OBSESSIVE–COMPULSIVE DISORDERS; PARANOID REACTIONS; PHOBIAS; PSYCHOPATHIC PERSONALITY; PSYCHOSOMATIC ILLNESS; SCHIZOPHRENIA. *Methods of assessing mental disorders are discussed in* ELECTROENCEPHALOGRAPHY; INTERVIEWING, *article on* PERSONALITY APPRAISAL; PERSONALITY MEASUREMENT; PROJECTIVE METHODS. *The treatment of mental disorders is discussed under* CLINICAL PSYCHOLOGY; COUNSELING PSYCHOLOGY; INTERVIEWING, *article on* THERAPEUTIC INTERVIEWING; MENTAL DISORDERS, TREATMENT OF; PSYCHIATRY; PSYCHOANALYSIS. *Social problems that can be considered as aspects of mental disorders are discussed in* DRINKING AND ALCOHOLISM; DRUGS; SEXUAL BEHAVIOR, *articles on* HOMOSEXUALITY *and* SEXUAL DEVIATION; SUICIDE.

I. GENETIC ASPECTS	*Eliot Slater*
II. ORGANIC ASPECTS	*Joseph M. Wepman*
III. BIOLOGICAL ASPECTS	*Joel Elkes*
IV. EPIDEMIOLOGY	*Ernest Gruenberg*
V. CHILDHOOD MENTAL DISORDERS	*Britton K. Ruebush*
VI. EXPERIMENTAL STUDY	*George Talland*

I
GENETIC ASPECTS

People who are related to one another by blood tend to resemble one another in, among other things, their mental make-up and their liability to mental illness. Both genetic and environmental factors may play a part in this resemblance. The most widely accepted view of the nature of the interaction between heredity and environment has been called the diathesis–stress theory (Rosenthal 1963). In its application to mental illness this view suggests that the susceptibility to mental illness, insofar as it is genetically based, varies along a continuum ranging from high to low extremes, most people clustering about an average of moderate susceptibility. Environmental stresses, also, vary from severe to slight. Accordingly, when a mental breakdown occurs, a combination of both factors is involved; thus, we should expect a high rate of breakdown among normal individuals subjected to severe stress, and a high rate also among very susceptible people placed under even mild stress. Such a quantitative relationship has been shown to hold in fact, e.g., in the neurotic illnesses of combat troops (Symonds 1943). Whether psychotic illnesses follow the same general law is a matter more difficult to decide.

Personality deviations and neurotic illness

Twin studies.   An important part of the work in the field of personality deviations and neurotic illness has been studies of twins. One-egg, or monozygotic (MZ), twins, whose entire genetic equipment is identical, are of the same sex and are very much alike in physical characteristics. Two-egg, or dizygotic (DZ), twins ordinarily resemble each other no more than any pair of brothers or sisters and are as likely to be of opposite sexes as of the same sex. As a rule only the same-sexed DZ twin pairs are taken by investigators for comparison with MZ pairs. Twin pairs are said to be concordant when it is found that the twin of a proband (index case) with a particular deviation also shows the same anomaly. Concordance rates are usually given as percentages. Genetic hypotheses lead one to suppose that concordance rates should be much higher in MZ than in DZ pairs and that variability within MZ pairs should be smaller than within DZ pairs. Table 1 lists the percentage of concordances found for a variety of conditions, in which the statistics are based on at least thirty pairs.

Criminality and delinquency.   Much effort has been put into the investigation of criminality and behavior disorder. The results of Rosanoff in juvenile delinquency are noteworthy (Rosanoff et al. 1934; 1941). There are high rates of concordance both in MZ and in DZ twin pairs, and little difference between them. This suggests that the similarity in the twins' behavior is due to common factors in their environment. It is at least possible that each of the twins constitutes part of the stress factor for his twin partner. The same suggestion arises from the observations of behavior disorder and neurotic traits in school children. Shields found that in these children the degree of neurotic reaction was more noticeably related to environmental factors than genetic constitution; the hereditary factor showed itself in the type of reaction (1954). [*See* CRIMINOLOGY; DELINQUENCY; PSYCHOPATHIC PERSONALITY.]

Adult neuroses.   Concordance rates are lower in neurotic adults, both in the MZ and in the DZ pairs. The greatly increased variability within both kinds of pairs can be put down to the much wider range of experience, and wider variety of stresses, to which adults are subjected.

Male homosexuality.   At the opposite extreme are Kallmann's findings of 100 per cent concordance in MZ pairs, as against 12 per cent concordance in DZ pairs, for male homosexuality. This would suggest that in these cases the genetic factors account for the greater part of the variance. Some caution in interpretation is needed, however. The importance that the genetic contribution acquires here may be due to the fact that there was a predominance of the more constitutional type of homosexual in the sample studied by Kallmann and his team. [*See* SEXUAL BEHAVIOR, *articles on* SEXUAL DEVIATION *and* HOMOSEXUALITY.]

Studies of relatives.   Attempts to estimate the importance of hereditary factors in causing neurotic illness have been made by investigating the frequency of such illnesses among the relatives of neurotic patients. Findings have varied greatly from observer to observer. One of the early workers, Brown (1942), started by investigating the first-degree relatives of patients who had been diagnosed as suffering from obsessional neurosis, anxiety neurosis, and hysteria, as well as those of a control group. Among the relatives of all groups he found individuals suffering from obsessional neurosis, anxiety neurosis, and hysteria, as well as from other personality deviations of a kind not easily named and classified. There were three significant findings: the relatives of the control group had much less psychiatric abnormality than the relatives of any of the other three groups; all three diagnoses were represented among the relatives of

Table 1 — Concordance rates for personality deviation and behavior disorders in monozygotic and same-sexed dizygotic twins

Deviation	Number of pairs	Investigator(s)	PER CENT OF CONCORDANCE MZ	DZ
Male homosexuality	63	Kallmann 1952	100	12
Adult crime	216	Lange 1929; Rosanoff et al. 1934; Kranz 1936; Stumpfl 1936; Borgstroem 1939	68	35
Juvenile delinquency	67	Rosanoff et al. 1934; 1941	85	75
Childhood behavior disorder	107	Rosanoff et al. 1934; 1941	87	43
Behavior disorder or marked neurotic traits in school children	41	Shields 1954	74	50
Neurosis, psychopathic personality	37	Slater 1953	25	14
Alcoholic addiction	82	Kaij 1960	65	30

Source: Shields & Slater 1960, p. 327, table 8.6.

all three patient groups; among those relatives who were classifiable under the three named diagnoses, it was found that there was a tendency for them to be in the same diagnostic category as the related patient. For example, of the nine obsessional relatives discovered, seven were related to the obsessional patients. This finding suggests a certain degree of specificity, which is best seen in the investigations which have been made on the relatives of obsessional patients (Luxenburger 1930; Lewis 1936; Rüdin 1953). Among the 100 parents of 50 obsessional patients Lewis found that 37 showed pronounced obsessional traits in one form or another; 21 per cent of the 206 siblings also showed obsessional traits. [See OBSESSIVE–COMPULSIVE DISORDERS.]

At the opposite pole are the findings in the relatives of patients diagnosed as suffering from "hysteria." The best family study was made by Ljungberg (1957), who found that among the fathers, brothers, and sons of hysterics, 2 per cent, 3 per cent, and 5 per cent respectively were themselves hysterics; and among the mothers, sisters, and daughters, 7 per cent, 6 per cent, and 7 per cent respectively. His observations also suggested that hysterical symptoms were not necessarily associated with hysterical personalities, and of the 363 hysterics whose personality structures were analyzed, 55 per cent were found to be nondeviant.

Similar conclusions were reached by the writer (Slater 1961) from a study of 24 pairs of twins, 12 MZ and 12 DZ, in which the proband had been diagnosed as suffering from hysteria. In none of these pairs was there a co-twin who had ever been diagnosed as suffering from hysteria, though abnormalities of personality and psychiatric illness were common. Among the relatives of these pairs the incidence of hysteria was even lower than in Ljungberg's material, and the anomalies found to be most noticeably in excess were manic–depressive and endogenous affective psychoses. [See HYSTERIA.]

It seems probable that environmental factors are more important than genetic ones in determining whether or not a man breaks down with a neurotic illness. But it would seem that genetic factors influence the predisposition to such breakdown, help to determine whether the personality is a stable one, and, in the event of breakdown, have a large effect on the type of symptoms which are likely to be shown.

Manic–depressive illness

The risk of affective psychoses in the first-degree relatives of manic–depressive patients is shown in

Table 2 — Per cent of manic–depressive disorders among relatives of manic–depressive patients

Investigator	NUMBER OF PROBANDS	NATURE OF RELATIONSHIP		
		Parents	Siblings	Children
Banse 1929	80	10.8	18.1	
Röll and Entres 1936	83	13.0		10.7
Slater 1938	138	15.5		15.2
Strömgren 1938	77	7.5	10.7	
Sjögren 1948	45	7.0	3.6	
Kallmann 1950	75	23.4	23.0	
Stenstedt 1952	216	7.4	12.3	9.4
Fonseca 1959	60	22.8	18.9	21.7

Table 2. It will be seen that there is much variation in the data reported by different observers. Nevertheless, these risk figures are all very much higher than would be expected of a sample taken from the general population, in which the incidence level is probably of the order of 0.4 per cent.

Approximately 15 per cent of the first-degree relatives of manic–depressives may themselves have affective disorders of the same generic group.

Single-gene explanation. One explanation suggests that there is a single dominant autosomal gene which predisposes a spontaneous variation in mood. Most people with such a tendency are likely to remain healthy throughout their lives, though their cyclothymic temperament may be clearly recognizable both to themselves and to their families. If such cyclothymic individuals are subjected to stresses, the spontaneous swing of mood into depression or elation may go so far and last so long that medical treatment becomes necessary; and then the patient may be stigmatized as a "manic–depressive." The genetic hypothesis proposes, in fact, to account for only a part of the causation. Environmental factors and threshold effects must also be playing a part. The theory requires that 50 per cent of the first-degree relatives of manic–depressives should be gene carriers; if only 15 per cent of the relatives show themselves as such, this can be put down to low penetrance of the gene. [See DEPRESSIVE DISORDERS.]

Polygenic explanation. A single-gene hypothesis, however, is not the only possibility; polygenic inheritance is an alternative explanation. Edwards (1960; 1963) has drawn attention to the fact that, in the case of common conditions, it is not easy to distinguish between the expected consequences of a single gene with diminished penetrance and of multifactorial inheritance with a threshold effect. Assuming that the predisposition to a condition, such as schizophrenia or diabetes, is quantitatively graded, with a normal distribution, Edwards suggests that when p = the frequency of the disorder, the incidence of the disorder in the first-degree relatives of persons suffering from the disorder will be approximately $\sqrt{p}$. If the frequency of manic–depressive illness in the general population is approximately 0.004, then the frequency of manic–depressive illness in the first-degree relatives of manic–depressives should be about 6 per cent to 7 per cent. The observations are about double that figure, but it is not possible to say that observation and expectation, on the multifactorial hypothesis, are irreconcilable.

Schizophrenia

Extensive investigations of the hereditary factor in schizophrenia have been made by Kallmann and his associates in the New York State Psychiatric Institute and Hospital (Columbia University). A synopsis of the results obtained is given in Table 3. These risk figures should be compared with the estimated risk of schizophrenia for a member of the general population of 0.9 per cent. Environmental effects show up: association with a schizophrenic proband in the same home virtually doubles the risk of schizophrenia for step-sibs and spouses; and there is a greater risk for the non-separated MZ co-twin of a schizophrenic than for an MZ co-twin who has lived apart from the proband for five years or more. However, the table also shows the risk of schizophrenia running up steeply with increasingly close degrees of blood relationship. In view of these figures it is difficult and, the writer feels, unrealistic to dispute the conclusion that genetic factors play a significant role in the causation of schizophrenia.

The risk figures published by Kallmann are somewhat higher than those obtained by other workers but are in the main reconcilable with them. The writer, for instance (Slater 1953), found a risk of

Table 3 — Per cent of risk of schizophrenia among relatives of schizophrenics

Nature of relationship	Per cent risk
Not related by blood, step-sibs	1.8
Not related by blood, spouses	2.1
First cousins	2.6
Nephews and nieces	3.9
Grandchildren	4.3
Half-sibs	7.1
Parents	9.2
Full-sibs	14.2
Dizygotic co-twins	14.5
DZ co-twins of same sex	17.6
Children with one schizophrenic parent	16.4
Children with two schizophrenic parents	68.1
Monozygotic co-twins	86.2
MZ co-twins living apart for at least 5 years	77.6
MZ co-twins not so separated	91.5

Source: Adapted from Kallmann 1950.

76 per cent for the MZ co-twin and 14 per cent for the DZ co-twin, in a sample of 41 MZ and 115 DZ pairs. However, it is noteworthy that Essen-Möller (1941) in Sweden found larger differences within MZ pairs than were found by other workers, and investigations in Norway and Finland show tendencies in the same direction. Thus Kringlen (1966) collected 50 MZ and 94 same-sexed pairs, with concordance rates of 38 per cent and 14 per cent; and Tienari (1963) found that none of the 16 male MZ pairs he studied were concordant. It is possible that what is diagnosed as schizophrenia in Scandinavia is not quite the same as schizophrenia in Germany, Britain, the United States, and Japan. That there may be peculiar features about the gene distributions in northern lands is also suggested by the work of Böök (1953). In a remote part of Sweden north of the Arctic circle, in a population of farmers and lumbermen, he found a high incidence of schizophrenia, in a predominantly catatonic form; the incidence of schizophrenia in the relatives of probands, however, was also high, suggesting an intermediate gene with 20 per cent penetrance in the heterozygote. The possible prevalence of different genetic predisposing factors for schizophrenia in different parts of the world is a possibility which deserves investigation.

The findings of Tienari, by themselves, are anomalous and should not be taken as throwing doubt on the results obtained by others; they should be considered in relation to those of other observers, summarized in Table 4. In this table the figures relating to schizophrenia are derived from work in Germany, the United States, Sweden, and England. To these should be added the results obtained by the Japanese workers Kurihara (1959) and Inouye (1961). Inouye found concordance for schizophrenia in 60 per cent of 55 MZ pairs and in 12 per cent (two pairs) of the DZ pairs. Kurihara also found that 29 of 45 MZ pairs were concordant for schizophrenic symptomatology, but none of the 9 DZ pairs were.

The twin work on schizophrenia has been analyzed and discussed critically by Rosenthal in a number of papers (1962a; 1962b; 1963). He concludes that concordance rates have been artificially inflated by the sampling methods employed. Cases have been largely taken from standing populations and include an unrepresentative proportion of severe cases; if genetic factors are connected with reduced chances of remission (which has yet to be shown), this sampling would obviously bias the results. Clearly, sampling from consecutive admissions, or better still from birth registers, would be an improvement. Rosenthal criticizes standards

Table 4 — Concordance rates for mental disorders in same-sexed dizygotic and monozygotic twins

Type of disorder	Number of studies	Pairs reported	PER CENT OF CONCORDANCE		Relative increase*
			MZ	DZ	
Mental defective	5	569	94	65	.83
Child and juvenile	5	209	87	53	.73
Schizophrenic	5	728	69	13	.63
Affective	6	184	70	28	.58
Epileptic	7	214	54	7	.50
Criminal	6	231	66	32	.50
Neurotic	5	103	43	23	.26
Senile	3	56	44	27	.24

* The relative increase in concordance associated with identity of genetical constitution, between theoretical limits of 1 and 0: (MZ − DZ)/(100 − DZ).

Source: Adapted from Essen-Möller 1963.

of diagnosis, both of zygosity and clinical classification, and considers that these diagnoses should be made independently of one another by different observers. Not all recorded work is equally open to such criticism; it is, for instance, a considerable safeguard to publish protocols in full, as the writer did, to make them available to rediagnosis by the reader. [See SCHIZOPHRENIA.]

Etiological theories. Rosenthal classifies the etiological theories of schizophrenia into (1) monogenic–biochemical, (2) diathesis–stress, and (3) life-experience theories, his own views inclining to a theory of the second type. This is no place for the discussion of the difficult problems involved, but the writer inclines to a theory of the first type. It can be shown (Slater 1958) that a monogenic theory fits fairly well with the empirically obtained figures for the frequency of schizophrenia in the siblings of schizophrenics, in the children of one schizophrenic parent, and in the children of parents both of whom had schizophrenic illnesses. These data can be reconciled with a gene of intermediate type, manifesting itself in all homozygotes but in only 26 per cent of heterozygotes; all but 3 per cent of schizophrenics would be heterozygous for the gene. This hypothesis clearly involves a massive environmental contribution in the causation of manifest illness and therefore differs from theories of type (2) only in supposing that the element of specificity in determining the type of psychosis is provided by the genetic constitution. One may expect that decisive support or refutation of type (1) theories will depend on biochemical investigations.

Presenile and senile dementias

Inheritance in Huntington's chorea is dependent on an autosomal dominant gene. Its incidence in the sexes is about equal. The age of onset, according

to Panse (1942), extends from early childhood to the late sixties, with a mean at age 36; Wendt and his colleagues estimate the mean age of onset at 44 (1960). These estimates mean that most of the children of gene carriers are born before the parent has developed the disease. Elimination of the pathogenic gene by processes of natural selection is, accordingly, very slow. The disease is slowly progressive and fatal, with a mean duration of 13 years (Wendt et al. 1960).

Unusual forms of presenile dementia are Pick's disease and Alzheimer's disease; both have a genetic basis. Compared with Huntington's chorea, they occur later in life, with a mean age of onset of 55, and with about seven years as the mean duration. Although the conditions are distinct pathologically, they are often difficult to distinguish clinically. According to Sjögren (Sjögren et al. 1952), the genetic factor in Pick's disease is most probably a dominant major gene, its manifestation subject to modifying genes; in Alzheimer's disease Sjögren thinks multifactorial inheritance more probable.

The problem of genetic determination in senile dementia is even more difficult. The most generally accepted opinion in the past has been that senile dementia is but one aspect of senescence and that specific genetic causation is improbable. However, this established viewpoint has been challenged by the work of Larsson, Sjögren, and Jacobson (1963). In a large study in Stockholm they found that senile dementia was not correlated with senescence. The relatives of patients suffering from senile dementia were not more than normally subject to other conditions, although their risk of senile dementia itself was increased; no instances of Pick's or Alzheimer's disease were found among them. There did not appear to be special factors for longevity whose presence or absence was connected with senile dementia. No evidence could be found of environmental factors of a sociomedical kind playing a part in determining the onset of senile dementia. Furthermore, there was no secular change in the incidence of the disease. Particularly in favor of an explanation in terms of a single gene rather than multifactorial inheritance were the variations in geographical distribution and the absence of intermediate states between senile dementia and normal aging in the siblings and children of the probands. [See AGING.]

The morbidity risk for senile dementia was found to be greatly increased among the relatives of the patients. These researchers consider that the best working hypothesis for the explanation of their findings is that of an autosomal major dominant gene. This gene would be subject to diminished penetrance, the manifestation rate increasing with age. Only a minority even of the gene carriers would ever develop senile dementia; and since the calculated gene frequency was 0.12, the great bulk of the population would be immune.

ELIOT SLATER

[Directly related are the entries GENETICS; PSYCHOLOGY, article on CONSTITUTIONAL PSYCHOLOGY. Other relevant material may be found in SCHIZOPHRENIA.]

BIBLIOGRAPHY

BANSE, J. 1929 Zum Problem der Erbprognosebestimmung: Die Erkrankungsaussichten der Vettern und Basen von Manisch–Depressiven. *Zeitschrift für die gesamte Neurologie und Psychiatrie* 119:576–612.

BÖÖK, J. A. 1953 A Genetic and Neuropsychiatric Investigation of a North-Swedish Population: I. Psychoses. *Acta genetica et statistica medica* (Basel) 4:1–100.

BORGSTROEM, C. A. 1939 Eine Serie von kriminellen Zwillingen. *Archiv für Rassen- und Gesellschaftsbiologie* 33:334–343.

BROWN, FELIX W. 1942 Heredity in the Psychoneuroses. Royal Society of Medicine, *Proceedings* 35:785–790.

EDWARDS, J. H. 1960 The Simulation of Mendelism. *Acta genetica et statistica medica* (Basel) 10:63–70.

EDWARDS, J. H. 1963 The Genetic Basis of Common Disease. *American Journal of Medicine* 34:627–638.

ESSEN-MÖLLER, ERIK 1941 Psychiatrische Untersuchungen an einer Serie von Zwillingen. *Acta psychiatrica et neurologica scandinavica* Supplement 23.

ESSEN-MÖLLER, ERIK 1963 Twin Research and Psychiatry. *Acta psychiatrica scandinavica* 39, fasc. 1:65–77.

FONSECA, ANTONIO F. DA 1959 *Análise heredo–clínica das perturbações afectivas: Estudo de 60 pares de gémeos a seus consanguíneos*. Universidad de Porto (Portugal): Faculdade de Medicina.

INOUYE, EIJI 1961 Similarity and Dissimilarity of Schizophrenia in Twins. Volume 1, pages 524–530 in World Congress of Psychiatry, Third, Montreal, *Proceedings*. Univ. of Toronto Press.

KAIJ, LENNART 1960 *Alcoholism in Twins: Studies on the Etiology and Sequels of Abuse of Alcohol*. Stockholm: Almqvist & Wiksell.

KALLMANN, FRANZ J. 1950 The Genetics of Psychoses: An Analysis of 1,232 Twin Index Families. *American Journal of Human Genetics* 2:385–390.

KALLMANN, FRANZ J. 1952 Comparative Twin Studies on the Genetic Aspects of Male Homosexuality. *Journal of Nervous and Mental Disease* 115:283–298.

KRANZ, HEINRICH 1936 *Lebensschicksale krimineller Zwillinge*. Berlin: Springer.

KRINGLEN, EINAR 1966 Schizophrenia in Twins: An Epidemiological–Clinical Study. *Psychiatry* 29:172–184.

KURIHARA, M. 1959 A Study of Schizophrenia by Twin Method. *Psychiatria et neurologia japonica* (Seishin shinkeigaku zasshi) 61:1721–1741. → Text in Japanese; title and summary in English.

LANGE, JOHANNES (1929) 1931 *Crime as Destiny: A Study of Criminal Twins*. London: Allen & Unwin. → First published as *Verbrechen als Schicksal*.

LARSSON, TAGE; SJÖGREN, TORSTEN; and JACOBSON, GEORGE 1963 *Senile Dementia: A Clinical Sociomedical and Genetic Study*. Copenhagen: Munsgaard.

LEWIS, AUBREY 1936 Problems of Obsessional Illness. Royal Society of Medicine, *Proceedings* 29:325–336.

LJUNGBERG, L. 1957 Hysteria: A Clinical, Prognostic and Genetic Study. *Acta psychiatrica et neurologica scandinavica* Supplement 112.

LUXENBURGER, H. 1930 Psychiatrisch–neurologische Zwillingspathologie. *Zeitschrift für die gesamte Neurologie und Psychiatrie* 56:145–180.

PANSE, FRIEDRICH 1942 *Die Erbchorea: Eine klinisch–genetische Studie*. Leipzig: Thieme.

RÖLL, A.; and ENTRES, J. L. 1936 Zum Problem der Erbprognosebestimmung: Die Erkrankungsaussichten der Neffen und Nichten von Manisch–Depressiven. *Zeitschrift für die gesamte Neurologie und Psychiatrie* 156:169–202.

ROSANOFF, AARON J.; HANDY, L. M.; and PLESSET, I. R. 1941 *The Etiology of Child Behavior Difficulties, Juvenile Delinquency and Adult Criminality, With Special Reference to Their Occurrence in Twins*. Sacramento: California State Printing Office.

ROSANOFF, AARON J.; HANDY, L. M.; and ROSANOFF, I. A. 1934 Criminality and Delinquency in Twins. *Journal of Criminal Law and Criminology* 24:923–934.

ROSENTHAL, DAVID 1962a Familial Concordance by Sex With Respect to Schizophrenia. *Psychological Bulletin* 59:401–421.

ROSENTHAL, DAVID 1962b Problems of Sampling and Diagnosis in the Major Twin Studies of Schizophrenia. *Journal of Psychiatric Research* 1:16–34.

ROSENTHAL, DAVID (editor) 1963 *The Genain Quadruplets: A Case Study and Theoretical Analysis of Heredity and Environment in Schizophrenia*. New York: Basic Books.

RÜDIN, EDITH 1953 Ein Beitrag zur Frage der Zwangskrankheit, insbesondere ihrer hereditären Beziehungen. *Archiv für Psychiatrie und Nervenkrankheiten* 191:14–54.

SHIELDS, JAMES 1954 Personality Differences and Neurotic Traits in Normal Twin Schoolchildren: A Study in Psychiatric Genetics. *Eugenics Review* 45:213–245.

SHIELDS, JAMES; and SLATER, ELIOT (1960) 1961 Heredity and Psychological Abnormality. Pages 298–343 in Hans J. Eysenck (editor), *Handbook of Abnormal Psychology: An Experimental Approach*. New York: Basic Books.

SJÖGREN, TORSTEN 1948 Genetic–Statistical and Psychiatric Investigations of a West Swedish Population. *Acta psychiatrica et neurologica scandinavica* Supplement 52.

SJÖGREN, TORSTEN; SJÖGREN, HAKON; and LINDGREN, AKE G. H. 1952 Morbus Alzheimer and Morbus Pick: A Genetic, Clinical and Patho-anatomical Study. *Acta psychiatrica et neurologica scandinavica* Supplement 82.

SLATER, ELIOT 1938 Zur Erbpathologie des manisch–depressiven Irreseins: Die Eltern und Kinder von Manisch–Depressiven. *Zeitschrift für die gesamte Neurologie und Psychiatrie* 163:1–47.

SLATER, ELIOT 1953 *Psychotic and Neurotic Illnesses in Twins*. Medical Research Council Special Report No. 278. London: H.M. Stationery Office.

SLATER, ELIOT 1958 The Monogenic Theory of Schizophrenia. *Acta genetica et statistica medica* (Basel) 8:50–56.

SLATER, ELIOT 1961 The Thirty-fifth Maudsley Lecture: Hysteria 311. *Journal of Mental Science* 107:359–381.

STENSTEDT, AKE 1952 A Study in Manic–Depressive

Psychosis. *Acta psychiatrica et neurologica scandinavica* Supplement 79.

STRÖMGREN, ERIK 1938 Beiträge zur psychiatrischen Erblehre. *Acta psychiatrica et neurologica scandinavica* Supplement 19.

STUMPFL, FRIEDRICH 1936 *Die Ursprünge des Verbrechens dargestellt am Lebenslauf von Zwillingen.* Leipzig: Thieme.

SYMONDS, C. P. 1943 The Human Response to Flying Stress. *British Medical Journal* [1943]:703–706, 740–744. → Lecture 1: "Neurosis in Flying Personnel." Lecture 2: "The Foundations of Confidence."

TIENARI, P. 1963 Psychiatric Illnesses in Identical Twins. *Acta psychiatrica scandinavica* 39 (Supplement 171). → The entire issue is devoted to Tienari's study.

WENDT, G. G.; LANDZETTEL, I.; and SOLTH, K. 1960 Krankheitsdauer und Lebenserwartung bei der Huntingtonschen Chorea. *Archiv für Psychiatrie und Nervenkrankheiten* 201:298–312.

II
ORGANIC ASPECTS

Traditionally, description of the organic syndromes, in relation to their effect upon the central nervous system and behavior generally, has included such generalizing conditions as cerebral arteriosclerosis, acute and chronic alcoholism, presenile and senile conditions, degenerative neural diseases, and developmental mental deficiencies, as well as conditions producing more focal disorders such as head injuries, brain tumor extirpations, and cerebrovascular accidents (the boxer who is punch-drunk or the stroke patient).

The trend in recent literature, however, confirms what is a notably progressive shift in emphasis away from strictly clinical or case description, as exemplified by texts in psychiatry and neurology, toward more varied studies, which consider psychodiagnostic and psycholinguistic phenomena in the context of clinical observations.

With these important changes in the study of organic pathology has also come a voluminous growth in the literature. Within this literature (see Wepman 1961) can be found the continuing traditional interest of the neurologist and psychiatrist, as seen, for example, in the recently published *American Handbook of Psychiatry* (Arieti 1959). However, the great breadth of the field can be noted in the work of experimental psychologists using both animal and human subjects; in the recent neurophysiologic research on such central nervous system areas as the reticular formation, the limbic lobes, and the association tracts; in the dramatic electrode stimulation studies of cortical reactions carried on during neurosurgery; in the elaboration of new psychodiagnostic signs by psychometric researchers; and in the growing group of neurophysiological theories related to brain function. Additional examples, from the more applied fields, are rehabilitation for brain-impaired persons and the not inconsiderable addition of research on language disabilities.

As can be seen, the literature of neuropsychology is rich and varied. Within it, the reader will find, however, that there are more unknowns than knowns, more questions than answers, more theories than facts. While a great deal has been written about the behavior of the brain-impaired, very few facts have been demonstrated. For example, it is generally accepted that in thought, emotional control, and intellection, the role of the central nervous system is crucial. Yet the precise manner in which the nervous system and the human brain work to fulfill this function is undetermined and vague. A leading neurophysiologist once described the human brain as a "black box" that must function in certain well-prescribed ways in order to produce all that it does in human behavior but unfortunately is not available for viewing.

Nevertheless, the great concentration of attention by so many trained observers, the extensive studies of clinical cases, the host of theories, the wide and growing application of differential diagnostic techniques, and the increasing activities of both language therapists and psychotherapists treating patients suffering from brain impairment have all produced a considerable body of knowledge available for better understanding of organic mental disorders. The following is an attempt to describe some of the more prominent behavioral phenomena commonly associated with neural impairment and includes major sources of data and references in order to facilitate and encourage further investigation by the reader.

Common behavioral manifestations

Alteration in thought, personality changes, and changes in language comprehension and usage take on many forms following cortical insult. By and large, however, most investigators agree that individual patterns of behavior in the brain-impaired differ from those of the unimpaired more in degree than in type. Table 1 presents the reader with a list of the most common indications of brain impairment.

While space limitations preclude extensive comment on the relative merit of individual signs of organicity as indicators of organic psychopathology, some generalizations about them are warranted. Many of these signs appear as the result of a disordering process producing abnormal behavior; others are the product of the retained ability to function of what is left of the nervous system; and

Table 1 — Behavioral symptoms of the brain-impaired

CLINICALLY OBSERVED SYMPTOMS	PSYCHODIAGNOSTICALLY ELICITED SYMPTOMS	LANGUAGE DISTURBANCES
Memory loss (especially immediate memory)	Poor attention and concentration	Aphasia
Reduced association of ideas	Memory loss	Agnosia
Perseveration of thought and language	Abstract–concrete imbalance	Apraxia
Feelings of inadequacy	Poor ability to organize and preplan	Dysarthria
Egocentricity	Difficulty in forming generalizations	
Hyperirritability	Inability to categorize	
Overfatiguability	Lowered general intelligence	
Euphoria	Psychomotor retardation	
Catastrophic overreaction	Perplexity (questioning one's own ability)	
Reduced initiative	Psychological impotence (recognition of errors without the ability to alter responses)	
Lack of spontaneity	Egocentricity	
Impulsive behavior	Anxiety	
Regressive behavior	Specific modality disabilities in learning	
Fluctuating ability	Body-image distortion	
Situational or fixed anxiety	Spiral afterimage reactions	
	Delayed response patterns	

still others derive from the altered self-concept of the people involved (their reactions to their impairment). At any rate, these signs, while not necessarily pathognomonic of the brain-injured, are rather useful indicators of the likelihood that a cortical impairment has occurred. Research comparing known brain-impaired subjects with normal individuals and subjects with thought disorders (for example, schizophrenics) has consistently shown that pathological conditions, while frequently unlike normal states, are most often like each other (Chapman 1960). In fact, the argument has been advanced that the very presence of so many so-called organic signs in schizophrenia may indicate that this psychiatric condition is indeed an organic psychosis. Thus, behavioral symptoms can be viewed as frequently occurring telltale indicators of pathology but cannot themselves be viewed as differentially diagnostic signs of organic pathology.

It should also be pointed out that most of the signs used as organic indicators have not been found by research studies to occur in every organic condition. In part this is true, the present writer feels, because few of the studies have been really comparable. Research populations differ in so many ways (for example, age of subjects and location and extent of lesion or impairment) that the signs said to be associated with brain pathology in one study may be completely lacking in an equally well attested study of another group of brain-injured patients. A final source of inconsistency is related to subjects with a known brain injury but who differ in behavior from other such subjects even though neuropathies may be alike, the location of damage is thought to be the same, and the amount or size of the lesion is thought to be

roughly equal. The generalization must be made, therefore, that brain-impaired patients differ from one another not only in the size and location of their structural defect but also in the behavioral aftereffects of similar neurological impairment.

Certain commonalities do exist, however, and it is to these that students of brain pathology turn in attempting to gain a greater understanding of cortical function and dysfunction. The remainder of this article will be concerned with a more particular discussion of the behavioral signs appearing in Table 1 in relation to organic disorder, with emphasis upon the literature and major sources of data. Shortage of space unfortunately limits consideration to only the most prominent and generally elicited signs appearing in each of the three categories arbitrarily designated as clinically observed behavior, psychodiagnostically elicited behavior, and psycholinguistic disturbance patterns.

Clinically observed behavior.   Many of the signs enumerated in the category of clinically observed behavior can be related to certain basic processes that seem to underlie the signs themselves.

Lack of control over behavior.   Most notable among these processes is the concept of "control." Since the central nervous system is generally considered a major determinant in the control of behavior as the individual seeks to adapt to his environment, loss of memory and similar behavior may be best understood, in this context, as a loss of selective control over recall of events from the past. Further, memory loss in organic conditions is said to be most severe in the area of recall of very recent events, for example, when the individual must select (control) the appropriate impressions from a variety of recent ones. Related to the recall aspect of memory loss is the loss of capacity to attend, concentrate, or exert simple control over one's ideas.

Impulsiveness, emotionality, and rigidity. Similarly, many clinicians have observed that the brain-impaired are often impulsive and emotionally labile. They react catastrophically to noncatastrophic events, or they become easily frustrated. At the other extreme, the brain-impaired often display tendencies toward rigidity or repetition in thought and language, find it difficult to shift from one idea to another, and are frequently inflexible in behavior. In each case then, these signs point to the patient's inability to regulate his behavior in a flexible fashion. Lack of adequate inhibition and sufficient control brings about these overt behavioral patterns, which have been termed symptoms of brain damage. With adequate control, the unimpaired behave with intent, behave appropriately, and behave purposively. The impaired, having lost control, show abnormalities of behavior in all three areas. (Note: The writer feels it is unnecessary to discuss clinically observed symptoms more extensively here, as they are generally self-explanatory; however, more detailed consideration may be found in the references cited in the bibliography.)

Psychodiagnostically elicited symptoms. The loss of perceptual ability is a basic process that frequently affects the brain-impaired. This loss of function is especially noticeable in the capacity to learn through specific sense modalities. Consequently, it is most often described in relation to problems of children with known neurological deficiencies. But it seems equally true in all adults with brain damage, where perceptual deficiencies have been noted as being modality-bound rather than generalized. Auditory perception, for example, may be affected by brain impairment or by failure of certain portions of the nervous system to develop, while other perceptual abilities may remain intact (Wepman 1960). Some children, it has been noted, fail to develop language at the time expected of them (that is, by two or three years of age). This is not because of any lack of general intelligence or because of deafness or emotional instability but rather because they are unable to learn in situations that involve the auditory pathway. Other children, who do speak adequately, have been observed having difficulty in learning to read at the expected age. Again, this may be caused by no other reason than their inability to use the visual modality in learning, and this despite the measurable adequacy of their visual acuity. [*See* HEARING; VISION.]

These auditory and visual agnosias in children are paralleled by similar disturbances of transmission of input stimuli following cortical insult in adults. Perceptual learning disability along specific modality lines has become the center of attention for many students of behavior in brain-impaired children and adults.

As Table 1 implies, many signs of organic brain impairment can be elicited by psychometric and projective assessment. In some instances these are found to duplicate the clinically observed signs. But in others, they are observed only when the subject is under the stress and scrutiny of formal testing.

Verbal and nonverbal functioning. The use of psychological tests as a means of isolating behavioral indicators of brain impairment continues to be a source of considerable research. Babcock (1941) noted in her studies of the brain-injured that certain intellectual faculties seem better retained after trauma than others. She then proposed to study subjects and evaluate their product in terms of these better retained areas (verbal behavior) as compared with the abilities that are less well retained (visually stimulated abstraction ability). A similar differentiation was used in the Shipley–Hartford Scale (Shipley 1940) and the Hunt–Minnesota Test for Brain Impairment (Hunt 1943). Some support for this notion also seemed to follow from the characteristics of the tests used. Vocabulary retention, or verbal ability, as measured by most tests, is statistically well equated with general intelligence, is known to have a high test–retest reliability, and is generally a stable measure. In contrast, the tasks of visual abstraction are less stable, have less reliability over time, and are therefore more likely to be susceptible to change as a result of organic conditions affecting the nervous system.

Wechsler followed the concept of retained as opposed to sensitive functions, not in a comparison of verbal versus nonverbal behavior, but in empirically determined responses to various subtests in his intelligence scale. From the results of his studies of an aging population, he devised a deterioration index (1955). By and large, this approach has fallen into disfavor among psychologists, however, since confirming research for the deficiencies found by the original author has been lacking (Kass 1949). Those who argue against the use of the verbal versus the nonverbal differential, or, as the believers in perceptual disabilities put it, "the differential between aurally stimulated verbal behavior and visually stimulated nonverbal behavior," seem to this writer to be correct in their conclusion —but for the wrong reasons. In none of the research reported on the many indexes of deterioration was any attempt made to isolate the location of the organic condition, even to the rather loose degree of determining the hemisphere affected. Yet many language studies (Wepman 1951; Ettlinger et al. 1956) and the work of such researchers as Reitan and Reed (1962), Milner (1954), Bauer and Wepman (1955), and others have reported each of the two hemispheres differentially responsible for various intellectual tasks. [*See* INTELLIGENCE AND INTELLIGENCE TESTING.]

In conclusion, therefore, it would be expected that the verbal–nonverbal paradigm would be successful. When damage has occurred to the left brain (the apparent site of integrations necessary for verbal behavior) it would seem that subjects should do less well with verbal than with nonverbal material. When, on the other hand, notable damage occurs in the right hemisphere, which, according to many studies, is the locus of control and integration for nonverbal thought, the expectancy would then be that nonverbal material would present greater difficulty. To the degree that such a distinction can be made in psychological tests— and it can be in many of them—the tendency for the effects of brain damage to be depicted seems high. Re-examining known organically impaired subjects from this viewpoint shows this differentiation to be a meaningful one. The degree to which this approach can be used in differential diagnosis where brain damage is suspected but not certain, however, still needs research verification.

The qualitative approach for the delineation of personality disorganization, using projective tests as the source of data, has proven of value in the hands of many psychologists (Aita et al. 1947; Baker 1956; Hughes 1948; Piotrowski 1937). Unfortunately, most of the results reported are the subjective interpretations of individual examiners and are barely or not at all confirmed in replicated studies. Where such studies have been attempted, few of the signs found diagnostic by one examiner have been elicited by others. For the purposes of demonstrating some of the psychodynamic processes affected in many brain-injured subjects, however, the different projective techniques have proven of considerable value. Yet even here it seems important to point out the individual variability in behavioral reactions. Since brain-injured subjects differ so markedly, for example, in their responses to their traumas, or with respect to their self-conceptions, it has been found to be of little value

to look for commonality of reaction in personality change.

Abstract and concrete functioning. Goldstein, perhaps more than any other student of brain disorders, has postulated both specific disabilities and changes in basic attitudes and thought processes as a result of organic conditions. He pointed out that ". . . even in cases of circumscribed cortical damage, the disturbances are scarcely ever confined to a single field of performance. In such intricate syndromes, we deal not only with a simple combination of disparate disturbances but also with more or less unitary, basic change that affects different fields homologously and expresses itself through different symptoms . . ." ([1934] 1939, pp. 15–16).

Of all the symptomatology noted in the study of the organic psychopathologies, none has had greater impact or perhaps stirred greater controversy than Goldstein's concept of the shift from the abstractive to the concrete mode of thought (Goldstein & Scheerer 1941). With his co-workers, he postulated both theory and methods for determining the loss of categorical, abstracting behavior. The concept, by and large, has received greater acceptance than the methods. Today almost every clinician studying the behavior of the brain-impaired patient concedes the correctness of Goldstein's observation that organic brain disease impairs abstract functioning. The many Goldstein tests, however, have been less successfully used by other examiners.

Changes in intellectual performance. Finally, some attention should be directed toward the concept of changes in general intellectual level as a consequence of brain impairment. Essentially, there are two types of change that have been widely noted. In some patients, over-all intellectual level seems grossly affected, as in conditions that to a certain degree affect the nervous system in its entirety. A good example is the deterioration that accompanies progressive cerebral disease and that is demonstrated by progressive generalized intellectual decline. In other patients, the condition is localized and affects intellectual ability within fairly circumscribed areas. It can be shown in most cases of brain disorder that one or the other of these two forms of intellectual loss occurs. In certain types of localized damage that affect only specific functions, as in the limited agnosias and apraxias affecting language, it may be held that no intellectual loss need be predicated. However, even here a loss must be considered to occur, since the deficiency in those functions immediately affected makes adaptation to the environment more difficult and more circumscribed. Thus, even very minor brain damage that functionally affects only the capacity to read or write and that might not affect the individual's capacity to think or perform on intelligence tests would still have its deleterious effect upon the totality of behavior and, consequently, upon intelligence. It would make the patient a less efficient organism and would thus make adaptation to life a more complex task for him.

Generalized deterioration, whether progressive or not, rarely permits alterations in behavior through therapy and rehabilitation. On the other hand, focalized injuries that produce limitations of intellectual ability can frequently be offset by proper training and therapeutic rehabilitation (Harlow 1953).

Organic language disturbances. Language function and dysfunction have also become the focus of attention of many researchers in recent years. Loss of the ability to comprehend and use language has an extensive literature of its own. Aphasia, a loss of ability to utilize verbal symbols, is a relatively common aftereffect of brain damage, especially when that damage affects the left cortical hemisphere. There have been widely different approaches to the study of the language syndromes. Schuell and Jenkins (1959) have postulated that language is a unitary process that may be lost in varying degrees. They have concluded from their studies that the language deficit may be measured along a continuum of severity of dysfunction. This would include difficulties with a variety of individual tasks, such as the abilities to speak, read, and write. Wepman and Jones (1961), on the other hand, contend that language is divisible into a series of different linguistic processes and that each process may be differentially affected. Five types of symbolic loss of language—five types of aphasia—have been described in this research: global, jargon, pragmatic, semantic, and syntactic.

Partial support for this viewpoint is seen in the insightful work of Jakobson (Jakobson & Halle 1956), who related certain observed aphasic disturbances, noted above as semantic and syntactic aphasia, to two basic linguistic processes. He pointed out that there are two basic types of aphasia, differentiated according to whether the deficiency is in the selection and substitution of words or in their combination and contexture.

Further support for this linguistic differentiation also comes from other sources. The research of Goodglass and his co-workers on agrammatism and paragrammatism (Goodglass & Hunt 1958; Goodglass & Mayer 1958) confirmed the Jakobson dis-

tinction. The work of Luriia (1947; 1958) in the Soviet Union goes far beyond the linguistic approach, identifying the process changes with neural constructs and specific localization of damage. Also included in his work is a description of five very similar types of language disturbance (1958).

The conception of aphasia as representing disorders along a continuum of severity and the psycholinguistic classification of aphasic types as discussed above are fairly recent developments. In contrast, traditional neurological literature treats language disturbances as receptive or expressive disorders, closely related to specific neurological substrata. Indeed, a fair proportion of the literature on the whole field of brain damage is given over to discussions of the question of localization of function in the nervous system. Harlow's review of literature dealing with the higher functions of the nervous system (1953) is devoted solely to the difference of opinion concerning localization. Discussing Hebb's brilliant *Organization of Behavior* (1949), the Hixon Symposium on *Cerebral Mechanisms in Behavior* (Jeffress 1951), and Fulton's *Functional Localization in Relation to Frontal Lobotomy* (1949), as well as research devoted to specific architectonic divisions of the cortex, Harlow concludes in part that "the data would appear to be almost overwhelmingly opposed to any theory of cortical localization of intellectual function which is anatomically precise or temporarily static" (1953, p. 512). Writers in the field vary from a position of extreme belief in punctate localization to the opposite view of equipotentiality or mass action. Somewhere between these two polar viewpoints rest the opinions of most present-day exponents of the role of the cortex in relation to behavior.

Recent reports of psychodiagnosticians studying the behavior of patients with known brain damage give some credence to a gross type of localization. Reitan and his co-workers (Reitan & Reed 1962), as mentioned earlier, have been able to show that subjects with left brain damage, when tested by such scaled instruments as the Wechsler Adult Intelligence Scale, show a greater deficit in performing verbal tasks, and less deficit, if any, in performing nonverbal tasks. The opposite findings were reported on patients with known right brain damage; that is, they did better on verbal tasks than on nonverbal ones. This general finding bears out what has previously been said about language disorders following brain injury; that is, symbolic verbal behavior is found to be disturbed only in left brain-injured subjects (Wepman 1951).

It is the viewpoint of most students of brain function that while there is a type of localization of function within the nervous system, the end product, which is an individual's behavior, is the result not of the functioning of any localized section or subsection but of the integrated nervous system as a whole. For example, Penfield and Rasmussen (1950), by their ingenious placement of electrodes during neurosurgery, have demonstrated that while aphasic arrest does occur more frequently when Broca's area (the third prefrontal convolution of the left cortex) is stimulated electrically, a similar arrest of language occurs when widely scattered areas of the parietal and even the temporal lobes are stimulated. From such studies it would appear that while a high concentration of cells in Broca's area may be responsible for a type of word-finding ability, other areas subserve the same function but in a less concentrated way. Behavior, it is held, is a far too complex process to be conceptualized as the product of any localized area of the brain. It is much more reasonably thought of as the integration of perceptual, conceptual, mnemonic, and motor processes—with factors of motivation, emotion, and the processes of feedback playing their various roles.

Organic mental disorders can thus be best described as the results of a variety of conditions— disease processes, traumas, agenesis, deteriorations, etc. These conditions in turn produce alterations in the consequent behavioral patterns of the brain-impaired. Certain specific signs of alteration are more commonly seen in the behavior of the impaired than in the unimpaired. These signs are recognizably not pathognomonic of the neural disorder. Yet, by their consistency of occurrence, they are often the best indicators available of brain damage in those in whom pathological behavior is noted. Many of these indications are admittedly seen only clinically and rarely verified by research. Others are elicited through more organized and scientific psychological and linguistic studies.

JOSEPH M. WEPMAN

[*Other relevant material may be found in* LANGUAGE, *article on* SPEECH PATHOLOGY; NERVOUS SYSTEM; SCHIZOPHRENIA.]

BIBLIOGRAPHY

AITA, JOHN A.; REITAN, RALPH M.; and RUTH, JANE M. 1947 Rorschach's Test as a Diagnostic Aid in Brain Injury. *American Journal of Psychiatry* 103:770–779.

ARIETI, SILVANO (editor) 1959 *American Handbook of Psychiatry.* 2 vols. New York: Basic Books.

BABCOCK, HARRIET 1941 The Level-efficiency Theory of Intelligence. *Journal of Psychology* 11:261–270.

BAKER, GERTRUDE 1956 Diagnosis of Organic Brain Damage in the Adult. Pages 318–428 in Bruno Klopfer (editor), *Developments in the Rorschach Technique.* Volume 2: Fields of Application. New York: World Book.

BAUER, ROBERT; and WEPMAN, JOSEPH M. 1955 Lateralization of Cerebral Functions. *Journal of Speech and Hearing Disorders* 20:171–177.

CHAPMAN, LOREN J. 1960 Confusion of Figurative and Literal Usages of Words by Schizophrenics and Brain Damaged Patients. *Journal of Abnormal and Social Psychology* 60:412–416.

ETTLINGER, GEORGE; JACKSON, C. V.; and ZANGWILL, O. L. 1956 Cerebral Dominance in Sinistrals. *Brain* 79: 569–588.

FULTON, JOHN F. 1949 *Functional Localization in Relation to Frontal Lobotomy.* New York: Oxford Univ. Press.

GOLDSTEIN, KURT [1934] 1939 *The Organism.* New York: American Book. → First published in German.

GOLDSTEIN, KURT; and SCHEERER, MARTIN 1941 Abstract and Concrete Behavior: An Experimental Study With Special Tests. *Psychological Monographs* 53, no. 2.

GOODGLASS, H.; and HUNT, J. 1958 Grammatical Complexity and Aphasic Speech. *Word* 14:197–207.

GOODGLASS, H.; and MAYER, J. 1958 Agrammatism in Aphasia. *Journal of Speech and Hearing Disorders* 23:99–111.

HALSTEAD, WARD C. 1947 *Brain and Intelligence.* Univ. of Chicago Press.

HARLOW, HARRY 1953 Higher Functions of the Nervous System. *Annual Review of Physiology* 15:493–514.

HEBB, DONALD O. 1949 *The Organization of Behavior.* New York: Wiley.

HUGHES, ROBERT M. 1948 Rorschach Signs for the Diagnosis of Organic Pathology. *Rorschach Research Exchange* 12:165–167. → Now called *Journal of Projective Techniques.*

HUNT, HOWARD F. 1943 A Practical Clinical Test for Organic Brain Damage. *Journal of Applied Psychology* 27:375–386.

JAKOBSON, ROMAN; and HALLE, MORRIS 1956 *Fundamentals of Language.* The Hague: Mouton.

JEFFRESS, LLOYD A. (editor) 1951 *Cerebral Mechanisms in Behavior: The Hixon Symposium.* New York: Wiley.

KASS, WALTER 1949 Wechsler's Mental Deterioration Index in the Diagnosis of Organic Brain Disease. Kansas Academy of Science, *Transactions* 52:66–70.

LASHLEY, KARL S. 1929 *Brain Mechanisms and Intelligence: A Quantitative Study of Injuries to the Brain.* Univ. of Chicago Press.

LURIIA, ALEKSANDR R. 1947 *Travmaticheskaia afaziia* (Traumatic Aphasia). Moscow: Academy of Medical Science.

LURIIA, ALEKSANDR R. 1958 Brain Disorders and Language Analysis. *Language and Speech* 1:14–34.

MILNER, BRENDA 1954 Intellectual Functions of the Temporal Lobes. *Psychological Bulletin* 51:42–62.

PENFIELD, WILDER; and RASMUSSEN, THEODORE 1950 *The Cerebral Cortex of Man.* New York: Macmillan.

PIOTROWSKI, ZYGMUNT A. 1937 The Rorschach Ink Blot Method in Organic Disturbances of the Central Nervous System. *Journal of Nervous and Mental Diseases* 86:525–537.

REITAN, RALPH M.; and REED, HOMER B. 1962 Consistencies in Wechsler–Bellevue Mean Values in Brain-damaged Groups. *Perceptual and Motor Skills* 15:119–121.

SCHUELL, HILDRED; and JENKINS, J. J. 1959 The Nature of Language Deficit in Aphasia. *Psychological Review* 66:45–67.

SHIPLEY, WALTER C. 1940 A Self-administering Scale for Measuring Intellectual Impairment and Deterioration. *Journal of Psychology* 9:371–377.

TEUBER, HANS L. 1950 Neuropsychology. Pages 30–52 in *Recent Advances in Diagnostic Psychological Testing.* Springfield, Ill.: Thomas.

WECHSLER, DAVID 1955 *Wechsler Adult Intelligence Scale (WAIS).* New York: Psychological Corp.

WEPMAN, JOSEPH M. 1951 *Recovery From Aphasia.* New York: Ronald Press.

WEPMAN, JOSEPH M. 1960 Auditory Discrimination, Speech and Reading. *Elementary School Journal* 60:325–333.

WEPMAN, JOSEPH M. 1961 *A Selected Bibliography on Brain Impairment, Aphasia, and Organic Psychodiagnosis.* Chicago: Language Research Associates. → Lists over a thousand items collected from 220 recent American journals and books.

WEPMAN, J. M.; and JONES, L. V. 1961 *The Language Modalities Test for Aphasia.* Chicago: Education–Industry Service.

III
BIOLOGICAL ASPECTS

In 1884 the founding father of neurochemistry, J. W. L. Thudichum, wrote:

Many forms of insanity are unquestionably the external manifestations of the effects upon the brain substance of poisons fermented within the body, [in the same way that] mental aberrations accompanying chronic alcoholic intoxication are the accumulated effects of a relatively simple poison fermented out of the body. These poisons we shall, I have no doubt, be able to isolate after we know the normal chemistry to its uttermost detail. And then will come in their turn the crowning discoveries to which all our efforts must ultimately be directed, namely, the discoveries of the antidotes to the poisons, and to the fermenting causes and processes which produce them. (1884, p. xiii)

Thudichum anticipated trends which we would regard as very modern in our day. Two premises are explicitly stated. An aberrant biological product (or "a product fermented in the body") leads to aberrant behavior; and knowledge of normal chemistry "to the uttermost detail" is an essential prerequisite to the isolation of such a product. Thudichum's own crowning achievement was an analysis of the brain in terms of its chemical building blocks, the so-called lipoproteins, which are complexes formed between fatty bodies (lipids) and proteins. This work still stands as a classic.

Yet this approach—what one might call a clockwork approach—reflects the hopes and limitations of an age. In the Victorian era, governed by the meter rule, the clock, and the kilogram, an understanding of the chemical machinery was regarded as a reasonable basis for the understanding of mental disorder and thus, by inference, of mental order. Attitudes have great viability; similar approaches (with somewhat better reason) are with us to this day. They aim at an understanding of the chemistry of the strange detector we carry in our skull. But of environment, forever playing upon this detector, and so often disrupting and distorting it, chemistry will tell us nothing. Nor can chemistry, in its old and classic form, tell us much of how environment is transcribed and coded by nervous tissue.

Yet in man the brain in some strange way internalizes and stores environment; it models it in sight and sound and uses these models as predictors; it transmits information from generation to generation by a symbolic (nongenetic) process, which is a radically new departure in evolution. Neurochemistry thus poses problems very different from those posed by classical chemistry or even by modern physical chemistry. It demands a revision of attitudes, and perhaps like no other field in biology is forcing a confrontation of biological process with the emerging concepts of system theory. In short, any attempt at understanding the brain as a chemically mediated organ of information forces an encounter between somatic transaction and symbolic process. This field one can, justifiably, term psychobiology.

Principles of regional brain organization

We may be a long way from understanding the nature of the chemical control processes which enable the brain to function as an integrating, "feeling," information-storing, predicting, and computing organ, but we have also come some way since Thudichum. Thudichum's analysis involved the analysis of the brain as a single organ. However, the brain, unlike the liver, is not a homogeneous organ; and in terms of anatomical arrangement, cell population, and chemistry it shows a regional economy which reflects the course of its own evolution. The distinctive attribute of the human and primate brain is the size and structure of its cortex. Its contribution to the analysis of secondary signaling (that is, symbolic) systems has been extensively studied by the Pavlovian school. Yet work since the 1940s has also emphasized the role of some developmentally older subcortical centers buried deep in the brain and the relationship of these structures to the cerebral cortex. The brain centers in question are the hypothalamus, the reticular activating system, the rhinencephalic ("smell brain") formation (also known as the limbic system), and the caudate and lentiform masses (the corpus striatum). Each of these systems has received its share of extensive review; and accumulated experience, using a variety of techniques with each, has steadily emphasized three separate, though related, trends. The first is the discrete neuroanatomic and cellular suborganization of these systems; the second, the interconnectedness between the systems themselves and between the systems and relatively distant elements at high cortical and spinal levels; and the third, the reciprocal, complementary, yet mutually exclusive relationship which some patterns represented in these systems bear to each other. These findings are relevant when considered in relation to the regional chemistry of these structures. [*See* NERVOUS SYSTEM, *article on* STRUCTURE AND FUNCTION OF THE BRAIN.]

There is little doubt of the anatomical heterogeneity and cytological differentiation of the hypothalamus, where small areas measuring hardly more than a few millimeters in diameter control the central representation of the autonomic nervous system and the appetitive drive systems (fight, flight, hunger, thirst, sex). Similarly, more recent studies have emphasized the remarkable anatomical and cytoarchitectonic differentiation within the reticular activating system, governing wakefulness, sleep, and focused attention. Elements in the structure of the limbic system have similar differentiation. Each of these systems thus encompasses a mosaic of subsystems which in a manner only poorly understood at present are fitted into one another. This understanding, however, is being steadily enhanced by mounting knowledge of the anatomical connections and electrophysiological properties. These connections are in both directions between the hypothalamus and the reticular formation, the limbic system and the hypothalamus, and between these structures and the cortex. [*See* ATTENTION; SLEEP.]

The term "limbic system midbrain circuit" is entirely apt (Nauta 1958). In a way still poorly understood, the limbic system would appear to be an intermediate between discrete analysis of diverse signals at high levels and the discharge of a limited genetically coded stereotyped response known as "affective" behavior. It appears to participate in and to modulate both.

There is a tremendous convergence of information in this area. There are structural counterparts of this convergence; in the olfactory bulb, for example (which in man can be regarded as a homologue of the hippocampus), the messages of about 50 million receptors are reduced to 150 thousand in mitral cells and finally reach the brain through the axons of a mere 45,000 pyramidal cells. These cells and their branchings thus have the structural features which make for an extraordinary funneling and filtering of information (Green 1964). It is, incidentally, in these areas too that a rich, tessellated, terrazzo-like apposition of shared membranes, a virtual mosaic, is found. These junctional areas are also highly localized electrical generators.

It is usually found convenient to speak of the reticular formation and the hippocampal amygdaloid cell assemblies as areas that control sleep, wakefulness, and the states between wakefulness and sleep. Yet there is evidence that these areas are pre-eminent in their relation to patterns of emotional expression of autonomic functioning and, also, that interference in these areas may be important for the process of "recall" and possibly for the process of registering the memory trace. Seen dimly, then, and in broadest silhouette, the functions covered by the terms "consciousness," "affect," and at any rate "recall" thus appear to be subserved by congruent or at least intimately connected systems (Elkes 1966). That we are "aware," that we are "responsive," that we are "appropriate," that we can *plan* a piece of behavior and be *sequent* rather than random, confused, and "in-con-sequent" in its execution may well be due to some elements and processes vested by evolution in these remarkable cell groups. Somehow, they appear to have the ability to build short-term representational systems of temporarily related events and to use them in the construction of appropriate responses. These models, these tiny maps in time, may be intercellular or cellular; at this stage we do not know.

We may thus regard the brain as a mosaic of what have appropriately been called "biased homeostats" (Pribram & Kruger 1954). The bias, handled by genetically coded "Yes–No" drive systems, keeps changing constantly in the light of ongoing events. To allow adequate comparison of events, slow-fading traces must be available to set up such transient comparisons. It is possible that the so-called after discharges (slow-fading electrical discharges) for which the cells—particularly of the hippocampus—are noteworthy provide a medium for the establishment of such traces. In a manner which is only just beginning to be understood, the *coincident* is detected and the *concurrent* arranged into an appropriate action that is *consequent*. Whereas internal perception and comparison may be multiple, action and preparation for action are essentially serial: it requires a rigorous regulation of construction of events at the time; it demands apprehension of the redundant and, above all, a selective inhibition of those elements which are judged irrelevant; a construction of subsets which carry meaning by ignoring but also can carry coded traces of what they ignore. Inhibition is thus the agent of structure in the central nervous system. This is borne out by all that we know of reciprocal inhibition in the spinal cord and all that is being learned of the organization of sensory processes. All evidence coming from visual, auditory, and the somatosensory fields points to the operation of highly patterned inhibitory processes reciprocating with the excitation. Delay of the immediate response—that is, the reduction of the immediate reactivity—is merely the giant child of inhibition, a vast and pervasive function woven by evolution into the nervous tissue as a device for judging relevance and for structuring time. Time, indeed, would appear to be the main axis around which the nervous system constructs its model of reality. It does so by judging what is relevant in time and "banking" what is irrelevant. The higher nervous system is remarkable for its ability to ignore; accurate adaptive performance is attained by ignoring all that is adjudged irrelevant.

Somehow, then, in such transactions the simultaneous has to be changed to the successive, and global or random apprehension likewise has to be transformed into rank-ordered sequential responses. It has been observed by Pribram and Kruger (1954) that it may be the role of the limbic system to provide the context in which drive stimuli are reinforcing and then to reverse the context–content relationship between the drive stimuli and reinforcing events. Thus affective connotation becomes a label and a gating device. Affect gates the emergence of memory traces into preconscious knowing and conscious action. The events and the internal representation may be highly varied and complex; the affective response patterns, however, are finite. Seen very broadly, the anatomy of the neuraxes reflects these requirements. For we are dealing here with two great vertical systems and one, so to speak, horizontal system.

First, there is the so-called specific afferent–efferent system which in particular preserves information coming from receptors in a point-to-point representation; second, there is the core of the midline structures comprising the massive facilitatory and inhibitory structures and characterized by a great variety of cells which serve as a mixing pool for each sense modality. Connected with both systems are the elements of the limbic system in which the indications for somewhat longer traces of activity (the so-called "after discharges") are located and which makes this information available for reference, for comparison, and for labeling. It is possible that the caudate and the striatal nuclei may have somewhat similar properties. In man the vast neocortical mantle provides a tremendous reservoir of cells for the storage of recorded traces of events and for their use in the shaping of new events, either symbolic or actual, i.e., those expressed in action. It is also well to recall that wherever we look in the central nervous system, extracellular space is scarce; nonneuronal (so-called) glial structures and membranes predominate. In fact (although this may prove to be an extravagant generalization), we may look upon the central nervous tissue as an array of growing, polymerizing protein fibers and a mosaic of lipid–protein membranes.

Studies have shown the power, the growth, and the specificity of connection formation in the peripheral nervous system. There is also evidence of the presence of nerve growth factors promoting the growth of nerve fibers (Levi-Montalcini & Angeletti 1961). It would seem that, scaled down and compressed to an enormously faster time scale, we may be dealing in the central nervous system with the growth and evolution of macromolecular forms, which by their interaction determine what we know as symbolic form. The junctional sites between cells, and particularly the enormous and highly ordered membranes existing in the central nervous system, may play a part in the initial construction of trace models capable of acting as recognizers, and hence as organizers and ultimately as decision points—organizers, that is, of coincidences, of sequences of pattern, that is, patterns in time. [*See* TIME, *article on* PSYCHOLOGICAL ASPECTS.]

Central neurohumoral substances

It may very well be asked why one should emphasize structural features in the context of a statement on the biological background of mental disorder. The partial answer is that the anatomical and functional attributes have some suggestive chemical correlates. For it is precisely in the areas just mentioned (the hypothalamus, the midline gray area, and elements of the limbic system, the amygdala, the hippocampus, the reticular activating system, and certain layers of the cortex) that one repeatedly encounters a number of small molecules which appear to have evolved for a role in the organization of control systems in the central nervous system. These molecules are acetylcholine, and possibly other choline esters; gamma aminobutyric acid, a derivative of glutamic acid; histamine, also found in the skin and released in injury of all tissues; catecholamines such as dopamine, norepinephrine, and epinephrine, mediators of sympathetic system responses at peripheral effector sites; and indoles such as serotonin. All these molecules show a regional gradient in their distribution. Histamine, for example, is found principally in the midline diencephalic structures; norepinephrine is present in the hypothalamus and in the periventricular gray matter; serotonin is present in both diencephalic and limbic structures. Two further features should be emphasized concerning these substances. First, they are representative members of *families* of compounds. As chemical mapping proceeds, related members of these various subgroups, their precursors, and their products are identified. Second, the metabolic pathways of each of these compounds—within and without the brain—are steadily being defined more clearly. New and elegant techniques are capable of demonstrating these materials *in situ* in the brain. These studies show that the intercellular and pericellular economies of these substances are organized very precisely. The molecules are transported into cells or their precursors by the energy-yielding system; once synthesized, they are transported and packaged into granular particles or "vesicles" inside cells; they are carefully stored in equilibrium at these sites and are released in response to electrical stimulation by mechanisms still poorly understood. Moreover, all work so far on how the psychoactive drugs act—be they tranquilizers, stimulants, or the so-called hallucinogenic compounds—suggests that all substances interfere in varying ways and to varying degrees with the uptake, storage, and release of the catecholamines (such as epinephrine and dopamine), indolic substances (such as serotonin), and possibly histamine in the areas that have been mentioned. The precise action profiles of these drugs are different, and it is upon such subtle differences in action that variation in therapeutic effect may well depend.

This, then, puts an end to the simple "clock model" of an earlier day. For we are not only dealing with *families* of compounds, but we are also considering multiple binding sites of organelles exquisitely sensitive to local subcellular conditions. The uneven distribution of these chemicals at neuronal decision points, the trigger (or selective suppressor) function of certain elements, and the anatomically imposed economy in terms of convergence and occlusion all suggest that we are dealing with transaction sites at highly localized subcellular levels which need not necessarily be reflected in gross over-all shifts. These sites are evidently unevenly distributed in nonhomogeneous cell populations. Their state at any one time depends exquisitely upon the short-term history of preceding or coincidental events. It is impossible to think in terms of a mechanistic spatial localization, i.e., in terms of points. Rather, one is forced to think in terms of convergence, coincidence, stochastic processes, and probabilities of interaction in time. It was earlier suggested that inhibition is the agent of structure in the nervous system and that the silence in the central nervous system is, so to speak, informed silence. The chemical computer we carry in our skulls apparently writes its chemical text of experience in proteins; and some small molecules appear to play a key part in the transcription or readout. Much work on the biology of mental disorder centers on the identification of the normal molecules mentioned above and of their deviant metabolites.

Chemical aspects of mental development

Chemical factors certainly operate in the development of the nervous system. Some of these are general; others are more special. Of the general factors, oxygen supply is one and hormones are another. Cerebral ischemia, i.e., restriction of blood supply, even for a short time in the developing animal, causes marked forms of mental deficiency. Yet in the adult animal, oxygen supply and fuel consumption are not necessarily related to mental functioning: they may be, but they need not be. A major advance in methodology (Kety & Schmidt 1948) has made it possible to make exact measurements of blood flow, oxygen consumption, and glucose consumption in the conscious human brain, in a variety of functional states in the normal brain and in various forms of mental disorder. These studies have shown quite clearly that in normal man the major substrate for oxidation is glucose and that the rate of energy utilization of the human brain is on the order of a mere 20 watts—eloquent testimony to the efficiency and miniaturization of the brain–computer, weighing about three pounds.

These same studies also showed that general anesthesia reduces cerebral oxygen consumption to about 40 per cent; in contrast, normal sleep did not show such reduced oxygen consumption. Similarly, in studies of schizophrenia and of the effects of LSD-25 and other hallucinogenic drugs there were no changes in over-all total oxygen consumption. First and last, the brain is an organ of information. To be sure, energy is needed to keep the living computer going, to synthesize the building blocks, particularly proteins and lipoproteins essential for its development. However, information storage and retrieval are evidently low-energy processes.

Another equally general factor concerned in intellectual development and mental functioning is presented by a number of hormones, of which thyroxin can serve as a useful example. Hypothyroidism due to an iodine deficiency leads to a mental deficiency syndrome known as cretinism. Hyperthyroidism (an excess of thyroxin) leads to striking hyperirritability and various signs of overactivity of the autonomic nervous system. There is much experimental evidence (Sokoloff & Kaufman 1959) that thyroxin may exert its action on the brain through influencing protein synthesis. It is relevant that although thyroxin does not stimulate protein synthesis in the mature brain, it does significantly do so in the newborn brain. The main structural defect in experimentally induced cretinism (produced by thyroid deficiency) is a deficiency in the proliferation of fine nerve *fibrils* (dendrites) in the immature cerebral cortex. Here again, a structural feature stresses the importance of *connectivity* between neurones (the so-called neuropile) rather than mere *number* of cells.

The pathology of phenylpyruvic oligophrenia (phenylketonuria, PKU) may serve as a useful example of the way in which a specific and genetically determined metabolic error—a so-called biochemical lesion—may profoundly affect the development of higher nervous function. In 1934 A. Z. Folling observed in the course of an investigation of mentally defective children that some of them excreted phenylpyruvic acid in the urine and that there appeared to be a relation between the anomaly and the imbecility. This was the first demonstration of a metabolic error definitely associated with a form of mental defect and also with physical characteristics (blond hair and blue eyes). In phenylketonuria the subject is unable to oxidize a normally occurring essential amino acid (phenylalanine) to tyrosine at a normal rate. Because of this inability, phenylalanine accumulates in the tissues, rises in the blood stream, and spills over in the urine. This error also mobilizes other metabolic routes which normally play little part in the metabolism of these amino acids. In 1953 it was definitely shown that enzymic extracts prepared from the livers of phenylketonuric patients failed to further the oxidation of phenylalanine to tyrosine (Jervis 1953; Wallace, Moldave & Meister 1957). Extracts of normal livers do so quite readily. Furthermore, the use of radioactively labeled phenylalanine showed that the phenylketonuric can convert this phenylalanine to tyrosine at only a fraction of the normal rate. The most striking result of this deficient oxidation mechanism is the appearance in the urine of phenylpyruvic acid, a compound which is readily detected through the greenish color it acquires when it reacts with ferric chloride. This provides a ready screening test for the deficiency in the newborn. The striking decreased pigmentation seen in phenylketonuria—blue eyes and blond hair—may be due to the decreased formation of melanin pigment, through inhibition of an enzyme known as tyrosinase. The abnormal metabolites of phenylalanine also apparently interfere with the synthesis of catecholamines important for brain functions. This may account for the lowered level of epinephrine and norepinephrine in the plasma of the phenylketonuric. Whether excess of phenylalanine or one of its breakdown products or an interference with some of the biosynthetic processes of catecholamines accounts for the mental defect remains uncertain. However, the concept opens up an inviting area for producing experimental phenylketonuria in the laboratory by means of "loading" the system with phenylalanine and also suggests a way of treating or preventing the disorder by withdrawing the offending amino acid from the diet.

The first attempt to relieve phenylketonuria by such dietary means followed only four years after the discovery of the syndrome (Penrose & Quastel 1937). A new approach to the problem was introduced in 1951, when, for the first time in the field of mental deficiency, diets specifically low in *one* amino acid (namely, phenylalanine) were introduced (Woolf & Vulliamy 1951). The so-called synthetic phenylalanine-low diets have now been used with varying success in a number of studies. They result in a sharp lowering of urinary phenylpyruvic acid and plasma phenylalanine. The patients so treated show a striking reduction in seizures and spasticity and increased responsiveness in motor development. There is also a darkening of the hair. Reversal to full phenylalanine natural diet leads to relapse. It has also become unambiguously clear that treatment must be introduced as early as possible and that improvement falls off sharply if this regimen is introduced beyond the stage of infancy. The developing nervous system is a vulnerable one. [*See* MENTAL RETARDATION.]

These studies are mentioned because in a sense they represent a prototype of approach which is now being applied, with some modest success, in other studies of the biological basis of mental disorder. The steps are as follows: An empirical finding—a deviant metabolite in urine—leads to a suspicion of a metabolic defect. The natural history of the disorder suggests a genetic basis for this defect. A biochemical lesion—a specific biochemical defect—is defined. Since the metabolic pathways are interrelated, this single defect leads to consequences only indirectly related to the primary defect, yet very pertinent to the total pathology. The correction of the defect by reducing the metabolic load forms the basis of therapy. An animal model for this disorder is developed, and, finally, the fit of the model in terms of detection and prevention is tested.

However, there is still a large no man's land between evidence and inference. The effects of the deviant metabolites on the development of the nervous system, and particularly those areas concerned with perception, coordination, control of motor activity, and maturation of intellectual function, remain largely unknown.

Schizophrenic disorders

The facts cited above point to the complexity of the field of disorder when it is seen in terms of available biochemical facts and biochemical hypotheses alone. These complexities are compounded many times over in an attempt to relate known biochemical facts to the group of disorders known as the schizophrenias. It is by now generally accepted that we may be dealing, in this group, with a number of very different disorders, sharing a general symptomatology but quite possibly in need of a radical regrouping. The role of genetic factors is reviewed elsewhere [see MENTAL DISORDERS, *article on* GENETIC ASPECTS]. Careful genetic psychosocial studies of twins, on a national and international scale, are now proceeding, and such studies (particularly of families in which twins are discordant for schizophrenia) may contribute some of the facts which are needed to separate, on a conceptual basis, nature from nurture. Equally, careful longitudinal studies—prospective rather than retrospective—are needed (starting, preferably, in early infancy) to establish the role of genetic "givens" in the autonomic reactivity patterns which have been claimed to be deviant among schizophrenics. These suggest an instability of hormonal control and diminished compensatory physiological responses: peripheral vasoconstriction, capillary abnormalities in the nail bed, and abnormal pupil responses have been implicated as such signals. Yet the one measure which reliably distinguishes schizophrenic populations from normal is their state of readiness in the face of oncoming stimuli (Rodnick & Shakow 1940). This anticipatory set or "set index" suggests that in schizophrenia one may be dealing with a disorder of the attention process. How much this disorder represents the collusion between a genetically determined insta-

bility in homeostatic control and a defensive homeostatic withdrawal from stressful stimulus situations and thus, ultimately, a learned pattern of adaptation (enhanced, for example, by the double message structure found in schizophrenogenic families) still remains a matter of conjecture. [*See* ATTENTION; REACTION TIME; SCHIZOPHRENIA; STRESS.]

Nor does the difficulty of relating biochemical varibles to clinical states end there. Even when the data are from the observation of schizophrenics in a hospital ward, there are a number of sources of errors which have seriously affected investigation (Kety 1959). These include long hospitalization, diet (including dietary iodine and protein deficiency), various therapeutic maneuvers (including medication), and the actual circumstances—stressful or otherwise—accompanying the drawing of the biochemical sample. Also, as in all other fields of psychobiology, subjective bias has cast a pall over many painstaking studies. All these reservations notwithstanding, there are, however, some findings largely attributable to the striking advances in present-day methodology. These advances are essentially three in number. First, the refinement of protein fractionation procedures (derived from the needs of blood transfusion and of plasma substitutes); second, the advance of microfluorometric techniques for the detection of very small quantities of catecholamines, indole derivatives, and their metabolites; and third, the development of radioactive tracer techniques and particularly the advent of the liquid scintillation counter, which makes it possible to follow a particular compound through a metabolic maze. As always, it is a moot question whether technical methods or intuitive insights are the more powerful propellants of science. Evidently, in our age they are inextricably connected.

In 1957 it was first reported that a serum fraction obtained from schizophrenic patients, when injected into carefully selected nonschizophrenic prisoner volunteers, led to the development of symptoms of thought disorder, autism, depersonalization, paranoid ideas, hallucinations, and catatonic stupor which were likened to schizophrenia (Heath et al. 1958). Attempts to replicate this finding by injection of material prepared according to similar instructions, however, were not successful (see Conference on Neuropharmacology 1959). This finding, however, seems to this writer less pertinent than the various lines of investigation which were stimulated by the finding. A number of groups have now independently obtained evidence which suggests at least the possibility that an abnormal protein may be present to a greater extent in the blood of schizophrenics than in normals and that this substance may be capable of producing behavioral metabolic changes in some animal tests. There is also evidence that there is an antigenic abnormality in the pooled serum of chronically ill schizophrenic patients (Haddad & Rabe 1963) and that plasma from schizophrenic patients affects learning and retention of learning in the rat (Bishop 1963). Similarly, serum of schizophrenic patients has been shown to affect cortical (electrically evoked) responses of animals (German 1963). However, it is of more than suggestive significance that in these various studies plasma derived from normal individuals put under stress produced somewhat similar responses. It is therefore possible that one may be dealing here with a small molecular constituent liberated during stress and attached to one of the plasma fractions; the constituent may not be a unique characteristic of schizophrenia.

Another approach to the problem is the characterization of various serum protein fractions, rather than total proteins, in terms of electrophoretic and immunochemical properties. There is evidence from double-blind studies that there may be abnormal protein fractions in a considerable proportion of schizophrenic patients (Fessel & Grunbaum 1961).

A cognate approach to the above are the findings of another group (Frohman et al. 1960), who reported that when red blood cells of chickens are incubated with plasma or plasma fractions of some schizophrenic patients, there is an increase, compared with normal controls, of the lactate–pyruvate ratio. This finding, however, still awaits full confirmation, for the difference (in the lactate–pyruvate ratio) is seen only when the subjects have been engaged in moderate exercise before the blood samples are drawn. It may be that these serum factors, while responsive to stress in normals, may be greatly increased in schizophrenics subjected to stress. The serum factor apparently influences the stability of the red cell membrane, the rupture of which may alone account for the changes in the lactate–pyruvate ratio.

Broadly, then, the conclusion at this stage is that there is evidence of a plasma protein abnormality in schizophrenia capable of producing measurable behavioral, immunological, electrophysiological, and biochemical responses in suitable test preparations; and that this abnormal constituent may in fact contain a small molecular substance released by, or related to, physiological stress.

There are, however, a number of other small molecules which are increasingly being implicated in the search for a biochemical factor (the so-called psychotoxic factor) in schizophrenia. As early as 1952 Osmond and Smythies pointed out that there is a close chemical similarity between the drug mescaline, derived from a Mexican cactus plant, and epinephrine and its precursor dopamine, both of which are usually found in the brain. Mescaline is a methylated derivative of dopamine. The mental changes produced by mescaline bear some resemblance to those seen in schizophrenia. The same paper concluded that "it is extremely probable that the final stage in the biogenesis of epinephrine is a transmethylation of norepinephrine, the methyl groups arising from methionine or choline" (a well-known methyl donor). It is just possible that a defective transmethylation of norepinephrine might lead to methylation of one or both of its hydroxyl groups instead of its amino group. This defective methylation could thus give rise to a mescaline-like toxic substance—Thudichum's "internally fermented psychotoxic." There is no denying the attractiveness of this hypothesis, for it relates the metabolism of epinephrine, a hormone liberated during stress, to the pathology of a condition in which stress tolerance and responsiveness to stress are markedly altered or reduced.

This suggestion that there may, in schizophrenia, be a disturbance of the transmethylation process is supported by the fact that a number of drugs (such as dimethyltryptamine, DMT) producing profound mental changes in man are in fact methylated congeners of normal body metabolites. On the basis of such findings it was indeed suggested by Hoffer and his colleagues (1957) that substances which would compete for methyl groups and act as methyl acceptors could competitively inhibit the abnormal process. The vitamins niacin and niacinamide are such substances, and some beneficial results following the administration of large doses of these vitamins in schizophrenia have been reported (Hoffer et al. 1957). These findings still await confirmation. A more direct approach to the problem was to administer large doses of L-methionine, a powerful methylating agent, and a number of other amino acids to chronic schizophrenic patients (Pollin et al. 1961). The changes seen in some patients following the administration of this material were striking; there was a brief and sharp intensification of the psychotic symptoms. This finding has since been confirmed by three other groups and suggests that methylation of aromatic compounds may indeed lead to substances which greatly affect brain function. Another piece of evidence along the same line is the reported occurrence in the urine of schizophrenic patients of a substance 3-4-dimethoxy-phenyl-ethyl-amine (Friedhoff & Van Winkle 1962), suggested in 1952 by Osmond and Smythies as possibly an abnormally methylated and toxic metabolite. This compound is indeed the dimethyl derivative of dopamine, the precursor of epinephrine, and in structure is closely related to mescaline (the trimethyl derivative of this substance).

It is only fair to say, however, that the finding of this compound in urine is still subject to confirmation. The presence of the compound may be related to dietary factors and there is, so far, only preliminary evidence that the substance identified in the urine is indeed produced in the body. Once again, then, one can but say that we are at the beginning; yet the pieces are showing some fit.

Affective disorders

The relation of the midbrain structures and certain elements of the limbic system to the regulation of the visceromotor and affective states has already been mentioned. It is also clear that catecholamines and indoles play a dominant role in these highly specialized and all-pervasive regulatory centers.

The past few years have seen increasing evidence to suggest a possible link between affective disorders (i.e., depression or elation of mood) and changes in the metabolism of catecholamines in the central nervous system. Most of the evidence so far is inferential, yet the advent of pharmacological agents which strikingly affect mood by interfering with the storage, release, and disposition of catecholamines in the central nervous system and at peripheral sites has added an important segment to the body of evidence. [See DEPRESSIVE DISORDERS.]

Quite early it was reported, in a carefully controlled metabolic study, that clinical manifestations of periodic catatonic excitement and stupor were correlated with a change in the nitrogenous constituents of the urine (Gjessing 1938; Gjessing et al. 1958). Longitudinal studies have shown that the urinary excretion of norepinephrine is increased in the manic phase and decreased in the retarded depression phase in manic–depressive ("cyclic") patients (Ström-Olsen & Weil-Malherbe 1958). Yet urinary epinephrine represents only a small fraction of the total metabolites of epinephrine. However, it is now possible to study and identify most other breakdown products of epinephrine and to draw up a full balance sheet of catecholamine metabolites in man. Such studies of urinary metabolites in depressed patients and normal controls suggest as a reasonable hypothesis that "some, if not all, depressions are associated

with an absolute or relative deficiency of catecholamines . . . at functionally important receptor sites in the brain" (Schildkraut 1965, p. 509).

The major inferential evidence so far derives not from physiological studies in the natural untreated states but from the results of pharmacological intervention. In this respect, three groups of drugs are of particular import, namely, reserpine (a major tranquilizer exerting its effect by depleting serotonin and norepinephrine sites in the brain and peripheral sites); the monoamine oxidase inhibitors, which are powerful antidepressants and inhibit the destruction of naturally occurring amines (epinephrine, serotonin, and the like) by oxidation; and various imipramine-like compounds which, in a way not yet clearly understood, interfere with the local economy of catecholamines at intracerebral sites. Reserpine has been found to induce severe depression in patients, yet whether reserpine-induced depression is a valid pharmacological model of the naturally occurring clinical state remains to be seen. In animals, reserpine induces sedation, which is associated with a decrease in the brain levels of norepinephrine, dopamine, and serotonin. The level of sedation correlates well with the depletion of catecholamines in the brain and, furthermore, shows a rise in level of catecholamines with a return of normal motor behavior. Furthermore, the administration of dihydroxy-phenylalanine and dopamine promptly reverses the reserpine-induced sedation in animals and restores normal behavior and norepinephrine level, while an administration of the corresponding serotonin precursor (5-hydroxy-tryptophan) does not. In man, dopamine has been reported to counteract the sedating effect of reserpine. Thus catecholamine depletion (i.e., depletion of dopamine, epinephrine, and norepinephrine) may be of major importance in reserpine-induced sedation in animals; reserpine-induced depression in man may possibly have a similar basis.

The gross picture is reversed for the antidepressive agents. Administration of monoamine oxidase inhibitors, such as iproniazid, and other clinically effective antidepressives both produced behavioral excitation in animals and correlated well with elevated levels of brain norepinephrine. The behavioral stimulation is less related to an elevation of brain serotonin. The mood-elevating properties of amphetamine (benzedrine) are well known. It may be that amphetamine acts by releasing active norepinephrine from its anchoring sites. Furthermore, the "rebound" effect following amphetamine intoxication (which shows clinically in depression) is reflected in a temporary depletion of norepinephrine stores available for continued release. Imipramine, another antidepressant, does not inhibit the enzymes involved in metabolic reactivation of norepinephrine and may interfere with the uptake of norepinephrine into peripheral tissue. There is also some evidence that imipramine inhibits norepinephrine uptake in the brain.

These findings are indicative of the kind of subcellular organization that one is compelled to consider. Little is known as yet of the physiological (rather than pharmacological) factors which govern the storage and release of substances at these subcellular sites. One would naturally suspect ionic shifts, although evidence in this respect so far is very circumstantial. The metallic ion lithium is used in the treatment of manic behavior. Evidence of the role of hormones in these transactions is also at present hardly more than suggestive. There is, however, a respectable body of evidence recently reviewed (Ramey & Goldstein 1957) which indicates a close physiological interaction between the adrenocortical steroids and the catecholamines. The two groups of stress hormones would seem to operate physiologically as one functional unit, the steroids maintaining the integrity and responsiveness of tissues in the process of reacting to norepinephrine. Indeed, many actions of epinephrine, norepinephrine, and dopamine are not elicitable in the absence of steroids. Equally, and perhaps more significantly, many actions attributable to the steroids may in fact be more accurately ascribed to the catecholamines. There is some clinical data available on the relation of plasma hydrocortisone levels to mood. There is, for example, a significant linear relationship between an increase in anxiety, anger, and plasma hydrocortisone levels; moreover, and perhaps less expected, severe depression is accompanied by elevated plasma hydrocortisone levels; and deeply retarded underactive patients show hormone levels higher than those of less depressed groups. Depression would thus appear to be an *active* stress response; the retarded tearless state, the final phase of an active, adaptive process. This phase is largely inhibitory, in contrast with the excitatory component commonly seen in the so-called agitated depressive syndromes. It would be idle to speculate at present on the possible effects of various degrees of adrenocortical mobilization on the binding and releasing of epinephrine and norepinephrine in trigger areas of the brain. It may even be that the reverse is true and that the differential proportion of amines in the brain may affect the degree of adrenocortical mobilization.

In closing, however, it would be safe to surmise that affective behavioral responses may have peculiar chemical topology in some nodal areas of the brain and that some small molecules, particularly catecholamines and indoles, may by virtue of differential storage, release, and disposition determine the particular pattern of response which is selected by the organism in the light of adaptive need. The affective responses are very simple and are relatively stereotyped. The symbols which produce them are infinitely more complex. We do not know what factors go into determining the responsiveness of the affective apparatus during an early developmental period, i.e., how much depends on certain genetic "givens" (enzyme proteins); how much is learned (incorporated into the plastic biological system during an early developmental period). Yet even in this area there is some suggestive evidence. For example, animals reared in isolation show a different pattern in the metabolism of actively labeled dopamine from animals which are forced to interact (Welch & Welch 1965).

Could, one might ask, the coldness and unresponsiveness of the sociopath have a biochemical basis? Could such an understanding yield, in time, appropriate additive therapies? Could learning be modified by chemical means, even in the adult? Could the affective disorders yield to specific chemotherapy? Is there a rational basis for a so-called biological theory of the schizophrenias? More important, could the slowly evolving principles of psychobiology be applied equally to states of mental *well*-being and ill-being? We know little about the physiology of these states, yet it is clear that whatever direction neurobiology takes, it cannot go it alone. It deals with the machinery and not with information; information is symbolic and social. Whatever hopes there may be for the brain sciences, they remain inseparable from education and social change. Human development, human learning, human communication, human social-field dependence remain the heart of the study of mental health. In these, the neurobiologist must take his modest place.

JOEL ELKES

[*Directly related are the entries* DRINKING AND ALCOHOLISM, *article on* PSYCHOLOGICAL ASPECTS; DRUGS, *articles on* PSYCHOPHARMACOLOGY *and* DRUG ADDICTION: ORGANIC AND PSYCHOLOGICAL ASPECTS; EVOLUTION, *article on* EVOLUTION AND BEHAVIOR; GENETICS, *article on* GENETICS AND BEHAVIOR; LEARNING, *article on* NEUROPHYSIOLOGICAL ASPECTS; MENTAL DISORDERS, TREATMENT OF, *article on* SOMATIC TREATMENT. *Other relevant material may be found in* ANXIETY; DEPRESSIVE DISORDERS; DRIVES,

article on PHYSIOLOGICAL DRIVES; EMOTION; HOME-
OSTASIS; INFANCY, article on THE EFFECTS OF EARLY
EXPERIENCE; MENTAL RETARDATION; NERVOUS SYS-
TEM; SCHIZOPHRENIA; SENSES; STRESS.]

BIBLIOGRAPHY

BISHOP, M. P. 1963 Effects of Plasma From Schizophrenic Subjects Upon Learning and Retention in the
Rat. Pages 77–91 in Robert G. Heath (editor), Serological Fractions in Schizophrenia: A Research Symposium. New York: Harper.

CONFERENCE ON NEUROPHARMACOLOGY, FOURTH, SEPTEM-
BER 25–27, 1957, PRINCETON, N.J. 1959 Neuro-
pharmacology: Transactions. Edited by Harold A.
Abramson. New York: Josiah Macy, Jr. Foundation.

ELKES, J. 1966 Psychoactive Drugs: Some Problems
and Approaches. Pages 4–21 in P. Solomon (editor),
Psychiatric Drugs. New York: Grune.

FESSEL, W. J.; and GRUNBAUM, B. W. 1961 Electrophoretic and Analytical Ultra-centrifuge Studies in
Sera of Psychotic Patients: Elevation of Gamma Globulins and Macroglobulins, and Splitting of Alpha
Globulins. Annals of Internal Medicine 54:1134–1145.

FØLLING, A. 1934 Excretion of Phenylpyruvic Acid in
Urine as Metabolic Anomaly in Connection With
Imbecility. Nordisk medicinsk tidskrift (Stockholm)
8:1054–1059.

FRIEDHOFF, A. J.; and VAN WINKLE, E. 1962 The Characteristics of an Amine Found in the Urine of Schizophrenic Patients. Journal of Nervous and Mental
Disease 135:550–555.

FROHMAN, CHARLES E. et al. 1960 Further Evidence of
a Plasma Factor in Schizophrenia. A.M.A. Archives
of General Psychiatry 2:263–267.

GERMAN, G. A. 1963 Effects of Serum From Schizophrenics on Evoked Cortical Potentials in the Rat.
British Journal of Psychiatry 109:616–623.

GJESSING, L.; BERNHARDSEN, A.; and FRØSHAUG, H. 1958
Investigation of Amino Acids in a Periodic Catatonic
Patient. Journal of Mental Science 104:188–200.

GJESSING, R. 1938 Disturbances of Somatic Functions
in Catatonia With a Periodic Course, and Their Compensation. Journal of Mental Science 84:608–621.

GREEN, J. D. 1964 The Hippocampus. Physiological Reviews 44:561–608.

HADDAD, R. K.; and RABE, AUSMA 1963 An Antigenic
Abnormality in the Serum of Chronically Ill Schizophrenic Patients. Pages 151–157 in Robert G. Heath
(editor), Serological Fractions in Schizophrenia: A
Research Symposium. New York: Harper.

HEATH, R. G. et al. 1958 Behavioral Changes in Non-
psychotic Volunteers Following the Administration of
Taraxein, the Substance Obtained From Serum of
Schizophrenic Patients. American Journal of Psychiatry 114:919–920.

HOFFER, A. et al. 1957 Treatment of Schizophrenia
With Nicotinic Acid and Nicotinamide. Journal of
Clinical and Experimental Psychopathology 18:131–
158.

JERVIS, G. A. 1953 Phenylpyruvic Oligophrenia Deficiency of Phenylalanine-oxidizing System. Society for
Experimental Biology and Medicine, Proceedings 82:
514–515.

KETY, SEYMOUR S. 1959 Biochemical Theories of
Schizophrenia. Science New Series 129:1528–1532,
1590–1596.

KETY, SEYMOUR S. 1960 Measurement of Local Blood
Flow by the Exchange of an Inert, Diffusable Substance. Volume 8, pages 228–236 in Methods in Medical Research. Edited by H. D. Bruner. Chicago: Year
Book Publishers.

KETY, SEYMOUR S.; and SCHMIDT, C. F. 1948 Nitrous
Oxide Method for the Quantitative Determination of
Cerebral Blood Flow in Man: Theory, Procedure and
Normal Values. Journal of Clinical Investigation 27:
476–483.

LEVI-MONTALCINI, RITA; and ANGELETTI, PIETRO U. 1961
Biological Properties of a Nerve-growth Promoting
Protein and Its Antiserum. Pages 362–377 in Inter-
national Neurochemical Symposium, Fourth, Varenna,
Italy, 1960, Regional Neurochemistry; the Regional
Chemistry, Physiology, and Pharmacology of the
Nervous System: Proceedings. Edited by Seymour S.
Kety and Joel Elkes. New York: Pergamon.

NAUTA, W. J. 1958 Hippocampal Projections and Related Neural Pathways to the Mid-brain in the Cat.
Brain 81:319–340.

OSMOND, H.; and SMYTHIES, J. 1952 Schizophrenia: A
New Approach. Journal of Mental Science 98:309–
315.

PENROSE, LIONEL; and QUASTEL, JUADA H. 1937 Metabolic Studies in Phenylketonuria. Biochemical Journal
31:266–274.

PERSKY, H. et al. 1958 Relation of Emotional Responses
and Changes in Plasma Hydrocortisone Level After
Stressful Interview. A.M.A. Archives of Neurology and
Psychiatry 79:434–447.

POLLIN, WILLIAM; CARDON, PHILIPPE V. JR.; and KETY,
SEYMOUR S. 1961 Effects of Amino Acid Feedings
in Schizophrenic Patients Treated With Iproniazid.
Science New Series 133:104–105.

PRIBRAM, K. H.; and KRUGER, L. 1954 Functions of the
"Olfactory Brain." New York Academy of Sciences,
Annals 58:109–138.

RAMEY, E. R.; and GOLDSTEIN, M. S. 1957 The Adrenal
Cortex and the Sympathetic Nervous System. Physiological Reviews 37:155–195.

RODNICK, E. H.; and SHAKOW, D. 1940 Set in the
Schizophrenic as Measured by Composite Reaction
Time Index. American Journal of Psychiatry 97:214–
225.

SCHILDKRAUT, JOSEPH J. 1965 The Catecholamine Hypothesis of Affective Disorders: A Review of Supporting Evidence. American Journal of Psychiatry 122:
509–522.

SOKOLOFF, LOUIS; and KAUFMAN, SEYMOUR 1959 Effects of Thyroxine on Amino Acid Incorporation Into
Protein. Science New Series 129:569–570.

STRÖM-OLSEN, R.; and WEIL-MALHERBE, H. 1958 Hu-
moral Changes in Manic–Depressive Psychosis With
Particular Reference to the Excretion of Catechol
Amines in Urine. Journal of Mental Science 104:
696–704.

THUDICHUM, JOHN W. L. 1884 A Treatise on the Chemical Constitution of the Brain. London: Ballière.

WALLACE, H. W.; MOLDAVE, K.; and MEISTER, A. 1957
Studies on Conversion of Phenylalanine to Tyrosine
in Phenylpyruvic Oligophrenia. Society for Experimental Biology and Medicine, Proceedings 94:632–
633.

WELCH, BRUCE L.; and WELCH, ANN MARIE 1965 An
Effect of Aggregation Upon the Metabolism of Dopa-

mine-1-H³. Pages 201–206 in Symposium on Binding Sites of Brain Biogenic Amines, Galesburg, Ill., 1963, *Biogenic Amines*. Progress in Brain Research, Vol. 8. Amsterdam: Elsevier.

WOOLF, L. I.; and VULLIAMY, D. G. 1951 Phenylketonuria With Study of Effect Upon It of Glutamic Acid. *Archives of Disease in Childhood* 26:487–494.

IV
EPIDEMIOLOGY

"Epidemiology" refers to the science which studies "the mass phenomena of disease" (Greenwood 1935) by determining the distribution of conditions or diseases and the factors which determine these distributions (Lilienfeld 1959); that is, it is "the study of the distribution and determinants of disease prevalence in man" (MacMahon et al. 1960). The analysis that epidemiology makes of these findings results in a "medical ecology" (Gordon 1952). Epidemiology relates observed distributions of disorders to the environments in which people live—the physical, biological, and social environments.

"Mental disorder" is used in this article to refer to the full range of psychic conditions identified by psychiatrists or competent social authorities as abnormal or needing improvement. This is a broader range than would be used in planning or conducting any single inquiry but permits consideration, where necessary, of studies of delinquency, criminality, military desertion, and group fads (such as fish swallowing), as well as any conventional psychiatric diagnostic category or an individual symptom or special syndrome recognized in psychiatry.

Uses of epidemiology

Seven uses of epidemiology can be distinguished (Morris 1957): (1) knowledge regarding *historical trends* helps to distinguish disorders that are on the increase from those that are disappearing; (2) *community diagnosis* of the size, location, and distribution of a condition aids in planning health programs for the community; (3) from accumulated records of the ages at which individuals contract a disease, *individual risks* can be calculated (a basic tool in calculating insurance premiums), and knowledge of contingency risks aids in estimating the effects of host factors in determining the distribution of cases; (4) knowledge of the attributes of cases not in treatment *enlarges the clinical picture* by making our concept of a disorder less dependent on the clinician's limited perspective on cases; (5) occasionally, new *syndromes are identified* because clinically dissimilar cases are found to arise from a particular common background or because clinically similar cases are found to arise in two or more distinct sets of circumstances; (6) the *working of health services* can be studied in terms of their successes and failures, their selection of cases for treatment, and their deleterious effects on the people they seek to serve; and (7) in the *search for causes* of disorders, data on the factors associated with the distribution of a disorder supplement laboratory and clinical data in the elucidation of causal mechanisms—at times the crucial breakthrough in our understanding of the way in which a condition is caused is made by epidemiological inquiry (this occurred with cholera, pellagra, and lung cancer).

Historical trends. Historical trends are important but difficult to study. The Group for the Advancement of Psychiatry reviewed psychiatric knowledge recently (1961). The use of old data gathered for another purpose is sometimes tried. It is difficult to identify two groups at two different points in time which can be considered different time samples of the same population. If the questions are asked broadly enough and if the population being considered has some sort of continuing dimensions, an approximation of trends can sometimes be established. Two studies are noteworthy because they are particularly well done.

Goldhamer and Marshall (1949), in a superb study of the admission of psychotics to mental hospitals in Massachusetts during a hundred-year period, found evidence to contradict the widely held view that schizophrenia is becoming more common. In spite of the work's excellence, the implications of the findings remain uncertain, mainly because the data depend entirely on records of cases admitted to mental hospitals and because the population "sample" was taken from an area (Massachusetts) that was the first in North America to be industrialized and was subject to gross emigration and immigration during the time period observed.

With the hope of showing that an inverse relationship between intelligence and fertility was leading to a decrement in the national average intelligence quotient (IQ), a survey of Scottish intelligence tested "all" 11-year-olds on one day in 1930 and repeated almost the same procedure on one day in 1949. The findings were negative, according to the publications (Scottish Council for Research in Education 1953), but reinterpretation of the differences between the methods used in the two surveys suggests that the prevalence of very low scores among Scottish 11-year-olds may actually have decreased (Gruenberg 1964).

Community diagnosis. Many studies of particular communities have been carried out for diagnostic purposes; some outstanding examples are mentioned later in this article, in the section on case-finding methods. Since community diagnosis, by its nature, is done for a particular community, it is no more reasonable to borrow the diagnosis of one community and apply it to another than to borrow a neighbor's X ray because he had a similar cough. The general picture will be more or less the same, but the details which differentiate one community from the other may be crucial. Techniques for making rapid and relevant surveys of communities to aid mental health planning are sadly lacking. A few demographic facts are often used (as in the American Psychiatric Association's consultations) to infer what the findings would be.

From the health service's point of view, enumeration of cases that do not distinguish preventable or curable conditions from nonpreventable or noncurable cases are of little value. One learns only that the problem is small, big, very big, or enormous, depending on how one defines the problem. The American Public Health Association's *Mental Disorders* (1962) is a milestone because it indicates the conditions for which it is currently important to be able to enumerate cases. As the technology of treatment and prevention grows, this list will grow. This analysis also indicates that the social-breakdown syndrome is important in evaluating the benefits of a comprehensive community mental health service (e.g., Gruenberg 1966). Similarly, future studies for community diagnosis, as well as for analysis of health services, will require techniques for counting cases of conditions for which something can be done.

The calculation of individual risks. The risk of a child's being Mongoloid is dependent on its mother's age at the time of birth, but not its father's (Penrose 1949). If a woman has German measles while pregnant, there is an increased risk of her child's being brain-damaged; this increased risk is highest if the infection occurs during the third month of pregnancy (Hill et al. 1958). If a young child is removed from his parental home for months, there is an increased risk of nightmares, bed-wetting, and some other neurotic symptoms; if the mother leaves the child's home for several months, the increased risk is much less or nonexistent (Douglas & Blomfield 1958, pp. 112–113).

Calculating individual risks is frequently helpful; it should not be confused with measuring the *incidence* of a condition (number of new cases arising during a unit of time in a defined population, divided by the number of people in the defined population), or with measuring the *prevalence* (number of cases present at one point in time in a defined population, divided by the number of persons in that population at that point in time).

Enlarging the clinical picture. The clinical picture of a condition is almost automatically enlarged by follow-up studies. Follow-up studies of persons identified at about the age of 12 or 13 as mentally retarded are needed now because many cross-sectional prevalence studies have shown an age distribution of cases indicating a rapid fall in prevalence after age 14 that is incompatible with the definition of the condition, which includes the concept of a fixed, permanent state. [*See* MENTAL RETARDATION.]

The Medical Research Council Unit for Research on the Epidemiology of Psychiatric Illness provides psychiatric care in a general hospital ward in Edinburgh to which are routinely brought, regardless of severity, all self-poisoning cases in the city of Edinburgh. This comprehensive experience has made the clinicians aware of self-poisoning cases with intent at self-destruction by people who do not exhibit evidence of any psychiatric disorder; they find that the severity of need for psychiatric attention has no relation to the probability that the self-poisoning would lead to death. Thus, looking at *all* cases of self-poisoning is beginning to provide a different picture of the range of clinical findings.

Syndrome identification. The study of population distributions of cases resulted in separating typhus ("jail fever") from typhoid (water- and food-borne). Psychiatry has not made progress this way. Yet, certain diagnostic categories have been set up in terms of the age or personal characteristics or situations of the cases (e.g., involutional melancholia, combat fatigue, dementia praecox, senile dementia); such a classification short-circuits epidemiological inquiry. The course of disorders has been a key criterion in characterizing manic–depressive psychoses, dementia praecox, and mental retardation. Patients discourteous enough to violate the rules have simply had their diagnoses changed. Such practices hinder progress. "Puerperal psychoses" have been in and out of fashion, but pregnancy has not yet been shown to be associated with psychoses (Pugh et al. 1963). Involutional melancholia is confined to certain age levels and is out of favor at present. These illustrations indicate the special problems of classification in psychiatry, where entities like the Ganser syndrome in prisoners and combat fatigue in soldiers gain currency in each generation.

The social-breakdown syndrome is a new sociogenic entity. Its identification arose from observations that can be loosely termed clinical epidemiology (Pickles 1939). A community served by a single mental hospital that undergoes radical reform of patient care and breaks down barriers between hospital and community services stops producing new cases of severely deteriorated, helpless, vegetating individuals. Similar reforms elsewhere lead to similar observations.

As a result of these observations, clinicians with a broad (population) perspective change their views of the disorders. Disturbances in capacities to fill social roles come to be seen as extrinsic to the mental disorders of the patients and of secondary importance in comparison with the society's customs and attitudes regarding mental disorders which result in rejections and degrading behavior toward the ill. This sequence of observations leads to a reformulation of clinical syndromes that puts together manifestations previously thought to be due to several different disorders and that attributes these manifestations to a series of particular social events likely to occur in the presence of any of these disorders.

Like any other conclusion derived from unsystematic observations, it may gain currency because it fits the prevailing preconceptions of many people, without being further established. Unless systematic evidence is obtained, its validity remains untested.

The new sociogenic social-breakdown syndrome is best examined as a promising hypothesis. In order to test the sociogenic hypothesis, the syndrome must be defined operationally and case-finding techniques developed. These must be kept separate from the specification of the social conditions suspected of favoring the syndrome's appearance. Recent investigations have shown that these are soluble problems and confirm the hypothesis in large part; further investigation will also make clearer which mental disorders make people particularly susceptible to the noxious social forces [Gruenberg 1966; *see also* PSYCHIATRY, *article on* SOCIAL PSYCHIATRY].

Working of health services. Much of the data gathered on the distribution of mental disorders can be studied to help us understand how hospitals and clinics work. This can be a productive approach to data gathered for other uses. When a population is surveyed for cases similar to those that have gone to a hospital, many unhospitalized cases are found. This suggests that social forces control admissions; if so, these social forces may account

partly, or entirely, for variations in admission rates. This proved to be a productive hypothesis in studying the distribution of admissions for the elderly (Mental Health Research Unit 1959–1960) and could be used to interpret many findings (e.g., Faris and Dunham 1939; Goldhamer and Marshall 1949). Readmission rates can also be looked at this way. Freeman and Simmons (1963) found that the types of homes to which mental hospitals released patients did not affect the probability of return to the hospitals; from this they concluded that reasons for rehospitalization are unrelated to the social environment. However, the same data can be approached by starting with the assumption that a hospital staff releases only certain patients and, in deciding which to release, takes the family situation into account; if this is true, the data can be used to argue that the observed lack of difference only shows that the various staffs are equally competent in evaluating the suitability of different types of homes for their patients.

Thus, the plan to see whether variations in home living arrangements affect the probability of rehospitalization by studying a cohort of patients released from hospitals to varying home situations is irrelevant to the question. The plan is suitable for an evaluation of the hospitals' release policies with regard to different types of home situations. Obviously, volunteer subjects cannot be assumed to be randomly selected subjects; it is just as important—but sometimes more difficult—to perceive that subjects have been selected by someone else or by some agency. It is necessary to realize that when a bureaucracy selects subjects, the data reflect the behavior of the bureaucracy. The same principle applies to analysis of first mental-hospital admission rates.

Preventive trials. The most important studies of health services are those which are carried out in the form of a preventive trial when the health services seek to prevent a particular disorder. The population given the service is selected so that there is a comparable control population to whom service is not given (Pasamanick et al. 1964). The study then becomes a crucial experiment for the health service; it can also be a crucial experiment, if all goes well, for testing an etiological hypothesis. The preventive trial is often thought to represent the last stage of inquiry and to be justified only when much other evidence has been accumulated. But when the preventive procedure advocated is believed to be harmless and generally thought to be desirable and when its supply cannot satisfy all demands, the preventive trial is justified even if prior evidence is very weak. It is wrong to assume that preventive trials are inherently more expensive, more dangerous, or more difficult than passive studies; such research can be easier and cheaper. However, creating the opportunity for preventive trials and ascertaining that the design of the study is being adhered to throughout pose difficult problems.

The search for causes. Each use described above generates data with implications for causes.

Outstanding today are the efforts to identify the mechanisms which lead to what Pasamanick has called the "continuity of fetal damage," ranging from death to mild brain damage followed by reading disabilities, impulsive behavior disorders, and other syndromes. Fetal damage has been linked to rubella, to the effects of poverty, and to early complications of pregnancy. Several lines of evidence suggest its linkage to very mild or moderate malnutrition of the mother during the first few months of gestation (MacMahon & Sowa 1961).

The hypothesis of schizophrenogenic mothering is being pursued (Lidz & Fleck 1960). Current work is clarifying the nature of the hypothesis and may do more [see SCHIZOPHRENIA].

Maternal deprivation, as Bowlby (Bowlby et al. 1956) named a hypothetically pathogenic experience, has been investigated a number of times (e.g., Douglas & Blomfield 1958). These studies, like those of Pasamanick, not only look for causes but relate dissimilar clinical syndromes to one set of causes. Many investigations are required before the relationships become clarified and before the credibility of the hypothesis can be appraised. Bowlby's own study has weakened the initial hypothesis. Hunt (1965) has recently pointed to some further weaknesses in the hypothesis [see INFANCY, article on THE EFFECTS OF EARLY EXPERIENCE].

Down's syndrome (Mongolism, trisomy-21) is not only a major cause of serious mental handicap, but the new and growing knowledge regarding the associated chromosomal abnormality supports the notion that some particular cause or group of causes must be at work and that other chromosomal abnormalities may have the same causes. It is complicated to investigate these conditions, and social phenomena have not yet been implicated.

Too often efforts to find the determinants of the distribution of a mental disorder are launched as one-shot investigations, without the researchers' knowing what the distribution of cases is. This procedure assumes that if the distribution is found to be that predicted in the hypothesis, then the hypothesis has been proved, and if not, then it has been disproved. Such a course is not absolutely doomed to failure, but it is not likely to lead to the gathering of data that can rule out alternative explanations of the observed distributions.

Tools and techniques

Case finding. Hospital and state school records, clinic outpatient records, records of private practitioners, and key-informant methods have all been used repeatedly in case finding.

Hospital records have been used to study first-admission rates in relation to various hypotheses. Faris and Dunham (1939) pioneered the analysis of first-admission rates in terms of the modern social ecology of a city. Using the census-tract classification of Chicago, based on the University of Chicago sociology department's methods of characterizing urban land use, they allocated the first admissions to mental hospitals to the census tract of origin. They predicted correctly the now well-established fact that the first-admission rates for schizophrenia are highest in the central, deteriorated section of the city and decline with the distance of neighborhoods from the center. This was a startlingly successful fusion of Durkheim's ideas, urban sociology, and a hypothesis about the social origins of schizophrenic syndromes. Even more startling were the failure of manic–depressive psychoses to fall into such a pattern and the existence of a different pattern for organic psychoses. These different patterns tend to confirm the importance of the psychiatric diagnosis in spite of the skepticism of many psychiatrists regarding the objective nature of their diagnoses.

These findings have been confirmed in other cities. A literature has developed seeking to account for the high first-admission rates of schizophrenics from the city's center. The straightforward notion that the depersonalized, socially isolated part of the city favored the development of schizophrenic disorders has not been universally accepted. Attempts to demonstrate that the disproportionate concentration of schizophrenic cases coming to hospitals from the central part of the city is due to consequences of schizophrenic disorders rather than the pathogenic nature of these neighborhoods can be thought of as studies of the "drift hypothesis." This states that schizophrenics tend to drift into the rooming-house areas of cities at a higher rate than do other people, producing the concentration of cases found there.

Sanua (1963) points to the main studies of this hypothesis and to the conflicting evidence, citing Morrison's (1959) finding that patients had a lower social-class status than their fathers, whose social-class distribution was similar to that of the general population. The inference that schizophrenia causes downward social mobility does not necessarily follow from this observation; since occupational levels tend to rise with age, schizophrenics may accumulate in lower occupational categories because they fail to climb the occupational ladder as fast as other young people.

If downward mobility (or failure to rise with one's generation) is really at the root of the phenomenon, then the etiological theory advanced by Faris and Dunham does not hold. Their observations would remain, however, and require explanation.

A more recent study, *Social Class and Mental Illness*, by Hollingshead and Redlich (1958), found that in New Haven the *prevalence* of treated cases was related to social class. The authors asserted that their data show a *gradient* of prevalence rates which falls from a high rate in the lowest social class to a low rate in the upper social classes. Miller and Mishler (1959), however, state (correctly, I believe) that the New Haven data show only a very high rate for the lowest social class and that the observed figures in other classes do not demonstrate a gradient of rates.

The difficulties of interpreting such studies are compounded by the reliance of the studies on clinical records of cases in treatment and by the social factors affecting hospital-utilization patterns. To obviate the weaknesses of relying solely on clinical records, a method centering on a structured household-interview questionnaire derived in part from the Cornell neuropsychiatric inventory has been developed; this method has not yet been systematically calibrated (Macmillan 1959), but it holds out a promising potential. Its first important use for case finding on a large scale was by Stouffer (Stouffer et al. 1949) in World War II. It was one of the methods used in the first large-scale metropolitan survey, the Midtown Manhattan Study (Langner & Michael 1963).

One population of over two thousand has been personally interviewed by psychiatrists at both the beginning and the end of a decade (Essen-Möller 1956). Participant-observers with a psychiatric background have been useful (e.g., Eaton 1955).

Finding cases of severe deterioration (severe social-breakdown syndrome) has been carried out by means of a semistructured interview by specially trained public health nurses, psychiatric social workers, and graduate behavioral-science students. Another method involves interviewers' filling out structured questionnaires—together with answers to open-ended questions—after they have been trained to complete the protocols following open-ended interviews; these protocols are then evaluated by psychiatrists, who categorize the individuals (Mental Health Research Unit 1959–1960). A method similar in principle was used in the following years in the age groups under 60 in Stirling County and in midtown Manhattan (A. Leighton 1959; Hughes et al. 1960; D. Leighton et al. 1963; Langner & Michael 1963).

Cases derived from nonmedical-service-agency records were identified by Lemkau and associates (1941–1942) in the Eastern Health District in Baltimore and in the survey of the mentally retarded in Onondaga County, New York State, by the Mental Health Research Unit staff, under the direction of the program director (Goodman et al. 1956). All of these are useful devices. In practice all are complicated to use and none are easily applied with precision and accuracy. None of them have been adequately calibrated against a standardized ultimate criterion. Such a criterion requires a set of explicit objective criteria for identifying a case, a standardized method of observation, and an estimate of observer variability (Cochrane et al. 1951).

The methods of household sampling of populations, highly developed by social scientists, have been used in a number of studies; their most extensive use currently is in the continuous National Health Survey (U.S. National Health Survey 1958).

Sorting populations.   The use of statistical techniques in planning and interpreting studies has developed to a very high level, borrowing from general statistical theory, agricultural research, genetic research, social science, and economics. Epidemiologic inquiries have contributed devices for age standardization and for adjustment of data, which have in turn been used by those fields (Hill 1937).

The study of case aggregations in neighborhoods, households, and families has developed a whole series of techniques. Some of these depend on the concept of primary-case (or proband) rates and secondary-case rates. In the study of mental disorders this has been most frequently associated with genetic hypotheses, and in these instances the concept of lifelong expectation of manifesting the disorder has been developed. In this field the formulas of Wilhelm Weinberg and the mathematician G. H. Hardy (1908) and of Stern (1943) are particularly appropriate. They depend, however, on estimates of differential death and migration rates, whose validity is hard to judge from existing data. The study of familial and household aggregations is not confined to genetic hypotheses, however, as is shown in a review of the literature

(Gruenberg 1950) and by Bleuler's review of studies on schizophrenia (1955); a review of the knowledge regarding group disorders brings together concepts from psychiatry, social psychiatry, and social psychology (Gruenberg 1957).

Populations have commonly been characterized by age and sex and time ever since the Hippocratic writings on times, places, and persons. Variations in incidence and prevalence rates by age and sex are frequently interpreted as though age and sex were causative factors. Generally they are not mechanisms by which disorders are produced but convenient ways of classifying populations which develop disorders at different rates. The suspected mechanisms which are distributed according to age and sex also need to be looked into, as was done recently by Langner and Michael (1963). Categorizing the population according to previous illnesses is a frequent but not highly standardized procedure. Except for body typing, the categorizing of populations according to physical characteristics has not been used in inquiries regarding mental disorders. Studies attempting to link genetic characteristics to certain disorders have focused on blood types. It is to be expected that in the next decade other physical characteristics will prove relevant to mental disorder epidemiology. Categorizing populations by their social characteristics is almost standard nowadays in epidemiological inquiry in all fields. The social environment has usually been regarded as important by epidemiologists, and this recognition has been increased greatly by advances in methods of characterizing socioeconomic status and other social variables. The complexity of socioeconomic classifications in a rapidly changing society has made this type of categorizing hard to standardize; attention will probably become more focused on specific characteristics of individuals, some of which are incorporated into indices of socioeconomic status. One study showed that hospital-admission rates for elderly persons were unrelated to economic levels of neighborhoods but were closely related to the frequency of multiple-family dwellings in neighborhoods; yet no correlations with socioeconomic status (a composite index) could be found [see Gruenberg 1953; see also AGING].

The conduct of studies. The list of references makes it clear that contributions to the epidemiology of mental disorder have been made by workers with various professional backgrounds; there is no reason to expect this to be altered in the future. Technical expertness in such work does not develop from any one course of professional training but is acquired by experience in conducting and interpreting the findings of investigations. Too many investigations have been conducted with the hope of testing a hypothesis about the determinants of the distribution of a disorder in a single investigation. The opportunity for refining a hypothesis and going back with experienced investigators to the same population rarely occurs. But such steps can be expected to yield larger returns in knowledge than a proliferation of single investigations. These defects in the social organization of research are being rectified by the creation of permanent laboratories for conducting investigations.

The first such laboratory was created at Syracuse, New York, in 1950, on a pilot basis, by the New York State Department of Mental Hygiene and was made permanent in 1955. Since then the Medical Research Council of Great Britain has created one in the University of Edinburgh department of psychiatry; the Danish government has set up one at Aarhus; and the Swedish government, one at Lund. The U.S. National Institute of Mental Health finances one at the Columbia University department of psychiatry.

These improvements in social support should lead to a more rapid exploitation of advances as they are made and thus should speed up the acquisition of knowledge. But it is to be expected that a larger number of contributions to our understanding of mental-disorder epidemiology will continue to come from workers who are not labeled epidemiologists and who will in many instances not regard their work as particularly relevant to mental health. The epidemiologist will continue to be interested in getting answers to his questions and will, hopefully, judge new contributions on their merits rather than on their author's school of thought or previous conditions of servitude (i.e., degree sequences).

In the context of this encyclopedia it may be well to point out that *all* disorders, whatever the causes, have distributions that reflect social factors. This universal proposition follows from the simple fact that all classes of causes have such social distributions.

For example, Goldberger (1964) showed that pellagra is due to a nutritional deficiency by studying its incidence in different social groups in southern mill towns. MacMahon and Koller (1957) showed that the higher leukemia death rate among whites, as compared to nonwhites, may well be due to more exposure to diagnostic radiation among Jews (who apparently use medical specialists at a higher rate). Gelfand and his associates (1957) showed that naturally acquired immunity to polio viruses occurs at early ages most frequently in low-income groups. Böök (1961) reviewed accumulations of genes in particular linguistic and social groupings.

Roueché (1954) describes how poisons can spread through socially isolated parts of a population.

Sometimes the social forces are considered the main factors (as in "diseases of poverty" and in "diseases of affluence," such as coronary heart disease) and sometimes the intermediate variables that help unravel the chain (as in pellagra). But in understanding every distribution of disorders, knowledge of social forces plays some role.

ERNEST GRUENBERG

[*Directly related are the entries* EPIDEMIOLOGY *and* PUBLIC HEALTH. *Other relevant material may be found in* POPULATION; PSYCHIATRY; SAMPLE SURVEYS.]

BIBLIOGRAPHY

AMERICAN PUBLIC HEALTH ASSOCIATION, TECHNICAL DEVELOPMENT BOARD, PROGRAM AREA COMMITTEE ON MENTAL HEALTH 1962 *Mental Disorders: A Guide to Control Methods.* New York: The Association.

BLEULER, M. 1955 Research and Changes in Concepts in the Study of Schizophrenia: 1941–1950. Isaac Ray Medical Library, *Bulletin* [1955]:1–132.

BÖÖK, JAN A. 1961 Genetical Etiology in Mental Illness. Pages 14–45 in Milbank Memorial Fund, *Causes of Mental Disorders: A Review of Epidemiological Knowledge, 1959.* New York: The Fund.

BOWLBY, JOHN et al. 1956 The Effects of Mother–Child Separation: A Follow-up Study. *British Journal of Medical Psychology* 29:211–247.

COCHRANE, A. L.; CHAPMAN, P. J.; and OLDHAM, P. D. 1951 Observers' Errors in Taking Medical Histories. *Lancet* 1B:1007–1009.

DOUGLAS, JAMES W. B.; and BLOMFIELD, J. M. 1958 *Children Under Five.* London: Allen & Unwin.

EATON, JOSEPH W. 1955 *Culture and Mental Disorders: A Comparative Study of the Hutterites and Other Populations.* Glencoe, Ill.: Free Press.

ESSEN-MÖLLER, ERIK 1956 Individual Traits and Morbidity in a Swedish Rural Population. *Acta psychiatrica et neurologica scandinavica* Supplement 100.

FARIS, ROBERT E. L.; and DUNHAM, H. WARREN (1939) 1960 *Mental Disorders in Urban Areas: An Ecological Study of Schizophrenia and Other Psychoses.* New York: Hafner.

FREEMAN, HOWARD E.; and SIMMONS, OZZIE G. 1963 *The Mental Patient Comes Home.* New York and London: Wiley.

GELFAND, HENRY M. et al. 1957 Studies on the Development of Natural Immunity to Poliomyelitis in Louisiana. *American Journal of Hygiene* 65:367–385.

GOLDBERGER, JOSEPH 1964 *Goldberger on Pellagra.* Edited by Milton Terris. Baton Rouge: Louisiana State Univ. Press. → Reprint of 17 papers.

GOLDHAMER, HERBERT; and MARSHALL, ANDREW W. (1949) 1953 *Psychosis and Civilization.* Glencoe, Ill.: Free Press. → First published as *The Frequency of Mental Disease: Long-term Trends and Present Status.*

GOODMAN, M. B. et al. 1956 A Prevalence Study of Mental Retardation in a Metropolitan Area. *American Journal of Public Health.* 46:702–707.

GORDON, JOHN E. 1952 The Twentieth Century—Yesterday, Today, and Tomorrow (1920–   ). Pages 114–167 in Franklin H. Top (editor), *The History of American Epidemiology.* St. Louis, Mo.: Mosby.

GREENWOOD, MAJOR 1935 *Epidemic and Crowd Diseases.* London: Williams & Norgate.

GROUP FOR THE ADVANCEMENT OF PSYCHIATRY, COMMITTEE ON PREVENTIVE PSYCHIATRY 1961 *Problems of Estimating Changes in Frequency of Mental Disorders.* New York: The Group.

GRUENBERG, ERNEST M. 1950 Review of Available Material on Patterns of Occurrence of Mental Disorders: Major Disorders. Pages 176–196 in Milbank Memorial Fund, *Epidemiology of Mental Disorder.* New York: The Fund.

GRUENBERG, ERNEST M. 1953 Community Conditions and Psychoses of the Elderly. *American Journal of Psychiatry* 110:888–896.

GRUENBERG, ERNEST M. 1957 Socially Shared Psychopathology. Pages 201–229 in Alexander H. Leighton, John A. Clausen, and Robert N. Wilson (editors), *Explorations in Social Psychiatry.* New York: Basic Books.

GRUENBERG, ERNEST M. 1964 Epidemiology. Pages 259–306 in Harvey A. Stevens and Rick Heber (editors), *Mental Retardation.* Univ. of Chicago Press.

GRUENBERG, ERNEST M. (editor) 1966 Evaluating the Effectiveness of Mental Health Services. *Milbank Memorial Fund Quarterly* 44, no. 1, part 2.

HARDY, G. H. 1908 Mendelian Proportions in a Mixed Population. *Science* 28:49–50.

HILL, A. BRADFORD (1937) 1961 *Principles of Medical Statistics.* 7th ed. London: Lancet.

HILL, A. BRADFORD et al. 1958 Virus Diseases in Pregnancy and Congenital Defects. *British Journal of Preventive and Social Medicine* 12:1–7.

HOLLINGSHEAD, AUGUST B.; and REDLICH, FREDERICK C. 1958 *Social Class and Mental Illness: A Community Study.* New York: Wiley.

HUGHES, CHARLES et al. 1960 *People of Cove and Woodlot: Communities From the Viewpoint of Social Psychiatry.* The Stirling County Study of Psychiatric Disorder and Sociocultural Environment, Vol. 2. New York: Basic Books.

HUNT, J. McV. 1965 Traditional Personality Theory in the Light of Recent Evidence. *American Scientist* 53: 80–96.

LANGNER, THOMAS S.; and MICHAEL, STANLEY T. 1963 *Life Stress and Mental Health.* Volume 2 of *The Midtown Manhattan Study.* New York: Free Press.

LEIGHTON, ALEXANDER H. 1959 *My Name Is Legion: Foundations for a Theory of Man in Relation to Culture.* The Stirling County Study of Psychiatric Disorder and Sociocultural Environment, Vol. 1. New York: Basic Books.

LEIGHTON, DOROTHEA et al. 1963 *The Character of Danger.* The Stirling County Study of Psychiatric Disorder and Sociocultural Environment, Vol. 3. New York: Basic Books.

LEMKAU, PAUL; TIETZE, CHRISTOPHER; and COOPER, MARCIA 1941–1942 Mental-hygiene Problems in an Urban District. *Mental Hygiene* 25:624–646; 26:100–119, 275–288.

LIDZ, THEODORE; and FLECK, STEPHEN 1960 Schizophrenia, and Human Integration, and the Role of the

Family. Pages 323–345 in Don D. Jackson (editor), *The Etiology of Schizophrenia*. New York: Basic Books.

LILIENFELD, ABRAHAM M. 1959 A Methodological Problem in Testing a Recessive Genetic Hypothesis in Human Disease. *American Journal of Public Health* 49: 199–204.

MACMAHON, BRIAN; and KOLLER, ERNEST K. 1957 Ethnic Differences in the Incidence of Leukemia. *Blood: The Journal of Hematology* 12:1–10.

MACMAHON, BRIAN; PUGH, THOMAS F.; and IPSEN, JOHANNES 1960 *Epidemiologic Methods*. Boston: Little.

MACMAHON, BRIAN; and SOWA, JAMES M. 1961 Physical Damage to the Fetus. Pages 51–110 in Milbank Memorial Fund, *Causes of Mental Disorders: A Review of Epidemiological Knowledge, 1959*. New York: The Fund.

MACMILLAN, ALLISTER M. 1959 A Survey Technique for Estimating the Prevalence of Psychoneurotic and Related Types of Disorders in Communities. Pages 203–218 in American Psychiatric Association, *Epidemiology of Mental Disorder*. Washington: The Association.

MENTAL HEALTH RESEARCH UNIT, NEW YORK STATE DEPARTMENT OF MENTAL HYGIENE, SYRACUSE, NEW YORK 1959–1960 A Mental Health Survey of Older People. Parts 1–3. *Psychiatric Quarterly Supplement* 33:45–99, 252–300; 34:34–75.

MILLER, S. M.; and MISHLER, E. G. 1959 Social Class, Mental Illness, and American Psychiatry: An Expository Review. *Milbank Memorial Fund Quarterly* 37: 174–199.

MORRIS, JEREMY N. (1957) 1965 *Uses of Epidemiology*. 2d ed. Baltimore: Williams & Wilkins.

MORRISON, S. L. 1959 Principles and Methods of Epidemiological Research and Their Application to Psychiatric Illness. *Journal of Mental Science* 105: 999–1011.

PASAMANICK, BENJAMIN et al. 1964 Home vs. Hospital Care for Schizophrenics. *Journal of the American Medical Association* 187:177–181.

PENROSE, LIONEL S. (1949) 1963 *The Biology of Mental Defect*. 3d ed. London: Sidgwick & Jackson.

PICKLES, WILLIAM N. 1939 *Epidemiology in Country Practice*. Bristol (England): Wright; Baltimore: Williams & Wilkins.

PUGH, THOMAS F. et al. 1963 Rates of Mental Disease Related to Childbearing. *New England Journal of Medicine* 268:1224–1228.

ROUECHÉ, BERTON 1954 *Eleven Blue Men*. Boston: Little.

SANUA, VICTOR D. 1963 The Etiology and Epidemiology of Mental Illness and Problems of Methodology, With Special Emphasis on Schizophrenia. *Mental Hygiene* 47:607–621.

SCOTTISH COUNCIL FOR RESEARCH IN EDUCATION, MENTAL SURVEY COMMITTEE 1953 *Social Implications of the 1947 Scottish Mental Survey*. Univ. of London Press.

STERN, CURT 1943 The Hardy–Weinberg Law. *Science* 97:137–138.

STOUFFER, SAMUEL A. et al. 1949 *The American Soldier*. Studies in Social Psychology in World War II. Vols. 1 and 2. Princeton Univ. Press. → Volume 1: *Adjustment During Army Life*. Volume 2: *Combat and Its Aftermath*.

U.S. NATIONAL HEALTH SURVEY 1958 *Health Statistics, Series A*. Volume I. Washington: Government Printing Office.

V

CHILDHOOD MENTAL DISORDERS

Early conceptions of mental disorders in children are reflected in several clinical papers on child-rearing practices from the sixteenth, seventeenth, and eighteenth centuries (see Kessen 1965). These precursors of present ideas about causality failed to receive widespread acceptance and scientific interest, however, until recently. Even Kraepelin's influential *Psychiatrie*, first published in 1893, did not discuss mental disorders in children in any of its many editions. Scientific interest in deviant mental processes in children has flowered in the twentieth century, stimulated in large part by theories of mental functioning advanced by Freud, Piaget, Watson, and others which emphasized developmental and dynamic factors as well as notions of environment causality and learning. Further, interest in mental disorders in children has increased with the resurgence of scientific interest in children's behavior in general in the twentieth century, particularly since the late 1940s.

Resources for the diagnosis and treatment of mental disorders in children have multiplied in the United States and in Europe since the 1950s. In the United States, the establishment of the National Institute of Mental Health and the National Institute of Child Health and Development and the allocation of federal funds for the development of plans for organizing and providing comprehensive mental health services in local communities have stimulated the growth of relevant programs of service, professional training, and research. A federally supported conference of professional organizations and interested agencies was held in 1964 to insure and to plan for the provision of diagnosis and treatment of mental disorders in children under federally sponsored community health programs (American Psychiatric Association 1964).

Definition, predisposition, precipitation. The definition of disorders of mental functioning in children varies depending upon one's conception of mental functioning in general. Most professionals—including psychologists, psychiatrists, and social workers—with special training in the diagnosis and treatment of mental disorders in children currently emphasize a multidimensional approach. This approach encompasses psychosomatic considerations; developmental capacities and vulnerabilities; constitutional and genetic factors; the internal personality system, including cognitive, perceptual, and affective mechanisms and the fluidity and plasticity of the child's personality characteristics; and psychosocial considerations, including parent–child relationships, family interactions, and sociocultural influences. This approach also stresses the need to assess and capitalize upon the healthy and adaptive facets of the child's personality.

A conceptual framework which encompasses all of the above aspects of the child's functioning inclusively and systematically has not been developed. However, the Committee on Child Psychiatry of the Group for the Advancement of Psychiatry has prepared (in unpublished form) what appears to be the best available approximation of such a framework (Committee on Child Psychiatry 1965). The present discussion of mental disorders in children leans heavily upon its work.

Mental disorder can be defined as a failure in the child's attempt to maintain an adaptive equilibrium between physiological, psychological, and interpersonal systems; there is a close relationship between physical and psychological factors. In the child with certain constitutional or experiential predispositions, disordered mental functioning may be precipitated and sustained by physical, psychological, or social stimuli.

Biochemical stimuli or stressful insufficiencies of chemical substances may disrupt the child's physiological equilibrium as well as associated perceptual, cognitive, and emotional systems. In addition, the child's restitutive efforts involve an interaction between physiological, psychological, and social systems.

Stimuli of a psychological nature may also precipitate mental disorder. Such stimuli include conscious or unconscious thoughts and feelings which arouse anxiety in the child because of their association with stressful past or present experiences. They involve the cognitive system in that they are represented in symbolic form in memory and thinking, and the perceptual apparatus. Thoughts, memories, and feelings triggered by anxiety-arousing psychological stimuli lead to the child's employment of psychological defenses or compensating behaviors as he seeks to avoid a breakdown in adaptation or equilibrium.

Stressful social stimuli in the child's environment may also precipitate disorder. Such stimuli include the loss, or threat of loss, of close interpersonal relationships and the frustration of basic needs resulting from disturbances in relationships within the family.

The nature and severity of the mental disorder precipitated by physical, psychological, or social stimuli, or of interactions among them, is contingent upon the stressfulness of the stimuli as well as upon genetic and constitutional factors (for example, temperament, body build), previous experience, and the developmental level of the child. Stressful stimuli initially disruptive of one of these systems may, and often do, have repercussions in other systems. Thus mental disorders in children may be precipitated by disruptions of a physical, social, or psychological nature, but the child's defensive efforts or attempts at restoration of ego functions or compensatory behavior almost always involve all three systems. For example, a stressful thought or fantasy may lead to emotional conflict which triggers "signal anxiety." This signal, warning of possible breakdown in adaptation or mental equilibrium, leads to the establishment of psychological defenses or adaptive interpersonal behaviors. If emotional conflict and anxiety are severe or become chronic, physiological concomitants may develop. Such physiological symptoms are reversible if the underlying emotional conflicts are resolved; chronic unresolved conflict and anxiety may lead, however, to serious strain and even breakdown of weakened physiological systems or organs. [*See* ANXIETY; CONFLICT, *article on* PSYCHOLOGICAL ASPECTS; STRESS.]

In the first several months of life the immaturity of the physical and mental systems results in the infant's responding in a global manner to lack of gratification of his needs or to stressful stimuli. The very young infant shows little differentiation of emotional response; he tends to respond to stressful stimuli with general symptoms of distress (for example, crying, global motor activity). However, there is increasing evidence of systematic individual differences in response even at this early level of development (Murphy 1962). Individual differences in stress thresholds, modes of expressing distress, and secondary reactions to distress—including the number of organ systems involved and the intensity of their involvement—may be prognostic in infants of a predisposition to mental disorder in later childhood (Korner 1964).

In children predisposed by stressful experiences and by personality structure, continued emotional conflict may lead to the chronic use of psychological defenses and maladaptive social behaviors known as symptoms of mental disorder. Particular constellations of such symptoms define the different types of mental disorder in children. In general, these clusters of clinical symptoms can be assigned to one of three general divisions: psychoneuroses, personality or character disorders, or psychoses.

Some of the physical or psychological symptoms in each cluster may result from the child's attempt to maintain equilibrium or adaptation in the face of *current* stressful events or to compensate for the disturbance, to make restitution, or to obtain gratification of physical, psychological, or interpersonal needs. Other symptoms in each clinical picture may define the new equilibrium resulting from the child's adaptive and compensating efforts. They may include partial restriction or malfunctioning of perceptual, cognitive, social, or physiological functions, rigid reliance upon defense mechanisms such as repression and denial, or a more severe breakdown in adaptive efforts.

Anna Freud (1965), Erik Erikson (1950), and many others have emphasized that in addition to the physical and personality characteristics and the experiences of the child, it is important to consider both his developmental level and "lines" or continuities of development. Thus, the notion of a state of psychological equilibrium in the child is only a relative one, with such states stable and definable only at cross-sectional points in time during his growth. These "states" interact systematically, and lines of development such as that from "dependency to emotional self-reliance and adult object relationships" may be observed (A. Freud 1965).

Interpersonal or psychological events may have stressful effects upon a relatively immature mental apparatus, whereas the same stimuli may be handled without disruptive anxiety by an older child or adult. In addition, the child may defend against anxiety resulting from such stimuli through regression to a more immature level of adaptation. Or, such stimuli may reinforce fixations of personality development which partially preclude further development in one or more areas of functioning (for example, learning). Thus the child's developmental level partially determines his capacities and modes of coping with potentially stressful stimuli of a physical, social, or psychological nature and partially determines the type and severity of mental disorder. For example, certain intrauterine viral infections during early pregnancy are more likely to produce congenital anomalies than such infections occurring later in gestation. In addition, a prolonged lack of adequate mothering is particularly damaging to infants in the second half of the first year. The research of Spitz (1946), Bowlby (1960*a*; 1960*b*), Provence and Lipton (1962), Piaget (Flavell 1963), Escalona and Heider (1959), and Heider (1960), as well as recent animal research by ethologists (Ostow 1959), suggests that serious and perhaps irreversible defects in social and intellectual development may follow if the child fails to receive sufficient interpersonal or perceptual stimulation during appropriate developmental phases, including those of early infancy. Such defects may predispose the child to one or another type of mental disorder, but knowledge of the specific nature of such relationships depends upon future research. [*See* INFANCY, *article on* THE EFFECTS OF EARLY EXPERIENCE.]

Freud's concept of emotional conflict as amplified by Anna Freud, Hartmann, Erikson, and others is central in contemporary theories of mental disorder in children, particularly with respect to the development of psychoneuroses. As the infant or preschool child develops relationships with people and as his mental functions become more complex, he may show a variety of *reactive disturbances* in behavior, such as temper tantrums, aggressive behavior, and crying. These disturbances are reactive to environmental stress, primarily conflicts with parents over the control (socialization) of basic sexual and aggressive drives, and are the early precursors of internalized emotional conflict. In the early years, these disturbances are generally transient and reversible in response to positive changes in the environment, although as a result of continued disturbances in parent–child relationships, they may become chronic and fixed. Reactive disorders are also seen in the older child; the symptoms may include anxiety, unrealistic fears, shyness, feelings of inadequacy or loneliness, disturbances in attentional processes and learning, and inappropriate social behavior.

If the child's emotional conflicts are especially anxiety-arousing and unresolved, they later lose their conscious nature and are repressed and internalized. The conflicts are then inaccessible to further attempts at resolution, including new efforts made possible by the development of more powerful and complex cognitive and other ego functions: the capacities for greater independence in the gratification of needs, a longer attention span, improved reality testing, increased ability to think abstractly as well as concretely, and further differentiation and integration of perceptual and motor functions—together with further differentiation of the emotions, more effective repression of anxiety and other affects, and the internalization and symbolic representation of conflict. Because of their relative inaccessibility to conscious problem-solving efforts, emotional conflicts in the child may become self-perpetuating and lead to the establishment of chronically maladaptive behavior learned in early periods of development.

Depending upon his experiences and his own developmental capacities, however, the child may instead resolve conflicts established earlier, or a new conflict facing him in a crisis situation, and thereby achieve a higher level of differentiation and structure of personality. If such resolution and mastery is prevented, temporary regression, long-term arrest in cognitive or emotional function and development, or decompensation or adaptive failure may occur. Thus, unconscious conflicts, with associated alternating experiences of anxiety and employment of maladaptive psychological defenses, may become firmly established components of the personality, leading to structural rigidity and brittleness and presenting the model of psychoneurosis in the child.

Psychoneurotic disorders. A variety of symptoms and patterns of symptoms may be observed in the psychoneurotic mental disorders of children. These symptomatic reactions to neurotic conflict may fluctuate and change with changes in development and socialization. The psychoneuroses are not characterized by extreme personality disorganization and grossly distorted reality testing. Although psychoneurotic symptoms of internalized emotional conflict may be observed in children as young as three or four years, fully structured neurotic disorders are not ordinarily seen in children until the early school-age period. The typical childhood neurosis develops in a youngster who has already evolved a conscience or superego, who has achieved an internalization of conflict and the use of a variety of defense mechanisms, including repression of affects from consciousness, and who manifests symptoms symbolically relevant to the underlying conflicts. Several relatively independent types of psychoneurotic disturbances in children have been defined, including anxiety, phobic, conversion, dissociative, obsessive–compulsive, and depressive disorders. Detailed descriptions of these disorders are discussed elsewhere [*see* ANXIETY; DEPRESSIVE DISORDERS; OBSESSIVE–COMPULSIVE DISORDERS; PHOBIAS; *see also* Committee on Child Psychiatry 1965].

The well-known cases of "Frankie" (Bornstein 1949) and "Little Hans" (Freud 1909) are illustrative of the phobic type of neurotic disorder in which the defense mechanism of *displacement* is prominent. Here the child unconsciously displaces the meaning or content of the underlying emotional conflict onto an object or situation in his environment which is symbolically relevant. The fears derived from the internalized conflict are experienced in a distorted and irrational manner. The child avoids stimuli which reactivate or intensify his displaced conflict, and he often projects his sexual, hostile, and other unacceptable feelings onto the external feared objects such as animals, dirt, elevators, or situations such as school. Mild

and transient fears, fearful reactions to stressful experiences (reactive disorders), and common developmental crises involving separation anxiety in children should be carefully distinguished from phobic psychoneurotic disorders, with their internalized and structured nature. [*See* DEFENSE MECHANISMS.]

Remission of symptomatic behaviors without treament may be observed in some of the milder psychoneurotic disorders as the child masters the developmental tasks and crises of later stages (Nagera 1966). However, such disorders ordinarily require psychotherapeutic intervention with the child and his family. The prognosis for response to treatment is good. Treatment requires assessment of the balance of external and internal forces involved in the disorder (Haworth 1964). Depending upon the balance of such forces, therapeutic intervention may be made primarily through manipulation of the environment, or the therapist may focus upon achieving intrapsychic changes in the child and other family members, leading to the resolution of interpersonal conflict, the relieving of neurotic symptoms, the promoting of further development in the mental apparatus, and the learning of more adequate social responses and modes of coping with stressful stimuli (Kessler 1966).

Personality disorders. The personality disorders differ from psychoneurotic disorders in children in the following ways. In personality disorders, chronic (fixed) pathological trends and traits are prominent, and they are ego-syntonic—that is, they are not perceived by the child as anxiety-arousing or as a source of distress. Most of the personality disorders in children appear to involve strong fixations and/or disturbances in earlier psychological and psychosexual development, related to crises and conflicts involving wishes for dependency and autonomy, the handling of sexual and aggressive impulses and behaviors, and sex role identification. The types of personality disorder which have been defined (Committee on Child Psychiatry 1965) include the anxious personality, compulsive personality, hysterical personality, overly dependent personality, oppositional personality, overly inhibited personality, overly independent personality, isolated personality, distrustful personality, personality with discharge disorder (impulse-ridden or neurotic types), and sociosyntonic personality disorder.

Discharge disorders. The discharge-disorder category includes many children who are classified in other systems as delinquent, acting-out, psychopathic, or sociopathic. Children in this general category tend to act out directly their feelings and impulses in an antisocial and often highly destructive manner. Two subcategories have been defined which distinguish between an impulse-ridden group and a group in whose discharge disorder neurotic conflict plays an important role. There is a central tendency in both of these subgroups to discharge rather than delay or inhibit antisocial impulses, but the sources of the tendency to discharge differ. The child with an impulse-ridden personality shows low frustration tolerance and difficulty in controlling or channeling sexual and aggressive impulses; his interpersonal relationships tend to be shallow, he experiences little anxiety or guilt, and there is considerable deficiency in conscience development and in the development of flexible and complex defense mechanisms. He tends to have a history of extreme emotional deprivation. The neurotic personality disorder subgroup, on the other hand, has achieved a more complex level of personality development. The child in this subgroup has developed the capacity to internalize conflict, and his antisocial behavior tends to be reactive to such conflicts and to have unconscious symbolic significance to such conflicts. These children experience some anxiety and guilt, and their interpersonal relationships, while ambivalent, are warmer and more meaningful than those of children with impulse-ridden personality [*see* DELINQUENCY, *article on* PSYCHOLOGICAL ASPECTS; PSYCHOPATHIC PERSONALITY].

Developmental deviations. It is important to distinguish between the diagnoses of psychoneurosis and personality disorder, and *developmental deviations.* Some behaviors (for example, sexual deviations), often part of a neurotic and personality disorder, may also be related primarily to delay, acceleration, or unevenness in development and should be classified as developmental deviations rather than as neuroses or personality disorders.

Psychotic disorders. Psychotic mental disorders in children are characterized by marked and pervasive deviations from mental functioning normal for the child's age. In general, these disorders usually include chronic and severe impairment or deterioration of emotional relationships, preoccupation with inanimate objects, failure to develop speech or loss of speech for purposes of communication, bizarre behavior and unusual motility patterns, extreme mood swings and intensity of affective experience and expression (as in sudden temper outbursts, panic, etc.), and failure to develop or loss of a sense of individual identity. There are generally severe disturbances in perceptual and cognitive development and functioning, but with onset in later childhood certain areas of intellectual functioning and achievement may be adequate or better. Some of the symptoms seen in childhood psychosis—such as some of the disorders in thinking, affect, perception, motility, speech, object relations, and reality testing—represent efforts at restitution or compensation for the psychotic process.

Autism and symbiotic psychosis. Childhood psychoses do not tend to crystallize into as many varieties or subtypes as is the case with adult psychoses (Kessler 1966). Two major subtypes have been defined in early childhood: infantile autism and symbiotic or interactional psychotic disorder. Age of onset in infantile autism is the first few months of life as the infant fails to develop a normal emotional attachment to a mother figure. He remains emotionally aloof, speech development is delayed or absent, feeding and sleeping problems and stereotyped motor and motility patterns are prominent, and the child responds to relatively slight changes in his environment with intense outbursts of anger or anxiety. Some intellectual functions are intact, but their use is impaired by the defective reality testing and lack of communication.

Age of onset of symbiotic psychosis is after the first year or two of life. The child develops a normal emotional attachment to his mother but fails to achieve separation and individuation. Intense and prolonged dependency upon the mother (or between mother and child) is prominent in the early history. The disorder is usually precipitated by some real or fantasied threat to the mother–child relationship. Symptoms include marked and severe separation anxiety, clinging (sometimes indiscriminately), regression (for example, giving up speech, loss of bowel control), gradual withdrawal from object relations, autistic behavior, and distortions in perceptual and cognitive functioning.

Childhood schizophrenia. Childhood schizophrenia or "schizophreniform" psychotic disorder occurs in middle childhood—ages 6 through 12 or 13. The disorder may be of gradual or relatively acute onset. Where onset of the disorder is gradual, the development of neurotic symptoms is followed by regression to use of the primitive defenses of marked denial and projection. Low frustration tolerance, hypochondriacal tendencies, and inappropriate outbursts of temper or panic are often observed, and these are followed by withdrawal, increasing involvement in private fantasy, emotional aloofness, disorders in thinking and perception, autistic behavior, and a breakdown in reality testing (e.g., Goldfarb 1961). The prognosis is more favorable if the psychosis is an acute reaction to a developmental crisis. Few adultlike hallucinations are experienced by psychotic children until ages 9 or 10 at least. However, bizarre motor behavior (for example, whirling), self-mutilation and suicidal attempts, and inappropriate mood swings are seen with some frequency in these cases. Occasionally, some of the symptoms more characteristic of adult psychoses are seen in children. These include ideas of reference, somatic delusions, catatonic behavior, and paranoia. [See SCHIZOPHRENIA.]

Parent–child relations. In diagnosing neurosis, personality disorder, or psychosis in children, the healthy, positive responses and capacities as well as psychopathological trends should be assessed, along with the positive and negative physical, social, and psychological determinants of the child's behavior (A. Freud 1965).

Current views of the diagnosis and treatment of mental disorders in children stress the importance of parent–child relationships, family processes, and sociocultural influences, while remaining cognizant of contributing and predisposing genetic and constitutional factors.

Disturbances in parent–child relationships have been implicated in a variety of children's mental disorders, including unusual fluctuations in mood, psychoneuroses, certain psychotic disorders, and "antisocial" personality disorders, as well as disorders in which both physical and psychological functions are disturbed, such as marasmus or failure to thrive in infants, ulcerative colitis, asthma, and disturbances in perceptual, cognitive, and sensory–motor functions related to structural changes in the central nervous system.

The connection between type of mental disorder and specific characteristics of parent–child relationships is complex and not clearly understood. Research on certain personality factors characteristic of parents of psychotic and neurotic children (such as that of Sarason et al. 1960) shows that parents of children with high anxiety differ in certain personality traits from parents of children with low anxiety, and the "superego lacunae" shown by Johnson and Szurek (1952) in the parents of some kinds of antisocial children indicate the probability of some specificity in the relationship between parent–child interaction variables and type and severity of mental disorder.

In addition to the quality of the parent–child relationship, other family variables may predispose and contribute to the development of mental disorders in children (e.g., Ross 1964). For example, loss of a family member, lack of family cohesiveness, distorted and neurotic communication patterns, deviant role functions, conflicting value orientations, or poor integration with the community may serve as stressful stimuli which upset the functioning of the family and lead to a reactive disorder, developmental deviation, neuroses, personality disorder, or psychoses in the child.

One of the characteristics of the healthy family is the capacity to respond adaptively to crisis. Serious illness, economic losses, death of a parent, removal to a new community, and other such stressful events tend to be disruptive of family equilibrium and established modes of functioning and relating. Such disruptions may be temporary and through mastery lead to a higher level of functioning, or they may continue and result in family disintegration or pathology in one or more family members.

There is some indication of a specific relationship between type of family disruption and type of mental disorder in the child. For example, certain types of delinquent acting-out tend to occur in families with little cohesiveness and faulty disciplinary practices (e.g., Bandura & Walters 1959; McCord et al. 1961). Certain patterns seem characteristic in families of children suffering from schizophrenia or certain types of autism (e.g., Lidz & Fleck 1960). However, as is the case with other variables which have been implicated to some degree in mental disorders of children, the establishment of clear-cut relations between family variables and individual child disorders depends upon further research.

Sociocultural variables have also been implicated in the etiology of children's mental disorders. Variations in child-rearing practices and attitudes have been noted in different ethnic and social-class groups and cultures, as have incidence and type of disorder and attitudes and responses to treatment (e.g., Whiting 1963; Clinard 1957). However, the social and psychological mechanisms mediating the relationship between sociocultural variables and mental disorder are still poorly understood. Potentially stressful events for families and individuals include movement from rural to urban areas; shifts in socioeconomic conditions and traditional customs, attitudes, and interpersonal functions; and the acculturation of primitive or previously relatively isolated cultures. Children who experience such events without adequate preparation are particularly vulnerable to mental disorder (Kessler 1966).

The economic, religious, and educational status of the family also seems related to the manner in which the other family members react to mental disorder in a child, just as stereotypes of these groups tend to affect the treatment plans and services offered by agencies and clinicians.

BRITTON K. RUEBUSH

[*Directly related are the entries* MENTAL RETARDATION; PSYCHIATRY, *article on* CHILD PSYCHIATRY. *Other relevant material may be found in* DEVELOPMENTAL PSYCHOLOGY; INFANCY.]

BIBLIOGRAPHY

AMERICAN PSYCHIATRIC ASSOCIATION 1964 *Planning Psychiatric Services for Children in the Community Mental Health Program.* Washington: The Association.

BANDURA, ALBERT; and WALTERS, RICHARD H. 1959 *Adolescent Aggression.* New York: Ronald Press.

BORNSTEIN, BERTA 1949 The Analysis of a Phobic Child: Some Problems of Theory and Technique in Child Analysis. *Psychoanalytic Study of the Child* 3/4:181–226.

BOWLBY, JOHN 1960a Separation Anxiety. *International Journal of Psycho-analysis* 41:89–113.

BOWLBY, JOHN 1960b Grief and Mourning in Infancy and Early Childhood. *Psychoanalytic Study of the Child* 15:9–52.

CHESS, STELLA 1959 *An Introduction to Child Psychiatry.* New York: Grune.

CLINARD, MARSHALL B. (1957) 1963 *Sociology of Deviant Behavior.* Rev. ed. New York: Holt.

COMMITTEE ON CHILD PSYCHIATRY, GROUP FOR THE ADVANCEMENT OF PSYCHIATRY 1965 A Proposed Classification of Psychological Disorders in Childhood. Unpublished manuscript.

CRAMER, JOSEPH B. 1959 Common Neuroses of Childhood. Volume 1, pages 797–815 in *American Handbook of Psychiatry.* Edited by Silvano Arieti. New York: Basic Books.

ERIKSON, ERIK H. (1950) 1964 *Childhood and Society.* 2d ed., rev. & enl. New York: Norton.

ESCALONA, SIBYLLE; and HEIDER, GRACE 1959 *Prediction and Outcome.* New York: Basic Books.

FLAVELL, JOHN H. 1963 *The Developmental Psychology of Jean Piaget.* Princeton, N.J.: Van Nostrand.

FREUD, ANNA 1965 *Normality and Pathology in Childhood: Assessment of Development.* New York: International Universities Press.

FREUD, SIGMUND (1909) 1955 Analysis of a Phobia in a Five-year-old Boy. Volume 10, pages 3–149 in Sigmund Freud, *The Standard Edition of the Complete Psychological Works of Sigmund Freud.* London: Hogarth; New York: Macmillan. → First published in German.

GOLDFARB, WILLIAM 1961 *Childhood Schizophrenia.* Cambridge, Mass.: Harvard Univ. Press.

HAWORTH, MARY R. (editor) 1964 *Child Psychotherapy: Practice and Theory.* New York: Basic Books.

HEIDER, GRACE 1960 Vulnerability in Infants. Menninger Clinic, *Bulletin* 24:104–114.

JOHNSON, ADELAIDE M.; and SZUREK, S. A. 1952 The Genesis of Antisocial Acting Out in Children and Adults. *Psychoanalytic Quarterly* 21:323–343.

KESSEN, WILLIAM 1965 *The Child.* New York: Wiley.

KESSLER, JANE W. 1966 *Psychopathology of Childhood.* Englewood Cliffs, N.J.: Prentice-Hall.

KORNER, ANNELIESE F. 1964 Some Hypotheses Regarding the Significance of Individual Differences at Birth for Later Development. *Psychoanalytic Study of the Child* 19:58–72.

LIDZ, THEODORE; and FLECK, STEPHEN 1960 Schizophrenia, Human Integration, and the Role of the Family. Pages 323–345 in Don Jackson (editor), *The Etiology of Schizophrenia.* New York: Basic Books.

McCORD, WILLIAM; McCORD, JOAN; and HOWARD, ALAN 1961 Familial Correlates of Aggression in Nondelinquent Male Children. *Journal of Abnormal and Social Psychology* 62:79–93.

MURPHY, LOIS 1962 *The Widening World of Childhood: Paths Toward Mastery.* New York: Basic Books.

NAGERA, H. 1966 *Early Childhood Disturbances, the Infantile Neurosis, and the Adult Disturbances.* New York: International Universities Press.

OSTOW, MORTIMER 1959 The Biological Basis of Human Behavior. Volume 1, pages 58–87 in Silvano Arieti (editor), *American Handbook of Psychiatry.* New York: Basic Books.

PROVENCE, SALLY; and LIPTON, ROSE 1962 *Infants in Institutions.* New York: International Universities Press.

ROSS, ALAN O. 1964 *The Exceptional Child in the Family.* New York: Grune.

SARASON, SEYMOUR et al. 1960 *Anxiety in Elementary School Children.* New York: Wiley.

SPITZ, RENÉ 1946 Anaclitic Depression. *Psychoanalytic Study of the Child* 2:313–342.

WHITING, BEATRICE B. (editor) 1963 *Six Cultures: Studies of Child Rearing.* New York: Wiley.

VI
EXPERIMENTAL STUDY

Mental disorders vastly extend the normal range and variety of human behavior available for psychological study. They present familiar patterns in exaggerated form or in unusual combinations, incompletely developed, or disorganized. Although these derangements are often accompanied by seemingly arbitrary and unique manifestations, there is enough regularity in them to allow for prediction from one occasion to another and for generalization within groups of persons. Experiments help to determine lawful relations in this area, as they do in other fields.

Since mental derangements are often accompanied by considerable discomfort or distress, they call first for caretaking and administrative action which, if feasible, includes treatment and rehabilitation. In addition, mental disorders provide a source of information about the mechanisms of normal, as well as impaired, function. We are apt to take for granted our ability to execute the many intricate operations necessary for the coordinated and complete performance of even quite simple movements and mental processes. Only when these operations break down, become inefficient, or fail to develop do we recognize the contribution of one or another mechanism to normal functioning. Any systematic examination of mental disorders involves the identification of the mechanisms or processes that are damaged in function. From this follows the determination of their part, typically in interaction with other mechanisms or processes, in the behavior disorder or symptoms. Such an analysis, often performed implicitly and schematically, constitutes the diagnosis. When it is explicit and precise, when it allows for prediction (i.e., prognosis) and is followed up by observations on the patient's progress, it can contribute to knowledge of mental function in general, as well as of psychopathology in particular.

Experimental techniques are better suited to the study of disorders in cognitive and motor function than to the study of disorders in emotions, but, with some ingenuity, these techniques have been made to serve in the exploration of affective and motivational anomalies as well. Experiments can serve to test a specific hypothesis or merely to verify the fact that some type of behavior does occur. More particularly, they are employed to determine the conditions under which such behavior occurs and the factors that influence its magnitude or frequency. Experimental techniques have been used not only to explore phenomena relevant to mental disorders but also to bring about such derangements (by drugs, fatigue, etc.) and to treat others that have emerged in the course of development or as a result of accident.

Thus, experimentation is appropriate at every stage of the evolution and remission of mental disorders. Its special virtue lies in its capacity to refine clinical observations, to evelute their accuracy and delineate the boundaries of their validity, and to sort out the several sources that contribute to the effects under investigation. An experiment may be necessary, for example in diagnosis, to decide whether a patient's sensory or motor function has been completely lost or is available in extreme emergencies, as happens with hysterical conversion symptoms. Experimental procedures are also widely used to determine the extent of an incapacity. These may include procedures such as perimetry of visual fields and determination of dark adaptation, or performance tasks, such as memorizing pairs of nonsense words and sorting designs.

Psychological tests used in diagnosis also have their origin in experimental procedure and retain some of its features—the objective tests more so than the projective. For example, certain aspects of the test situation are always standardized, e.g., the content and phrasing of the questions, the instructions given, the perceptual information presented, the method of recording the patient's responses, the format of the protocol taken for the record. In other respects clinical tests may not satisfy the requirements of control and reproducibility that distinguish the experimental from other methods of observation. Also, clinical test scores are evaluated against pre-established population norms, an advantage over the experimental method in determining the baseline and the extent of the deviation, that may have significance for psychopathology. In standardized tests, however, a significant clue could be missed if it emerges, not against the background of average performance, but in the unique pattern of the particular patient's function and dysfunction. Here the flexibility of the experimental method, its resources of manipulation and control, and, above all, its rationale of specifying functions by operations offer the investigator a considerable gain. [*See* PERSONALITY MEASUREMENT; PROJECTIVE METHODS.]

Although this article is concerned with the *psychological* study of mental disorders, it should be remembered that these disorders furnish subjects for experimental investigation by other disciplines, e.g., pathology, biochemistry, and neurophysiology. Even within psychology, the spectrum of experimental techniques and problem areas covers a wide range, from physiology to the social sciences. Experiments in autonomic and endocrine function, for instance, belong within its boundaries and have been of especial interest to students of unconscious psychic processes. At the other end, experiments in role playing, in group processes, and in the restructuring of social systems, such as hospital wards, have been undertaken jointly or alternately by psychologists and social scientists. The middle ground is marked by experiments in psychophysical measurement and perceptual judgment, by the several conditioning techniques, and by the immense variety of performance tasks—from simple motor responses to the solution of syllogistic problems, from the retention of nonsense syllables over a few minutes to the enduring acquisition of a new skill. [*See* PSYCHIATRY, *article on* SOCIAL PSYCHIATRY.]

As in other areas of research, in the study of mental disorders the experimental approach implies that as many as possible of the conditions that bear upon the subject under investigation are held constant, while the others are controlled by the design of the research. Only a few, and preferably only one, of the conditions is allowed to vary, and that one is varied systematically, so that its effect on the outcome can be evaluated, whenever possible in some quantified terms. The purpose of an experiment is not just to discover whether an anticipated result can be discerned but also to give an estimate of its magnitude and of the probability that it could be reproduced under similar circumstances.

In this methodological sense, "experiment" means something very different from the improvised trial or casual exploration to which the name is also applied. Ventures of that type are not unknown in the study of mental disorders, especially in the study of treatment and rehabilitation programs. They may be successful and even valuable in suggesting hypotheses or in demolishing an established misconception, but they are not experiments in the sense that their results can be attributed to a specific variable in the total situation. Certain guesses at the hidden meaning of a patient's obscure statement are experimental in this improvisational sense. Even though they may solve a riddle, there is no certainty that they hold the only solution or, indeed, that the riddle has been posed. Like other intuitive observations, such stabs at interpretation or intervention can supply hypotheses for subsequent testing.

Historical aspect.   The experimental method was introduced into the study of mental disorders soon after it appeared in general psychology. Kraepelin, the great system builder in clinical psychiatry, had worked with Wundt, and in due course he founded an experimental psychological laboratory at his research institute in Munich. Its program was outlined as far back as 1894, while Kraepelin was in Heidelberg, and appeared in print as the first in a series of reports under the title *Psychologische Arbeiten* (Kraepelin 1896). Periodic publications on research conducted by Kraepelin himself, and, under Kraepelin's editorship, on work done by his associates and students, followed during the first quarter of the twentieth century and constitute a record of eight volumes [*see* KRAEPELIN]. Kraepelin credited Gabriele Buccola, an Italian, with the first psychophysical experiments on patients with mental disorders and also noted the beginnings of such research in Russia and the United States. Another neuropsychiatrist whose prolific experimental activity started before the turn of the century was Paul Ranschburg, a Hungarian, most noted for his research in memory disturbances. By 1902 Ranschburg had established a permanent laboratory in Budapest, with government support, for the study of abnormal mental function.

In America, Shepard Ivory Franz set up the first laboratory dedicated to the experimental study of behavior in mental patients, at the McLean Hospital in Belmont, Massachusetts, in 1904. The apparatus came from Leipzig, and Franz's first experiments were concerned with the association areas in the brain, aphasia, memory defects, and especially with the physiology of manic–depressive psychosis. Psychological research was typically introduced into mental hospitals via physiology, with experiments on fatigue, speed of reaction, and time judgment. Significantly, Franz's laboratory was established for research in *pathological physiology*. When in 1907 he transferred his activities to the Government Hospital for the Insane in Washington, D.C., F. L. Wells succeeded him at McLean, heading a laboratory in *pathological psychology*. Wells was indeed less interested than Franz in cerebral localization, and his work in clinical psychology is best remembered for experiments in reaction time, the design of psychometric tests, and the pioneer use of psychogalvanic measurement.

Kraepelin's experimental program encompassed all the principal approaches to mental disorders. He studied normal function, in order to establish baselines, isolate distinct mental processes, and perfect techniques for their measurement. The same processes were also investigated in patients with various mental diseases and with mental disturbances brought on by drugs, fatigue, or sleep deprivation. The ultimate goal was to gain a clearer understanding of mental illness in order to determine its etiology and render its treatment more effective and more amenable to evaluation. Kraepelin's methodological goals have proved understandably uncongenial to the currently dominant school of psychiatry. One clue to his unpopularity is his definition of psychology as a branch of physiology, i.e., physiology of the mind. It is a definition that today few, even among his admirers, would accept, although the concepts underlying it inspired his research. The definition implied that mental function can be measured; that deranged mental function differs from the normal in some quantifiable properties; that operations allowing for the exact assessment of the speed, the regularity, or the frequency of certain incidents in performance can serve as diagnostic and prognostic devices.

This view entailed neither an atomistic model of personality nor a denial of psychogenic etiology. Kraepelin unequivocally declared that the physician concerned with mental disorders aims at forming a total picture of his patient and that the vast majority of these disorders originate from inside— genetic disposition being one of the prime determining factors. Experimental psychologists of the present day, while paying homage to his pioneer work, nonetheless adopt a critical attitude toward Kraepelin's contribution, for two reasons. One is the structuralist theory he inherited from Wundt, which has proved to be of limited value—especially Wundt's concept of apperception, which played an important part in the theory of Kraepelin's school. Second, Kraepelin himself and several of his associates—although not all, Ernst Grünthal being a notable exception—worked with extremely small samples of subjects. Typically, the investigator himself, not only dubiously representative of the general population but also far from naive in regard to the anticipated effects of the experimental treatment, was the only subject. Kraepelin and an associate's report of impaired performance attributed to a daily dose of alcohol no larger than two quarts of beer is the envy of later experimentalists who, like the author, have been unsuccessful in demonstrating impairment with much larger doses of alcohol [*see* DRINKING AND ALCOHOLISM, *article on* PSYCHOLOGICAL ASPECTS].

Theory and operationalism. While the program expounded by Kraepelin has been adapted by experimentalists to other psychological theories and to the requirements of representative sampling and stricter control, laboratory research on problems related to mental disorders has branched in other directions as well. Hughlings Jackson's hierarchic model of dissolution of function (1884) has stimulated innumerable experiments, especially with neurological patients, and Pavlov's theory of conditioning has been applied to mental disorders of every kind. Whether tied to a theoretical position or concerned only with the problem in hand, experimental studies of neurological patients have enriched, refined, and at times corrected our notions about sensory and motor function and higher mental processes. Since the purpose of most investigators has been to isolate the damaged function from those that remain intact or to arrive at a differential determination of deficit, the general approach to neurological disorders has been operational. The experimenter defines the function that seems impaired, selects operations that involve the function, and sets the patient experimental tasks that test these operations.

As a rule, the more closely defined these operations, the more informative they are to the investigator. This scale of value may, however, be reversed by his commitment to a theory couched in such global constructs that each and any derangement in function serves as an illustration of the general principle. A classical instance of that view, advanced by a clinician who was also a notable experimenter, is Goldstein's principle of abstraction. Goldstein conceived of abstraction as a composite function, central to which is the ability to categorize concrete instances. Its impairment is cited to account for disorders in speech and in thought, for the psychopathology associated with lesions in diverse areas of the brain, and for disorders that occur without known cerebral damage, such as schizophrenia. [*See* GOLDSTEIN.]

Werner's developmental principle was another such general concept, which inspired experimental attacks on mental derangements as diverse as aphasia, the psychoses, and mental deficiency. Implicit in Werner's principle is the notion that seemingly instantaneous events in perception and thought in fact evolve by steps over a microscopic time scale. The evolution of these processes is usually too rapid to be open to inspection, but with appropriate experimental techniques it can be demonstrated in some instances of disturbed mental function. This was done, for example, by Klaus Conrad, a clinical psychiatrist and ingenious experimenter, who derived quite specific neuropsychological formulations from the broad and formal gestalt laws of integration and differentiation.

In the aphasias, amnesias, and other cognitive derangements, experiments with the tachistoscope and memory drum (laboratory instruments for the regular, and very short, presentation of visual displays) merely extended the routine neurological examination and psychological testing. Students of the psychoses and psychoneuroses, on the other hand, could not always admit the relevance of experimental techniques. The psychoanalytic school, which in one version or another has undoubtedly been the most influential force in psychiatry and its ancillary professions in the United States, relies on analogy rather than on operational constructs. This applies even more emphatically to the existentialist and other metaphysical doctrines of psychiatry. In these theories explanation is more often by retrodiction than by prediction; the antecedent events are reconstructed without an exact weighting of the factors that contributed to the outcome or an analysis of their interaction. [*See* PSYCHOLOGY, *article on* EXISTENTIAL PSYCHOLOGY.]

Animal research. To be sure, certain key concepts in psychoanalytic theory, such as conflict, have been subjected to laboratory experiments. The effects of stress interviews, frustration, pain, and vexation have been studied with human subjects, but for obvious reasons the threat to health and human dignity had to be well below the level at which lasting mental disorders are likely to develop. Most of the laboratory studies, therefore, have been done with infrahuman species. A powerful stimulus to such studies was the almost undivided sway of learning theory in American experimental psychology following the behaviorist revolution. If mental disorders, or so many of them, are not diseases but, rather, clusters of maladaptive habits and drives, persistently faulty perceptions or thoughts, and stunted social skills, then the laws of learning and conditioning may explain the emergence of symptoms and lead to successful methods of treatment. Attempts to reconcile the clinical formulations of Freud with an experimentally based academic theory appealed strongly to Hull and his school, whose learning theory shared with psychoanalysis a hedonic principle of motivation. It is, perhaps, disappointing that experiments concerning the development of defense mechanisms have been largely equivocal (see Sears 1943; Miller 1944), although this is hardly surprising in view of the fact that most of them employed rats for subjects. [*See* CONFLICT, *article on* PSYCHOLOGICAL ASPECTS; LEARNING THEORY; STRESS; *and the biography of* HULL.]

While there is unquestionable elegance in the graphic representation of gradients and the equilibrium point between a rat's approach to food and avoidance of shock and there is quite live evidence of regression, fixation, and other maladaptive habits in the experimentally induced neuroses of cats, dogs, pigs, and sheep trapped in a physical or psychological harness (Liddell 1944), the leap from the laboratory to the human family setting is still a long one. It has been quite spectacularly shortened by Harlow's experiments with monkeys (1958; 1962). The affectionate display directed by infant monkeys toward their surrogate mothers— cloth dummies—was not only comparable with their responses to the natural mothers but also uncannily reminiscent of the behavior of human infants. Since these observations were made in a laboratory, several influences on the growth of affectional responses could be controlled and systematically varied. Furthermore, the situation seemed more likely to produce a lasting mental disturbance similar to those that afflict man than did the traditional procedure of inducing experimental neurosis in social isolation. As the monkeys grew up, some of them indeed developed marked personality disorders. Rather surprisingly, however, this outcome could not be traced to the artificial surroundings of the laboratory or to the substitution of a cloth dummy for the mother or, indeed, to her replacement by surrogates who rejected the clinging infant with a violent mechanical thrust or a concentrated blast of air. The infant experience that seemed chiefly to account for the adult monkey's psychopathology was deprivation of contact with other infants. [*See* AFFECTION; INFANCY.]

Mental disorders and brain function. The problems of generalizing from infrahuman animals to man will be briefly considered below. At this juncture another problem demands attention: the relationship of mental disorders to disturbed brain function. The conception that behavior disorders develop as a result of infantile deprivation or other stressful life experiences makes no explicit assumptions about alterations in the organism by which such effects could be mediated over time. It is, of course, tacitly assumed that learning, whether it results in greater efficiency or is maladaptive, involves some enduring organic changes, more particularly in the central nervous system. What these changes are is unknown, partly because of the inadequacy of current neurological techniques and partly because of the inadequacy of neuropsychological concepts. These two factors are as closely related as are technology and theory in other domains.

After many false attributions and an occasional correct guess in past centuries, it is now pretty universally agreed that the organ of the mind is the brain. The traditional metaphysical controversies about the relationship of body and mind have not been so completely resolved. They may be dismissed as irrelevant to the problem of mental disorders, but there survives a prejudice from the days when body and mind were regarded as two distinct substances, coordinate but not coequal in value or power. In the chain of being, man occupied a position intermediate between that of inanimate matter and the soulless animals, with whom he shared the bodily attributes, and that of the several classes of spiritual beings, whom he resembled by virtue of his mental faculties. His mind received credit for very extensive powers over the body, while control in the reverse direction was thought to be more limited in scope and also to be a likely avenue to sin. Moral judgments have changed, but clinicians are still apt to regard brain damage as but one of several causes of mental disorder and quite readily attribute disturbances in visible and tangible behavior to psychic processes that, at least by implication, take place outside the bodily dimensions.

The implication is made by the rough division between organic and functional disorders that has been established in the usage of psychiatrists and neurologists, as well as of clinical psychologists. "Organic" refers to brain damage, and that term is understood to stand for such structural impairment of brain tissue as can be observed directly or by means of currently available neurological techniques, e.g., electroencephalography, pneumography, angiography, etc. "Functional," by elimination, does not refer to organic or brain function. A classificatory principle as incompatible with present-day scientific notions as this is can be defended only on pragmatic grounds. It may, indeed, help with the prescription of treatment, but it introduces an unnecessary division into the research on mental disorders.

Localization of brain function. On the one hand, investigations of patients with brain lesions tend to be focused exclusively on the topographical localization of the damaged function. Preoccupation with specialized centers or areas discourages the search for functional systems in the brain or, for that matter, in behavior and experience. On the other hand, psychological concepts have been derived without reference to systems and processes within the organism, and it is hardly astonishing that they do not always fit exactly the neurologist's model. Derangement of function, especially when it can be determined independently by neurological techniques and by experimental studies of behavior, furnishes the most revealing clues about mechanisms and systems common to neurology and psychology. The concepts and patterns that will be meaningful in both disciplines need not correspond to those presently current in either. For example, if future research confirms the author's experimental and clinical observations about the close association of an extremely severe memory disorder with a general lack of spontaneity in the patient's behavior—although no comparable deficit in reasoning or intelligence is found—these two seemingly unrelated psychological functions could be properly subsumed under a common concept. Moreover, if evidence accumulates that this combined deficit occurs with lesions in a certain fairly well defined subcortical system of the brain, such a concept should be meaningful in the language of neural as well as of behavioral processes.

Although the accomplishment of experimental studies aimed at this objective is but modest to date, the advance has been considerable (a good share of that achievement being the result of investigations of disordered mental function; see Boring 1929; Flugel 1933; Hebb 1949; 1958) since G. Spurzheim, who ranks next to Franz Joseph Gall as the founder of phrenology, drew his spuriously detailed map of some thirty-odd brain areas that subserved as many mental faculties, with mirrorlike duplication in the two hemispheres. More reliable evidence for the functional subdivision of the brain came first from Paul Broca's clinical observations and shortly afterward from Luigi Rolando's experiments with electrical stimulation. Pierre Flourens, another pioneer in experimental research in this area, however, arrived at different conclusions in his studies using the extirpation technique. Phrenology survives today in the mosaic theory of the brain. An opposite point of view was forcefully advanced by Goldstein, whose concept of abstraction has already been mentioned, and, for a while, by Lashley, who derived the laws of mass action and equipotentiality from ablation experiments. These laws imply that the size, rather than the site, of brain damage determines the disturbance in behavior and that—outside the sensory and motor areas—any part of the cortex can potentially subserve any learned behavior. [*See* BROCA; FLOURENS; GALL; LASHLEY.]

Laboratory studies of human patients have led to formulations intermediate between the two poles. Teuber, who conducted extensive and carefully designed experiments on a group of patients with combat injuries, the majority with gunshot wounds in the brain, demonstrated that these lesions result in both specific and general impairment of perceptual function (Teuber & Liebert 1958). Halstead reached a somewhat different, intermediate position, from studies of patients with lesions in the various lobes of the cortex (1947). Statistical analysis of his experimental results showed that no intellectual function is uniquely dependent on a single region of the brain but that these areas differ in their importance for one or another function.

Experimental techniques have been extensively used to test hypotheses about cerebral dominance and the division of function between the hemispheres. In this context one again meets spokesmen of extreme as well as intermediate positions. At one pole is the opinion that man has two brains, that one hemisphere all but completely duplicates the function of the other. Indeed, experiments have repeatedly shown that the surgical removal of a diseased hemisphere or its decay through atrophy may cause little discernible loss of intellectual ability. Opponents of this view attribute a high degree of specialization to each half. Speech, for example, has been associated with the left hemisphere since Broca's time and, correspondingly, control over manipulative skills has been attributed to the right hemisphere. The proposition that cerebral dominance is thus manifested and that it is reversed in left-handed persons has been tested by many experimenters. Zangwill's survey (1960) of these studies reached the conclusion that the speech area is not invariably contralateral to the dominant hand. Nor is representation exactly identical in the two hemispheres when (as, for example, in sensory function) the rule of contralaterality obtains. Semmes and her associates (1960) have demonstrated this for somatosensory function, while experiments determining the two-point discrimination and pressure thresholds were used in Teuber's study of disabled veterans (Teuber & Liebert 1958).

Pathological damage to the brain that corresponds exactly to a functional impairment is the exception and so far has not been found typical of mental disorders. Lesions in the visual or auditory cortex offer the closest examples. Students of mental illness have been especially interested in the frontal lobe, which seems to play an important part in such emotional disturbances as depression and distress over pain. A functional severance of the prefrontal cortex from the central nervous system has been successfully applied in treating these complaints. Experimental studies, however, have been inconclusive in assigning a particular function or ability to the frontal lobe. Advocates of the mosaic theory of brain function have found more encouragement in the temporal lobe. Penfield, the neurosurgeon, exposed the temporal cortex in several patients while removing a focus of epileptic discharge (1954). Applying electric stimulation to clearly marked points, he was able to elicit repeatedly—although not always—the same sensation or evoke recall of the identical episode from the past. These recollections appeared to be as sensorially sharp as the original experience, even though the patient was fully aware of his immediate surroundings in the operating room. At first it seemed that the site where the organism stores its discrete memories had been discovered in the temporal lobe, and although later interpretations have been more cautious, they do not diminish the significance of these experimental findings, especially for the demonstration that experiences and memories are classified in the nervous system according to abstract principles.

This deeply hidden surface of the cortex and the adjacent subcortical regions are undoubtedly implicated in some of the processes of memory. Milner's reports with Penfield (Milner & Penfield 1955) and with Scoville (Scoville & Milner 1957), as well as other investigators' reports on patients who had lesions from surgery or disease in those areas, have noted grave defects in memory for recent events. Memory for remote events—like those which emerged under stimulation of the temporal cortex —is less consistently and less severely affected. Newer techniques in brain surgery, such as electro-

coagulation, have widened the area of experimental investigation of neuropsychological processes. Experiments performed with chronically implanted electrodes allow for the simultaneous recording of neuroelectric activity at deep brain centers and of overt behavior, as well as for electric stimulation. The subject in such investigations, however, is always a sick person, whose function is often influenced by drugs as well as the disease. Alternatively, the subject of an investigation may be a healthy monkey or cat, animals whose brains as well as behavioral repertoire have a good deal in common with man, although not quite as much as would satisfy many students of mental disorders. [See NERVOUS SYSTEM, *article on* BRAIN STIMULATION.]

Clinical research. There are well-established anatomical differences between the brain of man and that of even the highest subhuman primate; there is also reason to believe that some structures or neurophysiological systems are identical but serve different functions at the two different phylogenetic levels. Whether the accomplishments of the rat or the ape in learning and problem solving furnish an informative analogy for man's feats in forming unique memories and operating with symbols remains a debatable issue. Many experiments tracing the relationships between derangements in behavior and in the brain can be carried out only with human patients, because the psychological defect is entirely in the use of language. The variety of aphasias distinguished in clinical observation and confirmed by experimental tests are proof not so much of an ingenuity in classificatory exercises as of the scientific endeavor to expand our knowledge of significant lawful relationships. [See LANGUAGE, *article on* SPEECH PATHOLOGY; PERCEPTION, *article on* SPEECH PERCEPTION.]

Kinsbourne and Warrington's investigation of six patients with a reading disability (1962) is an example of the contribution experimental procedures can make in a clinical situation. These patients were right-handed, and they were known to have brain lesions in the right (i.e., minor) hemisphere. Paralexic errors, which their defects first seemed to exemplify, are regarded as aphasic in origin and are therefore attributed to damage in the dominant hemisphere. It appeared significant that the errors observed in these patients also differed from those commonly made in reading, in that they tended to occur with the first letters of a word. The investigators designed experiments to test the hypothesis that the reading errors arose from a perceptual derangement. By means of a tachistoscope, they exposed to the patients brief glimpses of whole and fragmented words and geometrical figures. It became apparent that the patients had an abnormal field of perception, in which fine discriminations were restricted to the right side, although gross operations, such as judging the length of words, were unaffected. Unaware of their disability, the patients attempted to complete what they could read of a word, always in a leftward direction. Experimental checks ruled out the possibility that the disability arose from faulty fixation or defective eye movements, and the investigators therefore attributed it to an abnormal distribution of visual attention—to an unconscious neglect of space. They also recognized that their findings may have implications for reading disabilities that originate from a failure to execute the normal operation of forward completion. [*See* READING DISABILITIES; VISION, *article on* EYE MOVEMENTS.]

Multidisciplinary contributions. Experiments following the trail between mental disturbances and cerebral dysfunction, in either direction, have the advantage of a clearly defined objective. The pursuit itself, however, may become exceedingly complex and involve—over and above the neurological and psychological considerations—such diverse disciplines as biochemistry, genetics, social science, and history (the patient's life history, as well as the history of the disease process). These disciplines have indeed appeared more promising for research in schizophrenia than have the neural sciences. Experimental studies of schizophrenia in the biochemistry laboratory, although varied, allow for a broad, threefold classification. Their goal is (1) to determine the chemical causes of the mental disorder; or (2) to assess metabolic, and particularly endocrine, function in patients, at different stages of their illness, under induced stress, special experimental conditions, or in the standard hospital setting; or (3) to form a part of a pharmacological treatment program. These experiments often include investigations of physiological and/or psychological function as well.

Experimental studies of schizophrenia, manic–depressive psychosis, and the neuroses are typically confined to the verification of clinical observations. The major exception to this trend has been research stimulated by theories that do not distinguish between functional disturbances attributed to brain damage and those due to psychological factors. Followers of Hughlings Jackson and Head, of Pavlov and the gestalt school, of Goldstein, Werner, and Schilder, have exerted an influence in that

direction. More recently, models built around the activating properties of a subcortical neural system have served as a comprehensive conceptual frame work for disordered mental function.

Theories that transcend the boundaries of established brain damage and psychogenic dysfunction employ loose and not fully operational constructs. Goldstein's principle of abstraction is an example, and, indeed, several experimenters have produced partial evidence against it. Some of these support Cameron's proposition (1947) that distractibility is an important source of concrete thinking in schizophrenia and that in several instances of mental disorder abstraction is manifested but is masked by the use of inappropriate, overinclusive, bizarre concepts, especially when they concern the social context. Of course, the conclusions of these experiments are limited by the extent to which their operations represent abstractness and concreteness in thinking. Uncertainty and disagreement about adequate correspondence between behavior under laboratory control and hypothetical mechanisms or processes—in personality dynamics or neural function alike—present the most difficult problem to the experimental psychologist investigating mental disorders.

Laboratory techniques. Experimental reports about the slow responses, sluggish work rate, and straying attention of depressed or schizophrenic patients are unlikely to arouse much controversy. In these instances, behavior observed in the laboratory does not conflict with clinical impressions, although inferences drawn from the two sets of data to underlying mechanisms may clash, whether they concern hypothetical psychic mechanisms, such as defenses against impulses, or hypothetical neural mechanisms, such as cortical arousal. Experimental techniques have also been used as a subsidiary procedure to clinical interviewing, e.g., the measuring of motor and autonomic responses in tests of word association or perception. If a patient seems to be unusually disturbed or ill at ease when discussing—or keeping silent about—certain topics, such suggestive impressions can be confirmed by the relatively exact measurement of his psychogalvanic response or hand movements. Evidence thus obtained may help in delineating and exploring his areas of conflict. This technique—popularly known as the lie detector—was systematically explored for the purpose of psychological research by Luriia in Moscow in the 1920s (1932). Other investigators, in the United States as well as in the Soviet Union, have further developed this technique, following clues from the patient's autonomic and skeletal behavior and measuring the latency, rhythm, and amplitude of his responses in structured interviews or during his performance of an experimental task.

Laboratory techniques have also been used in the study of the regularity of grossly distorted perceptions in patients with mental disorders. Estimates of the patient's body or of its parts; of the size and distance of objects, especially when the judgment involves the perceptual constancies; and of his dependence on external cues for accurate assessment of the vertical dimension have added to our knowledge of the effects of mental disease or of particular diagnostic types, but have neither promised nor succeeded in getting at the roots of these disorders.

Malmo and his associates (1951) have questioned the wisdom of resorting to tests of perception, and especially of concept formation, in order to establish characteristic differences between normal persons and neurotic or psychotic patients. In an experiment demanding difficult perceptual judgment under time pressure, it was demonstrated that groups representing these three classes barely differed in their accuracy. They did differ, though, in the regularity and duration of the motor response by which they indicated their judgment (this was simply pressing a button with the right thumb). They also differed in the frequency and magnitude of the synchronous response with the left hand and in the motor activity of their left hand between responses. The experimenters presented these results in support of the thesis that disproportionate motor disturbance is typical of patients with mental disorder under any stressful situation, and not only when the stress is specific to their emotional problem.

This line of reasoning is very congenial to Eysenck (1947; 1961), who has undertaken the most ambitious and extensive experimental research in mental disorders, with the purpose of establishing a reliable psychiatric nosology. Experimental studies have played an important part in this program and have contributed data to the factor analyses from which three personality dimensions were derived. One of these represents introversion–extroversion and accounts for certain individual differences in normal, healthy persons, as well as for the two types of disorders into which Eysenck groups the neuroses. The other dimensions represent the magnitude of a patient's neurotic and psychotic disturbance. The three dimensions are orthogonal to each other (i.e., independent), so that the extent of a patient's psychotic derangement is unrelated to the magnitude or type of his neurotic abnormality. Most of Eysenck's earlier experiments demanded performance of some task, but more recently he has preferred laboratory methods that call for judgments on perceptual illusions or aftereffects. Some of these procedures, such as assessing the afterimage of a rotating spiral, have been widely used by clinical psychologists for diagnostic as well as research purposes.

Induction and treatment. Experimental techniques have also been used for the induction and treatment of mental disorders. While the development of a lasting experimental neurosis in an animal may be a perfectly justified venture, with human subjects the derangement of mental function can be considered only if it is a reversible process of short duration. Various psychotomimetic drugs have been used for this purpose, producing effects that have been reported as pleasant by some, disagreeable by others, and weird by most persons undergoing the experience. Perception and thought processes are distorted in fairly predictable fashion, but it remains a matter of debate whether the abnormal effects thus induced are the same as, similar to, or different in character from those of, for example, schizophrenia. Sleep deprivation, extreme fatigue, anoxia, starvation, heat and cold, excessive sensory stimulation (e.g., continuous noise) and its opposite, sensory and social isolation, have been among the experimental devices used to induce transitory mental disorders. [*See* DRUGS; PERCEPTION, *article on* PERCEPTUAL DEPRIVATION.]

The application of experimental techniques to the treatment of mental disorders has received its strongest impetus from theories of conditioning. The therapeutic goal is to retrain the patient by progressive weakening of the maladaptive habit or symptom or by reinforcement of an adaptive response. From isolated experiments with laboratory techniques to cure enuresis or hysterical tics or paralysis, or to reach autistic or mentally defective children, there has now developed a recognized practice of behavior therapy. Its methods—desensitization, satiation, counterconditioning, reciprocal inhibition, operant and avoidance conditioning— were formulated and first tested with animals. Now they are applied by clinicians, whose relationship to the patient may not be very different from the psychotherapist's. Also, like the latter, the behavior therapist can combine psychological treatment with pharmacological treatment. [*See* LEARNING, *articles on* CLASSICAL CONDITIONING, INSTRUMENTAL LEARNING, *and* AVOIDANCE LEARNING; LEARNING THEORY; MENTAL DISORDERS, TREATMENT OF, *article on* BEHAVIOR THERAPY.]

Drug therapy and electroshock treatment have

many of the features of a research experiment. The agents administered to bring about certain effects, i.e., improvement in the patient's condition, are under control. The amount given, the duration of treatment, and the avenue by which the agent is administered can be varied, within limits, and the manifestation of side effects, as well as of the principal outcome, can be evaluated and related to the input variables. Opportunities to explore these relationships have been thoroughly exploited by experimenters. [*See* ELECTROCONVULSIVE SHOCK; MENTAL DISORDERS, TREATMENT OF, *article on* SOMATIC TREATMENT.]

The use of experiments in evaluating process and outcome in psychotherapy is far more limited. In individual and group therapy alike, too many of the relevant influences are outside the scope of controlled manipulation. Hypnotherapy offers more attractive possibilities; indeed, all research related to hypnosis seems to be relevant to an understanding of mental derangements and, in the light of Orne's findings, to an accurate assessment of experimental findings in psychology. Orne's experiments (1959) have shown that behavior under hypnosis depends very largely on the current notions about hypnotic effects and, also, that subjects volunteering for psychological experiments tend to have very definite ideas about how they are expected to behave in the laboratory, ideas which may exert a considerable influence on what they do or accomplish there. [*See* HYPNOSIS.]

Experiments in human behavior, whether they reflect normal or disordered mental function, pose certain problems that are of little or no concern to experimenters in other biological sciences. The patient or control subject does not ever merely react to stimuli. The best the experimenter can achieve is to elicit, with his instructions and setting, an unprejudiced cooperation and to rely on observations that allow the least possible latitude for subjective interpretation. In the course of his work he may make new and significant clinical observations or discover lawful relationships that explain some phenomena of the mental disorders. His special contribution, however, is the testing of such observations and the definition of clinical terms by operations that are reproducible and open to inspection by all who will take the trouble to look.

GEORGE TALLAND

[*Directly related are the entries* EXPERIMENTAL DESIGN; PSYCHOANALYSIS, *article on* EXPERIMENTAL STUDIES. *Other relevant material may be found in* ANXIETY; DEPRESSIVE DISORDERS; DRUGS; FATIGUE; MENTAL DISORDERS, TREATMENT OF; NERVOUS SYSTEM; SCHIZOPHRENIA; SLEEP; STRESS; *and in the biographies of* GOLDSTEIN; KRAEPELIN; LASHLEY.]

BIBLIOGRAPHY

BORING, EDWIN G. (1929) 1950 *A History of Experimental Psychology.* 2d ed. New York: Appleton. → See especially pages 50–60, "Phrenology and the Mind–Body Problem," and pages 61–79, "Physiology of the Brain: 1800–1870."

CAMERON, NORMAN A. 1947 *The Psychology of Behavior Disorders: A Biosocial Interpretation.* Boston: Houghton Mifflin.

CONRAD, KLAUS 1954 New Problems of Aphasia. *Brain* 77:491–509.

CONRAD, KLAUS 1960 Die Gestaltanalyse in der psychiatrischen Forschung. *Nervenarzt* 31:267–273.

EYSENCK, HANS J. 1947 *Dimensions of Personality.* London: Routledge.

EYSENCK, HANS J. (editor) 1961 *Handbook of Abnormal Psychology.* New York: Basic Books.

FLUGEL, JOHN C. (1933) 1964 *A Hundred Years of Psychology: 1833–1933.* With an additional part, *1933–1963,* by Donald J. West. New York: Basic Books.

GOLDSTEIN, KURT (1934) 1939 *The Organism: A Holistic Approach to Biology Derived From Pathological Data in Man.* New York: American Book. → First published as *Der Aufbau des Organismus.*

GOLDSTEIN, KURT 1942 *Aftereffects of Brain Injuries in War, Their Evaluation and Treatment: The Application of Psychologic Methods in the Clinic.* New York: Grune.

HALSTEAD, WARD C. 1947 *Brain and Intelligence.* Univ. of Chicago Press.

HARLOW, HARRY F. 1958 The Nature of Love. *American Psychologist* 13:673–685.

HARLOW, HARRY F. 1962 The Heterosexual Affectional System in Monkeys. *American Psychologist* 17:1–9.

HEAD, HENRY et al. 1920 *Studies in Neurology.* 2 vols. London: Hodder & Stoughton. → Consists mainly of papers published in *Brain* between 1905 and 1918. See especially Volume 2, pages 533–800, "The Brain."

HEBB, DONALD O. 1949 *The Organization of Behavior: A Neuropsychological Theory.* New York: Wiley.

HEBB, DONALD O. 1958 *A Textbook of Psychology.* Philadelphia & London: Saunders.

JACKSON, J. HUGHLINGS (1884) 1958 Evolution and Dissolution of the Nervous System. Volume 2, pages 45–75 in J. Hughlings Jackson, *Selected Writings* . . . . Edited by James Taylor. New York: Basic Books. → First published in 1884 in *Lancet.*

KING, HENRY E. 1954 *Psychomotor Aspects of Mental Disease.* Cambridge, Mass.: Harvard Univ. Press.

KINSBOURNE, M.; and WARRINGTON, ELIZABETH K. 1962 A Variety of Reading Disability Associated With Right Hemisphere Lesions. *Journal of Neurology, Neurosurgery, and Psychiatry* 25:339–344.

KRAEPELIN, E. 1896 Der psychologische Versuch in der Psychiatrie. Volume 1, pages 1–91 in E. Kraepelin, *Psychologishe Arbeiten.* Leipzig: Englemann.

KRECH, DAVID 1962 Cortical Localization of Function. Pages 31–72 in Leo Postman (editor), *Psychology in the Making.* New York: Knopf.

LASHLEY, KARL S. 1929 *Brain Mechanisms and Intelligence: A Quantitative Study of Injuries to the Brain.* Univ. of Chicago Press.

LIDDELL, H. S. 1944 Conditioned Reflex Method and Experimental Neurosis. Volume 1, pages 389–412 in Joseph McV. Hunt (editor), *Personality and the Behavior Disorders: A Handbook Based on Experimental and Clinical Research.* New York: Ronald.

LURIIA, ALEKSANDR R. 1932 *The Nature of Human Conflicts; or, Emotion, Conflict and Will: An Objective Study of Disorganization and Control of Human Behaviour.* New York: Liveright.

MAGOUN, HORACE W. (1958) 1963 *The Waking Brain.* 2d ed. Springfield, Ill.: Thomas.

MALMO, ROBERT B. et al. 1951 Motor Control in Psychiatric Patients Under Experimental Stress. *Journal of Abnormal and Social Psychology* 46:539–547.

MILLER, NEAL E. 1944 Experimental Studies of Conflict. Volume 1, pages 431–465 in Joseph McV. Hunt (editor), *Personality and the Behavior Disorders: A Handbook Based on Experimental and Clinical Research.* New York: Ronald.

MILNER, BRENDA; and PENFIELD, WILDER 1955 The Effect of Hippocampal Lesions on Recent Memory. American Neurological Association, *Transactions* 80: 42–48.

ORNE, MARTIN T. 1959 The Nature of Hypnosis: Artifact and Essence. *Journal of Abnormal and Social Psychology* 58:277–299.

OSGOOD, CHARLES E. (1953) 1959 *Method and Theory in Experimental Psychology.* New York: Oxford Univ. Press.

PENFIELD, WILDER 1954 Studies of the Cerebral Cortex of Man: A Review and an Interpretation. Pages 284–309 in Council for International Organizations of Medical Sciences, *Brain Mechanisms and Consciousness.* Edited by J. F. Delafresnaye. Oxford: Blackwell.

RANSCHBURG, PAUL 1939 Les bases somatiques de la mémoire. Pages 513–531 in *Centenaire de Th. Ribot: Jubilé de la psychologie scientifique française, 1839–1939.* Agen (France): Imprimerie Moderne.

SCHILDER, PAUL 1942 *Mind: Perception and Thought in Their Constructive Aspects.* New York: Columbia Univ. Press.

SCOVILLE, WILLIAM B.; and MILNER, BRENDA 1957 Loss of Recent Memory After Bilateral Hippocampal Lesion. *Journal of Neurology, Neurosurgery, and Psychiatry* 20:11–21.

SEARS, ROBERT R. 1943 *Survey of Objective Studies of Psychoanalytic Concepts.* Bulletin No. 51. New York: Social Science Research Council.

SEMMES, JOSEPHINE et al. 1960 *Somatosensory Changes After Penetrating Brain Wounds in Man.* Cambridge, Mass.: Harvard Univ. Press.

TALLAND, GEORGE A. 1965 *Deranged Memory.* New York: Academic Press.

TEUBER, HANS L. 1964 The Riddle of Frontal-lobe Function in Man. Pages 410–444 in Symposium on the Frontal Granular Cortex and Behavior, Pennsylvania State University, 1962, *The Frontal Granular Cortex and Behavior.* Edited by J. M. Warren and K. Akert. New York: McGraw-Hill.

TEUBER, HANS L.; and LIEBERT, ROBERT S. 1958 Specific and General Effects of Brain Injury in Man. *Archives of Neurology and Psychiatry* 80:403–407.

WEISENBURG, THEODORE; and McBRIDE, KATHARINE 1935 *Aphasia: A Clinical and Psychological Study.* New York: Commonwealth Fund.

WERNER, HEINZ (1926) 1957 *Comparative Psychology of Mental Development.* Rev. ed. New York: International Universities Press. → First published in German.

ZANGWILL, O. L. 1960 *Cerebral Dominance and Its Relation to Psychological Function.* Edinburgh: Oliver & Boyd.

MENTAL DISORDERS, TREATMENT OF

I
PSYCHOLOGICAL TREATMENT

Within the context of this article, the term "psychological treatment" means psychotherapy and "mental disorder" means mental distress. Psychotherapy consists of a group of communicative methods for exchanging semantic information with the aim of relieving mental distress. Mental distress consists of behavior patterns subjectively experienced as painful and judged by subjective and objective observers to be inappropriate to a context.

Although there are now several psychotherapeutic approaches in Western culture, only a few can be considered as seriously developed alternatives whose methods continue to be evaluated and improved through systematic study. These approaches can be subdivided into three schools—psychoanalytic–psychodynamic, learning theory, and client-centered. Although many similarities and differences can be found among these schools, depending upon how one compares them, there is agreement regarding a number of essential components in mental distress and its treatment by psychotherapy (Ford & Urban 1963).

Modern psychotherapy was derived mainly from the efforts of Josef Breuer and Sigmund Freud, toward the end of the nineteenth century, to systematize a "talking cure" from the hypnotic techniques of the time. From this beginning several methods have evolved, none showing a clear-cut superiority over the others. They share many presuppositions regarding the nature of man and a delineation of individual psychotherapy as a private two-person relationship limited to talking and listening, the intent of which is to relieve the mental suffering of a patient in an enduring way. This private and intimate relationship, peculiar to Western man at this time, is notable as much for what it does not contain as for what it does. For example, it is a regularly repeated human communion that is unaccompanied by food and drink.

Presuppositions are vaguely held and seldom

examined beliefs. Beliefs concerning the nature of man underlie the articulated suppositions of psychotherapy. This *Menschanschauung*, as it might be called, presupposes that man's suffering is an outcome of his experience, that mental suffering should be relieved, that man has some degree of freedom of choice and decision, that he can control himself to some extent, that he can be changed by experience, that one man can help another to change, and so on. A complete inventory of such presuppositions has never been attempted, and perhaps because of the tacit nature of such beliefs, no inventory could be complete. It is of obvious importance that these beliefs are held by both therapist and patient.

The more clearly held beliefs of therapists make up the specifiable suppositions and assumptions of psychotherapy theory. A therapist operates with a theory of the pathology (Greek, *pathos*, suffering) of mental processes and a theory regarding techniques that can bring about beneficial change in them.

Here the term "theory" refers to a rough framework of notions expressed in a language containing everyday and special terms. A therapist's theories do not represent formal systematized bodies of tested and established hypotheses, such as those found in some natural sciences. This is not so much due to the youth of the field as to its nature. Therapy is not a science but a practical healing art. Practical arts consist of techniques for achieving ends valued as good. Procedures and rules for achieving ends can be aided by basic scientific knowledge that increases our understanding of the subject matter or augments the power of techniques. The effective utilization of techniques remains in the hands of a skilled artisan whose work represents the conduct of an artistic rather than a scientific activity.

Theories of mental distress

A therapist's theories begin with conceptual notions about the subject matter to which his techniques will be applied. Mental suffering involves a set of conditions judged to be qualitatively or quantitatively inappropriate to a context. This judgment is made both by an internal observer, a patient, and by an external observer, a therapist, both of whom hold beliefs about ideal or desirable types of behavior for various contexts. The judgments that something is out of order are arrived at not by consulting experimental or statistical evidence, but by comparison of the patient's behavior with ideal types. This comparative method uses a concept of desirable behavior that represents an idealization, a useful fiction, and not the extreme of an observable range.

The chief empirical indications of mental distress, some or all of which are evident to both observers, are negative affects, thought distortions, and constrictions.

Common negative affects, subjectively experienced and reportable as intense and not in keeping with an external situation, are anxiety, anger, depression, shame, and guilt. For example, a person may experience great anxiety in a classroom where there is no evident threat. Or he may become repeatedly enraged at frustrations that he judges to be trivial. Or he may enter a prolonged depression over the death of a loved one and even feel, inexplicably, guilt over the loss.

Thought distortions have a great range of severity and variety of content. Common are beliefs that one is inferior, that one deserves admiration, that a disaster is about to occur, that one is being looked at or talked about, that people are dangerous, that one's body is defective, and that the opposite sex is hostile. These beliefs are often accompanied by the patient's own judgment that they are unwarranted or unjustified to this degree. Yet this judgment seems powerless to correct the thought distortion.

Constrictions involve limitations of feelings or behavior required by and congruent with contexts. These limitations include avoidance of the opposite sex, sexual impotence or frigidity, inability to enjoy life, and an incapacity to experience either joy or grief. Such constrictions have far-reaching consequences and lead to repetitions of old patterns in novel situations requiring discriminations and new behaviors.

There is great variation in how much distress an individual can stand. Most applicants for therapy have experienced enduring distress of more than mild severity which has not disappeared in the course of time. A patient seeks expert help for the negative affects, thought distortions, or constrictions that trouble him, and it is these phenomena from which a therapist attempts to release a patient by modifying the processes that generate them.

For more than five thousand years there have been attempts to classify symptoms, descriptions, and behavior patterns into disease categories (Menninger et al. 1963). All these efforts have failed to produce reliable categories. The growing modern view is that we are not dealing with disease entities in the medical sense but with states of experiencing that require conceptualizations different from those found in traditional medicine.

Today, various schools of psychotherapy have

reached moderate agreement on which elements are essential in descriptions of mental distress. Theories of the underlying pathological processes also agree insofar as they consider mental conflict, anxiety and other negative affect processes, and the ontogenesis of distress in parent–child relations to be crucial variables. The current uncertainty and disputes center on the problem of determining the best techniques for relieving distress and producing change. Although a crude theory of distress exists, we lack a theory both of mental change and of how change comes from external social influence. Hence there exists a profusion of techniques derived from clinical experience, but they lack a satisfactory theoretical underpinning.

Theories and techniques of therapy

Techniques of therapy are purely semantic, involving a communicative exchange of meaningful information. Treatment procedures are limited to conversations of various types, and there is a limit to what a therapist and patient can do with any purely semantic technique. These limitations are set by the nature of the therapist–patient relations, by what can take place in talking and listening, and by the topics chosen to be talked about. The relation between therapist and patient represents a working collaboration guided by a contract with stated and implied terms, usually involving payment of a fee for the therapist's services. Although the relation becomes intimate and emotionally arousing, it remains extremely one-sided, with the patient doing most of the talking. Disclosure is exchanged for confidentiality and neutral interest. The therapist's skills in listening and talking involve a general attitude of benevolent acceptance and specific acts of eliciting, focusing, clarifying, reflecting, and interpreting those relevant topics initiated by the patient. Criteria of relevance vary somewhat among therapy schools, but again there are limitations imposed by the regularities of deep human concerns—e.g., relations to significant other persons and the self to the self—and by what can in fact be said about them by therapists.

There exists a difficulty between and within schools of therapy in examining the facts of therapeutic conversation. When discussing therapeutic approaches, each school uses its own notions and language. But it is an open secret among *cognoscenti* that this talking *about* therapy is highly unrelated to the talking that takes place *in* therapy. Official discussions about therapy tend to call up school allegiances and personal commitments. With an increasing use of tape recordings, movies, and television, we are in a position to observe what

therapists actually do rather than relying on what they say they do.

As already emphasized, theories regarding processes of mental change are not as developed as theories of mental distress. Every therapy school could use a theoretically justified set of principles for achieving change. The technical rules and principles currently used have come from long clinical experience and common-sense knowledge about human behavior. As an example of the latter, if you want a person to tell you about his inner painful thoughts, do not frighten him. This simple but effective principle is used by all schools. For its skillful applications, a therapist must be able to accept and control himself when stirred by feelings that can lead one person to attempt to frighten another.

Most of the rules for conducting therapeutic conversations are of this simple type. Some schools try to justify their techniques by appealing to fanciful metatheories or to animal experiments having no relevance to human behavior. But thus far technical rules are entirely empirical and justified only by clinical experience. This does not mean they are all wrong or can be easily dismissed, but because they lack a theoretical basis, it is difficult to sort out which techniques are truly effective and which can be dispensed with. For the time being, then, techniques must be learned through the oral tradition of apprenticeships in which empirical knowledge is passed on from the more experienced to the less experienced in the course of studying representative examples of clinical problems. And like the skills of all practical arts, they are performed by some people better than by others.

Until theories of change are worked out, a therapist must rely, in his practice, on simple rules and on a tacit knowledge that comes with clinical experience. The type of guides he needs most are decision rules that tell him what to say and when and how to say it in order to achieve his short-range and long-range goals. It is important to distinguish techniques from goals. Much of the therapy literature is clear about goals (although what the language refers to may be obscured observationally), but it remains quite opaque as to how these ends are to be achieved technically. When one discusses the details of the therapist's utterances, all therapists say much the same things. And it is these utterances to which a patient responds, not the theory of the therapist's school. It is also noteworthy that statements about goals often refer to the way the patient should be rather than to what a therapist should do to help him become this way.

It is easy enough to state a goal of therapy as

an enduring relief of the mental distress a patient suffers. With such relief comes a positive gain in the form of a new ability to enjoy experiences. All schools, in addition, seek goals or subgoals assumed to be necessary to achieve the over-all end of enduring relief. They are variously termed as self-realization, personality growth, self-knowledge, full-functioning, enlightenment, etc. Here differing therapy approaches seem to be saying equivalent things about ideal types of mental functioning. Utopian or not, they play a part in the presuppositions and suppositions regarding therapy's ends. Statements about goals represent assertions of value systems striving to achieve the good (London 1964). A therapist's values regarding "the good" and "the right" in human conduct inevitably clash with other value viewpoints. Each therapist–patient pair must work out this difficult problem of values in a manner that provides some consonance with the values of the patient and the community in which he wants to live. It is this problem of values about what constitutes proper conduct, bound up with the ends of therapy, that contributes great difficulties in answering questions about the effectiveness of psychotherapy.

How the techniques of psychotherapy actually work to affect a patient remains mysterious. Changes observable to both subjective and objective observers take place in the form of reduction of negative affect, correction of thought distortions, liberation from constrictions, or a combination of these. Processes that generate such changes are difficult to understand and facilitate in our present state of knowledge. For far-reaching and enduring mental changes to occur, we assume some sort of scrutiny, and revision in belief systems must take place in which information is used to counteract and correct other information. This process is facilitated by the haven and support provided by a benevolent therapist, who functions as an ideal friend or parent and who occasionally can offer alternative views to be tried out by the patient first in safe thought-experiments and later in actual behavior. This is about as much as we think we know of mental change, an area in which dependable knowledge is very difficult to obtain.

Trends

Historically, the treatment of mental distress has involved the use of physical methods, such as drugs and electric shock, and semantic methods, such as individual psychotherapy (Walker 1957). Hospital treatment has mainly utilized the former methods, whereas outpatient clinics and private practice have relied mainly on the latter.

No great change in the techniques of semantic methods has gained much acceptance in the past few years. In classical psychoanalytic treatment a couch, free association, and several visits per week for two to three years, or more, are still used. In less-intensive therapies a patient is seen face-to-face for several weeks or months.

One trend in the field of psychotherapy concerns the matter of personnel and training. Since the early part of the twentieth century, the official (i.e., sanctioned by an accrediting organization) practice of psychotherapy has been by psychiatrists. But with the growing numbers of trained clinical psychologists and social workers, increasingly more therapeutic work is being carried on by individuals who do not have medical degrees. This trend is consistent with modern views regarding the nature of the "disease." If persons who seek therapy are not viewed as suffering from diseases in the medical sense, then it does not require medically trained personnel to deal with them. Medicine must either redefine "disease" to include human behavior patterns or concede some of its traditional territory to the nonmedical therapist. Since territorial dominance is what it is in male animals, the dispute will be a long one.

This issue will become crucial as more and more people seek therapy. The growth of therapy is not so much associated with the prestige of science as it is with a growing change in attitude that facilitates criticism of socially acquired beliefs. Therapy provides a sanctioned way of participating in social criticism within the microcosm of the self, of repudiating acquired beliefs, and of liberating the self. With our increasing prosperity and with a rapid lessening in shame over seeking help, it is estimated that one out of seven persons will eventually apply for therapy. Medicine, psychology, and social work alone will not be able to meet the demand of millions of people. It is obvious that other manpower resources must be trained (Schofield 1964).

Whether there has been any progress in the field of therapy over the past several years is an open question, partly because "progress" is such an evaluative term. Through clinical experience therapists have slowly learned much about what is not considered progress, and this represents a gain of information. It is agreed that we need more powerful and efficient methods as well as more knowledge about the differential application of semantic techniques. Furthermore, because patients tend to select therapists from schools about which they feel more comfortable, the various therapy approaches may be dealing with different classes of problems and patients, making outcome comparisons across schools worthless.

When a practical art tries to improve its methods, it often turns to science for help. Psychotherapy, relying purely on semantic techniques, turns to the behavioral sciences of psychology, sociology, ethology, etc. As yet there has been no great help for the therapist from these areas, but the hope is that scientific research can contribute to a therapist's knowledge in order to make therapy more effective.

Research

A historical example of mutually benefiting relations between science and practical art can be found in Louis Pasteur's contribution to wine making. Although the process of fermentation was not well understood, wine had been made for thousands of years, and the results had been unpredictable. At the request of wine makers, Pasteur undertook a systematic study of the process of fermentation and discovered the role of bacteria. With this understanding it became possible to control fermentation by regulating the activity of bacteria. Nowadays the making of a great wine still requires intuitive art, but the making of a predictably sound wine is rather straightforward.

Like a wine maker, a psychotherapist follows a set of rules for achieving his goal—the relief of mental distress. As mentioned, these rules come from a body of clinical knowledge accumulated through the empirical experience of thousands of practitioners over many years. Why does a therapist believe in these rules when so few (if any) of them rely on scientific knowledge? One must here consider the nature of scientific, clinical, and common-sense knowledge. Scientific knowledge consists of reliable data and tested and confirmed (i.e., not disproved) hypotheses. Depending heavily on measurement and replication, it is precise and highly plausible in the face of the evidence. But it is also limited, lacking in scope and full of errors as history has demonstrated. Clinical knowledge stems from the slow accumulation of data and rough conceptions deriving from the astute observations and powerful intuition of generations of practitioners. Consensus develops through trial and error, and clinicians gradually come to agreement about the suitability of a technique. Common-sense knowledge consists of everyday observations and inferences at a low degree of refinement; it is often fallible and dubitable, but since it is not entirely unevaluated knowledge, it is indispensable. Refined common-sense knowledge becomes scientific knowledge, which then becomes part of common sense

again. If we had no scientific or clinical knowledge, we would still be able to manage human affairs about as well as we do today, using only common-sense knowledge of human behavior. A person has powerful aids of introspection and empathy in thinking and feeling about the behavior of other persons.

Scientific research in the problems of therapy should be able to cast light on some of the difficulties in the art. Ideally, one would like to have explanations of everything regarding mental distress and its relief. But this is not likely, nor is it even necessary for the art to improve. Not everything in therapy is a major problem. Only certain aspects merit a scientific study, and only certain questions deserve the labor required to attain a satisfactory answer.

Is psychotherapy effective? A useful and apparently simple question to ask and answer would be, "Is psychotherapy effective?" This has turned out to be such a difficult question for research to answer that we now must consider the question unanswerable when posed in this form. Thousands of therapists by now have treated millions of patients. Some patients report they are better, a few that they are worse, and some say they are the same. Therapists believe they help a majority of their patients. Therapists continue to be trained and to practice, and patients continue to seek therapy. There seems to be no widespread doubt that therapy is helpful, or at least that it is in some cases. But there is no satisfactory statistical evidence as yet that therapy benefits a population of patients. Are all these people, therapists and patients, unwittingly deceiving themselves and one another?

The issue is reduced to statistical evidence versus clinical knowledge with its elements of common sense. The failure of statistical evidence to demonstrate a phenomenon may reflect the weaknesses in our current tools of demonstration. Also a failure to reject the null hypothesis (which is what statistics attempts) does not establish the null hypothesis. On the other hand, therapists should realize better than anyone the weaknesses and uncertainty of clinical and common-sense knowledge.

The question of therapy effectiveness should be rephrased, because what the terms "therapy" and "effectiveness" refer to has never been operationally explicit. On the one hand, the term "therapy" does not refer to a homogeneous set of events. Unless the therapy can be observed by others, there is no guarantee that a therapist is doing what he should be doing and no estimate of how competently he is doing it. On the other hand, the term "effectiveness" also initiates a snarl, because patients enter therapy with varying severity of mental distress and what is judged improvement for one patient may not be judged improvement for another. Furthermore, therapeutic goals contain values about desirable behavior, and unless judges share similar value systems, it is impossible for them to agree on whether the result of therapy was good or right.

Certainly every therapist has had at least one experience in which the outcome was judged favorable by himself, other clinicians, the patient, and others who know the patient. Such an experience carries the high conviction that therapy can benefit individual cases, and if it can happen to one patient, it should be able to happen to others. But to how many others in a population and what population? And perhaps it would have happened anyway "spontaneously." There is often mention of spontaneous remission in the literature, but as yet no one has presented any evidence that such a phenomenon exists.

Candid therapists admit they do not benefit all patients and wish that those who are helped could be helped more. The issue of effectiveness remains unsettled, but therapists are convinced that therapy has the potential to relieve mental distress. What is really needed is an improvement in methods to make therapy not only more powerful but more efficient.

Resistance and transference. If research is to help a practical art, it should address itself to crucial difficulties in that art. A crucial difficulty in all therapy involves a process known as "resistance." This term was derived from nineteenth-century electrodynamics, whose terms Freud used metaphorically in conceptualizing mental processes in terms of a flow of current through a circuit. The term refers to those hindrances a patient presents to explorations, scrutiny, and change. Clinical theory explains this phenomenon on the ground that a patient, although suffering distress, has achieved a mental state that is almost tolerable in many respects. Because the patient views any change in this state as a threat of even greater suffering, attempts to change are warded off and the state is defended for a long time. It is this fear of change and of being hurt that therapists believe to be a major factor in limiting the efficiency and effectiveness of therapy. Greater knowledge is needed about this process and its relation to "transference," i.e., the feelings and beliefs a patient develops about his therapist. Technical rules for dealing with transference and resistance may still be simple, but they should be based on a greater

understanding of what we are dealing with. Animal ethology and experimental psychology has already begun to indicate much about social bonds and social influence, especially between adults and their offspring (Scott 1962).

The future

Most research in therapy thus far has concentrated on the therapy situation itself, studying it directly as it exists in nature or studying experimental analogues. Naturalistic attempts to find common denominators among therapeutic approaches have not led us very far, because the comparisons have been too superficial and experimental attempts to duplicate the therapy situation have not brought about anything new. All this is ordinary research clearing up aspects of existing paradigms (Colby 1964). Sooner or later a new paradigm will appear, and extraordinary research will begin using surprisingly different presuppositions and suppositions. It is between the crevices of a *Menschanschauung* that new paradigms are discovered.

One attempts to forecast the future by extrapolating present trends and by predicting those discoveries or inventions needed to fulfill human wishes. The main trend in the profession of psychotherapy presently concerns the development of a therapist who is not a medical practitioner. With the admission that current training systems cannot meet the increasing social demand, a new type of therapist will emerge trained in the best way that can be agreed upon by psychiatry, clinical psychology, and social work. All kinds of impediments will be raised by organization officials, but the need is clear and reasonable men will eventually yield to it.

The second forecast involves discoveries and inventions needed by therapists who wish to improve their methods. The need for a theory of mental change has already been emphasized. This will be a fresh theory, not an amalgamation of current theories. For years there has been a demand for some sort of *rapprochement* between learning theory and psychoanalytic theory. A satisfactory combination seems unlikely as long as learning theory does not concern itself with such higher mental processes as symbol manipulation or with the fact that people think, talk meaningfully, and have awareness. Also, unless psychoanalytic theory develops novel concepts, no further contributions can be expected from it. The sorts of discoveries needed are those that can be provided by basic behavioral science or by a genius in the field of clinical observations and inference. Psychotherapy, as we know it now, will change markedly if vigorously and boldly worked on.

The inventions needed are recording apparatuses providing rapid information retrieval, voice-recognizing devices, automated analyses of natural language, and computerized training devices for the learning of therapy. There is also the interesting question of whether a future computer might do as well, if not better, than a person in providing individualized therapeutic conversation for certain classes of problems (Colby et al. 1966). If a computer will be able to treat with semantic techniques thousands of patients an hour, this would be one answer to the problems of (*a*) the countable hundreds of thousands of hospitalized patients who never have an opportunity to talk with a therapist and (*b*) the uncounted millions of patients who could benefit prophylactically or remedially from therapeutic conversation.

Kenneth M. Colby

[*See also* Clinical psychology. *Other relevant material may be found in* Anxiety; Interviewing, *article on* therapeutic interviewing; Psychiatry; Psychoanalysis, *article on* therapeutic methods; Stress.]

BIBLIOGRAPHY

Colby, Kenneth M. 1964 Psychotherapeutic Processes. *Annual Review of Psychology* 15:347–370.

Colby, Kenneth M.; Watt, James B.; and Gilbert, John P. 1966 A Computer Method of Psychotherapy: Preliminary Communication. *Journal of Nervous and Mental Disease* 142:148–152.

Ford, Donald H.; and Urban, Hugh B. 1963 *Systems of Psychotherapy: A Comparative Study.* New York: Wiley.

London, Perry 1964 *The Modes and Morals of Psychotherapy.* New York: Holt.

Menninger, Karl; Mayman, Martin; and Pruyser, Paul 1963 *The Vital Balance: The Life Processes in Mental Health and Illness.* New York: Viking.

Schofield, William 1964 *Psychotherapy: The Purchase of Friendship.* Englewood Cliffs, N.J.: Prentice-Hall.

Scott, J. P. 1962 Critical Periods in Behavioral Development. *Science* New Series 138:949–958.

Walker, Nigel (1957) 1963 *A Short History of Psychotherapy in Theory and Practice.* New York: Noonday Press.

II
CLIENT-CENTERED COUNSELING

Client-centered counseling and psychotherapy as a distinctive point of view and as a radical departure from current practices can be dated rather precisely to December 1940, when Carl R. Rogers, its leading exponent, presented a paper at the University of Minnesota on the attitude and orienta-

tion of the counselor. The paper later became the second chapter of his controversial book, *Counseling and Psychotherapy* (1942). The controversy engendered by this book centered as much upon what the counselor or psychotherapist *was not* to do in the psychotherapeutic situation as upon what he *was* to do. According to Rogers, he was not to guide or to reassure or support; he was not to interpret and was not to use an entire armamentarium of what were labeled "directive" standard techniques. Psychotherapeutic interventions, particularly interpretive explanations, were categorized as dangerous. It was recommended instead that the therapist stress what were called nondirective techniques, responding directly to the present, expressed attitudes of the client (reflection of feeling), and that the therapist convey his unequivocal respect for and acceptance of the client as he presented himself in the immediate present.

Rogers postulated that when the therapist demonstrates acceptance and permissiveness and shows understanding of the client's expressed attitudes and feelings, a process of personal change in the client would occur, in which the following stages could be observed: release of expression, achievement of insight, and development of capacities for making choices and of acting on the choices made. The main task of the therapist was to allow the stages to evolve, to facilitate a natural and inherent sequence, not to set the sequence into motion. Rogers also recognized that the therapist had his own propensities to become emotionally involved with his client in ways which resulted in directiveness and that, therefore, the therapist should work at circumscribing these propensities in himself. He stressed the complete abdication of power in the therapeutic relationship, in contrast with current and standard techniques, in a manner which seemed to many to strike directly at the heart of the current practice of psychotherapy in medicine, in social work, in nonmedical settings, and in vocational psychology as well. Pained and angry responses from the ranks of these helping professions were immediate, intense, and long-sustained.

Personal change in psychotherapy

Counseling and Psychotherapy was almost entirely theory-free and empirical in tone, and intentionally so. In 1942, Rogers was a clinical professor formulating his clinical experience for the benefit of clinical students; like many clinicians he was somewhat scornful of current psychological theories, regarding them as sparse and simplistic compared with the richness and complexity of the clients with whom he worked. The storm of controversy ensuing upon the publication of *Counseling and Psychotherapy* stimulated a flow of research and theoretical development by Rogers, his associates, and their students which has not yet abated. The development of theory and research in all areas until approximately 1956 was summarized and integrated by Rogers (1959, pp. 184–252). The approach to understanding personality, psychotherapy, and interpersonal relationships is entirely phenomenological. Technique is minimized and the necessary and sufficient conditions for inducing psychotherapeutic personality change are stated to be the following:

1. Client and therapist are in contact.

2. The client is in a state of incongruence: there is a discrepancy between his perceived self and his actual experience. He is vulnerable or anxious.

3. The therapist is congruent in the relationship with his client: his perceptions of this relationship are accurate symbolizations of the actual experience.

4. The therapist is experiencing unconditional favorable regard toward his client.

5. The therapist is experiencing an empathic understanding of the client's internal frame of reference.

6. The client perceives, at least to a minimal degree, the unconditional favorable regard of the therapist for him as well as the empathic understanding of the therapist.

It is noticeable that no techniques and no behavior prescriptions appear in this account. Everything is couched in terms of the experience of the client and of the therapist. Nonetheless, most responses of client-centered therapists continue to be reflections of feeling based on their perception of the internal frame of reference of the client. The behavior of client-centered therapists follows from this premise: The probability that the client will perceive the therapist as prizing (positively valuing) and understanding him is maximized when the therapist manages to convey his prizing attitude of unconditional favorable regard and when the therapist communicates his empathic understanding to the client in a consistent way.

Basic concepts. The theory of personality presented is also phenomenological and shows the influence of gestalt theory. The only motive postulated in the theoretical system is the actualizing tendency: the inherent tendency of the organism to develop all of its capacities in ways serving to maintain or enhance the organism. The actualizing tendency reflects in large part the tendency to develop autonomy and to lessen heteronomy, or

control by external forces. The actualizing tendency is a property of the total organism.

The self concept is the consistent conceptual gestalt (organization) derived from the perceptions of the "I" or the "me" that are developed in interaction with significant others. The ideal self concept denotes the self concept to which the individual aspires. The self-actualizing tendency is a subsystem of the basic organismic actualizing tendency and is a consequence of the development of the self concept. Self-actualization is the actualization of that portion of the experience of the organism which is symbolized in the self concept. When self-experience and the remainder of the experience of the organism are congruent, then the actualizing tendency remains relatively unified. If self concept and experience are incongruent, then self-actualization and actualization tendencies are incongruent. In this case, the individual is maladjusted: his self concept reflects a conflict between self-actualizing motives and actualizing motives. [See SELF CONCEPT.]

The self concept does not direct the organism; indeed, the self concept derives from the actualizing tendency and is but one aspect of the tendency of the organism to react and behave so as to maintain and enhance itself. Motives or needs such as the need for favorable recognition from others and the need for self-esteem arise out of the organism's experiences in relation to interpersonal transactions and their vicissitudes. In a broad sense, "experience," in Rogers' view, is the organism's receiving the impact of sensory or physiological events happening at the moment; experience is what happens to the organism, including what happens within it. However, in a more restricted meaning "to experience" for Rogers also denotes the accurate symbolization in awareness of the sensory or physiological events.

The theory presented by Rogers, although containing many propositions, is basically simple. It concerns the development and self-development of the organism, the accurate symbolization in awareness of experience, and the perception of threat, with consequent defenses and effects upon interpersonal behavior. The development of an accurate self concept is held to be a basic capacity of the organism.

An inaccurately symbolized self concept emerges because the individual, in the course of development, begins to have a need for favorable regard from others and an analogous and consequent need for favorable self-regard but perceives himself as being only conditionally prized or loved by others. He incorporates this conditional prizing into his self concept and subsequently evaluates experiences on the basis of conditional prizings instead of in terms of the basic actualizing tendency. Perception of unconditional prizing by others leads, on the other hand, to satisfaction of the needs for favorable regard and self-regard in a way that is congruent with the basic actualization tendency. Development under optimal conditions of unconditional prizing leads to a person who is fully functioning, open to experience, and psychologically adjusted.

Some comments on the theory are in order. As stated before, it is relatively simple, having neither the comprehensiveness, say, of psychoanalytic theory nor the seemingly rigorous and elegant simplicity of behavior theory. Not too much is said about motivation, and the defense mechanisms, such as repression, denial, and reaction formation, are taken for granted: they have been discussed and investigated elsewhere. The theory was developed to account for what other theories neglected and to stress a view of human nature and experience not currently dominant in Western culture, namely, that the individual inherently actualizes and self-actualizes, is personal and subjective, is not at the mercy of individual drives, and has inherent capacities for realistic adaptation and unrestricted experiencing. He is often conditionally valued by significant others early in life and often responds by evaluating his self in terms of these conditional prizings. The individual has a history that results in various degrees of congruence between the actualization and the self-actualization tendencies: the lower degrees of congruence are maladjustive; the higher degrees approximate the fully functioning, fully experiencing individual, who evaluates autonomously and is personally creative. [See DEFENSE MECHANISMS.]

Clinical and empirical foundations. Despite its phenomenological language, Rogers' theory has the virtue of being close to and being derived from clinical observation. When the client is in the psychotherapeutic situation, when he is unconditionally prized and is well understood by the therapist as he presents himself, he does change his self concepts, he does react more openly, he does abandon maladaptive strategies, maneuvers, and symptoms in relation to the therapist. He usually does not develop a "transference neurosis," and his expressive style changes. The organization and use of language changes, and the individual comes to act differently with others than before. Observations of such changes led to the theory. What is not observationally based is the theoretical prediction of the increase in congruence between self concepts and experience. What is observed is that self con-

cepts change and that the individual expresses himself as being in some ways more like the person he wants to be. However, the congruence of self concept and ideal concept is suspect because it is observed that some individuals claim to have congruent selves and ideals when obviously such is not the case; i.e., interpersonal behavior is not consistent with the claim, and worse, other persons, such as paranoid individuals, seem to have congruent self concepts and ideal concepts but are clearly psychologically maladjusted; thus the recourse by Rogers to the discrepancy between self concept and experience and between self-actualization and the actualization tendency, even though such discrepancies are not actually observed in the psychotherapeutic interaction.

In general, theoretical statements by writers within the client-centered orientation, with the exception perhaps of Raimy (1943) and Snygg and Combs (1949), have the same clinical–empirical and action-oriented flavor as those of Rogers. Complex behavior is considered. Little attempt is made to provide careful definitions in the sense in which terms such as stimulus, response, drive, and response generalization are carefully defined in, say, behavior theory because the primary referents can be pointed to in recordings, motion pictures, etc. This discriminability of primary referents is conceived to be an advantage. Considerable difficulty has been encountered by behavior theorists in defining such terms as stimulus, response, and response generalization unambiguously even for simple situations, and when they are applied as behavior therapy, the specification of reinforcing stimuli and of response generalization has been so vague that it seems safe to say that for some of the better-known studies it would be easy to obtain quite different results using the same reinforcing stimuli described by the investigators.

The therapy process. Rogers' specifications of the necessary and sufficient conditions of personality change in psychotherapy are to a large extent understood by client-centered therapists in terms of the predominant conduct of therapists: unconditional prizing behavior, mostly expressed nonverbally, and reflections of feeling as communications of manifest themes that occurred in the client's communications. The communicative behavior of clients includes the nonverbal, gestural, expressive components of communication which are linguistic in nature and which serve to modify the meaning of symbols and signs.

What happens in the psychotherapeutic hour when the therapist conducts himself in the manner mentioned above? Numerous studies, most of them cited by Rogers (1959), have been addressed to this question. While these studies are satisfactory in a certain sense, they do not really describe the events at all well. Hence, a naturalistic description will be attempted. The communicative behavior of the client usually, in contrast with psychotherapies in which the psychotherapist's responses are interventive, shows thematic unity. Thematic unity is also evident in the sequence of responses. Along with this, the voice qualities change, and language usage also changes in such a way that the client appears to be more expressive and integrated in his communicative behavior, to be using a richer and more figurative language. When the therapist accurately symbolizes the themes in a client response, he is in actuality amplifying and developing them through his own language and voice qualities. Often these responses of the therapist are met by the client with "Yes, yes," "That's it exactly," or "Exactly," spoken with considerable emphasis. The theme voiced by the therapist (but voiced by the client immediately before) is then elaborated and developed with considerably more differentiation in both language and voice, creating an impression of supple and spontaneous flexibility. This is true even for quite disturbed clients communicating initially in a passive way and with the passive voice, and using such phrases as "This comes to mind." As the therapist's language becomes richer and more apt, as he makes more use of his voice, as his expressive gestures become more explicit, the more thematic is the development, the more figurative is the speech, and the more closely knit, congruent, and spontaneous become the interchanges of the client and the therapist. This behavioral process, so difficult to describe but so denotable in audio and photographic reproductions of psychotherapy interviews, at its best has the kind of literary quality one might ascribe to recitations of the ancient Greek bards, whose recitations were worked out anew in each encounter with an audience. Published reports of client-centered therapy are, unfortunately, poor representations of the process described.

Later theoretical development

Theory development since 1956 has largely concentrated upon developing the phenomenological perspective (Shlien 1962), with much stress on the experiencing process in relation to personality change (Gendlin 1964). Gendlin (1962) has written a philosophical treatise on personal experiencing that stresses the relation of experiencing to the creation of meaning. This work developed out of his training as a philosopher and his extensive en-

counters with client-centered psychotherapy. In extending his concept of experiencing to the understanding of concepts and values (1963; 1964), psychotherapy (1961), and personality change (1964), Gendlin has concluded that changes may occur in psychotherapy even before concepts have been attained that accurately represent feelings referred to by the client. This occurs because the therapist's responses themselves may lead to symbolic completions, closures, and elaborated themata even when the client does not perceive the therapist as prizingly understanding. In emphasizing the influence of the therapist in promoting closure, Gendlin is in effect changing Rogers' conditions for personality change.

Dissatisfied with the postulational character of the actualization tendency, Butler and Rice (1963) have proposed that adient motivation, the need for experience, is the primitive base for the actualization and self-actualization tendencies. On the basis of studies of preference for complexity or novelty, of stimulus deprivation and of neurophysiological processes, they propose that adience is rewarded by thinking processes as well as by environmental transactions. The self-actualizing, fully functioning person autonomously creates experience for himself, and he can autonomously reinforce and extinguish behavior (learn) without moving a muscle. [See STIMULATION DRIVES.]

With respect to psychotherapy, Butler and Rice maintain that a stimulating, expressive communicative style on the part of the psychotherapist enriches the experience of the client, focuses associations by reflections of feeling, and leads to symbolic completions and thema development. A "difficult" client with a poor prognosis may lower the responsive participation of the therapist, thus creating an experientially impoverished environment matching his inner experiencing, with the consequence that enrichment of experience may not ensue. Clients with poor prognosis are just those who, in the therapeutic interaction, are likely to create the conditions leading to lack of progress and no constructive personality change. Butler and Rice maintain that the therapist who can sustain a participative, stimulating, and responsive expressive style is likely to induce progress in therapy even when such progress seems improbable. Evidence supporting their hypotheses has been presented by Wagstaff (see Butler et al. 1963) and Rice (1965.)

Research

Research on client-centered psychotherapy has been summarized or cited extensively in Rogers (1959; 1960), Seeman (1956; 1965), Butler

(1958), and Grummon (1965). Attention here will be centered on the proposition that the changes noted in psychotherapy are due to the psychotherapeutic encounter rather than to spontaneous remission or other extrapsychotherapeutic agents. All work cited has been discussed in Rogers (1959), except when cited by year.

Early studies tended to be confined to content analyses of transcripts of therapy interviews. These studies showed that, to a considerable extent, therapists did, indeed, consistently employ the techniques they claimed to use (Porter, Snyder, Seeman, Strom). Furthermore, for clients it was demonstrated that there was a change in the proportion of responses indicating insight, self-exploration, and integration (Porter, Snyder, Curran, Stock, Hoffman); that there were decreasing proportions of distress and discomfort responses and increasing proportions of favorable responses to self (Raimy, Assum, & Levy; Kauffman & Raimy; Zimmerman); that decreasing self-exploration was exhibited when therapists complied with requests for guidance, information, and support (Bergman 1951); that there occurred an increasing acceptance of self and others (Sheerer); and that there was an increased correspondence between ideal self and self concept for cases evaluated as successful, whereas this did not occur in cases evaluated as unsuccessful (Aidman 1951; Bowman 1951).

In later studies, control techniques and measuring devices suggested by theory and research results were employed. Self–ideal relations were found to increase during the course of psychotherapy for the client group as a whole, the increase being greater for the group of clients judged to be definitely improved in terms of both therapist ratings and Thematic Apperception Test (TAT) ratings (Butler & Haigh 1954). The therapist's judgments were made independently of the TAT ratings and of the tested self–ideal relations. There was a significant increase in the variability of the self–ideal correlations at the end of therapy and at the end of a follow-up period, indicating that self-acceptance was decreasing for some clients and increasing for others. The majority of the changes reflected increasingly self–ideal correspondence, however.

Butler showed that 11 of the clients serving as their own controls, to whom tests were administered 60 days prior to therapy, immediately before therapy, and 60 days or less after therapy began, changed their self-descriptions significantly more during the in-therapy period than during the no-therapy period (Butler 1964*a*).

Another control feature is the rating of clients

on a scale measuring maturity of behavior (Rogers 1954). Friends of the clients who were not informed that the clients were in therapy and who knew nothing of the research, made these ratings. In general, mean ratings on these scores did not change significantly between pretherapy, therapy termination, and follow-up testing. However, when the clients were stratified on the basis of therapist rating on a nine-point scale of success, the mean increase on maturity scores from pretherapy to therapy termination was statistically significant for clients whose ratings were in the 7–9 range, while there was a statistically insignificant decrease for clients rated in the 1–5 range. For the period between pretherapy and follow-up testings there was a significant increase in average maturity ratings for clients in the 7–9 range and a significant decrease in average maturity ratings for clients in the 1–5 range.

The findings are remarkable because the groups used were very small and the therapist rated clients solely on the basis of interview behavior, while the lay observers presumably did not know their friends were in psychotherapy and knew nothing of the research. Comparable ratings on normal controls showed no mean change in score between testing periods.

In a later study of many of the same clients, Butler (1964*b*) related self-reports, ratings by independent lay observers, and ratings by therapists. His results indicate that the vantage points of clients, therapists, and observers provide similar information, although the judgments are made on different bases.

While this particular group was small, cross validation with another group yielded the same conclusion about the effects of psychotherapy on self-description. Cartwright and Vogel (1960) reported on a group of clients for whom they individually matched periods of waiting for therapy with in-therapy testing points. The wait periods varied from 4 to 24 weeks. They found statistically significant differences in the variability of self-descriptions indicative of adjustment (highly related to self–ideal correspondence) during the treatment period over and above those obtaining in the waiting period. Psychotherapy was held to account for the increase in the variability of self-description scores.

In another study reported by Butler (1964*a*), the self–ideal correlations of clients with good and poor prognoses were compared with those of clients with good and poor prognoses who were not receiving psychotherapy. The treatment group received ten weeks or less of psychotherapy, whereas the control group received no psychotherapy for a ten-week period. Analysis of covariance of the self–

ideal correlations revealed that those of the treatment group changed more than those of the no-treatment control group and that the majority of the changes were in the direction of increased correspondence of self concepts and ideal concepts.

When clients are matched on prognosis and are randomly assigned, one can infer from these findings that self-acceptance does change in, and as a result of, client-centered psychotherapy. One can also infer that changes in self-acceptance are related in some way, not necessarily linearly, to changes in maturity of interpersonal behavior as seen by lay observers, to psychodynamic changes as reflected in indexes derived from projective tests, and to changes in personal integration and level of adjustment as perceived by therapists. No single study provides perfect control, but the progressive character of the results and the relationships of the measures lend considerable weight to the hypothesis that self-acceptance changes as a result of client-centered psychotherapy and that other changes, particularly maturity of interpersonal behavior, are associated with self-acceptance and the process of psychotherapy.

A particularly interesting study was conducted by Bills (1950). After a 30-day control period in which none of 18 third-graders who were retarded readers received play therapy, eight received client-centered play therapy and ten received no treatment. An analysis of covariance showed a statistically significant difference in gain in reading score for the treated group compared with the untreated group. Bills's study bears on the question of what kinds of behavior are affected by psychotherapy, adding reading to the list of self-regarding behavior, interpersonal behavior, and projective behavior. [*See* READING DISABILITIES.]

Research in client-centered psychotherapy since Rogers completed his survey (1959) has centered largely upon the conditions of psychotherapy as provided by the psychotherapist and upon therapist characteristics. Wagstaff has found three factors of expressive style in client verbal behavior, two of which are related to various criteria of outcome of psychotherapy (Butler et al. 1962; 1963); and Rice, analyzing responses of the therapists of the clients studied by Wagstaff, has found three factors of therapist vocal and lexical style, two of which are also related to various outcome criteria (1965). These studies support the hypothesis of Butler and Rice, alluded to earlier, that clients with poor prognoses deleteriously affect the responsiveness of their therapists.

Duncan (1965), studying a variety of discrete paralinguistic behaviors in both client and therapist, found significant relationships, on the one hand, between one aspect of therapy "process" (patterns of voice quality) and the therapist's judgments of the process, and, on the other hand, between this process and client test performance both before therapy and after 20 interviews.

Gaylin (1965) devised a Rorschach function score designed to measure psychological health. Obtaining this score for pretherapy and post-twentieth-interview Rorschachs, he found that those clients with high ratings of improvement by their therapists exhibited improved scores; those with low ratings, poorer scores. Gaylin's function score also correlated significantly with paralinguistic factors studied by Duncan.

Truax and Carkhuff (1963), working with Rogers, have presented evidence to show that when therapists dealing with hospitalized patients provided high levels of warmth, empathy, and congruence, patients improved; when they did not, patients became worse.

Client-centered psychotherapists hypothesize that the person is motivated largely by actualizing and self-actualizing tendencies which result in favorable personality change under proper interpersonal conditions initiated by the therapist. The results of studies of the psychotherapeutic situation and its effects strongly support these hypotheses. These studies also show that changes observed in psychotherapy are reflected in interpersonal relationships and in favorable and enduring changes in the structure of self concepts. In addition, the techniques and qualities of client-centered therapists significantly affect performances in other types of situations.

Although there are a few studies suggesting that client-centered psychotherapy compares favorably with other approaches (e.g., Shlien et al. 1962), it would be premature to claim that client-centered psychotherapy is more efficacious than other psychotherapies. This is due in part to the lack of systematic research on personal change in psychotherapy. Furthermore, different approaches to psychotherapeutic treatment, such as behavior therapy, apparently have goals somewhat different from those stated for client-centered psychotherapy. These circumstances render systematic comparisons difficult, if not impossible, at the present stage of development of research on psychotherapy. Currently, an opinion on the relative efficacy of various forms of psychotherapy must be regarded as just that and no more.

JOHN BUTLER

[*Directly related are the entries* CLINICAL PSYCHOLOGY; COUNSELING PSYCHOLOGY; IDENTITY, PSYCHOSOCIAL;

SELF CONCEPT. *Other relevant material may be found in* GESTALT THEORY; PERSONALITY, *article on* PERSONALITY DEVELOPMENT; PERSONALITY: CONTEMPORARY VIEWPOINTS, *article on* A UNIQUE AND OPEN SYSTEM; PHENOMENOLOGY; PSYCHOLOGY, *article on* EXISTENTIAL PSYCHOLOGY; SYMPATHY AND EMPATHY; THINKING, *article on* COGNITIVE ORGANIZATION AND PROCESSES.]

BIBLIOGRAPHY

AIDMAN, TED 1951 An Objective Study of the Changing Relationship Between the Present Self and Wanted Self-picture as Expressed by the Client in Client-centered Therapy. Ph.D. dissertation, Univ. of Chicago.

AXLINE, VIRGINIA M. 1947 *Play Therapy: The Inner Dynamics of Childhood.* Boston: Houghton Mifflin.

BARRINGTON, BYRON 1961 Prediction From Counselor Behavior of Client Perception and of Case Outcome. *Journal of Counseling Psychology* 8:37–42.

BERGMAN, DANIEL V. 1951 Counseling Method and Client Responses. *Journal of Consulting Psychology* 15:216–224.

BILLS, ROBERT E. 1950 Non-directive Play Therapy With Retarded Readers. *Journal of Consulting Psychology* 14:140–149.

BOWMAN, PAUL H. 1951 A Study of the Consistency of Current, Wish and Proper Self-concepts as a Measure of Therapeutic Progress. Ph.D. dissertation, Univ. of Chicago.

BUTLER, JOHN M. 1952 The Interaction of Client and Therapist. *Journal of Abnormal and Social Psychology* 47:366–378.

BUTLER, JOHN M. 1958 Client-centered Counseling and Psychotherapy. Volume 3, pages 93–106 in *Progress in Clinical Psychology.* Edited by Daniel Brower and Lawrence E. Abt. New York: Grune.

BUTLER, JOHN M. 1964a Self-acceptance as a Measure of Outcome of Psychotherapy. Unpublished manuscript. → Paper delivered at the First International Congress of Social Psychiatry.

BUTLER, JOHN M. 1964b Self Concept Change in Psychotherapy. *Acta psychologica* 23:119 only. → Volume 23 contains the *Proceedings* of the Seventeenth International Congress of Psychology held in Washington in 1963.

BUTLER, JOHN M.; and HAIGH, GERARD V. 1954 Changes in the Relation Between Self-concepts and Ideal Concepts Consequent Upon Client-centered Counseling. Pages 55–75 in Carl R. Rogers and Rosalind F. Dymond (editors), *Psychotherapy and Personality Change: Co-ordinated Research Studies in the Client-centered Approach.* Univ. of Chicago Press.

BUTLER, JOHN M.; and RICE, LAURA N. 1963 Adience, Self-actualization and Drive Theory. Pages 79–110 in Joseph M. Wepman and Ralph W. Heine (editors), *Concepts of Personality.* Chicago: Aldine.

BUTLER, JOHN M.; RICE, LAURA N.; and WAGSTAFF, ALICE K. 1962 On the Naturalistic Definition of Variables: An Analogue of Clinical Analysis. Volume 2, pages 178–205 in Conference on Research in Psychotherapy, *Research in Psychotherapy.* Edited by Lester Luborsky and Hans Strupp. Washington: American Psychological Association.

BUTLER, JOHN M.; RICE, LAURA N.; and WAGSTAFF, ALICE K. 1963 *Quantitative Naturalistic Research: An Introduction to Naturalistic Observation and Investigation.* Englewood Cliffs, N.J.: Prentice-Hall.

CARTWRIGHT, DESMOND 1957 Annotated Bibliography of Research and Theory Construction in Client-centered Therapy. *Journal of Counseling Psychology* 4:82–100.

CARTWRIGHT, ROSALIND D.; and VOGEL, JOHN 1960 A Comparison of Changes in Psychoneurotic Patients During Matched Periods of Therapy and No Therapy. *Journal of Consulting Psychology* 24:121–127.

DUNCAN, STARKEY D. JR. 1965 Paralinguistic Behaviors in Client–Therapist Communication in Psychotherapy. Ph.D. dissertation, Univ. of Chicago.

GAYLIN, N. L. 1965 Psychotherapy and Psychological Health: A Rorschach Structure and Function Analysis. Ph.D. dissertation, Univ. of Chicago.

GENDLIN, EUGENE 1961 Experiencing: A Variable in the Process of Therapeutic Change. *American Journal of Psychotherapy* 15:233–245.

GENDLIN, EUGENE 1962 *Experiencing and the Creation of Meaning: A Philosophical and Psychological Approach to the Subjective.* New York: Free Press.

GENDLIN, EUGENE 1963 Experiencing and the Nature of Concepts. *Christian Scholar* 46:245–255.

GENDLIN, EUGENE 1964 A Theory of Personality Change. Pages 100–148 in Symposium on Personality Change, University of Texas, *Personality Change.* Edited by Philip Worchel and Donn Byrne. New York: Wiley.

GENDLIN, EUGENE 1965 Values and the Process of Experiencing. Unpublished manuscript.

GRUMMON, DONALD L. 1965 Client-centered Therapy. Pages 30–90 in Buford Steffire (editor), *Theories of Counseling.* New York: McGraw-Hill.

RAIMY, VICTOR C. 1943 The Self-concept as a Factor in Counseling and Personality Organization. Ph.D. dissertation, Ohio State Univ.

RICE, LAURA N. 1965 Therapist's Style of Participation and Case Outcome. *Journal of Consulting Psychology* 29:155–160.

ROGERS, CARL R. 1942 *Counseling and Psychotherapy: Newer Concepts in Practice.* Boston: Houghton Mifflin. → See especially pages 19–47, "Old and New Viewpoints in Counseling and Psychotherapy."

ROGERS, CARL R. 1954 Changes in the Maturity of Behavior as Related to Therapy. Pages 215–237 in Carl R. Rogers and Rosalind F. Dymond (editors), *Psychotherapy and Personality Change: Co-ordinated Research Studies in the Client-centered Approach.* Univ. of Chicago Press.

ROGERS, CARL R. 1959 A Theory of Therapy, Personality, and Interpersonal Relationships, as Developed in the Client-centered Framework. Volume 3, pages 184–256 in Sigmund Koch (editor), *Psychology: A Study of a Science.* New York: McGraw-Hill.

ROGERS, CARL R. 1960 Significant Trends in the Client-centered Orientation. Volume 4, pages 85–99 in *Progress in Clinical Psychology.* Edited by Lawrence E. Abt and Bernard F. Riess. New York: Grune.

ROGERS, CARL R. 1961a *On Becoming a Person: A Therapist's View of Psychotherapy.* Boston: Houghton Mifflin.

ROGERS, CARL R. 1961b A Theory of Psychotherapy With Schizophrenics and a Proposal for Its Empirical Investigation. Pages 3–19 in J. G. Dawson, H. K. Stone, and N. P. Dellis (editors), *Psychotherapy With Schizophrenics: A Reappraisal.* Baton Rouge: Louisiana State Univ. Press.

ROGERS, CARL R.; and DYMOND, ROSALIND F. (editors) 1954 *Psychotherapy and Personality Change: Co-*

ordinated Research Studies in the Client-centered Approach. Univ. of Chicago Press.

ROGERS, CARL R.; and KINGET, G. MARIAN 1960 *Psychotherapie en menselijke verhoudingen: Theorie en praktijk van de non-directieve therapie.* Utrecht (Netherlands): Spectrum. → A French translation was published in Louvain by Presses Universitaires de France in 1962.

SEEMAN, JULIUS 1956 Client-centered Therapy. Volume 2, pages 98–113 in *Progress in Clinical Psychology.* Edited by Daniel Brower and Lawrence E. Abt. New York: Grune.

SEEMAN, JULIUS 1965 Perspectives in Client-centered Therapy. Pages 1215–1229 in Benjamin B. Wolman (editor), *Handbook of Clinical Psychology.* New York: McGraw-Hill.

SHLIEN, JOHN M. 1961 A Client-centered Approach to Schizophrenia: First Approximation. Pages 285–317 in Arthur Burton (editor), *Psychotherapy of the Psychoses.* New York: Basic Books.

SHLIEN, JOHN M. 1962 Toward What Level of Abstraction in Criteria? Pages 142–154 in Conference in Research in Psychotherapy 1961, *Research in Psychotherapy.* Washington: American Psychological Association.

SHLIEN, JOHN M.; MOSAK, HAROLD H.; and DREIKERS, RUDOLF 1962 Effect of Time-limits: A Comparison of Two Psychotherapies. *Journal of Counseling Psychology* 9:31–34.

SNYGG, DONALD; and COMBS, ARTHUR W. 1949 *Individual Behavior: A New Frame of Reference for Psychology.* New York: Harper. → A revised edition was published in 1959.

TRUAX, CHARLES B.; and CARKHUFF, ROBERT R. 1963 For Better or Worse: The Process of Psychotherapeutic Personality Change. Pages 118–157 in Academic Society on Clinical Psychology, Montreal, 1963, *Recent Advances in the Study of Behaviour Change: Proceedings of the Academic Assembly on Clinical Psychology.* . . . Montreal: McGill Univ. Press.

III
GROUP PSYCHOTHERAPY

Group psychotherapies are based on the recognition that, with proper guidance, certain types of persons with psychiatric disorders can help each other. In all forms of group therapy, patients and a therapist repeatedly meet to conduct certain activities within the framework of a special group structure and code. Their emotionally charged interactions with the leader and with each other may help to correct their faulty communication behavior and their distorted perceptions of themselves and others, leading to improved social and personal functioning and to relief of psychic distress.

Group healing methods are as old as individual ones. From earliest times, sufferers have sought relief through group activities at religious shrines, and many continue to do so. Group therapies began to emerge as recognized and legitimate forms of psychotherapy, however, only in the 1920s.

Many early practitioners exploited the instructional and inspirational potentialities of groups in a purely empirical way; but two pioneers, Trigant Burrow and J. L. Moreno, offered theoretical rationales that, although not in the mainstream of psychiatric thought, had considerable influence. According to Burrow (Riese & Syz 1963), mental disorder was a disturbance in communication, created largely by a person's "privately cherished and secretly guarded" image of himself; the aim of group therapy was to enable him to express himself as he really was by exposing the socially determined basis of his self-image. Moreno (1959) stressed the freeing of spontaneity through encouraging the patient to act out his problems, with the aid of other patients as well as of therapists, in the presence of a vicariously participating audience. In the 1930s psychoanalysts began to experiment with group therapy based on psychoanalytic theory. During World War II, psychotherapists in the armed forces were forced to resort to group methods to handle the enormous load of patients. These methods proved so successful that they spread with almost explosive rapidity. Many modifications were introduced and applied to an ever increasing variety of psychiatric conditions in many different settings. By the 1950s, group therapy in the United States had assumed the dimensions of a movement and had two professional associations, each with a journal devoted to promulgating it.

The wide popularity of group therapies may be partly due to the fact that they offer a type of intimacy characteristic of the family and other primary groups. The urbanization and mobility of modern life have reduced opportunities for such relationships, and the shallow, transient, competitive sociability of residential development, office, and club is not an adequate substitute.

Characteristics of group therapy

Therapeutic groups are conducted in outpatient clinics, private offices, social agencies, mental hospitals, and correctional institutions. Leaders are characteristically psychiatrists, psychologists, psychiatric social workers, or ministers. Some groups are conducted by their own members, without professional guidance. Most forms have a single leader, often with an observer to record what occurs; but some have cotherapists—usually a man and a woman—who try to take different functional roles, such as "father" and "mother."

Composition of therapy groups. Most therapy groups consist of from 7 to 25 strangers selected according to a principle such as age, institutional residence, or diagnostic category. Examples are groups composed of children, adolescents, mature adults, or the aged; of alcoholics, psychotics, or neurotics; or of persons whose only common feature is residence in the same mental hospital or correctional institution.

Increasing efforts are being made to group patients within these broad categories in such a way as to maximize their communication potential. It has been noted that groups tend to elicit certain group roles in predisposed members. For example, one repeatedly finds monopolists, nonparticipants, therapist's assistants, members who try to hold the stage by constantly complaining, and others who try to dominate by moralizing (Rosenthal et al. 1954). This raises the possibility of balancing groups by selecting prospective members with regard to their predilections for different group roles. Observation of patients' actual group behavior seems to be a more reliable way of determining this than individual interviews and psychological tests. To this end, assignment of patients to therapeutic groups may be based on their behavior in a diagnostic group, to which all patients are briefly assigned, where this is administratively possible.

A recent trend toward treatment of family groups as a unit is based on the view that the member officially labeled the patient is in reality the victim of a disturbed communication network in which other family members are also involved (Bell 1961; Satir 1964). This approach seems especially promising when the patient is chronologically or psychologically immature, as in the case of a child, an adolescent, or a schizophrenic.

Therapists meet privately with patients before the first group meeting to determine their suitability for inclusion and to prepare them for the group; they meet again, later, to evaluate the patients' readiness for discharge. The extent of private patient–therapist contacts at these and other times varies widely, depending on the therapist's conceptualization of treatment; but it is generally agreed that such meetings must be limited if they are not to drain important material from the group sessions.

This limitation also holds for meetings of patients between formal sessions, since such informal meetings create opportunities for antitherapeutic as well as therapeutic encounters. With family groups and married couples, such meetings are of course unavoidable; and they seldom can be completely prevented in groups of strangers. Extra group meetings foster growth of group cohesiveness and give members opportunities to interact away from the inhibiting presence of the therapist,

which may be advantageous. On the other hand, by diminishing the members' "social incognito," they may inhibit candid expression of feeling in the group and may foster "acting-out" of personal problems through, for example, exploitative or anxiety-relieving sexual behavior, thereby removing the problems from the helpful scrutiny of the group. Some therapists deal with this problem by prescribing meetings in their absence, so that these become part of treatment; all try to set the ground rule that there be no secrets from the group. The knowledge that anything occurring in an extra-group encounter may be reported to the group usually has an inhibitory effect on antitherapeutic activities.

Leader-centeredness or group-centeredness. Methods of group therapy can be ordered with reference to their degree of leader-centeredness or group-centeredness. Since group members are chosen by the therapist and initially expect help only from him, all groups begin as leader-centered. Throughout the duration of some groups the therapist continues to be seen as the sole therapeutic agent, and the group as merely the arena in which members interact with him and each other. Group-centered approaches attribute considerable therapeutic effects to properties of the group itself. Some groups have no official leader. In others, the leader encourages patients to rely increasingly on each other and deliberately tries to foster a group code and group attributes, such as cohesiveness, that have therapeutic potential. Actually, in therapy groups as in all others, leader behavior, member behavior, and group processes continuously interact. For example, a controlled study of group therapy with hospitalized patients found that intrapersonal exploration by the patients was associated with certain aspects of the therapist's style of leadership and with certain properties of the group itself (Truax 1961).

Degree of activity structure. Groups can also be roughly classified in terms of the extent to which their activities are organized. Some, such as Alcoholics Anonymous, therapeutic social clubs, and Recovery, Incorporated (Wechsler 1960), rely on tightly structured, prescribed activities; others, often termed interview or free-interaction groups, create an ambiguous situation and place responsibility for what occurs on the members. In general, the more structured the group, the larger its size can be.

Free-interaction groups. To illustrate the range of group therapies, three divergent types may be briefly described. Free-interaction groups typically consist of up to eight adult outpatients and a professional leader. These groups seek to create a code and a climate that foster development of greater self-reliance, spontaneity, and maturity in the members. They encourage free expression of feeling and discussion of personal problems, relying primarily on the shared experiences of the participants to help each find better solutions to his own problems. The responsibility for choice of topic and conduct of the meeting lies largely with the members. The therapist creates and maintains the ground rules and therapeutic atmosphere, facilitates members' interactions, and clarifies the meanings of their behavior (Foulkes & Anthony 1957; Mullan & Rosenbaum 1962).

Alcoholics Anonymous. Alcoholics Anonymous is a self-selected, group-oriented organization based on the single criterion of self-confessed alcoholism. Meetings are conducted by the members in a highly structured fashion, and consist chiefly of testimonials about how wretched they were when they drank and how much better they are since they have stopped. Other prescribed activities include making restitution to persons they have harmed and being available to alcoholics who ask for help. The considerable therapeutic effect of these groups lies in the unique degree of support and mutual understanding that alcoholics can give each other.

Therapeutic social clubs. Therapeutic social clubs, used chiefly for hospitalized patients or those making the transition back to the community, are run along parliamentary lines, and plan and conduct projects financed by dues. The therapist selects the members and attends all meetings, but remains in the background. The central purpose of these clubs is to combat the vicious circle of impaired social skills, withdrawal, and further social impairment by helping members to improve their social abilities (Bierer 1944).

Results of group therapies

Evaluation of the results of group therapies, as of all other forms of psychotherapy, is hampered by the absence of a satisfactory classification of psychiatric disorders and inadequate criteria of improvement, but certain clinical impressions are sufficiently widespread to warrant mention. Because of the tensions created by early meetings, especially in unstructured, group-centered approaches, the drop-out rate is higher than in individual psychotherapy, unless the therapist makes special efforts to maintain the patient's commitment to treatment. Particularly prone to leave are patients with such socially unacceptable problems as sexual deviations; those needing strong support from an authority figure; the excessively shy, sensitive, or suspicious; and those with high dominance but low popularity (Taylor 1961).

About two-thirds of those who remain in treatment improve, as in individual psychotherapy. Group therapy may be especially helpful to patients who are inadequately socialized, including those who express their personal problems in somatic symptoms rather than words, schizophrenics, and sociopaths. Certain obsessional patients, whose verbal and conceptual skills act as defenses against experiencing emotions in analytic-type therapies, may profit from the strong emotional reactions triggered by group processes.

Group treatment may aid families and married couples whose communications have become frozen in self-perpetuating, self-aggravating patterns, and who have become so busy defending themselves that they no longer "hear" each other. As they repeatedly display their pathological interaction patterns in a setting that offers support and encourages self-examination, each family member may come to understand how he contributes to the problems of the others and learn to modify his behavior.

Therapy groups and group dynamics

Although controlled experimentation with therapy groups obviously is very difficult, they provide a source for hypotheses concerning all small-group functioning; and some data obtained from experimental studies of small groups may cast light on the phenomena of therapy groups. The following discussion reviews some possible relationships between the two fields that afford areas for research (Kelman 1963).

Distinctive features. Most therapy groups represent subcultures that are demarcated from the culture of the community at large in certain important respects. One is the ground rule that what is said or done in a group meeting is confidential with respect to the outside world. In contrast to other types of groups, admission is secured by confession of failure in some aspects of living. Status within the group is related to skill in playing the role of patient, as defined by the group code, and to demonstration of clinical improvement. Another distinguishing feature of most therapy groups is that members are expected to express their feelings about themselves, persons outside the group, other group members, and the leader candidly and freely. At the same time, acting on feelings is interdicted or carefully controlled, as in psychodrama. Finally, therapy groups demand that patients in conflict keep in communication.

Such a group code maximizes opportunities for

learning and modification of attitudes and behavior. The protected atmosphere encourages patients to express their real feelings, uninhibited by the norms of ordinary social intercourse. Encouragement to verbalize feelings helps patients to differentiate them. Since the group is tolerant and there is little carry-over into daily life, penalties for failure are mitigated, thus encouraging freedom of experimentation. In daily life, antagonists customarily stop communicating, thereby leaving their mutual distortions unchanged. Maintenance of communication despite conflict encourages verbalization, enables each antagonist to gain fuller understanding of the other's position and his own, and helps each to learn to stand his ground despite opposition.

Member–leader and member–member interactions. All forms of psychotherapy support patients' self-esteem, arouse them emotionally, and offer them new cognitions. These features give them courage to examine and modify their habitual attitudes, supply the motive power for doing so, and guide their efforts, thereby enabling them to correct maladaptive attitudes and behavior and to progress in self-development. Therapeutic groups have certain potential advantages with respect to these goals.

Successful therapy groups overcome members' demoralizing sense of isolation by enabling them to discover that others have similar problems. Furthermore, in contrast to private treatment, in which all help flows from therapist to patient, members of therapy groups find that they can help each other. This counteracts the damage to self-esteem resulting from having been derogated by family and friends.

An important aspect of both the supportive and the influencing power of therapy groups lies in the cohesiveness successful ones develop, growing out of members' discovery of common problems, experience of mutual helpfulness, and a history of shared crises and triumphs. This is manifested by therapy groups' reluctance to disband and their resistance to the admission of new members. The danger that cohesiveness will produce pressure on members toward artificial conformity of behavior is reduced by the fact that the group task is to help each member develop in accordance with his own inner needs, so that the group norms encourage diversity.

Therapy groups arouse members emotionally in ways not available to individual therapy. One is rivalry for the leader's attention and approval, which, incidentally, seems to be more acute when the leader and members are of different sexes.

The central initial position of the therapist is illustrated by the finding that in a given group those patients who experience a "better" relationship with him relative to other patients show more improvement and are less likely to drop out than are those who experience a "worse" one, regardless of the absolute goodness of the relationship (Parloff 1961). The protective atmosphere of therapy groups and their norm of open expression of feelings facilitate expressions of anger toward the therapist. However, since members depend on him for help, prolonged, unanimous condemnation of him cannot occur. Whether a phase of scapegoating the leader is a necessary step in the development of group cohesiveness, as some believe, remains a question for research.

Members also arouse a wide range of hostile and friendly feelings in each other, based on more or less unconscious distortions as well as genuine differences or similarities in background, life experience, and values. In addition, many patients seem to benefit from vicarious emotional participation in problems of others.

From the cognitive standpoint, members also serve as models for each other; as sources of feedback, the value of which is increased by the fact that it is less distorted by the rules of social intercourse than are reactions from friends and acquaintances; and as representatives of attitudes existing outside the group. Acceptance by other members carries more weight than acceptance by the therapist, because they are viewed as being more like ordinary people.

Because group members represent the outside world, transfer of insights obtained through group experiences to daily life is easier than it is in private psychotherapy. Commitment to the group and awareness that one will report back to it help to sustain changes in attitude. On the other hand, the necessity of constantly dealing with the reactions of other members may hamper progress in patients who need to withdraw into reverie or fantasy or to subject their problems to leisurely scrutiny.

Group development and group issues. Well-established therapy groups differ from new ones in many ways, including greater freedom of expression among members and a greater tendency for topics to carry over from one session to the next; but whether therapy groups exhibit regularities of development similar to problem-solving groups remains open despite some experimental evidence in support of this possibility (Psathas 1960).

The developmental process in therapy groups

can be viewed from the standpoint of the progression of group preoccupations, or issues influencing the members at more or less unconscious levels. It has been suggested, for example, that initial meetings of therapy groups are dominated by three antitherapeutic "basic assumptions": dependency, fight–flight, and pairing, and that group progress can be judged by members' success in overcoming the obstacles these "basic assumptions" present to achievement of the therapeutic goal of increased self-realization (Bion 1961). Another theory conceptualizes group progress in terms of the successive emergence and resolution of "focal group conflicts." A well-nigh universal example of this in early meetings of free-interaction groups is the conflict between the desire to achieve therapeutic gain by becoming committed to the group and exposing one's feelings to it and the fear that by so doing one is exposing oneself to rejection and ridicule (Whitaker & Lieberman 1964).

Viewed in a larger perspective, group therapies exploit the universal human tendency to validate subjective experiences by comparing them with experiences of other persons who are perceived as similar. The standards, structure, and processes of therapy groups facilitate these comparisons and help members to correct the distortions thus brought to light. Since each group member deviates in a different way but shares attitudes consistent with the social norms of the community, the attitudes and values of the group as a whole tend to foster improved social adjustment of each member.

The advantages and limitations of group psychotherapy as compared with private methods of psychotherapy require further exploration, but it seems probable that the potentialities of group approaches have not yet been fully realized.

JEROME D. FRANK

[*Other relevant material may be found in* GROUPS *and* SOCIOMETRY.]

BIBLIOGRAPHY

BELL, JOHN E. 1961 *Family Group Therapy: Methods for Psychological Treatment of Older Children, Adolescents, and Their Parents.* U.S. Public Health Service Monograph. Publication No. 826. Washington: Government Printing Office.

BIERER, JOSHUA 1944 A New Form of Group Psychotherapy. *Mental Health* (London) 5:23–26.

BION, WILFRED R. 1961 *Experiences in Groups, and Other Papers.* New York: Basic Books. → Seven of these papers were published in *Human Relations* from 1948 to 1951.

CORSINI, RAYMOND J. 1957 *Methods of Group Psychotherapy.* New York: McGraw-Hill.

FOULKES, SIEGMUND H.; and ANTHONY, E. J. 1957 *Group Psychotherapy: The Psycho-analytic Approach.* Baltimore: Penguin.

KELMAN, HERBERT C. 1963 The Role of the Group in the Induction of Therapeutic Change. *International Journal of Group Psychotherapy* 13:399–451. → Includes discussion by Saul Scheidlinger.

MORENO, JACOB L. 1959 Psychodrama. Volume 2, pages 1375–1396 in *American Handbook of Psychiatry.* Edited by Silvano Arieti. New York: Basic Books.

MULLAN, HUGH; and ROSENBAUM, MAX 1962 *Group Psychotherapy: Theory and Practice.* New York: Free Press.

PARLOFF, MORRIS B. 1961 Therapist–Patient Relationships and Outcome of Psychotherapy. *Journal of Consulting Psychology* 25:29–38.

POWDERMAKER, FLORENCE B.; and FRANK, J. D. 1953 *Group Psychotherapy: Studies in Methodology of Research and Therapy.* Cambridge, Mass.: Harvard Univ. Press.

PSATHAS, G. 1960 Phase Movement and Equilibrium Tendencies in Interaction Process in Psychotherapy Groups. *Sociometry* 23:177–194.

RIESE, W.; and SYZ, H. 1963 Phyloanalysis: Theoretical and Practical Considerations on Burrow's Group-analytic and Socio-therapeutic Method. *Acta Psychotherapeutica et Psychosomatica: International Journal of Psychotherapy and Psychosomatics* (Basel) 11 (Supplement): 5–88. → Part 1, "Phyloanalysis (Burrow)—Its Historical and Philosophical Implications," by W. Riese, is on pages 5–36. Part 2, "Reflections on Group- or Phylo-analysis," by H. Syz, is on pages 37–88.

ROSENTHAL, DAVID; FRANK, J. D.; and NASH, E. H. 1954 The Self-righteous Moralist in Early Meetings of Therapeutic Groups. *Psychiatry* 17:215–223.

SATIR, VIRGINIA 1964 *Conjoint Family Therapy.* Palo Alto, Calif.: Science and Behavior Books.

SLAVSON, SAMUEL R. (editor) 1956 *The Fields of Group Psychotherapy.* New York: International Universities Press.

TAYLOR, FREDERICK K. 1961 *The Analysis of Therapeutic Groups.* Oxford Univ. Press.

TRUAX, CHARLES B. 1961 The Process of Group Psychotherapy: Relationship Between Hypothesized Therapeutic Conditions and Intrapersonal Exploration. *Psychological Monographs* 75, no. 7.

WECHSLER, HENRY 1960 The Self-Help Organization in the Mental Health Field: Recovery, Inc.; A Case Study. *Journal of Nervous and Mental Disease* 130:297–314.

WHITAKER, DOROTHY STOCK; and LIEBERMAN, MORTON A. 1964 *Psychotherapy Through the Group Process.* New York: Atherton.

IV
BEHAVIOR THERAPY

The term "behavior therapy" was introduced by B. F. Skinner and O. R. Lindsley in 1954 and popularized by H. J. Eysenck (1960). It refers to psychotherapeutic methods directly based on experimentally established learning principles. Although "behavior therapy" is broadly synonymous with "conditioning therapy" and "behavioristic psychotherapy," it more specifically denotes the methods that have developed from learning theory since the 1940s.

While the principles of learning upon which behavior therapy is based have stemmed mainly from the work of Clark L. Hull (1943)—who in many respects united the lines of study begun by Ivan P. Pavlov in Russia and by Edward L. Thorndike and John B. Watson in the United States—a distinctive group of techniques based on B. F. Skinner's operant conditioning paradigm (1938) has been emerging in recent years. Experimental neuroses, first produced in Pavlov's laboratories, provided the primary data from which Hullian learning theory evolved behavior therapy. Ironically, there could have been no such evolution in the Soviet Union because of the pervasive acceptance there of Pavlov's view that a neurosis is due to the establishment of a chronic pathological focus in the central nervous system.

Among those who in the 1920s and 1930s tried to apply principles of learning to clinical problems, foremost mention must be made of Mary Cover Jones (1924), who was the first deliberately to invoke the counterconditioning method that dominates present-day behavior therapy (and whose work moldered in the dust for most of the ensuing quarter of a century). She treated children's phobias by having the patient eat in the presence of a feared object. At first, the object was at a distance. Then, as his anxiety diminished, the patient was placed closer and closer to it. Guthrie (1935) realized the wide applicability of this principle, stating that the rule for overcoming an undesired response is to control the situation so that the cue to the undesired response is present while "other behavior prevails." Dunlap (1932) originated the technique of negative practice, in which the extinction mechanism is used to overcome unadaptive motor habits like tics through instigating their repeated evocation in the absence of reinforcement.

Approaching experimental neuroses from the standpoint of modern learning theory, Wolpe (1952; 1958) demonstrated that the behavior observed in neurotic states had all the attributes of learned behavior. The manifestations of anxiety and agitation were similar in detail to the behavior originally evoked in the situations of conflict or noxious stimulation that were used to precipitate the neurosis; the neurotic responses were conditioned to and remained under the control of stimuli present at the time of causation; and neurotic responses of smaller intensity could be evoked, in accordance with the principle of primary stimulus generalization, by other stimuli similar to those to which the neurotic reaction had been directly attached. The most marked and constant neurotic responses were *autonomic responses typical of anxiety*. These failed to undergo extinction no matter how often or for how long the animal was exposed to the experimental situation, but they could consistently be removed if the animal could be induced to eat in the presence of anxiety-evoking stimuli. Since the animal's eating was inhibited if anxiety was strong, food had to be offered first in the presence of generalized stimuli that aroused anxiety weakly; and then reciprocally, the eating would inhibit the anxiety, and repeated feedings would diminish it to zero. The same treatment in successively more "severe" situations eventually enabled the animal to eat without anxiety in the cage where the neurosis had been induced.

The methods of behavior therapy

These therapeutic experiments suggested the generalization that the reciprocal inhibition mechanism is the basis of the psychotherapeutic effects obtained by counterconditioning methods, so that if any response that inhibits anxiety can be made to occur in the presence of anxiety-evoking stimuli, it will on each occasion to some extent weaken the conditioned connection between these stimuli and the anxiety responses. This idea was subsequently widely applied in the treatment of human neuroses. Not only eating but a considerable number of other responses in human beings are incompatible with anxiety and thus lend themselves to therapeutic application. The use of some of these responses is briefly described below, followed by a short account of some methods employing different learning mechanisms. (For further details of many techniques of this type, see Wolpe 1958; Eysenck 1960; 1964; Wolpe & Lazarus 1966.)

Counterconditioning methods. The group of counterconditioning (reciprocal inhibition) methods is applied mainly, but by no means entirely, to the elimination of unadaptive anxiety-response habits such as fear of crowds, of praise, or of criticism. Such habits are the crux of most neuroses, and when they are overcome, treatment of "defenses against anxiety" and other secondary processes becomes irrelevant.

Assertive responses. Assertive responses are used to countercondition neurotic fears aroused in interpersonal interchanges. The term "assertive" is employed here a good deal more broadly than in common parlance and includes not only responses of a more or less aggressive nature but also others expressing affection, liking, admiration, and revulsion—almost any feeling *other than anxiety* (Salter 1949; Wolpe 1958). Aggressive kinds of assertion are, however, very commonly required. For example, there are many patients whom unjust criticism renders hurt and helpless. The therapist applauds the anger and resentment that they inevitably feel in the situations they inadequately handle and gives detailed instructions for the appropriate expression of these feelings. Such expression reciprocally inhibits the anxiety, and repetition of such expression brings about a cumulative conditioned inhibition of anxiety.

Sexual responses. Sexual responses are employed to overcome habits of anxiety inappropriately evoked in sexual situations. For example, the male patient usually complains of impotence or premature ejaculation, both of which are generally due to anxiety interfering with the predominantly parasympathetic responses that subserve penile erection. The emotional components of the sexual response (sexual feelings) usually remain adequate in the patient so afflicted. The therapist, having ascertained at what stage in the sexual approach anxiety begins to be experienced, instructs the patient (who must have secured the cooperation of his sexual partner) to take his sexual approach no further than this stage of minimal anxiety on repeated occasions—until the anxiety has decreased to zero. He is then directed to go on to the next stage in the same way. Advances continue to be made step by step until normal intercourse is achieved, usually from three to six weeks after the start of therapy. Although the principle is simple, the detailed tactics must always be adjusted to the individual case (see Wolpe 1958; Wolpe & Lazarus 1966).

Desensitization and muscle relaxation. Relaxation, long a popular prescription for nervous disturbances, first achieved scientific respectability through the work of Edmund Jacobson (1938), who showed its autonomic effects to inhibit those effects characteristic of anxiety. Jacobson treated neurotic patients by giving them very extensive training in relaxation and then instructing them to relax at all times all muscles not in use (differential relaxation). A similar program promulgated by Schultz (Schultz & Luthe 1950) has been widely adopted in Europe. It would seem that when improvement occurs, it is because persistent relaxation provides the possibility of reciprocal inhibition of anxiety aroused by stimuli that appear in the course of daily life.

Systematic desensitization, one method of using deep muscle relaxation to decondition neurotic anxiety, is much more economical of time and effort and affords detailed control of the therapeutic process. Training in deep muscle relaxation occupies only part of each of about six sessions. The greater part of these sessions is devoted to the construction of *anxiety hierarchies*. If a particular patient is neurotically anxious about high places and about being rejected, situations relating to each of these areas are listed in descending order of intensity of anxiety reaction, each list constituting a hierarchy.

In the actual desensitization procedure, the patient is made to relax as deeply as possible, and then the least disturbing scene from one of his hierarchies is presented to his imagination for a few seconds. Presentations are repeated until he no longer has any disturbance, and the same procedure is followed all the way up the hierarchy. Almost invariably there is transfer of this effect when the patient is exposed to the real situation. In individuals who are not disturbed upon imagining situations that disturb them in reality, desensitization requires the exploitation of real stimuli, being then called "desensitization in vivo."

Other modes of desensitization. Other inhibitors of anxiety may also be employed therapeutically in a systematic way. An anxiety-inhibiting effect is produced by the emotions spontaneously aroused in some patients by the therapeutic situation itself (see below). In behavior therapy this has been mainly used for desensitization in vivo. For example, in cases of anxiety in social situations characterized by tremor of the hand while lifting a teacup, patient and therapist repeatedly raise first an empty glass and then a progressively fuller one, until all signs of shaking disappear at each stage; and later they repeat the sequence before an audience.

Lazarus and Abramovitz (1962) have reported the desensitization of children's phobias by the use of what they call "emotive imagery." The patient is made to expose himself in imagination to phobic stimuli of increasing intensity in contexts of pleasant emotional excitement.

Recently, use has been made of the observation that anxiety can be inhibited through cutaneous stimulation by nonaversive galvanic shocks. The mechanism of this effect may well turn out to depend on afferent collateral inhibition (Eccles 1957) as may also that of the technique of inhibiting anxiety through the arousal of a dominating motor response evoked by mild electric current (Wolpe 1954; 1958).

Avoidance conditioning. Avoidance (aversive) conditioning is the application of the reciprocal-inhibition principle to the overcoming of responses other than anxiety. It is employed largely to treat obsessional behavior. The agents commonly used have been strong faradic stimulation of the forearm and drug-induced nausea, either of which must be administered in an appropriate time relation to the stimulus to which avoidance conditioning is desired. Avoidance conditioning has been effectively used in cases of obsessional thinking, compulsive acts, fetishism, and homosexuality. It has been least successful in homosexuality, which is often based on neurotic interpersonal anxiety and in such cases should be treated by deconditioning the anxiety (Stevenson & Wolpe 1960). Avoidance conditioning has also been applied with limited success in the treatment of addiction, especially alcoholism. [*See* LEARNING, *article on* AVOIDANCE LEARNING.]

Experimental extinction. Techniques based on the extinction mechanism—the breaking of habits through repeated performance of the relevant act without reinforcement—were introduced by Dunlap (1932) under the name "negative practice" and in recent years have again been employed occasionally in the treatment of such motor habits as tics. In the course of large numbers of forced evocations of the undesired movement, spontaneous evocations of it are progressively lessened.

Certain therapeutic measures have given the appearance of applying the extinction principle to the elimination of emotional reactions (e.g., Malleson 1959). The patient is exposed to anxiety-arousing stimuli, either in reality or in imagination, *at the greatest possible strength*. In some cases this leads to the decline and ultimate elimination of the anxiety response habit, but more often it does not. It is very doubtful that such improvement is really due to experimental extinction; and a form of inhibition has been suggested as the possible mechanism (Teplov et al. 1956). Both clinically and experimentally, the elicitation of a high-intensity anxiety response ordinarily tends to *increase* the habit strength of that response.

Positive reconditioning. While the overcoming of unadaptive autonomic response habits is usually the central task of behavior therapy, very frequently there is also a need to form adaptive motor habits. Such conditioning is often part and parcel of the measures employed to break down the anxiety habit, as, for example, in the case of assertive training. But motor habits often need to be changed even where anxiety is not involved. For instance, a man who has repeatedly spoiled courtships by over-eager behavior might be taught to "play it cool." If the new behavior is successful, it naturally tends to replace the old. In enuresis nocturna, waking is conditioned to the imminence of urination, and this makes possible the subsequent conditioned inhibition of urination during sleep (Eysenck 1960, p. 377).

In recent years Skinnerian operant conditioning techniques have been used to remove and replace undesirable habits. Anorexia nervosa has been successfully treated by providing social rewards—such as the use of a radio or permission to receive company—contingent upon the patient's eating, while withdrawing these rewards when the patient fails to eat (Bachrach et al. 1965). Several varieties of psychotic behavior have been treated on the same principle (e.g., Ayllon 1963), bringing about major and lasting changes in chronic schizophrenic patients, some of whom have been continuously hospitalized for decades.

The results of behavior therapy

The most distinctive feature of behavior therapy is that it enables the therapist to plan therapeutic strategy and control its details, in contrast to merely setting a framework for transactions with the patient and hoping that beneficial effects will emerge. The behavior therapist can specify the reactions to be overcome and the means to be employed in overcoming them, and he can often state the quantitative relations to be expected between defined therapeutic operations and amount of habit change (Wolpe 1963).

Statistical data. Two fairly extensive studies (Wolpe 1958; Lazarus 1963) have evaluated the results of behavior therapy in terms of R. P. Knight's five criteria: symptomatic improvement, increased productiveness, improved adjustment and pleasure in sex, improved interpersonal relationships, and the ability to handle ordinary psychological conflicts and reasonable reality stresses (Knight 1941). From these reports it appears that over 80 per cent of unselected neurotic patients exposed to the available techniques either recover or improve markedly.

These results must be compared with the 60 per cent "cured" or "greatly improved" among the *completely analyzed* patients studied by the Central Fact-Finding Committee of the American Psychoanalytic Association. While the psychoanalyzed patients were treated an average of four times a week for three to four years—i.e., about seven hundred sessions—the average course of behavior therapy covers about thirty sessions (Wolpe & Lazarus 1966, p. 156).

A fairly constant number of neurotic patients (about 40 per cent) improve markedly with therapies other than behavior therapy. It is suggested that these nonspecific improvements are due to emotional responses in the therapeutic situation that reciprocally inhibit the anxiety responses evoked by verbal stimuli during interviews. Such nonspecific effects presumably also account for part of the favorable results of behavior therapy.

Depth of the effects of behavior therapy. It is sometimes stated as a criticism of behavior therapy that it does not attempt to deal with the "basic dynamic conflict" that is alleged to underlie neurosis. This would be an important objection if a neurosis really had such a conflict as its basis. But there are facts that are hard to reconcile with this idea. For example, a corollary of such an objection would claim that unless the dynamic conflict is resolved, relapse or symptom substitution will sooner or later occur. But a survey (Wolpe 1961) of the results of follow-up studies on neuroses successfully treated by a variety of methods not concerned with the "dynamic conflict" *revealed only a 1.6 per cent incidence of relapse or symptom substitution.*

Weighing the evidence, it seems reasonably certain that neuroses can be considered to be nothing but habits and that therefore a therapy able to break these habits must be considered fundamental.

JOSEPH WOLPE

[*See also* LEARNING, *articles on* CLASSICAL CONDITIONING, INSTRUMENTAL LEARNING, REINFORCEMENT. *Other relevant material may be found in* ANXIETY; CLINICAL PSYCHOLOGY; CONFLICT, *article on* PSYCHOLOGICAL ASPECTS; NEUROSIS; PSYCHIATRY; *and in the biographies of* GUTHRIE; HULL; PAVLOV; THORNDIKE; WATSON.]

BIBLIOGRAPHY

AYLLON, T. 1963 Intensive Treatment of Psychotic Behaviour by Stimulus Satiation and Food Reinforcement. *Behaviour Research and Therapy* 1:53–61.

BACHRACH, A. J.; ERWIN, W. J.; and MOHR, J. P. 1965 The Control of Eating Behavior in an Anorexic by Operant Conditioning Techniques. Pages 153–163 in Leonard P. Ullmann and L. Krasner (editors), *Case Studies in Behavior Modification.* New York: Holt.

DUNLAP, KNIGHT 1932 *Habits.* New York: Liveright.

ECCLES, JOHN C. 1957 *The Physiology of Nerve Cells.* Baltimore: Johns Hopkins Press.

EYSENCK, HANS J. (editor) 1960 *Behaviour Therapy and the Neuroses: Readings in Modern Methods of Treatment Derived From Learning Theory.* Oxford. Pergamon.

EYSENCK, HANS J. 1964 *Experiments in Behaviour Therapy.* New York: Macmillan.

GUTHRIE, EDWIN R. (1935) 1952 *The Psychology of Learning.* Rev. ed. New York: Harper.

HULL, CLARK L. 1943 *Principles of Behavior.* New York: Appleton.

JACOBSON, EDMUND 1938 *Progressive Relaxation.* Univ. of Chicago Press.

JONES, MARY C. (1924) 1960 A Laboratory Study of Fear: The Case of Peter. Pages 45–51 in Hans J. Eysenck (editor), *Behaviour Therapy and the Neu-*

roses: Readings in Modern Methods of Treatment Derived From Learning Theory. Oxford: Pergamon.

KNIGHT, R. P. 1941 Evaluation of the Results of Psychoanalytic Therapy. *American Journal of Psychiatry* 98:434–446.

LAZARUS, ARNOLD A. 1963 The Results of Behaviour Therapy in 126 Cases of Severe Neuroses. *Behaviour Research and Therapy* 1:69–79.

LAZARUS, ARNOLD A.; and ABRAMOVITZ, ARNOLD 1962 The Use of "Emotive Imagery" in the Treatment of Children's Phobias. *Journal of Mental Science* 108:191–195.

MALLESON, NICOLAS 1959 Panic and Phobia: A Possible Method of Treatment. *Lancet* [1959], no. 1:225–227.

SALTER, ANDREW (1949) 1961 *Conditioned Reflex Therapy.* 2d ed. New York: Capricorn Books. → A paperback edition was published in 1961 by Putnam.

SCHULTZ, JOHANNES H.; and LUTHE, W. (1950) 1959 *Autogenic Training.* New York: Grune. → First published in German.

SKINNER, B. F. 1938 *The Behavior of Organisms.* New York: Appleton.

STEVENSON, IAN; and WOLPE, JOSEPH 1960 Recovery From Sexual Deviations Through Overcoming Nonsexual Neurotic Responses. *American Journal of Psychiatry* 116:737–742.

TEPLOV, BORIS M. et al. (1956) 1964 *Pavlov's Typology: Recent Theoretical and Experimental Developments From the Laboratory of B. M. Teplov, Institute of Psychology, Moscow.* Compiled, edited, and translated by J. A. Gray, with an editorial introduction by H. J. Eysenck. Oxford: Pergamon. → First published in Russian.

WOLPE, JOSEPH 1952 Experimental Neuroses as Learned Behavior. *British Journal of Psychology* 43:243–268.

WOLPE, JOSEPH 1954 Reciprocal Inhibition as the Main Basis of Psychotherapeutic Effects. *A.M.A. Archives of Neurology and Psychiatry* 75:205–226.

WOLPE, JOSEPH 1958 *Psychotherapy by Reciprocal Inhibition.* Stanford Univ. Press.

WOLPE, JOSEPH 1961 The Prognosis in Unpsychoanalyzed Recovery From Neurosis. *American Journal of Psychiatry* 118:35–39.

WOLPE, JOSEPH 1963 Quantitative Relationships in the Systematic Desensitization of Phobias. *American Journal of Psychiatry* 119:1062–1068.

WOLPE, JOSEPH; and LAZARUS, A. A. 1966 *Behavior Therapy Techniques.* Oxford: Pergamon.

V

SOMATIC TREATMENT

Somatic treatment comprises all therapeutic procedures which are based primarily on physical means of influencing the human organism. The agents employed may be mechanical, electromagnetic, or chemical in nature, but they are all characterized by their potential to change the energy balance within the physiochemical system of cerebral dynamics. Defined negatively, somatic treatment of mental disorders may be said to be essentially independent of social and psychological factors, and it would be expected to be generally effective regardless of individual differences in personality structure, in personal interactions, and in transactional processes inherent in the treatment situation.

Organic and functional mental disorders. Mental disorders are traditionally divided into two categories—the organic and the functional. Organic mental disorders are characterized by the presence of demonstrable morphological or metabolic abnormalities, which are necessary factors for the establishment of their clinical and pathological diagnosis. Mental disorders for which physical cerebral pathology cannot be demonstrated are defined as functional in nature.

Since it is in the organic mental disorders that somatic pathology has been clearly established, it would appear plausible to expect here the best results of somatic treatments. However, the most significant progress with somatic therapies has so far been made by psychiatry in the field of functional mental disorders, just since the mid-1930s.

The most spectacular exception to this statement was the discovery of malaria treatment for general paresis of the insane, or dementia paralytica, an inflammatory brain disease caused by syphilis. The discoverer of this therapy, Wagner-Jauregg, received the Nobel Prize in 1927, thus becoming the first psychiatrist to be so honored. However, because of the discovery of penicillin as the specific cure for syphilis, general paresis is no longer a significant mental disorder in many parts of the world.

It remains a fact that the major breakthroughs in the somatic treatment of mental disorders have occurred only fairly recently and in the field of functional psychoses—namely in schizophrenia and in manic–depressive psychosis and other depressions. These therapeutic advances have been achieved through shock therapies and still more recently through pharmacotherapy.

Throughout the history of psychiatry there have been those who have predicted that some day scientists will discover the physical substrate of all mental disorders. At that time, the argument goes, we might be able to approach all psychiatric treatment with the same scientific detachment that characterizes a surgeon performing an appendectomy or a physician treating a case of pneumonia with modern antibiotics. This hope of finding some kind of "magic bullet" for every mental disorder is not likely ever to be fulfilled.

First of all, it is by no means certain that physical substrates or lesions will be discovered for every psychological disorder. Even more important, however, is the well-established fact that in the realm of behavior, physical and psychological factors are so closely interwoven that a mental disorder—which is essentially a disorder of behavioral manifestations—will seldom respond to somatic therapy alone, without any consideration of psychological and interpersonal factors, even if its primary cause is clearly a physical one.

Are somatic treatments cures? The action of few of the major successfully employed somatic therapies is clearly understood, and none of the therapies are specific cures. This is not surprising, since these treatment methods are most effective in the functional psychoses, and this class of mental disorders is characterized by the fact that no definite physical or psychological cause has consistently been established by the many investigators who have searched intensively for the final common physical path of these disorders for nearly a century. A truly curative treatment, however, can be undertaken only if the cause of an illness is known. Otherwise, even the most successful treatment of a disease—for instance, insulin therapy of diabetes mellitus—can only be symptomatic, supportive, or compensatory in nature.

A comprehensive approach

Psychiatry is fundamentally a pragmatic science. Its *raison d'être* and essential goal are the improvement or cure of mentally disordered patients. While psychiatry has developed major theoretical frameworks of its own, e.g., psychoanalysis, and has assimilated others from behavioral sciences for its own use, e.g., learning theory, most of the major advances in psychiatric somatic therapy originated in empirical observations, and the underlying mechanisms through which these treatments became effective were usually inadequately or even erroneously understood.

The present methodological situation in the treatment of mental disorders is characterized by a highly dynamic state of flux. The two extreme positions of those who "believe" only in the psychodynamic approach to and resolution of the problems posed by mental disorders and regard a physical approach to mental disorders as methodologically naive and grossly inappropriate, and those who consider any other than a clearly somatic orientation and therapeutic approach to mental disorders as unscientific and doomed to failure, are no longer clearly defined. Today it is generally accepted that all psychodynamic processes depend on a neurophysiological substrate; consequently, psychoanalysts have in recent years shown much interest in neurophysiological research and the pharmacotherapeutic approach to mental disorders. On the other hand, even in their laboratory experiments, behavior researchers are now clearly acknowledging the important role of individual personality differences, nonquantifiable psychodynamic factors, and interpersonal transactions.

Therapeutic revolution in psychiatry. During the decade between 1950 and 1960 the therapeutic and administrative approach and the social attitudes toward the mentally ill underwent changes of such magnitude that one would be justified in speaking of a quiet revolution. In the United States there was a spectacular decrease of mental hospital populations. In the eight years between 1956 and 1964, i.e., since systematic drug therapy became widely established, there was a decrease of 54,000 patients instead of an anticipated increase of 82,000 patients confined in mental hospitals. One of the by-products of this decrease in mental illness and suffering is a probable saving of more than one billion dollars ("What Tranquilizers . . ." 1964).

Thousands of mental patients who only 15 years ago would have remained hospitalized for months, years, or often indefinitely, are now functioning in the community as the result of two new developments: (1) modern drug therapy for mental disorders for which there has been no precedent, and (2) a more progressive and tolerant attitude of mental hospital administrations coupled with increased social acceptance of the former mental patient. The second development is not entirely new, but in the past, if such liberal attitudes emerged they eventually disappeared because there were no effective physical treatments supporting them.

Historical treatment methods. During the more than two thousand years that elapsed between the time the somatic nature of mental disorders was first proclaimed by Alcmaeon and Hippocrates and the time it was reasserted by Wilhelm Griesinger at the beginning of the nineteenth century, medicine applied innumerable somatic treatment procedures and remedies, none of which survived because none was ever systematically explored and tested for its efficacy under controlled conditions (Zilboorg 1941; Haisch 1959; Kalinowsky & Hoch 1961). Bloodletting, purging, and induced vomiting were therapeutic mainstays in the treatment of mental disorders for many centuries. Physical threats, restraint, solitary confinement in the dark, whipping, periodic submersion under water, violent spinning of the mental patient on specially constructed revolving chairs, were all frequently applied. Many of these procedures, particularly when applied to severely excited patients, resulted, of course, in rapid "symptomatic improvement,"

because the patients fainted or became utterly exhausted and remained quiet for some time. Some of these uncritically employed treatment methods have sometimes been referred to as forerunners of modern shock therapies—for instance, the sudden pouring of ice water over the naked patient, burning of the scalp with scalding water, or the sudden plunging of the unsuspecting patient into a lake from a room with a trap-door device. However, the shock induced by these methods was primarily psychological. In contrast to this, modern somatic shock therapy is based on the induction of physiological shock.

A certain semantic confusion exists if no clear distinction is made between the biological and the experiential aspects of shock. The old treatments aimed at causing surprise and fear in the patient, while modern shock therapy tends to avoid conscious distress of the patient and aims at the production of a specific state of physiological stress.

Countless substances were prescribed as remedies for mental disorders, involving not only a great variety of the basic elements such as mercury, phosphorus, copper, iron, etc., but also chemical compounds—for instance, salts of silver, iodine, or lead. A host of organic chemical compounds was employed, most of which were derived from plants. In ancient times and during the Middle Ages the helleborus plant was thought to possess special powers for the treatment of mental illness.

Other treatments, which involved the drinking of the blood of a recently beheaded criminal or concoctions and distillates made from toads, snails, and salamanders, as well as the wearing of precious metals, crystals, and gems, were based on ideas and principles developed by magic and later elaborated on in the symbolic systems of alchemy.

Even in prehistoric times, surgical trepanations of the skull were performed, as a number of archeological findings prove. It is likely that the opening of the skull was not always undertaken because of increased intracranial pressure—the modern indication for such surgery—but more often to provide an escape for the evil spirits which were thought to possess the brain of an insane person.

Scientific rationale and evaluation. At first glance one might conclude that not much that is new has been added to the modern repertoire of somatic treatment methods in psychiatry, since basic patterns of shock therapy, chemotherapy, and even psychosurgery were traced out many centuries ago. However, it must be remembered that the number of possible physical treatment modalities at our disposal is limited and that the value of a therapeutic procedure does not lie in its incidental application but in the fact that its indication is based on a well-established rationale and that the results of the treatment have been assessed by scientific methods. Evidence of favorable results of any specific treatment procedure must be provided through objectively controlled and statistically evaluated clinical experiments. A rationale for psychiatric treatment was not seriously considered in scientific terms until the nineteenth century, and evaluation of treatment results based on controlled and statistically processed observations came into being only in the twentieth century.

The scientific groundwork for a successful therapeutic attack on mental disorders was laid at the turn of the twentieth century. This groundwork is founded on three major achievements: (1) the introduction of a clinically valid and useful classification of mental diseases by Kraepelin; (2) the discovery of the principles of a consistent and comprehensive psychodynamic theory by Freud; (3) the progress made by many researchers in bacteriology, cellular pathology, neurophysiology, and chemistry.

In the first decade of the twentieth century it was shown that the spirochete, which is the causative agent in syphilis, is present in the brains of patients with general paresis. Soon after the syphilitic etiology for this mental disorder became firmly established, August von Wassermann discovered a practical serological procedure which made it possible to prove objectively the presence or absence of syphilis. Until Wassermann's test became available, many patients, particularly those afflicted with dementia due to the effects of chronic alcoholism on the brain, had been misdiagnosed as suffering from general paresis.

Malaria treatment—first breakthrough. In 1917 Wagner-Jauregg, at the University of Vienna, announced results of tests using deliberately induced malaria fever as a treatment for nine patients diagnosed as suffering from general paresis. Six of these patients improved greatly and three of them were cured. Until then, general paresis had been an incurable disease which invariably led to complete dementia and a miserable death. For thirty years Wagner-Jauregg had thought about this kind of treatment, ever since he had observed that the course of a psychosis was often favorably influenced by intercurrent infectious diseases. However, this general observation and even Wagner-Jauregg's idea of imitating this "experiment of nature" and inoculating paretic patients with tertian malaria could not have assumed the status of a scientific procedure until he had, at his disposal, a reliable method—namely, Wassermann's serological test—

which enabled him to make an objective diagnosis and select a homogeneous sample of patients for his experiment. Had he tried the experiment twenty years earlier, he might have inadvertently chosen a group of patients whose diagnosis in 50 per cent of the cases was alcoholic dementia and only in the other 50 per cent, general paresis. Under those conditions, to draw valid conclusions about the efficacy of his malaria treatment in cases of general paresis he would have had to employ a much larger sample, and this would have proved difficult, since he was using an untried, somewhat hazardous procedure (Wagner-Jauregg 1946).

A variety of unsuccessful treatments. Around 1920 a group of clinicians conceived of focal infections in tonsils, teeth, and the intestines as the cause of many diseases, including the functional psychoses, and for a few years a great deal of unnecessary surgery was performed with the idea of removing the infectious foci. However, the theory was soon disproved, and this kind of surgical treatment was shown to be valueless or even harmful.

A number of other therapeutic efforts were aimed at duplicating the spectacular results of the malaria treatment of general paresis, and, in several places, particularly in Europe, fever was induced artificially through injections of sulfur, typhoid vaccine, or foreign protein in patients suffering from various functional psychoses. Other attempts in the same direction, namely, to produce a systemic irritation and thereby a general mobilization of biological defenses, consisted of producing large blisters on the skin through the use of vesicantia, of making sterile abscesses in the muscles through the injection of turpentine oil, and of creating an aseptic meningitis by means of horse-serum injections into the spinal canal. Although short-term improvements in psychotic states were often observed in response to some of the procedures, no lasting remissions in the major psychoses could be achieved by any of them.

The advances made in endocrinology suggested the therapeutic use of various hormones. Again, this approach did not prove to be fruitful. Most frequently employed in these therapeutic trials were the male sex hormone, testosterone, and the female sex hormones, estrogen and progesterone. However, some promising results in this field were obtained with the hormone of the thyroid gland in the treatment of mental and emotional disorders secondary to hypothyroidism.

Castration. Castration was used in the nineteenth century and earlier because of the mistaken belief that such surgery on the genital organs would prove beneficial in certain psychiatric disorders, particularly those with hysterical manifestations. In modern times, castration of recidivist male sex offenders is a legal therapeutically employed procedure in some countries, particularly in Scandinavia. A recent review of results of this procedure in this particular group of psychiatric patients has shown that the treatment is often effective, but since it has so many drawbacks of a moral, psychological, and medical nature—not the least being its irreversibility—it is not likely to become a widely accepted procedure (Tappan 1951).

Pharmacotherapy and psychopharmacology

Around 1930 new interest was aroused in the use of various drugs in mental disorders. Loevenhart and others (1929) reported interesting experiments with injections of small doses of potassium cyanate and with the inhalation of carbon dioxide in stuporous patients. Patients who had been mute and motionless for weeks would suddenly, under the influence of these drugs, begin to talk and move about. Within a short time, however, they would invariably relapse into their previous stuporous condition. These therapeutic procedures were hardly more than provocative laboratory experiments. Their mechanism of action was not well understood, and their therapeutic action could not be sustained.

New synthetic drugs which had become available at that time were given widespread application in psychiatric disorders. Benzedrine, one of the early representatives of the group of amphetamine compounds, produced marked stimulation of the central nervous system and had certain euphorizing effects (Myerson 1936). However, the early hopes that this drug might prove to be a specific agent counteracting depression were not fulfilled. Therapeutic experiments with photosensitization of depressed patients through the administration of hematoporphyrine, a hemoglobin derivative, seemed to give promising results at first but eventually proved to be disappointing. Amobarbital, a barbiturate, when given intravenously, was shown to produce the same tantalizing effect of relieving stupor states temporarily as did potassium cyanate injections and carbon dioxide inhalations.

Nitrogen metabolism. Gjessing, in a series of beautifully designed and very carefully controlled experiments conducted at a Norwegian mental hospital, demonstrated that a certain type of schizophrenia, which he named "periodic catatonia," was characterized by recurrent attacks of stupor or excitement and was associated with a defective regulation of nitrogen metabolism (Gjessing et al. 1958). Patients afflicted with it either accumulated

or lost nitrogen beyond the normally permitted biological limits, and at the critical points of change in the nitrogen balance of the body, psychotic episodes would occur. Gjessing showed that a small amount of thyroxin would enable these patients to maintain their nitrogen balance within normal limits and thus remain free from psychotic attacks. His brilliant work was greeted with great enthusiasm as another milestone on the road toward effective and scientifically grounded somatic treatment in psychiatry. Unfortunately, its practical importance is limited, since the mental disorder for which this treatment is indicated is comparatively rare.

Pellagra and phenylketonuria. Two more important therapies must be mentioned—both the outcome of systematic, scientific research. One has led to the almost complete disappearance of a mental disease that formerly was fairly frequent in certain parts of the world, while the other one has opened up exciting vistas for a practical therapeutic and preventive approach to mental deficiency.

In 1938 Elvehjem demonstrated that the so-called "black tongue" in dogs was a deficiency disease caused by a lack of nicotinic acid, a component of the vitamin B complex, in the food (see Woolley et al. 1938). Soon afterward, the first cases of pellagra in humans, which seemed to be closely related to the black-tongue disease, were successfully treated with nicotinic acid. Pellagra is a disease which produces manifestations in the skin, intestines, and the brain. In the past, many patients suffering from pellagra psychosis could be found in mental hospitals in certain parts of the world—for instance, in the south of the United States, where nutritional conditions were particularly bad among the lower classes. Today one rarely sees a patient with psychosis due to pellagra, and in the few instances where such a diagnosis is made, the condition readily responds to treatment with nicotinic acid.

The modern antibiotic treatment of general paresis with penicillin—which has superseded Wagner-Jauregg's original malaria treatment—and the supplementary vitamin therapy with nicotinic acid of pellagra psychosis are the only two truly curative treatments of mental disorders at our disposal today.

A recently developed treatment that has opened fresh possibilities for an attack on mental deficiency is really a preventive one. It consists of the reduction of a certain amino acid—phenylalanine—in the food intake of infants and young children in whom the diagnosis of phenylketonuria has been made. In 1934 Fölling showed that a certain small group of mental retardates was characterized by the excretion of an abnormal metabolite, namely, phenylpyruvic acid, in the urine. Later it was shown that these patients were afflicted with an "inborn error of metabolism," and, lacking certain essential enzymes—in particular, phenylalanine hydroxylase—were unable to metabolize phenylalanine, which is a component of normal food intake, to tyrosine. Because of this metabolic inadequacy, another metabolic product—phenylpyruvic acid— accumulates in their system. It seems that the increased blood level of phenylalanine is highly toxic for the developing brain. By carefully eliminating most phenylalanine from the food of a patient in whom the diagnosis has been made early enough —that is, before the toxic excess of phenylalanine can exercise its damaging influence on the developing brain, up until the fourth or fifth year of life— it is possible to prevent or at least reduce the intellectual damage inflicted upon individuals who carry this genetic error of metabolism [Ragsdale & Koch 1964; "Mental Deficiency . . ." 1961; *see* MENTAL RETARDATION].

Disulfiram in alcoholism.   When it was noted accidentally that people who had been exposed to a certain chemical (disulfiram) reacted during a period of several hours with considerable discomfort, flushing, nausea, palpitation, and vertigo to any amount of alcohol they consumed afterward, this substance was soon introduced into the therapeutic armamentarium of psychiatrists for treatment of alcoholism. The mechanism of disulfiram consists of the blocking of an enzyme which is essential for the metabolic breakdown of products of alcohol in the body. Accumulation of acetaldehyde in the body causes unpleasant toxic effects if any alcohol is taken while the enzyme action is blocked by disulfiram. This drug can serve as a self-imposed chemical restraint for the problem drinker. As long as he takes it, he knows he cannot drink alcohol without rapidly producing an alarming reaction. If the patient is motivated well enough to take his medication regularly, this treatment can be a valuable aid in the comprehensive treatment program required for the psychiatric management of alcoholics [*see* DRINKING AND ALCOHOLISM].

Psychotropic drugs and neuroleptic effects.   The latest chapter of somatic therapy in psychiatric disorders began in the early 1950s with the introduction of a new class of drugs. These drugs are designated as psychotropic or psychoactive substances, because their principal action is manifested in the realm of human behavior and experience. A whole new scientific discipline has

developed under the name of psychopharmacology. Its principal task is the study of psychoactive drugs [Lehmann 1963; *see* DRUGS].

Although psychoactive drugs are as old as civilization—alcohol, caffeine, and opium fall into this category—the new type of psychoactive drugs, first systematically applied in 1951, was characterized by a particular quality which has been termed "neuroleptic" by the French psychiatrists Jean Delay and Pierre Deniker, who were pioneers in proving the value of pharmacotherapy in psychiatry. A neuroleptic drug is a substance which produces distinct neurological effects in addition to its psychotropic action. The neuroleptic action may manifest itself in various ways, but it appears most frequently in the form of extrapyramidal symptoms. Extrapyramidal symptoms may occur as drug-induced Parkinsonism, which is characterized by muscular rigidity, a masklike face, tremor, and a shuffling gait, or sometimes they may occur as severe muscular dystonia or akathisia—a term denoting motor restlessness, which makes it impossible for the patient to sit or stand still.

Such a neuroleptic quality had never before been observed with any psychoactive drugs. In fact, there had been no experimental way of producing extrapyramidal symptoms consistently by pharmacological means. However, the neuroleptic action is only a side effect of the new drugs, whose principal action is their marked therapeutic effect on such psychotic symptoms as hallucinations, delusions, autistic thought-disorder, and psychotic stupor and withdrawal. For this reason, these drugs have often been referred to as antipsychotic or, more recently, as psychotostatic in their action. Up until a few years ago none of the clinically applied psychoactive drugs—mainly hypnotics, sedatives, and stimulants—had been effective in reducing specifically psychotic manifestations. In addition to their neuroleptic and their antipsychotic action some of the new drugs also possess an unusual sedative action which is characterized by their pronounced effect on psychomotor tension and agitation, without inducing any clouding of consciousness or impairment of cognitive processes. Until recently, clouding of consciousness and impairment of judgment had been almost synonymous with the notion of powerful sedation (Lehmann 1961; 1966).

Although the name "tranquilizer" was given to these new drugs and became a popular label for them soon after they appeared on the clinical scene, when generally applied it may sometimes be a misnomer, since a number of the new drugs which possess neuroleptic and antipsychotic properties may not tranquilize, but, instead, exercise a mild stimulant action.

Rauwolfia and phenothiazine derivatives. The first two substances which were clinically employed and systematically studied in the treatment of acute manic and schizophrenic psychoses were the rauwolfia and the phenothiazine derivatives. Rauwolfia derivatives are related to the principal active ingredient of the plant *R. serpentina*, which was used for centuries in India for the treatment of mental disorders. However, it was given in doses which today we would consider inadequate. The phenothiazine derivatives, on the other hand, are synthetic products of a systematic search by pharmacologists for certain compounds with pronounced effects on the central nervous system. The first rauwolfia derivative studied extensively in psychiatric patients was reserpine, and the first phenothiazine derivative was chlorpromazine. In the few years since their introduction into psychiatry a tremendous number of clinical and experimental observations has been reported, and a great number of other rauwolfia and phenothiazine derivatives with similar properties have been developed by the pharmaceutical industry. It has become evident that for clinical purposes the phenothiazine derivatives present the advantages of being more reliable and producing fewer undesirable side effects than the rauwolfia derivatives. The latter, however, still play an important role as standard drugs for certain psychopharmacological experiments.

Evaluation of neuroleptics. Many of these new drugs have the particular tranquilizing effect which has been described above, and they do not, like most other sedatives, lead to addiction, even in predisposed individuals. All of the clinically applied neuroleptics counteract specific psychotic manifestations in acute mental breakdowns, and they were soon found to be effective therapeutic agents even in chronic psychotic states. A considerable number of regressed, chronic schizophrenics, some of whom had vegetated for ten or twenty years as hopeless human derelicts in the back wards of mental hospitals, responded to treatment with the new antipsychotic drugs, although they had previously failed to show any favorable response to repeated courses of insulin-coma and electroconvulsive treatment.

The atmosphere of mental hospitals all over the world has changed rapidly since the new drugs were introduced, since treatment with phenothiazine derivatives often renders an acutely psychotic individual rational and cooperative within a matter of hours or days instead of weeks and months, as had been the rule prior to the drug era. As psychiatrists learned to employ the new tranquilizers it became possible to reduce violent and destructive behavior to a minimum. The construction of new hospitals has been profoundly influenced by these therapeutic developments in that facilities for seclusion and restraint are no longer considered to be essential features of every mental hospital.

Perhaps the most important function of the new drugs is their role in the maintenance treatment of psychotic patients in remission. It is now possible to maintain a psychotic patient who has been rendered symptom-free through the use of antipsychotic drugs indefinitely in this compensated, and for all practical purposes, recovered state, provided the patient is carefully observed and continues to take antipsychotic medication regularly and in adequate doses. There are as yet no objective methods to determine which patients may eventually be able to discontinue maintenance medication and which will have to remain on it indefinitely.

There are four therapeutic functions for neuroleptic drugs with antipsychotic or psychotostatic activity. The drugs may be used as: (1) symptomatic sedatives; (2) therapeutic agents in acute psychotic conditions; (3) therapeutic agents in chronic psychotic conditions; (4) maintenance agents in former psychotic patients in remission. Older somatic treatments had been known to provide sedation effectively (e.g., the barbiturates or scopolamine), and insulin-coma or electroconvulsive treatment was effective in acute psychotic conditions. However, there had been no therapeutic procedures which could promise any real hope for chronic schizophrenic patients, and there had never been any drug that could maintain former psychotic patients symptom-free.

At least 70 per cent of all patients suffering acute schizophrenic breakdowns respond favorably to modern pharmacotherapy. Pharmacotherapy is simpler and at least as effective as insulin-coma therapy and consequently has replaced the latter in most psychiatric clinics today. Drug treatment of functional psychoses is neither merely symptomatic nor capable of curing the mental disease. The function of such treatment has been characterized as compensatory in nature. In this respect it resembles such therapeutic procedures as insulin treatment for diabetes or anticonvulsant therapy for epilepsy: as long as the treatment is administered the patient's symptoms will remain in abeyance. The drugs seem to counteract and neutralize the behavioral effects of a somatic substrate in psychotic conditions without, however, being able to eliminate this physical substrate.

Today many different phenothiazine derivatives are used in the treatment of psychotic conditions—in particular in the therapy of schizophrenia. One may easily become confused by the many generic names and the innumerable trade names under which these drugs appear on the international markets. Common to most of them is the phenothiazine nucleus; their differences depend on the chemical structure of the side chain attached to this nucleus. Carefully controlled observations have shown that the therapeutic effectiveness of the great majority of phenothiazine derivatives appears to be roughly equal. The derivatives differ, however, in the dose which is required to produce therapeutic effects and also in the side effects which accompany their administration. Recently, another chemical class with neuroleptic and antipsychotic properties is being studied intensively—the butyrophenones. There seems to be little doubt that equally or more effective new psychotostatic drugs will be developed in the future.

Other psychoactive drugs. While the mainstream of therapeutic activity has been going in the direction of treating psychotic manifestations, a number of new chemical substances with other interesting psychoactive properties have also been developed since 1955. These new drugs can be considered under three headings: (1) minor tranquilizers, (2) antidepressants, (3) psychotomimetics.

Minor tranquilizers. Minor tranquilizers are sedatives which do not possess antipsychotic properties. In other words, they can sedate a tense and excited patient but they cannot counteract such specific psychotic manifestations in the cognitive and perceptual field as delusions, thought disorder, and hallucinations. Drugs which do have antipsychotic effects—for instance, phenothiazine or butyrophenone derivatives—are sometimes referred to as major tranquilizers. While a considerable number of new minor tranquilizers have appeared on the market, there is, so far, no convincing evidence that these new substances have accomplished anything that is essentially different from the achievement of the older well-known sedatives.

Minor tranquilizers which are useful adjuncts to the treatment of anxiety and emotional tension are also characterized by the fact that they usually induce drowsiness and postural ataxia, exert an anticonvulsant action, and may lead to habituation and psychological addiction. In contrast, major tranquilizers do not induce postural ataxia, and only rarely do they induce persistent drowsiness. Major tranquilizers also tend to lower the brain's convulsive threshold and they do not lead to habituation and addiction (Berger & Ludwig 1964).

Antidepressants. The early hopes that the new stimulants (such as the amphetamines), which had been introduced in the 1930s, would be useful in the treatment of severe depressive states were not fulfilled. A depressed person is frequently in a state of heightened arousal, and giving him stimulants might only increase his anxiety and agitation without affecting the fundamental symptom of all depression—namely, the depressive mood. To fill the gap that existed in the pharmacotherapy of mental disorders characterized by depression, another type of psychoactive substance was developed a few years after the discovery of the psychotostatic drugs (major tranquilizers)—the antidepressant drugs (Lehmann 1965). These may be divided into two major groups: (1) the mono-amine-oxidase inhibitors, (2) antidepressants with no mono-amine-oxidase inhibiting activity—also referred to as tricyclic antidepressants.

Mono-amine-oxidase is an enzyme which degrades the so-called neurohormones, noradrenalin and serotonin. There is indirect clinical and experimental evidence that the distribution and balance of these neurohormones in the brain is significantly related to emotional states. It has been observed clinically that chemical substances which inhibit mono-amine-oxidase and thereby allow noradrenalin and serotonin to build up in the brain may successfully reduce the duration of a depression from several months or years to a period of three or four weeks.

While this observation has provided a pharmacological model in the systematic search for new antidepressant drugs, the mono-amine-oxidase inhibitor model certainly does not account in full for the physical substrate of depressive states, since a number of other substances with no enzyme inhibiting activity but a close chemical resemblance to the phenothiazines have proved to be equally effective in the treatment of severe depression. Our knowledge of the specific indications for each type of antidepressant—for instance, which should be prescribed for reactive depressions and which for endogenous, agitated, or retarded depressive states—is still incomplete.

Nevertheless, antidepressant drug therapy represents a considerable step forward in psychiatric treatment, and antidepressant drugs are effective in about 60 per cent of all depressive conditions. This reduces the number of patients who otherwise would have to be given electroconvulsive therapy. It takes from one to three weeks for antidepressant drugs to manifest their therapeutic action, and they are, therefore, slower acting than the antipsychotic drugs. Some, but not all, antidepressants have stimulating effects. The mono-amine-oxidase-inhibiting drugs tend to produce mild euphoria, while the tricyclic antidepressants that do not inhibit mono-amine-oxidase merely eliminate depressive symptoms without inducing euphoria.

Like many other psychoactive drugs, antidepressants frequently produce side effects; the mono-amine-oxidase inhibitors are particularly prone to do this. It is interesting to note that all effective antidepressants may potentiate psychotic symptoms—for instance, hallucinations and delusions—and may sometimes even induce a toxic psychotic state.

Recently, the distinction between antipsychotic and antidepressant drugs, which at first appeared to be quite clear-cut, has lost some of its sharpness. There are depressed patients, particularly the anxious depressed, who respond to major tranquilizers, and there are schizophrenic psychotics who respond favorably to antidepressants. Patients who respond in this different manner cannot yet be clearly distinguished in advance from the patients who show average response tendencies.

Psychotomimetics. Psychotomimetics are drugs which experimentally induce states of psychotic disintegration accompanied by thought-disorder and perceptual disturbances. Some representatives of this class of drugs have been known for a considerable time—for instance, marijuana, an ingredient of the hemp plant, and mescaline, the active component of the Mexican peyote cactus (Unger 1963). Other psychotomimetic substances have been developed more recently—for instance, lysergic acid diethylamide, a synthetic ergot compound, and psilocybin, which is derived from Mexican mushrooms. These strange substances have received a great deal of public attention in recent years and have stirred up considerable controversy. Preliminary clinical trials with some of the psychotomimetics, or hallucinogens as they are sometimes called, suggest that they may prove to be useful in the treatment of alcoholism and character disorders. However, these results will have to be confirmed, and a methodology for systematic therapy with these substances still needs to be developed.

In the meantime, these substances provide interesting tools for the experimental study of the psychotic process, since it is possible to induce "model psychoses" in volunteer subjects, who will, for a period of hours, undergo experiences which seem to be closely related to the experiential world of the schizophrenic. Unfortunately, these chemicals, which, like any powerful drug, carry a dangerous physical potential, have become a rallying issue of almost political importance for a small but vociferous group of intellectuals who claim the right to administer these drugs to themselves and to others according to their own, nonmedical judgment. It appears that under the influence of such substances, states of ecstatic exaltation can be fairly easily induced.

Viewed in an objective clinical and psychopharmacological perspective, the development, understanding, and administration of psychotomimetic drugs must be judged to be still in the experimental stages.

Prolonged sleep treatment

In 1922 Klaesi introduced prolonged sleep therapy into the therapeutic armamentarium of the psychiatrist (Klaesi 1922). This treatment method, which consisted of keeping patients asleep with the help of hypnotic drugs throughout most of the day for a period of several weeks, has held its place in the treatment of certain psychiatric conditions. Originally introduced for the treatment of schizophrenia, depressions, and manic states, it is now mostly given to patients suffering from long-standing psychoneuroses and psychosomatic conditions. It is particularly popular with psychiatrists in Soviet Russia, where Pavlov's teachings determine the basic theoretical approach to psychiatry. In Pavlov's conceptual framework, prolonged sleep is viewed as a form of protective inhibition that can successfully counteract the pathological excitation of the higher central nervous processes that manifest themselves as symptoms of pathological behavior. A variety of hypnotic and sedative drugs are used for sleep therapy. They are given at regular intervals either by mouth or by injection. This therapy does not produce any unpleasant experiences for the patient, but it requires careful, continuous nursing care in order to avoid circulatory collapse or other untoward effects in the patient, who has to be kept inactive for long periods of time. [*See* SLEEP.]

The use of sleep-producing drugs in psychiatric patients may be variously determined according to the different theoretic orientations of the therapist. While the Russian psychiatrists think in terms of physiological protective inhibition, a psychiatrist from the West may be more interested in the psychodynamic aspects of sleep therapy—e.g., disinhibition, abreaction, or anaclitic dependency.

Another method of inducing therapeutic sleep makes use of a rather weak continuous electrical current that is passed through the brain and produces relaxation and sleep which may be sustained for several hours without eliciting pain, shock, or convulsions.

As with drug-induced prolonged sleep, Russian psychiatrists invoke the concept of protective inhibition for this kind of electrically induced alteration of consciousness, and the therapeutic procedure is more widely employed in countries in the Russian sphere of influence than in Western countries. However, neither its technical application nor its therapeutic effects are as reliable as electroconvulsive treatments. Recent claims for success with electrically induced sleep are made mainly for neurotic states and for a variety of psychosomatic disorders (see Clapp & Loomis 1950; Giljarowskii et al. 1956; Wageneder & Hafner 1965).

Shock therapies

A new era of somatic therapy in mental disorders began around 1935 with the discovery of two types of physiological shock therapy: (1) the hypoglycemic coma treatment, or insulin-shock therapy, developed by Sakel, a young German psychiatrist; and (2) the convulsive therapy, or pentylenetetrazol-shock treatment, developed by Meduna, a psychiatrist at the University of Budapest. Sakel started his experiments two years prior to Meduna's (Kalinowsky & Hoch 1961; Sakel 1958; Meduna 1935).

Insulin-coma treatment. The principle of insulin-shock treatment lies in the production of the deep coma that results from a severe lowering of the blood-sugar level following an injection of insulin. The brain depends for its metabolism mainly on carbohydrates. A reduction of the blood-sugar supply, therefore, lowers brain metabolism relatively more than that of any other organ. Sakel had been treating patients addicted to morphine with small doses of insulin as a relief measure during their withdrawal from the narcotic; he observed that sometimes they had inadvertently slipped into a deep coma and after having been aroused from it had appeared much improved. He was an imaginative man who, without much other justification, generalized from these specific observations to the bold hypothesis that schizophrenic patients would benefit from hypoglycemic coma therapy. He was also a courageous man, for, at that time, a coma produced by an overdose of insulin was still considered to be a dangerous complication. At any rate, in 1933 Sakel presented his first promising report with insulin-coma therapy in one hundred schizophrenic patients from the University Clinic of Vienna. His findings were soon confirmed in other European countries, and the treatment was rapidly adopted all over the world. It constituted

the first effective major therapeutic advancement in the management of schizophrenia (Sakel 1958).

Insulin-coma therapy of schizophrenia is most effective in patients who have been sick for not more than six months to a year. After this time it rapidly loses its effectiveness. Patients have to be treated in specially equipped hospital units for several months. They receive an injection of insulin while in the fasting state early in the morning. Within one to two hours they fall asleep and eventually go into a deep coma from which, at the end of three or four hours, they are aroused by an injection of glucose into the blood stream or by the infusion of a sugar solution into the stomach. A recent refinement of technique consists in the administration of glucagon, a substance which rapidly mobilizes available carbohydrate stores in the body and, therefore, reduces the need for large amounts of sugar to be administered through intravenous injection or stomach tube. The amount of insulin required for each patient to induce coma differs considerably and might change from day to day. The medical and nursing staffs administering insulin-coma treatment have to be well trained and experienced. Usually not more than ten or twenty patients can be treated on any one day. All these factors make the treatment a rather expensive procedure which requires considerable vigilance on the part of the staff and is by no means entirely without risk. Nevertheless, in competent hands, insulin treatment produces 70 per cent to 75 per cent remissions in acute schizophrenia, and it was the favored treatment for this disease until the advent of pharmacotherapy.

Subcoma insulin treatment. A modification of insulin-coma therapy consists of the administration of smaller doses of insulin, which will produce a state of lowered blood-sugar level (hypoglycemia) without, however, bringing about a deep coma. The patients are rendered sleepy, and a state of deep relaxation is produced. At the termination of each treatment—which lasts from two to three hours with the patient lying quietly in a darkened room—the patient feels hungry but relaxed. A course of subcoma insulin treatment usually lasts for several weeks. Indications for this type of therapy are conditions of neurotic anxiety and increased tension. Patients often respond to the treatment with improved sleep, gain of weight, a feeling of increased well-being, and a reduced need for sedatives.

Drug-induced convulsive treatment. Insulin-produced hypoglycemia sometimes leads to convulsions. It had been observed that patients often appeared to improve more rapidly after they had had a convulsion. Meduna theorized that there existed a biological antagonism between epilepsy and schizophrenia because these two diseases do not often occur simultaneously in the same patients. He had transfused schizophrenic patients with the blood of an epileptic and vice versa, hoping to see an improvement in the patients treated in this manner. When he obtained no results, he conceived of the idea of producing epileptiform convulsions in schizophrenic patients by injecting them intramuscularly with camphor in oil. Later he used the synthetically produced drug pentylenetetrazol, instead. This drug is water soluble and can be injected into a vein. When this is done the patient experiences for a short time an agonizing state of apprehension and panic and then, within a minute or two, loses consciousness and has a typical epileptiform convulsion of the *grand mal* type. The treatment is given every other day until a series of 10 to 25 or more convulsions has been produced. With his first group of schizophrenics treated with pentylenetetrazol, Meduna could report almost 90 per cent remissions. However, a considerable number of patients relapsed within a few weeks, and the over-all results of pentylenetetrazol-convulsive treatment in schizophrenia were not quite as favorable as those obtained with insulin-coma therapy. Often the two treatments could be combined for best results (Meduna 1935).

It did not take long before it became evident that convulsive therapy was highly effective in depressive states—in fact, more so than in schizophrenia—and in the treatment of severe depression convulsive therapy still plays an important role.

Electroconvulsive treatment (ECT). In 1938 Cerletti and Bini in Rome treated a patient with an improved modification of the convulsive treatment method, namely with convulsions produced through the application of an electrical current instead of the administration of convulsant drugs (Cerletti 1950). This method soon supplanted the pentylenetetrazol treatment, since it was simpler and, above all, did not produce the unpleasant subjective effects of the drug. A patient who receives electroshock therapy may remain comfortably in his own bed. Two electrodes are applied to the temples, and even if no anesthetic is given the patient never feels any pain, since the passage of the current—about 100 volts for 0.3–0.5 seconds—causes immediate loss of consciousness. After regaining consciousness the patient might remain rather confused for thirty minutes to an hour.

A depressed person usually begins to show defi-

nite improvement after the first four or five treatments, but additional treatments are required to prevent a relapse of depressive symptoms. Six to twelve treatments—administered over a period of two to four weeks—are the usual number for a course of ECT in acute depressions. If electroshock therapy is given to schizophrenic patients, twenty or more treatments are usually administered.

After three to five electrically induced convulsions, one observes a change in the patient's electroencephalogram in the direction of a general slowing of the electrical brain rhythms. At about the same time the patient develops an acute amnestic syndrome. He shows impairment of recent memory, and after a large number of treatments—or also if treatments are given at closely spaced intervals, for instance, every day or several times a day—the patient might become greatly confused. Sometimes such confusion is deliberately induced in the course of "regressive" or "depatterning" shock therapy, in the hope that the complete shattering of the patient's mental processes will be followed by a reconstitution and reintegration of his mental functioning but with a selective permanent destruction of the more recently acquired pathological manifestations [Cameron et al. 1962; *see* ELECTROCONVULSIVE SHOCK].

Within two to four weeks after discontinuation of electroshock therapy, memory functions and electroencephalographic indices tend to return to their normal levels. Although the human organism is able to tolerate convulsions amazingly well at any age, in elderly persons there is some danger of either producing or triggering off permanent impairment of memory due to physical brain changes. The aged are, of course, already predisposed to such organic brain damage. In younger persons there seems to be little or no danger of any permanent brain damage due to electroconvulsive treatment.

Several modifications of the standard treatment method have been proposed, mostly with the intention of reducing confusion and amnesia following ECT. One of the most promising is the unilateral application of the current, which seems to produce less memory impairment than the standard method (Cannicott 1962).

It has been demonstrated that the induction of paroxysmal seizure discharges in the brain is the essential factor in electroconvulsive therapy. All muscular, autonomic, and metabolic responses which can be observed during and after the convulsions seem to be secondary and carry little or no therapeutic value.

The violent muscular contractions which accompany the seizure discharges of the brain can easily lead to fractures of the vertebrae or of other bones in the trunk or the extremities, and for this reason electroconvulsive therapy today is almost always preceded by the administration of a muscle relaxant—either curare or one of its analogues, or more frequently, succinylcholine—which is injected into a vein together with a short-acting barbiturate to produce a superficial anesthesia as well as muscular relaxation. Immediately following these injections artificial respiration is established for a few minutes; the electrical shock is administered; and the convulsion ensues. However, suppressed by the muscle relaxant, the convulsion consists of hardly more than a flickering of the eyelids or a movement of the toes, although the electrical and physiological effects on the brain are not essentially altered.

Electroshock therapy, which should be referred to as electroconvulsive therapy (ECT), is today the most reliable treatment of severe depressive states. It produces favorable results in about 90 per cent of the cases, while treatment with antidepressant drugs is effective only in about 60 per cent of depressive conditions. Electroconvulsive treatment is most successful in involutional melancholia, an endogenous depressive condition usually associated with agitation and occurring in patients of the involutional age, i.e., between forty and sixty years. Electroconvulsive treatment is less effective when marked anxiety or many hypochondriacal symptoms are associated with the depressive state.

While ECT is still the most reliable treatment for severe depressive states and is also often remarkably effective in states of acute psychotic excitement or schizophrenic disintegration, it should be clearly understood that this type of therapy does not seem to influence the long-term development of a psychopathological process. Various studies have shown that ECT does not prevent depressive or psychotic relapses; nor does it seem to reduce the number of such relapses or prolong the normal intervals in recurrent mental diseases. The main value of this dramatic therapy lies in the fact that it leads to a rapid disappearance or amelioration of depressive or psychotic symptoms and that it may reduce the duration of a severe depression from nine to twelve months to three to six weeks. Although most manic–depressive episodes terminate eventually in spontaneous recovery, the ever-present danger of suicide in depressed patients can be eliminated with ECT, and the value of saving a patient a great deal of unnecessary suffering and restoring him early to useful functioning in the community is, of course, sufficient justification for employing this kind of therapy whenever it is indicated as the most suitable therapeutic approach. If the mental disease is not of a periodic nature, as in manic–depressive psychosis, but tends to be chronic, as for instance, schizophrenia, then ECT is much more limited in its value, because although regular repeated maintenance treatment with ECT is possible, it is more hazardous and not as practical as the continuous suppression of psychotic symptoms with pharmacotherapy.

Psychosurgery

In 1936, almost simultaneously with the introduction of the shock therapies, another dramatic somatic therapy was introduced into psychiatry by the Portuguese neuropsychiatrist Antonio Egas Moniz—the surgical procedure of prefrontal lobotomy. Basing his work on accumulated data from neurophysiological and experimental psychological research, Moniz theorized that the frontal lobes were essentially related to the higher mental processes, which were necessary components of normal cerebral and behavioral functioning. In particular, certain processes of abstraction, inhibition, and time projection had been thought to find their representation in the frontal and prefrontal lobes. Moniz severed the connections between the frontal lobes and the thalamus through small cuts of the fiber tracks responsible for these connections. He showed that his operation was often followed by improvement, particularly in early schizophrenia but also in chronic states of depression or in obsessive–compulsive ruminations that had not yielded to any other treatment. [*See* Nervous system, *article on* structure and function of the brain; Obsessive–compulsive disorders.]

This operation is not followed by any deterioration of intellectual performance, but it leads to a marked reduction in the intensity of the person's emotional involvement, imagination, and creative productivity. If an insufficient amount of brain substance is cut there will be no adequate relief of symptoms. If exactly the right amount of brain substance is destroyed, the therapeutic result might enable the patient to function better after the operation than he ever functioned before. If the surgeon destroys too much brain substance, the patient might develop into an apathetic slob or an irresponsible psychopath, being left either without ambition or without any consideration for others. Unfortunately, it is not possible to calculate precisely where and how much to cut. However, a great deal of progress has been made in perfecting this particular neurosurgical procedure, so that the probability of a good therapeutic response is heightened and the probability of personality deterioration is minimized.

Most of the results with this kind of therapy were collected in the United States prior to 1955 and particularly in Britain, where the interest in prefrontal lobotomies still persists and is probably higher than anywhere else. On the North American continent interest in psychosurgery has sharply declined since the introduction of modern drug therapy for mental disorders. There are probably two principal reasons for the disinclination of most American psychiatrists to submit their patients to a prefrontal lobotomy or to any other type of surgical interference with the brain: (1) Since neurons cannot regenerate, any artificially produced morphological changes in the brain—in particular any loss of substance—would be irreversible; (2) Several careful follow-up studies have brought out evidence that marked personality changes supervened eventually in almost all lobotomized patients, even if the therapeutic gain outweighed the personality deficit due to the operation (Greenblatt et al. 1950; Petrie 1952; Rylander 1939). One general consequence of a prefrontal lobotomy is a certain loss of subtleness and complexity in the patient's personality; he usually loses some of his creative imagination; he dreams less; and his dreams tend to become much simpler in structure; and on the whole he becomes less sensitive. However, for intractable conditions of chronic depression or for chronic obsessive–compulsive psychoneurosis which has been refractory to any other type of therapy, prefrontal lobotomy would still have to be seriously considered as a last resort, which, nevertheless, may often yield surprisingly good results.

Mechanisms of action

The rationale for a therapeutic procedure is easily understood if the etiological factors of the condition to be treated are known and if the treatment is specifically aimed at eliminating these etiological factors. This would apply to the modern penicillin treatment of general paresis, which kills the trepanoma pallidum and thus eliminates the causal factor of syphilis, which in turn is responsible for the psychosis. But the *modus operandi* of Wagner-Jauregg's malaria treatment of general paresis was not so easily understood because it constituted an unspecific attack on the disease, and a number of theories have been proposed to explain its effect. It was thought, for instance, that

the physical hyperthermia factor produced by malaria might kill the trepanoma pallidum, and it was also put forward that malaria therapy was effective because it mobilized general biological defenses in an unspecific manner, thus enabling the organism to deal successfully in its own way with the brain disease.

Many theories have been offered to explain the therapeutic action of insulin-coma treatment, ranging from a conception of reduced cerebral metabolism, which is equivalent to partial anoxia, to the idea that the artificially induced regression of the patient to an infantile level and the nursing care he is receiving during the coma treatment from doctor and nurse constitute a re-enactment of the patient's infantile situation without the traumatic factors which supposedly prevailed originally in his infancy. Theories to explain the effects of electroconvulsive treatment also involve physical and psychodynamic concepts and range from neurophysiological, biochemical, and endocrinological hypotheses to the proposal that the induced amnesia is responsible for the "unlearning" of recently acquired pathological behavior patterns and also to the suggestion that the patient experiences symbolic death and resurrection under the magic influence of the doctor administering the treatment.

There is no generally accepted theory for the action of modern psychopharmacological agents. It has already been mentioned that the therapeutic action of one group of antidepressants, namely the mono-amine-oxidase inhibitors, has been explained on the basis of competitive affinity of the drug and hormones to essential receptor sites on an enzyme. The neuroleptic major tranquilizers seem to act on the brain's reticular activating system, the diencephalon, and the extrapyramidal system and possibly produce their effects through an influence on synaptic transmission in the subcortical structures of the brain. Minor tranquilizers apparently affect more prominently the cerebral cortex and parts of the limbic system in the subcortical structures. The action of psychotomimetics still poses a very puzzling phenomenon: these drugs may lead to desynchronization and imbalance between the transmission of impulses through the primary sensory paths and their processing through the associative systems of the brain.

Treatment practices in clinical psychiatry

A general principle may be formulated, stating that somatic treatment is the primary therapeutic approach to the psychoses, with psychotherapy playing an auxiliary role, and that psychotherapy is the primary therapeutic approach to the psycho-neuroses, with somatic treatment serving as an adjutant (Kline & Lehmann 1962).

This would mean that the treatment of psychoses is less complex and demands less personal skill and experience from the therapist than the treatment of psychoneuroses. The recently developed pharmacotherapy of schizophrenia, manic states, and depressive conditions makes it now possible for a nonspecialist physician to treat a psychotic patient successfully outside a mental hospital. This is of particular significance for the organization of psychiatric services in underdeveloped countries, where the impossibility of constructing mental hospitals and finding enough well-trained specialists has prevented the build-up of such services until now. That modern pharmacotherapy can indeed provide the nucleus for a successful psychiatric service organization in a country where such services were nonexistent before has been demonstrated in Haiti, where a well-functioning psychiatric clinic with preventive, therapeutic, and rehabilitative functions has recently been set up within a short time and at minimum expense of financial means and trained manpower. Such shortcuts have become possible only since rapidly effective and self-administered therapeutic agents that can also maintain the patient symptom-free following the acute treatment phase have been made available in the form of antipsychotic and antidepressant medication.

Ready availability, ease, and continuity of administration are the main advantages of drug treatment over insulin-coma and electroconvulsive therapy. Insulin-coma therapy, although still a valuable treatment for schizophrenic patients who do not respond to drug therapy, is no longer given at most psychiatric treatment centers because the necessary, specially equipped insulin-treatment units have been dissolved. Electroconvulsive treatment is simple to administer but also requires some special apparatus and technical skill on the part of the therapist; besides, it cannot be given continuously because of its cumulative effects on a patient's memory. However, it is still widely used in the treatment of acute or chronic manic or schizophrenic psychoses, particularly when they do not respond to drug therapy. Prefrontal lobotomy—sometimes also referred to as leucotomy—is rarely performed today except in cases manifesting depressive or obsessive–compulsive symptoms which have failed to respond to any other treatment. Pharmacotherapy has in many instances replaced these older methods of somatic treatment.

Different national cultures seem to have shaped different therapeutic attitudes, and in certain countries preferences and dislikes for particular modes of treatment are clearly evident. In a very broad sense it may be stated that psychiatric orientation on the North American continent is characterized by a much heavier bias toward a psychodynamic—more specifically, Freudian psychoanalytic—approach to theory and practice than psychiatry in other parts of the world. European schools of psychiatry place more emphasis on genetic–constitutional and physicochemical factors in their speculation on the etiology of mental disorders as well as in their clinical approach to them.

In the Soviet Union, psychosurgery, in the form of prefrontal lobotomy, has been officially ruled out as a permissible treatment method. In Britain, on the other hand, there is still greater interest in this type of therapy than in most other countries. In German-speaking countries, where the influence of an existentialist orientation is fairly strong, electroconvulsive therapy seems to be disliked—possibly because of the radically disrupting effect such treatment has on the continuity of a patient's orientation toward his problems and his experience of the world in which he lives. In countries where psychiatric services must be created *de novo*, the practical advantages and the comprehensive effectiveness of modern pharmacotherapy have made it the favorite choice of somatic treatment for mental disorders.

It should again be recalled that the undoubted effectiveness of modern somatic treatment applies only to psychotic disorders, in particular to those of functional origin. Physical methods, including drug therapy, are of very limited value for the therapeutic management of psychoneuroses and character disorders.

In accordance with modern concepts one may view mental disorders as the resultants of multifactorial functions and forces. The complex factors interacting with each other may be categorized under the headings: (1) genetic factors—constitutional personality matrix, idiosyncratic and, within wide limits, independent of time; (2) situational factors—idiosyncratic and time-dependent; (3) physicochemical factors—general and independent of time.

Somatic treatment of mental disorders is aimed only at the physicochemical sector of the human behavioral complex. The indirect repercussions of physical treatment may, however, bring about a change of balance in the entire organism and thus result in therapeutic effects which seem to go far beyond simple physical changes.

HEINZ E. LEHMANN

[*Other relevant material may be found in* DEPRESSIVE DISORDERS; DRUGS; ELECTROCONVULSIVE SHOCK; NERVOUS SYSTEM, *article on* STRUCTURE AND FUNCTION OF THE BRAIN; NEUROSIS; PSYCHIATRY; PSYCHOSIS; SCHIZOPHRENIA.]

BIBLIOGRAPHY

BERGER, F. M.; and LUDWIG, B. J.   1964   Meprobamate and Related Compounds. Volume 1, page 103 in Maxwell Gordon (editor), *Psychopharmacological Agents*. New York: Academic Press.

CAMERON, D. E.; LOHRENZ, J. G.; and HANDCOCK, K. A.   1962   The Depatterning Treatment of Schizophrenia. *Comprehensive Psychiatry* 3:65–76.

CANNICOTT, S. M.   1962   Unilateral Electro-convulsive Therapy. *Postgraduate Medical Journal* 38:451–459.

CERLETTI, UGO   1950   Old and New Information About Electroshock. *American Journal of Psychiatry* 107:87–94.

CLAPP, JOHN S.; and LOOMIS, EARL A.   1950   Continuous Sleep Treatment: Observations on the Use of Prolonged, Deep, Continuous Narcosis in Mental Disorders. *American Journal of Psychiatry* 106:821–829.

FØLLING, A.   1934   Excretion of Phenylpyruvic Acid in Urine as Metabolic Anomaly in Connection with Imbecility. *Nordisk medicinsk tidskrift* (Stockholm) 8:1054–1059.

GILJAROWSKII, VASILII et al.   1956   *Elektroschlaf*. Berlin: VEB Verlag Volk und Gesundheit.

GJESSING, L.; BERNHARDSEN, A.; and FRØSHAUG, H.   1958   Investigation of Amino Acids in a Periodic Catatonic Patient. *Journal of Mental Science* 104:188–200.

GREENBLATT, MILTON; ARNOT, ROBERT; and SOLOMON, HARRY C. (editors)   1950   *Studies in Lobotomy*. New York: Grune.

HAISCH, ERICH   1959   Irrenpflege in alter Zeit. *Ciba-Zeitschrift* 8, no. 95:3142 only.

KALINOWSKY, LOTHAR B.; and HOCH, PAUL H.   1961   *Somatic Treatments in Psychiatry*. New York: Grune & Stratton.

KLAESI, J.   1922   Über die therapeutische Anwendung der "Dauernarkose" mittels Somnifen bei Schizophrenen. *Zeitschrift für die gesamte Neurologie und Psychiatrie* 74:557–592.

KLINE, NATHAN S.; and LEHMANN, H. E.   1962   *Handbook of Psychiatric Treatment in Medical Practice*. Philadelphia: Saunders.

LEHMANN, H. E.   1961   New Drugs in Psychiatric Therapy. *Journal of the Canadian Medical Association* 85:1145–1151.

LEHMANN, H. E.   1963   Psychopharmacology: A Discussion of Current Problems. *Ohio State Medical Journal* 59:1091–1097.

LEHMANN, H. E.   1965   The Pharmacotherapy of the Depressive Syndrome. *Journal of the Canadian Medical Association* 92:821–828.

LEHMANN, H. E.   1966   Pharmacotherapy of Schizophrenia. Pages 388–411 in American Psychopathological Association, *Psychopathology of Schizophrenia*. Edited by Paul Hoch and Joseph Zubin. New York: Grune.

LOEVENHART, ARTHUR S.; LORENZ, WILLIAM F.; and WATERS, RALPH M.   1929   Cerebral Stimulation. *Journal of the American Medical Association* 92:880–882.

MEDUNA, L. J.   1935   Versuche über die biologische Beeinflussung des Ablaufes der Schizophrenie. Part 1:
Campher- und Cardiazolkrämpfe. *Zeitschrift für die gesamte Neurologie und Psychiatrie* 152:235–262.

Mental Deficiency and Phenylketonuria.   1961   *Journal of the American Medical Association* 178:838 only.

MYERSON, ABRAHAM   1936   Effect of Benzedrine Sulphate on Mood and Fatigue in Normal and Neurotic Persons. *Archives of Neurology and Psychiatry* 36:816–822.

PETRIE, ASENATH   1952   *Personality and the Frontal Lobes: An Investigation of the Psychological Effects of Different Types of Leucotomy*. Philadelphia: Blakiston.

RAGSDALE, N.; and KOCH, R.   1964   Phenylketonuria Detection and Therapy. *American Journal of Nursing* 64, no. 1:90–96.

RYLANDER, GÖSTA   1939   Personality Changes After Operations on the Frontal Lobes. *Acta psychiatrica and neurologica* Supplement 20.

SAKEL, MANFRED   1958   *Schizophrenia*. New York: Philosophical Library.

TAPPAN, PAUL W.   1951   Treatment of the Sex Offender in Denmark. *American Journal of Psychiatry* 108:241–249.

UNGER, SANFORD M.   1963   Mescaline, LSD, Psilocybin and Personality Change: A Review. *Psychiatry* 26:111–125.

WAGENEDER, F. H.; and HAFNER, H.   1965   Elektroheilschlaf: Eine neue Therapieform. *Anaesthesist* 14:126–129.

WAGNER-JAUREGG, JULIUS VON   1946   The History of the Malaria Treatment of General Paralysis. *American Journal of Psychiatry* 102:577–582. → A translation by Walter L. Bruetsch of an earlier manuscript by Wagner-Jauregg.

What Tranquilizers Have Done.   1964   *Time* April 24:43–44.

WOOLLEY, D. W. et al.   1938   Anti-black Tongue Activity of Various Pyridine Derivatives. *Journal of Biological Chemistry* 124:715–723.

ZILBOORG, GREGORY   1941   *A History of Medical Psychology*. New York: Norton.

VI

THE THERAPEUTIC COMMUNITY

The term "therapeutic community" designates a method of treatment which attempts to use a hospital's social environment as an integral part of the treatment approach. It belongs to the general approach often referred to as "milieu therapy." As such, it is related to the field of social psychiatry, which attempts to incorporate sociocultural perspectives into psychiatry.

The first use of the term "therapeutic community" was by Thomas Main (1946) in his description of the experimental units developed during World War II in England for the treatment of various kinds of wartime psychological casualties. The felicitous phrase, mentioned almost casually in Main's report, was picked up and made into a self-conscious, organizing concept in the work of Maxwell Jones (1952), with whose name the concept is generally associated.

Although the idea of the therapeutic community was forged in the exigencies of war, it was developed to its fullest elaboration in its postwar applications. In essence, it represents a critique of prior psychiatric theories and practices in that it advocates radical changes in psychiatric hospitals to make them therapeutic rather than merely custodial or even psychologically damaging, and it is based on a new combination of ideas that have emerged from psychoanalysis and the social sciences. Accordingly, it is important to consider the complex of ideas associated with the term "therapeutic community" in the context of an appreciation of its precursors both in and out of psychiatry in Europe and America. There are two sets of precursors: those against which the therapeutic community idea represented a protest and those from which it drew its own creative elements.

Characteristics of therapeutic communities

There have been numerous attempts to find a quintessential definition of the therapeutic community idea as it has evolved and been applied in various settings (e.g., Jones 1952; Jones & Rapoport 1955; Rapoport et al. 1961; Research Conference . . . 1960; Schwartz et al. 1964). A number of key ideas are distinguishable that differentiate the therapeutic community approach from other forms of milieu therapy or administrative psychiatry. Some or all of the elements described below are employed in units designated as therapeutic communities. In any given setting, these elements may be part of a focal treatment method, they may be secondary elements with other methods more focally applied, or they may be a part of the general background or atmosphere against which various methods may be applied.

The holistic view.   Conceptualizing the organization in system terms, according to a "holistic" view of the entire hospital or unit, is an integral part of most therapeutic community ventures. As the concept suggests, the hospital or unit is seen as a "community," of more or less closed corporate character. The emphasis is on understanding how behavior is affected by and affects the over-all functioning of the hospital as a social system. This element of the therapeutic community idea is taken to contrast with the tendency of the old-fashioned mental hospital (with its associated theories emphasizing constitutional determination and therapeutic pessimism) to regard individual patients in depersonalized, asocial, atomistic terms. By conceptualizing the hospital as a special type of community in which the patient can be helped, therapeutic community practitioners seek, at the very least, to sustain a *social* definition of the nature of the patients' conditions and potentialities. They

hold that this social definition is a prerequisite of therapeutic effectiveness. The new community in the hospital is seen as belatedly providing a "good" substitute for the earlier pathogenic environment in which the patients' socially unadaptive tendencies developed. Identification with the hospital community is seen as a steppingstone to identification with society at large.

Permissiveness.   In contrast with the restrictive environment of the old-fashioned mental hospital, which was prisonlike or even punitive in character, the therapeutic community allows patients to express themselves relatively freely, even if this means the enactment of behavior that would be morally repugnant in ordinary settings. The degree to which this "acting out" can be tolerated is, of course, limited by several factors: the capacity of the institution to endure disruptive behavior, the exercise by the staff of their responsibilities for the care and protection of their patients, and the degree to which the expressive behavior may be taken to be in the interests of therapy. But some degree of permissiveness has become a hallmark of the therapeutic community.

Underlying the application of permissiveness is the theoretical viewpoint that psychiatric disorder is the manifestation of maladaptive responses to earlier situations which have formed a covert, often unconscious framework for the individual's contemporary behavior. Success in attempting to change the latter is seen as depending, to some extent, on uncovering the former. Permissive standards of patient role prescription thus create a deliberate, rather than a careless, set of ambiguities in the structuring of hospital role relationships. The hospital social structure can, in this context, be seen to act somewhat as a "social screen" onto which patients project their covert behavioral tendencies; these tendencies can then be subjected to group analysis. In addition, involvement of patients in one another's treatment responsibilities helps the staff to allow more permissiveness by providing a more diffuse base of social controls.

Increasing patient participation.   In old-fashioned mental hospitals the patients were treated as objects, led passive lives removed from ordinary social activities, and had little or no voice in the conduct of the affairs of the institution in which they lived. In therapeutic communities, by contrast, patient participation is encouraged. This trend seems to have several components: "democratization," which implies the increase of patient participation in policy decisions relating to the general administration of the organization (for example, by patient government); "egalitarianism," which implies a reduction of status differentiation between staff and patients, with an emphasis on sharing of the facilities and resources of the institution (usually accompanied by the use of familiar terms of address, the forgoing of titles, uniforms, etc.); and "harnessing of patients for therapy" through attempts to use their intimate knowledge of one another, their communications, and insight potentials (for example, by the emphasis on group therapy sessions as a major treatment method).

Broadening the base of therapy. In the therapeutic community a broader range of activities, relationships, and qualities of the patient's environment are considered relevant to the course of his treatment. Conventional medical thinking has always defined treatment in terms of what the doctor does—giving an injection, applying electrical shock therapy, or even subjecting the patient to "analysis" in a therapeutic "hour." Proponents of the therapeutic community, however, recognize that many experiences, relationships, and characteristics of the patient's life in the hospital can have a critical effect on his treatment. Activities previously thought of as purely diversionary or recreational have come to be seen as part of a program of treatment, and subordinate ranks of hospital personnel have become important links in the human communications network through which treatment is provided. Likewise, patient roles which had been seen as relatively unimportant or even troublesome, such as the leader of an informal patient clique, have become parts of the organizational and interactional process which therapeutic community practitioners seek to harness for therapy.

Rehabilitation. Another feature of therapeutic communities is their orientation toward patient rehabilitation, which is based on an optimistic view of therapeutic potentialities. Therapeutic communities seek to reproduce within the hospital a microcosm of the ordinary world of the patient so as to enhance the possibilities for rehearsing social roles while still in the hospital. Thus there is an emphasis on training or retraining individuals to take social roles outside the hospital, not by forcing conformity to ordinary role requirements but, rather, by providing the opportunity for learning what kinds of problems interfere with the individual's capacity to perform acceptably in these roles. This emphasis is seen in the development of "realistic" workshops in the hospital and in the tendency to confront patients continually with others' perceptions of their behavior.

This optimistic view of rehabilitation is reflected in what has come to be known as a "therapeutic atmosphere," which to some extent consists of a series of new attitudes toward the patient and the hospital. These attitudes emphasize, for example, the positive elements in personality rather than the sick parts and thinking from the outset in terms of pathways back to a normal existence in the community rather than in terms of a long and hopeless removal in the artificial and impersonal life of the mental hospital. To some extent this "atmosphere" seems to have been made up of a set of attitudes held by the psychiatric leader: a sense of innovative change, high valuation of the work and people involved in it, optimism, and a feeling for the social significance of the therapeutic enterprise. There has been an impression by some observers (for example, see World Health Organization, Expert Committee on Mental Health 1953) that this charismatic quality of the leader contributes a major share to the success of therapeutic communities. To the extent that sophisticated practitioners of the therapeutic community approach have been aware of the importance of this sense of innovative change (akin to the "Hawthorne effect" in industry), they have sought to develop a continuing sense of challenge. They have looked to positive elements of the therapeutic community concept on which to build after many of the inequities of the old hospital system have given way to widespread reform.

History of the concept

Ingredients of the therapeutic community concept within psychiatry stem from the reformist stance taken over a century ago, when, in keeping with the trends emanating from the French Revolution, mental patients in country after country were brought under the benign aegis of medicine. Philippe Pinel in France, William Tuke in England, Vincenzo Chiarugi in Italy, Johann Reil in Germany, and Benjamin Rush in the United States were leaders among scores of hospital superintendents who attempted to redefine the ailments of mental patients. With the development of "moral treatment," physicians sought to treat psychologically disturbed individuals with compassionate understanding and close attention to their personal needs, thoughts, and feelings.

The custodial system. The "moral treatment" approach declined in the latter part of the nineteenth century, to be replaced by a custodial, incarcerative system accompanied by deep-seated attitudes of therapeutic pessimism. The reasons for the change included the influx into urban areas of individuals who had few if any ties and who were disturbed and disfranchised through their experiences with urbanization and industrialization. Hospitals were overloaded, their patients were not integrated into the local communities, and as costs mounted, the tendency was to remove them to the outskirts of major urban concentrations. Patients were held there with prisonlike restraints for their own and society's security. Concurrently, a theory of psychopathology developed which attributed the more serious mental disorders (which were thought to be on the increase) to brain lesions, the cure of which was yet to be discovered by medicine. The fact that the moral treatment proponents had not developed a theory of etiology and therapy to underpin their efforts left them without a rationale to support a concerted program of care in the face of the new influx of intractable patients and competing etiological theories. Their effectiveness was based on their norms of personal conduct as genteel members of the relatively small, intimate communities of their times.

Reformist movements. Thus a combination of factors—ranging from fiscal to theoretical—led to the build-up of large custodial mental hospitals, which were stocked with chronically disturbed, neglected mental patients and ill-trained, pessimistic staffs. The therapeutic community approach found its immediate impetus in the reaction against this situation. The reformers were motivated in part by the ancient injunction *Primum non nocere*; as Florence Nightingale put it, "It may seem a strange principle to enumerate as the very first requirement in a hospital that it should do the sick no harm." The forces of institutionalization and neglect, as much as the innate pathology of the individual patients, were increasingly seen as having played a part in bringing them to their predicament.

As compared with their predecessors, the new reformist movements were better equipped by modern theory and research methods to implement new approaches to mental patient care. The new theoretical orientation stressed the growth potentialities of the mentally ill. One of the fortunate by-products of the great depression was a new recognition that individuals could not entirely control the social forces affecting their lives. This recognition negated the view that casualties of the social process were constitutionally defective. World War II led to the mobilization of new talents and energies, accompanied by a revised sense of federal responsibility for the care of the nation's casualties. The changes have been so great in the period following World War II, particularly in the fields of social psychiatry, that they have been termed by such partisans as Moreno (1934) and Dreikurs (1955) the "third revolution" in psychiatry—the first having been that associated with the early reformers and the second with the psychoanalytic movement.

Of particular relevance to the therapeutic community approach were the efforts of August Aichhorn in Austria, Jacob Moreno and Harry Stack Sullivan in America, Ernst Simmel in Germany, and Wilfred Bion and others associated with the Tavistock Clinic and Institute in England. Aichhorn's work (1925) was influential in applying the psychoanalytic conception of permissiveness to the administration of an adolescent treatment institution. His work has been carried on and developed in the United States by such men as Bettelheim (1950) and Redl (Redl & Wineman 1952); Moreno stressed the importance of "psychodrama," or the use of role playing for both diagnostic and therapeutic purposes. Harry Stack Sullivan's *Interpersonal Theory of Psychiatry* (1953) was a pioneering effort to revise psychoanalytic theory so that it would take sociocultural processes into account in therapy, and while he did not directly influence the early therapeutic community innovations, his work was important in the development of parallel efforts such as those of Rioch and Stanton (1959), Stanton and Schwartz (1954), and Artiss (1962) and in laying some of the groundwork for American acceptance of the therapeutic community idea. Ernst Simmel (1929) noted that the transference relationship, so vital to psychoanalytic therapy, could be developed in a hospital setting with reference to social roles and, therefore, be displaceable to some extent from one individual incumbent in the role to others. The Tavistock group, influenced particularly by Bion (1961), developed many of the notions of group dynamics that informed the efforts of Maxwell Jones and his colleagues with therapeutic community experiments.

A prior effort that resembled the therapeutic community method and provided ingredients for its subsequent development as a well-formulated approach was the "total push" method of Abraham Myerson (1939). This was an eclectic approach which optimistically sought to harness whatever resources and methods were at hand to reorient the staff's activity into a more holistic attack on the problems of psychiatric rehabilitation.

Ideology of the therapeutic community. It is interesting to consider the question of why such a movement, with its utopian emphasis on the healing power of the community, should have developed at this point in history. It may be conjectured that the movement to establish therapeutic communities is essentially a reaction against the anomic by-products of rapid social change attendant on increasing industrialization and urbanization. It represents an attempt to restore what Edward Sapir referred to as a "genuine culture," at least within the limited and more manageable sphere of the mental hospital world. The fact that the segregated mental hospital system displayed a remarkable degree of cultural lag and at the same time was associated with an idealistic, science-minded group of professional practitioners, gave unusual leverage for rapid implementation of this program once the conditions were favorable. The wartime mobilization of effort seems to have galvanized the profession to action that was directed toward reducing the cultural lag. The scientific ingredients of the new method were at hand, and the ideological emphasis on the corrective power of the tight-knit, intensively interacting community seems to be explainable in terms of a reaction against the anomic effects of modern society.

Social science and the therapeutic community

Social science has affected the development of therapeutic communities both indirectly, through the interest of innovating psychiatrists in social science concepts such as "culture" and "social structure," and directly, through the participation of social scientists in research on hospitals using this method of treatment.

The Rapoport study. Although there were several prior social science studies on mental hospitals of various kinds (see Belknap 1956; Dunham & Weinberg 1960; Rowland 1938; and Henry 1954 on the old-fashioned mental hospital; Stanton & Schwartz 1954 and Caudill 1958 on psychoanalytically oriented hospitals), the first social science study of a hospital styling itself a therapeutic community was the study by Robert N. Rapoport and his associates (1961) of the British unit under Maxwell Jones. The latter had advocated setting up such a unit, as a result of his wartime experiences with soldiers suffering from war neuroses and from the difficulties of returning to normal social life after such deprivations as prolonged prison camp internment. When the unit became established, it gained a wide reputation as the first fully developed therapeutic community.

In seeking to repeat their wartime successes with intensive resocialization methods, Jones and his staff developed a unit for the treatment of a variety of patients with problems of social maladjustment. They reported that their extension of the therapeutic community method was effective. Indeed, they advocated its application not only to the treatment of "psychopathic" personality disorders but also to the treatment of all sorts of behavioral adjustment problems, including those of imprisoned criminal offenders. Since the method was essentially one of harnessing the social processes of

institutional community life, the collaboration of a social scientist was sought.

Rapoport and his colleagues, following Caudill (1958) in viewing the hospital as a form of small society, observed that the culture of this society emphasized four principal themes—permissiveness, democratization, communalism, and rehabilitation (through reality confrontation). Analysis of the program of activities and prescriptions for social roles in relation to these themes led to certain conclusions of a structural–functional nature. For example, one structural recommendation focused on the importance of incorporating into the formal ideology a conceptual distinction between "treatment" (measures aimed at improving the organization of the individual personality structure) and "rehabilitation" (measures aimed at improving the individual's adjustment to his social role relationships). This distinction was shown to be important in avoiding certain potential conflicts between overt and covert role prescriptions, among ideological themes in their spheres of possible contradiction, and between intrahospital and external norms for social behavior.

One of Rapoport's functional recommendations was that treatment should concentrate on the hitherto relatively unrecognized process of "oscillations" in the state of over-all organization and functioning of the system. It was pointed out that all social systems are subject to variations in their state of organization and that systems with the properties of the unit are subject to particularly great swings in the state of "collective disturbance" —due to their permissiveness, the properties of their patients, and their emphasis on maximizing intercommunication. The tendency in the unit, as among practitioners generally, was to view these swings toward states of great collective disturbance with alarm and to attempt to avoid them wherever possible. However, Rapoport found evidence to support the view that the oscillatory process could be therapeutically very useful if appropriately harnessed. In the stage of social reorganization following the critical turning point of maximum disorganization, patients were observed to involve themselves more meaningfully in the constructive social processes and thereby to learn modes of social adaptation which could serve them in their subsequent relationships. The technique of managing these processes in the interests of therapy was shown to involve an interest in and alertness to their special properties; thus the Rapoport study recommended an avoidance of such pitfalls as "collusive anxiety" (premature intervention and imposition of authoritative staff social controls) and "collusive denial" (lack of recognition of the state of disorganization and consequently the failure to intervene at the social-psychologically critical point).

In addition, an analysis was made of the "careers" of a cohort of patients, and several conclusions were drawn, principal among which were the following. There was a relationship between the patient's acceptance of unit culture (as measured by change in profile scores on the ideological themes) and his perceived improvement in the unit (as measured by the patient, by the physician, and by the nursing staff); moreover, acceptance of unit cultural norms (and thus manifestation of clinical improvement) was far less likely to occur among patients who left the unit in less than six months than among those who stayed at least six months. The persistence of improvement in social functioning in the community for a year following discharge was more likely to be seen among certain types of "improved" patients than among others. Married patients did better than unmarried, and patients whose dominant personality defenses did not involve aggressive behavior did well in the permissive atmosphere of the unit. However, the fact that patients suffer setbacks in relationships outside the unit following discharge points up the importance of being alert to cultural discontinuities between treatment unit and community; in therapeutic communities the sense of contrast with the segregated mental hospitals may tend to obscure the contrast between such communities and their surrounding cultural context.

In conclusion, Rapoport and his colleagues listed 30 principles for the formation of therapeutic communities, attempting to formulate them in sufficiently flexible terms to make them adaptable to a wide range of therapeutic contexts (R. N. Rapoport et al. 1961).

Holistic and segmental studies. In considering the place of the Rapoport study of the therapeutic community among social science studies of the mental hospital generally, a useful distinction might be made between holistic studies and segmental studies. The study by Belknap (1956) and some other earlier studies of the state mental hospital, as well as Goffman's study (1961), may be thought of as cases at the custodial extreme of the continuum (described by Greenblatt et al. 1955) which ranges from custodial to therapeutic care; the Rapoport study is a holistic analysis of a case at the therapeutic extreme. Brown and Wing (1962) present a study of three hospitals representing three points along the continuum and provide further evidence to support the contention that changes in

the over-all organization of the hospital are reflected in changes in patients' behavior.

Segmental studies would be those which focus on part processes. Even the Stanton and Schwartz classic study, *The Mental Hospital* (1954), is essentially a collection of segmental analyses of part processes, most notable among which is the demonstration of a relationship between covert disagreement among staff members and clinical excitation of patients. Gilbert and Levinson (1956) are particularly concerned with the relationship between the espousal of a custodial ideology and certain personality types, notably the "authoritarian personality."

The other form of segmental research is seen in the replication studies, such as that of Carstairs and Heron (1957), who studied a British mental hospital, using the same measures as Gilbert and Levinson (1956) and their colleagues; they found that in Britain, as in the United States, higher-status staff members are more likely than lower-status members to have a low "custodial ideology" score. Working with a greater cultural contrast, Stein and Oetting (1964) found that the culturally prescribed role of the physician in Latin America countervails this tendency for liberalism to be easier for higher-status, relatively disengaged people. The role of the psychiatrist in Latin America is still oriented to the more authoritarian norms of physician conduct (reminiscent of the earlier period in Europe and the United States), and therefore their scores on the "custodial ideology" measures were less differentiated from their lower-echelon staff members than was found to be true in England and America.

Another type of segmental study involves focal concentration on *process.* Many of the processes indicated in the earlier holistic studies (e.g., Caudill's "linked open systems," or "transactions," Rapoport's "oscillations," and Stanton and Schwartz's "covert disagreements") have become the focuses for subsequent studies seeking to replicate, refute, or extend their relevance into other contexts. Some segmental process studies seek further development of these earlier insights, particularly of the dynamics of inducing changes in hospital structures. For example, a study by Isabel Menzies (1960) seeks to elucidate a specific type of psychological barrier to the accomplishment of social changes. She concentrates her attention on the deep intrapersonal functions served by the conventional role prescriptions, such as those of the nursing role, and the built-in resistances of participants in the change process that work against their conscious wishes for change and modernization. Agnew and Hsu

(1960–1961) approach the problem of understanding and overcoming resistances to change by using social structure as a point of departure; they suggest that the "democratization" theme of therapeutic communities may be most applicable to the phase of steady functioning following the institutionalization of the new system. In order to break through the rigidities of the older system, a measure of authoritative behavior may succeed where the democratic mode would be rejected.

Clinical applications.   Social science contributions of a more indirect kind can be seen in the clinical reports by psychiatrists on attempts to apply the therapeutic community idea to other contexts and in the course of so doing to evaluate and modify it to suit the circumstances (see Wilmer 1958; Scher 1958; Stainbrook 1955; Clark 1964). To some extent, the attention given to the therapeutic community idea in psychiatry has diminished as a consequence of the great development and immediate successes of new pharmacological treatments, even while the former was gaining general, if ancillary, acceptance. However, there is some reason to believe that interest in the therapeutic community dimensions of treatment will once again receive prominence as research reveals the limitations of a simplistic pharmacological approach (Klerman 1960).

Lessons of the therapeutic community

There are several ways in which the development of the therapeutic community emphasis in psychiatry may be seen as relevant to social science. Milieu therapists have provided opportunities for social scientists to observe the intimacies of an important form of institutional life that might otherwise have been inaccessible. Thus, the field of hospital studies and the entire field of comparative institutions have been enriched. Furthermore, the therapeutic community investigations have contributed to the already active trends in social science toward interdisciplinary collaboration. Epitomized in the work of Stanton and Schwartz (with their demonstration of the connection between structured conflict in the environment and emotional upset in the individual) and of Caudill (with his conception of "linked open systems"), research in the milieu therapy-oriented hospital demands interdisciplinary approaches.

The subsequent work by Robert N. Rapoport and his colleagues (1961) in the more labile environment of an innovating, experimental therapeutic community provided opportunities to examine unusually fluid social systems. This research has fed into the general trend toward developing more pro-

cessual modes of social science analysis and thus has become associated with numerous other approaches, such as general systems theories and the crisis theories. The experimental therapeutic communities were useful for such analyses because of their positive orientation toward flexibility and change and their relatively unstable functioning due to their tendency to de-emphasize authority hierarchies, to permit disruptive behavior by patients, and to encourage expressive communication. The resulting phenomenon, described in the mental hospital literature as "collective upsets," tends to be particularly notable in the therapeutic community. The "oscillatory tendency," as Rapoport termed it, was observed to have a discernible periodicity, to be affected by specific organizational events, and thus to have properties in common with other systems, as described, for example, in cybernetics.

The oscillatory process was also observed to engender therapeutic potentials if properly harnessed, particularly in its phase of social reorganization. This interest in harnessing the energies that become available at critical turning points is shared by those social scientists who have been studying the process of critical role transitions (Rhona Rapoport 1963). The importance of ritual at times of transition in primitive societies has long been recognized by sociologists and anthropologists, notably Arnold van Gennep. In the more complex situations of modern secular society, the mechanisms used to cope with these status transitions are of a more deliberate, rational kind, aiming at adaptation to changing situations as well as accommodating existing needs and expectations. The processes of oscillation within a complex organizational framework can, in this sense, be seen as resembling the pattern of alternation between periods of stable functioning and critical transition followed by reorganization that characterizes the life cycle.

From the viewpoint of the more analytic or fragmentary approaches, the quasi-experimental situation represented by the therapeutic community approach, particularly in its innovating stages, has been an attraction that has only begun to yield the kinds of results of which it is potentially capable.

Contemporary issues

As the therapeutic community concept has gained wider acceptance, the range of issues confronting social scientists in relation to research in this field has changed somewhat. There is still much to be desired by way of sheer evaluation of the effectiveness of the method; however, the types of research concern seem to be shifting. Rather than asking what the therapeutic community is and how well it works, the questions are being posed more in terms of what aspects of the approach are most relevant for what types of persons under what conditions, including conditions of concurrent use of other forms of therapy.

Furthermore, the possibility of the initial efficacy of the method as a novelty stimulus—akin to the medical "placebo effect" or the "Hawthorne effect" as recognized in industrial research—has relevance not only for evaluation of the method but also for the type of interest which it has for social scientists. Many of the early social scientists were interested in it as an innovating experiment with some of the characteristics of a utopian reformist movement. However, as the method has gained acceptance and has become to some extent routinized within the psychiatric profession, its appeal for social scientists has changed. The emphasis has shifted, to some extent, from the more macrosociological or holistic, anthropological type of approach to the more structured, quasi-experimental approaches that are more characteristic of the social psychologist. However, the holistic researcher still has scope for analyzing the range of problems associated with application of the concept in different subcultural and structural situations—in large state mental hospitals, prisons, delinquent groups, depressed slum neighborhoods, schools, and industrial work groups. The concept can also be applied to different national and cultural settings, and to functional processes related to the persistence of innovations.

In the context of these new and contrasting over-all situations, analyses will be fruitful on both the holistic level and on the level of part processes. Such issues as optimal size of the hospital unit, degree of social differentiation, type of authority structure, degree of interlinkage of subsystems, and flexibility versus fixity of value hierarchy can be tested in various contexts in relation to therapeutic effectiveness. The issues involved in doing systematic evaluative research in this field have hardly been broached and present a major challenge. On the side of implications for social theory, one can only note a great hiatus in work already done. Goffman's linking of the old-fashioned mental hospital to the larger class of "total institutions" (1961) is the most creative effort available in the hospital research field, but it relates not to therapeutic communities but, rather, to the polarity against which they are reactions.

Therapeutic communities of the future will probably turn out to be far more differentiated and can therefore be expected to provide materials for understanding many kinds of dynamic processes. It would seem that their contribution to social science might be expected to lie in two spheres: first, the reciprocal relationship between personality and social structure, and second, the relationship between stability and structure on the one hand, and fluidity and change on the other, in the functioning of institutions designed to "process" a continuous flow of people while the organization maintains continuity and reliable functioning. These are challenges faced by social scientists in increasingly numerous fields of investigation, and the degree to which the therapeutic community will be a fruitful arena for investigation of these issues will depend on a complex of many factors other than the intrinsic interest which it presents.

ROBERT N. RAPOPORT

BIBLIOGRAPHY

AGNEW, PAUL C.; and HSU, FRANCIS L. K. 1960–1961 Introducing Change in a Mental Hospital. *Human Organization* 19:195–198.

AICHHORN, AUGUST (1925) 1935 *Wayward Youth.* New York: Viking. → First published as *Verwahrloste Jugend.*

ARTISS, KENNETH 1962 *Milieu Therapy in Schizophrenia.* New York: Grune & Stratton.

BELKNAP, IVAN 1956 *Human Problems of a State Mental Hospital.* New York: McGraw-Hill.

BETTELHEIM, BRUNO 1950 *Love Is Not Enough: The Treatment of Emotionally Disturbed Children.* Glencoe, Ill.: Free Press.

BIERER, JOSHUA 1960 Past, Present and Future. *International Journal of Social Psychiatry* 6, no. 1/2:165–173.

BION, WILFRED 1961 *Experiences in Groups, and Other Papers.* New York: Basic Books.

BROWN, ESTHER L. 1961–1964 *Newer Dimensions of Patient Care.* 3 vols. New York: Russell Sage Foundation. → Volume 1: *The Use of the Physical and Social Environment of the General Hospital for Therapeutic Purposes.* Volume 2: *Improving Staff Motivation and Competence in the General Hospital.* Volume 3: *Patients as People.*

BROWN, G. W.; and WING, J. K. 1962 A Comparative Clinical and Social Survey of Three Mental Hospitals. Pages 145–168 in Paul Halmos (editor), *Sociology and Medicine.* Sociological Review Monograph No. 5. Univ. of Keele (England).

CARSTAIRS, G. M.; and HERON, ALASTAIR 1957 The Social Environment of Mental Patients: A Measure of Staff Attitudes. Pages 218–230 in Milton Greenblatt et al. (editors), *The Patient and the Mental Hospital.* Glencoe, Ill.: Free Press.

CAUDILL, WILLIAM 1958 *The Psychiatric Hospital as a Small Society.* Cambridge, Mass.: Harvard Univ. Press.

CLARK, DAVID 1964 *Administrative Therapy: The Role of the Doctor in the Therapeutic Community.* London: Tavistock.

CONFERENCE ON COMMUNITY MENTAL HEALTH RESEARCH, THIRD, WASHINGTON UNIVERSITY, ST. LOUIS, *1961* 1964 *The Psychiatric Hospital as a Social System: Proceedings.* Edited by Albert F. Wessen. Springfield, Ill.: Thomas.

DREIKURS, RUDOLF 1955 Group Psychotherapy and the Third Revolution in Psychiatry. *International Journal of Social Psychiatry* 1, no. 3:23–32.

DUNHAM, H. WARREN; and WEINBERG, S. KIRSON 1960 *The Culture of the State Mental Hospital.* Detroit, Mich.: Wayne State Univ. Press.

GILBERT, DORIS; and LEVINSON, DANIEL 1956 Ideology, Personality and Institutional Policy in the Mental Hospital. *Journal of Abnormal and Social Psychology* 53:263–271.

GOFFMAN, ERVING (1961) 1962 *Asylums: Essays on the Social Situation of Mental Patients and Other Inmates.* Chicago: Aldine.

GREENBLATT, MILTON; LEVINSON, DANIEL; and WILLIAMS, RICHARD (editors) 1957 *The Patient and the Mental Hospital: Contributions of Research in the Science of Social Behavior.* Glencoe, Ill.: Free Press.

GREENBLATT, MILTON; YORK, RICHARD H.; and BROWN, ESTHER L. 1955 *From Custodial to Therapeutic Patient Care in Mental Hospitals.* New York: Russell Sage Foundation.

HAMBURG, DAVID A. 1958 Therapeutic Hospital Environments: Experience in a General Hospital and Problems for Research. Pages 479–491 in *Symposium on Preventive and Social Psychiatry, Walter Reed Army Institute of Research, April 1957.* Washington: Government Printing Office.

HENRY, JULES 1954 The Formal Social Structure of a Psychiatric Hospital. *Psychiatry* 17:139–151.

JONES, MAXWELL (1952) 1953 *The Therapeutic Community: A New Treatment Method in Psychiatry.* New York: Basic Books. → First published as *Social Psychiatry: A Study of Therapeutic Communities.*

JONES, MAXWELL; and RAPOPORT, ROBERT N. 1955 Administrative and Social Psychiatry. *Lancet* [1955], no. 2:386–388.

KLERMAN, GERALD L. 1960 Staff Attitudes, Decision-making, and the Use of Drug Therapy in the Mental Hospital. Pages 191–214 in Research Conference on the Therapeutic Community, Manhattan State Hospital, Ward's Island, N.Y., 1959, *Proceedings of the Conference.* Edited by Herman Denber. Springfield, Ill.: Thomas. → Includes 2 pages of discussion.

LEVINSON, DANIEL; and GALLAGHER, EUGENE 1964 *Patienthood in a Psychiatric Hospital: An Analysis of Role, Personality, and Social Structure.* Boston: Houghton Mifflin.

MAIN, T. F. 1946 The Hospital as a Therapeutic Institution. Menninger Clinic, *Bulletin* 10:66–70.

MENZIES, ISABEL 1960 A Case-study in the Functioning of Social Systems as a Defense Against Anxiety. *Human Relations* 13:95–122.

MORENO, JACOB L. (1934) 1953 *Who Shall Survive? Foundations of Sociometry, Group Psychotherapy and Sociodrama.* Rev. & enl. ed. Beacon, N.Y.: Beacon House.

MYERSON, ABRAHAM 1939 Theory and Principles of the "Total Push" Method in the Treatment of Chronic Schizophrenia. *American Journal of Psychiatry* 95:1197–1204.

RAPOPORT, RHONA 1963 Normal Crises, Family Structure and Mental Health. *Family Process* 2:68–80.

RAPOPORT, ROBERT N. et al. 1961 *Community as Doctor: New Perspectives on a Therapeutic Community.* Springfield, Ill.: Thomas.

RAPOPORT, ROBERT N.; and RAPOPORT, RHONA 1957 Democratization and Authority in a Therapeutic Community. *Behavioral Science* 2:128–133.

RAPOPORT, ROBERT N.; and RAPOPORT, RHONA 1959 Permissiveness and Treatment in a Therapeutic Community. *Psychiatry* 22:57–64.

REDL, FRITZ; and WINEMAN, DAVID (1951) 1964 *Children Who Hate.* New York: Free Press.

REDL, FRITZ; and WINEMAN, DAVID 1952 *Controls From Within.* Glencoe, Ill.: Free Press.

RESEARCH CONFERENCE ON THERAPEUTIC COMMUNITY, MANHATTAN STATE HOSPITAL, WARD'S ISLAND, N.Y., 1959 1960 *Proceedings of the Conference.* Edited by Herman Denber. Springfield, Ill.: Thomas.

RIOCH, DAVID; and STANTON, ALFRED 1959 Milieu Therapy. *Psychiatry* 22:65–72.

ROWLAND, HOWARD 1938 Interaction Processes in the State Mental Hospital. *Psychiatry* 1:323–337.

SCHER, JORDAN M. 1958 The Structured Ward: Research Method and Hypothesis in a Total Treatment Setting for Schizophrenia. *American Journal of Orthopsychiatry* 28:291–299.

SCHWARTZ, MORRIS S. et al. 1964 *Social Approaches to Mental Patient Care.* New York: Columbia Univ. Press.

SIMMEL, ERNST 1929 Psycho-analytic Treatment in a Sanatorium. *International Journal of Psycho-analysis* 10:70–89.

SIVADON, PAUL 1958 Technics of Sociotherapy. Pages 457–464 in *Symposium on Preventive and Social Psychiatry, Walter Reed Army Institute of Research, April 1957.* Washington: Government Printing Office.

STAINBROOK, EDWARD 1955 The Hospital as a Therapeutic Community. *Neuropsychiatry* 3:69–87.

STANTON, ALFRED H.; and SCHWARTZ, MORRIS S. 1954 *The Mental Hospital: A Study of Institutional Participation in Psychiatric Illness and Treatment.* New York: Basic Books.

STEIN, WILLIAM; and OETTING, E. R. 1964 Humanism and Custodialism in a Peruvian Mental Hospital. *Human Organization* 23:278–282.

SULLIVAN, HARRY STACK 1953 *The Interpersonal Theory of Psychiatry.* Edited by Helen Swick Perry and Mary Ladd Gawel. New York: Norton.

WILMER, HARRY A. 1958 *Social Psychiatry in Action: A Therapeutic Community.* Springfield, Ill.: Thomas.

WORLD HEALTH ORGANIZATION, EXPERT COMMITTEE ON MENTAL HEALTH 1953 *Report, Third.* Technical Report Series, No. 73. Geneva: World Health Organization.

MENTAL HEALTH

I. THE CONCEPT — *Morris S. Schwartz and Charlotte Green Schwartz*

II. SOCIAL CLASS AND PERSONAL ADJUSTMENT — *William H. Sewell*

I
THE CONCEPT

The meaning of the term "mental health" is ambiguous; not only is it difficult to agree on its general application, but even in a single context it may be used in many different ways. This lack of agreement will probably continue because the term has been adopted for a variety of purposes. One conclusion, however, can be reached: "mental health" is not a precise term but an intuitively apprehended idea that is striving for scientific status while also serving as an ideological label.

Problems of definition

The word "mental" usually implies something more than the purely cerebral functioning of a person; it also stands for his emotional–affective states, the relationships he establishes with others, and a quite general quality that might be called his equilibrium in his sociocultural context. Similarly, "health" refers to more than physical health: it also connotes the individual's intrapsychic balance, the fit of his psychic structure with the external environment, and his social functioning. It is not surprising that the combination of two such terms produces an elastic and ambiguous concept. Another ambiguity attends this phrase. In common usage "mental health" often means both psychological well-being *and* mental illness.

Definitions obviously vary with the perspective of the definers, the point of reference used, and the values considered important. Thus, the *psychoanalytic* perspective focuses on the intrapsychic life of the individual. Freud defined mental health in his programmatic statement: "Where id was, there shall ego be" (1932, p. 112). Here the value is awareness of unconscious motivations and self-control based upon these insights. The *interpersonal* frame of reference, on the other hand, is more concerned with the functioning of individuals in interpersonal situations. Sullivan identifies a person's drive toward mental health as those "processes which tend to improve his efficiency as a human being, his satisfactions, and his success in living" (1954, p. 106) and places major value on effective and efficient social functioning. The *social relatedness* perspective is exemplified by Fromm, who focuses on the individual's relationship with the larger social environment.

The mentally healthy person is the productive and unalienated person; the person who relates himself to the world lovingly, and who uses his reason to grasp reality objectively; who experiences himself as a unique individual entity, and at the same time feels one with his fellow man; who is not subject to irrational authority, and accepts willingly the rational authority of conscience and reason; who is in the process of being born as long as he is alive, and considers the gift of life the most precious chance he has. ([1955] 1959, p. 275)

Here the values are humanism, individualism, freedom, and rationality.

The most comprehensive and definitive summary of the multiplicity of criteria used in defin-

ing mental health is that of Jahoda (1958). She rules out certain criteria as unsuitable because they are unsatisfactory for research purposes. "Absence of disease," for instance, is rejected as a criterion, not only because of the difficulty in circumscribing disease but also because common usage of the term "mental health" now includes something more than the mere absence of a negative value. "Statistical normality" is also considered unsuitable on the grounds that the term is unspecific, bare of content, and fails to come to grips with the question. Finally, "happiness" and "well-being" are ruled out because they involve external circumstances as well as individual functioning.

Jahoda then summarizes what are to her the acceptable sets of criteria in current use. These are *attitudes toward the self*, which include accessibility of the self to consciousness, correctness of the self concept, feelings about the self concept (self-acceptance), and a sense of identity; *growth, development, and self-actualization*, which include conceptions of self, motivational processes, and investment in living; *integration*, which refers to the balance of psychic forces in the individual, a unifying outlook on life, and resistance to stress; *autonomy*, which refers to the decision-making process, regulation from within, and independent action; *undistorted perception of reality*, including empathy or social sensitivity; *environmental mastery*, including the ability to love, adequacy in interpersonal relations, efficiency in meeting situation requirements, capacity for adaptation and adjustment, efficiency in problem solving, and adequacy in love, work, and play.

Since Jahoda's statement is a summary and not an attempt to integrate the criteria currently used in defining or identifying mental health, various difficulties (many recognized and discussed by her) attend her presentation. The criteria are overlapping, and the relationship between criteria is not spelled out (for example, the degree to which they are independent). Moreover, no method is indicated for identifying satisfactory indexes for the criteria, thus making it impossible to measure the degree of a particular criterion or even to discover its presence or absence. Ambiguities and different levels of specificity characterize the different criteria, and the impact of the social situation and the relevance of the society as context criterion are largely ignored.

Jahoda does not attempt a solution for these difficulties. She simply recognizes the impossibility of arriving at *a* "correct" definition and of attaining a consensus, because values underlie the definitions proposed and because the concept is used for different purposes. Jahoda's analysis of mental health as a concept deals mainly with the problems it poses for the empirical researcher: whether—and if so, how far—the various criteria can be integrated into one criterion or a set of criteria; the kinds of criteria that are required by different definitions; whether and how one might distinguish between "optimal" and "maximal" mental health; and operationalizing the definitions used. She deals minimally with the approach that the student of society would take: the meaning of this concept in society, its various functions, the ways in which it constitutes and expresses societal values, and the nature of the kinds of social environments that influence a person's psychological well-being. Nevertheless, her work represents the best summary of the current major definitions and the controversy connected with them.

Aspects of the mental health controversy

Discussions of the concept of mental health naturally reflect the interests of the principal groups involved in the mental health movement. One of the leading issues is whether "mental health" and "mental illness" should be conceptualized on the same continuum or on different continua that cut across each other. The conventional medical view holds that mental health is the absence of mental illness, that both terms represent the extreme ends of the same continuum, and that the difference between the two states is one of degree. A contrary view is that mental health is qualitatively different from mental illness and that a person can be both mentally healthy and mentally ill at the same time. Jahoda, as an advocate of the concept of "positive mental health," maintains that the absence of certain qualities does not imply the presence of others. For example, the absence of hallucinations does not imply the presence of accurate self-appraisal; conversely, the presence of creativity does not exclude the presence of severe anxiety. But if mental health and mental illness are placed on different continua, then it becomes necessary to specify their relationship. For this reason, Conrad (1952) has suggested that "negative health," or the absence of pathology, be used as an interstitial term.

A related issue is whether mental health is to be seen as a relatively constant and enduring function of personality or as a momentary function of person and situation. For instance, Klein (1960) distinguishes "soundness" from "well-being": the former refers to the level of integration of the general, more enduring personality structure, and the latter to the individual's current state of equilibrium. This distinction may be a useful way of identifying two different kinds of mental health.

There also are differences of opinion on whether the concept of mental health is ever value-free. Some authors—medically oriented professionals—view psychological health as analogous to physical health, which, they maintain, can be evaluated by objective medical standards, without regard to the patient's sociocultural context. Another view maintaining that mental health is a value-free concept equates it with the statistically normal: mentally healthy behavior is that which is considered average or conventional behavior for a particular population. Here, good mental health is evaluated in terms of adjustment to and acceptance of current societal norms. Clearly, these criteria are not value-free. Indeed, many students of the field maintain that criteria of mental health cannot be established in complete independence from the particular values and ideology of the society or group in which they are formulated and applied. According to this view, the study of definitions of mental health becomes a branch of the sociology of knowledge. But such an approach, although sociologically meaningful, cannot settle the question of which criteria are the most useful for therapy and mental health research.

Some of those who maintain that all definitions of mental health are culture-bound hold that multiple criteria should be used, depending upon the values cherished by each society or subculture. Thus, criteria for mental health in the lower classes may have to be different from those for the middle classes, and those for citizens of Japan would have to differ from those for India or the United States. The issue here is that of the relation of the mental health of a person to the nature of the society in which he lives. Although this issue is rarely discussed, its clarification and resolution are critical in identifying the field of interrelated variables that are relevant to the study of mental health. What is needed is nothing less than a complete theory of the relation between the individual and society.

Other students of the field hold that the criteria for mental health, though value-laden, can transcend situational or cultural boundaries and that an area of general value consensus can be arrived at. For example, M. B. Smith has suggested that universal criteria for mental health might be "identified with the stability, resilience, and viability—in a word the system properties—of these external and internal subsystems of personality" (1959, pp. 680–681). Similarly, Fromm (1955) insists that criteria for mental health must be based on some concept of a universal human nature rather than on the values of particular cultures or societies.

In summary, mental health can be viewed either as an ideal-type concept or as an empirical construct referring to a state that actually occurs. In the former view, mental health is an ideal to be striven for but never fully attained; it serves, however, as a standard against which to measure any particular individual. In the latter view, mental health is realistically attainable, though there is much dispute about the frequency with which it is encountered.

Mental health as a movement and a profession

The emergence of the concept of mental health is closely related to the growth of the mental hygiene movement in the United States and to the development of psychotherapeutic practice and personality research. As an explanatory construct, "mental health" emerged out of the concern with "mental hygiene" that gained its first adherents at the beginning of the twentieth century. Originally, this social movement focused on improving the wretched conditions in mental hospitals and providing better care and treatment for the mentally ill wherever they might be. In the 1920s interest shifted to promoting "mental hygiene" and establishing child-guidance clinics. The term "mental health" began to replace "mental hygiene" in the 1930s, and by the late 1940s it assumed an independent status with a growing and enthusiastic social movement operating in its name. This shift in terms signified the beginning of the era of concern with the prevention of mental disorders rather than merely care and treatment and the broadening of focus to include all forms of social and psychological maladjustment rather than just the severely emotionally disturbed or psychotic. The movement began to promote "positive" mental health as a goal distinct from the elimination of mental illness.

The popularity of mental health as a desired value in the United States is in part related to its advocacy by those in the mental health movement and in part to the growth of psychoanalytic theory and acceptance of psychotherapeutic practice in the past several decades. The orthodox psychoanalytic viewpoint that mental health is a property of individuals and a function of intrapsychic development and dynamics is still dominant. It maintains that an individual acquires good mental health as a consequence of fortunate early socialization; psychoanalysis or some other form of psychotherapy is a corrective for unfortunate early development. Thus, the individual remains the unit of analysis, and psychological health is seen as a function of the individual's unique, private intrapsychic development and life history. Subsequently, the unit of analysis was extended to include the patterning of an individual's interpersonal relations. Recently, another view of mental health was put forward by the proponents of social psychiatry [see PSYCHIATRY, *article on* SOCIAL PSYCHIATRY]. Only a few authors, such as Fromm (1955) and Frank (1948), take a comprehensive view of mental health as a function of the total society—its dominant ideologies, assumptions, norms, values, institutions, and general style of life. Such a perspective is largely ignored or considered irrelevant by the great majority of ideologists, practitioners, and researchers in the field of mental health.

Ideologists, practitioners, researchers. Action in the name of mental health has occasioned the development of three distinct groups whose membership may overlap but whose interests and functions are separable: they can be called the ideologists, the practitioners, and the researchers. The ideologists are primarily interested in promoting psychological well-being as a value and in encouraging action to prevent and eliminate mental illness. Well-developed mental health organizations, both private and public, now exist in the United States at the national, state, and local levels. In 1960 the National Association for Mental Health reported that, in addition to the state mental health associations, there were some eight hundred affiliated local mental health associations in 42 states, with a total registered membership and volunteer participation exceeding one million persons (Ridenour 1963). In addition, a network of federal governmental agencies, led by the National Institute of Mental Health (NIMH), spent a vast sum for research, training, education, demonstration, and the building and development of treatment facilities (during the fiscal year 1964/1965 the NIMH alone spent over $200 million). The NIMH also maintains links with the privately sponsored branches of the mental health movement. In addition to the federal government, each state and many cities and counties have a department of mental health or a mental health officer. Private and governmental agencies often join with practitioners to educate the public about mental illness and health, to urge persons to become concerned about their own and others' psychological health, and to collect funds for research.

The importance of the mental health movement has enhanced the prestige and power of its practitioners, who range from psychoanalysts to marriage counselors. They have gradually widened their sphere of operation and now function in institutions such as schools, courts, and industry. Although many of their activities are undertaken in the name of mental health, little work is directed toward mental health as distinct from mental illness. Primarily, their concern is treatment; secondarily, it is research; it is only minimally prevention.

The interests of researchers in mental health span the entire range of human behavior from circumscribed biochemical problems to existential problems of living. Despite the increasing number of research projects over the past decade, etiological problems remain unsolved and the field awaits conceptual clarification.

Mental health and American values

The mental health concept is related to current and traditional American values in three ways. First, it reflects and embodies many of these values; second, it functions to preserve certain of them; finally, it is a highly valued end in itself. In fact, mental health has become so esteemed that in some circles it has taken on the characteristics of a secular religion. In the twentieth century, human health is prized as it has been in no other. In the United States, in particular, we have moved from valuing sheer physical health to cherishing the psychological well-being of the total person. In pursuing these goals, we have relied on medicine, psychology, and social science to produce more valid knowledge and techniques with which to serve this value. Science and medicine, in turn, are values that are used to promote psychological health as a social and ethical goal. Thus, the importance of health, the faith in science and medicine, the reliance on technology to produce means for the ends declared desirable by experts, and the development of professional skill and specialization as attributes of the technology all combine to maintain and reinforce mental health as a value.

The high degree of acceptance of this value also seems related to its congruence with the Protestant ethic. Kingsley Davis (1938) has suggested that the mental health movement took over the Protestant ethic as a system of conscious preachment and unconscious premises and that it bases itself upon much the same values. But we suggest that the movement has done more than take over the Protestant ethic—it has dressed it up in a modern scientific cloak. Thus it serves as a new ideology that

recommends, in nonreligious, quasi-scientific terms, a way of dealing with personal troubles and anxieties without the necessity for becoming involved in broader social issues or societal reconstruction. In any case, its popularity among middle-class, college-educated Americans cannot be denied.

For some ideologists of the movement, "mental health" has become a mystique and a secular religion. Dicks, for example, proposes that it be conceived of as a new value in our world that is "comparable to the notions of 'finding God,' 'salvation,' 'perfection' or 'progress' which have inspired various eras of our history, as master-values which at the same time implied a way of life. . . . Some of the attributes of a secular priesthood or *therapeutae* are attached to us, and it is questionable whether we ought to divest ourselves of them even if the community would let us" (1950, pp. 3–4). Thus, for the mental health enthusiast, "mental health" becomes *the* standard for evaluating human behavior. Further, the mental health idea implies a new conception of moral and social progress in the form of self-correctability, self-perfectibility, inner growth, personal fulfillment, and inward and outward harmony, or the like. We are told that in the same way that we have achieved physical comfort—through the instrumental application of knowledge and understanding—we can achieve psychological mastery over the self. This idea of progress embodies a new conception of success. No longer is it sufficient to measure achievement in tangible coin; we are persuaded to evaluate ourselves in terms of self-development and maturity. But there are no clear guidelines as to the means of reaching this goal or even to knowing that one has reached it.

Orientations toward mental health.   Orientations toward mental health as a desirable objective, as a subject matter, and as a field of work, knowledge, and inquiry oscillate between two poles. On the one hand, mental health is seen as a restricted and circumscribed "state of being" and as the subject matter of a field of work that is a specialty among other specialties. The individual or his immediate social environment is the unit for analysis, attempted control, and change. On the other hand, mental health is seen as the sum total of the individual personality, and the field of work associated with it is a superordinate, all-inclusive science of man.

In the more restricted orientation, the acquisition of mental health is viewed as a technical problem that is to be solved under the direction and leadership of experts. Mental health technology is seen as being contained in and developed and transmitted by practitioners who claim special skills and expertise and who are legitimated by the society as the vehicle for the ethical application of knowledge about mental health. Operational techniques and procedures are established, and frames of reference and explanatory theories are developed and fiercely adhered to. In general this orientation stresses the separateness of persons and encourages them to seek inner tranquility and self-actualization on a private basis; psychological well-being is seen as a function of personality dynamics, which, in turn, are supposed to be primarily a function of early experience and only secondarily of later interpersonal relations. [*For an approach that stresses primarily social factors, see* PSYCHIATRY, *article on* SOCIAL PSYCHIATRY.]

By contrast, those who take an all-encompassing view of mental health phenomena claim as their province the entire range of human thought and behavior; they believe that the human panorama is to be interpreted within the mental health framework rather than vice versa.

These contrasting orientations have different advantages and disadvantages in achieving mental health objectives. The psychotherapeutic orientation is far more specific about the nature of the phenomena to be affected, be they biochemical, individual, or social; it therefore affords greater opportunity for intervention and control. However, by restricting the variables to be dealt with, it may neglect significant and, perhaps, crucial phenomena. By contrast, the broader orientation opens up greater possibilities of discovering the various interconnections between the variables involved. However, its very diffuseness and scope make it a poor guide for scientific research or social action.

The functions of mental health ideology. The mental health ideology and movement function, in general, whether deliberately or inadvertently, to preserve and enhance certain values in American society. Outstanding among these is the humanistic value that emphasizes the importance of the individual as well as his development and fulfillment. Thus, the mental health movement contributes to and reinforces certain aspects of American democratic ideals and also promotes a form of "inwardness" by emphasizing introspection and self-awareness. By focusing on changing the individual rather than the society, the mental health movement directs effort away from social reconstruction and thereby functions to preserve the *status quo* and those middle-class values that are an intrinsic part of it. This is not to deny that some practitioners use the mental health idea as a vehicle for achieving social reform; but they are interested only in specific social changes which they hope to effect in the name of mental health, such as changes in child-rearing practices in the family or in the ways in which students are handled in public school.

For the ideologists, the conception provides a *Weltanschauung* of self-betterment to which they can devote themselves at a time when sociopolitical ideologies are unfashionable in the United States. Thus mental health is put forward as the panacea for all social problems and for the wholesale improvement of mankind. For the practitioner, on the other hand, the concept of mental health usually serves as a goal—albeit an ambiguous one—against which he can measure the current functioning of his patients and toward which he can direct his and their efforts; it is an implicit or explicit standard against which he measures the success and failure of his efforts and those of his colleagues.

Problems for the future

Despite the expansion of the mental health movement and the prestige of the professionals involved with it, little is known about how to achieve mental health. Moreover, the mechanisms for applying this meager knowledge and effecting the ends sought are extremely inadequate. Of the many issues that need resolution, three are central. The first is the necessity for conceptual extension beyond the individual intrapsychic life, interpersonal relations, and limited social contexts. For no matter how sophisticated, discerning, or scientific is our understanding of human beings as individuals, this framework is insufficient for understanding mental health, which also needs to be seen as a function of social roles, institutions, and communities. The second problem concerns this very scope of the mental health conception, which, because it involves a number of aspects of human living, demands an integration of the biochemical, psychological, social, and philosophical disciplines that is not yet in sight. The third problem involves the difficulties in intervention, implementation, and control that would remain even if conceptual expansion and the integration of relevant disciplines were achieved. Even if mental health can be achieved by rational planning, how much planning of this kind is desirable? Would it not threaten other cherished values, or have consequences that we cannot now foresee? From one perspective, the problem of mental health is identical with the eternal question of how to lead the good life. Perhaps this is not subject matter for academic disciplines, whether they be expanded or integrated, but rather an emergent from the human condition, in its infinite complexity, only a part of which can be planned for. Perhaps we need to raise the issue of how much mental health can be achieved by science and planning. It may be that the ultimate goal of positive mental health for all will continue to elude us as one of our persistent human limitations.

MORRIS S. SCHWARTZ AND
CHARLOTTE GREEN SCHWARTZ

[Directly related are the entries on HEALTH; ILLNESS; LIFE CYCLE; MENTAL DISORDERS, TREATMENT OF, article on THE THERAPEUTIC COMMUNITY; PSYCHIATRY, article on SOCIAL PSYCHIATRY; PSYCHOANALYSIS. Other material relevant to the concept of mental health may be found in MENTAL DISORDERS; and in the biographies of FREUD; RANK; REICH; SULLIVAN.]

BIBLIOGRAPHY

CAPLAN, GERALD 1964 Principles of Preventive Psychiatry. New York: Basic Books.

CLAUSEN, JOHN A. 1956 Sociology and the Field of Mental Health. New York: Russell Sage Foundation.

CONRAD, DOROTHY C. 1952 Toward a More Productive Concept of Mental Health. Mental Hygiene 36:456–473.

DAVIS, KINGSLEY 1938 Mental Hygiene and the Class Structure. Psychiatry 1:55–65.

DICKS, HENRY V. 1950 In Search of Our Proper Ethic. British Journal of Medical Psychology 23:1–14.

EATON, JOSEPH W. 1951 The Assessment of Mental Health. American Journal of Psychiatry 108:81–90.

Educational Practices. 1960 Pages 111–170 in Pennsylvania Mental Health, Incorporated, Mental Health Education: A Critique. Philadelphia: The Corporation.

FELIX, ROBERT H. 1957 Evolution of Community Mental Health Concepts. American Journal of Psychiatry 113:673–679.

FRANK, LAWRENCE K. 1948 Society as the Patient: Essays on Culture and Personality. New Brunswick, N.J.: Rutgers Univ. Press.

FRANK, LAWRENCE K. 1953 The Promotion of Mental Health. American Academy of Political and Social Science, Annals 286:167–174.

FREUD, SIGMUND (1932) 1965 New Introductory Lectures on Psycho-analysis. New York: Norton. → First published as Neue Folge der Vorlesungen zur Einführung in die Psychoanalyse.

FROMM, ERICH 1947 Man for Himself: An Inquiry Into the Psychology of Ethics. New York: Holt.

FROMM, ERICH (1955) 1959 The Sane Society. New York: Holt.

GINSBURG, SOL W. 1955 The Mental Health Movement: Its Theoretical Assumptions. Pages 1–29 in Ruth Kotinsky and Helen Witmer (editors), Community Programs for Mental Health: Theory–Practice Evaluation. Cambridge, Mass.: Harvard Univ. Press.

GURSSLIN, O. R.; HUNT, R. G.; and ROACH, J. L. 1959–1960 Social Class and the Mental Health Movement. Social Problems 7:210–218.

HARTMANN, HEINZ 1939 Psychoanalysis and the Concept of Health. International Journal of Psycho-analysis 20:308–321.

JAHODA, MARIE 1955 Toward a Social Psychology of Mental Health. Pages 296–322 in Ruth Kotinsky and Helen Witmer (editors), Community Programs for Mental Health: Theory–Practice Evaluation. Cambridge, Mass.: Harvard Univ. Press.

JAHODA, MARIE 1958 Current Concepts of Positive Mental Health. Joint Commission on Mental Illness and Health, Monograph Series, No. 1. New York: Basic Books.

JAHODA, MARIE 1963 Mental Health. Volume 3, pages 1067–1079 in Encyclopedia of Mental Health. New York: Watts.

KLEIN, DONALD C. 1960 Some Concepts Concerning the Mental Health of the Individual. Journal of Consulting Psychology 24:288–293.

LEUBA, CLARENCE 1960 The Mental Health Concept. American Psychologist 15:554–555.

LEWIS, AUBREY 1953 Health as a Social Concept. British Journal of Sociology 4:109–124.

MASLOW, ABRAHAM H. 1962 Toward a Psychology of Being. Princeton, N.J.: Van Nostrand.

THE MIDTOWN MANHATTAN STUDY 1962 Mental Health in the Metropolis: The Midtown Manhattan Study, by Leo Srole et al. Vol. 1. New York: McGraw-Hill.

NUNNALLY, JUM C. JR. 1961 Popular Conceptions of Mental Health: Their Development and Change. New York: Holt.

OFFER, DANIEL; and SABSHIN, MELVIN 1966 Normality: Theoretical and Clinical Concepts of Mental Health. New York: Basic Books.

OPLER, MARVIN K. (editor) 1959 Culture and Mental Health: Cross-cultural Studies. New York: Macmillan.

REDLICH, F. C. 1952 The Concept of Normality. American Journal of Psychotherapy 6:551–569.

RIDENOUR, NINA 1963 The Mental Health Movement. Volume 3, pages 1091–1102 in Encyclopedia of Mental Health. New York: Watts.

RÜMKE, H. C. 1955 Solved and Unsolved Problems in Mental Health. Mental Hygiene 39:178–195.

SCOTT, WILLIAM A. 1958 Research Definitions of Mental Health and Mental Illness. Psychological Bulletin 55:29–45.

SEELEY, JOHN R. 1955 Social Values, the Mental Health Movement, and Mental Health. Pages 599–612 in Arnold Rose (editor), Mental Health and Mental Disorder. New York: Norton.

SMITH, M. BREWSTER 1950 Optima of Mental Health. Psychiatry 13:503–510.

SMITH, M. BREWSTER 1959 Research Strategies Toward a Conception of Positive Mental Health. American Psychologist 14:673–681.

SMITH, M. BREWSTER 1961 "Mental Health" Reconsidered: A Special Case of the Problem of Values in Psychology. American Psychologist 16:299–306.

SULLIVAN, HARRY STACK 1954 The Psychiatric Interview. Edited by Helen Swick Perry and Mary Ladd Gawel. New York: Norton. → Published posthumously.

WEGROCKI, HENRY J. (1948) 1953 A Critique of Cultural and Statistical Concepts of Abnormality. Pages 691–701 in Clyde Kluckhohn and Henry A. Murray (editors), Personality in Nature, Society, and Culture. 2d ed., rev. & enl. New York: Knopf.

WORLD FEDERATION FOR MENTAL HEALTH, SCIENTIFIC COMMITTEE 1962 Identity: Mental Health and Value Systems. Edited by Kenneth Soddy. London: Tavistock.

SOCIAL CLASS AND PERSONAL ADJUSTMENT

If personality is seen as referring to the relatively enduring needs, motives, attitudes, values, belief systems, and self-conceptions that characterize the behavior of the individual, there is good reason to expect a substantial relationship between social class (one's position in the stratification structure) and personality.

The basis for expecting such a relationship rests on widely accepted assumptions regarding man and society. Human personality is to a large extent a product of the social learning experiences that the individual undergoes in the sociocultural environment in which he lives. Moreover, there seems to be almost complete agreement among social scientists that the early experiences of the individual are of critical importance in personality development and in later adjustment, although there is considerable disagreement as to the dynamics of the relationship between early experience and later personality. It is also generally accepted that personality continues to develop throughout the life cycle (although probably at a less rapid rate than in childhood) in response to learning experiences and environmental pressures which the person encounters in the performance of his social roles. Finally, it is readily apparent that one of the most pervasive aspects of the social structures impinging on the individual throughout his life cycle is the stratification system of his society.

This last observation is true not only because all societies have a system of stratification in which the members are differentiated into strata of unequal status but also because of the unique function of the family as a status ascription and socialization agency. Because in all societies the child is accorded the same status as his parents, the family of origin serves as the main link between the child and society. Since the family is the major agency charged with the early socialization of the child, its position in the stratification structure will to a large extent determine the social learning influences to which the child will be subjected during the most formative periods of his life. Moreover, the family's position in the stratification structure will greatly affect the child's choice of associates outside of the family, which in turn will go far in determining the social opportunities he will encounter throughout his life. Thus the stratification system may be seen as one of the most important and continuous social contexts in which the individual's developmental history takes place; certainly, one's position in it should have a substantial bearing on his personality. This is not to say, however, that personality is wholly determined by social class. The possible influences on personality development to which the individual is subjected are many and varied and are by no means all class-linked.

The two principal sources of research evidence on the relationship between social class and personality are studies of social class and the socialization of the child and studies of social class and mental illness. In the past 25 years many studies in both of these areas have appeared. Fortunately, reviews of much of this literature are available (Bronfenbrenner 1958; Dunham 1961; Sewell 1962; Mishler & Scotch 1963) so that only major trends and more recent developments are covered here.

Social class and socialization

In one of the early studies of social class and personality, Davis and Dollard (1940) attempted to show how the social structure influences the nature of the learning process by which Negro children are trained to take on the behavior appropriate to their position in the social stratification system of the southern United States. The authors trace the process by which the child learns and acquires from his parents, his family's social clique, his peers, and his interactions with white adults the needs, motives, cognitions, attitudes, values, and behavior patterns of the class subculture of which he is a member. These results were based mainly on informal observational procedures and, consequently, are suggestive rather than definitive; but they stimulated many subsequent studies of social class and child rearing. Perhaps best known is the study by Davis and Havighurst (1946) of middle-class and lower-class Negro and white children in Chicago. Using interviewing procedures, they found that the social class differences were much greater than the race differences and clearly indicated that middle-class mothers were more restrictive than lower-class mothers in the critical early training of the child. For instance, middle-class mothers were more likely to bottle-feed, follow a strict nursing schedule, restrict the sucking period, wean earlier and more abruptly, and begin and complete toilet training earlier than lower-class mothers. They also followed stricter regimens in other areas and expected their children to assume responsibilities earlier.

These differences in early feeding and toilet training were widely interpreted by psychoanalytically oriented writers as evidence that middle-class child-training practices were baneful to middle-class children and were likely to produce maladjusted adults. Subsequent and more carefully designed studies of social class differences in child-rearing practices have failed to confirm the findings of the Chicago study. In fact, on many points, the results of later studies (see, for instance, Sears, Maccoby & Levin 1957) have contradicted those of the Chicago study—particularly on toilet-training and infant-feeding practices—and have shown that lower-class mothers are more restrictive and punitive in relation to basic needs than middle-class mothers. Urie Bronfenbrenner (1958), on the basis of a detailed examination of data from a number of studies covering a 25-year period, concluded that lower-class mothers have probably become more restrictive in infant feeding and toilet training since World War II, while middle-class mothers have become more permissive, with the result that the gap between them has tended to close. However, throughout this period, middle-class mothers have been consistently more permissive toward the child's expressed needs and wishes, less likely to use physical punishment, and more accepting and equalitarian in dealing with the child than have lower-class mothers. Thus, it would appear that there is little evidence from these studies to support the view that the lower-class child undergoes socialization experiences that are more favorable to his later personality than does the middle-class child; if anything, the evidence points in the opposite direction.

Possibly as a result of these findings, and because empirical research has cast doubt on the importance of toilet training and infant-feeding practices for later personality (Sewell 1952), recent studies of social class and personality development have tended to place less emphasis on infant training and more stress on parent–child relationships extending into childhood and adolescence. Several studies illustrating this trend may be briefly mentioned. Kohn (1959a; 1959b) finds that middle-class parents emphasize internalized standards of conduct, including honesty and self-control, while working-class parents stress respectability, obedience, neatness, and cleanliness. Middle-class parents tend to respond to misbehavior in terms of the child's intent and to take into account his motives and feelings, while lower-class parents focus on the child's actions and respond in accordance with the seriousness of the act. Moreover, there is evidence that middle-class parents are less authoritarian in their relations with their adolescent children than lower-class parents but have higher expectations of them (Elder 1962). Rosen (1961) finds that not only do middle-class junior-high-school boys have higher achievement motives and values than lower-class boys, but that middle-class parents put more pressure on them to succeed, teach them to believe

in success, and create conditions in which success is possible. Studies of lower-class adolescent boys, on the other hand, testify to the influence of peer groups and of the lower-class culture of the community, especially in socialization to delinquent roles (Miller 1958). Still other studies have shown that middle-class adolescents are trained to defer their gratifications and lower-class youths to satisfy their current needs (Schneider & Lysgaard 1953). Finally, many other studies show that middle-class parents, in comparison with lower-class parents, place more stress on values which result in high levels of aspiration and achievement in the educational and occupational spheres (Kahl 1953).

Another quite different recent emphasis in socialization research has been renewed interest in cognitive development. Studies thus far reported indicate that lower-class children suffer from cognitive deficits that may seriously impede their later adjustments to school and adult roles (Deutsch 1963; Hess & Shipman 1965).

Much more needs to be done to discover the full range of class differences in socialization practices and especially to determine their effects on personality development and adjustment in the various classes. Studies, not reviewed here, relating socioeconomic status to scores on personality tests indicate a low but positive correlation between social class and the personality adjustment of the child (Sewell 1962, pp. 348–349). Some good work on socialization and social class is being done, but much more is needed using better samples, a wider range of socialization practices, and better data-gathering and data-analysis techniques.

Social class and mental illness

The largest body of evidence on the relation of social class to personality comes from the findings of a number of studies of social aspects of mental illness. One of the most important of these is the study by Faris and Dunham (1939), who found, among other things, an inverse association between socioeconomic characteristics of Chicago census tracts and first admission rates for schizophrenia. Since the publication of this research, similar studies of American, European, and Asian cities have essentially replicated these results (Dunham 1961, pp. 274–290). Ecological studies of this kind have been criticized because of bias arising from socioeconomic selection in first admissions to mental hospitals; the possibility that mentally ill persons have drifted from the better into the poorer areas of the city after the onset of their illness; and reliance on purely ecological correlations. Studies (Clark 1948; Ødegaard 1956) based on the association between occupation or income and admission rates for psychoses, especially schizophrenia, generally confirm the results of the ecological studies, but are also subject to the criticism that admission rates to mental hospitals tend to be selective of lower-class persons.

Hollingshead and Redlich (1958), in their study of social class and mental illness in New Haven, improved on the earlier studies by obtaining detailed classifications of all cases in treatment with a psychiatrist or under the care of a psychiatric clinic or mental hospital, by carefully assessing individual socioeconomic status, by taking a city-wide control sample of normal persons for comparative purposes, and by computing rates for treated cases of various types of mental illness by class status. Most of their findings are for treated prevalence and therefore understate the total prevalence of mental illness in the community, but they clearly indicate that the lower classes have much higher rates for psychiatric illness, especially for psychoses.

Other evidence collected by Hollingshead and Redlich indicates that diagnosis and treatment favor the higher social classes, with the consequence that members of the lower social classes tend to be diagnosed more readily as psychotics, to receive less individually oriented treatment, and to remain in custodial care for much longer periods of time. Because this piling-up of cases might explain the higher treated prevalence rates of the lower classes, incidence rates (based on the number of patients who entered treatment during the interval of observation) were computed. Again the lowest social class had the highest rates, although the differences between the other classes were no longer as marked. Moreover, while there was no relationship between social class and the incidence of neuroses, the inverse relationship of class membership and psychoses remained, with the rate for the lowest class being twice that for the next highest class and almost three times as high as for the two highest classes. This finding is particularly impressive because it confirms the results of the earlier ecological and correlational studies.

But even the study just described is seriously defective because it is based only on treated cases. Evidence has been mounting for some time that the prevalence and incidence of mental illness in the community are much greater than the treated rates because many cases are either not treated or are handled by others than psychiatrists, mental health clinics, and mental hospitals. This is apparently true even for quite serious forms of mental illness. Recently, attempts have been made to obtain more satisfactory evidence concerning total prevalence of mental illness by means of sample surveys in which clinical examinations or symptoms inventories are used to determine mental health status. Obviously, the magnitude of the rate will depend on the inventories and the cutting points used in determining who is and who is not mentally ill. The results of the Midtown Manhattan Study (1962; 1963), based on a large probability sample of adults, are especially informative in that a consistent inverse relationship is found between socioeconomic status and poor mental health and a direct relationship between status and absence of significant symptoms of mental pathology. Of all of the many variables tested, socioeconomic status was the one most clearly associated with mental health. Moreover, this relationship held whether parental socioeconomic status or the person's own socioeconomic status was taken as the status measure, and it persisted when age and sex were controlled.

The finding of an inverse relation between socioeconomic status of parents and impaired mental health is particularly significant because it indicates that successively lower parental status carries for the child progressively greater likelihood of inadequate personality adjustment in adulthood. The finding that one's current socioeconomic status is even more closely related to one's mental health suggests that the effects of low socioeconomic status are probably cumulative in that the vulnerable personalities developed by some low-status children prevent their upward mobility and destine them to the further burdens and stresses that low socioeconomic status adults typically encounter in the United States. Moreover, lower-class persons tend toward socially disturbing psychotic adaptations that further complicate their adjustment to an already stressful environment, while higher-status persons tend to respond to stress with mild neurotic responses that are socially more adaptive. Thus, the cumulative effects of unfavorable childhood and adult experiences on the lower-class person may result in a higher degree of vulnerability not only to mental illness but also to the development of more serious psychiatric symptoms.

Another important finding of the Midtown Manhattan Study is that those who are downwardly mobile present more symptoms of mental disturbance than those who are nonmobile, with those who are upwardly mobile having the fewest symptoms of all. Evidence indicates that downward mobility is associated with the character disorders, or personality-trait disturbances, while upward mobility tends to be associated with neurotic behavior. These findings confirm the conclusions of earlier studies based on clinical observations (Hollingshead & Redlich 1958). The task of unraveling cause and effect in this area is indeed challenging and demands further research; whereas mobility may result in some types of psychiatric illnesses, it is also likely that certain personality characteristics —including psychiatric symptoms—may help determine who rises or falls in the stratification system (Dunham et al. 1966).

The one finding from the studies of social class and mental illness which comes through most clearly is that the lowest social class has the highest incidence and prevalence of major psychiatric illness. The explanations offered for this finding vary considerably, but they may be conveniently subsumed under three general notions. First is the claim that class variations in rates of mental illness are due to the way in which a social system functions over time to sort and sift persons with certain personality characteristics or vulnerabilities into social class positions. Second, it is argued that differences in the extent and nature of environmental stress in the various classes account for differences in rates. Finally, some authors argue that class differences in socialization, especially early socialization, are responsible for differing rates of mental illness among the various social classes. As we have seen in our examination of the research evidence so far available, it is clear that no one of these explanations has ever been subjected to anything approaching a scientifically adequate test.

It may be concluded that there are good theoretical reasons for expecting an association between social class and personality development and adjustment. However, studies to date do not indicate a sizable relationship but suggest that lower-class status is associated with socialization experiences that foster the development of needs, motives, attitudes, belief systems, self-conceptions, cognitive modes, and styles of coping with stress which result in personality maladjustment. Much more needs to be known about the socialization experiences that members of the various classes undergo, particularly how these affect personality systems. Finally, more systematic and theoretically informed studies of the role of social class in the etiology of mental illness are greatly needed.

WILLIAM H. SEWELL

[See also ACHIEVEMENT MOTIVATION; LIFE CYCLE; MENTAL DISORDERS, article on EPIDEMIOLOGY; PERSONALITY; PERSONALITY MEASUREMENT; PSYCHIATRY, article on SOCIAL PSYCHIATRY; SOCIAL MOBILITY; SOCIALIZATION; STRATIFICATION, SOCIAL.]

BIBLIOGRAPHY

BRONFENBRENNER, URIE 1958 Socialization and Social Class Through Time and Space. Pages 400–425 in Society for the Psychological Study of Social Issues, *Readings in Social Psychology.* 3d ed. New York: Holt.

CLARK, ROBERT E. 1948 The Relationship of Schizophrenia to Occupational Income and Occupational Prestige. *American Sociological Review* 13:325–330.

DAVIS, ALLISON; and DOLLARD, JOHN (1940) 1953 *Children of Bondage: The Personality Development of Negro Youth in the Urban South.* Prepared for the American Youth Commission. Washington: American Council on Education.

DAVIS, ALLISON; and HAVIGHURST, ROBERT J. 1946 Social Class and Color Differences in Child Rearing. *American Sociological Review* 11:698–710.

DEUTSCH, MARTIN 1963 The Disadvantaged Child and the Learning Process. Pages 163–179 in Work Conference on Curriculum and Teaching in Depressed Urban Areas, Columbia University, 1962, *Education in Depressed Areas.* Edited by Harry A. Passow. New York: Columbia Univ., Teachers College.

DUNHAM, H. WARREN 1961 Social Structures and Mental Disorders: Competing Hypotheses of Explanation. *Milbank Memorial Fund Quarterly* 39:259–311.

DUNHAM, H. WARREN et al. 1966 A Research Note on Diagnosed Mental Illness and Social Class. *American Sociological Review* 31:223–227.

ELDER, GLEN H. 1962 *Adolescent Achievement and Mobility Aspirations.* Chapel Hill: Univ. of North Carolina, Institute for Research in Social Sciences.

FARIS, ROBERT E. L.; and DUNHAM, H. WARREN (1939) 1960 *Mental Disorders in Urban Areas: An Ecological Study of Schizophrenia and Other Psychoses.* New York: Hafner.

HESS, ROBERT D.; and SHIPMAN, VIRGINIA C. 1965 Early Experience and the Socialization of Cognitive Modes in Children. *Child Development* 36:869–886.

HOLLINGSHEAD, AUGUST B.; and REDLICH, FREDRICK C. 1958 *Social Class and Mental Illness: A Community Study.* New York: Wiley.

KAHL, JOSEPH A. 1953 Educational and Occupational Aspirations of "Common Man" Boys. *Harvard Educational Review* 23, no. 3:186–203.

KOHN, MELVIN L. 1959a Social Class and the Exercise of Parental Authority. *American Sociological Review* 24:352–366.

KOHN, MELVIN L. 1959b Social Class and Parental Values. *American Journal of Sociology* 64:337–351.

THE MIDTOWN MANHATTAN STUDY 1962 *Mental Health in the Metropolis: The Midtown Manhattan Study,* by Leo Srole et al. Vol. 1. New York: McGraw-Hill.

THE MIDTOWN MANHATTAN STUDY 1963 *Life Stress and Mental Health: The Midtown Manhattan Study,* by Thomas S. Langner and Stanley T. Michael. Vol. 2. New York: Free Press.

MILLER, WALTER B. 1958 Lower Class Culture as a Generating Milieu of Gang Delinquency. *Journal of Social Issues* 14, no. 3: 5–19.

MISHLER, ELLIOT G.; and SCOTCH, NORMAN A. 1963 Sociocultural Factors in the Epidemiology of Schizophrenia. *Psychiatry* 26:315–351.

ØDEGAARD, Ø. 1956 The Incidence of Psychoses in Various Occupations. *International Journal of Social Psychiatry* 2:85–104.

ROSEN, BERNARD C. 1961 Family Structure and Achievement Motivation. *American Sociological Review* 26:574–585.

SCHNEIDER, LOUIS; and LYSGAARD, SVERRE 1953 The Deferred Gratification Pattern: A Preliminary Study. *American Sociological Review* 18:142–149.

Sears, Robert R.; Maccoby, E. E.; and Levin, H.   1957
  Patterns of Child Rearing. Evanston, Ill.: Row, Peterson.
Sewell, William H.   1952   Infant Training and the
  Personality of the Child. *American Journal of Sociology* 58:150–159.
Sewell, William H.   1962   Social Class and Childhood
  Personality. *Sociometry* 24:340–356.

MENTAL HOSPITALS

See Mental disorders, treatment of, *article on* the therapeutic community.

MENTAL ILLNESS

See Illness; Mental disorders; Mental health; Psychosomatic illness.

MENTAL RETARDATION

Mental retardation is a problem of serious social concern. In view of the large number of persons considered to be mentally retarded, such concern is certainly justified. Using the conventional criterion of 3 per cent of the population, the U.S. President's Panel on Mental Retardation (1963) estimated that almost 5.5 million children and adults in the United States are mentally retarded. The criterion for mental retardation established in the "Manual on Terminology and Classification in Mental Retardation" (Heber 1959) and adopted by the American Association on Mental Deficiency as well as the Biometrics Branch, National Institute of Mental Health, is that all those at least one standard deviation below the population mean intelligence quotient (IQ) are considered retarded. If one accepts this criterion, and many do not, there are almost 30 million mental retardates in the United States. If the more conservative estimate is employed, mental retardation is twice as prevalent as blindness, polio, cerebral palsy, and rheumatic heart conditions combined (Doll 1962).

The typical textbook pictures the distribution of intelligence as normal or Gaussian in nature, with approximately the lower 3 per cent of the distribution encompassing the mentally retarded. A common class of persons is thus constructed, a class defined by intelligence-test scores below 70. This schema has misled many laymen and students and has subtly influenced the approach of experienced workers in the area. For if one fails to appreciate the arbitrary nature of the cutoff point of 70, it is but a short step to the formulation that all those falling below this point compose a homogeneous class of "subnormals." Since the conceptual distance between "subnormal" and "abnormal," with

its age-old connotation of disease and defect, is minimal, the final step is to regard retardates as a homogeneous group of defective organisms, immutably different from those persons possessing a higher IQ.

The view that mental retardates represent a homogeneous group is seen in numerous research studies where comparisons between retardates and normals are made on the basis of IQ classification alone. The view that mental retardates, as a group, are "different" is most vividly encountered in comparative studies where mental retardates are conceptualized as occupying a position on the phylogenetic scale somewhere between monkeys and children of average intellect. It is of some interest to note that people deficient in respect to intelligence-test performance are usually not called "mental deficients" but rather are commonly referred to as "mental defectives."

The defect orientation to mental retardation originally emphasized the notion of moral defect and stemmed anywhere from the belief that retardates were possessed by a variety of devils to the empirical evidence of their exhibiting an inordinately high incidence of socially unacceptable behaviors, such as crime and illegitimacy. More recently, the notion of defect has referred to defects in either physical or cognitive structures. This defect approach has a certain unquestionably valid component. There is a sizable group of retardates who suffer from a variety of known physical defects. Mental retardation may be due to such factors as a dominant gene (as in epiloia), a single recessive gene (as in gargoylism, phenylketonuria, amaurotic idiocy), infections (such as congenital syphilis, encephalitis, rubella in the mother), chromosomal defects (as in mongolism), toxic conditions (such as radiation *in utero*, lead poisoning, and Rh incompatibility), and cerebral trauma. For a complete listing of the many types of mental retardation the reader is referred to the "Manual on Terminology and Classification in Mental Retardation" (Heber 1959).

The diverse etiologies noted above have one factor in common: in every instance examination reveals an abnormal physiological process, that is, there are specific or related defects in physiological functioning. Such persons *are* abnormal in the orthodox sense, since they suffer from a known disease defect. However, in addition to this group, which forms a minority of all retardates, there is the group labeled "familial," or more recently "undifferentiated," which comprises approximately 75 per cent of all retardates. This group presents the greatest mystery and has been the object of the most heated disputes in the area of mental retardation. The diagnosis of familial retardation is made when an examination does not reveal the physiological manifestations noted above and when retardation exists among parents, siblings, or other relatives. As will be seen in a later section, several theoreticians have extended the defect notion to this type of retardate. On the basis of differences in performance between retardates and normals on some experimental task rather than on physiological evidence, they have advanced the view that all retardates suffer from some specifiable defect over and above their general intellectual retardation. However, these theoreticians differ as to the specific nature of the defect. The experimental paradigm employed to demonstrate such defects involves equating groups of normals and retardates on Mental Age (MA), thus roughly controlling for general intellectual level, and demonstrating differences in performance between the two groups on some experimental task.

This more general defect approach thus lends support to the conceptualization of the mentally retarded as a homogeneous group of physiologically defective persons. Some order can be brought to the area of mental retardation if a distinction is maintained between physiologically defective retardates, with known etiologies, and familial retardates, whose etiology is unknown.

For the most part, work with physically defective retardates involves investigation into the exact nature of the underlying physiological processes, with prevention or amelioration of the physical and intellectual symptoms as the goals. Jervis (1959) has suggested that such "pathological" mental deficiency is primarily in the domain of medical sciences, whereas familial retardation represents a problem to be solved by behavioral scientists, including educators and behavioral geneticists. Diagnostic and incidence studies of these two types of retardates have disclosed two striking differences. The retardate having an extremely low IQ (below 40) is almost invariably of the defective type. (This does not mean that one cannot find defective retardates at every level of retardation. In fact, brain-damaged individuals may be found at every point along the IQ continuum.) Familial retardates, on the other hand, are almost invariably mildly retarded, usually with IQs above 50. The defect position emphasizes the innate, if not immutable, difference between retardates and normals.

The problem of definition. The decision of whether a person is considered retarded is often based not upon his intellectual characteristics but upon legal and occupational factors as well as his general level of social adjustment. The matter has been put most succinctly by Maher who stated:

What constitutes mentally retarded behavior depends to a large extent upon the society which happens to be making the judgment. An individual who does not create a problem for others in his social environment and who manages to become self-supporting is usually not defined as mentally retarded no matter what his test IQ may be. Mental retardation is primarily a socially defined phenomenon, and it is in large part meaningless to speak of mental retardation without this criterion in mind. (1963, p. 238)

This emphasis on social factors in defining mental retardation may lead to more confusion than clarity as indicated by the discrepancies found among various incidence and survey studies. The data of Table 1 would indicate that the incidence fluctuates not only across age categories but also according to the locality. If mental retardation is defined strictly in terms of IQ, and assuming a certain constancy of IQ score, we would expect no difference in the incidence of mental retardation at different ages. The standardization data of the Wechsler–Bellevue Scale confirm this expectation.

Table 1 — Percentage of persons classified as mentally retarded

| | | LOCALITY | |
AGE	England and Wales	Baltimore, Maryland	Onondaga County (Syracuse), New York
Under 5	0.12	0.07	0.45
5–9	1.55	1.18	3.94
10–14	2.65	4.36	7.76
15–19	1.08	3.02	4.49

Source: Jervis 1959, p. 1290.

The incidence figures reported in Table 1 are understandable if one realizes that they reflect diagnoses based on some combination of IQ and the success of the individual in meeting social demands. For example, the extremely low incidence under 5 years of age may reflect the minimal social demands made on young children. The highest incidence obtained at the 10–14 age level occurs when the child is faced with school and more demanding intellectual tasks. It is probably in this age range that the relationship between IQ scores and meeting societal expectancies (i.e., successful school performance) is greatest. Stated somewhat differently, it is probably in this age range where the use of either the IQ or the child's success in meeting social demands would result in his being classified as mentally retarded. A test-score orientation to mental retardation results in the view that approximately 3 per cent of the population is mentally retarded. The social competence viewpoint, however, results in a much smaller incidence. Data obtained through surveying representative samples of large populations or the entire population of certain limited regions in England and Scandinavia indicate that about 1 per cent or less of adults are classified as mentally retarded (e.g., Fremming 1947).

Armed with the information that a person's social adequacy has much to do with whether or not he is considered retarded, we begin to get some inkling of the arbitrariness involved in such a classification.

The nature of intelligence

Whether mental retardation is defined by an intelligence-test score or by the person's social competence, which many claim reflects his intelligence, the essential aspect of mental retardation is lower intelligence than that displayed by the modal member of an appropriate reference group. There is little agreement, however, when the question precipitated by this statement is raised, namely, "What is the nature of intelligence?" We cannot avoid this question by invoking the very unsatisfying cliché that "intelligence is what an intelligence test measures," since it is perfectly apparent that the test constructor must have some definition of intelligence in mind, either explicitly or implicitly, before he can select test items. However, some consensus can probably be found for the view that intelligence is a hypothetical construct which has as its ultimate referent the cognitive processes of the individual. Given this, we are still faced with the unresolved issue of whether intelligence represents some single cognitive process which permeates every intelligence test or nontest behavior or whether it represents a great variety of relatively discrete cognitive processes which can be sampled and then summated to yield some indication of the amount of intelligence a person possesses [see INTELLIGENCE AND INTELLIGENCE TESTING].

In either case, the more important questions involve an understanding of exactly how such cognitive processes develop over the life span and exactly how innate and environmental factors interact to influence such development. Approached in this way, the problem of defining intelligence becomes one with the problem of the nature of cognition and its development.

Cognitive versus psychometric approach. It follows that if we are to understand the nature of intelligence, we must consult those workers intent on investigating the nature and development of cognitive processes (e.g., thought, memory, concept formation, and reasoning) rather than focus on the work of test constructors and psychometricians. There has been little cross-fertilization between these two groups, which have approached the investigation of intellective functioning quite differently.

The former group of investigators utilizes a variety of techniques and, through extremely detailed analyses, attempts to tease out the intricacies of man's cognitive functioning. These theorists have tried to evolve a theory of human cognition and its development. If intelligence tests had been developed by this group, psychology might have avoided the perplexing state of affairs encountered in trying to define intelligence. Tests devised by such a group would, by necessity, be indicators of the formal features of the cognitive structure at various times in the life cycle. Recently, workers within this framework (e.g., Laurendeau & Pinard 1963) have taken an interest in the problem of assessment. Although the task of providing an acceptable theory of the development of cognition is far from finished, Laurendeau and Pinard have been able to take the first step toward the construction of an intelligence test based on the formal features of cognition that were isolated by Piaget [see DEVELOPMENTAL PSYCHOLOGY, *article on* A THEORY OF DEVELOPMENT].

From a historical point of view, the practical demands of society for a test which would measure intellectual functioning meant that intelligence became the province of the second group, namely, the testers and psychometricians. Furthermore, for a variety of reasons, American thinking was not receptive to the approach taken by the cognitive theorists. The practical and empirical nature of the work of the testers can be seen in the efforts of Alfred Binet, whose intent was not to investigate the nature of intelligence but rather to discover those test items which would discriminate between successful and unsuccessful school performance. As has been pointed out, Binet viewed his empirically selected tests as a social screening device rather than as a theoretical interpretation of the nature of intelligence. The success of Binet's tests in predicting school achievement led workers to the belief that such tests were inextricably bound to man's intelligence or cognitive functioning.

For the psychometricians, it then became clear that the nature of intelligence could be understood by examining the nature of the tests that were employed to measure it. By discovering the correlations obtained between subtests within a given battery or across different tests, it was felt that the structure of intellect would be revealed. Despite the statistical rigor involved, no very satisfactory theory of intelligence has come out of the correlational or factor-analytic methods. There is, in fact, little agreement among workers even with regard to the one constant theoretical issue throughout this body of work, namely, the global versus the specific nature of intelligent behavior.

It should be emphasized that the weakness of current theories of intelligence has led to a conceptual impasse in the area of mental retardation. If there is no satisfactory theory of intelligence, then the essential aspect of mental retardation must escape us and we must be content with superficial statistical and social approaches to this complex problem. We do not necessarily have to await a completed theory of intelligence, however, to cut through much of the complexity, disputation, and confusion encountered in the area of mental retardation. Some clarification appears possible through the simple process of reorienting or restructuring our approach to intellectual retardation. A rather sizable step forward is taken if our commitment to a simple test approach is abandoned in favor of a concern with cognitive processes.

The process–content distinction.   The plea is not that we abandon tests, for every cognitive theorist must eventually employ tests, as defined in the broadest sense. The plea is that workers in the field turn their attention from the superficial content of tests (i.e., the right or wrong answer) and come to grips with the problem of the cognitive structures and processes that give rise to content. It is this distinction between structure and content that has for too long escaped most workers in the area of mental retardation. Conventional tests are viewed by process-oriented cognitive theorists as too analytic and artificial in character and as measuring an end product and not a process (Laurendeau & Pinard 1963, p. 481).

In general, however, Piaget's approach, with its developmental and normative emphasis, has had very little appeal to workers in the area of mental retardation, since such workers are committed to the study of individual differences. In this context, the test-constructing efforts of Laurendeau and Pinard appear very promising, since these followers of Piaget have formulated the states of cognitive development in terms of the nature of the cognitive operations achieved, thus emphasizing the nature of the cognitive structure and its accompanying processes. In their work we thus see a bridge beween a truly cognitive approach to intelligence and the need in the area of mental retardation for an instrument with which to make individual comparisons.

The focus on the *content* of test behaviors has

been carried over to many nontest behaviors, and often an insufficient distinction is made between intelligence and intelligent behavior. It is the author's view that intelligence must refer to the formal characteristics of the cognitive structure and the processes that accompany it, whereas intelligent behavior should refer to the content of behavior in respect to the appropriateness (often defined in a relatively arbitrary manner) with which an organism carries out an act. (See Maher 1963, for another discussion of this distinction between intelligence and intelligent behavior.) For example, in a sheltered workshop the author recently encountered a retardate working with a surprisingly complex piece of machinery. His ability to use this machinery defied current knowledge concerning the capabilities of the retarded. The director of the workshop explained that the retardate had been taught to operate the machine through a shaping process not unlike that employed by B. F. Skinner in training pigeons to play Ping-pong. It was also learned that the retardate could handle the machine quite adequately provided its position was not changed. To emphasize this point, the machine was rotated on its axis approximately 90°; the retardate then became somewhat agitated and was no longer able to operate the equipment. (Piaget has also commented that remarkable intellectual feats performed by children on some task or other cannot be repeated following relatively minor alterations in the task stimuli.) In terms of the finished product, the retardate was behaving just as intelligently as an operator with a normal IQ. However, this accomplishment does not indicate that the retardate has become normal in intelligence. It is obvious that he is using a much more primitive cognitive process to achieve his intelligent behavior than is the normal person. This example should also make it clear that process analyses demand that the investigator make a more careful analysis of the content than that provided by a superficial "product" or criterion of correctness.

Social competence and mental retardation.   The content approach is expressed also in the social competence definition of mental retardation. What are the intellectual demands of social competence? We do not know, and very little effort is made to discover what they might be. In the area of mental retardation, social competence usually means the ability to maintain oneself without too frequent contact with state schools, state hospitals, welfare agencies, and police officers. Though social competence defined in this way reflects certain cognitive abilities, it may also reflect a variety of factors reminiscent of nonintellectual aspects of intelligence-test performance. We refer here to factors such as luck, social values, attitudes toward other people, and emotional needs that are relatively independent of intellectual level. Thus, present intelligence tests may predict social competence better than an ideal intelligence test because of the overlap of nonintellectual variables which influence both intelligence-test scores and social competence.

Social competence does not inevitably reflect normal intellectual functioning any more than its absence in the emotionally unstable, the criminal, or the social misfit reflects intellectual subnormality. Social competence is much too heterogeneous a phenomenon and reflects too many nonintellectual factors to be of great value in understanding mental retardation. The basic problem is that the concept of social competence is so value laden, and its definition so vague, that it has little heuristic utility. Windle (1962) has pointed out that the social competence definition of mental retardation is applicable only to institutionalized populations, whereas quite different definitional criteria must be employed with noninstitutionalized retardates. The only clear and acceptable operational definition of social competence would appear to be related to whether the individual has managed to function outside an institutional setting. Even Heber (1962), who has made the strongest case for employing social competence, has admitted that objective measures of adaptive behavior are presently unavailable. He has also stated that the present ambiguity of the social competence construct is such that in practice intelligence-test performance must remain "the most important and heavily weighted of the criteria used."

There is a further problem with the social competence construct related to a fallacy which has permeated much of our thinking concerning the retarded. We have somehow come to believe that it is impossible for anyone who is "truly" retarded to meet the complex demands of our society. The bulk of retardates who have MAs in the 9–12 range (remembering that an MA of 16 is the upper limit for an individual of average IQ), have the intellectual wherewithal to meet the minimal demands of our society. This becomes immediately apparent if one raises the question of how much intellectual ability is required to arise in the morning, dress oneself, catch a bus or walk to a single location, perform some undemanding sort of labor, and return home. Indeed in the 1920s and 1930s it was discovered that there were no less than 118 occupations in our society suitable for individuals having MAs from 5 to 12. As late as 1956 it was noted that 54 per cent of jobs require no schooling beyond the elementary level (Whitney 1956).

Another major aspect of social competence is the ability of the individual to abide by the values of the society, that is, obey laws, and so on. While the incidence of crime among the retarded is higher than among the nonretarded, this increase of incidence is not very great, especially if one controls for social class. Here again it is an error to view obedience to the law as somehow beyond the ability of the retarded. One simply has to apply the concept of the stages of moral development as investigated by Jean Piaget (1932): fairly young children are capable of a morality based on absolutism, that is, the rules inhere in the very fabric of existence and are not to be broken under any circumstances. Individuals who never achieve a higher stage of moral development are certainly not developmentally adequate, but neither are they likely to break many laws.

In order to make social competence a useful indicator of cognitive functioning, we must thus abandon some simplistic notion of social competence in favor of a variety of continua theoretically based upon the cognitive demands of the social requirements involved. Such indexes could then be considered independent indicators of intellectual functioning. Empirical efforts of this sort may be seen in the Vineland Social Maturity Scale and the Worcester Scale of Social Attainment. A more theoretical effort may be found in the work of Phillips and Zigler (1964) where both intelligence test scores and conventional social competence indexes are combined into an index of developmental or maturational level.

The nature–nurture issue

Attention is now turned to the role of cognitive capacity in mental retardation. Maher (1963) believes that the concept of capacity has considerable heuristic value for workers in the area of mental retardation. Intellectual capacity means something akin to Hebb's (1949) intelligence A, that is, an innate potential for the development of intellectual functions. Those who have argued that the intellectual capacity notion is a relatively useless one (e.g., Ferguson 1956) appear to be invariably committed to an environmentalistic or learning orientation.

Maher's position is that the capacity concept has value as related to "the differences between individuals in rate of acquisition of responses under similar learning conditions. Such a concept necessarily implies the existence of structural differences between individuals and is incompatible with a psychology of the empty organism . . ." (1963, p. 250). It is in this last sentence that we see the theoretical value of the capacity concept, since it forces us to conceptualize individuals as biological organisms innately differing in respect to the potential manifestation of a multitude of traits. Thus the concept of capacity is intimately related to the biological concept of the genotype.

There has been an interesting effort to make intelligence, and thus mental retardation, a matter of acquired skills and transfer phenomena in the classical learning theory sense (see Ferguson 1956). Although Ferguson appears to abhor a biological concept of intelligence, he nevertheless falls back upon it in dealing with those aspects of early learning which do not reflect transfer effects. In addition, his treatment of transfer as a uniformly manifested phenomenon overlooks differences in ability to transfer from one task to another which may very well be a reflection of biological capacity.

Given such an orientation, we can derive the optimistic view that complete control over learning experiences would do away with individual differences and, thus, mental retardation, at least of the nondefective variety. Such a view, though appealing, flies in the face of what has been observed. Herculean efforts of teaching and training have not resulted in marked change in the intellectual level of most retardates.

The environmentalist, while acknowledging the importance of biological capacity, treats human behavior as the outgrowth of an infinite number of experiences. It is of interest to note that one environmentally oriented theorist (McCandless 1964) has argued that although heredity and environment interact in the production of intelligent behavior, we need only concern ourselves with environment, since "we can do something about environment." This approach implies that the manipulations of environments are expected to have constant results and, furthermore, ignores the obvious possibility that children with particular capacities will need specific environmental events in order to maximize their cognitive development. The one group that has seriously considered the nature of the interaction between genotype and experiences in producing certain behaviors (phenotypes) has been the behavior geneticists. Employing infrahuman subjects, these investigators have presented evidence that the effects of particular experiences and the behaviors to which they give rise depend upon the biological nature of the organism (e.g., Hirsch 1963).

The attempt to determine the proportion of variance attributable to heredity or to environment is full of difficulties (H. Jones 1946). Despite the shortcomings of the nature–nurture work on intelligence, it is still possible to derive certain conclusions. (For more complete reviews of this work the reader is referred to H. Jones 1946; McCandless 1964.) Studies of parent–child and of sibling resemblances in intelligence, a variety of twin studies, and studies on children in foster homes have made it clear that inherited intellectual endowment is a much more important factor in intelligence than those who are environmentally oriented would have us believe.

At the same time one must not forget the importance of environmental factors to manifest intelligence. The role of environment is evident even in extreme cases where a known gene defect is the cause of mental retardation. In the case of genetically determined phenylketonuria, subnormal intelligence occurs only in an environment which provides phenylalanine in the diet of the affected individual. A specific change in the environment (i.e., withholding phenylalanine from the diet) will prevent the occurrence of subnormal intelligence.

An issue in the nature–nurture controversy of special pertinence to mental retardation concerns the degree to which the environment may produce individual differences in intelligence in contrast to affecting the absolute achievement level of man. It is one thing to assert that the environment may play a role in determining the range of individual differences found among men. It is another thing to assert that environmental events can cause the individual with a normal intellectual endowment to become retarded or, for that matter, shift the entire range of intelligence in such a way that no individual would display that degree of intellectual impairment that we now label retarded.

Different environments (e.g., rural versus urban, racial–cultural, social class) are associated with differences in intelligence. To what extent such differences reflect environmental as opposed to inherited factors remains an open issue. The position of the majority seems to be nurture oriented, and the argument advanced is that it is the social class or cultural environment which produces retardation. To state the matter more simply, the hereditarian asserts that one is in a lower socioeconomic class because one is less intelligent, whereas the environmentalist asserts that one is less intelligent because one is in the lower socioeconomic class. More specifically, mental retardation is sometimes seen as a major consequence of social deprivation. Such a view assumes that children are capable of "normal" intellectual functioning if we but expose them to enough "cultural enrichment."

Environmental factors and IQ changes. A matter of considerable import in testing the above hypotheses is the magnitude of change that could be effected as a result of changes in the environment. Many investigators have been relatively pessimistic in their conclusions. McClearn (1962) has pointed out that the magnitude of the difference in IQs attributable to environmental factors, though statistically significant, has been so minute as to be practically negligible.

In support of the environmentalistic point of view, however, instances can be found where rather marked improvements in IQ have been reported following some type of environmental manipulation. The reader is referred to the review by McCandless (1964), whose statement is perhaps one of the strongest in favor of the environmentalistic position.

Other studies have indicated that when a geographic area is subjected to social improvement, such as better schools and improved communication, there is a tendency for the IQs of all the inhabitants to improve. Wheeler's study of Tennessee mountain children (1942) is of considerable interest. Testing over three thousand subjects in 1930, he found that IQs progressively declined from a mean of 95 at age 6 to a mean of 74 at age 16. Testing a new sample ten years later, he found a mean increase in IQ of approximately 10 points at every age level. However, the steady decline with age, from a mean of 103 at age 6 to a mean of 80 at age 16, was again discovered, despite the general increase.

There has been a certain inconsistency in studies that have attempted to relate IQ changes to environmental factors. In some instances, significant correlations have been found between various subjective ratings of the "goodness" of the environment and increase in IQ (e.g., Thorpe 1946). But in other instances no environmental correlates could be found to account for changes in the IQ (e.g., H. Jones 1946). Jones has given some especially striking case histories of children who have manifested marked changes in IQ without the apparent involvement of environmental factors.

A continuing problem has been the failure to designate just what constitutes a good environment for optimal intellectual development. Little has been added to the implicit view that the American middle-class home represents some sort of standard. A related matter, of course, is the problem of defining cultural or social deprivation. The social deprivation concept has been loosely applied to certain events in early childhood which are characterized as antecedent to certain social behaviors. There is little agreement about either the early events or the resultant behaviors. Major

dimensions of childhood deprivations that have been suggested are social isolation, cruelty and neglect, institutional upbringing, adverse child-rearing practices, and separation experiences across a wide range of severity. Even factors such as these need much further definition and clarification.

The view that, given a fairly standard environment, it is extremely difficult to improve the quality of cognitive functioning is consistent with the bulk of findings resulting from efforts to improve children's performance on Piaget-type tasks. Of course, familial retardates do not come from what we consider standard environments. Even with these children there is considerable evidence that no great intellectual improvement is produced through environmental manipulation, and this holds true for a variety of techniques. The reader is referred to E. E. Doll's excellent history of mental retardation (1962) for evidence on this point. Binet, with his concept of "mental orthopedics," and Jean M. L. Itard, with his great faith in the possibility of improving the quality of intellect, were responsible for the philosophy underlying the early work with retardates in this country. After several years of employing a variety of techniques, many of which are today being rediscovered, it became apparent that this optimism was unwarranted. In the early days, training schools in this country were just what the name implies. They became custodial institutions only when it became apparent that many retardates could not be trained to a level that would make them self-sustaining in the society at large. A reaction appears to have set in at this time, and the view that we could do nothing for retardates except provide them with a comfortable domicile became dominant. There is much for contemporary workers to learn from this marked swing in attitude toward the retarded. It suggests that undue optimism is dangerous, since it breeds undue pessimism.

The conclusion that may be reached concerning the relevance of the heredity and environment controversy for mental retardation has been well stated by Penrose, who after a lifetime of work with the retarded wrote:

The most important work carried out in the field of training defectives is unspectacular. It is not highly technical but requires unlimited patience, good will and common sense. The reward is to be expected not so much in scholastic improvement of the patient as in his personal adjustment to social life. Occupations are found for patients of all grades so that they can take part as fully and usefully as possible in human affairs. This process, which has been termed socialization, contributes greatly to the happiness not only of the patients themselves but also of those who are responsible for their care.   ([1949] 1963, p. 282)

It is perhaps within this area of socialization that we can do a great deal to enhance the everyday effectiveness of the retarded. Personality and character traits were discovered to be more influenced by environment than was intellectual level (e.g., Leahy 1935). Such findings bolster the argument that there are many modifiable factors which are important in the determination of social adjustment. It is not rare to encounter individuals with the same intellectual make-up demonstrating quite disparate social adjustments. Perhaps the question is not how to improve the cognitive functioning of familial retardates but rather how to maximize the adjustment of such individuals, whatever their intellectual capacity may be. That considerable change in performance can result from the manipulation of nonintellective (i.e., motivational) factors will be made clear in subsequent passages.

A two-group conception. Hirsch has asserted that we will make little headway in understanding individual differences in intelligence and many other traits unless we incorporate into our thinking the fact that to a large degree such differences reflect the inherent biological properties of man. As Hirsch has noted, we can no longer make the "gratuitous uniformity assumption that all genetic combinations are equally plastic and respond in like fashion to environmental influences . . . ," and he added that "without an appreciation of the genotypic structure of populations, the behavioral sciences have no basis for distinguishing individual differences that are attributable to differences whatsoever where there is a common history" (1963, p. 1442).

Work in population genetics appears capable of bringing considerable order to the area of mental retardation. We need simply to accept the generally recognized fact that the gene pool of any population is such that there will always be variations in the behavioral or phenotypic expression of virtually every measurable trait or characteristic of man. From the polygenic model advanced by geneticists, we would deduce that the distribution of intelligence would be a symmetric bell-shaped curve, which is characteristic of such a large number of distributions that we have come to refer to it as the normal curve. This theoretical distribution is a fairly good approximation of what is actually encountered in the observed distribution of intelligence. In the polygenic model of intelligence (see Hirsch 1963; Penrose 1949), the genetic foundation of intelligence is not viewed as

dependent upon a single gene. Rather, intelligence is viewed as the result of a number of discrete genetic units. (This is not to assert, however, that single-gene effects are never to be encountered in mental retardation. As noted earlier, certain relatively rare types of mental retardation are the products of such simple genetic effects.)

A variety of specific polygenic models have been advanced that generate theoretical distributions of intelligence that are congruent with observed distributions (e.g., Burt & Howard 1956). Again caution is in order. An environmentalistic model positing five environmental factors acting additively would also generate an approximation to a normal curve. However, such a model appears much less capable of encompassing the raw data encountered in investigations of intelligence. An aspect of polygenic models of special interest for the area of mental retardation is that they generate IQ distributions ranging approximately from 50 to 150. Since an IQ of approximately 50 appears to be the lower limit for familial retardates, it has been concluded (e.g., Burt & Howard 1956; Penrose 1949) that the etiology of this form of retardation reflects the same factors that determine "normal" intelligence. Approached in this way, the familial retardate can be seen as normal, where "normal" is defined as representing an integral part of the distribution of intelligence that we would expect from the normal manifestations of the genetic pool in our population. Within such a framework, it is possible to refer to the familial retardate as less intelligent but it would make no sense to say that he is abnormal. He is just as integral a part of the normal distribution as are the 3 per cent of the population that we view as superior or that more numerous group of individuals that we consider to be average.

The two-group conception of mental retardation calls attention to the fact that the second group of retardates, those who have known physiological defects, represents a distribution of intelligence with a mean which is considerably lower than that of the familial retardates. Such children, for the most part, fall outside the range of normal intelligence, that is, they have an IQ below 50, although there are certain exceptions; brain-damaged children with IQs as high as 150 have been found. Thus the empirical distribution of intelligence may best be represented by two curves. Considerable clarity could be brought to the area of mental retardation if we were to do away with the practice of conceptualizing the intelligence distribution as a single continuous normal curve. The more appropriate representation is to depict the intelligence of the bulk of the population, including the familial retarded, as a normal distribution having a mean IQ of 100 with lower and upper limits of approximately 50 and 150. Superimposed on this curve would be a second nearly normal distribution having a mean IQ of approximately 35 and a range from 0 to 70. The first curve would represent the polygenic distribution of intelligence; the second would represent all those individuals whose intellectual functioning reflected factors other than the normal polygenic expression (i.e., those retardates for whom there is an identifiably physiological defect).

This two-group approach to the problem of mental retardation has been supported by Penrose (1949) among others. The very nature of the empirical distribution of IQs below the mean, especially in the 0–50 range (see Penrose 1949) seems to demand such an approach. This distribution is exactly what we would expect if we combined the two distributions discussed above, as is the general practice. This two-group approach is of particular significance to the issue of mental retardation, since it calls for a reappraisal of the entire concept of normality. Hirsch has pointed out that such a concept, as presently employed, is of little value:

Implicit in our use of "normal" is reference to some region of a distribution arbitrarily designated as not extreme—for example, the median 50 percent, 95 percent, or 99 percent. We choose such a region for every trait. Among n mathematically independent traits—for example, traits dependent on n different chromosomes—the probability that a randomly selected individual will be normal for all n traits is the value for the size of that region raised to the nth power. Where "normal" is the median 50 percent and $n = 10$, on the average only one individual out of 1024 will be normal (for ten traits).   (1963, p. 1437)

Thus, if we consider the whole person with his many variable physiological and psychological systems, it would be extremely rare to find an individual we would consider normal. Indeed, if we were to find him, his very normality would be considered abnormal in the sense that he represented a rare event. In the area of mental retardation the concept of abnormal should be confined to those cases with known physical defects wherever these cases may be found in the distribution of intelligence.

A two-group approach makes the problem of the etiology of the familial retarded just as assailable as the problem of etiology in pathological retardation. In respect to the etiology of familial retardates, McClearn has stated that "these individuals undoubtedly represent the lower tail of the distribution generated by assortment of the polygenes underlying 'normal' intelligence, and should no more be considered abnormal than those whose intelligences are an equal distance above the mean" (1962, p. 186).

Once we adopt the position that the familial mental retardate is not defective or pathological but is essentially a normal individual of low intelligence, then the problem of familial retardation becomes part of the general problem of developmental psychology. In terms of cognitive development, the familial retardate would then be viewed as progressing from one intellectual stage to the next in the same sequence as is encountered in other children. He would, of course, progress from stage to stage at a slower rate than other children, and the final stage that he achieves would be lower than that achieved by the more intelligent members of the population. In terms of cognitive functioning alone, the familial retardate with a chronological age (CA) of 10 and an MA of 7 would be conceptualized as being cognitively similar, that is, at the same developmental level as a child with a CA of 7 and an IQ of 100. (The reader must remember that the MA, which is invariably based on the IQ, can be considered only a very rough indicator of the cognitive or developmental level; however, to date, it represents the most adequate measure available.)

To say that two such hypothetical children are cognitively similar is not to assert that they will necessarily behave exactly the same on the intellective and nonintellective tasks with which society confronts them. If nothing else, the retardate is three years older, and if the performance involves lifting weights, or a task that he has encountered much more frequently than the 7-year-old normal child, we would expect the retardate to be superior. Furthermore, performance on even cognitive tasks reflects the wide variety of factors that are the product of the past history of the child rather than his cognitive ability alone. To the extent that these two children have different histories, have experienced different environments, and have developed different values and motives, we would expect differences in performance.

It is no great mystery that a group of children with IQs of 70 and a group with IQs of 100 matched on chronological age differ on a variety of tasks. These children are at different developmental levels, and such differences are exactly what a developmentalist would expect. The mystery is the repeated demonstration that even when groups are matched on MA, the retardate does less well, or at least behaves differently, than the MA-

matched "normal" child. Two distinctly different explanations for this phenomenon have been advanced. One view is that these differences reflect a variety of experiential or motivational differences. The second position is that the familial retardate is really not a normal individual developing at a slower rate but is rather an inherently different or abnormal type of organism who, at every level of development, is suffering from some defect in his physiological or cognitive structure. These hypothesized defects are then viewed as producing differences in behavior even in those instances where the MA is equated. In the next section we shall consider the defect orientation, and the motivational position will be discussed further in the final section.

The defect and difference orientation

This section deals with those theoretical and empirical efforts that have advanced the view that all retardates, including those conventionally diagnosed as familial, suffer from some specifiable defect. These efforts are in opposition to the view that the familial retardate suffers from nothing more than a slower and more limited rate of cognitive development. The evidence typically offered by the difference, or defect, theorist is that even when groups of normals and retardates are matched on MA, which grossly controls for differences in the rate of development, the two groups behave differently. This difference in behavior is advanced as proof of the existence of some physiological or cognitive defect which itself is responsible for the slower rate of development. Where the hypothesized defect is an explicitly physiological one, it would appear to be a simple matter to obtain direct validation for the defect's existence. Such evidence would come from biochemical and physiological analyses as well as from pathological studies of familial retardates. A number of such studies have, of course, been carried out. Although there is an occasional report of some physical anomaly, the bulk of the evidence has indicated that the familial retardate does not suffer from any gross physiological defects. Indeed, if such evidence were readily available, the defect theorist would give up his reliance on the more ambiguous data provided by studies examining molar behavior. The failure to find direct evidence for the existence of a physiological defect in the familial retarded has not deterred—and probably should not deter—theorists from postulating such defects.

In spite of the negative physiological evidence, such workers as Spitz (1963) maintain that all retardates, including familials, are physically defec-

tive and that our failure to discover defects in the familial retarded is due to the relatively primitive nature of our contemporary diagnostic techniques. It is perfectly legitimate for these workers to assert that, although presently not observable, the physical defect that causes familial retardates to behave differently from normals of the same MA will some day be seen. These theorists operate very much like the physicists of a not-too-distant era who asserted that the electron existed, even though it was not directly observable. Analogously, defect theorists in the area of mental retardation validate the existence of a defect by first asserting that its existence should manifest itself in particular phenomena, that is, in particular behaviors of the retarded. They then devise experiments in which, if the predicted behavior is observed, the existence of the hypothesized defect is confirmed. This approach is legitimate and has become increasingly popular.

The majority of theories in the area of mental retardation are basically defect theories. It should be noted that these theories differ among themselves. One difference involves the theoretician's effort to relate the postulated defect to some specific physiological structure. The theoretical language of some defect positions is explicitly physiological, that of others is nonphysiological, while that of others has remained extremely vague. Such differences are related to the specific nature of the defect postulated. Particular defects that have been attributed to the retarded include the relative impermeability of the boundaries between regions in the cognitive structure (Kounin 1941; Lewin 1926–1933); primary and secondary rigidity caused by subcortical and cortical malformations, respectively (Goldstein 1943); inadequate neural satiation related to brain modifiability or cortical conductivity (Spitz 1963); malfunctioning disinhibitory mechanisms (Siegel & Foshee 1960); improper development of the verbal system resulting in a dissociation between verbal and motor systems (Luria 1963; O'Connor & Hermelin 1959); and the relative brevity in the persistence of the stimulus trace (Ellis 1963).

Luria and verbal mediation theory. Some of the more influential of the defect positions will be examined here, turning first to the position of the Russian investigator, A. R. Luria, whose work has influenced investigators in England and the United States. In respect to Russian efforts it should be noted that, given the political philosophy of the U.S.S.R., workers in the area of mental retardation have no alternative but to accept a defect position. As in the United States, the Russians divide the retarded into three groups, although they use the older terms "idiot," "imbecile," and "debile." However, the generic term for mental retardation is "oligophrenia." The practice, followed in this article, of distinguishing between the group of approximately 25 per cent of retardates having known organic impairments and that larger group having unknown etiologies is simply not permitted by Soviet investigators.

Although this section of the article is directed at illuminating differences of opinion concerning this larger group, there is a general consensus in the United States that this type of retardate, which we conventionally classify as familial, is the product of complex genetic determinants and cultural deprivation. In contrast, as the subcommittee of the President's Panel which recently visited the U.S.S.R. has noted (see Mental Retardation in the Soviet Union 1964), Soviet philosophy does not accept the view that mental retardation is determined by genetic factors, nor is cultural causation considered a possible explanation. Thus workers in this area attribute all grades of mental retardation to central-nervous-system damage, suggesting that it occurs initially during the intrauterine period or during early childhood and then results in a disturbance of the child's subsequent mental development.

It is clear, then, that in the Soviet Union the diagnosis of mental retardation necessarily involves the specification of a defect in some neurophysiological system, and it is noteworthy that professionals, including researchers and teachers, working with the retarded are called "defectologists." Knowledgeable visitors (see "Mental Retardation in the Soviet Union" 1964) have pointed out that, given such an approach, diagnosticians will go to great lengths to "discover" some slight indication of possible organicity. However, in observing the pupils in the Soviet schools for the debile, it was apparent that those in attendance were primarily retardates who would be diagnosed as familial in the United States. With rare exceptions, these were the children of unskilled workers and in some instances were actually the children of the graduates of such schools.

Consistent with the over-all Russian philosophy, general intelligence tests have been banned since 1936 by the Communist party because such tests are considered to be methods which discriminate against the peasants and the working class in favor of the culturally advantaged. Diagnosis in mental retardation is made by neurologists and psychophysiologists, who rely heavily on gross

pathological signs in the case of the severely retarded and minor physical defects, minute examinations of electroencephalograph (EEG) patterns, and certain qualitative (nonstandardized) tests of perception, conditioning, and concept formation (with special emphasis on the identification of specific types of language disorders) in the case of the more mildly retarded.

Luria's efforts and the difficulties they pose for non-Russian workers can only be understood in terms of such an orientation toward mental retardation. In his work on verbal mediation, Luria has demonstrated that the behavior of retardates resembles that of chronologically younger normal children in that the verbal instructions do not result in the smooth regulation of motor behavior. His findings clearly indicate that on all his tasks requiring verbal mediation, the retarded subjects have considerable difficulty. In light of these behavioral data, Luria has inferred that the major defect in the retarded child involves both an underdevelopment or a general "inertness" of the verbal system and a dissociation of this system from the motor or action system. The general effect of this dissociation, vaguely conceptualized as a disturbance in normal cortical activity, is that a verbal response cannot serve as an adequate regulator of voluntary behavior.

Unfortunately, it is impossible to utilize Luria's data to throw any light on the issue of whether the cognitive processes of retardates, typically diagnosed as familial, differ from normal children of the same MA. As noted earlier, a Russian defectologist would not accept this as a legitimate question. Since there is no concern with the IQ, there is no way to determine the MAs of the retardates and normals compared in Luria's work. Furthermore, the etiological question of whether his retarded subjects are of the physiologically impaired or the familial–cultural type remains unanswered. However, in light of Luria's discussion of "profound atrophic changes . . . expressed in the underdevelopment of the complex neuron structures of the first and third strata of the cortex" and his classification of these retardates as imbeciles rather than debiles, it would appear that these subjects probably suffer from gross physiological impairment.

It must be concluded, then, that these data have extremely limited relevance to the issue of whether those retardates whom we conventionally classify as familial suffer from some physiological defect. We must therefore look to English and American workers for more adequate tests of the basic proposition that all retardates, including the familial, differ from normals in the degree to which they employ verbal cues in regulating voluntary behavior. For example, O'Connor and Hermelin (1959) have found no significant difference between normals and retardates in the number of trials required to learn a size discrimination. However the finding that retardates required significantly fewer trials to learn a reversal was interpreted as supporting Luria's position. O'Connor and Hermelin reasoned that on the original learning task the normal child employs both motor and verbal mediational responses in his learning, while the retarded child relies primarily on the motor response. When the reversal is introduced, the normal child must unlearn both the original motor and verbal responses. The retardate, having to unlearn only the motor response, would thus be expected to learn the reversal problem more easily. The findings of O'Connor and Hermelin are troublesome in light of their inconsistency with earlier studies (e.g., Stevenson & Zigler 1957) in which mental retardates were not found to be superior on a discrimination reversal task. In an effort to resolve this discrepancy, Balla and Zigler (1964) ran a reversal-learning study involving several different reversal tasks and different types of retardates at different MA levels. This study provided no support for the Luria position.

Milgram and Furth (1963) compared retarded and normal children of the same MA on a series of concept tasks assumed to vary in the degree to which language might facilitate performance. Their findings were consistent with expectations derived from Luria's position. However, in an experiment comparing retardates and normals of the same MA on their ability to employ verbal mediators, Rieber (1964) obtained findings that were inconsistent with those that would be derived from Luria's theory. It thus appears that the evidence to date which has been mustered to support Luria's position remains equivocal.

Spitz and cortical satiation theory. Another major defect position is that of Herman Spitz (1963), who has extended the Köhler–Wallach cortical satiation theory to the area of mental retardation. Spitz has argued that all retardates suffer from inadequate neural satiation which is related to brain modifiability or cortical conductivity, and has tested this position by comparing normals and retardates of the same CA. Again it should be noted that no direct physiological evidence has been presented to indicate that familial retardates suffer from inadequate neural or cortical function-

ing. Furthermore, there is direct physiological evidence (Lashley et al. 1951) which calls into question the validity of the entire Köhler–Wallach position [see GESTALT THEORY].

As in the case of the earlier gestalt workers, Spitz has primarily employed perceptual tasks to test his position. His extensive program of research has now been summarized (Spitz 1963), and any complete review would be beyond the scope of this paper. Spitz's most convincing evidence has been obtained on those perceptual tasks (e.g., figural aftereffects and Necker cube reversals) that are thought to be sensitive to hypothesized cortical satiation effects.

The heuristic value of Spitz's position can be seen in his recent efforts to extend his postulates beyond the visual perception area and to employ them to generate specific predictions concerning the phenomena of learning, transposition, generalization, and problem solving. Spitz has noted a number of studies in these various areas which lend credence to his basic position. He has also been quite explicit in noting the limitations of his view. He has pointed out that, contrary to his theory, cortical satiation as measured by his perceptual indexes does not "in general correlate with IQ, but rather only differentiates the average performance of two distinct groups." The extensive overlap between normals and retardates on his tests of satiation led him to conclude that "the satiation variable must be only a very small one in the total complex of intelligent behavior."

Spitz has also been appropriately concerned with the fact that the test–retest reliability of the scores of his retardates is not impressive. Furthermore, he has noted that the lack of any correlation of individual scores across certain of his satiation tasks is troublesome for his position. Across modalities and even in the same modality, correlations have been moderate or nonexistent. In addition to these concerns, Spitz has been sensitive to the issue of how accurately the subject's response, often a verbal report, reflects the perceptual response being investigated. (See Spivack 1963 for a discussion of this problem in respect to research with the retarded.)

Adding to these difficulties is the fact that several investigators have now discovered that responses to cognitive and perceptual tasks are influenced by a variety of motivational factors (e.g., Zigler & deLabry 1962; Zigler & Unell 1962). In addition certain aspects of Spitz's work have come in for criticism on the grounds that his findings are inconsistent with those of other investigators.

Spivack (1963) has voiced this concern in a review of research on perceptual processes in the retarded, noting that certain of Spitz's findings "are in marked contrast to the findings of others."

Of more importance to the central question of this section is the conclusion that Spitz's data throw little light on the issue of whether familial retardates are inherently different from normals of the same MA. Taking a stand reminiscent of the Russian position, Spitz has argued that the distinction between familial and organic retardates is misleading. In Spitz's view, all retardates suffer from brain damage in the broader sense, and he has argued (see Garrison 1966) that retardates be conceptualized as belonging to a common class. Therefore his work has been characterized by a relative lack of concern with the problem of etiology, and we have little way of assessing whether the differences he reports are a product of gross organic pathology or may actually reflect the cortical phenomena that Spitz postulates.

That one finds differences between normals and retardates matched on CA is not very surprising, since we are dealing with groups who are at different developmental levels (as defined by MA). One would be tempted to say that Spitz's work has little relevance to the central issue of this section except for the fact that he has been quite explicit in his view that the differences he obtains are not developmental phenomena but reflect a physical deficit that should manifest itself even in comparisons with MA-matched normals.

The Lewin–Kounin formulation. The final defect position that we shall discuss is that of Lewin (1926–1933) and Kounin (1941). This position is different from the other defect views in that the defect postulated is one in the cognitive structure rather than the physical structure of the retardate. The Lewin–Kounin formulation has had considerable impact not only on our conceptualization of the retarded but also on the treatment and training practices that have been employed over the years. (For a more complete historical review and critique of the Lewin–Kounin formulation, the reader is referred to Zigler 1962.)

In Lewin's general theory the individual is treated as a dynamic system with differences among individuals derivable from a diversity of (1) structure of the total system, (2) material and state of the system, or (3) meaningful content of the system. The first two of these factors play the most important role in Lewin's theory of retardation. Lewin viewed the retarded child as having a less-differentiated cognitive structure, that is, having fewer regions or cells, than a normal child of the

same CA. Thus, in terms of structure, the retarded child resembles a normal younger child. In relation to the material and state of the system, Lewin stated that even though a retarded child corresponded in degree of differentiation to a normal younger child, these children were not to be regarded as entirely similar. He considered "the major dynamic difference between a feebleminded and normal child of the same degree of differentiation to consist in a greater stiffness, a smaller capacity for dynamic rearrangement in the psychical systems of the former." (Degree of differentiation was later operationally defined as MA.)

Although Lewin undoubtedly felt that lack of differentiation could lead to rigid behaviors (e.g., pedantry, fixation, stereotypy, inelasticity, perseveration), he was quite clear that this lack of differentiation was not what he meant by rigidity. To Lewin, lack of differentiation referred to the number of regions within the total system, while rigidity was defined in terms of the fluidity between regions. (By rigidity, Lewin was referring to the nature of the boundary between cells in the cognitive structure.) It follows from Lewin's theory that an individual whose system is characterized by either lack of differentiation or rigidity, or both, is more likely to emit behaviors commonly referred to as rigid. The failure to draw a clear distinction between the meaning of rigidity as he employed it and rigid behaviors as such appears to be a major factor leading to the subsequent controversy in the area.

The clearest experimental support for the position that familial retarded individuals are more rigid than normal individuals having the same degree of differentiation is contained in the work of Kounin (1941; 1948). Kounin, building upon Lewin's work, advanced the view that rigidity is a positive, monotonic function of CA. Again, it is imperative to note that by rigidity Kounin, like Lewin, referred to "that property of a functional boundary which prevents communication between neighboring regions" and not to rigid behaviors as such.

Kounin (1941) offered the findings of five experiments in support of his theory. In these experiments he employed three groups, older familial retarded individuals, younger familial retarded individuals, and normals. Noting the inadequacies of Lewin's own experimental efforts, Kounin instituted certain experimental controls. He defined the degree of differentiation as the MA of an individual and controlled for this factor by equating the three groups on MA. He also attempted to reduce what he later referred to as "motivational factors (such as low success expectation and hesitance to enter unfamiliar regions) that might produce those very types of behavior that are sometimes lumped together in the pseudo-descriptive category of behavioral rigidity" (Kounin 1948). To control for these factors, Kounin attempted to make each subject feel confident and secure in the experimental tasks by having them engage in each of the activities prior to the experiment proper. As Kounin predicted, the three groups differed in certain instruction-initiated tasks (e.g., drawing cats until satiated and then drawing bugs until satiated, lowering a lever in order to release marbles and then raising the lever to release marbles). As predicted from the Lewin–Kounin formulation, the normals showed the greatest amount of transfer effects from task to task, the younger retarded a lesser amount of transfer, and the older retarded the least amount of transfer. That is, on the drawing task the retarded individuals drew longer on the second task following satiation of the first task than did normals, and the older retardates longer than the younger. On the lever-pressing task, the greatest number of errors, that is, lowering rather than raising the lever on part two, were made by the normals, the least number by the older retarded, with the younger retarded falling between these two groups.

One should note that on this last task the lesser rigidity, as defined by Lewin and Kounin, of the normals results in a higher incidence of a behavioral response often characterized as rigid (i.e., perseverative responses). Furthermore, this lack of influence of one region upon another in the performance of the retarded would only be predicted in those cases where the retarded individual is "psychologically" placed into a new region by employing an instructional procedure. In those instances where the individual must, on his own, move from one region to another, the Lewin–Kounin formulation would predict that such movement would be more difficult for the retarded than for the normal individual. This prediction was also confirmed by Kounin in his concept-switching experiment in which the child was asked first to sort a deck of cards, which could be sorted either on the basis of color or form, and then to put the cards together some other way. Here the normals evidenced the least difficulty in shifting, the older retarded the most difficulty, and the younger retarded group again fell between the other two groups. Thus, when a movement to a new region is self-initiated, it is the retarded who evidence the higher incidence of perseverative responses.

The Lewin–Kounin theory of rigidity is a con-

ceptually demanding one in that it sometimes predicts a higher and sometimes a lower incidence of "rigid" behaviors in retarded as compared to normal individuals. However, the fact that it generates specific predictions as to when one or the other state of affairs will obtain is a tribute to the theory. Kounin thus offered impressive experimental support for the view that, with MA held constant, the older or more retarded (or both) an individual is, the more will his behaviors be characterized by dynamic rigidity, that is, greater rigidity in the boundaries between regions.

This model and its experimental support was so impressive that until fairly recently very few further experimental tests were attempted. However, recent explicit tests of the model (Balla & Zigler 1964; Stevenson & Zigler 1957; Zigler & Unell 1962) have failed to provide support for it. Much evidence now indicates that the differences found by Kounin were not a product of the inherent rigidity of retardates, but rather reflected a number of motivational differences between normal children and institutionalized retardates of the same MA. These motivational factors will be discussed in the final section.

Motivational and emotional factors

A recurring theme in the present article has been the importance of a variety of nonintellective factors as determinants of the level at which the retarded functions. We shall never comprehend the behavior of the retarded if we assume that every behavior he manifests is the immutable product of his low intelligence. Furthermore, we must go beyond the overly simplistic theories that have been advanced, such as the view that all retardates manifest a highly similar pattern of behavior which is determined by their common defect. Indeed, a striking feature encountered when groups of retardates are observed is the variety of behavior patterns displayed. Clearly, we are not dealing with a homogeneous group of simple organisms. Once we concern ourselves with the total behavior of the retarded child, we find him an extremely complex psychological system. To the extent that his behavior deviates from the norms associated with his MA, he is even more difficult to understand than the normal individual.

It is unfortunate that so little work emanating from a personality point of view has been done with the retarded. Some progress has been made, however, and much of the recent work supports the view that it is not necessary to employ constructs other than those used to account for the behavior of normal individuals in explaining the behavior of the familial retarded. It appears that many of the reported differences between retardates and normals of the same MA are a result of motivational and emotional differences which reflect differences in environmental histories and are not a function of innate deficiencies.

That personality factors are as important in the retardate's adjustment as are intellective factors has been noted (e.g., Penrose 1949; see also Windle 1962 for an especially comprehensive review of the importance of nonintellective factors in the prognosis of mental retardation). Many of the early workers in this country felt that the difference between social adequacy and inadequacy in that large group of borderline retardates was a matter of personality and character rather than intelligence. A number of studies have confirmed this view (see Windle 1962). Perhaps the best of these is the comprehensive study by Weaver (1946) of the adjustment of 8,000 retardates inducted into the U.S. Army, most of whom had IQs below 75. Of the total group, 56 per cent of the males and 62 per cent of the females made a satisfactory adjustment to military life. The median IQs of the successful and unsuccessful groups were 72 and 68 respectively. Weaver concluded that "personality factors far overshadowed the factor of intelligence in the adjustment of the retarded to military service."

This tendency to overemphasize the importance of the intellect in adjustment has been made clear by Windle (1962). On the basis of a survey, he found that most institutions presume that intelligence is the critical factor in adjustment after release. Windle goes on to point out that the vast majority of studies (over 20) on outcome "after release from institutions have reported no relation between intellectual level and later adjustment." In examining this literature we find that the factors which led to poor social adjustment include anxiety, jealousy, overdependency, poor self-evaluation, hostility, hyperactivity, and failure to follow orders even when requests were well within the range of intellectual competence.

It is hardly surprising that retardates evidence such difficulties in light of their atypical social histories. The specific atypical features of their socialization histories and the extent to which they are atypical may vary from child to child. Two sets of parents who are themselves familially retarded may provide quite different socialization histories for their children. At one extreme we may find a familially retarded child who grows up in an abysmal home environment and who is ultimately institutionalized, not because of lack of intelligence but

because his own home represents such a poor environment. That many borderline retardates are institutionalized for just such reasons has been confirmed by Kaplun (1935) in a study of 642 high-grade retardates; Zigler's recent finding (1961) that a positive relationship exists between the institutionalized familial retardate's IQ and the amount of preinstitutional deprivation he experienced provides further support for this claim. This latter finding does not indicate that social deprivation produces greater intelligence but rather that our institutions contain borderline retardates who would not be institutionalized except for their extremely poor home environments.

At the other extreme, the familially retarded set of parents of an institutionalized child may have provided him with a relatively normal home, even though it might differ in certain important respects (e.g., values, goals, and attitudes) from the typical home in which the families are of average or superior intelligence. In the first example the child not only experiences a quite different socialization history while still living with his parents, but he also differs from the child in the second situation to the extent that institutionalization affects his personality structure. Given the penchant of many investigators for comparing institutionalized retardates with children of average intellect who live at home, the factor of institutionalization becomes an extremely important one. One cannot help but wonder how many differences discovered in such comparisons reflect some cognitive aspect of mental retardation as opposed to the effects of institutionalization, the factors that led to the child's institutionalization, or some complex interaction between these factors and institutionalization.

To add even more complexity, the socialization histories of both institutionalized and noninstitutionalized familial retardates differ markedly from the history of the brain-damaged retardates. The brain damaged do not show the same gross differences in the frequency of good versus poor environments as do familials. In the face of such complexity, we need not consider the problem unassailable, nor need we assert that each retarded child is unique and that it is therefore impossible for us to isolate the ontogenesis of those factors which we feel are important in influencing the retardate's level of functioning. Once we conceptualize the retardate as occupying a position on a continuum of normality, we can allow our knowledge of normal development to give direction to our efforts.

This does not mean that we ignore the importance of the lowered intelligence per se, since personality traits and behavior patterns do not develop in a vacuum. However, in some instances the personality characteristics of the retarded will reflect environmental factors that have little or nothing to do with intellectual endowment. For example, many of the effects of institutionalization may be constant regardless of the person's intelligence level. In other instances, we must think in terms of an interaction; that is, given his lowered intellectual ability, a person will have certain experiences and develop certain behavior patterns differing from those of a person with greater intellectual endowment. An obvious example is the greater amount of failure which the retardate typically experiences. But again what must be emphasized is that the behavior pattern developed by the retardate as a result of such a history of failure will not differ in kind or ontogenesis from those developed by an individual of normal intellect who, by some environmental circumstance, also experiences an inordinate amount of failure. By the same token, if the retardate can somehow be guaranteed a more typical history of success, we would expect his behavior to be more normal, independent of his intellectual level. Within this framework, the author will discuss the personality factors which have been known to influence the performance of the retarded.

Caution is needed in evaluating the role of motivational and emotional factors in the performance of the retarded. Performance on a task is most appropriately conceptualized as a function of two types of factors, intellective (i.e., cognitive) and nonintellective (i.e., motivational). The contribution of each factor will vary with the nature of the task. Motivational factors will more readily influence a perseveration task (e.g., how long a retardate will continue to put marbles into a box) than they will a discrimination-learning or concept-formation task. It has been demonstrated that the performance of retardates on tasks of the latter type is also influenced by motivational factors (Butterfield & Zigler 1965a; Zigler & deLabry 1962), but this should not be interpreted as evidence that basic intellectual capacity has been changed. Rather, these demonstrations suggest ways in which one may help the mentally retarded to utilize their intellectual capacity optimally. As such, they should not be viewed as manipulations which can make the retarded "normal" in their intellectual functioning.

Anxiety.   Considerable evidence has now been collected indicating the importance of anxiety on performance for a wide variety of tasks (Taylor 1956). The attenuating effects of anxiety on per-

formance appear to be a function of both the task-irrelevant defensive responses employed by the person to alleviate his anxiety and the drive features of anxiety itself. The drive approach to anxiety (Taylor 1956), which has received considerable confirmation, conceptualizes high anxiety as beneficial on extremely nondemanding tasks (e.g., classical eyelid conditioning) but detrimental on complex tasks where a variety of responses are available to the person. The higher anxiety level of retardates, as compared to normals, has now been noted by several investigators (e.g., Garfield 1963) who have either demonstrated or suggested that the heightened anxiety level of retardates could well have produced certain of the differences between retardates and MA-control normals reported in the literature. Work with retardates that has either focused on anxiety or raised the anxiety issue in a *post hoc* manner is of considerable value "in that it applies concepts and techniques to the study of retarded individuals, which for the most part had not been applied or seen as relevant for this group" (Garfield 1963, p. 594). [*See* ANXIETY.]

The facts that anxiety level affects the performance of retardates much as that of normals and that retardates might have higher levels of anxiety than normals tell us little about the ontogenesis of anxiety in retardates. To understand their atypical anxiety levels, we must examine the relatively atypical experiences of the retarded, as well as a variety of other motivational states which influence their performance.

Social deprivation.   It has now become increasingly clear that our understanding of the performance of the institutionalized familial retardates will be enhanced if we consider the inordinate amount of preinstitutional social deprivation they have experienced (Clarke & Clarke 1954; Kaplun 1935; Zigler 1961). A series of recent studies (Green & Zigler 1962; Zigler 1961; Zigler & Williams 1963) has indicated that one result of such early deprivation is a heightened motivation to interact with a supportive adult. (In the process of conducting these studies, a social deprivation scale was constructed which promises to bring some added objectivity to the social deprivation concept.) These studies suggest that, given this heightened motivation, retardates exhibit considerable compliance with instructions when the effect of such compliance is to increase or maintain the social interaction with the adult. Compliance is apparently reduced in those instances where it leads to terminating the interaction.

It now appears that the perseveration so frequently noted in the behavior of the retarded is primarily a function of this motivational factor rather than the inherent cognitive rigidity suggested by Lewin (1926–1933) and Kounin (1941). Evidence on this latter point comes from findings indicating that (1) the degree of perseveration is directly related to the degree of preinstitutional deprivation experienced (Zigler 1961) and (2) institutionalized children of normal intellect are just as perseverative as institutionalized retardates, while noninstitutionalized retardates are no more perseverative than noninstitutionalized children of normal intellect (Green & Zigler 1962). The finding that institutionalization (or the social history factors leading to institutionalization) is the crucial factor in determining the child's response to social reinforcement on a simple task has also been found by Stevenson and Fahel (1961). The heightened motivation to interact with an adult, stemming from a history of social deprivation, would appear to be consistent with the often-made observation of certain behaviors in the retarded, such as seeking attention and wishing for affection (Doll 1962).

It is impossible to place too much emphasis on the role of overdependency in the institutional familial retarded and on the socialization histories that give rise to such overdependency. Given some minimal intellectual level, the shift from dependence to independence is perhaps the single most important factor necessary for the retardate to become a self-sustaining member of our society. It appears that the institutionalized retardate must satisfy certain affectional needs before he can cope with problems in a manner characterized by individuals whose affectional needs have been relatively satiated. These affectional needs can best be viewed as ones which often interfere with certain problem-solving activities. Because the retardate is highly motivated to satisfy such needs through maximizing interpersonal contact, he is relatively unconcerned with the specific solution to these problems. Of course the two goals will not always be incompatible, but in many instances they will be. Some evidence that this attenuating aspect of retarded behavior can be overcome has been presented by McKinney and Keele (1963), who found improvement in a variety of behaviors in the mentally retarded following an experience of increased mothering.

Zigler and Williams (1963) have provided some evidence on the interaction between preinstitutional social deprivation and institutionalization in influencing the child's motivation for social interaction and support. It was found that although institutionalization generally increased this motivation, it was increased much more for children coming from relatively nondeprived homes than for those coming from more socially deprived backgrounds.

Change in IQ scores. An unexpected finding of the Zigler and Williams study was that a general decrease in the IQs of retardates was discovered between the administration of two IQ tests, the first of which occurred at the time of admission five years prior to this follow-up study. This change in IQ, discovered in the context of a study employing the amount of preinstitutional social deprivation as an independent variable, is reminiscent of a finding by Clarke and Clarke (1954). These investigators found that changes in the IQs of retardates following institutionalization were related to their preinstitutional histories. They discovered that children coming from extremely poor homes showed an increase in IQ which was not observed in children coming from relatively good homes. Zigler and Williams, however, found that the magnitude of the IQ change in their subjects was not significantly related to preinstitutional deprivation. Although this finding appears inconsistent with that of Clarke and Clarke, it should be noted that some support for a relationship was suggested, since the only subjects in the Zigler and Williams study who evidenced an increase in IQ were the highly deprived group. The failure of Zigler and Williams to replicate the findings of Clarke and Clarke may be due to two factors: the subjects used by Clarke and Clarke were older and had been institutionalized at a later age than the retardates employed by Zigler and Williams and the IQ changes reported by Clarke and Clarke took place during two years of institutionalization, while the IQ changes reported in the Zigler and Williams study were based on five years of institutionalization. This latter factor becomes increasingly important in view of E. C. Jones and Carr-Saunders' finding (1927) that normal institutionalized children show an increase in IQ early in institutionalization and then a decrease in IQ with longer institutionalization.

The work of Clarke and Clarke, Jones and Carr-Saunders, and others, dealing with changes in IQ following institutionalization has given central importance to the degree of intellectual stimulation provided by the institution in contrast to that provided by the original home. This orientation suggests that it is the actual intellectual potential of the person which is altered. The Zigler and Williams study, however, suggests that the change in IQ reflects a change in the child's motivation for social interaction. That is, as social deprivation, resulting from increased length of institutionalization, increases, the desire to interact with the adult experimenter increases. Thus, for the deprived child the desire to be correct must compete in the testing situation with the desire to increase the amount of social interaction. This argument would appear to provide the conceptual framework for Clarke and Clarke's finding that highly deprived subjects evidence an increase in IQ with relatively short institutionalization, while the less deprived subjects demonstrate no greater increase than a test–retest control group. One would further expect that with continued institutionalization all children would exhibit a decrease in IQ, the phenomenon found by Jones and Carr-Saunders (1927) and one that appears in the Zigler and Williams study. Direct support for this view comes from the finding in the Zigler and Williams study of a positive relationship between the magnitude of the decrease in IQ and the child's motivation for social interaction.

It should be noted that the Jones and Carr-Saunders (1927) study involved institutionalized children of approximately average intellect, thus indicating that the dynamics under discussion here are the same for both normal and retarded children. Furthermore, the position advanced here is quite consistent with the findings for normal children obtained by Barrett and Koch (1930); these investigators found that the greatest increase in IQ was obtained by children who showed the greatest improvement in their personality traits or by children who evidenced a marked change in the nature of their relationship with the examiner. Conversely, what must be emphasized in respect to lowered IQs is not the lowered test scores per se but rather that the factors which attenuate these test scores will, in all probability, reduce the adequacy of many problem-solving behaviors performed in a social situation.

Although there is considerable observational and experimental evidence that social deprivation results in a heightened motivation to interact with a supportive adult, it appears to have other effects as well. Again, the nature of these effects is suggested in those observations of the retarded that have emphasized their fearfulness, wariness or avoidance of strangers, or their suspicion and mistrust. The experimental work done by Zigler and his associates on the behavior of the institutionalized retarded has indicated that social deprivation results in both a heightened motivation to interact with supportive adults (positive-reaction tendency) as well as a reluctance and wariness to do so (negative-reaction tendency). That both of these tendencies are influenced by the quality of past relationships with adults and are amenable to ex-

perimental manipulations has been demonstrated in recent studies employing both normal and retarded children (e.g., Shallenberger & Zigler 1961). However, little work has been done on the range of behaviors that might be influenced by the negative-reaction tendency.

Failure and performance.   Another factor frequently mentioned as a determinant in the performance of the retarded is their high expectancy of failure (Cromwell 1963). This failure expectancy has been viewed as an outgrowth of a lifetime characterized by frequent confrontations with tasks for which the retarded are intellectually ill-equipped to deal. That failure experiences and the failure expectancies to which they give rise affect a wide variety of behaviors in the intellectually normal has now been amply documented. Of special interest to workers in the area of mental retardation is Lantz's finding (1945) that a relatively simple failure experience prevented children from profiting by practice which ordinarily leads to improvement on intelligence-test scores [see ACHIEVEMENT MOTIVATION].

The results of experimental work employing the success–failure dimensions with retardates are still somewhat inconsistent. The work of Cromwell and his students (reviewed in Cromwell 1963) has lent support to the general proposition that retardates have a higher expectancy of failure than do normals. This results in a style of problem solving for the retardate which causes him to be much more motivated to avoid failure than to achieve success. However, the inconsistent research findings suggest that this fairly simple proposition is in need of some further refinement. One investigator found that retardates performed better following success and poorer following failure as compared to a control group. Another investigator (Heber 1957) found that the performances of normals and retardates were equally enhanced following both a failure and a success condition, although in the success condition the performance of retardates was enhanced more than that of normals.

Conversely, Kass and Stevenson (1961) found that success enhanced the performance of normals more than that of retardates. Another study also found that failure had a general enhancing effect for both normals and retardates but that failure enhanced the performance of normals more than that of retardates (Gardner 1958). In a recent study by Butterfield and Zigler (1965a), one factor which may have produced this type of inconsistency was isolated. These investigators found that both normal and retarded children reacted differentially to success and failure experiences as a function of their responsivity to adults, that is, their desire to gain an adult's support and approval. The nature of the difference between normals and retardates in their reaction to success or failure experiences appeared to be determined by this desire for approval. Among high-responsive subjects, failure, as compared to success, attenuated the performance of retarded subjects while improving the performance of normal subjects. Among low-responsive subjects, failure, as compared to success, attenuated the performance of normals while improving the performance of retardates. Debilitating effects of prolonged failure on the performance of the retarded have been found by Zeaman and House (1962). These investigators discovered that following such failure, retardates were unable to solve a simple problem, although they had previously been able to do so. Assuming a failure set in retardates, Stevenson and Zigler (1958) confirmed the prediction that retardates would be more willing to "settle for" a lower degree of success than would normal children of the same MA. The fear of failure in the mentally retarded also appears to be an important factor in differences that have been found between normals' and retardates' achievement motivation (Jordan & DeCharms 1959).

Recent studies (Green & Zigler 1962; Turnure & Zigler 1964) have indicated that the high incidence of failure experienced by retardates generates a cognitive style of problem solving characterized by outer-directedness. That is, the retarded child comes to distrust his own solutions to problems and therefore seeks guides to action in the immediate environment. This outer-directedness may explain the great suggestibility so frequently attributed to the retarded child. Evidence has now been presented indicating that, compared to normals of the same MA, the retarded child is more sensitive to verbal cues given by an adult, is more imitative of the behaviors of both adults and peers, and engages in more visual scanning. Furthermore, certain findings (Green & Zigler 1962) suggest that the noninstitutionalized retardate is more outer-directed in his problem solving than the institutionalized retardate. This makes considerable sense if one remembers that the noninstitutionalized retardate does not reside in an environment adjusted to his intellectual shortcomings and should therefore experience more failure than the institutionalized retardate.

Turnure and Zigler (1964) have suggested that the distractability so frequently encountered in the retarded reflects, in part, this outer-directed style of problem solving. This interpretation is of particular interest, since distractability has often been viewed as a neurophysiologically determined characteristic of the retarded rather than the reflection of a style of problem solving emanating from the particular experiential histories of such children. Work on the outer-directedness of the retarded also appears related to the locus of control work done by Cromwell and his associates (Cromwell 1963). These investigators found that retardates, as compared to normals, manifest an external locus of control, that is, they attribute certain events caused by their own behavior to outside forces over which they have little control. (This internal-control versus external-control dimension has been employed by Cromwell to bring some further order to the inconsistent findings in the success–failure literature.)

The reinforcer hierarchy. Another nonintellective factor important in understanding the behavior of the retarded is the retardate's motivation under various types of incentives. That performance by normals and retardates on a variety of tasks is influenced by the nature of the incentive is certainly well documented. The social deprivation work discussed earlier in this section indicates that retardates have an extremely high motivation for attention, praise, and encouragement. Several investigators (e.g., Cromwell 1963; Zigler 1963) have suggested that in normal development the effectiveness of attention and praise as reinforcers diminishes with maturity and is replaced by the reinforcement inherent in the information that one is correct. This latter type of reinforcer appears to serve primarily as a cue for the administration of self-reinforcement [see LEARNING, *article on* REINFORCEMENT].

Zigler and his associates (Zigler 1962; Zigler & deLabry 1962; Zigler & Unell 1962) have argued that a variety of experiential factors in the history of the retarded cause them to be less motivated to be correct for the sake of correctness than normals of the same MA. Stated somewhat differently, these investigators have argued that the position of various reinforcers in the reinforcer hierarchies of normal and retarded children of the same MA differ. To date, the experimental work of this group has centered on the reinforcement which inheres in being correct. It is this reinforcer that is the most frequently dispensed, immediate incentive in most real-life tasks. Furthermore, it is a frequently used incentive in many experimental cognitive and perceptual tasks on which retardates and normals are compared, and it also seems to be the most important incentive in the typical test situation. When such an incentive is employed in experimental studies, one wonders how many of the differences found are attributable to differences in capacity between retardates and normals rather than to differences in performance which result from the different values that such incentives might have for the two types of subject.

Clearest support for the view that the retardate is much less motivated to be correct than is the middle-class child, so typically used in comparisons with the retarded, is contained in a study by Zigler and deLabry (1962). These investigators tested middle-class, lower-class, and retarded children equated on MA on a concept-switching task (Kounin 1941) under two conditions of reinforcement. In the first condition, similar to that employed by Kounin, the only reinforcement dispensed was the information that the child was correct. In the second condition, the child was rewarded with a toy of his choice if he switched from one concept to another. In the "correct" condition these investigators found, as Kounin did, that retardates were poorer in their concept switching than were middle-class children. That this was not a simple matter of cognitive rigidity was indicated by the finding that lower-class children equated with the middle-class children on MA were also inferior to the middle-class children. In the toy condition this inferiority disappeared, and retarded and lower-class children performed as well as the middle-class children. This study highlights an assumption that has been noted as erroneous by many educators; namely, that the lower-class child and the retarded child are motivated by the same incentives that motivate the typical middle-class child. An intriguing avenue of further research is the degree to which the position of various reinforcers in the hierarchy can be manipulated.

General effects of institutionalization. No discussion of motivational factors in the performance of the retarded would be complete without some mention of the effects of institutionalization. The institutionalization variable has probably contaminated more research in the area of mental retardation than any other single variable. Given our general lack of knowledge concerning the effects of institutionalization on human behavior, the extent of this contamination cannot be determined. That the effects of institutionalization on the behavior of retardates are considerable has been suggested by several investigators (e.g., McCandless 1964; Windle 1962). In view of the general consensus concerning the importance of institutionalization, it is amazing that more work has not been done to investigate its effects on retarded children.

Some fairly clear findings with retardates have demonstrated that institutionalization causes a decrement in the quality of language behavior (Lyle 1959), reduces the level of abstraction on vocabulary tests (Badt 1958), interferes with the ability to conceptualize an emotional continuum (Iscoe & McCann 1965), and increases the child's orientation toward punishment (Abel 1941). These studies, though suggestive, have shed little light on the specific aspects of institutionalization which affect such behaviors or on the exact nature of the process through which behaviors are affected. Whether the deficiencies in the behavior of the institutionalized retardate are motivational in nature or reflect an actual change in intellectual capacity is still an open question.

Evidence that institutions for the retarded differ in their effects on behavior has recently been reported by Butterfield and Zigler (1965*b*). It was found that children residing in a cold, restrictive institution showed a higher motivation for adult support and approval than children residing in an institution having a warm, accepting social climate. These investigators are presently conducting a cross-institutional longitudinal study of six state schools for the retarded in an effort to isolate the institutional factors and psychological processes underlying such effects.

Much of this work on motivational and emotional factors in the performance of the retarded is very recent. The research conducted on several of the factors discussed in this section is more suggestive than definitive. It is clear, however, that these factors are extremely important in determining the retardate's general level of functioning. Furthermore, these factors seem much more open to environmental manipulation than do the cognitive processes discussed earlier. An increase in knowledge concerning motivational and emotional factors and their ontogenesis and manipulation holds considerable promise for alleviating much of the social ineffectiveness displayed by that sizable group of persons who must function at a relatively low intellectual level.

EDWARD ZIGLER

[*Directly related are the entries* ACHIEVEMENT TESTING; INTELLIGENCE AND INTELLIGENCE TESTING; *other relevant material may be found in* CREATIVITY, *article on* GENIUS AND ABILITY; INFANCY, *article on* THE EFFECTS OF EARLY EXPERIENCE; SYSTEMS ANALYSIS, *article on* PSYCHOLOGICAL SYSTEMS; THINKING; *and in the biographies of* BINET *and* MONTESSORI.]

BIBLIOGRAPHY

ABEL, THEODORA M. 1941 Moral Judgments Among Subnormals. *Journal of Abnormal and Social Psychology* 36:378–392.

BADT, MARGIT 1958 Levels of Abstraction in Vocabulary Definitions of Mentally Retarded School Children. *American Journal of Mental Deficiency* 63:241–246.

BALLA, DAVID; and ZIGLER, EDWARD 1964 Discrimination and Switching Learning in Normal, Familial Retarded, and Organic Retarded Children. *Journal of Abnormal and Social Psychology* 69:664–669

BARRETT, HELEN E.; and KOCH, HELEN L. 1930 The Effect of Nursery-school Training Upon the Mental Test Performance of a Group of Orphanage Children. *Journal of Genetic Psychology* 37:102–122.

BURT, CYRIL; and HOWARD, MARGARET 1956 The Multifactorial Theory of Inheritance and Its Application to Intelligence. *British Journal of Statistical Psychology* 9:95–130.

BUTTERFIELD, EARL C.; and ZIGLER, EDWARD 1965a The Effects of Success and Failure on the Discrimination Learning of Normal and Retarded Children. *Journal of Abnormal Psychology* 70:25–31.

BUTTERFIELD, EARL C.; and ZIGLER, EDWARD 1965b The Influence of Differing Institutional Social Climates on the Effectiveness of Social Reinforcement in the Mentally Retarded. *American Journal of Mental Deficiency* 70:48–56.

CLARKE, A. D.; and CLARKE, A. M. 1954 Cognitive Changes in the Feebleminded. *British Journal of Psychology* 45:173–179.

CROMWELL, RUE L. 1963 A Social Learning Approach to Mental Retardation. Pages 41–91 in Norman R. Ellis (editor), *Handbook of Mental Deficiency: Psychological Theory and Research*. New York: McGraw-Hill.

DOLL, EUGENE E. 1962 A Historical Survey of Research and Management of Mental Retardation in the United States. Pages 21–68 in E. Philip Trapp and Philip Himelstein (editors), *Readings on the Exceptional Child*. New York: Appleton.

ELLIS, NORMAN R. 1963 The Stimulus Trace and Behavioral Inadequacy. Pages 134–158 in Norman R. Ellis (editor), *Handbook of Mental Deficiency: Psychological Theory and Research*. New York: McGraw-Hill.

FERGUSON, GEORGE A. 1956 On Transfer and the Abilities of Man. *Canadian Journal of Psychology* 10:121–131.

FREMMING, KURT H. (1947) 1951 *The Expectation of Mental Infirmity in a Sample of the Danish Population: (Based on a Biographical Investigation of 5,500 Persons Born in the Years 1883–1887)*. London: Eugenics Society. → First published in Danish.

GARDNER, WILLIAM I. 1958 *Reactions of Intellectually Normal and Retarded Boys After Experimentally Induced Failure: A Social Learning Theory Interpretation*. Ann Arbor, Mich.: University Microfilms.

GARFIELD, SOL L. 1963 Abnormal Behavior and Mental Deficiency. Pages 574–601 in Norman R. Ellis (editor), *Handbook of Mental Deficiency: Psychological Theory and Research*. New York: McGraw-Hill.

GARRISON, M. (editor) 1966 Cognitive Models and Development in Mental Retardation. *American Journal of Mental Deficiency* 70, no. 4 (Monograph Supplement).

GOLDSTEIN, KURT 1943 Concerning Rigidity. *Character and Personality* 11:209–226.

GREEN, CALVIN; and ZIGLER, EDWARD 1962 Social Deprivation and the Performance of Retarded and Normal Children on a Satiation Type Task. *Child Development* 33:499–508.

HEBB, DONALD O. 1949 *The Organization of Behavior: A Neuropsychological Theory*. New York: Wiley.

HEBER, RICK F. 1957 *Expectancy and Expectancy Changes in Normal and Mentally Retarded Boys*. Ann Arbor, Mich.: University Microfilms.

HEBER, RICK F. 1959 A Manual of Terminology and Classification in Mental Retardation. *American Journal of Mental Deficiency* 64, no. 2 (Monograph Supplement).

HEBER, RICK F. 1962 Mental Retardation: Concept and Classification. Pages 69–81 in E. Philip Trapp and Philip Himelstein (editors), *Readings on the Exceptional Child*. New York: Appleton.

HIRSCH, JERRY 1963 Behavior Genetics and Individuality Understood. *Science* 142:1436–1442.

ISCOE, IRA; and McCANN, BRIAN 1965 Perception of an Emotional Continuum by Older and Younger Mental Retardates. *Journal of Personality and Social Psychology* 1:383–385.

JERVIS, GEORGE A. 1959 The Mental Deficiencies. Volume 2, pages 1289–1313 in *American Handbook of Psychiatry*. Edited by Silvano Arieti. New York: Basic Books. → See especially Table 1 on page 1290.

JONES, E. CARADOG; and CARR-SAUNDERS, A. M. 1927 The Relation Between Intelligence and Social Status Among Orphan Children. *British Journal of Psychology* 17:343–364.

JONES, HAROLD E. (1946) 1954 The Environment and Mental Development. Pages 631–696 in Leonard Carmichael (editor), *Manual of Child Psychology*. New York: Wiley.

JORDAN, THOMAS E.; and DeCHARMS, RICHARD 1959 The Achievement Motive in Normal and Mentally Retarded Children. *American Journal of Mental Deficiency* 64:457–466.

KAPLUN, DAVID 1935 The High-grade Moron: A Study of Institutional Admissions Over a Ten Year Period. *Journal of Psychoasthenics* 40:69–91. → Now called the *American Journal of Mental Deficiency*.

KASS, NORMAN; and STEVENSON, HAROLD W. 1961 The Effect of Pretraining Reinforcement Conditions on Learning by Normal and Retarded Children. *American Journal of Mental Deficiency* 66:76–80.

KOUNIN, JACOB S. 1941 Experimental Studies of Rigidity. *Character and Personality* 9:251–282. → Part 1: The Measurement of Rigidity in Normal and Feebleminded Persons. Part 2: The Explanatory Power of the Concept of Rigidity as Applied to Feeble-mindedness.

KOUNIN, JACOB S. 1948 The Meaning of Rigidity: A Reply to Heinz Werner. *Psychological Review* 55:157–166.

LANTZ, BEATRICE 1945 Some Dynamic Aspects of Success and Failure. *Psychological Monographs* 59, no. 1; Serial no. 271.

LASHLEY, K. S.; CHOW, K. L.; and SEMMES, JOSEPHINE 1951 An Examination of the Electrical Field Theory of Cerebral Integration. *Psychological Review* 58:123–136.

LAURENDEAU, MONIQUE; and PINARD, ADRIEN 1963 *Causal Thinking in the Child: A Genetic and Experimental Approach*. New York: International Universities Press.

LEAHY, ALICE M. 1935 Nature–Nurture and Intelligence. *Genetic Psychology Monographs* 17:236–308.

LEWIN, KURT (1926–1933) 1935 *A Dynamic Theory of Personality: Selected Papers*. New York: McGraw-Hill.

LURIA, A. R.   1963   Psychological Studies of Mental Deficiency in the Soviet Union. Pages 353–387 in Norman R. Ellis (editor), *Handbook of Mental Deficiency: Psychological Theory and Research.* New York: McGraw-Hill.

LYLE, J. G.   1959   The Effect of an Institutional Environment Upon the Verbal Development in Imbecile Children. 1: Verbal Intelligence. *Journal of Mental Deficiency Research* 3:122–128.

McCANDLESS, BOYD R.   1964   Relation of Environmental Factors to Intellectual Functioning. Pages 175–213 in Harvey A. Stevens and Rick F. Heber (editors), *Mental Retardation: A Review of Research.* Univ. of Chicago Press.

McCLEARN, GERALD E.   1962   The Inheritance of Behavior. Pages 144–252 in Leo Postman (editor), *Psychology in the Making.* New York: Knopf.

McKINNEY, JOHN P.; and KEELE, TINA   1963   Effects of Increased Mothering on the Behavior of Severely Retarded Boys. *American Journal of Mental Deficiency* 67:556–562.

MAHER, BRENDAN A.   1963   Intelligence and Brain Damage. Pages 224–252 in Norman R. Ellis (editor), *Handbook of Mental Deficiency: Psychological Theory and Research.* New York: McGraw-Hill.

Mental Retardation in the Soviet Union.   1964   *Canada's Mental Health* Supplement no. 42.

MILGRAM, NORMAN A.; and FURTH, HANS G.   1963   The Influence of Language on Concept Attainment in Educable Retarded Children. *American Journal of Mental Deficiency* 67:733–739.

O'CONNOR, N.; and HERMELIN, B.   1959   Discrimination and Reversal Learning in Imbeciles. *Journal of Abnormal and Social Psychology* 59:409–413.

PENROSE, LIONEL S.   (1949) 1963   *The Biology of Mental Defect.* 3d ed. London: Sidgwick & Jackson.

PHILLIPS, LESLIE; and ZIGLER, EDWARD   1964   Role Orientation, the Action–Thought Dimension, and Outcome in Psychiatric Disorder. *Journal of Abnormal and Social Psychology* 68:381–389.

PIAGET, JEAN   (1932) 1948   *The Moral Judgment of the Child.* Glencoe, Ill.: Free Press. → First published in French.

RIEBER, MORTON   1964   Verbal Mediation in Normal and Retarded Children. *American Journal of Mental Deficiency* 68:634–641.

SHALLENBERGER, PATRICIA; and ZIGLER, EDWARD   1961   Rigidity, Negative Reaction Tendencies, and Cosatiation Effects in Normal and Feebleminded Children. *Journal of Abnormal and Social Psychology* 63:20–26.

SIEGEL, PAUL S.; and FOSHEE, JAMES G.   1960   Molar Variability in the Mentally Defective. *Journal of Abnormal and Social Psychology* 61:141–143.

SPITZ, HERMAN H.   1963   Field Theory in Mental Deficiency. Pages 11–40 in Norman R. Ellis (editor), *Handbook of Mental Deficiency: Psychological Theory and Research.* New York: McGraw-Hill.

SPIVACK, GEORGE   1963   Perceptual Processes. Pages 480–511 in Norman R. Ellis (editor), *Handbook of Mental Deficiency: Psychological Theory and Research.* New York: McGraw-Hill.

STEVENSON, HAROLD W.; and FAHEL, LEILA   1961   The Effect of Social Reinforcement on the Performance of Institutionalized and Noninstitutionalized Normal and Feebleminded Children. *Journal of Personality* 29:136–147.

STEVENSON, HAROLD W.; and ZIGLER, EDWARD   1957   Discrimination Learning and Rigidity in Normal and Feebleminded Individuals. *Journal of Personality* 25:699–711.

STEVENSON, HAROLD W.; and ZIGLER, EDWARD   1958   Probability Learning in Children. *Journal of Experimental Psychology* 56:185–192.

TAYLOR, JANET A.   (1956) 1963   Drive Theory and Manifest Anxiety. Pages 205–222 in Martha T. Mednick and Sarnoff A. Mednick (editors), *Research in Personality.* New York: Holt. → First published in the *Psychological Bulletin.*

THORPE, LOUIS P.   (1946) 1955   *Child Psychology and Development.* 2d ed. New York: Ronald Press.

TURNURE, JAMES; and ZIGLER, EDWARD   1964   Outer-directedness in the Problem Solving of Normal and Retarded Children. *Journal of Abnormal and Social Psychology* 69:427–436.

U.S. PRESIDENT'S PANEL ON MENTAL RETARDATION   1963   *A Proposed Program for National Action to Combat Mental Retardation.* Washington: Government Printing Office.

WEAVER, THOMAS R.   1946   The Incidence of Maladjustment Among Mental Defectives in Military Environment. *American Journal of Mental Deficiency* 51:238–246.

WHEELER, LESTER R.   1942   A Comparative Study of the Intelligence of East Tennessee Mountain Children. *Journal of Educational Psychology* 33:321–334.

WHITNEY, E. ARTHUR   1956   Mental Deficiency: 1955. *American Journal of Mental Deficiency* 60:676–683.

WINDLE, CHARLES   1962   Prognosis of Mental Subnormals. *American Journal of Mental Deficiency* 66, no. 5 (Monograph Supplement).

ZEAMAN, DAVID; and HOUSE, BETTY J.   1962   Approach and Avoidance in the Discrimination Learning of Retardates. *Child Development* 33:355–372.

ZIGLER, EDWARD   1961   Social Deprivation and Rigidity in the Performance of Feebleminded Children. *Journal of Abnormal and Social Psychology* 62:413–421.

ZIGLER, EDWARD   1962   Rigidity in the Feebleminded. Pages 141–162 in E. Philip Trapp and Philip Himelstein (editors), *Readings on the Exceptional Child.* New York: Appleton.

ZIGLER, EDWARD   1963   Social Reinforcement, Environmental Conditions and the Child. *American Journal of Orthopsychiatry* 33:614–623.

ZIGLER, EDWARD; and DELABRY, JACQUES   1962   Concept-switching in Middle-class, Lower-class, and Retarded Children. *Journal of Abnormal and Social Psychology* 65:267–273.

ZIGLER, EDWARD; and UNELL, EARL   1962   Concept-switching in Normal and Feebleminded Children as a Function of Reinforcement. *American Journal of Mental Deficiency* 66:651–657.

ZIGLER, EDWARD; and WILLIAMS, JOANNA   1963   Institutionalization and the Effectiveness of Social Reinforcement: A Three Year Follow-up Study. *Journal of Abnormal and Social Psychology* 66:197–205.

MENTAL TESTING
See INTELLIGENCE AND INTELLIGENCE TESTING.

MERCANTILISM
See under ECONOMIC THOUGHT.

MERCIER DE LA RIVIÈRE

Pierre Paul Mercier de la Rivière (1720–1793), French physiocrat, was born at Saumur (Indre et Loire), the son of a *président trésorier* of France. After studying law, at the age of 27 he became a member of the *parlement* of Paris and remained there for 12 years. He then served for several years as intendant of Martinique. Recalled as a result of policy differences with respect to free trade (he had admitted English ships to the island, in violation of the *pacte colonial*), he returned to the *parlement* in 1764 and in semiretirement wrote his masterpiece, *L'ordre naturel et essentiel des sociétés politiques* (1767).

The basic ideas of the physiocrats, and especially of Quesnay, their leader, are to be found in Mercier's work. In his *Ordre naturel*, Mercier built on the ideas presented by Quesnay in his "Despotisme de la Chine." Mercier stressed the political aspects of physiocracy rather than the agricultural ideas of the school. For him, the law of property, which is based on the physical order of nature, is unique and universal, underlying all other laws. It is a law that may be directly apprehended by all men, and one that governs the essential order of society. The proper character of political institutions derives from this basic importance of the law of property.

The sovereign, according to Mercier, is by definition co-owner of the fixed wealth of the society; in the eyes of his subjects he is no more than a large proprietor who has no privileges at the expense of others but, rather, is linked to his subjects by a common interest in maximizing the value of common property. The proportion of fixed wealth that is to be used as public revenue, or taxes, is thus determined by the natural law of property, provided that government takes the form of personal and legal despotism (as opposed to arbitrary despotism). Since under personal and legal despotism the despot embodies that fundamental unity of society which is based on the law of property, it is in the direct interest of such a despot to keep taxes within the limits of the portion required by the law of property.

Mercier proposed that the sovereign have both executive and legislative powers, for if legislative power is in the hands of a representative assembly, there necessarily arise parties with irreconcilable private interests. However, Mercier did advocate an independent judiciary, with the right to register laws, a suspensive veto of laws, and control of their constitutionality. In contrast with the law of property, which provides the security requisite to liberty, the laws enacted by the sovereign create no fundamental rights: they assure only the fulfillment of private contracts.

Thus Mercier envisioned a political order that is in harmony with nature. Every man becomes an instrument of the welfare of his fellows; no one can profit or become rich at the expense of others. Luxury, "that monster," will disappear, and peace will be established among nations.

The system of government that Mercier envisioned requires a mature public opinion as a final check on the consistency of the sovereign's conduct with the law of property. Mercier's *De l'instruction publique* (1775) described the system of national education necessary to raise public opinion to the appropriate level of maturity. To be sure, the "nation" that Mercier wished to educate was made up only of landowners and farmers; as a physiocrat, he considered commerce and industry as unproductive and unworthy of participation.

It is hard to assess the influence that Mercier had, since it merges with that of the entire school of Quesnay. Mercier is undoubtedly at least the most widely read of Quesnay's disciples, because his works have been most accessible to the general public. Mercier did not get along with Catherine the Great when he visited Russia at her invitation; however, the king of Sweden commissioned, and presumably profited from, Mercier's work on public education.

FRÉDÉRIC MAURO

[*For the historical context of Mercier's work, see* ECONOMIC THOUGHT, *article on* PHYSIOCRATIC THOUGHT; *and the biography of* QUESNAY.]

WORKS BY MERCIER

(1767) 1910 *L'ordre naturel et essentiel des sociétés politiques.* Paris: Geuthner.

1770 *L'intérêt général de l'état* . . . . Amsterdam and Paris: Desaint.

1775 *De l'instruction publique: Ou, considérations morales et politiques sur la nécessité, la nature et la source de cette instruction, ouvrage demandé pour le roi de Suède.* Stockholm and Paris: Didot.

1789 *Essais sur les maximes et loix fondamentales de la monarchie françoise* . . . . Paris: Vallat-La-Chapelle.

1790 *Palladium de la constitution politique: Ou, régénération morale de la France* . . . . Paris: Baudouin.

SUPPLEMENTARY BIBLIOGRAPHY

JOUBLEAU, F. 1858–1859 Notice sur P.-P. Lemercier de la Rivière. Académie des Sciences Morales et Politiques, Paris, *Séances et travaux* 46:439–455; 47:121–150, 249–265.

LARIVIÈRE, CHARLES DE (1897) 1909 Mercier de la Rivière à Saint-Pétersbourg en 1767. Pages 71–132 in Charles de Larivière, *La France et la Russie au XVIIIe siècle: Études d'histoire et de littérature franco-russe.* Paris: Soudier.

RICHNER, EDMUND 1931 *Le Mercier de la Rivière: Ein Führer der physiokratischen Bewegung in Frankreich.* Zurich: Girsberger.

SILBERSTEIN, LOTTE 1928 *Lemercier de la Rivière und seine politischen Ideen.* Berlin: Eberling.

WEULERSSE, GEORGES 1910 *Le mouvement physiocratique en France de 1756 à 1770.* 2 vols. Paris: Alcan.

WEULERSSE, GEORGES 1950 *La physiocratie sous les ministères de Turgot et de Necker (1774–1781).* Paris: Presses Universitaires de France.

WEULERSSE, GEORGES 1959 *La physiocratie à la fin du règne de Louis XV: 1770–1774.* Paris: Presses Universitaires de France.

MERGERS

A merger is the combination into a single business enterprise of two or more previously independent enterprises. The combination may take a number of forms. Among these are the outright purchase of the assets of one company by another for cash or for the stock or debt of the acquiring company. A holding company may be created, with the stock of the combining companies exchanged for that of the parent company. The stock of the merging companies may be held in trust, though this has been generally superseded by corporate arrangements. Combinations have been effected by long-term lease. The legal and financial forms the merger takes are governed largely by tax, corporate charter, and other legal provisions that introduce unique elements in each case. While such factors are of some influence in shaping the broad pattern of mergers, they are probably much less important than underlying forces of economic change and competition.

Mergers represent a formal, as against an informal, form of combination. Independent and competing enterprises may pursue a common course of action by various arrangements falling short of outright merger. These range from conscious parallelism of action to contractual agreements governing prices, production, conditions of sale, marketing, and other major business policies. Many of these less formal arrangements may achieve the same purpose as a merger in organizing an industry. However, their effects are likely to be less permanent, enforceability is less absolute, and they are vulnerable to the charge of conspiracy.

Probably only a small fraction of all mergers, certainly of recent mergers, have had the reduction or elimination of competition as a principal motive. Other reasons for merging are to achieve a more efficient integration of successive stages in production and marketing, to diversify into new products and markets, to take advantage of a favorable investment opportunity, to minimize taxes when liquidating a business, and to acquire a talented person or a promising patent. In the case of many mergers of very small enterprises, the purpose may be simply to gain the benefits of specialization in management, one partner to the merger becoming responsible for production, the other for marketing and sales.

The great variety of objectives in mergers suggests that convenient generalizations about their underlying causes may not be easy to find. Certain patterns in mergers have been observed, however, which offer some guides to promising lines of inquiry. The following discussion must be confined largely to the United States because of the lack of statistical information about other countries.

Merger movements. One outstanding characteristic of mergers in the United States is the highly episodic nature of their occurrence. In three periods—1898 through 1902, 1926 through 1930, and 1957 through 1961—industrial mergers occurred on so extensive a scale that they are best described as waves or movements (see Figure 1). This tendency of a fundamental form of enterprise expansion to show vast and widely separated peaks of activity has probably interested students more than the examination of individual mergers.

The first recorded merger movement of major proportions occurred as the United States entered the twentieth century, its peak years being 1898 through 1902. For a number of industries it represented the formal consolidation of companies that had already achieved a certain degree of policy coordination through agreements to avoid active competition, agreements that had shown distressing tendencies to break down. For a few important companies it represented merely a change in legal form, from trust to holding company, of an earlier merger. Most importantly, however, it involved the consolidation of companies in a large number of previously dispersed industries into single companies in which control was tightly centralized. It transformed many industries formerly characterized by many small and medium-size firms into those in which one or a few large corporations occupied dominant positions. During the first merger wave such industrial giants as U.S. Steel, American Tobacco, International Harvester, DuPont, Anaconda Copper, Corn Products, American Smelting and Refining, Otis Elevator, Allis-Chalmers, and American Sugar Refining were created.

The second large movement took place in the last half of the 1920s, its peak years being 1926 through 1930. To some degree it represented consolidation in the important new industries that had

Figure 1 — *Firm disappearances by merger, United States, annually, 1895–1961*

a. Logarithmic scale.

b. The two series are not directly comparable and are presented on the same chart only to provide historical perspective.

Sources: For 1895–1920, Nelson 1959, pp. 152–153; for 1919–1939, Thorp 1941, pp. 231–234; for 1940–1954, U.S. Federal Trade Commission 1955, p. 33; 1955–1961, U.S. Federal Trade Commission data.

appeared since the first merger wave. It also reflected attempts in some industries to restore the levels of concentration achieved three decades earlier by firms whose leading positions had been eroded in the meantime. Among the prominent companies created by merger in this period were National Steel, National Dairy Products, United Aircraft, Owens-Illinois, and Caterpillar Tractor.

As Figure 1 indicates, the third large movement was probably underway in the early 1960s. There was a short merger revival immediately following World War II, which was confined mainly to the two years 1946 and 1947. However, merger activity did not return to sustained high levels until the mid-1950s. The pattern of recent mergers has been more varied, with product diversification and tax minimization playing a more prominent role than in the earlier movements (Butters et al. 1951).

The current revival of merger activity, while large, is not as large as the earlier merger movements. In the five turn-of-the-century years, 1898 through 1902, at least 2,700 firms disappeared into the manufacturing and mining mergers reported in the financial press—and reporting was not as

comprehensive as it has since become. In the peak years of the late 1920s, 1926 through 1930, mergers claimed 4,800 firms. By contrast, in the five years 1957 through 1961 there were about 2,900 disappearances. Since the number as well as the size of industrial firms has grown considerably in the past six decades, the most recent levels of merger activity are relatively lower than suggested by the absolute comparisons.

Mergers and competition.   The three merger movements have had varied effects on the intensity and form of competition in markets. The turn-of-the-century movement, as indicated above, succeeded in consolidating thousands of small and medium-size companies into relatively few large ones. In literally dozens of cases the merged firm attained a dominant share of its industry. The avowed goal of many mergers was monopolistic control of a market, and this goal was realized in many instances. The effect was to transform competition from that among many firms into that in which one firm was large enough, through force of size, to maintain orderly, and profitable, conditions in a market. The result was a major reduction in the amount of competition as it had been known in the nineteenth century.

The merger wave of the late 1920s, superimposed on an industrial structure still showing the effects of its giant predecessor wave, had a necessarily different effect on competition. Some observers have speculated that its pattern was influenced by judicial interpretation. Antitrust policy, while generally permissive toward mergers in this period, may have made the largest companies in an industry less eager to engage in mergers which would markedly increase their leadership of an industry [see ANTITRUST LEGISLATION]. Such action might be considered predatory and lay the company open to the charge of being a "bad trust." Since well-behaved colossi were generally free from antitrust attention, an industry's largest company might think twice before taking action which might jeopardize its reputation. The second-, third-, or fourth-ranking companies might have felt less restricted. This may have accelerated the formation of industries in which the leadership was shared by several large firms. However, until direct evidence on the number and size of mergers in this period becomes available, such an interpretation must remain largely speculative.

The pattern of several-firm leadership of industry—oligopoly—is now characteristic of many of our leading industries [see OLIGOPOLY]. It is still a much-debated question whether the oligopolistic industry is competitive enough, though there is more general agreement that the existence of several big firms in an industry signifies more active competition than that of one huge, dominant firm. Certainly the merger wave of the 1920s produced an increase in industrial concentration, if by this is meant simply the centralizing of the control of markets into a smaller relative number of enterprises. It remains to be established, however, whether the more common result was the substitution of oligopoly for industries having only one clear leader or its substitution for decentralized industries having many firms and the more classical variety of competition.

The most recent merger revival has been even more complex in its effect on competition. Unlike the two earlier merger waves, the goal of most recent mergers has not been the union of two or more firms producing the same product at the same stage of fabrication. This type—the horizontal merger—has the immediate effect of reducing the number of independent firms selling the product in question. A study by the Federal Trade Commission suggests that horizontal mergers may be accounting for about two-fifths of recent merger activity (U.S.

Federal Trade Commission 1955, chapter 3). They amounted to about three-fourths of the turn-of-the-century merger activity (Nelson 1959, p. 103) and probably much more than half of that of the 1920s.

The over-all effect on competition of recent horizontal mergers has therefore been considerably less than the horizontal mergers of three and six decades earlier. It would be difficult to see how it could be greater. Given the existing levels of concentration, established in no small part in the earlier movements, the recent merger movement could only maintain or slightly increase this level. To change it greatly would mean the creation of monopolies or near-monopolies in many industries, and this is clearly contrary to public policy.

The strengthening of major oligopolies by merger has recently received greater discouragement from antitrust authorities. In 1958 the courts ruled against the proposed merger of the Bethlehem and Youngstown steel companies, whose effect would have been to make the second largest steel company, Bethlehem, more nearly equal to the largest company, U.S. Steel. Bethlehem, with 15 per cent of the industry, would have had 19 per cent had it acquired Youngstown, thus bringing it closer to U.S. Steel's share of 30 per cent. A comprehensive study by the National Industrial Conference Board has characterized recent antitrust orientation as follows:

The Board's study finds that, contrary to popular impression, enforcement has focussed, not on the size of the acquiring or acquired company, as such, but on market effects. Indeed, only 2% of the acquisitions recorded for 1958 and 1959 for the 300 largest manufacturing corporations had resulted in a merger case by March, 1960.

. . . up to the present time, a merger has been most vulnerable if the acquiring corporation's sales and assets exceed $10 million and it is *one* of the first companies in its field, if the acquired unit is also one of the major organizations in its field, and if a high percentage of the output of the products or services in question is concentrated in relatively few companies. Vulnerability is greatest if the two companies *operate in the same field.* (Bock 1960, pp. 9–10; italics added)

Approximately one-fifth of recent merger activity has involved the combining of firms at successive stages in the production and distribution of a particular product—the vertical merger. The effect of a vertical merger on competition is not likely to be great, unless it provides the merged company with a stranglehold on one of the stages of production. If this is the result, then the relevant combination is fundamentally a horizontal one. The relatively crude evidence available suggests that it is unlikely that the latest vertical mergers have produced any appreciable diminution in competition.

Finally, about two-fifths of recent mergers have had the diversification of products or production processes as a goal. In the first movement, by contrast, there were virtually no mergers for diversification. Diversification objectives cover a broad range. Some companies hope to achieve economies in marketing through production of a broader line of products. Others seek economies in production by acquiring products capable of being produced by the company's existing production facilities. Still others diversify simply to avoid having their fortunes dependent on a single product or industry. The competitive effects of a diversified merger are not likely to be great. If the merged products did not directly compete with one another before the merger, the fact that they are now produced by the same company can have only indirect effects on competition in their separate markets.

The above general review of the competitive consequences of the three merger movements should amply illustrate that we continue to possess only the crudest notions of the effect of mergers on competition. Considerable work remains to be done in classifying mergers; the simple horizontal–vertical–diversified taxonomy is only a beginning. Beyond this, however, lie challenging conceptual problems for which the tools of economic analysis are appropriate. Many problems are related to the appropriate economic sector in which to measure competition and have relevance to other factors in the structure and performance of industries. Many, however, have their basis in the unique characteristics of the merger and the role that considerations of competitive factors play in the merger decision.

Mergers and business cycles.   Although merger history has been dominated by the three large waves, mergers have occurred in measurable amount in every year. One of the periods of lowest activity observed in the twentieth century was the decade from 1905 through 1915, following the huge turn-of-the-century wave. Even during this period there were important mergers. In 1908 General Motors was formed, and in 1911 what is presently International Business Machines. Both were consolidations of several prominent firms in their fields. The great depression of the 1930s saw mergers at probably their lowest ebb; yet even then there were some important chemical and electronics mergers.

The historical pattern of merger activity is notable, therefore, not only for its great waves but also for the presence of cycles in mergers. The cycles are most pronounced as part of the great movements, but they also may be observed during the two-to-three-decade intervals of lowered activity. For the six-decade period from 1895 through 1954 12 clear merger cycles have been identified. During the same period the National Bureau of Economic Research identified 14 cycles in general economic activity, and the merger cycle conformed to the general business cycle in 11 of the 12 cases. When it did not conform, the cycle in general business was either very short, very mild, or both (Nelson 1959, chapter 5).

The cyclical responsiveness of mergers to business activity raises a number of questions. One set relates to the role of mergers as a form of business investment. The balancing of the cost of the firms to be acquired with the discounted expected value of the future earnings of the merged firm involves the same kind of calculation required when deciding to organize a new business or build another plant. Like private investment, merger activity has been shown to respond in a positive and sensitive fashion to the business cycle.

Both merger activity and private investment in new plant and equipment reach their highest points before the peak in general business activity. Both seem to bear a fairly close relationship to movements in stock prices, which suggests that an important factor is the possibility of financing the purchase of either a new plant or another company under conditions favorable to the issuance of new equity securities. Firms expanding by merger, as in other forms of firm growth, frequently turn to public sources for the needed extra funds. The issuance of new securities is most necessary when the acquired firm is purchased for cash; however, when the purchase is made by exchange of stock, new securities may be issued to increase working capital. Even when there is only the exchange of stock, the organizers of the merger are likely to be sensitive to the recent trend of the stock market, because ratios of exchange are often based on the relative market prices of the two securities.

Although both are generally responsive to stock price rises and other manifestations of economic expansions, merger activity and plant and equipment investment are not wholly synchronous. One examination has found that merger activity reaches its peak earlier in a cyclical expansion than do contracts for industrial and commercial construction and orders for manufacturers' durable equipment (Nelson 1966, p. 58). This pattern of timing refutes the theory that businesses turn to mergers only after other profitable forms of investment have been exhausted.

What might explain the earlier peak in mergers than in internal expansion? One hypothesis might be that, although nothing in the basic decision to invest in merger or new plant would predict when in an expansion each is more likely to occur, delays in the construction of new plants may result in merger plans coming to fruition sooner than plant-building programs. Indeed, delays encountered in plant-building may encourage firms to accelerate merger efforts in order to achieve growth targets on schedule.

Mergers by large firms. In the histories of a majority of the largest industrial corporations there has been at least one merger important enough to have had a significant effect on the subsequent rate and direction of company growth (Nelson 1959, p. 4). Some mergers have made companies leaders in their traditional industries, while others have created diversified enterprises. Some have given large companies commanding leads in expanding new industries, while others have consolidated into fewer firms the control of stationary or declining industries. One could claim that the attrition of time has nullified the effects of at least the earlier of these mergers, so that the structure and performance of these companies is now little different from what it would have been had no mergers taken place. This may have been true, almost by definition, of the least successful mergers, but it strains credibility to argue that the forces molding industry structures have been so pervasive as to make it generally true. Assuredly the structure of the aluminum industry from 1900 through 1940 would have been different had not early patent mergers succeeded in making Aluminum Company of America the only company in the field at that time.

A problem that continues to need solution is that of measuring with some precision the part that mergers have played in the growth of firms. Recent studies provide some idea of its magnitude, and evidently it has not been small. The most comprehensive examination made to date has been that of J. Fred Weston. Investigating 74 large industrial firms, he found that, at a minimum, 22.6 per cent of the 1900–1948 growth of these companies could be assigned to merger (1953, p. 14). Weston regards this as a minimum estimate because he explicitly counted as growth by merger only the addition of the acquired firm at the time of the merger. This assumes that the part of the now-enlarged company representing the new acquisition did not continue to grow after the merger, and so contributed nothing to the postmerger growth of the combined firm. While necessary in setting a lower limit

to the range of estimates, the assumption leads, among other things, to the unlikely inference that mergers are organized by pessimistic men.

It is difficult to measure the growth-enhancing effects of any major restructuring of an enterprise, and that produced by a merger is no exception. One approach to measurement might be to compare observed growth with that predicted by simple models of firm growth. One such model might assume that, for the merger to have been neutral in its effect on growth, the acquired firm would have grown at the same rate as its industry. Alternatively, one might assume that merging firms (acquiring and acquired) each would have grown at the same rate as the merged firm. Perhaps most plausible would be the assumption that the merging firms would have grown at the same rate as other similar firms that did not merge. Other models could be developed, and much could be learned of the effects of mergers in the process of developing and testing them. None has yet been used on a comprehensive scale to measure the merger component in large-firm growth.

The interest of many students has been in the role of mergers in producing high concentration in major industries, for this is where the implications for antitrust policy have greatest relevance [see INDUSTRIAL CONCENTRATION]. To study the role of mergers in concentration, one must focus on the firm's share of its industry and on horizontal mergers that directly affect this share. For 25 of his 74 companies Weston presented measures of mergers' effects on industry shares. In this formulation he assumed that, in the absence of merger, the acquiring firm would have maintained its pre-merger share of the industry, that is, it would have been able to grow as fast as the industry. This assumption probably assigns too little of postmerger growth to the acquired firm, for enhancement of growth potential must be a primary reason for acquiring a rival firm. Despite this bias toward understatement, the calculated contribution to growth was impressive. He found that, under the above assumption, most of the companies' increase in market share was assignable to merger. Indeed, for 11 of the 25 companies, mergers accounted for more than their increase in market share, that is, the companies witnessed a decline in the shares of markets that mergers had initially given them. These findings led Stigler, in his review of the Weston study, to conclude: "He [Weston] lends support to the opinion that merger has been the basic method by which individual firms have acquired high shares in major industries in the United States" (1956, p. 40).

International comparisons. Though crude and incomplete, merger statistics for the United States are incomparably more abundant than those for other countries. The only comprehensive time series on mergers known to the writer is that for Great Britain during the large wave of amalgamations it, too, experienced at the turn of the century (Macrosty 1907). Reasons for the paucity of merger statistics in other countries are not hard to find. Absence of antitrust laws, especially those directed at mergers, means that government agencies have had no need to collect data on which to base policy. Also, cartelization rather than amalgamation seems to have been the more common form of combination in European industry, and merger activity may not have been sufficiently large or widespread to engage the interest of economists.

With the acceleration of European economic integration, mergers may begin to receive more attention. The creation of a tariff-free market as large or larger than that of the United States may compel major changes in the firm-structures of industries, and it seems probable that mergers should emerge as important instruments for effecting any such change. The experience of the United States suggests that availability of data provides no sure guarantee that public policy toward mergers will always be enlightened. However, there are some indications that lags in assembling merger data have made the evolution of policy more tortuous, erratic, and probably less successful. An early beginning to the assembling of data on Common Market mergers could aid considerably in the development of appropriate public policies toward mergers; policies, one hastens to add, that may be expected to depart in significant respects from the United States example.

RALPH L. NELSON

BIBLIOGRAPHY

Current data on the number, size, and industry of mergers are available from the Office of Information of the Federal Trade Commission. Comprehensive lists of mergers may be found in National Industrial Conference Board, Conference Board Record (see Bock 1960, pages 107–119 for a discussion of these data).

BOCK, BETTY 1960 *Mergers and Markets: An Economic Analysis of Case Law.* Studies in Business Economics, No. 69. New York: National Industrial Conference Board. → See especially pages 107–119, "Data on Merging Companies."

BUTTERS, JOHN K.; LINTNER, JOHN; and CARY, WILLIAM L. 1951 *Effects of Taxation: Corporate Mergers.* Boston: Harvard Univ., Graduate School of Business Administration, Division of Research.

MACROSTY, HENRY W. 1907 *The Trust Movement in British Industry.* London: Longmans.

MARKHAM, JESSE W. (1955) 1966 Survey of the Evidence and Findings on Mergers. Pages 141–182 in Universities–National Bureau Committee for Economic Research, *Business Concentration and Price Policy: A Conference.* National Bureau of Economic Research, Special Conference Series, No. 5. Princeton Univ. Press.

NATIONAL INDUSTRIAL CONFERENCE BOARD *Conference Board Record.* → Published since 1944. Previously published under the titles *Conference Board Business Record* and *Conference Board Business Management Record.*

NELSON, RALPH L. 1959 *Merger Movements in American Industry: 1895–1956.* National Bureau of Economic Research, General Series, No. 66. Princeton Univ. Press.

NELSON, RALPH L. 1966 Business Cycle Factors in the Choice Between Internal and External Growth. Pages 52–70 in William W. Alberts and Joel E. Segall (editors), *The Corporate Merger.* Univ. of Chicago Press.

STIGLER, GEORGE J. 1956 The Statistics of Monopoly and Merger. *Journal of Political Economy* 64:33–40.

THORP, WILLARD L. 1941 *The Structure of Industry.* U.S. Temporary National Economic Committee, Investigation of Concentration of Economic Power, Monograph No. 27. Washington: Government Printing Office. → See especially pages 227–234, "The Merger Movement."

U.S. FEDERAL TRADE COMMISSION 1955 *Report on Corporate Mergers and Acquisitions: May 1955.* Washington: Government Printing Office.

WESTON, J. FRED 1953 *The Role of Mergers in the Growth of Large Firms.* Berkeley: Univ. of California Press.

MERRIAM, CHARLES E.

The life of Charles Edward Merriam, Jr. (1874–1953), American political scientist, represents and reflects many of the changes which have taken place not only in the field in which he achieved his reputation but also in American society in the twentieth century. His generation was perhaps the first to experience with enthusiasm the headlong rush of history and of industrial technology, which so depressed Henry Adams, and to return to the relentless faith in social study characteristic of eighteenth-century democratic thought. Merriam was determined to retain for America in the twentieth century the vision that Alexis de Tocqueville had had in the nineteenth: that the political course of Western society was set irrevocably toward ever more democratic government and that the United States could lead the way. To this vision Merriam added his own conviction that the observable weaknesses in modern government are the result of too little rather than too much democracy. His belief that the sources of such weaknesses can be found by an examination of the actual workings of politics, and that the methods of such examination have to be scientific, formed the basis of his approach to politics and of his efforts to reorganize political science. His commitment to democracy and to scientific method gave impetus to his lifelong efforts to bring scientific knowledge to the service of government, and his conception of scientific method facilitated the development of interrelationships among the social sciences.

Merriam was born in Hopkinton, Iowa, the second son of the local postmaster, who was also keeper of the general store. His mother, Margaret Campbell Kirkwood Merriam, was a devout Scottish Presbyterian who had been educated in Scotland to be a schoolteacher, although family responsibilities and chronic ill health prevented her from teaching. The Merriam family was deeply involved in Iowa politics; Merriam's father, however, never had the political career he hoped for. Like his father and his elder brother, Merriam was educated first at Lenox College in Hopkinton. His father planned a legal career for him, preparatory to a life in politics, but a brief period at the law school of Iowa State University convinced him that legal training lacked a proper concern for ethics, and he rebelled. He decided to study political economy and social science at Columbia University, then a rapidly growing center of American social science. At Columbia he was influenced by William A. Dunning, John W. Burgess, and E. R. A. Seligman, among many others. The introduction to the modern historical and comparative method that Merriam received at Columbia took much of the edge off his later pilgrimage to Germany to hear Otto von Gierke and Hugo Preuss.

Conception of political theory

Merriam's acceptance in 1900 of a position as docent in political science at the University of Chicago began his long career at that university. His doctoral thesis, *History of the Theory of Sovereignty Since Rousseau*, was published in 1900, but it was the publication, in 1903, of *A History of American Political Theories* that first established him in his profession. Dedicated to Dunning, the book follows Dunning's pseudo-biological methods of historical classification and description, grouping writers in orderly, if somewhat stilted, fashion by period and major concern. But it is the first work in which the practicing politicians of the colonial, early federal, and pre-Civil War periods are classified as "theorists." Merriam was also among the first to call attention to the fact that John Locke had exercised a stronger influence over American political history than had Rousseau. The work may now seem dated and quite static, but much of later discussion of American political thought is based on the analysis it contains. Like its sequel, *American Political Ideas* (1920), it demonstrates Merriam's particular interest in broadening the definition of political theory to include not only the more traditionally recognized theorists whose writings were already part of the canon of political thought, but also the practitioners of politics, whose actions and intentions permanently affect the life of the community even though they may have given little attention to the formulation of doctrine. Indeed, for Merriam political theory came to embrace the study of society itself, as is shown in the memorial volume for Dunning, *A History of Political Theories, Recent Times* (1924), that he and H. E. Barnes edited: the volume includes, in systematic arrangement, essays in philosophy, sociology, psychology, and anthropology, all of which fields Merriam considered directly relevant to political theory.

Involvement in politics

With his background of family involvement in Iowa politics, Merriam could scarcely have avoided a similar interest in Chicago. To be sure, his conception of involvement in the political life of the city hardly coincided with that of President William Rainey Harper of the University of Chicago and of successive university administrators. Harper preferred to exert influence on the community through adult education, while Merriam saw city politics as a suitable area for applying new technical skills to the operations of government. Merriam's first opportunity for direct involvement in Chicago politics came in 1905, when the City Club of Chicago asked him to do a study of the city's municipal revenues. The success of the report, particularly among the club's membership of prominent local businessmen, led to Merriam's appointment by the mayor in 1907 as secretary of the Chicago Harbor Commission, whose purpose was to study the city's water transportation facilities (part of an effort to make the new Chicago city plan effective). The work succeeded not only in bringing Merriam to public attention but also in acquainting him with some of the city's most complex problems of business policy and political obfuscation. The work raised issues of land use, public utilities, private enrichment at public expense, and graft. Chicago's unusually high consciousness of its physical layout and its growing determination to make use of its remarkable lake frontage gave Merriam a rich education in some of the newly developing problems related to urban planning.

As a result of his investigations, Merriam and his supporters were able to secure his nomination as alderman in the city's first primary and his election to the City Council in 1909. He promptly introduced an ordinance for a commission on city expenditures, becoming chairman of the commission upon its creation. By 1910, the commission had so successfully exposed fraud in Chicago city purchasing that it achieved a national reputation among reform groups interested in the reorganization of financing in local government. Merriam's work also came to the attention of Julius Rosenwald, who was already noted for his philanthropies but had hitherto avoided involvement in politics. Rosenwald financed the commission after the City Council angrily stopped its funds. He also backed Merriam's unsuccessful campaign for mayor in the 1911 election. Although Merriam ran on the Republican ticket, his identification as a progressive and a reformer alienated party regulars, who preferred the risk of Democratic victory to the possibility of party repudiation of their control of local politics.

Although Merriam was active in the formation of the national Progressive party in 1912, his unwillingness to support it after the election, even though he continued to respect and support its aims, was typical of the growing group of "realists" among the reformers. They had come to look upon a party as having a complex social base as well as a political one, and therefore as less amenable than some reformers had hoped to modification by such political methods as the initiative, referendum, recall, and direct primary elections. Merriam had published his *Primary Elections* in 1908. Unlike so many of the studies of structural reform, the book called attention to the fact that structural reorganization by itself is not enough, that politics ultimately depends upon which groups of citizens are interested, or willing to be made interested, in the outcome of political events.

Merriam's political activities, couched as they were in the imagery of the scholar–politician made popular by the successful candidacy of Woodrow Wilson, brought him also a national reputation. His desk became an informal clearinghouse of information for groups interested in the new methods of reform in local politics: primaries, budget and accounting systems, commissions of investigation and management, and the like. Re-elected to the Chicago City Council in 1913, he served until 1917, meanwhile continuing his teaching at the university. His career came to exemplify the new pragmatic voice of the academy, dedicated not only to the historical understanding of political structure but also to the discovery of useful methods for improving the conduct of politics.

World War I took Merriam to Italy, where he served briefly as the American high commissioner of public information, an office used by the Wilson administration to circumvent the more traditional diplomatic service. The position gave Merriam a sharp awareness of the problems involved in international exchanges of information, a field scarcely touched upon by Americans. Several of the postwar projects in which he was interested—most notably a series on civic education in various countries and a study of international reporting in American news media—were products of his months in Italy.

Organization of research

His return to Chicago politics after the war was unsuccessful; as an internationalist, he was swimming against the tide. The postwar period marked his ascendancy in the academic profession, an ascendancy which was nonetheless paralleled by an increasing sense of political frustration. His influence within the American Political Science Association was at its peak, and he led the movement for more research in politics and for closer relations with other disciplines, particularly psychology. He became president of the association in 1924. The founding of the Social Science Research Council in the same year was the culmination of his efforts to encourage greater interaction among the various fields.

During this period he also did his most successful graduate teaching, and the students from this period, among them V. O. Key, Jr., and H. D. Lasswell, have been among his most influential. Through his friendship with young Beardsley Ruml, Merriam had an influence on the Rockefeller Foundation, and Ruml's striking ability to give organizational reality to Merriam's ideas was the source of much of Merriam's effectiveness during the period. The Rockefeller Foundation financed a committee on local community research at the University of Chicago; a faculty board headed by Merriam and Leonard White used the funds to finance research projects by students and colleagues, often in fields far removed from local community study. The founding of the Public Administration Clearing House in 1931 fulfilled another dream of Merriam's: the bringing together of the research and reform organizations directly involved in professional work in public service. It also brought Louis Brownlow to Chicago, thereby establishing a working friendship which proved enormously influential to both men.

Yet the frustration of these years is also clear. Merriam's concern with the nature of leadership and the psychology of voting behavior was a response in part to his disappointment with the course taken by the Republican party after World War I. The years from 1920 to 1928 saw the tacit repudiation by successive administrations of most of the ideals and programs of the progressives. Only Secretary of Commerce Herbert Hoover seemed concerned with these ideals, and his election to the presidency raised some hope for a return to them. At the University of Chicago, successive presidents frustrated Merriam's efforts to finance research; they saw these efforts as a threat to their own more traditional fund-raising needs. Merriam was tempted, in 1923, to accept a chair at Columbia and again, in 1927, to take a post with the Rockefeller Foundation in Paris, but each time he ultimately decided to remain at Chicago.

Conception of a science of politics

New Aspects of Politics was published in 1925. More obviously characteristic of his method of work than many of his other books, *New Aspects* is a collection of papers written and revised between 1920 and 1924. The papers were, in turn, built on notes of his comments at meetings and conferences of social scientists. This method of gradual accretion, accumulation, and revision was the one most often employed by Merriam but it was usually obscured by the final revision. Other such books are *Chicago* (1929) and *Four American Party Leaders* (1926), the latter, again characteristically, paralleling work done by his students. More than any of his other writings, however, *New Aspects* reveals the hortatory Merriam, suggesting directions for future investigation and pointing out to colleagues and students the possibilities inherent in a science of politics that was one of the new sciences of society.

The essays also indicate his opposition to deterministic theories of history and politics, not only Darwinism and the economic theories of Charles A. Beard but also the behavioristic determinism in the very psychology, sociology, and anthropology whose methods he urged upon his colleagues. It was not the principles and predictions of these sciences which appealed to Merriam but the usefulness of their methods for the enrichment of the science of politics. Yet in spite of his rejection of deterministic views of history, he nonetheless depended upon a kind of "tendential" history that moves in trends and directions which are observable without being prescriptive. His attitude toward history is clearly related to the concepts of process then current in the pragmatic philosophies of John Dewey, George Herbert Mead, and, perhaps most of all, T. V. Smith. While the essays seem to describe new

directions of change, these directions are in effect consistent with the traditions of American government and the trends of American politics.

Merriam seems to have seen his own role in very classical terms: to provide a modern basis for the kind of "whole man" theories of politics that had marked the history of political theory. Theories of the state, such as those of Hobbes and Locke and of many of their predecessors, had been based on investigations under way in psychology and physics. By Merriam's day, psychology and physics, like all of the natural sciences, had changed far more radically since the eighteenth century than had theories of the democratic state. This lag meant that democracy seemed increasingly destined to bear the brunt of the critical disillusion produced by the more recent scientific investigations of the nature of man. Merriam sought to provide a basis for restating a theory of the democratic state which would be consistent both with the traditions of democratic theory and with the revolutions in scientific doctrine, aware all the while that no modern theorist could ever again claim the universal knowledge which had made possible the comprehensive ambitions of classical theory. Such an endeavor now required a social science community, ambitious for the same ends and willing to be tolerant of a multiplicity of approaches.

In *Political Power* (1934a) he sought to apply to American democracy European ideas about the sociological and psychological factors underlying political organization. European, and particularly German, theories of power analysis were given a specifically American setting and generalized in Merriam's characteristic fashion. Hitler's rise to power, like the ambitions of the Kaiser, shocked American scholars: Merriam had a deep respect for the quality of nineteenth-century German scholarship and sought to reconcile its traditional commitments with current events in Germany and in his own country.

National planning

By the 1930s, Merriam was once again in a position to exert political influence. He was a member of President Hoover's Research Committee on Social Trends, and the report of that committee, published in 1933, introduced Merriam's influence into the New Deal. The report had recommended the establishment of a high-level governmental agency for planning; and the appointment within the Department of the Interior of a national resources committee in 1933 brought Merriam a direct and influential role in the Roosevelt administration; it was a continuing role, since, in 1939, the committee became the National Resources Planning Board, with Merriam still a member.

In its own day the National Resources Planning Board was better-known to those who criticized it than to those who used the information it produced. Although more than two decades have passed since its demise in 1943, its place in the history of the New Deal has yet to be determined. Over seventy major and minor reports on subjects ranging from land and water resources to labor, industry, education, and science, to mention only the most obvious categories, are largely unknown to (or ignored by) historians, despite the fact that they represent perhaps the best example extant of the transformation of turn-of-the-century progressivism into the professionalized government and social science of the post-New Deal generation. President Roosevelt often used these reports as the basis for proposals to Congress and as a means of testing public response to far-reaching experimental programs. Roosevelt also considered giving the reports wider public circulation to stimulate public interest in government, but the necessity of keeping the board out of politics made any scheme difficult to realize.

Merriam was also a member in 1936 and 1937 of the President's Committee on Administrative Management, the so-called Brownlow Committee. His work on the report of the committee gave both practical structure and theoretical base to his concepts of national planning and the relation of national planning to executive organization.

The last decade of his life was spent in what might be called active retirement. He continued to influence policy in the department of political science at Chicago, and the loose intellectual community which had come to be known as the Chicago school was maintained. He spent a year, 1948–1949, on President Truman's Loyalty Review Board, and he undertook various lecture obligations, among them the Walgreen series at the University of Chicago (twice during this period) and a series on public administration at the Maxwell School of Syracuse University, in 1947. He intended these lectures to serve as first drafts for several books: an autobiography, a study of government and the economic order, and a work on politics and administration. They remained among the manuscripts left unfinished at his death.

Political theory and political behavior

Merriam's official retirement from the University of Chicago came in 1940. During the 1930s his writings reflected his gradual return to the problem he had considered fundamental earlier in his career but which had been overshadowed for a time by his interest in the study of political behavior, namely, the relation between political theory and democratic government. While Merriam's reputation remains bound to his work in political behavior, his fundamental interest throughout his life was theory. To be sure, theory, for him, needed ultimately to be based upon behavior, and behavior had been neglected by nineteenth-century students in the field: the bringing together of theory and behavior gave Merriam's work the appearance of shifts in focus—from theory to political behavior and back again to theory. His own experience in politics had led him to the observation and analysis of political action, using new methods and concepts imported from fields outside of politics. From the beginning it was his aim to bring new materials to the study of politics and to make it consistent with his ideals of political behavior; and in his later years he sought to fulfill this aim in his theoretical writings, an aim culminating in *Systematic Politics* (1945).

The title reflects what could be called the paradox of Merriam's intellectual life: that he viewed politics as systematic and scientific but could find successful elaboration of its organization only in descriptive statements of political experience, his own and others', rather than in the structure of political theory itself. Though committed to bridging what he felt to be the gap between theory and practice, his best formulations of theory were virtually indistinguishable from practical examples. His book *Chicago: A More Intimate View of Urban Politics* (1929) is the best example. In *Systematic Politics* he attempted explicitly to separate theory from practice, thereby extending theory. However, only to those who knew the practical politics in which it had properly been imbedded could the book reveal much; to those who did not, it seemed a bit antiquated. For the post-1945 political scientist, *Systematic Politics* seems either unsystematic or unpolitical, depending upon whether the critic is committed to the older sense of system which Merriam had sought to revise or to the newer sense of politics which Merriam had sought to create.

To assess the career of Merriam apart from the times in which he lived is apt to involve some rather complex distortions. His writings do not constitute a corpus of the importance ordinarily associated with the great in any field. Yet he deserves the accolade as few of his generation do. Merriam was in many ways a publicist of the persuasion of Walter Lippmann, Herbert Croly, and Walter Weyl, but instead of trying to give specialized knowledge of political science wide circulation, as they did, he sought to transcend the academic disciplines for their common benefit, to keep social scientists mindful not only of one another's increasingly specialized problems but also of the broad public responsibility which, as citizens, they shared.

Merriam is often called the father of behavioral study in politics, but he did not always relish recognizing his offspring, and his offspring in turn often looked upon him askance. Behavioral study emerged from World War II with a revised canon of method, often wholeheartedly committed to quantification (which Merriam had always viewed with much suspicion) and deeply influenced by the rapid development of new machinery for the collection and analysis of data. The war, too, had dampened reform ardor, as World War I had done. A shocking confrontation with reality had created a generation which, to Merriam, often seemed cynical and mechanistic. He had urged science upon them; but they were using science to question the very principles from which he himself had derived the necessity of scientific method.

His own interest in behavioral study was rooted in the conviction that the arena of politics is the proper source of information and generalization about politics and political reform. All of the newly developed social sciences should be brought to bear on the re-examination of old generalizations about politics, the destruction of demonstrably useless ones, and the construction of new ones whose utility would continue to be tested by experience. But it should always be recognized that the social sciences serve rather than control the process of democratic politics. In the continuing relationship between political science and practical politics, the political scientist will always question the adequacy of the politician's knowledge, while the politician will question the validity of the "science" offered to him. Merriam dealt with these reservations by subjecting science to politics and by basing politics on his unshakable belief in democracy. Democratic government, whatever the details of its form, was for him the only government ultimately consistent with the nature of man. He avoided the question of whether or not this principle can be determined behaviorally, convinced as he was that observable weaknesses in the operation of democratic governments were the result of the still-existing nondemocratic elements, not of the essential nature of democracy.

The accomplishments of Merriam's career rest as much on the insights to which he directed the attention of others as on the work which can be directly attributed to him. He used his optimism as a device for encouraging investigation and his entrepreneurial energies as a means of making that investigation possible. Through his efforts others were enabled to explore frontiers which he himself could see only dimly and to penetrate barriers which he himself could not reach. Much of his reputation must ultimately depend on the roads he marked and the maps he drew. More confident of the end than others were apt to be, and far more certain of the rightness of the direction, he pointed the way.

BARRY D. KARL

[*For the historical context of Merriam's work, see* POLICY SCIENCES; POLITICAL BEHAVIOR; POLITICAL SCIENCE; *and the biographies of* BEARD; DEWEY; MEAD. *For discussion of the subsequent development of Merriam's ideas, see the biography of* KEY.]

BIBLIOGRAPHY

A bibliography of Merriam's writings through 1941 can be found in White 1942. *Studies of aspects of his work can be found in the highly critical* Crick 1959 *and in* Karl 1963. *The Merriam papers at the University of Chicago contain a significant amount of unpublished material and constitute an extraordinarily rich source of information on the period during which he lived.*

WORKS BY MERRIAM

1900   *History of the Theory of Sovereignty Since Rousseau.* New York: Columbia Univ. Press.

1903   *A History of American Political Theories.* New York: Macmillan.

1906   *Report of an Investigation of the Municipal Revenues of Chicago.* City Club of Chicago.

(1908) 1928   MERRIAM, CHARLES E.; and OVERACKER, LOUISE *Primary Elections: A Study of the History and Tendencies of Primary Election Legislation.* Rev. ed. Univ. of Chicago Press.

1920   *American Political Ideas: Studies in the Development of American Political Thought, 1865–1917.* New York: Macmillan.

(1922) 1949   MERRIAM, CHARLES E.; and GOSNELL, HAROLD F. *The American Party System: An Introduction to the Study of Political Parties in the United States.* 4th ed. New York: Macmillan.

1924   MERRIAM, CHARLES E.; and BARNES, HARRY E. (editors) *A History of Political Theories, Recent Times: Essays on Contemporary Developments in Political Theory.* New York: Macmillan.

1924   MERRIAM, CHARLES E.; and GOSNELL, HAROLD F. *Non-voting: Causes and Methods of Control.* Univ. of Chicago Press.

(1925) 1931   *New Aspects of Politics.* 2d ed. Univ. of Chicago Press.

1926   *Four American Party Leaders.* New York: Macmillan.

1929   *Chicago: A More Intimate View of Urban Politics.* New York: Macmillan.

1931a   *The Making of Citizens: A Comparative Study of Methods of Civic Training.* Univ. of Chicago Press.

1931b   *The Written Constitution and the Unwritten Attitude.* New York: Smith.

1934a   *Political Power: Its Composition and Incidence.* New York: McGraw-Hill.

1934b *Civic Education in the United States.* Report of the Commission on the Social Studies, American Historical Association, Part 6. New York: Scribner.
1936 *The Role of Politics in Social Change.* New York Univ. Press.
1939a *The New Democracy and the New Despotism.* New York: McGraw-Hill.
1939b *Prologue to Politics.* Univ. of Chicago Press.
1941a *On the Agenda of Democracy.* Cambridge, Mass.: Harvard Univ. Press.
1941b *What Is Democracy?* Univ. of Chicago Press.
(1945) 1962 *Systematic Politics.* Univ. of Chicago Press.
1963 MERRIAM, CHARLES E.; PARRATT, SPENCER D.; and LEPAWSKY, ALBERT *The Government of the Metropolitan Region of Chicago.* Univ. of Chicago Press.

SUPPLEMENTARY BIBLIOGRAPHY

CRICK, BERNARD 1959 *The American Science of Politics: Its Origins and Conditions.* Berkeley: Univ. of California Press.
KARL, BARRY D. 1963 *Executive Reorganization and Reform in the New Deal: The Genesis of Administrative Management, 1900–1939.* Cambridge, Mass.: Harvard Univ. Press. → See especially pages 37–81, "Charles Edward Merriam: Politics, Planning, and the Academy."
The Limits of Behavioralism in Political Science: A Symposium. Edited by James C. Charlesworth. 1962 Philadelphia: American Academy of Political and Social Science.
RANNEY, AUSTIN (editor) 1962 *Essays on the Behavioral Study of Politics.* Urbana: Univ. of Illinois Press.
WHITE, LEONARD D. (editor) 1942 *The Future of Government in the United States: Essays in Honor of Charles E. Merriam.* Univ. of Chicago Press. → A bibliography of Charles E. Merriam's writings, complete through 1941, appears on pages 269–274.

MESMER, FRANZ ANTON

Franz Anton Mesmer (1734–1815) was the originator of the doctrine of animal magnetism, later called mesmerism. Son of a gamekeeper on the estate of a bishop, Mesmer studied divinity first at Dillingen and then at Ingolstadt, where he acquired the degree of doctor of philosophy. He next went to Vienna to study law, and there he appears to have obtained a second doctoral degree. He received his third and final doctoral degree, in medicine, in 1766. Having become by then a man of independent means, Mesmer for a time followed his inclination to be a dilettante in a variety of scientific fields and was especially active as a patron of the musical arts. Himself a versatile musician, he was a friend of Gluck and a patron of young Mozart.

What evidence there is shows Mesmer to have been a sensitive, sincere, well-educated man, of superior intelligence and possessed of an inquisitive and intuitive spirit, of imagination and enthusiasm, and of a genuine love for his fellow men.

Granted that he may have had unduly strong and erroneous convictions, that he may have been somewhat mystical and at times flamboyant, there is nevertheless little basis for believing that he was ever a charlatan or a quack.

Universal fluid and animal magnetism. The origins of Mesmer's notions of animal magnetism are often said to go back to his 1766 doctoral thesis in medicine, "De planetarum influxu," which was concerned with the influence of the planets on the human body. In it he attempted to apply the writings of Newton and Descartes to older ideas, propounded by such men as van Helmont, Paracelsus, and Wirtig. His thesis was that there is a universal fluid permeating all things; it is in a perpetual state of flux and reflux and serves as a medium through which all coexisting objects continuously interact. In particular, it is through this fluid that the planets influence human beings. As might be expected, Mesmer did have something to say in his thesis with regard to the medical aspects of this influence, but he did not then appear to have developed the notion of "animal magnetism." During the summer of 1774, however, he was given an opportunity to witness a remarkable cure effected through the application of magnets. Intrigued, he himself began to experiment on a few patients, with some remarkable successes. In his efforts to find the true basis of these cures, whose source, he hypothesized, must lie in something other than the scientifically known physical properties of magnets, he returned to some of his earlier ideas about the universal fluid. Strongly impressed by the success of Johann Gassner, a popular healer of the day, in obtaining cures solely through the touch of the hands, Mesmer arrived at the notion that the universal fluid manifests itself in living organisms, particularly man, in a way quite analogous to the manner in which physical magnetism manifests itself in natural magnets. According to this analogy, there are like and unlike animal magnetic poles, which can be transmitted (or induced), changed, destroyed, and reinforced. Health depends upon a proper distribution and balance of such poles or, in other words, upon a proper distribution or concentration of the vital fluid. Mesmer attributed to physical magnets powerful animal magnetic properties, parallel to their physical properties, which enable them to affect the distribution of animal magnetism in other objects, particularly human beings. Moreover, he believed that some human beings are like physical magnets, in that they are powerful sources of animal magnetism, and can influence objects and humans. Since illness is the result of an inadequate distribution or a lack of animal magnetism, a cure can be produced by altering the inadequate distribution through use of a powerful source of animal magnetism. This, in essence, is the doctrine of animal magnetism as Mesmer propounded and applied it.

Mesmerism.   However, in the hands of Mesmer's students and their students, at least three elements soon entered into the picture to distort the doctrine into "mesmerism." It is difficult to tell whether these were independent factors or whether each one followed more or less as a consequence of preceding ones. In any event, a critical departure was the discovery of "artificial somnambulism," a rather spectacular "nervous" condition that was presumably brought about by the use of animal magnetism and that produced in many individuals all sorts of unusual and often paranormal faculties. Another change was the increasing tendency to equate animal magnetism with the universal fluid discussed in Mesmer's thesis, rather than to consider it only one manifestation of that fluid. Last, animal magnetism became increasingly associated with various physical and paraphysical forces, so that, for instance, it was used to explain table tilting and turning during spiritualistic séances. In fact, in the hands of the mesmerists animal magnetism became a multifaceted biophysical entity which could account for just about anything. For Mesmer, animal magnetism was and remained a biophysical agency belonging to the Newtonian scheme of things, of interest primarily as a way to understand illnesses and a way to cure them rationally. For the mesmerists, animal magnetism became an occult agent, used primarily to bring about the somnambulistic state and other spectacular and extramedical effects. Mesmer himself noted this unfortunate development during the course of his life but was unable to stem its progress.

Charges of malpractice.   Mesmer's successful but unconventional use of magnets was unacceptable to the relatively small and select group of practicing Viennese physicians, and in 1778 he was forced to leave Vienna, following what now appear to have been poorly founded accusations of malpractice. From Vienna he moved to Paris, where he enjoyed great popularity as a practitioner for several years but again met with increasing opposition and hostility on the part of the medical profession, which labeled him an impostor and a charlatan. The final blow was dealt Mesmer when, in 1784, a commission, of which Benjamin Franklin was a member, was appointed by the French government to investigate Mesmer's claims and concluded that animal magnetism did not exist. The commission did recognize that Mesmer had effected numerous cures, but it preferred to ascribe them to as yet unknown physiological causes. It is worth noting that the commission itself never directly accused Mesmer of charlatanism; this accusation came from less well-informed professional men of his time. Forced to leave Paris by the attacks of the medical profession, Mesmer moved to Switzerland, where he lived out the remainder of his days as a medical doctor.

Assessment.   Today we know, of course, that Mesmer's animal magnetism is not a scientifically valid concept; but in the light of what constituted science, especially medical science, in his day, it probably seemed to have some validity. We cannot overlook the fact that Mesmer did observe the apparent cure of illnesses by some unknown principle or agent. He tried to find an explanation for these cures that was compatible with the best general scientific writings of his time, such as those of Descartes and Newton.

Seen in retrospect, Mesmer appears more a somewhat tragic figure—a product and a victim of his time—than a villain. He lived in an era of widespread superstitition, gullibility, and relative ignorance even among the upper classes, and of complete illiteracy among the common people. Black magic was still a thing to be feared, and wise men spoke seriously of the influence of the planets, advocated the intensive use of leeching, bleeding, and poultices as quasi-universal remedies, and talked learnedly of the circulation of the phlegm. Yet, significant strides were being made in the direction of modern science: Newton died just before Mesmer was born, and such men as Lavoisier, Gay-Lussac, Gauss, and Ampère were Mesmer's contemporaries. Most unfortunately for Mesmer, however, the comte de Saint Germain and Cagliostro also were his contemporaries. These charlatans succeeded in linking their names to the practice of mesmerism, thus bringing it into their own suspect orbit of intrigue and infamy. Finally, rather unwisely, Mesmer left much of the conduct of his affairs in the hands of students and friends who, however well-meaning they were, may have done him more harm than good through their overenthusiasm and personal inadequacies.

ANDRÉ M. WEITZENHOFFER

[*See also* HYPNOSIS.]

WORKS BY MESMER

(1779) 1957   *Memoir of F. A. Mesmer, Doctor of Medicine, on His Discoveries: 1799.* Mount Vernon, N.Y.: Eden. → First published as *Mémoire sur la découverte du magnétisme animal.*

1781   *Précis historique des faits relatifs au magnétisme-animal jusques en avril 1781.* London.

WORKS ABOUT MESMER

BERTRAND, ALEXANDRE   1826   *Du magnétisme animal en France et des jugements qu'en ont portés les sociétés savantes* . . . Paris: Baillière.

GOLDSMITH, MARGARET L.   1934   *Franz Anton Mesmer: A History of Mesmerism.* Garden City, N.Y.: Doubleday.

ZWEIG, STEFAN   (1931) 1932   *Mental Healers: Franz Anton Mesmer, Mary Baker Eddy, Sigmund Freud.* New York: Viking. → First published as *Die Heilung durch den Geist: Mesmer, Mary Baker Eddy, Freud.*

MESSIANIC MOVEMENTS

See MASS PHENOMENA; MILLENARISM; NATIVISM AND REVIVALISM; SECTS AND CULTS; SOCIAL MOVEMENTS.

METHODENSTREIT

See ECONOMIC THOUGHT, *article on* THE AUSTRIAN SCHOOL; *and the biographies of* MENGER *and* SCHMOLLER.

MÉTRAUX, ALFRED

Alfred Métraux (1902–1963) was a pioneer in South American ethnohistory, a student of African culture in the New World, and a specialist in the field of race relations. He was also instrumental in promoting the role of the social sciences in the United Nations and its specialized agencies.

Born in Lausanne, Switzerland, Métraux spent most of his childhood in Argentina, where his Swiss father was a well-known surgeon practicing in the city of Mendoza. He received his secondary and university education in Europe, studying at the Gymnasium in Lausanne, and in Paris at the École Nationale des Chartes, the École Nationale des Langues Orientales, the École Pratique des Hautes Études, and finally the Sorbonne, from which he received a doctoral degree in 1928. He also studied briefly in Göteborg, Sweden. Among his teachers were Marcel Mauss, Paul Rivet, and Erland Nordenskiöld. Métraux also acknowledged the influence of Father John M. Cooper of the Catholic University of America, Washington, D.C., with whom he corresponded for many years. It was Cooper who introduced him to the American school of cultural anthropology, and Métraux was to combine the best of both the European and the American traditions of historical anthropology in his work.

His professional career was equally cosmopolitan. He was the first director, from 1928 to 1934, of the Institute of Ethnology at the University of Tucumán in Argentina. In 1934/1935, he led a French expedition to Easter Island. From 1936 to 1938 he was a fellow of the Bishop Museum in Honolulu, and the following year he became the Bishop Museum visiting professor at Yale University. In 1939 he returned for a year to Argentina and Bolivia for field research as a fellow of the Guggenheim Foundation. Then he went back to Yale, where he worked with South American data on the Cross Cultural Survey (now Human Relations Area Files). In 1941 he joined the staff of the Bureau of American Ethnology of the Smithsonian Institution, and there he played an important role from 1941 to 1945 by editing and writing for the monumental *Handbook of South American Indians* (Steward 1946–1959). In addition, Métraux taught at the University of California at Berkeley, the Escuela Nacional de Antropología e Historia of Mexico, the Colegio Nacional de México, the Facultad Latino–Americana de Ciencias Sociales in Santiago, Chile, and the École Pratique des Hautes Études in Paris.

From 1946 until his retirement in 1962, Métraux served in various capacities for the United Nations and for UNESCO. As a representative of UNESCO he took part in the Hylean Amazon Project in 1947/1948 and in the Marbial Valley (Haiti) anthropological survey in 1949/1950. In cooperation with personnel from the International Labour Office, he studied the internal migrations of the Aymara- and Quechua-speaking Indians of Bolivia in 1954. He was primarily responsible for the publication by UNESCO, between 1950 and 1958, of a series of pamphlets, monographs, and books on the concept of race and on race and minority relations. As a staff member of the department of social science of UNESCO he was constantly in touch with social science research throughout the world.

Métraux contributed most to the social sciences in the field of ethnohistory. Perhaps no other writer contributed more pages to the *Handbook of South American Indians.* Most of these contributions are derived from documentary sources and are models of judicious historical reconstruction. His two books on the Tupinambá (1928a; 1928b) are classics in the ethnohistory of the South American Indian. In these two books, he drew upon a wide range of sixteenth- to eighteenth-century sources, written in French, Portuguese, and Spanish, to present a coherent picture of the material and socioreligious life of the extinct coastal tribes of Brazil known generically as the Tupinambá. His books are a contribution not only to South American ethnography but also to Brazilian history. The Tupinambá were the first Brazilian Indians encountered by the Portuguese upon their arrival in the New World. Their language, Tupí-Guaraní, became the lingua franca for missionaries, and their names for the flora, fauna, and topographical features became part of the Portuguese language as spoken in Brazil. From these coastal Indians, the Europeans learned to adapt to the New World environment, and much of the Indians' religious belief and mythology became a part of Brazilian folklore.

Métraux was also a sensitive and indefatigable field researcher among primitive and peasant societies of Latin America. He published numerous monographs and articles reporting upon his field research over a period of 25 years (see Wagley 1964 for his complete bibliography). His major field research was carried out in the Argentine Chaco and in Haiti. One piece of work in the Chaco stands out, his study of the mythology of the Toba and Pilagá Indians (1946), in which he made use of his vast knowledge of South American ethnology to draw parallels in theme and plot between Chaco mythology and that of the Andean region. *Making a Living in the Marbial Valley, Haiti* (1951) is a careful and detailed ecological study stressing the effects of *minifundia* (overparcelization), soil erosion, and overpopulation on the peasant society of one Haitian valley. In this report, such aspects of social life as cooperative work groups, marriage and household groups, and religion and religious organizations are shown in relation to the ecological adjustment.

He also wrote often for the public at large, both books and articles in a variety of journals. Most of his popular writing was originally in French, later translated into English. It was always solidly based upon his own bibliographical and field research; this is also true of his books on Easter Island (1940; 1941). In these books he disagreed with the theories both of American Indian and of Asian origin of the Easter Island stone sculpture. He took the view that the Easter Islanders are both physically and culturally Polynesian and that their art forms are likewise of local origin. Similarly, his book on Haitian voodoo (1958) is based upon many field trips to Haiti as well as on written sources. It is a study of the persistence of African fetish cults and African belief in Haiti and the relationship of this African religion, derived mainly from the Dahomeans of west Africa, to Catholicism. He gave an objective picture of voodoo as an orderly and complex religious system rather than a wild set of heathen orgies, as it had often been described [see CARIBBEAN SOCIETY].

CHARLES WAGLEY

[See also HISTORY, article on ETHNOHISTORY; and the biographies of COOPER; MAUSS; NORDENSKIÖLD; RIVET.]

WORKS BY MÉTRAUX

1928a *La civilisation matérielle des tribus Tupi-Guarani.* Paris: Geuthner.
1928b *La religion des Tupinamba et ses rapports avec celle des autres tribus Tupi-Guarani.* Paris: Leroux.
1940 *Ethnology of Easter Island.* Bernice P. Bishop Museum, Bulletin No. 160. Honolulu (Hawaii): The Museum.
(1941) 1957 *Easter Island: A Stone-age Civilization of the Pacific.* New York: Oxford Univ. Press. → First published as *L'Île de Pâques.*
1946 *Myths of the Toba and Pilagá Indians of the Gran Chaco.* American Folklore Society, Memoirs, Volume 40. Philadelphia: The Society.
1951 *Making a Living in the Marbial Valley, Haiti.* Paris: UNESCO.
(1958) 1959 *Voodoo in Haiti.* New York: Oxford Univ. Press. → First published as *Le voudou haïtien.*

SUPPLEMENTARY BIBLIOGRAPHY

STEWARD, JULIAN H. (editor) (1946–1959) 1963 *Handbook of South American Indians.* 7 vols. U.S. Bureau of American Ethnology, Bulletin No. 143. New York: Cooper Square.
WAGLEY, CHARLES 1964 Alfred Métraux, 1902–1963. *American Anthropologist* New Series 66:603–613.

METROPOLITAN GOVERNMENT
See under CITY.

MEYER, ADOLF

Adolf Meyer (1866–1950) was the dominant figure in American psychiatry during the first four decades of this century. He was a major force in molding psychiatry into its current form, but his teachings have become so solidly incorporated into American psychiatric theory and practice that the sweep and depth of his influence are often overlooked. He gave American psychiatry its pluralistic and instrumental orientation; its holistic approach to human problems; its conceptualization of psychiatric disorders, including schizophrenia, as reaction patterns rather than discrete disease entities; its concern with the psychotherapy of the psychoses. His contributions have been eclipsed, but not displaced, by those of Freud and by the ascendancy of psychoanalysis.

Meyer was born in Niederweningen, near Zurich, Switzerland, and emigrated to the United States soon after receiving his doctoral degree in 1892. He filled, in succession, the positions of neuropathologist at Kankakee State Hospital in Illinois, clinical director at Worcester State Hospital in Massachusetts, and chief of the Pathological Institute of New York's state mental hospitals. He increasingly became convinced that the essential pathology of mental disorders is to be found in the person and not in the brain cells. When the Johns

Hopkins Medical School decided to establish a department of psychiatry in 1908, Meyer was the obvious and unanimous choice for the new professorship. He remained at Hopkins until his retirement in 1941, by which time he had long been recognized as the dean of American psychiatrists.

The cultural setting may have determined the orientation of psychiatry in the United States. In a country in which people were undergoing rapid acculturation, the importance of environmental influences upon personality change was more apparent than in Europe. Even though Meyer was a Swiss, he was particularly suited by birth and training to introduce a characteristically American pragmatic, pluralistic, and instrumental approach into psychiatry. He was born into a family that considered itself the spiritual heir of Kleinjogg (Jakob Gujer), a folk philosopher who had practiced and taught an "instrumental" approach to farming and communal living, combating the superstitions and the confining traditional usages of the farmer. Meyer had gained an exceptional grounding in neuroanatomy and neuropathology under Constantin von Monakow and Auguste Forel and, while studying abroad, was attracted by Thomas H. Huxley's evolutionary and ecological approach to biology and by Hughlings Jackson's concepts of the integration of the nervous system. Soon after his arrival in the United States he came under the influence of those men who had shaped the American philosophical and sociological tradition—Charles Peirce, William James, John Dewey, G. H. Mead, and C. H. Cooley.

Meyer fused these various influences into a new conceptualization of human behavior, which he termed psychobiology, or ergasiology. He recognized that the Jacksonian concepts of the evolution and integration of the nervous system needed to be extended to include the highest level of integration through mentation: what man thinks affects his functioning down through the cellular and biochemical level, but, conversely, his thinking and feeling can be affected by the functioning of the organism at all levels of integration. Psychobiology offered an approach to the mind–body problem that obviated the need for the unsatisfactory mind–brain parallelism that had directed scientific attention to the study of the brain, to the neglect of the processes of living.

Meyer made a number of fundamental contributions to neuroanatomy and neuropathology, including the discovery of the temporal-lobe detour of the optic radiations, termed "Meyer's loop," and his studies of central neuritis and aphasia; and he introduced the construction of plasticine models into the teaching of neuroanatomy. However, he increasingly directed his attention to problems of the essentially human aspects of behavioral integration.

Although Meyer welcomed the development of psychoanalysis and particularly its emphasis upon early childhood experiences and upon the role of symbolization, he considered the focus upon instinctual vicissitudes and unconscious motivations as unduly limited and neglectful of the total person. He increasingly opposed the premature oversystematizations in Freud's theorizing. Meyer insisted upon studying the problems of human adaptation and integration in their total complexity.

Meyer's conception of psychiatric disorders as types of reaction patterns that are exaggerations of, aberrations from, or substitutions for, more normal and workable ways of living profoundly influenced the course of psychiatry. He turned away from psychiatry's efforts to become part of the mainstream of medical science by discovering some unknown biological or neuroanatomical basis for insanity, and chose instead to examine how people's ways of living and thinking can go astray. Of particular moment was his extension of this reaction-pattern concept to schizophrenia, as outlined in his 1906 paper "Fundamental Conceptions of Dementia Praecox" (*Collected Papers*, vol. 2, pp. 432–437), which emphasized that schizophrenia can result from deterioration of habit patterns, including habits of thinking. At the time, he stood almost alone in considering that schizophrenia may be a disorder of the personality rather than of the brain or its metabolism. His dynamic concept of schizophrenia also led to his insistence that patients suffering from schizophrenic reactions are amenable to psychotherapy and resocializing measures.

At the Henry Phipps Psychiatric Clinic of the Johns Hopkins Hospital, which opened in 1914, Meyer developed the first significant teaching and research psychiatric hospital that was an integral part of a medical school. It provided the model for medical school teaching and residency training in psychiatry for the next quarter century. A large proportion of the outstanding psychiatric teachers and investigators in the United States and Great Britain trained under Meyer, spreading his orientation throughout the English-speaking world.

Meyer was a man of broad vision, and his energy was sufficient to turn vision into reality. When he retired, psychiatry was on the verge of the vast expansion that followed World War II. Meyer had guided and nurtured it through its immaturity, propounding a psychiatry that had roots in both the biological and behavioral sciences, countering premature theoretical closures by his insistence upon a holistic and pluralistic approach, and fostering a psychotherapeutic approach to the psychoses.

THEODORE LIDZ

[*For the historical context of Meyer's work, see the biographies of* COOLEY; DEWEY; JAMES; MEAD; PEIRCE. *For discussion of the subsequent development of his ideas, see* MENTAL DISORDERS, *article on* BIOLOGICAL ASPECTS; PSYCHIATRY; SCHIZOPHRENIA.]

WORKS BY MEYER

Collected Papers. 4 vols. Edited by Eunice Winters. Baltimore: Johns Hopkins Press, 1950–1952. → Volume 1: Neurology. Volume 2: Psychiatry. Volume 3: Medical Teaching. Volume 4: Mental Hygiene.
The Commonsense Psychiatry of Dr. Adolf Meyer. Edited by Alfred Lief. New York: McGraw-Hill, 1948. → Consists of 52 selected papers.

WORKS ABOUT MEYER

BLEULER, M. 1962 Early Swiss Sources of Adolf Meyer's Concepts. American Journal of Psychiatry 119:193–196.
CAMPBELL, C. MACFIE 1937 Adolf Meyer. Archives of Neurology and Psychiatry 37:715–731.
EBAUGH, FRANKLIN G. 1937 Adolf Meyer: The Teacher. Archives of Neurology and Psychiatry 37:732–741.

MICHELS, ROBERT

Robert Michels (1876–1936) belongs to that generation of European sociologists which tried to apply the insights of the founders of sociology to the understanding of twentieth-century Western society. Michels' standing in sociology is assured by his brilliant monograph *Political Parties* (1911a), in which he formulated the problem of oligarchical tendencies in organizations. Like Schumpeter, Geiger, Mannheim, Lukács, de Man, and Ortega, he grappled with the problems of democracy, socialism, revolution, class conflict, trade unionism, mass society, nationalism, and imperialism, and with the role of intellectuals and of elites. He dealt more extensively than did these contemporaries of his with the politics of the working class, and he studied some topics that interested them little, such as eugenics, feminism, sex, and morality. More passionately committed than they were, he found himself deeply involved in the ideological and national conflicts of his time, and his work probably suffered from this involvement.

Michels' background was cosmopolitan: he was born in Cologne, into a bourgeois–patrician family with a German–French–Belgian background. He attended the Gymnasium in Berlin and, after serving in the army, studied in England and at the Sorbonne. He then went to Munich, where he attended lectures by the economist Lujo Brentano, and in 1897 he studied in Leipzig with Erich Brandenburg, Karl Lamprecht, and others. The following year he went to the University of Halle, studying with Michael Conrad and Hans Vaihinger and with Theodor Lindner, whose daughter he later married; in 1900 he completed his dissertation in history. Until World War I he was in close touch with the intellectual and political worlds of Belgium and France. Although he studied in England and taught in the United States, his interest in and understanding of the Anglo-Saxon world remained limited; his outlook was that of a continental European.

As a young *Dozent* at the University of Marburg, he became a socialist and participated in the Social Democratic party congresses of 1903, 1904, and 1905. He left the party in 1907 but attended the Stuttgart congress of that year as a delegate of the Italian Socialist party (he had become a *libero docente* at the University of Turin). A few months later he also resigned from the Italian Socialist party. Because of his socialist views, it was impossible for Michels to qualify for a position at a German university. Max Weber strongly deplored this stand on the part of the German universities and showed a great deal of personal interest in the young Michels. He admitted him to what he called the *salon des refusés* in Heidelberg, and in 1913 he asked Michels to become coeditor of the *Archiv für Sozialwissenschaft und Sozialpolitik*. Weber surely made a profound impression on Michels. It was partly Weber's influence and partly the security gained from his academic position at Turin that led Michels to shift from short and somewhat journalistic writings to more substantial publications in scholarly journals.

Michels described his own political evolution in an autobiographical essay, "Eine syndikalistisch gerichtete Unterströmung im deutschen Sozialismus" (1932a); he also recorded his perception of the external events of the first ten years of the twentieth century, in the introduction to the Italian edition of *Political Parties*. His political views were influenced by Arturo Labriola and Enrico Leoni, whom he met in 1902, and by the French syndicalists Georges Sorel, Hubert Lagardelle, Edouard Berth, Paul Delesalle, and Victor Griffuelhes, with whom he became increasingly friendly after 1904. Disturbed by the state of the labor movement, Michels was attracted to the idea of revitalizing it by fusing the ideas of Marx, Proudhon, and Pareto. In particular he deplored the way calculations of parliamentary advantage dominated party life and led to the abandonment of every vigorous idea and every energetic course of action. The contrast between the revolutionary statements that were made by the Social Democratic party in general and by August Bebel in particular and the cautious policy they actually pursued was brought home to him by the failure of the Ruhr strike in 1905 (Weber was also disturbed by this contrast). In a long and well-documented article (1907) Michels analyzed the socialist ideological position, particularly with respect to pacifism and the general strike to avert war; by a neat juxtaposing of texts, he made plain the extent to which radical statements and actual policy diverged.

Michels' involvement in German politics provided him with insights for his critique of the Social Democratic party and of the trade unions. It is clear from his autobiography that his descriptions of the demagogic orator, of party congresses, of the characteristics required for leadership, and, especially, of the intellectual in politics and of the class renegade are largely based on his own experiences. But his involvement was not motivated solely by intellectual concerns; it was related to his love for passion, for action, for youth, for principle irrespective of consequences, and for symbolic gestures. Indeed, his early political stance—his intellectual evolution toward a voluntaristic outlook—was the basis of his later affinity with fascism. His political life seems discontinuous and inconsistent if *Political Parties* is read only as the work of a disappointed democrat or a disillusioned regular member of the Social Democratic party. In fact, the life of a syndicalist Michels makes more sense than that of a purely Marxist-socialist Michels.

Michels refused to support Germany in World War I, and this led to what must have been a painful break with Weber. In 1914 he moved to Basel, where he became professor of economics. In 1926 he taught a course in political sociology at the University of Rome. The following year he was a visiting professor in the United States, and after that he became professor of economics at the University of Perugia. He died in 1936 in Rome. His life was that of a romantic, a frustrated politician, a patriot of an adopted country, and a scholar; it reflected as have few others the conflicts of loyalty and the intellectual ambivalences of the first decades of the twentieth century.

"Political Parties"

In the years between 1906, when he first published in Weber's *Archiv*, and 1910, when *Political Parties* was completed, Michels' life contained elements that have often produced classic works: a deeply felt and probably painful personal experience—his involvement with the revolutionary cause and its interference with his academic career—and the impact of major intellectual figures, particularly Max Weber and Mosca. (Michels had become friendly with Mosca in Turin.)

The starting point of Michels' classic study of political parties is the hypothesis that in organizations committed to the realization of democratic values there inevitably arise strong oligarchic tendencies, which present a serious if not insuperable obstacle to the realization of those values. "It is organization which gives birth to the domination of the elected over the electors, of the mandatories over the mandators, of the delegates over the delegators. Who says organization says oligarchy" ([1911a] 1962, p. 15). Thus Michels summed up his famous "iron law of oligarchy."

The nature of leadership. Michels was dissatisfied with "psychological" (i.e., motivational) explanations of the oligarchic tendencies in organizations. His whole analysis emphasized the constraints derived from organizational needs—the growth of the organization, the need to make rapid decisions, the difficulties of communicating with the members, the growth and complexity of the tasks, the division of labor, the need for full-time activity—and from the consequent processes of selection of leadership and development of knowledge and skills. These processes, in turn, lead to the emergence of stable leaders, whose professionalization, combined with their consciousness of their own worth, leads to oligarchy. The important point is that the leaders' deviation from norms they themselves accept is not the result of their motivation. The fact that conformity to certain norms may indirectly lead to deviation from other norms accepted by the same person has, of course, been emphasized by social scientists since Marx. Michels studied the special case of men who, despite their commitment to democracy, often acted in ways not conforming to their values because of the demands of organization and other factors of political life. While Michels often referred to the "psychological predispositions" of both the masses and the leaders, he saw these predispositions as fundamentally serving to reinforce or, occasionally, to weaken the organizational factors, even though at times they seemed to him to function independently. Significantly, when he presented his theory schematically in a chart (1911a, p. 382), he did not stress the manipulative or illegitimate actions of the leaders (which he discussed at length elsewhere in *Political Parties*) but concentrated instead on the factors influencing the active and effective participation of the members in decision making.

Leaders and followers. In organizations with formally democratic constitutions—such as the German working-class parties, which Michels examined closely—elections (and to a lesser extent referenda) determine who shall act in the name of the members. Elections presumably also assure the accountability of the leaders to the members. Michels' concern in a large part of *Political Parties* is with the way the leaders take advantage of the incompetence and emotionality of their followers to hold on to power and become a *de facto* oligarchy. When they establish such an oligarchy, they are no longer willing to submit their power to free electoral confirmation.

In his later writings (1927a; 1933a) Michels made a virtue of what initially he had seen only as an iron law; he was carried away by his preference for decisive leadership and an elite unhampered by the "numerical maximum, mortal enemy to all freedom of program and thought" (1927a, p. 765). By this time he saw no difference between elected representatives and charismatic leaders to whom the mass voluntarily sacrifices its will in conscious admiration and veneration (1928a, p. 291). Furthermore, he believed that "leaders never give up their power to the 'mass' but only to other, new leaders" ("die Führer weichen niemals der 'Masse' sondern immer nur anderen, neuen, Führern"; 1928a, p. 291).

He did not seem to realize that it does make a difference whether leaders are displaced by elections, in which the majority decides who shall lead, or by death or violent revolution. Furthermore, *de facto* oligarchy is not necessarily identical with *de jure* oligarchy, or dictatorship. The fact that *de facto* oligarchs need to manipulate their followers in the ways that Michels, Mosca, and Pareto described certainly makes "oligarchic" or corrupt democracies like Italy in the Giolittian period, from 1900 to 1914 very different from dictatorships like Italy under Mussolini. The inability of Michels to work out in his later writings a clear conception of the new elitist parties—the Fascists and the Bolsheviks—and his tendency to see them only as manifestations of the same general tendency to oligarchy are partly a result of this confusion.

Michels was not satisfied with electoral accountability as a criterion of democracy; in fact, he considered this *de jure* aspect insignificant compared to the *de facto* circumstances that affect the electoral process. He therefore constantly returned to another dimension: the degree of responsiveness

of (stable) leadership to the expectations and desires of the constituency. Presumably, if democratic leaders do not respond to the expectations and desires of their constituents, they will be defeated at the polls. Also, according to democratic theory, the wishes of the constituency will coincide with its interests, and democracy is the best way of assuring the satisfaction of those interests. Much of *Political Parties*, however, argues that leaders are responsive, not to the desires or interests of their constituents, but to the interests of the organization or to their own interests. (Michels noted perceptively that this identification is often unconscious.) This lack of responsiveness does not result, according to Michels, from a divergence between the interests of the leaders and those of their constituents but from the apathy and ignorance of the constituents—demonstrating what he called the incompetence of the masses—and from the general unwillingness of the leaders to overcome this passivity. (Only when new leaders challenge the old, raising real or spurious issues, are any attempts made to mobilize and inform the constituency.)

In his discussion of the responsiveness of the leadership to its followers, Michels was only dimly aware of what Carl Friedrich has called the "rule of anticipated reactions": when leaders have neither the time nor the technical means to ascertain the wishes of their constituency, or when those wishes have not crystallized, the leaders are generally guided by some sense of what their constituents' desires *might* be. This capacity to anticipate is characteristic of any leadership, but especially of democratic leadership.

Another dimension constantly present in Michels' analysis, as in all discussions of oligarchy and democracy, is the nature of the responsibility of the leaders to their followers: are leaders responsible only to their constituency, or are they responsible also to the larger whole of which their constituency is a part? are they responsible to the party membership or to the electorate? The problem of responsibility to a larger unit—the society as a whole—rather than to a particular constituency becomes especially acute when a party is in power, rather than in the opposition; this was a problem socialist leaders had not faced at the time *Political Parties* was written.

Party ideology and party policy. Michels was much concerned with two questions (which are somewhat confused in his brilliant chapter "The Conservative Basis of Organization"): can a revolutionary party follow a revolutionary policy? and can a democratic party follow a democratic policy? He felt that the answer to the first question is clearly negative if a revolutionary party hopes to achieve its goals by obtaining an electoral majority. To the question about democratic parties, his answer was less clear-cut. While he did assert that "within certain narrow limits, the Democratic Party, even when subject to oligarchic control, can doubtless act upon the state in the democratic sense" ([1911a] 1962, p. 333), he also tended to argue that if democratic parties are not internally democratic, then democracy is impossible. Lipset (1962) and Sartori (1960) have pointed out, however, that competition between parties makes the politically "organized" minority (within each party) dependent at times and to a degree on the "nonorganized" majority. This competition assures the citizen of a degree of participation and power.

Michels conceived of an ideal party as a purely ideological group, open only to those who share the goals of the founding members and identify their interests with the original conception of the interests of the group. According to Michels, the sole cause of deviation from party ideology is oligarchy. It is in the nature of oligarchy to sacrifice ideological purity to the methodical organization of the masses for electoral victory.

By such methods, not merely does the party sacrifice its political virginity, by entering into promiscuous relationships with the most heterogeneous political elements, relationships which in many cases have disastrous and enduring consequences, but it exposes itself in addition to the risk of losing its essential character as a party. The term "party" presupposes that among the individual components of the party there should exist a harmonious direction of wills towards identical objectives and practical aims. Where this is lacking, the party becomes mere "organization." ([1911a] 1962, p. 341)

The contrast between the party as an ideologically pure expression of interests (Michels had in mind primarily class interests) and the reality of modern mass parties is in many ways similar to that between sect and church in the sociology of religion of Ernst Troeltsch. Just as Troeltsch identified primitive Christianity with a sectlike conception, so did Michels identify the early socialist party with an ideal party.

Michels' ideal party is elitist—a group sharing a commitment to an ideological understanding of class interest. His conception did not encompass either organizations with specific substantive goals or modern mass parties. Lipset and Sartori have noted that the more specific the substantive goal of an organization, the more difficult it may be to find commitment to a procedural goal, such as democracy. The narrower the substantive goals, the less likely it is that the members have either the need or the time to participate and influence policy. This would explain why there is less democracy in trade unions than in parties. As for mass democratic parties, Michels believed that since these are "open" and do not require a declaration of faith in party principles, they cannot be "true" parties. He accurately pinpointed the open quality of modern parties as one of their basic characteristics, but his indignation at some of the consequences of this phenomenon prevented him from analyzing it and seeing that it is inevitable, given a society that has moved from closed and established status groups to voluntary, open organizations that compete for power in a system of universal suffrage.

Characteristics of oligarchy. Michels used the term "oligarchy" or "oligarchic tendency" to cover several aspects of political behavior that are conceptually quite distinct and that may or may not coexist in organizations, parties, or trade unions: (1) the emergence of leadership; (2) the emergence of professional leadership, and its stabilization; (3) the formation of a bureaucracy, that is, an appointed, regularly paid staff with distinct duties; (4) the centralization of authority; (5) the displacement of goals, particularly the shift from ultimate goals (e.g., achieving a socialist society) to instrumental goals (i.e., perpetuating the organization): with the growth of "conservative tendencies" in revolutionary parties, the survival of the organization takes precedence over the revolution itself, and increased emphasis is placed on satisfying the immediate needs of the members, through such activities as collective bargaining or participation in municipal government ("reformism"); and the addition of goals (e.g., ameliorating the condition of the working class); (6) increased ideological rigidity—conservatism, in the sense of adherence to policies and ideas that have been rendered obsolete by changed circumstances, and intolerance toward attempts to revise such policies or ideas; (7) the growing difference between the interests and/or points of view of the leaders and of the members, and the precedence of the leaders' interests over those of the members; (8) the decrease in the members' opportunities to participate in policy decisions, even when they are willing to participate; (9) the co-optation of emergent opposition leaders by the existing leadership; (10) the "omnibus" tendency of parties, the shift from appeals to the membership to appeals to the electorate and from appeals to a class electorate to appeals to a broader electorate—such shifts may produce a more moderate program, while opposition as a matter of principle is replaced by competition with other parties, and disloyal opposition to the social and political system is replaced by loyal opposition and even by participation in governing.

While the first nine of these characteristics may be found in very different types of organizations, the tenth is valid only for revolutionary parties or for organizations in a "democratically competitive political system" (and perhaps particularly in its parliamentary variety).

If, as the list suggests, the label "oligarchic tendencies" is used to cover so many different things, it becomes quite meaningless. Such critics as Cassinelli (1953) and Dahl (1958) therefore have tried to define the meaning of "oligarchy"— or of related concepts, like "ruling class"—in more precise and operational terms. They have also endeavored to show that some of the processes may be independent, rather than closely linked. Finally, they feel it is essential to clarify which of these tendencies are inherently incompatible with democracy and which can coexist with it.

Many factors favoring oligarchy seem to be especially characteristic of working-class organizations. In such organizations it is difficult for leaders to return to manual work in the factory after assuming leadership that implies a middle-class position; also, the workers' lack of education, their limited access to information, their frequent apathy, together with their predisposition to authoritarian attitudes, all contribute to the development of oligarchy. Evidence of such "oligarchic" tendencies in organizations with equalitarian, democratic, even revolutionary, ideology is nevertheless not proof of the validity of the iron law of oligarchy in all organizations.

Other works

In 1908 Michels published *Il proletariato e la borghesia nel movimento socialista italiano* (1908a), a work which he hoped would contribute to what is today called political sociology. Its content is similar to that of recent books in this field: discussions of the social composition of the Socialist party in parliament, of delegates to party congresses, of candidates in municipal elections, and of local party organizations, followed by an ecological analysis of electoral participation and of Socialist strength in the electorate. Michels was particularly original in his attempt to sketch what we would now call the "political culture" of Italy

in general and, specifically, that of the working class, making constant comparisons between Italian and German society. His combination of structural and psychological perspectives in this part of the book still stands as an example to sociologists who analyze the relationships between classes and the political manifestations of these relationships. The last part of the book is devoted to syndicalist currents and to comparisons between Italy and France. The discussion of the role of intellectuals in political parties, particularly in working-class parties, is linked with an analysis of the Italian occupational and academic structure.

In the same year that *Political Parties* was published, there also appeared Michels' *Die Grenzen der Geschlechtsmoral* (1911b). Such subjects as feminism, the female worker, sexual morality in different societies, and birth control had always interested him; many years later, in 1928, he published a book, *Sittlichkeit in Ziffern?* (1928b), presenting the available statistical data on various aspects of sex and family life and social deviance.

L'imperialismo italiano (1912) is concerned with the violent upheavals the Tripoli war of 1911–1912 (in which Italy took several coastal cities and towns from the Turks) produced in Italian values. (The war led to a crisis in Michels' life, which he described in the introduction.) In the book, he dealt with the suffering caused by war, the moral impact of war propaganda, and the sacrifice of long-held values to rhetorical appeals, as well as with the failure to see the similarity between the motives of the Arabs defending their homeland and those of the fighters for the Risorgimento. He interpreted Italian imperialism partly in politico-psychological terms but mainly as resulting from demographic pressure and from the social and cultural loss due to overseas migration. Thus, he asserted that the *imperialismo della povera gente* was qualitatively different from the imperialism of other nations.

In the 1920s and early 1930s he produced a number of books and many articles, dealing with nationalism, Italian socialism and fascism, elites and social mobility, the role of intellectuals, the history of the social sciences, and other subjects not so closely related to his central interests. "Psychologie der antikapitalistischen Massenbewegungen" (1925a) remains one of the most interesting and well-documented systematic treatments of working-class protest. He often returned to the problem of oligarchy and democracy (1927a; 1928a; 1933a) but added little to the original formulation of 1911; his writings merely became more antidemocratic in tone as a result of his tendency to see the new totalitarian parties as confirmation of his iron law of oligarchy.

Assessment of Michels' contributions

The chief basis of Michels' work, in addition to his personal experience, was secondary sources and contemporary accounts from magazines and newspapers. In many cases he did not analyze these secondary materials in a systematic way, and he never made an effort to develop a new methodology. His lack of sustained effort in the collecting of data and his reliance on scattered, piecemeal information gathered by others deprive his works of the unity characteristic of good monographs and of great books based on a single theme, although they often contain much valuable information.

Originality.   At the time that he wrote, Michels' work was not unique; a number of his contemporaries and immediate predecessors had formulated some of the same ideas and expressed similar sentiments. In footnotes, dedications, and later writings, he acknowledged the influence of, and intellectual affinity with, Mosca, Ostrogorskii, and Bryce; these men, in turn, acknowledged the coincidence of views.

Like his immediate predecessors—Sorel, Pareto, Mosca, and Weber—Michels challenged the prevalent democratic and socialist climate of opinion. But his basic confrontation was with Marx. Thus, he wrote:

> . . . the defects of Marxism are patent directly as we enter the practical domains of administration and public law, without speaking of errors in the psychological field and even in more elementary spheres. . . . The problem of socialism is not merely a problem in economics. In other words, socialism does not seek merely to determine to what extent it is possible to realize a distribution of wealth which shall be at once just and economically productive. Socialism is also an administrative problem, a problem of democracy, and this not in the technical and administrative sphere alone, but also in the sphere of psychology. [1911a] 1962, pp. 349, 350)

In underlining the sociopsychological aspects of political behavior—the problem of power and its abuse; the susceptibility of the masses, particularly of the lower classes, to charismatic appeals; and the importance of organization and its constraints in fostering oligarchic and dictatorial tendencies— Michels was trying to break away from the vulgar-Marxists, who saw the economic structure (of capitalism) only as a restriction of freedom.

Viability of democracy.   Michels' views on democracy have been the subject of much discussion.

Mosca (1912) presented Michels as an ademocratic theorist; others have gone further, arguing that his later writings and his attitude toward fascism provide evidence that he was actually antidemocratic; and finally, some have attributed to him a positive appraisal of the compatibility of organization and democracy.

Such very different interpretations suggest two possibilities that are not mutually exclusive. First, Michels had, in fact, no clear-cut assessment of the viability of democracy, although his more ambitious formulations of the iron law of oligarchy suggest that his view was predominantly negative. Second, the commentators do not have in mind the same problems Michels did. In common with many intellectuals, Michels tended to define democracy in terms of what he considered favorable to the interests of the people, and he concluded that if the people express preferences for, support, or acquiesce in policies not compatible with their interests, this must be the result of oligarchic manipulations. To some he has therefore appeared as a disappointed democrat whose disillusionment ultimately led him to adopt an ademocratic and even antidemocratic elitist stance (see May 1965).

Studies inspired by Michels

Michels' theories have inspired considerable empirical research intended to support, specify, or challenge them. Much of that research has been done in Anglo-Saxon countries or by scholars trained there. The recent interest in general theories of organization, concerned with such processes as bureaucratization, goal displacement, and co-optation—as distinct from a concern with specific groups, like parties, unions, pressure groups, government agencies, and corporations—has also contributed to a renewed interest in Michels.

In this theoretical development *Union Democracy*, a study of the International Typographical Union (I.T.U.) by Lipset, Trow, and Coleman (1956), has had a central place. Alone among American unions the I.T.U. has had, for over fifty years, a functioning two-party system at the national level. Its history seems to show that Michels' iron law of oligarchy is not, after all, universal: if even one exception can be found, there may be others. The study seeks to explain how the I.T.U. has maintained a system of democratic self-government. By examining the processes that have maintained democracy in a small society, the authors hoped to illuminate the relevant processes in the larger society.

Although *Union Democracy* represents an important challenge to Michels' ideas, a large number of studies of secular and religious organizations have confirmed Michels' theories, discovering processes similar to those he described. Thus, Harrison has shown (1959) that the American Baptist Convention, which is committed to the independence of its local churches and to the advisory nature of its larger organization, clearly manifests oligarchic tendencies. The growth of the organization and the increased complexity of tasks, the lack of means to ascertain the sentiments of the members on issues not directly relevant to them, specialization in pastoral work, the indifference of many of those concerned with organizational goals—all strengthen the leadership and increase its independence.

The recent literature on political parties has also been influenced by Michels' early classic. The basic books by Maurice Duverger (1951) and Sigmund Neumann (1956) have summarized and taken issue with it, while stressing its pathbreaking character. Monographic studies by Robert T. McKenzie (1955), Renate Mayntz (1959), and Samuel J. Eldersveld (1964) have been explicitly directed to the questions Michels raised. Although Eldersveld, on the basis of careful research, challenged Michels' thesis, research on political parties generally confirms Michels' observation that they are less oligarchic than single-purpose organizations concerned with more technical problems.

JUAN J. LINZ

[See also DEMOCRACY; ELITES; OLIGARCHY; PARTIES, POLITICAL. Other relevant material may be found in LEADERSHIP; ORGANIZATIONS; POLITICAL SOCIOLOGY; SOCIAL MOVEMENTS; VOLUNTARY ASSOCIATIONS; and in the biographies of BRYCE; MOSCA; OSTROGORSKII; PARETO; SOREL; WEBER, MAX.]

WORKS BY MICHELS

1905–1906 Proletariat und Bourgeoisie in der sozialistischen Bewegung Italiens: Studien zu einer Klassen- und Berufsanalyse des Sozialismus in Italien. Archiv für Sozialwissenschaft und Sozialpolitik 21:347–416; 22:80–125, 424–466, 664–726.

1906 Die deutsche Sozialdemokratie: I. Parteimitgliedschaft und soziale Zusammensetzung. Archiv für Sozialwissenschaft und Sozialpolitik 23:471–556.

1907 Die deutsche Sozialdemokratie im internationalen Verbande: Eine kritische Untersuchung. Archiv für Sozialwissenschaft und Sozialpolitik 25:148–231.

1908a Il proletariato e la borghesia nel movimento socialista italiano: Saggio di scienza sociografico–politica. Turin: Bocca.

1908b Die oligarchischen Tendenzen der Gesellschaft: Ein Beitrag zum Problem der Demokratie. Archiv für Sozialwissenschaft und Sozialpolitik 27:73–135.

1908c Le syndicalisme et le socialisme en Allemagne. Pages 21–28 in Syndicalisme et socialisme. Edited by Hubert Lagardelle. Paris: Rivière.

(1911a) 1962 Political Parties: A Sociological Study of the Oligarchical Tendencies of Modern Democracy. With an introduction by Seymour M. Lipset. New York: Free Press. → First published as Zur Soziologie des Parteiwesens in der modernen Demokratie. The 1911 German edition and the Italian translations include a graphic schema of Michels' theory, not included in the English editions.

1911b Die Grenzen der Geschlechtsmoral: Prolegomena, Gedanken und Untersuchungen. Grünwald: Frauenverlag.

(1912) 1914 L'imperialismo italiano: Studi politico–demografici. Rev. & enl. ed. Milan: Società Editrice Libraria. → First published in German.

1914 Probleme der Sozialphilosophie. Leipzig: Teubner.

1922 La teoria di C. Marx sulla miseria crescente e le sue origini: Contributo alla storia delle dottrine economiche. Turin: Bocca.

1924a Elemente zur Soziologie in Italien. Kölner Vierteljahrshefte für Soziologie 3:219–249.

1924b Lavoro e razza. Milan: Vallardi.

1925a Psychologie der antikapitalistischen Massenbewegungen. Section 9, part 1, pages 241–359 in Grundriss der Sozialökonomik. Tübingen: Mohr.

1925b Nachtrag zu Robert Michels' Aufsatz: Elemente zur Soziologie in Italien. Kölner Vierteljahrshefte für Soziologie 4:331 only.

1925c Sozialismus in Italien: Intellektuelle Strömungen. Munich: Meyer & Jessen.

1925d Sozialismus und Fascismus in Italien. Munich: Meyer & Jessen.

1926 Soziologie als Gesellschaftswissenschaft. Lebendige Wissenschaft, Vol. 4. Leipzig: Kröner.

(1927a) 1949 The Sociological Character of Political Parties. Pages 134–155 in Robert Michels, First Lectures in Political Sociology. Minneapolis: Univ. of Minnesota Press. → First published in Volume 21 of the American Political Science Review.

1927b Bedeutende Männer: Charakterologische Studien. Leipzig: Quelle & Meyer. → Biographical studies of Bebel, de Amicis, Lombroso, Schmoller, Max Weber, Pareto, Sombart, W. Müller—seven of whom Michels knew personally.

(1927–1936) 1949 First Lectures in Political Sociology. Translated with an introduction by Alfred de Grazia. Minneapolis: Univ. of Minnesota Press. → Includes a translation of Corso di sociologia politica.

1928a Grundsätzliches zum Problem der Demokratie. Zeitschrift für Politik 17:289–295.

1928b Sittlichkeit in Ziffern? Kritik der Moralstatistik. Munich: Duncker & Humblot.

1928c Die Verelendungs-theorie: Studien und Untersuchungen zur internationalen Dogmengeschichte der Volkswirtschaft. Leipzig: Kröner. → An excellent scholarly study of the historical development of the idea of immiserization.

1929 Der Patriotismus: Prolegomena zu seiner soziologischen Analyse. Munich: Duncker & Humblot.

1930a Authority. Volume 2, pages 319–321 in Encyclopaedia of the Social Sciences. New York: Macmillan.

1930b Italien von heute: Politische und wirtschaftliche Kulturgeschichte von 1860 bis 1930. Zurich: Füssli.

(1931) 1949 Patriotism. Pages 156–166 in Robert Michels, First Lectures in Political Sociology. Minneapolis: Univ. of Minnesota Press. → First published in Handwörterbuch der Soziologie.

1932a Eine syndikalistisch gerichtete Unterströmung im deutschen Sozialismus (1903–1907). Pages 343–

364 in *Festschrift für Carl Grünberg zum 70. Geburts-tag.* Leipzig: Hirschfeld.

1932b Intellectuals. Volume 8, pages 118–126 in *En-cyclopaedia of the Social Sciences.* New York: Mac-millan.

1933a *Studi sulla democrazia e sull'autorità.* Perugia, Università, Facoltà Fascista di Scienze Politiche, Collana di Studi Fascisti, 24–25. Florence: "La Nuova Italia."

1933b Historisch-kritische Untersuchungen zum politi-schen Verhalten der Intellektuellen. *Schmollers Jahr-buch für Gesetzgebung, Verwaltung und Volkswirt-schaft im Deutschen Reiche* 57:807–884.

1934 *Umschichtungen in den herrschenden Klassen nach dem Kriege.* Stuttgart: Kohlhammer.

SUPPLEMENTARY BIBLIOGRAPHY

BUKHARIN, NIKOLAI I. (1921) 1965 *Historical Material-ism: A System of Sociology.* Translated from the 3d Russian edition. New York: Russell. → First published as *Teoriia istoricheskogo materializma.*

BURNHAM, JAMES (1943) 1963 *The Machiavellians, Defenders of Freedom.* Chicago: Regnery.

CASSINELLI, C. W. 1953 The Law of Oligarchy. *Ameri-can Political Science Review* 47:773–784.

DAHL, ROBERT A. 1958 Critique of the Ruling Elite Model. *American Political Science Review* 52:463–469.

DUVERGER, MAURICE (1951) 1962 *Political Parties: Their Organization and Activity in the Modern State.* 2d English ed., rev. New York: Wiley; London: Me-thuen. → First published in French.

ELDERSVELD, SAMUEL J. 1964 *Political Parties: A Be-havioral Analysis.* Chicago: Rand McNally.

GOULDNER, ALVIN W. 1955 Metaphysical Pathos and the Theory of Bureaucracy. *American Political Science Review* 49:496–507.

HARRISON, PAUL M. 1959 *Authority and Power in the Free Church Tradition: A Social Case Study of the American Baptist Convention.* Princeton Univ. Press.

LINZ, JUAN J. 1966 Michels e il suo contributo alla so-ciologia politica. Pages vii–cxiii in Robert Michels, *La sociologia del partito politico nella democrazia moderna.* Bologna: Carlino.

LIPSET, SEYMOUR M. (1954) 1960 The Political Process in Trade-unions. Pages 357–397 in Seymour M. Lip-set, *Political Man: The Social Bases of Politics.* Garden City, N.Y.: Doubleday.

LIPSET, SEYMOUR M. 1962 Introduction. Pages 15–39 in Robert Michels, *Political Parties: A Sociological Study of the Oligarchical Tendencies of Modern De-mocracy.* New York: Free Press.

LIPSET, SEYMOUR M. 1964 The Biography of a Research Project: Union Democracy. Pages 96–120 in Phillip E. Hammond (editor), *Sociologists at Work: Essays on the Craft of Social Research.* New York: Basic Books.

LIPSET, SEYMOUR M.; TROW, MARTIN A.; and COLEMAN, JAMES S. 1956 *Union Democracy: The Internal Politics of the International Typographical Union.* Glencoe, Ill.; Free Press. → A paperback edition was published in 1962 by Doubleday.

McKENZIE, ROBERT T. (1955) 1963 *British Political Parties: The Distribution of Power Within the Con-servative and Labour Parties.* 2d ed. New York: St. Martins.

MAY, JOHN D. 1965 Democracy, Organization, Michels. *American Political Science Review* 59:417–429. → One of the most important studies of Michels' work.

MAYNTZ, RENATE 1959 *Parteigruppen in der Grossstadt: Untersuchungen in einem Berliner Kreisverband der CDU.* Cologne: Westdeutscher Verlag.

MOMMSEN, WOLFGANG 1959 *Max Weber und die deut-sche Politik, 1890–1920.* Tübingen: Mohr.

MOSCA, GAETANO (1912) 1949 La sociologia del partito politica nella democrazia moderna. Pages 26–36 in Gaetano Mosca, *Partiti e sindicati nella crisi del re-gime parlamentaro.* Bari: Laterza. → A review of Michels' *Political Parties.* First published in Volume 1 of *Il pensiero moderno.*

NEUMANN, SIGMUND (editor) 1956 *Modern Political Parties: Approaches to Comparative Politics.* Univ. of Chicago Press.

NIPPERDEY, THOMAS 1961 *Die Organisation der deut-schen Parteien vor 1918.* Düsseldorf: Droste.

PERUGIA, UNIVERSITÀ, FACOLTÀ DI GIURISPRUDENZA 1937 *Studi in memoria di Roberto Michels.* Annali, Vol. 49. Padua: CEDAM. → Contains a bibliography of Mi-chels' writings on pages 37–76.

RITTER, GERHARD A. 1959 *Die Arbeiterbewegung im Wilhelminischen Reich: Die Sozialdemokratische Par-tei und die freien Gewerkschaften, 1890–1900.* Berlin (West Berlin) Freie Universität, Friedrich Meinecke Institut, Studien zur Europäischen Geschichte, No. 3. Berlin-Dahlem: Colloquium Verlag.

ROTH, GUENTHER 1963 *The Social Democrats in Im-perial Germany: A Study in Working-class Isolation and National Integration.* Totowa, N.J.: Bedminster Press.

SARTORI, GIOVANNI 1960 Democrazia, burocrazia e oli-garchia nei partiti. *Rassegna di sociologia* 1:119–136.

SARTORI, GIOVANNI (1962) 1965 *Democratic Theory.* New York: Praeger. → Based on the author's transla-tion of his *Democrazia e definizione* (1957).

SCHORSKE, CARL E. 1955 *German Social Democracy, 1905–1917: The Development of the Great Schism.* Harvard Historical Studies, Vol. 65. Cambridge, Mass.: Harvard Univ. Press.

SCHUMPETER, JOSEPH A. (1942) 1950 *Capitalism, So-cialism, and Democracy.* 3d ed. New York: Harper; London: Allen & Unwin. → A paperback edition was published by Harper in 1962.

WEBER, MAX 1905 Bemerkungen im Anschluss an den vorstehenden Aufsatz. *Archiv für Sozialwissenschaft und Sozialpolitik* 20:550–553. → Comments on the article "Die soziale Zusammensetzung der sozialdemo-kratischen Wählerschaft Deutschlands," by R. Blank.

MIDDLE AMERICAN SOCIETY

Middle America is a cultural and geographical region comprising Mexico, Central America, and Panama. Central America is composed of Guate-mala, British Honduras (or Belize), Honduras, El Salvador, Nicaragua, and Costa Rica. Because of its size and many problems shared with the other countries, Panama is sometimes considered a part of Central America, although it was formerly a part of Colombia. The term *Mesoamerica*, coined by Paul Kirchhoff (1943), refers to a cultural sub-region within Middle America, specifically the areas occupied by the pre-Columbian high cultures [see URBAN REVOLUTION, *article on* EARLY CIVILI-ZATIONS OF THE NEW WORLD].

Mesoamerica was bordered on the south by a line that runs approximately from the Gulf of Nicoya (Costa Rica) to the mouth of the Motagua River (Guatemala). To the north, it included the areas set off by the northern borders of the Mexican states of Veracruz (including adjacent San Luis Potosí), Querétaro, Guanajuato, Jalisco, Durango, and the southern portions of Chihuahua and Sonora. Today Mesoamerica is a region of distinctive Indian populations surrounded by national civil populations. Culturally, the northern border of Middle America could be extended to include those portions of the southwestern United States that were formerly part of Mexico and that still have a significantly large and growing Spanish-speaking population.

The processes of economic and social development are presently affecting each inhabitant of Middle America, whether he cuts coupons in Mexico City's plush *pedregal* or cuts sugar cane in the Pacific lowlands of Central America. Inextricably woven into the process of development is the very high population growth rate and a social structure dominated by a concern for power but technologically still heavily primitive and agrarian. It is this challenge of primitive technology, on the one hand, and the growing concern for control of one's fellow man, on the other, that is shaping the development process in Middle America today. The heavily mercantilist export pattern that dominated the nineteenth-century political economy has continued, although industrialization and the national exploitation of mineral resources have made marked advances in Mexico.

Cultural components

Indians and mestizos. The contemporary Middle American population is predominantly mestizo, a mixture of Spanish and American Indian. (In much of this region, as elsewhere in Latin America, the term is also used to refer to the parallel cultural mixture.) In southern Mexico, Guatemala, and adjacent Honduras and El Salvador, the term *ladino* is used to refer to non-Indian peoples, especially to those of Spanish-American culture.

The concept of the plural society, often used in describing the societies of the Caribbean, is less applicable in Middle America, where its usage tends to obscure the continuing processes of integration and acculturation. In contrast to Guyana, where two distinctive ethnic groups contend for political dominance, Middle America is Spanish-American, and existing ethnic enclaves may be seen as a cultural pluralism that is gradually undergoing social integration. The term "ladino-ization" (*ladinización*) (Adams 1957) has been applied to this cultural process in those areas where *ladino* is in use; elsewhere, "mestizo-ization" (*mestizaje*) is the more general term for the acculturation process. The Indians now form a very minor percentage of the total population of all countries except Guatemala. "Indian," in the sense used here, refers to that sector of the population that retains the use of an Indian language (whether bilingually or monolingually) and specific forms of social organization that are considered by the Spanish-American population to be Indian. However, many of the specific customs that differentiate Indians from non-Indians today are of Spanish colonial origin, not indigenous origin—religious organizations such as the *cofradía;* many elements in the men's costume, such as short trousers and split-side trousers; representational dances of the Christians and the Moors; much of the paraphernalia of the church and its rituals, etc. Similarly, many cultural traits of Indian origin are now common to the way of life of the national population—the basic diet of corn tortillas, which is supplemented by beans, yucca, and squash; basic agricultural tools such as the digging stick; and rural constructions such as *ranchos*, which are made of adobe, poles, and wattle-and-daub and have grass or palm roofs. Traits of Indian origin have tended to survive in matters pertaining to direct adaptation to the habitat, whereas traits of Spanish origin have dominated in matters pertaining to social organization and ideas and values.

The decline of the Indian component of the total population has been steady since the conquest; however, three major aboriginal patterns may be distinguished, each with a separate history regarding relations with the non-Indian population. Numerically and culturally the most important of the three patterns has pertained to the sedentary agriculturalist population of Mesoamerica. This population was organized under native states, and at the time of the conquest some of these provided an already "domesticated" population which the Spanish empire was able to take over and harness to its needs. The process of adaptation to the requirements of Spanish colonial activity, however, led to a continuing and sometimes precipitous decline of the Indian population lasting until about the middle of the eighteenth century. At that time, the combination of forced labor, wars, and disease had completed its work. It is reasonable to suppose that the two and one-half centuries of conquest had led to a severe natural selection of the Indian population and that the survivors formed a genetically different population than had originally encountered the Spaniards. The Spanish empire itself became so weak that colonial segments were perforce acting with more local autonomy; the Indian population increased from that time on.

By the time of independence in 1821, the Spanish, creole, and mestizo populations were still outnumbered by the Indians, but they were increasing more rapidly. The ratio of non-Indians to Indians showed a relative decline of the Indian population in spite of its absolute growth, but this also meant that the Indian was increasingly brought into face-to-face contact with the growing mestizo population. This process, combined with government action of the nineteenth century designed to reduce the organizational strength of the Indian population, caused a series of sharp acculturation situations that continue into the present.

The aggressive retention of "Indian" cultural traits in the nineteenth century was in part a response to efforts to disorganize the Indians so as to convert them into a more controllable labor force. The Mexican reform laws and the later efforts of Justo Rufino Barrios in Guatemala sought to break the control that the church held over extensive lands as well as what might be termed the "eminent domain" over communal lands jealously guarded by the Indians. These efforts did succeed in challenging the church to a considerable degree and in shattering some Indian enclaves, but it also led many Indian communities to adopt a defensive posture with respect to the efforts of both government and private entrepreneurs to obtain the lands.

The over-all cultural result, however, is that while the Indian population continues to increase in number, sectors of it that have been subject to special economic disintegration or political penetration rapidly acculturate and cease, in a cultural sense, to be Indian. This evidently has happened in El Salvador, where in the early 1930s an abortive revolution among the Indians was put down with such violence that the Indians over a wide region gave up their Indian costumes and tried to become ladinos in order to avoid further reprisals.

The Mexican revolution caused severe acculturation in a number of instances, and Mexican government action against the Yucatán Indians and the Yaqui brought about similar shifts. The sudden progressive liberalism of the Arévalo–Arbenz period in Guatemala, from 1946 to 1954, caused a series of acculturative changes that continued thereafter.

The rapid decline of the Mexican Indian culture in recent years, coupled with growing nationalism, has led the national government to try to preserve certain of the native craft industries. Here again, the actual products in many instances are of colonial Spanish origin, but in the contemporary world they are marketed as "Indian." The Folk Art Museum of Mexico has achieved considerable success in providing a broader market for these industries, thereby strengthening their role in the local economy. Many of the Indian towns are becoming less and less distinctive as the demands and needs of the national scene impinge on the local organizational structure.

Although the tribes and lesser states to the south of Mesoamerica acculturated early to the efforts of the Spanish, in Costa Rica, Panama, and Honduras, where the population was much more sparse, the conquest and colonization led to severe losses in the aboriginal population, and, in many instances, flight into refuge areas. The contemporary Indians of Panama, especially the Cuna and Guaymí, are in fact the descendants of a number of distinctive groups, the remnants of which fled to avoid the pressures of European colonial rule. So far as can be determined, the surviving Jicaque, Sumu, Paya, and Mosquito of Honduras and the Nicaraguan Atlantic coast have somewhat similar histories. The last mentioned have long been racially mixed with Negroes, although their culture remains distinctively Indian.

To the north of Mesoamerica, the Spanish mission system brought under control various Indian populations, but as in the south, the Indian populations were sparse, and the effects of colonial control led to a much more severe destruction of the native cultures. By the nineteenth century, pressures from the north created by the expanding Anglo-American agricultural population increasingly forced bands of horse-riding "barbarians" into northern Mexico. Mexican efforts to control these bands, even with the loss of Texas and the greater southwest to the United States, were generally weak, since the northern frontier area was only sparsely settled by Mexicans far removed from the more central concerns of the government.

Culturally, the proximity of northern Mexico to growing centers of the United States led to an economic orientation toward the north, which tended by the early twentieth century to differentiate both the culture and society of northern Mexico from those in the center and south, and the continued interchange of population across the border has contributed to a growth of the Latin American population in the southwestern part of the United States. Northern Mexico, earlier a dry and sparsely populated area, today is one of the fastest-growing major regions in the republic, and one in which the Mexicans are achieving pronounced success in regional economic development.

In the general picture of ethnic distributions in Middle America today, the national mestizo, or Latin American, population is predominant in all but a few areas. Central Mexico, sectors of southern Mexico and Yucatán, and adjacent Guatemala contain the largest remaining Indian populations. Small enclaves are to be found scattered in western Mexico and in the remaining Central American countries.

Other ethnic groups. In addition to the Indian and mestizo populations, there are a number of other ethnic components that should be mentioned, either because of their past importance or because they remain today as ethnic enclaves. Negro slaves were brought into Mexico and various parts of Central America during the colonial period in an attempt to provide labor to substitute for the declining Indian population. In general, the settlement of these imported peoples was localized, and evidence of their presence survives today in a Negroid physical component in a few communities. Just prior to the end of the colonial period, the British shipped an entire population of "Black Caribs" from the Lesser Antilles to the northern coast of Honduras. Communities of these distinctive peoples today dot the littoral from British Honduras to southern Nicaragua. In spite of their name, they retain an Arawakan language and a culture that is more characteristic of the Antilles than the mainland. During the building of the Isthmian railway in Panama, the construction of the canal, and the two world wars, many English-speaking Antillean Negro laborers came to Panama and today form an important sector of the urban population. Their language and culture contrast with the Spanish-American culture of the mainland Negroid population. During the nineteenth and twentieth centuries, Chinese have settled in many areas along the west coast of the New World; in the early days they were imported as labor, and in more recent years they have immigrated for independent motives. This population is usually occupied in commerce in larger towns and cities. In recent years Chinese have mixed increasingly with the mestizo population.

European populations of more recent origin include the English Bay Islanders off Honduras, the English of British Honduras, and the English, Spanish, German, and North American agricultural and commercial entrepreneurs who have been investing in the countries of Middle America during the past 150 years. In some instances, these peoples have maintained strong connections with their homelands, and even though technically native-born nationals, they are considered by many mestizos to be still essentially foreign.

Indian culture change. The surviving Indian population of Middle America is being acculturated, although the process is uneven. It is hastened by economic and political events and slowed by the continuing social, commercial, or geographic isolation of many of the groups. Acculturation occurs as the individual removes himself from the context of the Indian community by migrating to the city or to a plantation as a laborer; it occurs also as entire communities undergo pressures leading to a breakup of the older social structure. Thus the decline of the religious and political system of the highland Indians has been due primarily to political pressure from the government and an inability of the older ritual organization to hold the community together. The formation of *sindicatos* and *gremiales* (labor unions and organized interest groups) and cooperatives that include Indians has led to a new patterning of relationships that is increasingly pertinent to the way of life in some regions.

A few community organizations have resisted the pressures for change. The *campesinos* (countrymen) of Jalapa, Guatemala, persist in regarding themselves as "Indian" although they have no distinctive Indian costume and speak only Spanish. In this case, the basis for cohesion lies in the *campesinos'* attempt to maintain their communal lands inviolate from the encroachments of neighboring *ladinos*. Generally speaking, however, poverty and political weakness characterize the Indians. This political inferiority is somewhat overcome when the Indian is economically successful. In a few places, such as Quezaltenango (Guatemala), and Tehuantepec (Mexico), a distinctive Indian middle class has emerged, composed of merchants who were long dominant in the market and are now among the major retailers in the city as well. This group has a heightened interest in forms of Indian organization that could prove politically viable within the nation.

Racial differences make almost no difference in the acculturation process. An individual is socially classified principally by his conduct. Indian physical appearance is significant only in terms of being one of a number of traits that may identify an individual as being "Indian." When behavior changes, however, physical appearance is taken as indicative of genetic history, not current social allocation. The same holds true concerning people of Negroid extraction in Panama. Although an Anglo-Caribbean background gives them some cultural differences, when they assimilate into the Spanish-speaking

Panamanian population their skin color carries no further social or cultural meaning.

Recent historical background

The termination of the Spanish empire in Middle America occurred in 1821. Mexico was formed of what had formerly been the viceroyalty of New Spain, but it also included Chiapas, the southern area that had been part of the captaincy-general of Guatemala. The Central American federation included the area from Guatemala through Costa Rica; and Panama was considered part of Gran Colombia. Politically, the federation disintegrated into its component parts in 1838. Although attempts have been made to reconstitute a Central American union, nothing has come of it to date.

Independence did not bring social or economic revolution to Middle America. Colonial mercantilism evolved naturally (and, in fact, had already done so through illicit trade) into an agrarian mercantilism whereby the Middle American countries gained their principal national income from the export of hacienda-produced crops, the extraction of forest and other products growing wild in the habitat, and from the continuing though much reduced mining. The governments alternated between a continuing conservatism, wherein the church played a strong stabilizing part and controlled a significant sector of the state territory, and the emergence of nineteenth-century liberalism, directed toward trying to exploit resources in order to foster economic growth. The collapse of the Central American federation marked the end of liberalism in Guatemala until the third quarter of the century, but liberalism continued in the other Central American states and in Mexico.

The private hacienda flourished during the nineteenth century; the *hacendado* essentially ran his private regional state when under the conservatives and received the overt support of the government when under the liberals. The condition of the mass of the population was basically of little concern to both conservatives and liberals. The last half of the century saw the ascendancy of liberalism, with the government of Porfirio Díaz in Mexico and that of Justo Rufino Barrios in Guatemala. The latter was killed in 1885, in an unsuccessful attempt to reconstitute the Central American union by force, but Díaz continued to lead Mexico until the revolution in 1910.

Middle America, like the rest of Latin America, constituted a part of the world's hinterland at the time of the industrial revolution in northern Europe and North America. Industrialization in Mexico was encouraged primarily by foreigners, since it was they who had direct contact and experience with the process. By 1880, 400 factories in Mexico employed 80,000 laborers, and the mining population had risen to 70,000. Heavy industry was underway by the turn of the century; there were steel plants in Monterrey, and oil was extracted under foreign concessions. Although there were a number of attempts, some fairly active, to establish labor organizations during the latter part of the nineteenth century, it was not until the revolution that they became significant. Although by 1900 some industry had begun, the predominant pattern of life in Middle America continued to be a rural one. The few nascent industries in a sense constituted an extension of the northern industrial effort into the Middle American region. Industrialization was not growing up within Middle America but rather being thrust upon it in a relatively advanced form. This led to a secondary development, wherein the technology was basically borrowed and the society had to make major readjustments to incorporate it. For example, the exploration for and extraction of oil were achieved with a well-developed technology, so that the labor force did not grow with the complexity of the industry but rather had to be trained specifically to handle certain kinds of tasks. The same was true for the steel plants. The development of labor organizations essentially followed European, and to some degree, North American counterparts: the organizations placed emphasis on anarchist philosophies, but they were unable to organize effectively much beyond the level of mutual benefit societies.

The entire process of industrialization involved an essentially rural laboring population. Differing from an urban proletariat, the laboring force moved to industry from the country and in many instances moved back to the country. Although the life of the workers in the countryside was extremely harsh, and perhaps even harsher in the mining sectors, conditions in the cities were not so much better that they attracted a great number of people. There was no enclosure movement to force people off the land; indeed, the growing haciendas had to compete for the available labor, and the rural population was needed in the rural area. The developing industries found that they had to adapt to the customs of the rural population rather than the reverse. The regional hegemony that provided haciendas with control over their labor was not so easily achieved by the new industries.

Involving as it does the adaptation of a population to different and complex cultural forms, the process of creating an organized and urbanized work force has proved to be the basic difficulty for the economic development of the Middle American countries, just as it has proved to be elsewhere in Latin America. The fact that the countries had been politically independent for over half a century did not have the same significance as in Europe and North America, where the societies had been evolving as an intrinsic part of the growing demands of the technological and economic changes and advances.

The very success of Díaz' economic development program can be measured to some extent by the degree of degradation to which the Mexican *campesino* was increasingly subjected. Mexico continued to be marked by strong regional ties and controls exercised as much by regional bosses as through derivative power of the central government. The Mexican revolution erupted in 1910 and shook the country for almost a decade. It is pertinent for understanding Middle America and its role in recent world history to recognize that this revolution was the first major successful social revolution to reflect the incredibly complex conflicts that were engendered by the industrial revolution. The fact that this occurred in a society controlled by an agrarian (although industrializing) oligarchy, not by the industrialists themselves, made the contrast between the conditions of the laboring population and those of the upper sector of the society especially visible. In the years that followed the initial outbreak, the Mexican revolution succeeded in eliminating much of the agrarian oligarchy, and it turned over much of the land to the hacienda laborers and neighboring communities of *campesinos*. It established a new set of community lands called after the earlier form, *ejido*, and, by retaining title, placed the recipients of this land under direct governmental control. The small subsistence landholder has not been supplanted, however, and the population expansion has brought increasing agrarian problems in its wake. None of the other Middle American countries has successfully undertaken such revolutionary reforms. The 1952 agrarian reform law of Guatemala lasted for two years and was then rescinded, and most of the expropriated lands were returned to their original owners.

The role of foreign countries in this process must be noted, especially that of the United States. During the nineteenth century, Middle America and the Caribbean continued to be objects of competition and some conflict between various European countries and the United States. The French intervention in Mexico came, significantly, after the United States' war with Mexico. In Central America, the British continued their territorial claims, which survive today in the colonial residue of British Honduras. U.S. policy in the Caribbean was an attempt to exclude European interests, and following the war with Spain at the end of the century, the United States began a program of "superpaternalism," developing complete economic control of Cuba, retaining Puerto Rico as U.S. territory, and attempting to control the external financial affairs of Haiti and Nicaragua. At the turn of the century the United States had developed its interests in the banana industry in a number of countries, and, following the separation of Panama from Colombia, the Panama Canal was built. The weakness of the Central American governments was reflected in the continuing action of the U.S. Marines in Nicaragua that led to the establishment of the Somoza dictatorship in the 1930s; the strong influence of the banana companies (and growing coffee interests) in the governmental affairs of Honduras, Guatemala, and Costa Rica; and the maintenance of U.S. control over the Panama Canal.

Mexico's concern for its own internal affairs and its desire to gain control of dominant foreign economic interests and nationalize its oil resources led that country to pay scant attention to the nations to the south, leaving the United States as the only major foreign power. Today, Mexico is finally capitalizing on its economic successes and in fact has challenged Guatemalan claims to the colony of British Honduras.

In a very real sense, the Mexican revolution culminated in the expropriation of foreign-held lands and interests under Cárdenas, head of state from 1934 to 1940, and in the great increase in agrarian reform activity. World War II brought to the Central American countries the same opportunity and cause for nationalistic development that occurred in Africa and Asia. During the period 1946–1954 Guatemala attempted to shed the controls exercised by the United States and to initiate strong national self-identification. This period in Guatemala was followed by a gradual shift toward the slower development that was occurring in Costa Rica and El Salvador after these two countries had ousted their dictators. Panama also has made a significant effort to provide national controls exclusive of foreign influence; Honduras and Nicaragua have showed somewhat less interest.

Among themselves, the five countries of Central America (Panama being excluded) have formed a "common market" organization that is scheduled, should things occur more or less as planned, to create a single economic entity of the entire region. Significantly, this union was initially encouraged by the Economic Commission for Latin America, an organization generally free of U.S. influences, although subsequently the United States has supported it with technical and economic aid.

Social organization

Although Middle America had several urban centers prior to the Spanish conquest and industry has become an integral part of the Mexican economy and a growing sector in the smaller Central American countries, the greater portion of the Middle American population is still agrarian in orientation, and much of the growing urban population has immediate rural origins. During the nineteenth century agrarian mercantilism created and perpetuated an upper class that lived on the land and a small service, commercial, and administrative class in the cities and towns. This pattern has continued. The middle-income group has expanded as the major cities have grown. The countryside and towns have an upper socioeconomic sector that is allied with the middle-income sector of the cities. The lower sector forms a continuous population from countryside to city, although there tends to be a sharp cultural differentiation between city dwellers of the second and later generations and those who have themselves made the move. Since so many migrants are recent, the poorer sectors of the city have a distinctly rural flavor. Guatemala City had no slums in 1950, but today it has a variety of shack towns. Mexico City has been the recipient of such migrants for some decades. Many are swallowed up in the older sections of the cities, moving in with earlier-arrived relatives until such time as they can be on their own. All the growing major Middle American cities are faced with the problem of rural migrants for whom there is not enough work and insufficient housing.

For the rural migrants, the major destinations other than the cities are frontier areas such as the Atlantic regions of Panama, Costa Rica, Nicaragua, Honduras, and Guatemala, and the northern and southern states of Mexico. Mexican migration to the United States over the past years has been large, although recent legislation has led to a severe restriction in numbers.

These population movements are creating broad kinship networks over great areas, extending from North American cities to the rural areas of Mexico. The household remains the basic kin unit, and migration to rural and urban areas establishes a chain of such households. Many Middle American rural communities have colonies in the major cities, and these serve to indoctrinate the newcomer, helping him to adjust to the exigencies of urban life. Advice from friends and relatives similarly leads

people to seek out a better life in the frontier areas. This kind of broad geographical network has been long established among wealthier peoples, but among the poor it is fairly new. It has not led to a disintegration of kinship as a major relational system, but many specific obligations and responsibilities have changed. In the middle-income groups, women are increasingly emancipating themselves from the pattern of male dominance and the traditional restrictions that limited the range of their contact to female relatives and the nuclear family. This older pattern has not entirely disappeared, but it has always been less effective among the poorer people, especially in the cities, where there is a high proportion of households headed by women who have to earn a living and support their children without the aid of a regularly employed man. Under these circumstances, when women carry the major economic responsibilities of the family, there is little room for the older restrictions.

Urban organization.   The plan of Middle American towns and cities generally follows a rectangular grid pattern, with one or more plazas. The major Catholic church and the municipal government building are found on the central or oldest plaza. In former years the houses of families in the upper social strata were generally located in or near this center. These houses were built with patios, the number of patios being some measure of the wealth and prominence of the family. The major cities today have grown far beyond this pattern; the automobile and bus have made possible middle-income and wealthy residential suburbs; projects have been developed for middle-income white-collar workers; and severe slums have grown up along the margins and in crevices of unoccupied land in almost all sections of the city. Workshops and house industries may be found in the older sections of the cities, but they are also scattered in the growing middle-income and lower-income districts.

The traditional centralism of Latin American countries is evident in the fact that the capital city in every Middle American country, with the possible exception of Honduras, is also the major commercial center, and it is five to ten times as large as the next largest center in the country. In Mexico some provincial centers have been growing more rapidly than the national capital. Regional industrial centers are of major importance, as are some regional educational institutions. In the Central American countries the national capital still dominates, although there is significant growth of some provincial centers, such as Escuintla in Guatemala and San Pedro Sula in Honduras.

Metropolitan Mexico City is one of the major cities of the world. Guadalajara, Monterrey, Puebla, Ciudad Juárez, Guatemala City, Panama, San Salvador, and Managua each exceed 200,000 in population. Industrial development in Mexico has been able to absorb a significant number of the rural and provincial immigrants, but there are still very many who lack basic skills and can enter the industrial labor force only in a completely unskilled capacity. This is also true in the smaller cities. The basically rural orientation of the migrants makes it difficult to organize them into syndicates or unions, although in Mexico such organizations have become large over the years and have played an important part in the consolidation of the single Mexican political party.

The organization of labor in Middle America dates back to the last century, but it has achieved strength mainly in Mexico, where well over two million men are involved. There are fewer than fifty thousand organized workers in each of the other countries, and of these, only in Costa Rica and El Salvador do unions have affiliations with an international organization. Unions have been under severe government control, and in Mexico especially the right to strike and the arbitration of demands are determined by what the government considers to be the national welfare. In many industrial and commercial firms there is still a strong paternalistic relationship between management and labor, but government action and the establishment of unions have done much to reduce this in Mexico and Guatemala.

While in Mexico and Guatemala government has attempted to balance industrial developments with the welfare of the general population, elsewhere private investment interests continue to be a stronger influence. In Panama and El Salvador the controlling oligarchies may not participate directly in political administration, but they effectively dominate the economic systems of the two countries. In Nicaragua, the Somoza family has, since the 1930s, exercised a political control that has enabled it to obtain ownership or interest in many of the enterprises of the country. In Guatemala, Honduras, and Costa Rica those who possess the wealth of the country exercise considerable influence, but they do not seem to have the same degree of political control as their counterparts in Panama, El Salvador, and Nicaragua.

Agrarian structure. Only in Mexico has industrialization advanced to a point where it has assumed a significant role in the national economy; industry and commerce have each equaled or bettered the agrarian portion of the gross domestic product. In the other countries, manufacturing is less than half as large as the agrarian production, and commerce seldom reaches even a third. Furthermore, the greater part of the national wealth in these countries is still dependent upon agrarian products, of which there is generally only one or a few export crops. In 1960 coffee was the principal agricultural export in four of the countries (Costa Rica, El Salvador, Guatemala, Nicaragua) and was the second most important export in all the rest. Bananas are the major export of Honduras and Panama and the second most important in Costa Rica and Guatemala. Cotton occupies first place in Mexico and second in Nicaragua.

This emphasis on one main crop in the Central American countries is a continuation of the nineteenth-century agrarian dependence, and much in the social structure reflects a similar continuation from that period. There has been a serious attempt to experiment with other crops that might require new forms of social organization, but except in Mexico it has had relatively little effect on the over-all picture.

In all countries of Middle America over half the economically active population is involved in agriculture, and in all but Mexico and Panama approximately one-half or more of all wage earners are so occupied. In Mexico, approximately one-third of the wage earners are in agriculture, and in Panama, because of the ready availability of free land, only 13 per cent are so employed. Subsistence agriculture, which emphasizes corn and beans (except in Panama, where rice is especially important), is still the basis of life for a large proportion of the population.

The subsistence agriculturalist still depends primarily on a few basic tools, such as the digging stick, the hoe, or the plow for planting, and the axe and the machete for clearing land, the last also being used for general work and occasionally as a weapon. The seasonal round of activity characteristically allows time for many subsistence farmers to earn wages as seasonal laborers on plantations or coffee *fincas;* there is also a period just before the first harvest that is known as the "hunger period." Those who do not migrate seasonally usually have some crop or craft that provides a cash income, and in many regions, whole communities will specialize in the production of squash, onions, wheat, vegetables, fruits, flowers, or some other marketable produce for the cities.

Scientific large-scale agriculture is increasing, but it has yet to achieve any degree of stabilization. Heavy dependence on a single crop makes the enterprise subject to the whims of the world market, and the use of pesticides, fertilizers, and herbicides is merely beginning. The most successful advance in this area has been the Mexican irrigation projects—the Rio Grande, the Fuerte, the Papaloapan, the Tepalcatepec, and the Grijalva–Usumacinta. Developments in agriculture are bringing economists, engineers, agronomists, and other technicians into important professional positions in Mexico, and they are assuming a new kind of control within the social structure.

While Mexico alone has taken the major steps toward industrialization of agriculture, it too has extensive areas populated by small-scale subsistence agriculturalists, and the number of these people is increasing. Although agrarian reform was instituted shortly after the Mexican revolution and well over 115 million acres of land have been reallocated to small holders, there are still some very large holdings. Cline (1962, p. 220) estimated that in 1950, fewer than one thousand landholders still received 35 per cent of the total agricultural income. None of the other Middle American countries has been able to carry through any significant land reform. Guatemala's attempt during the Arbenz regime, which lasted from 1950 to 1954, ended when Arbenz was exiled and has been replaced by rural colonization projects.

The contemporary agrarian structure is under three forms of pressure. First, the increase in rural population materially reduces the amount of land available per capita. Second, there is a demand for large-scale agricultural enterprises, since industrialization can best develop this way. Third, popular political efforts are aimed at reforming the entire tenure structure. To this, a fourth may be added, in Mexico—a gradual inflation that is making small-scale production increasingly noncompetitive at the national level.

Rural social organization. The lower sector of the agrarian social structure is composed of peasant farmers, small-scale subsistence agriculturalists (whether renting or owning land), and a variety of regular and seasonal agricultural wage laborers; the upper sector includes both corporately controlled agricultural entrepreneurs and individuals. The classic *latifundia* and *minifundia* are still in existence today, although the economic structure behind them has tended to change their appearance. Population increase in the rural areas has exacerbated the *minifundia* problem (i.e., the progressive diminution of land size due to equal inheritance in a population expanding through natural increase) and has led to an increase in demand for seasonal work. The *latifundia* is becoming more profit-oriented. The nineteenth-century-style hacienda, the private regional domain of its owners, has disappeared from much of the area. This development has occurred in part because of the laws protecting labor, but even more because of the appearance of younger aggressive agrarian entrepreneurs, who in some instances have developed large-scale plantations, often converted from the older haciendas and utilizing new crops. Others rent land and produce fast-growing crops that promise at the moment to be profitable on the world market. The speculator shows essentially no interest in the care of the land or the welfare of the laborer, and usually disappears, either wealthy or bankrupt, as soon as the market becomes unfavorable.

The basic landholding system is still private, with the exception of the *ejido* system in Mexico. This system, however, involves only about a quarter of the Mexican farming population. Community landholdings are found in scattered areas. They may be lands dating back to old grants, but probably just as common are those which have been more recently created out of land purchased by a community. Community land as such, however, must not be confused with the Mexican *ejido*. The former is controlled by the members of a community (not necessarily all members), whereas *ejido* lands are controlled by the federal government. The two are structurally different, just as the profit-oriented plantation is structurally distinct from the disappearing hacienda.

Except in very poor communities (and communities composed almost entirely of Indians) there tends to be a fairly evident local upper socioeconomic sector. Indian communities, especially those that have retained a corporate quality through collective interest in community lands or a strong local religious–political–administrative system, can seldom be differentiated into strata, although differences of wealth and prestige do exist and play an important role in the operation of the Indian community organization. In mestizo and *ladino* communities and those Indian communities with a significant non-Indian population, there is often a group of families that traditionally have taken responsibility for government and public leadership, and they usually have control of major local resources or manage them for those who do.

Rural community organization varies with many factors, but among the more important are whether the communities are composed primarily of landowning farmers or rural laborers; whether or not they are expanding rapidly; whether they are old or of fairly recent origin; and whether or not the farmers have rights to community land of some kind. Old communities of independent farmers with collective rights to the land tend to be fairly exclusive and maintain fairly close internal ties insofar as the land can support them. As the population grows and opportunities for wage labor become increasingly necessary for survival, there is a tendency to slough off population, sending people to plantations, the cities, or frontier areas. People in new communities, even when there is community land, tend to identify with the nation, neutralizing an otherwise strong attachment to the village. Where there is no basis for corporate community involvement, such as land held in common, the orientation of each of the members will be toward his own self-interest.

From the point of view of national growth, rural organizations not based on the community are more important. Among these are the *campesino* federations of Mexico and Guatemala, the rural labor unions, and cooperatives. The Confederación Nacional Campesina is the largest Mexican rural "interest" group and is fundamentally composed of all the *ejidatarios*. A similar attempt to organize peasants and wage laborers in Guatemala was made during the Arbenz period, but it collapsed with his downfall. Recently it has been reinitiated under Christian-Democratic efforts.

Rural labor unions, though underdeveloped, are usually organized on specific farms. Access to judicial action in protection of labor's rights has been established in all countries, although the bias of the courts varies considerably.

Recent years have seen a sudden proliferation of cooperatives, primarily of a producer type in handicrafts, and increased marketing of extractive products and farm produce. In Mexico the government has succeeded in obtaining and retaining a fairly strong degree of control over rural organizations; in the rest of Middle America landholders have a stronger lien on the government's interests and have been fearful of such organizations. As a result, they have been fewer in number and less successful.

Power and prestige structure

The liberal power structure of nineteenth-century Middle America had an agrarian base oriented toward the export of a few basic crops and depending on northern industrial centers for necessary tools and the luxuries enjoyed by the small upper sector. At the head of government there was in each country a strong individual who tried variously to develop the country or his own fortunes through encouraging the expansion of exportation. This was particularly true in Mexico

and Guatemala; less so elsewhere. In Nicaragua, power was thin and essentially balanced between the colonial cities of León and Granada; in Honduras the north coast was often beyond the effective control of the government of Tegucigalpa. The center of population in Costa Rica, the *meseta central*, and the population of Panama growing up around the transit zone were both effectively separated from all other centers by miles of uninhabited land. Local leaders, because of distance from the capital, often exercised more power than the central government could bring to bear. Economically, some regions were all but independent from the capital. In a country as small as Guatemala, coffee production in the western part of the country developed a regional society, which included many Germans in the administrative sector. The port of Champerico was used as the area's point of entry and exit. A similar society in the north, Alta Verapaz, exported directly through the Rio Dulce. The capital city had hardly any contact with people or products from either of these societies. Similarly, northern Mexico, Yucatán, and other regions were in many respects relatively independent of what was occurring in the country at large, and sometimes they had closer relations with foreign centers than with their own country's capital.

In the provincial areas, political control was generally held by large landholders, not necessarily having extraordinary wealth themselves, but relatively much wealthier than the rural population surrounding them. They either belonged, or considered themselves to belong, to a society that reached into urban parts of the world, and their homes usually were combinations of the special riches of their region and clothing, pianos, and other articles of varying luxury imported from Europe or the United States. Some areas were specifically under the control of members of the clergy, and others were still under the corporate control of organized Indian villages. The liberal governments were concerned with strengthening the central government, thereby weakening the local and regional power centers.

Strengthening of the central governments has come about through a number of means. Federal or national troops of police frequently were established to roam the country and keep order, helping the regional power holders but at the same time making them increasingly dependent upon central-government action. The church was neutralized by Barrios in Guatemala in the 1870s, and in Mexico it was effectively restricted in the nineteenth century and later most specifically by the expropriations following the revolution. Debt peonage was abolished in Guatemala, and a vagrancy law was substituted, thereby bringing the labor force under government control rather than control by local landholders. Alliances with foreign interests provided the government with an income independent of the rest of the country. While this substituted one kind of regional control for another, it placed governments in a position where they did have more funds. The professionalization of the military started in Mexico in the nineteenth century and in the Central American countries proceeded gradually, providing government with a more dependable military arm. In Mexico, however, military leaders had grown so powerful during the revolution that the immediate problem was how to extract the power from the military without destroying it as a necessary government arm. This was accomplished over the decades following the revolution, and now the Mexican military is essentially fragmented into a great number of small units; officers are rotated so that the possibility of collusion among them is severely reduced; and the early revolutionary generals are now replaced by younger officers. However, the trend toward a more powerful military, evident elsewhere, could occur in Mexico. More important than specific changes in the controls exercised by the Mexican government have been the significant gains in economic development that have established new bases of power within the country. In addition, the entire revolutionary situation created new political and governmental tasks and responsibilities and has led to an expanding bureaucracy and party organization, thereby providing thousands of positions by which individuals may participate in economic and political action. This may be thought of as an expansion of the base of power within the area and, as such, an increase in the amount of power that is available for people to manipulate.

In the Central American countries specific relations within the power structure are more varied. There have been no revolutions to completely displace the older landowning oligarchy, but in part this has been the case because such an oligarchy was not always dominant. In the early twentieth century, Nicaragua, Honduras, and Costa Rica had a fairly large proportion of small and medium farmers; concentration on export crops—first coffee, then cotton and other field products—has led to the accumulation of lands in relatively fewer hands. At the same time, however, the economic development that has occurred in the wake of cash cropping has provided the same expansion of the power base that has occurred in Mexico, and the sector of the society that operates in this framework has concomitantly expanded.

This broadening of the power structure has produced what many have considered to be an emerging middle class, middle sector, or middle mass. Considering economic measurements, i.e., the income gradient of the population, and the growing white-collar sector, these terms are applicable. This development, however, has been accompanied by an unfortunate tendency to attribute the origin of all new things to the members of this middle class: they are presumed to possess the ideology of nationalism; they are expected to produce industrial and commercial entrepreneurs; and they are thought to be the potential source of a stable political society in the Western tradition. While there is something to recommend these suggestions, they have become intellectual blinders to the fact that changing power bases have also served to perpetuate features of the nineteenth-century oligarchic structure.

The vast gulf between the ways of life of the older upper and lower classes produced a system of prestige behavior that identifies certain forms of behavior with the upper sector and certain others with the lower. Manual labor, or earning a living with one's hands, is generally regarded as the mark of a person of low prestige; work, in this sense, is not regarded as a goal of those individuals who aspire to a better way of life. Socially, this idea has led to a continuation of an apparent dichotomy between those who are satisfied with work as a means of employment of time and those who reject it. The idea is no longer clearly congruent with differences in income, because there are craftsmen and farmers with moderate holdings who, through the organization of workshops and employment of labor, have succeeded in achieving considerably more wealth, both in land and in cash, than the average white-collar worker. Also, while the per capita income of the countries has increased, there is no evidence of a significantly wider distribution of wealth among members of the lower classes. White-collar workers do not generally enjoy a large income but regard it as important that they not be marked as manual workers. The means to social mobility do not stem from the power that accrues from wealth but rather from the ability to control the behavior of others in a variety of ways. This, in turn, has perpetuated a series of what have been termed "vertical" relationships in the society. Through kinship, friendship, reciprocal help, influence, using one's position to achieve a slightly better one, and so on, there continues to be a strong set of interdependencies that relate people high in the power structure downward, in separate lines, to many people lower in the structure. Since power always works two ways, these are the very lines that are used by people lower down to better their positions.

In spite of new wealth and the growth of an economic middle class, Middle American society is still recognizably divided into two prestige sectors, many characteristics of which are derived from the past. While the power base has expanded, there seems to have been little to change the orientation toward work and wealth that has characterized the lower sector or the upper sector's orientation toward power manipulation in order to achieve a better position in the prestige system.

The orientation toward work in the lower sector is not necessarily manifested by a devotion to work. Among wage laborers it is often quite the reverse; the economic development process has not yet materially raised their standard of living, and they have recognized that work does not mean upward mobility. Work is seen as a necessary means to survival, measured by cash income. Working for additional income is not seen as crucial, since the amount of income such work makes available will have no material effect on the person's access to power. By the time a person may in fact achieve an income that will permit him such access, he has learned that money is still not enough: power is exercised through a variety of exchange devices and vertical relationships. The lower sector may be seen, then, as a survival sector, whereas the upper sector, having mastered survival, seeks political position, use of luxury goods (although not necessarily their ownership), ownership of land (the continuation of the old symbol of power), and leisure.

The power structure of the countries of Middle America has not fundamentally changed in shape, although there have been important shifts in emphasis. It has conserved certain features that used to be thought peculiar only to agrarian states. Many of these features appear to be viable in a situation of economic development and, as such, are responsible for many of the characteristics that have been called "Latin American" by those who have equated progress with the ways of life of Europe and the United States.

Government and political organization

The formal administrative structures of Mexico and the Central American countries differ in details, but they are basically the same in manner of operation. The Central American countries are divided into departments or provinces, the adminis-

tration of each of which tends to be nominal, since most power is vested in the national executive and the congress. The minimal unit of territorial and administrative organization within the national structure is the *municipio* (*distrito* in Panama, *cantón* in Costa Rica). There may be several small towns within a municipality, but they are completely subordinate to the capital, which gives its name to the entire territory.

All the Middle American countries are constitutional republics and have legal systems based on civil law. Only Mexico is technically a federal republic. Even in Mexico, however, the president has the power to remove any state government that is felt to be unequal to its tasks, and so in effect the central government exercises considerable power over the states.

The mode of election of the congresses and their specific breadth of responsibility and authority vary. Congresses are generally responsible for major legislation, usually supporting the executive policies. Situations such as have occurred in Brazil, Chile, and Argentina, where the congress may oppose the president for extended periods, have not been common in Middle America. Overt dictatorship began to decline following World War II, when some dictators resigned, as in Guatemala, El Salvador, and Honduras, and others were killed, as in the case of Somoza in Nicaragua. But violence has accompanied both constitutional and nonconstitutional rulers, with the recent exception of Mexico. Since World War II the military has played a central part in establishing or removing the executive in Guatemala, El Salvador, Honduras, Nicaragua, and Panama (where the national police function as an army). Following the 1948 revolution in Costa Rica the president disbanded the army entirely.

The judiciary operates at the local level through justices of the peace, who are in some instances also the local administrative officers. The courts of each country are based on civil law rather than constitutional law. There are special courts, such as labor courts, in some countries where the government felt that the regular courts would tend to operate unfairly with respect to a particular sector of the society.

Although all the countries of Middle America have political parties, these are by no means similar. Both Honduras and Nicaragua have a two-party system, Nicaragua's dating from the nineteenth century. For the past thirty years, however, Nicaragua has been controlled by the Somoza family. Mexico has had basically a single party for the past 35 years, but the party is so organized that it has sectors representing most of the major groups in the country—*ejido* families, rural unions, industrial and labor unions, civil servants, cooperatives, small proprietors, merchants, professionals, etc. While there have been opposition parties, none has been able to win sufficient support or success to retain a consistent front of opposition to the main party. There has been some continuity to party organization in the other countries, but for the most part, parties have arisen and been especially important at the time of elections.

The major political process of recent years has been that referred to as "politicization," the recognition of the state as the ultimate authority and the recognition of legitimacy of certain governmental processes. Elections in all countries have become regular events, even though in all but Mexico and Panama they have been interrupted by *coups d'état* that have displaced the duly elected officials or put off elections that apparently were not going to be favorable to the army. Since university education in Middle America is still available for relatively few people, it is in the secondary schools that the real politicization takes place. In the schools there are usually strongly nationalistic opinions, and the students are generally willing to turn out, or be turned out, for demonstrations of a political nature. University students also become involved in these activities, and frequently the police and army are called upon to restrain demonstrators. The party organization in Mexico has done much to facilitate the political participation of a wide segment of the population, as have the political events of recent years in Guatemala, Costa Rica, and Panama. Nevertheless, a large portion of the populations, especially the rural sectors, still do not participate in the political process because structures are not developed to keep an electorate interested and governments tend to inhibit popular participation, being afraid of a popular swing to support of either a demagogue or a leftist.

The major ideologies that operate in most countries involve some combination of nationalism (sometimes openly coupled with anti-U.S. positions, sometimes merely subtly so), promotion of economic development, and promotion of democratic and constitutional procedures (governments recently taken over by the military always immediately profess plans to return to these procedures). In general, all governments recognize, at least on paper, the need for social development and the responsibility the state has in this development.

Incumbent governments and the military in the Central American countries have dealt with opposition either by stopping an election if the opposition looked too promising or by outlawing the opposition's participation in the constitutional procedures.

The Roman Catholic church has played an important role in politics. It was restricted by the revolutionary government of Mexico, and only in the most recent years has it gradually become again a political influence of some importance. The Barrios regime set the number of priests to be permitted in Guatemala. As a result, Guatemala has the lowest ratio of priests to Catholic population of any country in the Western hemisphere, and during the Arbenz period the church's hostility did not deter much of the population from supporting the government. The efforts of Protestant missionaries have increased in recent years, and although they have not been marked with overwhelming success, they have stimulated the Catholic church to improve the quality of its own clergy. The role of Catholicism has remained one of participation by the clergy in political action rather than involvement with political ideology.

The influence of foreign powers in Middle America has a long history, but in recent years the United States has been most in evidence. The United States has retained the control over the Panama Canal and has exercised strong influence over a number of the governments, especially those of Guatemala and Nicaragua. Concerned that the incumbent Arbenz government was being taken over by "communists" the United States provided funds, equipment, and administrative aid in the "liberation" of Guatemala by Castillo Armas in 1954.

The Central American republics have increasingly been integrated into a Central American common market, and steps are taken annually to promote this development. This does not include either Panama or Mexico. Such a development does not mean that there will be a serious move toward Central American political union, since the conditions for this eventuality are not politically attractive for the external relations of the small countries, nor would it necessarily resolve their internal political problems. Mexico is a member of the Latin American Free Trade Association and therefore is not involved in the Central American Common Market. The smaller union has been undertaken with the view of providing a more viable entity that might ultimately participate in the Free Trade Association.

Research on Middle America

In the nineteenth century, most research in what today would be regarded as social science was natural-history reporting. Much of it was of high quality, such as the work of Alexander von Humboldt, John L. Stephens, Ephraim George Squier, A. P. Maudsley, and others. Otto Stoll, Eduard Seler, Walter Lehmann, Franz Blom, and Franz Termer have maintained a long tradition of Germanic scholarly work. French interest has concentrated more in Mexico, stemming in part from France's political interests during the period of Maximilian. Spanish scholarship, as well as that of the Middle Americans themselves, has until recent years focused on the colonial period. U.S. interest, while scattered through the nineteenth century, was marked by the major studies of Hubert H. Bancroft on Mexico and America. It matured into specific disciplinary concentrations in economics and anthropology early in the present century. The *indigenismo* movement stimulated work in Mexico, principally under Manuel Gamio, José Vasconcelos, Moises Saenz, and others. In Latin America this movement had little effect beyond the boundaries of Mexico, with the exception of the Andes region and Brazil. Interests stemming from philosophical traditions marked sociological studies until the period of World War II, when more empirical research began. Political science, marked by national and international biases, may be said to have started about the same time.

Besides the national libraries and archives of the region, other important research collections for the area are those at the University of California at Berkeley; the University of Texas in Austin; the Middle American Research Institute of Tulane University in New Orleans; the Library of Congress; the Instituto Ibero–Americano of Berlin; and the libraries of Seville, Barcelona, and Madrid. There are still many important private collections.

Research needs in Middle America are of two major types: (1) those concerned with preserving records of now disappearing entities; and (2) those emerging from concern with problems attendant on contemporary society. Among the first are ethnographic studies of gradually (and in some instances rapidly) disappearing indigenous cultures, especially in Mexico and Guatemala, as well as studies of ways of life that are being crowded out by population expansion and urbanization. The second includes the entire range of issues in economics, sociology, and political science having to do with the continuing adjustment of societies to the rapidly changing modern world. Contemporary understanding of Middle America is still fettered by a Euro–American intellectual inheritance that often obscures elements in the empirical situation. The advancing technology of the social sciences is gradually being applied to Middle American studies. What is most lacking is the development of new concepts for use in studying an increasingly complex evolutionary picture.

RICHARD N. ADAMS

BIBLIOGRAPHY

ADAMS, RICHARD N. 1957 *Cultural Surveys of Panama–Nicaragua–Guatemala–El Salvador–Honduras.* Pan American Sanitary Bureau, Scientific Publication No. 33. Washington: The Bureau.

AGUIRRE BELTRÁN, GONZALO 1946 *La población negra de México, 1519–1810: Estudio etnohistórico.* Mexico City: Ediciones Fuente Cultural.

ARRIOLA, JORGE LUIS (editor) 1956 *Integración social en Guatemala.* Guatemala City: Seminario de Integración Social Guatemalteca.

CLINE, HOWARD F. 1962 *Mexico: Revolution to Evolution, 1940–1960.* New York: Oxford Univ. Press.

COSÍO VILLEGAS, DANIEL 1955–1965 *Historia moderna de México.* Vols. 1–8. Mexico City: Editorial Hermes.

Handbook of Middle American Indians. Edited by Robert Wauchope. Vol. 1—. 1964—. Austin: Univ. of Texas Press. → Four volumes have been published to date.

KIRCHHOFF, PAUL (1943) 1952 Mesoamerica: Its Geographic Limits, Ethnic Composition and Cultural Characteristics. Pages 17–30 in Sol Tax et al., *Heritage of Conquest: The Ethnology of Middle America.* Glencoe, Ill.: Free Press. → First published in German in Volume 1 of *Acta americana.*

LEWIS, OSCAR 1961 *The Children of Sánchez: Autobiography of a Mexican Family.* New York: Random House.

MÉXICO, CINCUENTA AÑOS DE REVOLUCIÓN 1963 *Cincuenta años de revolución.* 4 vols in 1. Mexico City: Fondo de Cultura Económica.

MIRÓ, CARMEN A. 1964 The Population of Latin America. *Demography* 1, no. 1:15–41.

PARKER, FRANKLIN D. 1964 *The Central American Republics.* New York: Oxford Univ. Press.

SCOTT, ROBERT E. (1959) 1964 *Mexican Government in Transition.* Rev. ed. Urbana: Univ. of Illinois Press.

SILVERT, K. H. 1954 *A Study in Government: Guatemala.* Tulane University, Middle American Research Institute, Publication No. 21. New Orleans, La.: The Institute.

Statistical Abstract of Latin America. → Published since 1960 by the Center of Latin American Studies of the University of California.

TAX, SOL et al. 1952 *Heritage of Conquest: The Ethnology of Middle America.* Glencoe, Ill.: Free Press.

UNITED NATIONS 1964 *The Economic Development of Latin America in the Post-war Period.* New York: United Nations.

WEST, ROBERT C.; and AUGELLI, JOHN P. 1966 *Middle America: Its Lands and Peoples.* Englewood Cliffs, N.J.: Prentice-Hall.

WHETTEN, NATHAN L. 1948 *Rural Mexico.* Univ. of Chicago Press.

WHETTEN, NATHAN L. 1961 *Guatemala: The Land and the People.* New Haven: Yale Univ. Press.

WOLF, ERIC R. 1959 *Sons of the Shaking Earth.* Univ. of Chicago Press.

MIDDLE EASTERN SOCIETY

See NEAR EASTERN SOCIETY.

MIGRATION

I
SOCIAL ASPECTS

In its most general sense "migration" is ordinarily defined as the relatively permanent movement of persons over a significant distance. But this definition, or any paraphrase of it, merely begins to delimit the subject, for the exact meaning of the most important terms ("permanent," "significant") is still to be specified. A person who goes to another country and remains there for the rest of his life, we say, is a migrant; and one who pays a two-hour visit to the nearest town is not. Between these two extremes lies a bewildering array of intermediate instances, which can only partly be distinguished by more or less arbitrary criteria (Lacroix 1949).

Permanence of movement. What should be the minimum duration of stay that differentiates a migration from a visit? With respect to international migration, the recommendation of the United Nations (and the practice of a number of countries) is to define removal for one year or more as "permanent," and thus as migration, while a stay for a shorter period is classified as a visit. Note that the data reflect not behavior but statements about future behavior; and persons have been known to lie to immigration officials or to change their minds.

This kind of ambiguity often makes it difficult to interpret migration statistics. For example, according to a critical analysis of United States immigration statistics (Kuznets & Rubin 1954, table 7), during the height of the mass immigration of 1890–1910 about forty per cent of the foreign-born returned. Conclusions from uncorrected immigration data, therefore, are likely to be grossly inaccurate. Remigrants—those who leave their country of origin for a period and then return to it—ordinarily differ from the emigrants who remain abroad, but not necessarily according to any consistent pattern. Particularly during an economic depression, some immigrants left the new country when they lost their jobs (Berthoff 1953, p. 73). Sometimes, on the contrary, it was the relatively successful that returned, either to find wives (Borrie 1954) or to retire. The rise of nationalism in the old country often attracted back some of the incompletely assimilated migrants (Saloutos 1956). A small percentage of the subsidized emigrants to Australia and Canada have returned to Britain, and the especially careful studies made of these groups are largely inconclusive (Appleyard 1962a; 1962b; Richmond 1966). Almost by definition, remigrants are less able to acculturate to their new environment than immigrants who remain there, but few valid generalizations can be added to that truism.

The ambiguity pertains also to the definition of internal migrants (Hamilton 1961; Taeuber 1961). Particularly in a federal country like the United States, "permanence" of movement is defined, in effect, by laws stipulating the meaning of domicile with respect to marriage and divorce, suffrage, and other prerogatives reserved to "bona fide residents." Surveys by the U.S. Bureau of the Census show that each year approximately one person in five moves to a new residence (compare Wilber 1963). However, according to a detailed analysis of one particular community (Goldstein 1954), a sizable proportion of this large percentage is made up of persons who move more than once during a year and who are atypical also in other ways. A study of repeated migration in Denmark suggests that the phenomenon is not restricted to any one country (Goldstein 1964).

More generally, when one speaks of migratory birds, or migrant laborers, or nomads, the connotation is not of a permanent move from one area to another, but rather of a permanently migratory way of life, which often means a cyclical movement within a more or less definite area. Nomads (the word derives from the Greek for *pasturing*) typically follow their herds back and forth over a region delimited either by natural boundaries or by neighbors sufficiently powerful to repel incursions. Similarly, agricultural laborers often move with the growing season, and shepherds (in what is termed transhumance) alternate between high mountain pastureland in the summer and lowlands in the winter. Commutation, the daily "journey to work" (Liepmann 1944), constitutes a similar cycle within a smaller compass. One must not accept the common notion that such a separation of place of residence from place of work is peculiar to modern industrial societies. Many of the burghers of ancient Athens, fourteenth-century London, and preindustrial cities generally were part-time agriculturists (Petersen 1961, pp. 348–353). In many presently underdeveloped countries, particularly India and Pakistan, a peasant who migrates to the city often leaves his family in the village, to which he therefore returns periodically. In Africa south of the Sahara the temporary separation of male industrial or mine workers from village life has been institutionalized into the standard pattern (Mitchell 1961). In sum, whether short-term removals should be included in migration depends on the purpose of the statistics being collected. Thus, no particular specification of the duration of stay suits all purposes, and each analyst has to adapt the available data to his needs as best he can.

"Significant" distances.   The meaning of migration also varies according to how a "significant" distance is defined. The word derives from the Latin *migrare*, to change one's residence, but by current definitions it means rather to change one's community. A person who moves from one home to another in the same neighborhood, and who therefore retains the same social framework, is not deemed a migrant.

If we regard a nation as a community, then by this criterion all international movements are included under the rubric "migration." Partly because of this rationale, partly because the two sets of statistics are separately collected, the distinction between international and internal migration sets the framework of most analyses. It is worth emphasizing, therefore, that in a general discussion of the phenomenon the distinction is more or less irrelevant. Not only do some types of migration fall outside of this dichotomy (prehistoric wanderings, for instance), but some of the most important and interesting characteristics of migrants apply whether or not they cross an international border (labor mobility, urbanization, migratory selection, acculturation, etc.). Moreover, there are often greater cultural differences within the boundaries of a nation than between nations.

In practice, geographical distance is generally taken as a rough measure of whether the migrant crosses into another community. Thus, the U.S. Bureau of the Census divides the mobile population between "movers," who have changed their residence within a single county, and "migrants," who have crossed a county line, and it subdivides the latter category according to whether they move within a single state, to an adjacent state, or to a nonadjacent state. This kind of classification passes over the fact that a farmer who moves to a town in the same county probably changes his way of life more than one who crosses the nation but remains a farmer. To take a more striking example, the tens of thousands of refugees who fled from East to West Berlin have traversed the most significant boundary line in Europe while remaining within the confines of a single city.

Models of migration

It is reasonable to suppose that the number of migrants within any area homogeneous with respect to all the other factors that affect the propensity to migrate will be inversely related to the distance covered. One can express this relation in an equation, as follows: $M = aX/D^b$, where M stands for the number of migrants, D for the distance over the shortest transportation route, and X for any other factor that is thought to be relevant; a and b are constants, usually set at unity. In one version of this equation, the so-called P_1P_2/D hypothesis, the populations of the end points of the movement are taken as the X factor (Zipf 1949). Another variation is the familiar proposition that the number of persons going a given distance is directly proportional to the number of employment opportunities at that distance and inversely proportional to the number of intervening opportunities (Stouffer 1940). When "opportunities" were defined operationally as the number of in-migrants, the hypothesis could be validated in a number of instances. According to a detailed comparison of the two, Stouffer's formulation is better than Zipf's, since, in effect, measuring opportunities corrects the total population figures for the amount of unemployment in the two areas (Anderson 1955). (For other models, see Lövgren 1956; Thomlinson 1961; Heide 1963; Tabah & Cataldi 1963.)

A proposition about migration between only two points is too simplistic a unit, however, to be a useful building block for more elaborate theories. These have in general started from other premises. An important example is the three-volume study *Population Redistribution and Economic Growth: United States, 1870–1950* (Kuznets 1957–1964), in which the available data concerning the regional distribution of the developing national economy and data concerning internal migration are combined into a unified analysis of the interaction between the two.

This kind of analysis is not limited to migration within a single country. A shorter work in the same broad perspective analyzes the post-1945 migration to Switzerland (Mayer 1966). According to several studies of the transatlantic movement, if conditions in the home country build up a propensity to emigrate, the volume, direction, and timing of the movement are set largely by the business cycle in the receiving country (e.g., D. S. Thomas 1941). A later work, however, challenged this interpretation and placed more emphasis on the unity of "the Atlantic economy" and the importance of "push" factors (B. Thomas 1954).

Noneconomic motives.   In most of the supposedly general models of migration, it is presumed that movement is generated mainly by economic forces. This may not always be a reasonable postulate. Whether the correlation between business cycles and migratory movements is positive or neg-ative, for example, sometimes depends only on how broadly the study is conceived. While the rise of Europe's urban–industrial civilization brought a great increase in population and thus a pressure to emigrate, it also resulted in a general rise in the level of aspiration. Young men who were better off than their fathers were nonetheless dissatisfied, and many sought to better themselves overseas. Thus, it may be true to say that for certain periods the dominant motivation of emigrants from partic-ular countries was economic, even though these countries had, by and large, far better conditions than those from which very few persons left. This paradox is not limited to economic factors: reli-gious oppression, or the infringement of political liberty, was often a motive for European emigra-tion, but before the rise of modern totalitarianism those who left came predominantly from precisely those countries least marked by such stigmata. An increasing propensity to emigrate spread east and south from northwest Europe, together with demo-cratic institutions and religious tolerance. The anomaly that those who emigrated "because" of persecution tended to come from countries where there was less of it than elsewhere can be analyzed only by separating personal motivation from social causation. According to a recent survey of British emigrants' motives, they tended to rationalize their general feeling of insecurity and inadequacy into more specific economic factors (Appleyard 1964).

At least in the United States, internal migration is also less motivated by economic factors than is usually assumed. At one time, the U.S. Bureau of the Census asked a sample of migrants who had moved during one year why they had moved ("Postwar Migration" . . . 1947; compare "Reasons for Moving . . ." 1966, which showed similar re-sponses). Only 22.6 per cent said it was to take a job or to look for work. Family migration consti-tuted 61.7 per cent (i.e., moving with the head of the family or to join him, moving because of a change in marital status); 6.4 per cent said it was because of housing problems. Health, climate, edu-cation, and miscellaneous motives accounted for the remaining respondents. This conclusion has been generally validated by the few other studies made of internal migrants' motivation (e.g., Rossi 1955).

Migratory selection

That migration is both related to economic trends and yet not, in any simple sense, caused by them, should not occasion any surprise. The same is true of many other complex social phenomena. It would be no contribution to substitute for purely economic causes a list of other "factors," ranging from the spirit of adventure to the development of transportation facilities; nor would it be a great improvement to divide such a list between circum-stances at home that repel and those abroad that attract, that is, between "push" and "pull" factors. Given a sedentary population and an inducement to leave home, typically some persons go and some stay behind. Push and pull factors, in short, do not exert their force equally. The self-selection by which migrants differentiate themselves from the seden-tary population is called migratory selection (or, by some authors, selective migration). An analysis of this process can afford a better understanding of why a migration takes place.

It is a valuable extension of the Stouffer–Zipf generalization, for example, to go beyond the count-ing of heads and differentiate among the types of migrants. It is not sufficient, even in an analysis restricted to economically motivated migrations, to posit job opportunities in general: potential mi-grants with specific skills go to places where there are openings specifically for them. Thus, among white migrants within the United States, those seeking higher-status positions generally have to move greater distances than those with lower levels of skill. And some job-seeking migrants are also strongly motivated by noneconomic factors: among American Negroes important reasons for moving have been to get out of the rural South (hence the high rate of urbanization), and prefer-ably to get out of the South altogether (hence the shift to the North and West). Negroes, therefore, move greater distances than would be expected from the level of skill in the jobs that they typically seek (Rose 1958; compare Stub 1962; Taeuber & Taeuber 1965).

It is possible to analyze migratory selection by a number of demographic and social character-istics in addition to occupation and race; and al-though the conclusions from different studies vary widely, some tentative generalizations are possible (D. S. Thomas 1938; Petersen 1961, pp. 592–603). In both internal and international movements adolescents and young adults predominate; for not only do the young adapt more easily, but since they are close to the beginning of their working life, they can more readily take advantage of new op-portunities. It is feasible, therefore, to analyze mi-gration by cohorts (Eldridge 1964).

One can argue a priori that either the less or the more intelligent will tend to migrate: since the more intelligent will have succeeded at home, the less intelligent will seek their fortunes elsewhere; on the other hand, the more intelligent will respond first to any stimulus to migrate, while the duller will remain behind. Various studies have seemed to validate one or the other of these propositions. It is possible to reconcile the contradiction by postulating that a selection by intelligence is in fact one by actual or potential occupational level (Hofstee 1952; compare Lee 1966). Thus, since urban occupations are generally more demanding, rural–urban movements typically select the more intelligent. This is not true, however, of agriculturists who move to manual jobs in the cities, such as Negroes in the United States (D. S. Thomas 1938, pp. 111–121), or in general of migrants who make no substantial change in vocational level.

Effects on populations. For the two areas concerned, migratory selection determines the significance of the movement almost as much as the number of migrants. Consider the ramifications of what can be taken as the most fundamental question in migration theory: If X persons leave country A and migrate to country B, what changes take place in the size of the two populations (Petersen 1955, chapter 9)? The common-sense answer, that country A is decreased and country B is increased by X, is true only in the short run. If the typically young migrants have their children in their new country, its fertility rate may go up, while that of their native country goes down. Since the remaining population of country A will then be older on the average, its death rate may go up, while that of country B goes down. In short, after a generation the transfer of X persons will in fact amount to X plus a certain proportion based on the migration's effects on the population structures, and rates of population growth, of the two countries.

At a third level of analysis, however, this increment, and indeed X itself, may be canceled out. For Malthus, thus, emigration was a slight palliative, a partial and temporary expedient, with no permanent effect on population size (Malthus 1798, book 3, chapter 7). This is likely to be true of any country where the mortality of infants and children is high (so that emigration would reduce the mortality slightly), or where marriages and conceptions are put off because of economic pressure (so that a lesser pressure, the consequence of emigration, would result in a higher fertility). If one includes such indirect effects, the change in the population of the immigration country is also difficult to estimate. Immigration to the United States, for example, accelerated urbanization and

industrialization; and these changes, in turn, increased the upward social mobility of the native population and thus tended to accelerate the secular decline of the birth rate.

In sum, even the simplest question—How many persons migrated?—cannot be fully answered merely by counting heads. Unlike mortality and fertility, migration has no biological dimension: it cannot be analyzed, even in preliminary terms, independently of its cultural context. Accordingly, there are no "laws" of migration in the sense of universal generalizations; the highest level of abstraction possible is the contrast of various types of migrants (Heberle 1955).

Migration typologies

In a study of migrants to Aberdeen—that is, of movement within the single country of Scotland over only a few years—it was found useful to classify respondents into a number of types. These included professionals seeking careers, young persons seeking education, workers taking specific jobs, casual workers looking for employment, former commuters moving for greater convenience, family migrants joining heads of families, and return migrants (Illsley et al. 1963, pp. 238–240). The conclusions to be drawn differed for these various classes.

If this is so for movements within a relatively homogeneous area, then it is manifestly the case for migration in its most general terms, encompassing the whole world and all of human history. In constructing a general typology, one should begin by choosing the criteria by which the types are to be distinguished (Petersen 1964, pp. 271–290). Perhaps the most fundamental is the distinction between *innovating* migrants, who move in order to achieve the new, and *conservative* migrants, who move in response to a change in their circumstances, hoping by migrating to retain their way of life in another locus. Within each of these two broad classes, one can distinguish types of migration according to the force impelling the movement. An ecological push results in what might be termed a *primitive* migration—not a wandering of primitive tribes as such, but one dependent on a people's inability to cope with natural forces. When the activating agent is the state or some equivalent institution, the movement is *forced* or *impelled* migration, depending on whether the prospective migrants retain some power to decide whether to leave or not. A movement of adventurous pioneers, deviant religious or political groups, or similar individually motivated persons can aptly be termed *free* migration. Its importance is not in its size, which is never large, but in the example it sets for others. If the ensuing flow develops into a broad stream, an established pattern for whole social classes, an example of collective behavior, we speak of *mass* migration, similar to what has been termed "chain migration" (MacDonald & MacDonald 1964). Then individual motivations become correspondingly less important—indeed, the individuals involved may not be able to give a rational account of their decision to migrate. The motives they ascribe are likely to be trivial or, more probably, the generalities that they think are expected (Hansen 1940*a*, pp. 77–78).

Uses of typological method. The value of such a typology is in its utility: Does it help in solving analytical problems? The typology suggests, first of all, that migratory selection ranges along a continuum, from total migration at one extreme (food gatherers or nomads) to total nonmigration at the other. Intermediate instances, moreover, cannot be arranged along a single dimension. Sometimes it is the age or the sex or the occupation of the potential migrant that is relevant, but if an ethnic or social minority leaves to escape persecution or is shipped off to concentration camps, then the only pertinent characteristic is how the state defines "Jew" or "kulak," for example.

For more than a century various governments, concerned about the depopulation (real or supposed) of villages, have sought measures to counteract it. It would increase understanding of the process merely to ask whether this is a conservative or an innovating migration: Do these agriculturists want better conditions within their present way of life, or do they move to cities for the sake of urban amenities? Perhaps the most useful distinction in the typology is that between mass migration and all other types, for it emphasizes the fact that the nineteenth-century exodus from Europe does not constitute the whole of the phenomenon. When this type of migration declined after World War I, largely because of new political limitations imposed by both emigration and immigration countries, this was very often interpreted as marking the end of significant human migration altogether (e.g., Forsyth 1942). It was rather, in large part, a change to neomercantilist migration, in which the welfare of the national state becomes the main criterion for judging whether the movement is desirable and in which state agencies foster or impede, force or prevent, the migration. The "natural" right of the passportless person to move about has been supplanted by the "natural" right of the state to control that movement (Petersen 1955, chapter 1).

In the present age of total wars and totalitarian regimes, political motivations have set not only "Europe on the move" (Kulischer 1948) but also, partly as reverberations of European influences, much of the rest of the world. To take a notable example, the partition of British India into the nations of India and Pakistan was accompanied by one of the largest migrations in human history, in part induced by terrorists on both sides, in part arranged under state auspices. Many analysts prefer to omit this type of movement from their purview. In a United Nations publication, for example, international migration is defined as "the noncoerced migrations, which constitute the great majority of all migratory movements in normal times, and which are closely related to economic and social factors. . . . Specifically, 'migration' excludes population transfers, . . . deportations, refugee movements, and the movements of 'displaced persons'" (United Nations 1953, p. 98). That an international body which includes some of the states most responsible for forced migrations should exclude them from its demographic analyses is understandable; but there is no reason why independent scholars should accept this arbitrary and misleading definition.

The number of refugees in the world today depends of course on how that term is defined. Data on "refugees" are compiled mainly by the various agencies set up to aid them, and the resultant totals considerably understate the number of persons who have migrated because of political stress and sought refuge elsewhere. The major world-wide agency, the office of the U.N. High Commissioner for Refugees, has a narrowly restricted prime mandate: to assist persons who do not want to return to their country because of actual or feared racial, religious, or political persecution; and it may also extend its "good offices" to certain other limited categories. This definition does not include several numerically important classes of uprooted peoples: (1) those who have fled from local political disturbances but remain within the boundaries of the same state; (2) those who are forcibly moved about within the boundaries of a single state (see, for example, Conquest 1960); (3) those who have been forced to "return" to what is now defined as "their" country, after having lived "abroad" sometimes for generations. Thousands of refugees remain as hard-core cases from World War I, the Spanish Civil War, and World War II. It has been estimated, probably conservatively, that about forty million persons became refugees in the dozen years following 1945 (Rees 1957); the implication of the figure can be better grasped when it is recalled that the usual estimate for the total migration from all of Europe from 1800 to 1950 is only one and a half times as large, that is, sixty million.

WILLIAM PETERSEN

[See also POPULATION; REFUGEES; and the biographies of KULISCHER; WILLCOX.]

BIBLIOGRAPHY

ANDERSON, THEODORE R. 1955 Intermetropolitan Migration: A Comparison of the Hypotheses of Zipf and Stouffer. American Sociological Review 20:287–291.

APPLEYARD, R. T. 1962a The Return Movement of United Kingdom Migrants From Australia. Population Studies 15:214–225.

APPLEYARD, R. T. 1962b Determinants of Return Migration: A Socio-economic Study of United Kingdom Migrants Who Returned From Australia. Economic Record 38:352–368.

APPLEYARD, R. T. 1964 British Emigration to Australia. London: Weidenfeld & Nicolson.

BERTHOFF, ROWLAND T. 1953 British Immigrants in Industrial America: 1790–1950. Cambridge, Mass.: Harvard Univ. Press.

BORRIE, WILFRID D. 1954 Italians and Germans in Australia: A Study of Assimilation. Melbourne: Cheshire.

CANADA, DEPARTMENT OF CITIZENSHIP AND IMMIGRATION 1961 Citizenship, Immigration, and Ethnic Groups in Canada: A Bibliography of Research, 1920–1958. Ottawa: Queen's Printer.

CONQUEST, ROBERT 1960 The Soviet Deportation of Nationalities. New York: St. Martins.

ELDRIDGE, HOPE T. 1964 A Cohort Approach to the Analysis of Migration Differentials. Demography 1: 212–219.

FORSYTH, WILLIAM D. 1942 The Myth of Open Spaces: Australian, British and World Trends of Population and Migration. Melbourne Univ. Press.

GOLDSTEIN, SIDNEY 1954 Repeated Migration as a Factor in High Mobility Rates. American Sociological Review 19:536–541.

GOLDSTEIN, SIDNEY 1961 The Norristown Study: An Experiment in Interdisciplinary Research Training. Philadelphia: Univ. of Pennsylvania Press.

GOLDSTEIN, SIDNEY 1964 The Extent of Repeated Migration: An Analysis Based on the Danish Population Register. Journal of the American Statistical Association 59:1121–1132.

HAMILTON, C. HORACE 1961 Some Problems of Method in Internal Migration Research. Population Index 27: 297–307.

HANSEN, MARCUS L. 1940a The Immigrant in American History. Cambridge, Mass.: Harvard Univ. Press. → A paperback edition was published in 1964 by Harper.

HANSEN, MARCUS L. 1940b The Atlantic Migration: 1607–1860. Cambridge, Mass.: Harvard Univ. Press. → A paperback edition was published in 1961 by Harper.

HASKETT, RICHARD C. 1956 An Introductory Bibliography for the History of American Immigration: 1607–1955. Pages 85–295 in Stanley J. Tracy (editor), A Report on World Population Migrations. Washington: George Washington Univ.

HEBERLE, RUDOLF 1955 Theorie der Wanderungen. Schmollers Jahrbuch für Gesetzgebung, Verwaltung und Volkswirtschaft im Deutschen Reiche 75:1–23.

HEIDE, H. TER 1963 Migration Models and Their Significance for Population Forecasts. Milbank Memorial Fund Quarterly 41:56–76.

HOFSTEE, E. W. 1952 Some Remarks on Selective Migration. Research Group for European Migration Problems, Publications, No. 7. The Hague: Nijhoff.

HUTCHINSON, EDWARD P. 1956 Immigrants and Their Children: 1850–1950. New York: Wiley.

ILLSLEY, RAYMOND; FINLAYSON, ANGELA; and THOMPSON, BARBARA 1963 The Motivation and Characteristics of Internal Migrants: A Socio-medical Study of Young Migrants in Scotland. Milbank Memorial Fund Quarterly 41:115–143, 217–248.

INTERNATIONAL ECONOMIC ASSOCIATION 1958 Economics of International Migration. Edited by Brinley Thomas. New York: St. Martins; London: Macmillan.

INTERNATIONAL LABOR OFFICE 1928–1929 Migration Laws and Treaties. Vol. 1–3. Studies and Reports, Series O, No. 3. Geneva: The Office.

INTERNATIONAL LABOR OFFICE 1959 International Migration: 1945–1957. Studies and Reports, New Series, No. 54. Geneva: The Office.

KIRK, DUDLEY 1946 Europe's Population in the Interwar Years. Geneva: League of Nations.

KULISCHER, EUGENE M. 1948 Europe on the Move: War and Population Changes, 1917–1947. New York: Columbia Univ. Press.

KUZNETS, SIMON (editor) 1957–1964 Population Redistribution and Economic Growth: United States, 1870–1950. Memoirs, Nos. 45, 51, 61. Philadelphia: American Philosophical Society.

KUZNETS, SIMON; and RUBIN, ERNEST 1954 Immigration and the Foreign Born. National Bureau of Economic Research, Occasional Paper No. 46. New York: The Bureau.

LACROIX, MAX 1949 Problems of Collection and Comparison of Migration Statistics. Pages 71–105 in Milbank Memorial Fund, Problems in the Collection and Comparability of International Statistics. New York: The Fund.

LAVELL, C. B.; and SCHMIDT, WILSON E. 1956 An Annotated Bibliography on the Demographic, Economic and Sociological Aspects of Immigration. Pages 296–449 in Stanley J. Tracy (editor), A Report on World Population Migrations. Washington: George Washington Univ.

LEE, EVERETT S. 1966 A Theory of Migration. Demography 3:47–57.

LEE, EVERETT S.; and LEE, ANNE S. 1960 Internal Migration Statistics for the United States. Journal of the American Statistical Association 55:664–697.

LIEPMANN, KATE K. (1944) 1945 The Journey to Work: Its Significance for Industrial and Community Life. London: Routledge.

LÖVGREN, ESSE 1956 The Geographical Mobility of Labour: A Study of Migrations. Geografiska annaler 38:344–394.

MACDONALD, JOHN S.; and MACDONALD, LEATRICE D. 1964 Chain Migration, Ethnic Neighborhood Formation, and Social Networks. Milbank Memorial Fund Quarterly 42:82–97.

MALTHUS, THOMAS R. (1798) 1958 An Essay on Population. 2 vols. New York: Dutton. → First published as An Essay on the Principle of Population. A paperback edition was published in 1963 by Irwin.

MAYER, KURT B. 1966 The Impact of Postwar Immigration on the Demographic and Social Structure of Switzerland. Demography 3:68–89.

MILBANK MEMORIAL FUND 1947 *Postwar Problems of Migration.* New York: The Fund.

MILBANK MEMORIAL FUND 1958 *Selected Studies of Migration Since World War II.* New York: The Fund.

MITCHELL, J. CLYDE 1961 Wage Labour and African Population Movements in Central Africa. Pages 193–248 in K. M. Barbour and R. M. Prothero (editors), *Essays on African Population.* London: Routledge.

NATIONAL BUREAU OF ECONOMIC RESEARCH 1929–1931 *International Migrations.* Edited by Walter F. Willcox. 2 vols. New York: The Bureau. → Volume 1: *Statistics,* compiled on behalf of the International Labour Office, Geneva, with introduction and notes by Imre Ferenczi. Volume 2: *Interpretations,* by a group of scholars in different countries.

PETERSEN, WILLIAM 1955 *Planned Migration: The Social Determinants of the Dutch–Canadian Movement.* Berkeley: Univ. of California Press.

PETERSEN, WILLIAM 1961 *Population.* New York: Macmillan.

PETERSEN, WILLIAM 1964 *The Politics of Population.* Garden City, N.Y.: Doubleday.

Postwar Migration and Its Causes in the United States: August, 1945, to October, 1946. 1947 U.S. Bureau of the Census, *Current Population Reports* Series P-20, No. 4.

Reasons for Moving: March 1962 to March 1963. 1966 U.S. Bureau of the Census, *Current Population Reports.* Series P-20, No. 154.

REES, ELFAN 1957 Century of the Homeless Man. *International Conciliation* 515:193–254.

RICHMOND, A. H. 1966 Demographic and Family Characteristics of British Immigrants Returning From Canada. *International Migration* 4:21–26.

ROSE, ARNOLD M. 1958 Distance of Migration and Socioeconomic Status of Migrants. *American Sociological Review* 23:420–423.

ROSENFIELD, HARRY N. 1957 Historical Research as a Tool for Immigration Policy. American Jewish Historical Society, *Publications* 46:341–365.

ROSSI, PETER H. 1955 *Why Families Move: A Study in the Social Psychology of Urban Residential Mobility.* Glencoe, Ill.: Free Press.

SALOUTOS, THEODORE 1956 *They Remember America: The Story of the Repatriated Greek-Americans.* Berkeley: Univ. of California Press.

SHIMM, MELVIN G. (editor) 1956 Immigration. *Law and Contemporary Problems* 21, no. 2.

SHYOCK, HENRY S. 1964 *Population Mobility Within the United States.* Univ. of Chicago, Community and Family Study Center.

STOUFFER, SAMUEL A. 1940 Intervening Opportunities: A Theory Relating Mobility and Distance. *American Sociological Review* 5:845–867.

STUB, HOLGER R. 1962 The Occupational Characteristics of Migrants to Duluth: A Retest of Rose's Hypothesis. *American Sociological Review* 27:87–90.

TABAH, LÉON; and CATALDI, ALBERTO 1963 Effets d'une immigration dans quelques populations modèles. *Population* 18:683–696.

TAEUBER, KARL E. 1961 Duration-of-residence Analysis of Internal Migration in the United States. *Milbank Memorial Fund Quarterly* 39:116–131.

TAEUBER, KARL E.; and TAEUBER ALMA F. 1965 The Changing Character of Negro Migration. *American Journal of Sociology* 70:429–441.

THOMAS, BRINLEY 1954 *Migration and Economic Growth: A Study of Great Britain and the Atlantic Economy.* Cambridge Univ. Press.

THOMAS, BRINLEY 1961 *International Migration and Economic Development: A Trend Report and Bibliography.* Paris: UNESCO.

THOMAS, DOROTHY S. 1938 *Research Memorandum on Migration Differentials.* New York: Social Science Research Council.

THOMAS, DOROTHY S. 1941 *Social and Economic Aspects of Swedish Population Movements: 1750–1933.* New York: Macmillan.

THOMLINSON, RALPH 1961 A Model for Migration Analysis. *Journal of the American Statistical Association* 56:675–686.

TRACY, STANLEY J. (editor) 1956 *A Report on World Population Migrations.* Washington: George Washington Univ.

UNITED NATIONS, DEPARTMENT OF ECONOMIC AND SOCIAL AFFAIRS 1955 *Analytical Bibliography of International Migration Statistics, Selected Countries: 1925–1950.* U.N. Bureau of Social Affairs, Population Studies, No. 24. New York: United Nations.

UNITED NATIONS, DEPARTMENT OF SOCIAL AFFAIRS 1949 *Problems of Migration Statistics.* Population Studies, No. 5. New York: United Nations.

UNITED NATIONS, DEPARTMENT OF SOCIAL AFFAIRS 1953 *The Determinants and Consequences of Population Trends: A Summary of the Findings of Studies on the Relationships Between Population Changes and Economic and Social Conditions.* Population Studies, No. 17. New York: United Nations.

U.S. CONGRESS, HOUSE, COMMITTEE ON THE JUDICIARY 1950 *The Displaced Persons Analytical Bibliography.* House Report No. 1687. Washington: Government Printing Office.

WILBER, GEORGE L. 1963 Migration Expectancy in the United States. *Journal of the American Statistical Association* 58:444–453.

WILBER, GEORGE L.; and ROGERS, TOMMY W. 1965 Internal Migration in the United States, 1958 to 1964: A List of References. Sociology and Rural Life Series, No. 15. Unpublished manuscript, Mississippi State Univ., Agricultural Experiment Station.

ZIPF, GEORGE K. 1949 *Human Behavior and the Principle of Least Effort: An Introduction to Human Ecology.* Reading, Mass.: Addison-Wesley. → See especially "The Factor of Distance," pages 386–409.

ZUBRZYCKI, JERZY 1960 *Immigrants in Australia: A Demographic Survey Based Upon the 1954 Census.* 2 vols. Melbourne Univ. Press. → Volume 2 is a statistical supplement.

II

ECONOMIC ASPECTS

This article is mainly concerned with international migration, which may be defined, in the strict sense, as a permanent movement of people, of their own free will, from one sovereign country to another. Transfers of this kind, however, account for only a small part of the redistribution of world population in the last three centuries. A comprehensive view of international migration must therefore include forced as well as free movements, and temporary as well as permanent movements. It is also necessary to distinguish between intercontinental and intracontinental transfers.

Free and forced movements

Up to the beginning of the nineteenth century there were hardly any statistical records of international migration. Nevertheless, it is possible to indicate the main orders of magnitude. The first great Atlantic migration was the traffic in African slaves. It is estimated that over ten million slaves were transported to America between 1619 and 1776 and that 3.4 million of them went to the English colonies in America. The trade was initiated by the Portuguese and the Dutch. Britain also took part, beginning in the 1660s, mainly through the Royal African Company, which existed from 1672 to 1752. The plantation economies producing sugar in the West Indies, tobacco in Virginia, and rice and indigo in South Carolina entailed a growing demand for slave labor from Africa. In the West Indies white immigration was replaced by black on one island after another, until slaves constituted about four-fifths of the population.

In contrast, the white migration across the Atlantic in the seventeenth and eighteenth centuries was comparatively small. In the seventeenth century about 250,000 left the British Isles for the New World, and in the eighteenth century the outflow was perhaps 1,500,000, of whom about half a million were Ulster Presbyterians. An indication of the volume of Spanish emigration to the New World is given by the fact that 150,000 were recorded as having embarked at the port of Seville between 1509 and 1740, but this is a serious underestimate. The only other prominent group of trans-Atlantic migrants up to 1800 was the 200,000 Germans estimated to have left for America.

The nineteenth century was the great age of mass migration from Europe across the Atlantic of people who went of their own free will, and most of what we know about the economic and social determinants and consequences of international migration is based on the experience of that remarkable period. Between 1846 and 1932 about 52 million people left Europe for oversea destinations. When this redistribution was over, one-eleventh of the population of the world were people of European origin living outside Europe.

One of the most somber features of our time is that while there has been a sharp decline in free international mobility, the relative scale of forced transfers is reminiscent of the eighteenth century. The world picture has been dominated by movements of refugees, as shown by the following rough estimates. The partition of India and Pakistan led to the expulsion of more than 18 million people from their homes. Other outstanding examples of inflows of refugees after World War II are West Germany, 12 million; Japan, 6.3 million; South Korea, 4 million; Hong Kong, 1.3 million; Israel, 1 million; Arab refugees from Palestine, 1 million. About 1.5 million refugees were settled overseas by the International Refugee Organisation and the Intergovernmental Committee for European Migration [see REFUGEES, article on WORLD PROBLEMS]. This is only a partial account, for it is impossible to give estimates of the considerable forced movements which have taken place between countries controlled by the Soviet Union and China. Even this partial estimate of the international transfer of "political" migrants gives a total of 45 million for the ten years beginning in 1945. It is a sobering thought that the number of people expelled from one country to another in *the decade* after World War II was equal to the entire oversea emigration from Europe in *the century* ending in 1913.

Temporary and permanent movements

Of the large number of passengers who enter or leave any country in a given period, only a proportion are genuine migrants. Persons to be counted as migrants are those who move from one country to a *permanent* residence in another, and, in accordance with United Nations standards, the criterion generally adopted is a declared intention to stay in the receiving country for more than one year. Owing to the wide variety of methods used in different countries, it is not easy to obtain accurate statistics. It must be recognized, however, that much of the international mobility of labor which is of economic significance is of a temporary nature. This is particularly true on the European continent, where daily or weekly or seasonal movements over national frontiers occur on a considerable scale. For example, permanent immigration into Switzerland rose steadily from 1946 to 1957 and amounted to 690,000 workers for the period as a whole; during the same period there were 942,000 seasonal workers and 275,000 frontier workers. The *net* immigration for the period was, however, only 250,000; this demonstrates that a number of the aliens admitted as "permanent" immigrants (a great many being women) are in fact in the temporary category. On the American continent a similar case may be seen in the seasonal traffic across the border between Mexico and the United States.

Intercontinental and intracontinental movements

The distinction between intercontinental and intracontinental movements is illuminating when we are dealing with the phases in the migration of Europeans. With the exception of the movement of Russians into Asia, the story of the outpouring of Europe's population is largely one of oversea settlement, and it is noteworthy that the migrations which have had the deepest and most enduring effects have been those which were transoceanic and intercontinental. When migrants cross an ocean, there are strict limits to what they can take with them; their traditions, ideals, techniques, and material belongings, when applied in a distant and strange environment, yield a pattern of life quite different from the one they left behind. There is something irrevocable about crossing an ocean. The political, economic, and racial configuration of the United States today is very much the outcome of three transoceanic migrations—the Pilgrim Fathers and their successors, the slaves from Africa, and the European masses in the nineteenth century.

When we consider shifts of population in Asia, we find that intercontinental movements are not significant, for a journey by sea has often meant merely a transfer from one part of the same continent to another. The abolition of slavery in the British colonies in the 1830s saw the beginning of an outflow from the Far East to the countries of America, Oceania, and Africa; and throughout the nineteenth century the recruitment of indentured laborers from India, China, and Japan was a characteristic feature. This species of intercontinental migration came to an end in the 1920s, and its place was taken by interregional movements which have had important demographic and social effects. The chief suppliers of intracontinental migrants have been China, India, Pakistan, Japan, and Korea; the main recipients have been Malaya, Ceylon, Burma, Indonesia, Thailand, Vietnam, Laos, Cambodia, British Borneo, the Philippines, and Manchuria. In most of these countries the immigrants have been mainly Chinese and Indians. In the Far East internal migration has been more important than transfers across national boundaries. For example, in Japan in the period 1920–1940 the net exodus from rural areas to urban areas amounted to 17.5 million persons. This was more than the entire increase in the population of Japan in this period, and it was ten times greater than the net emigration from the country.

The measurement of migration

Countries did not begin to keep records of genuine international migration until the big modern movements had passed their peak. For most of the nineteenth century the available statistics were by-products of acts or regulations introduced to achieve some other purpose. For example, in the United States and the United Kingdom, records of passenger movements were the results of acts passed to regulate shipping. In Britain, statistics began to be furnished under an act in 1803. But it was not until over a century later, in 1912, that the British Board of Trade decided to adopt a sta-

Table 1 — Intercontinental migration, selected countries and periods (in thousands)

EMIGRATION			IMMIGRATION		
Country of emigration	Period covered	Number of emigrants	Country of immigration	Period covered	Number of immigrants
Austria and Hungary	1846–1932	5,196	Argentina	1856–1932	6,405
Belgium	1846–1932	193	Australia	1861–1932	2,913
British India	1846–1932	1,194	Brazil	1821–1932	4,431
British Isles	1846–1932	18,020	British West Indies	1836–1932	1,587
Denmark	1846–1932	387	Canada	1821–1932	5,206
Finland	1871–1932	371	Cuba	1901–1932	857
France	1846–1932	519	Hawaii	1911–1931	216
Germany	1846–1932	4,889	Mauritius	1836–1932	573
Holland	1846–1932	224	Mexico	1911–1931	226
Italy	1846–1932	10,092	New Zealand	1851–1932	594
Japan	1846–1932	518	South Africa	1881–1932	852
Norway	1846–1932	854	United States	1821–1932	34,244
Poland	1920–1932	642	Uruguay	1836–1932	713
Portugal	1846–1932	1,805			
Russia	1846–1924	2,253			
Spain	1846–1932	4,653			
Sweden	1846–1932	1,203			
Switzerland	1846–1932	332			

Source: Adapted from Carr-Saunders 1936, p. 49.

tistical classification which defined a migrant as a passenger who declares that he has lived for a year or more in one country and intends to remain for a year or more in another. Statistical tests have shown that, despite their obvious deficiencies, ". . . the Board of Trade statistics of aggregate net passenger movement are a surprisingly good measure of the course of total net emigration from the United Kingdom in the period ending in 1912" (Thomas 1954, p. 52). This would not hold good for recent times, because air travel has become important and Britain persists in not including air migrants in her statistics.

The primary data used by various countries to measure international migration can be grouped under six headings: those yielded by controls at ports, by transport contracts, by population registers, by control at land frontiers, by passports, and by coupons detached from certain documents. In North America, South America, Asia, and Africa the usual practice has been to base the records on controls at frontiers and ports; in Europe, however, countries have adopted one or another of the six systems. Each government has tended to organize its migration statistics in accordance with its own particular policy objectives, without any regard to the need for international comparability. The result has been a bewildering variety of definitions and classifications.

Valuable attempts have been made by the International Labor Office to point the way toward a common pattern (see, for example, International Labor Office 1932; 1952). In recent years the problem of improving migration statistics has been thoroughly explored by the United Nations. An inquiry in 1950 showed that only 16 out of 45 countries classified emigrants by country of future residence or destination and only 17 classified immigrants by country of last residence or origin, while only 16 distinguished between continental

Table 2 — World population, by continent, in 1946 and 1957, and balance of intercontinental migration in the intervening period (in millions)

Continent or major region	Population		Total population increase	Net migration
	1946	1957		
Africa	185.0	225.0	+40.0	+0.5
Americas	300.0	381.0	+81.0	+4.4
Asia	1,302.0	1,556.0	+254.0	−0.5
Europe	379.0	414.0	+35.0	−5.4
Oceania	11.8	15.4	+3.6	+1.0
U.S.S.R.	175.0	204.0	+29.0	*

* Not available.

Source: Adapted from International Labor Office 1959, p. 304.

Table 3 — Population growth and net migration for selected countries, 1946–1957 (in thousands)

ESTIMATED NET MIGRATION

Country	1946 population	Natural increase	Absolute number	Per cent of 1946 population	Per cent of natural increase
Canada	12,620	3,305	+1,000	+7.9	+30
United States	141,390	27,735	+2,200	+1.6	+8
Jamaica	1,300	348	−90	−6.9	−26
Mexico	23,180	8,689	−250	−1.1	−3
Argentina	15,650	3,358	+800	+5.1	+24
Brazil	47,310	16,000	+450	+1.0	+3
Uruguay	2,280	320	+110	+4.8	+34
Venezuela	4,390	1,812	+330	+7.5	+18
Australia	7,460	1,391	+930	+12.5	+67
New Zealand	1,660	351	+145	+8.7	+41

Source: Adapted from International Labor Office 1959, pp. 308, 312.

and intercontinental immigrants and 10 between continental and intercontinental emigrants. For the demographer it was disconcerting that only 16 countries gave information on the marital status of migrants, and in nine of these countries this information was not combined with age grouping. As a result of the work of the Economic and Social Council of the United Nations, most of the known statistics have been set out in two comprehensive monographs (United Nations, Bureau of Social Affairs 1953; 1958). These surveys cover 33 countries and include tables classifying migrants by occupation or industry, state of dependency, possession or nonpossession of a contract for employment, and, for the United States, Israel, and South Africa, the amount of money which immigrants bring in with them (for additional detailed information, see United Nations, Department of Economic and Social Affairs 1955).

Since progress in improving official sources on migration is inevitably a slow process, it is all the more necessary to check imperfect time series in the light of the more accurate population census data at decennial intervals. Thus, Kuznets and Rubin (1954) have compared the annual record of immigration into the United States over a long period with the estimates obtained from the census figures on resident foreign-born. Similarly, Keyfitz (1950) has drawn up a population balance sheet for Canada for the century 1851–1950, including the best possible estimates of immigration and emigration in each decade.

Some indications of the scale of intercontinental population movements from the middle of the nineteenth century to the middle of the twentieth can be found in tables 1–3.

Economic determinants of migration

The period 1840–1924 was in several respects unique in the history of migration. The evolution of the Atlantic economy in that era necessitated a considerable movement of population and capital from the Old World, which was relatively well endowed with these factors, to the New World, where they were relatively scarce. Over 45 million people crossed the ocean; the average rate of growth of population in each decade of the nineteenth century was 29 per cent in the United States, 34 per cent in Argentina, and 8 per cent in Europe. The world's chief provider of capital was Great Britain; of her foreign investments of over $17,000 million in 1913, nearly 70 per cent were located in North America, South America, and Oceania.

The motives which led these millions of people to leave their homelands were infinitely varied; a lengthy catalogue of them would be full of human interest but would not provide an interpretation of the phenomenon. At certain times and in certain places the operative force was political oppression or religious persecution or eviction by tyrannical landlords or the threat of starvation or evasion of military service or the love of adventure or the lure of gold or the attraction of a new country with limitless opportunities. But what has to be explained is why the individual decisions of millions of people resulted in four major upswings with intervening downswings, with an average interval of 15 to 20 years from peak to peak, in oversea emigration from Europe. The emigration upswings took place in 1845–1854, 1863–1873, 1881–1888, and 1903–1913. There can be no possible doubt about the explanation of the first of these: its inception had nothing to do with demand conditions in the United States. Calamity struck in Ireland in 1845, when the potato crop failed and a terrible famine followed; and as if this were not enough, the landlords added to the horrors by violently evicting thousands of peasants from their homes. In another part of Europe, southwest Germany, in the years 1848–1854 a severe crisis in the rural areas (in addition to the prevailing political unrest) brought population pressure to a head, and the only solution was emigration. In that period, of the 2,796,000 European immigrants who landed in the United States, no less than 80 per cent came from Ireland and Germany—1,283,000 from Ireland and 939,000 from Germany. This was essentially a Malthusian evacuation; both its timing and its magnitude were determined by exogenous driving forces in two stricken areas of Europe.

The explanation of the subsequent fluctuations in migration lies in a complicated process of interaction between the economies of the Old World and those of the countries of new settlement overseas. It is significant that when the receiving countries, notably the United States, Canada, and Australia, were absorbing immigrants on a large scale, they were also experiencing a long upswing in capital construction (such as railroads and housing), which is sensitive to population growth. When this cycle entered its downward phase, with both migration and capital imports dwindling, there was simultaneously an upsurge in capital construction in the United Kingdom, where the rural surplus was now absorbed in urban areas at home. This capital construction was financed by loanable funds which were no longer attracted abroad (Thomas 1954).

Thus, there was an inverse relation between long swings in population-sensitive capital formation in the United Kingdom and in the United States, and in the United Kingdom there was an inverse relation between external migration and internal migration. The mechanism of this inverse long swing between the United Kingdom and the United States can be seen most clearly in the period 1870–1913; it arose because a substantial part of total capital formation was sensitive to the rate of population growth and the rate of population growth was determined by the net migration balance. There are some grounds for thinking that the propensity to emigrate was in some way related to a cycle of births in Europe that caused a periodic recurrence of swollen numbers in the emigration age groups (Thomas 1954).

In the interwar period some of the basic trends of the pre-1913 era were reversed. The United States had become the world's leading exporter of capital, and the Immigration Restriction Act of 1924 virtually closed the doors to further immigration except on a very modest scale. From the turn of the century, British settlement in Canada, Australia, New Zealand, and South Africa had been expanding, and British emigration to the Empire considered as a proportion of British emigration to the United States, which had been only 43 per cent in 1881–1900, had risen to 245 per cent by 1911–1913. After World War I Britain embarked on a substantial program of Empire settlement, and in the decade 1922–1931, 400,000 emigrants received financial support to enable them to settle in the overseas dominions. However, this outflow did not survive the world depression, which had such severe consequences that it actually reversed the world currents of migration. In 1932, 11 European countries of emigration received a net inward balance of 102,000 persons, and Argentina, Australia, New Zealand, the United States, and Uruguay together had a net outflow of 65,000 (International Labor Office 1932). The international migration picture had become a perverse caricature of its former self.

Changes since World War II. The factors determining the volume, quantity, and direction of international migration since World War II are quite different from what they were in the nineteenth century. Profound structural changes have taken place in the Atlantic economy, and they have had far-reaching effects on the pattern of world migration. It is necessary to distinguish between the years immediately after the war and the period beginning in 1952. The correspondence between international flows of people and of private capital, which was the outstanding feature of the nineteenth century, disappeared. In its place there emerged in the years 1945–1952 an international circular flow based on the immense net transfer of $33,800 million of *public* capital (government loans and grants) from the United States, $22,800 million of which went to Europe. This recovery program made it possible for the exhausted countries of Europe, particularly the United Kingdom, France, the Netherlands, and Belgium, to resume exports of people and capital to the oversea territories with which they had a special relationship. It facilitated the revival of migration and mobility of capital within the British Commonwealth and strengthened the purchasing power of the less developed parts of the world. Perhaps the most significant effect of the recovery program was its contribution to basic capital formation in western Europe. This contribution was the prelude to the remarkable upsurge in economic growth in the 1950s [see FOREIGN AID].

After 1952 a new balance of economic forces emerged. American economic aid to Europe ended, but the volume of military aid rose considerably and the amount of private investment by American firms in Europe greatly increased, until in 1959 for the first time the flow of new American funds for direct investment was larger in western Europe than in either Canada or Latin America. Rapid economic growth in western Europe has meant a remarkable increase in intracontinental migration and a continued decline in emigration to oversea countries. Net immigration into the European Economic Community amounted to 288,000 in 1960 and 421,000 in 1961. The latter figure was particularly large because of the repatriation of French and Belgian nationals from Africa. Looking at the separate countries, we find that in 1961

West Germany had a net inflow of 421,000 and France 150,000, whereas Italy had a net outflow of 164,000. Over the five years 1956–1960 the net outward migration from Italy to other European countries was at an annual average of 83,000, and emigration from Italy to oversea countries fell from 111,000 in 1956 to 48,000 in 1960. Intracontinental migration is increasing at the expense of the traditional European outflow to countries such as those of Latin America, and this is basically determined by the economic resurgence of western Europe and the consequent change in the economic balance within the Atlantic economy.

New determinants are also operating on other continents. The complex problems of migration on the African continent have been explored in a comprehensive study by the International Labor Office (1958). The spread of industrial development draws Africans long distances from their rural homes, but they are often prevented from becoming members of a settled work force. They find themselves suspended with the maximum of insecurity between the village to which they are attached and the harsh conditions of the industrial labor market. This can have disastrous social consequences: the countryside is denuded of a large part of its labor, family life is broken up, the social structure disintegrates, and there is neither economic nor social security. The General Conference of the International Labor Office in 1955 adopted a recommendation on the protection of migrants in underdeveloped countries which is clearly relevant to Africa.

Most underdeveloped countries are detrimentally affected by current trends in the migration of qualified personnel. In the nineteenth century, skilled manpower tended to accompany capital flows from advanced to less developed countries: in the modern world the bulk of private investment is a circulatory process within the rich sector, and there is a suction of skilled labor from the poorer countries into the more advanced. Of the 9,245 immigrant engineers admitted to the United States in 1953–1956, 50 per cent came from Europe, 25 per cent from Canada, and 22 per cent from "other countries," which included a number in a low state of economic development. The same was true of natural scientists ([U.S.] National Science Foundation 1958). Unskilled labor is often complementary to skilled, and when there is a decline in the immigration of the latter into a developing country, as has occurred, e.g., in Latin America, the scope for the absorption of unskilled immigrants is automatically curtailed. Some of the international movements of relatively scarce human capital tend to widen the disparity between rates of economic growth in rich and poor countries. Such transfers could be on such a scale that some underdeveloped countries could never begin the process of growth. There seems to be a conflict here between the principle of freedom to migrate and the goal of reducing inequality. However, in assessing the economic effects of the migration of a factor of production, the relevant criterion is not marginal *private* productivity, but marginal *social* productivity. Judged by this criterion, some of the international migration of skill in the world today is perverse.

Impact on receiving countries

It used to be argued that immigration into the United States had not added to the American population because its effect had been counterbalanced by an induced decline in the fertility of native-born Americans (see, for instance, Walker 1891). This proposition has been disproved. Modern demographic analysis has demonstrated that the immigrations of the last century had hardly any net effect on the rate of natural increase of the native-born population in the receiving countries. It is estimated that in France between 1801 and 1936 net immigration was 3,960,000 and contributed only a third of the growth of population within the 1936 boundaries of the country during that period. The white population of the United States in 1790 was about 3.2 million; their descendants living in the United States in 1920 have been estimated at 41 million, and in the same year the number of descendants or survivors of immigrants since 1790 came to about 53 million. In that period net immigration into the United States was about 26.5 million (United Nations, Department of Social Affairs 1953, p. 139).

One of the most striking examples of mass immigration in recent times is that into West Germany, which absorbed 12 million immigrants in 12 years after the war. Although this influx increased the population of West Germany by one-third, it failed to make up for the gaps in the demographic structure caused by war losses, since the immigrant population had suffered the same kinds of losses in the same age groups (International Labor Office 1959, pp. 27–28).

In recent years there has been a dramatic change of trend in the United Kingdom, a traditional country of emigration. Since 1958 there has been an appreciable net *inward* movement of migrants. This reversal of trend was caused by the substantial inflow of colored Commonwealth citizens, mainly from the West Indies, India, and Pakistan.

This led the government to introduce legislation to regulate Commonwealth immigration; the Commonwealth Immigrants Act came into force on July 1, 1962. Although the total number of colored people living in the United Kingdom is only about 1 per cent of the population, the newcomers have tended to cluster in certain places, and this has given rise to difficult social problems. This is part of a wider phenomenon—compare, for instance, the situation of the Puerto Ricans in the United States or the north Africans in France. Where poor, overpopulated countries have special relationships with advanced countries, it is natural that an overflow of population will take place so long as channels of mobility remain open.

Impact on sending countries

Mass emigration can in certain circumstances turn into a self-reinforcing process with profound long-run effects on the sending country. This arises from one of the most significant of migration differentials, the fact that the incidence of migration is particularly heavy in the age group 15–30. Given a substantial initial outflow, the sequel can be as follows. There is a decline in the marriage rate and consequently a fall in the size of the age group 0–5; but, since the rate of emigration among children is relatively low, the 0–5 age group becomes a *relatively* large group ten years later. It is a paradox that countries which are heavy losers through emigration seem to be liberally endowed with teen-agers. The process is self-perpetuating because, after a lag of about 15 years from the original thinning out of the 15–30 age group, the number entering the high emigration age group of 15–20 is relatively high in relation to the total population.

The influence of mass emigration on age composition in the sending country can be observed most strikingly in the case of Ireland, from which the total outflow from 1850 to 1911 was 4,191,000. By 1951, 30 per cent of the population were aged 45 and over, as compared with 16 per cent in 1841, and 11 per cent were 65 and over, as compared with 3 per cent in 1841. The experiences of Ireland, Sweden, and Scotland show that substantial emigration tends to reduce the marriage rate, but we cannot be certain about the long-run effects on fertility. There can be little doubt that prolonged emigration helps to explain why there are so many spinsters in Ireland; however, the women who do get married have relatively large numbers of children. As to the death rate, the tendency is for the loss of good lives from the 15–35 age group through emigration to raise the average death rate in that group.

Assimilation

It is broadly agreed that assimilation is best regarded as a mutual process of integration. An American sociologist has well said that ". . . the United States has not assimilated the newcomer nor absorbed him. Our immigrant stock and our so-called 'native' stock have each integrated with the other. . . . It will be apparent that this concept of integration rests upon a belief in the importance of cultural differentiation within a framework of social unity. It recognizes the right of groups and individuals to be different so long as the differences do not lead to domination or disunity" (Borrie 1959, pp. 93–94). One of the difficulties of group settlement, e.g., in Latin America, is that there arises a conflict between the immediate interests of the migrant in his group and the long-run objective of cultural integration. Much benefit can be derived from the provision of instruction to the migrant before he has left his own country. The Intergovernmental Committee for European Migration has evolved effective means of selecting, educating, and pretraining European migrants. [See REFUGEES, article on ADJUSTMENT AND ASSIMILATION.]

Experts who have studied migration in Asia stress the importance of assimilation as a necessary condition of the diffusion of skills. In colonial regimes there was a tendency for skilled immigrants to remain a class apart, and they often sought to maintain the relative scarcity of their skill. The great need in Asian countries now is for the importation of skilled personnel who will assimilate easily and thereby facilitate the rapid spread of technical knowledge.

International migration no longer plays the role in economic growth that it did in the nineteenth century. Legislative restrictions, the changes in the economic determinants, and the population upsurge in different parts of the world have all tended to reduce the scale of movement. Countries which have been receiving a relatively large influx of migrants since World War II, e.g., Australia, will soon find that the rate of entry into the working population from the swollen lower age groups will make immigration on the old scale unnecessary. The international circulation of skilled manpower has become relatively more important. Intercontinental migrations have lost most of their significance and have been replaced by intracontinental movements.

Much more interdisciplinary research is needed into the problems of adjustment of immigrants, particularly where they are ethnically different from the population of the host country; the interaction between external and internal migration; the relation between immigration and the incidence of mental health; the determinants of the rate of increase of immigrant groups in multiracial societies; and the economic and social consequences of the changing pattern of the international circulation of skilled manpower.

BRINLEY THOMAS

[*Directly related are the entries* CAPITAL, HUMAN; REFUGEES. *Other relevant material may be found in* ASSIMILATION; POPULATION, *article on* POPULATION DISTRIBUTION; *and in the biographies of* GINI *and* KULISCHER.]

BIBLIOGRAPHY

BORRIE, WILFRID D. et al. 1959 *The Cultural Integration of Immigrants: A Survey Based Upon the Papers and Proceedings of the UNESCO Conference Held in Havana, April 1956 . . . With Case Studies.* Paris: UNESCO.

CARR-SAUNDERS, ALEXANDER M. 1936 *World Population: Past Growth and Present Trends.* Oxford: Clarendon.

EISENSTADT, SHMUEL N. (1954) 1955 *The Absorption of Immigrants: Comparative Study Based Mainly on the Jewish Community in Palestine and the State of Israel.* Glencoe, Ill.: Free Press.

GINI, CORRADO 1946 Los efectos demográficos de las migraciones internacionales. *Revista internacional de sociología* (Madrid) 4:351–388.

INTERNATIONAL ECONOMIC ASSOCIATION 1958 *Economics of International Migration: Proceedings of a Conference.* Edited by Brinley Thomas. New York: St. Martins; London: Macmillan.

INTERNATIONAL LABOR OFFICE 1932 *Statistics of Migration: Definitions—Methods—Classifications.* Geneva: The Office.

INTERNATIONAL LABOR OFFICE 1952 *International Classification of Occupations for Migration and Employment Placement.* 2 vols. Geneva: The Office. → Volume 1: *Occupational Tables, Codes and Definitions.* Volume 2: *Tables of Occupational Comparability: Major Occupational Groups 1 Through 6.*

INTERNATIONAL LABOR OFFICE 1958 *African Labour Survey.* International Labour Organization Studies and Reports, New Series, No. 48. Geneva: The Office.

INTERNATIONAL LABOR OFFICE 1959 *International Migration: 1945–1957.* International Labour Organization, Studies and Reports, New Series, No. 54. Geneva: The Office.

KEYFITZ, NATHAN 1950 The Growth of Canadian Population. *Population Studies* 4:47–63.

KUZNETS, SIMON; and RUBIN, ERNEST 1954 *Immigration and the Foreign Born.* National Bureau of Economic Research, Occasional Paper No. 46. New York: The Bureau.

LASKER, B. 1945 *Asia on the Move: Population Pressure, Migration, and Resettlement in Eastern Asia Under the Influence of Want and War.* New York: Holt.

MILBANK MEMORIAL FUND 1958 *Selected Studies of Migration Since World War II.* New York: The Fund.

NATIONAL BUREAU OF ECONOMIC RESEARCH 1929–1931 *International Migrations.* Edited by Walter F. Willcox. 2 vols. New York: The Bureau. → Volume 1: *Statistics,* compiled on behalf of the International Labour Office, Geneva, with Introduction and notes by Imre Ferenczi. Volume 2: *Interpretations,* by a group of scholars in different countries.

TAFT, D.; and ROBBINS, R. 1955 *International Migrations.* New York: Ronald.

THOMAS, BRINLEY 1954 *Migration and Economic Growth: A Study of Great Britain and the Atlantic Economy.* National Institute of Economic and Social Research, Economic and Social Studies, No. 12. Cambridge Univ. Press.

THOMAS, BRINLEY 1961 *International Migration and Economic Development: A Trend Report and Bibliography.* Paris: UNESCO.

UNITED NATIONS, BUREAU OF SOCIAL AFFAIRS 1953 *Sex and Age of International Migrants: Statistics for 1918–1947.* Population Studies, No. 11. New York: United Nations.

UNITED NATIONS, BUREAU OF SOCIAL AFFAIRS 1958 *Economic Characteristics of International Migrants: Statistics for Selected Countries, 1918–1954.* Population Studies, No. 12. New York: United Nations.

UNITED NATIONS, DEPARTMENT OF ECONOMIC AND SOCIAL AFFAIRS 1951–1952 International Migration in the Far East During Recent Times. *Population Bulletin* 1:13–30; 2:27–58.

UNITED NATIONS, DEPARTMENT OF ECONOMIC AND SOCIAL AFFAIRS 1955 *Analytical Bibliography of International Migration Statistics, Selected Countries: 1925–1950.* Population Studies, No. 24. New York: United Nations.

UNITED NATIONS, DEPARTMENT OF SOCIAL AFFAIRS 1953 *The Determinants and Consequences of Population Trends: A Summary of the Findings of Studies on the Relationships Between Population Changes and Economic and Social Conditions.* Population Studies, No. 17. New York: United Nations.

U.S. IMMIGRATION COMMISSION, 1907–1910 1911 *Abstracts of Reports of the Immigration Commission: With Conclusions and Recommendations and Views of the Minority.* 61st Congress, 3d Session, Senate Document 747, Vol. 1. Washington: Government Printing Office.

[U.S.] NATIONAL SCIENCE FOUNDATION 1958 Immigration of Professional Workers to the United States, 1953–1956. *Scientific Manpower Bulletin* No. 8.

WALKER, FRANCIS A. 1891 Immigration and Degradation. *Forum* 11:634–644.

MILITARISM

Militarism is a doctrine or system that values war and accords primacy in state and society to the armed forces. It exalts a function—the application of violence—and an institutional structure—the military establishment. It implies both a *policy* orientation and a *power* relationship.

Although militarists have used violence to silence domestic critics, their ideology rationalizes its use primarily in foreign affairs. War is held to be a divine commandment or an experience that ennobles by developing courage, patriotism, honor, unity, and discipline. Militarists seek to universalize such values by precept, symbol, and ceremony.

A fully militarized society also confers a privileged position on warriors. In the extreme case, possible only in centralized polities, the armed forces unilaterally determine the nature of basic institutions, the choice of regimes, the rights and duties of citizens, and the share of national resources allocated to military functions. In a less extreme but more common case military leaders exercise great power as partners or agents of other social groups rather than as relatively autonomous forces.

Ideal-type militarism was approximated in Japan from 1931 to 1945 and in Germany during the later stages of World War I.

Advocates of militarism. Militarists cannot be identified with military or uniformed personnel. In modern European history officers were often restrained in foreign policy and circumspect in domestic politics. Indeed, Huntington (1957, pp. 69–71) contends that such attributes define the genuinely professional officer.

The identification of militarists with men in uniform also fails because civilian militarists have long cherished war and warriors. D'Annunzio, Barrès, Carlyle, Theodore Roosevelt, and Treitschke stand as examples.

Because the policy and institutional aspects of militarism can be separated, it is quite possible to emphasize one without the other. For example, though the Nazis regimented Germany to facilitate foreign conquests, they also destroyed the vaunted autonomy of the professional army. Conversely, though officer–aristocrats of the nineteenth century exalted the army, they were not always bellicose. Their "enemies" were often fellow citizens, liberals, or socialists, against whom they sometimes made common cause with foreign officer–aristocrats. Such inward-looking militarism has also existed in Latin America.

Specialization of function. In ordinary usage "militarism" has a derogatory meaning. Like legalism or clericalism it suggests excess: a lack of proportion in policy or, when exhibited by warriors, a disregard for appropriate professional bounds. Since such disregard appears central to the concept, it is not rewarding to apply the term to societies in which professional bounds are invisible, that is, where roles are so fused that a distinctive military calling does not exist. Institutional militarism assumes a minimum differentiation of military from political, economic, and religious roles. At the same time it assumes that the differentiation is incomplete or that it has been challenged and stands in danger. The negative nuance in the term also implies that disregard for the bounds carries a penalty. The penalty is technical incompetence. Historically, for example, some European militarists failed to note the obsolescence of cavalry because they were less concerned with professional questions of maneuver and firepower than with a social question: the class status symbolized by cavalry. Japanese militarists exceeded their jurisdiction as strategic planners and, insisting on making their own diplomatic determination, embarked on a conflict that ultimately proved disastrous to their own forces. In both cases militarists actually jeopardized security ends by their inability to select means appropriate to their defense.

This inability is a function of inordinate power and forsaken expertise. In a nonmilitarized society the warrior is an agent and a specialist. In a militarized society he is a principal and a generalist. He feels competent to deal with the whole sweep of public policy, foreign and domestic. But in the long run so unconfined a jurisdiction impairs his professional military expertise without developing in the warrior the skills necessary to match experienced civilians in political bargaining or economic management.

Antimilitarism of the middle class. The term "militarism" appears to have been used first by middle-class liberals in nineteenth-century Europe. Possibly they sensed that militarism was incompatible with the specialization of functions demanded in an industrial era. Clearly they realized that standing armies had become citadels of aristocratic privilege. The values of officer–aristocrats conflicted with those of the middle class. The officers prized hierarchy, feudal honor, absolutism, prodigality, and organic unity; the middle class spoke of equality, material gain, parliamentary rule, thrift, and individualism. Inevitably, military institutions were suspect to such liberals as Locke, Ferrero, Voltaire, Jefferson, and Kant. Later they became equally suspect to Leninists, whose doctrine defined war as a disease of capitalism in its final, imperialist phase.

Given the problems that concerned them, it was natural that European critics of militarism rarely speculated about the danger that military expertise might be *inadequately* represented in the foreign policy process. Nor, despite examples of revolutionary armies in the Americas and France, did they theorize about the causes or consequences of military liberalism. Overgeneralizing from selected as-

pects of Western history, they merely identified the armed forces with unbridled power, social reaction, and war. Wherever representative democracy advanced, therefore, military power was curbed. Today, in the industrialized West such power tends to be confined to defense policy, the field of greatest professional concern to warriors. This generalization also holds for the Soviet Union and other totalitarian states, except possibly during crises of succession.

New approaches to militarism

Recent social research on militarism has dealt less with Europe and Japan than with southeast Asia, the Near East, and Latin America. The change in focus has had a perceptible impact on the term itself. It is no longer identified so closely with bellicose foreign policy. In these vast regions social revolution replaces war as the significant form of violence. To be sure, it is still identified with the primacy of the military establishment. But analysis of ideological views has been succeeded by interest in the actual degree of social and political power held by armed forces in different states. Efforts have been made to distinguish these levels and to analyze the variables that determine them. More sophistication is also displayed about the economic and social policies of military regimes.

The spectrum of power positions. The political power of armed forces reaches its nadir in countries which dispense with them altogether; Iceland and Costa Rica are modern examples. Next come societies in which the military establishment is dominated by authoritarian regimes: traditional autocracies or dictatorships supported by parties of mass mobilization. In stable constitutional democracies the armed forces, like other segments of the bureaucracy, press their claims through prescribed channels and procedures but ultimately comply with decisions made by civilian superiors.

Militarism begins when the armed forces accompany their advice with a threat of sanctions if the advice is unheeded. Finer (1962) has summarized the high-handed techniques sometimes used: threats to resign, to withdraw support, to announce disagreements publicly, to demonstrate disdain for the regime, to refuse to execute its orders, or to rise up in arms. Whenever such blackmail succeeds, the armed forces in fact begin to rule covertly, either by exercising a veto or by substituting policies and personnel of their own choice for those of the *de jure* government. From this point it is a short step to more extreme measures which take special advantage of a disciplined following, a superior communications net, and heavy weapons.

These measures include the manipulation or delay of elections, the deployment of troops to intimidate opponents or to seize key points, and the arrest or assassination of politicians.

In military interventions the armed forces may act alone or in coalition with civilians. They may take the initiative or respond, more or less eagerly, to pleas from politicians. These are important distinctions. It is equally important to distinguish sporadic from chronic intervention and brief from prolonged military rule. Military juntas frequently assume power with the statement that they will serve only as "caretakers" until a legitimate civilian regime can be installed. But such pledges are not always honored, and what appears to be withdrawal is sometimes merely a tactical retreat to a position from which covert rule can be attempted. On the other hand the examples of Atatürk, Franco, de Gaulle, and Ayub indicate that military leaders who serve as heads of government for long periods may in effect transform themselves into civilian politicians and thereby legitimize their rule.

Demands for military leadership. The degree of political power possessed by armed forces is determined first of all by the effective demand for military leadership. Response to such demand has been termed "reactive militarism" (Janowitz 1964, p. 16).

Demand for military leadership varies with the intensity of foreign or domestic social conflict. Prussia's history illustrates that armies become influential in countries which experience foreign pressure consistently. The theory of the "garrison state" (Lasswell 1941) elaborates this insight and applies it to industrial nations. It assumes that if such countries face continuing security crises they will subordinate all else to defense preparations and their social systems will be controlled rigorously by a combination of military and civilian leaders. Although this thesis has not been disproved, it is evident that the vitality of the political process can affect the outcome significantly. For example, military leaders have played a prominent role in American policy councils during the cold war, but at no time has military rule been likely. Soviet and British experiences in and after World War II also suggest that prolonged security crises need not generate military regimes where civilian government rests on a firm consensus. It is equally clear that military leaders can acquire great power in the absence of significant foreign pressure. Latin America and Tokugawa Japan provide examples. In the new states of Africa and Asia military primacy is more frequently a function of internal than of external security crises. In most cases the latter make themselves felt only indirectly. For example, military aid programs, initiated in response to global security crises, increase the political power of armed forces in recipient states by reducing their dependence on local political leaders and by stimulating more rapid modernization of the military bureaucracy than of the civil service.

Demands for military leadership can be generated by domestic events under three analytically distinct conditions, which can be understood with the aid of insights derived from the general theories of Hobbes, Marx, and Pareto respectively. In the first instance, once society becomes disorganized to the point of anarchy, military force seems essential to the restoration of public order, especially at the local level. In the second situation, a privileged social group, aided by control of the state, oppresses subordinate groups. If the latter cannot seek redress of grievances peacefully, their protests may take violent forms ranging from individual acts of terrorism to the organization of revolutionary armies. Since the dominant strata cannot rely on overarching loyalties to hold the community together, they in turn must call upon police and army to compel obedience. In the third situation, although the fundamental basis of the social order is not threatened, elites are at odds over such issues as corruption, constitutional procedure, or foreign policy, and one or another faction eventually turns to the military for help.

Countervailing forces. The strength of competing forces and institutions also affects the social and political power of the military establishment. Competition may, of course, emanate from within the armed forces themselves, but little is yet known about the conditions under which military influence in society is increased or decreased by factional rivalry. The effect of external forces seems clearer. In such stratified societies as Iran or Morocco, for example, the armed forces have long been regulated by autocratic rulers; in India they were controlled by colonial civil servants. Military primacy is more likely if the legitimacy of such traditional controls is challenged before influence can be acquired by other civilians. Military primacy varies inversely with the number and strength of private associations, with the integrity and skill of civilian bureaucrats, and with the prestige of political parties and legislatures. Especially in new states, if other public institutions are tarnished by corruption or if they are supported only by privileged social strata or only in the capital city, military leaders often assume the functions of mobilizing and representing social interests.

The strength of countervailing forces is sometimes weakened by disputes over legitimate authority. During civil strife or in crises of succession it is often unclear where rightful control over the armed forces is lodged and their discretionary power inevitably rises. Legislatures cannot always make good their claim to control military budgets or war ministers. Prime ministers and war ministers do not always possess full authority over senior command and staff officers. In some cases war ministers are ineffective agents of political authority because they, too, are professional officers, with strong ties to their military colleagues. This was often the case in Germany and France before 1914, in Japan through World War II, and in Argentina and Brazil in more recent times.

Finer has related the levels of military intervention to the demands for military leadership that are generated by domestic conditions or by what he terms "the order of political culture" (1962, p. 139). In mature political cultures the armed forces engage only in prescribed modes of influence. In developed but not fully mature cultures militarism emerges in the form of sporadic and usually covert intervention, the limits of which are set in part by countervailing social forces and institutions. In countries with low or minimal political culture military intervention is proportionately easier, more open, more frequent, and more enduring. However, a succession of military coups may also serve as a substitute for revolutionary warfare in propelling countries of low political culture toward political maturity.

National traditions. Military primacy is also a function of particular national traditions. Where leaders of the armed forces have formed part of a respected ruling class or where they have come to be respected as national heroes, saviors, or symbols, they recruit a disproportionate share of talented and ambitious men. Governments are readier to authorize these men the money and materials they desire. Citizens are also readier to tolerate their assumption of political and social leadership. Under such circumstances the armed forces develop corporate pride and confidence that translate into still greater influence. For such reasons the military in imperial Germany and Japan possessed greater social and political power than their counterparts in imperial China, nineteenth-century America, or twentieth-century Africa.

Values and internal policies. Given identical opportunities to acquire political primacy, not all military leaders are equally disposed to seize them. Readiness to do so depends on self-images and values, some of which in turn shape the internal policies of military regimes.

The most important inhibiting value is a commitment to the principle of civilian supremacy. As noted earlier, Huntington (1957) defines this as part of the professional military ethic, but Finer (1962, pp. 24–30) contends that it is an independent factor. The principle itself requires military leaders to serve all lawful regimes faithfully. Acceptance of such a commitment induces them to resist substantial temptations to intervene in politics; rejection makes intervention likely on little provocation. The strength of the commitment differs from country to country, from individual to individual, and probably from one branch of service to another.

Several kinds of values predispose military leaders to seek political power. From the praetorian guards of Rome to the *condottieri* of Italy and the janissaries of Turkey, blackmail and *coups d'état* have been attempted for personal aggrandizement, special privileges, and material benefits. These essentially personal motives or values are still important in many countries.

Institutional values are important wherever military careers provide a major outlet for ruling classes or upward-mobile persons; they are less important where good opportunities exist in business, learned professions, and other careers. Different institutional interests help explain the special affinity of navies for foreign politics and the special affinity of armies for internal politics. Although such interests may be either defensive or offensive, it is not always easy to distinguish the one from the other. A desire to preserve institutional criteria for promotion of personnel can shade off into a demand for autonomy so complete that the armed forces become "a state within the state." A desire to protect corporate values can induce an army to demand an enormous proportion of the nation's manpower and income.

Public or political values are nowadays most influential in prompting military men to seek political primacy. Such values involve conceptions of national security, aggressive as well as defensive; conceptions of nation building in the face of centrifugal forces; conceptions of efficiency and austerity in the face of corruption; conceptions of the rule of law in the face of arbitrary government; conceptions of social unity in the face of factional politics; and conceptions of social and economic justice—conservative, liberal, and eclectic.

A historical relationship has existed between armies and conservative regimes not only in western Europe but also in the traditional autocracies of Afro–Asia and under many Latin American dictatorships. Armed forces often assist in maintaining an existing system of social stratification and privilege. But it is impossible to ignore the tradition of military liberalism in the American and French revolutions, in the Napoleonic armies, among some Prussian military reformers, among the military republicans of Spain in 1820, and among the Latin American followers and heirs of Bolívar. It is equally impossible to dismiss as conservative the military elites of the underdeveloped world today. In the new states of Africa and Asia military conservatives in the classical European sense tend to be exceptions, in part because few such countries experienced feudal institutions and in part because colonial administrators monopolized high-status positions. Also, armies in emerging nations are heterogeneous. Countries as different in other respects as Brazil and Iraq are alike in having politically influential officers who represent both oligarchic and radical forces. The former are interested in fiscal responsibility, order, and legitimacy. The latter are more interested in welfare programs, tax and land reform, and the mobilization of youth, women, and peasants. Still other officers hold positions that can only be described as technocratic or pragmatic. Some change their ideologies in response to events. Many Latin American officers, for example, support modernization efforts up to the point at which the stratification system seems threatened and then recoil in alarm. On the other hand, in most of the new states of Afro–Asia there is little principled opposition to public enterprise, and the military regimes of Nasser in Egypt and Ne Win in Burma actually pledged major transformations of the social order.

Orientation of military leaders. Social origins and connections, age, and foreign influences are among the factors that shape the economic and social orientation of military leaders. When officership is primarily an ascriptive calling, it attracts the wellborn or the rich. However, when the entire military profession is open to men of talent on a competitive basis, men of the middle and lower middle class are more likely to enter it. A decision to recruit on the basis of merit has strengthened revolutionary elements in the officer corps in times and places as different as France in 1792 and Egypt in 1936. Moreover, popular military organizations, such as militia or national guards, are frequently more liberal than small professional armies.

In eighteenth-century and nineteenth-century Europe such relatively technical branches as artillery and engineers tended to attract middle-class liberals, while cavalry and infantry remained citadels of the aristocracy. Similarly, in the developing nations after World War II officers whose work had a relatively large technical component tended to be less conservative than their colleagues. In these countries, also, officers in the grade of colonel or lower tended to be more radical than their more senior colleagues.

Finally, economic and social orientations of military personnel are affected by foreign cultural impacts. In the armies of Latin America oligarchic tendencies were strengthened first by Iberian influences and later by fascist military advisers. In the nineteenth-century Turkish army, on the other hand, contact with France led to a diffusion of liberal ideas stemming from the Enlightenment and the French Revolution. Although it is extremely difficult to generalize, it is also probable that the net effect of post-1945 military aid programs—Soviet as well as Western—was to strengthen modernizing tendencies in the armed forces of developing nations.

LAURENCE I. RADWAY

[*See also* CIVIL–MILITARY RELATIONS; MILITARY; MILITARY POLICY. *Other relevant material may be found in* MODERNIZATION; NATIONAL SECURITY; PACIFISM; WAR.]

BIBLIOGRAPHY

ANDRZEJEWSKI, STANISLAW 1954 *Military Organization and Society.* London: Routledge; New York: Humanities.

ERICKSON, JOHN 1962 *The Soviet High Command: A Military–Political History, 1918–1941.* New York: St. Martins.

FINER, SAMUEL E. 1962 *The Man on Horseback: The Role of the Military in Politics.* New York: Praeger.

GIRARDET, RAOUL 1953 *La société militaire dans la France contemporaine: 1815–1939.* Paris: Plon.

HACKETT, ROGER F. 1964 The Military: A. Japan. Pages 328–351 in Conference on Political Modernization in Japan and Turkey, Gould House, 1962, *Political Modernization in Japan and Turkey.* Edited by Robert E. Ward and Dankwart A. Rustow. Princeton Univ. Press.

HUNTINGTON, SAMUEL P. 1957 *The Soldier and the State: The Theory and Politics of Civil–Military Relations.* Cambridge, Mass.: Harvard Univ. Press.

JANOWITZ, MORRIS 1964 *The Military in the Political Development of New Nations: An Essay in Comparative Analysis.* Univ. of Chicago Press.

LASSWELL, HAROLD D. 1941 The Garrison State. *American Journal of Sociology* 46:455–468.

LIEUWEN, EDWIN (1960) 1961 *Arms and Politics in Latin America.* Rev. ed. Published for the Council on Foreign Relations. New York: Praeger.

MAXON, YALE C. 1957 *Control of Japanese Foreign Policy: A Study of Civil–Military Rivalry, 1930–1954.* Berkeley: Univ. of California Press.

MILLIS, WALTER; MANSFIELD, HARVEY C.; and STEIN, HAROLD 1958 *Arms and the State: Civil–Military Elements in National Policy.* New York: Twentieth Century Fund.

RITTER, GERHARD 1954–1964 *Staatskunst und Kriegs-handwerk: Das Problem des "Militarismus" in Deutschland.* 3 vols. Munich: Oldenbourg. → Volume 1: *Die Altpreussische Tradition: 1740–1890.* Volume 2: *Die Hauptmächte Europas und das Wilhelminische Reich: 1890–1914.* Volume 3: *Die Tragödie der Staatskunst: Bethmann-Hollweg als Kriegskanzler, 1914–1917.*

SPEIER, HANS 1952 *Social Order and the Risks of War.* New York: Stewart.

VAGTS, ALFRED (1937) 1960 *A History of Militarism: Civilian and Military.* Rev. ed. London: Hollis & Carter.

MILITARY

As a sociological category, the term "military" implies an acceptance of organized violence as a legitimate means for realizing social objectives. Military organizations, it follows, are structures for the coordination of activities meant to ensure victory on the battlefield. In modern times these structures have increasingly taken the form of permanent establishments maintained in peacetime for the eventuality of armed conflict and managed by a professional military. Accordingly, the military professional is an officer who pursues a *lifetime* occupational career of service in the armed forces, where, to qualify as a professional, he must acquire the expertise necessary to help manage the permanent military establishment during periods of peace and to take part in the direction of military operations if war should break out. Career commitment and expertise, the hallmarks of any professional, set the professional military officer apart from those other personnel in the armed services who are merely carrying out a contractual or obligatory tour of duty or for whom officer status primarily represents, as it often did in former times, an honorific pastime into which military skill enters only as a secondary consideration.

Social organization and armed force

Throughout most of history the right to employ violence has been derived from membership in a special community or in one of its status groups. While societies everywhere have always regarded outsiders as legitimate targets for violence, societies whose internal relations are based on physical dominance of one group by another allow for fewer of the fine distinctions between brute force and other bases of social and political power. Thus the Roman legions both served imperial ambitions and became the major domestic political force. Indeed, war lords of all epochs have considered their armies a form of private property and have used

them to secure their tax base and to extend its boundaries. Under such conditions, the internal organization of the armed forces closely reflects the distribution of power within the society at large. In general, the more pervasive the prospect of violence against external or internal enemies of the regime, the more similar are the military and the civilian value hierarchies.

The concept of the military as a permanent establishment maintained solely in support of foreign policy objectives presupposes the development of a civil society based on consensus. In such a society, the armed forces are called upon to cope with domestic disorder only in extraordinary circumstances, this task being relegated largely to civilian police forces. However, the incapacity of party governments to resolve vexing internal problems, including an inability to mobilize the "home front" in support of national goals, has on many occasions led the military to do more than provide coercive power for use against external enemies. Their role in this regard has been especially important in those newly emerging nations whose civil institutions and sense of national identity have not yet had sufficient time to develop.

Professionalization of the military, with rank and authority granted on the basis of demonstrated competence rather than status, cannot evolve until the problem of military management has become separated from and subordinated to the more general problem of governing a society. Even so successful an innovator of strategy as Frederick II of Prussia, because he wanted to ensure the personal loyalty of his officers, insisted that they be drawn exclusively from the ranks of the aristocracy. Using this kind of power base inside the officer corps, the postfeudal nobility of many a European country was able to prolong its waning influence. It did so by preserving within the military certain archaic sentiments, ceremonial practices, and ideological beliefs that supported the social superiority of officers, and then proclaiming this superiority valid for the society as a whole (Vagts 1937). Militarism of this sort, because it hindered rather than helped the growth of expertise, was a major impediment to the professionalization called for by advances in military technology.

The possibility that certain strata of the society might use their monopoly of armed force to gain a disproportionate share of the values available within a society helps to explain why the right to bear arms has so frequently been declared one of the inalienable rights of a free citizenry. Such a right, when it becomes the prevailing military doctrine, may stand in the way of military efficiency.

In France the governments of the Third Republic, intent on curbing any possible political ambitions of military leaders, insisted on a short-term conscript force, and by this manpower policy they deprived the French army of the opportunity to develop a highly trained force. The doctrine of the "nation in arms" in this French version helped seal that country's fate when it had to confront better-trained and numerically superior German forces in two world wars.

Under modern conditions, lasting victory in war certainly can no longer—if it ever could—be achieved primarily through the sheer weight of a hastily assembled mass of manpower acting either under the command of their social superiors or of a very small professional cadre. Furthermore, a decided advantage now goes to the belligerent with the industrial and scientific base for developing more powerful weapon systems and with a labor force containing sufficient skilled personnel to maintain, repair, and replenish the products of military technology during hostilities. As research, development, technical maintenance, and the organization of logistic support become more important elements in strategic planning, military managers are forced to pay more attention to the implications of economic, social, and political policy for the state of military preparedness. Hence, the events to which they must be responsive have increasingly more to do with scientific–technical capabilities and sociopolitical forces, and proportionately less to do with direct encounters on a clearly delimited battlefield. The traditional wall of separation between strategy (the explicit domain of the professional military) and policy (the explicit responsibility of civil government) comes to be breached at many points.

This shift in perspective has been reinforced by the growing emphasis on deterrence, rather than counterviolence, as the major strategic goal of the nuclear powers. But similar tendencies are evident in the industrially backward nations, whose military leaders recognize that they must create an indigenous economic and educational base as a major condition for a complex military establishment. Their efforts to achieve this frequently propel them into major roles in the modernization of their countries. In general, where civilian agencies lack expertise or legal and political precedents for containing the military, the military can usurp the highest counsels not only through deliberate infiltration but also through lack of any opposing polical force.

The rapidity of technological progress in modern times often forces the abandonment of a whole weapon system before it can be operationally tested in battle. Thus there exist, within the military establishment, installations whose express function is to create and develop new and unorthodox concepts and procedures, including the application of computerized simulation techniques to the solution of strategic problems. In some ways, therefore, the military establishment begins to conform more to the pattern of a laboratory for testing the concepts and "hardware" underlying a new system, and relatively less to the pattern of a striking force whose permanent components are designed primarily to provide a basic framework for expansion in case of need. Here, again, the traditional boundaries between the civilian expert and the military professional tend to become blurred, in particular as the influence of the civilian expert ceases to be confined to the design and development of basic military "hardware" but begins to extend to matters related to its application. Civilian specialists have carried major responsibility for the introduction into the military of new managerial methods and training devices based on scientific evaluation rather than on traditional concepts. Perhaps the most significant development, however, is to be found in the number of civilians, either in the direct employ of the military or under contract, who have come to play major innovating roles that extend to the domain of strategy, which is traditionally a military preserve.

Military organization

The impact of modern technology notwithstanding, all military organizations continue to operate within a context of considerable uncertainty. The authority structure, work routines, and conceptions of discipline in the armed forces must be geared to the ever-present possibility, no matter how remote, that every member of the organization, whatever his job classification, may be called upon to perform his normal duties under battle conditions. Many specifically military practices explicitly express, or have as a latent point of reference, a concern about the capacity to make an adequate response under stress. The anxiety-reducing function of many routines is especially evident in the persistence of archaic ceremonial practices that have no apparent functional utility. These probably help instill confidence that, in the event of a crisis, officers and men at all levels of the organization will conduct themselves in a predictable manner.

Active warfare, moreover, is a highly seasonal occurrence that alternates with more or less prolonged periods of peace. As in the past, the military man must indulge in a certain amount of romanticism to justify his continuing dedication to the martial arts when no apparent need for them exists. Acclamation of selfless service to one's country as an ennobling ideal for all, emphasis on the manly virtues, and the sense of corporate eliteness implicit in these ideals have been basic ingredients of military *esprit de corps*. Thus, the tenacity with which European armies resisted motorizing their horse cavalry, even after its inutility in war had been fully demonstrated, derived not only from an aristocratic tradition, symbolized by the officer and his mount, but probably drew added vigor from a reluctance to countenance the replacement of heroic men by mechanized components.

By the same token, the massive resistance of military traditionalists to the formation of a separate air arm, to the introduction of the aircraft carrier and the atom-powered submarine as strategic naval weapons, to the replacement of manned bombers by missiles, and so forth, contains elements of a defensiveness that seems to be characteristic of the military, although it reflects rigidities and vested interests of a kind likely to develop in any large and complex organization. But military doctrines, in particular, are codifications of experiences gained in the past—experiences that are forever being reanalyzed. Since doctrinal modifications in time of peace cannot immediately be tested against new experiences, the remote advantages of change must inevitably be balanced against the confusion and uncertainty that attend reorientation of any sort. This organizational dilemma has been especially aggravated by acceleration of obsolescence. In this process, the reduction of "lag time" (the interval between the time a system becomes operationally feasible and its full acceptance by officers) becomes as important as the "lead time" between the drawing board and the operational stage. The concern about remaining up-to-date creates a real danger of innovation for its own sake rather than as a rational adaptation to changed circumstances. In turning toward science as a source of new ideas, the military may, under the guise of modernity, be searching for the same kind of procedural solutions that it once embraced because they were traditional. Reliance by the armed services in their internal management on highly rationalized procedures and computerized systems diverts some of the uncertainties inherent in the possibility of military failure into a quest for internal order. Scientific innovation, especially when the assumptions behind its adoption are not constantly tested by experience, can degenerate into an obsession with the latest gadgetry, as divorced from reality as the prescientific forms of ceremo-

nialism. Similarly, techniques as unorthodox, from a military point of view, as political warfare and counterinsurgency do not necessarily encourage objective evaluation of the limitations that political and social forces impose on the value of a strictly military success. To some enthusiasts within the military these techniques often appear merely as more effective alternatives to annihilation.

The military profession

Another effect of technological change has been to undermine the military profession's insularity, once the almost inevitable consequence of faraway missions, assignments at isolated posts, or duties on board ship, all of which tended to deprive officers of social contact outside their narrow professional world. Many tasks with which military personnel nowadays must cope as a matter of routine are only indirectly related to combat. Modern technology has so transformed the conditions of wartime service that to maintain a single soldier in combat takes many more men than it did when the martial arts were at a more primitive level. It follows that the most rapidly expanding military job categories are generally those involving scientific, technical, and administrative skills—categories for which there are near equivalents in the civilian economy. As a result, the experience gained during military service acquires transfer value for a subsequent career in civilian life, where these same skills are likewise in demand. In order to retain skilled personnel in military service beyond their obligatory tour, the armed forces must try to offer inducements comparable to those in alternative civilian employment.

Recruitment of officers. The traditional, ascriptive pattern of recruitment, especially the time-honored practices of giving preference to sons of officers in the selection of applicants to officer schools, and of fostering among candidates and junior officers a unique professional culture, was calculated to discourage all those not highly motivated toward an officer career. But higher skill requirements have more recently led to a wider search for talent and have opened new opportunities for social ascent to many ambitious young men of relatively modest origin. Sons of enlisted men, once likely to have been disqualified from officership on purely social grounds, are no longer at this great disadvantage. In France, their proportion among new officers has nearly tripled since World War II (Girardet 1964, pp. 38 ff.). There has been a similar broadening of the officer recruitment base, mostly under the impact of technology, in nearly every country. The proportion of the officer corps recruited from aristocratic and plutocratic elements has dropped off even more abruptly as political purges—especially in the Soviet Union, Germany, and many Latin American countries—have forced the separation or premature retirement of officers too closely identified with discredited political regimes.

Despite this general trend toward more representative recruitment, there are still many sons of officers who follow their fathers in choosing a military career and so to some extent maintain the social continuity of the occupation. For example, as opportunities for advancement were sharply curtailed in the contracted German army of the 1920s, the proportion of new officers who were sons of officers increased considerably. In the United States during the two decades after World War II, the proportion of "second generation" officers entering West Point remained at a nearly constant level of somewhat above 20 per cent (Janowitz 1964, p. 135).

The significance of this occupational continuity is debatable; as in any occupation, the amount of intergenerational mobility depends in part on changes within the entire occupational structure. It may be noted that in 1950 about 20 per cent of practicing lawyers were sons of lawyers, law having the highest amount of intergenerational continuity of any occupation in the United States (Warkov 1965, p. 43). But graduates of the major military schools, such as West Point, Sandhurst, and St. Cyr, have had, as a rule, stronger commitments to a military career and, partly for that reason, have contributed disproportionately to the higher officer ranks and leadership positions. Anticipatory socialization early in their family life, together with the experiences and contacts made in the academy, gives these officers a competitive advantage over others recruited directly from civilian life. Hence a hard core of traditionally military families, where they exist, probably exerts greater influence than is indicated by gross figures on occupational continuity. Even in the United States, where such families have not been especially conspicuous, intergenerational continuity of occupation among top military executives seems to have been greater than among their civilian counterparts in the federal government (Warner et al. 1963, chapter 2).

A significant ambiguity results from the fact that the officer corps is both a profession requiring the acquisition of certain skills and a corporate body through whose rank hierarchy each officer must advance. Many officers who have acquired educational and other professional skills of use to the military are not professional military men. In fact,

increases in officer allocations in recent years reflect in large measure the need for men qualified to take responsibility for complex equipment and to perform certain technical and administrative functions. While some old-fashioned armies, in order to provide positions for sons of the privileged classes, have had unusually high allocations of officers, in modern armies the increases have been greatest in branches with the most advanced technology and at levels of responsibility—usually intermediate ones—where experienced men with technical qualifications must be promoted in order to be retained. However, the authority of many officer specialists is severely limited, and in some instances their specific designation precludes advancement into positions of major responsibility. Also, the frequency with which officers in many specialties transfer out of the armed service into civilian employment indicates a primary commitment to a specialty that takes precedence over any commitment to the military.

Hierarchy of command. The implications of the diversification of skills and specialties extend beyond the character of officership as a profession. Diversification also affects the internal authority structure of military organization. Traditionally, military authority has been both hierarchical and collegial. On the one hand, military discipline prescribes unquestioning compliance with orders passed down through an unambiguous line-of-command authority, with only the details of implementation left to the discretion of individual commanding officers. On the other hand, military discipline means more than automatic compliance: it subsumes the imperative, binding on every officer, to inspire one's subordinates by personal example and to cultivate among all officers a strong respect for professional norms. The presence of specialists injects the element of technical knowledge into these authority relationships.

One source of strain stems from the fact that many unit commanders, even at the lower echelons, lack the technical knowledge necessary to direct all the diverse components for which they shoulder formal responsibility. Nor do they have officers on their staffs with sufficient knowledge. If such knowledge is not available at the level of the unit to which an individual officer is assigned, he has a strong incentive, when difficulties of a purely technical nature arise, to solicit information and advice directly from technical specialists attached to higher staffs. This enables him to resolve many routine difficulties while avoiding formal command channels and without involving his commanding officer in the details of every operational problem. However, commanding officers who tolerate such informal trouble-shooting activities, which clearly deviate from prescribed procedures, run the risk of teaching disrespect for the chain of command. In fact, they may inadvertently be discouraging their officers from keeping them fully informed on all matters under their own command.

Another source of strain is that many functions and policies come under the central administration of a staff from which detailed directives emanate. These directives often leave little leeway to a local commander and may actually usurp some of his traditional prerogatives. Staff officers, by definition, have no command authority in their own name, but only as delegated. Yet relatively junior officers can, and sometimes do, informally exercise a considerable amount of *de facto* authority, simply by virtue of the esoteric wisdom with which their position on the higher staff endows them. The hypertrophy of this kind of staff authority was reached by the Germany army in World War I, where general staff officers, in control of their own network of communication, came to issue orders that at times completely countermanded directives from commanding generals whom they formally served only as staff advisers. This development was evidently fostered by the past practice of favoring members of royal houses for command positions, the consequences of which staff intervention was intended to redress. Nevertheless, central direction, even when it accords with the best technical principles, tends toward the creation of a dual system of authority and inevitably generates some anxiety among unit commanders about what authority they actually have. The desire of commanding officers to retain firm personal control even over matters that are centrally directed can be seen in the frequency with which they use whatever discretion they have in implementing a centrally issued directive in such a manner as to subvert its intended purpose.

Strain also arises from the need to coordinate the activities of lower-echelon individuals or units that are components of different hierarchies. When the recognition of a work relationship does not in itself induce spontaneous collaboration, there can be considerable concern over limits of competence and of formal authority. Another version of this problem exists in the staffs of supernational forces, where the separate military hierarchies represented are associated with disparities of national power. Staff cooperation in NATO headquarters is said to have suffered considerably from the capacity of some officers to compensate for any lack of rank or formal authority by making use of the power of the nation they represented. Certainly, U.S. advisors in Vietnam were often able to use their country's control over certain weapons to gain compliance with their decisions, even when they were clearly outranked by their Vietnamese counterparts. Still a third and somewhat analogous version of this conflict, based on ideological disparity, has occurred between professional military officers and political commissars. Where the latter represent the political regime at the unit level, and are therefore assured of outside political support, they are often in a position to countermand certain orders of their nominal superiors if they wish to do so.

Combat

No authority structure can by itself ensure spontaneous cooperation under battle conditions, where confusion is inevitable and improvisation and unorthodox solutions are frequently called for. The makeshift character of front-line living arrangements inevitably gives rise to serious deviations from procedures learned in the training camp. A great deal has in fact been written on the displacement of motives to the immediate group: the "comrades" or "buddies" with whom each soldier shares the experience (Grinker & Spiegel 1945; Stouffer et al. 1949, vol. 2; Mandelbaum 1952; Janowitz 1964, pp. 195–224). This sense of solidarity, which in some ways extends to all combat men, usually engenders strongly deprecatory attitudes toward those echelons of lesser risk from which most regulations emanate. To the degree, therefore, that individual and interpersonal motives become determining factors, military units in combat tend to assume some of the characteristics of a primitive mass formation. The capacity of this formation to absorb stress is highly contingent on the strength of shared sentiments. Where organizational authority does not enjoy legitimacy, strong sentiments of this sort can facilitate the rapid spread of deviant tendencies. However, the prevalence of a sense of generalized obligation lends legitimacy to punitive discipline when it is invoked as a last resort.

The unavoidable presence of physical risk is a major source of disruption in combat units. Detailed investigations of the behavior of ground combat soldiers have convincingly documented the reluctance of many riflemen to discharge their weapons against a visible enemy target: during any single encounter, only a minority were found to have fired, irrespective of the chances the men had to engage the enemy (Marshall 1947; for the sources of the following remarks on reaction to combat stress, see Janowitz 1959, chapter 4; Lang 1965*a*). Evidently success in such encounters does not depend on the performance of every individual. Indeed, among U.S. interceptor pilots serving in Korea, only a small minority of aces accounted for an overwhelming majority of all enemy planes shot down, and most fliers were not even credited with a single plane. Air superiority was nevertheless maintained.

Containment of deviance. The old-fashioned practice of severely disciplining some men for "cowardice" to deter others from failing in their duty under fire at best promotes token compliance when opportunities for escape are lacking. As a means of instilling the motivation necessary for superior performance, it is hardly effective. Yet, under conditions of modern warfare, much depends on the initiative displayed by individuals operating in small units relatively removed from the influence of formal control. The problem under these conditions is how to contain deviance within certain tolerable limits so that it does not disrupt organizational effectiveness. Even in the normal engagement many men will not measure up to par. Since enemy fire causes casualties, rates of desertion, dereliction from duty, psychoneurotic breakdown, and other forms of deviance invariably begin to rise either after a prolonged stretch of uninterrupted combat or after an engagement in which a unit suffers particularly heavy losses. In these circumstances, any break in efficiency has cumulative implications because it tends to impair the motivations and efficiency of other men.

The major role in the control of deviance is increasingly being assigned to the medical specialist. In acknowledging anxiety in battle to be a natural and normal reaction, military psychiatry in general, but American and British military psychiatry in particular, has gone a long way toward treating its disruptive effects on behavior as primarily a medical and only secondarily a disciplinary problem. Although the literature provides regrettably few studies that permit reliable historical or crossnational comparisons, prevailing psychiatric theories certainly suggest that the reliance on rigid disciplinary controls would produce more lasting mental damage, with chances for ultimate recovery much diminished. In World War I, the number of severely impaired shell shock cases was certainly greater than in World War II, with its more enlightened practices of military medicine. Japanese soldiers in World War II, subject to the most unyielding discipline and supposedly indifferent to their own survival, seemed especially prone to severe attacks of hysteria. The possibility of culturally patterned reactions expressing differences in national character, especially tolerance for

anxiety, cannot, of course, be ruled out. Yet the apparent severity of the reactions among Japanese troops may have been provoked by the strong sanctions against the *open* expression of anxiety in any form.

Organizational correlates of breakdown. The availability of a legitimate medical evacuation channel has important implications for organizational behavior. Thus, some psychiatrists have pointed out that a collective belief among American troops in World War II in an objective "breaking point" beyond which a person could not go on may actually have contributed to an increase in the number of psychiatric breakdown cases who requested evacuation because of a typical symptomatology. Neuropsychiatric breakdown was far less frequent among British troops in north Africa, who, unlike the Americans, had no expectations of being permanently repatriated until the end of the war, but whose combat was interrupted by frequent periods of rest. Similarly, there were no neuropsychiatric casualties among South Korean troops until after their integration with American forces, when these same evacuation channels became available to them. Yet they had previously exhibited many other kinds of ineffectiveness.

The point is that evacuation statistics reflect not only psychiatric malaise but also a complex decision process. For the soldier who has had enough, the use of the evacuation channel with the approval of a psychiatrist offers a legitimate alternative to self-mutilation, letting himself be taken prisoner, temporary desertion, and other forms of escape. Thus, during the rapid retreat by U.S. troops from their advanced positions on the Yalu River during the winter of 1950/1951—a period of evident stress—the neuropsychiatric casualty rate exhibited a marked decline. Soldiers could not rely on evacuation, for all medical facilities were severely overtaxed. Even when ready to give up, they had a strong incentive to remain with their unit simply to avoid being captured or killed. Similarly, desertion, which had been a major problem in Europe with major cities nearby, was practically nonexistent among American troops engaged in island-hopping operations against Japan.

Although comparable data from other nations are not available, it is clear that the American combat soldier in World War II was inclined to take a rather lenient view of temporary desertion, consistent with his generally tolerant attitude toward a man who was suffering from symptoms of fear which he had made a genuine effort to control. One distinguishing characteristic of men who became neuropsychiatric casualties was their tendency, on the average, not to entertain favorable attitudes toward the less legitimate forms of escape provided by unauthorized absence from the battlefield. Conversely, many men guilty of desertion in combat left their units only after they had on one or more previous occasions been refused medical evacuation. There are indeed indications that the two forms of escape are in some respects interchangeable and also that the decision on whether a man is entitled to medical evacuation or should be returned to his unit is not only medical but nearly always involves judgments based on organizational criteria. The effect any disposition may have on the morale of the remaining men can rarely be kept from intruding into such decisions. If the tactical situation permits, a man's prior record of good performance can earn him evacuation for symptoms that might send another man back to the front. Particularly, officers and noncommissioned officers who carry responsibility for other men, whose safety might be jeopardized by their continued presence, are more readily evacuated (the technical reports on which the foregoing remarks are based can be found summarized in Janowitz 1959; Lang 1965a).

Units in combat are undergoing a constant process of attrition and replenishment, as evidenced by the continuous turnover in personnel. But the maintenance of logistic and organizational support is probably more important for maintaining the effectiveness of larger units than is keeping a particular man in battle, especially if he is suffering from evident symptoms of stress. Viewed in this context, military psychiatry as practiced nowadays reflects the same shift in orientation toward warfare that is often noted in connection with strategic planning: the long-term conservation and management of national resources and talent has become a more important military asset than victory in almost any local encounter. Again the picture of the whole world as a potential battlefield and of the possible involvement of whole populations is reflected in practices that reach into the lower units.

Understanding of combat goals is clearly essential to understanding the military and its organizational practices. Yet the battlefield itself is undergoing change, and the specific missions assigned to the military are changing with it. The new forms of warfare, including ideological war and nuclear deterrence, lead to new priorities in the mobilization of men and resources. Hence,

both the relationship between the armed forces and society and the internal structure of the military will undergo further change.

KURT LANG

[*Directly related are the entries* CIVIL–MILITARY RELATIONS; INTERNMENT AND CUSTODY; MILITARISM; MILITARY POLICY; MILITARY PSYCHOLOGY; NATIONAL SECURITY; WAR. *Other relevant material may be found in* ECONOMICS OF DEFENSE; INTELLIGENCE, POLITICAL AND MILITARY; MILITARY LAW; MILITARY POWER POTENTIAL; SCIENCE, *article on* SCIENCE–GOVERNMENT RELATIONS; STRATEGY; *and in the biographies of* CLAUSEWITZ; DOUHET; MAHAN.]

BIBLIOGRAPHY

ANDRZEJEWSKI, STANISLAW 1954 *Military Organization and Society.* London: Routledge.

DEMETER, KARL (1962) 1965 *The German Officer-corps in Society and State, 1650–1945.* New York: Praeger. → First published in German.

FOOT, MICHAEL R. D. 1961 *Men in Uniform: Military Manpower in Modern Industrial Society.* New York: Praeger.

GIRARDET, RAOUL 1953 *La société militaire dans la France contemporaine: 1815–1939.* Paris: Plon.

GIRARDET, RAOUL 1964 *La crise militaire française, 1945–1962: Aspects sociologiques et idéologiques.* Paris: Colin.

GRINKER, ROY R.; and SPIEGEL, JOHN P. 1945 *Men Under Stress.* Philadelphia: Blakiston. → A paperback edition was published in 1963 by McGraw-Hill.

GUTTERIDGE, WILLIAM F. 1965 *Military Institutions and Power in the New States.* New York: Praeger.

JANOWITZ, MORRIS (1959) 1965 *Sociology and the Military Establishment.* Rev. ed. New York: Russell Sage Foundation.

JANOWITZ, MORRIS 1960 *The Professional Soldier: A Social and Political Portrait.* Glencoe, Ill.: Free Press. → A paperback edition was published in 1965.

JANOWITZ, MORRIS (editor) 1964 *The New Military: Changing Patterns of Organization.* New York: Russell Sage Foundation.

JOHNSON, JOHN J. (editor) 1962 *The Role of the Military in Underdeveloped Countries.* Princeton Univ. Press. → Papers presented at a conference sponsored by the RAND Corporation at Santa Monica, Calif., in August 1959.

LANG, KURT 1965a Military Organizations. Pages 838–878 in James G. March (editor), *Handbook of Organizations.* Chicago: Rand McNally.

LANG, KURT 1965b Military Sociology: A Trend Report and Bibliography. *Current Sociology* 13, no. 1.

MANDELBAUM, DAVID G. 1952 *Soldier Groups and Negro Soldiers.* Berkeley: Univ. of California Press.

MARSHALL, SAMUEL L. A. 1947 *Men Against Fire: The Problem of Battle Command in Future War.* Washington: Infantry Journal.

MILLIS, WALTER; MANSFIELD, HARVEY C.; and STEIN, HAROLD 1958 *Arms and the State: Civil–Military Elements in National Policy.* New York: Twentieth Century Fund.

STOUFFER, SAMUEL A. et al. 1949 *The American Soldier.* Studies in Social Psychology in World War II, Vols. 1 and 2. Princeton Univ. Press. → Volume 1:

Adjustment During Army Life. Volume 2: *Combat and Its Aftermath*.

VAGTS, ALFRED (1937) 1960 *A History of Militarism: Civilian and Military*. Rev. ed. London: Hollis & Carter.

WARKOV, SEYMOUR 1965 *Lawyers in the Making*. Chicago: Aldine.

WARNER, W. LLOYD et al. 1963 *The American Federal Executive: A Study of the Social and Personal Characteristics of the Civilian and Military Leaders of the United States Federal Government*. New Haven: Yale Univ. Press.

MILITARY LAW

Military law, in the sense of a distinctive body of law relating to the armed forces and their activities, is probably as old as law and war themselves, which is to say about as old as organized human polities. The term embraces the codes that govern the members of a nation's armed forces (military justice), the relationship of the military to the civilian community (martial law or military government), and the conduct of belligerents in time of war (the law of war). In all of these areas the military, independently of civilian magistrates, may exercise some degree of jurisdiction, conferred by domestic legislation or international law or a combination of the two.

Military justice

It may be surmised that pre-Roman military codes amounted to little more than the complete subjection of the soldier to the will of the commander, the deprivation of whatever right to due process he might otherwise have had as a citizen. This was certainly the basic principle of Roman military law; the field commander and his delegates were empowered to inflict any punishment for any offense, military or civilian. The common military offenses were in general akin to those proscribed by modern codes—desertion, cowardice, insubordination, and the like. As was the case with most military codes until comparatively recent times, punishment was swift, severe, and often brutal. Corporal and capital punishment were very freely inflicted (in part, no doubt, because imprisonment was not available as an alternative), and resort was occasionally had to decimation and other punitive measures that have long been obsolete. Other Roman military penalties, such as ignominious expulsion, reduction in rank, and forfeiture of pay, are still standard features of military justice.

Medieval military justice was as simple and crude as medieval tactics and logistics: Richard I's Ordinance of 1190, intended to deter theft and fighting among his Crusaders, is probably a representative specimen. It provided, *inter alia:* "Whoever shall slay a man on shipboard, he shall be bound to the dead man and thrown into the sea. If he shall slay him on land, he shall be bound to the dead man and buried in the earth." Procedural provisions were entirely lacking; the court-martial, as a distinct tribunal, had not yet evolved. It probably traces its ancestry to the court of chivalry of the later Middle Ages. In late medieval and Renaissance times, there appeared in western Europe more elaborate and sophisticated military codes, in part derived from Roman precedents and in part based on the laws and customs of the Franks and other German nations. The best-known of these is the Constitutio Criminalis Carolina, promulgated by the Emperor Charles V in 1532, which served as a model for a number of other European codes. One of these was the Articles of War of Gustavus Adolphus, dated 1621, which was translated into English shortly before the English Civil War and may fairly be described as the direct ancestor of modern British and American articles of war, to which the following description is chiefly directed. The military codes of many other nations are, however, derived from, or strongly influenced by, the Anglo–American model, and even those which are based on other sources and traditions have many points of generic resemblance.

The basic reasons for the existence of a separate system of military justice may be summarized as (1) the need for swift and summary machinery for the maintenance of discipline; (2) the fact that the adjudication of military crimes may require military expertise by the court; and (3) the fact that the armed forces may be stationed abroad, outside the jurisdiction of their country's civil courts. The English Articles of War, from Richard I's Ordinance to James II's detailed Articles of 1688, were wholly exercises of the crown's prerogative, having no parliamentary sanction and, in time of peace, no lawful application in domestic territory. Military crimes, military punishments, and military courts had no place in the common law; in Macaulay's words, "A soldier, therefore, by knocking down his colonel, incurred only the ordinary penalties of assault and battery, and by refusing to obey orders, by sleeping on guard, or by deserting his colours, incurred no penalty at all" ([1849–1861] 1953, vol. 1, p. 222). Given the necessity of a standing army, such a situation was intolerable. Parliament dealt with it by the Mutiny Act of 1689, which permitted courts-martial to punish mutiny, sedition, or desertion by death or such lesser penalty as the court might adjudge. For nearly two centuries, the Articles of War, applicable only to troops stationed abroad, and the Mutiny Act, annually re-enacted, existed side by side. Not until 1881 were the two jurisdictions fused.

No such dichotomy exists in the history of the American Articles of War, which have always been statutory. Congress enacted the original articles, largely borrowed from the British, in 1775. Since the adoption of the constitution their enactment has been an exercise of Congress' power (art. I, sec. 8) "to make Rules for the Government and Regulation of the land and naval Forces." There have been several revisions, mostly with war in prospect or its lessons in retrospect. The principal ones are those of 1776, 1786, 1806, 1874, 1916, and 1920. In 1950 the Articles of War and the Articles for the Government of the Navy (basically similar, although differing in a number of details) were superseded by the Uniform Code of Military Justice, which applies alike to the army, navy, and air force. Like its predecessors, the Uniform Code specifies the persons who are amenable to military jurisdiction, defines offenses, prescribes punishments, and establishes trial and appellate procedure for courts-martial.

Jurisdiction over persons.   Courts-martial of the United States, like those of most nations, exercise criminal jurisdiction primarily over members of the armed forces on active duty, including cadets and midshipmen, in both peace and war. The U.S. code followed previous articles in subjecting to military law civilians accompanying or serving with the armed forces, such as dependents of military personnel and civilian employees, in time of war or outside the United States. Similarly the code attempted to deal with a serious problem that developed during and after World War II: it provided for the court-martial of discharged servicemen for serious offenses committed while the accused was subject to military law, offenses which could not be tried in an American court—for example, a murder committed in a foreign country. In a series of major decisions between 1955 and 1960, however, the Supreme Court held that Congress could not constitutionally subject to military jurisdiction either an honorably discharged serviceman who had severed all connection with the military or, in time of peace, any civilian. Whether such jurisdiction may be exercised in time of war and whether it is constitutional in regard to certain categories of quasi civilians (such as retired regulars, some reservists, and dishonorably discharged prisoners in military custody) must, in the

light of these decisions, be regarded as open to question. In time of war, courts-martial are empowered to try "any person" for aiding the enemy or espionage; the same constitutional question might, however, be raised if the act took place in the United States and particularly if the accused were an American citizen.

Military jurisdiction is not exclusive. If an offense committed by a soldier is denounced by both the code and state or federal law, he may be tried by either a court-martial or a civilian court. Moreover, since the constitutional prohibition against double jeopardy bans only a second trial by the same sovereign for the same offense, he may be tried by both a court-martial and a state court or (if the act embraces two distinct offenses—for example, the civilian offense of assault and the military offense of striking a superior officer) by both a federal court and a court-martial. As a general rule, however, the policy of the military, in peacetime and within the United States, is to leave to civilian justice a soldier who commits a civilian offense that does not directly affect the military. Soldiers stationed in friendly foreign countries are likewise subject to the jurisdiction of both courts-martial and the local civilian courts, although in the absence of agreement between the two sovereigns the jurisdiction of the host country is primary. In practice, the matter has been regulated by so-called status-of-forces agreements, which usually give American courts-martial primary jurisdiction over purely military offenses and other offenses not involving citizens, property, or other interests of the host nation.

Jurisdiction over offenses.   Courts-martial have, of course, long had jurisdiction over the traditional military offenses, such as desertion, absence without leave, mutiny, insubordination, disobedience, misbehavior before the enemy, drunkenness on duty, and a few whose interest is largely antiquarian, such as improper use of a parole or countersign, forcing a safeguard, and dueling. In 1916 American courts-martial were given jurisdiction in both war and peace over virtually all the common law crimes except the capital offenses of rape and murder committed in the United States in peacetime. The Uniform Code made even these offenses triable by court-martial. But court-martial jurisdiction of offenses is in reality still broader, for the "general article," which has no real analogue in civilian penal codes, covers "crimes and offenses not capital," which means acts that are not specifically covered by other articles of the code but are made criminal by other federal laws. Still more broadly, it denounces "disorders and neglects to the prejudice of good order and discipline in the armed forces" and "conduct of a nature to bring discredit upon the armed forces." The military authorities have traditionally been accorded broad, although not unlimited, discretion in giving content to these vague phrases; in practice almost any violation of the law of a state or foreign country can be fitted into one or the other category—or in the case of officers, cadets, and midshipmen, into "conduct unbecoming an officer and a gentleman."

Punishments. Courts-martial may impose a number of distinctively military punishments, such as dishonorable or bad-conduct discharge, reduction in rank or grade, forfeiture of pay, and reprimand. They may also impose sentences of death, imprisonment, and fine. In time of peace the death penalty is limited to mutiny, sedition, murder, and rape. In wartime, since the maintenance of discipline by deterrence is still the prime object of military justice, death may be inflicted for a number of military offenses, of which the chief are desertion, assaulting or willfully disobeying a superior officer, misbehavior before the enemy, aiding the enemy, and espionage; for the latter offense, the death sentence is mandatory. (It should be remarked, however, that during and since World War II there appears to have been only one case, involving a second desertion, in which an American soldier was actually executed for a military offense.) These punishments may be, and commonly are, combined in a single sentence, for example, dishonorable discharge, forfeiture of pay, and confinement at hard labor for a term of years.

General courts-martial may impose any authorized penalty. Special courts-martial are in substance limited to bad-conduct discharges and six months' imprisonment, and summary courts, to a month's confinement, plus corresponding forfeiture of pay. Although a court-martial may not inflict the death sentence unless explicitly authorized by the code itself, Congress has placed all lesser sentences within the court's discretion; in strict theory a soldier might be sentenced to life imprisonment for addressing rude language to his sergeant. The president, however, is empowered to prescribe maximum punishments for those offenses for which Congress has set no mandatory punishment—i.e., all save espionage (death) and premeditated or felony murder (death or life imprisonment). The "Table of Maximum Punishments," contained in the *Manual for Courts-Martial*, places limits that approximate civilian norms on the penalties for specific crimes. Corporal punishments, notably flogging and branding, which were a distinctive feature of military justice until well into the nineteenth century, have long been expressly prohibited, as has "any other cruel or unusual punishment."

The military authorities maintain their own prison system—in the case of the army, post stockades (for minor offenders) and disciplinary barracks—for those military convicts who are judged capable of rehabilitation and ultimate restoration to duty; others serve their confinement in federal reformatories and penitentiaries. If the authorities conclude that salvage is feasible, the execution of a punitive discharge will normally be suspended and ultimately, if the prisoner behaves himself, remitted.

Procedure. The Uniform Code regulates in detail the appointment, composition, jurisdiction, procedure, and appellate review of courts-martial. Authority to convene a *general court-martial* is normally given only to a commander of a division, a task force, or a comparable unit; a *special court-martial* may be convened by the commander of a regiment or of a naval vessel; and *summary courts-martial*, by commanders of detached companies. (Authority to convene a general or special court includes authority to convene the inferior types.) A general court consists of not fewer than five members plus a law officer; a special court, of not fewer than three members; and a summary court, of a single officer. Prior to the enactment of the Uniform Code, members of a court-martial were required to be commissioned officers, but an accused enlisted man may now request that a minimum of one-third of the members be enlisted men—a privilege rarely exercised in practice.

Traditionally the procedure of military courts has been swifter and more summary than that of civilian criminal courts; according to Macaulay again "a summary jurisdiction of terrible extent must, in camps, be entrusted to rude tribunals composed of men of the sword" ([1849–1861] 1953, vol. 2, p. 414). This splendid rhetoric is not applicable to the Uniform Code, whose protection of the rights of the accused is so extensive that some critics fear that it would be unworkable in time of war. Although the procedure of a court-martial differs in many respects from that of a civil court, an accused has—at least in a general court-martial—virtually all the substantial protections that he would have in a civil proceeding and even some that he might not have in many civil courts. The functions of the law officer—who must be a lawyer and is usually a member of the judge advocate general's corps, hence a specialist in military law—are roughly analogous to the functions of a trial judge; and the functions of the court-martial members, to those of the jury; the principal difference is that the members not only determine guilt or innocence but also assess the sentence. The rules of evidence are approximately the same as in a criminal trial in a federal court. The Uniform Code, like the bill of rights, prohibits compulsory self-incrimination, double jeopardy, and cruel or unusual punishments; the charges must be investigated before the accused is arraigned; he must be apprised of the charges against him; he is entitled to counsel of his choice and to compulsory process to obtain defense witnesses. His counsel must be a qualified lawyer, at least in a trial before a general court-martial, and pressure upon courts by commanders is forbidden—although it is not always easy to eradicate such influence. The principal differences are that the military accused is not entitled to bail and that he may be convicted and sentenced by vote of two-thirds of the members, although unanimity is required for a death sentence.

Appellate review under the code is probably more extensive than is common in civilian practice. All findings and sentences (other than acquittals) must be approved by the authority who convened the court-martial, after review of the record for legal sufficiency by his staff judge advocate. The convening authority may order a rehearing, or order the charges dismissed, or modify or remit the sentence in the exercise of clemency. Sentences that, as approved, include death, a punitive discharge, or confinement for a year or more are referred to a board of review (whose members must be lawyers) in the office of the judge advocate general of the service concerned. Death sentences or sentences involving general or flag officers require presidential approval; the dismissal of a commissioned officer requires the approval of the secretary or an assistant secretary of the department. At the top of the military appellate structure is the Court of Military Appeals, whose creation was the major innovation of the Uniform Code. Considering that the armed forces include some two million men, most of them in the age brackets in which crime is most frequent, it is perhaps the most important court of criminal appeal in the United States. Its three judges, who must be lawyers, are appointed by the president "from civilian life" and have no connection with the military establishment. They must review all death sentences and any cases certified to them by the judge advocate general of any of the services and may grant review of any case passed upon by a board of review. Their jurisdiction is otherwise essentially like that of a civilian appellate court, including power to set aside any conviction in which they find errors of law or insufficient evidence. Since its inception, the court has proved to be no rubber stamp. It has developed and applied a concept of "military due process," derived from both the code and the constitution and much influenced by the Supreme Court's holdings on constitutional due process. Experience so far indicates that a court-martial in which there has been substantial unfairness is unlikely to survive review by the Court of Military Appeals—although it should be recalled that its powers of review are in effect limited to fairly serious cases, those involving punitive discharges or confinement for a year or more. It is probable that many inferior courts-martial are still somewhat summary in operation, as are many inferior civilian criminal courts.

Although there can be no direct appeal to a civilian court from the decisions of the military reviewing authorities, there may be collateral review of the court-martial's jurisdiction by such proceedings as petition for a writ of habeas corpus in a federal district court or suit for pay in the Court of Claims.

Military nonjudicial or "disciplinary" punishments may be imposed by commanding officers without trial for offenses not deemed sufficiently serious to require reference to a court-martial. Depending on the rank of the commander and the offender, such punishments may include forfeitures, reduction in grade (of enlisted men), and comparatively short periods of additional fatigues or confinement. While the accused can always demand trial by court-martial, he is usually well-advised to accept company punishment in lieu thereof. Since punishments equivalent to (and in some cases slightly greater than) those within the competence of a summary court-martial may be imposed under the code's article on disciplinary punishment, the summary court has become more or less obsolete.

Martial law

The term "martial law" describes the exercise of military force to preserve order and insure the public safety in domestic territory in a time of emergency, when the civilian authorities are unable to deal with the situation. In one form or another, under such names as "state of siege" or "state of emergency," the concept is found in every country. In some countries it is almost the normal type of government. In Anglo–American law, its only proper purpose is to restore order with a view to the restoration of civilian government, and the degree to which the military may properly assume governmental functions depends entirely on the needs of the situation. In its mildest form martial law may amount to no more than the employment of troops, in aid of and under the direction of the civil authorities, to supplement the regular police in the control of riots and other public disorders and the enforcement of the law, as was done in connection with integration of the schools in Arkansas and Mississippi. At the other extreme, if the emergency is great enough, such as actual or imminent invasion, the military authorities may assume all the functions of government, including the legislative and judicial. In such a situation statutes and even the constitution may be suspended and replaced by ordinances of the military commander, and the civilian courts superseded by military tribunals. Such courts, although they bear a generic resemblance to courts-martial, are not bound to follow the same procedure, but may employ whatever rules are called for by the needs of the emergency. The best-known example of such a situation in recent American history is the declaration of martial law in Hawaii immediately after the Japanese attack on Pearl Harbor.

Martial law is nowhere explicitly mentioned in the constitution but is simply an inherent attribute of sovereignty, the right of every government to take whatever steps are necessary for its own preservation. As such it is a part, although an extraordinary part, of the common law. Although the constitution does not explicitly either authorize or limit the executive's invocation of martial law, it is now well established that there are constitutional checks upon the exercise of this power. To the extent that the measures of martial law encroach upon the citizen's rights under state and federal constitutions, the civil courts have jurisdiction to determine whether the measures taken are in fact commensurate with the emergency and to annul them to the extent that they are more drastic than the court deems requisite. Although the courts are usually disposed to give considerable weight to the executive's judgment of the crisis, there are numerous cases in which they have found martial law measures to be unjustified. Most such cases have involved the governors of states (some of whom have been tempted to use martial law whenever a political goal could not be achieved by lawful methods), but the Supreme Court has on occasion applied the same test to the exercise of war power by the president and Congress. One famous instance is Ex parte *Milligan* (71 U.S. 2, 1867), decided shortly after the Civil War, in which the Supreme Court freed a Copperhead leader who had been sentenced to death by a military commission

in Union territory at a time when the civil courts were open and functioning normally. Another is Ex parte *Endo* (323 U.S. 283, 1944), in which the court, having previously upheld most of the restrictive measures applied to American citizens of Japanese descent in World War II, finally concluded that certain relocation measures, involving drastic interference with normal constitutional rights, could not be justified by military need.

Military government

Military government is a belligerent's exercise, through its armed forces, of governmental powers in the conquered and occupied territory of another nation. It presupposes actual, effective physical control of the territory in question and ability to impose on its inhabitants the will of the military commander.

International law recognizes the occupant's right to govern the conquered territory, but it also imposes restrictions on the exercise of this right. The principal limitations are embodied in the Hague Convention of 1907 and the 1949 Geneva Convention Relative to the Protection of Civilian Persons in Time of War. Essentially, the occupant is required to preserve public order and to respect the laws in force "unless absolutely prevented"—a phrase of ambiguous content, which occupying powers have traditionally construed extremely broadly. The persons and property of inhabitants of the occupied territory are accorded some basic protections. Such aspects of former military occupations as pillage and the taking of hostages are forbidden. While the occupant may impose taxes and levy contributions for the needs of the occupying forces, he is bound also to defray the usual costs of government in the occupied territory. He may promulgate such ordinances as are reasonably necessary to protect his forces and govern the territory and may try violations thereof in his military government courts. Such trials must meet elemental standards of fairness, such as giving the accused the right to counsel and an interpreter and the right to call witnesses. Military government courts may supersede the indigenous courts and, to the extent authorized by the military governor, exercise criminal and civil jurisdiction over all persons in the occupied territory, including citizens of the occupying power and even members of its forces. In practice, matters which do not affect the interests of the occupant, its forces, or its nationals are usually left to the local courts—if they are open and can be trusted not to discriminate against persons friendly to the occupant.

The difficulty lies in the enforcement of the

rules designed to protect the inhabitants of occupied areas. It is common knowledge that in World War II, German, Japanese, and Russian occupations of conquered territory were marked by atrocities on an enormous scale. Such violations can, of course, be punished as are other violations of the law of war, discussed below, but for the duration of hostilities the degree of the occupant's compliance with the rules of international law regarding belligerent occupation must depend on his conscience and his estimate of the likelihood of retribution.

In normal circumstances an occupation endures until it is ended by the expulsion of the occupying forces, the annexation of the territory by a victorious belligerent, or the conclusion of a treaty of peace. The abnormally prolonged occupation of Berlin after World War II results simply from the inability of the victorious allies to agree on a peace treaty or any other method of bringing the occupation to an end. Upon the termination of the occupation and the return of the legitimate sovereign there are always difficult questions concerning the extent to which the restored courts and other authorities of the occupied nation should treat as valid the executive, legislative, and judicial acts of the occupant—the so-called problem of postliminium. In principle, those acts of the occupant which were within its lawful powers ought to be accorded as full force and effect by the returning sovereign as they would be if done under its own authority. In practice this has usually been done only with respect to routine governmental acts, such as the collection of normal taxes and the punishment of common crimes. Where an occupant has inflicted punishments, such as fines and imprisonment, for acts directed against the occupying forces, the returning sovereign can hardly be expected to give them effect—unless it has by treaty obligated itself to do so, as the Federal Republic of Germany did when the Western allies terminated their occupation of its territory.

Historically the powers of the United States as a military occupant have been exercised by the president as commander-in-chief of the armed forces, usually through the highest military commander in the occupied territory as the military governor thereof, but occasionally (as in Germany after 1949) through civilian officials. Congress has never attempted to control the president's discretion, and it is doubtful that it could constitutionally do so. Also uncertain is the extent, if any, to which the bill of rights and other parts of the constitution apply to the acts of American military government in foreign territory. The Supreme Court held in 1900 that the constitution had no application to a criminal trial in occupied Cuba, even though the accused was an American citizen. This must still be regarded as the orthodox view, although in recent years some members of the court have suggested that the powers of American military authorities in occupied territory are subject to the more basic provisions of the bill of rights.

It may be that the legal problems of military government are likely to be less important in the future than they have been in the past. They can be circumvented by the establishment of a friendly, or even a puppet, indigenous government and the recognition of that government as the legitimate sovereign. What would otherwise be occupation forces thus become merely visiting forces in the territory of a friendly power. The Soviet Union, although it did not invent the technique, brought it to a high degree of perfection after World War II, and the lesson has not been lost on other powers.

The law of war

The law of war comprises that branch of international law which governs the rights and obligations of belligerents. Its basic object is to protect combatants and noncombatants from unnecessary suffering and to safeguard the fundamental human rights of the victims of war, such as prisoners of war, the wounded and sick, and civilians, including the inhabitants of occupied territory. Its basic problem is to reconcile that policy with military necessity.

Belligerents in ancient times seem to have recognized few, if any, rules; the attitude of the Greeks and Romans is accurately summarized in Cicero's maxim, *Silent enim leges inter arma* ("When men fight, laws have no voice"). Customary limitations upon the conqueror's freedom to massacre, enslave, and loot began to evolve in the Middle Ages and to take coherent form in the sixteenth and seventeenth centuries, as exemplified by the writings of Hugo Grotius. The first really important and influential attempt to codify the rules recognized by the consensus of civilized nations was probably Francis Lieber's "Instructions for the Government of the Armies of the United States in the Field," drafted at President Lincoln's request and promulgated as a general order of the War Department in 1863. Lieber's "Instructions" were followed by a number of similar unilateral declarations by Italy, Russia, France, and other countries. The Brussels Conference of 1874 marked the beginning of an effort to embody the customary laws of war in international treaties, an effort which ultimately led to the Hague conventions of 1899 and 1907. The Hague conventions, still a basic source for the laws of war, have been supplemented by a number of other major treaties to which practically all of the great powers have acceded (sometimes with particular reservations). The most important of these are the Geneva Conventions of 1949 relating to the wounded and sick, prisoners of war, and the protection of civilians in time of war.

The law of war as established by custom and treaty, to the extent that it is observed and enforced, is calculated to mitigate the hardships of conventional war. Enforcement, however, is entirely unilateral. There is as yet no permanent international tribunal with jurisdiction to punish war crimes. The Nuremberg and Tokyo international tribunals, which tried violations of the laws of war committed by the German and Japanese defendants, were created *ad hoc*. If a belligerent is guilty of war crimes, the nation aggrieved may resort to protest and ultimately to reprisals in kind. The law of war may also be enforced by the punishment of captured violators. The Geneva Conventions of 1949 obligate each signatory to search out and try in its own courts persons guilty of "grave breaches" thereof, a provision which is essentially a declaration of the prior customary law. In theory, jurisdiction to try war crimes is universal—that is, any nation having physical custody of a war criminal may try and punish him. In practice, nations have not typically displayed much diligence or zeal in trying war criminals of their own nationality. Neither have they typically been concerned to punish violations which did not directly affect their own interests. The post-World War II trials of some German war criminals in the courts of the Federal Republic of Germany, although many criminals have gone unpunished and others have received sentences hardly commensurate with the enormity of the crimes, probably constitute the outstanding example of a nation punishing its own war criminals. In most of the cases in which war criminals have actually been tried and punished, the trials have taken place in the courts of a victorious enemy. Typically such jurisdiction is exercised by military tribunals; this has always been the practice of the United States. After World War II the United States tried before military commissions—tribunals akin to courts-martial but not bound by such rigid rules of procedure and evidence—many Germans and Japanese charged with offenses against prisoners of war or civilian nationals of the United States and its allies. The jurisdiction of military commissions to try such

offenses was upheld by the Supreme Court in Ex parte *Quirin* (317 U.S. 1, 1942), the case of nine saboteurs landed in Long Island and Florida by German submarines in 1942, and In re *Yamashita* (327 U.S. 1, 1946), which concerned the trial of the commanding general of Japanese forces in the Philippines. Under the Geneva Conventions of 1949, persons accused of war crimes are, however, afforded basic guarantees of a fair trial.

The laws of war as they now stand are open to the criticism that they do not deal with the realities of present-day wars. The use of nuclear weapons is not prohibited, and the Geneva Conventions could hardly do much to soften the impact of a hydrogen bomb. On the other hand, nonnuclear belligerency at the present time is likely to take the form of subversion, insurrection, and guerrilla warfare, covertly instigated and supported by nations that are not officially belligerents. The laws of war, being part of international law, are difficult to apply to domestic insurrection, short of a full-fledged civil war in which the parties are accorded belligerent status by other nations. Guerrillas, who wear no uniforms, do not carry arms openly, and usually do not obey the laws of war themselves, are not regarded as entitled to the benefit of those laws. In theory at least, every such guerrilla is an unlawful combatant, a war criminal, if not simply a violator of the laws of the recognized sovereign of the territory. However, article 3 of each of the Geneva Conventions of 1949 does apply to "armed conflict not of an international character occurring in the territory of one of the High Contracting Parties," and it does prescribe minimum human rights for persons involved in such insurrections by prohibiting, for example, murder, torture or other cruel treatment, and execution without fair trial.

JOSEPH W. BISHOP, JR.

[*See also* INTERNATIONAL LAW; LEGAL SYSTEMS; MILITARY.]

BIBLIOGRAPHY

BALDWIN, GORDON B. 1959 A New Look at the Law of War. *Military Law Review* 4:1–38.

BISHOP, JOSEPH W. JR. 1961 Civilian Judges and Military Justice: Collateral Review of Court-martial Convictions. *Columbia Law Review* 61:40–71.

FAIRMAN, CHARLES (1930) 1943 *The Law of Martial Rule.* 2d ed. Chicago: Callaghan.

FAIRMAN, CHARLES 1946 The Supreme Court on Military Jurisdiction: Martial Rule in Hawaii and the Yamashita Case. *Harvard Law Review* 59:833–882.

LAWYERS CO-OPERATIVE PUBLISHING COMPANY 1951 *Military Jurisprudence: Cases and Materials.* Rochester, N.Y.: The Company.

MACAULAY, THOMAS B. (1849–1861) 1953 *History of*

England From the Accession of James II. 4 vols. New York: Dutton.

McDougal, Myres S.; and Feliciano, Florentino P. 1961 *Law and Minimum World Public Order: The Legal Regulation of International Coercion.* New Haven: Yale Univ. Press.

Spaight, James M. 1911 *War Rights on Land.* London: Macmillan.

U.S. Department of Defense 1951 *Manual for Courts-martial: 1951.* Washington: Government Printing Office.

U.S. Department of the Army 1956 *The Law of Land Warfare.* Washington: Government Printing Office.

U.S. Department of the Army 1957 *Treaties Governing Land Warfare.* Washington: Government Printing Office.

Von Glahn, Gerhard 1957 *The Occupation of Enemy Territory: A Commentary on the Law and Practice of Belligerent Occupation.* Minneapolis: Univ. of Minnesota Press.

Wiener, Frederick B. 1958 Courts-martial and the Bill of Rights: The Original Practice. *Harvard Law Review* 72:1–49, 266–304.

Winthrop, William W. (1886) 1920 *Military Law and Precedents.* Rev. ed. Washington: Government Printing Office. → First published in two volumes as *Military Law.*

MILITARY POLICY

Military policy consists of those activities of a government which are primarily concerned with its armed forces. Military policy is thus defined in terms of its scope rather than its purpose. In Western nations reference is frequently made to "defense policy" and "national security policy." These terms define policy in terms of purpose— "defense" or "national security"—rather than in terms of scope. For this reason, they are less useful for research. In some states, defense and/or national security may not be the principal purpose of military policy: the armed forces may be designed for aggression rather than for defense or internal security and economic development, or they may be used to minimize the burden on the domestic economy rather than to maximize national security. In modern states, moreover, the scope of defense policy and national security policy is much broader than the scope of military policy. Diplomacy, economic mobilization, economic warfare, foreign economic assistance, political warfare, intelligence, and propaganda—all may be directed toward national security objectives, but they are not military policy. Military policy is, instead, a narrower field of governmental activity comparable to agricultural policy, labor policy, education policy, or tax policy.

Military policy differs from most other substantive policy areas in that it straddles the line between domestic policy and foreign policy. Domestic policy consists of those activities of a government which affect significantly the allocation of values among groups within its society; foreign policy consists of those activities of a government which affect significantly the allocation of values between it and other governments. Particular substantive policies may affect the allocation of values both within a society and between societies, but typically they have their primary impact in one field or the other. Foreign economic assistance affects the domestic allocation but has its primary impact on the international allocation. Agricultural subsidies affect the international allocation but have their primary impact domestically. Military policy, however, drastically affects the allocation of values both within the society and between societies.

The scope of military policy

Military policy can be divided generally into two broad categories: strategy and structure. Strategy concerns the units and uses of force; it is military policy viewed from the foreign-policy perspective. Strategy itself involves two broad types of issues. Program issues deal with the strength of the military forces, their composition and readiness, and the number, type, and rate of development of their weapons. Use issues deal with the deployment, commitment, and employment of military forces, and are manifested in alliances, war plans, declarations of war, force movements, and the like. A strategic concept identifies a particular need and implicitly or explicitly prescribes policies on the uses, strengths, and weapons of the armed services.

The structural side of military policy is its domestic component and deals with the acquisition and organization of the resources which are drawn from society and which go into the units and uses of force. Structural policy subsumes: budgetary policy, concerning the size and distribution of funds made available to the armed services; manpower policy, concerning the procurement, retention, pay, and working conditions of members of the armed services; procurement policy, concerning the acquisition and distribution of supplies to the military forces; and organizational policy, concerning the methods and forms by which the military forces are organized and administered.

Analytically these various elements of military policy are distinct. In actual practice, of course, any major decision in military policy involves a combination of many of them. The terms in which the decision is initially defined, however, often reflect the purposes which it is designed to realize. Decisions designed primarily to influence the international environment are formulated initially in strategic terms and must then be translated into structural policies. Conversely, decisions primarily designed to affect the allocation of domestic values are usually first formulated in structural terms, and their strategic implications are calculated later. For example, a decision to reduce the military budget is likely to be prompted by a concern with domestic factors: fear of the inflationary effects of high military spending, the desire to expand domestic welfare programs, concern over the undue influence of the military on the economy and in society, or the desire to balance the budget and reduce taxes. The reduction in military spending will require the elimination of some programs and forces and the reshaping of others. These changes will have implications for war plans and deployments, and they may make it difficult or impossible for the state to maintain its existing commitments in world politics. Hence, alliances may have to be negotiated, and what began as an effort to achieve certain domestic economic goals through the mediation of military policy comes to have a major impact on foreign relations. Conversely, a change in foreign policy, such as the assumption of a commitment to aid another state, may require increases and changes in military forces and programs and war plans which will eventually have their impact on military manpower and material procurement, which, in turn, may significantly redistribute goods and services in the domestic economy.

In theory the elements of domestic policy, foreign policy, and military policy should be congruent. In actual practice, of course, they never are. The purposes and goals of policies are always changing and always conflicting. If there are not major conflicts of purpose, however, the policies can be said to be in equilibrium. Periods of disequilibrium are typically periods following major changes in the domestic or international environments of a state. In some instances, changes in one environment and concomitant changes in foreign policy or domestic policy may not be transmitted into changes in military policy. In this event, the different elements may continue to operate at cross purposes for a long period of time. In some circumstances, such as France in the 1930s, such a disjunction between military policy and foreign policy may lead to disaster.

The elements of military policy

Strategy—programs and forces. Strategic programs deal with the over-all size, the weapons, and the composition of the military forces. The key issues normally concern the "mix" or relative strength and importance of different types of forces: land, sea, and air forces; offensive and defensive forces; active and reserve forces. After World War II, in the United States and in other major powers these traditional categories began to lose their significance. Increasingly, American military policy was concerned with the allocation of resources among strategic deterrent forces, continental defense forces, and general purpose or limited-war forces. Superimposed on these issues was the broader issue of the relative stress which should be placed on nuclear forces and conventional forces. In general, it is possible to analyze a country's policies on strategic programs in terms of the concepts of "strategic pluralism" and "strategic monism" (see Huntington 1954). A pluralistic strategy, such as that followed by the United States between 1950 and 1953 and after 1961, involves the maintenance of a variety of military forces so as to be able to make graduated and appropriate responses to different types of aggression and to serve a variety of foreign-policy objectives. Strategic pluralism in programs is usually accompanied by higher military budgets and a more restrained and "defensive" foreign policy. Strategic monism, on the other hand, involves primary emphasis on one particular type of military force (for example, strategic nuclear forces) which is well designed to serve certain foreign-policy objectives but not others. Consequently, strategic monism usually means a lower level of military spending, but it also requires a more active and positive foreign policy that attempts to prevent through diplomacy the appearance of challenges which the military forces of the state are not equipped to handle.

Major changes in a country's strategic programs occur only rarely and usually in combination with major changes in its foreign policy and domestic environments. Examples of such changes are the German decision in the late nineteenth century to create a sizable navy, the American decision in the 1950s to create a military system for the defense of North America against nuclear attack, and the Chinese decision in the mid-1950s to develop a nuclear-weapons capability. At a lower level, technological developments may lead to the innovation of new weapons without changes in major strategic purposes. Thus, between 1955 and 1965 the United States substantially changed the principal element in the weapons "mix" of its strategic deterrent forces from long-range bombers to intercontinental missiles. Weapons innovation is a continuing concern for all nations involved in prolonged international rivalries or arms races. In such situations the weaker power almost always has an interest in introducing new weapons, unless it thinks that such innovation will provoke the stronger power to an immediate attack. The stronger power, on the other hand, has a vested interest in the current level of weapons but must be prepared either to respond quickly to weapons innovation by the weaker power or to take the initiative in such innovation and thus in effect hasten the obsolescence of its existing superior weapons system.

Strategy—uses of force. A government can use or plan to use its military forces against another government in three ways (see Huntington 1961*a*, pp. 430–431). First, it can take the initiative in using force to secure some foreign-policy objective, such as the acquisition of territory or economic concessions. Second, it can use force responsively to counter or to reply to the initial use of force by another government. Third, it can use force as a deterrent in an effort to convince another government that it should not take some action. Any particular military action may, of course, serve all three purposes, but generally the strategy of a government gives primacy to one use. Have-not powers typically take the initiative in using force; *status quo* powers usually act responsively or deterrently. During much of its history the United States either took the initiative in the use of force, as in 1812 and 1898, or responded to the use of force by other governments, as in World War I. Since World War II, however, American military forces have been used primarily for deterrent purposes, although where deterrence has failed they have been used responsively (as in Korea in 1950) and in some cases initially (as in the Dominican Republic in 1965).

The uses of force are often analyzed in terms of the spectrum of violence. At one extreme is all-out war with thermonuclear weapons. At the other extreme are the terrorism and subversion of "sublimited" war and "wars of national liberation." In between are such forms of violence as guerrilla warfare, limited conventional war (restricted in geographical area, weapons, targets, or goals), general conventional war, tactical nuclear war, and limited nuclear war. At one time American thinking on war tended to hold that all war must be all-out war for total victory. During the twenty years after World War II, however, the American government became accustomed to the graduated use of force and came to accept the Clausewitzian dictum that political goals must determine the nature and the extent of the use of force in war as well as in peace. A recurring issue in military policy concerns the extent to which the use of force at any one level in the spectrum of violence is likely to escalate to higher levels in the spectrum. Escalation is most likely when one side appears about to suffer a total defeat at the lower level of violence. Communist China intervened in the Korean War in the fall of 1950 when North Korea was almost totally defeated; the United States expanded its military action in Vietnam in the winter of 1964–1965 when it seemed probable that the Saigon government would be defeated. The most important step in the escalation of a conflict would, of course, be the shift from conventional to nuclear weapons. While other forms of escalation may be gradual and difficult to identify clearly, this shift would be a dramatic qualitative change in the nature of the conflict.

A preventive war occurs when a government initiates hostilities because it is convinced that war is inevitable later and that it would then be fought under less favorable conditions than it would be if initiated immediately. A pre-emptive attack is an attack designed to forestall or to blunt an enemy attack already in the process of preparation and launching. Thus, a country could plan to launch a preventive attack against another country and at the same time be the target of a pre-emptive attack from its enemy.

After World War II, the development of nuclear weapons and of high-speed, long-range delivery capabilities brought to the fore new issues in the use of military force by the major powers. The crucial factors were the relative size and vulnerability of each side's strategic force. If both sides have relatively vulnerable strategic forces, in a crisis each will be under considerable pressure to launch a "first strike" and to destroy the other side's strategic force before it can attack. This is a situation of maximum instability. If one or both sides have relatively invulnerable strategic forces (as a result of concealment, dispersion, mobility, or sheer numbers), the incentive to launch a first strike is much less. The "balance of terror" is thus more stable when each side is capable of absorbing a first strike and then responding with an attack capable of dealing the other side unacceptable damage. These strategic issues are frequently formulated in terms of a choice between a counterforce and countervalue strategy. In a counterforce strategy the enemy's military forces are the principal target of the nuclear strike; in a countervalue (or countercity) strategy its population centers are the principal target.

The deterrence of military action may also be achieved through various combinations of diplomatic and military means. A defensive military alliance is a classic means of communicating the intention of one state to use force to protect another state. The North Atlantic Treaty Organization (NATO) is probably the most notable example of such an alliance in the mid-twentieth century. Deterrent intentions may also be communicated through formal or informal statements by government officials and by the deployment and maneuvering of military forces. The success of such deterrent moves depends upon the ability of the deterring state (a) to identify clearly the action which it wishes to deter; (b) to convince the potential military actor of its intention to respond if the identified action occurs; and (c) to suggest to the potential actor that a response will impose unacceptable costs upon the actor.

Structure—manpower. At its broadest level, manpower policy involves the nature of the military manpower procurement system. Four principal systems have been used by modern states: (1) a citizen militia (Israel, Switzerland), in which all those qualified serve a large part of their lives in the citizen reserve forces, which form the bulk of the country's military strength; (2) universal military service (France, the Soviet Union), in which all qualified men serve a short period (usually two or three years) in the active forces and then a longer period in the reserves; (3) volunteer service (Great Britain after 1960, Canada), in which efforts are made to recruit long-service professionals for the active forces; and (4) selective service (United States, Federal Republic of Germany), in which compulsory service typically for a two-year period is required of certain classes of young men, but liberal exemptions and deferments are granted, so that service is far from universal.

In addition to choice among these general systems, manpower policy concerns the recruitment, retention, pay, working conditions, promotion, education, training, and retirement of both officers and enlisted men. Among the more frequently debated issues of manpower policy are the following: To what extent should officers be recruited from special military schools, from civilian schools and colleges, or from enlisted ranks? What should be the criteria for promotion of officers—seniority, command ability, intellectual qualities? What types of education and training should officers and enlisted men receive during their military service? To what extent should military pay equal the pay for comparable work in civilian life?

Structure—procurement. Procurement and matériel policies concern the methods by which the military services acquire weapons and installations. A recurring issue is to what extent the military establishment should itself produce weapons within government-owned arsenals and to what extent it should procure them from private companies. If private procurement is preferred, to what extent is it desirable or possible to rely on competitive bidding as against negotiated bids? What policies should be followed with respect to maintaining production lines in existence on a stand-by basis: should a broad or a narrow "mobilization base" be maintained? Closely related to procurement are policies on the research and development of new weapons. To what extent should new weapons be developed in response to a previously determined "military requirement" or need for such a weapon? Or to what extent should scientists and technicians be encouraged to pursue broad-gauged research along the most promising scientific lines, with the expectation that these advances may lead to new weapons for which new appropriate uses could be found? A related issue concerns the extent to which weapons innovation is furthered by competition among several concerns or laboratories, each following a somewhat different path in attempting to develop a weapon to meet a military need. Or would weapons development be just as rapid and less costly if this duplication of effort were avoided and, at an early stage in the research, all resources were concentrated upon one approach to the problem?

Structure—organization. The key issues of military organization involve command and control, on the one hand, and mission and purpose, on the other. Both issues come together in the problem of "unification," or centralization, versus decentralization, a problem which continually troubled the major powers after World War II. In most countries the tendency was toward more and more centralized direction and control over the military forces. In the United States and Great Britain the previously separate services were brought within the framework of a single cabinet-level department. At the same time, in the United States in particular, the services were increasingly relegated to supporting rather than to combat roles. The principal combat units of the military establishment came to consist of the functional commands, which typically include forces from two or more services. These commands, such as the North American Air Defense Command, the European Command, the Strike Command, and the Strategic

Air Command, more directly reflected the missions and purposes of the military establishment than did the services organized simply in terms of the element in which they operated (land, sea, air, or sea–land). The civilian leaders of the services thus suffered a decline in prestige and power. The military leaders of the services avoided this decline in some degree through their participation in the central military staff organization (in the United States, the Joint Chiefs of Staff). Recurring in all countries is the issue of having a single military chief of staff or a chiefs of staff committee, and the problem of dividing responsibilities between the central military staff and the service staffs. The relations between the civilian secretary in charge of the military establishment and his civilian associates and subordinates, on the one hand, and the central military staff organization, on the other, raise other major organizational issues.

Structure—the budget. There are two major types of budgetary issues: substantive and procedural. Substantive issues concern the allocation of funds among different programs, weapons, and services. They are thus directly linked to program and force decisions on strategic programs. It is quite possible that decisions on strategic programs may be made only in the context of the budgetary process. In this event, no practical distinction exists between the strategic decision and the structural one. In other instances, however, decisions may be made to develop or to maintain certain types of forces and strategic programs, quite apart from the decisions on how much money should be devoted to those forces. Just as a decision to maintain a certain number of divisions may imply certain manpower decisions, so also it may imply certain budgetary decisions. Neither the manpower nor the budgetary decisions, however, are guaranteed as a result of the force-level decision. Indeed, they may be made by a substantially different group of people at a different time and with significantly different perspectives and priorities.

Procedural issues concern the nature and structure of the budget and the budgetary process. A major change in American military policy under the Kennedy administration was the reorganization of the budget in terms of major purposes or functions (that is, the output categories of the military establishment) rather than simply in terms of organizational categories (the services) or input categories (for example, men, hardware, soft goods). As a result of this change, it became possible to evaluate the costs of the major strategic programs. Since the budget is the one place where

military activities are expressed in a common denominator that makes them comparable to civilian activities, it is also the place where, typically, the civilian leaders of the defense establishment play a major role. Civilian control often is identified with budgetary control.

The making of military policy

In almost all countries the executive branch plays a decisive role in the formulation of military policy. In constitutional democracies, the predominance of the executive is particularly marked with respect to strategy, less so with respect to structure. In the United States, Congress has constitutional authority to determine the size and composition of the armed forces and to declare war. In actuality, however, after World War II, the effective decisions both on strategic programs and on the uses of force have been made by the president acting through and in consultation with the National Security Council, the civilian leadership of the State and Defense departments, the Joint Chiefs of Staff, and, at times, selected congressional leaders. Congressional groups can exert pressure on the executive decision makers, but they are seldom in a position to make decisions on strategy themselves. In effect, like Bagehot's queen, they have "the right to be consulted, the right to encourage, the right to warn." On the structural side of military policy, on the other hand, Congress retains an important role in the decision-making process. Typically, the executive presents its recommendations to Congress on legislation dealing with manpower, personnel, organization, pay, procurement, and reserve forces. Congress and its Armed Services Committees usually amend and at times even reject these executive proposals. With respect to the budget, Congress rarely makes any significant reductions in executive requests for funds. In many cases, Congress appropriates more money than the president requested for such particularly favored programs as the National Guard, bomber and missile procurement, and the Marine Corps. The president, however, can, and on occasion does, refuse to spend these extra funds. In general, Congress tends to be much more sympathetic to the requests of the military services than the top civilian leadership of the executive branch.

In parliamentary democracies, the legislature typically has much less control over military policy than does the United States Congress. Strategic and structural policies are determined by the cabinet in consultation with civil servants and military chiefs and are more or less automatically ratified by the legislature. In Great Britain the principal public debate on military policy occurs in connection with the approval of the defense estimates by Parliament. This is normally preceded by the issuance of a white paper which sets forth the government's over-all defense policies and strategy. At times in Great Britain, the presence of retired military officers in the House of Lords stimulates informed and caustic debates on military policy in that chamber.

Strategic programs and structural issues typically have fairly restricted publics; in some cases almost no groups outside of official government agencies play a significant role in the policy-making process. In the United States public opinion at large has been very favorably disposed toward the maintenance of large military forces; in other constitutional democracies the pattern of opinion is less clear, and the perception of serious conflicts between increased military spending and increased spending for social welfare programs often produces a more hostile attitude toward the former. In contrast to strategic programs, decisions on the use of force have obvious implications for the entire society. Consequently, in constitutional democracies public opinion has a much greater influence on such issues. In particular, efforts to initiate the use of force or to carry on the prolonged use of force for limited objectives overseas may arouse substantial opposition among broad groups in the population. This was true in France with respect to the Indochinese and Algerian wars, in Great Britain over Suez, and in the United States with respect to the Korean and Vietnamese conflicts. In such situations, a government may be caught between the realities of foreign politics and the pressures of domestic politics and thus be severely restricted in its ability to carry out a consistent policy.

In totalitarian states military policy is typically a major and continuing preoccupation of the top political leadership. In Nazi Germany the principal strategic decisions were made by Hitler and his immediate associates, frequently against the advice of, and over the opposition of, the principal professional military chiefs. In communist states the top leaders of the party shape military policy; often they have had considerable experience themselves in the conduct of military operations. In all totalitarian states ideological considerations are a major influence on military policy; these frequently run counter to the judgments of the professional military; and consequently the tension between "political" and "military" approaches is frequently more intense than it is in constitutional states. Ideologically oriented political leaders are often ready to pursue more expansionist or "adventurist" military policies than their more conservative professional military men are willing to support. Totalitarian political leaders also typically have more varied and more forceful means of asserting their authority over their military forces than do the political leaders of constitutional states.

In both modern constitutional states and in totalitarian states the dominant consideration in military policy is typically the need of the state in relation to other states. However, in many societies in Asia, Africa, and Latin America, domestic considerations and needs have a much more important influence on strategy and structure. Often the military forces play a key role in domestic politics; the size of the armed forces reflects their domestic political strength more than their external military function. Indeed, in many such states the armies, although large in terms of the governmental budget, seldom, if ever, engage in external warfare. Another important influence on military policy in these states comes from the more-developed countries which furnish military assistance and advice. In many cases these influences and the desire to appear "advanced" may lead a small and backward state to adopt a military policy more appropriate for a large and industrialized power. External support for the military forces of a state, of course, also tends to make those forces less dependent upon the political system of their own country and thus may well encourage tendencies toward "praetorianism."

SAMUEL P. HUNTINGTON

[*See also* CIVIL–MILITARY RELATIONS; FOREIGN POLICY; MILITARISM; MILITARY; NATIONAL SECURITY; PUBLIC POLICY; STRATEGY. *Other relevant material may be found under* INTERNATIONAL RELATIONS; WAR.]

BIBLIOGRAPHY

BERNARDO, C. JOSEPH; and BACON, EUGENE H. 1955 *American Military Policy: Its Development Since 1775.* Harrisburg, Pa.: Military Service Publishing Co.

BULL, HEDLEY (1961) 1965 *The Control of the Arms Race: Disarmament and Arms Control in the Missile Age.* 2d ed. New York: Praeger.

GARTHOFF, RAYMOND L. (1958) 1962 *Soviet Strategy in the Nuclear Age.* Rev. ed. New York: Praeger.

HALPERIN, MORTON H. 1963 *Limited War in the Nuclear Age.* New York: Wiley.

HAMMOND, PAUL Y. 1961 *Organizing for Defense: The American Military Establishment in the Twentieth Century.* Princeton Univ. Press.

HITCH, CHARLES J.; and MCKEAN, R. N. (1960) 1961 *The Economics of Defense in the Nuclear Age.* Cambridge, Mass.: Harvard Univ. Press.

HUNTINGTON, SAMUEL P. 1954 Radicalism and Conservatism in National Defense Policy. *Journal of International Affairs* 7:206–222.

HUNTINGTON, SAMUEL P. 1961a *The Common Defense: Strategic Programs in National Politics.* New York: Columbia Univ. Press. → A paperback edition was published in 1966.

HUNTINGTON, SAMUEL P. 1961b Equilibrium and Disequilibrium in American Military Policy. *Political Science Quarterly* 76:481–502.

KAHN, HERMAN (1960) 1961 *On Thermonuclear War.* 2d ed. Princeton Univ. Press.

KISSINGER, HENRY A. 1957 *Nuclear Weapons and Foreign Policy.* New York: Harper.

LEVINE, ROBERT A. 1963 *The Arms Debate.* Cambridge, Mass.: Harvard Univ. Press.

MILLIS, WALTER 1956 *Arms and Men: A Study in American Military History.* New York: Putnam. → A paperback edition was published in 1958 by New American Library.

MILLIS, WALTER; MANSFIELD, HARVEY C.; and STEIN, HAROLD 1958 *Arms and the State: Civil–Military Elements in National Policy.* New York: Twentieth Century Fund.

RIES, JOHN C. 1964 *The Management of Defense: Organization and Control of the U.S. Armed Services.* Baltimore: Johns Hopkins Press.

SCHELLING, THOMAS C.; and HALPERIN, MORTON H. 1961 *Strategy and Arms Control.* New York: Twentieth Century Fund.

SCHILLING, WARNER R.; HAMMOND, P. Y.; and SNYDER, G. H. 1962 *Strategy, Politics and Defense Budgets.* New York: Columbia Univ. Press.

STEIN, HAROLD (editor) 1963 *American Civil–Military Decisions: A Book of Case Studies.* University: Univ. of Alabama Press.

STERN, FREDERICK M. 1957 *The Citizen Army: Key to Defense in the Atomic Age.* New York: St. Martins.

U.S. LIBRARY OF CONGRESS, LEGISLATIVE REFERENCE SERVICE 1957 *United States Defense Policies Since World War II.* 85th Congress, 1st Session, House Document 100. Washington: Government Printing Office.

U.S. LIBRARY OF CONGRESS, LEGISLATIVE REFERENCE SERVICE 1958— *United States Defense Policies, 1945–1956.* Washington: Government Printing Office. → Kept up-to-date by annual supplements.

WOLFE, THOMAS W. 1964 *Soviet Strategy at the Crossroads.* Cambridge, Mass.: Harvard Univ. Press.

MILITARY POWER POTENTIAL

Military power potential consists in the resources that a nation-state can mobilize against other nation-states for purposes of military deterrence, defense, and war. This definition—which makes the term approximately synonymous with "defense potential" but renders it broader than the term "war potential"—follows a narrow definition of national power.

More broadly conceived, national power in interstate relations is the ability of nation-states to produce desired effects in the behavior of other nation-states. However, a wide variety of conditions and means, noncoercive as well as coercive, may be available to a nation-state to produce such effects. Indeed, since nation A may behave in certain ways toward nation B because it "respects" or "admires" nation B, such respect or admiration may be said to be part of B's power, broadly defined, over A. This inclusive perspective is useful, since it keeps us from neglecting or ignoring various factors affecting the behavior of nation-states toward others. However, as we know from the study of interpersonal relationships, a particular kind of behavior may result from different conditions or combinations of conditions and, for analytical, predictive, and manipulative purposes, we may be interested in distinguishing among particular conditions and their effects. One such condition, of prime importance in interstate relations, is power more narrowly defined as military power. This is in fact the most widely accepted definition of power in interstate relations. It is defined as the ability to affect the behavior of other nation-states through the actual or threatened exertion of force. As used in this article, then, national power is the ability to coerce other nations, and coercion refers to physical constraint rather than to such other means of pressure as economic reprisal.

National military power is, of course, relative. It pertains to a relationship between states, the military power of state A being great or small in relation to the military power of state B or of several other states. The importance of military power in shaping the behavior of nation-states toward one another is also relative to the importance of other means of generating desired results. Thus, the importance of national military power will vary between state actors and, over time, within the entire international system of action. The main conditions immediately accounting for this variability are: (1) the pattern of distribution of military power in the international system; (2) the values at stake in international conflicts; (3) the "costs"—in terms of such values as economic resources, personal self-direction, moral standards, and reputation—of producing and employing military power; and (4) the comparative availability and effectiveness of other means for resolving international conflict, and the "costs" of using these alternative means.

In studying the exertion and counterexertion of power, one approach is to concentrate on the results or on the means accounting for, or capable of accounting for, particular results. When we concentrate on the results, and perhaps equate power with particular effects, we are concerned with far more complex relationships than when we compare the particular power instruments available to different nation-states. Thus, state A may have twice as much military power to exert against states B or C than either can exert against A. Faced with the same threat and demand from A, B may give in and C may fight; and faced with the same threat, B may give in to one demand, but fight when confronted with a different demand. Conversely, A may use its military power against B or C in support of some demands but not in support of others. Such problems involve choices of action determined by the various advantages and disadvantages attached by state actors to the exertion or counterexertion of power.

In the following we are concerned not with the whole range and scope of power but with the availability of one particular instrument of power, namely, military power. Military power, however, may produce desired results without being exerted. State A may act in certain ways because it does not wish to risk the use of B's military power against itself. It is this silent effectiveness of national power that appears to be pervasive, even though it is hard to trace in terms of cause and effect and hence is easily ignored. In the real world, a nation's military power may be conditioned by its relations with friendly or allied states from which it may receive supplies, training for personnel, technological assistance, and financial aid, as well as military support in time of war. For the sake of simplicity, these international (and possibly supranational) phenomena will be disregarded in this discussion. We will assume that national power is self-generated.

If national military power is the ability of one nation to coerce other nations through the employment of military means, or to resist such coercion by other states, then this power may be said to have, at any one time, two components: first, mobilized military capabilities ready for immediate operational commitment; and, second, additional power potential, which is a nation's ability to produce further military capabilities. To be employed militarily, power potential must first be mobilized—that is, transformed into, or used in, the production of operational military force, although the very act of initiating the mobilization of potential is a demonstration of a nation's intentions and may of itself act as a coercive threat or counterthreat. The process of mobilizing military potential takes time, and the resources involved will add to operational military capability only to the extent that there actually is opportunity for their mobilization. Manpower and industrial re-

sources may obviously contribute to a nation's military potential, and most writers have in fact focused entirely or largely on economic potential when using the concept of war potential. In modern nations, however, a vast range of national resources is adaptable to the generation of military forces and it is, furthermore, possible to indicate certain administrative resources and political conditions that affect the magnitude of a nation's military potential and the speed with which it can be mobilized.

Since most authors refer to "war potential" rather than to "military power potential," they are usually concerned only with the part of a nation's power potential that has not yet been mobilized in the production of military forces and is still available for mobilization in pursuit of an arms race or in the event of war. However, in the nuclear age, as we shall see, the concept of power, or military, potential is of greater interest than that of war potential. Military power potential is the total ability of a nation to produce military power. Part of it is mobilized at any one time; part of it is unmobilized.

History of the concept

The concept of "war potential" did not gain appreciable currency until after World War II. However, thinking about the reality encompassed by the concept has been familiar in the literature of western Europe ever since the beginning of the mercantilist school. The mercantilist writers (for example, Charles Davenant, Josiah Tucker, and Jean Baptiste Colbert) were profoundly preoccupied with studying the bases—particularly the financial, commercial, industrial, and population resources—on which rested a nation's ability to prepare for war and to conduct it (Heckscher 1931). Mercantilist discussions of the "sinews of war" dealt with military power potential in the light of mercantilist perspectives. Despite the repudiation of mercantilist notions by the classical economists, there was a line of noted writers—for example, Adam Smith, Alexander Hamilton, Friedrich List, Friedrich Engels—who transmitted this preoccupation from the eighteenth to the twentieth century.

It is not surprising that the mercantilists were the first thinkers who undertook, although with inadequate analytical tools, the systematic study of military potential. They were themselves products of two momentous and interconnected events in the history of mankind—the emergence of the nation-state, which monopolized the organization of military power, and the beginnings of the industrial revolution, which was to have enormous effects on the nature and bases of military power.

The quickening evolution of pure modern science, the flourishing of applied science and technological innovation, and the rapid economic growth associated with the agricultural and, especially, the industrial revolution had even more revolutionary effects on the generation, form, and distribution of military power. These effects did not exhaust themselves in the forging of new weapons, such as constantly improved firearms; or even in such new devices as the steam engine and electrical apparatus, which were adapted to direct military use, lent themselves readily to the production of armaments, and vastly increased the mobility of heavily equipped military forces. More basic was the swift increase in the productivity of labor. In the preindustrial age, when communities were basically agrarian and farmers were unable, on the average, to produce much more than they consumed, the portion of resources available for military purposes as well as for other nonfarm activities was severely limited. Large military forces could be supported only temporarily, usually at the expense of plunder, capital depletion, and malnutrition or starvation. The Roman Empire began to decline when it attempted to place too heavy a burden of nonagricultural activities, including military ones, on a peasantry that, compared with today's, was poor in productive resources. What happened in modern times, and especially after 1800, was that farmers became able to feed an increasing number of nonfarm families, which were thus released to commerce, industry, government, and the military. Pigou ([1921] 1941, pp. 42–43) calculated that, by the beginning of the twentieth century, industrial nations were able to divert about one-half of their productive capacity to the conduct of war by means of augmented production, reduced personal consumption, reduced investment in new capital, and depletion of existing capital. Their ability to prepare for war had increased similarly.

The first push of modernization began in small local areas. It gave western Europe an enormous advantage in military capability, enabling that comparatively small region not only to inflict huge damage on itself in internecine warfare but also to conquer vast colonial empires overseas. The process of modernization was weak and halting at first, gathered rapid momentum during the second half of the nineteenth century, and—although still unevenly distributed over the globe—reached a stupendous acceleration after World War II.

The monopoly of coercion at the level of the modern nation-state brought about the "nationalization" of war. Advancing science, technology, and economic production resulted in what may be called the 'industrialization" of war. As war became nationalized and progressively industrialized, the concept of war, and warfare itself, tended to become "total." Although preindustrial and indeed preagrarian societies have been known to conduct wars of extermination, total war was widely recognized as a new development only after World War I. Thus, Oualid (Inter-parliamentary Union 1931, pp. 120–121) stated that modern war "implies the utilization of all the forces of the national collectivity: human, material, economic and moral." And General Douhet ([1921] 1942, p. 5) observed that "the prevailing forms of social organization" had given modern warfare "a character of national totality—that is, the entire population and all the resources of a nation are sucked into the maw of war." During World War I, the tendency for war to become "total" had expressed itself chiefly in the extension of the naval blockade to shipments of food and nearly all other civilian goods; in World War II, it led to the massive area-bombing of industries and cities, causing huge losses of civilian lives and assets. Making war "total" meant directing hostilities not only against the opponent's armed forces but also against his entire military potential.

Relevance in the nuclear age

Between World War I and World War II, military power potential was usually discussed in terms of "war potential"—that is, the ability of nations to mobilize resources *after* war had broken out. It was normal for nations to maintain military establishments in peacetime far smaller than those they could establish in time of war. Following the outbreak of hostilities, and in fact during the diplomatic crisis preceding it, there was usually time to mobilize potential power. Germany, for instance, in 1939 produced only 20 per cent of the volume of combat munitions that she produced in 1944 (Knorr 1956, p. 59); similarly, it took several years for the military production of the United States to reach a peak in World War II.

World War I and World War II were classical wars of attrition, won by the coalitions that possessed superior potential in manpower and economic resources. This outcome does not, of course, prove that war potential was decisive; the outcome of war is determined by other factors as well, such as the quality of generalship, strategic surprise, morale, and geography. One may surmise, however, that war potential became more important, in relation to other determinants, as warfare became industrialized and that very large asymmetries in these other conditions were then required to overcome a substantial difference in war potential, especially modern, industrial war potential. It is therefore not surprising that, in World War II, military fortunes turned with the balance of combat supplies (Knorr 1956, pp. 33–34).

The emergence of nuclear bombs, and of aircraft and rockets of high speed and vast range, has caused many analysts to regard the concept of war potential as obsolete. The new arms technology means that military destruction on an unprecedented and previously unimaginable scale could be visited on the interior of any country within days or even hours of the outbreak of war. A few penetrating weapons alone could wreak enormous damage, and there are no known or foreseeable defenses capable of preventing this. The only sure method of preventing a nuclear weapon from penetrating is to destroy it, by means of a first or preemptive strike, before it has taken off from its base. If *all-out* war occurred under these conditions, the decisive blows, it is assumed, would be struck within a matter of days. The preatomic age saw many cases in which an antagonist lacked sufficient time for mobilizing potential because he was quickly overrun by his opponent. Large-scale nuclear war, however, would permit no time at all to mobilize "war potential," and the constituents of this potential would be mostly destroyed or disorganized in the first waves of attack. The main object of defense in this situation is to deter attack by threatening retaliation; to do this requires forces fully mobilized before the outbreak of hostilities.

As long as these conditions of military technology prevail, "war potential," as distinct from "power potential," will be of less significance, although it remains important in the power relations of nonnuclear nations and in protracted nonnuclear disputes involving nuclear powers. (The Korean War required the United States to mobilize some margin of its war potential; and, in the early 1950s, the United States increased its capability for waging limited nonnuclear war.) However, the concept of military, as distinct from war, potential suffers no loss of significance whatever, since it refers to the capacity of nations to produce military power—nuclear and nonnuclear—whether in peace or war. The relative military power that nations are able to muster for deterrence and defense and their capacities for innovating in, and exploiting, a highly dynamic technology and for entering and sustaining arms races are basically matters of military potential.

Components of power potential

Nations have few, if any, properties—geographic, demographic, economic, political, social, or cultural—that do not directly or indirectly affect their ability to produce military forces. These factors are too numerous to permit detailed enumeration and too heterogeneous and interdependent to encourage exhaustive and meaningful classification. Analysts of power potential have therefore focused on what seem to them to be the important determinants and have described these in terms of broad categories, such as population and industrial resources, that have intricate structures and are capable of further differentiation and comparison.

The military sector may be regarded as a subsystem of the national society, receiving manpower, services, and other resources as inputs and producing from them the outputs—trained personnel, equipment, supplies, organization, doctrine, strategy, and deployment—that constitute the nation's military power.

Since virtually all nation-states maintain military establishments at all times, a varying portion of their total power potential is mobilized at any one time; and, in the case of the major nuclear powers at least, this portion has risen compared with previous peacetime periods. Clearly, the unmobilized portion, as well as the total, of a nation's ability to generate military power is subject to change.

It is possible to distinguish three major determinants of military power potential: *economic capacity* (in the past usually called "economic war potential"), *military motivation*, and *administrative competence*. The quantity and quality of the nation's manpower and other resources that are suitable as inputs for the military sector represent its economic military potential. The portion of this potential which, in time of peace or war, a nation is prepared to divert to the military sector depends upon military motivation. The efficiency with which the inputs are transformed into outputs depends on the nation's administrative military potential.

Economic capacity. Production for both civilian and military use depends upon the quantity, composition, and quality of available factors of production. These are the nation's labor force; land and other natural resources; material capital in such forms as farms, factories, railroads, and inventories; monetary capital in the form of net claims on foreigners; and organizations in which factors are combined for economic production. How large a volume of goods and services a nation produces depends, additionally, on the rate of factor employment (some resources may be idle voluntarily or involuntarily) and on resource productivity (that is, the productivity of labor, land, capital, and management). Productivity has a bearing on military potential, since the larger the volume of output per capita, the more resources can be diverted, if the community so chooses, to the military sector without causing intolerable hardship to the civilian sector.

A nation's resources, including its economic defense potential, tend to grow with the numbers in the labor force, additions to real capital, technological innovation, and improvements in productive human skills. Increases of the real gross national product (GNP), in the aggregate and per capita, are a rough index of such changes, although the benefits of rising labor productivity may be claimed, at least in part, in the form of increments to leisure rather than to goods and services. A country with a rapidly expanding national product, in the aggregate and per capita, tends to have an increasing economic potential for military purposes.

However, the magnitude of this economic potential is also conditioned by the composition and quality of resources. In time of peace, and especially in time of crisis and war, the value of potential is derived largely from the speed with which it can be mobilized. Therefore, whatever the size of the national product, the closer resources are to the forms required by the military sector, and the more flexible the economic system is in permitting a rapid shift of productive factors from civilian to military production, the larger a nation's economic defense potential will be. For instance, the larger the proportion of males in the age bracket preferred for military service and the greater the proportion of such males with previous military training, the more the labor force contributes to military potential. Similarly, the closer the products for the civilian sector are to the many products required by the military sector, the greater the nation's potential for military production. Output of energy in various forms and means of transportation are of course basic in the modern industrial age. Modern arms technology has made the military sector a voracious consumer of extremely complicated instruments and hence has put a high premium on such industries as electronics and on sophisticated metallurgical, chemical, and engineering production. Basic energy sources apart, a rich local base of raw materials has, on the other hand, become relatively less important, partly because modern technology has a startling capacity for creating new materials and for substituting one material or even one end product for another. Moreover, in view of the emphasis on military preparedness in peacetime and the improbability of large-scale and prolonged wars of attrition, productive nations can import many of the materials with which they are not endowed. With the acceleration of technological advance, notably in military technology, the most precious resource, especially among the leading military powers, is the capacity for endless scientific discovery and technological innovation and hence the number, skill, and genius of a nation's scientists and engineers.

As suggested, military potential depends not only on how close a nation's composition of total output is to the mixture required by the military sector but also on the rapidity with which output composition can be changed. This flexibility rests in large part on the mobility and versatility of labor and of other factors of production. It may be observed further that, assuming any given composition of national production, this mobility varies with the growth of the real GNP and with the stage of economic development. Rapid economic growth indicates a high rate of investment and of innovation, including product changes. It occurs in a society capable of initiating and absorbing frequent change. The stage of economic development is significant because the more advanced an economy, the richer it is in the kinds of skills and the variety of productive facilities that are conducive to rapid and continuous changes in output.

The quantity and quality of military potential are, of course, relative to the varying military needs and ambitions of the country. Relatively few countries have the potential resources for developing, on their own account, sophisticated nuclear weapons and vehicles for their delivery. Indeed, some of these nations do not intend to become nuclear powers and hence have no military use for nuclear energy production. Although these countries may possess a substantial potential for producing "conventional," that is, nonnuclear military forces, no single country can rival the United States and the Soviet Union in military power and military potential. One might, in fact, conjecture that there is now a greater diversity in the magnitude and quality of military economic potential than prevailed in the past. Differences in sheer size of population and territory have always existed, and so have differences in the state of the arts applicable to military activities. But one suspects that the qualitative differences between, for example, Afghanistan and the Soviet Union or between Haiti and the United States, are greater than formerly existed between comparable pairs of countries. These differences probably reflect, on the one hand, crucial differences in economic and technological development. On the other hand, they may also reflect a new implication of differences in the size of national outputs—namely, that certain very sophisticated lines of production (such as nuclear energy or nuclear weapons) demand a scale of effort that only large and highly developed countries can afford.

Military motivation. A nation may possess a large economic potential for military activities but refrain from mobilizing it for this purpose. Large economic potential for military power does not necessarily equal large military power. Power potential, therefore, depends on what may be called military motivation—that is, upon the will among members of society to supply men and other resources to the military subsystem. The production and employment of military power are organized, collective actions. Power potential is action potential, and action results from motivation. Since the production and use of military power are organized by government, it is through the political process that a society's military motivation is aggregated. However, that motivation expresses itself not only in determining the stream of men and resources made available to the military sector; it also conditions those other aspects of personal behavior that are relevant to the output of power and are often referred to as "morale." Broadly speaking, the military potential of a society depends upon the capacity of its members to forgo the satisfaction of wants and preferences—whether they are concerned with safety, income, consumption, status, leisure, respect, self-direction, or other values—that compete with the demands of the military subsystem (Knorr 1956, p. 67). This does not mean that the individual or group pursuit of such values necessarily conflicts with the production and use of national military power, for some individuals may gain in status, respect, income, and so forth from serving the military sector. Zero war potential would obtain if all the members of a nation were intensely dedicated to goals and preferences that, in every way, prevented military power from being produced or used and that they were completely unwilling to neglect even temporarily.

Military motivation is a concept beset with difficulties. Its systematic examination awaits further progress in relevant social science research. There is the additional difficulty that the willingness of a society to undertake a military effort obviously depends on the nature of international conflicts and of available choices for resolving them, and

on the way in which these conflicts and choices are perceived. However, societies also have a certain underlying disposition or readiness to accept military postures and actions, and the personal sacrifices they demand. Historians frequently refer to societies as "warlike" or "peaceful," and political leaders often speak of certain nations as highly likely or unlikely to fight—images obviously based on the record of past national behavior. We are concerned here with particular patterns of values, or cultural standards, that affect a society's attitudes toward international violence and national preparation for it. Since these standards are more or less internalized during the process of socialization—although they are no doubt susceptible to the impact of adult experience and learning—it is assumed that a society's underlying mode of readiness to react to military threats or opportunities usually undergoes only gradual change. This subject likewise stands in need of further conceptual and empirical research before important questions can find more than an intuitive answer. Thus, the dichotomy between "warlike" and "peaceful" is obviously far too simple. A "peaceful" nation may be basically and abidingly averse to the use of military power, or, although strongly preferring the peaceful resolution of international conflicts, it may reveal a high military motivation once it feels sufficiently provoked. In the latter case, a high threshold of provocation must be crossed before that society's underlying willingness to authorize military action is released—in other words, before its military motivation potential is mobilized.

The literature also lacks plausible hypotheses on the relation between military motivation potential and different political and social systems and, therefore, on whether the military motivation of nations tends to vary with forms of government. Two observations may be made. First, the willingness of a society to forgo the satisfaction of civilian wants and preferences competing with the demands of the military sector differs among groups that may also differ in formal and informal political influence. Second, whatever the structure of politics, political influence between government and governed is reciprocal, although the balance of influence may vary greatly from system to system. An authoritarian or totalitarian government (or elite) that is itself endowed with a strong military motivation and exerts a powerful influence on the relevant motivation of the rest of the population will tend to lend a high military motivation potential to the country involved and presumably will find it easy to mobilize this potential. In contrast, a democratic government that reflects or confronts a basically low military motivation in the electorate can do little to increase, and perhaps even to mobilize, the military potential of the nation. However, the historical record contains many democratic nations with a high potential and many authoritarian countries with a low one. The possible patterns are many and complex and do not encourage generalizations on the comparative power potential of nations with different forms of government. From this point of view, the military motivation potential of societies is an empirical question, which can be answered on the basis of empirical research.

Administrative competence. Whatever the military economic potential of a society and whatever its military motivation potential, its output of military power may be relatively large or small depending on the efficiency with which the military subsystem employs the resources supplied to it. The military sector uses inputs in the form of manpower, funds, industrial capacity, research physicists, in order to produce various military forces and supplies, military doctrine and strategy, and all the elements that, in the aggregate, constitute the nation's power.

In the modern age, the different production tasks are extraordinarily numerous and complex, involving difficult choices to be made in the face of various uncertainties. Moreover, the production processes are complicated and lengthy, requiring highly coordinated action and involving a great deal of time, often many years, for their completion. The efficiency problem is encountered on many levels. The industrial enterprises used for manufacturing military hardware may be more or less efficient in their employment of scarce resources; so may be the military services that must transform recruits into competent soldiers and officers; so is the planning and implementation of military research and development (which loom ever larger in the military power equation of modern nations); and so are the crucial choices of present and future weapons systems and strategies, intricately phased out and in over time as technology and strategic requirements change.

Efficiency is a matter not only of choosing the right military end products and components, and of producing them at the least cost in economic and bureaucratic resources, but also of the speed with which decisions are made and implemented. Until a few decades ago, military technology—and with it strategy and doctrine—changed only slowly. By the 1960s the pace of change had become explosive and the administration of the military sector far less able to rely on lessons from past experi-

ence. Since major weapon systems take years to develop and produce, a time lag of even one year may have an important bearing on national military power.

Administrative military potential resides essentially in the efficiency of several bureaucracies, especially in business, in the armed services, in special research organizations, and in various government departments. In these structures, competence depends on the conceptual realism with which tasks are understood, the intelligence and training of the directing and staff personnel, the efficiency with which information is procured and used, the efficiency with which many necessarily decentralized operations are coordinated, the quality of the analytical techniques and instruments employed for identifying and evaluating choices in problem solving, and all the other conditions that make for good and prompt decisions and their efficient and prompt execution.

Power potential in a changing world

As long as there is military power, power potential will, of necessity, remain important. However, the implications of power potential and, still more, the nature and relative weights of its constituents are notably sensitive to changes in the international system and to changes in technology and economic productivity. Industrialization and the accelerating progress of arms technology have had a revolutionary impact on the nature of national military power and power potential. As economic development and scientific and technological progress continue, the demands of the military sector on societies will tend to undergo further revision, and power potential will rise or fall depending on the society's ability to meet these changing demands for particular inputs of resources.

The future may also bring more or less radical changes in the properties of the international system and its parts. Thus, the consolidation of nation-states into larger units may have far-reaching effects on military power relationships, including comparative power potentials. Similarly, the establishment of various kinds of arms control and disarmament could affect the significance of power potential. It is interesting that the concept of war potential figured importantly in the exploration of disarmament during the 1920s and early 1930s (Inter-parliamentary Union 1931, chapters 3–5), because war potential was expected to become a more decisive factor in the international power balance as states limited their mobilized forces. Similarly, the military potential of nations would change in the future if nuclear weapons were abolished or drastically reduced in number. If general and complete disarmament occurred, and the disarmed world turned out to be highly unstable politically, rearmament or its threat might become a major political factor, and military potential would remain a major element in international relations.

The study of power potential

The importance of military potential in interstate power relations and in the calculations of statesmen stands in odd contrast to the paucity of rigorous social science literature on the subject. There are good reasons for this contrast. Although the basic concept of power potential is clear enough, it refers to a reality so complex and embracing so much of the political, social, economic, and cultural life of nations that it resists detailed definition and, on the whole and in many particulars, defies measurement. Who can measure the military motivation potential of a society, or its military administrative competence, or even its military economic potential? The first two are customarily regarded as "imponderables," and the important qualitative aspects of the last are not measured by the GNP or similar indices. Resistance to quantification is of course a common property of many social phenomena. It is lowest in the demographic and economic areas, where a great many data, although of greatly varying quality, are readily available. The structure of populations and labor forces can be roughly compared, and so can the capacity of many industries. It is nevertheless impossible, at least as yet, to compute comparable aggregate values for the economic war potential of nations.

Comparing military motivation potentials is much more problematical. Comparative defense budgets, terms of military service, and similar data are indicators of some interest. But it is patently difficult to infer motivation from behavior, and all we may be able to appraise in these instances is current rather than potential motivation. To estimate administrative military potential is yet more difficult, for to evaluate the outputs of the military sector, short of war, is even harder than to evaluate the inputs it receives.

But in this context, as in many others, "difficult" questions are not necessarily hopeless operations. Ingenious effort may yield worthwhile, although imperfect, results. The fact is that statesmen, government officials, and military men are continuously engaged in comparing the military power, including the power potential, of nations. If they did not do so, they would be unable to perform their tasks. Their comparisons may be extremely crude and largely represent intuitive judgment. Sound intuition, however, is anchored in observation, however haphazard, fragmentary, or impressionistic. Surely, whatever is done haphazardly and impressionistically can, in principle, be done more rigorously, or at least be greatly assisted, by means of empirical analysis and the formation and testing of hypotheses. The fact that this effort is lacking does not argue its impracticability. It is probable that the social sciences, especially as they progress further in analytical capability, could achieve a great deal more in this neglected area of application.

KLAUS KNORR

[See also ECONOMIC WARFARE; INTERNATIONAL POLITICS; STRATEGY. Other relevant material may be found in INTERNATIONAL RELATIONS; MILITARY; POWER; WAR.]

BIBLIOGRAPHY

ARON, RAYMOND 1962 Paix et guerre entre les nations. Paris: Calmann-Lévy.

BEATON, LEONARD; and MADDOX, JOHN R. 1962 The Spread of Nuclear Weapons. New York: Praeger.

BENOIT, ÉMILE; and BOULDING, KENNETH E. (editors) 1963 Disarmament and the Economy. New York: Harper.

DOUHET, GIULIO (1921) 1942 The Command of the Air. New York: Coward-McCann. → First published in Italian.

EARLE, EDWARD MEAD (editor) 1943 Makers of Modern Strategy: Military Thought From Machiavelli to Hitler. Princeton Univ. Press.

HECKSCHER, ELI F. (1931) 1955 Mercantilism. 2 vols., rev. ed. New York: Macmillan. → First published in Swedish.

HITCH, CHARLES J. 1941 America's Economic Strength. Oxford Univ. Press.

HITCH, CHARLES J.; and MCKEAN, R. N. 1960 The Economics of Defense in the Nuclear Age. Cambridge, Mass.: Harvard Univ. Press.

HUNTINGTON, SAMUEL P. (editor) 1962 Changing Patterns of Military Politics. New York: Free Press.

INTER-PARLIAMENTARY UNION 1931 What Would Be the Character of a New War? London: King. → A collection of essays.

KNORR, KLAUS 1956 The War Potential of Nations. Princeton Univ. Press.

KNORR, KLAUS 1957 The Concept of Economic Potential for War. World Politics 10:49–62.

KNORR, KLAUS 1966 On the Uses of Military Power in the Nuclear Age. Princeton Univ. Press.

PIGOU, ARTHUR C. (1921) 1941 The Political Economy of War. New & rev. ed. New York: Macmillan.

SCHLESINGER, JAMES R. 1960 The Political Economy of National Security: A Study of the Economic Aspects of the Contemporary Power Struggle. New York: Praeger.

SILBERNER, EDMUND 1946 *The Problem of War in Nineteenth Century Economic Thought.* Princeton Univ. Press.

SOKOLOVSKII, VASILII D. (editor) (1962) 1963 *Military Strategy: Soviet Doctrine and Concepts.* Introduction by Raymond L. Garthoff. New York: Praeger. → First published in Russian.

STEINMETZ, S. RUDOLF (1907) 1929 *Soziologie des Krieges.* Leipzig: Barth. → The 1929 publication is an enlarged and revised version of an earlier work published in 1907 under the title *Die Philosophie des Krieges.*

MILITARY PSYCHOLOGY

The application of psychology to military problems began in World War I, was revived in World War II, and has continued since then as a part of military research and development and in certain military staff activities.

It has had a major impact on military personnel procedures and on the design and use of military weapons, vehicles, and other equipment, as well as considerable effect on military training and on life-support activities. It is coming to have an important effect on what is known in the military as psychological or special operations: on all those military activities, that is, in which the knowledge of other customs and cultures is important. Finally, military psychology has been a major influence on psychology itself. During two generations, psychology's leaders served in the military, and a significant fraction of psychologists today are supported financially by the military. Military applications and activities tended, at least until the early 1960s, to associate psychology with the natural sciences and engineering rather than with the social sciences.

An understanding of military psychology may be facilitated by noting the nature of modern military operations and modern military duties. Even in peacetime, military operations are greatly varied. Practically the whole range of nonmilitary activities is represented, particularly if comparisons are in terms of kinds of activities rather than in terms of details. As Janowitz (1960, p. 65) has pointed out, modern military jobs, more often than not, are noncombat jobs. Increasingly they are specialized, technical jobs; in some instances they require knowledge from the very frontiers of science. Even in peacetime, however, the atmosphere is often one of crisis, danger, and stress. Operations are often conducted in environments that are exotic both physically and culturally, and involve complex, expensive, technically advanced, rapidly obsolescing equipment used by men whose terms of enlistment are short. Readiness to fight can be tested, and practice in the use of some weapons can be obtained, only in a simulation of war.

Thus it can readily be seen that the primary limit to the usefulness of psychology in military operations is the limit of psychology's knowledge of human behavior. It can quickly be appreciated, as Geldard (1953) has suggested, that it is difficult to think of an area of psychology which might not prove useful to the military. And Melton's definition of military psychology (1957) must be accepted: military psychology is coextensive with psychology and is defined primarily by the context of application.

The categories of information which are most helpful in understanding the work of military psychologists are the following: (1) the military problems for which solutions are needed; (2) the products or techniques to be developed or applied; (3) the military organization desiring help, i.e., the "client"; (4) the psychological organization offering help; (5) the relevant psychological concepts and theories; (6) the nature of the interdisciplinary team within which psychologists will probably work; (7) the place of the work in the research and development cycle; and (8) the impact on psychology more generally. These points will be considered in turn.

The first four—military problems, psychological products, military organizations with problems, and psychological organizations—can most profitably be considered together and in historical development. Except as specifically stated, the discussion will concern military psychology in the United States, since all types of development have taken place in this country and on a more organized basis than elsewhere.

World War I. As a significant activity, military psychology began in World War I. In several of the warring nations, psychologists used their professional talent to assist the military. The selection and classification of recruits and specialists by means of mental tests and the development of an over-all personnel system were of primary concern.

Robert M. Yerkes, president of the American Psychological Association, led in organizing a number of committees for war service. Most of these served under the auspices of the National Research Council. These committees were concerned with examination of recruits, acoustic problems, education and special training, incapacity, military training, emotional stability, motivation, recreation, special aptitudes, aviation, visual problems, psychological literature, tests for deception, a course in psychology for the Student Army Training Corps, and propaganda. (The most complete bibliographical source covering these and other World War I activities is Ferguson 1962.)

The Army Alpha Test. The outstanding accomplishment of the committees was the creation of the Army Alpha Test, a group-administered mental test given as a part of the medical examination to all recruits. A large number of the nation's leading academic and scientifically oriented psychologists served in the Sanitary Corps, administering Army Alpha. Results had been analyzed for more than 1.7 million men by the war's end.

Although the test was used to eliminate the unfit, to select for special duty, and to balance units in ability, its primary significance for today is its fascinating demonstration of the extent and significance of individual differences. Yerkes (1921) summarized the analyses. Laymen, military men, scientists, and even the psychologists themselves seem to have been greatly stimulated by the dramatic differences shown, by the possibilities of measuring individual differences, and by the potential impact on traditional ways of dealing with large numbers of people. [*See* INTELLIGENCE AND INTELLIGENCE TESTING.]

The Army's personnel system. Simultaneously with the development of the Army Alpha Test, Walter D. Scott, with the assistance of Walter V. Bingham, led a number of industrial psychologists and personnel men in a program which ultimately resulted in a modern personnel system for the United States Army (U.S. War Department 1919; Ferguson 1962). Scott, working independently of the committees described above, first developed a rating scale for selection and promotion of officers. This was enthusiastically received, and its success led to the creation, under Scott and Bingham, of the Committee on the Classification of Personnel in the Office of the Adjutant General. This committee guided the development of a complete personnel system for the army, including the analyses of civilian occupations and military jobs, the trade tests, the questionnaires and record forms, and the tables of organization, without which an army of specialists could not be created and maintained on a large scale. Late in the war, the committee was militarized and became the nucleus of the Personnel Branch of the Army General Staff. After the war, many of the individuals involved became prominent in industrial relations and scientific management. [*See* APTITUDE TESTING *and the biography of* BINGHAM.]

Between the world wars. Military psychology disappeared between the two world wars. At the close of World War I, the Advisory Committee on the Problems of Military Psychology was established in the Division of Anthropology and Psychology of the National Research Council. The division itself had just been created; in large part its existence was due to the success of military psychology. At the initial organization meeting of the division, Yerkes' list of those present showed that 11 of 22 individuals had a military title, and military problems were high on the list of items for which the division was needed. Nevertheless, the military psychology committee met with complete indifference to its task and finally went out of existence after years of inactivity.

World War II—personnel operations. One of the first activities to reappear in U.S. military psychology was the identification of similarities between civilian and military jobs, a function performed for the army in 1940 by the U.S. Employment Service. The army soon established a general personnel research and development program in the Adjutant General's Office. The Bureau of Naval Personnel later followed suit. (The navy's personnel program in World War II is described in U.S. Bureau of Naval Personnel 1947.) The army air forces and the navy established in their medical services special, very large psychological units to screen and classify flying officers, especially pilots. (See U.S. Army Air Forces 1947 for a description of work in this organization.) As in World War I, the academically and scientifically minded psychologists tended to move into mental testing while the industrial psychologists moved into other aspects of the personnel system.

Differing from the procedure in World War I, the military establishment rapidly created its own units. The National Research Council, through its Emergency Committee in Psychology (Dallenbach 1946), guided and assisted these personnel developments and the other developments to be described below. [*See* INDUSTRIAL RELATIONS, *article on* INDUSTRIAL AND BUSINESS PSYCHOLOGY.]

Contract research. In World War II, extensive use was made of contracts with academic and industrial institutions to support civilian research and development for military use. The Office of Scientific Research and Development (Baxter 1946) organized natural scientists and engineers through contracts with its National Defense Research Committee, and biologists and medical men through its Committee on Medical Research. The contractors often included psychologists in their interdisciplinary teams concerned with equipment and operating procedures for such military interests as night operations, underwater sound, communications, and stereoscopic range finding. Free from the organizational restraints which were placed on psychologists within the military establishment, the psychologists under contract contributed from the earliest days of the war not only to selection of special kinds of personnel but also to training and to the design and use of equipment.

Training. Research on the selection of personnel led generally to an interest in training because selection occurred before training, and the success of selection procedures was evaluated in terms of the success of the selected personnel in training for duty. The pattern of work established by Dean Brimhall and J. G. Jenkins in the prewar National Research Council Committee on the Selection and Training of [Civilian] Aircraft Pilots had a very considerable effect on the psychologists in military units, and even more on those of the National Defense Research Committee. Achievement and proficiency tests for use in training were developed and applied, industrial training methods were carried over to the military situation, and training devices were developed and evaluated.

Human engineering. The first step in research and development for selection and training is to analyze the jobs of the personnel concerned. This step draws attention to the impact of equipment design on personnel requirements, to the design of the displays and controls used by men. Closely associated are efforts to design efficient operating procedures. Out of these activities grew the field now known as human engineering.

In 1942 and 1943 the Applied Psychology Panel of the National Defense Research Committee was created to exploit any psychological approach to the military problems created by the advance of science and engineering. (Bray 1948 describes its work.) One of its projects on gunsights, under the direction of William E. Kappauf and Franklin V. Taylor, was absorbed at the war's end into the Naval Research Laboratory, ever since a leader in human engineering. Its other projects helped to establish the pattern for the human engineering research done by the psychology branch of the aero-medical laboratory at Wright Field, established late in the war under Paul M. Fitts.

In England a comparable series of developments occurred. Under the leadership of F. C. Bartlett and Kenneth Craik, and with the support of the Medical Research Council, attention soon turned to operating procedures and equipment design. According to Bartlett (1957), out of this work grew the Unit for Research in Applied Psychology at Cambridge and much of the present-day respect for scientific psychology in Britain.

Life support. British work, particularly that on night vision during the battle of Britain, was brought to the attention of the highest political authorities in the United States and was significant in the growth of physiological psychology in U.S. military medical laboratories. Since the war, this type of research has continued and now is part of the field known as life support. Included in the field today are psychophysiological studies on the effects of special and extreme environments, on sensory problems, on drugs, stress, fatigue, vigilance, and so on. [*See* ATTENTION; FATIGUE; STRESS.]

Attitudes and motivation. World War II provided the occasion for the first major organized program of military social psychology, a program on attitudes and motivation. Within the Information and Education Division of the U.S. Army, many leading psychologists and sociologists applied the recently developed techniques of attitude and opinion study to a host of topics. The range of the army studies may be illustrated by these examples: the reasons for soldiers' failure to use atabrine regularly in the Pacific, preferences for winter clothing, reactions to the military way of life, the probable number of neuropsychiatric casualties in particular units, and the probable cost (which turned out to be correct within a few percentage points) of the GI Bill of Rights.

The example also illustrate that this type of work leads into sensitive areas, that it is likely to be bound to a specific time and place, and that the information gathered is of interest in varying degree to any given military client. Thus the usefulness of the work depends greatly on calling it to the attention of the "right" user, one who is in the right place at the right time and is able and willing to put the information to use. As Stouffer (Social Science Research Council 1949–1950, vol. 1, p. 48) suggests, the army never found a systematic way to use this kind of information.

After World War II. Contrary to the experience after World War I, military psychology continued to be important after World War II. This resulted from the association during the war between psychology and the natural and biological sciences and from the outburst of military research and development following the atomic bomb and other scientific successes, particularly those of the Office of Scientific Research and Development. In consequence, psychological research, development, and application have continued in relation to military personnel operations, training, equipment design and use, and life support. The exception is the field of attitudes and motivation; in this instance basic research has received some continuing support, but development and application nearly died away after the Korean War. In the early 1960s, accelerating rapidly under the Kennedy administration, military social science began to develop again under the stimulus of the need for better communications with other peoples.

The postwar activities have been much influenced by organizational developments in the period, in particular by the rise in importance of the military laboratories, by the appearance of the nonprofit corporation for military research and development, by the organization and function of the Office of Naval Research, and by developments in the Office of the Secretary of Defense. The impact of each of these on military psychology will be considered.

The rise of military laboratories. By comparison with the prewar period, the postwar period has witnessed an enormous increase in the resources available for scientific laboratories and related institutions within the military establishment itself. Psychology has shared in this support. Personnel operations and psychological research and development units, laboratory-like in nature if not always in name, continue in each service. These have been given relatively large funds, facilities, professional positions, technician support, and access to "human guinea pigs." Research and development in military training likewise have found generous support through military laboratories since World War II. Human engineering units have appeared within a wider and wider range of military laboratories concerned with various types of equipment. The funding and the over-all control of these laboratories are normally a part of the more general scientific research and development activities of the services.

Nonprofit contract laboratories. A significant feature of the postwar period has been the creation of nonprofit corporations of a laboratory-like character to conduct military research under contract to some branch of the military establishment. For psychology and the social sciences the most significant of these have been the RAND Corporation and the System Development Corporation, both of Santa Monica, California; the Human Resources Research Office (HumRRO) of George Washington University; and the Special Operations Research Organization (SORO) of American University.

RAND was created by the air force to conduct long-range research and development in any of the sciences. It has provided continuous support for basic social science research for military purposes and has also been influential in the appearance of the system concept in military psychology. The significance of this concept is elaborated in Gagné (1962).

The RAND Corporation and the air force created the System Development Corporation to provide realistic synthetic training and exercise of the air defense system under attack. The System Development Corporation expanded into the world's largest employer of psychologists, using them chiefly in research and development relevant to the use of computers in training and in complex weapon systems. Both RAND and the System Development Corporation are contributing heavily to one of the most active modern fields of research, information processing and decision making in command and control activities.

In the 1960s HumRRO came to be the major psychological organization concerned with research and development in relation to training. Organized by the army, it has established small, laboratory-like activities at a number of army training centers. HumRRO's approach to training is described by Crawford (1962).

SORO is the army's main organization for research and development in the field of human interaction and communication across cultural boundaries. Windle and Vallance (1964) describe the content of its work and the military activities to which it is relevant.

Office of Naval Research. One of the most significant developments of the postwar period was military support of basic research in all scientific fields, including psychology. The U.S. Office of Naval Research (ONR) was the primary arm of the military establishment in this respect. ONR set a pattern which was widely followed in military laboratories and the other services. Darley (1957) describes its character. ONR operated through research contracts with civilian institutions, following the method used by the National Defense Research Committee during the war. ONR acted as the prototype of the National Science Foundation, now the federal government's principal agency for the support of basic research. ONR supported university research, and the research it supported was unrestricted. It accepted research plans from the country's leading scientists, rather than proposing research to them, and has been a major factor in U.S. military support for psychological research in other nations.

In recent years ONR has become somewhat more selective than it was originally in choosing to support those scientists who wish to do research related ultimately to navy interests, but it still imposes no direction or restrictions on those it supports. Within psychology, ONR has emphasized support for psychologists concerned with psychophysiology, psychometrics, learning, engineering psychology, and group behavior. In recent years the modeling of individual behavior and of social processes has become a major interest.

The Air Force Office of Scientific Research, set up in the mid-1950s on the pattern of ONR, has given continuing support to long-range social science research, as well as to psychological research. The army's research program has been more goal-oriented than those of the navy and air force.

Office of the Secretary of Defense. When, in 1947, the army, navy, and air force were brought together under the new Office of the Secretary of Defense, the Research and Development Board was established to review, evaluate, and plan for science and engineering in the military establishment as a whole. It established committees of consultants who served to integrate, or "couple," the military and scientific communities. One such was the Committee on Human Resources. Its panels on human engineering and psychophysiology, on personnel and training, on manpower, and on human relations and morale reflect the range of topics which were covered in military research in the postwar period. A report by Lyle H. Lanier, executive director of the Committee on Human Resources, gives the best available picture of military psychology in 1949.

Although the Research and Development Board was later abolished, there remains a planning and review officer for psychology and the social sciences under the director of defense research and engineering in the Office of the Secretary of Defense. Under the auspices of this officer, a number of consultants recently analyzed needs and opportunities for long-range research in military psychology and social science (see, for instance, Bray 1962). Some of the recommended programs have been activated by the Advanced Research Projects Agency in the Office of the Secretary of Defense.

The Office of the Secretary of Defense is significant not only because it is the prime center of power over all military research and development but also because it is a natural client for social science research oriented to military operations as an element in foreign policy. This office also represents the United States in NATO military psychology activities.

Conclusions. It seems likely that every type of military activity and every type of weapon is receiving some psychological attention. Effort has understandably been concentrated on topics for which traditional military solutions are not available. Short-term enlistments, like rapid mobilization, have led to attention to initial personnel processing

and training. Rapid change and increasing complexity of equipment have led to interest in human engineering. On the other hand, the inadequacy of traditional techniques and the proven superiority of new ones are not enough. Products must be easily used or embedded in an organizational structure.

Melton (1957) develops two related points. First, to change a person's behavior by psychological methods often requires that a commander or instructor change his own behavior. Second, the values of new products of natural science and engineering are readily appreciated, in contrast with the products of psychology. The significance of an increase in speed or power is evident. The advantages of improved maintenance work, which might produce an equivalent change in military effectiveness at less cost, are nevertheless hard to demonstrate.

No doubt, the lack of evident advantage in many products is responsible for the continuation of the practice in military psychology of conducting "demonstration experiments." To the extent—and it is usually considerable, or the demonstration would not be attempted—that the results of these experiments can be forecast, they are a waste of time, money, and talent. In the United States at least, products which conceptually and empirically are already known to be worth their cost must sometimes be demonstrated repeatedly in formal experiments to be accepted as superior to traditional methods.

The need for such demonstration experiments should be reduced as psychology becomes more technological. With improved scientific skill behind its concepts and products, demonstrations will no doubt give way to tests not of validity but of the degree to which the product meets the specifications laid down for it in advance of its development on the basis of sound scientific opinion. However, little progress can be expected in this respect unless the organizational relations of psychology and the other social sciences are also sound: the client organization and its relations to the research organization are significant.

Since the start of World War II, the personnel psychologist and the personnel and medical staffs have enjoyed a continuing and highly integrated relationship. Comparably, human engineering has an exceptionally close relation to its client; the user of human engineering information is the scientist or design engineer who incorporates the psychologist's product into the design of a weapon or other piece of hardware. Thus the routine users are professional people whose backgrounds are appropriate for the evaluation of the psychological contribution. Morgan's *Human Engineering Guide to Equipment Design* (1963) illustrates the extent to which human engineering information is adapted for use by other engineers.

For training the situation is different. In this instance the client is likely to be a professional military man with long experience and with a tradition of successful use of common-sense methods behind him. Probably for this reason, psychological work on training and training devices has not received very stable support in the navy and air force and has been very dependent on demonstration experiments in the army.

Social-psychological contributions appear to be even more affected by the presence or absence of an informed client and by the institutional relationships. The very successful work on attitudes and motivation in World War II expanded in the postwar period to include programs on military government, strategic planning and intelligence, and psychological warfare. By 1953 and 1954, however, this type of work was disappearing within the military establishment, although some relatively basic research studies continued under contract. There was little interest in the military and among natural scientists and engineers in defending this type of study against congressional attacks during a period in which economy in government was stressed.

Since 1960, with the revival of interest in civil defense, limited war, guerrilla war, disarmament, military aid, and nation building, behavioral science research relevant to these topics has also revived (Windle & Vallance 1964). Definite clients for this work now seem to exist in the Defense Department's civil defense and international security activities and the army's Special Forces.

Concepts and theories. From what has been said, it should be clear that the concepts and theories of concern to military psychology are those of psychology in general. As Hill (1955) suggests in his description of the content of military psychology at the end of the Korean War, contributions to theory are sent for publication to the scientific journals and do not appear in military reports.

It may be noted, however, that psychologists and their theories have an influence in the military far beyond that directly involved in the more obvious products. Concepts of individual differences, cultural differences, human error as determined by equipment design, and the need for motivation and reinforcement of learning have effects far beyond particular applications in aptitude tests, in military aid and guerrilla warfare, in aircraft altimeters, or in teaching machines. The very presence of significant numbers of psychologists in the military set-

ting helps to induce the "sleeper effect" by which new concepts come to affect behavior even though the concepts are not explicitly formulated. Perhaps the most important item in this relation is the psychologist's confidence that understanding of human behavior can be improved through the scientific approach.

Interdisciplinary relations. While specialization within psychology and within other disciplines has progressed, so too has the need to establsh interdisciplinary teams to deal comprehensively with problems of applied science. Interestingly, the various specialists within military psychology seem to form stronger alliances with nonpsychologists than with fellow psychologists.

Psychometricians seem to ally themselves with statisticians and not with job analysts. The latter tend to associate more closely with the management specialists than with training psychologists. And the human engineers, despite their current adherence to a doctrine of the importance of the complete system, rather definitely reject efforts to ally them with any but hardware engineers. These tendencies have probably contributed to the fact that no true profession of military psychology has emerged with special textbooks and graduate training of its own. Such unity as there is in military psychology today comes from common training in research methods rather than from training in application.

Place in research and development cycle. The role of the military in supporting basic research and the persistence of the demonstration experiment have been mentioned above. Recently, there has been a growth in the numbers of psychologists contributing to weapon development within defense industry. The growth has been directly spurred by the adoption, originally by the air force, of military specifications that require, first, that all new equipment receive adequate human engineering attention and, second, that the personnel requirements of new equipment and the ways of meeting these requirements be spelled out in detail. It is by no means clear that objective standards exist for the enforcement of these specifications. Enforcement depends heavily on the quality of psychologists available to inspect and test this new equipment.

Impact on psychology. Since World War II, the military establishment has consistently been a major source of funds for psychological research and development. The writer knows of no accurate estimate of the amounts involved, but they have certainly been large by any standard. Although, in the United States at least, the military establishment is becoming proportionately less of an influence in this respect, because of the rise of other government agencies to support research, it is still of the utmost importance to psychology that defense support be wisely administered.

Financial support is one way of suggesting the impact of military psychology on psychology more generally. A related type of estimation is based on a calculation of the number of psychologists involved. In 1957, Melton counted over seven hundred psychologist employees of the Department of Defense and its major nonprofit laboratory contractors. He estimated that some 5 per cent of the members of the American Psychological Association were working directly or indirectly for the department. There is reason to suppose that this figure was conservative.

It is more difficult to evaluate the impact on the quality of the development of psychology than on the quantity. There can be little doubt that military use and support of psychology was for many years a major force in associating psychology with the natural and biological, rather than the social, sciences. Psychology emerged from World War I with a position in the National Research Council. In World War II it was an organized activity in the Office of Scientific Research and Development. It emerged from World War II as part of the Office of Naval Research and the Research and Development Board. Military psychologists today are still primarily organized under technical and engineering activities.

Windle and Vallance (1964) suggest that a major shift within military psychology is now taking place and that social science aspects will be more prominent in the future. Certainly the association of psychology with social science in the higher levels of the military has been a factor in the reorganization of the Division of Anthropology and Psychology of the National Research Council into the Division of Behavioral Sciences. It seems probable, however, that such a development is better interpreted as a reflection of the need to incorporate social scientists into interdisciplinary teams of other scientists than as a simple association of psychology with social science.

Bartlett (1957, p. 49) suggests that military applications have been a major factor in establishing psychology as a science in Great Britain. He says that it took four crises—World War I, World War II, and the aftermaths of those wars—to convince the British that "unaided common sense observation is not by itself a good enough guide" to human behavior and that experiment is needed.

Issues of far-reaching importance may be raised about military psychology. Some psychologists react so strongly to the horrors of war as to wish no

involvement at all of their profession with the military. Many fear bureaucratic control. Others anticipate difficulties from authoritarianism, the sometimes unsatisfactory professional status of civil servants in military laboratories, the necessity to work as part of an organized research team, the subordination of research to application, and restrictions on the range of scientific activity of individual military psychologists.

There is no question that all of these fears are justified. Like most fears, however, little is to be gained by simple withdrawal from the source. Major opportunities are likely to be lost by doing so. Psychologists can help to meet their responsibilities with respect to the horrors of war, for example, by finding a way for their work to contribute to the military desire to take social, political, and ethical criteria into account, along with destructiveness, as components of a cost–effectiveness formula in choosing weapons and methods of war.

The other fears are by no means peculiar to the military. The problems involved have repeatedly been faced and dealt with by psychologists in the military service, just as they have been met in other fields. The problems are not insoluble, and they do not inevitably arise.

CHARLES W. BRAY

[*Directly related are the entries* INTERNATIONAL RELATIONS; MILITARY. *Other relevant material may be found in* CONFLICT; ENGINEERING PSYCHOLOGY; INDUSTRIAL RELATIONS; LEARNING, *article on* ACQUISITION OF SKILL; PSYCHOLOGY, *article on* APPLIED PSYCHOLOGY; SIMULATION; SPACE, OUTER; WAR; *and in the biography of* YERKES.]

BIBLIOGRAPHY

BARTLETT, FREDERIC C. 1957 *Some Recent Developments of Psychology in Great Britain.* Istanbul: Baha Matbaasi.

BAXTER, JAMES P. 1946 *Scientists Against Time.* Boston: Little.

BRAY, CHARLES W. 1948 *Psychology and Military Proficiency: A History of the Applied Psychology Panel of the National Defense Research Committee.* Princeton Univ. Press.

BRAY, CHARLES W. 1962 Toward a Technology of Human Behavior for Defense Use. *American Psychologist* 17:527–541.

CRAWFORD, MEREDITH P. 1962 Research and Development for Specific Training Programs. Pages 309–324 in Robert Gagné (editor), *Psychological Principles in System Development.* New York: Holt.

DALLENBACH, KARL M. 1946 The Emergency Committee in Psychology, National Research Council. *American Journal of Psychology* 59:496–582.

DARLEY, JOHN G. 1957 Psychology and the Office of Naval Research: A Decade of Development. *American Psychologist* 12:305–323.

FERGUSON, LEONARD W. 1962 *The Heritage of Industrial Psychology.* Hartford, Conn.: Finlay.

Gagné, Robert M. (editor) 1962 *Psychological Principles in System Development.* New York: Holt.

Geldard, Frank A. 1953 Military Psychology: Science or Technology? *American Journal of Psychology* 66: 335–348.

Hill, Charles W. 1955 Military Psychology. Pages 437–467 in Abraham A. Roback (editor), *Present-day Psychology.* New York: Philosophical Library.

Janowitz, Morris 1960 *The Professional Soldier: A Social and Political Portrait.* Glencoe, Ill.: Free Press.

Lanier, Lyle H. 1949 The Psychological and Social Sciences in the National Military Establishment. *American Psychologist* 4:127–147.

Melton, Arthur W. 1957 Military Psychology in the United States of America. *American Psychologist* 12: 740–746.

Morgan, Clifford T. et al. (editors) 1963 *Human Engineering Guide to Equipment Design.* New York: McGraw-Hill.

Social Science Research Council 1949–1950 *Studies in Social Psychology in World War II.* Vols. 1–4. Princeton Univ. Press. → Volume 1: *The American Soldier: Adjustment During Army Life,* by S. A. Stouffer et al. Volume 2: *The American Soldier: Combat and Its Aftermath,* by S. A. Stouffer et al. Volume 3: *Experiments on Mass Communication,* by Carl I. Hovland et al. Volume 4: *Measurement and Prediction,* by S. A. Stouffer et al.

U.S. Adjutant-General's Office 1919 *The Personnel System of the United States Army.* 2 vols. Washington: Government Printing Office.

U.S. Army Air Forces 1947 *Aviation Psychology Program: Research Reports.* Volumes 1–19. Washington: Government Printing Office.

U.S. Bureau of Naval Personnel 1947 *Personnel Research and Test Development in the Bureau of Naval Personnel.* Edited by Dewey B. Stuit. Princeton Univ. Press.

Windle, Charles; and Vallance, T. R. 1964 The Future of Military Psychology: Paramilitary Psychology. *American Psychologist* 19:119–129.

Yerkes, Robert M. (editor) 1921 *Psychological Examining in the United States Army.* National Academy of Sciences, Memoirs, Vol. 15. Washington: Government Printing Office.

MILL, JOHN STUART

<table>
<tr><td>i. Political Contributions</td><td>*John C. Rees*</td></tr>
<tr><td>ii. Economic Contributions</td><td>*V. W. Bladen*</td></tr>
</table>

I
POLITICAL CONTRIBUTIONS

John Stuart Mill (1806–1873) was born in London, the eldest son of James Mill, a leading disciple and friend of Jeremy Bentham. In his *Autobiography* (1873) the younger Mill described the remarkable education he received from his father, beginning Greek at the age of three and Latin at eight. At 15, massively instructed in a wide range of subjects, including economics, his-

tory, philosophy, and even some branches of natural science, he first read Bentham and emerged with a unifying conception of things and a sense of purpose in life. In 1823 he followed his father into the service of the East India Company and remained with the company until he retired in 1858.

For some years Mill vigorously promoted the Benthamite cause by speech and pen, but during a period of serious mental depression that started in 1826, he became convinced that there were serious weaknesses in his inherited opinions. At the same time he was subjected to new influences "which enlarged my early narrow creed," among them the ideas of Wordsworth, Coleridge, Carlyle, Goethe, the Saint-Simonians, and Comte. In these crucial years he came to value poetry and art, both for themselves and as a means of cultivating the feelings and character, and he developed a fuller conception of happiness as involving the rich and varied growth of personality. His conception of social and political affairs also underwent a change: he came to appreciate the Saint-Simonian division of history into organic and critical periods; to see that political institutions must be related to the state of society; and to accept the important role an intellectual elite can play in shaping and making coherent the attitudes and beliefs of a society in a stage of transition. It was at this time too that his fears about the growth of mass conformity and its stifling effect on individual freedom took firm root.

In the decade beginning in 1831 Mill published several articles containing clear signs of his changed outlook; notable among them are the series of articles entitled "The Spirit of the Age" (1831), the essay "Civilization" (1836), and his studies of Bentham (1838) and Coleridge (1840a). His judgment on Bentham is especially interesting, manifesting as it does some of the vital differences that were to distinguish Mill from his educators. He praised Bentham's contribution to the philosophy of law and his work for the reform of legal institutions; he greatly admired his methodological principle of breaking up wholes into their parts and abstractions into things; but he rejected a conception of man which, he claimed, has no room for the pursuit of spiritual perfection as an end in itself. Moreover, Bentham's theory of government, he argued, ignores the dangers arising from a despotic public opinion and the importance of establishing checks on the will of the majority. Mill's new attitude toward these two related matters was strongly confirmed by a careful reading of Tocqueville's *Democracy in America,* and he wrote lengthy reviews of the two parts of Tocqueville's work when they appeared (1835; 1840*b*).

Meanwhile, Mill had met Harriet Taylor, the wife of a London businessman, and there soon began what he called "the most valuable friendship of my life." They were married in 1851, two years after Mr. Taylor's death. Mill's extremely high estimate of his wife's abilities and of her contribution to his own writings has generally been regarded with skepticism, although quite recently, through works by Hayek (1951) and Packe (1954), there has been a reaction in her favor. However, it must be emphasized that the claims of Hayek and Packe for Mrs. Mill have been strongly contested.

Mill's first major work, *A System of Logic*, was published in 1843 and ran to several editions, as did the *Principles of Political Economy*, after it appeared in 1848. With these two works Mill's reputation as an outstanding thinker of his day was firmly established. The later editions of the *Political Economy* show a more pronounced sympathy for socialism and for the claims of the working class than Mill's early opinions would have permitted, and it is probably here that Mrs. Mill's influence is most generally allowed, when it is admitted at all. *On Liberty* (1859) came out in the year after Mrs. Mill's death, and Mill insisted that it was a joint product. Mill now spent much of each year in France, where his stepdaughter, Helen Taylor, managed a small house at Avignon, near her mother's grave. His main work on political institutions, *Considerations on Representative Government*, appeared in 1861, and in the same year he wrote for *Fraser's Magazine* a set of essays on moral philosophy (1861*b*) which came out as a book, *Utilitarianism*, in 1863. The most notable of his remaining works are *Auguste Comte and Positivism* (1865) and *The Subjection of Women* (1869). From 1865 to 1868 Mill represented Westminster in Parliament. He died at Avignon in 1873. His *Autobiography*, edited by Helen Taylor, was published later in the same year.

Mill's social and political thought can usefully be approached in terms of four major concerns: (1) the problem of method in the social sciences; (2) his elucidation of the principle of utility; (3) the freedom of the individual; and (4) his theory of representative government. All four are related, and the interdependence among the last three, at least, has long been recognized.

Method in the social sciences. In his *Essay on Government* (1820) James Mill had tried to demonstrate the necessity for representative government by arguing from the postulate that men's actions always conform to what they take to be their interests and that men's interests in turn can be analyzed in terms of pain and pleasure. Accordingly, a representative assembly should have sufficient power to check the rulers, who, like all other men, are concerned only with advancing their own interests, yet who will thus be made accountable to a body whose interests are identical with those of the whole community. This identity of interests between the representative assembly and the community is possible if the franchise is extended. John Stuart Mill and his circle of young utilitarian radicals initially regarded James Mill's essay as a masterpiece; yet when the new influences began streaming in upon the younger Mill, he began to have doubts which were considerably increased by Macaulay's famous attack on James Mill's essay in the *Edinburgh Review* (1829). But he became convinced that the various types of reasoning employed by his father and by Macaulay were both wrong, and he was thus led to his own conclusions about the proper methods of study in social matters, later published in Book 6 of *A System of Logic* (1843).

Mill denied that the actions of rulers can adequately be explained in terms of their interests. Such an explanation leaves out factors like a sense of duty, philanthropy, and the traditional attitudes of a community, as well as group or class sentiment and inherited standards of behavior among rulers themselves. The force of these traditional standards may override the personal interests of the rulers. Moreover, Mill believed, accountability to the governed is not the only way of ensuring an identity of interest between rulers and ruled, since to some extent their interests in fact coincide: it is in the interest of both, for example, that law and order be maintained. Nevertheless, the selfish interests of rulers do play an important, if by no means exclusive, part in shaping their conduct, and constitutional checks are therefore necessary.

Where James Mill and Bentham had gone wrong, according to the younger Mill, was in supposing that social phenomena depend on *one* causal factor or law of human nature, with others producing only trivial effects. In fact, the *several* aspects of human nature contribute to determining social phenomena, and none of these aspects is negligible. Mill believed that a science of society is possible. Its model should be astronomy, even though the science of society would never achieve the kind of precision in its predictive powers that astronomy has. James Mill's error was to adopt the deductive method of geometry; social science must rest on the laws of individual psychology which are discoverable by direct observation and experiment, and unless generalizations about social phenomena can be connected with, and shown to be derived from, these inductive laws, they cannot be regarded as having a scientific basis.

John Stuart Mill set great store by "ethology" (his term for knowledge of the formation of individual, group, and national character), whose laws are derived from those of psychology by deducing what sort of character will be produced, given the laws of mind and a specific set of circumstances. But psychological and ethological laws do not suffice to explain sociological phenomena, since the special circumstances of the society in which a particular phenomenon occurs must be taken into account. The propositions of sociology are therefore only crude, i.e., related to tendencies. The main aim of sociology must be to discover empirical generalizations about social development, generalizations that do not have the status of laws but that nevertheless can be related to the laws of human nature. Mill thought that an appreciation of the enormous importance of the state of intellectual knowledge as an agent of social change and as the chief cause of social progress might contribute to the discovery of such sociological "laws."

Mill's belief in the importance of knowledge explains his concern to ensure the existence of an active intellectual elite in an age of mass pressures. In his view the state of knowledge is the product of a small minority, and progress will give way to "Chinese stationariness" unless society secures to its potential innovators the means for their creative role; and among these means the first requirement is the freedom of the individual. Not that freedom is merely an instrumental value for Mill, but it is fundamental even as such.

Utility.   The principle of utility, as Mill expounded it in *Utilitarianism* (chapter 2), "holds that actions are right in proportion as they tend to promote happiness, wrong as they tend to produce the reverse of happiness." By "happiness" Mill meant pleasure and the absence of pain. "Pleasure and freedom from pain," he argued, "are the only things desirable as ends," and all desirable things are desirable "either for the pleasure inherent in themselves, or as means to the promotion of pleasure and the prevention of pain." On the evidence of this passage alone, Mill appears to be expounding the orthodox Benthamite creed. But it is well known that later in the same chapter he went on to maintain that the quality of pleasure is no less important than its quantity. Indeed, he insisted that the pleasure derived from the higher faculties is more valuable than any other sort and could even be said to have an "intrinsic superiority." Mill's elucidation

of the principle of utility is clearly inspired by, and intelligible only by reference to, an ideal of human development that he had earlier in his life explicitly contrasted with Bentham's narrow and constricting conception of man, with its failure to recognize adequately the role of such powerful factors as a sense of honor and a sense of personal dignity. Without ever retracting his affirmation that happiness is the sole desirable end, he so described its constituent elements that they reflected his own scale of values. Prominent in that scale was the Greek ideal of self-development, individual spontaneity, mental cultivation, and the importance of men "for ever stimulating each other to increased exercise of their higher faculties" (*On Liberty*, chapter iv).

One of Bentham's teachings that Mill never abandoned was that appeals to "the moral sense" or "right reason" merely serve to enthrone sentiment as its own reason and are incapable of providing a real solution to moral problems. Such appeals play the same sort of role in moral argument as reliance on intuition does in knowledge of truths in mathematics. Mill rejected the claim that truths of this kind can be known independently of observation and experience and was keen to demonstrate the falsity of this claim, since it seemed to him to support prejudices in favor of outdated institutions that have no backing in reason and rely on the alleged validity of intuition. Mill argued that if the principle of utility replaces "the moral sense," moral questions become amenable to rational consideration and the principle of utility itself supplies a tangible if not foolproof criterion for deciding moral issues.

Mill shared Bentham's conviction that moral values and the feeling of moral obligation can become purely secular phenomena, however much they may have owed to religion in the past. Every society, he contended, derives its cohesion from a common set of beliefs and values which have, until recent times, been supplied by supernatural religion. With the decline of the religious sanction, however, a secular vision of life must become the source of the necessary integrating beliefs and values. Mill did not conceal his hope that an elevated brand of utilitarianism, such as he sketched in his posthumously published essay, "Utility of Religion," would take the place of religion. He looked forward to a time when men would come to feel it their duty to serve humanity at large, when society would strive to cultivate in all its members a profound sense of unity with each other and a deep concern for the general good. While these are, to be sure, earthly goals, the conception and mode of life involved may well merit the name of religion, and Mill was sure that it was a better sort of religion than the supernatural one that was widely thought to have an exclusive right to the title. It was above all Comte who convinced him of the need for, and feasibility of, a "religion of humanity." While Mill thought that such a religion of humanity could secure a hold over men's minds, he did fear that it might militate against freedom and individuality.

Freedom of the individual.   Freedom of speech and publication are prominent among the conditions of good government in Benthamite political thought, and some of Mill's earliest journalistic efforts were based on this view. By the time he came to write *On Liberty*, his emphasis had changed: what had become central was the fear that society would become increasingly hostile to the full and varied expression of individual character. For his watchword Mill now took Wilhelm von Humboldt's assertion of the absolute importance of the rich and diverse development of the human personality, thereby provoking the charge that he (Mill) had abandoned the principle of utility. However, he took care to say in his introductory chapter that his ultimate standard for judging all ethical questions was still utility; but, he insisted, "it must be utility in the largest sense, grounded on the permanent interests of a man as a progressive being."

It was Mill's realization that popular government is no guarantee of freedom that gave much of the driving force to *On Liberty*. Tocqueville's account of democracy in America strengthened Mill's misgivings about the Benthamite assumption that to identify the interests of rulers and ruled is a necessary and sufficient condition of good government. Even a government based on the will of the people can exercise tyranny, and more than that, the informal pressures of society can become oppressive, especially in England, where, in contrast with France, the weight of public opinion was heavier than that of the law. Mill believed that the restrictions imposed on individuals, whether by law or by opinion, ought to be based on some recognized principle rather than on the preferences and prejudices of powerful sections of the public, and he set himself the task of formulating such a principle and of illustrating how it would work.

He described his principle in a number of different ways. At first he permitted social control only if it serves "to prevent harm to others" or to deter a person from inflicting "evil" on someone else; and here the line of division is between conduct which "concerns others," for which a person is answerable should it result in "harm," and conduct "which merely concerns himself," over which society has no jurisdiction at all. But later Mill talked about infringing "the interests" or "the rights" of others; and at other times he referred to the violation of "a distinct and assignable obligation" or a "perceptible hurt" to an "assignable individual." This variety of definitions of the sphere of liberty gives rise to complex problems of interpretation but should not obscure Mill's intention to make the area of freedom as large as possible and his clear recognition of the need for some restraint, both as a condition of social life of any sort and as a safeguard of freedom itself. Nor did Mill recommend indifference to conduct that falls short of accepted standards of private morality, even when it does not actually violate the interests of others; yet we should only try to *persuade* someone to give up his self-regarding vices, not to *coerce* him.

On Liberty is probably best known for the eloquent justification of liberty of thought and discussion contained in its second chapter. Mill contended that freedom of expression is no less necessary when an honest government is backed by the people than when the government is corrupt or despotic; and small minorities—even a single dissenter—have as much right to express their views as do large or overwhelming majorities. His case, argued at length, rests on the claim that to suppress an opinion is wrong, whether or not that opinion is true. For if it is true, we are robbed of the truth, and if it is false, we are denied that fuller understanding of the truth which comes from its conflict with error. And when, as often happens, the prevailing view is part truth and part error, we shall know the whole truth only by allowing free circulation of contesting opinions.

Mill's argument here is strictly utilitarian, in terms of the social benefits to be derived from a policy of freedom and access to truth. In his plea for individuality, however, there is an appeal to the idea of intrinsic goodness which he combined with instrumental arguments. The free development of individuality is indeed socially advantageous; it makes for improvement, progress, and variety in ways of living. But it means also that men may choose to live their own lives in their own distinctive ways, and Mill insisted that a man's own mode of "laying out his existence" is best simply because it is *his* own mode. Moreover, it is only by cultivating individuality that we can become well-developed human beings, and "what more or better can be said of any condition of human affairs than that it brings human beings themselves nearer to the best thing they can be?" Mill therefore believed in liberty both as a good in itself and as a means to happiness and progress: for him the ideas of happiness and progress were thoroughly infused with his conception of a freely choosing human agent.

It has often been said in criticism of Mill that in his zeal for liberty and his opposition to the extension of state interference, he attached too little importance to justice and welfare and failed to realize that these values can be promoted by government action without serious danger to freedom. It may not be possible to dismiss such a charge entirely, but in Mill's defense one can point to those passages of the *Principles of Political Economy* (especially book 2, chapters 1 and 2; book 4, chapters 6 and 7), where he showed himself to be fully aware of the injustices involved in the existing system of private property. One should also mention his fair-minded account of socialism and communism, his enthusiasm for the cooperative movement, and his idea of "the stationary state," in which there would be no more "trampling, crushing, elbowing, and treading on each other's heels, which form the existing type of social life" and where "while no one is poor, no one desires to be richer, nor has any reason to fear being thrust back, by the efforts of others to push themselves forward" (book 4, chapter 6, paragraph 2). He looked forward to the ultimate victory of socialism over the private property system, but it was to be a socialism which respected individuality. For the foreseeable future, the main task was so to improve the system of private property as to ensure that everyone shared in its benefits, and the measures on which Mill chiefly relied to achieve this end were a limitation on the inheritance of property, the restriction of the growth of population, and a great increase in the quantity and quality of education.

Representative government.   In his major work on political institutions, *Considerations on Representative Government*, the decline of individuality and the growing power of mass opinions are major reasons for Mill's advocacy of a number of reforms to protect minorities and to ensure that the influence exerted by educated minds on government is greater than that to which their numerical strength entitles them. But it is a wide-ranging book, and its interest lies as much in the discussion of general principles as in the particular recommendations regarding the ballot, proportional representation, and plural voting, not to mention the treatment of local government, federalism, and nationality.

If Mill's treatise has not stood the test of time as well as, say, Aristotle's *Politics* or Tocqueville's *Democracy in America*, nevertheless there is still much to admire; as when, for example, he asserts that institutions need to be adapted to the place where they have to work (his dealings with India had an important influence here) or that a despotic regime may not only help stabilize a society but may even prepare its people for the exercise of the responsibilities of a free electorate. Mill put heavy emphasis on a people's being properly equipped to assume these responsibilities; for representative government as he conceived it is the best possible form of government because, among other things, its very operation requires such activities of its citizens as are likely to increase both the desire and the capacity to make it work more effectively. One of its greatest virtues is that it puts power in the hands of those whose needs are sure to be considered only when they can voice them and whose rights and interests are sure of protection only when they can stand up for them. In saying this, Mill was surely stating an important part of the case for liberal democracy as it would commonly be made in the contemporary world.

JOHN C. REES

[*For the historical context of Mill's political thought, see* DEMOCRACY; FREEDOM; LIBERALISM; REPRESENTATION; UTILITARIANISM; *and the biographies of* BENTHAM; COMTE; SAINT-SIMON.]

BIBLIOGRAPHY

The bibliography for this article is combined with the bibliography of the article that follows.

II
ECONOMIC CONTRIBUTIONS

The essence of John Stuart Mill's economics is found in his *Principles of Political Economy*, published in 1848, and the best introduction to the *Principles* is Mill's *Autobiography* (1873). Here he described the strictly Ricardian economics taught him by his father, James Mill, and his later economic studies with a group of young men at George Grote's house. He also related the effect that Coleridge, Maurice and Sterling, Saint-Simon and Comte, Carlyle, and finally Harriet Taylor had in modifying his Ricardian Benthamite ideas. Highlighting the role that Harriet Taylor played in the writing of the *Principles*, he said that the chapter "On the Probable Futurity of the Labouring Classes" was "entirely due to her" (1873, p. 208). Insofar, at least, as the *Principles* were intended by Mill to be "more than a mere exposition of the abstract doctrine of Political Economy" (1848, p. xcii), the *Autobiography* does much to explain them.

Harold Laski, for one, realized that there was more to Mill's *Principles* than technical economics:

"The modern economist may use a technique more refined than that of Mill: he rarely conveys the same sense of generous insight into his material" (see Laski in Mill [1873] 1958, p. xix). Indeed, economists now answer with greater precision and certainty many of the questions that Mill asked, but there are many other questions that they have ceased to ask because, dissatisfied as they may be with Mill's answers, they see no better way of approaching them. Yet some of these questions are more important than those economists now deal with, and even Mill's answers would appear better if modern economists truly appreciated the questions he was in fact asking. In particular, he has been misinterpreted because it has been supposed that he was answering the questions posed by the neoclassical school of the later nineteenth century. Yet theirs was an economics of equilibrium; his was an economics of growth and development.

Method.   Mill had discussed the problems of method in the essay "On the Definition of Political Economy; and on the Method of Investigation Proper to It," published in the *Westminster Review* in 1836. This is an excellent statement of the value, character, and limitation of pure, abstract theory. In Book 4 of *A System of Logic* (1843) he discussed the problems of method in the social sciences generally: while still arguing the deductive character of political economy, he stressed the importance of the "inverse deductive or historical method." In the *Principles*, Mill decided to follow the example of Adam Smith, whose work "associates the principles with their applications" ([1848] 1965, p. xci). This approach, he saw, "implies a much wider range of ideas and of topics, than are included in Political Economy, considered as a branch of abstract speculation," for there are no practical questions which can be decided "on economical premises alone" (*ibid.*). Mill recognized that competition is limited in the real world (in part by custom), so that the results of analysis of a competitive model must be treated as "truths only in the rough" (*ibid.*, p. 422). He did not seem to notice that his doubts about the universality of self-interest raised doubts about the validity of any analysis based on the concept of the economic man. This economic man was defined as a "being who desires to possess wealth" (1844, p. 137), but Mill in the *Principles* indulged in some fine preaching against the obsessive pursuit of wealth: "it is only in the backward countries of the world that increased production is still an important object" ([1848] 1965, p. 755). Much of the interest in the *Principles* resides in its discussion of values:

policy can be determined only after a choice of ends, and problems arise out of a conflict of ends. What Mill did not notice, and what is still often ignored, is that the prediction of behavior depends on an understanding of the values held by society. Values are part of the data of the "science" of economics as well as a basis for the practical art.

Production.   However much Mill the preacher might doubt the importance of increasing production, Mill the economist was realistic enough to devote Book 1 of the *Principles* to the causes of productivity and of increasing productivity. Modern economists in developing countries, advanced or backward, would do well to study this book. Not least important is his concern with human resources and investment in people. Proper understanding of the book requires recognition that the problems he discussed are those of growth and development. For instance, the continued distinction between productive and unproductive labor is related to his concern for the liquidation of the primitive sector of the economy, in which menial servants are maintained in idleness on a more or less feudal basis, and for the development of industry, the advanced sector. Similarly, the propositions about capital, which have caused so much controversy ("the demand for commodities is not demand for labour" [(1848) 1965, p. 78]), make sense only in the context of the development of industry at the expense of the preindustrial sector.

Population.   The problems of population control crop up throughout the *Principles*. The possibility of "restraint" is the issue: "general improvement in intellectual and moral culture" or a rise in the "habitual standard of comfortable living" is necessary if an improvement in productivity is not to have as a consequence "a more numerous, but not a happier people" (*ibid.*, p. 159). Mill discussed the race between productivity and population further: he appeared less afraid of the effect of "communism" on population growth than was Malthus, but his advocacy of repression by public opinion of "this or any other culpable self-indulgence" (*ibid.*, p. 206) sounds more like Orwell's bad dream of 1984 than the sentiments of the author of the essay *On Liberty*. He recurred to the problem in his chapters on wages, where he effectively argued that what is needed is a dramatic improvement: "a system of measures which shall (as the Revolution did in France) extinguish extreme poverty for one whole generation" (*ibid.*, p. 374). Further discussion of the problem is found in Book 4, Chapter 3. All of this has a new relevance as economists become involved in the problems of the newly developing countries.

Distribution. Mill made a great point of distinguishing between the laws of production and the laws of distribution. The former, he said, "partake of the character of physical truths. . . . It is not so with the Distribution of Wealth. That is a matter of human institution solely" (*ibid.*, p. 199). Book 2, "Distribution," is, therefore, first concerned with the institution of property and with systems of socialism. Mill recognized that the "rules . . . are what the opinions and feelings of the ruling portion of the community make them." But these opinions and feelings are not "a matter of chance" (*ibid.*, p. 200); and how the chosen institutions work is as little arbitrary and "as much a subject for scientific enquiry as any of the physical laws of nature" (*ibid.*, p. 21). Although he insisted on the distinction between the laws of production and the laws of distribution, he in fact showed the importance of security and pecuniary incentive for productivity, in ideal forms of socialism and in actual institutions of peasant proprietorship and *métayage*. His interest in cooperatives (Book 4, Chapter 7) is partly based on the expectation of "a vast stimulus to productive energies" (*ibid.*, p. 792). The chapters on wages, profits, and rent are not without interest in the context of development, but they are unsatisfactory in the context of equilibrium analysis. His argument that distribution is not affected by exchange (Book 3, Chapter 16) is now hard to accept: he ignored the pricing process in the theory of distribution, and his successors were too readily content with his static solution. Yet Mill, in Book 2 and in Book 4, had some brilliant insights into the dynamics and the probable direction of change.

Exchange. Mill was injudicious in claiming that "there is nothing in the laws of Value which remains for the present or any future writer to clear up; the theory of the subject is complete" (*ibid.*, p. 456). Nevertheless, Book 3, "Exchange," is the most modern of the five books. The general theory of demand and supply is clearly stated. In this book are chapters on money, monetary theory and monetary policy, and international trade. Schumpeter in his *History of Economic Analysis* (1954, p. 689) has said that the chapters on money contain some of Mill's best work; and the chapters on international trade are described by Viner (1937, p. 535) as Mill's "chief claim to originality in the field of economics." Viner's favorable judgment refers to Mill's performance in the sphere of static analysis; in the context of growth and development Mill's discussion of "indirect benefits of commerce" is also noteworthy. "The opening of a foreign trade . . . sometimes works a sort of industrial revolution in a country whose resources were previously un-developed for want of energy and ambition in the people" ([1848] 1965, pp. 593–594). But Mill had political effects in mind too: "The great extent and rapid increase of international trade . . . is the great permanent security for the uninterrupted progress of the ideas, the institutions, and the character of the human race" (*ibid.*, p. 594).

Progress. Book 4, "Influence of the Progress of Society on Production and Distribution," contains the chapters on the dynamics of distribution referred to above and rated by Alfred Marshall as a short but profound study of the causes that govern the distribution of the national dividend; it also contains two important chapters involving social values. "Of the Stationary State" (Book 4, Chapter 6) ends with a magnificent plea for the preservation of natural beauty which may well have inspired Gissing's novel *Demos*. "On the Probable Futurity of the Labouring Classes" (Book 4, Chapter 7) contains a brilliant discussion of the "two conflicting theories respecting the social position desirable for manual labourers," the "theory of dependence and protection," and the theory of "self-dependence." The part played by industrialization in developing such self-dependence, thus providing the basis for democracy, had been stressed by Adam Smith and Malthus.

The functions of government. Book 5, "On the Influence of Government," in addition to six chapters on taxation, contains five chapters on the functions of government. The agenda of government changes with changes in the nature of the economy and with changes in the character (particularly the honesty and efficiency) of the government. We should not expect the English prescription for 1848 to be satisfactory for contemporary England, but Mill's discussion of the functions of government is not just material for the economic historian. He raised questions that still demand answers; and he reminds us that the appropriate answers depend on much more than economic effects, that liberty and democracy are at issue. The plea for "privacy" in the last chapter should not be ignored: it seemed to him necessary to develop "powerful defences, in order to maintain that originality of mind and individuality of character, which are the only source of any real progress" (*ibid.*, p. 940).

Strong as was his plea in Book 1 for security of property, he also argued in Book 2 that the rights of property are not absolute, and in Book 5 he argued for considerable restriction on the rights of inheritance and bequest. He noted with approval the endowment of charitable foundations in the United States and commented that a man would make a similar bequest in England "at the risk of being declared insane by a jury after his death" (*ibid.*, p. 226). The discussion of the economic importance of "limited liability" and of sound laws relating to insolvency (Book 5, Chapter 9) reminds us of the importance of examining some of the institutions we take for granted. The discussion of protection for infant industry (Book 5, Chapter 10) is still relevant; "the superiority of one country over another in a branch of production, often arises only from having begun it sooner" (*ibid.*, p. 918). Finally, attention is directed to education: public provision is defended but monopoly denounced (*ibid.*, pp. 949–950). He made a plea for support of research and scholarship, particularly for support of university professorships: "the greatest advances which have been made in the various sciences, both moral and physical, have originated with those who were public teachers of them" (*ibid.*, p. 969). This is a generous tribute from the servant of the East India Company who was developing the economics of the stockbroker Ricardo; but then Adam Smith and T. R. Malthus were professors.

V. W. BLADEN

[*For the historical background of Mill's economic thought, see the biography of* RICARDO.]

WORKS BY MILL

ECONOMIC WORKS

(1822) 1936 *Two Letters on the Measure of Value, Contributed to the* Traveller (*London) in December, 1822.* Reprint of Economic Tracts, No. 16. Baltimore: Johns Hopkins Press.

(1836) 1948 On the Definition of Political Economy; and on the Method of Investigation Proper to It. Pages 120–164 in John Stuart Mill, *Essays on Some Unsettled Questions of Political Economy.* London School of Economics and Political Science.

(1844) 1948 *Essays on Some Unsettled Questions of Political Economy.* London School of Economics and Political Science, Series of Reprints of Scarce Works on Political Economy, No. 7. London School of Economics and Political Science. → Five essays, of which the fifth was previously published in 1836.

(1848) 1965 *Principles of Political Economy, With Some of Their Applications to Social Philosophy.* 2 vols. Edited by J. M. Robson. Collected Works, Vols. 2–3. Univ. of Toronto Press. → This edition collates numerous earlier editions. The two volumes are paginated continuously.

POLITICAL AND OTHER WORKS

(1831) 1942 *The Spirit of the Age.* Introductory essay by Friedrich A. von Hayek. Univ. of Chicago Press. → Five articles first published in the *Examiner.*

(1835) 1962 Tocqueville on *Democracy in America* (Vol. I). Pages 187–229 in John Stuart Mill, *Essays on Politics and Culture.* Garden City, N.Y.: Doubleday. → First published in Volume 21 of the *Westminster Review.*

(1836) 1962 Civilization. Pages 51–84 in John Stuart Mill, *Essays on Politics and Culture.* Garden City, N.Y.: Doubleday. → First published in Volume 25 of the *Westminster Review.*

(1838) 1962 Bentham. Pages 85–131 in John Stuart Mill, *Essays on Politics and Culture.* Garden City, N.Y.: Doubleday. → First published in Volume 29 of the *Westminster Review.*

(1840*a*) 1962 Coleridge. Pages 132–186 in John Stuart Mill, *Essays on Politics and Culture.* Garden City, N.Y.: Doubleday. → First published in Volume 33 of the *Westminster Review.*

(1840*b*) 1962 Tocqueville on *Democracy in America* (Vol. II). Pages 230–287 in John Stuart Mill, *Essays on Politics and Culture.* Garden City, N.Y.: Doubleday. → First published in Volume 72 of the *Edinburgh Review.*

(1843) 1961 *A System of Logic, Ratiocinative and Inductive: Being a Connected View of the Principles of Evidence and the Methods of Scientific Investigation.* London: Longmans.

(1859) 1963 *On Liberty.* Indianapolis, Ind.: Bobbs-Merrill.

(1861*a*) 1962 *Considerations on Representative Government.* Chicago: Regnery. → A reprint of the original edition.

(1861*b*) 1957 *Utilitarianism.* Indianapolis, Ind.: Bobbs-Merrill. → First published in three parts in Volume 64 of *Fraser's Magazine.*

(1865) 1961 *Auguste Comte and Positivism.* Ann Arbor: Univ. of Michigan Press. → First published in two parts in Volume 83 of the *Westminster Review.*

(1869) 1911 *The Subjection of Women.* London and New York: Longmans.

(1873) 1958 *Autobiography.* With an appendix of hitherto unpublished speeches and a preface by Harold J. Laski. Oxford Univ. Press. → Published posthumously. There have been several editions of the *Autobiography,* including one in 1944 from the original manuscript in the Columbia University Library, published by Columbia University Press, and *The Early Draft . . . ,* published in 1961 by the University of Illinois Press.

(1874) 1958 Utility of Religion. Pages 45–80 in John Stuart Mill, *Nature* and *Utility of Religion.* New York: Liberal Arts Press. → Written between 1850 and 1858. Published posthumously.

COLLECTED WORKS

Bibliography of the Published Writings of John Stuart Mill. Edited from his manuscript, with corrections and notes, by Ney MacMinn, J. R. Hainds, and James McNab McCrimmon. Northwestern University Studies in the Humanities, No. 12. Evanston, Ill.: Northwestern Univ., 1945.

Collected Works. Univ. of Toronto Press, 1963—. → A projected multivolume publication.

Essays on Politics and Culture. Edited and with an introduction by Gertrude Himmelfarb. Garden City, N.Y.: Doubleday, 1962. → These essays were originally published between 1831 and 1874.

SUPPLEMENTARY BIBLIOGRAPHY

CANNAN, EDWIN (1893) 1953 *A History of the Theories of Production and Distribution in English Political Economy, From 1776 to 1848.* 3d ed. London and New York: Staples.

HALÉVY, ÉLIE (1901–1904) 1952 *The Growth of Philosophic Radicalism.* New ed. London: Faber. → First published in French.

HAYEK, FRIEDRICH A. VON (editor) 1951 *John Stuart Mill and Harriet Taylor: Their Correspondence* [i.e. *Friendship*] *and Subsequent Marriage.* Univ. of Chicago Press. → An errata slip indicates the correct title.

MACAULAY, THOMAS B. (1829) 1898 Mill on Government. Volume 7, pages 327–371 in Thomas B. Macaulay, *The Works of Lord Macaulay.* Albany ed. London: Longmans.

MILL, JAMES (1820) 1955 *Essay on Government.* New York: Liberal Arts Press.

MYINT, HLA 1948 *Theories of Economic Welfare.* Cambridge, Mass.: Harvard Univ. Press.

MYINT, HLA 1958 The "Classical Theory" of International Trade and Underdeveloped Countries. *Economic Journal* 68:317–337.

PACKE, MICHAEL ST. JOHN 1954 *The Life of John Stuart Mill.* London: Secker & Warburg.

SCHUMPETER, JOSEPH A. (1954) 1960 *History of Economic Analysis.* Edited by E. B. Schumpeter. New York: Oxford Univ. Press.

STEPHEN, LESLIE (1900) 1950 *The English Utilitarians.* London School of Economics and Political Science, Series of Reprints of Scarce Works on Political Economy, Nos. 9–11. 3 vols. London School of Economics and Political Science; Gloucester, Mass.: Smith. → A sequel to the author's *History of English Thought in the Eighteenth Century.* A detailed study of Bentham and the two Mills.

TAYLOR, OVERTON H. 1960 *A History of Economic Thought: Social Ideals and Economic Theories From Quesnay to Keynes.* New York: McGraw-Hill.

VINER, JACOB 1937 *Studies in the Theory of International Trade.* New York: Harper.

MILLAR, JOHN

John Millar (1735–1801), professor of civil law at the University of Glasgow from 1761 to 1801 and author of *The Origin of the Distinction of Ranks* and of *An Historical View of the English Government*, was born in the manse of the Kirk o' Shotts, Lanarkshire, Scotland. He was educated by an uncle and in the grammar school at Hamilton, where his father had by then been transferred. At the early age of 11 he entered Glasgow College, intended by his father for the Christian ministry. Five years later, he attended the first course of lectures given at Glasgow by Adam Smith, who soon discovered his promising qualities and later recommended him for a tutorship to the family of the distinguished jurist Lord Kames.

At the age of 25, just "passed advocate," he was appointed, on the recommendations of Smith and Kames, to the crown chair of civil law at Glasgow —a post he filled until his death. Here he lectured regularly on civil or Roman law (following the institutes and pandects of Justinian), on what he called "public law" or "the principles of government," and in alternate years on Scots and later also on English law.

The brilliance of his lectures soon attracted students from far and wide and gave great luster to a chair that had, at times, become almost defunct. Among his students were many who later came to hold places of the highest distinction at the bar, on the bench, in legal scholarship, in Parliament, and in the royal councils at Westminster.

His approach to the law was characterized by a comparative and historical, and in a sense sociological, orientation, by a lively attempt to reveal the relation of both law in general and the specific provisions of the law to the realities of everyday human experience, and by an unflagging effort to make law a genuine university subject rather than merely to furnish materials for the manual of the practitioner (Lehmann 1960, p. 48). This was true of his lectures on civil and municipal law as well as on public law or government.

Millar was, however, more than a teacher of law: he was first of all a teacher of youth. In line with the democratic, pragmatic, and broadly national aims of Scottish higher education in general, he always tried to make knowledge a vital thing in the lives of his students and a challenge to both their intellectual curiosity and their sense of moral responsibility in the affairs of the political community. "No individual, indeed, ever did more," Francis Jeffrey observed in the *Edinburgh Review*, "to break down the old and unfortunate distinction between the wisdom of the academician and the wisdom of the man of the world" (1806, p. 87). Jeffrey considered the informality of Millar's lectures—his "academic undress," as it were, his after-class and domestic hearthside discussions with the more promising of his students—to be an educational innovation of the highest order. John Rae, in the *Life of Adam Smith*, saw not indeed in the master but in his pupil, Millar, "the most effective and influential apostle of Liberalism in Scotland in that age" (1895, pp. 53–54).

In 1771, ten years after he began to lecture, Millar published his *Observations Concerning the Distinction of Ranks in Society*, entitled in the third and fourth editions *The Origin of the Distinction of Ranks*, with the revealing subtitle *An Inquiry Into the Circumstances Which Give Rise to Influence and Authority, in the Different Members of Society*. Sixteen years later (1787) he published *An Historical View of the English Government*. Both books brought him wide acclaim.

The former is essentially a historico–sociological analysis of social and political institutions from an evolutionary standpoint, focusing particularly on the relative position and the relations of the sexes in the various stages of civilizational development, on the rise of chieftaincy and of monarchical government, and on the "changes produced in the government of a people by their progress in arts, and in polished manners" ([1771] 1960, p. 284).

The latter book, somewhat more mature in scholarship and more purely historical in orientation, was dedicated to Charles Fox, whom Millar greatly admired. Millar himself viewed it as a "constitutional history of England," tracing its development from early Saxon institutions to the Norman Conquest; then, with the development of feudalism, to the end of the Tudor period; then to the Stuart period, with its struggles over the royal prerogative, and ending with the Revolution Settlement of 1688, which he considered the highest point in the development of British liberties; and, finally, to his own time. His own period he viewed as characterized by the growth of "the secret influence of the crown" and thus by a re-encroachment of the royal prerogative upon the legislative branch of the government, which was dangerous to established liberties. At the same time he saw that "rapid improvements of arts and manufactures . . . produced a degree of wealth and affluence, which diffused a feeling of independence and a high spirit of liberty, through the great body of the people" ([1787] 1818, vol. 4, p. 100). This work was often cited by James Wilson, a principal draftsman of the American constitution, in his lectures on law in 1790–1791, at what was later to become the University of Pennsylvania; it was one of the textbooks used by the elder Mill in the rigorous education of the young John Stuart Mill, who greatly preferred it to Hallam's *Constitutional History of England.*

Both of Millar's major works are characterized by a pervasive attempt to trace causes and effects in historical phenomena and by a strong emphasis upon the influence that economic factors have in shaping social and political institutions.

Because of this stress on economic factors, some have seen in Millar's work a marked anticipation of Marx's historical materialism. Perhaps it would be fairer to see in it, with A. L. Macfie of Glasgow (1961), both a further development of the thought of Adam Smith, with differences in emphasis, and an important bridge between eighteenth and nineteenth century social thinking in general.

WILLIAM C. LEHMANN

WORKS BY MILLAR

(1771) 1960 The Origin of the Distinction of Ranks. Pages 165–322 in William C. Lehmann, *John Millar of Glasgow: His Life, Thought and His Contributions to Sociological Analysis.* Cambridge Univ. Press. → First published as *Observations Concerning the Distinction of Ranks in Society.*

(1787) 1818 *An Historical View of the English Government, From the Settlement of the Saxons in Britain to the Revolution in 1688: To Which Are Subjoined Some Dissertations Connected With the History of the Government From the Revolution to the Present Time.* 4 vols. 4th ed. London: Mawman.

1796 *Letters of Crito, on the Causes, Objects, and Consequences, of the Present War.* Edinburgh: Johnstone.

SUPPLEMENTARY BIBLIOGRAPHY

CRAIG, JOHN 1806 Account of the Life and Writings of John Millar, Esq. Pages i–cxxxiv in John Millar, *The Origin of the Distinction of Ranks: Or, an Inquiry Into the Circumstances Which Give Rise to Influence and Authority, in the Different Members of Society.* 4th ed. Edinburgh: Blackwood.

FORBES, DUNCAN 1954 "Scientific" Whiggism: Adam Smith and John Millar. *Cambridge Journal* 7:643–670.

JEFFREY, FRANCIS 1806 [Review of] *The Origin of the Distinction of Ranks: Or, an Inquiry Into the Circumstances Which Give Rise to Influence and Authority, in the Different Members of Society,* by John Millar. *Edinburgh Review* 9:83–92.

LEHMANN, WILLIAM C. 1960 *John Millar of Glasgow: His Life, Thought and His Contributions to Sociological Analysis.* Cambridge Univ. Press. → Includes a bibliography of Millar's works on pages 417–418.

MACFIE, A. L. 1961 John Millar: A Bridge Between Adam Smith and Nineteenth Century Social Thinkers? *Scottish Journal of Political Economy* 8:200–210.

RAE, JOHN 1895 *The Life of Adam Smith.* London: Macmillan.

MILLENARISM

The Latin term *millennium* and its Greek equivalent, *chilias*, literally mean a period of a thousand years. According to the millenarian tradition, which is based on Jewish apocalyptic literature and the Revelations of St. John, Christ will reappear in the guise of a warrior, vanquish the devil, and hold him prisoner. He will then build the Kingdom of God and reign in person for a thousand years. Those saints who remained steadfast and gave their lives for their faith shall be raised from the dead and serve as his royal priesthood. At the end of this period Satan will be let loose again for a short while and will be finally destroyed. The victory will be followed by the general resurrection of the dead, the last judgment, and final redemption.

The term "millenarian" (or "chiliastic") is now used not in its specific and limited historical sense but typologically, to characterize religious movements that expect imminent, total, ultimate, this-worldly, collective salvation. Used thus, the term applies to a wide range of movements.

The millenarian tradition developed originally in Persian Zoroastrianism, and above all in Judaism, whence it was transmitted to Christianity and Islam (Mowinckel 1951). Millenarism has its roots in the messianic hopes and visions of the later days of prophetic Judaism (Klausner 1909). Belief in final redemption and expectation of the Messiah became firmly established tenets of Judaism. Messianism was a living force in Jewish history and gave rise to numerous popular movements. Many of these movements were of only local and passing importance, yet some of them had a very widespread appeal and left a lasting imprint. The most noteworthy of these movements are the Judean Desert Sect, which is a crucial link between Judaism and Christianity (*The Scroll of the War . . .*) and the seventeenth-century Sabbatean movement, which spread in most countries of the Diaspora and continued to exert considerable influence on Jewish communities even after its downfall (Scholem 1957).

Christianity derived its initial *élan* from radical millenarism. It is by its very name a form of messianism: the term *Christos*, or Christ, is a Greek translation of the Hebrew term *mashiah*. The most important aspects of the development of the messianic doctrine in Christianity are mythologization of the figure of the Messiah, universalization of the concept of redemption, and elaboration of the "suffering servant" motif. Jesus is conceived to be the incarnation of God and not just a God-ordained representative of the divine. In Christianity the conception of the golden age becomes transnational and metapolitical. The image of the Messiah as a king, warrior, or judge does not disappear, but it is overshadowed by the image of the suffering Messiah who redeems humanity by his tribulations and cruel death.

Millenarism was preserved in the Western church and was part of orthodoxy till the end of the fourth century. The change in the political position of the church, the penetration of Greek ideas, and the influence of Augustine led to its downfall. In the Concilium of Ephesus in 431 millenarism was denounced as error and fantasy and barred from official theology. The most important among the numerous heretical millenarian movements which developed within the aegis of the Catholic church during the Middle Ages are the movements which emerged during the crusades, the movements inspired by the ideas of Joachim de Fioris, who lived in the twelfth century, and the Cathari, or Universalists, who were prevalent in the south of France and went by the name of Albigenses and Waldenses (Cohn 1957).

Among the movements of the Reformation we find the Taborites, who were the extreme wing of the Hussites (Werner 1960), the Adamites, the Moravians, the followers of Münzer who joined the revolt of the German peasants against their landlords and made an attempt to establish the Kingdom of God on earth, and most important of all, the Anabaptists (Smithson 1935). In England we find the Fifth Monarchy Men, who during the days of Cromwell established the Parliament of Saints. The development in the Protestant church parallels that of the Greek Orthodox church and the Roman Catholic church. The German and Swiss reformers believed at first that final redemption was imminent, but this millenarian expectation was abandoned. Nevertheless, millenarism found its way into the churches of the Reformation through the influence of apocalyptic mysticism and Anabaptism. This influence is most noticeable in the reformed sects and in Pietism, but it left its mark on the Lutheran church as well. [*See* CHRISTIANITY.]

In Islam the millenarian tradition has developed under the name of Mahdism. The idea of final redemption was alien to Muhammad and his original followers. It was conceived only under Jewish and Christian influences during the civil wars and religious controversies attending the rise of the dynasty of the Ommaiades during the second half of the seventh century. The subsequent development of the caliphate and the decline of Muslim piety and power evoked a belief in the golden age of Islam and a longing for its restitution. A belief emerged that when injustice reached its acme the Mahdi (i.e., the rightly directed one), who was identified as a descendant of the prophet or as Isa (i.e., Jesus), would restore ancient glory and open a reign of abundance and justice. The theory of Mahdism has not been generally accepted in the Sunna and is not a fundamental dogma of orthodox Islam. It has, however, become a central idea of the Shi'ites, who have remained faithful to Ali, the son-in-law of Muhammad, and his descendants (Donaldson 1933). Millenarian Shi'ite sects were often constituted according to the belief in a particular descendant of Ali who was expected to emerge out of hiding as the deliverer. The most important Mahdi movements were those started by al-Mahdi Ubaidallah, who founded the dynasty of the Fatimites, Mohammed ibn-Tumart, a Berber of north Africa, and Mohammed Ahmed ibn Seyyid Abdullah, the Mahdi of Sudan (Holt 1958). [*See* ISLAM.]

The contact between primitive and modern societies and the processes of cultural interpenetration and assimilation have given rise to many millenarian movements in all developing countries. Prominent among these movements are the Ghost Dance movement of the North American Indians (Mooney 1896), the messianic movements of South

America (Métraux 1941; Ribeiro 1962), the "cargo" cults of the South Pacific (Worsley 1957; Burridge 1961; Lawrence 1964), and the numerous millenarian movements in Africa (Sundkler 1948; Balandier 1955; Price & Shepperson 1958).

There have been a number of important millenarian movements in modern societies as well. Most prominent among them are the sectlike Christadelphians (Wilson 1961), who expect a world-wide theocracy with Jerusalem at its center, the radical and proselytizing Jehovah's Witnesses (Stroup 1945; Pike 1954), and the Seventh Day Adventists (Froom 1946–1954). There is a strong millenarian element in Mormonism (O'Dea 1957). The extremist millenarian Black Muslim movement, which has developed among the American Negroes, views itself as anchored in the tradition of Islam (Essien-Udom 1962).

Each of the movements listed above has its unique, irreducible particularity and distinctiveness, yet they all manifest a set of common characteristics. Although the major recurrent themes appear in different constellations and there is considerable intratype variation, the basic pattern is reproduced in each of them.

Characteristics of millenarian movements

We have defined millenarism as the quest for total, imminent, ultimate, this-worldly, collective salvation. The terms of this definition require elucidation (see Mühlmann 1961; Sierksma 1961; Y. Talmon 1962; Thrupp 1962; Lanternari 1960).

The millenarian conception of salvation is total in the sense that the new dispensation will bring about not mere improvement but a complete transformation and perfection itself. Millenarian movements also view the impending redemption as ultimate and irrevocable. Time is conceived of as a process that leads to a final future. Millenarism is a merger between a historical and a nonhistorical conception of time. Salvation is viewed as imminent. The millennium is close at hand, and the believers live in tense expectation and preparation for it. Millenarism assumes that history has its predetermined, underlying plan, which is being carried to its completion, and that this predestined denouement is due in the near future. The millennial view of salvation is, in addition, revolutionary and catastrophic. Millenarism is dominated by a sense of deepening crisis that can be resolved only by ultimate salvation.

Another important element of millenarism is its terrestrial, this-worldly orientation. Its view of the divine is transcendent and imminent at the same time. The heavenly city is to appear on earth. Thus, the notion of perfect time is accompanied by the notion of perfect space.

Yet another major characteristic of millenarism is its collective orientation. Salvation is to be enjoyed by the faithful as a group. The aim of millenarism is not only the salvation of individual souls but the erection of a heavenly city for the chosen people, or the elect. The millenarian message may be directed to an already existing group, or it may call for the formation of a new group. Directly related to the collective orientation is the basic dualism of millenarism. A fundamental division separates the followers from nonfollowers. History is viewed as a struggle between saints and satans or, to use the terms coined by the millenarian Judean Desert Sect, as the "war between the sons of light and the sons of darkness."

Millenarian movements tend to be ecstatic. In most movements the ritual involves wild and often frenzied emotional display. We encounter in many millenarian movements cases of hysterical and paranoid phenomena, mass possession, trances, fantasies, and in others ecstatic dance figures prominently. Closely related to these phenomena are the antinomian tendencies, which appear in many guises. In some movements the antinomian element is moderate and mild, in others explicit and radical. Many millenarian movements deliberately break accepted taboos and overthrow hallowed norms. Sexual aberrations and excesses and unbridled expressions of aggression are very common. Sometimes aggression is turned inward; the members may destroy their own property and even commit mass suicide. The clearest example of the antinomian element inherent in millenarism is the doctrine of the "holiness of sin" developed by the Sabbatean movement after the apostasy of the Messiah (Scholem 1957).

The majority of millenarian movements are messianic (see Kroef 1952; Métraux 1941; Banton 1963). Salvation is brought about by a redeemer, who is a mediator between the human and the divine. Another important mediator between the divine and the movement is the leader. Leadership tends to be charismatic. The intense and total commitment required by millenarism is summoned forth by leaders who are considered to be set apart from ordinary men and endowed with supernatural power. Often there is also not just one charismatic leader but a multiple leadership. First, we find in a number of instances a division of leadership between the inspired prophet and the organizer who is concerned with practical matters. A second less prevalent line of bifurcation is the differentiation between the internal leader, who operates within the movement, and the external leader, who represents it in its relations with the outside world.

Organizationally, millenarian movements vary from the amorphous and ephemeral movement, with a cohesive core of leaders and ardent believers and a large ill-defined body of followers, to the fairly stable, segregated, and exclusive sectlike group. The organizational form of a more or less ephemeral movement is, however, more typical. This is no doubt closely related to the nature of the millenarian message. The promise of an imminent and total redemption awakes grandiose hopes and sweeps a large number of followers into the movement. However, its source of strength is also its source of weakness: by promising an imminent delivery and often even fixing a definite date, it brings about its own downfall. When the appointed day or period passes without any spectacular happenings or without the right apocalyptic events, the movement faces a serious crisis that often disrupts it or even breaks it up completely.

The crisis of nonmaterialization of the millennium is a severe one, but it need not always lead to disruption. In some cases the failures of prophecy have not caused disaffection or immediate disintegration (Festinger et al. 1956). Indeed, there are many cases of persistent recrudescence in spite of repeated failure. Radical millenarism became an ever-present though periodically dormant force in Andalusia for more than seventy years during the nineteenth century (Hobsbawm 1959). It suffered reversal after reversal, yet flared up repeatedly. The recurrent revival of the movement follows an almost cyclical pattern; the millennial outbursts follow one another at approximately ten-year intervals. Similar, though not as cyclical, patterns of disruption and revival can be found in studies of the medieval period, as well as in the literature on Melanesia and Africa. Sometimes there is a hidden continuity between the different phases of the movement. When the millenarian movement suffers a reverse, it goes under cover. It remains underground until it sees a better chance for its struggle, repeatedly hiding or going out into the open, but retaining its radical millenarism. It should be stressed, however, that often there is hardly any direct connection between what may seem to be recurrent phases of the self-same movement. Continuation of similar conditions often breeds similar yet independent reactions. In many cases there is no direct influence or any continuity of either tradition or personnel between successive movements (Guiart & Worsley 1958).

An alternative reaction to nonactualization is the switch from a short-range, radical millenarism to a long-range and more or less attenuated version of it. When the future becomes past and there is no fulfillment, the *Endzeit* is moved into the past and integrated into the present as a new *Urzeit*. Final redemption is either postponed to a more distant future or spiritualized. Thus, the millenarian dynamism solidifies into a new institutionalized religion. The histories of Zoroastrianism and of Christianity provide the best examples of this developmental pattern. The institutionalization of the Bahai movement and the gradual attenuation of its initial millenarism is another case in point (Berger 1957).

Dimensions of differentiation

So far we have underlined the main common characteristics of millenarian movements and only hinted at internal differentiation. Comparative analysis of millenarian movements is at its inception, and attempts to construct a systematic typology are partial and not very satisfactory (for example, see Mair 1959; Smith et al. 1959; Köbben 1960; Shepperson 1962; Wilson 1963). The following seem to be the major dimensions of intratype differentiation from the religious and sociological points of view.

(1) Millenarism combines a historical and a mythical time conception. The consciousness of time as a linear process of change, as a sequence of once-and-for-all events of unique character and particularity, is intertwined with the consciousness of time as cyclical and endlessly repetitive. Millenarism is in most cases posthistorical, in the sense that it is an outcome of a breakdown of historical consciousness, a flight from history to a mythical *Endzeit*. The historical perspective does not disappear. It is usually retained in an elaborate temporal scheme, in which a semihistorical or historical epoch ranges between the *Urzeit* and *Endzeit*. It should be noted, however, that in quite a number of cases the millennial conception is postmythical rather than posthistorical. The breakdown of the world view anchored in the metahistorical beginning leads to the displacement of the *Urzeit* and to its projection into the metahistorical future. There is in this type of millenarism a vague notion of time as duration and change, as well as recognition of a short semihistorical interim period, but the cyclical paradigmatic time conception of myth predominates.

(2) Millenarism combines the notion of perfect time with the notion of perfect space. The major emphasis may be on the notion of perfect time, in which case location in a specific place is subsidiary or in certain cases even nonexistent. The spatial element may, however, be crucial. The Jewish con-

ception of redemption is clearly localized: the return to the Promised Land and the rebuilding of Zion are an integral part of it.

(3) The millenarian process is two-phased: redemption is preceded by a premillennial catastrophe. The major emphasis may be on the preparatory struggle; in this case the tribulations of the period of breakdown are described in elaborate detail, and the fear of doom and hatred of the adversary are more prominent than hope and love. On the other hand, the dominant emphasis may be on redemption, and the catastrophe may be viewed as just a short prelude to eternal bliss. While the majority of millenarian movements combine catastrophe and redemption, in a number of cases one appears without the other.

(4) Millenarism usually involves messianism, but the two do not necessarily coincide. Expectation of a human–divine savior is not always accompanied by expectation of total and final redemption. Conversely, expectation of the millennium does not always involve the mediation of a messiah. Redemption is in certain cases brought about directly by the divine.

(5) Millenarism involves both inclusion and exclusion: there are always God's people within and the ungodly without. The divinely appointed group may be singled out on an ascriptive and particularist basis. Only those who belong—to the race, the ethnic group, the nation—will be redeemed and enjoy the new, happy life. The basis of selection may also be elective and universalist. The message is directed to the whole of mankind; everyone who will repent and who qualifies religiously and morally will be saved. The main emphasis may be either exclusive or inclusive.

(6) While expectation of imminent redemption is a constitutive element in millenarism, there is a certain range of variation in this respect. There are movements that are swept by a very strong sense of the immediacy and urgency of redemption. They set a very close date for the coming of the millennium or expect it any day. Other movements view the millennium as approaching and close at hand, yet not immediate.

(7) Millenarism is a future-oriented religious ideology. However, while its attitude to the present is outrightly and radically negative, there is considerable variation with respect to its orientation to the past. There are millenarian movements that are predominantly restorative. Their aim is a revival and revitalization of the indigenous culture, and their view of the future is largely traditional. Far more common, however, are predominantly innovative movements (Linton 1943). There is a strong antitraditional component in millenarism. Essentially millenarism is a bridge between past and future. There are many antitraditional elements in predominantly restorative movements. Some of the traditional myths and practices become symbols of the old order and acquire a new meaning and an exaggerated significance that they never enjoyed before. There is an ongoing process of selection and reinterpretation. To turn to the other pole, even the most antitraditional version of millenarism is, in fact, a synthesis of the external and the indigenous, of the new and the old. The strong antipast orientation of the innovative movements is mitigated when the millennium is envisaged as a return to a mythical golden age. Inasmuch as the millennium is regarded as "paradise regained," those elements of tradition that are viewed as embedded in it become also components of the new order. By establishing a connection between the metahistorical *Urzeit* and the metahistorical *Endzeit*, the millenarian movement can be radically change-oriented yet incorporate traditional elements in its view of the final future. Millenarian movements are thus both restorative and innovative. Classification of a given movement from the point of view of this dimension involves careful weighing of traditional versus nontraditional elements.

(8) Millenarism usually evokes extreme dedication and fervor. In the majority of cases this fervor is accompanied by abandonment of self-control and expressed in enthusiastic ritual, violent motion, and antinomian acts. However, in a minority of cases we encounter the direct opposite: religious fervor manifests itself in excessive self-discipline, stringent observation of rules, and extreme asceticism. The Black Muslims, for instance, insist on strict order and decorum; they prohibit any excess and any expression of religious enthusiasm.

(9) Another important dimension of differentiation is the definition of the role of the movement in bringing about the advent. There are many variations in this respect. Movements range from the fairly passive and nonviolent, on the one hand, to the extremely activist and aggressive, on the other. There are certain elements in the millenarian ideology that work against an outrightly active definition of the role of the follower. Salvation is preordained and inevitable. Thus, the followers are not makers of the revolution; they expect it to be brought about miraculously from above. Ultimately, initiative and actual power to bring about change rest with divine powers. All millenarian movements share a fundamental vagueness about the actual way in which the new order will be

brought about, expecting it to happen somehow by divine intervention.

It should be noted, however, that there is a strong militant ingredient in the millenarian ideology that more often than not outweighs the passive and pacifist elements in it. The assurance of operating in accordance with the predetermined divine plan and the passionate confidence in ultimate triumph may encourage heightened activity rather than passivity. Since the millennial view of redemption is both transcendent and terrestrial, paving the way for this redemption is usually not confined to the employment of ritual measures. Joining the movements affects participation and activity in the secular sphere as well. Total rejection of the social order leads in many cases to radical withdrawal and noncooperation. Cessation of economic activity, political nonparticipation, conscientious objection with regard to service in the army, strict segregation, and wholesale migration are frequent concomitants of millenarism.

An alternative and equally prevalent reaction is active revolt. Radical negation of the social order engenders, in many cases, open aggression and violence. Preparation for the future struggle often entails the introduction of military training for all members or the setting up of a selective secret military organization. Münzer's Elect, Joseph Smith's Apostolic Corps, and The Fruit of Islam organized by the Black Muslims are cases in point. There are numerous cases of eruption of violence: members of millenarian movements have swept over the country, devastating, burning, and massacring on their way. We also encounter many cases of planned and concerted assaults on the established authorities. Movements that have an essentially ritual and passive conception of their role are often pushed to active revolt by the inner dynamics of their millenarian position and as a result of persecution by the authorities.

Conditions of development

What are the conditions that account for the emergence and continuance of millenarian movements, and in which social groups are they anchored? By and large the data support the hypothesis that millenarism is the religion of deprived groups—the lower social strata and oppressed and persecuted minorities (Mannheim 1929–1931). It is usually engendered by severe and protracted suffering. At the root of it we often find multiple deprivation, that is, the combined effect of poverty, low status, and powerlessness. The effect of multiple deprivation accounts for the prominence of members of pariah groups and pariah people

among the promulgators and followers of millenarism (Weber 1920–1921; Troeltsch 1912; Mühlmann 1961). The low status of such groups derives from their despised ethnic origin and cultural tradition and from their limitation to menial and degrading occupations. Being at the bottom on so many counts, they are attracted to the myth of the elect and to the fantasy of reversal of roles, which are important elements in the millenarian ideology.

Millenarism flares up, in many cases, as a reaction to cumulative deterioration of life conditions and as a result of awareness of prospects for further decline in the future. We note also the precipitating effect of sudden and dramatic crises that aggravate endemic deprivation and at the same time symbolize and highlight it. Many of the outbursts of millenarism have taken place against a background of disaster: plagues, devastating fires, recurrent long droughts, economic slumps that caused widespread unemployment and poverty, and calamitous wars.

Deprivation, frustration, and isolation. The hypothesis of acute multiple deprivation provides an important clue. Yet, as it stands, it does not fully account for the emergence and development of millenarism and requires considerable modification and amplification.

First, it should be noted that the predisposing factor is, in quite a number of cases, not severe hardship but a markedly uneven relation between expectations and the means of their satisfaction (Aberle 1962). In many cases it is predominantly the inability to fulfill traditional expectations. In medieval Europe millenarism affected mainly people who were cut off from the traditional order and were unable to satisfy wants instilled in them by it. The insidious onslaught of the developing capitalistic order on a backward and isolated peasant economy created the same basic difficulty in Spain and Italy centuries later, although there it affected not only people who were cut off from the rural community but also the rural community itself (Hobsbawm 1959). We encounter the same type of frustration in primitive societies as well, but there it increasingly becomes not so much a problem of the lack of means to supply traditional wants as the development of a set of new expectations. The encounter with modern societies engenders enormously inflated expectations, without a concomitant and adequate development of institutional means for their fulfillment. This discrepancy creates a void that is often bridged by millenarian hope. That frustration may be much more important than actual hardship becomes evident when we consider the fact that millenarian unrest in certain parts of New Guinea was not caused by any direct contact with the white men. Although there were hardly any changes in the *status quo*, indirect contacts and impact by hearsay brought about changed expectations and acute frustration. It should be stressed that in many cases millenarian outbursts were caused not by a deterioration of conditions but by a limited amelioration that raised new hopes and new expectations but left them largely unfulfilled.

The incongruity between ends and means is not the only source of frustration. Much of the deep dissatisfaction stems from incongruities and difficulties in the realm of regulation of ends. Rapid social change and encounters with radically different systems of values result in more or less severe cultural disintegration and disorientation. The impinging cultural influences penetrate into the traditional setting and undermine the effectiveness of traditional norms as guides of action. Even central traditional values cease to be self-evident and sacred. Inasmuch as these traditional values are internalized and are an integral part of personal identity, the disintegration of the traditional system results in serious self-alienation. When the alien culture is that of a more prestigious upper class or that of a colonial ruling class, it is often—willingly or unwillingly, consciously or unconsciously—acknowledged as superior. This engenders a nagging feeling of inferiority and even self-hatred.

The effect of the incongruity between the indigenous and external influences is aggravated by the discrepancies between the values and policies of different external agencies. In most colonial countries there is constant conflict between the government, the traders, and the missions, as well as open and often bitter rivalry between the different missions. There are, in addition, inner contradictions and inconsistencies between different elements of religious doctrine and a split between religious ideals and reality. Since conflicting claims tend to neutralize and annul each other, the impinging influences weaken and destroy the traditional system without substituting a new system of values. Millenarism is often born out of the search for a tolerably coherent system of values, a new cultural identity, and a regained sense of dignity and self-respect (see Werblowsky 1965; Burridge 1961).

Another important factor operative in the emergence of millenarism is social isolation brought about by the disruption of traditional group ties. Analysis of the medieval material indicates that millenarism did not appeal much to people who were firmly embedded in well-integrated kinship groupings and effectively organized and protected in cohesive local communities. The people most exposed to the new pressures and therefore more prone to millenarian heresy were the malintegrated and isolated who could find no assured and recognized place in cohesive primary groups. Comparative historical analysis has underlined the important contribution of migrant groups and itinerant workers to the development and spread of millenarism.

The strains of transition. It is significant that millenarism occurs mainly in periods of transition. Millenarian movements in primitive societies provide the clearest proof of this hypothesis. Millenarism usually does not appear in areas largely untouched by modernization, and it appears only rarely in areas in which modernization has reached an advanced stage. It occurs mainly during the intermediate stages. This has given rise to the hypothesis that millenarism in primitive societies is a "half-way" or "quarter-way" phenomenon. (Belshaw 1950). While it is difficult to specify exactly at which point along the line millenarism begins or ceases to be feasible, the basic hypothesis that views it as a concomitant of transition is corroborated in other settings as well. In modern societies we find that those who have undergone the double transition of intercountry and intracountry migration and are both new immigrants and new urbanites are particularly prone to millenarism. Millenarian movements have proliferated during the transition between premodern and the modern way of life in rural Spain and Italy. Millenarian outbursts abounded toward the end of the Middle Ages and the beginning of modern times. The Judaeo-Christian formulation of millenarism developed during the stormy period that preceded the destruction of the Second Temple. The frustration, disorientation, and disruption engendered by these upheavals are the crux of the matter.

Millenarism and political helplessness. Even the combination of such factors as deprivation, frustration, and isolation does not supply us with an adequate answer to our question. The most important contribution of recent studies of millenarism to this analysis lies in their insistence that millenarism is essentially a prepolitical, nonpolitical and postpolitical phenomenon (Worsley 1957). Among primitive societies it appears mainly in so-called stateless segmentary societies, which have rudimentary political institutions or lack any specialized political institutions altogether [see STATELESS SOCIETY]. When it appears in societies with fairly developed or well-developed political institutions, it appeals mainly to strata that are politically passive and have no experience of political organization and no access to political power. Instances of such "nonpolitical" strata in societies with a more or less developed political structure are the peasants in feudal societies, the peasants in isolated and backward areas in modern societies, marginal and politically passive elements in the working class, recent immigrants, and malintegrated and politically inarticulate minority groups. Sometimes millenarism is "postpolitical," appearing after the downfall of a fairly developed political system. The collapse of an entire political system by a crushing defeat and the shattering of tribal or national hopes have sometimes led to widespread millenarism. It is the sense of blockage—the lack of effective organization, the absence of regular institutionalized ways of voicing their grievances and pressing their claims—that pushes such groups to a millenarian solution. Not being able to cope with their difficulties through concerted political action, they turn to millenarism. Millenarism is born out of great distress coupled with political helplessness.

The effect of the various predisposing economic and social factors is further clarified when we examine more closely the sources of recruitment to millenarian movements. The hypothesis that millenarism is a religious ideology of lower strata is based on an assumption that it is a concomitant of social and economic differentiation and is a manifestation of class society. Examination of the data indicates that this is true in most but not all cases. Millenarism is not confined to stratified societies. In quite a number of cases, it is the reaction of a largely undifferentiated primitive society to the unsettling impact of social change. Primitive societies undergo only gradual, almost imperceptible, social change. The dominant time dimension is the mythical past; life in the present is experienced as a repetition of the paradigmatic events of the *Urzeit*. The idea of *Endzeit* is either nonexistent or marginal. Swift and radical change disrupts this repetitive rhythm and transforms life conditions. The cosmic and social orders can no longer be grounded in the mythical beginning, and so the major emphasis shifts to the mythical future. The image of the future age of bliss may be largely an extrapolated replica of the former image of a past golden age. It may, on the other hand, be change-oriented and partly independent of this image of the mythical past. The main predisposing factor in such cases is the loss of anchorage in the life-giving myth of the *Urzeit*, and this loss affects society as a whole. Millenarism of this type is rooted in the

dilemma of stability and disruptive change and not so much in a polarization of underprivileged and overprivileged strata. This problem of breakdown of continuity is of central importance also in the emergence of "posthistorical" millenarism.

When we center our attention on stratified societies, we find that underprivileged groups predominate but do not have a complete monopoly. At one time or another millenarism has found support in all levels of society. There is, for instance, a distinctly middle-class element in British millenarism. It is true that such groups as those which built their hopes on Mother Ann Lee of Manchester were usually of humbler origin and that, from the days of Wesley through the initial period of the Salvation Army to the present-day frequenters of Kingdom Halls, the poor were in the majority. However, in most movements we find members, and especially leaders, of middle-class origin. There is even one distinctly middle-class movement: there were few, if any, underprivileged elements in the affluent "Irvingite" Catholic Apostolic church that developed in the middle of the nineteenth century in England (Shaw 1946; Taylor 1958).

It is also significant that adherents of millenarian movements are not always the worst off among the underprivileged. Those members of the deprived group who are somewhat better off are often better able to take stock of their situation, to react, and reorganize. The upper strata of a minority group or the indigenous aristocracy of a colonial country may identify with the dominant group in the society. They may, on the other hand, identify with their own membership group and want to share its destiny. An indiscriminate invidious evaluation of all members of the underprivileged group and the existence of an insurmountable barrier between it and the dominant group strengthen the solidarity of the underprivileged group and blur internal status differentiation. The tendency of members of the upper strata of deprived groups to join and lead millenarian protest movements is enhanced if their traditional status is threatened and bypassed.

Many studies underline the prominence of members of a frustrated secondary elite among the leaders of millenarian movements (see, for instance, Cohn 1957; Katz 1961). Many of the leaders of the medieval movements were members of the lower clergy who, for one reason or another, decided to turn their backs on the church; Thomas Münzer is the most famous example of such men.

Religious predispositions to millenarism. So far we have dealt mainly with the economic and social factors. That the combination of all the predisposing factors will actually lead to millenarism and not result in the development of other types of religious ideology is conditioned also by the type of religious beliefs that are prevalent in a society. The yearning for an earthly paradise and for final salvation is very widespread, and millenarian elements appear in most religions. It should be stressed, however, that certain types of religions are more conducive to millenarism than others. Clearly, religions in which history has no meaning whatsoever and religions which have a cyclical repetitive conception of time are not conducive to millenarism (Eliade 1949). Apocalyptic eschatology is essentially alien to religions of a philosophical and mystical cast that turn the eye of the believer toward eternity, where there is no movement and no process. This is certainly the case with some nature and cosmic religions that view the universe in terms of ever-recurring cycles of rise and decline. Another important factor operative in this sphere is a "this-worldly" emphasis. Religions with a radical, otherworldly orientation that put all the emphasis on the hereafter or on a purely spiritual and totally nonterrestrial salvation do not give rise to the vision of the Kingdom of God on earth. The myth of Kalki as an incarnation of Visnu in a period of abundance, as well as the doctrine of the future Buddha whose advent will bring a golden age, proves that even such basically non-millenarian religions as Hinduism and Buddhism are not devoid of millenarian conceptions. It should be noted, however, that there is hardly any millenarian tradition in Hinduism and that it has not occupied an important place in Buddhism.

It is mainly world views that are based on a notion of divine will working through history toward a preordained end which provide an overall scheme conducive to millenarism. The majority of millenarian movements have appeared in countries that have had direct or indirect contact with the Judaeo–Christian messianic traditions. The Christian missions have been the most important agency for the worldwide diffusion of millenarism. Several fundamentalist sects and millenarian movements have played a particularly important role in this process. The Kitawala movement, which is an African offshoot of the Jehovah's Witnesses, is a case in point (Cunnison 1958). It should be noted, however, that millenarism has also appeared in cases where the main contact was with less apocalyptic versions of Christianity. In such cases millenarism is reinstated to a central position by a process of selection and reinterpretation.

We should take into consideration the autochthonous religious concepts as well. Some primitive mythologies contain beliefs that are conducive to millenarism, such as the expectation of the future return of the culture hero or the idea of the return of all the dead as a prelude to a millennial era. It should be stressed, however, that these themes appeared in a rather embryonic form in primitive mythology and did not occupy a particularly important position. They were developed, reinterpreted, and elaborated into full-fledged millenarian conceptions only under the impact of new situations and after contact with Christianity or Islam.

The pre-existing primitive conceptions affected the development of millenarism in yet another way. The prevalence of millenarism in Melanesia and the importance of expectations of cargo in this view of the millennium are, it would seem, due to the almost exclusive emphasis that the indigenous religion puts on ritual activity oriented to the acquisition of material goods.

The most important ideological starting point of millenarism may be a new importation; it may be the native tradition that exists of old; and, in a number of cases, it seems to be predominantly a largely independent reaction to the pressure of circumstances. Availability of pre-existing millenarian precepts and patterns facilitates the development of a full-fledged millenarian ideology and the organization of a millenarian movement. Such millenarian precepts may be dormant for a long time until activated by suitable circumstances and by crisis. The readily found millenarian representations are invested with the particularity and immediacy necessary to convert them into an effective ideology that serves as a basis for collective action.

The Sabbatean movement. Comparative research underlines the close correspondence and interdependence between millenarism and economic and social conditions. At the same time, it indicates the potency and partial independence of the religious factor. The Sabbatean movement (so named after Sabbatai Zevi, a Jewish mystic of Smyrna, who in 1648 proclaimed himself Messiah) supplies us with clear proof of the inadequacy of a reductionist interpretation. In this respect the movement is a crucial case (Scholem 1941; 1957). It was preceded by two waves of unprecedented massacres and persecutions in Poland. Many thousands of Jews were slaughtered, and many more fled before the sword. Hundreds of communities were completely destroyed. Since the messianic movement erupted shortly after the massacres, it was assumed that it was a direct reaction to them. Examination of the differential appeal of messianism in different countries reveals, however, that the Sabbatean movement was not at its strongest in communities that bore the full brunt of the disaster and was just as powerful, and in certain cases more powerful, in countries in which the Jews lived in comparative peace. The calamity contributed to the emergence of the movement by emphasizing the fundamental precariousness of Jewish existence and by enhancing the consciousness of exile, yet in and by itself it cannot account for the development and differential impact of the movement. Moreover, it is significant that messianism spread in prosperous and expanding communities just as in destitute and declining ones. Intracommunity differentiation affected recruitment more than intercommunity differentiation. Part of the established elite distrusted and rejected Sabbatai Zevi as Messiah, and the secondary elite was more active than the primary one. It should be noted, however, that the majority of the elite and upper strata joined the movement and were as enthusiastic as the mass of the people. We find among the adherents members of all strata of society, ranging from wealthy merchants, who offered to donate their entire fortune to the Messiah, to the poorest of the poor.

The predominant predisposing factor that accounts for the deep and lasting impact and for the almost universal appeal of Sabbatai Zevi in all countries of the Diaspora was the very wide spread of the doctrines of Isaac Luria, the great Kabbalist teacher who died nearly a century before the Sabbatean movement reached its height. The aim of Luria and his followers was the restitution of cosmic harmony through the earthly medium of a spiritually elevated Judaism. Their doctrines laid far greater stress on the inner aspects of redemption than on its outward historical and political aspects; however, since they viewed liberation from the yoke of servitude and exile as a by-product of spiritual salvation and since they saw the coming of the Messiah as imminent, they engendered tense messianic expectations. To the large circles of Lurianic devotees, the coming of Sabbatai Zevi was an actualization of the promise and prediction of the Kabbala; indeed, Sabbatai chose to proclaim himself Messiah in the year that the Kabbalists had calculated as the year of salvation. The antinomian deviations of Sabbateanism were anchored in the nontraditional elements in the mystical conception of redemption. The inner dynamics of the movement, and especially its transformation during its later phases, are unintelligible without a detailed and full analysis of the precepts and symbols of the Lurianic Kabbala. [See JUDAISM.]

Causal analysis of millenarism. In concluding this causal analysis, it should be emphasized that the various predisposing factors are interrelated.

There is a low correlation between any one of them and the emergence of millenarism. It is only if we examine their intricate interplay and their combined effect that the results are more satisfactory. Moreover, to suggest that most millenarian movements arise in situations that have certain identifiable features in common is not to suggest that wherever such situations exist millenarian movements must inevitably arise. Inherent openness and indeterminacy remain even after we have considered all the major determinants. Examination of cases of occurrence, near-occurrence, and nonoccurrence, under basically similar conditions as far as degree of strain and structural and cultural conduciveness are concerned, indicates the considerable importance of historical accidents. Availability or nonavailability of leaders with strong suggestive powers, as well as occurrence or nonoccurrence of precipitating crises, affects the chances of the movement to emerge and develop. The variation in the reaction of the authorities to the movement's efforts to mobilize support is another important factor. Persistent and effective repression by the authorities may prevent the emergence of the movement or defeat and quench it soon after it appears. On the other hand, increased responsiveness and flexibility on the part of the authorities may open avenues of reform and thereby deflect the movement from its purpose. It is mainly when the authorities are not only unresponsive and inflexible but also somewhat ineffective, or at least permit some relaxation of control, that the millenarian movement has a chance to emerge and spread.

Functional analysis of millenarism

What are the consequences of millenarism? How does it serve the needs of the followers, and what does it contribute to the strata and societies in which it appears? We find two main, diametrically opposed, interpretations in the literature.

The first approach underlines the negative functions of millenarism and considers it as a dangerous collective madness (see, for instance, Cohn 1957). According to this viewpoint, millenarism is a paranoid fantasy, an outlet for extreme anxiety, and a delusion of despair. The megalomaniac view of oneself as wholly good and abominably persecuted, the attribution of demonic power to the adversary, the inability to accept the ineluctable limitations of human existence, as well as the excessive emotionality, the antinomian rituals, and the destructive activities, are all diagnosed as symptoms of mental illness. The millenarian ideology is considered as disruptive and destructive both from the point of view of the movement and from that of the over-all society.

The second approach rejects this negative evaluation of millenarism and underlines its positive functions (for the clearest expression of this viewpoint, see Worsley 1957). According to this view, the highly emotional and aggressive behavior is related to the revolutionary nature of the movement that strives to overthrow the old order and establish a new one. The severing of strong ties and the rejection of internalized norms demand an enormous effort and engender a deep sense of guilt, which causes much of the hysteria and the aggression. Many of the antinomian manifestations represent a deliberate overthrow of the accepted norms, not in order to throw morality overboard but in order to create a new brotherhood and a new morality. The "paranoid" manifestations are seen as stemming primarily from the contradictions inherent in the situation in which such movements appear and from the difficulties inherent in their revolutionary task rather than from the psychological aberrations of individual followers. If we take into consideration the social conditions and the cultural milieus that gave rise to these manifestations, they cease to be bizarre and fantastic and become fully understandable reactions. The promillenarian viewpoint emphasizes its underlying realism and its inherent, though hidden, rationality.

This viewpoint considers millenarism to be integrative on all levels. First, the millenarian ideology supplies the believers with invaluable safeguards and supports. The predominant element in millenarism is inner certainty and hope, not despair. Adherents are assured of "being in on history." They are in the know and are working on the winning side. The movement fosters a new collective identity and engenders a feeling of belonging and a sense of purpose. The promise that many of the first shall be last and the last first (Matthew 19.30) transforms inferiority into superiority and fosters self-confidence and a sense of ethical righteousness. The division of humanity into saints and devils enables the followers to focus and express their aggression and affirm the solidarity and integrity of their group. Vibrant expectation, pride, and hope lift them out of their apathy and bring about inner regeneration and rehabilitation.

The positive functions of millenarism become even more evident on the social level. Millenarism is an emancipating, activating, and unifying force in hitherto stagnant, politically passive, and segregated groups. In recent and contemporary history it has served as a precursor of political awakening and as a forerunner of political organization. Millenarism has played an important role in overcoming divisions and in joining previously isolated or even hostile groups together.

The revolutionary nature of millenarism makes it a very potent agent of change. It demands a fundamental transformation and not just improvement and reform. The radical versions of millenarism incite followers to active anticipation of the advent and even to active revolt. It invests their struggle with the aura of a final cosmic drama and interprets present difficulties as signs of the beginning of the end. Every small success is viewed as proof of invincibility and as a portent of future triumph. Millenarism arouses truly great hopes and therefore can make equally great demands on its followers. By promising complete salvation, it is able to liberate formerly untapped energies and generate a supreme effort without which no major break with the existing order can be achieved. Thus millenarism helps to bring about a breakthrough to the future, and its special efficacy lies in its power to bridge future and past (Wallace 1956).

Religion and politics.   While bridging the gap between future and past, millenarism also connects religion and politics. Operating in societies or in strata completely dominated by religion, millenarism couches its political message in the familiar and powerful language and images of traditional religion, employing and revitalizing its age-old symbols. In such milieus recruitment to new political goals is often possible only when expressed in religious terms. In many cases it is also the only means of establishing cooperation between leaders and followers. Millenarism provides an important mechanism of recruitment of new leaders. It opens up new avenues of ascent and develops a set of new statuses. Although some of the new leaders derive their authority from their central or marginal position in the traditional order, more often than not their authority stems at least in part from their comparatively superior knowledge and greater experience in nontraditional spheres of activity and has no traditional legitimation. Millenarism helps these leaders to establish their authority. Millenarism is, according to this view, a connecting link between prepolitical and political movements; it facilitates the passage from premodern religious revolt to a full-fledged revolutionary movement.

The process of transition from the one kind of movement to the other can actually be traced in both primitive and recent premodern movements. There are two main distinct avenues of transition. In some cases the movements gradually change their nature, slowly becoming less ritualized and more secular in emphasis. They start to pay much more attention to purely political and economic goals, attach far more importance to strategy and tactics, and organize more effectively. Yet they do not sever their ties with their millenarian tradition, and they continue to derive much of their revolutionary zeal from its promise of final salvation.

Positive and negative evaluations.   Assessment of the outcome of millenarism clearly reflects value premises. The two viewpoints on this matter stem at least in part from different ideological stands. The antimillenarian stream of research is gradualist and reformist, while the promillenarian stream is revolutionary and favors radical change. It should be noted, in addition, that the two viewpoints have emerged out of research in different historical and social settings. The positive evaluation grew mainly out of the research into those millenarian movements that were developed by rising groups at the upsurge of their efforts of emancipation. Such research deals mainly with movements that were precursors and concomitants of secular revolutionary action (see Tuveson 1949). These movements engender active change and leave their mark on the whole of society. Millenarism has, in fact, played an important role in all national and social liberation movements in premodern and modern Europe. It has also preceded and permeated many incipient nationalist and socialist movements in developing countries (Bastide 1961; Mühlmann 1961).

The negative evaluation of millenarism is based mainly on the study of movements developed by doomed or declining groups. Such movements have served as alternatives to, rather than as precursors or as concomitants of, secular collective action, and they have had few lasting social consequences. For example, most medieval millenarian movements were ephemeral outbursts. Since they had little chance to change the massive structure of medieval society, most of these revolutionary revivals "short-circuited" and disappeared. Material on the American Indians suggests that radical millenarism has played a limited and largely disruptive role in their history. Any movement with a revolutionary potential was quickly suppressed, leaving an aftermath of disillusion and disorganization. The task of rehabilitating and integrating the Indians was performed mainly by reformist cults oriented to peaceful accommodation to the white society (Voget 1956; Barnett 1957). Most millenarian movements in modern society are radically antipolitical. They conduct a violent campaign against secular movements and enjoin their members to keep away from them. In these cases religious and secular revolutionism are mutually exclusive, and they compete rather than mutually reinforce complementary solutions. [See NATIVISM AND REVIVALISM.]

The outcome of any millenarian movement depends on the historical circumstances, on the type of society, and on the nature of the group in which it occurs. Of crucial importance are the degree of differentiation of the society, the characteristics of the religious and political spheres, the position of the millenarian group in the changing balance of power, and the group's chances to promote its goals through political action.

Religious and secular revolutionism

The basic similarities and interconnections between religious and secular revolutionism is a major theme in most recent studies of millenarism, irrespective of their ideological position. First we note the typological affinity between these two kinds of movements. Secular revolutionary movements differ greatly from other types of secular political movements and have, in a certain sense, a semireligious character. Their world view is total and all-embracing. It purports to solve basic problems of meaning and to trace and interpret the unfolding of world history. The revolutionary ideology is a matter of ultimate concern and utmost seriousness; it demands from the followers unquestioning faith and unconditional loyalty. It is therefore all-pervasive and defines every aspect of life. Much like the great religious movements of the past, secular revolutionism has deeply stirred large masses of people, evoking intense fervor and dedication to its cause. Second, we find the similarity of predisposing factors. Like millenarism, secular revolutionism is brought about by a combination of deprivation, frustration, disorientation, and disintegration of primary groups. Last but not least are the dynamic interconnections between the two types of revolutionism. I have already mentioned that millenarism is often a precursor and concomitant of secular revolutionism.

The most important feature of millenarism seems to be its composite, "intermediate" nature. It combines components which are seemingly mutually exclusive: it is historical as well as mythical, religious as well as political, and, most significant, it is future-oriented as well as past-oriented. It is precisely this combination of a radical revolutionary position with traditionalism that accounts for the widespread appeal of millenarism and turns it into such a potent agent of change.

YONINA TALMON

[*Directly related are the entries* NATIVISM AND REVIVALISM; SECTS AND CULTS. *Other relevant material may be found in* COLLECTIVE BEHAVIOR; MASS PHENOMENA; RELIGIOUS ORGANIZATION; REVOLUTION; SOCIAL MOVEMENTS; *and in the biographies of* BUBER; KLUCKHOHN; MANNHEIM; TROELTSCH; WEBER, MAX.]

BIBLIOGRAPHY

ABERLE, DAVID F. 1962 A Note on Relative Deprivation Theory as Applied to Millenarian and Other Cult Movements. Pages 209–214 in Sylvia L. Thrupp (editor), *Millennial Dreams in Action: Essays in Comparative Study.* Comparative Studies in Society and History, Supplement No. 2. The Hague: Mouton.

BALANDIER, GEORGES (1955) 1963 *Sociologie actuelle de l'Afrique noire: Dynamique sociale en Afrique centrale.* 2d ed., rev. & enl. Paris: Presses Universitaires de France.

BANTON, MICHAEL 1963 African Prophets. *Race* 5, no. 2: 42–55.

BARNETT, HOMER G. 1957 *Indian Shakers: A Messianic Cult of the Pacific Northwest.* Carbondale: Southern Illinois Univ. Press.

BASTIDE, ROGER 1961 Messianisme et développement économique et social. *Cahiers internationaux de sociologie* 31:3–14.

BELSHAW, CYRIL S. 1950 The Significance of Modern Cults in Melanesian Development. *Australian Outlook* 22:116–125.

BENZ, ERNST (editor) 1965 *Messianische Kirchen, Sekten und Bewegungen im heutigen Afrika.* Leiden (Netherlands): Brill.

BERGER, PETER L. 1957 Motif messianique et processus social dans le Bahaïsme. *Archives de sociologie des religions* 2, no. 4:93–107.

BUBER, MARTIN (1932) 1936 *Königtum Gottes.* 2d ed., enl. Berlin: Schocken.

BURRIDGE, KENELM 1961 *Mambu: A Melanesian Millennium.* London: Methuen.

COHN, NORMAN (1957) 1961 *The Pursuit of the Millennium: Revolutionary Messianism in Medieval and Reformation Europe and Its Bearing on Modern Totalitarian Movements.* 2d ed. New York: Harper.

CUNNISON, IAN 1958 Jehovah's Witnesses at Work: Expansion in Central Africa. *The Times: British Colonies Review* 29, no. 1.

DESROCHE, HENRI 1963 Les messianismes et la catégorie de l'échec. *Cahiers internationaux de sociologie* 10:61–84.

DONALDSON, DWIGHT M. 1933 *The Shi'ite Religion: A History of Islam in Persia and Irak.* London: Luzac.

ELIADE, MIRCEA (1949) 1954 *Myth of the Eternal Return.* New York: Pantheon. → First published in French. A paperback edition was published in 1959 by Harper as *Cosmos and History: The Myth of the Eternal Return.*

ESSIEN-UDOM, ESSIEN U. 1962 *Black Nationalism: A Search for an Identity in America.* Univ. of Chicago Press. → A paperback edition was published in 1964 by Dell.

FESTINGER, LEON; RIECKEN, H. W.; and SCHACHTER, STANLEY 1956 *When Prophecy Fails.* Minneapolis: Univ. of Minnesota Press.

FIRTH, RAYMOND W. 1955 The Theory of "Cargo" Cults: A Note on Tikopia. *Man* 55:130–132.

FROOM, LE ROY E. 1946–1954 *The Prophetic Faith of Our Fathers: The Historical Development of Prophetic Interpretation.* Vols. 1, 3, 4. Washington: Review & Herald.

GUIART, JEAN; and WORSLEY, PETER 1958 La répartition des mouvements millénaristes en Mélanésie. *Archives de sociologie des religions* 3, no. 5:38–46.

HOBSBAWM, ERIC (1959) 1963 *Primitive Rebels: Studies in Archaic Forms of Social Movement in the 19th and 20th Centuries.* 2d ed. New York: Praeger.

HOLT, PETER M. 1958 *The Mahdist State in the Sudan, 1881–1898: A Study of Its Origins, Development and Overthrow.* Oxford: Clarendon.

HURWITZ, SIEGMUND 1958 *Die Gestalt des sterbenden Messiahs: Religions-psychologische Aspekte der jüdischen Apokalyptik.* Zurich: Rascher.

KATZ, JACOB 1961 *Tradition and Crisis: Jewish Society at the End of the Middle Ages.* New York: Free Press.

KLAUSNER, JOSEPH (1909) 1955 *The Messianic Idea in Israel: From Its Beginning to the Completion of the Mishnah.* 3d ed. New York: Macmillan. → First published in Hebrew.

KÖBBEN, A. J. F. 1960 Prophetic Movements as an Expression of Social Protest. *International Archives of Ethnography* 49:117–164.

KROEF, JUSTUS M. VAN DER 1952 The Messiah in Indonesia and Melanesia. *Scientific Monthly* 75:161–165.

KROEF, JUSTUS M. VAN DER 1962 Messianic Movements in the Celebes, Sumatra and Borneo. Pages 80–121 in Sylvia L. Thrupp (editor), *Millennial Dreams in Action: Essays in Comparative Study.* Comparative Studies in Society and History, Supplement No. 2. The Hague: Mouton.

LANTERNARI, VITTORIO (1960) 1963 *The Religions of the Oppressed: A Study of Modern Messianic Cults.* New York: Knopf. → First published as *Movimenti religiosi di libertà e di salvezza dei popoli oppressi.*

LAWRENCE, PETER 1964 *Road Belong Cargo.* Manchester Univ. Press.

LINTON, RALPH 1943 Nativistic Movements. *American Anthropologist* New Series 45:230–240.

MACRAE, DONALD G. 1961 *Ideology and Society: Papers in Sociology and Politics.* New York: Free Press. → See especially pages 181–198, "The Bolshevik Ideology."

MAIR, L. P. 1959 Independent Religious Movements in Three Continents. *Comparative Studies in Society and History* 1:113–136.

MANNHEIM, KARL (1929–1931) 1954 *Ideology and Utopia: An Introduction to the Sociology of Knowledge.* New York: Harcourt; London: Routledge. → A paperback edition was published in 1955 by Harcourt. A translation of *Ideologie und Utopie* (1929); Part 5 is a translation of the article "Wissenssoziologie" (1931).

MÉTRAUX, ALFRED (1941) 1957 Les messies de l'Amérique du Sud. *Archives de sociologie des religions* 2, no. 4:108–112.

MOONEY, JAMES 1896 The Ghost-dance Religion and the Sioux Outbreak of 1890. Part 2, pages 641–1110 in U.S. Bureau of American Ethnology, *Fourteenth Annual Report, 1892–1893.* Washington: Smithsonian Institution. → An abridged edition was published in 1965 by the University of Chicago Press.

MOWINCKEL, SIGMUND (1951) 1956 *He That Cometh.* Oxford: Blackwell. → First published in Norwegian.

MÜHLMANN, WILHELM E. 1961 *Chiliasmus und Nativismus: Studien zur Psychologie, Soziologie und historischen Kasuistik der Umsturzbewegungen.* Berlin: Reimer.

O'DEA, THOMAS F.   1957   *The Mormons*. Univ. of Chicago Press.

PIKE, EDGAR R.   1954   *Jehovah's Witnesses: Who They Are, What They Teach, What They Do*. London: Watts.

PRICE, THOMAS; and SHEPPERSON, GEORGE   1958   *Independent African: John Chilembwe and the Origins, Setting and Significance of the Nyasaland Native Rising of 1915*. Edinburgh Univ. Press.

RIBEIRO, RENÉ   1962   Brazilian Messianic Movements. Pages 55–69 in Sylvia L. Thrupp (editor), *Millennial Dreams in Action: Essays in Comparative Study*. Comparative Studies in Society and History, Supplement No. 2. The Hague: Mouton.

SCHOLEM, GERSHOM G.   (1941) 1961   *Major Trends in Jewish Mysticism*. 3d rev. ed. New York: Schocken.

SCHOLEM, GERSHOM G.   1957   *Shabtai Tsevi ve-hatnuah hashabtait* (Sabbatai Zevi and the Sabbatean Movement). 2 vols. Tel Aviv: Am Oved.

The Scroll of the War of the Sons of Light Against the Sons of Darkness. Edited by Yigael Yadin. Oxford Univ. Press, 1962.

SHAW, PLATO E.   1946   *The Catholic Apostolic Church, Sometimes Called Irvingite: A Historical Study*. New York: King's Crown Press.

SHEPPERSON, GEORGE   1962   The Comparative Study of Millenarian Movements. Pages 44–52 in Sylvia L. Thrupp (editor), *Millennial Dreams in Action: Essays in Comparative Study*. Comparative Studies in Society and History, Supplement No. 2. The Hague: Mouton.

SIERKSMA, FOKKE   1961   *Een nieuwe hemel en een nieuwe aarde: Messianistische en eschatologische bewegingen en voorstellingen bij primitieve volken*. The Hague: Mouton.

SMITH, MARIAN W.; WALLACE, ANTHONY F. C.; and VOGET, FRED W.   1959   Towards a Classification of Cult Movements. *Man* 59:8–12, 25–28.

SMITHSON, ROBERT J.   1935   *The Anabaptists: Their Contribution to Our Protestant Heritage*. London: Clarke.

STROUP, HERBERT H.   1945   *The Jehovah's Witnesses*. New York: Columbia Univ. Press.

SUNDKLER, BENGT G. M.   (1948) 1964   *Bantu Prophets in South Africa*. 2d ed. Published for the International African Institute. Oxford Univ. Press.

TALMON, JACOB L.   (1952) 1965   *The Rise of Totalitarian Democracy*. 2d ed. New York: Praeger. → The first British edition was entitled *The Origins of Totalitarian Democracy*.

TALMON, JACOB L.   (1960) 1961   *Political Messianism: The Romantic Phase*. New York: Praeger.

TALMON, YONINA   1962   Pursuit of the Millennium: The Relation Between Religious and Social Change. *Archives européennes de sociologie* 3:125–148.

TAYLOR, GORDON R.   1958   *The Angel Makers*. London: Heinemann.

THRUPP, SYLVIA L. (editor)   1962   *Millennial Dreams in Action: Essays in Comparative Study*. Comparative Studies in Society and History, Supplement No. 2. The Hague: Mouton.

TROELTSCH, ERNST   (1912) 1931   *The Social Teaching of the Christian Churches*. 2 vols. New York: Macmillan. → First published as *Die Soziallehren der christlichen Kirchen und Gruppen*. A paperback edition was published in 1960 by Harper.

TUVESON, ERNEST L.   1949   *Millennium and Utopia: A Study in the Background of the Idea of Progress*. Berkeley: Univ. of California Press.

VOGET, FRED W.   1956   The American Indian in Transition: Reformation and Accommodation. *American Anthropologist* New Series 58:249–263.

WALLACE, ANTHONY F. C.   1956   Revitalization Movements. *American Anthropologist* New Series 58:264–281.

WEBER, MAX   (1920–1921) 1922–1923   *Gesammelte Aufsätze zur Religionssoziologie*. 2d ed. 3 vols. Tübingen (Germany): Mohr.

WERBLOWSKY, ZWI R. J.   1965   A New Heaven and a New Earth: Considering Primitive Messianisms. *History of Religions* 5:164–172.

WERNER, ERNST   1960   Popular Ideologies in Late Medieval Europe: Taborite Chiliasm and Its Antecedents. *Comparative Studies in Society and History* 2:344–363.

WILSON, BRYAN R.   1961   *Sects and Society: A Sociological Study of the Elim Tabernacle, Christian Science, and Christadelphians*. Berkeley: Univ. of California Press.

WILSON, BRYAN R.   1963   Millennialism in Comparative Perspective. *Comparative Studies in Society and History* 6:93–114.

WORSLEY, PETER   1957   *The Trumpet Shall Sound: A Study of "Cargo" Cults in Melanesia*. London: MacGibbon & Kee.

MILLS, C. WRIGHT

C. Wright Mills (1916–1962) was at his death professor of sociology at Columbia University and one of the most controversial figures in American social science. He considered himself and was considered by his peers something of a rebel against the social science "establishment," and he attracted both admirers and critics for this role.

Shortly after his death, a series of essays, *The New Sociology*, was published in his honor. A central theme of these essays was the notion that Mills exemplified that spirit of social concern which he himself saw as the fundamental duty of the modern intellectual, in particular the social scientist—a duty, be it said, which he felt was not fulfilled by the majority of contemporary American social scientists (Horowitz 1964). His writings represented an attempt to open up paths of inquiry and analysis that would enable men to combat what he called the "main drift" of modern society to "rationality without reason," that is, the use of rational means in the service of substantively irrational ends. He found Marx and Weber to be the most helpful classical theorists, but he wanted to go "beyond" both of them to a new comparative world sociology that would seek to understand our time in terms of its historical specificity and by so doing renew the possibility of achieving human freedom. He thus set himself a large task, requiring research on the whole canvas of human (and particularly modern) history, but he died before he could present a full synthesis of his ideas.

He saw the present as a transition from the modern age to a postmodern period which he called the Fourth Epoch. If throughout his work there is a current of ultimate hope, it is equally suffused with pessimism about the more immediate future. He spoke of the "moral uneasiness of our time," a consequence throughout the Western world (including the Soviet Union) of what he called the "higher immorality," immorality encrusted in the structures and norms of the society, which he saw as particularly prevalent in the United States.

The basic problem of this era was that, unlike the eighteenth and nineteenth centuries, rationality no longer produced freedom, and since the two central ideologies which were developed in the modern West, liberalism and Marxism, assumed that it did, they no longer sufficed to explain and thus to control social change. Liberalism, being more heavily dependent on this assumption, was, he said, now irrelevant, and Marxism was inadequate.

What was even more unsettling to Mills was the "default" or "defeat" of the free intellectuals, especially deplorable at a time when the power of the intellectual had become potentially very great. His emphasis on the role of the intellectuals, on their failure, derived from his basic assumption that there is a great difference between the range of action possible to what he called "elites" and the range of action possible to the "masses." Men make their own history, but some are freer to do so than others. If the relatively free intellectuals fail to assert their moral leadership, other members of the elite, less qualified and less disinterested, will inevitably do so in their stead. This is in fact what had happened, according to Mills.

This failure is indicated by the nature of the problems studied by social scientists, and even more by the inadequate theory and methodology that underlie their work, an inadequacy he attributed to their deliberate abdication of social responsibility. Social theory, to be usable for Mills, had to deal in categories whose level of abstraction was not so high as to deprive them of all historical content or relevance. It should involve the search for causes of specific historical sequences and thereby explain shifts in the importance of and relations between the various "institutional orders" (politics, economics, the military, religion, and kinship). Mills took a strong stand against "principled monism or pluralism" and stated that the simple view of economic determinism must be "elaborated" by political and military determinism.

But more than theory was involved. Mills felt that the way in which the theory is used—the methodology of social research—is central to the results. He was not opposed to empirical research (indeed, he conducted a considerable amount of it), but he was against "abstracted empiricism," to which he contrasted the ideal of "craftsmanship." Craftsmanship is at once an ethos and an ideal which is only possible in a "properly developing society" but which also brings such a society into being. While Mills constantly called for such a conception of the role of the intellectual, he preferred to exemplify the skill rather than give an operational definition of it. It is perhaps as a result of this lack of definition that discussion of Mills's criticisms of his colleagues sometimes resembles a theological debate.

Mills's intellectual fathers in macrosociological theory were clearly Marx and Weber, as he himself acknowledged, and Freud and Mead in social psychology. It is sometimes said that he was the heir of Veblen. But while he called Veblen "the best social scientist America has produced," he was clearly critical of him, even in the introduction he wrote to *The Theory of the Leisure Class* (see Mills 1953). Mills called Veblen's views "oversimple" and "inadequate" and found the substance of his work less useful than the style. It is indeed in style and populist bias that Mills most resembles Veblen.

In his own research, he was more concerned with restating and advancing the Marx–Weber tradition than the Freud–Mead one. He accepted what he considered to be Weber's two most important revisions of Marx—the broadening of the concept of economic determinism to a wider social determinism and the "sophisticating" of the idea of class by the addition of the category of status or prestige. Mills thought that Marx's major political expectation about advanced capitalist societies—the progressive role of the proletariat—had "collapsed," and he railed against a "labor metaphysic," a faith in the progressive role of the working class (1960a), although an early monograph of his, *The New Men of Power* (1948), may be thought to exhibit this very view.

The shift in focus and methodology of Mills's empirical work over his life reflected his increasing discomfort with his peers in American sociology. *The New Men of Power* and *The Puerto Rican Journey* (Mills et al. 1950) rely in large part on survey data, especially the latter. They were both done under the aegis of the Bureau of Applied Social Research of Columbia University and under the methodological influence of Paul

Lazarsfeld. Nonetheless, even in these works Mills used the data to deal with problems of social change of the larger society, the United States; this was a feature of all his books, whatever their particular problems. In *White Collar* (1951), interview data became minor and government statistical data more important; he explicitly sought to locate the problems of the individual (in this case, the "new middle class") within the trends of the epoch, thus illustrating a methodological orientation he was later to insist upon in *The Sociological Imagination* (1959). *The Power Elite* (1956) represented a further evolution of this trend. The problem here was to explain the over-all power structure of the United States, not the role of out-groups that are relatively more accessible to being studied (labor leaders, migrants, white-collar workers). In this task, Mills asserted, national surveys are useless, and he relied upon "reasoning together." The data were largely historical, and the objective of the research was to explain the "moral uneasiness of our time."

In the three books that followed, *The Causes of World War Three* (1958), *The Sociological Imagination* (1959), and *Listen, Yankee* (1960b), Mills had moved one stage further. There was no question here of survey methods. There was even little question, as there still was in *The Power Elite*, of the systematic collection of data or the use of a research design and a research organization. These three books were historical interpretations—of the contemporary world system, of the evolution of the social sciences in the United States, of social revolution in Cuba—in the form of polemical essays. By then, Mills seemed to feel that methodological rigor was a trap which would prevent him or other scholars from dealing with significant problems. Thus, despite his critical view of Marxian theory, he grew more and more interested in Marxism as a "method of work," as his last published volume, *The Marxists* (1962), indicates. This was undoubtedly largely because he grew more and more unhappy with what he regarded as the ideological uses other scholars made of the Weberian critique—to defend an established order. And he came to fear the emphasis on science less as an illusion than as a diversion.

Mills ended as he began, a moralist preaching to his peers, the community of social scientists, throughout the world but especially in the United States. While he continued to accept the fundamentals of the Weberian modifications of Marx, he refused to accept Weber's "pessimistic world of a classic liberal." He thought the dominant apolitical or "value-free" bias of contemporary American sociology was an ideological mask, hiding value preferences which he did not share. In a basic sense, he was a utopian reformer. He thought that knowledge properly used could bring about the good society, and that if the good society was not yet here, it was primarily the fault of men of knowledge.

IMMANUEL WALLERSTEIN

[*See also* ASSIMILATION; ELITES; KNOWLEDGE, SOCIOLOGY OF; LEADERSHIP, *article on* SOCIOLOGICAL ASPECTS; MARXIST SOCIOLOGY; POLITICAL SOCIOLOGY; POWER; SOCIAL PROBLEMS; *and the biographies of* FREUD; MARX; MEAD; VEBLEN; WEBER, MAX.]

WORKS BY MILLS

1948   *The New Men of Power: America's Labor Leaders.* New York: Harcourt.

1950   MILLS, C. WRIGHT; SENIOR, C.; and GOLDSEN, R. K. *The Puerto Rican Journey: New York's Newest Migrants.* New York: Harper.

1951   *White Collar: The American Middle Classes.* New York: Oxford Univ. Press. → A paperback edition was published in 1956.

1953   Introduction. In Thorstein Veblen, *The Theory of the Leisure Class: An Economic Study of Institutions.* New York: New American Library.

1953   GERTH, HANS; and MILLS, C. WRIGHT *Character and Social Structure: The Psychology of Social Institutions.* New York: Harcourt.

1956   *The Power Elite.* New York: Oxford Univ. Press.

1958   *The Causes of World War Three.* New York: Simon & Schuster.

1959   *The Sociological Imagination.* New York: Oxford Univ. Press.

1960a   MILLS, C. WRIGHT (editor) *Images of Man: The Classic Tradition in Sociological Thinking.* New York: Braziller.

1960b   *Listen, Yankee: The Revolution in Cuba.* New York: McGraw-Hill.

1962   *The Marxists.* New York: Dell.

Power, Politics and People: The Collected Essays of C. Wright Mills. Edited and with an introduction by Irving Louis Horowitz. New York: Oxford Univ. Press, 1963.

SUPPLEMENTARY BIBLIOGRAPHY

APTHEKER, HERBERT 1960 *The World of C. Wright Mills.* New York: Marzani & Munsell.

HOROWITZ, IRVING LOUIS (editor) 1964 *The New Sociology: Essays in Social Science and Social Theory, in Honor of C. Wright Mills.* New York: Oxford Univ. Press.

WEBER, MAX (1906–1924) 1946 *From Max Weber: Essays in Sociology.* Translated and edited by Hans H. Gerth and C. Wright Mills. New York: Oxford Univ. Press.

MINISTRY

See RELIGIOUS SPECIALISTS.

MINNESOTA MULTIPHASIC PERSONALITY INVENTORY

See under PERSONALITY MEASUREMENT.

MINORITIES

Contemporary sociologists generally define a minority as a group of people—differentiated from others in the same society by race, nationality, religion, or language—who both think of themselves as a differentiated group and are thought of by the others as a differentiated group with negative connotations. Further, they are relatively lacking in power and hence are subjected to certain exclusions, discriminations, and other differential treatment. The important elements in this definition are a set of attitudes—those of group identification from within the group and those of prejudice from without—and a set of behaviors—those of self-segregation from within the group and those of discrimination and exclusion from without.

Among those who do not study minority groups, the common tendency is to take the word "minority" literally and simply to say that a minority is a small group of people who live in the midst of a larger group. At least two defects make this simple definition useless. First, groups are not "naturally" or "inevitably" differentiated: cultures (either of the minority or the majority, or—usually—both) must *define* them as differentiated before they are so. People of different races, nationalities, religions, or languages can live among one another for generations, amalgamating and assimilating or not doing so, without differentiating themselves. Like everything else that is social, minority groups must be socially defined as minority groups, which entails a set of attitudes and behaviors. Second, relative numbers in and out of the group have not been found to be definitionally important. Sociologically speaking, it makes no sense to say that Negroes are not a minority group in those few counties of Mississippi, Alabama, and South Carolina where they constitute a numerical majority of the population, but that they are a minority group in the rest of the South. Likewise, even though the Bantus constitute around 80 per cent of the population of South Africa, sociologists have defined them as a minority group because they occupy a subordinate position. Many nations have no single "majority group" in terms of numbers. Thus it is necessary either to counterpose a "minority" to a "dominant" group, in terms of power, or to abandon the term "minority" altogether and call it a "subordinate" group.

Origins of national minorities. The origin of the term "national minorities" can be traced to Europe, where it was applied to various national groups who were identified with particular territories by virtue of long residence in them but who had lost their sovereignty over these territories to some more numerous people of a different nationality. In some cases the minority groups ceased altogether to occupy their original territories and were dispersed throughout the nation of which they were now subjects. More often they stayed in the same place but in a subordinate position, since the dominant political and economic institutions were now run mainly for the benefit of the larger national group. The latter usually enacted laws to regulate the political existence of the minorities; for instance, they might have to send their own community leaders to the national assembly instead of being able to vote individually for candidates in a national election. Even the areas in which they could live or the occupations they could pursue might be determined by law; at the least, the dominant nationality regarded them with suspicion, as the Czechs were regarded under the Austro–Hungarian Empire.

Changing social definitions. A minority need not be a traditional group with a long-standing group identification. It can arise as a result of changing social definitions in a process of economic or political differentiation. The increasing saliency of a certain occupation, for example, can set apart the people who practice that occupation, if occupations are more or less hereditary in the society, and cause them to be considered a minority group. Language or religious variations in a society can be considered unimportant for thousands of years, but a series of political events can so sharpen the religious or linguistic distinctions that the followers of one variation who happen to be without much power in the society are thereafter considered a minority.

These processes can be illustrated by developments in India. The Marwaris, allegedly originating in Rajasthan, were until the late eighteenth century merely another occupational caste among the thousands of castes that make up India. They were moneylenders and small merchants, who were of no greater importance in the social structure than any other occupational caste until the rise of capitalism gave a great new importance to their economic functions. The new economic salience of the hereditary occupation created a salience for the people who practiced the occupation and made them into a despised, feared, and envied minority. The process was aided by the increased geographic dispersion of the group caused by a broader demand for their occupational services.

Language differentiation based on geographic dispersal has been going on in India since time immemorial within two great language stocks, the

Dravidian of southern India and the Indo-Aryan of northern India. The differentiation of Dravidian into Tamil, Telugu, Malayalam, and Kannada and several dozen lesser languages was not marked by definite historical events any more than was the differentiation of Latin into Italian, French, Spanish, and Rumanian. The modern development of political boundaries, which occurred at first under the British for administrative convenience and, after 1948, under the independent government of India, made language a salient basis of differentiation because the political boundaries were drawn as closely as possible to language boundary lines. Thus, it has been largely within the past few decades that language has become one of the most distinctive marks of a minority in India, and the basis of considerable group conflict.

Minority groups in the United States

In the United States, the term "minority groups" can be applied only in an extended sense. All citizens of the United States belong legally to a single American nationality; there are no laws that regulate the political status of any group of citizens according to their or their ancestors' national origin. Moreover, there is no single nationality group in the United States that either forms a numerical majority or enjoys a *de facto* political dominance; this state of affairs has existed at least since 1830.

This is not to say, however, that discrimination and prejudice are unknown in the United States, but that, since there is no one "majority group" with a special claim to American nationality, the handicaps faced by American "minority groups" cannot be explained in terms of their national origin as such. The crucial factor would appear to be the degree to which any group has been allowed to become assimilated into the mainstream of American life and to enjoy the same opportunities as the majority of Americans. Most immigrant nationality groups suffered some discrimination during their early years in the country but were later assimilated. Those groups that were not allowed to assimilate—notably, the Negroes—have continued to be objects of prejudice for most of their fellow citizens, and in this sense they constitute "minorities," even though the number of Negroes far exceeds that of many a group that does, indeed, have a common national origin outside the United States but now thinks of itself as "American."

This does not mean that members of assimilating groups in the majority completely lose all their memories of ancestry; they may pass along to successive generations selected aspects of traditional culture—often of a ceremonial nature—and at the very least they pass along knowledge of the name of the ancestral homeland. [*See* ASSIMILATION.]

Racial minorities. Racial groups are distinguished from each other by their possession of certain physical features inherited as the result of endogamy over a long period. Few races, however, are biologically pure, nor do most people use strictly biological criteria in deciding that a person belongs to one racial group rather than another. Thus, in the United States, a Negro is defined as someone of whom it is known that at least one of his ancestors was a Negro; the definition will hold even if, to all appearances, the individual is a "white." Moreover, although the principal racial minorities of the United States—the American Indians, the Chinese, the Filipinos, the Negroes, and the Japanese—all have members with some Caucasoid ancestry, they are still regarded as "nonwhite." The dominant white majority generally chooses to overlook the fact that they, too, are not "pure," since many whom they accept as white have some Negroid or Mongoloid ancestry.

Nationality groups. The principal nationality groups in the United States came originally from Europe and, in spite of some admixture from other races, can plausibly regard themselves as having a common racial ancestry. It is not race, therefore, but culture—and the history of each culture—that provides the most salient distinctions between them. Immigrants of the second and third generations generally adopt English as their major or only language and assimilate their values and manners —at least in the more socially visible aspects of their behavior—to those of the majority. There are thus no permanent physical reminders of their ancestors' minority status, and they are not usually regarded as belonging to a minority group.

The major exceptions to this are those groups— such as the Scandinavians of Wisconsin and Minnesota—that have remained in isolated rural areas, having little contact with the dominant American culture and therefore being under no pressure to assimilate themselves. Their status as national minorities is not the result of discrimination and prejudice on the part of the majority but of deliberate choice or sheer lack of opportunity. It cannot be said, however, that they suffer from their minority status, since they enjoy the full privileges of American citizenship and are not compelled to maintain their traditional way of life or to inhabit any particular territory.

Finally, a new type of nationality minority is being created by immigration of victims of political persecution; the best example is the Cubans, concentrated mainly in south Florida and New York City, who plan to return to their home country after an expected future political revolution there.

Language minorities. Some groups in the United States speak a language other than English, although they are not recent immigrants; indeed, they have continued to speak their own language over many generations. They are therefore best designated as "language minorities"; although they tend to have other distinctive cultural traits, it is principally their language that sets them apart from the majority of the population.

The outstanding example of such a minority is the Spanish-speaking people who live in the sparsely populated rural areas of New Mexico and southern Colorado. Their position is similar to that of some European national minorities, since most of their ancestors were originally Mexican citizens whose territories were incorporated into the United States after the Mexican War of 1846–1848. They have been able to maintain a distinctive way of life because they are both isolated and poor; this same isolation tends to protect them from the discriminatory attitudes of the dominant, English-speaking population, who have not, on the whole, found it necessary to impose any legal or political disabilities upon them.

Religious minorities. Discrimination on grounds of religion, although expressly forbidden by the constitution, has long been practiced in the United States with varying severity against a large number of groups. Chief among these groups are the Jews, the Muslims, Christians of the Eastern Orthodox church, and various Protestant and Orthodox sects. Roman Catholics, too, although their total number in the United States, according to some estimates, was more than forty million in 1960, share some of the disadvantages of minority-group status, though to a decreasing extent. One special feature of membership in a religious minority is that it can be acquired voluntarily, regardless of racial or national origin, though most members, of course, are following the religion of their parents.

The position of the Jews is unlike that of other religious minorities because there are more Jews than there are active believers in the Jewish religion. Indeed, it is likely that in the United States believers and nonbelievers are about equal in number, although most of the latter would undoubtedly regard themselves as Jews nonetheless. This raises the question of whether there is any single objective basis for classifying them as Jews. One criterion can be ruled out completely: there is no such thing as a Jewish race, as should be obvious from the endless variety of racial, national, and linguistic characteristics to be found among Jews. It therefore seems best to describe them, for summary purposes, as recent descendants of persons known to have followed the Jewish faith.

Minorities in other parts of the world

Outside the United States, racial minorities are found predominantly where race is considered important in the culture. This is mainly in Africa, where whites, Negroes, and immigrants from India variously consider themselves or each other as minorities. The Ainus are a racial minority in Japan, but the other group that is subjected to discrimination in that country—the *eta*—are to be considered a caste minority (some authors would prefer not to call castes "minorities" when they are of the same race, religion, nationality, and language as the majority group). To some extent, native Indians are considered minorities in parts of South America. But in a country like India, where race is not considered important, racial differences are not the basis for the formation of minority groups (religion and language are).

Nationality differences continue to provide the source of minorities throughout Europe (including the Soviet Union, which extends into Asia). Some of these are in the process of disappearing as distinctive minorities because of assimilation, such as the Scots, Irish, and Welsh in the British Isles. Some are of very ancient origin, and their minority status has not changed appreciably in centuries, such as the Basques in Spain and the Greeks in Turkey, who also use a language different from that of the majority in their respective countries. Other minorities are being newly created by virtue of recent migrations for economic reasons, such as the Italian minority in Sweden. Sometimes political refugees form a new nationality minority, such as the Poles in Great Britain and the Balts in Sweden. Some retain their status as minorities through language differences or through international conflict, such as the German-speaking, Austrian-backed Tyrolese in the Italian province of Alto Adige. Mainly outside Europe, some nationality minorities seems to maintain their distinction through political differences with the majority, such as the Karens of Burma.

Language is often closely associated with nationality, as we have seen. But there are some linguistic minorities which seem to owe their origin to differences of social class rather than of nationality; notable examples are the Swedish-speaking Finns and the German-speaking people of eastern Europe. Perhaps the contemporary nation with the most salient language minorities is India. When the states of India were divided mainly along linguistic boundaries, only the 14 languages spoken by the largest numbers of people could be assigned a state. As the states quickly assumed political importance and language became socially identified as the main basis for their differentiation, those who spoke languages other than the dominant one of their state became minorities. Such minorities included people who spoke one of the hundreds of "little" languages of India, for whom there was no state at all, including most of the "scheduled tribes," as the British administrators called the small "primitive" groups living outside the mainstream of Indian life. They also included those who spoke one of the major languages but were not residing in the state where their language was dominant. As language became a national issue in independent India, the language minorities usually became the objects of prejudice and discrimination.

Religious differences are still a prime source of minorities, although in Europe perhaps not as much as in past centuries. Perhaps the most destructive conflict of the post-World War II period has been the one between Muslims and Hindus in India, and a most bitter—though small-scale—conflict has been that between the Muslims and Jews in Palestine. Protestant minorities have been subject to a good deal of discrimination in Catholic Spain and parts of South America. Catholics feel themselves to be a minority in several countries where Protestants form a majority, although the prejudice or discrimination directed at them is not very strong, as it once was. The Jews, who have been the most persecuted minority in modern times, are still the subject of considerable prejudice and discrimination in several countries of Europe, particularly in the Soviet bloc. Religious minorities also include the Christians in Muslim countries, pagans and atheists in Christian countries, the Hutterites and Doukhobors in Canada, the minor religious groups of the Indian subcontinent, and several others.

The functioning of minorities in society

A minority's position involves exclusion or assignment to a lower status in one or more of four areas of life: the economic, the political, the legal, and the social–associational. That is, a minority will be assigned to lower-ranking occupations or to lower-compensated positions within each occupation; it will be prevented from exercising the full political privileges held by majority citizens; it will not be given equal status with the majority in the application of law or justice; or it will be partially or completely excluded from both the formal and the informal associations found among the majority. Not infrequently, the minority also voluntarily excludes itself partially or completely from participation in these areas of life, partly as a means of maintaining traditional cultural differences. Accompanying the objective subordination and segregation of the minorities are usually to be found some subjective attitudes of mutual hostility, although these may sometimes be publicly denied and camouflaged. Majority–minority relations invariably involve some conflict, although this may take varied forms and operate on different levels.

There seem to be three types of attitudes of hostility or prejudice with which the dominant group regards the minority and with which the minority may attempt to counter the dominant group. The complex etiologies of each of these, which differ somewhat from society to society, cannot be analyzed here. The first is an attitude in which *power* is the main element: the dominant group wishes to exploit the minority for economic, political, or sexual purposes, or for prestige, and the minority group seeks to escape their exploitation. While the achievement of ascendancy in terms of one or more of these scarce values may be brutal (including enslavement of the minority), it is seldom personal, nor does it, except accidentally, result in the death of a minority person. The second attitude is *ideological*: the dominant group believes that it has a monopoly on the "truth" (as may the minority group also). The achievement of ascendancy by one ideological group over the other results in drastic efforts to convert the minority to the dominant group's version of the "truth"; failing that, it banishes the minority by exile or death. The third attitude is *racist*: the dominant group believes itself to be biologically superior to the minority group, and it stereotypes the minority in terms of negatively valued characteristics. (The minority may have the same attitude toward the dominant group, but since it lacks power, this has few or no behavioral consequences.)

Different social systems of conflict accompany these three different attitudes of hostility. For example, the caste system is generally associated only with the racist attitude; this system prohibits mobility across group lines and equal-status relationships and requires endogamy, systematized displays of inferiority by the minority, and occupational division of labor. Racism also has a pathological form which insists on the physical extermination of the minority race because it is alleged to threaten the "purity" of the dominant race. Where power seems to be the main ingredient in the conflict between dominant and minority groups, there is one form or another of exploitation: for example, there may be slavery, piracy, tribute, suzerainty over the minority's political or military institutions, differential remuneration for work, or seizure of the minority group's women for sexual purposes. Where the ideological element seems to be the main factor in the hostility of the dominant group toward the minority, the majority group generally offers the minority the alternatives of conversion or extermination. Ideological conflict is at once the most brutal and the most generous toward the minority, depending on whether or not the minority will accede completely to the beliefs of the dominant group.

In the contemporary world, the religious minorities of India and Palestine offer examples of ideological conflict, as do the political minorities of some communist countries. Power conflict is most evident in dominant–minority relations in northern and central Africa and in South America. Racism is today most frequent in South Africa and in the United States, although it is apparently still strong in Germany and in eastern Europe.

Role of minorities in social change.   From the preceding discussion, it will readily be understood that the different roles of minorities in the society will affect their impact on general social change. In general, the existence of minorities in a society offers a constant stimulus and a constant irritant that for several reasons provoke social change. Minorities are often carriers of a culture different from that of the dominant group, and the contact and clash of cultures have long been hypothesized as sources of social change. Even when minorities carry no traditional alien culture, their partial exclusion from the general society serves as a basis for the development of some deviant culture.

In addition, apart from their cultural differences, minorities are sources of social dissatisfaction and social unrest, which are conditions for social change. As conflict groups, minorities tend to upset the *status quo*: they require the dominant to readjust to them regularly, and sometimes they are able to make coalitions with other minorities within the society or with outside societies in order to change the balance of power. Minorities will often join reform or revolutionary factions or parties among the dominant group, since often the best chance for improving their lot within the existing society is offered by a turnover of elites. Some minorities probably include a disproportionate number of inventive and otherwise creative individuals, because their alienation from the society in which they are forced to live without full participation gives such individuals a perspective that is not pos-

sible for the more fully integrated; the "marginal man" between two subsocieties has been identified by some sociologists as one type of "creative man" (Stonequist 1937). If necessity be the mother of invention (which it probably usually is not), minority members are more often beset by necessity than are dominant group members. At least in the limited area of seeking expedients to improve their unhappy lot, minority members are influenced by this creative aspect of necessity.

These general sources of social changes created by the existence of a minority in a society are probably best seen in that situation where power considerations by the dominant group maintain the existence of the minority. Where power and material exploitation are not involved, the dominant group is often either generous or unconcerned about letting the minority group go its own way, and that may often create the stimuli for social change. For example, while the powerful dominant group in the society is bent on accumulating wealth or retaining political ascendancy, the weak minority group can concentrate on acquiring knowledge and wisdom, which in the long run become stimulants of social change. The ideational tolerance often practiced by power-controlling groups sometimes results in their own destruction; for example, the historian Edward Gibbon held this to be true about the relations between Romans and Christians in the later stages of the Roman Empire.

On the other hand, where ideological or racist considerations maintain the existence of a minority in a society, there is less freedom for it to create conditions that are conducive to social change. Ideational deviation—cultural or individual—is not tolerated where it becomes open and obvious, and racists must constantly prove the incapacity of the minority group by squelching all evidence of creativity whenever it threatens to appear among minority members. Where the dominant group is either racist or believes it holds a monopoly on truth, it is likely to regulate closely the education, cultural expression, and other innovative tendencies of the minority group, thus severely inhibiting the minority as a source of social change. Yet, under these circumstances, the minority group becomes schooled in subtlety and ingeniousness and may stimulate change where it is least expected: the songs, humor, and folk tales of the Negro slaves in the nineteenth-century American South can be seen in retrospect to have had a leavening effect on the white society, and the Jews in medieval Europe—repressed as they were—invented a merchant capitalism which eventually was accepted by the whole society (Sombart 1911).

It should not be assumed that the existence of a minority in a society operates solely to create social change. Dominant–minority relations often inhibit change. They tend to make the dominant group rigid in maintaining the *status quo*. The existence of an exploited or repressed minority makes even the most powerful dominant group fearful, and fear can discourage all forms of social change. Dominant–minority relations are usually wasteful and inefficient—they waste the time and energy of the dominant group in maintaining the repression, and they prevent the minority group from producing at its maximum potential—and this waste of material and intellectual resources restricts creative social change.

Research on minorities

Research on minorities can be considered as having taken place within two frameworks. One is the framework of the ethnologist, who is concerned with describing the culture of a specific society where the society is the minority group. Whereas the usual ethnological study is of a geographically separated society, the ethnological study of a minority group has to consider its subject group living in physical proximity to one or more other groups. The institutions, the customs, and the daily life of the minority groups are considered under this approach. The second framework is that of the sociologist, who concentrates on the relationship between minority and majority groups, not on the distinctive cultural characteristics of either group, except insofar as they are pertinent to understanding the relationship. The relationship between majority and minority is analyzed in terms of general processes, such as conflict, accommodation, and assimilation. A variation on this approach has been one which treats minority–majority relations as social problems, with special emphasis on aspects (e.g., Brown & Roucek 1937), causes (e.g., Hughes & Hughes 1952), and results of discrimination and prejudice (e.g., Myrdal 1944).

There are other variations in the literature. J. H. Franklin (1947) has analyzed the American Negro problem as a historian, M. R. Konvitz (1946) has examined the position of the alien under American law, and Gordon Allport (1954) has analyzed majority–minority relations in terms of the psychological concept of prejudice. Yet these authors also treat their subject matter as social problems. Practically all monographic studies are limited to a single majority–minority group situation, as is Ruth Glass's study of the West Indians in London (1960). However, other empirical studies attempt to draw together the findings of a number of monographs: for example, A. H. Richmond's work *The Colour Problem* (1955) or Charles Wagley and Marvin Harris' more ethnologic *Minorities in the New World* (1958).

The largest number of empirical studies, usually published as articles in the professional social science journals, are highly specialized studies of the history, demography, economic status, political and legal rights, educational attainments, or other achievements of specific minorities. In addition, there are studies of prejudice, group identification, social change, or other such broad concepts, which are, however, usually based on very narrow and limited samples of the population.

Much of the literature soon becomes irrelevant, partly because it is limited to description and partly because of the value orientations guiding the research; these orientations are seldom made explicit and thus cannot be readily taken into account by the reader. There is a need for research using analytic concepts, thus permitting nomothetic rather than purely empirical generalizations. There is also a need for research that considers the dynamics of social change affecting and affected by minorities and majority–minority relations. The rapid changes in intergroup relations in contemporary life, occurring under a great diversity of cultural conditions, permit unrivaled opportunities for sociologists wishing to study the dynamic principles involved in all social change.

ARNOLD M. ROSE

[*See also* ANTI-SEMITISM; ASSIMILATION; CONSTITUTIONAL LAW, *article on* CIVIL RIGHTS; ETHNIC GROUPS; PREJUDICE; RACE; RACE RELATIONS; SECTS AND CULTS.]

BIBLIOGRAPHY

ALLPORT, GORDON W. 1954 *The Nature of Prejudice.* Reading, Mass.: Addison-Wesley. → An abridged paperback edition was published in 1958 by Doubleday.

BROWN, FRANCIS J.; and ROUCEK, JOSEPH S. (editors) (1937) 1952 *One America: The History, Contributions and Present Problems of Our Racial and National Minorities.* 3d ed. New York: Prentice-Hall.

BURMA, JOHN H. 1954 *Spanish-speaking Groups in the United States.* Durham, N.C.: Duke Univ. Press.

CLARK, KENNETH B. 1965 *Dark Ghetto: Dilemmas of Social Power.* New York: Harper.

CLAUDE, INIS L. 1955 *National Minorities: An International Problem.* Cambridge, Mass.: Harvard Univ. Press.

CONFERENCE ON RACE RELATIONS IN WORLD PERSPECTIVE, HONOLULU, 1954 1955 *Race Relations in World Perspective.* Edited by Andrew W. Lind. Honolulu: Univ. of Hawaii Press.

DRAKE, ST. CLAIR; and CAYTON, HORACE R. (1945) 1962 *Black Metropolis: A Study of Negro Life in a Northern City.* 2 vols., rev. & enl. New York: Harcourt.

FINKELSTEIN, LOUIS (editor) (1949) 1960 *The Jews: Their History, Culture and Religion*. 3d ed., 2 vols. New York: Harper.

FRANKLIN, JOHN H. (1947) 1956 *From Slavery to Freedom: A History of American Negroes*. 2d ed., rev. & enl. New York: Knopf.

FREEDMAN, MAURICE (editor) 1955 *A Minority in Britain: Social Studies of the Anglo-Jewish Community*. London: Vallentine.

GLASS, RUTH (1960) 1961 *London's Newcomers: The West Indian Migrants*. Center for Urban Studies, University College, London, Report No. 1. Cambridge, Mass.: Harvard Univ. Press. → First published as *Newcomers: The West Indians in London*. Chapters 2 and 3 analyze geographical distribution and discrimination in housing.

HUGHES, EVERETT C.; and HUGHES, HELEN M. 1952 *Where Peoples Meet: Racial and Ethnic Frontiers*. Glencoe, Ill.: Free Press.

KANE, JOHN J. 1955 *Catholic–Protestant Conflicts in America*. Chicago: Regnery.

KONVITZ, MILTON R. 1946 *The Alien and the Asiatic in American Law*. Ithaca, N.Y.: Cornell Univ. Press.

LINCOLN, CHARLES E. 1961 *The Black Muslims in America*. Boston: Beacon.

MYRDAL, GUNNAR (1944) 1962 *An American Dilemma: The Negro Problem and Modern Democracy*. New York: Harper. → A paperback edition was published in 1964 by McGraw-Hill.

RICHMOND, ANTHONY H. (1955) 1961 *The Colour Problem*. Rev. ed. Baltimore: Penguin.

ROSE, ARNOLD M.; and ROSE, CAROLINE B. (editors) 1965 *Minority Problems*. New York: Harper.

SCHERMERHORN, R. A. 1964 Toward a General Theory of Minority Groups. *Phylon* 25:238–246.

SHIBUTANI, TAMOTSU; and KWAN, K. M. 1965 *Ethnic Stratification: A Comparative Approach*. New York: Macmillan.

SIMPSON, GEORGE E.; and YINGER, J. MILTON (1953) 1965 *Racial and Cultural Minorities: An Analysis of Prejudice and Discrimination*. 3d ed. New York: Harper.

SOMBART, WERNER (1911) 1913 *The Jews and Modern Capitalism*. London: Allen & Unwin. → First published as *Die Juden und das Wirtschaftsleben*. A paperback edition was published in 1962 by Collier.

STONEQUIST, EVERETT V. (1937) 1961 *The Marginal Man*. New York: Russell.

SULKOWSKI, JÓZEF 1944 *The Problem of International Protection of National Minorities: Past Experience as a Basis for Future Solution*. New York: Privately published.

TAEUBER, KARL E.; and TAEUBER, ALMA F. 1965 *Negroes in Cities: Residential Segregation and Neighborhood Change*. Chicago: Aldine.

VANDER ZANDEN, JAMES W. (1963) 1966 *American Minority Relations: The Sociology of Race and Ethnic Groups*. 2d ed. New York: Ronald Press.

WAGLEY, CHARLES; and HARRIS, MARVIN 1958 *Minorities in the New World*. New York: Columbia Univ. Press.

WILLIAMS, ROBIN M. JR. 1964 *Strangers Next Door: Ethnic Relations in American Communities*. Englewood Cliffs, N.J.: Prentice-Hall.

MISES, LUDWIG VON

See VON MISES, LUDWIG.

MISES, RICHARD VON

See VON MISES, RICHARD.

MISSELDEN, EDWARD

Edward Misselden (fl. 1608–1654) was both an English merchant and a comparatively enlightened mercantilist. As a mercantilist, he made an important contribution to the development of the idea of the balance of trade as an analytical and measurable concept.

Concern over the state of England's foreign trade moved Parliament in 1622 to appoint a standing commission on trade, and this event stimulated Misselden to write his tract *Free Trade: Or, the Meanes to Make Trade Florish* (1622). The book attributed the alleged decay of English foreign trade to excessive imports, to the export of bullion by the East India Company, and to the defective enforcement of the regulations of the cloth trade. Misselden contended that the loss of bullion was partly due to the undervaluation of English coin. Consequently he proposed that its denomination be raised, in the hope that the ouflow of bullion would be checked and that, in "the plenty of money," trade would be quickened and exports increased. He conceded that too much bullion in the form of plate would cause scarcity of money; nevertheless, for a nation to have plate was considered preferable to turning it into coin and sending it out of the kingdom because of its undervaluation. He realized that landlords and creditors would suffer losses if the denomination were raised and advocated that they be protected by a provision that would make contracts negotiated before the raising of the currency payable at the value of the money when the contracts were made. Like other mercantilists, he did not regard higher prices as an evil if they are accompanied by at least an equal increase in money, stocks, employment, or incomes. In effect, this was his answer to the possible objection that raising the denomination of English coin would result in an increase in commodity prices.

Misselden's second book, *The Circle of Commerce: Or, the Ballance of Trade*, was written as a reply to Gerard Malynes—"a dastardly combatant"—who accused him of overlooking the role of foreign exchanges as the chief cause of England's distress. In this book, Misselden appears to have used in print for the first time the phrase "balance of trade," describing it as "an excellent and politique Invention, to shew us the difference of weight in the *Commerce* of one Kingdome with another"

(1623, p. 116). The notion of balance was well known; it was the actual measurement of trade in the absence of periodic trade statistics that he regarded as a novel idea. "The first End of our Balance of trade," he wrote, "is to shew us the state thereof" (1623, gloss on p. 133). Indeed, by multiplying the customs revenue by 20 (a tariff of 5 per cent), Misselden attempted to measure England's trade balance for the year 1621; he found it in deficit and, using mercantilist arguments, warned of the impoverishment of the people.

Recognizing that international balance does not consist of commodity exports and imports alone, Misselden added such items as re-exports, profits from fisheries, and freight earnings to commodity statistics in computing the balance. Accordingly, he denied Malynes' accusation that the East India Company had contributed to England's shortage of money by exporting "Reals of Plate" to the East Indies, asserting that England not only would benefit from increased employment and freight earnings related to these exports but also would, in the net, derive more bullion from the import of Indian commodities and their re-export to "all parts of the World" than it sent to India to purchase them (1623, p. 35).

In contrast to Malynes, who allegedly held the view that the relative value of internationally traded commodities depends upon the value of the exchanges, Misselden argued that the market value of the exchanges is itself dependent upon the relative demand and supply of the respective foreign currencies and, in turn, upon the relative demand and supply of commodities of the respective countries. Misselden did believe that there is a natural rate of exchange that can be determined by melting down metallic money into its pure form. This "fineness" of money is the "center"—or, in modern terminology, the mint par—"whereunto all *Exchanges* have their naturall propension" (1623, p. 97). In the last analysis, Misselden observed, the exportation or importation of bullion is to be explained by the general abundance or scarcity of commodities, and with some exaggeration, he accused Malynes of having stated the argument backwards.

This controversy probably represents the first time in English history that a question of economic policy produced a war of tracts which exerted an immediate and traceable influence on government policy. The new views of Misselden and Thomas Mun, an official of the East India Company whom he knew and cited with approval, won a definite victory over the older views of Malynes and Milles.

This is not to suggest that Misselden's writings on economics were the product of objective scholarship; while they represented an advance over those of earlier pamphleteers, his contributions to the balance-of-trade doctrine and to the theory of exchanges were steeped in pressure-group politics and in particular circumstances. His exaggerated emphasis on national objectives, combined with his failure to disclose his own private trade connections, lends support to those who see English mercantilism as a body of international trade doctrine primarily concerned with the importance of England's having an excess of exports over imports—and developed for the most part by merchants pleading for special interests.

Although there is a sharp and irreconcilable conflict between economic universalism and mercantilism, Misselden appears not to have been aware of any such conflict. He argued that England had to increase its exports and decrease its imports to achieve and maintain a positive balance of trade; otherwise its trade would decay and its bullion be lost. He failed to mention, however, that the continuous accumulation of the precious metals by one nation cannot but harm the economic interests of other nations. He simply asserted the natural harmony of private and public interests (1623, p. 17). His failure to understand the fundamental elements of a self-regulating mechanism of adjustment is explained by his confusion about interests, as well as by his generally limited conceptualization.

There is always danger in describing the thought of an earlier period by means of terms or concepts that have later taken on different meanings. Thus, when Misselden advocated greater economic freedom or "free trade" he was certainly not defending economic freedom in principle or in general but only specific forms and degrees of economic freedom. Similarly, when he objected to governmental regulation he was not objecting to it in principle but only to specific forms or degrees of regulation. The achievement of formulating a general doctrine of economic freedom, as distinguished from a selective advocacy of specific freedoms, belongs to the physiocrats and to Adam Smith. They, however, do appear to have built up their general case from earlier specific arguments for particular freedoms. Although never entirely original, Misselden, by advocating certain particular freedoms, made a genuine contribution to doctrinal advance. He pointed out elements in the physical and social order of nature that tend to produce a self-operating and beneficial pattern of human behavior; asserted, however naively, the harmony of private and public interests; stressed the role of invisibles and re-exports in the trade balance; achieved considerable generalization in his discussion of exchanges; and devoted particular attention to the rising role of the large-scale merchant and the important contribution he could make to society if left largely to his own devices. All these concepts served as antecedents in the development of the general doctrine of economic free trade.

JOHN M. LETICHE

[See also ECONOMIC THOUGHT, *article on* MERCANTILIST THOUGHT; INTERNATIONAL MONETARY ECONOMICS, *article on* BALANCE OF PAYMENTS.]

WORKS BY MISSELDEN

1622   *Free Trade: Or, the Meanes to Make Trade Florish.* London: Waterson.
1623   *The Circle of Commerce: Or, the Ballance of Trade, in Defence of Free Trade . . .* London: Dawson.

SUPPLEMENTARY BIBLIOGRAPHY

FRIIS, ASTRID 1927 *Alderman Cockayne's Project and the Cloth Trade: The Commercial Policy of England in Its Main Aspects; 1603–1625.* Copenhagen: Munksgaard.
GARDINER, SAMUEL R. (1883–1884) 1896–1901 *History of England From the Accession of James I to the Outbreak of the Civil War: 1603–1642.* 10 vols. London: Longmans.
HECKSCHER, ELI F. (1931) 1955 *Mercantilism.* 2 vols., rev. ed. London: Allen & Unwin; New York: Macmillan. → First published in Swedish.
HEWINS, WILLIAM A. S. 1892 *English Trade and Finance Chiefly in the Seventeenth Century.* London: Methuen.
HEWINS, WILLIAM A. S. (1894) 1953 Edward Misselden. Volume 13, pages 498–499 in *Dictionary of National Biography.* Oxford Univ. Press.
JOHNSON, EDGAR A. J. 1937 *Predecessors of Adam Smith: The Growth of British Economic Thought.* Englewood Cliffs, N.J.: Prentice-Hall. → See especially pages 57–69 on "Misselden, the Critic."
LETICHE, JOHN M. 1959 *Balance of Payments and Economic Growth.* New York: Harper.
SCHUMPETER, JOSEPH A. (1954) 1960 *History of Economic Analysis.* Edited by E. B. Schumpeter. New York: Oxford Univ. Press.
SUPPLE, BARRY E. 1959 *Commercial Crisis and Change in England, 1600–1642: A Study in the Instability of a Mercantile Economy.* Cambridge Univ. Press.
SUVIRANTA, BRUNO 1923 *The Theory of the Balance of Trade in England: A Study in Mercantilism.* Helsinki: Suomalaisen Kirjallisuuden Seura.
VINER, JACOB 1937 *Studies in the Theory of International Trade.* New York: Harper.
VINER, JACOB 1961 *The Intellectual History of Laissez Faire.* Univ. of Chicago Law School.

MITCHELL, WESLEY C.

Wesley Clair Mitchell (1874–1948), American economist, was born and raised in Illinois in modest and occasionally straitened circumstances. Entering the University of Chicago in 1892, he was soon attracted by the evolutionary view of the development of human thought and social institutions as advanced by John Dewey and Thorstein Veblen. His other teachers in economics influenced him less, but J. Lawrence Laughlin introduced him to problems in monetary theory and policy and also helped to sharpen his critical sense.

Mitchell's extensive early writing was devoted mainly to the role of money and its connection with price "revolutions" during the Civil War. He completed a doctoral dissertation on this subject in 1899 and later expanded it into a book entitled *A History of the Greenbacks* (1903), a major and in many respects still authoritative work on the monetary upheavals of 1862–1865. In 1908 he published *Gold, Prices, and Wages Under the Greenback Standard*, which carries the analysis of the *History* further and skillfully organizes a massive statistical investigation of the period 1862–1878.

From his studies of the greenbacks Mitchell derived some of the ideas that were to guide his economic thought. One of the earliest of these ideas was that economics, as one of the sciences concerned with the realities of human behavior and social institutions, must be grounded in observation and measurement. Statistics provide the principal means to ensure a cumulative growth of tested quantitative knowledge, and they are essential for testing hypotheses as well as for suggesting new ones. Mitchell's lifelong interest in the collection and improvement of economic data led him to make several influential studies, one of the best examples of which is *The Making and Using of Index Numbers* (a monograph published by the U.S. Bureau of Labor Statistics in 1915 and reissued as late as 1938). Such endeavors did much to increase and improve the output of statistical agencies in several areas, notably the preparation of indexes of commodity and security prices, indexes of production, measures of national income and its subdivisions, and measures of financial and other monetary transactions.

Another of Mitchell's guiding concepts was that "the use of money and the pecuniary way of thinking it begets is a most important factor in the modern situation." Throughout his working life, Mitchell conceived his central task to be the acquisition and the transmission of knowledge about how the "money economy" works—that is, how it did and does evolve and how it influences men's ideas and behavior.

Aiming ultimately at a tested dynamic theory of economic change, Mitchell was often critical of "orthodox" doctrines which dealt with essentially static problems (for example, relative prices, resource allocation, and income distribution, seen as interconnected and determined in equilibrium). He insisted that deductive reasoning must seek support from tests against observed facts; that logical determinacy and consistency of a theoretical system are not sufficient tests of its "truth"; that theorists are susceptible to, and should guard against, unconscious ideological preconceptions; and that methodologically convenient postulates may be misleading when indiscriminately applied. He thought, for example, that the "logic of pecuniary institutions"—the quest for profits or "making money"—fits tolerably well the activities of modern businessmen but not those of housewives who are engaged in the "backward art of spending money" on articles of family consumption. Occasionally, Mitchell's distrust of theoretical model-building seems too general and categorical; but his writings also clearly recognize the value of traditional theory and the complementarity of theoretical and empirical studies.

From 1903 to 1913 Mitchell taught at the University of California and engaged in particularly productive research. He completed his studies of the greenback episode, turned to a more general analysis of the evolution of the money system, discovered that this task required him to investigate the as yet scarcely explored "recurring readjustments of prices," and embarked upon a detailed study of this subject, which soon grew into a comprehensive account of cyclical movements in diverse economic variables. In 1913 his *Business Cycles* appeared, a large treatise which became an acknowledged precursor and guide for cyclical (and other quantitative) studies in economics for years to come. In particular, Part 3 of this work, reprinted several times between 1941 and 1959, remains one of the best analytical accounts of the processes that give rise to business cycles.

Theory of business cycles.   Mitchell found the then current theories of business cycles suggestive but fragmentary and uncertain; since none of them was clearly superior, he proposed to test them generally by studying the facts instead of making any one theory a separate object of research. He always conceived of the business cycle in evolutionary and comprehensive terms, and he believed that the study of cycles should encompass all the major parts and aspects of the money economy and should try to explain how they interact and participate in the process of cumulative change. Business cycles, he observed, appear only in those times and places where economic life has come to be organized on the basis of making and spending money incomes. They are not mere random disturbances that jolt the economy temporarily out of its equilibrium; instead, they are widely diffused, cumulative fluctuations generated by the modern economic system itself. Although not periodic, they recur in an unceasing round. Each cycle differs from its predecessors in many particulars, both because it is influenced by unique historical events and because the economy's structure and reactions change gradually over time. But the study of business annals and historical statistics leads to the conclusion that cycles do have sufficiently numerous and important features in common to constitute a distinct class of related phenomena, somewhat analogous to a biological genus of many species.

Thus conceived, there is no single cause, no simple—or even complex but complete and immutable—explanation of business cycles. Mitchell's "analytic description" does identify as the central issue the dependence of tides in business activity upon the prospects of profits or (in times of crisis) the quest for solvency. It emphasizes, therefore, such factors as the prices that enter into business receipts and expenses, the volume of sales effected at prevailing margins of profit, and businessmen's cash and credit requirements. But to explain business cycles it is not enough to know what each of these "factors of chief significance" is or does during such cycles; the "harder half of the battle" is to follow the complex interactions of these factors from one cycle stage to the next.

Thus, prosperity "cumulates" by spreading over enterprises, industries, regions, and types of economic activities in ever widening circles. Increases in prices accompany increases in the physical volume of business. But gradually, stresses also start to multiply. In many areas, costs begin to encroach upon selling prices. The rapid rise in prices of raw materials and goods for resale, the advance in interest rates on bank loans, the lowered efficiency of labor, the reactivation of older and poorer equipment, the increase in "incidental wastes of management"—all these contribute to the rise in costs. At the same time, the advance in selling prices is held back by contractual obligations, custom, and public regulation. In some industries, completion of new investment projects brings about increases in capacity outputs that cannot be sold at the high prices asked. The decline in their reserves makes the banks reluctant to expand loans further. A stringency in capital and money markets develops. These factors bring about postponements of investment projects by those who find current financing and construction costs abnormally high and who expect that they will soon decline. Prosperity, then, "breeds" a crisis or gives way to a contraction, which again cumulates and spreads over the economy for a time.

Even as the decline of activity continues, however, forces of recovery gradually gain strength. Marginal enterprises are reorganized or recapitalized, bad debts are charged off, and inventories are reduced, so that business can again be conducted more efficiently. Less efficient employees are weeded out, and those that remain are constrained to work harder to protect their jobs. The reserve position of banks improves, and costs of borrowing decline. Raw-material prices also fall, and a general realignment of costs and selling prices comes about. Meanwhile the demand for goods revives slowly, aided by the continuing growth of population, by the need to replace long-used durables and to replenish depleted inventories, and by improved investment opportunities (also, perhaps, by new tastes, products, and techniques, or some other favorable outside events). This is "how depression breeds prosperity" and a new cycle begins.

Mitchell attempted to reduce the intricacies of his subject, but he was even more anxious not to oversimplify it; his account of business cycles is, accordingly, complex. Even a brief and necessarily rough sketch of that analysis, however, must not fail to underscore that Mitchell viewed the business cycle as a process whose pervasiveness and continuity are due mainly to institutional responses of the economic system to a variety of unpredictable changes. The lags in these responses are of strategic significance in the dynamics of the cycle. Thus, the essential feature of the cumulative movements of expansion and contraction is that expenditures often are induced by, and lag behind, receipts and that selling prices lag behind buying prices. Also important are the lags of investment expenditures and deliveries behind investment decisions. Orders for new plant and equipment start expanding early during a business revival, when capacity reserves are still ample. Not knowing how much business their competitors are booking, contractors often sell to investors more construction than can readily be executed within the contract time. This is discovered later when efforts to get labor and materials needed to perform the work drive up the prices of these factors. Timely deliveries then become costly, some of the earlier contracts turn out to be less profitable than expected, and much higher prices are asked when new contracts are negotiated. The high costs of construction cause postponement of many new investment projects.

In his concept of a self-generating cycle and in his recognition of the need for empirical research, Mitchell had a forerunner in Clément Juglar. Writings akin to Mitchell's in spirit and approach, notably those by Aftalion and Spiethoff, appeared at about the same time as *Business Cycles* or in the following decade. But Mitchell's research was unique in its broad scope and continuity, and it proved particularly influential.

Teaching and research. The study of business cycles remained Mitchell's central scientific concern for the rest of his life, but he frequently also gave attention to other interests and duties. In 1913 he went to Columbia University, where he taught until his retirement in 1944 (except for 1919–1922, when he joined Alvin Johnson and others in organizing the New School for Social Research). His lectures attracted large audiences; one set, "Types of Economic Theory," was transcribed stenographically and issued in mimeographed form. This selective historical survey of the thought and activities of major economists from Adam Smith to Veblen and Commons gave rather scant attention to technical economic theory; instead, it emphasized the dependence of ideas on the main economic and social issues of the time, and also, conversely, the influence of ideas on the course of events. In several essays on individual men and doctrines—dealing with, among others, Ricardo, Bentham, and Wieser (see [1912–1936] 1937, chapters 10–12)—Mitchell showed also the interdependence of economic thought and political and moral philosophy.

In 1920 Mitchell assumed direction of the National Bureau of Economic Research in New York City, an organization for "exact and impartial investigations," whose founding was in a large measure due to his initiative. He served as director until 1945 and continued to be an active member of the Bureau's research staff until his death. He was author or coauthor of numerous National Bureau publications. Equally important was his role in inspiring and helping to carry out many other studies of the National Bureau. These included work on such diverse topics as seasonal fluctuations (Simon Kuznets), interest rates (Frederick Macaulay), production trends (Arthur F. Burns), national income (Kuznets), cyclical movements in transportation (Thor Hultgren), inventories (Moses Abramovitz), prices (Frederick Mills), consumption (Ruth Mack), business-cycle indicators (Geoffrey Moore), and others. In particular, the National Bureau's continuing series, Studies in Business Cycles, owes its existence to Mitchell's initiative, contributions, and guidance.

Resurvey of the field. *Business Cycles: The Problem and Its Setting* (1927) was the first book Mitchell wrote after he undertook a "resurvey of the field" to improve the analysis and to subject to extensive new tests the findings of his 1913 treatise. Although large, this book corresponds in scope only to the first of the three main parts of its predecessor. The statistical basis of the 1913 book covered four countries but was restricted to the brief period from 1890 to 1911 and to annual data, which often obscure cyclical movements. Furthermore, many economic processes were but poorly, or not at all, represented in the then available materials. By 1927 these deficiencies could be substantially reduced as new data accumulated at a fast pace. The 1927 study relies on a substantial collection of American and English "indexes of business conditions," which are monthly or quarterly and cover various periods between 1850 and 1925. It also uses reports by contemporary observers on each year's business in 17 countries; the oldest of these "business annals," compiled by Willard L. Thorp, goes back to 1790.

Drawing on a much larger mass of evidence than was previously accessible, Mitchell found no reason to alter his basic views on the nature of business cycles and the methods that are appropriate for their study. Of particular interest to the general economist is Chapter 2 of *The Problem and Its Setting*, which provides a comprehensive survey of the evolution and major features of the modern "economic organization," with particular reference to business cycles. One section of the book offers an important theoretical contribution by showing that the different elements in the equation of exchange must have differing dates if the equation is to be valid. The lags of deliveries and payments behind price agreements, which are reflected in these dating differences, are highly important for the short periods relevant for business-cycle analysis. Over longer periods, such as a year or more, the difference in dating can be disregarded. In the long run, the quantity of money was seen by Mitchell to be the major determinant of the price level, while in short periods its role is usually passive. This is because in contractions and moderate expansions the effective limit on business transactions is set by demand, whereas in "intense booms" a higher limit is reached, which is set by the monetary and banking systems. This accounts for the strong influence of changes in money supply over long periods of time. [*See* MONEY, *article on* QUANTITY THEORY.]

In the "tentative working plans" sketched at the end of the 1927 volume, the question, How do business cycles run their course? was put ahead of the question, What causes business cycles? It is necessary to answer the former question before one can see what the latter means and "in what sense it can be answered." But Mitchell found that the task of providing this answer required a much larger apparatus of research than he had at first expected: compilation of numerous time series to represent a variety of pertinent processes; development of new techniques of isolating and analyzing cyclical movements; and application of these methods to the accumulated data. Under Mitchell's direction, all these operations proceeded simultaneously at the National Bureau, each influencing the others.

Use of cyclical measures. The progress of Mitchell's researches can be traced through several brief preliminary reports, notably in the Bureau's *Annual Reports* and the *Bulletin* series, nos. 31 (Mitchell 1929), 57 (Mitchell & Burns 1935), and 69 (Mitchell & Burns 1938). The last of the above, "Statistical Indicators of Cyclical Revivals," deserves particular notice, since it paved the way for the more recent research on uses of cyclical measures in the analysis of current business conditions and in short-term forecasting.

A full account of their methods of analyzing cyclical behavior was presented by Burns and Mitchell in *Measuring Business Cycles* (1946). The working definition of business cycles used in Mitchell's 1927 volume is here adopted, with some modifications, as a tool of research. The book draws on the results of a systematic analysis of over 1,000 series, most of them monthly, for the United States, Great Britain, Germany, and France. The clustering of turning points in representative samples of these series, together with selected measures of aggregate economic activity, helps to determine the chronologies of general business expansions and contractions in the four countries. Two sets of measures for each series are computed, describing its behavior during the phases of the general business cycle and during its own "specific cycles," respectively; the differences between the two sets reflect the extent to which the turning dates in an individual series deviate from the turning dates in aggregate economic activity. These deviations also measure the cyclical leads or lags of different economic processes. In addition, measures of duration and amplitude of specific cycles are introduced, as well as "conformity indexes" that reflect the degree of directional agreement between the movements of a given series and those prevailing in the economy at large. Averages of these measures are struck for all the cycles covered by a series in order to bring out the features that are typical; but deviations from these averages are also presented in order to study how the cycles vary in duration, intensity, etc.

The last chapters of the volume contain tests of several hypotheses on the effects of secular trends, long-wave movements, and critical historic events upon business cycles. Some apparently systematic changes in the cyclical behavior of particular variables are indicated, but they seem to be rather weak. A tentative inference, qualified by acknowledged limitations of the data and methods used, is that these changes do not alter the typical course of business cycles appreciably.

Death prevented Mitchell from completing a final treatise in which he planned to give a comprehensive account of business cycles and their causes. His posthumous *What Happens During Business Cycles: A Progress Report* (1951) is only a fragment of this project. More than two-thirds of its text is given to a systematic analysis of the variety of cyclical attributes of individual economic processes. This part is preceded by a brief exposition entitled "Aims, Methods, and Materials" and is followed by the unfinished part called "The Consensus of Cyclical Behavior." The latter indicates the synthesis toward which Mitchell's work was directed. It aims at showing "how [the] measures of cyclical behavior in various parts of the economy fit together, and what composite picture they give of business cycles" (1951, p. 255).

A central theme of the *Progress Report* is that "both the similarities and the differences (among the cyclical patterns of a substantial sample of representative series) are explicable on the assumption that economic activities are functionally related to one another in the numberless direct and indirect ways suggested in fancy by the equations of Walras and the analyses of Marshall" (p. 112). The specific cycles of each activity depend in part on "factors peculiar to the activity itself" and in part on "those congeries of specific cycles in other activities which we call business cycles" (p. 113). An overwhelming majority of economic series fluctuate in sympathy with the cyclical phases in aggregate activity: only about one-tenth show "irregular" timing, that is, no systematic relation in time to business cycles. Countercyclical processes are not only far less numerous but also typically less regular than those that respond positively. But some conforming series tend to lead and others to lag by different intervals. Hence, business cycles consist not only of roughly synchronous expansions followed by roughly synchronous contractions in many activities: "they consist also of numerous

contractions while expansion is dominant, and numerous expansions while contraction is dominant" (p. 79). Mitchell not only put these observations in numerical form but also identified many of the leaders, coinciders, and laggers in the typical round of cyclical developments.

While business cycles provided the focus for Mitchell's studies, they were conceived by him as nothing less than the "economic process in motion," or the characteristic course of the money economy in a late stage of development. In this view, to understand business cycles is to understand also the structure and functioning of the economy. The interrelated movements of numerous economic variables reflect economic behavior in its current institutional setting, and their objective, quantitative analysis is the way to reach an understanding of that behavior. This view secured for Mitchell an outstanding place in the evolution of modern economics as a quantitative and empirical science. The theoretical thinking of our times may not seem strongly affected by the general institutionalist challenge of several decades ago, in which Mitchell participated. But Mitchell's own scholarly, empirical approach left a strong imprint on the growth and orientation of economic research. This applies to his critical attitude toward purely normative and deductive economics; his insistence on the need to improve and systematize observation of the economic manifestations of human behavior; and his belief that cumulation of tested knowledge will ensure that economics will have an important place in the deliberations of policy makers.

Mitchell had strong humanitarian sympathies and democratic convictions as well as a vivid awareness of the shortcomings of the contemporary social order. He believed that advances in economics and other social sciences can help to reduce such defects of the economic system as recurrence of depressions and unemployment, inequality of opportunity, concentration of power, and insufficient economic security. He recognized that "in the countries that have given wide scope to private initiative . . . , the masses of mankind attained a higher degree of material comfort and a larger measure of liberty than . . . under any other form of organization that mankind has tried out in practice" ([1912–1936] 1937, p. 94). But he also believed that government has social responsibilities which it should meet in the most practicable way. The "nation's full intelligence" should be organized "to deal seriously with social problems before they have produced national emergencies" (pp. 100, 131). National planning, thus conceived as a broad and continuous effort, would encounter many difficulties and doubtless have its share of failures; nevertheless, it would be preferable to the *ad hoc* "piecemeal planning," which Mitchell saw as "our common method of attempting to use the powers of government" (p. 130).

Although he treated scientific work as his prime commitment, Mitchell gave much of his time to public affairs. During World War I he was chief of the Price Section of the War Industries Board. Later, he served by presidential appointment on the Research Committee on Social Trends, 1929–1933, and the National Planning Board, 1933, and he prepared a report for the President's Committee on the Cost of Living, 1944.

VICTOR ZARNOWITZ

[*See also* BUSINESS CYCLES; ECONOMIC THOUGHT, *article on* THE INSTITUTIONAL SCHOOL; INDEX NUMBERS.]

WORKS BY MITCHELL

1903 *A History of the Greenbacks, With Special Reference to the Economic Consequences of Their Issue: 1862–1865.* Univ. of Chicago Press.
1908 *Gold, Prices, and Wages Under the Greenback Standard.* University of California Publications in Economics, Vol. 1. Berkeley: Univ. of California Press.
(1912–1936) 1937 *The Backward Art of Spending Money, and Other Essays.* New York: McGraw-Hill.
1913 *Business Cycles.* Berkeley: Univ. of California Press. → Part 3 was reprinted by the University of California Press in 1959 as *Business Cycles and Their Causes.*
(1915) 1938 *The Making and Using of Index Numbers.* 3d ed. U.S. Bureau of Labor Statistics, Bulletin No. 656. Washington: Government Printing Office.
1927 *Business Cycles: The Problem and Its Setting.* National Bureau of Economic Research, Publications, No. 10. New York: The Bureau.
1929 *Testing Business Cycles.* National Bureau of Economic Research, *Bulletin* 31.
1935 MITCHELL, WESLEY C.; and BURNS, ARTHUR F. *The National Bureau's Measures of Cyclical Behavior.* National Bureau of Economic Research, *Bulletin* 57.
1938 MITCHELL, WESLEY C.; and BURNS, ARTHUR F. *Statistical Indicators of Cyclical Revivals.* National Bureau of Economic Research, *Bulletin* 69.
1946 BURNS, ARTHUR F.; and MITCHELL, WESLEY C. *Measuring Business Cycles.* National Bureau of Economic Research, Studies in Business Cycles, No. 2. New York: The Bureau.
1951 *What Happens During Business Cycles: A Progress Report.* National Bureau of Economic Research, Studies in Business Cycles, No. 5. New York: The Bureau. → Published posthumously.

SUPPLEMENTARY BIBLIOGRAPHY

BURNS, ARTHUR F. 1951 Mitchell on *What Happens During Business Cycles.* Pages 3–14 in Conference on Business Cycles, New York, 1949, *Conference on Business Cycles.* New York: National Bureau of Economic Research. → Jacob Marschak's "Comment" and a reply by Arthur F. Burns appear on pages 14–33.
BURNS, ARTHUR F. (editor) 1952 *Wesley Clair Mitchell:*
The Economic Scientist. National Bureau of Economic Research, Publications, No. 53. New York: The Bureau. → Contains a list of Mitchell's publications.
DORFMAN, JOSEPH 1949 *The Economic Mind in American Civilization.* Vol. 3. New York: Viking. → See especially pages 455–473, on Mitchell.
HANSEN, ALVIN H. (1951) 1964 *Business Cycles and National Income.* Expanded ed. New York: Norton. → See especially pages 394–410, on Mitchell's work.

MOBILITY

See LABOR FORCE, *article on* MARKETS AND MOBILITY; MIGRATION; SOCIAL MOBILITY.

MODELS, MATHEMATICAL

Although mathematical models are applied in many areas of the social sciences, this article is limited to mathematical models of individual behavior. For applications of mathematical models in econometrics, see ECONOMETRIC MODELS, AGGREGATE. *Other articles discussing modeling in general include* CYBERNETICS, PROBABILITY, SCALING, SIMULATION, *and* SIMULTANEOUS EQUATION ESTIMATION. *Specific models are discussed in various articles dealing with substantive topics.*

Theories of behavior that have been developed and presented verbally, such as those of Hull or Tolman or Freud, have attempted to describe and predict behavior under any and all circumstances. Mathematical models of individual behavior, by contrast, have been much less ambitious: their goal has been a precise description of the data obtained from restricted classes of behavioral experiments concerned with simple and discrimination learning; with detection, recognition, and discrimination of simple physical stimuli; with the patterns of preference exhibited among outcomes; and so on. Models that embody very specific mathematical assumptions, which are at best approximations applicable to highly limited situations, have been analyzed exhaustively and applied to every conceivable aspect of available data. From this work broader classes of models, based on weaker assumptions and thus providing more general predictions, have evolved in the past few years. The successes of the special models have stimulated, and their failures have demanded, these generalizations. The number and variety of experiments to which these mathematical models have been applied have also grown, but not as rapidly as the catalogue of models.

Most of the models so far developed are restricted to experiments having discrete trials. Each trial is composed of three types of events: the presentation of a stimulus configuration selected by the experimenter from a limited set of possible presentations; the subject's selection of a response from a specified set of possible responses; and the experimenter's feedback of information, rewards, and punishments to the subject. Primarily because the response set is fixed and feedback is used, these are called choice experiments (Bush et al. 1963). Most psychophysical and preference experiments, as well as many learning experiments, are of this type. Among the exceptions are the experiments without trials—e.g., vigilance experiments and the operant conditioning methods of Skinner. Currently, models for these experiments are beginning to be developed.

Measures. With attention confined to choice experiments, three broad classes of variables necessarily arise—those concerned with stimuli, with responses, and with outcomes. The response variables are, of course, assumed to depend upon the (experimentally) independent stimuli and upon the outcome variables, and each model is nothing more or less than an explicit conjecture about the nature of this dependency. Usually such conjectures are stated in terms of some measures, often numerical ones, that are associated with the variables. Three quite different types of measures are used: physical, probabilistic, and psychological. The first two are objective and descriptive; they can be introduced and used without reference to any psychological theory, and so they are especially popular with atheoretical experimentalists, even though the choice of a measure usually reflects a theoretical attitude about what is and is not psychologically relevant. Although we often use physical measures to characterize the events for which probabilities are defined, this is only a labeling function which makes little or no use of the powerful mathematical structure embodied in many physical measures. The psychological measures are constructs within some specifiable psychological theory, and their calculation in terms of observables is possible only within the terms of that theory. Examples of each type of measure should clarify the meaning.

Physical measures. In experimental reports, the stimuli and outcomes are usually described in terms of standard physical measures: intensity, frequency, size, weight, time, chemical composition, amount, etc. Certain standard response measures are physical. The most ubiquitous is response latency (or reaction time), and it has received the attention of some mathematical theorists (McGill 1963). In addition, force of response, magnitude of displacement, speed of running, etc., can some-

times be recorded. Each of these is unique to certain experimental realizations, and so they have not been much studied by theorists.

Probability measures. The stimulus presentations, the responses, and the outcomes can each be thought of as a sequence of selections of elements from known sets of elements, i.e., as a schedule over trials. It is not usual to work with the specific schedules that have occurred but, rather, with the probability rules that were used to generate them. For the stimulus presentations and the outcomes, the rules are selected by the experimenter, and so there is no question about what they are. Not only are the rules not known for the responses, but even their general form is not certain. Each response theory is, in fact, a hypothesis about the form of these rules, and certain relative frequencies of responses are used to estimate the postulated conditional response probabilities.

Often the schedules for stimulus presentations are simple random ones in the sense that the probability of a stimulus' being presented is independent of the trial number and of the previous history of the experiment; but sometimes more complex contingent schedules are used in which various conditional probabilities must be specified. Most outcome schedules are to some degree contingent, usually on the immediately preceding presentation and response, but sometimes the dependencies reach further back into the past. Again, conditional probabilities are the measures used to summarize the schedule. [See PROBABILITY.]

Psychological measures. Most psychological models attempt to state how either a physical measure or a probability measure of the response depends upon measures of the experimental independent variables, but in addition they usually include unknown free parameters—that is, numerical constants whose values are specified neither by the experimental conditions nor by independent measurements on the subject. Such parameters must, therefore, be estimated from the data that have been collected to test the adequacy of the theory, which thereby reduces to some degree the stringency of the test. It is quite common for current psychological models to involve only probability measures and unknown numerical parameters, but not any physical measures. When the numerical parameters are estimated from different sets of data obtained by varying some independent variables under the experimenter's control, it is often found that the parameters vary with some variables and not with others. In other words, the parameters are actually functions of some of the experimental variables, and so they can be, and often are, viewed as psychological measures (relative to the model within which they appear) of the variables that affect them. Theories are sometimes then provided for this dependence, although so far this has been the exception rather than the rule.

The theory of signal detectability, for example, involves two parameters: the magnitude, d', of the psychological difference between two stimuli; and a response criterion, c, which depends upon the outcomes and the presentation schedule. Theories for the dependence of d' and c upon physical measures have been suggested (Luce 1963; Swets 1964). Most learning theories for experiments with only one presentation simply involve the conditional outcome probabilities and one or more free parameters. Little is known about the dependence of these parameters upon experimentally manipulable variables. In certain scaling theories, numerical parameters are assigned to the response alternatives and are interpreted as measures of response strength (Luce & Galanter 1963). In some models these parameters are factored into two terms, one of which is assumed to measure the contribution of the stimulus to response strength and the other of which is the contribution due to the outcome structure.

The phrasing of psychological models in terms only of probability measures and parameters (psychological measures) has proved to be an effective research strategy. Nonetheless, it appears important to devise theories that relate psychological measures to the physical and probability measures that describe the experiments. The most extensive mathematical models of this type can be found in audition and vision (Hurvich et al. 1965; Zwislocki 1965). The various theories of utility are, in part, attempts to relate the psychological measure called utility to physical measures of outcomes, such as amounts of money, and probability measures of their schedules, such as probabilities governing gambles (Luce & Suppes 1965). In spite of the fact that it is clear that the utilities of outcomes must be related to learning parameters, little is known about this relation. [*See* Gambling; Game theory; Utility.]

The nature of the models. The construction of a mathematical model involves decisions on at least two levels. There is, first, the over-all perspective about what is and is not important and about the best way to secure the relevant facts. Usually this is little discussed in the presentation of a model, mainly because it is so difficult to make the discussion coherent and convincing. Nonetheless, this is what we shall attempt to deal with in this section. In the following section we turn to the second level of decision: the specific assumptions made.

Probability vs. determinism. One of the most basic decisions is whether to treat the behavior as if it arises from some sort of probabilistic mechanism, in which case detailed, exact predictions are not possible, or whether to treat it as deterministic, in which case each specific response is susceptible to exact prediction. If the latter decision is made, one is forced to provide some account of the observed inconsistencies of responses before it is possible to test the adequacy of the model. Usually one falls back on either the idea of errors of measurement or on the idea of systematic changes with time (or experience), but in practice it has not been easy to make effective use of either idea, and most workers have been content to develop probability models. It should be pointed out that, as far as the model is concerned, it is immaterial whether the model builder believes the behavior to be inherently probabilistic, or its determinants to be too complex to give a detailed analysis, or that there are uncontrolled factors which lead to experimental errors.

Static vs. dynamic models. A second decision is whether the model shall be dynamic or static. (We use these terms in the way they are used in physics; static models characterize systems which do not change with time or systems which have reached equilibrium in time, whereas dynamic models are concerned with time changes.) Some dynamic models, especially those for learning, state how conditional response probabilities change with experience. Usually these models are not very helpful in telling us what would happen if, for example, we substituted a different but closely related set of response alternatives or outcomes. In static models the constraints embodied in the model concern the relations among response probabilities in several different, but related, choice situations. The utility models for the study of preference are typical of this class.

The main characteristic of the existing dynamic models is that the probabilities are functions of a discrete time parameter. Such processes are called stochastic, and they can be thought of as generating branching processes through the fanning out of new possibilities on each trial (Snell 1965). Each individual in an experiment traces out one path of the over-all tree, and we attempt to infer from a small but, it is hoped, typical sample of these paths something about the probabilities that supposedly underlie the process. Usually, if enough time is allowed to pass, such a process settles down —becomes asymptotic—in a statistical sense. This is one way to arrive at a static model; and when we state a static model, we implicitly assume that it describes (approximately) the asymptotic behavior of the (unknown) dynamic process governing the organisms.

Psychological vs. mathematical assumptions. Another distinction is that between psychological and formal mathematical assumptions. This is by no means a sharp one, if for no other reason than that the psychological assumptions of a mathematical model are ultimately cast in formal terms and that psychological rationales can always be evolved for formal axioms. Roughly, however, the distinction is between a structure built up from elementary principles and a postulated constraint concerning observable behavior. Perhaps the simplest example of the latter is the axiom of transitivity of preferences; if *a* is preferred to *b* and *b* is preferred to *c*, then *a* will be preferred to *c*. This is not usually derived from more basic psychological postulates but, rather, is simply asserted on the grounds that it is (approximately) true in fact. A somewhat more complex, but essentially similar, example is the so-called choice axiom which postulates how choice probabilities change when the set of possible choices is either reduced or augmented (Luce 1959). Again, no rationale was originally given except plausibility; later, psychological mechanisms were proposed from which it derives as a consequence.

The most familiar example of a mathematical model which is generally viewed as more psychological and less formal is stimulus sampling theory. In this theory it is supposed that an organism is exposed to a set of stimulus "elements" from which one or more are sampled on a trial and that these elements may become "conditioned" to the performed response, depending upon the outcome that follows the response (Atkinson & Estes 1963). The concepts of sampling and conditioning are interpreted as elementary psychological processes from which the observed properties of the choice behavior are to be derived. Lying somewhere between the two extremes just cited are, for example, the linear operator learning models (Bush & Mosteller 1955; Sternberg 1963). The trial-by-trial changes in response probabilities are assumed to be linear, mainly because of certain formal considerations; the choice of the limit points of the operators in specific applications is, however, usually based upon psychological considerations; and the resulting mathematical structure is not evaluated directly but, rather, in terms of its ability to account for the observed choice behavior as summarized in such observables as the mean learning curve, the

sequential dependencies among responses, and the like.

Recurrent theoretical themes.   Beyond a doubt, the most recurrent theme in models is independence. Indeed, one can fairly doubt whether a serious theory exists if it does not include statements to the effect that certain measures which contribute to the response are in some way independent of other measures which contribute to the same response. Of course, independence assumes different mathematical forms and therefore has different names, depending upon the problem, but one should not lose sight of the common underlying intuition which, in a sense, may be simply equivalent to what we mean when we say that a model helps to simplify and to provide understanding of some behavior.

Statistical independence.   In quite a few models simple statistical independence is invoked. For example, two chance events, *A* and *B*, are said to be independent when the conditional probability of *A*, given *B*, is equal to the unconditional probability of *A*; equivalently, the probability of the joint event *AB* is the product of the separate probabilities of *A* and *B*. A very simple substantive use of this notion is contained in the choice axiom which says, in effect, that altering the membership of a choice set does not affect the relative probabilities of choice of two alternatives (Luce 1959). More complex notions of independence are invoked whenever the behavior is assumed to be described by a stochastic process. Each such process states that some, but not all, of the past is relevant in understanding the future: some probabilities are independent of some earlier events. For example, in the "operator models" of learning, it is assumed that the process is "path independent" in the sense that it is sufficient to know the existing choice probability and what has happened on that trial in order to calculate the choice probability on the next trial (Bush & Mosteller 1955). In the "Markovian" learning models, the organism is always in one of a finite number of states which control the choice probabilities, and the probabilities of transition from one state to another are independent of time, i.e., trials (Atkinson & Estes 1963). Again, the major assumption of the model is a rather strong one about independence of past history. [*See* MARKOV CHAINS.]

Additivity and linearity.   Still another form of independence is known as additivity. If *r* is a response measure that depends upon two different variables assuming values in sets A_1 and A_2, then we say that the measure is additive (over the independent variables) if there exists a numerical measure r_1 on A_1 and r_2 on A_2 such that for x_1 in A_1 and x_2 in A_2, $r(x_1,x_2) = r_1(x_1) + r_2(x_2)$. This assumption for particular experimental measures r is frequently postulated in the models of analysis of variance as well as derived from certain theories of fundamental measurement. A special case of additivity known as linearity is very important. Here there is but one variable (that is, $A_1 = A_2 = A$); any two values of that variable, x and x' in A, combine through some physical operation to form a third value of that variable, denoted $x * x'$; and there is a single measure r on A (that is, $r_1 = r_2 = r$) such that $r(x * x') = r(x) + r(x')$. Such a requirement captures the superposition principle and leads to models of a very simple sort. These linear models have played an especially important role in the study of learning, where it is postulated that the choice probability on one trial, p_n, can be expressed linearly in terms of the probability, p_{n-1}, on the preceding trial. Other models also postulate linear transformations, but not necessarily on the response probability itself. In the "beta" model, the quantity $p_n/(1 - p_n)$ is assumed to be transformed linearly; this quantity is interpreted as a measure of response strength (Luce 1959).

Commutativity. The "beta" model exhibits another property that is of considerable importance, namely, commutativity. The essence of commutativity is that the order in which the operators are applied does not matter; that is, if A and B are operators, then the composite operator AB (apply B first and then A) is the same as the operator BA. Again, there is a notion of independence—independence of the order of application. It is an extremely powerful property that permits one to derive a considerable number of properties of the resulting process; however, it is generally viewed with suspicion, since it requires the distant past to have exactly the same effect as the recent past. A commutative model fails to forget gradually.

Nature of the predictions. As would be expected, models are used to make a variety of predictions. Perhaps the most general sorts of predictions involve broad classes of models. For example, probabilistic reinforcement schedules for a certain class of distance-diminishing models, i.e., ones that require the behavior of two subjects to become increasingly similar when they are identically reinforced, can be shown to be ergodic, which means that these models exhibit the asymptotic properties that are commonly taken for granted. A second example is the combining-of-classes theorem, which asserts that if the theoretical descriptions of behavior are to be independent of the grouping of

responses into classes, then only the linear learning models are appropriate.

At a somewhat more detailed level, but still encompassing several different models, are predictions such as the mean learning curve, response operating characteristics, and stochastic transitivity of successive choices among pairs of alternatives. Sometimes it is not realized that conceptually quite different models, which make some radically different predictions, may nonetheless agree completely on other features of the data, often on ones that are ordinarily reported in experimental studies. Perhaps the best example of this phenomenon arises in the analysis of experiments in which subjects learn arbitrary associations between verbal stimuli and responses. A linear incremental model, of the sort described above, predicts exactly the same mean learning curve as does a model that postulates that the arbitrary association is acquired on an all-or-none basis. On the face of it, this result seems paradoxical. It is not, because in the latter model, different subjects acquire the association on different trials, and averaging over subjects thereby leads to a smooth mean curve that happens to be identical with the one predicted by the linear model. Actually, a wide variety of models predict the same mean learning curve for many probabilistic schedules of reinforcement, and so one must turn to finer-grained features of the data to distinguish among the models. Among these differential predictions are the distribution of runs of the same response, the expected number of such runs, the variance of the number of successes in a fixed block of trials, the mean number of total errors, the mean trial of last error, etc. [See STATISTICAL IDENTIFIABILITY.]

The classical topic of individual differences raises issues of a different sort. For the kinds of predictions discussed above it is customary to pool individual data and to analyze them as if they were entirely homogeneous. Often, in treating learning data this way, it is argued that the structural conditions of the experiment are sufficiently more important determinants of behavior than are individual differences so that the latter may be ignored without serious distortion. For many experiments to which models have been applied with considerable success, simple tests of this hypothesis of homogeneity are not easily made. For example, when a group of 30 or 40 subjects is run on 12 to 15 paired-associate items, it is not useful to analyze each subject item because of the large relative variability which accompanies a small number of observations. On the other hand, in some psychophysical experiments in which each subject is run for thousands of trials under constant conditions of presentation and reinforcement, it is possible to treat in detail the data of individuals. The final justification for using group data, on the assumption of identical subjects, is the fact that for ergodic processes, which most models are, the predictions for data averaged over subjects are the same as those for the data of an individual averaged over trials.

Another issue, which relates to group versus individual data, is parameter invariance. One way of asking if a group of individuals is homogeneous is to ask whether, within sampling error, the parameters for individuals are identical. Thus far, however, more experimental attention has been devoted to the question of parameter invariance for sets of group data collected under different experimental conditions. For instance, the parameters of most learning models should be independent of the particular reinforcement schedule adopted by the experimenter. Although in many cases a reasonable degree of parameter invariance has been obtained for different schedules, it is fair to say that the results have not been wholly satisfactory.

For a detailed discussion of the topics of this section, see Sternberg (1963) and Atkinson and Estes (1963).

Model testing.   Most of the mathematical models used to analyze psychological data require that at least one parameter, and often more, be estimated from the data before the adequacy of the model can be evaluated. In principle, it might be desirable to use maximum-likelihood methods for estimation. Perhaps the central difficulty which prevents our using such estimators is that the observable random variables, such as the presentation, response, and outcome random variables, form chains of infinite order. This means that their probabilities on any trial depend on what actually happened in all preceding trials. When that is so, it is almost always impractical to obtain a useful maximum-likelihood estimator of a parameter. In the face of such difficulties, less desirable methods of estimation have perforce been used. Theoretical expressions showing the dependency on the unknown parameter of, for example, the mean number of total errors, the mean trial of first success, and the mean number of runs, have been equated to data statistics to estimate the parameters. The classical methods of moments and of least squares have sometimes been applied successfully. And, in certain cases, maximum-likelihood estimators can be approximated by pseudo-maximum-likelihood

ones that use only a limited portion of the immediate past. For processes that are approximately stationary, a small part of the past sometimes provides a very good approximation to the full chain of infinite order, and then pseudo-maximum-likelihood estimates can be good approximations to the exact ones. Because of mathematical complexities in applying even these simplified techniques, Monte Carlo and other numerical methods are frequently used. [*See* ESTIMATION.]

Once the parameters have been estimated, the number of predictions that can be derived is, in principle, enormous: the values of the parameters of the model, together with the initial conditions and the outcome schedule, uniquely determine the probability of all possible combinations of events. In a sense, the investigator is faced with a plethora of riches, and his problem is to decide what predictions are the most significant from the standpoint of providing telling tests of a model. In more classical statistical terms, what can be said about the goodness of fit of the model?

Just as with estimation, it might be desirable to evaluate goodness of fit by a likelihood ratio test. But, a fortiori, this is not practical when maximum-likelihood estimators themselves are not feasible. Rather, a combination of minimum chi-square techniques for both estimation and testing goodness of fit have come to be widely used in recent years. No single statistic, however, serves as a satisfactory over-all evaluation of a model, and so the report usually summarizes its successes and failures on a rather extensive list of measures of fit.

A model is never rejected outright because it does not fit a particular set of data, but it may disappear from the scene or be rejected in favor of another model that fits the data more adequately. Thus, the classical statistical procedure of accepting or rejecting a hypothesis—or model—is in fact seldom directly invoked in research on mathematical models; rather, the strong and weak points of the model are brought out, and new models are sought that do not have the discovered weaknesses. [*See* GOODNESS OF FIT; more detail on these topics can be found in Bush 1963].

Impact on psychology.   Although the study of mathematical models has come to be a subject in its own right within psychology, it is also pertinent to ask in what ways their development has had an impact on general experimental psychology.

For one, it has almost certainly raised the standards of systematic experimentation: the application of a model to data prompts a number of detailed questions frequently ignored in the past. A model permits one to squeeze more information out of the data than is done by the classical technique of comparing experimental and control groups and rejecting the null hypothesis whenever the difference between the two groups is sufficiently large. A successful test of a mathematical model often requires much larger experiments than has been customary. It is no longer unusual for a quantitative experiment to consist of 100,000 responses and an equal number of outcomes. In addition to these methodological effects on experimentation and on data analysis, there have been substantive ones. Of these we mention a few of the more salient ones.

Probability matching. A well-known finding, which dates back to Humphreys (1939), is that of probability matching. If either one of two responses is rewarded on each trial, then in many situations organisms tend to respond with probabilities equal to the reward probabilities rather than to choose the more often rewarded response almost all of the time. Since Humphreys' original experiment, many similar ones have been performed on both human and animal subjects to discover the extent and nature of the phenomenon, and a great deal of effort has been expended on theoretical analyses of the results. Estes (1964) has given an extensive review of both the experimental and the theoretical literature. Perhaps the most important contribution of mathematical models to this problem was to provide sets of simple general assumptions about behavior which, coupled with the specification of the experimenter's schedule of outcomes, predict probability matching. As noted above, investigators have not been content with just predicting the mean asymptotic values but have dealt in detail with the relation between predicted and observed conditional expectations, run distributions, variances, etc. Although this experimental paradigm for probability learning did not originate in mathematical psychology, its thorough exploration and the resulting interpretations of the learning process have been strongly promoted by the many predictions made possible by models for this paradigm.

The all-or-none model. A second substantive issue to which a number of investigators have addressed mathematical models is whether or not simple learning is of an all-or-none character. As noted earlier, the linear model assumes learning to be incremental in the sense that whenever a stimulus is presented, a response made, and an outcome given, the association reinforced by the outcome is thereby made somewhat more likely to occur. In contrast, the simple all-or-none model postulates that the subject is either completely conditioned to make the correct response, or he is not so conditioned. No intermediate states exist, and until the correct conditioning association is established on an all-or-none basis, his responses are determined by a constant guessing probability. This means that learning curves for individual subjects are flat until conditioning occurs, at which point they exhibit a strong discontinuity. The problem of discriminating the two models must be approached with some care since, for instance, the mean learning curve obtained by averaging data over subjects, or over subjects and a list of items as well, is much the same for the two models. On the other hand, analyses of such statistics as the variance of total errors, the probability of an error before the last error, and the distribution of last errors exhibit sharp differences between the models. For paired-associates learning, the all-or-none model is definitely more adequate than the linear incremental model (Atkinson & Estes 1963). Of course, the issue of all-or-none versus incremental learning is not special to mathematical psychology; however, the application of formal models has raised detailed questions of data analysis and posed additional theoretical problems not raised, let alone answered, by previous approaches to the problem.

Reward and punishment. The classic psychological question of the relative effects of reward and punishment (or nonreward) has also arisen in work on models, and it has been partially answered. In some models, such as the linear one, there are two rate parameters, one of which represents the effect of reward on a single trial and the other of which represents the effect of nonreward. Their estimated values provide comparable measures of the effects of these two events for those data from which they are estimated. For example, Bush and Mosteller (1955) found that a trial on which a dog avoided shock (reward) in an avoidance training experiment produced about the same change in response probabilities as three trials of nonavoidance (punishment). No general law has emerged, however. The relative effects of reward and nonreward seem to vary from one experiment to another and to depend on a number of experimental variables.

When using a model to estimate the relative effects of different events, the results must be interpreted with some care. The measures are meaningful only in terms of the model in which they are defined. A different model with corresponding re-

ward and nonreward parameters may lead to the
opposite conclusion. Thus, one must decide which
model best accounts for the data and use it for
measuring the relative effects of the two events.
Very delicate issues of parameter estimation arise,
and examples exist where opposite conclusions
have been drawn, depending on the estimators
used. The alternative is to devise more nonparametric methods of inference which make weaker
assumptions about the learning process. A detailed
discussion of these problems is given by Sternberg
(1963, pp. 109–116). [*See* LEARNING, *article on*
REINFORCEMENT.]

Homogenizing a group.   If one wishes to obtain
a homogeneous group of subjects after a particular
experimental treatment, should all subjects be run
for a fixed number of trials, or should each subject
be run until he meets a specific performance criterion? Typically it is assumed by those who use
such a criterion that individual subjects differ;
that, for example, some are fast learners and some
are slow. It is further assumed that all subjects
will achieve the same performance level if each is
run to a criterion such as ten successive successes.
Now it is clear that for identical subjects, it is
simpler to run them all for the same number of
trials and perhaps use a group performance criterion. It is, however, less obvious whether it would
be better to do this than to run each to a criterion.
An analysis of stochastic learning models has
shown that running each of identical subjects to a
criterion introduces appreciable variance in the
terminal performance levels. One can study individual differences only in terms of a model and
assumptions about the distributions of the model
parameters. When this is done, it becomes evident
that very large individual differences must exist to
justify using the criterion method of homogenizing
a group of subjects.

Psychophysics.   The final example is selected
from psychophysics. With the advent of signal detection theory it became increasingly apparent that
the classical methods for measuring sensory thresholds are inherently ambiguous, that they depend
not only, as they are supposed to, on sensitivity
but also on response biases (Luce 1963; Swets
1964). Consider a detection experiment in which
the stimulus is presented only on a proportion π of
the trials. Let $p(Y|s)$ and $p(Y|n)$ be the proba-
bilities of a "Yes" response to the stimulus and to
no stimulus respectively. If the experiment is run
several times with different values of π between 0
and 1, then $p(Y|n)$, as well as $p(Y|s)$, which is a
classical threshold measure, varies systematically

from 0 to 1. The data points appear to fall on a
smooth, convex curve, which shows the relation,
for the subject, between correct responses to
stimuli and incorrect responses to no-stimulus
trials (false alarms). Its curvature, in effect, characterizes the subject's sensitivity, and the location
of the data point along the curve represents the
amount of bias, i.e., his over-all tendency to say
"Yes," which varies with π, with the payoffs used,
and with instructions. Several conceptually different theories, which are currently being tested, account for such curves; it is clear that any new
theory will be seriously entertained only if it admits
to some such partition of the response behavior
into sensory and bias components. This point of
view is, of course, applicable to any two-stimulus–
two-response experiment, and often it alters significantly the qualitative interpretation of data. [*See*
ATTENTION; PSYCHOPHYSICS.]

Although one cannot be certain about what will
happen next in the application of mathematical
models to problems of individual behavior, certain
trends seem clear. (1) The ties that have been
established between mathematical theorists and
experimentalists appear firm and productive; they
probably will be strengthened. (2) The general
level of mathematical sophistication in psychology
can be expected to increase in response to the increasing numbers of experimental studies that
stem from mathematical theories. (3) The major
applications will continue to center around well-
defined psychological issues for which there are
accepted experimental paradigms and a considerable body of data. One relatively untapped area is
operant (instrumental) conditioning. (4) Along
with models for explicit paradigms, abstract principles (axioms) of behavior that have wide potential applicability are being isolated and refined,
and attempts are being made to explore general
qualitative properties of whole classes of models.
(5) Even though the most successful models to
date are probabilistic, the analysis of symbolic and
conceptual processes seems better handled by other
mathematical techniques, and so more nonproba-
bilistic models can be anticipated.

ROBERT R. BUSH, R. DUNCAN LUCE,
AND PATRICK SUPPES

[*See also* DECISION MAKING, *article on* PSYCHOLOGICAL
ASPECTS; SIMULATION, *article on* INDIVIDUAL BE-
HAVIOR. *Other relevant material may be found in*
ATTENTION; LEARNING; MATHEMATICS; PROBABIL-
ITY; PSYCHOMETRICS; PSYCHOPHYSICS; SCALING.]

BIBLIOGRAPHY

ATKINSON, RICHARD C.; and ESTES, WILLIAM K. 1963 Stimulus Sampling Theory. Volume 2, pages 121–268 in R. Duncan Luce, Robert R. Bush, and Eugene Galanter (editors), *Handbook of Mathematical Psychology.* New York: Wiley.

BUSH, ROBERT R. 1963 Estimation and Evaluation. Volume 1, pages 429–469 in R. Duncan Luce, Robert R. Bush, and Eugene Galanter (editors), *Handbook of Mathematical Psychology.* New York: Wiley.

BUSH, ROBERT R.; GALANTER, EUGENE; and LUCE, R. DUNCAN 1963 Characterization and Classification of Choice Experiments. Volume 1, pages 77–102 in R. Duncan Luce, Robert R. Bush, and Eugene Galanter (editors), *Handbook of Mathematical Psychology.* New York: Wiley.

BUSH, ROBERT R.; and MOSTELLER, FREDERICK 1955 *Stochastic Models for Learning.* New York: Wiley.

ESTES, WILLIAM K. 1964 Probability Learning. Pages 89–128 in Symposium on the Psychology of Human Learning, University of Michigan, 1962, *Categories of Human Learning.* Edited by Arthur W. Melton. New York: Academic Press.

HUMPHREYS, LLOYD G. 1939 Acquisition and Extinction of Verbal Expectations in a Situation Analogous to Conditioning. *Journal of Experimental Psychology* 25: 294–301.

HURVICH, LEO M.; JAMESON, DOROTHEA; and KRANTZ, DAVID H. 1965 Theoretical Treatments of Selected Visual Problems. Volume 3, pages 99–160 in R. Duncan Luce, Robert R. Bush, and Eugene Galanter (editors), *Handbook of Mathematical Psychology.* New York: Wiley.

LUCE, R. DUNCAN 1959 *Individual Choice Behavior.* New York: Wiley.

LUCE, R. DUNCAN 1963 Detection and Recognition. Volume 1, pages 103–190 in R. Duncan Luce, Robert R. Bush, and Eugene Galanter (editors), *Handbook of Mathematical Psychology.* New York: Wiley.

LUCE, R. DUNCAN; and GALANTER, EUGENE 1963 Psychophysical Scaling. Volume 1, pages 245–308 in R. Duncan Luce, Robert R. Bush, and Eugene Galanter (editors), *Handbook of Mathematical Psychology.* New York: Wiley.

LUCE, R. DUNCAN; and SUPPES, PATRICK 1965 Preference, Utility, and Subjective Probability. Volume 3, pages 249–410 in R. Duncan Luce, Robert R. Bush, and Eugene Galanter (editors), *Handbook of Mathematical Psychology.* New York: Wiley.

McGILL, WILLIAM J. 1963 Stochastic Latency Mechanisms. Volume 1, pages 309–360 in R. Duncan Luce, Robert R. Bush, and Eugene Galanter (editors), *Handbook of Mathematical Psychology.* New York: Wiley.

SNELL, J. LAURIE 1965 Stochastic Processes. Volume 3, pages 411–486 in R. Duncan Luce, Robert R. Bush, and Eugene Galanter (editors), *Handbook of Mathematical Psychology.* New York: Wiley.

STERNBERG, SAUL 1963 Stochastic Learning Theory. Volume 2, pages 1–120 in R. Duncan Luce, Robert R. Bush, and Eugene Galanter (editors), *Handbook of Mathematical Psychology.* New York: Wiley.

SWETS, JOHN A. (editor) 1964 *Signal Detection and Recognition by Human Observers: Contemporary Readings.* New York: Wiley.

ZWISLOCKI, JOZEF 1965 Analysis of Some Auditory Characteristics. Volume 3, pages 1–98 in R. Duncan Luce, Robert R. Bush, and Eugene Galanter (editors), *Handbook of Mathematical Psychology.* New York: Wiley.

MODERNIZATION

The articles under this heading deal with general social and political problems of modernizing societies. More specialized aspects are treated in AGRICULTURE, article on SOCIAL ORGANIZATION; COMMUNITY–SOCIETY CONTINUA; RURAL SOCIETY. For other relevant material see INDUSTRIALIZATION; POLITICS, COMPARATIVE; SOCIAL CHANGE; and the detailed guide under ECONOMIC GROWTH.

I. SOCIAL ASPECTS	*Daniel Lerner*
II. POLITICAL ASPECTS	*James S. Coleman*
III. THE BOURGEOISIE IN MODERNIZING SOCIETIES	*Ronald P. Dore*

I
SOCIAL ASPECTS

Modernization is the current term for an old process—the process of social change whereby less developed societies acquire characteristics common to more developed societies. The process is activated by international, or intersocietal, communication. As Karl Marx noted over a century ago in the preface to *Das Kapital*: "The country that is more developed industrially only shows, to the less developed, the image of its own future."

We need a new name for the old process because the characteristics associated with more developed and less developed societies and the modes of communication between them have become in our day very different from what they used to be. During the era of imperialism, "images," or pictures, of the future were transmitted mainly to colonial peoples by their colonizers. Accordingly, one spoke of India as Anglicized and of Indochina as Gallicized. As the long generations of colonization made evident certain important similarities among imperialist regimes, regardless of national origins, these parochial terms were abandoned, and one spoke of Europeanization. World War II, which witnessed the constriction of European empires and the diffusion of American presence, again enlarged the vocabulary, and one spoke, often resentfully, of the Americanization of Europe. But when one spoke of the rest of the world, the term was "Westernization."

The postwar years soon made plain, however, that even this larger term was too parochial to comprehend the communication mode that had spread regularly patterned social change so swiftly and so widely as to require a global referent. In response to this need, the new term "modernization" evolved. It enabled one to speak concisely of those similarities of achievement observed in all modernized societies—whether Western, as in Europe and North America, or non-Western, as in the Soviet Union and Japan—as well as of those similarities of aspiration observed in all modernizing societies regardless of their location and traditions.

The hard core of observed similarities was economic. It was along the continuum of economic performance that societies could most readily and unambiguously be aligned, compared, and rated. An important step was taken when development economists reached the consensus that their subject matter was, in the words of W. Arthur Lewis, "the growth of output per head of population" (1955, p. 9). This simple operational definition specified simultaneously the aspirational continuum of economic development and the comparative measure of achievement levels along this continuum. In so doing, it focused the analysis of economic development and anchored the more comprehensive analysis of modernization as a societal process.

Modernization, therefore, is the process of social change in which development is the economic component. Modernization produces the societal environment in which rising output per head is effectively incorporated. For effective incorporation, the heads that produce (and consume) rising output must understand and accept the new rules of the game deeply enough to improve their own productive behavior and to diffuse it throughout their society. As Harold D. Lasswell (1965) has forcefully reminded us, this transformation in perceiving and achieving wealth-oriented behavior entails nothing less than the ultimate reshaping and resharing of all social values, such as power, respect, rectitude, affection, well-being, skill, and enlightenment. This view of continuous and increasing interaction between economic and noneconomic factors in development produced a second step forward, namely, systematic efforts to conceptualize modernization as the contemporary mode of social change that is both general in validity and global in scope.

Criteria of modernity

Although no single theoretical formulation as yet commands consensus among social scientists, there has been steady convergence among scholars on certain key points concerning modernization. There appears to be general agreement, for example, that economic decisions on investment criteria and resource allocation must take close account of such noneconomic factors as population growth, urbanization rates, family structure, the socialization of youth, education, and the mass media. Indeed, the contemporary association of modernization with comprehensive social planning has obliged scholars to seek some consensus on the common characteristics of modern societies.

There appears to be a large area of agreement, despite conceptual and terminological differences of more or less importance, that among the salient characteristics (operational values) of modernity are (1) a degree of self-sustaining growth in the economy—or at least growth sufficient to increase both production and consumption regularly; (2) a measure of public participation in the polity— or at least democratic representation in defining and choosing policy alternatives; (3) a diffusion of secular–rational norms in the culture—understood approximately in Weberian–Parsonian terms; (4) an increment of mobility in the society—understood as personal freedom of physical, social, and psychic movement; and (5) a corresponding transformation in the modal personality that equips individuals to function effectively in a social order that operates according to the foregoing characteristics —the personality transformation involving as a minimum an increment of self-things seeking, termed "striving" by Cantril (1966) and "need-achievement" by McClelland (1961), and an increment of self-others seeking, termed "other-direction" by Riesman (1950) and "empathy" by Lerner (1958a).

Pictures of the future

Every nation that regards itself as more developed now transmits pictures of itself to those less developed societies that figure in its own policy planning. All the once-imperial nations of western Europe are involved—Britain, France, Belgium, the Netherlands, and even Portugal. Modernization has spread beyond the obsolete confines of Europe's once-imperial nations to the Soviet Union and Communist China, to Japan, and even to Israel. The United States, which André Siegfried (1927) judged to be presiding at a general reorganization of ways of living throughout the world, has for many years been spending between three and four billion dollars of its national income on modernization abroad.

Every nation that is less developed, but regards itself as developing, receives the pictures transmitted by these more developed societies and decides, as a matter of high priority for its own policy planning, which of them constitutes the preferred picture of its own future. This decision is the crucial turn in the direction of modernization; whatever its particular configuration, it spells the passing of traditional society and defines the policy planning of social change.

The decision is rarely clear-cut. Hence, the ensuing policy often is ambivalent, and the planning often works at cross purposes. Nevertheless, much of the world is now engaged in an unprecedented process of social change that seeks to govern itself by rational policy planning. The less developed societies want to achieve in years the modernization that more developed societies attained over centuries of haphazard, or at least unplanned, development. But we do not have available the evaluated experience needed to provide rational guidance for such unprecedented efforts to induce comprehensive social change. This is why modernization —the twentieth century's distinctive mode of accelerating social change by rational planning—presents to social scientists so great a challenge and so important an opportunity.

For modernization, as we have seen, presents a very complex matrix of experience to be evaluated. It is one thing to summarize the common characteristics of modern societies. It is quite another thing to plan the rational transfer of these "items" from more developed to less developed societies— for each such transfer from the sender involves a deep transformation in the receiver. There exists no rational formula for the transfer of institutions. Modernization operates rather through a transformation of institutions (Lerner 1964) that can only be accomplished by the transformation of individuals—the painfully complex process which W. H. Auden epitomized as "a change of heart."

Complexities of modernization

The complexities of modernization puzzle social scientists, who are indispensable for rational planning, because such complexities bring together varieties of institutional and individual behavior that have in the past been studied in very different ways under the specialized division of labor in the social sciences. The variation in the level of knowledge and the "state of the art" in the different social sciences has been so large that a major effort of reintegration is required to deal with the model of social change presented by the matrix of modernization. This "boomerang effect" upon the social sciences produced by their efforts to deal with modernization is relevant in two ways.

First, in seeking to account for variations in the responses of less developed societies to the picture of their own future presented by more developed societies, scholars have felt obliged to restudy the modernization paths of the more developed societies. Thus, W. Arthur Lewis (1955), building upon prior work on the conditions of economic progress by Colin Clark (1940) and others, has produced a theory of economic growth that measures less developed as well as more developed societies on the same continuum of aspiration and metric of achievement. David C. McClelland (1961), building upon prior work in the psychology of "achievement–aspiration ratios" since William James, has produced a synthetic construct of the achievement motive applicable to all recorded history. Seymour M. Lipset (1963), building upon prior work in sociology on the processes of social change since Karl Marx and Max Weber, has rewritten the history of the United States as "the first new nation." Walt W. Rostow (1960), reviving the latterly quiescent but newly relevant disciplines of economic history and political economy, has formulated a general theory of modernization that ranges all societies of the world along the stages of a single continuum of "self-sustaining growth."

These important efforts to conceptualize modernization have become, inevitably, objects of controversy in the modernized world of specialized scholars. However, the critique and correction of detailed relationships in these synthetic models, which is the proper business of scholarship, does not seem to have impaired either their conceptual validity or their policy utility. They have already enabled contemporary thinkers to recognize that economic development is a high priority objective of every modernizing society—the prime mover, when indeed it is not the only motivation, for modernization. Moreover, and this is the crux of the matter, the attainment of "self-sustaining growth" involves far more than purely economic processes of production and consumption. It involves the institutional disposition of the full resources of a society; in particular, its human resources. For an economy to sustain growth by its own autonomous operation, it must be effectively geared to the skills and values of the people who make it work. On this view, a society capable of operating an economy of "self-sustaining growth" is *ipso facto* a modernized society (Hagen 1962).

The apparent circularity of this statement is eliminated when one specifies the minimum conditions required to make a society capable of operating an economy of self-sustaining growth. Although no consensus has yet been reached on the full matrix of modernization, which requires explicit specification of interrelations and sequences among the components, a fair measure of agreement has been achieved on the identification and conceptualization of the components themselves. This has been the second large gain to accrue from recent attempts by social scientists to reintegrate their specialized ideas and tools in order to deal effectively with a general model of modernization (Millikan & Blackmer 1961).

All models of modernization that aim at generality have dealt in some way with the economic-development variables that affect rising output per head directly and visibly, such as industrialization, urbanization, national income, and per capita income. In their quest for a model sufficiently general to subsume the move from "rising output per head" to "self-sustaining growth," sociologists have added to these variables an enlightenment variable measured in terms of schooling, literacy, and media exposure; political scientists have added a power variable measured in terms of participation, party membership, and voting; psychologists have added a cross-cutting variable of personality (usually postulated as an explanatory variable for which other variables serve as behavioral indices) measured in terms of authoritarianism, empathy, and need achievement. Anthropologists have enriched the general model by obliging it to account for local–temporal variants—those "diverse cultures" which, in Kluckhohn's words (1959), shape the behavioral variations underlying our "common humanity."

The "Western model" reconsidered

The convergence of disciplined perspectives upon a general model of modernization has diffused among scholars the recognition that, in our time, social change has become the distinctive component of virtually every social system. There remain in the world today few "traditional" social systems that operate with low rates of change over long time periods. Most societies are in some phase of transition. These are social systems operating with high (and usually accelerating) rates of change over short (and usually decreasing) periods of time. It is this phenomenon which in our time documents the "acceleration of history" that for previous generations was merely an interesting speculation by philosophers of history. Acceleration, now an essential component that must be incorporated in the research designs of all empirical students of social change, has obliged us to reconsider as well the operational mode of social systems that are already "modern" on current indices of modernization.

This reconsideration of modern Western societies has occasioned considerable reorganization of their societal theories and policies. Such recon-

sideration, having modified the evaluation of historical paths from the past to the present, now shapes new ways of estimating policy paths from the present to the future. There exist few theoretical constructions of future states of the world that are based on present changes in social systems. Lasswell (1965) has outlined the dangers of a "garrison–prison state" that attend policies designed to make any nation more powerful than all others; Rostow (1960) has sketched the attractions of a "mass-consumption society" for peoples who now demand more comfort and fun than peoples dared to dream of in all previous history. These theoretical constructions are strong because they account for the ambivalent behavior of all "transitional" societies and the vigorous behavior of most "modern" societies.

These theoretical constructions are strong as well because they show that modern societies are better able to cope with perceived needs for change than less developed, transitional societies. The obvious examples are their concern with the population explosion and the expanding metropolis. These are the demographic and ecological variables that index fundamental mechanisms for the Want–Get ratios which govern "dynamic equilibrium" in any society. Modern Western societies have brought these two variables under policy control more rapidly and efficiently than any transitional society has been able to do. The reason is that modern societies restudy and reappraise themselves continuously with an eye to their future. Hence, it is no accident that contraceptives came into widespread use in modern Western societies a full century ago to prevent an unmanageable population explosion. Nor is it accidental that "the pill," invented in the Western societies, is still more widely used by Westerners than by the transitional peoples to whom it has been offered, virtually free of charge, since the 1950s. Modern societies, founding their societal policies on data-based estimations of the future, are readier to perceive the dangers of overpopulation and to take steps to prevent them (Spengler & Duncan 1956).

So it has been also with the dangers of overurbanization. The acceleration of history has produced everywhere, as a major manifestation, an accelerated movement of people from the village to the city (California, University of . . . 1959). The outcome has been the spread of slums in every modernizing society. But almost from the moment these slums appeared, social scientists in the Western world began to study them in empirical and policy terms. Over a century ago, Frédéric Le Play (1855) described the situation of the urban poor in France and elsewhere in Europe; Charles Booth (Booth et al. 1889–1891) and Jane Addams (*Hull-House* . . . 1895) did the same for England and the United States, respectively. Their studies led to social diagnosis, social legislation, and, finally, social programs aimed at improvement. The institutionalization of urban policy in modern society is now visible in American "urban renewal," British "new towns," and French "aménagement du territoire." Few such programs have been made effectively operative in the modernizing societies of the transitional world today (Hoselitz 1960).

Transformation, not transfer

The widespread failure of transitional societies to incorporate modernizing institutions of sufficient amplitude and durability has occasioned reconsideration of the theory and practice of social change under conditions of extreme acceleration. Among the conclusions that have emerged (many of them reminders of lessons brought by anthropologists from their early encounters with traditional societies a century and more ago) is this reciprocal proposition: Traditional societies can respond effectively to internally generated demands for institutional change articulated over a relatively long period, but they are typically incapable of rapid institutional changes to meet externally induced demands.

Such externally induced demands occur whenever a less developed society receives a picture of its own future from a more developed society. Since the start of international development programs in 1949 (with the Point IV program of the United States instituted by President Truman), we have understood that the transmission of such pictures is likely to constitute an intrusion into the less developed, traditional society. Only more recently, by way of hard and often unrewarding experience, have we concluded that such intrusions regularly are, and usually must be, disruptive in transitional societies—these being traditional societies that manifest an urgent will-to-change but are unable to incorporate rapidly an efficacious way-to-change. The disruptive effect, which is produced by the imbalance between the will and the way to modernize, emerges as a key problem of induced and accelerated social change.

Consider again the problem of overurbanization. The newly reviving civilizations of the East have always had more people living in their capital cities than could be productively employed. Hence, over many centuries there developed the institution (or at least the vocational jurisdiction) of begging. So ancient and venerable is this institution that its routinized practice is sanctified in the

holy books of most Eastern, and particularly Middle Eastern, religions. The practice of begging and the duty of charity are sanctified alike in the Mosaic code of the Jews, the Koranic verses of the Muslims, and the New Testament of the Christians. Yet, under intrusion from the antislum and antipoverty ideology of the modern West, modernizers in the Eastern world have grown ashamed of this venerable institution and have sought to transform it. Many Western travelers have witnessed, at the doors of the Nile hotels in Cairo and at the gates of the Taj Mahal in Agra, the often brutal consequences of the modernizing proscription of begging inflicted upon people who know no other trade. But the modernizing Eastern leaders, while speeding the obsolescence of begging, have not yet incorporated an efficient institutional replacement to relieve the urban poor, whose members swell at accelerating rates from year to year (Lerner 1962).

The great cities of the transitional world often have become massive impediments to orderly social change rather than productive centers of modernization. In much of Latin America, vast lands are deserted while the people are crushed into the megalopolis—for example, half of all Cubans live in and around Havana, half of all Uruguayans live around Montevideo, and about 80 per cent of the Venezuelan population lives on the 10 per cent of land located between Caracas and Maracaibo. In the transitional societies of Asia, which produce far less wealth than those of Latin America, the consequences of overurbanization are even more disruptive. No traveler in Cairo or Calcutta will forget the sights, sounds, and smells of debilitated peoples who perform no productive functions for themselves or their environment. These millions of hapless people who consume (however little) without producing are the psychic displaced persons of modernization—they have come to consider themselves useless for anything beyond survival and reproduction. Their futility is an expression of the disruptive imbalance, for their minuscule benefits are gained only at the disproportionately great costs to their society which overurbanization imposes upon all development efforts.

That the problem of overurbanization remains unresolved is the measure of our failure to develop a comprehensive theory and practice of modernization. This proposition is circular in one sense: since the urban explosion is systemic with the population explosion and the literacy explosion, true resolution of any one explosion will help resolve the others. These explosions are systemic in the sense that they derive from a common source, converge on a common demand, and produce a common failure to satisfy the demand. The common source is empathy; the common demand is well-being; the common failure is poverty. These terms denote the failures that explain why we are passing from a putative "revolution of rising expectations" (Staley 1954), which shaped the theory and practice of planned social change after World War II, to an incipient "revolution of rising frustration" (Conference . . . 1963, pp. 330–333) that may reshape our thinking in the future.

Empathy—mechanism of transformation

Empathy is the psychic mechanism that enables a person to put himself in another person's situation—to identify himself with a role, time, or place different from his own. Among the range of psychic mechanisms that supply imagination, empathy is distinctively the one that nourishes "upward mobility." For what greater stimulus is there to imagine oneself in another person's situation if not that his situation is "better" (in some sense) than one's own? The power to imagine oneself in a better situation rests upon the psychic mechanism of empathy. The mechanism may or may not be innate, but it can certainly be trained to operate more efficiently in people with a desire to better themselves. Since World War II such training has been supplied by the mass media of print, film, and radio. The mass media, which we call the "mobility multiplier" for this reason, accelerate the training in psychic mobility that enables people to imagine themselves in situations other than their own—and hence, since the alternatives invariably represent better situations, accelerate training in upward mobility.

The global spread of empathy has thus diffused a new demand for well-being among peoples who, over all previous centuries, had never even been exposed to the idea that well-being was theirs to demand. Wants have always been with the poor, and expectations have risen or fallen with the richness of the harvest or the goodness of the king, but demand is something new in the lives of poor peoples. It involves nothing less than a new sense of oneself, that is, the transformation of one's identifications that is accomplished by empathy and accelerated by the multiplier effect of the mass media. But the newly diffused sense of demand, which articulates and aggregates the age-old wants and needs of the poor, imposes a new condition upon the management of societies: that ways must be found to satisfy demand if a society is to maintain itself in a relatively durable state of equilibrium—or, more precisely, in a tolerable state of disequilibrium.

The new condition is imposed by the systemic quality of the new demand: its widespread dis-

tribution throughout the social system entails a comprehensive institutional response. Economic theory has taught generations of analysts in modernized societies that equilibrium can be maintained only in the measure that widespread and persistent demand is balanced by adequate supply. It is the failure of transitional societies to increase supply at a sufficient rate to balance accelerating demand that accentuates the new meaning of poverty as a key to the unsolved problems of modernization. Poverty, which was once accepted as an honorable estate (as in the Biblical theme of the "eye of the needle"), is now rejected as an abject condition unworthy of human acceptance. Poverty is now seen as the self-sealing mechanism of a vicious circle that deprives people of the means to obtain enough of the good things of life. As Hans W. Singer has succinctly summarized the situation, its core is "the dominant vicious circle of low production—no surpluses for economic investment—no tools and equipment—low standards of production. An underdeveloped country is poor because it has no industry; and it has no industry because it is poor" (1949, p. 5).

Economists agree that the root problem is that poor people in poor countries do not earn enough to raise their essential consumption (wants) and still have something left over to save (that is, invest). This is attributed to the series of "explosions"—population, urbanization, literacy—that consume all gains in production as soon as they are made, and often more rapidly than they are made. It is the worsening situation of the poor as compared to the rich countries that, as Gunnar Myrdal (1956) has shown, defeats the planning of modernization in our time. Despite large outlays of funds and skills for international development, the poor lands and peoples are continuously getting poorer relative to the rich lands and peoples. The latter have incorporated the individual and institutional mechanisms that make growth self-sustaining and thereby underwrite the stability of modern societies at high and rising levels of output and income. By the same token, transitional societies, which have not been able to incorporate the mechanisms needed for self-sustaining growth, tend to grow relatively poorer and less stable.

Recognition that the relative situation of transitional societies is worsening, despite their high expectations and despite substantial contributions of international aid, has stimulated new research and reflection on the mechanisms of self-sustaining growth. It has long been clear that surplus product for economic investment is necessary. What was *not* clear, until very recently, is that an external input of investment does not necessarily ignite the motor of modernization and almost never suffices to keep it running. It appears to be essential that the modernizing society, if its growth is to be self-sustaining, should incorporate internal means of generating the surpluses needed for investment. This apparently simple extension of thinking about economic development entails wide and deep consequences for the social theory and practice of modernization. For a transitional society to generate surpluses internally, it must work a profound transformation into its individual and institutional patterns of traditional behavior (Shannon 1957).

This is why we no longer speak of a "transfer of institutions" from more developed to less developed societies. Such transfer rarely occurs in fact. When it does, as in those transitional societies that have transferred electoral institutions based on universal suffrage from more developed societies, the effects have been not only intrusive and disruptive but often positively dysfunctional for societal modernization. The indispensable lesson taught by failures to transfer institutions is that modernization must be systemic if it is to be durable. It must involve indigenous people in behavioral transformations so manifold and profound that a new and coherent way of life comes into operation. Institutions cannot be transferred; they must be transformed. Lifeways cannot be adopted; they must be adapted.

Adaptive capacity, the most distinctive feature of societies that are genuinely modernized, is what enables them to develop more rapidly than the transitional societies they are aiding out of their own large surplus product. While such handouts alleviate hardship and encourage hope in some transitional societies, these societies do not modernize effectively until they develop an indigenous capacity for accelerating and sustaining growth. Among the requirements are indigenous surpluses that enable people to break out of the vicious circle of poverty and into the self-sustaining cycle of growth. The incorporation of an adaptive capacity of this magnitude can occur only in societies that diffuse widely among their peoples the lifeways and institutions of mobility, empathy, and participation. Mobility is the initial mechanism: people must be ready, willing, and able to move from where they are and what they are.

Physical and social mobility have always interacted closely in the societies now regarded as modernized. Horace Greeley's maxim "Go West, young man, go West" told aspiring Americans a century ago: If you want to move *up*, young man, move *out*! Among the millions of aspiring young men in the transitional world today, many are heeding some local variant of this advice—usually delivered by "pictures" from the mass media (Schramm 1964). Those who want to move up are, in rapidly swelling numbers, moving out. Physical mobility has become a characteristic of world society in our time. But social mobility has not kept pace. This is so in part because, as we have seen, poor lands have a built-in tendency to stay poor. This tendency is built in by the persistence of traditional lifeways among the peoples of the poor lands. When they move out, they are not adequately prepared to meet the other requirements for moving up. They are, in particular, unprepared to make efficient use of the empathic mechanism that shapes psychic mobility—the personality reagent that catalyzes the interaction between physical and social mobility. In a word, they lack a sufficient dose of empathy (Lerner 1958b).

The inadequate diffusion of empathy—psychic mobility—is a major source of failure for development programs. People everywhere have been moving out with the expectation of moving up, and everywhere they are being disappointed. Social mobility simply does not coincide with physical mobility often enough to produce widespread satisfaction. On the contrary, if we are facing an incipient "revolution of rising frustration," it is because the newly mobile peoples of the transitional world have not found—and, more critically, have not learned to produce from their own resources—adequate satisfactions for their accelerated expectations. The disruptive imbalance that weighs most heavily on traditional societies in our time is the imbalance between what people have been taught to want and what they have learned to get.

The Want–Get ratio

We refer to the disruptive imbalance, which is the global source of rising frustrations, as the Want–Get ratio. Adapting an ingenious formula of William James, this can be expressed as follows:

$$\text{Frustration} = \frac{\text{Want}}{\text{Get}}.$$

Frustration rises in the measure that the numerator of Want exceeds the denominator of Get. In traditional societies, frustration remained fairly constant and at a relatively low level because wants (at least in the form of articulated demands) were relatively few and unchanging. Frustration is accelerating in transitional societies because articulated wants are increasing, diversifying, and spreading at very rapid and erratic rates.

This way of putting the matter links the process of modernization directly to the problem of economic development. Economic development is critical because continuing and deepening poverty signals the failure to meet the accelerating demand for well-being (articulated Want) generated by the erratic diffusion of empathy that has accompanied increasing mobility. The economic model is also useful because it teaches us to analyze psychosocial states more exactly by submitting them to the metrics of supply and demand. For what has disrupted transitional societies so deeply that stable governance—and rational planning for growth—cannot become self-sustaining is precisely the worsening ratio between supply and demand. Transitional peoples are accelerating their manifold demands beyond the supply capacity of their institutions and resources, including the capacity of individuals with increasing demands to adapt their personal behavior in such ways as to increase supplies.

Public opinion—empathy to participation

A modern society depends so crucially upon its human resources because it must be, first and foremost, a *participant* society. This does not mean that all people must participate continuously in all societal activities, since it is unlikely that any society could survive this degree of interaction. It does mean that enough people must participate continuously in each major institution to make these institutions viable, adaptable, and durable. This optimum level of interaction between individuals and institutions can be sustained only when it produces outcomes that are reciprocally rewarding. Institutions cannot endure persistently excessive demands upon their capacity by their individual participants; nor will individuals continue to participate in institutions that consistently frustrate their wants (Shannon 1958).

Perhaps the most significant and subtle instance of self-sustaining interaction between individuals and institutions in modern society is public opinion—a distinctive interaction that is not found in traditional societies (Speier 1950). The evolution of public opinion in the modern West can be traced from the eighteenth century, when the institutions of free public education and inexpensive mass media (the so-called penny press, for example) began to expand in response to the direct demands of peoples who had gained a fair measure of empathy and literacy over preceding generations. This initiated a growth cycle of public enlightenment throughout the modern West, from which evolved the distinctive societal process known as public opinion—a process which, in turn, lubricates the self-sustaining mechanisms of a participant society.

For the adaptive capacity of a participant society resides in its institutionalized modes for registering, regulating, and responding to individual demands as well as their articulated and aggregated expression through manifold channels of collective demand. [*See* PUBLIC OPINION; *see also* Almond & Coleman 1960, chapter 1.]

Public demand is something new. Earlier societies were able to survive the sporadic expression of individual and collective demands, particularly during periods of affluence, when their institutions were able to make relatively satisfactory responses to such demands. But no society preceding those of the nineteenth-century West was able to incorporate public demand as a mechanism that continuously interacts with public policy on the shaping and sharing of all societal values—power as well as wealth, enlightenment as well as deference. Indeed, only the twentieth-century West has begun to develop the crude model of a polity in which public demand—in the institutionalized form of public opinion—participates as a matter of course in the making of public policy.

Public opinion has become the institutionalized expression of individual and collective demands because it has incorporated a significant measure of self-regulation. It avoids the persistent expression of demands that cannot be satisfied by existing institutions operating upon available resources—the outbursts of excessive demand that recurrently eventuate in the riots, rebellions, and revolutions of nonparticipant societies (Johnson 1962). It is responsible and self-regulating because it is based upon public enlightenment, which informs people about the current condition of public institutions and resources and thereby acts as a constraint upon their individual and collective demands. The effect of enlightenment, in this sense, is that people reconsider their felt private demands in the light of known public constraints and emerge with equilibrated (or otherwise balanced) opinions on the issues before them. It is this internal balancing of the Want–Get ratio by individuals that, ideally, corrects disruptive imbalances in their institutions and makes their society self-sustaining.

Next steps

The ideal type of a participant society does not yet exist in the modern West and may never be realized perfectly anywhere. As public-opinion polls have shown time and again, citizens are often ignorant of their past, voters are often ambivalent about their future, and consumers are often confused in making their present choices. The reliance of public opinion upon such routinized institutions of enlightenment as public schools and mass media tends to routinize its creative articulation and aggregation. Those alienated intellectuals from retrograde societies of the West who point to marginal black-marketing in austerity Britain and peripheral cheating on income taxes in the United States ignore the principal fact, which is that these skin rashes upon participant societies have not been permitted to become cancerous (Shils 1958). Public opinion in these countries, despite its putative ignorance and ambivalence, has judged that black-marketing and tax-cheating are "immoral"—that their cost to public welfare exceeds their benefit to private interests and, therefore, that adaptive institutions are needed to correct their potentially disruptive imbalance. Such institutions include public sanctions against private malfeasance.

This process is the key to the "self-sustaining" capacity of a participant society. Public opinion, despite its flaws, can be counted on to perform its system-sustaining functions in an environment that supplies satisfactions and explains frustrations of individual and collective demands. It is this subtle and continuous reciprocity between popular demand and public supply (or nonsupply)—between what people want and what they get (or fail to get) —that animates and sustains the participant society. Since this model represents the greatest advance in recorded history toward the ages-old ideal of social democracy, we must learn to assay its gains and measure its costs (Lerner & Schramm 1966).

These are tasks that lie ahead for social scientists concerned with modernization. Procedures for assaying gains and measuring costs must be perfected. As a precondition, our concepts of what constitutes a cost or a gain must be articulated in sufficiently explicit fashion to guide our measures. While our tasks as social scientists are important, they cannot count for much without the efforts of those social planners and decision makers who change the lifeways of transitional societies. For the modernized lands have learned to develop, however crudely, a participant society with self-sustaining growth capability. This is not yet the case in the lands that are seeking to modernize.

The modernized societies must now perfect the model for their own purposes—which include the "transfer" of the model in such fashion that it can be "transformed" by the modernizing societies. The modernizing societies must learn how transferred institutions may be transformed, how adopted lifeways may be adapted. As the modernized succeed in learning their own lesson, they will be better

equipped to teach the lesson to the modernizing. For the contemporary world has become interactive in the sense that *all* nations and peoples now are continuously exposed to each other.

Modernization, now occurring on an interactive global scale, will point the way to a future modernity in the measure that advanced and backward, developed and underdeveloped, societies arrive at an understanding of what they have in common. This achievement of consensus on the values of a commonwealth of human dignity will provide the ultimate motor of modernization—for those who think they are, as for those who wish to be, modern.

DANIEL LERNER

[*Directly related are the entries* ACHIEVEMENT MOTIVATION; ECONOMIC GROWTH; POVERTY.]

BIBLIOGRAPHY

ALMOND, GABRIEL A.; and COLEMAN, JAMES S. (editors) 1960 *The Politics of the Developing Areas.* Princeton Univ. Press.

BOOTH, CHARLES et al. (1889–1891) 1902–1903 *Life and Labour of the People in London.* 17 vols. London: Macmillan.

CALIFORNIA, UNIVERSITY OF, INSTITUTE OF INTERNATIONAL STUDIES, INTERNATIONAL URBAN RESEARCH 1959 *The World's Metropolitan Areas,* by Suzanne R. Angelucci et al. Berkeley: Univ. of California Press.

CANTRIL, HADLEY 1966 *The Pattern of Human Concerns.* New Brunswick, N.J.: Rutgers Univ. Press.

CLARK, COLIN (1940) 1957 *The Conditions of Economic Progress.* 3d ed., rev. London: Macmillan.

CONFERENCE ON COMMUNICATION AND POLITICAL DEVELOPMENT, DOBBS FERRY, N.Y., *1961* 1963 *Communications and Political Development.* Edited by Lucian W. Pye. Princeton Univ. Press.

HAGEN, EVERETT E. 1962 *On the Theory of Social Change.* Homewood, Ill.: Dorsey.

HOSELITZ, BERT F. 1960 *Sociological Aspects of Economic Growth.* Glencoe, Ill.: Free Press.

Hull-House Maps and Papers: A Presentation of Nationalities and Wages in a Congested District of Chicago, Together With Comments and Essays on Problems Growing Out of the Social Conditions. 1895 New York: Crowell.

JOHNSON, JOHN J. (editor) 1962 *The Role of the Military in Underdeveloped Countries.* Princeton Univ. Press. → Papers of a conference sponsored by the RAND Corporation at Santa Monica, Calif., in August 1959.

KLUCKHOHN, CLYDE (1959) 1964 Common Humanity and Diverse Cultures. Pages 245–284 in Daniel Lerner (editor), *The Human Meaning of the Social Sciences.* New York: Meridian.

LASSWELL, HAROLD D. 1965 The Policy Sciences of Development. *World Politics* 17:286–309.

LE PLAY, FRÉDÉRIC (1855) 1877–1879 *Les ouvriers européens.* 2d ed. 6 vols. Tours (France): Mame.

LERNER, DANIEL 1958a *The Passing of Traditional Society: Modernizing the Middle East.* Glencoe, Ill.: Free Press. → A paperback edition was published in 1964.

LERNER, DANIEL (editor) 1958*b* Attitude Research in Modernizing Areas. *Public Opinion Quarterly* Special Issue 22, no. 3.

LERNER, DANIEL 1962 The Reviving Civilizations. Pages 307–322 in Conference on Science, Philosophy, and Religion in Their Relation to the Democratic Way of Life, Fifteenth, New York, 1956, *The Ethic of Power: The Interplay of Religion, Philosophy, and Politics.* Edited by Harold D. Lasswell and Harlan Cleveland. New York: The Conference.

LERNER, DANIEL 1964 The Transformation of Institutions. Pages 3–26 in William B. Hamilton (editor), *The Transfer of Institutions.* Durham, N.C.: Duke Univ. Press.

LERNER, DANIEL; and SCHRAMM, WILBUR (editors) 1966 *Communication and Change in the Developing Countries.* Honolulu: East–West Center Press.

LEWIS, W. ARTHUR 1955 *The Theory of Economic Growth.* Homewood, Ill.: Irwin.

LIPSET, SEYMOUR M. 1963 *The First New Nation: The United States in Historical and Comparative Perspective.* New York: Basic Books.

McCLELLAND, DAVID C. 1961 *The Achieving Society.* Princeton, N.J.: Van Nostrand.

MILLIKAN, MAX F.; and BLACKMER, DONALD L. M. (editors) 1961 *The Emerging Nations: Their Growth and United States Policy.* A Study from the Center for International Studies, Massachusetts Institute of Technology. Boston: Little.

MYRDAL, GUNNAR (1956) 1957 *Rich Lands and Poor: The Road to World Prosperity.* Rev. ed. New York: Harper. → First published as *Development and Underdevelopment.*

RIESMAN, DAVID 1950 *The Lonely Crowd: A Study of the Changing American Character.* New Haven: Yale Univ. Press. → An abridged paperback edition was published in 1960.

ROSTOW, WALT W. (1960) 1963 *The Stages of Economic Growth: A Non-Communist Manifesto.* Cambridge Univ. Press.

SCHRAMM, WILBUR L. 1964 *Mass Media and National Development: The Role of Information in the Developing Countries.* Stanford Univ. Press.

SHANNON, LYLE W. (editor) 1957 *Underdeveloped Areas: A Book of Readings and Research.* New York: Harper.

SHANNON, LYLE W. 1958 Is Level of Development Related to Capacity for Self-government? *American Journal of Economics and Sociology* 17:367–381.

SHILS, EDWARD 1958 Intellectuals, Public Opinion, and Economic Development. *World Politics* 10:232–255.

SIEGFRIED, ANDRÉ (1927) 1928 *America Comes of Age: A French Analysis.* New York: Harcourt. → First published in French.

SINGER, HANS W. 1949 Economic Progress in Underdeveloped Countries. *Social Research* 16:1–11.

SPEIER, HANS (1950) 1952 The Historical Development of Public Opinion. Pages 323–338 in Hans Speier, *Social Order and the Risks of War: Papers in Political Sociology.* New York: Stewart.

SPENGLER, JOSEPH J.; and DUNCAN, OTIS DUDLEY (editors) 1956 *Population Theory and Policy: Selected Readings.* Glencoe, Ill.: Free Press.

STALEY, EUGENE (1954) 1961 *The Future of Underdeveloped Countries: Political Implications of Economic Development.* Rev. ed. Published for the Council on Foreign Relations. New York: Harper.

II
POLITICAL ASPECTS

The political aspects of modernization refer to the ensemble of structural and cultural changes in the political systems of modernizing societies. As an analytically separable subsystem of society the political system comprises all of those activities, processes, institutions, and beliefs concerned with the making and execution of authoritative policy and the pursuit and attainment of collective goals. Political structure consists of the patterning and interrelationship of political roles and processes; political culture is the complex of prevailing attitudes, beliefs, and values concerning the political system. The over-all process of modernization refers to changes in all institutional spheres of a society resulting from man's expanding knowledge of and control over his environment (Black 1962). Political modernization refers to those processes of differentiation of political structure and secularization of political culture which enhance the capability—the effectiveness and efficiency of performance—of a society's political system (Almond & Powell 1966).

Political modernization can be viewed from a historical, a typological, and an evolutionary perspective. *Historical political modernization* refers to the totality of changes in political structure and culture which characteristically have affected or have been affected by those major transformative processes of modernization (secularization; commercialization; industrialization; accelerated social mobility; restratification; increased material standards of living; diffusion of literacy, education, and mass media; national unification; and the expansion of popular involvement and participation) which were first launched in western Europe in the sixteenth century and which subsequently have spread, unevenly and incompletely, throughout the world. *Typological political modernization* refers to the process of transmutation of a premodern "traditional" polity into a posttraditional "modern" polity. (Since concrete polities are only more or less modern, the term "modern polity" is used here to refer to those polities which in the 1960s are typologically the most modern.) *Evolutionary political modernization* refers to that open-ended increase in the capacity of political man to develop structures to cope with or resolve problems, to absorb and adapt to continuous change, and to strive purposely and creatively for the attainment of new societal goals. From the historical and typological perspectives, political modernization is a process of development toward some image of a modern polity. From the evolutionary perspective, the growth process is interminable and the end state of affairs indeterminate.

Theoretical approaches

Efforts to depict the complex characteristics of a modern polity have tended to take three forms: descriptive trait lists, single-dimension reductionism, and ideal-type continua. Several studies have combined all three approaches in variant ways (e.g., Almond & Coleman 1960).

The trait list approach usually identifies the major structural and cultural features generic to those contemporary polities regarded as modern by the observer (Almond & Coleman 1960; Black 1962; Eisenstadt 1964a; Kornhauser 1964; Conference on Communication . . . 1963; Conference on Political Modernization . . . 1964). These efforts have been criticized for being temporally and culturally bounded, for being excessively multidimensional, and for including some traits which vary independently of one another (Holt & Turner 1966).

The reductionist approach focuses upon a single antecedent factor, explanatory variable, correlate, or determinant as the prime index or most distinguishing feature of modernization and, by implication, of political modernity. Single characteristics which have been highlighted include the concepts of capacity or capability (Brzezinski 1956; Holt & Turner 1966; Almond 1965), differentiation (Riggs 1963), institutionalization (Huntington 1965), national integration (Binder 1962), participation (Lerner 1958), populism (Fallers 1963), political culture (Almond & Verba 1963), psychological traits (Lerner 1958; Doob 1960; Conference on Communication . . . 1963), social mobilization (Deutsch 1961), and socioeconomic correlates (Lipset 1960; Coleman 1960; Cutright 1963). These reductive efforts do not imply a denial of multivariate causation; rather, they reflect either the timeless quest for a comprehensive single concept of modernity or simply the desire to illuminate a previously neglected or underemphasized variable.

The ideal-type approach is either explicit or implicit in most conceptualizations of both a modern political system and the process of political modernization. Descriptive trait lists of a generically modern polity tend unavoidably to be ideal-typical; indeed, the very notion of a "modern polity" implies an ideal-typical "traditional polity" as a polar opposite, as well as a "transitional polity" as an intervening type on a continuum of political modernization. Inspired by the original simple dichotomies of Maine (status–contract) and Tönnies (*Gemeinschaft–Gesellschaft*), and more directly by the pattern variables developed by Talcott Parsons, more complex ideal–typical dichotomous schemata of variable multidimensionality have been suggested for the study of comparative politics (Sutton 1959; Almond & Coleman 1960) and comparative administration (Riggs 1957). The essential differences between these schemata and the ideal–typical trait lists are that the attributes of the former are more logically interrelated in a unified construct and are specified for the two polar opposites (e.g., agrarian–industrial; traditional–modern). According to these schemata, the orientations governing the interactions characteristic of a traditional polity are predominantly ascriptive, particularistic, and diffuse; those of a modern polity are predominantly achievement-oriented, universalistic, and specific. Political modernization is viewed as the process of movement from the traditional pole to the modern pole of the continuum.

The three-stage (traditional–transitional–modern) approach to political modernization is vulnerable to at least three criticisms. First, like all such models used in the study of change in the social sciences, it tends to convey a false image of the traditional pole of the modernization continuum (Moore 1963). The static, sacred, undifferentiated character of chronologically traditional polities tends to be exaggerated. Many historically "traditional" political systems in fact had typologically "modern" structures, attributes, and orientations and vice versa. Indeed, the political structures of all empirical societies—historical and contemporaneous—are mixed; the degree of their modernity is determined by whichever tendency predominates within the mix. Although this fact is acknowledged, even stressed, by most users of the three-stage approach, the tendency to confuse, or at least to slur, the differences between historical and typological political modernity is a common fallacy in much of the literature. Second, this approach suggests that the movement between the two poles of traditionality and modernity is and must be irreversible, directional, and unilinear. It does not allow for political "breakdowns" in modernization (Eisenstadt 1964b), for "negative" political development or "prismatic" arrest (Riggs 1964), or for political "decay" (Huntington 1965). Third, at the modern end of the continuum, the three-stage model reinforces the image that the modernization process terminates, a notion implicit in the ordinary "present-day" meaning of the concept of modernity. It suggests the completion of a once-and-for-all and once-to-a-system process of transmutation. By implying that there cannot be any further or continuous modernization, it rules out the concept of evolutionary political modernization.

The evolutionary perspective emancipates the concept of political modernization from both its temporal (1500 to the present day) and its cultural and areal (Western world) constraints. It overcomes the implication of termination inherent in the idea of a "modern" polity and avoids the notion of "postmodern" political development. Although it does not becloud the fact that historically the major thrust in political modernization has occurred in the core area of western Europe in its postmedieval period, it allows us to reach back to the beginning of man's organized existence and to encompass the full range of structural diversity in man's experience in governing himself. Moreover, by viewing political modernization as an ongoing and continuous process, it encourages comparative trend analysis. Such a redefinition of the concept ties in with the revival and extension of evolutionary theory in cultural anthropology (Sahlins & Service 1960) and in sociology (Parsons 1964). Indeed, the distinction made by Sahlins between *specific evolution* (the historically continuous adaptation of particular societies to their environments) and *general evolution* (over-all, but discontinuous, development in human organization as manifested in the passage from lesser to greater capacity and all-round adaptability and from lower to higher levels of integration) is particularly crucial. [See EVOLUTION, *article on* CULTURAL EVOLUTION.] This dual character of the evolutionary perspective makes it possible to refer, on the one hand, to the specific process of political modernization (i.e., the acquisition of typologically modern traits and capabilities) in particular concrete societies, which through specialization and adaptation may in time cease modernizing, and, on the other hand, to general political modernization, as manifested in the successive acquisition by politically organized man of enhanced and new capacity to seek, change, and attain his goals. It is, in short, a perspective that allows us to conceptualize political modernization, political development, and political growth as synonymous.

Characteristics

In the growing body of literature on modernization and development, the major characteristics most often associated with the concept of a modern polity and the process of political modernization can be roughly grouped under three major headings: (1) *differentiation*, as the dominant empirical trend in the historic evolution of modern society; (2) *equality*, as the central ethos and ethical imperative pervading the operative ideals of all aspects of modern life; and (3) *capacity*, as the constantly increasing adaptive and creative potentialities possessed by man for the manipulation of his environment. The political modernization process can be viewed as an interminable contrapuntal interplay among the process of differentiation, the imperatives and realizations of equality, and the integrative, adaptive, and creative capacity of a political system. In these terms, political modernization is the progressive acquisition of a consciously sought, and qualitatively new and enhanced, political capacity as manifested in (1) the effective institutionalization of (*a*) new patterns of integration and penetration regulating and containing the tensions and conflicts produced by the processes of differentiation, and of (*b*) new patterns of participation and resource distribution adequately responsive to the demands generated by the imperatives of equality; and (2) the continuous flexibility to set and achieve new goals.

The process of differentiation. Differentiation refers to the process of progressive separation and specialization of roles, institutional spheres, and associations in the development of political systems. It includes such "evolutionary universals" (Parsons 1964) as social stratification and the separation of occupational roles from kinship and domestic life, the separation of an integrated system of universalistic legal norms from religion, the separation of religion and ideology, and differentiation between administrative structure and public political competition. It implies greater functional specialization, structural complexity and interdependence, and heightened effectiveness of political organization in both administrative and political spheres. [See POLITICAL ANTHROPOLOGY, *article on* POLITICAL ORGANIZATION.]

The ethos of equality. Equality is the ethos of modernity; the quest for it and its realization are at the core of the politics of modernization. It includes the notion of universal adult citizenship (equality in distributive claims and participant rights and duties), the prevalence of universalistic legal norms in the government's relations with the citizenry (equality in legal privileges and deprivations), and the predominance of achievement criteria (the psychic equality of opportunity to be unequal) in recruitment and allocation to political and administrative roles. Even though these attributes of equality are only imperfectly realized in the most modern polities, they continue to operate as the central standards and imperatives by which modernization is measured and political legitimacy established. Popular participation or involvement in the political system, either symbolically or determinatively, is a central theme in most definitions of political modernization. [*See* EQUALITY.]

The growth of political capacity. The acquisition of enhanced political administrative capacity is the third major feature of political modernization. It is characterized by an increase in scope of polity functions, in the scale of the political community, in the efficacy of the implementation of political and administrative decisions, in the penetrative power of central governmental institutions, and in the comprehensiveness of the aggregation of interests by political associations. Institutionalization of political organization and procedures, the development of problem-solving capabilities, centralization, and the ability to sustain continuously new types of political demands and organizations are among the varying ways in which the concept of capacity has been made central to the definition of political modernization and development. The sources of increased capacity include both differentiation (secularization, functional specialization, greater structural interdependence, motivation generated by status hierarchization) and equality (liberation of human energy and talent, universalism, achievement, rationalization, and civic identity and obligation); yet the tensions and divisiveness of differentiation and the demands of egalitarianism also constitute the main challenge to the capacity of a polity. The fact that the three aspects of modernization may sometimes conflict rather than reinforce one another explains why their contrapuntal interplay is central to any discussion of the modernization process.

Democracy and nation-state. Two other characteristics commonly attributed to a modern polity are democracy and the nation-state. In some instances, Western democratic institutions are used explicitly as the empirical referents for a model of political modernity; in others such an identification is only implicit. This infusion of the concept with an allegedly culture-bound element limits the utility of the concept as a cross-cultural analytical tool. Recognition of this fact has stimulated efforts to identify and specify traits generic to those political systems generally recognized as the most modern in the contemporary world. Ethnocentrism aside, however, there are those who defend a democratic component in any model of political modernization either on ethical grounds or because it demonstrably enhances the integrative and adaptive capacity and the flexibility of a political system. This latter rationale is the basis for identifying the "democratic association" as an "evolutionary universal," a major threshold in political modernization. [*See* DEMOCRACY.]

The nation-state is the second major controversial component in definitions of political modernization. Most studies assume that the nation-state is the essential, if not the natural, framework of political modernization. According to Black (1962), the essential effect of modernization has been the creation of national states. Indeed, "nation building" is commonly viewed as either a crucial dimension of or as a synonym for political modernization. Historically, of course, the centralized nation-state (existing or emerging) has been the empirical unit of modernization in all its aspects. Moreover, unlike democratic institutions, it is a form of political organization that has in fact become universalized. It has also been legitimated by prevailing norms of international law and organization. Therefore, it is the most convenient and logical unit for analysis in studies both of historical and of contemporary modernization. From the evolutionary and typological perspective, however, it need not and should not be included as a requisite component of political modernization. [*See* NATION.]

Patterns and variables

The autonomy of the polity. A prominent theme in various strands of Western social and political thought is the dependence of the polity upon other institutional spheres. This tradition of looking at political behavior and institutions as deriving from more fundamental social, economic, or psychological factors has been fortified in the social sciences—and particularly in political science—by a variety of other influences: behavioralism, systems theory, and structural-functionalism; the prominence in our image of modernization in the Western world of the laissez-faire period, in contrast with the earlier polity-dominant statist period; the pronounced economic determinism in America's post-World War II foreign aid policy, conditioned as it has been by the presumably successful democratization of West Germany and Japan; and several studies which suggest a positive correlation between political, social, and economic aspects of development (Lipset 1960; Coleman 1960; Cutright 1963; Banks & Textor 1963). In line with the continual rediscovery of lost or neglected variables in the pendulumlike evolution of the social sciences, the reaction against this polity-as-the-dependent-variable tradition is now in full swing (Montgomery & Siffin 1965; Spiro 1966).

The need for a critical re-examination of the

degree of autonomy and primacy of the polity in the modernization process has been given added impetus as a result of restrospective analysis of historical modernization in the West (Black 1966); the dominance of the political sphere in the modernization of the Soviet Union and mainland China, as well as Japan, Turkey, and Mexico (Black 1962; Tsou 1963; Conference on Political Modernization . . . 1964; Eisenstadt 1964*b*); and the pre-eminence of the political factor in the modernization of the developing countries. In virtually all of these instances political leadership and centralized political organization have been dominant and causal, rather than derivative. There are also historical instances where substantial changes have taken place in the political sphere without correspondingly significant changes in the social and economic spheres, and vice versa (see Paige in Montgomery & Siffin 1965), thus underlining the autonomy of the polity in the modernization process. The American experience, as Huntington (1966) emphasized, demonstrates conclusively that some institutions and some aspects of a society may become highly modern while other institutions and other aspects retain much of their traditional form and substance.

Patterns of modernization. The varying patterns in the relationship between the polity and the society (polity dominance, polity dependence, and polity autonomy) are only one aspect of the extraordinary diversity which has characterized the process of political modernization throughout history. There presumably is no single universal process, no uniform sequential pattern or common structural arrangement. The modernizing experience of each country is *sui generis*. According to one view, the only generalization one can make is that late modernizers ". . . will not follow the sequence of their predecessors, but will insist on changing it around or on skipping entirely some stages as well as some 'preconditions'" (Hirschman 1962). Nevertheless, certain patterns have been suggested. One typology (Black 1966), based on three criteria (the ascendance and consolidation of modernizing leadership, economic and social transformation, and the integration of society), identifies seven patterns of political modernization: (1) Britain and France, the early modernizers and models for later modernizers; (2) the United States, Canada, Australia, and New Zealand, the offshoots of Britain and France in the New World; (3) the other societies of continental Europe, in which the consolidation of modernizing leadership occurred after the French Revolution; (4) the independent countries of Latin America; (5) societies

that modernized without direct outside intervention but under the influence of early modernizers (Russia, Japan, China, Iran, Turkey, Afghanistan, Ethiopia, and Thailand); and (6) and (7) former and residual colonial territories differentiated according to the existence of precolonial institutions adaptable to modern conditions. Using different criteria, another schema (Eisenstadt 1964*b*) distinguishes six clusters (constitutional democracies; totalitarian states; indigenous revolutionary regimes such as Turkey and Mexico; dictatorships in eastern Europe, the Middle East, and Latin America; authoritarian regimes in Spain and Portugal; and the postcolonial new states). A third schema (Huntington 1966), primarily concerned with the earlier phases of political modernization in Europe and America, distinguishes three patterns (continental European, British, and American) according to three criteria (rationalized authority, differentiated political structure, and mass political participation). Actual or ideal–typical patterns of political modernization in late-modernizing new states as a special category have also been suggested (Shils 1959–1960; Apter 1965).

Variables affecting modernization. Among the many variables which can affect—and which historically have decisively affected—the course of political modernization, four seem to be particularly crucial: (1) the traditional political structure and culture, (2) the historical timing of the modernization thrust, (3) the character and orientation of political leadership, and (4) the sequence in which major system-development problems or "crises" generic to the political modernization process are encountered.

Tradition. Traditional institutions and values have an extraordinary resilience and persistence. "[The] form a modern society takes is the result of the interaction of its historically formed traditions with the universalizing effects of modernization" (Black 1962). For example, if prior to the modernization leap a national state, a centralized government, and a dominant value system supportive of innovation and change already exist, there can be a "reinforcing dualism" (Conference on Political Modernization . . . 1964) between the traditional system and the modernizing process.

Timing. The timing of the modernizing "take-off" is also crucial in many ways: it determines the significance of an array of other variables, such as the international environment, the range of modernizing models available for emulation, the political manipulability or obstructiveness of tradition, the degree of social and political mobilization of the population and the resultant demand load upon the polity, and the opportunities for modernizing short-cuts available to late starters favored by the so-called Law of Evolutionary Potential (Sahlins & Service 1960).

Leadership. The nature of a modernizing political leadership largely determines the extent to which tradition is harnessed to modernization if it is supportive or neutralized if it is obstructive. It also determines the degree to which the disadvantages of timing are minimized and the opportunities are exploited. Individual political leaders and political elites have been the prime movers in political modernization. The rate and direction of that process, as well as the political structures and culture which emerge, reflect in large measure the values and goal orientations of the leadership; its adaptive and creative capacities; and its reaction to the modernization crises it confronts.

Crises. The experience of the most highly developed contemporary polities has led to the identification of several critical "system-development problems" or "crises" which every modernizing polity encounters at least once and must cope with or surmount if it is to continue to modernize (Conference on Political Modernization . . . 1964; Black 1966; Almond & Powell 1966; Pye 1966). Although formulations vary, the following six problems illuminate this way of conceptualizing the political modernization process: (1) *national identity*, the transfer of ultimate loyalty and commitment from primordial groups to the larger national political system; (2) *political legitimacy*, the legitimation of modernizing elites and the authority structure of the new state; (3) *penetration*, the centralization of power, the establishment of a "determinate human source of final authority" transcending pre-existing subnational authority systems (Huntington 1966), the bridging of discontinuities in political communication, and the effectuation of policies throughout the society by the central institutions of government; (4) *participation*, the development of symbolic or participatory institutions and a political infrastructure to organize and channel the characteristically modern mass demand for a share in the decision-making process; (5) *integration*, the organization of a coherent political process and pattern of interacting relationships for the making of public policy and the pursuit and achievement of societal goals; and (6) *distribution*, the effective use of government power to bring about economic growth, mobilize resources, and distribute goods, services, and values in response to mass demands and expectations.

The modernization of a political system is meas-

ured by the extent to which it has developed the capabilities (symbolic, regulative, responsive, extractive, and distributive) to cope with these generic system-development problems (Almond 1965; Pennock 1966). It is argued not only that these capabilities are logically related but also that they suggest an order of development, that is, the development of one type of capability requires the development of another (e.g., increasing the extractive capability implies an increase in the regulative capability). Indeed, this approach could be the first step in the direction of a theory of political modernization, if the structural and cultural characteristics of political systems can be related to the ways in which these systems have confronted and coped with the crises common to all of them (Almond & Powell 1966).

Systematic comparative historical studies of political modernization in Western polities are increasingly feasible as a consequence of the development of data archives and the use of electronic computers in processing historical information (Rokkan 1966). One promising initial focus would be upon the growth in political participation: in most countries of the West the requisite political statistics are available as far back as the French Revolution. This rediscovery of the legitimacy and theoretical potentiality of the historical dimension in political research and in diachronic analysis has been one of the unintended consequences of the postwar concern with the modernization of the developing countries. Continued systematic study of the evolution of the latter, together with the retrospective analysis of the political modernization of older polities, should significantly enhance our capacity not only to generalize about the past but also to suggest probabilities regarding the future.

JAMES S. COLEMAN

[*See also* GOVERNMENT; POLITICAL ANTHROPOLOGY; POLITICAL CULTURE; POLITICS, COMPARATIVE; SOCIETAL ANALYSIS.]

BIBLIOGRAPHY

ALMOND, GABRIEL A. 1965 A Developmental Approach to Political Systems. *World Politics* 17:183–214.
ALMOND, GABRIEL A.; and COLEMAN, JAMES S. (editors) 1960 *The Politics of the Developing Areas.* Princeton Univ. Press.
ALMOND, GABRIEL A.; and POWELL, G. BINGHAM JR. 1966 *Comparative Politics: A Developmental Approach.* Boston: Little.
ALMOND, GABRIEL A.; and VERBA, SIDNEY (1963) 1965 *The Civic Culture: Political Attitudes and Democracy in Five Nations.* Boston: Little.
APTER, DAVID E. (1955) 1963 *Ghana in Transition.* Rev. ed. New York: Atheneum. → First published as *The Gold Coast in Transition.*

APTER, DAVID E. 1960 The Role of Traditionalism in the Political Modernization of Ghana and Uganda. *World Politics* 13:45–68.

APTER, DAVID E. 1961 *The Political Kingdom of Uganda: A Study in Bureaucratic Nationalism.* Princeton Univ. Press.

APTER, DAVID E. 1965 *The Politics of Modernization.* Univ. of Chicago Press.

BANKS, ARTHUR; and TEXTOR, ROBERT 1963 *A Cross-polity Survey.* Cambridge, Mass.: M.I.T. Press.

BARKER, ERNEST (1937) 1944 *The Development of Public Services in Western Europe: 1660–1930.* New York and London: Oxford Univ. Press. → First published as "The Development of Administration, Taxation, Social Services and Education" in Edward Eyre (editor), *European Civilization, Its Origin and Development.*

BENDIX, REINHARD 1961 Social Stratification and the Political Community. *Archives européennes de sociologie* 1:181–210.

BINDER, LEONARD (1962) 1964 *Iran: Political Development in a Changing Society.* Published under the auspices of the Near Eastern Center, University of California. Berkeley and Los Angeles: Univ. of California Press.

BLACK, CYRIL E. 1962 Political Modernization in Russia and China. Pages 3–18 in International Conference on Sino–Soviet Bloc Affairs, 3d, Lake Kawaguchi, 1960, *Unity and Contradiction: Major Aspects of Sino–Soviet Relations.* Edited by Kurt London. New York: Praeger.

BLACK, CYRIL E. 1966 *The Dynamics of Modernization: A Study in Comparative History.* New York: Harper.

BROOKINGS INSTITUTION, WASHINGTON, D.C. 1962 *Development of the Emerging Countries: An Agenda for Research.* Washington: The Institution.

BRZEZINSKI, ZBIGNIEW 1956 The Politics of Underdevelopment. *World Politics* 9:55–75.

CHICAGO, UNIVERSITY OF, COMMITTEE FOR THE COMPARATIVE STUDY OF THE NEW NATIONS 1963 *Old Societies and New States: The Quest for Modernity in Asia and Africa.* Edited by Clifford Geertz. New York: Free Press.

COLEMAN, JAMES S. 1960 The Political Systems of the Developing Areas. Pages 532–576 in Gabriel A. Almond and James S. Coleman (editors), *The Politics of the Developing Areas.* Princeton Univ. Press.

COLEMAN, JAMES S. (editor) 1965 *Education and Political Development.* Princeton Univ. Press.

CONFERENCE ON COMMUNICATION AND POLITICAL DEVELOPMENT, DOBBS FERRY, N.Y., *1961* 1963 *Communications and Political Development.* Edited by Lucian W. Pye. Princeton Univ. Press.

CONFERENCE ON POLITICAL MODERNIZATION IN JAPAN AND TURKEY, GOULD HOUSE, *1962* 1964 *Political Modernization in Japan and Turkey.* Edited by Robert E. Ward and Dankwart A. Rustow. Princeton Univ. Press.

CUTRIGHT, PHILLIPS 1963 National Political Development: Measurement and Analysis. *American Sociological Review* 28:253–264.

DAVIES, JAMES C. 1962 Toward a Theory of Revolution. *American Sociological Review* 27:5–19.

DEUTSCH, KARL W. 1953a The Growth of Nations: Some Recurrent Patterns of Political and Social Integration. *World Politics* 5:168–195.

DEUTSCH, KARL W. (1953b) 1966 *Nationalism and Social Communication: An Inquiry Into the Foundations of Nationality.* 2d ed. Cambridge, Mass.: M.I.T. Press; New York: Wiley.

DEUTSCH, KARL W. 1961 Social Mobilization and Political Development. *American Political Science Review* 55:493–514.

DEUTSCH, KARL W. 1963 *The Nerves of Government: Models of Political Communication and Control.* New York: Free Press.

DEUTSCH, KARL W. et al. 1957 *Political Community and the North Atlantic Area: International Organization in the Light of Historical Experience.* Princeton Univ. Press.

DOOB, LEONARD W. 1960 *Becoming More Civilized: A Psychological Exploration.* New Haven: Yale Univ. Press.

EASTON, DAVID 1965 *A Framework for Political Analysis.* Englewood Cliffs, N.J.: Prentice-Hall.

EISENSTADT, SHMUEL N. 1958 Bureaucracy and Bureaucratization: A Trend Report and Bibliography. *Current Sociology* 7:99–164.

EISENSTADT, SHMUEL N. 1961 *Essays on Sociological Aspects of Political and Economic Development.* The Hague: Mouton.

EISENSTADT, SHMUEL N. 1963a *The Political Systems of Empires.* New York: Free Press.

EISENSTADT, SHMUEL N. 1963b *Modernization: Growth and Diversity.* Bloomington: Indiana Univ., Department of Government.

EISENSTADT, SHMUEL N. 1964a Political Modernization: Some Comparative Notes. *International Journal of Comparative Sociology* 5:3–24.

EISENSTADT, SHMUEL N. 1964b Breakdowns of Modernization. *Economic Development and Cultural Change* 12:345–367.

EMERSON, RUPERT 1960a *From Empire to Nation: The Rise to Self-assertion of Asian and African Peoples.* Cambridge, Mass.: Harvard Univ. Press. → A paperback edition was published in 1962 by Beacon.

EMERSON, RUPERT 1960b Nationalism and Political Development. *Journal of Politics* 22:3–28.

FALLERS, LLOYD A. 1963 Equality, Modernity, and Democracy in the New States. Pages 158–219 in Chicago, University of, Committee for the Comparative Study of New Nations, *Old Societies and New States: The Quest for Modernity in Asia and Africa.* Edited by Clifford Geertz. New York: Free Press.

GINSBERG, MORRIS 1961 *Essays in Sociology and Social Philosophy.* Volume 3: Evolution and Progress. London: Heinemann.

HAGEN, EVERETT E. 1962 *On the Theory of Social Change: How Economic Growth Begins.* Homewood, Ill.: Dorsey.

HARRIS, DALE B. (editor) 1957 *The Concept of Development: An Issue in the Study of Human Behavior.* Minneapolis: Univ. of Minnesota Press.

HIRSCHMAN, ALBERT O. 1962 Comments on "A Framework for Analyzing Economic and Political Change." Pages 39–44 in Brookings Institution, *Development of the Emerging Countries: An Agenda for Research.* Washington: The Institution.

HOLT, ROBERT T.; and TURNER, JOHN E. 1966 *The Political Basis of Economic Development: An Exploration in Comparative Political Analysis.* New York: Van Nostrand.

HUNTINGTON, SAMUEL P. 1965 Political Development and Political Decay. *World Politics* 17:386–430.

HUNTINGTON, SAMUEL P. 1966 Political Modernization: America vs. Europe. *World Politics* 18:378–414.

Kilson, Martin 1963 African Political Change and the Modernisation Process. *Journal of Modern African Studies* 1:425–440.

Kornhauser, William 1959 *The Politics of Mass Society.* Glencoe, Ill.: Free Press.

Kornhauser, William 1964 Rebellion and Political Development. Pages 142-156 in Harry Eckstein (editor), *Internal War: Problems and Approaches.* New York: Free Press.

LaPalombara, Joseph G. (editor) 1963 *Bureaucracy and Political Development.* Studies in Political Development, No. 2. Princeton Univ. Press.

LaPalombara, Joseph G.; and Weiner, Myron (editors) 1966 *Political Parties and Political Development.* Princeton Univ. Press.

Lerner, Daniel 1958 *The Passing of Traditional Society: Modernizing the Middle East.* Glencoe, Ill.: Free Press. → A paperback edition was published in 1964.

Levy, Marion J. 1966 *Modernization and the Structure of Society: A Setting for International Affairs.* 2 vols. Princeton Univ. Press.

Lipset, Seymour M. 1960 *Political Man: The Social Bases of Politics.* Garden City, N.Y.: Doubleday. → A paperback edition was published in 1963.

Lipset, Seymour M. 1963 *The First New Nation: The United States in Historical and Comparative Perspective.* New York: Basic Books.

Marshall, T. H. (1934–1962) 1964 *Class, Citizenship, and Social Development: Essays.* Garden City, N.Y.: Doubleday. → A collection of articles and lectures first published in England in 1963 as *Sociology at the Crossroads and Other Essays.* A paperback edition was published in 1965.

Millikan, Max F.; and Blackmer, Donald L. M. (editors) 1961 *The Emerging Nations: Their Growth and United States Policy.* A Study from the Center for International Studies, Massachusetts Institute of Technology. Boston: Little.

Montgomery, John D.; and Siffin, William (editors) 1965 *Politics, Administration and Change: Approaches to Development.* New York: McGraw-Hill. → See especially the articles "The Rediscovery of Politics," by Glenn D. Paige, and "Political Development: Approaches to Theory and Strategy," by Alfred Diamant.

Moore, Wilbert E. 1963 *Social Change.* Englewood Cliffs, N.J.: Prentice-Hall.

Neufeld, Maurice F. 1965 *Poor Countries and Authoritarian Rule.* Ithaca: New York State School of Industrial and Labor Relations.

Organski, A. F. K. 1965 *The Stages of Political Development.* New York: Knopf.

Packenham, Robert A. 1964 Approaches to the Study of Political Development. *World Politics* 17:108–120.

Parsons, Talcott 1964 Evolutionary Universals in Society. *American Sociological Review* 29:339–357.

Pennock, J. Roland 1966 Political Development, Political Systems, and Political Goods. *World Politics* 18:415–434.

Pye, Lucian W. 1962 *Politics, Personality, and Nation Building: Burma's Search for Identity.* New Haven: Yale Univ. Press.

Pye, Lucian W. 1966 *Aspects of Political Development: An Analytic Study.* Boston: Little.

Pye, Lucian W.; and Verba, Sidney (editors) 1965 *Political Culture and Political Development.* Princeton Univ. Press.

Riggs, Fred W. (1957) 1959 Agraria and Industria: Toward a Typology of Comparative Administration. Pages 23–116 in William J. Siffin (editor), *Toward the Comparative Study of Public Administration.* Bloomington: Indiana Univ. Press.

Riggs, Fred W. 1963 Bureaucrats and Political Development: A Paradoxical View. Pages 120–167 in Joseph G. LaPalombara (editor), *Bureaucracy and Political Development.* Princeton Univ. Press.

Riggs, Fred W. 1964 *Administration in Developing Countries: The Theory of Prismatic Society.* Boston: Houghton Mifflin.

Rokkan, Stein 1966 Electoral Mobilization, Party Competition and National Integration. Pages 241–265 in Joseph G. LaPalombara and Myron Weiner (editors), *Political Parties and Political Development.* Princeton Univ. Press.

Rose, Arnold M. 1958 *The Institutions of Advanced Societies.* Minneapolis: Univ. of Minnesota Press.

Sahlins, Marshall D.; and Service, Elman R. (editors) 1960 *Evolution and Culture.* Ann Arbor: Univ. of Michigan Press.

Shils, Edward (1959–1960) 1962 *Political Development in the New States.* The Hague: Mouton.

Smelser, Neil J. 1964 Toward a Theory of Modernization. Pages 258–274 in Amitai Etzioni and Eva Etzioni (editors), *Social Change: Sources, Patterns and Consequences.* New York: Basic Books.

Spiro, Herbert J. (editor) 1966 *Africa: The Primacy of Politics.* New York: Random House.

Sutton, Francis X. 1959 Representation and the Nature of Political Systems. *Comparative Studies in Society and History* 2:1–10.

Tsou, Tang 1963 *America's Failure in China, 1941–1950.* Univ. of Chicago Press.

Ward, Robert E. 1963 Political Modernization and Political Culture in Japan. *World Politics* 15:569–596.

Wormuth, Francis D. 1949 *The Origins of Modern Constitutionalism.* New York: Harper.

III

THE BOURGEOISIE IN MODERNIZING SOCIETIES

Just as no pattern of late-developing industrialization is likely to repeat at all closely the history of those European nations where modern economic growth first began, so no non-Western country is likely to have a bourgeoisie identical with those groups whose self-conscious sense of collective identity first gave rise to the term. In many countries there have been, and are, recognizable groups which, by virtue of their intermediate position between a power-holding ascriptive upper class and a large peasant or wage-working mass, might be granted the minimum qualification of middleness required for the label "bourgeoisie." They are likely, however, to differ from the Western model by virtue of a variety of factors; the upper class from which they are differentiated may be not a landed nobility of military origins but a bureaucratic oligarchy, a theocratic court, or a colonial elite; within the middle class professionals or public servants may outnumber or outinfluence businessmen; the businessmen themselves may be more predominantly members of a corporation salariat than entrepreneurs; the state rather than the private firm may play the major role in industrialization; and the intellectuals of the middle class may function more as the importers and interpreters of ideologies than as their creators.

Japan

Japan, as the first non-Western country to achieve a high level of industrialization, provides an instructive illustration of some of these differences [see JAPANESE SOCIETY]. In Japan the drive to industrialize and the creation of a bourgeoisie were a consequence of a political revolution—the centralization of state power in the Meiji Restoration of 1868. In Europe, by contrast, causation ran mostly the other way: political change reflected the changed class relations resulting from economic growth.

Even before 1868 Japan already had a small merchant class which dominated interregional trade and controlled a good deal of handicraft production, but the majority of the crucially innovative entrepreneurs of the early stages of industrialization were drawn not from this old commercial middle class, but from the samurai—the warrior class that made up some 5–6 per cent of the population (Hirschmeier 1964). The samurai had been the retainers of the some 280 feudal lords, living in these lords' castle-towns and staffing their fief administrations, drawing rice stipends for their services. They were already, therefore, more bureaucratic than gentrylike, more urban than rural, more group-oriented than individualistic (Hall 1962; Smith 1966). This is one reason for the early bureaucratization of business organization in Japan, although there are other factors involved too: late-developing industrialization requires less individual inventiveness and more institutionalized learning—which enhanced the importance placed on formal educational qualifications (Smith 1960) —and a good deal of the initial phases of industrialization was undertaken directly by the state. By the end of the nineteenth century the business elite of Japan was located in a few large corporations, and by the 1950s the majority of business leaders had spent the whole of their careers as salaried officials rather than as independent entrepreneurs (Dore 1966).

Politically the role of the middle class reflected a crucial difference between the upper class of late nineteenth-century and early twentieth-century Japan and that of European countries in the early stages of industrialization—namely, that those who

held prestige and power in Japanese society did *not* hold a large proportion of their property in land and did *not* have personal interests in the protection of agriculture even at the expense of manufacturing industry. The Meiji land settlement had removed the feudal lords and their retainers from their fiefs and compensated them for their feudal revenues in government bonds. A few hundred of these feudal families were incorporated into a titled aristocracy, most of whom invested their large stocks of compensation bonds in banking and in industry. They formed a conspicuously consuming *rentier* class whose life revolved around the imperial court and which, though at the pinnacle of the prestige hierarchy, was almost completely divorced from participation in either business or political life. And insofar as they *were* able or concerned to insure the protection of their interests, those interests coincided with those of the industrial middle class, lying pre-eminently in the fostering of industrial growth.

Power rested initially with the bureaucracy and the army, both recruited from the samurai class. Both were therefore staffed by men who held little property but their commutation bonds, little source of income besides their salary, little power but what they enjoyed by virtue of their office. Both rapidly developed procedures for recruitment by academic examination which strengthened their sense of being elites that *deserved* to rule.

Because it was a bureaucracy selected for scholastic merit and because there were no restrictions based on heredity to bar promotion into the upper power-holding elite (except for the barrier between the administrative and clerical grades), middle functionaries could always aspire to be top functionaries and were consequently not an important source of middle-class consciousness: they produced no John Stuart Mill.

The professions also offered a different constellation from that of postfeudal Europe. Japanese feudalism did not dissolve gradually through the legal formalization of the customary property rights of subordinate members of the feudal hierarchy and the transformation of those rights into marketable assets. Consequently, there was no development of a powerful group of independent lawyers, necessarily led by their professional interests to be keenly concerned with politics. The law faculty dominated the new universities, but the pick of its graduates was drawn into the bureaucracy or into the ranks of the state prosecutors and judges. The civilian lawyer, consequently, was typically a failed bureaucrat who carried little prestige and influence —the more so since the habit of formal litigation in civil matters was less developed than in Christian, Hindu, or Muslim societies. The principal independent professions, therefore, were those of medicine, teaching, and journalism; the first was naturally apolitical, the second only slightly less so and in any case dominated by the professors of state universities closely allied to the bureaucracy. Journalism was the one profession of political importance, and its practitioners played a strong supporting role in the opposition political movement that developed.

For there *was* in the nineteenth century a kind of "middle-class" challenge to the military and bureaucratic elites strong enough to force the grant of a constitution, the gradual extension of the franchise, and an expansion of the powers of political parties (Ike 1950). This challenge came not chiefly from a rising business class but, first, from other ex-samurai who had failed to get a footing in the bureaucracy and, second, from the landlords —men of peasant origin and mostly still farmers themselves, sometimes also brewers, timber merchants or proprietors of small food-processing establishments—whose land taxes provided the bulk of government revenue and who demanded some say in its use. Thus, the dichotomies that roughly held for Europe—rural, aristocratic, agricultural, and power-holding versus urban, middle-class, industrial–commercial, professional, and power-demanding—did not apply to Japan.

In the initial stages of constitutional rule, indeed, the landlords largely dominated the opposition political parties, which were allowed to criticize but not to control the bureaucracy (Scalapino 1953). Later, urban commercial and industrial interests gained an increasing hold on the political parties and, *pari passu*, there was an increasing interpenetration of the bureaucracy and the parties—bureaucrats giving up office to become politicians and the parties influencing appointments in the bureaucracy—with a consequent sharing of power between the two. By the time, in the early 1920s, that industrial concentration, universal education, and imported ideologies had combined to produce a working-class consciousness and the beginnings of a self-styled proletarian political movement, there was no longer any meaningful sense in which the forces that rallied to contain the threat from the working class could be divided into patrician and bourgeois or even into the power-elite and the power-hungry. By then the effective power struggle was between groups that can only be defined in terms of occupation and outlook, not in terms of class or status group—between, on the one hand, the army and its allies in the bureaucracy, the parties, and the business world and, on the other, the bulk of the bureaucracy, politicians, and businessmen, whose interests were represented in the civilian cabinet.

However, if there was, by this time, no meaningful distinction between upper and middle to be drawn between the groups that dominated the country politically, it is possible to distinguish from them another group—in European terms the lower middle class—that was already of some importance politically, particularly inasmuch as its support helped the army to win the struggle for control in the 1930s. These were the shopkeepers and small businessmen, together with the products of the secondary grades of education who became primary and secondary school teachers and the clerical workers in government and private business. These, unlike the dominant metropolitan groups, were men with their roots in local communities, the natural opinion leaders of those communities —Japan's pseudo-intellectuals as one Japanese social scientist has dubbed them (Maruyama 1963) —leaders of reservists' associations, organizers of patriotic charities, and so on. They had enough causes for personal resentment against the dominant groups (there was only one educational ladder of success and they were the ones who had risen only halfway up it), and they were provided with enough moral grounds for expressing their resentment by the luxury and corruption of the business classes, the arrogance of the bureaucrats, the unpatriotic concern for sectional interests of the politicians, and the un-Japanese cosmopolitanism of them all.

The cosmopolitanism was a factor of some importance. In Europe and America national consciousness developed its real strength in the bourgeoisie, very often in partial reaction against the cosmopolitanism of the aristocracy (especially, for instance, in the countries culturally on the fringe of Europe, such as Russia and America). In Japan it was the new professional bureaucratic and business classes themselves that were cosmopolitan. Since educational selection played so big a role in their recruitment, a university education was the chief thing that distinguished them from the rest of the population. A high proportion of them had been to foreign universities, if only for a year or two. But even the culture of the Japanese universities, which provided the bulk of their education, was not something evolved out of Japanese traditions; it was an importation—overtly so in the technological fields, less obviously but more consequentially so in the humanities and social sciences, where knowledge and values could not be separated. A high proportion of the textbooks students read were translations or in foreign languages; their admired philosophers, physicists, jurists, novelists were German, French, and American; and they learned at the university not only about their subjects but also about Beethoven, whisky, animal protection societies, silk handkerchiefs, impressionism, waltzing, romantic love, anarchism, and all the other overt deviations from Japanese mores that the army (home-bred in much more quickly and wholly Japanized military academies) and the lower-middle groups (who had failed to get to a university) could denounce as cosmopolitan decadence (Bennett et al. 1958).

Nevertheless, even if an uncertain sense of cultural identity did prevent these new middle-upper groups from being the bearers of nationalism as opposed to cosmopolitanism, they were just as effective as their European counterparts in promoting nationalism at the expense of *regional* parochialism—and for the similar reason that they were geographically and socially mobile. Their mobility may have been different from that of the traveling late-medieval merchant—mobility from provincial home to metropolitan school, from one provincial bureaucratic appointment to another—but it had the same effect, of weakening local loyalties, which in Japan centered on the Tokugawa fiefs.

Equally, there were similarities between the cultural and ethical values of these groups and those of their European counterparts, determined by the very fact that their education was European in inspiration. The process was different, if the end results somewhat the same. Thus, for instance, a secular world view came *with* Western science, rather than giving birth to it. Like the steam engine, the Enlightenment did not have to be invented again. The effectiveness of this diffusion through *intellectual* channels depended, however, on the extent to which the traditional culture was receptive (the ground was already prepared, for instance, for greater stress on achievement at the expense of ascriptive criteria by changes within the samurai class (Smith 1966) and on the extent to which other structural changes supported the new values. The latter point may be illustrated by the contrast between two different elements of the Protestant ethic stereotype: "inner-worldly asceticism" and individualism. The first was a marked characteristic of the new Japanese middle classes, although the underlying mechanisms were different—the Japanese was trained to sacrifice immediate for future gratifications through the discipline of a strenuously purposeful education rather than

by the practice of thrift; the dream of success was sanctified by the approval not of God, but of the ancestors, the guardians of the family whose honor the success would adorn. By contrast, the other central feature of the Protestant middle-class ethic—individualism—was much less marked in Japan. The traditions of the family and the fief as institutions demanding a total loyalty and Japan's religious history (Buddhism did not have Christianity's emphasis on conviction, conscience, and principle, and on separating truth from error) are a partial explanation (Benedict 1946). Just as important were the early emphasis on occupational selection through education and the early bureaucratization of business. Even in the initial stages of industrialization most Japanese spent most of their lives firmly embedded either in a traditional community or in a large organization, and both school and firm (for labor mobility was low above the manual worker level) laid claims to a lifetime's loyalty. It was remarked in 1940 that in the sense of a flowering of individual creativity, the Chinese —who for a century had Western education but *no* stable development of modern corporate organizations—were more thoroughly "Westernized" than the Japanese (Hu 1940).

The priority of the firm, corporation, or government department as a focus of "belonging" is a reason not only for the lack of individuation but also for the lack of consciousness of class membership. Japan's society was more segmented than stratified. Thus, the tendency present in all advanced industrial societies for the lines of cleavage between status and class groups to become blurred into a gradual declension of income and prestige has been very marked in postwar Japan.

Consequently, one may say that the middle class has disappeared or, alternatively, that it has swallowed up an ever larger segment of the nation. The defeat and the elimination of the army as a significant political and cultural force ended polarization around the issues of cosmopolitanism or tradition. Power became more widely diffused among economic, political, and administrative groups in a pluralistic system. The corporation with its lifetime employment pattern came to embrace even larger groups of the population. Occupational selection became even more rigidly dependent on educational qualification. And rapid economic growth brought the same homogenizing effects—mass production of the consumer durables of prestige significance, wider diffusion of mass media of deeper impact, etc.—as in other societies. If one were to draw a major dividing line through the Japanese population today it would probably be to distinguish a lower class of poorer farmers and less skilled manual workers—perhaps 40 to 50 per cent of the population—from the remainder, who, though graded in income, differ little in standards (as opposed to levels) of living, in leisure tastes, reading habits, dress, accent, or aspirations. It is the broadening of this latter group and the relative homogeneity of its aspirations that have so intensified the pressure on the educational system that the intensely competitive entrance examinations for "the good schools" have become the events around which the whole lives of many families revolve (Vogel 1963; Plath 1964).

Sub-Saharan Africa

The ex-colonial countries of sub-Saharan Africa in some senses show the closest parallels to the Japanese pattern. It is rarely possible, for instance, to draw a meaningful distinction between an upper and a middle class, even where, as in the precolonial period, there was relatively marked social differentiation between the mass of the population and a chiefly stratum with dominant control over land and some degree of hereditary continuity [see AFRICAN SOCIETY]. Even in British Africa, where the power of the chiefs over land was strengthened by a system of indirect rule, they rarely achieved a sufficiently radical differentiation in culture and style of life to be termed a "landed aristocracy." (This is true even of Buganda, which is the nearest to an exception to this generalization [see Apter 1961; Fallers 1964].) And in those areas where the traditional political structure has survived into the postindependence period (as in Uganda and northern Nigeria), the chiefs or emirs tend to retain only local influence in a position of subordination to the new national or federal elites. When chiefs or the sons of chiefs themselves belong to this new political elite as civil servants, soldiers, or politicians, they most commonly do so by virtue of their education or professional training rather than by virtue of their heredity. (Again, even in Uganda there was a tendency for Gandan politicians to move into the national Ugandan majority party and away from a Bugandan identification [Lee 1965].)

The real upper class of these societies had been, of course, the group of white officials, teachers, and settlers. In the preindependence period the educated members of the professions who led the independence movements and now form the new national elites could well have been described as a "rising middle class." (The term "African bourgeoisie" was chosen by a sociologist to describe the South African counterparts of these professionals, precisely "to emphasise in terms of social change and prospective power their role at the apex of subordination" [Kuper 1965, p. 8].)

With independence and the removal of the colonial power the "apex of subordination" became the apex of the society. Those who were trained for teaching, the civil service, the army, the press, medicine, or the law, chiefs' sons educated to be better chiefs—men whose chief common characteristic was a shared experience of postprimary education in European, not African, traditions—have formed the relatively unstratified political elite of the new states. As in Meiji Japan, political struggles—when they are not still largely struggles between "primordial" local or ethnic groups—are usually struggles between the "ins" and the "outs," factional groups not distinguished by different social origins or a different constellation of material interests. ("When a developing country has two PH.DS, one will be prime minister and the other in exile.")

These educated professional groups as yet have few rivals for political or cultural influence, not least because the field of commerce was, and to a lesser extent remains, dominated by non-African immigrant communities—Asians and Arabs in east Africa, Levantines and Europeans in the west. Although in the colonial period these groups—particularly Asians in Kenya or Uganda—were sometimes more successful than Africans in pressing for political participation at an earlier stage, independence has seen a marked decline in their influence. They have become marginal minorities, culturally distinct and socially separated from Africans of similar income levels, tolerated for their essential services to the economy but (with a few exceptions, such as in Senegal) generally the object of discriminatory credit and fiscal policies designed to nurture an African trading class to replace them. Insofar as they translate their wealth into higher education for their sons, however, they may maintain their position by entry into the administrative and professional class itself—though without changing the nature of that class or the pattern of its dominance. Meanwhile, in only a few areas, such as Ghana and western Nigeria, have there emerged African traders of sufficient substance to acquire a notable share of political influence and thereby dilute the predominantly professional character of the elite (Hunter 1962).

India

Among ex-colonial countries, India stands out as being somewhat different because the colonial power took over a more developed literate civilization, because the land settlement created a landlord class of a modern rather than of a tribal–chieftainly kind, because a sizable business class—mostly commercial but partly industrial—had developed before independence, and because Western education and the devolution of power began so much earlier. There was even something similar to the European division between an upper and a middle class. On the one hand were the civil servants of the higher ranks, mostly drawn from the wealthiest (especially landed) families and identified with the colonial *status quo;* on the other were professional groups, such as physicians and, especially, lawyers, who were active in the independence movement (Misra 1961).

Postindependence India, however, is an even more striking example than Japan of the numerical and cultural predominance of the educationally qualified administrative and professional groups over mercantile and industrial elements within the occupations traditionally defined as bourgeois. The reasons are fairly clear: because state enterprise plays an even more dominant part in industrialization and because the bureaucracy has also expanded to accord with the dominant mid-twentieth-century notions of the role of the state in welfare, educational, and cultural, as well as in economic matters—notions that have evolved in response to the economic development of the advanced industrial societies but are now generally accepted also in societies at a much lower level of industrial development.

The diffusion of European middle-class values chiefly through the educational process is even more marked in India than it was in Japan, if only because British universities played such a large part in training the administrative elite and Indian universities were much more overtly modeled on the British. Even if they free themselves from the British model, Indian universities are bound to be modern institutions with a predominantly "Western" content and an entirely "Western" orientation in the techniques of research and scholarship. The problem of national identity—of accepting the alien origins of one's culture and at the same time accepting one's Indianness, of believing in the superiority of the imported alien to the traditional native values and ideologies and yet retaining one's national pride—this pull between tradition and modernity is acute (Shils 1961). It is especially so for intellectuals, but it has not, as in Japan in the 1930s, been brought to a point of traumatic exacerbation. In Japan the conflict with the West heightened the strain. India does not feel this strain so acutely, partly because of the syncretic

tradition of Hindu culture, partly because a *modus vivendi* between the traditional and the modern cultures has had time to become established, and finally because India and the West are not in political conflict. (In China, where the political hostility *has* been brought to a crucial pitch, the initial solution for intellectuals lay in the fact that by adopting one type of nineteenth-century European middle-class ideology, Marxism, they had a firm basis for confident denunciation of other types embodied in the modern American enemy. Later, as tensions developed in relations with other Marxist countries it became necessary to Sinicize Marxism itself.)

Middle East and Latin America

Other countries, by contrast, notably in the Middle East and in Latin America, show patterns much more similar to the European than to either the Japanese or the ex-colonial type, particularly inasmuch as they have—or until recently had—a recognizable landed upper class to provide a defining boundary for the "middleness" of the new professional and business groups. The political development of Egypt during this century can be interpreted, for instance, in terms familiar to European history. The Wafd, beginning in the 1920s as an alliance of the landlords and the business elites against the ruling house and its foreign protectors, became increasingly penetrated by the new white collar, professional, and small business groups in the 1930s. Finally, after it was allowed to share in power, it was increasingly weakened by tension between party oligarchy and rank and file to the benefit of the rival Muslim Brotherhood, a party whose center of gravity was at an even more popular level and which combined demands for social and economic reform with a reaffirmation of Islam (thus providing a solution to the late-developer's cultural dilemma by being modern while remaining traditional, accepting foreign models while remaining nationalist). Finally, the military revolution reconcentrated power in the hands of men predominantly of middle-class origin, though without government ever having been effectively exercised by men who were consciously representative of middle-class interests [see NEAR EASTERN SOCIETY; *see also* Vatikiotis 1961].

Similar processes may be observed in many Latin American countries, where again the "emergence of the middle sectors" has been looked on as the most hopeful source of political and economic progress [see LATIN AMERICAN POLITICAL THOUGHT; *see also* Johnson 1958]. In the Middle East and Latin America there has occurred a progressive fusion of the old upper and the newer middle groups. The successful lawyer, banker, or civil servant buys himself a prestige estate (to be used, also, for recreation, tax write-off, and sometimes genuinely agricultural profit-making purposes). The landlord invests in metropolitan business and puts his sons through professional training. The process of fusion is not unlike that, for example, in England, though with one crucial difference. In the English fusion the aristocracy absorbed bourgeois values in good measure—some becoming progressive commercial farmers, some of their sons going into trade, their schools developing the moral seriousness of purpose of the empire builder, and so on. In late-developing countries, by contrast, the aristocratic values are likely to emerge as the dominant ones for the following reasons: (1) professionals and the salariat predominate in the middle groups (expansion of government far beyond that of Europe at a similar stage of development; emergence of the modern corporation full-blown as the *initiator* of economic development; predominance in the business world of the foreign firm, whose managers and top technicians are outside the indigenous culture, society, and polity); (2) occupational aspirations are consequently concentrated on official or professional, rather than business or technological careers; (3) the universities (as opposed, for example, to the churches) play a dominant role in the formation of common values (the administrative and corporation salariat have above all to be *qualified;* education, like government, is more easily expanded to developed-country levels than is industry); (4) universities, designed primarily to train administrators, emphasize law, philosophy, the humanities, neglecting science, engineering, commerce; in other words they provide an education of a traditional consumption-oriented kind, reinforcing aristocratic values at the expense of those parts of the European (or Japanese) middle-class ethic—production-orientation, emphasis on diligence, objective standards of merit, dominance of nature, etc.—which were most important for economic development. Even the business world remains frozen in attitudes characteristic of the mercantilist period in Europe: the acquisition of wealth depends on political patronage and aristocratic connections; it is a function of power to get licenses and permits which are a source of money in themselves, requiring no production effort (Cochran 1959; van der Kroef 1956).

This does not prevent the new middle groups from effectively promoting new values and behavior patterns in some fields. In the Middle East, for instance, it is the middle, not the upper groups that

have been the pioneers in feminine education and the general emancipation of women (Berger 1958). In Latin America new literary movements have chiefly been promoted by and for the new middle groups (Ellison 1964).

Similarly, if the ethos of the new middle groups seems often directly inimical to economic development, they may still play a crucial role in promoting it insofar as middle-class intellectuals inspire, and men of middle-class origins in armies or revolutionary parties carry through, revolutionary political changes that destroy the existing correlation of power with wealth (both traditional landed and modern urban) to create a new regime that radically alters the dominant ethos, gives honor to the engineer, the manager, and the chemist, and uses state power to mobilize the resources necessary for developmental investment. To be sure, the gentlemanly antiscientific bias of the predominant culture may be such that even revolutionary regimes genuinely intent on economic development find it difficult to will the means to their economic ends. It was, for instance, some years after 1958 that the Cuban government recovered from a belief that revolutionary *élan* was all that was needed to build a new Jerusalem and began to recognize the essential importance of technological and economic skills (Dumont 1964).

Eventually the lesson is likely to be learned, however, and the exemplary effect of a few revolutionary regimes, together with the influence exerted by the expanding international organizations concerned with development, tend to promote in other countries as well the transformation of values that leads from aristocracy to technocracy. Whether that technocracy will be effective in its role of economic development, however—whether it can, as a salariat, show the same dedication as the legendary Puritan entrepreneur to the cause of growing two blades of grass where only one grew before—depends on whether it can find sufficient strength of motivation either in nationalism or in some reformist ideology to provide a substitute for the entrepreneur's more self-interested concerns (Gellner 1965).

RONALD P. DORE

[*See also* BUREAUCRACY; STRATIFICATION, SOCIAL.]

BIBLIOGRAPHY
APTER, DAVID E. 1961 *The Political Kingdom of Uganda: A Study in Bureaucratic Nationalism.* Princeton Univ. Press.
BENEDICT, RUTH 1946 *The Chrysanthemum and the Sword: Patterns of Japanese Culture.* Boston: Houghton Mifflin.
BENNETT, JOHN W.; PASSIN, HERBERT; and McKNIGHT,

ROBERT K. 1958 *In Search of Identity: The Japanese Overseas Scholar in America and Japan*. Minneapolis: Univ. of Minnesota Press.

BERGER, MORROE 1958 The Middleclass in the Arab World. Pages 67–71 in Walter Z. Laqueur (editor), *The Middle East in Transition*. London: Routledge.

COCHRAN, THOMAS C. 1959 *The Puerto Rican Businessman: A Study in Cultural Change*. Philadelphia: Univ. of Pennsylvania Press.

CHANG, CHUNG-LI 1962 *The Income of the Chinese Gentry*. Seattle: Univ. of Washington Press.

DORE, RONALD P. 1966 Individuation, Mobility and Equality in Modern Japan. Unpublished manuscript.

DUMONT, RENÉ 1964 *Cuba: Socialisme et développement*. Paris: Éditions du Seuil.

ELLISON, FRED P. 1964 The Writer. Pages 79–100 in John J. Johnson (editor), *Continuity and Change in Latin America*. Stanford Univ. Press.

FALLERS, LLOYD A. (editor) 1964 *The King's Men: Leadership and Status in Buganda on the Eve of Independence*. Oxford Univ. Press.

FEI, HSIAO-T'UNG (1947–1948) 1953 *China's Gentry: Essays in Rural–Urban Relations*. Univ. of Chicago Press.

GELLNER, ERNEST 1965 *Thought and Change*. Univ. of Chicago Press.

HALL, JOHN W. 1962 Feudalism in Japan: A Reassessment. *Comparative Studies in Society and History* 5: 15–51.

HIRSCHMEIER, JOHANNES 1964 *Origins of Entrepreneurship in Meiji Japan*. Cambridge, Mass.: Harvard Univ. Press.

HO, PING-TI 1954 The Salt Merchants of Yong-chon: A Study of Commercial Capitalism in Eighteenth-century China. *Harvard Journal of Asiatic Studies* 17: 130–168.

HODGKIN, THOMAS 1956 The African Middle Class. *Corona* 8: 85–88.

HU, SHIH 1940 The Modernisation of China and Japan: A Comparative Study in Cultural Conflict. Pages 243–251 in Caroline F. Ware (editor), *The Cultural Approach to History*. New York: Columbia Univ. Press.

HUNTER, GUY 1962 *The New Societies of Tropical Africa: A Selective Study*. London: Oxford Univ. Press.

IKE, NOBUTAKA 1950 *The Beginnings of Political Democracy in Japan*. Baltimore: Johns Hopkins Press.

INOKI, MASAMICHI 1964 The Civil Bureaucracy: Japan. Pages 283–300 in Conference on Political Modernization in Japan and Turkey, Gould House, 1962, *Political Modernization in Japan and Turkey*. Edited by Robert E. Ward and D. A. Rustow. Princeton Univ. Press.

JOHNSON, JOHN J. 1958 *Political Change in Latin America: The Emergence of the Middle Sectors*. Stanford Univ. Press.

KUPER, LEO 1965 *An African Bourgeoisie: Race, Class, and Politics in South Africa*. New Haven: Yale Univ. Press.

LEE, J. M. 1965 Buganda's Position in Federal Uganda. *Journal of Commonwealth Political Studies* 3: 165–181.

MARUYAMA, MASAO 1963 *Thought and Behaviour in Modern Japanese Politics*. London and New York: Oxford Univ. Press.

MISRA, BANKEY B. 1961 *The Indian Middle Classes: Their Growth in Modern Times*. Oxford Univ. Press.

NORMAN, E. HERBERT 1940 *Japan's Emergence as a Modern State: Political and Economic Problems of the Meiji Period*. New York: Institute of Pacific Relations, International Secretariat.

PLATH, DAVID W. 1964 *The After Hours: Modern Japan and the Search for Enjoyment*. Berkeley: Univ. of California Press.

SAFRAN, NADAV 1961 *Egypt in Search of Political Community: An Analysis of the Intellectual and Political Evolution of Egypt, 1804–1952*. Cambridge, Mass.: Harvard Univ. Press.

SCALAPINO, ROBERT A. (1953) 1962 *Democracy and the Party Movement in Prewar Japan: The Failure of the First Attempt*. Berkeley: Univ. of California Press.

SHILS, EDWARD 1961 *The Intellectual Between Tradition and Modernity: The Indian Situation*. The Hague: Mouton.

SMITH, THOMAS C. 1960 Landlords' Sons in the Business Elite. *Economic Development and Cultural Change* 9, no. 1, part 2: 93–107.

SMITH, THOMAS C. 1961 Japan's Aristocratic Revolution. *Yale Review* New Series 50: 370–383.

SMITH, THOMAS C. 1966 Merit as Ideology in Tokugawa Japan. Unpublished manuscript.

TIRYAKIAN, EDWARD A. 1959 Occupational Satisfaction and Aspiration in an Underdeveloped Country: The Philippines. *Economic Development and Cultural Change* 7, no. 4: 431–444.

VAN DER KROEF, JUSTUS M. 1956 Economic Development in Indonesia: Some Social and Cultural Impediments. *Economic Development and Cultural Change* 4, no. 2: 116–133.

VATIKIOTIS, PANAYIOTIS J. 1961 *The Egyptian Army in Politics: Pattern for New Nations?* Bloomington: Indiana Univ. Press.

VOGEL, EZRA F. 1963 *Japan's New Middle Class: The Salary Man and His Family in a Tokyo Suburb*. Berkeley: Univ. of California Press.

WEINER, MYRON 1957 *Party Politics in India: The Development of a Multi-party System*. Princeton Univ. Press.

MOHAMMEDANISM

See ISLAM.

MOIVRE, ABRAHAM DE

Abraham de Moivre (1667–1754) was born of French Protestant parents named Moivre. (He was also known as Demoivre; as part of the return address of a letter to Johann Bernoulli he himself wrote his name as deMoivre.) He studied mathematics and physics in Paris under Ozanam, and emigrated to England when he was 21 to escape religious persecution (Walker 1934). Although de Moivre was a mathematical genius of outstanding analytical power and was in contact by correspondence and in person (at the Royal Society) with many of the leading mathematicians of the day, he never succeeded in obtaining a university appointment. Instead, he had to live by tutoring noblemen's sons and by advising gamblers and speculators who dealt in annuities, which were a popular form of investment in the first half of the eighteenth century (Walford 1871). This misfortune for de Moivre is posterity's gain, for the problems he met in his consulting practice and his successful solution of them provided the material for his two great textbooks. In fact, during his last years de Moivre must have relied heavily on the sales of the later editions of his book on annuity calculations.

De Moivre's practical text on probability first appeared in 1718 as a translation and revision of his Latin article of 1711. It was dedicated to Isaac Newton, who is accorded the author's thanks for his writings and conversations. In its final form, published in 1756, this book is notable for its original treatment of the following topics, all of which play a central role in the modern theory of probability:

(1) The general laws of addition (David & Barton 1962, chapter 2) and multiplication of probabilities (Montucla [1758] 1802, part 5, book 1, chapter 39);

(2) The binomial distribution law (Cantor 1898, chapter 96);

(3) Probability-generating functions (Seal 1949a);

(4) Difference equations involving probabilities and their solution by means of recurring series (Czuber 1900);

(5) New and general solutions of problems on the duration of play, or "gambler's ruin" (Todhunter 1865, chapter 9);

(6) The limiting form of the binomial term

$$\binom{n}{x} p^x (1-p)^{n-x}, \qquad x = 0, 1, 2, \cdots, n;$$
$$0 < p < 1,$$

when (a) $n \to \infty$ with np remaining finite, and (b) $n \to \infty$ and $np \to \infty$. In case (a) only the term with $x = 0$ was considered (David 1962). In case (b) the result

$$\{2\pi np(1-p)\}^{-\frac{1}{2}} \exp[-(x-np)^2/2np(1-p)],$$

namely, the ordinate of the normal distribution, was obtained explicitly (in different notation). Included in this book were the trigonometrical theorem that goes by de Moivre's name and his approximation to the logarithm of a factorial which was improved by Stirling's discovery in the same year that the value of the series contained therein was 2π.

Some of the mathematical derivations of this probability text were published for a wider circle of readers in Latin (1730).

De Moivre's other textbook laid the foundations of the mathematics of life contingencies (Saar 1923). Although the first edition sold slowly, Thomas Simpson's plagiaristic text of 1742 spurred de Moivre to a complete revision published in the following year (Young 1908). The success of this edition is indicated by the two further editions, with minor changes, that followed within nine years. In 1756 a final, thoroughly revised edition was printed as the last section of the third edition of *The Doctrine of Chances*. In an appendix, reference is made to a paper published in 1755 by James Dodson, the father of scientific life insurance (Ogborn 1962) and possibly the "friend" who edited the posthumous edition.

The originality of this life contingency textbook is attested by its inclusion of the following:

(a) The recursion formula for calculating a life annuity at age x, given that at age $x + 1$ (though it is doubtful whether the author envisaged the calculation of the whole set of annuity values by starting at the "oldest age" [Young 1908]);

(b) General relations for survivorship and reversionary annuities in terms of single and joint life annuities;

(c) Use of the calculus to obtain the value of a continuous annuity-certain;

(d) A law of mortality, namely, that of uniform decrements in the number of survivors, which was in substantial agreement with the Breslau table, published by his friend Halley in 1693; and as a result:

(e) Easily computable values of single and joint life annuities for limited terms or for life;

(f) Expressions for the computation of complex survivorship probabilities;

(g) The value of a life annuity with a proportionate payment in the year of death.

All these results originated with de Moivre himself.

The earliest published works of de Moivre in the 1690s were influenced by Newton's method of fluxions and theory of series (Cantor 1898, chapter 86), and his interest in probability dates only from the first edition of Montmort's *Essay* (1708). Perhaps his most important contribution, first printed in 1733 as a supplement to the *Miscellanea analytica*, was his improvement of the wide limits obtained by Bernoulli (1713) in his statement of the law of large numbers. For this purpose de Moivre utilized the result mentioned in (6) to obtain the sum of the binomial probabilities from $x = np-\ell$ to $x = np+\ell$ with $p = \frac{1}{2}$ and $\ell = k(n/2)^{\frac{1}{2}}$, $k = 1,2,3$, by approximate quadrature (by ordinate summation and the three-eighths rule) of the normal ordinates. While this constitutes the first tabulation of the normal areas at one, two, and three standard deviations from the mean, there is no evidence that de Moivre thought in terms of a continuous probability distribution (Seal 1954; 1957).

Nevertheless, this work is clearly the basis for the subsequent demonstration by Laplace (1812, pp. 275–284) that the binomial tends to the normal when *n* is large (Pearson 1924).

It may be added that de Moivre was a pure mathematician little interested in the practical applications of his theory. Although he wrote on life contingencies, only in the final Appendix of the posthumous edition of 1756 is there a brief reference to mortality data later than those of the Breslau table. Actually, the early and middle years of the eighteenth century saw the publication of several collections of mortality statistics that would have been fertile ground for the application of de Moivre's improved version of Bernoulli's theorem (Seal 1949*b*). These data had led to a widespread belief in the divine regularity of demographic ratios, and a few paragraphs in the 1738 and 1756 editions of the *Doctrine* refer to a connection between this belief and Bernoulli's theorem. Unfortunately, the topic was not pursued by de Moivre or his contemporaries (Westergaard 1932, chapters 7, 10) and cannot be regarded as indicating that de Moivre was interested in theology (Walker 1929) or that he influenced the demographers of the eighteenth and early nineteenth centuries (Pearson 1926).

HILARY L. SEAL

[*For the historical context of de Moivre's work, see the article on the* BERNOULLI FAMILY. *For discussion of the subsequent development of de Moivre's ideas, see* DISTRIBUTIONS, STATISTICAL; LIFE TABLES; PROBABILITY; *and the biography of* LAPLACE.]

WORKS BY DE MOIVRE

In many reference works, de Moivre is alphabetized under D; however, in line with the cataloguing practice of major libraries, we have listed him under M. Consistent with this, we have used a lower-case "d" for the particle.

1711   De mensura sortis seu, de probabilitate eventuum in ludis a casu fortuito pendentibus. Royal Society of London, *Philosophical Transactions* 27:213–264. → Reprinted by Kraus (New York) in 1963.

(1718) 1756   *The Doctrine of Chances: Or, a Method of Calculating the Probabilities of Events in Play.* 3d ed. London: Millar.

(1725) 1752   *Annuities Upon Lives: Or, the Valuation of Annuities Upon Any Number of Lives, as Also, of Reversions.* 4th ed. London: Millar. → The Appendix concerns the expectations of life and the probabilities of survivorship.

1730   *Miscellanea analytica de seriebus et quadraturis.* . . . London: Tonson & Watts.

SUPPLEMENTARY BIBLIOGRAPHY

BERNOULLI, JAKOB (1713) 1899   *Wahrscheinlichkeitsrechnung: (Ars conjectandi).* 2 vols. Leipzig: Engelmann. → First published posthumously in Latin.

CANTOR, MORITZ   1898   *Vorlesungen über Geschichte der Mathematik.* Volume 3: Von 1668–1758. Leipzig: Teubner.

CZUBER, EMANUEL   (1900) 1906   Calcul des probabilités. Section 1, volume 4, pages 1–46 in *Encyclopédie des sciences mathématiques.* Paris: Gauthier-Villars. → First published in German in *Encyklopädie der mathematischen Wissenschaften.*

DAVID, F. N.   1962   *Games, Gods and Gambling: The Origins and History of Probability and Statistical Ideas From the Earliest Times to the Newtonian Era.* New York: Hafner.

DAVID, F. N.; and BARTON, D. E.   1962   *Combinatorial Chance.* New York: Hafner.

LAPLACE, PIERRE SIMON DE   (1812) 1820   *Théorie analytique des probabilités.* 3d ed., rev. Paris: Courcier.

[MONTMORT, PIERRE RÉMOND DE]   (1708) 1713   *Essay d'analyse sur les jeux de hazard.* 2d ed. Paris: Quillau. → First published anonymously.

MONTUCLA, JEAN É.   (1758) 1802   *Histoire des mathématiques dans laquelle on rend compte de leurs progrès depuis leur origine jusqu'à nos jours.* . . . Paris: Agasse.

OGBORN, MAURICE EDWARD   1962   *Equitable Assurances: The Story of Life Assurance in the Experience of the Equitable Life Assurance Society, 1762–1962.* London: Allen & Unwin.

PEARSON, KARL   1924   Historical Note on the Origin of the Normal Curve of Errors. *Biometrika* 16:402–404.

PEARSON, KARL   1926   Abraham de Moivre. *Nature* 117:551–552.

SAAR, J. DU   1923   De beteekenis van De Moivre's werk over lijfrenten voor de ontwikkeling van de verzekeringswetenschap. *Verzekerings archief* 4:28–45.

SEAL, H. L.   1949*a*   The Historical Development of the Use of Generating Functions in Probability Theory. Vereinigung schweizerischer Versicherungsmathematiker, *Mitteilungen* 49:209–228.

SEAL, H. L.   1949*b*   Mortality Data and the Binomial Probability Law. *Skandinavisk aktuarietidskrift* 32:188–216.

SEAL, HILARY L.   1954   A Budget of Paradoxes. *Journal of the Institute of Actuaries Students' Society* 13:60–65.

SEAL, HILARY L.   1957   A Correction. *Journal of the Institute of Actuaries Students' Society* 14:210–211.

SIMPSON, THOMAS   (1742) 1775   *The Doctrine of Annuities and Reversions, Deduced From General and Evident Principles.* . . . 2d ed. London: Printed for J. Nourse.

TODHUNTER, ISAAC   (1865) 1949   *A History of the Mathematical Theory of Probability From the Time of Pascal to That of Laplace.* New York: Chelsea.

WALFORD, CORNELIUS   1871   *The Insurance Cyclopaedia.* Volume 1. London: Layton. → See especially pages 98–169 on "Annuities."

WALKER, HELEN M.   1929   *Studies in the History of Statistical Method: With Special Reference to Certain Educational Problems.* Baltimore: Williams & Wilkins.

WALKER, HELEN M.   1934   Abraham de Moivre. *Scripta mathematica* 2:316–333.

WESTERGAARD, HARALD L.   1932   *Contributions to the History of Statistics.* London: King.

YOUNG, T. E.   1908   Historical Notes Relating to the Discovery of the Formula $a_x = v p_x (1 + a_{x+1})$: And to the Introduction of the Calculus in the Solution of Actuarial Problems. *Journal of the Institute of Actuaries* 42:188–205.

MONARCHY

The term "monarchy" has been used in both a broad and a narrow sense. The broad sense is found in the writings of the Ancients, especially Herodotus and the poets, where it denotes simply the rule of one man (or woman), whether good or bad, legitimate or unlawful, wise or incompetent. Plato and Aristotle introduced distinctions that narrowed the term by restricting it to rule by one good person; Plato defined the good by reference to law, and Aristotle did so by reference to happiness. In the modern West, another kind of narrowing has occurred in response to historical developments, especially feudalism. Here monarchy designates a particular type of one-person rule, characterized by legitimate blood descent, no matter how limited the extent of the governing functions; indeed, the term may even refer to regimes in which the monarch has no governing functions at all, as in Great Britain and the Scandinavian kingdoms.

Monocracy. Since Western historical associations cannot be applied to one-person rule in other cultures, comparative politics stands in need of a generic concept similar to the original Greek meaning of monarchy, a concept that would cover primitive kingship, Oriental despotism, tyranny, dictatorship, and the Western kind of monarchy.

The term "monocracy," or monocratic rule, first suggested by Max Weber, has been coming into use in recent years. When anthropologists discuss monocratic rule, they usually mean one-person rule among primitives, which prevails, or prevailed before the European conquest, in Polynesia, Africa, and parts of America as well as Asia. The economic, political, judicial, and priestly functions of monocratic rulers differ widely within the same culture area. These rulers are generally regarded as of divine origin, and their acts are invested with divine qualities. They are supposed to possess mana and in their persons are frequently taboo; to touch them constitutes treason. The power of such a ruler is typically related in a magical way to successful crops and wars: there can be little doubt that military leadership is often at the heart of his power.

When the rule of this kind of king-priest was extended over large territories, especially in the ancient Orient, it was accompanied by the development of a bureaucracy. Such a bureaucracy may and often does combine priestly and administrative functions. In Egypt, China, and elsewhere, such extended bureaucratic monocracy was often associated with an official doctrine, such as Confucianism, the mastery of which served as the principle for selecting participants in the regime.

The succession of empires from the Egyptian to the Persian shows how widespread was this form of governmental organization within very diverse culture patterns. Indeed, the extent and durability of such regimes suggest that monocratic rule is the usual form of governing extensive territorial domains. This fact may be related to a persuasive general proposition concerning the appearance of monocratic rule in a variety of social contexts: it appears whenever a group is engaged in a serious struggle for survival. The threat to survival may be internal or external: wars, floods, insurrections, and the crises of industrial society have all been "causes" of the appearance of one kind of monocracy or another.

Ancient monarchy. Primitive government in the historical perspective seems also to have been predominantly monocratic. In Greece, for example, chiefs of divine descent appear to have performed the key functions of military leader, high priest, and judge. But eventually the nobility secured, or perhaps recaptured, an effective share of government. These fluid situations are reflected in such poets as Homer and Pindar. Modern researches in anthropology, archeology, and prehistory have shown that the Greek situation exemplifies fairly universal and recurrent conditions of early government. It is worthy of note, however, that matriarchal or patriarchal monarchy occurs under conditions that call more for magical and arbitral abilities than for military prowess.

Tyranny. A marginal form of monocracy, rarely referred to as monarchy, is tyranny. It made its appearance in Greece, and elsewhere, when class warfare between the nobility and the plebs caused political order to dissolve into civil war and anarchy. According to Aristotle, tyranny is the least stable of all forms of government. The Romans sought to forestall such developments by institutionalizing tyranny in the form of dictatorship. Both forms have, of course, reappeared in more recent times. In Greece, aristocracies, democracies, and tyrannies were challenged by monarchy. Having successfully withstood the onslaught of the Persian kings, at least in Greece proper, the Greeks were overwhelmed by the Macedonian rulers. Philip and his brilliant son Alexander set the stage for a proliferation of dynasties, which had been traditional in Macedonia. These dynasties dominated Greece and Asia Minor during the Hellenistic age until their conquest by Rome.

Although deeply imbued with traditional antimonarchical sentiment nurtured by a triumphant aristocracy, Rome eventually became a monarchy of radically autocratic propensity. After an extended period of transition, during which republican trappings were deliberately cultivated by Augustus and his successors, the Roman Empire emerged as a full-fledged monarchy. It remained troubled by problems of succession throughout its long history, however, because the notion of legitimizing a ruler by blood descent remained unacceptable for many generations. Historians and political philosophers have speculated on why Roman republicanism should have been superseded by monarchical autocracy. In the works of writers from Machiavelli to Montesquieu, Gibbon, and Mommsen, to mention only the most famous, the explanations for this transformation were, variously, the decline in morals, in religion, and in traditional manners, the extension of Rome's sway and the corrupting influence of Oriental ways, and even the personal defects of Sulla, Pompey, and Caesar.

Actually, the emergence, or rather re-emergence, of monarchy in Rome occurred in response to the same forces that characteristically fashion monarchical government: civil dissension, breakdown of public order, and serious foreign setbacks and threats arising on Rome's far-flung frontiers. The continued pressure of outside enemies and internal dissensions operated in the direction of monocratic, and indeed autocratic, rule; when, in the third century, Diocletian openly proclaimed such rule, he was merely stating officially what had long been a fact.

Religious legitimation of monarchy. It has been said that the change in the status of the emperor reflected a fundamental transformation in all conceptions of life. This may be true, but the impending Christianization of the empire presumably had an even more profound significance. As against the pagan preoccupation with affairs of this world, the Christian emphasis on the life hereafter became the dominant interest. "Render unto Caesar that which is Caesar's" may be taken as the key symbolic utterance of a basic indifference toward politics. Soon the church was to claim complete autonomy, at least in the West, which spelled the end of monarchy in the priestly tradition; monarchy hereafter appeared as the secular arm of the one God, whose primary representative on earth was the monarchical head of the church.

It has rightly been said that the Roman Catholic church preserved and developed the great tradition of Roman law. This heritage had a profound impact upon the development of monarchy in the West. The crucial feature of the emerging monarchical pattern was, at first, not the doctrine of *legibus solutus*, but above all the emphasis on law as expressed in the principle *Quod placet principem,*

legis habet vigorem. Reinforced by the monotheistic conception of the deity in the Old Testament, which stressed the law-giving aspect, the monarch became primarily the dispenser of justice in the legal sense. This kind of monarch was epitomized in the symbolic figure of St. Louis sitting under an oak tree expounding the law. Such a monarch was a far cry from the omnipotent Oriental ruler, surrounded by pomp and circumstance. A monarch, confronted by ecclesiastical authorities ever ready to remind him of the natural and spiritual limits of the law and to back up their reminder with excommunication and the release of the ruler's subjects from their allegiance, needed to reinforce his position as an individual by the legitimation of monarchy as an institution. Such legitimation was provided by the hallowing of blood descent.

Absolutism and constitutional monarchy. There has been a great deal of learned controversy with regard to the details of the intertwining of Germanic and Roman traditions in the evolving of Western forms of political order. But there can be little question that a real amalgamation took place. The decisive event in this process was the crowning of Charlemagne by the pope in the year 800. This event, the result of ecclesiastical initiative, decisively shaped Western monarchy, especially in France, Germany, Austria, Bohemia, and Poland. After Charlemagne, and in contrast to the caesaro–papism of the Eastern Empire, which preserved the older pattern of monarchy and bequeathed it to Russia, Western monarchy was torn between the conception of the Holy Roman Empire and the folkways of Germanic kingship. The latter remained strong in England, Spain, and Scandinavia. In these countries the nobility successfully claimed a share in ruling and thereby provided the restraint that the church sought to exercise in the empire.

Nobility and clergy joined in shaping constitutional forms of monarchy, especially in England and Spain. These were "mixed" governments, rather than "pure" forms. But before they could become universal, most of Europe went through a phase of absolute monarchy. Absolutism, especially as practiced in France, at times turned into despotism. Absolutist regimes were at once the creators and the expressions of national unification. They did away with feudal impediments to economic growth and fostered national churches challenging the ultramontane bonds of Catholicism. What Protestantism accomplished by the complete break with Rome, Gallicanism provided in an indirect way: an ecclesiastical authority closely bound up with secular rule. The absolute power thus placed in the hands of the monarch "corrupted" men and regimes and eventually engendered the violent reaction of revolution. In due course, absolute monarchy was overthrown, never to reappear in the European West; it was replaced by various constitutionalist forms, which were inspired by the example of England but which rarely if ever achieved the stability that tradition lent to the British crown.

The French *Charte constitutionelle* is typical in that it contains a rather doctrinaire system of separation of powers, even though the theory underlying it was distrusted. Constitutional monarchies varied considerably in regard to the scope they allowed the monarchical element; the scope was gradually reduced, in stages punctuated by the revolutions of 1830 and 1848. In addition, a new form of monarchy made its appearance with the rise of Napoleon Bonaparte. Although at the outset he was more a dictator than a monarch, Bonaparte insisted upon acquiring the trappings of traditional monarchy and clearly hoped to found a dynasty. Although a more absolute ruler than the monarchs he emulated, he too acknowledged the persistent Western preoccupation with law in putting through his great codification. Still, his methods served to discredit absolutism, and the autocracy of the Russian tsars did nothing to rehabilitate it. Indeed liberalism, like the Enlightenment before it, rapidly undermined the bases of monarchical legitimacy.

The decline of monarchy. The extent of the corrosion of monarchy was laid bare by World War I. Its revolutionary sequels swept away the monarchy in Germany, Austria–Hungary, and Russia, a process later completed by the disappearance of monarchy in Spain, Italy, and Turkey. Only a few, largely ceremonial monarchs remain in Europe. The decline of monarchy is a world-wide trend. It has toppled in China and is in rapid retreat in Japan, India, the rest of Asia, and most of Africa. It has never been able to establish much of a foothold in America. If it is remembered that in Britain the monarch has long ceased to be in control of the government, one might venture the proposition that traditional monarchy, legitimized in terms of blood descent and ecclesiastical unction, is becoming extinct.

The rise of monocracy. Nothing of the kind can be said for monarchy in the sense of the monocratic rule of one man. This type of government is actually on the increase all over the world, not only in totalitarian dictatorships but in military and even constitutional regimes. The rising importance of executive power, linked as it is to the increasing complexity of the decisions required in a techno-

logical age, enhances the monocratic thrust inherent in bureaucratic structures. Not only men like Stalin, Hitler, Mao, Tito, and Gomulka but also Kemal Atatürk, Ayub Khan, Nasser, Nkrumah, and in a sense even de Gaulle and some of the more recent Latin American dictators, are the new monarchs in the original Greek meaning of the term. Rulers like the kings of Morocco and of Saudi Arabia are in fact becoming monocrats. The legitimacy of these rulers (as well as of their succession) varies. In the totalitarian states their legitimacy is based upon the party and its ideology; in other countries it rests upon military achievement and support; in still others it is linked to a broad plebiscitary appeal; and in all of them such rule is further legitimized by a rising standard of living and the furtherance of economic development. Nor is there any end to this trend in sight; rather the opposite. While hereditary monarchy is finished— even the movements trying to resuscitate it, like the Action Française, are dead or moribund— plebiscitary monarchy, as first instituted by Napoleon, seems destined to spread during the remainder of the twentieth century.

CARL J. FRIEDRICH

[*See also* AUTOCRACY; DICTATORSHIP; EXECUTIVE, POLITICAL; KINGSHIP; LEGITIMACY; SOVEREIGNTY.]

BIBLIOGRAPHY

BARKER, ERNEST 1923 The Conception of Empire. Pages 45–89 in Cyril Bailey (editor), *The Legacy of Rome*. Oxford: Clarendon.

BRYCE, JAMES (1864) 1956 *The Holy Roman Empire*. New ed., rev. & enl. London: Macmillan.

COULBORN, RUSHTON (editor) 1956 *Feudalism in History*. Princeton Univ. Press.

EISENSTADT, SHMUEL N. 1963 *The Political Systems of Empires*. New York: Free Press.

FIGGIS, JOHN N. (1896) 1922 *The Divine Right of Kings*. 2d ed. Cambridge Univ. Press. → First published as *The Theory of the Divine Right of Kings*. A paperback edition was published in 1965 by Harper.

FRANKFORT, HENRI 1948 *Kingship and the Gods: A Study of Ancient Near Eastern Religion as the Integration of Society and Nature*. Univ. of Chicago Press.

FRIEDRICH, CARL J. (1937) 1950 *Constitutional Government and Democracy: Theory and Practice in Europe and America*. Rev. ed. Boston: Ginn. → First published as *Constitutional Government and Politics: Nature and Development*.

FRIEDRICH, CARL J. 1963 *Man and His Government*. New York: McGraw-Hill. → See especially Chapter 10.

GIERKE, OTTO VON (1868–1913) 1954 *Das deutsche Genossenschaftsrecht*. 4 vols. Graz (Austria): Akademische Druck- und Verlagsanstalt. → Volume 1: *Rechtsgeschichte der deutschen Genossenschaft*. Volume 2: *Geschichte des deutschen Körperschaftsbegriffs*. Volume 3: *Die Staats- und Korporationslehre des Altertums und des Mittelalters und ihre Aufnahme in Deutschland*. Volume 4: *Die Staats- und Korporationslehre der Neuzeit*.

HOCART, ARTHUR M. 1927 *Kingship*. Oxford Univ. Press.

HOOKE, SAMUEL H. (editor) 1958 *Myth, Ritual, and Kingship*. Oxford: Clarendon.

KERN, FRITZ (1914) 1939 *Kingship and Law in the Middle Ages*. Oxford: Blackwell. → First published as *Gottesgnadentum und Widerstandsrecht im früheren Mittelalter.*

KOEBNER, RICHARD (1961) 1965 *Empire*. New York: Grosset & Dunlap.

LOEWENSTEIN, KARL 1952 *Die Monarchie im modernen Staat*. Frankfurt am Main (Germany): Metzner.

MAIR, LUCY P. (1962) 1964 *Primitive Government*. Baltimore: Penguin.

MAURRAS, CHARLES (1909) 1928 *Enquête sur la monarchie*. New ed. Versailles (France): Bibliothèque des Oeuvres Politiques.

MOMMSEN, THEODOR (1871) 1887–1888 *Römisches Staatsrecht*. 3d ed., 3 vols. Leipzig: Hirzel. → See especially Volume 2, Part 2.

NICOLSON, HAROLD G. 1962 *Kings, Courts and Monarchy*. New York: Simon & Schuster.

PETRIE, CHARLES A. 1952 *Monarchy in the Twentieth Century*. London: Dakers.

PINE, LESLIE G. 1958 *The Twilight of Monarchy*. London: Burke.

ROSTOVTSEV, MIKHAIL I. (1926) 1963 *The Social and Economic History of the Roman Empire*. New ed., 2 vols. Oxford: Clarendon.

SYME, RONALD (1939) 1960 *The Roman Revolution*. Oxford Univ. Press.

WEBER, MAX (1922) 1956 *Wirtschaft und Gesellschaft*. 4th ed., 2 vols. Tübingen (Germany): Mohr. → See especially Chapter 3 of Volume 1, Part 1.

WITTFOGEL, KARL A. 1957 *Oriental Despotism: A Comparative Study of Total Power*. New Haven, Conn.: Yale Univ. Press. → A paperback edition was published in 1963.

WOLFF-WINDEGG, PHILIPP 1958 *Die Gekrönten: Sinn und Sinnbilder des Königtums*. Stuttgart (Germany): Klett.

MONASTICISM

"Monasticism" is derived from the Greek word for "alone." Words like the Latin *monachus* ("monk") were first used to describe men who lived alone—hermits, solitaries who lived apart for the sake of God or a prayerful life. By a simple extension of meaning the word was applied to communities of monks (or of nuns) who retired within enclosures to separate themselves from other men for the purpose of seeking quiet for simple devotion and contemplation.

Monasteries are groups of men or women pursuing a religious ideal in retirement from society. The religious ideal pursued may differ between one religion and another. But in all the higher religions, examples are found of men or women retiring from society to contemplate truth and strive for purity of heart. The strains and noise of the world are believed to prevent the soul from concentrating upon the good: it must draw apart to direct its attention and eschew every distraction.

A universally accepted condition of this withdrawal has been celibacy, freeing the individual from the distractions of physical passions and the ties of family life. Another has been poverty, freeing the soul from concern for material possessions. When the withdrawal is to a community rather than to a hermitage, obedience to a superior is considered an important exercise in destroying self-will. In Roman Catholic monasticism the monk or nun takes a threefold vow of chastity, poverty, and obedience. In other religions there are rarely vows, but the threefold intention is almost universal.

The origin of the monastery was connected with the belief that the world is evil: existence is a burden, and the soul must be delivered from matter. The soul and body were believed to be opposed: the body must be mortified that the soul may find its true self, its "salvation," "perfection," "deliverance," "redemption." The most ancient forms of this doctrine are those found among the Hindus; the most ancient monasteries known appeared in the early years of Hinduism, when groups gathered to share a life of mortification and Vedic studies. Monasticism has flourished above all in Buddhism, for Gautama Buddha took the deliverance doctrine of Hinduism, spiritualized it, and thereby made withdrawal the only discipline that would lead to that state of perfection which was Nirvana. For Buddhists, monasticism is not a heightened form of the religious way of life, as it is for Catholic Christians; it *is* the religious life. At different times, monasteries have dominated religion, civilization, and culture in those countries where almost all the people profess Buddhism—Burma, Thailand, Tibet.

In the three religions with an interest in the Old Testament—Judaism, Christianity, Islam—monasticism has played a less dominant role. The God of Genesis is a living God, a ruler and a father, who created the world and saw that it was good. For none of these faiths is the body evil. The God of Mount Sinai demands a moral people and a moral society. His servants shall seek to secure a world free of injustice and oppression. Individuals and groups may be permitted to retire from society, but this never becomes a universal ideal. Moreover the monastic life is almost always associated with some form—however rudimentary or however advanced—of mysticism. In Hinduism and Buddhism the soul which mortifies the passions and directs its prayer may pass into union with the absolute good of the universe, possessing it and possessed by it. In the Old Testament, God is high and lifted up, transcendent and other. A Jewish soul cannot seek union with Jehovah, for the very conception appears blasphemous to it; the created being does not raise itself to equality with its creator.

Therefore, although monastic groups are found in all three religious traditions, all three also contain strands of thought that are antithetical to monasticism in the Hindu or Buddhist sense: the divine creation of the body; the salvation of society, as well as of the individual spirit; the faith in a transcendent God and its corollary, the distrust of any uncontrolled search for mystical unity.

Judaism and Islam have been less friendly to monasticism than has Christianity. Muhammad declared that there are no monks in Islam and made no mention of them in the Qur'an (Koran). Despite certain anticipations of monasticism among the Jews contemporary with Christ, there were no Christian monks, properly speaking, for two centuries after Christ's death. Monasticism is not inherent in Christianity, and monasteries have never been as integral to the practice of Christianity as they are to the practice of Buddhism. Partly for this reason Christianity has also produced many critics of monasticism. Even at the end of the fourth century, when monastic ideals were rapidly spreading throughout the Christian church, the Latin writer Vigilantius denounced the solitary life as a cowardly abandonment of responsibility. During the sixteenth-century Reformation half the western Christian church repudiated the monastic ideal; few examples of it are found among Protestant churches. Yet, the contemplative and hermit tradition was well represented in western Christendom, although the Benedictine Rule remained dominant. The most highly respected Western order of the quasi-hermit tradition is the Carthusians, founded by St. Bruno in 1084 at the Grande Chartreuse, in southeast France.

The mystical element in religion, however, is more diffused than those mysticisms that are dependent upon a division between body and soul. All three of the Old Testament religions came into touch with mystical doctrine and were affected. In Syria and Persia, Jewish, Christian, and Muslim doctrines of salvation were akin to those of Hinduism or Buddhism. The recently discovered Dead Sea Scrolls have proved the existence of a Jewish monastic community in the Dead Sea valley about the time of Christ. Within Judaism, the Essenes practiced a form of monastic life, with community of goods, silence, celibacy, poverty. Philo of Alexandria described a community in Egypt, the Therapeutae, whose way of life was so like that of Christian monks that for centuries Christian writers believed them to be Christians. Islam was not, on the whole, friendly to mysticism or to enclosed monasteries. But as Sufism developed in Persia it acquired strongly mystical doctrines, and monastic groups began to be founded.

Christianity assimilated monasticism into its system of religious life more readily than did Judaism or Islam. It was preaching its gospel in a Greek world where Platonic philosophy and religious dualism combined to welcome a doctrine of salvation through withdrawal from society. People who were educated in Greek thought and were later converted to the church sought to interpret Christian theology in accordance with their earlier philosophy. From Platonic philosophy, Christian teachers adopted the language used in speaking about the contemplation of supreme truth or the unity of the soul with the Divinity and in this sense interpreted the New Testament's statements concerning unceasing prayer. In the middle of the third century St. Anthony led a retreat into the Egyptian desert, and only a century later the movement was the strongest religious force in Christendom. The anarchic conditions of secular society helped it to remain so for six centuries.

The monks of the Eastern church looked back to St. Basil of Caesarea (who died in 379) as their chief organizer; the monks of the Western church to St. Benedict of Nursia, who founded the house of Monte Cassino, north of Naples, in the sixth century. In the West, the Benedictine Rule was an elementary framework to which other rules and customs were added. The ideal of life was simplicity, not excessive austerity, with seven or eight short services for worship at fixed points in the day and with time allotted to work in the fields and to spiritual reading. The orders descended from the Benedictine varied greatly in their customs. The first Christian monasteries were communities of laymen with a priest or two to celebrate the sacraments. As centuries passed, it was expected that all fully professed monks would be ordained. Slowly the forms of worship became more elaborate until they were the main work of the monk—especially among the Cluniacs, whose mother house, Cluny, in Burgundy, was founded in 910. The abbey church at Cluny was the grandest of any monastery in Europe. In reaction against these elaborations the Cistercians—called so after their mother house, of Cîteaux, Burgundy—sought to recall the monks to the simplicity of the Benedictine Rule. They restored the obligation to work in the fields and founded their houses in remote wildernesses, where they brought new land under cultivation or grazing.

In the Eastern church, there was no coherent

"Rule" of St. Basil similar to the Rule of St. Benedict. Monasticism in Russia and Greece always remained more individualistic in its ethos, nearer to the hermit tradition of Syria and Egypt, with a rich liturgical and contemplative tradition but more remote from society and less influential. Eastern Orthodoxy created a unique monastic republic on the peninsula of Mount Athos in northern Greece, where from the eighth or ninth century a great complex of communities and hermitages began to develop. No woman is yet allowed to set foot upon the peninsula.

Nuns are much more numerous in Christianity than in any other religion. The nuns of Buddhism are comparatively few. Every variety of Christian monasticism has made provision for women as well as men, and in modern Roman Catholicism nuns have greatly outnumbered monks.

The characteristic government of a monastery springs out of a personal relationship between a holy man and his disciple. A hermit goes into retirement to seek his salvation. He becomes known for his sanctity and moral wisdom. A disciple asks leave to sit at his feet or serve him in his cell, to advance his own salvation. More disciples come, and a group forms around a wise man. They partake of common meals and common worship and have simple rules. Most Hindu monasteries remained loose in organization and hardly passed beyond the stage of having a sage or saint and a few disciples. In many primitive Christian and modern Buddhist monasteries the government remained a loose administration by a group of "elders." Even when the constitution is highly organized, it never quite loses the flavor imparted by its remote origins; the relation is one of a novice to the director of his soul—the experienced elder imparting moral knowledge to the young in years or young in religious experience. Moreover, the disciple grows in grace by conquering his self-will, both by instant obedience to the commands of his director—even when he does not understand the reason—and by accepting without resentment punishment which looks like injustice. Therefore, the moral nature of this relationship has led to very authoritarian forms of constitution; abbots are superiors with absolute authority, except so far as they are limited by civil law or by a rule of life accepted by them at their entry as novices.

Some Buddhist communities grew so large that more elaborate forms of organization became necessary. In a country where every male must be a monk for part of his life, a monastery might rise to become a celibate township of ten thousand souls. However, as in Hindu monasteries, there was

flexibility, and a man might enter or leave the monastery without blame.

The most elaborate forms of organization are found in Christian monastic orders, where very early in Christian monastic practice the idea of stability became morally important. It was recognized that a man might try his experience in various directions. But it was also believed that the spiritual life demanded a long course of obedience and a continuity within the same brotherhood. The existence of vows and the demand for stability presented Christian thinkers with deeper constitutional problems. The characteristic Christian monastery, the Benedictine, had an elected abbot who possessed a permanent authority limited only by the provisions of the Rule of St. Benedict. Later medieval orders, such as the Cistercians and the Dominicans, experimented further in forms of organization, while retaining the absolute duty of obedience to the superior; the several houses of the order were placed under a single governing body in which each was represented.

All such societies used sanctions to preserve discipline, varying according to the country and century—flogging, confinement, deprivation of food, temporary exclusion from the social and especially from the religious meetings of the community, and, in the last resort, expulsion.

The first monks were holy men who sought retirement. They were devoted to poverty. But in both Christian and Buddhist monasticism, the poverty of the individual was compatible with the wealth of the community. Monasteries which began as societies of the poor sometimes ended as rich and powerful corporations.

Buddhist and Hindu monks were expected to live off charity. The begging bowl was almost indispensable as equipment, and the round for alms was an almost indispensable part of daily devotion. It was a devotional exercise to receive such alms with humility and tranquillity of spirit, eschewing worldly satisfaction if the alms were given and resentment if they were refused. In Christianity the Franciscan friar—especially of the stricter or spiritual group—expected God to provide in the same way. But Christianity possesses a stronger doctrine, that earthly vocations are God-given. Christian monks always believed that they should work for their living on simple tasks that did not distract devotion. Their characteristic work has been agriculture, but basket making, mat making, education, the copying of manuscripts, scholarship, and other forms of work have been accepted as suitable for Christian monks. Buddhist monks have likewise engaged in scholarship, education, agriculture, and the copying of manuscripts, but have not usually considered the earning of a livelihood to be a necessary element in religious devotion.

Sanctity attracted gifts. Rich novices might make over their funds to the community, although the practice has obvious dangers and monastic rules tried to regulate or even prevent it. Childless widows or widowers left money or lands; pious kings gave endowments; noblemen found in monasteries a worthy object for their alms. An accepted work was the maintenance of shrines, and pilgrims cast their offerings freely. In some countries monasteries have thus acquired over the centuries an astonishingly large proportion of the national land area. In western Europe between the eighth and eleventh centuries, in Russia between the thirteenth and fifteenth centuries, in Tibet between the seventeenth and twentieth centuries, the whole current of popular piety so flowed toward the monastic ideal that the monasteries came to be a major state institution. The climax of the process was attained in modern Tibet, where the monks formed something like a fifth of the population and where the government of the state was for three centuries controlled by the chief abbot, the Dalai Lama. In certain other countries, the abbots have held temporal prominence in the state. In Ceylon, the abbots were the secular judges and the king's cabinet. In medieval England and other European countries the abbots sat of right in the parliament.

Tibet is an example of how the social influence of monasteries has been strongest in countries where nearly all the population was, or is, Buddhist. The explanation probably lies in the doctrinal difference from Christianity. In the Christian churches the monastic way of life has always appeared as only one way to heaven among others— although seen by many as the surest way. The dogma that its practice was necessary to salvation appeared in a few early Christian sects but was always rejected as heretical and incompatible with the Bible. Buddhism, in contrast, has held that some institutionalized withdrawal is indispensable to the perfect life. In countries like Tibet and Burma almost the entire male population entered monasteries for a shorter or longer time (at least for three months) and wore the yellow robes. Before the Europeans opened schools in Burma and before the Chinese conquered Tibet, the monks were the only schoolmasters, and every educated layman was familiar with the life and devotion of the monastery. The absence in Buddhism of irrevocable vows, the freedom to leave a monastery without blame, made this possible. In western Europe of the early Middle Ages the monasteries

made important contributions to such education as existed, but in no Christian country were they for any length of time the sole instrument of education.

Monks have sometimes been of momentous importance in preserving and transmitting the cultural heritage of a people. From the seventh to the tenth centuries, Christian monasteries helped to preserve the libraries and knowledge inherited from Greco-Roman civilization. But monasticism has never possessed a social drive or consciousness and has acted as a main channel or focus of culture only by accident or as a by-product of other activities and in special (often anarchic) social circumstances. Nevertheless, the most notable of all monastic contributions to learning came from the Benedictine congregation of St. Maur, in France, during the late seventeenth and early eighteenth centuries, where a group of eminent scholars headed by Jean Mabillon laid the foundations for the modern critical study of historical sources.

On the edge of the monastic groups proper, brotherhoods have existed which accepted various monastic obligations, although their members lived in the world. In Catholicism the Jesuits accepted the threefold vows of poverty, chastity, and obedience but were nevertheless secular priests living in the world and engaged in pastoral care or in education; in modern times this sort of example led older and originally contemplative orders, like the Benedictine, to accept responsibility for education or pastoral duties outside the monastery.

In Tibet there were warrior–monks. Medieval Catholicism had its orders of crusading knights, like the Templars and Hospitalers, who took vows but were devoted to the defense of Christendom by force of arms. Such orders could achieve political authority, just as the Hospitalers ruled Malta and the Teutonic Knights founded the state which later became the duchy of Prussia. Under the Turkish empire the Baktashiyah were a similar military and quasi-monastic order connected with the Janissaries. In Islam—outside the mystical tradition of the Sufis—a majority of the "monasteries" have been of this quasi-monastic type of religious brotherhood with special duties in the world. A modern religious brotherhood of this kind, the Senusi, was founded as late as 1837 and came, in time, to achieve political control of part of the Sudan and nearly all the eastern Sahara.

The concern of Christian doctrine for this world and its society meant that the monastic ideal took forms very different from the original societies, which were directed to individual salvation and contemplative prayer. The most celebrated of these novel forms is found in the friars, founded by

St. Francis of Assisi and by St. Dominic at the beginning of the thirteenth century. Francis called for poverty and simplicity as a protest against the elaborate and powerful church of his day; Dominic wished to protect the church by confuting heretics. But both orders of friars which resulted from their initiative were devoted to saving the souls of others as well as their own souls. They are an important example of how monastic groups could become agents for evangelism and the propagation of the faith.

In modern times some secular governments, such as Mexico, Russia, and China, have confiscated much or all monastic property, whether Christian or Buddhist, as useless to the state and have secularized their inmates. Even in a still formally Christian country like Greece, where most of the inhabitants profess the Orthodox religion, there has been a spectacular decline, even on Mount Athos, in the number and the reputation of the monks. But as it is impossible to conceive of Buddhism without Buddhist monks, so the course of centuries has made it impossible to conceive of Catholic Christianity without varieties of Christian monks. Quiet withdrawal in the face of eternity appears to meet a need of the highest aspirations of the human conscience.

W. O. CHADWICK

[*See also* RELIGIOUS SPECIALISTS. *A guide to other relevant material may be found under* RELIGION.]

BIBLIOGRAPHY

BUTLER, EDWARD C. (1919) 1962 *Benedictine Monachism: Studies in Benedictine Life and Rule.* 2d ed. New York: Barnes & Noble.

CABROL, FERNAND 1916 Monasticism. Volume 8, pages 781–797 in *Encyclopaedia of Religion and Ethics.* Edited by James Hastings. New York: Scribner.

CHADWICK, OWEN (1950) 1967 *John Cassian: A Study in Primitive Monasticism.* 2d ed. Cambridge Univ. Press.

COULTON, GEORGE G. 1923–1950 *Five Centuries of Religion.* 4 vols. Cambridge Univ. Press.

FARQUHAR, JOHN N. (editor) 1916–1938 *The Religious Life of India.* 13 vols. London: Milford.

HEIMBUCHER, MAX (1896–1897) 1933–1934 *Die Orden und Kongregationen der katholischen Kirche.* 3d ed., rev. & enl. 2 vols. Paderborn (Germany): Schöningh.

KNOWLES, DAVID (1940) 1963 *The Monastic Order in England: A History of Its Development From the Times of St. Dunstan to the Fourth Lateran Council, 940–1216.* 2d ed. Cambridge Univ. Press.

KNOWLES, DAVID 1948–1959 *The Religious Orders in England.* 3 vols. Cambridge Univ. Press.

WADDELL, LAURENCE A. (1895) 1958 *The Buddhism of Tibet: Or, Lamaism, With Its Mystic Cults, Symbolism and Mythology, and in Its Relation to Indian Buddhism.* 2d ed. Cambridge: Heffer.

WARD, CHARLES H. S. (1934) 1947–1952 *Buddhism.* Rev. ed. 2 vols. London: Epworth. → First published as *Outline of Buddhism.* Volume 1: *Hīnayāna.* Volume 2: *Mahāyāna.*

WORKMAN, HERBERT B. (1913) 1927 *The Evolution of the Monastic Ideal From the Earliest Times Down to the Coming of the Friars: A Second Chapter in the History of Christian Renunciation.* London: Epworth. → A paperback edition was published in 1962 by Beacon.

MONETARY POLICY

In its broadest sense, monetary policy includes all actions of governments, central banks, and other public authorities that influence the quantity of money and bank credit. It therefore embraces policies relating to such things as choice of the nation's monetary standard; determination of the value of the monetary unit in terms of a metal or foreign currencies; determination of the types and amounts of the government's own monetary issues; establishment of a central banking system and determination of its powers and rules for its operation; and policies concerning the establishment and regulation of commercial banks and other related financial institutions. A few even extend the meaning of monetary policy to include official actions affecting not only the quantity of money but also its rate of expenditure, thus embracing government tax, expenditure, lending, and debt management policies.

It has become customary, however, to define monetary policy in a more restricted sense and to exclude from it choices relating to the broad legal and institutional framework of the monetary and banking system. This narrower concept will be employed here. Monetary policy in this sense refers to regulation of the supply of money and bank credit for the promotion of selected objectives.

Elements of monetary policy. Like all economic policies, monetary policy has three interrelated elements: selection of objectives, implementation, and at least an implicit theory of the relationships between actions and effects. All three elements present problems of choice and are continuing subjects of controversy.

Monetary policy can be directed toward achieving many different objectives. For example, the supply of money can be regulated to provide the government with cheap or even costless funds, to maintain interest rates at some selected level, to regulate the exchange rate on the nation's currency, to protect the nation's gold and other international reserves, to stabilize domestic price levels, to promote continuously high levels of employment, and so on. Such multiple objectives are unlikely to be fully compatible at all times. Rational policy making therefore requires identification of the various objectives, analysis of the extent to which they are or can be made compatible, and choices from among those that conflict with one another. A later section will stress changes in the objectives of monetary policy and some of the problems of reconciling them.

The role played by monetary policy in promoting selected economic objectives depends greatly on the nature of the economic system and on attitudes toward the use of other methods of regulation. This role is usually secondary in economies characterized by government operation of most economic enterprises and government control of resource allocation, distribution of output, and prices of inputs and outputs. Even in these economies monetary policy is not trivial. An excessive supply of money can create excessive demand and inflationary pressures, which are evidenced in black markets, hoarding, and bare shelves. On the other hand, a deficient supply of money can impede the flow of production and trade. Yet the major function of monetary policy in such economies is that of passive accommodation, that is, to provide the amount of money needed to facilitate the operation of other government controls; it is not to serve as a prime regulator.

Monetary policy usually plays a more positive regulatory role in economic systems that rely heavily on market forces to organize and direct processes of production and distribution. In such economies, decisions of business firms relating to rates of output, amounts of labor employed, rates of capital formation, and so on, are strongly influenced by relationships between costs and actual and prospective demands for output. If aggregate demands are deficient, firms will not find it profitable to employ all available labor, to utilize fully existing capacity, or to purchase all the new capital goods that could be produced. On the other hand, excessive aggregate demands for output are inflationary. A major function of monetary policy, therefore, is to regulate the behavior of aggregate demand for output in order to elicit a more favorable performance by the economy. This function is shared with fiscal policy in many countries and in many different combinations or "mixes." Although the deliberate use of fiscal policy for this purpose has increased considerably in recent decades, monetary policy continues to be a major instrument.

Primary responsibility for administering monetary policies is usually entrusted to central banks, although there are varying degrees of government control of central banks and their policies. Central banks regulate the money supply and influence the supply of credit in two principal separate but closely related capacities: as controllers of their own issues of money and as regulators of the amount of money created by commercial banks. Both are important, but their relative importance depends in part on the stage of financial development of the country and on the types of money employed. In countries where bank deposits have not yet come to be widely used, notes issued by the central bank often constitute a major part of the money supply. In such cases the central bank may regulate the money supply largely by controlling directly its own note issues. However, in countries that have reached a later stage of financial development, central bank notes constitute a smaller part of the money supply; deposits at commercial banks are the major component, and the actions of commercial banks directly account for a large part of the fluctuations of the money supply. In such countries, the central bank is primarily a regulator of the commercial banks, although control of its own money creation remains important and is a part of the process.

The terms "monetary policy" and "credit policy" are often used interchangeably or with only slightly different shades of meaning. This has come about primarily because in most modern systems the creation and destruction of money by central and commercial banks are so closely intertwined with their expansion and contraction of credit. They typically create and issue money (currency and deposits) by making loans or purchasing securities, usually debt obligations. Thus, one side of the transaction is the issue of money; the other is the provision of funds to borrowers or sellers of securities, which tends to lower interest rates. Central and commercial banks typically withdraw money (currency and deposits) by decreasing their outstanding loans or by selling securities, usually debt obligations. Thus there is both a decrease in the supply of money and a decrease in the funds available to borrowers and to purchasers of the securities sold by the banks, which tends to increase interest rates.

Those who speak of monetary policy tend to focus on the behavior of the stock of money, while those who speak of credit policy tend to focus on the quantity of loan funds available from the central and commercial banks. Such differences in focus need not lead to differences in either analysis or conclusions. Yet they sometimes do. Those who focus on the stock of money are more likely to stress "real balance effects" on both consumption and investment spending, while those who focus on credit are likely to put more stress on the direct effects on interest rates, the availability of funds, and investment. Monetary theory has made considerable progress in reconciling and integrating these approaches, but much remains to be done.

The third element in monetary policy is at least an implicit theory of the relationships between actions and effects. If its actions are to promote its objectives, the monetary authority needs some theory as to the nature, direction, magnitude, and timing of the responses. The relevant responses are numerous and on several levels. For example, they include the response of the supply of money and credit; the response of aggregate demand for output; and the responses of real output, employment, and prices. There are still disagreements among both economists and central bankers on many of these theoretical and empirical issues, and these disagreements underlie many continuing controversies over the proper nature and scope of monetary policy. Some of these will be treated in a later section.

Evolution of objectives. Monetary policy, in the modern sense of deliberate and continuous management of the money supply to promote selected social and economic objectives, is largely a product of the twentieth century, especially the decades since World War I. In the earlier period, when most countries were on either a gold or a bimetallic standard, the primary and overriding objective of monetary policy was to maintain redeemability of the nation's money in the primary metal, both domestically and internationally. A decline of the nation's metallic reserves to dangerously low levels, or any other threat to redeemability, became a signal for monetary and credit restriction, whatever might be its other economic effects. When redeemability seemed secure, monetary policy was used to promote other objectives—to deal with panics, crises, and other credit stringencies and even to expand money somewhat when business was depressed. But such intervention was sporadic rather than continuous and its purposes limited rather than ambitious. The international gold standard of the pre-1914 period was not purely automatic, but it was managed only marginally.

Many forces have contributed to the change and growth of monetary policy since World War I. One set of forces includes the breakdown of the international gold standard and other changes and crises in monetary systems—inflation during and following World War I and the long period of suspension of gold redeemability in most countries, the changed and insecure nature of the gold and gold exchange standards re-established in the 1920s, the renewed breakdown of gold standards during the great depression of the 1930s, and world-wide inflation during and following World War II. All these had profound effects on attitudes toward monetary policy. Both countries that had too little gold and those that had too much shifted to the view that the state of their gold reserves was no longer an adequate guide to policy and that new objectives and guides should be developed. Monetary actions became increasingly less sporadic and limited and more continuous and ambitious in scope.

The objectives of monetary policy have also been powerfully influenced by changes in attitudes concerning the responsibilities of central banks and governments for the performance of the economy. The 1920s witnessed growing demands that some central agency reduce instability of price levels and business activity. These demands were strengthened immeasurably by the economic catastrophe of the 1930s and by fears that World War II would be followed by another world-wide depression. Within a few years after that war the governments of almost all Western nations had formally assumed responsibility for promoting continuously high levels of employment and output. And within a few more years almost all of these governments had signified their intentions to promote economic growth. Monetary policy is required, in some cases by government and in others by the force of public opinion and pressure, to contribute to such objectives.

Although often phrased in different terms, it is now common for monetary authorities to state four major or basic objectives of monetary policy: (1) continuously high levels of employment and output, (2) the highest sustainable rate of economic growth, (3) relatively stable domestic price levels, and (4) maintenance of a stable exchange rate for the nation's currency and protection of its international reserve position. In some countries monetary policy is also influenced by other considerations, such as a desire to maintain low interest rates to facilitate government finance or other favored types of economic activity.

Conflicts of objectives. Some of the most basic problems of monetary policy relate to the compatibility of such multiple objectives. Can all these be achieved simultaneously and to an acceptable degree even if a nation has precise control of the behavior of aggregate demand for output? Of course, the answer depends in part on the ambitiousness of the goals; perfection in all respects is hardly to be expected.

The answer also depends to an important extent on the responses of output, employment, money wage rates, and prices to changes in aggregate demand. The most favorable case is that in which the supply of output is completely elastic at existing price levels up to the point of "full employment" and capacity output. In such cases, increases of demand would elicit only increases in output until the economy reached its maximum capacity to produce. Price inflation would appear only when demand became excessive relative to productive capacity.

Problems of reconciling objectives relating to output, employment, and price level stability arise, however, when the supply of output does not respond in such a favorable manner to increases of demand—when prices rise before the economy has neared its capacity to produce. Even in the face of considerable amounts of unemployment, average money wage rates may rise faster than average output per man-hour, thereby tending to raise costs of production. And for this, or other reasons, business firms may raise the prices of their products even though considerable amounts of excess capacity persist. Under such conditions it may be impossible to achieve all objectives, to acceptable degrees, solely by controlling aggregate demand. Levels of demand sufficient to elicit "full employment" and capacity output may bring inflation, while levels of demand low enough to assure stability of price levels may leave large amounts of unemployment and unused capacity.

Because of such difficulties, many economists and other observers have come to believe that objectives relating to output, employment, and price levels can be reconciled satisfactorily only if regulation of aggregate demand through monetary and fiscal policies is supplemented by measures designed to elicit more favorable responses by the economy. These measures are of several types, which can only be listed here: (1) reform of wage-making processes in order to avoid inflationary increases of money wage rates, (2) decrease of monopoly power in industry, and (3) increase of regional and occupational mobility of labor.

The above discussion related to possible conflicts among a nation's multiple domestic objectives. One, or more, of these domestic objectives may also conflict with the nation's international objectives of maintaining a stable exchange rate for its currency and of protecting its international reserve position. Fortunately, domestic and international objectives do not always conflict. For example, a nation may have a deficit in its balance of payments primarily because of excessive domestic demands and rising prices. In such cases, restrictive monetary policies may be appropriate for both domestic and international reasons. On the other hand, a nation may have a surplus in its balance of payments primarily because of unemployment and depressed output and incomes at home, which depress its demands for imports. In this case an expansionary monetary policy will promote both its domestic and international objectives.

Cases do arise, however, in which domestic objectives and the objectives of maintaining stable exchange rates and a balance in international payments come into conflict. For example, a nation may have a large and persistent surplus in its balance of payments while demands for its output are so large as to bring actual or threatened inflation. An expansionary monetary policy, aimed at reducing the surplus in its balance of payments, would increase inflationary pressures at home; while a restrictive policy, aimed at inhibiting domestic inflation, would continue, and perhaps even increase, the surplus in its balance of payments. A nation faced with this situation may be compelled to sacrifice its domestic objective of preventing inflation or to increase the exchange rate on its currency in order to decrease the value of its exports relative to its imports.

Considered by most countries to be even more serious is the situation in which there is a large and persistent deficit in the balance of payments combined with actual or threatened excess unemployment at home. Employing expansionary monetary and fiscal policies to increase domestic demand and eradicate excess unemployment would tend to widen the deficit in the nation's balance of payments and to drain away its international reserves. But employing restrictive policies to eradicate the deficit in its balance of payments would increase unemployment at home. The nation may be forced to sacrifice its domestic objectives relating to employment, output, and growth or to lower the exchange rate on its currency.

Because of such conflicts, many economists have become critical of arrangements under which exchange rates remain fixed over long periods of time. They see little merit in stable exchange rates as such and would alter them whenever they conflict with important economic objectives. However, their prescriptions vary widely. For example, some favor stability of exchange rates most of the time with adjustments only in case of "fundamental disequilibrium." Others favor continuously flexible exchange rates, with or without official intervention to influence their behavior. The entire field of exchange rate policy remains highly controversial. [See INTERNATIONAL MONETARY ECONOMICS, *article on* EXCHANGE RATES.]

Monetary policy and aggregate demand. The preceding sections dealt with some of the problems that would be encountered in promoting multiple economic objectives simultaneously, even if the monetary authority possessed precise control over the behavior of aggregate demand for output. But it is unsafe to assume without analysis that the monetary authority, or even the monetary authority together with the fiscal authorities, can control aggregate demand precisely. The monetary authority has no direct control over aggregate demand for output or over any of its major components, such as demands for consumption, for investment or capital formation, for government use, or for export. Its powers are largely confined to regulation of the supply of money and credit. Even at this level its controls may lack precision. Presumably the central bank can accurately control its own creation and destruction of money; but its control of the creation and destruction of money and credit by the commercial banking system, exercised largely through its control over the reserve position of the banks, may be less accurate. And even if the monetary authority has precise control of the money supply, aggregate demand for output may not respond in a uniform or precisely predictable manner; the income velocity, or rate of expenditure, of money may fluctuate. Thus there are many links in the chain of causation from central bank action to the reaction of aggregate demand and many possibilities of slippage.

The effectiveness of monetary policy as a regulator of aggregate demand does not depend on the existence of some fixed relationship between the supply of money and aggregate demand. It requires only that changes in the money supply influence aggregate demand in the desired direction and in a predictable way and that the monetary authority have power to change the money supply to the extent required to offset adverse variations in the income velocity of money. However, the possibility of control of aggregate demand does suffer to the extent that changes in money supply fail to affect aggregate demand, that the power of the monetary authority to change the money supply is limited, and that the relationship between the money supply and aggregate demand is unpredictable.

Few economists doubt the ability of monetary policy, in the absence of strong cyclical forces, to regulate effectively the secular behavior of both the money supply and aggregate demand for output. Secular changes in the velocity of money are usually gradual and can be allowed for in determining the appropriate rate of change of the money supply. There is much less agreement, however, concerning the effectiveness of monetary policy alone for offsetting cyclical forces and stabilizing aggregate demand over the various phases of the business cycle.

Monetary policy meets its most severe test in dealing with the strong forces that cause recessions or depressions. Consider the extreme case in which an economy has slipped into a severe depression with widespread unemployment and unused capacity. Under such conditions businessmen are likely to view the future pessimistically and to see few opportunities for investment in capital facilities that promise favorable rates of return. Their demand functions for output to be used for capital formation may be so low that only extremely low interest rates, perhaps rates approaching zero, would induce them to invest enough to lift the economy back toward full-employment levels.

But monetary policy may be incapable of depressing interest rates, and especially long-term rates, to such low levels. The monetary authority may encounter difficulties in increasing the money supply under such conditions because the banks prefer to hold excess reserves rather than lend and take risks. Interest rates, and especially long-term rates, may fall only sluggishly, even in the face of large increases in the money supply. One reason for this is the fear of default by borrowers under depression conditions. John Maynard Keynes suggested another reason—his famous "liquidity trap." He argued that there was some long-term rate of interest, not far below that previously prevailing, that the public considered "normal," in the sense that it would again prevail. No one would hold securities at lower yields because of fear of capital losses when interest rates returned to their normal levels. Below this normal rate the public would increase its holdings of money balances indefinitely rather than lend at a lower rate.

Thus monetary policy may be incapable of lowering interest rates enough to offset the decline of investment demand functions, and recovery may be delayed until something increases the expected profitability of private investment or until the government adopts expansionary fiscal policies.

In how many cases would a well-conceived and well-executed monetary policy prove incapable of dealing with depressive forces? On this there is still lack of agreement among economists. Some have argued that experience during the great depression proved the ineffectiveness of monetary policy. This experience is hardly relevant to the present question, however, because the monetary policies of that period were hardly exemplary. To protect gold standards or for other reasons, many countries actually followed deflationary monetary policies for a considerable period. Expansionary policies were in many cases initiated only after a long delay, during which excess capacity had become widespread, expectations had deteriorated, and the entire financial system had come under serious strain. It may well be that in this and other recessions an ambitious expansionary monetary policy introduced promptly after the downturn would have proved effective in arresting the decline of aggregate demand. However, many economists —including some who are optimists about the effectiveness of monetary policy—believe that monetary policy alone may not be potent enough to offset strong depressive forces and that expansionary fiscal policies should also be employed under such conditions.

It is generally conceded that well-conceived monetary policies can be more effective in restricting increases in aggregate demand during the prosperity phases of business cycles. However, such prosperity periods are usually characterized by increases in aggregate demand relative to the money supply. This increase in the income velocity of money, or "economizing of money balances relative to expenditures," reflects several forces that usually accompany prosperity—greater optimism on the part of both households and business firms concerning their future receipts of income, which decreases the amounts of money held against contingencies; more profitable opportunities for investing idle balances held by business firms; and rising interest rates. Theorists have tended to stress, perhaps to overstress, the role played by rising interest rates. The rise of investment demand during prosperity tends to raise interest rates, and the rise of rates is accentuated by a restrictive monetary policy. In turn, the availability of higher yields on other assets induces both business firms and households to economize their holdings of money balances that yield no interest.

Such increases of velocity—induced in part, but only in part, by restrictive monetary policy—do constitute a slippage in the operation of monetary policy. This does not mean that monetary policy is rendered ineffective; it means only that larger restrictive actions are required to achieve any specified amount of restriction of aggregate demand. Of course, the monetary authority may be unable or unwilling to restrict money to the required extent. For example, it may be inhibited by inadequacy of the control instruments currently at its disposal, fear that further restriction would precipitate a recession, dislike of high interest rates, or charges that credit restriction discriminates against both new and small business firms. However, these are not limitations on the capability of monetary policy to restrict aggregate demand. They are only considerations affecting the willingness of the monetary authority to use its powers of restriction.

Lags in monetary policy. The effectiveness of monetary policy as a countercyclical instrument depends heavily on the quickness of policy action and the quickness of response of the economy. Ideally, policy actions would be taken as soon as adverse developments appeared, or even in anticipation of such developments; and there would be an immediate and full response of aggregate demand and of such policy objectives as employment and output. Under such ideal conditions a high degree of stability might be maintained continuously. In practice, of course, such ideal performance is not realized. Economists have long recognized three lags in monetary policy: (1) the recognition lag—the interval between the time when a need for action develops and the time the need is recognized; (2) the administrative lag—the interval between recognition and the actual policy action; and (3) the operational lag—the interval between policy action and the time that the policy objectives, such as output and employment, respond fully.

Both the length and significance of these lags depend heavily on the reliability of economic forecasting. If developments could be reliably forecast well in advance, the first two lags could be eliminated and actions could be taken soon enough to allow for the operational lag. But when economic forecasting is unreliable the monetary authority is likely to wait until a development appears before taking action to deal with it. In such cases the length of the operational lag becomes highly important for countercyclical policy. Those who favor flexible countercyclical monetary policies implicitly assume that the operational lag is rather short, that all or most of the effects of a monetary action will be achieved within a few months or a year. [*See* PREDICTION AND FORECASTING, ECONOMIC.]

This view has been challenged by some economists, notably by Milton Friedman. These economists contend that the responses to a given monetary action are distributed over time and that the full effects are realized only after a lag of considerably more than a year. Because of this, monetary actions taken to counter cyclical fluctuations may actually produce, or at least accentuate, these fluctuations. For example, expansionary policy actions taken to counter recession may have little effect for several months and then achieve their full expansionary effects on aggregate demand only when the economy is in its next boom phase. And actions taken to restrict aggregate demand during a boom may in fact precipitate and accentuate an ensuing depression.

For this and other reasons, members of this school oppose flexible countercyclical monetary policies. They believe that a greater degree of stability will be achieved by a monetary policy aimed at a steady growth of the money supply, regardless of cyclical conditions. This growth should be at an annual rate approximating the growth rate of real gross national product.

This whole question, which is obviously crucial for countercyclical monetary policy, remains unresolved and controversial. Friedman's theoretical and statistical arguments have been strongly challenged but not wholly refuted. Much more research is needed on both the magnitude and timing of responses to monetary policy actions. The same applies to the various types of fiscal policy actions.

Monetary and fiscal policies.   Nations face complex problems in determining the relative roles to be played by monetary policies and by the various types of government expenditure and tax policies in promoting the economic objectives described earlier. Only a few of the considerations determining these relative roles can be mentioned here. One is, of course, the whole set of cultural, institutional, and political conditions determining the actual availability of these policy instruments. For example, in some countries it is in fact acceptable to use government tax and expenditure policies in a timely and flexible manner. Other governments are not yet in this position. Still others may find it possible to reduce taxes or increase expenditures to support aggregate demand but not to restrict it by fiscal measures. There can also be comparable differences in the actual availability of monetary policy instruments.

Also relevant are judgments concerning the relative effectiveness of monetary and fiscal policies in achieving some desired behavior of aggregate demand. For example, an expansionary fiscal policy may be judged to be necessary to promote quick recovery from depression conditions but to be no more effective than monetary policy in restricting increases of demand.

The optimum mix of monetary and fiscal policies also depends in part on the nature of economic objectives and on their relative priorities. Suppose that it is possible to achieve some selected level of aggregate demand with various combinations of monetary and fiscal policies—with, say, some restrictive fiscal policy and some expansionary monetary policy or with some expansionary fiscal policy and some restrictive monetary policy. This level of aggregate demand can reflect various combinations of consumption and capital formation. If the objective is only to achieve some selected level of total output and employment, without regard to the distribution of output between consumption and capital formation, many different combinations of monetary and fiscal policies may be equally acceptable. But this may cease to be true if promotion of economic growth through a higher rate of capital formation is also an objective. For this purpose a restrictive fiscal policy and an easy monetary policy may be most appropriate. Large taxes relative to government expenditures for current purposes can be used to force the nation to consume a smaller part, and to save a larger part, of its total income; and an easy monetary policy, instituted to lower interest rates, can encourage the use of savings for capital formation.

A somewhat different case is that in which a nation wishes to raise aggregate demand for its output while it faces an undesired deficit in its balance of payments. Both expansionary fiscal policies and expansionary monetary policies tend to increase the deficit in the balance of payments to the extent that they succeed in raising aggregate demand, which in turn increases imports. But an expansionary monetary policy, which lowers interest rates, will also tend to increase capital outflows or at least to reduce capital inflows. In such a situation, an optimum policy mix may require more expansionary fiscal policies to raise domestic demand, together with a less expansionary monetary policy to support interest rates and attract capital inflows or at least to retard capital outflows.

These are but a few of the many considerations that determine the relative roles of monetary and fiscal policies. These relative roles have changed markedly in recent decades and are likely to continue to change with changes in the nature and relative priorities of economic objectives, with changes in attitudes toward the flexible use of fiscal policies for stabilization purposes, and with changes in our knowledge concerning the magnitudes and timing of responses to various types of both monetary and fiscal actions.

LESTER V. CHANDLER

[See also FISCAL POLICY and MONEY.]

BIBLIOGRAPHY

COMMISSION ON MONEY AND CREDIT 1961 *Money and Credit: Their Influence on Jobs, Prices and Growth.* Englewood Cliffs, N.J.: Prentice-Hall.

CULBERTSON, J. M. 1960 Friedman on the Lag in Effect of Monetary Policy. *Journal of Political Economy* 68: 617–621.

CULBERTSON, J. M. 1961 The Lag in Effect of Monetary

Policy: Reply. *Journal of Political Economy* 69:467–477.

FRIEDMAN, MILTON 1961 The Lag in Effect of Monetary Policy. *Journal of Political Economy* 69:447–466.

GREAT BRITAIN, COMMITTEE ON THE WORKING OF THE MONETARY SYSTEM 1959 *Report.* Papers by Command, Cmnd. 827. London: H. M. Stationery Office. → Known as the Radcliffe Report.

SCAMMELL, W. M. (1957) 1962 *International Monetary Policy.* 2d ed. London: Macmillan; New York: St. Martins.

YEAGER, LELAND B. (editor) 1962 *In Search of a Monetary Constitution.* Cambridge, Mass.: Harvard Univ. Press.

MONETARY REFORM
See under MONEY.

MONEY

Monetary theory is discussed in the first two articles under this entry and in LIQUIDITY PREFERENCE *and* INTEREST. *For monetary policy and institutions, see the last article under this entry and* BANKING; BANKING, CENTRAL; CREDIT; FINANCIAL INTERMEDIARIES; *and* MONETARY POLICY. *Related material is covered in* INFLATION AND DEFLATION. *For the international aspects of money, see* INTERNATIONAL MONETARY ECONOMICS.

I. GENERAL — Albert Gailord Hart
II. QUANTITY THEORY — Milton Friedman
III. VELOCITY OF CIRCULATION — Richard T. Selden
IV. MONETARY REFORM — Fred H. Klopstock

I
GENERAL

The term "money" has accumulated such a wealth of connotations and variant uses that it is perhaps more serviceable as an adjective rather than as a noun. The most useful definition of the term as a noun seems to be *an extremely liquid asset, measured in a standard unit of account and capable with certainty of discharging debts expressed in that unit*. As applied to the United States at the present time, this definition includes in money the circulating stock of metallic small change, Federal Reserve Notes and other paper currency, and also the stock of commercial bank deposits with checking privileges.

Since the definition just proposed makes "moneyness" a matter of degree (because of the relativity inherent in the terms "extremely liquid" and "with certainty"), it may be construed either to include or to exclude from the stock of money in the United States such liquid claims as certificates of deposit issued by commercial banks, Treasury bills, savings deposits, and "shares" in savings and loan associa-

tions. Wherever the frontier between money and what the International Monetary Fund in its compilations calls "quasi money," we must always expect to find some types of quasi money which rank almost at the monetary extreme of the relativistic scales of "extremely liquid" and "capable with certainty of discharging debts."

The proposed definition implies differences in the list of things which constitute money—between different societies and through time within a given society. In rare cases where there are unusually sharp cleavages in attitudes and expectations within a given society, it may even imply different moneys for different groups within that society.

The underlying concepts "unit of account," "debt," and "liquid asset" obviously have to be interpreted to put content into the proposed definition of money. *Unit of account* means a unit (such as the U.S. dollar) which by convention (whether with or without supporting pressure from government) is accepted in a society to value commodities and services sold, to compute costs, to reckon wealth, and to state debts. Such units have been used to facilitate thinking about economic matters through much of human history. In Biblical annals, for example, we find as early as Genesis 23 an account of Abraham buying a field "for the full price . . . [of] four hundred shekels of silver according to the weights current among the merchants"; and the New Testament pictures Jesus as taking it for granted that the unsophisticated people to whom he addressed his parables could readily think in monetary units. As may be seen from the fact that the more venerable units of account (shekels, pounds, and the like) correspond to units of weight, most societies until recently have thought of their units of account as expressing the value of a stated weight of gold or silver; but since paper money came into general use in the nineteenth century, units of account have become more and more abstract. It should be noted that a society at a given time may be using one or more units of account.

A *debt* is an obligation on the part of one economic unit (person, firm, or government body) to another, expressed in a standard unit of account. For the debtor, a debt is negative wealth—but expressed in the unit of account, whereas other types of negative wealth (such as a contract to deliver 1,000 bushels of wheat next month) are expressed in physical units. Since every debt obligation is two-sided, the obverse of each debt payable is a claim receivable, which constitutes an asset (wealth) for the creditor. Money in most present-day societies consists chiefly of claims upon debtors who are central governments, central or commercial banks, or other credit institutions.

For an asset to be *liquid*, it must be either money or else something which quickly and with a high degree of certainty can be converted into a known amount of money. Since "quickly" and "with a high degree of certainty" are both relative expressions, assets can evidently be more or less liquid. The concept of a "liquid asset," furthermore, is subjective; it is defined from the point of view of the holder—the creditor, if the asset is a debt claim. In rating assets as more or less liquid, therefore, we should not ask whether *all units* of such a unit could *in fact* be converted into money, but whether *each unit* can be so converted *in the opinion of its holder*. This view admits of a shift of opinion through time. Such a shift may be quite sudden, with holders today viewing as illiquid assets which a short time ago they viewed as highly liquid. It seems clear that there were such sudden shifts in the liquidity attributed to deposits in individual banks during the great epidemic of bank failures in the United States in 1930–1933. There may also have been such a sudden shift in the liquidity attributed to government securities at the time of the "monetary accord" of 1951, which terminated the rigid support of government securities prices by the Federal Reserve.

Most liquid assets in the United States consist of short-term claims upon the national government, upon the Federal Reserve banks, upon commercial banks, or upon "nonbank credit institutions"—particularly mutual savings banks, savings and loan associations, and, in the view of some analysts, also credit unions and life insurance companies. For some holders and upon some occasions, liquid assets may include inventories of commodities, short-term claims upon firms which are not credit institutions, longer-term government securities, and even listed stocks. For holders in small countries, a large part of the stock of liquid assets may consist of claims upon banks, government bodies, etc., outside the country in question. Such use of foreign claims may or may not involve the use of foreign units of account in domestic dealings and calculations.

The meaning of money may be illuminated further by reference to two other terms, not used in the proposed definition. *Legal tender* is that which is established by governmental rules as a satisfactory medium for settling debts in case of dispute. Anything that is legal tender must be money; but often (as with checking deposits in the United States) large parts of the money stock may be excluded from legal tender. But one might paraphrase the definition of money as "that which is by custom treated like legal tender."

A *monetary standard* may be defined as a fixed relation between the unit of account and the standard commodity. Such a standard is, in the inspired definition of D. H. Robertson, an arrangement by which "a country keeps the value of its monetary unit and the value of a defined weight of gold [or other standard commodity] at an equality with each other" (1922, p. 134). In a "full" gold or silver standard, such as existed in many countries before World War I, this equality of value was maintained through the free convertibility of monetary metal, metal coins, and paper money. Such an arrangement based on gold (or possibly on a bimetallic standard with both gold and silver coins of full weight) was regarded as normal for a developed industrial economy. With the disappearance of gold coins, the restriction in most centers of dealings in monetary gold bars to "official" dealers, and the fading of the tradition of permanence in monetary arrangements, the standard has been modified. The United States today may be described as operating a "limited, provisional, gold-bullion standard," and similar descriptions would apply to the other major industrial countries. Many countries choose to treat the currency units of other countries as their "standard commodities" and may be described as on a "sterling-exchange standard" or a "dollar-exchange standard." [*See* INTERNATIONAL MONETARY ECONOMICS, *article on* INTERNATIONAL MONETARY ORGANIZATION.]

It should be noted that many economists prefer to define money more informally than is proposed above: simply as "that which constitutes means of payment." This is an easy and useful way to convey a correct general impression. But it is hard to give a precise meaning to "means of payment." Strictly, the immediate means of payment for most goods and services sold is the establishment of "book credit": the buyer recognizes a debt to the seller for merchandise supplied or for services rendered. (In the broad sweep of economic operations, "cash and carry" transactions are exceptional.) But no economist finds it convenient to regard book credit as the primary form of money. To adopt the means-of-payment definition without regarding book credit as money involves casuistry to the effect that goods are not "really" paid for until the book credit in question has been settled by check or by a transfer of paper currency.

Another often-proposed simple definition of money is "that which a seller will accept from a buyer whose credit standing is unknown." This may be a very useful formulation in countries where payments are normally made by *Giro* (a payments system used in parts of Europe). But it has the defect of ruling out checking deposits as a form of money—a defect which is fatal for analysis of the economy of the United States and a number of other advanced countries.

Analytical role of money in economics. One of the key problems of present-day economics is the role of money and other liquid assets in the structure of economic decisions—particularly in the decisions of firms and households to save and to invest in durable real assets, such as factories, machinery, houses, and vehicles. Broadly speaking, the funds available to a firm or household for investment within a stated period consist of its saving during the period (taking saving *gross*, to include depreciation charges and the like), plus its net borrowing, plus any reduction it may make in its holdings of liquid assets. In any stated situation, there is usually something to be gained for the firm or household by investing more, something to be gained by reducing rather than increasing debt, and also something to be gained (in the form of increased consumption, or of increased distribution of a firm's profits to its owners) by saving less. Given the size of current income, the more ample the stock of liquid assets, the more it is possible to realize all these benefits simultaneously. The scarcer the liquid assets, the more it is necessary to choose to forgo one benefit in order to reap another. Thus, adequacy of liquid assets in the possession of a firm or household is viewed as an incentive to invest, while inadequacy of liquid assets is viewed as an incentive to save and to curtail investment.

It is plain from experience that a "spendthrift" response to the possession of money and other liquid assets—that is, a course of management which outspends receipts so heavily as to bring liquid holdings down rapidly to a crisis point—is very rare. In most societies, the firms, households, and governments which account for the bulk of wealth holdings and of economic operations feel a need to maintain substantial holdings of money and other liquid assets. If we measure money by the sum of hand-to-hand currency plus checking deposits (which, as we saw at the outset, is a measurement which conforms fairly well to the proposed definition), the private sector of the U.S. economy in recent years has held a money stock roughly equivalent to a quarter-year's gross national product and, in addition, has held other liquid assets equivalent roughly to a half-year's product.

Motives for holding money. Monetary economists have developed an interesting array of hypotheses about the motives for holding money. Prior to the great depression of the 1930s, emphasis was placed primarily on the *transactions motive*— the need to hold a stock of money so as to smooth out the irregularities of inflow and outflow and to carry the holder past a foreseen trough in his money holdings. During the 1930s, under the leadership of John Maynard Keynes, emphasis shifted to the *speculative motive*—the benefit of holding money while one waits for an expected fall in the price of some alternative asset one may be interested in buying. Some such element in monetary theory was clearly needed to interpret the sharp fall during the 1930s of the "velocity of circulation of money"—the ratio of money payments to money stock—which would have to remain fairly constant if the transactions motive were dominant. Without abandoning either of these previously emphasized motives, monetary economists in recent years have put increasing emphasis on the *precautionary motive*—the benefit of holding money to mitigate uncertainty. An attractive explanation of the benefit derived from keeping a margin of safety in one's money holdings is the principle of linkage of risk. If a firm or household lacks such a margin, an unexpected unfavorable development is likely to create a crisis that will bring on further unfavorable events. But if the adverse effect of the first event can be taken in stride, the linkage of risk is weakened, and the further unfavorable events may be averted.

Except for very short-term aspects of the transactions motive, all these motives for holding money can be served at least moderately well by holding some type of nonmonetary liquid asset. Money as ordinarily defined consists of elements (paper currency and checking deposits) which yield no money income, while nonmonetary liquid assets do yield such income. Hence, it pays the holder to substitute other liquid assets for money up to the point at which the next remaining unit of money has net advantages equal to the interest income forgone. A practical consequence of this fact is that the financial institutions whose liabilities constitute the public's nonmonetary liquid assets have an incentive to design the claims they offer so as to present attractive combinations of liquidity and income. The working of this incentive to narrow the qualitative gap between money and money substitutes may be seen in the rapid development during the 1960s of "certificates of deposit" and "capital notes," which are offered on the open market by commercial banks. A theoretical consequence of the same fact is that it becomes interesting to view the demand for money in opportunity-cost terms. Developing a Keynesian insight, many monetary economists center their analysis on a *liquidity-preference function*, which treats the stock of money the public will choose to hold as an inverse function of the interest rate which could be earned on alternative uses of funds [see LIQUIDITY PREFERENCE].

Creation of money. The processes which bring stocks of money into being, and which distribute them among various holders, are best seen in terms of *transactions* among various sectors of a country's economy. In the first stage of analysis, it is convenient to recognize two sectors only. The first is called the "nonbank public"—made up of households, firms other than banks, and local governments; it is through effects upon incentives in this sector that monetary influences on saving and investment are supposed to work. The second sector is the "money-generating sector"—made up of the national government, the central bank (in the United States, the Federal Reserve System), and the commercial banks (those which include among their liabilities deposits that can be used in payment by check or *Giro* order). The stock of money constitutes an asset for the nonbank public and a liability for the money-generating sector.

A simple way to view the processes which generate money is to think of the flow of checks and its effect on the holdings of the nonbank public. Any check which is drawn by one member of the nonbank public and is payable to another member has a net effect of zero upon the total money stock. The payee enlarges his holding of money when he deposits the check, but the drawer's account is necessarily reduced by an identical amount, so the total is unchanged. (Transitory nominal changes may arise from variations in the "float" of checks which have been drawn and not yet debited, since there is often a spread of several days between the dates on which withdrawals and deposits are entered in bank records and in the checkbooks of depositors.) But net effects on the money stock are not zero when the checks cross the boundary between the two sectors. For example, when a government employee deposits his paycheck, it will not be debited against the account of any other member of the nonbank public, so that the transaction is money-increasing. In the other direction, if a business firm draws a check to repay a bank loan, this check is not deposited in the account of any other member of the nonbank public, so that the transaction is money-decreasing. Transactions in both directions across the frontier between the nonbank public and the money-generating sector go on continuously, and the net change in the money stock depends on the net difference between the money-increasing flow and the money-decreasing flow.

It should be noted in passing that the situation is complicated by the presence of liabilities of the money-generating sector which are not treated as part of the money stock. The government employee, for example, might have deposited his paycheck in a savings account at his bank instead of in his checking account. To deal with this complication, one may, like Milton Friedman (see Friedman & Schwartz 1963), adopt a working definition of money which includes as money the time deposits of commercial banks. Or one may (like the International Monetary Fund) adopt a concept of "quasi money," changes in which are viewed as an alternative use of "potential money" generated by net payments from the money-generating sector to the nonbank public.

Transactions in either direction between the two sectors may be *on income account* or *on wealth-transfer account*. The government paycheck referred to above is an income-account transaction; so is a check to pay for current products of the private sector which are bought for government use, or a dividend check to a bank stockholder. In the other direction, checks to pay taxes or to pay interest on bank loans may be regarded as income-account payments *from* the nonbank public *to* the money-generating sector. Wealth-transfer transactions may be represented by checks drawn by members of the nonbank public to pay for their subscriptions to newly issued government securities or, in the other direction, by checks drawn to pay for open-market purchases of government securities by the Federal Reserve from nonbank sellers. With minor exceptions, income-account transactions which affect the stock of money are transactions that figure in the social accounts among the receipts and expenditures of the central government and come into the domain of fiscal policy, while wealth-transfer transactions which affect the stock of money are bank-loan or government-debt transactions that clearly lie within the domain of monetary policy. A basic point of dispute between economists who think largely in terms of fiscal policy and those who are sometimes called "monetary monists" is whether the effect of an increment of money stock will be different according to whether it originates in an income-account or in a wealth-transfer-account transaction.

Theories of the supply of money. Theories of the supply of money center upon wealth-transfer transactions carried on by commercial banks. Income-account transactions of the government are seen as by-products of fiscal policy, and wealth-transfer transactions by the treasury and central bank are viewed in terms of policy decisions rather than of the more or less impersonal response mechanisms attributed to the banking subsector.

Particularly in the United States, with its wide dispersion of activity among unit banks, one must view the creation of money by bank activity as a mass phenomenon directed by incentives and restrictions, rather than as a simple decision of high policy like, for example, a cut in federal income tax rates. For this part of our analysis, we must look inside the "money-generating sector" and distinguish the commercial banks from the "bank-reserve-generating subsector" made up of the national government and the central bank. Commercial banks have a continuous incentive to carry out money-increasing transactions—that is, to expand their loans and investments—because their income arises as interest on these assets. Furthermore, there is ordinarily an available supply of such assets—for loans, a "fringe of unsatisfied borrowers"; for investments, a mass of bonds suitable for bank ownership that are held by the nonbank public and can be bought on the open market. Banks are free to respond to this incentive only insofar as they have a margin over reserve requirements in their holdings of reserve balances at Federal Reserve banks (plus their vault cash) or as they are willing to borrow reserves by discount at the Federal Reserve banks in the face of various deterrents [see BANKING, CENTRAL].

The central bank is able to facilitate the expansion of bank assets, and thus of the money stock, or to apply pressure toward contraction. The Federal Reserve System has authority within wide limits to vary legal reserve requirements. Furthermore, the total mass of reserves can be increased by Federal Reserve open-market purchases of government securities or decreased by open-market sales. The deterrents to discounting can be altered by varying the official discount rate or by official "moral suasion." True, there are certain forces outside central bank control which change the bank-reserve position—notably changes in the flow of international payments which expand or contract the reserve funds of commercial banks as well as the international-liquidity position of the country as a whole, and flows of hand-to-hand currency in and out of circulation. But on the whole, these forces can be offset or reinforced by measures at the disposal of the central bank.

For any individual commercial bank, the limits on its expansion of loans and investments within any short period are determined by its initial reserve position (the excess over requirements of the reserves it holds, plus the amount it is willing to borrow), plus the amount of additional deposits it can attract within the period, less the reserves required against those additional deposits. But if we shift our attention from the individual bank to the commercial banking system as a whole, the limits on expansion become less than one might think at first glance, because for the system as a whole the amount of additional deposits which can be "attracted" will be almost the same as the amount "created" by transactions which increase earning assets for the banks as a whole. (The only major difference between the amount created and the amount that can be attracted is the part of any increment in its total holding of money—hand-to-hand money plus commercial bank deposits—which the public will insist on taking in hand-to-hand currency.) The system as a whole can go on expanding so long as there are still commercial banks which have excess reserves or are willing to increase their discounts at the Federal Reserve. According to the assumptions one makes about the division of the increment into hand-to-hand money, checking ("demand") deposits, and time deposits, the unused lending power implied by a given amount of initial excess reserves may be calculated as anywhere between three and five times the initial excess reserves.

For any other class of credit institutions, the limits on expansion of earning assets are more like those for the individual commercial bank than like those for commercial banks as a whole. An acceleration of mortgage lending by savings and loan associations, for example, does very little to increase the amount of funds which savers hold at such associations. If these associations obtain a million dollars of excess reserves (for example, through discounts at a Federal Home Loan bank), the additional amount they can lend is increased by almost exactly a million dollars. Thus, the initiative in nonbank credit expansion comes largely from savers who decide to entrust their funds to these institutions—although of course the institutions have some scope for making themselves attractive to savers.

To the extent that society reorganizes itself to make more use of such financial intermediaries, liquid assets expand relative to activity. For example, suppose that a group of savers have been in the habit of using their flow of saving from year to year to erect apartment houses and rent flats to newly married couples. If these savers now decide to place their funds with savings-and-loan associations, which in turn lend to newly married couples who buy new houses, the amount of real activity in housing investment may be unaltered. But the savers (who have acquired savings-and-loan "shares" redeemable on short notice instead of the ownership of apartment houses) will have their assets in more liquid form, while the liquidity of the new homeowners will not be more impaired by the prospect of paying amortization and interest on their mortgages than it would have been by the prospect of paying corresponding apartment rent. Accordingly, the economy will be more liquid at the end of a period in which savings-and-loan mortgage financing is substituted for direct investment by savers in new buildings. The argument is similar for other kinds of credit-institution expansion. [*See* FINANCIAL INTERMEDIARIES.]

The economic impact of money. Monetary economics offers a wide range of competing views about the impact of monetary forces on prices and economic activity. In good part, differences of view relate to the interpretation of somewhat ambiguous historical and statistical evidence. In principle, the adherents of each of today's monetary schools admit the *conceivability* of a world in which the other schools' favorite channel of monetary influence would be of the highest importance, but each school tends to argue that *realistically and quantitatively* its favorite channel of influence is the most important by a decisive margin. Furthermore, the different schools disagree sharply at the level of monetary policy. Hence, a correct impression can probably be given by contrasting several distinct types of theory—disregarding the minor concessions made by each school to the others.

To clear the ground, we may examine briefly several discredited theories—held in the past by influential economists but without professional support today. A common element of these discredited theories, which today's monetary economists are at one in repudiating, is the view (stated explicitly by many of the older theorists and implied by the others) that the real volume of economic activity is governed entirely by nonmonetary forces, that the role of monetary analysis is solely to explain changes in the "purchasing power of money" (that is, the reciprocal of some broad index number of prices). Each of the discredited theories has in addition at least one other major element that today's monetary economists all find unacceptable. *Statist theories* viewed the value of money as determined by an act of will on the part of government, whereas observation suggests that changes in the price level ordinarily occur against the will of government. *Commodity theories* viewed the value of money as transferred from commodity markets for gold and silver, which could be interpreted by means of a supply-and-demand analysis essentially similar to that applicable to iron or cotton. In view of the increasingly abstract character of money and of peculiarities of the gold market which stem precisely from the monetary role of gold, it seems more reasonable to describe the commodity aspect of gold as dominated by the monetary aspect. The *classical quantity theory of money* (as it flourished before 1929) took the velocity of circulation as a constant. Today all schools, including the modern quantity theorists, regard velocity as a variable

whose behavior must be explained by monetary theory.

While each of the foregoing theories must be regarded as discredited as a general theory of money, present-day economists make much use of special-purpose theories which contain important elements of these older theories. For example, there is some affinity with statist theories in the widely used models which assume price levels to be constant or which take some key element of the price structure (for example, the level of wages) as a policy variable. In considering the probable long-run effects of suggestions that international monetary relations should be "reformed" along lines closer to the traditional gold standard, today's economists are not such purists as to refuse to take into account the costs of producing gold, as well as the speculative attitudes of private and governmental holders of gold. In taking these factors into account, they use market analysis techniques similar to those used for other durable commodities. The classical quantity theory can still be applied with confidence to situations in which changes in the money stock are of enormous magnitude. If, as sometimes happens, a country's money stock is multiplied by 10 or by 100 within a few years, monetary economists predict a change in the price level of the same order of magnitude—although many monetary economists would not be much surprised if some tenfold increases in the money stock were accompanied by fivefold increases in prices and others by twentyfold increases.

Present-day schools of monetary economics may be sorted out fairly well by their preferences in devising models that explain the general course of economic activity and prices in a market economy. At one extreme stands the "modern quantity theory" school, typified by Milton Friedman. It pictures changes in the stock of money as the dominant force in any explanation of the course of money payments and draws the policy inference that the sovereign prescription for steady growth without inflation is to engineer a steady growth rate for the money stock about equal to the growth of the economy's productive potential. In this theory, velocity is treated neither as a constant nor as an exogenous variable but, rather, as endogenous to the system of interrelations used in the theory. Nevertheless, the forces that govern velocity are not pictured as lending themselves to any sort of policy intervention which might usefully supplement the regulation of the quantity of money.

At the other extreme from quantity-theory models stand models that analyze the behavior of economic activity and the price level without including any variable that corresponds to the stock of money. It would be hard to name any economists who would make it a matter of principle to go to this extreme. But the stress, in teaching and in popularized statements about economic policy, on investment as an exogenous variable, and on the determination of activity by investment (mediated by a "propensity to consume"), is so heavy that this extreme view is likely to be taken as the sum of academic wisdom about macroeconomics by a large proportion of those who have been exposed to economic pedagogy or advice. The associated view of economic policy is that fiscal policy is all-sufficient and monetary policy is inconsequential.

Much more representative of professional opinion as the academic monetary economists would like it to be understood is what may be called the *interest rate school*. On the theoretical side, the models typical of this view present "the" rate of interest as a major influence on investment and, through investment, on economic activity. In policy terms, this school treats the interest rate as the monetary influence on activity par excellence and does not concern itself with any direct influence of the stock of money on activity. (In relation to fiscal policy, the position of this school is likely to be eclectic, looking to an interaction of interest rate policy with such fiscal-policy variables as public expenditure and tax rates.) In the analytical models of this school, a peripheral liquidity-preference function expresses a relation between the money stock and the interest rate. The policy implication drawn may be that the interest rate can be regulated through the stock of money, or that if an appropriate rate of interest is adopted, the stock of money can be allowed to adapt itself to this rate without disturbing other aspects of the economy.

Some variants of the interest-rate approach pay a good deal of attention to possible changes within the structure of interest rates: for example, possibilities of relative changes between the interest rates on home mortgages and those on foreign funds invested in treasury bills in New York. This view merges into another position, which in principle is quite distinct from the interest-rate school: that of the *credit-availability school*. The credit-availability doctrine is implicit in many official statements by the monetary authorities of the United States and other countries and has been usefully made explicit by Robert Roosa (1951). This view is that various types of investment may be powerfully influenced by the amount of funds the credit machinery makes available to finance home construction, inventory holding, exports, etc. Relative movements of interest rates may be useful indicators of the forces at work but will not themselves be the effective variable. The stock of money

as such does not figure in explanations of activity along these lines, but changes in the stock of money will be by-products of transactions called for to carry out appropriate financing. The size of the monetary expansion that accompanies a given course of economic activity and prices, in this view, may vary substantially according to the financing of the economic activity.

Despite the lively controversy among schools, it is hard to see their views as philosophically irreconcilable. "Pure" models of one or another of the types just sketched illuminate the implications of various hypotheses, can help guide the search for evidence, and may offer useful special-purpose models for work on economic diagnosis and economic policy. But advocacy of any of these views as all-sufficient can be seriously misleading. This is particularly true, in the judgment of the author, of the "monetary monism" shown by advocates of the modern quantity theory approach and of some variants of the interest-structure approach—advocates who try to explain the flow of payments and economic activity without reference to such variables as taxes, accelerator effects of activity upon investment, changes in the impact of the "rest of the world," and so forth. A certain healthy eclecticism, with willingness to be guided by the evidence in the choice of theoretical simplifications, would seem appropriate in the present stage of monetary economics.

ALBERT GAILORD HART

BIBLIOGRAPHY

FRIEDMAN, MILTON; and SCHWARTZ, ANNA J. 1963 *A Monetary History of the United States: 1867–1960*. National Bureau of Economic Research, Studies in Business Cycles, No. 12. Princeton Univ. Press.
KEYNES, JOHN MAYNARD (1930) 1958–1960 *A Treatise on Money*. 2 vols. London: Macmillan. → Volume 1: *The Pure Theory of Money*. Volume 2: *The Applied Theory of Money*.
KEYNES, JOHN MAYNARD 1936 *The General Theory of Employment, Interest and Money*. London: Macmillan. → A paperback edition was published in 1965 by Harcourt.
NUSSBAUM, ARTHUR (1939) 1950 *Money in the Law*. 2d ed. Chicago: Foundation Press.
PATINKIN, DON (1956) 1965 *Money, Interest, and Prices: An Integration of Monetary and Value Theory*. 2d ed. New York: Harper.
ROBERTSON, D. H. (1922) 1959 *Money*. Rev. ed. Univ. of Chicago Press.
ROOSA, ROBERT V. 1951 Interest Rates and the Central Bank. Pages 270–295 in *Money, Trade and Economic Growth: In Honor of John Henry Williams*. New York: Macmillan.

II

QUANTITY THEORY

Since men first began to write systematically about economic matters they have devoted special attention to the wide movements in the general level of prices that have intermittently occurred. Two alternative explanations have usually been offered. One has attributed the changes in prices to changes in the quantity of money. The other has attributed the changes in prices to war or to profiteers or to rises in wages or to some other special circumstance of the particular time and place and has regarded any accompanying change in the quantity of money as a common consequence of the same special circumstance. The first explanation has generally been referred to as the quantity theory of money, although that designation conceals the variety of forms the explanation has taken, the different levels of sophistication on which it has been developed, and the wide range of the claims that have been made for its applicability.

The broad outlines of the quantity theory of money were fully developed by the eighteenth century. The contemporary economist can still read David Hume's essay "Of Money" (1752) with pleasure and profit and find few if any errors of commission. Reasonably satisfactory attempts at mathematical formulation have been traced back to the eighteenth century (see the references in Marget 1938). And certainly the mathematical formulation given by Simon Newcomb, the eminent astronomer, in 1886 is entirely modern, excepting only the particular symbols used. Knut Wicksell published a highly sophisticated analysis in 1898 that, because it was written in German, had less influence than its excellence justified. The two formulations of the quantity theory that have most influenced modern thinking both date from the end of the nineteenth century (although the dates of their publication are later): Irving Fisher's transactions version (1911) and the Cambridge cash-balances version, attributed to Alfred Marshall (1923) and Arthur C. Pigou (1917). After some introductory remarks, this article discusses these two versions and then examines the Keynesian attack on the quantity theory, the post-Keynesian reformulation, empirical evidence bearing on the quantity theory, and finally some policy implications of the quantity theory.

In its most rigid and unqualified form the quantity theory asserts strict proportionality between the quantity of what is regarded as money and the level of prices. Hardly anyone has held the theory in that form, although statements capable of being so interpreted have often been made in the heat of argument or for expository simplicity. Virtually every quantity theorist has recognized that changes in the quantity of money that correspond to changes in the volume of trade or of output have no tendency to produce changes in prices. Nearly as many have recognized also that changes in the willingness of the community to hold money can occur for a variety of reasons and can introduce disparities between changes in the quantity of money per unit of trade or of output and changes in prices. What quantity theorists have held in common is the belief that these qualifications are of secondary importance for substantial changes in either prices or the quantity of money, so that the one will not in fact occur without the other.

The quantity theory in all its versions rests on a distinction between the *nominal* quantity of money and the *real* quantity of money. The nominal quantity of money is the quantity expressed in whatever units are used to designate money—talents, shekels, pounds, francs, lire, drachmas, dollars, and so on. The real quantity of money is the quantity expressed in terms of the volume of goods and services that the money will purchase.

There is no unique way to express the real quantity of money. One way of expressing it, one that is widely used, is in terms of some specified standard basket of goods and services. That is what is implicitly done when the real quantity of money is calculated by dividing the nominal quantity by a price index. The standard basket is then the basket whose components are used as weights in computing the price index—generally the basket purchased by some reference group in a base year.

Another way of expressing the real quantity of money is in terms of the time duration of the flows of goods and services the money could purchase. For a household, for example, the real quantity of money can be expressed in terms of the number of weeks of the household's average level of consumption that it could finance with its money balances or, alternatively, in terms of the number of weeks of its average income to which its money balances are equal. For a business enterprise, the real quantity of money it holds can be expressed in terms of the number of weeks of its average purchases or of its average sales or of its average expenditures on final productive services (net value added) to which its money balances are equal. For the community as a whole, the real quantity of money can be expressed in terms of the number of weeks of aggregate transactions of the community or aggregate net output of the community to which it is equal.

For the community, attention has generally centered not on the real quantity of money but on a velocity of circulation—which can be regarded as the reciprocal of a particular expression of the real quantity of money. The ratio, for example, of the aggregate annual transactions of a community to its stock of money is termed the "transactions velocity of circulation of money," since it gives the number of times the stock of money would have to "turn over" in a year to accomplish all transactions; similarly, the ratio of annual income to the stock of money is termed "income velocity." In every case the calculation of the real quantity of money or of velocity is made at the set of prices prevailing at the date to which the calculation refers. These prices are the bridge between the nominal and the real quantity of money.

The quantity theory takes for granted that what ultimately matters to holders of money is the real quantity rather than the nominal quantity of money they hold and that there is some fairly definite real quantity of money that people wish to hold under any given circumstances. Suppose the nominal quantity that people hold happens to correspond at current prices to a real quantity larger than that which they wish to hold. Individuals will then seek to dispose of what they regard as their excess money balances; they will try to pay out a larger sum for the purchase of securities, goods, and services, for the repayment of debts, and as gifts than they are receiving from the corresponding sources. However, one man's expenditures are another's receipts. One man can reduce his nominal money balances only by persuading someone else to increase his. The community as a whole cannot in general spend more than it receives.

The community's attempt to do so will nonetheless have important effects. If prices and income are free to change, the attempt to spend more will raise the nominal volume of expenditures and receipts, which will lead to a bidding up of prices and perhaps also to an increase in output. If prices are fixed by custom or by government edict, the attempt to spend more either will be matched by an increase in goods and services or will produce "shortages" and "queues." These in turn will raise the effective prices and are likely sooner or later to force changes in official prices. The initial excess of money balances will therefore tend to be eliminated, even though there is no change in the nominal quantity, by either a reduction in the real quantity held through price rises or an increase in the real quantity desired through output increases. Conversely, if nominal balances happen to correspond to a smaller real quantity at current prices than people wish to hold, people will seek to spend less than they are receiving. They cannot in the aggregate do so. But their attempt will in the process lower nominal expenditures and receipts, driving down prices or output and either raising the real balances held or lowering the real balances desired.

It is clear from this discussion that changes in prices and nominal income can be produced either by changes in the real balances that people wish to hold or by changes in the nominal balances available for them to hold. Indeed it is a tautology, summarized in the famous quantity equation (to which we shall return) that all changes in nominal income can be attributed to one or the other—just as a change in the price of any good can always be attributed to a change in either demand or supply. The quantity theory is not, however, this tautology. It is, rather, the empirical generalization that changes in desired real balances (in the demand for money) tend to proceed slowly and gradually or to be the result of events set in train by prior changes in supply, whereas, in contrast, substantial changes in the supply of nominal balances can and frequently do occur independently of any changes in demand. The conclusion is that substantial changes in prices or nominal income are almost invariably the result of changes in the nominal supply of money.

Variants of the quantity theory of money are distinguished by the variables that are regarded as most important in determining the real quantity of money that people desire to hold and by the analysis of the process whereby any discrepancy between actual and desired real balances works itself out. The chief issues that have occasioned controversy and conflict are perhaps the definition of money, the importance of transactions motives versus asset motives in the holding of money, the importance of substitution between money and other assets expressed in nominal terms as compared with substitution between money and real goods and services, and the speed and character of the dynamic process of adjustment. We shall have occasion to comment on these below.

Fisher's transactions approach

The quantity equation in transactions form. Every payment made by one economic unit in an economy—household, business enterprise, or governmental organization—to another can be regarded as the product of a price and a quantity: wage per week times number of weeks, price of a good times number of units of the good, dividend per share times number of shares, and so on. The total volume of transactions during a period of time can thus be regarded as equal to the sum of a large number of such products, say $\sum p_i t_i$, where p_i is the price and t_i the quantity for the ith transaction. Let P be a suitably chosen average of the prices, and let T be a suitably chosen aggregate of the quantities. We then have

(1)   Total volume of transactions $= PT = \sum p_i t_i$.

The total volume of transactions can also be viewed in terms of the medium of exchange used to effectuate them. Let M be the total quantity of money in the economy and V the average number of times each unit of money is used to effectuate a transaction during the year (the transactions velocity). We then have

(2)   Total volume of transactions $= MV$,

or, putting (1) and (2) together, the famous quantity equation

(3) $MV = PT$.

Each side of this equation can be broken into subcategories: the right-hand side into different categories of transactions and the left-hand side into payments in different form. Fisher and later writers emphasized in particular the subdivision of the left-hand side into two categories of payments, those effected by the transfer of hand-to-hand currency (including coin) and those effected by the transfer of deposits. Let M stand solely for the volume of currency and V for the velocity of currency, M' for the volume of deposits and V' for the velocity of deposits. We then can write

(4) $MV + M'V' = PT$.

One reason for the emphasis on this division was the persistent dispute about whether the term "money" should include only currency or deposits as well—this dispute was at the center of the banking school–currency school controversy that raged in England in the nineteenth century. Another reason was the direct availability of figures on $M'V'$ from bank records of clearings or of debits to accounts so that it was and is possible to calculate V' in a way that it is not possible to calculate V.

As they stand, equations (3) and (4) are identities: The V of (3) or the V and V' of (4) are defined as the numbers having the property that they render the equations correct. If P changes from one time period to the next, then so must one or more of the other terms in the equations. That is an arithmetic necessity, not an economic proposition. The identities are useful for economic analysis because they offer a useful classification of the factors at work, a classification into categories each of which contains factors largely independent of those in the other categories.

The categories in the quantity equation. Consider the fourfold classification in equation (3).

Transactions. The physical volume of transactions is denoted by T. It is determined by the resources available to the economy, the efficiency with which they are used, the degree of integration or disintegration of the economy (which determines the number of transactions involved in the production and sale of final goods), and so on. These are the basic physical and operational characteristics of the economy. All quantity theorists, at least since Hume, have recognized that changes in the stock of money may have transitional effects on T. However, they have generally regarded the average level of T and long-run changes in T as largely independent of the quantity of money, although not of the existence of a money economy.

Price level. The price level, which is the object of investigation, is denoted by P. It has generally been regarded as the resultant of other forces rather than as itself having any important element of autonomy. Cost-push or profit-push theories of inflation treat it as being to some extent independently determined. Under a regime of widespread government price fixing, it clearly does have some measure of autonomy.

Stock of money. The stock of money in nominal units is denoted by M. Its precise definition, as noted before, has been the subject of much controversy. The transactions approach makes it seem natural to define money in terms of its function as a medium of exchange and to include only those means of payments generally acceptable in discharge of debts. Under a gold standard, specie was regarded as money par excellence, and questions were raised about extending the definition to include paper money and then demand deposits transferable by check. Today these would generally be included in the definitions, but there is much controversy about the treatment of other deposits, such as time deposits and savings deposits. On transactions lines, it is argued that such deposits cannot be used to discharge debts without first being converted into either currency or demand deposits. One answer to this argument is that it is also true of some items that all are willing to regard as money. For example, in the United States, $10,000 is the largest denomination of currency. Such a currency note can be used to effectuate few transactions without first being converted into smaller denominations. No issue of principle is involved. However M is defined, equation (3) remains valid, provided V is appropriately defined. The issue is one of the usefulness of one or another definition: what definition of M will have the empirical property of rendering the forces determining the other symbols in the equation as nearly independent as possible of those determining M?

Whatever the precise definition of M, the factors determining it depend critically on the monetary system and are largely independent of the forces determining T. Two main cases should be distinguished: a commodity standard, of which a gold standard is the most important historical example, and a fiduciary standard.

Under a gold standard the amount of money in the gold standard world is determined by the total existing amount of gold, the fraction used as money, and the institutional arrangements determining the superstructure of claims to gold, in the form of currency or deposits, that can be erected on any given stock of gold. Changes in the amount of money depend on costs of producing various quantities of gold, the demand for gold for nonmonetary purposes, and the financial arrangements for issuing fiduciary claims to gold. For any one country the situation is somewhat different: the quantity of money is a dependent rather than an independent variable. It must be whatever quantity is consistent with levels of prices and incomes that will maintain balance in its international payments. Gold inflows or outflows tend to keep it at that quantity.

Under a fiduciary standard the amount of money is ultimately under the control of the monetary authorities. In practice these authorities have always been governmental agencies. Although they have had the power to control the stock of money, they frequently have not stated their objectives in these terms but have let the stock of money be whatever was consistent with some alternative objective (e.g., given exchange rates or given interest rates).

Under either the gold or the fiduciary standard the factors determining M are connected only loosely, if at all, with those we have considered as affecting directly either P or T. It is precisely this clearly perceived independence of the factors determining the quantity of money that has rendered the quantity theory so attractive to economists.

Velocity of circulation. We now come to V, the velocity of circulation. This is the core of the quantity theory. It is determined by whatever factors affect, on the one hand, the amount of money people want to hold and, on the other, their ability to make their actual money balances equal their desired balances.

The transactions approach makes it natural to emphasize payment practices: the frequency with which people are paid, the irregularity of receipts and payments, and so on. However, such payment practices themselves seem to be largely explained by the willingness of people to hold money. For example, during periods of rapid inflation, when it is costly to hold money, pay periods consistently tend to become more frequent.

It is convenient to postpone a fuller consideration of the factors determining velocity until we discuss the post-Keynesian formulation in terms of the demand for money. Here it suffices to point out that

Fisher and other earlier quantity theorists explicitly recognized that velocity would be affected by, among other factors, the rate of interest and also the rate of change of prices. They recognized that both high rates of interest and rapidly rising prices would give people an incentive to economize on money balances and so tend to raise velocity and that low rates of interest and falling prices would have the opposite effect. They were never guilty of the crude fallacy—with which critics have often charged them—of regarding velocity as something of a natural constant.

The quantity equation in income form.   One difficulty with equations (3) and (4) is that the magnitudes designated "transactions" and the associated "general price level" proved conceptually ambiguous and difficult to measure with available data. Despite the large amount of empirical work done on these equations, notably by Fisher and Carl Snyder, these ambiguities and deficiencies of data have never been satisfactorily resolved. Should capital transfers, such as purchases and sales of real estate and securities, be included? What about gifts? Money-changing transactions? What is the relevant price and quantity in these transactions?

As noted before, the data on volume of transactions have been satisfactory only for transactions effected by check. For these, debits to bank accounts (or bank clearings) provide a statistically reliable total, although even then there are problems involved in separating out money-changing transactions. Average deposits give a statistically reliable estimate of M', so that estimates of V' can be and are readily calculated for frequent time intervals and for many different geographical areas. However, even for check transactions, there is no satisfactory way to break down the other side of the equation into price and quantity components.

With the development of national or social accounting, which has stressed income transactions rather than gross transactions and which has explicitly and satisfactorily dealt with the conceptual and statistical problems of distinguishing between changes in prices and changes in quantities, there has been a tendency to express the quantity equation in terms of income rather than of transactions. Let Y be money national income, P the price index implicit in estimating national income at constant prices, and y national income in constant prices, so that

$$(5) \qquad\qquad Y = Py.$$

Let M represent, as before, the stock of money, but define V as the average number of times per year that the money stock is used in making *income* transactions (that is, payments for final productive services) rather than all transactions. We then can write the quantity equation in income form as

$$(6) \qquad MV = Py.$$

Although the symbols P and V are used both in eqs. (5) and (6) and in eqs. (1) through (4), they stand for different concepts in each group.

Equation (6) is both conceptually and empirically more satisfactory than equation (3). Nonetheless, the earlier discussion of the fourfold classification implicit in the quantity equation applies, except for changes that are nearly self-evident, such as the very different relevance for y than for T of the degree of integration or disintegration of industry. Equation (6) is also closer in conception to the Cambridge approach, to which we now turn.

The Cambridge cash-balances approach

The essential feature of a money economy is that it enables the act of purchase to be separated from the act of sale. An individual who has something to exchange need not seek out the double coincidence—someone who both wants what he has and offers in exchange what he wants. He need only find someone who wants what he has, sell it to him for general purchasing power, and then find someone else who has what he wants and buy it with general purchasing power.

In order for the act of purchase to be separated from the act of sale, there must be something which can serve as a temporary abode of purchasing power in the interim. It is this aspect of money which is emphasized in the cash-balances approach.

How much money will people or enterprises want to hold for this purpose? As a first approximation we may suppose that the amount one wants to hold bears some relation to one's income, since that determines the volume of purchases and sales in which one is engaged. We then add up the cash balances held by all holders of money in the community and express the total as a fraction of their total income. We can then write

$$(7) \qquad M = kPy,$$

where M, P, and y are defined as in equation (6) and k is the ratio of the money stock to income. We can regard k either as a constant so calculated as to make (7) an identity, or as the "desired" ratio, so that M is the "desired" amount of money, which need not be equal to the actual amount. In either case, k is clearly equal numerically to the reciprocal of the V of equation (6), the V in one case being interpreted as measured velocity and in the other as desired velocity.

Formally the Cambridge equation (7) is simply a transformation of Fisher's equation (6). Most writers who have used one of the two approaches regarded them in this way and tended to cover much the same ground. Yet to a far greater extent than is reflected in the writings of the early expositors, the two approaches stress different aspects of money, make different definitions of money seem natural, and lead to emphasis being placed on different variables and analytical techniques.

Consider the definition of money. The transactions approach makes it natural to define money in terms of whatever serves as the medium of exchange in discharging obligations. By stressing the function of money as a temporary abode of purchasing power the cash-balances approach makes it seem entirely appropriate to include also such stores of value as demand and time deposits not transferable by check, although it clearly does not require their inclusion.

Similarly, the transactions approach leads to stress being placed on such variables as payments practices, the financial and economic arrangements for effecting transactions, and the speed of communication and transportation as it affects the time required to make a payment—essentially, that is, to emphasis on the mechanical aspects of the payments process. The cash-balances approach, on the other hand, leads to stress being placed on variables affecting the usefulness of money as an asset: the costs and returns from holding money instead of other assets, the uncertainty of the future, and so on.

Stress on the first set of variables led most early writers—both those using the Fisher equation and those using the Cambridge equation—to predict that velocity would increase over time as a result of technological improvements in transportation and communication, which would facilitate the payments process. In fact, velocity has shown no tendency to rise over time. If anything it has rather tended to decline in economically progressive countries along with rises in real income, although this tendency is less pronounced when money is defined narrowly than when it is defined to include some deposits not transferable by check. The tendency for velocity to decline, along with the very size of money balances (equal in 1960 in the United States to about one month's income for currency outside banks alone, to nearly five months' income for currency plus adjusted demand deposits, and to about seven months' income for currency and all deposits at commercial banks) has contributed to a shift of emphasis from the function of money as a medium of exchange to its function as a temporary abode of purchasing power.

Finally, with regard to analytical techniques, the cash-balances approach fits in much more readily with the general Marshallian demand–supply apparatus than the transactions approach does. Equation (7) can be regarded as a demand function for money, with P and y on the right-hand side being two of the variables on which demand for money depends, and with k symbolizing all the other variables, so that k is to be regarded not as a numerical constant but as itself a function of still other variables. For completion the analysis requires another equation showing the supply of money as a function of other variables. The price level is then the resultant of the interaction of the demand and supply functions. From this point of view the quantity theory of money as embodied in equation (7) is a theory of the demand for money, not a theory of the price level or of money income.

The Keynesian attack

The Keynesian income–expenditure analysis developed in the *General Theory of Employment, Interest and Money* (1936) offered an alternative approach to the interpretation of changes in money income that emphasized the relation between money income and investment or autonomous expenditures rather than the relation between money income and the stock of money. The success of the Keynesian revolution in economic thought led to a temporary eclipse of the quantity theory of money and to perhaps an all-time low in the amount of economic research and writing devoted to monetary theory and analysis, narrowly interpreted. It became a widely accepted view that money does not matter, or, at any rate, that it does not matter very much, and that policy and theory alike should concentrate on investment, government fiscal policy, and the relation between consumer expenditures and income.

Keynes did not, of course, deny the validity of the quantity equation. What he did was something very different. He argued that *under conditions of underemployment equilibrium* the V in equation (6) and the k in equation (7) were highly unstable and would, for the most part, passively adapt to whatever changes independently occurred in money income or the stock of money. Hence, under such conditions these equations, although entirely valid, were largely useless for policy or prediction. Moreover, he regarded such conditions as prevailing much, if not most, of the time.

Keynes reached this conclusion by giving a highly specific form to equation (7). The quantity of money demanded, he argued, could be treated as if it were divided into two parts, one part, M_1, "held to satisfy the transactions- and precautionary-motives," the other, M_2, "held to satisfy the speculative-motive" (1936, p. 199). He regarded M_1 as

a roughly constant fraction of income. He regarded the demand for M_2 as arising from "*uncertainty* as to the future course of the rate of interest" and the amount demanded as depending on the relation between current rates of interest and the rates of interest expected to prevail in the future. (Keynes, of course, emphasized that there was a whole complex of interest rates. However, for simplicity, he spoke in terms of "the rate of interest," usually meaning by that the rate on long-term securities that were fixed in nominal value and that involved minimal risks of default—for example, government bonds.) In a "given state of expectations," the higher the current rate of interest, the lower would be the (real) amount of money people would want to hold for speculative motives for two reasons: first, the greater would be the cost in terms of current earnings sacrificed by holding money instead of securities, and, second, the more likely it would be that interest rates would fall, and hence bond prices rise, and so the greater would be the cost in terms of capital gains sacrificed by holding money instead of securities.

Although expectations are given great prominence in developing the liquidity function expressing the demand for M_2, they do not enter explicitly into that function. For the most part, Keynes and his followers in practice treated the amount of M_2 demanded simply as a function of the current interest rate, the emphasis on expectations serving only as a reason for their attribution of instability to the liquidity function.

Except for somewhat different language, the analysis up to this point differs from that of earlier quantity theorists, such as Fisher, only by its subtle analysis of the role of expectations about future interest rates and its greater emphasis on current interest rates and by restricting more narrowly the variables explicitly considered as affecting the amount of money demanded.

Keynes's special twist concerned the empirical form of the liquidity-preference function at the low interest rates that he believed would prevail under conditions of underemployment equilibrium. Let the interest rate fall sufficiently low, he argued, and money and bonds would become perfect substitutes for one another; liquidity preference, as he put it, would become absolute. The liquidity-preference function, expressing the quantity of M_2 demanded as a function of the rate of interest, would become horizontal at some low but finite rate of interest. Under such circumstances, he held, if the amount of money is increased by whatever means, the holders of money might seek to convert the additional cash balances into bonds. This would, however, tend to lower the rate of return on bonds. Even the slightest lowering would, he argued, lead holders of money to desist from trying to convert it into bonds. The result would simply be that people would be willing to hold the increased quantity of money; k would be higher and V lower. Conversely, if the amount of money were decreased, holders of bonds would seek to convert them into money, but this would tend to raise the rate of interest, and even the slightest rise would reconcile them to holding the bonds instead of the money. Or, again, suppose there is an increase in money income for whatever reason. That will require an increase in M_1, which can come out of M_2 without any further effects. Conversely, any decline in M_1 can be added to M_2 without any further effects. The conclusion is that *under circumstances of absolute liquidity preference* income can change without a change in M and M can change without a change in income. The holders of money are in metastable equilibrium, like a tumbler on its side on a flat surface; they will be satisfied with whatever the amount of money happens to be.

Keynes regarded absolute liquidity preference as a strictly "limiting case" of which, though it "might become practically important in future," he knew "of no example . . . hitherto" (1936, p. 207). But, since he regarded interest rates as frequently being not far above the level at which liquidity preference would become absolute, he treated velocity as if in practice its behavior frequently approximated that which would prevail in this limiting case.

Keynes's disciples went much farther than Keynes himself. They were readier than he was to accept absolute liquidity preference as the actual state of affairs. More important, many argued that when liquidity preference was not absolute, changes in the quantity of money would affect only the interest rate on bonds and that changes in this interest rate in turn would have little further effect. They argued that both consumption expenditures and investment expenditures were nearly completely insensitive to changes in interest rates, so that a change in M would merely be offset by an opposite and compensatory change in V (or a change in the same direction in k), leaving P and y almost completely unaffected. In essence their argument consists in asserting that only paper securities are substitutes for money balances—that real assets never are (see Tobin 1961).

The issues raised for the quantity theory by the Keynesian analysis are clearly empirical rather than theoretical. Is it a fact that the quantity of money demanded is a function primarily of current income and of the rate of interest on fixed-money-value securities? Is it a fact that the amount demanded is highly elastic with respect to the rate

of interest on such securities at a low but finite rate of interest? Is it a fact that expenditures are highly inelastic with respect to such a rate of interest? Or, to put the issue in an equivalent but more readily observable form, is it a fact that velocity is a highly unstable and unpredictable magnitude that generally varies in a direction opposite to that of the quantity of money?

The post-Keynesian reformulation

Experience with monetary policy after World War II very quickly produced a renewed interest in money and a renewed belief that money matters. Under the influence of Keynesian ideas, country after country followed an easy-money policy designed to keep interest rates low in order to stimulate, if only slightly, the investment regarded as needed to offset the shortage of demand that was universally feared. The result was an intensification of the strong inflationary pressure inherited from the war, a pressure that was brought under control only when countries undertook so-called orthodox measures to restrain the growth in the stock of money, as in Italy, beginning in August 1947, in Germany in June 1948, in the United States in March 1951, in Great Britain in November 1951, and in France in January 1960.

The effect of experience was reinforced by developments in economic theory, especially by the explicit analysis of the so-called real-balance effect as a channel through which changes in prices and in the quantity of money could affect income, even when investment and consumption were insensitive to changes in interest rates or when absolute liquidity preference prevented changes in interest rates (see Haberler 1937; Tobin 1947; Pigou 1943; 1947; Patinkin 1948).

Many economists continue to use Keynesian analysis but have revised their empirical presumptions. They grant that liquidity preference is not absolute and that investment does have a sizable elasticity with respect to interest rates. They continue, however, to regard analysis in terms of the quantity equation as less useful and meaningful than analysis in terms of autonomous expenditures and the multiplier, with monetary changes being taken into account as one factor among many that can affect these magnitudes.

The postwar period has also seen a return to analysis in terms of the quantity equation accompanied by a reformulation of the quantity theory that has been strongly affected by the Keynesian analysis of liquidity preference (Johnson 1962). The reformulation emphasizes the role of money as an asset and hence treats the demand for money as part of capital or wealth theory, concerned with the composition of the balance sheet or portfolio of assets.

From this point of view, it is important to distinguish between ultimate wealth-holders, to whom money is one form in which they choose to hold their wealth, and enterprises, to whom money is a producer's good like machinery or inventories.

Demand by ultimate wealth-holders. For ultimate wealth-holders the demand for money, in real terms, may be expected to be a function of the following variables.

(*a*) Total wealth. This is the analogue of the budget constraint in the usual theory of consumer choice. It is the total that must be divided among various forms of assets. In practice, estimates of total wealth are seldom available. Instead, income may serve as an index of wealth. However, it should be recognized that income as measured by statisticians may be a defective index of wealth because it is subject to erratic year-to-year fluctuations and that a longer term concept, like the concept of permanent income developed in connection with the theory of consumption, may be more useful. (Friedman 1957; 1959, p. 7; Meltzer 1963; Brunner & Meltzer 1963).

The emphasis on income as a surrogate for wealth, rather than as a measure of the "work" to be done by money, is conceptually perhaps the basic difference between the reformulation and the earlier versions of quantity theory.

(*b*) The division of wealth between human and nonhuman forms. The major asset of most wealth-holders is their personal earning capacity, but the conversion of human into nonhuman wealth or the reverse is subject to narrow limits because of institutional constraints. It can be done by using current earnings to purchase nonhuman wealth or by using nonhuman wealth to finance the acquisition of skills but not by purchase or sale and to only a limited extent by borrowing on the collateral of earning power. Hence, the fraction of total wealth that is in the form of nonhuman wealth may be an additional important variable.

(*c*) The expected rates of return on money and other assets. This is the analogue of the prices of a commodity and its substitutes and complements in the usual theory of consumer demand. The nominal rate of return on money may be zero, as it generally is on currency, or negative, as it sometimes is on demand deposits subject to net service charges, or positive, as it sometimes is on demand deposits on which interest is paid and generally is on time deposits. The nominal rate of return on other assets consists of two parts; first, any currently paid yield or cost, such as interest on bonds, dividends on equities, and storage costs on physical assets, and, second, changes in their nominal prices. The second part will, of course, be especially important under conditions of inflation or deflation.

(*d*) Other variables determining the utility attached to the services rendered by money relative to those rendered by other assets—in Keynesian terminology, determining the value attached to liquidity proper. One such variable may be one already considered—namely, real wealth or income, since the services rendered by money may in principle be regarded by wealth-holders as a "necessity," like bread, the consumption of which increases less than in proportion to any increase in income, or as a "luxury," like recreation, the consumption of which increases more than in proportion to any increase in income.

Another variable, one that is likely to be important empirically, is the degree of economic stability expected to prevail in the future. Wealth-holders are likely to attach considerably more value to liquidity when they expect economic conditions to be unstable than when they expect them to be highly stable. This variable is likely to be difficult to express quantitatively even though the direction of change may be clear from qualitative information. For example, the outbreak of war clearly produces expectations of instability, which is one reason why war is often accompanied by a notable increase in real balances—that is, a notable decline in velocity.

We can symbolize this analysis in terms of the following demand function for money for an individual wealth-holder:

$$(8) \qquad \frac{M}{P} = f(y, w; r_m, r_b, r_e, \frac{1}{P}\frac{dP}{dt}; u),$$

where M, P, and y have the same meaning as in equation (7) except that they relate to a single wealth-holder; w is the fraction of wealth in nonhuman form (or, alternatively, the fraction of income derived from property); r_m is the expected rate of return on money; r_b is the expected rate of return on fixed-value securities, including expected changes in their prices; r_e is the expected rate of return on equities, including expected changes in their prices; $(1/P)(dP/dt)$ is the expected rate of change of prices of goods and hence the expected rate of return on real assets; and u is a portmanteau symbol standing for whatever variables other than income may affect the utility attached to the services of money. Each of the four rates of return stands, of course, for a set of rates of return, and for some purposes it may be important to classify assets still more finely—for example, to distinguish currency from deposits, long-term from short-term fixed-value securities, risky from relatively safe equities, and different kinds of physical assets from one another.

The usual problems of aggregation arise in passing from equation (8) to a corresponding equation for the economy as a whole—in particular, they arise from the possibility that the amount of money demanded may depend on the distribution of such variables as y and w and not merely on their aggregate or average value. If we neglect these distributional effects, (8) can be regarded as applying to the community as a whole, with M and y referring to per capita money holdings and per capita real income, respectively, and w to the fraction of aggregate wealth in nonhuman form.

The major problems that arise in practice in applying (8) are the precise definitions of y and w, the estimation of *expected* rates of return as contrasted with actual rates of return, and the quantitative specification of the variables designated by u.

Demand by business enterprises. Business enterprises are not subject to a constraint comparable to that imposed by the total wealth of the ultimate wealth-holder. The total amount of capital embodied in productive assets, including money, is a variable that can be determined by the enterprise to maximize returns, since it can acquire additional capital through the capital market. Hence, there is no reason on this ground to include total wealth, or y as a surrogate for total wealth, as a variable in their demand function for money.

It may, however, be desirable to include a somewhat similar variable defining the "scale" of the enterprise on different grounds—namely, as an index of the productive value of different quantities of money to the enterprise. This is more nearly in line with the earlier transactions approach emphasizing the "work" to be done by money. It is by no means clear what the appropriate variable is: total transactions, net value added, net income, total capital in nonmoney form, or net worth. The lack of availability of data has meant that much less empirical work has been done on the business demand for money than on an aggregate demand curve encompassing both ultimate wealth-holders and business enterprises. As a result there are as yet only faint indications about the best variable to use.

The division of wealth between human and nonhuman form has no special relevance to business enterprises, since they are likely to buy the services of both forms on the market.

Rates of return on money and on alternative assets are, of course, highly relevant to business enterprises. These rates determine the net cost to them of holding the money balances. However, the particular rates that are relevant may be quite different from those that are relevant for ultimate wealth-holders. For example, rates charged by banks on loans are of minor importance for wealth-holders yet may be extremely important for businesses, since bank loans may be a way in which they can acquire the capital embodied in money balances.

The counterpart for business enterprises of the variable u in (8) is the set of variables other than scale affecting the productivity of money balances. At least one of these—namely, expectations about economic stability—is likely to be common to business enterprises and ultimate wealth-holders.

With these interpretations of the variables, equation (8), with w excluded, can be regarded as symbolizing the business demand for money and, as it stands, symbolizing aggregate demand for money, although with even more serious qualifications about the ambiguities introduced by aggregation.

The process of adjustment. Emphasis on the role of money as a component of wealth is important because of the variables to which it directs attention. It is important also for its implications about the process of adjustment to a difference between actual and desired stocks of money. Any such discrepancy is a disturbance in a balance sheet. As such it can be corrected in either of two ways: by a rearrangement of assets and liabilities through purchase, sale, borrowing, and lending or by the use of current flows of income and expenditure to add to or subtract from some assets and liabilities. The Keynesian liquidity-preference analysis stressed the first and, in its most rigid form, only one specific rearrangement: that between money and bonds. The earlier quantity theory stressed the second to the almost complete exclusion of the first. The reformulation enforces consideration of both.

The process of adjustment is important in particular for its implications about the time that readjustment may be expected to take. Balance-sheet adjustments can in general be expected to take considerable time, especially when they take the form of adjustments through alterations in flows and especially when they concern the money balance, M, whose function is precisely that of serving as a temporary abode of purchasing power, thereby permitting purchases to be separated from sales.

It is plausible that any widespread disturbance in money balances—through, say, an unanticipated increase or decrease in the quantity of money by the actions of monetary authorities—will initially be met by an attempted readjustment of assets and liabilities through purchase or sale. But such attempted readjustments will alter the prices of assets and liabilities, leading to the spread of the adjustment from one asset or liability to another. Such changes in prices will also alter the relative prices of capital items and the services they yield and so establish incentives to alter flows of receipts and expenditures. If the monetary change has altered the total nominal value of wealth, not simply its composition, this will introduce an additional reason to change flows. The effect of any monetary disturbance will thus spread in ever-widening ripples, and some of its most important effects may not be manifest for many months after the initial disturbance.

Empirical evidence

Empirical evidence about the relation between changes in the quantity of money and in prices, although it was sufficiently extensive to produce a widespread belief in the quantity theory, has seldom been systematically collated and organized. Until modern times, money was mostly metallic—copper, brass, silver, gold. The most notable changes in its nominal quantity under such circumstances were produced by sweating and clipping, by governmental edicts changing the nominal values attached to specified physical quantities of the metal, or by great discoveries of new sources of specie. Economic history is replete with examples of the first two and their coincidence with corresponding changes in nominal prices (see Cipolla 1956; Feavearyear 1931). The most important example of the third is the great specie discoveries in the New World in the sixteenth century. The association between this increase in the quantity of money and the price revolution of the sixteenth and seventeenth centuries has been well documented (see Hamilton 1934).

The nineteenth and early twentieth centuries offer another striking example, despite the much greater development of deposit money and paper money. The gold discoveries in Australia and the United States in the 1840s were followed by substantial price rises in the 1850s. When the rate of growth of the gold stock slowed down, and especially when country after country shifted from silver to gold (Germany in 1871–1873, the Latin Monetary Union in 1873, the Netherlands in 1875–1876, or returned to gold (the United States in 1879), world prices in terms of gold fell slowly but fairly steadily for about three decades. New gold discoveries in the 1880s and 1890s, powerfully reinforced by the development of improved methods of mining and refining, particularly the development of commercially feasible methods of using the cyanide process to extract gold from low-grade ore, reversed the trend. The world gold stock started to grow at a much more rapid rate, and no additional important countries shifted to gold, so there was no increase in demand from this source. The price trend also reversed itself. From the mid-1890s to 1914, world prices in terms of gold rose by 25 to 50 per cent, depending on the index used.

Evidence from great inflations. The most dramatic evidence about the role of the quantity of money comes from periods of great monetary disturbances, and among these the most striking are the periods of extremely rapid price rise, such as the hyperinflations after World War I in Germany, Austria, and Russia, those after World War II in Hungary and Greece, and the rapid rises, if not hyperinflations, in many South American and some other countries both before and after World War II. These twentieth-century episodes have been rather more systematically studied than earlier ones. The studies demonstrate almost conclusively the critical role of changes in the quantity of money (the most important study is Cagan 1956).

These studies also enable us to sketch with considerable accuracy a rather typical profile of an inflation that follows a period of fairly stable prices. The inflation often has its start in a period of war, but it need not. What is important is that something, generally the financing of extraordinary governmental expenditures, produces a much more rapid rate of growth of the money stock. Prices start to rise, but at a slower pace than the money stock, so that for a time the real stock of money increases. The reason for this is twofold. First, it takes time for people to readjust their money balances. Second, initially there is a general expectation that what goes up will come down, that the rise in prices is temporary and will be followed by a decline. Such expectations make money seem to be a desirable form in which to hold assets, and therefore they lead to an increase in desired money balances in real terms.

As prices continue to rise, expectations are revised. People come to expect prices to continue to rise. Desired balances decline. People also take more active measures to eliminate the discrepancy between actual and desired balances. The result is that prices start to rise faster than the stock of money, and real balances start to decline (that is, velocity starts to rise). How far this process continues depends on the rate of rise in the stock of money. If it remains fairly stable, real balances settle down to a level that is lower than the initial level but roughly constant—for a constant expected rate of rise in prices there will be a roughly constant level of desired real balances; in this case, prices ultimately rise at the same rate as the stock of money. A decline in the rate of rise in the stock of money is followed by a decline in the rate of rise in prices, and this is followed in turn by an increase in actual and desired real balances as people readjust their expectations; the converse also holds. The result is that once the process is in full swing, changes in real balances follow with a lag changes in the rate of change of the stock of money. The lag reflects the fact that people apparently base their expectations of future rates of price change on an average of experience over the preceding several years, the period of averaging being shorter the more rapid the inflation.

In the extreme cases, those which have degenerated into hyperinflation and a complete breakdown of the medium of exchange, rates of price change have been so high and real balances have been driven down so low as to lead to the widespread introduction of substitute moneys, usually foreign currencies. At that point completely new monetary systems have had to be introduced.

A similar phenomenon has occurred when inflation has been effectively suppressed by price controls, so that there is a substantial gap between the prices that would prevail in the absence of controls and the legally permitted prices. This gap prevents money from functioning as an effective medium of exchange and also leads to the introduction of substitute moneys, sometimes rather bizarre ones like the cigarettes and cognac used in post-World War II Germany.

Evidence from the United States.   Recent studies of the monetary history of the United States provide an especially full documentation of monetary relations (see especially Friedman & Schwartz

1963*a*). Some of the salient findings may be summarized briefly.

(*a*) The real stock of money, expressed in terms of months of income, has risen from about $3\frac{1}{2}$ months' income at the end of the Civil War in 1865 to over 7 months' income by 1960—that is, velocity has fallen (money is defined as currency held by the public plus all adjusted deposits in commercial banks, income is defined as net national product). One interpretation of this trend is that the rise in real balances reflects the contemporaneous rise in real income per capita. From the end of World War II to almost 1960, velocity rose rather than fell. It is not yet clear whether this was a temporary interruption or a change of trend.

(*b*) If allowance is made for the trend in velocity, there has been a very close connection between the stock of money per unit of output and prices. This is brought out clearly by Figure 1, which, to eliminate short-period fluctuations, plots the average stock of money per unit of output and average prices in successive reference-cycle phases.

(*c*) In the course of business cycles the stock of money has slowed up its rate of growth well before the date designated by National Bureau of Economic Research reference-cycle dates as the peak of the cycle and has increased its rate of growth well before the trough. In mild contractions these decelerations have generally produced not an absolute decline in the stock of money but only a lower rate of growth. Every severe contraction has been accompanied by an absolute decline in the stock of money, and the severity of the contrac-

Figure 1 — Implicit prices and stock of money per unit of output, reference-cycle phase averages, 1870–1961[a]

a. A phase is the trough-to-peak or peak-to-trough interval between reference-cycle turning points. (For a discussion of reference cycles, see Moore 1961.) Phase averages are computed by weighting initial and terminal years each at one-half and intervening years at unity. The trend lines are computed regressions based on phase-average values, 1882–1961.

b. The index of implicit prices is based on 1929 = 100. For the underlying figures, see Friedman and Schwartz (1963a, chart 62).

c. Stock of money per unit of output is the ratio of the money stock to real income, expressed as an index. For the underlying figures, see Friedman and Schwartz (1963a, table A-1, col. 8, and source notes to chart 62).

tion has been in roughly the same order as the size of the decline in the stock of money. Although changes in the rate of growth of the stock of money have to some extent reflected the contemporaneous course of business, on many occasions they have quite clearly been the result of independent forces, such as the deliberate decisions of monetary authorities. The clearest examples are probably the wartime increases and the decreases from 1920 to 1921, 1929 to 1933, and 1937 to 1938.

(*d*) Velocity as usually measured has tended to rise during business expansions and decline during business contractions. One explanation offered is that this pattern reflects the use of measured income in computing velocity rather than a longer term concept, such as permanent income (Friedman 1959). Another explanation offered is that it reflects the effect of interest rates.

(*e*) It is agreed that velocity is related to interest rates, higher interest rates being associated with higher velocity, and conversely, but there is wide disagreement about the magnitude and significance of the relation. One view is that changes in interest rates are either the primary or a major source of all cyclical and secular changes in velocity (Latané 1954; 1960; Brunner & Meltzer 1963). Another view is that changes in interest rates have been a minor factor, much less important than changes in real per capita income for secular changes in velocity and much less important than differences between measured and permanent income for cyclical changes (Friedman 1959; Friedman & Schwartz 1963a).

Evidence from underdeveloped countries. A few scattered figures for some of the less developed countries may help to indicate the broad range of applicability of the quantity theory of money.

Real balances of currency. In less developed countries, currency is often a more meaningful total than currency plus deposits for two reasons. One is that deposits are often used to a very limited extent and by highly selected groups in the population. The other is that governmental monetary intervention is more frequent and more important with respect to deposits, so that an erratic element is introduced into the conditions of supply of deposits.

Table 1 gives estimates for a recent year of the stock of currency expressed in number of weeks of personal disposable income for less developed countries and, for comparison, for the United States. These figures are subject to very wide margins of error, particularly because of the unreliability of income estimates for the less developed countries. It is, therefore, all the more

Table 1 — International comparison of real balances

	Year	Number of weeks of personal disposable income held in currency
India	1958–1959	6.9
Greece	1960	6.3
Yugoslavia	1960	6.2
Turkey	1961	5.2
Israel	1961	4.4
United States	1960	4.3

striking that for countries for which methods of economic organization vary so greatly and for which real income per capita must vary over a range of something well in excess of 20 to 1, real balances vary over a range of decidedly less than 2 to 1. And much of that variation is readily explained by different degrees of financial development: deposits are least widely used in India, Greece, and Yugoslavia, most widely used in Israel and the United States, and used to an intermediate extent in Turkey. Clearly, money-holding propensities have a great degree of uniformity under a wide range of circumstances.

Changes in quantity of money and in prices. If data like those in Table 1 are of questionable accuracy, year-to-year data are even more dubious for the underdeveloped countries. A recent study that was confined to the Middle East shows a variety of relations. In Egypt and Turkey the data for wholesale prices show the kind of close relationship between money supply and price changes that other experiences would lead one to expect. For the other countries the relation is loose or nonexistent (Penrose 1962). Rises in output may explain some part of the discrepancy. Much more likely explanations are the following: (*a*) The inclusion of rapidly expanding deposits whose significance is questionable. Currency figures alone show much less of a discrepancy. (*b*) Major defects in the price indexes. The countries have sought to suppress price increases, often have legal prices that are honored more in the breach than in the observance, and calculate price indexes in ways that understate the actual price rise. It is highly likely that revised and improved figures will remove much of the apparent discrepancy.

Stability of velocity and the multiplier. As pointed out above, the challenge to the quantity theory offered by Keynes rested entirely on differences in empirical presumptions, which can be summarized in terms of the stability attributed to the velocity of circulation, on the one hand, and the Keynesian multiplier (the ratio of changes in income to changes in autonomous expenditures), on the other.

A systematic comparison of the relative stability of velocity and the multiplier has been made for the United States from 1896 to 1958 (Friedman & Meiselman 1964a; 1964b; 1965). The results are striking: velocity is consistently more stable than the multiplier. These results have been challenged by other writers (Hester 1964; Ando & Modigliani 1965; DePrano & Mayer 1965), showing that this question is still far from settled.

Policy implications

On a very general level the implications of the quantity theory for economic policy are straightforward and clear. On a more precise and detailed level they are not.

Acceptance of the quantity theory clearly means that the stock of money is a key variable in policies directed at the control of the level of prices or of money income. Inflation can be prevented if and only if the stock of money per unit of output can be kept from increasing appreciably. Deflation can be prevented if and only if the stock of money per unit of output can be kept from decreasing appreciably. This implication is by no means a trivial one. Monetary authorities have more frequently than not taken conditions in the credit market— rates of interest, availability of loans, and so on— as criteria of policy and have paid little or no attention to the stock of money per se. This emphasis on credit as opposed to monetary policy accounts both for the great depression in the United States from 1929 to 1933, when the Federal Reserve System allowed the stock of money to decline by one-third, and for many of the post-World War II inflations.

The quantity theory has no such clear implication, even on this general level, about policies concerned with the growth of real income. Both inflation and deflation have proved consistent with growth, stagnation, or decline.

Passing from these general and vague statements to specific prescriptions for policy is difficult. It is tempting to conclude from the close average relation between changes in the stock of money and changes in money income that control over the stock of money can be used as a precision instrument for offsetting other forces making for instability in money income. Unfortunately there are many slips between this cup and this lip.

One slip is that a very close relationship *on the average* is consistent with much variation in the individual instance. A high correlation between changes relative to trend in the stock of money and in money income over many business cycles— involving, say, an average increase of 2 per cent in money income for every 1 per cent increase in money—is entirely consistent with the corresponding ratio varying in individual years or over single cycles from zero or a negative number to, say, 4 or 5. But for policy in a particular cycle, what is important is the relation in that cycle, not the relation on the average.

A second slip is the length of time it takes for changes in the stock of money to have their effect —this is one of the reasons for the variability that constitutes the first slip. A change in the stock of money today will have most of its effects some months from now, perhaps on the average as much as 12 to 15 months from now. A policy of using monetary changes to offset other forces making for instability therefore requires an ability to forecast a considerable time in advance what those forces will be—an ability that has so far been conspicuous by its absence. Moreover, the time it takes for monetary changes to be effective undoubtedly varies rather considerably. Hence it would also be necessary to forecast how long the lag would be in the specific instance.

These two slips mean that monetary changes intended to be stabilizing may in fact be destabilizing; they may introduce a random and erratic influence into economic affairs. It is a sobering thought that both the stock of money and economic activity displayed greater instability in the first two peacetime decades after the establishment of the Federal Reserve System (1919 to 1939) than in any other pair of decades in the whole of United States history. The blind, quasi-automatic forces that controlled monetary matters in earlier decades produced a higher degree of stability than a system specifically established to promote monetary and economic stability. The greater stability of prices and employment since the end of World War II may be a sign that we have learned how to avoid the mistakes of the interwar decades, but it is much too soon to have any confidence in that comfortable conclusion.

Other slips have to do with the indirect effects of methods used to control the stock of money; with possible conflicts between the objective of stable prices and such other objectives as stable exchange rates, stable employment at a high level, and low interest rates on government borrowing; and with the possible desire to use inflation as a means of imposing a tax on money balances.

One negative implication of the quantity theory, implicit in the above, is worth spelling out because of the continued widespread acceptance of the belief that fiscal policy is the key to control of the level of money income. The quantity theory implies that the effect of government deficits or surpluses depends critically on how they are financed. If a deficit is financed by borrowing from the public without an increase in the quantity of money, the direct expansionary effect of the excess of government spending over receipts will be offset to some extent, and possibly to a very great extent, by the indirect contractionary effect of the transfer of funds to the government through borrowing. Furthermore, the deficit will primarily affect income only while it lasts; a cessation of the deficit will mean a cessation of its effects. If a deficit is financed by printing money, there will be no offset, and the enlarged stock of money will continue to exert an effect after the deficit is terminated. What matters most is the behavior of the stock of money, and government deficits are expansionary primarily if they serve as the means of increasing the stock of money; other means of increasing the stock of money will have closely similar effects.

MILTON FRIEDMAN

[See also LIQUIDITY PREFERENCE; MONETARY POLICY.]

BIBLIOGRAPHY

ANDO, ALBERT; and MODIGLIANI, FRANCO 1965 The Relative Stability of Monetary Velocity and the Investment Multiplier. *American Economic Review* 55:693–728, 786–790.

BRUNNER, KARL; and MELTZER, ALLAN H. 1963 Predicting Velocity: Implications for Theory and Policy. *Journal of Finance* 18:319–354.

CAGAN, PHILLIP 1956 The Monetary Dynamics of Hyperinflation. Pages 25–117 in Milton Friedman (editor), *Studies in the Quantity Theory of Money*. Univ. of Chicago Press.

CIPOLLA, CARLO M. 1956 *Money, Prices, and Civilization in the Mediterranean World, Fifth to Seventeenth Century*. Princeton Univ. Press.

DEPRANO, MICHAEL E.; and MAYER, THOMAS 1965 Tests of the Relative Importance of Autonomous Expenditures and Money. *American Economic Review* 55:729–752.

FEAVEARYEAR, ALBERT E. (1931) 1963 *The Pound Sterling: A History of English Money*. 2d ed. Oxford: Clarendon.

FISHER, IRVING (1911) 1920 *The Purchasing Power of Money: Its Determination and Relation to Credit, Interest and Crises*. New ed., rev. New York: Macmillan.

FRIEDMAN, MILTON 1957 *A Theory of the Consumption Function*. National Bureau of Economic Research, General Series, No. 63. Princeton Univ. Press.

FRIEDMAN, MILTON 1959 The Demand for Money: Some Theoretical and Empirical Results. *Journal of Political Economy* 67:327–351.

FRIEDMAN, MILTON; and MEISELMAN, DAVID 1964a The Relative Stability of Monetary Velocity and the Investment Multiplier in the United States, 1897–1958. Pages 165–268 in *Stabilization Policies: A Series of Research Studies Prepared for the Commission on Money and Credit*. Englewood Cliffs, N.J.: Prentice-Hall.

FRIEDMAN, MILTON; and MEISELMAN, DAVID 1964b Reply to Donald Hester. *Review of Economics and Statistics* 46:369–377. → Includes a rejoinder by Donald D. Hester.

FRIEDMAN, MILTON; and MEISELMAN, DAVID 1965 Reply to Ando and Modigliani and to DePrano and Mayer. *American Economic Review* 55:753–785. → Contains a rejoinder by Ando and Modigliani on pages 786–790 and by DePrano and Mayer on pages 791–792.

FRIEDMAN, MILTON; and SCHWARTZ, ANNA J. 1963a *A Monetary History of the United States, 1867–1960*. National Bureau of Economic Research, Studies in Business Cycles, No. 12. Princeton Univ. Press.

FRIEDMAN, MILTON; and SCHWARTZ, ANNA J. 1963b Money and Business Cycles. *Review of Economics and Statistics* 45, no. 1, pt. 2:32–64.

HABERLER, GOTTFRIED (1937) 1958 *Prosperity and Depression: A Theoretical Analysis of Cyclical Movements*. 4th ed., rev. & enl. Harvard Economic Studies, Vol. 105. Cambridge, Mass.: Harvard Univ. Press; London: Allen & Unwin.

HAMILTON, EARL J. (1934) 1965 *American Treasure and the Price Revolution in Spain, 1501–1650*. Harvard Economic Studies, Vol. 43. New York: Octagon.

HESTER, DONALD D. 1964 Keynes and the Quantity Theory: A Comment on the Friedman–Meiselman CMC Paper. *Review of Economics and Statistics* 46:364–368.

HUME, DAVID 1752 Of Money. Discourse III. Pages 41–59 in David Hume, *Political Discourses*. Edinburgh: Fleming.

JOHNSON, H. G. 1962 Monetary Theory and Policy. *American Economic Review* 52:335–384.

KEYNES, JOHN MAYNARD 1936 *The General Theory of Employment, Interest and Money*. London: Macmillan. → A paperback edition was published in 1965 by Harcourt.

LATANÉ, HENRY A. 1954 Cash Balances and the Interest Rate: A Pragmatic Approach. *Review of Economics and Statistics* 36:456–460.

LATANÉ, HENRY A. 1960 Income Velocity and Interest Rates: A Pragmatic Approach. *Review of Economics and Statistics* 42:445–449.

MARGET, ARTHUR W. 1938 *The Theory of Prices: A Reexamination of the Central Problems of Monetary Theory*. Vol. 1. New York: Prentice-Hall.

MARSHALL, ALFRED (1923) 1960 *Money, Credit & Commerce*. New York: Kelley.

MELTZER, ALLAN H. 1963 Demand for Money: The Evidence From the Time Series. *Journal of Political Economy* 71:219–246.

MOORE, GEOFFREY H. (editor) 1961 *Business Cycle Indicators*. 2 vols. National Bureau of Economic Research, Studies in Business Cycles, No. 10. New York: The Bureau. → Volume 1: *Contributions to the Analysis of Current Business Conditions*. Volume 2: *Basic Data on Cyclical Indicators*.

NEWCOMB, SIMON 1886 *Principles of Political Economy*. New York: Harper.

PATINKIN, DON (1948) 1951 Price Flexibility and Full Employment. Pages 252–283 in American Economic Association, *Readings in Monetary Theory*. Homewood, Ill.: Irwin. → First published in Volume 38 of the *American Economic Review*.

PATINKIN, DON (1956) 1965 *Money, Interest, and Prices: An Integration of Monetary and Value Theory*. 2d ed. New York: Harper.

PENROSE, EDITH T. 1962 Money, Prices, and Economic Expansion in the Middle East, 1952–1960. *Rivista internazionale di scienze economiche e commerciali* 9:401–427.

PIGOU, A. C. (1917) 1951 The Value of Money. Pages 162–183 in American Economic Association, *Readings in Monetary Theory.* Philadelphia: Blakiston.

PIGOU, A. C. 1943 The Classical Stationary State. *Economic Journal* 53:343–351.

PIGOU, A. C. (1947) 1951 Economic Progress in a Stable Environment. Pages 241–251 in American Economic Association, *Readings in Monetary Theory.* Homewood, Ill.: Irwin. → First published in Volume 14 of *Economica* New Series.

TOBIN, JAMES (1947) 1960 Money Wage Rates and Employment. Pages 572–587 in Seymour Harris (editor), *The New Economics: Keynes' Influence on Theory and Public Policy.* London: Dobson.

TOBIN, JAMES 1961 Money, Capital and Other Stores of Value. *American Economic Review* 51, no. 2:26–37.

WICKSELL, KNUT (1898) 1936 Interest and Prices (*Geldzins und Güterpreise*). With an introduction by Bertil Ohlin. London: Macmillan. → First published in German.

III
VELOCITY OF CIRCULATION

At least since the time of William Petty the velocity of circulation of money—known also as the rate of turnover, rate of use, frequency of use, rapidity of circulation, or efficiency—has been recognized as an important dimension of monetary analysis. A given quantity of money can finance any volume of spending, depending on how frequently, on the average, each unit is used. Moreover, a change in the quantity of money will alter aggregate demand for goods and services only if it is not offset by an opposite change in velocity. An understanding of the factors governing velocity obviously is crucial to the formulation of effective monetary policy.

Nevertheless, the velocity concept has been surrounded by controversies throughout its long history. The concept found greatest acceptance during the opening decades of the twentieth century —particularly in the United States, through the influence of Irving Fisher (1911). During the 1930s and 1940s it was abandoned by most economists in favor of the new conceptual framework fashioned by J. M. Keynes [*see* LIQUIDITY PREFERENCE]. More recently, however, the older concept has been finding its way into monetary literature again.

The recent revival of interest in monetary velocity reflects a number of developments. It has become evident in the post–World War II period that the major behavior relations proposed in the New Economics are not as dependable as many Keynesian enthusiasts had hoped they would be. Meanwhile, velocity analysis has been improved significantly. The concept of velocity has been refined in various ways, and it has been integrated at last into the main body of economic theory. In addition, the statistical resources for study of velocity have been extended greatly. This combination of conceptual breakthroughs and improved statistics has been accompanied by a number of attempts to explain particular velocity movements over time or cross-sectional differences, or to fashion general theories of velocity.

The early history of thought relating to velocity has been traced quite fully elsewhere, particularly by Holtrop (1929) and Marget (1938). This article is confined to a review of fundamentals, along with a discussion of more recent developments in velocity theory.

Types of velocities

The concept of the velocity of circulation of money is clearly and easily defined in general terms. It is the average number of times that each unit of money is spent during any time period. From the equation of exchange,

$$MV = PT,$$

where M is the average stock of money in existence during the period, P the average price of items purchased, and T the number of items purchased, it is evident that velocity is the volume of spending per unit of money:

$$V = PT/M.$$

However, the definition does not uniquely define velocity, since it fails to specify the meaning of "spending" and "money." Actually, economists have worked with several broad types of velocities, and with countless minor variations thereof.

Fisher's approach was to include in spending all exchanges of money against goods, services, and securities throughout an economy during a period such as a year and to restrict money to actual means of payment (i.e., privately held demand deposits and currency). The resulting spending–money ratio can be called *aggregate transactions velocity*, V_t. For several reasons this velocity concept is not very useful, except for purposes of classroom exposition. In the first place, reliable measures of total spending in any economy—even for a single year—do not exist and would be extremely difficult to construct. Second, while study of V_t might help us to understand changes in total spending, the general price level (P), and the volume of transactions (T), these concepts have little interest from a welfare or policy point of view. Finally, the use of V_t could be defended, apart from its immeasurability, only if money were regarded mainly as a "medium of exchange"; the demand for money would then be sensitive to the volume of spending, and V_t would tend to be fairly stable. Most economists now emphasize the "store of wealth" function of money, and consequently they see no advantage in relating the stock of money to total spending, as V_t does.

A second approach, pioneered in the United States by the Federal Reserve System, is to focus on the velocity of demand deposits alone, in which case spending means "spending by check." This velocity is known as *deposit turnover*, V_d. Monthly estimates of V_d, based on data from a large sample of banks, are available for the United States since 1919 and are published each month in the *Federal Reserve Bulletin*. Although these estimates are a valued part of our monetary statistics, V_d, like V_t, does not directly relate to important policy variables such as the level of wholesale prices or the level of national income. And, like V_t, it assumes implicitly that the volume of spending is the major determinant of the demand for money.

Recognition of the shortcomings of V_t and V_d has led modern economists, beginning with Pigou (1927), to develop a third index of money use, *income velocity*, V_y. Since V_y is merely the ratio of spending for currently produced goods and services (i.e., gross or net national product) to the total money stock, it can be computed quite simply. Annual time series of V_y in the United States since 1867 have been constructed by Friedman and Schwartz (1963). Moreover, with the world-wide development of national income statistics, V_y estimates can now be made for a large number of other countries. Quarterly V_y series are also available for the United States since 1946.

In addition to its measurability, V_y has the important advantage of relating the money stock to national product, a concept of major interest to economists. Similarly, an index of the prices of final goods and services is much more meaningful than a general price index which includes prices of stocks and many other things that are not vitally important to most policy decisions. While V_y was attacked by Keynes (1930, vol. 2, p. 24) as a "hybrid conception having no particular significance" because some of the money included in its denominator is used to finance purchases other than those of final output, most contemporary economists would reject the criticism as placing too much emphasis on the "transaction motive" for holding cash. If the volume of spending does not dominate the demand for money, then it does not matter that V_y omits large segments of spending from the analysis.

One can obtain a fourth type of velocity by disaggregating whatever concept of spending one wishes to use and dividing each sector's spending by its money holdings. The sectors can be drawn according to any number of principles (e.g., by regions, industries, or size classes) and at any level of aggregation; hence, the number of conceivable *sector velocities* is indefinitely large.

The idea of sectoral velocity analysis is not new; Keynes (1930, vol. 2) advocated such an approach decades ago. Except for the Federal Reserve estimates of V_d, however, which have always been available by groups of cities as well as on an aggregate basis, sector velocities have been ignored for the most part until quite recently. One can compute annual velocities for business firms and households in the United States since the early 1930s and quarterly business velocities since the late 1940s (see Selden 1962).

The principal advantage of the sector approach is that it may facilitate analysis of aggregate velocity. Aggregate velocity is a weighted average of sector velocities, the weights being the share of the money stock that each sector holds. Let V_{ti} and M_i be transactions velocity and money holdings in the ith sector. Then,

$$V_t = \sum_i V_{ti}\, M_i / M.$$

Thus, changes in aggregate velocity reflect either changes in the weights of sectors or changes in sector velocities. Velocity changes may emanate from different sectors at different times; specific knowledge of the point of origin of a change should contribute to an understanding of its nature.

Another concept, the *velocity of active money*, V_a, was popularized by Keynes (1936). In a sense this may be regarded as a special kind of sector velocity, in which total spending, however defined, is divided by "active" balances only. The relationship of this velocity to aggregate velocity is then

$$V = V_a M_a / M,$$

where M_a is active money. Because of the difficulty in finding an appropriate basis for separating cash into active and idle components, most economists have found this concept, like V_t, useful mainly in abstract discussions of monetary theory. Angell (1936), Tobin (1947), Bronfenbrenner and Mayer (1960), and several others have attempted to solve this problem by (1) adopting the Keynesian hypothesis that V_a changes only gradually over time and (2) finding some period, such as 1929, in which all cash supposedly was drawn into active circulation. Such calculations are not without interest, but there has been a growing tendency in the 1950s and 1960s for economists to abandon the active–idle dichotomy and to work with total cash instead.

The behavior of velocity

It is doubtful whether any economist of recognized stature, from Petty's day to the present, has regarded the velocity of money as being rigidly fixed over time. Not until the twentieth century, however, did dependable time series become available, permitting close study of velocity movements.

U.S. data reveal the existence of fairly regular seasonal and cyclical velocity variations, as well as persistent secular changes. Seasonally, both V_d and V_y reach lows early in the year and highs in the closing months, despite the fact that the money stock has a similar seasonal pattern.

Cyclically, all velocity measures tend to rise during general business expansions and fall during contractions, with peaks and troughs in velocity coinciding with business cycle peaks and troughs. Cyclical amplitudes, interpreted as deviations from secular trends, are substantially greater in V than in M; indeed, the latter usually continues to rise during business contractions, although at a diminished rate. These cyclical changes in velocity can be seen in Figure 1, which reproduces two income velocity series constructed by Friedman and Schwartz, one referring to the velocity of money defined broadly (total adjusted deposits plus currency outside banks) for the period 1869–1960, the other referring to money defined more narrowly (adjusted demand deposits plus currency outside banks) for the period 1915–1960. Cyclical swings in velocity are characteristic of all major sectors of the economy, but they are much more severe for businesses than for households and governmental units.

Figure 1 also shows a pronounced and steady downtrend in velocity between the early 1880s and the late 1940s—a pattern that was first noted by

Figure 1

Source: Friedman & Schwartz 1963, p. 640.

Warburton (1945; 1949). The latter's studies, based on admittedly crude data, suggested that V_y has been declining at a rate of about $1\frac{1}{3}$ per cent per year since the beginning of the nineteenth century. It is interesting that the more elaborate study of Friedman and Schwartz (1963), covering nine decades ending in 1960, also found a declining trend of slightly over 1 per cent per year. These findings are particularly interesting because they are contrary to the expectation, held by Fisher (1911) and others, that velocity would rise over time. Comparable statistics over extended time periods are lacking for other countries, but fragmentary evidence compiled by Doblin (1951) strongly suggests that secular velocity declines have been a world-wide phenomenon, at least through the 1940s.

Since the end of World War II, on the other hand, V_d and V_y have been rising steadily, except for minor cyclical interruptions. The postwar rise shows up regardless of how spending and money are defined, although the rise is dampened considerably if one follows Friedman and Schwartz and defines M broadly to include commercial bank time deposits as well as demand deposits and currency. Moreover, sectoral studies reveal that the postwar velocity rise has taken place in every sector for which data are available.

There has been much controversy over the nature of postwar velocity movements—whether the rise represents a fundamental break with the past or is merely a readjustment from abnormally low levels in the 1930s and during World War II. We shall have more to say on this matter in the next section.

In addition to the temporal changes in velocity already mentioned, there are noteworthy cross-sectional differences at any point in time. Perhaps the most familiar of these differences are in V_d for New York City, for six other major centers, and for the remaining centers for which information is compiled. In 1963 these figures were 84.8, 44.6, and 29.0, respectively.

Among the major sectors covered by Federal Reserve flow-of-funds accounts, corporate business has consistently had higher velocity ratios than noncorporate business, which in turn has higher ratios than the consumer and nonprofit sectors. State and local governments, the farm sector, and nonbank financial intermediaries hold large amounts of cash per dollar of spending, while the federal government operates with relatively small cash balances, though not so small as that of corporate business.

Within the business sector there are further in-teresting differences by industry and by size of firm. Wholesale and retail trade are high velocity sectors, manufacturing is intermediate, and mining and public utilities maintain low velocity ratios. Until recently small firms have tended to have higher velocities than large firms; however, during the general velocity rise of the 1950s the velocities of very large firms rose much more rapidly than those of medium-size and small firms. By the end of the decade most of the earlier size differentials had been eliminated.

Determinants of velocity

Fisher, Marshall, Pigou, and Wicksell. Although a number of early thinkers gained important insights into the problem of what determines monetary velocity, it is fair to say that real progress dates from the first decade or two of this century, with the contributions of Fisher (1911), Marshall (1923), Pigou (1917), and Wicksell (1906). These men worked more or less independently (except Pigou, who was Marshall's student and colleague), and they developed rather different modes of analysis. In fact, Marshall and Pigou chose to work with the reciprocal of velocity, which they misleadingly designated k, rather than with velocity itself. Yet the substance of their analyses was remarkably similar. In each case emphasis was placed on more or less mechanical relationships between payments and receipts. This is evident from Fisher's formal listing of influences on velocity:

1. Habits of the individual.
     (*a*) As to thrift and hoarding.
     (*b*) As to book credit.
     (*c*) As to the use of checks.
2. Systems of payments in the community.
     (*a*) As to frequency of receipts and disbursements.
     (*b*) As to regularity of receipts and disbursements.
     (*c*) As to correspondence between times and amounts of receipts and disbursements.
3. General influences.
     (*a*) Density of population.
     (*b*) Rapidity of transportation.

However, implicitly or explicitly all of these economists assigned some role to the rate of interest as a velocity determinant. This comes out most clearly in Pigou's work (1917).

Perhaps the major stumbling block in these early analyses was the sterile manner in which velocity (or its reciprocal) was related to the demand for money. It was recognized that velocity and the demand for money are intimately related: a rise (fall) in V implies a fall (rise) in the demand for money. However, the neoclassical depiction of the demand for money necessarily took the form of a rectangular hyperbola. M was placed on the horizontal axis; the value of money, $1/P$, on the vertical. For given levels of V and T, M times $1/P$ is fixed; that is, real cash balances are constant. Variations in T/V would cause a shift in the demand curve, but the new curve would again be a rectangular hyperbola.

This pseudo integration of monetary theory with orthodox price theory was a cul-de-sac which impeded progress in velocity theory for a generation. To a large extent the theoretical advances made by Angell (1936; 1941), Ellis (1938), and others in the 1920s and 1930s were merely refinements of the technical payments factors isolated earlier by Fisher. The interesting contributions made more recently by Garvy (1959a; 1959b) represent a further development in this direction.

The Hicksian–Keynesian revolution. The transition into modern velocity analysis began with Hicks's famous article (1935) and Keynes's *General Theory* (1936). Both of these works proposed that the demand for money be analyzed by setting M against the *cost of holding it* rather than against its exchange value ($1/P$), cost being measured by forgone yields on other assets.

Unfortunately, the analysis was not carried much beyond this. Furthermore, Keynes's discussion, which attracted more attention than Hicks's, was built around the arbitrary distinction between active and idle cash—velocity received scant explicit attention. In fact, Keynes ridiculed "those who make sport with velocity." Many years passed, therefore, before it became generally recognized that the Keynesian discussion of "liquidity preference" was a disguised analysis of velocity.

Insofar as they have been expressly concerned with velocity theory, most Keynesian economists have emphasized the causal role of interest rates—low (high) rates being associated with low (high) velocities.

Postwar developments. The most significant advances in velocity theory in the postwar period have been, essentially, elaborations of Hicks's 1935 contribution. It is now widely accepted that velocity must be analyzed in the framework of the demand for money and that orthodox demand theory can be applied in a fairly straightforward manner to the demand for the services of money. However, the "price" variable—the cost of holding money—has been refined considerably, and attention has been directed increasingly to the impact of such nonprice determinants as income, wealth, money substitutes, tastes, and expectations.

The cost of holding money. Despite a number of interesting contributions, economists remain sharply divided over the role of the cost of holding money as a determinant of V. On the level of pure theory, Baumol (1952) and Tobin (1956) demonstrated that there are good reasons for thinking that, contrary to the earlier Keynesian emphasis, the demand for transactions balances *is* a function of interest rates. More significantly, several empirical studies were made. Cagan (1956) found striking relationships during hyperinflations in a number of countries between real balances (and presumably V) and the rate of change of the price level. On the basis of annual data for the United States for 1907–1958, Latané (1954; 1960) concluded that desired holdings of demand deposits plus currency, per dollar of gross national product, were fairly responsive to changes in corporate yields. Meltzer (1963b), using measures similar to those of Latané, also found a strong interest-rate effect on velocity for 1900–1958. In addition to these aggregate time series studies, Selden (1962) and Meltzer (1963a) made cross-section analyses of velocity and the demand for money among American business firms, and found strong indications of interest-rate effects.

On the other hand, Friedman (1959, p. 345), in a study of velocity movements over the period 1870–1954, concluded:

A rise in the bond yield tends to reduce the real stock of money demanded for a given real income—that is, to raise velocity—and conversely. Bond yields, however, play nothing like so important and regularly consistent a role in accounting for changes in velocity as does real income. The short-term interest rate was even less highly correlated with velocity than the yield on corporate bonds.

In part these differences in emphasis reflect differing concepts, measures, and time periods used in the various statistical tests. Friedman, in contrast with Latané and Meltzer, included commercial bank time deposits in the money stock, and his period of analysis is substantially longer. But the differences also reflect the fact that in Friedman's work the effect of interest rates on V was examined after allowing for the effect of changes in real income per capita.

Aside from these extensive empirical investigations, there was increasing concern, in general commentaries on monetary problems during the 1950s, with the interest elasticity of velocity. It was frequently contended that during periods of rising demand for goods and services, banks and other lenders can easily sell securities on the open market and use the proceeds to finance additional spending. Thus, while the monetary authorities can keep *M* from expanding at such times, they may be unable to prevent inflationary increases in *V*. However, the validity of this line of argument depends on (1) the terms on which the holders of cash are willing to acquire additional securities and (2) the terms on which prospective spenders are willing to incur additional debt. If the first of these relationships is highly interest-inelastic while the second is not, then lenders have little power to circumvent monetary policy. But the facts concerning these interest elasticities, and hence the interest elasticity of *V*, need much further study before any definite conclusions can be reached.

Other hypotheses. A number of economists, including Warburton (1949), Selden (1956), and Friedman (1959), have studied the role of per capita real income as a velocity determinant. Friedman's analysis is particularly interesting, in that he relies on income changes to explain not only broad secular movements in *V* but cyclical movements as well. This is done by use of a "permanent income" hypothesis. [*See* MONEY, *article on* QUANTITY THEORY, *for additional discussion*.] As income rises secularly, corresponding to rises in permanent income, the demand for money rises faster than income; hence, the ratio of income to the money stock (V_y) falls. On the other hand, during cyclical expansions measured income rises faster than permanent income; hence, V_y rises. Friedman was able to explain nearly all velocity movements in the United States between 1870 and 1954 in terms of this permanent income hypothesis. However, the persistent rise in V_y, despite rising real incomes, during the 1950s and early 1960s has created a problem for all of these income approaches.

The postwar rise in *V* has stimulated economists to propose other explanations as well. Some have stressed the greater sense of economic security in the postwar world because of the altered economic role of government. Others have pointed out the generally inflationary environment that characterized the 1940s and much of the 1950s, making cash an unattractive asset to hold. However, other than changes in interest rates and income, the factor that has received most attention as a velocity determinant has been wealth. The role of financial wealth has been singled out by Gurley and Shaw (1960, pp. 177–179), who point out that in its broad historical contours the ratio of income to all financial assets has followed a pattern similar to that of the ratio of income to the money stock.

Certainly the growth of money substitutes in the form of claims against nonbank financial intermediaries has been an outstanding feature of the postwar world. A different kind of wealth hypothesis has been put forth by Meltzer (1963*b*), who found a close multiple correlation between *V*, corporate bond yields, and nonhuman tangible wealth over the period 1900–1958.

It is clear from these various studies that economists are still some distance from reaching a consensus on the determinants of velocity. Nevertheless, the studies indicate that the velocity concept continues to preoccupy a large number of economists and that important progress has been made.

RICHARD T. SELDEN

BIBLIOGRAPHY

ANGELL, JAMES W. 1936 *The Behavior of Money: Exploratory Studies.* New York: McGraw-Hill.

ANGELL, JAMES W. 1941 *Investment and Business Cycles.* New York: McGraw-Hill.

BAUMOL, WILLIAM J. 1952 The Transactions Demand for Cash: An Inventory Theoretic Approach. *Quarterly Journal of Economics* 66:545–556.

BRONFENBRENNER, MARTIN; and MAYER, THOMAS 1960 Liquidity Functions in the American Economy. *Econometrica* 28:810–834.

CAGAN, PHILLIP 1956 The Monetary Dynamics of Hyperinflation. Pages 25–117 in Milton Friedman (editor), *Studies in the Quantity Theory of Money.* Univ. of Chicago Press.

DOBLIN, ERNEST 1951 The Ratio of Income to Money Supply: An International Survey. *Review of Economics and Statistics* 33:201–213.

ELLIS, HOWARD S. (1938) 1951 Some Fundamentals in the Theory of Velocity. Pages 89–128 in American Economic Association, *Readings in Monetary Theory.* Philadelphia: Blakiston.

FISHER, IRVING (1911) 1920 *The Purchasing Power of Money: Its Determination and Relation to Credit, Interest and Crises.* New ed., rev. New York: Macmillan.

FRIEDMAN, MILTON 1959 The Demand for Money: Some Theoretical and Empirical Results. *Journal of Political Economy* 67:327–351.

FRIEDMAN, MILTON; and SCHWARTZ, ANNA J. 1963 *A Monetary History of the United States: 1867–1960.* National Bureau of Economic Research, Studies in Business Cycles, No. 12. Princeton Univ. Press. → Copyright © 1963, by National Bureau of Economic Research.

GARVY, GEORGE 1959*a* *Deposit Velocity and Its Significance.* New York: Federal Reserve Bank of New York.

GARVY, GEORGE 1959*b* Structural Aspects of Money Velocity. *Quarterly Journal of Economics* 73:429–447.

GURLEY, JOHN G.; and SHAW, EDWARD S. 1960 *Money in a Theory of Finance.* With a mathematical appendix by Alain C. Enthoven. Washington: Brookings Institution.

HICKS, JOHN R. (1935) 1951 A Suggestion for Simplifying the Theory of Money. Pages 13–32 in American Economic Association, *Readings in Monetary Theory.* Philadelphia: Blakiston.

HOLTROP, MARIUS W. 1929 Theories of the Velocity of Circulation of Money in Earlier Economic Literature. *Economic History* 1:503–524.

KEYNES, JOHN MAYNARD (1930) 1958–1960 *A Treatise on Money.* 2 vols. London: Macmillan. → Volume 1: *The Pure Theory of Money.* Volume 2: *The Applied Theory of Money.*

KEYNES, JOHN MAYNARD 1936 *The General Theory of Employment, Interest and Money.* London: Macmillan. → A paperback edition was published in 1965 by Harcourt.

LATANÉ, HENRY A. 1954 Cash Balances and the Interest Rate: A Pragmatic Approach. *Review of Economics and Statistics* 36:456–460.

LATANÉ, HENRY A. 1960 Income Velocity and Interest Rates: A Pragmatic Approach. *Review of Economics and Statistics* 42:445–449.

MARGET, ARTHUR W. 1938 *The Theory of Prices: A Re-examination of the Central Problems of Monetary Theory.* Vol. 1. New York: Prentice-Hall.

MARSHALL, ALFRED (1923) 1960 *Money, Credit & Commerce.* New York: Kelley.

MELTZER, ALLAN H. 1963a The Demand for Money: A Cross-section Study of Business Firms. *Quarterly Journal of Economics* 77:405–422.

MELTZER, ALLAN H. 1963b The Demand for Money: The Evidence From the Time Series. *Journal of Political Economy* 71:219–246.

PIGOU, ARTHUR C. (1917) 1951 The Value of Money. Pages 162–183 in American Economic Association, *Readings in Monetary Theory.* Philadelphia: Blakiston.

PIGOU, ARTHUR C. (1927) 1929 *Industrial Fluctuations.* 2d ed. London: Macmillan.

SELDEN, RICHARD T. 1956 Monetary Velocity in the United States. Pages 177–257 in Milton Friedman (editor), *Studies in the Quantity Theory of Money.* Univ. of Chicago Press.

SELDEN, RICHARD T. 1962 *The Postwar Rise in the Velocity of Money: A Sectoral Analysis.* New York: National Bureau of Economic Research.

TOBIN, JAMES 1947 Liquidity Preference and Monetary Policy. *Review of Economics and Statistics* 29:124–131.

TOBIN, JAMES 1956 The Interest-elasticity of Transactions Demand for Cash. *Review of Economics and Statistics* 38:241–247.

WARBURTON, CLARK 1945 Volume of Money and the Price Level Between Two World Wars. *Journal of Political Economy* 53:150–163.

WARBURTON, CLARK 1949 The Secular Trend in Monetary Velocity. *Quarterly Journal of Economics* 63:68–91.

WICKSELL, KNUT (1906) 1935 *Lectures on Political Economy.* Volume 2: Money. London: Routledge. → First published in Swedish.

IV

MONETARY REFORM

In its broadest sense, the term "monetary reform" refers to any programs or measures intended to change basic features of a nation's monetary and banking system. Recently the term has been extended to include proposals for reform of the international financial mechanism through fundamental changes in the present system of operations under the gold exchange standard. But in its most commonly accepted sense, the term relates to the comprehensive stabilization programs adopted in many European countries after World War II with a view to ending monetary disorders or disorganization and re-establishing a well-functioning currency system.

Monetary reform programs after World War II typically provided for a reduction in varying degrees of the liquid asset holdings of the public. While differing in many respects from country to country, the reforms always involved a withdrawal of most, and on occasion all, of the outstanding currency and the issue of a new currency. In most countries that adopted such programs, only a small part of the currency holdings was directly converted into a new currency; the remainder had to be deposited in banks. All or a large part of the balances in bank accounts were usually blocked, with withdrawals or transfers permitted only up to specified amounts or for specified purposes. In some cases, a substantial proportion of the blocked deposits was eventually wiped out. Several reform programs were associated with fiscal measures of varying sorts, such as capital levies or war-profits taxes. In a few cases the compulsory exchange of some of the blocked deposits into nonmarketable government securities was required.

Background and objectives. The objectives of the reform programs can be readily understood given the monetary situation prevailing through most of continental Europe during World War II and immediately afterward. In German-occupied Europe, the diversion of goods and services to the occupation armies, and similar exactions, were typically financed by central banks. The same was true of the large export surpluses vis-à-vis Germany. In that country, only a relatively small part of the war effort was financed out of taxes and public subscriptions to government bonds. Following liberation of western Europe and the occupation of Germany and Austria, the Continent was subjected to new financial strains. The allies' military expenditures for local supplies and services, and particularly the spending of military currency by their armies, added to monetary disorders during a period of severe disruption of the civilian economy.

Yet, despite the vast accumulation of liquid reserves in the hands of the public throughout the Continent and the shrinkage of civilian production, the familiar signs of open inflation—rapidly rising prices and wages and skyrocketing currency circulation—were largely confined to France, Italy, and southeastern Europe. The reason was a rigid enforcement of comprehensive price, wage, and allocation controls. Experience in postwar Europe demonstrates that when shelves are bare of all save the most essential supplies and actual economic transactions are at a bare minimum, considerable scope exists for the effective enforcement of such controls. [See PRICES, *article on* PRICE CONTROL AND RATIONING.]

As conditions for a recovery of production were re-established, the effectiveness of controls rapidly diminished. Even then in some parts of Europe they were fairly effective in preventing price inflation. But it became apparent that repressed inflation was exerting a deactivating, if not disintegrating, effect on economic life. Farmers resisted selling in legal markets for money with which there was little to buy and which was likely to depreciate; they preferred to barter their produce for consumer goods, including jewelry and other valuables that could serve as hoarding media. Manufacturers were reluctant to use up their remaining stocks of raw materials and semiprocessed goods and preferred to produce not for sale but primarily for the purpose of adding to their inventories. Consumers with large hoards of unwelcome funds at their disposal had no incentive to work at legal wage rates, payment of which added little to their purchasing power in real terms and merely left them with so much more unusable cash holdings.

In some countries, notably Germany, money was thus increasingly repudiated as a medium for effecting transactions, and a growing segment of trade moved entirely outside the traditional money economy. Farmers and manufacturers, as well as traders, turned to barter and so-called "compensation trading," with sales of goods tied to the delivery of usable products. Elsewhere, several heterogeneous market spheres existed side by side, with gray and black markets taking over an ever larger share of the distribution of current output. Currency in circulation tended to be used only as one of several media of exchange in illegal market deals and as a supplement to the ration ticket in transactions at authorized prices. Especially in Italy and to a lesser extent in France, the control mechanism had largely broken down and open inflation taken hold. In some parts of southeastern Europe, particularly in Hungary and Greece, hyperinflation reigned after the end of the war.

Thus in much of postwar Europe a basic task for civilian and military governments was to mop up idle money before it leaked into illegal markets and undermined the control mechanism and to rehabilitate the monetary system so that producers, whether farmers or manufacturers, would again be responsive to incentives to sell for monetary compensation and workers would depend on current income instead of past savings. A longer-term objective was to make the economy more amenable to the traditional controls of monetary policy. In those parts of Europe where inflation was no longer repressed, the task of monetary reform was to re-establish public confidence in money as a store of value.

Several other major objectives of monetary reform programs had little to do with the removal of excess liquidity. Among such purposes were a census of wealth, the detection of war profiteering and tax evasion, the cancellation of currency held by the enemy, and the unification of the currency in countries where several currencies had been introduced during the war. In some countries, political objectives also played a major role; reforms were directed at depriving certain socioeconomic groupings of most or all of their savings. This was true particularly in the countries of Soviet-occupied Europe, where monetary reforms had the incidental aim of strengthening the planning and allocation system. In sharp contrast, one of the major objectives of the West German currency reform was to revitalize free market forces and to permit the price mechanism to reassert itself as the decisive determinant of economic behavior.

Types. Despite the variety of their purposes, monetary reform programs can be classified by a few basic types, although of course few programs fall wholly in any one category. A useful classification, based on the method of reform employed, distinguishes (1) those that reduce the money supply by canceling part of the currency in circulation and part of existing bank deposits; (2) those that reduce the money supply by directing part of it into bank deposits, which are then to some extent demonetized or deactivated; (3) those that provide for conversion of the outstanding currency into another currency, without any significant blocking of bank deposits; and (4) those that virtually replace the entire money circulation with a new unit of account, after the pre-existing unit has depreciated to an infinitesimal fraction of its original value. Further useful lines of distinction may be based on whether or not the programs include fiscal devices, such as capital levies directed at absorbing significant amounts of funds held by owners of real, rather than monetary, assets. (For a somewhat different typology of monetary reforms, see Gurley 1953.)

(1) Cancellation—Germany. Monetary reform programs of the first type—featuring a severe reduction of the money supply by simply wiping out

large portions of outstanding notes and deposits—were enacted in West Germany and several eastern European countries. West Germany's program, enacted in June 1948, is of special interest because it was a resounding success and a turning point in the postwar history of that country. Under a series of decrees by the occupation powers, individuals were issued Deutsche mark (DM) 60 in exchange for an equal amount of old reichsmark (RM) holdings, and DM60 per employee were paid out to businesses for payroll purposes. Business holdings and individual holdings in excess of the converted amount were credited to bank accounts. Only a small fraction of all bank deposits was eventually converted into Deutsche marks, the great bulk being simply wiped out. For individuals the ultimate conversion ratio was in effect one-to-one for original holdings of no more than RM60, between one-to-one and ten-to-one for those holdings between RM60 and RM600, and between ten-to-one and slightly over fifteen-to-one for those holdings over RM600. The effective conversion ratios were more favorable, however, for heads of families and for businesses with more than one employee, becoming less onerous with increasing size of family or firm.

All bonds, mortgages, annuities, and other forms of private indebtedness were written down by 90 per cent; but prices, wages, rentals, and similar payments had to be converted at the one-to-one ratio. Cash holdings of public bodies were canceled and replaced by Deutsche mark allotments based on average monthly receipts over a given period. The government security holdings of financial institutions were simply canceled. Banks received cash reserves and state equalization claims in amounts equal to their new liabilities plus an allotment of 5 per cent of deposit liabilities, the counterpart of which constituted the capital account of their balance sheets. Similar provisions applied to insurance companies and other financial institutions.

West Germany's monetary reform was not accompanied by a capital levy on real asset holdings. However, one of the military government laws providing for the reform called on appropriate German legislative bodies to frame the necessary legislation for the equalization of the war burden. Such legislation was subsequently adopted, along with laws that provided for special conversion rates applicable to deposit holdings of pensioners, refugees, savers, and selected groups of other liquid-asset holders.

(2) *Blocking—Belgium.* Belgium provides an example of the second type of monetary reforms—those that do not cancel any part of the money supply but reduce it by requiring the conversion of liquid holdings into illiquid assets and by imposing severe restraints on the spending of these illiquid assets. The Belgian program, executed in October 1944, was the forerunner of all other monetary reform measures in liberated Europe and probably the inspiration for several of the reform laws adopted elsewhere. For immediate needs, the head of each family could exchange old banknotes for new ones, on a one-to-one basis, up to the amount of 2,000 francs per family member; all remaining holdings of bank notes in denominations of 100 francs and higher had to be declared and deposited in blocked bank accounts. Simultaneously, all existing bank deposits were blocked. (A certain portion, representing either the amount held on the day preceding the German invasion or 10 per cent of the amount held immediately before the reform, was excepted; for business firms the exempted portion was 1,000 francs per employee.) A short time later, each deposit owner was permitted to withdraw an additional amount of up to 3,000 francs. Each blocked amount, whether arising from note deposits or from pre-existing deposits, was divided into two parts, with 40 per cent temporarily blocked and 60 per cent definitively blocked until a means for its disposition was determined. A series of general releases gradually deblocked the temporarily blocked deposits. At the end of 1945, the 60 per cent portion of previously deposited notes and frozen bank balances was converted into long-term nonnegotiable government bonds carrying an interest rate of 3.5 per cent; subsequently, a large part of these bonds was absorbed by a special tax program.

(3) *Simple conversion—Denmark, France.* Turning now to the third type of monetary reforms—those that convert the old currency into a new one, without significant contraction of the money supply—Denmark's currency exchange of July 1945 affords a good illustration. Its major objectives were to reduce currency holdings relative to bank deposits, to prevent the reimport into Denmark of German-held Danish currency, and to facilitate the taxation of war profits. The reform program called for a declaration of wealth, a limited exchange of banknote holdings, the depositing of excess holdings in blocked bank accounts, the blocking of existing bank deposits if in excess of 10,000 kroner or in excess of 150 per cent of deposit holdings on the day of Denmark's invasion by Germany. Within five months, however, the blocked deposits were released, except those of tax evaders.

The French currency reform of June 1945 had

MONEY: Monetary Reform

the same purposes as that of Denmark but did not call for even a temporary blocking of deposits. The reform was accompanied by a progressive capital levy and a capital gains tax, with payment of these taxes spread over several years. In February 1948 the French government withdrew all 5,000 franc notes in circulation, and amounts in excess of 10,000 francs were returned to their owners only after they had discharged certain tax liabilities. But this measure did little more than sterilize part of the money supply for a short period.

(4) Drastic conversion—Greece, Hungary. The monetary reform programs in Greece and Hungary, which exemplify the fourth type, were put into operation only after protracted periods of currency disturbances and not until inflation had brought about a depreciation of the currencies to an infinitesimal fraction of their prewar value. Special interest attaches to the Hungarian stabilization scheme of 1946, inasmuch as it brought to an end possibly the greatest inflation of history. Its special feature was that it provided for an internally consistent wage and salary structure designed to permit the distribution of scarce supplies at rigidly fixed prices. The program, executed in August 1946, called for the introduction of a new currency unit, the forint, to replace the pengö at the rate of 1 forint to 400 octillion pengö. (This conversion was preceded by the issue earlier in 1946 of a special currency, the so-called tax pengö, a monetary unit of account whose value was related to a price index expressed in terms of the regular pengö.)

The reform program was based on computations of the gross national product in relation to its prewar level. Proportionate ceilings were set on wages, somewhat less favorable ceilings were established for salaries, and the income to be allocated to farmers and to manufacturers was related to the new money supply. The architects of the reform were insistent on limiting total income to the money value of available goods and services. The program was reinforced by a balanced budget, by the central bank's acquisition of dollars circulating in the country, and by the return of the gold removed by the Nazi regime. (For details, see Nogaro 1948.)

Capital and increment levies. Many of the monetary reforms, notably those in western Europe, were accompanied by a census of both monetary and real assets. This served the purpose of laying the basis for capital levies and for taxes on capital increments and war profits—fiscal devices that in several countries, including Denmark and Norway, played a central role in the reform program. The motive, apart from the obvious desire to confiscate

profits resulting from trading with the enemy and illegal transactions, was to distribute the financial burden of monetary sanitation programs more equitably between holders of monetary and real wealth. By and large, monetary reforms that involve a cancellation of currency and bank deposit holdings affect solely households and businesses that have been unable or unwilling to dispose of their liquid funds. Capital and increment levies, on the other hand, can be laid on property owners in approximate proportion to their share in, or gains of, real wealth as well as monetary assets.

With few exceptions, capital levies and similar devices have failed to make a major contribution to achieving the objectives of monetary reforms, although some of them have produced handsome yields over time. Most of the nonmonetary property subject to such levies consists of real estate, buildings, plants, equipment, valuables, and securities. Quite apart from the valuation problems involved, such assets cannot be converted into cash with which to discharge the levy because of the absence of capital markets that could absorb large offerings. In actual practice, the collection of these levies had to be spread over many years, which meant that payment was usually made out of current income. The proceeds were rarely employed for the redemption of government debt and contraction of the money supply. In some countries, notably Belgium and the Netherlands, such levies were in part paid out of blocked accounts or nonnegotiable government securities into which blocked accounts had been converted. But even in these two countries, individual tax liabilities often substantially exceeded blocked or nonnegotiable asset holdings. Postwar experience has demonstrated that capital and increment levies, whatever their merit from the viewpoint of social justice and equity, give rise to highly complex assessment and collection problems. For this reason they do not commend themselves as an effective tool for the removal of a monetary overhang.

Evaluation. Not many additional generalizations about the efficacy of monetary reforms can be made with any assurance; there has been too much diversity in both the design and the execution of reform programs. On the whole, the preventive, ameliorative, and bracing effects of the more far-reaching measures, at least during the six months or year after their adoption, may be judged as quite impressive. In two or three countries, particularly in Germany, the effects of the reforms in stimulating the economy were truly remarkable; in several other countries they succeeded in eliminating black markets, at least temporarily, and in restoring the public's waning faith in the worth of money as a store of value. The resurgence of both open and repressed inflation and the re-emergence of black markets in many countries relatively soon after the completion of reforms should not be laid at their door, except in the few cases where the scope of the measures was so narrow as to cast doubt on the propriety of their designation as "reforms." In most cases, the reappearance of monetary maladies—which in several countries necessitated another sanitation program—should be attributed not to faulty or weak reforms but to subsequent inflationary monetary and fiscal policies and to the fact that in economies suffering from supply scarcities there was a low propensity to save and yet strong official pressures for investment.

This is not to deny that several of the reforms were marred by economic disturbances. A number of technical mistakes were made in the preparation and execution of reform programs, including premature announcements of details, too scanty or too liberal releases of deposits, and misjudgments of the public's transaction requirements. But this need not evoke surprise, since the architects of at least the initial programs had few if any precedents to draw on in their decision making.

From the viewpoint of equity, most monetary reform programs of the postwar period left much to be desired. The elimination or blocking of large proportions of the money supply without, or with scant, regard to the total wealth of its holders is a very crude device of the sledge-hammer variety, even if cushioned by exemptions for holders of small amounts of currency and bank deposits. But social justice would probably not have been served any better if the money surfeits of postwar Europe had been permitted to be absorbed by rising prices or if the authorities had continued their largely unsuccessful attempts to suppress the manifestations of excessive monetary expansion. On balance, the evidence justifies the conclusion that postwar monetary reforms made a major contribution to economic recovery in Europe.

FRED H. KLOPSTOCK

BIBLIOGRAPHY

Currency Reform in Eastern Europe. 1946 Federal Reserve Bank of New York, *Monthly Review* 28:39–43.
Currency Reform in the Netherlands. 1946 Federal Reserve Bank of New York, *Monthly Review* 28:8–9.
DE RIDDER, VICTOR A. 1948 The Belgian Monetary Reform: An Appraisal of the Results. *Review of Economic Studies* 16, no. 1:25–40.
DUPRIEZ, LÉON H. 1947 *Monetary Reconstruction in Belgium.* New York: King's Crown Press.
GROTIUS, FRITZ 1949 Die europäischen Geldreformen nach dem zweiten Weltkrieg. Parts 1–2. *Weltwirtschaftliches Archiv* 43:106–152, 276–325.
GURLEY, JOHN G. 1953 Excess Liquidity and European Monetary Reforms: 1944–1952. *American Economic Review* 43:76–100.
KLOPSTOCK, FRED H. 1946 Monetary Reform in Liberated Europe. *American Economic Review* 36, no. 4: 578–595.
KLOPSTOCK, FRED H. 1948a Monetary and Fiscal Policy in Post-liberation Austria. *Political Science Quarterly* 63, no. 1:99–124.
KLOPSTOCK, FRED H. 1948b Western Europe's Attack on Inflation. *Harvard Business Review* 26, no. 5:597–612.
KLOPSTOCK, FRED H. 1949 Monetary Reform in Western Germany. *Journal of Political Economy* 57, no. 4:277–292.
NOGARO, BERTRAND 1948 Hungary's Recent Monetary Crisis and Its Theoretical Meaning. *American Economic Review* 38, no. 4:526–542.
PESEK, BORIS P. 1958 Monetary Reform and Monetary Equilibrium. *Journal of Political Economy* 66, no. 5: 375–388.
SCHOUTEN, D. B. J. 1948 Theory and Practice of the Capital Levies in the Netherlands. Oxford University, Institute of Statistics, *Bulletin* 10, no. 4:117–122.

MONISM
See PLURALISM.

MONOPOLISTIC COMPETITION
See, *in order of relevance,* MONOPOLY; FIRM, THEORY OF THE; ADVERTISING, *article on* ECONOMIC ASPECTS.

MONOPOLY

In accordance with its etymological meaning of "one seller," the term "monopoly" in a strict sense refers to a situation in which a seller is the sole source of supply for an economic good that has no significant substitutes. The term is also applied more broadly, however, to any market in which the behavior of sellers is other than purely competitive. Since the price confronting the individual seller in pure competition, as determined by demand and supply in the market as a whole, is essentially independent of the quantity that he chooses to sell, monopoly in the broad sense characterizes the market position of any seller who has a significant degree of discretion about his price and whose quantity sold varies inversely with the price selected. In this sense, at least some degree of monopoly power is both widespread and practically unavoidable. Furthermore, monopoly and competition are not mutually exclusive elements but may both be present in any given market.

Finally, even when the behavior of individual sellers is purely competitive, any artificial restriction on their number or on the quantities that they are permitted to sell may also be classified as monopolistic.

Simple monopoly. The elementary static theory of the profit-maximizing equilibrium of a simple monopolist may be illustrated by Figure 1. With the monopolist's product quantity, q, measured on the horizontal axis and such magnitudes as his price, p, and his unit cost, c, on the vertical axis, the diagram depicts illustrative revenue and cost schedules, both average and marginal. The nature of these data can be briefly explained.

If the monopolist's total revenue and total cost are designated by R and C, respectively, the corresponding average magnitudes are defined as $AR = R/q = p$ and $AC = C/q = c$. The AR schedule reflects the demand confronting the seller, since it shows the quantities that customers are willing to buy from him at various alternative prices. Its significantly downward slope, the hallmark of the seller's monopoly power, is in contrast to the essentially horizontal demand that would apply to the individual seller in pure competition. Depending on the context of the analysis, the cost curves may refer to either (1) the long run, when a firm can vary all relevant factors of production, including the number and sizes of its plants, or (2) a short run, when certain components of the firm's plant and equipment are temporarily fixed (giving rise to the distinction between fixed and variable costs). In the long run the AC curve slopes downward, at least initially, as a reflection of the economies of large-scale production. If it turns upward at some point, that reflects an eventual dominance of diseconomies of scale. In the short run AC slopes even more sharply downward initially, as a reflection of the spreading of the fixed or overhead

costs over an increased output; it turns upward primarily because of plant-capacity limitations.

The concepts of marginal revenue and marginal cost refer to the rate of increase of the corresponding total magnitudes per unit of extra output. If output is increased by some finite amount, Δq, giving rise to similarly finite increments of total revenue, ΔR, and total cost, ΔC, marginal revenue and marginal cost in their discrete versions are defined as $MR = \Delta R/\Delta q$ and $MC = \Delta C/\Delta q$. For example, if Δq equals one unit, MR and MC reflect the increments of total revenue and total cost, respectively, occasioned by the production and sale of the one unit of extra output. If the basic variables are treated as continuous, the marginal concepts in their continuous versions become $MR = dR/dq$ and $MC = dC/dq$—the first derivatives of the corresponding total-revenue and total-cost functions, $R = R(q)$ and $C = C(q)$. In this version MR and MC again represent the additional R or C per unit of additional output, but only as the limiting values that are approached when the addition to output is viewed as becoming indefinitely small. It is this definition that is implied when MR and MC are represented by continuous curves, as in Figure 1. As can readily be proved, a marginal magnitude is less than, equal to, or greater than its corresponding average according as the average curve is decreasing, constant, or increasing.

The principal analytical significance of these marginal concepts is that the firm's profit-maximizing output is determined where the MR curve cuts the MC curve from above, as at the output q_0 in Figure 1. This follows from the definitions of MR and MC, which imply that the firm's total profit ($\pi = R - C$) is increased or decreased by an expansion of output according as MR is greater or less than MC. The profit-maximizing price, p_0, and unit cost, c_0, are then indicated on the AR and AC curves, respectively, at q_0. This identifies the equilibrium profit per unit as $\pi_0/q_0 = p_0 - c_0$; the maximized total profit, $\pi_0 = (p_0 - c_0)q_0$, is represented by the area of the shaded rectangle.

In a popular layman's phrase, monopolists are often represented as "charging what the traffic will bear," but this is, at best, ambiguous. Notice that a smaller "traffic" than q_0 would "bear" both a higher price and a higher profit per unit, whereas a lower price than p_0 would allow a "traffic" greater than q_0. In other words, to maximize total profit the monopolist must balance the favorable effect of a greater quantity against the unfavorable effect of a lower profit per unit, maximizing neither.

On the other hand, a positive profit is not a defining characteristic of monopoly. Thus, if the AR

Figure 1

Figure 2

curve is tangent to the AC curve at a single point (with $AR < AC$ everywhere else), as in Figure 2, total profit is merely zero when maximized. As may be relevant in a short run, furthermore, a maximized profit may also be negative—when AR lies below AC at all possible outputs. Conversely, a purely competitive firm may also have positive profit, not only in a short run but in the long run as well (provided only that "profit" is defined in a consistent manner, as the excess of total revenue over the *minimum* total cost that must be covered if the firm is to be willing to go on producing the given output indefinitely).

Monopoly broadly conceived.   "Simple" (sometimes called "pure") monopoly, implying essentially a complete absence of competitive influence, is a rare phenomenon, because of the strict conditions that must be met. First, there must be no significant relationship of substitution or complementarity with the products of any other firm or group of firms, save for the inevitable interdependence of all products in the economy as a whole. Second, there must be no threat of potential competition from the possible entry into the market of a supplier of a significantly substitutable product. Then, if the monopolist can vary the output that he produces and sells without having any appreciable effect on the situation or decisions of any other firm in the economy, his equilibrium can be treated in analytical isolation from the remainder of the economy—as that of a one-firm "industry."

Other forms of monopoly, to be distinguished from this simple species, include several forms of oligopoly, complementary monopoly, and the non-oligopolistic type of competition among a large number of suppliers of "differentiated" products— that is, products that are relatively close, but not perfect, substitutes.

Oligopoly exists when there are relatively few suppliers of at least relatively close substitutes or when relatively few suppliers account for the predominant part of the industry's total supply [*see* OLIGOPOLY]. It is classified as "pure" or "differentiated" oligopoly according as the oligopolists' products are perfect or imperfect substitutes. The distinctive feature of oligopoly is the appreciable effect that the individual firm has on the situation of its rivals through its own price, output, and other business decisions, since induced reactions of one kind or another on the part of the rivals are then highly likely. This means that it is highly unlikely that an oligopolist would suppose that the demand curve relevant for his market decisions would be one drawn on an assumption that either the prices or the outputs of his rivals were constant. Yet, since the reactions of rivals are, in general, uncertain, there is a corresponding uncertainty about the relevant demand confronting each oligopolist. This is why the oligopoly problem is such a conundrum, with a wide range of possible outcomes that embrace (1) various forms and degrees of collusion, whether explicit or tacit, toward one extreme and (2) various types and intensities of economic warfare toward the other. Except under conditions of warfare, however, the mutual awareness by oligopolists of their distinctive interdependence typically leads to higher prices and lower outputs than would be the case if that interdependence were ignored.

Although less important in reality and comparatively neglected by analysts, cases in which a small number of monopolists supply goods that are either perfect or imperfect complements involve essentially the same type of interdependence as in oligopoly. Here, however, collusion works in the direction of lower prices and greater quantities sold than is the case when the interdependence is ignored or imperfectly appreciated.

When differentiated products are supplied by a large number of small firms, oligopolistic relationships may be absent for much the same reason as in pure competition, because the small individual firm has only a negligible impact on the market position of any one of its many rivals even when it brings about a large relative change in its own sales. Accordingly, the demand relevant for this type of firm's decisions may be drawn on the assumption that all of its rivals' prices are constant— that is, independently determined. Given a sufficient degree of product differentiation, however, the demand confronting this type of firm slopes downward significantly, in contrast to the essentially horizontal demand facing the pure competitor. This market form may be called "differentiated competition," to distinguish it from pure competition in the same way that differentiated oligopoly is distinguished from pure oligopoly.

As to the equilibrium of the individual firm in differentiated competition, this is much the same as in simple monopoly. These two market forms differ, however, in that there is a problem of "group equilibrium" in differentiated competition, just as there is in pure competition. Differentiated competition typically involves not only a simultaneous equilibrium of each individual firm but also an equilibrium adjustment of the number of firms in the long run, through entry or exit in response to profits or losses. In a theoretically important, though hardly realistic, case in which all the actual and potential members of the group have like costs and face like demands, the ultimate long-run equilibrium is of the zero-profit type—with each firm's demand, or AR, curve just tangent to its AC curve, as in Figure 2. As emphasized by Edward H. Chamberlin (1933), the pioneer in the analysis of this and other forms of "monopolistic competition," this heroically simplified special case is merely a convenient illustration of the group-equilibrium concept. Realistically, various asymmetries of both demand and cost are overwhelmingly likely, with resulting differences of price, output, and profit among various firms in the group even in a state of long-run equilibrium.

Degree of monopoly power. In the sense that the situation of an individual seller may differ by much or little from that of a pure competitor, his monopoly power is a matter of degree. In the limiting case of pure competition, where the individual seller faces a horizontal demand so that AR and MR coincide, the maximizing of profit at the point where $MR = MC$ also implies an equating of AR and MC. When the AR curve slopes downward so that the MR curve lies below it, however, the equating of MR and MC implies that $AR > MC$. This led Abba P. Lerner (1934) to formulate as a quantitative measure of a firm's degree of monopoly power the ratio $M = (AR - MC)/AR$. That ratio is then zero for the profit-maximizing pure competitor, whereas for the profit-maximizing monopolist it is positive and would approach unity as an upper limit if his price or AR was visualized as becoming indefinitely large, relative to a given positive MC.

The degree of monopoly power of a firm in static profit-maximizing equilibrium is closely related to the "elasticity" of demand at the equilibrium point. That elasticity, defined as $E = (dq/dp)(p/q)$, measures the percentage change in quantity de-

manded, q, relative to the associated percentage change in price, p. It can then be shown that $E = AR/(MR - AR)$. Accordingly, when $MR = MC$ it follows that $M = -1/E$. This is consistent with the implication that the horizontal demand facing a purely competitive firm is "perfectly" or "infinitely" elastic, whereas the elasticity of the downward-sloping demand facing a monopolist is finite and greater than unity in absolute value at a point where profit is a maximum and MC is positive.

On the other hand, the relevance of M as a measure of the degree of monopoly power is not limited to situations of static equilibrium. Thus, whether or not MR is equated with MC or is determinate at all, the definition of M in terms of AR and MC makes it a measure of the degree of currently "exerted" monopoly power, even if its value would be different in some alternative position of static equilibrium. This is important, for sometimes (especially in oligopoly) MR may be basically uncertain or indeterminate, and very often monopolists of various types are persuaded by dynamic or "long run" considerations not to seek to maximize profit with respect to the demand and cost data that apply in a given short run. Furthermore, it is precisely the relationships of AR and MC in all of the firms throughout the economy that are of central interest in evaluating the efficiency of allocation of the economy's resources, as will be further discussed below.

Other comparative implications. As a reflection of the horizontal demand facing a pure competitor and the resulting equilibrium equality of AR and MC, each pure competitor sells all that it wishes to at the prevailing price. By contrast, since the firm that faces a downward-sloping demand regularly chooses to operate where $AR > MC$, it remains eager to sell more at its chosen price. If it could sell more at that price, its profit would rise by the amount $AR - MC$ for every extra unit of product sold. A variety of important implications follows from this basic contrast between monopoly and pure competition.

As an analytical matter, it means that only in pure competition can equilibrium price and quantity be explained by means of the famous law of supply and demand, for only in pure competition can the aggregate willingness of all eligible producers to sell be summarized in an industry supply curve, whose intersection with the industry demand curve then determines the equilibrium price and quantity. Under any form of monopoly, by contrast, supply regularly exceeds demand in the sense that each producer is willing to sell more than he actually sells at the price he chooses to set. Nor is it possible to analyze a monopolist's equilibrium with reference to any sort of quasi supply curve traced out by a series of hypothetically shifting demand curves, for a different locus of price–quantity equilibrium points would be traced out by every different set of shifting demands, as a reflection of the different relationships between AR and MR that apply when the slope and elasticity of demand are altered.

The monopolist's eagerness to sell more at his currently chosen price is also closely related to what is called "nonprice competition," including the two major categories of selling effort and product variation. Advertising, for example, is never relevant for a purely competitive firm, which can always sell what it pleases anyway, at a price over which it has no control. When $AR > MC$, however, advertising will pay if it induces a sufficient expansion of demand relative to the advertising expense. The higher is $M = (AR - MC)/AR$, moreover, the greater are the chances that this will be so. If $M = .1$, for example, an extra dollar spent on advertising will be profitable only if it raises the sales revenue R by more than ten dollars, but if $M = .25$, it will be profitable if it raises R by more than four dollars. This follows because an extra dollar of R, from expanded sales at an unchanged price, augments profit by a fraction of a dollar equal to the magnitude of M.

Naturally, advertising may also change the equilibrium price, and if it does so, the foregoing relationships apply with reference to the new price and the new value of M. In general, advertising may either raise or lower the profit-maximizing price. Thus, if MC is constant over the range of expanded output, the static-equilibrium price will rise or fall according as the elasticity of demand is lowered or raised in absolute value at the level of the original price—as can be proved from the relationship $E = AR/(MR - AR)$. Similarly, if E is unchanged at the original price as the demand curve is shifted to the right, the equilibrium price will rise or fall according as the MC curve is rising or falling. These relationships apply to the "comparative statics" of a spontaneous increase in demand as well as to an increase induced by advertising, since advertising expense is in the nature of a fixed cost, having no impact on marginal cost. At least as a matter of static analysis, it is worth emphasizing that the effect of a shift in demand on the equilibrium price depends on MC, not on AC, as popular discussions would usually have it. Since AC is much more likely to be downward sloping than MC

is, the correct analysis is less favorable to the possibility that price will fall as demand is increased than is the erroneous theory so widely held in the advertising profession.

When the products of rival firms are inherently homogeneous, as in pure competition or pure oligopoly, strategies of product variation are ruled out by definition. When there is scope for product differentiation, however, the "product" itself becomes a variable, so that deliberate variations in its characteristics become an eligible part of the total market strategy, with simultaneous effects on both cost and demand. From an economic standpoint, the "product" involves not just its physical features but all of those ancillary characteristics that influence its acceptability to customers, such as its packaging, the location and personality of its sellers, any accompanying services, and so on. This gives a very wide scope to the various possible strategies of product variation. Thus, some firms may seek to imitate as effectively as possible the more popular products of their rivals, while the rivals seek to maintain or increase the distinctiveness of theirs. Especially when the magnitude of M is great, consumers may be at least partially compensated for the weakness of price competition by an intensified effort by producers to improve quality and service. When consumers are relatively poor judges of quality differences, however, they may be victimized by deliberate product deterioration.

In general, the comparative strengths of price and nonprice competition often tend to be inversely related. Not only is nonprice competition wholly absent when $M = 0$ and price competition is of maximum effectiveness, but also, as price competition is increasingly inhibited, there is a natural tendency for the various forms of nonprice competition to be correspondingly intensified. To the extent that at least certain types of nonprice competition are deemed desirable, a difficult problem is posed for public policy as to the desirable degrees of both price and nonprice competition.

Bases and limitations of monopoly power. Restraints on competition may be natural, artificial, or both in some combination. Perhaps the simplest illustration of artificially created monopoly power is that based on the exclusive right granted by government in the form of a patent, whether as a gratuitous privilege bestowed by a monarch or, as in the more modern practice, as a reward for invention [see PATENTS]. The modern policy reflects another significant conflict between the social advantages and disadvantages of competition, for it is precisely when unrestrained competition is most likely to prevent the successful innovator from recovering adequate compensation for his costs and risks that some artificial incentive is most needed to induce his inventive and innovating activity. Although alternative forms of compensation would be possible, the patent systems of most modern nations reflect a judgment that, in the simplest and most favorable case, it is better to have a new product or process available under monopoly control than not to have it available at all. Similar considerations underlie the provisions for copyrighting literary and artistic productions.

Other types of franchise may be granted because of the inherent scarcity of an otherwise unappropriated resource. For example, the limited space on city streets may call for the limited licensing of taxicabs, and the limited number of television channels makes unique allocation necessary. More nearly absolute monopolies may also be enfranchised as a recognition of their status as "natural monopolies," where any relevant output can be produced much more efficiently by a single firm than by two or more. This is the case with a variety of "public utilities," which are then typically subjected to governmental regulation to limit their prices and profits [see REGULATION OF INDUSTRY]. Contrasting types of regulation of numbers of producers, outputs, or prices—as in agriculture, oil production, and even liquor retailing in some states—are designed only to limit competition in the interests of the existing producers.

Another possible source of monopoly power is the concentrated ownership of distinctive natural resources, such as ore deposits. Whether the consequences are monopolistic in the classical sense or just oligopolistic, such resource ownership frequently leads to monopoly power also over the products for which the distinctive resources are essential. On the other hand, the mere fixity of supply of a natural resource does not make it a monopoly. Modern economists do not follow Adam Smith's dictum that the rent of land is naturally a monopoly price.

In general, since pure competition requires that a homogeneous product be produced by a large number of firms, each large enough to exhaust all net economies of large-scale production, the more "natural" bases of monopoly power are to be found in the impediments to the fulfillment of these necessary conditions for pure competition. These impediments involve considerations that widen the scope for product differentiation, whether real or fancied, and also the conditions that underlie economies of scale, which limit the numbers of eligible producers of any given product and its relatively close substitutes.

Product differentiation would be important even if consumers were both exceedingly mobile and well informed about the inherent properties and relative prices of the various available products. It is all the more important in view of the actual imperfections of consumers' mobility and knowledge, which lead both to a good deal of inertia in consumer behavior and to the choice of products on the basis of reputation and prestige, whether deserved or not. Brand names and trade-marks, protecting the identity of given products, thus have the dual effects of guiding consumers to desired choices and fixing product differentiation in consumers' minds. Whatever its basis, strong consumer loyalty to a given brand strengthens the monopoly power of the supplier, against both existing and potential rivals.

Just as economies of scale sometimes produce natural monopolies, so under slightly weaker conditions they may cause some industries to be "natural oligopolies," when only a few firms at most can simultaneously achieve substantially all the potential economies of scale. In this connection there is an important distinction between the economies of the large-scale plant and the further possible economies of the large-scale, multiplant firm.

Given the number, sizes, and locations of firms producing a set of substitute products in a specified region, it should be emphasized that the market consequences further depend on the relative mobility of the customers, the products, or both. Thus, much retailing is inherently limited, as far as the spatial extent of the market is concerned, to relatively small neighborhoods. Toward the other extreme, there are meaningful "national" and "world" markets; but these markets are also inherently imperfect because of the costs and delays of communication and transportation. Just as space itself is a continuum, so are markets typically incapable of unique spatial definition.

The establishment, maintenance, and exercise of monopoly power also depend on the legal framework of permitted and prohibited acts. Clearly, mergers provide an easier path to monopoly than an increased market share that must be fought for competitively. Likewise, explicit agreements to limit competition among otherwise independent firms, whether in formal cartels or more informally, are consistently more effective techniques for achieving monopolistic behavior than the alternative of merely tacit collusion. Collusion, consisting of a mutual self-restraint from at least some forms of aggressively competitive behavior, frequently relies on one or more of such techniques as price leadership (the imitation of one firm's prices by the others) and market sharing (the policy on the part of each firm not to seek to increase its percentage of industry volume above some mutually recognized "normal" level). Full compliance with the "rules" of price leadership or market sharing is, however, typically difficult to achieve, especially on a lasting basis.

Although there is no necessary connection between a firm's degree of monopoly power (as reflected by the relationship of price and marginal cost) and its profitability, these are presumably linked in at least a rough empirical correlation. The persistence of profits through time depends, in turn, on barriers to the entry of potential rivals. Where entry is at least legally free, these barriers depend on net advantages of cost or product acceptance enjoyed by existing firms as compared with would-be entrants. The industries most difficult to enter are usually those with large absolute capital requirements for an efficient scale of production and product distribution, complex patentable technology, strong allegiance to existing brands by consumers, or some combination of these elements. When the nonrecurrent costs of building an efficient organization and achieving a sufficient degree of product acceptance are high, existing firms can continue to enjoy substantial profits without excessive danger of inviting actual attempts at entry.

Conversely, concern for potential competition is also a limiting factor on the degree of monopoly power that existing firms can afford to exert. Firms may also be deterred from the fullest possible exploitation of their monopoly power by the fear of government action and by other considerations, such as public, consumer, and employee relations.

Price discrimination. When a firm with monopoly power can divide its market into submarkets sufficiently distinct so that favored customers cannot readily resell to others, it is frequently more profitable for the monopolist to charge different prices in the different submarkets than to charge the same price throughout his whole market. In the limiting case where the various submarkets are wholly independent and costs per unit of product are the same, static profit-maximizing calls for equating marginal revenue in each submarket with the common marginal cost. This results in different prices when elasticities of demand differ from one submarket to another. Thus, from the previously noted relationship $E = AR/(MR - AR)$, it

follows that $AR = MR \cdot E/(1 + E)$, where $E < -1$. Hence, when MR is the same in each submarket, AR, or price, will be higher the closer is the elasticity, E, to -1.

When submarkets are not wholly independent, either because some limited resale among customers is possible or because the customers are themselves competing firms, the profit-maximizing rules are more complicated. Here, in addition to considerations of relative elasticities, it is also necessary to take into account the tendency of an increase in sales in a particular submarket, resulting from a price cut, to reduce sales in other submarkets.

Price discrimination is said to be "personal" when it depends on such features as the age, sex, income, and trade status of customers—as when different prices are charged to children and adults or to men and women at entertainments, or when rich and poor are charged different fees by physicians, or when different prices are charged to retailers and wholesalers even for like quantities of products, or when individual bargaining with customers results in different prices. Another category is "geographical" discrimination, as in the "dumping" of goods abroad at lower prices than at home or as a feature of "delivered-price systems" involving zone pricing or the use of basing points, where the net factory price differs for goods shipped to different localities. Price discrimination may also be either systematic or sporadic.

Not all price differences for the "same" product are necessarily discriminatory. Thus, if marginal costs vary for different quantities, and if prices reflect only those cost differences, there is no price discrimination. Similarly, when marginal costs vary between periods of peak and off-peak operation, price differences with the season of the year or even the time of day are not necessarily discriminatory. Indeed, when marginal costs differ and prices do not, that represents a concealed discrimination.

The concept of price discrimination is frequently expanded to cover the comparative prices of products that are related but not identical, such as different models of a generic product or physically comparable products marketed as different brands. The general test of price discrimination, covering these cases as well as the simpler ones, is whether the proportion of price to marginal cost is the same or different from one piece of business to another. Indeed, price discrimination may be defined as the firm's exertion of different degrees of monopoly power, as measured by the value of $M = (AR - MC)/AR$, from one submarket to another.

This formulation serves to emphasize that price discrimination is inherently a monopolistic phenomenon; in pure competition, where price necessarily equals marginal cost in equilibrium, price discrimination is impossible.

Of theoretical interest, though of limited practical importance, is the polar concept of "perfect" discrimination. This involves not only the monopolist's being able to treat each individual customer as a separate submarket but also his charging each customer, at least in effect, different prices for the different increments of product that he buys, in such a way that the monopolist arrogates to himself something approaching the entire potential gain from trade. Under appropriate continuity assumptions, the monopolist then maximizes his profit by equating with his marginal cost the price that he exacts from each customer for the final increment purchased (also equal to marginal revenue). As an alternative technique, the monopolist can achieve this result with an appropriate all-or-nothing offer to each customer for the appropriate aggregate quantity.

Monopsony.   In this section and the next some kindred concepts of monopoly will be briefly discussed.

Analogous to a seller's monopoly power, a buyer is said to have "monopsony" power when he can significantly affect the price of what he buys by varying the quantity bought. Typically, the monopsonist faces an upward-sloping supply schedule, showing the prices or average costs, AC, at which he may buy alternative quantities. There is then a related schedule of marginal cost, MC, lying above the AC curve when the AC curve is positively sloped. Examples of such schedules are shown in Figure 3.

Although a monopsonist might conceivably be a large ultimate consumer, the more important instances of monopsony concern the purchase of a factor of production by a firm. If the factor is passively supplied, as with unorganized labor or an intermediate product of a purely competitive industry, and if the buying firm is large enough to have the requisite influence on the factor price, the conditions for monopsony are fulfilled.

The monopsonist's equilibrium further depends on schedules of "average benefit," AB, and "marginal benefit," MB, as illustrated in Figure 3. In the rudimentary case where the factor in question is the only variable one, these concepts would correspond to what are called the factor's "average revenue product" and "marginal revenue product" —or R/f and dR/df, respectively, where R is the total revenue from the sale of the product and f is the factor quantity. When other factors are also variable, as in the firm's long-run equilibrium, similar concepts involving a "net revenue product" are used instead.

The monopsonist's equilibrium factor quantity is then determined where MC cuts MB from below, provided that AC does not exceed AB. In Figure 3, where the equilibrium factor quantity is at f_0, the corresponding equilibrium price is determined on the AC schedule at w_0, and the aggregate benefit from having that factor quantity (as compared with not producing at all) is indicated by the shaded area. In long-run equilibrium this would be the firm's total profit; in a short-run situation it would be necessary to subtract the fixed costs of the fixed factors to determine the profit.

Just as a monopolist would like to sell more at his equilibrium price and may therefore have a motive for exerting himself through advertising and other forms of nonprice competition to do so, so the monopsonist has a similar interest in buying more at his equilibrium price. This is so because his MB would exceed the price for a certain increment of hypothetical extra purchases. Similarly, the analogue of a seller's degree of monopoly power is the concept of a buyer's degree of monopsony power, which may be defined symbolically as $M' = (MB - AC)/MB$, with static-equilibrium values that lie between zero and one when the AC schedule is positive and positively sloped. A monopsony equilibrium with zero profit is also possible. This would be illustrated in a diagram such as Figure 3 if, in the long run, the positively sloped AC curve were shifted upward until it was just tangent to the AB curve.

Bilateral monopoly.   In monopoly or monopsony the discretionary power to set the price is uniquely on one side of the market, since the other side consists of passive price-takers. When compe-

Figure 3

tition is limited on both sides of the market at the same time, the usual consequence is a bargaining relationship. There are numerous possible patterns, involving either one or a few sellers, one or a few buyers, and homogeneous or differentiated goods. The application to union–management bargaining is obvious. Whether in the strict form of a single seller facing a single buyer or in the looser variants, this class of market relationships is known as "bilateral monopoly."

A basic theoretical case, first analyzed by Edgeworth (1881), concerns two persons who each possess fixed stocks of two homogeneous goods and who can trade only with one another. The problem is best formulated and analyzed with reference to the ingenious "box diagram" shown in Figure 4, first employed by Edgeworth himself.

Initial stocks of the two goods are designated as x_1 and y_1 for the first person and as x_2 and y_2 for the second. The dimensions of the box are then set at $x_1 + x_2$ on the horizontal axis and $y_1 + y_2$ on the vertical axis. When the first person's quantities are measured conventionally from the origin at I and the second person's are measured in

reverse directions from the origin at II, the point A represents the initial position and any other point within the box represents a possible redistribution of the fixed total quantities of the two goods. The tastes of the two traders are represented by selected indifference curves, such as those labeled I_{11}, I_{12}, and I_{13} for the first man and I_{21}, I_{22}, and I_{23} for the second. A person is made better off by any movement to another indifference curve lying farther away from his map's origin.

Since the indifference curves through point A—namely, I_{11} and I_{21}—are not tangent but, rather, intersect, mutually beneficial trade is possible. Specifically, any movement from A into the cigar-shaped area bounded by those two curves represents a simultaneous improvement for both parties —that is, a movement to "higher" indifference curves. The potential benefits of trade are fully exploited, however, only when the traders move to a point where their indifference curves are tangent —on a locus that Edgeworth called the "contract curve." The relevant range of this locus is depicted in Figure 4 by the curve drawn between D_1 and D_2. Naturally, the first person would prefer an

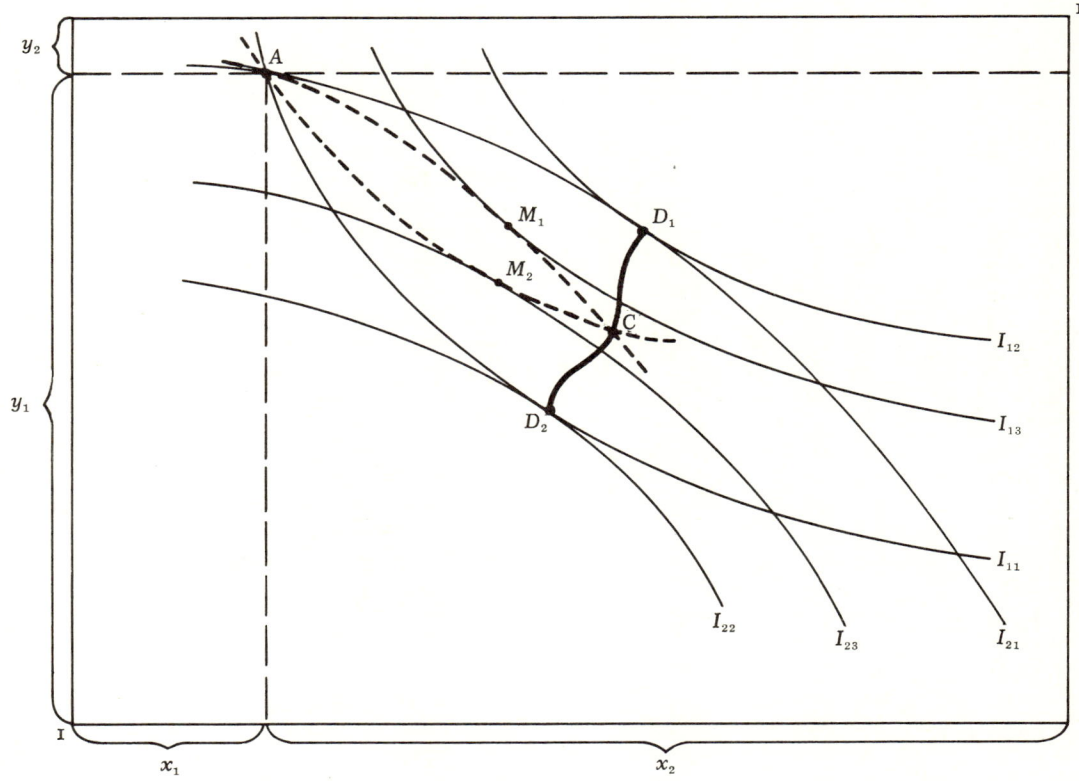

Figure 4

outcome as close as possible to D_1, and the second would prefer an outcome as close as possible to D_2. This conflict of interest is the source of the so-called indeterminacy of the bilateral-monopoly problem, since the analyst cannot confidently predict any unique outcome of the parties' bargaining.

In the course of that bargaining each party can threaten to refuse to trade at all unless the other is willing to grant sufficiently favorable terms. Hence, one possible outcome is that the parties may simply remain stubbornly at point A. If either can make a plausible take-it-or-leave-it offer to the other, however, an offer of the all-or-nothing type might achieve a result corresponding to perfect monopolistic discrimination, indefinitely close to D_1 or to D_2 (where the trader with the strategic initiative would reap all the potential gain and the passive trader none at all). Intermediate outcomes somewhere on the contract curve between D_1 and D_2 are, of course, more plausible under assumptions of a more nearly symmetrical bargaining process. Indeed, game theorists such as Nash (1950; 1953) and Harsanyi (1956), with the aid of further assumptions including the von Neumann–Morgenstern utility functions of the traders, claim to identify a unique solution point on the contract curve, but their reasoning is too complex for brief summary.

Other special outcomes, such as those at C, M_1, and M_2, also emerge from appropriately special assumptions. Thus, if each trader is assumed to be free to trade at some specified exchange ratio, along a straight line through A with a slope reflecting the given exchange ratio, he maximizes his benefit by moving to the point where the specified line is just tangent to one of his indifference curves. The locus of such points for various alternative exchange ratios is known as an "offer curve." It is illustrated in Figure 4 by the dashed curves through A, M_2, and C for the first person and through A, M_1, and C for the second.

The possible outcome at C, where the offer curves intersect, corresponds to the "competitive" solution, since it implies an equating of supply and demand. On the other hand, if either person has the privilege of setting the exchange ratio and the other then trades in accordance with his offer curve, the best ratio for the active strategist is the one implied at the point of tangency between one of his indifference curves and the offer curve of the other. These outcomes, corresponding to simple monopoly or monopsony solutions, are illustrated at M_1 and M_2, according as the first person or the second has the privilege of setting the exchange ratio. It should be noticed that these monopoly points fall short of the contract curve, in contrast to the competitive point which necessarily lies on it.

Bilateral monopoly in the context of a monopsonistic firm hiring organized labor or bargaining with a monopolistic supplier of an intermediate product is subject to similar analysis. By comparison with the monopsonistic equilibrium previously identified in Figure 3 (at f_0, w_0), for example, the competitive solution would call for the higher factor price and quantity at the intersection of AC and MB. Still higher prices and correspondingly reduced quantities along the MB schedule would illustrate a movement toward a monopolistic solution. A linear contract curve passing vertically through the intersection point of AC and MB is also implied in some cases, although not usually in the one involving labor.

Significance for welfare. The "evils" of monopoly and its kindred market situations, together with some possibly offsetting advantages, are at least to some extent in the eye of the beholder. This is especially so with respect to some of the sociopolitical issues involving "big" versus "small" business or the social implications of "economic power" —to the extent that these issues overlap with monopoly in the economic sense. Similarly, the tendency of monopoly to intensify the inequality of the distribution of income, though far from clear-cut, is in any event also subject to different evaluations.

The remaining aspect of monopoly and monopsony, on which economic analysis has had rather more to say, is the effect on the efficiency of resource allocation. Here the relevant analytical approach is that of welfare economics, with its central concept of "Pareto-optimality." As initially formulated by Vilfredo Pareto, a situation is said to be Pareto-optimal if there is no reallocation of resources or goods that can make one person better off without injury to at least one other person [see WELFARE ECONOMICS].

It is a principal theorem of welfare economics that a universally purely competitive general equilibrium is Pareto-optimal, provided that people's individual tastes are respected and that there are no "externalities," such as a dependence of any firm's output or any household's welfare on the factor employment of other firms or the goods consumption of other households. Short of a full demonstration of that theorem, it may be said that its essence lies in the implied equality of price and marginal cost for all produced goods and the similar equality of price and marginal benefit for all hired factors. By the same token, then, if these ideal conditions are disturbed by a monopolistic inequality of price and marginal cost or by a monopsonistic inequality of factor price and marginal benefit, the result is a departure from Pareto-optimality. Typically, the monopolist produces and sells too little at too high a price, and the monopsonist buys too little at too low a price.

Note that if excessive profit were the only evil of monopoly, the equating of price with average cost would be the remedy—as in the conventional philosophy of public-utility regulation. When average cost is decreasing, however, an excess of price over marginal cost is still implied. Under such circumstances the Pareto-optimal equating of price with marginal cost involves a loss, which must then be made good by external subsidy.

Even under the indicated ideal conditions, universally pure competition is only a sufficient—not a necessary—condition for Pareto-optimality. As already illustrated for the simplified two-person exchange economy portrayed in Figure 4, there are various ways in which the Pareto-optimal contract curve can be reached, including perfect discrimination as well as pure competition. At the same time, however, that analysis also showed how simple monopoly or monopsony systematically falls short of Pareto-optimality.

When universal pure competition is not naturally viable (for example because of persistently decreasing costs) or when externalities are present, Pareto-optimality cannot be achieved by simply preventing monopoly and monopsony. Furthermore, the attainment of that ideal by elaborate special regulations, though theoretically conceivable, obviously involves attendant difficulties and costs that force us to aim at less than the ideal. Under these circumstances there are no simple rules for attaining a "second-best" result. In this context, a blanket indictment of monopoly and monopsony as inefficient is no longer valid. In the wider context of a dynamic economy where technological progress is to be encouraged, this observation acquires still greater force.

ROBERT L. BISHOP

BIBLIOGRAPHY

BAIN, JOE S. 1956 Barriers to New Competition: Their Character and Consequences in Manufacturing Industries. Cambridge, Mass.: Harvard Univ. Press.

BURNS, ARTHUR R. 1936 The Decline of Competition: A Study of the Evolution of American Industry. New York and London: McGraw-Hill.

CHAMBERLIN, EDWARD H. (1933) 1962 The Theory of Monopolistic Competition: A Re-orientation of the Theory of Value. 8th ed. Cambridge, Mass.: Harvard Univ. Press.

COURNOT, ANTOINE AUGUSTIN (1838) 1960 Researches Into the Mathematical Principles of the Theory of Wealth. New York: Kelley. → First published in French.

EDGEWORTH, FRANCIS Y. (1881) 1953 Mathematical Psychics: An Essay on the Application of Mathematics to the Moral Sciences. New York: Kelley.

FELLNER, WILLIAM 1947 Prices and Wages Under Bilateral Monopoly. Quarterly Journal of Economics 61:503–532.

HARSANYI, JOHN C. 1956 Approaches to the Bargaining Problem Before and After the Theory of Games: A Critical Discussion of Zeuthen's, Hicks' and Nash's Theories. Econometrica 24:144–157.

LERNER, ABBA P. 1934 The Concept of Monopoly and the Measurement of Monopoly Power. Review of Economic Studies 1:157–175.

LERNER, ABBA P. 1944 The Economics of Control: Principles of Welfare Economics. New York: Macmillan.

MACHLUP, FRITZ (1952) 1964 The Economics of Sellers' Competition: Model Analysis of Sellers' Conduct. Baltimore: Johns Hopkins Press.

MASON, EDWARD S. (1957) 1964 Economic Concentration and the Monopoly Problem. New York: Atheneum.

NASH, JOHN F. JR. 1950 The Bargaining Problem. Econometrica 18:155–162.

NASH, JOHN F. JR. 1953 Two-person Cooperative Games. Econometrica 21:128–140.

PIGOU, ARTHUR C. (1920) 1960 The Economics of Welfare. 4th ed. London: Macmillan.

ROBINSON, E. A. G. 1941 Monopoly. Cambridge Univ. Press.

ROBINSON, JOAN (1933) 1961 The Economics of Imperfect Competition. London: Macmillan; New York: St. Martins.

STOCKING, GEORGE W.; and WATKINS, MYRON W. 1951 Monopoly and Free Enterprise. New York: Twentieth Century Fund.

TRIFFIN, ROBERT 1940 Monopolistic Competition and General Equilibrium Theory. Harvard Economic Studies, Vol. 67. Cambridge, Mass.: Harvard Univ. Press.

UNIVERSITIES—NATIONAL BUREAU COMMITTEE FOR ECONOMIC RESEARCH 1955 Business Concentration and Price Policy: A Conference of the Committee. National Bureau of Economic Research, Special Conference Series, No. 5. Princeton Univ. Press.

MONOPSONY
See MONOPOLY.

MONTE CARLO METHODS
See RANDOM NUMBERS.

MONTESQUIEU

Charles de Secondat, Baron de la Brède et de Montesquieu (1689–1755), made original contributions to social and political theory. He was viewed by Comte and Durkheim as the most important precursor of sociology; by Ernst Cassirer and Franz Neumann as the inventor of ideal-type analysis; by Sir Frederick Pollock as the "father of modern historical research" and of a "comparative theory of politics and law based on wide observation of . . . actual systems"; by Friedrich Meinecke as one of the founders of Historismus (historicism or historism) with its relativism, holism, and emphasis on the positive value of the irrational and the customary; and by Hegel, who did not find it easy to praise his predecessors, as the first to explain law and political institutions by reference to characteristics of the social system in which they function (Comte [1830–1842] 1877; Durkheim [1892–1918] 1960, p. 26; Cassirer [1932] 1951, p. 212; Neumann 1949, pp. xl–xli; Pollock [1890] 1960, pp. 86–87; Meinecke 1936, pp. 118–170; Hegel [1821] 1942, p. 16). Now that political sociology has become a recognized discipline, Montesquieu has also been given pride of place as its first modern practitioner (Aron [1960] 1965, pp. 55–56; Runciman 1963, pp. 24 ff.). Nor is there much question that Montesquieu's concept of the general spirit of a society anticipated modern cultural anthropology.

Thus, Montesquieu's position as social theorist would seem to be secure. Yet few other theorists of his order of achievement have combined such contributions with such defects: imprecise definition, lack of internal consistency, the tendency to generalize on the basis of inadequate evidence, and, in the *Spirit of the Laws*, a deplorable lack of organization. To discriminate what remains permanently valuable in Montesquieu from what is unacceptable—this is the difficulty complicating any critical exposition of his thought.

Other problems may perplex the modern reader. Montesquieu claimed to be breaking altogether new ground. He prefaced the *Spirit of the Laws* with the epigraph "prolem sine matrem" (a child born of no mother), yet it has been shown that his work in many ways carries on that of his predecessors and shares the concepts, attitudes, and political positions of his contemporaries (Dedieu 1909; Meinecke 1936; Ford 1953; Mauzi 1960; Shackleton 1961; Ehrard 1963; Rothkrug 1965). The genuine novelty of Montesquieu's work is to be found in its terms of analysis and its theoretical focus— the relations of a society's laws to its type of government, climate, religion, mores (*moeurs*), customs (*manières*), and economy. Such an approach is inconsistent with the older notion that there exists an eternal, natural law superior to positive law. Yet Montesquieu refused to abandon the theory of natural law, despite its patent incompatibility with his own.

Another difficulty arises from Montesquieu's insistence that his writings did not censure any established institution, that he took his principles not from his prejudices, but from the nature of things. Yet he condemned despotism, slavery, and religious persecution as contrary to natural law or human nature. Thus he wavered between a positivist, rela-

tivist concept of law on the one hand and a conventional acceptance of natural law on the other.

Montesquieu opposed intellectual systems, for he thought they falsify experience; he emphasized the irreducible diversity of human institutions and history. Yet he also asserted that he had laid down first principles from which all particular cases follow—the histories of all nations are only consequences of these first principles, and every particular law is connected with or depends on another law of a more general extent (1748, preface).

Montesquieu's family stemmed from both the nobility of the sword and the nobility of the robe; it could be traced back 350 years, which, in his view, made its name neither good nor bad. His childhood was a curious combination of aristocracy and rusticity. He was born in the castle at La Brède, but his godfather was a beggar, chosen to remind Montesquieu of his obligation to the poor. He was sent out to nurse with a peasant family for his first three years. His mother died when he was seven; her early death contributed to his detachment and to his distaste for enthusiasm; both qualities were equally prominent in his writing and in his character.

At the age of 11 he was sent away to Juilly, a school maintained by the Congregation of the Oratory. At Juilly Montesquieu acquired an education stronger in Latin than in Greek; it was relatively liberal for its day. The philosopher Malebranche was a member of the Congregation, and his influence made itself felt. Montesquieu's Latin studies impressed him with the value of civic virtue and stoicism. In 1705 Montesquieu returned to Bordeaux to study law. Between 1709 and 1713 he was a legal apprentice in Paris. There he came to know some of the most advanced thinkers of his time: Fréret, the Abbé Lama, and Boulainvilliers (Shackleton 1961, pp. 8–13).

On the death of an uncle in 1716, Montesquieu succeeded to considerable wealth, land, and the office of *président à mortier* in the Parlement of Guyenne. Montesquieu's office was not a sinecure. He worked seriously at his legal duties, but later confessed that he had not understood all the ancient procedures of his court. The truth was that he did not much enjoy his life as a magistrate. Nevertheless, in the *Spirit of the Laws* he supported the position of the *parlementaires* against the monarchy, defended venality of office, and condemned as despotism any attempt to divest the *parlements* of their political functions (1748, book 8, chapter 6).

During his residence in Bordeaux, Montesquieu participated in the work of its academy. At that time the provincial academies provided a setting within which the nobility of the robe could develop an intelligentsia of its own; their members included learned noblemen of the sword as well as educated commoners. Montesquieu did experiments in natural history and physiology. The academy gave him a distaste for prejudice, a priori reasoning, and teleological arguments; from it he acquired a predisposition to materialism.

The "Persian Letters." In his Bordeaux period Montesquieu began the *Persian Letters*, which was published anonymously in Amsterdam in 1721. An immediate and lasting success, it alone would have assured his reputation. The book is witty and delightful, but Montesquieu's irony and irreverence did more than amuse his readers. By depicting France as seen through the eyes of two Persians, he provided a double perspective, a revealing device used earlier by La Bruyère and Bayle. As Caillois has written, the positive construction later undertaken by Montesquieu in the *Spirit of the Laws* presupposed a prior sociological revolution— that of "daring to consider as extraordinary and difficult to understand those institutions, those habits, those *moeurs*, to which one has been accustomed since birth, . . . [which] are so powerfully, so spontaneously respected that in most situations, no alternative to them can be imagined" (*Oeuvres complètes*, vol. 1, p. v in the Gallimard edition). Relativism about values is among the most significant contributions of the *Persian Letters* to the early Enlightenment.

Certain points made in the *Persian Letters* anticipate what Montesquieu later argued more extensively—that men are always born into a society and that it is therefore meaningless to discuss the origin of society and government; that self-interest is not a sufficient basis for human institutions, as Hobbes had asserted; and that, instead, the possibility of good government depends on education and example, in short, on civic virtue.

Montesquieu did not believe that the absurdity and corruption in French society could be remedied by governmental action. His view of human nature put great stress on the passions, and he believed that jealousy and the desire for domination are among the mainsprings of despotism. He was already concerned with the structure and psychological basis of absolute rule. His models were taken from Louis xiv, as well as from what he read about the Near East and Far East.

Travel and later works. With the success of the *Persian Letters*, Montesquieu was accepted by the society of regency Paris and lived the life of an aristocratic rake. His Paris friends secured his elec-

tion to the French Academy in 1728. He sold his office of *président à mortier*, partly because of financial need and partly because he wanted to live in Paris. As a further result he was at last free to travel.

From 1728 to 1731 Montesquieu was away from France, visiting Austria, Hungary, Italy, Germany, Holland, and England. He came to think of himself as a man first and a Frenchman second, and claimed to regard "all the peoples of Europe with the same impartiality as I do the peoples of Madagascar" (*ibid.*, p. 997). The two years he spent in England had the greatest effect on his later work. There he made distinguished friends who taught him to view the English constitution through the eyes of the Whigs, although he was aware also of the Tories' point of view. During his stay he was elected a fellow of the Royal Society and became a Freemason as well. After his return to France he divided his time between his estate at La Brède and Paris; he became an independent scholar dedicated to producing his two great books, the *Considerations on the Causes of the Greatness of the Romans and Their Decline* (1734) and the *Spirit of the Laws* (1748). Much of his time was spent in Paris, where he shone among the luminaries of the intellectual salons, now more open to merit than before. Montesquieu encouraged the young *philosophes* he met there.

Personal religion. In 1775 Montesquieu fell victim to an epidemic sweeping Paris. As he lay dying, he asked to be given the last rites of the church. When he chose as confessor a Jesuit who had helped him publish the *Considerations*, the Society of Jesus insisted that he first accept certain conditions. Although Montesquieu denied ever having been in a state of disbelief, he was made to consent to having his final confession made public. It is reported that after receiving the last rites, he said, "I have always respected religion; the ethic of the evangelists is an excellent thing, and the most beautiful gift God could have made to man" (Shackleton 1961, p. 396). Certainly Montesquieu believed in the social and political utility of religion, nor is there any doubt that he held some form of belief compatible with natural religion. But it remains unknown to what degree he believed in the dogmas of his church. He never capitulated to the Jesuits' demands for control of his manuscripts.

Ideas about historical causation. The *Considerations*, perhaps the least known of Montesquieu's three major books, is notable for its style, clarity, and remarkable analysis of historical causation and of the nature of politics. Montesquieu was attracted to Roman history because it was the most complete record of a political society available to him. His study of Rome led him to concepts he later developed more fully in the *Spirit of the Laws*: although chance plays some part in human events, these may always be rationally analyzed; the orientation of political actors is in large part to be explained by religion, ideas, maxims, and public opinion (in the *Considerations* Montesquieu did not emphasize milieu); politics in a free society requires a degree of disunion and conflict; and every society has a "general spirit."

Perhaps the single most telling passage in the *Considerations* states Montesquieu's theory of causation:

It is not fortune that rules the world . . . The Romans had a series of consecutive successes when their government followed one policy, and an unbroken set of reverses when it adopted another. There are general causes, whether moral or physical, which act upon every monarchy, which create, maintain, or ruin it. All accidents are subject to these causes, and if the chance loss of a battle, that is to say, a particular cause, ruins a state, there is a general cause that created the situation whereby this state could perish by the loss of a single battle. (1734, chapter 18)

This statement, which received much attention after the fall of France in 1940, referred in its original context to the place held by war and conquest in Roman policy. Montesquieu reasoned, in what would later be called a dialectical manner, that Rome was first made and then ruined: "Here, in a word, is the history of the Romans. By following their original maxims, they conquered all other peoples. But after such success their republic could no longer be maintained. It became necessary to change the form of government. The new principles caused the Romans to fall from their former grandeur" (*ibid.*, chapter 18).

Montesquieu here combined judgments of fact and of value in a way dear to him. On the one hand he generalized about the effects of scale on governmental structure and functions; on the other he concluded that the Romans had fought too much and conquered too much. Violence, first used as a weapon against other nations, was in turn employed at home. Roman decadence was inherent in the means used to attain greatness. Montesquieu was recasting themes that had originated with opponents of Louis XIV's foreign policy and of mercantilism.

The *Considerations* contains a striking first formulation of Montesquieu's treatment of politics in a free society. The texture of relations among persons and groups is much looser in a free society than in a despotism. Under freedom, divergencies and even conflicts are essential, for such a society is based on the conciliation of recognized groups, each with its own interest. The virtues of consensus and unanimity are overrated:

Authors who write about the history of Rome never tire of asserting that its ruin was caused by internal division, by contending groups. But these writers fail to see that these divisions were necessary. . . . As a general rule, it may be assumed that whenever everyone is tranquil in a republic, that state is no longer free.

What constitutes a union in a political body is difficult to determine. True union is a harmony, in which all the parts, however opposed they may appear, concur in attaining the general good of the society, just as dissonances in music are necessary so that they may be resolved in an ultimate harmony. Union may exist in a state, where apparently only trouble is to be found. . . .

But underlying the unanimity of Asiatic despotism, that is to say every government that is not moderate, there is a division of another kind. The peasant, the soldier, the merchant, the noble are related only in the sense that some of them oppress others without meeting any resistance. If this is considered to be union, it can be so only in that sense in which corpses are united when buried in a mass grave. (*ibid.*, chapter 9)

The "Spirit of the Laws"

The *Spirit of the Laws*, the product of twenty years' work, is so sweeping in its scope that there can be no question of dealing here with all that it covers. Ostensibly a treatise on law, it spills over into a consideration of every domain affecting human behavior and into questions of philosophical judgment about the merit of various kinds of legislation. Its absence of organization is notorious, and many commentators have tried to rearrange the order of the separate books to produce a more coherent argument. Such schemes can be divided into those which pretend to have divined the true intent of the author and those with the more modest aim of reducing confusion. Behind these different approaches lie two different conceptions of Montesquieu as a thinker. Some argue that he based the *Spirit of the Laws* on general principles and a discernible over-all design; others that, whatever his intention, he fell far short of such an achievement because he composed the 31 books over so long a period. The supporters of the view that Montesquieu did formulate a distinctive and systematic theory tend to argue that for two reasons Montesquieu deliberately concealed his design: he feared the censure of the authorities, lay and ecclesiastical; and he believed that much of his public should be kept in ignorance of certain truths (about religion, for example).

Whatever Montesquieu's intent, the present value of the *Spirit of the Laws* depends upon two central topics: Montesquieu's classification of political structures and his comparative and historical political sociology.

Types of government. Montesquieu classified governments in terms of three types, each of which is characterized by a nature and a principle. By the "nature" of a government he meant the person or group holding sovereign power; by "principle," that passion which must animate those involved in a form of government if it is to function at its strongest and best. When a government is functioning properly, a legislator who violates the principle of government will provoke revolution. On the other hand, when a government is debilitated by the weakening of its essential principle, it can be saved only by a good legislator capable of strengthening it. The persona of the legislator is used by Montesquieu in the classical sense of an exceptional person called in by a society to give it basic laws. But the retention of this fiction produced an ambiguity when joined to what is novel in Montesquieu's thought, the limits placed upon legislation by the physical and moral causes that combine to form the general spirit of a society. Montesquieu was inconsistent in his recommendations to legislators: sometimes he suggested that the legislator adapt laws to the general spirit of the society, sometimes that he use laws and even religion to combat that spirit. Much depended on whether Montesquieu liked or disliked a particular institution or practice.

When classified by their nature, governments fall into three categories. A republic is that form in which the people as a whole, or certain families, hold sovereign power. A monarchy is that in which a prince rules according to established laws that create channels through which the royal power flows. (Montesquieu's examples of such channels include an aristocracy administering local justice, *parlements* with political functions, a clergy with recognized rights, and cities with historical privileges.) Despotism is the rule of a single person, who is directed only by his own will and caprice.

The principles of these governments differ: virtue is the principle of republics; honor, of monarchies; and fear, of despotism. Montesquieu subdivided republics into democracies and aristocracies. His image of the first was taken from classical Greece and Rome. When he assigned virtue to them as their distinctive principle, he meant those political qualities requisite to their maintenance: in the case of democracies, love of country, belief in equality, and the frugality and asceticism that lead men to sacrifice their personal pleasures to the general interest. Montesquieu found his model for aristocracy in contemporary republics such as Venice. Although aristocracies also require virtue, it takes the form of moderation in behavior and aspirations by members of the ruling class (the principal weakness of aristocracy being immoderate internal rivalry). Montesquieu thought that monarchy, as found in France and other European states of his time, was the characteristically modern way of ruling territories of intermediate size. The principle of monarchy is honor, that *esprit de corps* found only in a society based on preferment and distinctions for the few. Such privileges, when demanded and granted, sustain partially autonomous, intermediate groups between the crown and the people. In a famous phrase Montesquieu wrote, "Without a monarch, no nobility; without a nobility, no monarchy. For then there is only a despot" (1748, book 2, chapter 4). Despotism, in Montesquieu's view, has no offsetting virtues. Based on fear, it tolerates no intermediary powers and is moderated, if at all, only by religion.

Throughout this analysis Montesquieu used what Max Weber later called ideal types. As Montesquieu phrased it:

I have had new ideas; I have had to find new terms, or else to give new meaning to old ones. . . . It should be noted that there is a great difference between saying that a certain quality . . . or virtue is not the spring that moves a government, and saying that it is nowhere to be found in that government. If I say that this wheel, this cog are not the spring that makes this watch go, does it follow that they are not in this watch? . . . In a word, honor exists in a republic, although political virtue is its mainspring; political virtue, in a monarchy, although honor is its principle. (1748, "Avertissement de l'auteur")

Montesquieu's treatment of despotism is the most flagrant of his departures from his claim to have derived his principles not from prejudice but from the nature of things. Thus, he asserted that "it is impossible to speak of such monstrous governments without becoming infuriated" (*ibid.*, book 3, chapter 9). Yet he said much that was incisive about the patterns of authority in despotisms. Under this form of government unquestioning obedience is regarded as the only proper response to authority. Education is designed to produce the requisite type of character. The ruled must be ignorant, timid, broken in spirit, requiring little in the way of legislation. Family life is also regulated, and the members of one family are isolated from all others. Men, instead of being trained to live on the basis of mutual respect, are made to respond only to fear of violence. Furthermore, Montesquieu posed the question: Since men love liberty and hate violence, and will therefore presumably rise in rebellion against despotism, why in fact do most of the world's peoples live under despotisms? In part this is because large empires must be governed despotically if their administration is to be effective (*ibid.*, book 8, chapter 19); more important, it is because despotism has but one necessary condition, the human passions, and these exist everywhere.

The alternatives to despotism are more difficult to achieve (*ibid.*, book 5, chapter 15). The legislator who wishes to form a government that is free must have unusual skills. He must know how to combine political powers, subject them to rules, moderate them, and yet make them act together. In what are probably the best known and most influential sections of the *Spirit of the Laws*, those describing, or idealizing, the government of England (*ibid.*, book 11, chapter 6; book 19, chapter 27), Montesquieu went beyond Locke to distinguish clearly between the executive power (extended to foreign affairs), the legislative, and the judicial. He made their rigid separation the condition of liberty. "When the legislative power is united to the executive, there is no more liberty" (*ibid.*, book 11, chapter 6). Nor is there liberty if the judicial power is not separated from the legislative. "Power must check power" (*ibid.*, book 11, chapter 6). But can a government so constituted act effectively? Montesquieu simply asserted that it will because it has to.

Taken purely as constitutional doctrine, this theory does not appear to have had much factual basis, even when Montesquieu wrote. Taken as a guide to present-day practice, it is useless and even dangerous. Yet the theory of the division of powers is more plausible if understood in either a sociological or a psychological sense. Madison, for example, in the 51st *Federalist* paper, interpreted Montesquieu's doctrine in a psychological sense as involving not rigid separation, but the blending of powers. The means of resisting an attack on the powers given to an office by a constitution should be tied to the ambitions of the person holding office. Thus, Madison combined the formula "Ambition must be made to counteract ambition" with Montesquieu's formula "Power must check power."

The possibility of a sociological interpretation emerges clearly from the question, first asked by Bentham: What possible guarantee of liberty can there be in the separation of powers, if all three powers are controlled by the same group or class? Obviously there can be no guarantee unless each of the three powers is in the hands of a *different* group or class. In that case, liberty is the outcome of a struggle among groups. This is a struggle of a particular and limited kind that varies with the type of government. Intrigue is essential in a democracy, for when there is no intrigue, the people, whose nature it is to act by passion, become subject to bribery and corruption; in short, they calculate their own interest when they should be directed by patriotic passion (*ibid.*, book 2, chapter 2). In a monarchy, liberty exists when semiautonomous intermediate groups have the power to resist the will of the ruler, or at least to engage in negotiation with him when they feel their interests are threatened. Only in despotism is there no conflict among groups. Thus, even the most political part of Montesquieu's theory has a sociological dimension: conflict has positive functions—the prerequisite of liberty is the existence of groups that are at least partially independent groups set between the state and the individual.

Determinants of a society's spirit. The scope of Montesquieu's concern is global: "This work has for its object the laws, customs, and various usages of all peoples" (*Oeuvres complètes*, vol. 2, p. 1137 in the Gallimard edition). Such a subject can be treated adequately only by a method at once comparative and historical. Comparison, the single most valuable capacity of the human mind, is particularly useful when applied to human collectivities (*ibid.*, vol. 2, pp. 54, 57). For if we wish to explain why they have the characteristics they do, it is better to apply hypotheses to general effects known by comparison than to particular effects known from a single case. In making comparisons it should be remembered that in nature even members of the same class are not exactly alike, but only more or less so. Furthermore, such social phenomena as laws must be regarded as forming part of a system, within which they function in some relation to the other parts of the system. In order to understand a system properly, it is also essential to know how it developed over time: to explain why laws exist, it is necessary to follow the historical process by which they have acquired a function within the context of a system, even though the original system may have ceased to operate (*ibid.*, vol. 2, p. 1103).

What constitutes an adequate explanation of why a nation has a given set of laws, a given social and political structure? Montesquieu answered that a satisfactory explanation must include the two major types of causes, physical and moral, which together form a society's general spirit. Principal among physical causes is climate, which produces a number of physiological and mental consequences. Also to be taken into account are the quality of the terrain, the density of population, and the territorial extent of a society. Montesquieu, who made much of physical causes, nevertheless rejected the notion that they alone directly determine a society's mode of life. On the contrary, moral causes are more important than physical ones—a good legislator can, for example, minimize and overcome even the effects of climate (*ibid.*, vol. 2, pp. 61–62).

Many moral causes affect a society's general spirit: religion, laws, maxims, precedents, mores, customs, economy and trade, style of thought, and the atmosphere that is created in a nation's capital or court and then spreads to its outermost limits (1748, book 19, chapter 4). The general character of a society can also be seen in the style of education it gives to its members. There is nothing mystical, no notion of a *Volksgeist* for example, nothing transcending reason and experience, in Montesquieu's concept of the general spirit of a society. The general spirit results from a number of causes whose effects can be rationally assessed after empirical investigation.

Law. Montesquieu considered law to be among the most crucial determinants of human behavior. However, because his legal definitions in the first six books of the *Spirit of the Laws* are ambiguous and because he did not build on them in other parts of the book, it is best to seek to understand his use of the term "law" from its use in the work as a whole. For the most part he used "law" to mean any rule of conduct that is supported by governmental sanctions against those who disobey the rule. Montesquieu also used "law" to refer to rights and obligations protected or enforced by courts and to basic rules that must be followed by those who exercise power. Despite the confusion, Plamenatz was correct to conclude that Montesquieu, more than Hobbes or Locke, understood the social function of law—it is made up of rules that control the governors as well as the governed (1963, p. 263).

What is significant is Montesquieu's treatment of law as but one way of affecting human conduct. It is the method peculiar to the government. The society as a whole uses other means: religion, mores, and customs. Montesquieu did not underrate what can be done by laws that have behind them the coercive power of the state. But he wished to call attention to those forces outside the government that may limit the effectiveness of state action and thus serve a function equivalent to law

by using essentially social constraints to restrain human passions, wills, and imagination. Montesquieu did not attempt to reduce government to a derivative function of society, or vice versa; rather, he wished to specify the numerous and complex ways in which the political and social systems interact.

Religion. Among the essentially social forces that may affect government, religion ranks high. Montesquieu's treatment of religion wavers between the rationalist theory, which he found in Machiavelli, that elites manipulate the credulous, and a more sophisticated sociological theory, which he was one of the first to develop. When following Machiavelli's lead, Montesquieu treated religion as something used by rulers much as they use laws. Both religion and law, for example, can be employed to overcome the worst effects of climate, such as reluctance to work the land (1748, book 14, chapter 6). Montesquieu also agreed with Machiavelli that it is easier to enforce laws in a religious country than elsewhere. But Montesquieu developed this instrumental theory into the theory that to the extent that religion is an effective force in a society, there is less need for control by the state. Religion, Montesquieu argued, can even save a state that would be overturned if its survival depended upon the capacity of its police to coerce the population. He emphasized the political and social effects of religion, seen always as operating within a given type of social organization: thus, the most sacred and true dogmas may produce the worst consequences, if these dogmas should turn out to be incongruent with the general spirit of a society. In a despotism, religion is the only restraint upon the ruler. In a republic, it is dangerous to allow the clergy to gain strength, but in a monarchy, a strong clergy helps maintain liberty. Religion also can determine men's orientations toward politics, economic activity, population, and liberty. In a sentence that later engaged Max Weber's interest, Montesquieu called attention to the fact that the English had been the people who had most effectively combined religion, commerce, and liberty (*ibid.*, book 20, chapter 7).

Mores and customs. Two other causes affecting the general spirit are mores and customs, both of which closely resemble religion in their operation. They may be used as surrogates for laws of the state. "When a people has *bonnes moeurs*, its laws need not be complex" (*ibid.*, book 19, chapter 22). Mores (*moeurs*) apply internalized restraints on conduct not specifically prohibited by law; customs (*manières*) apply external restraints on such conduct, but the sanctions are social rather than legal. The distinctions among laws, mores, and customs are analytical. In practice they may be confused, as in China or Sparta. Yet even there one predominated: in Sparta it was mores, in China customs.

Implications of social theory. Montesquieu's social theory is especially significant because it emphasizes social determinants of behavior rather than legal sanctions. Hitherto, political theorists who had attempted empirical generalizations had concentrated almost exclusively on explanations based on the behavioral consequences of legal sanctions. Montesquieu offered instead a pluralist view of causation; he did not attempt to establish a hierarchy of causes, with priority assigned to non-governmental as against governmental action. Montesquieu believed that the general spirit might be determined by any one, or a combination, of the causes he had identified. (Tocqueville was very much in Montesquieu's style when he concluded the first part of *Democracy in America* with the argument that the success of the United States had been caused more by the constitution than the climate and terrain, but that most important of all had been the mores of the inhabitants.)

Montesquieu's emphasis on the general spirit also led him to discuss theories of national character. Every society has its own particular character, a mixture of good and bad qualities. Legislators ought not to fly in the face of this character, unless it violates principles necessary to the government's existence. Otherwise, apparently desirable innovations may produce disastrous consequences. Peoples have their own ways of reaching conclusions, their own style of thought, *leur manière de penser totale* (*Oeuvres complètes*, vol. 2, p. 1102 in the Gallimard edition).

There can be little doubt about the conservative implications of this theory. Some of them Montesquieu developed; others he did not. Inherent in his position is an appeal to the past or a vision of the past from a particular place in the society and politics of his time. Yet to the extent that he was a spokesman for the parliamentary nobility, "Montesquieu was not a true conservative, because he was not satisfied with the way the Bourbon monarchy had developed and was developing in his time" (Palmer 1959, p. 60). Although Montesquieu's work as a theorist should not be assessed simply in terms of his class position, it would be a mistake to ignore its influence on his political values, his theory of politics, and his scheme of analysis taken as a whole.

Conflict. The single most important doctrine in the *Spirit of the Laws* is Montesquieu's theory that intermediate bodies like the nobility, the *parlements*, the local courts of seigneurial justice, and the church are all indispensable to political liberty. These and other constituted bodies, such as provinces, towns, guilds, and professional associations, all have their rights, legal powers, and privileges, none of which can be removed, since they all derive from the original institutions of the realm. Their present function is to balance one another and to serve as barriers to despotism. Such constituted bodies are not to be treated as equal in value. To do so would violate the essential principle of monarchy, which rests upon honor derived from inequality. The great—those most distinguished by birth, wealth, or honor—should have a share in legislation equal to their advantages. This, Montesquieu specified, is the power necessary to check the enterprises of the people, and it is as important to the state as the people's power to check the enterprises of the great (1748, book 11, chapter 6). Montesquieu's analysis of the British constitution demonstrates that he did not believe in rule by one class (Palmer 1959, pp. 57–58). In addition to a body of nobles, there should also be a body representing the people, that is, those who are not noble. Classes should be distinct, with the nobility a vital element in the balance. A hierarchical form of society and a noble class jealous of its privileges are essential to the preservation of liberty.

Change. There is an ambivalence in Montesquieu's attitude toward political change. On the one hand he opposed large-scale innovations, especially if they were proposed as the implementation of a program deduced from abstract principles; on the other he himself suggested far-reaching reforms. In part his ambivalence derived from the fact that the legitimacy of his own class depended on historical rather than abstract arguments; in part from his belief that the reasons for the continued existence of a state are complex and probably unknowable. If the entire system were changed, unanticipated difficulties might arise. Piecemeal change is therefore best—precedents should guide policy (1734, chapter 18). Institutions of long standing tend to improve a people's mores, while new institutions tend to corrupt them (1748, book 5, chapter 7). Politics is an instrument that accomplishes its work by slowly wearing away resistance (*ibid.*, book 14, chapter 13). A prudent administration seldom proceeds to its ends by direct means. It changes by law only what has been established by law; it attempts to change the mores not by legislation, but by introducing new mores. The uniformity invariably sought by a centralized administration leads to despotism. Political wisdom consists in being able to discriminate those cases in which uniformity is preferable from those other instances in which diversity presents greater advantages (*ibid.*, book 29, chapter 18).

Montesquieu neither opposed all that was new nor defended all that existed. In addition to attacking slavery and religious persecution, he argued that the state owes its inhabitants an assured subsistence, nourishment, clothing, and good health. It is also the state's duty to provide for orphans, the sick, and the old; it should feed the people in the event of famine (*ibid.*, book 23, chapter 19). Much of this was based on a general aristocratic paternalism, but Montesquieu's values emerge clearly from his discussion of slavery. He took the position that slavery is incompatible with the general spirit of both republics and monarchies. Yet he added that emancipated slaves should be given only civil, not political, liberty. Even in popular governments, power should never be allowed to fall into the hands of the lowest classes (*le bas peuple*). Yet Montesquieu stressed the worth of education and denounced prejudice: knowledge makes men less cruel, prejudice leads them away from humanitarianism (*ibid.*, book 15, chapter 4).

Evaluation

Nothing is easier than to criticize Montesquieu, even in the most valuable parts of his writings. The concepts he used as ideal types are defective, and his typology is both abstract and incomplete. It is abstract in the sense that no existing government fitted his specifications, despite the great number of monarchies in his time. England, whose laws he claimed came closest to achieving liberty, was not a monarchy as he defined it, for intermediate bodies no longer existed there. Montesquieu's types are incomplete even on his own showing: Books 19, 26, and 29 of the *Spirit of the Laws* either modify or greatly amplify his initial types. Thus, in Book 19, while discussing the English constitution, he pointed out the advantages of representative over direct democracy. Yet he never included representation in his ideal type of democracy. Also in Book 19, he added political parties to his discussion of the politics of a free society, but again failed to explain how his types should be modified. And he virtually added a fourth type of government, the federative republic, formed by the confederation of a number of republics. It represented his solution to the puzzle of how republics could maintain their intimate scale and at the same time resist aggression by larger neighbors. Forgetfulness, inability or lack of willingness to revise, and absence of organization are everywhere evident in Montes-

quieu. To his intellectual faults may be added the fact that Montesquieu failed to emancipate his scheme of analysis from the perspective of his class. Yet in large part he triumphed over these defects. Montesquieu was extraordinarily imaginative in formulating general hypotheses designed to relate those variables that must be taken into account when explaining social and political behavior.

Montesquieu advanced a theory of politics and a conception of the relation between the political and social systems whose full usefulness made itself felt only later. He upheld the value of conflict in politics—the importance of pluralism in systems characterized by conciliation, compromise, and bargaining between intermediate groups and the central authority. He formulated the theoretical concepts that authority can be of diverse kinds and that order can be maintained by a variety of devices functionally equivalent to commands enforced by political and legal sanctions. He made comparison the central problem of political sociology and thus directed the focus of inquiry away from Europe to all the societies known, however imperfectly, to man.

MELVIN RICHTER

[*For the historical context of Montesquieu's work, see* CONSTITUTIONS AND CONSTITUTIONALISM; LEGAL SYSTEMS; POLITICAL THEORY; PUBLIC LAW, *article on* COMPARATIVE STUDY; *and the biographies of* BODIN; MACHIAVELLI; *for discussion of the subsequent development of Montesquieu's ideas, see the biographies of* COMTE; DURKHEIM; HEGEL; MEINECKE; TOCQUEVILLE.]

WORKS BY MONTESQUIEU

(1721) 1964 *The Persian Letters.* Translated by George R. Healy. Indianapolis: Bobbs-Merrill. → First published as *Lettres persanes.*

(1734) 1965 *Considerations on the Causes of the Greatness of the Romans and Their Decline.* Translated, with notes and an introduction by David Lowenthal. New York: Free Press. → First published in French. Translations of extracts in the text were provided by Melvin Richter.

(1748) 1950–1961 *De l'esprit des loix.* Vols. 1–4. Edited by Jean Brethe de la Gressaye. Paris: Société Les Belles Lettres. → The best critical edition. Translations of extracts in the text were provided by Melvin Richter. An English translation was published by Hafner in 1962.

Oeuvres complètes. Edited by Roger Caillois. 2 vols. Bibliothèque de la Pléiade, Vols. 81, 86. Paris: Gallimard, 1949–1951. → The most generally available edition. It does not contain Montesquieu's correspondence. Translations of extracts in the text were provided by Melvin Richter.

Oeuvres complètes. Vols. 1–3. Paris: Nagel, 1950–1955. → The best edition of Montesquieu; includes his correspondence.

SUPPLEMENTARY BIBLIOGRAPHY

ALTHUSSER, LOUIS 1959 *Montesquieu: La politique et l'histoire.* Paris: Presses Universitaires de France. → A provocative Marxist treatment.

ARON, RAYMOND (1960) 1965 *Main Currents in Sociological Thought.* Volume 1: Montesquieu, Comte, Marx, Tocqueville: The Sociologists and the Revolution of 1848. New York: Basic Books. → First published in French. Perhaps the best brief treatment of Montesquieu as a political sociologist.

BARCKHAUSEN, HENRI A. 1907 *Montesquieu: Ses idées et ses oeuvres d'après les papiers de La Brède.* Paris: Hachette.

BORDEAUX (France) 1948 *Montesquieu et L'esprit des lois: Exposition organisée dans les salons de l'Hôtel de Ville de Bordeaux pour célébrer le deuxième centenaire de la publication de L'esprit des lois.* Bordeaux: Delmas.

BORDEAUX (France) 1956 *Actes du Congrès Montesquieu, réuni à Bordeaux du 23 au 26 mai 1955 pour commémorer le deuxième centenaire de la mort de Montesquieu.* Bordeaux: Delmas. → Contains 31 critical essays.

CABEEN, DAVID C. 1947 *Montesquieu: A Critical Bibliography.* New York Public Library. → An annoted bibliography. Restricted to works by Montesquieu examined by the author at the Columbia University Library and the New York Public Library.

CABEEN, DAVID C. 1955 A Supplementary Montesquieu Bibliography. *Revue internationale de philosophie* 9: 409–434.

CARCASSONNE, E. 1927 *Montesquieu et le problème de la constitution française au XVIIIe siècle.* Paris: Presses Universitaires de France.

CASSIRER, ERNST (1932) 1951 *The Philosophy of the Enlightenment.* Princeton Univ. Press. → First published as *Die Philosophie der Aufklärung.*

COMTE, AUGUSTE (1830–1842) 1877 *Cours de philosophie positive.* 4th ed. 6 vols. Paris: Baillière.

DEDIEU, JOSEPH 1909 *Montesquieu et la tradition politique anglaise en France: Les sources anglaises de L'esprit des lois.* Paris: Gabalda. → An important study of English influences on Montesquieu.

DEDIEU, JOSEPH 1913 *Montesquieu.* Paris: Alcan.

DEDIEU, JOSEPH 1943 *Montesquieu, l'homme et l'oeuvre.* Paris: Boivin.

DURKHEIM, ÉMILE (1892–1918) 1960 *Montesquieu and Rousseau: Forerunners of Sociology.* Ann Arbor: Univ. of Michigan Press. → Part 1 is a translation of Durkheim's thesis *Quid Secundatus politicae scientiae instituendae contulerit* (1892); Part 2 was first published in Volume 25 of the *Revue de métaphysique et de morale.*

EHRARD, JEAN 1963 *L'idée de nature en France dans la première moitié du XVIIIe siècle.* 2 vols. Paris: S.E.V.P.E.N.

FLETCHER, FRANK T. H. 1939 *Montesquieu and English Politics (1750–1800).* London: Arnold.

FORD, FRANKLIN L. 1953 *Robe and Sword: The Regrouping of the French Aristocracy After Louis XIV.* Harvard Historical Studies, Vol. 64. Cambridge, Mass.: Harvard Univ. Press.

HEGEL, GEORG WILHELM FRIEDRICH (1821) 1942 *The Philosophy of Right.* Translated with notes by T. M. Knox. Oxford: Clarendon.

LEVIN, LAWRENCE M. 1936 *The Political Doctrine of Montesquieu's Esprit des lois: Its Classical Background.* New York: Columbia Univ., Institute of French Studies.

MAUZI, ROBERT 1960 *L'idée du bonheur dans la littérature et la pensée françaises du XVIIIe siècle.* Paris: Colin.

MEINECKE, FRIEDRICH (1936) 1959 *Werke.* Volume 3: Die Entstehung des Historismus. Munich: Oldenbourg.

NEUMANN, FRANZ (1949) 1962 Editor's Introduction. In Montesquieu, *The Spirit of the Laws.* New York: Hafner.

PALMER, ROBERT R. 1959–1964 *The Age of the Democratic Revolution: A Political History of Europe and America, 1760–1800.* 2 vols. Princeton Univ. Press.

PARIS, UNIVERSITÉ DE, INSTITUT DE DROIT COMPARÉ 1952 *La pensée politique et constitutionnelle de Montesquieu: Bicentenaire de L'esprit des lois 1748–1948.* Paris: Sirey.

PLAMENATZ, JOHN P. 1963 *Man and Society: Political and Social Theory.* Volume 2: Bentham Through Marx. New York: McGraw-Hill.

POLLOCK, FREDERICK (1890) 1960 *An Introduction to the History of the Science of Politics.* Boston: Beacon.

RICHTER, MELVIN 1963 [A Book Review of] *Montesquieu: A Critical Biography,* by Robert Shackleton. *History and Theory* 3:266–274.

ROTHKRUG, LIONEL 1965 *Opposition to Louis XIV: The Political and Social Origins of the French Enlightenment.* Princeton Univ. Press.

RUNCIMAN, W. G. 1963 *Social Science and Political Theory.* Cambridge Univ. Press.

SHACKLETON, ROBERT 1961 *Montesquieu: A Critical Biography.* Oxford Univ. Press. → The best biography in any language.

SOREL, ALBERT (1887) 1888 *Montesquieu.* Translated by Melville B. Anderson and Edward Playfair Anderson. Chicago: McClurg. → First published in French by Hachette. A German translation was published in Berlin in 1896 by Hofmann.

SPURLIN, PAUL M. 1940 *Montesquieu in America, 1760–1801.* Louisiana State Univ., Romance Language Series, No. 4. University: Louisiana State Univ. Press.

TOUCHARD, JEAN 1959 *Histoire des idées politiques.* 2 vols. Paris: Presses Universitaires de France.

MONTESSORI, MARIA

Maria Montessori (1870–1952), Italian educator, was born in the provincial town of Chiaravalle. Her father, a conservative army officer, had little sympathy with his daughter's desire for a career, but she received encouragement from her mother. Montessori attended a lay state school until she was 12, when the family moved to Rome for better educational opportunities. At 14, because of an interest in mathematics and engineering, she went to classes at the technical institute; this interest gave way to an interest in biology, which led ultimately to her decision to study medicine. She became the first woman graduate of a medical school in Italy, despite difficulties which surely enhanced her strong feminist leanings. (She attended several international feminist congresses.)

As an assistant doctor at the Psychiatric Clinic of the University of Rome, she had her first encounter with defective children, and this early experience convinced her that the problem of handicapped children is a pedagogical as well as a medical one. Previous advocates of this approach were Jean Itard, who worked with deaf-mutes as well as with "the wild boy of Aveyron," and Itard's student Edouard Séguin, who founded a school for defectives in Rome; their work reinforced her conviction that the difficulties of the handicapped could be ameliorated by special educational treatment.

In 1899 Montessori became the directress of the State Orthophrenic School in Rome, which served the "hopelessly deficient" children of the city, and later also the "idiot" children. There she taught the children and trained other teachers to work with them. She visited London and Paris to exchange ideas on methods of treatment with others in this field. The mentality of the children in the institution developed so remarkably and unexpectedly that she received considerable attention. Her success made her want to try the same methods and techniques with normal children, and the opportunity came when in 1906 the Italian government gave her the responsibility for 60 children aged three to six from the slums of the San Lorenzo quarter of Rome—the beginning of her famous Casa dei Bambini.

Meanwhile, in 1901 she had left the Orthophrenic School to resume studies at the University of Rome; she sought "further study and meditation" in psychology and philosophy. She was then holding the chair of hygiene at the Scuola di Magistero Femminile in Rome and was a permanent external examiner in the faculty of pedagogy. In 1904 she became a professor at the University of Rome, and from 1904 until 1908 held a chair of anthropology there. In addition to lecturing (some of her published works were based on her auditors' lecture notes), she was practicing not only in hospitals and clinics but also privately, and it was through this extensive practical application of her methods and principles that she came to formulate her conception of the nature of the child that underlay the program of the Casa dei Bambini.

The Montessori method.   It was in the early years of the Casa dei Bambini that the fundamentals of what we now know as the Montessori method were developed. This "Children's House," as well

as subsequent ones, proved to be an excellent way of dealing with cultural deprivation. The "prepared environment" set a basic atmosphere for learning, with room for "the liberty of the pupils in their spontaneous manifestations." In keeping with her belief that the teacher must be kept in the background, guiding and disciplining minimally, the entire staff consisted of herself and two untrained young women. The activity materials provided an opportunity for the child to acquire important percepts through sensory–motor means. Each "game" was designed to teach a skill or a fact. There were no benches, desks, or stationary chairs (standard equipment in schools prior to Montessori) but, rather, small chairs and tables, a low washstand, and low blackboards, all making the daily routine easy for the child. Long low cupboards contained the didactic materials, the care of which was entrusted to the children: these materials included counting beads in blocks of ten; two-dimensional geometric puzzles; graduated prisms, rods, and cubes; letters of the alphabet made of sandpaper, cardboard, and wood, for obtaining direct sensory impression of the letters; and series of tuned bells. In this "prepared environment" the child practiced the education of his senses, reading, metrics, grammar, music, manual training, and gymnastics, and he also learned cleanliness, order, poise, absorption, and patience. The pleasure the children took in silently concentrating on the materials was remarkable. Montessori had the ability to learn from observing the children at work on the apparatus and constantly made constructive changes in the "work situation."

Montessori made certain generalizations on the basis of her observations: that children go through a series of "sensitive periods" with their "creative moments," when they show spontaneous interest in learning and have maximal ability to do so; that children prefer "work" with creative materials to "play" with objects defined as toys; that they have an extraordinary capacity for mental concentration, a desire to repeat activities over and over, and a love of order, for which witness their concern that materials be returned where they "belong"; that "work is its own reward" and there is no need for external reward; and that since spontaneous self-discipline is created by the liberty and independence of the school situation, there is no need for punishment (other than isolation). Indeed, Montessori became quite mystical about this notion of self-discipline: she saw it as a continuation of the cosmic discipline that orders the stars. A further general pattern that she identified was the existence of spontaneous "advanced interests," for example, "the burst into writing," which precedes by several months the "burst into reading"; by virtue of these "advanced interests," three- and four-year-old children begin to read and write with the materials available to them in the classroom.

Influence. Montessori's work grew out of a dedication to individual self-expression that goes back to the eighteenth century; she belongs in the tradition of Rousseau, Froebel, and Pestalozzi. Also, her work is related to that strain in evolutionary thought which stresses development. But the hereditarian stress in Darwin's theory runs counter to her own emphasis on the importance of early experience, and her work was not in harmony with other strong intellectual trends of the first half of the twentieth century: behaviorism, with its emphasis on stimulus–response learning; the notion of fixed intelligence, based on intelligence testing; and the psychoanalytic emphasis on instinctual, and especially psychosexual, determination of personality and behavior. "Progressive education," as conceived primarily by John Dewey, was more in keeping with these trends, and as it came to dominate education, the Montessori system was all but forgotten.

Although the Montessori method did spread abroad from Rome after 1918—Montessori's publications were translated into 20 languages, and training courses were set up in England, Ireland, Germany, Spain, Ceylon, and Argentina—there was only a brief flurry of interest in it in the United States when Montessori visited there in 1913. Recently, beginning in the 1950s, there has been a resurgence of interest, related perhaps to such developments as reforms in the mathematics and science curricula in the schools and new concern for handicapped children—handicapped genetically or environmentally. This renewed interest has produced many new Montessori schools and training centers. It may well be that the Montessori method is more than a fad, that it deals, instead, with fundamental aspects of learning.

JACQUELINE Y. SUTTON

[See also DEVELOPMENTAL PSYCHOLOGY; EDUCATIONAL PSYCHOLOGY; INTELLECTUAL DEVELOPMENT; *and the* biographies of CLAPARÈDE; DEWEY; GESELL.]

WORKS BY MONTESSORI

(1909) 1964 *The Montessori Method: Scientific Pedagogy as Applied to Child Education in "The Children's Houses."* Cambridge, Mass.: Bentley. → First published as *Il metodo della pedagogia scientifica.* . . . A paperback edition was published by Schocken with an Introduction by J. McV. Hunt.

(1910) 1913 *Pedagogical Anthropology.* New York: Stokes. → First published as *Antropologia pedagogica.*

(1914) 1966 *A Montessori Handbook: "Dr. Montessori's Own Handbook."* Edited by R. C. Orem. New York: Putnam.

(1916–1917) 1964 *The Advanced Montessori Method.* 2 vols. Cambridge, Mass.: Bentley. → Volume 1: *Spontaneous Activity in Education.* Volume 2: *Montessori Elementary Material.* First published in Italian.

(1924) 1965 *Child in the Church: Essays on the Religious Education of Children and the Training of Character.* 2d ed. Edited by Edward M. Standing. St. Paul (Minn.) Catechetical Guild. → A collection of essays, excerpts, and conversations first published in Italian.

1936 *The Secret of Childhood.* London: Longmans. → A second edition was published in 1950 in Italian as *Il segreto dell' infanzia.*

1946 *Education for a New World.* Asundale Montessori Training Center, Adyar, Madras Publication Series, No. 1. Madras (India): Kalakshetra.

(1949a) 1964 *The Absorbent Mind.* 5th ed. Madras (India): Theosophical Publishing House.

(1949b) 1955 *The Formation of Man.* Madras (India): Theosophical Publishing House. → First published in Italian.

SUPPLEMENTARY BIBLIOGRAPHY

BRUNER, JEROME S. 1960 *The Process of Education.* Cambridge, Mass.: Harvard Univ. Press.

DONAHUE, GILBERT E. 1962 Dr. Maria Montessori and the Montessori Movement: A General Bibliography of Materials in the English Language, 1909–1961. Pages 141–175 in Nancy M. Rambusch, *Learning How to Learn: An American Approach to Montessori.* Baltimore and Dublin: Helicon.

ITARD, JEAN M. G. (1801) 1932 *Wild Boy of Aveyron.* New York: Century. → First published as *De l'éducation d'un homme sauvage, ou des premiers développements physiques et moraux du jeune sauvage de l'Aveyron.*

LEWIN, KURT (1931) 1935 Education for Reality. Pages 171–179 in Kurt Lewin, *A Dynamic Theory of Personality: Selected Papers.* New York: McGraw-Hill.

PIAGET, JEAN (1923) 1959 *The Language and Thought of the Child.* 3d ed., rev. New York: Humanities Press. → First published as *Le langage et la pensée chez l'enfant.*

RAMBUSCH, NANCY M. 1962 *Learning How to Learn: An American Approach to Montessori.* Baltimore and Dublin: Helicon.

SÉGUIN, EDOUARD 1846 *Traitement moral, hygiène et éducation des idiots.* Paris: Baillière.

STANDING, EDWARD M. 1959 *Maria Montessori: Her Life and Work.* Fresno, Calif.: Academy Library Guild.

STANDING, EDWARD M. 1962 *The Montessori Method: A Revolution in Education.* Fresno, Calif.: Academy Library Guild.

MOONEY, JAMES

James Mooney (1861–1921), author of "The Ghost-dance Religion and the Sioux Outbreak of 1890" (1896), *The Aboriginal Population of America North of Mexico* (1928), and other distinguished works on the American Indian, was born in a small town in Indiana of Irish immigrant parents. As a youth, he developed an intense interest in the Indian tribes of the Americas and early determined to be an ethnologist. After working briefly as a schoolteacher and newspaperman in Indiana, he went to Washington, D.C., where he met John Wesley Powell, the founder of the Bureau of American Ethnology in the Smithsonian Institution. Powell hired him as an ethnologist in 1885, and from then until his death Mooney worked for the bureau.

Mooney undertook many field trips among North American tribes, becoming an expert particularly on the Cherokee and the Kiowa. He collected historical and linguistic data which contributed heavily not only to his own work but also to the collaborative effort which led to the publication of the *Handbook of American Indians North of Mexico* (the famous Bulletin 30 of the Bureau of American Ethnology). He published extensively on the Cherokee and other American Indian tribal groups, always basing his publications on substantial personal field work and historical research. The value of his reports is enhanced today by the fact that his research was done at an early date, when some of the Oklahoma tribes still lived relatively independent of interference in Indian Territory and others, only recently confined to reservations, preserved customs and values of prior ages.

His most celebrated work, "The Ghost-dance Religion and the Sioux Outbreak of 1890," was a careful account of the religion which swept across the reservations west of the Mississippi in 1890 and the following years. Mooney talked to the Paiute prophet, Wovoka, and visited many of the tribes, including the Sioux, who were receptive to the ghost dance. The ghost dancers believed that a native millennium was about to arrive, in which the faithful dancers would be saved, to live in the ancient way in a world relieved of white men and their customs. The organization of the ghost dance among the Sioux, itself a response to various economic and political pressures, led to the killing of Sitting Bull, then chief, and to the massacre of Indians who resisted being disarmed. Mooney's sympathetic account of the dance generally and of Sioux resentments in particular has become a classic of early American ethnography. As a result, the ghost dance has achieved international fame and is often treated in secondary sources as the very prototype of nativistic or revitalization movements. His ability to understand the nativistic aspirations of the Indians and to see in their behavior a homologue with religious enthusiasms in other times and places (in the early phases of the great religions and the movement of Joan of Arc, as well as other Indian movements) was probably owing in part to his own vigorous interest in Irish nationalism.

ANTHONY F. C. WALLACE

[*See also* INDIANS, NORTH AMERICAN; MILLENARISM; NATIVISM AND REVIVALISM.]

WORKS BY MOONEY
1885   *Linguistic Families of the Indian Tribes North of Mexico, With Provisional List of the Principal Tribal Names and Synonyms.* U.S. Bureau of American Ethnology, Misc. Publ. No. 3. Washington: The Bureau.
1891   The Sacred Formulas of the Cherokees. Pages 301–397 in U.S. Bureau of American Ethnology, *Seventh Annual Report . . . 1885–1886.* Washington: The Bureau.
1894   Siouan Tribes of the East. U.S. Bureau of American Ethnology, *Bulletin* 22:1–101.
1896   The Ghost-dance Religion and the Sioux Outbreak of 1890. Part 2, pages 641–1136 in U.S. Bureau of American Ethnology, *Fourteenth Annual Report . . . 1892–1893.* Washington: The Bureau. → An abridged edition with an introduction by Anthony F. C. Wallace was published in 1965 by the Univ. of Chicago Press.
1898   Calendar History of the Kiowa Indians. Part 1, pages 129–445 in U.S. Bureau of American Ethnology, *Seventeenth Annual Report . . . 1895–1896.* Washington: The Bureau.
1900   Myths of the Cherokee. Part 1, pages 3–548 in U.S. Bureau of American Ethnology, *Nineteenth Annual Report . . . 1897–1898.* Washington: The Bureau.
1907   The Cheyenne Indians. American Anthropological Association, *Memoirs* 1:357–442.
1928   *The Aboriginal Population of America North of Mexico.* Smithsonian Miscellaneous Collections, Vol. 80, No. 7. Washington: Smithsonian Institution.

SUPPLEMENTARY BIBLIOGRAPHY
[HEWITT, J. N. B.] 1922 James Mooney. *American Anthropologist* New Series 24:209–214. → Includes a comprehensive bibliography of Mooney's works, prepared by his wife.
HODGE, FREDERICK W. (editor) (1907–1910) 1959 *Handbook of American Indians North of Mexico.* 2 vols. Smithsonian Institution, Bureau of American Ethnology, Bulletin No. 30. New York: Pageant.

MOORE, HENRY L.

Henry Ludwell Moore (1869–1958), American economist, made the first major attempts to combine economic theory and statistical techniques in the empirical estimation of theoretical economic relationships. Quantitative estimates of elasticities of demand and supply, of productivity changes and of the nature of strikes, of cost curves and of determinants of wage rates are so prominent in—even characteristic of—modern economics that it is difficult to remember that they were initiated only in the present century, and by Moore more than by any other economist.

Moore's life was that of a scholar wholehearted in his devotion to research. After receiving his PH.D. from Johns Hopkins University in 1896, he began teaching at Smith College, and in 1902 he went to Columbia University, where he remained until 1929; aside from two terms in Karl Pearson's statistical laboratory (in 1909 and 1913), he had no important association with any other institution or type of activity. His premature retirement was due to poor health.

His first professional interest was the history of economic thought. Moore's dissertation was a competent survey of the vast literature on von Thünen's celebrated natural rate of wages, $\sqrt{ap}$, where a is the subsistence of a workingman's family and p the total product per workingman (1895). A second study was devoted to Cournot, the great pioneer of the mathematical method in economics (1902). Soon, however, his interests shifted to what he called statistical economics and is now more commonly called econometrics.

His first publication in statistical economics was a set of essays, all connected with labor, *Laws of Wages* (1911). Several of the essays were devoted to a verification of the marginal productivity theory, as applied to the pattern of average wages in coal mining over time and space and to the differences between wages of individuals. In general these investigations displayed careful and (for that time) sophisticated statistical methodology, but the hypotheses were very loose in their theoretical formulation. Moore's contemporaries properly applauded the purpose and criticized the execution of these studies.

A second set of essays in this first volume proposed empirical uniformities, for which theoretical explanations might then be sought. One was a demonstration that within an industry or occupation, the larger the establishment, the higher the wage rates—a finding confirmed by later research. A second was an attempt to measure the influence of unions on the outcome of strikes, with much more ambiguous results.

Three years later Moore's *Economic Cycles* (1914) launched the most important of all his work, the empirical estimation of theoretical relationships. Yet these estimates were essentially only by-products of Moore's search for a truly fundamental explanation of fluctuations in the level of economic activity. The main theme, as he saw it, is as follows:

The principal contribution of this Essay is the discovery of the law and cause of Economic Cycles. The rhythm in the activity of economic life, the alternation of buoyant, purposeful expansion with aimless depression, is caused by the rhythm in the yield per acre of the crops; while the rhythm in the production of the crops is, in turn, caused by the rhythm of changing weather which is represented by the cyclical changes in the amount of rainfall. The law of the cycles of rainfall is the law of the cycles of the crops and the law of Economic Cycles. (p. 135)

The support for this bold claim consisted of four steps:

(1) The discovery of several cycles—the chief being of eight years' duration—in rainfall in Ohio.

(2) The argument that the rainfall cycles lead to cycles of equal duration in yields per acre (but lagged by half a cycle).

(3) The demonstration that yields per acre are inversely related to the prices of the grain products.

(4) The argument that demand curves for agricultural products shift upward in periods of rising industrial prices.

If, as Moore for a time believed, the demand curve for pig iron (a typical industrial good) is positively sloped and the volume of pig iron falls when crops decline, then the price of pig iron falls when crops are small, thus lowering the demand for the crops. The cycle in rain has thus been carried through to the cycles in outputs and prices of industrial goods.

Only the third step in this argument, in which statistical demand curves are estimated, was well founded, and it was this part of Moore's work which had the major impact on economics. Moore's first demand curve, that for corn from 1866 to 1911, illustrates his procedures. The historical series of prices and outputs are influenced by increasing population and fluctuations of price levels, so the annual price and quantity are expressed as ratios to the previous years' prices and quantities (link relatives). A linear demand equation then yields an elasticity of -1.12 (with $r = -.789$); a cubic equation yields an elasticity of $-.92$. Moore examined demand functions for periods of rising and of falling general prices—they differed little—but never introduced prices of substitutes or income (for which no satisfactory data existed).

The work on demand curves was extended in *Forecasting the Yield and the Price of Cotton* (1917). Here he developed predictions of the size of the cotton crop on the basis of early-season rainfall which were more reliable than the elaborate crop forecasting system of the U.S. Department of Agriculture. Subsequently Moore introduced the concept of the flexibility of prices (the relative change in price divided by the relative change in quantity—the reciprocal of the elasticity of demand in a two-variable relationship) and the partial elasticity of demand.

Two years later Moore extended this type of analysis to supply curves by correlating percentage changes in acreage with percentage changes in prices a year earlier (1919). This analysis assumes that farmers predict that this year's price (or price change) will continue next year, and this approach led Henry Schultz (who was Moore's chief disciple) to formulate the cobweb analysis.

Until 1923, however, Moore continued to consider his research on the extraterrestrial theory of cycles of primary importance. He found eight-year cycles almost everywhere and ultimately attributed them to the transits of Venus. Eventually he accepted the futility of this work, and he stopped working on the subject shortly after the book *Generating Economic Cycles* (1923) appeared.

Moore's final book, *Synthetic Economics* (1929), proposed the boldest of programs: the statistical estimation of Walras' equations of general equilibrium. But although Moore's vision continued to be superlatively farsighted, he had not the power to translate this vision into a workable research program.

The increasing rigor of economic theory, the expanding arsenal of statistical techniques, and the increasing intervention of the state in economic life all contributed to the cordial reception of Moore's work. The 1920s saw an extensive application of his techniques to agricultural products, and from this base empirical estimation of theoretical functions has spread over the entire corpus of economics.

GEORGE J. STIGLER

[*For the historical context of Moore's work, see the biographies of* COURNOT *and* THÜNEN. *For discussion of the subsequent development of Moore's ideas, see* DEMAND AND SUPPLY, *article on* ECONOMETRIC STUDIES; ECONOMETRICS; TIME SERIES, *article on* CYCLES; *and the biography of* SCHULTZ.]

WORKS BY MOORE

1895 Von Thünen's Theory of Natural Wages. *Quarterly Journal of Economics* 9:291–304, 388–408.
1902 Antoine-Augustin Cournot. *Revue de métaphysique et de morale* 13:521–543.
1911 *Laws of Wages: An Essay in Statistical Economics.* New York: Macmillan.
1914 *Economic Cycles: Their Law and Cause.* New York: Macmillan.
1917 *Forecasting the Yield and the Price of Cotton.* New York: Macmillan.
1919 Empirical Laws of Demand and Supply and the Flexibility of Prices. *Political Science Quarterly* 34:546–567.
1923 *Generating Economic Cycles.* New York: Macmillan.
1929 *Synthetic Economics.* New York: Macmillan.

SUPPLEMENTARY BIBLIOGRAPHY

STIGLER, GEORGE J. 1962 Henry L. Moore and Statistical Economics. *Econometrica* 30:1–21. → Contains a complete bibliography of Moore's work on pages 19–21, and references both to the leading reviews by his contemporaries and to the work on statistical demand curves in the 1920s.

MOORE, JOHN BASSETT

John Bassett Moore (1860–1947), the outstanding international lawyer of his generation, was born in Smyrna, Delaware. His father, John Adams Moore, was a prominent physician and for a time a member of the Delaware legislature; his mother, Martha Anne Ferguson, came from a family with classical interests, and Moore frequently said that one of his treasures was his mother's copy of Liddell and Scott's massive *Greek–English Lexicon*.

In 1870 Moore's father, who had moved to the town of Felton, was one of the principal founders of the Felton Institute and Classical Seminary. Moore attended the Felton Seminary, as it was popularly called, and when ready for college chose the University of Virginia, partly because of the climate. He spent three years there, from 1877 to 1880, then studied law privately, and in 1883 was admitted to the Delaware bar. Two years later, when civil service examinations were held to fill the position of law clerk in the Department of State at Washington, Moore was one of the four young men who passed the examination. His selection for the post was certain because the then secretary of state, Thomas F. Bayard of Delaware, was a friend of the family. From 1886 to 1891 Moore served as third assistant secretary of state and then left Washington to join the faculty of Columbia University where, until his retirement in 1924, he was Hamilton Fish professor of international law and diplomacy.

Although Moore was often on leave from the university to perform public services, he never neglected his students—a score who took their doctoral degrees under him did notable service in Washington, on the faculties of law schools, and in political science departments. For six months in 1898 he was again assistant secretary of state. In 1913 he became counselor of the Department of State with power to sign as secretary, but he resigned the next year because he was critical of some phases of Woodrow Wilson's foreign policy. He was repeatedly an American delegate to international conferences. He served as a member of the Permanent Court of Arbitration, The Hague, from 1912 to 1938 and (even though the United States was not a member of the League of Nations) was a judge of the Permanent Court of International Justice from 1921 to 1928. The first group, he remarked in 1943, was more distinguished than the second, as they constituted only an "eligible list" of persons nominated by their governments to serve as members of a panel of arbitrators and "were not required at once, if ever, to abandon their usual pursuits and live a sacrificial life abroad" (*The Collected Papers*, vol. 7, p. 348).

Before he went to Columbia, Moore had published a good deal, principally on extradition and extraterritoriality. In 1898 he brought out the *History and Digest of the International Arbitrations to Which the United States Has Been a Party*; in 1905 he published the textbook *American Diplomacy* and, the following year, the monumental *Digest of International Law*. Thereafter, every treatise writer relied on "Moore's Digest." He continued his interest in arbitration and between 1929 and 1933 edited six volumes of *International Adjudications, Ancient and Modern*. Moore edited a 12-volume edition of *The Works of James Buchanan* (1908–1911).

Most of Moore's minor writings were published in 1944 as *The Collected Papers of John Bassett Moore*. The arrangement is chronological: the first item is a previously unpublished Fourth of July speech that Moore had made in 1877 at the age of 17, and the last item a hitherto unpublished, brief monograph, "Peace, Law and Hysteria," described as "a 'dissertation' chiefly written prior to 1936 and completed in 1943" (vol. 7, pp. 220–349). In between are addresses, articles from the law reviews and popular journals, books (e.g., the 1924 "International Law and Some Current Illusions" [vol. 6, pp. 1–280]), legal opinions given to clients, letters to newspapers, and 125 book reviews, whose urbanity sometimes softens devastating criticisms. The much-discussed 1933 article, "An Appeal to Reason," is also included (vol. 6, pp. 416–464). Practically all of these "papers" demonstrate that Moore had a good classical education, that he was a learned historian, that he was steeped in great literature, that he had a keen wit, and that his career had enabled him not infrequently to participate in important events.

Moore did not seek involvement in the heated controversies over legal and political matters that followed World War I (he often asserted that this description was incorrect, that there had been previous world wars), but he never concealed his opinions. He adhered to traditional international law and was skeptical of attempts to "modernize" it. Throughout his life Moore was constantly aware of La Rochefoucauld's maxim "The mind is the dupe of the heart," and he seldom engaged in wishful thinking. His attitude toward the League of Nations Covenant was that expressed by Cardinal Fleury when he was shown the Abbé de Saint-Pierre's *Projet de paix perpétuelle*: "Admirable, Sire, save for one omission: I find no provision for sending missionaries to convert the hearts of the princes." Moore repudiated "the notion that every alleged violation of international law gives to every member of the international community a right of action against the supposed violator. . . ." This, he maintained, "is no less a counsel of anarchy and confusion than would be the claim that every alleged infraction of municipal law gives to every individual in the domestic community a right of action against the alleged wrongdoer" ([1937] 1944, p. 142).

Moore thought that the search for "collective security" was doomed to failure. He declared that the Kellogg Pact "constitutes with its record, experience and reservations, the most sweeping concession ever made to undefined claims of interest and the right to defend them by force" ([1935] 1944, p. 44) and for the "new neutrality" he had nothing but contempt. "The other day, when some one asked me what the 'new neutrality' meant," he wrote in a letter to the *New York Sun* on Dec. 10, 1935, "I replied that, as its limitations appeared to be wholly emotional, it perhaps might be best defined in the terms of the 'new chastity,' which encouraged fornication in the hope that it might reach the stage of legalized prostitution. In other words, the 'new neutrality' appears to be intended to get us into war, which is in a special legal category, by acts which cannot be defended on legal or moral grounds" (*ibid.*).

When, during the Wilson administration, the government of the United States departed from its traditional policy of extending recognition to any new government that controlled its territory and promised to fulfill its obligations, Moore was horrified. He never believed in refusing to recognize a certain regime in order to show disapproval of its character and policies. He outlined at length his views on this matter in an address "Candor and Common Sense" before the Association of the Bar of the City of New York in December 1930 (*The Collected Papers*, vol. 6, pp. 340–368).

Moore received many foreign decorations and honorary degrees and was a member of the principal learned societies. Fellow lawyers and corporations frequently retained him as special counsel, and from 1925 on he was a director of the Equitable Life Assurance Society. His private papers (including many boxes of correspondence) are in the Library of Congress and are much used by students of the diplomatic history of the period during which he was active.

LINDSAY ROGERS

[*For the context of Moore's work, see* INTERNATIONAL LAW.]

WORKS BY MOORE

1898   *History and Digest of the International Arbitrations to Which the United States Has Been a Party.* 6 vols. Washington: Government Printing Office.

1905   *American Diplomacy, Its Spirit and Achievements.* New York: Harper. → A revision and amplification of a series of articles that appeared in *Harper's Magazine.*

1906   *A Digest of International Law as Embodied in Diplomatic Discussion, Treaties and Other International Agreements* . . . . 8 vols. Washington: Government Printing Office.

1908–1911   BUCHANAN, JAMES *The Works of James Buchanan, Comprising His Speeches, State Papers, and Private Correspondence.* Collected and edited by John Bassett Moore. 12 vols. Philadelphia: Lippincott.

1929–1933   MOORE, JOHN BASSETT (editor) *International Adjudications, Ancient and Modern: Modern Series.* 6 vols. New York: Oxford Univ. Press.

(1935) 1944   The "New Neutrality" Defined. Volume 7, pages 43–45 in *The Collected Papers of John Bassett Moore.* Oxford Univ. Press; Yale Univ. Press.

(1937) 1944   The Dictatorial Drift. Volume 7, pages 136–149 in *The Collected Papers of John Bassett Moore.* Oxford Univ. Press; Yale Univ. Press.

The Collected Papers of John Bassett Moore. 7 vols. Oxford Univ. Press; Yale Univ. Press, 1944. → A comprehensive bibliography of Moore's works appears in Volume 7, pages 351–372.

MORAL DEVELOPMENT

The study of moral development has long been recognized as a key problem area in the social sciences, as indicated by McDougall's statement that "the *fundamental problem* of social psychology is the moralization of the individual by the society" (1908) or by Freud's statement that "the sense of guilt is the most important problem in the evolution of culture" (1930). However, it is hard to make clear distinctions between moral development and the broader area of social development and socialization (learning to conform to cultural standards). Such topics as the development of patterns of cooperation, of aggression, or of industry and achievement are generally studied under the broader rubric of *socialization,* although they may also be viewed as moral development insofar as cooperation or nonaggression are considered "good"

and insofar as they involve learning to conform to cultural rules. The past decade has witnessed a great deal of research on moral development (reviewed in Kohlberg 1963a; 1964; Hoffman 1966) viewed as the particular aspects of socialization involved in *internalization,* i.e., learning to conform to rules in situations that arouse impulses to transgress and that lack surveillance and sanctions. In this research literature, moral *development* has usually been conceived of as the increase in internalization of basic cultural rules. Various theories and researchers have stressed three different aspects of internalization: the behavioral, emotional, and judgmental aspects of moral action.

A *behavioral* criterion of internalization is that of intrinsically motivated conformity, or resistance to temptation. Such a conception is implicit in the common-sense notion of "moral character" which formed the basis of earlier American research on morality; Hartshorne and May (Columbia University 1928–1930) defined moral character as a set of culturally defined virtues, such as honesty, which could be measured by observing the child's ability to resist the temptation to break a rule (for example, against cheating) when it seemed unlikely that he would be detected or punished.

A second criterion of the existence of internalized standards is the *emotion* of *guilt,* that is, of self-punitive, self-critical reactions of remorse and anxiety after transgression of cultural standards. Both psychoanalytic and learning theories of conscience have focused upon guilt as the basic motive of morality. It has been assumed that a child behaves morally to avoid guilt.

In addition to conduct that conforms with a standard and to emotional reactions of remorse after transgression, the internalization of a standard implies a capacity to make judgments in terms of that standard and to justify maintaining the standard to oneself and to others. This *judgmental* side of moral development has formed the focus of the work and theory of Piaget (1932) and others (Kohlberg 1966).

In recent research, then, answers to the problems of moral development have been sought by examining how socialization factors, such as amount, type, and condition of punishment and reward, or opportunities for identification with parents, are related to individual differences in resistance to temptation, guilt, or moral judgment.

Internalization versus situational factors. Kohlberg has argued (1964; 1966) that the study of internalized socialization has cast a limited light upon the classical problems of moral development. Problems have arisen, in the first place, because internalization does not represent a clear dimension of temporal development. Experimental measures of resistance to temptation (honesty) do not indicate any clear age trends toward greater occurrence of honesty from the preschool years to adolescence. Projective measures of intensity of guilt or moral anxiety also do not indicate clear age trends, except in terms of rather rapid and cognitively based age changes in the years eight to twelve, and these changes are in the direction of defining moral anxiety as a reaction to moral self-judgment rather than to more diffuse external events. While clear trends of development have been found in moral judgment, these trends cannot be easily considered to be trends of internalized socialization as such.

In the second place, problems have arisen because a distinctive set of socialization factors has not been found that can be considered as an antecedent of moral internalization. Research results suggest that the conditions which facilitate moral internalization (e.g., parental warmth) are the same conditions which, in general, facilitate the learning of nonmoral cultural rules and expectations. In other words, this research does not indicate a distinct area of internalization or of "conscience"—of moral control linked to guilt feelings—that is distinct from general processes of social learning and social control.

Recent research findings, then, reinforce the skeptical conclusions about both common-sense and psychoanalytic conceptions of a faculty of conscience or superego. Such conclusions were the major results of Hartshorne and May's monumental studies of moral character. These scholars found that the most influential factors determining resistance to temptation to cheat or disobey were situational factors rather than a fixed, individual moral character trait of honesty. The first finding that led to this conclusion was the low predictability of cheating in one situation for cheating in another. A second finding was that children could not be divided into two groups—the "cheaters" and the "honest children." Children's cheating scores were distributed in bell-curve fashion around an average score indicative of moderate cheating. A third finding was the importance of the expediency aspect of the decision to cheat; that is, the tendency to cheat depends upon the degree of risk of detection and the effort required to cheat. Children who cheated in more risky situations also cheated in less risky situations. Thus, noncheaters appeared to act more from caution than honesty. A fourth finding was that even when honest behavior was not dictated by concern about punishment or de-

tection, it was largely determined by immediate situational factors of group approval and example (as opposed to determination by internal moral values). Some classrooms showed a high tendency to cheat, while other, seemingly identically composed classrooms in the same school showed little tendency to cheat. A fifth finding was that moral knowledge or values had little apparent influence on moral conduct, since the correlations between verbal tests of moral knowledge and experimental tests of moral conduct were low. A sixth finding was that where moral values did seem to be related to conduct, these values were somewhat specific to the child's social class or group. Rather than being a universal ideal, honesty was more characteristic of the middle-class child and seemed less relevant to the lower-class child.

The Hartshorne and May findings, then, suggested that honest behavior is determined by situational factors of punishment, reward, group pressures, and group values, rather than by an internal disposition of conscience or character. The general problem raised by these findings is whether moral traits describing moral character are simply value judgments of behavior made by the group or whether they correspond to some inner disposition in the person and hence help us to understand and predict his behavior. Psychologists have usually used "moral development" to mean the formation of internal standards that control behavior. This conception of an internalized standard seems to require some cross-situational generality. It is not useful to speak of behavior as being determined by an internalized rule like "Be honest" or "Don't cheat" if the rule does *not* predict the individual's behavior and situational forces *do*. We do not find it useful to speak of the morality of the dog or the rat, although both have been trained to "resist temptation" in specific situations. We do assume, however, that the animal's resistance to temptation is produced by anxiety aroused by situational cues, rather than by regard for a moral rule. To the extent that human resistance to temptation is not general across situations to which a moral rule pertains and must therefore be predicted by purely situational factors, it would seem to be no more useful to describe human behavior as the result of conscience than it is to describe animal behavior in these terms.

Since MacKinnon's research (1938), studies of morality have generally attempted to cope with Hartshorne and May's findings by defining moral internalization in terms of superego, rather than "moral character." Researchers have recognized that moral action was not the direct result of an internal disposition toward honesty or moral character and instead have assumed it to be the result of a complex balance of internal and external forces, including strength of drives aroused by temptation, defenses against these drives, situational fears, group pressures, etc. However, one distinctively moral force, guilt, was assumed to be a major determinant of action in situations of moral conflict or temptation. The disposition to feel guilt was assumed to be the result of early childhood identifications and experiences of punishment, rather than of situational forces. Accordingly, while moral behavior might be situation-specific, one might still be able to isolate a general process of moral internalization or guilt formation having the same childhood antecedents, regardless of the particular moral situation involved. These childhood antecedents should then have some value for predicting guilt and resistance to temptation in any situation, even though they did not produce a consistent disposition of moral character.

Subsequent research on parental antecedents of guilt and of resistance to temptation has fulfilled this hope only to a very limited extent. Usually the child-rearing correlates of children's resistance to temptation in one situation have not proven to be correlates of resistance in another, and the child-rearing correlates of projective test measures of guilt have not proven to be correlates of actual moral behavior. Finally, projective measures of guilt have not proven to predict consistently actual resistance to temptation behavior (reviewed in Kohlberg 1963a).

Kohlberg (1964) has argued that this more recent research evidence is consistent with the Hartshorne and May findings by suggesting that the variables leading to resistance to temptation arise primarily from the situation rather than from fixed habits, character traits like honesty, or permanent superego dispositions to feel guilt. Following Burton's analysis of honesty (1963), however, one would agree that there is some personal consistency in honest behavior or some determination of honest behavior by general personality traits. These traits, however, seem not to be traits of moral conscience but rather a set of ego abilities corresponding to common-sense notions of prudence and will. In a tradition of moral psychology dating back to the British associationists and utilitarians, moral character is believed to result from practical judgment or reason. In this view, moral action (action based on rational consideration of how one's action affects others) requires much the same capacities as does prudent action (action

based on rational consideration of how it affects the self's long-range interests). Both require empathy (the ability to predict the reactions of others to action), foresight (the ability to predict long-range consequences of action), judgment (the ability to weigh alternatives and probabilities), and capacity to delay (delay of response and preference for the distant, greater gratification over the immediate, lesser gratification). In psychoanalytic theory these factors are included with other aspects of decision making and emotional control in the concept of ego strength. Some of the ego abilities which have been found to correlate consistently with experimental and rating measures of children's honesty include the following: intelligence (IQ); delay of gratification (preference for a larger reward in the future over a smaller reward in the present); and attention (stability and persistence of attention in simple experimental tasks). [See DECISION MAKING, *article on* PSYCHOLOGICAL ASPECTS.]

These findings suggest that one can predict honesty about as well from an individual's behavior in cognitive-task or other nonmoral situations as one can from his behavior in other situations involving honesty. This, in turn, implies that the study of moral behavior in terms of early experiences centering on specifically moral training of honesty, guilt, etc., is less likely to be fruitful than is a study of moral behavior in terms of more general experiences relevant to ego development and ego control in nonmoral contexts.

Some specific moral determinants. While the findings stressed so far suggest the determination of moral action by nonmoral situational and personality forces, there are also some findings suggesting the determination of action by specifically moral values. This research conclusion should not be taken to mean that there is any direct correspondence between conformity of verbal moral beliefs or attitudes and conformity of moral action. Subjects who say that cheating is very bad or that they would never cheat are as likely to cheat in an experimental situation as are subjects who express a qualified view as to the badness of cheating (studies reviewed in Kohlberg 1966). Apparently, the same willingness to deceive in order to make a good appearance which impels cheating also impels the child to make pious moral statements about cheating.

A conclusion more consistent with actual research is that there is considerable correspondence between maturity of moral values (the possession of rational and internal reasons for moral action) and maturity of action in moral-conflict situations.

Clear relations between maturity of moral judgment and mature moral action are found in situations in which social norms are ambiguous or conflicting and in which developmentally advanced values clearly predispose toward one course of action rather than another. Such a correspondence is suggested only to a limited extent by Hartshorne and May's findings of moderate correlations between age-linked measures of moral knowledge and experimental measures of honesty. This limited correspondence occurred because they defined moral knowledge largely in terms of verbal conformity of attitudes rather than maturity of moral reasoning and because resistance to cheating is not clearly a developmentally more mature choice or a choice based on moral reasons in the young age group studied. There is evidence, however, suggesting that resistance to cheating does become a more mature alternative at older ages or higher levels of development than those involved in the Hartshorne and May study. Only 11 per cent of college subjects who were at the level of moral principle in a verbal moral-values test cheated in an experimental situation, whereas half the subjects at a level of conventional moral values cheated (this test is discussed later in this article; the findings cited are reviewed in Kohlberg 1966). With younger subjects, the same relations between moral judgment and cheating are not found, since few of the younger subjects are at the level in which not cheating may be defined as relevant to principles of contract, trust, and equity. While college-age subjects making principled moral judgments were more likely to conform to an experimenter in the matter of moral expectation about cheating, such subjects are markedly more autonomous, or less conforming to an experimenter, where the experimenter's expectations violate the subjects' moral values. Whereas 75 per cent of the morally principled subjects refused to give increasing levels of shock to an experimental "victim" when ordered to do so by an experimenter, only 13 per cent of the remaining subjects refused to do so.

Major questions. The evidence suggests, then, that the basic social science problem of moral development is not that of accounting for individual differences in moral character as revealed in behavior. Moral behavior that involves conformity to social rule is, on the whole, to be explained as the result of the same situational forces, ego variables, and socialization factors that determine behaviors which have no direct moral relevance. A more distinctive focus of analysis centers instead upon the direct study of the development of moral values, judgments and emotions. The study of actual conduct becomes relevant to problems of moral development insofar as research is able to find links between the child's conduct and the development of his moral values and emotions.

The major questions which may be asked about moral development, then, are as follows: What is the origin of distinctively moral concepts and emotions in the child? To what extent does the child's development indicate typical or regular trends of change in these concepts and sentiments? What causes or stimulates these developmental changes in moral concepts and sentiments? To what extent are these developmental changes in moral concepts and attitudes reflected in developmental changes in the child's moral action under conditions of conflict or temptation?

Culture and cultural agents. All of the questions may also be asked about the development of morality in cultures. The present article will not attempt to deal with the development of cultural moralities, a topic still most comprehensively treated in the work of Hobhouse (1906). It must be pointed out, however, that most recent psychological as well as sociological thought has assumed that the problem of the origin of moral values is a cultural problem. It has been assumed that morality is a system of rules and values defined by the culture and that the individual child acquires these ready-made values by general cultural-transmission mechanisms such as reinforcement learning or identification. If this were the case, our understanding of the content of the individual's moral beliefs and emotions should be based on seeing it as a cultural, rather than an individual, product. This culturological approach to moral development was first clearly outlined by Durkheim (1898–1911; 1925), who based it on assumptions about the cultural relativism of moral values which are still widely held but which do not seem to be supported by recent research findings. Durkheim developed his position out of a critique of the British utilitarians (e.g., Hume 1751; Smith 1759; and Mill 1861). The utilitarians assumed that moral values were the products of individual adults, possessed of language and intelligence, who judged the actions of other individual men. The utilitarians suggested that actions by the self or by others whose consequences to the self are harmful (painful) are naturally deemed bad and arouse anger or punitive tendencies, and actions whose consequences are beneficial (pleasant) are naturally deemed good and arouse affection or approving tendencies. Owing to natural tendencies of empathy, to generalization, and to the need for social agreement, acts are judged good (or bad) when their consequences to others are good (or bad), even if they do not help (or injure) the self. Logical tendencies lead these judgments of consequences to take the form of judging that act right which does the greatest good for the greatest number. [*See* UTILITARIANISM *and the biographies of* HUME; MILL; SMITH, ADAM.]

In his critique of the utilitarians Durkheim pointed to the following four phenomena: (1) Morality is basically a matter of respect for fixed rules (and the authority behind those rules), not of rational calculation of benefit and harm in concrete cases. (2) Morality seems universally to be associated with punitive sentiments, sentiments incompatible with the notion that the right is a matter of human-welfare consequences. (3) From group to group there is wide variation as to the nature of the rules arousing moral respect, punitiveness, and the sense of duty. (4) While modern Western societies divorce morality from religion, the basic moral rules and attitudes in many groups are those concerning relations to gods, not men, and hence do not center on human-welfare consequences.

According to Durkheim, these facts in turn implied the following: The mere fact of the existence of an institutionalized rule endows it with moral sacredness, regardless of its human-welfare consequences. Accordingly, moral rules, attitudes, and consequences originate at the group, rather than the individual, level. The psychological origin of moral attitudes, then, is in the individual's respect for the group, the attitudes shared by the group, and the authority figures who represent the groups. The values most sacred to the individual are those which are most widely shared by, and most closely bind together, the group.

While Durkheim's views of the group mind have been widely questioned, the essential implications of his position have been widely accepted. Assumptions common to Durkheim and Freud underlie the research studies of moral internalization previously discussed. Unlike Durkheim, Freud (1923; 1930) derived moral sentiments and beliefs from respect for, and identification with, individual parents, rather than from respect for the group. Furthermore, Freud derived this respect and identification from instinctual attachments (and defenses against these attachments) and viewed the central rules of morality as deriving their strength and rigidity from the need to counter these instinctual forces. In spite of these differences, Freud agreed in viewing morality (superego) as fundamentally a matter of respect for concrete rules which are culturally variable or arbitrary, since these rules are a manifestation of social authority, and he agreed in viewing punitive or (self-punitive) sentiments toward

deviation as the clearest and most characteristic expression of moral internalization or respect.

The research findings on individual moral judgments in a variety of cultures seem incompatible with either of the extreme views just contrasted (Kohlberg 1966). Moral judgments and decisions in all cultures are a mixture of judgments in terms of individual human-utility consequences and judgments in terms of concrete categorical social rules. The utilitarian derivation of respect for rules from utilitarian consequences is as psychologically unfeasible as Durkheim's derivation of concern for individual welfare consequences from respect for social rules as such. A culturally universal core of moral values and moral development may be found, but it is not based on a culturally universal acceptance of moral principles of the utilitarian variety. Individual moral beliefs and sentiments involving universal principles not directly embodied in concrete social rules often develop and often function at a level of conscious opposition and transcendence of group authority, as the utilitarians implied, but this development itself presupposes the development of respect for group authority discussed by Durkheim. Such, at least, seem the implications of recent research oriented to a third, or "developmentalist," concept of morality.

In general, the developmental approach to moral psychology (Baldwin 1897; Mead 1934; McDougall 1908; Hobhouse 1906; Piaget 1932; Kohlberg 1966) has attempted to mediate between the extreme positions represented by the utilitarians and by Durkheim. Moral judgment and emotion based on respect for custom, authority, and the group are seen as one phase or stage in the moral development of the individual rather than as the total definition of the essential characteristics of morality it was for Durkheim. Judgment of right and wrong in terms of the individual's consideration of social-welfare consequences, universal principles, and justice is seen as a later phase of development. This phase depends upon and integrates many of the emotional features of the earlier customary phase and does not spring directly from the minds of unsocialized rational adults, as it did for the utilitarians. Both a morality of respect for social authority and an autonomous rational morality are to be understood as arising from the development of a self through the process of taking the roles or attitudes of other selves in interactions occurring in institutionalized patterns.

Stages of moral development.   As elaborated in Piaget's developmental theory (1932), the child first moves from an amoral stage to Durkheim's stage of respect for sacred rules. This is not so much respect for the group as it is respect for the authority of individual elders such as the parents. Piaget believes that the cognitive limitations of the child of three to eight lead him to confuse moral rules with physical laws and to view rules as fixed external things, rather than as the instruments of human purposes and values. Piaget believes that the child sees rules as absolutes and confuses rules with things because of his "realism" (his inability to distinguish between subjective and objective aspects of his experience) and because of his "egocentrism" (his inability to distinguish his own perspective on events from that of others). In addition to seeing rules as external absolutes, the young child feels that his parents and other adults are all-knowing, perfect, and sacred. This attitude of unilateral respect toward adults, joined with the child's realism, is believed to lead him to view rules as sacred and unchangeable.

Piaget believes that intellectual growth and experiences of role taking in the peer group naturally transform perceptions of rules from external authoritarian commands to internal principles. In essence, he views internal moral norms as logical principles of justice. Of these, he says:

In contrast to a given rule, which from the first has been imposed upon the child from outside . . . the rule of justice is a sort of immanent condition of social relationships or a law governing their equilibrium. (Piaget [1932] 1948, p. 196). The sense of justice . . . is largely independent of [adult precept] and requires nothing more for its development than mutual respect and solidarity which holds among children themselves (p. 195).

By "the sense of justice," Piaget means a concern for reciprocity and equality between individuals. However, norms of justice are not simply matters of abstract logic; rather they are sentiments of sympathy, gratitude, and vengeance which have taken on logical form.

Piaget believes that an autonomous morality of justice develops in children of about age eight to ten and eventually replaces an earlier, heteronomous morality based on unquestioning respect for adult authority. He expects the autonomous morality of justice to develop in all children, unless development is fixated by unusual coerciveness of parents or cultures or by deprivation of experiences of peer cooperation.

Certain aspects of Piaget's theory have been supported by subsequent research findings, while others have not. Piaget's stage theory suggests a number of cross-culturally universal age trends in the development of moral judgment. At least three such trends have been found to occur in a variety of Western, Oriental, and aboriginal (American Indian and Malaysian) cultures (evidence summarized in Kohlberg 1966). These include: (1) *Intentionality in judgment.* Young children tend to judge an act as bad mainly in terms of its actual physical consequences, whereas older children judge an act as bad in terms of the intent to do harm. (2) *Relativism in judgment.* The young child views an act as either totally right or totally wrong and thinks everyone views it in the same way. If the young child does recognize a conflict in views, he believes the adult's view is always the right one. In contrast, the older child is aware of possible diversity in views of right and wrong. (3) *Independence of sanctions.* The young child says an act is bad because it will elicit punishment; the older child says an act is bad because it violates a rule, does harm to others, and so forth.

The young child's absolutism, nonintentionalism, and orientation to punishment do not appear to depend upon extensive parental use of punishment. Even the permissively reared child appears to have a natural tendency to define good and bad in terms of absolutism and punishment, a tendency which his awareness of punishment by teachers, police, and other parents seems sufficient to stimulate. While specific punishment practices or cultural ideologies do not appear necessary for the formation of the young child's moral ideology of punishment, they may lead to the persistence of this ideology into adolescence or adulthood. In other words, specific cultural factors appear to stimulate or retard age trends of development on the Piaget dimensions, but they do not appear to actually cause the age shifts or trends observed.

Piaget, then, appears to be correct in assuming certain characteristics of the young child's moral judgment in any society, characteristics which arise from the child's cognitively immature interpretation of acts labeled good and bad by adults, according to the derivation of their goodness or badness from their association with good and bad consequences of physical harm—punishment and reward. However, his interpretation of these aspects of the young child's morality—as deriving from the child's sense of the sacredness of the rules and of adult authority—has not been supported. Piaget (1932) attempts to demonstrate that the young child's attitude toward rules is one of unilateral sacredness by observations of children's behavior and beliefs about the rules of the game of marbles. Swiss children are quoted as saying that the rules of the game can never be changed, that the rules have existed from the beginning of time and have been invented and handed down by God, the head of the state, or the father. More systematic research suggests that attitudes of rigidity toward game rules seem to decline with age in American children of five to twelve but that attitudes expressing the rigidity or sacredness of moral rules or of laws increase in this period, rather than decline. The young child's ignoring of subjective factors such as intention, then, is not based on respect for sacred rule but on a more or less pragmatic concern for consequences. An example of the fact that young children orient more or less pragmatically to punishment rather than to sacred rule is indicated by a study by Kohlberg, Krebs, and Brener (Kohlberg 1963*b*). Young children were asked to judge a helpful, obedient act (attentively watching a baby brother while the mother is away) followed by punishment (the mother returns and spanks the baby-sitting child). Most four-year-olds, ignoring his act, say the obedient boy was bad because he got punished. By age seven, a majority say the boy was good, not bad, even though he was punished.

Piaget also appears to be incorrect in postulating a general trend from an authoritarian to a peer-group, or democratic, ethic. Postulated general age shifts from obedience to authority to peer loyalty, from justice based on conformity to justice based on equality, have not been generally found. Peer-group participation has not been found to be a factor facilitating development on the Piaget dimensions.

More broadly, however, Piaget is correct in assuming a culturally universal age development of a sense of justice, involving progressive concern for the needs and feelings of others and elaborated conceptions of reciprocity and equality. As this sense of justice develops, however, it reinforces respect for authority and for the rules of adult society; it also reinforces more informal peer norms, since adult institutions have underpinnings of reciprocity, equality of treatment, service to human needs, etc.

The last-mentioned conclusion is derived primarily from cross-cultural research by this writer and his colleagues on children's responses to a number of hypothetical moral dilemmas, such as whether to steal an expensive drug to save one's dying wife. In this research every sentence or response of a subject could be reliably classified into one of six stages that have also been divided into three major levels of development as follows:

Level I. Premoral:
  Stage 1. Punishment and obedience orientation.
  Stage 2. Naive instrumental hedonism.

Level II. Morality of conventional role conformity:
  Stage 3. Good-boy morality of maintaining good relations, approval by others.
  Stage 4. Authority maintaining morality.

Level III. Morality of self-accepted moral principles:
  Stage 5. Morality of contract, of individual rights, and of democratically accepted law.
  Stage 6. Morality of individual principles of conscience.

Each of these six general stages of moral orientation could be defined in terms of its specific stance on some 32 aspects of morality. For example, with regard to the aspect "motivation for rule obedience or moral action," the six stages were defined as follows:

Stage 1. Obey rules to avoid punishment.
Stage 2. Conform to obtain rewards, have favors returned, and so on.
Stage 3. Conform to avoid disapproval, dislike by others.
Stage 4. Conform to avoid censure by legitimate authorities and resultant guilt.
Stage 5. Conform to maintain the respect of the impartial spectator judging in terms of community welfare.
Stage 6. Conform to avoid self-condemnation.

It is evident that this aspect of moral development represents successive degrees of internalization of moral sanctions. Other aspects of moral development involve successive cognitive reorganization of the meaning of culturally universal values. As an example, in every society human life is a basic value, even though cultures differ in their definition of the universality of this value or of the conditions under which it may be sacrificed for some other value. With regard to the value of life, the six stages are defined as follows:

Stage 1. The value of a human life is confused with the value of physical objects and is based on the social status of physical attributes of its possessor.
Stage 2. The value of a human life is seen as instrumental to the satisfaction of the needs of its possessor or of other persons.
Stage 3. The value of a human life is based on the empathy and affection of family members and others toward its possessor.
Stage 4. Life is conceived as sacred in terms of its place in a categorical moral or religious order of rights and duties.

Stage 5. Life is valued both in its relation to community welfare and as a universal human right.

Stage 6. Life is valued as sacred and as representing a universal human value of respect for the individual.

It is evident that these stages represent a progressive disentangling or differentiation of moral values and judgments from other types of values and judgments. With regard to the particular aspect—the value of life—the moral value held by the person at stage 6 has become progressively disentangled from status and property values (stage 1), from his instrumental uses to others (stage 2), from the actual affection of others for him (stage 3), etc. While philosophers have been unable to agree upon any ultimate principle of the good which would define "correct" moral judgments, most philosophers agree upon the characteristics which make a judgment a genuine moral judgment (Hare 1952; Kant 1785). Moral judgments are judgments about the good and the right of action. However, not all judgments of "good" or "right" are moral judgments; many are judgments of aesthetic, technological, or prudential goodness or rightness. Unlike judgments of prudence or aesthetics, moral judgments tend to be universal, inclusive, consistent, and based on objective, impersonal, or ideal grounds. "She's really great; she's beautiful and a good dancer" and "The right way to make a martini is five to one" are statements about the good and right which are not moral judgments, since they lack these characteristics. If we say, "Martinis should be made five to one," we are making an aesthetic judgment; we are not prepared to say that we want everyone to make them that way, that they are good in terms of some impersonal ideal standard shared by others, and that we should all make five-to-one martinis whether we wish to or not. In a similar fashion, when a ten-year-old answers the "moral should" question "Should Joe tell on his older brother?"—in stage 1 terms of the probabilities of getting beaten up by his father and by his brother—he does not answer with a moral judgment that is universal (applies to all brothers in that situation and ought to be agreed upon by all people thinking about the situation) or one that has any impersonal or ideal grounds. In contrast, stage 6 statements not only use specifically moral words like "morally right" or "duty" but use them in a moral way: e.g., phrases such as "regardless of who it was" and "by the law of nature or of God" imply universality; "Morally, I would do it in spite of fear of punishment" implies impersonality and ideality of obligation, and so on. Thus, the responses of subjects at lower levels to moral-judgment matters fail to be moral responses the same way that the value judgments of subjects at higher levels about aesthetic or morally neutral matters fail to be moral responses.

In this sense we can define a moral judgment as "moral" without considering its content (the action judged) and without considering whether it agrees or not with our own judgments or standards.

It is also evident that moral development in terms of these stages is a progressive movement toward basing moral judgment on concepts of justice. To base a moral duty on a concept of justice is to base that duty on the right of an individual; to judge an act wrong is to judge it as violating such a right. The concept of a right implies a legitimate expectancy, a claim which I may expect others to agree I have. While rights may be grounded on sheer custom or law, there are two general grounds for a right—equality and reciprocity (including exchange, contract, and the reward of merit). At stages 5 and 6 all the demands of statute or of moral (natural) law are grounded on concepts of justice, i.e., on agreement, contract, and the impartiality of the law and its function in maintaining the rights of individuals.

It is apparent that the stages just defined are stages in the development of moral judgment. Rather similar stages, however, have been independently arrived at by Peck and Havighurst (1960), who include emotional and behavioral as well as judgmental traits in their stage definitions.

The progressions, or stages, just described imply something more than age trends. In the first place, they imply an invariant sequence in which each individual child must go step by step through each of the kinds of moral judgment outlined. It is, of course, possible for a child to move at varying speeds and to stop (become "fixated") at any level of development, but if he continues to move upward, he must move in accord with these steps. The longitudinal study of American boys at ages 10, 13, 16, and 19 suggests that this is the case (Kohlberg 1966).

Second, a stage concept implies universality of sequence under varying cultural conditions. It implies that moral development is not merely a matter of learning the verbal values or rules of the child's culture but reflects something more universal in development, which would occur in any culture. In general, the stages in moral judgment just described appear to be culturally universal. Middle-class urban, lower-class urban, and tribal or rural village boys aged 10 to 21 have been studied in Taiwan, Yucatan, Turkey, and the United States. In all groups, stage 1 appears first and becomes less prevalent with age. Stage 2 appears next and then stages 3 and 4, which increase with age. In all middle-class groups, and some lower-class groups, stages 5 and 6 appear at later ages (primarily ages 16 to 21). These last two stages are not found among tribal or village peasant groups. (Kohlberg 1966).

Factors in development. It seems obvious that moral stages must primarily be the products of the child's interaction with others, rather than the direct unfolding of biological or neurological structures. However, the emphasis on social interaction does not mean that stages of moral judgment directly represent the teaching of values by parents or direct "introjection" of values by the child. Theories of moral stages view the influence of parental training and discipline as only a part of a world or social order perceived by the child. The child can internalize the moral values of his parents and culture and make them his own only as he comes to relate these values to a comprehended social order and to his own goals as a social self.

Culturally universal invariant sequences in the child's social concepts and values imply that there are some universal structural dimensions or invariants in the social world analogous to those in the physical world. Universal physical concepts have been found because there is a universal physical structure which underlies the diversity of physical arrangements in which men live and the diversities of formal physical theories held in various cultures. In somewhat analogous fashion, the social stages imply universal structural dimensions of social experience; this is based on the fact that social and moral action involves the existence of a self in a world composed of other selves playing complementary roles organized into institutional systems. In order to *play* a social role in the family, school, or society, the child must implicitly *take* the role of others toward himself and toward others in the group. One side of such role taking is represented by acts of reciprocity or complementarity (Mead 1934), the other side by acts and attitudes of sameness, sharing, and imitation (Baldwin 1897). These tendencies, intimately associated with the development of language and symbolism, form the basis of all social institutions which represent various patternings of shared or complementary expectations. [*See* INTERACTION; LANGUAGE, *article on* LANGUAGE DEVELOPMENT; ROLE, *article on* PSYCHOLOGICAL ASPECTS.]

Such institutional expectations have per se a normative or moral component involving rights and duties and require moral role taking. While the concrete definitions of required behavior in given roles are relatively fixed throughout age development, the perspectives in which these behaviors are related to a moral order undergo successive stagelike transformation. Required behavior may be based upon power and external compulsion (stage 1), upon a system of exchanges and need satisfactions (stage 2), upon the maintenance of legitimate expectations (stages 3 and 4), or upon ideals or general logical principles of social organization (stages 5 and 6). The order in this development is largely the result of general aspects of cognitive development. Concepts of legitimate expectations presuppose concepts of reciprocity and exchange, while general principles of social organization and justice presuppose concepts of legitimate expectations.

The large cognitive component of moral role taking is suggested by correlations between the development of moral judgment and cognitive advance on intelligence tests or on Piaget's cognitive-stage tasks. Intelligence may be taken as a necessary, but not sufficient, cause of moral advance. All morally advanced children are bright, but not all bright children are morally advanced. Cognitive advance is associated with emotional aspects of moral role taking (e.g., the movement of moral motives from punishment to disapproval to self-condemnation) as well as with more intellectual forms of moral role taking in terms of the values and the rights of others (e.g., the movement from conceiving of life as a physical value to conceiving it as based on a universal respect for the human individual).

In addition to cognitive advance, opportunities for participation and role taking in all the basic groups to which the child belongs appear to be important for moral development. Piaget's theory (1932) has stressed the peer group as a source of moral role taking, while other theories (Mead 1934) stress participation in the larger secondary institutions or participation in the family itself (Baldwin 1897). Research results suggest that all these opportunities for role taking are important and that all operate in a similar direction by stimulating moral development rather than producing a particular value system. In three divergent cultures studied, middle-class children were found to be more advanced in moral judgment than matched lower-class children (Kohlberg 1967). This was not because the middle-class children heavily favored a certain type of thought which corresponded to the prevailing middle-class pattern.

Instead, middle-class and working-class children seemed to move through the same sequences, but the middle-class children seemed to move faster and farther. Similar but even more striking differences were found between peer-group participators (popular children) and nonparticipators (unchosen children) in the American sample. Studies underway suggest that these peer-group differences partly arise from, and partly add on to, prior differences in opportunities for role taking in the child's family (family participation, communication, emotional warmth, sharing in decisions, awarding responsibility to the child, pointing out consequences of action to others).

Our discussion has stressed the role of intellectual advance and of social participation and role-taking opportunities in family, peer group, and secondary institutions as they facilitate the development of moral judgment. While the evidence is less complete, these same factors appear to correlate with clinical ratings of maturity of moral character (Peck & Havighurst 1960) and experimental or rating measures of honesty and of moral autonomy (Kohlberg 1967; Columbia University 1928–1930).

Parental identification and guilt. It is important to note that some of the findings used here to argue for the centrality of role-taking opportunities in moral development have also been interpreted as indicating the centrality of parent identifications in conscience formation. In psychoanalytic and neopsychoanalytic discussions, identification has meant the general tendency to take the role of the punishing and criticizing other; that is, in order to criticize or punish himself after transgression, the child must take the role of another toward himself. Otherwise he would continue to view himself and the situation as he did when he performed the act. For self-criticism to be guilt, the child must "take the role of the other" in a deep or internalized sense, regardless of whether the other knows about his transgression. Such deep, fixed role taking or identification has been variously hypothesized to result from needs to substitute for an absent or rejecting love object (Freud 1930; Sears et al. 1957), from the need to defend against fear of aggression (A. Freud 1936), or from "status envy" needs (Whiting 1960).

It is evident that identification is a special or particular form of role taking as previously defined. As opposed to more general theories of role taking, identification theories of moral formation have assumed: (*a*) that the child's role taking of parents represents a unique, special, and necessary basis for conscience formation rather than one of a number of general role-taking relationships; (*b*) that the basic moral role-taking tendencies leading to conscience formation are formed in early childhood, when the child's weakness can create overwhelmingly strong tendencies to love, fear, and respect and lead to introjecting adult figures and their prescriptions; (*c*) that basic role taking of parents leads to direct introjection, transfer, or mimicking of fixed parental standards rather than being a step toward the development of general role-taking tendencies which move out into wider social realms and so promote moral advance.

In general the research findings suggest the importance of children's role taking of their parents in moral development, but they do not support the notion that conscience is a unique product of parent identifications (Kohlberg 1963*a*; 1963*b*; 1964; Hoffman 1966). Parental warmth, children's positive attitudes toward parents, and children's expressed desire to be like their parents correlate positively with acceptance of the conventional moral code as measured by tests of conventional expressions of guilt and of moral judgment. Little evidence, however, has been found to indicate that these variables are correlated with the fixed introjection of particular, individual parental moral values. Furthermore, little evidence has been found to suggest that a close bond to one or both parents is crucially necessary for conscience formation. The most relevant studies come from comparison of kibbutz-reared and family-reared children in Israel. While kibbutz children have regular contacts with parents in evenings and on holidays, parents are little involved in making or enforcing moral or socialization demands upon the child. This task is primarily the function of the nurse-caretaker, the teacher, and the peer group. Few clear differences have been found between these children and city children in moral judgment, in projective measures of guilt, or in naturalistic observations of moral control of behavior (studies reviewed in Kohlberg 1964). It would appear, then, that affectional relationships (or identification) with parents are important in moral development, more because positive and affectional relations to others are generally conducive to ego development and to role taking and acceptance of social standards than because they provide a unique and direct basis for conscience formation. [*See* AFFECTION.]

Common psychological notions that parental punishment and resultant guilt play a critical role in moral development seem even more questionable in the light of research findings. It seems self-evident that self-induced pain after transgression (guilt) must originate largely from experiences of transgression-related pain caused by others (punishment). Some core experiences of punishment, or at least of blame, are presumably necessary for the development of guilt reactions, and even the most permissively raised children experience them. Punishment, however, does not directly produce guilt, since the very young punished child does not experience guilt. Furthermore, there does not appear to be a direct relationship between amount of punishment and amount of guilt. We are also not able to say that the more psychologically painful the punishment, the more likely it is to produce guilt. Physical punishment seems to show a low positive correlation with children's use of punishment fantasies as consequences of transgression, but it does not relate positively to types of transgression reaction more representative of guilt. Even for punishment reactions, young children whose parents report they never use physical punishment may make heavy use of it in doll-play transgression stories.

Punishment by love withdrawal (ignoring, isolation, a mother's statements that she doesn't like her child when he is bad) has been thought to be especially critical in producing guilt, because loss of love is believed to be more psychologically painful or anxiety-arousing than physical punishment and because it would be expected to lead to implicit role taking or identification with the parent's disapproval. However, love withdrawal has not been found to relate to self-critical guilt (Hoffman 1966).

Rather than showing striking or unique relationships to punishment experiences, projective measures of internal guilt show the same general age trends and social correlates as measures of maturity of moral judgment in the school years. This suggests that the development of conscious internal standards of judgment and of empathic and role-taking capacities is the major factor in the genesis of guilt (Kohlberg 1964; Hoffman 1966).

The findings just reviewed, together with findings presented initially in this article, are inconsistent with the notion of a fixed moral structure (conscience–guilt) developing out of experiences of parental punishment and reward and determining moral behavior. This conclusion is not inconsistent with the obvious importance of punishment and reward in the short-term situational control of "moral" (conforming) behavior, as suggested by the Hartshorne and May findings. Experimental studies that manipulate punishment parameters show striking effects upon short-term resistance to temptation in given situations (Aronfreed 1966). In contrast, naturalistic correlational studies of parameters of parental punishment and reward suggests few clear or persisting effects of these parameters upon later moral behavior (findings reviewed in Kohlberg 1963a). Thus, S–R reinforcement theories may be useful in explaining short-run learning of behavioral conformity, without being adequate for the understanding of what we have considered as characteristic of moral development.

Neurotic behavior. In addition to distinguishing between moral development and situational conformity with regard to punishment–guilt factors, it is important to distinguish between moral development and the formation of neurotic inhibitions, anxieties, and punitive feelings resulting from punishment–guilt factors. It is obvious that neurotics suffer from strong feelings of anxiety, depression, low self-esteem, and inhibition. To a considerable extent, psychopathologists have held that these feelings result from guilt experiences resulting in turn from real or fantasied childhood transgressions and associated punishments, and they have developed general theories of moral development from these clinical data.

The research findings on guilt and moral factors in neurosis are sparse, but they do suggest limitations to the notion that neurotics suffer from too much general guilt or moral restraint. There is little reason to believe that neurotics are more scrupulous about moral ideals or more morally restrained in their conduct than normal people. Neurotic children have not been found to be higher (or consistently lower) than normal children in projective measures of guilt, in moral judgment, or in resistance to dishonest behavior. (In contrast, pathologically delinquent children are markedly lower on guilt and moral judgment than are either neurotic or normal children.) While neurotic symptoms do not seem to be explainable as the result of too much general guilt or moral concern resulting from childhood experiences, it does seem plausible to view distinctively "neurotic" moral anxieties and inhibitions (anxieties about matters viewed as morally permissible by the general culture) as the result of childhood experiences and fantasies of parental punishment. Clinical observations as to the genesis of these idiosyncratic moral anxieties may be valid, then, even though they have not provided a useful model for the general understanding of moral development. Such understanding rests on further elaboration of the processes of ego development as these interact with social experiences of which the moral is a universal dimension.

LAWRENCE KOHLBERG

[*Directly related are the entries* DEVELOPMENTAL PSY-CHOLOGY *and* SOCIALIZATION. *Other relevant material may be found in* CONFORMITY; DELINQUENCY; JUSTICE; LEARNING, *article on* REINFORCEMENT; PERSONALITY, *article on* PERSONALITY DEVELOPMENT; PSYCHOANALYSIS; ROLE; SYMPATHY AND EMPATHY; UTILITARIANISM; *and in the biography of* DURKHEIM.]

BIBLIOGRAPHY

ARONFREED, J. 1966 Conduct and Conscience: The Experimental Study of Internalization. Unpublished manuscript.

BALDWIN, JAMES M. (1897) 1906 *Social and Ethical Interpretations in Mental Development: A Study in Social Psychology.* 4th ed., rev. & enl. New York: Macmillan.

BOWERS, WILLIAM J. 1964 Student Dishonesty and Its Control in College. Cooperative Research Project No. OE 1672. Unpublished manuscript, Columbia Univ., Bureau of Applied Social Research.

BURTON, ROGER V. 1963 Generality of Honesty Reconsidered. *Psychological Review* 70:481–499.

COLUMBIA UNIVERSITY, TEACHERS COLLEGE 1928–1930 *Studies in the Nature of Character.* 3 vols. New York: Macmillan. → Volume 1: *Studies in Deceit,* by Hugh Hartshorne and Mark A. May. Volume 2: *Studies in Service and Self-control,* by Hugh Hartshorne, Mark A. May, and J. B. Maller. Volume 3: *Studies in Organization of Character,* by Hugh Hartshorne, Mark A. May, and F. K. Shuttleworth.

DURKHEIM, ÉMILE (1898–1911) 1953 *Sociology and Philosophy.* Glencoe, Ill.: Free Press. → Written between 1898 and 1911. First published posthumously in French.

DURKHEIM, ÉMILE (1925) 1961 *Moral Education: A Study in the Theory and Application of the Sociology of Education.* New York: Free Press. → First published posthumously in French.

FREUD, ANNA (1936) 1957 *The Ego and the Mechanisms of Defense.* New York: International Universities Press. → First published as *Das Ich und die Abwehrmechanismen.*

FREUD, SIGMUND (1923) 1961 The Ego and the Id. Volume 19, pages 12–63 in Sigmund Freud, *The Standard Edition of the Complete Psychological Works of Sigmund Freud.* London: Hogarth; New York: Macmillan. → First published as *Das Ich und das Es.*

FREUD, SIGMUND (1925) 1961 The Resistances to Psycho-analysis. Volume 19, pages 213–222 in Sigmund Freud, *The Standard Edition of the Complete Psychological Works of Sigmund Freud.* London: Hogarth; New York: Macmillan. → First published in German.

FREUD, SIGMUND (1930) 1958 *Civilization and Its Discontents.* Garden City, N.Y.: Doubleday. → First published as *Das Unbehagen in der Kultur.*

HARE, RICHARD M. 1952 *The Language of Morals.* Oxford: Clarendon.

HOBHOUSE, LEONARD T. (1906) 1951 *Morals in Evolution: A Study in Comparative Ethics.* With a new introduction by Morris Ginsberg. 7th ed. 2 vols. London: Chapman.

HOFFMAN, M. 1966 Childrearing Antecedents of Moral Internalization. Unpublished manuscript.

HUME, DAVID (1751) 1957 *An Inquiry Concerning the Principles of Morals.* New York: Liberal Arts Press.

KANT, IMMANUEL (1785) 1949 *Fundamental Principles of the Metaphysics of Morals.* New York: Liberal Arts Press. → First published as *Grundlegung zur Metaphysik der Sitten.*

KOHLBERG, LAWRENCE 1963a Moral Development and Identification. Pages 277–332 in National Society for the Study of Education, *Child Psychology.* 62d Yearbook. Edited by Harold Stevenson. Univ. of Chicago Press.

KOHLBERG, LAWRENCE 1963b The Development of Children's Orientations Toward a Moral Order. Part 1: Sequence in the Development of Moral Thought. *Vita humana* 6:11–33.

KOHLBERG, LAWRENCE 1964 Development of Moral Character and Moral Ideology. Volume 1, pages 383–431 in Martin Hoffman and Lois Hoffman (editors), *Review of Child Development Research.* New York: Russell Sage Foundation.

KOHLBERG, LAWRENCE 1966 Stage and Sequence: The Developmental Approach to Moralization. Unpublished manuscript.

KOHLBERG, LAWRENCE 1967 The Development of Children's Orientations Toward a Moral Order. Part 2: Social Experience, Social Conduct, and the Development of Moral Thought. Unpublished manuscript.

McDOUGALL, WILLIAM (1908) 1950 *An Introduction to Social Psychology.* 30th ed. London: Methuen. → A paperback edition was published in 1960 by Barnes and Noble.

MACKINNON, DONALD W. 1938 Violation of Prohibitions. Pages 491–501 in Henry W. Murray (editor), *Explorations in Personality.* New York: Oxford Univ. Press.

MEAD, GEORGE H. (1934) 1963 *Mind, Self and Society From the Standpoint of a Social Behaviorist.* Edited by Charles W. Morris. Univ. of Chicago Press. → Published posthumously.

MILL, JOHN STUART (1861) 1957 *Utilitarianism.* Indianapolis, Ind.: Bobbs-Merrill.

PECK, ROBERT F.; and HAVIGHURST, ROBERT J. 1960 *The Psychology of Character Development.* New York: Wiley.

PIAGET, JEAN (1932) 1948 *The Moral Judgment of the Child.* Glencoe, Ill.: Free Press. → First published in French. A paperback edition was published in 1965.

SEARS, ROBERT R.; MACCOBY, ELEANOR E.; and LEVIN, HARRY 1957 *Patterns of Child Rearing.* Evanston, Ill.: Row, Peterson.

SMITH, ADAM (1759) 1948 The Theory of Moral Sentiments. Pages 3–277 in *Adam Smith's Moral and Political Philosophy.* Edited by Herbert Schneider. New York: Hafner.

WHITING, JOHN W. M. 1960 Resource Mediation and Learning by Identification. Pages 112–126 in Ira Iscoe and Harold W. Stevenson (editors), *Personality Development in Children.* Austin: Univ. of Texas Press.

MORALE

See ATTITUDES; GROUPS, *article on* GROUP PERFORMANCE; INDUSTRIAL RELATIONS; LEADERSHIP; MILITARY PSYCHOLOGY; WORKERS.

MORALS

See MORAL DEVELOPMENT.

MORBIDITY

See EPIDEMIOLOGY; HEALTH; ILLNESS; MEDICAL CARE; MENTAL DISORDERS; PUBLIC HEALTH.

MORES

See NORMS; VALUES; *the biography of* SUMNER.

MORGAN, CONWY LLOYD

Conwy Lloyd Morgan (1852–1936), habitually known as Lloyd Morgan because of his common surname, was a British comparative psychologist and psychological philosopher who, coming under the influence of Thomas H. Huxley, interested himself in the philosophy of evolution and of human conduct and in the intelligent behavior of animals in their relation to each other and to man.

Lloyd Morgan, the son of a solicitor, James A. Morgan, was born in London. He received his early education at the Royal Grammar School in Guildford near London, after his parents had moved from the city. He was already reading philosophy, but to prepare himself to earn a living he enrolled in the School of Mines in London, with the intention of becoming a mining engineer. By chance, at a dinner at the school he found himself seated next to the great Huxley, 27 years his senior. Huxley quizzed the young student of mining about his intellectual interests and recommended that he finish his present training and then shift to work in biology with Huxley at the Royal College of Science. Thereafter Huxley had a new disciple.

Lloyd Morgan was much more interested in science than in mining. On completing his training at the school, he accepted a post as a tutor, which took him on tour through North America and Brazil. After that he did indeed go to study with Huxley; Adolf C. Bastian, later the defender of the doctrine of the spontaneous generation of life, was a fellow pupil. In 1878 he obtained the post of lecturer at the Diocesan College at Rondebosch in South Africa. There he taught physical science, English literature, and constitutional history but devoted his leisure to studying geology and natural history. It was becoming clear that teaching was his forte.

In 1883 he was appointed a lecturer in geology and zoology at University College, Bristol, where he was to remain for the rest of his professional life. In 1887 he was made principal of the college, a post equivalent to appointment to a permanent chair. Much later, in 1910, when the college became a university, he acted as vice-chancellor for a year but thereafter returned to teaching, the occupation that he greatly preferred, as professor of psychology and ethics. In 1919 he retired, continuing in the suburbs of Bristol his active life of writing. Then finally he withdrew to Hastings on the English Channel, where he died in 1936.

For fifty years at Bristol, Lloyd Morgan, besides being concerned with teaching and college administration, lived the life of a philosopher of nature, an observer of animal behavior, and a writer of many essays and a dozen books on evolution, especially the evolution of mind, as well as on comparative psychology, especially the emergence of consciousness and the growth of intelligence in the evolutionary scale. (The term "comparative psychology" had been coined by G. J. Romanes in 1882, the year of Darwin's death. Lloyd Morgan's best-known book, *An Introduction to Comparative Psychology*, was published in 1894, the year of Romanes' death.)

Lloyd Morgan was constantly on the alert for significant incidents in the behavior of animals: he brought together the reports of others on this topic, watched his own dogs and cats, and arranged little experiments with them and with newly hatched chicks and ducklings in order to study the distinction between instinctive and learned behavior. He wrote about instinct, learning, intelligence, association, imitation, reasoning, and the perception of relations. Always he compared animals with respect to one another and to man, with especial reference to the scale of mental evolution.

He is best known for what has come to be called Lloyd Morgan's canon, which demands parsimony in the inference of an animal's place on the scale of mind from its behavior: "In no case may we interpret an action [of an animal] as the outcome of the exercise of a higher psychical faculty, if it can be interpreted as the outcome of the exercise of one which stands lower in the psychological scale" (1894, p. 63). He used this canon consistently throughout his *Comparative Psychology* and his later books, always rejecting the inference of the more nearly human level of consciousness in favor of whatever simpler account seemed adequate.

Lloyd Morgan is also known for his support of the doctrine of emergent evolution, a view which he shared with his philosophical contemporary Samuel Alexander and which they derived in part from Henri Bergson's concept of *élan vital* and in part from the concept of entelechy as advocated by the vitalist Hans Driesch. Lloyd Morgan tells how quite early he tried to convince a skeptical Huxley that evolution occurs by discrete steps. Evolutionary emergence is equivalent to chemical emergence: the various observable properties of water cannot be predicted from the observable properties of hydrogen and oxygen. Lloyd Morgan presented this view as applied to new biological organizations in his Gifford lectures, published as *Emergent Evolution* in 1923, shortly after his retirement from Bristol, and again in *The Emergence of Novelty* of 1933, his last publication of importance, for he was then 81.

EDWIN G. BORING

[*For the historical context of Morgan's work, see* Evolution; *for discussion of the subsequent development of Morgan's ideas, see* Ethology; Instinct;
Psychology, *articles on* comparative psychology
and physiological psychology.]

WORKS BY C. L. MORGAN

1885 *The Springs of Conduct: An Essay in Evolution.*
London: Routledge.
1891 *Animal Life and Intelligence.* London: Arnold; New
York: Scribner.
(1894) 1906 *An Introduction to Comparative Psychology.*
London: Scott.
1896 *Habit and Instinct.* London and New York: Arnold.
1900 *Animal Behaviour.* London and New York: Arnold.
1912 *Instinct and Experience.* London: Methuen; New
York: Macmillan.
1923 *Emergent Evolution: The Gifford Lectures Delivered
in the University of St. Andrews in the Year 1922.* London: Williams & Norgate.
1926 *Life, Mind and Spirit: Being the Second Course of
the Gifford Lectures.* London: Williams & Norgate.
1929 *Mind at the Crossways.* London: Williams & Norgate.
1930 *The Animal Mind.* London: Arnold; New York:
Longmans.
1932 Autobiography. Volume 2, pages 237–264 in *A History of Psychology in Autobiography.* Worcester, Mass.:
Clark Univ. Press.
1933 *The Emergence of Novelty.* London: Williams &
Norgate; New York: Holt.

SUPPLEMENTARY BIBLIOGRAPHY

Conwy Lloyd Morgan. 1932 Volume 3, pages 952–955
in *Psychological Register.* Worcester, Mass.: Clark
Univ. Press; Oxford Univ. Press.
Field, G. C. 1949 Morgan, Conwy Lloyd: 1852–1936.
Pages 627–628 in *Dictionary of National Biography:
1931–1940.* Oxford Univ. Press.
Grindley, G. C. 1936 Professor C. Lloyd Morgan. *Brit-
ish Journal of Psychology* 27:1–3.
Parsons, J. H. 1936 Conwy Lloyd Morgan. Royal Society
of London, *Obituary Notices of Fellows* 2:25–27.

MORGAN, LEWIS HENRY

Lewis Henry Morgan (1818–1881), American
anthropologist, was born near Aurora, New York,
of a Welsh family who had settled in New England
as early as 1640. He attended Cayuga Academy in
Aurora before going to Union College, from which
he was graduated in 1840. He then returned to
Aurora, where he studied law. In 1844 he went
to Rochester and established himself as an attorney. In 1851 he married his cousin, Mary Elizabeth Steele, by whom he had three children. In the
1850s Morgan invested in mining and railroad ventures in the Upper Peninsula of Michigan. From
these investments he acquired a modest fortune
which he bequeathed to the University of Rochester.
He served two terms in the New York State legislature, one in the Assembly and one in the Senate.

He tried repeatedly, but without success, to obtain
a position as United States minister to a foreign
country. Morgan never served on the staff of a
scientific or educational institution; he declined
President A. D. White's offer of a chair of ethnology
at Cornell University. He retired from his legal
practice in 1862, although he continued to represent some of the Michigan corporations in which
he had invested. He resided in Rochester until his
death.

Morgan's ethnological career began when he
joined a young men's club, the Grand Order of the
Iroquois, in Aurora after graduating from college.
In order to pattern this club upon the famous Iroquois confederacy, Morgan undertook an exhaustive study of the Iroquois, their history, and their
culture, particularly of the Seneca tribe. The results
of his research were published in 1851 as *The
League of the Ho-dé-no-sau-nee, or Iroquois*, dedicated to his friend and co-worker Ely S. Parker, a
Seneca Indian. Morgan was adopted into the Seneca tribe in 1846, but he did not "live the life of an
Indian among them for years," as some have assumed. He was, however, a lifelong and stanch
champion of the American Indians in their losing
struggle against encroachment by the white man.

After a few fallow years, Morgan's interest in
ethnology was revived in 1856, when he attended
a meeting of the American Association for the Advancement of Science. He returned to further consideration of the Seneca method of designating
relatives, which differed radically from Anglo–
American usage at many points. In 1858 he discovered that the same system of terminology
existed among the Ojibway Indians who lived at
Marquette, Michigan. It occurred to Morgan that
this system might be widespread and that if it
could be found in Asia, the Asiatic origin of the
American Indians could be demonstrated. He at
once began a vigorous and comprehensive program of field research and circulated questionnaires to distant lands in the hope of obtaining
data. His monumental *Systems of Consanguinity
and Affinity of the Human Family*, published by
the Smithsonian Institution in 1871, was the result.
He believed that his data definitely proved that the
American Indians had migrated to America from
Asia. But, more important, his interpretation of the
kinship terminologies led him to formulate a comprehensive theory of social evolution, according to
which forms of the family evolved by stages from
an original state of promiscuity, culminating in
monogamy in the stage of civilization.

Morgan's researches and writings led to the publication in 1877 of his best-known and most influ-

ential work, *Ancient Society*. The book attempts to embrace culture in its entirety, but its emphasis is upon the evolution of society. It is divided into four parts, titled (1) "Growth of Intelligence Through Inventions and Discoveries"; (2) "Growth of the Idea of Government"; (3) "Growth of the Idea of the Family"; (4) "Growth of the Idea of Property." Two theories of evolution are used: an idealistic and a materialistic one. According to the idealistic one, institutions are explained as the accumulated product of germs of thought in the human mind; this concept was widely held by Morgan's predecessors and contemporaries. The second theory rests on zoological, ecological, and technological explanations. Man is seen as an animal species effecting life-sustaining adjustments to his habitat by technological means; culture evolves as control by these means is improved and extended.

Morgan tended to view the evolution of culture as the progress of the human mind, but he did not avoid the word "evolution" as some have claimed. He divided man's career, which is "one in source, one in experience, and one in progress," into three great stages: savagery, barbarism, and civilization. Each stage was subdivided into upper, middle, and lower "statuses." He likened stages of sociocultural development to successive geological strata.

Ancient Society has a number of defects and shortcomings. Morgan's whole theory of the evolution of the family has now been abandoned as obsolete. But this work was the first impressive attempt to provide a scientific account of the origin and evolution of civilization and to illustrate the successive stages of this development by the use of descriptions of specific cultures. For examples Morgan drew on ethnographic knowledge of such societies as the aborigines of Australia and America and on classical sources concerned with the ancient Greeks and Romans.

Ancient Society became a classic in Marxist literature. Marx and Engels were attracted to Morgan's writings: his emphasis on the role of property in the evolution of culture, his criticism of the "property career" of modern societies, and his predictions of a nobler and a more just social order to come unquestionably drew Marx and Engels to his work. Above all, *Ancient Society* provided the best available account in Marx's day of how culture had actually evolved, and emphasized—or called attention to—the revolutionary character of some cultural changes. Marx died before he was able to write a book he had planned about Morgan's work; in his stead Engels wrote *The Origin of the Family, Private Property and the State* (1884). Therein he credited Morgan with having independently formulated the Marxist materialist conception of history. Yet Morgan's lecture entitled *Diffusion Against Centralization* (1852) as well as several other writings make it clear that he had not clearly grasped the conception of a proletarian revolutionary overthrow of the capitalist order and that he was an enthusiastic admirer of the achievements of the so-called bourgeois revolution, that is, of the emergence and rise to predominance of the industrial and commercial classes as against the landed aristocracy.

Mention should be made of Morgan's work in Australian ethnology. He was the first anthropologist to publish a treatise on Australian kinship. Through correspondence, he taught the scientific principles of ethnology to Lorimer Fison, an English missionary in Fiji, and to A. W. Howitt, a police magistrate in Australia. He guided their field work and wrote the introduction to their book, *Kamilaroi and Kurnai* (1880), which was dedicated to him.

Morgan's ethnology was harshly criticized by John F. McLennan and was treated with some condescension by other British anthropologists. Nevertheless, he was recognized in England as a great pioneer in the field. On his European tour in 1870–1871 Morgan met Darwin, Huxley, McLennan, Lubbock, and Maine. He corresponded with these men and also with J. J. Bachofen on the Continent. In the United States, Morgan achieved great distinction. He knew all the leading anthropologists, many of whom came to him for advice and counsel. In 1879 the newly established Archaeological Institute of America asked Morgan to provide it with a comprehensive program for field research in the Americas (1879–1880). Union College awarded him an honorary degree. He was made a fellow of the American Academy of Arts and Sciences in 1868, elected to membership in the National Academy of Sciences in 1875, and elected president of the American Association for the Advancement of Science in 1879.

Morgan fell into disrepute in the United States when Franz Boas and his students rose to ascendancy in anthropological science. As an American he was looked down upon or ignored by the European-born members of the Boas school. The reaction against cultural evolutionism, which became vigorous in the United States under Boas, and in Europe under the leadership of Fritz Graebner and later of Schmidt and Koppers, took Morgan as its prime target. He was in turn ignored, belittled, and ridiculed. The fact that *Ancient Society* had become a Marxist classic unquestionably contributed to the hostility to and rejection of Morgan's work, but it is difficult to gauge the magnitude of this factor. The Catholic anthropologists of the *Kulturkreis* school, in the United States as well as in Europe, were especially venomous in their attacks upon Morgan's "crass materialism" and his "evolutionist vagaries."

The theory of evolution, however, has become respectable again, at least among many cultural anthropologists; the numerous Darwin centennials in 1959 did much to bring about this change of attitude. With this about-face has come a reconsideration and re-evaluation of Morgan and his work. *The League of the Iroquois* was reprinted for the fifth time in 1962. A new printing of *Ancient Society*, with an introduction and annotations by Eleanor Burke Leacock, was issued in 1963, and still another edition was published in 1964. The University of Rochester sponsored a series of Lewis Henry Morgan lectures in 1963 and 1964. The re-evaluation of Morgan and his work has contributed greatly to an appreciation of his full stature as one of the great pioneers in the science of anthropology.

LESLIE A. WHITE

[*For discussion of the subsequent development of Morgan's ideas, see* ANTHROPOLOGY, *article on* THE FIELD; CULTURE; EVOLUTION, *article on* CULTURAL EVOLUTION; FIELD WORK; INDIANS, NORTH AMERICAN; KINSHIP; SOCIAL STRUCTURE; *and the biographies of* BACHOFEN; BANDELIER; ENGELS; McLENNAN; MAINE; RIVERS; TYLOR; WESTERMARCK.]

WORKS BY L. H. MORGAN

(1851) 1962 *The League of the Iroquois*. New York: Citadel. → First published as *The League of the Ho-dé-no-sau-nee, or Iroquois*.

1852 *Diffusion Against Centralization*. Rochester, N.Y.: Dewey.

1868 *The American Beaver and His Works*. Philadelphia: Lippincott.

1871 *Systems of Consanguinity and Affinity of the Human Family*. Smithsonian Contributions to Knowledge, Vol. 17, Publication No. 218. Washington: Smithsonian Institution.

1872 Australian Kinship: From Original Memoranda of Reverend Lorimer Fison. American Academy of Arts and Sciences, *Proceedings* 8:412–438.

(1877) 1964 *Ancient Society*. Edited by Leslie A. White. Cambridge, Mass.: Belknap.

1879–1880 A Study of the Houses of the American Aborigines With a Scheme of Exploration of the Ruins in New Mexico . . . [and Elsewhere]. Archaeological Institute of America, *Annual Report* 1:27–80.

1881 *Houses and House-life of the American Aborigines*. Contributions to North American Ethnology, Vol. 4. Washington: Government Printing Office.

1937 Extracts From the European Travel Journal of Lewis H. Morgan. Edited by Leslie A. White. Rochester Historical Society, *Publications* 16:219–389.

1959 *The Indian Journals, 1859–1862*. Edited and with an introduction by Leslie A. White. Ann Arbor: Univ. of Michigan Press.

SUPPLEMENTARY BIBLIOGRAPHY

BANDELIER, ADOLPH F. A. 1940 *Pioneers in American Anthropology: The Bandelier–Morgan Letters, 1873–1883*. Edited by Leslie A. White. 2 vols. Albuquerque: Univ. of New Mexico Press.

EGGAN, FRED 1960 Lewis H. Morgan in Kinship Perspective. Pages 179–201 in Gertrude E. Dole and Robert L. Carneiro (editors), *Essays in the Science of Culture, in Honor of Leslie A. White*. New York: Crowell.

EGGAN, FRED 1966 *The American Indian: Perspectives for the Study of Social Change*. Chicago: Aldine. → This volume contains Eggan's "Lewis Henry Morgan Lectures" given at the University of Rochester in April 1964.

ENGELS, FRIEDRICH (1884) 1942 *The Origin of the Family, Private Property and the State*. New York: International Publishers. → First published in German.

FISON, LORIMER; and HOWITT, A. W. 1880 *Kamilaroi and Kurnai: Group-marriage and Relationship, and Marriage by Elopement, Drawn Chiefly From the Usage of the Australian Aborigines; Also the Kurnai Tribe, Their Customs in Peace and War*. With an introduction by Lewis H. Morgan. Melbourne: Robertson.

[Lewis Henry Morgan: A Bibliography.] 1923 Volume 2, pages 165–179 in Rochester Historical Society, *Publication Fund Series*. Rochester, N.Y.: The Society.

LOWIE, ROBERT H. 1936 Lewis H. Morgan in Historical Perspective. Pages 169–181 in Robert H. Lowie (editor), *Essays in Anthropology Presented to A. L. Kroeber*. Berkeley: Univ. of California Press.

RESEK, CARL 1960 *Lewis Henry Morgan: American Scholar*. Univ. of Chicago Press.

STERN, BERNARD J. 1931 *Lewis Henry Morgan: Social Evolutionist*. Univ. of Chicago Press.

WHITE, LESLIE A. 1944 Morgan's Attitude Toward Religion and Science. *American Anthropologist* New Series 46:218–230.

WHITE, LESLIE A. 1948 Lewis Henry Morgan: Pioneer in the Theory of Social Evolution. Pages 138–154 in Harry E. Barnes (editor), *An Introduction to the History of Sociology*. Univ. of Chicago Press.

WHITE, LESLIE A. (editor) 1957 How Morgan Came to Write *Systems of Consanguinity and Affinity*. Michigan Academy of Science, Arts, and Letters, *Papers* 42:257–268.

MORTALITY

Mortality statistics are by-products of the legal process of death registration [*see* VITAL STATISTICS]. These data serve various purposes, such as estimating a component of population growth and preparing population projections; delineating health problems, planning public health programs, and assessing health progress; and studying the natural history of disease.

The absolute numbers of deaths are useful as a direct measure of the attrition of the population due to deaths. However, for analytical purposes, death data are generally used in the form of ratios. Properly computed, a *death rate* expresses the force of mortality on the population at risk.

Types of death rate. The crudest form of death rate is the *total* or *general* death rate. This is the number of deaths occurring in a particular period of time, usually a year, for each 1,000 persons in the area or population. Because the general death rate (often called the *crude* death rate) is the mean of the death rates by age, sex, color, and other demographic variables weighted by the demographic composition of the population, an area with a young population, for example, would have a low general death rate, and an area with an old population a high general death rate, even if the set of age-specific death rates for the two areas were the same.

In order to take into account the differential mortality by age, sex, or other demographic variable, death rates are usually computed for a specific population class or group. The *age-specific* death rate is an example of this type of rate. In some cases, comparisons are based on death rates adjusted for differences in population composition. If the rate is standardized for differences in the age composition of two populations, it is called an *age-adjusted* death rate.

A special kind of death rate is the *life table* death rate. This is a hypothetical set of derived death rates based on certain assumptions of mortality in a stationary living population unaffected by migration or births. One function of the life table which is of interest is the expectation of life. This is the average number of years that will be subsequently lived by a group of persons who have attained a certain age. The expectation of life at birth is the average age at death of all the 100,000 who start life together in the life table cohort. Another important function is the survival rate, which is the probability that persons of a particular age will survive for a particular period of time, usually a calendar year [see LIFE TABLES].

Cause of death. An important aspect of mortality statistics relates to data derived from the medical information reported on death certificates. Despite their limitations, statistics on causes of death have contributed a great deal in the past to the field of public health [see PUBLIC HEALTH].

The present statistics on causes of death relate to the "underlying cause of death," which is the term used to denote the disease or injury that initiated the train of events leading directly to death; in the case of accident or violence, it may also include the circumstances which produced the fatal injury. These statistics have done good service for

public health in the past; but, with the lessening importance, at least in the United States, of the acute infectious diseases as compared with the chronic noninfectious diseases, the data have become less and less adequate. The selection of a single disease entity as the "underlying cause" poses a real problem in deaths involving chronic diseases, since in such cases it is frequently difficult, if not impossible, to identify a single underlying cause.

International comparison of cause-of-death statistics also presents a problem. In addition to differences arising from incompleteness of death registration in various countries, there are variations in proportion of deaths attended by a physician, in diagnostic acumen of the clinician in attendance, and in the recording of diagnostic information. International comparisons are further complicated by differences in medical concepts of diseases and in the methods of classifying causes of death. In fact, strict international comparability of cause-of-death statistics is at present a virtual impossibility, and too much significance should not be attached to small differences in rates between countries.

World mortality—situation and trends

The estimated annual death rate for the world population is 17 per 1,000 population for the period 1958–1962. As might be expected, the death rate varies over a wide range in different parts of the world (see Table 1).

If differences in the age composition of the population in various parts of the world were taken into account, the mortality differential would undoubtedly be much greater than that indicated by the crude death rates shown here. Unfortunately, the

Table 1 — Population estimates, birth rates, and death rates for major regions of the world

	Population[a]	Birth rate[b]	Death rate[b]
Africa	269	46	23
America	430	33	11
North	206	24	9
Middle	71	43	14
South	153	41	13
Asia	1,764	43	20
Europe	434	19	10
Oceania	17	24	8
U.S.S.R.	221	24	7
World total	3,135	37	17

a. 1962, in millions.
b. Annual average, 1958–1962, per 1,000 population.

Source: Computed from data in *Demographic Yearbook 1963*, p. 142. Copyright © United Nations 1964. Reproduced by permission.

data needed to compute age-adjusted death rates are not available for the various regions of the world. In fact, one of the serious problems in international mortality studies is the lack of adequate mortality statistics for a large part of the world. By and large, reliable data are available only for the countries of northern and western Europe, North America, and Oceania. With a few notable exceptions, data for countries in other regions are either very incomplete or nonexistent.

The estimated *birth rate* for the world population is a little more than twice the estimated death rate. The natural rate of population increase (the difference between the birth and death rates) is highest in the Latin American countries, followed by the countries on the African continent and in Asia. Traditionally, a major part of annual population growth comes from the contribution made by births, but one of the significant demographic developments in the recent postwar period is the sharp acceleration in population growth due to the rapid decline in mortality. Virtually all countries, and more particularly the developing countries, experienced unprecedented declines in mortality while their birth rates remained at a high level.

The rate of decline in world mortality following World War II was dramatic, but the death rate began to level off in the 1950s in a number of countries, such as the United States, England and Wales, Sweden, Norway, Finland, the Netherlands, Japan, and Chile. Intensive studies of the mortality trend for the United States (U.S. Dept. of Health, Education, and Welfare . . . 1964*a*), Chile (U.S. Dept. of Health, Education, and Welfare . . . 1964*b*), and England and Wales (U.S. Dept. of Health, Education, and Welfare . . . 1965) indicate that a large part of the acceleration in the decline of general mortality was due to the large reduction in the death rate for infective and parasitic diseases as a result of antimicrobial therapy. In the United States, for example, the death rate for infective and parasitic diseases reached a low level, and by the mid-1950s it was no longer significantly influencing the general mortality trend. At the same time, the mortality trend for chronic diseases and for violence was either rising, remaining unchanged, or declining very slowly. This combination of circumstances causes a marked deceleration in the downward trend of the general death rate.

Whether this change in the mortality pattern is transient or permanent is difficult to say. It is obviously not possible for the death rate to decline indefinitely. Further reductions in mortality appear possible in the United States, but it does not seem likely that large declines will occur until a major

breakthrough is made in the prevention of deaths from chronic diseases. On the other hand, if the age-specific death rates in the United States were to decline to levels already achieved by several other countries of low mortality, the crude death rate for the United States in 1960 would have been 7.3 per 1,000 population, as compared with the recorded death rate of 9.5 per 1,000 population. For males the expected death rate would have been 7.8, as compared with the recorded rate of 11.0 per 1,000 population. For females the corresponding rates would have been 6.9, as compared with 8.1 per 1,000 population.

The leveling off of the death rate as it reaches its irreducible minimum is readily understandable. However, there seems to be no ready explanation for the change in mortality trends at different levels. For example, the death rate for nonwhites in the United States is still considerably higher than that for whites. Yet the rate of decline of the mortality trend for nonwhites has slowed down in the same manner as that for the whites.

National death rates are also becoming stabilized at different levels. For example, the Scandinavian countries and the Netherlands have achieved much lower age-specific death rates than the United States, whereas the age-specific death rates for Japan and Chile are higher. Yet the death rates appear to be leveling off in all of these countries.

The experience of Chile appears to have important implications for the developing countries. It seems clear that the knowledge and technical means are available for securing significant reductions in the death rate even in developing countries. The institution of mosquito and fly control and/or the widespread introduction of antibiotics for therapeutic purposes will have an immediate impact upon the death rate. However, it would appear that a point of diminishing returns will soon be reached and the decline in mortality come to a halt. Accordingly, the study of mortality trends in Chile points to the importance of planning health activities as a part of the social and economic development of the country (U.S. Dept. of Health, Education, and Welfare . . . 1964*b*).

Death rates by age

Reference was made earlier to the unsatisfactory nature of the crude death rate, which is significantly affected by the age composition of the population to which it refers. Death rates computed for various age groups, as in Table 2, are, of course, free of this problem.

As indicated by these age-specific death rates, infancy is the most critical period of life, even for

Table 2 — Death rates by age group: United States, 1962

Age	Death rate*
Under 1 year	2,530.1
1–4	98.1
5–14	43.9
15–24	103.5
25–34	145.2
35–44	298.2
45–54	741.0
55–64	1,692.9
65–74	3,798.4
75–84	8,431.5
85 and over	20,510.0
Total population	945.4

* Per 100,000 population.

Source: U.S. Dept. of Health, Education, and Welfare, Public Health Service, National Vital Statistics Division 1964, pp. 1–5.

a developed country like the United States. Although data are not available to demonstrate this point, it would not be surprising if one-quarter or more of all live births in many of the developing countries fail to survive the first year of life.

For the developed countries it is possible to assess the progress made in the reduction of the infant mortality rate. A significant decline in infant mortality has occurred, and remarkably low rates have been achieved by the Netherlands (15.3 per 1,000 live births in 1962), Sweden (15.8 per 1,000 live births in 1961), and Norway (17.9 per 1,000 live births in 1961). A recent study (Shapiro & Moriyama 1963) of the international infant mortality trends indicates that the rate of decline is slowing up in many countries of low mortality.

From a relatively high death rate at infancy, the risk of death drops to a minimum at age ten or so. From then on, there is an increase in mortality with increasing age. This is the typical cross-sectional pattern of mortality in countries of low mortality. However, there are a number of countries where the infant mortality rates are lower than that for the United States. Except in extreme old age, lower death rates are also found at other ages in other countries of low mortality.

In countries of low mortality, most of the deaths occur in the older age groups. In the developing countries, by contrast, it would not be unusual for more than half of all deaths to occur among children under five years of age. Under these conditions, it is obvious that the expectation of life at birth could not be very great.

Expectation of life

The Biblical life span of "three-score years and ten" has become the norm for a number of countries. In Sweden, Norway, Denmark, the Netherlands, and Israel the life expectancy at birth is 70 years or more for both males and females. In other countries, such as the United States, Canada, Czechoslovakia, France, England and Wales, Australia, and New Zealand, the average length of life of 70 years or more for the total population has been attained only because of the favorable mortality experience of females. For example, the average expectation of life at birth in the United States for 1962 is 73.4 years for females and 66.8 years for males. If up-to-date life tables were available for all countries, it is probable that a few other countries could be added to the list above.

The world situation with regard to longevity cannot be described with any precision. However, it seems clear that longevity is at present greatest in the northern and western European countries, Canada and the United States on the North American continent, and Oceania. The average life expectancy is less favorable in the central, eastern, and southern European countries. Still lower on the scale are the Latin American countries. The average expectation of life for a large part of the Asian population is low, although an average length of life of 60 years or more may be found in such Asian countries as Japan, Nationalist China (Taiwan), and Ceylon. Life table values for many of the countries on the African continent are not available. The question in a good part of Africa, especially in the southern and tropical countries, is not longevity but survival through childhood.

The increase in longevity of the population in the developed countries has been considerable. For example, in the period 1900–1902 the average expectation of life at birth in the United States was 48 years for males and 51 years for females. In a period of some sixty years, the male population gained about 19 years in life expectancy at birth, while the gain for females was about 22 years.

The postwar increase in life expectancy has been spectacular for some countries. For example, the expectancy of life at birth in Ceylon increased from 46.8 years in 1945–1947 for males to 60.3 years in 1954. For females, the corresponding figures were 44.7 years and 59.4 years, respectively. The average annual gain in longevity in Ceylon, as compared with the experience in the United States, is therefore roughly five times greater.

Death rates by marital status

Almost without exception, the mortality among the married 20 years and over is lower, age for age, than the corresponding death rates for the single, widowed, or divorced. This is true for both males and females. Beyond this, the pattern of

Table 3 — Ratio of death rates of unmarried persons to death rates of married: Sweden, 1959

Age	MALE			FEMALE		
	Single	Widowed	Divorced	Single	Widowed	Divorced
20–24	2.00	*	*	2.00	*	*
25–34	2.50	2.50	4.13	2.40	2.00	2.40
35–44	2.12	1.56	2.31	2.23	1.77	2.15
45–54	1.53	1.82	2.58	1.50	1.34	1.59
55–64	1.27	1.42	1.87	1.28	1.19	1.35
65–74	1.21	1.29	1.47	1.09	1.17	1.17
75–84	1.26	1.30	1.41	1.13	1.16	1.10

* Too few cases for significant comparison with married.

Source: Computed from data in *Demographic Yearbook 1961*, pp. 592–593. Copyright ⓒ United Nations 1962. Reproduced by permission.

mortality differentials by marital status varies somewhat by country.

In countries like Sweden, the mortality among divorced males is higher by far than the corresponding rates for bachelors or widowers (see Table 3). For females, the differences in death rates between the single, widowed, and divorced are not so great as those observed for males. The higher mortality among the single has been explained on the basis of selection; that is, those who never marry because of some serious physical impairment or chronic disease have a higher risk of mortality than the married. The single may therefore include among their number a higher proportion of the poorer mortality risks than those who marry. The higher mortality among the widowed has been attributed to the high association of diseases from which both marital partners die or to a less favorable economic situation that they both share.

One of the problems in the interpretation of death rates by marital status is the fact that the informant may not always know the civil status of those living alone. Also, there is the problem of the lack of correspondence between the marital status reported on death certificates and on the census enumeration schedules. Because the married population constitutes a large part of the total population, errors in reporting of marital status affect the data for the married much less than the data for the single, widowed, and divorced.

Death rates by sex

One of the significant constants of mortality statistics in countries of low mortality is the favorable experience among females as compared with that of males. Examination of death rates by sex for a recent year indicates large sex differentials in mortality for the United States and Canada (36 and 38 per cent, respectively) and for New Zealand and Australia (23 and 26 per cent, respectively). In the countries of western Europe the male mortality exceeded the death rate for females by 10 to 20 per cent.

The death rate for females is lower than that for males in each age group from birth to the end of the life span in virtually every country of low mortality. Even in the developing countries the mortality experience among females is generally favorable as compared with males, except in the child-bearing ages. Maternal mortality is a significant public health problem in these countries, as it was in the developed countries some forty or fifty years ago.

It is not clear why female mortality is consistently lower than that among males. One obvious explanation is the biological difference between the sexes; however, biological differences do not appear to account for much of the sex differential in mortality. A good part of the difference in the death rate appears to be due to the increasing mortality among males or to the fact that the death rate among females is declining faster than that among males. Whatever the explanation for this phenomenon, the continued occurrence of the large sex difference in mortality as recorded in a number of countries will have important consequences in terms of the sex composition of the population of the future, especially in the older ages.

Death rates by cause of death

At the turn of the century, infective and parasitic diseases constituted the major public health problems in the world population. Pneumonia and influenza, tuberculosis, diarrhea and enteritis, and the childhood diseases were the principal causes of death in 1900, even in economically developed countries.

The large reduction in mortality since 1900 has been achieved primarily through control of the infective diseases. Although influenza and pneumonia still remain significant public health problems, mortality from the chronic diseases has

Table 4 — Death rate and proportionate mortality for the five leading causes of death: selected countries* of North America, Europe, and Oceania, 1961

Leading causes of death	Average death rate per 100,000 population	Per cent of total deaths
Heart disease	300	31
Malignant neoplasm	172	18
Vascular lesion of central nervous system	132	13
Accidents	48	5
Influenza and pneumonia	37	4

* Australia, Austria, Belgium, Canada, Denmark, Finland, France, German Federal Republic (including West Berlin), Hungary, Italy, Netherlands, New Zealand, Norway, Portugal, Republic of Ireland, Sweden, United Kingdom, and United States.

Source: Compiled from "The Ten Leading Causes . . ." 1964a.

come to the forefront. The results of the review of causes of death in selected countries of North America, Europe, and Oceania in 1961 are summarized in Table 4.

From Table 4 it may be seen that more than 60 per cent of all deaths in the developed countries are attributable to the cardiovascular diseases and to malignant neoplasms. Although accidents rank fourth, they constitute the leading cause of death in the age groups 1 to 44 years; malignant neoplasms are the most frequent cause of death in the age group 45 to 64 years; and heart disease the principal cause of death in the population 65 years and over. Similar data for selected countries of Africa, South and Central America, and Asia for 1960 are shown in Table 5.

The number of countries in Africa, Asia, and South and Central America that met the criteria for inclusion in the World Health Organization compilations is limited, and the 12 countries that were selected do not, by any means, represent the mortality problems in the vast population of these continents. Although gastritis, duodenitis, enteritis,

Table 5 — Death rate and proportionate mortality for the five leading causes of death: selected countries* of Africa, South and Central America, and Asia, 1960

Leading causes of death	Average death rate per 100,000 population	Per cent of total deaths
Gastritis, duodenitis, enteritis, and colitis	95	9
Heart disease	77	7
Influenza and pneumonia	67	7
Malignant neoplasms	48	5
Accidents	38	4

* Mauritius, United Arab Republic, Chile, Colombia, Costa Rica, Guatemala, Mexico, Panama, Trinidad and Tobago, Ceylon, Israel (Jewish population), and Japan.

Source: Compiled from "The Ten Leading Causes . . ." 1964b.

and colitis were the leading causes of death for half of the selected countries, their average death rate and the proportionate mortality are relatively low. A principal cause of death that accounts for only about 9 per cent of all deaths and five leading causes that constitute no more than one-third of all deaths do not suggest any major health problems. Actually, the averages conceal some of the problems indicated by the data for individual countries. For example, the death rate for gastritis, duodenitis, enteritis, and colitis was 700 per 100,000 population in the United Arab Republic, and 36 per cent of all deaths were charged to these intestinal infections.

Adequate mortality statistics for these regions would delineate existing public health problems more clearly. If such statistics were available, it is likely that other infective diseases, such as tuberculosis, dysentery, typhoid, and measles; parasitic diseases, such as schistosomiasis and malaria; and possibly malnutrition and other dietary deficiency diseases would figure prominently as causes of death.

With the availability of knowledge and means for controlling most of the important infective and parasitic diseases, prospects are good for rapid reduction in mortality from these diseases. The resultant increase in survival of the population will bring new problems to the regions affected. These are the problems of the chronic noninfectious diseases with which the developed countries are now struggling.

IWAO M. MORIYAMA

[See also FOOD, article on WORLD PROBLEMS; POPULATION; PUBLIC HEALTH.]

BIBLIOGRAPHY

CAMPBELL, HUBERT 1965 Changes in Mortality Trends: England and Wales, 1931–1961. U.S. National Center for Health Statistics, Vital and Health Statistics, Series 3, No. 3. Washington: Government Printing Office.

Demographic Yearbook 1961. 13th ed. 1961 New York: United Nations. → Special Topic: Mortality Statistics. Prepared by the Statistical Office of the United Nations in collaboration with the Department of Social Affairs.

Demographic Yearbook 1963. 15th ed. 1963 New York: United Nations. → Special Topic: Population Census Statistics II. Prepared by the Statistical Office of the United Nations in collaboration with the Department of Social Affairs.

SHAPIRO, S.; and MORIYAMA, I. M. 1963 International Trends in Infant Mortality and Their Implications for the United States. American Journal of Public Health and the Nation's Health 53, no. 5:747–760.

The Ten Leading Causes of Death for Selected Countries in North America, Europe and Oceania, 1954–1956,

1960, 1961. 1964a World Health Organization, *Rapport épidémiologique et démographique* 17:54–112.

The Ten Leading Causes of Death for Selected Countries in Africa, South and Central America and Asia, 1954–1956, 1960, 1961. 1964b World Health Organization, *Rapport épidémiologique et démographique* 17: 118–152.

U.S. Dept. of Health, Education, and Welfare, Public Health Service, National Center for Health Statistics 1964a *The Change in Mortality Trend in the United States.* Prepared by Iwao M. Moriyama. National Center for Health Statistics, Series 3, No. 1. Washington: Government Printing Office.

U.S. Dept. of Health, Education, and Welfare, Public Health Service, National Center for Health Statistics 1964b *Recent Mortality Trends in Chile.* National Center for Health Statistics, Series 3, No. 2. Washington: Government Printing Office.

U.S. Dept. of Health, Education, and Welfare, Public Health Service, National Center for Health Statistics 1965 *Changes in Mortality Trends in England and Wales, 1931–1961.* Prepared by H. Campbell. National Center for Health Statistics, Series 3, No. 3. Washington: Government Printing Office.

U.S. Dept. of Health, Education, and Welfare, Public Health Service, National Vital Statistics Division 1964 *Vital Statistics of the United States 1962.* Volume 2: Mortality. Part A. Washington: Government Printing Office.

MOSCA, GAETANO

Gaetano Mosca (1858–1941), Italian political scientist, was born in Palermo, Sicily. He took his law degree there in 1881 with the thesis *I fattori della nazionalità*. The thesis foreshadows some of the characteristics of Mosca's later writings: his detachment from the ideological climate of the *risorgimento* and his lively sense of history, which acted as a corrective to his strongly positivistic approach.

It is difficult to assess the extent to which Mosca's conceptual approach was influenced by the Sicilian environment of his youth. Sicily was, both socially and politically, the most backward region of Italy, and the introduction of representative government had, if anything, aggravated the political problems of the South. Hence, such diverse scholars as Antonio Gramsci, an Italian Marxist, and William Salomone, an American historian, have attributed to Mosca's Sicilian background his hostility toward democratic ideology and the parliamentary system, which was so evident in his first major work, the *Teorica dei governi e governo parlamentare* (1884; "On the Theory of Governments and Parliamentary Government"). The book is an outburst against contemporary Italian political life, which, Mosca alleged, had become arbitrary and corrupt as a necessary consequence of popular sovereignty. Such antiparliamentary polemics were common in Europe at the time; in Italy, however, feelings on this score were particularly intense because the difficulties of an enfeebled regime were exacerbated by problems created by the *risorgimento*. Mosca's criticism is, in part, simply an instance of the then prevailing antiparliamentarianism; but it stands apart because of its clear-cut distinction between the ideal of liberty on the one hand and the evils to the democratic "myth" on the other hand.

As an old man, Mosca used to blame certain failures in his early academic career on his denial of the principles of popular sovereignty and political representation. The fact is that he qualified to teach constitutional law very early—in 1885—but had no success in various competitions for fellowships for study abroad and for a chair of constitutional law. His writings during this period—e.g., his essay *Le costituzioni moderne* (1887; "Modern Constitutions")—were entirely in the field of public law; in the absence of chairs of political science in Italy at the time, this was the discipline closest to his interests and the one in which he hoped to make his career. In 1887 Mosca's setbacks at the universities led him to accept a position as editor of the proceedings of the Chamber of Deputies, a position he kept for ten years. It was, as he later said, an ideal observation post for a young man eager to understand the realities of politics. For most of that period he published little, but it must have been a time of intense study and meditation, decisive for the elaboration and ordering of his thought.

Basic to Mosca's thought was the conviction that only the substitution of scientific truth (such as the doctrine of "ruling class") for "metaphysical abstractions" (such as the democratic myth) would make it possible to purify and to heal political practice. His faith in the redeeming power of political science appears to have been fostered by the prevailing cultural atmosphere of his youth. At that time, in Italy as elsewhere, positivist philosophy was dominant, and Mosca believed he could transfer its inductive method from the study of nature to the study of human society.

The theory of the ruling class. Mosca's ideas were first systematically presented in *The Ruling Class* (1896), the work that may be said to mark the birth of political science in Italy. Mosca was never to change basically the theory he presented at that time, although by 1923, when the second edition of the work appeared, his doctrine had been in many respects deepened and elaborated. The main outlines of the second edition of *The Ruling Class* may be summarized as follows.

Whatever the form of government, power is always in the hands of an organized minority, the "ruling class," which has authority over the majority by virtue both of certain characteristics that vary according to the epoch and the situation and of the power derived from organization per se. In accordance with human nature, however, this ruling class always tries to justify its rule by a moral or legal principle, the "political formula," which, however abstract, must be consonant with the conception of life of the community that is governed. The concept of the political formula not only makes Mosca's theory a powerful tool for interpreting historical reality, in that the formula presumably reveals that reality, but also constitutes a reaffirmation of the value of consensus in the organization of the state.

As indicated by the title of Mosca's programmatic lecture "Il principio aristocratico ed il democratico nel passato e nell'avvenire" (1903; "The Aristocratic Principle and the Democratic One, in the Past and the Future"), he held that two opposite tendencies are inherent in society: the aristocratic tendency toward keeping power in the hands of the descendants of those who govern and the democratic tendency toward renewal by means of elements derived from the governed. (Mosca became involved in an acrimonious dispute with Pareto over the priority of the discovery of the concept of the circulation of elites; Mosca's priority is now generally acknowledged.) Paralleling these tendencies are two principles, likewise opposed to each other: the "autocratic," according to which authority is transmitted downward, and the "liberal," by which authority is delegated from below. The two antitheses are independent and may coexist.

The theory acquires a tighter articulation by its distinction between two levels within the ruling class, with government proper being at one level, and at the other, lower level all the existing political forces. Finally, the theory is crowned by the concept of "juridical defense," possible only when there exists a "balance of social forces" and therefore a government of law dispensing "relative justice" (Meisel 1958, p. 12). Juridical defense, that is, can be realized only when there is a plurality of forces, independent of and checking each other and sharing in the power of government [see CONSTITUTIONAL LAW].

Mosca's use of the concept of juridical defense clearly warrants his being classified as a liberal (in the European sense of the term), for it introduces a value judgment on political systems: those political systems are better which guarantee greater respect for the "moral sense." According to Meisel, what mattered to Mosca was less the substance of this moral sense than the existence of social mechanisms that allow it to flourish. These mechanisms are more likely to exist under conditions of political liberty. Moreover, a value judgment is also implied in the statement that an "open" ruling class is preferable to a "closed" one. By 1923 Mosca had in fact changed his position with regard to representative government, which he distinguished sharply from the parliamentary system (a degenerate form); he attributed to the representative system the highest degree of juridical defense ever attained in history [see REPRESENTATION].

It is not too clear how Mosca arrived at his theory of the ruling class and the political formula. It is known that from his boyhood he was an avid reader of history, and among historians there are, of course, some who more or less consciously realize that in human societies there is always a small group that does the actual governing. More specifically, it was Taine who influenced the development of Mosca's thinking, by his antiegalitarianism and his concept of a *bienfaisante* aristocracy in particular and in general by the pessimistic view of humanity to which his interpretation of history and politics is closely linked.

When Mosca first presented it, the theory of the ruling class had no influence whatever, either as an instrument of historical interpretation or as a lever for a new discussion of the nature of politics; only later, as a result of Pareto's writings, did the concept of a ruling minority take hold. Instead, Mosca's trenchant criticism of the parliamentary system did have wide repercussions, and it has not unfairly been charged that, although he was a liberal, his attack on the institutions that represent historically the attempt to realize the liberal ideal actually helped to undermine liberty.

Reception of Mosca's work. *The Ruling Class* did win for Mosca the chair of constitutional law at the University of Turin, where he remained until 1923. It is hard to say whether and to what extent the new environment influenced his subsequent political thinking. The intellectual atmosphere of Turin, more cosmopolitan than that of Rome, let alone Sicily, must surely have had an impact on him. Also, he came to know such outstanding men as the economist Luigi Einaudi, the ecclesiologist Francesco Ruffini, and the jurist and philosopher Gioele Solari, all of whom were then teaching at Turin and with whom he shared membership in the Liberal party. It was during the first part of his Turin period that Mosca seems to have become aware of the appeal that the doctrine of the political class had vis-à-vis the Marxist theory of the economic class.

Having reached high academic standing, Mosca went into active politics. He was elected to the

Chamber of Deputies in 1908 and took his seat among the conservatives (in 1912 he voted against extension of the suffrage). From 1914 to 1916 he was undersecretary for the colonies, and in 1919 he became a senator. In his attitude toward fascism he was typical of many of the most prominent Italian liberals of the time: he moved from an initial position of benevolently suspended judgment, and even outspoken hope, to one of open opposition. The fascists, for their part, never claimed that their ideology was related to Mosca's theories—as they did in the case of Pareto's—although around 1930 some young fascist intellectuals did maintain that Mosca's criticism of the majority principle and his vehement antiparliamentarianism entitled him to a prominent place among the ideological ancestors of fascism. They were, however, taking a one-sided view of Mosca's theory, which, as has been noted, ultimately led to a liberal position, mainly via the conception of juridical defense but also via the acknowledgment of the value of an "open" ruling class. It should be remembered, however, that although the events of the time had some influence on Mosca's formulation of a liberal position, he reached this position primarily by theoretical reasoning.

The new edition of *The Ruling Class* won for Mosca a call to the University of Rome in 1923, and there, from 1925 to 1933 (when he reached the mandatory retirement age), he occupied Italy's first chair of the history of political institutions and doctrines. The lectures he delivered in Rome were published as the well-known *Storia delle dottrine politiche* (1932a), remembered especially for its affirmation of the interdependence of political practice and political ideas.

Although the 1923 edition of *The Ruling Class* was well received, Mosca's doctrine continued to have little influence. In the case of Italy, at least, the reason for this was the predominance of the philosophy of idealism, which rejected the "generalizations" of the social sciences; although Mosca's work had won the approval of Benedetto Croce, the leader of Italian idealism, this did not move others to penetrate the positivist surface of his thought. Michels was the only one who used Mosca's theory of the ruling class, chiefly in his studies of the oligarchical structure of political parties. Not until after World War II did Mosca's doctrine have some success, in part because enlarged cultural contacts required notice of the Marxist doctrine of classes. Special mention should be made of the revision of Mosca's theories by Guido Dorso in *Dittatura, classe politica e classe dirigente* (1949), which evaluates the role of the masses in a new way. But it is especially in the United States, with its rich and deep-rooted tradition of research into the phenomena of association, that Mosca has received the attention he merits, from J. Burnham, J. H. Meisel, and others. Today in Europe as well, Mosca's central idea is considered a basic concept and has become common intellectual property.

MARIO DELLE PIANE

[*See also* ELITES *and* OLIGARCHY *and the biographies of* MICHELS; OSTROGORSKII; PARETO.]

WORKS BY MOSCA

1882   I fattori della nazionalità. *Rivista europea* 13, fasc. 4:703–720.

(1884) 1958   Teorica dei governi e governo parlamentare. Pages 15–328 in Gaetano Mosca, *Ciò che la storia potrebbe insegnare: Scritti di scienza politica.* Milan: Giuffrè.

(1884–1941) 1958   *Ciò che la storia potrebbe insegnare: Scritti di scienza politica.* Milan: Giuffrè. → A commemorative volume.

(1887) 1958   Le costituzioni moderne. Pages 445–549 in Gaetano Mosca, *Ciò che la storia potrebbe insegnare: Scritti di scienza politica.* Milan: Giuffrè.

(1896) 1939   *The Ruling Class (Elementi di scienza politica).* New York: McGraw-Hill. → An abridged edition, entitled *La classe politica*, was published by Laterza in 1966.

(1903) 1949   Il principio aristocratico ed il democratico nel passato e nell'avvenire. Pages 1–36 in Gaetano Mosca, *Partiti e sindacati nella crisi del regime parlamentare.* Bari: Laterza.

(1924) 1949   Lo stato-città antico e lo stato rappresentativo moderno. Pages 37–60 in Gaetano Mosca, *Partiti e sindacati nella crisi del regime parlamentare.* Bari: Laterza.

(1932a) 1962   *Storia delle dottrine politiche.* 8th ed. Bari: Laterza. → First published as *Lezioni di storia delle istituzioni e delle dottrine politiche.*

(1932b) 1958   The Final Version of the Theory of the Ruling Class. Pages 382–391 in James H. Meisel, *The Myth of the Ruling Class: Gaetano Mosca and the "Elite."* Ann Arbor: Univ. of Michigan Press. → First published as Chapter 40 of *Lezioni di storia delle istituzioni e delle dottrine politiche.*

Partiti e sindacati nella crisi del regime parlamentare. Bari: Laterza, 1949. → A posthumous volume, containing a large number of minor writings first published between 1897 and 1925.

SUPPLEMENTARY BIBLIOGRAPHY

BOBBIO, NORBERTO 1960 *Gaetano Mosca e la scienza politica.* Rome: Accademia Nazionale dei Lincei.

BOBBIO, NORBERTO 1962 Gaetano Mosca and the Theory of the Ruling Class. Banca Nazionale del Lavoro, Rome, *Quarterly Review* 60:3–23.

BURNHAM, JAMES 1943 Mosca: The Theory of the Ruling Class. Pages 79–115 in James Burnham, *The Machiavellians: Defenders of Freedom.* New York: Day.

CAPRARIIS, VITTORIO DE 1954 Profilo di Gaetano Mosca. *Mulino* 3:343–364.

COOK, THOMAS I. 1939 Gaetano Mosca's *The Ruling Class. Political Science Quarterly* 54:442–447.

CROCE, BENEDETTO (1923) 1947 Premessa. In volume 1 of Gaetano Mosca, *Elementi di scienza politica.* 4th ed. Bari: Laterza. → A book review of the 1923 edition of Mosca's *Elementi di scienza politica.*

DE PIETRI-TONELLI, ALFONSO 1935 Mosca e Pareto. *Rivista internazionale di scienze sociali* 43:468–493.

DELLE PIANE, MARIO 1949 *Bibliografia di Gaetano Mosca.* Florence: La Nuova Italia. → A comprehensive and annotated list of Gaetano Mosca's writings.

DELLE PIANE, MARIO 1952 *Gaetano Mosca: Classe politica e liberalismo.* Naples: Edizioni Scientifiche Italiane. → Contains a large and up-to-date list of Mosca's writings on pages 377–382.

DORSO, GUIDO 1949 *Dittatura, classe politica e classe dirigente.* Turin: Einaudi. → See especially pages 121–184 on "Classe politica e classe dirigente."

GRAMSCI, ANTONIO 1949 *Il risorgimento.* Turin: Einaudi. → See especially page 59.

HUGHES, H. STUART 1954 Gaetano Mosca and the Political Lessons of History. Pages 146–167 in H. Stuart Hughes (editor), *Teachers of History: Essays in Honor of Laurence Bradford Packard.* Ithaca, N.Y.: Cornell Univ. Press.

HUGHES, H. STUART 1958 *Consciousness and Society: The Reorientation of European Social Thought, 1890–1930.* New York: Knopf. → See especially pages 252–259.

LUCIOLLI, MARIO 1959 *G. Mosca y el pensamento liberal.* Santiago (Chile): Universidad de Chile, Instituto de Ciencias Políticas y Administrativas.

MALAGODI, GIOVANNI F. 1928 *Le ideologie politiche.* Bari: Laterza. → See especially Chapter 6.

MEISEL, JAMES H. 1958 *The Myth of the Ruling Class: Gaetano Mosca and the "Elite."* Ann Arbor: Univ. of Michigan Press.

MEISEL, JAMES H. 1964 Mosca "transatlantico." *Cahiers Vilfredo Pareto* 4:109–117.

PASSERIN D'ENTRÈVES, ALESSANDRO 1959 Gaetano Mosca e la libertà. *Politico* 24:579–593.

PIOVANI, PIETRO 1951 *Momenti della filosofia giuridico-politica italiana.* Milan: Giuffrè. → See especially pages 97–143.

RUNCIMAN, W. G. 1963 *Social Science and Political Theory.* Cambridge Univ. Press. → See especially Chapter 4.

SALOMONE, ARCANGELO WILLIAM 1945 *Italian Democracy in the Making: The Political Scene in the Giolittian Era, 1900–1914.* Philadelphia: Univ. of Pennsylvania Press. → See especially Chapter 2.

SPITZ, DAVID (1949) 1965 *Patterns of Anti-democratic Thought: An Analysis and a Criticism, With Special Reference to the American Political Mind in Recent Times.* Rev. ed. New York: Free Press.

VECCHINI, F. 1965 *La pensée politique de Gaetano Mosca et ses différentes adaptations au cours du XXe siècle en Italie.* Ph.D. dissertation, Univ. of Dijon.

MOTIVATION

I. THE CONCEPT   *Lawrence I. O'Kelly*
II. HUMAN MOTIVATION   *Robert C. Birney*

I
THE CONCEPT

The concept of motivation has had a comparatively short formal history in experimental psychology, figuring hardly at all in the systematic presentations of such forebears and founders as the English associationists Wundt, James, and Titchener. While space does not permit here adequate development of background or supporting documentation, it is probable that motivation became a central variable in behavior theories coincidentally with the change from viewing mind as "structure" to viewing mind as "function." This was the period of the emergence of the functionalism of Dewey and Angell, Freud's psychoanalysis, and McDougall's "hormic," or purposive, psychology. The notion that mind or behavior has directional and energetic components could only have occurred to students who regarded organisms as going and achieving, as desiring and searching, or as solving problems and adapting.

Philosophical antecedents. The philosophical heritage of experimental psychology was of little help in telling the functional psychologists how to think about these problems in dynamics. Philosophy had thought much about human values, but there seemed little possibility of generalizing ethical systems across the broad range of species and phyla that seemed to have motivational components in their behavior. Nor, except as a kind of confused background, do the nonhumans have much to contribute to the chronic debate over hedonism. The principles of "association," as contributions to theories of learning and memory, have had a long philosophical history, of course, but they never gave rise to concepts that could be called "motivational."

Biological contributions. A good deal more was available from the biologist, particularly concepts of instinct and physiological regulation and a knowledge of neurophysiological bases of behavior.

Instinct. Through many revisions, the concept of instinct as a directive force had achieved general acceptance among naturalists and was at hand for the now familiar uses in behavior theory to which it was put by McDougall and by Freud. Evolution, as Darwin saw it, made instinctive behavior clearly adaptive for either the individual or his species. Through the years, this concept of instinct has had an eventful career, being rejected out of hand by the radically empirical behaviorists and being dramatically revived into a new and fruitful usefulness by the zoological ethologists.

In the study of motivation the concept of instinct becomes useful when it is made to represent rather uniform, genotypically shaped behavior patterns operating in the context of self-maintenance or species maintenance. This, then, enables some of the fundamental characteristics of the motivational concept to be easily discerned. An animal's responses are triggered by some internal physiological change, usually acting conjointly with distinctive external stimulus patterns. The responses are selectively oriented to one or another aspect of the environment and show a flexibly shaped succession that is usually relevant to some adaptive end. There then ensues, if the animal is "successful," achievement of some state of affairs that ends the sequence.

Physiological regulation.   Another related set of facts and concepts from biology anticipated the psychologist's concern with motivation and gave him the framework of a model that has had long viability, not only within experimental psychology proper but also, as an inspiration for analogous models, within the social sciences generally. We refer to the facts of physiological regulation. Claude Bernard may properly be said to be their discoverer. In the middle of the last century he was demonstrating that the effective functioning of vertebrate organisms depends on maintenance of the physical and chemical state of body fluids within rather narrow zones of constancy. His maxim that "constancy of the internal environment is the condition of a free life" is among the most celebrated truths of modern physiology. While physiologists usually remained concerned with analysis of the internal mechanisms that ensured constancy, it was obvious that in many, if not all, instances the complete story would involve the behavioral capabilities of the animal.

To a working, machinelike body, the most usual and frequent threats to constancy come from the metabolic processes that make work possible, including those that labor themselves to maintain constancy. For example, body temperature may be controlled by using water for evaporative cooling or by using glycogen for warming through shivering. In these instances, stores of water and glucose are depleted. The only replacement sources are in the external world, and the animal must manifest behavior as it searches the environment to locate and to consume the needed substances. This whole cycle, which goes on endlessly throughout the animal's lifetime, provides a blueprint for theorizing about behavior which is basically and primarily motivational. Also, because animals depend for their very existence on the adequacy of both internal and external aspects of regulation, the structures mediating these functions are subjected to powerful selective biases in their evolution.

Neurophysiological bases.   In recent years the neurophysiologist and physiological psychologist have been increasingly successful in identifying the neural and endocrine bases for such important motivational conditions as hunger, thirst, and sex; but even before this actual demonstration the functional theories of behavior were assuming that

motivation was firmly anchored in the organic needs of the body. This is clearly illustrated in the following quotation from Dashiell's influential textbook of 1928:

The primary drives to persistent forms of animal and human conduct are tissue-conditions within the organism giving rise to stimulations exciting the organism to overt activity. A man's interests and desires may become ever so elaborate, refined, socialized, sublimated, idealistic; but the raw basis from which they are developed is found in the phenomena of living matter.   (1928, pp. 233–234)

Social motives.   The second sentence of the above quotation reflects one of the major problems of the contemporary motivational theorist: the nature and derivation of those human motives that do not seem to be connected in any obvious manner to the waxing and waning of organic needs. All possible positions are represented in the writings of psychologists, ranging from Dashiell's view that social motives simply grow out of physiological strivings to the assertion that social motives may be completely unrelated to biological needs in either their development or their full-fledged operation.

Experimental psychologists have been interested in the study of motivation for its own sake and because of the important role that motivational constructs have come to play in theories of learning and performance. Current developments in the psychology of motivation are taking place in a number of areas without a great deal of apparent interaction. Since the purpose of this article is to present an introductory overview of the field, some of the major fields of interest in motivation will be described, followed by a brief attempt at synthesis.

Physiological mechanisms in motivation

While the earliest and still most basic interest of the psychologist concerned with the physiological mechanisms in motivation is the nature of behavior resulting from alterations in internal physiological states, his study of underlying mechanisms has drawn him into an active partnership with the physiologist interested in regulatory processes and the neurophysiologist. The application of the Horsley–Clark stereotaxis technique for precise subcortical brain exploration has led to a vast number of discoveries of the importance of the hypothalamus and brain stem for regulation of the internal constancy of the body. It has further been demonstrated that these structures participate in the more external aspects of such regulation, as in the initiation and termination of eating and drinking. The underlying mechanisms of drive turn out to be complexly interrelated combinations of physical and chemical changes in cell membranes, endocrine secretion, and neural integration. As the sequence of operations underlying the various regulatory cycles becomes more clearly understood, a generalized schema is beginning to emerge—a pattern of processes not unlike the patterns psychologists and engineers are accustomed to deal with in the analysis of any type of behavior system. This schema is illustrated in Figure 1, a much simplified representation of the regulatory model of motivated behavior. When the physical or chemical constancies of the body are altered, correctional mechanisms are brought into play by either completely internal homeostatic adjustments or regulation that involves arousal of the animal to discriminatory awareness and to selective orientation with respect to corrective aspects of the environment. When system variables are restored to something approaching optimal levels, signals of restoration act to inhibit the behavioral and physiological processes of correction. Thus the familiar negative feedback principle of control can be applied to guidance of the organic system [*see* Cy-BERNETICS].

While regulation frequently is quite automatic and does not require any observable behavioral effort, such is not always the case. As was mentioned earlier, when restoration of system variables to an optimal range consumes substances which must be replaced from sources exterior to the animal or when the environment itself poses local conditions of stress, the animal must make dis-

criminative responses in that environment. That this is so has been recognized for a long time, as the quotation from Dashiell would indicate. What is essentially new is the identification of the mechanisms underlying the processes of the model. It is almost invariably true that significant variations from the optimum of any physiological system variable are signaled by changes in the physical or chemical characteristics of the extracellular body fluids. For example, oxygen lack is signaled by an increase in the carbon dioxide content of the plasma, dehydration is accompanied by an increase in extracellular osmotic pressure, etc. Either these changes or some of their secondary consequences are adequate stimuli for specialized detector cells which, functioning as quasi-sense organs, react to the index of system disturbance by hormonal and/or neural excitation and response. These responses are the direct cause of correctional activity in the case of the automatic regulations and instigate the discriminatory and orienting responses in the case where behavioral components are necessary. In the latter case it is obvious that docility, flexibility, and variability are introduced, furnishing survival criteria of a kind quite different in many ways from those inherent in the more automatic and internally sufficient type of regulatory mechanism. In short, it would appear that the phylogenetic modifications that have led to the superior mammalian nervous system were decisively determined by the demands of survival by external regulation.

Experimental verification of the essential points in this argument has been accomplished. Discrete

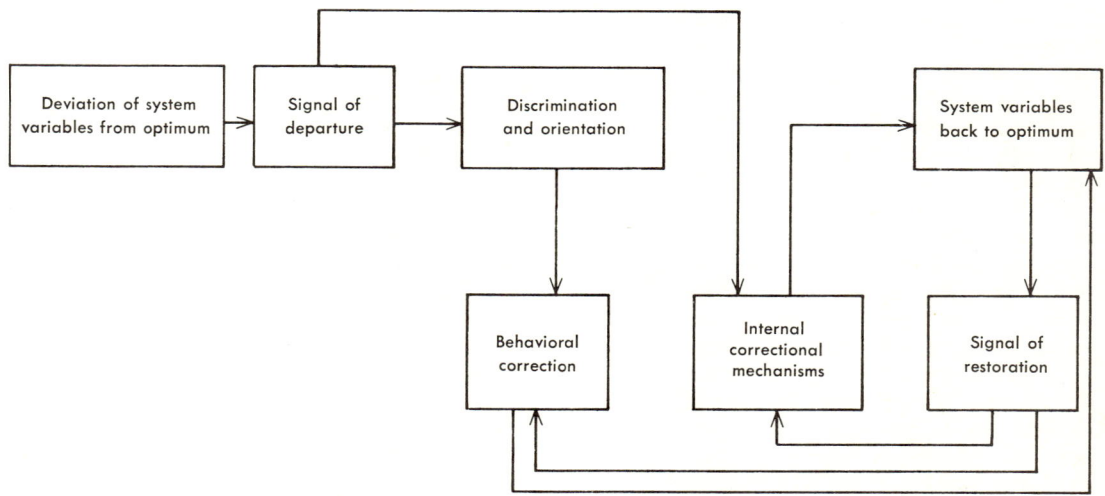

Figure 1 — A simplified representation of the regulatory model of motivated behavior

lesions produced in the lateral areas of the hypo-thalamus cause an animal to become aphagic; the animal will refuse food in the face of a growing and critical caloric need, and eventually, unless maintained by artificial feeding, will die of starva-tion. In a nearby region ablations can be made that will cause an animal to become adipsic; even when some water is placed in the mouth of such an animal it will refuse to swallow and will attempt to reject the water as if it were some ill-tasting or noxious substance. It has been reported (Andersson & McCann 1956) that aphagic animals will accept food if it is in liquid form and that adipsic animals will accept water if it is contained in fluid that has an acceptable taste and high caloric content. Such results tend to support the notion of relatively discrete neural systems con-trolling the urges to eat and to drink. Further sup-port for this point of view is gained by observing the results of lesions in the ventromedial nuclei of the hypothalamus. Animals so injured develop *hyperphagia*, eating ravenously and far beyond their caloric needs. Such animals, with unlimited supplies of palatable food, become obese, frequently weighing more than twice as much as would be normal for their age. Thus, there would appear to be a specific food-control system, the "need detec-tor" being critically involved with the lateral hypo-thalamus and the "satiation detector" with the ventromedial hypothalamus. Other parts of the nervous system are, of course, involved also, since the search for and consumption of food requires a vast amount of sensory apparatus, memory capac-ity, and ability to manage a repertoire of motor responses. But all of this apparatus, important as it is, appears to depend for its operation on signals instigated by the hypothalamic mechanisms. This would seem to be the closest we have yet come to locating a specifically physiological basis for a "pure" motivational component to behavior. While much remains to be done, it can be said with some confidence that the remaining problem in the phys-iological analysis of motivation is elucidating the organic basis for learning, memory, and percep-tion; the shape of the purely motivational compo-nent is now within our grasp.

Brain stimulation. One development that holds promise of relating the need-signaling and satia-tion-signaling systems to the systems governing learning, memory, and perception is the now well-known finding of Olds and his associates that animals will perform a wide variety of instrumental acts if rewarded by electrical stimulation in sub-cortical brain areas; still other areas are found to generate avoidance responses (see Olds 1962 for

a review of studies of the phenomenon). The "re-inforcing" areas are located in a somewhat diffuse path that extends from the midline septal nuclei down to the lateral and posterior hypothalamus. Under optimal stimulus conditions and with elec-trodes implanted in the most favorable hypo-thalamic loci, animals will continue pressing a lever to receive stimulation for an indefinitely long period, stopping only when apparently fatigued and resuming their efforts after brief periods of rest. Response rates are augmented by concur-rently operating tissue needs (Brady et al. 1957) and are modifiable by changes in the electrical parameters of the stimulus. The relations of this organic phenomenon to hedonic and other theories of motivation will be dealt with by other contribu-tors to this section. What appears inescapable is the fact that by quite artificial and nonphysiological means it is possible so to stimulate the brain as to instigate behavioral sequences that look for the most part like ordinary "motivated" behavior. Still an interesting and vital question is just what part of the regulatory mechanism is triggered by the elec-trical stimuli. Does the stimulation mimic the ade-quate need-detection stimuli, or does it operate on whatever system is responsible for determining the acceptability, palatability, or "hedonic tone" of peripheral stimuli? There is not yet enough evi-dence to decide between these alternatives. Perhaps neither possibility is true, and it might turn out that electrical stimulation of the brain creates a com-pletely unique motivational state having little to do with the central mechanism for other phys-iological drive states. Even if this were true, how-ever, the animal must marshal his sensory and motor equipment in the interest of repeating the instrumental acts leading to brain stimulation, and so at the perceptual and motor sectors of motivated behavior the over-all model is still sufficient [*see* NERVOUS SYSTEM, *article on* BRAIN STIMULATION].

Activation. In addition to the newly expanded knowledge of neural and hormonal variables in regulation, there has been another development in neurophysiology that has exercised a significant influence on concepts of motivation. The discovery by Horace Magoun (1950; 1958) and his co-work-ers of a second sensory and motor neural mediating system, working in conjunction with the classical afferent paths to the brain and the pyramidal ef-ferent motor outflow from the brain, has given the psychological theorist a wider range of phys-iological properties on which to base his thinking about the relation of brain to behavior. Magoun showed that the reticular formation of the brain stem received innervation from most of the afferent nerves leading from sense organs and that stimulation of sense organs caused excitation to be transmitted not only through the long-known "specific projection pathways" to the corresponding sensory areas of the cortex but also, by means of the reticular formation, diffusely to most or all other parts of the cortex.

Because the reticular formation receives excitation from all sensory channels and because any specificity appears lost in the diffuse transmission to the cortex, this system was called the "non-specific," or "diffuse," projection system. The major feature of the reticular formation seems to be the dependence of the higher regions of the brain on this diffuse excitatory consequence of sensory stimulation for proper transmission and integration of impulses that are carried over the specific projection system. In a classical experiment Moruzzi and Magoun (1949) showed that cats with the reticular formation ablated appeared unable to respond to peripheral stimulation, although electrical recording from the sensory areas of the cortex showed that the signals from the sensory nerves were arriving at the cortical sensory projection areas in a normal fashion. It had been known that the electroencephalogram (EEG) recording the spontaneous massed electrical activity of the cortex showed a regular alternation of a roughly sinusoidal character and of a frequency that was directly related to the degree of alertness of the subject—coma and sleep being accompanied by very slow waves; relaxed waking states, by an intermediate frequency; and a shift toward higher frequencies occurring when the subject either was attending to peripheral sensory stimulation, was actively engaged in tasks, or was disturbed by emotional thoughts. The shift from lower to higher frequencies was shown by Magoun and others to be closely related to activity in the diffuse projection system. The phenomenon of increased EEG frequency as a consequence of stimulation has been called activation and as such is an index of the widespread changes in the higher nervous system attending integrated behavior. More broadly, then, "activation" is a term used to denote the generalized, nondirectional alerting of the subject as a consequence of external or internal stimulation. In this sense, the concept has been called upon to bear an increasingly heavy theoretical load in discussions of motivated behavior [see ATTENTION].

Considering the importance of activation as a part of the physiological analysis of motivation, at least two main points should be made. To the extent that regulatory imbalance increases the activity level of the animal, it could be surmised that the various deficiency and excess detector mechanisms, like the peripheral sense organs, contribute to excitation in the diffuse projection system in addition to functioning as the origin of signals specific to the particular system out of equilibrium. If this is so, the diffuse projection system is at least a part of the physiological mechanism underlying "drive" and conforms nicely to some of the behaviorally observable properties of motivation. A second, and perhaps more important, possible property of the activation system is that, in its obvious importance for discriminatory awareness, it provides a common physiological mechanism for mediation of tissue-need motivation and the other more complex forms of motivation that appear to originate in peripheral sensory stimulation or in some relationship to the previous learning and memory of the individual. A number of years ago Morgan (1943) proposed that the essential physiological mechanism in motivation was a kind of general excitatory process, to which he gave the name "central motive state." It would seem that the central motive state could well be the diffuse activation process. To the extent that activation *is* nonspecific it is a process that can be equally at the service of *any* adequate stimulus situation, be it internal or external, be it changes in physical constants of plasma or changes in patterns of symbolic sensory input.

Instinctive behavior

The strongly empiricist bias of behavioral science in the United States and in Russia has led to a serious neglect by psychologists of some of the clearest examples of motivational models at work. Most animal species show, to varying degrees, complex behavioral sequences, the performance of which is so similar among members of a species as to suggest compellingly that some of the crucial determinants of the sequence are a part of the genetically transmitted characteristics of that species. Intensive field and laboratory studies of the behavior of members of many of the animal phyla have led to a renewed interest in instinctive behavior and to several important modifications in our concept of its characteristics. The most important insight is the recognition that instinctive behavior does not run itself off blindly and inflexibly, but rather occurs under an exquisitely balanced set of external and internal stimulus conditions, changes in any of which cause corresponding changes in the details of the instinctive acts; along with this there is a flexibility and adaptability of the activity to the existing conditions, and within the uniformity of the over-all ends, or goals, of the behavior, there is a variety of means employed that makes any given sequence of instinctive behavior well-nigh unique. Further, the physiological basis for instinctive behavior, so far as it is now known, seems to conform quite well to the general model for regulatory behavior.

All of these points can be made more vividly by briefly citing an example. Several species of Pacific salmon have a life cycle that starts with hatching from eggs laid in fresh-water streams at some distance from the ocean. After a few months of growth in the immediate vicinity of their birth site, the young salmon gradually drift downstream, foraging as they go and maintaining a predominant upstream body orientation. Upon reaching the ocean they range over a territory of many thousand square miles for periods that vary from one to four years. During this time, nourished by the plentiful food supply of the seas, they attain a large size. Then, for reasons still obscure, changes occur in the pituitary, the fish stop foraging for food, their digestive tracts start an active atrophic process, and the salmon start on the return trip to the river drainage from whence they came. With a high probability of success they locate the correct river, ascend it, select the correct branchings, and return to the particular stretch of water in which they were hatched. By this time the starvation and the pituitary-directed gonadal changes have produced marked structural alterations in the fish. Their skin pigmentation is changed, their jaw structure is modified, and they are immeasurably weaker. The female selects a favorable spot, scoops out a nest in the stream bottom, and lays her eggs. These are covered with the sperm-bearing fluid of the male. Soon both parents die. (Other closely related species, the steelhead trout and the Atlantic salmon, show the migratory sequence but live to spawn on several repeated occasions.) Noteworthy in this sequence is the interdependence of genetic inevitabilities, such as the digestive-tract atrophy and individually learned memories. In some very real sense the salmon must *learn* and *remember* a unique set of geographical coordinates and features. Its return from the ocean to the mouth of the main stream of its home drainage requires not only the capacity to use navigational techniques (it is probable that the salmon navigates by sun angles) but also a memory of these bearings in relation to particular sequences of temperatures, currents, salinities, odors, and other environmental features in order to return successfully to its spawning ground.

The complex interweaving of genotypic and phenotypic factors that are seen in patterns of instinctive behavior do not seem completely different from the types of variables underlying any physiological drive state. Nor is it beyond the realm of possibility that even the most complex and uniquely human motivational conditions may follow the same sort of pattern, in which cultural, individual, and genetic variables interact to produce resultants that have individual variability within a larger context of species uniformity. Modern concepts of instinctive behavior, then, may lend some support to a "neo-McDougallism," not by making culture and learning less important but by making "instincts" more susceptible to phenotypic variation [*see* INSTINCT].

Psychological aspects of motivation

Turning from the biological material we have been considering to the type of thinking and writing being done by the majority of experimental psychologists, we move from a search for organic substrates to an exercise in theoretically guided research, in which motivational concepts are treated as intervening variables and hypothetical constructs. These constructs are used as mediators between the observable and controllable aspects of stimulation and response, along with such nonmotivational constructs as habit.

The central issue in the theoretical psychology of motivation has been the relationship of motivational variables to those of learning. In what Hunt (1963) has called the traditionally dominant conceptual scheme, behavior is thought of as starting with general random activity, instigated by drive; the latter may be equivalent to painful or uncomfortable internal stimulation consequent to tissue needs. A behavior sequence, or cycle, is terminated when the drive is reduced by the animal coming into commerce with circumstances that terminate the uncomfortable internal stimulation. If, as is usually the case, the tissue need is recurrent, the animal *learns* quicker and more effective techniques for drive reduction. Thus, in its final form behavior becomes some sort of joint function of drive and habit. Important issues grow out of this simple basic conceptual scheme. Most influential in experimental psychology has probably been the treatment given to these problems by Hull (1943), in which drive reduction is viewed as a necessary condition for habit acquisition and in which performance is a joint function of habit as a directional component and drive as an energizing component. For well over a decade, almost every study reported in the experimental journals seemed oriented toward issues raised by this formulation or its obvious alternatives. Despite all the careful experimental work, however, it is still impossible to arrive at any simple specification of the role of motivation in learning. Nor, unfortunately, is it possible to make a clear decision about the correctness of the traditional formulation. There is, for example, enough experimental evidence to lead us to suspect that habits may be acquired quite independently (or even in the absence) of any concurrent drive state; that, while temporal contiguity of an action and drive reduction may facilitate learning, the role of drive reduction may be more apparent than real; that intensity of drive may be related to efficiency of performance by some sort of an inflected function, very high drive states being as detrimental to performance as are very weak drive levels; that decisions between alternative habit possibilities may be a function of perceptual structuring independent of the relative strength of the alternative habits *or* of the nature of the drive state; that quality and quantity of an incentive may be more important in determining acquisition or performance than any of the detectable properties of concurrent drive states; and that the intensity of a drive state under which a habit is acquired may be a determiner of the strength of the habit, as measured in later tests of retention [*see the biography of* HULL].

An over-all negative conclusion relevant to the problem of motivation, however, may be stated with some confidence: throughout the range of mammalian species explored (unfortunately almost exclusively rat, cat, dog, monkey, and man) *there are many sources for the energizing of behavior that are not easily and directly related to the needs that arise from regulatory processes.*

Space does not permit a thorough review of the facts or theoretical proposals concerning motivational sources of a nonregulatory nature, although Hunt provides an excellent summary (1963). One of the principal features of many "intrinsic" motivational proposals is their emphasis on the role of cognitive processes arising from one form or another of *incongruity*, either with or without the added assumption that the cognitive process is accompanied by or stimulates affective, or emotional, reactions. Thus, Montgomery (1954) and Berlyne (1960) have adduced evidence that behavior may be instigated by unfamiliar stimulus situations which arouse "curiosity" or "exploratory drive." Festinger (1957) has studied the motivational effects of what he terms cognitive dissonance, which refers to uncertain, unfamiliar, or unexpected relationships between stimulus elements and internally stored memories, beliefs, attitudes, etc. While not all of the "nonphysiological" theorists have made use of the concept of activa-

tion as the underlying energizing mechanism, Hebb (1955), Malmo (1959), Duffy (1962), and Hunt (1963) have each in his own way argued for the importance of the nonspecific projection system as the neural mediator of intrinsic motivation [*see* STIMULATION DRIVES].

The cognitive theories represent a departure from the classical formulation for the development of motives unrelated to primary needs. The older point of view maintained that drives could be acquired by the familiar process of conditioning and thus were derivable from primary drives. An earnest search for evidence of acquired drive and secondary reinforcement has been only partially successful. Recent summaries by Mowrer (1960) and by Brown (1961) discuss much of the evidence. Russian workers have reported a great many experiments which demonstrate that almost any internal "automatic" process, such as bile secretion, urine secretion, or gastric acidity, can be brought under the control of environmental stimulation by applying the methods of classical conditioning (see Razran 1961). The significance of these findings for the problem of higher-order motivational processes is potentially great.

What does the experimental psychology of motivation have to contribute to the social scientist? In the present writer's opinion, the strongest developments in motivation research of the past twenty years have been in the basic underlying physiological processes. Not only have mechanisms been specified for individual regulatory states, but an outline, at least of expectation for more general somatic integrating processes underlying complex perceptual and socially oriented behavior has been achieved. Socialized man, unique as he is, works within limits set by his anatomical characteristics, and a more precise prediction of his behavior may well emerge when his properties as a physiological system are assimilated with his properties as a social being.

LAWRENCE I. O'KELLY

[*Directly related are the entries* DRIVES; INSTINCT; LEARNING, *article on* REINFORCEMENT; STIMULATION DRIVES. *Other relevant material may be found in* EMOTION; HOMEOSTASIS; LEARNING; NERVOUS SYSTEM; PAIN; PERSONALITY: CONTEMPORARY VIEWPOINTS; *and in the biographies of* CANNON *and* McDOUGALL.]

BIBLIOGRAPHY

ANDERSSON, B.; and McCANN, S. M. 1956 The Effects of Hypothalamic Lesions on the Water Intake of the Dog. *Acta physiologica scandinavica* 35:312–320.
BERLYNE, D. E. 1960 *Conflict, Arousal, and Curiosity.* New York: McGraw-Hill.

BRADY, JOSEPH V. et al. 1957 The Effect of Food and Water Deprivation Upon Intracranial Self-stimulation. *Journal of Comparative and Physiological Psychology* 50:134–137.

BROWN, JUDSON S. 1961 *The Motivation of Behavior.* New York: McGraw-Hill.

DASHIELL, JOHN F. 1928 *Fundamentals of Objective Psychology.* Boston: Houghton Mifflin.

DUFFY, ELIZABETH 1962 *Activation and Behavior.* New York: Wiley.

FESTINGER, LEON 1957 *A Theory of Cognitive Dissonance.* Evanston, Ill.: Row, Peterson.

HEBB, DONALD O. 1955 Drives and the C.N.S. (Conceptual Nervous System). *Psychological Review* 62:243–254.

HULL, CLARK L. 1943 *Principles of Behavior: An Introduction to Behavior Theory.* New York: Appleton.

HUNT, J. McV. 1963 Motivation Inherent in Information Processing and Action. Pages 35–94 in O. J. Harvey (editor), *Motivation and Social Interaction.* New York: Ronald.

MAGOUN, HORACE W. 1950 Caudal and Cephalic Influences of the Brain Stem Reticular Formation. *Physiological Reviews* 30:459–474.

MAGOUN, HORACE W. (1958) 1963 *The Waking Brain.* 2d ed. Springfield, Ill.: Thomas.

MALMO, ROBERT B. 1959 Activation: A Neuropsychological Dimension. *Psychological Review* 66:367–386.

MONTGOMERY, K. C. 1954 The Role of Exploratory Drive in Learning. *Journal of Comparative and Physiological Psychology* 47:60–64.

MORGAN, CLIFFORD T. (1943) 1965 *Physiological Psychology.* 3d ed. New York: McGraw-Hill.

MORUZZI, G.; and MAGOUN, HORACE W. 1949 Brain Stem Reticular Formation and Activation of the E.E.G. *Electroencephalography and Clinical Neurophysiology* 1:455–473.

MOWRER, ORVAL H. 1960 *Learning Theory and Behavior.* New York: Wiley.

OLDS, J. 1962 Hypothalamic Substrates of Reward. *Physiological Reviews* 42:554–604.

RAZRAN, GREGORY 1961 The Observable Unconscious and the Inferable Conscious in Current Soviet Psychophysiology: Interoceptive Conditioning, Semantic Conditioning, and the Orienting Reflex. *Psychological Review* 68:81–147.

II

HUMAN MOTIVATION

The language of motivation is a workaday device for all of us in our social world. We speak of aims, purposes, desires, wants, needs, and compulsions in others and use the same language in testifying about ourselves. The language is descriptive, unqualified, contradictory, and misleading. It manifestly will not do for science, and yet, in a pragmatic fashion, we get it to work much of the time in our daily lives. For better or for worse, it has been the departure point for the development of scientific statements about human motivation.

From the outset, systematic writing about human motivation has had to accommodate the fact that our subjective sense of intention is an unreliable index of our behavior. Many behaviors show intentional organization which may be successfully identified by the observer when the behaving person himself cannot report or infer the intention. Efforts to cope with this feature of human motivation have led to a wide range of strategies of theorizing which, in turn, have stimulated rather distinctive styles of research tactics. One result of this state of affairs is that there is not yet any general theory of human motivation, nor does it seem likely that there will be one for quite some time. Let the reader thus be prepared for a certain amount of surveying here, with a special effort to mark numerous reference signs pointing to those sizable nexuses of literature which must be pursued in depth. (For a more extended survey, see Murphy 1954.)

Textbook treatments of social motivation from various viewpoints may be found in recent texts by Atkinson (1964), Brown (1961), and Cofer and Appley (1964). Atkinson provides an excellent historical review of the manner in which the framing of motivational questions has evolved and suggests an essentially cognitive resolution; Brown's book treats the topic from the point of view of Hullian drive theory, with its resultant absorption of motivational questions into the analysis of habit systems; while Cofer and Appley give an exhaustive and eclectic summary of the motivational literature, culminating in the suggestion that research will be best guided by an "equilibration" model focusing on the anticipation and/or sensitization invigoration mechanisms.

In these modern treatments of motivation, the fact of socialization is acknowledged but not given any special status beyond that given other sources of stimulus input. The same is true of the response concept, in which no qualitative distinction is made between subjective report and observed behavior. The effect of this sort of theorizing is to place the burden for distinguishing social classes of stimuli and responses upon spatial location, timing, intensity, association, and complexity. The power of such an approach lies in its reductionist implications, since the observer must give up his "area" terms, such as love, anxiety, ambition, etc., in favor of a step-by-step analysis of the motivated sequence. Such is the approach of Ford and Beach (1951) in describing the pre-conditions, body states, arousing stimuli, and preparatory, consummatory, and withdrawal movements which characterize sexual behavior across species, including man.

The limitations of the reductionist approach have been obvious for decades. McDougall (1908) warned against them and tried to provide an alternative that would preserve the value of social motivation in our common vocabulary. Contemporary writers have also pointed up the severe limitations of reducing the study of motivation to those behavioral sequences which focus on action "in order to" at the expense of action for its own sake of "being." Gordon Allport (1964) has reiterated his often expressed evaluation of theory and research unenlightened by a proper degree of eclecticism. When we add to these considerations the problems posed by the desire of many to write a truly social psychology of motivation—for example, Floyd Allport and Kurt Lewin—we must be prepared to find the literature of the field a disordered array of constructs, theories, methods, empirical findings, and research programs. There is a sense in which constructs and theories are answers to questions posed by observation. What are the origins of human motives? How do motives develop? What are the motives of men? How do motives affect behavior and experience? By organizing the remainder of this article around these questions, we will be surveying the literature on human social motivation.

The origins of motives

Nearly all serious observers of human behavior have had to frame a statement about the sources and wellsprings of motivated behavior. The early works of McDougall (1908), Freud (1915), and Thorndike (1927) use extensions of the philosophical discussions of hedonism and the role played by the affective dimensions of experience. The general notion is that those behaviors which result in changes in affect soon take on directional qualities, while those which have no observable affective components are not properly called motivational. However, both the Freudian postulation of unconscious affects and the difficulties of objective measurement of affects soon led to a willingness to assert that basic motivational tendencies may emerge as a natural component of behavior in the normal course of maturational development (e.g., White 1959). Gordon Allport has extended this position by postulating that new motives may develop from old by becoming "functionally autonomous"; that is, early motives produce a profusion of new experiences which transform and redirect them. Jung (1932–1936) extended the maturational change through the life span well beyond the middle years and asserted that new motives continue to appear late in life.

Learning theorists have progressively shown more interest in objective determinants of behavior. The two major research programs have been those of Clark Hull and B. F. Skinner [see HULL; LEARNING, *article on* INSTRUMENTAL LEARNING]. By emphasizing the role of response consequences ("rein-

forcers") in learning and the directing influence of stimuli associated with reinforcement, they reduced the motivational bases of behavior to those primary bodily conditions which drive the organism to a sufficient level of arousal to support learning. Thus Brown (1961) argues that all social motivation is based upon primary drive systems that have been elaborated by reinforcement into secondary systems.

The effect of these formulations has been to focus attention on the definition of primary systems. It is an empirical fact that hunger, thirst, pain, and affective arousal surrounding those body systems eventually integrated into adult sexuality have proved easiest to observe and manipulate. But other researchers, such as Sears, Maccoby, and Levin (1957), have demonstrated the feasibility of empirical studies of those systems devoted to cognition, mastery, empathy, and identification of value orientations. These "ego functions," as they are called, appear to be equally primary in driving the organism. Indeed, the difficulties of specifying the attributes of primary drive systems lend force to the models emerging in the discussions between psychologists and ethologists about the proper method of study of emergent patterns of behavior. Here we are warned against placing too much value on "area" terms such as "drive," "primary," etc., in favor of providing a closely specified, objective description of the sequence of events, both organismic and environmental, which contribute to the appearance of a behavior sequence (Bindra 1959). As this advice is more widely adopted, it appears likely that the origin of social motivation will be described as some unique arrangement of determinants known to characterize social motivation throughout the life span.

The development of social motivation. The earliest comprehensive statement of motivational development is Freud's theory of psychosexual stages (1932), wherein intense affects of pleasure and distress progressively focus on the emerging body functions of ingestion, elimination, and orgasm, as well as on fantasied castration threat. These maturational stages have been further supplemented by Erikson's "epigenetic ages" (1950), which emphasize psychosocial stages of development of trust, autonomy, initiative, industry, identity, intimacy, generativity, and ego integrity. Jung also conceives of psychological stages extending through the life span. The social factor in each of these schemes lies in the association of gratification or fear with other persons, acting within the area of interest to the developing human being. Since the focus is on the growing person, the "other" tends to be treated as an object or agent, and the sense of reciprocity found in social psychology is absent.

Also absent from the above formulations is a closely reasoned theory of learning. McClelland (1951) has presented a discussion of the importance of the first years of life in the formation of motives which points toward the objective analysis of those conditions of early environmental input, autonomic conditioning, undeveloped cognitive discrimination, absence of symbolic control, and failure of extinction due to the unreproducibility of the original learning situations. Recently more precise statements of early learning of social motives have been set out by Staats and Staats (1963), Bijou and Baer (1961), and Bandura and Walters (1963). The first two pairs of authors use recent developments in Skinnerian analysis of behavior to effect an exposition of the emergence of directed behavior according to the pattern of classical conditioning of "respondents," reinforcement schedules of "operants," use of "discriminant" stimuli, and eventual symbolization of such stimuli. From this point of view, motives appear because some stimuli and reinforcers are more common than others and are easier to discriminate and of greater importance to society. Important issues remain untouched in this analysis. The defining attributes of reinforcers, beyond their capacity to reinforce, go unanalyzed, thus placing a heavy environmental emphasis on the theory and separating it from the research discussed in the previous section on origins of motivation. The loss of objectivity which occurs when the child masters sufficient language to permit the chief dynamics of reinforcement and discrimination to take place as thought and decision points to the need for a theory of language, and the Skinnerian efforts in this direction have suffered heavy criticism as being too simplistic. Finally, the value of these theories in generating research on the development of motives remains to be seen. As yet the presentations are descriptive and largely speculative, being reminiscent of a previous effort by E. R. Guthrie [see GUTHRIE]. Judging by the capacity of such theory to stimulate research and by some of the preliminary efforts, considerable research will be produced.

Bandura and Walters (1963) write from the sociobehavioristic viewpoint and present a considerable array of research findings in support of their theorizing. They emphasize the importance of social imitation and vicarious reinforcement, that is, change in behavior through observing the reinforcement experience of another. By combining the effects of imitative experience with direct social reinforcement, they show that social learning may involve sudden "mastery" of whole patterns of behavior in brief periods of time. They further theorize that the establishment of behavior patterns of aggression, dependence, sexual behavior, and self-control follows directly from patterns of reinforcement and stimulus generalization. However, the inhibition of these behaviors by socially acceptable alternative behaviors requires a combination of reinforcement withdrawal, modeling of alternative responses by others, and perhaps cessation of punishment following a restitutive or prosocial response. Punishment alone is said to inhibit the expression of the response in the presence of the punishing agent, but nothing more. This monograph is an excellent example of the behaviorist's art of analyzing a behavioral sequence into those components of stimuli, responses, and environmental events for which reasonable estimates of relationship can be made.

There is the usual behavioristic sense of circumvention of the private, subjective interior of human experience in this writing, although Bandura and Walters devote considerable attention to learned verbal responses. "In contrast, a child may learn to criticize himself for transgression because self-criticism proved a successful means of securing the reinstatement of his parents' affection and approval. In this case, the child's behavior parallels that of an animal who learns to press a mildly charged lever in order to obtain food" (1963, pp. 186–187). The subjective sense of conflict, discrimination, interpretation, and decision—to say nothing of aspiration and purpose—continues to await an adequate theory of reinforcement. [See IMITATION.]

Standing in sharp contrast to the behavioristic approach is the work of McClelland in *The Achieving Society* (1961). He, too, attempts to trace the development of motivation, in this case the achievement motive, through an interlocking set of studies designed to focus on the value and meaning of various reinforcement situations as they impinge on the child. The emphasis is on the way parents interpret problem, work, and play situations to the child; on the problem-solving strategies of aspiration and effort which children adopt (Heckhausen 1963); on the effects of such experience as reflected in fantasy, self-evaluation, and choice of long-term interests; and on the eventual appearance in the adult personality of a coherent motivational system that continues to affect decision processes, performance characteristics, and belief systems. Such a program suffers from confusion of definitions, argument by analogy, numerous inadequate controls, and poorly defined construct validity. Its value lies in its holding close to the phenomenal world of the subject, as experienced, in the hope of laboriously introducing those methods uniquely required for the proper study of human motivation. [See ACHIEVEMENT MOTIVATION.]

The motives of men

Asking for a taxonomy of motives implies some sort of list. Thus it was that early writers on the subject (for example, Jeremy Bentham) felt that the naturalist's approach to motivational phenomena would lead to the proper definition of the subject. However, the proliferation of "instinct" theories, with their endless lists of motives, combinations, and hierarchies, eventually led to the discrediting (see Bernard 1926) of the work of men like McDougall (1908) and Troland (1928) and to the suppression of the question, What are the motives of men? In 1938 Henry Murray reopened the question with the publication of *Explorations in Personality*. This effort to re-establish the importance of the taxonomic approach to motives and situations seemed to renew interest in programs of research systematically directed at the study of single motive systems. The list of publications devoted to such study is growing steadily.

Generally speaking, the research strategy for the study of motive systems consists of identifying a reasonably finite set of behaviors designated by common-sense language under a single term, for example, affiliation. Efforts are then made to provide adequate measures of both the behavior—that is, an affiliative response—and the disposition so to respond—that is, the need for affiliation. Once the measure of the motive is established, a series of studies is begun to determine the motive's sensitivity to environmental and social arousal, its role in personality dynamics, and its effects on other specific behavior systems such as perception, cognitive processes, or learning sequences—and to abstract from all of these findings some general statements of motivational processes. Inevitably such research produces enough anomalies to require revision of the original conception of the motive construct itself, the set of behaviors initially said to define it, and some of the assumptions made in its measurement. The studies discussed below illustrate these conditions.

Since truly programmatic research is still not common in American social science and psychology, it should not be surprising to find that Murray's mapping of personality domains failed to guide motivational search. Broadly speaking, the programmatic literature does divide into "primary"

systems of sexual behavior and anxiety-driven behavior; "secondary" systems of curiosity, competence, and dependency; and acculturated systems of authoritarianism, affiliation, approval, ingratiation, conformity, achievement, and power. For each of the terms just mentioned, at least one volume or working paper has been published by researchers working continuously on the problem area with coherent methods and purposes. Certainly the literature on other motivational systems is quite large but fragmented to the point of defying integration. Frequently the study of a particular behavior pattern is accompanied by the invocation of the "need for _____" phrasing (Cofer and Appley index the need for identity, dreaming, rest, satisfaction, security, sex, and sleep) with no effort made to give the motive construct an independent definition and measurement. It is this practice which has led many writers to abandon the motive construct as unfruitful and redundant (e.g., Rogers 1963; Jones 1956–1962, esp. volume 8; Kelly 1962). However, the more naturalistic, descriptive analysis of motive systems continues to illuminate the nature of human experience in social situations.

Current studies of motivation

Sex. Given the extraordinary preoccupation of psychological studies with sexual behavior, we might expect to cite several comprehensive works on human sexual motivation. But in fact, the recent *Encyclopedia of Sexual Behavior* (Ellis & Abarbanel 1961) displays a wide diversity of investigation from every conceivable point of interest without providing a clear picture of sexuality as a motivational process. The early comparative study by Ford and Beach (1951) gave some hint of how such investigation might proceed, but we have only the Kinsey studies (Kinsey et al. 1948; 1953), exploratory reports by Maslow (1962), and the more recent intensive studies by Money, Hooker, and Masters (Money 1965) to show the beginnings of an assessment of sexual capacities, development, practice, and experience in humans. [See SEXUAL BEHAVIOR.]

Anxiety. The literature on anxiety undoubtedly exceeds that on any other motivational topic. It may be divided into studies of physiological processes, case studies, field studies, and laboratory studies of the effects of anxiety on behavior and experience, assessments of therapeutic procedures for its relief, and theoretical statements on its origin, nature, and role in personality functions. Psychopathology, work loss and impairment, much of the thematic content of contemporary works of art, and the focus of social commentary in both popular and scholarly writing all give testimony to the presence of anxiety in human affairs. Again, however, as with sex, we find a discursive literature remarkably deficient in programmatic intent and lacking in coherence. Hoch's assertions of 1950 remain true:

Today we know a great deal about where and when anxiety occurs, but we are still quite hazy as to how it originates and even what purpose it serves. . . . Some think that anxiety is secondary to an intraorganismic or interorganismic imbalance, being a symptom of a disturbed homeostasis in the organism due to conflicting drives within the individual and the environment; others support the point of view that anxiety itself is the cause of the disturbances we see in most neurotic and in some psychotic manifestations. (Hoch & Zubin 1950, p. 105)

The physiological mechanisms are outlined in the work of Selye (1956) on the "general adaptation syndrome," in Wolff (1953), and in papers delivered at the Symposium on Stress, held in 1953 by the National Research Council and Walter Reed Army Medical Center. The Funkenstein, King, and Drolette (1957) experimental studies of induced stress as it affects physiological and psychological indices reveal the complexity of individual mastery of stressor effects and their attendant anxiety. Janis' strategies (1958) for testing specific hypotheses of anxiety control in preoperative and postoperative patients stand as an excellent example of the careful field studies that are so badly needed. [See ANXIETY; STRESS.]

Aggression. An excellent example of the successful researching of a motivational process is found in Berkowitz' *Aggression*. By integrating his own research with the large body of material available, he was able to conclude:

. . . the habitually hostile person is someone who has developed a particular attitude toward large segments of the world about him. He has learned to interpret (or categorize) a wide variety of situations and/or people as threatening or otherwise frustrating to him. Anger is aroused when these interpretations are made, and the presence of relevant cues—stimuli associated with the frustrating events—then evokes the aggressive behavior. In many instances the anger seems to become "short-circuited" with continued repetition of the sequence so that the initial thought responses alone elicit hostile behavior. (1962, p. 258–259)

Thus a motive component surrounds the experience of threat, while the notion of latent aggression or need for aggression is abandoned in favor of a trait conception of more or less consistent aggressive reactions. However, Berkowitz clearly states that enduring motives may conflict with or support the aggressive response to threat as well as lie at the seat of the developmental course which leads to the aggressive personality pattern.

Berkowitz' findings probably have great generality for other motivational systems. By tracing the relative weights of the various sources of variance as they are found in capacity for emotional arousal, constitutional capability, early models for action and thought, social settings of support or inhibition, and the structure of interiorized moral standards, he has doubtless identified the basic sources of many important motivational systems. Not that the scheme is yet complete. Notably absent from the work is a treatment of the middle and late life changes which occur presumably from self-education, shifts in ideology, and a steadily lengthening course of experience. This deficit is a common one in the works we are reviewing. [See AGGRESSION.]

Ludic behavior. "Ludic behavior consists in large measure of what we are calling perceptual and intellectual activities—seeking out particular kinds of external stimulation, imagery, and thought" (Berlyne 1960, p. 5). There is a growing body of literature concerned with exploratory behavior, curiosity, manipulation, attention, and epistemic behavior. It is paralleled in the clinical literature by an increased emphasis on the analysis of ego functions. Berlyne's works (1960; 1965) constitute an impressive review of the studies of animals and men engaged in ludic behaviors. He suggests that exploration may be released by some specific stimulus event in the situation or may emerge from an ultrastable stimulus situation in an apparent effort to create "diversive" stimulation. Given these basic motivational dispositions, the processes of socialization, reinforcement, etc. may then produce more stable response patterns which are placed in the service of conflict reduction; these in turn lead to generalized epistemic behaviors designed to provide information and understanding suitable for adjustment to a wide range of choice and conflict situations. Thus ludic behaviors are usually found concurrently with the activation of other motivational systems, but they are distinct processes in their own right and not merely variants of anxiety, aroused drive states, etc. Thus far this research has not attempted to provide standardized measures of individual differences in ludic motivation. [See CREATIVITY; STIMULATION DRIVES.]

Affiliation. The complexity of human social attachments naturally leads to attempts to distinguish between the qualities of human association. The voluminous clinical and psychoanalytic literature on psychosexual development has generated numerous hypotheses about the sources of attraction, dependence, love, and identity between persons. For several years Sears and his associates have been studying the development of affiliative tendencies in children (Sears et al. 1957; Sears 1963). "For the child, the upshot of this infantile experience is that a certain number of operant responses become firmly established to the various instigators that have been commonly associated with primary gratifications or reinforcing stimuli. The child learns to 'ask' for the mother's reciprocal behavior. *These asking movements are the dependency acts whose frequency and intensity we use as a measure of the dependency trait (or action system)*" (Sears 1963, p. 31). It is the appearance, maintenance, growth, and elaboration of these dependency acts that concern Sears, and his studies demonstrate the complexities of tracing these processes. Thus for the sample of four-year-olds for whom data on early infancy was available, the prediction of negative or positive attention-seeking, touching or holding, being near, and seeking reassurance proved to differ for the sexes, with the girls' patterns related to level of maternal care, achievement demands, and sex anxiety for the father. Maternal coldness, slackness of standards, and neglect, without any real permissiveness, and paternal general nonpermissiveness—especially about sex— was related to boys' dependency (Sears 1963, p. 63). Sears is willing to refer to these patterns as motivational systems, but he makes it clear that the sheer complexity of variables requires more precise definition than a list of needs or motives can provide. It is perhaps for this reason that individual difference measures of the dependency disposition are not reported.

Shipley and Veroff (1952) have established a reliable measure of need for affiliation (*n Aff*), using the modified Thematic Apperception Test procedure of McClelland. For college student populations in particular, this measure has shown predicted positive relationship to suggestions for conformity (Walker & Heyns 1962), negative subjective reactions to rejection (Hardy 1957), and effort on achievement tasks when they are instrumental to social approval (French 1958), to cite a few salient findings. These studies have been primarily aimed at establishing the construct validity of the *n Aff* measure and do not constitute a comprehensive study of affiliative behavior.

Schachter (1959) set out to study the conditions which cause variation in affiliative action. It has been demonstrated that affiliative tendencies increase with increasing anxiety and hunger and that, for anxiety, ordinal position of birth is an effective discriminator of the magnitude of the affiliative tendency. The over-all findings warrant

the conclusion that affiliative tendencies are a manifestation of needs for anxiety reduction and self-evaluation (Schachter 1959, p. 132). Here we have an example of motive assignment from the observer's interpretation of the situation, supported by subjective report of the subjects.

Approval and ingratiation. A comprehensive program of research on affiliative behavior is found in *The Approval Motive* by Douglas P. Crowne and David Marlowe (1964). Starting with an interest in a measure of individual differences in the social-desirability response set to personality inventory items,

. . . we directed our search toward the goals and expectations that would impel one to evaluate himself in terms conditioned by the acceptance of others. To do so required us to postulate a motivational state [the approval motive], reflected in test-taking behavior [the Marlowe–Crowne Social Desirability Scale (MC)], and to seek its correlates in behaviors less harassed by the confusions of personality tests. Our findings have been confirmative, although in the process a major alteration of the concept of the approval motive—the defensiveness-and-vulnerable-self-esteem hypothesis— was necessary to account for some unanticipated and initially paradoxical results.   (1964, p. 206)

In this case the authors did find a significant correlation (+.55) between the projective *n Aff* score and the MC score, whose high scorers are

. . . more conforming, cautious, and persuasible, and [whose] behavior is more normatively anchored. . . . The greater amenability to social influence of persons who characterize themselves in very desirable terms is seen in (a) the favorability of their attitudes toward an extremely dull and boring task; (b) their greater verbal conditionability, both directly and vicariously; (c) social conformity; (d) a tendency to give popular word associations; (e) the cautious setting of goals in a risk-taking situation; (f) their greater reactivity . . . in a . . . perceptual-defense task; and (g) susceptibility to persuasion.   (1964, p. 190)

These authors chose to keep the concept "approval motive" while finding it useful, as did Schachter, to postulate underlying motivation to maintain and preserve self-esteem. Thus we see the manner in which the hierarchy of social motives must be uncovered by a coherent program of research.

The same experience is reported by Jones (1964). He reports a series of studies using instructional and situational manipulation designed to reveal the extent and variety of ingratiation behaviors as well as effects on attitudes, beliefs, and perceptions, especially as they focus on self-esteem. Given instructional or situational sets to enhance ingratiation behavior, subjects (*a*) emphasize their positive attributes over their weaknesses, (*b*) move toward greater public agreement with a target person's stated opinions, and (*c*) show an adaptive capacity for adjusting these actions to the status, awareness of the target of the subject's intentions, and requirements of the mutual task.

Each of these monographs approaches the affiliative process in particular response domains, demonstrates some of the determinants of the behaviors, and finds it useful to infer a generalized disposition having motivational properties. The data suggest that at the center of affiliative behavior lies a concern for self-confirmation, enhancement, esteem, or maintenance, which itself may imply a more basic personality disposition to stabilize, order, and control changes in one's position in the world.

Achievement.   A considerable part of one's lifetime is devoted to the performance of tasks whose outcomes provide important consequences for survival, well-being, social rewards, and self-esteem. Clearly understood standards of performance exist for these tasks, and to match or surpass the norm is considered an achievement. Murray gave the following definition of need Achievement (*n Ach*): "To accomplish something difficult. To master, manipulate, or organize physical objects, human beings, or ideas. To do this as rapidly and as independently as possible. To overcome obstacles and attain a high standard. To excel one's self. To rival and surpass others. To increase self-regard by the successful exercise of talent" (*Explorations in Personality* . . . 1938, p. 164).

In 1953 McClelland, Atkinson, Clark, and Lowell published *The Achievement Motive*—which presented a projective measure of *n Ach*, defined now as concern with success in competition with some standard of excellence—and a series of studies designed to establish the construct validity of the measure. This work was followed by Atkinson's *Motives in Fantasy, Action, and Society* (1958), which contains further studies of *n Ach* as well as new projective scoring systems for *n Sex, n Power,* and *n Aff.* McClelland's *Achieving Society* (1961) and Heckhausen (1963) have provided still more research and theory about the achievement motive and its avoidance opposite, fear of failure. The continuously growing body of literature is the subject of reviews by Heckhausen (1965) and Birney (1966) and a collection of papers edited by Atkinson and Feather (1966).

The body of knowledge growing out of this sustained research effort has slowly taken the following shape. The child's early efforts to master his world provide the parents with the opportunity to reward independent, self-propelled actions differentially. If such rewards come early in life and are accompanied by maternal praise and pacing and supportive paternal endorsement, task situations become the cue for realistic aspirations, capacity for delayed gratification, fantasies of success, and the desire for personal responsibility. These preferences lead to realistic occupational aspirations emphasizing moderate risks and personal freedom of decision. Authoritarian work situations are avoided and resisted, and these may include highly demanding academic situations. Vocational careers are marked by upward mobility, preference for moderate-risk business and managerial situations, and concentration on the instrumentalities of working situations.

It might be pointed out that this pattern of entrepreneurial features was not initially anticipated by the researchers, being only slowly understood as numerous studies showed that high task achievement did *not* necessarily denote a high need for achievement in most subjects. By focusing on the motivation measure, rather than on achieving behavior, the form of the motivational system has emerged.

This review of systematic studies of human motive systems illustrates the current phase of research now being pursued by persons interested in the identification, measurement, and functional properties of important social motives. Whether Murray's list of motives proves prophetic remains to be seen. As more of these systems are understood, the opportunity for writing a general theory of human motivation will arise. Whether that theory will resemble the many restrictive models of action and behavior also remains to be seen. At the present it appears that human motives play their major role in sensitizing persons to environmental possibilities, directing their choice among incentives, contributing to both their degree of involvement in the situation and their phenomenal sense of it, and ordering the sense of closure and history surrounding the past sequence of events. So long as these aspects of life remain denotable, the motive construct will retain its usefulness.

ROBERT C. BIRNEY

[*Directly related are the entries* ATTITUDES; DRIVES, *article on* ACQUIRED DRIVES; STIMULATION DRIVES. *Other relevant material may be found in* ACHIEVEMENT MOTIVATION; AFFECTION; AGGRESSION; ANXIETY; IMITATION; LEARNING, *article on* REINFORCEMENT; PERSONALITY, *article on* PERSONALITY DEVELOPMENT; PERSONALITY: CONTEMPORARY VIEWPOINTS; PROJECTIVE METHODS, *article on* THE THEMATIC APPERCEPTION TEST; SEXUAL BEHAVIOR; SOCIALIZATION; STRESS; *and in the biographies of* ALLPORT; LEWIN; MCDOUGALL.]

BIBLIOGRAPHY

ALLPORT, GORDON W. 1964 The Fruits of Eclecticism: Bitter or Sweet? *Acta psychologica* 23:27–44.

ATKINSON, JOHN W. (editor) 1958 *Motives in Fantasy, Action, and Society.* Princeton, N.J.: Van Nostrand.

ATKINSON, JOHN W. 1964 *An Introduction to Motivation.* Princeton, N.J.: Van Nostrand.

ATKINSON, JOHN W.; and FEATHER, NORMAN T. (editors) 1966 *A Theory of Achievement Motivation.* New York: Wiley.

BANDURA, ALBERT; and WALTERS, R. H. 1963 *Social Learning and Personality Development.* New York: Holt.

BERKOWITZ, LEONARD 1962 *Aggression: A Social Psychological Analysis.* New York: McGraw-Hill.

BERLYNE, D. E. 1960 *Conflict, Arousal, and Curiosity.* New York: McGraw-Hill.

BERLYNE, D. E. 1965 *Structure and Direction of Thinking.* New York: Wiley.

BERNARD, L. L. 1926 *Introduction to Social Psychology.* New York: Holt.

BIJOU, SIDNEY W.: and BAER, DONALD M. 1961 *Child Development.* Volume 1: A Systematic and Empirical Theory. New York: Appleton.

BINDRA, DALBIR 1959 *Motivation: A Systematic Reinterpretation.* New York: Ronald.

BIRNEY, R. C. 1966 Research on the Achievement Motive. Unpublished manuscript.

BROWN, JUDSON S. 1961 *The Motivation of Behavior.* New York: McGraw-Hill.

COFER, CHARLES N.; and APPLEY, MORTIMER H. 1964 *Motivation: Theory and Research.* New York: Wiley.

CROWNE, DOUGLAS P.; and MARLOWE, DAVID 1964 *The Approval Motive: Studies in Evaluative Dependence.* New York: Wiley.

ELLIS, ALBERT; and ABARBANEL, ALBERT (editors) 1961 *The Encyclopedia of Sexual Behavior.* 2 vols. New York: Hawthorne.

ERIKSON, ERIK H. (1950) 1964 *Childhood and Society.* 2d ed., rev. & enl. New York: Norton.

Explorations in Personality: A Clinical and Experimental Study of Fifty Men of College Age, by Henry A. Murray et al. 1938 London and New York: Oxford Univ. Press.

FORD, CLELLAN S.; and BEACH, FRANK A. 1951 *Patterns of Sexual Behavior.* New York: Harper.

FRENCH, E. G. 1958 Effects of the Interaction of Motivation and Feedback on Task Performance. Pages 400–408 in John W. Atkinson (editor), *Motives in Fantasy, Action, and Society.* Princeton, N.J.: Van Nostrand.

FREUD, SIGMUND (1915) 1959 Instincts and Their Vicissitudes. Volume 4, pages 60–83 in Sigmund Freud, *Collected Papers.* International Psycho-analytic Library, No. 10. New York: Basic Books; London: Hogarth.

FREUD, SIGMUND (1932) 1965 *New Introductory Lectures on Psycho-analysis.* New York: Norton. → First published as *Neue Folge der Vorlesungen zur Einführung in die Psychoanalyse.*

FUNKENSTEIN, DANIEL H.; KING, STANLEY H.; and DROLETTE, MARGARET E. 1957 *Mastery of Stress.* Cambridge, Mass.: Harvard Univ. Press.

HARDY, KENNETH R. 1957 Determinants of Conformity and Attitude Change. *Journal of Abnormal and Social Psychology* 54:289–294.

HECKHAUSEN, HEINZ 1963 *Hoffnung und Furcht in der Leistungsmotivation.* Meisenheim am Glan (Germany): Hain.

HECKHAUSEN, HEINZ 1965 Leistungsmotivation. Volume 2, pages 602–702 in *Handbuch der Psychologie.* Göttingen (Germany): Hogrefe.

HOCH, PAUL H.; and ZUBIN, JOSEPH 1950 *Anxiety.* New York: Grune.

JANIS, IRVING L. 1958 *Psychological Stress: Psychoanalytic and Behavioral Studies of Surgical Patients.* New York: Wiley.

JONES, EDWARD 1964 *Ingratiation: A Social Psychological Analysis.* New York: Appleton.

JONES, MARSHALL R. (editor) 1956–1962 *Nebraska Symposium on Motivation.* Vols. 4, 8, 10. Lincoln: Univ. of Nebraska Press.

JUNG, CARL G. (1932–1936) 1939 *The Integration of the Personality.* New York: Farrar. → Originally published in German in the 1932–1936 volumes of *Eranos Jahrbuch.*

KELLY, GEORGE A. 1962 Europe's Matrix of Decision. Volume 10, pages 83–125 in Marshall R. Jones (editor), *Nebraska Symposium on Motivation.* Lincoln: Univ. of Nebraska Press.

KINSEY, ALFRED C. et al. 1948 *Sexual Behavior in the Human Male.* Philadelphia: Saunders.

KINSEY, ALFRED C. et al. 1953 *Sexual Behavior in the Human Female.* Philadelphia: Saunders.

McCLELLAND, DAVID C. 1951 *Personality.* New York: Sloane.

McCLELLAND, DAVID C. 1961 *The Achieving Society.* Princeton, N.J.: Van Nostrand.

McCLELLAND, DAVID C. et al. 1953 *The Achievement Motive.* New York: Appleton.

McDOUGALL, WILLIAM (1908) 1950 *An Introduction to Social Psychology.* 30th ed. London: Methuen. → A paperback edition was published in 1960 by Barnes and Noble.

MASLOW, ABRAHAM H. 1962 *Toward a Psychology of Being.* Princeton, N.J.: Van Nostrand.

MONEY, JOHN (editor) 1965 *Sex Research: New Developments.* New York: Holt.

MURPHY, GARDNER 1954 Social Motivation. Volume 2, pages 601–633 in Gardner Lindzey (editor), *Handbook of Social Psychology.* Cambridge, Mass.: Addison-Wesley.

ROGERS, CARL 1963 The Actualizing Tendency in Relation to "Motives" and to Consciousness. Volume 11, pages 1–24 in Marshall R. Jones (editor), *Nebraska Symposium on Motivation.* Lincoln: Univ. of Nebraska Press.

SCHACHTER, STANLEY 1959 *The Psychology of Affiliation: Experimental Studies of the Sources of Gregariousness.* Stanford Studies in Psychology, No. 1. Stanford Univ. Press.

SEARS, ROBERT R. 1963 Dependency Motivation. Volume 11, pages 25–64 in Marshall R. Jones (editor), *Nebraska Symposium on Motivation.* Lincoln: Univ. of Nebraska Press.

SEARS, ROBERT R.; MACCOBY, E. E.; and LEVIN, H. 1957 *Patterns of Child Rearing.* Evanston, Ill.: Row, Peterson.

SELYE, HANS 1956 *The Stress of Life.* New York: McGraw-Hill.

SHIPLEY, THOMAS E.; and VEROFF, JOSEPH 1952 A Projective Measure of Need for Affiliation. *Journal of Experimental Psychology* 43:349–356.

STAATS, ARTHUR W.; and STAATS, CAROLYN K. 1963 *Complex Human Behavior.* New York: Holt.

THORNDIKE, EDWARD L. 1927 The Law of Effect. *American Journal of Psychology* 39:212–222.

TROLAND, LEONARD T. 1928 *The Fundamentals of Human Motivation*. New York: Van Nostrand.

WALKER, EDWARD L.; and HEYNS, ROGER W. 1962 *An Anatomy for Conformity*. Englewood Cliffs, N.J.: Prentice-Hall.

WHITE, ROBERT W. 1959 Motivation Reconsidered: The Concept of Competence. *Psychological Review* 66:297–333.

WOLFF, HAROLD G. 1953 *Stress and Disease*. Springfield, Ill.: Thomas.

MOTOR DEVELOPMENT

See SENSORY AND MOTOR DEVELOPMENT.

MOVEMENTS

See MILLENARISM; NATIVISM AND REVIVALISM; SOCIAL MOVEMENTS; VOLUNTARY ASSOCIATIONS.

MÜLLER, ADAM HEINRICH

Adam Heinrich Müller (1779–1829), German political economist of the romantic school, was born in Berlin and studied at Berlin and Göttingen. In 1802 he moved to Vienna, where he was an intimate friend of Friedrich von Gentz, a politician and writer associated with Metternich. In 1805 Müller was received into the Roman Catholic church, and as he grew older his ideas were increasingly influenced by Catholic thought.

He served from 1806 to 1809 in Dresden as a tutor to Prince Bernhard of Saxe-Weimar. There he was associated with the romantic dramatist Heinrich von Kleist in editing the literary journal *Phöbus*. His most creative book, *Die Elemente der Staatskunst* (1809), was based on lectures given at Dresden. He spent the years 1809–1811 in Berlin. Because he opposed the reforms of Stein and Hardenberg, opportunities for public service in Prussia were closed to him, and he returned to Vienna, where in 1813 he entered the Austrian government service. Through Gentz he became acquainted with Metternich, whom he served as an adviser and assistant in various posts.

Müller was a leading member of the German romantic school of political economy, composed of several political writers and literary figures affiliated with the early German romantic movement. Among them, in addition to Müller and Gentz, were Carl Ludwig von Haller, Johann Joseph von Görres, and Franz von Baader. In varying degrees these writers opposed the marked rationality, the individualism, and the emphasis on material values characteristic of the political economy of the Enlightenment. Inspired by the integrated social organization of the Middle Ages, they sought to develop a political economy based on an organic conception of society and, thus, to recapture the "German spirit." All were influenced by the philosophy of Fichte, and Müller and Gentz in particular were influenced by Edmund Burke.

Müller published copiously in the fields of political economy and social philosophy and served as a kind of intellectual spokesman for the reactionary forces of the post-Napoleonic period.

Müller's economic and political ideas were founded, then, on an organic conception of society. In such a form of society political, economic, religious, moral, and aesthetic elements would be merged indivisibly in the state, which would represent the "mysterious reciprocity of all the relationships of life." The state not only would unite all social elements at any given time but also would be the instrument that binds society together through time and fosters the development of national consciousness, or national spirit.

As a result of this conception of society, Müller opposed individual freedom in favor of central authority, he opposed competition in favor of cooperation and reciprocity, and he opposed free trade in favor of a national system of protection. He rejected the classical theory that value is determined by exchange in the market and argued that social as well as private usefulness be considered in determining the value of any good. He rejected also the classical concept of wealth as including only material objects and advanced his own, famous concept of spiritual capital. By this, he meant that the capital of a society includes not only material objects but also intangibles derived from the past, such as the national existence, the traditions of the society, the constitution, the language, the motivations and character of the people, the extant knowledge and technology, and other nonmaterial features of the culture.

Müller regarded money as a creature of the state and the value of money as derived from its role as a link between the individuals of the organic society rather than from its exchange value or its metallic content. Because of his organic theory of society, he was unwilling to isolate the economic aspect of society for study and insisted that society be studied as a comprehensive organic unity. This led him to point out some of the excessive narrowness, materialism, and individualism of classical economics, but it also led to diffuse and muddy analysis and exposition.

Müller's influence was never great. Despite the economic and political backwardness of the Germany of his time, the prevailing political trend was liberal, and his political position was distinctly counter to the trend. However, as indicated by the appreciative comments of Roscher and Hildebrand, he did have some influence on the older historical school of economists, who developed his more significant economic ideas. List, who knew Müller personally, acknowledged indebtedness to him. Various groups of socialists, especially Christian socialists (both Protestant and Catholic), have used his ideas. In recent times, Othmar Spann built his "universalist" system of economics on the foundation of Müller's ideas. The German National Socialists found Müller's ideas congenial and resurrected them from obscurity.

Many of Müller's ideas today appear quaint, fuzzy, or dangerously reactionary. Yet he stood in the van of a long line of critics whose work has been useful in countering the abstractness, the radical individualism, and the neglect of social values characteristic of the dominant classical economics. Müller's concept of spiritual capital, of the productive power imbedded in cultural factors as well as in the concrete physical wealth of a society, is being rediscovered in the mid-twentieth century, as economists face the problems of economic growth in the underdeveloped areas of the world.

HOWARD R. BOWEN

[*For discussion of the subsequent development of Müller's ideas, see* ECONOMIC THOUGHT, *article on* THE HISTORICAL SCHOOL; *and the biographies of* HILDEBRAND; LIST; ROSCHER.]

WORKS BY A. H. MÜLLER

(1806) 1920 *Vorlesungen über die deutsche Wissenschaft und Literatur.* New ed. Edited by Arthur Salz. Munich: Drei Masken.

(1809) 1922 *Die Elemente der Staatskunst: Öffentliche Vorlesungen.* 2 vols. New ed. Edited by Jakob Baxa. Vienna: Wiener Literarische Anstalt.

(1812a) 1931 *Ausgewählte Abhandlungen.* New ed. Edited by Jakob Baxa. Jena: Fischer. → First published as *Vermischte Schriften über Staat, Philosophie, und Kunst.*

1812b *Die Theorie der Staatshaushaltung und ihre Fortschritte in Deutschland und England seit Adam Smith.* Vienna: Schaumburg.

(1816) 1922 *Versuche einer neuen Theorie des Geldes mit besonderer Rücksicht auf Grossbrittannien.* Edited by Helene Lieser. Jena: Fischer.

(1817) 1920 *Zwölf Reden über die Beredsamkeit und deren Verfall in Deutschland.* Edited by Arthur Salz. Munich: Drei Masken.

Gesammelte Schriften. Munich: Franz, 1839.

SUPPLEMENTARY BIBLIOGRAPHY

BAXA, JAKOB 1923 *Einführung in die romantische Staatswissenschaft.* Jena: Fischer.

BAXA, JAKOB (editor) 1924 *Staat und Gesellschaft im Spiegel der deutschen Romantik.* Jena: Fischer.

BAXA, JAKOB 1930 *Adam Müller: Ein Lebensbild aus den Befreiungskriegen und aus der deutschen Restauration.* Jena: Fischer. → Contains a bibliography.

ROLL, ERICH (1938) 1942 *A History of Economic Thought.* 2d ed., rev. & enl. New York: Prentice-Hall. → See especially pages 154–202 on "Political Economy in Germany."

SPANN, OTHMAR (1911) 1930 *The History of Economics.* New York: Norton. → First published as *Die Haupttheorien der Volkswirtschaftslehre auf lehrgeschichtlicher Grundlage.* See especially pages 212–270 on "Reaction and Revolution."

TOKARY-TOKARZEWSKY-KARASZEWICZ, J. VON 1913 *Adam H. Müller, Ritter von Nittersdorf als Ökonom, Literat, Philosoph und Kunstkritiker: 1779 bis 1829.* Vienna: Gerold.

MÜLLER, GEORG ELIAS

Georg Elias Müller (1850–1934) was one of the leaders of the new experimental psychology when it was being "founded" in Germany, just after the middle of the nineteenth century. If Wilhelm Wundt at Leipzig was the founder and therefore first, Müller perhaps was second. Wundt's Leipzig laboratory was certainly the best, but Müller's at Göttingen was clearly second best. If most of the able students flocked to Wundt, still many important psychologists formed their values with Müller. Helmholtz had enormous influence, but he was a sense physiologist, who presently turned physicist. Fechner, the founder of psychophysics, was at heart a philosopher, with no loyalty to psychology as such. Hering was a physiologist, who influenced many by his thinking and his phenomenology of vision, but he was not quite a psychologist. Müller, throughout his forty years at Göttingen, was known for his clear thinking, his vigorous logic, his insistent polemics, and his indefatigable pursuit of theory and fact in each of his three chosen fields of research: psychophysics, memory and learning, and vision. He did not originate any of these fields, but in each he became the leader for a time. He took over psychophysics from Fechner when the latter died. He developed the experimental attack on learning and memory after the interests of Hermann Ebbinghaus, the pioneer, had moved elsewhere. From Hering he picked up the problems of visual sensation and color theory, and he became one of the three leading figures in that area of investigation, along with Hering and Helmholtz.

Müller was born on July 20, 1850, in Grimma, a small town 16 miles from Leipzig, which boasted a thirteenth-century castle. His father was a theologian and a professor of religion at the local royal academy, later becoming rector at another village near Leipzig. The son went first to the Gymnasium at Leipzig and then, at the age of 18, to the university there, to study history and philosophy. He had been a studious boy, with his thinking directed toward mysticism by his reading of Goethe, Byron, and Shelley but redirected later, by his discovery of Lessing, to the hard clarity that characterized his maturity. At Leipzig he was inducted into Herbartian philosophy; he then went to Berlin to study history. For two years he worried over the choice between history and philosophy, but when he became a soldier in the Franco–Prussian War, escaping from the worrisome dubieties of academic life, he saw clearly that he preferred philosophy. After the war he went back to Leipzig and then moved on to Göttingen to study with the great R. H. Lotze, in the days when Lotze was actively sponsoring the new scientific psychology and it was being said that all philosophy must be firmly founded upon a knowledge of science. He received his doctorate at the hands of Lotze in 1873 after having presented a psychological thesis on the theory of sensory attention, a basic analysis of this function that was still being cited in books on attention 35 years later.

After receiving his degree, Müller became a tutor, first at Rötha, near Leipzig, and then at Berlin. A severe illness caused him to return home, and there, during his convalescence, he became interested in Fechner and psychophysics. He wrote a critical monograph, which he presented when he applied at Göttingen in 1876 to become a *Dozent* and which was published in 1878 as *Zur Grundlegung der Psychophysik*. This and his critique the next year of the method of constant stimuli, a paper that contained a table of the well-known Müller weights, established Müller as a worthy successor to Fechner, who was then nearing the end of his eighth decade. In 1880 Müller accepted the chair in philosophy at Czernowitz; but in 1881 Lotze was persuaded to go to Berlin, where he died a few months later, and Müller succeeded him at Göttingen, remaining there for forty years of continuous service. Lotze had held the chair for 37 years—making a total of three-fourths of a century for the two of them. Actually, Müller's productive life extended to almost six decades, from 1873 to 1930.

We shall now consider separately the three lines of endeavor that he promoted so successfully through those many years.

Psychophysics. Müller's 1878 monograph was concerned mostly with a critique of Weber's law, the law of the relation of sensory intensity to its stimulus. In 1889—we can touch only the high points—he pursued this problem with Friedrich Schumann in an experimental study of the discrimination of weight. With an American, Lillian J. Martin, he published a classic paper (1899) on how anticipation affects the discrimination of weights, one of the early experimental papers on attitude. In 1903 appeared his elaborate study of psychophysical methods, the study that caused E. B. Titchener to delay the publication of his magnum opus on psychophysics for two years while he made revisions.

Memory and learning. In 1894 Müller and Schumann took up Ebbinghaus' work on learning, standardizing the method of complete mastery and working out rules for the use of the nonsense syllables that Ebbinghaus had invented as material for learning. In 1900 Müller, with Alfons Pilzecker, developed the use of reaction times in the memory method of right associates. Much later Müller, working alone, produced three huge volumes (1911–1917) on memory activity, which included much of his work with Rückle, the mathematical prodigy, and also his analysis of the method of introspection.

Vision. Müller's third line of interest was vision, particularly color vision. His classic papers of 1896 and 1897 contain his revision of Hering's theory of color, in which he eliminated some of the contradiction by assuming that the brain adds a constant gray to all the colors induced by the retina—a cortical gray, as he called it. At this time he also laid down his five "psychophysical axioms," principles of the relation of neural events in the brain to the corresponding events in perception. About twenty-five years later these axioms formed the basis for the gestalt psychologists' theory of isomorphism. In 1930, toward the end of his life, Müller published two large volumes on the psychophysics of color sensations; but these tomes made less of an impression than did his earlier work, because Müller was then 80 years old, nine years past his retirement, and the times were moving away from the patterns of his interests. Nevertheless it must be noted that not so many years before, in the period from 1909 to 1911, some of the important work on visual perception—work cast in the modes of the new experimental phenomenology—had been produced at Müller's laboratory by three soon-to-be-famous psychologists: E. R. Jaensch, David Katz, and Edgar Rubin.

Müller had retired in 1921. In 1923 he published a little book polemicizing against the new gestalt psychology, followed in 1924 by a short outline of general psychology as he then saw it. He died at Göttingen on December 23, 1934, an outstanding figure among the pioneers of the new experimental psychology.

EDWIN G. BORING

[For the historical context of Müller's work, see the biographies of EBBINGHAUS; FECHNER; HELMHOLTZ; HERING; LOTZE; TITCHENER; WEBER, E. H.; WUNDT; for discussion of the subsequent development of Müller's ideas, see FORGETTING; GESTALT THEORY; PSYCHOPHYSICS; VISION, especially the article on COLOR VISION AND COLOR BLINDNESS; and the biographies of KATZ and JAENSCH.]

WORKS BY G. E. MÜLLER

1873   Zur Theorie der sinnlichen Aufmerksamkeit. Leipzig: Edelmann.

1878   Zur Grundlegung der Psychophysik. Berlin: Grieben.

1889   MÜLLER, GEORG E.; and SCHUMANN, FRIEDRICH Über die psychologischen Grundlagen der Vergleichung gehobener Gewichte. Archiv für die gesammte Physiologie 45:37–112.

1894   MÜLLER, GEORG E.; and SCHUMANN, FRIEDRICH Experimentelle Beiträge zur Untersuchung des Gedächtnisses. Zeitschrift für Psychologie und Physiologie der Sinnesorgane 6:81–190, 257–339.

1896–1897   Zur Psychophysik der Gesichtsempfindungen. Zeitschrift für Psychologie und Physiologie der Sinnesorgane 10:1–82, 321–413; 14:1–76, 161–196.

1899   MÜLLER, GEORG E.; and MARTIN, LILLIAN J. Zur Analyse der Unterschiedsempfindlichkeit. Leipzig: Barth.

1900   MÜLLER, GEORG E.; and PILZECKER, ALFONS Experimentelle Beiträge zur Lehre vom Gedächtniss. Zeitschrift für Psychologie, Supplement No. 1.

1903   Die Gesichtspunkte und die Tatsachen der psychophysischen Methodik. Ergebnisse der Physiologie 2, part 2: 267–516.

1911–1917   Analyse der Gedächtnistätigkeit und des Vorstellungsverlaufes. 3 parts. Zeitschrift für Psychologie, Supplements no. 5, 8, 9.

1923   Komplextheorie und Gestalttheorie: Ein Beitrag zur Wahrnehmungspsychologie. Göttingen: Vandenhoeck & Ruprecht.

1924   Abriss der Psychologie. Göttingen: Vandenhoeck & Ruprecht.

1930   Über die Farbenempfindungen: Psychophysische Untersuchungen. 2 parts. Zeitschrift für Psychologie, Supplements no. 17, 18.

SUPPLEMENTARY BIBLIOGRAPHY

BORING, EDWIN G. (1929) 1950   A History of Experimental Psychology. 2d ed. New York: Appleton. → See especially pages 371–379; and the bibliography on pages 382–383.

BORING, EDWIN G. 1935   Georg Elias Müller: 1850–1934. American Journal of Psychology 47:344–348.

BORING, EDWIN G. 1936   Georg Elias Müller. American Academy of Arts and Sciences, Proceedings 70:558–560.

CLAPARÈDE, ÉDOUARD 1935   Georg Elias Müller: 1850–1934. Archives de psychologie 25:110–114.

KATZ, DAVID 1935a   Georg Elias Müller. Acta psychologica 1:234–240.

KATZ, DAVID 1935b   Georg Elias Müller. Psychological Bulletin 32:377–380.

VAN ESSEN, JACOB 1935   G. E. Müller ter gedachtenis. Nederlandsch tijdschrift voor psychologie 3:48–58. → Contains a bibliography.

WATSON, ROBERT I. 1963   The Great Psychologists: From Aristotle to Freud. Philadelphia: Lippincott. → See especially pages 269–270, "G. E. Müller."

MÜLLER, JOHANNES

Johannes Müller (1801–1858) is frequently referred to as the father of experimental physiology. While it might be argued that the title belongs more properly to Sir Charles Bell, the fact remains that during the first half of the nineteenth century Müller was the dominant figure in the rapidly developing science of physiology. Through his own researches, particularly on reflex action and on human and animal vision, through his massive Handbuch der Physiologie des Menschen (1834–1840; a translation, Elements of Physiology, appeared 1840–1843), which became the standard reference work for physiologists throughout Europe, and through his pupils he made a lasting impression on the biological sciences; and the doctrine for which he became most famous, the law of specific energies of nerves, continues in modified form to present a challenge.

Müller, the son of a shoemaker, was born in Koblenz. In 1819 he matriculated at the University of Bonn, where he received his medical degree in 1822. After a year of further study in Berlin he was habilitated at Bonn in 1823. Until 1830 he was Privatdozent in anatomy and physiology, at which time he was granted a professorship. In 1833 he was called to the chair of anatomy and physiology at the University of Berlin, which he occupied until his death in 1858. During his career he became prominent in international scientific circles, was an active leader in university affairs (being elected Dekan in 1835 and Universitätsrektor in 1838), and during the political upheaval of 1848 he was head of the "fliegende Korps der Universitätsangehörigen." Among his many pupils the best known are Ernst Brücke, Carl Ludwig, and Emil Du Bois-Reymond, the last of whom succeeded Müller in the Berlin chair. Even better known is Hermann von Helmholtz, who although not a pupil, was closely associated with Müller as a junior colleague and whose epoch-making contributions to sensory physiology are essentially extensions of Müller's pioneering studies. It is a tribute to Müller's greatness as a teacher that none of his pupils remained strictly faithful to their master's doctrine. In the empiricist–nativist controversy, for instance, Müller was on the nativist side of the argument, and Helmholtz became the spokesman for the empiricists; Müller's avowedly vitalist position was vigorously rejected by the younger generation of physiologists.

Müller's stature as a scientist is most evident in the Handbuch, in which he summarized and evaluated the physiological knowledge of his day, reported much of his own research, and defined problems for further investigation. Although his best-known contributions are in sensory physiology and what would now be called the experimental psychology of sensation and perception, he was interested in every aspect of human and animal physiology and even in the broader philosophical implications of natural science.

The famous law of specific energies was first formulated in the 1826 volume on the comparative physiology of vision, and it was amplified in Book 5 of the *Handbuch*. Briefly stated, it asserts that the basis of differentiation among sensory qualities is to be found not in the physical processes of the external world or in the receptors but in the condition of the sensory nerves. Our knowledge of the external world is thus an interpretation placed upon centrally aroused and immediately apprehended sensations. This is obviously not a totally new doctrine. The early British empiricist philosophers, notably George Berkeley, had made a similar distinction between sensation and interpretation, but without grounding it in anything more than a speculative physiology. A more direct anticipation is to be found in the independent discoveries by Charles Bell and François Magendie of the structural and functional differences between sensory and motor nerves, the sensory nerves being responsible for sensation and the motor nerves for muscular action. Müller extended the principle by according to each nerve its own unique sensory quality: color to the optic nerve, sound to the acoustic nerve, etc.; and a further refinement is to be found in Helmholtz' hypothesis that an even more specific differentiation exists among the constituent fibers of a given nerve. One of the physiological implications of his principle, which Müller recognized but did not fully explore, is that the ultimate correlates of sensory quality are to be sought not in the nerves themselves but in the specialized structures of the cerebral cortex. Müller's principle thus points towards a more generalized theory of cortical localization.

The *Handbuch* is a treatise on philosophy and psychology as well as on physiology. For Müller, both physiology and psychology are to be subsumed under a broader philosophy of nature. His philosophical views show the influence of the German metaphysical idealists, but he might be more properly classed as an Aristotelian in his conception of nature, and his approach to science was very close to that of Goethe. Purpose, he believed, is an observable fact of nature, without which the world of natural phenomena is unintelligible. Purpose is revealed in the forms of natural objects and events but emerges as conscious mind only with the differentiation of the specialized structures of the central nervous system, the brain being the special organ of consciousness. Causation in nature may be mechanical, chemical, or organic, the third of these involving a special life force (*Lebenskraft*) that is not reducible to the first two. A science which limits itself to the first two thus provides an incomplete account of nature. In Müller's philosophy of nature, as in Goethe's, the realm of natural law includes not only the mechanical processes of the physical world but also the phenomena of purposive striving, ideation, and reasoning. Müller was a staunch exponent of the experimental method in science, but also like Goethe, he insisted that the data of unconstricted observation (*unbefangene Beobachtung*) are fully as legitimate as are those of the laboratory. In this respect he might be considered one of the forerunners of the phenomenological movement in experimental psychology.

ROBERT B. MACLEOD

[*Directly related are the entries* NERVOUS SYSTEM, *especially the article on* STRUCTURE AND FUNCTION OF THE BRAIN; SENSES. *Other relevant material is found in* PSYCHOLOGY, *article on* PHYSIOLOGICAL PSYCHOLOGY; *and in the biographies of* BELL; HELMHOLTZ; LASHLEY. *The section of the biography of* FREUD *that deals with the historical background of his thought is also relevant.*]

WORKS BY J. MÜLLER

1826 *Zur vergleichenden Physiologie des Gesichtssinnes des Menschen und der Tiere, nebst einem Versuch über die Bewegungen der Augen und über den menschlichen Blick.* Leipzig: Cnobloch.

(1826) 1927 *Über die phantastischen Gesichtserscheinungen.* Leipzig: Barth.

(1834–1840) 1840–1843 *Elements of Physiology.* 2 vols. 2d ed. London: Taylor & Walton. → First published as *Handbuch der Physiologie des Menschen.*

SUPPLEMENTARY BIBLIOGRAPHY

BORING, EDWIN G. (1929) 1950 *A History of Experimental Psychology.* 2d ed. New York: Appleton.

BORING, EDWIN G. 1942 *Sensation and Perception in the History of Experimental Psychology.* New York: Appleton.

DRIESCH, HANS (1905) 1922 *Geschichte des Vitalismus.* 2d ed., rev. & enl. Leipzig: Barth. → An expansion of the main parts of *Der Vitalismus als Geschichte und als Lehre,* which was translated into English as *The History and Theory of Vitalism* and published in 1914 by Macmillan.

HABERLING, WILHELM 1924 *Johannes Müller: Das Leben des rheinischen Naturforschers.* Leipzig: Akademische Verlagsgesellschaft.

KOLLER, GOTTFRIED 1958 *Das Leben des Biologen Johannes Müllers, 1801–1858.* Stuttgart: Wissenschaftliche Verlagsgesellschaft.

Müller, Martin 1927 *Über die philosophischen Anschauungen des Naturforschers Johannes Müller.* Leipzig: Barth.

Post, Karl 1905 *Johannes Müller's philosophische Anschauungen.* Halle: Niemeyer.

MULTIPLE COMPARISONS
See under Linear hypotheses.

MULTIVARIATE ANALYSIS

I
OVERVIEW

Multivariate analysis in statistics is devoted to the summarization, representation, and interpretation of data when more than one characteristic of each sample unit is measured. Almost all data-collection processes yield multivariate data. The medical diagnostician examines pulse rate, blood pressure, hemoglobin, temperature, and so forth; the educator observes for individuals such quantities as intelligence scores, quantitative aptitudes, and class grades; the economist may consider at points in time indexes and measures such as per-capita personal income, the gross national product, employment, and the Dow-Jones average. Problems using these data are multivariate because inevitably the measures are interrelated and because investigations involve inquiry into the nature of such interrelationships and their uses in prediction, estimation, and methods of classification. Thus, multivariate analysis deals with samples in which for each unit examined there are observations on two or more stochastically related measurements. Most of multivariate analysis deals with estimation, confidence sets, and hypothesis testing for means, variances, covariances, correlation coefficients, and related, more complex population characteristics.

Only a sketch of the history of multivariate analysis is given here. The procedures of multivariate analysis that have been studied most are based on the multivariate normal distribution discussed below.

Robert Adrian considered the bivariate normal distribution early in the nineteenth century, and Francis Galton understood the nature of correlation near the end of that century. Karl Pearson made important contributions to correlation, including multiple correlation, and to regression analysis early in the present century. G. U. Yule and others considered measures of association in contingency tables, and thus began multivariate developments for counted data. The pioneering work of "Student" (W. S. Gosset) on small-sample distributions led to R. A. Fisher's distributions of simple and multiple correlation coefficients. J. Wishart derived the joint distribution of sample variances and covariances for small multivariate normal samples. Harold Hotelling generalized the Student *t*-statistic and *t*-distribution for the multivariate problem. S. S. Wilks provided procedures for additional tests of hypotheses on means, variances, and covariances. Classification problems were given initial consideration by Pearson, Fisher, and P. C. Mahalanobis through measures of racial likeness, generalized distance, and discriminant functions, with some results similar to the work of Hotelling. Both Hotelling and Maurice Bartlett made initial studies of canonical correlations, intercorrelations between two sets of variates. More recent research by S. N. Roy, P. L. Hsu, Meyer Girshick, D. N. Nanda, and others has dealt with the distributions of certain characteristic roots and vectors as they relate to multivariate problems, notably to canonical correlations and multivariate analysis of variance. Much attention has also been given to the reduction of multivariate data and its interpretation through many papers on factor analysis and principal components. [*For further discussion of the history of these special areas of multivariate analysis and of their present-day applications, see* Counted data; Distributions, statistical, *article on* special continuous distributions; Factor analysis; Multivariate analysis, *articles on* correlation *and* classification and discrimination; Statistics, descriptive, *article on* association; *and the biographies of* Fisher, R. A.; Galton; Girshick; Gosset; Pearson; Wilks; Yule.]

Basic multivariate distributions

Scientific progress is made through the development of more and more precise and realistic representations of natural phenomena. Thus, science, and to an increasing extent social science, uses mathematics and mathematical models for improved understanding, such mathematical models being subject to adoption or rejection on the basis of observation [*see* Models, mathematical]. In particular, stochastic models become necessary as the inherent variability in nature becomes understood.

The multivariate normal distribution provides the stochastic model on which the main theory of multivariate analysis is based. The model has sufficient generality to represent adequately many experimental and observational situations while retaining relative simplicity of mathematical structure. The possibility of applying the model to transforms of observations increases its scope [see STATISTICAL ANALYSIS, SPECIAL PROBLEMS OF, *article on* TRANSFORMATIONS OF DATA]. The large-sample theory of probability and the multivariate central limit theorem add importance to the study of the multivariate normal distribution as it relates to derived distributions. Inquiry and judgment about the use of any model must be the responsibility of the investigator, perhaps in consultation with a statistician. There is still a great deal to be learned about the sensitivity of the multivariate model to departures from that distributional assumption. [*See* ERRORS, *article on* EFFECTS OF ERRORS IN STATISTICAL ASSUMPTIONS.]

The multivariate normal distribution.   Suppose that the characteristics or variates to be measured on each element of a sample from a population, conceptual or real, obey the probability law described through the multivariate normal probability density function. If these variates are p in number and are designated by $X_1, \cdots, X_p$, the multivariate normal density contains p parameters, or population characteristics, $\mu_1, \cdots, \mu_p$, representing, respectively, the means or expected values of the variates, and $\frac{1}{2}p(p+1)$ parameters $\sigma_{ij}, i, j = 1, \cdots, p$, $\sigma_{ji} = \sigma_{ij}$, representing variances and covariances of the variates. Here σ_{ii} is the variance of X_i (corresponding to the variance σ^2 of a variate X in the univariate case) and $\sigma_{ij} = \sigma_{ji}$ is the covariance of X_i and X_j. The correlation coefficient between X_i and X_j is $\rho_{ij} = \sigma_{ij} / \sqrt{\sigma_{ii}\sigma_{jj}}$.

The multivariate normal probability density function provides the probability density for the variates $X_1, \cdots, X_p$ at each point $x_1, \cdots, x_p$ in the sample or observation space. Its specific mathematical form is

$$f(x_1, \cdots, x_p)$$
$$= (2\pi)^{-p/2}|\mathbf{\Sigma}|^{-\frac{1}{2}} \exp\left[-\tfrac{1}{2}(\boldsymbol{x} - \boldsymbol{\mu})'\mathbf{\Sigma}^{-1}(\boldsymbol{x} - \boldsymbol{\mu})\right],$$

$-\infty < x_i < \infty$, $i = 1, \cdots, p$. [*For the explicit form of this density in the bivariate case* ($p = 2$), *see* MULTIVARIATE ANALYSIS, *article on* CORRELATION (1).]

(Vector and matrix notation and an understanding of elementary aspects of matrix algebra are important for any real understanding or application of multivariate analysis. Thus, $\boldsymbol{x}'$ is the vector $(x_1, \cdots, x_p)$, $\boldsymbol{\mu}'$ is the vector $(\mu_1, \cdots, \mu_p)$, and $(\boldsymbol{x} - \boldsymbol{\mu})'$ is the vector $(x_1 - \mu_1, \cdots, x_p - \mu_p)$. Also, $\mathbf{\Sigma}$ is the $p \times p$, symmetric matrix which has elements σ_{ij}, $\mathbf{\Sigma} = [\sigma_{ij}]$, $|\mathbf{\Sigma}|$ is the determinant

of $\mathbf{\Sigma}$ and $\mathbf{\Sigma}^{-1}$ is its inverse. The prime indicates "transpose," and thus $(\boldsymbol{x} - \boldsymbol{\mu})'$ is the transpose of $(\boldsymbol{x} - \boldsymbol{\mu})$, a column vector.)

Comparison of $f(x_1, \cdots, x_p)$ with $f(x)$, the univariate normal probability density function, may assist understanding; for a univariate normal variate X with mean μ and variance σ^2,

$$f(x) = (2\pi)^{-\frac{1}{2}}(\sigma^2)^{-\frac{1}{2}} \exp\left\{-\tfrac{1}{2}(x - \mu)(\sigma^2)^{-1}(x - \mu)\right\}$$
$$= \frac{1}{\sqrt{2\pi}\sigma} e^{-(x-\mu)^2/2\sigma^2},$$

where $-\infty < x < \infty$.

The multivariate normal density may be characterized in various ways. One direct method begins with p independent, univariate normal variables, $U_1, \cdots, U_p$, each with zero mean and unit variance. From the independence assumption, their joint density is the product

$$(2\pi)^{-p/2} \exp\left\{-\tfrac{1}{2}(u_1^2 + \cdots + u_p^2)\right\},$$

a very special case of the multivariate normal probability density function. If variates $X_1, \cdots, X_p$ are linearly related to $U_1, \cdots, U_p$ so that $\mathbf{X} = \boldsymbol{A U} + \boldsymbol{\mu}$, in matrix notation, with $\mathbf{X}$, $\boldsymbol{U}$, and $\boldsymbol{\mu}$ being column vectors and $\boldsymbol{A}$ being a $p \times p$ nonsingular matrix of constants a_{ij}, then

$$X_i = a_{i1}U_1 + \cdots + a_{ip}U_p + \mu_i, \qquad i = 1, \cdots, p.$$

Clearly, the mean of X_i is $E(X_i) = \mu_i$, where μ_i is a known constant and E represents "expectation." The variance of X_i is

$$\mathrm{var}\,(X_i) = \sum_{k=1}^{p} a_{ik}^2 = \sigma_{ii},$$

and the covariance of X_i and X_j, $i \neq j$, is

$$\mathrm{cov}\,(X_i, X_j) = \sum_{k=1}^{p} a_{ik}a_{jk} = \sigma_{ij}.$$

Standard density function manipulations then yield the joint density function of $X_1, \cdots, X_p$ as that already given as the general p-variate normal density. If the matrix $\boldsymbol{A}$ is singular, the results for $E(X_i)$, $\mathrm{var}(X_i)$, and $\mathrm{cov}(X_i, X_j)$ still hold and $X_1, \cdots, X_p$ are said to have a singular multivariate normal distribution; although the joint density function cannot be written, the concept is useful.

A second characterization of the p-variate normal distribution is the following: $X_1, \cdots, X_p$ have a p-variate normal distribution if and only if $\sum_{i=1}^{p} a_i X_i$ is univariate normal for all choices of the coefficients a_i, that is, if and only if all linear combinations of the X_i are univariate normal.

The multivariate normal cumulative distribution function represents the probability of the joint occurrence of the events $X_1 \leqslant x_1, \cdots, X_p \leqslant x_p$ and may be written

$$P(X_1 \leqslant x_1, \cdots, X_p \leqslant x_p) = F(x_1, \cdots, x_p)$$
$$= \int_{-\infty}^{x_1} \cdots \int_{-\infty}^{x_p} f(u_1, \cdots, u_p) du_1 \cdots du_p,$$

indicating that probabilities that observations fall into regions of the p-dimensional variate space may be obtained by integration. Tables of $F(x_1, \cdots, x_p)$ are available for $p = 2, 3$ (see Greenwood & Hartley 1962).

Some basic properties of the p-variate normal distribution in terms of $\mathbf{X} = (X_1, \cdots, X_p)$ are the following.

(a) Any subset of the X_i has a multivariate normal distribution. In fact, any set of q linear combinations of the X_i has a q-variate normal distribution, a result following directly from the linear combination characterization, $q \leqslant p$.

(b) The conditional distribution of q of the X_i, given the $p - q$ others, is q-variate normal.

(c) If $\sigma_{ij} = 0$, $i \neq j$, then X_i and X_j are independent.

(d) The expectation and variance of $\sum_{i=1}^{n} a_i X_i$ are $\sum_{i=1}^{p} a_i \mu_i$ and $\sum_{i=1}^{p} \sum_{j=1}^{p} a_i a_j \sigma_{ij}$.

(e) The covariance of $\sum_{i=1}^{n} a_i X_i$ and $\sum_{i=1}^{n} b_i X_i$ is $\sum_{i=1}^{p} \sum_{j=1}^{p} a_i b_j \sigma_{ij}$.

A cautionary note is that $X_1, \cdots, X_p$ may be separately (marginally) univariate normal while the joint distribution may be very nonnormal.

The geometric properties of the p-dimensional surface defined by $y = f(x_1, \cdots, x_p)$ are interesting. Contours of the surface are p-dimensional ellipsoids. All inflection points of the surface occur at constant y and hence fall on the same horizontal ellipsoidal cross section. Any vertical cross section of the surface leads to a subsurface that is normal or multivariate normal in form and is capable of representation as a normal probability density surface except for a proportionality constant.

Characteristic and moment-generating functions yield additional methods of description of random variables [see DISTRIBUTIONS, STATISTICAL, *article on* SPECIAL CONTINUOUS DISTRIBUTIONS]. For the multivariate normal distribution, the moment-generating function is

$$M(t_1, \cdots, t_p)$$
$$= \int_{-\infty}^{\infty} \cdots \int_{-\infty}^{\infty} \exp(t_1 x_1 + \cdots + t_p x_p) \cdot$$
$$f(x_1, \cdots, x_p) \, dx_1 \cdots dx_p$$
$$= \exp(\mathbf{t'\mu} + \tfrac{1}{2} \mathbf{t' \Sigma \, t}),$$

where $\mathbf{t'} = (t_1, \cdots, t_p)$. The moment-generating function may describe either the nonsingular or

singular p-variate normal distribution. Note that, from its definition, the matrix $\mathbf{\Sigma}$ may be shown to be nonnegative definite. When $\mathbf{\Sigma}$ is positive definite the multivariate density may be specified as $f(x_1, \cdots, x_p)$. When $\mathbf{\Sigma}$ is singular, $\mathbf{\Sigma}^{-1}$ does not exist, and the density may not be given. However, $M(t_1, \cdots, t_p)$ may still be given and can thus describe the singular multivariate normal distribution. To say that $\mathbf{X}$ has a singular distribution is to say that $\mathbf{X}$ lies in some hyperplane of dimension less than p.

The multivariate normal sample. Table 1 illustrates a multivariate sample with $p = 4$ and sample size $N = 10$; the data here are head measurements.

Table 1 — *Measurements taken on first and second adult sons in a sample of ten families*

HEAD LENGTH		HEAD BREADTH	
First son	Second son	First son	Second son
X_1	X_2	X_3	X_4
191	179	155	145
195	201	149	152
181	185	148	149
183	188	153	149
176	171	144	142
208	192	157	152
189	190	150	149
197	189	159	152
188	197	152	159
192	187	150	151

Source: Based on original data by G. P. Frets, presented in Rao 1952, table 7b.2β.

One can anticipate covariance or correlation between head length and head breadth and between head measurements of first and second sons. Hence, for most purposes it will be important to treat the data as a single multivariate sample rather than as several univariate samples.

General notation for a multivariate sample is developed in terms of the variates $X_{1\alpha}, \cdots, X_{p\alpha}$ representing the p observation variates for the αth sample unit (for example, the αth family in the sample), $\alpha = 1, \cdots, N$. In a parallel way $x_{i\alpha}$ may be regarded as the realization of $X_{i\alpha}$ in a particular set of sample data. For multivariate normal procedures, standard data summarization involves calculation of the sample means, $\bar{x}_i = \sum_{\alpha=1}^{N} x_{i\alpha}/N$, $i = 1, \cdots, p$, and the sample variances and covariances,

$$s_{ij} = \sum_{\alpha=1}^{N} (x_{i\alpha} - \bar{x}_i)(x_{j\alpha} - \bar{x}_j)/(N-1)$$
$$= \left[\sum_{\alpha=1}^{N} (x_{i\alpha} x_{j\alpha}) - N\bar{x}_i \bar{x}_j \right]/(N-1),$$
$$i, j = 1, \cdots, p,$$
$$s_{ij} = s_{ji}.$$

Sample correlation coefficients may be computed from $r_{ij} = s_{ij}/\sqrt{s_{ii}s_{jj}}$. For the data of Table 1, the sample values of the statistics are given in Table 2.

Table 2 — Sample statistics for measurements taken on sons

MEANS, $\bar{x}_i$

Variate	1	2	3	4
	190.0	187.9	151.7	150.0

VARIANCES AND COVARIANCES, s_{ij}

Variate j / Variate i	1	2	3	4
1	81.56	42.00	29.56	18.67
2		72.32	11.86	33.11
3			20.01	7.78
4				20.67

CORRELATIONS, r_{ij}

Variate j / Variate i	1	2	3	4
1	1	.55	.73	.46
2		1	.31	.86
3			1	.38
4				1

The required assumptions for the simpler multivariate normal procedures are that the observation vectors $(X_{1\alpha}, \cdots, X_{p\alpha})$ are independent in probability and that each such observation vector consists of p variates following the same multivariate normal law—that is, having the same probability density $f(x_1, \cdots, x_p)$ with the same parameters, elements of μ and Σ. The joint density for the $p \times N$ random variables $X_{i\alpha}$ is, by the independence assumption, just the product of N p-variate normal densities, each having the same μ's and σ's. The joint density may be expressed in terms of μ and Σ and $\bar{x}$ and s, where s is the symmetric $p \times p$ matrix with elements s_{ij} and $\bar{x}' = (\bar{x}_1, \cdots, \bar{x}_p)$.

Elements of S, the matrix of random variables corresponding to s, and of the vector $\bar{X}$ constitute a set of sufficient statistics for the parameters in Σ and μ [see SUFFICIENCY]. Furthermore, it may be shown that S and $\bar{X}$ are independent.

Basic derived distributions. The distribution of the vector of sample means, $\bar{X} = (\bar{X}_1, \cdots, \bar{X}_p)$, is readily described for the random sampling under discussion. That distribution is again p-variate normal with the same mean vector, μ, as in the underlying population but with covariance matrix $N^{-1}\Sigma$.

There is complete analogy here with the univariate case.

The joint probability density function of the sample variances and covariances, S_{ij}, has been named the Wishart distribution after its developer. This density is

$$h(s_{11}, s_{12}, \cdots, s_{pp})$$
$$= \frac{[\frac{1}{2}(N-1)]^{\frac{1}{2}p(N-1)}|s|^{\frac{1}{2}(N-p-2)}\exp[-\frac{1}{2}(N-1)\operatorname{tr}\Sigma^{-1}s]}{\pi^{p(p-1)/4}|\Sigma|^{\frac{1}{2}(N-1)}\prod_{i=1}^{p}\Gamma[\frac{1}{2}(N-i)]},$$

where $-\infty < s_{ij} < \infty$, $i < j$, $0 \leqslant s_{ii} < \infty$, and $i, j = 1, \cdots, p$, and the matrix s is positive definite.

The Wishart density is a generalization of the chi-square density with $N-1$ degrees of freedom for $(N-1)S^2/\sigma^2$ in the univariate case, in which S^2 is the sample variance based on N independent observations from a univariate normal population. Anderson (1958, sec. 14.3) has a note on the noncentral Wishart distribution, a generalization of the noncentral chi-square distribution.

Procedures on means, variances, covariances

Many of the simpler multivariate statistical procedures were developed as extensions of useful univariate methods dealing with tests of hypotheses and related confidence intervals for means, variances, and covariances. Small-sample distributions of important statistics of multivariate analysis have been found; almost invariably the starting point in the derivations is the joint probability density of sample means and sample variances and covariances, the product of a multivariate normal density and a Wishart density, or one of these densities separately.

Inferences on means, dispersion known. If μ^* is a p-element column vector of given constants and if the elements of Σ are known, it was shown long ago, perhaps first by Karl Pearson, that when $\mu^* = \mu$, $Q(\bar{X}) = N(\bar{X} - \mu^*)'\Sigma^{-1}(\bar{X} - \mu^*)$ has the central chi-square distribution with p degrees of freedom [see DISTRIBUTIONS, STATISTICAL, *article on* SPECIAL CONTINUOUS DISTRIBUTIONS]. It was later shown more generally that $Q(\bar{X})$ has the noncentral chi-square distribution with p degrees of freedom and noncentrality parameter $\tau^2 = N(\mu^* - \mu)'\Sigma^{-1}(\mu^* - \mu)$ when $\mu^* \neq \mu$. (The symbol τ^2 is consistent with the notation of Anderson 1958, sec. 5.4.)

A null hypothesis, $H_{01}: \mu = \mu^*$, specifying the means of the multivariate normal density when Σ is known and when the alternative hypothesis is general, $\mu \neq \mu^*$, may be of interest in some experimental situations. With significance level α the critical region of the sample space, the region of rejection of the hypothesis H_{01}, is that region where $Q(\bar{x}) \geq \chi^2_{p;\alpha}$ ($\chi^2_{p;\alpha}$ being the tabular value of a chi-square variate χ^2_p with p degrees of freedom such that $P\{\chi^2_p \geq \chi^2_{p;\alpha}\} = \alpha$) [see HYPOTHESIS TESTING]. The power of this test may be computed when H_{01} is false, that is, when $\mu \neq \mu^*$, by evaluation of the probability, $P\{\chi'^2_p \geq \chi^2_{p;\alpha}\}$, where χ'^2_p is a noncentral chi-square variate with p degrees of freedom and noncentrality τ^2.

When the alternative hypotheses are one-sided, in the sense that each component of μ is taken to be greater than or equal to the corresponding component of μ^*, the problem is more difficult. First steps have been taken toward the solution of this problem (see Kudô 1963; Nüesch 1966).

Since μ is unknown, it is estimated by $\bar{x}$. Corresponding to the test given above, the confidence region with confidence coefficient $1 - \alpha$ for the μ_i consists of all values μ^* for which the inequality $Q(\bar{x}) \leq \chi^2_{p;\alpha}$ holds [see ESTIMATION, article on CONFIDENCE INTERVALS AND REGIONS]. This confidence region is the surface and interior of an ellipsoid centered at the point whose coordinates are the elements of $\bar{x}$ in the p-dimensional parameter space of the elements of μ.

Paired sample problems may also be handled. Let $Y_1, \cdots, Y_{2p}$ be $2p$ variates with means $\xi_1, \cdots, \xi_{2p}$ having a multivariate normal density, and let $y_{j\alpha}$, $j = 1, \cdots, 2p$, $\alpha = 1, \cdots, N$, be independent multivariate observations from this multivariate normal population. Suppose that Y_i and Y_{p+i}, $i = 1, \cdots, p$, are paired variates. Then $X_i = Y_i - Y_{p+i}$, $i = 1, \cdots, p$, make a set of multivariate normal variates with parameters that again may be designated as the elements of μ and Σ, $\mu_i = \xi_i - \xi_{p+i}$. Similarly, take $x_{i\alpha} = y_{i\alpha} - y_{p+i,\alpha}$ and $\bar{x}_i = \bar{y}_i - \bar{y}_{p+i}$. Inferences on the means, μ_i, of the difference variates, X_i, when Σ is known may be made on the same basis as above for the simple sample. In the paired situation it will often be appropriate to take $\mu^* = 0$, that is, $H_{01} : \mu = 0$. Here 0 denotes a vector of 0's. For example, in Table 1 the data can be paired through the association of first and second sons in a family; a pertinent inquiry may relate to the equalities of both mean head lengths and mean head breadths of first and second sons. For association with this paragraph, columns in Table 1 should have variate headings Y_1, Y_3, Y_2, and Y_4, indicating that $p = 2$; then $X_1 = Y_1 - Y_3$ measures difference in head lengths of first and second sons and $X_2 = Y_2 - Y_4$ measures difference in head breadths.

There are also nonpaired versions of these procedures. In a table similar to Table 1 the designations "first son" and "second son" might be replaced by "adult male American Indian" and "adult male

Eskimo." Then the data could be considered to consist of ten bivariate observations taken at random from each of the two indicated populations with no basis for the pairing of the observation vectors. Anthropological study might require comparisons of mean head lengths and mean head breadths for the two racial groups. The procedures of this section may be adapted to this problem. Suppose that $X_1^{(1)}, \cdots, X_p^{(1)}$ and $X_1^{(2)}, \cdots, X_p^{(2)}$ are the p variates for the two populations, the two sets of variates being stochastically independent of each other and having multivariate normal distributions with common dispersion matrix Σ^* but with means $\mu_1^{(1)}, \cdots, \mu_p^{(1)}$ and $\mu_1^{(2)}, \cdots, \mu_p^{(2)}$, respectively. The corresponding sample means are $\bar{x}_1^{(1)}, \cdots, \bar{x}_p^{(1)}$ and $\bar{x}_1^{(2)}, \cdots, \bar{x}_p^{(2)}$ based respectively on samples of independent observations of sizes N_1 and N_2 from the two populations. Definition of $\mu = \mu^{(1)} - \mu^{(2)}$, $\bar{x} = \bar{x}^{(1)} - \bar{x}^{(2)}$, and $N\Sigma^{-1} = [N_1N_2/(N_1 + N_2)]\Sigma^{*-1}$ permits association and use of $Q(\bar{x})$ and its properties for this two-sample problem. If the dispersion matrices of the two populations are known but different, a slight modification of the procedure is readily available.

Jackson and Bradley (1961) have extended these methods to sequential multivariate analysis [see SEQUENTIAL ANALYSIS].

Generalized Student procedures. In the preceding section it was assumed that Σ was known, but in most applications this is not the case. Rather, Σ must be estimated from the data, and the generalized Student statistic or Hotelling's T^2, $T^2(\bar{X},S) = N(\bar{X} - \mu^*)'S^{-1}(\bar{X} - \mu^*)$, comparable to $Q(\bar{X})$, is almost always used. (For procedures that are not based on T^2 see Šidák 1967.) It has been shown that $F(\bar{X},S) = (N - p)T^2(\bar{X},S)/p(N - 1)$ has the variance-ratio or F-distribution with p and $N - p$ degrees of freedom [see DISTRIBUTIONS, STATISTICAL, article on SPECIAL CONTINUOUS DISTRIBUTIONS]. The F-distribution is central when $\mu = \mu^*$, that is, when the mean vector of the multivariate normal population is equal to the constant vector μ^*, and is noncentral otherwise with noncentrality parameter τ^2 already defined.

The hypothesis $H_{01} : \mu = \mu^*$ is of interest, as before. The statistic $F(\bar{X},S)$ takes the role of $Q(\bar{X})$, and $F_{p,N-p;\alpha}$ takes the role of $\chi^2_{p;\alpha}$, where $F_{p,N-p;\alpha}$ is the tabular value of the variance-ratio variate $F_{p,N-p}$ with p and $N - p$ degrees of freedom such that $P\{F_{p,N-p} \geq F_{p,N-p;\alpha}\} = \alpha$. The confidence region for the elements of μ consists of all values μ^* for which the inequality $F(\bar{x},s) \leq F_{p,N-p;\alpha}$ holds; the region is again an ellipsoid centered at $\bar{x}$ in the p-dimensional parameter space, and the confidence coefficient is $1 - \alpha$.

Visualization of the confidence region for the elements of μ is often difficult. When $p = 2$, the ellipsoid becomes a simple ellipse and may be plotted (see Figure 1). When $p > 2$, two-dimensional elliptical cross sections of the ellipsoid may be plotted, and parallel tangent planes to the ellipsoid may be found that yield crude bounds on the various parameters. One or more linear contrasts among the elements of μ may be of special interest, and then the dimensionality of the whole problem, including the confidence region, is reduced. Some of the problems of multiple comparisons arise when linear contrasts are used [see LINEAR HYPOTHESES, *article on* MULTIPLE COMPARISONS].

For the simple one-sample problem, $s = [s_{ij}]$ is computed as shown in Table 2. For the paired sample problem, s in $F(\bar{x}, s)$ is the sample variance–covariance matrix computed from the derived multivariate sample of differences, and $\bar{x}$ is the sample vector of mean differences, as before. For the unpaired two-sample problem, it is necessary to replace Ns^{-1} in $F(\bar{x}, s)$, just as it was necessary to replace $N\Sigma^{-1}$ when Σ was known. Each population has the dispersion matrix Σ^{*}, and two sample dispersion matrices $s^{*}_{(1)}$ and $s^{*}_{(2)}$ may be computed, one for each multivariate sample, to estimate Σ^{*}. A "pooled" estimate of the dispersion matrix Σ^{*} is $s^{*} = [(N_{1} - 1)s^{*}_{(1)} + (N_{2} - 1)s^{*}_{(2)}]/(N_{1} + N_{2} - 2)$, the multivariate generalization of the pooled estimate of variance often used in univariate statistics. For the two-sample problem, Ns^{-1} in $F(\bar{x}, s)$ is replaced by $[N_{1}N_{2}/(N_{1} + N_{2})]s^{*-1}$. All of the assumptions about the populations and about the samples discussed in the preceding section apply for the corresponding generalized Student procedures.

An application of the generalized Student procedures for paired samples may be made for the data in Table 1. The bivariate $(p = 2)$ sample of paired differences (in Table 1, column 1 minus column 2, column 3 minus column 4) is exhibited in Table 3. The sample mean differences and sam-

Table 3 — Difference data on head measurements, first adult son minus second adult son

HEAD-LENGTH DIFFERENCE $X_1(d)$	HEAD-BREADTH DIFFERENCE $X_2(d)$
12	10
−6	−3
−4	−1
−5	4
5	2
16	5
−1	1
8	7
−9	−7
5	−1

Table 4 — Sample statistics for measurement differences on sons

MEANS, $\bar{x}_i(d)$

Variate	1	2
	2.1	1.7

VARIANCES AND COVARIANCES, $s_{ij}(d)$

Variate j \ Variate i	1	2
1	69.88	32.14
2		25.12

ELEMENTS OF $s^{-1}(d)$, $s^{ij}(d)$

Variate j \ Variate i	1	2
1	.0348	−.0445
2		.0967

ple variances and covariance of the difference data are given in Table 4, along with the elements s^{ij} of s^{-1}. The column headings and statistics in Table 3 and Table 4 have the arguments d simply to distinguish them from the symbols in tables 1 and 2. For a comparison of first and second sons, it may be appropriate to take $\mu^{*} = 0$ and compute

$$T^{2}(\bar{x}, s) = 10(2.1, 1.7)\begin{pmatrix} .0348 & -.0445 \\ -.0445 & .0967 \end{pmatrix}\begin{pmatrix} 2.1 \\ 1.7 \end{pmatrix}$$

$$= (21, 17)\begin{pmatrix} -.00257 \\ .07094 \end{pmatrix}$$

$$= 1.152.$$

$$F(\bar{x}, s) = 8(1.152)/2(9) = .512.$$

If a significance level $\alpha = .10$ is chosen, then $F_{2, 8; .10} = 3.11$ and the differences between paired means are not statistically significant; indeed, they are less than ordinary variation would lead one to expect. (For some sets of data this sort of result should lead to re-examination of possible biases or nonindependence in the data-collection process.)

To find those values μ^{*} in the confidence region for μ, μ^{*} must be replaced in $T^{2}(\bar{x}, s)$; thus,

$$T^{2}(\bar{x}, s)$$
$$= 10(2.1 - \mu^{*}_{1}, 1.7 - \mu^{*}_{2})\begin{pmatrix} .0348 & -.0445 \\ -.0445 & .0967 \end{pmatrix}\begin{pmatrix} 2.1 - \mu^{*}_{1} \\ 1.7 - \mu^{*}_{2} \end{pmatrix}$$
$$= .348(\mu^{*}_{1} - 2.1)^{2} - .890(\mu^{*}_{1} - 2.1)(\mu^{*}_{2} - 1.7)$$
$$+ .967(\mu^{*}_{2} - 1.7)^{2}.$$

The corresponding $F(\bar{x}, s) = \frac{4}{9}T^{2}(\bar{x}, s)$. The confidence region on μ_{1} and μ_{2} with confidence coefficient $1 - \alpha$ consists of those points in the (μ_{1}, μ_{2})-space inside or on the ellipse described by

$$.155(\mu^{*}_{1} - 2.1)^{2} - .396(\mu^{*}_{1} - 2.1)(\mu^{*}_{2} - 1.7)$$
$$+ 4.30(\mu^{*}_{2} - 1.7)^{2} = F_{2, 8; \alpha}.$$

This ellipse is plotted in Figure 1 for $\alpha = .05, .10, .25$, $F_{2,8;\alpha} = 4.46, 3.11, 1.66$, for clearer insight into the nature of the region.

A number of variants of the generalized Student procedure have been developed, and other variants are bound to be developed in the future. For example, one may wish to test null hypotheses specifying relationships between the coordinates of μ (see Anderson 1958, sec. 5.3.5). Again, one may wish to test that certain coordinates of μ have given values, knowing the values of the other coordinates. For another sort of variant, recall that it was assumed for the two-sample application that the dispersion matrices for the two parent populations were identical. If this assumption is untenable, then a multivariate analogue of the Behrens–Fisher problem must be considered (Anderson 1958, sec. 5.6). Sequential extensions of the generalized Student procedures have been given by Jackson and Bradley (1961).

Generalized variances. Tests of hypotheses and confidence intervals on variances are conducted easily in univariate cases through the use of the chi-square and variance-ratio distributions. The situation is much more difficult in multivariate analysis.

For the multivariate one-sample problem, hypotheses and confidence regions for elements of the dispersion matrix, Σ, may be considered. A first possible hypothesis is $H_{02}: \Sigma = \Sigma^*$, a null hypothesis specifying all of the elements of Σ. (This hypothesis is of limited interest per se, except when $\Sigma^* = I$ or as an introduction to procedures on multivariate linear hypotheses.) It is clear that a test statistic should depend on the elements S_{ij} of S; it is not clear what function of these elements might be appropriate.

The statistic $|S|$ has been called the generalized sample variance, and $|\Sigma|$ has been called the generalized variance. The test statistic $|S|/|\Sigma^*|$ was proposed by Wilks, who examined its distribution; simple, exact, small-sample distributions are known only when $p = 1,2$. An asymptotic or limiting distribution is available for large N; the statistic $\sqrt{N-1}\,[(|S|/|\Sigma|) - 1]/\sqrt{2p}$ has the limiting univariate normal density with zero mean and unit variance. It is clear that when $\Sigma = \Sigma^*$ under H_{02}, S estimates Σ^*, and the ratio $|S|/|\Sigma^*|$ should be near unity; it is not clear that the ratio may not be near unity when $S \neq \Sigma^*$. However, values of $|S|$ that differ substantially from $|\Sigma^*|$ should lead to rejection of H_{02} (see Anderson 1958, sec. 7.5).

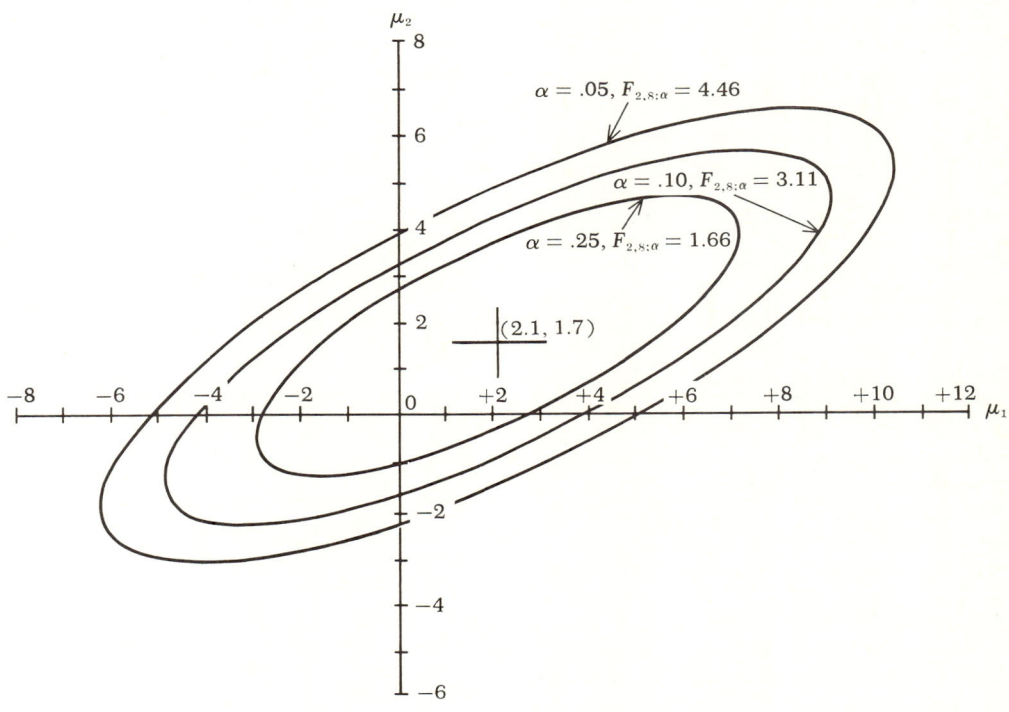

Figure 1 — Elliptical confidence regions on μ_1, μ_2:

$$.155(\mu_1 - 2.1)^2 - .396(\mu_1 - 2.1)(\mu_2 - 1.7) + .430(\mu_2 - 1.7)^2 = F_{2,8;\,\alpha}$$

Wilks's use of generalized variances is only one possible generalization of univariate procedures. Other comparisons of $\mathbf{S}$ and $\mathbf{\Sigma}^*$ are possible. In nondegenerate cases, $\mathbf{\Sigma}^*$ is nonsingular, and the product matrix $\mathbf{S\Sigma}^{*-1}$ should be approximately an identity matrix. All of the characteristic roots from the determinantal equation $|\mathbf{S\Sigma}^{*-1} - \lambda\mathbf{I}| = 0$, where $\mathbf{I}$ is the $p \times p$ identity matrix, should be near unity; the trace, $\mathrm{tr}\,\mathbf{S\Sigma}^{*-1}$, should be near p. Roy (1957, sec. 14.9) places major emphasis on the largest and smallest roots of $\mathbf{S}$ and $\mathbf{\Sigma}$ and gives approximate confidence bounds on the roots of the latter in terms of those of the former. A test of H_{02} may be devised with the hypothesis being rejected when the corresponding roots of $\mathbf{\Sigma}^*$ fail to fall within the confidence bounds. These and other similar considerations have led to extensive study of the distributions of roots of determinantal equations. Complete and exact solutions to these multivariate problems are not available.

Suppose that two independent multivariate normal populations have dispersion matrices $\mathbf{\Sigma}_{(1)}$ and $\mathbf{\Sigma}_{(2)}$, and samples of independent observation vectors of sizes N_1 and N_2 yield, respectively, sample dispersion matrices $\mathbf{S}_{(1)}$ and $\mathbf{S}_{(2)}$. The hypothesis of interest is $H_{03}: \mathbf{\Sigma}_{(1)} = \mathbf{\Sigma}_{(2)}$. In the univariate case ($p = 1$), the statistic $F = |\mathbf{S}_{(1)}|/|\mathbf{S}_{(2)}| = S_{11}^{(1)}/S_{11}^{(2)}$ is the simple variance ratio and, under H_{03}, has the F-distribution with $N_1 - 1$ and $N_2 - 1$ degrees of freedom. The general likelihood ratio criterion for testing H_{03} is, with minor adjustment,

$$\lambda = |\mathbf{S}_{(1)}|^{\frac{1}{2}(N_1-1)}|\mathbf{S}_{(2)}|^{\frac{1}{2}(N_2-1)}/|\mathbf{S}|^{\frac{1}{2}(N_1+N_2-2)},$$

where

$$\mathbf{S} = \frac{(N_1-1)\mathbf{S}_{(1)} + (N_2-1)\mathbf{S}_{(2)}}{N_1+N_2-2}.$$

If $p = 1$, then λ is a monotone function of F. By asymptotic theory for large N_1 and N_2, $-2\log_e \lambda$ may be taken to have the central chi-square distribution with $\frac{1}{2}p(p+1)$ degrees of freedom under H_{03}. Anderson (1958, secs. 10.2, 10.4–10.6) discusses these problems further.

Roy (1957, sec. 14.10) prefers again to consider characteristic roots and develops test procedures and confidence procedures based on the largest and smallest roots of $\mathbf{S}_{(1)}\mathbf{S}_{(2)}^{-1}$. Heck (1960) has provided some charts of upper percentage points of the distribution of the largest characteristic root.

Multivariate analysis of variance. Multivariate analysis of variance bears the same relationship to the problems of generalized variances as does univariate analysis of variance to simple variances. An understanding of the basic principles of the analysis of variance is necessary to consider the multivariate generalization. The theory of general linear

hypotheses is pertinent, and concepts of experimental design carry over to the multivariate case. [See EXPERIMENTAL DESIGN, *article on* THE DESIGN OF EXPERIMENTS; LINEAR HYPOTHESES, *article on* ANALYSIS OF VARIANCE.]

Consider the univariate randomized block design with v treatments and b blocks. A response, $X_{\gamma\delta}$, on treatment γ in block δ, $\gamma = 1, \cdots, v$, $\delta = 1, \cdots, b$, is expressed in the fixed-effects model (Model I) as the linear function $X_{\gamma\delta} = \mu + \tau_\gamma + \beta_\delta + \epsilon_{\gamma\delta}$, where μ is the over-all mean level of response, τ_γ is the modifying effect of treatment γ ($\sum_{\gamma=1}^{v}\tau_\gamma = 0$), β_δ is the special influence of block δ ($\sum_{\delta=1}^{b}\beta_\delta = 0$), and $\epsilon_{\gamma\delta}$ is a random error such that the set of vb errors are independent univariate normal variates with zero means and equal variances, σ^2. The multivariate generalization of this model replaces the scalar variate $X_{\gamma\delta}$ with a p-variate column vector $\mathbf{X}_{\gamma\delta}$ with elements $X_{\gamma\delta i}$, $i = 1, \cdots, p$, consisting of responses on each of p variates for treatment γ in block δ. Similarly, the scalars μ, τ_γ, β_δ, and $\epsilon_{\gamma\delta}$ are replaced by p-element column vectors, and the vectors $\mathbf{\epsilon}_{\gamma\delta}$ constitute a set of vb independent multivariate normal vector variates with zero means and common dispersion matrices, $\mathbf{\Sigma}$.

In univariate analysis of variance, treatment and error mean squares are calculated. If these are S_τ^2 and S_ω^2, their forms are

$$S_\tau^2 = b\sum_{\gamma=1}^{v}(\bar{X}_\gamma. - \bar{X}..)^2/(v-1)$$

and

$$S_\omega^2 = \sum_{\gamma=1}^{v}\sum_{\delta=1}^{b}(X_{\gamma\delta} - \bar{X}_\gamma. - \bar{X}._\delta + \bar{X}..)^2/(v-1)(b-1),$$

where $\bar{X}_\gamma. = \sum_{\delta=1}^{b}X_{\gamma\delta}/b$, $\bar{X}._\delta = \sum_{\gamma=1}^{v}X_{\gamma\delta}/v$, and $\bar{X}.. = \sum_{\gamma=1}^{v}\sum_{\delta=1}^{b}X_{\gamma\delta}/vb$. The test of treatment equality is the test of the hypothesis $H_{04}: \tau_1 = \cdots = \tau_v (= 0)$; the statistic used is $F = S_\tau^2/S_\omega^2$, distributed as F with $v-1$ and $(v-1)(b-1)$ degrees of freedom under H_{04} with large values of F statistically significant. When H_{04} is true, both S_τ^2 and S_ω^2 provide unbiased estimates of σ^2 and are independent in probability, whereas when H_{04} is false, S_ω^2 still gives an unbiased estimate of σ^2, but S_τ^2 tends to be larger.

The multivariate generalization of analysis of variance involves comparison of $p \times p$ dispersion matrices $\mathbf{S}_\tau$ and $\mathbf{S}_\omega$, the elements of which correspond to S_τ^2 and S_ω^2:

$$S_{\tau ij} = \frac{b\sum_{\gamma=1}^{v}(\bar{X}_{\gamma.i} - \bar{X}..._i)(\bar{X}_{\gamma.j} - \bar{X}..._j)}{(v-1)},$$

$$S_{\omega ij} = \frac{\sum_{\gamma=1}^{v}\sum_{\delta=1}^{b}(X_{\gamma\delta i} - \bar{X}_{\gamma.i} - \bar{X}._{\delta i} + \bar{X}..._i)(X_{\gamma\delta j} - \bar{X}_{\gamma.j} - \bar{X}._{\delta j} + \bar{X}..._j)}{(v-1)(b-1)},$$

for $i, j = 1, \cdots, p$. It can be shown that $\mathbf{S}_\tau$ and $\mathbf{S}_\omega$ have independent Wishart distributions with $v-1$

and $(v-1)(b-1)$ degrees of freedom and identical dispersion matrices, Σ, under H_{04}. Thus, the multivariate analysis-of-variance problem is reduced again to the problem of comparing two dispersion matrices, $\mathbf{S}_\tau$ and $\mathbf{S}_\omega$, like $\mathbf{S}_{(1)}$ and $\mathbf{S}_{(2)}$ of the preceding section. This is the general situation in multivariate analysis of variance, even though this illustration is for a particular experimental design.

Wilks (1932a; 1935) recommended use of the statistic $|\mathbf{S}_\omega|/|\mathbf{S}_\omega + \mathbf{S}_\tau|$, Roy (1953) considered the largest root of $\mathbf{S}_\tau \mathbf{S}_\omega^{-1}$, and Lawley (1938) suggested $\mathrm{tr}\,(\mathbf{S}_\tau \mathbf{S}_\omega^{-1})$. These statistics correspond roughly to criteria on the product of characteristic roots, the largest root, and the sum of the roots, respectively. They lead to equivalent tests in the univariate case (where only one root exists), but the tests are not equivalent in the multivariate case.

Pillai (1964; 1965) has tables and references on the distribution of the largest root. A paper by Smith, Gnanadesikan, and Hughes (1962) is recommended as an elementary expository summary with a realistic example.

Other procedures. Other, more specialized statistical procedures have been developed for means, variances, and covariances for multivariate normal populations, particularly tests of special hypotheses.

Many models based on the univariate normal distribution may be regarded as special cases of multivariate normal models. In particular, it is often assumed that observations are independent in probability and have homogeneous variances, σ^2. A test of such assumptions may sometimes be made if the sample is regarded as N observation vectors from a p-variate multivariate normal population with special dispersion matrix under a null hypothesis H_{05}: $\Sigma = \sigma^2 \mathbf{I}$, where $\mathbf{I}$ is the $p \times p$ identity matrix and σ^2 is the unknown common variance. This test and a generalization of it are discussed by Anderson (1958, sec. 10.7). See also Wilks (1962, problem 18.21).

Wilks (1946; 1962, problem 18.22) developed a series of tests on means, variances, and covariances for multivariate normal populations. He considered three hypotheses,

$$H_{06}: \mu_i = \mu, \quad \sigma_{ii} = \sigma^2, \quad \sigma_{ij} = \rho\sigma^2,$$
$$i \neq j, \quad i, j = 1, \cdots, p;$$
$$H_{07}: \sigma_{ii} = \sigma^2, \quad \sigma_{ij} = \rho\sigma^2,$$
$$i \neq j, \quad i, j = 1, \cdots, p;$$
$$H_{08}: \mu_i = \mu, \quad \text{given that } \sigma_{ii} = \sigma^2, \quad \sigma_{ij} = \rho\sigma^2,$$
$$i \neq j, \quad i, j = 1, \cdots, p.$$

H_{06} implies equality of means, equality of variances, and equality of covariances; H_{07} makes no assumption about the means but implies equality of variances and equality of covariances; H_{08} is a hy-

pothesis about equality of means given the special dispersion matrix, Σ, specified through equality of its diagonal elements and equality of its nondiagonal elements. In these hypotheses ρ is the intraclass correlation, which has been considered in various contexts by other authors [see MULTIVARIATE ANALYSIS, *article on* CORRELATION (1)]. Wilks showed that the test of H_{08} leads to the usual, univariate, analysis-of-variance test for treatments in a two-way classification. For H_{06} and H_{07}, likelihood ratio tests were devised and moments of the test statistics were obtained with exact distributions in special cases and asymptotic ones otherwise.

Other topics of multivariate analysis

This general discussion of multivariate analysis would not be complete without mention of basic concepts of other major topics discussed elsewhere in this encyclopedia.

Discriminant functions. Classification problems are encountered in many contexts [see MULTIVARIATE ANALYSIS, *article on* CLASSIFICATION AND DISCRIMINATION]. Several populations are known to exist, and information on their characteristics is available, perhaps from samples of individuals or items identified with the populations. A particular individual or item of unknown population is to be classified into one of the several populations on the basis of its particular characteristics. This and related problems were considered by early workers in the field and more recently in the context of statistical decision theory, which seems particularly appropriate for this subject [see DECISION THEORY].

Correlation. The simple product-moment correlation coefficient between variates X_i and X_j was defined above as ρ_{ij}, with similarly defined sample correlation, r_{ij} [see MULTIVARIATE ANALYSIS, *articles on* CORRELATION]. In the bivariate case ($p = 2$) the exact small sample distributions of r_{12} based on the bivariate normal model were developed by Fisher and Hotelling. The multiple correlation between X_1, say, and the set $X_2, \cdots, X_p$ may be defined as the maximum simple correlation between X_1 and a linear function $\beta_2 X_2 + \cdots + \beta_p X_p$, maximized through choice of $\beta_2, \cdots, \beta_p$.

Partial correlations have been developed as correlations in conditional distributions.

Canonical correlations extend the notion of multiple correlation to two groups of variates. If the variate vector, $\mathbf{X}$, is subdivided so that

$$\mathbf{X} = \begin{bmatrix} \mathbf{X}_{(s)} \\ \mathbf{X}_{(t)} \end{bmatrix},$$

$\mathbf{X}_{(s)}$ being the column vector with elements $X_1, \cdots, X_s$ and $\mathbf{X}_{(t)}$ being the column vector with elements $X_{s+1}, \cdots, X_p$ ($p = s + t$), the largest canonical correlation is the maximum simple correlation between two linear functions, $Y_{(s)} = \sum_{\alpha=1}^{s} \beta_\alpha X_\alpha$ and $Y_{(t)} = \sum_{\alpha=s+1}^{p} \beta_\alpha X_\alpha$. The second largest canonical correlation is the maximum simple correlation between two new linear functions, $Y'_{(s)}$ and $Y'_{(t)}$, similar to $Y_{(s)}$ and $Y_{(t)}$ but uncorrelated with $Y_{(s)}$ and $Y_{(t)}$, and so on. Distribution theory and related problems are given by Anderson (1958, chapter 12) and Wilks (1962, sec. 18.9).

The theory of rank correlation is well developed in the bivariate case [see NONPARAMETRIC STATISTICS, *article on* RANKING METHODS]. Tetrachoric and biserial correlation coefficients have been considered for special situations.

Principal components. The problem of principal components and factor analysis is a problem in the reduction of the number of variates and in their interpretation [see FACTOR ANALYSIS]. The method of principal components considers uncorrelated linear functions of the p original variates with a view to expressing major characteristic variation in terms of a reduced set of new variates. Hotelling has been responsible for much of the development of principal components, and the somewhat parallel treatments of factor analysis have been developed more by psychometricians than by statisticians. References for principal components are Anderson (1958, chapter 11), Wilks (1962, sec. 18.6), and Kendall ([1957] 1961, chapter 2). Kendall ([1957] 1961, chapter 3) gives an expository account of factor analysis.

Counted data. The multinomial distribution plays an important role in analysis when multivariate data consist of counts of the number of individuals or items in a sample that have specified categorical characteristics. The multivariate analysis of counted data follows consideration of contingency tables and relationships between the probability parameters of the multinomial distribution. Much has been done on tests of independence in such tables, and recently investigators have developed more systematically analogues of standard multivariate techniques for contingency tables [see COUNTED DATA].

Nonparametric statistics. There has been a paucity of multivariate techniques in nonparametric statistics. Except for work on rank correlation, only a few isolated multivariate methods have been developed—for example, bivariate sign tests. The difficulty appears to be that adequate models for multivariate nonparametric methods must contain measures of association (or of nonindependence) that sharply limit the application of the permutation techniques of nonparametric statistics [see NONPARAMETRIC STATISTICS].

Missing values. Only limited results are available in multivariate analysis when some observations are missing from observation vectors. Wilks (1932b), in considering the bivariate normal distribution with missing observations, provided several methods of parameter estimation and compared them. Maximum likelihood estimation was somewhat complicated, but two *ad hoc* methods proved simpler and yielded exact forms of sampling distributions. Basically, one may obtain estimates of means and variances through weighted averages of means and variances of the available data and estimate correlations from the available data on pairs of variates. If only a few observations are missing, usual analyses should not be much affected; if many observations are missing, little advice may be given except to suggest the use of maximum likelihood techniques and computers for the special situation. It is clearly inappropriate to treat missing observations as zero observations—as has sometimes been done.

Some useful references are Anderson (1957), Buck (1960), Nicholson (1957), and Matthai (1951).

Other multivariate results. In a general discussion of multivariate analysis, it is not possible to consider all areas where multivariate data may arise or all theoretical results of probability and statistics that may be pertinent to multivariate analysis. Many of the theorems of probability admit of multivariate extensions; results in stochastic processes, the theory of games, decision theory, and so on, may have important, although perhaps not implemented, multivariate generalizations.

RALPH A. BRADLEY

BIBLIOGRAPHY

Multivariate analysis is complex in theory, in application, and in interpretation. Basic works should be consulted, and examples of applications in various subject areas should be examined critically. The theory of multivariate analysis is well presented in Anderson 1958; *its excellent bibliography and reference notations by section make it a good guide to works in the field. Among books on mathematical statistics, other major works are* Rao 1952; Kendall & Stuart (1946) 1961; Roy 1957; Wilks 1946; 1962. Greenwood & Hartley 1962 *gives references to tables.* T. W. Anderson *is completing a bibliography of multivariate analysis. Books more related to the social sciences are* Cooley & Lohnes 1962; Talbot & Mulhall 1962. *Papers that are largely expository and bibliographical are* Tukey 1949; Bartlett 1947; Wishart 1955; Feraud 1942; *and* Smith, Gnanadesikan, & Hughes 1962. *Some applications in the social sciences are given in* Tyler 1952; Rao & Slater 1949; Tintner 1946; Kendall 1957.

ANDERSON, T. W. 1957 Maximum Likelihood Estimates for a Multivariate Normal Distribution When Some Observations Are Missing. *Journal of the American Statistical Association* 52:200–203.

ANDERSON, T. W.   1958   *An Introduction to Multivariate Statistical Analysis.* New York: Wiley.

BARTLETT, M. S.   1947   Multivariate Analysis. *Journal of the Royal Statistical Society* Series B 9 (Supplement): 176–190. → A discussion of Bartlett's paper appears on pages 190–197.

BUCK, S. F.   1960   A Method of Estimation of Missing Values in Multivariate Data Suitable for Use With an Electronic Computer. *Journal of the Royal Statistical Society* Series B 22:302–306.

COOLEY, WILLIAM W.; and LOHNES, PAUL R.   1962   *Multivariate Procedures for the Behavioral Sciences.* New York: Wiley.

FERAUD, L.   1942   Problème d'analyse statistique à plusieurs variables. Lyon, Université de, *Annales* 3d Series, Section A 5:41–53.

GREENWOOD, J. ARTHUR; and HARTLEY, H. O.   1962   *Guide to Tables in Mathematical Statistics.* Princeton Univ. Press. → A sequel to the guides to mathematical tables produced by and for the Committee on Mathematical Tables and Aids to Computation of the National Academy of Sciences–National Research Council of the United States.

HECK, D. L.   1960   Charts of Some Upper Percentage Points of the Distribution of the Largest Characteristic Root. *Annals of Mathematical Statistics* 31:625–642.

JACKSON, J. EDWARD; and BRADLEY, RALPH A.   1961   Sequential χ^2- and T^2-tests. *Annals of Mathematical Statistics* 32:1063–1077.

KENDALL, M. G.   (1957) 1961   *A Course in Multivariate Analysis.* London: Griffin.

KENDALL, M. G.; and STUART, ALAN   (1946) 1961   *The Advanced Theory of Statistics.* Rev. ed. Volume 2: Inference and Relationship. New York: Hafner; London: Griffin. → The first edition was written by Kendall alone.

KUDÔ, AKIO   1963   A Multivariate Analogue of the One-sided Test. *Biometrika* 50:403–418.

LAWLEY, D. N.   1938   Generalization of Fisher's z Test. *Biometrika* 30:180–187.

MATTHAI, ABRAHAM   1951   Estimation of Parameters From Incomplete Data With Application to Design of Sample Surveys. *Sankhyā* 11:145–152.

MORRISON, DONALD F.   1967   *Multivariate Statistical Methods.* New York: McGraw-Hill. → Written for investigators in the life and behavioral sciences.

NICHOLSON, GEORGE E. JR.   1957   Estimation of Parameters From Incomplete Multivariate Samples. *Journal of the American Statistical Association* 52:523–526.

NÜESCH, PETER E.   1966   On the Problem of Testing Location in Multivariate Populations for Restricted Alternatives. *Annals of Mathematical Statistics* 37:113–119.

PILLAI, K. C. SREEDHARAN   1964   On the Distribution of the Largest of Seven Roots of a Matrix in Multivariate Analysis. *Biometrika* 51:270–275.

PILLAI, K. C. SREEDHARAN   1965   On the Distribution of the Largest Characteristic Root of a Matrix in Multivariate Analysis. *Biometrika* 52:405–414.

RAO, C. RADHAKRISHNA   1952   *Advanced Statistical Methods in Biometric Research.* New York: Wiley.

RAO, C. RADHAKRISHNA; and SLATER, PATRICK   1949   Multivariate Analysis Applied to Differences Between Neurotic Groups. *British Journal of Psychology* Statistical Section 2:17–29. → See also "Correspondence," page 124.

ROY, S. N.   1953   On a Heuristic Method of Test Construction and Its Use in Multivariate Analysis. *Annals of Mathematical Statistics* 24:220–238.

ROY, S. N.   1957   *Some Aspects of Multivariate Analysis.* New York: Wiley.

ŠIDÁK, ZBYNĚK   1967   Rectangular Confidence Regions for the Means of Multivariate Normal Distributions. *Journal of the American Statistical Association* 62:626–633.

SMITH, H.; GNANADESIKAN, R.; and HUGHES, J. B.   1962   Multivariate Analysis of Variance (MANOVA). *Biometrics* 18:22–41.

TALBOT, P. AMAURY; and MULHALL, H.   1962   *The Physical Anthropology of Southern Nigeria: A Biometric Study in Statistical Method.* Cambridge Univ. Press.

TINTNER, GERHARD   1946   Some Applications of Multivariate Analysis to Economic Data. *Journal of the American Statistical Association* 41:472–500.

TUKEY, JOHN W.   1949   Dyadic ANOVA: An Analysis of Variance for Vectors. *Human Biology* 21:65–110.

TYLER, FRED T.   1952   Some Examples of Multivariate Analysis in Educational and Psychological Research. *Psychometrika* 17:289–296.

WILKS, S. S.   1932a   Certain Generalizations in the Analysis of Variance. *Biometrika* 24:471–494.

WILKS, S. S.   1932b   Moments and Distributions of Estimates of Population Parameters From Fragmentary Samples. *Annals of Mathematical Statistics* 3:163–195.

WILKS, S. S.   1935   On the Independence of k Sets of Normally Distributed Statistical Variables. *Econometrica* 3:309–326.

WILKS, S. S.   1946   Sample Criteria for Testing Equality of Means, Equality of Variances, and Equality of Covariances in a Normal Multivariate Distribution. *Annals of Mathematical Statistics* 17:257–281.

WILKS, S. S.   1962   *Mathematical Statistics.* New York: Wiley. → An earlier version of some of this material was issued in 1943.

WISHART, JOHN   1955   Multivariate Analysis. *Applied Statistics* 4:103–116.

II

CORRELATION (1)

CORRELATION (1) *is a general overview of the topic;* CORRELATION (2) *goes into more detail about certain aspects.*

The term "correlation" has been used in a variety of contexts to indicate the degree of interrelation between two or more entities. One reads, for example, of the correlation between intelligence and wealth, between illiteracy and prejudice, and so on. When used in this sense the term is not sufficiently operational for scientific work. One must instead speak of correlation between numerical measures of entities—in short, of correlation between variables.

If statistical inference is to be used, the variables must be random variables, and for them a probability model must be specified. For two random variables, X and Y, this model will describe the probabilities (or probability densities) with which

(X, Y) takes values (x, y); that is, it will describe probabilities in the (X, Y)-population. One of the characteristics of this population is the correlation coefficient; the available information concerning it is usually in the form of a random sample, $(X_1, Y_1), \cdots, (X_n, Y_n)$. Thus, correlation theory is concerned with the use of samples to estimate, test hypotheses, or carry out other procedures concerning population correlations.

Surprisingly enough, confusion occasionally sets in, even at this early stage. There are deplorable examples in the literature in which the authors of a study are concerned with whether a certain sample coefficient of correlation can be computed instead of with whether it will be useful to compute it in the light of the research goal and of some special model.

The so-called Pearson product-moment correlation coefficient—usually denoted by ρ in the population and r in the sample, and usually termed just the correlation coefficient—is the one most frequently encountered, and the purpose of this article is to survey the situations in which it is employed. Other sorts of correlation include rank correlation, serial correlation, and intraclass correlation. [*For a discussion of rank correlation, see* NONPARAMETRIC STATISTICS, *article on* RANKING METHODS; *for serial correlation, see* TIME SERIES. *Intraclass correlation will be touched on briefly at the end of this article.*]

First, simple correlation between X and Y will be considered, then multiple correlation between a single variable, X_0, and a set of variables, $(X_1, \cdots, X_p)$, and finally canonical correlation between two sets, $(Y_1, \cdots, Y_k)$ and $(X_1, \cdots, X_p)$. Partial correlation will be discussed in connection with multiple correlation. The case of two variables is a sufficient setting in which to discuss relationships with regression theory and to point out common errors made in applying correlation methods.

The two most important models for correlation theory are the linear regression model, discussed below (see also Binder 1959), and the joint normal model. The joint normal model plays a central role in the theory for several reasons. First, the conditions for its approximate validity are frequently met. Second, it is mathematically tractable. Finally, of those joint probability laws for which ρ is actually a measure of independence, the joint normal model is perhaps the simplest to deal with. For any two random variables, X and Y, it follows from the definition of ρ that if the variables are independent, they are uncorrelated; hence, to conclude that the hypothesis of zero correlation is false is to assert dependence for X and Y. In the other direction, if X, Y follow a bivariate normal law and

are uncorrelated, then X and Y are independent, but this conclusion does not hold in general—the assumption of normality (or some other, similar restriction) is essential; it is even possible that X and Y are uncorrelated and also perfectly related by a (nonlinear) function. If the probability law for X, Y is only approximately bivariate normal, conventional normal theory can still be applied; in fact, considerable departure from normality may be tolerated (Gayen 1951). For large samples, r itself is in any case approximately normal with mean ρ and with a standard deviation that can be derived if enough is known about the joint probability distribution of X, Y.

Many misconceptions prevail about the interpretation of correlation. These stem in part from the fact that early work in the field reflected confusion about the distinction between sample estimators and their population counterparts. For some time workers were also under the impression that high correlation implies the existence of a cause-and-effect relation when in fact neither correlation, regression, nor any other purely statistical procedure would validate such a relation.

Historically, research in the theory of correlation may be divided into four phases. In the latter part of the nineteenth century Galton and others realized the value of correlation in their work but could deal with it only in a vague, descriptive way [*see* GALTON]. About the turn of the century Karl Pearson, Edgeworth, and Yule developed some real theory and systematized the use of correlation [*see* EDGEWORTH; PEARSON; YULE]. From about 1915 to 1928, R. A. Fisher placed the theory of correlation on a more or less rigorous footing by deriving exact probability laws and methods of estimation and testing [*see* FISHER, R. A.]. Finally, in the 1930s first Hotelling and then Wilks, M. G. Kendall, and others, spurred on by psychologists, particularly Spearman and Thurstone, developed principal component analysis (closely related to factor analysis) and canonical correlation. [*For a discussion of principal component analysis, see* FACTOR ANALYSIS; *for a discussion of canonical correlation, see* MULTIVARIATE ANALYSIS, *article on* CORRELATION (2), *and the section "Canonical correlation" below. See also the biographies of* SPEARMAN *and* THURSTONE.] Along with the mathematical development there occurred an increasing realization among social scientists of the value of mathematics in their work. This produced better communication between them and statistical theorists and also led them to discard the older, and often incorrect, treatments of correlation on which they had relied.

Correlation theory is now recognized as an important tool in experimentation, especially in those situations involving many variables. Its main value is in suggesting lines along which further research can be directed in a search for possible cause-and-effect relations in complex situations [see CAUSATION].

In every field of application there are books describing correlation methods and, just as important, acquainting the reader with the types of data he will handle. Some examples are the works of McNemar (1949) in psychology, Croxton, Cowden, and Klein (1939) in economics and sociology, and Johnson (1949) in education. Mathematical treatments on several levels are also available. An excellent elementary work is the book by Wallis and Roberts (1956), which requires very little knowledge of mathematics, yet presents statistical concepts carefully and fully. Those equipped with more mathematics should find the books of Anderson and Bancroft (1952) and Yule and Kendall (1958), at an intermediate level, and Kendall and Stuart (1958–1966), at an advanced level, quite useful.

needed, one should note the important relation $\sigma^2_{cx+dY} = c^2\sigma^2_X + 2cd\rho_{XY}\sigma_X\sigma_Y + d^2\sigma^2_Y$, and in particular that variances are additive in the presence of zero correlation.

The usual estimator for ρ_{XY}, based on a random sample, $(X_1, Y_1), \cdots, (X_n, Y_n)$, is

$$r_{XY} = \frac{\sum(X_i - \bar{X})(Y_i - \bar{Y})}{[\sum(X_i - \bar{X})^2]^{\frac{1}{2}}[\sum(Y_i - \bar{Y})^2]^{\frac{1}{2}}} = \frac{s_{XY}}{s_X s_Y},$$

where $\bar{X}, \bar{Y}$ are the sample means and s_X, s_Y, s_{XY} are the sample standard deviations and covariance. Regardless of the specific model adopted, r_{XY} can be used to estimate ρ_{XY} and will have some desirable properties: r_{XY} lies between -1 and $+1$ and has approximately ρ_{XY} for its population mean; r_{XY} is a consistent estimator of ρ_{XY}, that is, if the sample size is increased indefinitely, $Pr(|r_{XY} - \rho_{XY}| < \epsilon)$ approaches 1, no matter how small a positive constant ϵ is chosen.

Normal model. If the joint probability law is bivariate normal, that is, probability is interpreted as volume under the surface

$$f(x, y) = \frac{1}{2\pi\sigma_X\sigma_Y(1 - \rho^2_{XY})^{\frac{1}{2}}} \exp\left\{ - \frac{1}{2(1 - \rho^2_{XY})}\left[\left(\frac{x - \mu_x}{\sigma_x}\right)^2 - 2\rho_{XY}\left(\frac{x - \mu_x}{\sigma_x}\right)\left(\frac{y - \mu_Y}{\sigma_Y}\right) + \left(\frac{y - \mu_Y}{\sigma_Y}\right)^2\right]\right\},$$

In the mathematical study of correlations between several variables the natural language is that of classical matrix theory; some knowledge of matrices, linear transformations, quadratic forms, and determinantal equations is required. This expository presentation, however, will not require background in these topics.

Simple correlation

For two jointly distributed random variables, X and Y, denote their population standard deviations by σ_X and σ_Y and their population covariance by σ_{XY}. The correlation coefficient is then defined as $\rho_{XY} = \sigma_{XY}/\sigma_X\sigma_Y$. (Both standard deviations are positive, except for the uninteresting case in which one or both variables are constant. Then the correlation coefficient is undefined.) As Feller has remarked, this definition would lead a physicist to regard ρ_{XY} as "dimensionless covariance."

Elementary properties of ρ_{XY} are that it lies between -1 and $+1$, that it is unchanged if constants are added to X and Y or if X and Y are multiplied by nonzero constants of the same sign (if the signs are different, the sign of ρ_{XY} will be changed), and that it takes one of its extreme values only if a perfect linear relation, $Y = a + bX$, exists (-1 for $b < 0$, $+1$ for $b > 0$). Also, since the variance of a linear combination is frequently

then $f(x, y)$ factors into an expression in x times an expression in y (the condition defining independence of X, Y) if and only if $\rho_{XY} = 0$.

Under normality, r_{XY} is the maximum likelihood estimator of ρ_{XY}. Further, the probability law of r_{XY} has been derived (Fisher 1915) and tabulated (David 1938). The statistic $(n - 2)^{\frac{1}{2}}r_{XY}/(1 - r^2_{XY})^{\frac{1}{2}}$ can be referred to the t-table with $n - 2$ degrees of freedom to test the hypothesis $H: \rho_{XY} = 0$. In addition, charts (David 1938), which have been reproduced in many books, are available for the determination of confidence intervals. The variable $z = \tanh^{-1}r_{XY}$ is known (Fisher 1925, pp. 197 ff.) to have an approximate normal law with mean $\tanh^{-1}\rho_{XY}$ and standard deviation $1/\sqrt{n - 3}$, even for n as small as 10; thus, the z-transformation is especially useful, for example, in testing whether two (X, Y)-populations have the same correlation. Also, it has the advantage of stabilizing variances —that is, the approximate variance of z depends on n but not on ρ_{XY}. The quantity r_{XY} itself, though approximately normal with mean ρ_{XY} and standard deviation $(1 - \rho^2_{XY})/\sqrt{n}$ for very large n, will still be far from normal for moderate n when ρ_{XY} is not near zero.

Even in the bivariate normal case currently under discussion, r_{XY} does not have population mean exactly ρ_{XY}, but the slight discrepancy can be greatly reduced (Olkin & Pratt 1958) by using $r_{XY}[1 + (1 - r_{XY}^2)/2(n - 3)]$ instead as an estimator for ρ_{XY}.

Biserial and point-biserial correlations. If one variable, say Y, is dichotomized at some unknown point ω, then the data from the (X, Y)-population appear in the form of a sample from an (X, Z)-population, with Z one or zero according as $Y \geqslant \omega$ or $Y < \omega$. If ρ_{XY} and ω are of interest, they can be estimated by r_b (biserial r) and ω_b, or by maximum likelihood estimators $\hat{\rho}_{XY}$ and $\hat{\omega}$ (Tate 1955a; 1955b). The latter estimators are jointly normal for large n, and tables of standard deviations are available (Prince & Tate 1966). If ρ_{XZ} is desired, it can be estimated by r_{XZ}, usually called point-biserial r. If, however, the assumption of underlying bivariate normality is correct, then $\rho_{XZ} \leqslant \sqrt{2/\pi}\, \rho_{XY}$, so r_{XZ} would be a bad estimator of ρ_{XY}. If one thinks in terms of models rather than data, there is no need for confusion on this point. Tate (1955b) gives an expository discussion of both models.

Tetrachoric correlation. If in the bivariate normal case both X and Y are observable only in dichotomized form, the sample values can be arranged in a 2×2 table, and one can calculate r_t, the so-called tetrachoric r. Unfortunately, the tetrachoric model is not amenable to the same type of simple mathematical treatment as is the biserial model. On this point the reader should consult Kendall and Stuart (1958–1966).

Relation of correlation to regression. The notion of regression is appropriate in a situation in which one needs to predict Y, or to estimate the conditional population mean of Y, for given X [see LINEAR HYPOTHESES, *article on* REGRESSION]. The discussion given here will be sufficiently general to bring out the meanings of the correlation coefficient and the correlation ratio in regression analysis and to indicate connections between them. The reader should keep two facts in mind: (1) predictions are described by regression relations, whereas their accuracy is measured by correlation, and (2) assumptions of bivariate normality are not required in order to introduce the notion of regression and to carry its development quite far.

A prediction of Y, $\phi(X)$, is judged "best" (in the sense of least squares), quite apart from assumptions of normality, if it makes the expected mean-square error, $E(Y - \phi(X))^2$, a minimum. It turns out that for best prediction, $\phi(X)$ must be $\mu_{Y|X}$, the mean of the conditional probability law (also often referred to as the regression function) for Y given X, but that if only straight lines are allowed as candidates, the "best" such gives the prediction $A + BX$, with $A = \mu_Y - \mu_X(\rho_{XY}\sigma_Y/\sigma_X)$,

$B = \rho_{XY}\sigma_Y/\sigma_X$. The basic quantities of interest, $\mu_{Y|X}$ and $A + BX$, lead to the following decomposition of $Y - \mu_Y$:

$$Y - \mu_Y = (Y - \mu_{Y|X}) + (A + BX - \mu_Y)$$
$$+ (\mu_{Y|X} - A - BX).$$

It can be shown that the right-hand terms are uncorrelated and that, therefore, by squaring and taking expected values they satisfy the basic relation

$$\sigma_Y^2 = E(Y - \mu_{Y|X})^2 + E(A + BX - \mu_Y)^2$$
$$+ E(\mu_{Y|X} - A - BX)^2.$$

These terms may be conveniently interpreted as portions of the variation of Y: the first is the variation "unexplained" by X, and the sum of the second and third is the variation explained by the "best" prediction, the second term being the amount explained by the "best" linear prediction. The quantity

$$\eta_{YX}^2 = [\sigma_Y^2 - E(Y - \mu_{Y|X})^2]/\sigma_Y^2,$$

the squared correlation ratio for Y on X, is the proportion of variation in Y "explained" by X (that is, by regression). Since it can be shown that $E(A + BX - \mu_Y)^2 = \rho_{XY}^2 \sigma_Y^2$, the basic relation may be rewritten as

$$\sigma_Y^2 = E(Y - \mu_{Y|X})^2 + \rho_{XY}^2 \sigma_Y^2 + (\eta_{YX}^2 - \rho_{XY}^2)\sigma_Y^2.$$

If the regression is linear, then $\mu_{Y|X} = A + BX$, the third term drops out of the decomposition of $Y - \mu_Y$, and η_{YX}^2, the proportion of "explained" variation, coincides with ρ_{XY}^2. If in addition $\sigma_{Y|X}^2$, the variance of the conditional law for Y given X, is constant, then this variance coincides with $E(Y - \mu_{Y|X})^2$, and

$$\rho_{XY}^2 = (\sigma_Y^2 - \sigma_{Y|X}^2)/\sigma_Y^2.$$

When X, Y follow a bivariate normal law, both conditions are met, and hence this last relation is satisfied. In any event one can see from the basic relation, and conditions of nonnegativity for mean squares, that $0 \leqslant \rho_{XY}^2 \leqslant \eta_{YX}^2 \leqslant 1$, with $\rho_{XY}^2 = \eta_{YX}^2$ if and only if the regression is linear; when that linearity of regression holds, both quantities equal zero if and only if the regression is actually constant, and both quantities equal one if and only if the point (X, Y) must always lie on a straight line. It should be noted that in general $\eta_{YX}^2 \neq \eta_{XY}^2$, whereas ρ_{XY} is symmetric: $\rho_{XY} = \rho_{YX}$. Traditional terms, now rarely used, are "coefficient of determination" for ρ_{XY}^2, "coefficient of nondetermination" for $1 - \rho_{XY}^2$, and "coefficient of alienation" for $(1 - \rho_{XY}^2)^{\frac{1}{2}}$.

The use of data to predict Y from X, by fitting a sample regression curve, evidently involves two types of error, the error in estimating the true regression curve by a sample curve and the inherent sampling variability of Y (which cannot be reduced by statistical analysis) about the true regression curve. (The reader may consult Kruskal 1958 for a concise summary of the above material, together with further interpretive remarks, and Tate 1966 for an extension of these ideas to the case of three or more variables and the consequent consideration of generalized variances.)

It cannot be too strongly emphasized that the correlation coefficient is a measure of the degree of *linear relationship*. It is frequently the case that for variables Y and X, the regression of Y on X is linear, or at least approximately linear, for those values of X which are of interest or are likely to be encountered. For a given set of data one can test the hypothesis of linearity of regression (see Dixon & Massey [1951] 1957, secs. 11–15). If it is accepted, then the degree of relationship may be measured by a correlation coefficient. If not, then one can in any event measure the degree of relationship by a correlation ratio. In some cases it may be desirable to give two measures (that is, to give estimates of both ρ_{XY}^2 and $\eta_{YX}^2 - \rho_{XY}^2$), one for the degree of linear relationship and one for the degree of additional nonlinear relationship. In the case of nonlinear relationship, however, $\mu_{Y|x}$ cannot be estimated satisfactorily for any specific value $X = x$ unless either a whole array of Y observations is available for that x or some specific nonlinear functional form is assumed for $\mu_{Y|x}$. In view of the advantages of using normal theory, it is best whenever possible to make the regression approximately linear by a suitable change of variable and to check the procedure by testing for approximate normality and linearity of regression. [See STATISTICAL ANALYSIS, SPECIAL PROBLEMS OF, *article on* TRANSFORMATIONS OF DATA.]

When X, Y follow a bivariate normal law, one has not only linear regression for Y on X but also normality for the conditional law of Y given X and for the marginal law of X. If the conditions of the bivariate normal model are relaxed in order to allow X to have some type of law other than normal, while the remaining properties just mentioned are present, some interesting results can be obtained. It is known, for example (Tate 1966), that for large n, r_{XY} is approximately normal with mean ρ_{XY} and standard deviation $(1 - \rho_{XY}^2)(1 + \frac{1}{4}\gamma\rho_{XY}^2)^{\frac{1}{2}}/\sqrt{n}$, with γ denoting the coefficient of excess (kurtosis minus 3) for the X-population. (For a general treatment of aspects of this case, see Gayen 1951.)

It is an important fact that there is value in r_{XY} even if there exists no population counterpart for

it. This arises in the following way: Let x be a fixed variable subject to selection by the experimenter, and let Y have a normal law with mean $A + Bx$ and standard deviation $\sigma_{Y|x}$. This is called the linear regression model. The usual mathematical theory developed for this model requires that $\sigma_{Y|x}$ actually not depend on x, although slight deviations from constancy are not serious. If a definite dependence on x exists, it can sometimes be removed by an appropriate transformation of Y [*see* STATISTICAL ANALYSIS, SPECIAL PROBLEMS OF, *article on* TRANSFORMATIONS OF DATA]. Note that the nonrandom character of x here is stressed by use of a lower-case letter.

The quantities A and B may be estimated, as before, by least squares, and the strength of the resulting relationship may be measured by r_{xY}. Distribution theory for r_{xY} is, of course, not the same as in the bivariate normal case, since r_{xY} is only formally the same as r_{XY}. In other words, it is important to take into consideration in any given case whether (X, Y) actually has a bivariate distribution or whether $X = x$ behaves as a parameter, an index for possible Y distributions.

Errors in correlation methods. Three common errors in correlation methods have already been mentioned: focusing attention on the data and ignoring the model, concluding that the presence of correlation implies causation, and assuming that no relation between variables is present if correlation is lacking. The literature contains many confused articles resulting from the first type of error and also many illustrations, some humorous, of what could occur if the second type of error were committed—for example, in connection with the high correlation between the number of children and the number of storks' nests in towns of northwestern Europe (Wallis & Roberts 1956, p. 79). The source of the correlation presumably is some factor such as economic status or size of house. As an artificial but mildly surprising example of the third type of error one should consider the fact that for a standard normal variable X, Y and X are uncorrelated if $Y = X^2$.

A different type of error arises when one tries to control some unwanted condition or source of variation by introducing additional variables. If $U = X/Z$ and $V = Y/Z$, then it is entirely possible that ρ_{UV} will differ greatly from ρ_{XY}. For example, ρ_{XY} may be zero but ρ_{UV} very different from zero. The difficulty is clear in this example, but similar difficulties can enter data analysis in insidious ways. Using percentages instead of initial observations can also produce gross misunderstanding. As a very simple example consider $U = X/(X + Y)$

and $V = Y/(X + Y)$ and the fact that $\rho_{UV} = -1$ even if X and Y are independent. Of course, if additional variables, say Z and W, are involved, the magnitude of the correlation between $X/(X + Y + Z + W)$ and $Y/(X + Y + Z + W)$ will not be so great. The adjective usually applied to this type of correlation is "spurious," though "artificially induced" would be better. A spurious correlation can in certain circumstances be useful; for instance, the idea of so-called part–whole correlation (see McNemar [1949] 1962, chapter 10) deserves consideration in certain situations. If, for example, a test score T is made up of scores on separate questions or subtests, say $T_1 + T_2 + \cdots + T_m$, a high correlation r_{TT_i} could not be ascribed wholly to spuriousness. It is altogether possible that T_i would serve as well as T for the purpose at hand.

Multiple and partial correlation

If more than two variables are observed for each individual, say $X_0, X_1, \cdots, X_p$, there are more possibilities to be considered for correlation relationships: simple correlations, ρ_{ij} ($i, j = 0, 1, \cdots, p$, $i \neq j$), multiple correlations between any variable and a set of the others, and partial correlations between any two variables with all or some of the others held fixed. (In this section capital letters for random variables will be omitted in subscripts; only the numerical indexes will be used.)

Multiple correlation.   The multiple correlation between X_0 and the set $(X_1, \cdots, X_p)$, denoted by $R_{0 \cdot 12 \ldots p}$, is defined to be the largest simple correlation obtainable between X_0 and $a_1 X_1 + \cdots + a_p X_p$, where the coefficients, a_i, are allowed to vary. It possesses the following properties: $R_{0 \cdot 12 \ldots p}$ is non-negative and is at least as large as the absolute value of any simple correlation; if additional variables, $X_{p+1}, X_{p+2}, \cdots$, are included, the multiple correlation cannot decrease. It thus follows that if $R_{0 \cdot 12 \ldots p} = 0$, all ρ_{0j} are zero. Also, if $R_{0 \cdot 12 \ldots p} = 1$, then a perfect linear relationship, $X_0 = a_0 + a_1 X_1 + \cdots + a_p X_p$, exists for some $a_0, a_1, \cdots, a_p$. The usual estimator of $R_{0 \cdot 12 \ldots p}$, based on a random sample of vector observations on $(X_0, X_1, \cdots, X_p)$, is the sample correlation $r_{0 \cdot 12 \ldots p}$ between X_0 and its least squares prediction based on $X_1, \cdots, X_p$. Under the joint normal model, $H: R_{0 \cdot 12 \ldots p} = 0$ can be tested by referring $[(n - p - 1)/p] r^2_{0 \cdot 12 \ldots p} / (1 - r^2_{0 \cdot 12 \ldots p})$ to an F-table with p and $n - p - 1$ degrees of freedom (Fisher 1928). Also, $r_{0 \cdot 12 \ldots p}$, like r_{XY}, is approximately normal for large n with mean $R_{0 \cdot 12 \ldots p}$ and standard deviation $(1 - R^2_{0 \cdot 12 \ldots p})/\sqrt{n}$, provided $R_{0 \cdot 12 \ldots p} \neq 0$; if $R_{0 \cdot 12 \ldots p} = 0$, then $nr^2_{0 \cdot 12 \ldots p}$ has approximately a chi-square law with p degrees

of freedom. Fisher's z-transformation applies as before—except when $R_{0 \cdot 12 \ldots p}$ is zero (Hotelling 1953). Note that $R_{0 \cdot 12 \ldots p}$ and $r_{0 \cdot 12 \ldots p}$ do not reduce to simple correlations if $p = 1$. Instead, one finds that $R_{0 \cdot 1} = |\rho_{01}|$ and $r_{0 \cdot 1} = |r_{01}|$.

Regression relationships, in which X_0 is predicted by $X_1, \cdots, X_p$, are analogous to those for simple correlation; for example, when regression is linear and conditional variances are constant, $R^2_{0 \cdot 12 \ldots p}$ is the portion of σ^2_0 which is "explained" by regression, namely $1 - (\sigma^2_{0 \cdot 12 \ldots p}/\sigma^2_0)$, with $\sigma^2_{0 \cdot 12 \ldots p}$ denoting the expected mean-square difference between X_0 and its best prediction based on $X_1, X_2, \cdots, X_p$: $\mu_{0 \cdot 12 \ldots p} = B_0 + B_1 X_1 + \cdots + B_p X_p$. Calculations are more difficult but follow the same principles. The coefficients, $B_1, B_2, \cdots, B_p$, are traditionally known as partial regression coefficients but are now usually termed just regression coefficients, as in the bivariate case. Each coefficient gives the change in $\mu_{0 \cdot 12 \ldots p}$ per unit change in the variable associated with that coefficient. It is clear that the relative importance of the contributions of the separate independent variables $(X_1, X_2, \cdots, X_p)$ cannot be measured by relative sizes of the coefficients, since the independent variables need not be measured in the same units. In chapters 12 and 13 of their book Yule and Kendall (1958) give many examples, along with interpretation and practical advice.

Statements made above in reference to simple correlation of biserial data carry over to multiple correlation (Hannan & Tate 1965), and the same tables (Prince & Tate 1966) are applicable.

Partial correlation.   The coefficient of partial correlation, $\rho_{01 \cdot 2}$, is, roughly speaking, what ρ_{01} would be if the linear effect of X_2 were removed. One can measure "X_0 with the linear effect of X_2 removed" and "X_1 with the linear effect of X_2 removed" by subtracting "best" linear predictions, $A_0 + A_2 X_2$ and $A'_0 + A'_2 X_2$, and obtaining the residuals, $X_0 - A_0 - A_2 X_2$ and $X_1 - A'_0 - A'_2 X_2$. Then $\rho_{01 \cdot 2}$ is defined to be the simple correlation between these two residuals. In the same way, the effect of more than one additional variable can be removed, and one may consider $\rho_{01 \cdot 23 \ldots p}$. Partials between any two other variables, with any of the remaining $p - 1$ "held fixed," are similarly defined by rearrangement of subscripts. For the case of three variables $\rho_{01 \cdot 2}$ can be expressed in terms of simple correlations as

$$\rho_{01 \cdot 2} = \frac{\rho_{01} - \rho_{02} \rho_{12}}{[(1 - \rho^2_{02})(1 - \rho^2_{12})]^{\frac{1}{2}}}.$$

Alternatively, if the joint probability law is normal, $\rho_{01 \cdot 2}$ can be defined as the simple correlation between X_0 and X_1, calculated from the conditional law for X_0 and X_1 given X_2, but this is not true in general. Also, since $\rho_{01 \cdot 2}$ is the ordinary correlation between the residuals defined above, $\rho_{01 \cdot 2}^2$ may be characterized in terms of the unexplained variance in one residual after linear prediction from the other, namely $1 - (\sigma_{0 \cdot 12}^2 / \sigma_{0 \cdot 2}^2)$.

To see an important relation between multiple and partial correlation, think of the variables $X_1, X_2, \cdots, X_p$ as being introduced one at a time and producing increases in multiple correlation with X_0. Then

$$R_{0 \cdot 12 \cdots p}^2 = 1 - (1 - \rho_{01}^2)(1 - \rho_{02 \cdot 1}^2) \cdots (1 - \rho_{0p \cdot 12 \cdots p-1}^2).$$

From this it follows that

$$1 - R_{0 \cdot 12 \cdots p}^2 = (1 - R_{0 \cdot 12 \cdots p-1}^2)(1 - \rho_{0p \cdot 12 \cdots p-1}^2),$$

which yields a recursion relation that allows for the correction of a multiple correlation when a variable is added or subtracted. Elaborate and useful computational schemes are available for adding and subtracting variables in correlation analysis. One viewpoint (see Ezekiel and Fox [1930] 1959, appendix 2) is that one should generally start with the largest feasible number of independent variables and then subtract one at a time those that are negligibly useful in predicting X_0. Other approaches begin with the best single predictor among $X_1, X_2, \cdots, X_p$ and then add others one at a time until further additions make no substantial improvement.

Many expressions and statements analogous to the above relationships can of course be obtained by rearrangement of subscripts, including those which employ only some of the $p + 1$ variables. Since all parameters involved in this discussion are actually only simple correlations between appropriate pairs of random variables, one can construct estimators by calculating the corresponding sample simple correlations. Thus, for example, $r_{01 \cdot 2}$ is calculable from the observation pairs, $(X_{0i} - \hat{A}_0 - \hat{A}_2 X_{2i}, X_{1i} - \hat{A}_0' - \hat{A}_2' X_{2i})$, of sample residuals.

Finally, it has been shown (Fisher 1928) that if the multivariate normal model is assumed, many results for $r_{01 \cdot 23 \cdots p}$ can be obtained from those for r_{01} by replacing $n - 2$ by $n - p - 1$. For example, $(n - p - 1)^{\frac{1}{2}} r_{01 \cdot 23 \cdots p} / (1 - r_{01 \cdot 23 \cdots p}^2)^{\frac{1}{2}}$ can be referred to the t-table with $n - p - 1$ degrees of freedom as a test of $H: \rho_{01 \cdot 23 \cdots p} = 0$.

An example.   As an example of the applications of multiple and partial correlation, consider an experiment in which X_0 represents grade point average, X_1 represents IQ, X_2 represents hours of study

per week, and the relationship is sought between X_0 and X_1, with X_2 held fixed (Keeping 1962, p. 363). Results based on a sample of 450 school children showed that $r_{0 \cdot 12} = 0.82$, $r_{01} = 0.60$, $r_{02} = 0.32$, $r_{12} = -0.35$, and $r_{01 \cdot 2} = 0.80$. The positive correlation between X_0 and X_1, together with the negative correlation between X_1 and X_2 (a more intelligent student need not study so long), obscured somewhat the strength of the relationship between X_0 and X_1. It should perhaps be mentioned that from the relation $1 - r_{0 \cdot 12}^2 = (1 - r_{02}^2)(1 - r_{01 \cdot 2}^2)$ it is clear that $r_{0 \cdot 12} \geqslant r_{01 \cdot 2}$, with equality if and only if $r_{02} = 0$. It is true in general, for parameters or sample estimators, that a multiple correlation between a given variable and others is at least as large in magnitude as any simple or partial correlation between that variable and any of the others.

Reduction of the number of variables

Yule and Kendall (1958, chapter 13) offer practical advice of an elementary nature in relation to economy in the number of variables to be considered. In this connection one thing is more or less certain: if the number of variables is, say, greater than ten, an attempt to analyze the interrelations between variables by using their whole correlation matrix offers too many possibilities for the mind to encompass, or for methods to isolate, and is therefore probably a waste of time.

There are less elementary techniques for dealing with problems involving large sets of variables, which have been treated in depth and are worthy of wide application. These include canonical correlation, principal components, and factor analysis.

Canonical correlation.   There are cases in which an experimenter wishes to study the interrelations between two sets of variables, $(Y_1, \cdots, Y_k)$ and $(X_1, \cdots, X_p)$. The purpose of canonical correlation theory (Hotelling 1936) is to replace these sets by new (and smaller) sets, at the same time preserving the correlation structure as much as possible. The method is as follows: Linear combinations, one from each set of variables, are so constructed as to have maximum simple correlation with each other. These linear combinations, denoted by U_1 and V_1, are called the first pair of canonical variables; their correlation, ρ_1, is the first canonical correlation. The process is continued by the construction of further pairs of linear combinations, with the provision that each new canonical variable be uncorrelated with all previous ones. If $k \leqslant p$, the process will terminate with $U_1, U_2, \cdots, U_k, V_1, V_2, \cdots, V_k$ and canonical correlations $\rho_1, \rho_2, \cdots, \rho_k$. If $k = 1$, the resulting single canonical correlation is the multiple correlation for Y_1 on $X_1, X_2, \cdots, X_p$. Since $\rho_1 \geqslant \rho_2 \geqslant \cdots \geqslant \rho_k \geqslant 0$ and since many canonical correlations may be small, it is clear that the canonical pairs worth preserving may be few.

The usual model specifies a joint normal law in $p + k$ variables, and estimation of canonical correlations can be carried out with a sample by a scheme which parallels that for the construction of $\rho_1, \cdots, \rho_k$. The joint probability law for sample canonical correlations is known both in exact form and in approximate form for large n.

Before canonical correlations are estimated, it may be wise to carry out an initial test for possible complete lack of correlation between the two sets of variables. The hypothesis that $\rho_1 = \rho_2 = \cdots = \rho_k = 0$, or, equivalently, that all correlations between an X_i and a Y_j are zero, may be tested essentially by a procedure of Wilks (see Tate 1966). The hypothesis being tested can be rewritten as $1 - (1 - \rho_1^2)(1 - \rho_2^2) \cdots (1 - \rho_k^2) = 0$, a form analogous to that of other, related tests. There are various tests available for this hypothesis; one should try to choose the one with highest power against the alternative hypotheses of interest. (See Anderson 1958, sec. 14.2; Hotelling 1936.)

Principal components and factor analysis. One of the central problems arising in the application of correlations is that of holding the variables considered down to a manageable number. This was mentioned above in connection with canonical correlation and is also the guiding principle underlying principal components analysis [*for a discussion of principal components, see* Hotelling 1933 *and* FACTOR ANALYSIS, *article on* STATISTICAL ASPECTS]. There one deals with a single set of variables, forming linear compounds that are uncorrelated with one another and arranged in order of decreasing variance. The basis of principal components analysis is the assumption that the more interesting observable quantities are those with larger variation. Factor analysis, which is of vast importance in psychological testing, utilizes a similar idea, except that the number of linear compounds to be considered is prescribed by the model. Connections between these two methods are discussed in a monograph by Kendall (1957).

Other methods of correlation

Intraclass correlation. In the discussion of sampling from an (X, Y)-population and the consequent use of the sample to estimate ρ_{XY}, there has been no question as to the separate identification of the X and Y for each observation. Thus, one can think of ρ_{XY} as a measure of the interrelation between two classes, an X-class and a Y-class, and hence the term *interclass correlation* may be used. As an example of a situation in which the identification of X and Y is not clear, consider measuring the correlation between the weights of identical twins at, say, age five. Here there is in effect only one class, that of pairs of weights of twins. Any establishment of two classes—for example, by considering X the weight of the taller twin and Y the weight of the shorter twin—would be wholly arbitrary and not helpful. The population of weight pairs has a correlation coefficient, and this gives the *intraclass correlation*, the correlation coefficient between the two weights of a pair in random order. The method for handling this situation works as well with data involving triplets (one is still, however, interested in correlation for weights in the same family) or any number of children. Consider n observations (families) on k-tuples, with $k \geqslant 2$. The method consists essentially in the averaging of products of deviations over all possible $k(k-1)$ pairs of children. If X_{ij} represents the weight of the jth child in the ith family, then the intraclass correlation, r, is given by $nk(k-1)s^2r = nk^2s_m^2 - nks^2$, with $s^2 = \sum\sum(X_{ij} - \bar{X})^2/nk$, the within-families sample variance, and $s_m^2 = \sum(\bar{X}_i - \bar{X})^2/n$, the between-families sample variance. Thus,

$$r = \frac{k(s_m^2/s^2) - 1}{k - 1}.$$

It is clear that $r \geqslant -1/(k-1)$ and that for a single family $(n = 1)$, $r = -1/(k-1)$. Intraclass correlation is closely related to components of variance models in the analysis of variance [*see* LINEAR HYPOTHESES, *article on* ANALYSIS OF VARIANCE].

Attenuation. Observations on random variables are frequently subject to measurement errors or, at any rate, are observable only in combination with other random variables, so that in attempting to observe U, V one must instead accept $X = U + E$, $Y = V + F$. Previous methods lead to information about ρ_{XY}, when what is relevant is information about ρ_{UV}. If E and F are assumed to be uncorrelated with U, V, and each other, then the relation between ρ_{UV} and ρ_{XY} is given by

$$\rho_{XY} = \frac{\text{cov}(U + E, V + F)}{\{(\sigma_U^2 + \sigma_E^2)(\sigma_V^2 + \sigma_F^2)\}^{\frac{1}{2}}}$$

$$= \frac{\rho_{UV}}{\{(1 + \sigma_E^2/\sigma_U^2)(1 + \sigma_F^2/\sigma_V^2)\}^{\frac{1}{2}}},$$

which shows that $\rho_{XY} \leqslant \rho_{UV}$, with equality occurring only in the trivial case in which E, F are both constant. The coefficient ρ_{UV} is said to be attenuated by the effect of E and F. Correction for attenuation consists in applying to the above relation known or assumed information relative to ρ_{XY}, (σ_E/σ_U), (σ_F/σ_V) in order to estimate ρ_{UV}. (For further discussion, see McNemar 1949.)

R. F. TATE

BIBLIOGRAPHY

ANDERSON, RICHARD L.; and BANCROFT, T. A. 1952 *Statistical Theory in Research.* New York: McGraw-Hill.

ANDERSON, T. W. 1958 *An Introduction to Multivariate Statistical Analysis.* New York: Wiley.

BINDER, ARNOLD 1959 Considerations of the Place of Assumptions in Correlational Analysis. *American Psychologist* 14:504–510.

CROXTON, F. E.; COWDEN, D. J.; and KLEIN, S. (1939) 1967 *Applied General Statistics.* 3d ed. Englewood Cliffs, N.J.: Prentice-Hall. → Klein became a co-author with the third edition.

DAVID, F. N. 1938 *Tables of the Ordinates and Probability Integral of the Distribution of the Correlation Coefficient in Small Samples.* London: University College, Biometrika Office.

DIXON, WILFRID J.; and MASSEY, FRANK J. JR. (1951) 1957 *Introduction to Statistical Analysis.* 2d ed. New York: McGraw-Hill.

EZEKIEL, MORDECAI; and FOX, KARL A. (1930) 1959 *Methods of Correlation and Regression Analysis: Linear and Curvilinear.* 3d ed. New York: Wiley.

FISHER, R. A. 1915 Frequency Distribution of the Values of the Correlation Coefficient in Samples From an Indefinitely Large Population. *Biometrika* 10:507–521.

FISHER, R. A. (1925) 1958 *Statistical Methods for Research Workers.* 13th ed. New York: Hafner. → Previous editions were published by Oliver & Boyd.

FISHER, R. A. 1928 On a Distribution Yielding the Error Functions of Several Well Known Statistics. Volume 2, pages 805–813 in International Congress of Mathematicians (New Series), Second, Toronto, 1924, *Proceedings.* Univ. of Toronto Press.

GAYEN, A. K. 1951 The Frequency Distribution of the Product-moment Correlation Coefficient in Random Samples of Any Size Drawn From Non-normal Universes. *Biometrika* 38:219–247.

HANNAN, J. F.; and TATE, R. F. 1965 Estimation of the Parameters for a Multivariate Normal Distribution When One Variable Is Dichotomized. *Biometrika* 52:664–668.

HOTELLING, HAROLD 1933 Analysis of a Complex of Statistical Variables Into Principal Components. *Journal of Educational Psychology* 24:417–441, 498–520.

HOTELLING, HAROLD 1936 Relations Between Two Sets of Variates. *Biometrika* 28:321–377.

HOTELLING, HAROLD 1953 New Light on the Correlation Coefficient and Its Transforms. *Journal of the Royal Statistical Society* Series B 15:193–225.

JOHNSON, PALMER O. 1949 *Statistical Methods in Research.* New York: Prentice-Hall.

KEEPING, E. S. 1962 *Introduction to Statistical Inference.* Princeton, N.J.: Van Nostrand.

KENDALL, M. G. (1957) 1961 *A Course in Multivariate Analysis.* London: Griffin.

KENDALL, M. G.; and STUART, ALAN 1958–1966 *The Advanced Theory of Statistics.* New ed. 3 vols. New York: Hafner; London: Griffin. → Volume 1: *Distribution Theory,* 1958. Volume 2: *Inference and Relationship,* 1961. Volume 3: *Design and Analysis, and Time Series,* 1966. The first edition, published in 1943–1946, was written by Kendall alone.

KRUSKAL, WILLIAM H. 1958 Ordinal Measures of Association. *Journal of the American Statistical Association* 53:814–861.

McNEMAR, QUINN (1949) 1962 *Psychological Statistics.* 3d ed. New York: Wiley.

OLKIN, INGRAM; and PRATT, JOHN W. 1958 Unbiased Estimation of Certain Correlation Coefficients. *Annals of Mathematical Statistics* 29:201–211.

PRINCE, BENJAMIN M.; and TATE, ROBERT F. 1966 The Accuracy of Maximum Likelihood Estimates of Correlation for a Biserial Model. *Psychometrika* 31:85–92.

TATE, R. F. 1955a The Theory of Correlation Between Two Continuous Variables When One Is Dichotomized. *Biometrika* 42:205–216.

TATE, R. F. 1955b Applications of Correlation Models for Biserial Data. *Journal of the American Statistical Association* 50:1078–1095.

TATE, R. F. 1966 Conditional-normal Regression Models. *Journal of the American Statistical Association* 61:477–489.

WALLIS, W. ALLEN; and ROBERTS, HARRY V. 1956 *Statistics: A New Approach.* Glencoe, Ill.: Free Press. → A revised and abridged paperback edition of the first section was published in 1962 by Collier.

YULE, G. UDNY; and KENDALL, M. G. 1958 *An Introduction to the Theory of Statistics.* 14th ed., rev. & enl. London: Griffin. → The first edition was published in 1911 with Yule as sole author. Kendall has been a joint author since the eleventh edition (1937), and the 1958 edition was revised by him. A 1965 printing contains new material.

III
CORRELATION (2)

Correlation, in a broad sense, is any probabilistic relationship between random variables (or sets of random variables) other than stochastic independence. Two random variables are said to be independent when the conditional distribution of one, given the other, does not depend on the given value. Viewed another way, independence means that the probability that both random variables are simultaneously in some given intervals is simply the product of the separate interval probabilities. Whenever independence does not hold, the two random variables are dependent, or correlated. (Terminology is not wholly standard, for the word "correlated" is sometimes used to refer to special kinds of dependence only.) [See PROBABILITY, *article on* FORMAL PROBABILITY.]

Two *sets* of random variables—that is, two random vectors—are independent when the conditional distribution of one set, given the other, does not depend on the given values.

The idea of a numerical measure of association between two random variables seems to have originated with Francis Galton, in the last part of the nineteenth century [*see* GALTON]. From crude beginnings at his hands, the concept passed into those of F. Y. Edgeworth and particularly into those of Karl Pearson, whose academic training had been in mathematical physics but who caught Galton's enthusiasm and devoted the rest of his life to statistics [see EDGEWORTH; PEARSON]. From them there came the definition and exploration of the important *correlation coefficient,*

$$r = \frac{(X_1 - \bar{X})(Y_1 - \bar{Y}) + (X_2 - \bar{X})(Y_2 - \bar{Y}) + \cdots + (X_N - \bar{X})(Y_N - \bar{Y})}{[(X_1 - \bar{X})^2 + (X_2 - \bar{X})^2 + \cdots + (X_N - \bar{X})^2]^{\frac{1}{2}} [(Y_1 - \bar{Y})^2 + (Y_2 - \bar{Y})^2 + \cdots + (Y_N - \bar{Y})^2]^{\frac{1}{2}}},$$

in sample form. Here $(X_1, Y_1), \cdots, (X_N, Y_N)$ are the members of an N-fold bivariate sample, and $\bar{X}$ and $\bar{Y}$ are the corresponding sample averages. Of course r may be written more compactly as

$$r = \frac{\sum\limits_{i=1}^{N} (X_i - \bar{X})(Y_i - \bar{Y})}{[\sum\limits_{i=1}^{N} (X_i - \bar{X})^2]^{\frac{1}{2}} [\sum\limits_{i=1}^{N} (Y_i - \bar{Y})^2]^{\frac{1}{2}}},$$

or still more compactly as

$$r = \frac{\sum\limits_{i=1}^{N} x_i y_i}{[\sum\limits_{i=1}^{N} x_i^2]^{\frac{1}{2}} [\sum\limits_{i=1}^{N} y_i^2]^{\frac{1}{2}}},$$

where $x_i = X_i - \bar{X}$ and $y_i = Y_i - \bar{Y}$ are the residuals, or deviations from the sample averages. Another way of expressing r is obtained by dividing the numerator and the denominator by $N - 1$:

$$r = \frac{S_{xy}}{\sqrt{S_{xx} S_{yy}}},$$

where S_{xx} and S_{yy} are the conventional modes of expressing sample variance and S_{xy} that of sample covariance.

The population, or underlying, correlation coefficient between random variables X and Y is

$$\rho = \frac{\text{cov}(X, Y)}{\sqrt{\text{var} X \cdot \text{var} Y}},$$

where $\text{var} X = E(X - EX)^2$, $\text{var} Y = E(Y - EY)^2$, and $\text{cov}(X,Y) = E[(X - EX)(Y - EY)]$. When the sample of (X_i, Y_i) is random, r is the usual estimator of ρ.

Instead of centering the quantities entering into the expressions for r and ρ on $(\bar{X}, \bar{Y})$ and (EX, EY), respectively, estimated or true conditional expectations, given other variables, may be used. Then the correlation coefficients are called partial correlation coefficients.

The adjectives "Pearsonian" and "product-moment" are sometimes used in naming the correla-

tion coefficient. Although Pearson was the first to study it with care, later workers, especially R. A. Fisher, pushed both the theoretical study and the applications of correlation much further [see FISHER, R. A.].

Applications of correlation

The initial application of correlation was to genetics, although that science remained at a rudimentary stage in England and other Western countries until the early 1900s, when the basic principles published in 1866 by the Austrian monk Gregor Mendel were rediscovered. Subsequent genetic research revealed specific correlations that result from various degrees of relationship, from the extent of random mating, and from other conditions. A substantial compendium of this correlational theory of genetics was published by Fisher (1918). These specific correlations made it important to compare certain hypotheses suggested by theoretical considerations about the value of a correlation coefficient with the observed results. For example, a theoretical correlation of $\frac{1}{2}$ between stature of father and stature of son is suggested by a hypothesis of random mating; this correlation may, however, be obscured by the fluctuations of random sampling. Because of such problems the probability distribution of r in samples from a basic distribution with correlation ρ became an object of mathematical inquiry, of which an account will be given below. Some of the mathematical problems of great complexity are still only partly solved.

Analysis of human abilities. Even before the rediscovery of Mendelian genetics, psychologists became interested in correlation with a view to detecting and analyzing variations in human abilities. A pioneer work was Charles E. Spearman's paper of 1904, which was later revised and expanded into his book *The Abilities of Man* (1927), leading to the theory that each of the various human abilities tested is the sum of a greater or less quota of "general intelligence" and another independent fraction of an ability special to the particular thing tested [see INTELLIGENCE AND INTELLIGENCE TESTING; *the biography of* SPEARMAN]. These special abilities were initially thought of as being independent of general intelligence and of each other [see FACTOR ANALYSIS]. If ρ_{ij} denotes the true, or population, correlation between the ith and *j*th test scores, the original Spearman theory holds, as a consequence of the assumptions that, for all different subscripts, i, j, k, l,

$$\rho_{ij}\rho_{kl} = \rho_{ik}\rho_{jl} = \rho_{il}\rho_{jk}.$$

The population correlations, ρ_{ij}, cannot, however, be derived from theory but must be estimated by the sample correlations, r_{ij}, obtained from actual test scores. After the problem was recognized, there ensued a long period of wrestling with the difficult mathematics and logic of this problem and of attempting to reformulate the early theory to apply with greater generality to situations involving group factors and other elaborations. Greatly enlarged testing programs supplied vast amounts of data. In the 1920s and 1930s new views of the problem were introduced—in numerous articles in journals, in the work of L. L. Thurstone, in a book by Truman L. Kelley (1928), and in a work of Karl Holzinger and Harry Harman (1941) that was the culmination of work done and papers published during the 1930s [see KELLEY; THURSTONE]. One of those who introduced new ideas and methods was Spearman himself, when he became convinced that his original formulation was inadequate (1927).

Rank-order correlation. Spearman introduced a correlation coefficient for ranked observations that avoids any assumption, either of normality or of any other particular form of distribution [see NONPARAMETRIC STATISTICS, *article on* RANKING METHODS]. It has been used extensively by statisticians unwilling to make assumptions of particular forms for their data. An exact standard error for the Spearman coefficient was published by Hotelling and Pabst in 1936. Maurice G. Kendall provided another rank correlation coefficient in *Biometrika* in 1938 and reviewed the subject at length in chapter 16 of his *Advanced Theory of Statistics* (1943–1946, vol. 1). See also Kendall's monograph on ranking methods (1948).

The correlation ratio. The correlation ratio was originally introduced to deal with nonlinear regression when the data are grouped. It has a strong formal similarity with analysis of variance in the one-way layout. Its theory is treated by Hotelling (1925) and Wishart (1932).

Effect of deviations from assumptions. The correlation coefficient, r, is sensitive to deviations from the usual basic assumptions of normality, independence of observations, and uniform variance among the observations. Extreme deviations in variance, particularly in the form of large deviations of both X and Y in the same term, may cause an exaggeration of r above ρ. Effects of nonnormality

may be serious and will be discussed later. These effects are generally ignored in the literature.

Lack of independence, another sort of deviation from assumptions, particularly between different observations on the same variate, has been felt to be so serious a menace as to impair deeply the reliability of many correlation coefficients, especially for economic time series. Partial correlation, equivalent to removal of a set of variables that are considered extraneous from both X and Y by least squares, is a useful method. A special case of it is the elimination of trends—best done by least squares—which may be combined with the elimination of seasonal variation, for which special methods have been devised. Caution is needed in such enterprises to obtain "models" that are truly reasonable and do not involve removing too much with the trend, throwing out the baby with the bath water. But the penalty for such a sin is often very light, usually being limited to a reduction in the number of degrees of freedom, whereas a failure to remove significant components of trend, such as secular and seasonal components, may grossly exaggerate the correlation.

Autocorrelation and serial correlation. Autocorrelation, in which each observation on X is matched with another observation on X, where there is a fixed time interval between the two observations, may be measured by the same formula as r or slight variations of it. Lag correlation is given by the usual formula with a fixed time interval between each X and the corresponding Y. In both these situations the distribution is different from that of r based on a random sample. The choice of suitable types of autocorrelations and serial correlations should be made with a view to what is known or believed about the interrelations of the actual observations. Since these interrelations are seldom known exactly, the choice of a particular statistic can often be made so as to relate it suitably both to the true matrix of correlation and to manageable forms for its own distribution. (For methods useful in finding some such distributions, see papers by Tjalling C. Koopmans 1942 and R. L. Anderson 1942.)

Other applications. Correlation enters biometrics in many places other than genetics. Areas in which it has been widely used are quality control and quantitative anthropology [see PHYSICAL ANTHROPOLOGY; QUALITY CONTROL, STATISTICAL].

The precision of *r*

The formula for r is the same as that used in solid analytic geometry for the cosine of the angle between two lines through the origin, one to each of the points with coordinates $(x_1, \cdots, x_N)$, $(y_1, \cdots, y_N)$, except that the formula given in the textbooks is usually confined to three dimensions. Since it is a cosine, r cannot exceed 1 or be less than -1, but when the variates are distributed under reasonable assumptions of continuity, r can take either of these extreme values. If (and only if) $r = \pm 1$, the Y's of the sample are linearly related to their corresponding X's, with the linear function increasing if $r = 1$ and decreasing if $r = -1$.

In order to make substantial use of r, it is necessary to have at least an approximation to its probability distribution, which will involve both the true value and the sample size. The probability distribution was first deduced for random samples with $\rho \neq 0$ from the bivariate normal population by Fisher (1915), but the results, although correct, were very difficult to use until simplifying transformations could be found. One simplification, which in the end proved too drastic, is to use the standard error of r, a function of ρ and N, and to treat r as normally distributed about ρ. This had been done by Karl Pearson and L. N. G. Filon (1898). An earlier version contained an error, whose cause it is instructive to examine: the two sample standard deviations in the denominator of r were regarded as fixed, or the same in all samples; this introduced into the denominator of the standard error of r an extraneous factor, $(1 + r^2)^{\frac{1}{2}}$. The error was corrected in the 1898 paper, which provided the equivalent of the formula

$$\sigma_r = (1 - r^2) n^{-\frac{1}{2}},$$

where $n = N - 1$, the number of so-called degrees of freedom in this case. (N could be used instead of n in the above expression, but it is useful and conventional to use the degrees of freedom.) The above expression appeared in textbooks for several decades, puzzling students by the obvious absurdity that the standard error of r appears as a function of r itself. Of course the meaning of the above formula is that the asymptotic (or large-sample) standard error of r is $(1 - \rho^2) n^{-\frac{1}{2}}$, which is estimated by substituting r for ρ in the expression. The notation of the period was one in which parameters and their estimators were often denoted by the same symbol, a pernicious practice that sometimes misled even those statisticians who presumably used it only as a convenient shorthand. The need for a notational distinction between the two concepts of parameter and estimator was not well understood, even by mathematical statisticians, until after the publication of Fisher's paper of 1915.

The development of mathematical theory

The first publication of an exact distribution of a correlation coefficient seems to have been by William S. Gosset (1908), a chemist publishing under the name "Student" because of his employers' opposition to publication [*see* GOSSET]. The data were supposed to represent a random sample from a bivariate normal population with correlation $\rho = 0$. Fisher's 1915 paper supplied for the first time an exact distribution of r with $\rho \neq 0$. This paper has led to others by various authors, and will stand as a great triumph.

The matter had been on Pearson's mind, and after the publication of Fisher's paper he mobilized the resources of his entire Biometric Laboratory in London to improve the results. In what has come to be referred to as the Cooperative Study (Soper et al. 1917), Pearson, with four collaborators, began with a series expression for the distribution which is remarkable in that although it converges, it does so with extreme slowness. When multiplied by an appropriate factor, however, and integrated to get the moments, the new series converges with great rapidity, especially for large samples. The Cooperative Study also effected other mathematical improvements and provided handsome plates showing the frequency function as a surface with horizontal coordinates r and ρ, with drawings and tables. But then came a fateful step.

Difficulties about the foundations of statistical inference were coming more clearly into view, partly as a result of all the work on r. It seemed only natural to Pearson to invoke Bayes' theorem of inverse probability to provide a solution of these unsolved problems. The Cooperative Study has a section on the application of the results, with a priori probabilities provided by Pearson's experience and judgment and with far-reaching inferences from hypothetical samples.

Fisher had already taken a stand against Bayesian inference and wrote a rebuttal to the inverse probability argument of the Cooperative Study. However, because of Pearson's opposition, Fisher, still a young man and comparatively unknown, was unable to publish his paper in England. It finally appeared in 1921 in Corrado Gini's new journal *Metron*, published in Rome. In the 1921 volume and in that of 1924, besides pointing out the absurdities arising from application of inverse probability by Pearson's methods to certain data, Fisher made an important constructive contribution regarding the application of the same distribution to partial correlations with a reduction in the number of degrees of freedom equal to the number of variates eliminated.

Florence N. David, a member of the Pearson group at University College, London, computed a very fine table (1938) of the correlation distribution in random samples from a normal distribution, using as a principal method the numerical solution of difference equations. It far exceeded in scope and accuracy the short tables previously published in Fisher's initial paper (1915) and in the Cooperative Study (Soper et al. 1917). She used as a principal computational tool the two second-order difference equations previously discovered, which she adapted.

The appropriate formula for the variance of the correlation coefficient, $\sigma_r^2 = (1 - \rho^2)^2/n$, equivalent to the 1898 result of Pearson and Filon, is only the first term of an infinite series of powers of n^{-1} with coefficients involving increasing powers of ρ. Additional terms may be computed by various methods—for example, by the rapidly convergent series for the moments of r used in the Cooperative Study (Soper et al. 1917) or by Hotelling (1953, p. 212).

All these approximations to the variance of r, however, require a knowledge of ρ, which is ordinarily not obtainable. Moreover, when $\rho \neq 0$, the distribution of r is skew, and if ρ is close to ± 1 and the sample is of moderate size, the distribution is very skew indeed. A serious problem is thus created for statisticians who wish to determine, for example, whether the values of r in two independent samples differ significantly from each other or to find a suitably weighted average of several quite different and independent values of r, corresponding either to distinct values of ρ or to one common value. Fisher proposed as a solution for such problems the transformation

$$r = \tanh z, \qquad z = \tanh^{-1} r = \tfrac{1}{2} \log_e \frac{1+r}{1-r},$$

abandoning an inferior transformation of his 1915 paper, and announced that, to a close approximation and with moderately large samples, z has a nearly normal distribution, with means and variances nearly independent of ρ. F. N. David examines, in her volume of tables (1938), the accuracy of these statements by Fisher and is inclined to consider them accurate enough for practical use. These descriptive terms are, however, relative, and it still seems that for some cases, especially with small samples, use of the z transformation is not sufficiently accurate.

In Fisher's original calculation there are small ·errors in the mean and variance of z, which are not carried beyond terms of order n^{-1}. These are corrected and the series are carried out to terms of order n^{-2} in a paper by Hotelling (1953). These series provide apparent improvements in the accuracy of z, at least for large samples. This paper also contains revised calculations on many other aspects of the correlation distribution.

A frequent practical problem is to test the null hypothesis $\rho = 0$ from a single observed correlation. Under normality this null hypothesis corresponds to independence. To this end, r is usually transformed into z, which is treated as normally distributed about 0. This practice, however, is not to be recommended. It is far more accurate in such cases to use one of the other three methods of testing the hypothesis $\rho = 0$ (given in the first part of Hotelling 1953).

This 1953 paper is a careful reworking of most of the earlier theory of correlation, with considerable additions. These include three new formulas for the distribution of r when $\rho = 0$ and one formula, involving a very rapidly convergent hypergeometric series, good for all $|\rho| < 1$. With these series there are easily calculated and usually small upper bounds for the error of stopping with any term. There are also attractive series for the probability integral and for the moments of r and of Fisher's transform, $z = \tanh^{-1} r$. Simple improvements are obtained for Fisher's estimates of the bias and variance of z. These eliminate certain small errors and go further in the series of powers of n^{-1} to terms of order n^{-3} and carry these through for moments of orders lower than 5. For moments of order 5 or more, all terms are of order n^{-4} or higher. The moments of r through the sixth are given through terms of order n^{-3}. The skewness and kurtosis are also given and differ slightly from Fisher's values.

Finally, it is proposed that z be modified, particularly for large samples, by using in its place either the first two or all three of the terms of

$$z - \frac{3z+r}{4n} - \frac{23z+33r-5r^3}{96n^2}.$$

Here, as throughout the 1953 paper, n means the number of degrees of freedom, which is ordinarily less by unity than the sample number.

A further method for testing $\rho = 0$ is to restate this hypothesis as asserting that the regression coefficient of one variate on the other is truly 0, and to test this by means of Student's t, the ratio of the estimated regression coefficient to its estimated standard error; this is a function of r.

All these methods are accurate only in the case of random sampling from a normal distribution.

However, even in this standard situation the use of z is more or less inaccurate, especially for small samples and large values of r.

As stated above, Fisher recommends the use of z instead of r also for purposes other than testing $\rho = 0$, such as testing the difference between two independent correlation coefficients or the dispersion among several such values of r or the weights to be applied in averaging them or the accuracy of the average. This idea was carried further by R. L. Thorndike (1933) in a study of the stability of the IQ. Each of his experiments resulted in a correlation between the results of the test given at an earlier and at a later date. With the magnitude of such a correlation coefficient is associated the number of persons in the sample and also the time elapsed between tests. Since the weights to be applied to the independent experiments are inversely proportional to the variances in the several cases, and since the reciprocals of the variances are approximately proportional to the number of cases in the samples when the correlations are transformed into values of z, essentially uniform variances are obtained. Thus, in fitting a curve to the several correlations, the method of least squares is appropriate because its assumptions are approximately satisfied. The weights are taken as the numbers of persons in the experiments. More accuracy could presumably be obtained by using instead of z the slightly different expressions z^* and z^{**} obtained by Hotelling (1953, pp. 223–224).

Variance of r in nonnormal cases

In addition to the unreliability of inferences involving correlation coefficients mentioned above, because of correlations between different observations on the same variate and because of nonuniform variances, a quite different source of errors is the nonnormal bivariate distributions that often affect observations. When these distributions, or their first four moments, are known or approximated, the variance of r is given, to a first approximation, by the formula

$$\sigma_r^2 = \frac{\rho^2}{n} \left\{ \frac{\mu_{22}}{\mu_{11}^2} + \frac{1}{4} \frac{\mu_{40}}{\mu_{20}^2} + \frac{1}{4} \frac{\mu_{04}}{\mu_{02}^2} + \frac{1}{2} \frac{\mu_{22}}{\mu_{20}\mu_{02}} - \frac{\mu_{31}}{\mu_{11}\mu_{20}} - \frac{\mu_{13}}{\mu_{11}\mu_{02}} \right\}$$

in which μ_{ij} $(i,j = 0,1,2,3,4)$ is the expectation $E[(X - EX)^i (Y - EY)^j]$. This formula was established by Arthur L. Bowley (1901, p. 423 in the 1920 edition) and later by Maurice G. Kendall (1943–1946, vol. 1, p. 211).

If the moments of the bivariate normal distribution are substituted in this formula, the result is $\sigma_r^2 = (1 - \rho^2)^2/n$, the well-known first approxima-

tion. A second approximation is found by multiplying this result by $1 + 11 \rho^2/(2n)$, as shown, with considerable extensions, by Hotelling (1953, p. 212).

If instead of being normal the distribution is of uniform density within an ellipse centered at the origin and tilted with respect to the coordinate axes if $\rho \neq 0$, and if the density is 0 outside this ellipse, the formula for the variance, given above, is multiplied by $\frac{2}{3}$. This is a substantial reduction.

Another case is a distribution over only four points, with probabilities

$$\begin{array}{ll} \frac{1}{4} + \frac{1}{4}\rho & \text{for } (1, 1) \text{ and } (-1, -1), \\ \frac{1}{4} - \frac{1}{4}\rho & \text{for } (1, -1) \text{ and } (-1, 1), \end{array}$$

and with ρ taking any value between -1 and 1. The moments needed are easily found; since $x^3 = x$ and $y^3 = y$ for the values ± 1, which are the only ones considered, any subscript of 2 or more may be reduced by 2 or 4. The result is $\sigma_r^2 = (1 - \rho^2)/n$, and ρ is the correlation. This variance is larger than that for samples from a normal distribution by the factor $(1 - \rho^2)^{-1}$.

A collection of such cases would be useful in practice because of the importance of nonnormality in correlation.

Partial and multiple correlation—geometry

Suppose that tests of arithmetical and reading abilities, yielding scores X_1 and X_2, are applied to a group of seventh-grade school children and the correlation between these abilities is sought. A difficulty is that proficiency in both tests depends on age, X_3, and general advancement, X_4.

In this case either or both of X_3 and X_4 may be incorporated in regression functions fitted by least squares to X_1 and X_2, and the deviations of X_1 and X_2 from these functions may be correlated in a way more nearly independent of age and general advancement than X_1 and X_2 by themselves. Such a correlation is called a *sample partial correlation* of order 1 or 2, according to the number of variables eliminated, and is denoted by $r_{12 \cdot 3}$, $r_{12 \cdot 4}$, or $r_{12 \cdot 34}$.

If all four variables are measured on each of N children, the results may be pictured as the N coordinates, in a space of N dimensions, of four points, and each of these determines a vector from the origin. If the coordinates are replaced by deviations from the respective four means, this is equivalent to projecting each of the four vectors orthogonally onto the flat subspace through the origin for which the sum of a point's coordinates is zero. Consider the four vectors from the origin to the four projections; the cosines of their angles are the correlations among the original variables. The above projections may be regarded as the original vectors, from each of which is subtracted its orthogonal projection on the equiangular line (the line of all points whose coordinates are equal among themselves). The sample partial correlations may be regarded similarly, except that the subtracted projection is onto a subspace that includes the equiangular line, and more. For example, $r_{12 \cdot 3}$ may be described geometrically as follows: Begin with the plane determined by the equiangular line and the vector from the origin to the point determined by the N observations on X_3 as coordinates. Project the vector from the origin to the X_1 point onto that plane, and subtract the resulting vector from the X_1 vector. This gives the residual values of the X_1 observations after best "removing" the effects of a constant and of X_3. Now go through the same procedure for X_2. Then $r_{12 \cdot 3}$ is the cosine of the angle between the two vectors of residuals. In order to compute $r_{12 \cdot 3}$ it is not necessary to go through this process arithmetically, for $r_{12 \cdot 3}$ is a simple function of the ordinary correlation coefficients

$$r_{12 \cdot 3} = \frac{r_{12} - r_{13} r_{23}}{(1 - r_{13}^2)^{\frac{1}{2}} (1 - r_{23}^2)^{\frac{1}{2}}}.$$

From this geometry, which was described by Dunham Jackson (1924), it is easy to see that if X_1 and X_2 have a joint normal distribution, with independence among the different persons, and X_3 is fixed or has an arbitrary distribution, then the deviations of X_1 and X_2 from their regressions on X_3 have a correlation distribution of the same kind, with the sample number reduced by unity.

The definition of $r_{12 \cdot 4}$ is equivalent to the formula above, with "3" replaced by "4." It may be given a geometrical interpretation like those above. In general, the subscripts before the dot, called primary subscripts, pertain to the variables whose correlation is sought; they are interchangeable. The subscripts after the dot are called secondary subscripts, refer to the variables being eliminated, and may be permuted among themselves in any order without changing the value of the partial correlation provided by the formula. If p variates and the arithmetic means are eliminated, with N values for each variable, the number of degrees of freedom is reduced to $n = N - 1 - p$.

Partial correlations may also be expressed as ratios of determinants of simple correlations. This fact is useful in proving theorems, but in numerical work the recursive formulas like those above are generally used.

Partial correlations were used extensively by Yule (see Yule & Kendall [1911] 1958) in investigations of social phenomena, generally on the basis of the poor-law union as a unit.

Multiple correlation is the correlation of one predictand ("dependent variate") with two or more predictor variables, with least squares as the method of prediction or estimation. The multiple correlation coefficient is the correlation between the observations, y, and the predicted values, Y [see LINEAR HYPOTHESES, *article on* REGRESSION]. The exact sampling distribution of the multiple correlation coefficient R, like that of r, was discovered by Fisher.

Canonical correlations

The situation of multiple correlation is generalized to the case where one has two sets of variables, with two or more variables in each set, and wishes to use and analyze the relations between the sets. The multiple correlation case is that in which one set consists of only a single variable, whereas in the new situation there are at least two variables in each set. This problem was dealt with in a brief paper by Hotelling (1935). A longer, definitive version of it and of many related problems appeared the following year (Hotelling 1936a). T. W. Anderson (1958), working with slightly different notation and subject matter, deals with canonical correlations and canonical variates in a population in chapter 12 and in a sample in chapter 13, with related subjects.

A primary objective of canonical correlation analysis is to determine two linear functions, one of variates in the first set, the other of those in the second set, so that the correlation between these two functions is as great as possible. Without loss of generality, one may require the variances of these two linear combinations to be unity, so that covariance is to be maximized. This permits use of the Lagrange multiplier approach, with two fixed conditions. The resulting equation for maximization is a determinantal equation in the Lagrange multiplier, λ, written in terms of all the original correlations. If there are s variates in the first set and t in the second, with $s \leqslant t$ as a matter of convention, it turns out that the determinantal equation has $2s$ real roots, all less than or equal to one in absolute value. (They come in pairs of equal magnitude and opposite sign.) If one of the roots is substituted for λ, the determinant of the determinantal equation is 0; then, if its matrix be used to form linear equations, their solution provides the coefficients of two linear functions of the s and t

variates, respectively. The correlations between those pairs of linear functions, lying between 0 and +1, constitute the *canonical correlations* of the system. The linear functions are the *canonical variates* and may be regarded either as determined only to within an arbitrary common multiplier or as determined by the conditions that their variance shall equal unity. The greatest root and its corresponding pair of linear functions provide the solution of the primary problem.

If all roots are 0, then every correlation of a variate in one set with a variate in the other is 0.

For $s = t = 2$ the calculations are easy by elementary methods. For larger values of s and t, however, elementary methods rapidly grow more laborious and may well be superseded by iterative procedures. Such processes are available; different but similar processes are described by Hotelling (1936a; 1936b).

Canonical correlations and variates may be computed for the population, if its correlation matrix is known, exactly as for the sample. If a population canonical correlation, ρ, is a single, not a multiple, root of its equation, then large-sample first approximations to it will tend to normality with a standard error that to a first approximation is $(1 - \rho^2)n^{-\frac{1}{2}}$, exactly as in the case of elementary correlation. For multiple roots the large-sample approximations have a distribution tending to the chi-square form, with the number of degrees of freedom equal to the multiplicity.

There is some awkwardness in using canonical correlations that may sometimes be avoided, according to the particular purpose, by using functions of them. Symmetric functions often bring special simplicity. If the roots are $r_1, r_2, \cdots$, two of the most useful symmetric functions are $q = r_1 r_2 \cdots r_s$ and $z = (1 - r_1^2)(1 - r_2^2) \cdots (1 - r_s^2)$; q has been called the *vector correlation coefficient* and z the *vector alienation coefficient*. They may be used to test different types of deviations from independence between the two sets, but the same is true of other functions of $r_1, \cdots, r_s$, for example, the greatest root.

Between the set (x_1, x_2) and the set (x_3, x_4) the vector correlation coefficient is

$$q = r_1 r_2 = \frac{r_{13} r_{24} - r_{14} r_{23}}{(1 - r_{12}^2)^{\frac{1}{2}}(1 - r_{34}^2)^{\frac{1}{2}}}.$$

This vanishes if the tetrad difference (the numerator) does so. Thus, the tetrad difference, of great importance in factor analysis, may sometimes be tested appropriately by testing q. It is shown by Hotelling (1936a, p. 362) that if complete independence exists between the two sets, the probability that q is exceeded in a sample of N from a quadrivariate normal distribution is exactly $(1 - |q|)^{N-3}$. (Many other matters involved in the statistics of pairs of variates are also included in Hotelling 1936a and other publications.)

A study of causes of death related to alcoholism in France carried out by Sully Lederman was the starting point of a utilization of canonical correlations and canonical variates by Luu-Mau-Thanh, of the Institut de Statistique de l'Université de Paris and the Institut National d'Études Démographiques (Luu-Mau-Thanh 1963). The first set of variates consisted of three causes of death: alcoholism, liver diseases, and cerebral hemorrhage. The other set consisted of seven other causes of death. The canonical correlations were found to be .812, .450, and .279. The author also calculated principal components for the two sets. He illustrated another kind of application of canonical analysis by some data on grain collected by Frederick V. Waugh (1942) and analyzed by Maurice G. Kendall (1957). Luu-Mau-Thanh commented that the progress of canonical correlation analysis has been hampered by the heavy computational labor required but that the arrival of modern electronic computers will abolish this difficulty.

HAROLD HOTELLING

[See also STATISTICS, DESCRIPTIVE, *article on* ASSOCIATION.]

BIBLIOGRAPHY

ANDERSON, R. L. 1942 Distribution of the Serial Correlation Coefficient. *Annals of Mathematical Statistics* 13:1–13.

ANDERSON, THEODORE W. 1958 *An Introduction to Multivariate Statistical Analysis.* New York: Wiley.

BOWLEY, ARTHUR L. (1901) 1937 *Elements of Statistics.* 6th ed. New York: Scribner; London: King.

DAVID, FLORENCE N. 1938 *Tables of the Ordinates and Probability Integral of the Distribution of the Correlation Coefficient in Small Samples.* London: University College, Biometrika Office.

FISHER, R. A. 1915 Frequency Distribution of the Values of the Correlation Coefficient in Samples From an Indefinitely Large Population. *Biometrika* 10:507–521.

FISHER, R. A. 1918 The Correlation Between Relatives on the Supposition of Mendelian Inheritance. Royal Society of Edinburgh, *Transactions* 52:399–433.

FISHER, R. A. 1921 On the "Probable Error" of a Coefficient of Correlation Deduced From a Small Sample. *Metron* 1, no. 4:3–32.

FISHER, R. A. 1924 The Distribution of the Partial Correlation Coefficient. *Metron* 3:329–333.

[GOSSET, WILLIAM S.] (1908) 1943 Probable Error of a Correlation Coefficient. Pages 35–42 in William S. Gosset, *"Student's" Collected Papers.* Edited by E. S. Pearson and John Wishart. London: University College, Biometrika Office.

HOLZINGER, KARL J.; and HARMAN, HARRY H. 1941 *Factor Analysis: A Synthesis of Factorial Methods.* Univ. of Chicago Press.

HOTELLING, HAROLD 1925 The Distribution of Correlation Ratios Calculated From Random Data. National Academy of Sciences, *Proceedings* 11:657–662.

HOTELLING, HAROLD 1935 The Most Predictable Criterion. *Journal of Educational Psychology* 26:139–142.

HOTELLING, HAROLD 1936a Relations Between Two Sets of Variates. *Biometrika* 28:321–377.

HOTELLING, HAROLD 1936b Simplified Calculation of Principal Components. *Psychometrika* 1:27–35.

HOTELLING, HAROLD 1943 Some New Methods in Matrix Calculation. *Annals of Mathematical Statistics* 14:1–34.

HOTELLING, HAROLD 1953 New Light on the Correlation Coefficient and Its Transforms. *Journal of the Royal Statistical Society* Series B 15:193–225.

HOTELLING, HAROLD; and PABST, MARGARET R. 1936 Rank Correlation and Tests of Significance Involving No Assumption of Normality. *Annals of Mathematical Statistics* 7:29–43.

JACKSON, DUNHAM 1924 The Trigonometry of Correlation. *American Mathematical Monthly* 31:275–280.

KELLEY, TRUMAN L. 1928 *Crossroads in the Mind of Man: A Study of Differentiable Mental Abilities.* Stanford Univ. Press.

KENDALL, MAURICE G. 1938 A New Measure of Rank Correlation. *Biometrika* 30:81–93.

KENDALL, MAURICE G. 1943–1946 *The Advanced Theory of Statistics.* 2 vols. London: Griffin. → A new edition, written by Maurice G. Kendall and Alan Stuart, was published in 1958–1966.

KENDALL, MAURICE G. (1948) 1955 *Rank Correlation Methods.* 2d ed. London: Griffin; New York: Hafner.

KENDALL, MAURICE G. (1957) 1961 *A Course in Multivariate Analysis.* London: Griffin.

KOOPMANS, TJALLING C. 1942 Serial Correlation and Quadratic Forms in Normal Variables. *Annals of Mathematical Statistics* 13:14–33.

LUU-MAU-THANH 1963 Analyse canonique et analyse factorielle. Institut de Science Économique Appliquée, *Cahiers* Series E Supplement 138:127–164.

PEARSON, KARL; and FILON, L. N. G. (1898) 1948 Mathematical Contributions to the Theory of Evolution. IV: On the Probable Errors of Frequency Constants and on the Influence of Random Selection on Variation and Correlation. Pages 179–261 in *Karl Pearson's Early Statistical Papers.* Cambridge Univ. Press. → First published in Volume 191 of the *Philosophical Transactions* of the Royal Society of London, Series A.

SOPER, H. E. et al. 1917 On the Distribution of the Correlation Coefficient in Small Samples: A Cooperative Study. *Biometrika* 11, no. 4:328–413.

SPEARMAN, CHARLES E. 1904 The Proof and Measurement of Association Between Two Things. *American Journal of Psychology* 15:72–101.

SPEARMAN, CHARLES E. 1927 *The Abilities of Man: Their Nature and Measurement.* London: Macmillan.

THORNDIKE, R. L. 1933 The Effect of the Interval Between Test and Retest Upon the Constancy of the IQ. *Journal of Educational Psychology* 24:543–549.

WAUGH, FREDERICK V. 1942 Regressions Between Sets of Variables. *Econometrica* 10:290–310.

WISHART, JOHN 1932 Note on the Distribution of the Correlation Ratio. *Biometrika* 24:441–456.

YULE, G. UDNY; and KENDALL, MAURICE G. (1911) 1958 *An Introduction to the Theory of Statistics.* 14th ed., rev. & enl. London: Griffin. → Maurice G. Kendall has been a joint author since the eleventh edition (1937). The 1958 edition was revised by Maurice G. Kendall.

IV

CLASSIFICATION AND DISCRIMINATION

Classification is the identification of the category or group to which an individual or object belongs on the basis of its observed characteristics. When the characteristics are a number of numerical measurements, the assignment to groups is called by some statisticians *discrimination*, and the combination of measurements used is called a *discriminant function*. The problem of classification arises when the investigator cannot associate the individual directly with a category but must infer the category from the individual's measurements, responses, or other characteristics. In many cases it can be assumed that there are a finite number of populations from which the individual may have come and that each population is described by a statistical distribution of the characteristics of individuals. The individual to be classified is considered as a random observation from one of the populations. The question is, Given an individual with certain measurements, from which population did he arise?

R. A. Fisher (1936), who first developed the linear discriminant function in terms of the analysis of variance, gave as an example the assigning of iris plants to one of two species on the basis of the lengths and widths of the sepals and petals. Indian men have been classified into three castes on the basis of stature, sitting height, and nasal depth and height (Rao 1948). Six measurements on a skull found in England were used to determine whether it belonged to the Bronze Age or the Iron Age (Rao 1952). Scores on a battery of tests in a college entrance examination may be used to classify a prospective student into the population of students with potentialities of completing college successfully or into the population of students lacking such potentialities. (In this example the classification into populations implies the prediction of future performance.) Medical diagnosis may be considered as classification into populations of disease.

The problem of classification was formulated as part of statistical decision theory by Wald (1944) and von Mises (1945). [*See* DECISION THEORY.] There are a number of hypotheses; each hypothesis is that the distribution of the observation is a given one. One of these hypotheses must be accepted and the others rejected. If only two populations are admitted, the problem is the elementary one of testing one hypothesis of a specified distribution against another, although usually in hypothesis testing one of the two hypotheses, the null hypothesis, is singled out for special emphasis [see HYPOTHESIS TESTING]. If a priori probabilities of the individual belonging to the populations are known, the Bayesian approach is available [see BAYESIAN INFERENCE]. In this article it is assumed throughout that the populations have been determined. (Sometimes the word *classification* is used for the setting up of categories, for example, in taxonomy or typology.) [See CLUSTERING; TYPOLOGIES.]

The characteristics can be numerical measurements (continuous variables), attributes (discrete variables), or both. Here the case of numerical measurements with probability density functions will be treated, but the case of attributes with frequency functions is treated similarly. The theory applies when only one measurement is available ($p = 1$) as well as when several are ($p \geqslant 2$). The classification function based on the approach of statistical decision theory and the Bayesian approach automatically take into account any correlation between variables. (Karl Pearson's coefficient of racial likeness, introduced in a paper by M. L. Tildesley [1921] and used as a basis of classification, suffered from its neglect of correlation between measurements.)

Classification for two populations

Suppose that an individual with certain measurements $(x_1, \cdots, x_p)$ has been drawn from one of two populations, π_1 and π_2. The properties of these two populations are specified by given probability density functions (or frequency functions), $p_1(x_1, \cdots, x_p)$ and $p_2(x_1, \cdots, x_p)$, respectively. (Each infinite population is an idealization of the population of all possible observations.) The goal is to define a procedure for classifying this individual as coming from π_1 or π_2. The set of measurements $x_1, \cdots, x_p$ can be presented as a point in a p-dimensional space. The space is to be divided into two regions, R_1 and R_2. If the point corresponding to an individual falls in R_1 the individual will be classified as drawn from π_1, and if the point falls in R_2 the individual will be classified as drawn from π_2.

Standards for classification. The two regions are to be selected so that on the average the bad effects of misclassification are minimized. In following a given classification procedure, the statistician can make two kinds of errors: If the individual is actually from π_1 the statistician may classify him as coming from π_2, or if he is from π_2 the statistician may classify him as coming from π_1. As shown in Table 1, the relative undesirability of

these two kinds of misclassification are $C(2|1)$, the "cost" of misclassifying an individual from π_1 as coming from π_2, and $C(1|2)$, the cost of misclassifying an individual from π_2 as coming from π_1. These costs may be measured in any consistent units; it is only the ratio of the two costs that is important. While the statistician may not know the costs in each case, he will often have at least a rough idea of them. In practice the costs are often taken as equal.

Table 1 — Costs of correct and incorrect classification

		Population	
		π_1	π_2
Statistician's decision	π_1	0	$C(1\|2)$
	π_2	$C(2\|1)$	0

In the example mentioned earlier of classifying prospective students, one "cost of misclassification" is a measure of the undesirability of starting a student through college when he will not be able to finish and the other is a measure of the undesirability of refusing to admit a student who can complete his course. In the case of medical diagnosis with respect to a specified disease, one cost of misclassification is the serious effect on the patient's health of the disease going undetected and the other cost is the discomfort and waste of treating a healthy person.

If the observation is drawn from π_1, the probability of correct classification, $P(1|1,R)$, is the probability of falling into R_1, and the probability of misclassification, $P(2|1,R) = 1 - P(1|1,R)$, is the probability of falling into R_2. (In each of these expressions R is used to denote the particular classification rule.) For instance,

$$(1) \quad P(1|1,R) = \int_{R_1} p_1(x_1, \cdots, x_p) \, dx_1 \cdots dx_p.$$

The integral in (1) effectively stands for the sum of the probabilities of measurements from π_1 in R_1. Similarly, if the observation is from π_2, the probability of correct classification is $P(2|2,R)$, the integral of $p_2(x_1, \cdots, x_p)$ over R_2, and the probability of misclassification is $P(1|2,R)$. If the observation is drawn from π_1, there is a cost or loss when the observation is incorrectly classified as coming from π_2; the expected loss, or risk, is the product of the cost of a mistake times the probability of making it, $r(1,R) = C(2|1)P(2|1,R)$. Similarly, when the observation is from π_2, the expected loss due to misclassification is $r(2,R) = C(1|2)P(1|2,R)$.

In many cases there are a priori probabilities of drawing an observation from one or the other population, perhaps known from relative abundances. Suppose that the a priori probability of drawing from π_1 is q_1 and from π_2 is q_2. Then the expected loss due to misclassification is the sum of the products of the probability of drawing from each population times the expected loss for that population:

$$(2) \quad \begin{aligned} &q_1 r(1,R) + q_2 r(2,R) \\ &= q_1 C(2|1) P(2|1,R) + q_2 C(1|2) P(1|2,R). \end{aligned}$$

The regions, R_1 and R_2, should be chosen to minimize this expected loss.

If one does not have a priori probabilities of drawing from π_1 and π_2, he cannot write down (2). Then a procedure R must be characterized by the two risks $r(1,R)$ and $r(2,R)$. A procedure R is said to be at least as good as a procedure R^* if $r(1,R) \leqslant r(1,R^*)$ and $r(2,R) \leqslant r(2,R^*)$, and R is better than R^* if at least one inequality is strict. A class of procedures may then be sought so that for every procedure outside the class there is a better one in the class (called a complete class). The smallest such class contains only *admissible* procedures; that is, no procedure out of the class is better than one in the class. As far as the expected costs of misclassification go, the investigator can restrict his choice of a procedure to a complete class and in particular to the class of admissible procedures if it is available.

Usually a complete class consists of more than one procedure. To determine a single procedure as optimum, some statisticians advocate the *minimax principle*. For a given procedure, R, the less desirable case is to have a drawing from the population with the greater risk. A conservative principle to follow is to choose the procedure so as to minimize the maximum risk [see DECISION THEORY].

Classification into one of two populations

Known probability distributions. Consider first the case of two populations when a priori probabilities of drawing from π_1 and π_2 are known; then joint probabilities of drawing from a given population and observing a set of variables within given ranges can be defined. The probability that an observation comes from π_1 and that the ith variate is between x_i and $x_i + dx_i$ $(i = 1, \cdots, p)$ is approximately $q_1 p_1(x_1, \cdots, x_p) dx_1 \cdots dx_p$. Similarly, the probability of drawing from π_2 and obtaining an observation with the ith variate falling between x_i and $x_i + dx_i$ $(i = 1, \cdots, p)$ is approximately $q_2 p_2(x_1, \cdots, x_p) dx_1 \cdots dx_p$. For an actual observation $x_1, \cdots, x_p$, the conditional probability that it comes from π_1 is

$$(3) \quad \frac{q_1 p_1(x_1, \cdots, x_p)}{q_1 p_1(x_1, \cdots, x_p) + q_2 p_2(x_1, \cdots, x_p)},$$

and the conditional probability that it comes from π_2 is

$$(4) \quad \frac{q_2 p_2(x_1, \cdots, x_p)}{q_1 p_1(x_1, \cdots, x_p) + q_2 p_2(x_1, \cdots, x_p)}.$$

The conditional expected loss if the observation is classified into π_2 is $C(2|1)$ times (3), and the conditional expected loss if the observation is classified into π_1 is $C(1|2)$ times (4). Minimization of the conditional expected loss is equivalent to the rule

$$(5) \quad \begin{aligned} R_1: \ &C(2|1) q_1 p_1(x_1, \cdots, x_p) \\ &> C(1|2) q_2 p_2(x_1, \cdots, x_p), \\ R_2: \ &C(2|1) q_1 p_1(x_1, \cdots, x_p) \\ &< C(1|2) q_2 p_2(x_1, \cdots, x_p). \end{aligned}$$

(The case of equality in (5) can be neglected if the density functions are such that the probability of equality is zero; if equality in (5) may occur with positive probability, then when such an observation occurs it may be classified as from π_1 with an arbitrary probability and from π_2 with the complementary probability.) Inequalities (5) may also be written

$$(6) \quad \begin{aligned} R_1: \ &\frac{p_1(x_1, \cdots, x_p)}{p_2(x_1, \cdots, x_p)} > k, \\ R_2: \ &\frac{p_1(x_1, \cdots, x_p)}{p_2(x_1, \cdots, x_p)} < k, \end{aligned}$$

where $k = [C(1|2) q_2]/[C(2|1) q_1]$. This is the Bayes solution. These results were first obtained in this way by Welch (1939) for the case of equal costs of misclassification.

These inequalities seem intuitively reasonable. If the probability of drawing from π_1 is decreased or if the cost of misclassifying into π_2 is decreased, the inequality in (6) for R_1 is satisfied by fewer points. Since the regions depend on q_1 and q_2, the expected loss does also. The curve A in Figure 1

EXPECTED LOSS

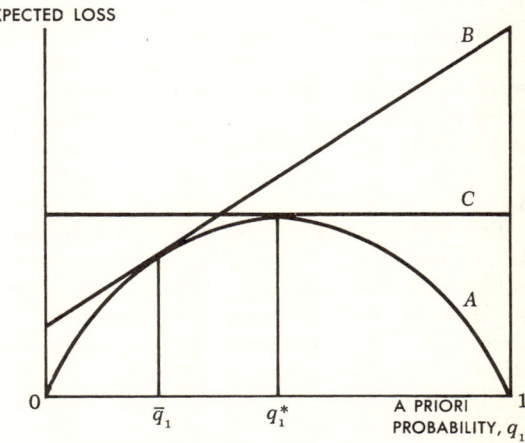

Figure 1 — Expected loss as a function of the a priori probability q_1 for three procedures indicates how the expected loss may vary with q_1 (and $q_2 = 1 - q_1$).

It may very well happen that the statistician errs in assigning his a priori probabilities. (The probabilities might be estimated from a sample of individuals whose populations of origin are known or can be identified by means other than the measurements for classification; for example, disease categories might be identified by subsequent autopsy.) Suppose that the statistician uses $\bar{q}_1$ and $\bar{q}_2$ ($= 1 - \bar{q}_1$) when q_1 and q_2 ($= 1 - q_1$) are the actual probabilities of drawing from π_1 and π_2, respectively. Then the actual expected loss is

$$q_1 C(2|1) P(2|1, \bar{R}) + (1 - q_1) C(1|2) P(1|2, \bar{R}),$$

where $\bar{R}_1$ and $\bar{R}_2$ are based on $\bar{q}_1$ and $\bar{q}_2$. Given the regions $\bar{R}_1$ and $\bar{R}_2$, this is a linear function of q_1 graphed as the line B in Figure 1, a line that touches A at $q_1 = \bar{q}_1$. The line cannot go below A because the best regions are defined by (6). From the graph it is clear that a small error in q_1 is not very important.

When the statistician cannot assign a priori probabilities to the two populations, he uses the fact that the class of Bayes solutions (6) is identical (in most cases) to the class of admissible solutions. A complete class of procedures is given by (6) with k ranging from 0 to ∞. (If the probability that the ratio is equal to k is positive a complete class would have to include procedures that randomize between the two classifications when the value of the ratio is k.)

The minimax procedure is one of the admissible procedures. Since R_2 increases as k increases, and hence $r(1, R)$ increases as k increases, and at the same time $r(2, R)$ decreases, the choice of k giving the minimax solution is the one for which $r(1, R) = r(2, R)$. This is then the average loss, for it is immaterial which population is drawn from. The graph of the risk against a priori probability q_1 is, therefore, a horizontal line (labeled C in Figure 1). Since there is one value of q_1, say q_1^*, such that $k = [C(1|2)(1 - q_1)]/[C(2|1)q_1]$, the line C must touch A.

Two known multivariate normal populations. An important example of the general theory is that in which the populations have multivariate normal distributions with the same set of variances and correlations but with different sets of means. [*See* MULTIVARIATE ANALYSIS: OVERVIEW.]

Suppose that $x_1, \cdots, x_p$ have a joint normal distribution with means in π_1 of $Ex_i = \mu_i^{(1)}$ and in π_2 of $Ex_i = \mu_i^{(2)}$. Let the common set of variances and correlations be $\sigma_1^2, \cdots, \sigma_p^2, \rho_{12}, \rho_{13}, \cdots, \rho_{p-1,p}$. It is convenient to write (6) as

$$R_1: \ln \frac{p_1(x_1, \cdots, x_p)}{p_2(x_1, \cdots, x_p)} > \ln k,$$

$$R_2: \ln \frac{p_1(x_1, \cdots, x_p)}{p_2(x_1, \cdots, x_p)} < \ln k,$$

where "ln" denotes the natural logarithm. In this particular case

(7)
$$\ln \frac{p_1(x_1, \cdots, x_p)}{p_2(x_1, \cdots, x_p)}$$
$$= \sum_{i=1}^{p} \lambda_i x_i - \sum_{i=1}^{p} \lambda_i (\mu_i^{(1)} + \mu_i^{(2)})/2,$$

where $\lambda_1, \cdots, \lambda_p$ form the solution of the linear equations

$$\sum_{j=1}^{p} \sigma_i \sigma_j \rho_{ij} \lambda_j = \mu_i^{(1)} - \mu_i^{(2)}, \qquad i = 1, \cdots, p.$$

The first term on the right side of (7) is the well-known *linear discriminant function* obtained by Fisher (1936) by choosing that linear function for which the difference in expected values for the two populations relative to the standard deviation is a maximum. The second term is a constant consisting of the average discriminant function at the two population means. The regions are given by

(8)
$$R_1: \sum_{i=1}^{p} \lambda_i x_i > \sum_{i=1}^{p} \lambda_i (\mu_i^{(1)} + \mu_i^{(2)})/2 + \ln k,$$

$$R_2: \sum_{i=1}^{p} \lambda_i x_i < \sum_{i=1}^{p} \lambda_i (\mu_i^{(1)} + \mu_i^{(2)})/2 + \ln k.$$

If a priori probabilities are assigned, then k is $[C(1|2)q_2]/[C(2|1)q_1]$. In particular, if $k = 1$ (for example, if $C(1|2) = C(2|1)$ and $q_1 = q_2 = \frac{1}{2}$), $\ln k = 0$, and the procedure is to compare the discriminant function of the observations with the discriminant function of the averages of the respective means.

If a priori probabilities are not known, the same class of procedures (8) is used as the admissible class. Suppose the aim is to find $\ln k = c$, say, so that the expected loss when the observation is from π_1 is equal to the expected loss when the observation is from π_2. The probabilities of misclassification can be computed from the distribution of

$$U = \sum_{i=1}^{p} \lambda_i x_i - \sum_{i=1}^{p} \lambda_i (\mu_i^{(1)} + \mu_i^{(2)})/2$$

when $x_1, \cdots, x_p$ are from π_1 and when $x_1, \cdots, x_p$ are from π_2. Let Δ^2 be the Mahalanobis measure of distance between π_1 and π_2,

$$\Delta^2 = \sum_{i=1}^{p} \lambda_i (\mu_i^{(1)} - \mu_i^{(2)}).$$

The distribution of U is normal with variance Δ^2. If the observation is from π_1 the mean of U is $\frac{1}{2}\Delta^2$; if the observation is from π_2 the mean is $-\frac{1}{2}\Delta^2$.

The probability of misclassification if the observation is from π_1 is

$$P(2|1,R) = Pr\{U \leqslant c|\pi_1\}$$

$$= Pr\left\{\frac{U - \frac{1}{2}\Delta^2}{\Delta} \leqslant \frac{c - \frac{1}{2}\Delta^2}{\Delta} \,\Big|\, \pi_1\right\}$$

$$= \Phi\left(\frac{c - \frac{1}{2}\Delta^2}{\Delta}\right),$$

where $\Phi(z)$ is the probability that a normal deviate with mean 0 and variance 1 is less than z. The probability of misclassification if the observation is from π_2 is

$$P(1|2,R) = Pr\{c \leqslant U|\pi_2\}$$

$$= Pr\left\{\frac{c + \frac{1}{2}\Delta^2}{\Delta} \leqslant \frac{U + \frac{1}{2}\Delta^2}{\Delta} \,\Big|\, \pi_2\right\}$$

$$= 1 - \Phi\left(\frac{c + \frac{1}{2}\Delta^2}{\Delta}\right) = \Phi\left(\frac{-c - \frac{1}{2}\Delta^2}{\Delta}\right).$$

Figure 2 indicates the two probabilities as the shaded portion in the tails. The aim is to choose c so that

$$r(2,R) = C(1|2)\left[1 - \Phi\left(\frac{c + \frac{1}{2}\Delta^2}{\Delta}\right)\right]$$

$$= C(2|1)\Phi\left(\frac{c - \frac{1}{2}\Delta^2}{\Delta}\right) = r(1,R).$$

If the costs of misclassification are equal, $c = 0$ and the common probability of misclassification is $\Phi(\frac{1}{2}\Delta)$. In case the costs of misclassification are unequal, c can be determined to sufficient accuracy by a trial-and-error method with the normal tables.

If the set of variances and correlations in one population is not the same as the set in the other population, the general theory can be applied, but $\ln[p_1(x_1, \cdots, x_p)/p_2(x_1, \cdots, x_p)]$ is a quadratic, not a linear, function of $x_1, \cdots, x_p$. Anderson and Bahadur (1962) treat linear functions for this case.

$$-\tfrac{1}{2}\Delta^2 \quad 0 \quad c \quad \tfrac{1}{2}\Delta^2$$

Figure 2 — Probabilities of misclassification as shaded areas under normal densities with means $\pm \frac{1}{2}\Delta^2$ and variance Δ^2

Classification with estimated parameters. In most applications of the theory the populations are not known but must be inferred from samples, one from each population.

Two multivariate normal populations. Consider now the case in which there are available random samples from two normal populations and in which the aim is to use that information in classifying another observation as coming from one of the two populations. Suppose the sample $(x_{1\gamma}^{(1)}, \cdots, x_{p\gamma}^{(1)})(\gamma = 1, \cdots, N^{(1)})$ is from π_1 and the sample $(x_{1\gamma}^{(2)}, \cdots, x_{p\gamma}^{(2)})(\gamma = 1, \cdots, N^{(2)})$ from π_2. Then $\mu_i^{(1)}$ can be estimated by the mean of the ith variate of the first sample $\bar{x}_i^{(1)}$ and $\mu_i^{(2)}$ by the mean of the second sample $\bar{x}_i^{(2)}$. The usual estimate of $\sigma_i\sigma_j\rho_{ij}$ based on the two samples is

$$s_{ij} = \frac{\sum\limits_{\alpha=1}^{N^{(1)}}(x_{i\alpha}^{(1)} - \bar{x}_i^{(1)})(x_{j\alpha}^{(1)} - \bar{x}_j^{(1)}) + \sum\limits_{\alpha=1}^{N^{(2)}}(x_{i\alpha}^{(2)} - \bar{x}_i^{(2)})(x_{j\alpha}^{(2)} - \bar{x}_j^{(2)})}{N^{(1)} + N^{(2)} - 2}.$$

These estimates may then be substituted into the definition of U, to obtain a new linear function of $x_1, \cdots, x_p$ depending on these estimates. The classification function is

$$\sum_{i=1}^{p} l_i x_i - \sum_{i=1}^{p} l_i(\bar{x}_i^{(1)} + \bar{x}_i^{(2)})/2,$$

where the coefficients $l_1, \cdots, l_p$ are the solution to

$$\sum_{j=1}^{p} s_{ij}l_j = \bar{x}_i^{(1)} - \bar{x}_i^{(2)}, \qquad i = 1, \cdots, p.$$

Since there are now sampling variations in the estimates of parameters, it is no longer possible to state that this procedure is best in either of the senses used earlier, but it seems to be a reasonable procedure. (A result of Das Gupta [1965] shows that when $N^{(1)} = N^{(2)}$ and the costs of misclassification are equal, the procedure with $c = 0$ is minimax and admissible.)

The exact distributions of the classification statistic based on estimated coefficients cannot be given explicitly; however, the distribution can be indicated as an integral (with respect to three variables). It can be shown that as the sample sizes increase, the distributions of this statistic approach those of the statistic used when the parameters are known. Thus for sufficiently large samples one can proceed exactly as if the parameters were known. Asymptotic expansions of the distributions are available (Bowker & Sitgreaves 1961).

A mnemonic device for the computation of the discriminant function (Fisher 1938) is the introduction of the dummy variate, y, which is equal to a constant (say, 1) when the observation is from

π_1 and is equal to another constant (say, 0) when the observation is from π_2. Then (formally) the regression of this dummy variate, y, on the observed variates $x_1, \cdots, x_p$ over the two samples gives a linear function proportional to the discriminant function. In a sense this linear function is a predictor of the dummy variate, y.

In practice the investigator might not be certain that the two populations differ. To test the null hypothesis that $\mu_i^{(1)} = \mu_i^{(2)}$, $i = 1, \cdots, p$, he can use the discriminant function of the difference in sample means

$$\sum_{i=1}^{p} l_i(\bar{x}_i^{(1)} - \bar{x}_i^{(2)}) = 2\left[\sum_{i=1}^{p} l_i\bar{x}_i^{(1)} - \sum_{i=1}^{p} l_i(\bar{x}_i^{(1)} + \bar{x}_i^{(2)})/2\right],$$

which is $(N^{(1)} + N^{(2)})/(N^{(1)}N^{(2)})$ times Hotelling's generalized T^2. The T^2-test may thus be considered as part of discriminant analysis. [See MULTIVARIATE ANALYSIS: OVERVIEW.]

Classification for several populations

So far, classification into one of only two groups has been discussed; consider now the problem of classifying an observation into one of several groups. Let $\pi_1, \cdots, \pi_m$ be m populations with density functions $p_1(x_1, \cdots, x_p), \cdots, p_m(x_1, \cdots, x_p)$, respectively. The aim is to divide the space of observations into m mutually exclusive and exhaustive regions $R_1, \cdots, R_m$. If an observation falls into R_g it will be considered to have come from π_g. Let the cost of classifying an observation from π_g as coming from π_h be $C(h|g)$. The probability of this misclassification is

$$P(h|g, R) = \int_{R_h} p_g(x_1, \cdots, x_p)dx_1 \cdots dx_p.$$

If the observation is from π_g, the expected loss or risk is

$$r(g, R) = \sum_{\substack{h=1 \\ h \neq g}}^{m} C(h|g)P(h|g, R).$$

Given a priori probabilities of the populations, $q_1, \cdots, q_m$, the expected loss is

$$\sum_{g=1}^{m} q_g r(g, R) = \sum_{g=1}^{m} q_g\left[\sum_{\substack{h=1 \\ h \neq g}}^{m} C(h|g)P(h|g, R)\right];$$

$R_1, \cdots, R_m$ are to be chosen to make this a minimum.

Using a priori probabilities for the populations, one can define the conditional probability that an observation comes from a specified population, given the values of observed variates, $x_1, \cdots, x_p$. The conditional probability of the observation coming from π_g is

$$\frac{q_g p_g(x_1, \cdots, x_p)}{q_1 p_1(x_1, \cdots, x_p) + \cdots + q_m p_m(x_1, \cdots, x_p)}.$$

If the observation is classified as from π_h, the expected loss is

$$(9) \qquad \sum_{\substack{g=1 \\ g \neq h}}^{m} \frac{q_g p_g(x)}{\sum_{k=1}^{m} q_k p_k(x)} C(h|g),$$

where x stands for the set $x_1, \cdots, x_p$. The expected loss is minimized at this point if h is chosen to minimize (9). The regions are

$$R_k: \sum_{\substack{g=1 \\ g \neq k}}^{m} q_g p_g(x)C(k|g) < \sum_{\substack{g=1 \\ g \neq h}}^{m} q_g p_g(x)C(h|g),$$
$$h = 1, \cdots, m,$$
$$h \neq k.$$

If $C(h|g) = 1$ for all g and h $(g \neq h)$, then $x_1, \cdots, x_p$ is in R_k if

$$(10) \qquad R_k: q_h p_h(x) < q_k p_k(x), \qquad h \neq k.$$

In this case the point $x_1, \cdots, x_p$ is in R_k if k is the index for which $q_g p_g(x)$ is a maximum, that is, π_k is the most probable population, given the observation. If equalities can occur with positive probability so that there is not a unique maximum, then any maximizing population may be chosen without affecting the expected loss.

If a priori probabilities are not given, an unconditional expected loss for a classification procedure cannot be defined. Then one must consider the risks $r(g, R)$ over all values of g and ask for the admissible procedures; the form is (10) when $C(h|g) = 1$ for all g and h $(g \neq h)$. The minimax solution is (10) when $q_1, \cdots, q_m$ are found so that

$$(11) \qquad r(1, R) = \cdots = r(m, R).$$

This number is the expected loss. (The theory was first given for the case of equal costs of misclassification by von Mises [1945].)

Several multivariate normal populations. As an example of the theory, consider the case of m multivariate normal populations with the same set of variances and correlations. Let the mean of x_j in π_g be $\mu_j^{(g)}$. Then

$$(12) \quad \begin{aligned} &\ln \frac{p_g(x_1, \cdots, x_p)}{p_h(x_1, \cdots, x_p)} \\ &= \sum_{i=1}^{p} \lambda_i^{(g,h)} x_i - \sum_{i=1}^{p} \lambda_i^{(g,h)}(\mu_i^{(g)} + \mu_i^{(h)})/2, \end{aligned}$$

where $\lambda_1^{(g,h)}, \cdots, \lambda_p^{(g,h)}$ are the solution to

$$\sum_{j=1}^{p} \sigma_i \sigma_j \rho_{ij} \lambda_j^{(g,h)} = \mu_i^{(g)} - \mu_i^{(h)}, \qquad i = 1, \cdots, p.$$

For the sake of simplicity, assume that the costs of misclassification are equal. If a priori probabilities, $q_1, \cdots, q_m$, are known, the regions are defined by

$$(13) \quad R_g : u_{gh}(x_1, \cdots, x_p) > \ln \frac{q_h}{q_g} = \ln q_h - \ln q_g,$$
$$h = 1, \cdots, m,$$
$$h \neq g,$$

where $u_{gh}(x_1, \cdots, x_p)$ is (12). If a priori probabilities are not known, the admissible procedures are given by (13), with $\ln q_h$ replaced by suitable constants c_h. The minimax procedure is (13), for which (11) holds. To determine the constants c_h, use the fact that if the observation is from π_g, $u_{gh}(x_1, \cdots, x_p)$, $h = 1, \cdots, m$ and $h \neq g$, have a joint normal distribution with means

$$(14) \quad Eu_{gh}(x_1, \cdots, x_p) = \sum_{i=1}^{p} \lambda_i^{(gh)}(\mu_i^{(g)} - \mu_i^{(h)})/2.$$

The variance of $u_{gh}(x_1, \cdots, x_p)$ is twice (14), and the covariance between the variables $u_{gh}(x_1, \cdots, x_p)$ and $u_{gk}(x_1, \cdots, x_p)$ is

$$\sum_{i=1}^{p} \lambda_i^{(g,h)}(\mu_i^{(g)} - \mu_i^{(k)}) = \sum_{i=1}^{p} \lambda_i^{(g,k)}(\mu_i^{(g)} - \mu_i^{(h)}).$$

From these one can determine $P(h|g,R)$ for any set of constants $c_1, \cdots, c_m$.

This procedure divides the space by means of hyperplanes. If $p = 2$ and $m = 3$, the division is by half-lines, as in Figure 3.

If the populations are unknown, the parameters may be estimated from samples, one from each population. If the samples are large enough, the above procedures can be used as if the parameters were known.

An example of classification into three populations has been given in Anderson (1958).

The problem of classification when $(x_1, \cdots, x_p)$ are continuous variables with density functions has been treated here. The same solutions are obtained when the variables are discrete, that is, take on a finite or countable number of values. Then $p_1(x_1, \cdots, x_p)$, $p_2(x_1, \cdots, x_p)$, and so on are the respective probabilities (or frequency functions) of $(x_1, \cdots, x_p)$ in π_1, π_2, and so on. (See Birnbaum & Maxwell 1960; Cochran & Hopkins 1961.) In this case randomized procedures are essential.

For other expositions see Anderson (1951) and Brown (1950). For further examples see Mosteller and Wallace (1964) and Smith (1947).

T. W. ANDERSON

[*Directly related are the entries* CLUSTERING; SCREENING AND SELECTION.]

BIBLIOGRAPHY

ANDERSON, T. W. 1951 Classification by Multivariate Analysis. *Psychometrika* 16:31–50.

ANDERSON, T. W. 1958 *An Introduction to Multivariate Statistical Analysis.* New York: Wiley.

ANDERSON, T. W.; and BAHADUR, R. R. 1962 Classification Into Two Multivariate Normal Distributions With Different Covariance Matrices. *Annals of Mathematical Statistics* 33:420–431.

BIRNBAUM, A.; and MAXWELL, A. E. 1960 Classification Procedures Based on Bayes's Formula. *Applied Statistics* 9:152–169.

BOWKER, ALBERT H.; and SITGREAVES, ROSEDITH 1961 An Asymptotic Expansion for the Distribution Function of the W-classification Statistic. Pages 293–310 in Herbert Solomon (editor), *Studies in Item Analysis and Prediction.* Stanford Univ. Press.

BROWN, GEORGE W. 1950 Basic Principles for Construction and Application of Discriminators. *Journal of Clinical Psychology* 6:58–60.

COCHRAN, WILLIAM G.; and HOPKINS, CARL E. 1961 Some Classification Problems With Multivariate Qualitative Data. *Biometrics* 17:10–32.

DAS GUPTA, S. 1965 Optimum Classification Rules for Classification Into Two Multivariate Normal Populations. *Annals of Mathematical Statistics* 36:1174–1184.

FISHER, R. A. 1936 The Use of Multiple Measurements in Taxonomic Problems. *Annals of Eugenics* 7:179–188.

FISHER, R. A. 1938 The Statistical Utilization of Multiple Measurements. *Annals of Eugenics* 8:376–386.

MOSTELLER, FREDERICK; and WALLACE, DAVID L. 1964 *Inference and Disputed Authorship: The Federalist.* Reading, Mass.: Addison-Wesley.

RAO, C. RADHAKRISHNA 1948 The Utilization of Multiple Measurements in Problems of Biological Classification. *Journal of the Royal Statistical Society* Series B 10:159–193.

RAO, C. RADHAKRISHNA 1952 *Advanced Statistical Methods in Biometric Research.* New York: Wiley.

SMITH, CEDRIC A. B. 1947 Some Examples of Discrimination. *Annals of Eugenics* 13:272–282.

TILDESLEY, M. L. 1921 A First Study of the Burmese Skull. *Biometrika* 13:176–262.

VON MISES, RICHARD 1945 On the Classification of Observation Data Into Distinct Groups. *Annals of Mathematical Statistics* 16:68–73.

WALD, ABRAHAM 1944 On a Statistical Problem Arising in the Classification of an Individual Into One of Two Groups. *Annals of Mathematical Statistics* 15:145–162.

WELCH, B. L. 1939 Note on Discriminant Functions. *Biometrika* 31:218–220.

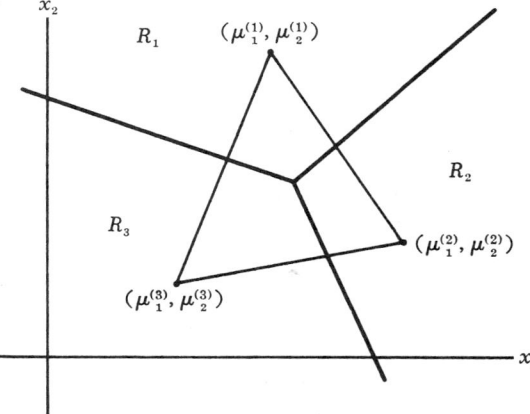

Figure 3 — Regions of classification into one of three multivariate populations

MUN, THOMAS

Thomas Mun (1571–1641), English writer on economics, was the third son of a substantial London family. His grandfather was an officer of the mint and acquired a coat of arms, his uncle was also an officer of the mint, and his stepfather was a director of the newly formed East India Company. Nothing is known of his education, but it is presumed, since there were close links between the Indian and the Mediterranean trades, that he served his apprenticeship in the latter. In fact, he says in one of his books that he lived for some time in Italy. He became a prominent and rich member of the East India Company, married the daughter of a Bedfordshire gentleman, and inherited and bought land in the country. One of his daughters married a baronet, another a merchant. His son appears to have lived the life of a country gentleman.

Mun came into the public eye during the economic depression which began in 1620. The books for which he is famous sprang entirely from that depression. The gravest symptom of the depression was the shortage of money, and, indeed, many regarded this shortage as a cause of the depression. In 1621 Mun wrote and published *A Discourse of Trade From England Unto the East-Indies* to answer the charge that the East India Company, which financed its trade largely by the export of silver coin, was responsible for the depression. His argument was that East Indian goods, when re-exported, earned more silver than that originally exported to pay for them.

Mun was one of the merchants consulted by the government about the causes of the depression and was a member of the great commission of trade set up in 1622 to make recommendations concerning economic policy. On the commission, he opposed successfully the advocates of two different policies, each based on a distinct theoretical analysis of the mechanism of foreign trade. One group of advocates held that the export of silver was caused by the undervaluation of silver coin in England and urged therefore that sterling be devalued: this view found articulate expression in Edward Misselden's *Free Trade* (1622). A second group believed that excessive export was intrinsic in foreign exchanges and advocated exchange control with a fixed exchange rate: this view was, in turn, forcibly presented by Gerard de Malynes in *The Maintenance of Free Trade* (1622) and elsewhere. Mun composed, or helped to compose, a series of papers directed against both these views, and these papers formed the substance of a book which he completed between 1626 and 1628 and which his

son published in 1664: *England's Treasure by Forraign Trade.*

Mun was a practicing professional merchant, which his opponents for the most part were not, and the book is much more a handbook for merchants and statesmen than an essay in theoretical economics. From the theoretical standpoint, Mun's criticism of de Malynes's views was inadequate. His central thesis was a tautological statement that money flows into or out of the country as the value of exports exceeds or falls short of the value of imports. He recognized the existence of invisible exports but was not original in this respect. Far from questioning in what sense treasure (that is, in the last resort, silver) is synonymous with wealth, he accepted as axiomatic that the balance of payments is the "rule" or "touchstone" of national wealth. He ignored the possibly inflationary effects of an indefinite influx of silver, took no account of international lending, and stated that the "overplus" of the balance and no more ought to be drawn off in taxation—as if government spending were economically irrelevant.

Nevertheless, *England's Treasure* remains a great book, even if it is not exactly a storehouse of the best economic ideas of the age and if its originality must be questioned at many points. It is an important book, first, because Mun's ideas prevailed —devaluation and exchange control were not attempted—and second, because in a single (admittedly partial) analysis it embraced with unrivaled lucidity all the economic variables under discussion at that time. Mun insisted that foreign trade is governed by the demand for commodities, that the flow of goods rules the exchange rate, and that silver itself is merely another commodity. He advocated low export prices, efficient commercial procedures, full exploitation of native skills and resources, low duties on exports, encouragement of re-exports, and the like: in sum, an export drive. Perhaps his most notable contribution to economic theory was to recognize and to insist on the principle of elasticity of demand, estimating that a reduction of 25 per cent in the price of cloth (England's chief export) would increase by 50 per cent the quantity sold. He dealt with the great but not insuperable difficulty of drawing up a balance of payments; such a balance was, in fact, established shortly after Mun's book was published.

Mun's originality lay in adjusting the conventional doctrine of the balance of trade (or rather of payments) to the new circumstances of rising foreign competition in the export market, especially of fierce economic rivalry with Holland, then the dominant commercial power; it is significant that the book was first published on the eve of the second Anglo–Dutch war. His practical liberalism, typical of the professional merchant of his day, commended him to later laissez-faire economists such as John R. McCulloch, who saw him as a tentative exponent of freedom of trade. He was, however, sharply divided from the laissez-faire economists and remained typically mercantilist in his reiterated distinction between the profit of the individual merchant and the general welfare of the national economy as a whole, as when he stated that the merchant's gain can be the commonwealth's loss and the merchant's loss the commonwealth's gain. His whole argument presupposes that a nation which gains by foreign trade does so at the expense of another.

R. W. K. HINTON

[*For the historical context of Mun's work, see* ECONOMIC THOUGHT, *article on* MERCANTILIST THOUGHT; *and the biography of* MISSELDEN.]

WORKS BY MUN

(1621) 1954 A Discourse of Trade From England Unto the East-Indies. Pages 1–47 in John R. McCulloch (editor), *Early English Tracts on Commerce.* Cambridge Univ. Press.

(1664) 1959 *England's Treasure by Forraign Trade.* Oxford: Blackwell.

SUPPLEMENTARY BIBLIOGRAPHY

GOULD, J. D. 1955a The Date of *England's Treasure by Forraign Trade. Journal of Economic History* 15:160–161.

GOULD, J. D. 1955b The Trade Crisis of the Early 1620's and English Economic Thought. *Journal of Economic History* 15:121–133.

HARDY, ALFRED L. 1894 Thomas Mun. Pages 1183–1186 in *Dictionary of National Biography.* London: Smith.

HINTON, R. W. K. 1955 The Mercantile System in the Time of Thomas Mun. *Economic History Review* Second Series 7:277–290.

MALYNES, GERARD DE 1622 *The Maintenance of Free Trade.* London: Sheffard.

MISSELDEN, EDWARD 1622 *Free Trade: Or, the Meanes to Make Trade Florish.* London: Waterson.

SUPPLE, BARRY E. 1959 *Commercial Crisis and Change in England, 1600–1642: A Study in the Instability of a Mercantile Economy.* Cambridge Univ. Press.

VINER, JACOB 1937 *Studies in the Theory of International Trade.* New York: Harper.

MÜNSTERBERG, HUGO

Hugo Münsterberg (1863–1916) made his greatest contribution by applying psychology to practical situations in education, medicine, law, and business. He pioneered in this field when most psychologists were still working only on basic theoretical principles. Münsterberg also did theoretical work, but he is best remembered for several books in special applied fields and for his very comprehensive (for his time) *Grundzüge* (1914a).

Most of these practical contributions were made in the eight or nine years prior to his untimely death. Münsterberg was born in Danzig in 1863, took his PH.D. under Wundt at Leipzig, and received a medical degree at Heidelberg. In 1892 William James arranged to bring him to Harvard as professor of psychology and director of the psychology laboratory. Except for a year as exchange professor at the University of Berlin in 1910/1911, the remainder of his career was spent at Harvard.

Münsterberg's initial academic interests were principally philosophical. His system was sometimes described as a "voluntaristic idealism." He placed a barrier between philosophy and science, philosophy the "real world" of purposes and science limited to causes. Later he tried to formalize this arrangement as causal psychology and purposive psychology. This dichotomy was included in his introductory textbook, but it was not received very well by students in the beginning course; nor did it have much impact on philosophers in general. The same thing was true of his "action theory," which stated that the vividness of experience depends on the amount of activity in the cerebral motor centers.

It was in applied psychology that Münsterberg's work had a lasting effect, although much of it was generated in the armchair rather than in the laboratory. His books mentioned numerous implications of psychology for problems in the workaday world and gave suggestions for further exploration and research. He did some experimental work himself and supervised research by students.

One field he explored was the use of psychology in business and industry. He made some of the first efforts toward validating aptitude tests. In an era when a correlation coefficient was something rarely understood or used, Münsterberg was in some fashion relating test results to a criterion of efficiency of workers on the job—motormen and telephone operators, for example—and he saw the implications of fatigue and monotony for industrial efficiency. He was one of the first to get in touch with business people to suggest ways psychology could help them. He was also in contact with aeronautical engineers regarding psychological problems connected with flying.

Another field which Münsterberg explored was education. His contributions here were less notable in the sense that he did not stand alone. Many academic educators had contacts with psychologists, and together they turned up problems of common interest.

With his medical background Münsterberg had

some experience with problems of mental health and did some work in therapy by suggestion. He was among the early users of hypnotism in psychotherapy. During his later years he kept on his desk as a symbol of his interest in hypnosis a paperweight consisting of four glass balls in the form of a tetrahedron. The center of this device provided a good fixation point for a patient being hypnotized.

In the field of law, and especially in regard to testimony, Münsterberg noted how mistakes in perception or lapses in memory contribute to the unreliability of a witness. Nobody else wrote along these lines for two decades. In the 1890s Münsterberg suggested that changes in blood pressure might have some relation to the veracity of testimony. The first experimental work on blood pressure in this context was done by a student in Münsterberg's laboratory. Records of blood pressure are now included in the measurements made by practically every polygraph used for "lie detection."

Münsterberg's contribution to applied psychology had two further facets: first, he let outsiders know how psychology might help them in practical problems; and second, he convinced a small group of psychologists that practical application of the science was a legitimate field for a career. This group has grown through the years.

Had Münsterberg lived longer, it is probable that he would have turned back to philosophy as his major interest. It is said that he had hoped to spend his later years in one of the endowed professorships of philosophy. If that had been possible, his professional life would have come full circle, but Münsterberg died suddenly while lecturing at Radcliffe College in 1916.

HAROLD E. BURTT

[For the historical context of Münsterberg's work, see the biography of WUNDT. For discussion of the subsequent development of his ideas, see APTITUDE TESTING; HYPNOSIS; INDUSTRIAL RELATIONS, article on INDUSTRIAL AND BUSINESS PSYCHOLOGY.]

WORKS BY MÜNSTERBERG

1908 *On the Witness Stand.* New York: Doubleday.
1909a *Psychology and the Teacher.* New York: Appleton.
1909b *Psychotherapy.* New York: Moffat.
1913 *Psychology and Industrial Efficiency.* Boston: Houghton Mifflin.
(1914a) 1928 *Grundzüge der Psychotechnik.* 3d ed. Leipzig: Barth.
1914b *Psychology, General and Applied.* New York: Appleton.

SUPPLEMENTARY BIBLIOGRAPHY

MÜNSTERBERG, MARGARETE 1922 *Hugo Münsterberg: His Life and Work.* New York: Appleton.

MURDER

See CRIME, *article on* HOMICIDE.

MUSIC

I
ETHNOMUSICOLOGY

The beginnings of ethnomusicology are usually traced back to the 1880s and 1890s, when studies were initiated primarily in Germany and in the United States. Early in this development there appeared a dual division of emphasis that has remained throughout the history of the field.

Definitions. Two polar positions on a definition of "ethnomusicology" are most frequently enunciated: the first is embodied in such statements as "ethnomusicology is the total study of non-Western music," and the second in "ethnomusicology is the study of music in culture." The first derives from a supposition that ethnomusicology should concern itself with certain geographical areas of the world; those who hold this point of view tend to treat the music structurally. The second stresses music in its cultural context, no matter in what geographical area of the world and is concerned with music as human behavior and the functions of music in human society and culture. Consequently, its emphasis on musical structure is not as great, although it does use objective techniques of detailing a musical style to effectuate comparison between song bodies and to attack problems of diffusion, acculturation, and culture history.

Thus one emphasis in ethnomusicology concerns the description and analysis of technical aspects of musical structure. In early writings this aim tended to be coupled with attempts to use the concept of social evolution to establish basic laws of the development of music structure through time. Particular attention was also directed toward the problem of the ultimate origin of music; and later, with the rise of *Kulturkreis* theories and particularly in connection with the study of musical instruments, detailed reconstructions of music diffusion from supposed basic geographical centers were attempted.

The second emphasis in ethnomusicology was directed toward the study of music in its ethnologic context, and research in this area was influenced by American anthropology. As a result, extreme theories of evolution and diffusion were strongly discounted.

Ethnomusicology has thus developed in two directions. On the one hand, music is treated as a structure that operates, it is presumed, according to certain principles inherent in its own construction. On the other hand, since music is produced by and for people, it must also be regarded as a product of human behavior operating within a cultural context and in conjunction with all the other facets of human behavior. The duality of music as a human phenomenon is thus emphasized in ethnomusicological studies; while musical sound has structure, that structure is produced by human behavior and operates in a total cultural context.

Ethnomusicology has also been shaped by various historical processes. Arising at a time when virtually nothing was known outside Western and, to a certain extent, Oriental cultures, ethnomusicology placed heavy emphasis on the unknown areas of the world—Africa, aboriginal North and South America, Oceania, inner Asia, Indonesia. Thus the development of ethnomusicology to a considerable extent paralleled that of anthropology: both disciplines were forced to deal with all these areas at once—the anthropologist with the total cultures of the so-called "primitive" peoples and the ethnomusicologist with the total study of their music. Thus there arose in ethnomusicology a body of techniques and a system of analysis, which, while drawing upon studies of Western music, have taken some unique turns.

Music structure. Ethnomusicologists are engaged in a search for the proper balance between the basic parts of their discipline, and this search tends to be made within the framework of three major responsibilities felt by scholars in the field.

The first of these areas is the technical study of music structure itself and of how it can best be learned, described, generalized, and compared in specific instances. Even here there is divergence of opinion, as one group of ethnomusicologists argues that the best way to learn a music system is by learning to perform in its style. Performance, most notably in Indonesian and Far Eastern orchestras and styles, is stressed by some scholars, and in many cases with notable results. On the other hand, this approach is criticized by those who hold that performance cannot be the ultimate goal of ethnomusicology and that the value of performance tends to be overstressed.

Ethnomusicologists are agreed, however, that musical sound must ultimately be reduced to notation. Notation by ear in the field is considered unreliable because of the many nuances that are lost, and the usual procedure is to work by ear from tape or disc recordings. In recent years the possibilities of constructing electronic equipment that will give a far more accurately detailed transcription have been explored, and preliminary results indicate that such equipment may, indeed, be both feasible and useful.

The precise transcription of scale systems tuned in intervals different from the Western scale remains somewhat difficult, although such measuring devices as the monochord, electronic equipment, and the cents system can, and do, bring a high degree of precision. Most ethnomusicologists, however, use the Western staff system for notation, employing various special signs to indicate pitch differences and discussing the precise tunings in the body of their report. Analysis is almost always couched in objective, arithmetical, and sometimes statistical terms, with frequencies of appearance of specific characteristics related to the total possibility of the sample. Those characteristics of the music usually considered include melodic range, level, direction, and contour; melodic intervals and interval patterns; ornamentation and melodic devices; melodic meter and rhythm; durational values; formal structure; scale, mode, duration tone, and (subjective) tonic; meter and rhythm; tempo; and vocal style. Other characteristics may be added by the individual student, and almost every body of song demands unique attention in some respects.

There remain, however, a number of difficulties in the technical analysis of music. The first of these concerns transcription itself and the accuracy that can be achieved through the use of the human ear. Closely connected with this is the unresolved question of how accurate a transcription must be; that is, can one generalize, or must the accuracy be as high as that presaged by the advent of electronic equipment? A third problem concerns sampling. Theoretically, at least, the musical universe of any given people is infinite, and the questions are thus how large a sample yields reliable results and whether a larger sample will yield significantly different results from a smaller one. It must also be decided whether one type of song in a given culture is significantly different from another and, if so, whether these types must be treated separately or lumped together into a general set of results for the entire body of music. Finally, there is the major problem of which elements of a musical style are significant, and whether those that are significant are also characteristic. Despite these questions, the technical analysis of musical style has reached a point at which a high degree of precision is possible, and the directions in which analysis has thus far moved seem clearly to be those that will be refined and more fully exploited in the future.

Musical instruments. Associated with the study of musical structure is the study of musical instruments, taken from both the technical and the distributional points of view. Ethnomusicology has supplied detailed studies of the construction and

tuning of instruments, as well as a precise classification of instruments according to the mechanism
of sound production (aerophones, chordophones,
idiophones, and membranophones). Distributional
and diffusion studies of instruments are found for
many parts of the world.

Music as human behavior.   Musical sound does
not and cannot constitute a system that operates
outside the control of human beings. It is thus a
product of the behavior that produces it. Behavior
includes a wide variety of phenomena, but within
the rubric four particularly important facets can
be segregated. The first of these refers to the physical behavior of the musician and his audience. In
order to produce vocal sounds, the musician must
control the vocal organs and the muscles of throat
and diaphragm in certain ways; likewise, in producing instrumental music his breath control and
manipulation of fingers or lips upon the instrument can only be achieved through training,
whether the musician trains himself or is trained
by others. It has further been noted that in performing, musicians take on characteristic bodily
postures, tensions, and attitudes, and attempts are
being made to correlate these with types of music
styles. Similarly, the audience responds to music
in physical and physiological ways, but little is
known of this phenomenon cross-culturally.

A second form of behavior in this context is the
social behavior that accompanies music. In response to his social role, the individual musician
behaves in specific ways according to his own concept of what that role entails, as well as in response to the pressures placed upon him by society
at large. Being a musician means behaving according to culturally defined values; for him, the attitudes and expectations of society, as well as his
own attitudes toward himself, define what is considered to be "musicianly." But society is shaped
also by the musician and his music, for it is often
the latter that gives the cues for proper behavior
in a given social situation.

The third important aspect of music behavior
concerns learning both on the part of the specialist
and the layman. The musician needs training,
whether it is achieved through imitation, apprenticeship, formal schooling, or some other device.
Similarly, the nonspecialist learns his music system sufficiently to participate to some extent and
certainly well enough to differentiate it from other
systems.

Finally, verbal behavior is involved in music to
the extent to which analytic comment is made by
members of a culture on their music system.

Theory of music.   Beneath the level of behavior
as such, however, lies a deeper level, that of the
conceptualization of music. The ethnomusicologist
deals with why music sounds the way it does, as
well as with the "musts" and "shoulds" of music.
Although little material of this kind is available as
yet, the problems lie in the nature of the distinctions made between music and nonmusic, the
sources from which music is drawn, techniques
of composition, the inheritance of musical ability,
and other questions of a similar nature. In other
words, before music behavior can be acted out,
there must be underlying concepts in terms of
which the behavior is shaped.

There exists, then, a continuum of levels of
analysis in the study of musical behavior: music
must begin with basic concepts and values, which
in turn are translated into actual behavior; this in
turn is directed toward the achievement of a specific musical product, or structural sound.

There remains one further aspect of the continuum, however, and this appears in the acceptance or rejection of the final product both by the
musician and by the members of the society at
large. If the product is acceptable to both, then the
concepts out of which it has arisen are reinforced
and the behavior perfected insofar as possible; if,
on the other hand, the product is not adjudged
acceptable, then concepts must be changed and
translated into different behavior in order to adjust the structured sound to what is considered
proper. The product thus inevitably feeds back
upon the concept, which in turn shapes behavior
so that the product, again, will be successful. Both
here and on the behavioral level, ideas and techniques of musical training are of the utmost importance.

Under the stimulation of anthropological problems, methods, and theory, the behavioral aspects
of ethnomusicology have begun to take on added
interest; and by 1950 "ethnomusicology" was replacing the older term "comparative musicology"
(*vergleichende Musikwissenschaft*).

Ethnomusicology and related fields.   Growing
out of the studies of those interested primarily in
music as human behavior has been a third area of
responsibility for ethnomusicologists, and this concerns the relationship of the field to other kinds
of studies. Two major avenues of research have
opened here, the first in the relationship of ethnomusicology to the study of the other arts, and the
second in its relationship to the social sciences.

Relations with the arts.   In respect to the arts
as a whole, ethnomusicologists have begun to turn
to problems of general aesthetics as these are illuminated by the cross-cultural perspective of comparative music studies. One such problem is the
nature of what is called the aesthetic in Western

culture, for those few ethnomusicologists who have considered the subject have in general agreed that the term does not translate well to other cultures, particularly those of nonliterate peoples where the underlying assumptions about music tend to run along different lines. There is a strong suggestion that for most peoples outside Western and Eastern civilization music may be a functional rather than an aesthetic complex in which major emphasis is placed upon what music does rather than philosophic speculation on what it is. This in turn has considerable bearing upon the Western assumption of the interrelatedness of the various arts. What empirical evidence is available seems to indicate that most other peoples do not conceive ideationally of the arts as structurally interrelated, and therefore this concept may well be applicable in the Western context alone. Similar problems that tend to bring evidence to these two major questions include synesthesia, intersense modalities, and so forth. The cross-cultural contribution of ethnomusicology in such problems is potentially considerable, and questions of this nature are being more and more widely considered.

Relations with the social sciences. The relationship of ethnomusicology to the social sciences has already been indicated in that an ethnologic component is inherent in the basic organization of the field. As ethnomusicology continues to expand its orientation, it becomes more and more apparent that both ethnomusicologists and social scientists have overlooked a number of possibilities for fruitful cooperation between the two broad areas. The entire study of music as human behavior, of course, lies well within the sphere of social science, as does the application even of technical music analysis to problems such as acculturation, but there are other applications as well.

Among these is the study of music as symbolic behavior, both in itself and as it relates to broader areas of the culture under study. Political, social, legal, economic, and religious concepts can all be symbolized in musical sound and behavior, and it is frequently to be noted that in the arts in general, among them music, symbolic expression tends to cut to the deepest levels of value and belief. The functions of music in any given culture tell much of the organization and processes of the culture at large, and reference is made here not only to "use" but to integrative function as well. Music operates for specific purposes in all cultures, and analysis of these processes reveals much about both specific and general behavior. Song texts are a badly neglected area of study, both in connection with music itself and with the wider culture. Studies have shown that language behavior in song

may differ sharply from that in everyday discourse, with the stress in song often being placed upon the expression of otherwise unutterable feelings, thoughts, attitudes, and ideas; texts are thus very often an extremely important index to basic values. Texts, too, reveal psychological processes in the life of any given culture, such as when they indicate mechanisms of repression or compensation. It is well known that songs can serve functions of social control, as well as educational and historiographical functions. The relevance of music studies to social science is indeed great, and both disciplines might derive considerable benefit from recognizing this fact.

Ethnomusicology, then, is currently in a phase of expansion and development wherein it is engaged in sorting out the kinds of studies of greatest importance to its development. By its very nature it is interdisciplinary, using the techniques, methods, and theories of both musicology and ethnology; from the fusion of the two it gains new and unique strengths.

ALAN P. MERRIAM

[*Directly related are the entries* CRAFTS; FOLKLORE; PRIMITIVE ART.]

BIBLIOGRAPHY

The works cited below have been chosen to give a broad rather than a selective coverage of widely divergent points of view and methods of approach.

ELLIS, ALEXANDER J. 1885 On the Musical Scales of Various Nations. *Journal of the Royal Society of Arts* 33:485–527.

HERZOG, GEORGE 1936 A Comparison of Pueblo and Pima Musical Styles. *Journal of American Folklore* 49:283–417.

HOOD, MANTLE 1963 Music, the Unknown. Pages 215–326 in Frank L. Harrison, Mantle Hood, and Claude V. Palisca, *Musicology.* Englewood Cliffs, N.J.: Prentice-Hall.

HORNBOSTEL, ERICH M. VON 1905 Die Probleme der vergleichenden Musikwissenschaft. *Zeitschrift der Internationalen Musikgesellschaft* 7:85–97.

KUNST, JAAP (1950) 1959 *Ethnomusicology.* 3d enl. ed. The Hague: Nijhoff. → First published under the title *Musicologica.* A supplement was published in 1960.

LOMAX, ALAN 1962 Song Structure and Social Structure. *Ethnology* 1:425–451.

McALLESTER, DAVID P. 1955 *Enemy Way Music: A Study of Social and Esthetic Values as Seen in Navaho Music.* Harvard University, Peabody Museum of American Archaeology and Ethnology, Papers, Vol. 41, No. 3. Cambridge, Mass.: The Museum.

MALM, WILLIAM P. 1959 *Japanese Music and Musical Instruments.* Rutland, Vt.: Tuttle.

MERRIAM, ALAN P. 1964 *The Anthropology of Music.* Evanston, Ill.: Northwestern Univ. Press.

NETTL, BRUNO 1964 *Theory and Method in Ethnomusicology.* New York: Free Press.

NKETIA, J. H. KWABENA (1963) 1965 *Drumming in Akan Communities of Ghana.* New York: Humanities Press.

SACHS, CURT 1940 *The History of Musical Instruments.* New York: Norton.

SCHAEFFNER, ANDRÉ 1936 *Origine des instruments de musique: Introduction ethnologique à l'histoire de la musique instrumentale.* Paris: Payot.

SEEGER, CHARLES 1953 Preface to the Description of a Music. Pages 360–370 in International Society for Musical Research, Fifth Congress, Utrecht, 1952, *Report.* Amsterdam: Alsbach.

WALLASCHEK, RICHARD 1893 *Primitive Music: An Inquiry Into the Origin and Development of Music, Songs, Instruments, Dances, and Pantomimes of Savage Races.* London: Longmans.

II
MUSIC AND SOCIETY

Music is an expression of inner life, an expression of feelings through the technique of composition, according to the rules of a certain musical style. As expression, music affects the listener as well as the player. It liberates feelings, but it also demands, on the part of the listener, receptiveness and an acquaintance with the style in question.

Music as communication

That music has affectual aspects was stressed in antiquity (in the Greek doctrine of the *ethos*), in the Middle Ages (*musica movet affectum*), and in the Baroque era (in the theory of emotions). Carl Philipp Emanuel Bach stated in 1753 that since a musician cannot move unless he himself is moved, he must be able to experience all the emotions that he wishes to awaken in his audience. He lets them know his feelings and, thus, arouses them to sympathy. This expressive character has been disputed by H. G. Nägeli (1826), who spoke of "arabesques," or an interplay of lines, in music, and by E. Hanslick (1854), who wrote that forms that are "moved tones" are the content of music and that the beautiful generates no emotions. This formal aesthetic is in contrast to the expressive aesthetic (Hausegger 1885). But, it seems that forms that are merely moved tones, such as arabesques, possess an expressive character, as do all forms (Wellek 1963). All music, even "empty [not aiming at expression] play music," such as Oriental music, is movement and, as such, the expression of demonstrable, nervous, physical sensations. The rhythm of this movement stimulates the listener elementally, causing him to move with it. This is especially evident in dancing. Groups or masses of people can be brought to uniform movement, extending to ecstasy, by endlessly repeated rhythms. A child spontaneously follows a musical movement he hears by making expressive motions, like those cultivated in the modern expressive dance. The educated concertgoer, to be sure, is trained from an early age to suppress these spontaneous sympathetic movements.

It follows, therefore, that music has the character of communication. Sound spontaneously uttered by an individual serves as a contact sound, as a first step toward a call or a shout, or as a decoy, wooing, or warning call. Both speech and music develop symbols. Speech evolves ideas, which lead to thinking and logic. Music begins with emotional sounds, which are followed by signals and calls that serve different social purposes. Yet, even in the animal world we find a play of sounds that is unrelated to social purpose, as in the songbirds. Here we have an instinctual root of purposeless, aesthetic enjoyment. But, much music is quite purposeful, integrated into a superordinate social process; it is so-called *Gebrauchsmusik*. March music enables a group to keep in step and in proper order (and also promotes *turgor vitalis*), as does dance music. The folk song even today reveals its social purposes in multifarious variety: cradle songs, war songs, courtship and love songs, serenades, religious songs, incantation and curing songs, and work songs. The last type has almost disappeared in our industrialized countries. Nor is it the oldest type of song, as K. Bücher believed (1896), for it presupposes the existence of rhythmic cooperative work. In present-day industry, music is employed as background music, not to speed up the working rhythm but to stimulate the autonomic nervous system and willingness to work. Schoolchildren doing their homework, and even scientists, employ allegedly soft background music, below the threshold of consciousness or aesthetic effect, as a stimulus to do their work.

Musical texts. In every musical performance the composer, the players, the singers, and the listeners interact with one another, often as semi-participants in popular and exotic music, as in rhythmic clapping. Even when the performer himself does not invent, or improvise (as was the case in the past and in most present-day performances of music by preliterate peoples), but more or less freely reproduces the music invented by others (learned by ear in folk music and in Oriental music), or accurately performs music written by others (*res facta*, in the Middle Ages), an interpersonal process takes place. The folk song is invented by an individual, but it is much modified ("taken apart") by the singer. The motets of the fourteenth century were also modified by the singers. A composition was not regarded as the individual property of a single composer. Everyone changed it ad lib, adding new voices with new texts, etc. Thus, the musical composition was regarded as common property, a notion that persisted into the seventeenth century and even the eighteenth, when George Frederick Handel took over the compositions of others. The concept of "plagiarism," applied to parts of a work as well as the whole work, is a modern concept.

The contemporary practice of copyright is the end product of a long development. To be sure, there were privileges of printing granted by a sovereign, but they were respected only in part. Today even a motif is protected by copyright, although protection is limited to a term of 50 years. Even primitive peoples have a law of musical property. Among the Andaman Islanders an invented song remains the intellectual property of the inventor, for which he is recompensed during festivals, and no one is permitted to sing the song after his death. The same was true among the Iroquois. The present-day law of property covers not only the right to reprint but also the right of performance and, in particular, mechanical reproduction.

The musical professions

Today the musical professions are highly specialized. The primeval musician was creator, singer, and performer in one, as shown in such mythological figures as Jubal and Orpheus. Composers were always performing musicians as well: singers (Josquin) in the fifteenth and sixteenth centuries; singers and conductors (Monteverdi) in the seventeenth century; and pianists (Mozart, Beethoven) and other instrumentalists (Viotti, Spohr) or professional conductors (Wagner, Mahler, Richard Strauss) in the eighteenth and nineteenth centuries and down into the twentieth century. Today, however, specialization characterizes the musical professions, even within a single profession, dividing them into entire categories, such as "serious" and "entertainment" music. There is a great diversity of musical roles, running from the highly paid star conductor down to the street musician and the beggar playing music, e.g., with a barrel organ. Moreover, each musical profession has a social scale of its own. The status of a musician is based upon one of two factors: (1) the professional role, which in turn derives from education, cultural level, and the prestige of his audience, and (2) income. There is no correlation between these two factors.

In addition to talent and endowment, career and success depend upon circumstances, which are often fortuitous, as well as upon reviews in the press. The occupational category of conductor covers all degrees of education, depending upon the kind of music; there are conductors of opera, church, military, jazz, and entertainment orchestras, each group being subdivided along an artistic scale. As the status of the church musician diminished during the nineteenth century, that of the conductor rose extraordinarily. In Verdi's time the conductor was unnamed, ranking behind the singers of the opera. After World War I his name might be printed on posters in conspicuous letters, above that of the composer. Singers, too, are categorized: opera singers, concert singers, jazz singers, and singers of popular tunes. Outstanding singers have always enjoyed substantial popularity and financial success. This was true in classical antiquity but has especially been the case since the eighteenth century, when prima donnas and *castrati* dominated the musical scene. The earnings of Caruso (who died in 1921), which were regarded as enormous in his day, have been overshadowed by the sensational success of more recent hit-tune singers who become millionaires overnight. This is due to mass responsiveness and particularly to the mechanical reproduction and distribution of hit tunes. Artistic reputation and prestige are greatly differentiated, for example, in the profession of the female singer. Female musicians and singers of the lower categories often led dubious lives, sometimes becoming prostitutes (the Syrian *ambubaiae* in Rome, the mistresses of princes during the Baroque, *chansonnières*). Instrumentalists also occupy many different positions on the social scale, ranging from the violinist in the orchestra, who is further differentiated according to his position in the orchestra and the quality of the orchestra, up to the eminent soloist, who can count on income from concerts of his own. The same holds true for pianists and other instrumentalists. The independent instrumentalist is often a teacher of his instrument—either privately or in schools, conservatories, etc.—thus, improving his financial status and his prestige (gaining the title of "professor"). It was common practice for masters of the past (Handel, Mozart, Beethoven) to make a living at times by giving lessons.

A musician's prestige, apart from the special prestige of his profession, has varied through the centuries and even today differs according to country and people. We know of whole hierarchies of musician castes in antiquity: in Babylon, in Egypt, in Judea. Music was often performed by slaves. What is strange is the frequently severe restrictions placed on the civic dignity of a musician in many countries and times, such as ancient Rome, in contrast with the high esteem in which musicians were held among the Germanic peoples. The *skald* of the Nordic peoples and the *skop* of the western Germans were the close confidants of princes. As the Nordic tribes became Westernized, the musician inherited the low status of the Roman *mimus*, becoming a vagrant minstrel, a tramp, or a street singer. In all of these cases, the individual musician was often able to secure high esteem, wealth, and status at the courts of secular and even ecclesiastical princes. Only with the establishment of cities did the domiciled musician obtain a civil occupation. Celebrated musicians gained high honors. Some of them were raised to the ranks of the nobility (Hofhaimer, Hassler); others were awarded papal decorations (Lasso and Mozart becoming knights; Dittersdorf, Gluck, and Spontini becoming *equites aurati*). The fact that universities awarded honorary doctorates to celebrated composers contributed to increasing the prestige of musicians. The title of professor gave the top level of musicians the right of presentation at court. A pianist, Ignace Paderewski, even became prime minister of Poland in 1919.

The status of the musician was just as indefinite in the eighteenth and nineteenth centuries as his prestige. Fame and riches did not always entail equal rights for many celebrated musicians. For example, Franz Liszt, a rich *grand seigneur*, who was raised to the ranks of the hereditary nobility, nevertheless encountered resistance at the court when he proposed to marry a princess. This discrepancy between fame as an artist and status in society prevails in parts of the Orient up to the present day. As recently as 1932, at a congress in Cairo, high government officials refused to sit at the same table with eminent musicians of their own country. The prejudice against the artist was reinforced when the "bohemian" type arose in the nineteenth century. Even today the artist is not highly respected among the bourgeois middle class. In a certain sense he is outside society.

Secondary musical professions. Alongside creating, performing, and directing there are many important professionals who serve the institutional structure of musical life, such as publishers, printers, music engravers, impresarios, and critics. The invention of the printing of music from movable type, in about 1500, made possible the spread of new musical styles and of music of high artistic merit. Nevertheless, in the eighteenth century the sale of handwritten music—music noted down by the copyist—still predominated over engraved notes. It was only toward the end of the eighteenth century that music publishing developed as a commercial enterprise and influenced the style, distribution, and acceptance of compositions.

Impresarios and agents. The impresario, or entrepreneur of public performances, played an important role in the history of opera, but his importance has lessened ever since the high cost of opera made it an unprofitable commercial undertaking, so that it now has to be managed as a subsidized public institution. On the other hand, the entrepreneur, manager, and agent are important elsewhere in the musical world, providing the talent employed in concerts and other musical performances.

Critics. Another related profession is that of the music critic, who works for newspapers, magazines, the radio, etc., either as his principal occupation or as a sideline. Critical evaluation of performed music is found as far back as antiquity, the Middle Ages, and the Age of Enlightenment. Yet, as late as the eighteenth century, critics dealt primarily with musical texts; good examples are Mattheson (1722–1725) in the *Critica musica* and the French Encyclopedists. Most representative critics of the second half of the nineteenth century, for example, in their battle against Wagner followed the same line. Contemporary criticism, on the other hand, emphasizes reproduction and performance. The critic is uncontradicted in the pages of his own newspaper, but public opinion, even when it goes against the opinions of the critic, usually triumphs in the end. No special study, no examinations are required for the profession of critic. His certificate of competence is the quality of his style, not special knowledge of the subject, which is often sadly lacking even in prominent critics. The history of criticism proves how greatly critics have erred.

Musicologists. Another musical profession is that of the musicologist who does his work in the quiet of the university. Musicology has made a significant contribution to the revival of music composed to order or on commission (Handel, Bach, and today Vivaldi and the music of the Baroque). Musical research in universities explores historical and aesthetic problems, as well as those dealing with instruments and performance.

Public musical life

The term "musical life" is generally taken to mean the total of all public and semipublic performances of music, rather than the private, intimate cultivation of music in the home. It involves, for the most part, the large musical institutions—that is, operas, orchestras, choruses. These events are sponsored by the government, the municipality, societies, associations, and commercial entrepreneurs.

Opera.   Today the opera is the biggest and most costly musical institution. As an art form, it is a stylized, special case of the theatrical play with music, which is to be found among all peoples and in all periods of history. Opera was begun in the West, by humanist circles in Florence, in 1594, as an aesthetic experiment in recreating the drama of antiquity, which used music to support the text. It developed in the sacred opera of the cardinals' palaces in Rome, in the impresario opera of Venice, including carnival farces and pantomimes, and in the royal opera of European sovereigns.

These last two types continue to exist. Opera managed by an impresario was started in Venice by Ferrarri in 1637, as a profit-sharing venture among the members of his company; later, in London, between 1720 and 1728, Handel's opera companies took the legal form of joint stock companies. Court opera—presented before members of the court seated hierarchically in the traditional tiered theater—was wholly subsidized by the crown.

The musical theater of the people took several forms: the *bagatelliste* drama, the *commedia dell'arte*, and the *Singspiel*. Starting with the caricature of Handel's *opera seria* in *The Beggar's Opera*, the *Singspiel* catered increasingly to the taste of the middle and petty bourgeois, especially in Germany. *Singspiel* troupes at first often played under the most wretched circumstances, but eventually this theater became a dangerous competitor to the court theater. The *Singspiel* disseminated the mood of the French Revolution in the theaters of the suburbs, but the political element was often secondary to pantomime and myth (e.g., E. Schikaneder's 1791 *Singspiel, Die Zauberflöte*, with music by Mozart). A combination of the two types of opera were the numerous traveling opera troupes of the impresarios, which were often engaged by princes to play in their court theaters.

The era of the Baroque court opera came to an end about 1760. Eight years earlier Empress Maria Theresa had turned her court theater over to the city of Vienna to be operated by the municipality. The French Revolution turned the opera into political propaganda, glorifying revolutionary ideas and heroes, a counterpart to the earlier glorification of princes during the Baroque era.

Most of the European monarchies established state opera houses in their principal cities. Many of these have remained active. Because of its many small principalities, Germany became the country with the largest number of opera houses and orchestras. In 1963 the German Federal Republic, including West Berlin, had 132 theaters with a total attendance of 6.3 million (including 2.4 million at operetta performances), 36 theater orchestras, and 41 independent orchestras, including 9 radio orchestras. East Germany had 86 theaters in 1962, with a total attendance of 3.4 million at the opera and 2.8 million at operettas. Russia had opera performances for the imperial court under Peter the Great, and a public state opera house was founded in Moscow in 1806. Alongside the state opera houses there were princely opera houses and, as late as 1900, private opera houses of princes. Bulgaria, Rumania, and Czechoslovakia have state opera houses. State opera houses were established in Scandinavia fairly late: in 1936, in Sweden, and in 1958, in Norway. Italy, the classic land of opera enterprise, established a royal opera house only in 1929.

The opera companies are subsidized on a very lavish scale from the receipts of the amusement tax, for the high cost of operas makes the running of an opera company financially unprofitable. La Scala, Milan, for example, has annual box-office receipts of 1,900 million lire and since 1936 has received an annual subsidy of some 880 million lire. In 1958 the Royal Opera House, Covent Garden, received an inadequate subsidy of £63,000, although £500,000 had been requested. The last big private opera company in Germany was Angelo Neumann's Wagnerian company in the 1880s. In France the major arts have always been centered in Paris, where the *grand opéra* received a subsidy of 20 million francs in 1958.

The oldest established opera company in the United States is the Metropolitan Opera in New York, founded in 1884. Like the opera in Chicago, it was initially financed by wealthy businessmen. American opera houses are still dependent upon patrons and foundations. In the 1950s there were about 600 opera organizations in 47 states, 25 per cent being professional organizations and the others affiliated with clubs, churches, studios, and colleges. Operas have been performed in colleges, in high schools, in conservatories, and even in elementary schools.

The support of large-scale artistic enterprises, whether by princes, institutions, wealthy patrons, or the state, means that these enterprises must conform, within varying limits, to the values of their patrons and publics. There are substantial differences between institutions in the type of financial support, the artistic achievement, and the intellectual level, depending upon the class of society that supports or attends them.

Operettas and musicals. The *Singspiel* troupes in the eighteenth century called their plays operettas. However, the modern operetta, which achieved popular success in the second half of the nineteenth century in the Viennese operettas of Johann Strauss and the Parisian ones of Jacques Offenbach and was performed in independent operetta theaters run by impresarios, tried to advance from a provincial style to a quasi-operatic style (e.g., Franz Lehár). In America there developed the musical comedy, designed as light entertainment in a popular musical idiom. *The Archers*, performed in 1796 in the John Street Theater, New York, may be regarded as the first of this type. Musical comedies have run for years with enormous success in the Broadway theater of the twentieth century, reaping millions for their investors (for example, *My Fair Lady*, book by A. J. Lerner after Shaw's *Pygmalion* and music by F. Loewe, ran for six years, from 1956 to 1962).

Orchestras. Orchestras are among the major public musical institutions; some of them are the most important components of the opera houses mentioned above. In the nineteenth and twentieth centuries large orchestras (a hundred men or more) acquired a mass audience in the concert halls of major cities. They are the outgrowth of the chamber orchestras of the seventeenth century, which often consisted of no more than twelve to sixteen men. Enlargement of the orchestras was promoted in Germany by the staging of patriotic celebrations of the Napoleonic Wars and the Congress of Vienna. In England large orchestras had played at the Handel festivals since 1784, and in France gigantic orchestras were assembled by Berlioz in connection with the political demonstrations and events of 1830, 1837 (an orchestra of 146 plus 4 auxiliary orchestras), 1841, 1848, and 1851. Speculative enterprises, such as the enormous orchestra used for an American performance of Johann Strauss, with 20,000 singers and players and 100 assistant conductors before an audience of 100,000, represented an extreme form of musical entertainment.

In 1965 the United States had 1,385 symphony orchestras of various sizes. Of the top 100 orchestras, 10 were in existence before 1900; 15 were founded between 1900 and 1920; 54 between 1920 and 1940; and 21 after 1940.

Of the 77 orchestras in the German Federal Republic today, 40 (not including the radio orchestras) have 60 to 100 players. The other European countries do not have as many large orchestras. In France there are five large orchestras, four in Paris and one in Strasbourg. In England, London has three orchestras, and there are orchestras in Liverpool, Birmingham, Bournemouth, and Glasgow; London also has one opera orchestra and three large radio symphony orchestras. Milan, Italy, has the orchestra of La Scala and a symphony orchestra; Rome has one symphony orchestra. There are two radio orchestras, one in Rome and the other in Turin.

Groups—in fact, masses—of performers have traditionally served as demonstrations of the power of kings, princes, and feudal lords, and more recently of governments. Musicians, usually trumpeters and drummers, announced the appearance of rulers in preliterate Africa and in advanced cultures on ceremonial occasions.

Alongside the highly trained orchestras we find orchestras of all musical and social ranks: opera, concert, operetta, vaudeville, circus, coffeehouse, and parade orchestras, as well as those playing at dances and in parks. The social status of orchestra members varies, ranging from those employed by the state or big private enterprises down to those employed by municipalities, to musicians in private employ either in institutions that receive government subsidies or guarantees or in unsubsidized theater orchestras, and finally to the less highly trained musicians, who have to depend on occasional employment. Military musicians often represent competition for independent orchestra players. Changes in the technology of public entertainment may have serious consequences for independent musicians; one instance was the catastrophe that hit musicians employed in movie theaters when the sound film was introduced in 1930.

Choral music. The evolution of the modern chorus parallels that of large-scale organizations in general in Western societies. The choruses of the sixteenth and seventeenth centuries cannot be compared in size with the choruses of today. They consisted of a few professional singers (as in the Sistine Chapel in Rome), with no more than two to four singers in each choir, except on special royal occasions.

The modern chorus received a mighty organizational impetus from the French Revolution, in which choruses played a political role. In 1795 it was proposed to the National Convention that national holidays be celebrated by *chœurs universels*. Mass choruses, with 2,400 men and women, were organized in Paris, in 1784. They set the example for mass choruses in subsequent revolutions. In Germany and France, between the Napoleonic Wars and the revolutions of 1830 and 1848, national enthusiasm and socialist trends led to the establishment of choruses, male choruses, and choral organizations, which performed at choral festivals. In choral activity of this period, the democratic ideal of a fusion of the various walks of life, from the commoner to the nobleman, seems to have been achieved in Germany. In the decades that followed, choruses were again divided according to class and occupation (e.g., teachers' choral societies, printers' choruses, etc.). The choral movement was furthered in France after the revolution, especially by G. Wilhem, and totaled 60,000 members in 1,500 *orphéons* by 1893. In the same period there were monster performances in England with over 4,000 participants, half of whom were singers.

Most contemporary choruses are organized as societies, which in turn are organized into associations. Germany has 15,000 choruses, with a total membership of 1.3 million, their social and civic significance outstripping their aesthetic achievements. The Scandinavian countries, Finland in particular, are also rich in choruses. In Italy large mixed choruses have evolved slowly because the association of adult men and women, which is so prominent a feature of choral life elsewhere, conflicted with the prevailing Italian pattern of the relations of the sexes. Only since the end of the nineteenth century have women been admitted to the church choirs in Roman Catholic countries. Choral singing has always been popular in England. The major choruses include the Royal Chorus Society, founded in 1873; the Bach Choir, founded in 1876; and the Goldsmith's Choir Union, founded in 1932. An international choral festival, the Eisteddfod, was founded in 1947 in Wales.

In addition to the choral societies, in which the artistic aim often is secondary to the desire for conviviality, there are the professional choruses. These include the little master choirs of the Roman Catholic and Protestant churches in the sixteenth and eighteenth centuries, the opera choruses of modern times, and outstanding national choirs, such as the Association Chorale Professionnelle in France and the Soviet State Chorus in Russia, which continues the tradition of the liturgical choirs and of the pre-1919 Moscow Synodal Choir. In Russia, there also are the first-class and highly paid choruses of the radio networks, newly established everywhere.

Ecclesiastical music. Churches are important in musical culture as public institutions, although here music is not an end in itself. They maintain choirmasters, organists, and musicians. They publish hymn books, and besides their significant influence upon broad, popular musical culture, they stage major events themselves, including services with orchestral and choral accompaniment and church concerts that are outside the liturgical framework (or else they make the churches available for such performances). Music has always been an element of religious worship. In ancient times the performance of music was reserved to persons of cultic importance: priests and magicians. Advanced theocratic civilizations—such as those of the Babylonians, the Sumerians, the Egyptians, and the Jews—had an extensive hierarchical system of religious musical culture. The recital of sacred texts by singing them is found throughout the world, not only because the singing voice enhances the texts but also because of music's magical effect.

From the days of the church fathers down to the present, there has been conflict between the concerns of the church musician, who wishes to elevate the faithful with his music, and the preachers, who regard music that is too copious as a distraction from religious meditation. That is why Calvin and Zwingli, for example, forbade all music with the exception of the chorale. Even today the playing of instruments is restricted in the Roman Catholic church, and their use has been governed by numerous edicts for centuries. In the Roman Catholic church, singing, except for the little permitted the congregation, was until recently reserved to the choir of priests, who, from the theological standpoint, are representatives of the angelic choir. Luther introduced singing by the whole congregation (again theologically based on the evangelical approach). Today, the significance of church music is confined to the church itself; yet, its influence is still great. Choirmasters (called church music directors in many churches) and organists train lay church choirs. In the missions (as well as in the Negro churches of the United States), the church makes considerable use of the performance of ethnic music. The basic conservatism of the churches in general entails greater cultivation of traditional music, discouraging the development of any generally effective new musical styles.

The training of musical taste and skill. Musical education is indispensable to the general cultivation of music. There is no doubt that here it fulfills an important function: bringing up children to be members of society. Musical education is conducted mostly in the schools, where a certain training of children to enjoy music made by singing together, as well as a modest degree of musical instruction, is an important factor in the development of the musical culture of any society. Little time, however, is scheduled for instruction in music in most countries, and only the wealthier classes of society can afford private teachers of music for their children.

Music schools serve primarily to train performing musicians. (The word "conservatory" is derived from the word for the orphan asylums in Venice and Naples during the eighteenth century, in which music gradually became the focus of activity.) In most countries there are "institutes of music" for training the musical elite.

Musicians' associations. Associations of musicians existed even in antiquity (e.g., the association of "Dionysian artists"). The first medieval organizations of musicians, founded in the twelfth and thirteenth centuries, were religious in nature (St. Bartholomew's Hospital in London, St. Nicolaibrüderschaft in Vienna). In 1657 the guilds and corporations of musicians in 43 localities of central Germany united in an "Instrumental-Musikalisches Collegium," sanctioned by Emperor Ferdinand III. Trumpeters and drummers constituted a separate caste, a "noble guild," in the royal courts and armies; this was so even in ancient Rome. Down to the nineteenth century, organized musicians tried to defend their privileges against the unorganized (for example, by playing at weddings, etc., with a restricted number of instruments).

Starting in 1808, the Prussian state contributed to the security of musicians and their families, and voluntary welfare agencies for widows, orphans, and pensioners were promoted by Spontini in Berlin in 1842 (and in Vienna by the Tonkünstlersociété of Gassmann as early as 1770). Like all social insurance, these programs signified a strengthening of the musical professions in their struggle for social recognition and, thus, strengthened the self-confidence of musicians in general.

Musicians' unions, as distinct from artistic organizations, are a comparatively recent phenomenon. In Germany, the Allgemeiner Deutscher Musikerverband was founded in 1872. Since 1952, the main organization is the Deutsche Orchester-Vereinigung in der Deutschen Angestellten-Gewerkschaft; it had a membership of 5,676 in 1960 out of a total of about 6,000 orchestra musicians. In England the Incorporated Society of Musicians was established in 1882; in France there is the Syndicat National des Artistes Musiciens, and in the United States, the American Federation of Musicians.

Alongside the professional organizations there are also associations of amateurs and patrons of music. At first, these societies did not intend to give public concerts, but only "practice concerts."

Later on, they were succeeded by organizations that gave public concerts (for example, the Concerts of Ancient Music between 1776 and 1848, in England; Le Concert Spirituel between 1725 and 1791, in France; and the Big Concerts in Leipzig, dating from 1743, which were continued in 1781 as the Gewandhaus Concerts). The Allgemeine Deutsche Musikverein, 1861–1937, had as its purpose the "cultivation of music and the advancement of musicians." The Gesellschaft der Musikfreunde was founded in 1771 in Vienna. In England, the New Philharmonic Society was active from 1852 to 1897, and the National Federation of Music Societies was started in 1935. In the United States, there were the Handel and Haydn Society (founded in 1915), the Musical Alliance of America (founded in 1917), and, for orchestral music, the Philharmonic Society of New York (founded in 1842).

There is hardly any aspect of musical life that has no organization; school musicians and teachers of music (the Music Teachers' Association, founded in 1876, in the United States), composers, music dealers, instrument makers, etc., all have their own organizations. There are even international bodies such as the International Music Council, established in 1949, which holds national and international congresses; 39 national committees are affiliated with this international organization. Other international organizations include: the Fédération Internationale des Jeunesses Musicales (founded in 1947), the International Folk Music Council (founded in 1947), the Confédération Internationale des Sociétés des Auteurs et Compositeurs (founded in 1926), and the Fédération Internationale des Musiciens (founded in 1948).

Audience and performance

There are various forms of music-playing for larger audiences. The playing of folk music unites the performers, singers, and players. Either there is no distinct audience at all or some of the listeners become participants, for instance, by clapping in rhythm or by joining in a song or its refrains. On a higher artistic plane, music is performed for an audience that does nothing but listen. At big dances, however, the listeners are also the dancers who express the music rhythmically.

This distinction among singers, players, and mere listeners is further subdivided into two categories: "familiar music-playing," represented in the past by the regular performance of music by town musicians, performances at church festivals, court music, music played at table, etc., and the modern "performance," which presupposes thorough study of the music to be played, by orchestras and ensembles. Mozart played his own piano concertos without any rehearsal, and Beethoven's symphonies were played (by amateurs) in big concerts without rehearsal. In these amateur concerts, practice concerts, and glee clubs of the eighteenth century, the relatives of the performers did not come only to hear the music but to play cards and smoke as well.

Concerts and publics. As early as the sixteenth and seventeenth centuries, musicians played private concerts and advertised them in the newspapers. Like the opera, which was sometimes open to the public upon payment of an admission fee, in the eighteenth century there were public concerts that were open to anyone upon payment of an admission fee. These concerts were held at the same time as the concerts for invited guests of the aristocracy and the wealthy of Paris and were often staged on a splendid scale. Ever since the middle of the eighteenth century, however, the concert open to the wide public has been the standard form for the performance of music. The admission ticket is a contract of sale. (The German youth music movement has criticized this form of concert since 1914, believing that it entails the danger that the listener, excluded from active participation, might become inwardly inactive as well. The youth movement advocated "open singing," with the active participation of all the listeners, in opposition to the concert form. It wanted to experience music in a community, with the participation of all those present.)

The musician presenting his art tries to gain a "public." This may be a homogeneous audience that is linked to the performers. Such is the case, for example, in a concert of active or passive members of a society, in a school concert, in a concert for a public united in support of a particular artistic goal, etc. However, the persuasiveness of music is required to establish a community of musical experience in a concert for a metropolitan public, which is brought together by interests not all of which are artistic and which is not at all uniform in taste. In this case, the purely creative social force, the "sociability" of music, is probably only transitory and hard to estimate. It is a hyperbole to speak of the creative social force of Beethoven's symphonies. Rather, like all works of art, these symphonies are the work of an individual genius, but they also express the general feelings of mankind (or at least those of a national group during a certain epoch).

The stratification of musical activity

Musical performances differ in the socially different strata of audiences according to the quality of the performance, the artistic and social strivings of the musicians, the magnitude of the performance (number of performers and type of music), and content of the repertoire, and the style and age of the works performed. They are further divided into two categories: serious and entertainment music. Serious-music performances include symphony concerts, choral concerts, oratorios, recitals, evenings of lieder, and programs of church music. Entertainment-music performances include folk-music and military-band concerts, concerts in public squares, and beer-garden concerts featuring light programs, dances, marches, jazz, and popular singing.

Public performances requiring tickets of admission constitute a classification of the listeners according to the price of admission, fixed by the listeners' means. The performances themselves differ, and the ticket effects a spatial stratification within the concert hall itself. The motive for opera-going or concertgoing often is the desire for social contacts and, in the case of expensive concerts and the higher-priced seats, the desire to be seen and to gain or maintain prestige, alongside the interest in the music and often ahead of it (in the case of the "snob"). The optional or frequently prescribed dress for the audience (black tie, evening gown) results in social gradations of the performance, as does the spatial allocation within the hall (orchestra seats versus balcony). Not only does the cost of admission act as a hindrance to lower-income groups, but the social level of the audience (education, dress) may hinder outsiders from attending the concert.

The statistics available on the stratification of the radio audience, however, indicate that the inexpensive opportunity of listening to music and the elimination of social shyness does *not* prevent a quite general stratification of the listeners. "Serious" or "heavy" music (usually called classical music for the sake of simplicity) is generally preferred by those of higher education. According to these statistics, the desire to hear serious music and the understanding thereof grow with the level of general education and, correspondingly, with musical training.

Audience organizations in all countries are endeavoring to lift the financial barriers for the bulk of the population. Yet, serious music cannot easily be made "accessible to the people." The problem of making "true folk music" widely accessible must also be regarded with skepticism in industrialized countries with a predominantly urban population. Folk music lives on in isolated regions and loses its character when it becomes a school song or is arranged for choral singing.

Mass communication, with some 300 million

radios in the world and about four times that many listeners, represents a totally new factor in bringing the masses into contact with different types of music. Programs are classified according to content and are broadcast at times that make allowance for the listeners' social status and working hours. (The phonograph record and the jukebox are related forms of mass communication.) Music is disseminated far more widely than at any previous time. This is paralleled by lower intensity; listening to music grows duller and shallower.

Mass communication is disseminating Euro–American music among non-Western peoples. Regrettably enough, exogenous entertainment music often displaces these peoples' indigenous music. A mixed style that approaches European music is already developing in the non-Western countries that have traditional musical styles of their own.

HANS ENGEL

BIBLIOGRAPHY

ADORNO, T. W. 1962 *Einleitung in die Musiksoziologie: Zwölf theoretische Vorlesungen.* Frankfurt am Main (Germany): Suhrkamp.

ALLEN, WARREN D. (1939) 1962 *Philosophies of Music History: A Study of General Histories of Music, 1600–1960.* New York: Dover.

BAB, JULIUS 1931 *Das Theater im Lichte der Soziologie.* Leipzig: Hirschfeld.

BAUMOL, WILLIAM J.; and BOWEN, WILLIAM G. 1966 *Performing Arts: The Economic Dilemma.* New York: Twentieth Century Fund.

BECKER, HOWARD S. 1951 The Professional Dance Musician and His Audience. *American Journal of Sociology* 57:136–144.

BLAUKOPF, KURT (1950) 1951 *Musiksoziologie: Eine Einführung in die Grundbegriffe mit besonderer Berücksichtigung der Soziologie der Tonsysteme.* Vienna: Verkauf.

BLAUKOPF, KURT 1952 Musiksoziologie, Bindung und Freiheit bei der Wahl von Tonsystemen. Pages 237–257 in Carl Brinkmann (editor), *Soziologie und Leben: Die soziologische Dimension der Fachwissenschaften.* Tübingen (Germany): Wunderlich.

BONNOT, RENÉ 1960 Sociologie de la musique. Volume 2, pages 297–298 in Georges Gurvitch (editor), *Traité de sociologie.* Paris: Presses Universitaires de France.

BÜCHER, K. (1896) 1902 *Arbeit und Rhythmus.* 3d ed. Leipzig: Teubner.

CROSTEN, WILLIAM L. 1948 *French Grand Opera: An Art and a Business.* New York: King's Crown Press.

ENGEL, HANS 1933 Musik, Gesellschaft, Gemeinschaft. *Zeitschrift für Musikwissenschaft* 17:175–185.

ENGEL, HANS 1942 Der Musiker: Beruf und Lebensformen. Pages 180–205 in *Von Deutscher Tonkunst: Festschrift zu P. Raabes 70. Geburtstag.* Edited by Alfred Morgenroth. Leipzig: Peters.

ENGEL, HANS 1952 Das Chorwesen in soziologischer Sicht. *Zeitschrift für Musik* 8:433–439.

ENGEL, HANS 1960 *Musik und Gesellschaft: Bausteine zu einer Musiksoziologie.* Berlin: Hesse.

FARNSWORTH, PAUL R. 1958 *The Social Psychology of Music.* New York: Dryden.

FELLERER, KARL G. 1963 *Soziologie der Kirchenmusik: Materialien zur Musik- und Religionssoziologie.* Cologne (Germany): Westdeutscher Verlag.

FISCHER, KARL A. 1951 *Kultur und Gesellung: Ein Beitrag zur allgemeinen Kultursoziologie.* Schriften der soziologischen Abteilung des Forschungsinstitutes für Sozial- und Verwaltungswissenschaften in Köln, No. 2. Cologne (Germany): Westdeutscher Verlag.

FRANCASTEL, P. 1960 Problèmes de la sociologie de l'art. Volume 2, pages 279–296 in Georges Gurvitch (editor), *Traité de sociologie.* Paris: Presses Universitaires de France.

GROUT, DONALD J. 1960 *A History of Western Music.* New York: Norton.

HANSLICK, EDUARD 1854 *Vom Musikalisch-Schönen: Ein Beitrag zur Revision der Aesthetik der Tonkunst.* Leipzig: Weigel.

HAUSEGGER, FRIEDRICH VON (1885) 1887 *Die Musik als Ausdruck.* 2d ed. Vienna: Konegen.

HOFSTÄTTER, PETER R. (1956) 1964 *Sozialpsychologie.* 2d ed. Berlin: Gruyter.

HONIGSHEIM, P. 1958 Soziologie der Kunst, Musik und Literatur. Pages 338–373 in Gottfried Eisermann (editor), *Die Lehre von der Gesellschaft: Ein Lehrbuch der Soziologie.* Stuttgart (Germany): Enke.

KLAUSMEIER, FRIEDRICH 1963 *Jugend und Musik im technischen Zeitalter: Eine representative Befragung in einer Westdeutschen Grossstadt.* Bonn: Bouvier.

KNEIF, TIBOR 1966 Gegenwartsfragen der Musiksoziologie: Ein Forschungsbericht. *Acta musicologica* 38: 72–118.

LENZ, FRIEDRICH 1952 *Einführung in die Soziologie des Rundfunks.* Emsdetten (Germany): Lechte.

MACKERNESS, ERIC D. 1964 *A Social History of English Music.* London: Routledge.

MATTHESON, JOHANN 1722–1725 *Critica musica.* 2 vols. Hamburg (Germany): No publisher given.

MEYER, ERNST H. 1952 *Musik im Zeitgeschehen: Grundprobleme der Musiksoziologie.* Berlin: Henschel.

MOSER, H. J. 1960 *Die Tonsprachen des Abendlandes: Zehn Essais als Wesenskunde der europäischen Musik.* Berlin: Merseburger.

MUELLER, JOHN H. (1951) 1958 *The American Symphony Orchestra: A Social History of Musical Taste.* London: Calder.

NÄGELI, HANS G. 1826 *Vorlesungen über Musik.* Tübingen (Germany): Cotta.

NETTEL, REGINALD 1946 *The Orchestra in England: A Social History.* London: Cape.

OLKHOWSKY, ANDREY V. 1955 *Music Under the Soviets: The Agony of an Art.* New York: Praeger.

PINTHUS, GERHARD 1932 *Das Konzertleben in Deutschland: Ein Abriss seiner Entwicklung bis zum Beginn des 19. Jahrhunderts.* Strassburg: Heitz.

PREUSSNER, EBERHARD (1935) 1950 *Die bürgerliche Musikkultur: Ein Beitrag zur deutschen Musikgeschichte des 18. Jahrhunderts.* 2d ed. Kassel and Basel: Bärenreiter.

PROESLER, HANS; and BEER, KARL 1955 *Die Gruppe; The Group; Le groupe: Ein Beitrag zur Systematik soziologischer Grundbegriffe.* Berlin and Munich: Duncker & Humblot.

REINOLD, H. 1955 Musik im Rundfunk. *Kölner Zeitschrift für Soziologie und Sozialpsychologie* 7:233–246.

RÉVÉSZ, GÉZA (1946) 1954 *Introduction to the Psychology of Music.* Norman: Univ. of Oklahoma Press. → First published in German.

SIEGMEISTER, ELIE (editor) 1938 *Music and Society.* New York: Critics group. → Also published in German in 1948.

SILBERMANN, ALPHONS (1957) 1963 *The Sociology of Music.* London: Routledge. → First published as *Wovon lebt die Musik? Die Prinzipien der Musiksoziologie.*

SLOTKIN, J. S. 1943 Jazz and Its Forerunners as an Example of Acculturation. *American Sociological Review* 8:570–575.

THOMAS, HANS A. 1962 *Die deutsche Tonfilmmusik: Von den Anfängen bis 1956.* Gütersloh (Germany): Bertelsmann.

[VIAN, BORIS] (1958) 1966 *En avant la zizique . . . et par ici les gros sous,* by Vernon Sullivan [pseud.]. Paris: Jeune Parque. → Essay on the popular music industry, by an experienced song writer and recording company executive.

WEBER, MAX (1921) 1958 *The Rational and Social Foundations of Music.* Carbondale: Southern Illinois Univ. Press. → First published in German.

WELLEK, ALBERT 1963 *Musikpsychologie und Musikästhetik: Grundriss der systematischen Musikwissenschaft.* Frankfurt am Main (Germany): Akademische Verlagsgesellschaft.

WOODFILL, WALTER L. 1953 *Musicians in English Society From Elizabeth to Charles I.* Princeton Univ. Press.

MYRES, JOHN LINTON

Sir John Linton Myres (1869–1954), a historian of classical antiquity, showed in his work a knowledge and competence gained from other disciplines—notably, from geography, anthropology, and archeology. The width of his interests led him to anthropology, at that time a broad, inclusive study that combined both humanist and scientific orientations, and he devoted much of his long life to furthering its cause in institutional ways—by his long association with the Royal Anthropological Institute, by founding and editing the journal *Man,* by helping to extend the teaching of anthropology at Oxford, and by organizing various national and international conferences and congresses.

For most of his life Myres lived and worked at Oxford, where from 1910 until 1939 he was Wykeham professor of ancient history. His central interest as a scholar was the origin and development of Greek civilization, and his most important book, *Who Were the Greeks?* (1930), was a contribution to this theme. First delivered as the Sather lectures at the University of California at Berkeley, this book might be described as an inquiry into the ethnological origins of Greek culture: Myres drew his data from geography, physical anthropology, comparative philology, and archeology, as well as from the traditions and beliefs recorded in Greek literature. In his general conclusions he emphasized the heterogeneity of Greek origins and the

processes of selection and adaptation that occurred to produce the seeming unity of the Greek people in its "great age." Myres excelled in this kind of cross-disciplinary study, his own particular contribution being to show the relevance of geography and history for the development of culture. It was this theme that he took up in his Frazer lecture, entitled "An Essay in Geographical History" (see 1943), and that underlay also the collection of essays published shortly before his death, *Geographical History in Greek Lands* (1953). His other notable books are *The Dawn of History* (1911) and *The Political Ideas of the Greeks* (1927). In the field of classics Myres' scholarly achievement was substantial, but in anthropology his influence lay perhaps to a greater extent in his enthusiasm for, and promotion of, the subject and in the opportunities that he created for others. Thus, when Myres was recorder of the anthropological section for the 1899 meeting of the British Association for the Advancement of Science, he wrote to another Oxford-trained classicist, R. R. Marett, asking him to enliven a potentially dull meeting with something "really startling"; for the occasion Marett produced his paper "Pre-animistic Religion," which had indeed the desired effect and brought fame to Marett [*see the biography of* MARETT]. In the following year, as honorary secretary to the Royal Anthropological Institute, Myres conceived the need for a journal which would report on recent work in the field of anthropological studies and would provide a place for general discussion through shorter articles and reviews. As a result, *Man: A Monthly Record of Anthropological Science* started publication in 1901. Myres became the first editor, and the form and policy of the journal were largely shaped by him. He was editor from 1901 to 1903 and again from 1931 to 1946. At Oxford, E. B. Tylor had been lecturing in anthropology since 1884, but there was no separate department or school until, in the first years of this century, Myres, with others, helped to create such a school and to establish the diploma course in anthropology. He became the first secretary to the committee for anthropology, which the university set up in 1905 to administer the teaching of the course. In 1908 he contributed to a course of public lectures that Marett (who had succeeded him as secretary to the committee) had arranged to stimulate an interest in anthropology. The lectures, published as *Anthropology and the Classics,* are an interesting reflection of the subject as it was then conceived; some of the other speakers were Arthur J. Evans, Andrew Lang, Gilbert Murray, and F. B. Jevons. In 1912 Myres, with Barbara Freire-Marreco, one of the first pupils in the diploma course, prepared a new edition of *Notes and Queries on Anthropology*. From 1919 to 1932 Myres was the honorary general secretary to the British Association for the Advancement of Science. He was vice-president of the Royal Anthropological Institute from 1921 to 1923 and thereafter continued to serve as an active member on committees until 1928, when he was elected president, an office he held for the very long period of three years. He was active in the creation of the International Congress of Anthropological and Ethnological Sciences and served as honorary general secretary of the group from its first meeting in 1934 until 1947.

M. J. RUEL

[*See also the biographies of* FRAZER; MARETT; TYLOR.]

WORKS BY MYRES

1908 Herodotus and Anthropology. Pages 121–168 in Robert R. Marett (editor), *Anthropology and the Classics.* Oxford: Clarendon.

1911 *The Dawn of History.* New York: Holt.

1912 BRITISH ASSOCIATION FOR THE ADVANCEMENT OF SCIENCE *Notes and Queries on Anthropology.* 4th ed. Edited by Barbara Freire-Marreco and J. L. Myres. London: Routledge. → First published in 1874. A sixth, revised edition was published in 1954.

1927 *The Political Ideas of the Greeks, With Special Reference to Early Notions About Law, Authority, and Natural Order in Relation to Human Ordinance.* London: Arnold; New York: Abingdon.

1930 *Who Were the Greeks?* Berkeley: Univ. of California Press.

1943 *Mediterranean Culture.* Cambridge Univ. Press.

1953 *Geographical History in Greek Lands.* Oxford: Clarendon. → Includes a bibliography of Myres' works.

SUPPLEMENTARY BIBLIOGRAPHY

John Linton Myres: 1869–1954. 1954 *Man* 54:37–43. → Memorial tributes by Raymond W. Firth and others.

MYTH AND SYMBOL

Myths treat of origins but derive from transitions. By "myths" I do not, of course, mean *Märchen*, fairy tales, folk tales, *Sagen*, or legends but sacred narratives telling, as Stith Thompson writes, "of sacred beings and of semi-divine heroes and of the origins of all things, usually through the agency of these sacred beings" (1946, p. 9). Myths relate how one state of affairs became another: how an unpeopled world became populated; how chaos became cosmos; how immortals became mortal; how the seasons came to replace a climate without seasons; how the original unity of mankind became a plurality of tribes or nations; how androgynous beings became men and women; and

so on. Myths are *liminal* phenomena: they are frequently told at a time or in a site that is "betwixt and between."

Myths as liminal phenomena

When Arnold van Gennep generalized the processual structure of *rites de passage* (1909), he opened up many lines of investigation that have not as yet been fully exploited. Van Gennep suggested a threefold progression of successive ritual stages: separation, margin (or limen), and aggregation. Many structural and cultural problems are posed by the liminal stage. The individual or group undergoing *rites de passage* is, during the liminal period, neither here nor there but in limbo. The individual initiand is no longer the incumbent of a culturally defined social position or status but has not yet become the incumbent of another. If a whole social group is in ritual transition, there is frequently an annulment or invalidation of the distinctive arrangement of specialized and mutually dependent positions that composed its preritual structure; nor as yet has its postritual structure been anticipated. The protracted liminal periods found to be marked by collective rites in preliterate societies are not without structure; rather there is a simplification and generalization of structure. The complexities of stratification and segmentation are replaced by dyadic oppositions of instructors and instructed: the interstructural situation often may also be an instructional situation. Initiators collectively confront initiands, and among the initiands there is usually complete equality of status. Preritual distinctions of kinship, wealth, rank, or age are temporarily invalidated.

Correlated with these structural changes, the symbols of liminality frequently represent such ideas as death and birth. The loss of preritual status or structural arrangements is interpreted as "death," the growth toward a new status or articulation as "birth" or "infancy." The loss of status may be emblematized by ritual nudity, or the group's social homogeneity may be emphasized by the wearing of some uniform ritual decoration or dress. The passive attitude of the male initiands may be symbolized by the wearing of female apparel. The absence of status distinctions may be shown further by the use of postures expressive of humility or by decorating the body with earth or ashes. The social invisibility of the initiands may be signified by their total or partial seclusion from the habitats and occasions of secular life, by rules enjoining them to be silent for long periods, and by strange disguises.

Liminality is thus a period of structural impoverishment and symbolic enrichment. It is essentially a period of returning to first principles and taking stock of the cultural inventory. To be outside of a particularized social position, to cease to have a specific perspective, is in a sense to become (at least potentially) aware of all positions and arrangements and to have a total perspective. What converts potential understanding into real gnosis is instruction. Instruction takes many forms: it is partly communicated through displays of *sacra* objects which are shown to the initiands and explained, sometimes with the aid of sacred myths; it partly takes the form of direct ethical instruction, although this is rarely the case in primitive ritual; and very often the cultural knowledge is transmitted by the recital of mythical narratives. It must be remembered that like all ritual phenomena and processes, such *sacra*, such gnosis, and such myths are felt by those who believe them to have ontological efficacy. They re-create or transform those to whom they are shown or told and alter the capacity of the initiand's being so that he becomes capable of performing the tasks of the new status ahead of him. It is not simply a cognitive restructuring that takes place, nor is it solely a ritual legitimization of the initiand's new social status; rather the rites, myths, and symbols are felt to have something akin to a salvific power—without the ontological aspect the initiand would be "lost"; he would not be able to perform even the physical acts appropriate to his new status nor to fulfill the ritual component of this new status. For example, unless a girl has been ritually "grown" into a woman, as the Bemba put it (Richards 1956), many aspects of adult sexuality will present dangers for her. Thus knowledge, including knowledge imparted by myth, "saves."

Even where myths are not bound to rites, they have a liminal character. Most of them have a genetic or critical reference. They refer to *how* things came to be *what* they are; they are not mere inventories or rules of behavior. They further refer, directly or indirectly, to the biological life-crises of birth, mating, disease, and death. They relate also to climatic or ecological changes, which always involve a restructuring of social relationships—with the possibility of conflict and disorder. The well-known amorality of myths is intimately connected with their existential bearing. The myth does not describe what ought to be done; it expresses what must be. The rhythms and outcomes of biology and climate are both amoral and non-logical, although they have form and order. To gain power the participant in ritual or the believer in myth (who enacts its episodes in imagination

by identification with its characters) must perform or feign to perform, in act or in fantasy, deeds of murder, cannibalism, adultery, or incest, since the generative processes of inner and outer nature are most directly expressed in such behavior. Liminal symbolism, both in its ritual and mythic expressions, abounds in direct or figurative transgressions of the moral codes that hold good in secular life, such as human sacrifice, human flesh eating, and incestuous unions of brother–sister or mother–son deities or their human representatives. Thus the theory that myths are paradigmatic (Eliade 1957) or that myths afford precedents and sanctions for social status and moral rules (Malinowski 1925) requires some sort of qualification. Myths and liminal rites are not to be treated as models for secular behavior. Nor, on the other hand, are they to be regarded as cautionary tales, as negative models which should not be followed. Rather are they felt to be high or deep mysteries which put the initiand temporarily into close rapport with the primary or primordial generative powers of the cosmos, the acts of which transcend rather than transgress the norms of human secular society. In myth is a limitless freedom, a symbolic freedom of action which is denied to the norm-bound incumbent of a status in a social structure. What the initiand seeks through rite and myth is not a moral *exemplum* so much as the power to transcend the limits of his previous status, although he knows he must accept the normative restraints of his new status. Liminality is pure potency, where anything can happen, where immoderacy is normal, even normative, and where the elements of culture and society are released from their customary configurations and recombined in bizarre and terrifying imagery. Yet this boundlessness is restricted—although never without a sense of hazard—by the knowledge that this is a unique situation and by a definition of the situation which states that the rites and myths must be told in a prescribed order and in a symbolic rather than a literal form. The very symbol that expresses at the same time restrains; through mimesis there is an acting out—rather than the acting—of an impulse that is biologically motivated but socially and morally reprehended.

The "reality" of myths

Many authorities on mythology have stressed the *reality*, as distinct from the fantastic or unreal aspects, of myth. Malinowski, for example, described how myth "as it exists in a savage community" is "not merely a story told but a reality lived." It is "not an idle tale, but a hard-worked active force" ([1925] 1948, pp. 100–101). Jung wrote that "the primitive mentality does not invent myths, it experiences them." Myths are "anything but allegories of physical processes. . . . Myths . . . have a vital meaning . . . not merely do they represent, they *are* the mental life of the primitive tribe, which immediately falls to pieces and decays when it loses its mythological heritage" ([1909–1946] 1953, p. 314). And we find Mircea Eliade writing that myth "is always the recital of a creation; it tells how something was accomplished, began to *be*. It is for this reason that myth is bound up with ontology; it speaks only of *realities*, of what *really* happened, of what was fully manifested" ([1957] 1959, p. 95). Now it is true that for each of these authors, reality or experience has a different meaning. Malinowski's primary intent was to relate the myths of the Trobriand Islanders to their social and cultural experience. Thus, myths of the emergence of clan ancestors from holes in the ground were related to actual topographical features, to the contemporary distribution of Trobriand clans, and to Trobriand kinship patterns and social stratification. By "reality" Malinowski meant that myths are charters of extant social institutions. Although they might mention fictitious beings, their details had a point-to-point correlation with social and cultural arrangements—which were real aspects of Trobriand experience. Jung, on the contrary, regarded myths not as indices of, or charters for, cultural institutions, but as "psychological realities," as expressions of the "archetypes" or "primordial images" of the "collective unconscious." These are real in the sense that they represent inherited forms or patterns (in the Platonic sense of ideas) present in every human being. At first these forms are without specific thought content; content is provided by the specific culture. Myths give "a local habitation and a name" to these general forms and give them "reality" by manifesting them to consciousness.

By "reality" Eliade means "sacred reality," for, he writes, "it is the *sacred* that is pre-eminently the real" ([1957] 1959, p. 95). His analysis hinges on a distinction between the sacred and the profane. The sacred for him is *sui generis;* like Rudolf Otto's *das Heilige*, the sacred presents itself as something "like nothing human or cosmic . . . a reality of a wholly different order from 'natural' (or 'profane') realities . . . saturated with being . . . equivalent to a *power*." Myth is a "sacred history" (and hence "saturated with being . . . and power"), and "to relate a sacred history is equivalent to revealing a mystery. For the persons of the myth are not hu-

man beings: they are gods or culture heroes, and for this reason their *gesta* constitute mysteries; man could not know their acts if they were not revealed to him" (*ibid.*, p. 95). We cannot get behind this theological language to the processes underlying myth. The sacred or sacred realm, for Eliade, is inaccessible to us except insofar as it chooses to reveal itself to us in the analogies of mythic or ritual symbolism.

Thus, for Malinowski, "reality," as an attribute of myth, is cultural, for Jung psychological, and for Eliade spiritual (as it is indeed for our preliterate interpreters). If, however, myth is merely a charter or precedent for the continuance of rites and customs, it has some weird and numinous features; if it is a bundle of archetypes, it also has close reference to specific cultural and social institutions and relations; while if it is "an irruption of the sacred, of creative energy into the world . . . a surplus of ontological substance" (*ibid.*, p. 97), it has a variety of profane cultural and psychological interconnections.

Analyzing liminal rites and symbolism

The social and cultural context. Possibly the best approach to the problem of cracking the code of myth is the *via negativa* represented by the liminal phase in initiation rites. But to analyze this adequately, we must take heed of all that Malinowski says concerning the necessity of studying such rites in the live context in which they occur. This context is in every given instance a social field: a structure of social positions and a set of cultural institutions and mechanisms. The specific initiation rite or myth must also be examined as a component of a total system of religious beliefs and practices. Its symbols and episodes, subdivided into such units as *significata*, stages, words, sentences, motifs, *personae*, objects and relationships, and the principles and themes underlying these, must be related to those found in other parts of the total religious system. Next, the properties and structure of the religious system must be compared and contrasted with the properties and structure of other cultural subsystems, such as the kinship system, the economic system, and the legal and political systems. In other words, we have to seek a part of the meaning of a myth in the idiosyncrasy of its cultural context, a context of many dimensions. Nor must we neglect the dynamics of that culture: we must see the rite and the myth as phases in social processes, as being performed or narrated at significant points in the seasonal cycle, at individual or group life-crises, at times of natural catastrophe, such as famine, drought, flood, and epidemic, or with reference to crises brought on by human law-breaking or "sinful" action. Before we can say with any certainty what this or that liminal phenomenon is, we must be able to state what it is not. It is not the state of cultural affairs that precedes it or that which follows. But since it is, in some sense, the antithesis of what precedes it, we must know the structure of that cultural state. And since it is, in some sense, a preparation for the state that is to follow, we must know the properties, conditions, and structural features of that state too. Liminality strains toward universality but never realizes it; a specific culture surrounds it in space and time and invades its innermost sanctum. Its very *sacra* bear the hallmarks of a particular historically derived culture.

Psychogenic factors. Nevertheless, simply because liminality, and the sacred myth which is one of its phenomena, does so strain toward universality, toward the dissolution of specific structural arrangements, there is a rich manifestation of psychical contents otherwise withheld from expression by a preoccupation with norm-governed or pragmatic activities. In many cultures the life-crises of birth, puberty, marriage, and death have been made the occasions of initiation ritual, and since these crises closely concern the experiences and relationships of the nuclear family, it is possible that Freudians and Neo-Freudians can shed much light on the unconscious semantic components of liminal symbolism, especially insofar as these may represent "the return of the repressed." The Jungians, whose therapy rests on the interpretation of symbols ejected from the "collective unconscious" under the pressure of an adult crisis, might discover in the relationship between ritual and crises found in primitive societies some justification for the use of their analytical procedures.

Jung himself uncompromisingly states that myths are first and foremost psychic manifestations that represent the nature of the psyche. All the myths concerned with occurrences of nature, such as summer and winter, the phases of the moon, and the rainy seasons, are definitely not allegories of these objective experiences, nor are they to be understood as explanations of the sunrise, the sunset, and other natural phenomena. Rather, they are symbolic expressions of the inner and unconscious psychic drama that becomes accessible to human consciousness by projection—that is, by being mirrored in the events of nature (Jung 1909–1946). This bluntly psychogenic explanation of myth denies to culture any formative

role in its symbolism. It also excludes the intellectualist variety of psychogenic explanation favored today by Lévi-Strauss, who holds that myths, and other religious manifestations, contain ideas that "give access to the mechanism of thought." Myths "pertain to the understanding, and the demands to which it responds and the way in which it tries to meet them are primarily of an intellectual kind" ([1962] 1963, p. 104). Lévi-Strauss finds in primitive religious phenomena "the emergence of a logic operating by means of binary oppositions and coinciding with the first manifestations of symbolism"; and in metaphor—which plays an important role in myth—he finds "a primary form of discursive thought" (p. 102). His emphasis is primarily on the "logic of oppositions and correlations, exclusions and inclusions, compatibilities and incompatibilities," which for him "explains the laws of association" found in mythic and ritual symbolism and discourse. When Lévi-Strauss analyzes myth, his main aim is to reveal the austere structure of this logic behind its symbolic and bizarre integument.

Depth psychologists generally would demur at the stress on logic in this realm; they hold that in unconscious thinking, logically incompatible ideas can coexist and even reinforce one another in a single situation, while symbols may have multiple disparate referents. The followers of Pareto, too, would assert that nonlogical or nonrational symbols must be distinguished from logical symbols, constituting a class whose members derive both form and semantic content from biotic and cultural processes of a noncognitive type; logical symbols are conceived in the conscious mind, as Pallas was in Zeus's head. Nonlogical symbols represent the impress on consciousness of factors external or subliminal to it. Such symbols may subsequently become objects of reflection, and from them many logical symbols may be derived by abstraction. But they are not generated by the consciousness, nor are they mutually interrelated in terms of the rules of logic. Many mythic and ritual symbols belong to the class of nonlogical symbols and cannot therefore be analyzed as though they operated by the rules of logic.

The cultural dynamics of ritual. Many of these dilemmas may be resolved if we take the cultural dynamics of ritual as our point of departure. Here we find more than the distinction between the profane and the sacred. In the liminal stage of *rites de passage*, we find not merely the sacred but the most sacred. And paradoxically this is where we also find the most human, indeed, the all-too-human. Particularly do we discover in this stage a crucial anchoring of ideas and symbols in the human body and in its somatic processes. The body (with its unconscious rhythms and orectic processes) is viewed as the epitome or microcosm of the universe. It becomes the metaphor or model which illustrates most vividly all other profane types of regularity—of nature, of culture, of society, and of thought. In the profane or secular realm—even though in multifunctional communities this too is saturated with religious ideas and imagery—utility and rationality guide behavior and lead to the classification of phenomena and processes, both of nature and society. This rational categorization of reality enables the human community to cope efficiently with the problems of obtaining its food supply and maintaining social order. These classifications "spill over" into the sacred realm and are particularly in evidence in the separation and aggregation phases of ritual, in which the sacred has to come to terms, so to speak, with the profane, where the two realms interdigitate. But in the liminal phase of separation and secret instruction in gnostic *sacerrima*, the nonlogical and biopsychical modes of thinking and acting prevail. The behavior in such phases is "inspired by things as they are and not by things as they ought to be" (Horton 1963, p. 98).

Trickster tales

In the liminal period we see naked, unaccommodated man, whose nonlogical character issues in various modes of behavior: destructive, creative, farcical, ironic, energetic, suffering, lecherous, submissive, defiant, but always unpredictable. One class of myths which throws into sharp relief many aspects of liminality is that represented by the widely distributed trickster tales. A considerable scholarly literature has accumulated on tricksters (see, for example, Radin 1955; Dumézil 1948; Wescott 1962; Herskovits 1938). They include the Greek god Hermes, the Norse god Loki, the Yoruba deity Eshu-Elegba, the Fon Legba, the Winnebago trickster Wakdjunkaga, and many others. Tricksters are clearly liminal personalities (threshold men or edge men). Joan Wescott, for example, describes the Yoruba Eshu-Elegba in the following terms: "[Eshu] is . . . described as a homeless wandering spirit, and as one who inhabits the market-place, the crossroads, and thresholds of houses. He is present whenever there is trouble and also wherever there is change and transition" (1962, p. 337).

In very similar terms Hermes, as the messenger of the gods, inhabits crossroads, open public places, and doorways, and is associated with commerce. He is the invincible child, well equipped with the powers of nature and instinct. Most tricksters have an uncertain sexual status: on various mythical occasions Loki and Wakdjunkaga transformed themselves into women, while Hermes was often represented in statuary as a hermaphrodite. On other occasions tricksters appear with exaggerated phallic characteristics: Hermes is symbolized by the herm or pillar, the club, and the ithyphallic statue; Wakdjunkaga has a very long penis which has to be wrapped around him and put over his shoulder in a box; Eshu is represented in sculpture as having a long curved hairdress carved as a phallus. In most trickster tales there are many scatological and even coprophagous episodes, exemplifying what Wescott has called the "katabolic nature of the trickster."

Tricksters are multiform and ambiguous. For example, myths about Eshu describe him as firstborn and as last-born, as old man and as child. In these four roles the individual normally has privileged freedom from some of the demands of the social code.

Other traits ascribed to tricksters include: combined black and white symbolism, aggression, vindictiveness, vanity, defiance of authority, willfulness, individualism, indeterminacy of stature (sometimes tall, sometimes dwarfish), destructiveness, creativeness (the Winnebago trickster transforms the pieces of his broken phallus into plants and flowers for men—hence he is both single and multiple), and libido without procreative outcome.

These liminal entities share an antinomian character. They behave as though there were no social or moral norms to guide them. Self-will, caprice, and lust impel them. In a rather different sense from Eliade's, they are "the opposite of the profane," if we include in the latter the notions of moral and jural order. Yet though wholly other, they are perfectly familiar to mankind, even jocularly so, for they represent what everyone would secretly like to do. Since their energies are untrammeled and unchanneled, they are supererogatory, and their surplus becomes the source of new substances and beings. They are raw, undomesticated bodily and collective power, undefinable, uncontainable, and compounded equally of polymorphous libido and aggression. It is true that in certain trickster myth cycles (especially in North America), the later tales describe the structuring of the trickster's life and activities: he marries, settles down, has children, obeys kinship and affinal norms, etc., but here he resembles the initiand who leaves the liminal scene and is "aggregated" once again to society. The unpredictable liminal *persona* becomes predictable again in terms of the norms and classifications of profane society. The interstructural transition stage is over. Creative chaos has become created cosmos.

Creation myths

But the concept of *limen* includes not only the Dionysian and polymorphous aspects of human normlessness; it also includes the notions of the mystical and the ascetical. In this regard, there is usually a feeling that the human cultural order is a kind of painted veil over a deeper, superhuman order, the mysteries of which begin to be accessible only to those who have been stripped during initiation of profane status and profane rank. The humility and discipline of the novice, his self-abnegation and self-denial, and his acceptance of the absolute authority of his instructors win for him true gnosis. This set of liminal attitudes is associated with a very different type of mythology than that represented by the trickster cycles. To this type belong such creation tales and chants as the Hebrew *Genesis*, the Greek *Theogony*, the Zoroastrian, Gnostic, and Mandaean cosmogonies, the Fon cosmogony, the Quiche Mayan *Popul Vuh*, the Norse *Elder Edda*, and the Hawaiian *Kumulipo*, or creation chant. These all reveal how the One became the Many, how in a series of orderly stages chaos became a cosmos of many dimensions and levels; most of these tell also how sin and death came into the world, and thus they provide a theodicy. These great myths are in many societies recited during liminal periods, the times that are rich in ritual. Every myth of this sort, Eliade holds, "shows how a reality came into existence, whether it be the total reality, the cosmos, or only a fragment—an island, a species of plant, a human institution . . . to tell how a thing was born is to reveal an irruption of the sacred into the world, and the sacred is the ultimate cause of all real existence" ([1957] 1959, p. 97).

At first glance, it might seem that these architectonic masterpieces have little in common with the trickster myths, in which "realities" come into being as the result of caprice or accident. Yet in many of these cosmogonies and theogonies, the deities and heroes mate incestuously, devour one another, and clearly transgress human and cultural norms of justice and equity. By these acts, despite priestly editing, the liminal character of the myth betrays itself. And, indeed, in most of these cycles of great myths, trickster figures may be found peeping grotesquely forth like the gargoyles on Gothic cathedrals.

Myths are not merely a guide to culture, although they are this as well; they point to the generative power underlying human life, a power which from time to time oversteps cultural limits. Surely these huge symbolizations of incest and crime at the level of the deity are more significant than Ruth Benedict supposed when she described their Zuñi manifestations as "distortions" due to "various fanciful exaggerations and compensatory mechanisms" (1935, pp. xx–xxi). They represent a return to the deep sources of psychosomatic experience in a legitimized situation of freedom from cultural constraints and social classifications. These relatively short "liminal instants" must counterbalance the long days of utilitarian and culture-bound experience. At the root of the rational is the nonrational, which gives it its meaning, and liminality is that root. Nature (and indeed spirit, the intelligent and immaterial part of man) is still the mentor of culture and the source of its often unpredictable changes. In myth we see nature and spirit at their shaping work—and this in the liminal moment in and out of time.

VICTOR W. TURNER

[*See also* FOLKLORE; POLLUTION; RELIGION; RITUAL; *and the biographies of* GENNEP; JUNG; MALINOWSKI; MAUSS; RADIN.]

BIBLIOGRAPHY

BAUMANN, HERMANN 1935 *Lunda: Bei Bauern und Jägern in Inner-Angola.* Berlin: Wurfel.

BENEDICT, RUTH 1935 *Zuñi Mythology.* 2 vols. Columbia University Contributions to Anthropology, Vol. 21. New York: Columbia Univ. Press.

DUMÉZIL, GEORGES 1948 *Loki.* Paris: Maisonneuve.

ELIADE, MIRCEA (1957) 1959 *The Sacred and the Profane.* New York: Harcourt. → A paperback edition was published in 1961 by Harper.

GENNEP, ARNOLD VAN (1909) 1960 *The Rites of Passage.* London: Routledge. → First published in French.

GLUCKMAN, MAX (1949) 1963 The Role of the Sexes in Wiko Circumcision Ritual. Pages 145–167 in Meyer Fortes (editor), *Social Structure: Essays Presented to A. R. Radcliffe-Brown.* New York: Russell.

HERSKOVITS, MELVILLE J. 1938 *Dahomey: An Ancient West African Kingdom.* 2 vols. New York: Augustin.

HORTON, ROBIN 1963 The Kalabari *Ekine* Society: A Borderland of Religion and Art. *Africa* 33:94–114.

JUNG, CARL G. (1909–1946) 1953 *Psychological Reflections: An Anthology of Writings.* Selected and edited by Jolande Jacobi. New York: Harper. → A paperback edition was published in 1961.

LÉVI-STRAUSS, CLAUDE (1962) 1963 *Totemism.* Boston: Beacon. → First published as *Le totémisme aujourd'hui.*

MALINOWSKI, BRONISLAW (1925) 1948 Magic, Science and Religion. Pages 1–71 in Bronislaw Malinowski,

"Magic, Science and Religion," and Other Essays. Glencoe, Ill.: Free Press.

OPLER, MORRIS 1938 Myths and Tales of the Jicarilla Apache Indians. Memoirs of the American Folklore Society, Vol. 31. Philadelphia: The Society.

RADIN, PAUL (1955) 1956 The Trickster: A Study in American Indian Mythology. London: Routledge; New York: Philosophical Library.

RICHARDS, AUDREY I. 1956 Chisungu: A Girls' Initiation Ceremony Among the Bemba of Northern Rhodesia. London: Faber.

THOMPSON, STITH 1946 The Folktale. New York: Dryden.

TURNER, VICTOR W. 1962 Three Symbols of Passage in Ndembu Circumcision Ritual. Pages 124–173 in Max Gluckman (editor), Essays on the Ritual of Social Relations. Manchester Univ. Press.

WESCOTT, JOAN 1962 The Sculpture and Myths of Eshu-Elegba, the Yoruba Trickster. Africa 32:336–354.

WHITE, CHARLES M. N. 1961 Elements in Luvale Beliefs and Rituals. Rhodes–Livingstone Paper No. 33. Manchester Univ. Press.